ISSN 0068-0141

Bookman's Price Index

VOLUME 102

A Guide to the Values of Rare and Other Out of Print Books

Edited by
Anne F. McGrath

GALE
CENGAGE Learning

Farmington Hills, Mich • San Francisco • New York • Waterville, Maine
Meriden, Conn • Mason, Ohio • Chicago

Bookman's Price Index, Vol. 102
Anne F. McGrath

Product Management: Michele LeMeau

Project Editor: Kristin B. Mallegg

Manufacturing: Rita Wimberley

© 2015 Gale, Cengage Learning
WCN: 01-100-101

ALL RIGHTS RESERVED. No part of this work covered by the copyright herein may be reproduced, transmitted, stored, or used in any form or by any means graphic, electronic, or mechanical, including but not limited to photocopying, recording, scanning, digitizing, taping, Web distribution, information networks, or information storage and retrieval systems, except as permitted under Section 107 or 108 of the 1976 United States Copyright Act, without the prior written permission of the publisher.

This publication is a creative work fully protected by all applicable copyright laws, as well as by misappropriation, trade secret, unfair competition, and other applicable laws. The authors and editors of this work have added value to the underlying factual material herein through one or more of the following: unique and original selection, coordination, expression, arrangement, and classification of the information.

For product information and technology assistance, contact us at Gale Customer Support, 1-800-877-4253.
For permission to use material from this text or product, submit all requests online at www.cengage.com/permissions.
Further permissions questions can be emailed to permissionrequest@cengage.com

While every effort has been made to ensure the reliability of the information presented in this publication, Gale, a part of Cengage Learning, does not guarantee the accuracy of the data contained herein. Gale accepts no payment for listing; and inclusion in the publication of any organization, agency, institution, publication, service, or individual does not imply endorsement of the editors or publisher. Errors brought to the attention of the publisher and verified to the satisfaction of the publisher will be

EDITORIAL DATA PRIVACY POLICY
Does this product contain information about you as an individual? If so, for more information about how to access or correct that information or about our data privacy policies please see our Privacy Statement at www.gale.cengage.com

Gale
27500 Drake Rd.
Farmington Hills, MI 48331-3535

LIBRARY OF CONGRESS CATALOG CARD NUMBER 64-008723

ISBN-13: 978-1-4103-1793-3
ISSN 0068-0141

Printed in the United States of America
1 2 3 4 5 6 7 19 18 17 16 15

Contents

Introduction vii
Dealers Represented in This Volume 1
Bookman's Price Index 9
Association Copies 835
Fine Bindings 1145
Fore-edge Paintings 1189

Introduction

With this 102nd edition, Bookman's Price Index marks over 50 years of providing comprehensive information on antiquarian books. Established in 1964, BPI is published twice each year as an index to both the prices and availability of antiquarian books in the United States, Canada, and the British Isles. Each issue of BPI reports the prices and availability of at least 10,000 different antiquarian books. Thus, in the course of an average calendar year, BPI reports the prices and availability of at least 20,000 antiquarian books that are important to readers in the North Atlantic portion of the English-speaking community.

Definition of Antiquarian Books

An antiquarian book is one that is, or has been, traded on the antiquarian book market. It is, or was, traded there because it is important (or in demand) and scarce.

Importance, in the case of antiquarian books, is national. American, Canadian, and British readers buy and sell the artifacts of their own literature and history, science and art as well as a select number of books that document the Continental and Classical origins of certain aspects of their cultures. There are special enthusiasms, too, such as children's books, sporting books, and books that are important principally for their physical beauty; but even the books of these special enthusiasms reflect the national preoccupations of English-speaking readers.

Scarcity means that the number of copies of any book that might come onto the market is measured, at most, in scores, and that only a dozen or a half-dozen, at most, come onto the market during any calendar year.

Lots of important books are not scarce, and lots of scarce books are not important. And, despite the word *antiquarian*, age is no guarantee of either scarcity or importance. Conversely, many books that are less than a generation old bring a handsome price on the market.

The antiquarian books that do appear on the North Atlantic market are a small percentage of the world's entire antiquarian book market, and, necessarily, they are the tiniest fraction of the total number of books published over the centuries.

Despite their thin ranks and scant number, antiquarian books are usually not outrageously expensive. They often range in price from $50 to $500, with most clustering between $100 and $200, and precious few enjoying four-figure prominence.

Prices Reported in *BPI*

The prices reported in *Bookman's Price Index* each year are established by some 100-200 antiquarian booksellers in the United States, Canada, and the British Isles. Usually, about 50 of these booksellers are represented in any one volume of *BPI*. By drawing information from a large number of antiquarian booksellers across English-speaking North America, as well as the British Isles, *BPI* is able to report broad, consistent, and reliable market patterns in the whole North Atlantic English-speaking community.

Within the ranks of the antiquarian booksellers whose prices are reported in *BPI*, the group most interesting is the specialist dealers, whose stock is limited to books in a single subject such as law, or psychiatry, or maritime studies, or horticulture. Such specialists provide readers of *BPI* with information that is not easily available elsewhere.

The prices that all of these antiquarian booksellers report are retail prices that they have established on the basis of their working experience and familiarity with current market conditions, including supply and demand and the effect upon price of the general physical condition of a book, as well as such extraordinary factors as the presence of important autographs.

The willingness of the various antiquarian booksellers to publish their prices in direct comparison with the prices of all other antiquarian booksellers serves as a general indication of the reliability of the prices reported in *BPI* as well as the probity of the antiquarian booksellers. These prices are public market prices, not private deals.

Availability of Books in *BPI*

Every one of the books in *Bookman's Price Index* was recently available in one of the shops of the antiquarian booksellers whose catalogs are included in this volume of *BPI*. It was upon the basis of a hands-on appraisal of each book that an antiquarian bookseller established its price. Thus, the prices reported in *BPI* are actual prices for specific books rather than approximate prices for probable or possible books.

While a particular book may no longer be in the shop of the antiquarian bookseller who established its price, the fact that the book stood on the shelf there recently means that the book is still to be found on the market and that the antiquarian bookseller who established its price may have access to another copy of the same book, or that a different antiquarian bookseller may price another copy of the book in the following issue of *BPI*. Thus, by reporting prices of actual books and their real availability, *Bookman's Price Index* serves as an index to the general market availability of a particular antiquarian book.

Conversely, *BPI* is an index to the absence of certain antiquarian books from the market: books not priced in *BPI* may be presumed to be generally unavailable on the antiquarian book market. *BPI* makes no effort to predict what such unavailable books might be worth if they were perhaps to someday come on the market; *BPI* reports only what is going on in the market, not what might go on.

For example, if a reader were to search the six most recent issues of *BPI* for the price of the first edition of Edgar Allan Poe's *Tamerlane,* he might not find it and could safely conclude that a first edition of *Tamerlane* was not generally available during the past two years or so. If, on the other hand, the same reader were to make a similar search for a first edition of *The Stand* by Poe's spiritual son Stephen King, he might discover that *The Stand* has been found in the shops from time to time and that it is worth about $1600 for a signed first edition, or between $200 and $400 for an unsigned first, depending on condition.

The Importance of Condition

Condition is critical in antiquarian books as in any other antiquarian artifact. The condition of all of the books priced in *Bookman's Price Index* is stated in elaborate detail because it is impossible to understand or justify the price of any antiquarian book without full knowledge of its condition.

Arrangement of *BPI*

The books priced in *Bookman's Price Index* are arranged in a single main alphabet according to the name of the author: in cases of personal authorship, the author's last name; in cases of books produced by corporate bodies such as governments of countries or states, the name of that corporation; in cases of anonymous books, the title; and in cases of anonymous classics such as the *Arabian Nights,* by customary title.

All names of authors, or titles, are standardized according to the usage of American libraries, thus gathering all works by an author.

The works of an author are arranged under his or her name in alphabetical sequence according to the first word of the title, excepting initial articles. However, editions of an author's collected works are listed, out of alphabetical sequence, at the end of the list of his or her individual works.

Different editions of a single work are arranged according to date of publication, with the earlier preceding the later even though this sequence sometimes disrupts alphabetical regularity. In such cases, the editor has sought to consult the reader's convenience rather than any rigid consistency.

The reasons for the occasional disruption of alphabetical regularity are two: the first is that in reporting prices, antiquarian booksellers sometimes refer to a book elliptically, leaving unknown the complete title. The second reason is that certain books change title without changing substance. The most obvious example of this particular editorial problem is the Bible. Title pages of Bibles can begin with such words as Complete, Holy, Sacred, New, Authorized, and so on: it is still the same book. Therefore all English Bibles appear, under the heading BIBLES – ENGLISH, in chronological order. Following the title of each book is its imprint: the place and date of publication and the name of the publisher (or the name of the printer in cases of certain books produced prior to the late eighteenth century).

Description of the Condition of Books

Following the author, title, and imprint of each book is a thorough description of the physical condition of the book, insofar as the bookseller has provided this information. While antiquarian booksellers do not always apply a standard formula in describing the condition of a book, they generally include, as appropriate, most of the following details:

Edition. *BPI* reports which edition of a book is being priced when this information is critical, as in cases when several editions were published in one year. If an edition was published in more than one issue, or state, *BPI* distinguishes among them and identifies them either by the order in which they appeared, or by the physical peculiarities that characterize them. When necessary, *BPI* even describes those obscure details, called "points," that are used to distinguish among issues or states. The points are often minute and consist of such details as one misspelled word buried in the text. Finally, *BPI* identifies limited editions, stating the number of copies in the press run and, if necessary, the types of paper used and the specific number assigned to the book being priced.

Physical Size. *BPI* describes the height and the bulk of each book when this information is available. Height is usually described in the traditional language of the antiquarian book trade: folio, for a tall book; quarto (4to) for a medium-size book; and octavo (8vo) or duodecimo (12mo) for a smaller book. Miniature books are usually described in inches top to bottom and left to right. The bulk of a book is described by stating its pagination, a custom that operates to assure the reader that the book in question is complete.

Illustrations. Since many antiquarian books are more valuable for their illustrations than for their text, *BPI* describes such illustrations carefully, sometimes in considerable detail, as in the case of a book with hand-colored plates.

Binding. All bindings are described fully as to the material used, be it paper, cloth or leather, and even as to the type and color of the material and the time at which it was applied. ("Contemporary tan calf" means that a binding of cattle hide was made for the book contemporaneously with its printing.) Decorations of the binding are also described, and in the cases of twentieth century books, the presence or absence of the dust jacket is always noted.

Authors' Signatures. These are always cited, as they have a significant effect on the price of a book.

General Physical Condition, Specific Flaws, and Relative Scarcity. Usually, *BPI* provides some advice on the general condition of a book by stating that its condition is good, very good, or fine. Additionally, specific flaws are usually listed; some of them are significant, as in the case of a missing leaf or a worn binding, while others are very minor, as in the case of a worm hole in an ancient tome.

Availability. Frequently *BPI* will point out that certain books are of unusual scarcity or rarity. As all antiquarian books are by definition scarce, a special remark that a book is uncommonly scarce should be noted carefully.

Prices. Following the description, *BPI* gives the price of the book along with the name of the antiquarian bookseller who established the price and provided the physical description. Accompanying the antiquarian bookseller's name is the number of the catalog in which he published the price and description of the book, plus the item number of the book in the catalog. The addresses of the antiquarian booksellers whose prices are reported in *BPI* are listed following this Introduction, in the section entitled Dealers Represented in This Volume.

Association Copies, Fine Bindings, and Fore-edge Paintings

Following the main section of *Bookman's Price Index* are three small sections of association copies of books, books in fine bindings, and books decorated with fore-edge paintings. The books in these three sections take on additional interest and value because of features peculiar to them that are not found in other copies of the same books. Their value, or some portion of it, derives from factors not inherent in the text and not identifiable through the name of the author, thereby requiring that they be isolated so that readers can search them out according to the factors that create, or influence, their worth: association, binding or fore-edge painting.

All books priced and described in one of the special sections are also priced and described in the main section of *BPI*, thus permitting the reader to compare an ordinary copy of a book with one that enjoys added attraction because of a unique feature.

Association Copies. Certain antiquarian books acquire added value because of their association with a prominent owner. For instance, an ordinary eighteenth century book would take on enormous extra worth if it had once belonged to George Washington. Association copies of books priced in the special section of *BPI* are arranged according to the name of the person with whom the book was associated rather than according to the name of the author. (The same book is listed in the main body of *BPI* under the name of the author.)

Fine Bindings. Some books are valuable because custom bindings were applied to them alone, and not to other copies of the same book. In the Fine Bindings section of *BPI*, books are gathered under the name of the binder, when known, and then listed according to author. (Each of the books so listed is also listed under the name of the author in the main section of *BPI*.)

Fore-edge Paintings. Fore-edge paintings are original watercolor drawings upon the vertical edges of the leaves of a book. The book is laid flat with the front cover open so that the vertical edges of the leaves slant a little when the painting is applied; when the book is closed, the painting is not visible. These unusual examples of book decoration are gathered in the Fore-edge section under the year of publication of the book, and then arranged according to the name of the author. Generally, fore-edge paintings are not signed and dated, and it is often difficult, if not impossible, to be sure a fore-edge painting was executed in the year of publication of the book. When there is conclusive evidence as to the name of the artist and the date of a fore-edge painting, the book is listed under the year in which the painting was executed. (All books listed in the Fore-edge section are also listed in the main section of *BPI* under the name of the author.)

Errors in *BPI*

The multiple volumes of *BPI* that appear each year combine to include millions of letters and numerals. The editor makes every effort to get them all right, and she asks the reader to be understanding about an occasional typo.

Suggestions Are Welcome

Comments on the *Bookman's Price Index* series and suggestions for corrections and improvements are always welcome. Please contact:

Editor, *Bookman's Price Index*
Gale
27500 Drake Rd.
Farmington Hills, MI 48331-3535
Phone: 248-699-GALE
Toll-free: 800-877-GALE

Antiquarian Book Dealers in Volume 102

Aleph-Bet Books, Inc.
85 Old Mill River Road
Pound Ridge NY 10576
USA

Telephone: (914) 764-7410
Fax: (914) 764-1356
e-mail: helen@alephbet.com
http://www.alephbet.com
Contact: Helen & Marc Younger
Specialties: Children's & illustrated books for the collector, first editions, pop-ups, picture books, fairy tales and more.

Andrew Isles Natural History Books
Rear 115 Greville Street
PO Box 2305
Pahran 3181
Australia

Telephone: 61 (0) 2 9510 5750
Fax: 61 (0) 3 9529 1256
e-mail: books@AmdrewIsles.com
http://www.AndrewIsles.com
Specialties: Natural history

Any Amount of Books
56 Charing Cross Road
London WC2H 0QA
England

Telephone: 0207 836 3697
Fax: 0207 240 1769
e-mail: charingx@anyamountofbooks.com
http://www.anyamountofbooks.com

Argonaut Book Shop
786-792 Sutter Street
San Francisco CA 94109
USA

Telephone: (415) 474-9067
Fax: (415) 474-2537
e-mail: argonautSF@PacBell.net
http://www.argonautbookshop.com

Athena Rare Books
424 Riverside Drive
Fairfield CT 06824
USA

Telephone: (203) 254-2727
Fax: (203) 254-3518
e-mail: bill@athenararebooks.com
http://www.athenararebooks.com
Contact: William H. Schaberg
Specialties: Philosophy, Psychology, Science, Literature, History, Alcoholism

B&B Rare Books
30 East 20th Street
Suite 305
New York NY 10003
US

Telephone: (646) 652-6766
e-mail: info@bbrarebooks.com
http://bbrarebooks.com
Contact: Joshua Mann, Sunday Steinkirchner
Specialties: 19th & 20th century literature; American literature, British literature, children's literature, drama,, espionage, fiction, fine bindings, illustrated books, Irish literature

Gene W. Baade
Books on the West
824 Lynnwood Ave., N.E.
Renton WA 98056-3805
USA

Telephone: (425) 271-6481
e-mail: bookwest@eskimo.com
Specialties: Western books relating to cattle/cowboy culture, Native American history, outlaws and lawmen, Western art and photography, and the whole range of subjects related to U.S. history west of the Mississippi River

Beasley Books
1533 W. Oakdale
Chicago IL 60657
USA

Telephone: (773) 472-4528
Fax: (773) 472-7857
e-mail: beasley@beasleybooks.com
http://www.beasleybooks.com
Contact: Paul and Beth Garon; hours by appointment.
Specialties: Modern first editiions, black literature, jazz & blues, radicalism, psychoanalysis.

Between the Covers Rare Books, Inc.
35 W. Maple Ave.
Merchantville NJ 08109
USA

Telephone: (856) 665-2284
Fax: (856) 665-3639
e-mail: mail@betweenthecovers.com
http://www.betweenthecovers.com
Contact: Tom Congalton, Heidi Congalton, Gwen Waring, Jessica Luminoso, Dan Gregory, Jennifer Gregory

Blackwell's Rare Books
48-51 Broad Street
Oxford OX1 3BQ
England

Telephone: 01865 333555
Fax: 01865 794143
e-mail: rarebooks@blackwell.co.uk
http://www.rarebooks.blackwell.co.uk

Bookworm & Silverfish
P.O. Box 639
Wytheville VA 24382
USA

Telephone: (276) 686-5813
Fax: (276) 686-6636
e-mail: bookworm@naxs.com
http://www.bookwormandsilverfish.com
Contact: Jim Presgraves, ABAA
Specialties: General antiquarian, appraisals, 19th & 20th century technology, trade catalogs.

The Brick Row Book Shop
49 Geary Street #230
San Francisco CA 94108
USA

Telephone: (415) 398-0414
Fax: (415) 398-0435
e-mail: book@brickrow.com
http://www.brickrow.com
Specialties: First Editions, Rare Books and Manuscripts of 17th, 18th & 19th Century English and American Literature

By the Book, LC ABAA-ILAB
1045 East Camelback Road
Phoenix AZ 85014
USA

Telephone: (602) 222-8806
Fax: (480) 596-1672
e-mail: bythebooklc@qwestoffice.net
http://bythebooklc.com
Specialties: Art, Children's China/Japan/Korea, History of Ideas, Literature, Medicine, Science &Technology, Signed Books

Buckingham Books
8058 Stone Bridge Road
Greencastle PA 17225-9786
USA

Telephone: (717) 597-5657
Fax: (717) 597-1003
e-mail: buckingham@pa.net
http://www.buckinghambooks.com
Specialties: Western Americana, mystery, detective, and espionage fiction.

L. W. Currey, Inc.
P. O. Box 187
Elizabethtown NY 12932
USA

Telephone: (518) 873-6477
http://www.lwcurrey.com
Contact: Lloyd Currey
Specialties: Popular fiction, with emphasis on science fiction and fantasy literature from the earliest times to end of the twentieth century.

John Drury Rare Books
Strandlands, Wrabness
Manningtree
Essex CO11 2TX
England

Telephone: 01255 886260
Fax: 01255 880303
e-mail: mail@johndruryrarebooks.com
http://www.johndruryrarebooks.com
Contact: David Edmunds, Jennifer Edmunds
Specialties: Economics, education. law, philosophy, social history.

Dumont Maps & Books of the West
314 McKenzie Street
P.O. Box 10250
Santa Fe NM 87504
USA

Telephone: (505) 988-1076
Fax: (505) 986-6114
e-mail: info@dumontbooks.com
http://www.dumontbooks.com

Peter Ellis, Bookseller
18 Cecil Court
London WC2N 4HE
England

Telephone: 20 7836 8880
Fax: 20 8318 4748
e-mail: ellisbooks@lineone.net
http://www.peter-ellis.co.uk

Joseph J. Felcone Inc.
P.O. Box 366
Princeton NJ 08542
USA

Telephone: (609) 924-0539
Fax: (609) 924-9078
e-mail: info@felcone.com
http://www.felcone.com

Gemini Fine Books & Arts, Ltd.
917 Oakwood Terrace
Hinsdale IL 60521
USA

Telephone: (630) 986-1478
Fax: (630) 986-8992
e-mail: art@geminibooks.com
http://www.geminibooks.com
Specialties: Art Reference Books, French Symbolism, Art Nouveau and Art Deco, German Expressionism, Modern Illustrated Books (Livres D'artistes)

Heritage Book Shop, LLC
9024 Burton Way
Beverly Hills CA 90211
USA

Telephone: (310) 659-3674
Fax: (310) 659-4872
e-mail: books@heritagebookshop.com
http://www.heritagebookshop.com
Contact: Ben Weinstein
Specialties: Illustrated books, bindings, literature, manuscripts, early printed books, first editions

Jeff Hirsch Books
39850 N. Dilleys Rd.
Wadsworth IL 60083
USA

Telephone: (847) 662-2665
e-mail: mail@jhbooks.com
http://www.jhbooks.com
Contact: Jeff or Susan Hirsch
Specialties: 20th Century Photography, Art Monographs, Drama, Modern Literary Firsts, Poetry, Signed Books, Broadsides

Ian Hodgkins & Co. Ltd.
Upper Vatch Mill
The Vatch
Stroud
Gloucestershire GL6 7JY
England

Telephone: 01453 764270
Fax: 01453 755233
e-mail: i.hodgkins@dial.pipex.com
http://www.ianhodgkins.com
Contact: Tony Yablon, Ian Hoy, Simon Weager

Honey & Wax Booksellers
540 President Street
Third Floor
Brooklyn NY 11215
USA

Telephone: (917) 974-2420
e-mail: info@honeyandwaxbooks.com
http://honeyandwaxbooks.com
Contact: Heather O'Donnell
Specialties: Literature, Graphic Design, the Arts

James S. Jaffe Rare Books
442 Montgomery Avenue
P.O. Box 496
Haverford PA   19041
USA

Telephone: (610) 949-4221
Fax: (610) 649-4542
e-mail: jaffebks@pond.com
http://www.literaryfirsts.com
Contact: James Jaffe, Ingrid Lin, Mark Lowe
Specialties: Rare books, literary first editions, poetry, livres d'artistes, association copies, letters and manuscripts, archives.

Jarndyce Antiquarian Booksellers
46, Great Russell Street
Bloomsbury
London WC1B 3PA
England

Telephone: 020 7631 4220
Fax: 020 7631 1882
e-mail: books@jarndyce.co.uk
http://www.jarndyce.co.uk
Contact: Brian Lake, Janet Nassau
Specialties: Specialty: 18th and particularly 19th century English literature and history; Dickens.

Priscilla Juvelis, Inc.
11 Goose Fair
Kennebunkport ME   04046
USA

Telephone: (207) 967-0909
e-mail: pf@juvelisbooks.com
http://www.juvelisbooks.com
Contact: Priscilla Juvelis
Specialties: Book arts, literary first editions

C. R. Johnson Rare Book Collections
4 Keats Grove
London NW3 2RT
England

Telephone: 20 7794-7940
Fax: 20 7433 3303
e-mail: chris@crjohnson.com
http://www.crjohnson.com
Contact: Chris Johnson, Chris Forster

Kaaterskill Books
PO Box 122
East Jewett NY   12424
USA

Telephone: (518) 589-0555
Fax: (518) 589-0555
e-mail: books@katerskillbooks.com
http://www.kaaterskillbooks.com
Contact: Joan Kutcher, Charles Kutcher
Specialties: Americana, Latin Americana, Asia, Art, Books on Books, History, Literature, Religion

The Kelmscott Bookshop
34 W 25th Street
Baltimore MD   21218
USA

Telephone: (410) 235-6810
Fax: (410) 366-9446
e-mail: info@kellmscottbookshop.com
http://www.kelmscottbookshop.com
Specialties: Artists' books, book arts, pre-raphaelites, private and fine press, victorian British literature, William Morris

John W. Knott, Jr., Bookseller
8453 Early Bud Way
Laurel, MD 20723
USA

Telephone: (301) 512-1300
e-mail: jwk@jwkbooks.com
http://www.jwkbooks.com
Contact: John W. Knott, Jr., Warren Bernard
Specialties: Fine first editions in popular fiction, science fiction, fantasy, supernatural and horror, mystery and detective, pulp magazines, letters and manuscripts, WWI – WWII: illustrated, cartoon, children's books & postcards.

Ken Lopez, Bookseller
51 Huntington Rd.
Hadley MA   01035
USA

Telephone: (413) 584-4827
Fax: (413) 584-2045
e-mail: klopez@well.com
http://www.lopezbooks.com
Specialties: Modern literary first editions, literature of the 1960's, Vietnam War, native American literature, nature writing.

Stephen Lupack
449 New Hanover Ave.
Meriden CT 06451
USA

Telephone: (203) 237-9198
e-mail: slupack@cox.net

M & S Rare Books.Inc.
P.O. Box 2594
East Side Station
Providence RI 02906
USA

Telephone: (401) 421-1050
Fax: (401) 272-0831
e-mail: dsiegel@msrarebooks.com
http://www.msrarebooks.com
Contact: Daniel G. Siegel
Specialties: Office hours by appointment

Maggs Bros Ltd.
50 Berkeley Square
London W1J 5BA
England

Telephone: 20 7493 7160
Fax: 20 7499 2007
e-mail: enquiries@maggs.com
http://www.maggs.com

Manhattan Rare Book Company
1050 Second Avenue
Gallery 90
New York NY 10022
USA

Telephone: (212) 326-8907
Fax: (917) 591-8980
e-mail: info@manhattanrarebooks.com
http://manhattanrarebooks.com
Contact: Michael DiRuggiero
Specialties: Literature, History, Culture and Ideas, Science & Technoloby, Art & Photobooks, Illuminated manuscripts

Marlborough Rare Books Ltd.
No, 1 St. Clement's Court
Clements Lane
London EC4N 7HB
England

Telephone: 020 7493 6993
e-mail: sales@mrb-books.co.uk
Contact: Jonathan Gestetner
Specialties: Art & architecture, English literature, early books on fine and applied arts, garden design, history of London.

Mordida Books
P.O. Box 79322
Houston TX 77279
USA

Telephone: (713) 467-4280
Fax: (713) 467-4182
e-mail: rwilson@mordida.com
http://www.mordida.com

Oak Knoll Books
310 Delaware Street
New Castle DE 19720
USA

Telephone: (302) 328-7232
Fax: (302) 328-7274
e-mail: orders@oakknoll.com
http://www.oakknoll.com
Specialties: Bibliography, book collecting, book design, book illustration, book selling, bookbinding, bookplates, fine press books, forgery, libraries, literary criticism, papermaking, printing history, publishing, typography, writing & calligraphy.

Phillip J. Pirages
Fine Books and Manuscripts
P.O. Box 504
2205 Nut Tree Lane
McMinnville OR 97128
USA

Telephone: (503) 472-0476; (800) 962-6666
Fax: (503) 472-5029
e-mail: pirages@onlinemac.com
http://www.pirages.com
Contact: Phil Pirages
Specialties: Early printing, bindings, illuminated manuscripts, illustrated books, private press books.

Bertram Rota Ltd.
31 Long Acre
Covent Garden
London WC2E 9LT
England

Telephone: 020 7836 0723
Fax: 020 7497 9058
e-mail: bertramrota@compuserve.com
http://www.bertramrota.co.uk

Royal Books
32 West 25th Street
Baltimore MD 21218
USA

Telephone: (410) 366-7329
Fax: (443) 524-0942
e-mail: mail@royalbooksonline.com
http://www.royalbooksonline.com
Contact: Kevin Johnson
Specialties: Modern first editions, books on film, jazz and the arts.

Schooner Books Ltd.
5378 Inglis Street
Halifax NSB3H 1J5
Canada

Telephone: (902) 423-8419
Fax: (902) 423-8503
e-mail: SchoonerBooks@schoonerbooks.com
http://www.SchoonerBooks.com
Specialties: Second hand and rare books, antique maps & prints.

Second Life Books, Inc.
P.O. Box 242
55 Quarry Road
Lanesborough MA 01237
USA

Telephone: (413) 447-8010
Fax: (413) 499-1540
e-mail: info@secondlifebooks.com
http://www.secondlifebooks.com

Ed Smith Books
P.O. Box 4785
Rolling Bay WA 98061
USA

Telephone: (206) 780-8168
e-mail: ed@edsbooks.com
http://www.edsbooks.com

Henry Sotheran Limited
Fine and Rare Antiquarian Books & Prints
2 Sackville Street
Piccadilly
London W1S 3DP
England

Telephone: 20 7439 6151
Fax: 20 7434 2019
e-mail: sotherans@sotherans.co.uk
Contact: Andrew McGeachin
Specialties: Fine and rare antiquarian books and prints.

Tavistock Books
1503 Webster Street
Alameda CA 94501
USA

Telephone: (510) 814-0480
Fax: (510) 814-0486
e-mail: vjz@tavbooks.com
http://www.tavbooks.com

Jeff Weber Rare Books
P.O. Box 3368
Glendale CA 91221-0368
USA

Telephone: (323) 344-9332
Fax: (323) 344-9267
e-mail: weberbks@pacbell.net
Contact: Jeff Weber, Linda Weber

Bookman's Price Index

A

A B C Book. New York: Doubleday Page, 1923. Limited to 100 copies signed by artist, C. B. Falls, folio, printed on handmade paper from original wood blocks, boards with color pictorial paste-on, paper worn at joints and spine ends chipped, else tight, clean and very good+, exceedingly rare in this edition.   Aleph-bet Books, Inc.   109 - 173   2015 $8000

A., T.   *Religio Clerici.*   London: for Henry Brome, 1681. 12mo., frontispiece, small piece 55 x 5mm. neatly sliced away from lower margin of l2, minor ink spots just touching fore-edge of G3, G4, E5 and E6, small rust spot to C10 and I7, early 19th century calf, gilt spine, upper joint cracked, lower joint rubbed, corners worn, from the library of James Stevens Cox (1910-1997).   Maggs Bros. Ltd.   1447 - 1   2015   £240

A. E. Farr Ltd.   *A Selection of Civil engineering & building Contracts Complete by A. E. Farr Ltd. Between 1921-1939.*   London: First printed 1939, reprinted, 1950. 4to., half tone plates with captions, original black patterned wrappers, lettered in red.   Marlborough Rare Books   List 53 - 9   2015   £125

Abagnale, Frank W,   *Catch Me If You Can.*   New York: Grosset & Dunlap, 1980. First edition, fine in dust jacket.   Mordida Books   March 2015 - 010110   2015 $275

Abbatius, Baldus Angelius   *De Admirabili Viperae Natura et de Mirificis Eiusdem Facultatibus.*   The Hague: Sam Broun, 1660. Dudodecimo, 186 pages, index engraved titlepage, four wood engraved plates, early papered boards, old library stamp on verso of titlepage, excellent copy, contained in half calf and marbled boards, solander box.   Andrew Isles   2015 - 36425   2015 $1850

Abbe, Dorothy   *The Dwiggins Marionettes, a Complete Experimental Theatre in Miniature.*   New York: Harry N. Abrams, 1970. Small folio, cloth, printed plastic wrappers soiled with wrinkling, photos.   Oak Knoll Books   306 - 18   2015 $100

Abbey, Edward   *Desert Solitaire. A Season in the Wilderness.*   New York: McGraw Hill, 1968. First edition, drawings by Peter Parnall, fine, touch of foxing to top edge, nearly fine dust jacket, crisp copy.   Ed Smith Books   83 - 1   2015 $750

Abbey, Edward   *Slickrock: the Canyon Country of Southeast Utah.*   San Francisco: Sierra Club, 1971. First edition, folio, 67 color photos, maps, owner's name on blank flyleaf, else very fine, pictorial dust jacket, very scarce.   Argonaut Book Shop   Holiday Season 2014 - 1   2015 $350

Abbey, John Roland   *Scenery of Great Britain and Ireland in Aquatint and Lithography 1770-1860. With Life in England. With Travel.*   London: privately printed, 1952. 1953. 1956. 1957. First edition, limited to 500, 400 and 400 copies respectively, 4to., cloth, spine labels, top edge gilt, leather spine labels, dust jackets, many plates in color, jacket of volume one chipped, with spot on front cover, lower corner chipped with spot on front cover, lower corner clipped off of jacket of first volume, unusual to find preserved in jackets.   Oak Knoll Books   306 - 65   2015 $2500

Abbot, Anthony   *The Shudders.*   New York: Farrar & Rinehart, 1943. First edition, some light staining of front and rear channel area, else fine, bright copy in price clipped dust jacket with one small (1/4) closed tear to bottom edge of front panel.   Buckingham Books   March 2015 - 9469   2015 $275

Abbot, Samuel   *The Proceedings and Documents Relative to Certain Members Separating from the Church in Wilton (NH).*   Concord: Isaac Hill, 1824. First edition, 8vo., removed, traces of original dark green wrapper.   M & S Rare Books, Inc.   97 - 210   2015 $100

Abbott, Benjamin   *Cone Cut Corners: the Experiences of a Conservative Family in Fanatical Times.*   New York: Mason Bros., 1855. First edition, 8vo., 456 pages, illustrations, contemporary calf backed marbled boards, text browned, otherwise very nice.   M & S Rare Books, Inc.   97 - 1   2015 $750

Abbott, John S. C.   *The History of Napoleon Bonaparte.*   New York: Harper and Bros., New edition, 4 volumes, green hardcover with gilt lettering on spine and gilt top edge, very good, slight wear, tight, clean text.   Stephen Lupack   March 2015 - 2015 $75

Abbott, Keith   *An American Mystery with Ernest Hemingway, Gertrude Stein & Friends.*   Berkeley: Blue Wind Press, 1979. First edition, #26 of 50 copies, signed by author, fine in red cloth with gold lettering in fine dust jacket.   Ed Smith Books   83 - 2   2015 $75

Abbott, Othman A.   *Recollections of a Pioneer Lawyer.*   published by the Nebraska State Historical Society, 1929. First edition, 8vo., inked presentation inscription from granddaughter of author, red cloth, gold gilt stamped decoration on front cover and titles stamped in gold and gilt on spine, frontispiece, illustrations, fine.   Buckingham Books   March 2015 - 36908   2015 $300

Abdullah, Achmed *The Honourable Gentleman and Others.* New York: Putnam, 1919. First edition, fine in very good dust jacket with slightly faded spine, chips at spine ends, small chip on front panel, couple of chips on back panel, few tiny tears.   Mordida Books   March 2015 - 012689   2015 $300

Abell, William *A True Discovery of the Protectors of the Wine Project, Out of the Vintners Owne orders made at Their Common Hall Whereby it Clearley Appeares that This Project was Contrived at Vintners Hall by the drawing Vintners of London...*   London: Thomas Walkley, 1641. First edition, small 4to., titlepage shaved at head and some loss to first line dampstaining to lower corner sof C3-4 and D1-2, early 20th century half calf and marbled boards, boards slightly faded, from the library of James Stevens Cox (1910-1997).   Maggs Bros. Ltd.   1447 - 2   2015   £750

Abercrombie, Lascelles *The Art of Wordsworth.*   London: Oxford University Press, 1952. Original red cloth, slightly spotted and torn dust jacket, Geoffrey Tillotson's signed copy with correspondence with Frederick Page, review cutting &c., pencil notes.   Jarndyce Antiquarian Booksellers CCVII - 575   2015   £20

Abraham H. Maslow: a Memorial Volume.   Monterey: Brooks/Cole, 1972. First edition, hardcover, fine, photos, handsome slipcased volume.   Beasley Books   2013 - 2015 $45

Abraham, R. M. *Winter Nights Entertainments.*   New York: Dutton, 1933. Later printing?, very good, owner's bookplate.   Beasley Books   2013 - 2015 $125

Abrams, Meyer Howard *The Milk of Paradise: The Effect of Opium Visions on the Works of De Quincey, Crabbe, Francis Thompson and Coleridge.*   Cambridge: Harvard University Press, 1934. First edition, one of 300 copies, 8vo., original decorated wrappers with printed paper label on upper wrapper, fine.   The Brick Row Book Shop Miscellany 67 - 1   2015 $300

Abramson, Harold A. *The Use of LSD in Psychotherapy and Alcoholism.*   Indianapolis: Bobbs Merrill, 1967. First edition, large 8vo., some offsetting to endpapers from news clippings, otherwise near fine in very good+ jacket with tiny tears at spine ends.   Beasley Books   2013 - 2015 $45

Abridgment of the New Testament; or the Life Miracles and Death of Our Lord and Saviour Jesus Christ.   Glasgow: Lumsden, n.d. circa, 1815. 24mo., grey wrappers, 8 full page illustrations. 16 very fine etchings printed in red, beautiful copy.   Aleph-bet Books, Inc.   109 - 153   2015 $200

An Abstraction of the Accounts of the Overseers of Dorking from the 28th of March 1824 to the 27th of March 1825... Dorking Langley: n.d.?, 1825. 8vo., recent marbled boards lettered on spine, very good, apparently very rare.   John Drury Rare Books   March 2015 - 24518   2015 $221

Abstraction Creation Art Non figuratif 1 1932. Paris: Editions les Tendances Nouvelles, 1932. 4to., wrappers, handsome, very good+ to near fine, tiny chip at foot of spine.   Beasley Books   2013 - 2015 $500

Abstraction Creation Art Non figuratif 2 1933. Paris: Association Abstraction Creation, 1933. 4to., wrappers, very good+ to near fine with just little darkening to spine and edges.   Beasley Books   2013 - 2015 $500

Abstraction Creation Art Non figuratif 3 1934. Paris: Association Abstraction Creation, 1934. 4to., wrappers, very good+ to near fine with little darkening to spine and 1/16 inch chip at foot of spine, upper right corner slightly bumped.   Beasley Books   2013 - 2015 $500

Academy of Dramatic Art *Memorandum and Articles of Association of the Academy of Dramatic Art Registered the 5th Day of December 1913.*   London: 1913. Folio, original cloth backed printed card covers, fine.   John Drury Rare Books   2015 - 19349   2015 $133

Acconci, Vito Hannibal *Double Bubble. Poems by Vito Hannibale Acconci and E. Lagomarsino.*   New York: E. Lagomarsino, 1966. First edition, 24 pages, original paper wrappers, fine, rare in commerce.   Maggs Bros. Ltd. Gathering of 26 Countercultural items Oct. 2013 - 4   2015   £2500

An Account of the Culture of Potatoes in Ireland.   London: Shepperson and Reynolds, 1796. First edition, 8vo., 28 pages, some general paper browning, final page little soiled, rebound recently in marbled boards, spine lettered, very good, surprisingly rare.   John Drury Rare Books 2015 - 25552   2015 $1049

Accum, Frederick *A Treatise on the Art of making Wine from Native Fruits...*   London: Longman &c, 1823. Second edition, 12mo., engraved vignette on titlepage, half title and final 24 pages of reviews of Accum books, original boards, rebacked and restored, uncut, very good, contemporary signature of Robert Ridsdale 1828.   John Drury Rare Books 2015 - 23552   2015 $699

Ackermann, Rudolph 1764-1834 *A History of the University of Cambridge.* London: printed for R. Ackermann, 1815. First edition, 2 volumes, 4to., 95 hand colored aquatint or stipple engraved plates and one uncoloured engraved portrait, some offsetting of plates onto text, good and complete copy with portraits of founders and list of plates, which is usually missing, contemporary full russia gilt, border of a 'cathedral' roll with similar corner fans of gothic tracery in blind, spines with five wide bands, lettered in two panels, other panels tooled in gilt marbled edges, some minor cracking to joints and spines, sunned, unsigned by very redolent of workshop of Taylor & Hessey, tall copy of splendid book. Marlborough Rare Books List 54 - 9 2015 £3500

Ad-----l M----ws's Conduct in the Late engagement Vindcated. London: M. Cooper, 1745. First edition, 8vo., recent plain wrapper, very good. John Drury Rare Books 2015 - 20407 2015 $177

Adair, James Makittrick *Curious Facts and Anecdotes, Not contained in the Memoirs of Philip Thickness, esq. Formerly Gunner of Landguard Fort and Now Censor General of Great Britain, Professor of Empiricism and Animal Mangetism....* London: J. Ridgway, 1790. Only edition, 8vo., engraved frontispiece, although now supplied in excellent facsimile, bound recently in marbled wrappers with printed label on upper cover, fault apart a very good copy, very rare. John Drury Rare Books March 2015 - 24038 2015 £306

Adair, Robert *The Declaration of England Against the Acts and Projects of the Holy Alliance.* London: James Ridgway, 1821. First edition, 8vo., recent marbled boards lettered on spine, very good. John Drury Rare Books March 2015 - 24416 2015 £266

Adam, William *Observations respecting the further extension of Trial by Jury to Scotland in Civil Causes.* Edinburgh: printed by J. Hay and Co., 1819. First edition, 8vo., recent marbled boards lettered on spine, very good, scarce. John Drury Rare Books March 2015 - 24523 2015 £266

Adam, William *A Treatise and Observations on Trial by Jury in Civil Causes as Now Incorporated with the Jurisdiction of the Court of Session.* Edinburgh: Thoms Clark, 1836. First edition, 8vo., recently rebound in half leather, marbled boards, lettered gilt on spine, 5 raised bands, all edges gilt, from the library of the Dukes of Bedford with 2 page signed letter dated 1836 to the then Duke from William Adam tipped in, slight foxing to prelims, otherwise sound, clean, near fine. Any Amount of Books March 2015 - A71748 2015 £325

Adams, Ansel *Examples. The Making of 40 Photographs.* Boston: NYGS/Little Brown, 1983. First edition, 4to., fine in fine dust jacket. Beasley Books 2013 - 2015 $40

Adams, Ansel *These We Inherit. the Parklands of America.* San Francisco: Sierra Club, 1962. First edition, folio, 42 black and white photos, blue cloth, very fine, pictorial dust jacket (tiny tear to bottom edge). Argonaut Book Shop Holiday Season 2014 - 2 2015 $125

Adams, Ansel *Yosemite and the Range of Light.* Boston: New York Graphic Society, 1979. First edition, 2nd printing, boldly signed by Adams under half title, oblong folio, frontispiece, 116 halftones, blue cloth, red cloth, gilt, minor little surface rub mark to front cover, else very fine, boldly signed by Adams under half title. Argonaut Book Shop Holiday Season 2014 - 3 2015 $400

Adams, Charles Francis *An Address on the Occasion of Opening the New town Hall in Braintree (Mass.) July 29 1858.* Boston: William Smith, 1858. First edition, 8vo., original front printed wrapper (only), lightly soiled, spine partly perished, internally clean, about very good, lacks map. M & S Rare Books, Inc. 97 - 2 2015 $85

Adams, Daniel *The Medical and Agricultural Register for the Years 1806 and 1807.* Boston: Loring and Manning et al, 1806-1807. Volume 1 #1-24, all published, contemporary leather backed boards, front endpaper little loose, otherwise nice, tight copy, scarce. Second Life Books Inc. 190 - 1 2015 $400

Adams, Frank R. *Arizona Feud.* Garden City: Doubleday Doran, 1941. First edition, fine in dust jacket. Mordida Books March 2015 - 000067 2015 $100

Adams, Hannah *An Abridgment of the History of New England for the Use of Young Persons...* Boston: Etheridge & Bliss, 1807. Second edition, 8vo., contemporary calf, chipped leather label, leaves toned, but very good. Second Life Books Inc. 189 - 2 2015 $150

Adams, Herbert *The Golf House Murder.* Philadelphia: Lippincott, 1933. First edition, spine slightly darkened and light fraying at top of spine, otherwise near fine without dust jacket. Mordida Books March 2015 - 007453 2015 $100

Adams, Herbert *The Secret of Bogey House.* London: Methuen, 1924. First edition, fine, some scattered light spotting on fore-edge and on prelims, otherwise fine. Mordida Books March 2015 - 011340 2015 $450

Adams, Herbert *Signal for Invasion.* London: Collins - The Crime Club, 1942. First edition, 8vo., 192 pages, original publisher's orange cloth, lettered black on spine, from the Donald Rudd collection of detective fiction, rare, especially in dust jacket, one closed tear and very slight chipping at spine ends and very slightly edge worn, decent copy. Any Amount of Books 2015 - C8632 2015 £150

Adams, Jane *The Greenway.* London: Macmillan, 1995. First edition, very fine in dust jacket, signed by author. Mordida Books   March 2015 - 000004   2015 $95

Adams, Leonie *Those Not Elect.* New York: Robert M. McBride, 1925. First edition, one of just 10 copies on Inges paper which are not for sale, signed by author, 8vo., 50 pages, little soiled, paper over boards, near fine,.   Second Life Books Inc.   189 - 3   2015 $700

Adams, Samuel Hopkins *Average Jones.* Bobbs Merrill Co., 1911. First edition, cloth, lightly rubbed at fore edge of front panel, else near fine, clean copy, lacking elusive dust jacket, uncommon.   Buckingham Books   March 2015 - 33285   2015 $750

Adams, Tomas R. *English Maritime Books Printed Before 1801 Relating to Ships Their Construction and Their Operation at Sea.* Providence and Greenwich: John Carter Brown Library and the National Maritime Museum, 1995. First edition, 4to., very slightly rubbed at corners, otherwise fine hardback.   Any Amount of Books   2015 - A922914   2015   £280

Addams, Jane *Twenty Years at Hull-House.* New York: Macmillan, 1910. Autograph edition, limited to 210 signed copies, this no. 107, recased with new endpapers, recased with new endpapers, small 4to., original vellum spine and paper covered boards with gilt lettered spine and front cover, top edge gilt, mild cover edgewear, small 4to, scarce. By the Book, L. C. Special List 10 - 40   2015 $1000

Addey, Markinfield *The Life and Military Career of Thomas Jonathan Jackson, Lieutenant General in the Confederate Army.* New York: 1863. First edition, 12mo, 240 pages, old damp spot to cover front and small abrasion to top of backstrip, bookplate removed, two inner cancelled library stamps, no outside marks, possible CSA soldier signature.   Bookworm & Silverfish   2015 - 5331828264   2015 $175

Addison, Alexander *Reports of Cases in the County Courts of the Fifth Circuit and in the High Court of Errors & Appeals of the State of Pennsylvania and Charges to Grand Juries of Those County Courts.* Washington: John Colerick and May, 1800. First edition, new covers, contemporary spine and label.   M & S Rare Books, Inc.   97 - 107   2015 $750

Addison, Henry Robert *Recollections of an Irish Police Magistrate.* London: John & Robert Maxwell, circa, 1885. Initial ad leaf, 6 pages ads, 'yellowback', original yellow printed paper boards, rubbed and little worn with some glueing to head and tail of spine, good, sound copy.   Jarndyce Antiquarian Booksellers   CCXI - 1   2015   £120

Addison, Joseph 1672-1719 *A Letter from Italy, to the Right Honourable Charles, Lord Halifax...* London: printed and sold by H. Hills, 1709. First separate edition, 8vo., disbound, some soiling first and last leaves detached.   C. R. Johnson   Foxon R-Z - 1211r-z   2015 $38

Addison, Joseph 1672-1719 *The Letters...* Oxford: Clarendon Press, 1941. Half title, frontispiece, plate, original maroon cloth, Geoffrey Tillotson's copy with some pencil and ink notes, typescript review by Donald Bond and contrasting printed review by Marjorie Williams with card from her and from Harold Williams about review.   Jarndyce Antiquarian Booksellers   CCVII - 1   2015   £30

An Address to the Electors of England. London: M. Cooper, 1758. Only edition, 8vo., 54 pages, modern unlettered wrappers, very good, scarce.   John Drury Rare Books   March 2015 - 16190   2015 $221

An Address to the Inhabitants of Great Britain: Occasioned by the Late Earthquake at Lisbon. London: printed for J. Buckland, T. Field, E. Dilly and J. Robinson..., 1755. First edition, 8vo., well bound recently in linen backed marbled boards lettered, very good, rare.   John Drury Rare Books   March 2015 - 19399   2015   £306

An Address to the Proprietors of Bank Stock, the London and country Bankers and the Public in General, on the Affairs of the Bank of England. London: Saunders and Otley, 1828. First edition, 8vo., recent cloth backed marbled boards with morocco label on upper cover lettered gilt, very good.   John Drury Rare Books   March 2015 - 25608   2015   £306

An Address to the Public, in Behalf of the Association among Protestant Schoolmasters in the North of England for the Support of their aged brethren, widows and orphans... Newcastle: printed by M. Angus Drury Lane...., 1788. Probably second edition, 8vo., well bound fairly recently in marbled boards, spine lettered on a paper label, very good. John Drury Rare Books   2015 - 26134   2015 $874

The Addresses, Squibs and Other Publications, Issued by all Parties During the Late Election for the Borough of Boston. Also a Correct copy of the poll book as taken on Tuesday and Wednesday the 7th and 18th of March 1820. Boston: printed and sold by Jackson, 1820. First edition, 8vo., well bound in mid 20th century maroon cloth with printed title labels, very good, rare.   John Drury Rare Books   March 2015 - 23477   2015   £306

Ade, George *Fables in Slang.* Toronto: George J. McLeod, 1900. Half title, double page illustrated title, illustrations, uncut in original decorated mustard cloth, dulled and slightly rubbed, hinges slightly weak, ownership stamp. Jarndyce Antiquarian Booksellers   CCXI - 2   2015   £40

Adey, Robert *Locked Room Murders and Other Impossible Crimes: a Comprehensive Bibliography.* Minneapolis & San Francisco: Crossover Press, 1991. First edition, large 8vo., original grey cloth lettered red on spine and cover, signed by author, issued without dust jacket. Any Amount of Books 2015 - C4966 2015 £240

Adirondack Sutra. Canton: Caliban Press, 2013. Artist's book, one of 48 copies, all on various handmade papers, mostly from La Papeterie St. Armand, initialled and numbered by publisher, Mark McMurray on colophon, 12 3/4 x 3 15/16 inches, some smaller, 50 pages, 25 leaves, plus 2 pages, text printed from metal and wood types in Caliban Press collection, many of the papers used have been dyed, dipped and or floated in an indigo dye bath, done with the assistance of Velma Bolyard. Priscilla Juvelis - Rare Books 61 - 2 2015 $375

Adler, Carl *Souvenir of Baker City, Oregon.* Baker City: Carl Adler and Brooklyn: The Albertype Co., circa, 1905. Assumed first edition, oblong silver stamped and cord tied hardbound, 5 3/8 x 7 1/4 inches, 15 photogravure images, one folding, wear to top and bottom of spine and very moderately so to other extremities, good+, rare. Baade Books of the West 2014 - 2015 $208

Adrian, Arthur A. *Georgina Hogarth and the Dickens Circle.* London: Oxford University Press, 1957. First edition, half title, frontispiece, plates, original yellow cloth, purple label, dulled and slightly marked, Kathleen Tillotson's copy with notes, given her by OUP. Jarndyce Antiquarian Booksellers CCVII - 204 2015 £30

Aeolus; or the Constitutional Politician. London: printed for S. Bladon, 1770. First and only edition, 8vo., half title, late 19th century half calf over marbled boards, some wear, particularly to corners, upper joint cracked but sound, good copy, rare. John Drury Rare Books 2015 - 25089 2015 $1136

Aeschylus *Aeschyll Tragoediae, ad Optimorum Librorum Fidem Recensuit...* Lipsiae: Sumtibus Frid. Chr. Guil. Vogelii, 1823. 1824. First edition thus, octavo, 2 volumes bound in 1, 19th century full calf with raised bands, gilt decoration to spine, gilt armorial crest on each cover covers little scuffed in places, spine slightly faded, very good. Peter Ellis, Bookseller 2014 - 019626 2015 £285

Aesopus *The Fables of Aesop.* London: Hodder and Stoughton, n.d., 1909. First edition, presumable second issue, no gilt on cover and plain endpapers, Thick 4to., pictorial cloth stamped in colors, fine in publisher's box, very good, some soil, rubbing and flaps repaired, 23 magnificent tipped in color plates by Edmund Detmold, mounted on heavy stock, plus black and whites in text, grey copy, rarely found with box. Aleph-bet Books, Inc. 109 - 123 2015 $1650

Afterem, George *Silken Threads.* Boston: Cupples Upham, 1885. First edition, some wear along edges, otherwise very good in green cloth covered boards with gilt titles. Mordida Books March 2015 - 008921 2015 $200

Agassiz, Louis 1807-1873 *An Introduction to the Study of Natural History in a Series of Lectures Delivered in the Hall of the College of Physicians and Surgeons, New York.* New York: Greeley & McElrath, 1847. First edition, 8vo., 58 pages, printed in double columns, scores of small text illustrations, removed, corners of title browned, sheets of first half of text lightly browned, very good. M & S Rare Books, Inc. 97 - 200 2015 $150

Agassiz, Louis 1807-1873 *On Extraordinary Fishes from California.* New Haven: B. L. Hamlen, printer to Yale College, 1853. First separate edition, 8vo., 12 pages, original printed wrappers. M & S Rare Books, Inc. 97 - 7 2015 $100

Agee, James 1909-1955 *James Agee: Let Us Now Praise Famous Men, A Death in the Family, & Shorter Fiction.* New York: Library of America, 2005. First edition thus, small 8vo., fine in fine dust jacket. Beasley Books 2013 - 2015 $40

Agee, James 1909-1955 *Permit Me Voyage.* New Haven: Yale University Press, 1934. First edition, scarce first book, tipped to front free endpaper is slip of paper inscribed note from Stephen Vincent Benet for Miss Locke, spine little faded, inch deep strip at top of back cover faded as well, otherwise near fine. James S. Jaffe Rare Books Modern American Poetry - 1 2015 $1,250

Agricola, Georgius *De Re Metallica.* London: The Mining Magazine, 1912. Facsimile reprint of 1556 edition, no. 2175 of 3000 copies, large 4to., original vellum boards, lettered black on spine, some soiling, scuffing and marking to boards with scarring at rear board and light foxing to endpapers not affecting text, otherwise sound, used, very good minus copy. Any Amount of Books 2015 - C13330 2015 £275

Ahlback, Tore *Old Norse and Finnish Religions and Celtic Place-Names: Based on Papers Read at the Symposium on Encounters Between Religions in Old Nordic Times ....* Abo & Stockholm: Donner Institute for Research in Religious and Cultural History, Almquvist & Wiksell International, 1990. First edition, wrappers, large 8vo., 507 pages, original white wrappers, lettered black on spine and covers, fine in very good+ dust jacket. Any Amount of Books March 2015 - C4792 2015 £350

Aickman, Robert *Sub Rosa: Strange Tales.* London: Victor Gollancz, 1966. First edition, 8vo., original maroon cloth lettered gilt on spine, fine in very good+ dust jacket, very slightly rubbed at edges with one short closed tear and no loss. Any Amount of Books 2015 - A99780 2015 £225

Aiken, Conrad *Blue Voyage.* New York: Scribner's, 1927. First edition, limited issue, one of 125 numbered copies signed by author, 8vo., decorated endpapers, original cloth backed textured paper over boards, top edge gilt, publisher's slipcase, top and bottom edges lightly rubbed from slipcase, otherwise fine.   James S. Jaffe Rare Books   Modern American Poetry - 2 2015 $175

Aiken, P. F. *A Comparative View of the Constitutions of Great Britain and the United States of America in Six Lectures.*   London: Longman and Co., Hamilton Adams and Co., 1842. First edition, 8vo., original green cloth lettered gilt on spine, few scattered white marks to covers, otherwise very good with some light wear, presentation copy from Thomas Kington to Alexis de Tocqueville, very good with some light wear.   Any Amount of Books   2015 - C16194 2015   £160

Aikin, Arthur *An Address Delivered on the 27th of May 1817 at the Annual Distribution by the Hands of His Royal Highness the Duke of Sussex &c...*   London: printed by T. Woodfall, Assistant Secretary to the Society, 1817. First edition, 8vo., titlepage rather foxed and dust soiled, with 'wine glass' ring at foot otherwise good copy in fairly recent cloth backed boards, rare.   John Drury Rare Books   March 2015 - 21059 2015   £266

Aikin, John   1747-1822 *Vie de Jean Howard. Celebre Philanthrope Anglais ou Caractere et Services Publics de Ce Bienfaiteur des Prisonniers.*   Paris: chez le Directeur de la Decade Philosophique, 1796. First edition in French, 8vo., half title, contemporary sheep backed boards, spine fully gilt and labelled but worn, good copy nonetheless.   John Drury Rare Books   March 2015 - 23283   2015 $266

Ainsworth, William Harrison   1805-1882 *Crichton.* London: Richard Bentley, 1837-1849. First edition, 3 volumes, half titles, extra illustrated with engraved portrait, engraved title and 17 plates by Phiz, small tear to upper corner of pages 127-28 volume I, plates trimmed close, partly uncut in slightly later full brown rushed morocco by Morrell, triple ruled gilt borders, raised bands, gilt compartments and dentelles, all edges gilt, handsome copy.   Jarndyce Antiquarian Booksellers   CCXI - 3   2015   £450

Ainsworth, William Harrison   1805-1882 *Hilary St. Ives.* London: George Routledge & Sons, 1881. Illustrations by Frederick Gilbert, contemporary half red roan, spine faded and slightly rubbed, bookplate with crest of A. J. Constable over another, from the library of Geoffrey & Kathleen Tillotson.   Jarndyce Antiquarian Booksellers   CCVII - 2 2015   £20

Ainsworth, William Harrison   1805-1882 *Merry England; or Nobles and Serfs.*   London: published by Tinsley Brothers, 1874. First edition, 8vo., 16 page publisher's catalog dated March 1873 at end of volume 2 and four page catalog at end of volume 3, the 3 volumes in highly attractive navy blue half leather, marbled boards, raised bands at spine which are richly gilt decorated, top edge gilt, binding by Bickers, original grass green cloth covers and spines laid in on 3 pages at rear of each volume, showing this to be first state with spelling 'Merry' on spines, bright very good+ set in slightly rubbed and slightly scuffed at corners and text very slightly browned.   Any Amount of Books   2015 - A40494   2015   £175

Airship Panorama Book.   London and New York: Nister & Dutton, n.d. circa, 1910. Oblong 4to., cloth backed pictorial boards, slightest bit of cover rubbing, else fine, 4 fabulous pop-up pages, rarely found in such nice intact condition. Aleph-Bet Books, Inc.   108 - 358   2015 $2750

Aitken, Richard *The Oxford Companion to Australian Gardens.*   South Melbourne: Oxford University Press, 2002. First edition, large 8vo. black and white illustrations, very good+ in like dust jacket with slight abrasion to front. Any Amount of Books   2015 - A91005   2015   £150

Aken, David *Pioneers of the Black Hills or Gordon's Stockdale Party of 1874.*   Allied Printing, n.d. circa, 1911. First edition, 16mo., pictorial wrappers, frontispiece, illustrations, little light soiling, else near fine.   Buckingham Books   March 2015 - 34502   2015 $275

Akins, Zoe *The Hills Grow Smaller.*   New York: Harper, 1937. First edition, decorated boards, worn at spine ends, otherwise near fine.   Stephen Lupack   March 2015 - 2015 $60

Akweks, Aren *Migration of the Iroquois.*   Hogansburg: Akwesasne Mohawk Counselor Organization, 1947. First edition, edge sunned, otherwise near fine in stapled wrappers.   Ken Lopez, Bookseller   164 - 151   2015 $300

Akwesasne Notes.   Rooseveltown: Mohawk Nation, 1980. First edition, 24 issues, year/copies - 1970/2, 71/4, 72/5, 3/6 (complete), 77/1, 78/2, 79/3, 80/1.   Beasley Books   2013 - 2015 $250

Al-Furat, Ibn *Ayyubids Mamlukes and Crusaders: Selections from the Tarikh Al-Duwal Wa'l Muluk of....* Cambridge: W. Heffer and Sons, 1971. First edition, 2 volumes, large 8vo., original red cloth lettered gilt on spine, fine in clean, very good dust jackets with some fading.   Any Amount of Books   2015 - A96286   2015   £300

Alabone, Edwin William *Poly-Cyclo-Epicycloidal and Other Geometric Curves.* London: John Swain & Son 89-90 Shoe Lane Fleet Street E.C., 1912. Second edition, royal 8vo., half tone portrait, 86 colored plates, original decorative red cloth, upper cover lettered gilt, gilt edges, presentation from author to Dr. L. L. Lake.   Marlborough Rare Books   List 54 - 1   2015   £800

Alba, Nanina *The Parchments II. A book of verse.* N.P.: Tuskegee? Nanina Alba, 1967. First edition, octavo, stapled printed wrappers, modest age toning and soiling on wrappers, very good or better, signed by author and dated in year of publication.   Between the Covers Rare Books   197 - 3   2015 $200

Albee, Edward *Who's Afraid of Virginia Woolf?* New York: Atheneum, 1962. First edition, wrapper issue, signed by author, very good with some light wear and creases to spine, wrapper lightly toned, includes promo flyer from Albee's talk and signing at NY Times Speaker Series.   B & B Rare Books, Ltd.   234 - 1   2015 $650

Albert, Neil *The January Corpse.* New York: Walker, 1991. First edition, very fine in dust jacket.   Mordida Books   March 2015 - 008194   2015 $100

Alberti, Rafael *Selected Poems.* New York: New Directions, 1944. First edition, wrappers, fine in fine dust jacket.   Beasley Books   2013 - 2015 $45

Alberti, Rafael *Sobre los Angeles.* Buenos Aires: Editorial Losada, 1962. One of 400 numbered copies, this copy numbered 189, folio, near fine in like dust jacket, lovely copy with tiny bumps at spine ends, very good slipcase.   Beasley Books   2013 - 2015 $350

Albin, Eleazar *A Natural History of Insects.* London: printed for the author and sold by William and John Innys, 1720. First edition, 100 hand colored engraved plates, plates colored by watercolors, plate number 84 with one butterfly heightened in gold, quarto, original decorative red morocco, rebacked and recornered, boards and spine beautifully ruled in and tooled in gilt, spine lettered gilt, gilt dentelles, all edges gilt, newer Dutch patterned gold endpapers, inner hinges reinforced with repair, bit of light offsetting and one, one of the prelim blanks with two inch closed tear, professionally repaired, clean and handsome.   Heritage Book Shop   Holiday 2014 - 1   2015 $7500

Albright, Horace M. *The Birth of the National Park Service. The Founding Years 1913-1933.* Salt Lake City: Howe Bros., 1985. First edition, photos, early engravings, blue cloth lettered in silver, very fine with pictorial dust jacket.   Argonaut Book Shop   Holiday Season 2014 - 7   2015 $45

Alciati, Andrea *Andreae Alciati. V. C. Emeblemata.* Lugduni: Apud Aeredes Gulielmi Rouilli, 1614. 8vo., red and black titlepage, separate titlepage after page 704, with same printer's device as first, 211 woodcut emblems, contemporary full calf, spine with four raised bands decorated gilt with heraldic devices, early handwritten paper labels on spine, earlyish ownership stamps and other marks on front endpapers, few tiny early words inked on titlepage, few small ink blots to some pages, otherwise excellent, clean copy, sturdily bound.   Any Amount of Books   2015 - C13997   2015   £750

Alcoholics Anonymous. the Story of How More than One Hundred Men Have Recovered from Alcoholism. New York: Works Pub. Co., 1939. First edition, one of approximately 500 copies, large octavo, publisher's original bright red cloth, front board and spine lettered gilt, fine, bright, crisp, square and completely unused, pristine, near fine dust jacket with several short closed tears at top of spine, one tear at base of spine hat has been reinforced from inside with tape and minor loss at corners.   Heritage Book Shop   Holiday 2014 - 2   2015 $40,000

Alcott, Louisa May   1832-1888 *Aunt Jo's Scrap-Book.* Boston: Roberts, 1842. First edition, 12mo., inserted double frontispiece, rubbing at extremities of spine, contemporary inscription on flyleaf, blue cloth, stamped in gilt, very good, tight copy.   Second Life Books Inc. March 2015 - 191   2015 $250

Alcott, Louisa May   1832-1888 *Flower Fables.* Boston: Briggs, 1855. First edition, 6 wood engravings, 12mo., brown cloth stamped in blind and gilt, cloth little dust marked and lacks bit of cloth at extremities of spine, some light stains on endpapers, very good, usually found in rough condition, rare.   Second Life Books Inc.   189 - 4   2015 $2000

Alcott, Louisa May   1832-1888 *Good Wives: a Story for Girls.* London: Ward Lock & Tyler, 1871? First English edition, 12mo., 313 pages, contemporary calf backed marbled boards, repeated ink inscriptions dated May 22 (18) 72, early ownership, inscribed by Warren to Ticknor.   M & S Rare Books, Inc.   97 - 8   2015 $450

Alcott, Louisa May   1832-1888 *Old Fashioned Thanksgiving (in) St. Nicholas Magazine Volume 9 Part 1 - November 1881 - May 1882.* New York: Century Co., 1881-1882. 4to., three quarter leather and cloth, near fine, with the first appearance of this story, heavily illustrated in black and white.   Aleph-bet Books, Inc.   109 - 15   2015 $500

Alcott, Louisa May   1832-1888 *Under the Lilacs.* Boston: Roberts Brothers, 1878. First edition, 12mo. dark tan pictorial cloth, binding slightly leaning else very good+, 4 black and white plates.   Aleph-bet Books, Inc.   109 - 16   2015 $600

Alcott, Louisa May 1832-1888 *Under the Lilacs.* Boston: Roberts, 1878. First edition, 8vo., frontispiece, 3 illustrations inserted, brown cloth stamped in black and bright gilt, several fascicles starting to pull a bit, some very little rubbing to hinges, little rubbed at extremities of spine, former owner's name in pencil on endpaper, very good plus. Second Life Books Inc. 191 - 3 2015 $300

Aldan, Daisy *Folder 4.* New York: Tiber Press, 1956. First edition, folder with parts laid-in, covers some soiled, internally very good with Felix Pasilis Serigraph "Still Life" laid in. Second Life Books Inc. 191 - 4 2015 $85

Aldin, Cecil *Dogs of Character.* London & New York: Eyre & Spottiswoode and Charles Scribner, 1927. Limited to only 250 numbered copies, signed and with drawing, 4to., quarter vellum and printed white boards, all edges gilt, slight bit of cover soil, fine, 7 full page illustrations, 70 large partial page illustrations and 2 color plates. Aleph-bet Books, Inc. 109 - 17 2015 $2000

Aldin, Cecil *Merry Puppy Book.* London: Henry Frowde & Hodder & Stoughton, n.d. circa, 1913. First edition, 4to., cloth backed pictorial boards, slightest bit of edge rubbing, fine and bright, 36 full page color illustrations plus numerous black and whites, great copy, rare. Aleph-bet Books, Inc. 109 - 18 2015 $1200

Aldington, Richard *Love and the Luxembourg.* New York: Covici Friede, 1930. First edition, one of 475 numbered copies signed by author and designer, Frederic Warde, title vignette printed in green, original red cloth gilt, top edge gilt, others uncut, spine trifle dulled, very nice in marked and somewhat worn slipcase, from the collection of Gavin H. Fryer. Bertram Rota Ltd. 308 Part II - 124 2015 £30

Aldington, Richard *Soft Answers: Stories.* London: Chatto & Windus, 1932. First edition, cloth little marked and bumped, spine faded, otherwise nice, inscription on front free endpaper and bookseller's small label on front pastedown, from the collection of Gavin H. Fryer. Bertram Rota Ltd. 308 Part II - 125 2015 £20

Aldiss, Brian W. *An Age.* London: Faber and Faber, 1967. First edition, octavo, cloth. John W. Knott, Bookseller Selected New Arrivals Jan. 2015 - 16873 2015 $125

Aldiss, Brian W. *The Helliconia Trilogy: Helliconia Spring; Helliconia Summer; and Helliconia Winter.* London: Jonathan Cape, 1982-1985. First British edition, 3 volumes, boards, each volume signed by Aldiss. John W. Knott, Bookseller Selected New Arrivals Jan. 2015 - 16875 2015 $350

Aldiss, Brian W. *Hothouse.* London: Faber & Faber, 1962. First edition, octavo, cloth, signed by author. John W. Knott, Bookseller Selected New Arrivals Jan. 2015 - 16872 2015 $1250

Aldiss, Brian W. *Non-Stop.* London: Faber and Faber, 1958. First edition, octavo, board. John W. Knott, Bookseller Selected New Arrivals Jan. 2015 - 16871 2015 $950

Aldiss, Brian W. *Trillion Year Spree: the History of Science Fiction.* London: Victor Gollancz Ltd., 1986. First edition, octavo, boards. John W. Knott, Bookseller Selected New Arrivals Jan. 2015 - 16877 2015 $65

Aldrich, T. B. *The Stillwater Tragedy.* Boston: Houghton Mifflin, 1880. First edition, very nice, bright copy, hardcover. Beasley Books 2013 - 2015 $45

Alembert, Jean Lerond D' 1717-1783 *Miscellaneous Pieces in Literature, History and Philosophy.* printed for C. Henderson, 1764. First edition in English, uniformly slightly browned, few spots and stains, last leaf torn at upper inner corner (caused by adhesion of free endpaper), 8vo. modern marbled boards, stamp of Lynn Free Pub. Library on title, accession number ink on verso with note 'Auction, Leonard's June 1879', accession number repeated at head of text, few 19th century pencil notes, good. Blackwell's Rare Books B179 - 1 2015 £750

Alembert, Jean Lerond D' 1717-1783 *Melanges de Litterature, d'Histoire, et de Philosophie.* Leiden: Brothers Murray, 1783. New edition, 5 volumes, 12mo., contemporary speckled calf, gilt rules on either side of raised bands on spines, contrasting lettering pieces, initial "CVK" in gilt on black strip at foot of spines, red edges, little trivial damage to leather, very good, attractive copy, scarce edition. Blackwell's Rare Books B179 - 2 2015 £500

Alexander, Arabel Wilbur *Light through Darkened Windows.* Cincinnati: Jennings & Pye, 1901. First edition, very good+ to near fine. Beasley Books 2013 - 2015 $45

Alexander, Edwin P. *Down at the Depot. American Railroad Stations from 1831 to 1920.* New York: Bramhall House, 1970. Later printing, quarto, 320 pages, black and white photos, elevations and floor plans, half cloth and boards, upper edge of boards bit faded, very good, tattered pictorial dust jacket. Argonaut Book Shop Holiday Season 2014 - 8 2015 $40

Alexander, Franz *Psychoanalytic Pioneers.* New York: Basic Books, 1966. First edition, fine in lightly used dust jacket. Beasley Books 2013 - 2015 $45

Alexander, William Lindsay *A Discourse on the Qualities and Worth of Thomas Chalmers...* Edinburgh: John D. Lowe, 1847. First edition, 8vo., wanting half title, recently well bound in linen backed marbled boards lettered, good, uncommon.   John Drury Rare Books   2015 - 18497   2015 $133

Alexie, Sherman *"Architecture" in Black Bear Review Issue 9.* Croyden: Black Bear Publications, 1989. Very faintly sunned, near fine in wrappers.   Ken Lopez, Bookseller   164 - 152   2015 $125

Alexie, Sherman *Indian Killer.* New York: Atlantic, 1996. First edition, very fine in dust jacket, signed by author.   Mordida Books   March 2015 - 002488   2015 $100

Alfieri, Bruno *Pagina: International Review of Graphic design 5.* Milano: Socita Italiana de Grafica, 1964. Text in English, Italian and French, 4to. stiff paper wrappers, tipped in lithographed tin sheet, originally used in printing tests for product labels, table of contents, illustrations, mostly black and white but some in color, with 45 rpm record commemorating the tenth anniversary of the television in Italy, description of this item laid in, wrappers soiled with shelf and edgewear.   Oak Knoll Books   306 - 247   2015 $100

Alger, John Goldworth *Englishmen in the French Revolution.* London: Sampson Low, 1889. First edition, half title, 4 pages ads, 32 page catalog (Sept. 1888), few leaves roughly opened, original olive green cloth, spine slightly dulled, little rubbed, contemporary signature of J. C. Hussey on half title.   Jarndyce Antiquarian Booksellers   CCXI - 5   2015   £50

Algren, Nelson *The Man with the Golden Arm.* Garden City: Doubleday, 1949. First edition, very good, little fraying to head of spine, in very good dust jacket with shallow chipping at spine head, this copy signed by author on tipped in leaf, less common issue than trade editions signed or inscribed.   Beasley Books   2013 - 2015 $175

Algren, Nelson *The Neon Wilderness.* Garden City: Doubleday & Co., 1947. First edition, 8vo., original green cloth lettered brown on spine, signed, first state dust jacket with ads for other Doubleday books on rear, very good in near very good dust jacket with slight chips and creasing at edges, slight soiling to rear panel.   Any Amount of Books   2015 - A96980   2015   £245

Alison, Archibald *Free Trade and a Fettered Currency.* Edinburgh and London: William Blackwood and Son, 1847. First edition, 8vo., recently well bound in linen backed marbled boards lettered, very good.   John Drury Rare Books   March 2015 - 16659   2015 $221

Allbeury, Ted *The Alpha List.* London: Granada, 1979. First edition, fine in dust jacket.   Mordida Books   March 2015 - 000174   2015 $75

Allbeury, Ted *A Choice of Enemies.* New York: St. Martin's Press, 1972. First edition, fine in dust jacket, scarce.   Buckingham Books   March 2015 - 36678   2015 $200

Allbeury, Ted *Snowball.* Peter Davies, 1974. First edition, fine in dust jacket with light wear to extremities.   Buckingham Books   March 2015 - 36653   2015 $225

Allemagne, Henry Rene D' *Les Cartes Jouer de Quatorzieme au Vingtieme Siecle...* Paris: Librairie Hachette et Cie, 1906. First edition, 2 volumes, large quarto, 3200 reproductions of historical playing cards, 956 of which are in color, five mounted color plates, 456 intertextual illustrations, titlepage in red and black, quarter 19th century brown calf over marbled boards, spines and decorated in gilt with five raised bands, marbled endpapers, original front and rear wrappers bound in, board extremities rubbed, bit of toning to top of front cover on volume I, overall very good.   Heritage Book Shop   Holiday 2014 - 45   2015 $2000

Allen & Ginter *50 Decorations of the Principal Orders of Knighthood and Chivalry of the World.* Richmond: Allen & Ginter, n.d., circa 1880's, First edition, large 8vo., rebound in dark red cloth, lettered gilt at front, original paper covers bound in, new endpapers, copiously illustrated in color, slight marking and foxing to new prelims, otherwise clean, very good, original contents near fine.   Any Amount of Books   2015 - C11921   2015   £180

Allen, A. H. Burlton *Pleasure and Instinct. A Study in the Psychology of Human Action.* New York: Harcourt, 1930. First US edition, near fine, hardcover.   Beasley Books   2013 - 2015 $40

Allen, Grant *An African Millionaire. Episodes in the Life of the Illustrous Colonel Clay.* London: Grant Richards, 1897. First edition, first printing, 8vo., original dark green cloth with gilt titles and illustration to front cover and spine, illustrations, top edge gilt, minor rubbing to spine ends and corners, else very good, pictorial gilt stamped front cover, rare first edition, superb copy.   Buckingham Books   March 2015 - 37646   2015 $1250

Allen, Grant *Hilda Wade.* London: published by Grant Richards, 1900. First edition, 8vo. original blue cloth lettered gilt on spine and cover with gilt illustration on cover, illustrations by Gordon Browne, slight signs of label removal at rear, no other marks, very good+.   Any Amount of Books   2015 - A99137   2015   £275

Allen, Henry *The Management of the Linnet. How to Train Them, How to Moult Them. How to get them to Sing with Wings Down.* Leeds: signed by Harry Allen City Aviary 40 Beckett Street, n.d. circa., 1900. 12mo., printed on blue paper, ink stamp of Harry Allen in two places, stapled as issued, staple now rusty and leaves have become loose, in good state of preservation nonetheless.   John Drury Rare Books   2015 - 22331   2015 $89

Allen, James S. *The Negro Question.* New York: International, 1936. First edition, fine in lightly chipped dust jacket. Beasley Books 2013 - 2015 $45

Allen, Jeffrey *Nursery Mrs. Rat.* New York: Viking Kestrel, 1985. First edition, first printing, with correct number code, 4to., glazed pictorial boards, as new in as new dust jacket, illustrations by artist, illustrations in color on every page by James Marshall, this copy has large and detailed full page drawing of Mrs. Rat, inscribed by Marshall and dated Oct. 1985. Aleph-Bet Books, Inc. 108 - 283 2015 $600

Allen, Leslie *Murder in the Rough.* New York: Five Star, 1946. First edition, paperback original, very good in wrappers with wear along edges, small chip along front edge and couple of faint creases on covers. Mordida Books March 2015 - 009727 2015 $85

Allen, Lewis *The Allen Press Bibliography, a Facsimile with Original leaves and Additions to date Including a Checklist of Ephemera.* San Francisco: Book Club of California, 1985. Limited to 750 copies, printed in black and red with tipped-in specimens, 4to., cloth. Oak Knoll Books 306 - 156 2015 $150

Allen, Lewis *The American Herd Book containing Pedigrees of Short-Horn Cattle Volume IX Part II - Cows.* Buffalo: 1870. First edition, abundantly illustrated with plates, inner joints repaired, gilt bright. Bookworm & Silverfish 2015 - 6016531074 2015 $75

Allen, Martha M. *Coca Cola, a Drug Drink.* Evanston: Woman's Christian Temperance Union, n.d., First separate printing, single sheet, 7 3/4 x 6 1/4 printed on both sides and intended to be folded in half (this example unfolded), light toning, negligible scuff to very bottom edge, else fine. Tavistock Books Temperance - 2015 $75

Allen, Rex *The Arizona Cowboy-Rex Allen "My Life" "Sunrise to Sunset".* Scottsdale: Rex Gar Rus Press, 1989. First edition, quarto, presentation inscription by Allen, brown cloth, gold stamping on front cover and spine, extensively illustrated with color and black and white photos, exceptional copy. Buckingham Books March 2015 - 29220 2015 $225

Allen, Willis Boyd *The Lion City of Africa: a Story of Adventure.* Boston: D. Lothrop Co., 1890. First edition, 38 illustrations, inserted plates, original pictorial green cloth, front and spine panels stamped in light blue, brown and gold. L. W. Currey, Inc. Boy's Adventure Fiction 2015 - 77 2015 $100

Allerton, Mark *The Girl on the Green.* London: Methuen, 1914. First edition, 8vo., original green cloth lettered gilt on spine and cover, review copy with small circular "presentation copy" stamp bottom of titlepage and printed review slip noting publication date as 26 March 1914, faint handling wear, covers very slightly bumped, otherwise very good. Any Amount of Books 2015 - A775623 2015 £240

Allestree, Richard *The Ladies Calling.* Oxford: printed at the Theater, 1673. First edition, 8vo., 2 parts in 1, early 18th century panelled calf with marbled endpapers, frontispiece, the copy of Barbara Dobell with her signature, and below is "Sally Harrison/June 11th 1797" with note about her marriage and on facing blank is 19th century inscription "the gift of S. Mitchell to her niece Mary Best December 1855, in lower margin of final page of text is note in Dobell's hand about binding and cost charged by a Mr. Double on March 30 1706, edges little rubbed, marbled endpapers have cleanly lifted from boards, firmly held in place by sewing, fine. The Brick Row Book Shop Miscellany 67 - 3 2015 $500

Allestree, Richard *The Ladies Calling in Two Parts.* Oxford: at the Theater, 1676. Fourth impression, 8vo., engraved frontispiece, vignette on title, some minor rust spotting to B2, I3 and S4 (forming small hole), occasional marginal dampstaining and small (30mm) closed tear to blank fore-margin of Z1, contemporary brown morocco, covers gilt panelled with floral tool at each corner, spine divided into six gilt tool panels, joints lightly worn, attractive copy, from the library of James Stevens Cox (1910-1997). Maggs Bros. Ltd. 1447 - 3 2015 £450

Allestree, Richard *The Ladies Calling. In Two Parts.* Oxford: at the Theater, 1677. Fifth impression, 8vo., engraved frontispiece, vignette of the Sheldonian theatre on the title, light marginal browning and occasional spotting, very small paper flaw in lower blank margin of B2, contemporary black morocco, covers with fillet border, gilt panel with small floral tool at corners, spine with five raised bands, panels tooled in gilt, marbled endleaves and gilt edges (corners lightly bumped, few minor bumps and scuffs), from the library of James Stevens Cox (1910-1997), with ink signature (J(ane) Dymoke (of Scriveldaby, Yorkshire). Maggs Bros. Ltd. 1447 - 4 2015 £500

Allhands, J. L. *Gringo Builders.* N.P.: privately printed, 1931. First edition, signed by author, 8vo., dark blue cloth, gold stamping on front cover and spine, illustrations, bit of light rubbing to spine ends, else near fine. Buckingham Books March 2015 - 28808 2015 $275

Allingham, Helen *Happy England.* London: published by Adam and Charles Black, 1904. Reprint, 8vo., original florally illustrated blue cloth lettered gilt on spine and front cover, uncut, unopened, 81 illustrations, endpapers slightly browned, otherwise fine in near fine, complete, unchipped dust jacket that is faintly browned, exceptional condition, original mailing box somewhat worn and used but has printed list of books in same series on inside card. Any Amount of Books   2015 - A47324   2015   £180

Allingham, Margery *Dancers in Mourning.* London: Heinemann, 1937. First edition, page edges slightly darkened, else near fine without dust jacket. Mordida Books   March 2015 - 009590   2015 $125

Allingham, Margery *Dancers in Mourning.* Doubleday Doran, 1938. First American edition, stamp on front pastedown, otherwise fine in very good dust jacket with slightly faded spine, spine chipped at ends and corners and wear along edges and folds. Mordida Books   March 2015 - 010107   2015 $150

Allingham, William *Flower Pieces and Other Poems.* London: Longmans, Green and Co., 1893. First edition, 8vo., original white parchment backed green cloth lettered gilt on spine, frontispiece and one other illustration by Dante Rossetti, pages uncut, sound, decent, very good copy with slight mottling and slight soiling to spine, otherwise very good or better. Any Amount of Books   2015 - A76083   2015   £160

Allingham, William *Life and Phantasy.* London: Longmans Green and Co., 1893. 8vo., white vellum under light green paper boards, lettered gilt at spine, signed presentation by Allingham's widow, Helen, very slight soiling and very slight spotting to endpapers, otherwise clean, very good. Any Amount of Books   2015 - C8507   2015   £240

Allott, Miriam *Novelists on the Novel.* London: Routledge, 1959. Half title, few pencil notes, original brown cloth in slightly torn dust jacket, Kathleen Tillotson's copy with note that she reviewed in review of English Studies in 1960. Jarndyce Antiquarian Booksellers   CCVII - 3   2015   £20

Allsop, William *Guide Book to Allsop's Splendid and Unrivalled Wax-Work Exhibition, Sculpture Galleries...* N.P.: but Liverpool: Matthews, n.d. circa, 187-. 8vo., original pink wrappers, overprinted in black with graphic view of front elevation of Teutonic Hall and Allsop's Waxworks on upper cover and scene, wrappers themselves little worn and creases and with some careful restoration, good copy, probably rare. John Drury Rare Books   March 2015 - 25348   2015 $266

Allsopp, Bruce *Decoration and Furniture.* London: Pitman, 1952. First edition, 2 volumes, very good+, in very good dust jackets. Beasley Books   2013 - 2015 $85

Allston, Washington *Description of the Grand Historical Picture of Belshazzar's Feast... Now Exhibiting at the Corinthian Gallery...* Boston: Eastburn's Press, 1844. Second edition, 8vo., original printed wrappers, top of wrappers waterstained. M & S Rare Books, Inc.   97 - 14   2015 $225

Almack, Henry *A Plea for Deacons.* London: Rivingtons, 1868. First edition, 8vo., well bound fairly recently in linen backed marbled boards lettered, very good, presentation inscribed and initialled by author for Revd. Hugh Pearson, uncommon. John Drury Rare Books   2015 - 20936   2015 $80

Almendros, Nestor *A Man with a Camera.* New York: FSG, 1984. First edition, review copy with slip and promo letter, nearly fine book and dust jacket. Stephen Lupack   March 2015 -   2015 $150

Alphonso di Borgo; or a Sentimental Correspondence of the Sixteenth Century. printed (By S. Gosnell for J. and T. Carter), 1800. First edition, 8vo., uncut in original cream paper backed blue paper covered boards, spine darkened and little defective at foot, lacking label, lower cover bit soiled and slightly worn, very good. Blackwell's Rare Books   B179 - 79   2015   £2000

Alsted, Johann Heinrich *Templum Musicum; oro the Musical Synopsis of the Learned and Famous Johannes Henricus Alstedius, Being a Compendium of the Rudiments both of the Mathematical and Practical part of Musick...* London: by Will. Godbid for Peter Dring, 1664. First edition in English, 8vo., without final blank leaf, emblematic engraved frontispiece (inner margin torn at head and an ink blot on lyre of Orpheus), without final blank leaf, some light soiling to titlepage, margins browned throughout and with some marginal staining, small piece torn away from upper blank margin of G7, contemporary sheep (old rebacking, now very worn again and with joints split and upper cover detached), corners worn, 19th century endleaves, from the library of James Stevens Cox (1910-1997). Maggs Bros. Ltd.   1447 - 5   2015   £450

Altara, Edina *Libro Giocattoli. (The Book of Toys).* Milano: Hoepli, 1945. Folio, pictorial wrappers, fine and unused, 8 page instructional booklet to be used as a guide to construct a variety of toys from nearly 50 leaves of color lithograph pages, several thick card pages used at bases, lavish book. Aleph-bet Books, Inc.   109 - 335   2015 $875

Altrocchi, Julia Cooley *Black Boat: a True Story Melodrama in Verse about a tragic Negro Incident.* Berkeley: the author, n.d., First separate edition, 32 mimeographed leaves printed rectos only, stapled into unprinted wrappers hand titled and signed by author, extremely uncommon. Between the Covers Rare Books   197 - 2   2015 $750

Amazing Alphabet. Le Jardin. D'Acclimation. The Zoological Garden. London: Darton & Dodge, n.d. circa, 1880. Small octavo, approximately 90 x 5 1/2 inches, original decorated boards, illustrations in color on front cover and with black decorative paper on rear cover, foldout format with 24 hand colored engravings, illustrating letters of alphabet, text in English and French, housed in original decorative cover, binding covered with laminated adhesive backed acetate, rubbed on edges, but in good condition, long folding plates laid in loosely, might have been published with plates loosely inserted, some light marking a few small nicks or splits on folds, two corners with minor repair, plates in very good condition, very rare.   Heritage Book Shop   Holiday 2014 - 46   2015 $2750

Ambler, Eric *The Ability to Kill.* London: Bodley Head, 1963. First edition, 2nd issue, fine in dust jacket, Mordida Books   March 2015 - 011405   2015 $85

Ambler, Eric *Background to Danger.* New York: Alfred A. Knopf, 1937. First American edition, fine in exceptionally fresh, about fine dust jacket with only tiny bit of rubbing to couple of corners to note, from the collection of Duke Collier. Royal Books   36 - 135   2015 $2500

Ambler, Eric *A Coffin for Dimitrios.* New York: Alfred A. Knopf, 1939. First US edition, near fine in unusually bright dust jacket with none of the usual fading, light professional restoration to spine ends, corners and extremities, sharp collector's copy.   Buckingham Books   March 2015 - 27760   2015 $2250

Ambler, Eric *The Mask of Dimitrios.* London: Hodder & Stoughton Ltd., 1939. First edition, signed and inscribed on titlepage in ink by author to fellow mystery writer and journalist Wayne Warga, 25 Feb. 1982, bookplate of mystery collector Adrian Homer Goldstone, near fine, bright, square copy in dust jacket with light professional restoration by expert paper conservationist, housed in cloth clamshell case with leather label on spine and titles stamped in gold gilt, rare.   Buckingham Books   March 2015 - 37292   2015 $22,500

Ambler, Eric *Passage of Arms.* New York: Knopf, 1960. First American edition, fine in advance copy dust jacket which is darkened at spine and is chipped at top of spine and along top edge of front panel.   Mordida Books   March 2015 - 006466   2015 $75

Ambulance Train in the Great War: Selections from the Pages of La Vie Sanitaire August 1916 to February 1919. No. 5. Blackburn: Geo. Toulmin & Sons, 1919? frontispiece, illustrations, original black boards with paper label, cream cloth spine, inner hinges cracking, Kathleen Tillotson's copy with signature and 'my father Eric Constable's copy'.   Jarndyce Antiquarian Booksellers   CCVII - 4   2015   £125

The American Bee: a Collection of Entertaining Histories. Leonminster: printed by and for Charles Prentiss, 1797. First edition, 12mo., contemporary tree calf, red leather label, gilt lettering, portion of label lacking edges, bit rubbed, very good.   The Brick Row Book Shop   Miscellany 67 - 6   2015 $1750

American Druggists' Circular and Chemical Gazette: a Practical Journal of Chemistry, as Applied to Pharmacy, Arts and Sciences... Volume 8 for, 1864. Volume 17 for 1873, Folio, 2 volumes, contemporary half roan, both fine. Joseph J. Felcone Inc.   Science, Medicine and Technology - 46   2015 $400

American Fashionable Letter Writer... Troy: Merriam Moore, 1850. 16mo., black leather stamped in gilt, front hinge near tender, some foxing, slight worm damage to rear pastedown and one leaf, cover scuffed, otherwise very good.   Second Life Books Inc.   189 - 165   2015 $45

American Historical Association *Records of the American Historical Association.* Washington: 1889-1922. 57 volumes, 4 in leather, covers loose or gone, 6 with some hinge looseness, most with privately library bookplate, no stamps.   Bookworm & Silverfish   2015 - 6016045182   2015 $750

American Journal of Nursing. Concord: 1942-1974. 34 volumes, good in wrappers.   Bookworm & Silverfish   2015 - 6016085673   2015 $350

American Medical Botany. Boston: Cummings and Hilliard, 1821. 4to., later quarter leather, cloth, title gilt stamped on spine, back original paper wrapper, top edge cut, other edges uncut, endpapers tanned, pencilled notation on back pastedown, Treadwell Library (Boston) ex-libris and regulations of the Public Library of the city of Boston laid in.   Oak Knoll Books   306 - 14   2015 $950

American Red Cross Society *The War-time Manual.* Chicago: Service Publishers, n.d., First edition, 16mo., wrappers, very good, offsetting from clipping to two pages. Beasley Books   2013 - 2015 $45

American Saw Company *Organized Under the Laws of the State of New York, Jan. 1866. Captial $250,000 Officers, James C. Wilson... President (et al)... Office No. 2 Jacob Street, New York.* Trenton: Murphy & Bechtel, 1868. 8vo., profusely illustrated, original printed and pictorial wrappers, worn but sound, hole punched in upper left hand corner, not affecting text, faint stain on fore-edge of front wrapper and lightly on title, some corners curled &c., good, sound, owner's signature on front wrapper.   M & S Rare Books, Inc.   97 - 302   2015 $225

American State Papers and Correspondence: Between Messrs. Smith, Pinkney, Marquis Wellesley, General Armstrong, M. Champagny, M. Turreau... London: reprinted for Longman, Hurst, Rees, Orme and Brown and J. M. Richardson by J. G. Barnard, 1812. First edition thus, 8vo., 3 folding charts, Ex-British Foreign Office library with few library markings, else very good, modern blue cloth lettered in gilt at spine, clean text, most pages unopened.   Any Amount of Books   2015 - A67940   2015   £250

America's Blue Yodeler.   Lubbock: Jim Evans, 1952-1954. First 6 issues (Volume 1, Nos. 1-4; Volume 2, Nos. 1 & 2), each newsletter is one sheet folded to make four pages, first two issues are folded in sixths and fourths, respectively, last four issues folded in half vertically, each has small price in ink in upper right corner, set very good.   Ken Lopez, Bookseller   164 - 178   2015 $150

Ames, Richard   *Fatal Friendship; or the Drunkards Misery; Being a Satyr Against Hard Drinking.*   London: for and sold by Randal Taylor, 1693. First edition, small 4to., final ad leaf, final two leaves uncut at tail, penultimate leaf closely shaved along upper edge, touching pagination, disbound, from the library of James Stevens Cox (1910-1997).   Maggs Bros. Ltd.   1447 - 6   2015   £400

Amidei, Sergio   *Tales of Ordinary Madness.*   Rome: Nuova Stampa, 1981. Screenplay by Amidei and Ferreri, this copy signed by Charles Bukowski on front cover, velo-bound with gray cardstock covers and typed label on front cover, near fine, scarce, signed by Charles Bukowski on front cover.   Ken Lopez, Bookseller   164 - 23   2015 $3500

Amiel, S.   *Jonathan the Sailor. (Yonatan Ha Sapan).*   Palestine: 1945. 12mo., pictorial wrappers, slight edge wear, else very good+, illustrations by Lev Dickstein with full page color linoleum cuts.   Aleph-Bet Books, Inc.   108 - 251-1   2015 $325

Amiel, S.   *Nira's Story - Firefighting. (Ma Aseh B'nira).*   Palestine: circa, 1945. 12mo., pictorial wrappers, slight edge wear, else very good+, illustrations by Lev Dickstein with full page color linoleum cuts.   Aleph-Bet Books, Inc.   108 - 251-4   2015 $325

Amiel, S.   *The Red Nurse.(Ha Achot Ha Aduma).*   Palestine: circa, 1945. 12mo., pictorial wrappers, slight edge wear, else very good+, illustrations by Lev Dickstein with full page color linoleum cuts.   Aleph-Bet Books, Inc.   108 - 251-3   2015 $325

Amiel, S.   *What Will Ram Become - Trades. (Ram calba).*   Palestine: circa, 1945. 12mo., pictorial wrappers, slight edge wear, else very good+, illustrations by Lev Dickstein with full page color linoleum cuts.   Aleph-Bet Books, Inc.   108 - 251-2   2015 $325

Amis, Kingsley   *A Frame of Mind. Eighteen Poems.*   Printed at the School of Art, University of Reading, 1953. First edition, one of 150 numbered copies (this unnumbered, but penned 'Proof Copy'), 8vo., original printed cream wrappers over card, with less than the usual darkening to covers, very faint stain to front cover fore-edge, good.   Blackwell's Rare Books   B179 - 124   2015   £200

Amis, Kingsley   *Lucky Jim.*   London: Victor Gollancz, 1953. First edition, 8vo., finely bound in full green leather lettered gilt on spine, 5 raised bands and gilt at spine, marbled endpapers, fine.   Any Amount of Books   2015 - A98802   2015   £275

Amis, Martin   *Other People: a Mystery Story.*   London: Jonathan Cape, 1981. First edition, fine in dust jacket.   Buckingham Books   March 2015 - 24093   2015 $165

Amis, Martin   *Success.*   London: Jonathan Cape, 1978. First edition, octavo, fine in fine dust jacket with just hint of inevitable fading to spine.   Peter Ellis, Bookseller   2014 - 021807   2015   £275

Ammons, A. R.   *Ommateum with Doxology.*   Philadelphia: Dorrance & Co., 1955. First edition, rare first book, one of 300 copies printed of which only 100 were bound, small 8vo., original salmon cloth dust jacket, very fine, essentially as new.   James S. Jaffe Rare Books   Modern American Poetry - 3   2015 $2500

Anacreon   *Anacreon Done into English out of the Original Greek.*   Oxford: by L. Litchfield, Printer to the University, for Anthony Stephens, 1683. First edition of this translation, 8vo., leaf (c)1 is duplicated; (c)2 was also duplicated, but the second leaf has been torn away, lightly browned, damp-staining along lower edge of a1-4, corners of K2-L2 and fore margin of P1-2 and in top half of last few leaves, small rust hole in D2 (affecting one letter on each side), marginal rust spot on H1, contemporary calf, spine gilt and lettered (head-cap damaged and with upper joint slightly split at head), from the library of James Stevens Cox (1910-1997), inscribed "Sum Philippi Ayresij 1683" on titlepage (Philip Aryes (1638-1712), signature of Madam. Mary Redman, ink signature under bookplate of John Holmes (1702/03-1760) of Holt, Norfolk, Master of Gresham School and writer on education, with his signature, early 19th century circular label with manuscript lot number 12/4 pasted to foot of front flyleaf, the pencil mark of Christie-Miller Britwell Court with pencil shelf mark.   Maggs Bros. Ltd.   1447 - 7   2015   £1500

Anacreon *(in Greek) Anakreontos Teiou Mele (then) Anacreontis Teii Odaria (i.e. The Odes).* Parmae: Ex Regio typographeio, 1785. One of 250 copies on 'blue' paper (of a total of 310 copies), 305 x 222mm., splendid contemporary crimson morocco, handsomely gilt by Derome Le Jeune (with his ticket), covers framed with double gilt rules, inner rule with scalloped corners, raised bands, compartments with very appealing all-over diaper pattern, chain pattern (asterisk and four petal flower) on board edges, endleaves of lavender watered silk, very wide and intricate inner dentelles extending (in an unusual way) from turn-ins onto silk pastedowns, all edges gilt, small author portrait in style of ancient coin on titlepage, large and elaborate armorial vignette on dedication page engraved by Cagnoni, tiny bit of wear at spine ends, few leaves with very minor tear or paper flaw at fore edge, especially fine, beautiful book with elegant original binding scarcely worn, text very clean and bright and fresh with margins nothing short of immense. Phillip J. Pirages 66 - 48 2015 $8500

Anacreon *Odes.* Paris: Chez Du Pont, 1795. 171 x 102mm., fine contemporary black straight grain morocco gilt by Bozerian (stamp-signed at foot of spine), covers framed with undulating grape vine enclosed by double rules, starburst cornerpieces, raised bands, spine gilt in densely stippled compartments with gilt leaves and flowers emanating from central inlaid red morocco dot, turn-ins with gilt bead and star roll, pink watered silk endleaves embellished with their own cresting floral border, all edges gilt, large paper copy, bookplate of Raoul Simonson (and faint dampstain under it, indicating removal of previous one); one faint scratch on back cover, especially fine, text, clean, smooth and bright, in unworn sparkling binding. Phillip J. Pirages 66 - 61 2015 $2250

Andersen, Hans Christian 1805-1875 *Fairy Tales.* London: Sampson Low, Marston, 1872. First edition, 4to., brownish maroon cloth extensively illustrated in black and gold, beveled edges, all edges gilt, spine ends inconspicuously strengthened and slight cover soil, near fine, 12 magnificent and almost indescribably beautiful, large, full page chromolithographs done in rich colors by E. V. Boyle, very scarce. Aleph-bet Books, Inc. 109 - 68 2015 $3250

Andersen, Hans Christian 1805-1875 *Faery Tales from Hans Andersen.* New York: and New York: Dent & Dutton, 1910. First edition with these illustrations, 4to., gilt pictorial cloth, top edge gilt, 329 pages, light spotting on endpaper, else near fine, illustrations by Maxwell Armfield with 24 beautiful color plates plus pictorial chapter head and tailpieces and pictorial endpapers. Aleph-bet Books, Inc. 109 - 21 2015 $600

Andersen, Hans Christian 1805-1875 *Fairy Tales.* New York: Brentanos, n.d., 1916. First American edition, tall thick 4to., grey cloth with black and white paste-on surrounded by intricate cloth decoration in black, top edge gilt, spine slightly sunned, else fine, 16 color plates mounted on heavy stock with lettered tissue guards, 24 full page black and white plates plus many decorative tailpieces, all by Harry Clarke, increasingly scarce. Aleph-bet Books, Inc. 109 - 96 2015 $2950

Andersen, Hans Christian 1805-1875 *Fairy Tales.* New York: Thomas Nelson, n.d. circa, 1920. First edition, blue pictorial cloth, as new in publisher's pictorial box (box very good with flaps repaired), large 4to., pictorial endpapers, 12 magnificent color plates plus numerous detailed pen and ink drawings by Honor Appleton, outstanding copy, rarely found with box. Aleph-bet Books, Inc. 109 - 25 2015 $1250

Andersen, Hans Christian 1805-1875 *Fairy Tales by Hans Andersen.* London: Harrap (McKay on spine), 1932. First edition, 4to., 288 pages, red gilt cloth, top edge gilt, lettering dulled else fine in dust jacket and pictorial box (neatly strengthened), illustrations by Arthur Rackham with pictorial endpapers, 12 color plates and a profusion of black and whites in text, mounted color plate on wrapper that is repeated on box does not appear in text, extraordinary copy of truly beautiful book. Aleph-Bet Books, Inc. 108 - 384 2015 $1500

Andersen, Hans Christian 1805-1875 *Fairy Tales and Legends.* London: Cobden Sanderson, 1935. First edition, 8vo., original cream cloth, decorated and lettered gilt on spine and cover, all edges gilt, copiously illustrated, signed by artist, Rex Whistler, very faintly bumped at head of spine and very very slight browning, otherwise fine. Any Amount of Books March 2015 - C8306 2015 £425

Andersen, Hans Christian 1805-1875 *The Sand-Hills of Jutland.* Boston: Ticknor and Fields, 1880. First edition, very good, wear to extremities, clean, text tight. Stephen Lupack March 2015 - 2015 $150

Andersen, Hans Christian 1805-1875 *Stories from Hans Andersen.* London: Hodder & Stoughton, 1911. Limited to only 750 numbered copies signed by artist, Edmund Dulac, large thick 4to., full vellum, decorated in gold, top edge gilt, tips bumped, else fine copy with original ties, housed in custom cloth case, 28 wonderful tipped in color plates with lettered guards plus decorative borders on each page of text, all by Edmund Dulac, great copy, quite scarce in such nice condition. Aleph-bet Books, Inc. 109 - 142 2015 $4500

Andersen, Hans Christian 1805-1875 *Stories from Hans Andersen.* London: Hodder & Stoughton, n.d., 1911. First trade edition, large thick 4to., gold cloth stamped in gold, fine in dust jacket with mounted color plate, illustrations by Edmund Dulac, 28 magnificent tipped-in color plates with separate captioned page guards plus decorative border on text pages, beautiful copy, rarely found so bright in dust jacket.   Aleph-Bet Books, Inc.   108 - 157   2015 $1500

Andersen, Hans Christian 1805-1875 *Stories from Hans Andersen.* New York and London: Hodder & Stoughton, 1911. First edition, large thick 4to., goldish tan gilt decorated cloth, tiny edge bump else fine, 28 wonderful tipped in color plates with lettered guards plus decorative border on each page, beautiful copy.   Aleph-bet Books, Inc.   109 - 146   2015 $975

Andersen, Hans Christian 1805-1875 *The Ugly Duckling.* New York: Macmillan, Aug., 1927. First edition, square 12mo., pictorial boards, slight fading on bottom of cover, else near fine in soiled dust jacket with some edge chipping, color lithographs by Berta and Elmer Hader.   Aleph-bet Books, Inc.   109 - 216   2015 $275

Andersen, Hans Christian 1805-1875 *Wonderful Stories for Children.* New York: Wiley and Putnam, 1847. Early U.S. edition, 12mo, frontispiece and one other illustration, original green cloth, lettered and decorated gilt on spine and on front cover, small bookplate with arts and crafts style lettering reading "From the Library of Janet Ashbee and C. R. Ashbee", and pictorial bookplate of Janet designed by her husband C.R., sound, clean, very good, slight wear at head of spine, slight foxing, very slight shelfwear and some family note, press cutting about author's chair on blank prelims.   Any Amount of Books   2015 - A466337   2015   £160

Anderson, Alexander *Early American Wood Engravings by Dr. Alexander Anderson and Others.* New York: Burr & Boyd, 1877. First edition, 8vo., modern gray boards and printed paper label, 65 wood engravings printed on rectos only, very good.   The Brick Row Book Shop Miscellany 67 - 19   2015 $650

Anderson, Anne *The Anne Anderson Fairy Tale Book.* New York: Thomas Nelson, First American edition, 4to., 190 pages, drawings, 12 full page color plates, gray cloth with color illustration applied to front, cover some scuffed, little worn at corners and ends of spine, hinge little tender, otherwise very good.   Second Life Books Inc.   191 - 5   2015 $225

Anderson, Gary J. *Salar: the Story of the Atlantic Salmon.* St. Andrews & New York: Published in cooperation with the Atlantic Salmon Association and The International Atlantic Salmon Foundation, 1976. Limited first edition of 150, this #99 signed by both authors, blue cloth with silver titles to spine and front cover, numerous color and black and white illustrations as well as line drawings by Lin Paul, some light shelfwear to edges.   Schooner Books Ltd.   110 - 155   2015 $100

Anderson, Ho Che *King, A Comics Biography of Martin Luther King Jr.* Seattle: Fantagraphics Books, 2005. First printing, small 4to., wrappers, fine.   Beasley Books   2013 - 2015 $250

Anderson, Isabel *The Great Sea Horse.* Boston: Little Brown, Dec., 1909. First edition, 4to., red gilt pictorial cloth, top edge gilt, near fine, beautiful color plates by John Elliott (24 with guards), color endpapers and decorative chapter heads by Frank Downey.   Aleph-Bet Books, Inc.   108 - 184   2015 $225

Anderson, James 1662-1728 *Royal Genealogies; or the Genealogical Tables of Emperors, Kings and Princes from Adam to these Times...* London: printed by James Bettenham for Charles Davis in Pater Noster Row, 1736. Second edition, folio, addenda, corrigenda, 540 tables, collated complete, full contemporary brown leather with elaborate gilt at spine and 6 raised bands, covers somewhat rubbed and scuffed, hinges worn slightly but holding, very good.   Any Amount of Books   2015 - A77608   2015   £650

Anderson, Mary *A Few Memories.* New York: Harper, 1896. First edition, 8vo., with tipped-in 2 page Autograph letter, 6 photos, moderate wear, front hinge going, top edge gilt, other edges uncut.   Second Life Books Inc.   189 - 6   2015 $135

Anderson, Maxwell *Valley Forge.* Washington: Anderson House, 1934. First edition, limited issue, one of 200 numbered copies, full leather gilt as issued, signed by Anderson and inscribed by him to actress Margalo Gillmore thanking her for performing beautifully in the Play.   Between the Covers Rare Books, Inc.   187 - 1   2015 $275

Anderson, Poul *Earthman's Burden.* New York: Gnome Press Inc., 1957. First edition, first binding, light blue boards, spine panel lettered in dark blue, octavo.   John W. Knott, Bookseller   Selected New Arrivals Jan. 2015 - 16885   2015 $100

Anderson, Poul *The High Crusade.* Garden City: Doubleday & Co., 1960. First edition, octavo, cloth.   John W. Knott, Bookseller   Selected New Arrivals Jan. 2015 - 16880   2015 $1250

Anderson, Poul *Murder Bound.* New York: Macmillan, 1962. First edition, pages slightly darkened, otherwise fine in dust jacket with some light stains on back panel and tiny wear at base of spine. Mordida Books March 2015 - 000214 2015 $100

Anderson, Poul *Perish the Word.* New York: Macmillan, 1959. First edition, pages darkened, otherwise fine in dust jacket with couple of internal tape mends. Mordida Books March 2015 - 000187 2015 $100

Anderson, Poul *Tau Zero.* Garden City: Doubleday & Co., 1970. First edition, octavo, cloth, signed by author. John W. Knott, Bookseller Selected New Arrivals Jan. 2015 - 16883 2015 $300

Anderson, Poul *Virgin Planet.* New York: Avalon Books, 1956. First edition, octavo, cloth. John W. Knott, Bookseller Selected New Arrivals Jan. 2015 - 16879 2015 $250

Anderson, Robert M. *American law of Zoning.* Rochester & San Francisco: 1976. Second edition, five volumes complete, each with 1983 supplement. Bookworm & Silverfish 2015 - 5622270207 2015 $225

Anderson, Sherwood 1876-1941 *Perhaps Women.* New York: Liveright, 1931. First edition, 8vo., 144 pages, frontispiece woodcut by J. J. Lankes, fine in dust jacket (lacks small piece at upper corner and extremities of spine). Second Life Books Inc. 189 - 8 2015 $100

Anderson, Sherwood 1876-1941 *6 Mid-American Chants and 11 Midwest Photographs.* Highlands: Jargon 45/Jonathan Williams, 1964. First edition, an edition of 1550 copies, oblong 8vo., spiral bound original stiff thin card brown covers with photographic illustration, slight crease at front and back otherwise very good+. Any Amount of Books 2015 - A90774 2015 £300

Andre, Yves Marie *Essai Sur la Beau ou L'on Examine en Quoi Consiste Precisement le Beau dans le Physique...* Paris: Hippolyte-Louis Guerin, 1741. First edition, woodcut device on title, engraved headpiece at start of text, woodcut tailpieces, contemporary mottled calf, gilt panelled spine, little craquelure, very good, crisp copy. Blackwell's Rare Books B179 - 3 2015 £300

Andrew, John A. *An Address to the Graduating Class of the Medical School in the University at Cambridge.* Boston: Ticknor and Fields, 1864. First edition, 8vo., original printed wrappers, light wear, presentation inscription by author for E. P. Whipple. M & S Rare Books, Inc. 97 - 184 2015 $175

Andrew, Roy Chapman *On the Trail of Ancient Man.* New York: Putnam, 1926. First edition, 8vo., inscribed by author for John D. Rockefeller, very good++, mild cover edgewear, top edge gilt, in good+ dust jacket with pieces missing along top edge. By the Book, L. C. 44 - 61 2015 $2500

Andrew, William *A Masterpiece on Politics, in Ten Letters: Addressed to Mr. G. Beaumont, Minister of the Gospel at Norwich.* London: printed for R. Carlile, 1819. First edition, apparently rare, 8vo., recent marbled boards lettered on spine, very good. John Drury Rare Books March 2015 - 24996 2015 £306

Andrewes, Lancelot *Two Sermons of the Resurrection.* Cambridge: University Press, 1932. Half title, Geoffrey Tillotson's copy with corrections and some ms. marginal and inserted notes, GT's paper wrappers made from 18th century Latin printed text, color stained blue,. Jarndyce Antiquarian Booksellers CCVII - 6 2015 £25

Andrews, James P. *Cases Argued and Determined in the Supreme Court of Errors of the State of Connecticut.* New York: Banks Law Pub., 1913-1917. 5 volumes, from July 1912-July 1916, full tan leather (3 volumes) with raised bands and red and black leather labels and tan cloth (2 volumes) with raised bands and red and black leather labels, leather volumes show some light shelfwear, but are otherwise near fine as are the cloth volumes. Stephen Lupack March 2015 - 2015 $100

Andrews, James P. *Cases Argued and Determined in the Supreme Court of Errors of the State of Connecticut.* New York: Banks Law Pub. Co., 1918-1921. 5 volumes, from July 1916 to February 1921, tan cloth with raised bands and red and black leather labels, near fine set. Stephen Lupack March 2015 - 2015 $100

Andrews, James P. *Cases Argued and Determined in the Supreme Court of Errors of the State of Connecticut.* New York: Banks Law Pub. Co., 1922-1924. 5 volumes, Feb. 1921-June 1924, tan cloth with raised bands and red and black leather labels, near fine set, attractive in appearance. Stephen Lupack March 2015 - 2015 $100

Andrews, James P. *Cases Argued and Determined in the Supreme Court of Errors of the State of Connecticut.* New York: Banks Law Pub. Co., 1925-1927. 5 volumes from June 1924-March 1927, tan cloth with raised bands and red and black leather labels, near fine set, attractive in appearance. Stephen Lupack March 2015 - 2015 $100

Angelo, Valenti *Look Out Yonder.* New York: Viking, 1943. First edition, signed, near fine in fine dust jacket,. Stephen Lupack March 2015 - 2015 $75

(Animals). Tel Aviv: B(inyamin) Barlevy, n.d. circa, 1945. 8vo., pictorial boards, slight stain on blank verso of a panel, very good+, opening accordion style, each page features a different animal, illustrations are lovely color lithographs, scarce. Aleph-Bet Books, Inc. 108 - 250 2015 $275

Annals: Nineteenth Century. n.p.: circa, 1920-1960? Original maroon cloth boards, rubbed and dusted with blue paper ms. title, cloth tabs attached to pages, marking decades, given to Geoffrey Tillotson by Kathleen Tillotson. Jarndyce Antiquarian Booksellers CCVII - 7 2015 £45

Anniversary Volume Dedicated to Professor Hantaro Nagaoka by His Friends and Pupils on the Completion of Twenty-Five Years of His Professorship. Tokyo: privately published, 1925. One of 1280 copies, 4to., 19 half tone plates, tissue guards (few with tissue overlays), figures, tables, maroon cloth, gilt stamped cover and spine titles, spine ends frayed, covers lightly faded, former library copy with usual markings and defects, signature of George Ellery Hale, fair, scarce with 4 page errata sheet loosely placed in. Jeff Weber Rare Books 178 - 816 2015 $200

Annual Review of Jazz Studies. Metuchen: Scarecrow Press, 1991. First edition, 8 volumes (No. 5-12), 8vo., original cloth, lettered gilt on spine and cover, illustrations, all near fine or very good+. Any Amount of Books 2015 - A97761 2015 £175

Anouilh, Jean *Le Bal Des Voleurs.* Le Belier: 1952. #56 of 40 numbered copies, with an extra suite of illustrations, fine, 4to., unbound signatures laid into wrappers, protected by custom slipcase. Beasley Books 2013 - 2015 $400

Ansell, Charles *A Treatise on Friendly Societies, in Which the Doctrine of Interest of Money and the Doctrine of Probability are Practically Applied to the Affairs of Such Societies...* London: Baldwin and Cradock, 1835. First edition, with errata, 2 folding statistical charts, contemporary half calf over marbled boards, spine simply gilt and lettered, some general but minor wear, very good, sound copy with later 19th century booklabel of Mr. Thomas Bell. John Drury Rare Books 2015 - 26253 2015 $221

An Answer to Mr. B----w's Apology, as Itr Respects His King, His Country, His Conscience and His God. London: W. Bizett, 1755. First edition, 8vo., digit '8' in crayon on title, modern plain wrappers, good copy. John Drury Rare Books 2015 - 14859 2015 $177

Answer to the Considerations on the Establishment of a regency. London: J. Debrett, 1788. First edition, pretty scarce, 8vo., half title, preserved in modern wrappers with printed title label on upper cover, fine. John Drury Rare Books 2015 - 22457 2015 $133

An Answer to the Discourse on Free-thinking: Wherein the Absurdity and Infidelity of the Sect of Free-Thinkers is Undeniable Demonstrated. London: printed and sold by John Morphew and A. Dodd, 1713. First and only edition, 8vo., very good in later plain wrappers, scarce. John Drury Rare Books 2015 - 14742 2015 $221

Anthropologie Abstracted; or the Idea of Humane Nature Reflected in Briefe Philosophicall and Anatomicall Collections. London: for Henry Herringman, 1655. First edition, 8vo., small chip from blank corner of A2, minor rust spot in blank fore-margin of A3, light stain at head in first part, text lightly browned, large (5mm) rust hole in lower blank inner margin of I1, closely trimmed along upper edge in places, contemporary sheep, rebacked, corners repaired, lower cover scuffed, new endleaves, from the library of James Stevens Cox (1910-1997), "Lo. Aston" contemporary ink signature, probably Walter Aston, 2nd Baron Aston of Exeter. Maggs Bros. Ltd. 1447 - 9 2015 £700

An Antidote to revolution; or a Practical Comment on the Creation of Privilege for Quadrating the Principles of Consumption and Thereby Creating Stimulu for the Unlimited Production of National Wealth Neutralizing the Motives for Political Discontent... Dublin: printed for the author by M. Goodwin, 1830. First edition, 8vo., 16 pages, bound in modern rather oversized green cloth boards, spine lettered gilt, good copy, rare outside Ireland. John Drury Rare Books March 2015 - 20942 2015 $221

Antipas: a Solemn Appeal to the Right Reverend the Archbishops and Bishops of the United Churches of England and Ireland... London: William Stockdale, 1821. First edition, 4to., well bound in later 19th century cloth backed marbled boards, very good, large copy, scarce. John Drury Rare Books March 2015 - 23910 2015 £306

Antiquelades Mexicanas. Mexico: Officina Tiografico de la Secretaria de Fomento, 1892. Large folio, half red morocco over marbled paper boards, gilt stamped at spine with five raised bands, 80 pages of text bound in front, chromolithograph title and 149 plates, some double page, some in color, bit of dampstaining to few pages, small location sticker on bottom of spine and two small location stickers on top right corners of front free endpapers, previous owner's bookplate on front pastedown of Hans Lenz (German politician), few spots on spine, otherwise fine. Heritage Book Shop Holiday 2014 - 41 2015 $2500

Anton, John *American Precedents of Declarations.* Boston: Manning and Loring for Barnard B. Macauly, Salem, June, 1802. First edition, 8vo., errata leaf, new quarter leather and marbled boards. M & S Rare Books, Inc. 97 - 295 2015 $450

Antoninus, Brother 1912-1994 *The Last Crusade.* Berkeley: Oyez, 1969. One of 165 numbered copies signed by author, from a total edition of 180, first edition, fine in original acetate dust jacket.   Ed Smith Books   83 - 21   2015 $200

Antoninus, Brother 1912-1994 *Single Source. The Early Poems (1934-1940).* Berkeley: Oyez, 1966. One of 25 numbered copies, specially bound and signed by author, with copies of this issue, second corrected state, with 'language' on page ix, 8vo., original quarter leather and boards, dust jacket, very fine.   James S. Jaffe Rare Books Modern American Poetry - 83   2015 $850

Antoninus, Brother 1912-1994 *Tendril in the Mesh.* N.P.: Cayucos Books, 1973. printed in an edition limited to 250 numbered copies, signed by author, tall 4to., quarter leather with decorated paper covered boards, printed in Goudy thirty on handmade paper from English Wookey Hole Mill, titles and section numbers finely printed in tan and brown, bookplate of Steven Corey on front pastedown. Oak Knoll Books   306 - 148   2015 $125

Antonioni, Michaelangelo *Que Bowling Sul Tevre.* Torino: Einaudi, 1983. First edition, very good plus in like dust jacket, jacket bright with some creasing at extremities, inscribed by Antonioni.   Royal Books   46 - 25   2015 $475

Antonozzi, Leopardo *Trajan Letters De Caratteri di Leopardo Antonozzi Libro Primo Rome MDCXXXVIII.* Madison: Meles Vulgaris Press, 1972. Limited to 50 numbered copies signed by Donald Anderson and Phillip Hamilton and Robert Rodini, oblong 8vo., cloth, bottom edge cut, other edges uncut.   Oak Knoll Books   Special Catalogue 24 - 1   2015 $650

Antrim, Doran K. *Secrets of Dance Band Success.* New York: Famous Stars Publishing, 1936. First edition, 8vo., fine in fine dust jacket with two color mail order brochure laid in.   Beasley Books   2013 - 2015 $200

Apgar, John F. *Frank E. Schoonover, Painter - Illustrator. A Bibliography.* Morristown: Mark Lithographers, 1969. First edition, limited to 50 copies signed by author and artist, this no. 4, oblong 8vo., fine, bright copy, illustrations, housed in cloth slipcase.   Buckingham Books   March 2015 - 32555   2015 $275

Apidta, Tinga *The Hidden History of New York: A Guide for Black Folks.* New York: Reclamation Project Publishers, 1998. First edition, trade paperback, pictorial wrappers bit scuffed and faded, light creases on front jacket, still very good, scarce.   Between the Covers Rare Books   197 - 91   2015 $200

Apollinaire, Guillaume *The Poet Assassinated.* New York: Holt Rinehart Winston, 1968. First American edition translated by Ron Padgett, small 4to., original pictorial boards, dust jacket, fine in slightly sunned dust jacket, inscribed by artist, Jim Dine for Burt (Britton) 1978, also inscribed with drawing by Ron Padgett (translator) to same. James S. Jaffe Rare Books   Many Happy Returns - 192 2015 $50

Apollinaire, Guillaume *The Poet Assassinated.* London: Rupert Hart Davis, 1968. First English edition, small 4to., translated by Ron Padgett, original pictorial boards, fine in slightly tanned, price clipped dust jacket.   James S. Jaffe Rare Books   Many Happy Returns - 190   2015 $50

Apollinaire, Guillaume *The Poet Assassinated.* New York: Holt Rinehart & Winston, 1968. First American edition, translated by Ron Padgett, small 4to., original pictorial boards, dust jacket, fine in slightly sunned and dust soiled jacket, illustrations by Jim Dine, inscribed by Dine with drawing for Burt Britton, also inscribed with drawing by Padgett. James S. Jaffe Rare Books   Many Happy Returns - 191 2015 $350

An Appeal to the Common Sense of Scotsmen, Especially Those of the Landed Interest and More Especially Freeholders, If Their Own conduct be not the Source of their Misery? Edinburgh: printed by W. Sands, A. Murray and J. Cochran, sold by J. Traill and other booksellers, 1747. First edition, only edition, 8vo., half title, lower margins trimmed (nowhere near printed surface), removing ms. ink notes, half title bit soiled, 19th century half calf, spine gilt, some wear to marbled paper sides, good, crisp copy.   John Drury Rare Books   2015 - 24361   2015 $830

Appeal of the Trustees of Bradford Academy to the Friends of the female Education. Boston: Adams & Torrey, 1836. First edition, 8vo., removed, foxed.   M & S Rare Books, Inc.   97 - 323   2015 $250

Appleton, George S. *A Catalogue of Illustrated and Entertaining Juvenile Works.* Philadelphia: George S. Appleton, circa, 1850. First edition, 12mo., 8 leaves with vignette title and 7 other illustrations, sewn as issued, small chip in gutter of title leaf, some light stains and soiling, quite sound.   M & S Rare Books, Inc.   97 - 131   2015 $225

Appleton, Victor *Tom Swift and His Talking Pictures or the Greatest Invention on Record.* New York: Grosset & Dunlap, 1928. Early printing, 12mo., frontispiece, mustard cloth with 4 vignette front board, four color dust jacket with blue spine lettering, very good+, slight lean, personal ownership signature, very good+, colors bright, light wear. Tavistock Books   Bah, Humbug? - 21   2015 $235

Apuleius *Lamour de Cupido et de Psiche mere de Volupte...* Paris: avec privilege du roy, 1586. First edition of Leonard Gaultier's illustrated version, small 4to., engraved architectural titlepage, with standing figures of Venus, with Cupid and Psyche, signed by Gaultier and 12 numbered engraved plates 115 x 75mm., early 19th century green vellum over pasteboards, covers with triple gilt fillet and ornate gilt border in neo-classical style, flat spine gilt with red morocco label, joints just split but sound, extremities rubbed, some edges uncut, very lightly toned but generally very good. Maggs Bros. Ltd. Illustrated Books 2014 - 2015 £8500

Apuntes Para la Historia de la Guerra Entre Mexico y Los Estados-Unidos. Mexico: Tipografia de Manuel Payno, 1848. First edition, 28 litho maps and plates, small 4to., contemporary quarter morocco over marbled boards, four raised bands, gilt title on spine, extremely rare, Nelson Osgood Rhoades bookplate, about very good, small chip to foot of spine, edges worn, scattered foxing, title line on top fore margin of first dozen or so leaves, armorial bookplate on front free endpaper, few leaves with old reinforcement repairs on top inner edge affect a few words, one map with few repairs affecting neat line at one corner and blank areas, one leaf with two wear holes to lower margin, otherwise quite solid. Kaaterskill Books 19 - 143 2015 $4000

Arabian Nights *Aladin or the Wonderful Lamp.* New York: McLoughlin Bros., n.d. circa, 1865. 12mo., pictorial wrappers, highlighted in gold, mounted on linen, slightest edge soil and small crease, near fine, 8 brightly colored half page illustrations, beautiful copy. Aleph-Bet Books, Inc. 108 - 173 2015 $300

Arabian Nights *The Arabian Nights.* London: Hodder and Stoughton, 1925. Limited to numbered copies signed by Detmold, large thick 4to., full vellum, gilt pictorial covers, slightest cover browning and blank endpapers foxed as usual, else fine and bright in custom vellum backed box, 12 exquisite tipped in color plates with tissue guards, beautiful book, rare in limited edition. Aleph-bet Books, Inc. 109 - 121 2015 $6500

Arabian Nights *The Arabian Nights.* London: Hodder & Stoughton, 1925. Large thick 4to., white gilt pictorial cloth, slight soil on rear cover and slight foxing on fore edge, else near fine in original box with color plate on cover (box flaps repaired), illustrations by Edward Detmold with 12 exquisite tipped in color plates and tissue guards, exceptional copy, rare in box. Aleph-Bet Books, Inc. 108 - 133 2015 $2500

Araki, Noobuyoshi *Araki.* Cologne: Taschen, 2002. Limited to 2500 numbered copies signed by Araki, elephant folio, fine, numerous color and black and white plates, pink silk over boards housed in original silk over boards clamshell case, still in original card shipping box. Any Amount of Books 2015 - C8220 2015 £850

Arblay, Frances Burney D' 1752-1840 *Brief Reflections Relative to the Emigrant French Clergy, Earnestly Submitted to the Humane Considerations of the Ladies of Great Britain.* London: Thomas Cadell, 1793. First edition, 8vo., bound in later plain non printed wrappers, slight nick a spine, titlepage little dusty, otherwise clean, very good+. Any Amount of Books 2015 - C14397 2015 £300

Arblay, Frances Burney D' 1752-1840 *Evelina.* London: Macmillan, 1903. Illustrations by Hugh Thomson. Honey & Wax Booksellers 2 - 42 2015 $125

Archer, Thomas *Pictures and Royal Portraits Illustrative of English and Scottish History...* London: Blackie & Son, Old Bailey, 1880. First edition, 4to., 2 volumes, 2 frontispieces, 67 full page engravings, original full red morocco, Blackie presentation luxury binding with bevelled edges, extensive and elaborate gilt tooling and blind stamping with various English and Scottish heraldic gilt crests on front and back boards, spines with 6 raised bands, elaborate gilt decoration, inner gilt dentelles, all edges gilt, marbled endpapers, some slight rubbing at hinges, cover and edges, otewise very good+ with small label on rear pastedown. Any Amount of Books 2015 - A68988 2015 £260

Ardene, Jean Paul De Rome D' *Traite des Renoncules, qui Contient, Outre ce Qui Regarde ces Fleurs, Beaucoup D'Observations, Physiques & De Remarques Utiles...* Avignon: Louis Chambeau, 1763. Third and last edition, 6 folding engraved plates, trifle browned, small 8vo., contemporary green boards, rebacked in matching morocco with part of original gilt spine preserved, monogram of AS in gilt on upper cover, bookplate of NY Horticultural Society Bequest of Kenneth Mackenzie, inside front cover. Blackwell's Rare Books B179 - 6 2015 £600

Aretino, Pietro *Les Sonnets Luxurieux de L'Aretin...* Paris: n.p., 1907. First edition, number 32 of 310 and of 300 printed on Velin de Rives,, oblong 4to., erotic frontispiece, 16 erotic illustrations, tissue guards, text set within decorative architectural borders, half black morocco over marbled boards, spine lettered black, marbled endpapers, top edge gilt, other page edges untrimmed, edges slightly rubbed, otherwise very nice, notably scarce. Any Amount of Books March 2015 - C7491 2015 £480

Argences, Tanneguy Joseph Cauvin, Sieur D' *The Countess of Salisbury; or the Most Noble Order of the garter.* London: R. Bentley and S. Magnes, 1683. 1682. First edition, 12mo., small piece torn away from upper edge of titlepage, blank lower fore-corner of D1-2 torn, a number of slightly short uncut lower edges, long closed tear across centre of F10, paper flaw corner of I1, contemporary blind ruled sheep (leather torn away from upper cover exposing the board, headcaps torn away, all edges heavily worn), rare, from the library of James Stevens Cox (1910-1997), contemporary signature of Anne Whyte. Maggs Bros. Ltd. 1447 - 10 2015 £750

Ariosto, Lodovico *Orlando Furiosa in English Heroical Verse.* London: Richard Field, 1607. Second English edition, folio, period style full sprinkled calf gilt, engraved title by Thomas Cockson, 46 plates, bound by Riviere.   Honey & Wax Booksellers   3 - 3   2015 $8500

Ariosto, Lodovico *Orlando Furioso.* Birmingham: Da' Torch di G. Baskerville per P. Molini, 1773. One of 100 large paper copies, 4 volumes, with subscriber list at end of volume IV, contemporary red morocco by Derome Le Jeune (his ticket on titlepage of volume I), covers gilt with French fillet borders and with FitzGibbon family arms of Earl of Clare at Center, raised bands, spines gilt in double ruled compartments with simple lozenge centerpiece, gilt titling, densely gilt turn-ins, marbled endpapers, all edges gilt, frontispiece by Eisen after Titian and 46 fine engraved plates, large paper copy, vellum bookplate of Burnham Abbey and engraved armorial bookplate of Charles Tennant, The Glen, spines slightly and evenly sunned, hint of rubbing to extremities, titles faintly browned and with an inch of slightly darker browning to edges from binder's glue), a dozen other leaves with pale browning or spotting, occasional very faint offsetting from plates, isolated light spots of foxing, small marginal smudges or other trivial imperfections with just handful of plates affected, still an elegant set in fine condition, impressive bindings lustrous and scarcely worn, leaves clean and smooth, margins enormous and with strong impressions of the engravings.   Phillip J. Pirages   66 - 49   2015 $19,500

Aristoelian Society *Proceedings.* London: Methuen/Compton Press/Aristotelian Society, 1969-1987. First edition, Run from 1969-1987, lacking volumes 72, 75-78, 81, together 13 volumes, most about 300 pages, 8vo., from the library of philosophy professor J. N. Findlay (1903-187), with no sign of his ownership apart from train times written in his hand on front endpaper, all volumes complete and good.   Any Amount of Books   2015 - B26238   2015   £175

Aristophanes *The Comedies of...* London: John Murray, 1820. First edition thus, 8vo., 2 volumes bound as one, neat name on endpaper of poet Ernest Downson, disbound, i.e. lacking covers, otherwise in decent, sound condition with clean text, very good.   Any Amount of Books   2015 - A96146   2015   £225

Aristotle, Pseud. *Aristoteles Master-Piece, or the secrets of Generation Displayed in all Parts Thereof.* London: for J. How and are to be sold next to the Anchor Tavern in Sweeting Rents in Cornhill, 1684. First or second edition, 12mo., woodcut frontispiece (3rd line of text beneath slightly shaved and with catchword 'Jovia' cropped off), 6 woodcuts at end, initial engravings slightly chipped, torn in lower gutter margin and trimmed along lower edge (just touching caption), very light staining to A9-B8, D1-D2, E6v, E12, G4 and H11, 3mm. hole through blank fore-margin of d4, small (20mm.) closed tear to fore-margin of final leaf I6 (just missing text and woodcut) and with a number of edges and corners lightly bumped, otherwise good unsophisticated copy, contemporary sheep (slightly worn), inscriptions "Charles Roane His Booke January ye 15 1697", from the library of James Stevens Cox (1910-1997).   Maggs Bros. Ltd.   1447 - 11   2015   £7500

Arkin, David *Black and White.* Los Angeles: Ward Ritchie Press, 1966. Square 4to., pictorial cloth, fine in slightly worn dust jacket, illustrations by author in black and white, this copy inscribed by Arkin.   Aleph-bet Books, Inc.   109 - 61   2015 $200

Arkwright, Ruth *Brownikins and Other Fancies.* London: Wells Gardner Darton, n.d., 1910. First edition, 4to., pictorial cloth, slight bit of cover soil, near fine, magnificent full color pictorial cover, pictorial endpapers, 5 tipped in color plates plus 35 illustrations in text by Charles Robinson, beautiful copy.   Aleph-bet Books, Inc.   109 - 410   2015 $1200

Arlington, Henry Bennet, Earl of *The Right Honourable the Earl of Arlington's Letters to Sir W. Temple.* London: Thomas Benner, 1701. First edition, 2 volumes, small 8vo., full leather with blindstamped designs on covers, ex-British office Library with library markings, slight splitting at spines, slight shelfwear else, very good.   Any Amount of Books   2015 - A66990   2015   £150

The Armies Remembrancer. London: for Stephen Bowtell, 1649. First edition, small 4to., titlepage slightly soiled and with remnants of small circular sticker to upper inner margin (affecting type ornament frame), closely trimmed long lower edge throughout (touching catchwords and signatures in places), some occasional light foxing, early 19th century half green morocco and marbled boards, covers rubbed and corners bumped, from the library of James Stevens Cox (1910-1997).   Maggs Bros. Ltd.   1447 - 96   2015   £100

Armour & Co. *Armour & Company, Chicago.* Armour Printing Works, 1920. 9 1/2 x 6 1/4 inches, printed wrappers, 28 pages, illustrations, full page color plates by Charles Winter, top edges of front cover darkened and oversized wrappers lightly worn, else near fine.   Buckingham Books   March 2015 - 34933   2015 $275

Armstrong, R. A. *A Gaelic Dictionary in Two Parts.* London: printed for James Duncan, 1825. First edition, 4to., attractively bound in recent dark green leather, marbled boards, lettered gilt at spine, 5 raised bands, clean, very good, small discreet stamp on titlepage, slight occasional foxing to text, slight wear to edges of couple of pages not affecting text and neat, small old scholarly note in margin, uncommon.   Any Amount of Books   March 2015 - C15974   2015   £480

Armytage, Lewis *Out of Tune.* London: Swan Sonnenschein, Lowrey & Co., 1887. First edition, 2 volumes, 16 pages catalog in both volumes, loosely inserted in both volumes is single sheet ad 'Armytage's Spindle and Shears', published by W. H. Allen in 1891, original blue cloth, front boards blocked and lettered in black, spines lettered and ruled in gilt, very good, crisp copy, presentation inscription, news cutting relating to Paganini from John O'London is partially laid down on leading f.e.p. volume I.   Jarndyce Antiquarian Booksellers   CCXI - 12   2015   £450

Arnay, Jean Rodolphe D' *The Private Life of the Romans; Wherein Several of the Customs of Modern Times are Traced to Their Origin...* Edinburgh: printed by J. Orphoot, Blackfriars Wynd, for Peter Cairns, 3 College Street, 1808. 12mo. in sixes, full contemporary calf, gilt banded spine, red gilt morocco label, slight damp marking to back board, very good.   Jarndyce Antiquarian Booksellers   CCXI - 13   2015   £75

Arness, James *James Arness: an Autobiography.* McFarland & Co., 2001. First edition, first printing, signed and dated in month of publication by Arness and co-author James Wise, also included is T shirt and several promotional leaflets from the signing, and photo of Matt Dillon/Arness, blue cloth, gilt stamped front cover and spine, frontispiece, as new.   Buckingham Books   March 2015 - 17626   2015 $750

Arnold-Forster, Frances *Studies in Church Dedications; or, England's Patron Saints.* London: Skeffington, 1899. First edition, octavo, 3 volumes, full white buckram lettered in red and black, all edges red, armorial pictorial bookplates and ownership signature of one of the book's subscribers, Harriet A. Simpson, loosely inserted is short ALS to her from author, endpapers little spotted, red lettering on spines slightly faded, still near fine, remarkably bright set.   Peter Ellis, Bookseller   2014 - 005500   2015   £350

Arnold, Edwin *The Light of Asia.* Philadelphia: David McKay, 1932. First edition, 4to., black cloth, silver decorations, pictorial paste-on, mint in publisher's box (fine), 12 beautiful full page gravure plates by Willy Pogany.   Aleph-Bet Books, Inc.   108 - 355   2015 $275

Arnold, Julian T. Biddulph *Palms and Temples Being Notes of a Four Months' Voyage Upon the Nile.* London: Tinsley Bros., 1882. First edition, octavo, frontispiece and titlepage drawing, original turquoise blue cloth gilt decorated spine, pages unopened, armorial bookplate, spine just trifle scuffed, inner hinges little cracked, very good.   Peter Ellis, Bookseller   2014 - 012449   2015   £350

Arnold, Lloyd R. *High on the Wild with Hemingway.* Caldwell: Caxton, 1968. First edition, very fine in dust jacket.   Mordida Books   March 2015 - 012746   2015 $150

Arnold, Matthew **1822-1888** *Culture and Anarchy: an Essay In Political and Social Criticism.* London: Smith, Elder & Co., 1869. First edition, half title, original brown cloth, bevelled boards, spine slightly worn at head and tail, inner hinges splitting, decent copy, from the library of Geoffrey & Kathleen Tillotson.   Jarndyce Antiquarian Booksellers   CCVII - 11   2015   £220

Arnold, Matthew **1822-1888** *Culture and Anarchy...* London: Smith, Elder & Co., 1875. Second edition, half title, inserted ad leaf, original brown cloth, slightly dulled, from the library of Geoffrey & Kathleen Tillotson.   Jarndyce Antiquarian Booksellers   CCVII - 12   2015   £85

Arnold, Matthew **1822-1888** *Culture and Anarchy...* Cambridge: University Press, 1935. Half title, original orange cloth, dulled, piece cut from leading f.e.p., signed by Kathleen Tillotson Jan. 1940 with ink and pencil notes.   Jarndyce Antiquarian Booksellers   CCVII - 13   2015   £20

Arnold, Matthew **1822-1888** *Discourses in America.* London: Macmillan, 1885. First edition, half title, original dark green cloth, slightly dulled, few pencil notes, from the library of Geoffrey & Kathleen Tillotson.   Jarndyce Antiquarian Booksellers   CCVII - 14   2015   £65

Arnold, Matthew **1822-1888** *Essays in Criticism.* London: Macmillan, 1865. First edition, half title, 2 pages ads, 32 page catalog, original brown cloth, dark green endpapers, slightly dulled, signed by Geoffrey Tillotson.   Jarndyce Antiquarian Booksellers   CCVII - 16   2015   £45

Arnold, Matthew **1822-1888** *Essays in Criticism.* London: Macmillan, 1869. Second edition, half title, 2 pages ads, original brown cloth, dark green endpapers, dulled and rubbed, inner hinges, strengthened with paper, working copy, signed by Geoffrey Tillotson 14 Jan. 142, with numerous ink and pencil notes, insertions, including cuttings, causing slight browning.   Jarndyce Antiquarian Booksellers   CCVII - 17   2015   £75

Arnold, Matthew   1822-1888   *Essays in Criticism: Second Series.*   Leipzig: Tauchnitz, 1892. Copyright edition, without half title, uncut, later red buckram with note 'bound 1942', notes in pencil, ink and red ink, from the library of Geoffrey & Kathleen Tillotson.   Jarndyce Antiquarian Booksellers   CCVII - 18   2015   £60

Arnold, Matthew   1822-1888   *Essays, Including Essays in Criticism 1865, on Translating Homer.*   London: Oxford University Press, 1914. Frontispiece, original red cloth, spine rubbed and dulled, with signature of Arthur Tillotson 1931 and few notes by Geoffrey Tillotson.   Jarndyce Antiquarian Booksellers   CCVII - 15   2015   £20

Arnold, Matthew   1822-1888   *A French Eton; or Middle-Class Education and the State.*   London & Cambridge: Macmillan, 1864. First edition, half title, 6 pages ads, 24 page catalog (25.4.64), original red brown cloth, spine defective, inner hinges splitting, signed by Geoffrey Tillotson Xmas 43, with pencil marginal marks and part of original text from Macmillan's Magazine inserted.   Jarndyce Antiquarian Booksellers   CCVII - 20   2015   £20

Arnold, Matthew   1822-1888   *A French Eton.*   London: Macmillan, 1892. Half title, original dark blue cloth, endpaper causing some browning, otherwise very good, from the library of Geoffrey & Kathleen Tillotson.   Jarndyce Antiquarian Booksellers   CCVII - 21   2015   £25

Arnold, Matthew   1822-1888   *Friendship's Garland; Being the Conversations, Letters and Opinions of the Late Arminius, Baron von Thunder-Ten-Tronckh.*   London: Smith Elder, 1871. First edition, 2 pages ads, half title removed, original white cloth by Hanbury & Simpson, spine sunned, slightly discolored, attractive bookplate of Leonard Courtney, 15 Cheyne Walk, with inserted letters and cuttings including exchange between R. H. Super and Geoffrey Tillotson.   Jarndyce Antiquarian Booksellers   CCVII - 22   2015   £35

Arnold, Matthew   1822-1888   *Friendship's Garland.*   London: Smith, Elder, 1897. Second edition, half title, 4 pages ads, original white cloth, spine slightly dulled, few spots, bookplate of C. F. Mason, presented to Geoffrey Tillotson by WEB.   Jarndyce Antiquarian Booksellers   CCVII - 23   2015   £30

Arnold, Matthew   1822-1888   *Friendship's Garland...*   London: Smith Elder, 1903. Popular edition, 2 pages ads, half title removed, original crimson cloth, spine faded, signed by Geoffrey Tillotson 1932 with few notes.   Jarndyce Antiquarian Booksellers   CCVII - 24   2015   £20

Arnold, Matthew   1822-1888   *God & the Bible: a Review of Objections to 'Literature & Dogma'.*   New York: Macmillan, 1875. First American edition, half title, 2 pages ads, spotting caused by endpapers, name erased from title, original brown cloth, rubbed, inner hinges cracking, signed by Geoffrey Tillotson, with pencil notes and marginal marks.   Jarndyce Antiquarian Booksellers   CCVII - 25   2015   £30

Arnold, Matthew   1822-1888   *God and the Bible.*   London: Smith, Elder, 1885. Popular edition, initial ad leaf, half title, original brown cloth, signed by Geoffrey Tillotson 1942, with pencil notes and marginal marks.   Jarndyce Antiquarian Booksellers   CCVII - 26   2015   £20

Arnold, Matthew   1822-1888   *Higher Schools and Universities in Germany.*   London: Macmillan, 1874. Second edition, 83 pages, catalog Oct. 1873, browning caused by endpapers, original brown cloth, dulled, signed by Geoffrey Tillotson.   Jarndyce Antiquarian Booksellers   CCVII - 27   2015   £35

Arnold, Matthew   1822-1888   *Irish Essays and Other.*   London: Smith, Elder, 1891. Popular edition, half title, 2 pages ads, original brown cloth, signature of Ernest de Selincourt Sept. 24 1891, very good.   Jarndyce Antiquarian Booksellers   CCXI - 14   2015   £25

Arnold, Matthew   1822-1888   *Irish Essays and Others.*   London: Smith, Elder, 1891. Popular edition, half title, 2 pages ads, original crimson cloth, spine slightly faded, few pencil notes, from the library of Geoffrey & Kathleen Tillotson.   Jarndyce Antiquarian Booksellers   CCVII - 28   2015   £20

Arnold, Matthew   1822-1888   *Last Essays on Church and Religion.*   London: Smith, Elder, 1885. First edition, half title, text slightly browned, original brown cloth, signed by Geoffrey Tillotson 25.11.47.   Jarndyce Antiquarian Booksellers   CCVII - 29   2015   £30

Arnold, Matthew   1822-1888   *The Letters of Matthew Arnold to Arthur Hugh Clough.*   London: Oxford University Press, 1932. Half title, replacement label at end, uncut in original dark blue cloth, paper label slightly chipped, spine faded, Kathleen Tillotson's copy, signed and heavily annotated with few insertions.   Jarndyce Antiquarian Booksellers   CCVII - 31   2015   £40

Arnold, Matthew   1822-1888   *Literature and Dogma...*   London: Smith, Elder & Co., 1873. First edition, half title, inserted slip, final ad leaf, original brown cloth, slight rubbing, signed by Geoffrey Tillotson 6/x/44 with pencil notes.   Jarndyce Antiquarian Booksellers   CCVII - 32   2015   £40

Arnold, Matthew   1822-1888   *Literature and Dogma.*   London: Smith, Elder & Co., 1900. Popular edition, half title, 4 pages ads, original crimson cloth, spine rubbed, signed by Geoffrey Tillotson Xmas 1924 with ink and pencil notes.   Jarndyce Antiquarian Booksellers   CCVII - 33   2015   £20

Arnold, Matthew 1822-1888 *Merope.* London: Longmans, 1858. First edition, half title, 2 pages ads, 32 pages partly unopened catalog (Jan. 1877), plain grey endpapers, original deep blue green wavy grained cloth, ownership inscription "H. Crossley 1878", fine, bright, in Carter's C binding.   Jarndyce Antiquarian Booksellers   CCXI - 15   2015   £150

Arnold, Matthew 1822-1888 *Merope.* London: Longmans, 1858. First edition, half title, 3 pages ads, 32 page catalog (Nov. 1857), odd spot, original green cloth by Westleys, orange endpapers with printed ad, very good, inscribed "From the author" on verso of leading pastedown and signed by Geoffrey Tillotson.   Jarndyce Antiquarian Booksellers   CCVII - 37   2015   £150

Arnold, Matthew 1822-1888 *Mixed Essays.* London: Smith Elder, 1879. First edition, half title, few spots, original dark blue cloth, dulled, inner hinges splitting, from the library of Geoffrey & Kathleen Tillotson.   Jarndyce Antiquarian Booksellers   CCVII - 38   2015   £20

Arnold, Matthew 1822-1888 *New Poems.* London: Macmillan and Co., 1867. First edition, original green cloth by Burn, slightly marked, following inner hinge slightly cracked, Geoffrey Tillotson's copy.   Jarndyce Antiquarian Booksellers   CCVII - 39   2015   £150

Arnold, Matthew 1822-1888 *Matthew Arnold's Notebooks.* London: Smith Elder, 1902. First edition, half title, frontispiece, facsimile, few spots, original white cloth, marked, spine darkened, signed by Geoffrey Tillotson. Jarndyce Antiquarian Booksellers   CCVII - 36   2015   £20

Arnold, Matthew 1822-1888 *The Note-Books.* London: Oxford University Press, 1952. Half title, original red buckram, from the library of Geoffrey & Kathleen Tillotson, inscribed by same, with copy of Geoffrey's review or reviews.   Jarndyce Antiquarian Booksellers   CCVII - 40   2015   £35

Arnold, Matthew 1822-1888 *On The Study of Celtic Literature.* London: Smith, Elder & Co., 1867. First edition, half title, without ads, original brown cloth, bevelled boards, brick red endpapers, inner hinges noticeably strengthened with blue paper, presentation from H. S. King to the Hon. Mrs. Gordon, with Kathleen Tillotson's booklabel.   Jarndyce Antiquarian Booksellers   CCVII - 41   2015   £35

Arnold, Matthew 1822-1888 *On Translating Homer: Three Lectures Given at Oxford.* London: Longman, 1861. First edition, half title, 32 page catalog (July 1864), original green cloth, spine torn & chipped at head, signed by Geoffrey Tillotson 1942.   Jarndyce Antiquarian Booksellers   CCVII - 42   2015   £40

Arnold, Matthew 1822-1888 *On Translating Homer: Last Words; a Lecture Given at Oxford.* London: Longman, 1862. First edition, half title, 12 pages ads (August 1878), original turquoise green cloth, ownership inscription, Samuel Pearson Lanc.16 Md. Coll. 1880", fine, Carter variant B.   Jarndyce Antiquarian Booksellers   CCXI - 16   2015   £125

Arnold, Matthew 1822-1888 *On Translating Homer: Last Words a Lecture Given at Oxford.* London: Longmans, 1862. First edition, half title, original turquoise green cloth, slight wear to spine, damp marks on endpapers, pencilled note by Geoffrey Tillotson.   Jarndyce Antiquarian Booksellers   CCVII - 43   2015   £38

Arnold, Matthew 1822-1888 *Passages from the Prose Writings.* London: Smith, Elder, 1880. 2 pages ads, original dark blue cloth, slight marked, signed by Geoffrey Tillotson.   Jarndyce Antiquarian Booksellers   CCVII - 44   2015   £30

Arnold, Matthew 1822-1888 *Poems.* London: Longmans, 1853. New edition, half title, 32 page catalog (March 31 1853), unexplained erasure of edition statement, original green cloth by Westleys, yellow endpapers with printed ads, spine quite worn at head and tail, trace of lending library label, novelist S. R. Crockett's copy, signed by him, H. J. Macrory and Geoffrey Tillotson.   Jarndyce Antiquarian Booksellers   CCVII - 45   2015   £35

Arnold, Matthew 1822-1888 *Poems.* London: Longmans, 1853. New edition, half title, 24 page catalog (Nov. 1854), original green cloth by Westleys, orange endpapers with printed ads, spine faded and worn, hinges splitting, signed by Geoffrey Tillotson, April 1944 with few notes and cuttings inserted.   Jarndyce Antiquarian Booksellers   CCVII - 46   2015   £35

Arnold, Matthew 1822-1888 *Poems.* London: Longman, Brown, Green and Longmans, 1853. New edition, 8vo., original green cloth lettered gilt at spine and decorated in blind on cover, handwritten signed letter from author to his friend Edmond Scherer the writer, slight splitting at front hinge, minor scuffing to covers, otherwise sound, about very good.   Any Amount of Books   March 2015 - C14214   2015   £350

Arnold, Matthew 1822-1888 *Poems. Second Series.* London: Longmans, 1855. First edition, vi & 24 page catalog. (Nov. 1854), original green cloth by Westley's, orange endpapers with printed ads, spine faded, with splits in hinges, bookplate of Oxford Young, signed by Geoffrey Tillotson April 1944.   Jarndyce Antiquarian Booksellers   CCVII - 47   2015   £50

Arnold, Matthew 1822-1888 *The Poems.* London: Longmans, 1965. Half title, frontispiece, original turquoise cloth, very good in creased dust jacket, signed by Geoffrey Tillotson 1965 with few notes and few insertions including miscellaneous notes, etc.   Jarndyce Antiquarian Booksellers   CCVII - 48   2015   £25

Arnold, Matthew 1822-1888 *Poetical Works.* London: Macmillan, 1924. Reprint, half title, original half brown calf, darkened and rubbed, top edge gilt, signed by Geoffrey Tillotson with many ink and pencilled notes and inserted ALS to Tillotson about Arnold from Frederick Page.   Jarndyce Antiquarian Booksellers   CCVII - 49   2015   £35

Arnold, Matthew 1822-1888 *Reports on Elementary Schools 1852-1882.* London: Macmillan, 1889. First edition, half title, 2 pages ads, original dark blue cloth, dulled, inner hinges splitting, leading f.e.p. slightly chipped, from the library of Geoffrey & Kathleen Tillotson.   Jarndyce Antiquarian Booksellers   CCVII - 52   2015   £25

Arnold, Matthew 1822-1888 *St. Paul and Protestantism...* London: Smith Elder, 1870. First edition, half title, browning caused by endpapers, original brown cloth, small tear on back board, slight rubbing, traces of library label in leading endpapers, from the library of Geoffrey & Kathleen Tillotson.   Jarndyce Antiquarian Booksellers   CCVII - 55   2015   £30

Arnold, Matthew 1822-1888 *Schools and Universities on the Continent.* Ann Arbor: University of Michigan Press, 1964. Original green cloth, very good in dust jacket, Geoffrey Tillotson's presentation copy with carbon copy of TL presumably from him, sending praise for the project.   Jarndyce Antiquarian Booksellers   CCVII - 54   2015   £20

Arnold, Matthew 1822-1888 *The Strayed Reveller and Other Poems.* London: B. Fellowes, 1849. First edition, original green blindstamped cloth, spine lettered gilt, half title, cloth little marked and rubbed, else very nice, armorial bookplate of R. E. Bartlett, scarce, from the collection of Gavin H. Fryer.   Bertram Rota Ltd.   308 Part II - 126   2015   £500

Arnold, William Delafield *Oakfield; or Fellowship in the East.* London: Longman, 1854. Second edition, 2 volumes, contemporary half calf, tooled in blind and gilt, black labels, bookplates of Tarradale House & earlier signatures of H. F. Bishop, very good.   Jarndyce Antiquarian Booksellers   CCXI - 17   2015   £225

Around the World with Santa Claus. New York: McLoughlin Bros., 1891. Large 4to., cloth backed pictorial boards, neat mend to margin of one page and spine. edges and corners worn else tight and very good, pages mounted on thick board, 14 fabulous chromolithographs, illustrations all by R. Andre, rare+.   Aleph-Bet Books, Inc.   108 - 97   2015 $1200

The Arraignments, Tryals and Condemnations of Charles Cranburne and Robert Lowick, for the Horrid ... London: printed for Samuel Heyrick and Isaac Cleave, 1696. First edition, folio, initial imprimatur leaf, fine, crisp copy, recently bound in boards, lettered.   John Drury Rare Books   March 2015 - 23938   2015   £306

Arredondo, Antonio de *Arredondo's Historical Proof of Spain's Title to Georgia.* Berkeley: University of California Press, 1925. First edition, very scarce, 10 photographic plates, maps, some folding, publisher's navy blue cloth, gilt, very fine and bright copy, very scarce.   Argonaut Book Shop   Holiday Season 2014 - 15   2015 $300

Arrelannes, Audrey *Tagore's Fireflies.* Alhambra: Audrey Arrelanes, 1968. Limited to 200 numbered copies, 8.6 x 4.5cm., quarter cloth, paper covered boards, miniature booklabel of Kathryn Rickard.   Oak Knoll Books   306 - 102   2015 $150

Arrington, Fred *A History of Dickens County, Ranches and Rolling Plains.* N.P.: Nortex, 1971. First edition, quarto, decorated cloth, frontispiece, photos, map, former owner's neat bookplate, small inked date, six tiny black ink spots and one small spot to front cover, else near fine, tight copy, without dust jacket.   Buckingham Books   March 2015 - 31187   2015 $185

Arseniev, V. K. *Dersu the Trapper.* New York: E. P. Dutton, 1941. First American edition, very good in yellow cloth stamped in blue, neat ownership signature to front endpaper, very good- dust jacket with shallow chipping at spine crown and foot with short tear to top front spine fold, still solid.   Ed Smith Books   82 - 2   2015 $350

The Art Journal Illustrated Catalogue. The Industry of All Nations 1851. London: published for the Proprietors by George Virtue, 1851. Folio, frontispiece, illustrations, final ad leaf, slightly later half maroon calf by J. Carss & Co., Glasgow, leading hinge rubbed, corners slightly bumped, later paper label partially removed.   Jarndyce Antiquarian Booksellers   CCXI - 127   2015   £145

Art and Archeology. 1915-1921. 42 issues, all very good with minor soil.   Bookworm & Silverfish   2015 - 3654002697   2015 $295

The Art Journal for 1876 New Series Volume 2. New York: D. Appleton & Co., 1876. First edition, 4to, contemporary black three quarter leather, some rubbed, some very minor soiling inside but very good tight, clean copy, 36 steel-cut full page engravings.   Second Life Books Inc.   191 - 6   2015 $250

The Art of Governing a Wife; with Rules for Batchelors. printed and old by J. Robinson, 1747. New edition, bit foxed or browned in places, 12mo., modern calf, signature on old flyleaf and another at head of text, latter dated 1815, sound.   Blackwell's Rare Books   B179 - 69   2015   £950

Art Work of Delaware. N.P.: Charles Madison Co., 1898. First edition, quarto, contemporary leather, 22 pages of text, 70 pages of photos, with ink binding stamp indicating that this copy was bound by R.T. Stuart 615 Shipley Street, Wilmington, Del." and with name "Isaac C. Elliott" stamped in gilt on lower portion of front cover, spine replaced and stamped with author's name and title, professional restoration to original front and rear covers, new front and rear endpapers, some tissues replaced, else near fine, housed in cloth slipcase with leather label on spine and titles stamped in gilt.   Buckingham Books   March 2015 - 23961   2015 $1250

Arthur, Chester A. *Message from the President of the United States. transmitting a Communication from the Secretary of war in Relation to Building Quarters for Troops at Fort Leavenworth, Kansas.* Washington: GPO, 1882. First edition, 8vo., hardcover binder, titles stamped in gold gilt on front cover, 3 pages, plus 3 large foldout diagrams, both text and diagrams fine.   Buckingham Books   March 2015 - 35686   2015 $300

Arthur, T. S. *Uncle Ben's New-Year's Gift and Other Stories.* Philadelphia: 1869. First edition, 4 plates, some cover spotting and some rubbing to backstrip, gilt generally legible.   Bookworm & Silverfish   2015 - 6016855992   2015 $45

The Arthurian Romances The Vulgate Version edited from the Manuscripts in the British Museum. Washington: Carnegie Institution, 1908-1916. First edition, wrappers, 8 volumes, 4to., bright, clean set with occasional slight edgewear to some volumes, slight staining to printed wrappers of few volumes, text clean and bright, most pages uncut, excellent, unread copy.   Any Amount of Books   March 2015 - A6848   2015   £375

Arthurs, Stanley *The American Historical Scene as Depicted by Stanley Arthurs and Interpreted by Fifty Authors.* Philadelphia: University of Pennsylvania Press, 1935. First edition, tall quarto, quarter leather and linen, frontispiece, illustrations, fine, without dust jacket, as issued, housed in matching cloth slipcase with leather label and titles stamped in gold.   Buckingham Books   March 2015 - 20233   2015 $250

Articles of Agreement and Association of the Emigrant Aid Company. Boston: Alfred Mudge & Son, 1854. First edition, 8vo., 8 pages, sewn as issued, edges lightly browned, very good fragile pamphlet.   M & S Rare Books, Inc.   97 - 140   2015 $350

Artistic Pussy and Her Studio. Chicago: L. W. Walter Co., n.d. circa, 1890. 4to., cloth backed pictorial boards, some edge wear and cover soil, else very good+ in good working order, 7 tab operated plates with jointed parts and with few illustrations in brown, rare.   Aleph-Bet Books, Inc.   108 - 292   2015 $2900

Artzybasheff, Boris *Poor Shaydullah.* New York: Macmillan Co., Nov., 1931. First edition, 4to., grey pictorial cloth, cover slightly faded else fine in nice wrapper with 1 closed tear, this copy signed by Artzbasheff with bold woodcuts.   Aleph-bet Books, Inc.   109 - 26   2015 $425

Ashbee, Felcitiy *The W.A.A.F. Magazine.* Walford: H. Q. F. C. Unit, 1939. First edition, 8vo., possibly all published, some illustrations, slight wear, otherwise very good.   Any Amount of Books   2015 - A63895   2015   £150

Ashbery, John *Art and Literature.* Lausanne: Societe Anonyme d'Editions Litteraire March 1946- Spring 1947, Complete run, 12 issues, large 8vo., illustrations, original printed wrappers, volumes 1-3 limited to 5500 copies, volumes 4-6, 5000 copies and volumes 7-12 4500 copies, occasional light use, some dust soil, otherwise fine.   James S. Jaffe Rare Books   Many Happy Returns - 371   2015 $450

Ashbery, John *Description of a Masque.* New York: Limited Editions Club, 1998. Limited to 300 numbered copies, signed by author and artist, folio, illustrations by Jane Freilicher, cloth, inlaid leather label on front cover, top edge gilt, other edges uncut, cloth clamshell box with inlaid leather label on spine, dent on fore-edge of clamshell box, Monthly letter loosely inserted, watercolor woodblock prints printed by Keiji Shinohara paper for this edition.   Oak Knoll Books   25 - 68   2015 $595

Ashbery, John *The Double Dream of Spring.* New York: E. P. Dutton & Co., 1970. First edition, first issue, 8vo., original cloth backed boards, dust jacket, fine, jacket slightly rubbed, two short closed tears and some minor wear to top edge, presentation copy inscribed by author for Daisy Aldan, editor of "Folder", with original invitation to book's publication party at Gotham Book Mart on Feb. 9 1970 laid in.   James S. Jaffe Rare Books   Modern American Poetry - 13   2015 $1500

Ashbery, John *The Double Dream of Spring.* New York: E. P. Dutton & Co., 1970. First edition, first issue, signed by author, 8vo., original cloth backed boards, dust jacket, fine in lightly rubbed dust jacket.   James S. Jaffe Rare Books   Modern American Poetry - 9   2015 $150

Ashbery, John *Faster than Birds Can Fly.* New York: Granary Books, 2009. First edition, one of 40 numbered copies signed by author and artist, oblong 4to., full page illustrations in colors by Trevor Winkfield, original cloth over boards, color onlay on both covers, publisher's acetate dust jacket, as new.   James S. Jaffe Rare Books   Modern American Poetry - 20   2015 $2500

Ashbery, John *Hotel Lautreamont.* New York: Alfred A. Knopf, 1993. First edition, faint sticker shadow on front pastedown, else fine in fine dust jacket, pencil signature of Ashbery's editor Elizabeth Sifton.   Between the Covers Rare Books, Inc.   187 - 4   2015 $65

Ashbery, John *Houseboat Days. Poems.* New York: Viking, 1977. First edition, erratum slip laid in, 8vo., original cloth backed boards, contemporary, presentation copy inscribed by Ashbery for Ted Berrigan and wife Alice Notley, 9/20/77, fine.   James S. Jaffe Rare Books   Many Happy Returns - 352   2015 $3500

Ashbery, John *Locus Solus.* France: Locus Solus, 1960-1962. First edition, second (trimmed) state of first volume, 4 volumes, 8vo., original printed wrappers, fine set, the artist, Nell Blaine's set with her ownership signature on titlepage of each volume.   James S. Jaffe Rare Books Modern American Poetry - 22   2015 $1250

Ashbery, John *A Nest of Ninnies.* New York: Dutton, 1969. First edition, one of 6000 copies, 8vo., cloth backed boards, dust jacket, small spot of dampstaining at head of spine, spine little cocked, otherwise fine in slightly dust soiled, and nicked dust jacket, with one tiny closed tear and bit of wear to head of spine, presentation from James Schuyler for Trevor Winkfield.   James S. Jaffe Rare Books Modern American Poetry - 12   2015 $1750

Ashbery, John *A Nest of Ninnies.* Calais: Z Press, 1975. First wrapper edition, 8vo., original wrappers, one of 26 lettered copies signed by Ashbery and Schuyler, fine.   James S. Jaffe Rare Books   Modern American Poetry - 16   2015 $3500

Ashbery, John *Novel.* New York: Grenfell Press, 1998. First edition, limited to 100 copies signed by Ashbery and Winfield (entire edition), 4to., 10 drawings by Trevor Winkfield, original silk screened cloth, very fine.   James S. Jaffe Rare Books   Modern American Poetry - 19   2015 $1000

Ashbery, John *Self Portrait in a Convex Mirror.* New York: Viking, 1975. First edition, one of 3500 copies, 8vo., original cloth backed boards, dust jacket, fine.   James S. Jaffe Rare Books   Modern American Poetry - 15   2015 $750

Ashbery, John *Some Trees.* New Haven: Yale University Press, 1956. First edition, fine in very near fine, price clipped dust jacket.   Between the Covers Rare Books   196 - 61   2015 $600

Ashbery, John *Some Trees.* New Haven: Yale University Press, 1956. First edition, one of only 817 copies, small 8vo., original black cloth, dust jacket, presentation copy inscribed to poet Barbara Guest, covers slightly soiled, otherwise fine in dust jacket.   James S. Jaffe Rare Books Modern American Poetry - 10   2015 $2500

Ashbery, John *The Tennis Court Oath. A Book of Poems.* Middletown: Wesleyan University Press, 1962. First edition, one of only 750 copies, 8vo., original boards, dust jacket, presentation copy inscribed by poet to artist Nell Blaine, fine.   James S. Jaffe Rare Books   Modern American Poetry - 11   2015 $2500

Ashbery, John *Three Plays.* Calais: Z Press, 1978. First edition, one of 26 lettered copies signed by Ashbery, out of a total hardcover edition of 500 copies, 8vo., original cloth, dust jacket, fine, cover design by Joe Brainard. James S. Jaffe Rare Books   Modern American Poetry - 18 2015 $350

Ashbery, John *Tumadot and Other Poems.* New York: Tibor De Nagy Gallery, 1953. First edition, one of 300 copies printed under supervision of Nell Blaine, 4 drawings by Jane Freilicher, 8vo., original decorated stitched wrappers with printed paper label on front cover, fine, bright copy of this fragile pamphlet with few tiny nicks and closed edge tears in wrappers.   James S. Jaffe Rare Books   Modern American Poetry - 8   2015 $5000

Ashendene Press *A Chronological List, With Prices of the Forty Books printed at the Ashendene Press MDCCCXCV-MCMXXXV.* Ashendene Press, 1935. Sole separate edition, printed in red and black, 4to. original stitched blue wrappers, upper stitching, loose from centre, discolored at edges, edges untrimmed, good, with ALS by C. H. St. John Hornby loosely inserted, written in black ink on headed paper and dated 13 Feb. 1939.   Blackwell's Rare Books B179 - 125   2015   £150

Ashton-Wolfe, H. *The Thrill of Evil.* Houghton Mifflin, 1930. First edition, fine, bright copy in price clipped dust jacket with professional restoration to the spine ends and extremities.   Buckingham Books   March 2015 - 37545 2015 $400

Ashton, Herbert *The Locked Room: a comedy Mystery in three Acts.* New York: Samuel French, 1934. First edition, fine in wrappers, nicks at top of spine and small corner chips on back cover.   Mordida Books   March 2015 - 005207   2015 $125

Ashton, James *The Book of Nature; Containing Information for Young People Who Think of Getting Married on the Philosophy of Procreation and Sexual Intercourse...* New York: Brother Jonathan Office, 1870. First edition, 18m., five colored plates (presumably of 8), of which one is folding, original flexible pictorial cloth, some plates contain hand coloring, all in good condition, some light soiling to covers, some leaves loose, leaf 49/50 lacking, very rare. M & S Rare Books, Inc.   97 - 79   2015 $200

Ashworth, John *An Account of the Rise and Progress of the Unitarian Doctrine; in the Societies at Rochdale, Newchurch in Rossendale and other Places...* Rochdale: printed for the author and sold by J. Westell; also by Rowland Hunter and David Eaton, London, 1817. First edition, 8vo., 80 pages, recent marbled boards lettered on spine, very good very scarce.   John Drury Rare Books   March 2015 - 24709   2015 $266

Asimov, Isaac   1920-1992   *The Caves of Steel.* Garden City: Doubleday and Co., 1954. First edition, octavo, boards.   John W. Knott, Bookseller   Selected New Arrivals Jan. 2015 - 16887   2015 $4500

Asimov, Isaac   1920-1992   *The End of Eternity.* Garden City: Doubleday & Co., 1955. First edition, octavo, illustrations by mel Hunter, cloth.   John W. Knott, Bookseller Selected New Arrivals Jan. 2015 - 16897   2015 $1250

Asimov, Isaac   1920-1992   *The Foundation Trilogy.* New York: Gnome Press, 1951-1953. First edition, first bindings and dust jacket where required, first 3 volumes of the Foundation series, octavo, first volume in cloth, others in boards.   John W. Knott, Bookseller   Selected New Arrivals Jan. 2015 - 16893   2015 $4500

Asimov, Isaac   1920-1992   *The Naked Sun.* Garden City: Doubleday & Co. Inc., 1957. First edition, octavo, jacket illustration by Ruth Ray, cloth.   John W. Knott, Bookseller   Selected New Arrivals Jan. 2015 - 16888   2015 $4500

Asimov, Isaac   1920-1992   *Robot Dreams: Masterworks of Science Fiction and Fantasy.* New York: Berkley Books, 1986. First edition, one of 300 numbered copies signed by author, octavo, illustrations by Ralph McQuarrie.   John W. Knott, Bookseller   Selected New Arrivals Jan. 2015 - 16899 2015 $500

Asimov, Isaac   1920-1992   *Robots and Empire.* West Bloomfield: Phantasia Press, 1985. First edition, one of 605 numbered copies, signed by author, octavo, cloth. John W. Knott, Bookseller   Selected New Arrivals Jan. 2015 - 17210   2015 $250

Asimov, Isaac   1920-1992   *The Robots of Dawn.* Huntington Woods: Phantasia Press, 1983. First edition, one of 750 numbered copies signed by author, octavo, cloth. John W. Knott, Bookseller   Selected New Arrivals Jan. 2015 - 16889   2015 $350

Asimov, Isaac   1920-1992   *The Union Club Murders.* Garden City: Doubleday, 1983. First edition, fine in dust jacket with light wear at spine ends and at corners. Mordida Books   March 2015 - 002191   2015 $75

Asquith, Cynthia   *The Black Cap: new Stories of Murder & Mystery.* London: Hutchinson, 1828. First edition, some slight fading along cover edges, offsetting on endpapers, some scattered spotting on page edges, otherwise very good in dust jacket with closed tear at base of spine and attendant internal tape mends that have been removed, small stain on front panel.   Mordida Books   March 2015 - 001521   2015 $500

Association for the Religious Instruction of the Negroes in Liberty County, Georgia   *Ninth Annual Report.... Together with the Address to the Association by the President the Rev. Robert Quarterman.* Savannah: Thomas Purse, 1844. First edition, 12mo., 44 pages, removed, numerous stab holes in gutter, some dust soiling and spotty foxing, vertical crease &c., about good sound.   M & S Rare Books, Inc.   97 - 27   2015 $400

Astrup, Arne   *The Revised Stan Getz Discography.* Karlslunde: Per Meistrup, 1984. First edition, inscribed by author, spiral bound wrappers, very good+ with few old corner creases.   Beasley Books   2013 - 2015 $45

At Duty's Call. London: John F. Shaw & Co. n.d., 1904. First edition, large octavo, inserted chromolithograph frontispiece, other illustrations, original pictorial bevel edged red cloth, stamped in green, blue, black and silver, chromolithograph mounted on front cover, endpaper ads.   L. W. Currey, Inc.   Boy's Adventure Fiction 2015 - 78   2015 $100

ATF   *American Specimen Book of Type Styles Complete Catalogue of Printing Machinery and Printing Supplies.* New York: American Type Founders, 1912. Thick 4to., original cloth, color printed section headings, some use of color in ornament section, covers rubbed, especially on spine with fading to back cover, better preserved than most copies. Oak Knoll Books   306 - 206   2015 $450

ATF   *Specimen Book and Catalogue.* Jersey City: American Type Founders Co., 1923. Thick 4to., two toned cloth, section headings in color, some use of color in illustration part, color in borders, covers rubbed with some spotting.   Oak Knoll Books   306 - 207   2015 $365

Atherton, Faxon Dean *The California Diary of Faxon Dean 1836-1839.* San Francisco: California Historical Society, 1964. First edition, one of 325 copies of the deluxe edition, signed by editor, printed on rag paper, numbered and signed by editor, frontispiece, maps, illustrations, folding map, facsimiles, gilt lettered and decorated blue-gray cloth, very fine, lightly faded, publisher's slipcase. Argonaut Book Shop   Holiday Season 2014 - 16   2015 $125

Atherton, Gertrude *Adventures of a Novelist.* New York: Liveright, July, 1932. First edition, 2nd printing, frontispiece, 18 photo portraits, black cloth stamped in red and gold, very fine with slightly chipped dust jacket. Argonaut Book Shop   Holiday Season 2014 - 17   2015 $50

Atkins, Francis Henry *The Black Opal: a Romance of Thrilling Adventure.* London: John F. Shaw & Co., 1914. First edition, octavo, 3 inserted plates, original decorated blue cloth, front panel stamped in black, spine panel stamped in black and gold. L. W. Currey, Inc.   Boy's Adventure Fiction 2015 - 30   2015 $250

Atkins, Francis Henry *By Airship to Ophir.* London: John F. Shaw & Co., n.d., 1911. Octavo, 3 inserted plates with color illustrations by A. Pearse, original decorated olive green cloth, front and spine panel stamped in forest green, black and gold pictorial paper inlay on front panel, plain endpapers, edges not gilt. L. W. Currey, Inc.   Boy's Adventure Fiction 2015 - 7   2015 $750

Atkins, Francis Henry *A Trip to Mars.* London: Edinburgh: W. & R. Chambers Ltd., 1909. First edition, octavo, six inserted plates with color illustrations by W. C. Groome, original red pictorial cloth stamped in blue, cream, black and gold, slate coated endpapers. L. W. Currey, Inc.   Boy's Adventure Fiction 2015 - 4   2015 $1000

Atkins, Kathryn A. *Masters of the Italic letter Twenty-Two Exemplars from the Sixteenth Century.* Boston: David R. Godine, 1988. First edition, oblong 4to., cloth, dust jacket, well illustrated. Oak Knoll Books   306 - 231   2015 $100

Atkins, Maurice *Cataplus or, Aeneas His Descent to Hell. A Mock Poem...* London: for Maurice Atkins, 1672. First edition, small 8vo., number of small discreet repairs and some light staining to cancel titlepage, titlepage little browned and some light dampstaining to edges, mid 20th century red morocco, small hole in upper joint, this copy preserved an additional unique cancel title at front with imprint "London, printed for Abisha Brocas, Bookseller in Exiter (sic) 1672", from the library of James Stevens Cox (1910-1997). Maggs Bros. Ltd.   1447 - 12   2015   £1100

Atkinson, Charles *The Life and Adventures of an Eccentric Traveller.* York: printed for the author by M. W. Carrall, 1818. First edition, 8vo., two whole-page woodcut plates and six smaller woodcuts in text, original boards, rebacked, entirely uncut, very good. John Drury Rare Books   2015 - 23462   2015 $830

Atkinson, Frank H. *Atkinson's Sign Painting Up to Now.* Chicago: Frederick J. Drake & Co., 1909. First edition, oblong small 4to., light brown cloth, decorative lettering in orange, green and black, covers rubbed, minor spotting, inside hinges cracked but solid. Oak Knoll Books   Special Catalogue 24 - 2   2015 $450

Atkinson, James *Epitome of the Whole Art of Navigation.* London: by J. D. for James Atkinson and R. Mount, 1695. Second edition?, 12mo., 8 (of 10) folding engraved diagram plates (Plates 1-6, a fragment of 7, 8, 9 torn and loose, 10 lower third missing and volvelle missing, plates generally bit tatty and frayed at fore-edges), titlepage dusty, edges occasionally ragged and torn throughout, closely shaved along fore-edge throughout (occasionally touching text), final gathering M detached from book block and M1 damaged in inner margin, last page dusty), contemporary sheep, panelled in blind, very worn, heavily rubbed and bumped, corners scuffed and holed, headcaps torn, marks of two catches/ties?), 18th century signature "Thos. Gandin" and "Geo. Matthew", from the library of James Stevens Cox (1910-1997). Maggs Bros. Ltd.   1447 - 13   2015   £950

Atlantic Radio Company *"Listen In" at the Boston Radio Exposition.* Boston: 1922. 4to., 64 pages, very good. Bookworm & Silverfish   2015 - 5496748107   2015 $45

Aubert, Rosemary *Free Reign.* Bridgehampton: Bridge Works, 1997. First edition, very fine in dust jacket. Mordida Books   March 2015 - 000010   2015 $75

Auden, Wystan Hugh 1907-1973 *About the House.* New York: Random House, 1965. Fifth printing, signed by author, 8vo., near fine, little sunning to top edge, lightly sunned dust jacket with tiny chip at head of spine. Beasley Books   2013 - 2015 $300

Auden, Wystan Hugh 1907-1973 *The Old Man's Road.* New York: Voyage Press, 1956. First edition, octavo, one of 750 copies (of which 50 had been numbered and signed by author), signed by author, presentation copy from publisher, inscribed to Mr. John Hayward, fine in near fine dust jacket with hint of darkening to spine. Peter Ellis, Bookseller   2014 - 012140   2015   £350

Auden, Wystan Hugh 1907-1973 *Poems.* London: Faber and Faber, 1930. One of 1000 copies, signed by author, small quarto original stiff wrappers with little edgewear, rear wrapper with few indentations and little rubbing, rare signed. Manhattan Rare Book Company   Literature 2014 - 2015 $4300

Audette, A. *Verses Written in the Trenches.* N.P.: n.p., 1918. 12mo., wrappers, 3 maps, very good. Schooner Books Ltd. 110 - 145   2015 $45

Audry, Andre *Arcadie: revue Litt Raire et Scientifique.* Paris: Arcadie, 1954-1972. First edition, circa 210 issues, bound volumes are 1957-1961 and 1963-1972, loose issues 2-5 from the library of Tim D'Arch Smith (the first bound volume has pencilled instructions with his name), 15 bound volumes slightly rubbed, top edge gilt, all bound volumes have front wrappers bound in, loose issues 2-5, 10, 17-24, 25 to 31/32, 229-240, 241-250, 252, odd issue of 311, very good. Any Amount of Books   2015 - A98793   2015   £650

Audubon, John James 1785-1851 *The Birds of America.* New York: Abbeville Press, 1985. Double elephant folio, 435 colored plates, publisher's spectacular full grteen morocco, four volumes, fine set. Andrew Isles 2015 - 28479   2015 $32,500

Aulnoy, Marie Catherine Lejumel De Barnville, Comtesse De *Histoire D'Hypolite Comte De Douglas.* A La Haie: Chez Jean Swart, R. Christ. Alberts, 1726. Reprint, small 8vo., 2 parts in 1, 22 copperplates, one a frontispiece, frontispiece signed D. Coster, other plates unsigned, titlepage of part one printed in red and black, contemporary calf with morocco label, some minor external rubbing, very good, scarce. Second Life Books Inc. 189 - 16   2015 $600

Aumont, Jean Pierre *Sun and Shadow. An Autobiography.* New York: Norton, 1977. First edition, inscribed by author, near fine in like dust jacket but for short tear on rear panel, lower corner of dust jacket flap clipped, but price still unclipped at upper corner (9.95). Beasley Books   2013 - 2015 $45

Austen, Jane 1775-1817 *Emma.* London: printed for John Murray, 1816. First edition, 3 volumes, 12mo., without without half title in volume I, which is very common, contemporary and almost certainly Continental, possibly German original quarter red paper, spines over marbled boards, gilt stamped on spines in Gothic style, overall fine, fresh and entirely uncut in contemporary binding, wanting one rear flyleaf, minor rubbing to upper joints of volume I and II and lower joint of volume II, housed in red morocco back clamshell. Heritage Book Shop   Holiday 2014 - 7   2015 $45,000

Austen, Jane 1775-1817 *Jane Austen's Letters to Her Sister Cassandra and Others.* Oxford: Clarendon Press, 1932. 2 volumes, half titles, frontispieces, plates, maps, uncut, original marbled boards, pale blue cloth spines, paper labels, spines slightly faded, from the library of Geoffrey & Kathleen Tillotson. Jarndyce Antiquarian Booksellers CCVII - 77   2015   £85

Austen, Jane 1775-1817 *Mansfield Park.* Belfast: Simms & M'Inyre, 1846. Half title, 4 pages ads, original maroon cloth, spine slightly faded, nice, from the library of Geoffrey & Kathleen Tillotson. Jarndyce Antiquarian Booksellers CCVII - 78   2015   £200

Austen, Jane 1775-1817 *Mansfield Park.* London: Dent, 1922. Reissue, octavo, 16 color plates by C. E. Bock, very near fine in scarce dust jacket which is near fine, slightly tanned at spine and with couple of small nicks. Peter Ellis, Bookseller   2014 - 019113   2015   £285

Austen, Jane 1775-1817 *Northanger Abbey and Persuasion.* London: John Murray, 1818. First edition, 12mo., 4 volumes, bound with old and incorrect half titles, each 20th century full smooth tan morocco by Riviere, covers ruled in gilt, spines decoratively tooled in gilt, gilt turn-ins, black and red morocco gilt lettering labels, all edges gilt, bookplate pastedown of each volume, light foxing throughout, some light rubbing to spine extremities and outer hinge repair to all volumes, all in all handsome set. Heritage Book Shop   Holiday 2014 - 6   2015 $8500

Austen, Jane 1775-1817 *The Novels of Jane Austen.* Edinburgh: John Grant, 1906. First edition thus, Winchester edition, large 8vo., 9 volumes only, lacking Persuasion, original green cloth lettered gilt at spine, gilt titles and decorated gilt, top edge gilt, tissue protected frontispiece, clean, tight, bright cloth set, very good. Any Amount of Books   March 2015 - C12105   2015   £375

Austen, Jane 1775-1817 *Pride and Prejudice.* London: printed for T. Egerton, 1813. First edition, 3 volumes, 12mo., fine early 20th century full brown crushed morocco Riviere binding, gilt titles and decorations to spines, all edges gilt, marbled endpapers, gilt inner dentelles, binding shows very minor wear, few light scuffs to corners and few small spots to volume III, while often lacking, half titles present in volumes I and III they appear to be supplied from a second edition; volume 1 with minor chips to pages 143/144 and 15/158 and few minor creases to gatherings M and N, volume II with tiny tear to rear flyleaf, small tear to outer margin of page 77, some very minor scattered spotting, volume III, small repair to upper corner of page 129, repair to lower corner of page 137/138, tiny pin hole to page 259/260, beautiful, clean, very attractive. B & B Rare Books, Ltd. 234 - 2   2015 $60,000

Austen, Jane 1775-1817 *Pride and Prejudice; a Novel.* London: T. Egerton, 1813. Second edition, 3 volumes, occasional spotting, small hole in F4 volume II not affecting text, lacking following free endpapers, contemporary half green calf, raised bands, elaborate gilt compartments, marbled paper boards, slight rubbing, with some loss of marbled paper on boards, each volume inscribed 'Priory' in contemporary hand, attractive, well preserved copy, bound without half title. Jarndyce Antiquarian Booksellers   CCXI - 18 2015   £7500

Austen, Jane 1775-1817 *Pride and Prejudice.* London: Standard Pub. Co. circa, 1895. Odd spot, original blue green pictorial cloth, fine, bright copy.   Jarndyce Antiquarian Booksellers   CCXI - 19   2015   £200

Austen, Jane 1775-1817 *Pride and Prejudice.* New York: Limited Editions Club, 1940. Limited to 1500 numbered copies signed by artist, 8vo., full leather stamped in blind, top edge gilt, slipcase rubbed with wear along edges, book with minor wear at spine ends, with monthly letter loosely inserted.   Oak Knoll Books   25 - 25   2015 $350

Austen, Jane 1775-1817 *Sense and Sensibility.* London: 1811. First edition, 3 volumes, 12mo., bound without half titles as is common, with prelim and final blank leaves in volume I and II (bound without final blank in volume III, but with prelims blank), half calf over marbled boards, rebacked to style, each volume with two morocco spine labels, one red and one green, spines stamped and lettered gilt, later endpapers, volume I leaf C11 with two inch closed tear, professionally repaired and with no loss of text, volume II, leaves H7 and H8 with tiny hole, leaf k8 with lower margin torn, only affecting catchword, volume III with paper flaw to page 252, but no loss of text, small holes to leaves B8, B11, D8, F3 and N5, some light foxing throughout, overall very good set.   Heritage Book Shop   Holiday 2014 - 8   2015 $30,000

Austen, Jane 1775-1817 *Sense and Sensibility.* Philadelphia: Carey & Lea, 1833. First American edition, 2 volumes, original drab paper boards over purple cloth with white paper spine labels, ad leaf to volume II inserted before title as called for (often lacking), corner worn, light spotting to boards, paper spine labels heavily rubbed, still partially intact, spines rubbed and faded, but without any tears of fraying to ends, former owner's name to titlepages, volume I with heavy foxing to title page through page 156, remaining leaves and original endpapers clean, small bookseller's label to front pastedown, volume II with few stains to front board, pages clean but for few light spots to fore edge, well preserved without any restoration or repairs, clean and sturdy set in original boards of first American edition, very scarce in original unsophisticated original binding.   B & B Rare Books, Ltd.   234 - 3   2015 $9500

Austen, Ralph *A Treatise of Fruit-Trees Shewing the Manner of Grafting, Setting, Pruning and Ordering of Them in all Respects.* Oxford: for Tho. Robinson, 1653. First edition, small 4to., engraved title with image of ornamental walled garden, small wormtrail in inner margin L4-T4 (partially repaired M2-R1), contemporary calf, spine stamped with gilt shelf mark '393', spine rubbed and scuffed, boards slightly warped, pastedowns unstuck, with "Robert Stone his book/ Anne Coombar 1677" and various pen trials of his name on front flyleaf and on last blank page, signature John Stone, from the library of James Stevens Cox (1910-1997).   Maggs Bros. Ltd.   1447 - 14   2015   £600

Austin, Mary *California the Land of the Sun.* New York: Macmillan, 1914. First American edition, 32 mounted color plates, folding map, green pictorial cloth stamped in black, orange, blue, white, lavender, yellow and gilt, slightest of rubbing to spine ends and corners, previous owner's ink inscription on half title, fine.   Argonaut Book Shop   Holiday Season 2014 - 19   2015 $400

Austin, Mary *Taos Pueblo.* Boston: 1977. Facsimile of 1930 edition, limited to 950 numbered copies, signed by Ansel Adams, folio, quarter leather cloth boards, 12 full page plates reproducing in duotone photos by Ansel Adams, near fine in slipcase.   Dumont Maps & Books of the West   131 - 34   2015 $1950

Austin, William "Peter Rugg the Missing Man." (in) *Tales of Terror Or the Mysteries of Magic.* Boston: Charles Gaylord, 1833. First edition, 8vo. original printed and pictorial boards, rebacked, new label on spine, browned and foxed.   M & S Rare Books, Inc.   97 - 17   2015 $1250

Australia: its Scenery, Natural History and Resources... London: Religious Society, n.d., 1854. First edition, 24mo., original decorated boards, front cover decoration and spine titles stamped in gold, cream colored endpapers, 192 pages, covers lightly soiled, light waterstain to bottom corner edges, else very good.   Buckingham Books   March 2015 - 28199   2015 $225

Automobile Blue Book Publishing Co. *Official Automobile Blue Book 1920 Volume Seven.* New York: 1920. 872 pages plus ad inserts, illustrations, folding map, original limp leather, some rubbing, binding starting in few plates, sound, minor separations to folds of map, overall very good, obviously never used for intended purpose.   Dumont Maps & Books of the West   131 - 35   2015 $150

Aux Origines De L'Abstraction: 1800-1914. Paris: Musee De Orsay, 2003. First edition, 4to., color illustrated wrappers, copiously illustrated in color and black and white, excellent copy, rare.   Any Amount of Books   March 2015 - A72950   2015   £325

Avedon, Richard *In the American West.* New York: Harry N. Abrams Inc., 1985. First edition, small folio, pictorial brown cloth, trimmed and lettered in black, photos on front and rear covers, numerous full page black and white photos, words "Christmas 1985" on front free fly leaf, else fine.   Buckingham Books   March 2015 - 31441   2015 $350

Aveillan, Bruno *Savoir et Faire: Louis Vuitton.* N.P.: Louis Vuitton, n.d. circa, 2013. Folio, 12 pages, original brown fold out case, lettered black and gilt on front cover, 12 loose photos with tissue guards, fine.   Any Amount of Books   2015 - C5187   2015   £150

Avrahami, A. *Guri the Dog with Ruthi and Uri. (Ha Kelev Guri Im Ruti Ve Uri).* Tel Aviv: B(inyamin) Barlevy, n.d. circa, 1945. Oblong 8vo., pictorial boards, light cover soil, very good+, printed on thick boards, each page with different animal.   Aleph-bet Books, Inc.   109 - 235   2015 $300

Ayer, A. J. *The Foundations of Empirical Knowledge.* London: Macmillan, 1940. First edition, 8vo., original blue cloth lettered gilt on spine, signed presentation from author, for his nurse Miss Clark-Jervaise, endpapers very slightly browned, otherwise very good+ in like dust jacket, complete with faint shelfwear, excellent condition.   Any Amount of Books   2015 - A92758   2015   £675

Ayer, A. J. *Part of My Life.* London: Collins, 1977. First edition, 8vo., illustrations, signed presentation from author to Lady Caroline Gilmour, Nov. 3rd 1977, in price clipped dust jacket with slight edgewear.   Any Amount of Books   2015 - A74370   2015   £175

Ayres, Philip *Cupids addresse to the Ladies.* London: sold by R. Bently, 5 Tidmarsh, 1683. First edition, small 8vo., engraved throughout, 44 engraved emblem plates, without final blank leaf, small chip torn from fore-margin of titlepage, titlepage lightly soiled, small unobtrusive waterstaining to upper blank margin of first third of the work, short tear to foot of L1, contemporary calf, gilt spine with brown morocco label, corners, head and foot of spine repaired, this copy includes, presumably autograph, 20 line commendatory poem by poet and playwright Nahum Tate addressed "To My Honb. Friend Philip Ayres esqe on his book of Emblems in four Languages", 18th century signature Henry Burt, large bookplate removed, from the library of James Stevens Cox (1910-1997).   Maggs Bros. Ltd.   1447 - 15   2015   £3500

Ayres, Philip *Lyric Poems, Made in Imitation of the Italians.* London: by J. M. for Jos. Knight and F. Saunders, 1687. First edition, 8vo., single wormhole to upper right blank, corner throughout touching an occasional letter and small tear to lower blank margin of D3, contemporary calf over thin, wooden boards, (usually characteristic of American bindings), gilt tooled spine, printed waste pastedowns, lacking label, top half of front joint split, cords holding, lower corners worn), from the library of James Stevens Cox (1910-1997).   Maggs Bros. Ltd.   1447 - 16   2015   £1500

Azara, Felix De *Essais sur l'Histoire Naturelle des Quadrupedes de la Province du Paraguay.* Paris: C. Pougens, 1801. First edition, 8vo., modern quarter brown cloth over marbled boards, brown morocco spine labels, from the Swann NY Historical Society Sale 1978, lot 523, very good, untrimmed, recent binding with new endpapers, half titles repaired, institutional stamps on half titles and titles, last 7 leaves of volume I in facsimile on matching, period paper, handsome set.   Kaaterskill Books   19 - 9   2015 $900

B

Babou, Henry *Jacques Touchet. Les Artistes Du Livre.* Paris: Henry Babou, 1932. First edition, number 614 of 650 copies, unbound signatures laid into wrappers, fine but for sunned spine and mild offsetting to front and rear blanks, 15 full page plates in color and black and white, small 4to. Beasley Books 2013 - 2015 $125

Baby's Book. London: Raphael Tuck, n.d. circa, 1920. 4to., cloth backed pictorial boards, edges rubbed, else very good, pages mounted on thick boards, pictorial titlepage, decorative border around each page of text, 16 fine full page color illustrations by Mabel Lucy Attwell. Aleph-bet Books, Inc. 109 - 28 2015 $850

Baby's Pets. London: Dean's Rag Book Co. Ltd. n.d. circa, 1938. 8vo., pictorial cloth, illustrations by Valerie Sweet, each page features children with their pets, well printed. Aleph-bet Books, Inc. 109 - 97 2015 $150

Bach, Hugo *Ultra Violet Light by Means of the Alpine Sun Lamp: Treatment and Indications.* New York: 1916. 114,12 pages, five full and part page illustrations, very good. Bookworm & Silverfish 2015 - 3730530687 2015 $75

Bach, Johann Sebastian *Brandenburg Concertos 1-5.* Harmondsworth: Penguin, 1949-1956. 4 volumes, all published, bound in signature patterned wrappers. Honey & Wax Booksellers 2 - 28 2015 $60

Bach, Johann Sebastian *The Complete Organ Works.* Bury St. Edmunds: Kevin Mayhew, 1994. First edition, oblong 4to., 4 volumes, original burgundy cloth, lettered gilt on spines and front covers, fine in very good+ slipcase. Any Amount of Books 2015 - C10019 2015 £225

Bacheller, Irving *Vergilius: a Tale of the Coming of Christ.* New York: Harper & Bros., 1904. First edition, lightly edgeworn, near fine, without dust jacket, bookplate of collector Frederick W. Skiff and later book label of Estelle Doheny collection, inscribed by Bacheller to Skiff Dec. 22 1916. Between the Covers Rare Books, Inc. 187 - 5 2015 $125

Bachiller Y Morales, Antonio *Antiguedades Americanas.* Habana: Oficina del Faro Industrial, 1845. First edition, 8vo., plate, 1 folding map, in text engravings, later half marbled calf over brown cloth boards, four raised bands, red and brown morocco spine labels titled in gilt decorative endpapers, original wrappers bound in, very good, mostly unopened (uncut) copy with spine rubbed, small tears and chips to original wrappers, occasional foxing. Kaaterskill Books 19 - 19 2015 $1000

Bachiller Y Morales, Antonio *Apuntes para la Historia de las Letras y De La Instruction Publica de la Isla de Cuba.* Habana: Impr. de P. Massana/Impr. del Tiempo, 1859-1861. First edition, 8vo., modern quarter speckled calf over green marbled boards, four raised bands, red morocco spine label tilted in gilt, marbled endpapers, very good the copy of Mario Guiral Moreno (1882-1964), titlepage foxed, owner's stamp on margin, few small holes to top edge, notations on few pages, leaves browned and edges foxed, more heavily to first volume, binding quite fine, handsome copy of a rare and important work. Kaaterskill Books 19 - 11 2015 $1000

Bacon, Francis, Viscount St. Albans 1561-1626 *Historia Vitae et Mortis.* Amsterdam: Joannem Ravesteinium, 1663. Fifth separate edition, 12mo., contemporary mottled calf covers ruled in gilt, rebacked, new endleaves, old flyleaves preserved, inscription "Guil Rayner Aedis Ch. Alummus 1683" (William Rayner of London 1664-1730), signature of W. Leigh, from the library of James Stevens Cox (1910-1997). Maggs Bros. Ltd. 1447 - 17 2015 £120

Bacon, Francis, Viscount St. Albans 1561-1626 *Sermones Fideles, Ethici, Politici, Oeconomici...* Leiden: F. Hackium, 1644. Second Latin edition, 12mo., engraved allegorical frontispiece, small rust spot to inner margin of H9 and with some light occasional foxing in places (F1-G1), contemporary French or Low Countries calf, ruled in gilt, gilt spine (lightly worn, edges bumped, upper and lower headcaps damaged), signature "A M J J Dupin" (Andre Marie Jean Jacques Dupin 1783-1865), from the library of James Stevens Cox (1910-1997). Maggs Bros. Ltd. 1447 - 18 2015 £200

Bacon, Francis, Viscount St. Albans 1561-1626 *Opera Omnia.* Frankfurt: Impensis Joannis Baptistae Schonwetteri typis Matthaei Kempfferi, 1665. One of only two issues with variant titles printed in 1665, folio, browned throughout, heavily in many places, due to poor paper quality, contemporary English calf, covers with floral cornerpieces in blind, joints split, wear to head and foot of spine, edges rubbed, from the library of James Stevens Cox (1910-1997). Maggs Bros. Ltd. 1447 - 19 2015 £200

Bacon, Peggy *Cat-Calls.* New York: McBride, 1935. Stated first edition, fine in tattered dust jacket, illustrations by Bacon with many lovely black and white illustrations in text, with fabulous half page drawing inscribed by Bacon. Aleph-bet Books, Inc. 109 - 29 2015 $650

Bacon, Roger *The Cure of Old Age and Preservation of Youth.* London: for Tho. Flesher and Edward Evets, 1683. First edition in English, 8vo., early 19th century half russia, drab boards, gilt edges, ribbon marker (joints cracked), bookplate of George Field (1777-1854), with occasional pencil notes, from the library of James Stevens Cox (1910-1997).   Maggs Bros. Ltd. 1447 - 20   2015   £300

Bacon, Thomas *The Orientalist; Containing a Series of Tales, Legends and Historical Romances...* London: Thomas Arnold, 1842. First and second series, 2 volumes, double frontispiece, plates, slight creasing to lower corners volume II, original purple fine diaper cloth, gilt spines, boards decorated with central vignette in gilt and elaborate borders in blind, spines slightly faded, all edges gilt, very attractive.   Jarndyce Antiquarian Booksellers   CCXI - 20   2015   £180

Badcock, Benjamin *Tables Exhibiting the Prices of Wheat from the Year 1780 to 1830...* London: Longman, Rees, Brown and Green, and Henry Slatter, Oxford, 1832. Folio, tables, engraved frontispiece and two hand colored engraved graphs, uncut in original burgundy half roan over cloth boards, upper cover with a label lettered in gilt, rare.   Marlborough Rare Books   List 53 - 2   2015   £4500

Badger, Clarissa Munger *Floral Belles from the Green-House Garden.* New York: Charles Scribners, 1867. First edition, folio, publisher's blind and gilt decorated black morocco with gilt floral borders, inner dentelles and lettering, all edges gilt, hand colored lithographed frontispiece and 15 hand colored plates, with stunning hand colored lithographs, some faint foxing to blank leaves, unusually fine.   The Brick Row Book Shop   Miscellany 67 - 5   2015 $4500

Badger, Joseph Edward *The Lost City.* Boston: Dana Estes & Co., 1898. First edition, octavo, 8 inserted plates, illustrations by L. J. Bridgman, original pictorial blue cloth, front panel stamped in white, brown and gold, spine panel stamped in brown and gold.   L. W. Currey, Inc. Boy's Adventure Fiction 2015 - 35   2015 $225

Badham, Charles David *The Question concerning the sensibility, Intelligence and Instinctive Actions of Insects by Scarabaeus.* Paris: printed by A. Belin n.d., 1837. First edition, 8vo., with final blank leaf, original upper wrapper preserved, little dust marked, holograph presentation inscription in ink from author to Dr. Charles Price.   John Drury Rare Books   2015 - 15141   2015 $133

Baedeker, Karl *Egypt and the Sudan - Handbook for Travellers.* Leipzig: Karl Baedeker, 1929. Eighth edition, 12mo., 106 maps and plans, 56 woodcuts, small ownership inscription on front pastedown under dust jacket flap, very good in scarce dust jacket which is rubbed, chipped, marked and stained, heavily repaired on reverse.   Peter Ellis, Bookseller   2014 - 019011   2015   £300

Baedeker, Karl *Egypt: Handbook for Travellers Part 1....* Leipsic & London: Karl Baedeker, 1895. Third edition, 8vo., original red cloth, lettered gilt on spine and on front cover and lined in blind, 14 maps, 33 plans, 7 views, 78 vignettes, very slight fading at spine, slight bumping at lower corners, otherwise sound, very good+, excellent condition.   Any Amount of Books   2015 - C13685   2015   £160

Baedeker, Karl *Egypt - Handbook for Travellers.* Leipzig: Karl Baedeker, 1898. Fourth edition, revised by Georg Steindorff, small octavo, 22 maps, 55 plans, 66 views and vignettes, presentation copy from Prof. Steindorff for John H. Gretton, good, scarce inscribed, front hinge cracking, covers bit bumped at edges and marked.   Peter Ellis, Bookseller   2014 - 10317   2015   £350

Baedeker, Karl *The United States with an Excursion into Mexico.* Leipsic: Karl Baedeker, 1899. Second edition, 8vo., flyleaf loose, owner's name and date on it, cover little worn, spine faded, otherwise very good.   Second Life Books Inc.   191 - 7   2015 $190

Baif, Lazare De *Annotationes in L. II. De Captivis et Postiliminio Reversis in Quibus Tractatur de re Navali (and three other works).* Paris: Robert Estienne, 1536. First edition of De Re Navali, first printing of this collection, 216 x 140mm., striking 16th century English calf, heavily and beautifully gilt, covers gilt with border formed by two plain rules flaking a floral roll, this frame enclosing a central field of very many tiny star tools, intricate strapwork cornerpieces and large central arabesque composed of strapwork interspersed with lilies and volutes, flat spine divided into latticed gilt panels by double plain rules and floral bands, newer (17th or 18th century?) black morocco label, binding almost certainly with some restoration (joints probably worked on, though repairs executed with such skill as to make difficult identifying exactly what has been done), old stock used for replacement endpapers 32 fine woodcuts in text, 11 of them full page or nearly so, 4 woodcut diagrams, decorative initials, covers with minor discoloration, little crackling and minor scratching, gilt bit dulled and eroded, one corner somewhat bumped, half a dozen leaves with faint damp-stains to lower outer corner, hint of soil in isolated places, but extremely pleasing copy, binding solid, no serious wear, still very attractive, text clean, fresh and bright, margins generous.   Phillip J. Pirages   66 - 4   2015 $7500

Bailey Rawlin's Expanding View of the Great Exhibition Transept. London: published for the Proprietor Chas. Moody, High Holborn, 1851. Concertina-folding peepshow printed in chromolithograph with four cut-out sections, front face (180 x 162mm.), peepshow extends by linen bellows to approximately 464mm.   Marlborough Rare Books Ltd.   List 49 - 25   2015   £950

Bailey, H. C. *Dead Man's Effects.* London: MacDonald, 1945. First English edition, fine in dust jacket.   Mordida Books   March 2015 - 006479   2015 $125

Bailey, H. C. *Meet Mr. Fortune.* Garden City: Doubleday, 1942. First Omnibus edition, fine in price clipped dust jacket with fading on spine and scattered nicks along edges. Mordida Books   March 2015 - 007816   2015 $125

Bailey, H. C. *The Red Castle Mystery.* New York: Doubleday Crime Club, 1932. First American edition, red topstain mottled, else near fine in like, price clipped dust jacket with professional restoration to spine ends, and extremities, from the collection of Duke Collier.   Royal Books   36 - 136   2015 $750

Bailey, H. C. *Slippery Ann.* London: Gollancz, 1944. First edition, fine in lightly soiled dust jacket.   Mordida Books   March 2015 - 000218   2015 $135

Bailey, Nathan *Dictionarium Britannicum or a More Compleat Universal Etymlogical English Dictionary Than an Extant...* printed for T. Cox, 1736. Variant with publisher's address and date in Roman numerals, title printed in red and black, text printed in double columns, numerous woodcut illustrations in text, 1 engraved plate, tear in second leaf emanating from lower inner corner and ascending first vertically then diagonally, entering the text for 10 lines but without loss, some dampstaining in lower margins towards end, folio, contemporary panelled calf, double gilt fillets on sides, double gilt fillets on either side of raised bands on spine, red lettering piece, rebacked preserving original spine, bookplate of J. A. Gotch, good copy.   Blackwell's Rare Books   B179 - 7   2015   £750

Bailik, H. N. *Sefer Hadvarim. (A Book of Things).* Berlin: Ophir, 1922. First edition, square 8 1/4 inch, cloth backed pictorial boards, some cover soil and rubbing, matching newer endpapers, light finger soil, clean and tight, very good+, 16 full page hand colored illustrations by Freud, rare.   Aleph-bet Books, Inc.   109 - 185   2015 $4000

Baillie, Joanna *Epilogue to the Theatrical Representation at Strawberry Hill.* N.P.: n.p., 1800. First edition, 2nd issue with paper watermarked 1804, folio, single leaf folded to make 4 pages, paper little browned, fore edges little chipped, very good.   The Brick Row Book Shop Miscellany 67 - 23   2015 $350

Baird, Frank *Parson John of the Labrador.* London: Religious Tract Society, 1924. 8vo., illustrations by George Soper, frontispiece and 7 other full page illustrations, some dampstaining throughout, one plate torn at top, bookplate partially removed, generally good, dark green cloth with gilt titles to front and spine.   Schooner Books Ltd.   110 - 31   2015 $45

Baker, Estelle *The Rose Door.* Chicago: Charles H. Kerr, 1911. First edition, illustrations, green cloth, very good+ copy.   Beasley Books   2013 - 2015 $150

Baker, John *The Oxford History of the Laws of England: Volume Six 1483-1558.* Oxford: Oxford University Press, 2003. First edition, 8vo., original black cloth lettered gilt at spine, fine in fine dust jacket.   Any Amount of Books   2015 - C948-   2015   £160

Baker, M. *A Word for Scientific Theology in Appeal from the Men of Science and the Theologians.* London: Williams and Norgate, 1868. First edition, 8vo., 32 pages, title bit foxed, else very good, recently well bound in linen backed marbled boards, lettered.   John Drury Rare Books   2015 - 5336   2015 $168

Baker, Nicholson *A Box of Matches, with Matches.* London: Chatto & Windus, 2002. Advance reading copy of first British edition, fine in wrappers, with a Chatto & Windus promotional book of matches with author and title (and pet duck) printed on front cover, all matches present - fine.   Ken Lopez, Bookseller   164 - 8   2015 $75

Baker, Silvia *Journey to Yesterday.* London: Peter Davies, 1950. First edition, top corner little bumped, near fine in near fine dust jacket, author Ralph Hodgson's copy, unsigned but with Baker's London address with date in 1953 on front fly annotated on (p. 138) and supplied the book with further handmade and hand lettered brown paper dust jacket.   Between the Covers Rare Books, Inc.   187 - 6   2015 $125

Baker, Thomas *The Geometrical Key or the Gate of Equations Unlock'd.* London: by J. Playford for R. Clavel, 1684. First edition, small 4to., 10 leaves of folding engraved diagrams, very occasional light spotting, paper flaw in blank corner of K2, a number of leaves uncut in tail, minor dampstaining to lower fore-corner of folded plates, mid 18th century polished calf, gilt spine (joints split but held by cords, boards little scuffed, label half missing, lower corners bumped), from the library of James Stevens Cox (1910-1997).   Maggs Bros. Ltd.   1447 - 21   2015   £400

Baker, Thomas Barwick Loyd *War with Crime: Being a Selection of Reprinted Papers on Crime, Reformatories, etc.* London: Longmans Green and Co., 1889. First edition, 8vo., fine frontispiece, half title, contemporary half calf, gilt over marbled boards, very good.   John Drury Rare Books   2015 - 18936   2015 $177

Balazs, Bela *Duke Bluebeard's Castle.* Llandogo: Old Stile Press, 2006. 39/150 copies, signed by translator, John Lloyd Davies and by artist, Susan Adams, frontispiece and 17 further full page illustrations, 4to., original illustrated red and black boards, backstrip lettered grey, top edge black, others untrimmed, illustrated cloth and paper slipcase, fine.   Blackwell's Rare Books   B179 - 202   2015   £200

Baldwin, George *Political Recollections Relative to Egypt...* London: T. Cadell and W. Davies, 1801. First edition, 8vo., recent blue cloth lettered gilt with Foreign and Commonwealth Office with their small oval stamp and accession number, blindstamped on cover, bound with half title, handwritten presentation from author, pages faintly browned, overall decent very good copy. Any Amount of Books 2015 - A49989 2015 £225

Baldwin, George P. *The Black Hills Illustrated.* N.P.: Black Hills Mining Men's Association, 1904. First edition, tall quarto, decorated wrappers in gold and black, illustrated with original photos, corners lightly bumped, else near fine, tight, clean copy, scarce. Buckingham Books March 2015 - 32320 2015 $1250

Baldwin, James *Blues for Mister Charlie.* New York: Dial, 1964. First edition, 8vo., blue cloth, edges little chipped, otherwise very good, tight copy in price clipped and somewhat soiled and chipped dust jacket. Second Life Books Inc. 191 - 8 2015 $85

Baldwin, James *Going to Meet the Man.* New York: Dial, 1965. First edition, 8vo., fine, dust jacket little crinkled. Second Life Books Inc. 190 - 2 2015 $325

Baldwin, James *The Price of the Ticket. Collected Nonfiction 1948-1985.* New York: St. Martin's Press/Marek, 1985. First edition, inscribed by author, fine in near fine dust jacket with tiny tear, large 8vo., 690 pages. Beasley Books 2013 - 2015 $450

Baldwin, James *Tell Me How Long the Train's Been Gone, a Novel.* New York: Dial, 1968. First edition, 8vo., 484 pages, nice in very good, price clipped dust jacket. Second Life Books Inc. 190 - 3 2015 $125

Balfour, Arthur James *Criticism and Beauty: a Lecture Rewritten...* Oxford: Clarendon press, 1910. publisher's slip, original blue printed wrappers, slightly creased, 48 pages, from the library of Geoffrey & Kathleen Tillotson. Jarndyce Antiquarian Booksellers CCVII - 81 2015 £20

Ball, John *In the Heat of the Night.* New York: Harper & Row, 1965. First edition, fine in price clipped, otherwise fine dust jacket, superb copy, scarce especially in this condition, from the library of Kate Stettner Lobell and Carl D. Lobell. Between the Covers Rare Books 196 - 43 2015 $1200

Ball, John *In the Heat of the Night.* New York: Harper & Row, 1965. First edition, fine in price clipped dust jacket, exceptional copy. Buckingham Books March 2015 - 35864 2015 $1250

Ball, John *A New Compendious Dispensatory; or a Select Body of the Most Useful, Accurate and Elegant Medicines...* London: T. Cadell, 1769. First and only edition, very scarce, contemporary calf, neatly rebacked to match with raised bands and label, very good, very scarce. John Drury Rare Books 2015 - 24960 2015 $830

Ball, Robert *An Atlas of Astronomy: a Series of Seventy-Two Plates.* New York: D. Appleton and Co., 1892. First American edition, square 8vo., 72 plates, some color lithograph and tissue guards, reinforced hinges, original full blind and silver stamped cloth, extremities rubbed and abrasions to hinges, inner joints neatly reinforced with kozo, endleaves scarred due to tape pulled from surface, very good, rare. Jeff Weber Rare Books 178 - 773 2015 $375

Ball, Robert *In the High Heavens.* London: Isbister and Co., 1894. Small 8vo., color frontispiece, 41 figures, modern red cloth, maroon gilt stamped spine label, bookplate, fine. Jeff Weber Rare Books 178 - 774 2015 $45

Ballantine, James *The Gaberlunzie's Wallet.* London: Tilt & Bogue, R Tyas, 1843. First book edition, tall 8vo., plates and illustrations, cream endpapers, original purple brown horizontal ribbed cloth, blind borders and ornaments on boards, gilt pictorial spine with title reversed out on gilt banner, spine slightly faded, top edge gilt, very good, crisp copy. Jarndyce Antiquarian Booksellers CCXI - 22 2015 £120

Ballantyne, Robert Michael *The Giant of the North or Pokings Round the Pole.* Toronto: A. G. Watson; Toronto: Willard Tract Depository Ltd., n.d., 1882? First Canadian edition?, octavo, five inserted plates plus engraved title leaf, illustrations by H. Pearson, one map in text, original pictorial brown cloth, front and spine panels stamped in orange yellow, green and black, yellow coated endpapers. L. W. Currey, Inc. Boy's Adventure Fiction 2015 - 31 2015 $250

Ballard, J. G. *Myths of the Near Future.* London: Published by Jonathan Cape, 1982. First edition, 8vo., signed by author, fine in fine dust jacket. Any Amount of Books 2015 - A92720 2015 £160

Balliett, Whitney *Alec Wilder and His Friends.* Boston: Houghton Mifflin, 1974. First edition, advance review copy with slip laid in, fine in near fine dust jacket, this copy inscribed by Balliett, 8vo. Beasley Books 2013 - 2015 $175

Balliett, Whitney *New York Notes.* Boston: Houghton Mifflin, 1976. First edition, 8vo., signed by Balliett, fine in near fine dust jacket. Beasley Books 2013 - 2015 $150

Balmford, William *The Seaman's Spiritual Companion or Navigation Spiritualized.* London: for Benj. Harris, 1678. First edition, small 8vo., variant state of title with double rule border and price on titlepage, A2 shaved at foot affecting signature and catchword on recto, minor worming in upper outer corner of D4-K8 (affecting end of text in places), stain to B3-E2 affecting three lines, occasional foxing, small hole from paper flaw in lower margin of E2, short tear at foot of F3 slightly affecting last line on recto and catchword on verso, small hole from paper flaw in centre of I2 touching two lines, actually reasonable and much loved copy, contemporary sheep (rubbed, covers scuffed, fore edge of lower cover worn exposing board, corners worn), several pen trials, scribbles, ownership inscriptions John Allab(on) His Booke October ye 24th 16, Charles Canning his book 1679, James Purnell His Booke Anno Domini (deleted), "Thomas Nichols His Book May ye 10 1718", "James Croome His Book March ye 9th 1757" "Jane Hanley", from the library of James Stevens Cox (1910-1997). Maggs Bros. Ltd. 1447 - 21 2015 £2800

Balwhidder, Micah *Annals of the Parish; or the Chronicle of Dalmailing; During the Ministry of...* Edinburgh: William Blackwood, 1821. First edition, 8vo., recent half brown leather lettered gilt on spine, 5 raised bands, marbled boards, text clean, very good. Any Amount of Books 2015 - A75416 2015 £220

Balzac, Honore De *La Belle Fille De Portillion.* Paris: L'Enseigne De La Trireme, 1944. #18 of only 25 copies from an edition of only 125, with Colucci's illuminations hand colored by Ferrariello, on Auvergne rag paper with extra suite of black and white illustrations at rear, stunning book, unbound signatures laid into printed wrappers, fine in very good hardcover chemise and box, folio. Beasley Books 2013 - 2015 $750

Balzac, Honore De *La Duchesse De Langeais.* Paris: Editions Rombaldi, 1942. #22 of 100 copies from an edition of 410, illustrations by Dignimont, with an extra set of plates, wrappers fine in original glassine (slightly sunned) in repaired, lightly sunned and lightly soiled chemise in sunned box, 8vo. Beasley Books 2013 - 2015 $200

Balzac, Honore De *La Fille Aux Yeux D'Or.* Paris: Editions Rombaldi, 1942. #142 of 410 copies, wrappers, unbound signatures fine in fine chemise with sunned spine in near fine box, small 8vo. Beasley Books 2013 - 2015 $150

Bambay, Cuthbert *James Cope: the Confessions of a United States District Attorney.* New York: New Amsterdam, 1899. First edition, label on front pastedown, fine in pictorial cloth covered boards. Mordida Books March 2015 - 000223 2015 $100

Bangs, John Kendrick *The Dreamers; a Club.* New York: Harper, 1899. First edition, fine, ownership stamp, fine in pictorial brown cloth covered boards with gold stamped titles. Mordida Books March 2015 - 007427 2015 $125

Bangs, John Kendrick *The Enchanted Type-Writer.* New York: Harper, 1899. First edition, lower front cover slightly bumped and spine slightly darkened, otherwise fine in pictorial cloth covered boards with gold stamped titles. Mordida Books March 2015 - 007428 2015 $125

Bangs, John Kendrick *The Pursuit of the House Boat.* New York: Harper, 1897. First edition, illustrations by Peter Newell, spine darkened, else very good in pictorial cloth covered boards. Mordida Books March 2015 - 002641 2015 $100

Bangs, John Kendrick *R. Holmes & Co.* New York: Harper, 1906. First edition, very good in light pictorial cloth covered boards with gild stamped titles. Mordida Books March 2015 - 007429 2015 $175

Bangs, Merwin & Co. *Catalogue of a Collection of American Silver and Copper Coins and medals, Colonial, Pattern and Washington Pieces...to be sold by auction in New York... Thursday 29th June 1865...* Philadelphia: Myers, Graham & McFarland printers, No. 36 South Third Street, 1865. 8vo., 16 pages, original dark green printed wrappers, light wear, close to fine. M & S Rare Books, Inc. 97 - 227 2015 $150

Bangs, Merwin & Co. *Catalogue of Coins, Autographs and Paper Money, Comprising a Large Lot of Roman Silver, English Silver and Gold Coins in Medals, in Fine Condition... to be sold at auction Thursday Afternoon Nov. 25th 1869.* New York: C. C. Shelley, printer, 68 Barclay St., 1869. First edition, 8vo., sewn, edges little browned, tiny nick top margin, very good, fragile. M & S Rare Books, Inc. 97 - 226 2015 $150

Bangs, Merwin & Co. *Catalogue of Mr. John A. Rice's Library to be Sold by Auction on March 21 1870 and or five following Days by Bangs Merwin & Co.* New York: J. Sabin & Sons, 1870. First edition, original cloth, little flaked, priced in pencil, printed price list at rear, original wrappers bound in. M & S Rare Books, Inc. 97 - 30 2015 $325

Banham, Reyner *The Aspen Papers.* London: Pall Mall Press, 1974. First edition, 8vo., black and white illustrations, fine in fine dust jacket. Any Amount of Books 2015 - A42089 2015 £150

Banks, Iain M. *Consider Phlebas.* London: Macmillan, 1987. First edition, one of 176 numbered copies signed by Banks, octavo, cloth. John W. Knott, Bookseller Selected New Arrivals Jan. 2015 - 16906 2015 $750

Banks, Iain M. *The Player of Games.* London: Macmillan, 1988. First edition, octavo, boards. John W. Knott, Bookseller   Selected New Arrivals Jan. 2015 - 16907   2015 $250

Banks, John *The Destruction of Troy, a Tragedy Acted at His Royal Highness the Duke's Theatre.* London: by A. G. and J. P. are to be sold by Charles Blount, 1679. First edition, small 4to., lightly dampstained throughout, shaved close at head with occasional cropping of headlines, light ink staining to recto of final and verso penultimate leaves, holes from early stitched in gutter throughout, 19th century half morocco and marbled boards, from the library of James Stevens Cox (1910-1997).   Maggs Bros. Ltd.   1447 - 23   2015   £150

Banks, Joseph *Banks' Florilegium.* London: Alecto Historical Editions, 1980-1990. One of 100 numbered copies, 738 copper engraved plates in titled window mounts, color printed a la poupee in up to 17 colors with additional watercolor touches from the original plates, supplement with five copper engraved plates in titled window mounts, the catalogue with 8 copper engraved uncolored duplicate plates, 35 solander boxes (including supplement), broadsheet folio, and one volume catalogue, folio, the Florilegium and supplement in 101 original cloth covered solander boxes by G. Ryder and Co., the catalog bound in half dark green morocco, top edge gilt.   Andrew Isles   2015 - 25871   2015 $125,000

Banks, Joseph *Banks' Florilegium... Madeira Section only.* London: Alecto Historical Editions, 1985. 22 copper engraved plates finished by hand, each with publisher's and printer's blindstamp, numbered and initialed by printer in window mounts with title, loosely contained in cloth backed portfolios in publisher's spectacular solander box as issued. Andrew Isles   2015 - 31283   2015 $2250

Banks, Joseph *Banks' Florilegium... Tierra del Fuego section only.* London: Alecto Historical Editions, 1988. 65 copper engraved plates, la poupee and finished by hand, each with publisher's and printer's blindstamp, numbered and initialled by printer in window mounts with title, loosely contained in cloth backed portfolios, in three publisher's spectacular solander boxes as issued.   Andrew Isles   2015 - 31284   2015 $4850

Banks, Russell *Family Life.* New York: Avon, 1975. First edition, wrappers, advance uncorrected proofs, near fine with small faded spot on rear wrapper, unusual format. Beasley Books   2013 - 2015 $200

Banks, Thomas Christopher *The Detection of Infamy: earnestly Recommended to the Justice and Deliberation of the Imperial Parliament of Great Britain.* London: printed and published for the author by H. K. Causton, 1816. First (only?) edition, 8vo., 28 pages, including half title, folding table, modern plain wrappers, very good.   John Drury Rare Books   2015 - 16385   2015 $133

Banner, Angela *Ant & Bee & Kind Dog.* New York: Franklin Watts, 1963. First American printing, 110 pages, decorated avocado green boards, illustrations by Bryan Ward, very good plus in very good dust jacket (some wear, staining to verso, price clipped), bookplate.   Stephen Lupack   March 2015 - 2015 $125

Bannerman, David Armitage *The Birds of Tropical West Africa.* London: Crown Agents for the Colonies, 1931-1951. Octavo, 8 volumes, 86 (85 colored) plates, text illustrations, folding maps, publisher's cloth, apart from few minor corner bumps, fine set.   Andrew Isles   2015 - 5239   2015 $1250

Bannerman, Helen *The Story of Little Black Quibba.* London: James Nisbet, n.d., 1903. First edition, full page color illustrations, scarce, light binding and wear, very good+.   Aleph-bet Books, Inc.   109 - 34   2015 $1200

Bannerman, Helen *Little Black Sambo.* London: Grant Richards, 1899. First edition, 16mo., green striped cloth covers lightly soiled and rubbed, else near fine, color illustrations engraved on wood and printed by Edmund Evans, nice copy, rare.   Aleph-bet Books, Inc.   109 - 31   2015 $12,500

Bannerman, Helen *The Story of Little Black Sambo.* New York: Frederick Stokes, n.d., 1900. 16mo., gold cloth, spine pictorial board covers lettered in blue, corners worn and normal, light cover soil, else unusually clean, tight and very good+, full page color illustrations, nice.   Aleph-bet Books, Inc.   109 - 32   2015 $1500

Bannerman, Helen *Little Black Sambo.* Racine: Whitman, n.d. circa, 1930. folio, stiff linen-like pictorial wrappers, very good+, illustrations by Terry and Mary Smith with bold colors printed on various colored papers, very scarce.   Aleph-bet Books, Inc.   109 - 33   2015 $675

Bannerman, Helen *The Story of The Teasing Monkey.* New York: Stokes, 1907. First American edition, 12mo., cloth backed pictorial boards, some cover soil and corners worn, else very good, illustrations by author, very scarce. Aleph-bet Books, Inc.   109 - 35   2015 $875

Bannister, Saxe *Humane Policy; or Justice to the Aborigines of New Settlements Essential to a Due Expenditure of British Money...* London: Thomas and George Underwood, 1830. First edition, 8vo., fine folding lithographic map, colored by hand, with half title but without ads found in some copies, mid 19th century half calf gilt with raised bands, red morocco label, very minor wear to extremities, very good, recently from the library of the late Quentin Keynes, originally belonging to the Aborigines Protection Society (name in ink at head of title).   John Drury Rare Books   2015 - 19428   2015 $2185

Banns, William *The Cabinet of Jewels; or Repository of Truth.* Diss: printed by E. E. Abbott bookseller, 1836. 12mo., half title, original cloth, faded, label removed from upper cover, early signature (Mary Willis 1841), good copy, apparently rare.   John Drury Rare Books   2015 - 23516   2015 $133

Baouir De Lormian, Pierre Marie Francois Louis *Veillees Poetiques et Morales Suivies Des Plus Beaux Fragmens D'Young en Vers Francais.* Paris: printed by P. Didot for Latour Delanay and Brunot Abbot, 1811. First edition, 156 x 89mm., extremely pretty contemporary green calf, gilt, covers with delicate floral frame enclosing gilt compartments separated by inlaid red morocco bands, two compartments with rose sprig centerpiece and two compartments with densely interlocking rows of circles, red morocco label, turn-ins with decorative gilt roll, marbled endpapers, all edges gilt (lower joint apparently with very neat expert repair at tail), with etched vignette on titlepage and 3 engraved plates, original tissue guards; bookplate of Raoul Simonson, leather bookplate of Laurent Mecus; front joint with very short thin crack at tail, one opening with faintest freckled foxing, otherwise beautiful copy, text exceptionally clean, fresh and bright, scarcely worn, lustrous binding glistening with gold, especially pleasing gold dusted or "Saupoudrage" binding.   Phillip J. Pirages   66 - 78   2015 $1500

Baptista Mantuanus, Giovanni   1448-1516 *De Patientia.* Basel: Johann Bergmann de Olpe, 17 Aug., 1499. First printing of this edition, 222 x 165mm., 118 unnumbered leaves, 30 lines in roman type, pleasing contemporary blindstamped calf by the Trier Matthiaskloster (Abbey of Saint Matthias in Trier) , covers with frames formed by triple blind rules, typographic banners at head and foot of frame, frame and central panel decorated with floral tools and medallions of various sizes containing representations of St. Catherine, the Agnus Dei, crossed halberds, pomegranates, foliage, rosettes and floral sprays, raised bands, original brass foreedge clasp, front pastedown a vellum manuscript leaf circa 1100, with early form of neumes, rear pastedown removed but with remnants of manuscript text still visible, with 5 large initials written by hand in red, 3 tiny cracks to spine, head of rear joint with quarter inch wormhole exposing band, joints little worn, couple of short worm trails, handful of small patches of lost patina due to insect activity, but contemporary binding still sound, only modest wear and generally very appealing, isolated mild foxing, two pages with small inkblot affecting a couple of letters, other minor defects, almost entirely a fine copy, unusually fresh and clean internally.   Phillip J. Pirages   66 - 2   2015 $22,500

Baraclough, John *James Bond for Your 007 Eyes Only.* London: Marvel, 1981. First edition, fine, without dust jacket as issued.   Mordida Books   March 2015 - 008062   2015 $85

Baraka, Amiri *Jello.* Chicago: Third World Press, 1970. First edition, wrappers, fine.   Beasley Books   2013 - 2015 $45

Baraka, Amiri *The Music Reflections on Jazz and Blues.* New York: Morrow, 1987. First printing, 8vo., 332 pages, illustrations, paper over boards with cloth spine, edges little soiled, else very good, tight copy, presentation (from author?).   Second Life Books Inc.   190 - 4   2015 $150

Barbaro, Francesco *De Re Uxoria Libelli Duo.* Paris: Vaenundantur in aedibus Ascensianis June 2, 1514. Second edition, 4to., printer's device on titlepage, contemporary vellum with marbled endpapers, blindstamped centerpiece with date '1513' (probably added later), marbled endpapers, upper margin bit short, occasionally touching the running title, otherwise fine, ruled throughout, large woodcut initials colored in red, blue, green and gold, fine.   Second Life Books Inc.   189 - 17   2015 $6500

Barbash, Jack *Labour Unions in Action.* New York: Harper, 1948. First edition, inscribed by author, fine and bright in lightly chipped dust jacket (one chip retained), inscribed to labor lawyer Joe Jacobs.   Beasley Books   2013 - 2015 $45

Barber, John *The Life and Character of John Barber, Esq; Late Lord Mayor of London, Deceased.* London: T. Cooper, 1741. First edition, 8vo., engraved portrait, perhaps wanting a half title, titlepage little spotted and browned, some mainly marginal browning throughout, worm track or wormholes in lower blank margins (not touching printed surface), disbound, very scarce.   John Drury Rare Books   2015 - 15016   2015 $177

Barbette, Paul *Opera Chirurgico-Anatomica ad circularem Sanguinis Motum...* Lugd. Batav. (Leiden): Ex Officina Hackiana, 1672. First Latin edition, 12mo., engraved titlepage, letterpress titlepage with woodcut vignette, and one full page engraving, contemporary full vellum, title in manuscript on spine, edges sprinkled brown, Bookplate of Dr. Pierre Broca, small contemporary owner's name in ink on titlepage, two later ownership signatures on front pastedown, vellum moderately darkened with light bowing to front board, very good, scarce, ture first Latin edition, 2 fine copperplate engravings.   Between the Covers Rare Books   196 - 112   2015 $2000

Barbour, Ralph Henry *The Adventure Club with the Fleet.* New York: Dodd Mead, 1918. First edition, illustrations, brown cloth with embossed flag on front cover and spine and with orange lettering on cover and spine, near fine, very scarce.   Stephen Lupack   March 2015 - 2015 $175

Bard, Samuel *Enquiry into the Nature, Cause and Cure of the Angina Suffocativa or Sore Throat Distemper....* New York: S. Inslee and A. Car at the New printing Office, 1771. First edition, 12mo., 33 pages, recent cloth backed boards, some folios trimmed, otherwise very nice, Haskell F. Norman bookplate.   M & S Rare Books, Inc.   97 - 18   2015 $4000

Barger, Ralph L. *A Century of Pullman Cars. Volume I: Alphabetical List.* Skykesville: Greenberg Pub. Co., 1988. First edition, oblong quarto, green cloth, photos, drawings, owner's ink name to top border of endpaper, very fine with pictorial dust jacket.   Argonaut Book Shop   Holiday Season 2014 - 20   2015 $175

Barham, Joseph Foster *Substance of a Speech Delivered in the House of Commons by J. F. Barham on Monday May 23 1808 on the Motion for Prohibiting Corn and the Substitution of Sugar, in the Distilleries.*   London: John Stockdale, 1808. First edition, 8vo., half title rather soiled and with small inkstamp of Dutch social policy library on blank verso, disbound, good, apparently scarce.   John Drury Rare Books   2015 - 19552   2015 $133

Barham, Richard Harris   1788-1845   *The Jackdaw of Rheims.*   Philadelphia: John Winston, 1914. First edition, folio, illustrations by Charles Folkard with 12 beautiful large tipped-in color plates on heavy stock, plus black and whites in text, printed on quality paper, purple gilt pictorial cloth, some fading on edges and marks on endpaper, else near fine, lavish picture book.   Aleph-bet Books, Inc.   109 - 176   2015 $450

Baring-Gould, Sabine   1834-1924   *Grettir the Outlaw: a Story of Iceland.*   London: Glasgow: Edinburgh: and Dublin: Blackie & Son, 1890. First edition, 10 inserted plates with illustrations by M. Zeno Diemer plus inserted foldout two-color topographical map of Iceland, original pictorial brown cloth, front and spine panels stamped in black, gold and dark brown, rear panel ruled in blind, plum coated endpapers, all edges stained green.   L. W. Currey, Inc.   Boy's Adventure Fiction 2015 - 49   2015 $150

Baring-Gould, Sabine   1834-1924   *Mehalah a Story of the Salt Marshes.*   London: Smith Elder & Co., 1880. First edition, 2 volumes, 8vo., with both half titles and final ad leaf in volume 1, bound uniformly in contemporary dark blue half morocco gilt over boards, with overall pattern of leaves and flowers, spines with raised band, gilt lettered and tooled, others uncut, excellent copy, of great rarity.   John Drury Rare Books   2015 - 24031   2015 $6119

Barker, Elliott S.   *Beatty's Cabin.*   Albuquerque: 1970. Second edition, photos, map endpapers, near fine in lightly rubbed dust jacket, signed by author.   Dumont Maps & Books of the West   131 - 36   2015 $55

Barker, Elliott S.   *When the Dogs Bark 'Treed'.*   Portale: 1975. Later edition, illustrations, map endpaper, near fine in like dust jacket, signed by author.   Dumont Maps & Books of the West   131 - 37   2015 $75

Barker, Eugene C.   *Mexico and Texas 1821-1835. University of Texas Research Lectures on the Causes of the Texas Revolution.*   P. L. Turner Co., 1928. First edition, 8vo., maroon cloth, titles stamped in gold gilt on spine, errata, pages edges uniformly tanned, spine lettering lightly faded, light wear to head of spine, else very good.   Buckingham Books   March 2015 - 36906   2015 $285

Barnard, John   *A Defence of Several Proposals for raising of Three Millions for the Service of the Government for the Year 1746.*   London: J. Osborn, 1746. First edition, modern plain wrappers, 8vo., very good.   John Drury Rare Books   2015 - 19551   2015 $89

Barnard, Robert   *Death of an Old Goat.*   Collins, 1974. First edition, presentation inscription by author, fine in dust jacket that is lightly soiled on back cover panel.   Buckingham Books   March 2015 - 36589   2015 $450

Barnard, Robert   *The Disposal of the Living.*   London: Collins Crime Club, 1985. First edition, fine in dust jacket, signed by author.   Mordida Books   March 2015 - 000228   2015 $75

Barnard, Robert   *Death on the High C's.*   London: Collins, 1977. First edition, small label removed from front cover, otherwise fine in wrappers, uncorrected proof copy.   Mordida Books March 2015 - 002755   2015 $100

Barnard, Robert   *Mother's Boys.*   New York: Collins Crime Club, 1981. First edition, fine in dust jacket.   Mordida Books   March 2015 - 010123   2015 $125

Barnard, Robert   *Sheer Torture.*   London: Collins Crime Club, 1981. First edition, fine in dust jacket.   Mordida Books   March 2015 - 010124   2015 $100

Barnard, Robert   *Unruly Son.*   London: Collins Crime Club, 1978. First edition, some slight spine fading, otherwise fine in dust jacket, signed by author.   Mordida Books March 2015 - 010122   2015 $150

Barnard, Samuel   *The Hearer's Remembrancer; Containing a View of the Leading ideas, of a Number of Sermons, Preached at New Chapel, Dagger-Lane, Hull.*   Sheffield: printed and sold by S. & E. Slater, 1822. 12mo., frontispiece, original printed boards, minor wear at extremities, else very good, uncut.   John Drury Rare Books   2015 - 24372   2015 $133

Barnes, Julian   *Duffy.*   London: Cape, 1980. First edition, very fine in price clipped dust jacket with price sticker.   Mordida Books   March 2015 - 002358   2015 $75

Barnes, Julian *Flaubert's Parrot.* London: Jonathan Cape, 1984. First edition, octavo, 190 pages, fine in very near fine dust jacket with hint of creasing in laminate. Peter Ellis, Bookseller 2014 - 017378 2015 £325

Barnes, Julian *Metroland.* London: Jonathan Cape, 1980. First edition, review copy with publisher's slip loosely inserted, review slip for 27 march 1980, 8vo., fine in fine dust jacket. Any Amount of Books 2015 - A92923 2015 £240

Barnes, Linda *A Trouble of Fools.* New York: St. Martin's, 1987. First edition, very fine in dust jacket. Mordida Books March 2015 - 007536 2015 $85

Barnes, Ralph *A Letter to Henry Gervis Esqr., Portreeve of Ashburton, on Agricultural Labour and Wages 1831.* Exeter: printed by W. Roberts, 1831. First edition, 8vo., little staining on titlepage and occasionally elsewhere, preserved in modern wrappers with printed label on upper cover, good copy, rare. John Drury Rare Books March 2015 - 25421 2015 $266

Barnes, William S. *The Life of Count Rumford, a Lecture Given in the Lyceum Course of 1872-3 at Woburn, Mass. Jan. 21st 1873.* Woburn: John L. Parker, 1873. Original printing, 8vo., 24 pages, original printed wrappers, very good, rare. Jeff Weber Rare Books 178 - 1060 2015 $45

Barnett, C. Z. *A Christmas Carol, or the Miser's Warning.* British Columbia: Barbarian Press, 1984. Printed in an edition of 350 copies, large 8vo., scarlet cloth, paper cover and spine labels, top cloth, paper cover and spine labels, top edge cut, fore and bottom edges, uncut, cloth covered slipcase, handset in 14 point Scotch roman and italic and printed on Zerkall Cream wove, 6 illustrations, printer's marks and press device were printed from Edwina Ellis's wood engravings, slight fading of spine and along edges of slipcase. Oak Knoll Books 306 - 126 2015 $225

Barney, James M. *Tales of Apache Warfare. True Stories of Massacres. Fights and Raids in Arizona and New Mexico.* privately printed, 1933. First edition, stiff printed wrappers, 45 pages, light wear to spine and small crease to lower corner of front cover, else near fine, very scarce. Buckingham Books March 2015 - 37209 2015 $300

Barney, Libeus *Letters of the Pike's Peak Gold Rush (or Early Day Letters from Auraria): Early-Day Letters by Libeus Barney.* San Jose: Talisman Press, 1959. Reprint from original edition, one of 975 copies, frontispiece, folding facsimile map in rear pocket, half cloth and printed boards, very fine with dust jacket. Argonaut Book Shop Holiday Season 2014 - 21 2015 $100

Barnfield, Richard *Sonnets.* Llandogo: Old Stile Press, 2001. 57/200 copies signed by artist Clive Hicks-Jenkins, printed on Somerset Printmaking paper, line drawing to each recto, enhanced by blocks of gold, blue or green in various shades, oblong imperial 8vo., original illustrated boards, backstrip lettered in silver, patterned endpapers, top edge black, fore-edge untrimmed, cloth slipcase with poet's signature stamped to front and a 'spyhole', fine. Blackwell's Rare Books B179 - 203 2015 £200

Barnham, Henry D. *The Khoja Tales of Nasr-Ed-Din.* New York: D. Appleton and Co., 1924. First edition, bookplate of designer P. K. Thomajan, some offsetting on front board, about very good, in poor, internally repaired dust jacket with some chips and tears. Between the Covers Rare Books, Inc. 187 - 7 2015 $65

Barnhardt Bros. *Book of Type Specimens Comprising a Large Variety of Superior Copper Mixed Types... Specimen Book No. 9.* Chicago: Barnhart Bros. & Spindler, n.d. circa, 1907. Thick 8vo., cloth, ugly binding as original covers are very worn along edges and spine has been taped with silver fabric tape, pages at beginning are darkened along edge, with one excised piece. Oak Knoll Books 306 - 208 2015 $200

Barnitz, Albert *Life in Custer's Cavalry. Diaries and Letters of... 1867-1868.* New Haven: Yale University Press, 1977. First edition, illustrations, tan cloth, lettered in black, very fine, pictorial dust jacket. Argonaut Book Shop Holiday Season 2014 - 303 2015 $50

Barnum, Phineas Taylor 1810-1891 *Dick Broadhead. A Tale of Perilous Adventures.* New York: G. W. Dillingham, 1888. First edition, octavo, 2 inserted plates, original decorated brown cloth, front panel stamped in black, spine panel stamped in black and gold, rear panel stamped in blind, salmon endpapers. L. W. Currey, Inc. Boy's Adventure Fiction 2015 - 49 2015 $150

Barnum, Phineas Taylor 1810-1891 *A Full and Interesting Account of the Great Hippopotamus, or River Horse, from the White Nile.* New York: Steam Book and Job Printer, 1861. 8vo., 32 pages, vignette title and several cuts in text, sewn, retaining original yellow back wrapper (only) containing a full page illustration of two hippos with palm tree and pyramid in background, title and text somewhat foxed, corners curled &c., but good, sound copy. M & S Rare Books, Inc. 97 - 19 2015 $250

Barnum, Phineas Taylor 1810-1891 *Jack in the Jungle: a Tale of Land and Sea.* New York: G. W. Carleton& co., London: S. Lowe, 1880. First edition, octavo, five inserted plates, original decorated brown cloth, front panel stamped in black, spine panel stamped in black and gold, rear panel stamped in blind, brown endpapers. L. W. Currey, Inc. Boy's Adventure Fiction 2015 - 50 2015 $150

Baron, Stanley *Benny, King of Swing.* New York: Morrow, 1979. First edition, fine in fine dust jacket. Beasley Books   2013 - 2015 $45

Barr, Nevada *Track of the Cat.* New York: Putnam, 1993. First edition, fine in dust jacket. Buckingham Books   March 2015 - 18907   2015 $225

Barr, Robert *The Mutable Many.* New York: Stokes, 1896. First edition, some staining on fore-edge, otherwise near fine in decorated grayish green cloth covered boards with some goldstamped titles and gilt top page edges. Mordida Books   March 2015 - 008926   2015 $125

Barratt, F. Layland *Lycanthia.* London: Herbert Jenkins, 1935. First edition, 8vo., original light red cloth lettered black on spine and cover, slight rubbing at head of spine, lower edge slightly scuffed, prelims very slightly used, otherwise clean, bright, very good.   Any Amount of Books   2015 - C520   2015   £240

Barres, Maurice *Un Jardin Sur L'Oronte.* Paris: Javal & Bourdeaux, 1927. of 490 this one marked 'hors commerce', unbound signatures with 17 watercolor plates and numerous illustrations, wrappers have very minor crease to front wrapper, otherwise fine in near fine chemise with sunned spine, box sunned on edges, bumped corner, 4to. Beasley Books   2013 - 2015 $500

Barrett, Neal *Long Days and Short Nights: a Century of Texas Ranching on the Yo a1880-1980.* Mountain Home: Y-O Press, 1980. First edition, octavo, pictorial cloth, 192 pages, printed and already becoming scarce, fine in dust jacket.   Buckingham Books   March 2015 - 32359   2015 $175

Barrett, Theodosia Wells *Pioneers on the Western Waters.* Bristol: 1978. First edition, wrappers, sunfaded at backstrip and some damp spotting, inscribed and signed by author.   Bookworm & Silverfish   2015 - 6017016966   2015 $45

Barrie, James Matthew   1860-1937 *Peter and Wendy.* New York: Charles Scribner's Sons, 1911. First American edition, octavo, original olive cloth, gilt, original dust jacket, very good, inscribed by author and accompanied by note to recipient.   Honey & Wax Booksellers   2 - 8   2015 $12,500

Barrie, James Matthew   1860-1937 *Peter Pan and Wendy.* New York: Charles Scribner's Sons, 1921. First U. S. edition with these illustrations, illustrations by Mabel Lucy Attwell with 12 beautiful color plates and many black and whites in text, nice, 4to., green gilt pictorial cloth, endpapers toned, else near fine in original dust jacket with piece off lower right corner, rare in dust jacket.   Aleph-bet Books, Inc.   109 - 36   2015 $750

Barrie, James Matthew   1860-1937 *Peter Pan In Kensington Gardens.* London: Hodder & Stoughton, 1906. First Rackham edition, first printing, original red cloth, spine and front cover lettered gilt, decoration to front cover, 49 color illustrations and frontispiece by Arthur Rackham, bright copy, some rubbing to edges, corners lightly worn, former owner bookplate to front pastedown, some light scattered foxing, else lovely copy, free of any repairs.   B & B Rare Books, Ltd.   234 - 4   2015 $2500

Barrie, James Matthew   1860-1937 *The Works.* New York: Charles Scribner's Sons,, 1929-1931. Limited to 1030 copies, signed by author on colophon of first volume, Peter Pan edition, 8vo., quarter cloth, paper covered boards, labels with printed titles on spine, gilt stamped, Peter Pan emblem on front cover, unopened, slipcases lightly soiled, worn at edges.   Oak Knoll Books   306 - 251   2015 $1000

Barrigner, Tim *Art and Emancipation in Jamaica: Isaac Mendes Belisario and His Worlds.* New Haven and London: Yale Center for British Art/Yale University Press, 2007. First edition, 4to., original bright blue cloth lettered black on spine, copiously illustrated in color and black and white, fine in very good+ dust jacket with very slight surface wear, excellent condition.   Any Amount of Books   2015 - C16316   2015   £230

Barrow, William *An Essay on Education: in Which are Particularly Considered the Merits and the Defects of the Discipline and Instruction in our Academies.* London: F. And C. Rivington, 1804. 2 volumes, 12mo., stain in lower corner of last few leaves volume I, contemporary green half calf, carefully rebacked, spines gilt with labels, stain on lower cover of volume I, good copy, complete with ad leaf in first volume.   John Drury Rare Books   2015 - 13939   2015 $221

Barry Du Barry & Co. *The Natural Restorer of Perfect Health to the Most Enfeebled or Shattered Constitution.* London: Barry Du Barry & Co. 77 Regent St., 1861. First edition, 12mo., original blind stamped maroon cloth, short title in gilt letters on upper cover, cloth little faded, but fine, apparently of some rarity.   John Drury Rare Books   March 2015 - 26009   2015   £306

Barry, Theodore Augustus *Men and Memories of San Francisco in the "Spring of '50".* San Francisco: A. L. Bancroft & Co., 1873. First edition, 12mo., green cloth gilt stamped title lettering to spine and front board, green endpapers, withal a good copy, gilt bright, slight lean, small abrasion to cloth at top front joint, foxing to edges, bookplate of James D. Phelan (mayor of San Francisco), ownership signature of Mrs. M. G. Wilson.   Tavistock Books   Bah, Humbug? - 28   2015 $275

Bart, Harriet *The Poetry of Chance Encounters.* Minneapolis: Mnemonic Press, 2003. One of 35 numbered copies, all on Rives BFK, from a total edition of 40, 9 x 6 1/8 inches, 42 pages, bound by Jill Jevne, full brown box calf, matching calf edged and gold paste paper by Claire Mariarcyzk, matching calf over boards slipcase, book contains 16 visual poems on multi-color fields, each imprinted with an icon in 22 karat gold, each printed page has a total of five press runs, including varnish over the icon and field with impression of the gold leaf imparting embossed effect to the icon, basic typeface is Lydian, a stressed sans serif chosen to complement the treatment of image and type throughout the book.   Priscilla Juvelis - Rare Books   61 - 1   2015 $3200

Barth, George H. *The Mesmerist's Manual of Phenomena and Practice with Directions for Applying Mesmerism to the Cure of Diseases and the methods of Producing Mesmeric Phenomena.* London: H. Bailliere, 1850. First edition, half title, original blindstamped cloth, short title in gilt on upper cover, rebacked, endpapers renewed, good copy, very scarce.   John Drury Rare Books   March 2015 - 21041   2015   £266

Bartholomew, J. G. *The Survey Atlas of Scotland.* Edinburgh: Edinburgh Geographical Institute, 1912. First edition, large folio, 68 double page maps, folio, original quarter blue morocco, gilt title, rules and lion device on spine, blue cloth, gilt decorations, leather spine little rubbed and slightly scuffed at lower spine, cloth bumped and rubbed at corners, text and maps very clean, book handsome, very good.   Any Amount of Books   March 2015 - C12185   2015   £400

Bartlett, Ichabod *Address of the Great State Convention of Friends of the Administration Assembled at the Capitol in Concord, June 12 1828.* Concord: published by Order of the Convention, 1828. First edition, 12mo., 24 pages, including front wrapper, sewn with original front printed wrapper (only), sheets very browned and foxed, otherwise very good with fore and bottom margins untrimmed.   M & S Rare Books, Inc.   97 - 3   2015 $150

Bartlett, N. Grey, Mrs. *Mother Goose of '93.* Boston: Joseph Knight, 1893. Oblong 4to., quarter cloth and patterned paper, tips worn a bit, else near fine, printed rectos only, each leaf printed on delicate rice paper mounted on heavier stock, illustrations by Bartlett with superb mounted photo illustrations, line illustrations, very scarce.   Aleph-bet Books, Inc.   109 - 302   2015 $600

Bartlett, Samuel C. *An Appeal for Ministers: a Discussion on the Necessity for a Great Effort to Supply the Country with Preachers of the Gospel.* Chicago: Dunlop, Sewell & Spalding, 1865. First edition, 8vo, 19 pages, original printed wrappers.   M & S Rare Books, Inc.   97 - 56   2015 $375

Barto, A. *Brateshki. (Little Brothers).* Moscow: Ogiz, 1935. 4to., pictorial wrappers, color lithographs by Georgi Echeistov, fine.   Aleph-bet Books, Inc.   109 - 421   2015 $850

Barton, O. S. *Three Years with Quantrell: a True Story Told by His Scout John McCorkle.* Armstrong: Armstrong Herald Print, n.d. circa, 1914. First edition, 8vo., variant black, unprinted cloth binding, 157 pages, frontispiece, illustrations, plates,.   Buckingham Books   March 2015 - 23459   2015 $1750

Bartruse, Grace *The Children in Japan.* New York: McBride Nast, 1915. 4to., boards, slight cover soil, very good+, 16 fine color plates by Pogany and 16 black and whites, quite scarce.   Aleph-Bet Books, Inc.   108 - 354   2015 $350

Barzun, Jacques *A Catalogue of Crime.* New York: Harper, 1971. First edition, fine in dust jacket.   Mordida Books   March 2015 - 010966   2015 $100

Basler Bauten des 18. Jahrhunderts. Ingenieur & Arachitekten Verein Basel, 1897. Marbled boards and leather spine, lovely patterned endpapers, very good, corners rubbed, small chip at spine bottom, owner stamp of Bern architect Oscar Weber.   Stephen Lupack   March 2015 - 2015 $100

Bass, Michael Thomas *Street Music in the Metropolis. Correspondence and Observations on the Existing Law and Proposed Amendments.* London: John Murray, 1864. First edition, 8vo. half title, original maroon cloth, fine presentation copy from 19th century library of Edward Strutt, Lord Belper, with author's compliments, scarce.   John Drury Rare Books   2015 - 25788   2015 $1049

Bassett, Samuel Clay *Buffalo County. Nebraska and Its People. A Record of Settlement, Organization, Progress and Achievement.* S. J. Clarke Pub. Co., 1916. First edition, quarto, three quarter leather and cloth, gold stamping to spine, raised bands, marbled endpapers, frontispiece, all edges marbled, illustrations, cosmetic restoration to spine ends, corners and extremities, else very good, housed in slipcase with titles stamped in gold on spine.   Buckingham Books   March 2015 - 28985   2015 $1275

Bastian der Faulpelz. Frankfurt a.m,: Litterarische Anstalt (Rutten und Loning), circa, 1860. 4to., hand colored pictorial boards, some wear to spine paper, generally very good+, 24 leaves printed on rectos only, each page with fine hand colored illustration, rare.   Aleph-Bet Books, Inc.   108 - 241   2015 $1200

Bate, Walter Jackson *Coleridge.* London: Collier MacMillan, 1968. Half title, uncut, original dark green cloth, very good in dust jacket, from the library of Geoffrey & Kathleen Tillotson, presentation from same with inserts. Jarndyce Antiquarian Booksellers   CCVII - 152   2015   £35

Bate, Walter Jackson *Samuel Johnson.* New York: Harcourt Brace Jovanovich, 1977. Half title, frontispiece and plates, original dark blue cloth, slightly dusted in slightly torn dust jacket, 2 ALS's from author to Kathleen Tillotson with photo, notes and cuttings of her reviews.   Jarndyce Antiquarian Booksellers   CCVII - 338   2015   £45

Bateman, Thomas *A Treatise on Agistment Tithe in Which the Nature, Right, Objects, Mode of Payment and method of Ascertaining the Value of Each Species Of It are fully Stated and Explained.* London: S. Crowder and N. Frobisher, York, n.d. or, 1778? 1775. First edition, variant issue, 8vo., stitched as issued in early marbled wrappers, fine, rare. John Drury Rare Books   March 2015 - 9868   2015 $266

Bates, Henry Walter *The Naturalist on the River Amazon...* London: John Murray, 1863. First edition, 2 volumes, 8vo., original brown cloth lettered gilt on spines and front covers, illustrations, final fold missing from map, browned, chipped at torn edges, ownership signature of Theodore Rathbone and circulating library plates mounted on rear endpapers, top margin of titlepage on volume one torn, edges rough and some leaves loose, rebacked with original spines laid down, inner hinges rubbed and cracked with some foxing to prelims, otherwise good, somewhat used copy.   Any Amount of Books   2015 - C14402   2015   £280

Bates, Wesley W. *In Black and White, a Wood Engraver's Odyssey.* Newtown: Bird and Bull Press, 2005. Limited to 140 numbered copies, this copy not numbered, Japanese cloth, cloth covered slipcase, written in pencil in this copy by Henry Morris 'Sample binding 2/9/5. Move label 1/8" to spine o.w. ok", book printed on Zerkall mouldmade paper, includes fold-out 4 color woodcut print which was made for a book Bird & Bull published in 2001, loosely inserted are 3 signed woodcuts by Bates and the prospectus.   Oak Knoll Books   306 - 127   2015 $300

Batey, Mavis *Jane Austen and the English Landscape.* London: Barn Elms, 1966. First edition, large 4to., 135 pages, original grey cloth lettered gilt at spine, copiously illustrated in color and black and white, fine in fine dust jacket.   Any Amount of Books   2015 - C8479   2015   £150

Bath Penitentiary and Lock Hospital *The Collective Reports of the Bath Penitentiary and Lock Hospital from 1816 to 1824...* Bath: printed by Wood, Cunningham and Smith, 1824. First edition, 8vo., contemporary dark blue calf, gilt borders, spine gilt in compartments, fine presentation copy inscribed by chairman of the Penitentiary to Lord Eldon with his armorial bookplate and signature, apparently rare.   John Drury Rare Books   2015 - 25027   2015 $1136

Bath, William Pulteney, 1st Earl of   1684-1764 *An Enquiry into the Conduct of our Domestick Affairs from the Year 1721 to Christmas 1733.* London: H. Haines of Mr. Francklin's, 1734. 8vo., 68 pages, erratum at foot of page 68, first and last pages just little dust marked, preserved in recent plain wrappers with label on upper cover, good. John Drury Rare Books   2015 - 21467   2015 $89

Bath, William Pulteney, 1st Earl of   1684-1764 *A Letter from a Member of Parliament to a Friend in the Country, Concerning the Sum of £115,000 Granted for the Service of the Civil List.* London: J. Walker, 1729. First edition, first issue, 8vo., large folding table bound in between pages 12 and 13, some leaves little dampstained, modern boards with label on upper cover, good.   John Drury Rare Books   2015 - 7944   2015 $177

Bath, William Pulteney, 1st Earl of   1684-1764 *A Report from the Committee Appointed by Order of the House of Commons to Examine Christopher Layer and Others...* London: printed for Jacob Tonson, Bernard Lintot and William Taylor, 1722. First edition, initial licence leaf, stab holes in inner blank margins of last 3 leaves, contemporary calf with double gilt fillets on sides, spine with gilt lines, raised bands and label, minor splits in joints at head and foot but very good, 18th century armorial bookplate of John Schutz, Esq. and armorial bookplate (early 19th century?) of Horace Walpole.   John Drury Rare Books   2015 - 17995   2015 $874

Battye, Christine *The Brewhouse Private Press 1963-1983.* Wymondham: Syacmore Press, 1984. First edition, limited to 120 numbered copies, 4to., cloth, many illustrations.   Oak Knoll Books   306 - 144   2015 $135

Baudelaire, Charles *Three Poems from Les Fleurs Du Mal. (The Flowers of Evil).* New York: Limited Editions Club, 1997. Limited to 500 numbered copies, signed by artist, folio, cloth, inset label on front cover, fore-edge uncut, cloth clamshell box with title stamped on spine, designed and set in Monotype Walbaum and printed by Michael and Winifred Bixler, 4 photogravures by Jon Goodman, photos by Henri Cartier-Bresson, clamshell box lightly sunned on spine.   Oak Knoll Books   25 - 67   2015 $3000

Baudelaire, Charles *Petits Poemes en Prose.* Aux Depens D'un Groupe de Bibliophile, 1934. #88 of a very limited edition, 4to., illustrations by Maurie Lalau with lithographs, unbound signatures laid into wrappers, fine in fine glassine, slipcase has dampstain at one lower edge. Beasley Books   2013 - 2015 $300

Baudelaire, Charles *Poemes de Baudelaire.* Paris: Textes Pretextes, 1946. No. 198 of 330 copies, 4to., unbound signatures laid into wrappers, illustrations by Louise Hervieu, fine in fine wrappers, lightly sunned and lightly soiled clamshell box.   Beasley Books   2013 - 2015 $300

Baudelaire, Charles *Oeuvres Poetiques Completes De Charles Baudelaire.* Paris: Editions Vialetay, 1960-1961. #1289 of 2500 copies, 5 volumes, near fine, blue cloth slipcases, 8vo.   Beasley Books   2013 - 2015 $150

Baudouin, Benoit *B. Balduinus de Calceo Antiquo et Ju. Nigronus De Caliga Veterum...* Amstelodami: sumpt. A. Frisi, 1667. New edition, 2 volumes in 1, 28 full page engraved plates, of which 7 are folding, 12mo., bound in later three quarter calf with leather labels and modest gilt on spine, engraved general titlepage with another titlepage for each work, fine.   Second Life Books Inc.   190 - 299   2015 $1800

Baum, Lyman Frank *The Emerald City of Oz.* Chicago: Reilly & Britton Co., 1910. First edition, first state, 16 full page color plates embellished with emerald green, original light blue cloth with color pictorial paper label on front board, Reilly & Lee dust jacket, minor rubbing, corners bumped, otherwise near fine.   Heritage Book Shop   Holiday 2014 - 9   2015 $1850

Baum, Lyman Frank *John Dough and Cherub.* Chicago: Reilly & Britton, 1906. First edition first state without correction line 10 on page 275 (cage instead of cave), 4to., tan cloth stamped in red, black and brown on front and in black on rear, fine in dust jacket (repaired on verso, some pieces off edges), and with contestant blank intact, 40 fantastic full page color illustrations, 20 color pictorial chapter heads, 100 black and whites in text plus pictorial endpapers and title by J. R. Neill, super rare with dust jacket.   Aleph-bet Books, Inc.   109 - 40   2015 $6500

Baum, Lyman Frank *The Marvelous Land of Oz.* Chicago: 1904. First edition, second state with July 1904 copyright page, binding A but with second issue text, 16 full color plates inserted throughout, exceptionally clean copy, scarce.   Heritage Book Shop   Holiday 2014 - 10   2015 $3000

Baum, Lyman Frank *The Navy Alphabet.* Chicago: Geo. Hill, 1900. First and only edition, printed rectos only, full color illustrations by Harry Kennedy, folio, cloth backed pictorial boards, slight cover soil, edges rubbed a bit as usual, corner of blank endpaper repaired, else very good+, nice clean, very scarce, especially in such nice condition. Aleph-bet Books, Inc.   109 - 42   2015 $2750

Baum, Lyman Frank *Sky Island.* Chicago: Reilly & Britton, 1912. First edition, first issue, 4to., red cloth, pictorial paste-on, slightest bit of shelf wear, else near fine, illustrations by J. R. Neill with beautiful color pictorial endpapers plus 12 color plates and many black and whites, very scarce in such nice condition.   Aleph-bet Books, Inc.   109 - 43   2015 $1200

Baum, Lyman Frank *The Visitors from Oz.* Chicago: Reilly & Lee, 1960. First edition, illustrations in color and black and white by Dick Martin, 4to., green pictorial composition binding, dust jacket which replicates binding design, splay to boards, otherwise very good in similar dust jacket. Tavistock Books   Bah, Humbug? - 27   2015 $75

Baum, Lyman Frank *The Woggle-Bug Book.* Chicago: Reilly & Britton, 1905. First edition, secondary binding, green cloth spine, stiff pictorial card covers with yellow stippled background and title in yellow on rear cover, light cover soil and tips worn else, tight and near fine, large fragile book consequently very few copies have survived in such nice condition, rare. Aleph-bet Books, Inc.   109 - 39   2015 $3500

Baum, Lyman Frank *The Wonderful Wizard of Oz.* Chicago: Geo. M. Hill Co., 1900. First edition, 2nd state, quarto, 24 inserted color plates, original light green cloth pictorially stamped and lettered in red, serified type with the "C" of "Co." (encircling the 'o'), pictorial pastedown endpapers issued without free endpapers, cloth very clean and bright, minimal rubbing to top and bottom of spine and corners, previous owner's old ink signature on copyright page, professional restoration to front inner hinge, overall very good or better, housed in custom full green morocco clamshell. Heritage Book Shop   Holiday 2014 - 11   2015 $16,500

Baum, Lyman Frank *The Wonderful Wizard of Oz.* Chicago: George M. Hill Co., 1900. First edition, illustrations by W. W. Denslow, original pictorial cloth, binding state "C" with 'o' inside the 'C' at foot of spine, text and illustrations in second (corrected state), light soiling to cloth, some rubbing along spine, light fraying along margin of front cover and spine, spine mildly toned, extremities bit rubbed, hinges cracked with some evidence of repair, without any other repairs or restoration, nicer than usual example.   B & B Rare Books, Ltd.   234 - 5   2015 $8000

Baumann, Walter *Roses from the Steel Dust: Collected Essays on Ezra Pound.* Orono: National Poetry Foundation, 2000. First edition, 8vo., fine in near fine dust jacket, very slight creasing at rear top edge.   Any Amount of Books   2015 - A96724   2015   £180

Bauwens, Emile *Livre de Cocktails.* Bruxelles: Zux Zeditions au coup de, 1949. First edition, trade issue, color ads inserted for various liquors, original paper wrappers printed in blue and black, little light wear to edges, old (possibly original) acetate with tidy tape reinforcements at front hinge, else near fine, this copy 2122 of 2175 copies, wonderfully inscribed by author.   Between the Covers Rare Books   196 - 134   2015 $950

Baxter, John *A New and Impartial History of England, from the most early period of genuine historical evidence to the present important and alarming crisis...* London: printed by the proprietors and sold by H D. Symonds, n.d., 1796. Only edition, occasional very minor foxing, few leaves with mild old dampstain, rebound fairly recently in quarter calf over marbled boards, spine gilt with raised bands and morocco label lettered gilt, good, well bound copy, rare.   John Drury Rare Books   2015 - 24828   2015 $3409

Baxter, Stephen *Raft.* London: Grafton Books a Division of Harper Collins, 1991. First edition, octavo, boards, review copy with publisher's promotional letter laid in.   John W. Knott, Bookseller   Selected New Arrivals Jan. 2015 - 16910   2015 $450

Baxter, Stephen *The Time Ships.* London: Harper Collins, 1995. First edition, octavo, boards, signed by author.   John W. Knott, Bookseller   Selected New Arrivals Jan. 2015 - 16916   2015 $300

Bayer, Friedrich *Praktisch Erprobte Druck-Recepte bei Benutzung der Alizarin-Anilin, und Azo-Farbstoffe der farbenfabriken Vorm.* Friedr. Bayer & Co. Elberfeld, 1896. 8vo., pink errata slip, entirely printed in red and black, numerous specimens of printed textiles, very lightly spotted in places, original brown cloth, front cover lettered gilt, patterned endpapers, little rubbed.   Marlborough Rare Books List 54 - 4   2015   £450

Baylis, Thomas Henry *An Answer to the Attack of the 'Daily News' of the 1st July, 1856, on the Unity Fire Insurance Association, Together with some Remarks on the Position and Progress of the Unity Institutions.* London: Chief Offices of Unity, 1856. First edition, 8vo., 36 pages, preserved in modern wrappers with printed title label on upper cover, very good, rare.   John Drury Rare Books   2015 - 23676   2015 $177

Bayly, Thomas *Witty Apophthegms Delivered at several Times and Upon Several Occasions by King James King Charls (sic) the Marquess of Worcester, Francis Lord Bacon and Sir Thomas Moor.* London: printed by W(illiam) R(awlins) for Matthew Smelt, 1669. Second edition, 12mo., engraved frontispiece, browned throughout, staining to C2 and c6, closed tear to fore margin of #12 and with small piece missing from corner of B6 and blank fore margin of F3, contemporary sheep, ruled in gilt, gilt lettered spine, rubbed, corners bumped, from the library of James Stevens Cox (1910-1997).   Maggs Bros. Ltd.   1447 - 24   2015   £550

Bazin, Germain *L'Architecture Religieuse Baroque au Bresil.* Sao Paolo: Paris: Musseu De Arte/Librairie Plon, 1955. First edition, 2 volumes, handsomely bound in maroon and brown leather with gilt titlings, 4 raised bands, lettered gilt on red spine labels, 180 plates, prelims slightly foxed, otherwise fine.   Any Amount of Books   March 2015 - A90988   2015   £330

Bazucha, Robert *Let's Play House: 3 Rooms with Complete Furnishings.* Racine: Whitman, 1932. Giant folio, pictorial wrappers, some rubbing, unused, with 250 pieces on 6 card stock pages and with die-cuts of the three rooms, as well, rare.   Aleph-Bet Books, Inc.   108 - 321   2015 $800

Beach, Joseph Perkins *The Log of Apollo: Joseph Perkins Beach's Journal of the Voyage of the Ship Apollo from New York to San Francisco 1849.* San Francisco: Book Club of California, 1986. First edition, limited to 550 copies, tipped in color frontispiece, illustrations, map, facsimile, cloth paper labels on spine and front cover, very fine.   Argonaut Book Shop   Holiday Season 2014 - 22   2015 $150

Beach, Marion *Come Ride with Me.* Chicago: DMAAH, 1970. First edition, warmly inscribed by author to well-known writer and activist Walter Lowenfels, with two page signed manuscript poem "The Theft of Two Continents" folded and tipped inside front cover, light staining to covers, very good in stapled wrappers.   Ken Lopez, Bookseller   164 - 12   2015 $125

Beale, Edward F. *Letter of the Secretary of War, Transmitting the Report of Mr. Beale Relating to the Construction of a Wagon Road from Fort Smith to the Colorado River.* Washington: GPO, 1860. First edition, 8vo., binder, 91 plates plus folding map bound in at end, old waterstain affects the top and bottom corners of every page with folded map having no waterstain at all, else very good, cloth binder with titles stamped on spine.   Buckingham Books   March 2015 - 33121   2015 $675

Bear, Elizabeth *Avalanche - Number One.* New York: Willoughby Sharp, Kineticism Press, 1970. First issue of this journal, square small quarto, 71 pages plus ads, glossy card wrappers, photos, laid in is publisher's subscription card, inside front cover is an ownership signature which is barely discernible, being in dark blue ink on black background, spine slightly rubbed, near fine, scarce.   Peter Ellis, Bookseller   2014 - 011579   2015   £350

Beard, George M. *A Practical Treatise on Nervous Exhaustion.* New York: William Wood, 1880. First edition, very good, little wear to spine ends, owner's name at head of title.   Beasley Books   2013 - 2015 $450

Beard, J. S. *Plant Life of Western Australia.* Kenthurst: Kangaroo Press, 1990. First edition, 4to., copiously illustrated in color, very slightly rubbed, otherwise fine in fine dust jacket, excellent condition.   Any Amount of Books   2015 - A99676   2015   £270

Beard, Mark *Manhattan Third Year Reader.* New York: Vincent FitzGerald & Co., 1984. First edition, one of only 30 copies, on 28 different papers, each copy signed by artist/author, page size 1 x 11 inches, 16 signatures, unique binding by Donald Glaister, red and black morocco with onlays of goatskin and laminated mylar and gold painted tooling composed to reader a view of the urban landscape, featuring obscured subway cars, altered grid paper imagery and a corregated leather keystone shape that transverses the spine and extends to both boards, doublures of painted cork, top edge gilt with eccentric gold shapes echoing shapes found on covers, binding signed by binder, Glaister, 2014 in blind with usual gold dot on inner rear hinge, housed in black linen clamshell box.   Priscilla Juvelis - Rare Books   63 - 5   2015 $15,000

Beard, Mary R. *On Understanding Women.* New York: Longmans Green, 1931. First edition, 8vo., very good, laid in is TLS about the book from author to Mrs. Margaret Wadsworth Gensmer.   Second Life Books Inc.   189 - 18   2015 $275

Beard, Peter *Peter Beard.* New York: Taschen, 2006. First edition, limited to 2500 copies signed by Beard, large elephant folio, this no. 536, full page color photos, half burgundy morocco over burgundy cloth, housed in cloth clamshell with elephant gilt stamped on front, some minor scuffing to book and slipcase, almost fine.   Heritage Book Shop Holiday 2014 - 12   2015 $3750

Beardsley, Aubrey Vincent   1872-1898 *The Early Work of Aubrey Beardsley.* London: John Lane, 1912. Reprint of 1899 edition, rebound in green cloth, ex-library with perforation on title and label on spine, little rippled on few pages, otherwise very good, tight copy.   Second Life Books Inc.   190 - 11   2015 $250

Beardsley, Aubrey Vincent   1872-1898 *Fifty Drawings by Aubrey Beardsley.* New York: Nichols, 1920. One of 500 copies signed by H.S. Nichols, 4to., top edge gilt, very good in chipped dust jacket.   Second Life Books Inc.   190 - 9   2015 $500

Beasley, Conger *Spanish Peaks: Land and Legends.* Boulder: 2001. Near fine in like dust jacket, well illustrated with black and white photos.   Dumont Maps & Books of the West   131 - 39   2015 $50

Beaton, M. C. *Death of a Gossip.* New York: St. Martins, 1985. First edition, very fine in dust jacket.   Mordida Books   March 2015 - 012625   2015 $200

Beattie, James   1735-1803 *Dissertations Moral and Critical.* London: W. Strahan, T. Cadell and W. Creech at Edinburgh, 1783. First edition, 4to., half title, intermittent very minor foxing, contemporary tree calf gilt, neatly rebacked to match retaining original label, very good, late 19th century armorial bookplate of Oldhams of Doverdale in Worcestershire.   John Drury Rare Books   2015 - 23062   2015 $1311

Beatty Bros. Limited *Beatty Bros. Limited "Direct Drive Pumps and Water Pressure Systems". Catalog No. 22.* Toronto: Beatty Bros. ltd., 1938. Quarto, color illustrated card covers, illustrations throughout, very good, revised price list laid in.   Schooner Books Ltd.   110 - 157   2015 $40

Beatty, Bessie *A Political Primer for the New Voter.* San Francisco: Whitaker & Ray-Wiggin, 1912. First edition, small 8vo., paper over boards, cover little soiled, slightly torn at top of spine, little worn at edges, otherwise very good.   Second Life Books Inc.   189 - 19   2015 $225

Beauchamp, Joan *Working Women in Great Britain.* New York: International Publishers, 1937. First edition, 8vo., very good, dust jacket little chipped and worn.   Second Life Books Inc.   189 - 20   2015 $45

Beaugrand, Honore *Six Mois Dans Les Montagnes-Rocheuses. Colorado - Utah - Novueau Mexique.* Granger Freres, 1890. First edition, light blue printed wrappers, several illustrations and large folding map, moderate uniform browning to wrappers and pages as well as moderate chipping to wrappers, spine and some page corners, paper slightly brittle, overall still very good, 15 x 18 inch map is shaded in blue and has one 1 inch closed tear to left edge of map at fold, very nice and attached at front.   Buckingham Books   March 2015 - 37981   2015 $400

Beauman, S. G. Hulme *Out of the Ark Books.* London: Warne, n.d. circa, 1930. 6 books, color pictorial wrappers housed in pictorial box, 5 x 6 inches, books fine, box has edge stain, illustrations by author.   Aleph-Bet Books, Inc.   108 - 320   2015 $500

Beaumont, Charles *A Treatise on the Coal Trade.* London: J. Crowder for G. G. J. and J. Robinson, 1789. First edition, 4to., blank final page attached to original rear wrapper, early 19th century half calf over marbled boards, neatly rebacked and lettered, with armorial bookplate of Ferguson of Raith, very good, inscribed by author for William Ferguson Esqr.   John Drury Rare Books   2015 - 24872   2015 $1311

Beaumont, Cyril W.   *The Wonderful Journey a Fairy Tale.* London: C. W. Beaumont, 1927. Special edition, #46 of 110 copies signed by author and artist, white vellum boards with gold stamped figures are sunned on spine and lightly on front edges, else close to fine, previous owner's slipcase and half chemise, William Maxwell bookplate was designed by John Fairleigh, 8vo.   Beasley Books   2013 - 2015 $150

Beaumont, Francis   *Comedies and Tragedies written by Francis Beaumont and John Fletcher.* London: for Humphrey Robinson and Humphrey Moseley, 1647. First edition, small folio, lacking final leaf of text, engraved portrait, second state with "Vates Duplex" in fourth line of the inscription and "J. Berkenhead' in smaller letters (backed with old paper, at time of rebinding, slightly cropped at foot, ink blot in inscription) titlepage stained and slightly dusty, loose at upper inner margin, margins bit frayed, small hole in blank area near outer edge, lower outer corner of F3 torn away with loss to five lines, few words on 7 lines on Dd1v have adhered to blank page opposite upper corner 3U4 torn away affecting pagination, loss at foot of 7A1 from paper flaw affecting a few letters, closed vertical tears, minor spots and stains throughout, some ink blots, upper inner margin of first few leaves and lower outer corner of last few leaves dampstained, late 17th/early 18th century sheep, covers ruled in blind (headcaps and top and bottom of spine torn away, covers somewhat scuffed, cup ring on lower cover, upper corner of lower cover chewed and dampstained), from the library of James Stevens Cox (1910-1997), name Wyndham Harbin, 2nd son of William and Elizabeth Harbin of Newton Surmaville, Somerset with his signature, name Elizabeth (probably Harbin).   Maggs Bros. Ltd.   1447 - 25   2015   £600

Beaumont, Francis   *Fifty Comedies and Tragedies...* London: printed by J. Macock for John Martyn, Henry Herringman, Richard Marriot, 1679. With scarce portrait frontispiece, 19th century full calf blind and gilt stamped front and rear with decorative borders respined with little later calf blind and gilt stamped with decorations with red spine label, lettered gilt, two brass clasps, page edges red, binding by Alex Patterson of Knotty Ash, binding slightly rubbed, two neat ownership signatures, one in corner of titlepage, page numbers neatly inked alongside certain titles in tables of contents, one short closed tear to edge of one page not affecting text.   Any Amount of Books   2015 - C13431   2015   £1650

Beaumont, Francis   *Salmacis and Hermaphroditus.* London: Golden Cockerel Press, 1951. No. 321 of 380 copies in ivory paper covered boards stamped in gilt, 4to., 10 color engravings by John Buckland Wright, but for minor browning to pages edges, fine.   Beasley Books   2013 - 2015 $300

Beaumont, George   *The Beggar's Complaint, Against Rack-Rent Landlords, Corn Factors, Great Farmers, Monopolizers, Paper Money Makers and War and Many Other Oppressors and Oppressions.*   Sheffield: printed for the author by J. Creme, 1813. (1812). Second edition, 12mo., with final errata leaf, prelim leaves rather stained, margins soiled, original printed wrappers, soiled and stained, whole preserved in later plain wrappers, entirely uncut, in spite of the above, not a bad copy, scarce.   John Drury Rare Books   2015 - 23451   2015 $656

Beaumont, John   *The Present State of the Universe...* London: for William Whitwood, 1696. First edition, 2nd issue, small 4to., browned, dampstained and with some worming (particularly severe near centre) in inner margin, edges dusty, uncut, stitched as issued, Maggs catalog note tipped onto inside front cover with price of £8 and old Maggs cost code pencilled verso final leaf, from the library of James Stevens Cox (1910-1997).   Maggs Bros. Ltd.   1447 - 26   2015   £380

Beaumont, William   1785-1853   *Experiments and Observations on the Gastric Juice and the Physiology of Digestion.*   Plattsburgh: printed by F. P. Allen, 1833. 8vo., 280 pages, 3 woodcut illustrations, original tan paper covered boards, purple-brown linen spine, rebacked retaining 95 per cent of original spine but largely obscuring the original printed paper spine label, gathering 21 browned as always, usual scattered foxing, else very good copy of fragile book.   Joseph J. Felcone Inc.   Science, Medicine and Technology - 29   2015 $3000

The Beautes Architecturals De Londres.   Paris: H. Mandeville; London: Ackermann & co. and Read and Co., 1851. Oblong 4to., parallel text in three languages, 35 engraved plates, including engraved vignette title, each measuring 203 x 160mm. occasional spotting, original red cloth, upper cover blocked with image of Crystal Palace, spine lettered gilt.   Marlborough Rare Books   List 53 - 27   2015   £1150

Beauvoir, Simone De   *Le Deuxieme Sexe. (The Second Sex).*   Paris: Gallimard, 1949. First edition, one of 2000 numbered copies from an edition of 2150 on alfa Marais paper, volume 1 numbered 479 and volume 2 numbered 1478, octavo, bound in original boards with design by Mario Prassinos, minor wear to exterior with half inch circular 'dent' to lower spine volume 2, otherwise lovely copy.   Athena Rare Books   15 - 1   2015 $1500

The Beaver State Almanac 1908 for Circulation in the State of Oregon. Brooklyn: Lyon Manufacturing Co. & C. Molloy, 1908. First thus, 12mo., cream wrappers with green print, printed seal of Mexican Mustang Liniment on front cover (14) pages, couple of illustrations, worn but complete copy with some cover corner chips, binding staples gone and rust spots present from same, all pages appear to be present, although there is no pagination, rare promotional booklet, along with circa 1890 blown glass Mexican Mustang Liniment, fair.   Baade Books of the West   2014 - 2015 $180

Bechdolt, Frederick R.   *Riot at Red Water.*   New York: Doubleday Doran, 1941. First edition, endpapers slightly darkened, otherwise fine in dust jacket with small chip at top of spine.   Mordida Books   March 2015 - 000063   2015 $100

Becher, B.   *Anonyme Skulpturen.*   New York: Wittenborn and Co., 1970. First edition, fine in near fine dust jacket with short closed tear and few small nicks, signed by Hilla and Bernhard Becher, very uncommon thus.   Jeff Hirsch Books   E-62 Holiday List 2014 - 1   2015 $5500

Becher, B.   *Typologies of Industrial Buildings.*   Cambridge: MIT, 2004. First edition, 4to., fine in fine dust jacket.   Beasley Books   2013 - 2015 $150

Beck, Samuel J.   *Personality Structure in Schizophrenia.*   New York: Nervous and Mental Disease Monograph 1, 1938. First edition, small 4to., very good, little fraying at head of spine, issued without dust jacket.   Beasley Books   2013 - 2015 $40

Becker, George   *Becker's Ornamental Penmanship. A Series of Analytical and Finished Alphabets by George J. Becker.*   Philadelphia: Uriah Hunt & son, 1854. First edition, oblong 12mo., original calf backed cloth, 4 pages text and 33 engraved plates, one being titlepage, spine worn and tape repaired, internally fine.   Oak Knoll Books   Special Catalogue 24 - 3   2015 $250

Becker, Robert H.   *Disenos of California Ranchos. Maps of thirty-Seven Land Grants 1822-1846.*   San Francisco: Book Club of California, 1964. First edition, one of 400 copies, folio, 37 maps, including 24 folding and 27 in color, text illustrations, decorated boards in yellow, red and white, grey linen back stamped in red, spine slightly darkened, spine lettering faded, small scar top of inner cover from removed sticker, top and bottom edges of decorated boards, slightly faded, slight spotting to rear board, very good, internally fine.   Argonaut Book Shop   Holiday Season 2014 - 23   2015 $300

Beckett, Samuel   1906-1989   *The Theatrical Notebooks of Samuel Beckett....*   London: Faber & Faber, 1992-1993. First edition thus, 3 volumes, fine in fine dust jackets and card mailing slipcases.   Peter Ellis, Bookseller   2014 - 019231   2015   £275

Beckett, Samuel   1906-1989   *The Theatrical Notebooks of Samuel Beckett: Krapp's Last Tape.*   London: Faber and Faber, 1993. First edition, large 8vo., some illustrations, fine in fine dust jacket and in plain slipcase.   Any Amount of Books   2015 - A88702   2015   £220

Beckwith, Martha Warren   *Jamaica Folk-lore.*   New York: Kraus, 1969. Ex-library, original binding, pencilling in chapter intros, good+.   Beasley Books   2013 - 2015 $40

Becquart, Paul   *Musiciens Neerlandais a La Cour De Madrid: Philippe Rogier et Son Ecole (1560-1647).*   Brussels: Palais des Academies, 1967. 8vo., stiff paper wrappers, unopened, wrappers faded at edges and chipped at bottom.   Oak Knoll Books   306 - 66   2015 $125

Becvar, Antonin   *Atlas of the Heavens: Atlas Coeli 1950.0 Scientific Editor: Prof. Dr. J. M. Mohr: Reviewer: Pavel Mayer.*   Praha & Cambridge: Czechoslovak Academy and Sky Pub., 1962. Folio, 16 folded sheets of colored star charts/maps, navy blue silver stamped boards with binder-form rings, spine ends show wear, rubbed, bookplate, very good.   Jeff Weber Rare Books   178 - 775   2015 $50

Bedini, Silvio A.   *Early American Scientific Instruments and Their Makers.*   Washington: Museum of History and Technology Smithsonian Inst., 1964. First edition, illustrations, photos, rust cloth, very fine copy.   Argonaut Book Shop   Holiday Season 2014 - 24   2015 $75

Bedtime Stories.   New York: Simon & Schuster, 1942. First edition of Golden Book number 2, 12mo., pictorial boards, blue cloth spine, fine in very slightly worn dust jacket, extremely scarce in this condition with dust jacket.   Aleph-Bet Books, Inc.   108 - 212   2015 $1500

Beebe, Lucius   *Narrow Gauge in the Rockies.*   Berkeley: Howell North, 1958. First edition, limited to 850 copies signed, this no. 725 of the Clear board edition, quarto, black cloth, gold stamped front cover and spine, pictorial endpapers, frontispiece, illustrations, housed in original pictorial paper over boards slipcase, moderate wear to spine ends and corners.   Buckingham Books   March 2015 - 27923   2015 $200

Beebe, Lucius   *The Overland Limited.*   Berkeley: Howell North, 1963. First edition, photos, portraits, facsimiles, maps, drawings, 2 color plates, very fine, pictorial dust jacket.   Argonaut Book Shop   Holiday Season 2014 - 25   2015 $50

Beebe, Lucius *The Trains We Rode.* Berkeley: Howell-North, 1965-1966. First editions, 2 volumes, quarto, lavishly illustrated with over 1500 photographic illustrations, including 11 in color and 7 paintings by Howard Fogg, gilt lettered black cloth, fine set, slightly chipped pictorial dust jackets, slight wrinkling to rear of jacket volume I. Argonaut Book Shop   Holiday Season 2014 - 26   2015 $140

Beecham, Thomas *Beecham's Photo-folio.* St. Helens, Lancashire: Thomas Beecham, 1898. First edition, 120 parts in 5 volumes, oblong octavo, each part is booklet of 24 views, original published in paper wrappers (not present), each album bound in contemporary pale red textured cloth with gilt lettering to spine and with patterned endpapers, boards slightly faded, some light toning to index pages, otherwise excellent, clean, sound set.   Any Amount of Books   2015 - A89026   2015   £240

Beeding, Francis *Hell Let Loose.* New York: Harper and Bros., 1937. First US edition, cloth moderately mottled on front and rear cloth panels, else good in dust jacket with professional restoration to spine ends, corners and extremities. Buckingham Books   March 2015 - 29520   2015 $250

Beeding, Francis *Mr. Bobadil.* London: Hodder & Stoughton, 1934. First edition, cloth lightly rubbed, spine slightly faded, else very good, lacking original dust jacket. Buckingham Books   March 2015 - 29521   2015 $300

Beeding, Francis *The Two Undertakers.* Boston: Little Brown, 1933. First American edition, label removed from front endpaper, otherwise fine in very good dust jacket with chipping at top of spine, several tears and wear at corners. Mordida Books   March 2015 - 006496   2015 $75

Beer, Georg Joseph *The Art of Preserving the Sight Unimpaired to an Extreme Old Age.* London: Henry Colburn, 1813. First edition, 8vo., frontispiece, original boards with original printed spine label, entirely uncut, fine, pretty scarce.   John Drury Rare Books   2015 - 25729   2015 $656

Beer, Gillian *Darwin's Plots; Evolutionary Narrative in Darwin, George Eliot and Nineteenth Century Fiction.* London: Routledge, 1983. Half title, illustrations, original red cloth, very good in dust jacket, initialled to Kathleen Tillotson with card from her inserted.   Jarndyce Antiquarian Booksellers   CCVII - 83   2015   £20

Beerbohm, Max 1872-1956 *A Christmas Garland.* London: William Heinemann, 1912. First edition, blue cloth gilt, boards quite stained, particularly rear board, which extends to final leaf, fair copy only, bookplate of Beerbohm's contemporary, author and politician, Augustine Birrell. Between the Covers Rare Books, Inc.   187 - 12   2015 $150

Beerbohm, Max 1872-1956 *The Dreadful Dragon of Hay Hill.* London: Heinemann, 1928. First edition, 8vo., original red cloth backed grey boards, lettered gilt on spine, signed presentation from author, sound, very good- with boards little marked and soiled.   Any Amount of Books   2015 - A97339   2015   £240

Beerbohm, Max 1872-1956 *The Works of Max Beerbohm.* London: William Heinemann, 1922. First edition thus, 10 volumes, one of 780 sets, first volume numbered 153 and signed on limitation by author, various colored cloth with paper spine labels, all but one with second labels tipped in, somewhat dulled and rubbed and some very small nicks and splits at spine ends, some pages unopened, slight foxing to few pages, spine labels mottled with slight chips, 2 volumes with armorial bookplate of James F. N. Lawrence.   Any Amount of Books   2015 - A86207   2015   £275

Beerbohm, Max 1872-1956 *Zuleika Dobson or an Oxford Love Story.* London: Heinemann, 1911. First edition, 8vo., handsomely bound in half blue leather lettered and decorated gilt on spine, marbled boards, 5 raised bands, prelims very slightly foxed and fore edges slightly browned, otherwise fine, excellent condition.   Any Amount of Books   2015 - A99416   2015   £280

Beerbohm, Max 1872-1956 *Zuleika Dobson, or an Oxford Love Story.* London: William Heinemann, 1922. New impression, half title, title in brown and black, uncut in original brown cloth, slightly dulled, and marked, signed by Kathleen Tillotson as Constable.   Jarndyce Antiquarian Booksellers   CCVII - 85   2015   £25

Beeson, John *Are We Not Men and Brethren? An Address to the People of the United States in Behalf of the Indians.* Boston: Bela Marsh, 1859. First edition, large 8vo., leaflet (4) pages, illustrations, map, sheets browned, some separations but without serious loss along a number of folds.   M & S Rare Books, Inc.   97 - 124   2015 $225

Beeton, S. O. *The Boy's Own Volume of Fact, Fiction, History and Adventure Christmas 1865.* London: S. O. Beeton, 248 Strand, W. C., Christmas, 1865. Octavo, profusely illustrated with full page illustrations on inserted plates, smaller illustrations and diagrams in text, original decorated cloth stamped in bold and blind.   L. W. Currey, Inc.   Boy's Adventure Fiction 2015 - 80   2015 $100

Begbie, Matthew Baillie *Partnership 'en Commandite' or Partnership with Limited Liabilities...* London: Effingham Wilson, 1848. First edition, 8vo., half title, original embossed brown cloth, spine lettered gilt, slight signs of wear, still very good.   John Drury Rare Books   March 2015 - 25501   2015 $266

Behan, Brendan 1923-1964 *The Scarperer.* London: Hutchinson, 1966. First English edition, fine in dust jacket. Mordida Books   March 2015 - 008200   2015 $85

Behn, Aphra 1640-1689 *Miscellany, Being a Collection of Poems by Several Hands.* London: for J. Hindmarsh, 1685. Only edition, 8vo., corner of Y4 torn away with loss of catchword and two or three letters of text, blank corner D8 torn away (no loss of text), light dampstain lower right corner of last half of work, some light soiling, later calf rebacked, new endleaves, from the library of James Stevens Cox (1910-1997), 'with "J.W." contemporary initials to titlepage.   Maggs Bros. Ltd.   1447 - 27   2015   £1800

Behn, Aphra 1640-1689 *The Widdow Ranter, or the History of Bacon in Virginia.* London: printed for James Knapton, 1690. First edition, small 4to., titlepage lightly soiled, light dampstain to blank fore margins throughout, odd page number just touched by binder, late 19th century brown morocco by Pratt, gilt edges, joints and corners shipped, fore edge of front cover slightly bowed, good copy, inkstamp "J. W. Bouton, Bookseller NY", from the library of James Stevens Cox (1910-1997).   Maggs Bros. Ltd.   1447 - 28   2015   £4500

Behrman, S. N. *The Burning Glass.* Boston: Little Brown, 1968. First edition, fine in very good dust jacket that has been trimmed along bottom edge, dedication copy, nicely inscribed by author to Brigitta and Goddard Lieberson on dedication page.   Between the Covers Rare Books 196 - 66   2015 $650

Bekker, Balthasar *De Betoverde Weereld... (The Bewitched World).* Amsterdam: Daniel van den Dalen, 1691-1693. First edition, quarto, with rare engraved 1691 portrait of Balthasar Beeker created by Johannes Hilarides, 4 books in one volume, contemporary darkened and speckled vellum binding with lovely handwritten title on spine, page opposite the portrait has two chips taken out of front edge, not affecting type, all four books have been hand signed by Bekker in ink, lovely authentic and unsophisticated copy.   Athena Rare Books   15 - 2   2015 $2800

Bekker, Balthasar *Die Bezauberte Welt.... (The Bewitched World...).* Amsterdam: but Hertel, Hamburg, 1693. First German edition, quarto, 4 books in 1 volume, quarto, contemporary vellum with light (but still gorgeous) hand lettering to spine, binding with bit of outer wear, but much less than one would expect in a book over 300 years old, former owner's bookplate "Ex Libris E. B. Waller/Amsterdam 1893", all pages lightly uniformly browned, lovely copy.   Athena Rare Books   15 - 3   2015 $2400

Belfield, H. Wedgwood *"Piston Payne's Jungle Submotank." in Champion Library.* London: Amalgamated Press 5 November, 1936. Number 188, octavo, pictorial wrappers.   L. W. Currey, Inc.   Boy's Adventure Fiction 2015 - 91   2015 $100

Bell, Alexander Graham *Growth of the Oral method and Instructing the Deaf. An Address Delivered November 10 1894 on the Twenty-fifth Anniversary of the Opening of the Horace Mann School, Boston, Mass.* Boston: Press of Rockwell and Churchill, 1896. First separate edition, 8vo., folding chart, original printed wrappers, label of institutional library on lower cover, very good, perhaps fine.   John Drury Rare Books   2015 - 19346   2015 $133

Bell, Alexander Graham *The Mystic Oral School. An Argument in Its Favor.* Washington: Gibson Bros., 1897. First edition, 8vo., 38 pages, original printed card covers, leaves lightly creased in outer margins, label of institutional library on lower cover, good, clean copy.   John Drury Rare Books   2015 - 19347   2015 $133

Bell, Alexander Graham *The Question of Sign-Language and the Utility of Signs in the Instruction of the Deaf.* Washington: Sanders Printing Office, 1898. First separate edition, 8vo., original printed card covers, label of institutional library on lower cover, still fine.   John Drury Rare Books 2015 - 19348   2015 $133

Bell, Horace *Reminiscences of a Ranger or Early Times in Southern California.* Santa Barbara: Wallace Hebard, 1927. First edition thus, fine, bright copy, internally reinforced dust jacket.   Buckingham Books   March 2015 - 28848   2015 $175

Bell, Hugh *An Impartial Account of the Conduct of the Excise Towards the Breweries in Scotland, Particularly in Edinburgh.* Edinburgh: Printed in the year, 1791. First edition, 8vo., including final blank F4, some light marginal dust soiling, recent cloth backed marbled boards, morocco label on upper cover, lettered gilt, very good, uncut, scarce. John Drury Rare Books   March 2015 - 25485   2015   £306

Bell, James *Influence of Physical Research on Mental Philosophy.* Edinburgh: Adam and Charles Black, 1839. First edition, 12mo., few very small minor spots and rustmarks, original cloth, original printed spine label, uncut, very good, presentation inscription by author for Mr. Thomas Henderson, Haddington Dec. 1843, rare.   John Drury Rare Books   2015 - 19901   2015 $177

Bell, James G. *A Log of the Texas-California Cattle Trail 1854.* Reprinted from the Southwestern Historical Quarterly, 1932. first book edition of only 100 copies, 8vo., original blue printed wrappers, minor wear to extended edges of front and rear covers, else near fine, clean, inscribed by James Evetts Haley for Mr. John Thomas Lee, June 29 1934.   Buckingham Books   March 2015 - 37237   2015 $1750

Bell, James G. *A Log of the Texas California Cattle Trail 1854.* Austin: Southwestern Historical Quarterly, 1932. First edition, in Southwestern Historical Quarterly, Volume XXXV No. 3 Jan. 1932, Volume XXXV No. 4 April 1932, Volume XXXVI No. 1 July 1932, 8vo., original tan printed wrappers, near fine, from the collection of Al Lowman. Buckingham Books   March 2015 - 29639   2015 $750

Bell, Julian *Work for the Winter More or Less for Christmas.* N.P.: Charleston, 1935. First edition, 8vo., original white stapled wrappers, lettered black on cover with small illustration/vignette at centre, uncommon, signed presentation from author to Robert, sound, about very good copy with slight toning to covers, very faint shelfwear and slight creasing at top corners of some pages, very good. Any Amount of Books   2015 - C14990   2015   £1050

Bell, Madison Smartt *Doctor Sleep.* New York: Harcourt Brace Jovanovich, 1991. First edition, fine in fine dust jacket, inscribed by author for Nicholas Delbanco and his wife. Between the Covers Rare Books, Inc.   187 - 13   2015 $100

Bell, Quentin *An Introductory History of England in the 18th Century.* Charlbury: Senecio Press, 2013. First edition, 32/500 copies, illustrations, all text reproduced in facsimile, imperial 4to., original quarter brown leather with green patterned boards in facsimile of original binding, introduction by Julain Bell laid in at front, slipcase with print label to front, fine. Blackwell's Rare Books   B179 - 232   2015   £195

Bell, Robert *Lectures on the Solemnities Used in Scotland.* Edinburgh: sold by A. Guthrie and A. Lawrie, 1795. First edition, 8vo., 19th century half calf, neatly rebacked, spine lettered, very good, rare.   John Drury Rare Books   March 2015 - 19309   2015 $266

Bell, Steve *Steve Bell: Im Auge Des Zeichners; Eine Ausstellung Im Deutschen Museum fur Karikatur und Zeichenkusnt...* Hannover: Wilhelm-Busch, 2011. First edition, oblong 4to., original illustrated matt boards, lettered white on spine and in red on front cover, copiously illustrated in color and black and white, signed presentation from author for Ronald and Monica, written note in Ronald Searle's hand on front endpaper "Rec'd from Steve 8 April 2011", fine.   Any Amount of Books   2015 - C7346   2015   £150

Bell, Vanessa *Recent Paintings by Vanessa Bell.* London: London Artists' Association, 1930. One of an unstated limitation of 500 copies, two folded sheets stapled, pages little spotted, staples little rusted, one tiny (1cm.) closed tear, very good.   Any Amount of Books   March 2015 - C14471   2015   £350

Bellamy, Edward *Looking Backward 2000-1887.* London: William Reeves, 1889? Nineteenth edition, 16mo., 6 pages ads, ads on leading pastedown, original green cloth, lettered in red ink, very good.   Jarndyce Antiquarian Booksellers   CCXI - 23   2015   £30

Bellamy, Edward *Looking Backward 2000-1887.* Boston and New York: Houghton Mifflin, 1889. First edition, later printing, with "One Hundred and Second Thousand" on titlepage, 8vo., original brown cloth, gilt lettering, top edge of upper board and first few signatures bumped, fine, signed "With compliments of / Edward Bellamy", heraldic bookplate with names John Haley Bellamy and John W. P. Frost typed in lower margin.   The Brick Row Book Shop   Miscellany 67 - 24   2015 $500

Bellet, Isaac *Lettres Sur le Pouvoir De L'Imagination Des Femmes Enceintes.* Paris: Freres Guerin, 1745. First edition, contemporary stamped calf little worn, very good copy. Second Life Books Inc.   189 - 21   2015 $500

Belloc, Hilaire 1870-1953 *The Missing Masterpiece.* London: Arrowsmith, 1929. First edition, fine, bright, tight copy in dust jacket, 41 drawings by G. K. Chesterton, exceptional copy.   Buckingham Books   March 2015 - 24326   2015 $850

Bellow, Saul *Herzog.* London: Weidenfeld & Nicolson, 1964. First British edition, 8vo., uncorrected proof, author's name on cover, publication date change in neat hand (by publisher's office) from Nov. 6th 1964 to Jan. 22nd 1965, orange printed wrappers very slightly soiled, hinges slightly rubbed, otherwise sound, tight, very good.   Any Amount of Books   2015 - A70527   2015   £250

Bellow, Saul *Herzog.* London: Weidenfeld & Nicolson, 1964. First British edition, foxing to page edges, very good in very good dust jacket, John Fowles copy with his bookplate.   Ken Lopez, Bookseller   164 - 13   2015 $300

Bellow, Saul *Mr. Sammler's Planet.* New York: Viking Press, 1970. First printing, complimentary copy with publisher slip laid in, fine in very near fine dust jacket with some minute wear, signed in full by Bellow on titlepage, lovely copy.   Jeff Hirsch Books   E-62 Holiday List 2014 - 2   2015 $300

Bellow, Saul *Nobel Lecture.* New York: Targ Editions, 1979. First edition, one of 350 copies, numbered and signed by Bellow, large 8vo., printed by Ronald Gordon on Rives Heavyweight, fine in fine dust jacket.   Beasley Books 2013 - 2015 $150

Bellow, Saul *Ravelstein.* New York: Viking Press, 2000. First edition, 8vo., very good++, mild cover edgewear, near fine dust jacket.   By the Book, L. C.   Special List 10 - 23   2015 $120

Bellow, Saul *A Silver Dish.* New York: Albondocani Press, 1979. First edition, number 297 of 300 copies, numbered and signed by author, fine in acetate dust jacket, 8vo. Beasley Books   2013 - 2015 $125

Bellwood, Peter S. *South Asia 2005.* London: Europa Publications, 2005. Second edition, 4to., color illustrated map endpapers, very good.   Any Amount of Books   2015 - A64361   2015   £150

Beloof, Robert *The One Eyed Gunner and Other Portraits: a Book of Poems.* London: Villiers Pub., 1956. First edition, fine in near fine dust jacket with small nicks and tears at crown, inscribed by author to fellow poet, Karl Shapiro.   Between the Covers Rare Books, Inc.   187 - 14   2015 $45

Belsham, Thomas *A Letter to the Unitarian Christian in South Wale, Occasioned by the Animadversions of the Right Reverend the Lord Bishop of St. David's...* London: printed for R. Hunter successor to Mr. Johnson, 1816. First edition, 8vo., recently well bound in boards with printed title label on spine, very good.   John Drury Rare Books   2015 - 24705   2015 $221

Belsham, Thomas *The Right and Duty of Unitarian Christians to from Separate Societies for Religious Worship.* London: sold by J. Johnson and by Knot and Lloyd and by James Belcher, 1802. First edition, 8vo., recently well bound in linen backed marbled boards lettered, very good, very scarce.   John Drury Rare Books   March 2015 - 21122   2015 $221

Bemelmans, Ludwig *Madeline and the Bad Hat.* New York: Viking, Dec., 1956. Limited to 885 copies for sale, signed by Bemelmans, large 4to., beautifully illustrated in color, green pictorial cloth, fine in plain slipcase that is slightly cracked, extremely scarce.   Aleph-bet Books, Inc.   109 - 47   2015 $1850

Bender, Henry E. *Uintah Railway: the Gilsonite Route.* Forest Par: Heimburger House n.d. circa, 1995. First corrected edition, signed by author, quarto, 29 black and white photos, maps, yellow cloth gilt, very fine with pictorial dust jacket.   Argonaut Book Shop   Holiday Season 2014 - 29   2015 $75

Bendix, Hans *The Lady Who Kept Her Promise.* New York: American Artists Group, 1941. First edition, 12mo., illustrated paper covered boards, slight edgewear, else near fine, inscribed by author for Gurmar Leistikow(?).   Between the Covers Rare Books, Inc.   187 - 15   2015 $75

Benedek, Therese *Psychosexual Function in Women.* New York: Ronald, 1952. First edition thus, hardcover, some internal library signs, binding clean, very good+, much of dust jacket laid in.   Beasley Books   2013 - 2015 $45

Benedikt, Michael *Serenade in Six Pieces.* Huntington: M. Sabados, 1958. First edition, 24mo., first edition, trifle age toned, corners little bumped, still very near fine in wrappers, one of 55 numbered copies, this copy inscribed by author to poet Howard Moss.   Between the Covers Rare Books, Inc.   187 - 16   2015 $450

Benefield, Barry *Short Turns.* New York: Century Co., 1926. First edition, spine lettering bit worn, faint dampstain on fore edge, very good plus in very good example of scarce dust jacket with some shallow chipping at spinal extremities, not affecting any lettering, Gloria Swanson's copy with her ownership signature and stamp, this copy was given by Swanson to Van Heflin who later gave it to a friend.   Between the Covers Rare Books, Inc.   187 - 17   2015 $475

Benett, John *An Essay on the Commutation of Tithes; to Which as Adjudged the Bedfordean Gold Meald by the Bath and West of England Society for the Encouragement of Agriculture, Arts, Manufactures and Commerce at their Annual Meeting December 13th 1814.* Bath: printed by Richard Cruttwell, 1814. First edition, 8vo., preserved in modern wrappers, printed title label on upper cover, very good, scarce.   John Drury Rare Books   2015 - 18612   2015 $133

Benezit, E. *Dictionnaire Critique et Documentaire des Peintres, Sculpteurs, Dessinateurs et Graveurs.* Libraire Grund, 1966. Fourth printing, Nouvelle edition redesigned, 8 volumes, 32 photograuvres, maroon cloth, gilt lettering on spine and front cover, very fine set, as new, with original glassine jackets.   Argonaut Book Shop   Holiday Season 2014 - 74   2015 $600

Benford, Gregory *Timescape.* New York: Simon and Schuster, 1980. First edition, octavo, cloth backed boards.   John W. Knott, Bookseller   Selected New Arrivals Jan. 2015 - 16918   2015 $150

Bengal (India). Supreme Court Of Judicature *Report on the Proceedings of the Supreme Court of Judicature at Fort William in Bengal, in Its Admiralty Jurisidiction in the Case of George Collier as Well from Himself as for the King, Versus the Cutter Dispatch on Tuesday the 4th Feb. 1817.* Calcutta: printed by desire and on account of the merchants of this city, by T. Watley, 1817. Uncut, sewn as issued, first and last leaves slightly dusted, inscription "presented to Messrs. J. & R. Gladstone, Liverpool with Palmer & Co's. Comps", with 'Fasque' written in different hand on title, additional signature of H. Howeitt.   Jarndyce Antiquarian Booksellers   CCXI - 57   2015   £180

Bennet, Robert Ames *Go-Getter Gary.* Published by A. C. McClurg, 1926. First edition, fine in dust jacket with one small chip missing from bottom edge of rear panel.   Buckingham Books   March 2015 - 71   2015 $275

Bennet, William *The Case of Orphans Stated a Sermon: preached in St. Andrew's Church, Edinburgh, Before the Society of the Orphans' Hospital, Tuesday 14th July 1801....* Edinburgh: printed by C. Stewart & Co., 1801. First edition, 8vo., neatly bound fairly recently in dark blue cloth boards, printed title label, very good, rare outside usual Scottish libraries.   John Drury Rare Books   March 2015 - 24594   2015 $221

Bennet, William *Report of the Trial by Jury, Anderson Against Rintoul and Other, for Libels, Spoken at Public Meetings in Dundee and Published in the Dundee, Perth and Cupar Advertiser Newspaper.* Edinburgh: John Lothian, 1824. First edition, rare, 8vo., titlepage little dust soiled, contemporary half calf over marbled boards, rebacked and labelled, good copy.   John Drury Rare Books   2015 - 19293   2015 $656

Bennett, Charles *Adventures of Young Munchausen.* London: Routledge, Warne and Routledge, 1865. First edition, 12 fine full page engravings, 4to., blue cloth stamped in gold and blind, slight wear to bottom of spine and occasional light spot, else near fine, very scarce.   Aleph-bet Books, Inc.   109 - 48   2015 $1200

Bennett, George *Wanderings in New South Wales, Batavia, Pedir Coast, Singapore and China.* London: Richard Bentley, 1834. Octavo, 2 volumes, uncolored frontispieces, attractive early binder's cloth, few spots, otherwise bright, pleasant copy.   Andrew Isles   2015 - 5337   2015 $750

Bennett, George F. *Early Architecture of Delaware.* Wilmington: Historical Press Inc., 1932. First edition, limited to 120 numbered copies, 4to., cloth, chipped at head of spine, back cover spotted.   Oak Knoll Books   306 - 252   2015 $100

Bennett, Whitman *A Practical Guide to American Book Collecting 1663-1940.* New York: Bennett Book Studios, 1941. First edition, one of 1250 copies (1150 bound in cloth), tan cloth, spine printed in black with printed paper label on front cover, errata pasted to front endpaper as issued, fine.   Argonaut Book Shop   Holiday Season 2014 - 30   2015 $60

Benschoter, George E. *1837-1897 Book of Facts Concerning the Early Settlement of Sherman County.* Loup City: Northwestern Print, 1897. First edition, 12mo., printed wrappers, rare, light wear to spine panel, else near fine, tight, clean copy, clamshell case.   Buckingham Books   March 2015 - 20695   2015 $1875

Benson, Allan L. *Inviting War to America.* Girard: Appeal to Reason, 1916. First edition, wrappers, near fine with crease on rear wrapper (also issued in cloth).   Beasley Books   2013 - 2015 $45

Benson, E. F. *Pharisees and Publicans.* London: Hutchinson & Co., n.d. circa, 1926. First edition thus, 8vo., original red cloth, lettered black on spine and cover, from the Donald Rudd collection, publisher's catalog dated Autumn 1926, very slight and faint creasing at spine, otherwise very good+, excellent condition.   Any Amount of Books   2015 - C4965   2015   £300

Benson, Lawrence S. *Philosophic Reviews. Darwin Answered; or Evolution a Myth.* New York: James S. Burton, 1875. First collected edition, 8vo., few text diagrams, original glazed paper printed wrappers, light wear, upper corner of first few leaves gnawed, but not affecting text, solid copy, sheets very darkly browned throughout, title and text dampstained.   M & S Rare Books, Inc.   97 - 86   2015 $175

Benson, Raymond *The World is Not Enough 007.* London: Hodder & Stoughton, 1999. First edition, very fine in dust jacket.   Mordida Books   March 2015 - 011589   2015 $125

Bentham, Jeremy *Traites de Legislation Civile et Penale, Precedes de Principes Generaux de Legislation..* Paris: Chez Bossange, 1802. First edition, 8vo., 3 volumes, half title in each volume, little spotting and general paper browning, contemporary uniform tree sheep, neatly rebacked to match with contrasting labels and gilt lines, very good, really quite scarce.   John Drury Rare Books   2015 - 141   2015 $1049

Bentley, E. C. *Clerihews Complete.* London: Werner Laurie, 1951. First edition, some tiny light spotting on page edges, else fine in price clipped dust jacket with nick at top of spine and couple of closed tears.   Mordida Books   March 2015 - 000244   2015 $75

Bentley, John *The Eyes of Death.* Garden City: Doubleday Doran & Co., 1934. First US edition, fine, bright copy in dust jacket with light wear to spine ends and corners.   Buckingham Books   March 2015 - 25841   2015 $425

Bentley, John *Mr. Marlow Chooses Wine.* Boston: Houghton Mifflin, 1941. First American edition, fine in fine dust jacket.   Mordida Books   March 2015 - 010619   2015 $275

Bentley, John *Mr. Marlow Takes to Rye.* Boston: Houghton Mifflin, 1942. First American edition, fine in dust jacket.   Mordida Books   March 2015 - 007818   2015 $275

Bentley, Joseph *Health and Wealth: How to Get, Preserve and Enjoy Them or Physical and Industrial Training for the People.* London: Joseph Bentley, 1858. Fifth edition, illustrations, unopened ads pages 299-328, original brown cloth by Richmond & Son, blocked in blind, neat library number foot of spine, ex-libris Manchester & Salford Bank Ltd., very good.   Jarndyce Antiquarian Booksellers   CCXI - 24   2015   £75

Bentley, Nicolas *The Floating Dutchman.* London: Michael Joseph, 1950. First edition, fine in dust jacket with publisher's wraparound intact.   Mordida Books   March 2015 - 000247   2015 $90

Bentley, Richard *A Full and True Account of the Dreadful and Melancholy Earthquake which Happened Between Twelve and One O'Clock in the Morning on Thursday the Fifth Instant.* London: Tim Tremor, 1750. Fifth edition, folio, woodcut ornament on title, 8 paes, very small stain on outer margin, but fine, crisp, simply folded and unbound as issued, rare.   John Drury Rare Books   2015 - 15181   2015 $177

Benyowsky, Mauritius Augustus, Count De *Memoirs of Travels of...* London: printed for G. G. J. and J. Robinson, 1790. First edition, 2 volumes, quarto, 23 engraved plates, maps and plans, both volumes with half titles, titlepage of volume 1 with engraved portrait vignette of author, original quarter parchment over drab blue boards, pages uncut and volume II partially unopened, boards bit rubbed and bumped, delicate spines with expected chipping and flaking, hinges cracked by holding, leaf YY of volume 1 with small tear to top margin, not affecting text, previous owner's bookplate on front pastedown of both volumes, overall very good set, internally very clean with large margins each volume housed in two cloth clamshell cases, clamshells worn and probably need to be replaced.   Heritage Book Shop   Holiday 2014 - 14   2015 $9500

Benzing, Josef *Buchdrucker des 16 und 17 Jahrhunderts Im Deutschen Sprachgebiet.* Wiesbaden: Otto Harrassowitz, 1963. Thick 8vo., cloth, leather spine and cover labels, spine label rubbed and small piece chipped off edge, from the library of Rudolf Hirsch with his name and comment.   Oak Knoll Books   306 - 182   2015 $125

Beowulf *The Tale of Beowulf.* Hammersmith: Kelmscott Press, 1895. One of 300 copies printed on Perch paper, quarto, bound in limp vellum, inscribed by translator, A. J. Wyatt to his wife Catherine, custom slipcase, woodcut borders and initials designed by William Morris, "Not to Reader" slip laid in, with pencil annotations to verso, lovely association copy.   Honey & Wax Booksellers   1 - 55   2015 $8200

Berendt, John *Midnight in the Garden of Good and Evil.* New York: Random House, 1994. True first edition, first state with dust jacket flap price of $23.00, the word 'for' misspelled on page 11, line 7 from bottom to read 'fmmr' and black cloth spine with green paper over boards with 'JB' stamped in silver on front cover, fine in dust jacket.   Buckingham Books   March 2015 - 8692   2015 $175

Berendt, John *Midnight in the Garden of Good and Evil.* New York: Random House, 1994. First edition, very fine in dust jacket.   Mordida Books   March 2015 - 002366   2015 $250

Berenson, Bernard *Italian Pictures of the Renaissance: a List of the Principal Artists and their Works with an Index of Places.* New York: Phaidon, 1968. First edition thus, 3 volumes, small 4to., illustrations, occasional faint foxing to prelims, otherwise handsome very good+ in like dust jackets.   Any Amount of Books   2015 - A79097   2015   £300

Beresford-Hope, A. J. B. *The Social Influence of the Prayer Book; a lecture Delivered in the Town Hall at Hanley, Before the Members of the Hanley Branch of the Church of England Young Men's Society. Feb. 2th 1863, the Right Rev. the Lord Bishop of Lichfield in the Chair.* London: William Ridgway, Hanley: printed by William Timmis, 1863. First edition, 8vo., contemporary half calf, spine lettered gilt, fine, from author's own library with signature on front pastedown and arms in gilt at head of spine, uncommon.   John Drury Rare Books   March 2015 - 19253   2015 $221

Beresford, Leslie *"The Flying Fish." in The Boys' Friend Library.* London: Amalgamated Press, 11 May, 1931. number 311 new series, octavo, 64 pages, pictorial wrappers.   L. W. Currey, Inc.   Boy's Adventure Fiction 2015 - 83   2015 $100

Berg, Karl *The Sadist.* London: Heinemann, 1945. Reissued, 8vo., original black cloth lettered grey at spine, 9 plates, 3 tables, very good in like dust jacket, price clipped with slight rubbing, tanning and surface wear, slight creasing at edges and two closed tears, decent copy of rare book.   Any Amount of Books   2015 - C2308   2015   £300

Berg, Stephen *With Akhmatova at the Black Gates.* Urbana: University of Illinois Press, 1981. First edition, fine in fine dust jacket but for tiny tear at top of front flap fold, inscribed by Berg to author and translator Bertrand Mathieu, scarce hardcover issue.   Between the Covers Rare Books, Inc.   187 - 18   2015 $200

Bergamo, Ilarione Da *Daily life in Colonial Mexico. The Journey of Friar Ilarione da Bergamo 1761-1768.* Norman: University of Oklahoma Press, 2000. First edition in English, 20 illustrations, 4 maps, blue cloth, gilt, very fine with pictorial dust jacket.   Argonaut Book Shop   Holiday Season 2014 - 31   2015 $45

Bergengren, Ralph *David the Dreamer.* Boston: Atlantic Monthly Press, 1922. Oblong 4to., green gilt cloth, pictorial paste-on, edge of cover pale slightly rubbed, attractive bookplate on endpaper, near fine, color plates by Tom Freud. Aleph-Bet Books, Inc. 108 - 196 2015 $1200

Berger, Edward *Annual Review of Jazz Studies 10 1999.* Lanham: Scarecrow & Jazz Studies, 2001. First edition, very slight spine slant, otherwise fine, issued without jacket. Beasley Books 2013 - 2015 $45

Berger, Eliezer *Dan the Painter and a Cow. (Dan Ha Tzayar Ve Ha Parah).* Palestine: circa, 1945. 12mo., pictorial wrappers, slight edge wear, else very good+, illustrations by Lev Dickstein with full page color linoleum cuts. Aleph-Bet Books, Inc. 108 - 251-7 2015 $325

Berger, Eliezer *Dan the Painter and Chickens. (Dan Ha Tzayarve Ha Ophot).* Palestine: circa, 1945. 12mo., pictorial wrappers, slight edge wear, else very good+, illustrations by Lev Dickstein with full page color linoleum cuts. Aleph-Bet Books, Inc. 108 - 251-6 2015 $325

Berger, Eliezer *Dan the Painter and Sheep. (Dan Ha Tzayar Ve Ha Keyes).* Palestine: circa, 1945. 12mo., pictorial wrappers, slight edge wear, else very good+, illustrations by Lev Dickstein with full page color linoleum cuts. Aleph-Bet Books, Inc. 108 - 251-8 2015 $325

Berger, Eliezer *Dan the Painter and Transportation. (Dan Ha Tzayar Vve Kley Ha Rechev).* Palestine: circa, 1945. 12mo., pictorial wrappers, slight edge wear, else very good+, illustrations by Lev Dickstein with full page color linoleum cuts. Aleph-Bet Books, Inc. 108 - 251-5 2015 $325

Berger, Sidney E. *Forty-Four Years of Bird & Bull. A Bibliography 1958-2002.* Newtown: Bird & Bull Press, 2002. Limited to 150 numbered copies, this copy not numbered but bears Henry Morris's handwritten note on colophon "Binding sample rec'd 6-19-02. Book looks fine - box not so - he's making new box for this copy, Later decided the labels had to be remade - lighter type face, stamp clearer and rectangular spine label as I have rec'd. Looks better. He sent samples", large 4to., quarter morocco with japanese cloth sides, leather spine label, Japanese cloth portfolio, cloth covered clamshell box, leather spine label, 99 pages plus not paginated inserts, with prospectus. Oak Knoll Books 306 - 128 2015 $525

Berghaus, Heinrich *Physikalischer Atlas.* Gotha: J. Perthes, 1845-1848. First edition variant, oblong folio, 90 colored plates, some plates loose, smoky aroma, contemporary half calf over marbled paper boards, modern beige and black cloth box (binding is remnant), spine torn and coming free, boards with open tears, loose atlas maps are easy to view and handle regardless of condition of the binding, scarce, internally very good, fine box, rare. Jeff Weber Rare Books 178 - 776 2015 $1000

Berington, Simon *Geschichte des Gaudentio di Lucca: Oder Merkwrdige Nachricht Seiner sonderbahren reise Durch die Sandwusteneyen...* Frankfurt und Leipzig: Van Duren, 1751. First edition, 2 volumes in 1, 8vo., titles printed in red and black, contemporary German half calf over marbled boards, spine fully gilt with raised bands and contrasting morocco label, red edges, fine. John Drury Rare Books 2015 - 25671 2015 $1005

Berkeley, Anthony *The Layton Court Mystery.* New York: Doubleday Doran and Co., 1929. First US edition, near fine in fine dust jacket, beautiful copy of scarce title. Buckingham Books March 2015 - 37161 2015 $1250

Berkeley, Anthony *The Poisoned Chocolates Case.* Doubleday Doran and Co., 1929. First US edition, light waterstain to toe of spine, else very good in bright dust jacket with minor wear to head of spine, exceptional copy, scarce. Buckingham Books March 2015 - 26203 2015 $1275

Berkeley, George, Bp. of Cloyne 1685-1753 *Bishop Berkeley's Querist Republished with Notes, showing How Many of the Same Questions Still remain to be Asked, Respecting Ireland.* London: T. Bretell for James Ridgway, 1829. First edition thus, 8vo., wanting half title, early 19th century half calf over marbled boards, neatly rebacked and lettered, armorial bookplate of Ferguson of Raith, seemingly rare. John Drury Rare Books 2015 - 24874 2015 $787

Berkeley, George, Bp. of Cloyne 1685-1753 *Siris; a Chain of Philosophical Reflexions and Inquiries Concerning the Virtues of Tar Water and Divers other Subjects Connected Together and Arising One from Another.* London: for W. Innys and C. Hitch and C. Davis, 1744. Second English edition, variant with author's name on titlepage, removed from bound volume, very good. Joseph J. Felcone Inc. Science, Medicine and Technology - 10 2015 $275

Berkeley, Maurice Frederick Fitzhardinge *A Letter Addressed to Sir John Barrow, Bart on the System of war and Peace Complements in Her Majesty's Ships.* London: J. Ridgway, 1839. First edition, recently well bound in linen backed marbled boards, lettered, very good, uncommon. John Drury Rare Books 2015 - 18003 2015 $151

Berkman, Pamela *The History of the Atchison, Topeka & Santa Fe.* Greenwich: Bonanza, 1988. First edition, quarto, 129 pages, illustrations in color and black and white, black and white photos, maps, blue cloth, covers dulled and bit spotted, creases to front endpaper, else fine, pictorial dust jacket. Argonaut Book Shop Holiday Season 2014 - 32 2015 $35

Berman, Wallace *A Retrospective.* Los Angeles: Fellows of Contemporary Art, 1978. First edition, perfect bound 4to., illustrations in color black and white and color, fine, price sticker to rear.   Ed Smith Books   83 - 3   2015 $200

Bermudez De Castro, Manuel *Bombardment of Valpariso. Speech of the Spanish Minister for Foreign Affairs.* London: printed by J. H. Scrader, 1866. First edition, 8vo., stitched paper wrappers, nicks to spine, else near fine.   Kaaterskill Books   19 - 18   2015 $400

Bernanos, Georges *The Star of Satan.* London: Published by John Lane, 1927. First edition, 8vo., original green cloth lettered black on spine and front cover, clean, very good in pink purple patterned dust jacket, slight wear with tiny nick at lower spine hinge, excellent condition.   Any Amount of Books   2015 - C12520   2015   £180

Bernard, Thomas *The New School: Being an Attempt to Illustrate Its Principles, Detail and Advantages.* London: printed by W. Bulmer and Co. for the Society for Bettering the Condition of the Poor and sold by J. Hatchard Dec., 1809. First edition, 8vo., contemporary half calf over marbled boards, gilt lines and red label on spine, joints neatly repaired, very good, scarce.   John Drury Rare Books   2015 - 24088   2015 $699

Bernhard, Josephine *Cry-Baby Dolls.* New York: Roy, 1945. First edition, oblong 4to., pictorial boards, fine in slightly worn dust jacket, illustrations by Irena Lorentowicz.   Aleph-Bet Books, Inc.   108 - 148   2015 $150

Bernstein, Charles *Rough Trades.* Los Angeles: Sun & Moon Press, 1991. First edition, paperback original, small octavo, glossy wrappers, fine, inscribed by author to Ray DiPalma.   Between the Covers Rare Books, Inc.   187 - 19   2015 $50

Bernstock, Judith E. *Joan Mitchell.* New York & Ithaca: Hudson Hills Press in association with Herbert F. Johnson Museum of Art, Cornell University, 1988. First edition, 118 color plates, 8 black and white illustrations, fine in fine dust jacket, fresh copy.   Jeff Hirsch Books   E-62 Holiday List 2014 - 3   2015 $250

Berosus, The Chaldean *Berosi Sacerdotis Chaldaici, Antiquitatum Libri Quinque: Clim Commentariis Ioannis Anni Viterbensis.* Antwerp: printed by Johannes Grapheus for Heirs of Joannes Steels, 1545. 171 x 114mm., contemporary calf by Pecking Crow Binder, covers with blind ruled frame, oblique gilt fleur-de-lys cornerpieces and binder's signature gilt stamps - a hand clutching spray of flowers, bird perched on top-at the center, raised bands, later but well chosen endpapers, ink titling to fore edge (expertly rebacked in the style of the period with simple blind and gilt decoration, corners neatly restored), printer's device on titlepage, later pasted on manuscript note regarding forgery on front pastedown, contemporary ownership inscription Fr(ater) Augustinus (illegible), first and last page with shallow (and scarcely visible) blindstamp of (now defunct) Theological Institue of Connecticut, covers little marked and with minor staining (a narrow inner strip of upper board somewhat darkened and crackled because of rebacking), text printed on inferior stock (and so with overall faint browning), otherwise excellent example with only insignificant defects, carefully restored binding sound and pleasing, text fresh and clean.   Phillip J. Pirages   66 - 5   2015 $7800

Berrigan, Ted *Back in Boston Again.* Philadelphia: Telegraph Books, 1972. First edition, small 8vo., original pictorial wrappers with cover by Rudy Burckhardt, very good, inscribed by Berrigan.   James S. Jaffe Rare Books   Many Happy Returns - 202   2015 $350

Berrigan, Ted *Bean Spasms.* New York: Kulchur Press, 1967. First edition, paperback issue, signed by all three (Berrigan, Ron Padgett and artist, Joe Brainard with a note by Berrigan for Burt Britton), fine.   James S. Jaffe Rare Books   Many Happy Returns - 212   2015 $1250

Berrigan, Ted *Bean Spasms.* New York: Kulchur Press, 1967. First edition, small 4to., presentation copy inscribed by Berrigan to one of his publishers, Ted and Joan Wilentz, original pictorial boards, illustrations and drawings by Joe Brainard, covers slightly rubbed, otherwise fine.   James S. Jaffe Rare Books   Many Happy Returns - 211   2015 $1500

Berrigan, Ted *Carrying a Torch.* Brooklyn: Clown War, 1980. First edition, limited to 500 copies (474 regular copies), oblong 8vo., reproductions of engravings by Jan Vredeman de Vries, original wrappers, fine.   James S. Jaffe Rare Books   Many Happy Returns - 51   2015 $125

Berrigan, Ted *Carrying a Torch.* Brooklyn: Clown War, 1980. First edition, limited to 500 copies, oblong 8vo., illustrated with reproductions of engravings by Jan Vredeman de Vries, original pictorial wrappers, presentation copy inscribed on dedication page (cc#1) to Lewis (Warsh), 25 Jan. 80 NYC, fine.   James S. Jaffe Rare Books   Many Happy Returns - 52   2015 $1750

Berrigan, Ted *Clear the Range.* New York: Adventures in Poetry, 1977. First edition, one of 750 copies, 8vo., original wrappers, fine, inscribed by author for Burt (Britton). James S. Jaffe Rare Books   Many Happy Returns - 41   2015 $225

Berrigan, Ted *Clear the Range.* New York: Adventures in Poetry, 1977. First edition, one of 750 copies, 8vo., original wrappers, signed by author NYC 1966-7, very fine.   James S. Jaffe Rare Books   Many Happy Returns - 42   2015 $250

Berrigan, Ted *Clear the Range.* New York: Adventures in Poetry, 1977. First edition, one of 750 copies, 8vo., original wrappers, top right corner bumped, else fine, presentation copy inscribed by author for Keith Abbott.   James S. Jaffe Rare Books   Many Happy Returns - 40   2015 $375

Berrigan, Ted *Doubletalk.* Iowa City: Miller, 1969. First edition, limited to 240 copies signed by Berrigan and Anselm Hollo, tall narrow 8vo., portraits, wrappers, very fine. James S. Jaffe Rare Books   Many Happy Returns - 207 2015 $250

Berrigan, Ted *The Drunken Boat.* New York: Adventures in Poetry, 1974. First edition, 4to., original pictorial stapled wrappers, fine.   James S. Jaffe Rare Books   Many Happy Returns - 28   2015 $150

Berrigan, Ted *The Drunken Boat.* New York: Adventures of Poetry, 1974. First edition, one of 26 numbered copies, signed by author and artist, Joe Brainard, this copy numbered '26', 4to., stapled original pictorial wrappers, fine. James S. Jaffe Rare Books   Many Happy Returns - 30 2015 $750

Berrigan, Ted *The Drunken Boat.* New York: Adventures in Poetry, 1974. First edition, inscribed by author and artist, Joe Brainard for Burt (Britton), fine.   James S. Jaffe Rare Books   Many Happy Returns - 29   2015 $350

Berrigan, Ted *A Feeling for Leaving.* New York: Frontward Books, 1975. First edition, limited to 400 copies, 4to., original wrappers with hand colored front cover by Rochelle Kraut, fine.   James S. Jaffe Rare Books   Many Happy Returns - 31   2015 $150

Berrigan, Ted *A Feeling for Leaving.* New York: Frontward Books, 1975. First edition, limited to 400 copies, 4to., wrappers, hand colored front cover by Rochelle Kraut, very fine, inscribed by author for Burt (Britton).   James S. Jaffe Rare Books   Many Happy Returns - 32   2015 $300

Berrigan, Ted *A Feeling for Living.* New York: Frontward Books, 1975. First edition, mimeographed, limited to 400 copies, this one of 25 numbered and signed by author, this numbered '1' an signed by author, 4to., original stapled hand colored pictorial wrappers by Rochelle Kraut, fine, presentation copy inscribed by author for George and Katie (Schneeman), wonderful association.   James S. Jaffe Rare Books   Many Happy Returns - 33   2015 $2500

Berrigan, Ted *Guillaume Apollinaire Ist Tot. Tedichte, Prosa, Kollaborationen Mit Notizen von Tom Clark, Allen Kaplan und Rod Padgett.* Frankfurt: Marz Verlag, 1970. First edition, 8vo., photos of Berrigan and friends, original yellow printed wrappers, inscribed by author for Burt, fine. James S. Jaffe Rare Books   Many Happy Returns - 18 2015 $400

Berrigan, Ted *In a Blue River.* New York: Little Light Books, 1981. First edition, one of 26 lettered copies, signed by author, original wrappers, with manuscript poem by him also signed, out of an edition of 500 copies, colophon calls for this issue to be signed by artist, but we cannot find Cataldo's signature, fine, cover design by Cataldo. James S. Jaffe Rare Books   Many Happy Returns - 56 2015 $2250

Berrigan, Ted *In a Blue River.* New York: Little Light Books, 1981. First edition, limited to 500 copies, 8vo., original wrappers, signed by author, lightly soiled, otherwise very good, uncommon.   James S. Jaffe Rare Books   Many Happy Returns - 55   2015 $450

Berrigan, Ted *In the Early Morning Rain.* New York: Cape Goliard Press in Association with Grossman Publishers, 1970. First American edition, simultaneous paperback issue, review copy with publisher's slip laid in, inscribed by author for Burt Britton, cover and drawings by George Schneeman, fine.   James S. Jaffe Rare Books Many Happy Returns - 25   2015 $150

Berrigan, Ted *In the Early Morning Rain.* New York: Cape Goliard Press in association with Grossman, 1970. First American edition, simultaneous paperback issue, 8vo., original wrappers, fine, cover and drawings by George Schneeman.   James S. Jaffe Rare Books   Many Happy Returns - 21   2015 $50

Berrigan, Ted *In the Early Morning Rain.* London: Cape Golliard, 1970. First edition, tall 8vo., original pictorial boards, fine, presentation copy inscribed by author for Ted and Joan Wilentz, cover and drawings by George Schneeman.   James S. Jaffe Rare Books   Many Happy Returns - 24   2015 $850

Berrigan, Ted *In the Early Morning Rain.* London: Cape Goliard Press, 1970. First edition, 8vo., original boards, although not called for, signed by author, fine, cover and drawings by George Schneeman.   James S. Jaffe Rare Books   Many Happy Returns - 22   2015 $250

Berrigan, Ted *In the Early Morning Rain.* New York: Cape Goliard Press in association with Grossman Pub., 1970. First American edition, review copy with publisher's slip laid in, 8vo., original boards, inscribed by author for Burt Britton, fine, cover and drawings by George Schneeman. James S. Jaffe Rare Books   Many Happy Returns - 20   2015 $200

Berrigan, Ted *In the Nam What Can Happen?* New York: Granary Books, 1997. First edition, limited to 70 copies printed letterpress from magnesium plates on Rives 300 gm paper by Philip Gallo at the Hermetic Press, signed by artist, George Scheeman, of which 50 copies were for sale, square 4to., loose sheets in clear plastic slipcase, as new. James S. Jaffe Rare Books   Many Happy Returns - 70   2015 $1000

Berrigan, Ted *Living with Chris.* N.P. but New York: A Boke Press Publication, n.d. but, 1968. First edition, mimeographed, inscribed by Berrigan and Joe Brainard to Burt (Britton), 4to., original stapled wrappers, cover slightly dust soiled, otherwise fine.   James S. Jaffe Rare Books   Many Happy Returns - 13   2015 $1250

Berrigan, Ted *Living with Chris.* No Place, but New York: A Boke Press Publication, n.d. but, 1968. First edition, mimeographed, in gutter of first titlepage is handwritten "N. Blaine copy" in what appears to be Nell's hand, fine. James S. Jaffe Rare Books   Many Happy Returns - 1   2015 $1000

Berrigan, Ted *Living With Chris.* N.P., but New York: A Boke Press Publication, n.d. but, 1968. First edition, 4to. original stapled pictorial wrappers, covers little sunned, otherwise fine.   James S. Jaffe Rare Books   Many Happy Returns - 11   2015 $750

Berrigan, Ted *Many Happy Returns.* New York: Corinth Books, 1969. First edition, one of 1500 copies, review copy with publisher's slip laid in, 12mo., original illustrated wrappers by Joe Brainard, inscribed by author for Burt Britton, titlepage also signed by Brainard, mint.   James S. Jaffe Rare Books   Many Happy Returns - 17   2015 $350

Berrigan, Ted *Many Happy Returns.* New York: Corinth Books, 1969. First edition, one of 1500 copies, 12mo., original illustrated wrappers by Joe Brianrd, fine.   James S. Jaffe Rare Books   Many Happy Returns - 15   2015 $100

Berrigan, Ted *Many Happy Returns.* New York: Corinth Books, 1969. First edition, one of 50 numbered copies signed by Berrigan and Brainard, 12mo., original illustrated wrappers by Joe Brainard, very fine.   James S. Jaffe Rare Books   Many Happy Returns - 15   2015 $450

Berrigan, Ted *Memorial Day. A Collaboration by Anne Waldman & Ted Berrigan.* New York: Poetry Project, 1971. First edition, mimeographed, 4to., original stapled wrappers by Donna Dennis, fine, signed by Berrigan and Waldman. James S. Jaffe Rare Books   Many Happy Returns - 224   2015 $750

Berrigan, Ted *Memorial Day. A Collaboration by Anne Waldman & Ted Berrigan.* New York: The Poetry Project, 1971. First edition, mimeographed, 4to., original stapled pictorial wrappers by Donna Dennis, fine, inscribed by author for Burt (Britton).   James S. Jaffe Rare Books   Many Happy Returns - 223   2015 $450

Berrigan, Ted *Memorial Day. A Collaboration by Anne Waldman & Ted Berrigan.* New York: Poetry Project, 1971. First edition, mimeographed, 4to. original stapled pictorial wrappers by Donna Dennis, fine.   James S. Jaffe Rare Books   Many Happy Returns - 221   2015 $250

Berrigan, Ted *Memorial Day. A Collaboration by Anne Waldman & Ted Berrigan.* London: Aloes Books, 1974. First English edition, limited to 500 copies, although Fischer specifies 479 copies, the projected signed limited edition never having been done, 8vo., original pictorial wrappers, signed by Waldman on titlepage, acidic paper discolored as usual, otherwise fine.   James S. Jaffe Rare Books   Many Happy Returns - 226   2015 $350

Berrigan, Ted *The Morning Line.* Santa Barbara: Am Here Books/Immediate Editions, 1982. First edition, 4to., original stapled pictorial wrappers by Tom Clark, in acetate binder with white plastic spine, special issue, with manuscript poem by Berrigan bound in at back, cover signed by artist and at back, between two pieces of stiff paper matching the cover paper is holograph poem by Berrigan, "Three Lost Years" signed by Berrigan at end, acetate somewhat discolored, otherwise fine.   James S. Jaffe Rare Books   Many Happy Returns - 58   2015 $3500

Berrigan, Ted *Nothing for You.* Lenox: Angel Hair Books, 1977. First edition, limited to 1000 copies, 8vo., illustrations, original wrappers, fine.   James S. Jaffe Rare Books   Many Happy Returns - 43   2015 $100

Berrigan, Ted *Nothing for You.* Lenox: Angel Hair Books, 1977. First edition, one of 1000 copies, 8vo., illustrations, original wrappers, covers slightly dust soiled, else fine, inscribed by author for Burt (Britton).   James S. Jaffe Rare Books   Many Happy Returns - 46   2015 $250

Berrigan, Ted *Selected Poems.* New York: Penguin Poets, 1994. Advance uncorrected proof, signed by Ron Padgett, Alice Notley, Sandy & Edmund Berrigan, Lewis Warsh, Anne Waldman, Anselm Hollo, Bill Berkson, Dick Gallup and Johnny Stanton, 8vo., original wrappers, very fine, publisher's letter laid in.   James S. Jaffe Rare Books   Many Happy Returns - 68   2015 $1000

Berrigan, Ted *The Collected Poems of Ted Berrigan.* Berkeley: University of California Press, 2005. First edition, thick 8vo., original cloth boards, very fine, dust jacket.   James S. Jaffe Rare Books   Many Happy Returns - 72   2015 $125

Berrigan, Ted *Red Wagon.* Chicago: Yellow Press, 1976. First edition, one of 26 lettered copies, signed with holograph poem by author, 8vo., original boards, dust jacket, fine.   James S. Jaffe Rare Books   Many Happy Returns - 38   2015 $850

Berrigan, Ted *Red Wagon.* Chicago: Yellow Press, 1976. First edition, 8vo., original boards, dust jacket, fine, inscribed by author for Lewis (Warsh), fine.   James S. Jaffe Rare Books   Many Happy Returns - 36   2015 $1250

Berrigan, Ted *Red Wagon.* Chicago: Yellow Press, 1976. First edition, review copy with publisher's materials laid in, 8vo., original boards, dust jacket, fine, inscribed by author for Burt Britton.   James S. Jaffe Rare Books   Many Happy Returns - 37   2015 $450

Berrigan, Ted *Red Wagon.* Chicago: Yellow Press, 1976. First edition, simultaneous paperback issue, 8vo., original wrappers, fine, inscribed by author with small self portrait for Burt (Britton).   James S. Jaffe Rare Books   Many Happy Returns - 34   2015 $150

Berrigan, Ted *Red Wagon.* Chicago: Yellow Press, 1976. First edition, simultaneous paperback issue, 8vo., original wrappers, Jim Carroll's copy with his ownership signature and date 1977, inscribed to him by author, with Carroll's notations throughout and with fragment of poem in Carroll's hand on separate folded sheet of paper laid in, covers bit rubbed and sunned, otherwise fine.   James S. Jaffe Rare Books   Many Happy Returns - 35   2015 $1750

Berrigan, Ted *Red Wagon.* Chicago: Yellow Press, 1976. First edition, 8vo, original boards, dust jacket, very fine, presentation copy inscribed by author for poet Barbara Guest.   James S. Jaffe Rare Books   Many Happy Returns - 39   2015 $1000

Berrigan, Ted *Seventeen.* N.P.: Ted Berrigan & Ron Padgett, 1964. First edition, 4to., stapled wrappers, inscribed by Berrigan and signed by Padgett, pages little age darkened, else fine.   James S. Jaffe Rare Books   Many Happy Returns - 210   2015 $1250

Berrigan, Ted *So Going Around Cities. New and Selected Poems 1958-1979.* Berkeley: Blue Wind Press, 1980. First edition, paperback issue, 8vo., original pictorial wrappers bit dust soiled, otherwise fine, inscribed by author for Rosemary.   James S. Jaffe Rare Books   Many Happy Returns - 53   2015 $450

Berrigan, Ted *So Going Around Cities. New and Selected Poems 1958-1979.* Berkeley: Blue Wind Press, 1980. First edition, one of 75 specially bound copies, numbered and signed by author, 8vo., original red cloth, slipcase, fine.   James S. Jaffe Rare Books   Many Happy Returns - 54   2015 $850

Berrigan, Ted *Some Things.* New York: n.p. late 1963 or 1964, First edition, drawings by Joe Brainard, one of probably fewer than 100 copies printed, signed by all authors (presumably) as issued, on this copy the artist, Joe Brainard signed two times.   James S. Jaffe Rare Books   Many Happy Returns - 208   2015 $1250

Berrigan, Ted *The Sonnets.* New York: Lorenz & Ellen Gude, 1964. First edition, limited to 300 numbered copies, this one out of series, small chip in wrappers, otherwise fine, with back cover that is almost always missing.   James S. Jaffe Rare Books   Many Happy Returns - 4   2015 $1750

Berrigan, Ted *The Sonnets.* New York: Grove Press, 1964. First trade edition, original wrappers, review copy with publisher's slip laid in, mint.   James S. Jaffe Rare Books   Many Happy Returns - 5   2015 $125

Berrigan, Ted *The Sonnets.* New York: Lorenz & Ellen Gude, 1964. First edition, limited to 300 numbered copies 'plus an unspecified number of unnumbered copies, 4to., mimeographed sheets stapled together, original wrappers, presentation copy inscribed by author to Aram (Saroyan), rear wrapper missing as usual, front wrapper lightly foxed and dust soiled, otherwise very good.   James S. Jaffe Rare Books   Many Happy Returns - 3   2015 $4500

Berrigan, Ted *Sonnets.* New York: Grove Press, 1964. First trade edition, paperback original, inscribed by author for Jim Carroll, pen scribbles, covers somewhat rubbed, upper corner of front wrapper dampstained, still good.   James S. Jaffe Rare Books   Many Happy Returns - 6   2015 $1500

Berrigan, Ted *The Sonnets.* New York: Grove Press, 1964. First trade edition, paperback original inscribed by author with elaborate pen and ink self portrait for John Clark, fine.   James S. Jaffe Rare Books   Many Happy Returns - 8   2015 $450

Berrigan, Ted *The Sonnets.* New York: Grove Press, 1964. First trade edition, paperback original, one page smudged, otherwise very good, inscribed by author for Keith Abbott, with Abbott's ownership signature.   James S. Jaffe Rare Books   Many Happy Returns - 7   2015 $1000

Berrigan, Ted *The Sonnets.* New York: Lorenz & Ellen Gude, 1964. First edition, limited to 300 numbered copies plus an unspecifed number of unnumbered copies, this copy (as with most copies) unnumbered, laid in is 1 page TLS from Ted Berrigan to Conrad Aiken sending him the book, unlike the majority of copies seen, this copy has the back wrapper, letter is creased, otherwise fine, book exceptionally fine.   James S. Jaffe Rare Books   Many Happy Returns - 2   2015 $4500

Berrigan, Ted *The Sonnets.* New York: United Artists Books, 1982. First edition thus, signed by author, 8vo., frontispiece by Joe Brainard, original pictorial wrappers, very fine.   James S. Jaffe Rare Books   Many Happy Returns - 61   2015 $350

Berrigan, Ted *The Sonnets.* New York: United Artists Books, 1982. First edition thus, 8vo., frontispiece by Joe Brainard, original cloth, pictorial dust jacket by Louise Hamlin, fine in dust jacket with small triangular tear and short closed tear on back.   James S. Jaffe Rare Books   Many Happy Returns - 60   2015 $45

Berrigan, Ted *The Sonnets.* New York: United Artist's Books, 1982. First edition thus, with handwritten colophon by Berrigan, "this special limited edition consists of 20 hardbound copies numbered 1 thru 20, signed by poet and covers artist and containing handwirtten Sonnett, excluded from his final (trade edition), copies by the poet", colophon signed by author Louise Hamlin, fine with holograph poem signed by author.   James S. Jaffe Rare Books   Many Happy Returns - 63   2015 $2500

Berrigan, Ted *The Sonnets.* New York: United Artists Books, 1982. First of this edition, inscribed by author to one of the publisher's Lewis (Warsh) and wife Bernadette Mayer.   James S. Jaffe Rare Books   Many Happy Returns - 62   2015 $1250

Berrigan, Ted *Train Ride (February 18th 1971) for Joe.* New York: Vehicle Editions, 1978. First edition, one of 256 lettered hardcover copies, this one being copy A, 12mo., original red cloth with front cover illustration by Joe Brainard tipped-on, fine.   James S. Jaffe Rare Books   Many Happy Returns - 50   2015 $750

Berrigan, Ted *Train Ride (February 18th 1971) for Joe.* New York: Vehicle Editions, 1978. First edition, simultaneous paperback issue, limited to 1500 copies, 12mo., original illustrated wrappers by Joe Brainard, presentation copy inscribed by author for Keith Abbott, fine.   James S. Jaffe Rare Books   Many Happy Returns - 47   2015 $450

Berrigan, Ted *Yo-Yo's With Money.* Hennicker: United Artists (Bernadette Mayer & Lewis Warsh), 1979. First edition, mimeographed, limited to 500 copies, 4to., original pictorial wrappers with cover drawing by Rosina Kuhn and photographs by Rochelle Kraut, fine, presentation copy inscribed by author and Harris Schiff for Steve.   James S. Jaffe Rare Books   Many Happy Returns - 217   2015 $1250

Berrigan, Ted *Yo-Yo's With Money.* Hennicker: United Artists (Bernadette Mayer & Lewis Warsh), 1979. First edition, mimeographed, limited to 500 copies, 4to., original picctorial wrappers with cover drawing by Risna Kuhn and photographs by Rochelle Kraut, fine.   James S. Jaffe Rare Books   Many Happy Returns - 216   2015 $750

Berry, Cecilla Ray *Folk Songs of Old Vincennes.* Chicago: Fitsimmons, 1946. First edition, 4to., fine in near fine dust jacket with short tears top edge.   Beasley Books   2013 - 2015 $45

Berry, Chuck *The Autobiography.* New York: Harmony Books, 1987. First edition, signed by author, 8vo., fine in fine dust jacket.   Beasley Books   2013 - 2015 $175

Berry, Chuck *Chuck Berry: the Autobiography.* Harmony Books, 1987. First edition, signed presentation from author to his business attorney, couple of pages have indentation from paper clip, else fine, bright copy in dust jacket.   Buckingham Books   March 2015 - 11943   2015 $650

Berry, Ira *The Liberty of the Press Vindicated and Truth Triumphant!* Augusta: 1832. First edition, tall 8vo., 20 pages, sewn, uncut, foxed.   M & S Rare Books, Inc.   97 - 149   2015 $375

Berry, W. Turner *Catalogue of Specimens of Printing Types by English and Scottish Printers and Founders 1665-1830.* London: Oxford University Press, 1935. First edition, 4to., 24 full page plates, including some foldouts, half cloth over boards, covers rubbed with small mark at bottom of spine where label was removed, bookplate of Frederic Melcher and remnants of another bookplate on front pastedown, supplement is unbound signatures as issued.   Oak Knoll Books   306 - 209   2015 $300

Berry, Wendell *Another Turn of the Crank.* Washington: Counterpoint, 1995. Uncorrected bound galleys, 8vo., fine in original printed wrappers, scarce.   Second Life Books Inc.   190 - 14   2015 $125

Berry, Wendell *Distant Neighbors. the selected Letters of Wendell Berry and Gary Snyder.* Berkeley: Counterpoint, 2014. First edition, 8vo., fine in dust jacket, signed by Berry.   Second Life Books Inc.   191 - 12   2015 $75

Berry, Wendell *Home Economics, Fourteen Essays by...* San Francisco: North Point Press, 1987. First edition, near fine in dust jacket, non authorial presentation on endpaper, scarce, only 973 copies printed.   Second Life Books Inc.   191 - 13   2015 $150

Berry, Wendell *Jayber Crow, a Novel.* Washington: Counterpoint, 2000. First edition, 8vo., fine in dust jacket, this was issued in an edition of just 5000 copies, inscribed by author.   Second Life Books Inc.   191 - 14   2015 $85

Berry, Wendell *The Kentucky River: Two Poems.* Monterey: Larkspur Press, 1976. First edition, limited to 1026 numbered copies (this #226), original wrappers, fine, inscribed by author.   Second Life Books Inc.   190 - 15   2015 $125

Berry, Wendell *The Memory of Old Jack.* New York: Harcourt Brace, 1967. First edition, 8vo., fine in dust jacket.   Second Life Books Inc.   190 - 16   2015 $165

Berry, Wendell *Nathan Coulter, a Novel.* Boston: Houghton Mifflin, 1960. First edition, endpapers little foxed, little wear at extremities of dust jacket spine, waterstain at bottom of spine of dust jacket, book near fine, scarce.   Second Life Books Inc.   190 - 17   2015 $300

Berry, Wendell *A Place on Earth.* New York: Harcourt Brace, 1967. First edition, 8vo., excellent copy in dust jacket with couple of small chips at extremities of spine (little faded), couple of creases to rear dust jacket.   Second Life Books Inc.   190 - 18   2015 $400

Berry, Wendell *Traveling at Home.* Lewisburg: Bucknell University the Press of Appletree Alley, 1988. First edition, wood engravings by John De Pol, cloth backed boards, fine, signed by author, issue A of the binding with spine bound in lighter green cloth, fine, printed on Rives lightweight mould made paper and set in Spectrum type.   Second Life Books Inc.   190 - 19   2015 $600

Berry, Wendell *The Unforeseen Wilderness.* Lexington: University Press of Kentucky, 1971. First edition, 1 of 1500 copies of a total edition of 3000 first prinitng, (with text block on copyright page -iv- flushed to the right margin), white cloth with flat spine, dust jacket, ex-library with couple of small stamps on titlepage, circulation pocket on rear endpaper and tape holding glassene over dust jacket,.   Second Life Books Inc.   190 - 20   2015 $150

Berryman, John 1914-1972 *Homage to Mistress Bradstreet.* New York: Farrar, 1956. First edition, fine in very good+ dust jacket with tiny chips and tears at spine head and spine fold.   Beasley Books   2013 - 2015 $45

Berryman, John 1914-1972 *Love & Fame.* New York: Farrar Straus Giroux, 1968. First edition, 8vo., limited to 250 copies signed by author, 8vo., original cloth, fine.   James S. Jaffe Rare Books   Modern American Poetry - 33   2015 $250

Berryman, John 1914-1972 *Poems.* Norfolk: New Directions, 1942. First edition, one of 1500 copies in wrappers out of a total edition of 2000 copies, 8vo., original unprinted wrappers, dust jacket, spine portion faintly sunned, otherwise fine, presentation copy inscribed by author for Allan Covici.   James S. Jaffe Rare Books   Modern American Poetry - 29   2015 $1000

Berryman, John 1914-1972 *Stephen Crane. The American Men of Letters.* New York: William Sloane Associates, 1950. First edition, 8vo., original cloth, dust jacket, inscribed by author to his teacher Mark Van Doren, fine, dust jacket neatly reinforced on verso at couple of places along flap folds.   James S. Jaffe Rare Books   Modern American Poetry - 31   2015 $4500

Berssenbrugge, Mei-Mei *Four Year Old Girl.* Berkeley: Kelsey St. Press, 1998. First edition, oblong octavo, decorated wrappers, very near fine, inscribed by poet to Ray DiPalma.   Between the Covers Rare Books, Inc.   187 - 20   2015 $85

Berssenbrugge, Mei-Mei *Sphericity.* Berkeley: Kelsey St. Press, 1993. First edition, Deluxe issue, one of 50 numbered copies signed by author and artist from an entire edition of 2000, original hand colored drawing by Richard Tuttle, bound in at back of book, large square 8vo., illustrations, original illustrated wrappers, lower fore-corner of wrappers and text block lightly bumped, otherwise fine.   James S. Jaffe Rare Books   Modern American Poetry - 35   2015 $1500

Berthold, Victor M. *The Pioneer Steamer California 1848-1849.* Houghton Mifflin Co., 1932. First edition, limited to 550 copies of which 500 are for sale, brief generic inscription by author, blue cloth, titles on paper label affixed to upper spine, frontispiece, illustrations, map, former owner's bookplate, front and rear endpapers uniformly tanned, else fine, bright square, uncut copy, housed in matching slipcases with titles on paper label affixed to upper spine panel, slipcase rubbed at spine ends and corners.   Buckingham Books   March 2015 - 32363   2015 $250

Berto, Frank *The Dancing Chain. History and Development of the Derailleur Bicylce.* San Francisco: Van der Plas, 2000. First edition, inscribed by author, 4to., fine in fine dust jacket.   Beasley Books   2013 - 2015 $45

Bertolt, Brecht *The Seven Deadly Sins of the Lower Middle Class.* New York: Vincent FitzGerald & Co., 1992. Artist's book, one of 50 copies only, all on rives paper, each signed by artist, Mark Beard, and translator Michael Feingold, over 100 hand collaged and watercolored images of etchings and lithographs, with each of the seven sins a separate gate fold, printed letterpress in Garamond in at least 14 different colors by Dan Keleher at Wild Carrot Letterpress, calligraphy by Jerry Kelly, page size 12 1/2 x 21 inches, bound by Zahra Partovi in association with BookLab, cloth over boards, three quarter leather spine, protective box with game board map of America.   Priscilla Juvelis - Rare Books   62 - 4   2015 $7500

Best, Gerald M. *Nevada County Narrow Gauge.* Berkeley: Howell North, 1965. First edition, 284 photos, maps, diagrams, orange cloth, fine with slightly chipped pictorial dust jacket.   Argonaut Book Shop   Holiday Season 2014 - 33   2015 $50

Beste, John Richard *Alcazar; or the Dark Ages.* London: Hurst & Blackett, 1857. 3 volumes, original dark green horizontal fine ribbed moire cloth by Edmonds & Remnants, boards blocked in blind, spine decorated and lettered in gilt, fine, half titles, ownership inscription of Henry Elwell. Jarndyce Antiquarian Booksellers   CCXI - 25   2015   £480

Bester, Alfred *The Demolished Man.* Chicago: Shasta Publications, 1953. First edition, octavo, quarter cloth with boards.   John W. Knott, Bookseller   Selected New Arrivals Jan. 2015 - 16919   2015 $650

Bester, Alfred *The Stars My Destination.* Boston: Gregg Press, 1975. First edition, octavo, cloth.   John W. Knott, Bookseller   Selected New Arrivals Jan. 2015 - 16920   2015 $450

Besterman, Theodore *World Bibliography of Bibliographies and of Bibliographical Catalogues, Calendars, Abstracts, Digest, Indexes and the Like.* Totowa: Rowman and Littlefield, 1971. Second printing of fourth and best edition, thick small 4to, cloth, thousands of pages, 5 volumes, some silver speckling of front cover volume one. Oak Knoll Books   306 - 67   2015 $450

Bethune, Thomas G. *The Marvelous Musical Prodigy, Blind Tom, the Negro Boy Pianist...* New York: French & Wheat, 1876. 8vo., later plain wrappers, foxed.   M & S Rare Books, Inc. 97 - 24   2015 $275

Betjeman, John   1906-1984 *Continual Dew.* London: Murray, 1937. First edition, printed on pale blue paper, 4 leaves printed on tissue paper in black and red also present, illustrations, signatures strained, 8vo., original black cloth stamped in gilt to front with clasp decoration overlapping onto backstrip, backstrip worn and corners rubbed, all edges gilt foxing to rear free endpaper, sound, from the library of Barbara Pym, signed and dated by Pym, footnote in her hand, 2 further Betjeman poems written out by Pym on blanks at rear.   Blackwell's Rare Books   B179 - 224   2015 £950

Betjeman, John   1906-1984 *High and Low.* London: John Murray, 1966. First edition, 51/100 copies signed by author, foolscap 8vo., original white buckram, backstrip lettered gilt, marbled endpapers, top edge gilt others untrimmed and unopened, glassine jacket, fine. Blackwell's Rare Books   B179 - 128   2015   £575

Betjeman, John   1906-1984 *High and Low.* London: John Murray, 1966. First edition, small octavo, 81 pages, full white buckram lettered gilt, marbled paper endpapers, printed on handmade-paper, pages unopened, one of 100 numbered copies signed by author, titlepage little tanned at outer edge, otherwise fine.   Peter Ellis, Bookseller   2014 - 015915   2015   £300

Betjeman, John   1906-1984 *A Nip in the Air.* London: Murray, 1974. Second impression, 16mo., original bright yellow cloth, backstrip gilt lettered, faint, insignificant free endpaper foxing, dust jacket, near fine, inscribed by author for Keith Miller.   Blackwell's Rare Books   B179 - 130 2015   £135

Betjeman, John   1906-1984 *An Oxford University Chest, Comprising a Description of the Present State of the Town and University of Oxford...* Miles, 1938. First edition, 54 plates, line drawings by Osbert Lancaster and reproductions of engravings from earlier works, titlepage and frontispiece bordered in red, 4to., original quarter dark blue buckram, lightly faded backstrip gilt blocked, cream, black and red marbled boards, very light tail edge rubbing, very good, very good, with author's presentation inscription on front free endpaper to Greta Wyndham (widow of Richard Wyndham). Blackwell's Rare Books   B179 - 131   2015   £500

Betjeman, John   1906-1984 *An Oxford University Chest - Comprising a Description of the Present State of the Town and University of Oxford with Itinerary...* London: John Miles, 1938. First edition, quarto, numerous black and white photos and line drawings, buckram backed marbled boards, top edge gilt, edges faintly spotted, near fine in very good, chipped nicked and slightly torn dust jacket.   Peter Ellis, Bookseller   2014 - 019507   2015   £350

Better Farming with Atlas Farm Powder. The Safest Explosive. Philadelphia: privately printed for Atlas Powder Co., 1919. First edition, 8vo., color lithograph pictorial wrappers, 128 pages, illustrations, former owner's faint inked name at top margin of front cover, else vey good copy. Buckingham Books   March 2015 - 32706   2015 $200

Betts, Emmett *Big Book Stories.* New York: American Book Co., 1958. 19 x 26 inches, one page margin mend, else very good-fine, illustrations in bright colors by Erna Ward, rare.   Aleph-bet Books, Inc.   109 - 126   2015 $650

Betty Crocker's New Picture Book. New York: McGraw Hill, 1961. First printing, illustrations, often from photos, drawings and decorations by Joseph Pearson, 9 7/8 x 8 7/8 inches full color 5 ring notebook binding, light wear and soiling, faint vertical crease to front cover, spine slightly separating at bottom of binding, prior owner signature to front pastedown, page 187 with personal owner's pencil annotations to recipe, withal very good to very good+.   Tavistock Books   Bah, Humbug? - 2   2015 $375

Beveridge, William *De Linguarum Orientalium...(bound with) Grammatica Linguae Domini Nostri Jesu Christi...* London: Thomas Roycroft, 1664. London: Thomas Roycroft for Humphrey Robinson, 1664., First edition 2nd issue, 8vo., show-through of print on B2-6 in first work, contemporary mottled calf panelled in blind, joints split, lower cover almost detached, rubbed, spine label missing, from the library of James Stevens Cox (1910-1997).   Maggs Bros. Ltd.   1447 - 29   2015   £220

Bewick, Thomas   1753-1828 *A History of British Birds.* Newcastle: R. E. Bewick, 1805. Second edition, octavo, 2 volumes, 746 pages, wood engravings, contemporary half calf and marble boards, some wear, stain in volume two but not affecting text, very good.   Andrew Isles 2015 - 20514   2015 $600

Bewick, Thomas   1753-1828 *A Memoir of Thomas Bewick. Written by Himself.* Newcstle on Tyne: printed by Robert Ward for Jane Bewick; London: Longman, Green Longman and Roberts, 1862. First edition, 8vo., frontispiece, wood engraving on titlepage and further wood engravings in text, illustrations of fishes and one tipped-in engraving by R. E. Bewick, original bright green morocco cloth lettered gilt on spine, loosely inserted 4 prospectuses, extremely rare, very slightly creased at head and foot of spine, corners bit rubbed, near fine.   Any Amount of Books   March 2015 - C13442   2015   £450

Beyle, Marie Henri   1783-1842 *L'Abbesse De Castro.* Paris: La Tradition, 1946. No. 25 of 46 copies with an extra suite of illustrations on China paper and original drawing, from an edition of 200 with striking engravings by C. P. Josso, 4to., unbound signatures laid into wrappers, fine, titled chemise (boards in matching box), both near fine. Beasley Books   2013 - 2015 $400

Bezzerides, A. I. *Thieves Market.* Bantam Books, 1950. First paperback edition, signed by author, front cover lightly rubbed, minor chip to head of spine, else very good, clean copy.   Buckingham Books   March 2015 - 33326   2015 $200

Bianco, Margery *Hurdy Gurdy Man.* London: Toronto: Oxford University Press, 1933. First edition, square 8vo., pictorial boards, very good-fine in dust jacket with several large edge chips, illustrations by Robert Lawson.   Aleph-Bet Books, Inc.   108 - 265   2015 $300

Bianco, Margery *Poor Cecco.* New York: George Doran, 1925. Limited to 105 numbered copies signed by author, 4to., vellum like backed blue boards, spine very slightly toned, owner bookplate, fine in original slipcase with limitation number of book also inked on case (flaps mended but very good), 7 very large tipped in color plates with tissue guards, plus pictorial endpapers and black and whites in text by Arthur Rackham.   Aleph-bet Books, Inc.   109 - 400   2015 $9500

Bianco, Margery *Poor Cecco.* New York: Doran, 1925. First US edition, first issue with pictorial endpapers, 4to., blue gilt cloth, fine in dust jacket with piece off bottom edge and top of spine, illustrations by Arthur Rackham, 7 fabulous color plates plus black and whites in text, scarce with dust jacket.   Aleph-bet Books, Inc.   109 - 396   2015 $850

Bianco, Margery *The Velveteen Rabbit.* Mount Vernon: Press of A. Colish, 1974. Limited to 1500 copies, printed on arches paper and illustrated by Marie Angel with 6 magnificent mounted color illustrations, very scarce, 8vo., brown velvet covers, fine with original plain paper wrapper.   Aleph-bet Books, Inc.   109 - 52   2015 $800

Bible. English - 1640 *The Holy Bible: Containing the Old Testament and the New. (Bound with) The Whole Book of Pslames.* London: by Robert Barker, 1640. 1639, 191 x 127mm., superb contemporary dark brown morocco, elaborately gilt, covers with intricate frame and central lozenge composed of many fleurons, volutes and other small tools, silver cornerpieces and centerpiece, engraved "Recor/dare/matrem?Johanna Strode" (To Remeber Mother, Johanna Strode"), original silver clasps and catches, raised bands, spine densely gilt in compartments with fleurons radiating from concentric circles, marbled pastedowns (apparently lacking marbled free endpapers), all edges gilt, ornate woodcut titles and headpieces for each testament, full page royal coat of arms opposite dedication; slight rubbing to joints and extremities, occasional mild browning, isolated rust spots or small stains, other trivial imperfections, exceptionally fine, clean and fresh internally, sparkling binding.   Phillip J. Pirages   66 - 25   2015 $17,500

Bible. English - 1684 *The Holy Bible. (bound with) The Whole Book of Psalms Collected into English Metre.* London: printed by the Assigns of J. Bill, T. Newcombe and Henr. Hills, 1684. 1683. Printed for the company of stationers, 1683, 127 x 64mm., 2 separately published works bound in 1 volume, 2 leaves (Eee3 and 4) bound in reverse order, very appealing contemporary red morocco, elaborately gilt and painted, covers with an ornate design of drawer handle tools, semi-circle at head and tail and wedge tool at side, both shapes filled with floral tools, top spine end raised, higher than board edges in stylized a la grecque design, marbled endpapers, all edges gilt, velvet lined modern maroon clamshell box with black morocco label, engraved titlepage with architectural frame, engraved bookplate of Gaspard Ernest Stroehlin showing Calvin preaching, with motto "Mente Libera", early (binder's?) pin inserted behind the upper headband; extremities bit rubbed, spine little crackled and with tiny split at bottom, faint faded in several spots, gilt on front cover just slightly dulled but binding still extremely pleasing, with no significant wear, titlepage with minor soil and corner crease, head margin trimmed with little close (no loss), otherwise fine internally, text especially smooth, fresh and clean.   Phillip J. Pirages   66 - 29   2015 $3500

Bible. English - 1713 *The Holy Bible Containing the Old Testament and the New.* London: John Baskett, 1713. 159 x 95mm., 2 volumes, charming contemporary burgundy morocco, elaborately gilt, covers with French fillet border and floral roll frame, large central filigree lozenge surrounded by flowers, stars and other small tools, raised bands, spine compartments with central fleuron incorporating saltire, four silver cornerpieces on each cover, two silver clasps and catches (all original), marbled endpapers, all edges gilt, very expert repairs to portions of joints, in quite pretty elaborately gilt morocco box made to look like a similar but larger two volume Bible; joints slightly worn, opening leaves lightly browned, isolated tiny rust spots, otherwise fine set, clean and fresh text with no signs of use, pretty bindings without significant wear.   Phillip J. Pirages   66 - 32   2015 $2500

Bible. English - 1736 *The Holy Bible Containing the Old and New Testaments.* Edinburgh: Robert Freebairn, 1736. 178 x 144m., animated contemporary red morocco, heavily gilt in characteristically Scottish design, covers framed by dogtooth rolls and densely tooled with gilt flowers, foliage turnips, swirls and dots, central panel with vaguely herringbone design formed by interlocking full and half circles accented by floral tools, fleurons and dots, panel framed by very prominent densely cross-hatched pear shaped ornaments, each containing a stylized thistle within it, raised bands, spine intricately gilt in compartments with scrolling cornerpieces and large fleuron centerpiece incorporating a saltire, patterned paper pastedowns (lacking free endpapers), all edges gilt (boards with shallow, thin blind rules as part of the design or else added later demarcating central panel as well as extending from top to bottom and side to side along exact center of the cover, very expert repairs to head of joints, tiny restoration to corners, bookplate of Hans Furstenberg, hint of splaying to front board, joints and extremities little rubbed (though carefully refurbished), gilt bit muted in places, but once spectacular binding still extremely appealing with nothing approaching a major condition issue, mild browning throughout, occasional trivial foxing, marginal stains, or other trivial imperfections, still excellent copy, internally few signs of use, fresh, clean leaves with comfortable margins.   Phillip J. Pirages   66 - 41   2015 $13,000

Bible. English - 1743 *The Holy Bible Containing the Old and New Testaments.* Edinburgh: printed by Richard Watkins, 1743. 140 x 70mm., 2 volumes, extremely pleasing period black morocco, very elaborately gilt in Scottish Herrigbone design, covers bordered by garland roll and double gilt rules, central panel framed by decorative roll and plain rules enclosed by dotted half circles alternating with fleurs-de-lys and with oblique tulip cornerpieces, central panel with herringbone pattern formed by turnip tools and accented by other small ornaments, raised bands, spine gilt in compartments quartered by saltire and tooled with fleurons, small flowers and circlets, gilt turn-ins, Dutch endpapers of green, white and gold, all edges gilt, tiny expert repairs at spine ends, front flyleaf of each volume with 19th century? ownership inscription of H. Gordon; bit of rubbing to joints and corners, but this well masked with dye, otherwise very appealing set in fine condition, bindings bright and showing no serious wear and especially smooth, clean text with virtually no signs of use.   Phillip J. Pirages   66 - 42   2015 $4500

Bible. English - 1875 *Isaiah XL-LXVI with the shorter prophecies ... edited with notes by Matthew Arnold.* London: Macmillan, 1875. First edition, original brown cloth, signed by Geoffrey Tillotson 30.iii.42 with note that it was given to him by Prof. Hermann Levy.   Jarndyce Antiquarian Booksellers   CCVII - 58   2015   £38

Bible. English - 1883 *Isaiah of Jerusalem in the Authorised English Version... notes by Matthew Arnold.* London: Macmillan, 1883. First edition, half title, 32 page catalog (1883), original brown cloth, slightly dulled, from the library of Geoffrey & Kathleen Tillotson.   Jarndyce Antiquarian Booksellers   CCVII - 59   2015   £38

Bible. English - 1947 *The Book of Ruth from the Translation Prepared at Cambridge in 1611 for King James I.* New York: Limited Editions Club, 1947. Limited to 1500 numbered copies and signed by Szyk, 4to., quarter leather, gold foil covered slipcase (minor rubbing of foil), very colorful mounted illustrations. Oak Knoll Books   25 - 31   2015 $275

Bible. English - 1995 *The Revelation of Saint John the Divine.* New York: Limited Editions Club, 1995. Limited to 300 numbered copies, signed by artist, Allan Rohan Crite, folio, cloth, title gilt stamped on front cover, cloth clamshell box with inlaid leather label gilt stamped with title and velvet endpapers, engravings printed on Japanese Kitikata paper, text set in Monotype Caslon with Romulus heads by Julia Ferrari at Golgonooza Letter Foundry with special numerals hand cut by Dan Carr, Monthly Letter loosely inserted. Oak Knoll Books   25 - 64   2015 $1875

Bible. English - 1995 *The Song of Songs Which is Solomon's.* Alton: Clarion Press, 1995. 38/199 copies of an edition of 499 copies, this for Anthony Dowd, signed by artist Henry Fuller and designer Trevor Weston and with folder containing a set of color illustrations, each numbered and signed by artist Henry Fuller and designer Trevor Weston and with a folder containing a set of color illustrations each numbered and signed by artist, line drawings throughout with occasional splashes of gold, 8 panel foldout color illustrations tipped-in to inside read cover, original illustrated wrappers, slight bump at head of upper joint, slipcase, near fine.   Blackwell's Rare Books   B179 - 139   2015   £140

Bible. English - 2012 *The Book of Jonah.* New York: Russell Maret, 2012. One of 80 copies, oblong folio, grey cloth over patterned paper boards, accompanied by printer's prospectus,.   Honey & Wax Booksellers   3 - 27   2015 $400

Bible. German - 1784 *Biblia das ist; Die Ganze Heilige Schrift Alten Und Neuen Testamentes.* Basel: Johann Rudolf Im-Hof und Sohn, 1784. 197 x 121mm., 2 volumes bound 'dos-a-dos', very appealing contemporary red morocco Dos-a-Dos binding, covers gilt with delicate roll border featuring calligraphic flourishes at corners, at center a pineapple like oval ornament flanked by curling acanthus leaves from which a floral garland is draped, flap spines divided into compartments by multiple plain and decorative gilt rules, floral spring centerpiece and small tools at corners and sides, gilt turn-ins, all edges gilt, original (somewhat rubbed) marbled paper pull-off case, front pastedowns with booklabel of Jean Furstenberg, isolated trivial spots of foxing, really excellent specimen and virtually no internal signs of use in very bright binding with only very superficial wear. Phillip J. Pirages   66 - 47   2015 $6500

Bible. Greek - 1590 *Metaphrasis tou Psalteros dia Stichon Heroikon.* Excudebat Georgius Bishop, 1590. First printing in England, ownership embossment to titlepage causing small hole affecting two characters, intermittent light dampmarks to fore-edge, 8vo., contemporary blind ruled sheep, rebacked preserving original spine, few other tidy repairs, hinges lined with printed binder's waste, bookplate of Shirburn Castle, good.   Blackwell's Rare Books   B179 - 9   2015   £600

Bible. Hieroglyphic - 1849 *A New Hieroglyphical Bible with Devotional Pieces for Youth.* New York: John C. Riker, 1849. First edition, 12mo., 210 pages, frontispiece, original gilt stamped cloth, hinges cracking, this copy has not half title but does have illustrated title, very good, rare, containing 400 cuts by J. A. Adams.   M & S Rare Books, Inc.   97 - 130   2015 $500

Bible. Hieroglyphic - 1859 *A New Hieroglyphical Bible.* Halifax: Milner & Sowerby, 1859. 16mo., frontispiece, illustrations, original brown cloth, slightly rubbed, very good. Jarndyce Antiquarian Booksellers   CCXI - 139   2015   £60

Bible. Latin - 1489 *Biblia cum Concordantis et Terminoorii Hebraicorum Interpretationibus.* Strassburg: Johann Press, 1489. Small folio, rubricated initials in red and blue, edges stained red, period full darkened pigskin over wooden boards intricately blindstamped with pictorial biblical scenes, raised bands, brass bosses for clasps (clasp lacking), binding with contemporary owner's initials GSM and date 1577.   Argonaut Book Shop   Holiday Season 2014 - 132   2015 $2750

Bible. Latin - 1529 *Textus Biblie.* Lyons: per Johanem Crespin, 1529. Second Crespin edition, reprinted from 1527 edition, folio, complete with final blank leaf, Gothic type, text in double columns within rule borders, title printed in red and black with small woodcut of St. Jerome (repeated three times in text with Jerome's prefaces), within a four part woodcut border, large woodcut at beginning of Genesis, half page woodcut at beginning of Proverbs, full page Nativity woodcut at beginning of New Testament, 121 small text woodcuts, 91 Old Testament woodcuts within strip borders, 30 New Testament woodcuts without borders, decorative woodcut initials, contemporary pigskin over wooden boards roll tooled in blind to a panel design, lacking clasps, original index tabs, binding worn with some loss of pigskin on upper corner of front cover, title soiled, lower margin of first few leaves wormed and frayed with some loss to woodcut titler border, few short marginal tears, some mostly marginal dampstaining, minor worming to lower inner margins, few inkstains, slight discoloration throughout, despite these minor flaws, this is beautiful example of a French woodcut Bible, complete unsophisticated, contemporary ink inscription dated 1534, contemporary ink inscription on recto of d4 beneath the Nativity cut, 18th or 19th century inscription, some early underlining and coloring of woodcuts in red and few early ink marginalia, housed in cutom quarter brown morocco clamshell case.   Heritage Book Shop   Holiday 2014 - 15   2015 $9500

Bible. Latin - 1726 *Biblia Scacra ex Sebastiani Castellionis Interpretatione Ejusque Postrema Recognitione (Volume I).* Londoni: Excudebat Jacob Bettenham, Impensis J. Knapton, R. Knaplock..., 1726. First edition, volume one only, 12mo., text in Latin, from the library of American book collector Ralph Isham with his engraved bookplate, dust jacket inscription to Mrs. Hester Lynch Thrale from Dr. Samuel Johnson, contemporary full sheep, dark red morocco spine label, gilt edges light cracking to joints, very good, housed in dark red full morocco box, gold silk interior and gold edges, presumably commissioned by Isham, with the Johnston presentation "Bible presented to Mrs. Thrale by Dr. Johnson" in gilt on front cover, front joint of box professionally repaired, very good.   Between the Covers Rare Books, Inc.   187 - 44   2015 $3000

Bible. Latin - 1785 *Bibliorum Sacorum Vulgatae Versionis Editio.* Parisiis: Excudebat Fr. Amb. Didot, 1785. 2 volumes, 318 x 235mm, superb crimson straight grain morocco by Bozerian, covers with distinctive wide frame incorporating arches, Grecian urns, floral garlands and sunburst cornerpieces, the outer and inner edge of the frame flanked by thick and thin gilt rules and cresting and floral rolls, double raised bands separated by a gilt tooled inlaid strip of black morocco, spines densely gilt in compartments filled with much foliage and many flowers against a stippled background, turn-ins with interlacing flame roll, light green glazed endpapers, all edges gilt, wood engraved bookplate of Ellic Howe (1910-1991) with faint evidence of earlier bookplate removal, verso of rear flyleaf with small engraved heraldic book label; half a dozen or so faint scratches or small spots to boards, occasional mild browning or small marginal spots, couple of gatherings in second volume with faint overall browning, otherwise an excellent copy internally, clean and smooth with generous margins, elegant bindings in fine condition, especially lustrous and with only insignificant wear.   Phillip J. Pirages   66 - 62   2015 $6500

Bible. Manx - 1819 *Yv Vible Casherick, NY Yn Chenn Chonaant as Yv Connaant ...* London: printed by George Eyre and Andrew Strahan for the British and Foreign Bible Society, 1819. First edition thus, 8vo., original full leather with blind patterning and oval blindstamp of British and Foreign Bible Society, corners rubbed, spine lightly patterned but no (discernibly) lettered, corners rubbed, spine ends, very slightly worn, splitting at front hinge (repaired), overall sound, decent very good copy with clean text.   Any Amount of Books   March 2015 - A75894   2015   £400

Bible. Polyglot - 1554 *Le Noveau Testament De Nostre Seigneur Jesus Christ.* Lyon: Guillaume Rouille, 1554. 127 x 83mm., pleasing contemporary calf decorated in an Entrelac design, boards ornamented in the Lyonnaise style with intricate interlacing strapwork and foliage in dark brown and gray outlined in gilt on a background of tiny gilt dots, flat spine with similar decoration (these 16th century designs expertly laid down onto modern calf), all edges gilt, elaborate historiated woodcut frame enclosing each of the two title pages, some decorative and historiated woodcut initials and headpieces in text, embossed armorial bookplate of Daniel Sickles, covers with trivial marks and worm traces, text printed on inexpensive (and consequently yellowed) paper, first few leaves and last leaf little thumbed, isolated minor soiling, but excellent example, carefully restored binding entirely solid and quite bright and text smooth and fresh.   Phillip J. Pirages   66 - 10   2015 $8500

Bickham, George *Alphabets and Sentences, In all the Hands Now Practised in Great Brtiain.* London: printed for John Bowles & Son at the Black Horse in Cornhill, n.d. after, 1754. First and only edition, 8vo., original plain paper covers, 14 engraved plates, plate 2 missing, occasional staining and parts of back cover chipped away, inscribed 'John Park his book. Francis Murphy Schoolmaster".   Oak Knoll Books Special Catalogue 24 - 4   2015 $650

Bickham, George *The Universal Penman or the Art of Writing Made useful to the Gentleman and Scholar as Well as the Man of Business.* London: H. Overton, 1743. First edition, issue number iii of the imprint as noted by Heal in his English Writing Masters, folio, later quarter leather with paper covered boards, frontispiece, 212 engraved plates, magnificent book, front hinge broken with cover close to coming loose, wear at spine ends.   Oak Knoll Books Special Catalogue 24 - 5   2015 $2000

Bickham, George *The Universal Penman.* printed for and sold by H. Overton, 1743. Fourth edition, engraved frontispiece, each leaf a full page engraving, one leaf with closed tear touching couple of letters, frontispiece offset onto titlepage, some light age browning, old ink mark to verso final plate, folio, modern brown calf in period style, boards bordered in blind, red morocco lettering piece to spine, very good.   Blackwell's Rare Books   B179 - 11   2015   £950

Bickham, George *The Universal Penman.* New York: Paul A. Struck, 1941. Reprint of 1743 first edition, limited to 1000 numbered copies, facsimile reprint, folio, cloth, dust jacket has pieces missing along edges and bottom of spine,.   Oak Knoll Books   306 - 233   2015 $125

Bidart, Frank *The Book of the Body.* New York: Farrar, Straus and Giroux, 1977. First edition, tiny spot on front fly, else fine in fine dust jacket, very warmly inscribed to Alan Helms in year of publication.   Between the Covers Rare Books, Inc.   187 - 22   2015 $250

Bidart, Frank *Golden State.* New York: George Braziller, 1973. First edition, one of 500 copies, fine in fine dust jacket with bit of age toning at extremities, inscribed by author for essayist, author and academic Alan Helms, June 23 1973.   Between the Covers Rare Books, Inc.   187 - 21   2015 $375

Bierce, Ambrose   1842-1914 *The Devil's Dictionary.* New York and London: Bloomsbury, 2003. Fourth printing, small 8vo., fine in fine dust jacket, signed and inscribed by Ralph Steadman for Beef (Torrey), he has added a illustration on same page, small blank sheet of stationery laid in from Jerome Hotel in Aspen CO, fine in fine dust jacket.   Ed Smith Books   82 - 26   2015 $250

Biggers, Earl Derr *Behind that Curtain.* New York: Grosset & Dunlap, n.d. circa 1930's, Later edition, bright square copy in dust jacket with light professional restoration to spine ends.   Buckingham Books   March 2015 - 30757   2015 $200

Biggers, Earl Derr *Behind that Curtain.* Indianapolis: Bobbs Merrill, 1928. Later edition, without the bow-and-arrow symbol on copyright page, fine in very good dust jacket with twin inch piece missing from back panel, chipping at spine ends, several short closed tears.   Mordida Books   March 2015 - o11463   2015 $150

Biggers, Earl Derr *The Black Camel.* New York: Grosset & Dunlap, n.d. circa, 1931. First edition thus, fine, bright, tight copy in blue cloth and black lettering on front cover and spine, dust jacket with light professional restoration to spine ends, corners and extremities.   Buckingham Books   March 2015 - 30759   2015 $250

Biggers, Earl Derr *The Chinese Parrot.* New York: Grosset & Dunlap, n.d. circa, 1932. Later edition, three tiny holes along channel of front cover, else fine, bright, square copy in lightly rubbed dust jacket, exceptional copy.   Buckingham Books   March 2015 - 32340   2015 $350

Biggers, Earl Derr *Keeper of the keys.* Indianapolis: Bobbs Merrill Co., 1932. First edition, near fine with all lettering on front cover and spine bright and unchipped, bright dust jacket with few short closed tears to extremities and light wear to corners.   Buckingham Books   March 2015 - 38450   2015 $800

Biggers, Earl Derr *Love Insurance.* Indianapolis: Bobbs Merrill, 1914. First edition, very good in cloth covered boards with embossed illustration on front cover, without dust jacket.   Mordida Books   March 2015 - 002369   2015 $75

Bijlmer, H. J. T. *Outlines of the Anthropology of the Timor-Archipelago.* Wiltevreden: G. Kolff & Co., 1929. First edition, large 8vo., 234 pages, original flexible burgundy cloth, lettered gilt on spine and front cover, illustrations, very slight wear, otherwise clean, sound, very good+.   Any Amount of Books   2015 - C2154   2015   £150

Billboard Encyclopedia of Music. 1946-1947. Eighth annual edition, hardcover, illustrations, 4to., very good, owner's name stamped.   Beasley Books   2013 - 2015 $125

Billingham, Mark *Sleepyhead.* London: Little Brown, 2001. First edition, very fine in dust jacket with publisher's around intact.   Mordida Books   March 2015 - 009584   2015 $80

Binet, Rene *Esquisses Decoratives.* Paris: Librairie Centrale des Beaux Arts, n.d. circa, 1905. Folio, 60 plates printed in black or sepia of which 16 ar pochoir colored, 43 text illustrations, some plates soiled and occasionally abraded in lower margins, loose as issued in publishers cloth backed decorative portfolio, little spotted, fine portfolio.   Marlborough Rare Books   List 54 - 5   2015   £875

Bingham, Clifton *Fun and Frolic.* London: Nister, 1902. 4to., cloth backed pictorial boards, 144 pages, few tiny margin mends, some cover soil, very good+, illustrations by Louis Wain with 6 fabulous color plates with marvelous black and whites one very page, very scarce.   Aleph-bet Books, Inc.   109 - 482   2015 $1500

Bingley, William *Travels in Asia, from Modern Writers, with Remarks and Observations Exhibiting a Connected View of the Geography and Present State of the Quarter of the Globe.* London: Harvey & Darton, 1822. First edition, half title, frontispiece, vignette title and 3 further plates, final ad leaf, little foxed, original drab boards, light brown glazed cloth spine, paper label, spine slightly dulled, slight rubbed, very good.   Jarndyce Antiquarian Booksellers   CCXI - 26   2015   £150

Binyon, Laurence   1869-1943 *Arthur: a Tragedy.* London: Heinemann, 1923. First edition, 8vo., with programme of first public performance loosely inserted (March 1923 at the Old Vic), signed inscription by author, head of spine slightly frayed, slight rubbing, otherwise sound, near very good with small press cutting about Binyon pasted to f.e.p.   Any Amount of Books   2015 - C3225   2015   £300

Binyon, Laurence   1869-1943 *The Engraved Designs of William Blake.* London: Ernest Benn Ltd., 1926. First edition, one of 1000 copies, in addition there was a deluxe edition limited to 20 copies, extra color plate, 4to., quarter cream linen over decorative paper covered boards, titled dust jacket, 62 collotype plates and 20 color plates, each with caption tissue guard, occasional light scattered spotting, otherwise near fine in lightly tanned dust jacket.   Henry Sotheran Ltd.   William Blake Exhibition 17th Oct.-7th Nov. 2014 - 89   2015   £145

Biquard, P. *Deux Heures de Physique.* Paris: Editions KRA, 1930. First edition, signed and inscribed by P. Biquard and F. Joliot, very good++, original printed wrappers, 8vo., mild cover edge wear, spotting to covers, 247 pages.   By the Book, L. C.   Special List 10 - 1   2015 $200

Bird, Isabella *Unbeaten Tracks in Japan...* London: Newnes, 1900. New edition, royal octavo, illustrations, folding map, original dark blue pictorial buckram stamped in black, pink and gilt, bevelled edges, all edges gilt, contemporary calligraphic and florally decorated prize inscription for the winner of a 'Bouquet Competition'.   Peter Ellis, Bookseller   2014 - 020283   2015   £350

Bird, Will R.   *Done at Grand Pre.*   Toronto: Ryerson Press, April, 1955. Small 8vo., 14 photo illustrations, light green cloth, dust jacket.   Schooner Books Ltd.   110 - 57   2015 $40

Bird, Will R.   *Thirteen Years After: the Story of the Old Front Revisited.*   Toronto: McLean Pub. Co., 1932. 8vo., pebbled cloth boards, gilt title to front, photo illustrations plus sketch map, edges slightly worn.   Schooner Books Ltd.   110 - 146   2015 $55

Bird, William Wilberforce   *State of the Cape of Good Hope in 1822.*   London: John Murray, 1823. First edition, 8vo., 2 folding maps, both rather foxed, small repair to titlepage, not affecting printed surface, contemporary green half calf over marbled boards, spine fully gilt with raised bands and label, minor wear to extremities, overall very good, pleasing binding.   John Drury Rare Books   March 2015 - 24113   2015 $874

Birdsall, Byron   *Byron Birdsall's Alaska and Other Exotic Worlds.*   Seattle/Portland: Epicen/Graphic, 1993. First edition, oblong small 4to., fine in fine dust jacket, neatly inscribed by author.   Beasley Books   2013 - 2015 $45

Birdwood, James   *Heart's-Ease in Heart-Trouble.*   printed for W. Johnston, 1762. Woodcut frontispiece of Bunyan, some spotting and dampstaining, one page creased, frontispiece, 12mo., contemporary canvas over paste boards, split in spine, one cord broken, good.   Blackwell's Rare Books   B179 - 12   2015   £350

The Birmingham Register or Entertaining Museum. Birmingham: printed by and for J. Sketchley sworn appraiser auctioneer and salesman in the High Street and sold by Mr. Luckman printer in Coventry, Mr. Pryse Shrewsbury, Mr. Clare Bewdley; Mr. Guest Dudley...., 1764-1765. 2 volumes in 1, complete run of 40 issues, large folding plan, little general light foxing and some minor soiling, overall good in very good condition, old half calf, gilt over marbled boards, skillfully rebacked and labelled, exceptionally rare.   John Drury Rare Books   2015 - 19043   2015 $2185

Bishop, Bonnie   *Furies. Poetry and Original Prints.* Cornville: 2013. Artist's book, one of 7 copies, all on handmade paper by Katie MacGregor, each copy signed and numbered by artist/author, page size 5 3/4 x 8 1/2 inches, 64 pages, bound by artist, handsewn

Coptic style binding, single thread sewn through each of the 8 signatures, red wrappers stiffened with archival paper, title blind embossed on front panel, housed in grey paper box, images printed silkscreen for the vermilion and monoprint in gold gilt, text handset in Optima and printed letterpress by Scott Vile at Ascensius Press, each page spread, gold monoprint textures overprinted with red silkscreens or white pages with gold gilt silkscreens (white page serving as negative space and creating images), highlight the text by allowing printing of text within images of the human form, strong line of silkscreen repeated over three pages, each time on different grounds, provoking different responses.   Priscilla Juvelis - Rare Books   63 - 1   2015 $1250

Bishop, Elizabeth   *The Ballad of the Burglar of Babylon.* New York: FSG, 1968. First edition, 8vo., original pictorial boards, dust jacket, very good.   James S. Jaffe Rare Books   Modern American Poetry - 38   2015 $150

Bishop, Elizabeth   *Geography III.*   New York: Farrar & Giroux, 1976. First edition, one of 7500 copies, thin 8vo., original brown cloth, dust jacket, signed by author, very fine. James S. Jaffe Rare Books   Modern American Poetry - 42   2015 $2500

Bishop, Elizabeth   *North & South.*   Boston: Houghton Mifflin, 1946. First edition, 1000 copies printed, 8vo., original cloth, dust jacket, near fine.   James S. Jaffe Rare Books   Modern American Poetry - 36   2015 $3500

Bishop, Elizabeth   *North & South - a Cold Spring.* Boston: Houghton Mifflin, 1955. First edition, one 2000 copies, 8vo., original cloth, dust jacket, inscribed by author for Phyllis Armstrong, faint offsetting to endpapers, covers little spotted, otherwise fine in trifle rubbed and dust soiled dust jacket.   James S. Jaffe Rare Books   Modern American Poetry - 37   2015 $7500

Bishop, Elizabeth   *Poem.*   New York: Phoenix Book Shop, 1973. First edition, one of author's copies from the lettered issue, copy "L" (presumably chosen for Loren) of 26 lettered copies from a total edition of 126, signed by author, this copy with presentation from author for Loren MacIver & Lloyd Frankenberg, housed in custom green cloth clamshell box with black morocco spine label, superb association copy.   James S. Jaffe Rare Books   Modern American Poetry - 41   2015 $10,000

Bishop, Elizabeth   *Poem.*   New York: Phoenix Book Shop, 1973. First edition, one of 16 lettered copies, out of a total edition of 126, signed by Bishop, thin oblong 12mo., decorated wrappers, as new.   James S. Jaffe Rare Books Modern American Poetry - 40   2015 $2750

Bishop, Elizabeth *The Complete Poems.* New York: Farrar Straus & Giroux, 1969. First edition, one of 5500 copies, 8vo., original blue cloth, signed by author, fine in slightly sunned dust jacket with spot of soiling on front panel.   James S. Jaffe Rare Books   Modern American Poetry - 30   2015 $2500

Bishop, Elizabeth *Questions of Travel.* New York: Farrar, Straus & Giroux, 1965. First edition, trifle rubbed, else fine in price clipped, otherwise fine dust jacket, ownership stamp and signature of poet Sandra McPherson by Bishop who was then studying under Bishop at the University of Washington, two small corrections in text by Bishop and small pencil note, probably in McPherson's hand, beautiful copy.   Between the Covers Rare Books   196 - 68   2015 $2500

Bishop, Elizabeth *12 O'Clock News.* Octon: Verdigris Press, 2006. One of 40 copies fro a total edition of 50, all on Hahnemuhle paper, signed by artist, Judith Rothchild and printer/binder, Mark Lintott, 10 of the 50 are deluxe copies with an original copper plate and additional mezzotint, 40 regular copies (this copy) in additional 20 suites of prints from original copper plates were printed, page size 11 1/2 x 16 7/8 inches, bound by Mark Lintott, original gray-green paper over boards, paper has been silkscreened with yellow moon and title printed in khaki green with exposed sewing in ivory linen thread, blood red cloth hinges, red paper spine with title printed in black with author and artist's name, blood red endpapers, housed in publisher's matching slipcase, fine, illustrations by Judith Rothchild and designed by Rothchild and Mark Lintott, including two original mezzotints, pulled from two copper plates, one full page and the other copper plate cut into 8 sections and each of the eight plates separately reprinted and inserted in text.   Priscilla Juvelis - Rare Books   61 - 53   2015 $1300

Bishop, J. Michael *How to Win the Nobel Prize.* Cambridge: Harvard University Press, 2003. First edition, fine in near fine, price clipped dust jacket.   By the Book, L. C.   Special List 10 - 71   2015 $125

Bishop, John Peale *Selected Poems.* New York: Charles Scribner's Sons, 1941. First edition, top corner bumped, bit of rubbing, very good without dust jacket, Mary Sarton's copy with her ownership signature.   Between the Covers Rare Books, Inc.   187 - 24   2015 $125

Bisselius, Joannis *Argonauticon Americanorum sive Historiae Periculorum Petri de Victoria ac Sociorum ejus Libris XV.* Monachii: Lucae Straubii Johann Wagner, 1647. First Latin edition, 12mo., bound in old calf, all edges red, some minor soiling and foxing, engraved titlepage (signed "Wolf. Kilian 1647 fecit) and map of America, woodcut vignette on titlepage.   Second Life Books Inc.   190 - 30   2015 $950

Bjorkman, Frances Maude *Woman Suffrage, History, Arguments and Results.* New York: National Woman Suffrage Publishing Co., 1915. 12mo., blue cloth, covers nicked along edges, stamp of Mass. woman Suffrage Association, good.   Second Life Books Inc.   189 - 23   2015 $45

Blacam, Aodh De *The Druid's Cave: a Tale of Mystery and Adventure for Young People Aged Seven to Seventy.* Dublin: Whelan & Son, 1920. First edition, octavo, 12 full page illustrations in text by George Monks, original red cloth, front and spine panels stamped in black.   L. W. Currey, Inc.   Boy's Adventure Fiction 2015 - 51   2015 $150

The Black Dispatch. Volume I No. 3 April 15 1970. Schenectady: Union College Black Alliance, 1970. Mimeographed quarto leaves stapled in corner, one page printed upside down, oxidation marks on first couple of leaves, small chip on front leaf, overall very good, very scarce.   Between the Covers Rare Books   197 - 50   2015 $250

The Black Nation: Position of the Revolutionary Communist League (MLM) on the Afro-American National Question. Newark: n.p., 1978. Quarto, 57 pages, photomechanically reproduced sheets with stapled printed wrappers, about very good with wear at extremities, price sticker and heavy staining to front and rear wrapper affecting few interior pages, Amiri Baraka's personal copy, signed on first page, numerous comments, deletions and additions in his hand.   Between the Covers Rare Books   197 - 55   2015 $4500

Black, Matthew *New Testament Studies: an International Journal....* Cambridge: University Press, 1955. First edition, volumes 1-12, large 8vo., soundly bound in red buckram, gilt lettered on spine, very good.   Any Amount of Books   2015 - A89775   2015   £160

Black, William *The Privileges of the Royal Burrows as contained in their particular rights and the Ancient laws and Records of Parliament and their General Convention.* Edinburgh: printed by the heirs and successors of Andrew Anderson, 1707. First edition, 8vo., 2 pages of errata on pages 42/3, contemporary sprinkled calf, ruled in blind, neatly rebacked and labeled to match, 18th century armorial bookplate of "Ad Rolland Advocat", fine, crisp copy.   John Drury Rare Books   March 2015 - 21389   2015 $656

Blackett, Patrick *Cloud Chamber Researches in Nuclear Physics and Cosmic Radiation.* Stockholm: Kungl. Boktrychkeriet P. A. Norstedt & Soner, 1949. 8vo., offprint, original printed wrappers with staple rust stains spine, soil to covers, with TLS by author laid-in.   By the Book, L. C. Special List 10 - 51   2015 $350

Blackmore, Richard 1654-1729 *Instructions to Vander Bank, a Sequel to the advice to the Poets...* Pirated edition, 8vo., 16 pages, disbound, misprint on titlepage has been corrected to 'Flanders', very good.   C. R. Johnson Foxon R-Z - 12124r-z   2015 $77

Blackmore, Richard 1654-1729 *King Arthur. An Heroick Poem.* London: for Awnsham and John Churchil at the Black Swan in Pater Noster-Row and Jacob Tonson at Judges Head in Fleet-Street, 1697. Third edition, 4to., small hole close to inner margin of A2, large piece torn away from blank margin of Nn2, otherwise very clean, contemporary speckled calf, spine divided into 6 panels tooled in gilt and with red morocco label in second (joints split - upper board held by one cord - covers little scuffed), early signature effaced from front pastedown leaving only date 1758, from the library of James Stevens Cox (1910-1997).   Maggs Bros. Ltd.   1447 - 31   2015 £300

Blackmore, Richard 1654-1729 *The Kit-Cats, a Poem.* London: printed and sold by H. Hills, 1709. 8vo., disbound, very good.   C. R. Johnson Foxon R-Z - 1214r-z   2015 $115

Blackwell, Alice Stone *Lucy Stone, Pioneer of Woman's Rights.* Boston: Little Brown, 1930. Second printing, 8vo., very good copy.   Second Life Books Inc.   189 - 25   2015 $75

Blackwell, Antoinette Brown *The Physical Basis of Immortality.* New York: Putnam, 1876. First edition, 8vo., ex-library with bookplate, wear at extremities of spine, (lacks small piece of cloth on spine above title), first signature little loose, very good, tight, scarce.   Second Life Books Inc.   191 - 16   2015 $650

Blackwell, Elizabeth *The Laws of Life, with Special Reference to the Physical Education of Girls.* New York: George P. Putnam, 1852. First edition, slate-gray cloth, edges stained red, spine bit faded, few very tiny spots, else remarkably fresh, tight copy, as close to fine as one could hope for, contemporary signature of E. H. Cressey on front endpaper.   Joseph J. Felcone Inc.   Science, Medicine and Technology - 12   2015 $12,000

Blackwell, John *A Compendium of Military Discipline, As It Is Practised by the Honourable the Artillery Company of the City of London, for the Initiating and Instructing the Officers of the Trained-Bands of the Said City.* London: printed for the author and are to be sold at his house in Well Court in Queen Street near Cheapside, 1726. First and only edition, 8vo., 3 large double folding engraved plates, old name inked out on titlepage and later ownership signature in upper margin, 20th century armorial bookplate of John Gretton of Stapleford, contemporary calf, gilt, appropriately rebacked with raised bands, gilt lines and label, very good, crisp, quite rare.   John Drury Rare Books   2015 - 25303   2015 $3324

Blackwood, Algernon *John Silence, Physician Extraordinary.* London: Eveleigh Nash, 1908. First edition, 8vo., original red cloth, lettered gilt on spine and on front cover, ownership signature of gardener Reginald Farrer, slight browning to endpapers, some fading at spine with rubbing at corners and spine ends, else sound, very good- with clean text.   Any Amount of Books   2015 - C16278   2015 £280

Blades, William *An Extract from the Enemies of Books.* New York: n.d., 1934. 12mo., illustrations, full leather decorated binding in slipcase, case rubbed, book fine, 12mo. illustrations by Philip Reed.   Dumont Maps and Books of the West   130 - 35   2015 $75

Blaine, Gilbert *Reflections on the Present Crisis of Publick Affairs...* London: Ridgway and Sons and Hatchard, 1831. First edition, 8vo., one gathering foxed and rather browned, recent marbled boards, lettered, good copy.   John Drury Rare Books   March 2015 - 6634   2015 $221

Blair, Robert *The Grave.* R. H. Cromek, 1808. First quarto edition, 4to., later half calf over contemporary marbled paper covered boards, spine divided into seven compartments with raised bands, frontispiece, etched titlepage, plates engraved by Luigi Schiavonetti after Blake's designs, with ticket of Liverpool bookseller, W. Robinson to front pastedown, Neva and Guy Littell copy with their gilt and red morocco book label to upper edge, of considerable rarity in early boards.   Henry Sotheran Ltd.   William Blake Exhibition 17th Oct.-7th Nov. 2014 - 72   2015   £3000

Blake, Nicholas *The Whisper in the Gloom.* London: Collins Crime Club, 1954. First edition, page edges darkened, otherwise near fine in dust jacket with slightly darkened spine and light wear at top of spine.   Mordida Books   March 2015 - 009781   2015 $90

Blake, William 1757-1827 *All Religions are One.* Trianon Press, 1970. Limited to a total of 662 copies, this one of 36 deluxe copies numbered I-XXXVI, 4to., original full leaf green morocco, spine faded to olive, marbled paper covered slipcase, 10 collotype plates with hand colored washes, a further 32 collotype plates showing plates in various states, near fine.   Henry Sotheran Ltd.   William Blake Exhibition 17th Oct.-7th Nov. 2014 - 81   2015   £965

Blake, William 1757-1827 *Auguries of Innocence.* Flansham: Pear Tree Press, 1914. First edition thus, limited to 25 copies, this number '7', scarce title, 8vo., original blue grey card wrappers with printed label to upper corner of upper cover, preserved in recent cloth covered fall downback box, etched frontispiece, titlepage and one other plate, light dust marks to wrappers and f.f.e.p., A. J. Symons with his neat booklabel to verso of upper wrapper.   Henry Sotheran Ltd.   William Blake Exhibition 17th Oct.-7th Nov. 2014 - 62   2015   £800

Blake, William   1757-1827   *Blake Trust: William Blake's Watercolour Inventions in Illustration of the Grave by Robert Blair.*   William Blake Trust, 2009.   One of 36 copies numbered I-XXXVI, of the portfolio, plates and book contained within cloth covered double slipcase, this copy number XX, folio, gilt lettered quarter deep scarlet calf over black moire silk covered boards, deep scarlet leather label blocked in gilt to centre of upper board, 96 plates, illustrated with color and black and white reproductions, with portfolio 35 x 28 x 2.8cm. bound in maroon calf with tongue-and-strap closure blocked in gold, flap blind embossed with double rule border lined in red, all in close replication of portfolio made sometime after 1822 to contain 19 (of) watercolor inventions, mounted on thick beige paper within ruled and tinted borders trimmed to 33.3 x 26.7cm.   Henry Sotheran Ltd.   William Blake Exhibition 17th Oct.-7th Nov. 2014 - 86   2015   £3700

Blake, William   1757-1827   *The Book of Los.*   Trianon Press, 1976.   Limited to a total of 512 copies, this one of 32 deluxe copies, numbered I-XXXII, this copy numbered XII, 4to., original full tan morocco, marbled paper covered slipcase, 5 collotype plates hand colored by stencil, 20 further collotype plates showing progressive states, guide sheet, zinc stencil and original copper plate for titlepage, fine.   Henry Sotheran Ltd.   William Blake Exhibition 17th Oct.-7th Nov. 2014 - 84   2015   £800

Blake, William   1757-1827   *The Book of Thel.*   Edmonton: William Muir, 1885.   Limited to 50 copies, this copy numbered '21' in ink, 4to., original titled blue paper wrappers, cream paper backstrip as issued, preserved in green cloth covered chemise and slipcase, 8 delicately hand colored plates, each tissue guarded, upper portion of backstrip very lightly spotted, otherwise an especially bright copy.   Henry Sotheran Ltd.   William Blake Exhibition 17th Oct.-7th Nov. 2014 - 55   2015   £2895

Blake, William   1757-1827   *The Book of Thel. Songs of Innocence and Songs of Experience.*   printed at the Ballantyne Press and sold by Hacon and Ricketts, 1897.   One of 210 copies, small 8vo., original blue paper covered boards, printed paper labels to upper board and backstrip, printed on upper board and backstrip, printed on handmade paper with illustration and decorative border to titlepage and two historiated initials, all by Charles Ricketts.   Henry Sotheran Ltd.   William Blake Exhibition 17th Oct.-7th Nov. 2014 - 61   2015   £625

Blake, William   1757-1827   *Jerusalem. The Emmanation of the Giant Albion.*   John Pearson, 1877.   Fine facsimile of copy D, limited to 100 copies, large 4to., original blue grey paper wrappers, backstrip worn at head and tail, 100 plates printed in black and white with black borders, text block untrimmed.   Henry Sotheran Ltd.   William Blake Exhibition 17th Oct.-7th Nov. 2014 - 54   2015   £965

Blake, William   1757-1827   *Europe a Prophecy.*   Trianon Press, 1969.   Limited to 536 copies printed on Arches pure rag paper, present copy one of 20 de-luxe copies numbered I-XX, this number XV, folio, original full brown morocco, top edge gilt, preserved in original marbled paper covered card slipcase, 17 color plates, printed collotype and hand colored using stencil process, 9 pages descriptive commentary and a further 47 color plates, color collotype proofs and a set of hand colored plates, original guide sheet and zinc and stencil for one of the applications of color to plate 15, mounted to rear pastedown, spine lightly faded as usual, otherwise fine, scarce.   Henry Sotheran Ltd.   William Blake Exhibition 17th Oct.-7th Nov. 2014 - 80   2015   £2075

Blake, William   1757-1827   *The Gates of Paradise. For Children. For the Sexes.*   Trianon Press, 1968.   From an edition totalling 726 copies, including 700 numbered 1 to 700 of which the first 50 contain additional material and are in special binding, this copy numbered 25, 4 volumes, 8vo. for volume I, with volumes II-IV 12mo., first three volumes bound in tan morocco, volume I bound in full cloth, all four volumes preserved in original brown cloth covered card slipcase, pages and a negative and a copper plate.   Henry Sotheran Ltd.   William Blake Exhibition 17th Oct.-7th Nov. 2014 - 79   2015   £1350

Blake, William   1757-1827   *Illustrations of Dante.*   Trianon Press, 1978.   One of 440 copies printed on Lan Rag paper, this copy being number 17 of the first 18 (numbered I-XVIII) which included a recent restrike of one of the original copperplates and an additional set of the facsimile engravings.   Henry Sotheran Ltd.   William Blake Exhibition 17th Oct.-7th Nov. 2014 - 85   2015   £3500

Blake, William   1757-1827   *Illustrations of the Book of Job.*   Limited to 100 sets on wove paper with word 'Proof' removed and one hundred and fifty sets on India paper and 65 on "French paper' were also lettered at the same time, latter two having word "Proof" on every plate except title,, 1825.   folio, late 19th century full red morocco, boards panelled gilt with gilt fleurons at corners, spine in seven compartments with raised bands, olive green morocco lettering piece to second compartment, remainder panelled gilt and tooled with gilt floral motifs, decorated gilt turn-ins, all edges gilt, marbled endpapers, engraved title and 21 engraved plates printed on handmade paper, five of which are watermarked 'J. Whatman Turkey Mill 1825', the copy of Henry Cunliffe with his engraved bookplate, exceptionally fine set with sparkling impressions of the plates,.   Henry Sotheran Ltd.   William Blake Exhibition 17th Oct.-7th Nov. 2014 - 51   2015   £57,000

Blake, William 1757-1827 *Illustrations of the Book of Job...* London: published by the author and Mr. J. Linnell, 1874. One of 100 sets printed on india paper, folio, line engraved title and 21 line and stipple engraved plates by and after Blake, also with an additional letterpress titlepage, not issued with the book, quarter reverse calf over black cloth, spine lettered and ruled gilt, black and red morocco spine labels lettered gilt, marbled endpapers, corners bit bumped and cloth lightly scuffed, sheets mounted on stubs, bit of very light foxing to some sheets, generally not affecting engravings, fine, strikingly clean copy.   Heritage Book Shop   Holiday 2014 - 16   2015 $32,500

Blake, William 1757-1827 *Jerusalem.* Cobham: Trianon Press for the William Blake Trust, London, 1951. Limited to 526 copies, 250 copies numbered 1-250 for Britain, 250 copies for America numbered 251 to 500 and 16 copies lettered A to P reserved for the Trustees of the William Blake Trust and the publishers, this copy numbered 240, large 4to., original navy blue cloth, gilt lettered spine, preserved in quarter cloth and marbled paper covered card solander box, spine titled in blue, 100 plates printed by collotype and hand colored by pochoir method, box trifle worn, small areas of light spotting to few prelim leaves, otherwise fine, printed on pure rag paper.   Henry Sotheran Ltd.   William Blake Exhibition 17th Oct.-7th Nov. 2014 - 75   2015   £1995

Blake, William 1757-1827 *Jerusalem. The Emanation of the Great Albion.* Trianon Press, 1976. Limited edition of 558 copies, this copy one of 32 copies numbered I-XXXII, this copy numbered XXIX, folio, original full dark tan morocco preserved in original marbled paper covered slipcase, 25 collotype plates, hand colored by stencil, 8 collotype trial proof plates, 14 page descriptive commentary, further 16 collotype plates C and D of the trial proof plates, guide sheet and zinc stencil mounted to rear pastedown, fine facsimile.   Henry Sotheran Ltd.   William Blake Exhibition 17th Oct.-7th Nov. 2014 - 83   2015   £1450

Blake, William 1757-1827 *The Marriage of Heaven and Hell.* John Camden Hotten, 1868. Limited to 150 copies, 4to., original quarter dark green morocco gilt over claret cloth covered boards, backstrip gilt lettered, marbled endpapers, 27 lithographic plates with extensive hand coloring, spotted as usual, else good.   Henry Sotheran Ltd.   William Blake Exhibition 17th Oct.-7th Nov. 2014 - 53   2015   £1450

Blake, William 1757-1827 *The Marriage of Heaven and Hell.* Edmonton: William Muir, 1885. Limited to 50 copies, this copy numbered 35 and signed by Muir, 4to., original printed wrappers, lacking greater part of paper backstrip, but stitching strong, 27 plates in color, 3 leaves at rear printed in facsimile, small chips to lower edge of upper wrapper, one or two very small old ink splashes to same, internally bright, fresh copy.   Henry Sotheran Ltd.   William Blake Exhibition 17th Oct.-7th Nov. 2014 - 57   2015   £2875

Blake, William 1757-1827 *Milton a Poem.* Clairvaux: Trianon Press for the William Blake Trust, London, 1967. Limited edition of 426 copies, this one of 380, numbered 264, 4to., original quarter brown morocco over marbled paper covered boards, top edge gilt, marbled paper covered card slipcase, 50 colored facsimile plates printed by collotype in two colors and hand colored by pochoir method and 1 monochrome plate reproducing original preface, spine of volume evenly sunned, otherwise very good.   Henry Sotheran Ltd.   William Blake Exhibition 17th Oct.-7th Nov. 2014 - 78   2015   £575

Blake, William 1757-1827 *The Poems of William Blake.* London: Basil Montagu Pickering, 1874. First edition, octavo, early 20th century crimson crushed morocco gilt, bound by Roger De Coverly.   Honey & Wax Booksellers   2 - 5   2015 $550

Blake, William 1757-1827 *Songs of Experience.* Edmonton: William Muir, 1885. Limited to 50 copies, signed by Muir and Numbered 32, 4to., original blue paper wrappers as issued, chipping to lower edges, 28 finely hand colored plates, each tissue guarded, limitation leaf, particularly fine, preserved in grey card portfolio.   Henry Sotheran Ltd.   William Blake Exhibition 17th Oct.-7th Nov. 2014 - 56   2015   £6500

Blake, William 1757-1827 *Songs of Innocence and Experience, Shewing the Two Contrary States of the Human Soul.* London: W. Pickering and W. Newbery, 1839. First edition, octavo, original plum cloth lettered in gilt.   Honey & Wax Booksellers   2 - 3   2015 $9500

Blake, William 1757-1827 *Songs of Innocence. (and) Songs of Experience.* Edmonton: William Muir, 1885. Limited to 50 numbered copies of each, Innocence #35, Experience #50, signed by Muir, 4to., 2 volumes, each bound in 20th century half brick red morocco, spines gilt lettered, original wrappers bound into both volumes, 34ff and 30ff., hand colored plates.   Henry Sotheran Ltd.   William Blake Exhibition 17th Oct.-7th Nov. 2014 - 58   2015   £6850

Blake, William 1757-1827 *Songs of Innocence and Experience.* Trianon Press in collaboration with the William Blake Trust, 1955. Limited to 526 copies, this being unnumbered 'Review copy', superb color facsimile of Rosenwald LC copy (Z), 8vo., quarter sea-green crushed morocco, some fading to spine, spine gilt lettered, top edge gilt, preserved in marbled paper covered slipcase, 54 hand color collotype plates hand colored by pochoir process, very good.   Henry Sotheran Ltd.   William Blake Exhibition 17th Oct.-7th Nov. 2014 - 76   2015   £1995

Blake, William 1757-1827 *There is No Natural Religion (and All Religions are One).* Quartich, 1886. Limited to 50 copies, 4to, original pale blue paper wrappers, chipped at extremities, buff paper backstrip lacking in a number of places, but binding itself tight and sound, 21 hand colored plates.   Henry Sotheran Ltd.   William Blake Exhibition 17th Oct.-7th Nov. 2014 - 60   2015   £1750

Blake, William 1757-1827 *Visions of the Daughters of Albion.* Edmonton: William Muir, 1885. Limited to 50 numbered copies, this number 34, 4to, mid 20th century half brick red morocco over cloth cover boards, gilt lettered spine, original blue printed wrappers bound in, 11 lithographed plates, with extensive hand coloring, fine, bright copy.   Henry Sotheran Ltd.   William Blake Exhibition 17th Oct.-7th Nov. 2014 - 59   2015   £2875

Blake, William 1757-1827 *Visions of the Daughters of Albion.* Trianon Press, 1959. Limited to 446 copies, printed on Arches pure rag paper, this one of 20 numbered I-X, this copy number II, folio, original full deep orange morocco, top edge gilt, preserved in the original marbled paper covered slipcase, 11 color plates, including frontispiece and title, printed in collotype and hand colored using stencil process, further 38 plates composed of color collotype proofs, set of hand colored plates showing progressive stages an original guide sheet and zinc stencil for one of the applications of color to frontispiece, very light spotting to endpapers and fore-edges, else fine.   Henry Sotheran Ltd.   William Blake Exhibition 17th Oct.-7th Nov. 2014 - 77   2015   £2395

Blake, William 1757-1827 *William Blake's Water-Colour Designs for the Poems of Thomas Gray.* Trianon Press, 1971. Limited to 28 copies, signed and numbered by Keynes, this number 2, small folio, original quarter tan morocco over marbled paper covered boards, preserved in original marbled paper covered card slipcase, 16 color facsimile plates, suites of progressive plates and 116 black and white illustrations, fine.   Henry Sotheran Ltd.   William Blake Exhibition 17th Oct.-7th Nov. 2014 - 82   2015   £795

Blake, William 1757-1827 *William Blake's Water-Colour Designs for the Poems of Thomas Gray.* London: Trianon Press, 1972. First edition, one of 518 copies, this number 92, large quarto, 25 pages of text and 116 color facsimile leaves, 3 volumes, folio, quarter brown morocco over marble boards, matching marbled slipcases, fine set.   Heritage Book Shop   Holiday 2014 - 17   2015 $2750

Blake, William 1757-1827 *The Wit's Magazine or Library of Momus.* Harrison and Co., 1784-1785. First edition, 8vo., 2 volumes in one, contemporary marbled boards, sometime rebacked in full calf, folding engraved, frontispiece (second version), numerous folding engraved plates.   Henry Sotheran Ltd.   William Blake Exhibition 17th Oct.-7th Nov. 2014 - 65 2015   £3665

Blake, William 1757-1827 *The Writings of William Blake.* London: Nonesuch Press, 1925. First edition of the single volume Nonesuch Blake, one of 75 copies, royal octavo, original full limp vellum lettered in gilt, 58 black and white plates.   Honey & Wax Booksellers   2 - 4   2015 $1500

Blakeney, Thomas S. *Sherlock Holmes: Fact or Fiction?* London: John Murray, 1932. First edition, small chip along fore-edge of page 55, else near fine in dust jacket, lightly tanned on spine and with one small closed tear to top edge of front panel, laid-in is promotional booklet titled Six Omnibus Volumes of Outstanding Value done by publisher, John Murray.   Buckingham Books   March 2015 - 725   2015 $675

Blakiston, John *Twenty Years in Retirement.* London: James Cochrane and Co., 1835. First edition, 2 volumes, 8vo., half title in volume 1, contemporary half calf over marbled boards, sides rather worn, still sound, now rebacked with gilt lines and labels, good, scarce.   John Drury Rare Books   March 2015 - 21000   2015 $266

Blakiston, Peyton *A Lecture on the Diffusion of Scientific Knowledge, in Large Towns; Delivered to the Members of the Birmingham Philosophical Institution Dec. 18 1837.* London: Simpkin Marshall & Co. and Allen & Lyon, Birmingham, 1837. First edition, preserved in modern wrappers, 8vo., printed title label on upper cover, very good, very rare.   John Drury Rare Books   2015 - 22663   2015 $133

Blanchard, Edward Litt Leman *Freaks and Follies of Fabledom; a Little Lempriere.* London: John Ollivier, 1852. Title in red and black, original dark green cloth, front board slightly marked with one small nick to cloth, spine little rubbed at head and tail, nice.   Jarndyce Antiquarian Booksellers   CCXI - 27   2015   £125

Blanchard, Jean Pierre *An Exact and Authentic Narrative of M. Blanchard's Third Aerial Voyage.* London: C. Heydigner, 1784. First edition, small folio, frontispiece, early dark brown paper wrappers, housed in dark blue cloth folder by Sangorski & Sutcliffe for E. P. Dutton, gilt lettering on outside of folder, balloon themed bookplate of previous owner William G. Gerhard =, lacking half title, slight offsetting to titlepage from frontispiece and some light foxing to final leaf, very good.   Heritage Book Shop   Holiday 2014 - 18   2015 $2750

Bland, Alden *Behold a Cry.* New York: Scribner's, 1947. First edition, near fine in very good dust jacket with wear, tears and tiny chips at spine head.   Beasley Books   2013 - 2015 $45

Bland, Alexander *The Nureyev Iamge.* London: Studio Vista, 1976. First edition, quarto, 288 pages, over 300 photos, boldly signed by Nureyev on half titlepage, loosely inserted is programme for the memorial tribute performance staged at Royal Opera House in 1993, fine in near fine dust jacket with just hint of rubbing to edges.   Peter Ellis, Bookseller   2014 - 010136   2015   £350

Bland, Alexander *The Royal Ballet: the First 50 years.* London: Threshold Books, 1981. Deluxe edition, no. 212 of 250 copies signed by Dame Ninette De Valois, 4to., red half leather lettered gilt on spine, all edges gilt, copiously illustrated in color and black and white, slight rubbing at fore edges, otherwise very good+.   Any Amount of Books   2015 - A78159   2015   £160

Blandy, Alfred A. *Cheoplastic Process, an Improvement in Mechanical Dentistry.* Baltimore: 1857. 8 pages, wrappers, very good.   Joseph J. Felcone Inc.   Science, Medicine and Technology - 20   2015 $150

Blankeney, Thomas S. *Sherlock Holmes: Fact or Fiction?* London: John Murray, 1932. First edition, former owner's name on front flyleaf, else very good in dust jacket with small closed tear to top edge of front panel, small closed tear to top edge of rear panel and lightly foxed on dust jacket flap folds, laid in is promotional card.   Buckingham Books   March 2015 - 17844   2015 $400

Blanshard, Henry *An Appeal to the Inhabitants of Great Britain on Behalf of the Native Population of India in a Letter to Sir Charles Forbes, Bart.* London: Thomas Bumpus, 1836. First edition, 8vo., 24 pages, recently well bound in cloth, spine lettered gilt, very good.   John Drury Rare Books   2015 - 5608   2015 $150

Blatch, Harriot Stanton *Challenging Years: the memoirs of...* New York: Putnams, 1940. First edition, 8vo., very nice in dust jacket, inscribed by Nora Stanton Barney (author's daughter) to Winifred A. Tyler.   Second Life Books Inc.   189 - 26   2015 $150

Blechman, R. O. *The Juggler of Our Lady.* New York: Holt, 1953. First edition, hardcover, inscribed by author, very good.   Beasley Books   2013 - 2015 $45

Blesh, Rudi *Shining Trumpets.* New York: Knopf, 1946. First edition, fine in yellow cloth in near fine dust jacket, this copy has been inscribed with two inscriptions by Blesh to two people on the same occasion, March 1948.   Beasley Books   2013 - 2015 $175

Blish, James *Earthman Come Home.* New York: G. P. Putnam's Sons, 1955. First edition, octavo, boards.   John W. Knott, Bookseller   Selected New Arrivals Jan. 2015 - 16922   2015 $350

Blish, James *A Life for the Stars.* London: Faber and Faber, 1964. First edition, octavo, cloth.   John W. Knott, Bookseller   Selected New Arrivals Jan. 2015 - 16921   2015 $350

Bliss, Carey S. *Julius Firmicus Maternus and the Aldine Edition of the Scriptores Astronomici Veteres.* Los Angeles: Kenneth Karmiole, 1981. First edition, number 56 of 164 copies printed by Patrick Reagh, small folio, decorated titlepage plus 6 illustrations, gray cloth, paper spine label, very fine, presentation inscription by publisher.   Argonaut Book Shop   Holiday Season 2014 - 160   2015 $800

Bloch, Robert *The Couch.* Greenwich: Fawcett, 1962. First edition, paperback original, booksellers' stamp on first page, otherwise fine, unread copy in wrappers, signed by author.   Mordida Books   March 2015 - 000276   2015 $75

Bloch, Robert *Psycho.* New York: Simon and Schuster, 1959. First edition, octavo, original half cloth, browning to paper as always (poor paper stock), just hint of edgewear to beautiful dust jacket, outstanding copy.   Manhattan Rare Book Company   Literature 2014 - 2015 $2800

Bloch, Robert *Screams.* San Rafael: Underwood Miller, 1989. First edition, one of 300 numbered copies signed by Block, fine in dust jacket with tiny rubbing on spine in slipcase.   Mordida Books   March 2015 - 000289   2015 $125

Bloch, Robert *The Selected Stories of Robert Bloch...* Los Angeles: Columbia: Underwood-Miller, 1987. First edition, one of 500 numbered sets signed by author, this number 345, octavo, 3 volumes, cloth.   John W. Knott, Bookseller   Selected New Arrivals Jan. 2015 - 16925   2015 $200

Bloch, Robert *The Skull of the Marquis De Sade and Other Stories.* London: Hale, 1975. First hardcover edition, some tiny spotting on page edges, otherwise fine in dust jacket.   Mordida Books   March 2015 - 008203   2015 $130

Bloch, Robert *The Undead in the Book Sail 16th Anniversary Catalogue.* Orange: McLaughlin, 1984. First edition, signed by author, one of 100 copies reserved for presentation by publisher numbered in Martian numerals, front cover displays 3-D portrait of Elvira, who has signed the first page, also signed by Rowena for her illustration, extensively illustrated, very fine, without dust jacket as issued.   Mordida Books   March 2015 - 012475   2015 $250

Blochman, Lawrence G. *Diagnosis: Homicide the Casebook of Dr. Coffee.* Philadelphia: J. B. Lippincott, 1950. First edition, signed by author on titlepage, presentation from author for Doc. Hasse, lightly rubbed at spine ends, else near fine in dust jacket lightly rubbed at spine ends and corners.   Buckingham Books   March 2015 - 27777   2015 $2500

Blochman, Lawrence G. *See You at the Morgue.* New York: Duell, Sloan and Pearce, 1941. First edition, signed by author on titlepage, presentation inscription from author to Lee & Mike Klinger, cloth little faded on spine, light offsetting to front and rear pastedown sheets, else very good, tight, price clipped dust jacket with light professional restoration to spine ends and corners.   Buckingham Books   March 2015 - 29112   2015 $875

Block, Laurie *An Odd Bestiary.* Easthampton: Cheloniidae Press, 1982. First edition, one of 50 deluxe copies, illustrations by Alan James Robinson, with original watercolor of the Tortoise in addition to extra suite of engraved called for, on Rives lightweight, signed by artist, hand numbered by him on colophon page, he has also signed and numbered each print in additional suite and signed the drawing and watercolor, page size 13 1/2 x 9 3/4 inches, 158 pages, including 6 page introduction and 13 page bibliography, bound by Gray Parrot, red quarter leather and light tan cloth over boards, tan cloth over boards folder for extra suite of engravings, clamshell box of tan linen over boards with red morocco spine stamped in gilt with title, fine, each letter of the alphabet exemplified by animals whose name represents the letter, each letter has its own page with small wood engraving, followed by original full page wood engraving of the animal with caption, first letter of each of the 26 text sections printed in red, original calligraphy by Betse Curtis in Old English gothic, (letters surrounding the debossed turtle) with colophon text printed in Arrighi, text of book in Centaur as well as Arrighi, set in monotype by Mackenzie-Harris, some handsetting by Arthur Larson.   Priscilla Juvelis - Rare Books   63 - 2   2015 $2500

Block, Lawrence *After Hours.* Albuquerque: University of New Mexico, 1995. First edition, one of 350 numbered copies, signed by both authors, very fine in dust jacket.   Mordida Books   March 2015 - 002878   2015 $78

Block, Lawrence *Ariel.* New York: Arbor House, 1980. First edition, one of 500 numbered copies signed by Block on card front endpaper, fine in dust jacket.   Mordida Books   March 2015 - 003020   2015 $75

Block, Lawrence *The Burglar in the Closet.* New York: Random House, 1978. First edition, fine and unread, very lightly rubbed, near fine dust jacket, from the collection of Duke Collier.   Royal Books   36 - 139   2015 $450

Block, Lawrence *The Burglar Who Painted Like Mondrian.* New York: Arbor House, 1983. First edition, fine in dust jacket.   Mordida Books   March 2015 - 007349   2015 $125

Block, Lawrence *The Burglar Who Studied Spinoza.* New York: Random House, 1980. First edition, fine in dust jacket.   Mordida Books   March 2015 - 007348   2015 $125

Block, Lawrence *Burglars Can't be Choosers.* New York: Random House, 1977. First edition, fine in dust jacket.   Mordida Books   March 2015 - 008271   2015 $175

Block, Lawrence *Eight Million Ways to Die.* New York: Arbor House, 1982. First edition, lightly rubbed at foot of spine with light evidence of erasure to front flyleaf, lettering on spine lightly worn, else near fine in fine dust jacket.   Buckingham Books   March 2015 - 23373   2015 $400

Block, Lawrence *Eight Million Ways to Die.* New York: Arbor House, 1982. First edition, slight lean, else near fine in fine dust jacket, bright, clean copy, from the collection of Duke Collier.   Royal Books   36 - 140   2015 $325

Block, Lawrence *Even the Wicked.* London: Orion, 1996. First edition, precedes American edition, publisher's bookplate signed by Block laid in, very fine in dust jacket.   Mordida Books   March 2015 - 000013   2015 $300

Block, Lawrence *Hope to Die.* Galdestry: Scorpion, 2001. One of 99 numbered copies signed by Block, very fine in acetate dust jacket.   Mordida Books   March 2015 - 008612   2015 $150

Block, Lawrence *Ronald Rabbit is a Dirty Old Mane.* New York: Geis, 1971. First edition, fine in dust jacket.   Mordida Books   March 2015 - 008205   2015 $500

Block, Lawrence *Ronald Rabbit is a Dirty Old Man.* New York: Bernard Geis Assoc., 1971. First edition, fine and unread in fine dust jacket, from the collection of Duke Collier.   Royal Books   36 - 138   2015 $400

Block, Lawrence *The Specialists.* Mission Viejo: Cahill, 1996. First American hardcover edition, one of 200 numbered copies signed by Block,, very fine in dust jacket with slipcase.   Mordida Books   March 2015 - 011604   2015 $125

Block, Lawrence *A Stab in the Dark.* New York: Arbor House, 1981. First edition, fine, unread copy in fine dust jacket, exceptional copy.   Buckingham Books   March 2015 - 31318   2015 $750

Block, Lawrence *A Stab in the Dark.* New York: Arbor House, 1981. First edition, bump along base of front cover edge otherwise fine in dust jacket with faint short crease on inner front flap. Mordida Books March 2015 - 009686 2015 $600

Block, Lawrence *Such Men are Dangerous: a Novel of Violence.* New York: Macmillan, 1969. First edition, signed by author as Block, fine and unread, in very good plus dust jacket with couple of closed tears, from the collection of Duke Collier. Royal Books 36 - 142 2015 $325

Block, Lawrence *Threesome.* Mission Viejo: ASAP/Subterranean, 1999. First hardcover edition, one of 300 numbered copies signed by Block and artist, Phil Parks, very fine, without dust jacket as issued. Mordida Books March 2015 - 011606 2015 $125

Block, Lawrence *The Topless Tulip Caper.* London: Allison & Busby, 1984. First hardcover edition, very fine in dust jacket, signed by author. Mordida Books March 2015 - 008208 2015 $125

Block, Lawrence *The Triumph of Evil.* New York: World, 1971. First edition, scrape on front endpaper otherwise fine in dust jacket with corner crease on inner front flap. Mordida Books March 2015 - 007346 2015 $300

Block, Lawrence *A Week as Andrea Benstock.* New York: Arbor House, 1975. First edition, fine and unread in fine dust jacket, signed by author as Jill Emerson, executed with his left hand, from the collection of Duke Collier. Royal Books 36 - 141 2015 $675

Block, Lawrence *Writing the Novel: from Plot to Print.* Cincinnati: Writer's Digest, 1979. First edition, fine in dust jacket. Mordida Books March 2015 - 011501 2015 $100

Bloemaert, Abraham *Oorpronkelyk En Vermaard Konstryk Tekenboek.* Amsterdam: Reiner & Josua Ottens, 1740. Engraved title added, engraved dedication plate, portrait of author and plates numbered 1 (engraved title) to 166; engraved title, portrait and duplicates of plates 80, 94, 95, 108, 137, 144 & 145 overprinted with chiaroscuro blacks to ochre, making a total of 175 plates by Frederick Bloemaert after Abraham Bloemaert; folio, contemporary half calf, speckled boards, remains of label on upper cover, rubbed, from the library of Lord Gretton. Maggs Bros. Ltd. Illustrated Books 2014 - 2015 £7500

Bloomfield, Robert *Wild Flowers; or Pastoral and Local Poetry.* London: printed for Vernor Hood and Sharpe, Poultry and Longman, Hurst Rees and Orme, 1806. First edition, contemporary speckled calf, ruled and spine heavily gilt, spine rubbed, some loss of leather at corners, handsome, very good, engraved bookplate of Lady Frances Compton. Between the Covers Rare Books, Inc. 187 - 25 2015 $375

Bloor, Ella Reeve *We Are Many, an Autobiography by...* New York: International, 1940. First edition, 8vo., fine in dust jacket (little chipped). Second Life Books Inc. 189 - 27 2015 $65

Blount, Thomas Pope 1649-1697 *Essays on Several Subjects.* London: for Richard Bentley, 1691. First edition, F8vo., lacking A4, blank, intermittently foxed, mor pronounced in gatherings M and N, contemporary calf, rebacked, corners repaired, from the library of James Stevens Cox (1910-1997). Maggs Bros. Ltd. 1447 - 33 2015 £300

Blount, Thomas Pope 1649-1697 *De Re Poetica; or Remarks Upon Poetry with Characters and Censures of the Most Considerable Poets, Whether Ancient or Modern.* London: for Ric(hard) Everingham, 1694. First edition, small 4to., occasional spotting and browning, small marginal tear to L1, contemporary calf, covers panelled in blind, spine with late 18th century elaborate gilt tooling with armorial crest of Bunbury (Sir Henry Edward Bunbury, 7th Baronet 1778-1860) in top panel (joints and corners rubbed), bookplate and gilt crest, from the library of James Stevens Cox (1910-1997). Maggs Bros. Ltd. 1447 - 32 2015 £220

The Blue Bag; or Toryana; an Address to the Electors and Election Committees of the United Kingdoms. London: Effingham Wilson, 1832. First edition (only edition?), small 8vo., half title, recently well bound in linen backed marbled boards, lettered, very good, very scarce. John Drury Rare Books March 2015 - 16394 2015 $266

Bluett, J. C. *Duelling and the Laws of Honour Examined Upon Principles of Common Sense and Revealed Truth.* London: published by R. B. Seeley and W. Burnside, 1835. First edition, 12mo., half title, final 2 ad leaves, original cloth, neatly rebacked and lettered to match, very good. John Drury Rare Books 2015 - 25172 2015 $1180

Blunt, Anthony *The James A. De Rothschild Collection at Waddesdon Manor: Furniture Clocks and Gilt Bronzes.* London: National Trust by Office Du Livre, 1974. First edition, 2 volumes, large 4to., original blue cloth, lettered gilt on spine and on front cover, copiously illustrated in color and black and white, fine in about fine dust jackets, slightly faded, excellent condition in very good+ plain slipcases. Any Amount of Books 2015 - C6991 2015 £160

Bly, Robert *In the Month of May.* New York: Red Ozier Press, 1985. First edition, copy 23 of 140 numbered copies, signed, 12mo., printed self wrappers, neat ownership signature of woodcut artist John DePol, wrappers trifle soiled, else fine. Between the Covers Rare Books, Inc. 187 - 26   2015 $75

Blyth, R. H. *Senryu. Japanese Satirical Versus.* Japan: Hokuseido Press, 1949. First edition, 8vo., near fine, minimal foxing to edges, in very good dust jacket with small pieces missing, tape, 2 inch piece missing, dust jacket spine lower tip, profusely illustrated by Sobun Taniwaki with black and white drawings and color plates with printed tissue guards, including foldout color frontispiece. By the Book, L. C.   44 - 67   2015 $300

Blyton, Enid *A Day with Noddy.* London: Sampson Low Marston, 1958. First edition, 4to., cloth backed pictorial boards, light cover soil and wear, brightly colored picture book, each page completely covered with bright color illustrations full of dolls, minimal text. Aleph-bet Books, Inc. 109 - 65   2015 $75

Bobby Benson's B-Bar B Riders. No. 1, 2, 3, 4, 5 and 6. New York: Parkway Pub. Co., 1950. First edition, 4to., wrappers, original illustrated wrappers, lettered black on covers, illustrations, all very good+, volume one slightly worn at spine. Any Amount of Books   2015 - C10165   2015   £160

Boccaccio, Giovanni 1313-1375 *Amorosa Visione.* (bound with) *Urbano.* Milan: Zanottie Castiglione per Andrea Calvo 10 Feb., 1521. Bologna: Franciscus Plato de Benedictis circa, 1492-1493. First printing of both works, 210 x 133mm., 2 separately published works in one volume; handsome Renaissance intricately decorated blindstamped calf by Claes Van Doermaele, covers with outer frame of medallion and foliate roll, inner frame of long stemmed lilies and scrolling vines, large central panel containing a medallion with three quarter portrait of Holy Roman Emperor of Charles V, binder's small 'CvD' escutcheon stamp below central panel, raised bands, early ink titled paper label, small paper shelf number of private library at foot of spine, unobtrusive repairs to head of front joint, tail of both joints and upper corners, lacking ties, in (slightly worn) linen clamshell box, 16th century ink ownership inscription of Johannes Hoyel, inscription of A(ndrew) Fletcher (of Saltoun), titlepage just slightly soiled, two leaves with minor browning to lower corners, two tiny marginal stains, otherwise fine, fresh copy in very well preserved binding, leather lustrous and blindstamped details remarkably sharp. Phillip J. Pirages   66 - 6   2015 $35,000

Boccaccio, Giovanni 1313-1375 *Del Decamerone...* Amsterdam: N.P., 1718. 2 volumes, 8vo., contemporary calf, rather worn at joints and corners, patches of loss from spines, neat oval armorial stamps to both titlepage, text blocks nice and clean. Any Amount of Books   2015 - 5634   2015   £150

Boccaccio, Giovanni 1313-1375 *The Decameron.* London: Henry F. Bumpus, 1906. 2 volumes, small 4to., original half leather, marbled paper covered boards, gilt tooled spine with five raised bands, top edge gilt, other edges uncut, marbled endpapers, frontispiece in first volume, slightly bumped at corners and light scuffing at edges of spine, scattered foxing on endpapers and portions of text. Oak Knoll Books   306 - 253   2015 $350

Boccaccio, Giovanni 1313-1375 *The Decameron.* New York: Limited Editions Club, 1940. Limited to only 530 numbered copies signed by artist, woodcuts by Fritz Kredel, 2 volumes, tall 8vo., quarter leather with cloth sides, top edge gilt, slipcase, designed by George Macy, minor rubbing of slipcase. Oak Knoll Books   25 - 70   2015 $650

Boccaccio, Giovanni 1313-1375 *Laberinto D'Amore D M. Giovanni Boccaccio.* Vinegia: Appresso Giolit, 1582. 12mo., decorative woodcuts to titlepage and colophon and decorated initials in text, speckled page edges, early marbled paper boards with leather, spine lettered and decorated gilt, somewhat rubbed and faded but clean and sound, few millimetres of worming in first half of book not affecting text. Any Amount of Books   2015 - C4949   2015   £280

Boessenecker, John *Badge and Buckshot. Lawlessness in Old California.* Norman: University of Oklahoma Press`, 1988. First edition, very scarce thus, 2 maps, 57 photos, red cloth, very fine, pictorial dust jacket. Argonaut Book Shop   Holiday Season 2014 - 34   2015 $50

Bogan, Louise *Body of This Death.* New York: Robert M. McBride, 1923. First edition, very good+ (mild tanning to spine and extremities). Stephen Lupack   March 2015 - 2015 $150

Bogan, Louise *Dark Summer Poems.* New York: Charles Scribner's Sons, 1929. First edition, 8vo., blue cloth with green spine and paper label, rear board little faded, very good, tight copy. Second Life Books Inc.   189 - 28   2015 $75

Bogan, Louise *Poems and New Poems.* New York: Charles Scribner's Sons, 1941. First edition, sunned at spine ends, else very good in about very good dust jacket with internal repairs and chips that correspond to the sunning on spine, presentation copy inscribed by author for friend Fred Dupee, May 13 1942, with autograph postcard dated Sept. 18 1944 from Botang to Dupee laid in. Between the Covers Rare Books, Inc.   187 - 27   2015 $475

Bogle, Donald *Brown Sugar Eighty Years of America's Black Female Superstars.* New York: Harmony, 1980. First edition, 4to., uncommon in cloth, fine in near fine dust jacket (slight curl at edges). Beasley Books   2013 - 2015 $45

Bogue, Thomas *A Treatise on the Structure, Color and Preservation of the Human Hair.*   Philadelphia: 1845. Second edition, portrait, 2 plates, cloth, hint of foxing on plates, else near fine.   Joseph J. Felcone Inc.   Science, Medicine and Technology - 26   2015 $125

Bohr, Niels *Atomteori Og Naturbeskrivelse.*   Copenhagen: Bianco Lunos Bogtrykkeri, 1929. First edition, inscribed and signed by author, 8vo., very good+, original printed wrappers, spine archivally repaired, lettering intact.   By the Book, L. C.   Special List 10 - 52   2015 $950

Bohun, William *The Law of Tithes.*   London: in the Savoy: printed by E. and R. Nutt and R. Gosling assigns of Edw. Sayer Esq. for Weaver Bickerton, 1730. First edition, 8vo., contemporary blind ruled calf, very good, crisp copy.   John Drury Rare Books   March 2015 - 24013   2015   £306

Bohun, William *The law of Tithes: Shewing their Nature, Kinds, Properties and Incidents...*   London: in the Savoy, printed by Catherine Lintot for W. Meadows and others, 1760. Fourth edition, 8vo., contemporary blind ruled calf with raised bands, very little wear at extremities, very good.   John Drury Rare Books   March 2015 - 19865   2015 $266

Bois, William Pene *Giant Otto.*   New York: Viking, 1936. First edition, square 12mo., pictorial boards, fine in dust jacket, color lithos.   Aleph-Bet Books, Inc.   108 - 153   2015 $400

Bois, William Pene *Great Geppy.*   New York: Viking, 1940. First edition, 4to., striped cloth, very good+ in slightly worn dust jacket, 22 color drawings and 48 black and whites by Du Bois, nice.   Aleph-Bet Books, Inc.   108 - 154   2015 $250

Boitard, Pierre *Le Jardin des Plantes. Description et Moeurs des Mammiferes de la Menagearie et du Museum d'Histoire Naturelle.*   Paris: G. Barba, 1851. 4to., 56 plates, numerous illustrations, folding plate torn and missing lower left section, very occasional closed marginal tears, contemporary half gilt stamped green morocco over marbled boards, place keeping ribbon, extremities worn, corners showing, front hinge mended with colored Kozo, good.   Jeff Weber Rare Books   178 - 777   2015 $125

Bokks London *Anthology of Luxury Volume One.*   London: published by Bokks, 2005. First edition, 4to., color illustrated wrappers, copiously illustrated throughout, about fine luxury goods catalog.   Any Amount of Books   2015 - A68709   2015   £160

Bolderwood, Rolf *A Colonial Reformer.*   London: Macmillan and Co., 1891. Second edition, half title, contemporary half maroon morocco, little rubbed, bookplate of J. Monro Walker.   Jarndyce Antiquarian Booksellers   CCXI - 28   2015   £35

Bolderwood, Rolf *The Crooked Stick; or Pollie's Probation.*   London: Macmillan and Co., 1895. First edition, half title, contemporary half maroon morocco, little rubbed, bookplate of J. Monro Walker.   Jarndyce Antiquarian Booksellers   CCXI - 29   2015   £35

Bolderwood, Rolf *A Modern Buccaneer.*   London: Macmillan and Co., 1894. Second edition, half tittle, frontispiece, folding map, contemporary half maroon morocco, little rubbed, bookplate of J. Monro Walker.   Jarndyce Antiquarian Booksellers   CCXI - 30   2015   £35

Bolderwood, Rolf *Nevermore.*   London: Macmillan and Co., 1892. First one volume edition, half title, contemporary half maroon morocco, some wear to following hinge, little rubbed, bookplate of J. Monro Walker.   Jarndyce Antiquarian Booksellers   CCXI - 31   2015   £40

Bolderwood, Rolf *Robbery Under Arms.*   London: Macmillan and Co., 1889. Half title, contemporary half maroon morocco, little rubbed, bookplate of J. Monro Walker.   Jarndyce Antiquarian Booksellers   CCXI - 32   2015   £65

Bolderwood, Rolf *The Squatter's Dream.*   London: Macmillan and Co., 1890. New edition, half title, contemporary half maroon morocco, little rubbed, bookplate of J. Monro Walker.   Jarndyce Antiquarian Booksellers   CCXI - 33   2015   £35

Bolmer, Paul *Eine Sammlung von neuen Rezepten und Erporbten Kuren fur Menschen und Thiere.*   Deutschland: 1831. Stitched in printed wrappers, scuffy, edges torn and dog eared, but no loss of text.   Joseph J. Felcone Inc.   Science, Medicine and Technology - 30   2015 $125

Bolton, Robert *An Answer to the Question Where are Your Arguments Against What you Call, Lewdness if you Make no Use of the Bible?*   London: R. and J. Dodsley and J. Whiston and B. White, 1755. First edition, 8vo., small old library stamp (Yale withdrawn) in lower blank margin of final leaf, preserved in modern wrappers, printed title label on upper cover, very good, scarce.   John Drury Rare Books   March 2015 - 22321   2015   £266

Bolton, Robert *Deity's Dealy in Punishing the Guilty, Considered, on the Principles of Reason.*   London: printed for J. Whiston and B. White and R. Dodsley, 1751. First and only edition, 8vo., preserved in modern wrappers with printed title label on upper cover, very good.   John Drury Rare Books   2015 - 18162   2015 $133

Bolton, Robert *A Letter to a Lady, on Card-Playing on the Lord's Day.*   London: printed for J. Leake at Bath and sold by M. Cooper and R. Dodsley, 1748. First edition, 8vo, with half title and final blank H2, preserved in modern wrappers, printed label on upper cover, very good, uncommon.   John Drury Rare Books   2015 - 25508   2015 $612

Bombal, Maria Luisa *La Amortajada.* Santiago: Sociedad Bibliofils Chilenos, 1966. First edition, signed by artist on each illustration, number 43 of 100 special copies (of a total run of 235) with two extra etchings that were for Society members only and dropped from the normal edition, near fine, uncut, unopened copy, spine tanned, slipcase rubbed with small split on lower edge.   Kaaterskill Books   19 - 23   2015 $500

Bonaparte, Lucien *Charlemagne ou L'Eglise Delivree Poeme Epique en Vingt Quatre Chants.* London: Hurst, Rees, Orme and Brown, 1814. True first edition, 2 volumes, 4to., frontispieces, portrait,, original dun boards with white printed spine labels, uncommon, well preserved, slight foxing to frontispieces and slight offsetting to titlepages, slight splitting and tenderness to front outer hinge of first volume, minor wear at top of spine of first volume.   Any Amount of Books   March 2015 - B29452   2015   £360

Bonaparte, Marie *Five copy Books.* London: Imago, 1950. First edition, no. 250 of 1030 sets, 4 volumes, lacking volume V which contained facsimiles of the handwritten copy books, lavish production, near fine copies.   Beasley Books   2013 - 2015 $325

Bonaparte, Napoleon I, Emperor of the French   1769-1821 *Napoleon Peint par lui-meme. Extraits du Veritable Manuscrit de Napoleon Bonaparte par un Americain.* Londres: chez Colburn, 1818. First edition, 8vo., half title, original marbled wrappers, printed title label on upper cover below near contemporary Dublin bookseller's ticket (C. P. Archer), entirely uncut, very good, uncommon.   John Drury Rare Books   March 2015 - 23374   2015 $221

Bonaparte, Napoleon III, Emperor of the French   1808-1873 *Fragmens Historiques 1688 et 1830.* Paris: Administration De Librairie, 1841. Inscribed on slip pasted to half title "Baron Le Crespy-Le Prince", the dedicatee is presumably the artist Charles Edouard Le Prince, Baron de Crespy (1784-1850), note pasted to front endpaper states that the inscription is the autograph of Napoleon III, but is more likely that of an amanuensis, red buckram quarter bound with red calf spine ruled and lettered gilt, from the library of Allan Heywood Bright, with his calling card loosely inserted, neat 19th century ownership inscription to titlepage, some light foxing, especially to first few pages, binding little rubbed and scuffed, otherwise very good.   Any Amount of Books   2015 - C11782   2015   £240

Bond, Richmond P. *English Burlesque Poetry 1700-1750.* Cambridge: Harvard University Press, 1932. Half title original red cloth, spine faded, signed by Geoffrey Tillotson, Mr 1933, with few pencil notes and proof copy of his review.   Jarndyce Antiquarian Booksellers   CCVII - 90   2015   £45

Bondelli, Bernardino *Glossarium Azteco-Latinum et Latino-Aztecum cura et Studio Bernardini Biondelli Collectum ac Digestum.*   Mediolani: Valentienr et Mues, 1869. First edition thus, one of 200 copies, 4to., paper wrappers, later spine, front wrapper repaired, rear edge worn, still about very good.   Kaaterskill Books   19 - 51   2015 $1250

Bondy, Louis W. *Small is Beautiful.* Morrow Bay: Miniature Book Society, 1987. Limited to 400 copies, printed at the Tabula Rasa Press, 6.5 x 6 cm., cloth, gilt lettering on front cover and gilt design on spine.   Oak Knoll Books   306 - 103   2015 $125

Bonham, Frank *Blood on the land.* New York: Ballantine Books, 1952. First edition, pages uniformly browned, else fine in dust jacket with light wear to head of spine.   Buckingham Books   March 2015 - 45   2015 $225

Bonington, Chris *Kongur, China's Elusive Summit.* London: Hodder and Stoughton, 1982. First edition, profusely illustrated, most color and black and white photos, maps, black cloth, very fine, unclipped pictorial dust jacket.   Argonaut Book Shop   Holiday Season 2014 - 35   2015 $75

Bonnefons, Nicolas De *The French Gardiner...*   London: by T. B. for B. Took and are to be sold by J. Taylor, 1691. Fourth (i.e. fifth edition) translated by John Evelyn, 12mo., engraved frontispiece, 4 engraved plates, browned throughout, except plates which are on different paper, slight worming in lower margin at front, mid 20th century blue buckram, armorial bookplate of Isaac Borrow (1673-1745), from the library of James Stevens Cox (1910-1997).   Maggs Bros. Ltd.   1447 - 34   2015   £750

Bonner, Mary Graham *The Magic Music Shop.* New York: Macauley, 1929. First edition, 4to. orange and green cloth, 95 pages, small stain on lower edge of front cover and few pages, else very good+ in dust jacket (frayed with 2 pices of top edge and spine), illustrations by Luxor Price, very scarce in dust jacket.   Aleph-Bet Books, Inc.   108 - 375   2015 $475

Bonomo, Joe *The Strongman: a True Life, Pictorial Autobiography of the Hercules of the Screen, Joe Bonomo.* New York: Bonomo Studios, 1968. First edition, quarto, red cloth gilt, some posting to boards, small stain on page edges, good copy, without dust jacket, inscribed by author 12-2-67 for friend William Abner.   Between the Covers Rare Books, Inc.   187 - 28   2015 $85

Bontemps, Arna *American Negro Poetry.* New York: Hill & Wang, 1963. Uncorrected proof copy, tall, comb bound galley sheets without Bontemps introduction that appeared in published text, publicity information taped inside front cover, this may be what was once tipped to front cover and is now absent, minor sunning and creasing, couple of small tears, very good.   Ken Lopez, Bookseller   164 - 6   2015 $275

Bontemps, Arna *Drums at Dusk.* New York: Macmillan, 1939. First printing, 8vo., black cloth, two cuts in front endpaper, otherwise very good, tight copy in worn dust jacket. Second Life Books Inc.   190 - 33   2015 $325

Bontemps, Arna *The Harlem Renaissance Remembered.* New York: Dodd, Mead, 1972. First edition, portraits, signed on flyleaves Roy L. Hill, poet and professor, fairly extensive underlining and marking, edges little stained, otherwise very good, tight copy in worn dust jacket.   Second Life Books Inc.   190 - 34   2015 $100

Bontemps, Arna *Popo and Fifina.* New York: Macmillan Co., 1949. Sixth printing, illustrations by E. Simms Campbell, cloth, considerable edge wear to cloth at extremities, presentable and sound copy, inscribed by Langston Hughes for the Second Grade Class of Alexander Street School, Charlotte, Nov. 15, 1950.   Between the Covers Rare Books   197 - 7   2015 $450

Bonvalot, Gabriel *Across Thibet Being a translation of "De Pris Au Tonkin a Travers le Tibet Inconnu".* London: Cassell, 1891. First edition in English, large 8vo., photos, folding map, decent, sound set in original illustrated putty green cloth, lettered gilt on spine and gilt heightened illustration on covers, copies known in red cloth also, light handling wear, slight rubbing and slight tanning to spines, otherwise very good, f.e.p. slightly foxed, text and illustrations very clean.   Any Amount of Books   March 2015 - A74376   2015   £450

The Book-Lover. A Magazine of Book Lore. New York: Book-Lover's Press, 1899-1902. San Francisco: 1899, 10 consecutive issues, Autumn 1899 to January 1902, bound in 2 small folio volumes, gray cloth and marbled boards, fine. Stephen Lupack   March 2015 - 2015 $150

The Book of Martyrs with an Account of the Acts and Monuments of Church and State from the Time of Our Blessed Saviour to the Year 1701. London: privately printed, 1702. First edition, 2 volumes, 8vo., 8 copperplates, clean and vivid, some rubbing, some wear, pronounced splitting at hinges, one board detached, corners worn, spine unlettered, overall near very good, text occasionally slightly browned, some worming at edges of pages.   Any Amount of Books   2015 - B29636   2015   £180

Boole, George *A Treatise on Differential Equations.* Cambridge: Macmillan, 1859. First edition, full brown leather, rebacked with new leather spine and endpapers, seal of University of Aberdeen on front cover, likely a prize binding, raised bands spine, gilt lettering on black leather spine label, marbled edges, cover edge wear, scuffs, 12mo., errata slip and foldout plate.   By the Book, L. C.   44 - 26   2015 $550

Booth, Stephen *Blood on the Tongue.* London: Harper Collins, 2002. First edition, advance review copy with review slip laid in, very fine in dust jacket, signed by author. Mordida Books March 2015 - 008212   2015 $185

Boothby, Guy *Farewell Nikola.* Philadelphia: J. B. Lippincott, 1901. First US edition, 8vo., original gray cloth, titles decorated in white and black on front cover and stamped in white on spine, frontispiece, full page plates, white spine lettering largely worn, few light rubs to covers, else very good, clean copy.   Buckingham Books   March 2015 - 32077   2015 $175

Boothby, Guy *The Kidnapped President.* London: Ward Lock, 1902. First edition, very good, illustrations by Stanley Wood, foxing on page edges and light spotting on endpapers, otherwise near fine in cloth covered boards with gold stamped titles.   Mordida Books   March 2015 - 000300 2015 $75

Bordelon, Laurent *The Management of the Tongue.* London: printed by D. L. (ie. D. Leach for H. Rhodes, 1707. Second edition, 8vo., some minor dust marking and light soiling, contemporary panelled calf with 20th century mismatched rebacking and fairly recent replaced free endpapers, good.   John Drury Rare Books   March 2015 - 18170 2015   £306

Bordier, Henri *Une Fabrique de Faux Autographes ou Recit de laffaire Vrain Lucas.* Paris: Leon Techener Libraire, 1870. First edition, 4to., original printed wrappers bound in, contemporary black quarter morocco, decorated cloth boards, gilt lettering, top edge gilt, others untrimmed, 7 leaves of lithographed facsimiles, bookplate of book collector Charles Walker Andrews, with his notation this was purchased from James Tregaskis in London, Dec. 1935, edges little rubbed, very good, inscribed "A Monseiur... S. Turner/ Hommage des editeurs/H. Bordier".   The Brick Row Book Shop   Miscellany 67 - 44   2015 $750

Borges, Jorge Luis *Borges at Eighty, Conversations.* Bloomington: Indiana University Press, 1982. First edition, signed by Borges on titlepage, fine in fine dust jacket, lengthy conversations with Willis Barnstone, many photos by Barnstone, small 4to.   Beasley Books   2013 - 2015 $300

Borges, Jorge Luis *Ficciones.* New York: Limited Editions Club, 1984. Limited to 1500 numbered copies, signed by Sol Lewitt, square 4to. 22 geometric illustrations (silkscreens) by Sol Lewitt, full black cowhide, fine in slipcase, Monthly Newsletter laid in, strikingly beautiful. Aleph-bet Books, Inc. 109 - 266 2015 $650

Borges, Jorge Luis *Ficciones.* New York: Limited Editions Club, 1984. Limited to 1500 numbered copies, signed by artist and book designer Sol Lewitt, with finely printed silk screens by Jo Wantabe for Lewitt, square 8vo., full black cowhide, slipcase. Oak Knoll Books 25 - 53 2015 $485

Borges, Jorge Luis *Jorge Luis Borges. My Work in Prose. Jorge Luis Borges. My Life in Books.* Black River Falls: Obscure Publications, 2010. First edition, both limited edition os 60 only, both no. 39, 2 booklets, 8vo., illustrated wrappers, pages 30 and 33, fine. Any Amount of Books 2015 - A84631 2015 £180

Borges, Jorge Luis *Poemas (1922-1923).* Buenos Aires: Editorial Losada, 1943. First edition, some tiny spotting on page edges, otherwise fine in soft covers with dust jacket which has few tiny spots on front panel. Mordida Books March 2015 - 006456 2015 $1250

Borie, Lysbeth Boyd *More Poems for Peter.* Philadelphia: 1931. First edition, very good, yellow cloth with expected age soil, illustrations by Lisi Hummel. Bookworm & Silverfish 2015 - 6016652547 2015 $60

Borissow, Michael *The Naked Fairways.* Crankbrook Golf Club, 1984. First edition, fine, paperback original, some wear along edges, otherwise near fine in wrappers. Mordida Books March 2015 - 010753 2015 $85

Boruwlaski, Joseph *Memoirs of the Celebrated Dwarf, Joseph Boruwlaski. A Polish Gentleman.* Kelso: James Ballantyne at the Kelso Mail Printing Office, 1801. First edition thus, 8vo., inscribed by author for Christ. Ebdon (1744-1824), full contemporary calf, front board detached, bears 1797 Thomas Bell bookplate, spine rather chipped and faded, small chip at top of f.f.e.p., otherwise very good. Any Amount of Books March 2015 - C13206 2015 £450

Bosanquet, Charles *A Letter to W. Manning, Esq. M.P. On the Causes of the Rapid and Progressive Depreciation of West India Property.* London: printed by S. & C. McDowell and sold by Richardsons &c, n.d?, 1807. Second edition, 8vo., 54 pages, modern maroon quarter morocco, spine lettered in gilt, very good. John Drury Rare Books March 2015 - 5499 2015 $221

Bose, Amalendu *Chronicles of Life Studies in Early Victorian.* London: Longmans, 1962. Original pale grey cloth, very good in torn and marked dust jacket, Geoffrey Tillotson's copy with typewritten copy of his letter to author. Jarndyce Antiquarian Booksellers CCVII - 91 2015 £35

Bosschere, Jean De 1878-1953 *Arabesques.* Paris: Bibliothque de L'Occident, 1909. First edition, one of 250 numbered copies out of a total edition of 260, quarto, 27 illustrations, decorations and initials, contemporary three quarter morocco, raised bands, marbled endpapers, preserving original wrappers, presentation copy from author, inscribed on second blank in black and red for S. Alexandridi, head of spine splitting, leather partially faded at upper cover, very good. Peter Ellis, Bookseller 2014 - 014048 2015 £235

Bosschere, Jean De 1878-1953 *Folk Tales of Flanders.* New York: Dodd Mead, 1918. First edition, 4to., green gilt and blindstamped cloth, fine, 12 color plates and a profusion of wonderful black and whites. Aleph-Bet Books, Inc. 108 - 124 2015 $300

Boston Female Anti-Slavery Society *Annual Report of the Boston Female Anti-Slavery Society...* Boston: published by the Society, Isaac Knapp, Printer, 1836. First edition, 12mo., printed brown wrappers, slight staining and modest overall use to wrappers, else attractive and pleasing, near fine copy. Between the Covers Rare Books 197 - 68 2015 $2250

Boston, Charles K. *The Silver Jackass.* New York: Reynal & Hitchcock, 1941. First edition, 3 small numbers in ink on rear pastedown sheet, else fine, bright copy in lightly rubbed dust jacket with light wear to head and toe of spine and extremities. Buckingham Books March 2015 - 12597 2015 $275

Boston, Charles K. *The Silver Jackass.* New York: Reynal Hitchcock, 1941. First edition, fine in very good dust jacket with scraping on front panel, light wear at spine ends and several short closed tears. Mordida Books March 2015 - 009051 2015 $200

Boswell, Edward *The Civil Division of the County of Dorset, Methodically Digested and Arranged Containing Lists of the principal Civil magistrates and Officers...* Sherborne: printed by W. Crutwell, 1795. First edition, tall 8vo., folding engraved map, half title, contemporary black half morocco flat spine gilt and lettered in compartments, little wear to extremities and joints, else very good, crisp copy, 19th century armorial bookplate of Sir John Smith, Bart, scare. John Drury Rare Books 2015 - 182768 2015 $168

Boswell, George *A Treatise on Watering Meadows: wherein Are Shewn some of the Many Advantages Arising from that Mode of Practice....*   London: for J. Debrett, 1801. Fourth edition, 6 plans, on five folding plates, 8vo., contemporary marbled paper boards, quarter bound, leather spine, ruled and lettered gilt, two neat ownership inscriptions, otherwise slight handling wear only, very good.   Any Amount of Books   March 2015 - C14291   2015   £350

Boswell, James   1740-1795 *An Account of Corsica, the Journal of a Tour to that Island and Memoirs of Pascal Paoli...*   Glasgow: printed by Robert and Andrew Foulis for Edward and Charles Dilly, 1768. First edition, folding engraved map, little wear at one fold junction and a short handling tear at rear guard invisibly repaired, small abrasion to first two leaves of Introduction (affecting one letter with no loss of sense), engraved vignette on titlepage, half title present, ownership stamp of M.P. Carter to titlepage, 8vo., contemporary speckled calf, red morocco lettering piece, rubbed, little wear to joint ends, pencilled ownership inscription of broadcaster Frank Muir, modern bookplate to flyleaf, very good.   Blackwell's Rare Books   B179 - 13   2015   £1200

Boswell, James   1740-1795 *The Journal of a Tour to the Hebrides, with Samuel Johnson...*   London: printed by Henry Baldwin for Charles Dilly, 1785. Second edition, half title, final leaf advertising Boswell's Life of Johnson, occasional light spotting, light marginal stain to last few leaves, early 19th century quarter calf, marbled paper boards, spine decorated and lettered gilt, slightly rubbed, marbled endpapers, red sprinkled edges, bookplate of Charles William Kennedy, University College, Oxford, attractive copy.   Jarndyce Antiquarian Booksellers   CCXI - 34   2015   £420

Boswell, James   1740-1795 *Boswell's Journal of a Tour to the Hebrides with Samuel Johnson, LL.D.*   London: William Heinemann, 1936. Half title, folding map, plates, original red cloth, spine faded, copy given to Kathleen Tillotson by family members with her name altered from Constable to Tillotson.   Jarndyce Antiquarian Booksellers   CCVII - 92   2015   £35

Boswell, James   1740-1795 *Letters Collected and Edited by Chauncey Brewster Tinker.*   Oxford: Clarendon Press, 1924. 2 volumes, half titles, frontispiece volume I, plates, old pencil mark, original brown cloth, from the library of Geoffrey & Kathleen Tillotson, given by Geoffery to Kathleen 3.IV.38, with note and cutting inserted.   Jarndyce Antiquarian Booksellers   CCVII - 93   2015   £35

Boswell, James   1740-1795 *The Life of Samuel Johnson, LL.D. Including a Journal of His Tour to the Hebrides.*   London: John Murray, 1835. Croker's second edition, 10 volumes, small octavo, each with engraved frontispiece and vignette title, extra illustrated with over 100 engraved plates, bound by Morrell, full tan polished calf, gilt double rule border on covers, spines decoratively tooled gilt in compartments with maroon and green morocco gilt lettering labels, gilt board edges and turn-ins, top edge gilt, others uncut, marbled endpapers, about fine set.   Heritage Book Shop   Holiday 2014 - 19   2015 $2500

Boswell, James   1740-1795 *Boswell's Life of Johnson...*   Oxford: at the Clarendon Press, 1934-1950. Revised and enlarged edition, 6 volumes, half titles, frontispieces, plates, original maroon cloth, very good, volumes I-II with marked dust jacket, Geoffrey Tillotson's copy with cuttings, correspondence and ALS.   Jarndyce Antiquarian Booksellers   CCVII - 339   2015   £125

Boswell, Ruth *A Historical Compilation of Victoria by the Sea Our Legacy and Trust Centennial Year 1973.*   Prince Edward Island: pub. by authors, 1973. 8vo., black and white illustrations, maps and street layout in rear, very good, previous owner's name on front cover, small stain to front cover.   Schooner Books Ltd.   110 - 126   2015 $45

Bosworth, Newton *The Accidents of Human Life; with Hints for their Prevention or the Removal of their Consequences.*   London: printed for Lackington, Allen and Co., 1813. 12mo., frontispiece, plates, slightly later half brown calf, gilt spine, slight rubbing at extremities, corners slightly bumped, nice attractive copy, scarce.   Jarndyce Antiquarian Booksellers   CCXI - 35   2015   £580

Botsford, Keith *Benvenuto.*   London: Hutchinson of London, 1961. First edition, endpapers foxed, corners trifle bumped, very good in very good dust jacket (rubbed with small chip on front panel), stamp of Helga Greene Literary Agency of London, beneath which is Botsford's inscription to author George Garrett and Susan.   Between the Covers Rare Books, Inc.   187 - 29   2015 $200

Boucher, Anthony *The Case of the Seven of Calvary.*   New York: Simon & Schuster, 1937. First edition, very good in dust jacket with internal tape mends, wear along folds, several short closed tears and nicks at spine ends.   Mordida Books   March 2015 - 012604   2015 $200

Boucher, Anthony *The Case of the Solid Key.*   New York: Simon and Schuster, 1941. First edition, near fine, lower front corner bumped and couple of small discolored spots on front cover, otherwise near fine in price clipped dust jacket with small chip at top of spine, slightly faded spine, couple of tiny closed tears.   Mordida Books   March 2015 - 012606   2015 $400

Boucher, Anthony *On the Nomenclature of the Brothers Moriarty.* San Francisco: Beaune Press, 1966. Reprint edition, one of 225 numbered copies, in three groups of 75, numbered in red, blue and green respectively, this copy number 64 in green and has been signed by author, fine. Mordida Books   March 2015 - 012467   2015 $100

Bouchette, Joseph *The British Dominions in North America; or a Topographical and Statistical Description of the Provinces of Lower and Upper Canada, New Brunswick, Nova Scotia, Islands of Newfoundland, Prince Edward and Cape Breton.* London: Longman, Rees, Orme, Brown, Green and Longman, 1832. 2 volumes, modern brown quarter calf with cloth boards and red labels to spine, quarto, volume I with frontispiece, 10 plates and 8 plans, volume II with 5 plates and 2 plans, both volumes rebound with new endpapers, small tear to bottom inner corner of titlepage expertly repaired, frontispiece has light waterstain, interior to volume II in very good condition.   Schooner Books Ltd. 110 - 159   2015 $1250

Bouchette, Joseph *A Topographical Description of the Province of Lower Canada, with Remarks Upon Upper Canada and on the Relative Connexion of Both Provinces with the United States of America.* London: published by W. Faden, 1815. Contemporary half brown calf with brown cloth boards, gilt borders and title to spine, quarto, frontispiece, 7 plates, 3 folding maps, 5 plans, wear to edges of binding and bottom of spine frayed, frontispiece foxed, on plate cropped to top edge image, some pen notations and underlining to appendix.   Schooner Books Ltd.   110 - 158 2015 $875

Bougeant, Guillaume Hyacinthe De *Amusuement Philosophique sur le Langage des Bestes.* Paris: Chez Gissez, 1739. First edition, 12mo., titlepage and 153 pages (with "fin"), contemporary calf, worn, with George Gibson Jr. bookplate and Gibson family embossed stamp. Stephen Lupack   March 2015 - 2015 $125

Bouland, D. L. *Marques de Livres Anciennes et Modernes Francaises et Etrangeres.* Paris: Librairie Henri Leclerc, L. Girau Badin, 1925. First edition, 8vo., rebound in burgundy cloth lettered gilt on spine, copiously illustrated in black and white, attractive bookplate 'FM', very good.   Any Amount of Books   2015 - C2424   2015   £150

Boulanger, C. *Bronzes D'Eclairage Electricite.* Paris: circa, 1905. Oblong folio, 252 heliotype plates divided by 8 section titles, some minor chipping to few plates, original blue cloth, upper cover blocked in silver, slightly bumped at extremities, very large elaborately produced catalog. Marlborough Rare Books   List 53 - 23   2015   £950

Boulay, Anthony Du *Christie's Pictorial History of Chinese Ceramics.* Oxford: Phaidon, 1984. First edition, 8vo., 319 pages, original black cloth lettered gilt at spine, review copy with publisher's printed review slip loosely inserted, copiously illustrated in color and black and white throughout, very good+ in very good+ dust jacket, slightly bumped at lower spine, not price clipped, excellent.   Any Amount of Books March 2015 - C7120   2015   £450

Boulenger, George Albert *Catalogue of the Snakes in the British Museum.* London: British Museum, 1893-1896. Octavo, 3 volumes, 73 uncolored lithographs, publisher's cloth, some slight wear, primarily to top of spine of volume 3 which has split along upper edge, library accession numbers in copperplate hand on titlepages and endpapers, very good set, scarce.   Andrew Isles   2015 - 25316   2015 $2850

Boulle, Pierre *La Planete des Signes: Roman.* Paris: Le Cercle du Nouveau Livre, 1963. First edition, number 507 of an unstated limitation, gold and blindstamped green cloth. John W. Knott, Bookseller   Selected New Arrivals Jan. 2015 - 16926   2015 $1250

Bourchier, John *The History of Valiant Knight Arthur of Little Britain: a Romance of Chivalry.* London: printed for White, Cochrane & Co., 1814. Limited to 200 copies, 25 on large paper with plates in two states, this one of 175 regular copies, from the library of Allan Heywood Bright (1862-1941), with his attractive bookplate (by Downey), 4to., 25 leaves of plates, green paper covered boards with darker green cloth spine and red leather spine label, lettered gilt, possibly original publisher's binding, slight rubbing to covers and marking with foxing to prelims an slight foxing to plates, otherwise pleasing, sound, very good, copy, scarce.   Any Amount of Books   2015 - C11873   2015   £900

Bourdon, Georges *The German Enigma, Being an Inquiry Among Germans as to What They Think What They Want, What They Can Do.* Paris and London: Georges Cres and J. M. Dent, 1914. First edition, 8vo., original red cloth lettered gilt at spine, slight sunning at edges, endpapers browned, else very good+ in like dust jacket (clean, slightly chipped at head of spine), rare in dust jacket.   Any Amount of Books   2015 - A63088   2015   £180

Bouret, Jean *Eloge De Louis Neillot.* Editions Manuel Bruker, 1962. First edition, 4to., limited to 200 copies, no. XV with 'Ex collaborateur' signed in pencil by Bouret?, unbound signatures laid into wrappers, 8 original lithographs including 6 double page spreads and 3 in color, near fine in slightly worn glassine.   Beasley Books   2013 - 2015 $300

Bourinot, John G. *Builders of Nova Scotia.* Toronto: Copp-Clark, 1900. Large 8vo., green cloth with gilt decorations and title to front and spine, frontispiece, illustrations, cloth quite worn with inner front hinge cracked, author's presentation copy.   Schooner Books Ltd.   110 - 58   2015 $45

Bourne, George *A Condensed Anti-Slavery Bible Argument.* New York: S. W. Benedict, 1845. First edition, 8vo., original printed wrappers (faded), spine backed with paper strip at early date, wrappers with some wear to extremities, text block bit browned, scattered foxing, good. M & S Rare Books, Inc. 97 - 281 2015 $375

Boursier-Mougenot, A. *Doudou Flies Away.* New York: Grosset & Dunlap, 1937. Folio, cloth backed pictorial boards, near fine in slightly soiled dust jacket, brightly colored illustrations, very lovely. Aleph-Bet Books, Inc. 108 - 346 2015 $250

Bousteau, Fabrice *In the Arab World Now.* Paris: Galerie Enrico Navarra, 2005. First edition, 4to., 3 volumes in slipcase, copiously illustrated in color and black and white, fine in slipcase. Any Amount of Books 2015 - A73017 2015 £220

Bouvier, Hannah M. *Bouvier's Familiar Astronomy; or an Introduction to the Study of the Heavens.* Philadelphia: Childs & Peterson, 1857. 8cvo., 2 double page blue star maps, 219 figures, original bluish green blind and gilt stamped cloth, some minor wear to corners, top edge gilt and top edge ink ownership signature, mark of James H. Graff, Baltimore. Jeff Weber Rare Books 178 - 778 2015 $45

Bouwstenen Voor Een Geschiedenis Nederlanden. Utrecht: Vereniging voor Nederlandse Muziekgeschiedenis, 1965. 8vo., 3 volumes, cloth, title and volume number gilt stamped on spine, black and white illustrations. Oak Knoll Books 306 - 85 2015 $250

Bowcock, William *The Life, Experience and Correspondence of William Bowcock, the Lincolnshire Drillman: late Deacon of the Particular Baptist Church....* London: Houlston and Stoneman, 1851. First edition, 12mo., 168 pages, original blindstamped cloth, spine lettered gilt, pretty good copy, rare. John Drury Rare Books 2015 - 18809 2015 $177

Bowdich, Thomas Edward *Mission from the Cape Coast Castle to Ashantee, with a Statistical Account of that Kingdom and Geographical Notices of Other Parts of the Interior of Africa.* London: 1819. First edition, quarto, with half title, 2 engraved maps, folding plate, 7 hand colored aquatint plates, uncut, original boards, original printed paper spine label, minor offsetting from second map, contemporary owner's declaration on front free endpaper (dated 1820), head of spine with small repair, slight extremity and joint wear, paper spine label with small chip, cloth clamshell case, previous owner's bookplate inside case, superb copy, tall, clean and uncut. Heritage Book Shop Holiday 2014 - 20 2015 $8500

Bowdler, John *Remarks on the Rev. Dr. Vincent's Defence of Public Education; with an Attempt to State Fairly the Question, Whether the Religious Instruction and Moral conduct of the Rising Generation...* London: J. Hatchard, 1802. 8vo., two old inkstamps of an institutional library of titlepage, not a lending library, disbound, good. John Drury Rare Books 2015 - 20578 2015 $80

Bowen, Catherine Drinker *Biography: the Craft and the Calling.* Boston: Little Brown, 1969. First edition, light offsetting to front endpapers from clipping or letter, else fine in near fine dust jacket with little light wear at spinal extremities, inscribed by author for her editor Barbara Rex, with Rex's ownership signature. Between the Covers Rare Books, Inc. 187 - 22 2015 $350

Bower, Samuel *A Sequel to the Peopling of Utopia; or the Sufficiency of Socialism for Human Happiness...* Bradford: printed by C. Wilkinson, 1838. First and only edition, 8vo., 20 pages, recently well bound in blue boards, upper cover lettered. John Drury Rare Books 2015 - 5620 2015 $656

Bowles, Jane *The Collected Works of Jane Bowles.* New York: Noonday Press, 1966. First edition, inscribed to Arab-American poet, Sam Hazo. Honey & Wax Booksellers 2 - 58 2015 $1000

Bowles, John *A View of the Moral State of Society at the Close of the Eighteenth Century....* London: F. and C. Rivington, J. Hatchard, J.Asperne and J. Spragg, 1804. Third edition, 8vo., half title, rebound fairly recently in plain boards, spine lettered, very good inscribed in ink on half title, Right Hon. Lord Aucklan(d) from the author. John Drury Rare Books March 2015 - 23137 2015 £266

Bowles, William *Pamphlets on Naval Subjects.* London: James Ridgway, 1854. First collected edition, contemporary or slightly later half calf, spine fully gilt incorporating an anchor device in compartments with title label lettered gilt, joints carefully restored, top edge gilt, very good, with late 19th armorial bookplate of United Service Club (London). John Drury Rare Books March 2015 - 24765 2015 $656

Bowman, David *Let the Dog Drive.* New York: New York University, 1992. First edition, very fine in dust jacket. Mordida Books March 2015 - 002377 2015 $165

Box, Edgar *Death in the Fifth Position.* New York: Dutton, 1952. First edition, cloth lightly rubbed, else near fine in dust jacket with some light professional restoration to spine ends and corners. Buckingham Books March 2015 - 26733 2015 $400

Boyd, Harriet *Bedtime Stories About Cabbages and Peanuts.* Akron: Saalfield, 1930. Large 8vo., cloth backed pictorial boards, very good, illustrations in color and black and white by Fern Bisel Peat, very scarce.   Aleph-Bet Books, Inc.   108 - 340   2015 $200

Boyd, James *Drums.* New York: Charles Scribners, 1928. First edition, 4to, black cloth, pictorial paste-on, fine in dust jacket with mounted color plate, dust jacket lightly frayed at spine ends, illustrations by N. C. Wyeth.   Aleph-bet Books, Inc.   109 - 496   2015 $850

Boyd, William *A Good Man in Africa.* London: Hamish Hamilton, 1981. First edition, 8vo., review copy with slip, fine in fine dust jacket.   Any Amount of Books   March 2015 - A92591   2015   £400

Boyd, William H. *Boyd's Philadelphia City Business Directory Containing the names of Banks, Insurgance Companies, Railroads, Newspapers, Corporations, Manufacturers &c.* Philadelphia: Central News Co., 1882. 12mo., original cloth, boards scuffed and rubbed, especially at edges inside hinges repaired with archival tape, small spot at top of titlepage, stamp of previous owner on fore-edge.   Oak Knoll Books   306 - 255   2015 $200

Boydell, James *A Treatise on landed Property, In Its Geological, Agricultural, Chemical, Mechanical and Political Relations.* London: published by the author, 1849. First edition, 8vo., errata leaf, original blindstamped cloth, spine gilt lettered, very good, surprisingly scarce.   John Drury Rare Books   March 2015 - 23164   2015 $221

Boyer, Rick *Billingsgate Shoal.* Boston: Houghton Mifflin, 1982. First edition, fine in dust jacket.   Mordida Books   March 2015 - 010285   2015 $80

Boyle, James *The Minimum Wage and Syndicalism.* Cincinnati: Stewart & Kidd, 1913. First edition, hardcover, dulling to spine gilt, otherwise tight and bright.   Beasley Books   2013 - 2015 $45

Boyle, Robert   1627-1691 *Certain Physiological Essays and Other Tracts.* London: Henry Herringman, 1669. Second edition, 4to., without final blank leaf, small wormhole through upper blank margin, long wormtrail in inner margin and into text around line 14 of Pp1(3)E2, leaf B1 dusty at head, small piece torn away from blank corner of T2 and with tear to foot of O3, contemporary sprinkled calf, covers panelled in blind, paper label in second panel of spine, covers affected by worm damage, in particular they have chewed out corner ornaments of panels, early inscription of George Sampson, 18th century signature J. W. Hawker, from the library of James Stevens Cox (1910-1997).   Maggs Bros. Ltd.   1447 - 35   2015   £950

Boyle, Robert   1627-1691 *An Essay of the Great Effects of Even Languid and Unheeded Motion.* London: by M. Flesher, for Richard Davis, 1685. First edition, first state titlepage (without Boyle's name), 8vo., neat modern calf, antique, retaining original front flyleaf with signature of Mr. Jocelyn, light dust soiling of first few leaves, else fine, clean copy.   Joseph J. Felcone Inc.   Science, Medicine and Technology - 13   2015 $2800

Boyle, Robert   1627-1691 *Essays of the Strange Subtilty, Great Efficacy, Determinate Nature of Effluviums.* London: by W(illiam) G(odbid) for M. Pitt, 1673. First edition, first issue, 8vo., lightly browned in places, mostly in margins, rust mark of head of E1-3, contemporary calf, covers ruled in blind, marbled edges (rebacked, new endpapers), from the library of James Stevens Cox (1910-1997).   Maggs Bros. Ltd.   1447 - 36   2015   £1200

Boyle, Robert   1627-1691 *The Excellency of Theology.* London: by T. N. for Henry Herringmann, 1674. 8vo., titlepage badly defective having been affected by damp and stuck to front pasteboard (where some of it still remains) and has large (145 x35mm) piece torn away and two (approximately 50mm) closed tears caused by leaf being torn away from pastedown, first sheet dampstained, continuing less severely in places throughout, final blank and binders blank little ragged and stained by turn-ins, contemporary sheep, large piece torn away from leather exposing book block, covers almost detached, holes and scuffs to both boards, no pastedowns, late 20th century brown cloth folding box, the duplicate copy of John Evelyn (1630-1706), from the library of James Stevens Cox (1910-1997).   Maggs Bros. Ltd.   1447 - 37   2015   £550

Boyle, Robert   1627-1691 *Experiments, Notes, &c. about the Mechnical Origine or Production of Divers Particular Qualities...* London: by E. Flesher for R. Davis bookseller in Oxford, 1675. First edition, 8vo., without leaf of 'Directions to Binder' and errata, general title dusty, light browning stronger in margins throughout, small chip at head of title, contemporary calf, covers panelled in blind, rebacked, new endleaves, contemporary signature of Thos. Smith, few marginal ink notes, some with chemical signs, from the library of James Stevens Cox (1910-1997).   Maggs Bros. Ltd.   1447 - 38   2015   £1100

Boyle, Robert   1627-1691 *Hydrostatical Paradoxes made Out by New Experiments.* Oxford: by William Hall for Richard Davis, 1666. First edition, with all 3 folding engraved plates, but lacking contents and imprimatur leaves, some very light dampstaining to edges throughout, late 19th century tree calf, rebacked, later endleaves, from the library of James Stevens Cox (1910-1997).   Maggs Bros. Ltd.   1447 - 39   2015   £600

Boyle, Robert 1627-1691 *Medicinal Experiments or a Collection of Choice Remedies for the most Part Simple, and Easily Prepared...* London: for Sam. Smith, 1692. First edition, 12mo., very lightly foxed, contemporary sheep (worn, edges rubbed and bumped, text block split down centre and loose in case), from the library of James Stevens Cox (1910-1997). Maggs Bros. Ltd. 1447 - 40 2015 £500

Boyle, Robert 1627-1691 *New Experiments and Observations Touching Cold, or an Experimental History of Cold, Begun.* London: for John Crook, 1665. First edition, 8vo., without final blank leaf, two folding plates, bound at end, tightly bound, text-block starting to split in places, title little stained very small piece torn away from blank corner of d4, contemporary calf (rebacked, corners worn, 19th century endleaves), old front flyleaf (stained), preserved, late 18th/early 19th century signature Edward Kendall, from the library of James Stevens Cox (1910-1997). Maggs Bros. Ltd. 1447 - 41 2015 £3500

Boyle, Robert 1627-1691 *Some considerations Touching the Style of the H. Scriptures.* London: for Henry Herringman, 1663. Second edition, 8vo. in 4's, light marginal browning with some occasional spotting, contemporary sheep ruled in blind, front cover detached, worn, scuffed, bumped and with small pieces missing from upper and lower headcaps, contemporary signature "Dan(ie)l Williams, ex-libris J. Kembler Anno 1755, from the library of James Stevens Cox (1910-1997). Maggs Bros. Ltd. 1447 - 42 2015 £180

Boyle, Robert 1627-1691 *Some considerations Touching the Usefulnesse of Experimental naturall Philosophy...* Oxford: by Henry Hall printer to the University for Ric. Davis, 1664. Second edition, London issue A, 4to., some minor intermittent light dampstaining to blank margins, verso of g2 and recto of G3 lightly soiled, closed, vertical paper flaw near gutter at edge of printed text on L2, small closed paper flaw to blank corner of H4, verso of K2 and recto of k3 soiled, small rusthole to lower blank margin of Mm4-Nn2, contemporary calf, covers with double gilt fillet border and small floral tool at corners, worn edges and corners chipped, turn-ins coming unglued, spine chipped at head and foot, from the library of James Stevens Cox (1910-1997). Maggs Bros. Ltd. 1447 - 43 2015 £600

Boyle, Robert 1627-1691 *Some Motives and Incentives to the love of God, pathetically Discorus'd of in a Letter to a friend.* London: for Henry Herringman, 1665. Fourth edition, title browned by turn-ins, one or two wormholes in lower margin, extending to a short trail from C4 to D3 each leaf throughout, H2 trimmed along lower edge, small piece torn away and a close tear I3 (touching text), 8vo., contemporary sheep (heavily worn and scuffed, upper joint split but holding, headcaps missing, pastedowns unstuck torn and stained by turn-ins), from the library of James Stevens Cox (1910-1997), 19th century bookplate William Warren, Bristol, signature A. S. Quick 17 may 1883, number of pencil markings by him. Maggs Bros. Ltd. 1447 - 44 2015 £150

Boynton, Peter *Black Shoes a Christmas Story.* Printed at the Sun-Up Press, First edition, green paper wrappers, inscribed by author to Bill & Katchen, nearly fine, very scarce. Stephen Lupack March 2015 - 2015 $95

The Boy's Realm June 14 1902-May 30 1903. London: privately published, 1902. Large 4to., blue cloth lettered gilt on spine, 51 consecutive issues, well illustrated, some wear, slight tear bottom of spine, slight rubbing, slight edgewear, otherwise sound, very good. Any Amount of Books 2015 - A67971 2015 £220

Boyson, V. F. *The Falkland Islands: with Notes on the Natural History.* Oxford: Clarendon Press, 1924. First edition, 8vo., original navy blue cloth, lettered gilt at spine, folding ap at rear, press cutting with poem by V. F. Boyson, slight browning to endpapers, slight marking to blue cloth on front board, some foxing to rear folding map, otherwise very good+, excellent. Any Amount of Books 2015 - C11657 2015 £750

Brackenridge, Henry Marie 1786-1871 *History of the Western Insurrection in Western Pennsylvania Commonly Called the Whiskey Insurrection.* Pittsburgh: W. S. Haven, 1859. First edition, 8vo., publisher's cloth (lacks 1 inch piece at top of spine and half inch on bottom). Second Life Books Inc. 191 - 17 2015 $300

Bracker, Jurgen *Alster, Elbe and the Sea.* Hamburg: Topographikon/Rolf Mullr, 1981. First edition, hardcover, oblong 4to., fine in fine dust jacket. Beasley Books 2013 - 2015 $45

Brackett, Anna C. *The Education of American Girls, Considered in a Series of Essays.* New York: Putnam's, 1874. First edition, 8vo., 401 pages, green cloth stamped in gilt, pencil ownership signature on endpaper, near fine. Second Life Books Inc. 191 - 18 2015 $250

Brackett, Leigh *An Eye for an Eye.* Garden City: Doubleday, 1957. First edition, very good in dust jacket with several closed tears, nicks at spine ends and wear along edges. Mordida Books March 2015 - 007351 2015 $85

Brackett, Leigh *The Starmen.* New York: Gnome Press, 1952. First edition, octavo, cover art by Ric Binkley, boards. John W. Knott, Bookseller Selected New Arrivals Jan. 2015 - 16927 2015 $250

Bradburn, Samuel *Methodism set Forth and Defended in a Sermon on Acts XXVII 22 Preached at the Opening of Portland-Chapel, Bristol August 26 1792.* Bristol: printed and sold by Lancaster and Edwards sold also at the Methodist Chapels, n.d, 1792. First edition, 8vo., 56 pages, title and last leaf bit dusty, waterstaining in upper margins of first three or four leaves stitched as issued, entirely uncut, minor fault apart, very good copy, very scarce.   John Drury Rare Books   March 2015 - 14799   2015 $221

Bradbury, Ray *The Aqueduct.* Glendale: Roy A. Squires, 1979. First edition, octavo, wrappers with printed paper label affixed to front cover, laid into marbled paper dust jacket.   L. W. Currey, Inc.   Featured Author: Ray Bradbury (Oct. 2014) - 151283   2015 $150

Bradbury, Ray *The Anthem Sprinters and Other Antics.* New York: Dial Press, 1963. First edition, octavo, cloth.   L. W. Currey, Inc.   Featured Author: Ray Bradbury (Oct. 2014) - 112192   2015 $450

Bradbury, Ray *The Collected Stories of Ray Bradbury: a Critical Edition Volume I: 1938-1943.* Kent: Kent State University Press, 2010. First edition, cloth, octavo.   L. W. Currey, Inc.   Featured Author: Ray Bradbury (Oct. 2014) - 139259   2015 $65

Bradbury, Ray *Dandelion Wine.* Garden City: Doubleday & Co., 1957. First edition, octavo, cloth.   L. W. Currey, Inc.   Featured Author: Ray Bradbury (Oct. 2014) - 140685   2015 $1750

Bradbury, Ray *Dandelion Wine.* London: Rupert Hart Davis, 1957. First edition, octavo, boards.   L. W. Currey, Inc.   Featured Author: Ray Bradbury (Oct. 2014) - 150288   2015 $850

Bradbury, Ray *Dark Carnival.* Sauk City: Arkham House, 1947. First edition, octavo, cloth.   L. W. Currey, Inc.   Featured Author: Ray Bradbury (Oct. 2014) - 1530834   2015 $6500

Bradbury, Ray *Dark Carnival.* London: Hamish Hamilton, 1948. First British edition, octavo, cloth.   L. W. Currey, Inc.   Featured Author: Ray Bradbury (Oct. 2014) - 140687   2015 $850

Bradbury, Ray *Dark Carnival.* New York: Ballantine Books, 1953. First edition, octavo, red boards, front and spine panels stamped in yellow.   L. W. Currey, Inc.   Featured Author: Ray Bradbury (Oct. 2014) - 149056   2015 $6500

Bradbury, Ray *Dark Carnival.* Springfield: Gauntlet Publications, 2001. Limited edition, octavo, imitation leather.   L. W. Currey, Inc.   Featured Author: Ray Bradbury (Oct. 2014) - 127869   2015 $750

Bradbury, Ray *The Day It Rained Forever.* London: Rupert Hart-Davis, 1959. First edition, presumed first binding, blue boards, spine panel stamped in silver.   L. W. Currey, Inc.   Featured Author: Ray Bradbury (Oct. 2014) - 151276   2015 $2000

Bradbury, Ray *Death is a Lonely Business.* New York: Alfred A. Knopf, 1985. First trade edition, first printing, octavo, cloth backed boards.   L. W. Currey, Inc.   Featured Author: Ray Bradbury (Oct. 2014) - 759   2015 $45

Bradbury, Ray *Death is a Lonely Business.* New York: Alfred A. Knopf, 1985. First trade edition, octavo, full black cloth, front and spine panels stamped in gold, all edges gilt.   L. W. Currey, Inc.   Featured Author: Ray Bradbury (Oct. 2014) - 89130   2015 $350

Bradbury, Ray *The Dragon.* Round Top: Bill Munster Publisher, 1988. First separate edition, small octavo, illustrations by Ken Snyder, pictorial wrappers.   L. W. Currey, Inc.   Featured Author: Ray Bradbury (Oct. 2014) - 151278   2015 $100

Bradbury, Ray *Fahrenheit 451.* New York: Ballantine Books, 1953. First edition, octavo, white asbestos boards.   L. W. Currey, Inc.   Featured Author: Ray Bradbury (Oct. 2014) - 151231   2015 $22,500

Bradbury, Ray *Fahrenheit 451.* New York: Ballantine Books, 1953. First edition, octavo, red boards, front and spine panels stamped in yellow, hardboard trade issue, Currey binding D (no priority).   John W. Knott, Bookseller Selected New Arrivals Jan. 2015 - 16931   2015 $7500

Bradbury, Ray *Fahrenheit 451.* New York: Ballantine Books, 1953. First edition, octavo, red boards, front and spine panels stamped in yellow.   L. W. Currey, Inc.   Featured Author: Ray Bradbury (Oct. 2014) - 111876   2015 $10,000

Bradbury, Ray *Fahrenheit 451.* New York: LEC, 1982. First edition thus, limited to 2000 copies, this no. 1497, monthly letter laid in, color illustrations by Joseph Mugnaini, tall 8vo., full aluminum foil binding, silk screened in black and white and scarlet, silver paper slipcase, title printed in black to spine, mild wear to binding, slight rubbing and soiling to slipcase, very good + in very good slipcase, title printed in black to spine, mild wear to binding, slight rubbing and soiling to slipcase, title printed in black to spine, mild wear to binding. slight rubbing and soiling to slipcase, very good+ in very good slipcase, monthly letter laid.   Tavistock Books Bah, Humbug? - 29   2015 $500

Bradbury, Ray *Futuria Fantasia Summer 1939. Volume 1 Number 1.* Los Angeles: Ray Bradbury Summer, 1939. Large octavo, single issue, mimeographed, pictorial self wrappers, stapled.   L. W. Currey, Inc.   Featured Author: Ray Bradbury (Oct. 2014) - 129094   2015 $1250

Bradbury, Ray *The Golden Apples of the Sun.* Garden City: Doubleday & Co. Inc., 1953. First edition, octavo, boards.   L. W. Currey, Inc.   Featured Author: Ray Bradbury (Oct. 2014) - 89132   2015 $1250

Bradbury, Ray *The Golden Apples of the Sun.* Garden City: Doubleday & Co, 1953. First edition, octavo, cloth.   L. W. Currey, Inc.   Featured Author: Ray Bradbury (Oct. 2014) - 81884 2015 $850

Bradbury, Ray *The Golden Apples of the Sun.* Garden City: Doubleday and Co., 1953. First edition, octavo, jacket and interior illustrations by Joe Mugnaini, boards, signed by author and artist.   John W. Knott, Bookseller   Selected New Arrivals Jan. 2015 - 16930   2015 $1500

Bradbury, Ray *A Graveyard for Lunatics.* New York: Alfred A. Knopf, 1990. Advance copy, uncorrected proof, of the first edition, octavo, printed light blue wrappers.   L. W. Currey, Inc.   Featured Author: Ray Bradbury (Oct. 2014) - 112196   2015 $45

Bradbury, Ray *I Sing the Body Electric! Stories.* New York: Alfred A. Knopf, 1969. First edition, octavo, cloth.   L. W. Currey, Inc.   Featured Author: Ray Bradbury (Oct. 2014) - 140690   2015 $150

Bradbury, Ray *The Illustrated Man.* Garden City: Doubleday and Co., 1951. First edition, octavo, cloth.   L. W. Currey, Inc.   Featured Author: Ray Bradbury (Oct. 2014) - 148487   2015 $1000

Bradbury, Ray *The Illustrated Man.* London: Rupert Hart-Davis, 1952. First British edition, octavo, boards.   L. W. Currey, Inc.   Featured Author: Ray Bradbury (Oct. 2014) - 148489   2015 $1000

Bradbury, Ray *The Last Circus and Electrocution.* Northridge: Lord John Press, 1980. First edition, octavo, cloth.   L. W. Currey, Inc.   Featured Author: Ray Bradbury (Oct. 2014) - 140693   2015 $100

Bradbury, Ray *Long After Midnight.* New York: Alfred A. Knopf, 1976. First edition, octavo, cloth backed boards.   L. W. Currey, Inc.   Featured Author: Ray Bradbury (Oct. 2014) - 140694   2015 $100

Bradbury, Ray *Long After Midnight.* New York: Knopf, 1976. First edition, fine in dust jacket with crease tear on back panel.   Mordida Books   March 2015 - 011489   2015 $125

Bradbury, Ray *Long After Midnight.* London: Hart-Davis, MacGibbon, 1977. First British edition, octavo, boards.   L. W. Currey, Inc.   Featured Author: Ray Bradbury (Oct. 2014) - 112201   2015 $100

Bradbury, Ray *The Love Affair; A Short Story and Two Poems.* Northridge: Lord John Press, 1982. First edition, octavo, cloth, green skivertex shelf back.   L. W. Currey, Inc.   Featured Author: Ray Bradbury (Oct. 2014) - 140695   2015 $75

Bradbury, Ray *The Machineries of Joy: Short Stories.* London: Rupert Hart Davis, 1964. First British edition, octavo, boards.   L. W. Currey, Inc.   Featured Author: Ray Bradbury (Oct. 2014) - 140697   2015 $100

Bradbury, Ray *The Machineries of Joy: Short Stories.* New York: Simon & Schuster, 1964. First edition, octavo, cloth backed boards.   L. W. Currey, Inc.   Featured Author: Ray Bradbury (Oct. 2014) - 89139   2015 $300

Bradbury, Ray *The Martian Chronicles.* Garden City: Doubleday & Co., 1950. First edition, octavo, cloth.   L. W. Currey, Inc.   Featured Author: Ray Bradbury (Oct. 2014) - 148490   2015 $2500

Bradbury, Ray *The Martian Chronicles.* New York: Time Incorporated, 1963. First printing of this edition, octavo, pictorial wrappers.   L. W. Currey, Inc.   Featured Author: Ray Bradbury (Oct. 2014) - 64   2015 $140278

Bradbury, Ray *The Martian Chronicles.* Avon: Limited Editions Club, 1974. limited to 2000 numbered copies, signed by author and artist, illustrations by Joseph Mugnaini, with monthly letter loosely inserted, well preserved, tall 8vo., cloth, slipcase.   Oak Knoll Books   25 - 45   2015 $275

Bradbury, Ray *A Medicine of Melancholy.* Garden City: Doubleday & Co., 1959. First edition, octavo, cloth.   L. W. Currey, Inc.   Featured Author: Ray Bradbury (Oct. 2014) - 150465   2015 $250

Bradbury, Ray *No Man is an Island.* Beverly Hills: National Women's Committee of Brandeis University, Los Angeles Area Chapter, 1952. First edition, small octavo, printed wrappers.   L. W. Currey, Inc.   Featured Author: Ray Bradbury (Oct. 2014) - 151281   2015 $350

Bradbury, Ray *The October Country.* New York: Ballantine Books, 1955. First edition, probable earliest state of hardcover trade binding with publisher's monogram stamped upside down on spine panel, Currey Binding B1.   L. W. Currey, Inc.   Featured Author: Ray Bradbury (Oct. 2014) - 111877   2015 $3500

Bradbury, Ray *The October Country.* New York: Ballantine Books, 1955. First edition, probable second state of hardcover trade binding with publisher's monogram stamped correctly on spine panel, Currey binding B2.   L. W. Currey, Inc.   Featured Author: Ray Bradbury (Oct. 2014) - 127887   2015 $2500

Bradbury, Ray *Old Ahab's Friend and Friend to Noah, Speaks His Piece: a Celebration.* Glendale: Roy A. Squires, Apollo Year Two, i.e., 1971. First edition, octavo, printed wrappers. L. W. Currey, Inc. Featured Author: Ray Bradbury (Oct. 2014) - 151284   2015 $100

Bradbury, Ray *R is for Rocket.* Garden City: Doubleday & Co., 1962. First edition, octavo, boards. L. W. Currey, Inc. Featured Author: Ray Bradbury (Oct. 2014) - 150442   2015 $650

Bradbury, Ray *R is for Rocket.* Garden City: Doubleday and Co., 1962. First edition, octavo, boards. L. W. Currey, Inc. Featured Author: Ray Bradbury (Oct. 2014) - 140702   2015 $450

Bradbury, Ray *S is for Space.* Garden City: Doubleday & Co. Inc., 1966. First edition, octavo, cloth. L. W. Currey, Inc. Featured Author: Ray Bradbury (Oct. 2014) - 150582   2015 $450

Bradbury, Ray *The Silver Locusts.* London: Rupert Hart Davis, 1951. First British edition, octavo, boards. L. W. Currey, Inc. Featured Author: Ray Bradbury (Oct. 2014) - 140699   2015 $750

Bradbury, Ray *Something Wicked This Way Comes.* New York: Simon & Schuster, 1962. First edition, octavo, cloth. L. W. Currey, Inc. Featured Author: Ray Bradbury (Oct. 2014) - 150100   2015 $750

Bradbury, Ray *Something Wicked This Way Comes.* New York: Simon and Schuster, 1962. First edition, octavo, cloth. John W. Knott, Bookseller   Selected New Arrivals Jan. 2015 - 16932   2015 $1500

Bradbury, Ray *The Stories of Ray Bradbury.* New York: Alfred A. Knopf, 1980. First edition, octavo, decorated black cloth stamped in blind, top edge gilt. L. W. Currey, Inc. Featured Author: Ray Bradbury (Oct. 2014) - 140707   2015 $750

Bradbury, Ray *The Stories of Ray Bradbury.* New York: Alfred A. Knopf, 1980. First edition, octavo, cloth. L. W. Currey, Inc. Featured Author: Ray Bradbury (Oct. 2014) - 128593   2015 $85

Bradbury, Ray *The Stories of Ray Bradbury.* New York: Knopf, 1980. First edition, large 8vo., fine in fine dust jacket, signed by author. Beasley Books   2013 - 2015 $200

Bradbury, Ray *Sun and Shadow.* Berkeley: Quenian Press, 1957. First separate edition, small octavo, decorated wrappers, sewn. L. W. Currey, Inc. Featured Author: Ray Bradbury (Oct. 2014) - 151280   2015 $850

Bradbury, Ray *Switch on the Night.* New York: Pantheon Books, 1955. First edition, first printing, octavo, illustrations by Madeleine Gekiere, gray pictorial boards. L. W. Currey, Inc. Featured Author: Ray Bradbury (Oct. 2014) - 103485   2015 $450

Bradbury, Ray *That Son of Richard III: a Birth Announcement.* Glendale: Roy A. Squires, 1974. Octavo, printed wrappers, sewn with marbled paper overlay. L. W. Currey, Inc. Featured Author: Ray Bradbury (Oct. 2014) - 141586   2015 $250

Bradbury, Ray *That Ghost, that Bride of Time: Excerpts from a Play-in-Progress...* Glendale: Roy A. Squires, March, 1976. First edition, octavo, printed wrappers with unprinted paper overlay. L. W. Currey, Inc. Featured Author: Ray Bradbury (Oct. 2014) - 139168   2015 $250

Bradbury, Ray *The Toynbee Convector: Stories.* New York: Alfred A. Knopf, 1988. First edition, octavo, cloth backed marbled boards. L. W. Currey, Inc. Featured Author: Ray Bradbury (Oct. 2014) - 140709   2015 $150

Bradbury, Ray *The Toynbee Convector: Stories.* New York: Alfred A. Knopf, 1988. First edition, octavo, cloth backed boards. L. W. Currey, Inc. Featured Author: Ray Bradbury (Oct. 2014) - 140710   2015 $75

Bradbury, Ray *Twice Twenty-Two; The Golden Apples of the Sun. (and) A Medicine for Melancholy.* Garden City: Doubleday & Co., 1966. First edition, octavo, cloth. L. W. Currey, Inc. Featured Author: Ray Bradbury (Oct. 2014) - 127876   2015 $450

Bradbury, Ray *Twin Hieroglyphs that Swim the River Dust.* Northridge: Lord John Press, 1978. First edition, octavo, cloth backed boards, printed paper label affixed to front panel. L. W. Currey, Inc. Featured Author: Ray Bradbury (Oct. 2014) - 149842   2015 $75

Bradbury, Ray *The Wonderful Ice Cream Suit and Other Plays for Today, Tomorrow and Beyond Tomorrow.* London: Hart-Davis, MacGibbon, 1972. First British (and first hardcover) edition, octavo, boards. L. W. Currey, Inc. Featured Author: Ray Bradbury (Oct. 2014) - 112226   2015 $150

Braddon, Mary Elizabeth *Phantom Fortune.* London: John & Robert Maxwell, 1883. First edition, 3 volumes, original green cloth, spines lettered gilt, slight rubbing and marking with some minor expert repairs, good plus. Jarndyce Antiquarian Booksellers   CCXI - 36   2015   £380

Bradley, Lonnie *Off the Battlefield of War on the Battlefield of Destitution.* 1944. First edition, signed by author, wrappers, very good. Beasley Books   2013 - 2015 $45

Bradley, Richard *A Philosophical Account of the Works of Nature Endeavouring to Set Forth the Several Graduations Remarkable in the Mineral, Vegetable and Animal parts of the Creation.* London: W. Mears, 1721. Quarto, 28 hand colored engraved plates, contemporary full calf and maroon leather label, some wear and corners bumped, all edges colored, sound.   Andrew Isles   2015 - 23992   2015 $2850

Bradley, Will *Wonder Box Stories.* New York: Century, Oct., 1916. First edition, 8vo., decorative cloth, 154 pages, some soil on rear cover, very good+, many full and partial page illustrations.   Aleph-bet Books, Inc.   109 - 69   2015 $700

Brady, Buckskin *Stories and Sermons.* Toronto: William Briggs, 1905. First edition, 8vo., maroon cloth, portrait label of cowboy affixed to front cover, frontispiece, plates, portraits, 19.8 cm., scarce minor wear to spine ends, else fine, rare.   Buckingham Books   March 2015 - 26865 2015 $1875

Braeme, Charlotte M. *The Coquette's Victim. Coralie. The Tragedy of the Chair Pier. My Mother's Rival. Marion Arleigh's Penance.* Chicago: Everyday Life, n.d., 5 pamphlets, wrappers, each about 30 pages, 8vo., each very good.   Beasley Books   2013 - 2015 $45

Brain, Walter Russell, Baron *Some Reflections on Genius and Other Essays.* London: Pitman Medical Pub., 1960. Original purple cloth, illustrations by Norman Smith, half title, very good in slightly spotted dust jacket, from the library of Geoffrey & Kathleen Tillotson, Geoffrey's gift to Kathleen, with AL from Geoffery congratulating Brain on his peerage and Brain's ALS in reply.   Jarndyce Antiquarian Booksellers   CCVII - 96   2015   £20

Brainard, Joe *The Banana Book.* New York: Siamese Banana Press, 1972. First edition, 4to., illustrations by author, original wrappers, covers little darkened, otherwise fine, inscribed by author for Burt Britton.   James S. Jaffe Rare Books   Many Happy Returns - 95   2015 $500

Brainard, Joe *Bolinas Journal.* Bolinas: Big Sky Books, 1971. First edition, one of 300 copies, 4to., illustrations by author, original patterned wrappers stapled as issued, fine, inscribed by author to Burt Britton.   James S. Jaffe Rare Books   Many Happy Returns - 88   2015 $250

Brainard, Joe *Bolinas Journal.* Bolinas: Big Sky Books, 1971. First edition, one of 26 lettered copies signed by author (out of a total edition of 326), 4to., illustrations by author, original patterned wrappers, stapled as issued, fine.   James S. Jaffe Rare Books   Many Happy Returns - 89   2015 $750

Brainard, Joe *Brainard-Freeman Notebooks.* New York: Gegenschein Quarterly, 1975. First edition, 4to. original illustrated wrappers, covers lightly sunned, otherwise fine.   James S. Jaffe Rare Books   Many Happy Returns - 255   2015 $125

Brainard, Joe *C Comics No. 1-2.* New York: Lorenz Gude, 1964-1965. First editions, 2 volumes, 4to., original pictorial wrappers, covers and edges lightly foxed, staples bit rusted, otherwise fine.   James S. Jaffe Rare Books   Many Happy Returns - 379   2015 $3000

Brainard, Joe *The Cigarette Book.* New York: Siamese Banana Press, 1972. First edition, 4to., illustrations by author, original illustrated wrappers by author, stapled as issued, inscribed by author for Burt Britton, fine.   James S. Jaffe Rare Books   Many Happy Returns - 96   2015 $450

Brainard, Joe *The Cigarette Book.* New York: Siamese Banana Press, 1972. First edition, special issue, one of 26 lettered copies signed by author (out of an unspecified total edition), 4to., illustrations and original illustrated wrappers by author, stapled as issued, fine.   James S. Jaffe Rare Books   Many Happy Returns - 97   2015 $750

Brainard, Joe *Flesh Game.* N.P.: n.p., n.d., First edition of this booklet, 4to., illustrations by Brainard, original wrappers, fine.   James S. Jaffe Rare Books   Many Happy Returns - 228   2015 $150

Brainard, Joe *The Friendly Way.* New York: Siamese Banana Press, 1972. First edition, regular issue, 4to., original illustrated wrappers, cover design by author, stapled as issued, light soiling, but very good, scarce.   James S. Jaffe Rare Books   Many Happy Returns - 100   2015 $250

Brainard, Joe *The Friendly Way.* New York: Siamese Banana Press, 1972. First edition, special issue, one of 26 lettered copies, signed by author (of an unspecified edition), 4to., original illustrated wrappers with cover design by author, stapled as issued, fine.   James S. Jaffe Rare Books   Many Happy Returns - 102   2015 $750

Brainard, Joe *The Friendly Way.* New York: Siamese Banana Press, 1972. First edition, regular issue, signed by author, original illustrated wrappers with cover design by author, stapled as issued, signed by author, light soiling and foxing to covers, very good.   James S. Jaffe Rare Books   Many Happy Returns - 101   2015 $500

Brainard, Joe *I Remember.* New York: Angel Hair Books, 1970. First edition, one of 26 lettered copies signed by author, small 4to., original wrappers, covers little dust soiled, otherwise fine.   James S. Jaffe Rare Books   Many Happy Returns - 87   2015 $1250

Brainard, Joe *I Remember.* New York: Angel Hair Books, 1970. First edition, limited to 700 copies, small 4to., original wrappers, fine, inscribed by author for Burt Britton. James S. Jaffe Rare Books   Many Happy Returns - 86   2015 $450

Brainard, Joe *I Remember.* New York: Angel Hair Books, 1970. First edition, small 4to., original wrappers, presentation inscribed by Brainard to artist Nell Blaine, fine. James S. Jaffe Rare Books   Many Happy Returns - 85   2015 $1000

Brainard, Joe *I Remember.* New York: Full Court Press, 1975. First edition, simultaneous paperback issue, 8vo., original wrappers, signed by author, fine. James S. Jaffe Rare Books   Many Happy Returns - 111   2015 $150

Brainard, Joe *I Remember.* New York: Full Court Press, 1975. First edition fo the expanded version, one of only 100 copies signed by author, 8vo., original cloth, fine in dust jacket. James S. Jaffe Rare Books   Many Happy Returns - 112   2015 $350

Brainard, Joe *I Remember Joe.* New York: Full Court Press, 1975. First edition, 8vo., original cloth, fine, dust jacket, inscribed by author for Burt (Britton). James S. Jaffe Rare Books   Many Happy Returns - 110   2015 $250

Brainard, Joe *I Remember Christmas.* New York: Museum of Modern Art, 1973. First edition, 8vo., illustrations and original pictorial wrappers by Brainard, inscribed by author for Burt Britton, fine. James S. Jaffe Rare Books   Many Happy Returns - 104   2015 $650

Brainard, Joe *I Remember Christmas.* New York: Museum of Modern Art, 1973. First edition, 8vo., illustrations and original pictorial wrappers by author, fine. James S. Jaffe Rare Books   Many Happy Returns - 103   2015 $150

Brainard, Joe *I Remember More.* New York: Angel Hair Books, 1972. First edition, one of 26 lettered copies, signed by author, small 4to., original wrappers, small 4to.. original wrappers, covers little age darkened, otherwise fine. James S. Jaffe Rare Books   Many Happy Returns - 99   2015 $750

Brainard, Joe *I Remember More.* New York: Angel Hair Books, 1972. First edition, one of 800 copies, small 4to., original wrappers, inscribed by author for Burt Britton, covers little age darkened, otherwise fine. James S. Jaffe Rare Books   Many Happy Returns - 98   2015 $450

Brainard, Joe *Joe Brainard, Retrospective March 20-April 19 1997.* New York: Tibor de Nagy Gallery, 1997. First edition, 4to., illustrations, original pictorial wrappers, fine. James S. Jaffe Rare Books   Many Happy Returns - 123   2015 $50

Brainard, Joe *Little Caesar Magazine #6.* Los Angeles: Little Caesar Magazine, 1978. First edition, 8vo., original pictorial wrappers, covers bit soiled and discolored, otherwise very good. James S. Jaffe Rare Books   Many Happy Returns - 380   2015 $250

Brainard, Joe *More I Remember More.* New York: Angel Hair Books, 1973. First edition, one of 700 copies, small 4to., original wrappers, spine little tanned, otherwise fine, inscribed by author for Burt Britton. James S. Jaffe Rare Books   Many Happy Returns - 105   2015 $450

Brainard, Joe *The Nancy Book.* Los Angeles: Siglio Press, 2008. First edition, 4to., illustrated, original pictorial boards, as new. James S. Jaffe Rare Books   Many Happy Returns - 120   2015 $50

Brainard, Joe *The Nancy Book.* Los Angeles: Siglio Press, 2008. First edition, limited to 100 numbered copies including a hand pulled photo litho (6 1/2 x 9 1/4 inches of an original mixed media collage by Brainard, c. 1964, stamped by the Estate of Brainard, intialled by publisher and accompanied by a certificate of authenticity, print housed in foil stamped portfolio and slipcase with trade edition of the book. James S. Jaffe Rare Books   Many Happy Returns - 121   2015 $500

Brainard, Joe *New Work.* Los Angeles: Black Sparrow Press, 1973. First edition, one of 200 hardcover numbered copies signed by author, 8vo., original cloth backed boards, covers slightly foxed, otherwise fine. James S. Jaffe Rare Books   Many Happy Returns - 109   2015 $150

Brainard, Joe *New Work.* Los Angeles: Black Sparrow Press, 1973. First edition, one of 1000 copies, paperback issue, original wrappers, 8vo., review copy with publisher's slip laid in, covers lightly foxed, otherwise fine. James S. Jaffe Rare Books   Many Happy Returns - 107   2015 $75

Brainard, Joe *New Work.* Los Angeles: Black Sparrow Press, 1973. First edition, one of 26 lettered copies signed by author with original drawing by author in envelope tipped-in, fine. James S. Jaffe Rare Books   Many Happy Returns - 108   2015 $1500

Brainard, Joe *New Work.* Los Angeles: Black Sparrow Press, 1973. First edition, 8vo., original wrappers, review copy with publisher's slip laid in, fine, inscribed for Burt (Britton). James S. Jaffe Rare Books   Many Happy Returns - 106   2015 $250

Brainard, Joe *Nothing to Write Home About.* Los Angeles: Little Caesar Press, 1981. First edition, fine, scarce, 8vo., original pictorial wrappers. James S. Jaffe Rare Books   Many Happy Returns - 117   2015 $750

Brainard, Joe *Reading at the Poetry Project: Flyers by Joe Brainard.* New York: Boke Press, 1997. First edition, one of 250 numbered sets, reproducing 15 flyers, 4to., 19 loose sheets in printed paper envelope, fine.   James S. Jaffe Rare Books   Many Happy Returns - 119   2015 $150

Brainard, Joe *Recent Visitors.* N.P.: Best & Co./Boke Press, 1971. first edition of these comic strips, 4to., illustrations by Brainard, loose sheets with original pictorial cover, stapled as issued, covers lightly soiled at margins, otherwise fine, surprisingly scarce.   James S. Jaffe Rare Books   Many Happy Returns - 228   2015 $250

Brainard, Joe *The Sand Burg. Poems by Thomas Clark.* London: Ferry Press, 1966. First edition, limited to 500 copies, 4to., original wrappers, cover by Joe Brainard, fine. James S. Jaffe Rare Books   Many Happy Returns - 230   2015 $50

Brainard, Joe *Selected Writings 1962-1971.* New York: Kulchur Foundation, 1971. First edition, small 4to., original wrappers, review copy with publisher's slip laid in, inscribed by author for Burt Britton, fine.   James S. Jaffe Rare Books Many Happy Returns - 90   2015 $350

Brainard, Joe *Selected Writings 1962-1971.* New York: Kulchur Foundation, 1971. First edition, hardcover issue, small 4to., original boards, acetate dust jacket, boards slightly bowed, touch of wear at corners, otherwise very fine, very scarce, especially in this condition.   James S. Jaffe Rare Books   Many Happy Returns - 91   2015 $750

Brainard, Joe *Selections from the Butts Collection at UCSD Feb. 19-March 22, 1987.* La Jolla: Mandeville Gallery of University of California, San Diego, 1987. Square 8vo., illustrations, original wrappers, fine exhibition copy.   James S. Jaffe Rare Books   Many Happy Returns - 122   2015 $75

Brainard, Joe *Self Portrait.* New York: Siamese Banana Press, 1972. First edition, 4to., self portraits, original wrappers, fine.   James S. Jaffe Rare Books   Many Happy Returns - 261   2015 $150

Brainard, Joe *Self Portrait.* New York: Siamese Banana Press, 1972. First edition, 4to., original wrappers, fine, signed by Anne Waldman and inscribed by Brainard for Burt Britton.   James S. Jaffe Rare Books   Many Happy Returns - 262   2015 $350

Brainard, Joe *Some Drawings of Some Notes to Myself.* New York: Siamese Banna Press, 1971. First edition, 4to., original printed wrappers, stapled as issued, although not called for signed by author, covers lightly dust soiled, otherwise fine.   James S. Jaffe Rare Books   Many Happy Returns - 92   2015 $225

Brainard, Joe *Some Drawings of Some Notes to Myself.* New York: Siamese Banana Press, 1972. First edition, one of 26 lettered copies signed by author, 4to., original wrappers, fine.   James S. Jaffe Rare Books   Many Happy Returns - 93   2015 $750

Brainard, Joe *Ten Imaginary Still Lifes.* New York: Boke Press, 1997. First edition, one of 1000 copies, 12mo., frontispiece by author, wrappers, fine.   James S. Jaffe Rare Books   Many Happy Returns - 118   2015 $250

Brainard, Joe *Twelve Postcards.* Calais: Z Press, 1975. First edition, one fo 26 lettered copies signed by author, 16mo., 12 illustrated postcards, original mailing envelope, fine.   James S. Jaffe Rare Books   Many Happy Returns - 114   2015 $450

Brainard, Joe *29 Mini-Essays.* Calais: Z Press, 1978. First edition, one of 50 copies signed by author from a total edition of 500, oblong 16mo., original wrappers, fine. James S. Jaffe Rare Books   Many Happy Returns - 116   2015 $250

Brainard, Joe *29 Mini-Essays.* Calais: Z Press, 1978. First edition, one of 500 numbered copies, oblong 16mo., original wrappers, inscribed by author for Burt (Britton), covers slightly sunned, otherwise fine.   James S. Jaffe Rare Books   Many Happy Returns - 115   2015 $250

Brainard, Joe *Twelve Postcards.* Calais: Z Press, 1975. First edition, 16mo., 12 illustrated postcards, original mailing envelope.   James S. Jaffe Rare Books   Many Happy Returns - 113   2015 $75

Branch, E. Douglas *The Hunting of the Buffalo.* D. Appleton and Co., 1929. First edition, 8vo., cloth, decorated paper labels on front cover and spine, frontispiece, illustrations, former owner's neat bookplate, else fine, tight, bright copy in elusive dust jacket with light wear to head of spine, exceptional copy.   Buckingham Books   March 2015 - 33524   2015 $250

Brand, Christianna *The Crooked Wreath.* New York: Dodd Mead, 1946. First edition, fine in dust jacket with couple of short closed tears and tiny wear at spine ends and at corners.   Mordida Books   March 2015 - 007664   2015 $165

Brand, Christianna *The Rose in Darkness.* London: Michael Joseph, 1979. First edition, fine in dust jacket with some spotting on inner flaps. Mordida Books March 2015 - 002375 2015 $75

Brand, Christianna *The Three Cornered Halo.* London: Michael Joseph, 1957. First edition, full page inscription by author, fine in dust jacket with light wear to spine ends and extremities. Buckingham Books March 2015 - 20457 2015 $275

Brand, Max *Call of the Blood.* New York: Macaulay, 1934. First edition, very good in dust jacket with chipping at spine ends and at corners, several closed tears and some spine fading. Mordida Books March 2015 - 002376 2015 $125

Brand, Max *The Happy Valley.* Dodd Mead & Co., 1931. First edition, 8vo., fine, bright square copy in lovely fine dust jacket. Buckingham Books March 2015 - 37934 2015 $450

Brand, Max *The Killers.* New York: Macaulay, 1931. First edition, fine in very good dust jacket with faded spine and several short closed tears. Mordida Books March 2015 - 000041 2015 $325

Brand, Max *Red Devil of the Range.* New York: Macaulay, 1934. First edition, some staining on front cover, otherwise very good in dust jacket with chips at corners and several short closed tears. Mordida Books March 2015 - 000042 2015 $250

Brand, Max *Timbal Gutch Trail.* New York: Dodd Mead, 1934. First edition, fine in dust jacket with several short closed tears and nicks at corners. Mordida Books March 2015 - 005215 2015 $450

Brand, Max *Valley Thieves.* New York: Dodd Mead, 1946. First edition, fine in dust jacket. Mordida Books March 2015 - 0065509 2015 $250

Brandelius, Jerilyn Lee *Grateful Dead Family Album.* New York: Warner Books, 1989. First edition, 'Grateful Dead All Area Access sticker laid down to jacket, this copy signed by band members Jerry Garcia, Mickey Hart and Bob Bralove as well as long time road crew members Ram Rod Shurtliff, Bill 'Kid' Candelario, Steve Parish and Robbie Taylor among others, hundreds of intimate photos and stories, very good plus to near fine with little soil and handling marks, in very good plus to near fine dust jacket with short closed tear to bottom of front flap. Ed Smith Books 83 - 34 2015 $950

Brandt, Bill *Behind the Camera, Photographs 1928-1983.* New York: Aperture, 1985. First edition, 4to., fine in fine dust jacket. Beasley Books 2013 - 2015 $45

Brandt, Bill *The English at Home - Sixty-Three Photographs.* London: B. T. Batsford, 1936. First edition, pictorial boards, 63 photos, some rubbing and flaking but with lettering almost all intact, corners bit bumped, very good. Peter Ellis, Bookseller 2014 - 020153 2015 £325

Branen, Jeff *Denison's Minstrel Opening Choruses and Finales/Plantation.* Chicago: T. S. Denison, 1922. First edition, wrappers, near fine. Beasley Books 2013 - 2015 $45

Brannon, George *Brannon's Picture of the Isle of Wight: or, The Expeditious Traveller's Index to Its Prominent Beauties and Objects of Interest.* Wooton, Isle of Wight: George Brannon, 1844. First edition, 8vo., half red leather lettered gilt at spine, frontispiece, 20 engravings, spine and marbled little rubbed, endpapers slightly marked, neat name on front endpaper "Wm. Somerton Lowe, Grenoble House Nelson St. Ryde", plates slightly foxed, folding map dated 1844 in good shape, overall sound, very good. Any Amount of Books 2015 - A35754 2015 £150

Brassai *The Artists of My Life.* New York: Wilken Berley Ltd., 1982. First edition, large 4to., full page reproductions of photos of artists at work, pictorial patterned paper covered boards over cloth lettered silver at spine, special presentation folder housing photogravure, deluxe edition, this number 11 of 150 copies signed and numbered by Brassai, issued with hand pulled dust grained 'photogravure 21 x 15.9cm' also signed by Brassai, book in special binding designed by Sage Reynolds and executed at the Four Hands Bindery, fine in plain buff very good slipcase. Any Amount of Books 2015 - A68259 2015 £750

Bratt, John *Trails of Yesterday.* University of Publishing Co., 1921. First edition, pictorial cloth, top edge gilt, frontispiece, drawings, photos, fine, bright, tight, unread copy housed in clamshell case with design on front panel and spine matching the book, exceptional copy. Buckingham Books March 2015 - 29731 2015 $750

Braun-Fock, Beatrice *Die Puppe Pimpernell.* Munchen: Schreiber, n.d. circa, 1940. 4to., pictorial boards, paper slightly aging, else fine, illustrations in color by Braun-Fock. Aleph-Bet Books, Inc. 108 - 206 2015 $225

Brautigan, Richard *A Confederate General from Big Sur.* New York: Grove Press, 1964. First edition, signed by author with drawing of a trout and dated Sept. 11 1966, slight offsetting to endpages and little bit of foxing to top edge, near fine in near fine dust jacket with some top edge creasing to rear panel. Ken Lopez, Bookseller 164 - 19 2015 $2500

Brautigan, Richard *Dreaming of Babylon.* New York: Delacorte, 1977. First edition, very fine in dust jacket. Mordida Books March 2015 - 011402 2015 $100

Brautigan, Richard *Rommel Drives on Deep into Egypt Poems.* New York: Seymour Lawrence/Delacorte Press, 1970. First edition, signed by author on front endpaper and underneath his signature he has added date May 2 1970, fine in photo illustrated cloth in which would be near fine bright jacket except for small chip to top of spine.   Ed Smith Books   82 - 5   2015 $450

Brautigan, Richard *Trout Fishing in America, The Pill Versus The Springhill Mine Disaster and In Watermelon Sugar.* New York: Seymour Lawrence/Delacorte Press, 1972. Fifth printing of this edition, signed by author, from the estate of Beef Torrey, friend of author, near fine in very good plus dust jacket (price clipped).   Ed Smith Books   82 - 6   2015 $300

Brautigan, Richard *Willard and His Bowling Trophies.* New York: Simon & Schuster, 1975. First edition, very fine in dust jacket.   Mordida Books   March 2015 - 011401   2015 $100

The Brave Little Tailor. London: Raphael Tuck, n.d. circa, 1900. 2 x 3 1/2 inches, very good- fine, opening accordion style, 6 chromolithographed panels with die-cut openings, lovely.   Aleph-Bet Books, Inc.   108 - 174   2015 $150

Bravo, Manuel Alvarez *100 Years, 100 days.* Madrid: Turner Publications SI, 2001. First edition, 1/1000 copies, folio, fine in fine dust jacket.   Beasley Books   2013 - 2015 $200

Braybrooke, Neville *The Idler.* London: Secker & Warburg, 1961. Paperclip mark to first few pages, else fine in very good, spine tanned dust jacket, inscribed by author to Richard Lattimore.   Between the Covers Rare Books, Inc.   187 - 32   2015 $40

Brayer, Yves *Yvves Brayer.* Paris: Galerie Romanent/ Librairie Fischbacher, First edition, no. 221 of 500 (of an edition of 2500 copies), wrappers, dust jacket, fine in fine dust jacket, 4to., 30 illustrations, many in color and tipped in, romanet imprint is cancelled on titlepage with pasted over sticker from Librairie Fischbavcher and there is also a piece of blank black tape on rear wrapper, presumably cancelling another mention of Galerie Romanent.   Beasley Books   2013 - 2015 $350

Brayley, Edward Wedlake   1773-1854 *Historical and Descriptive Accounts of the Theatres of London...* London: printed for J. Taylor, Architectural Library, High Holborn, 1826. First edition, original colored issue, 4to., hand colored aquatint plates, 2 plans, final leaf with marginal tear, minor spotting in places, uncut in original grey boards, skillfully rebacked.   Marlborough Rare Books   List 53 - 3   2015   £4250

Bready, Charles J. *Red Alley.* Cedar Rapids: Torch Press, 1938. First edition, near fine in very good++ dust jacket with few tiny tears.   Beasley Books   2013 - 2015 $45

Breckinridge, Sophonisba *Madeline McDowell Breckinridge.* Chicago: University of Chicago Press, 1921. First edition, 8vo., very good, little worn at extremities of spine, else very good, tight copy.   Second Life Books Inc.   189 - 32   2015 $75

Bredero, Gebrand Adriaensz *Boertigh Amoreus en Aendachtigh Groot Lied-boeck.* Amsterdam: Cornelis Lodowijcksz vander Plasse, 1622. First collected edition, 3 parts in 1, oblong 4to., 19th century vellum over pasteboards, engraved title added, engraved portrait of Bredero by Hassel Gerritsz, 20 engravings, full page calligraphic woodcut, tear on page 89/90 of part 2 neatly repaired, bookplate of G. S. Overdiep.   Maggs Bros. Ltd.   Illustrated Books 2014 - 2015   £6000

Bree, Charles Robert *A History of the Birds of Europe Not Observed in the British Isles.* London: George Bell & sons, 1875-1876. Second edition, octavo, 5 volumes, 252 chromolithographs, publisher's blindstamped cloth with gilt design, library stamps of Royal Zoological Society of New South Wales, mainly on prelims, sound working set.   Andrew Isles   2015 - 34090   2015 $659

Breeskin, Adelyn Dohme *Mary Cassatt, a Catalogue Raisonne of the Oils, Pastels, Watercolors and Drawings.* Washington: Smithsonian Institution, 1970. First edition, very good, few small chips and tears, dust jacket slightly shorter than book as issued, previous owner's gift inscription to "The Bentons" (either the family of William Benton (1900-1973) or that of his son Charles (1949-1953).   Beasley Books   2013 - 2015 $200

Breiter, Christian August *Hortus Breiterianus Oder Verzelchniss aller Derjenigen Gewachse, Weiche im Breiterschen Botanischen Garten zu Leipgiz...* Leipzig im Verlag: bey C. F. Franz, 1817. 8vo., engraved frontispiece, early 19th century ink inscriptions on titlepage and flyleaf, little general paper toning, original boards with gilt lettering piece on spine, boards lightly worn at extremities, else very good.   John Drury Rare Books   2015 - 25546   2015 $1049

Bremer, Frederika *The Homes of the New World.* New York: Harper, 1853. First American edition, 8vo., pages 651, 654, 2 volumes, hinge loose, little split to cloth on hinges and some soiling internally, generally very good.   Second Life Books Inc.   191 - 19   2015 $325

Bremner, Robert H. *Children and Youth in America: a Documentary History. Volume II: 1866-1932 Parts 1-6 and Parts 7-8.* Cambridge: Harvard, 1971. First edition, 2 volumes, large 8vo., illustrations, gray cloth, edges slightly soiled, otherwise very good, tight copies little chipped and soiled dust jackets.   Second Life Books Inc.   189 - 33   2015 $75

Brenner, Sydney   *Theories of Biological Pattern Formation.* London: Royal Society, 1981. First separate edition, 4to., original printed wrappers, signed by author, fine.   By the Book, L. C.   44 - 22   2015 $200

Brent, Humphry   *Report to the Right Honourable the Lords Commissioners of His Majesty's Treasury by Humphrey Brent...* N.P.: London? n.d.?, 1722. First edition, folio, stitched as issued, but stitching now loose, unbound and uncut, slightly dusty, very good, large copy.   John Drury Rare Books   March 2015 - 23006   2015 $656

Brereton, Charles David   *Observations on the Administration of the Poor Laws in Agricultural Districts.* Norwich: J. Hatchard & Son, 1824. Second edition, half title uncut, sewn as issued, original brown paper wrappers, ink title on front wrapper, very good.   Jarndyce Antiquarian Booksellers   CCXI - 37   2015   £180

Brereton, Frederick Sadleir   *The Great Aeroplane: a Thrilling Tale of Adventure.* London: Glasgow: and Bombay: Blackie and Son Ltd., 1911. First edition, first printing with recto of title leaf dated 1911, 8 inserted plates with illustrations by Edward Hodgson, original pictorial blue cloth, front and spine panels stamped in black and gold, all edges stained green, gray endpapers.   L. W. Currey, Inc.   Boy's Adventure Fiction 2015 - 69   2015 $125

Brereton, Frederick Sadleir   *The Great Aeroplane: a Thrilling Tale of Adventure.* New York: Boston: H. M. Caldwell Co., 1911. First edition, US issue with title leaf dated 1911 on recto, tipped in on a stub, octavo, 8 inserted plates, illustrations by Edward Hodgson, original pictorial green cloth.   L. W. Currey, Inc.   Boy's Adventure Fiction 2015 - 68   2015 $125

Brereton, Frederick Sadleir   *The Great Aeroplane: a Thrilling Tale of Adventure.* London: Glasgow and Bombay: Blackie and Son Ltd., 1911. first edition, first printing with recto of title leaf dated 1911, octavo, 8 inserted plates with illustrations by Edward S. Hodgson, original pictorial red cloth, front and spine panels stamped in black and gold, all edges stained green, gray endpapers.   L. W. Currey, Inc.   Boy's Adventure Fiction 2015 - 70   2015 $125

Brereton, Frederick Sadleir   *The Great Airship: a Tale of Adventure.* London: Glasgow and Bombay: Blackie and Son Ltd., 1914. First edition, first printing with title leaf dated 1914, octavo, 6 inserted plates, original pictorial blue cloth, front and spine panels stamped in white, black, yellow and gold, gray coated endpapers, all edges stained green. L. W. Currey, Inc.   Boy's Adventure Fiction 2015 - 85   2015 $100

Bresson, Robert   *Notes on Cinematography.* New York: Urizen Books, 1977. First edition, 8vo., original black cloth lettered gilt at spine, very good+ in very good dust jacket with faint surface soiling, decent copy.   Any Amount of Books   2015 - C13301   2015   £180

Breton, Nicholas   1545-1626   *A Poste with a Packet of mad letters.* London: for George Badger, 1653. Small 4to., lacking title to part 2, lacking final leaf of text, woodcut on title (block much wormed), inner margin of title and first few leaves and final leaf of part 1 dampstained, dampstain in lower margin of pages 31-42 and 59-68, short wormtrail (breaking into holes in places) in inner margin of first part (old patch over worming on final leaf of part 1), final leaf somewhat soiled and slightly short at lower margin, late 19th century half maroon morocco, marbled boards slightly rubbed, signature, J. S. Hasted, bookplate of Allan D. MacDonald, from the library of James Stevens Cox (1910-1997).   Maggs Bros. Ltd.   1447 - 46 2015   £950

Brett, David   *Tales of the 3 Pigs and 3 Bears.* London: Dean and Son, n.d. circa, 1910. 4to., gilt cloth, pictorial paste-on, light cover soil, very good+, illustrations by David Brett.   Aleph-bet Books, Inc.   109 - 171   2015 $400

Brett, David   *Three Tiny Pigs.* London: Dean and son, n.d. circa, 1910. 4to., pictorial boards, some wear to rear cover and spine, very good+ condition, full page color illustrations, untearable book with sheets mounted on linen. Aleph-bet Books, Inc.   109 - 172   2015 $225

Brett, Simon   *Simon Brett: an Engraver's Progress. A Selection of Engravings...* Mission: Barbarian Press, 2013. 1 of 55 deluxe copies with signed and numbered print by Brett, 134 engravings printed from wood on Zerkall White Smooth, texts printed in Joanna with Fry's Ornamented for display in green and black on Zerkall cream laid, bound in quarter green leather with skived leather spine label, patterned green and white paper by artist over boards, housed in slipcase along with stiff paper folder containing signed and numbered strike of the commissioned frontispiece for the book, this being number 23 of 55 copies, fine.   The Kelmscott Bookshop   11 - 2   2015 $1700

Brettell, Richard   *Commentary the Art of Paul Gaugin.* Washington and Chicago: National Gallery of Art and Art Institute of Chicago, First edition, 4to., wrappers, laid in is the 8 page supplement supplied by the Art Institute, fine very good+ supplement.   Beasley Books   2013 - 2015 $45

Breuer, Lee *The Warrior Ant.* New York: Vincent FitzGerald & Co., 1992. Artist's book, one of 40 copies, all on handmade paper by Paul Wong of Dieu Donne Papermill, each copy signed by artist, Susan Weil and author, page size 10 x 10 inches, bound in handmade paper wrappers in custom box by BookLab, fine, etchings editioned by Marjorie Van Dyke and Vincent FitzGerald at Printing Workshop and text printed letterpress in Bembo by Dan Keleher at Wild Carrot Letterpress, calligraphy is by Jerry Kelly.   Priscilla Juvelis - Rare Books   62 - 5   2015 $3500

Brewer, J. Mason *Aunt Dicy Tales: Snuff Dipping Tales of the Texas Negro.* privately printed for J. Mason Brewer, 1956. Limited to 400 copies, this #39 and signed by Brewer, this copy given as gift by then Governor of Texas Allan Shivers with his gift card laid in and inked presentation, original green gold gilt stamped padded leatherette, beautiful black and white front and rear endpaper, frontispiece on brown enamel stock, illustrations by John Biggers with 13 full page plates, fine, clean, square copy.   Buckingham Books   March 2015 - 37618   2015 $2000

Brewster, David *A Farewell Address to the Inhabitants of the Parish of Stockton upon Tees.* Stockton: printed by Christopher and Jennett, 1805. First edition, 8vo., 16 pages, preserved in recent plain wrappers, very good, extremely rare.   John Drury Rare Books   2015 - 20031   2015 $177

Brewster, David *A Treatise on Optics.* Philadelphia: Carey, Lea & Blanchard, 1833. First American edition, text diagrams, contemporary linen backed paper covered boards, printed paper spine label, text untrimmed, scattered foxing, spine bit faded, book was owned by Aaron Brainard Jerome (1813-1839) who has dated his signature "Nassau Hall March 2 1835", and several pencil drawings and a poem poking fun at Jerome.   Joseph J. Felcone Inc. Science, Medicine and Technology - 14   2015 $300

Brewster, Francis *New Essay's on Trade, Wherein the present State of Our trade, It's Great Decay in the Chief Branches of It and the Fatal Consequence Thereof to the Nation...* London: W. Walwyn, 1702. First edition, 8vo., folding table, contemporary plain ruled sheep, patches of general surface wear, neatly rebacked and labelled, very good, crisp copy with good margins.   John Drury Rare Books   2015 - 23496   2015 $1486

Brewster, John *The Duty and Advantage of Attending the Divine Services of the Church; a Sermon Preached in the Church of the Holy Trinity at Seaton Carew Oct. 2 1831 the Sunday after its Consecration.* Stockton: printed by T. Jennett, 1831. First edition, preserved in recent plain wrappers, very good.   John Drury Rare Books   2015 - 20036   2015 $177

Brewster, John *A Memoir of the Late Reverend Hugh Moises, M.A. Head Master of the Royal Grammar School, Newcastle upon Tyne.* Newcastle: printed by Edward Walker Private impression, 1823. First edition, first issue, 8vo., preserved in recent plain wrappers, very good, uncommon.   John Drury Rare Books   2015 - 20034   2015 $133

Brewster, John *On the Religious Improvement of Prisons: a Sermon Preached in the Cathedral Church of Durham at the Assizes, Holden There August 10, 18108.* London: F. C. and J. Rivington, 1808. First edition, 8vo., preserved in recent plain wrappers, very good, first edition, rare.   John Drury Rare Books   March 2015 - 20032   2015   £266

Brewster, John *On the Spiritual Character of the Christian Church. A Sermon Preached in the Parish Church of St. Andrew's Auckland at the Visitation of the Archdeacon of Durham July 2th 1832.* Stockton-upon-Tees: printed by t. Jennett and sold by J. G. and F Rivington, 1832. First edition, 8vo., 26 pages, preserved in recent plain wrappers, very good, very rare.   John Drury Rare Books   2015 - 20037   2015 $133

Brewster, John *The Restoration of Family Worship Recommended in Two Discourses...* London: F. C. and J. Rivington, 1804. First edition, 8vo., with half title, preserved in recent plain wrappers, very good, very rare.   John Drury Rare Books   2015 - 20030   2015 $89

Brewster, John *A Thanksgiving Sermon for the Peace; Preached in the Parish Church of Stockton Upon Tees June 1 1802.* Stockton: printed by Christopher and Jenentt sold by F. and C. Rivington and W. Clarke, London, 1802. First edition, rare, 8vo., preserved in recent pali wrappers, very good.   John Drury Rare Books   2015 - 20029   2015 $133

Brewster, John *Thoughts on Residing in Villages, with respect to the Observations of Religious Duties and Obligations...* London: printed for F. C. and J. Rivington, 1820. First edition, 8vo., 44 pages, preserved in recent plain wrappers, very good, very rare.   John Drury Rare Books   March 2015 - 20033   2015   £266

Brewster, Patrick *The Seven Chartist and Military Discourses Libelled by the Marquis of Abercorn and other Heritors of the Abbey Parish.* Paisley: pub. by author and sold by M. Paterson and others, 1843. First edition, 8vo., occasional light spotting and soiling, old ownership inscription in pencil, contemporary black half calf, spine gilt, slightly rubbed, rebacked, preserving original spine.   John Drury Rare Books   March 2015 - 25568   2015 $656

Breyer, Stephen *Active Liberty.* New York: Alfred A. Knopf, 2005. Stated first edition, signed by author, small 8vo., fine in fine dust jacket.   By the Book, L. C.   44 - 51   2015 $140

Bridel, Pascal *Foundations of Price Theory.* London: Pickering & Chatto, 2001. First edition, 8vo., about fine, 6 volumes, hardback.   Any Amount of Books   2015 - A15865   2015   £280

Bridges, Robert   1844-1930 *Poems.* London: Basil Montagu Pickering, 1873. First edition, original blue cloth, uncut, spine with printed label (rubbed), cloth somewhat soiled, endpapers severely browned as always, otherwise nice, Logan Pearsall's copy, with his ownership signature, from the collection of Gavin H. Fryer.   Bertram Rota Ltd.   308 Part II - 127   2015   £280

Bridges, Thomas *A Burlesque Translation of Homer.* London: printed for G. G. & J. Robinson, Paternoster Row, 1797. Fourth edition, 2 volumes, frontispiece, titlepage devices, 23 engraved plates, fine contemporary calf with double gilt banded spine, red morocco title labels, small circular dark green volume labels, pencil signature of Richard Thornton Duff, 1807.   Jarndyce Antiquarian Booksellers   CCXI - 38   2015   £280

Bridges, Thomas Charles *Men of the Mist.* London: Calcutta: Sydney: George G. Harrap & Co. Ltd., 1923. First edition, octavo, 4 inserted plates, illustrations by G. Henry Evison, original pictorial olive green cloth, front and spine panels stamped in black and white, fore and bottom edges rough trimmed.   L. W. Currey, Inc.   Boy's Adventure Fiction 2015 - 86   2015 $100

The Bridgewater Treatises: on the Power, Wisdom and Goodness of God as Manifested in the Creation. London: William Pickering, 1833-1839. London: John Murray 1838. Mixed set, Treatises I-IX in 13 volumes, 8vo., all plates and engravings present, occasional light foxing to first and last few pages, contemporary half black calf over marbled paper backed boards, gilt stamped spines and brown leather spine labels, extremities rubbed, some spine labels missing, corners showing, armorial bookplates of Francis Frederick Fox, signature of John Usborne (volume II), very good.   Jeff Weber Rare Books   178 - 779   2015 $1850

Bright, George *Religionis, Seu Legis Christianae Tabula Undecim Dogmata Omnia Quae Libris Quo Novum Testamentum Vocamus Canonicis Reperiuntur...* London: John Darby, 1687. First edition, folio, 19th or 20th century half brown calf over matching buckram, spine lettered gilt, endpapers reinforced at joints, light scuffing only, otherwise excellent.   Any Amount of Books   2015 - C11923   2015   £300

Bright, Henry Arthur *Free Blacks and Slaves. Would Immediate Abolition be a Blessing?* London: Athur Hall Virtue and Co., 1853. First edition, 8vo., recently well bound in linen backed marbled boards lettered, very good, inscribed in ink "J. Ramsay with author's kind regards".   John Drury Rare Books   2015 - 18038   2015 $168

Brighton Constitutional and Conservative Association *The Brighton Constitutional and Conservative Association Offices 28 Duke Street Brighton.* Brighton: E. Lewis steam printer 126 St. James's Street, 1870. 8vo., general light foxing, preserved in modern wrappers with printed label on upper cover, probably rare.   John Drury Rare Books   2015 - 23282   2015 $133

Brimhall, John *Charlie Brown and Friends, a Piano Party, the Music of Vince Guaraldi.* N.P.: Lee Mendelson Film Productions, 1997. First edition, wrappers, 4to., fine.   Beasley Books   2013 - 2015 $45

Brin, David *Earth.* New York: Toronto: London: Sydney: Auckland: Bantam Books, 1990. First edition, limited to 342 (unnumbered) copies signed by Brin, octavo, full black leather, spine panel stamped in gold, dust jacket.   John W. Knott, Bookseller   Selected New Arrivals Jan. 2015 - 16938   2015 $75

Brin, David *Startide Rising.* West Bloomfield: Phantasia Press, 1985. First hardcover edition, octavo, one of 375 numbered copies signed by author, cloth.   John W. Knott, Bookseller   Selected New Arrivals Jan. 2015 - 16936   2015 $450

Brine, Percival *The Revolution and Siege of Paris: with the Elections and Entry of the Prussians in 1870-1871.* London: printed by A. Lewis, 1871. First edition, 8vo., color tinted plate, tinted map, color plate diagram, original publisher's purple cloth lettered, gilt on spine and on front covers, some sun fading at spine and edges, slight rubbing and browning, otherwise decent very good copy.   Any Amount of Books   March 2015 - A86326   2015 $375

Brininstool, E. A. *The Custer Fight. Capt. Benteen's Story of the Battle of Little Big Horn...* E. A. Brininstool, 1932. First edition, 8vo., one of 500 autographed copies printed for the author at his expense, each numbered, this copy #430, inscribed by author for L. H. Spragle of Cresco, PA, cream colored printed wrappers, 36 pages, frontispiece, illustrations, bit of age toning to covers, else near fine, scarce, clamshell case.   Buckingham Books   March 2015 - 29469   2015 $450

Brininstool, E. A. *The True Story of the Killing of "Billy the Kid".* Los Angeles: privately printed by E. A. Brininstool, 1923. Second edition, 8vo. limited to 250 numbered copies, this number 169, tan printed wrappers, illustrations, very scarce.   Buckingham Books   March 2015 - 30993   2015 $400

Britannicus *Friendly Admonitions to the Inhabitant of Great Britain, in General...* London: printed for R. Baldwin, 1758. First edition, 8vo., half title, preserved in recent plain wrappers, very good, rare.   John Drury Rare Books   March 2015 - 19840   2015 $266

The British Catholic Colonial Quarterly Intelligencer No. 1. London: Keating and Brown, 1833. No. 1 only of 4, 8vo., 80 pages, original printed wrappers, uncut and unopened, fine.   John Drury Rare Books   2015 - 20144   2015 $89

British Jurist   *Thoughts on the Elements of Civil government Tending to Prove as a Fundamental Principle on the Authority of the Jurists...(bound with) Second Part of Thoughts on Civil government...by a British Jurist.*   London: B. Fellowes Milliken and Son, Dublin, 1836. 1838., 8vo., errata slip tipped in, contemporary half calf over marbled boards, spine simply gilt with raised bands and label lettered gilt, marbled boards, excellent copy.   John Drury Rare Books   2015 - 25091   2015 $1136

British Sports and Sportsmen, Shooting and Deerstalking. London: British Sports and Sportsmen, 1913. Limited edition (630 of 1000), Large 4to., numerous illustrations, mostly from photos, 9 portrait plates in photogravure, very slight fading at spine, hinges lightly rubbed, handsome, sound clean, very good copy, original full red morocco with bevelled edges, gilt lettered and decorated on spine, gilt titles and lines on front boards, inside front boards gilt bordered with marbled endpapers, all edges gilt, black and white plates with tissue guards and photos in text.   Any Amount of Books   2015 - C6906   2015   £285

British Sports and Sportsmen, big Game Hunting and Angling.   London: British Sports and Suportsmen, 1914. First edition, limited edition (555 of 1000), large 4to., original gilt tooled full red morocco, all edges gilt, marbled, endpapers (very light wear), top edges of spine slightly rubbed and slightly faded at spine, but gilt lettering bright and clear, very good, black and white plates with tissue guards and photos. Any Amount of Books   2015 - C6905   2015   £325

British University Education.   London: Thoemmes Press, 2000. Reprint, 8vo., 6 volumes, about fine.   Any Amount of Books   2015 - A16286   2015   £275

Briton's Own Library.   London: Aldine Pub. co. Inc. Ltd. n.d., 1918. Number 9, 16mo., pictorial wrappers.   L. W. Currey, Inc.   Boy's Adventure Fiction 2015 - 87   2015 $100

Britton, David   *Lord Horror. No. 1-14. Lord Horror 1 & 2. Hard Core Horror 1-5 & Reverbstorm 1-7.*   Manchester: Savoy, 1989. First edition, wrappers, 14 volumes, quarto, copiously illustrated in black and white, occasional very slight rubbing to edges and creasing to corners, otherwise near fine.   Any Amount of Books   March 2015 - C5279   2015   £450

Broadbent, R. J.   *Stag Whispers.*   London: Simpkin Marshall, 1901. First edition, original blue decorated cloth, dulled, pencil markings and rudimentary index on endpapers, signature of Bernard Miles.   Jarndyce Antiquarian Booksellers   CCXI - 40   2015   £40

Broadgrin, Godfrey, Pseud.   *The Convivial Jester, or Bane of Melancholy...*   London: printed for the Proprietor and published by H. D. Symonds & T. Hurst, n.d., 1800. 12mo., engraved frontispiece dated 1 July 1800, 48 pages, in fairly recent marbled boards, entirely uncut, very good, crisp copy, apparently very rare.   John Drury Rare Books 2015 - 19940   2015 $874

Broager, Bendt   *Spinal Neurinoma.*   Copenhagen: Munksgaard, 1953. First edition, wrappers, this copy inscribed to Percival Bailey, very good, library marks, pocket, stickers inside.   Beasley Books   2013 - 2015 $45

Broch, Hermann   *The Death of Virgil.*   London: Routledge, 1946. First English edition, 8vo., dust jacket by McKnight Kauffer, very good+ in slightly tanned and very slightly soiled, otherwise very good or better dust jacket.   Any Amount of Books   2015 - A48849   2015   £150

Broch, Hermann   *Der To Des Vergil.*   New York: Pantheon Books, 1945. First German edition, 8vo., cloth, covers very lightly soiled, corners bumped.   Oak Knoll Books   306 - 256   2015 $350

Brock, Lynn   *The Slip-Carriage Mystery.*   New York: Harper & Bros., 1928. First US edition, cloth spine faded at spine with mottling to rear cover and cloth at bottom of spine bit frayed, else very good in fine dust jacket.   Buckingham Books   March 2015 - 32203   2015 $275

Brome, Alexander   *Rump: or an Exact Collection of the Choycest Poems and Songs Relating to the late Times.* London: for Henry Brome and Henry Marsh, 1662. First edition, 8vo., lacking longitudinal half title final blank, Oo4 with added etched titlepage by Wenceslaus Hollar and additional engraved plate, circa 1850, of the Rump bound at front, small burn-hole to gutter of K2 affecting one letter to verso, light discoloration to K3 from burn-hole on preceding leaf, light spotting to O2-O4, small burn-hole to O6 affecting a letter of text on recto, very light dampstain to lower blank margin of gatherings S-X, repaired burn-hole to gutter of X3 affecting three letters on recto, some occasional discoloration, lightly pressed, late 19th century emerald morocco by Bedford, spine lightly sunned, lower edges lightly chipped, couple of minor scrapes to front cover, good copy, from the library of James Stevens Cox (1910-1997).   Maggs Bros. Ltd.   1447 - 50   2015   £575

Brome, James *An Historical Account of Mr. Rogers's Three Years Travels over England and Wales.* London: by J. Moxon and B. Bearwell, 1694. First (unauthorized) edition, 8vo., large folding map of England and Wales (closely trimmed), light dampstain to fore edge of first few leaves, occasional minor worming to blank fore margin, final four leaves browned, early 19th century russia, extremities rubbed, signature of Henry Cope with inscription "given me by Sr. Richard Middleton 1697 H. Cope", (Sir Richard Middleton, 3rd Bart - 1655-1716) of Chirk Castle Co. Denbigh, Wales, label of R. Beckley bookseller, JSC's signature, from the library of James Stevens Cox (1910-1997). Maggs Bros. Ltd.   1447 - 48   2015   £1200

Brome, Richard *Five New Plays, Viz. The English Moor, or The Mock-Marriage. The Love Sick Court, or The Ambitious Politique. Covent Garden Weeded. The New Academy or the New Exchange. The Queen and Concubine.* London: A. Crook and for H. Brome, 1659. First edition, lacking A1, paper flaw to lower right corner of C4 affecting a letter or two of text on recto and verso, blank corner of K1 torn away without loss, occasional headline cropped and lightly browned throughout, old rembottage binding of early 17th century vellum with early manuscript title written vertically to spine partly recoverable, vellum lightly soiled, later endpapers, label removed from foot of spine, lacking ties, from the library of James Stevens Cox (1910-1997).   Maggs Bros. Ltd.   1447 - 49   2015   £450

Bronaugh, W. C. *The Youngers' Fight for Freedom. A Southern Soldier's Twenty Years' Campaign to Open Northern Prison Doors...* E. W. Stephens Pub. Co., 1906. First edition, 8vo., original blind tooled maroon cloth with gilt stamping on front panel and spine and with crossed Union and Confederate flags in color on rear panel, frontispiece, plates, portraits, rubbed at spine ends, corners and extremities, else very good, tight copy.   Buckingham Books   March 2015 - 22516   2015 $325

Bronson, F. W. *Nice People Don't Kill.* New York: Farrar & Rinehart, 1933. First edition, fine in handsome, very good dust jacket with some modest chips at crown and few tears, very scarce, from the library of Kate Stettner Lobell and Carl D. Lobell.   Between the Covers Rare Books   196 - 44   2015 $650

Bronte, Charlotte   1816-1855   *Jane Eyre; an Autobiography.* London: Smith, Elder and Co., 1848. Second edition, half titles, 3 volumes, slight foxing, some pencil marking in margins, original purple vertical fine grained cloth, boards blocked in blind, spines lettered gilt, faded and slightly rubbed, very carefully recased, nice in original cloth, neat ownership inscription on leading free endpaper of C. L. Petre Jany. 17th 1848 Holly Lodge".   Jarndyce Antiquarian Booksellers   CCXI - 46   2015   £6500

Bronte, Charlotte   1816-1855   *Jane Eyre.* Oxford: Clarendon Press, 1969. Half title, original dark blue cloth, very good in slightly marked dust jacket, with ad leaflet, TLS from Ian Jack to Kathleen Tillotson asking for advice and copy of note from Kathleen to Margaret Smith inserted.   Jarndyce Antiquarian Booksellers   CCVII - 103   2015   £70

Bronte, Charlotte   1816-1855   *The Letters... Volume I: 1829-1847.* Oxford: Clarendon Press, 1995. Half title, original dark blue cloth, very good in dust jacket, presentation from editor, Margaret Smith, for Kathleen Tillotson, with earlier card and ALS thanking KT for kind comments, she has made 2 pencil corrections in text.   Jarndyce Antiquarian Booksellers   CCVII - 104   2015   £50

Bronte, Charlotte   1816-1855   *The Professor.* New York: Harper and Bros., 1857. First American cloth edition, 12mo., original ribbed cloth, title and publisher gilt stamped on spine, previous owner's name on front free endpaper, light foxing in text.   Oak Knoll Books   306 - 257   2015 $150

Bronte, Charlotte   1816-1855   *The Professor.* Oxford: Clarendon Press, 1987. Half title, original dark blue cloth, very good in dust jacket, presentation from editor for Kathleen Tillotson.   Jarndyce Antiquarian Booksellers   CCVII - 105   2015   £50

Bronte, Charlotte   1816-1855   *Shirley.* London: Smith Elder and Co., 1849. First edition, 3 volumes, edges faintly browned, integral ad at end, volume iii present but inserted ads discarded, 8vo., modern dark green morocco by Bayntun-Riviere, backstrips with gilt wavy line-decorated raised bands between double gilt rules, gilt lettered direct in second and fourth compartments, gilt fillet border on sides, wide turn-ins, marbled endpapers, all edges gilt, slipcase, modern bookplate in volume i, very good.   Blackwell's Rare Books   B179 - 20   2015   £2500

Bronte, Charlotte   1816-1855   *Shirley.* London: Smith, Elder and Co., 1849. First edition, 3 volumes, 16 page catalog (Oct. 1849) volume I, signed by Geoffrey Tillotson and with pencil notes and marginal marks, card wrappers made by Tillotson retaining original f.e.p., slightly dusty blue ms. paper labels, volumes I and II labelled upside down.   Jarndyce Antiquarian Booksellers   CCVII - 106   2015   £125

Bronte, Charlotte   1816-1855   *Shirley.* Oxford: Clarendon Press, 1979. Half title, original dark blue cloth, very good in slightly marked dust jacket, with note by Kathleen Tillotson.   Jarndyce Antiquarian Booksellers   CCVII - 107   2015   £50

Bronte, Charlotte 1816-1855 *Villette.* London: Smith Elder & Co., 1853. First edition, 3 volumes, few leaves proud and damaged at fore-edge, from the library of Geoffrey & Kathleen Tillotson, with note by Kathleen, card wrappers made by Geoffrey, many pencil notes and marginal marks.   Jarndyce Antiquarian Booksellers   CCVII - 108   2015   £250

Bronte, Charlotte 1816-1855 *Villette.* London: Smith Elder and Co., 1853. First edition, publisher's ads in volume ii discarded, leaf L1 in volume I remargined, some toning, 8vo., modern green morocco by Bayntun-Riviere, backstrips with gilt wavy line decorate raised bands between double gilt rules, gilt lettered direct to second and fourth compartments, gilt fillet border on both sides, wide turn-ins, marbled endpapers, all edges gilt, slipcase, modern bookplate volume i, very good.   Blackwell's Rare Books   B179 - 21   2015   £2000

Bronte, Charlotte 1816-1855 *Villette.* Boston: Houghton Mifflin Co., 1971. Riverside edition, original printed card wrappers, slightly marked, very good, from the library of Geoffrey & Kathleen Tillotson, edited by Geoffery with inserted correspondence.   Jarndyce Antiquarian Booksellers   CCVII - 109   2015   £20

Bronte, Charlotte 1816-1855 *Villette.* Oxford: Clarendon Press, 1984. half title, original dark blue cloth, very good in slightly marked dust jacket, from the library of Geoffrey & Kathleen Tillotson, with 3 page ALS from editor about this edition.   Jarndyce Antiquarian Booksellers   CCVII - 110   2015   £50

Bronte, Emily 1818-1848 *The Complete Poems.* New York: Columbia University Press, 1947. Second printing, half title, frontispiece, original green cloth, signed by Kathleen Tillotson, April 1950, few notes in text and relevant cutting.   Jarndyce Antiquarian Booksellers CCVII - 133   2015   £20

Bronte, Emily 1818-1848 *Wuthering Heights.* Oxford: Clarendon press, 1976. Half title, original dark blue cloth, very good in dust jacket, presented to Kathleen Tillotson by Press delegates.   Jarndyce Antiquarian Booksellers CCVII - 114   2015   £75

Bronte, Emily 1818-1848 *Wuthering Heights.* New York: Limited Editions club, 1993. Limited to 300 numbered copies, signed by artist, folio, leather, title stamped on front cover, top edge cut, other edges uncut, cloth clamshell box with leather label on spine, set in Monotype Dante, printed by Michel and Winifred Bixler, frontispiece and lithographs in text by Balthus, lithographs printed by Bruce Porter, monthly letter loosely inserted.   Oak Knoll Books   25 - 62 2015 $4500

Bronte, The Sisters *Poems by Currer, Ellis and Action Bell.* London: Smith, Elder & Co., 1846. First edition, second issue, octavo, contemporary brown morocco gilt over marbled boards,.   Honey & Wax Booksellers   2 - 12   2015 $4200

Brook, George *Catalogue of the Madreporian Corals in the British Museum.* London: British Museum, 1893. Large quarto, 7 volumes, 240 uncolored photos, publisher's cloth, some wear, upper spine of volume 7 repaired, titlepages with stamp of Royal Zoological Sosciety of New South Wales, plus a few stamps, sound set, scarce.   Andrew Isles   2015 - 20821   2015 $1650

Brooke, H. B. *Annals of the Revolution or a History of the Doans.* Philadelphia: John B. Perry, New York: Nafis and Cornish, 1848. First edition, 16mo., extensively illustrated, original pictorial boards, very bright, slight wear.   M & S Rare Books, Inc.   97 - 256   2015 $750

Brooke, Henry *The History of a Reprobate; being the Life of David Doubtful.* Printed for the Booksellers, 1784. First edition, bit browned and spotted, first few leaves brittle at fore-edge, small hole in one leaf with loss of part of a word on recto and touching four letters on verso, small 8vo., original sheep, worn, spine defective at head, lower cover nearly detached, ownership inscription of John Georges (25 July 1793 price 1/3) and some annotations in text, sound.   Blackwell's Rare Books   B179 - 22   2015   £1100

Brooks, Charles Timothy *Bread from God.* Philadelphia: American Sunday School Union, 1869. First edition, 4to., original green cloth, gilt decorations and lettering, all edges gilt, titlepage and 11 chromolithographed pages, printed rectos only, each leaf has decorated gold frame printed border around an onlaid chromolithographed illustrations, in lower margin of each leaf is imprint of F. Moras Lith. Phil.", inscribed by Brooks for Brooksie Stevens, grandchild, edges little rubbed, fine.   The Brick Row Book Shop   Miscellany 67 - 25   2015 $1500

Brooks, E. Searles *The Antlered Man.* London: George G. Harrap & Co., 1935. First edition, advance proof, printed green wrappers lettered in black, uncommon edition, slight surface wear, slight chip at foot of spine, pencilled price on spine, overall sound close to very good with clean text.   Any Amount of Books   2015 - A93758   2015   £240

Brooks, Gwendolyn *Annie Allen.* New York: Harper, 1949. First edition, 8vo., black cloth, frontispiece, paper band around cover noting "Winner of the Pulitzer Prize for Poetry", owner's note on pastedown, front cut from dust jacket(?) laid in, very good, tight.   Second Life Books Inc.   190 - 36   2015 $125

Brooks, Gwendolyn *Annie Allen.* New York: Harper & Bros., 1949. First edition, hardcover, 8vo., inscribed by author, very good, dulled spine, lacking most of dust jacket, present are rear panel, much of spine and rear flap. Beasley Books   2013 - 2015 $150

Brooks, Gwendolyn *Maud Martha.* New York: Harper, 1953. First edition, 8vo., paper boards with cloth spine, top edges little soiled, edges of cover scuffed and slightly worn, otherwise very good, tight copy in little scuffed and chipped dust jacket.   Second Life Books Inc.   190 - 37   2015 $150

Brooks, Gwendolyn *A Street in Bronzeville.* New York: Harper, 1945. First edition, 8vo., little offsetting to titlepage, contemporary ownership signature on endpaper, else near fine in unclipped, very good plus dust jacket.   Second Life Books Inc.   189 - 35   2015 $500

Brooks, James J. *Adventures of a U. S. Detective.* Philadelphia: Souder, 1876. Later edition, near fine in cloth backed boards.   Mordida Books   March 2015 - 000327   2015 $100

Brooks, John Graham *American Syndicalism, The I.W.W.* New York: Macmillan, 1913. First edition, hardcover, very good+ with owner's name and slight wear at head of the bit dulled spine.   Beasley Books   2013 - 2015 $45

Brooks, Juanita *John Doyle Lee: Zealot - Pioneer Builder - Scapegaot.* Glendale: Arthur H. Clark Co., 1961. First limited edition of 209 copies, this copy was released one year prior to red cloth trade edition, blue cloth, blue foil stamping on spine and rules, top edge stained blue, frontispiece, portraits, former owner's bookplate on front free flyleaf and inked name and address on front pastedown sheet, lightly rubbed along edges and corners else near fine in custom made cloth slipcase with leather label on spine, very scarce edition.   Buckingham Books   March 2015 - 24726   2015 $2100

Brooks, Tim *Lost Sounds. Blacks and the Birth of the Recording Industry 1890-1919.* Urbana: University of Illinois Press, 2004. First edition, fine in fine dust jacket. Beasley Books   2013 - 2015 $45

Brooks, Walter *Freddy and the Space Ship.* New York: Knopf, 1953. Stated first edition, 8vo., cloth, fine in very slightly worn dust jacket, illustrations in black and white by Kurt Wiese, nice, sold with fine 1 page letter from Brooks. Aleph-bet Books, Inc.   109 - 72   2015 $1200

Brookshaw, George *Groups of Flowers Drawn and Accurately Coloured after Nature with Full Instructions for the Young Artist.* London: printed for Longman Hurst, Rees, Orme and Brown, 1817. First edition, 343 x 267mm., striking red straight grain morocco gilt in unusual design, covers framed by decorative gilt rules and creating roll, large central lozenge formed by two very elaborately gilt and blind tooled triangular 'curtains', wide bases of which meet at center of each board, large gilt butterfly at peak of each triangle (seeming to pull the curtains upward and downward toward the top and bottom edge of covers), flat spine in densely tooled panels, gilt titling, gilt chain roll on turn-ins, all edges gilt, with 11 (of 12) excellent engravings of flowers in two states, colored and uncolored, without color plate of the Moss Rose, joints and extremities little rubbed, two small abrasions to boards, spine uniformly darkened, touch of faint yellowing to uncolored plates, couple of marginal smudges but still very appealing example in most excellent condition, binding with lustrous covers, and text fresh and smooth, rare example of a 'curtain' binding, based on Spanish style 'cortina' binding.   Phillip J. Pirages   66 - 72   2015 $2400

Brookshaw, George *Groups of Flowers (Groups of Fruit... Six Birds) Drawn and Accurately Coloured After Nature with Full Instructions for the Young Artist.* London: published by Thomas McLean, 1819. Second edition, 368 x 273mm., 3 parts in one volume, splendid contemporary English red straight grain morocco elaborately tooled in gilt and blind, covers with concentric filigree frames in alternating gilt and blind tooling, raised bands, spine panels intricately gilt with two large lozenges formed by rectangular and triangular tools surrounded by curling botanical ornaments, turn-ins gilt, all edges gilt, excellent recent matching morocco lipped slipcase, 36 very appealing illustrations, being 18 engravings, each in two states (monochrome and fully hand colored), text leaves with faint mottled foxing and minor browning and offsetting, just few plates with negligible faint spots or smudges, otherwise beautiful copy, original sparkling binding in amazing state of preservation.   Phillip J. Pirages   66 - 73   2015 $15,000

Brookshaw, George *Pomona Britannica or a Collection of the Most esteemed Fruits of Present Cultivated in Great Britain...* London: printed by Bensley and Son, 1817. First quarto edition, 2 volumes, large quarto, 60 line and stipple engraved plates partially printed in color and finished by hand, contemporary maroon straight grain morocco, covers elaborately paneled in gilt and blind, spine elaborately tooled and lettered in gilt in compartments, gilt board edges and dentelles, all edges gilt, some light foxing, mostly to text leaves and generally, not affecting plates, previous owner's bookplate and front pastedown of each volume and previous owner's old ink signature front free endpaper, excellent copy.   Heritage Book Shop   Holiday 2014 - 22   2015 $20,000

Broonzy, William *Big Bill Blues.* London: Cassell, 1955. First edition, 8vo., in Grove Press dust jacket, (is this the US edition or a made up copy?), photos and drawings by Paul Olliver, donor's presentation on flyleaf, author's presentation under his frontispiece for Mrs. Martha King, black cloth, top edges slightly soiled, otherwise very good, tight copy in little chipped and somewhat soiled dust jacket, scarce signature. Second Life Books Inc.   190 - 38   2015 $2500

Brough, Robert B.   *The Life of Sir John Falstaff...* London: Longman, Brown, Green, Longmans and Roberts, 1858. Royal 8vo., 20 etched plates and duplicate hand colored set, text illustrations by George Cruickshank, full red morocco, spine decorated gilt by Riviere, preserving the original wrapper for part 1, also upper wrapper for the separate publication 'Twenty Etchings" by Cruikshank, and original decorated cloth, upper cover and spine for book issue. Marlborough Rare Books   List 54 - 7   2015   £1100

Brough, Robert B.   *The Life of Sir John Falstaff.* London: Longman, Brown, Green, Longmans and Roberts, 1858. Royal 8vo., 20 etched plates and duplicate hand colored set, text illustrations, full red morocco, spine decorated in gilt by Riviere, preserving original wrapper for 'part 1' also upper wrapper for the separate publication, 20 etchings by George Cruikshank and original decorated cloth upper cover and spine for book issue.   Marlborough Rare Books   List 53 - 4   2015   £1100

Brougham & Vaux, Henry Peter Brougham, 1st Baron 1778-1868   *Lord Brougham's reply to Lord John Russell's Letter to the Electors of Stroud, on the Principles of the Reform Act.*   London: Ridgway, 1839. First edition, 8vo., 16 pages of Ridgway ads, recently well bound in linen backed marbled boards, lettered, very good.   John Drury Rare Books   2015 - 22446   2015 $133

Brougham & Vaux, Henry Peter Brougham, 1st Baron 1778-1868   *The Speech of H. Brougham, Esq. on the Education of the Poor, Spoken in the House of Commons June 29 1820.*   London: 1820. First edition, 8vo., preserved in plain wrappers, ink stamp of British Library of Economic and Poltical Science verso of titlepage, good copy, rare.   John Drury Rare Books   March 2015 - 20693   2015   £262

Brougham & Vaux, Henry Peter Broughan, 1st Baron 1778-1868   *Critique from the Edinburgh Review on Lord Byron's Poems.*   London: printed by W. T. Sherwin, 1820. One of two separate editions published in 1820, priority unknown, 8vo., original printed wrappers, uncommon, wrappers worn and splitting at fold, small imperfection in upper wrapper which also effects letter 'P' imprint on titlepage, good copy.   The Brick Row Book Shop   Miscellany 67 - 29   2015 $350

Brougham & Vaux, Henry Peter Broughan, 1st Baron 1778-1868   *Practical Observations Upon the Education of the People, Addressed to the Working Classes and their Employers.*   London: Mechanics Institution, 1825. First separate edition, Large 8vo., recent marbled boards lettered on spine, very good.   John Drury Rare Books   March 2015 - 24418   2015   £266

Broughton, James   *Odes for Odd Occasions: Poems 1954-1976.*   South San Francisco: Manroot, 1977. First edition, illustrated wrappers, toning on spine, else near fine, Ruth Witt-Diamant's copy, signed by her twice, and signed by Broughton, nice association.   Between the Covers Rare Books, Inc.   187 - 33   2015 $100

Broumas, Olga   *Caritas.*   N.P.: White Camel Press, 1985. First edition thus, one of 40 copies printed in Romulus Roman and Italic type on Gutenberg laid paper, tall 8vo., original paste paper boards with printed label on spine, signed by binder Mary Patrick Bogan, very fine, lovely edition.   James S. Jaffe Rare Books   Modern American Poetry - 43   2015 $250

Brower, David   *Manual of Ski Mountaineering.*   San Francisco: Sierra Club, 1962. Third edition, small octavo, photos and drawings, blue pictorial cloth stamped in silver, very fine with pictorial dust jacket.   Argonaut Book Shop Holiday Season 2014 - 37   2015 $60

The Brown Reader: 50 Writers Remember College Hill. New York: Simon & Schuster, 2014. Advance reading copy, scarce, trace wear to spine ends, very near fine in wrappers. Ken Lopez, Bookseller   164 - 177   2015 $125

Brown, Abbie Farwell   *The Lonesomest Doll.*   Boston & New York: Houghton Mifflin, 1928. First Rackham edition, 8vo., tan pictorial cloth, some rubbing to endpaper (not visibile under dust jacket), else fine in dust jacket (chipped on edges), color pictorial titlepage plus 3 full page color illustrations in rose and blue, 25 text drawings in black and white including silhouettes by Arthur Rackham, very scarce in pictorial wrapper.   Aleph-Bet Books, Inc.   108 - 385   2015 $1250

Brown, Alphonse   *La Station Aerienne.*   Paris: A La Librairie Illustree et aux Bureau du Journal des Voyages, n.d., 1894? First edition, octavo, numerous full page illustrations by Charles Clerice, original pictorial light gray-green cloth, front and spine panels stamped in black, brown, orange, blue and gold, all edges gilt, gray coated endpapers.   L. W. Currey, Inc.   Boy's Adventure Fiction 2015 - 36   2015 $225

Brown, Charles B. *Reports on the Physical, Descriptive and Economic Geology of British Guiana.* London: Longmans Green and Co., 1875. First edition, 8vo., original blindstamped red cloth, numerous folding illustrations, including map in pocket at rear, very slight rubbing, very good+, handsome copy.   Any Amount of Books   2015 - A83602   2015   £220

Brown, Dan *The Da Vinci Code.* New York: Doubleday, 2003. First edition, very fine in dust jacket, first issue with 'skitoma' on page 243, line 25.   Mordida Books   March 2015 - 009374   2015 $400

Brown, Frank London *The Myth Maker.* Chicago: Path Press, 1969. First edition, hardcover, fine in very good dust jacket with small chips, very scarce.   Beasley Books   2013 - 2015 $150

Brown, Fredric *The Case of the Dancing Sandwiches. Frederic Brown in the Detective Pulps. Volume 4.* Volcano: Dennis McMillan, 1985. First edition, limited to 400 copies, each signed and numbered by author of introduction, Lawrence Block, fine in dust jacket.   Buckingham Books   March 2015 - 17878   2015 $225

Brown, Fredric *The Freak Show Murders.* Belen: Dennis McMillan, 1985. First edition, one of 350 numbered copies signed by author of introduction, Richard Lupoff, some very tiny scattered light spotting on page edges, otherwise very fine.   Mordida Books   March 2015 - 010385   2015 $150

Brown, Fredric *Happy Ending.* Missoula: Dennis McMillan, 1990. First edition, one of 450 numbered copies, very fine in dust jacket.   Mordida Books   March 2015 - 003030   2015 $85

Brown, Fredric *Knock Three-One-Two.* New York: Dutton, 1959. First edition, very fine in dust jacket.   Mordida Books   March 2015 - 003023   2015 $400

Brown, Fredric *The Lights in the Sky are Stars.* New York: E. P. Dutton & Co., 1953. First edition, octavo, boards.   John W. Knott, Bookseller   Selected New Arrivals Jan. 2015 - 16940   2015 $350

Brown, Fredric *Madman's Holiday.* Volcano: Dennis McMillan Publications, 1985. First edition, limited to 350 copies, each signed and numbered by author, this no. 118, fine in dust jacket.   Buckingham Books   March 2015 - 31420   2015 $800

Brown, Fredric *The Murderers.* New York: E. P. Dutton, 1961. First edition, fine, fresh dust jacket with slightest bit of rubbing, beautiful copy, from the library of Kate Stettner Lobell and Carl D. Lobell.   Between the Covers Rare Books   196 - 45   2015 $350

Brown, Fredric *The Office.* New York: Dutton, 1958. First edition, fine in dust jacket with some very slight spine fading.   Mordida Books   March 2015 - 007827   2015 $250

Brown, Fredric *The Office.* Miami Beach: Dennis McMillan, 1987. First edition, limited to 425 copies, numbered and signed by Philip Jose Farmer, author of introduction, fine in dust jacket.   Buckingham Books   March 2015 - 17871   2015 $165

Brown, Fredric *Science Fiction Carnival: Fun in Science-Fiction.* Chicago: Shasta, 1953. First edition, octavo, cloth backed pictorial boards.   John W. Knott, Bookseller Selected New Arrivals Jan. 2015 - 16942   2015 $350

Brown, Fredric *The Shaggy Dog and Other Murders.* New York: E. P. Dutton & Co. Inc., 1963. First edition, fine in dust jacket with hint of wear to foot of spine,.   Buckingham Books   March 2015 - 31417   2015 $650

Brown, Fredric *Space on My Hands.* Chicago: Shasta, 1951. First edition, fine in dust jacket.   Mordida Books   March 2015 - 007359   2015 $350

Brown, Fredric *Thirty Corpses Every Thursday.* Belen: Dennis McMillan, 1986. First edition, one of 375 numbered copies, signed by author of introduction, William Campbell Gault, very fine in dust jacket with very slight fading to spine lettering.   Mordida Books   March 2015 - 011704   2015 $125

Brown, H. Rap *Die Nigger Die!* New York: Dial Press, 1969. First edition, near fine with slight soiling on boards, little foxing and stamp of the Liberation Book Store of Harlem on front blank, slightly rubbed, near fine dust jacket, very warmly inscribed by author to Angela Davis using most of the blank page facing half title.   Between the Covers Rare Books   197 - 52   2015 $8000

Brown, J. H. *Spectropia or Surprising Spectral Illusions, Showing Ghosts Everywhere and of any Colour... First series.* London: Griffith and Faran, H. & C. Treacher, Brighton, 1864. First edition, 4to., 16 colored plates, 6 text figures, original cloth backed pictorial boards, fine, fresh, scarce.   John Drury Rare Books   2015 - 25305   2015 $1530

Brown, J. P. S. *The Outfit. A Cowboy's Primer.* Dial Press, 1971. First edition, inked presentation inscription by author, brown fabricoid, titles stamped in gold title on spine, brown endpapers, illustrations, fine, tight copy in dust jacket with small chip to head of spine and another to top corner edge of rear cover.   Buckingham Books   March 2015 - 36783   2015 $250

Brown, John *The Mysteries of Neutralization; or the British Navy Vindicated from the Charges of Injustice and Oppression Towards Neutral Flags.* London: printed for the author and sold by Jordan and Maxwell, 1806. First and only edition, 8vo., well bound recently in cloth, spine lettered gilt, entirely uncut, very good, large copy, uncommon. John Drury Rare Books   2015 - 19099   2015 $177

Brown, John Henry *History of Dallas County, Texas from 1837 to 1887.* Milligan, Cornett & Farnham, 1887. First edition, 18mo., printed wrappers, errata, very light wear to edges of front cover, small chip to top corner of rear cover, else interior clean and bright and solid, very good. Buckingham Books   March 2015 - 36178   2015 $750

Brown, John Mason *George Pierce Baker - a Memorial.* New York: Dramatists Play Service, 1939. First edition, octavo, 46 pages, frontispiece, marbled paper boards, title label on front cover, signed on front free endpaper by all authors, John Mason Brown, Eugene O'Neill, Sidney Howard, Allardyce Nicoll, Stanley R. McCandless, drawing by Gluyas Williams, frontispiece, marbled paper boards, title on label on front cover, covers rubbed at head and tail of spine, corners bruised, very good in chipped and torn original tissue jacket, largely defective at bottom edge. Peter Ellis, Bookseller   2014 - 018199   2015   £300

Brown, John W. *An Abridged History Alabama.* Press of Gateway Printing Co., 1909. First edition, stiff pictorial wrappers, illustrations, photos, tables, 2 maps, scarce, light general soiling to wrappers, internally clean and tight. Buckingham Books   March 2015 - 37426   2015 $300

Brown, Jonathan *The History and Present Condition of St. Domingo.* Philadelphia: William Marshall and Co., 1837. First edition, 2 volumes, 12mo, original ribbon embossed cloth with printed spine labels, early owner's bookplate on front pastedowns, ex-library with spine letters, bookplate to rear pocket and perforated stamps, light foxing and light wear on spines, overall very good set. Between the Covers Rare Books   197 - 53   2015 $150

Brown, Julia *The Mermaid's Gift.* Chicago: Rand McNally, 1912. First edition, 4to., blue gilt cloth, pictorial paste-on, light shelfwear, very good-fine, 8 very beautiful color plates by Maginel Wright Enright. Aleph-Bet Books, Inc.   108 - 169   2015 $250

Brown, Margaret Wise *The Dark Wood of the Golden Birds.* New York: Harper & Bros., 1950. First edition, nicely illustrated by Leonard Weisgard, cloth backed decorated boards, illustrated endpapers, very nearly fine in like dust jacket, uncommon. Stephen Lupack   March 2015 - 2015 $125

Brown, Margaret Wise *Little Fur Family.* New York: Harper Bros., 1946. First edition, pictorial box with circular cut-out in bear's stomach through which the fur protrudes, minimal wear, near fine, illustrations by Garth Williams with full and partial page color illustrations. Aleph-bet Books, Inc.   109 - 74   2015 $1250

Brown, Matthew Cullerne *A Dictionary of Twentieth Century Russian and Soviet Painters 1900-1980.* London: Izomar, 1998. First edition, 4to., original red leather lettered gilt at spine, illustrations in color and black and white, fine in near fine dust jacket, very slight edgewear. Any Amount of Books   2015 - C13657   2015   £220

Brown, Olympia *Democratic Ideals. A Memorial Sketch of Clara B. Colby.* Racine: Carrie Stebbins?, 1917. First edition, 8vo., blue cloth stamped in gilt on cover, frontispiece, very nice. Second Life Books Inc.   189 - 36   2015 $450

Brown, Paul *3 Rings: a Circus.* New York: Scribner, 1938. A. First edition, 4to., cloth backed pictorial boards, fine in dust jacket with some soil and fraying, illustrations on every page by Brown, this copy inscribed by Brown with drawing of Dog's head dated 1938, special copy, scarce. Aleph-bet Books, Inc.   109 - 75   2015 $850

Brown, R. Allen *Proceedings of the Battle Conference 1978-1981. And Anglo-Norman Studies. Volumes V-X.* Woodbridge: Boydell Press, 1978-1987. First editions, 11 volumes, including index, copiously illustrated in black and white, slight rubbing at edges, some light pencil underlinings and markings, very slight damp staining, otherwise about very good in slightly very good- tatty dust jackets. Any Amount of Books   2015 - A65015   2015   £180

Brown, Richard *A History of the Island of Cape Breton with some Account of the Discovery and Settlement of Canada, Nova Scotia and Newfoundland.* Belleville: Mika Publishing, 1979. Facsimile edition, green cloth, 8vo., frontispiece, folding map in rear, very good. Schooner Books Ltd.   110 - 60   2015 $85

Brown, Robert *Letters on the Distressed State of Agriculturists Originally Published in the Edinburgh Courant and other Newspapers.* Edinburgh: printed for the author by David Willison, 1816. First separate edition, 8vo., recently well bound in calf backed marbled boards, spine gilt lettered, uncut, good, rare. John Drury Rare Books   March 2015 - 21696   2015   £306

Brown, Robert 1842-1895 *Biographical Sketch of the Late Professor Oersted, Copenhagen.* Edinburgh: Transactions of the Botanical Society of Edinburgh, 1872-1873. Original paper wrappers, signed presentation from author, very good. Jeff Weber Rare Books   178 - 854   2015 $45

Brown, Robert Carlton *My Marjonary.* Boston: Luce, 1916. First edition, front endpaper excised, otherwise nice, lightly sunned spine, very good+. Beasley Books 2013 - 2015 $150

Brown, Ruth *Miss Rhythm.* New York: Donald Fine, 1996. Second edition, 8vo., fine in dust jacket, inscribed by Brown. Second Life Books Inc. 190 - 39 2015 $125

Brown, Sterling *The Collected Poetry of Sterling A. Brown.* New York: Harper & Row, 1980. First edition, fine in fine dust jacket, 8vo. Beasley Books 2013 - 2015 $40

Brown, Sterling *The Negro Caravan.* New York: Citadel, 1941. First edition, 8vo., tan cloth, cover slightly worn at ends of spine and corners, edges slightly soiled, otherwise very good, tight copy in chipped and spotted dust jacket. Second Life Books Inc. 190 - 224 2015 $125

Brown, Sterling *Southern Road.* New York: Harcourt, Brace and Co., 1932. First edition, octavo, original dust jacket, inscribed in year of publication, illustrations by E. Simms Campbell. Honey & Wax Booksellers 3 - 11 2015 $3000

Brown, Thomas *Amusements Serious and Comical, Calculated for the Meridian of London.* London: for John Nutt, 1700. First edition, 8vo., some light dampstaining (Particularly to sheet B), contemporary sprinkled calf, joints split at head and foot of spine, corners bumped and with front flyleaves coming loose), from the library of James Stevens Cox (1910-1997), signature of Russell Robartes, with armorial bookplate, another signature roughly deleted. Maggs Bros. Ltd. 1447 - 51 2015 £220

Brown, W. Henry *Co-operation in a University Town - with the Seventh Years' Record of the Cambridge & District Co-operative Society Limited.* London: Co-operative Printing Society, 1939. First edition, octavo, 11 drawings by Ronald Searle, photos, edges slightly spotted, very good in very scarce, very good dust jacket little chipped and nicked on edges and on upper panel of which someone has written 'may be cut up'. Peter Ellis, Bookseller 2014 - 916249 2015 £325

Browne, Albert G. *"The Growing Power of the Public of Chile." in Bulletin of the American Geographical Society 1884. No. 1.* New York: printed for the Society, 1884. First edition, small 4to., paper wrappers, inscribed by author to publisher George Haven Putnam, rear wrapper with small repaired tear, else contents fine and unopened, uncut. Kaaterskill Books 19 - 27 2015 $100

Browne, Harold *Warrior of Dawn.* Chicago: Reilly & Lee, 1943. First edition, fine in price clipped dust jacket with some light wear at top of spine and along edges. Mordida Books March 2015 - 008757 2015 $150

Browne, Howard *Incredible Ink.* Tucson: Dennis McMillan, 1997. First edition, one of 350 numbered copies signed by author, very fine in dust jacket with slipcase. Mordida Books March 2015 - 000017 2015 $85

Browne, Howard *Return of Tharn.* Providence: Grandon, 1956. First edition, some spotting on top of page edges and on top cover edges, otherwise near fine in dust jacket with slightly darkened spine. Mordida Books March 2015 - 008758 2015 $150

Browne, John Ross 1821-1875 *Relacion de los Debates de la Convecion de California Sobre la Formacion de la Constitucion de Estado, en Setiembre y Octubre de 1849.* Nueva York: Imprenta de S. W. Benedict, 1851. First edition, Spanish issue, exceptional copy in original blind and gilt stamped brown cloth, portion of front free endpaper lacking, but exceptionally bright and clean copy, no foxing, fine and clean. Argonaut Book Shop Holiday Season 2014 - 38 2015 $1100

Browne, John Ross 1821-1875 *Reports Upon the Mineral Resources of the United States.* Washington: GPO, 1867. First edition, original brown pebbled cloth, gilt lettered spine, index, light wear to head of spine and small area of upper edge of cover, two small areas worn at lower cover edges, else very nice, tight and clean. Argonaut Book Shop Holiday Season 2014 - 39 2015 $250

Browne, Joseph *The Circus; or British Olympicks, a Satyr on the Ring in Hide-Park.* London: printed and sold by booksellers of London and Westminster, 1709. Pirated edition, 8vo., disbound, very good. C. R. Johnson Foxon R-Z - 1215r-z 2015 $192

Browne, Joseph *St. James's Park; a Satyr.* London: printed and sold by H. Hills, 1708. The second of two piracies b Hills, 16 pages, 8vo., disbound, very good. C. R. Johnson Foxon R-Z - 1216r-z 2015 $192

Browne, Thomas 1605-1682 *Hyrdriotaphia, Urne Buriall or a Discourse of the Sepulchral Urnes Lately found in Norfolk...* London: printed for Hen(rey) Brome, 1658. First edition, 8vo., lacking errata leaf found in some copies, titlepage lightly soiled, spotted, some occasional light foxing, 19th century olive morocco by Ramage, gilt edges, few minor chips to spine, 19th century pencil notes in margins, early 20th century signature S. A. Pope, from the library of James Stevens Cox (1910-1997). Maggs Bros. Ltd. 1447 - 54 2015 £1200

Browne, Thomas 1605-1682 *Pseudeodoxia Epidemica...* London: Edward Dod, and are to be sold by Andrew Crook, 1658. Fourth edition of Pseudodoxia, second edition of Hydriotaphia and the Garden of Cyrus, 4to., longitudinal half title before second section, titlepage very lightly browned small dampstain in lower margin of sheet 'a' and with occasional spotting, pastedown and endleaves stained by turn-ins, contemporary calf ruled in blind, early manuscript paper label on spine, endleaves from printed sheets from an edition of Aristotle and another work in Latin, joints rubbed, handsome copy, probably an Oxford binding with diagonal blind hatching at head and tail of spine, from the library of James Stevens Cox (1910-1997).   Maggs Bros. Ltd.   1447 - 53   2015   £450

Brownell, Elizabeth *Really Babies.* Chicago: Rand McNally, 1908. 4to., gilt cloth, photo paste-on, 6 pages, fine, photo illustrations.   Aleph-Bet Books, Inc.   108 - 345   2015 $275

Browning, Elizabeth Barrett 1806-1861 *Poems.* London: Edward Moxon, 1844. First edition, mixed issue as usual, first impression of volume I, with "let the flood/of your salt scorn" to page 141, 2nd impression of volume II with 161 & 163 page numbers battered and with 'the end' to page 175, publisher's green cloth, near fine with some toning to spines, few tiny closed tears to spine ends, spine head of volume II rubbed and worn, clean bindings, former owner's bookplate to front pastedown, spines very lightly cracked inside rear covers, otherwise sturdy spines and secure binding, clean and pleasing set. free of any repairs or restoration, housed in custom light brown slipcase with dark brown morocco spine, with matching chemises.   B & B Rare Books, Ltd.   2015 - 2015 $2250

Browning, John *How to Work the Spectroscope: a Manual of Practical Manipulatin with Spectroscopes of all Kinds.* London: John Browning, n.d., 1882. Second edition, 8vo., original green cloth lettered black on spine and front cover, color frontispiece, 30 black and white engravings, inner hinge slightly cracked with signs of label removal from front pastedown and press cutting attached to first blank page, otherwise very good+.   Any Amount of Books   2015 - C14392   2015   £220

Browning, Robert 1812-1889 *Ferishtah's Fancies.* London: Smith, Elder and Co., 1884. First edition, inscribed "To G F Watts From Robert Browning Dec. 1884" not in Browning's hand, in very good original dark brown cloth boards with gilt title to spine and black decoration to front board, rubbing to hinges, edges and corners with short open tear to book along front hinge, foxing to first and last few pages with light pencil bracket marks to text and occasional folded corners, blue endpages, 143 pages plus 8 pages of ads, from the collection of Stuart B. Schimmel, very good.   The Kelmscott Bookshop   11 - 7   2015 $450

Browning, Robert 1812-1889 *Men and Women.* Oxford: Clarendon Press, 1920. Original dark blue cloth, slightly dulled, Geoffrey Tillotson's signed secondhand 'working copy' with some text emendations, notes and insertions.   Jarndyce Antiquarian Booksellers   CCVII - 118   2015   £40

Browning, Robert 1812-1889 *Parleyings with Certain People of Importance in Their Day...* London: Smith, Elder & Co., 1887. First edition, octavo, brick cloth stamped in black and gilt, small leather bookplate of English author and dramatist Alfred Sutro, previous bookplate removed, modest rubbing at extremities, very good or better.   Between the Covers Rare Books, Inc.   187 - 34   2015 $85

Browning, Robert 1812-1889 *The Pied Piper of Hamelin.* New York: Grosset & Dunlap, 1936. Probable first edition, folio, cloth backed pictorial boards, slight wear, near fine in soiled dust jacket, illustrations on every page in full color or detailed black and whites by Roger Duvoisin.   Aleph-bet Books, Inc.   109 - 147   2015 $200

Browning, Robert 1812-1889 *The Ring and the Book.* London: Smith, Elder, 1872. Second edition, 4 volumes, original brown cloth, bevelled boards, contemporary gift inscription on leading f.ep. "Ellen E. Cumpstore from J. S. Wood 1882", very good.   Jarndyce Antiquarian Booksellers   CCXI - 48   2015   £110

Browning, Robert 1812-1889 *The Ring and the Book.* London: Oxford University Press, 1912. Frontispiece, original brown cloth, inner hinge cracking, signed by Geoffrey Tillotson 6.II.45 with notes and marks.   Jarndyce Antiquarian Booksellers   CCVII - 119   2015   £22

Browning, Robert 1812-1889 *Sordello.* London: Edward Moxon, 1840. First edition, half title, 1 page ads, 15 page catalog Jan. 1840, Geoffrey Tillotson's copy with pencil markings by previous owner, with notes and inserted markers, stiff paper wrappers with paper label made by Geoffrey.   Jarndyce Antiquarian Booksellers   CCVII - 120   2015   £75

Bruccoli, Matthew J. *Kenneth Millar/Ross MacDonald: a checklist.* Detroit: Gale Research Co., 1971. First edition, 8vo., photos, inscribed by author to his lawyer Harris Seed, also laid-in is bookmark issued by publisher that prints the poem by author that also bears his holograph signature in ink, fine, bright copy.   Buckingham Books   March 2015 - 27904   2015 $1250

Bruccoli, Matthew J. *Kenneth Millar/Ross MacDonald: a Checklist.* Detroit: Gale Research, 1971. First edition, very fine.   Mordida Books   March 2015 - 008395   2015 $90

Bruccoli, Matthew J. *The Romantic Egoists.* New York: Scarecrow, 1974. First edition, very fine in dust jacket. Mordida Books   March 2015 - 012747   2015 $200

Bruccoli, Matthew J. *Ross MacDonald/Ken Millar: a Descriptive Bibliography.* Pittsburgh: University of Pittsburgh, 1983. First edition, very fine without dust jacket as issued.   Mordida Books   March 2015 - 008160   2015 $100

Bruce, Alexander *The Tutor's Guide...* Edinburgh: printed by M. Robert Freebairn..., 1714. First edition, 8vo., title printed in red and black, errata on verso of final leaf, contemporary panelled calf, raised bands, dark red spine label lettered gilt, very good, crisp copy with 18th century armorial bookplate of Simon Mackenzie of Scotsburn.   John Drury Rare Books   2015 - 23128   2015 $787

Bruen, Ken *Cross.* Gladestry: Scorpion Press, 2007. First edition, limited to 77 numbered copies signed by author, fine in quarter leather and marbled boards in transparent dust jacket.   Buckingham Books   March 2015 - 25249   2015 $175

Bruen, Ken *The Dead Room.* Mission Viejo: ASAP Press, 2005. First edition, one of 26 lettered copies signed by Bruen, Jason Starr (provided introduction and Phil Parks (artist), fine in publisher's green linen covered boards and matching clamshell box, wooden cross and printed bronze plate affixed to inside front panel, from the collection of Duke Collier.   Royal Books   36 - 144   2015 $1500

Bruen, Ken *The Dead Room.* Mission Viejo: ASAP Press, 2005. First edition, one of 150 numbered copies signed by Bruen, Jason Starr (provided introduction) and Phil Parks (the artist), fine in publisher's green linen covered boards, from the collection of Duke Collier.   Royal Books   36 - 143   2015 $750

Bruff, P. S. *Sunbonnet Babies.* London: Dean, n.d. circa, 1905. 4to., light corner stain, light soil, else very good, illustrations in color on every page by G. Hall, quite scarce. Aleph-bet Books, Inc.   109 - 456   2015 $475

Bruker, Manuel *Elogue De Lucien Mainssieux.* Manuel Bruker, 1950. First edition, no. 191 of 200 copies, 4to., unbound signatures laid into wrappers, 11 original lithographs including color frontispiece, spine of wrappers sunned, otherwise near fine.   Beasley Books   2013 - 2015 $300

Bruner, Helen Marcia *California's Old Burying Grounds.* San Francisco: National Society of Colonial Dames of America, 1945. First edition, very scarce, thin octavo, 24 pages, three text photos, printed tan wrappers, very fine copy, very scarce.   Argonaut Book Shop   Holiday Season 2014 - 40   2015 $60

Bruner, Peter *A Slave's Adventures Toward Freedom: Not Fiction, but the True Story of a Struggle.* Oxford: The author, 1919. First edition, small octavo, frontispiece, 3 plates blue and yellow lettered cloth, pencil notes on titlepage, little worn at extremities, near fine, signed by author beneath his portrait, uncommon.   Between the Covers Rare Books   197 - 58   2015 $550

Brunhoff, Jean De   1899-1937 *Babar et Le Pere Noel.* New York: Random House, 1941. First French language edition, folio, cloth backed pictorial boards, inconspicuous mend on two leaves, else very good+ in dust jacket chipped with some soil, calligraphic text and wonderful color lithos, scarce in dust jacket.   Aleph-bet Books, Inc.   109 - 117   2015 $1875

Brunhoff, Jean De   1899-1937 *Histoire De Babar.* Paris: Jardin des Modes, 1931. First edition, first issue of the first Babar book, folio, cloth backed pictorial boards, spine and edge of each cover faded and light cover soil, else clean, tight and very good+ color illustrations on every page, quite scarce.   Aleph-Bet Books, Inc.   108 - 125   2015 $2850

Brunhoff, Jean De   1899-1937 *The Travels of Babar.* New York: H. Smith & R. Haas, 1934. First US edition, folio, cloth backed pictorial boards, very slight cover soil, else very good+.   Aleph-Bet Books, Inc.   108 - 126   2015 $375

Brunhoff, Jean De   1899-1937 *Zephir's Holidays.* New York: Random House, 1937. First edition, folio, cloth backed pictorial boards, slight rubbing, near fine in edge frayed and chipped dust jacket, calligraphic text with some wonderful color illustrations.   Aleph-bet Books, Inc.   109 - 118   2015 $600

Brunhoff, Laurent De *Babar Visits Another Planet.* New York: Random House, 1972. 4to., slight edgewear, else very good+, signed twice by author with small sketch, full color illustrations by author.   Aleph-Bet Books, Inc.   108 - 126   2015 $250

Brunhoff, Laurent De *La Fete De Celesteville.* Paris: Hachette, 1954. First edition, folio, cloth backed pictorial boards, fine, wonderful and vivid color illustrations on every page by author, scarce in this condition.   Aleph-bet Books, Inc.   109 - 119   2015 $600

Brunner, John *The Shockwave Rider.* New York: Evanston: San Francisco: London: Harper & Row, 1975. First edition, octavo, cloth backed boards.   John W. Knott, Bookseller   Selected New Arrivals Jan. 2015 - 16943   2015 $150

Brunnow, Franz *Spherical Astronomy.* Berlin: Fred. Dummler (Harrwit & Grossman), 1865. First edition in English, contemporary half morocco and marbled paper covered boards, some rubbing and edgewear to boards, very good, tipped to titlepage is small pink slip with inscription "Professor Peck with much love the author" (almost certainly William Guy Peck).   Between the Covers Rare Books, Inc. 187 - 35 2015 $450

Bryant, Sara Cone *Epaminodas and His Auntie.* Boston: Houghton Mifflin, 1938. Square 8vo., pictorial cloth, cloth slightly faded, else very good in lightly soiled and frayed dust jacket, illustrations by Inez Hogan with silhouettes and yellow line illustrations.   Aleph-bet Books, Inc. 109 - 63 2015 $175

Bryant, William Cullen 1794-1878 *Picturesque America or the Land We Live In.* New York: 1872. First edition, 2nd issue, with Bryant's name on titlepage, massive quarto, full embossed leather, inner dentelles gilt as are all edges, last 20 pages and last two plates with fore edges damped, beveled edges, five raised bands on each backstrip mildly rubbed (one bruised but intact), backstrip gilt bright, modest rubbing, rear cover volume 1 with large very mild discoloration, both volumes firm and tight, 49 steel engraved plates, many full and partial page illustrations, remarkably free of foxing, tissue guards present, some with ghosting. Bookworm & Silverfish 2015 - 6014951925 2015 $650

Bryers, Duane *The Bunkhouse Boys from the Lazy Daisy Ranch.* Flagstaff: Northland Press, 1974. First edition, 4to., fine in fine dust jacket, artist has penned portrait of a cowboy on f.e.p. and he and Dee Ray have inscribed this copy.   Beasley Books 2013 - 2015 $150

Buc'Hoz, Pierre Josph *The Toilet of Flora; or a Collection of the Most Simple and Approved Methods of Preparing Baths, Essences, Pomatums, Powders, Perfumes and Sweet-scented Waters.* London: J. Murray and W. Nicoll, 1784. One of four early editions, 12mo., frontispiece, with half title, little, mainly marginal, browning and spotting, some light soiling, early ownership names on endpapers, contemporary mottled sheep, appropriately rebacked to match, gilt lettered, good copy.   John Drury Rare Books 2015 - 25294 2015 $830

Buchan, John 1875-1940 *The Gap in the Curtain.* London: Hodder and Stoughton, 1932. First edition, octavo, near fine in very good, slightly marked dust jacket with few nicks.   Peter Ellis, Bookseller 2014 - 018107 2015 £325

Buchan, John 1875-1940 *The King's Grace 1910-1935.* London: Hodder & Stoughton, 1935. Special Canadian edition, limited to 250 copies, this #209 signed by author, royal blue cloth with beveled edges, presentation box with title label and limitation number on front box, large 8vo., color frontispiece and other illustrations, fine.   Schooner Books Ltd. 110 - 161 2015 $200

Buchan, John 1875-1940 *Prester John.* London: Edinburgh: Dublin: Leeds: and New York: Thomas Nelson and sons, 1910. First edition, inserted frontispiece map, original green cloth, spine stamped in white and gold, decorated endpapers.   L. W. Currey, Inc. Boy's Adventure Fiction 2015 - 23 2015 $350

Buchan, John 1875-1940 *Prester John.* London: Edinburgh: Dublin and New York: Thomas Nelson and Sons, n.d., 1911. First illustrated edition, inserted frontispiece map and 7 inserted plates and illustrations in color by Stephen Reid, titlepage printed in red and black, original green cloth, front and spine panels stamped in red, white and gold, pictorial paper onlay affixed to front panel, gray endpapers.   L. W. Currey, Inc. Boy's Adventure Fiction 2015 - 39 2015 $200

Buchan, John 1875-1940 *Sick Heart River.* London: Hodder & Stoughton, 1941. First edition, very good, some spotting on front cover, otherwise very good in price clipped dust jacket with internal tape mends and spotting on back panel.   Mordida Books March 2015 - 000337 2015 $85

Buchan, William 1729-1805 *Every Man His Own Doctor or a Treatise on the Prevention and Cure of Diseases by Regimen and Simple Medicines.* New Haven: Nathan Whiting, 1816. Contemporary sheep, minor foxing and soiling, good, sound copy.   Joseph J. Felcone Inc. Science, Medicine and Technology - 31 2015 $250

Buchanan, A. W. Patrick *The Bench and Bar of Lower Canada Down to 1850.* Montreal: Burton's Limited, 1925. 8vo., card covers, cover edges chipped and worn, generally very good, some pages uncut.   Schooner Books Ltd. 110 - 162 2015 $75

Buchanan, George 1506-1582 *Octupla; hoc est Octo Paraphrases Poeticae Psalmi CIV.* Edinburgh: Excudebant Haeredes & Successores Andreae Anderson, 1696. One of two reissues, 8vo., contemporary sprinkled panelled calf, spine with gilt crowned orange device of the Earl of Marchmont (joints cracking, spine rubbed), bound for Patrick Hume, 1st Earl of Marchmont, 1641-1724, signature of Lord Polwarth, from the library of James Stevens Cox (1910-1997).   Maggs Bros. Ltd. 1447 - 55 2015 £280

Buck, Frank *Wild Cargo.* New York: Simon and Schuster, 1932. First edition, nicely inscribed by author for Nicholas Delbanco, fine in slightly soiled but fine dust jacket. Between the Covers Rare Books, Inc. 187 - 36 2015 $225

Buck, Pearl S. *Of Men and Women.* New York: John Day, 1941. First edition, inscribed by author to Philadelphia bookseller Mabel Zahn, small stain at spine crown corresponding to jacket chip, very good in very good, spine tanned dust jacket with very minor edge loss.   Ken Lopez, Bookseller 164 - 21 2015 $375

Buck, Pearl S. *To My Daughters, with Love.* New York: John Day Co., 1967. First edition, 8vo., near fine in very good++, signed by author, price clipped dust jacket with minimal sun spine, scarce signed. By the Book, L. C. Special List 10 - 24   2015 $150

Buckbee, Edna Bryan *The Saga of Old Tuolumne.* New York: Press of the Pioneers, 1935. First edition, frontispiece, 18 photos, gilt lettered red cloth, very fine and bright, pictorial dust jacket. Argonaut Book Shop   Holiday Season 2014 - 291   2015 $250

Buckingham, James Silk *An Earnest Plea for the Reign of Temperance and Peace as Conducive to the Prosperity of Nations; submitted to the Visitors of the Great Exhibition...* London: Peter Jackson, Late Fisher Son & Co. Angel Street, St. Martin's-le-Grand, n.d., 1851. First edition, presentation copy, 8vo., lithographed frontispiece and folding colored chart on taxation at rear, strangely paginated, as noted in an apology at end of work, but would appear to be complete, apart from few minor marks and cancelled library stamp at foot of title (not touching text), clean throughout, original blindstamped cloth, upper cover lettered and tooled gilt, spine lettered in white, lightly sunned, still very good, inscribed by author to poet and writer Edwin Atherstone, dated July 26 1851. Marlborough Rare Books Ltd.   List 49 - 3   2015   £300

Buckingham, James Silk *Inaugural Lecture, Written for the Opening of the British Foreign Institute and Delivered in a Abridged Form, Before the members and Friends of that Association on Wednesday the 2nd of August 1843 at the Hanover Square Rooms.* London: Fisher Son & Co., 1843. First edition, 8vo., last few leaves little foxed, original blindstamped blue cloth with title in gilt on upper cover, neatly rebacked, all edges gilt, very good presentation copy inscribed in ink by author for members of the Royal Yacht Squadron bookplates and press marks, rare. John Drury Rare Books   March 2015 - 17734   2015 $266

Buckingham, John Sheffield, 1st Duke of   1648-1721 *The Temple of Death a Poem...* London: printed and sold by H. Hills, 1709. First of two printings by Hills, with siganture A2 under words "which it" as opposed to first letters of "which", 16 pages, 8vo., disbound, trimmed bit close at top, affecting some page numbers, otherwise good copy. C. R. Johnson   Foxon R-Z - 1228r-z   2015 $77

Buckingham, John Sheffield, 1st Duke of   1648-1721 *The Temple of Death, a Poem...* London: printed and sold by H. Hills, 1709. Second of two printings, with signature A2 under the word "which", 8vo., disbound, bit browned, otherwise good. C. R. Johnson   Foxon R-Z - 1229r-z   2015 $77

Buckland Wright, John *Sensuous Lines. A Catalogue Raisonne of the Intaglio Prints....* Upper Denby: Fleece Press, 2014. One of 220 copies (from an edition of 360 copies), with original tipped-in copper engraving frontispiece, over 400 illustrations, oblong 4to., original quarter red cloth with 'false Suminagashi marbled paper' sides, backstrip with grey paper label printed in black, errata slip tipped into front pastedown, slipcase with original prospectus laid in, fine. Blackwell's Rare Books   B179 - 149   2015   £292

Buckland, Francis Trevelyan *Log-Book of a Fisherman and Zoologist.* London: Chapman & Hall, 1875. First edition, wood engraved frontispiece, 3 plates, illustrations in text, endpapers through-set on to outside of flyleaves, 8vo., original cloth, slightly darkened an worn, neat repair to front inner hinge and spine ends, inscribed by author on inside front cover, good, presentation from author to friend Henry Lee Aug. 12 1875, the copy of Dr. Emile Louis Bruno Clement (1844-1928). Blackwell's Rare Books   B179 - 23   2015   £225

Buckland, Gail *Who Shot Rock & Roll: a Photographic History 1955-the Present.* New York: Knopf, 2009. First edition, more than 200 photos, this copy signed by Buckland and by photographers Bob Gruen and Godlis, fine in fine dust jacket, uncommon with signatures. Ken Lopez, Bookseller   164 - 167   2015 $300

Bucknell, William *The Eccaleobion; a Treatise on Artificial Incubation.* London: printed and published for the author, 1839. First edition, 8vo., 2 parts in one volume, errata slip tipped in, bound recently in grey boards with printed title on upper cover, very good. John Drury Rare Books   2015 - 20523   2015 $656

Budd, Henry *A Petition Proposed to be Presented Respectively to the Three Estates of the Legislature on the Subject of Church Reform.* London: L. B. Selley and Sons, 1833. First edition, 8vo., half title creased and foxed, slight foxing at foot of titlepage, preserved in modern wrappers with printed title label on upper cover, good, very rare. John Drury Rare Books   March 2015 - 23054   2015 $221

Budden, Maria Elizabeth *True Stories from Ancient History...* London: 1822. First illustrated edition, 2 volumes, 12mo., period style full crushed morocco gilt by Bayntun, 72 hand colored plates. Honey & Wax Booksellers   3 - 8   2015 $2500

Budden, Maud *Curly Wee in Further Exciting Episodes of His Adventures.* Madras: The Mail, 1950. 4to., pictorial boards, as new in publisher's printed mailer (faded), illustrated with cartoon panels in color by Roland Clibborn, outstanding copy, rare in this condition. Aleph-Bet Books, Inc.   108 - 90   2015 $400

Buechner, Frederick *A Long Day's Dying.* New York: Alfred A. Knopf, 1950. First edition, fine, crisp copy in near fine dust jacket caused by slight ghost on verso from removal of strip of cellophane tape.   Buckingham Books   March 2015 - 37936   2015 $275

Buel, J. W. *Russian Nihilism and Exile Life in Siberia.* Philadelphia: Historical Pub., 1889. First edition, hardcover, damping to rear board and fore-edge of front board, good to very good.   Beasley Books   2013 - 2015 $150

Buffon, Louis Leclerc De *Histoire Naturelle Des Oiseaux.* Paris: 1780+, 12mo., volumes 12-15 containing 66 full page plates, full marbled 18th century calf, backstrips gilt extra, all edges rubricated, marbled endpapers, backstrip end wear.   Bookworm & Silverfish   2015 - 5621156705   2015 $385

Buffum, E. Gould *Six Months in the Gold Mines: from a Journal of three Years' Residence in Upper and Lower California 1847-8-9.* Lea and Blanchard, 1850. First edition, 12mo., original decorated black cloth, light wear to spine ends, small old waterstain to bottom edge of first four pages, inked name on front pastedown sheet and few ink spots to front and rear fly leaf, text block clean with no foxing, attractive binding, very good.   Buckingham Books   March 2015 - 34571   2015 $1250

Bukowski, Charles *Shakespeare Never Did This.* San Francisco: Cty Lights Books, 1979. First edition, numerous photos by Michael Montfort, inscribed by author for Silvanna, with self caricature, with address label of director Barbet Schroeder on inside front cover, along with coffee spot that has been circled, labeled 'Authentic!' and signed by Barbet, laid in is NS from Schroeder to Silvana presenting the book as a birthday gift, near fine wrapper issue.   Ken Lopez, Bookseller   164 - 22   2015 $1250

Bulfinch, Thomas *Legends of Charlemagne.* New York: Cosmopolitan book, 1924. First Wyeth edition, 4to., maroon cloth, pictorial paste-on, top edge gilt, fine, illustrations by N. C. Wyeth.   Aleph-bet Books, Inc.   109 - 495   2015 $350

Bullar, John *The Brothers: a Brief Narrative of the Character and Death of Pretor and Thomas Whitty (First Part)....(Second Part).* Southampton: printed by and for T. Baker, 1821. First edition, 2 parts in one volume, 8vo., few leaves lightly browned, few spots, contemporary polished calf gilt, spine gilt with morocco lettering piece, chip at head and rubbed at extremities, still pleasing copy.   Marlborough Rare Books   List 53 - 5   2015   £225

Buller, A. H. *Selecta Fungorum Carpologia of the Brothers L. R. and C. Tulasne.* Oxford: Clarendon, 1931. Folio, 3 volumes, 61 uncolored plates, fine set, slightly chipped dust jackets.   Andrew Isles   2015 - 13391   2015 $950

Bulliet, C. J. *Venus Castina. Famous Female Impersonators, Celestial and Human.* New York: Covici Friede, 1928. First edition, one of 960 numbered copies, #754, 4to., black cloth and patterned boards, housed in publisher's original slipcase with large label with title, etc., very good plus with occasional spotting to pages, couple of snags to slipcase spine.   Ed Smith Books 83 - 6   2015 $350

Bullivant, Cecil Henry *The Woman Wins.* London: C. Arthur Pearson, 1919. First edition, half title, 3 pages ads, original blue cloth, spine slightly faded, slightly dulled pictorial dust jacket, signature of M. J. Bancroft.   Jarndyce Antiquarian Booksellers   CCXI - 49   2015   £35

Bulloch, John *George Jamesone the Scottish Vandyck.* Edinburgh: David Douglas, 1885. First edition, No. 187 of 250 copies initialled by author, 8vo., original green cloth lettered gilt on spine and front cover, uncut, frontispiece, one plate, slight marks to cover, slight soiling, otherwise decent, very good copy.   Any Amount of Books   2015 - A6y1722   2015   £150

Bullock Shan, F. *Mors et Vita.* London: T. Werner Laurie, 1923. Limited to 350 copies, 8vo., original cream quarter vellum style lettered black over green boards, very slight foxing to prelims, otherwise near fine, very slightly discolored dust jacket, excellent condition.   Any Amount of Books   2015 - A9715   2015   £300

Bulteel, John *The Apophthegems of the Ancients...* London: for William Cademan, 1683. First edition, 8vo., first blank leaf, small paper flaw to lower blank margin of N6, light browning and some light spotting, contemporary sheep, joints rubbed, wormhole to top joint, tiny chip to headcap, pastedowns unstuck, from the library of James Stevens Cox (1910-1997).   Maggs Bros. Ltd.   1447 - 56   2015   £360

Bunau-Varilla, Philippe *Panama - The Creation, Destruction Resurrection.* London: Constable, 1913. First UK edition, octavo, illustrations, 2 folding plans, original brown cloth lettered gilt, cloth snagged at head of spine, fore-edge spotted, very good, scarce.   Peter Ellis, Bookseller   2014 - 019213   2015   £300

Bunge, Mario *Treatise on Basic Philosophy.* Dordrecht: Boston: D. Reidel Pub., 1974. First edition, 9 volumes, 8vo., illustrations, all about very good with some chips and nicks to jackets but clean with clean text.   Any Amount of Books   2015 - A91417   2015   £240

Bunn, Alfred *Old England and New England, in a Series of Views Taken on the Spot.* London: Richard Benley, 1853. First edition, 2 volumes, 12mo., half title volume I only, color frontispiece, folding table, prelims slightly foxed, original green cloth, elaborate gilt borders and decorated gilt spine, corners slightly rubbed, uneven fading on lower board volume II, very good, all edges gilt.   Jarndyce Antiquarian Booksellers   CCXI - 52   2015   £250

Buntline, Ned *Buffalo Bill. The King of Border Men.* J. S. Ogilvie & Co., 1881. First edition,, First edition, 11 3/4 x 8 5/8 inches, printed wrappers, spine reinforced with paper tape, tears and chips to front page, old waterstain to top edge of few pages, reinforced at a number of points with adhesive backed paper tape, entire rear cover completely backed and reinforced, overall good, entire contents legible. Buckingham Books   March 2015 - 36105   2015 $650

Bunyan, John 1628-1688 *The Pilgrim's Progress...* London: Routledge, 1862. New edition, illustrations by John Gilbert, frontispiece and plates, ads on endpapers, original dark green cloth, color paper pasted on by Geoffrey Tillotson, inner hinge splitting, rubbed, ms. label defective, presentation to Joseph Tillotson, with Kathleen Tillotson's notes and Geoffrey's notes and marginal marks, from the library of Geoffrey & Kathleen Tillotson.   Jarndyce Antiquarian Booksellers   CCVII - 123   2015   £30

Burchell, William John *Travels in the Interior of Southern Africa.* London: printed for Longman, Hurst, Rees, Orme and Brown, 1822-1824. First edition, 2 volumes, quarto, bound without half titles and final blank in first volume but with the 4 page "Hints on Emigration to the Cape of Good Hope" (which was printed separately in 1824 and not found in all copies), with half page errata slip to beginning of volume 1, largely folding engraved map, 20 hand colored aquatint plates, 96 wood engraved vignettes, inscribed by author for niece Ruth Burchell, contemporary purple morocco, expertly rabacked to style over blue morocco, covers with elaborate gilt panels, spines with gilt on compartments and lettering, all edges gilt, some offsetting from plates, map with some minor fold tears, ZZ4 volume two with one inch tear to upper blank margin (not affecting any lettering), hinges starting, previous owner's bookplate of each volume, overall very good, tight and clean.   Heritage Book Shop   Holiday 2014 - 23   2015 $12,500

Burden, Philip D. *The Mapping of North America. A List of Printed Maps 1511-1670.* Rickmansworth: Raleigh Publications, 1996. Small folio, cloth, dust jacket, corners bumped, 11 color plates, 418 black and white plates.   Oak Knoll Books   306 - 82   2015 $195

Burden, Philip D. *The Mapping of North America II. A List of Printed Maps 1671-1700.* Rickmansworth: Raleigh Publications, 2007. Small folio, dust jacket, 12 color plates, 392 black and white plates, corners bumped.   Oak Knoll Books   306 - 83   2015 $195

Bureau of American Ethnology *Twenty-Fourth Annual Report.* 1907. Front cover creased, mildly ex-library.   Bookworm & Silverfish   2015 - 3447169482   2015 $175

Burges, Mary Anne *The Progress of the Pilgrim Good-Intent in Jacobinical Times.* Charlestown: Samuel Etheridge, 1801. Fifth English edition, 8vo., removed, sheets uniformly browned, title foxed, otherwise foxing and age stains most confined to ample margins.   M & S Rare Books, Inc.   97 - 44   2015 $85

Burges, Tristam *Remarks... at the Celebration of the Fourth of July in Clayville.* Providence: printed at the office of the Daily Advertiser, 1829. First edition, 8vo., sewn as issued, sheets browned, title stained, sound, fore and bottom margins, untrimmed.   M & S Rare Books, Inc.   97 - 267   2015 $100

Burgess, Gelett *The Master of Mysteries.* 1912. First edition, near fine, tight, bright copy, illustrations by Karl Anderson and George Brehm, sharp copy.   Buckingham Books   March 2015 - 37309   2015 $750

Burgess, Jack A. *Trains to Yosemite.* Berkeley & Wilton: Signature Press, 2004. First edition, quarto, color and black and white photos, technical drawings, maps, black cloth lettered in white on spine, very fine, as new, with pictorial dust jacket.   Argonaut Book Shop   Holiday Season 2014 - 41   2015 $250

Burgess, Thornton 1866-1951 *A Box of Burgess Books.* Racine: Whitman, 1927. 4 books, each 5 1/2 x 4 5/8 inches, contained in original brightly illustrated publisher's box 11 x 5 inches, pictorial boards, fine in dust jackets few closed tears but very good+.   Aleph-bet Books, Inc.   109 - 77   2015 $1200

Burgess, Thornton 1866-1951 *Happy Jack Squirrel's Bright Idea.* New York: Eggers, 1928. 8vo., stiff pictorial wrappers, near fine, illustrations by Harrison Cady.   Aleph-bet Books, Inc.   109 - 78   2015 $90

Burgoyne, John *A State of the Expedition from Canada, As laid before the House of Commons by Lieutenant General Burgoyne and Versified by Evidence...* London: printed for J. Almon, 1780. First edition, quarto, 6 folding maps, including frontispiece, all maps have some contemporary hand coloring in outline, two of the maps with overslips all maps engraved by William Faden, 19th century half black morocco over marbled boards, spine stamped and lettered gilt, all edges speckled brown, green silk place holder, edges bit rubbed, bit of light offsetting to maps, generally very clean, previous owner F. A. Crownshield's bookplate, overall very good.   Heritage Book Shop   Holiday 2014 - 24   2015 $8500

Burgoyne, Michael Hamilton *Mamluk Jerusalem: an Architectural Study.* N.P. (United Kingdom): pub. on Behalf of the British School of Archaeology in Jerusalem by the World of Islam Festival Trust, 1987. First edition, 4to., illustrations in black and white, folding map loosely inserted, neat name on front endpaper (2410 of 3000 copies), otherwise fine in fine dust jacket and slipcase. Any Amount of Books 2015 - A82787 2015 £275

Burke, B. W. *A Compendium of the Anatomy, Physiology and Pathology of the Horse...* Philadelphia: James Humphreys, 1806. First American edition, 12mo., 2 plates, contemporary mottled sheep, plates moderately foxed, upper spine cap partly chipped, small chip from spine label, else very attractive in handsome period binding, ownership signature of Wm. Gunkle 1818. Joseph J. Felcone Inc. Science, Medicine and Technology - 15 2015 $1000

Burke, Bill *Portraits.* New York: Ecco Press, 1987. First edition, signed by Ray Carver and inscribed by Carver, photos by Burke, fine in near fine dust jacket. Ed Smith Books 83 - 8 2015 $500

Burke, Edmund 1729-1797 *An Account of the European Settlements in America.* London: R. and J. Dodsley, 1757. First edition, 2 volumes, octavo, 2 engraved folding maps, modern full calf to style, black morocco spine labels lettered in gilt, 2 small paper repairs to title volume II and marginal repair to one other leaf, overall near fine. Heritage Book Shop Holiday 2014 - 25 2015 $1500

Burke, Edmund 1729-1797 *Bemerkungen uber die Franzosische Revoluzion und das Betragen Einiger Gesellschafte in London bey Diesen Ereignissne...* Wien: Joseph Stahel, 1791. First edition in German, 8vo., engraved portrait, tiny localised stain in extreme lower corners of several leaves, contemporary ownership signature of Ladislai Melizer, contemporary German half calf over marbled boards, flat spine with blind lines and three contrasting labels including oval label with Melizer's initials, slight wear to fore edges of boards, else fine in handsome binding. John Drury Rare Books 2015 - 23546 2015 $1005

Burke, Edmund 1729-1797 *Correspondence of the Right Honourable Edmund Burke between the Year 1744 and the Period of His Decease in 1797.* London: Francis & John Rivington, 1844. First edition, 4 volumes, original brown cloth, decorations on spine and rules in blind, covers scuffed and marked and bruised at corners, covers volume I little waterstained, very good, internally bright set. Peter Ellis, Bookseller 2014 - 014534 2015 £275

Burke, Edmund 1729-1797 *Letters, Speeches and Tracts on Irish Affairs Collected and Arranged by Matthew Arnold.* London: Macmillan, 1881. Half title 2 pages ads, original dark blue cloth, slightly chipped, spine faded, inner hinges cracking, from the library of Geoffrey & Kathleen Tillotson. Jarndyce Antiquarian Booksellers CCVII - 60 2015 £35

Burke, Edmund 1729-1797 *Reflexions sur la Revolution de France.* Paris: Adrien Egron, 1819. Nouvelle edition, half title, some slight borning, unusual contemporary continental marbled paper boards, brown spine label lettered in gilt, gilt decoration head and tail of spine, very nice. Jarndyce Antiquarian Booksellers CCXI - 53 2015 £180

Burke, James Lee *Bitterroot.* New Orleans: B. E. Trice, 2001. First edition, one of 150 specially bound copies, numbered and signed by Burke, fine in fine slipcase, still sealed. Beasley Books 2013 - 2015 $125

Burke, James Lee *Black Cherry Blues.* Boston: Little Brown and Co., 1989. First edition, signed, fine in dust jacket. Buckingham Books March 2015 - 18918 2015 $250

Burke, James Lee *Cadillac Jukebox.* New Orleans: Trice, 1995. Limited, numbered edition, one of 175 specially bound numbered copies signed by Burke, very fine in slipcase, without dust jacket as issued. Mordida Books March 2015 - 010050 2015 $175

Burke, James Lee *Cadillac Juke Box.* New York: Hyperion, 1996. Special American Bookseller's Association Collectors Edition, with embossed juke box on plain white front panel of jacket, very fine. Mordida Books March 2015 - 011662 2015 $100

Burke, James Lee *Cimarron Rose.* London: Orion, 1997. First edition, very fine in dust jacket, signed by author. Mordida Books March 2015 - 009662 2015 $100

Burke, James Lee *The Convict.* Baton Rouge: Louisiana University Press, 1985. First edition, signed by author, fine in fine dust jacket, from the collection of Duke Collier. Royal Books 36 - 146 2015 $4000

Burke, James Lee *The Convict and Other Stories.* London: Orion, 1995. First English edition, very fine in dust jacket. Mordida Books March 2015 - 011650 2015 $150

Burke, James Lee *Half of Paradise.* Boston: Houghton Mifflin, 1965. First edition, small faint stain on fore-edge, otherwise fine in dust jacket with tiny closed tears at spine ends, couple of short closed tears, scrape on inner front flap, signed by author. Mordida Books March 2015 - 000019 2015 $2000

Burke, James Lee *Heaven's Prisoners.* New York: Henry Holt and Co., 1988. First edition, signed, pages evenly browned, else fine in dust jacket. Buckingham Books March 2015 - 18917 2015 $275

Burke, James Lee *In the Electric Mist with Confederate Dead.* New York: Hyperion, 1993. First edition, one of 150 numbered copies signed by author, gilt lettering on spine, fine in shrink wrapped slipcase.   Buckingham Books   March 2015 - 18921   2015 $200

Burke, James Lee *Lay Down My Sword and Shield.* New York: Thomas Y Crowell, 1971. First edition, inscribed by author, review copy with publisher's slip and promotional letter laid in, fine in fine dust jacket, from the collection of Duke Collier.   Royal Books   36 - 145   2015 $2000

Burke, James Lee *The Lost Get-Back Boogie.* Baton Rouge: Louisiana State University Press, 1986. First edition, signed by author, fine in fine dust jacket.   Ken Lopez, Bookseller   164 - 24 2015 $500

Burke, James Lee *The Lost Get Back Boggie.* Baton Rouge and London: Louisiana State University Press, 1986. First edition, signed by author, fine, crisp copy in like dust jacket.   Ed Smith Books   82 - 7   2015 $750

Burke, James Lee *A Morning for Flamingos.* Boston: Little Brown, 1990. First edition, very fine in dust jacket.   Mordida Books   March 2015 - 009682   2015 $145

Burke, Thomas *The Bloomsbury Wonder.* London: Mandrake, 1929. First edition, fine in lightly soiled dust jacket.   Mordida Books   March 2015 - 000350   2015 $200

Burke, Thomas *Limehouse Nights. Tales of Chinatown.* London: Grant Richards, 1916. First edition, lightly foxed on front and rear endpapers, else very good, tight.   Buckingham Books   March 2015 - 3511106   2015 $750

Burke, Thomas *The Sun in Splendour.* New York: Doran, 1926. First edition, fine in lightly soiled dust jacket with couple of closed tears on front panel.   Mordida Books   March 2015 - 000349   2015 $75

Burke, Thomas *Vagabond Minstrel: the Adventures of Thomas Dermody.* London: Longmans, Green and Co., 1936. First edition, 8vo., original blue cloth lettered purple on spine, file copy stamp on front endpaper "File copy/Not to be Taken Away", endpapers with some browning, covers very slightly faded, otherwise very good+ in very good, slightly rubbed and slightly edgeworn (with no loss), dust jacket, pleasing copy, rare.   Any Amount of Books   2015 - C742   2015   £240

Burke, Thomas *Whispering Windows: Tales of the Waterside.* London: Grant Richards, 1921. First edition, 8vo., original burnt sienna cloth lettered black on spine and cover, very good in somewhat used dust jacket (which is very good- - chipped at head of spine, slightly discolored at spine, front panel of jacket very good showing some abrasion, possibly from label removal).   Any Amount of Books   2015 - C1896   2015   £160

Burke, Thomas *Whispering Windows.* London: Richards, 1921. First edition, near fine in dust jacket with slightly darkened spine and several internal tape mends, signed by author.   Mordida Books   March 2015 - 008225   2015 $475

Burley, W. J. *To Kill a Cat.* London: Gollancz, 1970. First edition, former owner's name on front flyleaf, else very good in lightly soiled dust jacket with light wear to head of spine.   Buckingham Books   March 2015 - 9530   2015 $325

Burn, John Southerden *Registrum Ecclesiae Parochialis. The History of the Parish Registers in England, also of the Registers of Scotland, Ireland, the East and West Indies...* London: Edward Suter, 1829. First edition, 8vo., complete with final leaf (errata on recto, imprint on verso), original boards, neatly rebacked, entirely uncut, very good, from the library of Henry Alworth Merewether (1780-1864), the distinguished lawyer, with his signature, notes of purchase in 1829, with ms. notes in text.   John Drury Rare Books   2015 - 14897   2015 $221

Burnaby, Anthony *Two Proposals, Humbly Offer'd to the Honourable House of Commons, Now Assembled in Parliament.* London: printed in the year, 1696. First edition, old burnhole in leaf A3 affecting one word on verso, recently well bound in old style quarter calf gilt, very good.   John Drury Rare Books   March 2015 - 8119   2015 $656

Burne-Jones, Edward *Drawings of Sir Edward Burne-Jones.* London and New York: George Newnes and Charles Scribner's Sons, n.d., 1905. 4to., (46) plates, original green cloth spine over brown illustrated boards, lettered gilt at spine, copiously illustrated, very early jacket, faint offsetting to front endpaper, otherwise near fine in very good, printed and illustrated dust jacket, slightly marked and slightly chipped at head of spine.   Any Amount of Books   2015 - C13480   2015   £175

Burnet, Gilbert *The Life of William Bedell, D.D., Bishop of Kilmore in Ireland. (bound with) An Abstract of the Number of Protestant and Popish families in the Several Counties and Provinces of Ireland.* Dublin: M. Rhames for R. Gunne, Bookseller in Capel Street, 1736. Second edition, 8vo., full brown leather, plain spine, 5 raised bands, lacks spine label but has title in blindstamp, some rubbing, slight marks and scuffing but sound, about very good with pleasing, clean text.   Any Amount of Books   March 2015 - A72900   2015   £400

Burnet, Thomas *The Theory of the Earth...* London: R. Norton for Walter Kettilby, 1684. First edition, folio, engraved frontispiece, 12 engraved plates in text and 2 double page engraved plates, 80mm. tear along fold of second plate from lower margin, occasional spotting and light browning, contemporary sprinkled calf, covers panelled in blind, front joint split but firm, covers little scuffed, headcaps broken, lower corner on front cover damaged, other corners and edges rubbed, from the library of James Stevens Cox (1910-1997).   Maggs Bros. Ltd.   1447 - 58   2015   £750

Burnett, Frances Hodgson *Sara Crewe: or What Happened at Miss Minchin's.* New York: Charles Scribner's Sons, 1888. First edition, 8 1/2 x 6 7/8 inches, frontispiece + 5 black and white wood engravings by Reginald Birch, light brown cloth with gilt, red and black stamped lettering and design to spine and cover, average wear and rubbing to spine and board edges, light soiling to boards, spine ends significantly worn, gilt to cover bright, very good.   Tavistock Books   Bah, Humbug? - 3   2015 $275

Burnett, W. R. *Little Caesar.* New York: Lincoln MacVeagh, Dial Press, 1929. First edition, fine, bright square copy in neatly price clipped dust jacket with some light professional restoration at edges, exceptional copy.   Buckingham Books   March 2015 - 32777   2015 $7500

Burnett, William G. *Better a patriot Soldier's Grave the History of the Sixth Ohio Volunteer Cavalry.* N.P.: 1982. First edition, 257 pages, fine in fine, unclipped dust jacket.   Bookworm & Silverfish   2015 - 6017543349   2015 $45

Burnham, Carrie *Woman Suffrage. the Argument of... Before Chief Justice Reed and Associate Justices Agnew, Sharswood and Mercur of the Supreme Court of Pennsylvania in Banc, on the Third and Fourth of April 1873.* Philadelphia: Citizen's Suffrage Assoc., 1873. First edition, 8vo., contemporary sheep, some stained, expertly rebacked, very good, clean, tight, scarce.   Second Life Books Inc.   189 - 37   2015 $750

Burnham, Leavitt *Guide to the Union Pacific Railroad Lands. 12,000,000 Acres. 3,000,000 Acres in Central and Eastern Nebraska Now for Sale.* Omaha: Land Department Union Pacific Railroad Co., 1879. First edition, 8vo., pictorial wrappers, map on back cover, 32 pages, illustrations, maps, two engraved views from Elkhorn & Platte, light stamp of Union Pacific Railroad on upper portion of front cover, else fine, bright copy.   Buckingham Books   March 2015 - 30999   2015 $1750

Burns, Robert   1759-1796 *Poems, Chiefly the Scottish Dialect.* London: printed for A. Strahan, T. Cadell in the Strand, W. Creech, Edinburgh, 1787. frontispiece, bound without half title, contemporary half calf, marbled boards, spine with raised and gilt bands, red morocco label, very slightly rubbed, slight wear to marbled paper on edges of following board, very good, clean, attractive contemporary binding.   Jarndyce Antiquarian Booksellers   CCXI - 54   2015   £1500

Burns, Robert   1759-1796 *Poems Chiefly in the Scottish Dialect.* Kilmamock: James McKie, 1869. 1886. First edition thus, limited to 600 copies, all signed by publisher James McKie, 4 volumes, 8vo., original blue paper covered boards with white parchment style spine complete with printed title labels, sound clean, very good, minor shelf wear and slight tanning at spine, decent set.   Any Amount of Books   2015 - C16551   2015   £300

Burns, Robert   1759-1796 *The Works of...* London: printed for T. Cadell and W. Davies and W. Creech at Edinburgh, 1814. 5 volumes, frontispiece in volume I, closed tear to titlepage in volume i, crown 8vo., mid 20th century brown straight grained morocco, French fillets on sides, spines gilt in compartments, citron lettering pieces, gilt inner dentelles, for Aspreys, spines trifle faded.   Blackwell's Rare Books   B179 - 24   2015   £350

Burns, William *The Crevice.* New York: Watt, 1915. First edition, fine, illustrations by Will Grefe, bright pictorial covers, lightly soiled dust jacket with nicks at spine ends and light wear at corners.   Mordida Books   March 2015 - 006539   2015 $300

Burnup, Henry *The Carriage Tax. A Letter to the Right Hon. Sir Charles Wood, Bart. Chancellor of the Exchequer.* London: printed by J. King, 1851. First edition, 8vo., modern wrappers, printed title label on upper cover, apparently very rare.   John Drury Rare Books   March 2015 - 23678   2015 $221

Burr, Hattie A. *The Woman Suffrage Cook Book.* Boston: in aid of the Festival and Bazaar, December 13-19, 1886. "Country Store" April 21-26, 1890. Second edition, 8vo., printed paper covered boards with cloth spine, cover very little soiled, but near fine, scarce.   Second Life Books Inc.   190 - 40   2015 $950

Burroughs, Charles *A Discourse Delivered in the Chapel of the New Alms-House in Portsmouth, N.H. Dec. XV MDCCCXXXIV on the Occasion of its Being First Opened for Religious Services.* Portsmouth: J. W. Foster, 1835. First edition, 8vo., 108 pages, including half title, very minor foxing on last couple of leaves, well bound recently in cloth backed marbled boards with printed title label on upper cover, very good, very scarce outside US.   John Drury Rare Books   March 2015 - 21405   2015   £266

Burroughs, Edgar Rice   1875-1950   *A Fighting Man of Mars.*   New York: Metropolitan Books, 1931. First edition, octavo, frontispiece, original red cloth lettered in green on front cover and spine, top edge stained green, near fine in original pictorial dust jacket by Hugh Hutton, price clipped with small tear neatly repaired to front panel, spine very slightly chipped along extremities.   Heritage Book Shop   Holiday 2014 - 26   2015 $1750

Burroughs, Edgar Rice   1875-1950   *Jungle Tales of Tarzan.*   Leipzig: Bernhard Tauchnitz, 1921. Copyright edition, half title, leaves little browned, original beige cloth, morocco label, slightly dulled.   Jarndyce Antiquarian Booksellers   CCXI - 55   2015   £30

Burroughs, Edgar Rice   1875-1950   *New Adventures of Tarzan "Pop-Up".*   Chicago: Pleasure Books/Blue Ribbon, 1935. Square 4to., pictorial boards, fine, fabulous pop-ups by Stephen Sleisinger and 2 black and whites on each page of text, nice.   Aleph-bet Books, Inc.   109 - 369   2015 $875

Burroughs, Edgar Rice   1875-1950   *Tamar of Pellacidor.*   New York: Metropolitan Books, 1930. First edition, octavo, frontispiece, original bright blue cloth lettered in black on front cover and spine, spine very slightly rubbed at extremities, otherwise fine, original color pictorial dust jacket.   Heritage Book Shop   Holiday 2014 - 27   2015 $2250

Burroughs, Edgar Rice   1875-1950   *Tarzan: the Lost Adventure.*   Milwaukee: Dark Horse, 1995. First edition, very fine, signed by author, soft covers.   Mordida Books   March 2015 - 005324   2015 $100

Burroughs, Margaret T. G.   *Life with Margaret, the Official Autobiography.*   Chicago: Time Pub. and Media Group, 2003. First edition, glossy printed boards, issued without dust jacket, 8vo., fine, inscribed by author.   Beasley Books   2013 - 2015 $125

Burroughs, Stephen   *Memoirs of Stephen Burroughs.*   Hanover: Benjamin True, 1798. Boston: Caleb Bingham, 1804, First editions, 2 volumes 8vo, volume I original tree calf, errata at bottom of page 296, title in red leather on spine, bookplate of William L. Clements Library of American History of the University of Michigan, top edge of titlepage repaired with old paper, name in ink of Charles Miller Feb. 14 1848 on titlepage, small hole on pages 111 and 112, affecting few letters, minor foxing throughout, else very good, exceedingly rare book, volume II 16mo., original calf with title gilt on red leather label on spine, five gilt bands on spine, former owner's name, waterstain to bottom third of front endpapers and titlepage, moderately rubbed at spine ends and extremities, else very good, exceedingly rare.   Buckingham Books   March 2015 - 25797   2015 $6750

Burroughs, William S.   *The Naked Lunch, The Soft Machine, The Ticket that Exploded.*   Paris: Olympia Press, 1959. 1961. 1962. First editions, with Naked Lunch in first state, 3 volumes, each fine in fine dust jacket, price of Soft Machine neatly crossed out in black pen, beautiful copies, all 3 housed in very nice cloth clamshell case with morocco spine label gilt, Soft Machine inscribed, although not marked in any way, this copy from distinguished modern first collection of Bruce Kahn.   Between the Covers Rare Books   196 - 67   2015 $5500

Burroughs, William S.   *The Naked Lunch.*   New York: Grove Press, 1959. First American edition, first printing, near fine, lightly rubbed with some minor spots, unclipped first issue dust jacket with minor rubbing to upper spine, tiny tear to front panel, some spotting to rear panel, otherwise bright, crisp copy.   B & B Rare Books, Ltd.   234 - 7   2015 $400

Burroughs, William S.   *Naked Lunch.*   Paris: Olympia, 1959. First edition, 5000 copies, this the copy of Peter Matthiessen with his ownership signature, slight fore-edge foxing and minor sunning to spine and rear panel, near fine in very dust jacket with just few small edge chips.   Ken Lopez, Bookseller   164 - 25   2015 $3000

Burroughs, William S.   *The Naked Lunch.*   Paris: The Olympia Press, 1959. First edition, first issue with original price of 'Francs 1500' (later issues have and '18NF' price sticker), original publisher's green wrappers, dust jacket, about fine with some spotting to top edge and small stain to fore-edge, fine jacket, free of any wear, chips or loss, excellent copy.   B & B Rare Books, Ltd.   234 - 6   2015 $2800

Burroughs, William S.   *some of it.*   London: Knullar Ltd. copyright, 1969. First edition, 4to., blank, illustrated with black and white photo plate, illustrations in text and overprinted in a variety of colors and some in split fountain, perfect bound into original red card covers, red tape backstrip, fitted mylar dust jacket with onlaid oval paper 'eyes' label on upper right corner of upper portion printed in black, erratum slip/authorial notice loosely inserted, 1969, very good, clean and crisp, slip fine, mylar losing color and transparent around sharp bit of covers, eyes looking bit tired and creased.   Maggs Bros. Ltd.   Gathering of 26 Countercultural items Oct. 2013 - 25   2015   £150

Burroughs, William S.   *The Ticket that Exploded.*   Paris: Olympia Press, 1967. First edition, wrappers, fine in fine dust jacket.   Beasley Books   2013 - 2015 $400

Burroughs, William S.   *Time.*   New York: "C" Press, 1965. First edition, one of 100 numbered copies signed by Burroughs and Gysin (out of entire edition of 1000), 4to., 4 drawings by Brion Gysin, original pictorial wrappers, back cover lightly dust soiled, otherwise fine.   James S. Jaffe Rare Books   Many Happy Returns - 355   2015 $1250

Burrus, Ernest J. *Kino and Manje, Explorers of Sonora and Arizona, Their Vision of the Future.* Rome and St. Louis: Jesuit Historical Institute, 1971. First edition, thick 8vo., 4 facsimiles, large folding map in rear, navy blue cloth, gilt, fine. Argonaut Book Shop Holiday Season 2014 - 42 2015 $250

Burt, Struthers *Powder River, Let 'er Buck.* New York: Farrar & Rinehart, 1938. First edition, 8vo., inscribed by author, and artist, Ross Santee, cloth, red top edges, discoloration to bottom edge of rear cloth, about size of half dollar, cloth somewhat soiled, else very good, tight copy in second issue dust jacket with light wear to spine ends and corners. Buckingham Books March 2015 - 24983 2015 $250

Burtis, Thomson *Flying Blood.* New York: Fiction League, 1932. First edition, owners' names, otherwise near fine in very good dust jacket with small chip at foot of faded spine. Beasley Books 2013 - 2015 $45

Burton, John Edward Bloundelle *The Desert Ship: a Story of Adventure by Sea and Land.* New York: Frederick Warne & Co., 1895. First US edition, octavo, illustrations by Hume Nisbet and W. Buckley including a vignette on titlepage, original pictorial red cloth, front and spine panels stamped in brown, orange, white and black, cream endpapers. L. W. Currey, Inc. Boy's Adventure Fiction 2015 - 40 2015 $200

Burton, Katherine *The Bibliolatrous Series.* Norton: Periwinkle Press, 1938-1939. 8 volumes, small octavo, custom slipcase. Honey & Wax Booksellers 1 - 33 2015 $450

Burton, Miles *Death in a Duffle Coat.* London: Collins Crime Club, 1956. First edition, fine in dust jacket. Mordida Books March 2015 - 007363 2015 $300

Burton, Miles *The Hardway Diamonds Mystery.* New York: Mystery League Inc., 1930. First US edition, fine in dust jacket lightly rubbed at corners and lightly foxed along top edges, sharp copy. Buckingham Books March 2015 - 29146 2015 $200

Burton, Richard Francis 1821-1890 *Arabian Nights Entertainments...* New York: Limited Editions club, 1954. Limited to 1500 numbered copies, 4 volumes, small 4to., cloth, illustrations by Arthur Szyk, well preserved, with slipcases. Oak Knoll Books 25 - 38 2015 $375

Burton, Richard Francis 1821-1890 *The Book of a Thousand Nights and a Night.* New York: Heritage Press, 1934. Illustrated edition, 6 volumes in 3 books, illustrations by Valenti Angelo, cream colored spine covers, decorative boards, attractive nearly fine set, with 3 slipcases. Stephen Lupack March 2015 - 2015 $95

Burton, Richard Francis 1821-1890 *The Book of the Thousand Nights and a Night, a Plain and Literal Translation of the Arabian Nights Entertainments.* New York: Limited Editions Club, 1934. Limited to 1500 numbered copies signed by artist, Valenti Angelo, 6 volumes, 8vo., leather backed decorated paper covered boards, three slipcases rubbed and worn along edges, leather spines age darkened. Oak Knoll Books 25 - 13 2015 $600

Burton, Richard Francis 1821-1890 *The Book of the Thousand Nights and a Night.* Norwalk: Easton Press, 1994. First edition thus, 17 volumes, Collector's Edition, bound in genuine leather with fancy tooling and gilt decorations, all edges gilt, with ribbon markers, some minor rubs here and there, nearly fine set overall, each volume housed in original plastic bag. Ed Smith Books 83 - 7 2015 $750

Burton, Robert *A New View and Observations on the Ancient and Present State of London and Westminster....* London: A. Bettesworth & Charles Hitch, 1730. First edition, small 8vo., full brown leather with red spine label, lettered gilt on spine, illustrations, covers somewhat rubbed and scuffed, otherwise clean, sound, very good, occasional spotting to illustrations and browning to pages but very decent. Any Amount of Books March 2015 - C4885 2015 £400

Burton, William *A Commentary on Antoninus His Itinerary or Journies of the Roman Empire...* London: Tho. Roycroft and are to be sold by Henry Twyford and T. Wyford, 1658. First edition in English, folio, etched portrait of Burton by Hollar, double page etched map by Hollar, few woodcut illustrations in text, small stain on titlepage, very lightly spotted in places, contemporary sheep, old reback, corners repaired, area of loss to leather at head of lower cover, new endleaves, from the library of James Stevens Cox (1910-1997). Maggs Bros. Ltd. 1447 - 59 2015 £350

Burtynsky, Edward *Before the Flood: Photographs by Edward Burtynsky.* San Francisco: Robert Koch Gallery, 2003. First edition, oblong softcover, 32 pages, 21 color images and two black and white illustrations, close to near fine in wrappers with some slight wear, uncommon. Jeff Hirsch Books E-62 Holiday List 2014 - 4 2015 $150

Bury, Shirley *Jewellery 1789-1910. The International era volume I 1789-1861.* Antique Collector's Club, 1991. First edition, 4to., fine but for two store stickers, one on pastedown, one on half title, near fine dust jacket, just lacking freshness at spine head. Beasley Books 2013 - 2015 $200

Busby, Richard *Rudimentum Grammaticae Latinae Metricum.* London: Ex Officina Eliz Redmayne, 1699. Early edition, 8vo., interleaved with blanks, woodcut Westminster School arms on title, small circular stain just touching titlepage coat of arms and minor spotting throughout, errata page has been misprinted with some loss to text, top corners beginning to fold between gatherings B-D but generally clean copy, contemporary sprinkled calf, covers panelled in blind (worn, corners bumped, pastedowns unstruck), signed by John and Robert Bere, annotations on only two of the blank interleaves, from the library of James Stevens Cox (1910-1997). Maggs Bros. Ltd. 1447 - 60 2015 £240

Busby, Thomas *The Cries of London. Drawn from Life.* London: Artists' Depository, 21 Charlotte Fitzroy Square and by Simpkin and Marshall..., 1823. First edition, separate engraved pictorial title coloured by hand, 23 hand coloured engraved plates, later half green morocco over marbled boards by Tout, green silk marker, all edges gilt, 16.8 x 10.5cm., bookplate of noted collector Eric Quayle. Marlborough Rare Books   List 53 - 6   2015   £3250

Busch, Frederick *Harry and Catherine.* New York: Alfred A. Knopf, 1990. First edition, top corner little bumped, near fine in slightly spine sunned, thus near fine, warmly inscribed by author for Nicholas Delbanco. Between the Covers Rare Books, Inc.   187 - 38   2015 $150

Bush, Christopher *The Case of the Grand Alliance.* London: MacDonald, 1964. First edition, fine, dust jacket. Mordida Books   March 2015 - 00810   2015 $95

Bush, Christopher *Dead man Twice.* Grosset & Dunlap, 1930. Later edition, fine, bright, unread copy in spectacular dust jacket, red top edge coloring bright and in 'as new' condition. Buckingham Books   March 2015 - 38227   2015 $175

Bushman, Claudia L. *A Good Poor Man's Wife being a Chronicle of Harriet Hanson Robinson and Her Family in Nineteenth Century New England.* Hanover: University Press of New England, 1981. First edition, 8vo., illustrations, blue cloth, nice, little chipped and soiled dust jacket. Second Life Books Inc.   189 - 38   2015 $65

Bushnell, Horace *Woman Suffrage; Reform Against Nature.* New York: Scribner, 1869. First edition, 8vo., bound in publisher's green cloth, lacks half inch of cloth at bottom of spine, small piece at top, ex-libris with labels on front pastedowns and pocket in rear, couple of small stamps, good copy.   Second Life Books Inc.   189 - 39 2015 $125

Butcher, David *The Whittington Press: a Bibliography 1982-1993.* Leonminster: Whittington Press, 1996. No. 224 of 244 copies of Zerkall paper, quarter green cloth and green leaf patterned boards, copiously illustrated in color and black and white, fine in sound slipcase, slight rubbing, otherwise near fine.   Any Amount of Books   2015 - A73501   2015   £175

Butler, Arthur Gray *The Three Friends: a Story of Rugby in the Forties.* London: Henry Frowde, 1900. Original maroon cloth, spine slightly faded, signed by A. F. Buxton, Christmas 1900 and Kathleen Tillotson Oct. 1594, ALS from Dorothy Ward to Kathleen.   Jarndyce Antiquarian Booksellers   CCVII - 124   2015   £40

Butler, Elias *Grand Obsession. Harvey Butchart and the Exploration of Grand Canyon.* Flagstaff: Puma Press, 2007. First edition, first printing (so stated), illustrations, photos, maps, reproductions, black cloth, gilt, very fine, superior copy with pictorial dust jacket, very, very scarce hardcover version in unread condition.   Argonaut Book Shop   Holiday Season 2014 - 43   2015 $500

Butler, James D. *Nebraska. It's Characteristics and Prospects.* n.d. circa, 1873. Printed self wrappers, 40 pages, illustrations, charts, tables, some light general soiling to wrappers, former owner's name top front panel, else very good.   Buckingham Books   March 2015 - 29791   2015 $250

Butler, Octavia *Kindred.* Garden City: Doubleday, 1979. First edition, 8vo., author's presentation flyleaf, newspaper obit for Butler laid in, paper over boards, cloth spine, very good, tight copy in little soiled dust jacket, scarce.   Second Life Books Inc.   190 - 43   2015 $350

Butler, Octavia *Kindred.* Garden City: Warner, 1995. First Warner Books printing, 12mo, paper wrappers, author's signature on title, nice.   Second Life Books Inc.   190 - 42 2015 $150

Butler, Octavia *Pattern-Master.* New York: Warner, 1995. First Warner Books printing, 12mo., 202 pages, paper wrappers, author's signature on title, nice.   Second Life Books Inc.   190 - 42   2015 $150

Butler, Octavia *Survivor.* Garden City: Doubleday, 1978. First edition, paper over boards, nice, dust jacket.   Second Life Books Inc.   189 - 40   2015 $375

Butler, Octavia *Wild Seed.* Garden City: Doubleday, 1980. First edition, 8vo., paper over boards, nice, soiled dust jacket.   Second Life Books Inc.   189 - 41   2015 $150

Butler, Richard *Italian Assets.* London: Peter Davies, 1976. First edition, fine in dust jacket. Buckingham Books March 2015 - 29243   2015 $275

Butler, Richard *Where all the Girls are Sweeter.* London: Peter Davies, 1975. First edition, tiny inked letter "C" top of front flyleaf, else fine in dust jacket. Buckingham Books March 2015 - 29668   2015 $275

Butler, Samuel   1612-1680 *Genuine Remains in Verse and Prose of Mr. Samuel Butler.* London: J. and R. Tonson, 1759. 2 volumes, 8vo., leather, five raised bands on spine, tooled gilt lines surround borders, boards scuffed and rubbed, previous owner's bookplate on front pastedown of both volumes, joints and hinges cracked, borders of endpapers tanned. Oak Knoll Books   306 - 305   2015 $200

Butler, Samuel   1612-1680 *Hudibras. (bound with) Hudibras, the second part.* London: printed in the year, 1663. London: T(homas) R(oycrofts) for John Martyn and James Allestry, 1664. Fourth pirated edition and second authorized edition of second part, small 8vo., imprimatur verso of title lacking final blank H8, some minor repairs to margins of titlepage of first work, first work lightly soiled and foxed, second work with minor dampstain to lower right corner of first three or four gatherings, 19th century half calf and marbled boards, spine rubbed and chipped, corners chipped, boards rubbed, from the library of James Stevens Cox (1910-1997). Maggs Bros. Ltd.   1447 - 61   2015 £150

Butler, Samuel   1835-1902 *Luck or Cunning as the Main means of Organic Modification?* London: Longmans, 1890. Half title, final ad leaf, original brick brown cloth, bevelled boards, slightly rubbed, presentation from author to Mr. and Mrs. Crookshank with author's very kind regards Jul 11 1898. Jarndyce Antiquarian Booksellers   CCXI - 86 2015   £280

Butt, John *Dickens at Work.* London: Methuen, 1957. First edition, half title, frontispiece, plates, half brown morocco by Sangorski & Sutcliffe, spine in compartments, slight rubbing to leading hinge, top edge gilt, publisher's specially bound copy to Kathleen Tillotson with ANS from Peter Wait inserted. Jarndyce Antiquarian Booksellers   CCVII - 207 2015   £40

Butt, John *Dickens at Work.* London: Methuen, 1957. First edition, half title, frontispiece, facsimile, plates, original green cloth, very good in slightly torn and dusted dust jacket, from the library of Geoffrey & Kathleen Tillotson, with Kathleen's presentation to Geoffrey. Jarndyce Antiquarian Booksellers   CCVII - 208   2015   £35

Butt, John *Imagined Worlds: Essays on Some English Novels and Novelists in Honour of John Butt...* London: Methuen, 1968. Half title, frontispiece, original brown cloth, very good in slightly torn dust jacket, Kathleen Tillotson's copy May 1968, with inserted reviews and correspondence. Jarndyce Antiquarian Booksellers   CCVII - 126   2015 £35

Butt, John *Pope, Dickens and Others: Essays and Addresses.* Edinburgh: University Press, 1969. First edition, half title, original pink cloth, very good, with correspondence between editor, Geoffrey Carnall and Kathleen Tillotson. Jarndyce Antiquarian Booksellers   CCVII - 127 2015   £25

Butterworth, Elizabeth *Parrots and Cockatoos.* London: Fischer Fine Art, 1979. Limited to 60 numbered copies, with the separately printed booklet by Rosemary Low supplied in photocopy, folio, 20 uncolored aquatints, each signed and numbered by artist, all plates printed on deckle edge paper and contained in cloth covered folio box, fine. Andrew Isles   2015 - 15401   2015 $2650

Buttinger, Joseph *The Smaller Dragon. A Political History of Vietnam.* New York: Praeger, 1958. First edition, signed by author, very good in like dust jacket with multiple small chips, uncommon signed. Ken Lopez, Bookseller 164 - 224   2015 $250

By Land: a Trip Personally Conducted by McLoughlin Bros. New York: McLoughlin Bros., 1889. 4to., pictorial wrappers, neat spine strengthening, few very small mends, very good, each leaf fully illustrated in rich colors by R. Andre. Alephbet Books, Inc.   109 - 281   2015 $350

Byatt, A. S. *Babel Tower.* London: 1996. First edition, as new, dust jacket. Stephen Lupack March 2015 - 2015 $40

Bye, Reed *Some Magic at the Dump.* New York: Angel Hair Books, 1978. First edition, one of 500 copies, illustrated wrappers, inscribed by author to the three sons of artist and poet, George Schneeman "for Paul, Elio, Emilio..."". Between the Covers Rare Books, Inc.   187 - 40   2015 $225

Byington, Margaret F. *Homestead: the Households of Mill Town.* Kellogg: Charities Publication Committee, 1910. First edition, photos, foldout photo frontispiece, green cloth stamped in gilt, hinges tender, over worn at edges and torn at one side of spine, else good. Second Life Books Inc. 189 - 42   2015 $250

Byrne, Muriel St. Clair *Somerville College 1879-1921.* London: Oxford University Press, 1922. Frontispiece, illustrations, music, original dark blue cloth, slightly rubbed, Kathleen Tillotson's copy with note 'Helen Darbishire's copy given me by Nesta Clutterbuck, May 1878". Jarndyce Antiquarian Booksellers   CCVII - 128   2015   £22

Byron, George Gordon Noel, 6th Baron   1788-1824 *Childe Harold's Pilgrimage.*   London: John Murray, 1841. First extensively illustrated edition, large 8vo., dark red morocco by Riviere, elaborate gilt decorations and inner dentelles, gilt lettering, top edge gilt, frontispiece portrait, engraved title, folding map, 59 engravings binding slightly rubbed, fine.   The Brick Row Book Shop   Miscellany 67 - 28   2015 $850

Byron, George Gordon Noel, 6th Baron   1788-1824 *Sardanapalus. The Two Foscari. Cain.* London: John Murray, 1821. First edition, half leather and marbled boards and endpapers, raised bands, spine decorations, maroon labels, half title present, very good, little rubbing to corners, nice, tight, clean text, attractive spine.   Stephen Lupack   March 2015 - 2015 $250

Byron, May *Jack and Jill.* New York: Hodder & Stoughton, n.d., 1914. First US edition, large 4to., cloth backed pictorial boards, light edge rubbing and slight cover soil, clean and tight and very good++, 24 color plates and color pictorial titlepage by Cecil Aldin, great copy, scarce in such nice condition.   Aleph-bet Books, Inc.   109 - 19   2015 $850

Bysshe, Edward   *The Art of English Poetry.*   London: printed for Sam. Buckley at the Dolphin in Little Britain, 1710. Fourth edition, top corner of front endpaper clipped, otherwise internally very good, clean and crisp, contemporary unlettered panelled calf, blindstamped floral cornerpieces, raised bands, very slight chip to base of spine, bottom 2cm. of upper joint cracked, very good, attractive, E. Libris Chris Clitherow March 21 1709, later armorial bookplate of Sir Edward B. Baker, Bart.   Jarndyce Antiquarian Booksellers   CCXI - 56   2015   £280

C

The C-------ll Volunteer Corps. A Farce in Two Acts. Colchester: printed and sold by I. Marsden, sold also by all booksellers in the United Kingdom, n.d. circa, 1804. 8vo., engraved folding plate (bit soiled, one blank corner removed, mounted) 6 woodcut vignettes, 32 pages, few short marginal tears, not touching printed surface, uncut, stitched as issued, preserved in modern wrappers with printed title label on upper cover, very rare.   John Drury Rare Books   March 2015 - 20577   2015   £266

Cable, George Washington 1844-1925 *Bonaventure. A Prose Pastoral of Acadian Louisiana.* New York: Charles Scribner's Sons, 1899. 8vo., 314 pages, original cloth, very good ex-library, fine ink presentation inscription from Cable to Edward J. Canning, head gardener at Smith College, Mass.   M & S Rare Books, Inc.   97 - 46   2015 $225

Caddel, Richard *Burnt Acres and the Shangri-la....* Sunderland: Ceolfrith Press, 1978. Folio, illustrations, ad leaf slightly browned, original grey printed wrappers, from the library of Geoffrey & Kathleen Tillotson, with press cutting of reviews.   Jarndyce Antiquarian Booksellers   CCVII - 129   2015   £85

Cafky, Morris *Colorado Midland.* Denver: Rocky Mountain Railroad Club, 1965. First edition, limited to 6000 volumes, signed by author and numbered, this copy 5617, thick quarto, black cloth, gold stamping on front cover and spine, timetables on endpapers, frontispiece, maps, full color paintings, five folding maps in pocket affixed to rear flyleaf, fine in dust jacket, lightly rubbed at spine ends.   Buckingham Books   March 2015 - 23280   2015 $400

Cage, John *Diary: How to Improve the World (You Will Only Make Matters Worse).* New York: Something Else Press, 1967. First edition, 8vo., original publisher's stapled white wrappers, lettered blue, pink, red on front cover, slight surface wear and slight fading, otherwise sound, very good-slightly used copy.   Any Amount of Books   2015 - C10002   2015   £220

Cahun, Leon *The Adventures of Captain Mago; or a Phoenician Expedition BC 1000.* New York: Scribner, Armstrong & Co., 1876. First US edition, octavo, 73 illustrations by P. Philippoteaux, inserted large folded map, original bevel edged pictorial green cloth, front and spine panels stamped in black and gold, rear panel ruled in blind, yellow endpapers.   L. W. Currey, Inc.   Boy's Adventure Fiction 2015 - 88   2015 $100

Cain, James M. *The Butterfly.* New York: Knopf, 1947. First edition, fine in dust jacket with some internal tape and tiny color restoration at spine ends.   Mordida Books   March 2015 - ooo372   2015 $100

Cain, James M. *Mildred Pierce.* New York: Alfred A. Knopf, 1941. First edition, near fine in about near fine, lightly rubbed dust jacket, much brighter than usually found, from the collection of Duke Collier.   Royal Books   36 - 147   2015 $1500

Cain, James M. *The Moth.* New York: Knopf, 1948. First edition, fine in price clipped dust jacket.   Mordida Books   March 2015 - ooo373   2015 $75

Cain, James M. *Our Government.* New York: Alfred A. Knopf, 1930. First edition, fine in very good or better example of the second issue dust jacket (with the bloated plutocrat on front panel), very small chip on front panel, couple of tears and faint horizontal line from old jacket protect, still much nicer than usual.   Between the Covers Rare Books   196 - 139   2015 $1200

Cain, James M. *The Postman Always Rings Twice.* London: Cape, 1934. First English edition, some small spotting on page edges, otherwise fine in soiled dust jacket with spotting along inner flap edges.   Mordida Books   March 2015 - 005227   2015 $1500

Cain, James M. *The Postman Always Rings Twice.* New York: Penzler, 1996. Facsimille of Knopf first edition of 1934, very fine in dust jacket still in original shrinkwrap.   Mordida Books   March 2015 - 010141   2015 $100

Cain, James M. *Sinful Woman.* Avon Publications, 1957. Fourth edition, paperback original, Avon 768, with one of the two (or perhaps3?) master copies of this contract, signed in ink by Cain, By Avon's executive v.p. Joseph Mann and by someone from Cain's Literary Agents, is included with this very good+ copy.   Buckingham Books   March 2015 - 18201   2015 $400

Cain, Paul *Seven Slayers.* Hollywood: Saint Enterprises Inc., 1946. First edition, digest size PBO, reader's crease and small diagonal crease to rear panel, else very good in pictorial wrappers.   Buckingham Books   March 2015 - 17847   2015 $175

Cain, Peter J. *The Empire and It's Critics 1899-1939.* London: Thoemmes Press, 2000. Reprint, 8vo., 8 volumes, about fine.   Any Amount of Books   2015 - A16320   2015   £240

Cairncross, A. S. *Modern Essays in Criticism.* London: Macmillan, 1938. Half title, final ad leaf, original green cloth, slightly marked, Geoffrey Tillotson's copy with caricature of himself? partly laid down and embellished. Jarndyce Antiquarian Booksellers   CCVII - 130   2015   £25

Cairnes, John Elliot   *The Slave Power: Its Character, Career and Probable Designs...*   London and Cambridge: Macmillan, 1863. Second edition, original green pebbled cloth lettered in gilt, ownership signature on verso of front free endpaper, cloth little rubbed at head and tail of spine, corners little bruised, inner hinges starting to crack, very good.   Peter Ellis, Bookseller   2014 - 013891   2015   £295

Cairnes, John Elliot   *Some Leading Principles of Political Economy Newly Expounded.*   London: Macmillan and Co., 1874. First edition, 39 page publisher's catalog dated March 1879, original cloth, gilt, fine.   John Drury Rare Books   March 2015 - 26292   2015   £306

Calhoun, W. C.   *Gold and How to Find It... Being a True Prospector's Guide.*   W. C. Calhoun, 1900. Third edition, 3.5 x 3 inches, green printed wrappers, covers lightly soiled and rubbed along with splitting to top and bottom of spine to staples and with library stamp inside front cover, very good. Buckingham Books   March 2015 - 35969   2015 $225

California a Guide to the Golden State.   New York: Hastings House, 1939. First edition, many photos and maps large folding map in rear pocket, light green cloth, lettered in dark green, fine.   Argonaut Book Shop   Holiday Season 2014 - 89   2015 $90

California Perfume Company   *Color Plate Catalogue of Perfumes, Toliet Waters, Sachet Powders, Complexion Creams, Talcum Powders....*   New York: Stockinger Photo Eng. & Ptd. Co. n.d. circa, 1915. Oblong folio, 39 indexed and tabbed full page color plates, original black boards, front cover lettered and ruled gilt, corners slightly bumped, top edge gilt with small chip to top right corner of margin, not affecting text, last leaf with tape repair to bottom right corner, still very good, scarce sample book.   Heritage Book Shop   Holiday 2014 - 28   2015 $1000

California Perfume Company   *Issued Only to the Representatives of the California Perfume Company.*   New York: Kansas City: San Francisco: Luzern: Montreal; New York: Scless & Co. for the California Perfume Company, circa, 1914-1915. Oblong folio, title printed in red and black followed by 42 chromolithographically illustrated plates and one final page of index, occasionally little spotted, some prizes masked out, original screw-bound black cloth portfolio, front cover lettered gilt, cloth tabs with printed numbers to fore-edges, extremities little worn, lettering faded. Marlborough Rare Books   List 54 - 64   2015   £750

Call, William Timothy   *Blackmail.*   Brooklyn: Call, 1915. First edition, fine, original tissue dust jacket partially intact. Mordida Books   March 2015 - 005232   2015 $200

Callimachus   *Callimaco Greco-Italiano Ora Pubblicato.*   Parma: Nel Regal Palazzo Co' Tipi Bodiani, 1792. 311 x 229mm., handsome early 19th century red straight grain morocco by Charles Hering (his ticket on verso of front free endpaper), covers with thick and thin gilt rule border, raised bands flanked by gilt rules, gilt titling and turn-ins, all edges gilt, booklabel of Steven St Clair Smallwood; joints bit rubbed and flaked, though refurbished with considerable success, two corners little bumped, spine faded toward rose, few minor marks in morocco, isolated faint marginal foxing, still extremely pleasing copy   high quality binding with no serious defects, text printed on thick paper, creamy paper with enormous margins.   Phillip J. Pirages   66 - 66   2015 $6500

Calmet, Augustine   *The Phantom World; or the Philosophy of Spirits, Apparitions &c.*   London: Richard Bentley, 1850. 2 volumes, occasional slight foxing, small label removed from lower margin of pastedown, volume II, original purple horizontal wavy grained cloth by Remnant & Edmonds, fading to brown, spine embossed in blind, boards slightly rubbed, very good.   Jarndyce Antiquarian Booksellers CCXI - 58   2015   £485

Calnek, W. A.   *History of the County of Annapolis...*   Toronto: William Briggs, 1897. Large 8vo., cloth boards, gilt titles to front and spine, 18 illustrations and maps, including folding frontispiece map, cloth slightly scuffed and stained, worn along edges, some ink markings to f.e.p., interior generally good.   Schooner Books Ltd.   110 - 63   2015 $75

Calverley, C. S.   *The Complete Works...*   London: George Bell & Sons, 1901. Half title, frontispiece, titles in red and black, browning caused by endpapers, original dark brown cloth, signed by Geoffrey Tillotson 1942 with cuttings inserted and 4 page photocopy of original ms. "Lovers and a Reflection".   Jarndyce Antiquarian Booksellers   CCVII - 131   2015   £20

Calvin, Ross   *River of the Sun. Stories of the Storied Gila.*   Albuquerque: University of New Mexico Press, 1946. First edition, presentation inscription signed by author, title map, 10 illustrations from photos, gilt lettered rust cloth, slight wear to lower corners, else fine with decorated dust jacket. Argonaut Book Shop   Holiday Season 2014 - 45   2015 $90

Calvin, Ross *Sky Determines.* Albuquerque: The University of New Mexico, 1948. Revised edition, illustrations by Peter Hurd, tan cloth decorated and lettered in brown, some very light 'blotchy' foxing to front cover cloth, overall, near fine copy with pictorial dust jacket, light chipping to top edge of jacket, minor stain to foot of jacket spine, presentation inscription signed by author, original publisher's order form laid in.   Argonaut Book Shop   Holiday Season 2014 - 46   2015 $150

The Cambridge Quarterly. Cambridge: Cambridge University Press, 1965. First edition, 24 volumes, wrappers, complete 10 year run, 5 index pamphlets loosely inserted, most volumes clean, very good+, occasional slight soiling and tanning to white printed covers.   Any Amount of Books   2015 - A68979   2015   £180

Camden, William *Annals Rerum et Hibernicarvm Regnante Elizabetha.* Leiden: Ex Officina Elzeviriana, 1625. First complete edition, 8vo., finely engraved portrait, engraved titlepage, contemporary calf, rubbed along hinges, calf split but hinges tight, contemporary name on endpaper 'N. J. Woodcock', very good, clean copy.   Second Life Books Inc.   189 - 44   2015 $1500

Camden, William *Remains Concerning Britain....* London: Charles Harper, 1674. Seventh impression, small 8vo., frontispiece, full brown leather, 4 raised bands, red spine lettered gilt, respined at some point with board appearing slightly later, sound, clean, decent, very good copy with cover slightly tender at top front hinge, text very clean.   Any Amount of Books   March 2015 - C4863   2015   £450

Camoens, Luis De *The Lusiad or Portugals Historicall Poem.* London: by Thomas Newcombe for Humphrey Moseley, 1655. Folio, A5 with paper repair top corner and loss of about a dozen letters in total, few minor stains, 2 small wormholes in lower blank margin throughout, contemporary panelled calf, covers with gilt arms block of Sir William Boothby, rebacked lower right corner of cover repaired, covers rather worn and faded, front flyleaf repaired, from the library of James Stevens Cox (1910-1997).   Maggs Bros. Ltd.   1447 - 62   2015   £4000

Camp, Charles *Muggins, the Cow Horse.* Denver: Welsh Haffner Printing Co., 1928. First edition, 8vo., stiff wrappers, label pasted on front cover, illustrations, laid in is 4 page printed flyer titled Horse Sense by Muggins, rare book with rare brochure, fine.   Buckingham Books   March 2015 - 34338   2015 $875

Campbell, Alex *Rose Gay, Wanted!* New York: Macaulay, 1933. First edition, rear endpaper missing, otherwise near fine in lightly soiled dust jacket with couple of short closed tears.   Mordida Books   March 2015 - 008947   2015 $85

Campbell, Alice *Murder in Paris.* New York: Farrar & Rinehart, Inc., 1930. First US edition, former owner's name and bookplate, else near fine in dust jacket with light wear to head of spine, exceptional copy.   Buckingham Books March 2015 - 24614   2015 $300

Campbell, Allan *Report of a Direct Route for the Eastern Termination of the Erie Canal, with Estimates of Its Expense and the Comparative Expense of the Proposed Enlargement of the Present Line.* Albany: printed by Packard and Van Benthuysen, 1836. First edition, large 8vo., sewn (leather thread) with stab holes in gutter, vertical crease, few spots of foxing.   M & S Rare Books, Inc.   97 - 222   2015 $125

Campbell, Archibald James *Nests and Eggs of Australian Birds...* Sheffield: the author, 1901. Octavo, 28 chromolithographs by Brittlebank, photos, publishers' brown decorated cloth, bright, crisp copy, scarce in this condition.   Andrew Isles   2015 - 36417   2015 $1500

Campbell, Diana A. G. *Miss Sellon and the Sisters of Mercy. Further Statement of the Rules, Constitution and Working of the Society Called "The Sisters of Mercy".* London: T. Hatchard and J. B. Rowe Plymouth, 1852. First edition, fourth thousand, 8vo., half title, recent marbled boards lettered on spine, very good.   John Drury Rare Books   2015 - 24589   2015 $221

Campbell, Harry H. *The Early History of Motley County.* San Antonio: Naylor Co., 1958. First edition, 8vo., brown cloth, illustrations, fine in dust jacket.   Buckingham Books March 2015 - 30903   2015 $250

Campbell, Hector *The Impending Ruin of the British Empire; Its Cause and Remedy Considered.* London: E. Wilson, 1813. First edition, 8vo., fairly modern paper wrappers, title on upper cover, good presentation copy inscribed by author for Francis Jeffrey.   John Drury Rare Books March 2015 - 25606   2015   £306

Campbell, Iain *Ian Fleming: a Catalogue of a Collection.* Liverpool: Campbell, First edition, short corner crease at top of covers and pages, otherwise fine in soft covers. Mordida Books   March 2015 - 012621   2015 $85

Campbell, John   1779-1861 *The Lives of the Lord Chancellors and Keepers of the Great Seal of England, from the Earliest Times till the Reign of King George IV. (with) Lives of Lord Lyndhurst and Lord Brougham.* London: John Murray, 1845. Volumes 1 and 7 third edition, others first editions, 8 volumes, 8vo., hardback sound, clean, very good, soundly bound in black cloth lettered gilt on spine with red spine labels and new endpapers.   Any Amount of Books   March 2015 - A97210   2015   £350

Campbell, John 1779-1861 *Speeches of Lord Campbell at the Bar and in the House of Commons with an Address to the Irish Bar as Lord Chancellor of Ireland.* Edinburgh: Adam and Charles Black, 1842. 8vo., little foxing of early leaves later 19th century polished calf gilt, raised bands and crimson label, top edge gilt, others uncut, joints worn, still handsome copy, bookplate and inscription "The Early of Portsmouth, Hurstbourne Park Library 1880". John Drury Rare Books   March 2015 - 17815   2015 $221

Campbell, John Francis *Popular Tales of the West Highlands.* Edinburgh: Edmonston and Douglas, 1860-1862. First edition, 4 volumes, 8vo., contemporary tan half calf, marbled boards, matching endpapers, red and black leather labels, gilt decorations and lettering, top edge gilt, others untrimmed, two plates and 44 illustrations in text, half titles present, edges little rubbed, very good set.   The Brick Row Book Shop   Miscellany 67 - 80   2015 $500

Campbell, John W. *Who Goes There?: Seven Tales of Science Fiction.* Chicago: Shasta Pub., 1948. First edition, octavo, illustrations by Hannes Bok, cloth, one of an undetermined number of subscriber copies signed.   John W. Knott, Bookseller   Selected New Arrivals Jan. 2015 - 16945   2015 $950

Campbell, Maurice *Sherlock Holmes and Dr. Watson: a Medical Digression.* London: Ash, 1935. First edition, pages foxed, otherwise very good, soft covers.   Mordida Books   March 2015 - 008992   2015 $100

Campbell, Roy 1901-1957 *The Flaming Terrapin.* New York: Dial Press, 1924. First US edition, fine in very good dust jacket with quarter inch chip at head of spine, removing word "The" , 8vo.   Beasley Books   2013 - 2015 $45

Campbell, Roy 1901-1957 *Pomegranates.* London: Boriswood, 1932. First edition, no. 76 of 99 copies, numbered and signed by author, 2 drawings by James Boswell, fine in near fine, bit shrunken glassine, 8vo.   Beasley Books   2013 - 2015 $150

Campbell, Steven *The Caravan Club: New Paintings by Steven Campbell.* Edinburgh: Talbot Rice Gallery: London: Marlborough Fine Art, 2002. First edition, large 8vo. color illustrated wrappers, illustrations in color, very slight handling wear, otherwise very good+.   Any Amount of Books   2015 - C1368   2015   £160

Campion, J. S. *On the Frontier; Reminiscences of Wild Sports, Personal Adventure and Strange Scenes.* London: 1878. Stated second edition, illustrations, rebound in tan cloth, library stamp on f.f.e.p. and titlepage, else very good.   Dumont Maps & Books of the West   131 - 40   2015 $125

Camus, Albert *Le Minotaure ou La Halte d'Oran.* Paris: Charlot, 1950. Limited edition, edition was 1343 copies, this one of 120 copies reserved for use of author, this copy inscribed by author for Nicole et Jean, most certainly Nicole & Jean-Marie Domenach, French intellectuals and friends of author, this issue in vellum on rives paper, remarkable rarity.   Ken Lopez, Bookseller   164 - 28   2015 $4500

Canadian General Electrical Co. *Supplies Catalogue No. 20 1920-1921.* Toronto: Canadian General Electrical Co., 1921. 8vo., green cloth, illustrations, cloth worn, interior good.   Schooner Books Ltd.   110 - 165   2015 $45

Candy & Co. Ltd. *The Devon Fire.* London: circa, 1935. 4to., 12 color plates, original buff wrappers with onlaid coloured plate.   Marlborough Rare Books   List 53 - 15   2015   £75

Canfield, Joseph M. *Badger Traction.* Chicago: Central Electric Railfans Association, 1969. First edition, quarto, photos, car plans, maps, blue cloth, gilt, some light spotting to covers, very good, pictorial dust jacket, jacket lightly foxed and chipped, errata sheet laid in.   Argonaut Book Shop   Holiday Season 2014 - 48   2015 $60

Canfield, Joseph M. *TM: The Milwaukee Electric Railway and Light Company.* Chicago: Central Electric Raillans Association Inc., 1972. First edition, quarto, illustrations throughout with color and black and white photos, as well as maps, diagrams, gilt lettered green leatherette, very fine in lightly tattered pictorial dust jacket.   Argonaut Book Shop   Holiday Season 2014 - 47   2015 $80

Canfield, Mary Cass *Lackeys of the Moon: a Play in One Act.* New York: Edmond Byrne Hackett, Brick Row Book Shop Inc., 1923. First edition, thin octavo, black paper over boards with printed labels, bit of sunning and rubbed, inscribed by author to Papa.   Between the Covers Rare Books, Inc.   187 - 41   2015 $65

Cannan, Edwin *A History of the Theories of Production and Distribution in English Political Economy from 1776 to 1848.* London: Rivington Percival & Co., 1894. 8vo., half title and Rivington's lengthy book catalog of 1893, original dark blue cloth, spine lettered gilt, uncut, very good, from the library of Abram Piatt Andrew, with his signature.   John Drury Rare Books   2015 - 24402   2015 $177

Cannan, Gilbert *The Joy of The Theatre.* New York: E. P. Dutton, 1913. First American edition, stamp on front fly, releasing the book from a library, but with no other library markings and corners little rubbed, near fine, bookplate of lawyer and collector John Quinn.   Between the Covers Rare Books, Inc.   187 - 42   2015 $65

Canning, George *Speech of the Right Hon. George Canning to His Constituents at Liverpool on Saturday March 18th 1820 at the Celebration of his Fourth election.* London: John Murray, 1820. First edition, 8vo., half title, errata slip tipped in, preserved in modern wrappers with printed title label on upper cover, very good.   John Drury Rare Books   2015 - 18353   2015 $89

Canning, Victor *The Limbo Line.* London: Heinemann, 1963. First edition, fine in price cllipped dust jacket.   Mordida Books   March 2015 - 010893   2015 $85

Cannon, Curt *I Like 'Em tough.* Fawcett Publications Inc., 1958. First edition, Gold Medal Book 743 POB, pictorial wrappers.   Buckingham Books   March 2015 - 38253   2015 $200

Cannon, Curt *I'm Cannon-for Hire.* Fawcett Pub., 1958. First edition, PBO Gold Medal Books 814, signed, light reader's crease else fine in color pictorial wrappers.   Buckingham Books   March 2015 - 35892   2015 $185

Cantrell, Dallas *Youngers' Fatal Blunder, Northfield, Minnesota.* Naylor Co., 1973. First edition, decorated fabricoid, illustrations, fine, unread copy in lightly soiled dust jacket.   Buckingham Books   March 2015 - 35478   2015 $325

Capek, Karel *R.U.R. a Play (Rossum's Universal Robots).* London: Humphrey Milford, Oxford University Press, 1923. First edition, wrappers, small 8vo., decent, clean copy, plain white sheet pasted to verso of titlepage as in other copies (possibly covering erroneous or outdated copyright information) inner hinge very slightly cracked, titlepage slightly wrinkled, lower spine slightly rubbed, else decent copy, scarce, very good.   Any Amount of Books   2015 - A39605   2015   £175

Capel, Arthur *Excellent Contemplations, Divine and Moral.* London: for Nath(aniel) Crouch, 1683. First edition, 12mo., engraved portrait of Capel (mounted and repaired along inner margin), small piece torn from blank lower margin of F1, small hole (paper flaw?) to blank corner of F6, 19th century sprinkled calf by Bedford, William Twopenny late 19th/early 20th century label, from the library of James Stevens Cox (1910-1997).   Maggs Bros. Ltd.   1447 - 63   2015   £350

Capern, Edward *Sungleams and Shadows.* London: Kent & Co.; Birmingham: Cornish Bros. &c, 1881. First edition, title browned by endpapers, 12 pages ads, original green cloth, inscription on title for Frank Denton, Esq. from friend the author May 10th 1881, signed by Denton.   Jarndyce Antiquarian Booksellers   CCXI - 59   2015   £50

Capote, Truman 1924-1985 *Breakfast in Tiffany's.* New York: Random House, 1958. First edition, octavo, original cloth, little toning to spine and partially erased ink inscription, original dust jacket in outstanding condition, tiny closed tear top rear panel and slightest fading to spine (much less than usual).   Manhattan Rare Book Company   Literature 2014 - 2015 $2400

Capote, Truman 1924-1985 *A Christmas Memory.* New York: Random House, 1958. First edition thus, 4to., one of 600 numbered copies signed by Capote, #159 with corresponding number to publisher's slipcase, green cloth with glassine wrapper (one chip to top rear panel), publisher's photo illustrated slipcase, fine in near fine slipcase.   Ed Smith Books   82 - 9   2015 $850

Capote, Truman 1924-1985 *In Cold Blood.* New York: Random House, 1965. Limited to 500 copies, signed by author, octavo, original black cloth, original slipcase, original acetate, little edgewear and chip at bottom of acetate, book and original slipcase fine.   Manhattan Rare Book Company Literature 2014 - 2015 $2600

Capote, Truman 1924-1985 *In Cold Blood.* New York: Random House, 1965. First edition, fine in maroon cloth with gilt lettering, small bookseller label to rear pastedown, near fine dust jacket with lightest browning to spine.   Ed Smith Books   82 - 8   2015 $400

Capote, Truman 1924-1985 *In Cold Blood...* New York: Random House, 1965. First edition, octavo, head of spine slightly faded, very good in very good, price clipped dust jacket slightly nicked and rubbed at edges.   Peter Ellis, Bookseller   2014 - 017325   2015   £350

Capote, Truman 1924-1985 *The White Rose.* Newton: Tamzaunchale Press, 1987. Limited to 250 numbered copies, miniature book, 6.5 x 4.5 cm., vellum, gilt stamped spine and front cover, all edges gilt frontispiece tissue protected, with miniature bookplate of Kathryn Rickard.   Oak Knoll Books   306 - 104   2015 $210

Capra, Frank *Largely a Pictorial Representation of Frank Capra's Production of Lost Horizon...* N.P.: Columbia Pictures, 1937. First edition, folio, copiously illustrated in black and white, 18 color illustrations, boards worn at edges, covers and corners rubbed, faded at edges and waterstained, some foxing, sound, complete, used, near very good-, scarce.   Any Amount of Books   2015 - A85368   2015   £160

Caprilli, Frederico *The Caprilli Papers: Principles of Outdoor Equitation.* London: J. A. Allen & Co. Ltd., 1967. First edition, large 8vo., frontispiece, illustrations, original red cloth with white lettering on spine, dust jacket , slightly bumped at lower spine, otherwise very good+ in like dust jacket but with some ink underlining on 8 pages by former owner, this was Lt. Col. A. J. B. McFarland, he has neatly pasted article by Florence Wassell to rear pastedown, scarce.   Any Amount of Books   2015 - A72285   2015   £160

Carbajal Y Lancaster, Isidro De, Bp. of Cuenca *Memorial Ajustado Hecho de Orden del Consejo-Pleno a Instancia de los Senores Fiscales, del Expediente Consultivo Visto por Remision de Su Magestad a el Sobre el Contenido y Expresiones de Diffentes Cartas del Rev. Obispo de Cuenca D. Isidro de Carbajal y Lancaster.* Madrid: En la officina de Joachin de Ibarra, 1768. First edition, 4to., old paper covered boards, crude leather spine, faint dampstain to front board and corner of first few leaves, rare board with larger dampstain as well as last leaves, occasional soil spot on leaves, bookseller label at rear, untrimmed, wide margined, strong impressions, certainly good or better copy, the copy of Alberto Parreno, the Sann Parreno sale 9 Feb. 1978.   Kaaterskill Books   19 - 30   2015 $500

Carco, Francis *Les Jours et Les Nuits.* Paris: Textes Pretextes, 1946. First edition, no. 163 of 250 copies, 8vo., unbound signatures laid into wrappers, illustrations by original lithographs by Daragnes, fine in fine wrappers, publisher's lightly soiled clamshell box.   Beasley Books   2013 - 2015 $250

Carco, Francis *Notre Ami Louis Jou with a Bibliography by Raymond Cogniat.* Paris: M-P Tremois, 1929. First edition, #454 of 460 copies in wrappers, woodcuts by Jou, including colored frontispiece, 4to., some wear and wrinkling to spine which has been nicely repaired sometime in the past, thus very good.   Beasley Books   2013 - 2015 $250

Card, Orson Scott *Ender's Game.* New York: Tor, 1985. First edition, octavo, boards, signed by Card.   John W. Knott, Bookseller   Selected New Arrivals Jan. 2015 - 16949   2015 $2750

Card, Orson Scott *First Meetings: Three Stories from the Enderverse.* Burton: Subterranean Press, 2000. First edition, one of 350 numbered copies signed by Card, octavo, cloth.   John W. Knott, Bookseller   Selected New Arrivals Jan. 2015 - 16958   2015 $75

Card, Orson Scott *Xenocide.* New York: Tor, 1991. First edition, octavo, limited to 325 copies, this one of 30 numbered copies signed by author, full black leather, front and spine panels stamped in gold.   John W. Knott, Bookseller   Selected New Arrivals Jan. 2015 - 16952   2015 $250

Carew, Thomas   1595-1639 *Poems.*   Printed by I(ohn) D)awson) for Thomas Walkley, 1640. First edition, first issue with G7 not cancelled, 7 line errata,, neat repairs to fore-margin of titlepage, old ink ownership inscription crossed out, ink blot at top of title (not affecting text), closed tear in fore-margin of B4 (mis-signed A4), small hole in C4 with loss of catchword on page 23 (this seems to down to a paper flaw), lower outer corner of H2 torn away (no loss), few other leaves with paper weaknesses, few spots or minor soiling, contemporary calf, rebacked, surface of covers crackled, preserved in morocco backed folding box, sound.   Blackwell's Rare Books   B179 - 25   2015   £5000

Carew, Thomas   1595-1639 *Poems, Songs and Sonnets, Together with a Masque.*   London: Henry Herringman, 1670. Fourth edition, 8vo., foxed and browned, heaviest in margins, occasional repairs to fore and upper edge, closely shaved along lower edge, touching catchwords and signatures on a number of leaves, early 20th century half calf and cloth boards, with W(illia)m Gates 18th century signature, pencil signature of H. F. B. Brett Smith (1896-1942), ink inscription March 20th 1922 of Francis K. W. Needham, signature John (?Harr)ison dated 1926, from the library of James Stevens Cox (1910-1997).   Maggs Bros. Ltd.   1447 - 64   2015   £180

Carey, Eustace *Vindication of the Calcutta Baptist Missionaries in Answer to "A Statement Relative to Serampore" by J. Marshman, D.D. with introductory Observations.*   London: Wightman & Co. and Parbury Allen & co., 1828. First edition, 8vo., recently well bound in linen backed marbled boards lettered, very good, rare outside UK libraries.   John Drury Rare Books   March 2015 - 23069   2015   £266

Carey, H. C. *The Past, The Present and the Future.* London: Longmans, Brown, Green and Longmans, 1848. First edition, 8vo., original green blind patterned cloth lettered gilt at spine, 32 page publisher's catalog at rear, sound, clean copy with unsightly chip at head of spine and loss of about 2 inches of cloth, affecting part of lettering, lesser chip at foot of spine, otherwise near very good, text very clean.   Any Amount of Books   2015 - A45215   2015   £175

Carey, William Paulet *Both Sides of the Gutter; or, all Parties Laughing at Each other.* Dublin: printed by P. Byrne, 1789. First edition, 8vo., 19th century marbled boards, quarter bound with burgundy morocco spine lettered gilt, spine somewhat scuffed and chipped with lettering worn and obscured, little loss to head and foot of spine, some light foxing, within, otherwise nice and clean.   Any Amount of Books   2015 - C11781   2015   £240

Cargill, Leslie *The Man from the Rhine.* London: Jenkins, 1943. First edition, fine in dust jacket with closed tears and light wear along folds.   Mordida Books   March 2015 - 008013   2015 $85

Cargill, William *An Examination of the Origin, Progress and Tendency of the Commercial and Political Confederation Against England and France, called the Prussian League.* Newcastle: printed at the Courant office by J. Blackwell and Co., 1840. First edition, 8vo., 50 pages, errata slip tipped in after title, occasional very minor spotting in recent plain wrappers, very good. John Drury Rare Books 2015 - 19458 2015 $106

Caricatures Pertaining to the Civil War; Reproduced from a Private Collection of Originals Designed for Currier & Ives, New York and Published by Them in Sheets from 1856 to 1872.... New York: 1892. One of an edition of 150 published Dec. 1892, on heavy plate paper, oblong 4to., original red morocco, rebacked, old tape marks. M & S Rare Books, Inc. 97 - 68 2015 $1650

Carion, Johann *Newe Volkommene Chronica.* Frankfurt am Mayn: Martin Lechler Sigmund Feyerabend 1566, i.e., 1569. 340 x 219mm., contemporary blindstamped German pigskin chained binding, original boards with large heraldic device at center enclosed by multiple rolls (on front, a pineapple roll and two rolls with heads and foliage on back, three rolls, one each with pineapples, heads among foliage and captioned panels showing Lucretia, Suavitas, Prudentia and Justica), 8 brass corner bosses, brass claps and catches with pigskin thongs (all hardware original and delicately tooled), early inked titling on fore-edge, original nine-link iron chain fastened to eyelet in back cover, with iron fastening ring at end, pigskin with minor worming, soiling and rubbing (though blind decoration still readily apparent), front hinge partly cracked and expertly marked (on weakness), few very tiny round wormholes at beginning and end, usual browning to paper characteristic of the time and place (never unsightly), small wax stain and other trivial defects, but excellent specimen, text smooth and mostly quite clean, and binding solid and pleasing, chain in outstanding condition. Phillip J. Pirages 66 - 17 2015 $29,000

Carleton, George *Astrologomania; the Madnesse of Astrologers.* London: by R. C. for John Hammond, 1651. Second edition, 8vo., first blank leaf (inner margin with old guard), closely shave date head, contemporary sheep ruled in blind, rebacked, corners chewed, upper edge front cover slightly wormed, signature of Ni(cholas?) Saunderson, from the library of James Stevens Cox (1910-1997). Maggs Bros. Ltd. 1447 - 65 2015 £400

Carleton, William 1794-1869 *The Emigrants of Ahadarra a Tale of Irish Life.* London: Simms & M'Intyre, 1848. Engraved series title, slightly dusted, recent half black cloth, marbled boards. Jarndyce Antiquarian Booksellers CCXI - 60 2015 £150

Carlisle, Anthony *An Essay on the Disorders of Old Age and on the Means of Prolonging Human Life.* Philadelphia: by Edward Earle, W. Myer, printer, New Brunswick, 1819. First American edition, original paper covered boards, paper covered spine and printed spine label, covers moderately worn and soiled, particularly along spine, faint dampstain on first few leaves, but withal very good copy in fragile original boards, signature of Wm. B. Magruder 1824. Joseph J. Felcone Inc. Science, Medicine and Technology - 16 2015 $300

Carlow, Viscount *On Collecting Books and Printing Them Two.* Quenington: Reading Room Press, 2013. 54/110 copies, tipped-in frontispiece by Eric Kennington, titlepage printed in brown, small 4to., original quarter beige cloth with patterned boards, backstrip and upper cloth lettered gilt, fore edge untrimmed, fine. Blackwell's Rare Books B179 - 225 2015 £44

Carlson, Chip *Tom Horn. Blood on the Moon, Dark History of the Murderous Cattle Detective.* High Plains Press, 2001. First edition, 8vo., limited to 500 numbered copies, signed by author, also signed by Larry Ball who provided foreword, this copy 489, red cloth, gold stamping on front cover and spine, illustrations. Buckingham Books March 2015 - 20965 2015 $250

Carlson, Raymond *Arizona Highways. Volume XXII Numbers 1-12 1946.* Phoenix: Arizona Highways, 1946. First edition, quarto, light blue buckram, titles stamped in gold gilt on front cover and spine, illustrations, full page colored pen and ink drawing by Ross Santee and addressed to Louis P. Merrill (Texas ranchman), fine, bright, tight copy. Buckingham Books March 2015 - 28365 2015 $1000

Carlson, Raymond *Arizona Highways. Volume XXIII Numbers 1-12 1947.* Phoenix: Arizona Highways, 1947. First edition, quarto, red buckram, titles stamped ingold gilt on front cover and spine, illustrations, full page ink drawing on front flyleaf by Ross Santee and addressed to Louis P. Merrill (noted Texas ranchman), fine, bright, tight copy. Buckingham Books March 2015 - 28366 2015 $1000

Carlson, Raymond *Arizona Highways. Volume XXIV. Numbers 1-12 1948.* Phoenix: Arizona Highways, 1948. First edition, quarto, red buckram, titles stamped in gold gilt on front cover and spine, illustrations, full page color pen and ink drawing by Ross Santee addressed to Louis P. Merrill (Texas ranchman), fine, bright, tight copy. Buckingham Books March 2015 - 28367 2015 $1000

Carlyle, Joseph Darce *Specimens of Arabian Poetry from the Earliest Time to the Extinction of the Khaliphat, with Some Account of the authors.* London: T. Cadell and W. Davies, 1810. Second edition, large 8vo., original paper covered blue boards over paper covered brown spine, lettered at spine on printed label, sound, near very good with some edgewear and browning at spine and slight wear at head of spine, very slight foxing to prelims, otherwise clean text.   Any Amount of Books   March 2015 - C16113   2015   £325

Carlyle, Thomas 1795-1881 *Critical and Miscellaneous Essays...* London: Chapman & Hall, 1842. Second edition, 5 volumes, half titles original dark blue green cloth, slightly damp marked, small nick to lower margin spine volume I, nice set.   Jarndyce Antiquarian Booksellers CCXI - 61   2015   £110

Carlyle, Thomas 1795-1881 *The French Revolution a History.* London: James Fraser, 1837. First edition, 3 volumes, octavo, half titles and integral ad leaf in volume II, uncut, publisher's brown boards, expertly rebacked in style and with original printed spine labels laid down, some expectable rubbing to boards, still remarkable copy, very difficult to find in original boards and complete, housed in blue cloth clamshell case with red morocco gilt spine label.   Heritage Book Shop   Holiday 2014 - 29   2015 $5000

Carlyon, Philip *A Sermon Preached in the Parish Church of Nayland, Suffolk for the Benefit of the National School....* Ipswich: printed and published by R. Deck, 1837. Only edition, 8vo., 18 pages, well bound recently in dark blue cloth boards with printed title label, excellent copy, very scarce.   John Drury Rare Books   2015 - 24388   2015 $133

Carman, Bliss 1861-1929 *Later Poems.* Toronto: McClelland & Stewart, 1921. First edition, near fine, inscribed by author in year of publication, lovely decorated cloth, bright, near fine.   Stephen Lupack   March 2015 - 2015 $100

Carnac, Carol *Upstairs and Downstairs.* Doubleday & Co., 1850. First US edition, pages browned, else fine in beautiful, fine dust jacket.   Buckingham Books   March 2015 - 37183   2015 $250

Carnap, Rudolf *Logical Foundations of Probability.* Chicago: University of Chicago Press, 1951. Second printing, 8vo., very good++ hardback, red cloth binding with gilt lettering to spine, minimal sun spine, cover edge wear.   By the Book, L. C.   44 - 27   2015 $750

Carnevali, Emanuel *A Hurried Man.* Paris: Contact Editions, 1925. First edition, wrappers, very good+ to near fine.   Beasley Books   2013 - 2015 $550

Caron, Francois *A True Description of the Mighty Kingdoms of Japan and Siam.* London: Argonaut Press, 1935. First edition, large 8vo., quarter white vellum, red cloth lettered gilt on spine with gilt illustration on covers, 13 plates, 7 maps, pages uncut, cloth little mottled and rubbed, vellum spine at rubbed and slightly soiled, corners bumped, bookplate, very good.   Any Amount of Books   2015 - A89169   2015   £250

Carr, Caleb *The Alienist.* New York: Random House, 1994. First edition, very fine in dust jacket with internal stain.   Mordida Books   March 2015 - 011694   2015 $85

Carr, Dan *Gift of the Leaves.* Ashuelot: Trois Fontaines, 1997. Limited to 80 numbered and 26 lettered copies signed by author and artist on colophon, 4to., decorated cloth, top edge gilt, other edges uncut, illustrations and cover design, postcard notice and invoice ot Henry Morris laid in.   Oak Knoll Books   306 - 151   2015 $1200

Carr, John Dickson *Death Watch.* New York: Harpers, 1935. First edition, fine, without dust jacket.   Mordida Books   March 2015 - 010143   2015 $185

Carr, John Dickson *He Who Whispers.* New York: Harper, 1946. First edition, spine slightly darkened, otherwise near fine in very good dust jacket with internal tape mends, chipped and frayed spine ends, several closed tears and wear at corners.   Mordida Books   March 2015 - 006565   2015 $75

Carr, John Dickson *It Walks by Night.* New York: Harpers, 1930. First edition, very good, scrape at base of front pastedown and small holes on front endpaper and first prelim, otherwise very good.   Mordida Books   March 2015 - 010142   2015 $150

Carr, John Dickson *The Life of Sir Arthur Conan Doyle.* London: Murray, 1949. First edition, initials on front endpaper and page edges foxed, otherwise very good in price clipped dust jacket with internal tape mends, darkened spine and foxing on inner flap.   Mordida Books   March 2015 - 002689   2015 $75

Carr, John Dickson *The Man Who Could Not Shudder.* New York: Harper & Bros., 1940. First edition, fine, bright, square copy, in fine, bright dust jacket, exceptional copy.   Buckingham Books   March 2015 - 32066   2015 $875

Carr, John Dickson *The Murder of Sir Edmund Godfrey.* New York: Harper, 1936. First edition, bookplate, tape residue on front endpapers and page edges darkened, otherwise near fine in very good price clipped dust jacket with slightly darkened spine, chips at corners and chips and fraying at top of spine.   Mordida Books   March 2015 - 002391   2015 $300

Carr, John Dickson *The Nine Wrong Answers.* New York: Harper, 1952. First edition, page edges slightly darkened, otherwise fine in dust jacket with chip at top corner of front panel.   Mordida Books   March 2015 - 007381   2015 $90

Carr, John Dickson *The Problem of the Wire Cage.* New York: Harper and Bros., 1939. First edition, very good in very good plus dust jacket with light wear at spine ends and corners and edges, from the collection of Duke Collier.   Royal Books   36 - 150   2015 $500

Carr, John Dickson *The Sleeping Sphinx.* London: Hamilton, 1947. First English edition, fine in very good price clipped dust jacket with nicked and frayed spine ends, couple of closed tears and wear at corners.   Mordida Books   March 2015 - 00739   2015 $85

Carranco, Lynwood *Steam in the Redwoods.* Caldwell: The Caxton Printers, 1988. First edition, 4to., profusely illustrated with photos, maps, drawings, very fine with pictorial dust jacket, very scarce.   Argonaut Book Shop   Holiday Season 2014 - 49   2015 $150

Carriego, Evaristo *Misas Herejes - La Cancion Del Barrio. (Heretic Masses - the Neighbourhood's Song).* Buenos Aires: Ediciones Dos Amigos, 1992. One of 17 copies, total edition, 15 on cream Richard de Bas paper and 2 on white Richard de Bas paper, all signed by artist, Mirta Ripoll, the publisher, Samuel Cesar Palui and the printer, Ruben R. Lapolla on colophon page, page size 15 1/4 x 11 1/4 inches, 64 pages, loose in original wrappers as issued with etching by Aida Barballo on front wrapper, housed in publisher's brown cloth over boards clamshell box with cork paper on front and spine, reverse printed with title and author, artists and publishers' names on front and author's and artists name on spine, text printed in 20 pt. Erasmus in soft brown, initial letters designed by Mirta Ripli in elegant blue with title of each poem letterpress printed in same blue, titlepage printed in black as are dedication, table of contents and colophon, 12 original full page etchings printed in color.   Priscilla Juvelis - Rare Books   61 - 9   2015 $3200

Carrington, Margaret Irving *Ab-Sa-Ra-Ka Land of Massacre Being the Experience of an Officer's Wife on the Plains with an Outline of Indian Operations and Conferences of an Officer's wife on the Plains...* Philadelphia: J. B. Lippincott & Co., 1878. Fourth edition, 8vo, 15 plates, two fold-out maps, brown cloth stamped in black and gilt, little rubbed at extremities of spine, very good, clean copy.   Second Life Books Inc.   189 - 45   2015 $600

Carroll, Jim *4 Ups and 1 Down.* New York: Angel Hair Books, 1970. First edition, one of 13 numbered copies signed by Caroll and Dona Dennis (cover art), with strands of their hair tipped in, out of a total edition of 313 copies, 4to., pictorial wrappers, inscribed by Carroll to Ted Berrigan, very fine.   James S. Jaffe Rare Books   Many Happy Returns - 354   2015 $3500

Carroll, Jim *Living at the Movies.* New York: Grossman, 1973. First edition, near fine in near fine Larry Rivers designed dust jacket with small black sticker on front flap over price, Viking Press catalog clipping announcing the forthcoming book is laid in.   Ken Lopez, Bookseller   164 - 30   2015 $350

Carroll, John M. *Custer in Periodicals. A Bibliographic Checklist. Together with John M. Carroll's Custer in Periodicals: Corrections and Additions.* Old Army Press, 1974. First edition, autographed edition of 500 copies, signed by author and by Jeff Dykes, two-tone cloth, decoration on front cover and titles on spine in gold, gilt, light blue endpapers, fine, cloth slipcase, housed in cloth slipcase with titles stamped gold on red leather label and affixed to spine.   Buckingham Books   March 2015 - 34026   2015 $250

Carroll, John M. *Eggenhofer: the Pulp Years.* Old Army Press, 1975. First edition, limited to 250 signed copies, cloth, 145 pages, numerous illustrations by Eggenhofer, fine in original slipcase.   Buckingham Books   March 2015 - 28063   2015 $200

Carroll, Paul *The Young American Poets: a Big Table Book.* Chicago & New York: Follett Pub. Co., 1968. First edition, thick 8vo., illustrations, original cloth, dust jacket, fine, scarce hardcover issue in lightly rubbed, spine faded jacket.   James S. Jaffe Rare Books   Many Happy Returns - 381   2015 $125

Carruth, Hayden *Aura. A Poem by Hayden Carruth...* West Burke: Janus Press, 1977. First edition, limited to 50 copies, tall folio, imprinted handmade folder enclosed in linen folding box with printed paper label on spine, folded paperwork landscape by Claire Van Vliet and Kathryn and Howard Clark, enclosed in paper folder on which text is printed, paperwork illustration made from 12 variously colored handmade paper pulps, housed in clam box covered and lined with natural linen, sides of dull red -orange Seta cloth, very fine, rare.   James S. Jaffe Rare Books   Modern American Poetry - 47   2015 $5000

Carruth, Hayden *Journey to a Known Place.* Norfolk: New Directions, 1961. First edition, large 8vo., original cloth and patterned paper over boards, dust jacket, very fine, presentation copy inscribed by author for Barnard Taylor.   James S. Jaffe Rare Books   Modern American Poetry - 44   2015 $450

Carruth, Hayden *Journey to a Known Place.* Norfolk: New Directions, 1961. First edition, one of 300 numbered copies, small quarto, printed on Hayle paper by Harry Duncan and Kim Merker, prospectus laid in, this copy inscribed by Carolyn Kizer to fellow poet Leonie Adams, Christmas 1962.   Between the Covers Rare Books, Inc.   187 - 43   2015 $450

Carruth, Hayden *North Winter.* Iowa City: Prairie Press, 1964. First edition in book form, large 8vo., original cloth and patterned paper over boards, dust jacket, very fine, inscribed by author to Barnard Taylor. James S. Jaffe Rare Books   Modern American Poetry - 46   2015 $400

Carruthers, George *Paper-Making. Part I. First Hundred Years of Paper Making by Machine. Part II First Century of Paper Making in Canada.* Toronto: Garden City Press Co-Operative, 1947. Red buckram with gilt titles to spines and front cover, 2 folding maps, diagrams, numerous black and white illustrations, some shelf wear and top corner of 1st flyleaf cropped, otherwise very good.   Schooner Books Ltd.   110 - 168   2015 $125

Carryl, Charles E. *The River Syndicate.* New York: Harper, 1890. First edition, fine in pictorial cloth covered boards with gold stamped titles.   Mordida Books   March 2015 - 000392 2015 $100

Carson, Rachel *The Sea Round Us.* New York: Oxford, 1951. First edition, less than 100 sent out for review, correct first state of the first printing, correct dust jacket, previous owner has penned, a Louisville bookseller, "This is a 'true' first as all this printing was recalled because of an error in binding. I kept mine anyway", bookseller has penned his name and date June 1951, boards have dull texture that was soon replaced by shiny plastic impregnated version, jacket has all the correct points according to Bob Maddox and Steve Messier.   Beasley Books   2013 - 2015 $2000

Carstairs, Henry *Secretary of State for Death.* London: Ward Lock, 1946. First edition, fine in dust jacket with couple of short closed tears and tiny wear at corners.   Mordida Books   March 2015 - 008021   2015 $85

Carte, Thomas *A Collection of Original Letters and Papers, Concerning the Affairs of England from the Year 1641 to 1660.* London: James Bettenham at the Expense of the Society for the Encouragement of Learning, 1739. First edition, 2 volumes, full brown tree calf lettered gilt at spine, ex-Foreign and Commonwealth Office library with 2 small stamps to each volume, covers somewhat used and rubbed, chipping at spine and hinges worn and splitting, very good- with clean text.   Any Amount of Books   2015 - A49990   2015   £200

Carter, Carrol Joe *Pike in Colorado.* Fort Collins: 1978. Author's edition of 500 autographed copies, 83 pages, illustrations, book near fine in lightly rubbed dust jacket. Dumont Maps & Books of the West   131 - 41   2015 $50

Carter, Edmund *The Artificer's Looking-Glass Containing an Exact and Diverting Representation of the Lives, Conduct, Characters and Various Humours of the following professors...* London: printed for J. Wilford at the three Flower De Luces in Little Britain, 1726. Only edition, 8vo. in half sheets, without ad leaf, upper margins cropped up to page 24 with loss or partial loss of several page numbers (but in no case affecting text), bound in early 20th century black half roan over marbled boards, neatly rebacked to match, spine gilt lettered, sometime in the library of the Surveyors' Institution with its 1908 bookplate, but with no other obvious marks of ownership, rare.   John Drury Rare Books   2015 - 24504   2015 $2185

Carter, Forrest *The Rebel Outlaw: Josey Wales.* London: Jonathan Cape, 1957. First edition, copyright page states First Published 1957, fine in dust jacket with correct price of 13s.6d, superior copy, very scarce.   Buckingham Books   March 2015 - 37453   2015 $7500

Carter, James *Two Lectures on Taste, read before the Philosophical Society of Colchester in the Years 1825 and 1827.* Colchester: Geo. Dennis and sold by Simpkin and Marshall, London, 1834. First edition, 12mo., errata leaf, old half cloth and orange boards, unlettered, rebacked, wanting rear free endpaper, hinges strained but reasonably good copy, scarce.   John Drury Rare Books   2015 - 16539 2015 $133

Carter, Jimmy *Negotiation; an Alternative to Hostility.* Macon: Mercer University Press, 1984. First edition, 8vo., 15 illustrations, fine, hardback signed presentation from Jimmy Carter to Marrack Goulding (1936-2010) UK's Ambassador to Angola until 1985.   Any Amount of Books 2015 - A82989   2015   £180

Carter, Matthew *Honor Rediviuus (sic) or an Analysis of Honor and Armory.* London: by E(llen) Coates, 1655. First edition, one of two issues, 8vo., engraved frontispiece, 7 etched portraits, numerous armorial woodcuts with four in contemporary hand color, possibly a thick paper copy, some light foxing and occasional staining, contemporary calf, covers ruled in gilt, expertly rebacked, covers worn, chipped especially at corners and edges, mid 19th century endleaves, presentation by author to William Dugdale (1605-1686), the copy of James Robinson Planche (17696-1880) with bookplate, from the library of James Stevens Cox (1910-1997).   Maggs Bros. Ltd.   1447 - 66   2015   £3200

Carter, Matthew *Honor Rediviuus (sic) or an Analysis of Honor and Armory.* London: for Henry Herringman, 1660. Second edition, engraved frontispiece, 7 etched plates, numerous woodcut coats of arms in text, very minor foxing to blank margins of B1-2 and with some early inked hash markings in margins, 19th century calf, covers with gilt tooled border, rebacked, corners repaired, new endleaves, 19th century manuscript family tree from Thomas Carter (d. 1603) (family of author) to children of Mary Toke d. 1875 and Charles Frederick Jarvis d. 1903, from the library of James Stevens Cox (1910-1997). Maggs Bros. Ltd. 1447 - 67 2015 £200

Carter, Robert G. *The Old Sergeant's Story. Winning the West from the Indians and Bad Men in 1870-1876.* Frederick H. Hitchcock, 1926. First edition, cloth, 8 plates, previous owner's bookplate, else fine, bright copy in protective slipcase. Buckingham Books March 2015 - 34300 2015 $750

Carter, Samuel *Legal Provisions for the Poor; or a Treatise of the Common and Statute Laws Concerning the Poor..* London in the Savoy: printed by John assignee of Edward Sayer Esq. for John Walthoe, 1710. 12mo., contemporary blind ruled calf, fine, crisp, rare. John Drury Rare Books 2015 - 21506 2015 $1486

Cartwright, Bert *The Bible in the Lyrics of Bob Dylan.* Wanted Man, 1985. First edition, 8vo., wrappers, about fine. Any Amount of Books 2015 - A68194 2015 £200

Cartwright, William *Comedies, Tragi-Comedies with other Poems.* London: for Humphrey Mosely, 1651. First edition, 8vo., engraved portrait by Lombart (small rust hole at foot of image repaired), G8v stained, otherwise occasional small stains, early 19th century calf, covers ruled in gilt, gilt spine, armorial bookplate of Sir Frances Freeling, 1st Bart. 1764-1836, 19th century armorial bookplate of Francis Darby, from the library of James Stevens Cox (1910-1997). Maggs Bros. Ltd. 1447 - 68 2015 £600

Carvella, Venturino *Sulla Educazione Della Donna.* Catania: Tipografia di C. Galatola, 1876. First edition, 12mo., bound in recent green wrappers, presentation from author, rare. Second Life Books Inc. 191 - 21 2015 $425

Carver, Raymond *At Night the Salmon Move.* Santa Barbara: Capra Press, 1976. Hardcover issue, of a total edition of 1100 this one of 100 numbered hardcover copies, signed by author, fine, without dust jacket, as issued, drawings by Marcia. Ken Lopez Bookseller E-list # 82 - 912310 2015 $750

Carver, Raymond *Carnations: a Play in One Act.* Vineburg: Engdahl Typography, 1993. Of a total edition of 200 copies, this one of 124 numbered copies bound in full cloth, fine. Ken Lopez Bookseller E-list # 82 - 914824 2015 $275

Carver, Raymond *Early for the Dance.* Concord: Ewert, 1986. Of a total edition of 136, this one of 10 sets of advance sheets prepared by publisher, twelve 9 x 12 inch double flat gatherings printed on rectos only, laid into gray folding cardstock case with card laid in representing the sheets with compliments, indicating the limitation and signed by publisher, fine set, rare advance issue. Ken Lopez Bookseller E-list # 82 - 012110 2015 $350

Carver, Raymond *Elephant and other Stories.* London: Collins Harvill, 1988. Uncorrected proof, tiny shiny spot to front cover, else fine in wrappers. Ken Lopez Bookseller E-list # 82 - 912320 2015 $175

Carver, Raymond *If It Please You.* Northridge: Lord John Press, 1984. Limited edition, of a total edition of 226 copies, this one of 26 lettered copies signed by author, fine, without dust jacket as issued. Ken Lopez Bookseller E-list # 82 - 912325 2015 $500

Carver, Raymond *In a Marine Light.* London: Collins Harvill, 1987. Fine in fine dust jacket. Ken Lopez Bookseller E-list # 82 - 912326 2015 $175

Carver, Raymond *Intimacy.* Concord: Ewert, 1987. One of 12 advance copies, signed by publisher, William Ewert, fine in wrappers. Ken Lopez Bookseller E-list # 82 - 912329 2015 $325

Carver, Raymond *A New Path to the Waterfall.* London: Collins Harvill, 1989. Uncorrected proof copy of the first British edition, corner crease to front cover, near fine in wrappers. Ken Lopez Bookseller E-list # 82 - 012741 2015 $85

Carver, Raymond *A New Path to the Waterfall.* New York: Atlantic Monthly Press, 1989. One of 200 numbered copies, signed by Tess Gallagher, full blue cloth stamped in gold, fed cloth slipcase, fine. Ken Lopez Bookseller E-list # 82 - 001337 2015 $125

Carver, Raymond *No Heroics Please.* London: Harvill, 1991. True first edition, signed by editor, William Stull fine in fine dust jacket. Ken Lopez Bookseller E-list # 82 - 912331 2015 $70

Carver, Raymond *No Heroics, Please.* New York: Vintage, 1992. Uncorrected proof copy of American edition, fine in wrappers. Ken Lopez Bookseller E-list # 82 - 912333 2015 $45

Carver, Raymond *The Pheasant.* Worcester: Metacom Press, 1982. Limited edition of 176 copies, this one of 26 lettered hardcover copies, signed by author, fine, without dust jacket, as issued. Ken Lopez Bookseller E-list # 82 - 914634 2015 $2000

Carver, Raymond *Put Yourself in My Shoes.* Santa Barbara: Capra Press, 1974. One of 500 copies, fine copy of issue in wrappers.   Ken Lopez Bookseller   E-list # 82 - 912334   2015 $200

Carver, Raymond *Raymond Carver Remembered: Three Early Stories.* One of 15 tear sheet reprints of an offprint from Studies in Short Fiction, Volume 25 No. 4 1988, signed by William Stull, stapled, fine.   Ken Lopez Bookseller   E-list # 82 - 019153   2015 $125

Carver, Raymond *"Sixty Acres". in Best Little Magazine Fiction 1970.* New York: New York University Press, 1970. Scarce hardcover issue, uncommon, fine in very good, rubbed dust jacket.   Ken Lopez Bookseller   E-list # 82 - 012679   2015 $100

Carver, Raymond *The Stories of Raymond Carver.* London: Picador/Pan, 1985. Only issued in wrappers, slight age toning to page edges and mild spine creasing, near fine.   Ken Lopez Bookseller   E-list # 82 - 912347   2015 $45

Carver, Raymond *This Water.* Concord: William B. Ewert, 1985. One of 36 copies, quarterbound in grey linen with spine label and blue boards and signed by author, fine.   Ken Lopez Bookseller   E-list # 82 - 912351   2015 $500

Carver, Raymond *The Toes.* Concord: Ewert, 1988. Limited to 136 copies, this one of 36 specially bound in red wrappers, pages uncut, fine.   Ken Lopez Bookseller   E-list # 82 - 9122348   2015 $100

Carver, Raymond *Two Poems.* Salisbury: Scarab, 1982. Of a total edition of 100 numbered copies, this one of 25 copies were reserved for author's use, signed by author, fine in saddle stitched wrappers.   Ken Lopez Bookseller   E-list # 82 - 912354   2015 $500

Carver, Raymond *Two Poems.* Concord: Ewert, 1986. There were 100 copies issued, this one of 26 lettered copies, this letter M, signed by Carver, and were bound in brown wrappers, fine.   Ken Lopez Bookseller   E-list # 82 - 012353   2015 $325

Carver, Raymond *Ultramarine.* New York: Random House, 1986. Uncorrected proof, signed by author, with poem "This Morning" pasted in, several poems checked off in text, nickel sized stain to front cover, near fine.   Ken Lopez Bookseller   E-list # 82 - 912355   2015 $325

Carver, Raymond *Ultramarine.* New York: Random House, 1986. Uncorrected proof, near fine in wrappers.   Ken Lopez Bookseller   E-list # 82 - 011391   2015 $100

Carver, Raymond *Where I'm Calling From.* Franklin Center: Franklin Library, 1988. Correct first edition, leatherbound, page edges gilt, silk ribbon marker bound in, Franklin Library's "Signed First Edition" series, signed by author, fine in publisher's original shrinkwrap.   Ken Lopez Bookseller   E-list # 82 - 0110491   2015 $100

Carver, Raymond *Where I'm Calling From.* New York: Atlantic Monthly, 1988. Uncorrected proof copy of the trade edition, fine in wrappers.   Ken Lopez Bookseller   E-list # 82 - 912358   2015 $175

Carver, Raymond *Where Water Comes Together with Other Water.* New York: Random House, 1985. First edition, signed by author, laid in is press release about book printed on cardstock with Random House letterhead, fine in fine dust jacket.   Ed Smith Books   82 - 10   2015 $250

Carver, Raymond *Will You Please Be Quiet, Please?* New York: McGraw Hill, 1976. First edition, signed by author, trifle spotting to top stain, still fine in fine dust jacket, beautiful copy from the Bruce Kahn collection.   Ken Lopez Bookseller   E-list # 82 - 911022   2015 $5000

Carver, Raymond *Winter Insomnia.* Santa Cruz: Kayak, 1970. One of 1000 copies, illustrated with prints by Robert McChesney, this is the issue in rare white wrappers, exceedingly scarce, inscribed by author 3 - 3- 83, spine and edge sunning to covers, near fine.   Ken Lopez Bookseller   E-list # 82 - 914629   2015 $3000

Carver, Raymond *Winter Insomnia.* Santa Cruz: Kayak, 1970. One of 1000 copies, this issue bound in yellow wrappers printed in green, signed by author, fine.   Ken Lopez Bookseller E-list # 82 - 912361   2015 $750

Cary, John *An Account of the Proceedings of the Corporation of Bristol in Execution of the Act of Parliament for the Better Employing and maintaining the Poor of that City.* London: by F. Collins and are to be sold by John Nutt, 1700. Scarcer of two editions, 8vo., light spotting, small wormhole and short tear (not touching text) to titlepage, mid 20th century quarter morocco and cloth boards, from the library of James Stevens Cox (1910-1997).   Maggs Bros. Ltd.   1447 - 69   2015   £750

Cary, John *Cary's British Traveller; or an Abridged Edition of His New Itinerary...* London: J. Cary, 1803. 2 initial folding plates, a page illustrated ad for Cary's New Globes on verso of final leaf, uncut in original blue paper boards, cream paper spine, orange printed paper label, some slight wear to spine, overall very good.   Jarndyce Antiquarian Booksellers   CCXI - 63   2015   £380

Cary, John *A Discourse Concerning the East India Trade.* London: for E. Baldwin, 1699. Small 4to., lightly browned and with small faint ink splash on titlepage, disbound, from the library of James Stevens Cox (1910-1997).   Maggs Bros. Ltd.   1447 - 70   2015   £750

Cary, John *A Discourse Concerning the Trade of Ireland and Scotland as they Stand in Competition with the Trade of England...*   Reprinted at London, 1695. First separate edition, small 4to., small hole through titlepage and second leaf, A2-3 heavily soiled and with some dampstaining to upper fore-corner throughout, stitched as issued, edges trimmed, light pencil notes on blank verso of final leaf, from the library of James Stevens Cox (1910-1997).   Maggs Bros. Ltd.   1447 - 71   2015   £750

Cary, John *An Essay on the Coyn and credit of England.* Bristol: by Will. Bonny and sold by booksellers of London and Bristo., October 22d, 1696. First edition, small 8vo. half title, light staining to inner margin on verso of half title and with final leaf slightly foxed, mid 20th century half brown pigskin and marbled boards, from the library of James Stevens Cox (1910-1997), JSC's pencil signature.   Maggs Bros. Ltd.   1447 - 72   2015   £2000

Cary, John *A Vindication of the Parliament of England...* London: Freeman Collins and to be sold by Sam. Crouch and Eliz. Whitlock, 1698. First edition, 8vo., lightly browned, mid 19th century half calf and marbled boards, one corner scuffed, early 20th century label Charles Wells, from the library of James Stevens Cox (1910-1997).   Maggs Bros. Ltd.   1447 - 73   2015   £250

Cary, Joyce 1888-1957 *The Horse's Mouth.*   New York: Harper & Brothers, 1944. First edition, signed by author on tipped-in leaf dated 1949, fine in near fine, lightly rubbed dust jacket, exceptionally nice copy.   Ken Lopez, Bookseller   164 - 31   2015 $450

Cary, Melbert B.   *War Cards.*   New York: Press of the Wooly Whale, 1937. First edition, very fine, quarter red leather and gray cloth with gilt titles and gilt top page edges, without dust jacket as issued.   Mordida Books   March 2015 - 012622   2015 $250

Caryll, John   *Naboth's Vinyard; or the Innocent Traytor...* London: for C. R., 1679. Second edition, small 4to., 20 pages, title lightly browned with two small (55 20mm) circular dampstains at foot of B1 and b2, 19th century marbled wrappers, from the library of James Stevens Cox (1910-1997).   Maggs Bros. Ltd.   1447 - 74   2015   £100

Casdorph, David G. *Plastic-Pellet Hopper Cars. A Catalog of Modern Plastics Cars.* N.P.: Society of Freight Car Historians, 1994. First edition, number 8 of a limited edition, photos, line drawings, blue pictorial laminated boards, slight rubbing to spine ends, fine.   Argonaut Book Shop Holiday Season 2014 - 50   2015 $60

The Case of Seduction; Being an Account of the Late Proceedings at Paris as well as Ecclesiastical as Civil Against the Reverend Abbee, Claudius Nicholas des Rues for Committing Rapes Upon 133 Virgins... London: printed for E. Curll over against Catherine Street in the Strand, 1726. First edition in English, rare, 12mo., little general soiling including on titlepage which has some wear to outer margins (not affecting printed surface) well bound in mid 19th century half calf over marbled boards, neatly rebacked and lettered, good copy, rare.   John Drury Rare Books   2015 - 23340   2015 $1486

The Case of the Island of Minorca; Being the Credentials and Instructions as well as the Generality of the Whole Island, as of the Four Universalities thereof, Unto Don John De Bayarte, their Lawful and General Deputy to the Crown of England. N.P.: London? n.d.?, 1717. First edition, Folio, two of the leaves with professionally repaired closed tears (no loss of printed surface), well bound fairly recently in quarter calf gilt over marbled boards, vellum tips, rare.   John Drury Rare Books   2015 - 24014   2015 $656

Caspar, Horst   *Horst Caspar.*   Berlin: Verlag A. Daehler, 1955. First edition, thin folio, fine in lightly worn, near fine dust jacket, photos, laid in four page ALS by Caspar's muse and wife, Antje Weisgerber.   Between the Covers Rare Books, Inc.   187 - 212   2015 $200

Caspari, Gertrud   *Lustiges Kleinkinderbuch.*   Leipzig: Hahn, 1907. Oblong 4to., cloth backed thick boards, edges rubbed, else very good, printed on thick boards, wonderfully illustrated in rich color on every page by Adolf Holst.   Aleph-Bet Books, Inc.   108 - 207   2015 $450

Caspary, Vera   *Bedelia.* London: Eyre & Spottiswoode, 1945. First English edition, name on titlepage, near fine in lightly soiled dust jacket with stains on back panel and couple of short closed tears.   Mordida Books   March 2015 - 000395   2015 $85

Caspary, Vera   *Evvie.* London: Allen, 1960. First English edition, lower corners slightly bumped, otherwise fine in dust jacket with some tiny tears.   Mordida Books   March 2015 - 008848   2015 $85

Caspary, Vera   *Thicker than Water.*   New York: Liveright, 1932. First edition, 8vo., original textured beige cloth under mauve paper covered board, lettered black on spine, signed and dated presentation from author to Pauline Levy, slight fading and rubbing to boards, otherwise very good.   Any Amount of Books   2015 - C2223   2015   £850

Cassidy, James F.   *The Women of Gael.*   Boston: Stratford Co., 1922. First edition, 8vo., green cloth stamped in gilt, little faded on spine, very good.   Second Life Books Inc.   189 - 46   2015 $65

Cassin, John *Illustrations of the Birds of California, Texas, Oregon, British and Russian America...* Philadelphia: 1856. First edition, large octavo, 50 hand colored lithographed plates, including frontispiece, tissue guards, original full brown morocco, boards ruled in blind, blind central device on both boards, spine lettered gilt, board edges and turn-ins stamped in blind, all edges gilt, marbled endpapers, front outer hinge cracked and repaired, minor corner and edge wear, few tiny chips to spine, old dampstain to upper margins of pages 191-298 not affecting text or plates and hardly visible on plate margins affected, previous owner's old ink signature on top margin of titlepage, previous owner's bookplate, overall excellent copy in handsome contemporary binding.   Heritage Book Shop   Holiday 2014 - 31   2015 $5000

Casson, Mark *Entrepreneurship and Industrial Revolution.* London: Thoemmes Press, 2001. Reprint, 8vo., 7 volumes, very clean set, very good.   Any Amount of Books   March 2015 - A69648   2015   £340

Castamore *Conjugium Languens; or the natural, Civil and Religious Mischiefs Arising from Conjugal Infidelity and Impunity.* London: printed by R. Roberts, 1700. First edition, 4to., blank portions of titlepage torn away (not near printed surface), fore-edges generally cut close touching letters of some sidenotes (loss of all or part of single letter in five cases), disbound and now preserved in recent plain wrappers, scarce.   John Drury Rare Books   March 2015 - 20189   2015   £306

Castelli, Carlo *L'Arte di Filare la Serta a Freddo ossia Senza Fuoco Sotto le Bacine Delle Filatrici...* Venice: Domenico Fracasso, 1795. 8vo., 2 folding charts, original stiff paper wrappers, very fine fresh copy.   Joseph J. Felcone Inc.   Science, Medicine and Technology - 48 2015 $450

Castelli, Vittorio *The Bix Bands.* Milan: Raretone, 1972. First edition, wrappers, fine.   Beasley Books   2013 - 2015 $45

Castro, Casimiro *Album Mexicano. Coleccion de Paisajes Monumentos Costumbres y Ciudades Principales de la Republica.* Mexico: Antique Lithografia Debray Sucs, C. Montaurol, n.d. c., 1880-1885. First collected edition, oblong folio, lithographed titlepage, 28 colored or tinted lithographed plates, publisher's three quarter brown cloth, pictorial paper boards, front cover with lithographed title and pictorial scene of the Plaza de Gaudalupe in black on light green boards, rear cover with lithographed pictorial scene of the Plaza de St. Domingo, spine and corners renewed, titlepage bit toned and soiled, front cover with minor loss to small area of lower corner, expertly restored, small spot to lower border of few plates, which are generally bright and clean.   Argonaut Book Shop   Holiday Season 2014 - 51   2015 $10,500

A Catalogue of Early Colour Printing from Chiaroscuro to Aquatint. Culham, Oxford: Colin & Charlotte Franklin, 1977. 4to., cloth, number of full color plates.   Oak Knoll Books   306 - 71   2015 $125

Catalogue Officiel de La Grande Exposition des Produits de l'Industrie de Toutes les Nations a 1851. Londres: Spicer freres papetiers, W. Clowes et fils imprimeurs, 1851. First French edition, 4to., titlepage with border of Coats of Arms, original printed powder blue wrappers similar in design to titlepage, loosely inserted plan, unidentified monogram TC surmounted with crown and motto 'per vias rectas', preserved in black cloth box, upper cover with red label lettered gilt.   Marlborough Rare Books Ltd.   List 49 - 4   2015   £550

The Catechism for the Curats, Compos'd by the Decree of the Council of Trent... London: printed by Henry Hills for Him and Matthew Turner, 1687. First edition translated into English by John Bromley, contemporary speckled calf with designs blindstamped to front and rear boards, ex-library (Franciscan Friary, Crawley, Sussex), several of their inkstamps and more recent ownership signs to front blank, front board detached, otherwise very sound, clean example. Any Amount of Books   2015 - C7305   2015   £300

Cather, Willa Sibert 1873-1947 *April Twilights.* Boston: Richard G. Badger/The Gorham Press, 1903. First edition, 8vo., paper covered boards, paper spine label, uncut, some minor spotting to boards, small tear in lower joint and spine, neatly repaired, otherwise fine, internally, untrimmed, better than average copy, scarce.   Second Life Books Inc.   189 - 50   2015 $1400

Cather, Willa Sibert 1873-1947 *Death comes for the Archbishop.* New York: Alfred A. Knopf, 1927. First edition, one of 175 copies on Borzoi all rag paper, this being number 81, signed by author, octavo, titlepage an half title verso printed with blue border, publisher's quarter green cloth over marbled paper boards, black leather spine label, lettered gilt, edges ncut, mostly unopened, very light amount of sunning to spine, front board lightly rubbed, very good. Heritage Book Shop   Holiday 2014 - 32   2015 $2750

Cather, Willa Sibert 1873-1947 *December Night. A Scene from Death Comes for the Archbishop.* New York: Knopf, 1933. First edition, thin octavo, 12 pages, illustrations, original boards, title and rules blindstamped on front cover, owner's ink inscription on blank jacket flap, very fine with very elusive decorated dust jacket chipped at lower spine, less so to upper spine and lower corners.   Argonaut Book Shop   Holiday Season 2014 - 52   2015 $125

Cather, Willa Sibert 1873-1947 *Lucy Gayheart.* New York: Knopf, 1935. First edition, one of 749 large paper copies, signed by author, 8vo., blue cloth, spine and part of cover faded, uncut, very nice.   Second Life Books Inc. 189 - 47   2015 $365

Cather, Willa Sibert   1873-1947   *Novels and Stories of Willa Cather.*   New York: Houghton Mifflin Co., 1937.   First edition, limited signed edition, one of 950 (of 970) total copies, signed by author in volume 1, 13 volumes, 8vo., very slight darkening to spines, some light overall wear to cloth, chipping to spine labels of several volumes, heavily to volume 8 and affecting spine title of volume 9, puncture to center spine of volume 12, just below spine label (about 1/4), sound decent set.   Any Amount of Books   2015 - A97643   2015   £850

Cather, Willa Sibert   1873-1947   *The Professor's House.*   New York: Knopf, 1925.   First edition, 8vo., fine in dust jacket that shows little wear at tips and extremities, rare in dust jacket.   Second Life Books Inc.   189 - 48   2015 $1200

Cather, Willa Sibert   1873-1947   *The Professor's House.*   New York: Knopf, 1925.   First edition, limited edition, one of 40 on Imperial Japon vellum, 8vo., fine, large paper copy, signed by author, titlepage, small owner's bookplate, custom clamshell case.   Second Life Books Inc.   189 - 40   2015 $3000

Catholic Church. Liturgy & Ritual - Breviary   *Breviarium Romanum.*   Venetiis: Ex Typographia Balleoniana, 1744.   4 volumes, 184 x 121mm., 4 volumes, very attractive contemporary Italian dark brown crushed morocco, handsomely gilt, covers with simple border of plain and stippled gilt rules and fleuron cornerpieces, raised bands intricately and elegantly gilt in compartments formed by plain and decorative gilt rules and featuring cornerpieces of leaves and volutes framing a central curling lozenge incorporating palmettes and a fleur-de-lys, marbled endpapers, all edges gilt with gauffering on top and bottom edges next to endbands, apparently original elaborate ribbon markers comprised of four silk strands held together at top by a large tassel, woodcut tailpieces and floriated initials, engraved printer's device of titlepages, 14 engravings by M. Beylbrouck printed in red and black, one opening with small wax(?) stain, other very trivial imperfections, but nearly flawless copy, binding with only faintest signs of age and clean, fresh and bright text, virtually no signs of use.   Phillip J. Pirages   66 - 36   2015 $1500

Catholic Church. Liturgy & Ritual - Hours   *Use of Rome (Printed book of Hours on Vellum in Latin and French).*   Paris: Thielman Kerver, May, 1510.   Calendar covering years 1506-1530, 171 x 108mm., titlepage (A1) in very good paper facsimile (though blank on verso, so lacking Anatomical man engraving that should appear there), pleasing mid 16th century dark calf, gilt, covers framed by multiple blind rules, central panel formed by a gilt fillet with acorn fillet with acorn tools extending obliquely from outer corners, gilt vegetal tools at inner corners, central gilt arabesque, raised bands, expertly rebacked preserving original backstrip (as well as recornered?), spine in blind ruled compartments with saltire, unusual later 17th century?) brass clasps and catches, hardware extending some 90mm. (or three quarters of the way) across each board, extensions held in place by small brass nails, numerous one and two line initials in colors and gold, each page with decorative and/or historiated frames featuring charming and sometimes fascinating scenic metal-cut border panels at bottom and fore edge, 34 small miniatures and 18 richly detailed full page cuts, a diagram explaining the concept of Trinity and Christ with the symbols of the Passion, 17th century engraved and hand painted holy card on vellum by Cornelius Galle tipped in at front, early engraved heraldic bookplate, inkstamp "Kon. Kupferstich Cabinet Stuttgart" on verso of holy card and of last leaf, last (blank) page with early ink ownership signatures and pen trials and dated 1679; spine slightly cocked, backstrip little roughened, but carefully restored binding quite lustrous with very little wear and generally well preserved, trimmed cloth at top, decorative border just touched on several leaves containing full page miniatures, half dozen leaves with faint but noticeable brown stains, minor signs of use, vellum generally not very bright, other trivial imperfections, still reasonable copy internally with many pages quite pleasing, no fatal condition issues.   Phillip J. Pirages   66 - 11   2015 $16,000

Catholic Church. Liturgy & Ritual - Hours   *Heures du Roy Loys XIII. (bound with) Formulaire De Confession Pour Cleux Qui Freqentent les Sacrements.*   Paris: Eustache Foucault, 1615.   2 works in one volume, 187 x 114mm., without blank final leaf, very pleasing contemporary reddish brown armorial morocco gilt, covers with border formed by double gilt rules enclosed by dotted rolls, oblique fleuron cornerpieces, center panel with rules enclosed by dotted rolls, oblique fleuron cornerpieces, center panel with "CHV" (or "GHV") cipher at corners and central oval containing two lined "V's" surrounded by four "S" ferme characters, flat spine with panelling similar to that on cover, remnants of ribbon ties, all edges gilt, spine expertly rebacked with original spine laid down, tips of corners carefully renewed, engraved titlepage with elaborate frame, 12 emblematic illustrations, 10 full page copperplate engravings, first volume printed in black and red, pastedown with bookplate "HB" (collector Heribert Boeder), very light rubbing to joints and extremities, otherwise fine with only trivial imperfections internally and with expertly restored binding lustrous and showing little wear.   Phillip J. Pirages   66 - 23   2015 $2500

Catich, Edward M. *Letters Redrawn from the Trajan Inscription in rome.* Davenport: Catfish Press, 1961. 8vo., cloth, with 93 4to. broadside plates, two sections enclosed in cloth bound case specially constructed to hold the two different sized parts, presentation "Dr. J. C. McMillan, E. Catich", preface signed and dated by Dwiggins.   Oak Knoll Books   306 - 145   2015 $410

Catich, Edward M. *Letters Redrawn from the Trajan Inscription in Rome.* Davenport: Catfish Press, 1961. 8vo., cloth, with 93 4to. broadside plates, two sections enclosed in cloth bound case specially constructed to hold the two differently sized parts, signed by Catich, first plate age yellowed as usual from cloth case, presentation from Catich to John Michael.   Oak Knoll Books   Special Catalogue 24 - 7   2015 $400

Catich, Edward M. *The Origin of the Serif Brush Writing & Roman Letters.* Davenport: Catfish Press St. Ambrose College, 1968. First edition, 4to., cloth, top edge gilt, dust jacket, jacket chipped with small pieces missing along edge, large foldout prospectus loosely inserted (pencil notes on it), many illustrations in green and red.   Oak Knoll Books   Special Catalogue 24 - 8   2015 $300

Catich, Edward M. *Reed Pen & Brush Alphabets for Writing and Lettering.* Davenport: Catfish Press, 1972. 2 volumes, 8vo and 4to., quarter grey cloth over marbled paper covered boards, paper cover labels, 32 pages in book and 28 heavy leaves printed on both sides loosely inserted in 4to. portfolio, beautifully printed in red, blue and black.   Oak Knoll Books   Special Catalogue 24 - 9   2015 $200

Catledge, Oraien *Cabbagetown.* Austin: University of Texas Press, 1985. First edition, 67 black and white photos, clean, near fine with small crease to top corner of first two pages in very good dust jacket with closed tear to top front panel, another to the bottom of rear panel and longer tear to bottom of spine, still nice.   Jeff Hirsch Books   E-62 Holiday List 2014 - 5   2015 $125

Cat's Cradle. Berkeley: Flying Fish Press, 2013. Artist's book, one of 50 copies, all on Mohawk Superfine paper, signed and numbered by artist/author/publisher, Julie Chen, page size 5 3/8 x 8 1/16 x 1 inches, bound by artist, carousel style book with grey cloth over boards, title printed on paper on front cover and on spine, grey gros-grain ribbon ties.   Priscilla Juvelis - Rare Books   61 - 17   2015 $950

Catt, Carrie Chapman *Woman Suffrage and Politics.* New York: Scribner's, 1923. First edition, 8vo., pieces of dust jacket laid in, signature on flyleaf, very good, laid in is ribbon from "American Youth Party" Woman Suffrage Day July 7 1907z", torn at extremities but not affecting any text.   Second Life Books Inc.   189 - 51   2015 $750

Catton, Eleanor *The Rehearsal.* London: Granta, 2009. First British and first hardcover edition, signed by author in 2013, fine in very near fine dust jacket nicked at upper rear spine fold.   Ken Lopez, Bookseller   164 - 32   2015 $200

Catton, Eleanor *The Rehearsal.* London: Granta, 2009. First British edition, advance reading copy, (identified on front cover as an uncorrected proof), signed by author, fine in wrappers, scarce, especially signed.   Ken Lopez, Bookseller   164 - 33   2015 $350

Causley, Charles *Johnny Alleluia.* N.P.: Heron Court Press, n.d. circa, 1958. First separate edition, 2 folded sheets, titles being printed in red, author's holograph manuscript of it alongside number 14 of 15 copies, signed and dated October 1968 by author at end of text, fold crease, very good+.   Peter Ellis, Bookseller   2014 - 002735   2015   £300

Causley, Monroe S. *Arthur W. Rushmore and the Golden Hind Press.* Madison: Madison Public Library, 1994. First edition, one of 500 copies, stapled pastepaper style wrappers, with applied printed label, fine, Artist John DePol's copy with his ownership signature and notations on pages his woodcuts appear.   Between the Covers Rare Books, Inc.   187 - 45   2015 $150

Caussin, Nicolas *De Symbolica Aegyptiorum Sapientia i Qua Symbola Parabolae Historiae Selectae, Quae ad Omnem Emblematu(m)....* Coloniae Agrippinae: Apud Ioannem Kinckium Sub Monocerote, 1623. 8vo.,fine engraved titlepage, contemporary vellum, yapp fore edges and handwritten title at head of spine, very nice, sound.   Any Amount of Books   2015 - C4724   2015   £700

Cavalcanti, Guido *Sonnets & Ballate of Guido Cavlcanti.* London: Stephen Swift & Co. Ltd., 1912. First English edition translated by Ezra Pound, bulk of which was destroyed by a fire at the binders, 8vo., original gray streaked cloth, spine a shade darkened, otherwise fine, unopened copy with publisher's ads at back.   James S. Jaffe Rare Books   Modern American Poetry - 231   2015 $1000

Cave, Estella *Ant Antics.* London: John Murray, 1933. First edition, 8vo., cloth backed pictorial boards, spine ends slightly faded and some spotting on endpaper and flyleaf, else fine in dust jacket (some tape marks and rubbing), 12 marvelous color plates, black and white plates and line illustrations.   Aleph-Bet Books, Inc.   108 - 92   2015 $150

Cave, Stephen *A Few Rods on the Encouragement Given to Slavery and the Slave Trade by Recent Measures and Chiefly by the Sugar Bill of 1846.* London: John Murray, 1849. Second edition, 8vo., modern wrappers with printed label on upper cover, very good, presentation copy, inscribed 'with the authors compts'.   John Drury Rare Books   March 2015 - 25442   2015   £306

Cayley, Cornelius *The Riches of God's Free Grace, Displayed in the Life and Conversion of Cornelius Cayley, Clerk in the Late Princess Dowager of Wales's Treasury, to the Faith of Jesus Chirst...* Leeds: printed by J. Bowling and sold by him and all booksellers, 1778. Third edition, 8vo., frontispiece, titlepage and much of text soiled, wanting back free endpaper, contemporary sheep, worn, spine very worn and boards now loose, complete, but poor copy. John Drury Rare Books 2015 - 21333 2015 $133

A Celebration for Stanley Kunitz on His Eightieth Birthday. Sheep Meadow Press, 1986. First edition, 8vo., original wrappers, signed by Kunitz on titlepage, fine. James S. Jaffe Rare Books Modern American Poetry - 172 2015 $75

Celiere, Paul *The Startling Exploits of Dr. J. B. Quies.* London: Sampson Low Marston, Searle & Rivington, 1886. First edition in English, 32 page pub. catalog dated October 1886, 120 illustrations by F. Lix, original pictorial blue cloth, publisher's monogram on rear cover, cream coated endpapers, all edges gilt. L. W. Currey, Inc. Boy's Adventure Fiction 2015 - 89 2015 $100

Celiere, Paul *The Startling Exploits of Dr. J B. Quies.* New York: Harper & Bros., 1887. First US edition, octavo, 120 illustrations by F. Lix, original pictorial blue cloth, front panel stamped in gold, silver, gray and red, spine panel stamped in gold and silver, brown coated endpapers. L. W. Currey, Inc. Boy's Adventure Fiction 2015 - 52 2015 $150

Celine, Louis Ferdinand *Journey to the End of the Night.* Boston: Little Brown and Co., 1934. First US edition, 8vo., original black cloth lettered gilt on spine, very good+ in clean, very good- dust jacket with slight edgewear and slight chips at edges and head of spine and slight creasing, decent copy. Any Amount of Books March 2015 - C1657 2015 £360

Cellius, Erhard *Imagines Professorum Tubingenium...* Tubingen: typis auctoris, 1596. First and only edition, 2 parts in 1, small 4to., five woodcut portraits of Johann Friedrich, Duke of Wurtemberg and Augustus the Younger, Duke of Brunswick, 35 stunning woodcut bust portraits of the Tubingen professors by Jakob Lederlein after Jacob Zuberlin within a variety of ornamental frames and 2 ornamental woodcut borders for the titlepages, contemporary gilt (now large oxidised) panelled vellum over thin boards, with lozenge shaped ornaments in centre of covers, flat spine gilt in compartments, remains of three ties (lower cover little stained), first few leaves with little dust soiling in upper margin, but very good. Maggs Bros. Ltd. Illustrated Books 2014 - 2015 £11,000

Cenac-Moncaut, M. *Histoire Des Chanteurs et Des Artistes Ambulants.* Saint German en Laye: L. Toinon et Cie, 1866. First edition, text in French, printed wrappers, 30 pages, uncut and untrimmed, some foxing, small slits at spine, about very good, inscribed by author to Charles Augustine Sainte-Beuve. Between the Covers Rare Books, Inc. 187 - 46 2015 $1250

Cendrars, Blaise *Kodak.* New York: Adventures in Poetry, 1976. First edition translated by Ron Padgett, 4to., original black wrappers, inscribed by Padgett for Burt, mint. James S. Jaffe Rare Books Many Happy Returns - 195 2015 $150

Cendrars, Blaise *Kodak.* New York: Adventures in Poetry, 1976. First edition translated by Ron Padgett, one of 26 lettered copies signed by Padgett, 4to., original black wrappers, fine. James S. Jaffe Rare Books Many Happy Returns - 194 2015 $350

Centennial Anniversary Canton, Oklahoma. Rich Hill: Bell Books, 2005. First edition, 4to., gilt stamped pictorial cloth, 216 pages, illustrations, portraits, fine, gift inscription on rear pastedown, scarce. Baade Books of the West 2014 - 2015 $46

Central Railroad of Iowa *The Central Railroad of Iowa Forming, with Its Connections, a Direct and Unbroken Line from St. Louis to S. Paul...* Brown & Hewitt Printers Nov. 15, 1870. 9 x 6 inch printed wrappers, 32 pages, frontispiece, wrappers printed on each panel, light vertical crease, creasing to bottom corners, as well as small blue stamp to front cover and with minor chipping to spine. Buckingham Books March 2015 - 35116 2015 $700

Ceravolo, Joseph *Fits of Dawn.* New York: "C" Press, 1965. First edition, 4to., original cloth over boards, gilt title on front cover, original illustrated wrappers (with cover design by Rosemary Ceravolo) bound in, this copy 1 of 1 Hor Commerce, publisher Ted Berrigan's copy annotated by him, signed by Berrigan, laid in is ALS from Ceravolo to Berrigan, letter folded from mailing, otherwise it and original mailing envelope fine, gutters and margins of pastedowns in book are variably darkened from binding adhesive, otherwise fine, rare. James S. Jaffe Rare Books Modern American Poetry - 48 2015 $500

Ceravolo, Joseph *Fits of Dawn.* New York: "C" Press, 1965. First edition, 4to., original illustrated wrappers, wrappers lightly to moderately soiled, otherwise fine, presentation copy inscribed by author to Frank and Sheyla Lima. James S. Jaffe Rare Books Modern American Poetry - 49 2015 $2250

Ceravolo, Joseph *Fits of Dawn.* New York: "C" Press, 1965. First edition, 4to., original cloth over boards, gilt title on front cover, original illustrated wrappers bound in, publisher Ted Berrigan's copy, specially bound for Berrigan and annotated by him, signed by Berrigan, laid in is ALS 4to., from Ceravolo to Berrigan, letter folded from mailing, otherwise it and envelope fine, gutters and margins of pastedowns in book variably darkened from binding adhesive, otherwise fine.   James S. Jaffe Rare Books   Many Happy Returns - 360   2015 $5000

Ceremonial for the Private Internment of His Late Royal Highness Frederick Duke of York and of Albany in the Royal Chapel of St. George at Windsor on Saturday evening the 20th Day of January 1827. London: privately printed by S. and R. Bentley, 1827. First edition, folio, printed throughout within black mourning borders, ms. annotations, some minor creasing, sewn but now loose within original black glazed paper wrappers, fore-edge of upper wrapper frayed, good copy, very rare.   John Drury Rare Books   March 2015 - 21660   2015   £306

Certain Observations Upon the new League or Covenant as It Was Explained by a Divine of the New Assembly in a Congregation at London. Bristol: for Rich. Harsell, 1643. First edition, small 4to., without final blank, first gathering loose, C3-D4 dampstained and with a number of uncut leaves, disbound, from the library of James Stevens Cox (1910-1997).   Maggs Bros. Ltd.   1447 - 87   2015   £100

Cerutti, Gustave *Discographie John Technical.* Sierre: Jazz 360, 1982. First edition, wrappers, 16 pages, fine.   Beasley Books   2013 - 2015 $40

Cervantes Saavedra, Miguel De   1547-1616 *The History of Don Quixote.* London: Cassell Petter and Galpin, circa 1870's, Illustrated edition, illustrations by Gustave Dore, with frontispiece, plates and illustrations, half leather and boards, raised bands, all edges gilt, very good overall, prelim sheets have some old closed tears with old tape, some mild shelfwear, old paper shows some mild age toning, tight, essentially clean text.   Stephen Lupack   March 2015 - 2015 $250

Cervantes Saavedra, Miguel De   1547-1616 *El Ingenioso Hidalgo Don Quixote de la Mancha.* Madrid: J. Ibarra, 1780. Deluxe edition, 4 volumes, 4to., frontispieces, portrait of Cervantes, 31 plates, 14 ornamental capital letters, 22 vignettes, 20 culs-de-lampe and folding engraved map, contemporary Spanish binding of green stained calf, covers 'marbled' with octagonal panel of pale brown calf set in gilt tooled border, spines gilt in compartments, red morocco labels, marbled endpapers, gilt edges, slight worm damage to foot of spine volume 1, head of volume 4 slightly chipped, armorial bookplate of Sarah Sophia Child (Villiers), Countess of Jersey (1785-1867) with old pressmarks of Osterley Park Library, bookplate of Jonathan and Phillida Gili (by Reynolds Stone).   Maggs Bros. Ltd.   Illustrated Books 2014 - 2015   £12,000

Cervantes Saavedra, Miguel De   1547-1616 *Don Quixote de la Mancha.* London: printed for T. M'Lean, 1819. 24 highly finished engravings from drawings, 8vo., 4 volumes, contemporary full calf with gilt tooling to spine compartments and boards, red speckled page edges, neatly rebacked with new endpapers, tight set with light rubbing to corners, clean internally with light foxing to few leaves only.   B & B Rare Books, Ltd.   234 - 9   2015 $1900

Cervantes Saavedra, Miguel De   1547-1616 *The Spirit of Cervantes; or Don Quixote Abridged.* London: printed for F. C. and J. Rivington, 1820. 4 hand colored plates, titlepage little browned and stained, occasional spotting elsewhere, light offsetting from plates, 8vo., contemporary half black calf, red morocco lettering piece, marbled boards, terracotta endpapers, rubbed, slight wear to joint ends.   Blackwell's Rare Books   B179 - 26   2015   £400

Cervantes Saavedra, Miguel De   1547-1616 *Don Quixote.* London: Macmillan, 1900. 3 volumes, contemporary blue morocco gilt over cloth boards.   Honey & Wax Booksellers   2 - 37   2015 $1000

Cesaire, Aime *Toussaint Louverture - La Revolution.* Paris: Presence Africaine, 1962. New edition, octavo, 312 pages, 2 full page maps at rear, wrappers, presentation from author inscribed for Francois Erval, very scarce thus, covers little creased and slightly bruised at spine, very good in very good dust jacket, little creased and rubbed at edges, small internal repair at head of spine.   Peter Ellis, Bookseller   2014 - 019786   2015   £350

Chabody, Philip *The 86 Proof Pro.* New York: Exposition, 1974. First edition, fine, embossing label on rear endpaper and staining on endpapers, otherwise fine in lightly rubbed dust jacket with some staining on lower part of front and rear flaps and short closed tear.   Mordida Books   March 2015 - 011344   2015 $185

Chabon, Michael *The Yiddish Policemen's Union.* New York: Harper Collins Pub., 2007. First edition, one of 1000 numbered and signed copies, octavo, boards.   John W. Knott, Bookseller   Selected New Arrivals Jan. 2015 - 16962   2015 $150

Chabot, Frederick G. *The Alamo Altar of Texas Liberty.* Naylor Printing Co., 1936. First edition, stiff printed wrappers, 141 pages, illustrations, facsimiles, diagrams, maps, signed by author plus 16 other Texans, including Mary Maverick, very good, clean copy.   Buckingham Books   March 2015 - 35160   2015 $175

Chaff, Gumbo, Pseud. *The Ethiopian Flute Instructor.* Boston: Elias Howe, Stereotyped by A. B. Kidder No. 7 Cornhill, 1848. First edition, oblong octavo, 48 pages, original canvas spine and printed yellow wrappers, faint crease on front wrapper, modest age toning, near fine.   Between the Covers Rare Books   197 - 85   2015 $1950

Chandler, Raymond 1886-1959 *The Big Sleep.* New York: Alfred A. Knopf, 1939. First edition, fine, bright, square copy with top edge dark blue and unfaded in dust jacket with tiny (1/8") closed tear to top edge of rear panel and tiny (1/8") closed tear and one inch wrinkle to bottom, edge of rear panel, housed in two-tone quarter leather and cloth clamshell case with leather label to spine and titles stamped in gold gilt.   Buckingham Books   March 2015 - 33775 2015 $25,000

Chandler, Raymond 1886-1959 *The Big Sleep.* San Francisco: Arion Press, 1986. First printing of this edition, one of 425 non-numbered copies signed by photographer, fine in cream lucite boards with beveled edges, blue silk-screened titles and design, 10 x 8 inches, 40 duotone photo illustrations, printed in Monotype scotch Roman and handset Futura Black by letterpress on Mohawk Superfine paper, from the collection of Duke Collier.   Royal Books   36 - 8   2015 $950

Chandler, Raymond 1886-1959 *The Brasher Doubloon.* Cleveland: World, 1946. Second Tower Books edition, pages darkened as usual, otherwise fine in dust jacket with short tear along rear flap-fold crease, particularly fine, fragile item.   Mordida Books   March 2015 - 01683 2015 $250

Chandler, Raymond 1886-1959 *The Finger Man.* New York: Avon, 1946. First edition, paperback original, some fading on front cover and crease on front and back panels, otherwise near fine in wrappers,.   Mordida Books   March 2015 - 009793   2015 $150

Chandler, Raymond 1886-1959 *Five Sinister Characters.* New York: Avon, 1945. First edition, scrape on back cover, wear along edges, some faint creasing on covers, very good, tight square copy in wrappers.   Mordida Books   March 2015 - 009792   2015 $125

Chandler, Raymond 1886-1959 *Killer in the Rain.* Boston: Houghton Mifflin, 1964. First American edition, fine in dust jacket with several short closed tears and some scattered rubbing. Mordida Books   March 2015 - 011381   2015 $350

Chandler, Raymond 1886-1959 *Killer in the Rain.* London: Hamilton, 1984. some very light spotting on top of page edges, otherwise fine in dust jacket with some very slight darkening on spine.   Mordida Books   March 2015 - 011333   2015 $500

Chandler, Raymond 1886-1959 *The Lady in the Lake.* New York: Alfred A. Knopf, 1943. First edition, near fine in like dust jacket with miniscule wear at spine extremities, scarce in such outstanding condition, from the collection of Duke Collier.   Royal Books   36 - 6   2015 $8500

Chandler, Raymond 1886-1959 *"The Little Sister."* in *Cosmopolitian magazine, April 1949 issue.* New York: Hearst Magazine, 1949. Abridged version and first publication of the novel, English price stamp on front cover, otherwise fine, fine in fine, price clipped dust jacket.   Mordida Books   March 2015 - 008620   2015 $250

Chandler, Raymond 1886-1959 *The Little Sister.* Hamish Hamilton, 1949. First edition, UK edition is true first edition, spine very slightly faded (but less so than is often the case with sensitive orange cloth), else fine in near fine dust jacket with several small chips and tears, professionally restored.   Buckingham Books   March 2015 - 38451   2015 $875

Chandler, Raymond 1886-1959 *The Little Sister.* Boston: Houghton Mifflin, 1949. First American edition, first issue with correct date on titlepage and in the orange first issue binding, fine in fine, crisp dust jacket that shows only trace of usual sunning to spine and has couple of tiny dings at edges, far superior to most copies one encounters, from the collection of Duke Collier.   Royal Books   36 - 7   2015 $2000

Chandler, Raymond 1886-1959 *The Notebooks of Raymond Chandler and English Summer.* New York: Ecco, 1976. First edition, fine in dust jacket, illustrations by Edward Gorey.   Mordida Books   March 2015 - 002976   2015 $75

Chandler, Raymond 1886-1959 *Playback.* Boston: Houghton Mifflin Co., 1958. First American edition, cloth trifle rubbed at foot, else fine in fine dust jacket with almost none of the usual rubbing.   Between the Covers Rare Books   196 - 140   2015 $250

Chandler, Raymond 1886-1959 *Playback.* Boston: Houghton Mifflin, 1958. First American edition, bookseller's small label on rear pastedown, fine in dust jacket with wear along front panel/front flap fold.   Mordida Books   March 2015 - 009797   2015 $300

Chandler, Raymond 1886-1959 *Playback.* Boston: Houghton Mifflin, 1958. First American edition, very good, names on front endpaper, otherwise fine in very good, price clipped dust jacket with crease on front panel, wear along folds and edges, nicked and frayed spine ends.   Mordida Books   March 2015 - 010011   2015 $175

Chandler, Raymond 1886-1959 *Playback.* London: Hamilton, 1958. First edition, some scattered light spotting on top of page edges, otherwise fine in dust jacket with slight spine fading and nicks at base of spine and at corners.   Mordida Books   March 2015 - 010010   2015 $300

Chandler, Raymond 1886-1959 *Raymond Chandler's Unknown Thriller, The Screenplay of Playback.* New York: Mysterious Press, 1985. First edition, one of 250 copies numbered and signed by author, this copy 187, fine in dust jacket housed in original cloth slipcase.   Buckingham Books   March 2015 - 21266   2015 $175

Chandler, Raymond 1886-1959 *Raymond Chandler Speaking.* London: Hamilton, 1962. First edition, fine in dust jacket with lightly soiled back panel, slightly faded spine and tiny wear at corners.   Mordida Books   March 2015 - 008233   2015 $125

Chandler, Raymond 1886-1959 *The Simple Art of Murder.* Boston: Houghton Mifflin, 1950. First edition, fine in dust jacket with some spine fading, short closed tear and tiny wear at corners.   Mordida Books   March 2015 - 010717   2015 $1250

Chandler, Samuel *The Dispute Better Adjusted, About the Proper Time of Applying for a Repeal of the Corporation and Test Acts.* London: J. Roberts and John Gray, 1732. First edition, well bound recently in plain grey boards, spine lettered, very good.   John Drury Rare Books   March 2015 - 24691   2015 $221

Chandrasekhar, S. *The Highly Collapsed Configurations of a Stellar Mass.* Royal Astronomical Society, 1935. First separate edition, 8vo., original printed wrappers, minimal staple rust stains to front cover, foxing to edges, 8vo., inscribed by author, near fine.   By the Book, L. C.   Special List 10 - 54   2015 $300

Chandrasekhar, S. *The Occurrence of Negative Density Gradients in Stars and Allied Problems.* Royal Astronomical Society, 1936. First separate edition, 8vo., signed and inscribed by author, near fine in original string bound wrappers from the Monthly Notices of the Royal Astronomical Society Volume 97 no. 2.   By the Book, L. C.   Special List 10 - 55   2015 $450

Chandrasekhar, S. *Stochastic problems in Physics and Astronomy.* Reviews of Modern Physics, 1943. First separate edition, offprint in original orange printed wrappers, small 4to., inscribed by author to David Schoenberg.   By the Book, L. C.   Special List 10 - 53   2015 $250

Chanukoff, Lon *(title in Yiddish) Di submarin Z-1.* New York: Bayonne: Bidermans Farlag/Jersey Printing, 1932. First edition, illustrations by Note Kozlovski, octavo, pebble grained cloth gilt, text in Yiddish, trifle rubbed, near fine, attractive, very good or better dust jacket with triangular chip at crown, exceptionally scarce in dust jacket.   Between the Covers Rare Books   196 - 70   2015 $650

Chapin, Frederick H. *The Land of the Cliff Dwellers.* Boston: 1892. First edition, illustrations, original illustrated cloth, ink number on f.f.e.p., library stamp on page 25, back hinge starting, else very good.   Dumont Maps and Books of the West   130 - 36   2015 $150

Chapin, James P. *The Birds of the Belgian Congo.* New York: American Museum of Natural History, 1932-1954. Octavo, 4 volumes, 3054 pages, 3 color plates, photos, illustrations, binder's red cloth, all edges specked, bookplate and signatures of Stephen Marchant, very good, scarce.   Andrew Isles   2015 - 12104   2015 $1200

Chapin, Maud H. *Rush-Light Stories.* New York: Duffield and Co., 1918. First edition, octavo, quarter cloth and paper covered boards, gilt, nice gift inscription from American artist Geraldine Spalding to radio pioneer and storyteller Ted Malone (pseudonym of Alden Russell), some cloth eroded on spine, about very good.   Between the Covers Rare Books   196 - 151   2015 $125

Chapman, George *A Treatise on Education.* Edinburgh: A Kincaid & W. Creech, sold by London by T. Cadell, 1773. First edition, 12mo., wanting front free endpaper, contemporary calf, spine with raised bands, gilt lines and crimson morocco label, very good, scarce.   John Drury Rare Books   2015 - 17948   2015 $787

Chapman, William *Observations on the Various Systems of Canal Navigation with Inferences Practical and Mathematical in Which Mr. Fulton's Plan of Wheel-Boats...* London: by I. and J. Taylor, 1797. First edition, 4to., 4 engraved plates, modern cloth (bit amateur), half title heavily dust soiled with few stains, verso of folding plate also bit dust soiled, inner hinge opening, otherwise a large and internally clean copy, entirely untrimmed, mostly unopened.   Joseph J. Felcone Inc.   Science, Medicine and Technology - 17   2015 $900

Chardiet, Bernice *C is for Circus.* New York: Walker and Co., 1971. First edition, oblong quarto, slight wear to corners, near fine in like dust jacket with vertical line rubbed on front panel, warmly inscribed by artist Brinton Tinkle to publisher, Beth and Sam Walker.   Between the Covers Rare Books, Inc.   187 - 47   2015 $225

Chardon, Francis *Chardon's Journal at Fort Clark 1834-1839.* State of South Dakota, 1932. First edition, cloth, 3 plates, bump to lower fore corner of front cover, else exceptionally fine, bright, clean copy.   Buckingham Books   March 2015 - 3444   2015 $250

Charity School at Bamburgh Castle *Rules for the Government of the Charity School for Sixty Poor Girls at Bambrugh Castle, Established on the Appointment of a New Mistress, Assistant and Usher to the Said School Dec. 1st 1794.* Alnwick: printed by J. Catnach, 1794. First edition, 8vo., light waterstaining throughout, attractively bound in late 19th/early 20th century chocolate morocco by Hatchards with title in gilt on upper cover, mid 19th century ownership inscription in ink on title margin, good, well bound, apparently very rare.   John Drury Rare Books   2015 - 25751   2015 $2622

Charles I, King of England *Eikon Basilike.* London: by W(illiam) D(ugard) (for Francis Eglesfield) in R.M., Anno dom, 1649. 8vo., lacking final blank, 2 engraved plates laid down and mounted on stub opposite the title, small piece torn away from upper corner of titlepage (not touching text but removing in ink name or price), inscription cut from head of first leaf, light browning to margin throughout, dampstain to inner margin of (2)A1-(2)B4, book-block split at page 160, contemporary black morocco, covers elaborately tooled gilt with border and panel, inside corners filled with flower and scroll tools and small hearts and central lozenge with crown and initials 'CR' in middle, smooth spine (once handsome binding, covers still bright, spine badly worn and defective at head and tail, corners worn, some rubbing on lower cover), late 19th century marbled endleaves, from the library of James Stevens Cox (1910-1997).   Maggs Bros. Ltd.   1447 - 78   2015   £200

Charles I, King of England *The King's Maiesties Declaration to His Subjects Concerning Lawfull Sports to Bee Used.* London: Richard Barker and by the Assignes of John Bill, 1633. First edition, 4to., woodcut device on titlepage, large woodcut royal arms on verso, woodcut head and tailpieces, wanting final blank, few minor stains and rust marks, near contemporary ms. annotation in ink, ownership signature of 'Sam. Ware" with 19th century armorial bookplates of Richard Clark Esq. Chamberlain of London (1739-1831) and of William Henry Drummond, 9th Viscount Strathallan (1810-1886), bound, presumably for Richard Clark in late 18th or early 19th century half russia gilt, good copy, wanting only final blank.   John Drury Rare Books   2015 - 25124   2015 $2185

Charles II, King of England *His Majesties Commission for the Rebuilding of the Cathedral Church of St. Paul in London.* London: printed by the Assignes of John Bill and Christopher Barker ..., 1674. First edition, folio, title printed with double ruled borders, woodcut of royal arms, bound recently in fine old style quarter calf gilt over marbled boards by Trevor Lloyd, fine, very scarce.   John Drury Rare Books   2015 - 25352   2015 $2185

Charlottetown. The Beautiful City of Prince Edward Island. Charlottetown: Published for Carter & Co. Ltd., 1903. 64 black and white photo engravings, light waterstain to top inside corner into text and images, card covers.   Schooner Books Ltd.   110 - 127   2015 $45

Charteris, Leslie *The Avenging Saint.* Garden City: Doubleday Crime Club, 1931. First American edition, previous owner's stamps on endpapers and spotting on top of page edges, otherwise fine, bright without dust jacket.   Mordida Books   March 2015 - 000412   2015 $75

Charteris, Leslie *Call for the Saint.* Garden City: Doubleday Crime Club, 1948. First edition, pages darkened, otherwise fine in dust jacket with slight spine fading and nicks at corners.   Mordida Books   March 2015 - 008765   2015 $200

Charteris, Leslie *Call for the Saint.* London: Hodder & Stoughton, 1948. First English edition, spine faded, otherwise very good in dust jacket with internal tape mend, closed tear at base of spine, scattered light wear along edges.   Mordida Books   March 2015 - 010930   2015 $85

Charteris, Leslie *Lady on a Train.* Hollywood: Shaw, 1945. First edition, very good in soft covers.   Mordida Books   March 2015 - 006551   2015 $100

Charteris, Leslie *The Last Hero.* London: Hodder & Stoughton, 1930. First edition, spine soiled, otherwise very good without dust jacket.   Mordida Books   March 2015 - 011421   2015 $200

Charteris, Leslie *Saint Errant.* London: Hodder & Stoughton, 1949. First English edition, pages 11-22 roughly opened, otherwise fine in dust jacket with tiny internal tape mend.   Mordida Books   March 2015 - 010932   2015 $150

Charteris, Leslie *The Saint Goes West.* Garden City: Doubleday Crime Club, 1942. First American edition, very good, bookplate on front endpaper, near fine in very good dust jacket with chipped and frayed spine ends, some chipping and wear along edges, several short closed tears and wear at corners.   Mordida Books   March 2015 - 007668   2015 $165

Charteris, Leslie *The Saint Goes West.* London: Hodder & Stoughton, 1942. First English edition, very good in dust jacket with half inch piece missing at top of spine, small chips along edges, several short closed tears.   Mordida Books   March 2015 - 010926   2015 $85

Charteris, Leslie *The Saint in the Sun.* Garden City: Doubleday Crime Club, 1963. First edition, some slight spotting and darkening on endpapers and tiny spotting on top of page edges, otherwise fine in dust jacket with tiny wear at top of spine.   Mordida Books   March 2015 - 008766   2015 $100

Charteris, Leslie *The Saint on Guard.* Garden City: Doubleday Crime Club, 1944. First edition, near fine, pages slightly darkened, otherwise fine in near fine dust jacket and slightly faded and rubbed spine.   Mordida Books   March 2015 - 011410   2015 $300

Charteris, Leslie *The Saint On Guard.* London: Hodder & Stoughton, 1946. First English edition, very good, lower back corner bumped, otherwise fine in very good dust jacket with internal tape mends, chip at top corner of spine, several short closed tears.   Mordida Books   March 2015 - 010928   2015 $85

Charteris, Leslie *The Saint on the Spanish Main.* Garden City: Doubleday Crime Club, 1955. First edition, inscribed by author, some darkening on endpapers and small light stain on top of spine, otherwise fine in very good dust jacket with closed, three inch tear on front panel which has had internal tape repair removed, but has lightly bled through, couple of other tape repairs with tape removed, some wear along folds.   Mordida Books   March 2015 - 011513   2015 $350

Charteris, Leslie *The Saint Sees It Through.* London: Hodder & Stoughton, 1947. First English edition, top of page edges lightly spotted, otherwise very good in dust jacket with internal tape mend, quarter inch chip top of spine, several closed tears, nicks at base of spine, and at corners.   Mordida Books   March 2015 - 010922   2015 $85

Charteris, Leslie *The Saint Steps In.* Garden City: Doubleday Crime Club, 1943. First edition, some darkening on front endpaper, otherwise fine in very good dust jacket with chipped and frayed top of spine, small chips along top of front panel and some light wear along folds.   Mordida Books   March 2015 - 011001   2015 $175

Charteris, Leslie *The Saint Steps In.* London: Hodder & Stoughton, 1944. First English edition, bookseller's small label front pastedown, some light spotting top of page edges, small label removed from front endpaper, else very good in price clipped dust jacket with internal tape emdns, chip at top of spine, several short closed tears.   Mordida Books   March 2015 - 010927   2015 $85

Charteris, Leslie *The Saint to the Rescue.* Garden City: Doubleday Crime Club, 1959. First edition, page edges slightly darkened, otherwise fine in dust jacket with faint stain on front panel, short closed tar and minor wear at spine ends.   Mordida Books   March 2015 - 011400   2015 $100

Charteris, Leslie *The Saint to the Rescue.* London: Hodder & Stoughton, 1961. First English edition, fine in dust jacket.   Mordida Books   March 2015 - 010933   2015 $85

Charteris, Leslie *Senor Saint.* London: Hodder & Stoughton, 1959. First English edition, lower corner back cover bumped, else fine in dust jacket.   Mordida Books   March 2015 - 010935   2015 $85

Charteris, Leslie *Trust the Saint.* London: Hodder & Stoughton, 1962. First English edition, fine in lightly soiled dust jacket, with some internal spotting.   Mordida Books   March 2015 - 00934   2015 $85

Charters, Sam *Jazz: a History of the New York Scene.* Garden City: Doubleday, 1962. First edition, very good, few little bumps, tall 8vo., very good dust jacket with wear and tiny chips at top edge, somewhat ornately inscribed by Leonard Feather in 1964, nice association.   Beasley Books   2013 - 2015 $200

Chartrand, Rene *Canadian Military Heritage. Volume II (1755-1871).* Montreal: Art Global, 1995. Quarto, lavishly illustrated in color, two four page sections dedicated to uniforms and weapons, maps on endpapers, very good, previous owner's name on 2nd fly leaf, glossy hardcovers.   Schooner Books Ltd.   110 - 148   2015 $45

Chase, Arthur M. *Peril at the Spy Nest.* New York: Dodd Mead, 1945. First edition, page edges darkened, otherwise fine in dust jacket with light wear at spine ends and at corners.   Mordida Books   March 2015 - 000418   2015 $150

Chase, James Hadley *My Laugh Comes Last.* London: Hale, 1977. First edition, fine in dust jacket with some spotting on inner flaps, inscribed by author.   Mordida Books   March 2015 - 012614   2015 $100

Chase, James Hadley *No Orchids for Miss Blandish.* New York: Howell Soskin, 1942. First US edition, author's first book, near fine, tight copy in dust jacket, professionally restored at spine ends and corners with two small closed tears at bottom edge of rear panel, exceptional copy.   Buckingham Books   March 2015 - 24956   2015 $2500

Chassepol, Francois De *The History of the Grand Visiters, Mahomet and Achmet Coprogli, of the Three Last Grand Signiors...* printed for H. Brome, 1677. First edition in English, engraved frontispiece, worming in lower margins, on a few occasions affecting a letter or two, small 8vo., original sheep, blind ruled borders on sides, corner ornaments, compartments blind ruled on spine, worn at extremities but sound.   Blackwell's Rare Books   B179 - 26   2015   £800

Chatto, W. A. *A Treatise on Wood Engraving, Historical and Practical...* London: Charles Knight and Co., 1839. First edition, 4to., half leather, marbled paper covered boards, marbled endpapers, boards scuffed and rubbed, especially along edges and spine, previous owner's bookplate, leaves including preface and list of illustrations loose, back hinge cracked, page 449 torn, some tanning along edges of text. Oak Knoll Books 306 - 15 2015 $300

Chatwin, Bruce *The Viceroy of Ouidah.* London: 1980. First edition, fine in near fine, price clipped dust jacket. Stephen Lupack March 2015 - 2015 $45

Chaubry De Troncenord *Des Gouvernemens et de l'Homme Public: Du Suffrage Universel.* Paris: de l'Imprimerie de Crapelet, 1834. First edition, 8vo., 43 pages, uncut, unopened, stitched in pink wrapper as issued, corner creased, fine. John Drury Rare Books March 2015 - 17856 2015 $266

Chaucer, Geoffrey 1340-1400 *The Workes of Geffrey Chaucer.* London: imprinted by Jhon Kyngston for Jhon Wight, 1561. First collected edition, first issue, 22 woodcuts in The Prologues, folio, title within woodcut border, 22 woodcuts of Pilgrims in "The Prologues" and woodcut of knight on horse at head of "The Knightes Tale", large and small historiated and decorative initials and other ornaments, Black letter, fifty-six lines, double columns; late 19th century crimson morocco by Riviere, covers with gilt fillet and roll tool border enclosing central olive wreath and elaborate cornerpieces composed of scroll-work and spreading olive branches, remaining field seme with cinquefoils, spine in 7 compartments with six raised bands, lettered gilt in two compartments, rest decoratively tooled gilt with repeated olive leaf motif, board edges and turn-ins decoratively tooled in gilt, all edges gilt, marbled endpapers (pastedowns with decorative gilt tooling), title creased and lightly soiled, small repair to outer blank margin, lower corner of second leaf renewed, affecting catchword on recto and two letters on verso, closed tear through lower half of divisional title to "The Caunterburie Tales", closed tear to A2 of "The Prologues" affecting 8 lines of text to first column and another closed tear at lower margin, F2 with small paper repair to margin and closed tear just touching text, 2U2 with paper fualt affecting one word in bottom line of text on recto and verso, few additional small marginal tears or repairs not affecting text, occasional early ink underlining and markings, early signature of James Rea (faded) on title, wonderful copy, from the libraries of C. W. Dyson Perrins and William Foyle, with bookplates. Heritage Book Shop Holiday 2014 - 36 2015 $65,000

Chaucer, Geoffrey 1340-1400 *The Works of Our Ancient and Learned and Excellent English Poet...* London: 1687. Folio, frontispiece, Black Letter, some browning and light foxing throughout and with small ink blot on Yy3, touching two lines of text, fore margin rather narrow, early 19th century calf, rebacked. large armorial bookplate of Francis Thomas de Grey Cowper, 7th and last Earl Cowper (1834-1905), from the library of James Stevens Cox (1910-1997). Maggs Bros. Ltd. 1447 - 80 2015 £1100

Chaucer, Geoffrey 1340-1400 *The Works.* London: printed for Bernard Lintot, 1721. First edition, engraved frontispiece, fine portrait of Chaucer, title vignette and 27 excellent headpiece vignettes, just little light browning, folio, 19th century diced Russia, boards panelled and framed in blind with gilt roll tool border, neatly rebacked preserving original spine decorated in gilt and blind, corners renewed, old leather somewhat scratched and rubbed around edges, bookplate of R. St. John Mathews and pencil inscription of J. Henry Stormont (dated 1901), good. Blackwell's Rare Books B179 - 28 2015 £900

Chaucer, Geoffrey 1340-1400 *The Works of Geoffrey Chaucer.* London: Folio Society, 2002. First edition thus, limited edition facsimile of 1896 first edition, #544 of 1010 copies, accompanied by 16 page booklet on Kelmscott Chaucer by Peterson as well as a 'care' leaflet, illustrations after original, elephant folio, full creme colored nigerian goatskin binding with elaborate gilt stamping after original, raised bands, top edge gilt, blue ribbon page markers, blue cloth clamshell case, fine, near fine case. Tavistock Books Bah, Humbug? - 8 2015 $1750

Chaumereix, Jean Hughes De *Narrative of M. de Chaumereix who Escaped from the Massacres of Aruai and Vannes After the Expedition of Quiberon.* London: T. Baylis, 1795. first edition in English, 8vo., printed on tinted paper, recently well bound in linen backed marbled boards, lettered, very good. John Drury Rare Books March 2015 - 18107 2015 £306

Cheddleton Association *Rules of the Cheddleton Association for the Prosecution of Felons.* Leek: printed by James Rider, 1859. 8vo. sewn but unbound as issued, fine. John Drury Rare Books 2015 - 14262 2015 $89

Chen, Julie *Panorama.* Berkeley: Flying Fish Press, 2008. Number 67 of 100 copies signed and numbered by Chen, letterpress printed from wood blocks and photopolymer plates and assembled at Flying Fish Studio, bound in dark grey cloth with yellow title label and cutout design to front cover, box has same grey cloth and title label, book measures 9 1/2 x 20 1/4 x 1 1/4 inches, opening to a width of 60 inches, box is 10 1/4 x 20 5/8 x 1 1/4 inches, fine. The Kelmscott Bookshop 11 - 9 2015 $2400

Chen, Julie *Praxis*. Sarasota: and Berkeley: Flying Fish Press and Ringling College of art and Design, 2013. One of 45 copies, all on Mohawk Superfine paper, hand numbered and signed by author/artist, Julie Chen, page size 7 x 10 inches, 14 pages, two of which are double page gatefolds, one page with pull-out tab to add color to images of page, plus one of double page gatefolds with three volvelles, bound by artist/author, Julie Chen in orange flecked blue cloth with citrus yellow and green paper illustration overlay on first third of fore edge, exposed orange paper tab spine, label printed in black on orange paper, housed in custom made gold cloth over boards, four sided portfolio case with magnetic closures, lined with orange cloth printed with diagram schematic of inspiration for text on inside cover, pastedowns from Cave Papers.   Priscilla Juvelis - Rare Books   62 - 6   2015 $1250

Chen, Julie *True to Life*. Berkeley: Flying Fish Press, 2005. First edition, limited to 100 copies, each signed and numbered by author/artist, Julie Chen, printed letterpress, using a combination of pressure plates, woodblocks and photopolymer plates, assembled and bound at Flying Fish Press with assistance from Macy Chadwick, book is a tablet that sits on its own easel, housed within box holding the book, tablet, covered in deep red silk, fastened with brass in each corner, has an opening 10 1/2 x 6 7/8 inches covered with plexi, through which is viewed the text, along each vertical side of box are wooden 'arrows' each numbered in turquoise on an orange ground, reading 2-12, each representing a page, box measures 14 7/8 x 8 1/4 inches, reader must push up both 'arrows' marked 2 or 3, etc., each page illustrated with abstract images, very organic in nature as well as a partial view of a long, continuous visual timeline, covers right and left, fold open and there is an only image, 6 7/8 x 1 7/8 inches in shades of green on board with title and author printed in black on tobacco colored paper the same width of the image.   Priscilla Juvelis - Rare Books   61 - 19   2015 $1800

Chen, Julie *View*. Berkeley: Flying Fish Press, 2007. One of 100 copies, each signed and numbered on inside of box by author, artist and designer, Julie Chen, box 13 3/4 x 6 1/4 x 4 3/4 inches, wrapped in dull gold and oyster white Japanese book cloths with title printed in black on green paper label, closure in green paper and oyster colored book cloth over book board with title printed in black, closure with magnet and corresponding magnet in case, box contains two books "Mise en Scene" and "After-Image" both printed letterpress, "Mise" printed on single long sheet of grey paper with laser cut outs, the page inserted between top lighter grey page and bottom grey-green page, the cut-out text on gray paper gives illusion of floating freely in space when the book is opened and is bound accordion style with green cloth over boards with lighter grey-green cloth and paper label in green printed with title in black and sewn with grey thread on exterior edge, "After" text printed in black on grey-green paper that is bound accordion style between double fold of green paper silkscreen printed with tree limbs in darker green, text is behind Mylar and appears in laser cut outs in page spread, two books housed on each side of box, center of box is a still life of water and trees, this diorama is made of concrete, resin with trees made for architectural models and is behind Plexiglas that is hinged top and can be opened from bottom.   Priscilla Juvelis - Rare Books   61 - 20   2015 $1675

Cheny, John *An Historical List of Horse Matches Run and of Plates and Prizes Run for in Great Britain and Ireland in 1744*. London: printed in the year, 1744. 12mo., first couple of leaves slightly chipped at head not near printed surface, contemporary ruled calf, neatly rebacked to match, spine having gilt lines, raised bands and red morocco label lettered gilt, very good, very rare.   John Drury Rare Books   2015 - 24123   2015 $787

Cherke, John *De Pronuntiatione Graecae Potissimum Linguae Disputationes cum Stephano Vuintoniensi Episcopo, Septem Contrariss Epistolis Comprehensae, Magna Quadam Elegantia & Eruditionere Sertae*. Basel: per Nicol. Episcopium iuniorem, 1555. First edition, few minor creases and small splashmarks, blindstamp of Earls of Macclesfield to first few leaves, early ownership inscription of Arthur Hilder, 8vo., contemporary English blind-stamped dark calf, boards with decorative frame inside set of blind rules, vellum pastedowns, from an older manuscript with music and red and blue initials, ties removed, joints little rubbed, spine ends slightly defective, front hinge cracking and flyleaf lost, bookplate of Shirburn Castle, good.   Blackwell's Rare Books   B179 - 19   2015   £1500

Cheronnet, Louis *Algerie*. Paris: Duchartre, 1930. Folio, cloth backed pictorial boards, some cover soil and toning of paper, very good, illustrations by Maurice Tranchant with hand colored illustrations.   Aleph-Bet Books, Inc.   108 - 349   2015 $750

Cherryh, C. J. *Cyteen*. New York: Warner Books, 1988. First edition, octavo, cloth backed boards.   John W. Knott, Bookseller   Selected New Arrivals Jan. 2015 - 16967   2015 $100

Chertok, Leon *A Critique of Psychoanalytic Reason.* Stanford: Stanford, 1992. First US edition, fine in fine dust jacket. Beasley Books 2013 - 2015 $45

Chesbro, George C. *The Beasts of Valhalla.* New York: Atheneum, 1985. First edition, very fine in dust jacket. Mordida Books March 2015 - 009378 2015 $150

Chesbro, George C. *Shadow of a Broken Man.* New York: Simon and Schuster, 1977. First edition, page edges slightly darkened, otherwise fine in dust jacket. Mordida Books March 2015 - 009760 2015 $100

Cheshire, Joseph Blount *Diocese of North Carolina. The Early Conventions: Held at Tawborough, Anno domini 1790, 1793 and 1794.* Raleigh: Spirit of the Age Print, 1882. First edition, 29 pages, stitched printed yellow wrappers, light foxing, near fine, inscribed by author's son to Bishop Pevick in 1951. Between the Covers Rare Books, Inc. 187 - 48 2015 $125

Chesnutt, Charles W. *The House Behind the Cedars.* Boston and New York: Houghton Mifflin, 1900. First edition, later issue with undated titlepage, 8vo., light green cloth stamped in silver and black, endpapers unevenly browned, fine, bright copy. Second Life Books Inc. 190 - 48 2015 $150

Chester, George Randolph *Get-Rich-Quick Wallingford.* Henry Artemus Co., 1908. First edition, inscribed by author's daughter, Alida for Mr. and Mrs. Geo. R. Chester, College Hill, Cincinnati May 21 -09, spine letters faded out, else very good, elusive title. Buckingham Books March 2015 - 37310 2015 $750

Chester, George Randolph *The Wonderful Adventures of Little Prince Toofat.* New York: James McCann, 1922. First edition, 4to., blue-grey gilt and pictorial cloth, cover very slightly soiled, else near fine, exceedingly scarce, pictorial headpieces, decorative initials, pictorial endpapers and 6 color plates by Robert Lawson. Aleph-Bet Books, Inc. 108 - 263 2015 $3500

Chester, George Randolph *Young Wallingford.* Indianapolis: Bobbs Merrill, 1910. First edition, some light foxing on top of page edges and shelfwear along bottom cover edges, otherwise fine in blue cloth covered boards, gold stamped titles and decorations. Mordida Books March 2015 - 008953 2015 $85

Chesterfield, Philip Dormer Stanhope, 4th Earl of 1694-1773 *Letters written by the Late Right Honourable Philip Dormer Stanhope, Earl of Chesterfield to his Son Philip Stanhope...* London: J. Dodsley, 1774. First edition, 2 volumes, frontispiece volume I, contemporary boards, calf backs and tips, rubbed, worn at joints and edges, some foxing, soiling and minor stains, generally very good, tight copy, first issue with half title, errata leaf at end of volume 2, first issue with 'quia uroit' line 16 page 55 in volume I, contemporary ownership inscription and bookplates of Sir Archibald Grant of Monymoske, housed in custom cloth slipcase. Second Life Books Inc. 189 - 54 2015 $2000

Chesterfield, Philip Dormer Stanhope, 4th Earl of 1694-1773 *Letters Written by the Late Right Honourable Philip Dormer Stanhope, Earl of Chesterfield to his Son, Philip...* London: printed for J. Dodsely, 1774. First edition, first state with 'quia uroit error on line 16 page 55 of volume 1, 2 large octavo volumes, engraved frontispiece, half titles and errata, early full tan calf boards, rebacked to style, front hinge volume I cracked but firm, unprofessionally reinforced boards ruled in gilt, spine labels printed in red and green and lettered in gilt, spines stamped gilt in compartments, board edges gilt, all edges dyed red, marbled endpapers, volume 1 with some minor chipping to headcap and some cracking along outer. Heritage Book Shop Holiday 2014 - 37 2015 $1500

Chesterton, Gilbert Keith 1874-1936 *Four Faultless Felons.* London: Cassell and Co. Ltd., 1930. First edition, 8vo., some light foxing to page edges and corners slightly bumped, else near fine, bright, tight copy, crisp dust jacket that has been professionally internally restored along flap folds and spine ends, exceptional copy, scarce. Buckingham Books March 2015 - 24907 2015 $2000

Chesterton, Gilbert Keith 1874-1936 *The Incredulity of Father Brown.* London: Cassell, 1926. First edition, crown 8vo., original black cloth stamped in red to upper board, backstrip lettered in red, slight lean to spine, top tail edges rough trimmed, bookplate tipped in to flyleaf, dust jacket with very short closed tear at foot of rear panel and odd nick lightest of rubbing to extremities, very good, scarce in dust jacket. Blackwell's Rare Books B179 - 134 2015 £2000

Chesterton, Gilbert Keith 1874-1936 *The Innocence of Father Brown.* London: Cassell, 1911. First edition, frontispiece and 7 further plates by Sidney Seymour Lucas, very light creasing to top corner of middle portion of textblock, faint foxing to prelims with occasional spot further in, crown 8vo., original red cloth stamped in gilt to upper board, backstrip lettered in gilt, hint of fading, bookplate tipped in to pastedown, good. Blackwell's Rare Books B179 - 135 2015 £700

Chesterton, Gilbert Keith 1874-1936 *The Poet and the Lunatics.* London: Cassell, 1929. First edition, fine in very good dust jacket with glue residue along internal flap edges, edge of rear flap partially torn away without affecting any text, several short closed tears and small chips.   Mordida Books   March 2015 - 2015 $600

Chesterton, Gilbert Keith 1874-1936 *The Poet and the Lunatics.* London: Cassell, 1929. First edition, fine in near fine dust jacket, very light wear at base of spine and both corners of front panel, from the collection of Duke Collier.   Royal Books   36 - 151   2015 $1500

Chesterton, Gilbert Keith 1874-1936 *The Scandal of Father Brown.* London: Cassell, 1935. First edition, crown 8vo., original blue cloth, backstrip lettered gilt, bookplate tipped to flyleaf, dust jacket with chipping to corners and at head of backstrip panel, edges little frayed and creased, few short closed tears and chip at head of front panel, light soiling to rear panel, very good.   Blackwell's Rare Books   B179 - 136   2015   £1000

Chesterton, Gilbert Keith 1874-1936 *The Scandal of Father Brown.* London: Cassell, 1935. First edition, some scattered light foxing on page edges, otherwise near fine in dust jacket with internal tape mends, small chip at top of spine and chip at top corner of front panel.   Mordida Books   March 2015 - 00421   2015 $1150

Chesterton, Gilbert Keith 1874-1936 *The Secret of Father Brown.* London: Cassell, 1927. First edition, crown 8vo., original black cloth with single fillet blindstamped order to upper board, backstrip lettered gilt, bookplate tipped in to flyleaf, dust jacket with few nicks and light rubbing to extremities, corners trifle chipped, some very light creasing around head, very good.   Blackwell's Rare Books   B179 - 137   2015   £2000

Chesterton, Gilbert Keith 1874-1936 *The Secret of Father Brown.* London: Cassell & Co. Ltd., 1927. First edition, moderate mottling to front and rear boards, else very good in fine facsimile dust jacket.   Buckingham Books   March 2015 - 26323   2015 $275

Chevreul, Michel Eugene *Des Couleurs et Leurs Applications aux Arts Industriels a l'Aide des Cercles Chromatiques.* Paris: J. B. Bailliere et Fils Libraires de l'Academie Imperiale de Medecine Rue Hautefeuille 19 (and others), 1864. First edition, large 4to., 27 colored engraved plates, one folding, some occasional foxing, original blindstamped red cloth, upper cover and spine lettered in gilt, some light wear to extremities, good copy.   Marlborough Rare Books   List 54 - 14   2015   £2250

Chevreul, Michel Eugene *The Laws of Contrast and Colour.* London: G. Routledge & Co. Farrington Street, New York: 18 Beekman Street, 1857. First edition of this translation, small 8vo., colored frontispiece and 3 plates with overlay, original blue decorated cloth, gilt.   Marlborough Rare Books   List 54 - 11   2015   £250

Chevreul, Michel Eugene *The Laws of Contrast of Colour.* London: Routledge, Warne and Routledge, 1859. New edition, small 8vo., 13 colored plates, including colored frontispiece, 2 wood engraved plates with overlay, original green decorated cloth, gilt brown blindstamped cloth, spine with letter in gilt.   Marlborough Rare Books   List 54 - 12   2015   £100

Chevreul, Michel Eugene *The Laws of Contrast of Colour.* New York: 419 Broome Street, after, 1868. New edition, small 8vo., 17 plates including 15 colored and one with overlay, original green blindstamped cloth, spine lettered in gilt.   Marlborough Rare Books   List 54 - 15 2015   £75

Chevreul, Michel Eugene *The Laws of Contrast of Colour.* London: G. Routledge and Co. Farrington Street, New York: 18 Beekman Street, 1883? Third edition of this translation, small 8vo., 17 plates, 15 colored and one with overlay, original green blindstamped cloth, spine lettered in gilt.   Marlborough Rare Books   List 54 - 16   2015   £75

Chevreul, Michel Eugene *De La Loi Du Contraste Simultane Des Couleurs... (Laws of the Contrast of Colour).* Paris: Imprimerie Nationale Librairie Gauthier Villars et fils..., 1889. Centenary edition, large 4to., 2 folding tables, 40 engraved and lithograph plates on 22 sheets, including 37 printed in colour, one with overslip, one facsimile of autographs, 9 samples of colored paper and 2 printed tables, contemporary green morocco backed green pebble grained cloth, sprinkled edges.   Marlborough Rare Books   List 54 - 17   2015   £1500

Chevreul, Michel Eugene *The Principles of Harmony and Contrast of Colours and Their Application to the Arts, Including Painting....* London: Longman, Brown, Green and Longmans, 1855. Second edition in English, 8vo., 4 double page engraved folding plates, one with overlay, original blue cloth blocked in blind, spine lettered gilt.   Marlborough Rare Books   List 54 - 10   2015   £200

Chevreul, Michel Eugene *The Principles of Harmony and Contrast of Colours and Their Application to the Arts...* London: Henry G. Bohn, York Street, Covent Garden, 1860. Third edition of the first English translation, 8vo., 15 chromolithograph plates and 4 engraved folding plates, folding wood engraving, original red cloth blocked in blind, spine lettered in gilt.   Marlborough Rare Books   List 54 - 13   2015   £185

Cheyne, George 1671-1743 *The English Malady or a Treatise of Nervous Diseases of All Kinds as Spleen, Vapours, Lowness of Spirits, Hypochrondriacal and Hysterical Distempers.* London: printed for G. Strahan and J. Leakeat Bath, 1733. First edition, 8vo., contemporary panelled calf with raised bands, spine label renewed, short cracks in joints, still near fine, crisp and sound, early ownership inscription in ink on front free endpaper of Thos. Welman of Lowe(e)r Poundisford 1735.   John Drury Rare Books   2015 - 26183   2015 $874

Cheyney, Peter *Dark Hero.* London: Collins, 1946. First edition, special commemoration edition, one of 250 numbered copies, signed by author, fine in dust jacket with nicks on spine and heavily stained back panel.   Mordida Books   March 2015 - 005234   2015 $165

Chicago; Her Commerce and Railroads: Two Articles Published in the Daily Democratic Press Book and Job Steam Printing Office 1853. Chicago: Democratic Press Book and Job Steam Printing Office, 1853. 8vo., 29 pages, institutional stamps top of first text page, else clean text, reinforced spine, good+.   M & S Rare Books, Inc.   97 - 54   2015 $475

Chicago Medical Journal and Examiner. 1876-1879. First edition, very nice run, broken at beginning, of 132+ issues.   Beasley Books   2013 - 2015 $150

Chicago, Burlington & Quincy Railroad *Great Opportunities for Farmers, Business Men and Investors in Nebraska, Northwestern Kansas and Eastern Colorado.* Privately printed, 1892. First edition, 12mo., printed wrappers, 32 pages, maps, rear cover has map of Burlington Route's system, large folding map affixed to rear cover, perimeter edges of front cover tanned, small closed tear to fore-edge of rear cover, else internally clean and folding map fine, unused condition, overall near fine, rare booklet.   Buckingham Books   March 2015 - 37210   2015 $750

Child, Frank S. *South Dakota.* Baker & Taylor, 1888. First edition, 8vo., while bound in to a cloth binder, this copy lacks original wrappers, else very good, housed in clamshell case.   Buckingham Books   March 2015 - 28200   2015 $775

Child, Graham *World Mirrors 1650-1900.* London: Sotheby's Publications, 1990. First edition, 4to., original grey cloth lettered gilt at spine, slight rubbing to lower edges, otherwise very good+ in clean slightly used dust jacket with slight shelfwear and a closed tear at rear.   Any Amount of Books   2015 - C16304   2015   £160

Child, Josiah 1630-1699 *A New Discourse about Trade, Wherein the Reduction of Interest of Money to 4 1. per Centrum is Recommended.* London: printed by A. Sowle, 1690. First edition, small 8vo., with initial license leaf A1 but lacking errata leaf P8, some occasional light soiling and ink markings to blank margins throughout the occasional headline shaved by the binder, lower fore-corners of first few leaves chipped away, modern quarter blue morocco and marbled boards, from the library of James Stevens Cox (1910-1997).   Maggs Bros. Ltd.   1447 - 81   2015   £1100

Child, Josiah 1630-1699 *A New Discourse of Trade, Wherein is recommended Several Weighty Points Relating to Companies of Merchants.* London: printed and sold by T. Sowle, 1698. Fourth edition, 8vo., final blank titlepage heavily browned, following seven leaves less severely marked, contemporary sheep ruled in blind, rebacked, corners repaired, corners worn and leather affected by damp, (new endleaves), from the library of James Stevens Cox (1910-1997).   Maggs Bros. Ltd.   1447 - 82   2015   £280

Child, Lee *Killing Floor.* New York: Putnam, 1997. First edition, signed by author, fine in fine dust jacket.   Buckingham Books   March 2015 - 27538   2015 $275

Child, Lydia Maria 1802-1880 *An Appeal in Favor of the Class of Americans Called Africans.* Boston: Allen and Ticknor, 1833. First edition, 8vo., frontispiece inserted with two full page plates in text, light stain to flyleaves, some foxing to margins of frontispiece, otherwise text good and clean, contemporary ownership of Mary Ann Ingalls on top of titlepage, bound in original cloth, little rubbed and couple of nicks to cloth and edge of spine label, which is complete, better than average copy of a book usually found in tough condition, with errata slip noted by BAL, scarce.   Second Life Books Inc.   190 - 40   2015 $2500

Child, Lydia Maria 1802-1880 *A New Flower for Children...* New York: C. S. Francis, 1856. First edition, 12mo., original blindstamped black cloth, gilt decorations and lettering, frontispiece, pictorial title and illustrations in text, 12 page publisher's catalog at end, contemporary gift inscription from a father to his son Feb. 9 1856, cloth little spotted and worn, some light foxing, very good.   The Brick Row Book Shop   Miscellany 67 - 31   2015 $425

Children's Hour with Peter Rabbit. n.p., n.d., 10 illustrations in color, 11 in black and white, pink and white 'checked' boards with color illustration, 5 1/4 x 4 1/4 inches, small surface rub top corner front free endpaper, fine in dust jacket.   Ian Hodgkins & Co. Ltd.   134 - 244   2015   £65

Childress, Alice *A Hero Ain't Nothing' but a Sandwich.* New York: Coward McCann & Geoghegan, 1973. Ninth printing, fine in near fine dust jacket with rubbing and short tears, nicely inscribed by author.   Between the Covers Rare Books   197 - 8   2015 $65

Child's First Primer, or A B C Book. New York: H. & S. Raynor circa, 1845. 3 5/8 x 4 5/8 inches, 23 pages, blue pictorial wrappers, fine, 4 woodcuts, charming primer in excellent condition.   Aleph-bet Books, Inc.   109 - 11   2015 $275

Chimot, Edouard *Les Belles Que Voila, Mes Modeles De Montmartre a Sebville.* Paris: Le Livre Du Bibliophile, 1958. No. 93 of 831 copies on Rives paper, 4to., unbound signatures laid into wrappers, fine in fine wrappers, little darkening to glassine, illustrations by Chimot.   Beasley Books   2013 - 2015 $400

Chinese Ivories from the Shang to the Quing. London: Oriental Ceramic Society and the British Museum, 1984. 4to., 20 color and 320 black and white illustrations, cloth, dust jacket.   Oak Knoll Books   306 - 69   2015 $250

Chinese Porcelain: the S. C. Ko Tianminlou Collection. Hong Kong: Hong Kong Museum of Art, 1987. 2 volumes, small folio, cloth, decorated endpapers, slipcase, plates, pines of both volumes slightly sunned, illustrated paper band around slipcase includes title in both Chinese and English and has been repaired at edges.   Oak Knoll Books   306 - 70   2015 $950

Chisholm, Hugh *Several Have Lived.* New York: Gemor Press, 1942. First edition, 500 copies printed, very good, large 8vo., unnumbered, about 50 pages, black wrappers, small illustration pasted to cover printed title label at spine, 3 tipped in illustrations in black and white, loosely inserted is rear printed flier for book.   Any Amount of Books   2015 - A39537   2015   £170

Chisholm, Louey *Enchanted Land.* New York and London: Putnam & Jack, 1906. First edition, 4to., green cloth with elaborate gilt pictorial cover by Katharine Cameron, all edges gilt, gold endpapers, 30 magnificent color plates by Cameron.   Aleph-bet Books, Inc.   109 - 81   2015 $600

Chittenden, Hiram Martin *The American Fur Trade of the Far West.* Press of the Pioneers, 1935. 2 volumes, cloth, titles stamped in gilt on front cover and spine, frontispieces, illustrations, large folding map in pocket affixed to rear pastedown, fine, attractive set in original slipcase.   Buckingham Books   March 2015 - 34350   2015 $175

Chittenden, Hiram Martin *History of Early Steamboat Navigation on the Missouri River, Life and Adventures of Joseph La Barage...* Francis P. Harper, 1903. First edition, limited to 950 copies, 8vo., 2 volumes, blue cloth, gilt stamping on spine, frontispiece, illustrations, exceptionally fine, bright, uncut set.   Buckingham Books   March 2015 - 34297   2015 $850

Choi, Sunu *The World's Great Collections: Oriental Ceramics. volume 2.* Tokyo: Kodansha International, 1982. folio, cloth, slipcase, ad brochure laid in, 100 color and 327 monochrome plates.   Oak Knoll Books   306 - 258   2015 $150

Chonz, Selina *Florina and the Wild Bird.* New York: Oxford University Press, 1953. First edition, large oblong 4to., cloth backed pictorial boards, fine in dust jacket with several chips, illustrations in full color by Alois Carigiet.   Aleph-bet Books, Inc.   109 - 89   2015 $150

Christian Frederick VIII, King of Denmark *Disposiciones Tomados el Gobierno de S.M. el Rey de Dinamarca en Favor de los Negros Esclavos en las Antillas Danesas Fecha de 18 de Febrero de 1844.* Madrid: 1844. First edition, (3) pages, 8 1/2 x 13 inches, very good.   Kaaterskill Books   19 - 49   2015 $1500

Christie's, New York *Dresses from the Collection of Diana, Princess of Wales.* New York: Christie's, 1997. First edition, folio, original purple linen cloth, without lettering, illustrations in color and black and white, fine in very good+ dust jacket, short closed tear at head of spine hinge of jacket.   Any Amount of Books   2015 - C11093   2015   £260

Christie Manson & Woods *Catalogue of the Very Select Collection of Modern Pictures of the English and Continental Schools. The Property of Mr. Gambart...* London: Printed by W. Clowes & Sons, 1861. First edition, 8vo., rebound, quarter black calf crocodile effect patterned boards lettered gilt on spine, marbled endpapers, very slightly rubbed at head and foot of spine, very good+, slight rubbing, otherwise very good.   Any Amount of Books   2015 - C8173   2015   £150

Christie, Agatha   1891-1975 *The Body in the Library.* London: Collins crime Club, 1942. First edition, very good, bookseller's small label on front pastedown, spine slightly faded and lightly soiled, otherwise, near fine in very good restored dust jacket which has been completely backed with plain white paper.   Mordida Books   March 2015 - 011512   2015 $450

Christie, Agatha   1891-1975 *Cards on the Table.* London: Collins Crime Club, 1936. First edition, spine slightly faded and covers slightly soiled, otherwise near fine, without dust jacket.   Mordida Books   March 2015 - 008957   2015 $650

Christie, Agatha   1891-1975 *Death Comes as the End.* Crime Club (by Collins), 1945. First edition, crown 8vo., original red cloth, backstrip lettered in black, edges little dust soiled, light bump to fore-edge, contemporary ownership inscription to flyleaf, dust jacket very lightly dust soiled, overall with small amount of spotting at foot of rear panel and to borders of rear flap, very good.   Blackwell's Rare Books   B179 - 138   2015   £200

Christie, Agatha 1891-1975 *Death Comes as the End.* London: Collins Crime Club, 1945. First English edition, near fine in very good, slightly darkened dust jacket with internal tape mend, nicks at spine ends and wear along folds.   Mordida Books   March 2015 - 011516   2015 $200

Christie, Agatha 1891-1975 *The Hound of Death and Other Stories.* Odhams Press Limited, 1933. First edition, spine faded but lettering legible, cloth lightly spotted, lightly foxed along fore-edges, former small owner's stamped name on front flyleaf and top of titlepage, else good, internally clean copy in dust jacket, moderately soiled on rear panel, light wear to spine ends and internally reinforced with archival tape.   Buckingham Books   March 2015 - 33544   2015 $750

Christie, Agatha 1891-1975 *The Labours of Hercules.* London: Collins Crime Club, 1947. First edition, fine in very good dust jacket with chipping at spine ends and corners. Mordida Books   March 2015 - 011514   2015 $200

Christie, Agatha 1891-1975 *The Murder of Roger Ackroyd.* London and Glasgow: Collin's Clear Type Press, 1934. Thirteenth edition, 8vo., original publisher's red cloth lettered black on spine, slight lean, otherwise very good+ in very good clean dust jacket (very slightly chipped at top of spine and front bottom corner of dust jacket).   Any Amount of Books   2015 - A98800   2015   £160

Christie, Agatha 1891-1975 *The Mystery of the Blue Train.* New York: Dodd Mead, 1928. First American edition, near fine in fine dust jacket, backstrip very slightly toned, else book quite clean and bright, jacket is exceptional, without wear, bright and colorful, from the collection of Duke Collier.   Royal Books   36 - 152   2015 $2000

Christie, Agatha 1891-1975 *Poirot Loses a Client.* Dodd Mead & Co., 1937. First US edition, 8vo., fine, bright, tight copy in bright dust jacket, few tiny chips at extremities, beautiful copy.   Buckingham Books   March 2015 - 37456   2015 $1500

Christie, Agatha 1891-1975 *The Seven Dials Mystery.* London: Collins, 1929. First edition, stamp on titlepage and spine slightly faded, otherwise very good.   Mordida Books   March 2015 - 011517   2015 $300

Christie, Agatha 1891-1975 *Towards Zero.* London: Collins, 1944. First edition, first printing, very good, bright copy with stain to front panel, unclipped dust jacket with soiling, staining, spine tone, few small chips to spine ends, good copy.   B & B Rare Books, Ltd.   234 - 10   2015 $300

Christie, Agatha 1891-1975 *Towards Zero.* London: Collins Crime Club, 1944. First edition, name on front endpaper, otherwise near fine in price clipped dust jacket with darkened spine and nicks at corners.   Mordida Books   March 2015 - 011518   2015 $250

Christie, Agatha 1891-1975 *The Witness for the Prosecution and Other Stories.* Dodd Mead & Co., 1948. First edition, tiny bump to top corner of front cover, else near fine, internally clean copy in dust jacket, lightly soiled on white rear panel, light wear to spine ends and corners and some light rubbing to spine, bright sharp copy. Buckingham Books   March 2015 - 36940   2015 $2500

Christmas. Chicago: Le Petit Oiseau Press, 1963. Limited to 150 copies, frontispiece tipped in, signed by publishers, illustrations in text, half cloth, paper covered boards, paper spine label, miniature bookplate of Kathryn Rickard.   Oak Knoll Books   306 - 105   2015 $150

Christmas Improvement or Hunting Mrs. P. A Tale founded on facts. London: printed for N. Hailes, 1834. First edition, 12mo. lithograph frontispiece, half title, 6 page catalog of new works, original maroon quarter roan over marbled boards, spine gilt lettered, minor wear, spine with slight loss at foot, good copy, very scarce.   John Drury Rare Books   March 2015 - 25803   2015   £306

Christmas Poems and Pictures: A collection of Songs, Carols and Descriptive Poems relating to the Festival of Christmas. New York: James G. Gregory, 1864. Previous owner inscription Christmas 1863, 4to., green cloth stamped in gold, all edges gilt, 96 pages, slight wear to spine ends and tips, foxing, mainly in margins, else tight and embellished with beautiful full page and smaller engravings by leading artists of the time.   Aleph-bet Books, Inc.   109 - 90   2015 $1350

Christmastide in Ancient Britain. Berkeley: Poole Press, 1987. Limited to 51 numbered copies signed by designer, printer and binder, Maryline Poole Adams, 7.4 x 5.5 cm., quarter leather, decorated paper covered boards, title gilt stamped on spine, illustrated with British postage stamps, miniature bookplate of Kathryn Rickard.   Oak Knoll Books   306 - 106   2015 $350

Christopher, John *The Death of Grass.* London: Michael Joseph, 1956. First edition, octavo, boards.   John W. Knott, Bookseller   Selected New Arrivals Jan. 2015 - 16968   2015 $1000

Christopher, John *The World in Winter.* London: Eyre & Spottiswoode, 1962. First edition, octavo, boards.   John W. Knott, Bookseller   Selected New Arrivals Jan. 2015 - 16969   2015 $200

Chuinard, E. G. *Only One Man Died. The Medical Aspects of the Lewis and Clark Expedition.* Arthur H. Clark Co., 1979. First edition, cloth, numerous illustrations, fine, bright copy in near fine dust jacket.   Buckingham Books   March 2015 - 29886   2015 $325

Chukovski, K. *Mukha Tsokotooka. (The Chattering Fly).* 1933. Small 4to., pictorial wrappers, corner creases, else very good, black and white illustrations by V. Konashevich on every page.   Aleph-bet Books, Inc.   109 - 424   2015 $1500

Chukovski, K. *Fedorino Gore. (Fedora's Troubles).* Leningrad: Ogiz, 1935. 8vo., pictorial wrappers, light rear cover soil, else near fine, 3-color drawings on every page by N. Kekarenko.   Aleph-Bet Books, Inc.   108 - 400   2015 $275

Church of England. Book of Common Prayer *The Book of Common Prayer and Administration of the Sacraments and Other Rites & Ceremonies of the Church...* London: printed by His Majesties Printers, 1662. Small folio, printed in gothic black letter, Kalendar printed in red and black, numerous elaborate woodcut head and tailpieces and initials, engraved title mounted, Psalms of David with separate titlepage, lacks frontispiece, some minor edge repairs to few leaves, leaf Cc6 supplied in early manuscript, slip of early manuscript music tipped in at R3, slightly later full calf, covers paneled in blind with decorative tooling and corner fleurons, spine compartments, blind ruled and stamped with gilt leather title label, front hinge expertly restored, handsome and clean.   Argonaut Book Shop   Holiday Season 2014 - 54   2015 $2500

Church of England. Book of Common Prayer *The Book of Common Prayer. (bound with) The Whole Book of Psalms Collected into English Metre.* London: John Bill and Christopher Barker, 1676. 184 x 127mm., very animated contemporary black morocco, elaborately gilt and with many inlays and onlays, covers with large central panel framed by citron morocco in a modified cottage-roof design, (including a peaked roof and protruding eaves under vertical supports but with scalloped interruptions on all four sides), vertical sidepieces entwined with gilt and black morocco vines bearing gilt leaves and acorns, panel within filled with lowers and geometrical designs accented with and surrounded by delicate gilt tooling, raised bands, spine compartments gilt and inlaid and either geometric shapes or a rosette, marbled endpapers, all edges gilt and gauffered, with floral vine painted in pinks and blues, fine modern black morocco clamshell box, extra illustrated with 55 hand colored engravings, rear flyleaf with handwritten list of five children born into the Man family between 1745 and 1752 verso of same with pencilled inscription of the eldest child, Robert Man, front flyleaf with pencilled note identifying the family as relatives of Admiral Man, hint of rubbing to joints, very small stain to foot of titlepage, edges of leaves slightly browned, trimmed close at top, isolated minor foxing, other trivial imperfections, but extremely pleasing copy, immensely appealing binding with only insignificant wear and text smooth and clean.   Phillip J. Pirages   66 - 28   2015 $22,500

Church of England. Book of Common Prayer *The Book of Common Prayer... Together with the Psalter or Psalms of David.* Cambridge: Printed by John Baskerville, 1762. Third edition, 241 x 165mm., excellent contemporary Irish red morocco, very elaborately gilt and inlaid, covers with central white morocco lozenge inlaid and tooled with gilt flowers, plumes and birds beak, whole framed by undulating floral sprigs, raised bands, spine gilt in compartments quartered by a saltire and tooled with roses and other flowers, gilt turn-ins, marbled endpapers, all edges gilt, (small expert repair along top of spine), titlepage with ink inscription of A. Wolseley dated 1772 at top with small decorative printed paper strip pasted over price at bottom, covers less dark than the spine (and so somehow faded?), slight flaking but no cracking to joints, corners little worn, but the once splendid binding still extremely attractive, without serious wear, and with its very animated gilt still bright, despite the loss of color in the morocco background, many leaves with faint browning and muted foxing (one gathering conspicuously toned), some other trivial imperfections, but fresh and clean and generally pleasing internally.   Phillip J. Pirages   66 - 40   2015 $12,500

Church of England. Book of Common Prayer *The Book of Common Prayer... together with The Psalter or Psalms of David.* Oxford: Clarendon Press, 1783. 1784, 140 x 83mm., very appealing contemporary vellum over boards, almost certainly by Edwards of Halifax, covers bordered by a neoclassical pentaglyph and metope roll against a blue wash, center of each board with large gilt bordered medallion containing gilt monogram "M L C" on a blue background, flat spine divided into panels by gilt pentaglyph and metope border (the one at bottom over blue wash), panels with classical urn centerpiece and volute cornerpieces, second panel with gilt titling on blue background, turn-ins with gilt chain roll, marbled endpapers, all edges gilt, with fine fore-edge painting, very probably by Edwards, depicting Fountains Abbey In Yorkshire, in original (rubbed and soiled but quite intact) soft green leather slipcase, titlepage with ink ownership inscription of M. L. Carey, spine gilt slightly dulled in places, rear turn-in lifting a little at one corner, title and couple of gatherings with moderate foxing, still quite excellent copy binding showing no wear, text clean and fresh and painting well preserved.   Phillip J. Pirages   66 - 46   2015 $5500

Church of England. Book of Common Prayer *The Book of Common Prayer. (with) A New Version of the Psalms of David.* London: Eyre and Strahan, 1820. 1818, 222 x 140mm., exceptionally fine contemporary black straight grain morocco, extravagantly black straight grain morocco, extravagantly gilt, covers framed by wide, delicate gilt dentelle roll within thick and thin rules, central panel enclosed by gilt chain roll with volutes at corners, space between the two frames blind tooled in wavy pattern large gilt sunburst centerpiece containing a dove and the Tetragrammation, raised bands, spine heavily gilt in panels with floral centerpiece and volutes at corners, gilt titling, turn-ins with decorative gilt roll, marbled endpapers, all edges gilt, engraved frontispiece, hint of browning internally but in amazing condition, text remarkably clean, fresh and smooth, binding unworn and glittering, like new.   Phillip J. Pirages   66 - 74   2015 $2500

Church of England. Book of Common Prayer *The Book of Common Prayer...* Cambridge: printed by C. J. Clay for SPCK, circa, 1880. small 4to., original full black morocco with embossed device, slight rubbing, stamp of Thomas Davidson, Fritchley Nr. Derby and Kathleen Tillotson's note that he was her grandfather, ink and pencil notes.   Jarndyce Antiquarian Booksellers   CCVII - 156   2015   £35

Church of Scotland *Account of the Proceedings and Debate in the General Assembly of the Church of Scotland 27th May 1796 on the Overtures from the Provincial Synods of Fife and Moray...* Edinburgh: printed for Alex. Lawrie bookseller no. 28, Parliament Close, 1796. First edition, 8vo., recent marbled boards lettered on spine, very good, rare.   John Drury Rare Books   March 2015 - 24277   2015 $266

Church of Scotland *Report from the Committee to Whom the Petition of the Commissioners of the General assembly of the Church of Scotland and also the Petition of James Earl of Morton and others....* London: printed in the year, 1751. First edition, London issue, final blank 2K2, recent plain wrappers, very good.   John Drury Rare Books   March 2015 - 18239   2015   £306

Churchill, W. A. *Watermarks in Paper in Holland, England, France, Etc. in the XVII and XVIII Centuries and Their Interconnection.* Nieuwkoop: B. de Graaf, 1990. Reprint of 1935 edition, thick 4to., cloth, 432 plates.   Oak Knoll Books   306 - 91   2015 $275

Churchill, Winston Leonard Spencer   1874-1965 *The River Wars: a Account of the Reconquest of the Sudan.* London: Longmans, Green & Co., 1899. First edition, first printing, one of only 2000 copies, 2 volumes, original blue cloth, lettered with pictorial illustrations in gilt, frontispieces, folding maps and plans, line drawings by Angus McNeill, photogravure portraits, some rubbing mostly to edges, spines bright, hinges tender but secure, some light foxing, former owner signature to first blank of volume II, else bright, much nicer than usual, very good set, each volume preserved in custom folding case and housed in slipcase.   B & B Rare Books, Ltd.   234 - 11   2015 $3000

Churchill, Winston Leonard Spencer   1874-1965 *The Second World Ward.* London: Cassell & Co. Ltd., 1948-1954. First edition, 6 volumes, small quarto, numerous maps and diagrams, some folding, throughout, finely bound for Brentano's, probably by Sangorski in full crimson morocco, covers double ruled in gilt, spines decoratively tooled and lettered gilt with five raised bands, gilt stamped with flower motif to compartments, top edge gilt, gilt turn-ins, slightest of sunning to spines, otherwise fine, housed in custom open ended red cloth slipcase, slipcase bit worn and repaired.   Heritage Book Shop   Holiday 2014 - 39   2015 $3500

Churchward, James *The Children of Mu.* New York: Ives Washburn, 1931. First edition, spine sunned and lettering dull, about very good, without dust jacket, pencilled ownership signature of boxing great Gene Tunney.   Between the Covers Rare Books, Inc.   187 - 53   2015 $225

Cicero, Marcus Tullius *Cato der Atler Uber Das Greisenalter.* Munchen: 1924. Limited to 200 numbered copies, titlepage and initials by Ana Simons, small 4to., paper covered boards, spine and front cover gilt stamped.   Oak Knoll Books   306 - 142   2015 $125

Cicero, Marcus Tullius *Orations and Essays.* New York: Limited Editions Club, 1972. One of 1500 copies signed by artist, this marked HC (hors commerce), titlepage printed in black and red, 12 full page color portraits, royal 8vo., original patterned cloth, backstrip with black leather label lettered gilt, top edge lavender, others untrimmed, faint soiling to cloth, very good.   Blackwell's Rare Books   B179 - 190   2015   £40

Cinderella *Cinderella or the Glass Slipper.* Baltimore: Bayly & Burns, 1837. 8vo., pictorial wrappers, very good+, pictorial cover plus 8 fine half page hand colored woodcuts, nice, uncommon.   Aleph-bet Books, Inc.   109 - 149   2015 $600

Cinderella *Cinderella.* New York: McLoughlin Bros., 1891. Large 4to., stiff pictorial wrapper, light soil and crease on rear cover, else very good to fine, book shaped like a Theatre Stage which opens from center to reveal full page chromolithographed scenes from Cinderella.   Aleph-bet Books, Inc.   109 - 164   2015 $450

Cinderella *Cinderella and Other Tales.* New York: Blue Ribbon, 1933. Thick 8vo., pictorial boards, binding slightly cocked, else fine in frayed dust jacket, illustrations by Harold Lentz.   Aleph-Bet Books, Inc.   108 - 360   2015 $900

A Circular Letter to the Practitioners of Physic and Surgery in the State of New York, form the Practitioners of Physic and Surgery in the County and City of New York... New York: printed by James Smith, 1829. 8vo., some marginal fraying and soiling, some creases, overall very good, entirely uncut, stitched as issued in crease wrappers.   John Drury Rare Books   March 2015 - 25700   2015 $266

Circus. No publishing information except made in Holland, circa, 1948. Cut in the shape of circus tent, 9 1/2 x 6 1/2 inches, cloth backed pictorial boards, light rubbing, near fine, 3 dimensional pop-out circus scenes.   Aleph-bet Books, Inc.   109 - 370   2015 $400

Cirque d'Amateurs Lille 1913. Lille: No. 7 Monsieur Hector, 1913. Oblong folio, title, 18 plates with translucent paper guard printed with descriptive title and names, as issued in original grey wrappers, upper cover lettered in gilt, tied with cotton chord, rare.   Marlborough Rare Books   List 53 - 8   2015   £950

Ciscar, Francisco *Reflexiones Sobre las Maquinas y Maniobras del Uso de a Bordo.* Madrid: en la Imprenta Real, 1791. First and only edition, folio, 23 folding plates, folding table, contemporary sprinkled calf, red morocco spine label, spine ends chipped, hinges scuffed but solid, occasional marginal dampstaining, near very good.   Joseph J. Felcone Inc.   Science, Medicine and Technology - 18   2015 $2200

Cistiaga, Jose Hilario *Memoria del Senor Secretario de Hacienda al Congreso de Venezuela de 1831.* Valencia: n.p., 1831. First edition, 8vo., 167 pages, three quarter morocco over marbled boards, good copy, front board detached, backstrip mostly worn away, otherwise contents about fine.   Kaaterskill Books   19 - 38   2015 $400

The City Alarum; or the Weeke of Our Miscarriages, Which Have Hitherto Obstructed Our Proceedings and Will Now Retard the if not speedily removed. London: printed for Joshua Kirton, 1645. First edition, title printed within ornamental border and with printer's woodcut device, most flyleaves lightly dampstained, but good, crisp copy in old calf backed boards, spine lettered in gilt, nonetheless worn and chipped.   John Drury Rare Books   March 2015 - 21452   2015 $874

Claiborne, F. L. *Address Before the Several Lodges of the Independent Order of Odd fellows of the City of Natchez.* Natchez: Free Trade Office, 1842. First edition, 8vo., 16 pages, sewn, wear and edges and staining to upper corners.   M & S Rare Books, Inc.   97 - 193   2015 $250

The Claims of the People of England, essayed in a letter from the country. London: A. Baldwin, 1701. First edition, 8vo., titlepage neatly repaired at head affecting part of the ruled border, contemporary sprinkled sheep with blind ruled fillets on sides, sometime neatly rebacked, unlettered, excellent, crisp copy.   John Drury Rare Books   March 2015 - 16654   2015   £306

Clancy, Tom *Patriot Games.* New York: Putnam, 1987. First edition, fine in printed wrappers, uncorrected proof copy.   Mordida Books   March 2015 - 000432   2015 $85

Clandon, Henrietta *Inquest.* London: Bles, 1933. First edition, some scattered foxing on page edges, otherwise fine in lightly soiled dust jacket.   Mordida Books   March 2015 - 008241   2015 $275

Clare, John *The Later Poems of John Clare 1837-1864.* Oxford: Clarendon Press, 1985. Reprint, 2 volumes, 8vo., frontispiece, hardback.   Any Amount of Books   2015 - A07534   2015   £220

Clare, John *Madrigals & Chronicles: Being Newly Found Poems Written by John Clare.* London: Beaumont Press, 1924. First edition, one of 310 numbered copies on handmade paper of a total of 400, octavo, quarter cloth and decorated paper covered boards, bookplate of Leonard Clark, corners rubbed, very good, this copy inscribed by Edmund Blunden for editor Leonard Clark.   Between the Covers Rare Books, Inc.   187 - 54   2015 $250

Clark, Barrett H. *Eugene O'Neill.* New York: Robert M. McBride & Co., 1926. First edition, slight wear at crown and spine lettering little dull, very good or better without dust jacket, inscribed by author in year of publication to journalist Walter Lippmann, 8 Sept. 1926. Between the Covers Rare Books, Inc. 187 - 55 2015 $275

Clark, Charles *An Antarctic Queen.* London and New York: Frederick Warne and Co., n.d., 190-. Later edition, octavo, 8 inserted plates with illustrations by J. B. Greene, original non-bevel edged blue pictorial cloth, front and spine panels stamped in black, white and gold decorated endpapers with floral pattern printed in orange. L. W. Currey, Inc. Boy's Adventure Fiction 2015 - 71 2015 $125

Clark, George *Target Trials of Armour Plating for Ships and Batteries.* London: W. F. Tubby...n.d., 1862. First edition, 8vo., titlepage bit dust soiled, unbound, sewn as issued, good copy with small 'withdrawn' inkstamp, apparently very rare. John Drury Rare Books March 2015 - 23987 2015 $266

Clark, J. J. *The Manufacture of Pulp and Paper.* New York & London: 1921. First edition, 5 volumes, near fine. Bookworm & Silverfish 2015 - 3278846523 2015 $250

Clark, John *Self-Annihilation; Being the Substance of a Sermon, Preached at the Funeral of Mrs. Joanna Turner, wife of Mr. Thomas Turner, who died Dec. 24 1784 at Trowridge, Wilts.* Bath: printed and sold by S. Hazard sold also by Balance and Conder; London: T. Mills, Bristol and W. Sleigh, Trowbridge, 1785. Only edition, 8vo., errata on final page, few very minor edge nicks, piece torn away from margin of last leaf (not touching printed surface), rebound recently in lettered cloth, good copy. John Drury Rare Books March 2015 - 24699 2015 $266

Clark, Robert *Mr. White's Confession.* New York: Picador, 1998. First edition, very fine in dust jacket, signed by author. Mordida Books March 2015 - 012594 2015 $125

Clark, Thomas *The Sand Burg. Poems by Tom Clark.* London: Ferry Press, 1966. First edition, limited to 500 copies, 4to., original wrappers with cover by Joe Brainard, fine, presentation copy inscribed by Clark for Tom Veitch. James S. Jaffe Rare Books Many Happy Returns - 229 2015 $150

Clark, Tom *Air by Tom Clark.* New York: Harper & Row, 1970. First edition, 8vo., original cloth backed boards, dust jacket designed by Joe Brainard, inscribed and signed by Clark, very fine. James S. Jaffe Rare Books Many Happy Returns - 232 2015 $125

Clark, Tom *Late Returns: a Memoir of Ted Berrigan.* Bolinas: Bo Tombouctou, 1985. First edition, hardcover issue, one of an unspecified number of limited hardbound copies, signed by Clark, mint. James S. Jaffe Rare Books Many Happy Returns - 75 2015 $50

Clark, Tom *The Once Series.* Brightlingsea, Essex: 1966-1968. First editions, 11 issue, large 4to., illustrations, original illustrated wrappers stapled as issued, light to moderate overall use, occasional small tide mark, terminal leaf of a couple of issues detached, otherwise complete run in very good to fine condition. James S. Jaffe Rare Books Many Happy Returns - 382 2015 $2500

Clark, Tom *Selecting Aircraft Timber.* Toronto: De Havilland Aircraft Co. Ltd. n.d. 1950's, 12mo., card covers, line diagrams, very good, card laid in, "Compliments of DH Toronto Mosquito news service Plant Publicity Dept". Schooner Books Ltd. 110 - 169 2015 $45

Clark, Tom *Sugar Mountain. Whole number 1(all published).* Bolinas: August, 1970. First edition, small folio, original photographic wrappers, stapled as issued, lightly rubbed, otherwise fine. James S. Jaffe Rare Books Many Happy Returns - 383 2015 $100

Clark, Zachary *An Account of the Different Charities Belonging to the Poor of the County of Norfolk, Abridged from the Returns Under Gilbert's Act, to the House of Commons in 1786...* Bury St. Edmonds: printed by Gedge and Barker for Longman &c London, 1811. First edition, 8vo., last couple of leaves rather foxed, wanting flyleaf and free endpaper at front, original boards, neatly rebacked, entirely uncut, good copy. John Drury Rare Books 2015 - 18842 2015 $133

Clarke, Amy *The Bushranger's Secret.* Blackie & Son, 1892. First edition, frontispiece, 2 plates, 32 page catalog, original brown pictorial cloth, school prize label dated 1900, very good. Jarndyce Antiquarian Booksellers CCXI - 68 2015 £48

Clarke, Arthur C. *Astounding Days: a Science Fictional Autobiography.* London: Victor Gollancz, 1989. First edition, ownership signature of Ian Macauley who made a few notations in text, on front fly, else fine in near fine dust jacket, with faint crease on spine, signed by Clarke on his own bookplate. Between the Covers Rare Books, Inc. 187 - 250 2015 $750

Clarke, Arthur C. *The City and the Stars.* New York: Harcourt Brace and Co., 1956. First edition, octavo, boards, signed by author. John W. Knott, Bookseller Selected New Arrivals Jan. 2015 - 16973 2015 $1500

Clarke, Arthur C. *Expedition to Earth.* New York: Ballantine Books, 1953. First edition, octavo, boards, signed by author.   John W. Knott, Bookseller   Selected New Arrivals Jan. 2015 - 16971   2015 $2000

Clarke, Arthur C. *The Exploration of the Moon.* London: Frederick Muller Ltd., 1954. First edition, large octavo, 45 full page drawings, 8 in color, by R. A. Smith, original black boards stamped in gold.   John W. Knott, Bookseller   Selected New Arrivals Jan. 2015 - 16975   2015 $500

Clarke, Arthur C. *Greetings, Carbon-Based Bipeds" Collected Essays 1934-1998.* New York: St. Martin's Press, 1999. First edition, fine in fine dust jacket with touch of rubbing, editor Ian Macauley's copy with his ownership signature, Macauley was Clarke's protege and one-time secretary and longtime friend.   Between the Covers Rare Books, Inc.   187 - 248   2015 $400

Clarke, Arthur C. *The Songs of Distant Earth.* New York: Ballantine Books, 1986. First edition, one of 500 numbered copies signed by author, octavo, cloth,.   John W. Knott, Bookseller   Selected New Arrivals Jan. 2015 - 16980   2015 $200

Clarke, Arthur C. *2001 a Space Odyssey.* London: Hutchinson, 1968. First edition, crown 8vo., original black boards, backstrip lettered in silver, dust jacket, fine.   Blackwell's Rare Books   B179 - 140   2015   £300

Clarke, Arthur C. *2001: a Space Odyssey.* London: Hutchinson, 1968. First British edition, octavo, boards, signed by author with Arthur C. Clarke Foundation blindstamp and Foundation's secretary inkstamp to half titlepage.   John W. Knott, Bookseller   Selected New Arrivals Jan. 2015 - 16976   2015 $750

Clarke, Arthur C. *2010: Odyssey Two.* New York: Ballantine Books/Del Rey, 1982. First edition, fine in fine dust jacket, inscribed by Arthur C. Clarke to his protege and one time secretary and longtime friend Ian Macauley.   Between the Covers Rare Books, Inc.   187 - 249   2015 $950

Clarke, Charles Cowden *The Riches of Chaucer...* London: Effingham Wilson, 1835. First edition, 2 volumes, 8vo., 19th century brown half calf, marbled paper boards and matching endpapers, red morocco labels, gilt decorations and lettering, frontispiece, vignette titlepages and 16 plates, half titles present, inscribed by author for Jones Esqre., edges little rubbed, fine.   The Brick Row Book Shop   Miscellany 67 - 33   2015 $500

Clarke, Edward H. *The Building of a Brain.* Boston: Ogsood, 1874. First edition, 8vo., excellent, rare.   Second Life Books Inc.   189 - 57   2015 $225

Clarke, Ida Clyde *Record No. 33.* New York: D. Appleton and Co., 1915. First edition, contemporary gift inscription front fly, small stain on front board, else near fine in good dust jacket with chip on front panel and at crown some stains, very scarce in dust jacket.   Between the Covers Rare Books   196 - 141   2015 $400

Clarke, John Cooper *Directory 1979.* London: Omnibus, 1979. First edition, small quarto, illustrated, mostly with photos, glossy card wrappers, signed by author, near fine.   Peter Ellis, Bookseller   2014 - 017252   2015   £325

Clarke, John Henrik *The Middle Passage: Our Holocaust.* Detroit: Dr. Walter O. Evans, 1991. First edition, 8vo., pages, string-bound with surgical silk, one of just 250 copies signed by Clarke and Lawrence, rare included is an invitation to the NY Premiere of the film "John Henry Clarke: a Great and Mighty Walk June 1 1997".   Second Life Books Inc.   190 - 50   2015 $1250

Clarke, Samuel 1599-1683 *A True and Faithful Account of the Four Chiefest Plantations of the English in America.* London: for Robert Clavel, Thomas Passenger, William Cadman, William Whitwood, Thomas Saiwbridge and William Birch, 1670. Small folio, occasional light browning and soiling, blank fore-margin of 7A2 stained, contemporary calf, rebacked, recornered and with new endpapers, from the library of James Stevens Cox (1910-1997).   Maggs Bros. Ltd.   1447 - 100   2015   £250

Clarke, Susanna *Jonathan Strange & Mr. Norrell.* London: Bloomsbury, 2004. First British edition, one of 1450 numbered copies signed by author, octavo, boards.   John W. Knott, Bookseller   Selected New Arrivals Jan. 2015 - 16982   2015 $150

Clarke, W. B. *Narrative of the Wreck of the 'Favorite' on the Island of Desolation...* London: William Edward Painter, 1850. First edition, 8vo. folding chart, frontispiece, 56 woodcut illustrations, 16 page Painter catalogue, part of blank upper margin on titlepage neatly excised (not affecting printed surface), original embossed dark blue cloth, decorated in blind, spine gilt and lettered, Association copy (bookplate and small blindstamp.   John Drury Rare Books   2015 - 25865   2015 $656

Clarke, W. K. Lowther *Eighteenth Century Piety.* London: SPCK, 1944. Half title, plates, original brown cloth, very good in slightly worn dust jacket, Geoffrey Tillotson's review copy with part of his m.s review.   Jarndyce Antiquarian Booksellers   CCVII - 136   2015   £20

Clason, George S. *Free Homestead Lands of Colorado Described: a Handbook for Settlers.* Denver: 1915. 318 pages, map, large folding map in pocket, no dust jacket (as issued?), contemporary pencilled notes, binding shaken but intact, tear to rear map pocket, repairs to fold separations on map, laid in is 8 panel illustrated leaflet put out by Denver Chamber of Commerce touting 18,899,441 acres of homestead land.   Dumont Maps & Books of the West   131 - 42   2015 $250

Clater, Francis *Every Man His Own Farrier; or the Whole Art of Farriery Laid Open.* London: by Assignment of A. Tomlinson, Newark, for B. Crosby and Co., 1809. Late edition, 2 text woodcuts, removed, very good.   Joseph J. Felcone Inc.   Science, Medicine and Technology - 22   2015 $125

Clater, Francis *Every Man His Own Cattle Doctor: Containing the Causes, Symptoms and Treatment of All the Diseases Incident to Oxen, Sheep and Swine...* Philadelphia: Lea and Blanchard, 1844. First US edition, cloth, paper label on spine, light foxing and all pages uniformly browned, else very good, tight copy with all pages intact, slipcase.   Buckingham Books   March 2015 - 5816   2015 $250

Claude and Francois-Xavier Lalanne. London: Reed Krakoff, Paul Kasmin and Ben Brown, 2007. First edition, 4to, copiously illustrated in color and black and white, fine in fine dust jacket.   Any Amount of Books   March 2015 - A83008   2015   £350

Clausewitz, Karl *Von Kriege... (in) Hinterlassene Werke...* Berlin: Ferdinand Dummler, 1832-1834. First edition, 3 volumes, octavo, few woodcut diagrams throughout, later half black morocco over green speckled paper boards, red paper spine labels, spines ruled and lettered in gilt, front board of volume I with small black ink spot, some minor marginalia in volume 1, volumes with stamps, overall very good.   Heritage Book Shop   Holiday 2014 - 40   2015 $6000

Claviere, Etienne *De la France et des Etats-Unis, ou de l'Importance de la revolution de l'Amerique Pour Le Bonheur de la France...* Londres (i.e. ?Paris): 1787. First edition, 8vo., uncut and partly unopened (towards the end) in original pink wrappers, paper label on spine hand lettered, minor wear, contemporary signature on title of Baron du Soleil, red stamp of Charles B. Vincent on verso of title at end, preserved in cloth foldover sleeve, leather booklabel of Frederick Spiegelberg, brown morocco backed slip-pin case, very good.   Blackwell's Rare Books   B179 - 30   2015   £1200

Clavis Virgiliana or a Vocabulary of all the words in Virgil's Bucolics, Georgics and Aeneid... Oxford: printed by W. Baxter, 1824. Scarce printing, 8vo., contemporary straight grained olive brown roan, spine divided by wide raised bands with tight gilt cross hatching, black morocco lettering piece, other compartments with scale pattern in blind, rubbed, front joint cracking but strong, good.   Blackwell's Rare Books   Greek & Latin Classics VI - 112   2015   £75

Clay, Henry *Remarks of Mr. Clay of Kentucky on Introducing His Propositions to Compromise on the Slavery Question. in the Senate of the United States Jan. 29 1850. (bound with) Speech... on taking up His Compromise Resolutions of the Subject of Slavery Delivered in the Senate Feb. 5th and 6th 1850.* New York: Stringer & Townsend, 1850. First editions, 8vo., 2 pamphlets, 16, 32 pages, removed, contemporary signature head of first title cropped.   M & S Rare Books, Inc.   97 - 283   2015 $125

Clay, John Cecil *The Lover's Mother Goose.* Indianapolis: Bobbs Merrill, 1905. 4to., pictorial cloth stamped in gold, very good+, 8 beautiful color plates and many full page 3 color illustrations as well as with decorations on text pages, printed on heavy coated paper.   Aleph-Bet Books, Inc.   108 - 305   2015 $225

Cleaver, Eldridge *A Hit Squad of Chinks.* Stanford: C. P. Times Press, 1984. First edition, 12mo., stapled wrappers, staples slightly rusty, else fine, signed by author.   Between the Covers Rare Books   197 - 5   2015 $150

Cleland, James *The Rise and Progress of the City of Glasgow, Comprising an Account of Its Public Buildings, Charities and Other Concerns.* Glasgow: James Brash and Co., 1820. First edition, 8vo., engraved map, folding table, 296 pages, wanting half title, later 19th century half calf over marbled boards, raised bands and spine label, marbled edges, minor general wear, but very good, sound.   John Drury Rare Books   2015 - 23165   2015 $177

Clemens, Samuel Langhorne   1835-1910 *The Adventures of Tom Sawyer.* New York: Limited Editions Club, 1949. Limited to 1500 numbered copies, 4to., blue denim, paper spine label, slipcase slightly rubbed, fine with slight chip on spine label, very slight sunning of spine, illustrations by Thomas Hart Benton and signed by him, newsletter laid in.   Oak Knoll Books   25 - 24   2015 $400

Clemens, Samuel Langhorne   1835-1910 *A Double Barrelled Detective Story.* New York: Harper, 1902. First edition, one of 7 plates missing, spine slightly darkened, small stain on back cover, otherwise near fine in red cloth covered boards, gilt top edges, near fine.   Mordida Books   March 2015 - 007442   2015 $250

Clemens, Samuel Langhorne   1835-1910 *The Innocents Abroad.*   Hartford: American Publishing Co., 1869. First edition, first issue, with pages xvii-xviii lacking page reference numbers, xviii lacking 'Conclusion' in last entry, page 129 without illustration, "XLI" to page 643, "Personal History" ad to page 654, publisher's black cloth with beveled edges, gilt illustrations and decorative lettering to front board and spine, publisher's device to rear board in blind, brown speckled edges, brown coated endpapers, pleasing copy with minor wear to extremities, spine rebacked with original cloth laid on, hinges repaired inside both covers, bright and clean pages, overall bright and presentable copy with all first issue points.   B & B Rare Books, Ltd.   2015 - 2015 $2250

Clemens, Samuel Langhorne   1835-1910 *The Innocents Abroad or the New Pilgrims' Progress.*   Hartford: American Pub. Co., 1869. First edition, 2nd issue with page reference numbers on pages xvii-xviii, 8vo., cloth, spine and front cover, gilt stamped, all edges gilt, previous owner's name with date of Nov. 13 1869 on front free endpaper, also includes gift inscription dated July 2, 1877, professionally recased in original binding.   Oak Knoll Books   306 - 308   2015 $1850

Clemens, Samuel Langhorne   1835-1910 *The Jumping Frog.*   Easthampton: Cheloniidae Press, 1985. One of 15 Artist Proof copies, with one extra suite of wood engravings plus a suite of 15 state proof engravings, plus one rejected engraving, plus three proofs of portrait etchings of Twain, plus 2 pencil drawings of frogs by the artist, plus one original watercolor of the jumping frog, each signed and numbered by the artist, plus a copy of the prospectus, inscription by artist on front flyleaf below pencil sketch of Jim Smiley by the artist, regular edition was limited to 250 copies and is bound in green paper wrappers, all editions printed on Saunders paper in Centaur and Arighi types at Wild Carrot letterpress with assistance of Arthur Larson, 15 wood engravings printed by Harold Patrick McGrath, page size 6 x 8 1/2 inches, bound by Daniel Kelm, full undyed Oasis with onlays of the frog in repose - before the jump on front panel and after the jump on back panel, with doublures showing the front in mid-jump, onlays in green oasis of the frog, jumping are on front and back pastedowns, housed in linen clamshell box with pull-out portfolio for extra suites and book.   Priscilla Juvelis - Rare Books   61 - 6   2015 $4000

Clemens, Samuel Langhorne   1835-1910 *The Prince and the Pauper: a Tale for People of All Ages.*   Boston: James R. Osgood, 1882. First edition, first state binding (rosette 1/8" below fillet), second state of text with corrections on pages 124, 263 and 362 4to., green cloth stamped gold and black very slight cover soil and rubbing, really near fine in custom cloth box with leather label, 192 engravings.   Aleph-bet Books, Inc.   109 - 468   2015 $775

Clemens, Samuel Langhorne   1835-1910 *Pudd'nhead Wilson a Tale.*   London: Chatto & Windus, 1894. First English edition, (catalog in rear dated Sept. 1894), 8vo., red cloth stamped in black, few tiny black dots on cover, else very good+, illustrations by James Mapes Dodge with photo frontispiece and 6 black and white plates by Louis Loeb.   Aleph-bet Books, Inc.   109 - 469   2015 $500

Clemens, Samuel Langhorne   1835-1910 *The Oxford Mark Twain.*   New York: Oxford University Press, 1996. First edition thus, 29 volumes, frontispieces, illustrations, burgundy cloth, dust jackets, fine and unread in fine dust jacket, few near fine, excellent condition.   Any Amount of Books   March 2015 - C2842   2015   £375

Clement, Simon *Remarks Upon a late Ingenious Pamphlet, Entituled. A Short but Thorough Search into What May Be the Real Cause of the Present Scarcity of Our Silver Coin.*   London: printed For S. Baker, 1718. Second edition, 8vo., recently well bound in cloth, spine lettered gilt, good copy.   John Drury Rare Books   March 2015 - 18015   2015   £306

Clement, Walter B. *Alphabets and Others.*   Alabama: Armstrong Press and Slow Loris Press, 1988. Limited to 125 numbered copies, a type specimen of woodtypes,, oblong 4to., cloth, paper cover label, loosely inserted in pocket in back are various pieces of printed ephemera.   Oak Knoll Books   306 - 212   2015 $300

Clerke, Agnes Mary *The Concise Knowledge: Astronomy.*   London: Hutchinson & Co., 1896. 4 plates, 99 figures, frontispiece, prelims and rear endpapers showing offsetting, original quarter red calf, maroon gilt stamped cloth, leather heavily damaged, fragmented, with circa 1970's plastic covering applied over original binding - if removed will further damage the leather (though cloth with not be affected), bookplate of George H. Billson (Times Book Club, London).   Jeff Weber Rare Books   178 - 782   2015 $75

Clerke, Agnes Mary *Problems in Astrophysics.*   London: Adam & Charles Black, 1903. First edition, frontispiece and 30 plates, 50 figures, original dark green gilt stamped cloth, endleaves both with offsetting and rubbing, small nick on spine, corners bumped, very good.   Jeff Weber Rare Books   178 - 781   2015 $50

Cleveland, John *Clievlandi Vindiciae or Cleveland's Genuine Poems, Orations, Epistles &c.*   London: for Obadiah Blagrave, 1677. 8vo., engraved portrait (small piece missing from lower margin), tear to lower inner margin of L2, light worming to lower fore-corner between a1-N1 and with minor spotting and dampstaining in places, late 19th century mottled calf, rebacked, corners repaired, new endpapers, from the library of James Stevens Cox (1910-1997).   Maggs Bros. Ltd.   1447 - 101   2015   £150

Cleveland, John *The Idol of the Clownes or Insurrection of Wat the Tyler with His Priests Baal and Straw...* London: in the Year, 1654. Second edition, small 8vo., without engraved portrait found in some copies and without final blank, light dampstaining to first few leaves, closely shaved at head (just touching pagination in places), early 19th century calf, covers ruled in gilt, spine tooled in gilt and blind, marbled edges and endpapers, small stain on front cover and minor repair on rear, old front flyleaf preserved, from the library of James Stevens Cox (1910-1997), with late 17th/early 18th century inscription "Thomas Browne/His booke", not that of Sir Thomas Browne (1605-1682), with bookplate of Albert M. Cohn, posthumous sale, Christie 26/2/1934 lot 176 (as Sir Thomas Browne's copy), £5 to Charles H. Stonehill.   Maggs Bros. Ltd.   1447 - 102   2015   £200

Clevenger, Shobal V. *A Treatise on the method of Government Surveying.* New York: D. Van Nostrand, 1874. First edition, bound in wrap-around leather binding, insert flap, suitable for field use, all edges gilt, very good, binding worn, some chips, rubbing and little repair, text nice and clean, scarce.   Stephen Lupack   March 2015 - 2015 $200

Clifford, Francis *Amigo, Amigo.* London: Hodder and Stoughton, 1973. First edition, fine in dust jacket.   Buckingham Books   March 2015 - 29003   2015 $200

Clifford, Francis *The Grosvenor Square Goodbye.* London: Hodder & Stoughton, 1974. First edition, fine in dust jacket.   Buckingham Books   March 2015 - 29004   2015 $175

Clifford, Hugh Charles *A Statement of the Reasons why the Right Rev. Bench of Bishops of the established Church of England Ought Not to be required by the Friends of that Establishment to Oppose the Bill Brought into the House of Lords by Earl Grey, for the Abolition of the Declarations of the 25th and 30th of Charles the Second.* London: printed by Keating Brown and Co., 1819. First edition, 8vo., unbound, uncut and unopened, fine, fresh copy.   John Drury Rare Books   2015 - 16617   2015 $80

Clifford, James L. *Eighteenth Century English Literature: Modern Essays in Criticism.* New York: Oxford University Press, 1959. Half title, original printed card wrappers, from the library of Geoffrey & Kathleen Tillotson, Geoffrey's presentation to Kathleen.   Jarndyce Antiquarian Booksellers   CCVII - 137   2015   £20

Clifton, Mark *They'd Rather Be Right.* New York: Gnome Press, 1957. First edition, octavo, boards.   John W. Knott, Bookseller   Selected New Arrivals Jan. 2015 - 16984   2015 $350

Clines, David J. A. *The Dictionary of Classical Hebrew.* Sheffield: Sheffield Academic Press, 1993. First edition, 5 volumes, small 4to., fine, hardback.   Any Amount of Books   March 2015 - A89891   2015   £375

Close, Francis *An Examination of Witnesses and their Evidence Given Before a Royal Commission Upon the Administration and Operation of the "Contagious Diseases Acts 1871".* London: Tweedie & Co., 1872. First edition, uncommon, 8vo, 46 pages, recent marbled boards lettered on spine, very good.   John Drury Rare Books   March 2015 - 25058   2015   £266

Close, Francis *Pauperism Traced to Its True Sources, by the Aid of Holy Scripture and Experience.* London: John Hatchard and Son, 1837. First edition, 8vo., preserved in modern wrappers with printed title label on upper cover, good copy, rare.   John Drury Rare Books   March 2015 - 18094   2015 $221

Clough, Arthur Hugh *Bothie of Toper-Na-Fuosich.* Oxford: Francis Macpherson, 1848. First edition, very good in original blue cloth flexible boards with gilt title to front cover, minor wear to edges of covers, few small chips to edges of several pages, binding split in few places, all pages remain bound in, bookplate of Mark Samuels Lasner, 55 pages plus 1 page of ads, very good.   The Kelmscott Bookshop   11 - 10   2015 $400

Clough, Arthur Hugh *Emerson-Clough Letters.* Cleveland: Rowfant Club, 1934. No. 52 of 165 copies, half title, original marbled paper boards, paper labels, brief pencil note by Geoffrey Tillotson, but unsigned.   Jarndyce Antiquarian Booksellers   CCVII - 140   2015   £40

Clough, Arthur Hugh *Letters and Remains.* London: Spottiswoode & Co., 1865. Half title, original green patterned cloth, inner hinges rather crudely strengthened, presented to Miss Rankin, sent by her to Joseph Hutton 1888, signed by Geoffrey Tillotson 12.v.47.   Jarndyce Antiquarian Booksellers   CCVII - 141   2015   £40

Clough, Arthur Hugh *Poems.* London: Macmillan, 1862. First edition, half title, 16 page catalog, original green patterned cloth by Burn, spine darkened with split in leading hinge, Geoffrey Tillotson's copy signed 1944.   Jarndyce Antiquarian Booksellers   CCVII - 142   2015   £50

Clough, Arthur Hugh *Poems...* London: Macmillan, 1885. Eleventh edition, half title, full dark green calf, prize binding from Marlborough College, small chip from head of spine, inner hinges splitting, from the library of Geoffrey & Kathleen Tillotson.   Jarndyce Antiquarian Booksellers   CCVII - 143   2015   £20

Clough, Blanche Athena *A Memoir of Anne Jemima Clough by her niece.* London: Edward Arnold, 1897. Frontispiece and plates, 32 page catalog (Ot. 1897), uncut in original dark green cloth, small split at head of spine, from the library of Geoffrey & Kathleen Tillotson.   Jarndyce Antiquarian Booksellers   CCVII - 138   2015   £35

Clum, John P. *It All Happened in Tombstone.* Flagstaff: Northland Press, 1965. First edition, signed by John Gilchriese, two-toned decorated cloth, fine, unread copy in unused dust jacket, exceptional copy.   Buckingham Books   March 2015 - 26743   2015 $175

Clymer, R. Swinburne *The Rosicrusians Their Teachings.* Allentown: Philosophical Pub. Co., 1910. Second edition, tall octavo, red cloth stamped in gilt and blind, ownership signature (twice) of Elsa Barker (American novelist and poet), extensive pencil notes and several pencil markings in text, bottom corners rubbed through, still very good, bright copy.   Between the Covers Rare Books, Inc.   187 - 56   2015 $225l

Clyne, Geraldine *The Jolly Jump-Ups see the Circus.* Springfield: McLoughlin Bros., 1944. First edition, pictorial paper over boards, illustrations, 6 color pop-ups showing intricate scenes, pop-ups complete and in fine condition, pages clean and free of marking.   Buckingham Books   March 2015 - 28166   2015 $300

Co-Operative Wholesale Society *Annual for 1906.* Manchester: Co-operative Wholesale Societies Limited, 1906. Plates, presentation binding of dark green crushed morocco, bevelled boards, bordered gilt, front board elaborately decorated in gilt with inscription, raised bands, spine decorated and lettered gilt with floral gilt dentelles, spine very slightly rubbed at head and tail, front board slightly marked, all edges gilt, very good, inscribed for His Royal Highness Prince of Wales 1906.   Jarndyce Antiquarian Booksellers   CCXI - 74   2015   £125

Coates, Robert M. *Wisteria Cottage.* Harcourt, Brace and Co., 1948. First edition, fine in dust jacket lightly soiled on rear panel, light wear to spine ends and corners and extremities.   Buckingham Books   March 2015 - 37513   2015 $175

Coatsworth, Elizabeth *Night and the Cat.* New York: Macmillan, 1950. State first printing, 4to., two tone cloth, near fine in dust jacket (rubbed with small strip off rear flap at fold), 12 beautiful full page lithographs by Foujita, laid in is handwritten letter from Coatsworth to a fan on her Personal 'Chimney Farm' pictorial card in which she discusses the book.   Aleph-bet Books, Inc.   109 - 177   2015 $950

Cobb, Irvin S. *Faith, Hope and Charity.* Indianapolis: Bobbs Merrill, 1934. First edition, 8vo., former owner's inked name on front flyleaf, else near fine with chip missing from head of spine affecting letter "F" and partially affecting letter "A", tiny chip at base of spine and small chip at top edge of front panel at corner of front flap fold.   Buckingham Books   March 2015 - 22719   2015 $300

Cobban, James MacLaren *The Tyrants of Kool-Sim.* London: H. Henry & Co. Ltd., 1896. First edition, variant (probably first) binding, octavo, 6 inserted plates with illustrations by J. Brewster Fisher, original pictorial red cloth, front panel stamped in black and gold, spine panel stamped in gold, all edges untrimmed.   L. W. Currey, Inc.   Boy's Adventure Fiction 2015 - 24   2015 $350

Cobbe, Frances Power *Essays on the Pursuits of Women.* London: Emily Faithfull, printer ad publisher in Ordinary to Her Majesty, 1863. First edition, 8vo., 239 pages, bound in brown buckram with gilt title, new endpapers with cutting from The Spectator dated 16 June 1866 of a letter written by Cobbe to editor of Women's petition for votes attached to rear pastedown, ownership signature of her partner Mary Lloyd on pastedown, with 11 lines of holograph written by Cobbe or Lloyd on endpaper.   Second Life Books Inc.   191 - 24   2015 $350

Cobbett, William   1763-1835 *The Bloody Buoy, Thrown Out as a Warning to the Political Pilots of all Nations.* Philadelphia printed: London: reprinted and sold by J. Wright`, 1797. 12mo., 2 leaves of prelims bound out of order, contemporary half calf over marbled boards, neatly rebacked with gilt lines and label, some wear to marbled paper sides, still sound and very good.   John Drury Rare Books   2015 - 22856   2015 $612

Cobbett, William   1763-1835 *Cobbett's Legacy to Peel; or an Inquiry with Respect to What the Right Honourable Baronet will Now Do the House of Commons with Ireland with the English Church and Dissenters with swarms of Pensioners....* London: published at Cobbett's Register Office 11 Bolt court Fleet Street, 1836. First edition in book form, 16mo., titlepage lightly browned and with couple of small edge nicks and corner crease, rebound some years ago in plain unlettered dark blue morocco, good copy, scarce.   John Drury Rare Books   March 2015 - 22841   2015   £266

Cobbett, William   1763-1835 *Cobbett's Sermons on 1. Hypocrisy and Cruelty. 2. Drunkenness. 3. Bribery. 4. Oppression. 5. Gaming. 9. Public Robbery. 10. The Unnatural Mother. 11. Forbidding Marriage. 12. Parsons and Tithes.* London: printed and published by C. Clement no. 183 Fleet Street, 1822. First collected edition, 12mo., few minor spots, contemporary half calf, neatly rebacked, spine gilt and labelled, excellent copy.   John Drury Rare Books   March 2015 - 22842   2015   £306

Cobbett, William   1763-1835 *Cobbett's Two-Penny Trash; or Politics for the Poor.* London: printed for the author, 1831-1832. 12mo., original blue boards, purple cloth spine, rubbed paper label, spine faded, library numbers removed, small chip to following hinge, little worn.   Jarndyce Antiquarian Booksellers   CCXI - 69   2015   £150

Cobbett, William 1763-1835 *A Collection of Facts and Observations Relative to the Peace with Bonaparte Chiefly Extracted...* London: Cobbett and Morgan, Pall Mall, 1801. First edition, 8vo., ex-British Foreign Office library with 2 small old oval stamps and their library bookplates + a further stamp on verso of new endpaper, later blue cloth lettered gilt at spine, spine faded and slightly chipped at top, rear cover faded, else sound, near very good with clean text, of some rarity.   Any Amount of Books   2015 - A49984   2015   £220

Cobbett, William 1763-1835 *A History of the Protestant Reformation in England and Ireland; Showing How that Event Has Impoverished the Main Body of the People in Those Countries.* London: published by the author, 1829. 2 volumes, large 8vo., contemporary black half roan, spines gilt and lettered with raised bands, some wear to extremities and short split at head of spine volume I, still good copies. John Drury Rare Books   2015 - 19472   2015 $159

Cobbett, William 1763-1835 *Important Considerations for the People of This Kingdom.* London: T. Davidson printer White Friars published July and sent to the officiating minister of every parish in England, 1803. First separate edition, first issue, vairant, 8vo., 16 pages, woodcut of royal arms on titlepage, unbound and uncut as issued, outer leaves just little dust marked, still fine.   John Drury Rare Books   March 2015 - 19132   2015 $221

Cobbett, William 1763-1835 *Important Considerations for the People of This Kingdom.* London: printed by C. Rickaby Peterborough Court Fleet Street, n.d. but, 1803. First separate edition, 1st issue, 8vo., stitched as issued, minor spotting and rust marking, generally bit dust soiled, still good, uncut. John Drury Rare Books   March 2015 - 18270   2015 $266

Cobbett, William 1763-1835 *Paper Against Gold.* London: printed by W. Molineux published by W. Cobbett June, 1817. First edition, 8vo., occasional paper browning and foxing, contemporary, perhaps original boards, rebacked, edges of boards worn, entirely uncut, good, large copy but bound without Clement's ads sometimes found. John Drury Rare Books   March 2015 - 17853   2015 $266

Cobbett, William 1763-1835 *Rural Rides in the Counties of Surrey, Kent, Sussex, Hans, Berks, Oxford Bucks, Wilts, Somerset, Gloucester, Hereford, Salop, Worcester, Stafford, Leicester, Hertford, Essex, Suffolk, Norfolk, Cambridge, Huntingdon, Nottingham Lincoln, York, Lancaster, Durham, and Northumberland in the Years 1821, 1822, 1823, 1825, 1826, 1829, 1830 and 1832...* London: published by A. Cobbett, 1853. New edition, 12mo., frontispiece, errata on verso of final leaf, but without addenda found in other copies, original patterned green cloth, spine gilt lettered, faded and repaired at head, good copy.   John Drury Rare Books   March 2015 - 22857   2015   £266

Cobbett, William 1763-1835 *A Treatise on Cobbett's Corn.* London: Published by William Cobbett, 183 Fleet Street, 1828. First edition, 12mo., 3 woodcut plates, prelims printed on corn paper, contemporary half calf, marbled boards, board of spine chipped, burgundy morocco label lettered in gilt.   Marlborough Rare Books   List 53 - 10   2015   £85s

Cobbett, William 1763-1835 *The Woodlands; or a Treatise on the preparing of Ground for Planting...* London: William Cobbett, 1825-1828. First edition, 8vo., 2 woodcut figures, titlepage little soiled, contemporary green half calf, spine fully gilt with good replacement label, joint repaired, very good.   John Drury Rare Books   March 2015 - 22862   2015   £306

Cobbett, William 1763-1835 *The Woodlands; or a Treatise on the Preparing of Ground for Planting; on the Planting; on the Cultivation; on the Pruning; and on the Cutting Down of Forest Trees and Underwoods...* London: William Cobbett, 1828. Illustrated, 2 pages ads, ads on endpapers, uncut in original olive green cloth, blind double ruled border boards decorated in blind, spine lettered gilt, small mark to spine below 'Cobbett', boards little marked, otherwise very good, handsome, armorial bookplate of James Watts, Cheshire.   Jarndyce Antiquarian Booksellers   CCXI - 70   2015   £225

Cobden-Sanderson, Thomas James 1840-1922 *City Planned.* Hammersmith: Doves Press, n.d. but, 1911. First edition, limited to about 300 copies, first issue with two errors in text, errors are both correct with proof reader's marks in margin, well preserved copy, 8vo., brown paper wrappers.   Oak Knoll Books   306 - 150   2015 $175

Cobden-Sanderson, Thomas James 1840-1922 *The Ideal Book or Book Beautiful: a Tract of Calligraphy printing and Illustration and On the Book Beautiful as a Whole.* Hammersmith: Doves Press, 1900. First edition, one of 300 copies, small quarto, original full vellum, gilt lettering, bookplate of American collector Charles Walker Andrews, with his notation in pencil that this was purchased from Slocum Hyde's library in 1924, fine.   The Brick Row Book Shop   Miscellany 67 - 36   2015 $1250

Cochran, Charles B. *First International Rodeo or Cowboy Championships June 14th to 28th 1924...* printed and published by Freeway Press Ltd., 1924. First edition, 8vo., pictorial wrappers, 16 pages, illustrations, cream colored covers lightly soiled, else very good.   Buckingham Books   March 2015 - 34768   2015 $750

Cochrane, Basil *An Expose of the Conduct of the Victualling Board to the Honorable Basil Cochrane as Contractor and Agent Victualler to His Majesty's Ships on the East Indian Station.* London: printed by J. Davy, 1824. First and only edition, 8vo., half title, text followed by 5 large folding tables of contract accounts, contingent accounts, abstracts, and disbursements, original boards, printed label (slightly defective) on upper cover, printed spine label, head of spine chipped, upper joint splitting but fine, crisp, presentation copy inscribed by author for Robert Wm. Newman Esq. M.P. (1776-1848), seemingly of great rarity.   John Drury Rare Books   2015 - 25406   2015 $1311

Cochrane, Basil *An Improvement in the Mode of Administering the Vapour Bath, and in the Apparatus Connected With It.* London: John Booth, 1809. First edition, 4to., 11 engraved plates, well bound recently in holland backed boards, spine lettered, entirely uncut, fine.   John Drury Rare Books   2015 - 25971   2015 $1049

Cockburn, Alexander *Corruptions of Empire: Life Studies and the Reagan Era.* London: Verso Books, 1987. First edition, top edge foxed, else near fine in lightly rubbed, near fine dust jacket, warmly inscribed by author to journalist Jonathan Kwitney.   Between the Covers Rare Books, Inc.   187 - 56   2015 $125

Cocquiel, Charles Chevalier De *Industrial Instruction in England, Being a Report Made to the Belgain Government.* London: Chapman and Hall, 1853. First edition in English, erratum leaf, original printed wrappers sometime respined, very good, uncommon.   John Drury Rare Books   2015 - 16758   2015 $133

Cocteau, Jean *A Call to Order.* London: Faber and Gwyer, 1926. First English edition, 2 small stains on boards and corners bit bumped, else very good or better, lacking dust jacket, anthropologist, Eslanda Goode Robeson's copy with her ownership signature.   Between the Covers Rare Books, Inc.   187 - 58   2015 $350

Code, Henry Brereton *The Insurrection of the Twenty-Third July 1803.* Dublin: printed by Grassberry and Campbell 10 Black lane, 1803. First edition, 8vo., few leaves little creased, recent marbled boards, lettered on spine, very good, from the 20th century library of George Gilbertson (1915) with his signature, uncommon.   John Drury Rare Books   2015 - 24817   2015 $1049

Cody, John *Empty Holsters.* New York: Godwin, 1936. First edition, fine in dust jacket.   Buckingham Books   March 2015 - 11601   2015 $185

Cody, Liza *Culprit: a Crime Writer's Annual.* London: Chatto & Windus, 1992. First edition, 3 annual volumes, first volume signed by Robert Barnard, Liza Cody, Michael Lewin, Susan Moody and H. R. F. Keating, fine in soft covers and pictorial dust jackets.   Mordida Books   March 2015 - 008749   2015 $150

Cody, Liza *Head Case.* London: Collins, 1985. First edition, fine in dust jacket, signed by author.   Mordida Books   March 2015 - 002407   2015 $125

Cody, Liza *Stalker.* London: Collins, 1984. First edition, signed, fine in dust jacket with light chipping to fore-edges.   Buckingham Books   March 2015 - 24693   2015 $275

Cody, Liza *Stalker.* London: Collins Crime Club, 1984. First edition, back cover edge bumped, else fine in dust jacket, signed by author.   Mordida Books   March 2015 - 011720   2015 $100

Coe, Charles Francis *G Man.* J. P. Lippincott Co., 1935. First edition, cloth lightly soiled, else very good in beautiful wraparound dust jacket with light wear to head of spine.   Buckingham Books   March 2015 - 33067   2015 $275

Coe, Jonathan *The Accidental Woman.* London: Duckworth, 1987. First edition, 8vo., signed on titlepage, fine in fine dust jacket.   Any Amount of Books   2015 - A38068   2015   £175

Coel, Margaret *The Eagle Catcher.* University Press of Colorado, 1995. First edition, signed by author, fine in dust jacket, author's first book.   Buckingham Books   March 2015 - 33198   2015 $250

Coel, Margaret *The Woman Who climbed to the sky.* ASAP Press, 2001. First edition, limited to 300 numbered copies signed by author, Tony Hillerman and Phil Parks, illustrations by Parks, fine in transparent dust jacket.   Buckingham Books   March 2015 - 19279   2015 $250

Coetzee, J. M. *Diary of a Bad Year.* London: Harvill Secker, 2007. Limited edition, Copy no. 87 of 100 copies, signed by author, bound in goatskin, fine copy, housed in custom slipcase.   Ken Lopez, Bookseller   164 - 38   2015 $550

Coetzee, J. M. *Dusklands.* Johannesburg: Ravan Press, 1974. True first edition, near fine in nearly fine, clean dust jacket.   Ed Smith Books   83 - 9   2015 $750

Coetzee, J. M. *"Hero and Bad Mother in Epic" in Staffrider, a South African Literary Journal...* Braamfontein: Ravan Press, 1978. Advance or trial copy of Volume I No. 1, some foxing to pictorial covers, in all very good, now housed in folding chemise and slipcase, special copy.   Ken Lopez, Bookseller   164 - 40   2015 $750

Coetzee, J. M. *His Man and He. Nobel Lecture December 7 2003.* London: Rees & O'Neill, 2004. First edition, one of 87 copies of which 75 were signed and numbered by author, this #36, small 4to., fine in brick red dark cloth with acetate dust jacket.   Ed Smith Books   83 - 10   2015 $500

Coetzee, J. M. *A House in Spain.* Amsterdam: Cossee, 2003. Bilingual (English/Dutch) limited edition, one of 1500 copies, hardbound, yellow cloth very mildly dusty, still fine. Ken Lopez, Bookseller   164 - 37   2015 $150

Coetzee, J. M. *In the Heart of the Country.* London: Secker & Warburg, 1977. First edition, signed by author for publisher, Tom Rosenthal, laid in is ANS signed by Rosenthal dated in 2007 stating "John Coetzee signed this book for me when he came here for dinner...", mild toning to endpages near fine in like dust jacket with original price intact and no sticker, with tanning to spine lettering and trace edge wear, very nice copy.   Ken Lopez, Bookseller 164 - 34   2015 $850

Coetzee, J. M. *The Nobel Lecture in Literature 2003.* New York: Penguin, 2004. American edition, signed by author, fine, without dust jacket as issued.   Ken Lopez, Bookseller   164 - 36   2015 $375

Coetzee, J. M. *Waiting for the Barbarians.* London: Secker & Warburg, 1980. First British edition and true First edition, signed by author, signed by publisher Tom Rosenthal with ANS laid in dated 2007 "John Coetzee signed this book for me when he came here for dinner...", couple of faint spots to top edge, else fine in near fine dust jacket with usual spine fading, text, white faint, still visible and readable, unlike some other copies we have seen. Ken Lopez, Bookseller   164 - 35   2015 $3500

Coffield, Glen *The Horned Moon.* Waldport: Untide Press, 1944. First edition, wrappers, one of 600 copies, very good with much of the tattered dust jacket laid in. Beasley Books   2013 - 2015 $150

Coffin, Charles Carleton *The Seat of Empire.* Boston: 1870. Large folding map, with some separations on folds and a repaired tears, but complete and bright, slight wear to extremities and fading to spine, front hinge reinforced, else very good,.   Dumont Maps & Books of the West   131 - 43   2015 $150

Coghlan, Margaret *Memoirs of Mrs. Coghlan... Written by Herself.* New York: T. & J. Swords, 1795. First American edition, 12mo., full brown morocco by Riviere, gilt lettering, all edges gilt, hinges just starting but firm, fine.   The Brick Row Book Shop   Miscellany 67 - 34   2015 $875

Cohen, Octavus Roy *Jim Haney, Detective.* Dodd Mead and Co., 1823. First edition, original green cloth, titles stamped in orange on front cover and spine, 283 pages, light wear to spine ends, else very good, lacking elusive dust jacket.   Buckingham Books   March 2015 - 37496   2015 $250

Cohn, Albert M. *George Cruikshank, a Catalogue Raisonne of the Work Executed During the Years 1806-1877...* London: The Bookman's Journal, 1924. First edition, limited to 500 numbered copies, thick 4to., brown cloth, top edge gilt, others uncut, well illustrated, some rubbing along hinges.   Oak Knoll Books   306 - 17   2015 $250

Coke and Birch. The Paper War, Carried on at the Nottingham Election 1803, Containing the Whole of the Addresses, Songs, Squibs &c... Nottingham: W. and M. Turner, n.d., 1803. First edition, 12mo., minor soiling of few leaves at beginning, contemporary blue boards, these soiled, neatly rebacked, printed spine label, good, complete and large, uncut copy.   John Drury Rare Books   March 2015 - 22076   2015 $266

Coke, Roger *A Treatise Wherein is Demonstrated that the Church and state of England are in Equal Danger with the Trade of It.* London: by J. C. for Henry Brome, 1671. First edition, small 4to., two small wormholes in blank corner of A1-3 reducing to a single hole A4-B2, occasionally closely shaved along upper edge, large ink blot in centre of A2v-A34, contemporary sprinkled sheep, rebacked, lower corner of board heavily bumped, from the library of James Stevens Cox (1910-1997).   Maggs Bros. Ltd.   1447 - 103   2015   £700

Colchester *The New Charter Granted to the Mayor and Commonalty of Colchester in Essex, in the third year of the reign of King George III and in the year of Our Lord 1763.* Colchester: by permission printed for W. Keymer bookseller in Colchester, 1764. First edition, 8vo., stitched into old blue wrappers torn and defective at spine, very good, apparently very rare.   John Drury Rare Books   2015 - 21353   2015 $612

Cole, Elizabeth *Jottings from Overland Trip to Arizona and California 1908.* Poughkeepsie: Hansman & Pralow, Printers, 1908. First edition, 8vo., original printed wrappers, 18 black and white photo illustrations in text, fine.   The Brick Row Book Shop   Miscellany 67 - 91   2015 $275

Cole, G. D. H. *The Blatchington Tangle.* New York: Macmillan Co., 1926. First US edition, light foxing to front and rear interior pages, cloth moderately rubbed and somewhat faded at spine, else very good in dust jacket, professionally restored at spine ends and extremities, uncommon. Buckingham Books   March 2015 - 24427   2015 $450

Cole, G. D. H. *The Walking Corpse.* New York: William Morrow & Co., 1931. First US edition, fine, bright, tight copy in striking dust jacket with only hint of rubbing to spine ends, exceptional copy.   Buckingham Books   March 2015 - 25856   2015 $850

Cole, G. D. H. *The Walking Corpse.* New York: William Morrow & Co., 1931. First edition, 8vo., original orange cloth, lettered black on spine and front cover, very slightly rubbed, otherwise very good+ in used, near very good- dust jacket with thumbsized chip at head of spine (loosing title), slight edgewear and fraying at edges, front panel of jacket in good order.   Any Amount of Books   2015 - C6963   2015   £160

Cole, John *Bookselling Spiritualised. Books and Articles of Stationery Rendered Monitors of Religion.* Scarborough: imprinted by John Cole Newborough St., 1826. First edition, limited impression of only 60 copies, printed on thick paper extended with many blank leaves, contemporary dark red morocco by gilt extra by J. MacKenzie, gilt edges with gilt cypher on each cover and 19th century armorial bookplate of James Cornerford on pastedown, extremities lightly rubbed, fine, handsome.   John Drury Rare Books   2015 - 25207   2015 $830

Coleridge, Hartley *Letters.* Oxford University Press, 1941. Half title, frontispiece, from the library of Geoffrey & Kathleen Tillotson, erratum slip, original buff cloth, marked, inscribed by Kathleen for Geoffrey, with original 4 line comic verse, but not signed by him.   Jarndyce Antiquarian Booksellers   CCVII - 146   2015   £20

Coleridge, Samuel Taylor 1772-1834 *Biographia Literaria; or Biographical Sketches...*   London: Rest Fenner, 1817. First edition, 2 volumes, half titles, without final ad leaf volume II, some spotting, few leaves rather browned, half red calf, spines chipped, hinges weak, signed S. Palmer and with his pencil notes at end of Chapter I, inserted is ALS of inquiry to Geoffrey Tillotson from Geoffrey Grigson.   Jarndyce Antiquarian Booksellers   CCVII - 147   2015   £850

Coleridge, Samuel Taylor 1772-1834 *The Poems...*   London: Oxford University Press, 1924. Half title, frontispiece, original red cloth, spine dulled, Geoffrey Tillotson's copy signed with ms. notes and various insertions.   Jarndyce Antiquarian Booksellers   CCVII - 148   2015   £40

Coleridge, Samuel Taylor 1772-1834 *The Rime of the Ancient Mariner.*   New York: Crowell, 1910. First US edition, folio, green gilt pictorial cloth, titlepage. others trimmed, gilt on spine dulled, else fine, illustrations by Willy Pogany.   Aleph-Bet Books, Inc.   108 - 353   2015 $1600

Coleridge, Samuel Taylor 1772-1834 *Shakespeare, Ben Jonson, Beaumont and Fletcher: Notes and Lectures.*   Liverpool: Edward Howell, 1875. New edition, half title, final ad leaf, original olive green cloth, spine slightly bubbled, signed K. M. Constable, April 1926 with some marginal marks and inserted reviews, from the library of Geoffrey & Kathleen Tillotson.   Jarndyce Antiquarian Booksellers   CCVII - 149   2015   £35

Coleridge, Samuel Taylor 1772-1834 *Specimens of the Table Talk of the late Samuel Taylor Coleridge.*   London: John Murray, 1835. First edition, small octavo, frontispieces, period binding in leather backed marbled paper boards, raised bands, gilt decorated spines, red leather title labels in gilt, black leather title labels lettered in gilt, covers little marked and slightly rubbed at edges, lower edges little rubbed, very good.   Peter Ellis, Bookseller   2014 - 018801   2015   £275

Coleridge, Samuel Taylor 1772-1834 *Zapolya; a Christmas Tale in Two Parts.*   London: Printed for Rest Fenner, 1817. First edition, 8vo., 19th century half red morocco, marbled paper boards, matching endpapers, gilt rules, decorations and lettering, top edge gilt, half title present, edges somewhat rubbed, very good.   The Brick Row Book Shop   Miscellany 67 - 35   2015 $750

Coleridge, Sarah *Phantasmion, a Fairy Tale.*   Henry S. King & Co., 1874. 8vo., first titlepage spotted, 8vo., original grass green sand grain cloth blocked in silver and gold and lettered in gold on front, ruled and lettered in gold on spine, bevelled boards, some loss to silver on front cover, slight wear to extremities, inner hinges strained, ownership inscription of Sir J(ohn) T(aylor) Coleridge, of Heath's Court, Ottery St. Mary Aril 8 1874 and below this an inscription 'Amy ?Metson with the affectionate regards of her cousin ?Coleridge, Heath's Court, September 1876", good.   Blackwell's Rare Books   B179 - 31   2015   £750

Coles, Elisha *Christologia or a Metrical paraphrase on the History of Our Lord and Saviour Jesus Christ.*   London: for Peter Parker, 1671. First edition, 8vo., without first blank leaf, light browning particularly in margins, words "OR A" on title deleted with ink and replaced with "a" in later manuscript, closely shaved, mid 20th century blue quarter morocco and marbled boards, from the library of James Stevens Cox (1910-1997), inscribed by Lewis Caesar Hill, 19th century signature George R. Hales, signature R. Betts dated "Silverhill 15.1 (18)90", booklabel of Gerald P Mander (d. 1951) of Tettenhall Wood, Staffordshire.   Maggs Bros. Ltd.   1447 - 105   2015   £240

Coles, Elisha *An English Dictionary Explaining the Difficult terms that are Used in Divinity, Husbandry, Physick, Philosophy, Law, Navigation, Mathematicks and Other Arts and Sciences.*   London: for Peter Parker, 1696. Sixth edition, titlepage lightly soiled and with margins browned by turn-ins, single wormhole to A1-B1, H1-L1 and short worm trail to Z6-2A3, minor ink staining to Q6 and 2C2-4, lower edge of H1 little ragged, with small spider neatly pressed between R3-4, cut fairly close at head, contemporary calf, ruled in blind, spine creased, upper headcap split and short crack at head of upper joint, small hole in foot of spine, corners and edges worn, no pastedowns, rear flyleaf only, ink inscription of William Cheyney, from the library of James Stevens Cox (1910-1997).   Maggs Bros. Ltd.   1447 - 104   2015   £500

Coles, Elisha *An English Dictionary Explaining the Difficult Terms that are Used in Divinity, Husbandry and Other Arts.* London: Peter Parker, 1708. Early edition, 8vo., sound full calf with rather rubbed raised bands and lettering only just detectable, some general wear to covers, slight chipping and indentation, text has slight browning and occasional worming at top corner margins with no loss of legibility of dictionary text, reasonable towards very good copy.   Any Amount of Books   2015 - C15768   2015   £160

Coles, Manning *The Fifth Man.* London: Hodder & Stoughton, 1946. First edition, some tiny light spotting on page edges, otherwise fine in dust jacket (tiny wear at corners).   Mordida Books   March 2015 - 008964   2015 $85

Coles, Manning *A Toast to Tomorrow.* New York: Doubleday Doran and Co., 1941. First US edition, fine, bright copy in dust jacket with light professional restoration to spine ends and corners.   Buckingham Books   March 2015 - 29536   2015 $675

Coles, Manning *A Toast to Tomorrow.* New York: Doubleday Doran Co., 1941. First US edition, fine, bright copy in dust jacket with hint of wear to spine ends.   Buckingham Books   March 2015 - 29526   2015 $1275

Colette, Sidonie Gabrielle   1873-1954 *Paris de Ma Fenetre.* Paris: Editions Literaires de France, 1951. No. 155 of 159 numbered copies, folio, illustrations by Buchaguqes, unbound signatures in wrappers, fine in fine wrappers and slightly sunned chemise, in striking box decorated by artist.   Beasley Books   2013 - 2015 $399

Colette, Sidonie Gabrielle   1873-1954 *La Vagabonde.* Paris: Les Editions Nationales, 1945. #191 of 300 copies, 16 full page color prints by Berthomee Saint Andre, numerous black and white illustrations, this copy has an extra suite of prints printed in black, wrappers fine in publisher's glassine, small 4to., chemise is near fine with slightly sunned spine, in close to fine box.   Beasley Books   2013 - 2015 $400

Collado, Luigi *Prattica e dell' Artiglieria.* Milan: Girolamo Bordoni & Pietromartire Locarni, 1606. Later printing, small quarto, 15 folding woodcut plates plus abundance of full page and half page woodcut text illustrations, decorated initials, old full paneled calf, minor extremity wear to binding, few marginal repairs to prelims, old ink scored names on blank portion of titlepage, lower corner of title restored with imprint date supplied in manuscript, light marginal dampstaining to few endleaves, small bookplate, fine.   Argonaut Book Shop   Holiday Season 2014 - 55   2015 $2250

A Collection of Addresses Transmitted by Certain English Clubs and Societies to the National Convention of France; the Decree of the Executive Council Respecting the Scheldt.... London: J. Debrett, 1793. 8vo., tear in one leaf but no loss of printed surface, recent marbled boards lettered on spine, very good.   John Drury Rare Books   2015 - 25736   2015 $656

A Collection of Interesting, Authentic Papers, Relative to the Dispute Between Great Britain and America... London: printed for J. Almon, 1777. First edition, dated bookplate "Woburn Abbey 1873", contemporary three quarter marbled sides, lacking one leaf, corners worn, spine very rough, some scattered light foxing, internally clean overall.   Argonaut Book Shop   Holiday Season 2014 - 9   2015 $900

A Collection of Poems by Several Hands. Paris: printed by J. G. A. Stoupe, 1779. half title, titlepage slightly soiled, few minor patches of browning, 12mo., original sheep, double gilt fillets on sides, red lettering piece on spine, headcap defective, corners slightly worn, good.   Blackwell's Rare Books   B179 - 5   2015   £600

A Collection of Pslams and Hymns for Public Worship. Wednesbury: printed ad sold by Joshua Booth, 1830. 8vo., generally little soiled through use, little foxing and some staining on prelim blanks, ownership inscription, bound in contemporary plain black calf, just bit worn at extremities, good copy, apparently rare.   John Drury Rare Books   March 2015 - 25195   2015   £266

College De Geneve *Projet d'une Ordonnance Provisionelle Concernant l'Education Publique du College.* N.P.: Geneva: n.d., 1792. 8vo., folding table, well bound recently in cloth lettered in gilt, very good, together with No. 1 Tableau characterstque 1792, unbound, very good.   John Drury Rare Books   March 2015 - 17866   2015   £306

Collier, Calvin L. *The War Child's Children. The Story of the Third Regiment, Arkansas Cavalry, Confederate States Army.* Little Rock: 1965. First edition, 139 pages, fine in fine, unclipped dust jacket.   Bookworm & Silverfish   2015 - 6018515133   2015 $75

Collier, Jeremy *Essays Upon Several Moral Subjects.* London: for R. Sare and H. Hindmarsh, 1697. Second edition, 8vo., small piece torn from B8 with loss to 3 words, small hole to C8 with loss of letter or two, some occasional light foxing and staining, contemporary calf, rebacked, corners repaired, from the library of James Stevens Cox (1910-1997).   Maggs Bros. Ltd.   1447 - 106   2015   £120

Collier, Jeremy *A Short View of the Immorality and Profaneness of the English Stage together with the Sense of Antiquity Upon the Argument.* London: for S. Keble, R. Sare and H. Hindmarch, 1698. Second edition, 8vo., light dampstain to blank fore-margin of sheet #, two tears to blank margins of E7 and E8 (just touching a sidenote or two), light worming to blank lower right corner of G4-T8, some discoloration due to poor paper quality, contemporary calf, covers panelled in blind, spine tooled in gilt and with red morocco label, covers slightly scuffed, from the library of James Stevens Cox (1910-1997) with bookplate.   Maggs Bros. Ltd.   1447 - 107   2015   £350

Collingwood, Harry *The Cruise of the "Flying-Fish" the Airship-Submarine.* London: Sampson Low, Marston & Co. Ltd. n.d., 1924. First edition, octavo, inserted frontispiece, original red pictorial cloth, front and spine panels stamped in black.   L. W. Currey, Inc.   Boy's Adventure Fiction 2015 - 92   2015 $100

Collingwood, Harry *Geoffrey Harrington's Adventures.* London: Society for Promoting Christian Knowledge/New York: E. S. Gorham, n.d., 1907. First edition, 6 inserted plates with color illustrations by Harold Piffard, original pictorial red cloth, front panel stamped in black, white and tan, spine panel stamped in black, white tan and gold.   L. W. Currey, Inc.   Boy's Adventure Fiction 2015 - 72   2015 $125

Collingwood, Harry *The Log of the 'Flying Fish".* London: Glasgow: Edinburgh: and Dublin: Blackie & son, 1887. First edition, first printing, octavo, 12 inserted plates with illustrations by Gordon Browne, original pictorial terra cotta brown cloth, front panel stamped in light brown, black and silver, spine panel stamped in light brown, black and gold, rear panel stamped in blind, brown coated endpapers, all edges yellow glazed.   L. W. Currey, Inc.   Boy's Adventure Fiction 2015 - 12   2015 $650

Collingwood, Harry *Through Veld and Forest: an African Story.* London: Glasgow: Bombay: Blackie and Son, 1914. First edition, octavo, 6 inserted plates, illustrations by Arch Webb, original pictorial green cloth, front and spine panels stamped in black, gray, yellow and gold, all edges stained green, tan coated endpapers.   L. W. Currey, Inc.   Boy's Adventure Fiction 2015 - 53   2015 $150

Collins, Billy *Pokerface.* Los Angeles: Kenmore Press, 1977. Limited first edition, 1/400 copies, signed by Billy Collins, oblong octavo, Japanese stab binding with exposed sewing, pictorial wrappers, custom cloth box, cover silk screened from original photo by Judy Lane, fine, scarce.   Manhattan Rare Book Company   Literature 2014 - 2015 $2500

Collins, Hunt *Cut Me In.* Abelard Schuman, 1954. First edition, fine in dust jacket with light wear to spine ends and corners, small crease and closed tear to front cover, scarce.   Buckingham Books   March 2015 - 37211   2015 $1250

Collins, Jennie *Nature's Aristocracy; or Battles and Wounds in Time of Peace.* Boston and New York: Lee and Shepard, 1871. First edition, 8vo., publisher's cloth dust soiled, some minor foxing and staining, hinges repaired, good copy.   Second Life Books Inc.   189 - 58   2015 $200

Collins, Max Allan *Jim Thompson: the Killers Inside Him.* Cedar Rapids: Fedora Press, 1983. First edition, limited edition of 425 copies, this number 3, fine, unread copy in pictorial wrappers.   Buckingham Books   March 2015 - 29374   2015 $225

Collins, R. M. *Chapters from the Unwritten History of the War Between the States...* Dayton: Limited edition, #241 of 300 copies, fine.   Bookworm & Silverfish   2015 - 6017624331   2015 $100

Collins, Wilkie 1824-1889 *Man and Wife.* New York: Harper, 1870. First American edition, spine cocked, otherwise very good in soft covers.   Mordida Books   March 2015 - 000485   2015 $100

Collins, Wilkie 1824-1889 *The New Magdalen. The Moonstone. Poor Miss Finch. the Dead Secret. & The Woman in White. Volume 2.* New York: Scribners, 1908. Later edition, 5 volumes, spine slightly darkened, otherwise near fine in red cloth covered boards, gold stamped titles gilt to page edges, very good.   Mordida Books   March 2015 - 011828   2015 $85

Collins, Wilkie 1824-1889 *The Woman in White.* Boston: Houghton Mifflin, 1969. Riverside edition, half title, illustrations, original card wrappers, slightly creased and marked, Kathleen Tillotson's copy with note, with inserted TLS of appreciation for the loan from Gordon (Haight?) 1987.   Jarndyce Antiquarian Booksellers   CCVII - 155   2015   £20

Collins, William *The Poems of William Collins.* London: Frederick Etchells & Hugh MacDonald, 1929. First edition thus, one of 50 numbered copies, octavo, frontispiece portrait, original quarter brown morocco, gilt decorated boards, pages unopened, printed on Van Gelder's Japon paper and signed by Blunden, spine bruised at tail, corners bruised, free endpapers tanned, frontispiece image offset onto titlepage, very good.   Peter Ellis, Bookseller   2014 - 015651   2015   £325

Colombia. Laws, Statutes, etc. *Coleccion de las Leyes Dadas por el Congreso Constitucional de la Republica de Combia en las sesiones de los anos 1825 i 1836.* Bogota: Imp. de P. Cubiddes, 1827. First edition, signed by Agustin Guerrero (1817-1902) President of the Provisional government of the Republic of Ecuador, very good, two tiny wormholes in spine, scuffing to boards, partial label on spine, minor dampstaining to rear leaves, last leaf soiled.   Kaaterskill Books   19 - 39   2015 $1250

Colquhoun, John Campbell *The System of National Education in Ireland: its Principle and Practice.* Cheltenham: published by William Wight, 1838. First edition, 12mo., original publisher's cloth, sides embossed in blind, spine gilt and lettered, fine, from the 19th century library of John Eardley Wilmot 1783-1847 with his signature. John Drury Rare Books   March 2015 - 21788   2015   £306

Colquhoun, Patrick 1745-1820 *A Treatise on Indigence: Exhibiting a General View of the National Resources for Productive labour...* London: J. Hatchard, 1806. First edition, 8vo., complete with final leaf with ads on recto and directions to binder on verso, one large folding table, contemporary half calf over boards, flat spine with gilt lines and title, just little wear to spine head and slight crack down centre of spine, otherwise fine, crisp copy.   John Drury Rare Books   2015 - 25448   2015 $1311

Colquhoun, Patrick 1745-1820 *A Treatise on the Wealth, Power and Resources of the British Empire in every Quarter of the World, including the East Indies...* London: Joseph Mamman, 1814. First edition, endpapers little foxed, contemporary half calf over marbled boards, sometime rebacked reusing original gilt backstrip, labelled and lettered, some general wear to binding, overall very good, sound, good, contemporary binding.   John Drury Rare Books   March 2015 - 23883   2015 $874

Colton, James *Strange Marriage.* New York: Paperback Library Inc., 1966. First paperback edition, signed by author, few tiny nicks to edges and small corner crease on back panel, else very good, apparently unread copy. Buckingham Books   March 2015 - 19078   2015 $175

Columbus. London: Bancroft, 1960. Folio, cloth backed pictorial card covers, few wheel nubs on cover damaged, else very good+, illustrations in color by Kubasta and moveable ships wheel on cover and on absolutely stunning, large pop-up scene.   Aleph-Bet Books, Inc.   108 - 363   2015 $325

Colvil, Samuel *Whiggs Supplication.* Edinburgh: by Jo. Reid for Alexander Ogston, 1687. Second edition, 8vo., very small chip from upper fore corner with four minor circular stains on titlepage, some occasional staining throughout, dampstaining just touching corners of F4-F6, some heavy modern pencil markings in a number of margins, and with a number of gatherings beginning to come loose from book block, signed by author sheep (worn, large piece torn away from foot of spine and with upper headcap damaged, boards heavily rubbed and corners bumped, early signature of Geo(rge) Dundas, bookplate of Frederick Locker-Lampson (1821-1895), given by him to Lytton Strachey (1880-1932), from the library of James Stevens Cox (1910-1997). Maggs Bros. Ltd.   1447 - 108   2015   £150

Combe, William 1742-1823 *The Tour of Doctor Syntax in Search of the Picturesque.* London: George Routledge, n.d. circa, 1860. Ninth edition, 80 fine colored aquatint plates by Thomas Rowlandson, beautiful set, 3 volumes, 4to., red cloth stamped in black and gold, tips bumped, very slightly rubbing, very good-fine.   Aleph-bet Books, Inc. 109 - 419   2015 $850

Comber, Thomas *A Companion to the Temple or a Help to Devotion in the Use of the Common Prayer divided into four parts.* London: printed by Miles Flesher for Charles Brome at the Gun at the West end of St. Paul's Cathedral, 1688. Third edition, small folio, collated complete, newer full brown calf, black blindstamped spine label, some browning or staining, especially to gutter of part II, very good. Argonaut Book Shop   Holiday Season 2014 - 56   2015 $500

Comber, Thomas *The Occasional Offices of Matrimony, Visitation to the Sick, Burial of the Dead, Churching of Women...* London: by M. C. for Henry Brome and Robert Clavel, 1679. 8vo., dampstaining to fore-margin of Q2-Z-4 and lower fore corner Ff1-Kk8, contemporary black morocco 'semi sombre' binding, covers finely tooled with double gilt fillet containing blind tooled fronds, sequins and daisies, central gilt panel with vase and flower tool at each corner and containing further blind tooling and central lozenge, spine in six panels, tooled in gilt with red morocco label in second panel, gilt edges and marbled endleaves, early 20th century marbled slipcase (slight worm damage at foot of spine, slightly rubbed, corners very lightly bumped), from the library of James Stevens Cox (1910-1997).   Maggs Bros. Ltd.   1447 - 110   2015   £550

Comber, William Turner *An Inquiry into the State of National Subsistence, as Connected with the Progress of Wealth and Population...* London: printed for the author and sold by J. M. Richardson, 1822. 8vo., half title and appendix original boards, printed spine label (slightly chipped), entirely uncut, fine, from the library of Lord Eldon with his circular armorial bookplate and signature in ink. John Drury Rare Books   2015 - 25037   2015 $1049

Comes, Natalis *Natalis Comitis Mythologiae, Siue Explicatonu Fabularum Libri Decem.* Venetiis: 1568. Early printing, 340 numbered leaves, small 4to., original limp vellum with paper label, title handwritten on spine, few very light short contemporary inscriptions, small area of worming in some pages, not affecting text, some pages mottled, most very bright and clean.   Any Amount of Books   2015 - C5075   2015   £750

The Comic Adventures of Old Mother Hubbard and Her Dog. Part I. York: Kendrew, n.d. circa, 1820. 16mo., yellow wrappers, fine, 15 fine and well printed half page woodcuts to accompany this.   Aleph-bet Books, Inc.   109 - 154 2015 $300

Conrad, Joseph 1857-1924 *Typhoon and Other Stories.* London: William Heinemann, 1903. First English edition, first binding, original grey cloth gilt, ad leaf beginning and 32 pages at end, corners bumped and light browning to endpaper, otherwise very nice, from the collection of Gavin H. Fryer.   Bertram Rota Ltd.   308 Part II - 136   2015   £500

Conrad, Joseph 1857-1924 *Under Western Eyes.* London: Methuen & Co., 1911. First edition, original red cloth, spine gilt, spine touch faded and with minor damage at foot, sides little marked, endpapers browned and little foxing, otherwise very nice, from the collection of Gavin H. Fryer.   Bertram Rota Ltd.   308 Part II - 139   2015   £250

Conrad, Joseph 1857-1924 *Victory.* New York: Doubleday Page, 1915. First American edition prior to the English edition by 6 months, very good, some shelfwear at extremities, some dulling of spine, gilt, tight, clean text. Stephen Lupack   March 2015 - 2015 $45

Conrad, Joseph 1857-1924 *Victory; an Island Tale.* London: Methuen & Co., 1915. First English edition, original red cloth, spine gilt, spine little faded and upper cover marked, prelims foxed, but nice, ownership inscription, from the collection of Gavin H. Fryer.   Bertram Rota Ltd.   308 Part II - 142   2015   £150

Conrad, Joseph 1857-1924 *Within the Tides.* London: J. M. Dent & Sons, 1915. First edition, original green cloth, spine gilt, sides faded as usual, spine bright and fresh, browning to free endpapers and little foxing, but very nice in dust jacket, professionally restored at hinges and little browned at spine panel, from the collection of Gavin H. Fryer.   Bertram Rota Ltd.   308 Part II - 143   2015   £1750

Conrad, Joseph 1857-1924 *The Works of Joseph Conrad.* London: William Heinemann, 1921. 1926. 1927. Limitation leaf signed by Conrad, this no. 658 of 780 sets, 750 for sale, 30 for presentation, 20 volumes, half titles, uncut in original cream boards, cream cloth spines, Conrad's printed signature on front boards, slight rust marking to back board volume 5, slight bump to near edge of front board, volume 6, bookplate of Cuthbert Headlam in all volumes except volumes 11, 12, 19 & 20, overall very good set.   Jarndyce Antiquarian Booksellers   CCXI - 71   2015   £1500

Conrad, Joseph 1857-1924 *The Works of Joseph Conrad.* London: J. M. Dent & Sons, 1923-1928. Uniform edition, octavo, 22 volumes (complete), contemporary three quarter crimson morocco over marbled boards, marbled endpapers, top edges gilt, little rubbing to some spine ends and joints, handsome.   Manhattan Rare Book Company Literature 2014 - 2015 $2900

Conrad, Joseph 1857-1924 *Youth.* London: William Blackwood and Sons, 1902. First edition, first issue with earliest ads (dated 10/02), original green cloth, excellent copy with trace of rubbing to extremities, some very faint soiling to covers, few small spots to page edges, former owner bookplate, tipped-in to front pastedown, else near fine.   B & B Rare Books, Ltd.   234 - 12   2015 $4500

Conrad, Joseph 1857-1924 *Youth: a Narrative and Two Other Stories.* Edinburgh and London: William Blackwood and Sons, 1902. First edition, publisher's catalog at end dated "11/02 ("10/02" first state), original green cloth lettered and decorated black and gilt, spine little dulled, damage to head and foot, minor tears to margin of final ad leaf, corners little rubbed, hinges cracked and endpapers little foxed, still nice, ownership inscription, from the collection of Gavin H. Fryer.   Bertram Rota Ltd.   308 Part II - 133   2015   £1200

Conrad, Joseph 1857-1924 *Youth: a Narrative and two other stories.* London: J. M. Dent & Sons Ltd., 1917. Second English edition, original green cloth lettered and decorated in gilt and black, corners bumped and gilt lettering to spine somewhat dulled, sides very slightly marked and light browning to free endpapers, else very nice, inscription and ownership stamp, bookseller's small label, from the collection of Gavin H. Fryer.   Bertram Rota Ltd.   308 Part II - 134   2015   £250

Conselman, Deirdre *Keedle.* New York: Hillman - Curl, 1940. First edition, 4to., pictorial boards, near fine in dust jacket with some soil, full page color illustrations by Fred Fox.   Aleph-bet Books, Inc.   109 - 491   2015 $350

Conservative and Unionist Women's Franchise Association *The Unjust Laws of England as They Affect Women.* N.P.: but London, n.d. circa, 1908. Folding 8vo. leaflet, 4 pages, unbound as issued, fine, probably rare. John Drury Rare Books   2015 - 26056   2015 $177

Considerations Concerning the Nature and Consequences of the Bill Now Depending In Parliament, Relating to the Peerage of Great Britain in a Letter from One Member of the House of Commons to Another. London: printed for J. Roberts, 1719. First edition, 28 pages, recent plain wrappers, very good.   John Drury Rare Books   2015 - 17719   2015 $177

Considerations on a Letter to the Mayor ---, in Relation to a Bill Now Depending in Parliament, for the Encouragement of Seamen Employed in the Royal Navy.... London: William Lewis, 1758. First and only edition, scarce, woodcut vignette of martial symbols on titlepage, wanting half title, very good, large copy, uncut in recent plain wrappers with printed label on upper cover, scarce.   John Drury Rare Books   March 2015 - 19839   2015   £306

Considerations on the Bill for the Better Government of the navy. London: M. Cooper, 1749. First edition, 8vo., half title, preserved in recent marbled endpapers with printed label, very good.   John Drury Rare Books   March 2015 - 25471   2015   £306

Considerations Touching Trade, with the Advance of the Kings Revenue and Present Reparation of His Majestie... London?: printed in the yeare, 1641. First and only edition, 4to., 16 pages, some dust soiling, recently well bound in old style quarter calf gilt, fine, wide margined copy.   John Drury Rare Books   2015 - 8082   2015 $1661

Considerations Upon the Intended Navigable Communication Between the firths of Forth and Clyde In a Letter to the Lord Provost of Edinburgh. Edinburgh: n.d. but April 11, 1767. First edition, 4to., last few leaves rather foxed, old ink splash in title margin, old ink inscription in upper margin, preserved in modern wrappers with printed label on upper cover, good, scarce.   John Drury Rare Books   March 2015 - 25243   2015   £306

The Conspiracy of Aeneas & Antenor Against the State of Troy. London: for John Spicer, 1682. First edition, small 4to., 20 pages, titlepage and recto of B3 lightly soiled, lower margins uncut, late 19th century half calf and marbled boards (foot of spine lightly chipped, one or two bumps to top edge of both boards), 20th century signature of James Bell, from the library of James Stevens Cox (1910-1997). Maggs Bros. Ltd.   1447 - 112   2015   £450

Constantine, K. C.   *The Rocksburg Railroad Murders.* New York: Saturday Review Press, 1972. First edition, small label on front pastedown sheet with initials 'BTP' else fine in fine first state dust jacket with $5.95 price mark and ads on rear cover.   Buckingham Books   March 2015 - 37305   2015 $750

Contemporary Western Artists. New York: Bonanza, 1985. Reprint, but nicely produced on decent paper, fine in fine dust jacket.   Beasley Books   2013 - 2015 $45

Convention Between His Britannick Majesty and the Empress of Russia. London: printed by Edward Johnston in Warwick Lane, 1793. First published edition, 4to., woodcut of royal arms on title, preserved in modern wrappers with printed title label on upper cover, very good, rare.   John Drury Rare Books   March 2015 - 22874   2015   £306

Conway, George Robert Graham   *An Englishman and the Mexican Inquisition 1556-1560.* Mexico: privately printed, 1927. First edition, inscribed by author, 14 black and white plates, plans and facsimiles, cloth, uncommon, very good+, clean, crisp and unmarked, little foxing on fore edge, no dust jacket.   Kaaterskill Books   19 - 150   2015 $400

Cook, James   *Sentence, Confession and Execution of James Cook for the Murder of Mr. Paas, at Leicester on Wednesday the 30th of May 1832, Rendered more Remarkable by the Horrid manner in which the murderer disposed of the body...* Manchester: printed by W. D. Varey, 1832. Third edition, 12mo., 12 pages, fine woodcut frontispiece, preserved in modern wrappers with printed label on upper cover.   John Drury Rare Books   March 2015 - 25756   2015   £306

Cook, James   1728-1779   *The Journals of Captain James Cook on His Voyages of Discovery.* Cambridge: The Hakluyt Society, Cambridge at the University Press and London, 1968-1974. 4 volumes in 5, printed card wrappers, fine, many black and white and color illustrations and maps, fold-outs, uniform navy cloth lettered gilt at spines with gilt bust portrait of Cook on upper panels, all in original dust jackets, jackets variously faded and various slight discolorations to page edges, one 1 x 0.5 inch hole in rear of first jacket rear panel, otherwise very clean, smart set.   Any Amount of Books   March 2015 - C16438   2015   £340

Cook, Joel   *America.* New York: Merrill and Baker, 1900. First edition thus, 6 volumes, illustrations, frontispiece and tissue guards in place, very good set, mild shelfwear, little color disturbance/spotting to size of cloth, nice.   Stephen Lupack   March 2015 - 2015 $75

Cook, John   *Redintegratio Amoris, or a Union of Hearts...* London: for Giles Calvert, 1647. First edition, small 4to., without first and final blank leafs, dark circular dampstain (45 x 25mm) in upper fore-corner of titlepage (from deleted signature), some spotting and browning throughout and with small (15mm) closed tear to margin of F2, some minor worming in inner margin dampstain in top margin at end, late 19th century calf, covers panelled blind, red edges, spine defective at head and tail, corners bumped, signature of Rev. Richard Grosvenor Bartelot, FSA, earlier signature deleted from titlepage, from the library of James Stevens Cox (1910-1997).   Maggs Bros. Ltd.   1447 - 113   2015   £350

Cook, John R.   *The Border and the Buffalo. an Untold story of the Southwest Plains...* Crane & Co., 1907. First edition, 8vo., tan pictorial cloth, brown illustration on cover, frontispiece, illustrations, fine, bright, tight copy. Buckingham Books   March 2015 - 28822   2015 $250

Cook, Stanley   *Alphabet.* Cheshire: Harry Chambers/ Peterloo Poets, 1976. First edition, 12mo., printed wrappers, fine, illustrations in black.   Aleph-bet Books, Inc. 109 - 10   2015 $75

Cook, Tennessee Celeste, Lady   1845-1923
Constitutional Equality a Right of Woman...   New York: Woodhull and Claflin, 1871. First edition, 8vo., frontispiece, green cloth stamped gilt, little foxing on front and rear leaves, cover scuffed, little soiled and little worn at edges, otherwise very good, scarce.   Second Life Books Inc.   189 - 56   2015 $500

Cook, Tennessee Celeste, Lady   1845-1923
Constitutional Equality a Right of Woman or a Consideration of the Various Relations Which She Sustains as a necessary part of the Body of Society and Humanity.   New York: Woodhull, Claflin & Co., 1871. First edition, 8vo., original cloth, few chips on spine, bookplate removed from inside front cover, inner front joint starting.   M & S Rare Books, Inc.   97 - 69   2015 $750

Cook, Thomas H.   *The Orchids.*   Boston: Houghton Mifflin, 1982. First edition, signed by author, very fine in dust jacket.   Mordida Books   March 2015 - 008972   2015 $90

Cook, Thomas H.   *The Orchids.*   Boston: Houghton Mifflin, 1982. First edition, very fine in dust jacket.   Mordida Books   March 2015 - 011732   2015 $85

Cook, William   *The Ploughboy's Harrow Number Three....*   Salem: William Cook, Jan., 1860. First edition, 8vo., pages 9-16, bound in original pictorial wrappers, stitched as issued, with two plates, little chipped and worn, very good, scarce, fragile.   Second Life Books Inc.   191 - 25   2015 $350

Cooke, Henry   *Turpin the Second; or Cooke Caught at Last.*   London: printed for A. Ilive, 1741. Only edition, outer leaves soiled and stained, 3 holes in last leaf affecting the text but only with loss of 7 or 8 letters and a small hole with loss of 4 letters, tear at head of B1 entering text but without loss, small piece missing from upper margin, pages 24, 8vo., disbound.   Blackwell's Rare Books   B179 - 43   2015   £550

Cooke, James   *Mellificium Chirurgiae or the Marrow of Many Good Authors.*   London: for Samuel Cartwright, 1648. First edition, 12mo., upper fore corners of B6-7 and P5 torn from paper flaws (affecting rule border not touching text), some worming in inner margin (heavily between Q5-R11), contemporary sheep ruled in blind (rubbed, 30mm piece torn at head of spine, a number of loose gatherings, bumped and rubbed, pastedowns unstuck), early ink initials "E K", late 18th century signature Isaac Webster/Hull, signature Isaac Raines 1802, by descent to Rev. George Francis Twycross-Raines, vicar and antiquary of Hull, with ink inscription, of "H. Page from his old friend G. F. Twycross-Raines Sept. 11, 1911", from the library of James Stevens Cox (1910-1997).   Maggs Bros. Ltd.   1447 - 114   2015   £750

Coolbrith, Ina   *California.*   San Francisco: Book Club of California, 1918. First edition, one of 500 copies, despite limitation a very scarce book, small thin quarto, mounted frontispiece, printed in green by Dan Sweeney, printed with green ruled borders throughout with orange floral decorations by Lawrence Haste, handset type on handmade paper, linen backed pale green boards, printed paper spine label, lower corners jammed, upper corner just slightly showing, spine slightly darkened, slight darkening to front and rear inner hinge, from binder's glue (common), near fine, extremely fragile.   Argonaut Book Shop   Holiday Season 2014 - 58   2015 $250

Coole, Benjamin   *Honesty the Truest Policy, Shewing the Sophistry, Envy and Perversion of George Keith, in His Three Books...*   Bristol?: by W. Bonny for the author, 1700. First edition, small 8vo., very small stain in inner margin of A8-B4, 19th century half red calf and marbled boards, early 20th century label of K. G. Pittard, inkstamp of George's bookshop in Bristol, from the library of James Stevens Cox (1910-1997).   Maggs Bros. Ltd.   1447 - 115   2015   £200

Cooney, Barbara   *Chanticleer and the Fox.*   New York: Crowell, 1958. First edition, 4to., fine in dust jacket, slight fraying at spine ends, else very good+, brightly illustrated in color by Cooney, Caldecott Award winner (no medal), signed by Cooney.   Aleph-bet Books, Inc.   109 - 103   2015 $800

Coonley, Lydia Avery   *Singing Verses for Children.*   New York: 1897. First edition, oblong 4to., cloth, pictorial paste-on, printed on heavy coated paper, each page individually hinged into book preventing the pages from separating at spine, full color illustrations, brilliant copy, rare.   Aleph-Bet Books, Inc.   108 - 107   2015 $400

Cooper, G. Kersey   *The Two Prize Essays of the Suffolk Agricultural Association on the Elevation, Improvement and Education of the Labouring Classes.*   Ipswich: William Hunt for the Suffolk Agricultural Association, 1859. First edition, 8vo., original printed wrappers, very good, largely unopened, very rare.   John Drury Rare Books   2015 - 12908   2015 $133

Cooper, James Fenimore   1789-1851   *The Deerslayer; a Tale.*   London: Richard Bentley, 1841. Second edition, 3 volumes, half titles, original drab boards, brown horizontally ribbed cloth spines, paper labels, slightly chipped, signatures of J. and Elizabeth Bell, recent labels of Ronald George Taylor.   Jarndyce Antiquarian Booksellers   CCXI - 72   2015   £125

Cooper, James Fenimore   1789-1851   *The Pioneers or the Sources of the Susquehanna; a Descriptive Tale.*   New York: Charles Wiley, 1823. First edition, first printing of volume I, first state of volume II, 2 volumes, 12mo., original drab boards, uncut, boards detached, most of paper gone from one spine, portions of printed paper labels intact.   M & S Rare Books, Inc.   97 - 80   2015 $1000

Cooper, Merian C. *Grass.* New York: G. P. Putnam's Sons, 1925. First edition, inscribed by author to Sidney Williams, scarce thus, very good plus in very good dust jacket, spine slightly toned and couple of faint smudges to boards, jacket spine and folds toned, few faint dampstains and tiny chips and tears (several cellophane repairs on verso). Royal Books 46 - 24 2015 $3750

Cooper, Susan *Sea Under Stone.* New York: Harcourt Brace World, 1966. Stated First American edition, 8vo., tan pictorial cloth, fine in very good+ dust jacket frayed at spine ends, illustrations in line by Margery Gill. Aleph-bet Books, Inc. 109 - 104 2015 $1750

Cooper, Susan Rogers *Houston in the Rearview Mirror.* New York: St. Martin's, 1990. First edition, fine in dust jacket with tiny wear at base of spine. Mordida Books March 2015 - 000508 2015 $75

Cooper, Thomas *A Treatise on the Law of Libel and the Liberty of the Press showing the Origin, Use and Abuse of the Law of Libel.* New York: printed by G. F. Hopkins & son, 1830. First and only edition, 8vo., well bound in strong mid 20th century cloth, spine lettered gilt, very good. John Drury Rare Books 2015 - 23989 2015 $1049

Cooper, W. D. *The History of South America, Containing the Discoveries of Columbus, the Conquest of Mexico and Peru...* London: E. Newbery, 1789. First edition, 16mo., 14 x 9cm., frontispiece, 5 engraved plates, full brown tree calf with plain leather gilt lettered spine with 7 gold bands, sound clean, very good copy with few marks to leather, front endpaper excised, bookplate of one Cecil Byshopp and note dated 1791 in neat sepia ink about the gifting of the book from Katherine Byshopp, first blank has modern neat name, plates and text noticeably clean and bright. Any Amount of Books 2015 - A66548 2015 £320

Copernicus, Nicolai *De Revolutionibus Orbium Coelestium Libri VI.* Brussels: Culture et Civilisation, 1966. Facsimile of the first edition, 4to., leatherette, maroon spine labels, very good. Jeff Weber Rare Books 178 - 783 2015 $100

Cope's Smoke-Room Booklets. Numbers 1-14. Liverpool & London: Cope Bros. & Co., 1889-1896. 8vo., 2 volumes, half leather lettered in gilt at spine, top edge gilt, gilt crest of Society of Writers to Signet on marbled boards, preserving original chromolithographed wrappers with gilt highlighting, illustrations in text, excellent clean set. Any Amount of Books March 2015 - A68705 2015 £350

Copley James S. *The James S. Copley Library.* New York: Sotheby's, 2010. 4to., stiff paper wrappers, color illustrations. Oak Knoll Books 306 - 72 2015 $125

Copley, Frederick S. *A Set of Alphabets of all the Various Hands in Modern Use with Examples in Each Style.* New York: Geo. E. Woodward, 1870. First edition, engraved by Korff Bros. of NY, oblong 12mo., 47 plates, original green cloth stamped in gilt, covers show some minor spotting, wear at spine ends, well preserved. Oak Knoll Books Special Catalogue 24 - 10 2015 $200

Copley, Heather *Drawings of the Katydid.* Bainbridge: Katydid Press, 1958. First edition, 24mo., printed paper covered boards, fine in near fine, unprinted dust jacket, ownership signature of wood engraved John De Pol, with ALS from publisher John Lehmann to De Pol presenting the book. Between the Covers Rare Books, Inc. 187 - 61 2015 $450

Coppard, Alfred Edgar 1878-1957 *Polly Oliver.* London: Jonathan Cape, 1935. Stated first edition, very nearly fine in very good dust jacket, piece of tape at spine top, closed tear, not chipped. Stephen Lupack March 2015 - 2015 $125

Coppola, Giovanni Carlo *Le Nozze Degli Dei; Favola... Rappresentata in Musica in Firenze nelle Reali Nozze de Serenissimi Gran Duchi di Toschana Ferdinando II e Vittoria Principessa d'Urbino.* Florence: A. Massi & L. Landi, 1637. First edition, 4to., large and handsome copy, etched titlepage and 7 double page etched plates by Stefano della Bella after Alfonso Parigi, 4to., 104 pages, expertly rebound in vellum over pasteboards, bookplate of Professor John Ramsay Allardyce Nicoll (1894-1976). Maggs Bros. Ltd. Illustrated Books 2014 - 2015 £9000

Corbet, Richard *Poems.* London: by J. C for William Crook, 1672. Third edition, 12mo., without first blank leaf, woodcut publisher's device of a dragon on title, some spotting on titlepage, wormed at head up to page 28 then declining to a single tiny pinhole, affecting headlines (repaired on first six leaves), closely shaved (touching some headlines and catchwords), fore margin of A6 (The Table) unevenly trimmed with slight loss on recto), early 20th century brown morocco, tooled in blind, by Riviere, from the library of James Stevens Cox (1910-1997). Maggs Bros. Ltd. 1447 - 116 2015 £240

Corlett, Charles H. *Cowboy Pete: the Autobiography of Major General Charles H. Corlett.* Santa Fe: 1974. 127 pages, illustrations, original printed wrappers, wrappers worn, previous owner's name on titlepage, internally clean, inscribed by Corlett's wife. Dumont Maps and Books of the West 130 - 37 2015 $45

Corman, Cid *For Good.* Kyoto: Origin Press, 1964. First edition, 16mo., string-tied wrappers, fine, nicely inscribed by author to poet John Ciardi, and his wife, Judith. Between the Covers Rare Books, Inc. 187 - 62 2015 $150

Corman, Cid *Hearth.* Kyoto: Origin Press, 1968. First edition, 8vo., unpaginated, signed and numbered, no. 63/100 by Corman with three signed and numbered etchings by Ryohei Tanaka with original guards, original green and gilt cloth, paper label on spine, mint green endpapers and pastedowns, dust jacket designed by Tetsuo Yamada, stapled cardboard slipcase and original stamped, franked and addressed mailing box with roundels and ties.   Maggs Bros. Ltd.   Gathering of 26 Countercultural items Oct. 2013 - 17   2015   £200

Corman, Cid *In Good Time.* Kyoto: Origin Press, 1964. First edition, one of 300 copies, small octavo, fine in wrappers, sunned, else near fine dust jacket, this copy inscribed by author to poet John Ciardi and wife Judith.   Between the Covers Rare Books, Inc.   187 - 63   2015 $250

Corneille, Pierre *Les Chefs-D'Oeuvre De P. Corneille.* Paris: P. Didot l'aine, 1814. 3 volumes, 210 x 165mm., superb contemporary deep blue polished calf by Thouvenin (stamp signed in gilt at foot of spine of volume), covers with triple gilt fillet border, central panel with large blindstamped floral frame, highlighted with gilt, raised bands, spine panels with delicate stippled and tooled cruciform ornament, gilt titling, turn-ins with cresting gilt roll, marbled endpapers, all edges gilt, one gathering somewhat foxed, otherwise splendid set in pristine condition.   Phillip J. Pirages   66 - 76   2015 $1400

Corning, Frederick Gleason *Papers from the Notes of an Engineer.* New York: Scientific Pub. Co., 1889. First compiled edition, 103 pages, maps, diagrams, plates, text illustrations, blind and gilt stamped brown cloth, rubbing to extremities, inner front hinge just starting, very good, internally fine.   Argonaut Book Shop   Holiday Season 2014 - 59   2015 $125

Cornwall, Bruce *Life Sketch of Pierre Barlow Cornwall.* San Francisco: A. M. Robertson, 1906. First edition, 8vo., three quarter leather and marbled paper, frontispiece, illustrations, light wear to spine ends, front and rare pages moderately foxed, else very good.   Buckingham Books   March 2015 - 29625   2015 $200

Cornwall, L. Peter *Ride the Sandy River.* Edmonds: Pacific Fast Mail, 1973. First edition, quarto, color frontispiece, illustrated with photos, rosters, detailed drawings, maps, timetables, etc., index, brown cloth, gilt very fine, spine faded pictorial dust jacket.   Argonaut Book Shop   Holiday Season 2014 - 60   2015 $125

Cornwell, Bernard *Sharpe's Company. Richard Sharpe and the Siege of Badajoz January to April 1812.* London: Collins, 1982. First edition, inscribed by author, fine in price clipped dust jacket.   Buckingham Books   March 2015 - 23692   2015 $875

Cornwell, Bernard *Sharpe's Gold.* London: Collins, 1981. First edition, signed by author, fine in price clipped dust jacket.   Buckingham Books   March 2015 - 9558   2015 $750

Cornwell, Bernard *Sharpe's Gold.* Viking Press, 1982. First US edition, signed by author, fine in price clipped dust jacket.   Buckingham Books   March 2015 - 37656   2015 $175

Cornwell, Bernard *Sharpe's Honour.* London: Collins, 1985. First edition, signed by author, page edges, uniformly tanned, former owner's name, else near fine in dust jacket.   Buckingham Books   March 2015 - 27543   2015 $275

Cornwell, Bernard *Sharpe's Regiment.* London: Collins, 1986. First edition, signed by author, page edges beginning to tan evenly, else fine in price clipped dust jacket.   Buckingham Books   March 2015 - 9576   2015 $250

Cornwell, Bernard *Sharpe's Regiment.* London: Collins, 1986. First edition, signed by author, page edges beginning to tan evenly, else fine in dust jacket.   Buckingham Books   March 2015 - 24175   2015 $350

Cornwell, Patricia D. *All that Remains.* London: Little Brown and Co., 1992. First edition, fine in dust jacket.   Buckingham Books   March 2015 - 19041   2015 $200

Cornwell, Patricia D. *Body of Evidence.* New York: Scribner's, 1991. First edition, fine in near fine dust jacket with few streaks on rear panel.   Beasley Books   2013 - 2015 $45

Cornwell, Patricia D. *The Body Farm.* New York: Scribners, 1994. First edition, very fine in dust jacket, signed by author.   Mordida Books   March 2015 - 009678   2015 $100

Coronado Quarto Centennial 1540-1940 - New Mexico "Land of Enchantment". Santa Fe: n.p., 1940. Colorfully illustrated wrappers, 9 x 8 inches, corners bumped, else unusually nice as the leaflet has not been folded vertically for mailing as is usually seen, lavishly illustrated.   Dumont Maps & Books of the West   131 - 30   2015 $40

A Correct Account of the Visit of His Royal Highness the Prince Regent and His Illustrious Guests to the University and City of Oxford in June 1814. Oxford: Printed and sold by N. Bliss, 1814. First edition, 8vo., half title, recent plain wrappers, very good, scarce.   John Drury Rare Books   2015 - 17682   2015 $151

Corrie, Edgar *Considerations on the Corn Laws with remarks on the Observations of Lord Sheffield on the Corn Bill....* London: John Stockdale, 1791. First edition, without half title, with 3 tables, one folding, titlepage little soiled, recently well bound in linen backed marbled boards, good copy. John Drury Rare Books March 2015 - 16429 2015 £288

Corry, John *The Detector of Quackery; or Analyser of Medical, Philosophical, Political, Dramatic, and Literary Imposture.* London: printed for B. Crosby R. Ogle, J. Hughes, C. Chapple and Ogle and Aikman, Edinburgh, 1802. 12mo., later 19th century half calf over marbled boards, spine lettered in gilt, obvious evidence of removal of label from foot of spine and from upper cover, internally in very good state of preservation, scarce. John Drury Rare Books 2015 - 20289 2015 $656

Cortez Cruz, Ricardo *Straight Outta Compton.* Boulder: Fiction Collective 2, 1992. First edition, octavo, fine in near fine dust jacket with minor rubbing, inscribed by Cortez Cruz to feminist/philosopher/critic Bell Hooks. Between the Covers Rare Books 197 - 6 2015 $375

Cory, William *Ionica with Biographical Introduction...* London: George Allen, 1905. Third edition, half title, final colophon leaf, original light blue cloth, marked, top edge gilt, Geoffrey Tillotson's copy May 46 which had belonged to Wilfred Granville. Jarndyce Antiquarian Booksellers CCVII - 159 2015 £120

Coryat, Thomas *Coryat's Crudities: Hastily Gobbled Up in Five Moneth's Travels.* London: printed by W. S., 1611. First edition, quarto, full period style dark brown morocco gilt, elaborately tooled, fine copy bound by Ramage. Honey & Wax Booksellers 2 - 1 2015 $25,000

Costard, George *The History of Astronomy, with Its Application to Geography, History and Chronology, Occasionally Exemplified by the Globes.* London: printed by James Lister...and sold by J. Newery..., 1767. First edition, 4to., half title, textual diagrams throughout, corrective slips pasted to pages 222 and 223, bound without final errata leaf, free endpapers removed, uncut in original pale blue boards, drab paper spine lettered in ms, slight wear to upper leading hinge and head of spine, front board slightly cracked, very nice in original boards. Jarndyce Antiquarian Booksellers CCXI - 75 2015 £500

Coston, W. Hilary *The Spanish-American War Volunteer: Ninth United States Volunteer Infantry Roster and Muster Biographies Cuban Sketches.* Camp Meade: published by author, 1899. Second edition, tall octavo, frontispiece, charts, photos, gray decorated cloth, substantial bump at bottom of front board bit of edgewear, modest cracking at edges of hinges at frontispiece and bookplate, remnant on front pastedown, still nice, very good. Between the Covers Rare Books 197 - 108 2015 $1500

Cotes, Roger *Hydrostatical and Pneumatical Lectures.* London: for the editor and sold by S. Austen, 1738. First edition, 5 engraved folding plates, contemporary sprinkled calf, neatly rebacked, name clipped from top corner of front endpaper and repaired with old paper very good. Joseph J. Felcone Inc. Science, Medicine and Technology - 19 2015 $1200

Cother, E. *A Serious Proposal for Promoting Lawful and Honourable Marriage. Address'd to the Unmarried of both Sexes.* London: printed for W. Owen, 1750. First edition, 8vo., first and last leaves rather dust soiled, short closed tear in title (no loss), old maroon half morocco over marbled boards, neatly rebacked to match, gilt lines and old label, good copy, very scarce. John Drury Rare Books 2015 - 25344 2015 $2622

Cotten, Bruce *Housed on the Third Floor Being a Collection of North Caroliniana.* Baltimore: Horn-Shafer Co., 1941. Limited to 250 copies, signed and inscribed by author for F. C. Latrobe, Sept. 4th 1941, original brown cloth with gilt title to spine, very subtle damp stain to front cover, offsetting to endpages and few small spots of foxing to interior, overall clean and bright, 100 facsimiles impressions of titlepages, 66 pages plus 101 plates, very good. The Kelmscott Bookshop 11 - 11 2015 $350

Cotton, Charles *Scarronnides; or, Virgile Travestie.* London: by E. Cotes for Henry Brome, 1666. 1665. Reprint of Book 1, first edition of book 4, 8vo., first ad last leaves blank except for bookseller's woodcut device of a crowned cannon, long closed tear from paper flaw down D5 (touching seven lines of text), small spot at head of E1, contemporary sheep ruled in blind, smooth spine with red morocco and gilt label, no pastedowns, parts of two printed leaves from 17th century English 8vo. Bible as binder's waste (lower headcap torn, joints little rubbed), armorial bookplate of Hon. Shute Barrington, Bp. of Salisbury, from the library of James Stevens Cox (1910-1997). Maggs Bros. Ltd. 1447 - 118 2015 £700

Cotton, Charles *The Wonders of the Peake.* London: W. Everingham and Tho. Whitledge, 1694. Third edition, 8vo., engraved vignette of cannon on title, first sheet browned, rest less so with some spotting, A6 with two holes from paper flaw (affecting a few letters), red sprinkled edges have occasionally spread onto leaf and a number of lower edges uncut, contemporary sheep (small wormtrail to front board and large scuff on rear board), lower joint split at head, pastedowns unstuck, Lady Anne Coventry's signature, from the library of James Stevens Cox (1910-1997). Maggs Bros. Ltd. 1447 - 117 2015 £300

Cottrell, Sue *Hoof Beats North and South Horses and Horsemen of the civil War.* New York: 1975. First edition, fine in fine, unclipped dust jacket, scarce, illustrations by author. Bookworm & Silverfish 2015 - 6017988750 2015 $100

Coues, Elliott *History of the Expedition Under the Command of Lewis and Clark.* Francis P. Harper, 1893. New edition, faithfully reprinted from the only authorized edition of 1814, 4 volumes, nicely rebound in brown cloth, ex-library with small blindstamp of Huntington Memorial Library on titlepage of each volume, 2 large folding maps professionally reinforced, 4 leaves professionally tipped in at front of volume I, else near fine. Buckingham Books March 2015 - 34449 2015 $2500

Count Teleki. A Story of Modern Jewish Life and Customs. London: Frederick Warne; New York: Scribner, Welford, 1869. First edition, 8vo., original decorated terra cotta cloth, gilt lettering, cloth little worn and soiled, some light foxing, very good. The Brick Row Book Shop Miscellany 67 - 21 2015 $1250

Country Farm. New York: G. P. Putnam, 1984. 6 1/2 inch square, peepshow, with peephole on cover and viewer can see 8 tiered, detailed three dimensional farm scene, wonderfully illustrated in color by Tomie De Paolo. Aleph-bet Books, Inc. 109 - 347 2015 $150

Country Life Illustrated Volume I. No. 1. London: Hudson & Kearns, 1897. Original first issue dated 8th Jan. 1896, large folio, illustrations, unbound and stapled as issued, very good state of preservation. John Drury Rare Books 2015 - 25250 2015 $133

The Country Spectator. Gainsborough: printed by Messrs. Mozley and Co. and sold by Todd, York: Tessyman...., 1792. 8vo., comprising all 33 issues and including half title, with bold ink inscription on title page (Job Lousley's book Hampstead Norris Berks 1842), very scarce, well bound in early/mid 20th century cloth backed boards, spine simply labelled, excellent, crisp copy. John Drury Rare Books 2015 - 26136 2015 $874

The Country Well governed; or, Plain Questions on the Perplexed State of Parties in Opposition. London: Hatchard and Son, 1830. First edition, 8vo., half title, recently well bound in linen backed marbled boards, lettered, very good presentation copy, inscribed "With the author's compts.". John Drury Rare Books March 2015 - 22720 2015 £306

Courtney, Abraham *The Moderate Use of Intoxicating Drinks, Being the Substance of a Lecture Delivered at a Meeting of the Isle of Thanet Temperance Society...* London: published by Permission of the author by The New British and Foreign Temeprance Society, n.d., 1840. First edition, 12mo., prelim leaf misnumbered, few page numerals just shaved, recent plain wrappers, good copy, rare. John Drury Rare Books 2015 - 20677 2015 $133

The Courtship, Merry Marriage and Feast of Cock Robin and Jenny Wren to which is added the Doleful Death of Cock Robin. New York: Holiday House, 1935. 16mo., cloth backed pictorial boards, fine, illustrations by Anne Heyneman, scarce. Aleph-Bet Books, Inc. 108 - 101 2015 $225

Cousin, Victor *Report on the State of Public Instruction in Prussia; Addressed to the County De Montalivet, Peer of France, Minister of Public Instruction and Ecclesiastical Affairs.* London: Effingham Wilson, 1834. First edition in English, 8vo., half title, 5 engraved folding plates, 2 large folding charts, corner torn from one leaf not affecting printed surface, small 19th century inkstamp of Bibliotheca Edinensis, original dark green cloth backed boards, printed spine label, good, uncut. John Drury Rare Books March 2015 - 17974 2015 $266

Cousins, Sheila *To Beg I Am Ashamed.* Allahabad: Kitabistan, 1938. First edition thus, 8vo., original crimson cloth , lettered in black on spine an cover, some very slight fading at top and bottom of spine, otherwise sound, clean, very good+ in slightly chipped and nicked, near very good jacket with inch or more loss at lower spine, still handsome. Any Amount of Books 2015 - C15741 2015 £240

Cousteau, Jacques *Whales.* New York: H. Abrams, 1988. First edition, 4to., this copy signed by author on special bound-in signature leaf, fine in dust jacket. Beasley Books 2013 - 2015 $300

Covarrubias, Miguel *Negro Drawings.* New York: Alfred A. Knopf, 1921. First edition, one of 100 numbered copies with original pen drawing and signed by artist, quarto, dark blue cloth backstrip over royal blue cloth boards stamped in gilt, excellent copy very scarce, housed in custom blue cloth slipcase. Heritage Book Shop Holiday 2014 - 44 2015 $5000

Coventry Sabbath Observance Society *An Appeal to the Friends of Religion on the Establishment of Societies for Promoting the observance of the Christian Sabbath.* London: Seeley & Co., Wightman & Cramp; H. Merridew Coventry, 1829. First (only?)edition, 8vo., 16 pages, preserved in recent wrappers, printed title label on upper cover, very good, apparently very rare. John Drury Rare Books March 2015 - 21587 2015 $266

Coventry, Andrew *Notes on the Culture and Cropping of Arable Land.* Edinburgh: printed by J. Johnstone, 1812. First edition, 2nd issue, 8vo., half title, appendix, well bound in blue cloth, printed paper label on spine, very good. John Drury Rare Books 2015 - 14440 2015 $89

Cowan, Robert Ernest *A Bibliography of the History of California and the Pacific West 1510-1906.* Columbus: Long's College Book Co., 1952. Reprinted from the edition of Book club of California in 1914, quarto, original peach cloth, gilt lettered spine, slightest of rubbing to corners, fine. Argonaut Book Shop   Holiday Season 2014 - 61   2015 $150

Cowan, Robert Granniss *A bibliography of the History of California 1510-1930. Volume IV.* Los Angeles: Torrez Press, 1964. First edition, quarto, cloth backed boards, paper spine label, small light stain near fore-edge of front cover, spine area slightly faded, near fine.   Argonaut Book Shop   Holiday Season 2014 - 62   2015 $50

Coward, Noel   1899-1973 *The Plays of Noel Coward: First Series: Sirocco/Home Chat/The Queen was in the Parlour.* Garden City: Doubleday & Doran, 1928. First edition, 8vo., original grey cloth lettered grey on black label on spine and cover, signed by author, spine label slgthtly chipped, slight surface wear covers slightly bumped, else very good.   Any Amount of Books   2015 - A08342   2015   £220

Cowe, James *Religious and Philanthropic Tracts...* London: J. Robson, 1797. First edition, 8vo., including half title, entirely unopened and uncut in original blue wrappers, inscribed 'From the author", minor edge wear and staining to wrappers and defective at spine (loss of paper), overall near fine in original state, very scarce.   John Drury Rare Books   2015 - 26330   2015 $787

Cowe, Martha *Witchcraft: Catalogue of the Witchcraft Collection in the Cornell University Library.* Millwood: Kto Press, 1977. First edition, 4to., original crimson cloth lettered gilt at spine, about fine.   Any Amount of Books   2015 - A64805   2015   £280

Cowley, Abraham   1618-1667 *Poemata Latina.* London: T. Roycroft, Impensis Jo. Martyn, 1668. First collected edition, 8vo., engraved frontispiece by Faithorne, small hole to blank inner gutter of O1-O4 some occasional light soiling, contemporary blind ruled calf, red morocco label to spine (half of label has perished), from the library of James Stevens Cox (1910-1997), contemporary signature of Benjamin Spann, a contemporary signature of Richard Inett, contemporary signature of John Leslie, early18th century auction or fixed price lot number, acquisition note of John Loveday, by descent to Loveday family library at Willamscote, Banbury, Oxfordshire dispersed in the 1960's.   Maggs Bros. Ltd.   1447 - 119   2015   £240

Cowley, Abraham   1618-1667 *The Works of Mr. Abraham Cowley.* London: by J(ohn) M(acock) for Henry Herringman, 1668. First edition, small folio, engraved portrait by William Faithorne, stain along lower margin of A1, inksplash on H1, margins of H1-H4 creased (by binder?), uncut corner of (2)Q4 folded, contemporary calf, spine with partial remains of red morocco label (heavily rubbed, covers scuffed and worn, corners worn, endleaves dusty, lower front third of front flyleaf torn away, pastedowns coming loose), ink initials A B H on front flyleaf, handsome engraved bookplate of Dominick Trant has come detached from pastedown and loosely inserted, from the library of James Stevens Cox (1910-1997).   Maggs Bros. Ltd.   1447 - 120   2015   £200

Cox, Nicholas *The Gentleman's Recreation.* London: by Jos. Phillips and Hen. Rodes (part 4 Oxford by L. Lichfield for Nicholas Cox), 1685-1686. Third edition, 4 engraved plates, engraved frontispiece by W. Sherwin, large folding engraved plate (old repair to a long tear), double page plate of hawking and double page plate of fish, both by Dolle, lightly browned, light marginal dampstaining throughout, minor worming to top of gatherings C-G that touches the headlines and occasionally the first line of text, contemporary calf, front cover with 19th century arms of Duke of Sutherland and blindstamped to front cover, covers worn, front cover detached, spine split at head and tail; armorial bookplate of Sir John Levenson-Gower (1675-1609) 1st Baron Gower by descent to John Levenson-Gower (1694-1754, 1st Earl Gower with early 19th century armorial bookplate, by descent to George Granville Levenson-Gower, 1st Duke of Sutherland with his arms stamped in blind on front cover, from the library of James Stevens Cox (1910-1997). Maggs Bros. Ltd.   1447 - 121   2015   £1500

Cox, Palmer *The Brownies Around the World.* Century Co., 1894. First edition, 4to., glazed pictorial boards, very slight rubbing, else near fine in dust jacket frayed on edges and folds but very good, particularly nice.   Aleph-bet Books, Inc.   109 - 109   2015 $1250

Cox, Palmer *The Brownies at Home.* New York: Century Co., 1893. First edition, 4to., glazed pictorial boards, fine in near fine dust jacket, illustrations on every page, beautiful copy, rare in such nice dust jacket.   Aleph-bet Books, Inc. 109 - 110   2015 $1500

Cox, Thomas *Learning a Necessary Accomplishment for All Men. A Sermon Preach'd at the Parish Church of Felstead in Essex, on Tuesday the 30th of August 1709.* London: printed for W. Carter, 1709. Only edition, 4to., title and last page just bit soiled, margins cut close, just shaving some headlines and side-notes, several catchwords cropped, last line on 3 pages cropped or partially lost, preserved in recent plain wrappers, very rare.   John Drury Rare Books   2015 - 18503   2015 $133

Coxe, George Harmon *Four Frightened Women.* New York: Knopf, 1939. First edition, fine in very good dust jacket with chip at top of darkened spine and some scattered nicks on front panel.   Mordida Books   March 2015 - 011522   2015 $135

Coxe, George Harmon *The Jade Venus.* New York: Knopf, 1945. First edition, bookplate on front pastedown, fine in dust jacket.   Mordida Books   March 2015 - 010449   2015 $100

Coxe, George Harmon *The Lady is Afraid.* New York: Knopf, 1940. First edition, fine in dust jacket with nicks and tiny wear at spine ends and along front flap fold.   Mordida Books   March 2015 - 010158   2015 $200

Coxe, George Harmon *Lady Killer.* New York: Knopf, 1949. First edition, fine in dust jacket with tiny wear at corners.   Mordida Books   March 2015 - 010453   2015 $85

Coxe, George Harmon *The Reluctant Heiress.* New York: Knopf, 1965. First edition, advance review copy with review slip laid in, also laid in is Typed personal note from the desk of George Harmon Coxe dated 2 29 68 and signed by Coxe requesting addressee send his copy of this book to author for him to sign, fine in dust jacket.   Mordida Books   March 2015 - 010442   2015 $100

Coxe, John Redman *Practical Observations on Vaccination or Inoculation for the Cow-Pox.* Philadelphia: James Humphreys, 1802. First edition, 8vo., color frontispiece, original two toned boards, paper spine chipped, title foxed, small piece lacking from outer margin of title leaf, fore and bottom margins uncut, partially unopened, very scarce.   M & S Rare Books, Inc.   97 - 82   2015 $750

Coxe, William *Letter to John Benett, Esq. of Pyt House, Wilts. on his Essay relative to the Commutation of Tythes to which was adjudged the Bedfordian Gold Medal by the Bath and West of England Society...* Salisbury: printed and sold by Brodie and Dowding on the Canal n.d., 1815. First edition, 8vo., preserved in modern wrappers with printed title label on upper cover, very good.   John Drury Rare Books   2015 - 20223   2015 $80

Coyner, David H. *The Lost Trappers: a Collection of Interesting Scenes and Events in the Rocky Mountains.* Cincinnati: J. A. & U. P. James, 1847. First edition, 12mo., recased with original spine and blind tooled covers relaid, original spine title gilt, foxed throughout, else very good, scarce.   Buckingham Books   March 2015 - 27293   2015 $750

Crabbe, George *Peter Grimes from the Borough.* Llandogo: Old Stile Press, 1985. 90/220 copies signed by artist, printed on all-rag mouldmade paper, 20 linocuts in green and brown by J. Martin Pitts, imperial 8vo., original beige canvas with design in green by Pitts, backstrip lettered in green, top edge green, cloth and patterned paper slipcase, fine.   Blackwell's Rare Books   B179 - 204   2015   £60

Cracking the Color Line Non-Violent Direct Action Methods of Eliminating Racial Discrimination. New York: Congress of Racial Equality, 1960. First edition, 8vo., hardcover.   Beasley Books   2013 - 2015 $45

Craig, James Gibson *Answer to Dr. Mitchell's Statement of Facts.* Edinburgh: Neill & Co., 1808. 4to., final leaf little smudged and with tear, preserved in modern wrappers with printed label on upper cover, apparently rare.   John Drury Rare Books   March 2015 - 24885   2015   £266

Craig, John *Newton at the Mint.* Cambridge: Cambridge University Press, 1946. First edition, 8vo., 128 pages, frontispiece medal of Newton, 3 plates, index, neatly written notes in pen, red cloth, blindstamped cover illustration and silver stamped spine title, dust jacket, rear hinge split (now preserved neatly in Mylar), bookplate, generally very good.   Jeff Weber Rare Books   178 - 834   2015 $40

Craig, John C. *The Recipe Book of Lillie Hitchcock Coit.* Berkeley: Friends of the Bancroft Library, 1998. First edition, one of 1800 copies, frontispiece, stiff wrappers printed in black, very fine.   Argonaut Book Shop   Holiday Season 2014 - 64   2015 $60

Craig, John R. *Ranching with Lords and Commons or Twenty Years on the Range.* Toronto: William Briggs, 1903. First edition, 8vo., illustrations, plates, former owner's inked name on front flyleaf, white ink on cover unchipped but white ink to spine panel moderately chipped, overall much better than most copies, very good, tight copy.   Buckingham Books   March 2015 - 30843   2015 $2000

Craig, Philip R. *A Beautiful Place to Die.* New York: Scribner, 1989. First edition, small stain bottom of page edges, otherwise fine in dust jacket.   Mordida Books   March 2015 - 009473   2015 $85

Craigie, Dorothy *Victorian Detective Fiction: a Catalogue of the Collection Made by Graham Greene and Dorothy Glover.* London: Bodley Head, 1906. First edition, one of 500 numbered copies signed by Greene and Glover, publisher's announcement and order form laid-in fine in fine dust jacket.   Mordida Books   March 2015 - 009490   2015 $500

Crais, Robert *The First Rule.* New York: Mysterious Bookshop, 2010. First edition, one of 26 lettered copies signed by author, fine in quarter leather and marbled boards and transparent dust jacket. Buckingham Books   March 2015 - 28607   2015 $275

Crais, Robert *Lullaby Town.* New York: Bantam Books, 1992. First edition, presentation inscription by author, laid in is typed letter and envelope dated April 20 1992, to same collector, fine in dust jacket. Buckingham Books   March 2015 - 28955   2015 $1000

Crais, Robert *Lullaby Town.* New York: Bantam, 1992. First edition, fine in dust jacket with slightly faded spine. Mordida Books   March 2015 - 011018   2015 $450

Crais, Robert *Lullaby Town.* New York: Bantam Books, 1992. First edition, signed by author, fine and unread in fine dust jacket, from the collection of Duke Collier. Royal Books   36 - 153   2015 $450

Crais, Robert *The Monkey's Raincoat.* London: Piatkus, 1987. First hardcover (UK) edition, presentation by author, fine in dust jacket. Buckingham Books   March 2015 - 28957   2015 $650

Crane, Hart   1899-1932 *The Bridge.* Paris: Black Sun Press, 1930. First edition, one of 200 numbered copies on Holland paper, 4to., original white printed wrappers, original glassine, publisher's silver gilt paper covered slipcase, touch of discoloration to glassine where slipcase accommodates finger pulls, original silver foil slipcase edge little cracked at head of spine, otherwise exceptionally fine, photos by Walker Evans. James S. Jaffe Rare Books   Modern American Poetry - 51   2015 $15,000

Crane, Hart   1899-1932 *Three Poems by Hart Crane from The Bridge.* Bremen and New York: Red Angel Press, 2004. First edition, oblong quarto, original ecru cloth lettered in silver, original prospectus, fine. Honey & Wax Booksellers   2 - 23   2015 $1000

Crane, Hart   1899-1932 *White Buildings: Poems.* New York: Boni & Liveright, 1926. First edition, 8vo., original cloth backed decorated paper over boards, dust jacket, very fine, virtually as new, extremely rare thus. James S. Jaffe Rare Books   Modern American Poetry - 50   2015 $10,000

Crane, Richard Teller *The Autobiography of Richard Teller Crane.* privately published, 1927. First edition, illustrated with photos, pebbled black cloth embossed and gilt stamped, bit musty, otherwise near fine. Beasley Books 2013 - 2015 $150

Crane, Stephen   1871-1900 *The Black Riders and Other Lines.* Boston: Copeland and Day, 1895. First edition, small 8vo., original boards printed in black with floral design, exceptional copy, in specially made cloth dust jacket and slipcase, spine lettered gilt, from the collection of Gavin H. Fryer. Bertram Rota Ltd.   308 Part II - 146   2015   £700

Crane, Stephen   1871-1900 *Maggie. A Girl of the Streets.* New York: printed for author, 1893. First edition, one of 35 known copies, Crane had 1100 copies printed but only two were sold through Brentano's, bound in paper wrappers which have been expertly restored, original front wrapper has been backed and missing areas have been filled in, spine and rear wrapper are modern, but have colored to match original front wrapper, edges of first few pages are chipped and several corners clipped, few spots of foxing to interior, otherwise remains very clean, housed in modern clamshell box with rounded leather spine titled in gilt, very good. The Kelmscott Bookshop   11 - 12   2015 $12,000

Crane, Stephen   1871-1900 *Maggie: a Girl of the Streets.* New York: printed for the author, 1893. First edition, one of 1100 copies of which less than 50 are known to exist today, rebound in light tan cloth with original wrappers bound into rear of text, some light soiling to titlepage and last few pages of text, discreet repairs to edges of titlepage, few faint hints of scattered spotting, tiny nicks to top corners of pages 3-7, otherwise bright and clean interior, lovely copy. B & B Rare Books, Ltd.   2015 - 2015 $8500

Crane, Stephen   1871-1900 *The Red Badge of Courage.* New York: D. Appleton and Co., 1896. 12mo., original cloth stamped in red, black and gold, light rubbing and darkening of binding, title leaf printed in red and black, last two leaves of text slightly damaged in outer margins, very rare. M & S Rare Books, Inc.   97 - 83   2015 $425

Crane, Walter   1845-1915 *Triplets. Baby's Own Opera. Baby's Bouquet and the Baby's Own Aesop.* London: Routledge, 1899. Number 17 of 20 copies printed on Japan vellum, square 4to., original buckram, spine label, covers soiled, interior tight and fine, printed in full color on vellum with wide margins, paper quality is fine, color reproductions particularly beautiful, rare. Aleph-Bet Books, Inc. 108 - 114   2015 $1500

Cranidge, John *A Mirror for the Burgesses and Commonalty of the City of Bristol...* Bristol: printed by Jonathan Bailer & Co. for the author and sold at his Academy Upper Easton, n.d., 1818. First edition, 8vo., well bound in early 20th century quarter vellum with crimson morocco lettering piece, very good. John Drury Rare Books   March 2015 - 18375   2015 $266

Craven, W. F. *The Army Air Forces in World War II.* Chicago: University of Chicago Press, 1948. First edition, 7 volumes, original blue cloth lettered gilt at spine and covers, sound, very good in used, slightly rubbed and chipped dust jackets, some with larger tears (volume 1 lacks jacket). Any Amount of Books   2015 - C8450   2015   £220

Crawford, Alan   *By Hammer and Hand: the Arts and Crafts Movement in Birmingham.*   Birmingham: Birmingham Museums and Art Gallery, 1984. Square 8vo., stiff paper wrappers, black and white illustrations.   Oak Knoll Books 306 - 16   2015 $100

Crawford, Bryce L.   *Cultivating Sherlock Holmes.*   La Crosse: Sumac Press, 1978. First edition, one of 400 copies, fine, in fine dust jacket, laid in is a copy of 'the Norwegian Explorers of Minnesota... (1982)', fine.   Beasley Books   2013 - 2015 $150

Crawford, C. H.   *Scenes of Earlier Days in Crossing the Plains to Oregon and Experiences of Western Life.*   J. T. Studdert, 1898. First edition, cloth covered boards, portrait and illustrations, some light edgewear, else clean, near fine, very scarce.   Buckingham Books   March 2015 - 34524   2015 $750

Crawford, Francis Marion   1854-1909   *Uncanny Tales.* London: T. Fisher Unwin, 1911. First edition, 8vo., original blue cloth, lettered gilt at spine and front cover, neat name on front endpaper with bookplate and inscription, blind-stamped on titlepage 'presentation copy' with some wear at top inside hinge, some rubbing at edges and spine, little used and slightly worn, very good- with text clean.   Any Amount of Books   March 2015 - Ca14287   2015   £350

Crawford, Iain   *Scare the Gentle Citizen.*   London: Hammond, 1966. First edition, some light spotting on page edges, otherwise near fine in very good dust jacket with darkened spine, chipping at top of spine and several tiny closed tears.   Mordida Books   March 2015 - 010754   2015 $150

Crawford, Jack   *Camp Fire Sparks.*   Charles H. Kerr, 1893. First edition, printed wrappers, 48 pages, portrait on front wrapper, closed tear to titlepage and next page, address of original bookseller (?) lightly stamped on lower portion of front wrapper and titlepage, otherwise clean, tight copy, scarce, fragile work.   Buckingham Books   March 2015 - 36736   2015 $275

Crawford, Medorem   *Journal of Medorem Crawford. an Account Of His Trip Across the Plains with the Oregon Pioneers of 1842.*   State Job Office, 1897. First separate edition, 8vo., front cover lightly foxed, rear cover missing, internally clean with light corner crease to top edges, else very good.   Buckingham Books   March 2015 - 37483   2015 $350

Crawfurd, George   *A Sketch of the Rise and Progress of the Trades' House of Glasgow its Constitution, Funds & Bye-laws.*   Glasgow: printed by Bell & Bain, 1858. First edition, folding plate, partially unopened in wavy rained dark green cloth, slightly rubbed at head of spine, very good. Jarndyce Antiquarian Booksellers   CCXI - 77   2015   £60

Crawley, Michael J.   *Natural Enemies the Population Biology of Predators Parasites & Diseases.*   London: Blackwall Scientific, 1992. First edition, very good+, some wrinkle at upper right front corner, tight, clean text, scarce. Stephen Lupack   March 2015 - 2015 $95

Creasey, John   *Blue Mask Strikes Again.*   Philadelphia: J. B. Lippincott, 1940. First American edition, very good pus in like (scarce) dust jacket, jacket bright and complete, minor rubbing and nicking at extremities, from the collection of Duke Collier.   Royal Books   36 - 154   2015 $325

Creeley, Robert   *The Class of '47.*   New York: Bouwerie Editions, 1973. First edition, one of 100 copies numbered and signed by author and artist, 4to., illustrations by Joe Brainard, original wrappers, very fine.   James S. Jaffe Rare Books   Many Happy Returns - 234   2015 $350

Creeley, Robert   *Le Fou. Poems.*   Columbus: Golden Goose Press, 1952. First edition, scarce first book, limited to 500 copies, 12mo., frontispiece by Ashley Bryan, original stiff wrappers, opalescent tissue dust jacket, top of spine and bottom fore-tips slightly bumped, otherwise very fine. James S. Jaffe Rare Books   Modern American Poetry - 52   2015 $1500

Creeley, Robert   *The Island.*   New York: Charles Scribner's Sons, 1963. First edition, 8vo., original cloth, dust jacket, spine discolored, top edge faintly foxed, otherwise fine in slightly rubbed dust jacket with bit of wear to head and heel of spine, presentation copy inscribed by author to his mother.   James S. Jaffe Rare Books   Modern American Poetry - 53   2015 $1500

Creeley, Robert   *Numbers.*   West Germany: Edition Domberger Stuttgart-Schmela Dusseldorf, 1968. First edition, one of 2500 copies signed by author and artist, small 8vo., illustrations by Robert Indiana, original printed wrappers, fine copy of the regular issue.   James S. Jaffe Rare Books   Modern American Poetry - 55   2015 $1750

Creeley, Robert   *The Collected Poems of Robert Creeley 1945-1975.*   Berkeley: University of California Press, 1975. First edition, thick 8vo., original cloth, dust jacket, cloth-bound issue, signed by author, fine.   James S. Jaffe Rare Books   Modern American Poetry - 56   2015 $350

Creeley, Robert *Words. Poems.* New York: Scribner's, 1967. First edition, 8vo., original cloth, top corner bit bumped, horizontal crease on front cover, otherwise fine, dust jacket trifle rubbed, presentation copy inscribed by author for his mother. James S. Jaffe Rare Books Modern American Poetry - 54   2015 $1500

Cresson, Elliott *Reports of the Board of Managers of the Pennsylvania Colonization Society....* Philadelphia: printed for the Society, London: John Miller, 1831. First edition, 8vo., 48 pages, recent marbled boards lettered on spine, very good, uncommon. John Drury Rare Books   March 2015 - 24424   2015   £306

Cresy, Edward *Report to the General Board of Health on a Preliminary Inquiry into the Sewerage, Drainage and Supply of Water and the Sanitary Condition report of the Inhabitants of the Town of Braintree.* London: printed by W. Clowes & Sons for HMSO, 1850. First edition, folding engraved map, old waterstain in lower margin of titlepage, stitched as issued, good. John Drury Rare Books   2015 - 26095   2015 $133

Crews, Harry *This Thing Don't Lead to Heaven.* New York: William Morrow, 1970. First edition, inscribed by author to Paul Bartel, fine in dust jacket. Ed Smith Books 83 - 13   2015 $350

Crews, Judson *The Southern Temper.* Waco: Motive, 1946. First edition, inscribed by author in 1952 to Mary Shore, painter and friend of Charles Olson, near fine in stapled wrappers and very good, dampstained dust jacket with two small holes on rear panel. Ken Lopez, Bookseller 164 - 41   2015 $125

Crichton, Michael *The Terminal Man.* New York: Knopf, 1972. First edition, fine in dust jacket. Mordida Books March 2015 - 008254   2015 $85

Crispin, Edmund *The Long Divorce.* London: Gollancz, 1961. First edition, fine in dust jacket with slightly faded spine. Mordida Books   March 2015 - 010012   2015 $400

Cristoforis, Luigi De *Relazione Letta Alla Camera Di Commercio E D'Industria Della Provincia Di Milano... Alcune Macchine da lui Specialmente esaminate all'Esposizione di Londra del 1851...* Milano: presso Giuseppe Bernardoni, 1852. First edition, 8vo., folding lithographed frontispiece, apart from some minor light foxing, clean copy, recent mottled boards, appealing copy, rare. Marlborough Rare Books Ltd.   List 49 - 5   2015   £300

Critien, L. *The Malta Almanack and Directory 1890 to 1907.* Valetta: L. Critien, Strada San Giovanni, Small 8vo., 6 volumes, each about 150 pages, ex-British Foreign Office library with some slight library markings, occasional stamp, gilt numbers on spine, else very good+ clean set in green cloth with clean text, highly uncommon. Any Amount of Books   2015 - A85497   2015   £275

Crittenden, H. H. *The Crittenden Memoirs.* G. P. Putnam's Sons, 1936. First edition, 8vo., original brown cloth, gold stamped front cover and spine, frontispiece, illustrations, chart, some light foxing to few prelim pages, else near fine, tight copy, scarce. Buckingham Books   March 2015 - 29501   2015 $450

Crofton, Francis Blake *Hairbreadth Escapes of Major Menda...* Philadelphia: Hubbard Brothers, 1889. First edition, octavo, 15 full page black and white illustrations by Bennett, titlepage printed in orange and black, original bevel edged chocolate brown pictorial cloth, front and spine panels stamped in black and gold, light green floral patterned endpapers. L. W. Currey, Inc.   Boy's Adventure Fiction 2015 - 32   2015 $250

Crofts, Freeman Wills *Anything to Declare?* London: Hodder & Stoughton, 1957. First edition, fine in dust jacket with slightly darkened spine, tiny wear at top of spine and lightly soiled back panel. Mordida Books   March 2015 - 008783   2015 $250

Crofts, Freeman Wills *Death of a Train.* London: Hodder & Stoughton, 1946. First edition, fine in very good dust jacket, soiled with nicks at spine ends, wear along edges, chips at corners and several short closed tears. Mordida Books   March 2015 - 000559   2015 $175

Crofts, Freeman Wills *Double Tragedy. An Inspector French Story.* New York: Dodd, Mead & Co., 1943. First US edition, 8vo., light offsetting to rear endpapers from a news clipping, else fine, bright copy in bright, unfaded dust jacket, lightly rubbed at head of spine and to top edge of front panel. Buckingham Books   March 2015 - 23245 2015 $400

Crofts, Freeman Wills *Fear Comes to Chalfont.* New York: Dodd Mead & Co., 1942. First US edition, fine in dust jacket with light wear to spine ends. Buckingham Books March 2015 - 21139   2015 $450

Crofts, Freeman Wills *The Four Gospels in One Story.* London: Longmans, Green, 1949. First edition, some light spotting on endpapers, otherwise fine in price clipped dust jacket with some scattered light spotting. Mordida Books March 2015 - 000557   2015 $100

Crofts, Freeman Wills *Golden Ashes.* London: Hodder & Stoughton Ltd., 1940. First edition, moderate wear to cover, non-authorial gift inscription, else very good in fine, bright dust jacket, exceptional copy.   Buckingham Books   March 2015 - 25854   2015 $2500

Crofts, Freeman Wills *Man Overboard.* London: Collins Crime Club, 1936. First edition, export copy without price on spine, small stain on front cover, otherwise fine in lightly soiled dust jacket with chips at corners, small chip along front fold edge and couple of short closed tears.   Mordida Books   March 2015 - 000558   2015 $850

Crofts, Freeman Wills *Silence for the Murderer.* New York: Dodd Mead, 1948. First edition, fine in near fine dust jacket with slightly faded spine, nicks at spine ends and chip at lower corner back panel.   Mordida Books   March 2015 - 010745   2015 $150

Crommelin, May *Louis Wain's Little Soldiers.* London: Hutchinson, 1916. First edition, 39 color illustrations by Louis Wain, original pictorial boards, bookplate on front pastedown, small faint stain to front cover, text block slightly bumped at top corner, very good, scarce in such bright condition.   Peter Ellis, Bookseller   2014 - 016670   2015   £350

Cronin, A. J. *Hatter's Castle.* London: Victor Gollancz, 1931. First edition, crown 8vo., original black cloth, backstrip lettered in gilt, light dust soiling to top edge, Dennis Wheatley's Frank Pape designed bookplate with further bookplate to flyleaf, dust jacket with backstrip panel touch faded and some light dust soiling overall, little fraying to edges and short tear to head of rear panel, original Book Society band, very good.   Blackwell's Rare Books   B179 - 141   2015   £800

Cronin, A. J. *The Keys to the Kingdom.* Boston: Little Brown, 1941. Fourth printing, 8vo., very good, lacking dust jacket, this the copy of Grace Hall Hemingway (Ernest's mother) with her name and address in her hand.   Beasley Books   2013 - 2015 $45

Cros, Charles *The Salt Herring.* New York: Gotham Book Mart, 1971. Limited to 326 copies of which 300 are numbered, this is no. 90, illustrations by Edward Gorey, signed by Gorey, 24mo., near fine in original printed wrappers, minimal stain at spine.   By the Book, L. C.   44 - 93   2015 $250

Crosby, T. *This is Tomorrow.* London: Whitehchapel Gallery, 1956. First edition, issued in an edition of 1300 copies, light paint-smudging to front and rear covers with few light smudges to first few pages, corners slightly rubbed, two very faint short creases, otherwise very good, ring bound printed wrappers.   Any Amount of Books   2015 - C1949   2015   £750

Cross, Amanda *The Question of Max.* New York: Knopf, 1976. First edition, fine in price clipped dust jacket.   Mordida Books   March 2015 - 000570   2015 $75

Cross, Joe *Cattle Clatter. A History of Cattle From the Creation to the Texas in Centennial in 1936.* Walker Publications, 1938. First edition, 8vo., pictorial cloth, frontispiece, illustrations, scarce, lightly rubbed at spine ends, light foxing to few prelim pages and former owner's inked name and date at top of front flyleaf, else very good, tight copy.   Buckingham Books   March 2015 - #2896   2015 $400

Cross, Odo *The Snail that Climbed the Eiffel Tower and Other Stories.* London: John Lehmann, 1947. First edition, first issue binding of cloth backed color pictorial boards, quarto, 86 pages, 6 color plates, black and white headpieces and tailpieces by John Minton, endpapers and color cover design by John Minton, fine in very good, price clipped dust jacket with thumbnail sized chip to base of spine.   Peter Ellis, Bookseller   2014 - 018567   2015   £350

Cross, Thomas *The Autobiography of a Stage Coachman.* London: Hurst & Blackett, 1861. First edition, 3 volumes, half titles, frontispieces, 4 pages ads volume II, some occasional slight spotting, original red morocco grained cloth, boards blocked in blind, spine blocked and lettered gilt, slightly dulled, few small marks to boards, volume III little unevenly faded, overall very good, scarce.   Jarndyce Antiquarian Booksellers   CCXI - 78   2015   £480

Crossman, Francis Geach *A Sermon Preached in Behalf of the Distressed manufacturers at Queen's Square Chapel, Bath on Sunday the 11th Day of February 1827.* Bath: printed by and for Anne E. Binns, London: Hamilton Adams and Co., 1827. Only edition, 8vo., 20 pages, sewn into old (original?) wrappers, uncut, very good, apparently rare.   John Drury Rare Books   2015 - 18391   2015 $89

Crouch, John *The Man in the Moon, Discovering a World of Knavery Under the Sun...* Colophon: London: printed in the World in the Moon for J. Jones..., 1663. Small 4to., (8) pages, occasionally little spotted and marked with small tear from fore-edge of A3, disbound, strip of old paper pasted along spine as a strengthener, from the library of James Stevens Cox (1910-1997).   Maggs Bros. Ltd.   1447 - 122   2015   £750

Crouch, Nathaniel *Admirable Curiosities Rarities and Wonders in England Scotland and Ireland.* London: for Nath. Crouch, 1697. Fifth edition, 12mo., engraved frontispiece, 6 woodcut illustrations lightly browned, printer's crease across B10 (touching three lines of text) and F2 (touching to lines), fore-margin of G2 little frayed, small piece torn away from corner of G4 and G6 (with loss to ends of four lines), fore margin of C1 creased and with some light staining to E11 and G9, mid 19th century half calf and marbled boards, label of Upham and Beet, 46 New Bond Street, rebacked with original spine laid down, covers faded, early signature of J. Hathway, from the library of James Stevens Cox (1910-1997). Maggs Bros. Ltd. 1447 - 123 2015 £250

Crouch, Nathaniel *The English Empire in America.* London: Nath(aniel) Crouch, 1692. Second edition, 12mo., engraved frontispiece map of New England, engraved map of the Caribbean and one of two engraved plates of "Strange Creatures in America", lacking one plate and text leaves D6-7, wormed in gutter throughout, fore-edges chipped and bumped, piece torn away from corner of d4 (touching four lines of text), large stain in inner margin of D4-D5, pencil markings on rear pastedown, contemporary sheep, garment from unidentifiable broadside showing royal arms and "by the Queen (Anne) has been used as front pastedown, 20mm. piece torn away from top of spine, hole lower down spine, covers and spine rubbed, chipped and corners heavily bumped, signature 'John Topping his booke 1710', early 18th century signature Joseph A. Lingom, from the library of James Stevens Cox (1910-1997). Maggs Bros. Ltd. 1447 - 124 2015 £500

Crowe, Catherine *Uncle Tom's Cabin for Children.* London: George Routledge and Sons, 1867. Second edition, 12mo., original blue cloth, gilt decorations and lettering, frontispiece and pictorial titlepage, 8 page publisher's catalog at end, cloth little worn but very good. The Brick Row Book Shop Miscellany 67 - 86 2015 $150

Crowne, John *Caligula. A Tragedy...* London: by J. Orme for R. Wellington, 1698. First edition, small 4to., browned and dampstained throughout, early 20th century blind ruled calf slightly stained and scuffed on rear board, from the library of James Stevens Cox (1910-1997). Maggs Bros. Ltd. 1447 - 126 2015 £220

Cruden, Alexander *A Complete Concordance to the Holy Scriptures of the Old and New Testament or a Dictionary and alphabetical Index to the Bible.* London: Longman, T. Cadell, 1838. 4to., frontispiece, silk doublures, contemporary full brown morocco decorated in gilt, elaborate gilt dentelles, gilt inscription on leading pastedown "Presented to Mr. James Keyden...Glasgow 15 February 1839", booklabel of James Keyden, all edges gilt, handsome copy. Jarndyce Antiquarian Booksellers CCXI - 79 2015 £150

Cruden, William *Nature Spiritualised in a Variety of Poems.* London: printed by J. and W. Oliver for the author, 1766. First edition, 12mo., general intermittent soiling and finger marking, some minor dampstaining, contemporary calf, unlettered, ms. ownershp inscription on lower free endpaper of Jane Gall her book 1802. John Drury Rare Books March 2015 - 23201 2015 £306

Cruikshank, George 1792-1878 *George Cruikshank's Fairy Library.* London: George Bell, 1885. Limited to 500 copies printed on india paper, 4to., calf backed boards, edges rubbed, else fine, 4 volumes bound into one, with 24 etched plates by Cruikshank. Aleph-Bet Books, Inc. 108 - 116 2015 $350

Cruikshank, George 1792-1878 *George Cruikshank's Omnibus.* London: Tilt and Bogue, 1841-1842. First edition, 100 engravings on steel and wood, half title, frontispiece, plates and illustrations, some plates slightly browned and spotted, illustrations, front wrappers numbers I-IX bound in at front of volume, slightly dusted, some expert paper repair, uncut in later full light brown crushed morocco by Zaehnsdorf, very good, handsome copy, 11 line ALS from Cruikshank to Mr. Eales tipped in. Jarndyce Antiquarian Booksellers CCXI - 80 2015 £850

Cruikshank, George 1792-1878 *Sir John Falstaff Knight.* London: Longman & Co., 1857. First edition, small oblong 4to., 20 leaves of plates drawn and etched by Cruikshank, contemporary half green morocco green cloth boards lettered gilt on upper cover and spine, all edges gilt by Webb & Hunt, Liverpool, marbled endpapers, extremities little rubbed, some occasional scattered foxing, very good, slight rubbing, some occasional foxing, otherwise very good, tipped in handwritten signed letter from Cruikshank to H. A. Bright. Any Amount of Books March 2015 - C16212 2015 £375

Crumley, James *Bordersnakes.* Tucson: Dennis MacMillan, 1996. First edition, one of 300 numbered copies signed by author, very fine in dust jacket with slipcase. Mordida Books March 2015 - 008976 2015 $200

Crumley, James *Dancing Bear.* New York: Random House, 1963. First edition, signed by author, fine in dust jacket with three quarter inch crease to bottom of rear flap. Buckingham Books March 2015 - 24293 2015 $175

Crumley, James *Dancing Bear.* New York: Random House, 1983. First edition, fine in fine dust jacket. Buckingham Books March 2015 - 19359 2015 $250

Crumley, James *Dancing Bear.* New York: Random House, 1983. First edition, very fine in dust jacket. Mordida Books March 2015 - 008785 2015 $150

Crumley, James *The Final Country.* Tucson: Dennis McMillan, 2001. First edition, one of 400 numbered copies signed by Crumley, very fine in dust jacket with slipcase. Mordida Books   March 2015 - 007858   2015 $125

Crumley, James *The Last Good Kiss.* New York: Random House, 1978. first edition very fine in dust jacket, Mordida Books   March 2015 - 011774   2015 $125

Crumley, James *The Last Good Kiss.* New York: Random House, 1978. First edition, fine in dust jacket. Buckingham Books   March 2015 - 19358   2015 $175

Crumley, James *The Mexican Tree Duck.* Bristol: Scorpion, 1993. Limited to 75 numbered copies, signed by author, very fine in very fine acetate dust jacket.   Mordida Books   March 2015 - 008788   2015 $250

Crumley, James *The Muddy Fork.* Northridge: Lord John Press, 1984. First edition, limited to 50 deluxe numbered copies signed by author, fine in quarter leather and marbled boards as issued, gold stamping on spine.   Buckingham Books   March 2015 - 19361   2015 $400

Crumley, James *The Muddy Fork and Other Things.* Northridge: Lord John Press, 1984. First edition, preceding trade edition by 7 years, one of 200 numbered copies signed by Crumley, this is designated an unnumbered 'Presentation Copy' and additionally inscribed to his friend, writer Andre Dubus, fine, with no dust jacket, as issued, from the collection of Duke Collier.   Royal Books   36 - 156   2015 $850

Crumley, James *One to Count Cadence.* New York: Random House, 1969. First edition, signed on card and laid-in, fine in dust jacket with tiny rub mark to top edge of front panel, minor wear to head of spine and light wear to corners, scarce.   Buckingham Books   March 2015 - 20584   2015 $375

Crumley, James *The Wrong Case.* New York: Random House, 1975. First edition, about very good in very good plus dust jacket, spine lean and with light shelfwear and edge toning, jacket bright with little toning at extremities, crease to rear flap, small dampstain at bottom of front flap fold, inscribed by author June 16th '76 for Steve, from the collection of Duke Collier.   Royal Books   36 - 155   2015 $1250

Crump, Paul *Burn, Killer, Burn!* Chicago: Johnson, 1962. First edition, residue from removed label on front endpaper, otherwise fine in very good dust jacket with faded spine, nicks at spine ends and several closed tears.   Mordida Books   March 2015 - 008977   2015 $85

Crumpe, Samuel *An Essay on the Best Means of Providing Employment for the People.* Dublin: printed by Bonham, published by Mercier & Co., 1793. First edition, 8vo., printed on thick paper with half title and errata leaf, some prelim leaves and several text margins lightly dampstained, but overall fine, crisp copy in contemporary tree calf, spine simply gilt with crimson lettering piece, with 19th century armorial bookplate of William Mussenden.   John Drury Rare Books   March 2015 - 19609   2015 $874

Cruse, Thomas *Apache Days and After.* Caxton Printers Ltd., 1941. First edition, original green decorated cloth, frontispiece, photos, bright copy in dust jacket with light wear to extremities and chipping to top and bottom of spine, attractive collector's copy of very scarce work. Buckingham Books   March 2015 - 35979   2015 $275

Cuckoo; or the Welsh Embassadour's Application to the Raven, in Behalf of the Mag-pies and Jack-Dawes. London: J. Orme for R. Wellington, 1698. First edition, small 4to., browned and dampstained throughout, early 20th century blind ruled calf, slightly stained and scuffed on rear board, from the library of James Stevens Cox (1910-1997). Maggs Bros. Ltd.   1447 - 127   2015   £950

Cudworth, William *Life and Correspondence of Abraham Sharp, the Yorkshire Mathematician and Astronomer and Assistant of Flamsteed...* London & Bradford: Sampson Low, Marston, Searle & Rivington & Thos. Brear, 1889. Tall 8vo., frontispiece with tissue guard, 9 unnumbered plates, 19 figures, half vellum with marbled paper sides, gilt stamped black morocco spine labels, top edge gilt, soiled, extremities worn, author's presentation for Rev. Addison Croft.   Jeff Weber Rare Books   178 - 1006   2015 $300

Cullen, Countee *The Lost Zoo.* New York: Harper, 1940. First edition, 8vo., illustrations in color by Charles Sebree, yellow cloth, edges of cover scuffed, edges and endpapers little browned but very good, tight, in chipped and browned dust jacket.   Second Life Books Inc.   190 - 52   2015 $225

Cullinan, Elizabeth *Yellow Roses.* New York: Viking Press, 1977. First edition, fine in fine dust jacket, this copy inscribed by author to her editor at the New Yorker, Rachel MacKenzie.   Between the Covers Rare Books, Inc.   187 - 64   2015 $125

Cullum, Ridgwell *Sheets in the Wind.* Philadelphia: Lippincott, 1932. First edition, pages edges foxed, otherwise fine in dust jacket with couple of tiny closed tears and tiny wear at corners.   Mordida Books   March 2015 - 000577   2015 $100

Culpeper, Nicholas 1616-1654 *Culpeper's Semeiotica Uranica; or an Astrological Judgment of Diseases...* London: for N. Brook and are to be sold by Benj. Billingsley, 1671. Fourth edition, 8vo., engraved portrait, small engraved astrological charts of the crises at page 34 and 44 and two hand drawn charts of the crises, some minor rust spotting, small inkstain just touching fore-edge of D3-D5, table on D7, just shaved at fore-edge, inner margin of M5v-M64, stained, small spot on verso of first chart, contemporary calf, covers scuffed, rubbed and chipped, front pastedown unstuck, no rear pastedown on flyleaf, very neat ink manuscript table of astrological signs and parts of the body they influence, few contemporary ink annotations, partial remains of later bookplate inside front cover, from the library of James Stevens Cox (1910-1997).   Maggs Bros. Ltd.   1447 - 128   2015   £750

Culpeper, Nicholas 1616-1654 *A Directory for Midwives; or a guide for Women in Their Conception, Bearing and Suckling their Children...* London: for George Sawbridge, 1681. Small 8vo., 2 parts in 1 volume, lacking longitudinal half title to second part, somewhat browned, grubby and thumbed throughout, some occasional spotting and few torn edges on creased corners, contemporary calf covers panelled in blind, spine creased down center, backstrips torn, joints rubbed and worn, new front endleaves covering old bookplate, rear flyleaf cut away, from the library of James Stevens Cox (1910-1997).   Maggs Bros. Ltd.   1447 - 129   2015   £950

Cumberland, Marten *The House in the Forest.* Garden City: Doubleday Crime Club, 1950. First edition, pages darkened, otherwise fine in dust jacket.   Mordida Books   March 2015 - 010746   2015 $85

Cumberland, Marten *Out of this World.* London: Hutchinson, 1958. First edition, small light stain on bottom of page edges, otherwise fine in lightly soiled dust jacket with short closed tear.   Mordida Books   March 2015 - 007400   2015 $85

Cumberland, Marten *Remains to be Seen.* London: Hutchinson, 1960. First edition, name and address on front endpaper, else fine in dust jacket.   Mordida Books   March 2015 - 012684   2015 $85

Cumberland, Richard *Arundel.* printed for C. Dilly, 1791. Second edition, 2 volumes, scorch mark to first age of text volume ii, no loss, very minor browning and spotting here and there, contemporary calf, spines gilt in compartments, contrasting labels on spines, those for the volume nos. circular, numbering piece on volume ii lacking, that on volume i slightly defective, without flyleaf in volume I, slight wear to extremities, engraved armorial bookplate of Sir John Eden inside front covers, attractive copy, rare edition. Blackwell's Rare Books   B179 - 34   2015   £500

Cumberland, Richard *A Few Plain Reasons Why We Should Believe in Christ and Adhere to His Religion...* London: Lackington Allen and Co., 1801. First edition, 8vo., uncut and stitched as issued, fine.   John Drury Rare Books   March 2015 - 19886   2015 $266

Cumin, Patrick *The Popular Education of the Bristol and Plymouth Districts with Special Reference to Ragged Schools and Pauper Children.* London: Longman, Green, Longman and Roberts, 1861. First edition, 8vo., 6 lithographic plates, 'reserve stock' ink stamped on blank margin of title, original embossed cloth, neatly rebacked, printed spine label, corners of boards worn, new endpapers, entirely unopened and uncut, good, scarce.   John Drury Rare Books   March 2015 - 20805   2015   £306

Cuming, E. D. *Three Jovial Puppies.* London: Blackie & Son, n.d., 1908. Folio, cloth backed pictorial boards, slight tip and edge rubbing, else near fine, illustrations by J. A. Shepherd in color on every page and with pictorial endpapers, printed Frenchfold on quality paper.   Aleph-bet Books, Inc.   109 - 133   2015 $600

Cumming, Alexander *Observations of the Effects Which Carriage Wheels with Rims of Different Shapes, Have on the Roads...* London: printed by W. Bulmer and Co., 1799. Second edition, 4to., 2 folding engraved plates, the first which is mounted on a stub as frontispiece, one small text figure, 66 pages, contemporary half calf over marbled boards with coroneted monogram on upper cover, neatly rebacked gilt, very good, sometime in the library of the Franklin Institute, very rare.   John Drury Rare Books   2015 - 22684   2015 $1311

Cumming, Alexander *A Sketch of the Properties of the Machine Organ, Invented, Constructed and Made by Mr. Cumming for the Earl of Bute...* London: printed by E. and H. Hudson Cross Street Hatton Garden, 1812. First edition, printed rectos only, contemporary red half roan gilt, neatly rebacked, original backstrip retained, very good, of great rarity, from the library of Lord Stuart de Rothesay at Highcliffe Castle with his coat of arms stamped in blind on covers, signature (1952) and one amendement by him in red ink of American composer Bernard Herrmann and NY Public Library.   John Drury Rare Books   2015 - 22640   2015 $8741

Cumming, Robert *The Weight of Franchise Meat.* Orange County: privately printed, 1971. First edition, softcover, one of 500 copies, with black and white photos, very good plus with some minor spotting to wrappers, signed by Cumming, laid in is Mike Mandel's baseball card of Robert Cumming which has been signed by Cumming.   Jeff Hirsch Books   E-62 Holiday List 2014 - 7   2015 $1250

Cummings, Edward Estlin 1894-1962 *& (ampersand).* privately printed, 1925. First edition, 1/333 numbered copies, this being 149, f.e.p. bears Cummings's inscription for 'W. L./ from the author', very good with soiling and foxing of paper covered boards and wear to spine. Beasley Books 2013 - 2015 $300

Cummings, Edward Estlin 1894-1962 *50 Poems.* New York: Duell Sloan & Pearce, 1940. First trade edition, one of 1000 copies, 8vo., original cloth, very fine in dust jacket which is trifle nicked near head of spine, rare in this condition. James S. Jaffe Rare Books Modern American Poetry - 61 2015 $1000

Cummings, Edward Estlin 1894-1962 *Him.* New York: Liveright, 1927. First edition, deluxe issue, one of 160 copies signed by author, 8vo., original half vellum and black paper boards, untrimmed, publisher's glassine, very good, lacking publisher's slipcase. James S. Jaffe Rare Books Modern American Poetry - 58 2015 $500

Cummings, Edward Estlin 1894-1962 *Is 5.* New York: Liveright, 1926. First edition deluxe issue, one of 77 copies on special paper, specially bound and signed by author, 8vo., original cloth backed decorated paper over boards, publisher's matching slipcase with paper label, presentation copy inscribed by author, Montgomery Evans bookplate, otherwise fine in slipcase with two short cracks. James S. Jaffe Rare Books Modern American Poetry - 57 2015 $1500

Cummings, Edward Estlin 1894-1962 *Six Nonlectures.* Cambridge: Harvard University Press, 1953. First edition, limited to 350 copies, signed by author, tall 8vo., original two-toned cloth, black dust jacket is slightly rubbed and price clipped as usual with limited signed issue of this title, otherwise fine. James S. Jaffe Rare Books Modern American Poetry - 62 2015 $750

Cummings, Edward Estlin 1894-1962 *Tom.* New York: printed by The Rydal Press for Arrow Editions, 1935. First edition, one of 1500 copies printed, 8vo., frontispiece by Ben Shahn, original cloth, dust jacket, very fine in uncommon jacket in which there are a couple of short closed tears. James S. Jaffe Rare Books Modern American Poetry - 60 2015 $450

Cummings, Edward Estlin 1894-1962 *W.* New York: Horace Liveright, 1931. First edition, one of only 95 numbered copies printed on special paper and signed by author, narrow 4to., original cloth backed acetate dust jacket, publisher's slipcase, very fine, largely unopened, copy in slipcase which is inexpertly repaired at a few places along spine panel, rare, especially in this condition. James S. Jaffe Rare Books Modern American Poetry - 59 2015 $2250

Cummins, Sarah J. *Autobiography and Reminiscences of Sarah J. Cummins.* Walla Walla Bulletin, 1914. First edition, 8 x 5.5 inches, printed wheat wrappers, 61 pages, illustrations, four printings were issued in 1914 but with different impressions, light tanning to wrapper edges, else very good. Buckingham Books March 2015 - 35760 2015 $350

Cundall, H. M. *A History of British Water Colour Painting with Biographical List of Painters.* New York: 1908. First US edition, 279 pages, very good gilt bright, one corner abraded, 58 color plates. Bookworm & Silverfish 2015 - 6017219421 2015 $55

Cunnignham, Thomas *A New Treatise on the Laws Concerning Tithes....* London: printed by His Majesty's Law Printers for W. Griffin, 1766. First edition, 8vo., half title, contemporary ruled calf with raised bands, unlettered, very good. John Drury Rare Books March 2015 - 19993 2015 £306

Cunningham, A. B. *The Strange Death of Manny Square.* New York: Dutton, 1941. First edition, fine in dust jacket with tiny wear at corners. Mordida Books March 2015 - 008626 2015 $200

Cunningham, Henry Stewart *Late Laurels.* London: Longman, 1864. First edition, 2 volumes, half titles, final ad leaf volume II, original dark green pebble grained cloth, boards blocked in blind, spines lettered gilt, decorated boards at head and tail, signatures on titles of Arthur A. Morison 1864. Jarndyce Antiquarian Booksellers CCXI - 83 2015 £180

Cunningham, Peter Miller *Two Years in New South Wales: a Series of Letters.* London: Henry Colburn, 1827. First edition, 8vo., attractively rebound in modern hafl buckram and marbled boards, lettered gilt on spine, volume one only, very good+. Any Amount of Books 2015 - C5078 2015 £150

Cunningham, Valentine *Everywhere Spoken Against: Dissent in the Victorian Novel.* Oxford: Clarendon Press, 1975. Half title, original dark blue cloth, very good in dust jacket, from the library of Geoffrey & Kathleen Tillotson. Jarndyce Antiquarian Booksellers CCVII - 161 2015 £20

Cupid and Bacchus; or Love and the Bottle. London: printed and sold by E. Palmer No. 7 at the Bible in Middle Row Holborn and by most booksellers, 1770. Oblong 12mo, wanting five leaves, one leaf cropped at foot with loss of catchword, original very worn sheep, now preserved in specially made book box of watered cloth over boards, morocco spine label lettered gilt, incomplete but of great rarity. John Drury Rare Books 2015 - 24102 2015 $1661

The Curious Book. Edinburgh: printed by John Pillans for John Thomson and Baldwin, Cradock and Joy, London, 1826. First edition, 8vo., later green half calf, green cloth boards, red morocco label, gilt decorations and lettering, top edge gilt, others untrimmed, half title and errata leaf present, some smudges and stains in text, very good.   The Brick Row Book Shop   Miscellany 67 - 20   2015 $400

Curious Enquiries. London: Randal Taylor, 1688. First edition, small 4to., with license to print leaf (1), all edges uncut, minor spotting to B1-4 two circular stains in blank lower margin of d2 where paper flaws have been repaired, fore-margin of final leaf cut away and renewed, mid 20th century half calf and marbled boards, from the library of James Stevens Cox (1910-1997), with cipher and pencil rice £5-5-0.   Maggs Bros. Ltd.   1447 - 130   2015   £600

Curly Heads and Long Legs. London: Raphael Tuck, n.d., 1914. 4to., cloth backed pictorial boards, pictorial paste-on, as new in publisher's box, illustrations by Hilda Cowham, with 12 bright color plates plus black and whites.   Aleph-Bet Books, Inc.   108 - 110   2015 $1200

Currie, Barton   *Officer 666.*   New York: Fly, 1912. First edition, very good in dust jacket with internal tape mends, chips at corners, wear along folds.   Mordida Books   March 2015 - 006594   2015 $250

Curtis, Edward S.   *North American Indian, the Southwest.* Santa Fe: 1980. Edition of 288 copies, frontispiece, errata slip, full leather, folio, still in original shipping box, very, very slight rubbing to leather, else fine.   Dumont Maps and Books of the West   130 - 38   2015 $595

Curtis, James   *The Gilt Kid: a Novel.*   London: Jonathan Cape, 1936. First edition, 8vo., original yellow cloth, lettered green on spine and cover, neat name in pencil on front endpaper, slight surface wear and slight rubbing, otherwise sound, very good.   Any Amount of Books   2015 - C3229   2015   £650

Curtis, Wardon   *The Strange Adventures of Mr. Middleton.* Chicago: Herbert S. Stone and Co., 1903. First edition, first state, pictorial gray cloth, titles in white and tan on front and spine panels, publisher's monogram stamped in white on rear panel, top edge gilt, lightly rubbed at spine ends, former owner's name stamped on front pastedown sheet and on page 1, else very good, bright copy.   Buckingham Books   March 2015 - 32459   2015 $225

Curtiss, Thomas Quinn   *Von Stroheim.*   New York: Farrar, Straus and Giroux, 1971. First edition, fine in very near fine dust jacket, inscribed by author to film actor, Ricardo Cortez.   Between the Covers Rare Books, Inc.   187 - 65   2015 $250

Curwood, James Oliver   *The Flaming Forest.*   New York: Cosmopolitan, 1921. First edition, lower corners slightly bumped, otherwise fine in dust jacket with several short closed tears and small scrape on front panel.   Mordida Books   March 2015 - 008980   2015 $200

Cushman, Karen   *The Midwife's Apprentice.*   New York: Clarion, 1995. First edition, 8vo., cloth, as new in dust jacket with no award medal, color dust jacket by Trina Schart Hyman, scarce in first edition.   Aleph-Bet Books, Inc.   108 - 117   2015 $200

Cussans, John E.   *Handbook of Heraldry with Instructions for Tracing Pedigrees and Deciphering Ancient Mss. Rules for the Appointment of Liveries &c.*   London: Chatto & Windus, 1893. Fourth edition, 32 page catalog Sept. 1901, half title, frontispiece, illustrations, slightly browned, original olive green cloth, spine faded to brown, from the library of Geoffrey & Kathleen Tillotson.   Jarndyce Antiquarian Booksellers   CCVII - 162   2015   £25

Cussler, Clive   *Iceberg.*   New York: Dodd Mead and Co., 1975. First edition, fine in fine, price clipped dust jacket with one tiny rub to top front corner.   Buckingham Books   March 2015 - 28696   2015 $1250

Cussler, Clive   *Pacific Vortex!*   Mission Viejo: James Cahill, 2000. Limited numbered edition, one of 300 numbered copies signed by author and dust jacket artist, David Monette, very fine as new in dust jacket with slipcase.   Mordida Books   March 2015 - 011399   2015 $400

Customs and Privileges of the manors of Stephney and Hackney in the County of Middlesex.   London: in the Savoy printed by E. and R. Nutt and R. Goslign for J. Worral and C. Corbett and R. Wellington, 1736. 12mo., very minor browning and slight dampstaining in margins of couple of leaves beginning and end, mid 19th century morocco with blank morocco title label on upper cover, very good.   John Drury Rare Books   March 2015 - 16204   2015 $266

Cuthbertson, Bennett   *A System for the Compleat Interior of management an Oeconomy of a Battalion of Infantry.* Dublin: printed by Boutler Grierson, 1768. First edition, 17 tables, 3 are folding, one of the text leaves torn in lower margin (not affecting printed surface), contemporary marbled boards, neatly rebacked in calf, raised bands, original lettering piece reused, very good, rare.   John Drury Rare Books   2015 - 24859   2015 $1224

Cutright, Paul Russell   *Lewis and Clark: Pioneering Naturalists.*   University of Illinois Press, 1969. First edition, cloth, illustrations, increasingly scarce, very very light bump to upper fore-corners, as new, dust jacket with slightest of wear to top corner front panel, light sunning to edges of back panel, barely visible half inch closed tear to edge of back panel, else fine and bright.   Buckingham Books   March 2015 - 34170   2015 $200

Cutten, George B. *The Silversmiths of North Carolina.* Raleigh: 1948. First edition, wrappers, small spots, signed and inscribed by author.   Bookworm & Silverfish   2015 - 5399772162   2015 $100

Cutter, George Washington *Buena Vista and Other Poems.*   Cincinnati: Morgan & Overend Printers,   1848. First edition, 12mo., original blindstamped red cloth, gilt decorations and lettering, all edges gilt, frontispiece, fine presentation copy inscribed by author for Maj. Gen'l. John E. Wool (1784-1869), cloth little worn, slight foxing, fine.   The Brick Row Book Shop   Miscellany 67 - 14   2015 $800

Cutts, James M.   *The Conquest of California and New Mexico by the Forces of the United States in the Years 1846 and 1847.*   Philadelphia: Carey & Hart, 1847. First edition, 8vo., 264 pages, bound in black cloth, rebacked with binder's cloth, numeral crossed out from bottom of titlepage, water 'tide-mark' through titlepage and prelim matter, library stamp crossed out at bottom of page 50, very good, tight copy.   Second Life Books Inc.   191 - 27   2015 $850

Cyclists' Touring Club   *British Road Book 1-5.*   London: E. R. Shipton, 1897. Mixed editions, Volumes 1-4 with companion to volume 1 in 5 volumes, 8vo., original dark green cloth lettered gilt on spines and covers, color folding maps in front pockets, slight wear and rubbing, else very good, exceptional set.   Any Amount of Books   2015 - A94433   2015   £225

D

D'Aulaire, Ingri *Abraham Lincoln.* New York: Doubleday Doran and Co., 1939. Stated first edition, first issue with errata slip, large 4to., cloth backed pictorial boards, fine in dust jacket, worn at folds, chipped at spine folds, chipped at spine ends, full color lithos throughout. Aleph-Bet Books, Inc. 108 - 121 2015 $1500

D'Aulaire, Ingri *Animals Everywhere.* New York: Doubleday, Doran, 1940. Stated first edition, large 4to., cloth, slight fading, else fine in dust jacket (chipped all along bottom edge with 2 inch piece off spine) one side of the large accordion, folded sheet with beautiful full color lithographs of more than 50 animals, very scarce. Aleph-bet Books, Inc. 109 - 115 2015 $600

D'Aulaire, Ingri *Buffalo Bill.* Doubleday & Co., 1952. First edition, quarto, color pictorial paper over boards, cloth spine, color pictures and map on front and rear endpapers, illustrations in color and black and white, fine, lacking dust jacket. Buckingham Books March 2015 - 34329 2015 $175

D'Aulaire, Ingri *D'Aulaire's Trolls.* New York: Doubleday & Co., 1972. Stated first edition, folio, pictorial boards, color illustrations. Aleph-bet Books, Inc. 109 - 116 2015 $100

D'Esme, Jean *Thi-Ba Fille D'Annam.* Paris: Editions Haussmann, 1956. First edition, no. 469 of 2000 copies on velin Fleur 'alfa, color lithographs by Jacques Boullaire, 4to., wrappers, near fine. Beasley Books 2013 - 2015 $45

D'Israeli, Isaac 1776-1843 *Curiosities of Literature.* London: printed for J. Murray, 1793. Third edition, volume II second edition, 2 volumes, folding facsimile, large uncut and unpressed copy with corner of Hh3 in volume I torn with loss not affecting text, contemporary quarter calf, marbled boards, slight wear to head of one spine and corners, boards rubbed, ownership label of A. Benson, Reading, who has also created manuscript half titles on endpapers, the first with naive roundel portrait, he has also neatly added calligraphic subject headings to few pages. Jarndyce Antiquarian Booksellers CCXI - 92 2015 £125

D'Ivray, Jehan *Promenades a Travers Le Caire.* Paris: J. Peyronnet & Co., 1928. No. 235 of 335 numbered copies, 28 full color illustrations and decorative initials by Louis Cabanes, 4to., unbound signatures in wrappers, quite lovely, fine in fine wrappers, in previous owner's chemise and slipcase. Beasley Books 2013 - 2015 $750

D., A. *Proposals to Supply His Majesty with Twelve to Fourteen Millions of Money (or more if required) for the Year 1697 without subscriptions or Advancing the Present Taxes.* London: printed for the author and sold by Peter Parker and John Waltho and John Gouge, 1697. First edition, 4to., including supplement, titlepage dusty, final leaf (verso blank) worn with perforations just affecting single letter of word 'Finis', large, uncut copy, well bound in recent, but old style, quarter calf over marbled boards. John Drury Rare Books 2015 - 20740 2015 $1049

Da Costa, Esther *Schoenberg, Kandinsky and the Blue Rider.* London: Scala Publishers for the Jewish Museum, New York, First edition, fine in fine dust jacket, with CD in pocket on rear pastedown. Stephen Lupack March 2015 - 2015 $60

Da Vaz, Jurg *Psychospheres 1975-1978.* Washington: The Artist, 1978. First edition, copy #4 of 300 numbered and handbound copies, monogrammed and dated by Da Vaz, nicely inscribed by Da Vaz to co-editor, Herman Kamenetz and his wife, very large oblong folio,. Between the Covers Rare Books, Inc. 187 - 2 2015 $1500

Dahl, Roald *Charlie and the Chocolate Factory.* New York: Knopf, 1964. First edition, first issue with 6 line colophon, illustrations by Joseph Schindelman, publisher's red cloth, lacking ISBN number to rear panel, dust jacket, near fine with gilt just touch dimmed and few faint spots to topstain, unclipped dust jacket with few closed tears to spine ends, creasing and nicks to top edge of rear panel, vertical creasing to front panel and vertical creasing, minor soiling and light dampstain to rear panel, overall bright and unfaded, unclipped dust jacket without usual chipping and fading. B & B Rare Books, Ltd. 2015 - 2015 $2800

Dahl, Roald *Charlie and the Chocolate Factory.* New York: Alfred Knopf, 1964. First edition, 8vo., red cloth blindstamped on cover, fine in very good dust jacket with few closed margin tears and creases, black and white illustrations by Joseph Schindelman, later copies have same original published price but have ISBN# on rear cover, laid-in is black and white glossy photo of Dahl, inscribed by Dahl. Aleph-Bet Books, Inc. 108 - 118 2015 $3500

Dahl, Roald *Danny the Champion of the World.* London: Puffin Books, 1979. Reprint, paperback, fine in wrappers, inscribed by author to children's book reviewer Helen Heinrich. Between the Covers Rare Books, Inc. 187 - 49 2015 $350

Dahl, Roald *Matilda.* London: Jonathan Cape, 1988. First edition, illustrations by Quentin Blake, inscribed by author. Honey & Wax Booksellers 2 - 26 2015 $5000

Dahl, Roald *Sometime Never.* London: Collins, 1949. First edition, 8vo., handsome blue leather with marbled boards lettered and decorated gilt at spine, five raised bands, about fine.   Any Amount of Books   2015 - C3226 2015   £150

Dahlberg, Edward *Can These Bones Live.* New York: New Directions, 1960. First revised edition, illustrations by James Kearns, fine in like dust jacket, nicely inscribed by author for Ned Erbe, head of publicity at New Directions.   Between the Covers Rare Books, Inc.   187 - 67   2015 $150

Dahlberg, Edward *The Flea of Sodom.* Norfolk: New Directions, 1950. First edition, fine in fine dust jacket with little rubbing at spine, inscribed by author for bandleader Artie Shaw.   Between the Covers Rare Books, Inc.   187 - 66   2015 $250

Dakota Territory. Dept. of Immigration & Statistics *1887. Resources of Dakota. An Official Publication Compiled by the Commissioner of Immigration.* Sioux Falls: Argus Leader Co., 1887. First edition, 8vo., decorated cloth, blindstamped on covers, stamped in gold on spine, 498 pages, frontispiece, scarce, words "Dakota State Bindery Co." stapled on front pastedown sheet and flyleaf respectively, else near fine.   Buckingham Books   March 2015 - 26001   2015 $450

Dale, Harrison C. *The Ashley Smith Explorations and the Discovery of a Central Route to the Pacific 1822-1829.* A. H. Clark Co., 1918. First edition, cloth, 2 maps, few small spots on back cover, residue from removal of bookplates on front pastedown and free endpaper, remnants of small book review tipped on rear endpaper, very good.   Buckingham Books   March 2015 - 34458   2015 $275

Dale, Samuel *The History and Antiquities of Harwich and Dovercourt, Topographical, Dynastical, and Political.* London: C. Davis and T. Green, 1730. First edition, large paper copy, 4to., large paper copy, 14 engraved plates, printed on thick paper, contemporary panelled calf, some wear to extremities, neatly rebacked retaining original labels (although one label worn), very good, sometime in the library of the Dukes of Leinster at their country house Carton or Carten House with their armorial bookplate and shelf number and arms in gilt at head of spine, of great rarity.   John Drury Rare Books   2015 - 24774   2015 $787

Dali, Salvador *50 Secrets of Magic Craftsmanship.* New York: Dial Press, 1948. First American edition, 4to., 192 pages, 2 color plates, many text illustrations, black cloth, little dusty, but very good, tight copy.   Second Life Books Inc.   191 - 28   2015 $125

Dallas, W. S. *A Natural History of the Animal Kingdom...* London: Houlston & Stoneman, 1856. First edition, 8vo., recently rebound in green half leather, marbled boards, gilt on spine, illustrations, color frontispiece and titlepage, inscription presumably by author's son James Dallas 8 March 1898, very slight foxing to prelims, very good+.   Any Amount of Books   2015 - A88401   2015   £300

Dalrymple, John *Three Addresses by Sir John Dalrymple, Baronet, Lately Baron of Exchequer in Scotland to the Seamen, Soldiers and Great Mess of the People of England, Scotland and Ireland.* Edinburgh: printed by J. Robertson, 1808. 8vo., 5 woodcut illustrations in text, wanting half title but with final blank (F4), light marginal dampstain in several leaves at end, titlepage little dust soiled, recent marbled boards, lettered on spine, entirely uncut, good, large copy, apparently rare.   John Drury Rare Books   2015 - 25987   2015 $787

Dalton, Charles *English Army Lists and Commission Registers 1661-1714.* London: Eyre & Spottiswoode, 1892. First edition, large 8vo., 6 volumes, original red half leather over red cloth lettered gilt at spine, bookplate to front pastedowns, some wear and rubbing to covers, slight splitting at spine of volume 4, front board of volume 5 almost detached with most of backstrip missing, otherwise decent run, bindings sound, contents clean.   Any Amount of Books   2015 - C14055   2015   £300

Daly, Carroll John *Murder Won't Wait.* Ives Washburn, 1933. First edition, cloth slightly faded at edges, else clean, near fine, dust jacket faded at spine with shallow chipping at spine ends, scarce.   Buckingham Books   March 2015 - 38458   2015 $875

Daly, Elizabeth *An Elizabeth Daly Mystery Omnibus.* Rinehart & Co. Inc., 1960. First edition thus, green cloth, titles stamped in dark blue on spine, fine in dust jacket with light wear to spine ends.   Buckingham Books   March 2015 - 35902   2015 $185

Daly, Kathleen *A B C Around the House.* New York: Simon & Schuster, 1957. First edition, paper toned as in all copies, else near fine, illustrations by Violet Lamont, with 3 windows cut out of cover and moveable wheel inside cover so that when wheel is turned a picture of the object, the word spelled out and the capital letter that begins the word appear in the windows, scarce.   Aleph-bet Books, Inc.   109 - 201   2015 $150

Dan Dare, Pilot of the Future. London: Titan Books, 2004-2009. 12 facsimile reproductions of the Dan Dare stories, each 296 x 220mm., near fine in hardcovers in near fine dust jackets with some very slight discoloration and tiny amount of edgewear.   Any Amount of Books   2015 - A91732   2015   £240

Dana, Julian *Sutter of California. A Biography.* New York: Press of the Pioneers, 1934. First edition, signed by author, illustrations, map, red pictorial cloth gilt, some offsetting to front ends, but very fine with pictorial dust jacket (short tears, slight fading, protected with plastic cover). Argonaut Book Shop Holiday Season 2014 - 65 2015 $75

Dana, Richard Henry 1815-1882 *To Cuba and Back: a Vacation Voyage.* Boston: 1859. Original cloth, spine faded, owner's name on f.f.e.p., quarter inch loss of cloth at top of spine, else clean and very good. Dumont Maps & Books of the West 131 - 45 2015 $150

Dana, Richard Henry 1815-1882 *Two Years Before the Mast.* New York: Harper and Bros., 1840. First edition, first issue, 16mo., binding B (no priority) in original printed paper over boards, contemporary pencil signature and small and attractive later bookplate, original spine perished, professionally replaced with appropriate cloth, some staining and rubbing on boards, sound, good copy, housed in custom clamshell case, laid in is leaf of paper with Dana's signature dated 1852. Between the Covers Rare Books 196 - 71 2015 $2500

Dana, Richard Henry 1815-1882 *Two Years Before the Mast.* Los Angeles: Ward Ritchie, 1964. 2 volumes, 8 color plates, 108 reproductions of vintage photos and charts, pictorial cloth, very fine set with slipcase. Argonaut Book Shop Holiday Season 2014 - 66 2015 $125

Dancing Dolls. London: Raphael Tuck, n.d. circa, 1910. Oblong large 4to., flexible card covers with pages 'untearable', except for slight chipping on paper spine and cover, very good+ clean condition, color covers, 6 full page chromolithographs, 6 full pages in orange and black plus 6 full pages in green and black. Aleph-bet Books, Inc. 109 - 353 2015 $450

Daniel Boone: Les Aventures D'un Chasseur American Parmi les Peaux Rouges. Paris: Domino Press, 1931. First book done by Domino Press, one of 25 numbered copies in French signed by Rojankovsky containing an extra suite of illustrations printed without text, printed on high quality velin d'Arches paper, this edition limited to 50 numbered copies, 25 in French and 25 in English, beautiful, richly colored lithographs by Fedor Rojankovsky. Aleph-bet Books, Inc. 109 - 416 2015 $2500

Daniel, Walter C. *Black Journals of the United States.* Westport: Greenwood, 1982. First edition, large 8bvo., very good, ex-library copy in original boards. Beasley Books 2013 - 2015 $45

Daniels, Bebe *282 Ways of Making a Salad...* London: Cassell and Co., 1950. First edition, slightly cocked, else near fine in attractive, very good dust jacket with little bit of chipping at crown and extremities, signed by Daniels and Jill Algood, as well as 2 others. Between the Covers Rare Books 196 - 137 2015 $450

Daniels, Les *Teacher's Manual for Thirteen Tales of Terror.* New York: Scribner's, 1977. First edition, this copy inscribed by Daniels to an interviewer, near fine in stapled wrappers. Ken Lopez, Bookseller 164 - 43 2015 $100

Dante Alighieri 1265-1321 *The Divine comedy of Dante Alighieri.* New York: Limited Editions Club, 1932. Limited to 1500 numbered copies, signed by printer, Hans Mardersteig, thick 4to., patterned cloth, paper spine label, dust jacket, slipcase rubbed, jacket chipped along edges, unusual to find in rather flimsy jacket and slipcase. Oak Knoll Books 25 - 8 2015 $400

Dante Alighieri 1265-1321 *L'Enfer.* Paris: Editions De La Pleiade, 1930. Number IV of 50 copies not for sale, the full edition was 1360 copies, 8vo., wrappers in glassine, full page illustrations by Edy Legrand, fine in fine glassine, protected by previous owner's box. Beasley Books 2013 - 2015 $150

Dante Alighieri 1265-1321 *L'Enfer.* Paris: Chez Jean Porson, 1950. No. 81 of 250 copies, the first 127 of which are printed on velin blanc, 2 volumes, all with 108 stunning etchings, 34 hors-texte by Edouard Georg, unbound signatures laid into wrappers, in handsome red and black chemise and matching boxes, one box has slight ding on one top edge and tiny split starting on same edge, beautiful set, folio. Beasley Books 2013 - 2015 $900

Dante Alighieri 1265-1321 *The New Life.* London and New York: George Harrap, n.d. circa, 1910. 4to., publisher's full leather, top edge gilt, fine, publisher's pictorial box, binding termed 'antique leather' on box meant to simulate medieval binding, with faux leather hinge straps and nail heads, title and decorative box are blindstamped in center of which color is raised and sculpted image of medieval woman, tipped in and printed color plates plus pictorial embellishments one very page of text in Art Nouveau style, rare in this binding with box. Aleph-bet Books, Inc. 109 - 343 2015 $600

Daragnes, Jean Gabriel *L'Enfance Du Christ.* Paris: Elaine Norberg, 1952. First edition, one of 380 numbered copies printed entirely on polyvinyl chloride plastic, blue and white, manufactured especially for this project, soft flexible wrappers, this one of only 160 copies disitributed to the trade, no. 330, with 23 engravings in color by Jean Boutet, fine in clamshell box with see-through plastic cover, 4to. Beasley Books 2013 - 2015 $600

Daragnes, Jean Gabriel *Terres Chaudes Tableaux De L'Ocean Indien et De L'Indo-Chine Ecrits et Peints.* Societe Du Livre D'Art, 1940. Limited to 129 signed and numbered copies, this copy signed but not numbered, although it is designated 'pour Monsieur Alfred Perrot', 15 full page color illustrations by Daragnes, folded gatherings, with very minor foxing to titlepage, wrappers fine and chemise fine, but for sunned spine, very good+ box, signed on colophon, folio. Beasley Books   2013 - 2015 $500

Darlow, Biddy *Fifteen Old Nursery Rhymes.* Bristol: Perpetua Press, 1935. Limited to 1500 copies, hand colored linocuts.   Honey & Wax Booksellers   2 - 29   2015 $700

Darwin, Charles Robert   1809-1882 *The Descent of Man and Selection in Relation to Sex.* London: John Murray, 1874. Second edition, 8vo., denoted 10th thousand, original green cloth lettered gilt at spine, library label on pastedown and remains of label on rear pastedown, no other ex-library signs, sound, close to very good, used copy with covers slightly rubbed at spine and hinges and corners, very slight marking, inner hinges cracked but holding.   Any Amount of Books   2015 - A94346   2015   £300

Darwin, Charles Robert   1809-1882 *The Descent of Man and Selection in Relation to Sex.* London: John Murray, 1888. Second edition, 21st thousand, 8vo., original green cloth lettered gilt at spine, illustrations, faint rubbing to covers and spine, very slight creasing, otherwise near fine, excellent condition.   Any Amount of Books   2015 - C13677   2015   £160

Darwin, Charles Robert   1809-1882 *Journal of Researches into the Natural History and Geology of the Countries Visited During the Voyage of the HMS Beagle Round the Wold Under the Command of Capt. Fitz Roy.* London: John Murray, 1860. 10th thousand, illustrations, 32 page catalog (Jan. 1863), original green cloth, by Edmonds & Remnant, neatly recased, little dulled, contemporary signature of G. M. Gibson.   Jarndyce Antiquarian Booksellers   CCXI - 84   2015   £580

Darwin, Charles Robert   1809-1882 *On the Origin of Species by Means of Natural Selection.* New York: D. Appleton and Co., 1860. First American edition, first state with two notices opposite titlepage, octavo, original brown blindstamped cloth, gilt stamped on spine previous owner's bookplate, minor scattered foxing, fine,.   Heritage Book Shop   Holiday 2014 - 47   2015 $12,500

Darwin, Charles Robert   1809-1882 *On the Origin of Species by Means of Natural Selection.* London: John Murray, 1891. 41st thousand, half title, folding plate, final ad leaf, original green cloth, slightly rubbed at head and tail of spine, contemporary signature of James Bell, very good. Jarndyce Antiquarian Booksellers   CCXI - 85   2015   £380

Darwin, Charles Robert   1809-1882 *On the Origin of Species by Means of Natural Selection or the Preservation of Favoured Races...* New York: Limited Editions Club, 1963. Limited to 1500 numbered copies signed by artist, small 4to., wood engravings by Paul Landacre, quarter leather, slipcase, monthly letter loosely inserted.   Oak Knoll Books   25 - 41   2015 $250

Darwin, Charles Robert   1809-1882 *The Variation of Animals and Plants Under Domestication.* London: John Murray, 1875. Second editions, 1st volume 4th thousand, 2nd 5th thousand, 2 volumes, 8vo., original green blind-stamped cloth lettered gilt on spine, 43 illustrations, both volumes have neat names J. R. Sowerby 1880 and J. B. Muirhead; both volumes very nice, very good+ bright copies with slight abrasion and short closed tear to front endpaper second volume.   Any Amount of Books   2015 - A82987   2015   £325

Darwin, Erasmus   1731-1802   *The Botanic Garden. (with) The Botanic Garden Part II.* J. Johnson, 1795. 1794. Third and Fourth edition, 4to., 2 volumes in one, recent full calf, engraved frontispiece to each volume, 10 engraved plates in volume I, 8 engraved plates in volume II, occasional light spotting as usual, William Blake plates being exceptionally clean and wide margined.   Henry Sotheran Ltd. William Blake Exhibition 17th Oct.-7th Nov. 2014 - 66   2015   £2395

Dary, Michael   *The Complete Gauger.*   London: for Robert Horne and Nathaniel Ponder, 1678. First and only edition, 12mo., license to print on verso of title, worming to lower inner margin occasionally touching a word and with small stain on D6v and D7r, contemporary sheep, rebacked, later pastedowns, edges lightly rubbed, from the library of James Stevens Cox (1910-1997), the copy of Thomas Strode (d. 1697) by descent to his niece, signature of Abigail Swayne (d. 1723).   Maggs Bros. Ltd.   1447 - 131   2015   £2000

Daubeny, Charles   *Lecture on the Application of Science to Agriculture, Delivered Before the Members of the Royal Agricultural Society of England on Thursday Dec. 9 1841.*   London: 1842. First separate edition, Offprint from Journal of Royal Agricultural Soceity of England, 1842 Volume III Part I, 8vo., modern wrappers with printed title label on upper cover, very good presentation copy inscribed "Ashmolean Society from the authors".   John Drury Rare Books   2015 - 23226   2015 $89

Daubeny, Charles   *On the Public Institutions for the Advancement of Agricultural Science Which Exist in Other countries and on the Plans which Have Been Set on Foot by Individuals with a Similar Intent in our Own.* London: 1842. First separate edition, 8vo., very good, inscribed "Ashmoleaon Society from the author".   John Drury Rare Books   2015 - 23228   2015 $168

Daubeny, Charles *Supplement to the Introduction to the Atomic Theory...* London: J. Murray and J. H. Parker, Oxford, 1840. First edition, 8vo., including both original and cancel titlepage and final postscript, very good, recently well bound in linen backed marbled boards lettered, presentation copy inscribed by author for Ashmolean Society. John Drury Rare Books   March 2015 - 23224   2015 $221

Daubeny, Charles *Three Lectures on Agriculture, Delivered at Oxford on July 22nd and Nov. 25th 1840 and on Jan. 26th 1841, in which the Chemical Operation of manures is Particularly Considered, and the Scientific Principles Explained, Upon which their efficacy Appear to Depend.* Oxford: John Murray and J. H. Parker, 1841. First edition, 8vo., recently wel bound in linen backed marbled boards, lettered, very good, inscribed "Ashmolean Society presented by the author", very scarce.   John Drury Rare Books   March 2015 - 23230   2015   £306

Daudet, Alphonse *Aventures Prodigieuses de Tartarin de Tarascon.* Paris: E. Dentu, 1872. First edition, 8vo., half title but without ad in contemporary vellum backed boards, vellum soiled, very good.   Second Life Books Inc.   191 - 29   2015 $750

Daugherty, James *Daniel Boone.* New York: Viking Press, 1939. First edition, first printing, 4to., brown cloth, fine in dust jacket (two 1 inch pieces off front edge, ward seal), Newbery award winner, laid in is one page TLS by author, letter has 2 old tape marks and he has made several sloppy corrections and few spelling errors in text.   Aleph-Bet Books, Inc.   108 - 129   2015 $850

Davenant, Charles   1656-1714 *An Essay Upon the Probable Methods of making a People Gainers in the Ballance of Trade.* London: for James Knapton, 1700. Second edition, five folding tables, few sidenotes slightly shaved, sheet D foxed, occasional minor spotting throughout, late 18th century calf, covers with gilt arms of William Stuart, rebacked, corners repaired, edges worn, new endleaves, arms of William Stuart (1798-1874) on covers, stringently and critically underlined and marked throughout in pencil in early 20th century hand, some occasional longer annotations and mathematical calculations, from the library of James Stevens Cox (1910-1997).   Maggs Bros. Ltd.   1447 - 132   2015   £500

Davenant, Charles   1656-1714 *An Essay Upon the Probable Methods of making a People Gainers in the Balance of Trade.* London: James Knapton, 1700. Second edition, 8vo., 6 folding tables as called for, contemporary mottled calf with old rebacking, small patches of surface wear to joints, later endpapers, very good, sound.   John Drury Rare Books   2015 - 25505   2015 $1311

Davenant, William   1606-1668 *Gondibert: an Heroick Poem.* London: John Holden, 1651. Second edition, 8vo., marginal browning some spotting and with paper fault in lower margin of O4, contemporary sheep, covers ruled in blind, rebacked, corners repaired, new endleaves, old flyleaves preserved, 17th century inscription of John Wallis, below another deleted signature, from the library of James Stevens Cox (1910-1997).   Maggs Bros. Ltd.   1447 - 133   2015   £240

David, Elizabeth *An Omelette and a Glass of Wine.* New York: Viking, 1985. First U. S. edition, fine in fine dust jacket.   Beasley Books   2013 - 2015 $45

David, J. C. *David's Display of the Specific Distinctions (on prominent Principles or Essence of the Soul) of the Executive and Each Individual of the Executive Council Also of all the Members.* Philadelphia: printed for the author, 1836. First edition, 8vo., original rear printed wrapper only (detached), title browned, blank corner chipped away, tide mark across top margin of first few leaves.   M & S Rare Books, Inc.   97 - 248   2015 $225

Davidson, Bruce *East 100th Street.* Los Angeles: St. Ann's Press, 2003. First edition thus, copy 4 of only 100 copies, expanded edition, very fine in very fine acetate jacket and in fine slipcase, includes original silver gelatin print that along with book are both signed and numbered by Davidson.   Jeff Hirsch Books   E-62 Holiday List 2014 - 8   2015 $1250

Davidson, George *Pacific Coast. Coast Pilot of California, Oregon and Washington Territory 1869.* Washington: GPO, 1869. First edition, small quarto, 32 engraved plates, publisher's dark brown cloth, gilt lettered on front cover, rebacked to match, paper spine label, corners show light wear, hint of occasional foxing, some soiling to title and one other page, overall fine.   Argonaut Book Shop   Holiday Season 2014 - 67   2015 $450

Davidson, Jo *Spanish Portraits.* New York: Georgian Press, 1939. Reissue of 1938 NY exhibition catalog, off white covers now bit smudged, near fine in stapled wrappers.   Ken Lopez, Bookseller   164 - 85   2015 $65

Davidson, Laura *Vaso.* Boston: 1994. One of 20 copies signed and numbered by artist, page size 6 1/4 x 4 1/4 inches, printed red boards with black leather spine, ceramic laid onto front panel in white with beige border surrounding a black antique vase with title in black lettering, screwed on with two brass screws, 10 woodcuts that cut-out and onlaid onto black french-fold paper with text written by artist on white, fine.   Priscilla Juvelis - Rare Books   61 - 7   2015 $850

Davidson, Lionel *A Long Way to Shiloh.* London: Gollancz, 1966. First edition, lower corners slightly bumped, otherwise fine in price clipped dust jacket with closed tear on back panel and small chips at corners. Mordida Books   March 2015 - 000595   2015 $75

Davidson, Lionel *Making good Again.* London: Cape, 1968. First edition, corner creasing on front endpaper, otherwise fine in dust jacket with couple of short closed tears. Mordida Books   March 2015 - 011394   2015 $100

Davidson, William *The Sources and Mode of Propagation of the Continued Fevers of Great Britain and Ireland.* London: John Churchill, 1841. First edition, 8vo., half title, original green cloth, embossed in blind, fine, uncut, presentation copy from author for John Welsh, esquire.   John Drury Rare Books   March 2015 - 25531   2015   £306

Davies, Robertson *An Introduction to the Twenty-First Toronto Antiquarian Book Fair.* Letters an Coach House, 1993. First edition, one of 100 numbered copies, signed by author, fine.   Beasley Books   2013 - 2015 $85

Davies, William Henry   1871-1940 *The Soul's Destroyer and Other Poems.* London: privately printed for the author, 1905. First edition, octavo, wrappers, scarce, spotting, mainly to prelims and last few leaves, covers detached, chipped and creased, spine defective, in need of attention, but internally sound.   Peter Ellis, Bookseller   2014 - 017438   2015   £350

Davis, E. *Elsie's Trip in the Rocky Mountains.* New York: n.d., 1888. 49 pages, illustrations, original decorative wrappers with string binding, wrappers soiled, internally clean and very good.   Dumont Maps and Books of the West   130 - 22   2015 $75

Davis, Eliza Jeffries *The University Site, Bloomsbury.* Cambridge: 1936. Reprinted from London Topographical Record Volume XVII, Folding map, photos, maps, plans, uncut in blue paper wrappers, marked, front wrapper detached, presentation by author for Geoffrey Tillotson. Jarndyce Antiquarian Booksellers   CCVII - 163   2015   £35

Davis, George *Black Life in Corporate America: Swimming in the Mainstream.* Garden City: Anchor/Doubleday, 1982. First edition, fine in near fine dust jacket with usual rubbing, inscribed by Davis and co-author, Glegg Watson for novelist Barry Beckham.   Between the Covers Rare Books, Inc.   187 - 68   2015 $250

Davis, Herbert *Stella: a Gentlewoman of the Eighteenth Century.* New York: Macmillan Co., 1942. First edition, boards trifle soiled near fine, bookplate of Hallie Flanagan Davis, with bookplate.   Between the Covers Rare Books, Inc.   187 - 69   2015 $125

Davis, Hewitt *The Sources Farmers Possess for Meeting the Reduced Prices of their Produce.* London: F. Waller, 1844. First edition, 8vo., 46 pages, recent plain wrappers, very good.   John Drury Rare Books   2015 - 15304   2015 $89

Davis, Lindsey *The Iron Hand of Mars.* London: Hutchinson, 1992. First edition, top corners bumped, else fine in dust jacket.   Mordida Books   March 2015 - 005334   2015 $225

Davis, Lindsey *Shadows in Bronze.* London: Sidgwick & Jackson, 1990. First edition, signed by author, fine, unread copy in fine dust jacket.   Buckingham Books   March 2015 - 29214   2015 $275

Davis, Lindsey *Shadows in Bronze.* London: Sidgwick & Jackson, 1990. First edition, very fine in dust jacket. Mordida Books   March 2015 - 005238   2015 $500

Davis, Lindsey *Shadows in Bronze.* London: Sidgwick and Jackson, 1990. First edition, signed by author, fine in fine dust jacket, from the collection of Duke Collier.   Royal Books   36 - 157   2015 $500

Davis, Lindsey *Shadows in Bronze.* London: Sidgwick & Jackson, 1990. First edition, fine in fine dust jacket. Buckingham Books   March 2015 - 19446   2015 $300

Davis, Lindsey *A Time to Depart.* Blakeney: Scorpion Press, 1955. First edition, limited to 15 lettered copies signed by author and Ellis Peters, fine in quarter leather with raised bands and marbled boards in transparent dust jacket. Buckingham Books   March 2015 - 20459   2015 $425

Davis, Lindsey *Venus in Cooper.* Hutchinson, 1901. First edition, very fine in dust jacket, signed by author. Mordida Books   March 2015 - 005239   2015 $200

Davis, Lydia *Blind Date.* Tucson: Chax Press, 1998. Copy number 66 of 100 numbered copies, although not called for, this copy signed by author, cover illustration by Cynthia Miller, approximately 6 x 10 1/2 inches, erratum slip laid in, with additional note stating that the initial plan was to paste the over illustration on to silk tissue paper, and only in second half of the print run did they change to using the uncovered boards, as they 'felt that was appropriate', this being number 66, this one of the 'appropriate' copies, scarce, fine.   Ken Lopez, Bookseller   164 - 44   2015 $550

Davis, Lydia *The Cows.* Louisville: Sarabande, 2011. First edition, thirty plus pages, including photos, this copy signed by author, tiny lower outer corner bump, else fine in stapled wrappers, uncommon signed.   Ken Lopez, Bookseller   164 - 45   2015 $125

Davis, Lynn *Monument.* Santa Fe: Arena Editions, 1999. First edition, fine, fine dust jacket, signed by Davis in year of publication, lovely copy. Jeff Hirsch Books E-62 Holiday List 2014 - 9   2015 $125

Davis, Norbert *The Mouse in the Mountain.* Morrow, 1943. First edition, fine, bright, tight copy, dust jacket with light professional restoration to spine ends. Buckingham Books March 2015 - 32999   2015 $1250

Davis, Paxton *Two Soldiers.* New York: Simon & Schuster, 1956. First edition, pages age toned, else near fine in very good or better dust jacket with two small chips at crown and some rubbing, inscribed by author for fellow author George Garrett 12 Dec. 1962, typed slip laid-in with request to send the book to Garrett. Between the Covers Rare Books, Inc. 187 - 70   2015 $125

Davis, Perry *The People's Pamphlet.* Providence: 1846. First edition, 8vo., 16 pages, on back wrapper is an illustration of the author in flames, self wrappers illustrated with large three quarter bust of author, sheets browned, foxed, fore-edge little frayed. M & S Rare Books, Inc. 97 - 36   2015 $275

Davis, Robert H. *Breathing in Irrespirable Atmospheres and In Some Cases, also Under Water, Including a Short History of Gas and Incendiary Warfare from Early Times to the Present Day...* London: St. Catherine Press, n.d. circa, 1948. First edition, 8vo., original brown cloth lettered gilt on spine and on front cover, copiously illustrated in black and white, very good. Any Amount of Books 2015 - A48848   2015   £170

Davis, Robert H. *Efficiency: a Play in One Act.* New York: George H. Doran, 1917. First edition, wrapped issue (simultaneous with board issue), printed flexible card covers, little soiled, else near fine, signed by Davis. Between the Covers Rare Books 196 - 152   2015 $650

Davis, Ronald L. *Phyllis Diller's Oral History Interview Transcript.* Dallas: Southern Methodist University, 1982. First edition, 4to., near fine, attractively bound in blue cloth, from the estate of Phyllis Diller. Ed Smith Books 83 - 14   2015 $200

Davis, S. C. H. *Motor Racing.* London: Iliffe, 1932. First edition, octavo, 32 photos, 6 maps and sketches by author, tail of spine slightly faded, very good in like dust jacket, with few short tears and chips. Peter Ellis, Bookseller 2014 - 017685   2015   £285

Davis, W. W. H. *El Gringo: or New Mexico and Her People.* New York: 1857. First edition, 432 pages, illustrations, original cloth stamped, extremities worn, spine faded, gilt title barely legible, bookplate on front pastedown, binding sound, internally clean and very good. Dumont Maps & Books of the West 131 - 46   2015 $175

Davis, Winfield J. *History of Political Conventions in California 1849-1892.* Sacramento: California State Library, 1893. First edition, handsomely bound in new dark brown cloth, leather spine label, errata slip, very fine. Argonaut Book Shop Holiday Season 2014 - 69   2015 $325

Davison, David *Remarks on the Best Means of School Education.* London: printed by W. Hughes Islington. n.d., 1833. Only edition, 8vo., titlepage bit dust marked, label removed from final (blank) page, recent plain wrappers, good, very scarce. John Drury Rare Books 2015 - 20550   2015 $177

Davy, Humphry 1778-1829 *A Lecture on the Plan Which is Proposed to Adopt for Improving the Royal Institution and rendering It Permanent. Delivered at the Theatre of the Royal Institution March 3d 1810.* London: William Savage Printer to the Royal Inst itutiton, 1810. First edition, final page lightly smudged, recent marbled boards lettered on spine, very good. John Drury Rare Books 2015 - 24890   2015 $787

Dawdy, Doris Ostrander *Artists of the American West. A Biographical Dictionary.* Chicago: Sage Books, Swallow Press, 1974. 1981. 1987. First edition of volumes 1 and 2, second printing of volume 3, signed by artist, Nick Eggenhofer, 3 volumes, black cloth gilt, slight rubbing to dust jacket volume I, else very fine set with printed dust jackets. Argonaut Book Shop Holiday Season 2014 - 70   2015 $125

Dawes, Manasseh *An Essay on Crimes and Punishments with a View of and Commentary Upon Beccaria, Rousseau, Voltaire, Montesquieu, Fielding and Blackstone.* London: C. Dilly and J. Debrett, 1782. First and only edition, 19th century bookplate on front pastedown of Worcester Library instituted 1790, with its blindstamp on titlepage and occasionally elsewhere, contemporary half calf over marbled boards, neatly rebacked and labelled, very good, rare. John Drury Rare Books 2015 - 23951   2015 $3060

Dawson, Coningsby *The Vanishing Point.* New York: Cosmopolitan, 1922. First edition, some foxing on page edges, otherwise fine in dust jacket with short closed tear. Mordida Books March 2015 - 000605   2015 $200

Dawson, E. Rumley *The Causation of Sex.* London: H. K. Lewis, 1909. First edition, hardcover, fine, lightly rubbed spine ends, bookplate. Beasley Books 2013 - 2015 $45

Dawson, Fielding *The Dirty Blue Car a Long Story.* Fresno: Wake Up Heavy, 1999. First edition, one of 30 numbered copies signed by author, from an edition of 200 copies, this being no. 14, 8vo., fine, wrappers. Beasley Books 2013 - 2015 $45

Dawson, Nicholas *Narrative of Nicholas 'Cheyenne' Dawson.* San Francisco: Grabhorn Press, 1933. Second edition, although not indicated, one of 500 copies, color drawings by Arvilla Parker, cloth backed decorated boards, paper spine label, some offsetting as usual to free endpapers, fine.   Argonaut Book Shop   Holiday Season 2014 - 71   2015 $125

Dawson, William Harbutt *Matthew Arnold and His Relation to the Thought of Our Time...* New York: G. P. Putnam's Sons, 1904. Frontispiece, few marginal marks, original dark blue cloth, from the library of Geoffrey & Kathleen Tillotson.   Jarndyce Antiquarian Booksellers CCVII - 62   2015   £20

Dawson, William Leon *The Birds of California.* San Diego: South Moulton Co., 1923. Patron's edition deluxe, limited to 250 numbered copies, signed by author, 4 volumes, large quarto, original green hard grain morocco, front covers lettered gilt, spines decoratively stamped in gilt and black, lettered in gilt with inlaid bird designs, top edge gilt, about fine in original box, which shows some fading.   Heritage Book Shop   Holiday 2014 - 48   2015 $5000

Day, Lionel *"The Buried World." in The Boys' Friend Library.* London: Amalgamated Press Oct. 4, 1928. Number 162 (new series), octavo, 64 pages, pictorial wrappers.   L. W. Currey, Inc.   Boy's Adventure Fiction 2015 - 81   2015 $100

De Acosta, Mercedes *Archways of Life.* New York: Moffat Yard and Co., 1921. First edition, paper covered boards with printed label, small label of Churchill Book and print shop in L, erosion of spine, sunning and corners of board rubbed, good copy, Mabel Normand's copy with her bookplate and inscribed by her to herself, additionally she has made comments at a couple of poems.   Between the Covers Rare Books, Inc.   187 - 71   2015 $3000

De Angeli, Marguerite *The Door in the Wall.* Garden City: Doubleday and Co., 1949. 8vo., brown cloth, fine in dust jacket (no award seal, not price clipped, frayed at spine ends), black and white illustrations by de Angeli, this copy inscribed by De Angeli.   Aleph-Bet Books, Inc.   108 - 123   2015 $300

De Baca, Manuel C. *Vicente Silva and his 40 Bandits.* Edward McLean, Libros Escogidos, 1947. First edition, 4to., limited of 500 copies, signed by Lane Kauffmann, the translator and Fanita Lanier, who did the illustrations, further inscribed to Carl Hertzog by Edward McLean, the publisher, two-tone cloth, titles in red on front cover, bookplate of Carl Hertzog, illustrations, fine, clean, bright copy in original dust jacket with chips at spine ends and light wear to extremities.   Buckingham Books   March 2015 - 35962   2015 $200

De Belabre, Baron *Rhodes of the Knights.* Oxford: Clarendon Press, 1908. First edition, 4to., original black buckram lettered gilt at spine with shield decoration on front cover, copiously illustrated in color and black and white with maps, inscriptions, shields and photos by author, rebacked with new endpapers, handsome, very good+.   Any Amount of Books   2015 - C7941   2015   £240

De Camp, L. Sprague *A Gun for Dinosaur and Other Imaginative Tales.* Garden City: Doubleday & Co., 1963. First edition, octavo, cloth backed boards.   John W. Knott, Bookseller   Selected New Arrivals Jan. 2015 - 16990   2015 $250

De Coste, John A. *A History of Aylesford and District.* Hantsport: Lancelot Press, 1986. 8vo., map and numerous black and white photo illustrations, card cover slightly worn and darkened along edges.   Schooner Books Ltd.   110 - 68   2015 $45

De Grazia, Ted *Father Junipero Serra. Sketches of His Life in California.* Los Angeles: Ward Ritchie Press, 1969. First edition, profusely illustrated with sketches by De Grazia, tan pictorial cloth stamped in dark brown, very fine with pictorial dust jacket.   Argonaut Book Shop   Holiday Season 2014 - 72   2015 $60

De Grey, William *The Compleat Horse-Man and Expert Feerrier.* London: by J. and R. and R. H. for Samuel Lowndes, 1684. Fifth edition, small 4to., some minor staining and spotting throughout, small piece torn away from fore-corner of I2, minor tearing to edges of some, small hole through centre of M3 affecting 4 words, contemporary sheep (covers rubbed, corners worn, large piece torn away from lower headcap, flyleaves bit torn and stained, pastedowns unstuck, signatures of William Ebourne and Ann Ebourne 1689, from the library of James Stevens Cox (1910-1997).   Maggs Bros. Ltd.   1447 - 134   2015   £300

De Hass, Wills *History of the Early Settlement and Indian Wars of Western Virginia...* H. Hoblitzell, 1851. First edition, 8vo., original embossed front and rear panels, gold image on front cover, titles stamped in gold on spine, frontispiece, illustrations, plates, cloth professionally reinforced on spine with original title laid down, little foxing to few pages, light wear to corners and extremities, else very good, tight copy, very rare.   Buckingham Books   March 2015 - 29566   2015 $2250

De Holden-Stone, Geoffrey *The Automobile Industry.* London: Methuen, 1904. First edition, numerous diagrams and illustrations, small spot on front board, corners just little rubbed and worn, near fine, exceptionally scarce.   Between the Covers Rare Books   196 - 62   2015 $750

De La Gorce, Jerome *Berain: Dessinateur Du Roi Soleil.* Paris: Herscher, 1986. First edition, 4to., copiously illustrated in color and black and white, fine in fine dust jacket.   Any Amount of Books   2015 - C1455   2015   £150

De La March, John *A Complaint of the False Prophets Marin(ers) Upon the Drying Up of Their Hierarchical Euph(rates).* London: Thomas Payne, 1641. First edition, small 4to., engraved titlepage by John Droeshout (cropped at fore-edge with loss of text to two words affecting figure on right and folded-in at foot, frayed at foot with loss of second line of imprint with date and engraver's name), folding letterpress table, B1 has been cancelled, first leaf repaired at outer corners and mounted on a stub, title damaged at upper corner, third leaf damaged in inner margin, mounted on stub and short at fore-margin, first few leaves dampstained, minor staining to lower fore-corner of E3-4, mid 20th century unfinished binding of quarter morocco and pasteboards, spine unlettered, boards unlined, from the library of James Stevens Cox (1910-1997). Maggs Bros. Ltd. 1447 - 135 2015 £350

De La Mare, Walter 1873-1956 *Down-Adown-Derry.* London: Constable, 1922. Limited to 325 numbered copies, signed by De La mare, 4to., printed on handmade paper and illustrated by Lathrop with 3 magnificent color plates with guards, plus a profusion of beautiful black and whites, white imitation vellum paper binding top edge gilt, gilt pictorial cover, covers aged as is common with this title, few small spots else tight, clean and very good+. Aleph-bet Books, Inc. 109 - 251 2015 $750

De La Mare, Walter 1873-1956 *Down a Down Derry.* London: Constable, 1922. First edition, 4to., blue cloth, top edge gilt, slight cover soil and rubbing, near fine, slight cover soil and rubbing, near fine, illustrations by Dorothy Lathrop. Aleph-Bet Books, Inc. 108 - 262 2015 $300

De La Mare, Walter 1873-1956 *Songs of Childhood.* London: Longmans, Green and Co., 1902. First edition, frontispiece by Richard Doyle, original quarter parchment, spine lettered and decorated gilt, gilt ruled pale blue linen sides with gilt publisher's device stamped on upper cover, top edge gilt, spine little rubbed and browned, sides slightly soiled and light spotting to endpapers, label removed from front pastedown, otherwise nice in worn and partly defective slipcase, bookplate, scarce, from the collection of Gavin H. Fryer. Bertram Rota Ltd. 308 Part II - 148 2015 £400

De La Mare, Walter 1873-1956 *Told Again.* Oxford: Basil Blackwell, 1927. Limited to only 260 numbered copies signed by author, 8vo., white cloth stamped in gold, edges uncut (one roughly), cloth very lightly soiled, else fine, illustrations by A. H. Watson, 8 lovely color plates plus many full page black and whites. Aleph-Bet Books, Inc. 108 - 128 2015 $500

De La Torre, Lillian *The Detections of Dr. Sam. Johnson.* Garden City: Doubleday, 1960. First edition, fine in price clipped dust jacket with nick at top corner, inscribed by author. Mordida Books March 2015 - 006608 2015 $125

De Lolme, John Louis *The Constitution of England, or an Account of the English Government....* London: printed by T. Spilsbury and sold by G. Kearsley, 1775. First edition in English, small blindstamp on title and cancelled inkstamp on verso of title of Maidstone Museum, first and final leaves just bit spotted or browned, contemporary half calf gilt over marbled boards, little wear to spine, but very good, 19th century armorial bookplate of Julius Lucius Brenchley. John Drury Rare Books 2015 - 22812 2015 $787

De Monti, Hurka *Strictures on Mr. Logier's System of Musical Education.* Glasgow: printed by James Hedderwick, sold by William Burnbull and Charles J. A. De Monti, Glasgow, 1817. First edition, 8vo., one double page engraved plate of music, 80 pages, well bound recently in red watered cloth, spine lettered gilt, very good. John Drury Rare Books March 2015 - 25400 2015 £306

De Morgan, Augusta *A Budget of Paradoxes.* London: Longmans, 1872. First edition, half title, contemporary half red morocco, spine darkened, scarce, with Geoffrey Tillotson's initials 1953 and Kathleen Tillotson's marker denoting special interest. Jarndyce Antiquarian Booksellers CCVII - 164 2015 £120

De Quincey, Thomas 1785-1859 *The Collected Writings of...* Edinburgh: Adam & Charles Black, 1889. New edition, 14 volumes, frontispieces to some volumes, sound, about very good with some volumes slightly faded or tanned at spine and slight rubbing. Any Amount of Books 2015 - A82592 2015 £240

De Regniers, Beatrice Schenk *May I Bring a Friend?* New York: Atheneum, 1964. Stated first edition, 4to., cloth, slight bit of rubbing to top of spine, else fine in dust jacket (2 small holes and some fading to spots, no medal, not price clipped), bright color illustrations and detailed black and whites by Beni Montresor, very scarce edition. Aleph-bet Books, Inc. 109 - 298 2015 $525

De Rousiers, Paul *La Vie Americaine.* Paris: Librairie De Firmin Didot Et Cie, 1892. First French edition, thick quarto, three quarter leather and cloth, titles stamped in gold on spine, raised bands, marbled endpapers, frontispiece, illustrations, maps, chapter notes, light cosmetic restoration to spine ends and corners, else very good. Buckingham Books March 2015 - 31037 2015 $400

De Vinne, Theodore Low 1828-1914 *Historic Printing Types, a Lecture Read Before the Grolier Club of New York Jan. 25, 1885.* New York: Grolier Club, 1886. First edition, limited to only 202 copies, 4to., original half creme colored cloth over boards, top edge gilt, others uncut, 54 illustrations, covers rubbed and spotted, wear at head of spine. Oak Knoll Books 306 - 213 2015 $225

De Vinne, Theodore Low 1828-1914 *Specimens of Printing Types Made at Bruce's New York Type Foundry Established in 1813....* New York: George Bruce's Son & Co., 1882. 1878., thick 4to., 2 volumes in one as issued, later blue cloth with leather spine label, a number of pages have been skillfully repaired along edges using rice paper, this copy contains the 7th supplement to general catalog dated 1891 and containing pages 381-384. Oak Knoll Books 306 - 211 2015 $2500

De Volpi, Charles P. *Newfoundland a Pictorial.* Toronto: Longman, 1972. Quarto, half title, 181 plates, cloth, reproductions of 181 woodcuts, engravings, lithographs, previous owner's name and a notation on back of half title and there is light scuff mark to titlepage. Schooner Books Ltd. 110 - 34 2015 $60

De Windt, Harry *Through the Gold-fields of Alaska to Bering Straits.* Harper & Bros., 1898. 8 1/2 x 6 inches, grey cloth stamped in gilt, black and white, illustrations, errata sheet still attached, folding map, 32 plates, spine darkened, bookplate on front pastedown sheet with offsetting to free front flyleaf, good. Buckingham Books March 2015 - 37032 2015 $295

Deacon, Samuel *On the Choice of a Wife, Illustrated by Many Curious Examples in the History of the Frugals...* Leicester: printed and sold by J. F. Winks; London: G. Wightman, n.d.?, 1836. Second edition but first with this title, 12mo., frontispiece, half title, stitching broken, original dark green cloth with original printed title label on upper cover, rare. John Drury Rare Books 2015 - 23130 2015 $177

Dean, John W. *Flying Saucers and the Scriptures.* New York: Vantage, 1964. First edition, many diagrams, tables, photos, charts, maps, near fine in very good dust jacket with small chips. Beasley Books 2013 - 2015 $125

Dean, Johnny *The Beatles Book.* London: Best Publicans, Ealing, 1976-2003. Complete run from first issue, 321 monthly issues in all, all very good, clean, complete condition in 22 original red folders. Any Amount of Books March 2015 - A72990 2015 £400

Dean, Robert George *Murder in Mink.* New York: Charles Scribner's Sons, 1941. First edition, former owner's small embossed name stamp on front fly, else fine in dust jacket with minor wear to head of spine. Buckingham Books March 2015 - 33100 2015 $250

Dearborn, Nathaniel *American Text Book for Letters.* Boston: Nathl. Dearborn, 1846. Third edition, oblong tall 12mo., original leather backed printed paper covered boards, engraved titlepage and dedication page, leather spine worn and front cover detached, covers spotted, boxed. Oak Knoll Books Special Catalogue 24 - 11 2015 $250

Dearmer, Mabel *The Book of Penny Toys.* London & New York: Macmillan, 1899. First edition, 4to., cloth backed pictorial boards, some cover rubbing and scattered internal foxing, else very good, 14 color illustrations, exceedingly scarce. Aleph-Bet Books, Inc. 108 - 128 2015 $1400

Deaver, Jeffery *Blue River Blues.* London: Hodder & Stoughton, 2001. First edition, very fine in dust jacket. Mordida Books March 2015 - 008794 2015 $90

Deaver, Jeffery *Mistress of Justice.* New York: Doubleday, 1992. First edition, signed by author, fine in dust jacket, exceptional copy. Buckingham Books March 2015 - 24153 2015 $375

Deaver, Jeffery *Praying for Sleep.* New York: Viking, 1964. First edition, signed by author, very fine in dust jacket. Mordida Books March 2015 - 008263 2015 $80

Debussy, Claude *La Boite a Joujoux. Ballet pour Enfants.* Paris: Durand et Cie, 1913. Published in hardbound and softbound editions, this copy recased in tan paper covered boards with digital reproduction of Andre Helle's illustrated title affixed to front cover, original paper covers bound in, very good plus with few small closed tears to lower margin of few pages, 10 x 13 inches, very good+. The Kelmscott Bookshop 11 - 15 2015 $850

Declamationes, quae ex CCCLXXXVIII supersunt CXLV ex Vetere Exemplari Restitutae. Paris: Apud Mamertum Patissonium Typographum Regium in officina Roberti Stephani, 1580. First printing, some toning and spotting, neatly reinforced old tear to blank margin of four leaf, frequent old marginal notes and underlining in last quarter of text (and occasionally elsewhere), early ownership inscriptions to title, 8vo., contemporary limp vellum wrappers using Hebrew manuscript (with German printed binder's waste visible under pastedowns), sometime (probably 17th century) backed with pigskin, yapp edges, top edge and spine lettered in ink, old paper label at foot, ties removed, somewhat soiled, couple of short splits to edge of vellum, 17th century bookplate of Viennese monastery with shelfmarks, good. Blackwell's Rare Books Greek & Latin Classics VI - 88 2015 £700

The Declaration of Independence by the Citizens of Mecklenburg County on the Twentieth Day of May 1775 with Accompanying Documents and the Proceedings of the Cumberland Association. Raleigh: Lawrence & Lemay, Printers to the State, 1831. First edition, 8vo., 32 pages, original printed wrappers, light wear, foxed, very good, signature of A. B. Hamilton and 'Alexander' family, NC. M & S Rare Books, Inc. 97 - 225 2015 $225

A Definition of True Religion, by the Authors of Different Religious Denominations. Stockport: printed at the office of J. Lomax Great Bunderlank, 1816. First edition, 12mo., 24 page, preserved in modern wrappers, printed label on upper cover very good, very rare.   John Drury Rare Books   2015 - 24311   2015 $133

Defoe, Daniel *A Brief State of the Inland or Home Trade, of England; and of the Oppressions It Suffers and the Dangers Which Threaten It from Invasion of Hawkers, Pedlars and Clandestine Traders of all Sorts, Humbly Represented to the Present Parliament.* London: printed for Tho. Warner at the Black Boy in Pater Noster Row, 1730. First edition, 8vo., 70 pages, bound in later plain cream boards, printed paper label on spine, very good crisp copy.   John Drury Rare Books   2015 - 25504   2015 $2185

Defoe, Daniel *Robinson Crusoe.* Boston: L. Prang, n.d. circa, 1864. 8vo., pictorial wrappers, some edge wear, die-cut in shape of Crusoe, every page delicately illustrated in color, rare.   Aleph-bet Books, Inc.   109 - 442   2015 $750

Defoe, Daniel *The Life and Adventures of Robinson Crusoe.* London & Edinburgh: William & Robert Chambers, circa, 1880? Frontispiece, original green cloth, hinges little rubbed, prize label from All Saints' Schools, Bradford to John H. Tillotson, Christmas 1882 and note from Arthur Tillotson, aged 10 with page of notes inserted, crossed through.   Jarndyce Antiquarian Booksellers   CCVII - 166   2015   £35

Defoe, Daniel *Robinson Crusoe.* London: Humphrey Milford, n.. circa, 1910. Thick 4to., pictorial cloth, top edge gilt, fine, publisher's pictorial slipcase (scuffed), 24 color plates, pictorial titlepage and pictorial endpapers by Noel Pocock.   Aleph-Bet Books, Inc.   108 - 130   2015 $550

Defoe, Daniel *Queries to the New Hereditary Right-Men.* London and Westminster: printed and sold by the booksellers, 1710. First edition, 8vo., stitched as issued, uncut, unbound, fine large copy.   John Drury Rare Books   March 2015 - 9823   2015 $266

Defoe, Daniel *The Religious Courtship being Historical Discourses, on the Necessity of Marrying Religious Husbands...* Montpelier: Derick Sibley for Josiah Parks, 1810. Third American edition, 8vo., contemporary calf little worn, leather label, pencil scribbling on endpaper, some toning and light foxing, very good tight copy.   Second Life Books Inc.   189 - 60   2015 $225

Defoe, Daniel *The Shakespeare Head Edition of the Novels and Selected Writings of Daniel Defoe.* Oxford: Basil Blackwell, 1974. Reprint of 1927 Shakespeare Head edition, limited to 750 copies, 14 volumes, original pale blue cloth, gilt, top edge gilt, fore-edges untrimmed, spines slightly faded, otherwise sound and clean, very good.   Any Amount of Books   2015 - A72449   2015   £280

Deford, Miriam Allen *The Theme is Murder.* Abelard Schuman, 1967. First edition, former owner's inked name and small inked later "M" to top edge of front flyleaf, else very good in rubbed black dust jacket.   Buckingham Books   March 2015 - 37489   2015 $200

Deford, Miriam Allen *Up-hill all the Way. The Life of Maynard Shipley.* Yellow Springs: Antioch Press, 1956. First edition, inscribed by author, near fine, one tiny spot, very good+ dust jacket with shallow chipping.   Beasley Books   2013 - 2015 $40

Defouri, James H. *The Martyrs of New Mexico; A Brief Account of the Lives and Deaths of the Earliest Missionaries in the Territory.* Las Vegas: 1893. 78 pages, original printed wrappers, spine and gutters taped, pages browned with some edge chipping but no loss of text, very fragile.   Dumont Maps & Books of the West   131 - 47   2015 $250

Degerando, Baron *The Visitor of the Poor.* Boston: Hilliard, Gray, Little & Wilkins, 1832. First edition translated by Elizabeth Palmer Peabody, 8vo., publisher's cloth with paper label (faded out), untrimmed, little wear at extremities of spine, library bookplate, small blank label on rear blank, little foxing and toning, very good, tight copy.   Second Life Books Inc.   189 - 194   2015 $450

Deighton, Len *Billion Dollar Brain.* London: Jonathan Cape, 1966. First edition, laid in are a facsimile of Deighton notebook and a facsimile of a TLS from Deighton describing the notebook, fine in near fine example of the fragile foil dust jacket, exceptional copy, from the collection of Duke Collier.   Royal Books   36 - 158   2015 $1850

Deighton, Len *Billion Dollar Brain.* London: Cape, 1966. First edition, fine in dust jacket with tiny wear at spine ends and crease on front panel.   Mordida Books   March 2015 - 009829   2015 $85

Deighton, Len *An Expensive Place to Die.* New York: Putnam, 1967. First edition, advanced reading copy, fine in plain soft covers with pictorial dust jacket bound into spine.   Mordida Books   March 2015 - 006603   2015 $125

Deighton, Len *Funeral in Berlin.* London: Jonathan Cape, 1964. First edition, fine in price clipped dust jacket.   Buckingham Books   March 2015 - 28635   2015 $200

Deighton, Len *Horse Under Water.* London: Cape, 1963. First edition, 2nd state with plain black endpapers, name on half titlepage, otherwise fine in dust jacket slightly darkened at spine and short crease on inner rear flap. Mordida Books   March 2015 - 012695   2015 $85

Deighton, Len *Introduction to the Adventure of the Priory School.* Santa Barbara: Santa Teresa, 1985. First edition one of 25 copies, bound in stapled wrappers printed for copyright purposes, very fine.   Mordida Books   March 2015 - 002629   2015 $250

Deighton, Len *Yesterday's Spy.* London: Cape, 1975. First edition, fine in dust jacket.   Mordida Books   March 2015 - 012693   2015 $100

Dekobra, Maurice *Serenade to the Hangman.* New York: Payson & Clarke, 1929. First American edition, very good in dust jacket with chipping at spine ends and wear along folds.   Mordida Books   March 2015 - 008523   2015 $125

Dekobra, Maurice *The 13th Lover.* Payson & Clarke, 1928. First American edition, some tiny spotting on page edges, otherwise fine in dust jacket with some wear at corners, publisher's wraparound intact.   Mordida Books   March 2015 - 007413   2015 $125

Delano, Alonzo *A Sojourn with Royalty and Other Sketches by Old Block (Alonzo Delano.* San Francisco: George Fields, 1936. First book edition, one of 500 copies, Small octavo, illustrations by Charles Lindstrom, 7 initials in sepia, 8 headpieces and titlepage illustration in color, orange pictorial boards, tan cloth spine, orange spine label printed in black, very light offsetting to ends from jacket flaps, but fine.   Argonaut Book Shop   Holiday Season 2014 - 73   2015 $75

Delany, Samuel R. *Nova.* Garden City: Doubleday & Co., 1968. First edition, octavo, cloth.   John W. Knott, Bookseller   Selected New Arrivals Jan. 2015 - 16992   2015 $150

Delaware's Industries. an Historical and Industrial Review. Philadelphia: Keighton, 1891. First edition, 8vo., original decorated cloth, frontispiece, illustrations, tiny bit of old light water staining to few pages at top of fore-edges, else very good.   Buckingham Books   March 2015 - 20169   2015 $200

Delepierre, Octave *Histoire Litteraire des Fous.* London: Trubner, 1860. First edition, octavo, original cloth, decorated in blind, lettered gilt, rare, pages unopened, spine faded bottom edge of lower cover little waterstained, very good. Peter Ellis, Bookseller   2014 - 002103   2015   £350

Delillo, Don *Underworld.* New York: Scribners, 1997. First edition, special signed copy that was not for sale, very near fine with some slight bumping to to rear corner in very near fine advanced state dust jacket, signed by author on publisher slip tipped in.   Jeff Hirsch Books   E-62 Holiday List 2014 - 10   2015 $150

Delillo, Don *White Noise.* N.P.: Viking, 1985. Advance reading copy, light foxing to rear cover and edges of text block, near fine in wrappers, from the library of National Book Award-winning author Peter Matthiessen.   Ken Lopez, Bookseller   164 - 46   2015 $250

Delillo, Don *The Word for Snow.* New York: Karma; Easthampton: Glen Horowitz, 2014. Limited edition, of a total edition of 1000, this one of 125 clothbound copies signed by Dello and co-author, Richard Prince, fine in publisher's acetate.   Ken Lopez, Bookseller   164 - 48   2015 $375

Dellon, Gabriel *Relation de L'Inquisition De Goa.* Paris: Daniel Horthemels, 1688. First edition thus, 12mo., 6 engraved plates, including 3 foldouts, woodcut vignettes and devices, contemporary full vellum, title inked at head of spine, boards little bowed and grubby as typical, some of the engraved plates have been cropped with minimal loss of printed matter, otherwise pleasing.   Any Amount of Books   March 2015 - C16379   2015   £450

Demainbray, Stephen George Francis Tribondet *The Poor Man's Best Friend; or land to Cultivate for His Own Benefit.* London: James Ridgway, 1831. First edition, 8vo., 38 pages, wanting half title and final leaf of ads, recent marbled boards, lettered on spine, very good.   John Drury Rare Books   March 2015 - 25857   2015 $221

Demidoff, Anatole *Voyage dans la Russie Meridonale & la Crime...* Paris: Dublie par Gihout Freres, 1838-1848. First edition, large folio, half title, lithographed title with plate list on verso and 100 contemporary hand colored lithographed plates by August Raffet, with descriptive text (issued separately) bound in, unusual thus; contemporary half red morocco over marbled boards, boards ruled gilt, spine lettered and decoratively tooled in gilt, minimal wear to extremities, including thumbnail size peeling to bottom edge of front marbled board, overall very clean except for dampstaining to back endpapers and occasionally to upper corner of some plates, but only occurring on title verso, not affecting plates, some light marginal browning and closed crack to upper outer hinge, with no loss, previous owner, Baron de Northmont's armorial bookplate, overall wonderful copy. Heritage Book Shop   Holiday 2014 - 49   2015 $45,000

Demille, Nelson *Cathedral.* New York: Delacorte Press, 1981. First edition, fine in dust jacket with light wear to extremities.   Buckingham Books   March 2015 - 29488   2015 $200

Deming, Therese *Red People of the Wooded Country.* Chicago: Laidlaw, 1932. 8vo., cloth, fine in chipped dust jacket, illustrations by Edwin Deming with 40 full page color illustrations, plus few smaller illustrations in text, beautiful copy, rare in dust jacket.   Aleph-Bet Books, Inc.   108 - 247   2015 $350

Deming, William Chapin *Roosevelt in the Bunk House. Visits of the Great Rough Rider to Wyoming in 1903 and 1910.* privately printed, n.d. circa, 1926. First edition, 8vo., tan printed wrappers, illustrations, rare first edition, very good.   Buckingham Books   March 2015 - 29027   2015 $1500

Deming, William Chapin *Roosevelt in the Bunk House and Other Sketches.* Laramie: Laramie Printing Co., 1927. Second edition, 8vo., blue printed wrappers, frontispiece, illustrations, scarce, fine, bright copy, very scarce. Buckingham Books   March 2015 - 25003   2015 $650

The Democratic Platform for 50 Years. The Immortal Kentucky and Virginia Resolutions of 1798, with their History and Application. Chicago: Aug., 1864. First edition, 8vo., (8) pages, folded, dusted, rubberstamp on titlepage and release on blank verso, good+.   M & S Rare Books, Inc. 97 - 62   2015 $625

Denby, Edwin *Aerial.* New York: Eyelight Press, 1981. First edition, one of 26 lettered copies, signed by most contributors on tipped-in sheet, 4to., illustrations, original pictorial wrappers, fine.   James S. Jaffe Rare Books   Many Happy Returns - 384   2015 $1250

Denham, John *Poems and Translations with the Sophy.* London: for H. Herringman, 1668. First collected edition, 2nd issue, 8vo., small dampstain and some very minor worming to lower inner margin of A1-K6, 2 small holes in lower part margin of Hh6, with paper flaw in lower corner of M3, 2B1 and lower edge of I2, stain on Aa8, slight rust spotting to Cc3, small slip of paper glued to lower corner of cc4 covering old neat repair, contemporary sheep (20mm. piece torn away from foot of spine, lower corners worn and boards lightly rubbed, old label missing, pastedowns unstuck), Alex Henderson 16?84 signature, early 19th century bookplate of Morough O'Bryen, purple ink oval library stamp of George Stawell, solicitor Torrington, from the library of James Stevens Cox (1910-1997).   Maggs Bros. Ltd.   1447 - 137   2015   £500

Denham, John *Poems and Translations with the Sophy.* London: for H. Herringman, 1668. First collected edition, first issue, 8vo., small ink stain to lower margin of titlepage and fore-edges of D1-D7, small rust spots to 2E5 and 2E8, with small piece torn away from lower blank margin of I1, contemporary polished mottled calf, covers with double gilt fillet and gilt floral tool in each corner, smooth spine ruled in gilt, gilt edges joints rubbed, three small wormholes in upper joint, slight surface crazing to covers, from mottling acid, one corner slightly worn, bottom corner of front flyleaf torn away, errata has been corrected by hand, signature of Edmund Smith (16)88, inscription of Jenks Lutley Esquire 1729, early 18th century armorial bookplate of Richard Barneby of Brockhampton, Herefordshire, from the library of James Stevens Cox (1910-1997).   Maggs Bros. Ltd.   1447 - 136   2015   £600

Denham, Thomas *The Temporal Government of the Pope's State.* London: J. Johnson, 1788. First edition, very good, scarce, 8vo., wanting front free endpaper contemporary calf, spine simply gilt and labelled, very good. John Drury Rare Books   2015 - 24103   2015 $656

Dennett, Mary Ware *Birth Control Laws Shall We Keep Them Change Them or Abolish Them?* New York: Hitchcock, 1926. First edition, 8vo., very good, little chipped and worn dust jacket.   Second Life Books Inc. 189 - 62   2015 $75

Dennis, John *The Pioneer of Progress; or the Early Closing Movement in Relation to the Saturday in Relation to the Saturday Half-Holiday and the Early Payment of Wages...* London: Hamilton Adams & Co., circa, 1861. (1860). Second edition, 8vo., including half title with erratum slip tipped in, original blindstamped lilac cloth, spine gilt lettered, fine.   John Drury Rare Books   2015 - 25758 2015 $177

Dennis, John *Rinaldo and Armida; a Tragedy...* London: Jacob Tonson, 1699. First edition, small 4to., lacking half title and without errata slip pasted below 'Dramatis Personae' in some copies, heavily browned and stained throughout, repair to upper corner of B4 touching first letter on verso, large repair to upper blank corner of d4 and with a number of leaves mounted on stubs, early 20th century full black morocco, signature of Dr. Thomas Loveday (d. 1968), from the library of James Stevens Cox (1910-1997). Maggs Bros. Ltd.   1447 - 138   2015   £220

Denny, Henry *Monographia Pselaphidarum et Seydmaenidarum Britanniae or an Essay.* Norwich: S. Wilkin, 1825. Octavo, 74 pages, 14 hand colored engraved plates, publisher's cloth, respined, very good, scarce. Andrew Isles   2015 - 37174   2015 $650

Dennys, Joyce *Our Hospital Anzac British Canadian.* London: John Lane, The Bodley Head, New York: John Lane Co., Toronto: S. B. Gundy, 1916. Half title, illustrations in color, few marginal tears, signs of previous tape repair to gutter of 2 leaves, original grey boards, pictorially blocked in white, red and blue, lettered in red and white, blue cloth spine, slightly marked and scratched, signs of old repair to leading inner hinge. Jarndyce Antiquarian Booksellers CCXI - 88 2015 £75

Denslow, W. W. *When I Grow Up.* New York: Century, Sept., 1909. First edition, 4to., tan pictorial cloth, slight finger soil on rear cover, else fine. Aleph-bet Books, Inc. 109 - 120 2015 $1200

Dent, Edward John *A Treatise on the Aneroid, a Newly Invented Portable Barometer.* London: published by the author, 1840. First edition, 8vo., printed on blue paper, complete with final ad leaf, 10 figures in text and 2 further figures, preserved in modern. John Drury Rare Books March 2015 - 25239 2015 £266

Derby, Edward Henry Smith Stanley, 15th Earl of *Memorandum on Suggested Improvements in the Patent Laws of 1852. 1853.* London: T. & W. Boone, 1856. First edition, 8vo., 18 pages, recent plain wrappers, very good, very scarce. John Drury Rare Books 2015 - 16762 2015 $106

Dereme, Tristan *Songes Du Papier.* Paris: Papeteries Du Marais, 1944. No. 65 of 400 copies on velin pur fil, unbound signatures, fine in fine wrappers, fine board chemise shows some foxing in near fine box, issued by the Marais paper company to display the suitability of their papers for typography, aquatints, woodcuts and lithographs, this copy printed for Monsieur Guido Colucci, 4to. illustrations by Daraganes, Galanis and Moreau. Beasley Books 2013 - 2015 $225

Dering, Edward Heneage *Freville Chase.* London and Leamington: Art and Book Co., 1890. Second edition, 6 pages ads, 2 volumes bound in one, original cream morocco grained cloth, boards with borders in blind, spine decorated and lettered in gilt, slightly dulled. Jarndyce Antiquarian Booksellers CCXI - 89 2015 £150

Derleth, August *The Casebook of Solar Pons.* Sauk City: Mycroft & Moran, 1965. First edition, small stain on fore-edge, otherwise fine in dust jacket. Mordida Books March 2015 - 008281 2015 $165

Derleth, August *In re: Sherlock Holmes.* Sauk City: Mycroft & Moran, 1945. First edition, fine in price clipped dust jacket. Mordida Books March 2015 - 008277 2015 $175

Derleth, August *In Re: Sherlock Holmes.* Sauk city: Mycroft & Morgan, 1945. First edition, fine in dust jacket with tiny tear at spine ends. Mordida Books March 2015 - 002426 2015 $200

Derleth, August *Mischief in the Lane.* New York: Scribner, 1944. First edition, very fine in dust jacket, inscribed by author. Mordida Books March 2015 - 007860 2015 $300

Derleth, August *The Reminiscences of Solar Pons.* Sauk City: Mycroft & Moran, 1961. First edition, fine in dust jacket. Mordida Books March 2015 - 008280 2015 $140

Derleth, August *The Return of Solar Pons.* Sauk City: Mycroft & Moran, 1958. First edition, fine in dust jacket. Mordida Books March 2015 - 008279 2015 $175

Derleth, August *Sentence Deferred.* New York: Scribners, 1939. First edition, fine in dust jacket. Mordida Books March 2015 - 006592 2015 $350

Des Brisay, Mathers *History of the County of Lunenburg.* Bridgewater: The Bridgewater Bulletin Ltd., 1967. Third edition, 8vo., blue buckram, photo, cloth slightly worn, top edges lightly stained. Schooner Books Ltd. 110 - 69 2015 $45

Desai, Anita *Cry, the Peacock.* London: Peter Owen, 1963. First edition, octavo, inscribed by author, fine in very good dust jacket with few nicks. Peter Ellis, Bookseller 2014 - 013711 2015 £350

Desaint, A. *Ideas & Studies in Stencilling & Decorating.* London: Charles Griffin, 1927. First edition, very good, old cloth shows some toning and wear, especially to spine, nice text and plates. Stephen Lupack March 2015 - 2015 $125

Descartes, Rene *Epistolae, Partim ab Auctore latino Sermone Conscriptae, Partim ex Gallico Translatae... (and) Epistolae, Parim Latino Sermone, Conscriptae, Partim & Gallico Latinim Versae.* Amstelodami: Danielem Elzevirium, 1668. and 1678. Blauiana: Amstelodami, 1683, 3 volumes, small quarto, numerous woodcuts in text, small quarto, 3 matching volumes in full contemporary vellum, spine titles in manuscript hand, small armorial stamp in mid right hand edge of each titlepage, truly gorgeous. Athena Rare Books 15 - 4 2015 $5200

Descartes, Rene *Renati Descartes Epistolae...* London: Joh(n) Dunmore & Octavian Pulleyn, 1668. First London edition, small 4to., 14 folding plates and numerous illustrations, endpapers little stained by original turn-ins, some light dampstaining to first three leaves of sheet O, contemporary calf, covers panelled in blind, rebacked new endpapers, John Wheeler with inscription, 18th century armorial bookplate of Johnstone family of Westerhall, Dumfries, from the library of James Stevens Cox (1910-1997). Maggs Bros. Ltd. 1447 - 141 2015 £750

Descartes, Rene *Renatus Descartes Excellent Compendium of Musick.* London: by Thomas Harper for Humphrey Moseley and Thomas Heath, 1653. First edition in English, small 4to., later engraved portrait, dampstaining to lower margins throughout, dark ink stain to upper margins of a1-b1- (not touching text), worming to lower margin of I4-M4 and with small piece torn away from margins of B3, G3 and L3 (not touching text), contemporary sheep, covers ruled in blind, spine worn and with some worm damage, edges and corners worn and chewed, 18th century inscription William Wilsons, 19th century signature G. U. Hart, Killderry, from the library of James Stevens Cox (1910-1997). Maggs Bros. Ltd. 1447 - 139 2015 £1500

Descartes, Rene *Six Metaphysical Meditations, Wherein It is proved that There is a Gold.* London: by B G. for Benj. Tooke, 1680. First edition in English, 12mo., titlepage soiled in margins and with small piece torn away from blank upper margin (to delete signature), soiling and dampstaining to margins throughout, small closed tear to lower blank margin of C1 (not touching text), some minor rust spots, mid 19th century calf, gilt ruled, rebacked, corners repaired, new endleaves, old signature torn away from upper margin of titlepage, from the library of James Stevens Cox (1910-1997). Maggs Bros. Ltd. 1447 - 140 2015 £1500

Description Des Travaux Entrepis Dans la Construction de La Tonnelle ou Passage Sous La Tamise Entre Rotherhithe et Wapping. London: Warrington & Co., 1851. Oblong 12mo., 10 plates, folding frontispiece map (torn along hinge), 1 folding plate, 1 tinted plate, 3 folding plates, 1 plate with overlay, 3 engraved plates, printed pictorial wrappers, old paper repairs to spine. Marlborough Rare Books Ltd. List 49 - 35 2015 £300

Description Exacte de Tout ce Qui S'est Passe Dans Les Guerres Entre Le Roy D'Angleterre Le Roy De Frances, Les Estats Des Provinces... Amsterdam: Jacques Benjamin, 1668. First French edition, small 4to., half brown leather lettered and decorated in gilt on spine with marbled boards, large engraved illustration on titlepage, 8 engraved illustrations in text, slightly worn with small chip missing from head of spine, some pronounced browning of text at middle (8 pages) but text legible and plates clean, slight loss to corner of one page but not affecting text, overall pleasing, very good. Any Amount of Books 2015 - C11647 2015 £800

A Description of Stonehenge, Abiry & c. In Wiltshire. Salisbury: printed and sold by Collins and Johnson, sold also by J. Wilkie, London, 1776. First edition, 6 woodcut plates (on leaves which form part of the gatherings, but are not included in pagination), 12mo., original mottled sheep, double gilt fillet borders on sides, rebacked preserving most of original red lettering piece, armorial bookplate of James Comerford placed over another, good. Blackwell's Rare Books B179 - 101 2015 £600

Descriptive Guide. 1000 Mile Excursion! By Rail, Sound & Ocean, to the Sea Islands... Stork Wright & Co., 1878. 7.5 x 5 inches, pictorial wrappers, 24 pages, engraved views, folded map on light blue parchment paper, penciled figuring on front wrapper along with light crease to bottom corner and light round stain to bottom of first 2 pages as well as to bottom of front cover, very good or better. Buckingham Books March 2015 - 34971 2015 $795

A Descriptive Historical Guide to the Valley of Lake Champlain and the Adirondacks. Burlington: R. S. Styles Starn Printing House, 1871. First edition, original gilt stamped dark pebbled paper over boards, illustrations, lacking map, rebacked, front hinge broken but reasonably closed by previous owner with archival material, same inside rear free leaf, gilt bright, minor edgewear to covers, text in very good condition, very scarce, good+. Baade Books of the West 2014 - 2015 $95

Design & Style 2. Cohoes: Mohawk Paper Mills, 1987. 4to., stiff paper wrappers in mailing envelope, 34 pages, envelope lightly worn along edges, illustrations. Oak Knoll Books 306 - 260 2015 $100

Desilver's Philadelphia Directory and Stranger's Guide for 1833. Philadelphia: Robert Desilver, 1833. 8vo., later quarter leather, paper covered boards, tanning and foxing, spine faded, original front wrapper laid down on front free endpaper,. Oak Knoll Books 306 - 261 2015 $300

Desmarest, Marie Anne *Torrents.* Paris: Editions De Gringoire, 1948. Unnumbered copy of an edition of 2980, wrappers fine in chemise with sunning to spine, box has stains to top edge, otherwise near fine, this copy with extra suite of prints, showing the four states of the litho color process for each print, interesting addition (total of 44 prints for the 11 prints shown in the book), small 4to. Beasley Books 2013 - 2015 $135

Desnos, Louis Charles *Dissertation Historique sur l'Invention des Lettres ou Caracteres E'Ecriture sur les Instruments dont les anciens se Sont Serevi Pour Ecrire & Sur les Matieres Qu'ils ont Employees.* Paris: Denos, 1771. First edition, 12mo. contemporary stiff paper wrappers, title written in pencil on front wrapper, wrappers bent and chipped at edges and soiled, pencilled notations on inside back wrapper, light foxing. Oak Knoll Books 306 - 93 2015 $575

Destruction of Life by Snake, Hydrophobia, etc. in Western India.   London: W. H. Allen, 1880. Duodecio, 120 pages, publisher's green cloth with titles, few blemishes otherwise very good, rare.   Andrew Isles   2015 - 36183   2015 $500

Detrosir, Rowland   *The Benefits of General Knowledge More Especially, the Sciences of Mineralogy, Geology, Botany and Entomology....*   London: J. Cleave, n.d.?, 1834. First edition, 8vo., very good, recent plain wrappers, very scarce.   John Drury Rare Books   March 2015 - 17952   2015 $266

Deulin, Charles   *Contes D'Un Buveur De Beire.*   Paris: Marcel Seheur, n.d., No. 90 of 187 copies, signed by publisher and by artist, Lucien Boucher, unbound signatures in wrappers, fine in wrappers in glassine, in titled board chemise and printed box depicting a drinking man, 4to.   Beasley Books   2013 - 2015 $300

Deutsches Bucherverzeichnis: Eine Zusammenstellung Der Im Deutxhen Buchhandel Erfchienennen Bucher...   Leipzig: Verlag des Borsenvereins der Deutschen Buchhandler, 1916-1937. 19 volumes, volume 3 in two parts, volume 6 missing from this set, ex-library with markings, most volumes have normal wear associated with age.   Oak Knoll Books   306 - 73   2015 $450

Devambez, Andre   *Auguste a Mauvais Caractere.*   Paris: Devambez Editeur, 1914. Large square folio, cloth backed pictorial boards, boards rubbed and bit toned, else fine, rare, printed on handmade paper, with each page hinged into book, fabulous vibrant hand colored illustrations.   Aleph-Bet Books, Inc.   108 - 191   2015 $4000

Development and Resources of Beadle County in the New State of South Dakota.   N.P.: published and endorsed by the County Commissioners, 1889. First edition, 8vo., pink wrappers printed in black ink illustrations, maps, rare, former owner's inked name along top edge of front cover, else fine, tight copy.   Buckingham Books   March 2015 - 32828   2015 $1750

Deveria, Laure   *Fleurs Dessinees D'Apres Nature et Lithographiees.*   Paris: Jeannin, 1833-1838. First and only edition, folio, contemporary dark green half morocco, cloth boards with blind floral pattern, gilt spine with raised bands, titlepage and 24 hand colored lithographs after Deveria printed by Lemercier, some with original publisher's blindstamp, no text, rubbing to spine, repair to front hinge, occasional faint spots, very good, ink stamp of Ohrhybus Castle to front pastedown with pencil inscription attribution ownership to Gustav Bonde, exceptionally rare.   Henry Sotheran Ltd.   Natural History: Rarities 2015 - 2015   £17,500

The Devil's Diamond, or The Fortunes of Richard of The Raven's Crest.   London: Hogarth House, n.d. circa, 1885. Later edition?, large 12mo., 4 full page black and white illustrations, plus pictorial titlepage, original pictorial wrappers, printed in red and blue, side stapled.   L. W. Currey, Inc.   Boy's Adventure Fiction 2015 - 46   2015 $150

Devon and Exeter Hospital   *Statutes and Constitutions of the Devon and Exeter Hospital at Exeter; with the Rules and Orders for the Government and Conduct of the House...*   N.P.: Exeter? printed in the year, 1741. First edition, apparently of significant rarity, 4to., remains of old blue wrappers adhering to the blank recto of first leaf and blank verso of final leaf, fairly recent cloth backed boards with morocco label on upper cover, lettered gilt, fine, crisp copy.   John Drury Rare Books   2015 - 25573   2015 $1311

Dew, Robb Forman   *Dale Loves Sophie to Death.*   New York: Farrar Straus and Giroux, 1981. First edition, fine in fine dust jacket with very slight sunning to spine, with ALS sending the book to Nicholas Delbanco Dec. 1989.   Between the Covers Rare Books, Inc.   187 - 72   2015 $350

Dewey, John   *A Common Faith.*   New Haven: Yale University Press, 1934. First edition, 2nd printing, boldly signed by author on front free endpaper, octavo, original blue cloth with beautifully intact printed spine label, very slightest of sun toning to spine, overall tight, bright and clean copy.   Athena Rare Books   15 - 5   2015 $450

Dewey, John   *Impressions of Soviet Russia and the Revolutionary World.*   New York: New Republic Books, 1929. First edition, wrappers, close to fine.   Beasley Books   2013 - 2015 $45

Dewey, Thomas B.   *Hue and Cry.*   New York: Jefferson House, 1944. First edition, fine in price clipped dust jacket with nicks at spine ends, short internal tape repair and couple of short closed tears.   Mordida Books   March 2015 - 000640   2015 $135

Dexter, Colin   *Last Bus to Woodstock.*   London: Macmillan, 1975. Uncorrected proof, good to very good in publisher's plain green wrappers with black titles, spine lean, some vertical creasing to spine panel, light soil, lengthily inscribed by author for Staffan, from the collection of Duke Collier.   Royal Books   36 - 159   2015 $6500

Dexter, Colin   *Last Bus to Woodstock.*   London: Macmillan, 1975. First UK edition, very good in like dust jacket, slight spine lean, bumped at corners with mild shelfwear, jacket shows some fading along left edge of front panel, with 2 inch closed tear top of same and light soil overall, inscribed by author for Joan Spencer (colleague of author at Oxford), from the collection of Duke Collier.   Royal Books   36 - 160   2015 $3500

Dexter, Colin *Last Seen Wearing.* New York: St. Martin's, 1976. First US edition, fine in dust jacket with one small closed tear to bottom edge of front cover. Buckingham Books   March 2015 - 2015 $875

Dexter, Colin *Service for all the Dead.* London: Macmillan, 1979. First edition, 8vo., slight rubbing, slight spotting to fore-edges, otherwise very good+ in like dust jacket, signed presentation from author for Roger, Xmas 1979, from the Donald Rudd collection of detective fiction. Any Amount of Books   2015 - A93457   2015   £300

Dexter, Colin *Service for all the Dead.* St. Martin's Press, 1980. First US edition, fine in price clipped dust jacket. Buckingham Books   March 2015 - 36254   2015 $175

Dexter, Colin *Service of all the Dead.* St. Martin's Press, 1980. First US edition, fine in dust jacket. Buckingham Books   March 2015 - 36255   2015 $250

Dexter, Dave *Jazz Cavalcade.* New York: Criterion, 1946. First edition, hardcover, near fine with date on rear blank, very nice, dust jacket with small chip on spine. Beasley Books   2013 - 2015 $45

Dexter, Pete *Brotherly Love.* New York: Random House, 1991. First trade edition, fine in very good dust jacket with small chip on rear panel, signed by author, laid in TLS by author to Gary Will. Between the Covers Rare Books, Inc.   187 - 73   2015 $125

Diaz Del Castillo, Bernal 1496-1584 *The Discovery and Conquest of Mexico 1517-1521.* New York: Limited Editions Club, 1942. Limited to 1500 numbered copies signed by Block, Covarrubias and Chavez, printed by Chavez in Mexico, tall 4to., full marbled leather, leather spine label, slipcase with wear along edges. Oak Knoll Books   25 - 29   2015 $300

Dibdin, Michael *Dark Spectre.* London: Faber, 1995. First edition, very fine in dust jacket signed by author. Mordida Books   March 2015 - 002987   2015 $75

Dibdin, Thomas Frognall 1776-1847 *The Bibliographical Decameron or Ten Days Pleasant Discourse Upon Illuminated Manuscripts...* London: printed for the author by W. Bulmer and Co., Shakespeare Press, 1817. First and only edition, limited to 750-800 regular and 50 large paper copies, 3 volumes, 8vo., engraved plates, two double page, 35 text illustrations printed on Indian paper and mourned on pages, one mounted gilt lettered specimen of red pared calf, hundreds of engraved and woodcut text illustrations, several colored, bookplates, bound in later three quarter brown morocco, all edges marbled some minor foxing, soiling and offsetting, nice. Second Life Books Inc.   190 - 228   2015 $500

Dibdin, Thomas Frognall 1776-1847 *The Library Companion; or the Young Man's Guide and Old Man's Comfort in the Choice of a Library.* London: Harding Triphook and Lepard and J. Major, 1824. First edition, 2000 copies of this small paper edition printed, thick 8vo., full calf stamped in blind and gilt all edges gilt marbled, rubbing along edges and hinges. Oak Knoll Books   306 - 262   2015 $300

Dibdin, Thomas John *The Wigwam or, The Red Men of Wilderness.* London: John Dicks, 1884. Vignette title, sewn as issued, 15 pages. Jarndyce Antiquarian Booksellers   CCXI - 73   2015   £35

Dick Whittington and His Cat. New York: Holiday House, 1937. 16mo., cloth backed pictorial boards, very good-fine, color and black and white woodcuts by Fritz Eichenberg. Aleph-Bet Books, Inc.   108 - 167   2015 $200

Dick Whittington & His Cat. Beauty & the Beast. Saint George & the Dragon. New York: Limited Editions Club, 1949. Limited to 2500 numbered copies, Dick Whittington signed by Lawson and editor, Jean Hersholt, 3 volumes, folio, cloth, fine in slipcase, illustrations in color. Aleph-Bet Books, Inc.   108 - 266   2015 $425

Dick, Philip K. *Deus Irae.* Garden City: Doubleday & Co., 1976. First edition, octavo, boards. John W. Knott, Bookseller   Selected New Arrivals Jan. 2015 - 17011   2015 $150

Dick, Philip K. *Flow My Tears, The Policeman Said.* Garden City: Doubleday & Co. Inc., 1974. First edition, octavo, cloth. John W. Knott, Bookseller   Selected New Arrivals Jan. 2015 - 17007   2015 $850

Dick, Philip K. *The Man in the High Castle.* New York: G. P. Putnam's Sons, 1962. First edition, publisher's review slip laid in, octavo, cloth. John W. Knott, Bookseller   Selected New Arrivals Jan. 2015 - 17002   2015 $4500

Dick, Philip K. *Now Wait for Last Year.* Garden City: Doubleday & Co., 1966. First edition, octavo, cloth. John W. Knott, Bookseller   Selected New Arrivals Jan. 2015 - 17216   2015 $650

Dick, Philip K. *'The Skull' (in) If: Worlds of Science Fiction.* Buffalo: Quinn Pub. September, 1952. 12mo., perfectbound in illustrated wrappers, bit browned, little rubbing to wrappers, very good, signed by Dick, rare thus. Between the Covers Rare Books   196 - 153   2015 $850

Dick, Philip K. *The Collected Stories of Philip K. Dick.* Los Angeles: Columbia: Underwood Miller, 1987. First edition, octavo, 5 volumes, one of 500 numbered sets, this one of 100 specially bound in imitation leather with marbled endpapers and inserted limitation leaf with mounted Dick signature (cut from canceled check), laid in is leaflet (single sheet, folded to make four pages) "Brief Synopsis for Alternate World Novel: The Acts of Paul", imitation leather. John W. Knott, Bookseller   Selected New Arrivals Jan. 2015 - 17010   2015 $2000

Dickens, Charles   1812-1870   *American Notes for General Circulation.* London: Chapman and Hall, 1842. First edition, first issue, 2 volumes, original reddish brown cloth, spines lettered in gilt, covers stamped in blind, spines lightly faded, corners bumped, very minor wear to spine ends and small tear to upper spine of volume I, few minor spots to covers, prelim leaves in volume II unopened, excellent and very bright set, housed in custom folding quarter morocco folding case.   B & B Rare Books, Ltd.   234 - 16   2015 $2000

Dickens, Charles   1812-1870   *American Notes for General Circulation.* London: Chapman & Hall, 1842. First edition, original brown vertically ribbed blindstamped cloth, spines lettered gilt, original pale yellow coated endpapers, spines very slightly sunned, otherwise exceptional cloth, cloth bright and fresh, housed together in custom quarter red morocco slipcase, gilt stamped.   Heritage Book Shop Holiday 2014 - 50   2015 $1500

Dickens, Charles   1812-1870   *American Notes.* London: Chapman & Hall, 1842. First edition first issue, 2 volumes, half titles, ad leaf preceding half title volume I, 6 page catalog volume II, few marks in text, original purple cloth, blocked in blind, spines lettered gilt, expertly recased, bought by Kathleen Tillotson.   Jarndyce Antiquarian Booksellers   CCVII - 168   2015   £850

Dickens, Charles   1812-1870   *Barnaby Rudge: a Tale of the Riots of 'Eighty.* London: Chapman & Hall, 1841. First edition, first separate issue, large 8vo., variant binding of olive-green fine diaper cloth, covers and spine stamped in blind, covers with borders, leaf and chain-like design, spine lettered gilt, vignette illustrations and initials, excellent, near fine copy with very slight fading to spine and very slight bumping at corners.   Any Amount of Books   2015 - A98249   2015   £850

Dickens, Charles   1812-1870   *Barnaby Rudge.* Paris: Baudry's European Lib., 1842. 2 volumes, half titles, 4 page catalog volume I, some spotting, original brown paper wrappers, slightly torn, ink mark, original paper labels, nice, from the library of Geoffrey & Kathleen Tillotson.   Jarndyce Antiquarian Booksellers   CCVII - 169   2015   £85

Dickens, Charles   1812-1870   *Bleak House.* London: Bradbury and Evans, 1853. Frontispiece, added engraved title and plates, contemporary half dark blue calf, crimson label, rather rubbed but sound, internally very clean, Kathleen Tillotson's copy with note.   Jarndyce Antiquarian Booksellers   CCVII - 170   2015   £320

Dickens, Charles   1812-1870   *Bleak House.* London: Bradbury and Evans, 1853. First edition with all points and date in Roman numerals at foot of spine, original olive blindstamped cloth, rebacked with new endpapers preserving original spine gilt, spine somewhat browned, some soiling to cloth, one plate oddly trimmed, only affecting blank margin and plates, some foxing, but nice, from the collection of Gavin H. Fryer.   Bertram Rota Ltd.   308 Part II - 149   2015   £850

Dickens, Charles   1812-1870   *The Chimes.* London: Chapman & Hall, 1845. First edition, 2nd state with publisher's name outside title vignette, fine, in beautiful Kelliegram binding (so stamped on inside rear cover), full crimson morocco with inlaid leather picture on cover after one of John Leech's illustrations in book, lovely gilt decorative border on both covers, in the six compartments and on the turn-ins as well, all edges gilt. original covers and spine bound in at end, beautiful book.   Aleph-Bet Books, Inc.   108 - 136   2015 $2850

Dickens, Charles   1812-1870   *The Chimes.* London: Limited Editions Club, 1931. Limited to 1500 numbered copies, 4to., full tan cloth with beveled boards, with Rackham design printed in black and gold on front cover, spine lettered gilt, slipcase decorated with red and gold design by the artist, signed by the artist, Arthur Rackham, printed on Japon vellum in brown and black, endpapers printed with Rackham drawing in brown, each recto page has title and author printed in pale tan at bottom of page, title page and frontispiece decorated with Rackham designs printed in black and brown, many full page illustrations, chapter headings, beautiful book, slipcase soiled and spotted with cracking along hinges, spine of book age darkened and covers abraded along spine, endpapers show light foxing, series announcement loosely inserted.   Oak Knoll Books   25 - 5   2015 $250

Dickens, Charles   1812-1870   *A Christmas Carol in Prose.* London: Chapman & Hall, 1843. First edition, first issue, i.e. "Stave 1",, text entirely uncorrected, green coated endpapers, blue half title, red and blue title, foolscap 8vo., four inserted handcolored steel engraved plates and four black and white text wood engravings, original cinnamon vertically ribbed cloth, covers decoratively stamped and lettered gilt, all edges gilt, binding matches Todd's first impression, first issue, with smallest interval between blindstamped border and gilt wreath equal to 14mm. and with perfect 'D' in 'Dickens', previous owner's inscription on half title, some soiling to covers, mostly to front cover, bottom of spine little rubbed, small amount of chipping to top of spine, good, clean copy.   Heritage Book Shop   Holiday 2014 - 51   2015 $10,000

Dickens, Charles 1812-1870 *A Christmas Carol in Prose.* London: Chapman & Hall, 1843. First edition, first issue i.e. 'Stave I', text entirely uncorrected, blue half title and red and blue title, small octavo, four hand colored steel engraved plates by and after Leech and 4 wood engraved illustrations by Linton after Leech, bound by Bayntun Riviere of Bath (stamp signed in gilt on front turn-ins), full red morocco, covers gilt stamped with holly, gilt single rule border, spines decoratively tooled an decorated in gilt compartments, board edges with gilt dotted rule, gilt inner dentelles, all edges gilt, marbled endpapers, original covers bound in rear, a very attractive copy, housed in custom red cloth clamshell.   Heritage Book Shop   Holiday 2014 - 52 2015 $7500

Dickens, Charles 1812-1870 *A Christmas Carol.* Philadelphia: Carey & Hart, 1844. First American edition, 12mo. in 6's, four hand colored lithographed plates, including frontispiece and 4 hand colored wood engraved plates, original gilt binding by "J. C. Russell Binder" in dark brown vertically ribbed cloth with front cover decoratively stamped in gilt, rear cover decoratively stamped in blind and spine decoratively stamped and lettered gilt, original buff endpapers, spine gilt lightly rubbed, headcap and tailcap chipped, rear outer hinge repaired, very good in scarce gilt binding, housed in brown cloth clamshell case.   Heritage Book Shop   Holiday 2014 - 54   2015 $10,000

Dickens, Charles 1812-1870 *A Christmas Carol in Prose.* London: Chapman & Hall, 1844. First edition, first issue the very rare so called 'trial issue' with titlepage printed in red and green and half title in green, 'Stave 1', text entirely uncorrected, yellow coated endpapers, small octavo, 4 hand colored steel engraved plates by and after Leech and 4 wood engraved text illustrations by W. J. Linton after Leech, original cinnamon vertically ribbed cloth, outer hinge repaired, covers decoratively stamped in blind, front cover and spine decoratively stamped and lettered gilt, all edges gilt, binding matching Todd's first impression, first issue with closest interval between blindstamped border and gilt wreath, equal to 14mm. and with the 'D' in 'Dickens' in perfect condition, spine little faded, previous owner's signature on front free endpaper, overall wonderful copy, of great rarity, exceptionally clean and bright, housed in half red morocco clamshell case.   Heritage Book Shop   Holiday 2014 - 53   2015 $30,000

Dickens, Charles 1812-1870 *A Christmas Carol in Prose.* East Aurora: Roycroft Shop, 1902. First edition thus, #84 of 100 copies, signed by Elbert Hubbard, printed on Japanese vellum, 8vo., frontispiece, titlepage decorations, headbands and tailpieces by Samuel Warner, three quarter blue morocco with marbled boards and endpapers, spine gilt decorated, top edge gilt, light wear, handsome, very good+.   Tavistock Books   Bah, Humbug? - 1   2015 $1500

Dickens, Charles 1812-1870 *A Christmas Carol.* Chicago: Reilly & Lee, 1915. 8vo., pictorial boards, fine in dust jacket (chips on both cover edges), full page color illustrations by John Neill, rare in dust jacket.   Aleph-Bet Books, Inc.   108 - 315   2015 $400

Dickens, Charles 1812-1870 *A Christmas Carol.* N.P.: Micawber Fine Editions, 2000. First edition thus, #III of 10 cc hors commerce, total limitation of 85 copies signed by Findeiss & Dean, illustrations in color by Amy Findeiss, with additional suite of 11 numbered/signed loose plates, 8vo., full green morocco leather binding with gilt stamped title lettering to spine, full color pictorial onlay to front board, silk moire endpapers, custom chamshell case, fine in near fine case with small bump to upper corner.   Tavistock Books   Bah, Humbug? - 13   2015 $950

Dickens, Charles 1812-1870 *The Cricket on the Hearth.* London: Bradbury & Evans, 1846. First edition, first printing, with second issue Oliver Twist ad at rear, original crimson cloth stamped in blind, all edges gilt, engraved frontispiece, 12 in text illustrations by John Leech and others, some light wear to lower extremities, fraying to upper spine without loss, former owner bookplate ad bookseller slip to front pastedown, former owner gift inscription to front endpaper, bright, clean and very tight copy, free of any repairs or restoration.   B & B Rare Books, Ltd.   234 - 17   2015 $550

Dickens, Charles 1812-1870 *The Cricket on the Hearth. A Fairy Tale of Home.* London: printed and published for the author by Bradbury Evans, 1846. First edition, 2nd state of OT ad, 14 illustrations by Leech et al, 8vo., original red cloth with gilt stamping to front board and spine, all edges gilt, pale yellow endpapers, bookseller ticket (Robert Weir/Harley Street), bright gilt to front board, spine faintly sunned, square and tight, minor wear, pleasing very good+.   Tavistock Books   Bah, Humbug? - 9   2015 $435

Dickens, Charles 1812-1870 *Dealings with the Firm of Dombey and Son, Wholesale, Retail and for Exportation.* New York: Wiley and Putnam, 1846-1848. First US edition, 20 parts in 19, last two parts with imprint 'John Wiley', 36 plates after Phiz, 7 /12 x 5 inches, printed grey brown paper wrappers, occasional soiling and staining to wrappers with some modest chipping to spine paper, first 9 numbers with previous owner signature, parts XIX/XX lacks rear wrappers, some foxing, overall very good.   Tavistock Books   Bah, Humbug? - 5   2015 $5000

Dickens, Charles   1812-1870   *Dombey and Son.* London: Bradbury & Evans, 1848. First edition in book form, octavo, engraved frontispiece, engraved titlepage and 38 plates, with two original pen and ink drawings by the artist, Phiz, inserted, each signed "Phiz", extremely rare with drawings, each drawing is on a sheet of onion skin measuring 138 x110mm and then inlaid into later sheet to match size of other leaves, original front wrapper for part iv bound in at end, without half title and list of plates, full olive morocco bound by Sangorski & Sutcliffe, boards decoratively stamped in black, gilt lettered on spine, gilt ruled dentelles, marbled endpapers, top edge gilt, with two previous owner's bookplates, "Kenyon Starling" and "Self" and spine lightly sunned, near fine.   Heritage Book Shop   Holiday 2014 - 55   2015 $16,500

Dickens, Charles   1812-1870   *Dombey and Son.* Oxford: Clarendon Press, 1974. Half ttile, frontispiece and illustrations, original dark blue cloth, slightly damp marked in dusted and slightly torn dust jacket, advanced copy signed by Kathleen Tillotson 9 May 1974 with TLS's from Press about publication and note by Kathleen.   Jarndyce Antiquarian Booksellers   CCVII - 174   2015   £100

Dickens, Charles   1812-1870   *Dombey and Son.* Oxford: Clarendon Press, 1974. Half title, frontispiece and illustrations, original dark blue cloth in dusted and slightly torn dust jacket, from the library of Geoffrey & Kathleen Tillotson.   Jarndyce Antiquarian Booksellers   CCVII - 175   2015   £85

Dickens, Charles   1812-1870   *Great Expectations.* Oxford: Clarendon Press, 1993. Half title, illustrations, original dark blue cloth, very good in slightly torn dust jacket, from the library of Geoffrey & Kathleen Tillotson with Kathleen's note, several inserted letters.   Jarndyce Antiquarian Booksellers   CCVII - 177   2015   £120

Dickens, Charles   1812-1870   *Hard Times.* London: Bradbury and Evans, 1854. First edition, half title, few spots, original olive green horizontal ribbed cloth, sunned, spine torn and worn at tail, slight damp marking at foreedge, inner hinges cracking, armorial bookplate of George Jacob Bosanquet, Kathleen Tillotson's copy, signed 1949 with pencil notes , in Kathleen's brown paper wrappers.   Jarndyce Antiquarian Booksellers   CCVII - 178   2015   £350

Dickens, Charles   1812-1870   *Hard Times and Pictures from Italy.* London: Chapman & Hall, 1866. Frontispiece, original green pebble grained cloth, few marks on leading pastedown, split in following hinge, otherwise bright, clean copy, from the library of Geoffrey & Kathleen Tillotson.   Jarndyce Antiquarian Booksellers   CCVII - 179   2015   £45

Dickens, Charles   1812-1870   *The Letters Volumes I-V (1820-1852).* Oxford: Clarendon, 1965-1988. Pilgrim edition, original pink (volume I) and red cloth, dulled and marbled, volume I with spine strip torn away, volumes III & IV slightly loose, from the library of Geoffrey & Kathleen Tillotson.   Jarndyce Antiquarian Booksellers   CCVII - 199   2015   £480

Dickens, Charles   1812-1870   *The Letters.* Oxford: Clarendon Press, 1969. Pilgrim edition, Volume II 140-1841, original red cloth, very good in very slightly torn dust jacket, from the library of Geoffrey & Kathleen Tillotson.   Jarndyce Antiquarian Booksellers   CCVII - 202   2015   £85

Dickens, Charles   1812-1870   *The Letters.* Oxford: Clarendon Press, 1981. Volume V 1847-1849, original red cloth, very slightly torn dust jacket, from the library of Geoffrey & Kathleen Tillotson.   Jarndyce Antiquarian Booksellers   CCVII - 203   2015   £110

Dickens, Charles   1812-1870   *The Letters.* Oxford: Clarendon Press, 1982? Pilgrim edition, volume I, 1820-1839, original red cloth, near mint in very slightly creased dust jacket, from the library of Geoffrey & Kathleen Tillotson.   Jarndyce Antiquarian Booksellers   CCVII - 200   2015   £85

Dickens, Charles   1812-1870   *The Letters.* Oxford: Clarendon Press, 1989. Volume I 1820-1839, original red cloth, near mint in slightly creased dust jacket, from the library of Geoffrey & Kathleen Tillotson.   Jarndyce Antiquarian Booksellers   CCVII - 201   2015   £85

Dickens, Charles   1812-1870   *The Library of Fiction or Family Story-Teller.* London: Chapman and Hall, 1836. 1837. First edition, 2 volumes, octavo, full 19th entury crushed morocco gilt, fine, bound by Ramage, illustrations by George Cruikshank.   Honey & Wax Booksellers   2 - 14   2015 $5000

Dickens, Charles   1812-1870   *The Life and Adventures of Nicholas Nickleby.* London: Chapman & Hall, 1839. First book edition, this copy with 36 of 41 first issue points as noted in Smith, frontispiece and first two plates with Chapman and Hall imprint (first state), third and fourth without imprint, octavo, scarce publisher's deluxe green morocco, rebacked with original spine laid down, some rubbing to upper joint of binding, browning to margins of plates (as usual), very good.   Manhattan Rare Book Company   Literature 2014 - 2015 $2900

Dickens, Charles 1812-1870 *The Life and Adventures of Nicholas Nickleby.* London: Chapman and Hall, 1839. First edition in book form, illustrations by Phiz, later issue 'latter' has not been corrected on page 160, 'Chapman & Hall' imprint on a few plates prior to page 45, 'visiter' has been corrected to 'sister' on line 17, page 13, with 39 etchings, beautifully bound in three quarter maroon morocco with raised bands on spine and gilt lettering, light rubbing on front board at spine, as well as to corners, else very good, without dust jacket as issued.   Buckingham Books   March 2015 - 23023   2015 $850

Dickens, Charles 1812-1870 *Little Dorrit.* London: Bradbury & Evans, 1857. First edition, frontispiece, added engraved title and plates, odd spot, contemporary half dark green calf, rubbed, split in leading hinge, wear at head of spine, clean copy, Kathleen Tillotson's ownership.   Jarndyce Antiquarian Booksellers   CCVII - 180   2015   £185

Dickens, Charles 1812-1870 *Martin Chuzzlewit.* Oxford: Clarendon Press, 1982. Half title, frontispiece, illustrations, original dark blue cloth, very good in slightly torn dust jacket, Kathleen Tillotson's copy with few pencil notes.   Jarndyce Antiquarian Booksellers   CCVII - 181   2015   £90

Dickens, Charles 1812-1870 *Mr. Pickwick: Pages from the Pickwick Papers.* London: Hodder & Stoughton, n.d. circa, 1910. First edition, 4to., red cloth stamped in gold and black, few fox spots, else nearly as new in publisher's box (flaps repaired), illustrations by Frank Reynolds with 25 colored tipped-in color plates with lettered guards.   Alephbet Books, Inc.   109 - 408   2015 $500

Dickens, Charles 1812-1870 *The Mystery of Edwin Drood.* London: Chapman & Hall, April - September, 1870. First edition in original monthly parts, original wrappers, engraved portrait, vignette titlepage and 12 engraved plates by Samuel Luke Fildes, part 6 in the earliest state with eighteen pence slip pasted over the one shilling price on front wrapper, most of inserted ads present, Edwin Drood Advertiser present in each part, part 4 with 8 page Chapman & Hall ads at end which is often lacking part 2 with All the Year Round Slip and without the Gaimes, Sanders and Nicol ad on cork, as usual; wrappers lightly soiled, some wear along edges, chips and some loss to spine, some leaves loose at front of part 6, very pleasing, completely unsophisticated set, free of repairs or restoration, housed in custom slipcase with folding chemise.   B & B Rare Books, Ltd.   234 - 18   2015 $1350

Dickens, Charles 1812-1870 *The Mystery of Edwin Drood.* Oxford: Clarendon Press, 1972. Half title, frontispiece, plates, original dark blue cloth, very good in torn dust jacket, Kathleen Tillotson's spare copy.   Jarndyce Antiquarian Booksellers   CCVII - 184   2015   £75

Dickens, Charles 1812-1870 *Oliver Twist or the Parish Boy's Progress.* London: Richard Bentley, 1838. First edition, first issue, with the 'Fireside' plate and 'Boz' on all three titles, octavo, contemporary full calf by William Lewis (binder's sticker), gilt decorated spines in six compartments, red and green leather labels, gilt ruled boards, gilt dentelles, all edges gilt, with half title to volume I, bound without volume II half title and ads, toning to plates (as often), text generally very clean, only occasional scattered foxing, almost invisible repairs to spine tops and volume 3 label, with 25 plates including 'Fireside' and 'Church' plate.   Manhattan Rare Book Company   Literature 2014 - 2015 $4800

Dickens, Charles 1812-1870 *The Adventures of Oliver Twist.* London: Chapman and Hall, 1853. Half title, original light green cloth, one mark, spine slightly sunned, otherwise very good, from the library of Geoffrey & Kathleen Tillotson with note by Kathleen.   Jarndyce Antiquarian Booksellers   CCVII - 185   2015   £50

Dickens, Charles 1812-1870 *Oliver Twist or the Parish Boy's Progress. (bound with) Pollock's Characters and Scenes.* London: B. Pollock, n.d. circa, 1860. Octavo, full 19th century mottled calf, 23 double page plates, all brilliantly hand colored.   Honey & Wax Booksellers   2 - 13   2015 $3500

Dickens, Charles 1812-1870 *The Adventures of Oliver Twist.* London: Chapman and Hall, 1861. illustrations by George Cruikshank, half title, frontispiece and plates, original red cloth spine slightly dulled & rubbed, clean, with few notes by Kathleen Tillotson.   Jarndyce Antiquarian Booksellers   CCVII - 186   2015   £60

Dickens, Charles 1812-1870 *The Adventures of Oliver Twist.* London: Chapman & Hall, 1867? 8 illustrations, half title, frontispiece and plates, original red cloth, spine worn at head and tail, dulled, internally good, from the library of Geoffrey & Kathleen Tillotson.   Jarndyce Antiquarian Booksellers   CCVII - 186   2015   £45

Dickens, Charles 1812-1870 *The Adventures of Oliver Twist.* London: Oxford University Press, 1953. Half title, frontispiece and plates, original red cloth, spine worn at head and tail, dulled, internally good, signed by Kathleen Tillotson, TLS about new edition from OUP dated 1955.   Jarndyce Antiquarian Booksellers   CCVII - 188   2015   £25

Dickens, Charles 1812-1870 *Oliver Twist.* Oxford: Clarendon Press, 1966. Half title, frontispiece, illustrations, map, original dark blue cloth in slightly worn dust jacket, from the library of Geoffrey & Kathleen Tillotson.   Jarndyce Antiquarian Booksellers   CCVII - 189   2015   £120

Dickens, Charles 1812-1870 *Oliver Twist.* Oxford: Clarendon Press, 1966. Half title, frontispiece, illustrations, map, original blue cloth, very good in dust jacket, from the library of Geoffrey & Kathleen Tillotson, inscribed by her for Geoffrey.   Jarndyce Antiquarian Booksellers   CCVII - 190   2015   £90

Dickens, Charles 1812-1870 *Oliver Twist.* Oxford: Clarendon Press, 1974. Half title, frontispiece, illustrations, map, original blue cloth in slightly torn dust jacket with notes, Kathleen Tillotson's copy, als inserted Geoffrey Tillotson's copy of her paper 'Oliver Twist from Essays and Studies" 1959.   Jarndyce Antiquarian Booksellers   CCVII - 191   2015   £110

Dickens, Charles 1812-1870 *Our Mutual Friend.* London: Chapman & Hall, 1865. First edition, 2 volumes, octavo, 4 engraved plates including frontispiece by by Marcus Stone, 20 in each volume, each volume with all the internal flaws called for by Smith, original purplish brown sand grain cloth, stamped in blind, spines decoratively stamped and lettered gilt, endpapers coated pale yellow, top of spines lightly frayed, front inner hinges of volume I and both inner hinges of volume II with hairline crack, small repair to inner hinge of volume II, small embossed bookseller's label on front endpaper of each volume, very superior copy of book usually found in remainder bindings or rebound, housed in cloth slipcase.   Heritage Book Shop   Holiday 2014 - 56   2015 $9500

Dickens, Charles 1812-1870 *The Personal History of David Copperfield.* London: Bradbury & Evans, 1850. First edition in book form, octavo, full 19th century polished calf, gilt, illustrations by Phiz, bound by Riviere.   Honey & Wax Booksellers   2 - 16   2015 $2800

Dickens, Charles 1812-1870 *The Personal History of David Copperfield.* London: Bradbury & Evans, 1850. First edition, first issue in book form, octavo, 40 inserted plates, including frontispiece and vignette titlepage and the second of Browne's famous 'dark plates', contemporary three quarter smooth black calf over patterned brown cloth, decoratively gilt stamped on spine, marbled edges, very good, text and plates generally clean, overall very good, scarce in first edition first printing.   Heritage Book Shop   Holiday 2014 - 57   2015 $2000

Dickens, Charles 1812-1870 *David Copperfield.* Oxford: Clarendon Press, 1981. Half title, frontispiece, illustrations, original dark blue cloth, very good in torn dust jacket, Kathleen Tillotson's unmarked copy with correspondence inserted.   Jarndyce Antiquarian Booksellers   CCVII - 173   2015   £120

Dickens, Charles 1812-1870 *David Copperfield.* Oxford: Clarendon Press, 1981. First edition, 8vo., original navy blue cloth, lettered gilt at spine, illustrations, fine in very good+ dust jacket with faint edgewear, excellent condition.   Any Amount of Books   2015 - C13718   2015 £160

Dickens, Charles 1812-1870 *The Pickwick Papers.* Oxford: Clarendon Press, Half title, frontispiece, illustrations, original dark blue cloth, very good in creased dust jacket, from the library of Geoffrey & Kathleen Tillotson, relevant papers inserted including browned proof article by Kathleen Tillotson for TLS.   Jarndyce Antiquarian Booksellers   CCVII - 195   2015   £120

Dickens, Charles 1812-1870 *The Posthumous Papers of the Pickwick Club.* London: 1837. First edition in book form, mixed issue, thick 8vo., 43 illustrations, including frontispiece and vignette titlepage, extra illustrated with an additional 31 plates by Thomas Onwhyn, with 7 plates by Seymour and the remaining ones by Phiz, also 2 plates by Buss (page 69 and page 74) which were later replaced by two of Browne's, originally illustrated in 20 parts; with half title, 'Directions to Binder' and errata leaf, includes 'Weller' sign and 'Phiz fecit' and marginal note on page 9 that was suppressed in later issues, contemporary half calf over marbled boards, gilt stamped spine with red morocco label, extra illustrated with 31 inserted plates by Thomas Onwhyn, 43 engraved plates, including frontispiece, engraved titlepage, with half title, previous owner's contemporary signature, very good, housed in custom green cloth clamshell gilt stamped.   Heritage Book Shop   Holiday 2014 - 59   2015 $1000

Dickens, Charles 1812-1870 *Pickwick Papers.* London: Chapman & Hall, 1837. First edition, early issue with no imprint on plates, Weller title, half title, frontispiece, engraved title, plates by Seymour & Phiz, offsetting and spotting signature of M. Weale, Leamington, pencil notes by Kathleen Tillotson, records loans, with inserted notes.   Jarndyce Antiquarian Booksellers   CCVII - 194   2015   £150

Dickens, Charles 1812-1870 *Sikes and Nancy....* London: Henry Sotheran, 1921. Half title, frontispiece, final ad leaf, original black boards, paper label, dulled, from the library of Geoffrey & Kathleen Tillotson.   Jarndyce Antiquarian Booksellers   CCVII - 193   2015   £45

Dickens, Charles 1812-1870 *Sketches by Boz. First Series.* London: John Macrone, 1837. Third edition, 2 volumes, frontispiece and plates by George Cruikshank, original dark green cloth, slight rubbing, good, clean, attractive copy, from the library of Geoffrey & Kathleen Tillotson.   Jarndyce Antiquarian Booksellers   CCVII - 196   2015   £350

Dickens, Charles 1812-1870 *Sketches By Boz.* Philadelphia: Lea and Blanchard, 1842. New edition, from the library of Geoffrey & Kathleen Tillotson, tall 8vo., frontispiece and 18 plates after George Cruikshank, one missing, some browning, lacking pages 29-32, blue paper wrappers made by Geoffrey his note on wrappers, text annotated throughout by Kathleen in ink and pencil.   Jarndyce Antiquarian Booksellers   CCVII - 197   2015   £45

Dickens, Charles 1812-1870 *Sketches by Boz... (bound with) American Notes for General Circulation.* London: Chapman and Hall, 1850. 1850, 2 volumes in 1, frontispiece, half title, contemporary half maroon calf, spine slightly rubbed and faded, from the library of Geoffrey & Kathleen Tillotson. Jarndyce Antiquarian Booksellers CCVII - 198 2015 £35

Dickens, Charles 1812-1870 *Sketches of Young Couples.* London: Chapman & Hall, n.d. circa, 1870. 12mo., frontispieces, 3 volumes in 1, 6 x 3 3/4 inches, beautifully bound by H. Sotheran in full crimson morocco, decoratively tooled in gilt on covers and spine, original red cloth covers bound in at rear, all edges gilt, gilt turn-ins, bookplate, minor rubbing to spine extremities, else near fine. Heritage Book Shop Holiday 2014 - 61 2015 $750

Dickens, Charles 1812-1870 *The Works of Charles Dickens.* London: Chapman and Hall, 1929. Limited to 150 copies, 40 volumes, 8vo., blue cloth stamped in gilt, gray dust jackets on each volume, well preserved many of the jackets chipped. Oak Knoll Books 306 - 263 2015 $2000

Dickens, Charles 1837-1896 *Doom's Day Camp. Being the Extra Christmas Number of All the Year Round. Conducted by Charles Dickens (Jr.) for Christmas 1872. (wrapper title).* London: published at the Office 26 Wellington St. Strand, C. Whiting, Printer, 1872. First edition, large 8vo., 48 pages, original blue printed wrappers, light wear. M & S Rare Books, Inc. 97 - 87 2015 $85

Dickerson, K. *The Philosophy of Mesmerism, or Animal Magnetism.* Concord: Morrill Silsby & Co., 1843. First edition, 8vo., removed. M & S Rare Books, Inc. 97 - 190 2015 $150

Dickey, James *Poems 1957-1967.* London: Rapp & Caroll, 1967. First British edition, bound up from US sheets, 8vo., original cloth, dust jacket, fine, jacket price clipped. James S. Jaffe Rare Books Modern American Poetry - 64 2015 $150

Dickey, James *Poems 1957-1967.* Middletown: Wesleyan University Press, 1967. First edition, 8vo., original cloth, dust jacket, presentation copy inscribed by author, fine. James S. Jaffe Rare Books Modern American Poetry - 63 2015 $150

Dickinson, Emily Elizabeth 1830-1886 *Poems of Emily Dickinson.* New York: Limited Editions Club, 1952. Limited to 1500 numbered copies, signed by artist, drawings, tall 8vo., full leather, slipcase, well preserved, monthly letter loosely inserted ownership inscription in ink. Oak Knoll Books 25 - 36 2015 $350

Dickinson's Comprehensive Pictures of the Great Exhibition of 1851 from the Originals Painted for H. R. H. Prince Albert. London: Dickinson,, 1854. First edition, 2 volumes, large folio, titles in red and black 55, chromolithograph plates, hand colored and highly finished with egg white, 22.75 x 16.5 inches (page size), few plates and leaves little foxed, modern red half morocco to style over marbled boards, spines in seven compartment separated with raised bands, lettered gilt in two compartments with date at foot, all edges gilt. Marlborough Rare Books Ltd. List 49 - 6 2015 £12,500

Dickson, Carter *My Late Wives.* New York: Morrow, 1946. First edition, fine in dust jacket with tiny fraying at spine ends and wear at corners. Mordida Books March 2015 - 010166 2015 $250

Dickson, Gordon R. *Necromancer.* Garden City: Doubleday & Co., 1962. First edition, octavo, boards. John W. Knott, Bookseller Selected New Arrivals Jan. 2015 - 17013 2015 $250

Diebert, Timothy S. *Southern Pacific Company Steam Locomotive Compendium.* Huntington Beach: Shade Tree Books, 1987. First edition, quarto, photos, black cloth lettered in gilt, very fine with slightly chipped pictorial dust jacket. Argonaut Book Shop Holiday Season 2014 - 75 2015 $225

Dietz, F. Meredith *The Southern Literary Messenger.* Richmond: 1939+, 11 issues, first has cover soil, three with covers loose and wear at edges, some library stamps. Bookworm & Silverfish 2015 - 6014061123 2015 $45

Digby, George *A Choice Collection of Rare Chymical Secrets and Experiments in Philosophy.* London: for the publisher (George Hartman), 1682. First edition, second issue, 8vo., 4 engraved plates, lower edge of titlepage shaved, just touching border, very slight browning to final few leaves, contemporary calf, ruled in blind, 19th century reback and endpapers, corners bumped and headcaps torn, inscription R. Sydney Marsden University of Edin. 1882, later pencil note, from the library of James Stevens Cox (1910-1997), with his pencil notes "Bought 1930 (Douglas) Cleverdon. Maggs Bros. Ltd. 1447 - 43 2015 £350

Digby, George *Letters Between the Ld. George Digby and Sr Kenelm Digby, Kt. Concerning Religion.* London: for Humphrey Moseley, 1651. First edition, small 8vo., printer's crease across top corner to final leaf disturbing top four lines, small semi circular ink spot touching upper edge of A1-B8, page numbers occasionally shaved at upper edge, contemporary calf, rebacked, new endpapers, boards little scuffed, some occasional underlinings, from the library of James Stevens Cox (1910-1997). Maggs Bros. Ltd. 1447 - 142 2015 £220

Digby, John *Incantations: Poems and Collages.* Roslyn: Stone House Press, 1987. First edition, ownership signature of noted engraver John De Pol, fine copy, inscribed to De Pol by publisher Morris Gelfand with complimentary slip, signed by Gelfand.   Between the Covers Rare Books, Inc.   187 - 74   2015 $150

Digby, Kenelm 1603-1665 *Castrations from the Private Memoirs of Sir Kenelm Digby.* London: not published, 1828. First edition, 8vo., later grey buckram beveled edges, spine gilt ruled, from the library of Allan Heywood Bright (1862-1941), Liberal politician and book collector, pictorial bookplate (by Downey) on front pastedown showing coats of arms and motto "Post Tenebras Lucem" and view of the valley with hills beyond, a church and rising sun, printed as a supplement to "Private memoirs of Sir Kenelm Digby..." London Saunders and Otley 1827, text bound with additional leaves, near fine.   Any Amount of Books   2015 - C13447   2015   £180

Digby, Kenelm 1603-1665 *A Late Discourse made in a Solemne Assembly of nobles and Learned Men at Montpellier in France.* London: R. Lownes and (T) Davies, 1658. First edition in English, 12mo., inner margin of title little stained with some loss ot imprint due to adhesion of flyleaf, contemporary sheep tightly rebacked, large repair to front cover and corners repaired, from the library of James Stevens Cox (1910-1997).   Maggs Bros. Ltd.   1447 - 144   2015   £240

Digby, Kenelm 1603-1665 *A Late Discourse made in a Solemne assembly of Nobles and Learned Men at Montpellier in France.* London: for R. Lowndes and T. Davies, 1658. Second edition in English, 12mo., browned and spotted throughout, a number of leaves faintly printed, small burn-hole to blank margin of F1, early 19th century russia, ruled in gilt, upper head cap damaged and joints rubbed and just starting to crack, marbled endleaves stained by turn-ins, bookplate of Henry Montagu Digby, 1874-1934, from the library of James Stevens Cox (1910-1997). Maggs Bros. Ltd.   1447 - 145   2015   £180

Digby, Kenelm 1603-1665 *Of Bodies and of Mans Soul.* London: by S(arah) G(riffin) and B(ennet) G(riffin) for John Williams, 1669. First collected edition, 4to., some light dampstaining and spotting throughout, small closed tear to upper edge of L8 (just touching pagination), 2 minor chips to fore margin of 2F1-2, contemporary calf, covers ruled in blind, later spine label and small gilt ornament in each panel (surface of leather on covers crazed by damp, some surface rubbing and slight insect damage on lower cover chipped and rubbed), bookplate of Helyar family of Coker Court, Somerset, from the library of James Stevens Cox (1910-1997).   Maggs Bros. Ltd.   1447 - 147   2015   £400

Digby, Kenelm 1603-1665 *Two Treatises. In the One of Which the Nature of Bodies: in the Other the Nature of Mans Soule.* Paris: printed by Gilles Blaizot, 1644. First edition, folio, signatures Ggg iij and Ggg if are transposed, otherwise complete and correctly bound, very scarce first printing, ornamental woodcut initials, head and tailpieces, brown 19th century half morocco over marbled paper, gilt lettering, rules and fluer-de-lis ornaments to spine, corner of first five leaves have been diagonally cropped but not near text, slight wave in the lie of the pages tightens almost to a couple of creases near the end of book, overall remarkably dry and clean, binding only slightly worn.   Any Amount of Books   2015 - C12071   2015   £2600

Digby, Kenelm Henry *The Children's Bower; or what you like.* E. S. Ellis, 1868. Re-issue with cancel titles, 2 volumes, original blue cloth, spines slightly dulled, little rubbed.   Jarndyce Antiquarian Booksellers   CCXI - 90   2015   £125

Dignimont, Andre *Femmes, fleurs et Branches.* Paris: Michele Trinckvel, 1968. First edition, unbound signatures laid into wrappers, fine, 12 illustrations by artist, with text tributes to him, 4to., handsome blue cloth clamshell box with blindstamped cover and gilt stamped spine.   Beasley Books   2013 - 2015 $300

Dillard, Annie *Tickets for a Prayer Wheel.* Columbia: University of Missouri, 1974. First edition, 8vo., author's presentation to poet and editor William Claire and his wife Helen, orchid cloth over flexible boards, top edges little spotted, otherwise very good, tight copy in somewhat toned dust jacket.   Second Life Books Inc.   190 - 56   2015 $350

Dillard, Richard *The Day I Stopped Dreaming About Barbara Steele and Other Poems.* Chapel Hill: University of North Carolina, 1966. First edition, 8vo., author's presentation on flyleaf, blue cloth, clipping laid in, top edges little soiled, otherwise very good, tight copy in scuffed and chipped dust jacket.   Second Life Books Inc.   190 - 57   2015 $125

Dinesen, Isak 1885-1962 *Out of Africa.* New York: Random House, 1938. First American edition, darkening to joints and fading to top stain, near fine in like dust jacket (mildly tanned with trace rubbing near crown).   Ken Lopez, Bookseller   164 - 54   2015 $500

Dinesen, Isak 1885-1962 *Out of Africa.* New York: Random House, 1938. First American edition, text block shaken, very good in like dust jacket, mildly sunned spine with small snagged tear at rear panel.   Ken Lopez, Bookseller   164 - 55   2015 $375

Dinesen, Isak 1885-1962 *Out of Africa.* New York: Random House, 1938. First American edition, small ink stamp '59233' on rear flyleaf, darkening to pastedown from binder's glue, mostly near hinges, rich top stain, near fine in very near fine dust jacket with mild tanning to spine, attractive copy.   Ken Lopez, Bookseller   164 - 53   2015 $750

Dinges, Bruce J. *Arizona 100 a Centennial Gathering of Essential Books on the Grand Canyon State.* Tucson: Arizona Historical Society, 2012. First book edition, number 56 of 100 copies, signed by all 7 contributors, portrait, 26 plates reproducing covers, cover illustrations from a painting by Maynard Dixon, stiff wrappers, slight wrinkling to last leaf from pasted-on limitation notice, else fine and clean. Argonaut Book Shop   Holiday Season 2014 - 14   2015 $75

Dinnean, Lawrence *Nineteenth Century Illustrators of California Sights and Scenes.* Berkeley: University of California, 1986. First edition, 31 illustrations, stiff printed wrappers, very fine.   Argonaut Book Shop   Holiday Season 2014 - 76   2015 $35

Dinsdale, Alfred *Television.* London: Television Press ltd., 1928. Second edition, signed presentation inscribed by John Baird, inventor of TV to G. G. Mulligan 12th April 1929, frontispiece also inscribed "J. H. Baird", octavo, original blue cloth, lightly sunned on spine, title and author embossed in black on front cover and spine, first few leaves bit foxed, lovely copy.   Athena Rare Books   15 - 6   2015 $3800

Diodorus Siculus *The History of Diodorus Siculus.* London: by John Macock for Giles Calvert, 1653. First edition in English, small folio, longitudinal half title has been cut-out leaving a stub, 271 pages, small circular stain in inner margins of first few leaves and Kk4-L12, rust spot on Kk4, contemporary sheep, smooth spine ruled in blind and with red morocco and gilt label, covers heavily scuffed, piece missing from top corner of lower cover, upper headcap torn, front pastedown torn away at head, early inscription on flyleaf heavily deleted, early signature Nic. Hare, signature on title Edm. Sex. Pery, 1st and last Viscount Pery (1719-1806) by descent to his elder daughter Diana Jane, Countess of Ranfurly to Earls of Ranfurly, with 19th century bookplate, from the library of James Stevens Cox (1910-1997).   Maggs Bros. Ltd.   1447 - 148   2015   £380

Diogenes Laertius *Digenous Laertiou Peribion Dogmaton Kai Apophthegmaton Ton en Philosophia Eudokimesanton Biblia...* Geneva: Henri Estiene, 1593. Second edition, 12mo., contemporary full vellum, boards soiled at edges, ink notations on front free endpaper.   Oak Knoll Books   306 - 264   2015 $1500

Dioscorides *The Greek Herbal of Dioscorides.* Oxford: printed by John Johnson for the author at University Press, 1934. First edition by Robert Gunther, large 8vo., limited to 350 copies, original white buckram lettered black on spine, 396 illustrations, ownership signature writer Wilfred Blunt, very slight surface wear, otherwise very good, decent copy, A Wheldon & Wesley catalog clipping on pastedown.   Any Amount of Books   2015 - C5776   2015   £225

Diringer, David *The Alphabet, a Key to the History of Mankind.* New York: Funk & Wagnall, 1968. Third edition, 2 volumes, 4to., cloth, slipcase faded in spots, illustrations.   Oak Knoll Books   Special Catalogue 24 - 12   2015 $125

The Discontented Frogs. New York: McLoughlin Bros., n.d. circa, 1875. Oblong 4to., fine, fine, rare, chromolithographed illustrations.   Aleph-bet Books, Inc.   109 - 282   2015 $600

Discours de son Excellence Monsieur Jean Hancock, President du Congres de Philadelphie. Philadelphia: 1776. First edition, 8vo., 32 pages, contemporary European calf backed boards, spine with label and gilt (worn), all edges red.   M & S Rare Books, Inc.   97 - 113   2015 $2000

Discours Prononce dans le Temple de St. Pierre a Geneve par le Jeune Orateur des Classed du College le 20 Juin 1814.... Geneve: chez J. J. Paschoud, 1814. Small 8vo., 21 pages, ink smudge on lower edge of title, small marginal snag/stain on page 10, recent plain wrappers, very good.   John Drury Rare Books   2015 - 17869   2015 $89

Disney, Walt *Adventures of Mickey Mouse Book I.* Philadelphia: McKay, 1931. First edition, 8vo., red cloth, pictorial paste-on, owner's inscription on margin of titlepage, else very fine, color illustrations on every page.   Aleph-Bet Books, Inc.   108 - 139   2015 $1800

Disney, Walt *Adventures of Mickey Mouse Book Number Two.* Philadelphia: McKay, 1932. First edition, 8vo., pictorial boards, edges slightly rubbed, else fine in dust jacket (few pieces off edges), color pictorial endpapers and color illustrations on every page, very scarce.   Aleph-Bet Books, Inc.   108 - 140   2015 $1500

Disney, Walt *Bambi Hankies.* Walt Disney Productions, 1942. 7 x 9 1/4 inches, flexible pictorial card covers with original string binding, hankies slightly toned, else fine, tucked into slits on four of the pages are color printed handkerchiefs.   Aleph-bet Books, Inc.   109 - 131   2015 $750

Disney, Walt *Donald Duck.* New York: Grosset and Dunlap, 1936. 4to., pictorial boards, very good+ in soiled and frayed dust jacket, bright full color illustrations plus black and whites and pictorial endpapers, rare.   Aleph-Bet Books, Inc.   108 - 142   2015 $600

Disney, Walt *Mickey Mouse and his Friends.* Whitman, 1936. Large 4to., stiff pictorial wrappers, owner's name on back cover, slightest of cover wear, else fine, printed on heavy linen like paper and illustrated in bold color on every page, nice, quite scarce.   Aleph-bet Books, Inc.   109 - 128   2015 $450

Disney, Walt *Mickey Mouse Book/Hello Everybody.* New York: Bibo and Lang, 1930. 4to., green pictorial wrappers, fine, intact copy with no soil or wear, illustrations by Disney Studios with full page and partial page drawings.   Aleph-bet Books, Inc.   109 - 127   2015 $7500

Disney, Walt *Mickey Mouse Has a Busy Day.* Racine: Whitman, 1937. Square 4to., pictorial wrappers, some normal shelfwear, very good, illustrations in color and black and white, very scarce.   Aleph-Bet Books, Inc.   108 - 141   2015 $275

Disney, Walt *Micky maus Am Hofe Konig Arthurs. (Mickey Mouse in King Arthur's Court).* Zurich: Bollmann, n.d., 1933. 4to., glazed pictorial boards, very fine in fine dust jacket, color pictorial endpaper, 4 double page pop-up scenes, plus full page and partial page black and whites, rare.   Aleph-bet Books, Inc.   109 - 371   2015 $2500

Disney, Walt *Mickey Mouse on Tour.* London: Birn Bros., n.d. circa, 1936. 4to., pictorial boards, near fine, great color covers with nearly full page illustrations.   Aleph-bet Books, Inc.   109 - 129   2015 $350

Disney, Walt *Mickey Mouse Waddle Book.* New York: Blue Ribbon, 1934. 4to., pictorial boards, near fine in dust jacket, this copy includes the 4 Waddle figures unpunched, the ramp and the pictorial band that goes around the ramp (brass fasteners in plastic envelope and instructions for assembling ramp are in Xeroxed format), book illustrated by Disney Studios.   Aleph-Bet Books, Inc.   108 - 138   2015 $12,000

Disney, Walt *Pop-Up Silly Symphonies Containing Babes in the Woods and King Neptune.* New York: Blue Ribbon, 1933. 4to., pictorial boards, near fine, very scarce, color endpapers, full page and in text illustrations, plus 4 glorious double page pop-ups.   Aleph-bet Books, Inc.   109 - 372   2015 $850

Disney, Walt *The Victory March or the Mystery of the Treasure Chest.* New York: Random House, 1942. 4to., spiral backed pictorial boards, slightest bit of rubbing, else fine, complete with savings book in rear pocket with stamp affixed, nearly every page has a moveable wheel or tab operated mechanism, color illustrations by Disney Studio.   Aleph-bet Books, Inc.   109 - 130   2015 $950

Disraeli, Benjamin 1804-1881 *The Revolutionary Epick.* Paris: Longman, Green, Longman, Roberts and Green, 1864. First edition, 8vo., original bright copper brown cloth lettered gilt at spine, uncut, very good+ bright clean copy with triangle excised from top corner of front endpaper.   Any Amount of Books   2015 - A47684   2015   £200

Disraeli, Benjamin 1804-1881 *Vindication of the English Constitution in a Letter to a Noble and Learned Lord.* London: Saunders and Otley, 1835. First edition, half title, final leaf of ads and rare errata slip, few very minor blemished and some light marginal soiling, old ink shelf or reference number on lower blank margin of one prelim leaf, old, probably original boards, little worn and soiled, rebacked sometime in maroon patterned cloth, good large copy with generous margins, uncut, scarce.   John Drury Rare Books   2015 - 15118   2015 $699

Disraeli, Benjamin 1804-1881 *Vivian Grey.* London: Henry Colburn, 1826-1827. First edition of volumes III-V, new edition, i.e. second edition of volumes I & II, complete with half titles and ads, as called for, 8vo., 5 volumes, untrimmed in original boards, volumes iii-v with pink paper backstrips, small puncture to front board of volume v resulting in tiny hole to first 1- leaves and a dent detectable as far as page 50, otherwise just little worn overall, modern bookplate to volume I, very good, scarce first novel, each volume with contemporary inscription of E(lizabeth) M. Geough.   Blackwell's Rare Books   B179 - 35   2015   £600

Disraeli, Benjamin 1804-1881 *Vivian Grey.* London: Henry Colburn, 1826-1827. First edition, 5 volumes, contemporary half calf, gilt rules on spines and eagle crest, very good.   Jarndyce Antiquarian Booksellers   CCXI - 91   2015   £450

Disturnell, John *A Trip Through the Lakes of North America...* J. Disturnell, 1857. First edition, 12mo., original blindstamped light green cloth, gold stamped front cover and spine, blindstamped rear cover, illustrations, one large folding map affixed to rear pastedown sheet, very good.   Buckingham Books   March 2015 - 29072   2015 $1250

Ditchfield, P. H. *The Cottages and the Village Life of Rural England.* London & New York: J. M. Dent & Sons/E. P. Dutton & Co., 1912. First edition, 8vo., original light brown cloth, lettered gilt at spine and black on front cover, copiously illustrated in color by A. R. Quinton, very slight rubbing at lower corners and very slightly bumped with slight foxing to prelims, otherwise near fine in near very good, complete dust jacket (slightly spotted and slightly used) with some tape reinforcement.   Any Amount of Books   2015 - C11819   2015   £160

Dixon, Charles *Fifteen Hundred Miles an Hour.* London: Bliss, Sands and Foster, 1895. First edition, octavo, six inserted plates, with illustrations by Arthur Layard, original pictorial blue gray cloth, front panel stamped in black, gold and white, spine panel stamped in gold, publisher's monogram stamped in blind on rear panel, all edges gilt, olive green floral patterned endpapers.   L. W. Currey, Inc.   Boy's Adventure Fiction 2015 - 2   2015 $1250

Dixon, Charles *Fifteen Hundred Miles an Hour.* London: Bliss, Sands and Foster, 1895. First edition, Colonial issue, octavo, six inserted plates with illustrations by Arthur Layard, original decorated yellow cloth, front and spine panels printed in black.   L. W. Currey, Inc.   Boy's Adventure Fiction 2015 - 5   2015 $850

Dixon, E. *Fairy Tales from the Arabian Nights.* London: J. M. Dent & Co., 1893. Limited edition, no. 14 of 160 copies, 4to., plates, original blue cloth, lettered gilt on spine and on front cover with bevelled edge, copiously illustrated in black and white, neat gift inscription dated 1895, slight browning to endpapers, some marking and some staining to covers, otherwise sound, used fair copy.   Any Amount of Books 2015 - C11660   2015   £160

Dixon, Edward H. *Scenes in the Practice of a New York Surgeon.* New York: Robert M. De Witt, 1856? Second edition, 8vo., 407 pages plus ads, original cloth, personal ink presentation from Dixon on titlepage.   M & S Rare Books, Inc.   97 - 91   2015 $500

Dixon, Franklin W. *Over the Ocean to Paris or Ted Scott's Daring Long-Distance Flight.* New York: Grosset & Dunlap, 1927. First edition, original pictorial red cloth stamped in black and brown.   L. W. Currey, Inc.   Boy's Adventure Fiction 2015 - 73   2015 $125

Dixon, Robert M. W. *Blues and Gospel Records 1902-1943.* Chigwell: Storyville, 1982. Third edition, near fine, stout 8vo.   Beasley Books   2013 - 2015 $135

Dixon, Stephen *Time to Go.* Baltimore: Johns Hopkins University Press, 1984. Second edition, fine in fine dust jacket, very warmly inscribed by author to Raymond Federman.   Between the Covers Rare Books, Inc.   187 - 75   2015 $125

Dixon, William Hepworth *Her Majesty's Tower.* New York: Thomas Y. Crowell and Co., n.d. circa, 1900. Reprint, green cloth, gilt, 2 volumes in 1, small nick at crown, some staining to rear board, tight, about very good copy, Edward Everett Horton's copy with bookplate, pencil note indicating it was purchased at Dawson's in LA in 1913.   Between the Covers Rare Books, Inc.   187 - 77   2015 $150

Dobbs, Betty Jo Teeter *The Foundations of Newton's Alchemy or "The Hunting of the Green Lyon".* Cambridge, et al: Cambridge University Press, 1975. First edition, 4 plates, tables, yellow cloth gilt stamped black spine label, dust jacket, very good, rare.   Jeff Weber Rare Books   178 - 835   2015 $225

Dobell, Sydney *The Poetical Works of Sydney Dobell.* London: Smith Elder & Co., 1875. First edition thus, 2 volumes, 8vo., original black cloth lettered gilt on spine, ownership signature of author's wife, Emily Dobell dated Jan. 1st 1901, with good signed letter in plain envelope which is pasted to front endpaper, sound, clean, very good set with very slight shelfwear and slight nick at spine of one volume.   Any Amount of Books   2015 - A88049   2015   £160

Dobias, Frank *The Picture Book of Flying.* New York: Macmillan, 1928. First edition, 4to., pictorial cloth, slight rubbing else fine in dust jacket with some closed tears, illustrations by Dobias, with full page color lithographed illustrations, quite scarce.   Aleph-bet Books, Inc.   109 - 132 2015 $375

Dobie, James *Memoir of William Wilson of Crummock...* Edinburgh: privately printed, 1896. First edition, no. 12 of 60 copies, 'George Sheden Esq/With the editor's kind regards', loosely inserted is note probably from book's publisher, 8vo., original quarter leather lettered gilt on spine and on front cover, uncut, slight wear at rear corner, slight splitting at head of spine, otherwise about very good+.   Any Amount of Books   2015 - A47872   2015   £170

Dobie, James Frank   18401-1921 *John C. Duval. First Texas Man of Letters. His Life and some of His Unpublished Writings.* Dallas: Southwest Review, 1939. First edition, 8vo., limited to 1000 copies, two tone cloth, illustrations by Tom Lea, fine in fine dust jacket.   Buckingham Books March 2015 - 20577   2015 $375

Dobie, James Frank   18401-1921 *John C. Duval. First Texas Man of Letters. His Life and Some of His unpublished writings.* Dallas: Southwest Review, 1939. First edition, limited to 1000 copies, two tone cloth, 105 pages, frontispiece, illustrations by Tom Lea, fine in dust jacket. Buckingham Books   March 2015 - 20842   2015 $250

Dobie, James Frank   18401-1921 *Mustangs and Cow Horses.* Austin: Texas Folk Lore Society, 1940. First edition, cloth, pictorial endsheets, illustrations, former owner's bookplate, else very good.   Buckingham Books   March 2015 - 16758   2015 $275

Dobie, James Frank   18401-1921 *The Mustangs.* Boston: Little Brown, 1952. First edition, 8vo., two tone pictorial cloth, pictorial endsheets, illustrations by Charles Banks Wilson, fine in fine dust jacket.   Buckingham Books March 2015 - 19766   2015 $375

Dobie, James Frank   18401-1921 *Stories of Christmas and the Bowie Knife.* Austin: Steck Co., 1953. First edition thus, 8vo., maroon cloth, silver stamping on front cover and spine, gray endpapers, frontispiece, illustrations, fine in original glassine dust jacket and fine original slipcase. Buckingham Books   March 2015 - 20851   2015 $250

Dobie, James Frank 18401-1921 *A Texan in England.* Boston: Little Brown & Co., 1945. First edition, 8vo., signed by author, cloth, fine, bright tight copy in fine dust jacket. Buckingham Books   March 2015 - 21121   2015 $300

Doblin, Alfred *Nocturno.* Los Angeles: Pazifischen Presse, 1944. Limited to 250 numbered copies, 150 signed by author on colophon, this copy is thus, 8vo., quarter leather, paper covered boards, fore-edge uncut, spine gilt stamped, spine covering detached, bumped at bottom corners. Oak Knoll Books   306 - 160   2015 $200

Dodd, William *The Visitor. By Several Hands...* London: printed for Edward and Charles Dilly, 1764. First edition, 2 volumes, 12mo., frontispiece in volume I, contemporary full brown calf, gilt lined with 5 raised bands, spine unlettered or most probably lacking spine labels, faint gilt volume numbers, hinges slightly tender, neat name at head of title pages "Ann May Vansittart 1825", overall very good, scarce. Any Amount of Books   2015 - A34298   2015   £175

Doddridge, Philip 1702-1751 *Deliverance Out of the Hands of Our Enemies Urged as a Motive to Obedience in the Substance of Two Sermons Preached at Northampton Feb. 9 1745-46.* London: printed and sold by J. Waugh, 1746. Only edition, 8vo., including final leaf of ads (G2) neatly bound recently in lettered boards, good, crisp copy. John Drury Rare Books   2015 - 24697   2015 $221

Dodge, David *Death and Taxes.* Macmillan and Co., 1941. First edition, lightly foxed on front and rear endpapers, else very good in price clipped dust jacket with light professional restoration to spine ends, corners and extremities. Buckingham Books   March 2015 - 32998   2015 $750

Dodge, David *It Ain't Hay.* New York: Simon and Schuster, 1946. First edition, page edges uniformly browned, else fine in dust jacket with light professional restoration to spine ends. Buckingham Books   March 2015 - 30650   2015 $200

Dodge, Richard Irving *Our Wild Indians: Thirty-Three Year Personal Experience Among the Red Men of the Great West.* Hartford: Worthington, 1883. Second edition, 8vo., recased, nice, little offsetting to titlepage, some small numerals on tape on several pages. Second Life Books Inc.   191 - 30   2015 $125

Dodgson, Charles Lutwidge 1832-1898 *Alice's Adventures in Wonderland 1872. and Through the Looking Glass 1877.* London: Macmillan and Co., Later printings, 2 volumes, 8vo., all edges gilt, silk endpapers, original covers bound in rear, illustrations by John Tenniel, each volume in lovely Kelliegram binding stamped inside each rear cover, bound in full green morocco with inlaid leather figure on both covers after Tenniels illustrations, elaborate gilt border featuring crown on both covers and spine compartments, each have a different figure, gilt turn-ins triple ruled with spade motif, except for some darkening on edge of back cover, this fine as well, handsome set. Aleph-Bet Books, Inc.   108 - 87   2015 $5250

Dodgson, Charles Lutwidge 1832-1898 *Alice's Adventures in Wonderland. (with) Through the Looking-Glass and What Alice Found There.* London: Macmillan, 1870-1873. Later printings, illustrations by John Tenniel, finely bound in full red calf by Root and Son, boards stamped after original cloth bindings with illustrations of Alice and Cheshire Cat and the Red and White Queens, with the original cloth bound into rear of texts, very good with some light wear and rubbing to extremities, minor toning to spine and board edges, light rubbing to spines and hinges, Looking Glass with shallow chip to spine head, bookplates of noted art collector and art historian, J. Frederic Byers, bright and clean pages, overall lovely, finely bound copy. B & B Rare Books, Ltd.   2015 - 2015 $1500

Dodgson, Charles Lutwidge 1832-1898 *Alice's Adventures in Wonderland.* London: William Heinemann & New York: Doubleday Page & Co., 1907. First trade edition, original green gilt pictorial, copy with Gryphon and Mock Turtle to front board, signed by Rackham on half titlepage and with original pen and ink drawing of a Gryphon and dated 23.3.08, very good, some rubbing and light wear to extremities, gilt decorated custom brown half morocco fleece lined folding box. B & B Rare Books, Ltd.   234 - 8   2015 $6000

Dodgson, Charles Lutwidge 1832-1898 *Alice's Adventures in Wonderland. (with) Through the Looking Glass and What Alice Found There.* New York: Limited Editions Club, 1912. 1935. Both limited to 1500 numbered copies, signed by the original Alice, Alice Hargraves, signed by Frederic Warde, this copy of of the few signed by the 'original Alice', octavo, original text illustrations by Tenniel re-engraved on wood by Bruno Rollitz, printed by members of the LEC by the Printing House of William Edwin Rudge, typography and binding design by Frederic Warde, publisher's full red morocco by George McKibbin & Son, NY. covers decoratively bordered in gilt, smooth spine decoratively tooled and lettered gilt in compartments, some rubbing to spine, near fine, housed in original blue cloth slipcase (some browning and light wear); Looking Glass with original text illustrations by Tenniel, Re-engraved (in metal) by Frederick Warde, publisher's full blue morocco by McKibbin, covers decoratively bordered gilt, smooth spine decoratively tooled and lettered in gilt in compartments, all edges gilt some rubbing, some scuffing to spine, near fine copy, housed in original red cloth slipcase, fine.   Heritage Book Shop   Holiday 2014 - 30   2015 $4000

Dodgson, Charles Lutwidge 1832-1898 *Alice's Adventures in Wonderland.* London: Philip Lee Warner for The Medici Society, 1914. First edition thus, number 172 of 1000 copies, large 8vo. original cloth spine, floral patterned boards, printed spine label and printed title label on cover (spares at rear), slight browning to covers, slight rubbing, else very good, dust jacket little tanned and marked with some nicks and slight chipping at edges, illustrations by John Tenniel, greeting and name on front free endpaper dated 1918.   Any Amount of Books   2015 - A90216   2015   £240

Dodgson, Charles Lutwidge 1832-1898 *Alice in Wonderland.* Paris: Black Sun Press, 1930. Limited to only 350 copies for America printed on Rives paper, illustrations by Marie Laurencin, 6 magnificent color plates, oblong 4to., white wrappers, covers and flyleaves lightly foxed, else fine in original slipcase and chemise (case scuffed and soiled some).   Aleph-bet Books, Inc.   109 - 82   2015 $3500

Dodgson, Charles Lutwidge 1832-1898 *Alice's Adventures in Wonderland and Through the Looking-Glass.* New York: Limited Editions Club, 1932. Limited to 1500 numbered copies, signed by typographer and binder, Frederic Warde and by Alice Hargreaves, 2 volumes, 8vo., leather, covers and spine gilt stamped, all edges gilt, slipcases, gilt stamped spine, front and rear covers with pictorial vignettes, title, author and publisher on spine.   Oak Knoll Books   25 - 7   2015 $5500

Dodgson, Charles Lutwidge 1832-1898 *Alice in Wonderland.* New York and London: North - South Books, 1999. (1-10 code), 4to., pictorial boards, as new in like dust jacket, first printing, illustrations by Lisbeth Swerger.   Aleph-bet Books, Inc.   109 - 84   2015 $150

Dodgson, Charles Lutwidge 1832-1898 *The Hunting of the Snark.* London: Macmillan, 1876. First edition, unrecorded binding, 8vo., bright red cloth with gilt vignettes on covers, surrounded by 3 gilt ruled circles and triple gilt rules on edges, all edges gilt, some finger soiling on covers and slightest of fraying to spine extremities, else nice, tight copy, binder's ticket Burn and Co., 9 incredibly detailed full page illustrations by Henry Holliday, this copy from the Lewis Carroll collection of Philip C. Blackburn with his notation and note to him laid in.   Aleph-Bet Books, Inc.   108 - 88   2015 $1950

Dodgson, Charles Lutwidge 1832-1898 *The Hunting of the Snark and Other Poems.* New York: Harper & Bros., 1903. First edition with Peter Newell's illustrations, 8vo., white imitation vellum boards, gilt decoration, top edge gilt, fine in original cloth backed dust jacket, jacket very good+ with some fading, spine fraying and mends on verso, tissue guarded color frontispiece plus 39 other fabulous plates, beautiful copy.   Aleph-bet Books, Inc.   109 - 85   2015 $500

Dodgson, Charles Lutwidge 1832-1898 *Through the Looking Glass.* London: Macmillan, 1872. First edition, first printing with 'wade' to page 21, illustrations by John Tenniel, finely bound in full crimson morocco by Bayntun-Riviere, gilt, original cloth bound in at rear, about fine, with former owner's 1872 inscription to half title, few hints of scattered light spotting to otherwise fresh pages, book in fine binding.   B & B Rare Books, Ltd.   2015 - 2015 $4500

Dodgson, Charles Lutwidge 1832-1898 *Through the Looking Glass and What Alice Found There.* New York: Harper, 1902. First edition thus, 8vo., signed and inscribed by the artist, Peter Newell on titlepage, very good+, original white paper covered boards with gilt lettering to spine and front cover, gilt illustration of Alice on front cover, top edge gilt, soil, toning and scuffs to covers, cover edgewear, mild soil to endpapers, binding intact, rare.   By the Book, L. C.   44 - 76   2015 $1000

Dodsley, Robert 1703-1764 *The Chronicle of the Kings of England.* London: printed for T. Cooper, 1741. 8vo., half title, bound fairly recently in cloth with printed title label, good copy.   John Drury Rare Books   March 2015 - 24680   2015   £266

Dodsley, Robert   1703-1764   *A Collection of Poems... by several hands.*   London: for J. Dodsley, 1782. 6 volumes, 178 x 108mm., with half titles, superb contemporary sprinkled calf, flat spines, wide gilt bands forming elegantly gilt compartments with scrolling cornerpieces and large sunburst centerpiece, red and green morocco labels, engraved vignette titlepage, engraved and woodcut headpieces and tailpieces, two engraved plates, perhaps 20 leaves with moderate foxing, small dent and puncture in fore edge of four gatherings of first volume, text unaffected, frequent offsetting in text, otherwise only insignificant defects internally, leaves quite fresh and clean, covers with only trivial imperfections, especially attractive bindings in very fine condition.   Phillip J. Pirages   66 - 45   2015 $1900

Dodsley, Robert   1703-1764   *Economie De La Vie Humaine, Divise en Deaux Partie.*   D. N. Shury and 'Se vend au Magasin des Enfans, chez didier et Co., 1805. Obscure edition, 10 woodcut plates, few spots here and there and minor offsetting of plates, 12mo., original red roan backed drab boards, worn at extremities, elegantly inscribed 'Miss Ward with C. M. Mikels kind regards', good.   Blackwell's Rare Books   B179 - 36   2015   £800

Doherty, P. C.   *The Assassin the Greenwood.*   London: Headline, 1993. First edition very fine in dust jacket,   Mordida Books   March 2015 - 008985   2015 $100

Doherty, P. C.   *The Fate of Princes.*   London: Robert Hale, 1990. First edition, fine in dust jacket.   Buckingham Books   March 2015 - 24590   2015 $325

Doig, Ivan   *This House of Sky.*   New York: Harcourt Brace Jovanovich, 1978. First edition, inscribed in year of publication, with 5 x 7 photo of author laid in, fine in fine dust jacket.   Ed Smith Books   83 - 18   2015 $250

Doig, Ivan   *This House of Sky.*   New York: Harcourt Brace Jovanovich, 1978. First edition, tall galleys, signed by author, perfect bound in blue wrappers, very good.   Ed Smith Books   83 - 17   2015 $300

Dolby, George   *Charles Dickens as I Knew Him...*   London: T. Fisher Unwin, 1885. Second thousand, half title, 32 page catalog 1885, pin holes in title, original red cloth, dulled, from the library of Geoffrey & Kathleen Tillotson, press cuttings inserted including obit of Dolby 1900.   Jarndyce Antiquarian Booksellers   CCVII - 212   2015   £40

The Dolphin.   New York: Limited Editions Club, 1933. 1935. 1938. 1940-1941, Limitations vary from 1200 to 2000 copies, 4to., first part of volume four bound in cloth, not in paper wrappers, cover soiled, volume I has stain on front cover, volume 2 and 3 have fraying at spine ends.   Oak Knoll Books   25 - 69   2015 $500

Dolzali, Gary W.   *Monan the Hoosier Line.*   Glendale: Interurban Press, 1987. First edition, quarto, black and white and color photos, diagrams, maps, gray cloth lettered red, very fine, pictorial dust jacket.   Argonaut Book Shop   Holiday Season 2014 - 78   2015 $75

Dolzali, Gary W.   *Steel Rails Across America. The Drama of Railroading in Spectacular Photos.*   Waukesha: Kalmbach Books, 1989. First edition, signed by Dolzali and co-author Mike Danneman, full page color photos, endpaper map, quarto, blue cloth, slight rubbing to lower edge of boards, else fine, pictorial dust jacket.   Argonaut Book Shop   Holiday Season 2014 - 77   2015 $45

Domett, Alfred   *The Diary of Alfred Dommett 1872-1885.*   London: Oxford University Press, 1953. Half title, frontispiece, original green cloth, very good, dust jacket, inscribed by Kathleen Tillotson from EAH.   Jarndyce Antiquarian Booksellers   CCVII - 223   2015   £20

Dominguez, Patrice   *Roland Garros 2001: Vu Par Les Plus Grands Photogaphes de Tennis.*   N.P.: Roland Garros Productions, 2001. First edition, oblong box, containing 3 booklets (unstapled) with rectangle open in centre of box cover revealing image of wrappers cover, pages 76, 20 and 22, copiously illustrated, fine in fine dust jacket.   Any Amount of Books   2015 - A97951   2015   £180

Donaldson, D. J.   *Cajun Nights.*   New York: St. Martin's, 1988. First edition, very fine in dust jacket.   Mordida Books   March 2015 - 000673   2015 $150

Donaldson, James   *Husbandry Anatomized, or an Enquiry into the Present Manner of Teiling and Manuring the Ground in Scotland for Most Part...*   Edinburgh: printed by John Reid, 1697. Second edition, 8vo. (in half sheets), tiny pinhole touching one letter of date, contemporary ownership inscription in ink on titlepage of James Bennet, later endpapers, contemporary morocco, sides panelled gilt in Cambridge style, spine fully gilt within compartments with overall geometric pattern, all edges gilt, joints and extremities worn, very good.   John Drury Rare Books   2015 - 22402   2015 $3409

Donan, P.   *Utah. A Peep Into a Mountain-Walled Treasury of the Gods.*   Matthews-Northrop Co., 1891. First edition, stiff gilt stamped wrappers, profusely illustrated, including many photos, full page map, near fine and very scarce.   Buckingham Books   March 2015 - 37193   2015 $200

Donatus, Alexander *Constantinus Romae Liberator.* Romae: Ex Typographia Manelfi, 1640. First edition, 184 x 121mm., fine contemporary Italian honey brown morocco, ornately gilt, covers framed by multiple plain and dotted rules and elaborate jewel-and-flower roll, central panel with delicate dentelle border enclosing elaborate cornerpieces of scrolling floral vines and central oval with filigree frame formed by fleurons and small tools, at center the 'Sede Vacante' arm of the Holy See comprising crossed keys beneath an umbraculum (i.e. a papal umbrella), this symbol flanked here by the letters "S" and "R", flat spine decorated with a chain of fleurons within an elongated frame of multiple plain and decorative rules, old ink titling, holes for ties (now lacking) all edges gilt (new but suitable endpapers, some small repairs presumably made to joints and corners though obviously with expert hands), extra engraved titlepage with arms of Duke of Etruria and engraved allegorical portrait of Constantine I, just bit of wear to joints and extremities, title page slightly soiled and with careful repairs to edges, faint browning and minor foxing throughout (two gatherings somewhat browned, conspicuous foxing on a dozen or so leaves), little worming to final two (index) leaves, other minor defects, still reasonable copy internally, consistently fresh and clean and splendidly gilt binding lustrous and no serious signs of use. Phillip J. Pirages 66 - 26 2015 $3900

Donellan, John *The Trial of John Donellan, Esq. for the Willful murder of Sir Theodosius Edward Allesley Boughton, Bart at the Assize at Warwick on Friday March 30th 1781 before the Honorable Francis Buller, Esq. one of the Justice of His Majesty's Court of King' Bench.* London: sold by George Kearsley and Martha Gurney, 1781. First edition, folio, 58 pages, generous margins, neatly bound recently in cloth backed marbled boards, spine lettered gilt, good, large copy, scarce. John Drury Rare Books March 2015 - 20974 2015 £306

Donne, John 1571-1631 *Biathanatos (First word in Greek).* Printed by John Dawson, circa, 1647. First edition, first issue, with undated titlepage, woodcut initials, woodcut and typographic headpieces, initial blank, last 4 leaves with few short marginal tears, light browning at edges of titlepage (offset from binding turn-ins), 4to., contemporary blind ruled calf with corner ornaments, spine gilt, rebacked preserving original spine, lacking lettering piece, preserved in full brown morocco pull-off case, early signature of Wm. Vernon at head of initial blank, engraved bookplate of Henry Greenhill dated 1911, inside front cover, bookplate of H. Bradley Martin inside rear cover, modern bookplate recto of initial blank very good. Blackwell's Rare Books B179 - 37 2015 £5000

Donne, John 1571-1631 *The Divine Poems.* Oxford: Clarendon Press, 1952. Half title, frontispiece, original dark blue cloth, torn dust jacket, Kathleen Tillotson's copy 1953 with few pencil marginal notes. Jarndyce Antiquarian Booksellers CCVII - 224 2015 £30

Donne, John 1571-1631 *The Elegies and Songs and Sonnets.* Oxford: Clarendon Press, 1965. Half title, music, original dark blue cloth, very good in slightly torn and marked dust jacket, with 4 related cuttings inserted, from the library of Geoffrey & Kathleen Tillotson. Jarndyce Antiquarian Booksellers CCVII - 2245 2015 £35

Donne, John 1571-1631 *The Extasie.* London: privately printed at the Department of English at University College London, 1934. Unopened, original blue printed wrappers, from the library of Geoffrey & Kathleen Tillotson. Jarndyce Antiquarian Booksellers CCVII - 226 2015 £50

Donne, John 1571-1631 *The Holy Sonnets of John Donne.* London: J. M. Dent & Sons, 1938. First edition, limited to 500 copies, original black cloth lettered gilt on spine and front cover, engravings by Eric Gill, signed by Gill, slight offsetting to front and rear endpapers and slight browning to rear pages, otherwise very good+ in somewhat tatty, good only dust jacket with large chunk from top edge of front panel and split at spine. Any Amount of Books 2015 - C14002 2015 £260

Donne, John 1571-1631 *Poems &c. With Elegies on the Authors Death.* London: printed by T. N. for Henry Herringman, 1669. Fifth edition according to Keynes, seventh edition according to Wing, octavo, contemporary full brown calf, expertly rebacked, covers decoratively ruled in blind, spine decorated in gilt, red morocco label on spine, gilt stamped with five raised bands, previous owner's bookplate, signatures on front free endpapers, corners worn, minor foxing, very good. Heritage Book Shop Holiday 2014 - 62 2015 $5500

Donne, John 1571-1631 *The Poems.* Oxford: Clarendon Press, 1912. 2 volumes, original brown buckram, paper labels slightly split at edges, with inserted, notes, probably by J. B. Leishman, the editor to whom correspondence is addressed, from the library of Geoffrey & Kathleen Tillotson. Jarndyce Antiquarian Booksellers CCVII - 227 2015 £60

Donne, John 1571-1631 *The Poems.* London: Oxford University Press, 1929. Half title, frontispiece, uncut in original blue cloth, covered in thick striped paper, paper label, Kathleen Tillotson's copy 1930 as KMC, Geoffrey Tillotson added 1934, many notes, mostly marginal on endpapers and inserted articles. Jarndyce Antiquarian Booksellers CCVII - 228 2015 £50

Donne, John 1571-1631 *Where Many Shipwreck.* Llandogo: Old Stile Press, 2004. 679/190 copies (from an edition of 216 copies), signed by artist, Robert MacDonald, printed on Velin Arches paper, 25 woodcuts, 4to., original quarter blue leather with purple boards illustrated in silver, backstrip lettered in silver, top edge purple, others untrimmed. Blackwell's Rare Books B179 - 205 2015 £180

Donoho, M. H. *Circle dot. A True Story of Cowboy life Forty Years ago.* Crane and Co., 1907. First edition, 8vo., cloth, frontispiece, very scarce, fine, bright, tight copy, scarce. Buckingham Books March 2015 - 30015 2015 $275

Donovan, Dick *Eugene Vidocq.* London: Hutchinson, 1895. First edition, spine slightly darkened, otherwise near fine, green decorated cloth covered boards, gilt top of page edges. Mordida Books March 2015 - 000678 2015 $100

Donovan, Dick *The Man Hunter. Stories from the Note-Book of a Detective.* New York: Frank F. Lovell & Co., 1889. First US edition, this copy in cloth binder with original front and rear covers affixed to front and rear panels, with original front and rear inside panels affixed to front and rear pastedown sheets, first four pages fragile and have been reinforced at fore-edges, fifth page has small piece removed from top corner edge that does not affect text, all page edges uniformly browned, else very good, tight, well protected copy in new cloth binder, titles stamped in blue on spine, very scarce. Buckingham Books March 2015 - 31370 2015 $750

Doolittle, Hilda 1886-1961 *Hymen.* New York: Holt, 1921. First edition, wrappers, very good with little discoloration to wrinkling edges and few tiny tears. Beasley Books 2013 - 2015 $125

Doolittle, Hilda 1886-1961 *Kora and Ka.* Paris: privately printed, 1934. First edition, one of only 100 copies, octavo, wrappers, pages unopened, covers slightly creased at edges, one small nick, near fine. Peter Ellis, Bookseller 2014 - 017656 2015 £300

Doolittle, Hilda 1886-1961 *Selected Poems.* New York: 1957. First edition, number 27 of a specially bound numbered edition of 50 copies signed by author, 8vo., original quarter brown cloth lettered in gilt to upper board, backstrip lettered gilt, very slightly sunned, very good, excellent condition, signed by author (she as added "Kussnacht, Zurich, March 17 1957"). Any Amount of Books 2015 - C7936 2015 £175

Dorn, Edward *The Newly Fallen.* New York: Totem Press, 1961. First edition, drawings by Fielding Dawson, illustrated wrappers, bit of age-toning to wrappers, thus near fine, poet Robert Creeley's copy with his ownership signature. Between the Covers Rare Books, Inc. 187 - 78 2015 $150

Dorr, Rheta Childe *Susan B. Anthony, the Woman who Changed the Mind of a Nation, Illustrated from Photographs.* New York: Stokes, 1928. First edition, 8vo., spine little faded, otherwise very good. Second Life Books Inc. 189 - 63 2015 $75

Dostoevskii, Fyodor Mikhailovich 1821-1881 *Crime & Punishment.* New York: Limited Editions Club, 1948. Limited to 1500 numbered copies, signed by artist, Fritz Eichenberg, wood engravings by Eichenberg, 4to., black and red cloth with gilt decorated inset on front cover, corner of slipcase bumped. Oak Knoll Books 25 - 32 2015 $250

Dostoevskii, Fyodor Mikhailovich 1821-1881 *The Grand Inquisitor.* London: Elkin Matthews, 1930. First edition, limited to 300 numbered copies, this no. 267, 4to., original ultra modernist decorated pigskin, lettered black on spine and front cover, signed presentation from S. S. Koteliansky for Raphael Salaman (1906-1993 and wife Miriam Polianovsky, very faint surface soiling, otherwise fine in sound, used slipcases, excellent copy. Any Amount of Books 2015 - C11380 2015 £225

Dostoevskii, Fyodor Mikhailovich 1821-1881 *L'Idiot.* Paris: Gallimard NRF, 1966. One of 10,250 numbered copies, 20 illustrations by Andre Masson, large 8vo., near fine in publisher's acetate dust jacket which is also near fine and near fine publisher's slipcase. Beasley Books 2013 - 2015 $45

Dostoevskii, Fyodor Mikhailovich 1821-1881 *Die Sanfte.* Berlin: Erich Reiss, 1920. First edition, 4to., illustrations by Bruno Krauskopf, number 4 of 70 copies with each print signed, non-authorial inscription, slight bowing to rear board, very slight scuffing to rear cover, some slight staining to front endpapers otherwise sound, very good. Any Amount of Books 2015 - A93760 2015 £300

Doty, M. R. *An Alphabet.* Ithaca: Alembic Press, 1979. First edition, one of 600 copies, initials by Teresa McNeil, wrappers as issued, modest age toning, at least near fine, very warmly inscribed by co-author, Ruth Doty for Michael Benedikt. Between the Covers Rare Books, Inc. 187 - 79 2015 $450

Doubleday, H. Arthur *The Victoria History of the Counties of England: Warwickshire.* London: Archibald Constable/ University of London Institute of Historical Research/Oxford University Press, 1904. First edition, 4to., 6 volumes, original red cloth lettered gilt on spines and covers, copiously illustrated in black and white, slight unobjectionable mottling to covers of 2 volumes, tape ghost marks to endpapers of some volumes, slight foxing, inner hinges starting of volumes 1 & 2, 1 & 4 rubbed at spine with resultant fading of gilt, otherwise close to very good, sound set with clean text. Any Amount of Books 2015 - A90528 2015 £240

Doughty, Arthur G. *Report of the Work of the Public Archives for the Year 1914 and 1915.* Ottawa: King's Printer, J. De L. Tache, 1916. 8vo., printed wrappers, 3 maps, front and rear covers missing, spine creased. Schooner Books Ltd. 110 - 181 2015 $100

Douglas, F. *An Essay on Certain Points of Resemblance Between the Ancient and Modern Greeks.* London: John Murray, 1813. Second edition, 8vo., full tree calf lettered and decorated gilt on spine, handsome, with very slight splitting at spine but holding well and looking good.   Any Amount of Books   2015 - A85673   2015   £240

Douglas, James *Methodism Condemned; or Priestcraft Detected.* Newcastle upon Tyne: printed for the author by J. Mitchell, 1814. At least 3 editions were printed in 1814, all pretty scare, 12mo., 24 pages, recent plain wrappers, good copy.   John Drury Rare Books   2015 - 20797   2015 $159

Douglas, Janet Mary Stair *The Life and Selections from the Correspondence of William Whewell, D.D.* Bristol & Tokyo: Thoemmes & Kinokuniya, 1991. Facsimile reprint of 1881 edition, 8vo., frontispiece portrait, black cloth, gilt stamped spine title, fine, scarce.   Jeff Weber Rare Books   178 - 1143   2015 $100

Douglas, Kirk *Dance with the Devil.* New York: Random House, 1990. First edition, signed by author and Jack Valenti, very fine in dust jacket.   Mordida Books   March 2015 - 000684   2015 $100

Douglas, Norman 1868-1952 *Looking Back: an Autobiographical Excursion.* London: Chatto & Windus, 1934. First edition in one volume, thick large volume, boards bit soiled, thus very good without dust jacket, publisher Martin Secker's copy with his small bookplate.   Between the Covers Rare Books, Inc.   187 - 80   2015 $125

Douglas, Roy *Who is Nemo?* Philadelphia: Lippincott, 1937. First edition, very good in dust jacket with nicke and frayed spine ends, wear along folds and edges, several short closed tears.   Mordida Books   March 2015 - 000685   2015 $75

Douglass, Royal *Prison Verse by Royall Douglass No. "19173".* San Quentin: Palo Alto: Altruria Press, 1911. First edition, tall 4to., original pictorial wrappers, sewn as issued with red cords, 32 pages, text in brown ink on cream colored paper with gold ruled borders, small photo of San Quentin on upper wrapper within scene of a wall and gate, edges little worn, fine copy.   The Brick Row Book Shop Miscellany 67 - 78   2015 $250

Douton, Agnes May Maud *A Book with Seven Seals.* London: Cayme Press, 1928. Half title, illustrations, original brown boards, brown cloth spine, slight rubbing, given to Kathleen Tillotson by Margaret Blom, with Kathleen's notes of her research included.   Jarndyce Antiquarian Booksellers   CCVII - 229   2015   £110

Dove, Rita *Selected Poems.* New York: Pantheon, 1993. Uncorrected proof, little sunned on spine thus, near fine in pale green wrappers, signed by Dove on front wrapper.   Between the Covers Rare Books   197 - 14   2015 $85

Dove, Rita *Through the Ivory Gate.* New York: Pantheon, 1992. Uncorrected proof, fine in printed buff wrappers, inscribed by author.   Between the Covers Rare Books   197 - 13   2015 $100

Dow, Arthur Wesley *Composition: a Series of Exercises in Art Structure for the Use of Students and Teachers.* Garden City: Doubleday Page and Co., 1923. Ninth edition, quarto, illustrations, quarter cloth and decorated paper over boards, ownership signature of artist Mary Blackford Fowler, corners rubbed, small tear on spine, else near fine in edgeworn, good dust jacket with several tears and modest chipping at and near crown, scarce in jacket.   Between the Covers Rare Books, Inc.   187 - 81   2015 $250

Dow, Lorenzo *The Opinion of Dow or Lorenzo's Thoughts on Different Religious Subjects...* Windham: J. Byrne, 1804. First edition, 18mo., contemporary calf, text browned, lacks front endpaper.   M & S Rare Books, Inc.   97 - 93   2015 $600

Doyle, Arthur Conan 1859-1930 *The Adventures of Sherlock Holmes. (with) The Memoirs of Sherlock Holmes.* Newnes, 1892-1894. First editions, 104 and 90 text illustrations by Signey Paget, royal 8vo., original blue (Adventures dark, Memoirs pale), bevel edged cloth backstrips and boards blocked in gilt and black (street name absent on 'Adventures' but present on 'Memoirs'), both volumes recased with backstrips reinforced (hinges notoriously fragile), rear flyleaf of 'Adventures' replaced, spine gilt rubbed, 'Adventures' with two lines of staining to front board matching gift inscription to front flyleaves, gift inscriptions dated 1892 and 1894 from George Baker to his father Thomas.   Blackwell's Rare Books   B179 - 143   2015   £2000

Doyle, Arthur Conan 1859-1930 *The Adventures of Sherlock Holmes. (with) The Later Adventures of Sherlock Holmes. (with) The Final Adventures of Sherlock Holmes.* New York: Limited Editions Club, 1950. 1952. 1952. Limited to 1500 numbered sets, 8vo., black cloth spine with decorated paper covered boards, black cameo of Holmes center of each cover, original slipcases rubbed along edges, bookplate, illustrations.   Oak Knoll Books   25 - 35   2015 $750

Doyle, Arthur Conan 1859-1930 *The Dealings of Captain Sharkey. Black Doctor. The Croxley Master. Last of the Legions. Man from Archangel. The Great Keinplatz Experiment.* New York: 1919. All have Doran colophon on titlepage, two have light vertical crease to front cover, Doctor has backstrip reglued, all have top edges with minor abrasion, all have backstrips with some fading, issued in various covers, these are all cloth, together 6 volumes.   Bookworm & Silverfish   2015 - 5631947556   2015 $225

Doyle, Arthur Conan 1859-1930 *The Exploits of Brigadier Gerard.* New York: D. Appleton and Co., 1896. First American edition, decorated maroon cloth, contemporary owner's name on front of Capt. W. T. Duggan 10th Inty, bookplate of noted Sherlockian Edgar W. Smith with his pencil notation.   Between the Covers Rare Books, Inc. 187 - 192   2015 $450

Doyle, Arthur Conan 1859-1930 *The Field Bazaar.* Summit: Pamphlet House, 1974. First American separate edition, copy 85 of 250 numbered copies, fine, some darkening on endpapers, otherwise fine in original glassine dust jacket.   Mordida Books   March 2015 - 011806   2015 $125

Doyle, Arthur Conan 1859-1930 *The Hound of the Baskervilles.* London: George Newnes, 1902. First edition, original cloth, frontispiece and 15 full page illustrations by Signey Paget, armorial bookplate of Gilbert A. Tonge, later bookplate of Henry Rouse Viets, little bit of wear to extremities, few spots of bubbling to cloth (as usual), very faint ring on rear panel, gilt on cloth sharp and bright, exceptionally nice.   Manhattan Rare Book Company   Literature 2014 - 2015 $4800

Doyle, Arthur Conan 1859-1930 *The Hound of the Baskervilles.* London: George Newnes, 1902. First edition, illustrations by Sidney Paget, publisher's red cloth by Alfred Garth Jones, unusually fine, only hint of wear to extremities, spine almost completely unfaded, bright gilt, hint of spotting to endpapers, bright and fresh, unsophisticated copy.   B & B Rare Books, Ltd.   2015 - 2015 $8000

Doyle, Arthur Conan 1859-1930 *The Hound of the Baskervilles.* London: George Newnes Ltd., 1902. First edition, 16 full page illustrations by Sidney Paget, original red cloth with gilt decorations and lettering on front cover and spine, former owner's inked name and street address on flyleaf and inked initials on front pastedown sheet, minor wear to spine ends, top edge lightly soiled, else near fine, bright, clean, housed in bright cloth clamshell case, with hound like the one on book's front cover on front panel and titles stamped in gold gilt on leather spine label, attractive.   Buckingham Books   March 2015 - 37647   2015 $6500

Doyle, Arthur Conan 1859-1930 *The Memoirs of Sherlock Holmes.* London: George Newnes, 1894. First edition, first state, dark blue cloth, black illustrations of The Strand Library on front cover, titles stamped in gold gilt on front cover and spine, all edges gilt, frontispiece, illustrations, housed in cloth slipcase with leather label on spine and titles stamped in gold gilt, illustrations by Sidney Paget, brief non-authorial inscription front and rear covers have been professionally reinforced which makes this a nice, tight square copy, very good.   Buckingham Books   March 2015 - 36739   2015 $1950

Doyle, Arthur Conan 1859-1930 *Micah Clarke: His Statement as Made to His Three Grandchildren Joseph, Gervas & Robert during the hard winter of 1734...* London: Longmans, 1889. Half title, final ad leaf, few leaves roughly opened, original navy blue cloth, bevelled boards, little rubbed, booklabel of Christopher Clark Geest on leading pastedown, signature on half title of Vincent Starrett, 1886-1974.   Jarndyce Antiquarian Booksellers   CCXI - 93   2015   £220

Doyle, Arthur Conan 1859-1930 *The Sign of the Four.* Spencer Blackett, 1890. First edition, second state with Griffith Farran & Co. Standard Library at bottom of spine, lightly spotted on rear cover, else very good, tight copy, housed in quarter leather and cloth clamshell case with titles stamped in gold gilt on spine.   Buckingham Books   March 2015 - 36743   2015 $9750

Doyle, Arthur Conan 1859-1930 *The Tragedy of Korosko.* London: Smith Elder, 1898. First edition, very good, some internal splitting along hinges, otherwise very good in red cloth covered boards with gold stamped titles.   Mordida Books   March 2015 - 002663   2015 $200

Doyle, Arthur Conan 1859-1930 *The Valley of Fear. A Sherlock Holmes Novel.* New York: George H. Doran, 1914. True first edition, octavo, 7 full page illustrations by Keller (including frontispiece), publisher's red cloth with gilt lettering on spine and front board, rare original dust jacket, small bookseller's blindstamp on front endpaper, book fine, jacket completely unrestored, jacket with some wear to edges and front flap fold with longer chip at foot of fold, some small chips to edges and corners, crease line to lower front panel, spine and back panel of jacket bit foxed, overall bright, fine, very good dust jacket.   Heritage Book Shop Holiday 2014 - 63   2015 $10,000

Doyle, Arthur Conan 1859-1930 *White Company.* New York: Cosmopolitan Book Co., 1922. First Wyeth edition, 4to., maroon gilt cloth, pictorial paste-on, top edge gilt, very fine in dust jacket (white paper wrapper has quarter size piece off mid spine), 3 small chips off bottom edges, else very good, rear panel with correct first edition ads for only Robinson Crusoe and a Tale of Two Cities, illustrations by N. C. Wyeth with cover plate, pictorial paste-on, pictorial endpapers and titlepage, plus 13 color plates, rare in such nice dust jacket.   Aleph-bet Books, Inc.   109 - 494   2015 $1350

Doyle, Richard 1824-1883 *Richard Doyle's Pictures of Extra Articles and Visitors to the Exhibition.* London: Chapman and Hall, 1852. Oblong crown 8vo., title and leaf of contents, 8 double page engraved plates by Doyle, original blue boards, new endpapers, scarce.   Marlborough Rare Books   List 53 - 12   2015   £350

Doyle, Richard 1824-1883 *Richard Doyle's Pictures of Extra Articles and Visitors to the Exhibition.* London: Chapman and Hall, 1852. Oblong 8vo., 8 double page lithographic plates by Doyle, modern brown half calf over pebble grained cloth covered boards, front cover lettered gilt, scarce.   Marlborough Rare Books Ltd.   List 49 - 7   2015   £500

Doyle, Richard 1824-1883 *The Story of Jack and Giants.* London: Cundall & Addey, 1851. First edition, small 4to., 56 pages, frontispiece, pictorial titlepage, 6 plates, 27 illustrations and initials all by Doyle, all uncolored, wood engraved, original cream cloth, lettered gilt on spine and cover with blind decoration to edges, covers slightly soiled and tanned at spine with inner hinge slightly cracked, otherwise decent, close to very good.   Any Amount of Books   2015 - C5104   2015   £175

Drake, Daniel 1824-1883 *A Systematic Treatise... on the Principal Diseases of the Interior Valley of North America. (First and Second Series).* Cincinnati: Winthrop B. Smith and Co., Philadelphia: Lippincott Grambo & Co., 1850. First edition, thick 8vo., one folding map, numerous charts, volume II in contemporary calf, volume I in closely matching new calf, moderate foxing and occasional dampstaining.   M & S Rare Books, Inc.   97 - 94   2015 $2000

Drake, Judith *An Essay in Defence of the female Sex.* London: for A. Roper and R. Clavel, 1697. Third edition, large 8vo., frontispiece, light waterstaining to lower right corner of second half of work, section cut from top of titlepage (62 x 25mm) removing 'An' from title, contemporary panelled calf, corners and edges slightly chipped, joints cracked, pencil inscription Frances Cotton Anne Fleming Aug 14 1715, H. Hall 18th century red ink stamp, from the library of James Stevens Cox (1910-1997).   Maggs Bros. Ltd.   1447 - 150   2015   £1500

Dramatic Characters or Different Portraits of the English Stage. London: printed for Robert Sayer and John Smith, 1770. First edition, 24 hand colored plates, square 12mo., full contemporary calf, gilt.   Honey & Wax Booksellers   2 - 22   2015 $6000

Drayton, Michael 1563-1631 *Endimion and Phoebe. Ideas Lamos.* N.P.: 1870? 4to., privately printed facsimile, original purple wrappers with title, front wrapper detached and creased, spine defective, from the library of Geoffrey & Kathleen Tillotson, with few pencil notes by Geoffrey.   Jarndyce Antiquarian Booksellers   CCVII - 232   2015   £120

Drayton, Michael 1563-1631 *England's Heroical Epistles.* London: printed for J. Johnson, 1788. Some leaves slightly browned, 19th century half dark green morocco, slightly rubbed with scars on marbled boards, with early note on page 308, with names of Geoffrey and Kathleen Tillotson, inserted correspondence shows Kathleen offered this to British Library which in fact had acquired a copy, ALS from John Betjeman probably to Bernard Newdigate.   Jarndyce Antiquarian Booksellers   CCVII - 233   2015   £280

Drayton, Michael 1563-1631 *Ideas Mirrour.* London: printed by James Roberts for Nicholas Linge, 1928? Facsimile, 4to., photographic facsimile, from Huntington Library copy with label, dark green binder's cloth, signed by Kathleen Tillotson 1928.   Jarndyce Antiquarian Booksellers   CCVII - 234   2015   £40

Drayton, Michael 1563-1631 *Minor Poems.* Oxford: Clarendon Press, 1907. 4to., original cream card imitation vellum wrappers, very slightly dusted, very good, signed by Geoffrey Tillotson 1928 with very few pencil notes.   Jarndyce Antiquarian Booksellers   CCVII - 236   2015   £40

Drayton, Michael 1563-1631 *Minor Poems...* Oxford: Clarendon Press, 1907. 4to., original cream card imitation vellum wrappers, spine and edges browned, signed, Kathleen M. Constable (Tillotson) may 1927, later pencil notes, letter by Tillotson.   Jarndyce Antiquarian Booksellers   CCVII - 235   2015   £45

Drayton, Michael 1563-1631 *Nimphidia the Court of Fayrie.* Stratford-upon-Avon: printed at the Shakespeare Head Press, 1924. 4to., half title, original decorated paper wrappers, spine slightly browned with small chips, with Christmas greetings from F. H. R. Dix, Hemingford or Stratford-on-Avon sending this poem, from the library of Geoffrey & Kathleen Tillotson.   Jarndyce Antiquarian Booksellers   CCVII - 237   2015   £50

Drayton, Michael 1563-1631 *Poems.* London: Routledge, 1953. 2 volumes, half titles, frontispieces, original dark blue cloth, very good in dust jacket, Kathleen Tillotson's review copy with few pencil notes and galley proof of her favourable review of volume I inserted.   Jarndyce Antiquarian Booksellers   CCVII - 238   2015   £20

Drayton, Michael 1563-1631 *Poly-Olbion.* London: printed for M. Lownes, I. Browne, A. Helme, J. Bushbie, 1612-1622. Engraved maps, 19th century half black calf, rubbed with split at head of leading hinge, armorial bookplate of Bernard Henry Newdigate, somewhat defective copy with few pencil marks, from the library of Geoffrey & Kathleen Tillotson.   Jarndyce Antiquarian Booksellers   CCVII - 239   2015   £950

Drayton, Michael 1563-1631 *The Works.* Oxford: printed at Shakesepare Head press, 1931-1941. Tercentary edition, 5 volumes, half titles, frontispieces, facsimiles, uncut, original dark blue cloth, inner hinges volume I splitting, good set, Kathleen Tillotson's copy with notes and insertions.   Jarndyce Antiquarian Booksellers   CCVII - 230   2015   £480

Drayton, Michael 1563-1631 *The Works.* Oxford: published for the Shakespeare Head Press, 1961. 1941, Volumes I-IV with Volume V 1941, half titles, frontispieces, facsimiles, uncut in original dark blue cloth, very good, from the library of Geoffrey & Kathleen Tillotson.   Jarndyce Antiquarian Booksellers   CCVII - 231   2015   £300

Dreier, Edward *The Lure Book of Michigan's Upper Peninsula.* N. P.: Upper Peninsula Development Bureau, 1943. First edition thus, folio, green stapled pictorial wrappers 100 pages, illustrations, photos, very light fading to covers, very good, mighty scarce.   Baade Books of the West   2014 - 2015 $40

Dreikurs, Rudolf *The Challenge of Parenthood.* New York: Duell Sloan, 1958. Later printing, signed by author, near fine hardcover, tiny tear at spine head.   Beasley Books   2013 - 2015 $45

Dresser, Christopher *The Art of Decorative Design.* London: Day and Son, Lithographers to the Queen..., 1862. First edition, royal 8vo., original decorated red cloth, gilt with design by author, red edges, recased, armorial bookplates of James O'Byrne.   Marlborough Rare Books   List 54 - 22   2015   £950

Dresser, Christopher *Japan, Its Architecture, Art and Art Manufactures.* London: Longman, Green and Co., 1882. Dresser proof copy "To Keep for Reference", 8vo., profusely illustrated, with proof of decorated title and temporary printed title, contemporary half calf, spine with labels, lettered gilt, somewhat rubbed.   Marlborough Rare Books   List 54 - 24   2015   £1500

Dresser, Christopher *Japan, Its Architecture, Art and Art Manufactures.* London: Longman Green and Co., 1882. First edition, 8vo., title printed in red and black, profusely illustrated, original decorated hessian.   Marlborough Rare Books   List 54 - 25   2015   £450

Dresser, Christopher *Popular Manual of Botany...* Edinburgh: Adam and Charles Black, 1860. First edition, 8vo., 12 hand colored plates, original brown cloth, blocked in blind, intertwined leaves, gilt lettered spines, binders ticket on pastedown, bound by Burn, London, clean copy of the colored issue.   Marlborough Rare Books   List 54 - 21   2015   £185

Dresser, Christopher *Studies in Design.* London: Cassell, Peter and Galpin, 1874. First edition, folio, chromolithograph title, 60 chromolithographs by A. Goater, Nottingham, plates, including frontispiece, each with tissue guard, original burgundy cloth, cover blocked key pattern border and lettered in gilt, gilt edges, skillfully recased.   Marlborough Rare Books   List 54 - 23   2015   £2500

Drexel, Jeremias *Hieremiae Drexelii E Societate Iesu Opera Cum Indice Quadruplici & Symbolis Aenesis.* Munich: Apud Melchioren Sege bibliopolam et Nicolaum Henricum Electoralem Typographum, 1628. First edition, 4to., original thick vellum covered boards, blindstamped with decorative panels front and rear, bevelled edges, some contemporary hand lettering at head of spine, remains of 2 early metal and leather clasps, small bookplate and two stamps, library of Rev. C. T. Showronski, about 18 tiny metal clips have been fastened as page markers to various page fore-edges, now immoveable and rusted, nevertheless do not affect even lie of text block, very occasional blotch or small ink mark, overall very decent clean and extremely sturdy.   Any Amount of Books   March 2015 - C16614   2015   £450

Dreyer, John Louis Emil *Tycho Brahe; a Picture of Scientific Life and Work in the Sixteenth Century.* Edinburgh: Adam and Charles Black, 1890. First edition, 8vo., frontispiece, 4 plates, original navy blue gilt stamped cloth, somewhat rubbed, still very good, color added to endleaves, inscribed by author to Thomas Heath, bookplate of Herbert Kraus.   Jeff Weber Rare Books   178 - 787   2015 $450

Dreyfus, John *A History of the Nonesuch Press.* London: Nonesuch Press, 1981. Limited to 950 numbered copies, 4to., cloth, dust jacket, printed on specially made paper from Dalmore Mill of William Sommerville, Edinburgh, many illustrations, some black and white, few with color, various news reviews laid in, presentation from Dreyfus for Joshua Heller, toning to inside flaps of jacket.   Oak Knoll Books   306 - 157   2015 $350

Dreyfus, John *The Work of Jan Van Krimpen, a Record in Honour of His Sixtieth Birthday.* London: Sylvan Press, 1952. First edition, small 4to., cloth, dust jacket, later cardboard slipcase, illustrations, jacket chipped with small tears along edges, ink inscription.   Oak Knoll Books   306 - 63   2015 $150

Drug Markets Catalog and Directory 1931. New York: Drug Markets Inc., 1931. illustrations, very nearly fine, very scarce.   Stephen Lupack   March 2015 - 2015 $100

Drury, Allen *Advise and Consent.* London: Collins, 1960. Uncorrected proof of the first British edition, near fine in unprinted, cloud themed wrappers, laid into very good dust jacket, with typed letter from publisher laid in, very uncommon in this advance issue and very nice.   Ken Lopez, Bookseller   164 - 56   2015 $750

Dryden, John 1631-1700 *Absalom and Achitophel.* London: printed and sold by H. Hills, 1708. Second and more common of two printings by Hills in 1708, identifiable by signature C under 'trade' as opposed to 'his' in the other edition, 8vo., disbound, very good. C. R. Johnson Foxon R-Z - 1204r-z 2015 $115

Dryden, John 1631-1700 *Elenora: a Panegyrical Poem...* London: printed and sold by H. Hills, 1709. Reprint, 8vo., disbound, narrow blank strip clipped from lower margin of titlepage, removing price of one penny perhaps deliberately, otherwise good. C. R. Johnson Foxon R-Z - 1218r-z 2015 $38

Dryden, John 1631-1700 *Fables Ancient and Modern.* London: Jacob Tonson, 1700. First edition, large paper copy, folio, contemporary paneled calf, rebacked with early spine label laid down, handsome large paper copy. Honey & Wax Booksellers 3 - 25 2015 $2500

Dryden, John 1631-1700 *Hymns Attributed to John Dryden.* Berkeley: University of California Press, 1937. Frontispiece, original brown cloth, very good in slightly dusted dust jacket, signed by Geoffrey Tillotson, with pencil notes, copies of his review, correspondence about the questioned ascription, long TLS from Professor Noyes and ms. copy of the reply. Jarndyce Antiquarian Booksellers CCVII - 248 2015 £30

Dryden, John 1631-1700 *The Medal. A Satyr Against Sedtion.* London: printed and sold by H. Hills, 1709. Reprint, 8vo., 16 pages, good, light browning, otherwise good. C. R. Johnson Foxon R-Z - 1219r-z 2015 $77

Dryden, John 1631-1700 *Of Dramatick Poesie, an Essay.* Printed for Henry Heringham, 1668. First edition, uniformly browned, various minor paper repairs, but including a tear in middle of titlepage (very neatly done), 4to., full crushed red morocco by Riviere and Son, lettered in gilt on upper cover and in minuscule letters on spine, gilt edges, cloth slip-in case, upper joint skillfully repaired, lower corners slightly bumped, good. Blackwell's Rare Books B179 - 38 2015 £1500

Du Boccage, Marie Ann Le Paget *La Colombiade ou la foi portee au nouveau monde.* Paris: Chez Desait & Saillant-Durant, 1756. First edition, 8vo., frontispiece, 10 engraved plates by Chedel, engraved vignette on title, headpiece and 10 engraved tailpieces, bound in original uncut marbled wrappers, lacks paper on spine, Swedish bookplate, fine, untrimmed, housed in cloth clamshell case. Second Life Books Inc. 190 - 58 2015 $750

Du Boccage, Marie Ann Le Paget *La Colombiade ou la Foi Portee au Nouveau Monde.* Paris: et se Vende a Francfort en Foire Chez Bassompierre & Vanden Berghen -Liege & Bruxelles, 1758. Second edition, 8vo., frontispiece, 10 engraved plates, vignette on title, headpiece and 10 engraved tailpieces, top edge gilt printed in red and black, little rubbed later half calf. Second Life Books Inc. 191 - 31 2015 $325

Du Bois, Henri Pene *American Bookbindings in the Library of Henry William Poor...* Jamaica: printed at the Marion Press, published by George D. Smith, 1903. First edition, number 164 of 200 numbered copies on Dutch handmade paper, 8vo., original grey green cloth, gilt lettering, frontispiece and 39 chromolithographed plates, striking color plates, bookplate of American book collector Charles Walker Andrews, binding slight worn and soiled, some offsetting from plates, very good. The Brick Row Book Shop Miscellany 67 - 4 2015 $450

Du Bois, William Edward Burghardt 1868-1963 *The Black Flame, a Trilogy, Consisting of The Ordeal of Mansart, Mansart Builds a School, Worlds of Color.* New York: Mainstream Publishers, 1957. 1959. 1961. First edition, 8vo., very good copies. Second Life Books Inc. 190 - 58 2015 $750

Du Bois, William Edward Burghardt 1868-1963 *The Crises. A Record of the Darker Races. volume 24 no. 4. whole number 142.* New York: NAACP, August, 1922. 8vo., original pictorial wrappers, some foxed and stained very good, rare. Second Life Books Inc. 190 - 60 2015 $175

Du Bois, William Edward Burghardt 1868-1963 *The Crises. A Record of the Darker Races. Volume 24 no. 5. Whole number 143.* New York: NAACP Sept., 1922. 8vo., original wrappers, very good, rare. Second Life Books Inc. 190 - 51 2015 $200

Du Bois, William Edward Burghardt 1868-1963 *The Crises. A Record of the Darker Races. Volume 30 No. 1. Whole Number 175.* New York: NAACP May, 1925. 8vo., original pictorial wrappers, covers tender, very good, rare. Second Life Books Inc. 190 - 66 2015 $175

Du Bois, William Edward Burghardt 1868-1963 *The Crises. A Record of the Darker Races. Volume 31 no. 2. whole number 182.* New York: NAACP. Dec., 1925. 8vo., original pictorial wrappers, cover separate, good copy, rare. Second Life Books Inc. 190 - 62 2015 $165

Du Bois, William Edward Burghardt 1868-1963 *The Crises. A Record of the Darker Races. Volume 31 No. 3. Whole number 183.* New York: NAACP, Jan., 1926. 8vo., original pictorial wrappers, covers tender, very good, rare. Second Life Books Inc. 190 - 65 2015 $175

Du Bois, William Edward Burghardt 1868-1963 *The Crises. A Record of the Darker Races. Volume 31. No. 5 Whole number 185.* New York: NAACP March, 1926. 8vo., original pictorial wrappers, covers separate, good. Second Life Books Inc.   190 - 63   2015 $165

Du Bois, William Edward Burghardt 1868-1963 *Darkwater.* New York: Harcourt Brace, 1920. First edition, 8vo., publisher's blue cloth with couple of small blemishes, with publisher's dust jacket, lacks small chip on lower right of cover, couple of small pieces at top of cover, top two inches of spine and part of monogram on bottom of spine along bottom of rear cover, not affecting any of the text on rear cover, quite scarce in any form of dust jacket.   Second Life Books Inc.   190 - 67   2015 $1500

Du Bois, William Edward Burghardt 1868-1963 *I Take My Stand for Peace.* New York: Masses & Mainstream, 1951. First edition, 16mo., printed self wrappers, fine, rare. Second Life Books Inc.   190 - 68   2015 $150

Du Bois, William Edward Burghardt 1868-1963 *The Negro Artisan: a Social Study Made Under the Direction of Atlanta University by the Seventh Atlanta Conference.* Atlanta: Atlanta University Press, 1902. First edition, brown wrappers, 192 pages, paper eroded at spine ends, tiny nicks and tears but handsome, very good or better copy. Between the Covers Rare Books   197 - 15   2015 $950

Du Bois, William Edward Burghardt 1868-1963 *The Souls of Black Folk.* Chicago: McClurg, 1903. First edition, front hinge repaired, moderate loss to the corners and spinal extremities, contemporary owner's signature (Solomon Carrington of Walden, Massachusetts) and later embossed stamp of well-known collector, both on front fly, very good with spine and front board lettering legible and clear, very uncommon.   Between the Covers Rare Books   197 - 16   2015 $4000

Du Bois, William Edward Burghardt 1868-1963 *The World and Africa.* New York: Viking Press, 1947. First edition, 8vo., fine in dust jacket (little worn).   Second Life Books Inc.   190 - 69   2015 $150

Du Bois, William Pene *The Forbidden Forest.* New York: Harper & Row, 1975. Stated first edition, 4to., pictorial boards, fine in frayed dust jacket, color illustrations.   Aleph-bet Books, Inc.   109 - 139   2015 $75

Du Bois, William Pene *Giant Otto. (and) Otto at Sea.* New York: Viking, 1936. First editions, 2 books, square 8vo., pictorial boards, light cover soil, else near fine in dust jackets in original pictorial box, jackets frayed, box sides repaired, fabulous color lithographs, nice set, quite rare. Aleph-bet Books, Inc.   109 - 138   2015 $1600

Du Maurier, Daphne *Rebecca.* London: Victor Gollancz, 1938. First edition, some very faint foxing to margins of prelims, crown 8vo., original black cloth stamped gilt to upper board, light rubbing to extremities, backstrip lettered gilt lightly rubbed, bookplates, dust jacket lightly soiled overall, backstrip panel darkened and chipped at head and tail, minor dampstaining to front fold, good.   Blackwell's Rare Books   B179 - 144   2015   £100

Du Plessix Gray, Francine *Lovers & Tyrants.* New York: Simon & Schuster, 1976. Uncorrected proof, signed by author, heavily foxed covers and fragile, tall padbound wrappers, with cover detaching, good copy.   Ken Lopez, Bookseller   164 - 201   2015 $100

Du Tillet, Jean *Chronicon de Regibus Francorum a Faramundo Usque ad Franciscum Primum.* Paris: Apud Vascosanum, 1551. Third edition, little light foxing, 8vo., early 20th century red morocco, boards bordered with triple gilt fillet, spine divided by a solid rule between dashed rules, second and third compartments gilt lettered direct, rest with central urn tools, marbled endpapers, edges gilt, just slightly rubbed at extremities, very good.   Blackwell's Rare Books   B179 - 39   2015   £400

Du Verney, Joseph Guichard *Tractatus de Organo Auditus Continens Structuram Usum et Morbos Omnium Auris Partium.* Nuremberg: Johann Zieger, 1684. First Latin edition, 4to., 16 engraved folding plates, 19th century paper wrappers, plate 16 neatly backed, title very lightly soiled, else very good, Joseph Friedrich Blumenbach's copy with his signature on verso of titlepage, in fine morocco backed clamshell box.   Joseph J. Felcone Inc.   Science, Medicine and Technology - 32   2015 $4800

Dubois, Cardinal *Memoires Du Cardinal Dubois.* Paris: Edmond Vairel, 1949-1950. #584 of 1000 copies, 4 volumes, all unbound signatures laid into wrappers in chemise and slipcases, many fine color illustrations by Jean Gradassi, all volumes have wrappers that are fine but for mild sunning to spine, chemise with soiled spines and some creasing, slipcases somewhat soiled and worn, small 4to. Beasley Books   2013 - 2015 $385

Duclos-Arkilovitch, Jonathan *Jazzin' Riviera. 70 Ans de Jazz sur la Cote d'Azur.* Nice: ROM Editions, 1997. First edition, wrappers, heavily illustrated, 8vo., near fine with mild corner bump to upp3r right corner, many photos. Beasley Books   2013 - 2015 $40

Dudden, Faye E. *Serving Women Household Service in Nineteenth Century America.* Middletown: Wesleyan University, 1983. First edition, 8vo., maroon cloth, two leaves creased, otherwise nice in very slightly chipped dust jacket.   Second Life Books Inc.   189 - 64   2015 $45

Dudley, Carrie *Let's Play Circus.* Minneapolis: Buzza, a Gordon Volland Book, 1928. Large oblong 4to., cloth backed pictorial boards, nearly as new in publisher's box (with some soil and flap repair, but very good+), 8 thick cardboard scenes with holes cut out in various places, any one of these scenes can be placed over any one of 6 paper pages so reader can change text and illustrations, illustrations by Carrie Dudley. Aleph-bet Books, Inc. 109 - 311 2015 $775

Dudley, Carrie *My Peek-a-Book Show Book.* Minneapolis: Buzza, a Gordon Volland Book, 1928. Large 4to., cloth backed pictorial boards, very fine, original box (flaps repaired), 8 thick cardboard scenes with holes cut out in various places, any of these scenes can be placed over any one of 6 paper pages so reader can change text and illustrations to create a number of stories, scarce, rare in box. Aleph-bet Books, Inc. 109 - 312 2015 $775

Dudley, Owen Francis *The Tremaynes and the Masterful Monk.* New York: Longmans, Green, 1940. First edition, fine in dust jacket with some nicks at spine ends and few short closed tears. Mordida Books March 2015 - 009480 2015 $100

Duerer, Albrecht 1471-1528 *The Construction of Roman Letters.* Cambridge: Dunster House, 1924. Limited to 350 copies, designed by Bruce Rogers, 12mo., later quarter leather and blue cloth covers, exquisite book, original fragile covers have been replaced with modern tasteful binding. Oak Knoll Books Special Catalogue 24 - 44 2015 $350

Duff, E. Gordon *William Caxton.* Chicago: Caxton Club, 1905. Limited to 252 copies on American handmade paper, one of 148 copies to include original Caxton leaf, 118 pages, 25 plates with tissue guards, also publisher's prospectus laid in, publisher's quarter red cloth over gray paper boards, printed paper spine label, top edge rough trimmed, others untrimmed, partially unopened, board edges bit rubbed and bumped, top edge of spine bit frayed, paper label, slightly rubbed, internally very clean, overall about fine, laid in rear pocket is original leaf from first edition of William Caxton's Canterbury tales printed Westminster 1478, the leaf has faint dampstain to inner margin an slightly toned along edges, otherwise very good. Heritage Book Shop Holiday 2014 - 33 2015 $12,500

Dugan, Alan *Poems.* New Haven: Yale University Press, 1961. First edition, 8vo., original cloth, dust jacket, presentation copy inscribed by author for Norman Thomas DiGiovanni, top and fore edges of text block lightly foxed, otherwise fine. James S. Jaffe Rare Books Modern American Poetry - 65 2015 $1500

Dugdale, F. *Book of Baby Birds.* London: Humphrey Milford/Oxford University Press, n.d., 1919. First edition, 4to., cloth backed boards, pictorial paste on, fine in dust jacket, illustrations by Detmold with 19 magnificent mounted color plates. Aleph-bet Books, Inc. 109 - 122 2015 $950

Duggleby, John *Story Painter. The Life of Jacob Lawrence.* San Francisco: Chronicle, 1998. First printing, illustrations by Jacob Lawrence, signed on title by Lawrence, paper over boards, about as new in dust jacket. Second Life Books Inc. 191 - 32 2015 $225

Duhring, E. *Die Überschatzung Lessing's und Dessen Anwaltschaft fur die Juden. (The Overevaluation of Lessing and His Advocacy of the Jews).* Karlsruhe und Leipzig: Verleg von H. Reuther, 1881. First edition, octavo, green cloth gilt, spine bit faded and little foxing in text, very good or better, signed by Duhring at conclusion of introduction, bookplate of Friedrich Lessing (presumably a descendant of the subject), with much pencil marginalia. Between the Covers Rare Books, Inc. 187 - 82 2015 $950

The Duke of York. A Plain Statement of the Conduct of the Ministry and the Opposition, Towards His Royal Highness the Duke of York. London: printed by B. McMillan printer to His Royal Highness the Prince of Wales, 1808. First edition, 8vo., tiny hole in E3 with loss of one letter and partial loss of 2 others, titlepage rather soiled and stained, otherwise good, disbound. John Drury Rare Books 2015 - 20580 2015 $71

Duke, Arthur *The Larke: a Seventeenth Century Poem Ascribed to Dr. Arthur Duke.* London: privately printed in the Department of English at the University College London, 1934. original blue printed wrappers, slightly faded and creased, printed by Geoffrey Tillotson on departmental hand press, inscribed by him to Kathleen Tillotson, inserted is ALS from Priscilla (Preston) to Kathleen. Jarndyce Antiquarian Booksellers CCVII - 251 2015 £60

Duke, Donald *Electric Railways Around San Francisco Bay.* San Marino: Golden West Books, 1999-2000. First editions, 2 volumes, oblong octavo, photos, maps, reproductions, stiff pictorial wrappers, very fine set. Argonaut Book Shop Holiday Season 2014 - 79 2015 $75

Dulac, Edmund *Contes et Legendes Des Nations Allies.* N.P: n.p., 1917. First edition, 4to., 15 plates by Dulac loosely inserted in patterned folder designed by Dulac, folder worn and slightly creased and chipped at edges, plates in good shape with slight nicks. Any Amount of Books 2015 - A67853 2015 £180

Dulac, Edmund *Edmund Dulac's Fairy Book: Fairy Tales of the Allied Nations.* London, et al: Hodder & Stoughton, n.d., 1916. First edition, 4to., cloth, extensive decoration, mint in dust jacket and publisher's box, near fine dust jacket has light wear, box has flaps repaired with some toning, 15 very beautiful tipped in color plates with gilt rules plus a pictorial titlepage, amazing copy, rare in dust jacket and box. Aleph-bet Books, Inc.   109 - 141   2015 $1500

Dulac, Edmund *Lyrics Pathetic & Humorous from A to Z.* London and New York: Frederick Warne, 1908. First edition, 4to., cloth backed pictorial boards, beveled edges, slight edge rubbing, else near fine, illustrated with cover, pictorial endpapers and 24 very wonderful full page color illustrations printed on one side of paper only,.   Aleph-bet Books, Inc.   109 - 143   2015 $1050

Dulac, Jean *Pierre Brissaud. Les Artistes Du Livre.* Paris: Henry Babou, 1929. First printing, no. 335 of 650 copies, small 4to., unbound signatures laid into wrappers, fine but for slightly sunned spine, many color plates and black and white illustrations.   Beasley Books   2013 - 2015 $125

Dumas, Alexandre   1802-1870   *Celebrated Crimes.* London: H. S. Nichols, 1895. 8 volumes, octavo, contemporary three quarter red crushed morocco gilt over marbled boards.   Honey & Wax Booksellers   3 - 16   2015 $4200

Dumas, Alexandre   1802-1870   *The Count of Monte Cristo.* London: Chapman and Hall, 1846. First edition in English, 2 volumes, original blue cloth, 20 wood engraved illustrations by Henry Valentin, both volumes very lightly worn and rubbed, spine ends repaired with minor restoration, small split at upper joint of volume II, hinges neatly reinforced, internally very clean, only few minor spots, bookplates and former owner signatures July 1852, very scarce in original cloth.   B & B Rare Books, Ltd.   234 - 19 2015 $15,000

Dumas, Alexandre   1802-1870   *The Forty-Five Guardsmen.* London: Henry Lea, circa, 1860. 2 pages, frontispiece, original red publisher's cloth, spine lettered gilt, boards blocked in blind, dulled and stained on front board. Jarndyce Antiquarian Booksellers   CCXI - 102   2015   £65

Dumas, Alexandre   1802-1870   *The Three Musketeers.* London: G. Vickers, 1846. First illustrated edition, 16 wood engraved illustrations, bound in 20th century three quarter calf over contemporary mottled boards, red speckled edges, some very light soiling, generally very clean and fresh.   B & B Rare Books, Ltd.   234 - 20   2015 $7500

Dumas, Alexandre   1825-1895   *Camille (La Dame Aux Camelias).* New York: Limited Editions Club, 1937. Limited to 1500 numbered copies, signed by artist, Marie Laurencin, 4to., cloth, top edge gilt, 12 drawings by Laurencin, slight rubbing of slipcase.   Oak Knoll Books   25 - 18   2015 $400

Dumas, Henry *Rope of Wind and Other Stories.* New York: Random House, 1979. First edition, 8vo., fine in fine dust jacket.   Beasley Books   2013 - 2015 $40

Dunayevskaya, Raya *Philosophy and Revolution from Hegel to Sartre and from Marx to Mao.* New York: Delta, 1973. First edition, wrappers, very good, inscribed by author.   Beasley Books   2013 - 2015 $45

Dunbar, Charles F. *Reply to Dr. Stille's Strictures on the Harvard Examinations for Women.*   Philadelphia: 1878? First separate edition, large 8vo., 12 pages, tipped-in errata slip at end, original dark blue printed wrappers, little chipped an dust stained at edges with red, text clean and very good. M & S Rare Books, Inc.   97 - 96   2015 $300

Dunbar, Margaret *Bern! Porter! Interview! Conducted by Margaret Dunbar.* N.P.: Dog Ear Press, n.d., First edition, octavo, illustrations, stiff wrappers, front wrapper with one interior tape mend, covers lightly rubbed, else near fine, inscribed by Porter, but unsigned to noted scholar Bertrand Mathieu, Belfast 6.24.90, few annotations by Mathieu in text, five APS's from Porter to Mathieu dated from May 29 1990 to June 25 1991 laid in.   Between the Covers Rare Books, Inc.   187 - 218   2015 $375

Dunbar, Paul Laurence *Candle-Lightin' Time.* New York: Dodd, Mead & Co., 1901. First edition, photos, decorative cloth and decorations by Margaret Armstrong, trifle rubbed at bottom of the boards, just about fine in about very good example of rare dust jacket with shallow loss at crown and some slight loss at top of front flap fold, very nice example of fragile dust jacket.   Between the Covers Rare Books   197 - 17   2015 $2500

Dunbar, Paul Laurence *The Jest of Fate.* London: Jarrold & Sons, 1902. First English edition, ownership signature of author's half brother, William L. Murphy, corners little bumped, some slight discoloration at base of spine, still handsome and sound, very good or better, exceptionally uncommon title.   Between the Covers Rare Books   197 - 18   2015 $1500

Dunbar, Paul Laurence *Li'l' Gal.* New York: Dodd, Mead, 1904. First edition thus, large 8vo., frontispiece, 63 photos, olive cloth stamped in gilt, blue, cream and gold designed by Margaret Armstrong, binding little rubbed at extremities, former owner's name in pencil on endpaper, very good, clean copy.   Second Life Books Inc.   190 - 71   2015 $325

Dunbar, Paul Laurence *The Strength of Gideon and Other Stories.* New York: Dodd Mead, 1900. First edition, small 8vo., bound in brown cloth stamped in gilt, white, black and brown, some slight rubbing to extremities of spine, else near fine, frontispiece and 5 plates inserted. Second Life Books Inc.   190 - 72   2015 $225

Duncan, David Douglas *Picasso's Picassos.* New York: Harper & Brothers, 1961. First edition, folio, endpapers little foxed, little cocked, very good in chipped, fair only dust jacket, inscribed by author to author James Jones 19 May 63, Paris. Between the Covers Rare Books, Inc. 187 - 213 2015 $600

Duncan, Robert *As Testimony: the Poem and the Scene.* San Francisco: White Rabbit Press, 1964. First edition, stapled wrappers, about fine, inscribed by author to Charles Olson, Sept. 8 1964. Between the Covers Rare Books, Inc. 187 - 83 2015 $1750

Duncan, Robert *Caesar's Gate. Poems 1949-1950.* Palma de Mallorca: Divers Press, 1955. First edition, one of 200 copies signed by author, 8vo., original white pictorial laminated wrappers slightly rubbed, otherwise fine, uncommon. James S. Jaffe Rare Books Modern American Poetry - 66 2015 $750

Duncan, Robert *Caesar's Gate: Poems 1949-1950.* Palma de Majorca: Divers Press, 1955. First edition, one of 10 copies of original collage by Jess and original manuscript poems by Duncan, signed by poet and artist, entire edition was 213 copies of which 200 were for sale and 13 special copies Marked A to C and 1 to 10 for private distribution, illustrations, fine. James S. Jaffe Rare Books Modern American Poetry - 67 2015 $15,000

Duncan, Robert *Faust Foutu: Act One (-Act Four).* San Francisco: privately printed by author, 1953. First privately printed edition, one of 100 copies printed, this copy accompanied by large manila envelope addressed by Mary Fabilli to Robert Duncan in Stinson Beach, where he was living at the time the play was written, fine, rare. James S. Jaffe Rare Books Modern American Poetry - 68 2015 $2500

Duncan, Robert *Letters.* Highlands: Jonathan Williams, 1958. First edition, one of 450 copies on Arches paper out of a total edition of 510 copies printed at Banyan Press, signed by Duncan, 8vo., original plain wrappers with marbled paper dust jacket with printed spine label, with 5 drawings by author, bit of wear to head and foot of spine, otherwise fine. James S. Jaffe Rare Books Modern American Poetry - 69 2015 $350

Duncan, Robert *Medea at Kolchis. The Maiden Head.* Berkeley: Oyez, 1965. First edition, hardbound issue, one of 28 numbered copies signed by Duncan (out of a total edition of 500), 8vo, original unprinted linen over boards, dust jacket, although not called for, this copy signed by Graham Mackintosh, book's designer and printer, this copy also with second dust jacket with same design (as first) but printed on white enameled stock with design of first jacket embossed on front cover, covers slightly splayed, otherwise fine. James S. Jaffe Rare Books Modern American Poetry - 71 2015 $1250

Duncan, Robert *The Opening of the Field.* New York: Grove Press, 1960. First edition, Ted Berrigan's copy with his ownership signature in pencil, 1962, fine copy, presentation from author to Berrigan. James S. Jaffe Rare Books Modern American Poetry - 78 2015 $1500

Duncan, Robert *A Paris Visit. Five Poems.* New York: Grenfell Press, 1985. First edition, one of 115 numbered copies printed on handmade Indian paper signed by author and artist, out of a total edition of 130 copies, large 4to., frontispiece and 9 full page illustrations by R. B. Kitaj, original quarter red morocco and pictorial boards, glassine dust jacket, few very short closed edge tears to glassine, fine, beautiful book. James S. Jaffe Rare Books Modern American Poetry - 76 2015 $375

Duncan, Robert *A Paris Visit. Five Poems.* New York: Grenfell Press, 1985. First edition, one of 15 deluxe copies printed on J. Barcham Greene's handmade DeWint paper, numbered in Roman and specially bound by Claudia Cohen, accompanied by two mounted illustrations not included with regular issue, book signed by author and artist, from a total edition of 130, small folio, 2 mounted illustrations printed on linen by R. B. Kitaj, original full scarlet morocco lettered and ruled in blind, publisher's line tray case with morocco lettering piece, very fine, beautiful book. James S. Jaffe Rare Books Modern American Poetry - 77 2015 $5000

Duncan, Robert *Six Prose Pieces.* Rochester: Perishable Press Limited, 1966. One of only 150 copies printed on handmade paper made by Walter Hamady, printer and signed by author, out of a total edition of 70 copies, 8vo., illustrations by author, unbound folded and gathered signatures in natural linen cloth, chemise with facsimile signature printed in red, matching slipcase, presentation copy inscribed by author, slipcase very slightly soiled, otherwise fine. James S. Jaffe Rare Books Modern American Poetry - 72 2015 $6000

Duncan, Robert *Writing Writing.* Albuquerque: Sumbooks, 1964. First edition, deluxe issue one of 25 numbered copies signed by author (out of entire edition of 375) with original ink & colored crayon drawing, small 4to., original stapled blue wrappers, printed in black after design by Duncan, signed and dated by Duncan, additional bifolium printed with errata and an additional poem is laid in, spine portion very lightly sunned, tiny nick in fore-edge of front wrapper, narrow three quarter inch long faint splash mark back wrapper, otherwise fine. James S. Jaffe Rare Books Modern American Poetry - 74 2015 $2500

Duncan, Robert *Writing Writing.* Portland: Trask House, 1971. First Trask House edition, large 8vo., original stapled printed wrappers, presentation from author for book's publisher Carlos Reyes, with TLS from author to same, with typed receipt signed by Duncan and Reyes for advance royalty, spine portion of book lightly sunned, otherwise book, letter and receipt in fine condition. James S. Jaffe Rare Books Modern American Poetry - 73 2015 $2500

Duncan, Robert *The Years as Catches. First Poems (1939-1946).* Berkeley: Oyez, 1966. First edition, deluxe hardbound issue, one of 30 numbered and signed hors commerce copies with original endpaper decorations by Duncan (out of 200 copies comprising hardbound issue), very fine, 8vo., pictorial boards, dust jacket. James S. Jaffe Rare Books Modern American Poetry - 75 2015 $2500

Duncombe, John *Dramatic Tales and Romances.* London: J. Duncombe & Co., 1831-1832. 59 separate tales in 7 volumes, all but one with folding color frontispiece, all but 7 with separate titlepage, partly bound from original parts in contemporary half black calf, marbled boards, spines lettered gilt, volume II with maroon morocco label, very good. Jarndyce Antiquarian Booksellers CCXI - 104 2015 £3200

Dundee Town Council *Report of the Committee of the Magistrates and Town Council of Dundee, Appointed to Examine into the Report Upon the Report of the Select Committee of the House of Commons...* Dundee: Alex Colville, 1820. First edition, apparently rare, half title and final blank, recently well bound in cloth, gilt lettered, very good. John Drury Rare Books March 2015 - 25858 2015 $221

Dundonald, Archibald Cochrane, Earl of *Description of the Estate and Abbey of Culrosss.* Edinburgh: 1793. First edition, 8vo., near contemporary scoring through the words 'and abbey' on titlepage and on A2, recent marbled boards lettered on spine, very good, very scarce. John Drury Rare Books 2015 - 25903 2015 $656

Dunham, N. J. *A History of Jerauld County South Dakota from the Earliest Settlement to January 1st 1909.* Wessington Springs: privately printed, 1910. First edition, 8vo., cloth, illustrations, few top edges of page corners bent, cloth lightly soiled, else very good. Buckingham Books March 2015 - 26005 2015 $375

Duniway, Abigail Scott *From the West to the West. Across the Plains to Oregon.* Chicago: McClurg, 1905. First edition, 8vo., pictorial cloth, hinge repaired, cloth of binding rubbed, good only, inscribed by author, scarce. Second Life Books Inc. 189 - 65 2015 $450

Duniway, Abigail Scott *Path Breaking an Autobiographical History of the Equal Suffrage Movement in Pacific Coast States.* Portland: by the author, 1914. First edition, 8vo., covers bowed, rear little bent, small cut to cloth of spine, good copy, usually found in poor condition, scarce. Second Life Books Inc. 189 - 67 2015 $300

Duniway, Abigail Scott *Path Breaking an Autobiographical History of the Equal Suffrage Movement in Pacific Coast States.* Portland: by the author, 1914. Second edition, 8vo., covers little browned, near fine, contemporary name Jessie M. Ellis, scarce. Second Life Books Inc. 189 - 66 2015 $250

Dunlap, Susan *Karma.* Toronto: Raven, 1981. First edition, very fine, unread copy in wrappers. Mordida Books March 2015 - 006838 2015 $85

Dunlop, Alex *A Treatise on the Law of Scotland Relative to the Poor.* Edinburgh: William Blackwood and T. Cadell, London, 1825. First edition, 8vo., wanting half title, fairly recently in boards, printed label on spine, entirely uncut, very good, scarce. John Drury Rare Books March 2015 - 20085 2015 £306

Dunn, Brenda Dunn *A History of Port Royal Annapolis Royal 1605-1800.* Halifax: Nimbus Pub. Ltd. & The Historical association of Annapolis Royal, 2004. 8vo., green cloth in dust jacket with map illustrated endpapers, half title, black and white illustrations, fine. Schooner Books Ltd. 110 - 71 2015 $45

Dunn, J. B. *Perilous Trails of Texas.* Dallas: Southwest Press, 1932. First edition, original green cloth with titles stamped in red ink on front cover and spine, frontispiece, illustrations, housed in custom made slipcase. Buckingham Books March 2015 - 32617 2015 $750

Dunning, John *Booked to Die.* New York: Charles Scribner's Sons, 1992. First edition, fine in fine dust jacket, from the collection of Duke Collier. Royal Books 36 - 161 2015 $850

Dunning, John *Booked to Die.* New York: Charles Scribner's Sons, 1992. First edition, fine in fine dust jacket, from the library of Kate Stettner Lobell and Carl D. Lobell. Between the Covers Rare Books 196 - 46 2015 $600

Dunning, John *Deadline.* London: Gollancz, 1982. First UK edition, 8vo., highly uncommon, very slight lean at spine, one edge slightly bumped, else near fine in very close to fine, bright, clean yellow Gollancz jacket with very slight creasing to edges, excellent condition. Any Amount of Books 2015 - A48700 2015 £250

Dunning, John *Two O'Clock Eastern Wartime.* Santa Barbara: Santa Teresa, 2001. First edition, one of 100 specially bound numbered copies, signed by author, containing one page of the book's original working manuscript which has also been signed and authenticated by Dunning, hand bound by Harcourt Bindery of Boston in quarter leather with marbled boards, very fine in slipcase, without dust jacket as issued. Mordida Books March 2015 - 007445 2015 $650

Dupin, Andre Marie Jean Jacques *Effets la Convention Militaire du 3 Juillet 1815 et du Traite du 20 Novembre 1815, Relativement a l'Accusation de M. le Marechal Ney.* Paris: Carpelet, 1815. First edition, 4to., lightly spotted in places, preserved in modern wrappers with printed label on upper cover, apparently rare. John Drury Rare Books 2015 - 24927 2015 $612

Dupin, Charles *Institut Royal der France, Influence des Sciences sur l'Humanite des Peuples. Discours Prononce dans la Seance Publique des Quatre Academies le 24 Avril 1819.* Paris: Firmin Didot, 1819. First separate edition, apparently rare, 8vo., half title and final blank, early 19th century half calf over marbled boards, neatly rebacked and labelled with armorial bookplate of Ferguson of Raith, fine presentation copy inscribed and signed in ink, apparently rare. John Drury Rare Books 2015 - 24467 2015 $787

Duplaix, Georges *Gaston and Josephine in America.* New York: Oxford University Press, 1934. First edition, 4to., pictorial boards, neat spine mend and light fading and rubbing, very good++, illustrations by Duplaix, inscribed by Duplaix for Elizabeth with drawing, rare thus, special copy of scarce first edition. Aleph-Bet Books, Inc. 108 - 158 2015 $850

Duppa, R. *Travels in Italy, Sicily and the Lipari Islands.* London: Longman, Rees, Orme and Col., 1828. First edition, 8vo., modern green buckram lettered gilt on spine, 224 pages, numerous woodcut illustrations by A. J. Morgan, one folding plate, ex-library with usual markings, few stamps and nicks to spine and endpapers, no half title, text of book has 3 rectangular discreet stamps only (one on folding plate). Any Amount of Books March 2015 - A76646 2015 £360

Durham, David *The Exploits of Fidelity Dove.* London: Hodder and Stoughton Ltd., 1924. First edition, true first, very good, clean copy without dust jacket,. Buckingham Books March 2015 - 33704 2015 $2250

Durham, Philip *The Boys in the Black Mask: an Exhibit in the UCLA Library.* Los Angeles: UCLA Library, 1961. First edition, fine in printed wrappers. Mordida Books March 2015 - 010052 2015 $85

Durrell, Lawrence 1912-1990 *The Alexandria Quartet.* London: Faber & Faber, 1952. First One volume edition, fine in fine acetate dust jacket, cardboard slipcase, rubbed at joints, one of 500 numbered copies, signed by author, 8vo. Beasley Books 2013 - 2015 $600

Durrell, Lawrence 1912-1990 *Beccafico.* Montpelier: L'Imprimerie Nouvelle, 1963. Limited edition, one of 150 numbered and signed copies, 16mo., wrappers. Beasley Books 2013 - 2015 $125

Durrell, Lawrence 1912-1990 *The Black Book.* Paris: Olympia Press, 1959. Second edition, wrappers, near fine with few little bumps in very good dust jacket, 12mo. Beasley Books 2013 - 2015 $40

Durrell, Lawrence 1912-1990 *Nunquam.* London: Faber & Faber, 1970. First edition, uncorrected proof, 8vo., wrappers, very good, few old corner creases. Beasley Books 2013 - 2015 $45

Durrell, Lawrence 1912-1990 *On Seeming to Presume.* London: Faber & Faber, 1948. First edition, 8vo. signed presentation from author to John Waller, with Waller ownership signature, fine in slightly darkened else bright, near fine jacket. Any Amount of Books 2015 - A68493 2015 £270

Durrell, Lawrence 1912-1990 *The Red Limbo Lingo a Poetry Notebook.* New York: Dutton, 1971. First edition, one of 1200 copies, 100 of which were signed for UK issue and 100 were signed for US issue, this copy 167, signed by Durrell, there were also 500 trade copies for each country, fine in fine acetate dust jacket, fine slipcase, small 4to. Beasley Books 2013 - 2015 $125

Durrell, Lawrence 1912-1990 *The Tree of Idleness.* London: Faber, 1955. First edition, fine with usual browning of endpapers, near fine dust jacket but for slightly sunned spine, bookplate of Joyce Scudamore, 48 pages. Beasley Books 2013 - 2015 $200

Durrell, Lawrence 1912-1990 *Tunc.* New York: Dutton, 1968. First edition, signed by author on tipped in leaf, near fine very lightly used dust jacket showing mild wear at edges 8vo. Beasley Books 2013 - 2015 $40

Dury, Andrew *A Collection of Plans of the Principal Cities of Great Britain and Ireland...* London: printed and sold by A. Dury in Dukes Court, St. Martin's Lane, 1764. 12mo., engraved title, dedication and index with 41 hand colored maps and city plans, all mounted on guards, each measuring 115 x 140mm. but London and Edinburgh folding out to 115 x 220mm and 115 x 200mm., upper margin of one plan scorched, contemporary vellum, slightly soiled with 19th century armorial bookplate of A. A. Edge. Marlborough Rare Books List 54 - 25 2015 £3800

Dutens, Louis *Tables Genealogiques des Heros des Romans.* A Londres: chez M. Edwards, 1794? 22 leaves, mounted on stubs to form double page spreads, few spots and minor soiling, 4to., folded to 8vo., contemporary mottled calf, sometime crudely rebacked, worn. Blackwell's Rare Books B179 - 40 2015 £500

Duvar, John Hunter *De Roberval, a Drama; also the Emigration of the Fairies and the Triumph of Constancy, a Romaunt.* St. John: J. & A. McMillan, 1888. First edition, brown cloth, gilt design and title to front cover, 8vo., front cover has light stain, interior very good.   Schooner Books Ltd.   110 - 14   2015 $45

Duvigneau, Volker *Ludwig Hohlwein 1874-1949.* Munchen: Klinkhardt & Biermann, 1996. 4to., cloth, dust jacket, frontispiece, color and black and white illustrations. Oak Knoll Books   306 - 269   2015 $100

Dybek, Stuart *The Coast of Chicago.* New York: Alfred A. Knopf, 1990. First edition, fine in fine dust jacket, in nicely inscribed by author for Nicholas Delbanco, signed in full. Between the Covers Rare Books, Inc.   187 - 84   2015 $225

Dybek, Stuart *I Sailed with Magellan.* New York: Farrar, Straus & Giroux, 2003. First edition, fine in fine dust jacket, nicely inscribed by author for Nicholas Delbanco, additionally signed in full.   Between the Covers Rare Books, Inc.   187 - 85   2015 $225

Dyer, D. B., Mrs. *Fort Reno or Picturesque Cheyenne.* 8vo., dark blue embossed decorated cloth, gold stamping on front cover and spine, frontispiece, illustrations, former owner's pencilled name, front cover has linear indentation, else very good copy.   Buckingham Books   March 2015 - 25966   2015 $650

Dykes, Jeff C. *High Spots in Western Illustrating.* Kansas City Posse, The Westerners, 1964. First edition, limited to 250 autographed copies, cloth, frontispiece, fine. Buckingham Books   March 2015 - 9144   2015 $250

Dykes, Jeff C. *Western High Spots. Reading and Collecting Guides.* Flagstaff: Northland, 1977. First edition, inscribed by author, cloth, fine in dust jacket. Buckingham Books   March 2015 - 23972   2015 $175

Dyson, Anthony *Pictures to Print, the Nineteenth Century Engraving Trade.* London: Farrand Press, 1984. One of 100 special copies thus, signed by Anthony Dyson, Paula Allerton and R. A. Farrand, square 8vo., half brown leather and brown buckram over boards, title in gilt on front cover and spine, top edge gilt, brown silk ribbon marker, prospectus laid-in as well as signed letter from publisher.   Oak Knoll Books   306 - 19   2015 $125

Dyson, Freeman J. *A Many Colored Glass. Reflections on the Place of Life in the Universe.* Charlottesville: University of Virginia, 2007. First edition, fine in fine dust jacket, 8vo., signed by author.   By the Book, L. C.   44 - 11   2015 $95

Dyson, H. V. D. *Augustans and Romantics 1689-1830.* London: Cresset Press, 1940. Half title, original grey green cloth, inscribed to Geoffrey and Kathleen Tillotson by John Butt.   Jarndyce Antiquarian Booksellers   CCVII - 253   2015   £20

E

Eardley-Smith, Culling *The Romanism of Italy.* London: John Snow, 1845. First edition, 8vo., 2 folding plates, several text figures, recent marbled boards, lettered on spine, good copy, uncommon. John Drury Rare Books March 2015 - 24588   2015 $221

Earle, Joe *Flower Bronzes of Japan.* London: Michael Goedhuis, 1995. First edition, 4to., copiously illustrated in color, fine in fine dust jacket. Any Amount of Books 2015 - A86232   2015   £225

The Earwig or an Old Woman's Remarks on the Present Exhibition of Pictures of the Royal Academy. London: printed for G. Kearsly, 1781. First edition, 4to., recent red quarter morocco period style by Philip Dusel, marbled paper boards, gilt rules, decorations and lettering, fine. The Brick Row Book Shop Miscellany 67 - 41   2015 $1500

Eassie, William *Cremation of the Dead, Its History and Bearings Upon Public Health.* London: Smith Elder & Co., 1875. First edition, 8vo., 6 lithographic plates, little foxing and spotting at beginning and end of volume, occasional rubber inkstamps of Royal College of Surgeons of Ireland, original cloth, title in gilt on spine and upper cover, good, bright copy, uncommon. John Drury Rare Books March 2015 - 26205   2015   £306

East of the Sun and West of the Moon. London: Hodder & Stoughton, n.d., 1914. First edition, large 4to., blue cloth with extensive gilt decoration, very fine with gilt bright, pictorial endpapers, 25 magnificent tipped in color plates with lettered guards as well as numerous detailed black and whites throughout by Kay Nielsen, beautiful copy. Aleph-bet Books, Inc.   109 - 329   2015 $6000

East India Company *Appendix to the Comment on the Petition of the British Inhabitants of Bengal, Bahar and Orissa to Parliament.* London: circa, 1780. five parts issued and bound together, 4to., recent marbled boards lettered on spine, rare first appearance of these papers. John Drury Rare Books   March 2015 - 24894   2015 $656

Eastern Anecdotes of Exemplary Characters with Sketches of the Chinese History. London: printed by Sampson Low, 1799. First edition, 12mo., very good+, modern full leather with raised bands, gilt lettering, leather spine label, new endpapers, owner name page 25, pages with light dampstain. By the Book, L. C.   44 - 62   2015 $1250

Eastern Steamship Company *Along the Coast: Maine and the Maritime Provinces.* John C. Sherman, n.d. circa, 1925. 4 x 9 inches, color pictorial wrappers, 40 panels (including covers), photos, spine panel lightly rubbed, light wear to fore-edges, else very good. Buckingham Books March 2015 - 34986   2015 $175

Eastman, Charles A. *Red Hunters and the Animal People.* New York: Harper & Brothers, 1905. Later printing, signed by author, owner name in pencil on flyleaf along with Eastman's signature, cocked, very good, lacking dust jacket. Ken Lopez, Bookseller   164 - 155   2015 $250

Eaton, Charlotte Anne *Continental Adventures.* Boston: Wells and Lily, 1826. First American edition, 3 volumes, 8vo., original tan paper spines and blue paper boards, spines lettered by hand, untrimmed, boards worn with some pieces chipped from spines, text foxed, good, sound in original state. The Brick Row Book Shop   Miscellany 67 - 40   2015 $250

Eaton, Seymour *The Roosevelt Bears Abroad.* Philadelphia: Stern, 1908. 4to., cloth backed boards, pictorial paste-on, light edge rubbing, spine faded and very faint small edge soil on several pages, else tight and very good, illustrations by R. K. Culver with15 color plates plus many black and whites. Aleph-Bet Books, Inc.   108 - 166   2015 $550

Eaton, Seymour *Teddy-B and Teddy-G the Bear Detectives.* New York: Barse & Hopkins, 1909. 4to., cloth backed boards, pictorial paste-on, 178 pages, near fine, illustrations by Francis Wightman and William Sweeny with 15 great color plates plus a profusion of line illustrations, remarkable copy. Aleph-bet Books, Inc.   109 - 157   2015 $875

Eatwell, John *The New Palgrave: a Dictionary of Economics.* London: & New York: Macmillan, 1994. Reprint, small 4to., original faux green leather over green boards, lettered gilt at spines, 4 volumes. Any Amount of Books   2015 - C16099   2015   £180

Ebbutt, Percy G. *Emigrant Life in Kansas.* Swan Sonnenschein and Co., 1886. First edition, original green pictorial cloth, frontispiece with tissue guard, 12 plates, slightly cocked, else very good with minor edgewear, very scarce. Buckingham Books   March 2015 - 33833   2015 $225

Eberhard, Frederick G. *The Secret of the Morgue.* New York: Macaulay Co., 1932. First edition, former owner's inked name on front pastedown sheet, else very good in price clipped dust jacket with light professional restoration to spine ends and front flap fold. Buckingham Books   March 2015 - 33033   2015 $300

Eberhart, Richard *Collected Poems 1930-1960.* New York: Oxford University Press, 1960. First edition, fine in spine faded, otherwise very good dust jacket, inscribed by author for Barbara Guest and her husband, military historian Trumbull Higgins.   Between the Covers Rare Books, Inc.   187 - 86   2015 $225

Eberstadt, Edward, and Sons *Catalog 162. Texas. Being a Collection of Rare & Important Books & Manuscripts relating to the Lone Star State.* New York: Edward Eberstadt & Sons, 1963. First edition, 220 pages, 30 reproductions of facsimiles, cream wrappers printed in black and green, very slight crunching to upper rear wrapper, fine.   Argonaut Book Shop   Holiday Season 2014 - 287   2015 $75

Eco, Umberto *Foucalt's Pendulum.* New York: Harcourt, 1989. First edition, fine in dust jacket.   Mordida Books   March 2015 - 000717   2015 $100

Eco, Umberto *Semiotics and the Philosophy of Language.* Bloomington: Indiana University, 1948. First edition, 8vo., near fine in fine dust jacket, minimal foxing to edges, cover edge wear.   By the Book, L. C.   44 - 52   2015 $600

Eddy, John W. *Hunting the Alaska Brown Bear. The Story of a Sportsman's Adventure in an Unknown Valley After the Largest Carnivorous Animal in the World.* New York: G. P. Putnam's Sons, 1930. First edition, 8vo., red cloth, gold stamped front cover and spine, maps on endpapers, frontispiece, 44 illustrations, 3 maps, light foxing to few prelim pages and lightly rubbed at spine ends and corners, else fine.   Buckingham Books   March 2015 - 22669   2015 $385

Eddy, Mary Baker Glover *Science and Health. Volume II (all published).* Lyn: Dr. Asa G. Eddy, 1878. Second edition, 8vo., leaf of errata, frontispiece, inserted errata leaf, probably not required, original cloth, recased, original spine laid down, cased, very nice, rare edition, presentation from author to Mr. Thomson.   M & S Rare Books, Inc.   97 - 95   2015 $2250

Edgar, Alfred *"Invaders from Mars." in The Boys' Friend Library.* London: Amalgamated Press 7 May, 1931. Number 287 New Series, octavo, 64 pages, pictorial wrappers.   L. W. Currey, Inc.   Boy's Adventure Fiction 2015 - 84   2015 $100

Edgeworth, Anthony *Brandywine: a Legacy of Tradition in Du Pont-Wyeth Country.* Charlottesville: Tomasson-Grant Publishers, Signed by artist, fine in fine dust jacket.   Stephen Lupack   March 2015 -   2015 $100

Edgeworth, Maria *1768-1849 Castle Rackrent; an Hibernian Tale. Essays on Irish Bulls. Leonora, a Tale.* Paris: Baudry's European Library, 1841. Half title, contemporary half speckled calf, spine lettered and decorated in gilt, good plus.   Jarndyce Antiquarian Booksellers CCXI - 105   2015   £65

Edinburgh Almanack for the Year 1751. Edinburgh: printed by R. Fleming and sold by the widow of James Voy in Craig's Close..., n.d., 1751. 12mo., 24 leaves + 24 pages, one or two ruled borders just shaved and couple of page numerals cropped, but overall very good, complete copy with red paper duty stamp on titlepage, preserved in original vellum wallet style binding with flap, rare.   John Drury Rare Books   March 2015 - 21859   2015 $266

Edinburgh School of Arts *First Report of the Directors of the School of Arts of Edinburgh for the education of Mechanics in Such Branches of Physical Science as are of Practical Application in their Several Trades.* Edinburgh: printed by George Ramsay and Co., May, 1822. First edition, 8vo., early 19th century half calf over marbled boards, neatly rebacked and labelled, armorial bookplate of Ferguson of Raith, fine.   John Drury Rare Books   2015 - 24514 2015 $787

Edison, Julian I. *Miniature Books.* St. Louis: Julian I. Edison, 1970. Limited to 100 copies, 6.7 x 5.4 cm., leather, title and author gilt stamped on spine, decoration gilt stamped on front board, all edges gilt, black and white illustrations, miniature bookplate of Kathryn Rickard.   Oak Knoll Books   306 - 108   2015 $200

Edmonds, Walter D. *Drums Along the Mohawk.* Little Brown and Co., 1936. First edition, 8vo., very fine in dust jacket, brilliant and exceptional copy.   Buckingham Books   March 2015 - 38457   2015 $750

Edson, Russell *The Brain Kitchen.* Stamford: Thing Press, 1965. First edition, limited to 250 copies, quarto, illustrated wrappers, one corner bumped, spine bit faded, otherwise near fine, inscribed by author to publisher of Corinth Books, Ted Wilentz.   Between the Covers Rare Books, Inc.   187 - 87   2015 $225

Edwards, George *The True original Scheme of Human Economy, Applied to the Completion of the Different Interests and Preservation of the British Empire.* Newcastle upon Tyne: printed for the author by S. Hodgson, 1808. First edition, 8vo., well bound in cloth, spine lettered gilt, very good, early annotations in ink and pencil, scarce. John Drury Rare Books   March 2015 - 17900   2015 $221

Edwards, I. E. S. *The Cambridge Ancient History.* Cambridge: Cambridge University Press, 1970-1977. Third edition, 8vo., 4 volumes, original burgundy cloth lettered gilt at spines, plates, inscriptions, all clean, very good in very good dust jackets.   Any Amount of Books   2015 - C9801 2015   £160

Edwards, J. B. *Early days in Abilene.* Abilene: Abilene Daily Chronicle, 1938. Reprint of 1896 edition with added material, pictorial wrappers, 16 pages, illustrations, near fine, scarce.   Buckingham Books   March 2015 - 29630   2015 $750

Edwards, William *Sketches in the Scinde...* London: Henry Graves & Co., Printsellers to Her Majesty the Queen and His Royal Highness prince Albert 6 Pall Mall April 20th 1846, 1846. Folio, hand colored tinted lithograph title, 10 tinted hand colored lithograph plates each mounted on card, without dedication leaf and 'description of plates' original burgundy morocco backed cloth portfolio decorated and lettered gilt, few minor repairs, presentation from author with label mounted on inside cover.   Marlborough Rare Books   List 54 - 26   2015   £14,500

Edwin Austin Abbey, Royal Academician, The Record of His Life and Work. New York: Charles Scribner's Sons, 1921. First edition, 4to, 2 volumes, quarter cloth, paper covered boards, paper spine labels, covers rubbed at bottom corners, front inside hinges of both volumes cracked, previous owner's bookplate in each volume, foxing and tanning to endpapers and in parts of text.   Oak Knoll Books   306 - 13   2015 $175

Edye, John *Calculations Relating to the Equipment, Displacement etc. of Ships and Vessels of War.* London: Samuel and Richard Hodgson, 1832. First edition, 4to, 31 steel engraved plates, some folding, very few early ink annotations, contemporary maroon morocco, sides panelled in gilt, neatly rebacked with original gilt lettered backstrip replaced, all edges gilt, very good, originally presented to the Royal Yacht Squadron by the author, with RYS 19th century booklabel on endpaper, no significant RYS marks except for gilt stamp foot of spine.   John Drury Rare Books   2015 - 21341   2015 $612

Eells, Myron *Marcus Whitman, Pathfinder and Patriot.* Seattle: Alice Harriman Co., 1909. First edition, 349 pages, frontispieces, 20 plates, folding map, gilt lettered blue cloth, light spotting on front cover, else fine and clean.   Argonaut Book Shop   Holiday Season 2014 - 80   2015 $90

Een Bezoek Aan De Diergaarde. Amsterdam: J. Vileger, n.d., Owner dated 1899, small 8vo., cloth backed pictorial boards, slight rubbing, rear fine, 6 wonderful chromolithographed pop-ups, scarce, very fine, great copy.   Aleph-Bet Books, Inc.   108 - 359   2015 $900

Egan, Gregory *Axiomatic.* London: Millenium an Orion Book, 1995. First edition, octavo, boards.   John W. Knott, Bookseller   Selected New Arrivals Jan. 2015 - 17014   2015 $250

Egerton, Michael *Airy Nothings; or Scraps and Naughts and Odd-cum Shorts...* London: Pyall and Hunt 18 Tavistock Street, Covent Garden, 1825. 4to., 23 colored engraved plates, few outer margins, slightly shaved with minimal loss of plate mark, some light foxing and nothing in contemporary half green calf over cloth boards, spine ruled and decorated in gilt with morocco label lettered in gilt.   Marlborough Rare Books   List 54 - 27   2015   £1250

Eggenhofer, Nick *Wagons; Mules and Men: How the Frontier Moved West.* New York: Hastings House, 1961. First edition, illustrations, publisher's brown cloth, very fine with slightly chipped pictorial dust jacket, presentation inscription signed by author/artist.   Argonaut Book Shop   Holiday Season 2014 - 81   2015 $350

Eggenhofer, Nick *Wagons, Mules and Men. How the Frontier Moved West.* Hastings House, 1961. First edition, 184 pages, cloth, illustrations, fine in near fine dust jacket, neatly signed.   Buckingham Books   March 2015 - 12795   2015 $250

Eggers, Dave *Timothy McSweeney's Quarterly Concern, a.k.a "Gegenshein". Issue 1.* Brooklyn: McSweeney's, 1998. Signed by Eggers, covers slightly dusty, very near fine in wrappers.   Ken Lopez, Bookseller   164 - 58   2015 $450

Eggers, Dave *Timothy McSweeney's Blues/Jazz Odyssey? Issue II.* Brooklyn: McSweeney's, 1999. Inscribed by editor, Eggers, 'Paid' stamp inside rear cover, some handling evident to covers, near fine in wrappers.   Ken Lopez, Bookseller   164 - 59   2015 $250

Eggers, Dave *Timothy McSweeney's Windfall Republic. Issue III.* Brooklyn: McSweeney's, 1999. inscribed by Eggers, fine in wrappers.   Ken Lopez, Bookseller   164 - 60   2015 $250

Eggers, Dave *Timothy McSweeny's Trying, Trying, Trying, Trying, Trying. Issue IIII.* Brooklyn: McSweeney's, 2000. Issue 4, With individually bound works, all 14 along with extremely entertaining subscriber agreement laid into fine folding pictorial box, signed by Jonathan Lethem at his contribution and signed by Eggers on front of box.   Ken Lopez, Bookseller   164 - 61   2015 $200

Eggers, Dave *Timothy McSeeney Is Staring Like That Why Does He Keep Staring? Issue No. 5.* Brooklyn: McSweeney's, 2000. this being the state with text printed on boards and partially dissected face on dust jacket, signed (initialled) by Eggers on dust jacket, fine in fine dust jacket.   Ken Lopez, Bookseller   164 - 62   2015 $75

Eggleston, William *Ancient and Modern.* New York: Random House, 1992. First edition, fine in fine dust jacket and still in publisher's shrinkwrap, terrific copy.   Jeff Hirsch Books   E-62 Holiday List 2014 - 11   2015 $200

The Egyptian Struwwelpeter...   New York: Stokes, n.d., Inscribed 1897, 4to., cloth backed pictorial boards, title plus (16) leaves, light rubbing and soil, very good+, printed on rectos only, each leaf simulates aged paper and is illustrated in color, rare.   Aleph-Bet Books, Inc.   108 - 240   2015 $1875

Ehernberger, James L.   *Sherman Hill.*   Callaway: E. & G. Publications,   1978. First edition, 2nd printing, quarto, black and white photos, maps, drawings, portraits, blue pictorial boards, slight rubbing to spine ends, fine.   Argonaut Book Shop   Holiday Season 2014 - 82   2015 $45

Ehrhart, W. D.   *Channel Fever.*   Long Island: Backstreet, 1982. Copy no. 100 of 526 numbered copies, text block threatening to separate from covers due to frying of glue, near fine in wrappers.   Ken Lopez, Bookseller   164 - 63   2015 $50

Ehrich, Paul Von   *Historisches zur Frage Der Immunisierung per OS.*   Wiener: Klinischen Wochenschrift, 1908. First separate edition, offprint, 8vo., very good+, self wrappers, minimal creases and edgewear, inscribed and signed by author to his long time collaborator Hans Sachs.   By the Book, L. C.   44 - 32   2015 $500

Ehrlich, Gretel   *Facing the Wave. A Journal in the Wake of the Tsunami.*   New York: Pantheon, 2013. Uncorrected proof, leatter laid in to well known writer from the Editorial Director, soliciting a comment for the book, fine in wrappers.   Ken Lopez, Bookseller   164 - 64   2015 $100

Eichtal, A. D'   *De La Monnaie de Papier et des Banques d'Emission.*   Paris: Guillaumin et Cie, 1864. First edition, 8vo., half title, contemporary red quarter morocco, spine lettered gilt, raised bands.   John Drury Rare Books   2015 - 5662   2015 $177

Eide, Asbjorn   *Economic Social Cultural Rights: a Textbook.*   Dordrecht and London: M. Nijohff,   1995. Second revised edition, illustrated laminated boards, issued without dust jacket, neat name on front endpaper, otherwise very good+.   Any Amount of Books   2015 - C10683   2015   £150

Eigert, Robert Armand   *Costumes et Modes D'Autrefois: Horace Vernet: Incroyables et Merveilleuses.*   Paris: Editions Rombaldi, 1955. Folio, stiff printed pink wrappers folder, 24 loose color plates, plain pale green slipcase, fine in very good slipcase.   Any Amount of Books   2015 - C366   2015   £180

1890. Facts About South Dakota: an Official Encyclopedia Containing Useful Information in Handy form for Settlers, Home-Seekers and Investors, in Regard to Soil, Climate, Productions, Advantages and Development....   Aberdeen News Co., 1890. 8 1/2 x 5 3/4 inches, printed brown wrappers, 64 pages, front wrapper with 2 inch closed tear to bottom along with chipping to spine and to extremities, title is printed at spine edge of front panel with portions of title missing, very good.   Buckingham Books   March 2015 - 37684   2015 $350

Einthoven, Willem   *Der Dondersche Druck und Die Gasspannungen in Der Pleurahohle.*   Bonn: Verlag vom Emil Strauss, 1888. First separate edition, 8vo., inscribed and signed by author, rare thus, good, original printed front wrapper (rear wrapper missing), spine repaired, chips cover edges, in modern brown leather and marbled paper custom made clamshell with raised bands spine and gilt lettering on red leather title labels spine and front cover.   By the Book, L. C.   Special List 10 - 72   2015 $1000

Eire Nua. The Social and Economic Programme of Sinn Fein.   Eanair Sinn Fein, 1971. First edition, wrappers, 54 pages, fine.   Beasley Books   2013 - 2015 $45

Eisenstein, Elizabeth   *The Printing Press as an Agent of Change: Communications.*   Cambridge: Cambridge University Press, 1979. First edition, 8vo., cloth, dust jackets with some chipping and small piece missing from top edge of back cover of volume one, bookplate each volume, name and acquisition date in ink.   Oak Knoll Books   306 - 186   2015 $150

Eisler, Robert   *Man into Wolf.*   London: Routledge and Kegan Paul, 1951. First edition, nearly fine in very good+ dust jacket.   Stephen Lupack   March 2015 - 2015 $45

Eldridge, Elleanor   *Elleanor's Second Book.*   Providence: Albro, 1842. First edition, 12mo., cloth backed boards, little foxed, portrait, very good.   Second Life Books Inc.   189 - 70   2015 $350

Eleska   *Three Tall Tales.*   New York: Macmillan, 1947. First edition, 4to., pictorial boards, near fine illustrations by Helen Sewell.   Aleph-bet Books, Inc.   109 - 440   2015 $100

Elffers, Dick   *Biljetletters.*   Amsterdam: Dick Elffers, n.d. but circa,   1971. Square 4to., stiff paper wrappers, color illustrations, covers sunned at edge, handwritten and printed insert with date of Feb. 1971 laid in, text partly separated from wrappers, light tanning in text.   Oak Knoll Books   306 - 210   2015 $350

Eliot, George, Pseud. 1819-1880 *Adam Bede.* Edinburgh & London: William Blackwood & Sons, 1859. Second edition, 3 volumes, half titles, occasional light foxing, contemporary half dark green morocco, green cloth boards, gilt spines, very good. Jarndyce Antiquarian Booksellers CCXI - 107 2015 £300

Eliot, George, Pseud. 1819-1880 *Daniel Deronda.* Oxford: Clarendon Press, 1984. Half title, original black cloth, very good in slightly marked dust jacket, Kathleen Tillotson's copy from the editor, Graham Handley, with TLS of explanation from him inserted 1985, with draft copy of the introduction and notes in response to criticism by General editor, Gordon Haight. Jarndyce Antiquarian Booksellers CCVII - 254 2015 £60

Eliot, George, Pseud. 1819-1880 *Felix Holt the Radical.* Edinburgh and London: William Blackwood & Son, 1866. First edition, Carter's 'A' binding, 3 volumes, half titles, original cinnamon cloth, spines lettered and decorated in gilt, covers in blind, excellent set, spines lightly rubbed with minor wear, corners bumped, front hinge of volume I slightly cracked and secure, very bright and completely unsophisticated set in earliest publisher binding. B & B Rare Books, Ltd. 234 - 21 2015 $2000

Eliot, George, Pseud. 1819-1880 *The George Eliot Letters.* New Haven: Yale University Press, 1954-1955. First American edition, 7 volumes, large octavo, no dust jackets, this set belonged to novelist Graham Greene who has signed the front free endpaper of each volume and scrupulously marked text throughout. Honey & Wax Booksellers 1 - 57 2015 $5200

Eliot, George, Pseud. 1819-1880 *The Mill on the Floss.* Edinburgh: William Blackwood and Sons, 1860. First edition, original publisher's cloth with gilt spines, covers stamped in blind, pale yellow endpapers, half titles present in each volume, 16 page publisher's catalog at rear of volume III, Carter's first state lacking the ad leaf at end of volume I, some wear and fraying to spine ends and corners, hinges cracked and secure, 19th and 20th century former owner inscriptions, some spotting and soiling to pages, overall good set, free of any repairs or restoration, housed in custom folding cloth box. B & B Rare Books, Ltd. 234 - 22 2015 $1500

Eliot, George, Pseud. 1819-1880 *Romola.* Leipzig: Bernhard Tauchnitz, 1863. Copyright edition, extra illustrated with numerous photos, elaborate gilt binding, contemporary full vellum, bevelled boards, embossed in maroon, finely tooled gilt, gilt endpapers, small bookseller's ticket, G. Giannini, Florence, very good, handsome copy in red cloth jacket now broken red cloth box, presentation by Graham Handley for Kathleen Tillotson, with his inscription, his appreciation, occasional ink marginal notes and accompanying letter and copy of Kathleen's reply. Jarndyce Antiquarian Booksellers CCVII - 256 2015 £65

Eliot, George, Pseud. 1819-1880 *Scenes of Clerical Life.* Edinburgh and London: William Blackwood & Sons, 1859. Second edition, 2 volumes, half titles, 16 page catalog volume II, original burgundy pebble grained cloth by Edmonds & Remnants, little rubbed and dulled with small splits in hinges, lacking leading f.e.p.'s, from the library of Geoffrey & Kathleen Tillotson. Jarndyce Antiquarian Booksellers CCVII - 257 2015 £68

Eliot, George, Pseud. 1819-1880 *Scenes of Clerical Life.* London: Macmillan, 1906. Illustrations by Hugh Thomson. Honey & Wax Booksellers 2 - 27 2015 $125

Eliot, George, Pseud. 1819-1880 *Selections from George Eliot's Letters.* New Haven: Yale University Press, 1985. Original olive green cloth, very good in dust jacket, presentation for Kathleen Tillotson, TLS from Gordon Haight for Kathleen. Jarndyce Antiquarian Booksellers CCVII - 258 2015 £30

Eliot, George, Pseud. 1819-1880 *Silas Marner, the Weaver of Raveloe.* London: William Blackwood & Sons, 1861. First edition, half title, contemporary half dark green crushed morocco, green marbled boards, spine gilt in compartments, black leather labels, all edges gilt, very good. Jarndyce Antiquarian Booksellers CCXI - 108 2015 £650

Eliot, George, Pseud. 1819-1880 *Silas Marner, the Weaver of Raveloe.* Edinburgh & London: William Blackwood & Sons, 1861. First edition, 16 page catalog and 4 pages ads, little spotting, original orange brown cloth by Burn, slightly rubbed, one hinge cracking, good, from the library of Geoffrey & Kathleen Tillotson. Jarndyce Antiquarian Booksellers CCVII - 259 2015 £500

Eliot, George, Pseud. 1819-1880 *The Spanish Gypsy; a Poem.* Edinburgh: William Blackwood, 1868. First edition, Half title, contemporary half dark green crushed morocco, green marbled boards, spine gilt in compartments, very slight rubbing to spine, all edges gilt, very good. Jarndyce Antiquarian Booksellers CCXI - 109 2015 £250

Eliot, Thomas Stearns 1888-1965 *Four Quartets.* London: Faber and Faber, 1940-1942. First editions, 4 volumes, thin 8vo., original printed wrappers, wrappers very slightly soiled, otherwise fine set, far superior to usual. James S. Jaffe Rare Books Modern American Poetry - 81 2015 $2250

Eliot, Thomas Stearns 1888-1965 *Marina.* London: Faber and Faber, 1930. First edition, large paper issue, limited to 400 copies, printed on English handmade paper and signed by author, thin 8vo., original blue gray boards very slightly rubbed, otherwise unusually fine. James S. Jaffe Rare Books Modern American Poetry - 79 2015 $750

Eliot, Thomas Stearns 1888-1965 *Triumphal March.* London: Faber, 1931. First edition, one of 30 large paper edition copies printed on English handmade paper and signed by author, 8vo., original gray boards, fine.   James S. Jaffe Rare Books   Modern American Poetry - 80   2015 $500

Eliot, Thomas Stearns 1888-1965 *The Waste Land.* New York: Boni & Liveright, 1923. First edition, 2nd impression, octavo, 64 pages, no dust jacket, boxed, ownership signature of American photographer Walker Evans with note "New York/March, 1926" in his hand.   Honey & Wax Booksellers   1 - 34   2015 $7000

Eliot, Thomas Stearns 1888-1965 *The Waste Land.* London: Faber & Faber, 1961. First limited signed edition, limited to 100 copies, hand printed on Dante type on Magnani paper by Giovanni Mardersteig at the Officina Bodoni in Verona and signed by Eliot, 8vo., original quarter vellum & marbled board, publisher's marbled board slipcase, very fine in slightly rubbed slipcase.   James S. Jaffe Rare Books   Modern American Poetry - 82   2015 $4000

Elizabeth, Queen of Great Britian *The Queen's Book of the Red Cross.* London: Hodder & Stoughton, 1939. First edition, fine in lightly rubbed dust jacket with light wear to spine ends and extiemities, handsome copy.   Buckingham Books   March 2015 - 18684   2015 $250

Elkin, Benjamin *The King's Wish.* New York: Beginner books a Division of Random House, 1960. Stated first printing, 8vo., pictorial boards, very good in dust jacket, illustrations in color by Leonard Shortall.   Aleph-bet Books, Inc.   109 - 46   2015 $125

Elkin, Stanley *George Mills.* New York: E. P. Dutton, 1982. First edition, fine in fine dust jacket with tiny tear at crown, inscribed by author to fellow author Nicholas Delbanco and his wife, Elena.   Between the Covers Rare Books, Inc.   187 - 88   2015 $350

Elkins, Aaron J. *Fellowship of Fear.* New York: Walker and Co., 1982. First edition, inscribed by author for John Curtis, review copy with slip laid-in, fine in dust jacket with very small professional restoration spot to top edge of front panel,.   Buckingham Books   March 2015 - 28627   2015 $1275

Elkins, Aaron J. *Fellowship of Fear.* New York: Walker and Co., 1982. First edition, fine in fine dust jacket, splendid copy of elusive title.   Buckingham Books   March 2015 - 35826   2015 $750

Ellet, Charles *The Position and Prospects of the Schuylkill Navigation Company.* Philadelphia: 1845. First edition, 36 pages, removed, vertical crease, minor wear to title edges, some age stains.   M & S Rare Books, Inc.   97 - 102   2015 $175

Ellin, Stanley *The Eighth Circle.* New York: Random House, 1958. First edition, pages darkened as usual, name on front endpaper, otherwise near fine in fine unfaded dust jacket.   Mordida Books   March 2015 - 01067   2015 $250

Ellin, Stanley *Mystery Stories.* New York: Simon & Schuster, 1956. First edition, page edges uniformly browned, else fine in dust jacket with some minor internal professional restoration at spine ends.   Buckingham Books   March 2015 - 21782   2015 $275

Ellin, Stanley *Mystery Stories.* New York: Simon & Schuster, 1956. First edition, pages edges uniformly browned, else fine in dust jacket.   Buckingham Books   March 2015 - 24993   2015 $300

Elliot, Daniel Giraud *The Life and Habits of Wild Animals Illustrated by Designs by Joseph Wolf.* London: Alexander MacMillan, 1874. Folio, 72 pages, 20 woodcut plates, handsome contemporary (publisher's) full morocco with gilt design, all edges gilt, some minor wear, very good.   Andrew Isles   2015 - 15412   2015 $1350

Elliot, Nathaniel *Occasional Letters on the Present Affairs of the Jesuits in France.* London: printed by R. Balfe opposite Surgeons-Hall in the Old Baily, n.d.?, 1765. First edition, 12mo., half title and final blank rather dust soiled, entirely uncut and partly unopened, lacking original stitching and now preserved in marbled wrapper case, very good.   John Drury Rare Books   March 2015 - 24618   2015   £306

Elliott, James William *National Nursery Rhymes and Nursery Songs Set to Original Music.* London: Novello & Co. circa, 1875. Large 8vo., signed in 4's, half title, frontispiece, vignette title, illustrations engraved by brothers Dalziel, slight tear to lower inner margin of pages 3-8, original brown cloth, beveled boards, pictorially blocked and lettered in black and gilt, slight rubbing, all edges gilt, very good.   Jarndyce Antiquarian Booksellers   CCXI - 110   2015   £65

Ellis-Fermor, Una Mary *The Jacobean Drama: an Interpretation.* London: Methuen, 1936. Half title, original black cloth, crease along spine, with few inserted and marginal pencil notes by Geoffrey Tillotson.   Jarndyce Antiquarian Booksellers   CCVII - 254   2015   £25

Ellis-Fermor, Una Mary *Shakespeare the Dramatist and Other Papers.* London: Methuen, 1961. Half title, frontispiece, original maroon cloth, slightly faded in torn dust jacket, from the library of Geoffrey & Kathleen Tillotson, signed by Kathleen with few comments, letter from her to Kenneth Muir and his reply, with two papers presented by author to Kathleen and Geoffrey.   Jarndyce Antiquarian Booksellers   CCVII - 461   2015   £25

Ellis, Erl H. *The Gold Dredging Boats Around Breckenridge, Co.* Boulder: Johnson Pub. Co., 1967. Number 155 of a limited edition of 1000 copies, 173 pages, signed by author, fine in near fine, price clipped dust jacket. Stephen Lupack   March 2015 - 2015 $150

Ellis, F. S. *Poems Chosen Out of the Works of Samuel Taylor Coleridge.* Hammersmith: Kelmscott Press, 1896. printed in an edition of 308 copies, this being one of 300 copies printed on paper, small 8vo., original publisher's limp vellum with silk ties, ornamented with woodcut borders and six and ten-line initial letters throughout the text, some soiling of vellum along edges, bookplate of Anna H. Wilmarth, some leaves foxed along edges, ribbon ties well preserved. Oak Knoll Books   306 - 154   2015 $2000

Ellis, John *Instructions for collectors of Excise, in Prosecutions Before Justices of the Peace for Forefeitures Incurred or Offences committed.* London: J. Tonson, 1735. Second edition, 8vo., 2 parts in one volume, few minor stains and ink marks, contemporary panelled calf, neatly rebacked with label, very good, crisp copy.   John Drury Rare Books   2015 - 7955   2015 $787

Ellison, Harlan *Dangerous Visions: 33 Original Stories.* Garden City: Doubleday and Co., 1967. First edition, octavo, cloth.   John W. Knott, Bookseller   Selected New Arrivals Jan. 2015 - 17015   2015 $250

Ellison, Harlan *Watching.* Los Angeles: Underwood Miller, 1989. First edition, one of 600 numbered copies signed by author, very fine in dust jacket with slipcase. Mordida Books   March 2015 - 006645   2015 $135

Ellison, Ralph *Invisible Man.* New York: Random House, 1952. First edition, octavo, original beige cloth, wear between front free endpaper and title, otherwise fine, original dust jacket with one horizontal crease across spine only, attractive copy, scarce.   Manhattan Rare Book Company Literature 2014 - 2015 $2500

Ellison, Ralph *Invisible Man.* New York: Vintage, 1972. First Paperback edition?, small 8vo., paper wrappers, ink markings on front edges, cover creased and scuffed, but very good, tight copy, author's presentation for Joe Reed family.   Second Life Books Inc.   190 - 73   2015 $700

Ellroy, James *The Big Nowhere.* New York: Mysterious Press, 1988. First edition, fine in dust jacket.   Mordida Books   March 2015 - 007888   2015 $125

Ellroy, James *Blood on the Moon.* New York: Mysterious Press, 1984. First edition, presentation inscription on front endpaper to Lew Buckingham, by author, fine, unread copy in dust jacket.   Buckingham Books   March 2015 - 32057 2015 $275

Ellroy, James *Brown's Requiem.* New York: Avon, 1981. First edition, couple of scrapes on front cover, otherwise fine, unread copy in wrappers.   Mordida Books   March 2015 - 009487   2015 $125

Ellroy, James *Clandestine.* New York: Avon, 1982. First edition, near fine in pictorial wrappers.   Buckingham Books March 2015 - 19787   2015 $200

Ellroy, James *The Hilliker Curse. My Pursuit of Women.* New York: Mysterious Bookshop, 2010. First edition, True first edition, one of a limited edition of 26 lettered copies, signed by author, this copy "V", red quarter leather and red marbled paper over boards, titles stamped in gold on spine, as new in unprinted dust jacket.   Buckingham Books March 2015 - 30035   2015 $275

Ellroy, James *Silent Terror.* New York: Avon Books, 1986. First edition, generic inscription by author, near fine in pictorial wrappers.   Buckingham Books   March 2015 - 19788   2015 $175

Ellroy, James *Suicide Hill.* New York: Mysterious Press, 1986. First edition, full page inscription, fine in fine dust jacket.   Buckingham Books   March 2015 - 19823   2015 $250

Ellsworth, R. S. *The Giant Sequoia; An Account of the History and Characteristics of the Big Trees of California.* Oakland: 1914. 167 pages, 12 full page illustrations from photos, extremities lightly rubbed, gift inscription, signed by author.   Dumont Maps & Books of the West   131 - 49 2015 $45

Ellsworth, Whitney *Adventure Comics No. 138 March 1949.* New York: DC National Comics, 1949. First edition, 4to., original illustrated wrappers, lettered yellow and white on front cover, copiously illustrated in color, slight wear and soiling to cover, slight tear at head of spine and slightly around staples with tape reinforcement, contents slightly age toned, otherwise near very good.   Any Amount of Books   2015 - C10663   2015   £150

Elmslie, Kenward *Album.* New York: Kulchur Press, 1969. First edition, cover and drawings by Joe Brainard, 4to., original decorated wrappers, spine faded, otherwise fine.   James S. Jaffe Rare Books   Many Happy Returns - 244   2015 $50

Elmslie, Kenward *Album.* New York: Kulchur Press, 1969. First edition, cover and drawings by Joe Brainard, 4to., original coated patterned paper over boards, photographic endpapers, scarce hardcover issue, fine.   James S. Jaffe Rare Books   Many Happy Returns - 245   2015 $150

Elmslie, Kenward *Album.* New York: Kulchur Press, 1969. First edition, cover and drawings by Joe Brainard, small 4to., original coated patterned paper over boards, photographic endpapers, scarce hardcover issue, presentation copy, inscribed by author for poet Tony Towle, fine. James S. Jaffe Rare Books   Many Happy Returns - 248   2015 $450

Elmslie, Kenward *Album.* New York: Kulchur Press, 1969. First edition, 4to., original decorated wrappers, cover and drawings by Joe Brainard, covers little sunned, otherwise fine, although not called for, this copy signed by author and artist.   James S. Jaffe Rare Books   Many Happy Returns - 246   2015 $350

Elmslie, Kenward *The Baby Book.* New York: Boke, 1965. First edition, one of 40 numbered copies signed by author and artist, out of a total edition of 500 copies, 4to., illustrations, original wrappers, fine, illustrations by Joe Brainard.   James S. Jaffe Rare Books   Many Happy Returns - 235   2015 $250

Elmslie, Kenward *The Baby Book.* N.P.: n.p., 1965. First edition, one of 40 numbered copies signed by author and artist, out of a total edition of 500 copies, 4to., illustrations by Joe Brainard, original wrappers, fine, this copy inscribed by author and artist for Burt Britton.   James S. Jaffe Rare Books   Many Happy Returns - 236   2015 $375

Elmslie, Kenward *The Champ.* Los Angeles: Black Sparrow Press, 1968. First edition, one of 26 lettered copies, illustrations by Joe Brainard, handbound in boards by Earle Gray with original ink drawing by Brainard and signed by author and artist, fine.   James S. Jaffe Rare Books   Many Happy Returns - 242   2015 $1250

Elmslie, Kenward *The Champ.* Los Angeles: Black Sparrow Press, 1968. First edition, limited to 750 copies, signed by author and artist, small 4to., original wrappers, illustrations by Joe Brainard, wrappers trifle rubbed, otherwise fine.   James S. Jaffe Rare Books   Many Happy Returns - 240   2015 $150

Elmslie, Kenward *Circus Nerves.* Los Angeles: Black Sparrow, 1971. First edition, one of 26 lettered copies, handbound in boards by Earle Gray, illustrations by Joe Brainard, with original drawing by Brainard and signed by author and artist, original cloth backed boards, fine.   James S. Jaffe Rare Books   Many Happy Returns - 250   2015 $1250

Elmslie, Kenward *Circus Nerves.* Los Angeles: Black Sparrow Press, 1971. First edition, one of 200 numbered copies, handbound in boards by Earle Gray, signed by author, 8vo., original cloth backed boards with front cover illustration by Joe Brainard, acetate dust jacket, fine.   James S. Jaffe Rare Books   Many Happy Returns - 249   2015 $100

Elmslie, Kenward *Circus Nerves.* Los Angeles: Black Sparrow Press, 1971. First edition, 8vo., cover and illustrations by Joe Brainard, original wrappers, review copy with publisher's materials laid in, signed by author and artist, back cover lightly sunned and dust soiled, otherwise fine.   James S. Jaffe Rare Books   Many Happy Returns - 249   2015 $350

Elmslie, Kenward *The 1967 Game Calendar.* N.P.: n.p., 1967. First edition, 4to., original wrappers, drawings by Joe Brainard, fine, signed by Elmslie and Brainard.   James S. Jaffe Rare Books   Many Happy Returns - 239   2015 $500

Elmslie, Kenward *The 1967 Game Calendar.* N.P.: n.p., 1967. First edition, 4to., original wrappers, drawings by Joe Brainard, fine.   James S. Jaffe Rare Books   Many Happy Returns - 23   2015 $150

Elmslie, Kenward *The Orchid Stories.* Garden City: Doubleday & Co., 1973. First edition, review copy with publisher's materials laid in, 8vo., original cloth, dust jacket by Joe Brainard, fine in lightly dust soiled jacket, signed by author and artist.   James S. Jaffe Rare Books   Many Happy Returns - 253   2015 $250

Elmslie, Kenward *Pay Dirt.* Flint: Bamberger Books, 1992. First edition, one of 26 lettered copies signed by author and artist, 4to., illustrations by Joe Brainard, original glossy wrappers, price label on back cover, otherwise very fine.   James S. Jaffe Rare Books   Many Happy Returns - 254   2015 $650

Elmslie, Kenward *Shiny Ride.* N.P.: Boke Press, 1972. First edition, one of 26 lettered copies signed by author and artist, this being copy "A", 4to., illustrations by Joe Brainard, 4to., original wrappers, fine.   James S. Jaffe Rare Books   Many Happy Returns - 252   2015 $750

Elmslie, Kenward *Shiny Ride.* N.P.: Boke Press, 1972. First edition, 4to., illustrations by Joe Brainard, original wrappers, fine, signed by author and artist.   James S. Jaffe Rare Books   Many Happy Returns - 251   2015 $250

Elmslie, Kenward *The Sweet Bye and Bye: an Opera.* New York: Boosey & Hawkes, 1966. First edition, 8vo., original wrappers, cover design by Joe Brainard, signed by author and Brainard, fine.   James S. Jaffe Rare Books   Many Happy Returns - 237   2015 $750

Elmslie, Kenward *Z.* New York: Z Press, 1973-1977. First editions, 6 volumes, 8vo., illustrations, original pictorial white wrappers, spines of few volumes sunned, otherwise fine.   James S. Jaffe Rare Books   Many Happy Returns - 385   2015 $500

Elskamp, Max *Enluminures - Paysages - Heures - Views - Chansons - Grotesques.* Bruxelles: Paul Lacomblez, 1898. Limited to 256 numbered copies, 250 on papier de Hollande, this copy thus, 8vo., later quarter vellum, marbled boards gilt stamped leather label on spine with original vellum covers bound in, 80 original woodcuts in color, by author, unopened, covers lightly soiled and rubbed at corners.   Oak Knoll Books   306 - 265   2015 $1250

Elson-Gray *Dick and Jane Basic Pre-Primer.* Chicago: Scott, Foresman, 1936. 8vo., pictorial wrappers, illustrations in color on every page, scarce, slight wear, near fine. Aleph-Bet Books, Inc.   108 - 134   2015 $400

Elsum, John *The Art of Painting After the Italian Manner.* London: Printed for D. Brown at the Black Swan Without Temple Bar, 1703. First edition, first issue, 8vo., some browning and foxing, 19th century Spanish calf by J. Leighton, skillfully rebacked to style with red label, lettered gilt, covers embossed with heraldic device of William Stirling Maxwell with his earlier heraldic bookplate, and on rear paste down location label of Keir designated under "Art and Design" press marks 13.3' scored through and relocated at 'D4'.   Marlborough Rare Books   List 53 - 13   2015   £1350

Elton, Ben *Popcorn.* London: Simon & Schuster, 1996. First edition, fine in dust jacket.   Mordida Books   March 2015 - 000027   2015 $75

Elton, Oliver *Michael Drayton: a Critical Study with Bibliography.* London: Constable & Co., 1905. Half title, frontispiece and plates, original brown cloth, dulled and ink marked, Kathleen Tillotson's copy, signed Kathleen M. Constable Nov. 12 1927, with few notes, bookplate of Sidney Colvin.   Jarndyce Antiquarian Booksellers   CCVII - 241   2015   £20

Elwood, Anne Katharine *Memoirs of the Literary Ladies of England from the Commencement of the last Century.* London: Henry Colburn, 1843. First edition, 2 volumes, 8vo., contemporary black quarter calf, marbled boards, red leather labels, gilt rules and letters, 2 frontispiece portraits, edges somewhat rubbed, very good.   The Brick Row Book Shop   Miscellany 67 - 96   2015 $450

Ely, Richard T. *Property and Contract in Their Relations to the Distribution of Wealth.* London: Macmillan, 1914. London edition using American printed sheets, 8vo., 2 volumes, 8vo., discreet blindstamp to dust jackets and lower front boards, bright, very good+ with very slight shelfwear (boards slightly bowed) in very good- dust jacket with some soiling and some slight chips and some nicks.   Any Amount of Books   2015 - A45291   2015   £300

Emberley, Barbara *One Wide River to Cross.* Englewood Cliffs: Prentice Hall, 1966. First edition, 8 x 10.5 inches, very good++ dust jacket with short closed tear, mild soil, edge wear, no Caldecott medal on dust jacket or mention of award.   By the Book, L. C.   44 - 82   2015 $125

Emelin, Gabriel *Considerations Pysiologiques et Generales sur les Diverses Epoques de la vie de la Femme Suivies de Quelques Regles d'Hygiene sur la Grossesse....* Paris: de l'Imprimerie de Didot Jeune, 1811. 4to, 44 pages, preserved in modern wrappers, printed title label on upper cover, very good, crisp copy, apparently rare.   John Drury Rare Books   2015 - 20257   2015 $177

Emerson, Joseph *The Evangelical Primer...* Charlestown: Samuel T. Armstrong, 1809. First edition, small 8vo., bound in some worn original marbled wrappers, some staining and toning, good.   Second Life Books Inc.   190 - 179   2015 $325

Emerson, Sarah Hopper *Life of Abby Hopper Gibbons.* New York: Putnam's, 1897. 8vo., 2 volumes portraits, presentation on endpaper, hinges starting, some dust soiling, good.   Second Life Books Inc.   189 - 71   2015 $125

Emery, C. *Twinkie Town Tales Book 1.* St. Louis: Brown Hamilton, 1926. 8vo., pictorial boards, top edge of rear cover rubbed, else near fine, color illustrations.   Aleph-Bet Books, Inc.   108 - 237   2015 $250

Emily Faithfull, Printer and Publisher in Ordinary to Her Majesty. A Welcome. Original contributions in Poetry and Prose. London: 1863. First edition, 8vo., publisher's green cloth stamped gilt, all edges gilt, some foxing throughout as usual, very good, contemporary inscription.   Second Life Books Inc.   189 - 72   2015 $700

Emin, Tracey *Tracey Emin: Works 1963-2006.* New York: Rizzoli, 2006. First edition, 4to., copiously illustrated in color and black and white, signed and date on front endpaper by Emin, fine in fine dust jacket.   Any Amount of Books   2015 - A83877   2015   £225

Emmett, George *Captain Jack; or One of the Light Brigade.* London: Hogarth House, 1873? First edition, frontispiece, illustrations, few spots, without wrappers, purple brown binder's cloth, slightly faded, inner hinge splitting, booklabel of Arthur Edward Waite,.   Jarndyce Antiquarian Booksellers   CCXI - 111   2015   £75

Emmett, Ross B. *Chicago Tradition in Economics 1892-1945.* London: Routledge, 2002. First edition, 8vo., 8 volumes, hardback, about fine.   Any Amount of Books   March 2015 - B15837   2015   £450

Empson, William *Seven Types of Ambiguity.* London: Chatto & Windus, 1930. First edition, half title, inserted errata list, original orange cloth in torn and dusted dust jacket, with Geoffrey Tillotson's paper label Oxford 1931 and with ms. index compiled by him inserted, pencil marginal corrections by Kathleen Tillotson.   Jarndyce Antiquarian Booksellers   CCVII - 264   2015   £20

The Emu. Melbourne: Royal Australasian Ornithologists Union, 1909-1994. Quarto, 84 volumes, one and three in binders cloth, volumes two and all volumes up to volume forty in quarter calf and blue cloth with speckled edges, remaining volumes in wrappers, excellent set.   Andrew Isles   2015 - 36512   2015 $7500

The Emu. Melbourne: Royal Australasian Ornithologists Union, 1909-1994. Octavo, volumes 1-92, first 3 volumes are the Hyett/Cooper facsimile, volume 6 unbound, volume 8 part one only (lacks three parts) and volume nine is in shabby 'Emu' binding, all other volumes in neat binder's cloth, very good run.   Andrew Isles   2015 - 36419   2015 $5000

The Enchanted Forest. New York: G. P. Putnam, 1984. 6 1/2 inch square, 'Magic window' book is peepshow modeled after the 19th century devices that open accordion fashion, though the peephole on cover the viewer can see on 8 tiered detailed three dimension scenes, wonderfully illustrated by Trina Schart Hyman.   Aleph-Bet Books, Inc.   108 - 343   2015 $150

The Encyclopaedia Britannica. A Dictionary of Arts, Sciences, Literature & General Information. London and New York: Encyclopaedia Britannica Co., 1926. Thirteenth and best edition, quarto, 32 volumes in 16, photos, maps, dark green cloth, gilt lettered spine, first two leaves of volume I with minor wrinkles, very slight extremity rubbing to few volumes, overall fine and clean set.   Argonaut Book Shop   Holiday Season 2014 - 83   2015 $750

Enders, John F. *The Cultivation of the Poliomyelitis Viruses in Tissue Culture.* Stockholm: Kungl. Boktryckeriet P. A. Norstedt & soner, 1955. Offprint, 8vo., original printed wrappers, fine, signed by author.   By the Book, L. C.   Special List 10 - 73   2015 $600

Enfantin, Barthelemy Prosper *Religion Saint-Simonienne. Economie Politique et Politique.* Paris: Bureau du Globe Mars, 1823. First edition, 8vo.,half title, light paper browning and spotting, original printed blue wrappers, uncut and unopened, good copy.   John Drury Rare Books   2015 - 14993   2015 $177

Engelbrecht, Martin (*Perspectivische Vorstessung Eines mahs und Kunst Zimers*). Augsburg: C. P. Maj. Mart. Engelbrecht excud. A. V. circa, 1750. Set of 6 engraved card backed cut away sheets, 100 x 140mm., with contemporary hand coloring, fine series with first three-dimensional imagery.   Marlborough Rare Books   List 54 - 3   2015   £2500

Engels, Frederick *The Condition of the Working-Class in England in 1844.* London: Swan Sonnenschein & Co., 1892. First edition, 8vo., original red cloth with title in black on upper cover and in gilt on spine, few minor stains on upper cover, in all other respects very good, scarce.   John Drury Rare Books   2015 - 25015   2015 $612

Engels, Frederick *The Origin of the Family, Private Property and the State.* Chicago: Charles H. Kerr & Co,., 1902. 7 pages ads, original light brown cloth blocked in black and blind, contemporary signature, very good.   Jarndyce Antiquarian Booksellers   CCXI - 112   2015   £40

England and Wales. Laws, Statutes, etc. - 1657 *An Act for Raising of Fifteen Thousand Pounds Sterling in Scotland. At the Parliament Begun at Westminster the 17th Day of Sept. An. Dom. 1656.* London: printed by Hen. Hills and John Field printers to His Highness the Lord Protector, 1657. Folio, woodcut of the Commonwealth arms on titlepage, black letter, tiny wormtrack in lower margins, stitching renewed, preserved in 20th century in specially made dark blue quarter morocco fitted box, gilt and lettered, silk marker, silk ties, fine.   John Drury Rare Books   March 2015 - 23406   2015   £306

England and Wales. Parliament - 1642 *A Declaration of the Lords and Commons Assembled in Parliament, with their Resolution, That if Captaine Catesby, Captaine Lilborne, Captaine Vivers or any Others Which are or shall be Taken Prisoners, by His Majesties Army Shall be Put to Death...* London: Decemb. 19 printed for John Wright, 1642. First edition, small 4to, 8 pages, nasty marks along inner margin of title where a cloth backing has been removed, last leaf stained with white blob obscuring parts of two words, type ornament border at foot of title shaved, disbound, the copy of Sidney Russell, of Fairway, Gorway Rad, Walsall, circa 1936, from the library of James Stevens Cox (1910-1997).   Maggs Bros. Ltd.   1447 - 92   2015   £150

England and Wales. Parliament - 1642 *A Declaration of the Lords and Commons Assembled in Parliament that all such Persons Who Shall Advance Present Moneyes Upon the Credit of their Late Ordinance for the Carrying on the Great Affaires of this Kingdome...* London: Dec. 3 printed by John Wright in the Old Bailey, 1642. First edition, 4to., title printed within typographical border, very good, crisp copy with good margins, rebound in early 20th century in cloth backed boards, spine lettered, from the Fairfax of Cameron Library with armorial bookplate.   John Drury Rare Books   2015 - 24358   2015 $612

England and Wales. Parliament - 1643 *An Ordinance of the Lords and Commons Assembled in Parliament for the Better Raising, Leavying and Impresting of Mariners Saylers and Others...* London: for L. Blaiklock, Jan. 15, 1643-1644. Small 4to., browned, early 20th century half blue roan and marbled boards, slightly rubbed, from the library of James Stevens Cox (1910-1997). Maggs Bros. Ltd. 1447 - 93 2015 £180

England and Wales. Parliament - 1660 *A Declaration of the Parliament Assembled at Westminster January 23 1659 Ordered by the Parliament, that this Declaration be Forthwith Printed and Published Thomas St. Nicholas, Clerk of the Parliament.* London: printed by John Streeter and John Macock..., 1660. (1659). First edition, 4to., final leaf misnumbered (16) on recto, blank on verso, modern grey boards, spine lettered, very good, crisp copy. John Drury Rare Books 2015 - 24378 2015 $1049

Englander, Nathan *For the Relief of Unbearable Urges.* New York: Knopf, 1999. First edition, advance, uncorrected proofs, wrappers, fine. Beasley Books 2013 - 2015 $45

Engleheart, Gardner D. *Journal of the Progress of H.RH. The Prince of Wales through British North America and His Visit to the United States 10th July to 15 November 1860.* London: privately printed, 1860. First edition, 8vo., blue pressed cloth with gilt titles to front, frontispiece vignette, 2 color folding maps, 8 colored plates, 22 engraved vignettes, two gutters repaired, resewn on cords with endpapers and spine repaired, some minor staining to plates, mainly along edges. Schooner Books Ltd. 110 - 172 2015 $875

Enos, Randall *The Life and Death of Mocha Dick.* Brooklyn: Strike Three Press, 2009. First edition of this tribute, one of 32 copies, 11 linoleum cuts with facing text, original ecru cloth. Honey & Wax Booksellers 3 - 26 2015 $350

Enslin, Theodore *Agreement and Back: Sequences.* New York: Elizabeth Press, 1969. First edition, fine in slightly spine faded, else very near fine dust jacket, inscribed by author to Clayton Eshleman. Between the Covers Rare Books, Inc. 187 - 89 2015 $250

Entick, John *A New History or Complete View of the British Marine.* London: Printed for R. Manby et al, 1757. First edition, folio, five copper engraved full page plates, copper engraved folding map, few tables within text, modern three quarter orange brown morocco, marbled boards, raised spine bands, marbled endpapers, new flyleaves, frontispiece and titlepage adhered at gutter margin, affecting inner edge of engraved frontispiece image, frontispiece with minor wrinkles and short tear to bottom border, inner hinge cracked at dedication page, occasional marginal pencil notations, few latter pages with minor edge tears or paper clip marks, page 843 with two tiny repairs, some wear to lower edge of marbled boards, exceptions noted, clean, crisp and complete copy. Argonaut Book Shop Holiday Season 2014 - 84 2015 $1250

Ephron, Nora *I Remember Nothing and Other Reflections.* New York: Knopf, 2010. First edition, inscribed by author, fine in fine dust jacket. Ed Smith Books 83 - 19 2015 $125

Epictetus *Epicteti Enchiridion. The Morals of Epictetus Made English.* London: printed by W. Bowyer for S. Keble and R. Goslin, 1716. 12mo., engraved frontispiece, contemporary panelled sheep, top of spine little worn, very good. C. R. Johnson Foxon R-Z - 1059r-z 2015 $153

Epipyhtic Plant Study Group *Journal.* Bristol: A. J. S. Macmillan, 1968. First edition, 100 issues complete in 7 volumes, 8vo., nicely bound in green cloth lettered gilt at spine tipped in full color plates, very good. Any Amount of Books 2015 - A40550 2015 £200

Epstein, M. *The Annual Register: a review of Public Events at Home and Abroad 1931-1938.* London: Longmans, Green and Co., 1932. First edition, 8 volumes, 8vo., original purple cloth lettered gilt on spine, new series, all clean, very good copies, slightly sunned at spine, bookplates of 11th Duke of Bedford, Woburn Abbey. Any Amount of Books 2015 - A70517 2015 £180

Erasmus, Desiderius 1466-1536 *Eloge De La Folie.* Paris: Editions Litteraires de France, 1946. One of 440 copies, unbound signatures, not numbered, this with original color woodcut signed by artist, Lucien Boucher, fine in fine wrappers, chemise has owner's decoration on spine, else fine in near fine box, 4to. Beasley Books 2013 - 2015 $200

Erikson, Erik H. *Life History and the Historical Moment.* New York: W. W. Norton, 1975. First edition, 8vo., signed by author, near fine in like dust jacket, price clipped, scarce signed first. By the Book, L. C. 44 - 53 2015 $400

Ernest, Edward *Alphablock Books.* New York: Grosset and Dunlap, 1943. 26 miniature books, each 4 inch square, housed in publisher's pictorial box measuring 9 1/2 inch square, books are fine, box slightly dusty and near fine, each book has illustrations and words for a different letter illustrated in typical 40's style by Lee Morse, covers of book have large black letters. Aleph-bet Books, Inc. 109 - 9 2015 $450

Ernst, Donna B. *Sundance, My Unle.* Early West Creative Pub. Co., 1992. First edition, 8vo., limited to 1500 copies, signed by author and by her husband, Paul Ernst, a descendant of the Longabaugh family, red cloth titles stamped in black on spine, red pictorial endpapers, illustrations, as new, unread in like dust jacket. Buckingham Books March 2015 - 34087 2015 $175

Ernst, Max *La Femme 100 Tetes.* New York: Editions De L'Oeil/George Wittneborn, 1956. First edition thus, one of 1000 copies, this unnumbered, wrappers, 8vo., illustrations, glassine jacket, 12 text pages, 147 illustrations, very slight tanning to cream illustrated wrappers, very good+, excellent. Any Amount of Books March 2015 - A78155 2015 £350

Ernst, Robert *Immigrant Life in New York City 1825-1863.* New York: King's Crown Press, Columbia University, 1949. First edition, octavo, blue cloth, little spotting on boards, else fine without dust jacket, dedication copy inscribed for Harry James Carman, Dean of Columbia College. Between the Covers Rare Books, Inc. 187 - 90 2015 $300

Errazuriz, Paz *Agenda Cochrane 1994: Fotografias de Pas Errazuriz.* Santiago De Chile: Editorial Lord Cochrane, 1993. First edition, large oblong 8vo., original publisher's black cloth and internally spiral bound, copiously illustrated in color and black And white, signed presentation from photographer, few early calendar entries written in pencil, otherwise about fine in fine dust jacket. Any Amount of Books 2015 - C16450 2015 £180

Erskine, Firth *Naked Murder.* London: Butterworth, 1935. First English edition, fine in dust jacket with slight wear at spine ends, at corners and along edges. Mordida Books March 2015 - 000733 2015 $75

Erskine, Gladys Shaw *Broncho Charlie. A Saga of the Saddle.* Thomas Y. Crowell Co., 1934. First edition, cloth, 21 plates, 3 maps, very good in dust jacket with moderate wear to edges and corners, two 1 x 1 inch chips to top edge of spine and front panel, numerous news clippings from late 1930's through early 1950's laid-in. Buckingham Books March 2015 - 29603 2015 $200

Erskine, James *The Fatal Consequences of Ministerial Influence or the Difference Between Royal Power and Ministerial Power, Truly Stated.* London: printed for A. Dodd, 1736. First edition, variant issue, 8vo., wanting half title, inner margin of title strengthened, recently well bound in linen backed marbled boards lettered, very good with blank spaces in the 13 page appendix completed with all names added in contemporary manuscript. John Drury Rare Books March 2015 - 18048 2015 £306

Erskine, John *Collected Poems 1907-1922.* New York: Duffield and Co., 1922. First edition, lacks front free endpaper, else very good, without dust jacket, Du Bose and Dorothy Heyward's copy with their joint bookplate. Between the Covers Rare Books, Inc. 187 - 91 2015 $45

Erwin, Edward *The Freud Encyclopedia. Theory, Therapy and Culture.* New York: Routledge, 2002. First edition, 4to., fine, hardcover, issued without dust jacket. Beasley Books 2013 - 2015 $195

Escobal, Patricio *Death Row: Spain 1936.* Indianapolis: Bobbs Merrill, 1968. First edition, fine in fine dust jacket, slightly dulled spine. Beasley Books 2013 - 2015 $45

Eshleman, Clayton *Everwhat.* La Laguna: Zasterele, 2003. First edition, illustrated wrappers, inscribed by author to Jerome and Diane Rothenberg. Between the Covers Rare Books, Inc. 187 - 92 2015 $250

Espinasse, Isaac *The Five Acts Called Mr. Peel's Acts (7 & 8 Geo. IV, C 27 28, 29, 30, 31) Reduced to Distinct Heads and Adapted to the Arrangement of Burn's Justice...* London: printed by A. Strahan for T. Cadell and others, 1827. 8vo., extensive near contemporary ms. notes in ink on flyleaf, original boards rebacked in cloth with printed title label on upper cover, with contemporary label of "Kirton Sessions", uncut. John Drury Rare Books 2015 - 21445 2015 $133

An Essay on Political Lying &c. London: sold by S. Hooper, 1757. First edition, 8vo., 2 pages rather weakly printed, wanting half title, but very good with generous margins recently well bound in linen backed marbled boards, lettered. John Drury Rare Books 2015 - 9857 2015 $221

An Essay on the Polity of England with a View to Discover the True Principles of the Government. London: printed by T. Cadell, 1785. First edition, 8vo., half leather, marbled boards, 4 raised bands at spine, corners rubbed, spine ends rubbed, very slight fraying at top of spine, spine rubbed, gilt lettering faded, bookplate of Henry Beaufort on pastedown, inner spine hinges slightly cracked, otherwise sound, very good with clean text. Any Amount of Books 2015 - A97612 2015 £180

Essays on The Principles of Charitable Institutions: Being an Attempt to Ascertain What are the Plans Best Adapted to Improve the Physical and Moral Condition of the Lower Orders in England. London: Longman, Rees Orme Brown & Longman, 1836. First edition, 8vo., original green cloth with printed spine label, uncut, very good, uncommon. John Drury Rare Books   March 2015 - 20516   2015 $874

Essex Resolutions. (fly title). Newburyport: E. W. Allen, 1808. First edition, 8vo., sewn as issued, sheets lightly toned, else fine and unopened, fore and bottom margins uncut. M & S Rare Books, Inc.   97 - 103   2015 $175

Estes, Eleanor   *The Lollipop Princess.* New York: Harcourt Brace, 1967. Stated first edition, oblong 4to., cloth, fine in dust jacket, illustrations by Estes. Aleph-Bet Books, Inc.   108 - 170   2015 $150

Estes, George   *The Stagecoach.* George Estes' Pub., 1925. First edition, limited to 1000 copies inscribed to one who helped pull the stagecoach through by paying for this number the sum of ten pinches of gold dust, this copy 103 signed by author, three quarter leather, gold stamped front cover and spine, illustrations, rebacked with original spine laid down, else near fine tight copy, original color artwork "Undine" tipped in, rare. Buckingham Books   March 2015 - 25469   2015 $1000

Estienne, Charles   1504-1564   *Praedium Rusticum.* Lutetiae: Apud Carolum Stephanum, 1554. First edition of this collection, 178 x 114mm., fine period French calf, covers with blind ruled borders and attractive gilt chain roll frame with fleuron cornerpieces pointing obliquely outward, ornate central arabesque, raised bands flanked by plain gilt rules, spine panels with small gilt fleuron apparently original green morocco label, titlepage with printer's device, front pastedown with bookplate of Cholmondeley Library, little wear to joints and extremities (three corners rubbed, one of them with loss of its leather tip), half inch cracks at head of joints, shallow chip out of top of backstrip, titlepage with hint of soiling, isolated minor marginal spots or smudges, elsewhere in text but still excellent, contemporary copy with ample margins, binding solid and without any serious condition problems, very fine internally, unusually fresh, clean, smooth and bright. Phillip J. Pirages   66 - 15   2015 $8000

Etchison, Dennis   *Lord John Ten.* Northridge: Lord John Press, 1988. First edition, limited to 250 numbered copies, signed by contributors, fine, without dust jacket as issued, photos. Buckingham Books   March 2015 - 21524   2015 $250

Euclides   *Les Elemens D'Euclide du R. P. Dechalles...* Paris: Ch. Ant. Jombert, 1753. 12mo., 20 folding engraved plates, contemporary French calf, spine gilt, spine ends chipped, else fine, tight copy. Joseph J. Felcone Inc. Science, Medicine and Technology - 21   2015 $275

Eudaly, Kevin   *The Chesapeake & Ohio Railway West End: PM District, Chicago Division, Cincinnati & Russell Divisions.* Hart: White River Productions, 1999. First edition, color photos, black cloth, gilt, very fine, pictorial dust jacket. Argonaut Book Shop   Holiday Season 2014 - 86   2015 $60

Eudaly, Kevin   *Missouri Pacific Diesel Power.* Kansas City: White River Productions, 1994. First edition, quarto, 192 pages, profusely illustrated with color and black and white photos, blue cloth, gilt, very fine with pictorial dust jacket. Argonaut Book Shop   Holiday Season 2014 - 85   2015 $60

Euler, Leonhard   *Methodus Inveniendi Lineas Curvas Maximi Minimive Properietate Gaudentes.* Lusanne and Geneva: Marcum-Michaelem Bousquet, 1744. First edition, near fine, late 19th century qaurter leather marbled board binding, gilt lettering and decorations spine, binding with edge wear, label residue spine, owner's name and bookplate, f.f.ep., stamp r.f.e.p., text shows mild scattered toning, volume complete with five foldout engraved plates at rear, 4to., scarce. By the Book, L. C.   44 - 4   2015 $9250

Europe's Catechism. To Which are Added. The New Elect Catechis'd and the Catechist Catechis'd. London: printed and sold by the Pamphlet Shops of London and Westminster, 1741. First edition, variant issue, 8vo., wanting half title, outer leaves bit dusty, recent plain wrappers, good copy, scarce. John Drury Rare Books   2015 - 14884   2015 $89

Evans-Wentz, Walter   *The Tibetan Book of the Dead or the After Death Experiences...* London: Oxford University Press, 1957. Third edition, octavo, green cloth, gilt, bookplate of Gordon MacFarlane, some foxing on fore edge and first and last few leaves, some light spotting on front board, very good or better in price clipped, about very good, second edition dust jacket (presumably married to the book or a publisher's extra), with some spotting on spine and some misfolding, inscribed by author to MacFarlane. Between the Covers Rare Books, Inc.   187 - 94   2015 $1500

Evans-Wentz, Walter   *The Tibetan Book of the Great Liberation or the method of Realizing Nirvana through Knowing the Mind.* London: Oxford University Press, 1954. First edition, octavo, green cloth, gilt, bookplate of Gordon B. MacFarlane, some foxing on fore edge and first and last few leaves, some light foxing on fore edge and first and last few leaves with some light spotting on front board, very good or better in price clipped, very good dust jacket, inscribed by author for MacFarlane. Between the Covers Rare Books, Inc.   187 - 93   2015 $1750

Evans, Abel   *The Apparition. A Poem.* London: printed and sold by H. Hills, 1710. Piracy, 8vo., disbound, price 2d on titlepage, first few leaves rather stained, small wormhole catching few letters. C. R. Johnson   Foxon R-Z - 1234r-z   2015 $38

Evans, Edmund *My Diary Illustrated.* London: Cassell, Petter, Galpin & Co., 1892. Engraved half title and title, color frontispiece, 11 other color plates, black and white illustration for each day of the year, 16 page catalog, staples rusted causing some marking to gutter and loosening of few leaves, text pages rubricated, original red printed cloth, some surface wear, spine faded.   Jarndyce Antiquarian Booksellers   CCXI - 113   2015   £75

Evans, F. W. *A Short Treatise on the Second Appearing of Christ in and Through the Order of the Female.* Boston: Bazin & Chandler, 1853. First edition, 8vo., printed wrappers, very good.   Second Life Books Inc.   189 - 73   2015 $200

Evans, Frederick H. *William Blake's Illustrations to Thornton's Pastorals of Virgil in Ambrose Phillips' Imitation of Vergil's First Eclogue. 1821.* privately printed, 1912. Enlarged facsimiles in Platinotype from scarce original edition, limited to two copies, from a total of 25, this copy inscribed by Evans as one of two 'unnumbered presentation copies' and was his own copy, letter from Cecil Smith of the V & A accepting the other presentation copy tipped-in to front of volume, tipped in rear is review of the present volume from The Athenaeum dated Jan. 25th 1903, large 4to., original half midnight blue morocco gilt, spine lettered gilt and stamped with Evans's initials, 38ff., 17 woodcuts by Blake enlarged and mounted, frontispiece by John Linnell, photo of the life marks of Blake by Deville, Frederick Evans copy with his engraved bookplate.   Henry Sotheran Ltd. William Blake Exhibition 17th Oct.-7th Nov. 2014 - 74   2015   £3500

Evans, G. W. *Slash Ranch Hounds.* University of New Mexico Press, 1951. First edition, 8vo., photos, former owner's neat inked name on front flyleaf, else near fine in dust jacket with light wear to spine ends and corners and moderate wear to top edges of front and rear panels.   Buckingham Books   March 2015 - 33451   2015 $275

Evans, J. B. *Some facts about Suffrage Leaders. A Case is No Stronger that Its leaders.* Montgomery: Brown Publishing, circa, 1920. First edition, 14 x 8 1/2 inches, rare.   Second Life Books Inc.   189 - 74   2015 $400

Evans, Liz *Who Killed Marilyn Monroe?* London: Rion, 1997. First edition, signed by author, very fine in dust jacket.   Mordida Books   March 2015 - 006656   2015 $100

Evans, Walker *American Photographs.* New York: Museum of Modern Art, 1962. Second edition, quarto, bookplate designed by Johnathan Shahn, fine in slightly spine toned dust jacket, with tiny tear, otherwise fine, inscribed by author to Ben and Bernarda Shahn, May 1962.   Between the Covers Rare Books, Inc.   187 - 214   2015 $5000

Evenson, Brian *Altmann's Tongue. Stories and a Novella.* New York: Knopf, 1994. First edition, proof copy of author's first book, near fine in printed wrappers, sticker ghost to front cover.   Ed Smith Books   83 - 20   2015 $150

Everett, Edward *Workingmen's Library.* Boston: Leonard C. Bowles; Cambridge: Brown, Hattuck, 1833-1834. 5 parts, original printed wrappers, rare, wrappers little worn and soiled, lacking lower wrapper on two parts, very good set.   The Brick Row Book Shop   Miscellany 67 - 43   2015 $750

Evers, Helen *This Little Pig.* New York: Ferrar & Rinehart, 1932. Oblong 4to., pictorial boards, fine in dust jacket with some soil and fraying, 2 lines of calligraphic text on each page surrounding 2 color illustrations.   Aleph-bet Books, Inc.   109 - 359   2015 $100

Everyman His Own Brewer; or a Compendium of the English Brewery. London: printed for the author and sold by J. Almon and Mess. Robinson and Roberts, 1768. First edition, 12mo., half title, two final leaves of ads, contemporary plain sheep, spine gilt with raised bands and red label, joints and corners worn, upper cover coming loose, else good, crisp copy, very scarce.   John Drury Rare Books   2015 - 25093   2015 $1136

Evison, Vera I. *The Fifth-Century Invasions South of the Thames.* London: University of London, Athlone Press, 1865. 4to., half title, frontispiece, plates, illustrations, maps, original red cloth, very good in dated dust jacket, inscribed by author for Geoffrey Tillotson.   Jarndyce Antiquarian Booksellers   CCVII - 267   2015   £25

Ewart, David *Memoir of the late Mahendra La'l Basa'k Catechist of the Free Church of Scotland, Calcutta.* Calcutta: published for the Committee of the Bengal Mission of the Free Church of Scotland by Carey and Mendes Lall Bazar, 1846. First edition, 12mo., original maroon blind-stamped cloth, spine rather faded, but fine, crisp copy, rare.   John Drury Rare Books   March 2015 - 23398   2015 $221

Ewart, John S. *The Kingdom of Canada Imperial Federation The Colonial Conferences the Alaska Boundary and Other Essays.* Toronto: Morgan and Co., 1908. Red cloth, 8vo., cloth worn, some unerlining of text, generally good.   Schooner Books Ltd.   110 - 173   2015 $45

An Examination of the Justice and Expediency of a Bill "an Act for building and promoting the Building of Additional Churches in Scotland. Edinburgh: printed for Archibald Constable and Co. and John Smith and Son Glasgow, 1818. First edition, 8vo., small abrasure and spot on title, preserved in modern wrappers with printed label on upper cover, scarce.   John Drury Rare Books   March 2015 - 24935   2015   £306

Examiner, Pseud. *Some Thoughts on Examinations, by an Examiner.* London: privately printed in the Department of English at University College, London, 1936. 4to., original blue printed wrappers, slightly creased, 7 pages, inscribed to Geoffrey Tillotson by Hilda Holme and L. Paulin, with quotation inserted by Tillotson.   Jarndyce Antiquarian Booksellers   CCVII - 268   2015   £60

The Exclusives.   London: Henry Colburn & Richard Bentley, 1830. First edition, 8vo., 3 volumes, half light brown leather with pink paper covered boards, lettered gilt at spines with four raised bands, all half ties and rear ad leaves, neat name on front endpapers dated 1851, some wear and splitting at spines of first two volumes, slight loss at spine head on volume one and slight rubbing to boards, otherwise sound, very good- set with clean text.   Any Amount of Books   2015 - C14048   2015   £280

Exercises Instructive & Entertaining in False English... Leeds: printed for T. Binns by Edward Baines and sold by J. Johnson, Crosby & Cox and Vernor & Hood, London, 1802. Seventh edition, original hessian cloth, slight ink marking to back board, but very good, crisp copy, contemporary inscription 'R. Wells July 31 1804', later signature on leading pastedown.   Jarndyce Antiquarian Booksellers   CCXI - 6   2015   £120

An Exhibition of Books on Papermaking, a Selection of Books from the Collection of Leonard B. Schlosser. Philadelphia: Free Library of Philadelphia, 1968. One of 300 copies, large 8vo., double salmon colored paper wrappers, self paper wrappers with both pieces in clamshell red cloth box with title in gilt on spine, 24 pages.   Oak Knoll Books   306 - 129   2015 $175

Experiments on the Polarization of Electrons.   Philosophical Magazine Ser. 7 Volume XVII , May, 1934. Offprint, 8vo., near fine in original printed wrappers, inscribed and signed by author.   By the Book, L. C.   Special List 10 - 64   2015 $40

Exter, Alexandra   *Panorama Du Fleuve.*   Paris: Flammarion, 1937. Square 9 3/4 inches, opening to 8 feet, slight bit of edge rubbing, else near fine, illustrations by Exter.   Aleph-bet Books, Inc.   109 - 161   2015 $525

Extracts from the Information Received by His Majesty's Commissioners as to the Administration and Operation of the Poor-Laws.   London: B. Fellowes, 1833. First edition, 8vo., original oatmeal linen with title printed in black on spine, very slight fraying at head of spine, else very good, from the library of W. Jex Blake with his signature dated 1834.   John Drury Rare Books   March 2015 - 23624   2015   £306

F

F., W. *An Account of Some Strange Apparitions Had by a Godly Man in Kintyre, who hath been blind six years...* Edinburgh?: printed in the year, 1730. First edition, 8vo., 8 pages, paper just little soiled, bound in 19th century half calf over marbled boards, spine gilt lettered "Predictions", very good with 19th century armorial bookplate of John Whiteford Mackenzie, of some rarity.   John Drury Rare Books   2015 - 25872   2015 $2622

Faces in a Bookshop. Irish Literary Portraits. Galway: Kennys of Galway, 1990. First edition, 4to., black leather, fine in fine dust jacket.   Ed Smith Books   83 - 49   2015 $75

Fagnani, Federigo *Errori e Pregiudizj Sopra La Sanita dei Bigatti con Alcune Osservazioni relative alla Materia.* Milan: Gio. Bernardoni, 1818. 104 pages, contemporary wrappers, lightly dust soiled, untrimmed, fine.   Joseph J. Felcone Inc.   Science, Medicine and Technology - 50   2015 $175

Fair, A. A. *Traps Need Fresh Bait.* New York: Morrow, 1967. First edition, inscribed "To Helen Moore, my Hollywood Della Street. With love from 'Uncle Erle' Erle Stanley Gardner, fine in dust jacket with short closed tear on front panel.   Mordida Books   March 2015 - 011705   2015 $300

Fairbank, Alfred *Beacon Writing.* Portland: Alcuin Press, 1978. 11 volumes, 8vo., stiff paper wrappers, later cardboard slipcase.   Oak Knoll Books   Special Catalogue 24 - 13   2015 $250

Fairlie, Gerard *Bulldog Drummond Attacks.* London: Hodder & Stoughton, 1939. First edition, name and date on front pastedown, endpapers darkened and tiny spotting on page edges, otherwise near fine in dust jacket with darkened spine, soiled back panel, few tiny nicks.   Mordida Books   March 2015 - 000740   2015 $250

Fairly, Adam *A Half Hour's Crack with a Glasgow Radical Reformer, Rehearsed in a Letter to a Friend by Adam Fairly, Weaver in Camlachie.* Edinburgh: William Whyte and Co and John Smith & Son, Glasgow, 1820. First edition, 12mo., 12 pages, preserved in modern wrappers with printed label on upper cover, excellent, uncut copy, apparently rare.   John Drury Rare Books   2015 - 25899   2015 $177

Falkner, Thomas *A Description of Patagonia and the Adjoining Parts of South America.* Chicago: Armann & Armann, 1935. Facsimile edition, first edition thus, illustrations, 2 large folding maps, 2 facsimiles plates, small 4to., cloth with gilt titles, fine.   Kaaterskill Books   19 - 56   2015 $100

Falopii, Gabrielis *Neu Eroffnete Vortreffliche und rare Geheimisse der Natur'Darinnen in Zehen Buchern Gehandelt wird...* Frankfurt am Main: Verlegt in Christian Genschen Buchhandlung, 1715. 3 volumes in one, frontispiece, 3 engraved woodcut plates, woodcut head and tailpieces throughout, second volume bound first, but all three volumes collated complete, early full calf, blindstamped title panel on spine, head of spine, lightly worn, light rubbing to extremities, some overall foxing or toning to leaves, very good.   Argonaut Book Shop   Holiday Season 2014 - 88   2015 $1500

Fane, Robert George Cecil *Ministry of Justice: Its Necessity as an Instrument of Law Reform.* London: Spottiswoode and Shaw, 1848. First separate edition, 8vo., half title, recent plain wrappers, very good presentation copy inscribed by author for P. J. Locke King 38 Dover St.   John Drury Rare Books   2015 - 16769   2015 $133

Fannie, Cousin *Every Beginning is Easy for Children Who Love to Study.* Boston: Phillips Sampson and Co., 1856. 4to., cloth backed pictorial boards inner corner stain, else very good+, 7 very fine color lithographs.   Aleph-Bet Books, Inc.   108 - 160   2015 $300

Fargo, Frank F. *A Full and Authentic Account of the Murder of James King...* San Francisco: J. W. Sullivan, 1856. First edition, 8vo., 24 pages, original printed and pictorial front wrapper (frayed, soiled), lower right hand corner chewed on most leaves, affecting several words on each page.   M & S Rare Books, Inc.   97 - 48   2015 $500

Fargue, Leon Paul *Contes Fantastique.* Paris: Galerie Charpentier, 1944. Number 128 of 230 copies, 4to., unbound signatures laid into wrappers, fine in near fine, board chemise in near fine box.   Beasley Books   2013 - 2015 $300

Farjeon, Eleanor *The Soul of Kol Nikon.* privately printed, n.d., 1914. First edition, royal octavo, 107 pages, original black cloth lettered gilt on spine, presentation copy inscribed by author Feb. 26th 1914, spine little rubbed, small stain at outer edge of upper cover, free endpapers tanned, very good.   Peter Ellis, Bookseller   2014 - 014244   2015   £350

Farjeon, J. Jefferson *The Oval Table.* London: Collins Crime Club, 1946. First edition, fine in lightly soiled dust jacket.   Mordida Books   March 2015 - 006660   2015 $95

Farjeon, J. Jefferson *Peril in the Pyrenees.* London: Collins Crime Club, 1946. First edition, fine in price clipped dust jacket with tiny wear at base of spine.   Mordida Books   March 2015 - 006659   2015 $125

Farley, John *The London Art of Cookery and Housekeeper's Complete Assistant.* London: J. Scratchard and J. Whitaker and J. Fielding, 1784. 8vo., frontispiece, 12 engraved plates, portrait slightly offset, contemporary sheep, neatly and sympathetically rebacked with gilt lines and old label, very good.   John Drury Rare Books   2015 - 24207   2015 $1049

Farley, Walter *The Blood Bay Colt.* New York: Random House, 1950. First edition, signed by author, very good plus, nick to bottom of back board, very good, bright dust jacket with some tears and wear to spine crown.   Ed Smith Books   83 - 23   2015 $125

Farley, Walter *The Island Stallion Races.* New York: Random House, 1955. First edition, 8vo., near fine, minimal cover edge wear, very good++ dust jacket with mild edge wear, minimal creases, beautiful dust jacket illustration. signed by author.   By the Book, L. C.   44 - 77   2015 $200

Farmer, Philip Jose *The Best of Philip Jose Farmer.* Burton: Subterranean Press, 2006. First edition, one of 100 numbered copies, signed by author, octavo, boards.   John W. Knott, Bookseller   Selected New Arrivals Jan. 2015 - 17024   2015 $350

Farmer, Philip Jose *The Fabulous Riverboat.* New York: G. P. Putnam's Sons, 1971. First edition, octavo, boards, signed label by Farmer laid in.   John W. Knott, Bookseller   Selected New Arrivals Jan. 2015 - 17018   2015 $650

Farmer, Philip Jose *Pearls from Peoria.* Burton: Subterranean Press, 2006. First edition, one of 126 copies, this one of 100 numbered and signed copies, octavo, boards.   John W. Knott, Bookseller   Selected New Arrivals Jan. 2015 - 17021   2015 $250

Farmer, Philip Jose *River of Eternity.* Huntington Woods: Phantasia Press, 1980. First edition, one of 500 numbered copies signed by author, octavo, cloth.   John W. Knott, Bookseller   Selected New Arrivals Jan. 2015 - 17218   2015 $100

Farmer, Philip Jose *Up from the Bottomless Pit.* Burton: Subterranean Press, 2007. First edition, octavo, one of 276 copies, this one of 25 numbered copies signed by author, cloth.   John W. Knott, Bookseller   Selected New Arrivals Jan. 2015 - 17023   2015 $150

Farmer, Philip Jose *The World of Tiers: The Maker of the Universes, The Gates of Creation; a Private Cosmos; Behind the Walls of Terra; and the Lavalite World.* Huntington Woods: Phantasia Press, 1980-1983. Second hardcover edition of book one, first hardcover editions of books two and three and first separate editions of books four and five, octavo, 5 volumes, first book one of 200 numbered signed copies, rest are one of 250 numbered and signed copies by Farmer.   John W. Knott, Bookseller   Selected New Arrivals Jan. 2015 - 17062   2015 $500

Farnol, Jeffery *A Book for Jane and Every Other Jane with All Children Large and Small, Old and Young.* London: Sampson Low, Marston & Co., 1937. First edition, crown 8vo., few fox spots to borders of prelims, original brown cloth, stamped in cream to upper board, backstrip lettered in cream, very slight lean to spine, some very faint offsetting of black ink to lower board, free endpapers with strip of browning to inner margin, edges lightly spotted, dust jacket with couple of short closed tears, light crease at head of front panel and touch of rubbing at corners and tips of backstrip, very good.   Blackwell's Rare Books   B179 - 147   2015   £400

Farnol, Jeffery *Murder by Nail.* London: Sampson Low Marston, 1942. First edition, near fine, small stain on front pastedown and page edges foxed, otherwise near fine, lightly soiled dust jacket with several short closed tears.   Mordida Books   March 2015 - 008632   2015 $175

Farrell, Henry *What Ever Happened to Baby Jane?* Rinehart & Co., 1960. First edition, pages uniformly browned, else fine in fine, bright dust jacket, exceptional copy.   Buckingham Books   March 2015 - 36579   2015 $750

Farren, George *A Treatise on Life Assurance; in which the Systems and Practice of the Leading Life Institutions are Stated and Explained...* London: printed for the author and published by Butterworth and Son, 1823. First edition, 8vo., half title and final leaf (imprint only), 19h century dark blue half calf, spine gilt and lettered with raised bands, marbled edges, slight wear to extremities, else very good, near fine, from the library of the Institute of Actuaries with its Armorial bookplate and with ms. note in ink that it was 'Given to the Equitable Life March 1949", uncommon.   John Drury Rare Books   2015 - 19408   2015 $1311

Farrere, Claude *Les Civillises Eaux-Fortes Originales en Noir 35 en Couleurs de Henri Le riche.* Paris: Librairie De La collection Des Dix, 1926. First edition, no. 118 of 300 copies, 200 of which were on velin d'arches and 100 on Japan, 53 etchings by Henri le Riche, although this is one of the 200 on velin d'Arches, it includes two extra suites, previous owner's very good chemise and worn box, 4to.   Beasley Books   2013 - 2015 $500

Farshchian, Mahmoud *Painting and Drawing of Mahmoud.* Tehran: Bongahe Tarjomeh Va Nashre Ketab, 1976. First edition, folio, original brown cloth, lettered white on spine and front cover, copiously illustrated in color and black and white, fine in close to near fine dust jacket, very faintly rubbed at edges in servicable packing case. Any Amount of Books   March 2015 - C16231   2015   £450

Father Tuck's Rocking Animals. London et al: Rapahel Tuck, n.d. circa, 1905. Housed in original pictorial box are 10 large chromolithographed animal figures 9 x 7 1/2 inch high, box has some wear, but sound and in very good condition, animals fine with minor repair to tiger's ear, figures printed with exquisite and detailed chromolithographs, each has rounded base with section that can be moved apart enabling each animal to stand up and rock back and forth. Aleph-bet Books, Inc.   109 - 306   2015 $900

Fatherless Fanny; or the Memoirs of a Little Mendicant and Her Benefactors. London: James Taylor & Co., 1811. First edition, 4 volumes in 2, slightly later half calf, raised gilt bands, dark green labels, slight rubbed, good plus. Jarndyce Antiquarian Booksellers   CCXI - 114   2015   £580

A Father's Advice to His Son, Written Chiefly for the Perusal of Young Gentlemen. London: printed and sold by John Marshall and Co...., 1789? (1779). Only edition, 12mo., wanting free endpapers, contemporary sheep backed marbled boards, generally rubbed or rather worn, nonetheless, good copy, sound and crisp, rare.   John Drury Rare Books   2015 - 25071   2015 $1005

Faucher, Leon *Etudes sur l'Angleterre.* Bruxelles: Wouters Freres, 1845. Published the same year as the Paris first edition, 2 volumes in 1, 8vo., half title in each volume contemporary half calf spines gilt with raised bands, contrasting labels, top edge gilt, little wear to joints and corners, but good, uncut.   John Drury Rare Books   2015 - 15934   2015 $133

Fauchier-Delavigne, Marcelle *A Propos de Chansons...* Paris: Berger-Levrault Nov. 1918, Large 4to., cloth backed pictorial boards, near fine, illustrations by Guy Arnoux with fabulous full page and in text vibrant hand colored illustrations.   Aleph-bet Books, Inc.   109 - 183   2015 $500

Faulding, Gertrude *Nature Children: a Flower Book for Little Folks.* London: Henry Frowde, 1911. 8vo., boards with pictorial paste-on, small chip at base of spine, endpaper spotted, else very good, illustrations on every page by Eleanor March, charming book.   Aleph-bet Books, Inc.   109 - 24   2015 $200

Faulkner, Thomas *An Historical and Topographical Description of Chelsea and Its Environs.* London: T. Egerton, Messrs. Sherwood, Neeley and T. Faulkner, 1810. First edition, quarto, folding map, frontispiece, plates and vignettes, quarter leather, lettered gilt, marbled boards, top edge gilt, scarce, spine and corners rubbed, split at top of upper hinge, boards scuffed, offsetting from plates onto facing pages including titlepage, good.   Peter Ellis, Bookseller   2014 - 020446   2015   £300

Faulkner, William Harrison   1897-1962 *Absalom, Absalom.* New York: Random House, 1936. First edition, owner's neat name stamp, evidence of dust jacket flaps having been detached and pasted to pastedowns, thus very good, lacking dust jacket.   Beasley Books   2013 - 2015 $250

Faulkner, William Harrison   1897-1962 *Go Down, Moses.* New York: Random House, 1942. First edition, original black cloth, red top edge, very good plus, bookplate, little general age wear, fine facsimile dust jacket.   Stephen Lupack   March 2015 - 2015 $150

Faulkner, William Harrison   1897-1962 *Go Down, Moses.* New York: Random House, 1942. First edition, original red cloth, very good plus, little light disturbance to cloth sizing, near spine.   Stephen Lupack   March 2015 - 2015 $125

Faulkner, William Harrison   1897-1962 *Hunting Stories.* N.P.: Limited Editions Club, 1988. Limited to 850 numbered copies signed by artist, 4to., etchings by Neil Welliver, quarter green Nigerian Oasis goatskin, slipcase, well preserved copy, handset at Out of Sorts Letter Foundry on paper Arches paper by Peter Pettengill and Paul and Clary Taylor, bound by Jensen Bindery, with Monthly Letter.   Oak Knoll Books   25 - 57   2015 $350

Faulkner, William Harrison   1897-1962 *Idyll in the Desert.* New York: Random House, 1931. First edition, limited to 400 copies signed by author, original marbled paper boards, excellent, lightly edge rubbed copy in superb example of original glassine jacket with only few tiny nicks. B & B Rare Books, Ltd.   234 - 23   2015 $2000

Faulkner, William Harrison   1897-1962 *Light in August.* New York: Harrison Smith & Robert Haas, 1932. First edition, first printing, fine in extremely bright and crisp jacket, spine slightly nicked, exceptional copy with original glassine outer jacket which is perfectly intact and without any loss, very seldom found so well preserved with original glassine. B & B Rare Books, Ltd.   234 - 24   2015 $9000

Faulkner, William Harrison 1897-1962 *The Sound and the Fury.* New York: Jonathan Cape and Harrison Smith, 1929. First edition, first printing in first issue dust jacket with 'Humanity Uprooted' priced at $3.00, near fine with some light wear to extremities, hint of light toning to spine head, otherwise bright spine, fresh and clean interior, unclipped dust jacket with some wear and rubbing to extremities, few minor chips to spine head, closed tear extending from top edge of rear panel to front hinge below spine's title panel, short closed tear to front hinge at spine head, bright and unfaded spine, few light spots of minor soiling to otherwise fresh panels, overall tight and clean in scarce first issue jacket, free of any repairs or restoration, housed in custom quarter leather box.   B & B Rare Books, Ltd.   2015 - 2015 $27,500

Faulkner, William Harrison 1897-1962 *The Unvanquished.* New York: Random House, 1938. First edition, limited to 250 copies signed by author, drawings by Edward Shenton, original publisher's cloth backed patterned boards, from the library of Hogarth scholar Ronald Paulson bearing his bookplate to front pastedown, excellent copy, spine very slightly faded, few small stains to endpaper, else fine, author's scarcest signed limited edition.   B & B Rare Books, Ltd.   234 - 25   2015 $4000

Faulks, Sebastian *Charlotte Gray.* London: Hutchinson, 1998. First edition, signed by author, beneath his printed name, 8vo., original blue boards, backstrip lettered in gilt, dust jacket, near fine.   Blackwell's Rare Books   B179 - 145   2015   £50

Faust, Bernhard *Catechism of Health; for the Use of Schools and Domestic Instruction.* London: J. Dilly, 1794. First edition in English, 12mo., engraved woodcut frontispiece, colored by hand, other text figures on 3 pages, one with hand tinting, title and frontispiece both with red ruled borders, contemporary half calf over marbled boards, recently rebacked and lettered, good, near contemporary annotations in ink in several places.   John Drury Rare Books   2015 - 21036   2015 $1224

Faust, Bernhard *Gesundheits Katechismus zum Gebranche in den Schulen und Behm Hauslichen Unterrichte...* Leipzig: Paul Gotthelf Kummer, 1800. 8vo., frontispiece, original blue wrappers, entirely uncut, fine.   John Drury Rare Books   March 2015 - 16109   2015 $266

Favorite Fairy Tales: the Childhood Choice of Representative Men and Women. New York: Harper and Brothers, 1907. First edition, 8vo., gilt stamped paper covered boards, frontispiece and 15 plates by Peter Newell, decorative borders by Francis Bennett, covers and spine soiled, endpapers tanned, gilding on top edge worn, previous owner's name.   Oak Knoll Books   306 - 36   2015 $125

Fawcett, Edward Douglas *The Secret of the Desert or How We Crossed Arabia in the 'Antelope'.* New York: Edward Arnold, n.d., 1895. First edition, octavo, 6 inserted plates with illustrations by A. Twidle, original pictorial red cloth, front and spine panels stamped in brown, black and silver, rear panel stamped in black.   L. W. Currey, Inc.   Boy's Adventure Fiction 2015 - 9   2015 $750

Fawcett, Henry *Endowed Schools act Amendment Bill, Speech Delivered in the House of Commons July 20 1874.* London: Unwin Brothers, 1874. First edition, 8vo., 22 pages, preserved in modern wrappers with printed title label on upper cover, very good.   John Drury Rare Books   2015 - 15291   2015 $89

Fawcett, Millicent Garrett *Women's Suffrage a Short History of a Great Movement.* London: Jack, 1912. First edition, 12mo., green cloth printed in black, very good.   Second Life Books Inc.   189 - 78   2015 $125

Fawkes, Walter Ramsden Hawkesworth *The Englishman's Manual.* London: Longman Hurst and Co. for the booksellers in York, Leeds, Hull, Halifax, Huddersfield, Bradford, Wakefield &c, 1817. Second edition, 8vo., well bound in modern quarter leather over marbled boards, spine lettered gilt, very good, uncommon.   John Drury Rare Books   March 2015 - 23849   2015   £306

Fearing, Kenneth *The Big Clock.* New York: Harcourt Brace, 1946. First edition, near fine in strong, very good plus dust jacket, jacket bright and lovely, none of the spine fading nearly always found on this title, only short closed tear and associated crease at top front panel and some rubbing to crown, from the collection of Duke Collier.   Royal Books   36 - 162   2015 $1500

Fearing, Kenneth *Dagger of the Mind.* New York: Random House, 1941. First edition, review copy with slip laid-in, fine in price clipped dust jacket with some professional at spine ends and along flap folds.   Buckingham Books   March 2015 - 37464   2015 $750

Fearing, Kenneth *The Generous Heart.* New York: Harcourt, 1954. First edition, Goldstone bookplate, some offsetting on endpapers, otherwise fine in dust jacket with couple of closed tears and tiny wear at corners.   Mordida Books   March 2015 - 000746   2015 $85

Fearnside, Henry Gray *Picturesque Beauties of the Rhine, Displayed in a Series of Eighty Splendid Views...* London: Black and Armstrong, 1860. First edition, 8vo., handsomely rebound in half brown leather, marbled boards, lettered gilt on spine, 5 raised bands at spine, all edges gilt, tissue guards to plates, 80 engravings by H. G. Fearnside, neat name verso of frontispiece, slight foxing to plates almost all at edges of pages, very good.   Any Amount of Books   March 2015 - A72601   2015   £360

Fearon, Henry Bradshaw *Sketches in America.* London: Longman et al, 1818. First edition, contemporary calf backed marbled boards, early rebacking, armorial bookplate, hinges reinforced, nice, clean copy.   Second Life Books Inc.   190 - 74   2015 $600

Feather, John *English Book Prospectuses, an Illustrated History.* Newtown: Bird & Bull Press and Minneapolis: Daedalus Press, 1984. Limited to 325 copies, 8vo., quarter morocco with tips, Dutch gilt sides reproduced from an 18th century German decorated paper plus 1 larger facsimiles in separate accompanying portfolio, 109 pages, prospectus loosely inserted.   Oak Knoll Books   306 - 130   2015 $175

Feather, Leonard *The Encyclopedia of Jazz in the Sixties.* New York: Horizon, 1966. First edition, fine in lightly used dust jacket.   Beasley Books   2013 - 2015 $45

Feather, Leonard *The Encyclopedia Yearbook of Jazz.* New York: Horizon, 1956. First edition, signed by author, very good in like dust jacket.   Beasley Books   2013 - 2015 $85

Feather, Leonard *From Satchmo to Miles.* New York: Stein and Day, 1972. First edition, advance review copy with slip laid in, fine but for light dusting to spine, close to fine dust jacket.   Beasley Books   2013 - 2015 $45

Fellenberg, Philipp Emanuel Von *Vues relatives a l'Agriculture de la Suisse et aux Moyens de la Perfectionner.* Geneve: chez J. J. Paschoud, 1808. First edition in French, uncommon, 8vo., half title, large uncut copy in contemporary wrappers of printers' waste, wrappers worn and dust soiled, uncommon.   John Drury Rare Books   March 2015 - 12663   2015 $266

Fenelon, Francois De Salignac De La Mothe, Abp. 1651-1715 *Les Aventures De Telemaque.* Paris: Imprimerie de Monsieur (i. e. Pierre Francois Didot), 1785. 340 x 264mm., 2 volumes bound in 1, elegant red contemporary straight grain morocco, elaborately gilt by Staggemeier and Welcher, covers with wide gilt border composed of inlaid strips of blue goatskin tooled with Greek-key roll with square green goatskin inlay at corners tooled with a medallion and with inner frame composed of an inlaid citron goatskin band and large, graceful gilt impressions of flowers, foliage and ears of wheat, smooth spine divided into four unequal compartments by a strip of inlaid green goatskin tooled with gilt pentaglyph and metope roll, gilt lettering on green goatskin label in second compartment and directly at foot of backstrip, first compartment tooled with face-in-the-sun, third (elongated) compartment featuring a strange figure with winged helmet holding festoons of flowers, balancing on top of flower issuing from large neoclassical vase, vase in turn perched on candelabrum, edges of boards and turn-ins tooled with gilt rolls, marbled endpapers, all edges gilt; with fore-edge painting very probably contemporary, of two boats sailing on a lake , a stately home in the background; with engraved printer's device on titlepages and two frontispiece portraits and mounted, hint of wear to corners, spine little darkened, slight variation in color of leather covers, other minor defects, but extremely handsome binding entirely solid with nothing approaching a significant fault, and covers especially lustrous with bright gilt, intermittent pale foxing in text (a few gatherings with faint overall browning or more noticeably foxed), but leaves remarkably fresh, they crackle as you turn them, very clean and printed with vast margins.   Phillip J. Pirages   66 - 51   2015 $9500

Fenichel, Otto *The Psychoanalytic Theory of the Neurosis.* New York: Norton, 1945. First edition, very good, shaken.   Beasley Books   2013 - 2015 $45

Fenisong, Ruth *Murder Needs a Face.* Garden City: Doubleday Crime Club, 1942. First edition, dust jacket with slightly faded spine.   Mordida Books   March 2015 - 011879   2015 $85

Fenley, Florence *Oldtimers: their Own Stories.* Hornby Press, 1939. First edition, 8vo., cloth, frontispiece, portraits, plates. 22.5cm., scarce, fine, bright square copy in dust jacket with light wear to spine ends and two tiny chips to top edge of rear panel.   Buckingham Books   March 2015 - 35028   2015 $350

Fensch, Thomas *The Lions and the Lambs: Pool Players and the Game Today.* South Brunswick and New York and London: A. S. Barnes and Co./Thomas Yoseloff, 1970. First edition, 8vo, 167 pages, illustrations, fine in slightly creased and slightly rubbed, otherwise clean, very good dust jacket.   Any Amount of Books   2015 - A91075   2015   £180

Ferguson, Adam *An Essay on the History of Civil Society.* Dublin: printed by Boutler Grierson, 1767. First Irish edition, 8vo., intermittent worming in many lower margins (but nowhere touching letters), sometimes a single perforation, at others a worm track, contemporary catspaw calf, raised bands and morocco spine label, very good, well bound and crisp copy from contemporary library of Michael Kearney 1734-1814, with his armorial bookplate, very scarce. John Drury Rare Books   2015 - 21158   2015 $1005

Ferguson, Helen *Rich Get Rich.* London: John Lane, Bodley Head, 1937. First edition, 8vo., original green cloth lettered gilt on spine, page 302, spine toned, front cover slightly mottled, Book Club scroll stamp on front endpaper, otherwise sound, close very good with clean text. Any Amount of Books   March 2015 - C1656   2015   £350

Ferguson, W. B. M. *The Pilditch Puzzle.* New York: Liveright, 1932. First American edition, fine in dust jacket with nicks at spine ends and at corners and several short closed tears. Mordida Books   March 2015 - 005243   2015 $125

Fergusson, B. Menzies *Through Holland and Belgium on Wheels.* Stirling: Messrs James Hogg and Co., 1904. First edition, octavo, pale red cloth, (penciled ownership "Mary Fergusson Ellis") volume appears to lack front fly, corners little bumped, near fine. Between the Covers Rare Books   196 - 172   2015 $350

Fergusson, James *The Parthenon. An Essay on the Mode by Which Ligh was Introduced into Greek and Roman Temples.* London: John Murray, 1883. First edition of author's own copy, quarto, half title and titlepage with engraved vignette, frontispiece, 4 other engraved plates, numerous woodcuts blank sheet of paper bound between each leaf, this copy being author's own copy with his numerous additions and corrections in manuscript in margins and on blank sheets, in author's hand, original full maroon pebble grained cloth over beveled boards, rebacked with original spine, front board with gilt lettering and gilt vignette of the Parthenon, also heavily tooled in gilt, spine lettered in gilt, back board tooled to blind, black coated endpapers, some rubbing to board edges an corners, back board with some scrapes, cloth on top of front boards a bit rubbed and discolored, bit of finger smudging, repair to inner hinges, overall very good. Heritage Book Shop   Holiday 2014 - 64   2015 $4500

Fergusson, William *Notes and Recollections of a Professional Life by the late William Fergusson, Esq.* London: Longman, Brown, Green and Longmans, 1846. First edition, 8vo., contemporary half calf over marbled boards spine gilt with raised bands and label, very good. John Drury Rare Books   March 2015 - 24009   2015   £306

Ferlinghetti, Lawrence *Endless Life.* San Miniaro & Berkeley: Edizioni Canopo, 1999. First of this edition, limited to only 35 copies printed on Magnani paper in Atheneum type by Franco Palagini in San Miniato, Italy and signed by poet and artist, 11 drypoint etchings and aquatints by Stephanie Peek, loose sheets in decorated wrappers, publisher's folding box, very fine copy of this beautiful book. James S. Jaffe Rare Books   Modern American Poetry - 84   2015 $1500

Ferlinghetti, Lawrence *The Mexican Night: Travel Journal.* New York: New Directions, 1970. First edition, trade paperback, very near fine in pictorial wrappers, inscribed by author to fellow poet Margaret Randall, 9 21 78. Between the Covers Rare Books, Inc.   187 - 95   2015 $300

Ferrars, Elizabeth *The Seven Sleepers.* London: Collins Crime Club, 1970. First edition, fine in near fine dust jacket with tiny wear at spine ends and creases at top corner front panel. Mordida Books   March 2015 - 011343   2015 $85

Ferrell, Mallory Hope *The Gilpin Gold Tram. Colorado's Unique Narrow Gauge.* Boulder: Pruett Pub. Co., 1970. First edition, quarto, photos, detailed drawings, maps, black cloth decorated and lettered gold, very fine with spine faded pictorial dust jacket. Argonaut Book Shop   Holiday Season 2014 - 90   2015 $75

Ferry, Nancy *Russes et Francais.* n.d., 19th century, 4 1/4 x 6 1/2 inches, pictorial wrappers, small repair on cover, some soil, very good, hole cut in each page through which a different face can appear, 14 full page hand colored illustrations, hand colored covers. Aleph-bet Books, Inc. 109 - 334   2015 $500

Feuillet, Octave *The Marquis d'Hauterive; or the Romance of a Poor Young Man.* London: Cassell, Petter & Galpin, 1860. First English edition, original brown pebble grained cloth, very good, W. T. R. Powell (Nanteos) booklabels. Jarndyce Antiquarian Booksellers   CCXI - 116   2015   £90

A Few Plain Questions to the working People of Scotland. N.P.: Edinburgh?, 1793. New edition, 8vo., half title, recent cloth backed marbled boards with morocco label lettered in gilt on upper cover, very good. John Drury Rare Books   March 2015 - 25386   2015   £306

Fforde, Jasper *The Eyre Affair.* Hodder & Stoughton, 2001. First edition, signed, fine in dust jacket. Buckingham Books   March 2015 - 35272   2015 $200

Fickewirth, Alvin A. *California Railroads.* San Marino: Golden West Books, 1992. First edition, quarto, black and white photos, gilt lettered black cloth, fine, pictorial dust jacket (yellow jacket evenly faded to white). Argonaut Book Shop   Holiday Season 2014 - 91   2015 $60

Field, Eugene *Dibdin's Ghost.* Salem: Beaverdam Press, 1986. Limited to 135 numbered copies, 5.4 x 7.1cm., cloth, silhouette stamped on front cover, title stamped on spine, frontispiece. Oak Knoll Books 306 - 109 2015 $125

Field, Eugene *The Sugar Plum Tree.* Akron: Saalfield, 1930. First edition, folio, cloth backed pictorial boards, spine slightly faded, tiny bit of corner wear, else near fine, illustrations by Fern Bisel Peat. Aleph-Bet Books, Inc. 108 - 341 2015 $200

Field, George *Chromatics, or an Essay on the Analogy and Harmony of Colours.* London: printed for the author by A. J. Valpy, Tooke's Court, chancery Lane and sold by Mr. Newman, Soo Square, 1817. One of 250 copies, 4to., 20 hand colored examples including 5 on engraved plates and 15 further examples in text, original brown ribbed cloth, upper cover blocked in blind and lettered gilt, worn at extremities. Marlborough Rare Books List 54 - 29 2015 £1850

Field, George *Chromatics, or, the Analogy Harmony and Philosophy of Colours.* London: David Bogue Fleet Street, 1845. Second edition, 11 engraved plates, 7 are hand colored, text illustrations, few hand colored, modern green and black half cloth. Marlborough Rare Books List 54 - 31 2015 £450

Field, George *Chromatography or a Treatise on Colours and Pigments and of their Power in Painting &c.* London: Charles Tilt, Fleet Street..., 1835. First edition, 4to., hand colored engraved frontispiece, 2 leaves loose, uncut in original green cloth, spine title gilt, repaired at foot, green and gold lettered printed booklabel of British banker, poet and literal politician William Henry Leathen and his wife Pricilla. Marlborough Rare Books List 54 - 30 2015 £1250

Field, Rachel *Hitty Her First Hundred Years.* New York: Macmillan, Oct., 1929. First edition, 4to., patterned cloth, fine in very nice dust jacket (moderate sunning else very good+), illustrations by Dorothy Lathrop with 3 color plates plus many full page and in text-black and whites, quite scarce with dust jacket. Aleph-Bet Books, Inc. 108 - 186 2015 $1350

Fielding, Henry 1707-1754 *The History of the Adventures of Joseph Andrews.* London: A. Millar, 1742. First edition, 12mo., 2 volumes, contemporary full calf rebacked with original spines laid down, 4 pages ads at end of volume 1, volume 2 with one ad leaf opposite title and two pages of ads at rear, early bookplate, without spine label on volume I, discoloration to margin of few leaves in volume 1, volume 2 clean, very handsome. Manhattan Rare Book Company Literature 2014 - 2015 $5000

Fielding, Henry 1707-1754 *The History of Tom Jones a Foundling.* London: A. Millar, 1749. Second edition, published same year as the first, 12mo., contemporary full calf, rebacked, 6 volumes, only very minor occasional foxing, very handsome, clean set. Manhattan Rare Book Company Literature 2014 - 2015 $4500

Fielding, Henry 1707-1754 *The History of Tom Jones a Foundling.* London: printed for C. Cooke, n.d., 1801. Cooke's edition, 13 super engraved plates, 12mo., 3 volumes, contemporary tree calf, red and green leather labels to spine, blue speckled page edges, titlepages present in each volume, letter to George Lyttleton in volume I, two pages of ads in volume III, titles with former owner inscriptions of John Ogilvy, bright and sturdy set with minor rubbing to corners, some hinges worn but secure, pages clean, volume I titlepage with "Printed" misprint, Volume II light staining to margins, small loss to bottom corner of page 51, lacking rear endpapers (appears to have been bound without them, rather than removed), volume III with small touch of loss to head of spine, 18th century set in attractive tree calf, with all 13 plates. B & B Rare Books, Ltd. 234 - 26 2015 $450

Fielding, Henry 1707-1754 *The Complete Works of Henry Fielding.* New York: Croscup & Sterling, 1902. 16 volumes, 8vo., very good+ set, nicely bound in tan cloth. Beasley Books 2013 - 2015 $450

Fielding, Henry 1707-1754 *The Works of Henry Fielding.* New York: Jargon Society, 1905. Limited edition, one of 1000 sets, 12 volumes, complete set, light green cloth with paper spine labels to each volume (fading/soiling to paper spine labels, slight wear, fraying to upper or lower edges of spines), each volume with frontispiece and one black and white plate, clean text and tight bindings, except for some fading and toning to paper labels, near fine set, tight and clean. Stephen Lupack March 2015 - 2015 $150

Fife, James Duff, Earl of *Hints for a Reform, Particularly in the Gambling Clubs.* London: printed for R. Baldwin, 1784. First edition, seemingly pretty rare, wanting half title, very small stain on final leaf, recent cloth backed marbled boards with morocco label on upper cover lettered gilt, very good. John Drury Rare Books March 2015 - 25455 2015 $656

Fifty State Birds and Flowers on Stamps. Mill Valley: Splendid Press, 1982. Limited to 70 copies, 50 numbered, signed by printers/designers, Susan Acker and Carol Cunningham on colophon, on which this is one, with US postage stamps illustrating the birds and flowers of the 50 states, 7.2 x 7.5cm., quarter leather, illustrated cloth boards, title gilt stamped on spine, fore edge uncut, pictorial stiff paper slid-on wrapper, spine sunned. Oak Knoll Books 306 - 110 2015 $125

Figaro in Chesterfield. Volume I issue no. 1 July 21 1832 - no. 24 December 29, 1832. Chesterfield: T. Ford, 1833. Contemporary quarter cloth, marbled boards, worn but sound. Jarndyce Antiquarian Booksellers CCXI - 66 2015 £250

Figueroa, Virgilio *Diccionario Historico, biografico y Bibliografico de Chile 1800-1931.* Santaigo de Chile: Imprenta y litografia, Balcells (Volume IV), 1925-1931. Small 4to., 5 volumes in 4, black and white photos and reproductions, cloth with gilt titles, marbled endpapers, spine ends chipped, front hinges starting, one volume scuffed at joints, one torn along joints, one with backstrip tender, leaves browning, clean and unmarked, still good solid set. Kaaterskill Books 19 - 59 2015 $400

Filcher, J. A. *Untold Tales of California.* privately printed for the author, 1903. First edition, 16mo., pictorial wrappers, illustrations, former owner's nameplate neatly affixed to inside front panel, small old cellophane tape repair to top inside portion of front cover, light chipping to bottom of front cover, one small closed tear to front cover, corner chips, text block clean, overall good copy, rare. Buckingham Books March 2015 - 33662 2015 $750

The Finances of Egypt. London: William Ridgway, 1874. First edition, 8vo., preserved in modern wrappers with printed label on upper cover, very good, scarce. John Drury Rare Books 2015 - 25650 2015 $133

Fink, Sheri *Five Days at Memorial.* New York: Crown, 2013. Advance reading copy, with textual changes between this version and final, published book, "July 13" written in marker on lower edge of text block (book published in September), fine in self wrappers. Ken Lopez, Bookseller 164 - 66 2015 $100

Finley, Helen *Martha Elsie Series.* New York: 1868+, Lacking 6 volumes from being a complete set, together 21 volumes, good working set all but one with good shelf backs and lettering gilt bright, several volumes have some facsimiles of missing leaves inserted some gluing. Bookworm & Silverfish 2015 - 4273514997 2015 $346

Finley, Helen *Santa Claus a Musical Play for Juveniles in Four Acts.* Cincinnati: 1931. Very good in paper covers, expected aging. Bookworm & Silverfish 2015 - 6018798570 2015 $125

Finnegan, Robert *The Bandaged Nude.* New York: Simon & Schuster, 1946. First edition, fine in fine dust jacket with touch of rubbing, lovely copy, from the library of Kate Stettner Lobell and Carl D. Lobell. Between the Covers Rare Books 196 - 47 2015 $250

Finney, Patricia *A Shadow of Gulls.* London: Collins, 1977. First edition, fine in dust jacket. Buckingham Books March 2015 - 17313 2015 $285

Fiol, Ignacio *Razones Para Convencer Al Pecador Pare que Salga De Pecado Se Ponga i Gracia De Dios...* Barcelona: Maria Marti, n.d. probably early part of 1700's, First edition, Small 8vo., very scarce, text has no loss, some pages have some browning and few have some water marking or slight spotting, titlepage little rubbed at inner edge, overall internally very good with worn soft vellum covers, somewhat browned, slightly chipped and with one small hole and evidence of where vellum ties had been. Any Amount of Books 2015 - B22289 2015 £175

Firmin, Thomas *Some Proposals for the Imploying of the Poor, Especially in and About the City of London.* London: printed for Barbazon Aylmer at the three Pigeons in Cornhill, 1678. First edition, 20th century marbled boards with gilt, gilt on red morocco spine label, very good, crisp copy. John Drury Rare Books 2015 - 25447 2015 $4371

Firmin, Thomas *Some Proposals for the Imployment of the Poor and for the Prevention of Idleness and the Consequence Thereof, Begging.* London: printed by J. Grover and are to be sold by Francis Smith at the Elephant and Castle and Brab. Aylmer at the Three Pigeons in Cornhill, 1681. Second edition, 4to., engraved frontispiece, fine, crisp copy with good margins in old (18th century?) marbled wrappers. John Drury Rare Books 2015 - 24362 2015 $5245

The First Prize. A Tale. London: Seeley, Jackson & Halliday, 1869. Hand colored frontispiece and one additional plate, illustrations, final ad leaf, original green cloth, slightly dulled, ownership signature of Eustace on title, 46 pages, very good. Jarndyce Antiquarian Booksellers CCXI - 7 2015 £125

Fischer, Aaron *Ted Berrigan: An Annotated Checklist.* New York: Granary Books, 1998. First edition, one of 26 numbered copies signed by George Schneeman, Lewis Warsh and Fischer, 8vo., illustrations, original cloth, pictorial plate on front cover, printed spine label, including original comic strip similar to frontispiece tipped in, very fine. James S. Jaffe Rare Books Many Happy Returns - 77 2015 $250

Fischer, Bruno *The Restless Hands.* Dodd, Mead & Co., 1949. First edition, fine, bright, tight copy in dust jacket with minor wear to foot of spine and top fore corner. Buckingham Books March 2015 - 33128 2015 $275

Fischer, E. S. *Elements of Natural Philosophy.* Boston: Hilliard, Gray, Little and Wilkins, 1827. First American edition, quarter cloth, gilt and paper covered boards, dampstain tidemarks on some pages, most pronounced in final quarter of book, one corner of boards worn through, still tight, very good, ownership signature of Joseph Ray, professor of mathematics. Between the Covers Rare Books, Inc. 187 - 97 2015 $375

Fischer, Hans *Pitschi*. Harcourt Brace, 1953. Oblong 4to., pictorial boards, very good+ in frayed dust jacket, illustrations in color.   Aleph-bet Books, Inc.   109 - 174   2015 $100

Fish, H.   *Animals of the Bible*. New York: Frederick Stokes, 1937. First edition, first state (name mis-spelled on dust jacket), 4to., aqua cloth, offset on endpapers, else near fine in chipped dust jacket with small pieces off spine ends, cover design, pictorial endpapers and partial page lithographs by Dorothy Lathrop.   Aleph-bet Books, Inc.   109 - 250   2015 $1100

Fish, Helen Dean   *Four and Twenty Black Birds: Old Nursery Rhymes Collected by...*   New York: Stokes, 1937. First edition, 4to., green cloth, fine in dust jacket with some soil, wear to spine ends and corners, illustrations by Robert Lawson.   Aleph-Bet Books, Inc.   108 - 264   2015 $750

Fish, Robert L.   *The Incredible Schlock Homes*. New York: Simon & Schuster, 1966. First edition, signed by author, fine in lightly soiled dust jacket.   Buckingham Books   March 2015 - 30269   2015 $300

Fish, Robert L.   *The Incredible Sherlock Holmes*. New York: Simon & Schuster, 1966. First edition, fine in dust jacket.   Buckingham Books   March 2015 - 13717   2015 $375

Fish, Robert L.   *Mute Witness*. New York: Doubleday, 1963. First edition, incredibly scarce, fine in near fine dust jacket with trace of rubbing to corners and some sunning to small bit of orange coloring on spine, from the collection of Duke Collier.   Royal Books   36 - 223   2015 $1750

Fisher, Harrison   *A Garden of Girls*. New York: Dodd Mead, 1910. First edition, folio, cloth backed boards with large pictorial paste on of a woman, top edge gilt, 2 tiny corner creases, else fine in original pictorial box, corners reinforced, 16 large tipped in plates, beautiful copy, scarce.   Aleph-bet Books, Inc.   109 - 175   2015 $1250

Fisher, Leona Weaver   *Lemon, Dickens and Mr. Nightingale's Diary a Victorian Farce*. Victoria: University of Victoria, 1988. Original card wrappers, marked, presentation by Reg Terry in 1989 for Kathleen Tillotson.   Jarndyce Antiquarian Booksellers   CCVII - 213   2015   £35

Fisher, M. D.   *Colton's Traveler and Tourist's Guide-Book through the Western States and Territories...*   J. H. Colton and Co., 1857. First edition, 18mo., original red embossed cloth, titles stamped in gold gilt on front cover, lightly rubbed at spine ends, front interior hinge to show wear, tiny closed tear to top edge of front flyleaf, maps in fine, unused condition, overall near fine.   Buckingham Books   March 2015 - 38032   2015 $1875

Fisher, Rudolph   *The Conjure-Man Dies*. New York: Covici Friede, 1932. First edition, few small stains to cloth, else near fine in dust jacket that has been restored at extremities and presents as fine, from the collection of Duke Collier.   Royal Books   36 - 2   2015 $7500

Fiske, John   *Edward Livingston Youmans: Interpreter of Science for the People. A Sketch of His Life with Selections from His Published Writings and Extracts from His Correspondence with Spencer, Huxley, Tyndall and Others*. New York: D. Appleton, 1894. 8vo., 2 plates, 1 facsimile sample of Youmans handwriting, brown cloth, gilt stamped cover and spine titles, top edge gilt, extremities speckled, bit rubbed, former library copy with usual markings, and defects, signed presentation inscription by author for Petersham Library June 3/94, blindstamped.   Jeff Weber Rare Books   178 - 1182   2015 $50

Fitzgerald, Arthur   *Thoroughbreds of the Crown*. Hedley: Genesis, 1999. First edition, one of 950 deluxe copies, small folio, collector's leather bound limited edition book, fine in quarter red leather with purple buckram, gilt tooling and gilded page edging, printed on heavyweight archival acid free paper and housed in publishers' original purple cloth covered slipcase with gilt tooling.   Ed Smith Books   83 - 24   2015 $300

Fitzgerald, Francis Scott Key   1896-1940   *"The Cruise of the Rolling Junk." complete in three issues of 'Motor: the National Magazine of Motoring'*. New York: Motor: the National Magazine of Motoring, Feb. - April, 1924. 3 issues, large quartos, pictorial wrappers, all illustrated by Howard Chandler Christy, photos, light erosion at spinal extremities, one faint crease on front wrapper, near fine, custom cloth slipcase with morocco spine label gilt.   Between the Covers Rare Books   196 - 66   2015 $6000

Fitzgerald, Francis Scott Key   1896-1940   *F. Scott Fitzgerald: Novels and Stories 1920-1922*. New York: Library of America, 2000. First edition thus, small 8vo., book fine in close to fine dust jacket.   Beasley Books   2013 - 2015 $40

Fitzgerald, Francis Scott Key   1896-1940   *Flappers and Philosophers*. New York: Charles Scribner's Sons, 1920. First edition, original cloth, spine in gilt, front cover in blind, very good or better with only very slight rubbing to spine, gilt bit dimmed but brighter than usual, lighty rubbed to lettering at lower spine, some foxing to first few pages and endpaper, short early former owner inscription to front endpaper, attractive copy.   B & B Rare Books, Ltd.   234 - 27   2015 $700

Fitzgerald, Francis Scott Key   1896-1940   *The Great Gatsby*. New York: Charles Scribner's Sons, 1925. First edition, first printing, publisher's dark green cloth, fine, only hint of wear to spine ends, very slight lean to spine, else fine, beautiful copy, free of any repairs or restoration.   B & B Rare Books, Ltd.   2015 - 2015 $4750

Fitzgerald, Francis Scott Key   1896-1940   *The Great Gatsby.*   New York: Charles Scribner's Sons, 1925. first edition, first printing, with all first issue points present, fine, extremely bright and clean, spine gilt, completely intact and unfaded, only some light foxing to top edges, contemporary (1925) former ownership signature, else absolutely superb copy.   B & B Rare Books, Ltd.   234 - 28   2015 $4500

Fitzgerald, Francis Scott Key   1896-1940   *The Great Gatsby.*   London: Chatto & Windus, 1926. First English edition, dark blue cloth gilt, primary binding (there were two later bindings, tan and light blue, thought to be remainder bindings), minuscule tear at crown and bit of rubbing on board, still very good or better, lacking very rare dust jacket.   Between the Covers Rare Books   196 - 76   2015 $9500

Fitzgerald, Francis Scott Key   1896-1940   *The Last Tycoon.*   New York: Charles Scribner's Sons, 1941. First edition, octavo, original blue cloth, gilt stamped front board and spine in first issue dust jacket, jacket with small chips to top and bottom of spine as well some chips to front cover, along spine extremity in few short tears to bottom of rear dust jacket, very scarce.   Heritage Book Shop   Holiday 2014 - 65   2015 $1250

Fitzgerald, Francis Scott Key   1896-1940   *The Letters.*   New York: 1963. First edition, near fine in very good dust jacket.   Stephen Lupack   March 2015 - 2015 $40

Fitzgerald, Francis Scott Key   1896-1940   *Tales of the Jazz Age.*   New York: Charles Scribner's Sons, 1922. First edition, with 'and' on page 232 line 6 (priority undetermined), original cloth, spine lettered gilt, front cover stamped in blind, bright, about fine with extremely bright gilt, former owner bookplate to front pastedown, light offsetting to pastedowns, excellent copy.   B & B Rare Books, Ltd.   234 - 29   2015 $800

Fitzgerald, Francis Scott Key   1896-1940   *Tender is the Night.*   New York: Scribner, 1934. First edition, signed by author, one of 190 copies signed by author in his home at the behest of book buyer for Baltimore Department Store Hochschild, Kohn, trace foxing to edges of text block, shallow insect paths to covers, very good, lacking dust jacket, small Hochschild Kohn label, notable rarity signed rather than inscribed.   Ken Lopez, Bookseller   164 - 67   2015 $25,000

Fitzgerald, George Robert   *An Appeal to the Public by George Robert Fitzgerald, Esq.*   Dublin: Printed in the year, 1782. First edition, with errata leaf, text with numerous neat contemporary ink amendments, contemporary tree calf gilt, flat spine fully gilt in compartments, spine rather dull, patch of old worm damage to corner of upper cover, in spite of this, good, sound, scarce.   John Drury Rare Books   2015 - 25090   2015 $612

Fitzgerald, Penelope   *Offshore.*   London: Collins, 1979. First edition, near fine with little foxing to edges in very good jacket that would be fine except for a snag at top of rear panel.   Ed Smith Books   83 - 25   2015 $100

Fitzhugh, Percy Kesse   *Roy Blakeley Up in the Air.*   New York: Grosset & Dunlap, 1931. First edition, 8vo., several illustrations, red cloth, edges little soiled, cover little scuffed and slightly worn at edges, otherwise very good, tight copy in some worn dust jacket.   Second Life Books Inc.   191 - 36   2015 $125

Fitzsimmons, Cortland   *Sudden Silence.*   New York: Stokes, 1938. First edition, very good in price clipped dust jacket with wear at spine ends and along folds and several short closed tears.   Mordida Books   March 2015 - 000761   2015 $75

Five on Paper, a Collection of Five Essays on Papermaking, Books and Relevant Matters.   North Hills: Bird & Bull Press, 1963. Limited to 169 numbered copies, small 4to., original full morocco, 6 wood engravings, browning along edges of paper and inner margin as is common with all copies presentation from Lessing Rosenwald dated 1963.   Oak Knoll Books   306 - 131 2015 $1000

Fix, Betty   *Adventures of Idabell and Wakefield: What Would You Do?*   Oklahoma City: Crosby House, 1946. 4to., pictorial boards, fine in dust jacket, illustrations by Kenneth McClellean.   Aleph-bet Books, Inc.   109 - 158   2015 $100

Flaminius, Marcus Antonius   *Carmina Quinque Illustrium Poetarum.*   Florence: Apud Larentium Torrentium, 1552. 8vo., 18th century full panelled calf, rebacked with spine labels lettered gilt, later endpapers, red page edges, several small 17th and 18th century ink inscriptions on titlepage the printers device of which has been stained light red, binding somewhat rubbed and worn with slight chipping to head of spine, otherwise very sound, clean.   Any Amount of Books   March 2015 - C12498   2015   £350

Flanagan, Richard   *The Narrow Road to the Deep North.*   New York: Knopf, 2014. Uncorrected proof of first American edition, with letter from publisher laid in, presenting the book to another writer and soliciting any comment, fine in blue wrappers, scarce.   Ken Lopez, Bookseller   164 - 70   2015 $200

Flanagan, Richard   *Wanting.*   North Sydney: Knopf, 2008. Advance reading copy of true first Australian edition, inscribed by author in 2008 to another writer, several notations by recipient in text, near fine in wrappers, uncommon advance copy.   Ken Lopez, Bookseller   164 - 68   2015 $500

Flanagan, Sue *Trailing the Longhorns: a Century Later.* Austin: Madrona Press, 1974. First edition, one of a limited edition of 250 numbered copies, this no. 182, signed by author and by Robert Weddie, quarto, two-tone leather and cloth with illustration mounted on front cover, tinted endpapers, photos by author, 3 pictorial maps by Jose Cisneros, as new in original slipcase.   Buckingham Books   March 2015 - 32558   2015 $300

Flanner, Hildegarde *In Native Light.* Calistoga: n.p., 1970. First edition, engravings by Frederick Monhoff, cloth with printed paper spine label toned and rubbed, touch of edgewear to cloth, else near fine, inscribed by Flanner and Monhoff to their editor at the New Yorker, Rachel MacKenzie.   Between the Covers Rare Books, Inc.   187 - 99   2015 $100

Flanner, Janet *The Cubical City.* New York: G. P. Putnam's Sons, 1926. First edition, first printing, very good with some rubbing to extremities, faint staining to rear cover and early former owner gift inscription dated '1927'.   B & B Rare Books, Ltd.   234 - 30   2015 $500

Flaubert, Gustave   1821-1880 *Bouvard et Pecuchet.* Paris: Les Editions Nationales, 1949. Number 432 of 2500 numbered copies, bound in embossed leather-look boards, stamped in gilt and brown, illustrations by Jacques Boullaire's watercolors and drawings, large 8vo., fine.   Beasley Books   2013 - 2015 $45

Flaubert, Gustave   1821-1880 *Herodias.* London: Eragny Press, 1901. 1 of 226 copies of which 200 were for sale, early full crimson morocco binding with five raised bands to spine, title, author and date in gilt to spine, slight rubbing to hinges, leather turn-ins gold tooled and endpapers are marbled paper, red handsewn endbands with three color silk ribbon marker and top edge in gilt, interior pages bright and clean save for evidence of bookplate on verso of front free endpaper that has lightly offset on opposite page, woodcut frontispiece by Lucien with borders and initials done by Esther, near fine, lovely fine binding.   The Kelmscott Bookshop   11 - 16   2015 $1350

Flaubert, Gustave   1821-1880 *Herodias.* Paris: A. Plicque & Cie, 1926. No. 355 of 475 numbered copies, small 4to., 12 illustrations, fine but for one tiny spot lower right corner front wrapper.   Beasley Books   2013 - 2015 $375

Flaubert, Gustave   1821-1880 *Madame Bovary Moeurs De Province.* Paris: Michel Levy, 1857. First edition, first issue with dedicatee's name misspelled 'Senart for Senard, 2 volumes, original green cloth, covers paneled in blind, spines lettered in gilt, yellow coated endpapers, extremities lightly worn and rubbed, hinges of volume 1 cracked and rear hinge tender, former owner bookplate of novelist Louis Auchincloss, cracked at front hinge, very good and unsophisticated set and extremely scarce in cloth, housed in custom folding case.   B & B Rare Books, Ltd.   234 - 31   2015 $12,500

Flaubert, Gustave   1821-1880 *Madame Bovary.* London: Vizetelly & Co., 1886. First edition in English, octavo, original green cloth stamped in gilt and black.   Honey & Wax Booksellers   2 - 61   2015 $8500

Flaubert, Gustave   1821-1880 *Novembre Illustre De vingt Et Une Eaux-Fortes et Pointes Seches Gravee Edgar Chahine.* Paris: Les Editions d'Art Devambez, 1928. No. 186 of 238 copies on velin d'Arches, loose gatherings in wrappers in glassine, in slipcase, with chemise, trace of darkening to glassine wrappers in glassine, slipcase with chemise, trace of darkening to glassine which has two tiny tears at upper spine fold, slipcase has leather spine, slightly scuffed with rubbing to top and bottom (shelf wear), book remains lovely, 21 etchings and dry point engravings by Chahine, 4to.   Beasley Books   2013 - 2015 $450

Flaubert, Gustave   1821-1880 *Salambo: a Realistic Romance of Ancient Carthage.* London: Vizetelly, 1886. First UK edition, 8vo., yellowback format with color illustrated covers, sound, slightly used, very good, slight abrasion to cover, some wear at spine hinges, illustrated spine mostly complete, corners rubbed, text very clean.   Any Amount of Books   2015 - A92757   2015   £175

The Fleet Papers Being Letters to Thomas Thornhill, Esq. of Riddlesworth in the County of Norfolk... London: W. J. Cleaver and John Pavey, 1841-1844. First collected edition, Jan. 2, 1841-Sept. 7 1844, 4 volumes, 8vo., 4 engraved plates, bound in 4 volumes, including duplicate of volume III, in non-uniform half roan, gilt lettered with general wear, foot of spine of volume I defect, good, textually complete set.   John Drury Rare Books   2015 - 22533   2015 $2185

Fleetwood, John *The Life of Our Blessed Lord and Saviour Jesus Christ...* London: Thomas Kelly & Co., 1857. 4to., frontispiece, additional engraved title, plates, contemporary full brown crushed morocco by Hammond, inlaid with red morocco cornerpieces, border and diamond shaped central labels initial "GJS" decorated in gilt, raised bands, compartments in gilt with central floral design in red morocco, loss of red morocco & some gilt to one floral cornerpiece of rubbing to edge of front board, all edges gilt, very handsome.   Jarndyce Antiquarian Booksellers   CCXI - 118   2015   £380

Fleetwood, William *An Essay Upon Miracles in two discourses.* London: printed for Charles Harper, 1701. First edition, 203 x 146mm., 203 x 146mm., fine contemporary crimson morocco gilt by Robert Steel, covers with French fillet border, central floral frame with triangular filigree sidepieces and oblique fleuron cornerpieces, raised bands, spine heavily gilt in compartments adorned with curls and small tools, black morocco label, gilt rolled turn-ins, marbled endpapers, all edges gilt, large paper copy, front joint bit rubbed and with three very short cracks (spine ends and rear joint minimally worn), darkened areas on front board but binding entirely solid with shining gilt and extraordinarily fine internally, almost preternaturally clean, fresh and bright. Phillip J. Pirages 66 - 30 2015 $1900

Fleming, Ian Lancaster 1908-1964 *Casino Royale.* New York: NAL, 1960. First Signet paperback edition, Signet No. s1762, tiny wear at top of spine, otherwise fine, unread copy in wrappers. Mordida Books March 2015 - 011100 2015 $100

Fleming, Ian Lancaster 1908-1964 *Diamonds are Forever.* London: Jonathan Cape, 1956. First edition, binding A, fine in just about fine price clipped dust jacket with small tear on front panel, seldom found in this condition, from the library of Kate Stettner Lobell and Carl D. Lobell. Between the Covers Rare Books 196 - 52 2015 $5000

Fleming, Ian Lancaster 1908-1964 *Dr. No.* London: Jonathan Cape, 1958. First edition, first printing, about fine with dancing woman on front cover, some minor spotting to edges in very close to fine, unclipped dust jacket with slightest trace of wear to extremities, excellent copy. B & B Rare Books, Ltd. 234 - 32 2015 $3000

Fleming, Ian Lancaster 1908-1964 *For Your Eyes Only.* London: Jonathan Cape, 1960. First edition, fine in dust jacket. Buckingham Books March 2015 - 37452 2015 $2250

Fleming, Ian Lancaster 1908-1964 *For Your Eyes Only.* London: Jonathan Cape, 1960. First edition, binding A, top corners little bumped, else fine in very attractive, near fine dust jacket with small rubbed spot at crown and very slight age toning, exceptional copy, from the library of Kate Stettner Lobell and Carl D. Lobell. Between the Covers Rare Books 196 - 55 2015 $2500

Fleming, Ian Lancaster 1908-1964 *For Your Eyes Only.* London: Jonathan Cape, 1960. First edition, first printing, fine, extremely bright in crisp, unclipped and lightly soiled jacket with spine still bright and only slightly faded, minor rubbing to extremities, else near fine. B & B Rare Books, Ltd. 234 - 33 2015 $1250

Fleming, Ian Lancaster 1908-1964 *From Russia with Love.* London: Jonathan Cape, 1957. First edition, 8vo., recently rebound in full blue calf lettered gilt at spine and gilt raised bands, fine. Any Amount of Books 2015 - A34143 2015 £300

Fleming, Ian Lancaster 1908-1964 *From Russia, with Love.* London: Jonathan Cape, 1957. First edition, binding A, fine in very near fine dust jacket with very slight age toning at spine, very nice, from the library of Kate Stettner Lobell and Carl D. Lobell. Between the Covers Rare Books 196 - 53 2015 $8500

Fleming, Ian Lancaster 1908-1964 *Goldfinger.* London: Jonathan Cape, 1959. First edition, first impression, publisher's black cloth, skull stamped on front board, original pictorial dust jacket, about fine with bright gilt, unclipped jacket with very minor wear and light rubbing to spine ends, bright in bright, attractive dust jacket. B & B Rare Books, Ltd. 234 - 34 2015 $1500

Fleming, Ian Lancaster 1908-1964 *Goldfinger.* London: Jonathan Cape, 1959. First edition, first issue, second state (with 'skull' design on front board), small London bookseller's label front pastedown, corners slightly bumped, small rubbed spot bottom of front board, still near fine, attractive good plus only dust jacket that has been trimmed along edge of titlepage, attractive copy, from the library of Kate Stettner Lobell and Carl D. Lobell. Between the Covers Rare Books 196 - 54 2015 $1000

Fleming, Ian Lancaster 1908-1964 *Ian Fleming Introduces Jamaica.* London: Deutsch, 1966. First edition, fine in dust jacket with short closed tear. Mordida Books March 2015 - 008299 2015 $100

Fleming, Ian Lancaster 1908-1964 *Live and Let Die.* London: Jonathan Cape, 1954. First edition, first issue, 2nd state, fore edge and top edge trifle toned, slight tarnish on gilt lettering, very near fine in attractive, near fine, second state dust jacket (with artist's name centered between bottom of blurb and bottom of front flap), price clipped and with some modest age-toning to rear panel, from the library of Kate Stettner Lobell and Carl D. Lobell. Between the Covers Rare Books 196 - 51 2015 $12,000

Fleming, Ian Lancaster 1908-1964 *Live and let Die.* New York: Macmillan, 1955. First American edition, label removed from back and paper and name on front endpaper, otherwise very good in dust jacket with internal dampstain, faint dampstain on back panel and some very slight fading on spine. Mordida Books March 2015 - 010940 2015 $450

Fleming, Ian Lancaster 1908-1964 *The Man with the Golden Gun.* London: Cape, 1965. First edition, small scrape on front endpaper, else fine in dust jacket. Mordida Books March 2015 - 011446 2015 $350

Fleming, Ian Lancaster 1908-1964 *The Man with the Golden Gun.* New York: American Library, 1965. First American edition, fine in dust jacket with closed tear on back.   Mordida Books   March 2015 - 010936   2015 $100

Fleming, Ian Lancaster 1908-1964 *The Man with the Golden gun.* New York: NAL, 1965. First American edition, fine in dust jacket.   Mordida Books   March 2015 - 009865   2015 $135

Fleming, Ian Lancaster 1908-1964 *Moonraker.* London: Jonathan Cape, 1963. Sixth printing, octavo, 256 pages, small spot to fore-edge of rear free endpaper, fine in fine dust jacket.   Peter Ellis, Bookseller   2014 - 020115   2015   £350

Fleming, Ian Lancaster 1908-1964 *Octopussy and the Living Daylights.* London: Cape, 1965. First edition, fine in brown cloth with gilt lettering in fine dust jacket with price sticker to bottom of front flap.   Ed Smith Books   83 - 26   2015 $200

Fleming, Ian Lancaster 1908-1964 *On Her Majesty's Secret Service.* London: Cape, 1963. First edition, fine in price clipped dust jacket with small spot on front panel and light soiling on back panel.   Mordida Books   March 2015 - 011447   2015 $500

Fleming, Ian Lancaster 1908-1964 *On Her Majesty's Secret Service.* London: Jonathan Cape, 1963. First edition, binding A, fine in fine, price clipped dust jacket, beautiful copy, from the library of Kate Stettner Lobell and Carl D. Lobell.   Between the Covers Rare Books   196 - 58   2015 $1250

Fleming, Ian Lancaster 1908-1964 *The Property of a Lady in the Ivory Hammer: the Year at Sotheby's.* London: Longmans Green, 1963. First edition, fine in dust jacket with some darkening along edges and light wear at spine ends.   Mordida Books   March 2015 - 008635   2015 $175

Fleming, Ian Lancaster 1908-1964 *The Spy Who Loves Me.* New York: Viking, 1961. First edition, bookplate, fine in dust jacket.   Mordida Books   March 2015 - 010937   2015 $175

Fleming, Ian Lancaster 1908-1964 *The Spy Who Loved Me.* London: Jonathan Cape, 1962. First edition, black cloth, blindstamped Wilkinson dagger with silver gilt blade on front cover, titled in silver gilt on spine, bright red front and rear endpapers, fine in dust jacket with bit of light foxing to rear cover panel, attractive copy, first state of book and dust jacket.   Buckingham Books   March 2015 - 37323   2015 $1500

Fleming, Ian Lancaster 1908-1964 *The Spy Who Loved Me.* London: Jonathan Cape, 1962. First edition, very faint foxing on fore-edge, still easily fine in fine dust jacket with just touch of toning on rear panel, from the library of Kate Stettner Lobell and Carl D. Lobell.   Between the Covers Rare Books   196 - 57   2015 $1500

Fleming, Ian Lancaster 1908-1964 *Thunderball.* London: Jonathan Cape, 1961. First edition, first issue, binding A, fine in fine dust jacket, handsome copy.   Between the Covers Rare Books   196 - 56   2015 $3800

Fleming, Ian Lancaster 1908-1964 *Thunderball.* London: Cape, 1962. First edition, tiny spot on top of page edges, otherwise fine in dust jacket with closed tear on back panel and tiny wear at base of spine.   Mordida Books   March 2015 - 011445   2015 $750

Fleming, Ian Lancaster 1908-1964 *You Only Live Twice.* London: Cape, 1964. First edition, some offsetting on endpapers, otherwise fine in price clipped dust jacket with tiny wear at corners, first state without the month on copyright page.   Mordida Books   March 2015 - 009863   2015 $350

Fleming, Ian Lancaster 1908-1964 *You Only Live Twice.* London: Jonathan Cape, 1964. First edition, 2nd state with 'March 1964' on copyright page, Japanese lettering in gilt on upper cover, spine lettered in silver, ownership signature on front free endpaper, tail of spine slightly bumped, near fine in very good, slightly nicked dust jacket, bit rubbed at edges and faintly tanned at spine.   Peter Ellis, Bookseller   2014 - 002817   2015   £300

Fleming, Ian Lancaster 1908-1964 *You Only Live Twice.* London: Cape, 1964. Second state of first edition with March 1964 on copyright page, some light staining on page edges, otherwise fine in dust jacket with tiny wear at corners and some slight darkening.   Mordida Books   March 2015 - 011448   2015 $200

Fletcher, J. S. *The Burma Ruby.* London: Benn, 1932. First edition, very good in soft covers.   Mordida Books   March 2015 - 00831   2015 $125

Fletcher, J. S. *The Heaven-Sent Witness.* Garden City: Doubleday Doran, 1930. First edition, fine in very fine as new dust jacket.   Mordida Books   March 2015 - 010716   2015 $200

Fletcher, J. S. *The Malachite Jar.* London: Collins, 1930. First edition, pages edges lightly foxed, otherwise very good in dust jacket with half inch piece missing from back panel, chips on front panel edges and several short closed tears, very good.   Mordida Books   March 2015 - 011885   2015 $250

Fletcher, J. S. *The Pinfold.* Garden City: Doubleday Doran, 1928. First American edition, fine in very fine, as new dust jacket. Mordida Books March 2015 - 008641 2015 $85

Fletcher, J. S. *The Time-Worn Town.* New York: Alfred A. Knopf, 1924. First US edition, fine with top edges red color bright, dust jacket with light wear to spine ends and one tiny closed tear to bottom edge of rear panel. Buckingham Books March 2015 - 27241 2015 $300

Fletcher, J. S. *The Wrist Mark.* New York: Knopf, 1928. First American edition, spotting on spine and scattered spotting on fore edge, otherwise very good in very fine dust jacket. Mordida Books March 2015 - 008810 2015 $125

Fletcher, R. A. *In the Days of the Tall ships.* London: Brentano's, 1928. First edition, decorated cloth, nicely illustrated, neat 1930 Nantucket inscription, nearly fine, tight and bright. Stephen Lupack March 2015 - 2015 $45

Fletcher, W. *National Education. An Address to the Nation on the Education of the Children of the Poor...* Oxford: J. Vincent, 1848. First edition, 8vo., original printed wrappers with old institutional stamp on upper wrapper, paper spine bit worn, still good copy, rare. John Drury Rare Books March 2015 - 18528 2015 $266

Fleury, Joseph Abraham Bernard *The French Stage and French People as Illustrated in the Memoirs of M. Fleury.* London: Henry Colburn, 1841. First English edition, 2 volumes, half titles, 6 pages volume I, original green cloth, slight crease to spine beneath volume I, slight fading to spines, very good, bright copy. Jarndyce Antiquarian Booksellers CCXI - 119 2015 £150

Flick, Charles Leonard *The Ballad of Vimy Ridge.* Dawlish: Channing Press, 1937. 8vo, card covers sunned at spine and chipped at edges, generally very good, Victoria Bookstore stmap on back cover. Schooner Books Ltd. 110 - 149 2015 $125

The Flight of the Pretender, with Advice to the Poets. London: printed and sold by H. Hills, 1708. Piracy, 8vo., disbound. C. R. Johnson Foxon R-Z - 1205r-z 2015 $153

Flip the Frog Annual. London: Dean, 1931. Thick 8vo., pictorial boards, some edge and spine rubbing, else very good+, illustrations in black and white on every page. Aleph-Bet Books, Inc. 108 - 91 2015 $900

Flitner, Johann *Nebulo Nebulonum: hoc est, locoseria Modernae Nequitiae Censura....* Francofurti: Apud Iaocobu(m) De Zetter, 1620. First edition, 8vo., missing one leaf, decorative titlepage and 33 subsequent woodcuts, early patterned paper covered boards quarter bound with leather spine, five raised bands and title label, spine slightly rubbed with minor chipping and splitting at head, bookplate, otherwise very good, clean. Any Amount of Books March 2015 - C16615 2015 £375

Flitner, Johann *Nebulo Nebulonum: Hoc Est, loco-Seria Vernaculae Nequitiae Censura Carmine Iambico Depicta Tipisque Exomata Aeneis A Iohanne Flintero.* Leeuwarden: Joanne Coopmans, 1634. Second edition, 8vo., handsome half red leather, marbled boards, five raised bands and lettered gilt at spine, binding by Alfred Matthews, text in Latin, slight rubbing, else very good, exquisite binding. Any Amount of Books 2015 - C11840 2015 £750

Flora Europaea. Cambridge: University Press, 1964. First edition, 3 volumes, 4to., very good+ in very good dust jackets with slight edgewear. Any Amount of Books 2015 - A4096 2015 £150

Florian, Jean Pierre Claris De 1755-1794 *The Adventures of Numa Pompillus Second King of Rome.* Brussels: printed by B. Le Francq book-seller, 1790. 4 volumes, 12mo., frontispiece in volume 1, 3 further engraved plates in each volume (13 plates in all), text in English and French, uniformly bound in late 18th century catspaw calf, spines fully gilt with contrasting labels, silk markers, bindings all with wear and some insect damage, but all volumes fine and crisp internally, rare. John Drury Rare Books March 2015 - 25301 2015 $656

Florian, Jean Pierre Claris De 1755-1794 *Oeuvres Completes.* Leipzig: Gerard Fleischer, 1810. 13 volumes, frontispiece in volume I and engraved frontispiece in each volume, small 8vo., contemporary half calf, contrasting lettering pieces on spines, crowned stamp on titles with initials E. L. . G. P., very good. Blackwell's Rare Books B179 - 42 2015 £300-

Florilege Du Livre Francais Imprime aux Pays-Bas. N.P.: L'Imprimerie Nationale des Pays-Bas, 1954. First edition, limited to 400 copies of which this is one of 100 numbered copies printed on Van Gelder paper, light cover rubbing. Oak Knoll Books 306 - 197 2015 $125

Florus, Publius, Pseud. *Modern Patriots a Poetical Letter to T. S. W. Samwell.* London: J. J. Stockdale, 1816. First and only edition, 8vo., occasional very slight foxing, well bound in 20th century cloth, short title gilt on upper cover, few small paint (?) splashes on upper board, else very good, apparently very rare. John Drury Rare Books March 2015 - 25631 2015 £306

Flory, Jane *How Many?* New York: Henry Holt, 1944. Square 6 inches, pictorial wrappers, near fine, color lithographs.   Aleph-bet Books, Inc.   109 - 106   2015 $150

Floyd, William *Observations on Dog-Breaking.* London: Henry Wright Agricultural and Sporting Library, n.d.?, 1835. Probably third printing, 8vo., 16 pages, modern wrappers, printed title label on upper cover, very good.   John Drury Rare Books   2015 - 18615   2015 $71

Fludd, Robert *Philosophia Moysaica.* Gouda: Petrus Rammazenius, 1638. First edition, folio, engraved titlepage vignette, woodcut text illustrations, panelled sprinkled calf, mixed paper stocks, some gatherings lightly browned, some very lightly foxed, lovely, fresh, near fine copy.   Joseph J. Felcone Inc.   Science, Medicine and Technology - 23   2015 $8000

Fly-Sheets in Defence of the Rev. James Everett, Against the Aspersions and Slanders of Conference Calumniators. London: John Kaye and Co., 1852. First edition, 8vo., 32 pages, some old stains on final page, unbound and sewn as issued, very good, apparently of considerable rarity.   John Drury Rare Books   2015 - 26272   2015 $133

Fogel, Robert William *The Fourth Great Awakening.* Chicago: University of Chicago, 2000. First edition, 8vo., fine in fine dust jacket.   By the Book, L. C.   Special List 10 - 12   2015 $350

Fogel, Robert William *Time on the Cross.* Boston: Little Brown, 1974. Stated first edition, 2 volumes, fine in near fine dust jackets with mild edgewear.   By the Book, L. C.   Special List 10 - 10   2015 $950

Fogel, Robert William *Without Consent or Contract.* New York: Norton, 1898. First edition, 8vo., signed and inscribed by author, very good++, mild foxing, soil to edges, near fine dust jacket with mild soil, housed in custom made black cloth covered slipcase.   By the Book, L. C.   Special List 10 - 11   2015 $450

Foley, Robert *Laws Relating to the Poor, from the Forty-Third of Queen Elizabeth to the Third of King George II.* London: in the Savoy: printed by E. and R. Nutt and R. Gosling assigns of E. Sayer Esq. for T. Woodward, 1739. First edition, 8vo., including initial ad leaf, contemporary calf with raised bands and label, little wear and cracking of top portion of upper joint (but binding absolutely sound, else fine, crisp copy.   John Drury Rare Books   2015 - 23202   2015 $787

Follett, Ken *Triple.* London: MacDonald and Jane's, 1979. First edition, fine in dust jacket, uniformly tanned at extremities, small crease to top edge of rear panel.   Buckingham Books   March 2015 - 21456   2015 $175

Fontenelle, Bernard Le Bovier De *The Life of Sir Isaac Newton with an Account of His Writings.* London: James Woodman and David Lyon, 1728. First edition, 8vo., very good++, modern quarter leather and marbled boards, gilt lettered spine, minimal scattered foxing.   By the Book, L. C.   44 - 13   2015 $1200

Foot, Jeffery Robert *National Education; a Paper Read before the Ruridecanal Chapter of Tutbury.* Burton-on-Trent: printed by Richard Darnley, 1867. 8vo., 52 pages, recent plain wrappers, very good, inscribed by author, apparently rare.   John Drury Rare Books   2015 - 16718   2015 $133

Foote, A. H. *The African Squadron. Ashburton Treaty. Consular Sea Letters.* Philadelphia: William F. Geddes, 1855. First edition, wrappers, several old library stamps, very good.   Beasley Books   2013 - 2015 $125

Forbes, Alexander *The Radio Gunner.* Boston and New York: Houghton Mifflin, 1924. First edition, octavo, 4 inserted plates with illustrations, original decorated blue cloth, front and spine panels stamped in orange.   L. W. Currey, Inc.   Boy's Adventure Fiction 2015 - 54   2015 $150

Forbes, Colin *The Stone Leopard.* London: Collins, 1976. First edition, fine in dust jacket with small wear at lower corner of front panel.   Mordida Books   March 2015 - 003726   2015 $75

Forbes, Colin *Taget Fine.* London: Collins, 1973. First edition, fine in dust jacket with nicks at spine ends.   Mordida Books   March 2015 - 003725   2015 $75

Forbes, Leslie *Bombay Ice.* London: Phoenix House, 1908. First edition, very fine in fine dust jacket.   Mordida Books   March 2015 - 003084   2015 $250

Ford, Julia Ellsworth *Snickerty Nick and the Giant.* New York: Moffat Yard, 1919. First edition, 4to., blue pictorial cloth, near fine, illustrations by Arthur Rackham with 3 color plates, 10 full page black and whites, lovely inscription from Julia Ford Ellsworth and signed by Witter Bynner.   Aleph-bet Books, Inc.   109 - 404   2015 $850

Ford, Edward *David Rittenhouse Astronomer - Patriot 1732-1796.* Philadelphia: University of Pennsylvania Press, 1946. First edition, 8vo., frontispiece, blue cloth, gilt stamped over initials and spine title, printed portions of dust jacket have been cut apart and tipped in onto endleaves, very good.   Jeff Weber Rare Books   178 - 946   2015 $45

Ford, Ford Madox *The Good Soldier.* London: and New York: John Lane, Bodley Head, 1915. First edition, 8vo., 294 pages, original russet blind patterned cloth, lettered gilt at spine and on cover, name and date on front pastedown, some rubbing at spine hinges, slight split at lower hinge of spine and some marks and slight staining to covers and spine, overall sound used near very good copy, scarce, clean text. Any Amount of Books 2015 - C13088 2015 £1500

Ford, G. M. *Who in the Hell is Wanda Fuca?* New York: Walker, 1995. First edition, one of 200 numbered copies, this no. 21, signed by author, in special Seattle Mystery Bookshop dust jacket fine in fine dust jacket with trade dust jacket also fine. Beasley Books 2013 - 2015 $125

Ford, Leslie *Murder in the O.P.M.* New York: Scribner, 1942. First edition, top rear corner bumped, otherwise fine in price clipped dust jacket with couple of internal tape mends. Mordida Books March 2015 - 009869 2015 $85

Ford, Leslie *Siren in the Night.* New York: Scribner, 1943. First edition, covers lightly spotted, otherwise fine in dust jacket with faded spine. Mordida Books March 2015 - 009870 2015 $85

Ford, Richard *The Sportswriter.* London: Collins Harvill, 1986. First UK edition, 8vo., signed by Richard Rayner, review copy with slip, fine in fine dust jacket. Any Amount of Books 2015 - A97053 2015 £160

Ford, Simon *Wreckers of Civilisation....* London: Black Dog Pub., 1999. First edition, original issued as a trade softcover original, this copy rebound by Wiering Books in gray cloth with black titles and rule and original Throbbing Gristle thunderbolt patch inset onto front board, inscribed by COUM founder Genesis P-Orridge (nee Neil Megson), small bindery label to rear pastedown, near fine overall. Royal Books 46 - 28 2015 $950

Ford, St. Clair *Scraps from Indian and Other Journals.* Cheltenham: printed by R. Edwards circa, 1858. (1857), 8vo., headings printed in red, contemporary crushed red morocco, fully gilt, sides with extravagant gilt panelling, spine fully gilt with raised bands, all edges gilt, cream silk doublures, superb but unsigned binding, lettered in gilt "Lady Ford" on upper cover. John Drury Rare Books 2015 - 25666 2015 $1049

Fording. Volume I no. I (April 1917) - no. 12 (March 1918). Fording Pub. Co., 1917-1918. 12 issues, illustrations and ads, large tear to first leaf of no. 6, original red cloth, spine faded. Jarndyce Antiquarian Booksellers CCXI - 231 2015 £220

Foreman, Grant *Indian Removal, the Emigration of the Five Civilized Tribes of Indians.* Norman: University of Oklahoma Press, 1932. First edition, signed by author, red cloth, gold stamping on spine, frontispiece, illustrations, maps, front and rear hinges becoming loose, three small check marks in red ink by former owner at list of illustrations, light foxing to fore-edges, moderate wear to frnt cover and spine, else good in price clipped, lightly rubbed jacket with pink holes along front and rear flap folds. Buckingham Books March 2015 - 23086 2015 $175

Forester, Cecil Scott 1899-1966 *Love Lies Dreaming.* London: John Lane, The Bodley Head, 1927. First edition, 8vo., signed presentation from author for Peggy, pencilled note in hand of respected dealer Peter Jolliffe to wife of C. E. Bechofer Roberts, endpapers slightly browned, original jade green cloth lettered gilt on spine and on front cover, slight tanning at spine, slight sunning, else very good or better. Any Amount of Books 2015 - A63488 2015 £220

Forester, Cecil Scott 1899-1966 *Poo-Poo and the Dragons.* Boston: Little Brown, Aug., 1942. Stated first edition, 8vo., green cloth, fine in dust jacket (touch of fraying at head of spine, else near fine), illustrations by Robert Lawson with pictorial endpapers and titlepage, plus many fabulous black and whites. Aleph-bet Books, Inc. 109 - 256 2015 $850

Forman, Charles *Mr. Forman's Letter to the Right Honourable William Pulteney, Esq...* London: printed for and sold by S. Buffey, 1725. First edition, 8vo., with half title, outer margin of leaf E3 (pages 37-38) just shaved affecting single letter at end of few lines (but sense unimpaired), recently well bound in linen backed marbled boards, lettered, good. John Drury Rare Books 2015 - 14635 2015 $221

Forms of Prayer, for the Use of a Congregation of Protestant Dissenters, in Bradford. Trowbridge: printed by Abraham Small, 1793. First edition, page 48 misnumbered 8, contemporary sheep, with 'Grove Meeting 39', gilt on upper cover, binding neatly rebacked and repaired, spine gilt lettered, very good, crisp copy, very rare. John Drury Rare Books 2015 - 24149 2015 $1136

Forrest, Earl R. *Lone War Trail of Apache Kid.* Pasadena: Trail's End Pub. Co., 1947. First edition, 143 pages, cloth, inscribed by author, near fine in dust jacket with moderate wear to spine ends and extremities. Buckingham Books March 2015 - 17961 2015 $250

Forrest, Leon *There is a Tree More Ancient than Eden.* New York: Random House, 1973. First edition, hardcover, inscribed by author, fine in fine dust jacket. Beasley Books 2013 - 2015 $150

Forrester, Alfred Henry 1804-1872 *Seymour's Humorous Sketches.* London: T. Miles & Co., 1888. 86 caricature etchings, decorated red cloth, very good, spine faded, some cracking and loss at inner paper hinges, tight, essentially clean. Stephen Lupack March 2015 - 2015 $75

Forster, Edward Morgan 1879-1970 *The Eternal Moment.* New York: Harcourt, 1928. First American edition, hardcover, fine in lightly chipped dust jacket, latter quite uncommon. Beasley Books 2013 - 2015 $150

Forster, Frederick *On the Road to Make Believe.* Chicago: Rand McNally, 1924. Folio, cloth, pictorial paste-on, light soil, near fine, full page color plates, smaller color illustrations on every page of text by Uldine Trippe. Aleph-Bet Books, Inc. 108 - 347 2015 $200

Forster, John *Dramatic Essays: Reprinted from the 'Examiner' and the 'Leader'.* London: Walter Scott, 1896. Half title, frontispiece, 4 pages ads, original maroon cloth, spine slightly faded, lacking leading free endpaper, stitching slightly weakening, top edge gilt, extensive ms. notes by Kathleen Tillotson. Jarndyce Antiquarian Booksellers CCVII - 361 2015 £35

Forsyth, Frederick *The Biafra Story.* Biafra: Penguin Books, 1969. First edition, author's scarce first book, paperback original, fine in pictorial wrappers. Buckingham Books March 2015 - 24168 2015 $375

Forsyth, Frederick *The Day of the Jackal.* New York: Viking, 1971. First American edition, fine in dust jacket. Mordida Books March 2015 - 012694 2015 $150

Forsyth, Frederick *The Odessa File.* New York: Viking, 1972. First American edition, fine in dust jacket. Mordida Books March 2015 - 011889 2015 $85

Forsyth, James W. *Report of an Expedition up the Yellowstone River Made in 1875.* Washington: GPO, 1875. First edition, 8vo., illustrations, large folding map, printed wrappers, some professional restoration to spine, folding map has been professionally reinforced on verso at folds, else very good, clean copy, very scarce. Buckingham Books March 2015 - 27083 2015 $1250

Forsyth, William *A Treatise on the Culture and Management of Fruit-Trees.* Albany: Whiting el al, 1803. Second US edition, 13 plates, most folding, rebacked contemporary calf, very good, name excised from top of titlepage, little light foxing, but very good, tight copy. Second Life Books Inc. 191 - 37 2015 $250

Fortescue, Hugh, 2nd Earl of *Memorandum of two Conversations Between the Emperor Napoleon and Viscount Erbrington at Porto Ferrajo on the 6th and 8th of December 1814.* London: James Ridgway, 1823. First edition?, 8vo., errata slip tipped in after title, 19th century half calf over marbled boards, rebacked to match, spine lettered gilt, very good from the 20th century library of Clement King shorter. John Drury Rare Books March 2015 - 22159 2015 £306

Fortescue, J. W. *A History of the British Army.* London: Macmillan, 1899-1930. First edition, 20 volumes complete, 6 map volumes with colored maps, original red cloth, lettered gilt at spine, very good or better, sound copies with some slight fading, some volumes have mottling to covers/ and or edges, contents text and maps clean and sound, bookplate of Lieut. Colonel. J. R. Harvey in many volumes, occasional label of Officer's Mess 5th Battalion of S. Staffordshire Regiment or small oval stamp of 2nd Battalion. Any Amount of Books 2015 - C5522 2015 £750

Foskett, Henry *The Rights of the Army Vindicated; in an Appeal to the Public...* London: J. M. Richardson, J. Ebers and J. Bell, 1810. First edition, 8vo., half title, recently well bound in cloth lettered gilt, very good, very scarce. John Drury Rare Books March 2015 - 19655 2015 £306

Fossett, Frank *Colorado Its Gold and Silver Mines, Farms and Stock Ranges and Health and Pleasure Resorts.* New York: 1879. Third edition, expanded text, folding maps and folding view not in first two editions, 3 folding maps, 1 folding view, illustrations, front hinge starting, minor chip to f.f.e.p., else clean, very good. Dumont Maps and Books of the West 130 - 39 2015 $150

Foster, B. F. *Foster's System of Penmanship or the Art of Rapid Writing Illustrated and Explained.* Boston: Perkins, Marvin & Co., 1835. First edition, 8vo., 15 plates present, modern cloth, few ink spots and foxing marks but altogether a well preserved copy. Oak Knoll Books Special Catalogue 24 - 14 2015 $350

Foster, B. F. *Penmanship, Theoretical and Practical, Illustrated and Explained.* Boston: Benjamin Perkins, 1843. First edition, 12mo., original embossed cloth, title gilt stamped on front cover, wood engraved frontispiece, 36 engraved illustrations, cover faded in spots, rubbed and scuffed at edges, previous owner's name stamped on front pastedown, written in ink on front free endpaper, light foxing on endpapers, frontispiece an illustrated examples. Oak Knoll Books Special Catalogue 24 - 15 2015 $300

Foster, Edward *Code of the West; a Memoir of Ted Berrigan.* Boulder: Rodent Press, 1994. First edition, one of 300 copies, 8vo., original pictorial wrappers, fine. James S. Jaffe Rare Books Many Happy Returns - 78 2015 $100

Foster, Elena *Blood on Paper.* London: Ivory Press/ Victoria and Albert Museum, 2008. First edition, 4to., wrappers, booklabels, house in cloth covered box printed in blind, with strip of gauze (Natural Scoured muslin cotton) folded neatly on top, in publisher's card casing, 38 loose 6 page folded booklets + 2 booklets, many color illustrations, fine.   Any Amount of Books   2015 - A94247   2015   £260

Foster, Elena *Blood on Paper.* London: Ivory Press/ Victoria & Albert Museum, 2008. First edition, 4to., wrappers, 38 loose 6 page folded booklets + 2 text booklets, wrappers, housed in cloth covered box printed in blind, with strip of gauze folded neatly on top, without publisher's outer card casing which was possibly used for mailing, many color illustrations, fine, printed publisher's card casing very slightly used, boxes inside fine.   Any Amount of Books   2015 - C13284   2015   £235

Foster, Genevieve *George Washington's World.* New York: Charles Scribner's Sons, 1941. A. First edition, thick 4to., blue cloth, fine in dust jacket (repaired on verso, 2 inch piece of spine, no award seal), many color illustrations.   Aleph-Bet Books, Inc.   108 - 188   2015 $200

Foster, John *Speech of the Right Honorable John Foster, Speaker of the House of Commons of Ireland, Delivered in Committee on Monday the 17th Day of February 1800.* Dublin: printed for James Moore, 1800. First edition, 8vo., half title, penultimate leaf being a folding table, very good, recently well bound in linen backed marbled boards, lettered.   John Drury Rare Books   March 2015 - 19378   2015 $221

Foster, Michael *A Report of Some Proceedings on the Commission for the Trial of the Rebels in the Year 1746 in the County of Surry and of Other Crown Cases...* London: E. and R. Brooke, 1792. Third edition, 8vo., contemporary calf, crimson spine labels lettered gilt, very good, edges lettered in red ink, Chester Circuit Library.   John Drury Rare Books   2015 - 18739   2015 $133

Foster, William Z. *The Great Steel Strike and Its Lessons.* New York: Huebsch, 1920. First edition, wrappers, very good, 266 pages, more uncommon than cloth.   Beasley Books   2013 - 2015 $45

Foulkes, Nicholas *Bals De Legende & Bals: Legendary Costume Balls of the Twentieth Century.* New York: Assoulien/Van Cleef & Arpels, 2011. First edition, 2 volumes, folio, special presentation set, illustrated pink boards lettered gilt, copiously illustrated in color and black and white, ornate black silk covered presentation box, black ribbon and magnetic clasp, fine in near fine slipcase with slight rubbing.   Any Amount of Books   March 2015 - C6766   2015   £350

Four Satires. Viz. 1. On National Vices... II. On Writers.... III. On Waucks... IV. O Religious Disputes. London: printed for T. Cooper, 1737. First edition, woodcut headpieces, initials and ornaments, small hole at head of A4 and B1 without loss, tear at head of B4, entering text but without loss, bit stained and soiled, 8vo., modern half calf, contemporary signature of Edw. Elliott, sound.   Blackwell's Rare Books   B179 - 4   2015   £450

Fournier, Alain   1886-1914 *Le Grand Meaulnes.* Paris: Editions Emile Paul, 1961. Reprint of 1913 publication, uncommon, small 4to., wrappers, full page color illustrations by Grau-Sala, near fine with wrinkle to spine.   Beasley Books   2013 - 2015 $45

Fournier, Pierre Simon   1712-1768 *Fournier On Typefounding the text of the Manual Typographique (1764-1766).* London: Fleuron Books, 1930. Limited to 26 numbered copies and printed at Socino Press, small 8vo., cloth, 16 double page plates, slipcase worn with tape repairs along edges, spine of book faded.   Oak Knoll Books   306 - 214   2015 $350

Fowles, John *The Collector.* Boston: Little Brown, 1963. First US edition, 8vo., signed by author, near fine in like dust jacket with barely darkened spine.   Beasley Books   2013 - 2015 $275

Fox, Charles *Jazz on Record. A Critical Appreciation.* London: Hutchinson, 1960. First edition, fine but for one-line copyright oblit, in fine dust jacket.   Beasley Books   2013 - 2015 $45

Fox, Charles James *Speech of the Right Honourable Charles James Fox on Mr. Whitbread's Motions on the Russia Armament Thursday March 1 1792.* London: J. Debrett, 1792. First separate edition, 8vo., recent marbled boards lettered on spine, very good, surprisingly scarce.   John Drury Rare Books   March 2015 - 23664   2015 $221

Fox, George E. *Excavations on the Site of the Roman City at Silchester, Hants.* London: Nichols and Sons, 1891-1910. First edition, 19 volumes, 4to., printed blue wrappers, copiously illustrated in black and white, very good or better, some earlier issues have edgewear and slight chipping, later issues in excellent condition.   Any Amount of Books   2015 - A49581   2015   £250

Fox, John *The Little Shepherd of Kingdom Come.* New York: Charles Scribner's Sons, 1931. First Wyeth edition, 8vo., cloth, illustrated label on front cover, illustrated endpapers, fore edge uncut, endpapers, over label, title and 14 color plates by N. C. Wyeth, cover illustration rubbed, light rubbing at edges and corners.   Oak Knoll Books   306 - 43   2015 $100

Fox, Joseph *A Vindication of Mr. Lancaster's System of Education from the Aspersions of Professor Marsh, the Quarterly, British and Anti-Jacobin Reviews &c &c.* London: printed at the Royal Free School Press, 1812. Second edition, 8vo., burn mark lower blank margin of 3 or 4 leaves and resultant hole in one margin, not near printed surface, well bound in good library cloth, spine lettered gilt, University 'withdrawn' stamp on endpaper, good, uncut copy. John Drury Rare Books   March 2015 - 24340   2015 $656

Foxworth, Nilene *Ajinde.* Denver?: Nilene Foxworth, 1974. First edition, octavo, 8 pages, stapled purple wrappers with illustrations by author, slight fading on wrappers, else fine, very scarce.   Between the Covers Rare Books   197 - 21   2015 $200

France *The New Constitution of France.* London: n.p., printed in the year, 1793. First edition in English, small 8vo., marbled wrappers, title inked at spine, titlepage soiled but text of titlepage complete and legible, text of rest of book clean, scarce, slight wear, otherwise very good.   Any Amount of Books   2015 - A63416   2015   £800

France, Anatole *Le Mannequin D'Osier. L'Anneau D'Amethyste. L'Orme Du Mail.* Paris: Les Editions Nationales, 1947. One of 300 numbered copies and each with extra suite of color lithographs, 3 volumes, 4to., wrappers, illustrations by Edy Legrand, in very good chemise and very good boxes with occasional short splits, some have little fading to spine.   Beasley Books   2013 - 2015 $350

France, Anatole *Thais.* Paris: A. Plicque & Cie., 1924. No. 644 of 780 numbered copies, full color illustrations by Ralph Frieda, fine with some vertical wrinkling to spine from age and glue shrinkage, 4to.   Beasley Books   2013 - 2015 $275

France, Anatole *The Works of Anatole France.* London: Library Press, 1925. First edition, 18 volumes, 8vo., brown cloth lettered gilt on spine and cover with portrait of author on cover, frontispiece to each volume, very good.   Any Amount of Books   2015 - A89377   2015   £180

Francis, Dick 1920- *Blood Sport.* London: Michael Joseph, 1967. Uncorrected proof, very good plus in plain brown wrappers as issued, very slightly cocked, small stray red pen mark near fore edge of front wrapper, vertical wrinkling at spine, from the collection of Duke Collier.   Royal Books   36 - 170   2015 $300

Francis, Dick 1920- *Blood Sport.* New York: Harper, 1968. First American edition, fine in dust jacket with some slight spine fading.   Mordida Books   March 2015 - 010180   2015 $150

Francis, Dick 1920- *Bonecrack.* London: Michael Joseph, 1971. First edition, fine in dust jacket with some slight staining on inner flaps.   Mordida Books   March 2015 - 010186   2015 $200

Francis, Dick 1920- *Dead Cert.* London: Michael Joseph, 1962. First edition, boards very slightly browned, else book clean and bright, near fine in about near fine dust jacket, jacket shows none of the usual fading, nor any chips or tears, just a bit of uniform rubbing, inscribed by author for Elaine and Michael, from the collection of Duke Collier.   Royal Books   36 - 163   2015 $8500

Francis, Dick 1920- *Enquiry.* New York: Harper, 1970. First American edition, fine in dust jacket with nicks at top of spine and couple of short closed tears.   Mordida Books   March 2015 - 0100183   2015 $150

Francis, Dick 1920- *Flying Fish.* London: Michael Joseph, 1966. First edition, staining on page edges and on a number of pages and number of page edges darkened, otherwise very good in dust jacket.   Mordida Books   March 2015 - 10109   2015 $100

Francis, Dick 1920- *Flying Finish.* New York: Harper, 1967. First American edition, fore edge lightly spotted, otherwise fine in price clipped dust jacket with crease on front inner flap.   Mordida Books   March 2015 - 009871   2015 $175

Francis, Dick 1920- *For Kicks.* London: Michael Joseph, 1965. First edition, very good in price clipped dust jacket with three quarter inch pieces missing at top and base of spine, chips at corners, several closed tears.   Mordida Books   March 2015 - 011461   2015 $150

Francis, Dick 1920- *For Kicks.* New York: Harper and Row, 1965. First American edition, signed by author on half titlepage, near fine in near fine dust jacket with only touch of usual fading to jacket spine, diagonal crease fold at top of front flap, from the collection of Duke Collier.   Royal Books   36 - 167   2015 $425

Francis, Dick 1920- *Forfeit.* New York: harper, 1969. First American edition, fine in dust jacket with some slight spine fading.   Mordida Books   March 2015 - 10184   2015 $100

Francis, Dick 1920- *High Stakes.* London: Michael Joseph, 1975. First edition, "Xmas 1975" written on endpaper, otherwise fine in price clipped dust jacket.   Mordida Books   March 2015 - 010194   2015 $100

Francis, Dick 1920- *In the Frame.* London: Michael Joseph, 1976. Uncorrected proof, very good in plain brown wrappers as issued, spine roll and associated vertical wrinkling to spine, from the collection of Duke Collier.   Royal Books   36 - 171   2015 $300

Francis, Dick 1920- *In the Frame.* London: Michael Joseph, 1976. First edition, inscription and date on front endpaper, else fine in dust jacket.   Mordida Books   March 2015 - o1o198   2015 $90

Francis, Dick 1920- *Knock Down.* London: Michael Joseph, 1974. First edition, very fine in dust jacket.   Mordida Books   March 2015 - 010192   2015 $150

Francis, Dick 1920- *Nerve.* New York: Harper, 1964. First American edition, fine in very good, rubbed, price clipped dust jacket and wrinkled back panel and tiny fraying at spine ends.   Mordida Books   March 2015 - 010175   2015 $200

Francis, Dick 1920- *Nerve.* London: Michael Joseph, 1964. First edition, fine, some tiny scattered spotting on page edges, otherwise fine in dust jacket with some very slight spine fading and some scattered stains on back panel.   Mordida Books   March 2015 - 011435   2015 $800

Francis, Dick 1920- *Nerve.* London: Michael Joseph, 1965. Uncorrected proof, very good in plain brown wrappers as issued, spine lean, some vertical wrinkling to same, generic bookplate signed by author laid in, earliest state of this title, from the collection of Duke Collier.   Royal Books 36 - 168   2015 $1850

Francis, Dick 1920- *Nerve.* London: Michael Joseph, 1965. First edition, signed by author, near fine in like dust jacket, price clipped, touch of foxing to page edges, else book bright and clean, jacket exceptionally nice, only small amount of toning usually found, from the collection of Duke Collier.   Royal Books   36 - 154   2015 $1500

Francis, Dick 1920- *Odds Against.* New York: Harper & Row, 1965. First US edition, lightly rubbed at base of spine, else fine in dust jacket.   Buckingham Books   March 2015 - 28684   2015 $175

Francis, Dick 1920- *Odds Against.* London: Michael Joseph, 1965. Uncorrected proof, very good in plain brown wrappers as issued, spine roll and associated vertical wrinkling to same, generic bookplate signed by author laid in, from the collection of Duke Collier.   Royal Books   36 - 169 2015 $425

Francis, Dick 1920- *Odds Against.* New York: Michael Joseph, 1965. First edition, some light spotting on top page edges, otherwise fine in dust jacket with some light soiling on back panel.   Mordida Books   March 2015 - 010178   2015 $500

Francis, Dick 1920- *Odds Against.* London: Michael Joseph, 1965. First edition, near fine in bright, easily very near fine dust jacket, inscribed by author, from the collection of Duke Collier.   Royal Books   36 - 166   2015 $825

Francis, Dick 1920- *Odds Against.* New York: Harper, 1966. First American edition, fine in dust jacket.   Mordida Books   March 2015 - 010177   2015 $250

Francis, Dick 1920- *Rat Race.* London: Michael Joseph, 1970. First edition, fine in price clipped dust jacket.   Buckingham Books   March 2015 - 33580   2015 $275

Francis, Dick 1920- *Rat Race.* New York: Harper, 1971. First American edition, fine in dust jacket.   Mordida Books   March 2015 - 010187   2015 $85

Francis, Dick 1920- *Reflex.* London: Michael Joseph, 1980. First edition, fine in dust jacket.   Mordida Books March 2015 - 008306   2015 $85

Francis, Dick 1920- *Risk.* London: Michael Joseph, 1977. First edition, fine in price clipped dust jacket. Mordida Books   March 2015 - 010199   2015 $100

Francis, Dick 1920- *Second Wind.* Blakeney: Scorpion Press, 1999. First edition, limited to 110 numbered copies signed by author.   Buckingham Books   March 2015 - 13772   2015 $175

Francis, Dick 1920- *Slay-Rider.* London: Michael Joseph, 1973. First appearance, fine in price clipped dust jacket with slightly faded spine.   Mordida Books   March 2015 - 010190   2015 $100

Francis, Dick 1920- *Smokescreen.* London: Michael Joseph, 1972. First edition, fine in dust jacket.   Mordida Books   March 2015 - 010189   2015 $200

Francis, Dick 1920- *The Sport of Queens.* London: Michael Joseph, 1957. First edition, signed by author, fine in fine dust jacket, truly superior copy, scarce first book, from the collection of Duke Collier.   Royal Books   36 - 165 2015 $850

Francis, George William *The Dictionary of Practical Receipts....* London: D. Francis White Horse Lane Mile End Road, W. Strange Paternoster Row, 1848. First edition, 8vo., text figurs, contemporary half calf, spine simply gilt with label, rubbing and wear to joints and extremities but good copy, scarce.   John Drury Rare Books   2015 - 16646   2015 $177

Franck, Peter *A Lost Link in the Technique of Bookbinding and How I Found It.* Gaylordsville: Hawthorne House, 1941. Limited to 150 numbered copies, small 8vo., marbled cloth, scarce.   Oak Knoll Books   306 - 1   2015 $100

Francois *Chansons de France.* Paris: Plon Nourrit, 1928. 48 pages, oblong 4to., decorative cloth stamped in gold and black, fine, clean and bright, original dust jacket very chipped and worn, 24 songs, beautiful color illustrations, beautiful copy.   Aleph-bet Books, Inc.   109 - 67   2015 $225

Frank, Anne *Anne Frank: The Diary of a Young Girl.* London: Constellation Books, 1952. First UK edition, 8vo., original green cloth lettered gilt on spine, gilt flower illustration on front cover, frontispiece, one plan, 5 plates, covers slightly marked and slightly stained, very good- sound copy with clean text.   Any Amount of Books   2015 - A92155   2015   £280

Frank, Jane *The Frank Collection. A Showcase of the World's Finest Fantastic Art.* London: Paper Tiger, 1999. First edition, quarto, cloth, 112 pages, illustrations in color, fine in fine dust jacket.   Buckingham Books   March 2015 - 14423   2015 $225

Frank, Leonhard *Mathilde.* Los Angeles: Pazifischen Presse, 1943. Limited to 250 numbered copies, 150 signed by author, this copy thus, 8vo., quarter leather, paper covered board, fore-edge uncut, spine gilt stamped, covers lightly soiled.   Oak Knoll Books   306 - 161   2015 $135

Frank, Pat *Alas, Babylon.* Philadelphia: and New York: J. B. Lippincott Co., 1959. First edition, octavo, cloth.   John W. Knott, Bookseller   Selected New Arrivals Jan. 2015 - 17022   2015 $1250

Frankau, Gilbert *The Seeds of Enchantment.* Garden City: Doubleday Page, 1921. First American edition, fine in light soiled dust jacket with some tiny closed tears.   Mordida Books   March 2015 - 007704   2015 $100

Frankau, Gilbert *Wine, Women and Waiters.* London: Hutchinson, 1932. First edition, inscription, fine without dust jacket.   Mordida Books   March 2015 - 010581   2015 $100

Franklin, Benjamin   1706-1790 *Experiments and Observations on Electricity Made at Philadelphia in America.* London: for F. Newbery, 1774. Fifth and final edition, 4to., 7 engraved plates, several woodcut text illustrations, lacks half title, contemporary marbled paper covered boards, calf spine, very skillfully rebacked in period style, later endpapers, occasional foxing of both text and plates, some offsetting from a few plates, light stains on H3-4 and 2M3-4, withal very good.   Joseph J. Felcone Inc.   Science, Medicine and Technology - 24   2015 $8500

Franklin, Benjamin   1706-1790 *The Life of the Late Dr. Benjamin Franklin written by himself.* Philadelphia: 1811. 12mo, original blue printed paper boards.   Honey & Wax Booksellers   3 - 6   2015 $500

Franklin, Benjamin   1706-1790 *Works of the late...* London: printed for G. G. J. and J. Robinson, 1793. First edition, first issue with errata leaf at end volume one, 2 volumes, 8vo., contemporary calf rebacked with original spines laid on, black leather labels, gilt rules and lettering, engraved titlepages with vignette portrait of Franklin, titlepages little foxed, very good.   The Brick Row Book Shop   Miscellany 67 - 46   2015 $5000

Franklin, Colin *The Ashendene Press.* Dallas: Bridwell Library, 1986. First edition, limited to 750 copies, well printed and designed, small 4to., cloth backed boards, paper spine label, illustrations.   Oak Knoll Books   306 - 124   2015 $150

Franklin, Margaret Ladd *The Case for Woman Suffrage a Bibliography.* New York: National College Equal Suffrage League sold by the National American Woman Suffrage Assoc., 1913. First edition, 8vo., mustard cloth stamped in black, soiled, good, useable and clean inside.   Second Life Books Inc.   189 - 79   2015 $135

Franklin, Moses *Stolen Jobs and the Thief.* Pueblo: the author, 1915. First edition, wrappers, very good, little tearing at spine, 8vo.   Beasley Books   2013 - 2015 $45

Franks, J. M. *Seventy Years in Texas. Memories of the Pioneer days...* privately printed, 1924. First edition, original printed wrappers, frontispiece, lightly soiled on front cover, perimeter of covers uniformly tanned, else near fine.   Buckingham Books   March 2015 - 34506   2015 $195

Franzen, Jonathan *How to Be Alone.* New York: FSG, 2002. Advance reading copy, signed by author at NY book store, store's bookmark laid in, fine in wrappers, uncommon advance issue, especially signed.   Ken Lopez, Bookseller   164 - 71   2015 $250

Franzoni, David *Gladiator: the Film Screenplay.* Dream Works Pictures, 2000. First edition, 8 1/2 x 11 inches, bradbound printed wrappers, specially printed for distribution to members of Academy of Motion Pictures Arts Sciences, fine, bright. Buckingham Books March 2015 - 28976 2015 $400

Frasconi, Antonio *See and Say.* New York: Harcourt Brace and co., 1955. Stated first edition, 4to., cloth, fine in very slightly worn dust jacket, color woodcuts, this copy inscribed by Frasconi. Aleph-Bet Books, Inc. 108 - 190 2015 $350

Fraser, A M. *The Newfoundland Industrial Development Board and Its Work 1942-1949.* St. John's: Robinson & Co. Ltd., 1950. 8vo., blue cloth with dust jacket, very good in dust jacket with two small white marks to spine. Schooner Books Ltd. 110 - 36 2015 $45

Fraser, Alexander *The Account of the Proceedings at the Festival of the Society of Freemasons at their Hall on Wednesday the 27th of Jan. 1813...* London: printed for Brother James Asperne, 1813. First edition, 8vo., 2 engraved portraits, engraved plate, double page engraved facsimile of ticket of admission to the festival, minor foxing and slight paper browning, contemporary half calf over marbled boards, general light wear to binding, good, sound with early 19th century ownership signature of James Bygott and later ms. note that this copy was presented in 1868 to the Witham Lodge, very rare. John Drury Rare Books March 2015 - 21853 2015 $874

Fraser, William *The State of Our Educational Enterprises.* Glasgow: Edinburgh and London: Blackie and Son, 1858. First edition, 8vo., errata slip tipped in at end, recently wel bound in linen backed marbled boards, lettered, very good, scarce. John Drury Rare Books March 2015 - 22963 2015 $221

Frederic, Harold *The Copperhead.* New York: Scribner's, 1893. First edition, 8vo., brown cloth stamped in black and gilt, cover little scuffed at edges and slightly worn at corners and ends of spine, otherwise very good, tight copy. Second Life Books Inc. 190 - 75 2015 $150

Frederic, Harold *The Deserter and Other Stories.* Boston: Lothrop, 1898. First edition, illustrations, gray cloth with pictorial stamping in black, gilt and pale green, front hinge starting tender, cover somewhat browned at spine and edges, else very good in plastic dust jacket. Second Life Books Inc. 190 - 76 2015 $185

Frederic, Harold *Gloria Mundi.* Chicago: Herbert S. Stone, 1898. First edition, red cloth stamped in black, edges and cover somewhat darkened cover little worn at ends of spine, hinges beginning tender, otherwise very good. Second Life Books Inc. 190 - 77 2015 $175

Frederic, Harold *Mrs. Albert Grundy Observations in Philistia.* New York: Merriam, 1896. First American edition, 'A' issue, 8vo., pale green cloth stamped in dark green, gilt and red, top edge gilt, unopened, cover very slightly yellowed at spine, otherwise fine. Second Life Books Inc. 190 - 78 2015 $225

Frederick, J. V. *Ben Holladay. The Stagecoach King.* Glendale: Arthur H. Clark Co., 1940. First edition, 8vo., green cloth, gold stamping on spine,. Buckingham Books March 2015 - 30787 2015 $300

Frederick, J. V. *Ben Holladay. The Stagecoach King.* Glendale: Arthur H. Clark Co., 1940. First edition, 8vo., green cloth, gold stamped spine, frontispiece, 8 plates, folding map, fine, bright, unread copy. Buckingham Books March 2015 - 22813 2015 $375

Fredericks, Arnold *One Million Francs.* W. J. Watts & Co., 1912. First edition, near fine in cloth, pictorial cover printed in gilt, illustrations by Will Grefe. Buckingham Books March 2015 - 38478 2015 $175

Free Trade to India. Letters Addressed to the Merchants and Inhabitants of the town of Liverpool, Concerning a free Trade to the East Indies. by a member of Parliament. Liverpool: printed and sold by E. Smith and Co., 1812. First edition, 8vo., 32 pages, recent marbled boards lettered on spine, very good, very rare. John Drury Rare Books 2015 - 24477 2015 $612

Freedom School Poetry. Atlanta: Student Nonviolent Coordinating Committee, 1965. 8vo., 47 pages, paper wrappers, owner's name on cover, cover very slightly soiled and yellowed, else very good, tight copy. Second Life Books Inc. 191 - 85 2015 $75

Freeling, Nicolas *The King of the Rainy Country.* Victor Gollancz, 1966. First edition, fine in dust jacket with light wear to top of spine, spine darkened and lightly soiled on front and rear panels. Buckingham Books March 2015 - 35649 2015 $185

Freeling, Nicolas *Valparaiso.* New York: Harper & Row, 1965. First US edition, near fine in dust jacket, very lightly rubbed at extremities and white back panel beginning to uniformly tan, presentation copy from his literary agent, inscribed to Juliet (O'Hea). Buckingham Books March 2015 - 27167 2015 $200

Freeman, Don *Dandelion.* New York: Viking Press, 1964. First edition, oblong 4to., pictorial cloth, fine in dust jacket (chip on spine and few closed tears), full page multi color drawing inscribed by author. Aleph-bet Books, Inc. 109 - 178 2015 $1200

Freeman, Don *A Pocket for Corduroy.* New York: Viking Press, 1978. First edition, oblong small quarto, slight bend at spine and small spot on rear pastedown, near fine in near fine dust jacket with light wear at edges and some waviness, lovely copy, uncommon-. Between the Covers Rare Books 196 - 160 2015 $750

Freeman, G. D. *Midnight and Noonday or the Incidental History of Southern Kansas and the Indian Territory...* G. D. Freeman, 1892. second edition, 8vo., red cloth, frontispiece, illustrations, very good, tight copy, all editions rare. Buckingham Books March 2015 - 26480 2015 $750

Freeman, Lucy *The Why Report, A Book of 45 Interviews with Psychiatrists.* Purchase: Arthur Bernhard, 1964. First edition, 602 pages, fine in tissue dust jacket. Beasley Books 2013 - 2015 $45

Freeman, R. Austin *The Case of Oscar Brodski.* New York: Detective Story Book, 1923. First separate edition, spine and corners worn, otherwise very good without dust jacket. Mordida Books March 2015 - 000812 2015 $75

Freeman, R. Austin *The Cat's Eye.* Dodd Mead and Co., 1927. First US edition, former owner's inked name on front pastedown sheet but completely covered by dust jacket flap, else near fine in jacket with two tiny closed tears to top and bottom edges, rear cover, attractive copy. Buckingham Books March 2015 - 38243 2015 $850

Freeman, R. Austin *For the Defense: Dr. Thorndyke.* New York: Dodd Mead, 1934. First American edition, very good, inscription on front endpaper, otherwise fine in very good dust jacket with restoration at top of spine. Mordida Books March 2015 - 000808 2015 $175

Freeman, R. Austin *Mr. Pottermack's Oversight.* New York: Dodd Mead, 1930. First American edition, fine, name and date on front endpaper, else fine in very fine, as new dust jacket. Mordida Books March 2015 - 000805 2015 $400

Freeman, R. Austin *Mr. Pottermack's Oversight.* New York: Dodd Mead, 1930. First American edition, spine slightly faded, otherwise very good in dust jacket with nicked and frayed spine ends, chip on back panel and couple of short closed tears. Mordida Books March 2015 - 000811 2015 $150

Freeman, R. Austin *The Penrose Mystery.* New York: Dodd Mead & Co., 1936. First US edition, very good in bright dust jacket with one small closed tear to top edge of front panel. Buckingham Books March 2015 - 11863 2015 $385

Freeman, R. Austin *The Red Thumb Mark.* New York: Dodd, Mead, 1924. First printing of this edition, fine, bight copy in equally fine dust jacket, from the collection of Duke Collier. Royal Books 36 - 178 2015 $1500

Freeman, R. Austin *A Savant's Vendetta.* London: Pearson, 1920. First English edition, name on front endpaper, bookseller's label on front pastedown and covers faded, otherwise very good in dust jacket with internal tape mends, faded spine, several closed tears, chip on front panel and at top of spine. Mordida Books March 2015 - 000809 2015 $1350

Freeman, R. Austin *The Surprising Experiences of Mr. Shuttlebury Cobb.* London: Hodder & Stoughton, 1927. First edition, page edges foxed and scattered internal foxing, otherwise very good, tight clean copy without dust jacket. Mordida Books March 2015 - 009883 2015 $150

Freeman, R. Austin *The Uttermost Farthing.* Philadelphia: Winston, 1914. First edition, near fine, spine slightly soiled, otherwise near fine, red pictorial cloth covered boards with gold stamped titles. Mordida Books March 2015 - 009882 2015 $150

Freeman, R. Austin *The Uttermost Farthing.* Philadelphia: Winston, 1914. First edition, precedes English edition, fine without dust jacket. Mordida Books March 2015 - 000807 2015 $300

Freeman's Address to the North Americans, proving that Their Present Embarrassments are Owning to Their Federal Union... N.P.: 1846? First edition, 8vo., 29 pages, uncut, modern wrappers. M & S Rare Books, Inc. 97 - 245 2015 $400

Freemantle, Brian *Charlie Muffin's Uncle Sam.* London: Cape, 1980. First edition, very fine in dust jacket. Mordida Books March 2015 - 000820 2015 $75

Freemantle, Brian *The Inscrutable Charlie Muffin.* London: Cape, 1979. First edition, very fine in dust jacket. Mordida Books March 2015 - 000821 2015 $75

Freemantle, Brian *The Man Who Wanted tomorrow.* Jonathan Cape, 1975. First edition, former owner's inked name on flyleaf, else fin in dust jacket. Buckingham Books March 2015 - 36652 2015 $225

Frees, Harry *Circus Day at Catnip Center.* Chicago: Manning, 1932. 4to., stiff pictorial card covers, owner name on top edge of cover, else very good+, photo illustrations, scarce. Aleph-bet Books, Inc. 109 - 351 2015 $250

Freiligrath-Kroeker, Kate *Alice through the Looking Glass and Other Fairy Plays for Children.* London: Swan Sonnenschein, n.d. circa, 1883. 8vo., brown cloth stamped in gold and black with pictorial scene of Alice, all edges gilt, binding has light soil, very good+, engraved frontispiece signed by Elta, quite scarce.   Aleph-bet Books, Inc.   109 - 86   2015 $500

Freind, John *Emmenologia in Qua Fluuxus Muliebris Menstrui.* Paris: Apud Guillelmum Cavelier Filium, 1727. Eighth edition?, 12mo., contemporary mottled calf with gilt spine, unobtrusive renewal of headcaps and corners.   Second Life Books Inc.   189 - 290   2015 $600

Freind, John *Emmenologia.* London: printed for T. Cox, 1752. Second edition, handsomely bound by Star Bookworks in full modern brown calf with gilt stamped decorations to boards and spine, raised spine bands and red title label, interior pages have waterstaining to first several pages and some foxing and aging throughout, margin cut from endpaper, several ink ownership signatures of Littleton Weatherly, dated 1817, other signatures and stamp to titlepage, very good.   The Kelmscott Bookshop   11 - 20   2015 $400

Freke, John *The History of Insipids, a Lampoon...* London: printed and sold by H. Hills, 1709. 8vo., disbound, good, this with 6 type flowers on titlepage as opposed to 14 in slightly earlier printing, titlepage loose, otherwise good.   C. R. Johnson   Foxon R-Z - 1220r-z   2015 $77

French, Gerald *When Steam Was King. Railroads of the Central Mother Lode Region of California.* Petaluma: Eureka Pub., 2005. First edition, signed by author, quarto, profusely illustrated with historic photos, maps, route maps, green pictorial boards, very fine, bright.   Argonaut Book Shop   Holiday Season 2014 - 93   2015 $95

French, John *The Art of Distillation; or a Treatise of the Choicest Spagyrical Preparations, Experiments and Curiosities Performed by Way of Distillation.* London: printed by E. Cotes for T. Williams at the Bible in Little Britain, 1664. Third edition, 16mo., numerous woodcuts, title and first two leaves and last two leaves mounted with loss to borders and bit of text, leaves uniformly toned, pages 87-88 with later repair at fore-edge and bottom border, newer full calf, red leather spine label, gilt, very good.   Argonaut Book Shop   Holiday Season 2014 - 94   2015 $1250

French, Nicci *Killing My Softly.* London: Michael Joseph, 1999. First edition, very fine in dust jacket.   Mordida Books   March 2015 - 002446   2015 $85

French, Nicci *The Memory Game.* London: Heinemann, 1997. First edition, very fine in dust jacket.   Mordida Books   March 2015 - 003086   2015 $85

French, Tana *In the Woods.* New York: Viking, 2007. First American edition, very fine in dust jacket.   Mordida Books   March 2015 - 012591   2015 $85

Freud, Anna *Infants without Families.* New York: IUP, 1944. First edition, fine in near fine dust jacket with few short tears.   Beasley Books   2013 - 2015 $45

Freud, Sigmund   1856-1939 *Eine Teufelsneurose Im 17 Jahrhundert.* Leipzig: IPV, 1924. First edition, gray wrappers, near fine with one roughly opened page, institutional library stamps and pocket.   Beasley Books   2013 - 2015 $150

Freud, Sigmund   1856-1939 *Gesammelte Schriften.* Vienna IPV: 1925. First printings, 11 volumes, volume V has one hinge point, very tender joints, includes the uniform Volume XII containing papers from 1928-1933.   Beasley Books   2013 - 2015 $1200

Freud, Sigmund   1856-1939 *Aus der Geschichte Einer Infantilen Neurose.* Leipzig: Internationaler Psychoanalytischer Verlag, 1924. First edition, hardcover, browned and fragile, spine reattached, otherwise very good+ in gray paper covered boards.   Beasley Books   2013 - 2015 $45

Freud, Sigmund   1856-1939 *The Origins of Psychoanalysis, Letters to Wilhelm Fliess...* New York: Basic Books, 1954. First edition, fine but for small bumps at head of boards, remarkably fresh dust jacket with few tiny chips.   Beasley Books   2013 - 2015 $45

Freud, Sigmund   1856-1939 *Zur Einfuhrung des Narzissmus.* Vienna: IPV, 1924. First edition, very good, front joint just starting.   Beasley Books   2013 - 2015 $125

Freud, Sigmund   1856-1939 *Zur Geschichte Der Psychoanalytischen Bewegung.* Leipzig: Internationler Psychoanalytischer Verlag, 1924. First German edition, gray paper covered boards, good to very good with chipping to spine, little staining thre, pencilling on early prelims.   Beasley Books   2013 - 2015 $45

Freud, Tom Seidmann *Play Primer.* Racine: Whitman, 1932. Unauthorized American edition, 4to., flexible pictorial card covers, near fine, illustrations by author with simple black and white pictures, rare.   Aleph-Bet Books, Inc.   108 - 195   2015 $1350

Freud, Tom Seidmann *Das Zauberboot.* Berlin: Herbert Stuffer, 1929. First edition, 4to., cloth backed pictorial boards, covers slightly dusty, else fine and complete, rare moveable book, with a variety of moveable pages, there is also a grid with cut-outs that enables the reader to develop 4 different stories from one page. Aleph-bet Books, Inc. 109 - 184   2015 $2000

Friede, Marcia *New Guinea Art: Masterpieces from the Jolika Collection of Marcia and John Friede.* San Francisco: Fine Arts Museum, 2005. First edition, 2 volumes, large 4to., original black cloth lettered silver on spine, illustrations in color and black and white, large folding map, fine in fine dust jacket and slipcase. Any Amount of Books 2015 - C2022   2015   £225

Friedman, Isaac Kahn *Poor People: a Novel.* Boston and New York: Houghton Mifflin, 1900. First edition, 8vo., original pictorial grey cloth, black lettering, fine. The Brick Row Book Shop   Miscellany 67 - 7   2015 $225

Friedman, Kinky *Musical Chairs.* New York: Morrow, 1991. First edition, fine in dust jacket. Mordida Books March 2015 - 011077   2015 $100

Friedman, Milton *Two Lucky People.* Chicago: University of Chicago, 1998. Stated first edition, signed and inscribed by Milton and Rose Friedman, fine in fine dust jacket, 8vo. By the Book, L. C.   Special List 10 - 13   2015 $1000

Friedman, Richard *15 Chicago Poets.* Chicago: Yellow Press, 1976. First edition, 8vo., illustrations, original boards, fine in lightly rubbed dust jacket with one short closed tear, review copy with publisher's slip laid in, signed by Ted Berrigan on page 3 and dated "London 1973". James S. Jaffe Rare Books   Many Happy Returns - 387 2015 $150

Friedman, William F. *The Shakespearean Ciphers Examined: an Analysis of Cryptographic Systems...* Cambridge: Cambridge University Press, 1957. First edition, 8vo., 10 plates, 17 figures, hardback, ownership signature of Martin Pares, with few pages of notes by him loosely inserted, signed presentation to Pares from author, very good+ in like dust jacket with very slight edgewear. Any Amount of Books   March 2015 - A78928   2015   £350

Friend, John *The Tryal and Condemnation of Sir John Friend, Knight, for Conspiring to Raise Rebellion in These Kingdoms.* London: printed for Barbazon Aylmer, 1696. First edition, folio, wanting initial imprimatur leaf, edges little browned, bound fairly recent in marbled boards, spine labelled and lettered, good copy. John Drury Rare Books March 2015 - 23940   2015   £306

Friends of the Land *The Land.* Washington: 1941. Volume 1 numbers 1-4, 412 pages, illustrations, 4 issued bound in hardcover, exterior quite soiled (smoked?), interior good. Dumont Maps & Books of the West   131 - 50 2015 $65

Frieze, Jacob *A Concise History of the Efforts to obtain an Extension of Suffrage in Rhode Island from the year 1811 to 1842.* Providence: Benjamin F. Moore, 1842. First edition, small 8vo., paper over boards, donor's presentation to fly-leaf, some foxing, cover little worn at edges, otherwise very good, tight copy. Second Life Books Inc.   190 - 79   2015 $225

Frigge, Karli *Marbled Landscapes.* Buren: Frits Knuf, 1988. First edition, limited to 99 numbered copies signed by author, oblong 8vo., vellum spine stamped in gold, parchment backed marbled covered boards, paper cover label, 12 plates with mounted marbled paper specimens. Oak Knoll Books   306 - 278   2015 $1850

Frigge, Karli *Marbled Papers.* Buren: Frits Knuf, 1985. Limited to only 200 numbered copies signed by Frigge, 33 actual specimens, oblong 4to., full calf in harness leather binding with laced leather straps after Dutch style of binding, cardboard slipcase, 22 pages of text in English and Dutch, 33 mounted samples of marbled paper. Oak Knoll Books 306 - 279   2015 $2250

Frisbie, W. A. *ABC Mother Goose.* Chicago: Rand McNally, 1905. Large 4to., tan pictorial cloth, fine, clean copy, bold full color illustrations on every page by Bart, super copy, rarely found so clean. Aleph-bet Books, Inc. 109 - 7   2015 $600

Frith, Henry *UNAC the Indian: a Tale of Central America.* London and New York: George Routledge and Sons, 1884. First edition, octavo, inserted frontispiece, chromolithograph color illustration and 21 black and white illustrations in text, original pictorial green bevel edged cloth, front and spine panels stamped in gold, brown and dark green, rear panel stamped in blind. L. W. Currey, Inc.   Boy's Adventure Fiction 2015 - 21   2015 $375

Frohne, Michael *Subconscious-lee. 35 Years of Records and Tapes. The Lee Konitz Discography.* Freiburg: Jazzrealities, 1983. First edition, wrappers, 4to., 132 pages, near fine with slight bump at top edge. Beasley Books   2013 - 2015 $45

From a Lover's Garden: More Rondeaux and Other Verses of Boyhood. London: privately printed, 1924. First edition, limited to 200 copies, small 8vo., original green boards, paper labels to spine and cover, photo frontispiece, very slight mottling to green boards, dust jacket, very good+. Any Amount of Books   2015 - A73076   2015   £160

From the Bottom Up. N.P.: n.d. published by Mutual Broadcasting Co., n.d. circa, 1940. (based upon mention of 1940 world Series), folio, pictorial boards, edges and covers rubbed, some else tight and very good+, 4 large pop-ups, illustrations by Scott Johnston, rare.   Aleph-bet Books, Inc. 109 - 376   2015 $2000

Frome, David   *The Hammersmith Murders.*   Doubleday Doran & Co., 1930. First edition, neat inked non-authorial gift inscription on front flyleaf, else fine, bright copy in price clipped dust jacket with small rubs to front panel and tiny chip to bottom edge of front cover.   Buckingham Books March 2015 - 37227   2015 $1250

Frost, Joseph   *A List of the Books, with Part of Their Title Pages and the Price of Each Book of the Third and last Testament of the Only God, Our Lord Jesus Christ.* London: printed by R Feeny, 1843. First edition, 8vo., 16 pages, original printed wrappers, pen trial on upper wrapper, else fine, fresh copy, scarce.   John Drury Rare Books 2015 - 21216   2015 $133

Frost, Joseph   *The Testament of the Twelve Patriarchs, the Sons of Jacob.*   London: reprinted for James Frost and Joseph Frost and Isaac Frost from a copy printed at London for the Company of Stationers, printed by R. Feeny, 1837. Reprint of 1693 edition, 8vo. original boards, printed spine label, entirely unopened and uncut, fine, fresh copy.   John Drury Rare Books   2015 - 21221   2015 $133

Frost, Robert Lee   1874-1963   *A Boy's Will.*   London: David Nutt, 1913. First edition, first issue in earliest binding, of approximately 1000 copies of this edition, less than 350 copies were issued by Nutt, small 8vo., original bronzed brown pebbled cloth, front cover lettered gilt, spine very slightly faded, extremities bit rubbed, otherwise fine, half morocco slipcase.   James S. Jaffe Rare Books   Modern American Poetry - 85   2015 $12,500

Frost, Robert Lee   1874-1963   *A Boy's Will.*   London: David Nutt, 1913. First edition, first printing in Crane's "A" binding, signed and inscribed by Frost to a former student (Emma Pearl Goldsmith) one month after publication, very good with few light spots of minor soiling to otherwise clean boards, edges with light rubbing, some toning to spine, spine head touch frayed, spine foot showing light signs of starting inside front cover, otherwise sturdy and intact spine, minor toning to endpapers, Goldsmith's inscription, former owner's pencil inscription to front free endpaper, annotations from multiple owners throughout, bright and fresh pages, attractive copy, housed in custom quarter leather box.   B & B Rare Books, Ltd.   2015 - 2015 $27,500

Frost, Robert Lee   1874-1963   *A Boy's Will.*   London: David Nutt, 1923. Second issue, binding D, 8vo., original printed cream line laid paper wrappers, one of 716 copies out of a total edition of 1000, this one of the 686 with "Printed in Great Britain" rubber stamped on copyright page, although not called for, this copy signed by author, fine.   James S. Jaffe Rare Books   Modern American Poetry - 86   2015 $3500

Frost, Robert Lee   1874-1963   *A Boy's Will.*   New York: Henry Holt, 1934. First edition thus, reissue with minor changes from previous editions, 8vo., original cloth, dust jacket, inscribed by author for Marion Sheridan.   James S. Jaffe Rare Books   Modern American Poetry - 96   2015 $2500

Frost, Robert Lee   1874-1963   *From Snow to Snow.* New York: Henry Holt, 1936. Second edition, small 8vo., facsimile, original light brown cloth, essentially first hardcover trade edition following the privately printed pamphlet issue that was limited to 300 copies, binding B according to Crane, 'about 1200 sets of sheets' from privately printed issue were so bound.   James S. Jaffe Rare Books   Modern American Poetry - 98   2015 $100

Frost, Robert Lee   1874-1963   *A Further Range. Book Six.*   New York: Henry Holt & Co., 1916. First edition, one of 803 specially printed, bound and numbered copies signed by Frost, 8vo., original cloth, printed leather spine label, slipcase, fine.   James S. Jaffe Rare Books   Modern American Poetry - 99   2015 $750

Frost, Robert Lee   1874-1963   *The Gold Hesperidee.* Corland: Bibliophile Press, 1935. First edition, first state, one of only 37 copies with "A" on copyright page and with second line from bottom on page 7 consisting of 9 words, small 8vo., original illustrated wrappers, stitched as issued, very fine.   James S. Jaffe Rare Books   Modern American Poetry - 97   2015 $450

Frost, Robert Lee   1874-1963   *In the Clearing.*   New York: Holt, Rinehart and Wisnton, 1962. First edition, slightly rubbed bottom of boards, near fine in like dust jacket with little rubbing, bookplate of author Alan Pryce-Jones. Between the Covers Rare Books, Inc.   187 - 102   2015 $125

Frost, Robert Lee   1874-1963   *The Lone Striker.*   New York: Alfred A. Knopf, 1933. Limited to 2000 copies, 12mo., original cream stitched illustrated wrappers, illustrations by W. A Dwiggins, signed by author, booklabel.   James S. Jaffe Rare Books   Modern American Poetry - 95   2015 $1500

Frost, Robert Lee 1874-1963 *A Masque of Mercy.* New York: Henry Holt and Co., 1947. First edition, limited to 751 copies printed at the Spiral Press and signed by author, tall 8vo., original cloth backed boards, slipcase, very fine. James S. Jaffe Rare Books   Modern American Poetry - 103   2015 $750

Frost, Robert Lee 1874-1963 *A Masque of Reason.* New York: Henry Holt, 1945. First edition, trade issue, about fine, mildly chipped, very good dust jacket with slight nicking, inscribed by author for friend Daniel Smythe, Oct. 30 1945 Cambridge.   Between the Covers Rare Books, Inc.   187 - 101   2015 $475

Frost, Robert Lee 1874-1963 *A Masque of Reason.* New York: Henry Holt and Co., 1945. First edition, limited to 800 numbered copies, printed at the Spiral Press and signed by Frost, tall 8vo., original cloth backed boards, publisher's slipcase, very fine.   James S. Jaffe Rare Books   Modern American Poetry - 101   2015 $750

Frost, Robert Lee 1874-1963 *Mountain Interval.* New York: Henry Holt & Co., 1916. First edition, first sate with uncorrected readings on pages 88 and 93, one of 4000 copies, including both states of the edition, 8vo., original blue cloth, dust jacket, ownership inscription on front fre endpaper and there's largely closed and wrinkled tear in fore-edge of titlepage.   James S. Jaffe Rare Books   Modern American Poetry - 90   2015 $2500

Frost, Robert Lee 1874-1963 *New Hampshire. A Poem with Notes and Grace Notes.* New York: Henry Holt & Co., 1923. First edition, one of 350 numbered copies signed by author, large 8vo., original gilt decorated black cloth, top edge gilt, bookplate, 2 small newsprint clippings affixed to colophon page offset to facing leaf, otherwise very good. James S. Jaffe Rare Books   Modern American Poetry - 91   2015 $1500

Frost, Robert Lee 1874-1963 *New Hampshire.* New York: Henry Holt, 1923. First edition, limited to 350 copies signed by Frost, this copy additionally inscribed by Frost to his friend and Allegheny College English professor, Stanley Swartley, woodcuts by J. J. Lankes, excellent copy with only very minor rubbing to extremities.   B & B Rare Books, Ltd.   234 - 38   2015 $3500

Frost, Robert Lee 1874-1963 *North of Boston.* New York: Henry Holt, 1914. First edition, American issue, 8vo., original brown cloth backed drab gray brown boards with printed labels on spine and cover, binding B, one of 150 copies, very fine.   James S. Jaffe Rare Books   Modern American Poetry - 89   2015 $4500

Frost, Robert Lee 1874-1963 *North of Boston.* London: David Nutt, 1914. First edition, binding A, one of 350 copies in original coarse green linen, out of a total of 1000 copies, 8vo., inscribed twice by poet in 1941 and in 1948, contemporary owner's neat initials (AWH) and date (1915) on endpapers, spine slightly darkened, several pages smudged, otherwise fine.   James S. Jaffe Rare Books   Modern American Poetry - 87   2015 $7500

Frost, Robert Lee 1874-1963 *North of Boston.* London: David Nutt, 1914. First edition, binding A, one of 350 copies in original coarse green linen, out of a total edition of 1000 copies, 8vo., fine, preserved in black cloth slipcase with chemise, presentation copy inscribed by author for Earle Bernheimer.   James S. Jaffe Rare Books   Modern American Poetry - 88   2015 $12,500

Frost, Robert Lee 1874-1963 *Selected Poems.* New York: Henry Holt, 1923. First edition, one of 1025 copies, 8vo., dark green cloth backed patterned boards, dust jacket, presentation copy inscribed by author for friend Llewellyn Jones, beautiful copy, virtually as new in rare dust jacket which is splitting at one of the folds, in half morocco slipcase.   James S. Jaffe Rare Books   Modern American Poetry - 92   2015 $4500

Frost, Robert Lee 1874-1963 *Selected Poems.* New York: Henry Holt, 1928. First expanded edition, 8vo., original cloth backed boards, fine in very slightly worn and torn dust jacket, signed by author.   James S. Jaffe Rare Books   Modern American Poetry - 93   2015 $2500

Frost, Robert Lee 1874-1963 *Complete Poems of Robert Frost.* New York: Henry Holt and Co., 1949. First edition, thick 8vo. portrait original buckram, glassine dust jacket, publisher's slipcase, beautiful copy, glassine with few small chips and creases.   James S. Jaffe Rare Books   Modern American Poetry - 105   2015 $2500

Frost, Robert Lee 1874-1963 *The Complete Poems of Robert Frost.* New York: Limited Editions Club, 1950. Limited to 1500 copies, signed by Frost and book designer, Bruce Rogers and artist, Thomas Nason, quarto, original blue cloth, original marbled slipcase, 2 volumes, books fine, slipcase with toning to spine and wear to extremities, as usual, with LEC newsletter laid in, beautiful copy, rare in such good condition.   Manhattan Rare Book Company   Literature 2014 - 2015 $2850

Frost, Robert Lee 1874-1963 *Steeple Bush.* New York: Henry Holt, 1947. First edition, limited to 751 copies printed at the Spiral Press and signed by author, tall 8vo., original cloth, glassine dust jacket, very fine.   James S. Jaffe Rare Books   Modern American Poetry - 104   2015 $750

Frost, Robert Lee 1874-1963 *West-Running Brook.* New York: Henry Holt, 1928. First edition, first issue (no statement of "First Edition" on copyright page), 8vo., illustrations by J. J. Lankes, original cloth backed boards, inscribed by author in 1929, fine.   James S. Jaffe Rare Books   Modern American Poetry - 94   2015 $1500

Frost, Robert Lee 1874-1963 *A Witness Tree.* New York: Henry Holt, 1942. First edition, Limited to 735 copies, printed at the Spiral Press and signed by author, tall 8vo., frontispiece, original cloth backed paste paper boards, fine, slipcase.   James S. Jaffe Rare Books   Modern American Poetry - 100   2015 $750

Fry, Edmund *Pantographia; Containing Accurate Copies of All the Known Alphabets in the World...* London: John and Arthur Arch et al, 1799. First edition, 8vo. recased with most of original cloth preserved, newer leather spine label, finely printed letterpress, signed and dated "William Tooke 1799:, his name crossed out and "E. West" is written under it, book recased, preserving original cloth sides and spine and all laid down on newer cloth with leather spine label.   Oak Knoll Books   Special Catalogue 24 - 16   2015 $850

Fry, Elizabeth *Memoir of the Life of Elizabeth Fry with Extracts from her Journal and Letters.* London: John Hatchard and Son, 1848. Second edition, 2 volumes, half titles, frontispieces, errata slip volume II, some slight foxing in prelims, uncut in original purple cloth, borders in blind, spines little faded, bookplates of W. M. Mason, very good.   Jarndyce Antiquarian Booksellers   CCXI - 120   2015   £125

Fry, Elizabeth *Observations on the Visiting, Superintendence, and Government of Female Prisoners.* London: John and Arthur Arch and W. Wilkin Norwich, 1827. First edition, 12mo., contemporary red straight grain morocco, sides panelled gilt, spine fully gilt with raised bands, joints and extremities rubbed, else handsome copy, all edges gilt, from the library of Prince George, Duke of Cambridge, Earl of Tipperary, Baron Culloden (1850-1904) with his posthumous bookplate Dec. 1904, and subsequent armorial bookplate of Wigan Free Public Library with blindstamp at foot of titlepage, ink stamp on blank verso and further blindstamp on final leaf, uncommon, particularly pleasing copy.   John Drury Rare Books   2015 - 25151   2015 $1136

Fry, Frederick Morris *An Illustrated Catalogue of Silver Plate of the Worshipful Company of Merchant Taylors.* London: printed for private circulation by Burrup Mathieson & Co., 1929. First edition thus, 4to., 47 plates, full navy blue leather with gilt spine and gilt coat of arms on front board, illustrations, quite scarce, very good, slight rubbing at hinges and edges with few marks, bookplate and ownership signature on first blank page of Jean Schofield (1922-1988).   Any Amount of Books   2015 - C14049   2015   £225

Fry, Joseph Storrs *An Essay on the Construction of Wheel Carriages as they Affect both the Roads and the Horses.* London: J. and A. Arch., Baldwin & Co. and Harding and T. J. Manchee, Bristol, 1820. First edition, 8vo., ornamental dedication leaf, few woodcuts in text, signs of erasure on blank verso of title with small brown mark showing on recto, generally very good, crisp copy, bound in boards sometime in 20th century, spine lettered.   John Drury Rare Books   March 2015 - 25452   2015 $656

Fryer, Jane Eayre *The Mary Frances Cook Book of Adventures Among the Kitchen People.* Philadelphia: John C. Winston, 1912. 4to., blue cloth, pictorial paste-on, 175 pages, cover plate worn in corner, else very good+, illustrations by Jane Allen Boyer with color frontispiece plus profusion of color and line illustrations by Margaret Hays.   Aleph-Bet Books, Inc.   108 - 198   2015 $450

Fryer, Jane Eayre *The Mary Frances First Aid Book.* Philadelphia: Winston, 1916. 4to., blue cloth, pictorial paste-on, some cover rubbing, very good.   Aleph-bet Books, Inc.   109 - 186   2015 $275

Fryer, Jane Eayre *The Mary Frances Housekeeper: Adventures Among the Doll People.* Philadelphia: Winston, 1914. 4to., cloth, pictorial paste-on, few minor margin mends, else fine, silhouettes by Julia Greene, frontispiece by Albert Mowitz, 9 paper dolls, rare in complete condition.   Aleph-Bet Books, Inc.   108 - 197   2015 $800

Fryer, Michael *The Trial and Life of Eugene Aram: Several of His Letters and Poems and His Plan and Specimens of an Anglo-Celtic Lexicon...* Richmond: printed by and for M. Bell, 1832. 8vo., frontispiece, half title, final postscript leaf, well bound in early 20th century sheep over marbled boards, spine lettered gilt, very good, crisp copy.   John Drury Rare Books   2015 - 21758   2015 $106

Fuchs, Leonhart *The Great Herbal of Leonhart Fuchs: De Historia Stripiu Commentarii Insignes. 1542...* Stanford: Stanford University Press, 1999. First edition thus, 2 volumes, black and white photographic facsimile, 2 volumes uniformly browned in off white linen covered boards with brown cloth spines and black and gilt spine labels, burgundy endpapers, housed in matching line covered slipcase, both volumes fine with light rubbing to spine labels, near fine slipcase with very slight shelfwear only.   Any Amount of Books   2015 - A89025   2015   £180

Fuentes, Carlos *Terra Nostra.* New York: Farrar Straus and Giroux, 1976. First American edition, fine in very good dust jacket with some rubbing and light wear to spinal extremities and edges of panel, inscribed by author fellow author Barry Beckham.   Between the Covers Rare Books, Inc.   187 - 104   2015 $175

Fuentes, Carlos *Where the Air is Clear.* New York: Ivan Obolensky, 1960. First edition, fine in very lightly used, price clipped dust jacket with spine bit sunned, this copy inscribed by author, laid in is mimeographed announcement about a Fuentes appearance where he will read in English from his novel-in-progress 'Christopher Unborn' folded once, very good+. Beasley Books 2013 - 2015 $125

Fuentes, Manual *Memorias de los Vireyes que han Gobernado el Peru Duranate el Tiempo del Coloniaje Espanol.* Lima: Libreria Central de Feilipe Bailly, 1859. First edition, 6 volumes one folding map, 12 plates, 4to., original dark brown pebbled cloth, ruled in blind, gilt titles on spine, and front board with armorial device, gift copy with note on official letterhead dated 1867 tipped in from Felipe Masias, Director of Administration of the Ministerio de Hacienda and later Finance Minister of Peru, good or better, boards rubbed, few joints split but quite solid, corners heavily worn, spines chipped, especially at heads with repairs, cloth separating from boards on one volume, free endpapers heavily offset, pencil notations in last volume, otherwise contents clean and very good, plates sharp and map fine but for tiny marginal tear along crease line. Kaaterskill Books 19 - 117 2015 $600

Fugger, Wolffgang *Wolffgang Fugger's Handwriting Manual Entitled a Practical and well Grounded Formulary for Divers Fair Hands...* London: Lion and Unicorn Press, 1955. Limited to 200 numbered copies, first book from the press, oblong small 8vo., boards, slipcase faded and foxed, front free endpaper and pastedown foxed, prospectus loosely inserted, scarce. Oak Knoll Books Special Catalogue 24 - 17 2015 $195

Fukase, Masahisa *The Soltidue of Ravena.* San Francisco: Bedford Arts, 1991. First U. S. edition, softcover, very near fine in French wrappers, lovely copy, uncommon. Jeff Hirsch Books E-62 Holiday List 2014 - 13 2015 $450

A Full and Genuine History of the Inhuman and Unparallel'd Murders of Mr. William Galley, a Custom-House Officer at the Port of Southampton and Mr. Daniel Chater, a Shoemaker at Fordingbridge in Hampshire by Fourteen Notorious Smugglers... London: printed for and sold by G. Robinson, J. Russell at Guildford, T. Ford at Southampton..., 1779. Early edition, 12mo., 7 engraved plates, with generally pretty minor dust marking or soiling, contemporary calf, neatly and sympathetically rebacked, with gilt lines and raised bands and original lettering piece, good, perhaps very good copy, very scarce. John Drury Rare Books 2015 - 25115 2015 $2185

Fullarton, William *A Letter, Addressed to the Right Hon. Lord Carrington.* London: J.. Debrett, 1801. First edition, half title, rebound in mid 20th century cloth backed boards, very good. John Drury Rare Books 2015 - 14101 2015 $177

Fuller, Henry C. *Adventures of Bill Longley.* printed for the author by Baker Printing Co., n.d. circa, 1820. First edition, 8vo., stiff printed wrappers, frontispiece, illustrations, very scarce, fine. Buckingham Books March 2015 - 23092 2015 $350

The Funny Little Darkies. New York: McLoughlin Bros. circa, 1870. 4to., pictorial wrappers, inconspicuous spine strengthening and few minor margin mends, else near fine, printed on one side of paper and illustrated with 6 full page brightly colored lithographs that have to be seen to believed, wonderful black and white illustrations, rare. Aleph-bet Books, Inc. 109 - 56 2015 $1500

Furer-Haimendorf, Christoph *The Aboriginal Tribes of Hyderabad.* London: Macmillan & Co., First edition, 4to., original green cloth, lettered gilt at spines, illustrations, 10 maps, clean, very good+ in serviceable, near very good dust jackets, volume one has remains of dust jacket included. Any Amount of Books March 2015 - C6971 2015 £425

Furness, Horace Howard *"The Gloss of Youth:" an Imaginary Episode in the Lives of William Shakespeare and John Fletcher.* Philadelphia: J. B. Lippincott, 1920. First edition, quarter cloth a decorated paper covered boards with applied printed title label, corners rubbed, very good, without dust jacket, bookplate of Eva Le Gallienne. Between the Covers Rare Books, Inc. 187 - 105 2015 $100

Furness, William Henry *The Home-Life of Boreno Head-Hunters: its Festivals and Folk-Lore.* Philadelphia: J. B. Lippincott, 1902. First edition, large 8vo., original red cloth lettered gilt on spine and cover and gilt decorated on cover, 88 plates, slight rubbing at hinges and spine ends, corners very slightly bumped, stitching slightly weak, otherwise clean, very good, neat name onf ront endpaper. Any Amount of Books 2015 - C1897 2015 £750

Furst, Alan *The Caribbean Account.* New York: Delacorte Press, 1981. First edition, spine ends tapped, else fine in fine dust jacket, from the collection of Duke Collier. Royal Books 36 - 176 2015 $500

Furst, Alan *The Caribbean Account.* London: Quartet Quime, 1983. First UK edition, fine in fine dust jacket. Beasley Books 2013 - 2015 $150

Furst, Alan *The Caribbean Account.* London: Quartet, 1983. First English edition, fine in dust jacket. Mordida Books March 2015 - 008525 2015 $150

Furst, Alan *Dark Star.* Boston: Houghton Mifflin, 1991. First edition, fine and unread in fine dust jacket, from the collection of Duke Collier. Royal Books 36 - 177 2015 $400

Furst, Alan *Night Soldiers.* Boston: Houghton Mifflin, 1988. First edition, fine and unread in fine dust jacket, from the collection of Duke Collier.   Royal Books   36 - 174   2015 $500

Furst, Alan *The Paris Drop.* Garden City: Doubleday, 1980. First edition, fine in about fine dust jacket, jacket has faintest crease at heel, else lovely, uncommon second book, from the collection of Duke Collier.   Royal Books   36 - 173   2015 $850

Furst, Alan *Shadow Trade.* New York: Delacorte, 1983. First edition, signed by author, fine in near fine dust jacket, touch of rubbing to jacket corners, one of the usual fading, from the collection of Duke Collier.   Royal Books   36 - 175   2015 $500

Furst, Alan *Your Day in the Barrel.* New York: Atheneum, 1976. First edition, fine in fine dust jacket, lengthily inscribed to Joan and Morris Alhadeff, from the collection of Duke Collier. Royal Books   36 - 172   2015 $1500

Fuseli, Henry *Remarks on the Writings and Conduct of J. J. Rousseau.* London: printed for T. Cadell, J. Johnson, Be. Davenport and J. Payne, 1767. First edition, 8vo., brown half calf period style by Philip Dusel, marbled paper boards, orange morocco label, gilt rules and lettering, frontispiece engraved by Charles Grignon after Fuseli, fine.   The Brick Row Book Shop   Miscellany 67 - 47   2015 $1500

G

Gabaldon, Diana *Drums of Autumn.* New York: Delacorte, 1997. First edition, inscribed and signed, fine book and dust jacket.   Stephen Lupack   March 2015 - 2015 $45

Gabor, Dennis *Diffraction Microscopy.* Research, 1951. Offprint, 8vo., original white wrappers, string tied with mild cover soil, signed by author.   By the Book, L. C.   Special List 10 - 57   2015 $160

Gabrielle, Roy *Rue Deschambault.* Paris: Flammarion, 1955. First edition, 8vo., wrappers, pages uncut and unopened, long presentation in French from Roy for M. Marks, spine very slightly toned, covers faintly foxed, pages browned, otherwise sound, clean very good or better.   Any Amount of Books   March 2015 - A98113   2015   £400

Gaddis, William *A Frolic of His Own.* New York: Poseidon Press, 1994. Advance copy, in the form of tape-bound 8 1/2 x 11 inch galleys, earliest issue of the novel, spine slant, handling apparent to covers, very good.   Ken Lopez, Bookseller   164 - 73   2015 $200

Gaer, Joseph *Bibliography of California Literature. Pre-Gold Rush Patrol.* San Francisco: SERA Project, California Library Research, circa, 1935. First edition, quarto, printed rectos only, mimeographed, later stiff wrappers, small gouge to upper edge of first leaf, else fine.   Argonaut Book Shop Holiday Season 2014 - 96   2015 $200

Gag, Wanda *The ABC Bunny.* New York: Coward McCann, 1933. Stated first edition, 4to., pictorial boards, fine in dust jacket with old tape repairs but not offensive, illustrations are original lithographs by Gag on paper especially made for this edition.   Aleph-bet Books, Inc.   109 - 187   2015 $2000

Gag, Wanda *The Funny Thing.* New York: Coward McCann, 1929. First edition, oblong 8vo., yellow pictorial boards, fine in very slightly soiled dust jacket, full page and in text black and white lithos.   Aleph-Bet Books, Inc.   108 - 200   2015 $600

Gag, Wanda *Millions of Cats.* New York: Coward McCann, 1928. First edition, first issue, oblong 4to., yellow pictorial boards, slightest bit of dusting, else fine in very good, lightly soiled dust jacket, slight fraying at spine ends, pictorial endpapers, black and white lithos.   Aleph-Bet Books, Inc.   108 - 199   2015 $2000

Gaiman, Neil *Adventures in the Dream Trade.* Framingham: The NESFA Press, 2002. First edition, one of 290 numbered copies signed by author and artist, Stephen Hickman.   John W. Knott, Bookseller   Selected New Arrivals Jan. 2015 - 17026   2015 $200

Gaiman, Neil *American Gods.* New York: William Morrow, an Imprint of Harper Collins, 2001. First edition, octavo, boards, one of 500 (un-numbered) signed copies.   John W. Knott, Bookseller   Selected New Arrivals Jan. 2015 - 17025   2015 $150

Gaiman, Neil *The Graveyard Book.* London: Bloomsbury, 2008. First edition, signed by author, dated "28 Oct. '08", fine in fine dust jacket.   Ed Smith Books   82 - 11   2015 $250

Gaines, Ernest J. *The Autobiography of Miss Jane Pittman.* New York: Dial, 1971. First printing, 8vo., paper over boards, clipping from book laid in, edges slightly soiled, otherwise nice copy in little scuffed nicked dust jacket. Second Life Books Inc.   190 - 80   2015 $300

Gaines, Ernest J. *Catherine Carmier.* New York: Atheneum, 1964. First edition, 8vo., paper over boards with cloth spine, very good, tight copy in little scuffed dust jacket (remnants of price sticker on rear dust jacket). Second Life Books Inc.   190 - 81   2015 $425

Gaines, Ernest J. *Catherine Carmier.* New York: Atheneum, 1964. First edition, very good+ with front hinge just starting, owner's name on pastedown, lightly used dust jacket with tiny chips at folds, inscribed by Gaines. Beasley Books   2013 - 2015 $500

Galassi, Peter *Friedlander.* New York: Museum of Modern Art, 2005. First edition, stout 4to. fine in fine dust jacket.   Beasley Books   2013 - 2015 $150

Gale, Leah *Nursery Songs.* New York: Simon & Schuster, 1942. First printing of Golden Book no. 7, blue cloth spine, owner name on endpaper, else near fine in nice dust jacket with slight faying at spine ends, illustrations in color by Corinne Malverne, rare in dust jacket.   Aleph-Bet Books, Inc.   108 - 213   2015 $875

Galien, Madame De Chateau-Thierry *Apologie Des Dames Appuyee sur L'Histoire.* Paris: Chez Didot, 1737. First edition, 12mo., lacks top one inch of front blank, names written in pencil, ink ownership signature on top of titlepage, contemporary full calf, spine gilt, some light water staining, very good, tight, clean copy, ornaments and initial letters. Second Life Books Inc.   189 - 80   2015 $800

Gallagher, Simon Felix *A Brief Reply to a Short Answer to a True Exposition of the Doctrine of the Catholic Church...* New York: printed for the author by Sherman & Pudney, 1815. First edition, disbound, 176 pages, foxing on titlepage, else very good or better, the copy of Bishop Henry Treadwell Onderdonk with his ownership signature twice. Between the Covers Rare Books, Inc.   187 - 106   2015 $300

Gallaudet, T. H. *An Address on Female Education, Delivered Nov. 21st 1827 at the opening of the Edifice Erected for the Accommodation of the Hartford Female Seminary.* Hartford: H. & F. J. Huntington, 1828. First edition, 8vo., 34 pages, removed, foxed.   M & S Rare Books, Inc.   97 - 100   2015 $150

Gallup, Carol *Poet's Home Companion.* N.P.: Carol Gallup, n.d. but, 1968. First edition, mimeographed sheets, stapled as issued, covers by George Schneeman, one of 100 copies, date June 11 1968 written in ink top of table of contents, covers soiled, contents very good, scarce.   James S. Jaffe Rare Books   Many Happy Returns - 388   2015 $500

Gallup, Dick *Above the Tree Line.* Bolinas: Big Sky, 1976. First edition, one fo 26 lettered copies, signed by author (out of a total of 750), very fine, large 8vo. original illustrated wrappers.   James S. Jaffe Rare Books   Many Happy Returns - 133   2015 $750

Gallup, Dick *The Bingo.* New York: Mother Press, 1966. Limited to 500 copies, 12mo., original wrappers by Joe Brainard, covers little browned, otherwise fine.   James S. Jaffe Rare Books   Many Happy Returns - 129   2015 $125

Gallup, Dick *Hinges. Poems.* New York: C Press, 1965. First edition, 4to., original illustrated wrappers, some light foxing, covers slightly tanned, otherwise fine.   James S. Jaffe Rare Books   Many Happy Returns - 127   2015 $250

Gallup, Dick *Plumbing the Depths of Folly: Poems, Conundrums and Statements.* Bolinas: Smithereens Press, 1983. First edition, one of 100 copies, 4to., original stapled wrappers, fine.   James S. Jaffe Rare Books   Many Happy Returns - 134   2015 $100

Gallup, Dick *Plumbing the Depths of Folly: Poems, Conundrums and Statements.* Bolinas: Smithereens Press, 1983. First edition, one of 10 numbered copies signed by Gallup out of an edition of 100 copies, this number 10, 4to., stamped wrappers, fine.   James S. Jaffe Rare Books   Many Happy Returns - 135   2015 $250

Gallup, Dick *Where I Hang My Hat.* New York: Harper & Row, 1970. First edition, large 8vo., original cloth and paper over boards, dust jacket design by George Schneeman, two small dents, one in each cover, that in front cover affecting first few pages of text and adjacent portion of dust jacket, otherwise fine, presentation inscribed by Gallup to fellow author Tom Veitch, with Gallup's accompanying ink drawing.   James S. Jaffe Rare Books   Many Happy Returns - 130   2015 $650

Galsworthy, John   1867-1933   *The White Monkey.* London: Heinemann, 1924. First edition, signed by author, moderate foxing to text block, offsetting to front flyleaf, very good in very good dust jacket (spine tanned with several small edge chips), quite uncommon.   Ken Lopez, Bookseller   164 - 74   2015 $375

Galt, John   1779-1838   *The Entail; or the Lairds of Grippy.* Edinburgh: Blackwood, London: Cadell, 1822. First edition, octavo, 3 volumes, original boards, recent sympathetic reback retaining original labels, covers rubbed at edges, very good set.   Peter Ellis, Bookseller   2014 - 08719   2015   £325

Galton, Arthur *Two Essays Upon Matthew Arnold with Some of His Letters to the Author.* London: Elkin Mathews, 1897. Uncut in original blue boards, printed cloth spine, slightly marked and dusted, from the library of Geoffrey & Kathleen Tillotson.   Jarndyce Antiquarian Booksellers   CCVII - 65   2015   £25

Gamel, Thomas W. *Life of Thomas W. Gamel.* privately printed, n.d. circa, 1932. First edition, 8vo., printed wrappers, rare.   Buckingham Books   March 2015 - 23539   2015 $275

Gamow, George *Constitution of Atomic Nuclei and Radioactivity.* Oxford: Clarendon Press, 1931. First edition, near fine, mild toning to endpapers, in very good+ dust jacket, with age toning, sun spine, mild edge wear, chips, rare first edition in dust jacket, 8vo., folding periodic table.   By the Book, L. C.   44 - 12   2015 $500

Gandarillas Y Guzman, Manuel Jose *Refutacion de la breve exposicion del S. D. Jose Maria Novoa ex Ministro de Estado en los Departmentos de Guerra y Marina.* Santiago de Chile: Imprenta de la Biblioteca, 1826. First edition, small 8vo., removed from a larger volume, very good, small chip to lower inner margin of titlepage, small duplicate release stamp on margin of last leaf.   Kaaterskill Books   19 - 60   2015 $350

Ganter, Regina *The Pearl-Shellers of Torres Strait: Resources Use, Development and Decline.* Carlton: Melbourne University Press, 1994. First edition, 8vo., original illustrated wrappers.   Any Amount of Books   2015 - C4489   2015   £220

Garces, Francisco Tomas   1738-1781   *On the Trail of a Spanish Pioneer: The Diary and Itinerary of Francisco Garces (Missionary Priest) in his Travels through Sonora, Arizona and California 1775-1776.*   New York: 1900. 2 volumes, illustrations, folding map, original cloth, shelfwear, else clean and very good.   Dumont Maps & Books of the West   131 - 44   2015 $275

Garcia Lorca, Federico   *Chant Funebre Pour Ignacio Sanchez Mejias.*   Paris: Krol, 1949. Number 118 of 160 copies on BFK Rives, numbered and signed by Krol (from an edition of 225 + 26 HC), illustrated with 20 engravings by Abram Krol, fine, although gutter edge of half title is bit rolled, chemise bears portrait by Roger Tarrov, nice in near fine matching box, folio.   Beasley Books   2013 - 2015 $2500

Garcia Marquez, Gabriel   *La Mala Hora. (The Evil Hour).*   Madrid: Premio Literario Esso, 1962. First Spanish edition, wrappers, very good+ with rubbing to front spine fold, mild signs of edgewear and owner's name to blank prelim.   Beasley Books   2013 - 2015 $950

Garcia Marquez, Gabriel   *El General en su Laberinto.*   Bogota: Editorial Oveja Negra, 1989. First edition, fine in fine dust jacket.   Beasley Books   2013 - 2015 $45

Garcia Marquez, Gabriel   *El Amor en Los Tiempos de Colera.*   Bogota: Editorial Oveja Negra, 1985. First edition, limited issue of 100 copies signed by author and stamped and signed by Colombian authorities on limitation page, near fine in like dust jacket.   B & B Rare Books, Ltd.   2015 - 2015 $5000

Garcia Marquez, Gabriel   *Love in the Time of Cholera.*   New York: Alfred A. Knopf, 1988. First edition, limited issue of 350 numbered copies, signed by author on limitation page, fine in fine acetate dust jacket.   B & B Rare Books, Ltd.   2015 - 2015 $3000

Garcia Marquez, Gabriel   *One Hundred Years of Solitude.*   New York: Limited Editions Club, 1982. Limited to 2000 numbered copies, signed by translator, Gregory Rabassa, artist, Rafael Ferrer, and introducer Alastair Reid, calligraphy by G. G. Laurens, 4to., quarter leather, slipcase, illustrations, with Monthly Letter loosely inserted, and with original lithograph loosely inserted.   Oak Knoll Books   25 - 49   2015 $275

Garcia, Carlos   *L'Art Kota: Les Figures De Reliquaire.*   Meudon: Alain & Francoise Chaffin, n.d. circa, 1979. First edition thus, large 4to., original pale peach cloth, lettered in brown on spine and cover, copiously illustrated in black and white, near fine rear top corner slightly bumped, slightly yellowed, slightly creased, very good dust jacket.   Any Amount of Books   March 2015 - C3082   2015   £900

Gardenstone, Francis Garden   1721-1793   *Letter to the People of Laurencekirk on Occasion of Presenting the King's Charter...*   Edinburgh: printed by Murray and Cochran sold by J. Sibbald & Co. and Other booksellers, 1780. First edition, 8vo., plain mid 20th century cloth boards with printed spine label, good copy, scarce.   John Drury Rare Books   2015 - 23391   2015 $656

Gardiner, Henry   *Essays on Currency and Absenteeism &c &c...*   Liverpool: printed for G. and J. Robinson and sold by Hatchard & Son, Picadilly and J. M. Richardson Cornhill, London, 1827. First and only edition, 8vo., 188 pages, errata slip (11 errata) tipped in, two with ms. notes in ink referring to Sraffa's Ricardo on pages 102 and 108, original boards, uncut, original printed spine label (chipped however), excellent copy with 19th century ownership inscription of Henry Booth, very scarce.   John Drury Rare Books   2015 - 25944   2015 $5682

Gardiner, Howard C.   *In Pursuit of the Golden Dream.*   Stoughton: Western Hemisphere Inc., 1970. First trade edition, first issue in red cloth, frontispiece, 7 illustrations, 2 maps, red cloth, gilt lettered spine and front cover, fine.   Argonaut Book Shop   Holiday Season 2014 - 98 2015 $90

Gardiner, Robert William   *Considerations on the Military Organization of the British Army; Respectfully addressed to the Honourable the Members of the House of Commons.*   London: Byfield Hawksworth and Co., 1858. First edition, large 8vo., original red cloth, embossed in blind and lettered in gilt on upper cover, gilt edges, fine, presentation inscription by author for Sir William Jolliffe, Bart.   John Drury Rare Books   March 2015 - 16415   2015 $266

Gardner, Erle Stanley   *The Case of the Backward Mule.*   New York: William Morrow, 1946. First edition, fine in fine, price clipped dust jacket, inscribed by author for Raymond Chandler, from the collection of Duke Collier.   Royal Books   36 - 10   2015 $20,000

Gardner, Erle Stanley   *The Case of the Baited Hook.*   New York: William Morrow, 1940. First edition, bit of staining at lower edges of cover, else near fine in near fine dust jacket with light wear along edges, inscribed by author to early assistant, Noni (Bibler), from the collection of Duke Collier.   Royal Books   36 - 21   2015 $3000

Gardner, Erle Stanley   *The Case of the Black-Eyed Blonde.*   New York: Morrow, 1944. First edition, fine, bookplate, dust jacket.   Mordida Books   March 2015 - 010203   2015 $250

Gardner, Erle Stanley *The Case of the Caretaker's Cat.* New York: William Morrow, 1935. First edition, fine in near fine, lightly rubbed dust jacket with light wear to top of spine and corners and tiny closed tear on front panel, inscribed by author for Noni (Bibler), one of author's early assistants, from the collection of Duke Collier.   Royal Books   36 - 14   2015 $3500

Gardner, Erle Stanley *The Case of the Counterfeit Eye.* New York: William Morrow, 1935. First edition, publisher's file copy with 'OFFICE FILE COPY' stamped on rear panel of jacket and several pencilled notations and deletions on front flap and front endpaper, near fine in very good or better dust jacket, evidence of removal on front pastedown, else book quire clean, jacket has no significant loss, only some rubbing at folds, light fading to spine panel, small chips at corners, very presentable copy, from the collection of Duke Collier.   Royal Books   36 - 13   2015 $3500

Gardner, Erle Stanley *The Case of the Curious Bride.* New York: William Morrow, 1934. First edition, fine in bright, very good dust jacket with several modest chips, largest being at top of spine, affecting word 'The', inscribed by author for Noni Bibler, one of author's early assistants, from the collection of Duke Collier.   Royal Books   36 - 12   2015 $3000

Gardner, Erle Stanley *The Case of the Dangerous Dowager.* New York: William Morrow, 1937. First edition, very good plus in good dust jacket, 1 3/4 inch loss to top portion of jacket spine, else very good in couple of droplet stains on rear panel and light rubbing overall, warmly inscribed by author to early assistant, Noni (Bibler), from the collection of Duke Collier.   Royal Books   36 - 17   2015 $1250

Gardner, Erle Stanley *The Case of the Drowsy Mosquito.* New York: Morrow, 1943. First edition, fine in very good dust jacket with chipped and frayed spine ends, wear and nicks along edges and at corners, couple of closed tears.   Mordida Books   March 2015 - 012500   2015 $125

Gardner, Erle Stanley *The Case of the Empty Tin.* New York: William Morrow, 1941. First edition, fine in bright, unrubbed dust jacket, lightly chipped at top of spine and corners, from the collection of Duke Collier.   Royal Books   36 - 23   2015 $1750

Gardner, Erle Stanley *The Case of the Goldigger's Purse.* New York: Morrow, 1945. First edition, date on front pastedown, otherwise fine in dust jacket with small chips at base of spine and at corners.   Mordida Books   March 2015 - 008817   2015 $200

Gardner, Erle Stanley *The Case of the Haunted Husband.* New York: William Morrow, 1941. First edition, near fine in about very good scarce dust jacket, jacket rubbed with small chips at spine ends and folds one triangular chip at bottom right corner front panel, affecting part of author's name, from the collection of Duke Collier.   Royal Books   36 - 25   2015 $450

Gardner, Erle Stanley *The Case of the Haunted Husband.* Philadelphia: Philadelphia Inquirer, 1942. Reprint, tabloid folio in size with 19 triple columned pages, illustrations by Harry Weinert, uniform browning along page edges, else near fine.   Buckingham Books   March 2015 - 22572   2015 $175

Gardner, Erle Stanley *The Case of the Howling Dog.* New York: William Morrow, 1934. First edition, near fine in very good and scarce dust jacket (couple of neat repairs along two of the folds, fading to reds on spine panel, chipping at spine ends affecting a portion of word 'The' in title, warmly inscribed by author for Noni Bibler, one of author's early assistants, from the collection of Duke Collier.   Royal Books   36 - 11   2015 $3250

Gardner, Erle Stanley *The Case of the Lame Canary.* New York: William Morrow, 1937. First edition, very good in like dust jacket, dampstain along fore-edges of boards (and conversely along flap folds of jacket at verso) and top right corner of text block, jacket has two chips, one at the crown and one at bottom rear panel, neither affecting any titling, despite noted flaws, bright copy, warmly inscribed by author to early assistant Noni (Bibler), from the collection of Duke Collier.   Royal Books   36 - 18   2015 $2250

Gardner, Erle Stanley *The Case of the Rolling Bones.* New York: William Morrow, 1939. First edition, about fine in bright, near fine dust jacket, which is lightly worn at top of spine and corners, with fingernail sized chip at base of spine, affecting publisher's logo, inscribed by author to early assistant Noni (Bibler), from the collection of Duke Collier.   Royal Books   36 - 20   2015 $3000

Gardner, Erle Stanley *The Case of the Silent Partner.* New York: William Morrow and Co., 1940. First edition, fine, bright, tight copy in fine, unfaded dust jacket, exceptional copy.   Buckingham Books   March 2015 - 25205   2015 $775

Gardner, Erle Stanley *The Case of the Silent Partner.* New York: William Morrow, 1940. First edition, fine in bright, unrubbed dust jacket, jacket lightly worn at spine tips, small chip top of front hinge, inscribed by author for early assistant, Noni (Bibler), from the collection of Duke Collier.   Royal Books   36 - 22   2015 $3000

Gardner, Erle Stanley *The Case of the Sleepwalker's Niece.* New York: William Morrow, 1936. First edition, fine in near fine dust jacket, very lightly rubbed, lightly chipped at top of spine, inscribed by author to early assistant Noni (Bibler), from the collection of Duke Collier.   Royal Books   36 - 15   2015 $3500

Gardner, Erle Stanley *The Case of the Smoking Chimney.* New York: William Morrow, 1942. Uncorrected proof, about very good in publisher's self wrappers with publication date of Jan. 6 1942 and projected price of $2.00 rubber stamped on front endpaper, slight lean, vertical creasing to spine panel, some splitting to front flap fold, from the collection of Duke Collier.   Royal Books   36 - 28   2015 $950

Gardner, Erle Stanley *The Case of the Stuttering Bishop.* First edition, small mark on front cover, else about fine in bright, unrubbed, price clipped dust jacket, gorgeous copy, inscribed by author for Louise Weisberger, Aug. 1936, from the collection of Duke Collier.   Royal Books   36 - 16   2015 $3000

Gardner, Erle Stanley *The Case of the Substitute Face.* New York: William Morrow, 1938. First edition, fine in bright, unrubbed dust jacket with trivial rubbing to spine tips, inscribed by author for early assistant, Noni (Bibler), from the collection of Duke Collier.   Royal Books   36 - 19   2015 $3500

Gardner, Erle Stanley *The Case of the Sulky Girl.* William Morrow and Co., 1933. First edition, light spotting to front and rear pastedown sheets, else near fine, bright copy in dust jacket, professionally restored at spine ends, corners and extremities.   Buckingham Books   March 2015 - 33542   2015 $7500

Gardner, Erle Stanley *The Case of the Velvet Claws.* First edition, near fine in very good plus example of rare dust jacket, jacket is quite nice with slight loss at crown, just barely touching word 'The' in title, light wear at heel, corners and top of back panel and couple of closed tears, otherwise bright and clean, inscribed by author for Capt. Joe Shaw, editor, from the collection of Duke Collier.   Royal Books   36 - 9   2015 $37,500

Gardner, Erle Stanley *The Case of the Velvet Claws.* New York: William Morrow, 1936. Second printing, near fine in very good dust jacket (both clearly state 'Second Printing'), jacket lightly rumpled along spine panel, with small bit of loss at crown and heel in (not titling affected), shallow rectangular chip at top rear panel, light general overall rubbing and nicking, very presentable copy, inscribed by author for early assistant Noni (Bibler), from the collection of Duke Collier.   Royal Books   36 - 24   2015 $2500

Gardner, Erle Stanley *The Case of the Worried Waitress.* New York: William Morrow and Co., 1966. First edition, review slip tipped in, signature of American crime writer and literary critic Dorothy B. Hughes on front blank in red ink, near fine in red cloth with black spine lettering in very good plus to near fine dust jacket with wear to spine crown.   Ed Smith Books   83 - 28   2015 $250

Gardner, Erle Stanley *The Court of Last Resort.* William Sloane Associates, 1952. First edition, near fine in dust jacket lightly sunned on spine and with professional restoration to spine ends, corners and extremities, inked presentation from author to June 1955.   Buckingham Books   March 2015 - 37508   2015 $450

Gardner, Erle Stanley *The D. A. Breaks a Seal.* New York: Morrow, 1946. First edition, endpapers darkened, otherwise fine in very good price clipped dust jacket with slightly faded spine, small chips at top of spine, several closed tears and nicks at corners.   Mordida Books   March 2015 - 008421   2015 $125

Gardner, Erle Stanley *The D. A. Cooks a Goose.* New York: William Morrow, 1942. First edition, fine in dust jacket with light wear to corners and evenly sunned on spine. Buckingham Books   March 2015 - 24786   2015 $650

Gardner, Erle Stanley *The D. A. Draws a Circle.* New York: William Morrow, 1939. First printing of this edition, near fine in very good or better dust jacket, dampstain bottom right corner of front board, affecting jacket verso in same spot, otherwise only lightly rubbed overall, inscribed by author to early assistant, Noni (Bibler), from the collection of Duke Collier.   Royal Books   36 - 30   2015 $1850

Gardner, Erle Stanley *The D. A. Draws a Circle.* New York: William Morrow and Co., 1939. First edition, fine in lightly rubbed dust jacket with light wear to spine ends, two tiny closed tears to top edge of rear top panel, light vertical crease to front flap fold.   Buckingham Books   March 2015 - 24788   2015 $650

Gardner, Erle Stanley *The D. A. Goes to Trial.* New York: William Morrow & Co., 1940. First edition, lower front and rear corners lightly bumped, else near fine, tight crisp copy in lightly rubbed dust jacket, light wear to foot of spine and some ink loss to bumped corner of front panel. Buckingham Books   March 2015 - 24787   2015 $750

Gardner, Erle Stanley *The D. A. Goes to Trial.* New York: William Morrow, 1940. First edition, dampstain bottom right corner of front board, endpapers toned, else near fine in about very good dust jacket with small chips at extremities and some of the usual color-fading to pink spine title, warmly inscribed by author to early assistant, Noni (Bibler), from the collection of Duke Collier.   Royal Books   36 - 31   2015 $1850

Gardner, Erle Stanley *The D. A. Holds a Candle.* New York: William Morrow, 1938. First edition, very slightly cocked, else very good plus in very good dust jacket with small chips at extremities and some of the usual color fading to pink spine title, warmly inscribed by author to early assistant, Noni (Bibler), from the collection of Duke Collier. Royal Books   36 - 29   2015 $2250

Gardner, Erle Stanley *Murder Up My Sleeve.* New York: William Morrow, 1937. First Canadian edition, fine in bright, price clipped dust jacket, lightly worn at spine ends and with three small chips on back panel, exceptional copy, very scarce in jacket, from the collection of Duke Collier.   Royal Books   36 - 32   2015 $2000

Gardner, Erle Stanley *Over the Hump.* London: Gordon Martin Publishing, 1945. First UK edition, and first separate edition, near fine in very good example of scarce dust jacket, jacket has light rubbing and few small cellophane repairs at verso, attractive copy, most uncommon, from the collection of Duke Collier.   Royal Books   36 - 33   2015 $1250

Gardner, Erle Stanley *The World of Water. Exploring the Sacramento Delta.* William Morrow, 1965. First edition, inked presentation inscription by author, minor tiny bump to top front corner, else fine in lightly soiled and rubbed dust jacket with light wear to spine ends, extremities and top, front corner, numerous photos.   Buckingham Books   March 2015 - 37507   2015 $250

Gardner, George Peabody *E1/2S. Some Harbors in Nova Scotia and Thereabouts.* Salem: Peabody Museum, 1953. Small 8vo., map, cloth, photos and sketches, covers stained, interior good.   Schooner Books Ltd.   110 - 74   2015 $45

Gardner, John *Every Night's a Bullfight.* London: Michael Joseph, 1971. First edition, fine in dust jacket.   Mordida Books   March 2015 - 000847   2015 $75

Gardner, John *The Garden of Weapons.* London: Hodder & Stoughton, 1980. First edition, fine in dust jacket. Mordida Books   March 2015 - 000846   2015 $75

Gardner, John *Grendel.* New York: Alfred A. Knopf, 1971. First edition, octavo, cloth.   John W. Knott, Bookseller   Selected New Arrivals Jan. 2015 - 17029   2015 $750

Gardner, John *Icebreaker.* London: Jonathan Cape and Hodder & Stoughton, 1983. First edition, pages very lightly toned, crown 8vo., original black boards, backstrip lettered gilt, dust jacket with little rubbing to top corners and rear panel, very good.   Blackwell's Rare Books   B179 - 151   2015   £30

Gardner, John *Jason & Medeia.* New York: Knopf, 1973. First edition, signed by Gardner, little spine sunning to jacket, fine in very good dust jacket.   Ed Smith Books   83 - 31   2015 $350

Gardner, John *The King's Indian. Stories & Tales.* New York: Knopf, 1974. First edition, illustrations by Herbert L. Fink, signed and inscribed by author, near fine in near fine dust jacket.   Ed Smith Books   83 - 30   2015 $350

Gardner, John *No Deals Mr. Bond.* Wellingborough: September Press, 1988. One of 480 copies (of an edition of 600), printed on mouldmade papers, supplemented with reproductions of 4 photos and essays by Christopher Skelton and Robert Gibbings, folio, original black cloth, backstrip with fawn morocco label, lettered gilt, top edge gilt, cream cloth, slipcase, small blue mark, fine, prospectus, sample leaves, order form laid in at rear.   Blackwell's Rare Books   B179 - 153   2015   £450

Gardner, John *The Revenge of Moriarty.* London: Weidenfeld, 1975. First edition, fine in dust jacket. Mordida Books   March 2015 - 002684   2015 $75

Gardner, John *Role of Honor.* New York: Putnam, 1984. First edition, review copy with 5 x 7 inch black and white photo of author laid in, as well as press release, fine in blue cloth and boards, would be fine jacket but for some spine sunning.   Ed Smith Books   83 - 29   2015 $100

Garis, Howard *Uncle Wiggily Drawing Master.* New York: Fred Wish, 1923. Folio, stiff card covers, fine, rare, full color cover, 8 line illustrations, by Lang Campbell.   Aleph-Bet Books, Inc.   108 - 202   2015 $325

Garis, Howard *Uncle Wiggily's Picture Book.* New York: A. L. Burt, 1922. Large 8vo., cloth, 161 pages, some shelf-wear and offsetting from mounts that hold plates, else very good, 32 fine color plates on 16 leaves by Lang Campbell. Aleph-bet Books, Inc.   109 - 191   2015 $650

Garland, Hamlin 1860-1940 *The Book of the American Indian.* New York: and London: Harper and Bros., 1923. First edition, tall quarto, quarter cloth and paper over boards, Remington drawing on front cover, illustrations, 4 in color, all be Remington, light cosmetic restoration to corners and front flyleaf moderately soiled, else very good. Buckingham Books   March 2015 - 31038   2015 $225

Garland, Hamlin 1860-1940 *Trail-Makers of the Middle Border.* New York: Macmillan, 1926. First edition, decorated cloth, bright, nearly fine copy, quite attractive, illustrations, by Constance Garland.   Stephen Lupack   March 2015 - 2015 $45

Garner, Alan *Owl Service.* New York: Walck, 1968. First American edition, 8vo., cloth, fine in slightly worn dust jacket.   Aleph-bet Books, Inc.   109 - 192   2015 $200

Garnett, Louis A. *For Private Circulation. the Paris Monetary Conference of 1881 and Bi-Metallism.* San Francisco: May 28, 1881. First edition, large 8vo., original printed wrappers, fine presentation copy inscribed by author to professor George Davidson in August 1881.   John Drury Rare Books   2015 - 26236   2015 $177

Garnett, Louise Ayres *Creature Songs.* Boston: Oliver Ditson, n.d. circa, 1912. Large 4to., green gilt cloth, pictorial paste on, 2 small blemishes on side of paste-on, else very good-fine, illustrations by Peter Newell with 10 wonderful large half page illustrations in various shades of green, original poem written by Garnett on free endpaper, special copy, very uncommon.   Aleph-bet Books, Inc.   109 - 327   2015 $500

Garrett, Randall *Too Many Magicians.* Garden City: Doubleday & Co., 1967. First edition, octavo, cloth.   John W. Knott, Bookseller   Selected New Arrivals Jan. 2015 - 17030   2015 $350

Garrett, William *From Dusk to Dawn.* New York: Appleton, 1929. First American edition, fine in dust jacket with slightly faded spine, several short closed tears and tiny wear at corners.   Mordida Books   March 2015 - 008074   2015 $175

Garrison, William Lloyd *Sonnets and Other Poems.* Boston: Oliver Johnson, 1843. First edition, 16mo., 96 pages, original cloth, some browning, near fine, inscribed in ink by publisher, O(liver) Johnson to his sister.   M & S Rare Books, Inc.   97 - 108   2015 $600

Garston, Guy *The Champagne Mystery.* London: Muller, 1935. First edition, some light spotting on page edges, otherwise fine in dust jacket, tiny fraying at spine ends and water at corners.   Mordida Books   March 2015 - 010668   2015 $100

Garth, Samuel *The Dispensary: a poem in six cantos.* London: printed by H. Hills and sold by the booksellers of London and Westminster, 1709. 8vo., woodcut frontispiece, disbound, some light browning, but very good.   C. R. Johnson   Foxon R-Z - 1221r-z   2015 $230

Garver, Thomas H. *The Last Steam Railroad in America.* New York: Harry N. Abrams, 2000. First Abrams edition, square quarto, 144 pages, black and white and color photos, black boards, very fine, pictorial dust jacket.   Argonaut Book Shop   Holiday Season 2014 - 99   2015 $45

Gascoigne, Bamber *Images of Richmond: a Survey of the Topographical Prints of Richmond in Surrey up to the Year 1900.* Richmond-upon-Thames: Saint Helena Press, 1978. First edition, number 67 of 200 copies signed by Gascoigne, 4to., original full light bright leather lettered gilt on spine and decorated in gilt on front cover with image of Richmond on cover, pages 237 with many illustrations, fine in fine handsome slipcase, marbled covers and full leather spine lettered gilt.   Any Amount of Books   2015 - A69200   2015   £225

Gash, Jonathan *The Gondola Scam.* New York: St. Martin's, 1984. First American edition, fine in fine dust jacket.   Mordida Books   March 2015 - 010065   2015 $1984

Gash, Jonathan *The Lies of fair Ladies.* Bristol: Scorpion, 1991. Limited edition, one of 99 numbered copies signed by Gash, very fine in acetate dust jacket.   Mordida Books   March 2015 - 000868   2015 $135

Gash, Jonathan *Moonspender.* London: Collins Crime Club, 1986. First edition, fine in dust jacket.   Mordida Books   March 2015 - 000858   2015 $75

Gaskell, Elizabeth Cleghorn   1810-1865 *Mary Barton: a Tale of Manchester Life.* Leipzig: Bernhard Tauchnitz, 1849. Copyright edition, half title, bookseller's stamps, contemporary half calf, rebacked, retaining original spine strip with red label and initials A.I.T., bookplate of Anthony Philip Martineau Walker, ownership inscription of Anne Thackeray (Ritchie), with note by Kathleen Tillotson that Captain Walker gave her the book.   Jarndyce Antiquarian Booksellers   CCVII - 273   2015   £50

Gaskell, Elizabeth Cleghorn   1810-1865 *Mary Barton and Other Tales.* London: Smith, Elder & Co., 1891. New edition, half title, frontispiece, 4 pages ads, from the library of Geoffrey & Kathleen Tillotson, home made paper wrappers with paper label, Kathleen has made few notes in text and marginal marks and inserted handwritten copy of preface to first edition in envelope affixed to half title, with postcard portrait of author.   Jarndyce Antiquarian Booksellers   CCVII - 274   2015   £20

Gaspey, William *Tallis's Illustrated London; in Commemoration of the Great Exhibition of all Nations in 1851...* London: John Tallis & Co., 1851-1852. First edition, 2 volumes, 8vo., engraved frontispieces, additional vignette titlepages and 154 engraved views, many with 2 scenes per plate and including 3 folding views, contemporary half calf, spines decorated gilt with red and black labels, marbled edges.   Marlborough Rare Books Ltd.   List 49 - 10   2015   £450

Gassendi, Pierre *Three Discourses of Happiness, Virtue and Liberty.* printed for Awnsham and John Churchill, 1699. First and only (printed) edition in English, 8vo., some browning and spotting, paper thin in places but scarcely affecting text, B5 frayed at fore-edge and dust soiled there, contemporary panelled calf, rebacked (little crudely), sound. Blackwell's Rare Books B179 - 44 2015 £1500

Gatty, Margaret *The Fairy Godmothers and Other Tales.* London: Bell & Daldy, 1860. Third edition, engraved frontispiece, contemporary half blue calf, maroon leather label, spine faded, slightly rubbed, Ratherspeck Parsonage library label, very good. Jarndyce Antiquarian Booksellers CCXI - 121 2015 £35

Gauden, John *The Case of Ministers Maintenance by Tithes...* London: printed by Thomas Maxey for Andrew Crook...., 1653. First edition, 4to., edges bit browned and outer leaves little dust marked, recently well bound in cloth, spine lettered gilt, good, large copy. John Drury Rare Books March 2015 - 18595 2015 $266

Gaudin, Abbe Jacques *Les Inconveniens du Celibat des Pretres, Prouves par des Recherches Historiques.* Geneva: J. L. Pellet, 1781. First edition, 8vo., half title, title and half title coming loose, tear in one leaf (no loss), old plain orange card covers, unlettered, short splits in joints, entirely uncut, good, large copy. John Drury Rare Books March 2015 - 16110 2015 £306

Gault, William Campbell *County Kill.* New York: Simon and Schuster, 1962. First edition, fine in dust jacket with some minor light rubbing. Mordida Books March 2015 - 006729 2015 $75

Gautier, Theophile *Jettatura.* Paris: Romangol, 1904. #85 of 105 from an edition of 300, wrappers, slightly soiled and lightly wrinkled, interior foxed throughout, two extra suites of plates are in badly damaged chemise, first plate is quite tanned from offsetting, small 4to. Beasley Books 2013 - 2015 $185

Gautier, Theophile *Nature at Home from the French of...* London: Bradbury Agnew, 1883. First edition, 4to., 12 x 9 inches, frontispiece with tissue guard and 24 fine double page black and white illustrations by Karl Bodmer and numerous illustrations in text, all edges gilt, very attractive with grey, green and gilt illustrated covers in almost fine condition, clean, bright and fresh, very slightly bumped at lower spine, exceptional condition. Any Amount of Books 2015 - A32984 2015 £300

Gay, John 1685-1732 *The Beggar's Opera as it is acted at the Theatre Royal in Lincolns Inn Fields.* London: printed for John Watts, 1728. Second edition, 8vo., 18th century red quarter roan, salmon paper boards, gilt lettering, handsomely bound copy, small dampstain in lower corner of inner margins, paper little foxed, very good. The Brick Row Book Shop Miscellany 67 - 48 2015 $400

Gay, John 1685-1732 *Fables.* London: John Stockdale, 1793. First edition with plates by William Blake, royal 8vo., 2 volumes, contemporary full calf, light worn in places, single gilt roll tooled floral border to both boards, repeated on turn-ins, spines divided into 6 compartments, gilt panelled with Greek key device and floral central tool, all edges marbled, marbled endpapers, engraved titles to each volume, engraved frontispiece to volume I and 70 engraved plates, including 12 by Blake, usual light browning and offsetting, otherwise very good set, very tall, possibly large paper copy. Henry Sotheran Ltd. William Blake Exhibition 17th Oct.-7th Nov. 2014 - 63 2015 £965

Gay, John 1685-1732 *The Fables of.* published and sold by the booksellers and (printed) by T. Wilson and R. Spence... York, 1806. 12mo., woodcut vignette on title and numerous 'cuts' in text by T. Bewick, minor spotting and staining, red crushed morocco, elaborate gilt tooled borders on sides of leafy tendrils punctuated with flowers, spine gilt with leaf sprays in 6 compartments between raised bands, wide gilt turn-ins, gilt edges signed F. G. and dated 1906, booklabel of Peter Summers inside front cover, very good in early Arts & Crafts binding by Frank Garrett. Blackwell's Rare Books B179 - 45 2015 £750

Gay, John 1685-1732 *Polly. An Opera.* London: printed for the author, 1729. First edition, 4to., contemporary quarter calf marbled paper boards, red leather label, gilt rules and lettering, 31 pages of engraved sheet music, contemporary armorial bookplate of Henry Streatfield, his library was later sold by W. H. Robinson Ltd., bookplate of American collector Charles Walker Andrews, noted in pencil above bookplate that he purchased this from Robinson in 1935, binding bit worn and stained, some light dampstains in text, very good, large copy. The Brick Row Book Shop Miscellany 67 - 49 2015 $500

Gay, John 1685-1732 *Polly: an Opera.* London: Heinemann, 1923. Limited to 380 copies signed by artist, 4to., blue gilt cloth, blank corner of two plates missing (frontispiece and last plate), else very good+ condition, 9 lovely tipped-in color plates by William Nicholson, scarce. Aleph-Bet Books, Inc. 108 - 317 2015 $275

Gaze, Harold *Copper Top.* New York: Harper Bros., 1924. B-Y, First American edition, thick 4to., blue cloth stamped in gold, last illustration slightly out of register, else fine in dust jacket (chipped on spine ends), illustrations by Gaze with 12 beautiful color plates plus many full and partial page fanciful line illustrations, scarce in dust jacket. Aleph-bet Books, Inc. 109 - 194 2015 $650

Gaze, Howard *The Chewg-Um-Blewg-Um.* Melbourne: Auckland: Christchurch; Dunedin and Wellington and London: whitcombe & tombs Limited, 1919. 4to., wrappers, color plate on cover, string ties, erasure mark on 2 pages of text, else fine, 2 tipped-in color plates, 1 tipped-in black and white plate and 8 pen ink drawings in text, great copy of rare book. Aleph-Bet Books, Inc. 108 - 203 2015 $1850

Gazzadi, Domenico *Zoologia Morale Esposta in Cento Venti Discorsi in Versi o in Prosa.* Florence: Vincenzo Batelli e Compagni, 1843-1846. First and only edition, 2 volumes, contemporary quarter brown morocco, marbled boards, elaborate gilt tools and lettering to spines, 93 hand colored engraved plates, binding little rubbed to edges, browning to 3 plates on volume II, closed tear not affecting image to bottom margin of plate of St. Bernard's in volume I, occasional marking elsewhere, generally very clean and bright indeed, very good, with ownership stamps of Giovanni Bosari, Bosari's stamp and two censors' stamps to half title volume I.   Henry Sotheran Ltd.   Natural History: Rarities 2015 - 2015   £20,000

Gebhardt, A. G. *State Papers Relating to the Diplomatic Transactions Between the American and French Governments from the Year 1793 to the Conclusion of the Convention to the 30th of September 1800.* London: J. E. Vogel, 1816. First edition, 3 volumes, half leather gilt at spine, ex-British Foreign Office Library with few library markings, slight general wear, spine hinges little cracked, otherwise sound, very good.   Any Amount of Books   2015 - A49589   2015   £200

Gedge, Adam *On the Abuses of Civil Incorporations: in a Letter to Hudson Gurney, Esq. M.P.* London: Sherwood Gilbert and Piper and W. Alexander, Great Yarmouth, 1830. First edition, half title, well bound in fairly recent watered cloth, spine lettered in gilt, very good.   John Drury Rare Books   2015 - 16193   2015 $133

Gee, John *Bunnie Bear.* Gordon Volland, 1928. Third printing, square 8vo., pictorial boards, fine in original box with part of one flap restored, illustrations by author, this copy signed by Gee and inscribed, very scarce.   Aleph-bet Books, Inc.   109 - 476   2015 $300

Gee, Joshua *The Trade and Navigation of Great Britain Considered: Shewing that the Surest Way for a Nation to Increase in Riches, is to Prevent the Importation of Such Foreign Commodities...* London: printed by Sam. Buckley, 1730. 8vo., endpapers defective, contemporary calf, spine gilt with raised bands, wanting label, small loss to leather on lower cover, still very good, crisp copy.   John Drury Rare Books   March 2015 - 25016   2015 $874

Gee, Joshua *The Trade and Navigation of Great Britain Considered.* London: J. Almon and S. Bladon, 1767. 12mo., contemporary calf, spine gilt with raised bands and label, joints and head and foot of spine worn, otherwise very good, crisp copy, early 19th century armorial bookplate of Sir Abraham Hume bart, with later 19th century ink stamp of the board of Trade Library with a government withdrawn stamp on blank flyleaf.   John Drury Rare Books   March 2015 - 16811   2015   £306

Geiger, Leroy *How to Make your Own Violin.* Cleveland: Ernst Heinrich Roth, 1963. First edition, 4to., spiral bound wrappers fine with two folded templates laid in at rear. Beasley Books   2013 - 2015 $125

Geikie, James *Outlines of Geology: an Introduction to the Science for Junior Students and General Readers.* London: Edward Stanford, 1896. Third edition, 8vo., 400 illustrations, gilt stamped maroon calf presentation binding, front cover Reading School emblem, 5 raised bands, gilt stamped black leather spine label, extremities lightly rubbed, corners showing, Reading School presentation bookplate with holograph ink inscription awarding the book to F. H. Stainton, additional ownership signature of A. A. Quelch, very good. Jeff Weber Rare Books   178 - 790   2015 $40

Geisel, Theodor Seuss   1904-1994 *And to Think That I Saw It on Mulberry Street.* New York: Vanguard Press, 1937. First edition, earliest issue with boys pants on cover and on dust jacket white instead of blue), 4to., pictorial boards, fine in very good dust jacket with few repairs to chips on edges and old tape residue on 2 areas, very scarce, brightly illustrated in color.   Aleph-bet Books, Inc. 109 - 434   2015 $10,000

Geisel, Theodor Seuss   1904-1994 *The Eye Book.* New York: Random House, 1968. First edition, 8vo., glazed pictorial boards, fine in near fine dust jacket which is slightly soiled, illustrations by Roy McKie in color, great copy. Aleph-bet Books, Inc.   109 - 437   2015 $1350

Geisel, Theodor Seuss   1904-1994 *More Boners.* New York: Viking, 1931. First edition, near fine in very good price clipped dust jacket with 1 inch tear at head of spine. Beasley Books   2013 - 2015 $125

Geisel, Theodor Seuss   1904-1994 *Secrets of the Deep. (and) Secrets of the Deep Volume II.* Standard Oil, Essomarine, 1935. 1936, 2 volumes, 8vo., pictorial wrappers, small margin mend and crease to volume 2, else both very good+, illustrations in color by author, both volumes inscribed by author, rare thus.   Aleph-bet Books, Inc.   109 - 439   2015 $2700

Geisel, Theodor Seuss   1904-1994 *The Seven Lady Godivas.* New York: Random House, 1939. Stated first edition, 4to., cloth, fine in very slightly frayed dust jacket, color illustrations, laid in is full page handwritten letter from author.   Aleph-bet Books, Inc.   109 - 436   2015 $2000

Geisel, Theodor Seuss   1904-1994 *Ten Apples Up in Top.* New York: Random House, 1961. First edition, first printing, 8vo., glazed pictorial boards, fine in nice very good+ dust jacket that is slightly rubbed at spine ends, illustrations by Ray McKie, great copy.   Aleph-bet Books, Inc. 109 - 438   2015 $1500

Gellius, Aulus *Auli Gelii Luculentissimi Scriptoris Noctes Atticae. (Attic Nights).* Lugduni: Apud Antonium Gryphium, 1591. 124 x 76mm., handsome contemporary Venetian red morocco richly gilt in armorial design, upper cover with central coat of arms flanked by oval to right containing an eagle and one to left enclosing a star, the background a riot of foliage, grotesques, crescents and gilt dots, "ALOYS" in a cartouche at top, "ZABAR" at bottom, lower cover with similar design but with different coat of arms, "TIBER" in a cartouche at head, "CINC" at foot, raised bands, spine panels tooled in gilt in a chain pattern, all edges gilt and gauffered in a diapered design, holes for ties (apparently some very expert repairs at spine ends), Printer's griffin device on titlepage, short marginal wormhole to first four leaves, E1 with light (wax?) stain obscuring a couple of words on four lines, text on inferior paper and consequently with light overall browning throughout, occasional minor foxing, other trivial defects but still very good internally, joints and corners little rubbed, but resplendent binding in excellent condition, quite bright and showing only insignificant wear. Phillip J. Pirages 66 - 20 2015 $6500

Gelis: Peintures-Serigraphies-Lithographies. Orleans: W. Meliet/Copie 45, 1884. First edition, 4to., copiously illustrated in color and black and white throughout, text in English and French, stamp of Atelier Gelis on half titlepage, very good in like dust jacket, excellent. Any Amount of Books 2015 - A84060 2015 £175

Gem ABC and Picture Book. New York: McLoughlin Bros., 1898. Folio, cloth backed pictorial boards, some edge rubbing and finger soil, tight and very good+, printed on coated paper, each page has 2 lines of text printed in gold above which is very, very fine, large chromolithograph, very scarce. Aleph-bet Books, Inc. 109 - 5 2015 $750

General Rules for the Government of the Cheshire County Asylum at Parkside, near Macclesfield in the County of Chester. Macclesfield: Swinnerton and Brown, 1875. 8vo., small piece torn from blank margin of last two leaves, sewn and unbound as issued, good, apparently rare. John Drury Rare Books 2015 - 20838 2015 $133

Gentillet, Innocent *Discours sur els Moyens de Bien Gouerneur et Maintenir en Bonne Paix un Royaume ou Autre Principaute.* N.P.: Geneva: Jac. Stoer?, 1576. First edition in French, 8vo., woodcut title vignette, final blank with printer's device on recto, blank verso, very small worm track piercing all leaves from page 431 but affecting generally no more than a couple of letters on most of these leaves, contemporary calf gilt with raised bands and another label, corners and joints worn with joints shaken, good, crisp copy with early 20th century bookplate of Dr. Von Raven. John Drury Rare Books 2015 - 24834 2015 $1311

Gentle, Mary *Ash: a Secret History.* London: Gollancz, 2000. First combined and first hardcover edition, octavo, boards, signed and dated 7/12/200 by author. John W. Knott, Bookseller Selected New Arrivals Jan. 2015 - 17031 2015 $150

The Gentleman's Magazine and Historical Chronicle Volume XLVI for the Year MDCCLXXVI. London: printed at St. John's Gate, 1776. First English printing of the American Declaration of Independence, full maroon cloth, rebacked original spine preserved, lacking most maps and plates, else fine and clean. Argonaut Book Shop Holiday Season 2014 - 10 2015 $2500

George II, King of Great Britian *His Majesty's Most Gracious Speech to Both Houses of Parliament On Thursday the Seventeenth Day of October 1745.* London: printed by Thomas Baskett and by the Assigns of Robert Baskett, 1745. Folio, woodcut royal arms on titlepage, large woodcut initial, sometime folded several times, slight soiling to upper leaf, good. Blackwell's Rare Books B179 - 46 2015 £600

George, Andrew L. *A Texas Prisoner.* Charlotte: Elam & Dooley, 1895. First edition, 16mo., original pictorial wrappers, illustrations, moderate wear to spine panel, covers lightly soiled, first two pages top corner edges torn, else very good, scarce. Buckingham Books March 2015 - 32670 2015 $750

George, H. B. *The Oberland and Its Glaciers: Explored and Illustrated with Ice-Axe and Camera.* London: Alfred W. Bennett, 1866. First edition, 4to., double page map and 28 photo plates, the 9 larger plates with tissue guards, original brown cloth with gilt lettering and decoration, all edges gilt, cloth somewhat rubbed and scuffed with patchy fading to gilt and very small hole in spine at rear joint, slight chipping with partial loss of spine label, spine rebacked and hinges strengthened, very sound, internally some light foxing and some very pale blotching but generally very clean text and plates, occasional closed tear not affecting text or photographic images. Any Amount of Books 2015 - A86936 2015 £320

George, Lyman F. *The Naked Truth of Jesusism.* Pittsburgh: George Bk. Pub., 1914. First edition, bound by Kerr in their standard tan binding and with stamping on spine and front boards, fine but for tear to f.e.p. Beasley Books 2013 - 2015 $45

George, Waldemar *Larionov.* Paris: La Bibliotheque Des Arts, 1966. First edition, fine in fine dust jacket, mounted color plates, 4to., fine cardboard slipcase. Beasley Books 2013 - 2015 $45

Geraldy, Paul *Clindindin.* Paris: Calmann Levy, 1937. 4to., cloth backed pictorial boards, fine, illustrations by Andre Helle. Aleph-Bet Books, Inc. 108 - 236 2015 $600

Gerard De Neval Labrunie, Known as   1808-1855
Aurelia. Monaco Club: International De Bibliophile/Jaspard, Polus, 1960. No. 140 of 250 copies from an edition of 300, 4to., unbound signatures laid into wrappers, 34 etchings by Leonor Fini, lovely copy, fine in fine wrappers in publishers titled clamshell box.   Beasley Books   2013 - 2015 $1200

Gerard, John   1545-1612   *The Herball or Generall Historie of Plantes.*   London: by Ada Islip, Joice Norton and Richard Whitakers, 1633. Folio, engraved title, over 2500 woodcuts of plans, early 19th century panelled calf, neatly rebacked retaining original fully gilt spine, title lightly soiled but complete and free of any repair, blank fore and bottom edges of A4-5 neatly extended, few marginal tears neatly closed, intermittent faint dampstain in top margin becoming bit more noticeable toward the end of text, marginal repair to 7A1 (index) costing several page numbers, blank lower corner of 7B5 replaced, very good, most attractive copy, ownership inscription and cost dated 1634.   Joseph J. Felcone Inc.   Science, Medicine and Technology - 25   2015 $8000

Gerber, Dan   *The Chinese Poems: Letters to a Distant Friend.*   Fremont: Sumac Press, 1978. First edition, number 89 of 300 hardcover copies, signed by author, drawings by Jack Smith, octavo, fine in fine dust jacket, inscribed by poet to Galen Williams, laid in is a brief ANS from Gerber to Williams.   Between the Covers Rare Books, Inc.   187 - 107   2015 $150

Gerhart, Isaac   *Choral Harmonie. Enthaltend Kitchen Melodien.*   Harrisburg: John Wyeth, 1818. First edition, oblong 8vo., contemporary calf backed boards, small piece torn from margin of title, leaves age darkened, very good, repeated ownership signature in ink of Henry Landis Jan. 20 1818.   M & S Rare Books, Inc.   97 - 197   2015 $750

Germain, Claudio   *Icon Philosophiae Occultae, Sive Vera methodus Componendi Magnum Antiquorum Philosophorum Lapidem.*   Paris: Apud Edmundum Couterot, 1672. First edition, scarce, text in Latin, original limp vellum with slightly chipped spine, joints between endpapers front and rear neatly reinforced, few small ink blots and inscriptions not affecting text, nice example.   Any Amount of Books   2015 - C4954   2015   £700

Gerstein, Mordicai   *The Man Who Walked Between the Towers.*   Brookfield: Roaring Brook, 2003. First edition, signed and dated 9/11/11 exactly 10 years after the 9/11 tragedy by Gerstein and with original drawing of a man in top hat on tight rope, additionally signed by the tightrope walker, Philippe Petit with small tight rope drawing, as new in like dust jacket, 4to, no Caldecott medal or mention of award on dust jacket.   By the Book, L. C.   44 - 83   2015 $400

Gerstner, Karl   *Compendium for Literates, a System of Writing.*   N.P.: MIT, 1974. First US edition, square 12mo., cloth, dust jacket, 180 pages printed french-fold, very scarce.   Oak Knoll Books   306 - 44   2015 $175

Gettmann, Royal A.   *A Victorian Publisher: a Study of the Bentley Papers.*   Cambridge: University Press, 1960. Half title, plates, original blue cloth in torn dust jacket, inscribed by Kathleen Tillotson with few internal marks, inserted notes, draft and typescript review.   Jarndyce Antiquarian Booksellers   CCVII - 87   2015   £40

Getz, Mike   *Baseball's 3000-Hit Men: a Book of Stats, Facts and Trivia.*   Brooklyn: Gemmeg Press, 1982. First edition, fine in fine dust jacket, inscribed by author to Cliff Kachline.   Between the Covers Rare Books, Inc.   187 - 8   2015 $550

Giannone, Pietro   *Opera Postume di Pietro Giannone in Difesa Della Sua Storia Civile de Regno di Napoli con la sue Professione di Fede si Aggiungono in Questa Edizione le Annotazioni Critiche del Padre Paoli, Sopra il IX. Libro del Tomo Secondo Della Storia Civile...*   Venezia: Giambattista Pasquale, 1768. New edition, volumes, quarto, engraved titlepages, head and tailpieces, contemporary quarter leather with patterned boards, contemporary engraved bookplate of William Parsons on each front pastedown, covers rubbed at spines and edges, very good, internally bright and clean.   Peter Ellis, Bookseller   2014 - 016080   2015   £325

Gibbon, Edward   1737-1794   *The History of the Decline and Fall of the Roman Empire.*   Dublin: William Hallhead, 1777. Pirated Dublin edition, 10 Volumes, Volume 1 states that it is the Fourth edition, it was printed in Dublin for Hallhead in 1777, Volumes 2- were also printed in Dublin for Hallhead and are dated 1781, Volumes 7-10 were printed in Dublin for Luke White in 1788, lacks volumes 11 and 12, Volume 2 has folding map, bookplate of Charles Chauncey to front pastedown of each volume, bound in full leather with title and volumes labels to spines, however, one volume lacks volume label, volumes 1-6 have matching full calf and volumes 7-10 are bound in matching mottled calf bindings, very good.   The Kelmscott Bookshop   11 - 21   2015 $1200

Gibbon, Edward   1737-1794   *The History of the Decline and Fall of the Roman Empire.*   New York: Limited Editions Club, 1946. Limited to 150 numbered copies, 7 volumes, small 4to., quarter leather, marbled paper covered boards, gilt spines, slipcase, etchings of Giovanni Battista Piranesi, marginal notes throughout text, two of the volumes worn along hinges with some loss of leather.   Oak Knoll Books   25 - 30   2015 $450

Gibbons, Floyd *The Red Napoleon.* New York: Jonathan Cape and Harrison Smith, 1929. First edition, very good plus, solid copy with faint letter and number to front endpaper, usual darkening of cloth at gutters in very good plus dust jacket with shallow chipping to spine crown and foot. Ed Smith Books 82 - 12 2015 $200

Gibbons, Kaye *One the Occasion of My Last Afternoon.* New York: G. P. Putnam's Sons, 1998. First edition, small bump bottom rear board, else fine in fine dust jacket, inscribed by author for Reynolds Price July 1 1998. Between the Covers Rare Books, Inc. 187 - 108 2015 $350

Gibbons, Thomas *Memoirs of Eminently Pious Women Who were Ornaments to their Sex, Blessings to their Families and Edifying Examples to Their Church and the World.* London: J. Buckland, 1777. First edition, 8vo., 12 full page engraved portraits, engraved arms of dedicatee, Countess of Huntingdon at beginning, occasional foxing and browning, bound in contemporary scuffed boards, later presentations on endpapers, scarce. Second Life Books Inc. 190 - 22 2015 $1250

Gibbons, William *A Reply to Sir Lucius O'Brien, Bart. In Which that part of his letter to the author which most particularly respects the present state of the iron trade between England and Ireland is considered.* Bristol: printed by Cocking and Rudhall for J. B. Becket &c, 1785. First edition, 8vo., half title, (marginal tear repaired), recent plain wrappers, very good, early ownership name 'Garbett' in ink at head of title. John Drury Rare Books March 2015 - 17709 2015 $266

Gibbs, Barbara *The Meeting Place of the Colors. Poems.* West Branch: Cummington Press, 1972. First edition, one of 300 copies printed on Arches text paper, 4 plates from drawings by Ulfert Wilkie, octavo, black cloth with printed spine label, spine slightly sunned, else fine. signed by Wilke, printer' A. D. Moore's copy with gift inscription. Between the Covers Rare Books, Inc. 187 - 109 2015 $150

Gibbs, George *The Castle Rock Mystery.* New York: D. Appleton and Co., 1927. First edition, 8vo., near fine in dust jacket. Buckingham Books March 2015 - 21893 2015 $375

Gibbs, George *The Triangle Man.* New York: Appleton-Century, 1939. First edition, fine in dust jacket with nicks at top of spine and several short closed tears. Mordida Books March 2015 - 002447 2015 $125

Gibbs, John Arthur *The History of Anthony and Dorothea Gibbs and of their Contemporary Relatives...* London: Saint Catherine Press, 1922. 4to., original publisher's dark blue cloth, lettered gilt on spine and on front cover, excellent condition, slight browning to endpapers, otherwise very good+, from the library of Allan Heywood Bright (1862-1941). Any Amount of Books 2015 - C11662 2015 £285

Gibbs, N. H. *Grand Strategy.* London: HMSO, 1956-1976. Mixed editions, large 8vo., 7 volumes, ex-British Foreign Office Library with few library markings, inner hinges of 2 volumes cracked but holding else very good set. Any Amount of Books 2015 - C1196 2015 £320

Giblett, Paul *A Refutation of the Calumnies of George Harrower, Lately Convicted at the Old Bailey Sessions on a Charge of Bigamy.* London: printed by and for Paul Giblett, 1816. Second edition, 8vo., brown spots on last couple of leaves, recently well bound in linen backed marbled boards lettered, good, rare. John Drury Rare Books March 2015 - 19810 2015 $266

Gibson, Colin *Art and Society in the Victorian Novel.* London: Macmillan Press, 1989. Half title, few notes by Kathleen Tillotson, her signed copy, original olive brown cloth, very good in dust jacket, with inserted postcard from Philip (Collins?). Jarndyce Antiquarian Booksellers CCVII - 277 2015 £25

Gibson, Walter B. *Looks that Kill.* New York: Atlas, 1948. First edition, page edges strengthened, otherwise fine in wrappers. Mordida Books March 2015 - 009042 2015 $100

Gibson, Walter B. *The Shadow and the Golden Master.* New York: Mysterious Press, 1984. First edition, limited to 250 copies numbered and signed by author, this copy 153, signed as Walter Gibson and Maxwell Grant, fine, without dust jacket, as issued and housed in matching cloth slipcase. Buckingham Books March 2015 - 29530 2015 $225

Gibson, Walter B. *The Shadow: Jade Dragon & House of Ghosts.* New York: Mysterious Press, 1981. First edition, limited to 300 numbered and signed copies, very fine in decorated cloth, original very fine slipcase. Buckingham Books March 2015 - 27856 2015 $175

Gibson, Walter B. *The Shadow Scrapbook.* New York: Harcourt Brace Jovanovich, 1979. First edition, quarto, signed by author, paperback original, illustrations in black and white and color. Buckingham Books March 2015 - 24592 2015 $375

Gibson, William *The Difference Engine.* New York: Toronto: London: Sydney: Auckland: Bantam Books, 1991. First US edition, one of 350 numbered copies signed by Gibson and Sterling, octavo, cloth. John W. Knott, Bookseller Selected New Arrivals Jan. 2015 - 17035 2015 $250

Gibson, William *Neuromancer.* West Bloomfield: Phantasia Press, 1986. First US hardcover edition, octavo, illustrations by Barclay Shaw, cloth. John W. Knott, Bookseller Selected New Arrivals Jan. 2015 - 17034 2015 $850

Gibson, William *The Peripheral.* New York: Putnam's, 2014. First edition, signed by author, fine in dust jacket. Ed Smith Books 83 - 118 2015 $75

Giffen, Helen S. *Trail-Blazing Pioneer: Colonel Joseph Ballinger Chiles.* San Francisco: John Howell Books, 1969. First edition, although not indicated, one of 750 copies printed by Lawton and Alfred Kennedy, frontispiece, 6 plates, red cloth, gilt, very fine, mostly uncut, pictorial dust jacket. Argonaut Book Shop Holiday Season 2014 - 100 2015 $90

Gifford, John *A Maximum; or the Rise and Progress of Famine. Addressed to the British People by the author of a Residence in France during the Years 1792, 1793, 1794, 1795 &c.* London: J. Wright, 1801. First edition, 8vo., recent marbled boards lettered on spine, very good, apparently rare outside UK libraries. John Drury Rare Books March 2015 - 25510 2015 $266

Gifford, William *The Anti-Jacobin; or Weekly Examiner.* London: printed for J. Wright, 1799. Fourth edition, 8vo., half brown leather with dark orange boards lettered gilt on black spine label, 2 volumes, no. 1-36 dated 20 Nov. 1797-9 July 1798, with index, clean, very good, neat name on first blank page and bookplate of John Hopton. Any Amount of Books 2015 - C11845 2015 £220

Gil Y Garces, Martin *El Doctor Don martin Gil y Garces, dean de la Santa Iglesia Catedral de Michoacan...* Mexico: Impr. del ciudadano A. Valdes, 1831. First edition, 8vo., black and white photos, three quarter red morocco over blue cloth boards, scarce, about fine, minor rubbing on board, few old erasures. Kaaterskill Books 19 - 99 2015 $450

Gilbert, Anthony *The Case Against Andrew Fane.* New York: Dodd Mead & Co., 1931. First US edition, fine in dust jacket with closed tear and wrinkling to bottom edge of rear panel. Buckingham Books March 2015 - 11125 2015 $325

Gilbert, Anthony *The Murder of Mrs. Davenport.* New York: Dial, 1928. First American edition, covers lightly soiled and slight crease on prelims, otherwise near fine in very fine dust jacket. Mordida Books March 2015 - 008076 2015 $200

Gilbert, Colleen B. *A Bibliography of the Works of Dorothy L. Sayers.* London: Macmillan, 1979. First edition, fine in price clipped dust jacket with publisher's price sticker and some scattered slight spotting. Mordida Books March 2015 - 009159 2015 $95

Gilbert, Jack *Views of Jeopardy.* New Haven London: Yale University Press, 1962. First edition, 8vo., original cloth, dust jacket, fine, very scarce. James S. Jaffe Rare Books Modern American Poetry - 106 2015 $1750

Gilbert, John *The Crystal Palace that Fox Built, a Pyramid of Rhyme.* London: David Bogue 86 Fleet Street, 1851. square 8vo., 9 plates engraved on wood by H. Vizetelly after John Gilbert, original buff boards, slight abrasions to extremities. Marlborough Rare Books Ltd. List 49 - 11 2015 £250

Gilbert, Michael *The Black Seraphim.* New York: Harper, 1984. First U.S. edition, signed by author, fine in near fine dust jacket with few tiny nicks. Beasley Books 2013 - 2015 $45

Gilbert, Michael *The Mathematics of Murder.* London: Robert Hale, 2000. First edition, fine in fine dust jacket. Buckingham Books March 2015 - 29491 2015 $275

Gilbert, Paul *Bertram's Trip to the North Pole.* Chicago: Rand McNally, 1940. First edition (later editions are so stated), 8vo., cloth, fine in very good+ dust jacket with 2 tiny chips on rear panel, illustrations by Anne Stossel with color endpapers and numerous full and partial page black and whites, scarce in this condition. Aleph-Bet Books, Inc. 108 - 211 2015 $375

Gilbert, Thomas *A Plan for the Better Relief and Employment of the Poor...* London: G. Wilkie, 1781. First edition, including half title, early 19th century half calf over marbled boards, neatly rebacked and label, armorial bookplate of Ferguson of Raith, fine, large, crisp copy, partially unopened. John Drury Rare Books 2015 - 24432 2015 $1311

Gilbert, Thomas *A Plan for the Better Relief and Employment of the Poor...* London: G. Wilkie, 1781. First edition, 8vo., half title, contemporary marbled boards, rebacked in calf, spine fully gilt labelled and with raised bands, fine and large crisp copy in excellent binding. John Drury Rare Books 2015 - 21196 2015 $1311

Gilbert, William Schwenck 1836-1911 *The Pinafore Picture Book.* London: George Bell and Sons, 1908. Deluxe edition, 4to., white cloth with pictorial gilt covers, top edge gilt, fine, printed on handmade paper and illustrated by Alice B. Woodward, 16 mounted color plates, 2-color pictorial titlepage and pictorial endpapers and 12 very fine pen and inks in text, rare edition. Aleph-bet Books, Inc. 109 - 490 2015 $850

Gilchrist, Alexander *Life of William Blake. "Pictor Ignotus".* London: and Cambridge: Macmillan and Co., 1863. First edition, 8vo,. 2 volumes, 19th century full calf expertly rebacked, presumably to accommodate extra-illustrations, preserving original spine, triple gilt fillet borders to upper and lower boards, spine divided into six compartments with raised bands gilt, red morocco and gilt lettering pieces to second compartment, green morocco and gilt lettering pieces to the third compartments, remainder attractively gilt tooled turn-ins, all edges gilt, marbled endpapers, frontispiece in volume I, folding frontispiece in volume 2, numerous illustrations, this is an extra illustrated copy with 34 bound, tipped-in or loosely inserted engravings, front flyleaf in volume I with chip at upper right corner, occasional light spotting.   Henry Sotheran Ltd.   William Blake Exhibition 17th Oct.-7th Nov. 2014 - 87   2015   £2200

Gilchrist, Alexander *Life of William Blake.* London: Macmillan and Co., 1880. Second edition, 8vo., 2 volumes, original blue cloth, upper boards and spine gilt blocked with elaborate design after Blake, frontispiece to each and numerous illustrations, boards lightly rubbed in plates, lower hinge volume 2, expertly repaired, otherwise bright set.   Henry Sotheran Ltd.   William Blake Exhibition 17th Oct.-7th Nov. 2014 - 88   2015   £500

Gilchrist, Ellen *The Land Surveyor's Daughter.* Fayetteville: Lost Road, 1979. First edition, first book, paperback original, 8vo., original wrappers, presentation copy inscribed by author for Denise Levertov.   James S. Jaffe Rare Books   Modern American Poetry - 107   2015 $1500

Gilder, William H. *Schwatka's Search. Sledging in the Arctic in Quest of the Franklin Records.*   New York: Charles Scribner's Sons, 1881. First edition, frontispiece 29 woodcut illustrations, 2 maps outlined in color, dark brown pictorial cloth stamped in black and gilt, dark blue coated endpapers, expertly recased, corners lightly rubbed, fine.   Argonaut Book Shop   Holiday Season 2014 - 101   2015 $375

Gildersleeves, Elena *Baby Epicure: Appetizing Dishes for Children and Invalids.*   New York: E. P. Dutton & Co., 1937. First edition, fine in near fine with rubbing and several tiny tears along extremities, very attractive.   Between the Covers Rare Books   196 - 138   2015 $150

Gildzen, Alex *Six Poems/Seven Prints. Poems by John Ashbery, James Bertoline, Gwendolyn Brooks, Denise Levertov, Steven Oserland & Gary Snyder.*   Kent: Kent State University Libraries, 1971. First edition, one of 50 sets signed by authors and by Smithson, Porter, Quaytman, Sacco and Piene out of a total edition of 500 sets, 4to., 14 loose sheets laid into paper portfolio, fine.   James S. Jaffe Rare Books   Modern American Poetry - 6   2015 $5000

Gill, Eric   1882-1940 *From the Palestine Diary of Eric Gill.* London: Harvill Press, 1949. First edition, small 8vo., attractively bound in blue cloth with blue leather spine lettered gilt, 70 pages, uncut, rare, spine slightly faded, otherwise sound, very good neat name pencilled on front endpaper.   Any Amount of Books   March 2015 - A99139   2015   £350

Gill, Merton *The Collected Papers of David Rappaport.* New York: Basic Books, 1967. First edition, fine in near fine dust jacket with short tear at spine fold.   Beasley Books   2013 - 2015 $45

Gillespie, Dizzy *To Be or Not to Bop.*   Garden City: Doubleday, 1979. First edition, signed by author and dated '79, large 8vo., near fine in very good+ dust jacket with two clean tears at top edge, jacket spine has not been sunned and dust jacket is near fine, other than faults listed above.   Beasley Books   2013 - 2015 $250

Gillet, Alexis Francois *Titan and Volcan: a story Woven into the Lives of Two Young Men.*   Boston: Meador Pub. co., 1933. First edition, octavo, inserted frontispiece, original pebbled maroon cloth, front panel stamped in gold and ruled in blind, spine panel stamped in gold.   L. W. Currey, Inc.   Boy's Adventure Fiction 2015 - 55   2015 $150

Gillette, William *The Painful Predicament of Sherlock Holmes.*   Chicago: Ben Abramson, 1955. First edition, fine, without dust jacket as issued, with publisher's flyer.   Mordida Books   March 2015 - 008799   2015 $85

Gilliland, Maude T. *Rincon (Remote Dwelling Place) A Story of life on a South Texas Ranch at the Turn of the Century.*   Brownsville: Springman-King Lithograph Co., 1964. First edition, presentation inscription by author, cloth, lightly foxed on fore edges and endpapers, else fine in fine dust jacket.   Buckingham Books   March 2015 - 28748   2015 $300

Gillis, Donald *Inverness: History, Memoirs, Anecdotes, Centennial 1904-2004.* Antigonish: Casket Pub. Co., n.d., 2004. Trade paperback, 8vo., illustrations, very good.   Schooner Books Ltd.   110 - 75   2015 $40

Gillmore, Parker *The Amphibion's Voyage.* London: W. H. Allen & Co., 1885. First edition, octavo, 48 page publisher's catalog dated 'December 1884' inserted at rear, 8 inserted plates with illustrations by A. T. Elwes, original pictorial green cloth, front and spine panels stamped in gold and black, all edges untrimmed.   L. W. Currey, Inc.   Boy's Adventure Fiction 2015 - 37   2015 $225

Gilman, Charlotte Perkins *Concerning Children.* Boston: Small Maynard, 1900. First edition, 8vo., blue cloth stamped in green and gold and signed MLP, spine rubbed, hinge tender, name label blocked out, good copy.   Second Life Books Inc.   189 - 86   2015 $350

Gilman, Charlotte Perkins *The Forerunner Volume 3 no. 1 January 1912 to Volume 3 no. 12 December 1912.* New York: Charlton, 1913. First edition, large 8vo., publisher's cloth, little spotted and worn, very good, rare.   Second Life Books Inc.   190 - 84   2015 $1200

Gilman, Charlotte Perkins *The Forerunner Volume 4 #1 January 1913 to Volume 4 #12, December 1913.* New York: Charlton, 1914. First edition, large 8vo. bound in publisher's cloth, little spotted and worn, very good, rare. Second Life Books Inc.   190 - 85   2015 $1200

Gilman, Charlotte Perkins *The Forerunner. Volume 5 # 1 (January 1914) to volume 5 #12 December 1914.* New York: Charlton, 1915. First edition, large 8vo., publisher's cloth, covers show effects stains which affects endpapers, top margin of endpaper and first seven leaves have some paper torn (or eaten away, this does not affect text), rare. Second Life Books Inc.   189 - 84   2015 $900

Gilman, Charlotte Perkins *The Forerunner Volume 6 # 1 January 1915 to Volume 6 #12 December 1915.* New York: Charlton, 1915. First edition, large 8vo., publisher's cloth that show moisture damage to upper right of front cover, and upper rear of rear cover, includes some waterstaining to rear endpapers that affects somewhat the contents page. Second Life Books Inc.   189 - 85   2015 $1250

Gilman, Charlotte Perkins *Gems of Art for the Home and Fireside.* Providence: J. A. & R. A. Reid, 1888. First edition, 4to., mustard yellow cloth cover with faint stampings in Victorian styling, covers badly waterstained, soiled and bent, endpapers waterstained and soiled, staining stops before titlepage, which is quite clean as is the text and illustrations, rare.   Second Life Books Inc.   189 - 90   2015 $3750

Gilman, Charlotte Perkins *Gems of Art for the Home and Fireside.* Providence: J. A. & R. A. Reid, 1890. Second edition, 4to., grey cloth stamped in gilt and black, stamped red and green, edges stained yellow, hinges tender but connected, 50 black and white plates, rare.   Second Life Books Inc.   189 - 91   2015 $1500

Gilman, Charlotte Perkins *In This Our World.* Boston: Small Maynard, Oct., 1899. Second edition, 12mo., top edge gilt, hinge loose, covers rubbed along edges, just good, uncut, closed tear to one leaf, otherwise very nice in stamped binding, scarce.   Second Life Books Inc.   189 - 87   2015 $225

Gilman, Charlotte Perkins *Women and Economics.* Boston: Small Maynard, 1899. Second edition, 8vo., chipped spine label, bookplate, very good, untrimmed, scarce.   Second Life Books Inc.   189 - 88   2015 $85

Gilman, Charlotte Perkins *Women and Economics.* Boston: Small Maynard, 1900. Third edition, 8vo., maroon cloth, ex-library with stamps and bookplate, owner's name, hinges tender, few pencil marks in margins, cover spotted and little worn at corners and edges of spine, otherwise very good.   Second Life Books Inc.   189 - 89   2015 $75

Gilmore, Florence *For the Faith Life of Just De Bretenieres.* Maryknoll, Ossing: Catholic Foreign Mission Society, 1918. First edition, tan cloth with inlaid picture to upper portion of front cover, photos, very good minutest color loss to portions of boards, nice, clean tight set. Stephen Lupack   March 2015 - 2015 $125

Gilson, Charles *The Pirate Aeroplane.* London: Henry Frowde Hodder and Stoughton, 1913. First edition, octavo, 6 inserted plates with color illustrations by Christopher Clarke, original pictorial light blue cloth, front and spine panels stamped in cream, tan, brown and blackc, gray endpapers, all edges stained black.   L. W. Currey, Inc.   Boy's Adventure Fiction 2015 - 41   2015 $200

Gilson, Charles *The Race Round the World: Being the account of the Contest for £100,000 Prize Offered by the Combined Newspaper League....* London: Henry Frowde Hodder and Stoughton, 1914. First edition, octavo, inserted folded map, original pictorial blue cloth, front panel stamped brown, white and black, spine panel stamped in brown, white, black and gold, all edges stained black.   L. W. Currey, Inc.   Boy's Adventure Fiction 2015 - 42   2015 $200

Gimlett, F. E. *Over Trails of Yesterday.* Salida: Hermit of Arbor Villa, 1943-1951. First editions, 8vo., all printed wrappers, each volume 64 pages, illustrations, 9 volumes. Buckingham Books   March 2015 - 31048   2015 $350

Gingerich, Owen *The Nature of Scientific Discovery.* Washington: Smithsonian Institution, 1975. First edition, signed by author, 8vo., near fine, mild soil and foxing to edges in very good++, price clipped dust jacket with mild soil , short closed tears, 8vo.   By the Book, L. C.   44 - 54   2015 $50

Ginsberg, Allen *Careless Love.* Madison: Red Ozier Press, 1978. First edition, limited to 280 copies signed by author, thin 8vo., original marbled wrappers, very fine, preserved in custom folding box.   James S. Jaffe Rare Books   Modern American Poetry - 110   2015 $100

Ginsberg, Allen *Howl and Other Poems.* San Francisco: City Lights Pocket Bookshop, 1956. First edition, one of 1000 copies printed letterpress at Villiers Publications Ltd. in England, 12mo., printed wrappers, presentation copy inscribed by author for poet Jack Gilbert, printed cover label lightly soiled, otherwise fine.   James S. Jaffe Rare Books   Modern American Poetry - 108   2015 $15,000

Ginsberg, Allen *Making It Up: Poetry Composed at St. Mark's Church on May 9 1979.* New York: Catchword Papers, 1994. First edition, one of only 60 roman numeraled copies signed by Ginsberg, 8vo., original cloth, dust jacket with front panel illustration by Larry Rivers, fine. James S. Jaffe Rare Books   Many Happy Returns - 189   2015 $250

Ginsberg, Allen *Siesta in Xbalba and Return to the States.* Near Icy Cape, Alaska: At the Sign of the Midnight Sun as published by the author July, 1956. First edition, small 4to., original mimeographed self wrappers stapled as issued, trifle soiled, but fine, rare, Jack Gilbert's copy signed by Ginsberg, with Gilbert's ownership signature dated 5ix1956 in upper left hand corner of same page.   James S. Jaffe Rare Books   Modern American Poetry - 109   2015 $25,000

Ginsberg, Allen *White Shroud. Poems 1980-1985.* New York: Harper & Row, 1986. First edition, 8vo., original cloth, dust jacket, signed by author on titlepage, fine in price clipped dust jacket.   James S. Jaffe Rare Books   Modern American Poetry - 111   2015 $150

Gioia, Dana *Journeys in Sunlight.* Cottondale: Ex Ophidia, 1987. First edition, one of 90 copies printed by Richard Gabriel Rummonds and signed by Gioia & Testa, 4to., original quarter morocco and hand painted boards, glassine dust jacket, cloth box, exquisite book, last book printed with Ex Ophidia imprint, as new, 3 etchings by Fulvio Testa.   James S. Jaffe Rare Books   Modern American Poetry - 113   2015 $1750

Gioia, Dana *Two Poems/Due Poesie.* Verona: Edizioni Ampersand, 1987. First edition, text in English & Italian, limited to 50 press numbered copies printed by Alessandro Zanella and Linda Samson-Talleur in Monotype Dante on handmade paper from Cartiere Magnani in Pescia, and signed by Gioia and Bacigalupo, folio, 2 illustrations cut by Linda Samson-Talleur, original paste paper boards, fine, rare.   James S. Jaffe Rare Books   Modern American Poetry - 114   2015 $1500

Giono, Jean *Menagerie Enigmatique.* Paris: Aux Depens d'un Amateur, 1961. #CVII of 260 copies, signed by author and artist, Assia (Henri Prince de Hesse), 27 lovely color illustrations, unbound signatures laid into wrappers, fine in fine wrappers, orange clamshell box with waterstains, folio. Beasley Books   2013 - 2015 $375

Girvin, Ernest Alexandner *Domestic Duels or Evening talks on the Woman Question.* San Francisco: Bronson, 1898. First edition, 8vo., grey cloth stamped in green and gilt, hinge little tender, but very good, tipped in slip "Compliments of E. E. Washburn personal friend of author", contemporary ownership signature "Mary Dudley Dozier Nov. 23rd 1898", scarce.   Second Life Books Inc.   189 - 92   2015 $300

Gisborne, Thomas *An Enquiry into the Duties of the Female Sex.* London: Cadell, Davies, 1797. First edition, 8vo., uncut and unopened, contemporary three quarter calf and marbled boards, little light foxing, titlepage toned and cropped affecting the contemporary ownership signature of A. Barclay, otherwise very good, clean tight copy.   Second Life Books Inc.   189 - 93   2015 $650

Gisborne, Thomas *Walks in a Forest.* London: printed by J. Davis for B. and J. White, 1796. Second edition, 191 x 127mm., fine contemporary red straight grain morocco handsomely gilt by Charles Hering Sr. (his ticket), covers with frame of bead and flower roll within thick and thin gilt rules, daisy cornerpieces, scalloped central panel with delicate gilt rule frame inset with garlands at sides and corners, flat spine lavishly gilt in compartments with oval centerpiece surrounded by small circles and many gilt dots, decorative gilt roll to turn-ins, marbled endpapers, all edges gilt, vague hints of soiling to covers, endpapers with minor smudges and faint browning, occasional light spots of foxing leaves a shade less than bright, otherwise excellent internally, text clean and fresh, lovely binding in very fine condition, bright morocco and gilt, virtually no wear.   Phillip J. Pirages   66 - 67   2015 $1500

Gissing, George *Thyrza: a Tale.* London: John Murray, 1907. New edition, half title, original pink cloth, little faded, leading f.e.p. cut out, from the library of Geoffrey & Kathleen Tillotson, marked from Kathleen to Geoffrey, 1937 with 2 notes and 2 press cuttings inserted.   Jarndyce Antiquarian Booksellers   CCVII - 278   2015   £20

Giustiniani, Luigi *The Missionary or the Life of a Wesleyan.* London: printed by S. Fawcett, 1834. First (only) edition, 8vo., 48 pages, recent marbled boards lettered on spine, very good, presentation copy inscribed by author to M. Rawlins, apparently rare.   John Drury Rare Books   March 2015 - 25009   2015   £306

Gladstone, John *Letters Addressed to the Right Honourable the Earl of Clancarty, President of the Board of Trade &c &c...* London: J. M. Richardson, 1813. First edition, wanting half title, recent plain wrappers, very good. John Drury Rare Books   2015 - 16432   2015 $177

Glaister, Donald *A Few Questions.* Vashon: 2009. Artist's book, one of 10 copies, each signed and numbered by author, page size 8 inches square, 15 pages, bound by artist, Donald Glaister, exposed sewn spine, Mylar and collage, text laser printed in gill sans, pages are Mylar encapsulated, with interior collages of various materials.   Priscilla Juvelis - Rare Books   61 - 21   2015 $3500

Glasgow, Ellen 1874-1945 *The Descendant.* New York: Harper and Brothers, 1897. First edition, first printing and binding with single NY imprint on titlepage and spine without Glasgow's name, 8vo., original decorated tan cloth, gilt lettering, 6 pages of publisher's terminal ads, fine.   The Brick Row Book Shop   Miscellany 67 - 50   2015 $275

Glasgow, Ellen 1874-1945 *Vein of Iron.* New York: Harcourt Brace, 1935. First edition, with signed by author (letter nearly fine), fine in very good+ dust jacket.   Stephen Lupack   March 2015 - 2015 $100

Glashow, Sheldon *Interactions. A Journey through the Mind of a Particle Physicist and the Matter of This World.* New York: Warner, 1988. First edition, 8vo., fine in near fine dust jacket, signed, inscribed and dated by author.   By the Book, L. C.   Special List 10 - 58   2015 $200

Glaspell, Susan *A Jury of Her Peers.* London: Ernest Benn Ltd., 1927. First edition, one of only 250 copies signed by author, fine in printed wrappers.   Buckingham Books   March 2015 - 24421   2015 $675

Glass, I. I. *Shock Waves and Man.* Toronto: University of Toronto, Institute for Aerospace Studies, 1974. First edition, 8vo., signed presentation from author for John Brunner, attractive Brunner bookplate, very good+ in like jacket. Any Amount of Books   2015 - A66971   2015   £150

Glendinning, Robert *Practical Hints on the Culture of the Pine Apple.* Exeter, Pollard: for Longman and Co. in London, sold by W. Spear 263 High Street Exeter,..., 1839. 18mo., folding lithograph plate, original green cloth, upper cover blocked with title in gilt, lower cover with slight damp marks.   Marlborough Rare Books   List 53 - 19   2015   £500

Glimpses of North Dakota. David Bartlett, 1901. First edition, oblong 16mo., original purple printed wrappers, very good.   Buckingham Books   March 2015 - 32871   2015 $750

Glover, Edward *The Technique of Psycho-Analysis.* London: Institute of Psy./Balliere, 1928. First edition, paperback.   Beasley Books   2013 - 2015 $45

Glover, Jesse R. *Bruce Lee: Between Wing Chung and Jeet Kune Do.* Seattle: Jesse R. Glover, 1976. First edition, octavo, 96 pages, illustrated wrappers, illustrations with drawing and from photos, some modest rubbing on wrappers, small old price label inside front cover, very good or better copy.   Between the Covers Rare Books   197 - 59   2015 $1200

Gluck, Louise *Firstborn.* New York: NAL, 1968. First edition, scarce, 8vo., original cloth, white dust jacket faintly discolored with touch of rubbing at head of spine, otherwise fine.   James S. Jaffe Rare Books   Modern American Poetry - 115   2015 $750

Gluck, Louise *Firstborn.* Middlesex: Anvil Press, 1969. First British edition, limited to 50 copies, 8vo., printed on Glastonbury Antique rose paper, signed by poet, fine. James S. Jaffe Rare Books   Modern American Poetry - 116   2015 $350

Gluck, Louise *The Garden.* N.P.: Anateus Editions, 1976. First edition, one of 50 numbered copies signed by author out of total edition of 500 copies, tall 8vo., original green printed wrappers, very fine.   James S. Jaffe Rare Books   Modern American Poetry - 117   2015 $350

Goddard, Jeanne M. *A Catalogue of the Frederick W. & Carrie S. Beinecke Collection of Western Americana.* New Haven: Yale University Press, 1925. First edition, small quarto, frontispiece, 12 photo plates, half black cloth, red boards, red spine label, very fine, dust jacket (short closed tear to bottom edge).   Argonaut Book Shop   Holiday Season 2014 - 27   2015 $50

Godden, Geoffrey A. *Minton Pottery & Porcelain of the First Period 1793-1850.* London: Barrie & Jenkins, 1978. First edition, small 4to., fine in fine, but price clipped dust jacket.   Beasley Books   2013 - 2015 $45

Godey, John *The Gun and Mr. Smith.* Garden City: Doubleday, 1947. First edition, pages darkened, otherwise very good in dust jacket.   Mordida Books   March 2015 - 003878   2015 $75

Godfrey, Ambrose *An Account of the New Method of Extinguishing Fires by Explosion and Suffocation.* N.P.: London: printed in the year, 1724. 8vo., small engraving, very small fault affecting tiny part of ruled border of title (no where near letters), but excellent copy in fine recent 18th century style quarter calf gilt over marbled boards, scarce. John Drury Rare Books   2015 - 25349   2015 $1661

Godfrey, Thomas *Murder for Christmas.* New York: Mysterious Press, 1982. First edition, one of 250 numbered copies signed by author and artist, Gahan Wilson, very fine, slipcase.   Mordida Books   March 2015 - 010013   2015 $85

Godoy, Armand *Les Litanies De La Vierge.* Paris: A. Blaizot et Fils, 1934. #32 of 131 copies, wrappers near fine with one tear at foot of spine fold, in publisher's glassine, near fine with few tears, 48 color illustrations by Lydis, small 4to., protective chemise and slipcase.   Beasley Books   2013 - 2015 $500

Godwin, Francis *The Man in the Moone and Nuncius Inanimatus...* Northampton: Smith College, 1937. pages 25-30 torn without loss, original grey printed wrappers, slightly marked with splits at tail of spine, Kathleen Tillotson's marked copy, with typescript proofs and copy of her review.   Jarndyce Antiquarian Booksellers   CCVII - 279   2015   £20

Godwin, William   1756-1836   *Enquiry Concerning Political Justice and Its Influence on Morals and Happiness.*   London: Robinson, 1796. Second edition, 8vo., half titles, new three quarter calf and marbled boards, clean set.   Second Life Books Inc.   189 - 94   2015 $3500

Godwin, William   1756-1836   *The History of England for the Use of Schools and Young persons by Edward Baldwin.*   London: M. J. Godwin, 1815. Stereotype edition, 12mo., frontispiece and 7 plates in rubbed, contemporary calf, contemporary name on endpaper.   Second Life Books Inc.   189 - 96   2015 $325

Godwin, William   1756-1836   *History of the Commonwealth of England.*   London: Colburn, 1824. 1826. 1827. 1828. First edition, 4 volumes, three quarter calf and marbled boards, morocco labels, little rubbed, very good, clean set.   Second Life Books Inc.   189 - 98   2015 $950

Godwin, William   1756-1836   *The History of England for the Use of Schools and Young Persons by Edward Baldwin.*   London: Baldwin and Cradock, 1833. New edition, portraits, 12mo., frontispiece, 3 plates, contemporary calf rubbed, 1834 ad leaf tipped to endpapers.   Second Life Books Inc.   189 - 95   2015 $325

Godwin, William   1756-1836   *History of Rome.*   London: M(ary) J(ane) Godwin Skinner Street, 1824. Fourth edition, 12mo., little worn contemporary calf, front cover nearly separate, 2 folding maps and 4 engraved plates, very good.   Second Life Books Inc.   189 - 97   2015 $325

Godwin, William   1756-1836   *Memoirs of the Author of a Vindication of the Rights of Woman.*   London: Johnson, 1798. First edition, 8vo., lacks half title and final leaf of ad, engraved frontispiece, former owner J. H. Anthony, 1854 ownership signature on endpaper, early 19th century three quarter calf, spine somewhat dry and rubbed, upper joint partially cracked, very nice, clean, scarce.   Second Life Books Inc.   189 - 99   2015 $4500

Godwin, William   1756-1836   *Memoirs of the Author of a Vindication of the Rights of Woman.*   Philadelphia: James Carey, 1799. First American edition, 8vo., front blank tissued and remounted, bound in new boards with calf spine, some little marginal staining, very good, this copy was owned and annotated by a contemporary American reader, Nathaniel Pendleton Taylor, who signed and dated titlepage, Philadelphia July 17, 1812 and made occasional comments in text and on titlepage.   Second Life Books Inc.   189 - 270   2015 $1500

Godwin, William   1756-1836   *The Pantheon or Ancient History of the Gods of Greece and Rome for the Use of Schools and Young Persons of Both Sexes...*   London: M(ary) J(ane) Godwin Skinner Street, 1810. Third edition, 12mo., frontispiece and 11 plates in rubbed contemporary calf, large bookplate on endpaper, good, ownership signature of Frances Elizabeth Milford on titlepage.   Second Life Books Inc.   189 - 100   2015 $325

Godwin, William   1756-1836   *Thoughts on Man, His Nature.*   London: Effingham Wilson, 1831. First edition, tall 8vo., contemporary three quarter calf and marbled boards, spine chipped and banged, lacks some of the lower label, old bookseller label on endpaper, some offsetting, some toning to titlepage, very good, lacks ad in front and rear.   Second Life Books Inc.   189 - 101   2015 $950

Godwin, William   1756-1836   *Thoughts on Man, His Nature, Productions and Discoveries Interspersed with Some Particulars Respecting the Author.*   London: Effingham Wilson, 1831. First edition, half bound in leather over marbled paper covered boards, original spine laid back down, hinges repaired and tightened, new endpapers, old f.e.p. detached and chipped, trimmed during rebinding, just very good-, 8vo.   Beasley Books   2013 - 2015 $175

Goebel, Julius   *History of the Supreme Court of the United States.*   New York and London: Cambridge University Press, Macmillan Co., 1971. Mixed editions, large 8vo., 8 volumes in 7 books, original teal and burgundy cloth boards, lettered gilt at spines and front covers, all clean, very good+ copies.   Any Amount of Books   2015 - C8485   2015   £300

Goedeke, Karl   *Grundrisz zur Geschichte der Deutschen Dichtung aus Den Quellen.*   Dresden: L. Ehlermann, 1862-1881. Second edition, 8vo., quarter leather, cloth, gilt stamping and four raised bands on spine, decorated endpapers, previous owner's stamp on front free endpaper of first volume, some pencil notations in text, covers scuffed and lightly worn at edges. Oak Knoll Books   306 - 75   2015 $125

Goethe, Johann Wolfgang Von   1749-1832   *The Auto-Biography. Truth and Poetry from My Own Life.*   London: Henry G. Bohn, 1848-1849. 2 volumes, frontispiece, contemporary half green morocco, spines ribbed, decorated and lettered gilt, marbled edges and endpapers, slightly rubbed.   Jarndyce Antiquarian Booksellers   CCXI - 123   2015   £85

Goethe, Johann Wolfgang Von   1749-1832   *Faust: a Dramatic Poem.*   London: Edward Moxon, 1834. Second edition, octavo, contemporary half leather with marbled sides, bookplate, endpapers tanned, covers slightly rubbed at edges, very good.   Peter Ellis, Bookseller   2014 - 010644   2015   £275

Goethe, Johann Wolfgang Von 1749-1832 *Goethe Ausmeinem Leben.* Frankfurt am main: Dichtung und Wahrheit, 1921. 4 volumes, illustrations, foldouts, color frontispieces, decorated boards, very good set, wear at extremities. Stephen Lupack   March 2015 - 2015 $100

Goethe, Johann Wolfgang Von 1749-1832 *Hermann Und Dorothea.* Munchen: 1922. printed in an edition limited to 500 numbered copies, small 4to., paper covered boards, paper title label on cover, deckled fore and bottom edges, printed on laid paper, toning along edges of covers and spine.   Oak Knoll Books   306 - 143   2015 $125

Goetzmann, William H. *Exploration and Empire. The Explorer and Scientist.* Knopf, 1966. First edition, cloth, numerous maps and illustrations, increasingly scarce, fine, bright, dust jacket near fine with very slight wear at spine ends.   Buckingham Books   March 2015 - 34914   2015 $200

Gogarty, Oliver St. John 1878-1957 *It Isn't This Time of Year at All! An Unpremeditated Autobiography.* New York: Doubleday and Co., 1964. First U. S. edition, 8vo., prelims very slightly marked (from press cuttings?), otherwise very good+ in bright, clean, slightly edgeworn (otherwise very good) dust jacket, signed presentation from author to Alice Tyldesley Kendall, a Canadian artist, loosely inserted are 2 good short TLS's from author to Kendall.   Any Amount of Books   2015 - A84548   2015   £160

Gogol, Nicolas *Tarass Boulba.* Lyon: Edition D'Art Les Emeraudes, 1949. Number 203 of 320 numbered copies, folio, unbound signatures in wrappers, drawings and etchings by P. Arcangioli, frontispiece and 20 full page illustrations, each on separate leaf, signed in pencil by artist, fine but for trace of offsetting to half title, fine wrappers and glassine, in chemise with slightly sun darkened spine and very good box with one joint starting to split.   Beasley Books   2013 - 2015 $160

Goines, Dabvif Lance *A Constructed Roman Alphabet, a Geometric Analysis of the Greek Roman Capitals and of the Arabic Numerals.* Boston: David R. Godine, 1982. First edition, 4to., cloth, dust jacket, plates, jacket chipped long edges and spine toned.   Oak Knoll Books   306 - 215   2015 $125

Goldberg, Rube *Rube Goldberg Memorial Exhibition: Drawings from the Bancroft Library.* Berkeley: Friends of the Bancroft, 1971. First edition, wrappers, fine, 32 pages. Beasley Books   2013 - 2015 $45

Golden Sunbeams. London: Society for Promoting Christian Knowledge, 1896. First edition, one year run, 4to., each issue about 16 pages on handmade style uncut paper heavily illustrated with woodcuts in black and red, some signed or initialled contributions by artists, 12 issues stoutly bound in red unlettered cloth, slight wear, very good. Any Amount of Books   2015 - B10051   2015   £175

Golden ABC. New York: McLoughlin Bros. n.d. circa, 1870. Large 12mo., pictorial wrappers, near fine, printed in deep orange and black with word lists for each letter in large type, each letter has fine engraving with letter in red superimposed on illustration.   Aleph-bet Books, Inc.   109 - 6   2015 $275

The Golden Book of Fairy Tales. New York: Simon & Schuster, 1942. First printing of LGB #9, beautiful color lithos by Winifred Hoskins, rare in this condition, fine in fine dust jacket.   Aleph-bet Books, Inc.   109 - 202   2015 $650

Goldenveizer, Aleksandr Borisovich *Talks with Tolstoi.* Richmond: Leonard & Virginia Woolf at The Hogarth Press, 1923. First edition, 8vo., original plain beige grained cloth, printed spine label, lettered in black, some browning to endpapers, otherwise very good+.   Any Amount of Books   2015 - C14279   2015   £180

Goldin, Nan *The Devil's Playground.* London: Phaidon, 2003. Special edition individually signed and numbered, number 17 of 100 presented in a specially made box together with an original large Cibachrome print, signed and numbered By Goldin, book is placed within a larger box with photo in its own compartment and strong dark grey covers, containing the book and print, book as new in unopened plastic wrapper, print fine, untouched.   Any Amount of Books   2015 - A86359   2015   £975

Goldman, Judith *Windows at Tiffany's. The Art of Gene Moore.* New York: Abrams, 1980. First edition, folio, fine in fine dust jacket.   Beasley Books   2013 - 2015 $45

Goldman, William 1911-1993 *Marathon Man.* Delacorte Press, 1974. First edition, fine in dust jacket. Buckingham Books   March 2015 - 33821   2015 $225

Goldman, William 1911-1993 *Marathon Man.* New York: Delacorte, 1974. First edition, fine in dust jacket with couple of tiny tears.   Mordida Books   March 2015 - 008536   2015 $100

Goldman, William 1911-1993 *The Princes Bride.* New York: Harcourt Brace Jovanovich, 1973. First edition, signed by author on titlepage, octavo, original full gray cloth, spine lettered in black and red, original dust jacket not price clipped, orange endpapers, fine in fine dust jacket. Heritage Book Shop   Holiday 2014 - 67   2015 $2250

Goldman, William 1911-1993 *The Princess Bride.* New York: Harcourt Brace Jovanovich, 1973. First edition, first printing, near fine in bright, unclipped dust jacket with crease to rear flap, else fine.   B & B Rare Books, Ltd.   234 - 39   2015 $1000

Goldsmid, Edmund *A Treatise of Magic Incantations.* Edinburgh: privately printed, 1886. First edition, one of 275 copies, 8vo., 54 pages, original stiff printed parchment wrappers, sound, clean, very good, few spots and slight tanning but with clean text, no chips. Any Amount of Books 2015 - C6391 2015 £150

Goldsmith, Oliver 1730-1774 *The History of Little Goody Two-Shoes.* Surrey: Genesis, 1985. First edition thus, facsimile of first edition, one of 250 copies bound in publisher's deluxe leather binding and slipcase, 32mo., fine in near fine slipcase. Ed Smith Books 83 - 33 2015 $200

Goldsmith, Oliver 1730-1774 *The Miscellaneous Works.* London: printed for W. Griffin, 1775. First collected edition, 8vo., contemporary sheep, rebacked with original spine retained, red morocco label, gilt rules and lettering, half title present, uncommon first collected edition, bookplate of collector Charles Walker Andrews, edges little rubbed, outer margins of endpapers browned, very good. The Brick Row Book Shop Miscellany 67 - 51 2015 $500

Goldsmith, Oliver 1730-1774 *She Stoops to Conquer.* New York: Hodder & Stoughton, n.d., 1912. First US edition, thick 4to., blue cloth, extensive gilt decoration, as new in publisher's box with color plate on cover, 26 beautiful tipped in color plates plus many illustrations in text, incredible copy with ornate binding in beautiful condition. Aleph-bet Books, Inc. 109 - 460 2015 $600

Goldsmith, Oliver 1730-1774 *The Vicar of Wakefield.* Salisbury: printed by B. Collins for F. Newbery, 1766. First edition, a number of variants exist for this book with no priority, this copy with catchword on page 213, volume 1, the incorrected catchword on page 39 volume II and the correctly numbered page 159 in volume II, 2 volumes, 12mo., charming full crushed morocco by Bedford with gilt detailing in spine compartments, all edges gilt, inner gilt dentelles and marbled endpapers, bindings excellent condition, fine but for slight scuff to edge of spine on volume II, internal contents bright and clean with few nearly invisible repaired closed tear in all lovely set, housed in cloth and marbled paper slipcase. Heritage Book Shop Holiday 2014 - 68 2015 $4500

Goldsmith, Oliver 1730-1774 *The Vicar of Wakefield.* Halle: printed and sold by Friedrich Daniel Francke, 1787. 8vo., engraved frontispiece and engraved vignette on title, original paper boards, gilt lettered spine label, few chips, very good. Blackwell's Rare Books B179 - 47 2015 £600

Goldsmith, Oliver 1730-1774 *Vicar of Wakefield.* Philadelphia: David McKay, 1929. First US edition, 4to., gilt cloth, top edge gilt, fine in dust jacket (light soil, few closed tears but very good), illustrations by Arthur Rackham with jacket design, cover design, pictorial endpapers, 12 color plates, 22 black and whites, beautiful copy. Aleph-bet Books, Inc. 109 - 401 2015 $225

Goldsmith, Oliver 1730-1774 *The Miscellaneous Works of Oliver Goldsmith, M.B.* London: printed for Richardson & Co., 1821. Later edition, Volume IV only, later 19th century half leather and cloth, original spine laid down with some loss at extremities, good copy, this the copy of author Clement C. Moore with his ownership signature. Between the Covers Rare Books, Inc. 187 - 110 2015 $1750

Gole, Susan *Maps of the Mediterranean Regions Published in British Parliamentary Papers 1801-1921.* Nicosia: Bank of Cyprus Cultural Foundation, 1996. First edition, 4to., copiously illustrated in color and black and white, small neat name on front endpaper, otherwise fine. Any Amount of Books 2015 - A77032 2015 £160

Golgi, Camillo *Appunti Intorno Alla Struttura Delle Cellule Nervose.* Milan: Ulrico Hoepli, 1898. Offered in a very good+ full issue of Reale Instituto Lombaro Di Scienze E Lettere rendiconti Series II Volume XXXI Fasc. XIII 1898, 8vo., pages uncut, original printed wrappers with minimal soil and stains to covers, cover edge and spine wear, inkstamp to front cover verso. By the Book, L. C. 44 - 34 2015 $650

Golovnin, Vasilii *Recollections of Japan.* London: printed for Henry Colburn, 1819. First edition, 8vo., near fine, later 19th century half calf, marbled boards with red leather spine label, gilt lettering, rare. By the Book, L. C. 44 - 70 2015 $1800

Gonzalez Obregon, Luis *Memoria Historica, Tecnica y Administrativa de las Obras del Desague del Valle Mexico 1449-1900.* Mexico: Tipografia de al Oficina Impresora de Estampillas, 1902. First edition, 2 volumes, black and white plates, plans, maps, folio, three quarter morocco over cloth boards, five raised bands, gilt title decoration and rules on spine, very good with soiled spot on front board of first volume, boards and spines lightly rubbed with occasional small scuff, bookseller's sticker and owner's bookplate on front pastedowns. bookplate of Joseph M. Gleason. Kaaterskill Books 19 - 65 2015 $600

Good, Milt *Twelve Years in a Texas Prison.* Amarillo: Russell Stationery Co., 1935. First edition, 8vo., stiff pictorial wrappers, frontispiece, illustrations, some moderate staining to front and rear panels adjacent to spine, else fine, unread copy. Buckingham Books March 2015 - 29632 2015 $250

Goodchild, George *The Monster of Grammont.* New York: Mystery League Inc., 1930. First US edition, lightly foxed at edges, former owner's inked name on front flyleaf, else fine in fine dust jacket. Buckingham Books March 2015 - 29144 2015 $275

Goodis, David *Fire in the Flesh.* New York: Gold Medal Books, 1957. First edition, PBO Gold Medal 691, pages uniformly browned, faint reader's crease, slight spine lean, and small corner crease to bottom edge of rear panel, else very good, tight copy in pictorial wrappers.   Buckingham Books   March 2015 - 23366   2015 $175

Goodis, David *4 Novels.* London: Zomba, 1983. Omnibus edition, fine in dust jacket.   Mordida Books   March 2015 - 008314   2015 $100

Goodis, David *Night Squad.* Greenwich: Fawcett, 1961. First edition, stamp on top of page edges, otherwise fine in wrappers.   Mordida Books   March 2015 - 000940   2015 $75

Goodrich, Samuel Griswold 1793-1860 *The Story of the Trapper: One of (Peter) Parley's Winter Evening Tales.* Boston: S. G. Goodrich, 1830. First edition, 16mo., 16 pages, including frontispiece and 1 other full page illustration, both crude, original printed and pictorial wrappers, imprint on printed slip pasted down on title, wrapper imprint also on slip pasted down, worn and little soiled but still sound, whip-stitched, titlepage bit grubby, scattered stains in text &c, fair to good only, but intact and complete, youthful ownership signature of one Charlotte M. Doty.   M & S Rare Books, Inc.   97 - 135   2015 $250

Goody Two Shoes. Boston: L. Prang, n.d. circa, 1863. 12mo., pictorial wrappers, slight wear, very good to fine, die cut in shape of Little Goody Two Shoes, every page delicately illustrated by Lydia Very, rare.   Aleph-bet Books, Inc.   109 - 444   2015 $750

Gordley, James *The Philosophical Origins of Modern Contract Doctrine.* Oxford: Clarendon Press, 1991. First edition, 8vo., fine in fine dust jacket.   Any Amount of Books   2015 - A97044   2015   £240

Gordon, Alexander Hamilton *Remarks on National Defence, Volunteers and Rifles...* London: Peter Furnivall & Parker, 1853. First edition, 2 parts in 1 volume, 8vo., text figures on some 13 pages, titlepage and final page of text somewhat dust marked, few early ms. annotations in margins cropped by previous binder, recently well bound in linen backed marbled boards lettered, good copy.   John Drury Rare Books   March 2015 - 16508   2015 $221

Gordon, Anna A. *The Just-in-the-Middle Girl.* Evanston: National WCTU Pub. House, n.d. circa, 1940. 20 pages, 4 1/2 x 7 inches, just hint of soiling and wear to stapled wrappers, else near fine.   Tavistock Books   Temperance - 2015 $40

Gordon, Elizabeth *The Turned Into's.* Chicago: Volland, 1920. 16th edition, 8vo., pictorial boards, fine in original box, illustrations by Janet Laura Scott with pictorial endpapers plus many full page and in-text bold and beautiful color illustrations, beautiful copy.   Aleph-Bet Books, Inc.   108 - 412   2015 $300

Gordon, Elizabeth *Wild Flower Children: the Little Playmates of the Fairies.* Chicago: Volland, 1918. 20th printing, 4to., green pictorial boards, offsetting on spine paper from binding glue, else fine in original box, flaps repaired, illustrations by Janet Laura Scott with pictorial endpapers plus color illustrations on every page, excellent copy. Aleph-bet Books, Inc.   109 - 478   2015 $500

Gordon, Ernest *Russian Prohibition. Studies and Documents of the Anti-Alcohol Movement, No. 1.* Westerville: American Issue Pub. Co., 1916. First edition, original printed red paper wrappers, small stain to bottom edge of rear wrapper and last few leaves spine sun faded, tiny nick to fore-edge, else very good.   Tavistock Books   Temperance - 2015 $40

Gordon, George *The History of Our National Debts and Taxes from the Year MDCLXXXVIII to the Present Year MDCCLI.* London: M. Cooper, 1753. 1751. First edition, four volumes in one, 8vo., 8 folding tables, complete with half title and title to each part, each part with its own pagination and register, contemporary calf, gilt, rebacked, very good.   John Drury Rare Books   2015 - 7860   2015 $874

Gordon, Mike *I Arrested Pearl Starr and Other Stories of Adventures as a Policeman in Forth Smith, Arkansas for 40 Years.* Press Atgus, n.d. circa, 1958. 9 x 6 inches, tan printed wrappers.   Buckingham Books   March 2015 - 35299   2015 $300

Gore, Montague *Has Ireland Gained or Lost by the Union with Great Britain?* London: James Ridgway, 1831. First edition, bound without half title, preserved in modern wrappers with printed label on upper cover.   John Drury Rare Books   March 2015 - 24903   2015   £266

Gore, Montague *The Repeal of the Legislative Union of Great Britain and Ireland Considered.* London: James Ridgway, 1831. 8vo., preserved in modern wrappers with printed label on upper cover,.   John Drury Rare Books   March 2015 - 24904   2015   £266

Gores, Joe *A Time of Predators.* New York: Random House, 1969. First edition, fine in dust jacket with tiny rub to top corner point of front panel.   Buckingham Books   March 2015 - 25217   2015 $275

Gores, Joe *A Time of Predators.* New York: Random House, 1969. First edition, inscribed twice by author, fine in dust jacket with tiny rub to top corner point of front panel. Buckingham Books   March 2015 - 35851   2015 $450

Gorey, Edward *Amphigorey: Fifteen Books.* New York: Putnam, 1972. First edition, 4to., original cream illustrated boards, lettered black and red on spine and covers, copiously illustrated in color and black and white, signed presentation from author for Robert Baker, edgewear, lower spine very slightly creased, otherwise near fine in near very good dust jacket nicked with slight edge wear.   Any Amount of Books   March 2015 - C6715   2015   £375

Gorey, Edward *Amphigorey I-III: Amphigorey, Amphigorey Two and Amphigorey Also.* New York: G. P. Putnam's Son/ Congdon & Weed Inc., 1972-1983. First editions, first printings, 3 volumes, publishers' pictorial cloth, 12 square titles with Gorey's pictorial lettering to boards, in original pictorial dust jackets, illustrated to match bindings, about near fine with minor wear and light rubbing to extremities else fine, fresh and clean interiors, unclipped dust jacets with some light wear and rubbing to extremities, bright spines, clean panels, first volume with small triangular chip to bottom panel at spine tail and hint of rubbing to hinges, 2nd volume with small triangular chip top edge of front panel, third volume with hint of soiling to rear panel, else fine, overall bright and attractive set.   B & B Rare Books, Ltd.   2015 - 2015 $900

Gorey, Edward *Betrayed Confidence. Seven Series of Dogear Wryde Postcards.* Orleans: Parnassus Imprints, 1992. Limited to 250 signed copies, with adddditional plate laid in which is also signed, both book and plate are no. 84 of 250 copies, signed by Gorey, 8vo., original illustrated wrappers, fine original black slipcase, as issued, scarce.   By the Book, L. C.   44 - 91 2015 $650

Gorey, Edward *The Black Doll.* New York: Gotham Book Mart, 1973. Limited to 100 numbered copies signed by author, 8vo., black boards, pictorial label, fine in slipcase. Aleph-Bet Books, Inc.   108 - 215   2015 $600

Gorey, Edward *The Blue Aspic.* New York: Meredith Press, 1968. Stated first edition, oblong 8vo., pictorial boards, fine in fine, price clipped dust jacket, signed by Gorey.   Aleph-Bet Books, Inc.   108 - 216   2015 $400

Gorey, Edward *Dancing Cats and Neglected Murderesses.* New York: Workman Publishing, 1980. Limited to 300 numbered copies (of a total 326) with special cover design by Gorey, signed by Gorey, publisher's pale blue and black laid paper wrappers, about near fine, some light toning to spine and panel edges, hint of light rubbing to hinges, bright and fresh interior, clean and attractive copy. B & B Rare Books, Ltd.   2015 - 2015 $800

Gorey, Edward *Dancing Cats and Neglected Murderesses.* New York: Workman Publishing, 1980. First edition, limited to 300 signed and numbered copies, this no. 259, 16mo., signed by Gorey, fine in original printed wrappers, original mailing envelope.   By the Book, L. C.   44 - 94 2015 $600

Gorey, Edward *The Fantod Pack.* New York: Gotham Book Mart, 1995. Limited to 26 signed lettered sets, this is set "G", 20 laminated cards with booklet of card interpretations, signed by Gorey, fine housed in fine original printed paper covered box with Gorey illustration on box top, 24mo. By the Book, L. C.   44 - 95   2015 $850

Gorey, Edward *The Helpless Doorknob.* No publishing information, 1989. Limited to 500 copies signed by Gorey, 20 illustrated cards with captions plus folded pictorial titlepage and colophon, all housed in clear plastic box, cards fine, box has small side chip, else near fine.   Aleph-Bet Books, Inc.   108 - 217   2015 $500

Gorey, Edward *Prune People.* New York: Albondocani Press, 1983. Limited to 400 numbered copies signed by Gorey, first edition, 6 x 5 inches, pictorial wrappers, fine, printed on fine paper and handsewn, printed on one side of the paper, with a full page illustration on every page. Aleph-Bet Books, Inc.   108 - 218   2015 $475

Gorey, Edward *The Sopping Thursday.* New York: Gotham Book, Mart & Gallery, 1970. First edition, limited issue of 300 (of 326 total) numbered copies, signed by Gorey on limitation page, publisher's white paper wrappers with illustrations to front wrapper in black and gray, lettered in black, very good or better, some light wear and rubbing to extremities, minor toning to spine, light soiling to rear wrapper, faint creasing to top corners of front wrapper and first few pages, otherwise bright and fresh interior, overall bright and pleasing.   B & B Rare Books, Ltd.   2015 - 2015 $275

Gorey, Edward *Tragedies Topiares: Dogear Wryde Postcards.* 1989. Limited to 250 sets, numbered and signed by Gorey, 12 postcards, original pictorial envelope, all in fine condition, rare.   Aleph-bet Books, Inc.   109 - 204 2015 $800

Gorey, Edward *Tragedies (Tragedies) Topiares Series. Dogear Wryde Postcards.* 1989. Limited to 250 sets, this No. 230, 12 illustrated cards and colophon card, 13 fine cards in original printed envelope.   By the Book, L. C.   44 - 96   2015 $400

Gorey, Edward *The Unstrung Harp; or Mr. Earbrass.* New York: Duell Sloan and Pearce; Boston: Little Brown and Co., 1953. First edition, first printing, publisher's mustard yellow cloth, original mustard yellow dust jacket, illustrated to match binding, very good or better with minor wear to extremities, hint of toning to page edges, otherwise bright and clean pages, unclipped dust jacket with some wear and rubbing to extremities, light rubbing to hinges, few minor nicks to spine head, else clean and bright.   B & B Rare Books, Ltd.   2015 - 2015 $200

Gorey, Edward *Whatever Next? Series Dogear Wryde Postcards.* 1990. Limited to 250 sets, this no. 178, 12 illustrated cards and colophon card, 13 fine cards in original fine printed envelope.   By the Book, L. C.   44 - 97   2015 $365

Gorman, James Thomas *Gorilla Gold.*   London and Glasgow: Blackie & son ltd. n.d., 1937. First edition, octavo, 4 inserted plates, illustrations by John de Walton, original yellow cloth, front and spine panels stamped in brown.   L. W. Currey, Inc.   Boy's Adventure Fiction 2015 - 56   2015 $150

Gorton, John *A General Biographical Dictionary.*   London: Whittaker and Co., 1833. 3 substantial volumes, 8vo., original maroon/pink pebbled dash cloth, spines lettered gilt but cloth color little faded, fine, uncut, from the library of Lord Gretton of Stapleford (1867-1947).   John Drury Rare Books   2015 - 26214   2015 $106

Gosse, Edmund   1849-1928   *Some Diversions of a Man of Letters.*   London: William Heinemann, 1919. First edition, cheap paper browned, else near fine, Carl Van Vechten's copy with his bookplate.   Between the Covers Rare Books, Inc.   187 - 111   2015 $150

Gotch, Phyllis *Tuffy and the Merboo - More Boo-Birds.* London: R. Brimley Johnson, n.d. circa, 1905. 4to., pictorial boards, covers soiled and small scrape of paper on rear board, else tight, internally clean and very good.   Aleph-Bet Books, Inc.   108 - 185   2015 $350

Gottfredson, Peter *History of Indian Depredations in Utah.*   Salt Lake City: privately printed, 1919. Original light blue decorated cloth, frontispiece, illustrations, light wear to spine ends and corners, else very good, tight copy.   Buckingham Books   March 2015 - 29396   2015 $250

Gottlieb, Martin *The Foundling: the Story of the NY Foundling Hospital.*   New York: Norfleet Press Book, 2001. First edition, photos by Claire Yaffa, inscribed by author, scarce.   Stephen Lupack   March 2015 - 2015 $195

Goudge, Elizabeth *The Little White Horse.*   New York: Coward McCann, 1947. Stated first American edition, 8vo., cloth very slightly faded in areas, else fine in dust jacket (slight crease), illustrations by C. Walter Hodges with color dust jacket, pictorial endpapers plus black and whites in text.   Aleph-Bet Books, Inc.   108 - 219   2015 $275

Goudy, Frederic William   1865-1947   *Elements of Lettering.*   New York: Mitchell Kennerley, 1922. First edition, 4to., cloth, inserted in original cardboard mailing slipcase, paper spine label, 13 plates, signed and dated by Goudy, slipcase defective, yet intact, with piece missing along top and is tape repaired, former owner has signed this copy, well preserved, chipped original glassine wrapper. Oak Knoll Books   Special Catalogue 24 - 18   2015 $300

Gougen, J. A. *Journal of Consciousness Studies: Controversies in Science and the Humanities.*   Devon: Keith Sutherland, 1994-2004. First edition, 72 large 8vo., wrappers, illustrations, all clean bright very good+ condition. Any Amount of Books   2015 - A47858   2015   £300

Gough, J. W. *John Locke's Political Philosophy: Eight Studies.*   Oxford: Clarendon Press, 1950. First edition, small label from London bookseller Blackwell's, near fine without dust jacket, Graham Greene's ownership signature, which has been lightly struck through with another name beneath it.   Between the Covers Rare Books, Inc.   187 - 158   2015 $350

Gougle, William *Panoplia Tou Theou (Greek). The Whole Armor of God or the Spirituall Furniture Which God hath provided to Keepe Safe Every Christian Souldier from all the Assaults of Satan. (bound with) The Saints Scrifice....* London: John Beale/George Miller for Edward Brewster, 1632. Small quarto, decorative woodcuts, original full calf, somewhat scuffed, few light 17th century ink annotations, whimsical 20th century ownership stamp to inner cover, light tidemark to some pages, few pages affected by spots of worming, not affecting text, some pages slightly cropped affecting few page numbers and running titles, withal sound, clean book.   Any Amount of Books   March 2015 - C7189   2015   £350

Gould, Chester *Dick Tracy: The Capture of Boris Arson.* Chicago: Pleasure Books, 1935. 4to., pictorial boards, covers lightly soiled, else fine, 3 great color-pop ups and many black and white illustrations, scarce.   Aleph-bet Books, Inc. 109 - 367   2015 $650

Gould, F. J. *The Divine Archer, Founded on the Indian Epic of Ramayana.*   London: Dent, 1911. 12mo., very good++, quite nice.   Beasley Books   2013 - 2015 $45

Gould, John   1804-1881   *Birds of Australia.*   Melbourne: Hill House, 1989. Facsimile, Volume five, folio, 92 color plates, publisher's green cloth, fine.   Andrew Isles   2015 - 13579   2015 $1500

Gould, John 1804-1881 *Hummingbirds.* Secaucus: Wellfleet Press, 1990. First edition, fine, includes supplementary volume completed after Gould's death in 1881, fine book and dust jacket.   Stephen Lupack   March 2015 - 2015 $125

Gove, Mary Sargeant Nichols *Mary Lyndon or Revelations of a Life.* New York: Stringer and Townsend, 1855. First edition, 8vo., recased and partially rebacked with spine laid down, very good, tight, clean, scarce.   Second Life Books Inc.   189 - 102   2015 $650

Gowar, Edward *A Child's Book of Verse: Being the Thoughts of a Small Boy.* Kansas City: Frank T. Riley, 1920. Large 8vo., fine in chipped dust jacket, illustrations by Muriel Mattocks with very fine 2-color frontispiece and many full and partial page detailed pen and inks, uncommon.   Aleph-bet Books, Inc.   109 - 276   2015 $125

Goya Y Lucientes, Francisco *Los Caprichos.* Madrid: 1881-1886? Fifth edition, limited to 210 copies, this one of those printed on thick paper measuring 365 x 260mm and probably cut down by binder, folio, 80 etched and aquatint plates on which thick paper, bound without original grey cover in modern brown morocco, gilt spine, slipcase, printed in sepia ink and with plates bevelled they are numbered 1-80, first being portrait of Goya, which was also printed on upper cover not found here, some plates show signs of wear, most very well preserved, margins somewhat foxed in places, bookplate of Jonathan and Phillida Gili by Reynolds Stone.   Maggs Bros. Ltd.   Illustrated Books 2014 - 2015   £10,000

Graber, H. W. *The Life Record of H. W. Graber.* privately printed by H. W. Graber, 1916. First edition, 8vo., three quarter leather and cloth, frontispiece, original spine professionally laid down, new front and rear endpapers, else very good, tight, square copy of a rare book.   Buckingham Books   March 2015 - 32655   2015 $2000

Grabhorn Press *Grabhorn Press, a Catalogue of Imprints in the Collection... Wagner.* Los Angeles: Ward Ritchie Press, 1938. First edition, limited to 250 copies, 8vo., cloth spine, boards, paper spine label, dust jacket, jacket chipped with small pieces missing at bottom of spine and along top of front cover, endpapers foxed, two versions of bookplate of Robert Voris with woodcuts on front pastedown.   Oak Knoll Books   306 - 152   2015 $126

Grabo, Carl *Peter and the Princess.* Chicago: Reilly & Lee, 1920. First edition, 4to., great gilt cloth, pictorial paste-on top edge gilt, as new in original box with color plate on cover, illustrations by John R. Neill, rarely found in box.   Aleph-Bet Books, Inc.   108 - 314   2015 $800

Grace, Fran *Carry A. Nation: retelling the Life.* Bloomington and Indianapolis: Indiana University Press, 2001. First edition, presentation copy inscribed by author for Paul B. Scott, octavo, original blue cloth, black titles, fine in fine dust jacket.   Tavistock Books   Temperance - 2015 $50

Gracian y Morales, Baltasar 1601-1658 *The Art of Prudence, or a Companion for a Man of Sense.*   printed for D. Browne... J. Walthoe... and W. Mears and Jonas Browne, 1714. 8vo., contemporary panelled calf, lettered gilt on front cover 'I. Phelipps Y', (Rev. John Phelipps), red lettering piece, cracks at head of spine, very good, delightful copy, this copy from Newton Surmaville, in Somerset, the home of Robert Harbin, it remained in the library which remained untouched for hundreds of years (until it was sold in 2007), when the last member of the family, Sophia Wyndham died.   Blackwell's Rare Books   B179 - 48   2015   £600

Gradus ad Parnassum: sive, Noveus Synonymorum, Epithetorum Parasium Poeticarum ac Versuum Thesaurus. Impensis Benj. Tooke, 1687. Second recorded surviving English printing, titlepage dust soiled with little adhesion damage at inner margin (just touching a couple of letters), few rust spots and other soiling elsewhere, several leaves with marginal tears (only once causing loss to one word), fore-margin trimmed bit close in places, but always clear of text, old ownership inscription (illegilbe) to titlepage, 12mo., contemporary dark calf, boards ruled in blind, leather rubbed an worn, especially at corners and joints, endpapers excised, joints cracking, sound.   Blackwell's Rare Books   Greek & Latin Classics VI - 65   2015   £750

Grady, James *Six Days of the Condor.* New York: W. W. Norton & Co., 1974. First edition, bit of light foxing to front and rear endpapers, else fine in corner clipped dust jacket.   Buckingham Books   March 2015 - 30267   2015 $300

Graeme, Bruce *Passion, Murder and Mystery.* Doubleday Doran and Co., 1928. First US edition, few pages roughly opened, moderate foxing and covers moderately soiled, else very good in dust jacket.   Buckingham Books   March 2015 - 36201   2015 $175

Graf, Oskar Maria *Die Eroberung Der Welt.* Munchen: Kurt Desch, 1949. 12mo., quarter cloth, paper covered boards, dust jacket lightly soiled and chipped at edges, tanning at edges of text.   Oak Knoll Books   306 - 266   2015 $200

Graff, Everett D. *Fifty Texas Rarities. Selected from the Library of Mr. Everett D. Graff for an Exhibition to Commemorate the Hundredth Anniversary of the Annexation of Texas by the United States.* Ann Arbor: William L. Clements Library, 1946. First edition, limited to 50 copies, inscribed by Graff for Herbert Brayer, laid in is TLS by Graff for Brayer, light wear to head of spine and minor wear to extremities, else very good.   Buckingham Books   March 2015 - 31539   2015 $300

Grafton, C. W. *The Rat Began to Gnaw the Rope.* New York: Farrar & Rinehart, 1943. First edition, fine in near fine dust jacket with short crease tears at spine ends, nicks at corners and along edges and tears along flap folds. Mordida Books   March 2015 - 010205   2015 $400

Grafton, Sue *"A" is for Alibi.* New York: Holt Rinehart, Winston, 1982. First edition, very fine in dust jacket, signed by author.   Mordida Books   March 2015 - 011453   2015 $2500

Grafton, Sue *"A" is for Alibi.* London: Macmillan, 1986. First English edition, pages slightly darkened, otherwise fine in dust jacket.   Mordida Books   March 2015 - 010867   2015 $500

Grafton, Sue *"B" is for Burglar.* New York: Holt Rinehart Winston, 1985. First edition, library labels removed from endpapers and library stamp on copyright page where small label has been removed, otherwise fine in dust jacket, inscribed by author.   Mordida Books   March 2015 - 010868   2015 $150

Grafton, Sue *"B" is for Burglar.* London: Macmillan, 1986. First English edition, pages slightly darkened, otherwise fine in dust jacket, signed by author.   Mordida Books   March 2015 - 010866   2015 $350

Grafton, Sue *D is for Deadbeat.* London: Macmillan, 1987. First edition, 8vo., signed for collector Donald Ross on titlepage, near fine in like dust jacket with very slight foxspotting to endpapers and dust jacket, excellent condition. Any Amount of Books   2015 - A99152   2015   £220

Grafton, Sue *"D" is for Deadbeat.* New York: Holt, 1987. First edition, very fine in dust jacket, signed by author. Mordida Books   March 2015 - 011003   2015 $350

Grafton, Sue *"D" is for Deadbeat.* London: Macmillan, 1987. First English edition, pages slightly drkened, otherwise fine in dust jacket, signed by author.   Mordida Books   March 2015 - 010872   2015 $100

Grafton, Sue *"F" is for Fugitive.* New York: Holt, 1989. First edition, very fine in dust jacket, inscribed by author. Mordida Books   March 2015 - 000959   2015 $75

Grafton, Sue *Keziah Dane.* New York: Macmillan, 1967. First edition, fine in fine dust jacket, beautiful copy, author's scarce first book.   Between the Covers Rare Books   196 - 143   2015 $400

Graham, Caroline *The Envy of the Stranger.* London: Century, 1984. First edition, fine in price clipped dust jacket.   Mordida Books   March 2015 - 002449   2015 $185

Graham, Caroline *Murder at Madingley Grange.* London: Mysterious Press, 1990. First edition, fine in dust jacket. Mordida Books   March 2015 - 006743   2015 $90

Graham, Catharine Macaulay *The History of England from the Revolution to the Present Time in a Series of letters to a Friend.* Bath: printed by R. Cruttwell and sold by E. & C. Dilly, T. Cadell and J. Walter, London, 1778. First edition, 4to., engraved portrait and additional engraved titlepage (foxed as usual), contemporary speckled calf, spine gilt, contrasting labels, spine numbered "Volume 6), spine rather rubbed and eroded, joints cracked, despite wear to spine, an excellent copy, with wide margins, bookplate of Sir John Eden, Bart of West Auckland Co. Durham. Second Life Books Inc.   189 - 103   2015 $2500

Graham, Catharine Macaulay *Observations on the Reflections of the Right Hon. Edmund Burke on the Revolution in France in a Letter to the Right Hon. the Earl of Stanhope.* London: C. Dilly, 1790. First edition, 8vo., without half title removed from bound volume, little foxed and stained, very good, lower edge of title leaf folded to preserve the MSS annotation, first and last leaves with minor spots, titlepage has contemporary mss. annotation, scarce. Second Life Books Inc.   189 - 104   2015 $1500

Graham, Frank *The New York Yankees.* New York: Putnam, 1943. First edition, fine without dust jacket. Mordida Books   March 2015 - 009578   2015 $100

Graham, Jorie *All things.* Iowa City: Empyrean Press, 2002. First edition, one of 15 special copies printed on Center for the Book hemp paper made by Lynn Amlie, signed by poet, 4to., pastel frontispiece by Ronald Cohen, original vellum and two-toned alum tawed navy blue goatskin over boards by Mick Le Tourenaux, navy blue linen folding box with printed paper labels.   James S. Jaffe Rare Books   Modern American Poetry - 125   2015 $1500

Graham, Jorie *The Dream of the Unified Field: Selected Poems.* Hopewell: Ecco Press, 1995. First edition, 8vo., signed by author, original cloth backed boards, dust jacket, fine.   James S. Jaffe Rare Books   Modern American Poetry - 124   2015 $100

Graham, Jorie *The End of Beauty.* Hopewell: Ecco Press, 1987. First edition, 8vo., original cloth backed boards, dust jacket, clothbound issue, signed by author. James S. Jaffe Rare Books   Modern American Poetry - 120   2015 $75

Graham, Jorie *Erosion.* Princeton: Princeton University Press, 1983. First edition, 8vo., original black cloth, dust jacket, fine.   James S. Jaffe Rare Books   Modern American Poetry - 119   2015 $500

Graham, Jorie *Hybrids of Plants and of Ghosts.* Princeton: Princeton University Press, 1980. First edition, 8vo., original boards, presentation copy, inscribed by poet, fine.   James S. Jaffe Rare Books   Modern American Poetry - 118   2015 $650

Graham, Jorie *Materialism. Poems.* New York: Ecco Press, 1993. First edition, signed by author, 8vo., original cloth backed boards, fine.   James S. Jaffe Rare Books   Modern American Poetry - 121   2015 $100

Graham, Jorie *The Turning.* Atlanta: Emory University, 1994. First edition, one of 200 copies printed on handmade paper at Shadowy Water Press, although not called for, this copy signed by poet, 4to., original handmade marbled paper wrappers with printed paper label, very fine.   James S. Jaffe Rare Books   Modern American Poetry - 122   2015 $200

Graham, Margaret *Swing Shift.* New York: Citadel Press, 1951. First edition, fine in slightly spine toned, near fine dust jacket, tipped in to fly is TLS by author to Earl Dickerson using her real name (Grace McDonald) about the pattern of violence in labor struggles.   Between the Covers Rare Books, Inc.   187 - 112   2015 $200

Graham, Robert Bontine Cunninghame   1852-1936 *Economic Evolution.* Aberdeen: James Leatham and London: William Reeves, 1891. First edition, 16mo., original grey wrappers, ad leaf at end, upper wrapper with small brown mark, some foxing, nice, fragile, rare, from the collection of Gavin H. Fryer.   Bertram Rota Ltd.   308 Part II - 147   2015   £250

Graham, William *Socialism New and Old.* London: Kegan Paul, 1908. Fifth impression, half title, original red cloth by Hugh Rees, boards decorated and lettered in blind, very good, bright copy.   Jarndyce Antiquarian Booksellers CCXI - 124   2015   £20

Graham, Winston *Crimson Hairs.* New York: Grove, 1970. First edition, fine in dust jacket.   Mordida Books March 2015 - 000965   2015 $75

Grahame, James *Thoughts on Trial by Jury in Civil Causes...* Edinburgh: William Blackwood, 1806. First edition, uncommon, title and final page bit dust marked, recently well bound in linen backed marbled boards, lettered, good copy.   John Drury Rare Books   March 2015 - 19918   2015 $266

Grahame, Kenneth   1859-1932 *The Golden Age.* New York: John Lane Bodley Head, 1921. First edition thus, 8vo., green pictorial cloth, scattered spotting, else fine, 4 tipped in color plates with lettered tissue guards plus many delicate black and whites in text by Lois Lenski.   Aleph-bet Books, Inc.   109 - 261   2015 $150

Grahame, Kenneth   1859-1932 *The Wind in the Willows.* London: Methuen, 1927. First edition thus, 8vo., blue cloth, top edge gilt, very slight lean, else fine in dust jacket (slight soil and some chips), illustrations by Wyndham Payne with color dust jacket plus 20 plates in black and yellow.   Aleph-bet Books, Inc.   109 - 206   2015 $700

Grahame, Kenneth   1859-1932 *The Wind in the Willows.* London: Methuen, 1931. Limited to only 200 numbered copies signed by author and artist, 4to., cloth backed boards, 312 pages, very slight cover soil, else very good-fine, illustrations by E. H. Shepard, rare.   Aleph-bet Books, Inc.   109 - 295   2015 $8000

Grahame, Kenneth   1859-1932 *The Wind in the Willows.* New York: Limited Editions Club, 1940. Limited to 2020 numbered copies, signed by designer Bruce Rogers, small 4to.,cloth backed paper covered boards, top edge gilt, slipcase, illustrations by Arthur Rackham in color and printed on different paper stock and mounted on separate pages, extra mounted print loosely inserted, slipcase has wear along edges, spine of book slightly age darkened, with few spots.   Oak Knoll Books   25 - 71   2015 $850

Gramatky, Hardie *Loopy.* New York: Putnam, 1941. First edition, 4to., fine, pictorial cloth, dust jacket worn at folds, piece off end of spine and some fraying.   Aleph-Bet Books, Inc.   108 - 220   2015 $250

Grand D'Hauteville, Paul Daniel *Report of the D'Hauteville Case: the Commonwealth of Pennsylvania at the Suggestion of Paul Daniel Gonsalve Grand D'Hauteville versus David Sears, Miriam C. Sears and Ellen Sears Grand D'Hauteville...* Philadelphia: printed by William S. Martien and for sale by the booksellers generally, 1840. First edition, 8vo., contemporary black quarter calf over marbled boards, spine gilt and lettered, slight abrasion on lower cover but very good.   John Drury Rare Books   March 2015 - 19971   2015 $266

La Grande Esposizione Di Londra. No. 1 (-25) Sabato 24 Maggio 1851-(Martedi 2 Dicembre 1851). Turin: Tipographia Subalpina, 1851. First edition, folio, apart from some minor light foxing and dust soiling in places, clean copy throughout, contemporary calf backed mottled boards, spine tooled and lettered in gilt, minor cracking to joints and rubbing to extremities, one corner weak but holding, otherwise appealing copy, rare.   Marlborough Rare Books Ltd. List 49 - 17   2015   £950

Grandineau, Francois *Conversations Familieres or Conversational Lessons for the use of Young Ladies from Nine to Twelve Years of Age.* Kensington: 1832. First edition, 12mo., contemporary full straight grained morocco gilt, this copy inscribed from Kensington Palace by Victoria's mother to her young grandson by her first marriage.   Honey & Wax Booksellers   3 - 5   2015 $2500

Granit, Ragnar *Receptors and Sensory Perception. A Discussion of Aims, Means, and Results of Electrophysiological Research into the Process of Reception.* New Haven: Yale University, 1956. Second printing, 8vo. minimal soil to edges, minimal cover edge wear. By the Book, L. C. Special List 10 - 75 2015 $80

Grant, Brewin *Christianity and Secularism, Report of a Public Discussion Between the Rev. Brewin Grant and George Jacob Holyoake, Held at the Royal British Institution, Cowper Street London on Six Successive Thursday Evenings Commencing Jan. 20 and ending Feb. 24 1853 on the Question "What Advantages would Accrue to Mankind Generally and the Working Classes in Particular, by the Removal of Christianity and the Substitution of Secularism in Its Place?* London: Ward and Co., 1853. with 2 final ad leaves, 12mo., original embossed cloth, lettered gilt, very good. John Drury Rare Books 2015 - 12919 2015 $133

Grant, George Munro *The Easternmost Ridge of the Continent Historical and Descriptive Sketches of the Scenery and Life in New Brunswick, Nova Scotia, Prince Edward Island and Along the Lower St. Lawrence and Saguenay.* Chicago: Alexander Belford & Co., 1899. Quarto, cloth, wood engravings from original drawings, missing front endpaper, cloth worn, interior good. Schooner Books Ltd. 110 - 174 2015 $40

Grant, Kenneth *Nightside of Eden.* London: Frederick Muller, 1977. First edition, 8vo., original black cloth lettered silver on spine, 18 illustrations, 7 line drawings in text, fine in very good dust jacket, rubbed at spine ends, slightly scratched at rear panel, otherwise excellent condition. Any Amount of Books 2015 - C1887 2015 £160

Grant, Maxwell *The Living Shadow.* New York: Street & Smith Publications, 1931. First edition, moderate rubbing to front and rear panels, spine and extremities of illustrated boards, else very good tight, without dust jacket as issued. Buckingham Books March 2015 - 25557 2015 $375

Grant, Maxwell *Norgil the Magician.* New York: Mysterious Press, 1977. First edition, one of 250 numbered copies signed by author, very fine in dust jacket with slipcase. Mordida Books March 2015 - 006744 2015 $200

Grant, Maxwell *Norgill: More Tales of Prestidigitection.* New York: Mysterious Press, 1979. First edition, one of 250 numbered copies signed by author Grant and Walter Gibson, very fine in dust jacket with slipcase. Mordida Books March 2015 - 002453 2015 $100

Grant, Robert *East River Worthies.* New Glasgow: Scotia Printers, n.d., 192-? First edition in book form, printed card covers, small 8vo., frontispiece portrait of author, covers worn and stained, interior good. Schooner Books Ltd. 110 - 77 2015 $45

Grapewin, Charley *The Bronze Bull.* Boston: Christopher Pub. House, 1930. First edition, front fly lacking, else near fine, lacking dust jacket, inscribed by author on dedication page to film actor, Ricardo Cortez. Between the Covers Rare Books, Inc. 187 - 113 2015 $350

Grass, Gunter *Cat and Mouse.* London: Secker & Warburg, 1963. First edition, 8vo., original green cloth, lettered red at spine, fine in fine dust jacket, price clipped by publisher with two 'new' price labels, 21/- and £1.05 at corner, exceptional condition, boldly signed by author. Any Amount of Books 2015 - C10635 2015 £280

Grass, Gunter *Drawings and Words 1954-1977.* London: Secker & Warburg, 1983. Copy B77 of 250 copies, signed by Grass with original etching "Sign in the Sky" signed in pencil by artist, with tissue guard in specially designed pocket with printed description, fine, folio, in fine dust jacket, original plain slipcase, worn, is present. By the Book, L. C. Special List 10 - 25 2015 $395

Grass, Gunter *The Flounder.* New York: Limited Editions Club, 1985. Limited to 1000 numbered copies, oblong 4to., quarter natural eelskin with cloth covered boards, paper cover labels, slipcase, Monthly Letter loosely inserted, touch of wear along bottom of slipcase, finely illustrations by author. Oak Knoll Books 25 - 55 2015 $300

Graves, John *Goodbye to a River.* New York: Knopf, 1960. First edition, special copy signed by author on titlepage, on second blank page there is original ink drawing by Russell Waterhouse, below drawing is two-line inscription in ink by Waterhouse that is signed by him and dated Sept. 1 1961, very good plus to near fine, nudge to bottom front corner, salmon colored illustrated cloth, in very good plus dust jacket with small closed tear to top of spine fold, some minor wear around edges. Ed Smith Books 83 - 35 2015 $750

Graves, Robert 1895-1985 *Adam's Rib and Other Anomalous Elements in the Hebrew Creation Myth.* Jura: Trianon Press, 1955. First edition, copy "R" of 26 lettered copies signed by Graves and Metcalf, large 8vo., original red cloth lettered gilt at spine, wood engravings by James Metcalf, signed presentation from book's designer Arnold Fawcus, fine in slightly browned but very good plani slipcase. Any Amount of Books 2015 - A49568 2015 £280

Graves, Robert 1895-1985 *Count Belisarius.* London: Cassell, 1938. First edition, former owner's name and some light foxing to fore-edges, else fine in price clipped dust jacket with moderate wear to extremities.
Buckingham Books   March 2015 - 7454   2015 $250

Graves, Robert 1895-1985 *Mockbeggar Hall.* London: Hogarth Press, 1924. First edition, small quarto, original paper boards, pictorial bookplate of W. MacDonald MacKay, Scottish historian and bookman and name plate of Douglas Grant, Prof. of American Lit. at Leeds University, spine little bruised at foot, lower corners slightly bumped, very good.
Peter Ellis, Bookseller   2014 - 006488   2015   £325

Graves, Robert 1895-1985 *The Nazarene Gospel Restored.* London: Cassell, 1953. First edition, royal octavo, black bukram covers, bottom corner of front cover bit bumped, very good in like dust jacket, slightly nicked and crease dust jacket with some spotting to rear panel, uncommon in such presentable condition.   Peter Ellis, Bookseller 2014 - 019537   2015   £350

Graves, Robert 1895-1985 *Over the Brazier.* London: Poetry Bookshop, 1916. First edition, wrappers, 8vo., original illustrated wrappers, yapped edges slightly creased and slightly chipped at rear, titlepage very slight foxed otherwise text clean, sound, very good.   Any Amount of Books   2015 - C5361   2015   £300

Graves, Robert 1895-1985 *Ten Poems More.* Paris: Hours Press, 1930. First edition, quarto, 17 pages, leather backed boards with brilliant photographic design by Len Lye, one of 200 copies signed by author, this being unnumbered, front endpapers faintly spotted, cover slightly rubbed at spine and edges, very good.   Peter Ellis, Bookseller   2014 - 018278   2015   £325

Gray, Charles Glass *Off at Sunrise. The Overland Journal of...* San Marino: Huntington Library, 1976. First edition, title illustration, plus 5 text illustrations, map endpapers, blue cloth, very fine in pictorial dust jacket.   Argonaut Book Shop   Holiday Season 2014 - 102   2015 $60

Gray, E. H. *Assaults Upon Freedom! Or, Kidnapping an Outrage Upon Humanity and Abhorrent to God.* Shelbourne Falls: D. B. Gunn, 1854. First edition, 8vo., 22 pages, library boards, ex-library, perforated library stamp to title and one leaf, lacks wrappers, rare.   M & S Rare Books, Inc.   97 - 45   2015 $1600

Gray, Frank S. *"For Love of Bears." A Description of a Recent Hunting Trip with a Romantic Finale.* Chicago: Frank S. Gray, 1886. First edition, oblong 4to., 139 pages plus ads, pencil sketches reproduced and cabinet photo, original printed and pictorial wrappers, front wrapper reattached near spine and lacking lower corner, affecting one letter in imprint, small blank corner lacking from back wrapper as well, early owner's signature with his stamp as passenger agent for Northern Pacific Railroad.   M & S Rare Books, Inc.   97 - 112   2015 $650

Gray, John *The Person in Question.* Buenos Aires: F. A. Colombo, 1958. Number 22 of 50 copies of which 10 were reserved for the press, presentation copy inscribed by Patricio Gannon to bookseller (librarian and collector) Herbert Faulkner West, fine in white paper wrappers with black title and illustration to front cover, clean, bright interior printed on handmade paper in black with red initials, loose and unopened as issued, fine in original slipcase, fine.
The Kelmscott Bookshop   11 - 5   2015 $450

Gray, John Edward *Catalogue of Reptiles... in the Collection of the British Museum.* London: British Museum, 1844-1845. Duodecimo, 2 volumes, original (?) blue wrappers with title labels on upper covers and hand written paper label on spine, fine set contained in handsome modern half calf solander box.   Andrew Isles   2015 - 36424   2015 $850

Gray, Nicolete *Nineteenth Century Ornamented Typefaces.* Berkeley: University of California Press, 1976. Revised edition, 4to., cloth, dust jacket, well preserved.
Oak Knoll Books   306 - 216   2015 $150

Gray, Sylvester *The United States License Policy and Its Crimes or the Magnitude of Each Voter's Rime for the License Law as Foretold in Prophecy.* N.P.: n.p., n.d. circa, 1890. Presumed first and only edition, original printed paper wrappers some minor creasing to rear flyleaf and front panel, some mild soiling and toning to wrappers, else very good.   Tavistock Books   Temperance - 2015 $50

Gray, Thomas 1716-1771 *Correspondence.* Oxford: Clarendon Press, 1935. 3 volumes, half titles, frontispieces, original red cloth, spines faded, Geoffrey Tillotson's signed copy with notes, correspondence, copies of his reviews and list of corrections, &c.   Jarndyce Antiquarian Booksellers   CCVII - 287   2015   £65

Gray, Thomas 1716-1771 *Designs by Mr. R. Bentley for Six Poems by Mr. T. Gray.* London: printed for R. Dodsley, 1753. Second edition, folio, brown quarter contemporary calf, marbled paper boards, gilt rules, 6 engraved plates and 13 vignettes by Richard Bentley, bookplate of collector Charles Walker Andrews, edges little rubbed, some light foxing, very good.   The Brick Row Book Shop   Miscellany 67 - 52   2015 $1250

Gray, Thomas 1716-1771 *Elegia Inglese di Tommaso Gray Sopra un Cimietero Campestre Trasportata in Verso Italiano da Giuseppi Torello Veronese.* Parma: Nel regel Palazzo Co' tipi Bodoniani, 1793. First Bodoni edition, 4to., 19th century black quarter morocco, marbled paper boards, gilt decorations and lettering, text interleaves with blank paper and ruled by hand in red throughout, bookplate of Charles Walker Andrews, notations in ink about edition by another previous owner on front blank, edges bit rubbed, some foxing, very good. The Brick Row Book Shop Miscellany 67 - 53 2015 $750

Gray, Thomas 1716-1771 *L'Elegia di Tommaso Gray un Cimitero di Campagna.* Verona: Dalla Tipografia Mainardi, 1817. First edition, 8vo., contemporary dark green morocco, gilt rules, decorations and lettering, all edges gilt, edges little rubbed, some light foxing and stains, very good. The Brick Row Book Shop Miscellany 67 - 54 2015 $500

Gray, Thomas 1716-1771 *An Elegy Written in a Country Churchyard.* London: printed by Edward Walters & Geoffrey Miller at Primrose Hill, 1933. 4to., title in red, uncut in original grey printed boards, cream buckram spine, spine label defective, dusted, complimentary copy of the 125 copies on handmade paper, 125 also on machine paper, from the library of Geoffrey & Kathleen Tillotson, review copy for the TLS with inserted notes by Geoffrey. Jarndyce Antiquarian Booksellers CCVII - 285 2015 £50

Gray, Thomas 1716-1771 *An Elegy Wrote in a Country Church Yard (1751) and the Eton College Manuscript...* Los Angeles: William Andrews Clark Memorial Lib., 1951. 4to., plates, facsimiles, original orange printed wrappers, dusted, from the library of Geoffrey & Kathleen Tillotson. Jarndyce Antiquarian Booksellers CCVII - 286 2015 £25

Gray, Thomas 1716-1771 *Ode Performed in the Senate-House at Cambridge July 1 1769 at the Installation of His Grace Augustus-Henry Fitzroy, Duke of Grafton, Chancellor of the University.* Cambridge: printed by J. Archdeacon for T. and J. Merrill, J. Dodsley, J. Johnson and B. White, in London, 1769. Second edition, 4to., disbound, 8 pages, few small stains in margins, very good. The Brick Row Book Shop Miscellany 67 - 55 2015 $200

Gray, Thomas 1716-1771 *Poems by Mr. Gray.* London: printed for J. Murray, 1778. illustrations, full tan calf with raised bands, gilt spine decorations and maroon leather spine label, small bookplate of Yale Professor and Hardy scholar, Richard Little Purdy, very good, little rubbing to board edges, tight clean text. Stephen Lupack March 2015 - 2015 $150

Gray, Thomas 1716-1771 *The Poems of Mr. Gray.* London: printed for G. Kearsley, 1786. from the library of Geoffrey & Kathleen Tillotson. red paper covered card wrappers by Geoffrey Tillotson, with calligraphic "prize label" at front "reward of merit Thos. Hodges 1795". Jarndyce Antiquarian Booksellers CCVII - 281 2015 £45

Gray, Thomas 1716-1771 *Poems by Mr. Gray.* Parma: printed by Bodoni, 1793. First Bodoni edition, 4to., contemporary brown quarter calf, marbled paper boards, gilt rules and lettering, edges little rubbed, some light foxing, very good. The Brick Row Book Shop Miscellany 67 - 56 2015 $450

Gray, Thomas 1716-1771 *The Poems.* Printed for White, Cochrane & Co. by S. Hamilton, Weybridge, Surrey, 1814. Contemporary half red calf, spine tooled gilt and blind, green labels, attractive copy, few pencil marks, from the library of Geoffrey & Kathleen Tillotson. Jarndyce Antiquarian Booksellers CCVII - 282 2015 £45

Gray, Thomas 1716-1771 *The Complete Poems.* Oxford: Clarendon Press, 1966. Half title, frontispiece, original dark blue cloth, very good, strengthened dust jacket, review copy signed by Geoffrey Tillotson, June 1966, with note of his review. Jarndyce Antiquarian Booksellers CCVII - 284 2015 £25

Gray, Thomas 1716-1771 *The Poetical Works of Gray and Collins.* London: Oxford University Press, 1926. Second edition, frontispiece and plates, original red cloth, rubbed with small split at head of leading hinge, Geoffrey Tillotson's copy 1930 with copious notes and insertions. Jarndyce Antiquarian Booksellers CCVII - 283 2015 £45

Gray, William S. *New We Come and Go.* Chicago: Scott Foresman, 1956. 8vo., cloth backed pictorial wrappers, 72 pages, some cover soil, very good+. Aleph-Bet Books, Inc. 108 - 135 2015 $250

Gray, William S. *We Come and Go.* Chicago et al: Scott Foresman & Hall, 1940. 8vo., pictorial wrappers, bookplate, slight cover rubbing, very good+, illustrations in color by Miriam Hurford, scarce. Aleph-Bet Books, Inc. 108 - 136 2015 $300

Graydon, William Murray *The River of Darkness or Under Africa.* Chicago: Thompson & Thomas, 1902. First edition, octavo, 3 inserted plates, original pictorial gray cloth, front and spine panels stamped in black and white. L. W. Currey, Inc. Boy's Adventure Fiction 2015 - 57 2015 $150

The Great London Exhibition of Industry 1851. London: Great exposition industrielle au Palais de Verre a Lodres, 1851. First issue, concertina folding hand colored peepshow, with four cut-out sections front facing measuring 145 x 160mm., forming lid of the box containing the peepshow, which extends by paper bellows to approximately 630mm., box little worn and discolored, housed in custom made cloth box.   Marlborough Rare Books Ltd.   List 49 - 26   2015   £1500

Great Britain. Board of Agriculture - 1816 *Agricultural State of the Kingdom, in February March and April 1816 Being the Substance of the Replies to a Circular letter Sent by the Board of Agriculture to Every Part of the Kingdom.* London: printed by Sherwood Neely and Jones, 1816. First edition, 8vo., evidence of erasure on verso of title and foot of final leaf, contemporary half calf gilt, neatly rebacked, good copy, 19th century armorial bookplate of Sir Robert Johnson Eden, Bart.   John Drury Rare Books   March 2015 - 16526   2015 $266

Great Britain. Laws, Statutes, etc. - 1660 *Anno XII. Caroli II. Regis. An Act for regulating of the Trade of Bay-making in the Dutch Bay-Hall in Colchester.* London: printed by John Bill and Christopher Barker, 1660. Folio 8 pages, printed throughout in black letter woodcut of royal arms on title, little paper browning, preserved in recent plain wrappers with label on upper cover, good crisp copy.   John Drury Rare Books   2015 - 21456   2015 $133

Great Britain. Laws, Statutes, etc. - 1696 *Anno Septimo & Octavo Gulielmi III. Regis. An Act for Continuing to His Majesty Certain Duties Upon Salt, Glass Wares, Stone and Earthen Wares and for Granting Several Duties Upon Tobacco Pipes and Other Earthen Wares...* London: printed by Charles Bill and the Executrix of Thomas Newcomb, 1696. Folio, royal arms on title, black letter, small hole in final leaf affecting couple of letters o recto and verso, preserved in recent plain wrappers lettered on upper cover, good, crisp copy.   John Drury Rare Books   2015 - 21460   2015 $133

Great Britain. Laws, Statutes, etc. - 1772 *An Act for Better Regulating the Poor, Maintaining a Nightly Watch...* London: printed in the year, 1772. Second printing, 8vo., 112 pages, old ink doodle on titlepage, contemporary calf backed marbled boards, raised bands, little wear to extremities, very good, rare.   John Drury Rare Books   2015 - 25809   2015 $830

Great Britain. Laws, Statutes, etc. - 1778 *An Act for Dividing and Inclosing the Common or Waste Ground Called Brislington, Otherwise Bussleton, Common, in the Parish of Brislington, otherwise Bussleton in the County of Somerset.* London: 1778. First edition, original printing, folio, final blank on recto and with docket title on verso, stitched as issued, folded and final leaf worn and dust soiled, uncut, very good.   John Drury Rare Books - 18392   2015 $177

Great Britain. Laws, Statutes, etc. - 1786 *Anno Regni Georgii III Vicesimo Tertio. An Act for the Better Regulation of the Office of the Paymaster General of His Majesty's Forces and the More Regular Payment of the Army...* London: printed by C. Eyre and the executors of W. Strahan, 1786. 8vo., old, probably original marbled wrappers, very good, rare.   John Drury Rare Books   2015 - 16358   2015 $177

Great Britain. Laws, Statutes, etc. - 1790 *An Act for Making and repairing the Road from Newmiln Bridge by Foodie's Mill, Inverkeithing, Aberdour, Kirkcaldy, Gallatown and Cameron Bridge to Craill...* Edinburgh: 1790. First edition, 4to., wanting final leaf called for by NLS, recent marbled boards lettered on spine, fault apart very good.   John Drury Rare Books   March 2015 - 24899   2015   £306

Great Britain. Laws, Statutes, etc. - 1828 *Acts and Votes of Parliament Relating to the British Museum with the Statutes and Rules Thereof and the Succession of Trustees and Officers.* London: G. Woodfall, 1828. Contemporary full dark grey calf, triple ruled gilt borders and additional blind decorated border, raised gilt bands, compartments ruled gilt, slightly rubbed, contemporary inscription, bookplate of Stuart B. Schimmel.   Jarndyce Antiquarian Booksellers   CCXI - 39   2015   £180

Great Britain. Laws, Statutes, etc. - 1839 *An Act for Regulating the Police in the city of London 2 & 3 Vict. Cap (xciv). With an abstract.* London: printed by Arthur Taylor 39 Coleman Street..., 1839. First edition thus, 8vo., woodcut of City of London arms on title, original boards, neatly rebacked with recent spine label, uncut, very good, apparently rare.   John Drury Rare Books   March 2015 - 25677   2015 $266

Great Britain. Parliament - 1789 *The History and Proceedings of the Lords and Commons of Great Britain, in Parliament, with Regard to the Regency, Containing a full Account of all Their Speeches on the Proposed Regency Bill from Nov. 20 1788 to March 10 1789...* London: John Stockdale, 1789. 8vo., very occasional minor spotting, generally little just bit foxed, contemporary tree calf, sympathetically rebacked, flat spine gilt and labelled, excellent copy, 19th century library of John Scott, Lord Eldon with his circular armorial bookplate and signature.   John Drury Rare Books   2015 - 25069   2015 $1136

Great Britain. Parliament - 1794 *First Report from the Committee of Secrecy Ordered to be printed 17th May 1794 (bound with) The Second Report from the Committee of Secrecy of the House of Commons to whom the Several Papers Referred to His Majesty's Message of the 12th day of May 1794 and Which were Presented (Sealed up) to the House by Mr. Secretary Dundas...* London: J. Debrett, 1794. 8vo., 2 volumes in one, one plate, minute hole in one leaf with loss or partial loss of one or two letters on recto and verso, contemporary calf backed marbled boards, original morocco label lettered gilt, fine with early 20th century bookplate of Robert A. N. Petrie, complete set.   John Drury Rare Books   2015 - 26175   2015 $787

Great Britain. Parliament - 1889 *A Bill to Extend the Parliamentary Franchise to Women. No. 2.* London: 1889. Folio, single sheet folded to make 4 pages, professional repair at fold, very good.   Second Life Books Inc.   189 - 34   2015 $75

Great Britain. Parliament. House of Commons - 1812 *An Abstract of the Evidence Lately taken in the House of Commons Against the orders in Council...* London: printed by J. McCreery, 1812. First edition thus, 8vo., errata leaf and index, additional editor's slip tipped in, recent marbled boards lettered on spine, very good.   John Drury Rare Books   March 2015 - 24436   2015   £306

Great Britain. Parliament. House of Commons - 1815 *Minutes of the Evidence Taken Before the Committee Appointed by the House of Commons to Inquire into the State of Mendicity and Vagrancy in the Metropolis and Its Neighbourhood.* London: printed for Sherwood Neely and Jones and others, 1815. First edition, 8vo., occasional foxing, original boards with paper spine, spine itself chipped and worn (with loss, entirely uncut, very good.   John Drury Rare Books   March 2015 - 25789   2015 $266

Great Britain. Parliament. House of Commons - 1817 *Report from the Committee of the Honourable the House of Commons on the Employment of Boys in Sweeping of Chimneys together with the Minutes of Evidence Taken Before the Committee and an Appendix....* London: Baldwin Cradock & Joy, 1817. First edition thus, 8vo., engraved frontispiece, 142 pages, occasional light spotting, frontispiece slightly offset, very good copy, bound recently in red cloth, spine lettered in gilt,.   John Drury Rare Books   March 2015 - 26241   2015 $962

Great Britain. Parliament. House of Commons - 1832 *Report from the Select Committee of the House of Commons on the Observations of the Lord's Day with Extracts from the Evidence taken by the Committee.* Edinburgh: printed by Neill & Co., 1832. 8vo. 32 pages, preserved in modern wrappers, printed label on upper cover, good.   John Drury Rare Books   2015 - 26216   2015 $133

Great Britain. Parliament. House of Commons - 1838 *Report from the Secret Committee on Joint Stock Banks; Together with the Minutes of Evidence, Appendix and Index.* London: ordered by the House of Commons to be printed, 25 July, 1838. First edition, folio, without index, printer's slip tipped in at end notifying purchaser that 'the index will be delivered as soon as completed 28 July 1838", ownership marks of Institute of Bankers including small inkstamp at foot of title and bookplate on front pastedown, 19th century black half roan, gilt, joints rather worn, still good.   John Drury Rare Books   March 2015 - 18765   2015 $221

Great Britain. Parliament. House of Commons - 1852 *Report from the Select Committee on Postage Label Stamps; Together with the Proceedings of the Committee, Minutes of Evidence and Index.* London: Ordered by the House of Commons to be printed 21 May, 1852. First edition, large 8vo., few old emphasis marks and annotations in pencil, paper generally lightly browned, rebound recently in boards with original printed wrappers laid down, very good. John Drury Rare Books   2015 - 26026   2015 $787

Great Britain. Parliament. House of Lords - 1814 *First and Second Reports from the Committees of the House of Lords, Appointed to Inquire into the State of the Growth, Commerce and Consumption of Grain and all the Laws Relating Thereto...* London: James Ridgway, 1814. First 8vo. edition, several folded tables, original boards, neatly rebacked, entirely uncut, very good, crisp copy.   John Drury Rare Books   March 2015 - 22890   2015   £306

Great Britain. Treaties, Etc. - 1725 *Treaty of Peace Between His Imperial and His Catholick Majesty Charles VI and His Royal Catholick Majesty Philip V. concluded at Vienna the 30th of April 1725.* London: printed by Sam. Buckley, 1725. 4to., some leaves lightly dampstained, title bit dust marked, stitched as issued, some marginal fraying, else large, uncut copy, uncommon.   John Drury Rare Books   2015 - 12712   2015 $221

Great Britain. War Office - 1811 *A List of the Officers of the Local Militia of Great Britain 1811.* London: printed by C. Roworth for the War Office, 30th September, 1811. 8vo., contemporary red morocco with triple gilt borders to spines, flat spine gilt in compartments with Catherine wheel tools and a green morocco lettering piece, inner gilt dentelles and all edges gilt, handsome copy in fine, early 19th century binding, later armorial bookplate of William Allen Potter.   John Drury Rare Books   2015 - 21575   2015 $1049

Great Western Gun Works *Wholesale Priced Catalogue of Guns, Rifles, Revolvers and Ammunition, Manufactured & for sale at the Great Western Gun Works.* Pittsburgh: Seibert Sloan & Co. Print, n.d. circa, 1871. 16mo., 32 pages, original printed pink wrappers, very good, rather nice.   John Drury Rare Books   2015 - 23899   2015 $133

Greaves, James Pierrepont *A Brief Account of the First Concordium or Harmonious Industrial College, a Home for the Affectionate, Skilful and Industrious Uncontaminated by False Sympathy, Avaricious Cunning or Excessive Labour.* Ham Common Surrey: published at the Concordium price one penny and sold by all bookseller, n.d.?, 1840. First edition, variant issue, 8vo., in page, rather foxed and browned, well bound in old style quarter calf, gilt, attractively bound. John Drury Rare Books   2015 - 16537   2015 $1311

Grebenstein, Maryanne *Trinity.* Hingham: Maryanne Grebenstein, 2012. Number 3 of 20 copies, one unique hand lettered copy was also issued, 3 x 3 inches, in this limited edition the black text is printed and decorations are hand colored and illuminations in gold or silver pen, each book is hand bound and colored differently so that the 20 copies all have completely different look, this copy bound in lavender leather with inlaid cross to both covers and title in gold, bound by Samuel Feinstein, fine.   The Kelmscott Bookshop   11 - 22   2015 $800

Greeley, Horace *The American Conflict.* Hartford: O. D. Case, 1866. 2 volumes, leather, engravings, maps, covers worn, hinges weak on volume 1, volume 2 quite solid, some foxing, very good.   Second Life Books Inc.   190 - 87   2015 $350

Greeley, Horace *An Overland Journey from New York to San Francisco in the Summer of 1859.* New York: Saxton Barker, 1860. First edition, 8vo, brown cloth with some minor wear, ex-library with spine label, bookplate and pockets, little foxing, one hinge tender, otherwise very good copy. Second Life Books Inc.   190 - 88   2015 $250

Green Mountain White Ribbon Cook Book. N.P.: Woman's Christian Temperance Union of Vermont, n.d. circa, 1895. First edition, 7 4/7 x 5 1/8 inches, green crepe paper style printed wrappers, wrappers almost completely faded to tan/buff (green on inside wrappers), textblock detached from wrappers, staples rusted and rust clearly visible on pages and wrappers, good plus example.   Tavistock Books Temperance - 2015 $95

Green, Anna Katharine *The Circular Study.* New York: McClure Phillips, 1900. First edition, page edges slightly darkened, otherwise fine in dark green pictorial cloth covered boards with gold stamped titles.   Mordida Books March 2015 - 002454   2015 $85

Green, Anna Katharine *A Difficult Problem and Other Stories.* New York: Lupton, 1909. First edition, light wear at corners, otherwise fine in pictorial olive green cloth covered boards with gold stamped titles and decorations. Mordida Books   March 2015 - 000974   2015 $150

Green, Ben K. *Horse Conformation as to Soundness Performance-Ability. (and) Hoss Trades of Yesteryear.* privately printed by the author, 1963. One of 1000 copies, of which 944 were offered for sale, 8vo., presentation to Dr. Mattingly from author, illustrations, lightly foxed along edges, else very good in lightly rubbed black dust jacket with light wear to spine ends and corners.   Buckingham Books March 2015 - 30902   2015 $400

Green, Ben K. *The Last Trail Drive through Downtown Dallas.* Published by Northland Press, 1971. First edition, limited to 100 copies signed by author, oblong 8vo., original drawing by Joe Beeler and signed by him, this copy #18, two-tone quarter leather and cloth brown front and rear endpapers, illustrations by Beeler, very fine, without dust jacket as issued, housed in original slipcase.   Buckingham Books March 2015 - 350333   2015 $1250

Green, Ben K. *Wild Cow Tales.* New York: Alfred A. Knopf, 1969. First edition, one of 300 copies on special paper, specially bound, numbered and signed by author, this copy 300, cloth with morocco label on spine, illustrations by Lorence Bjorklund, fine in slipcase as issued.   Buckingham Books   March 2015 - 25987   2015 $400

Green, Charles H. *The Headwear Workers. A Century of Trade Unionism.* New York: United Hat, Cap and Millnery, 1944. First edition, fine in torn dust jacket with sunned spine and few small chips.   Beasley Books   2013 - 2015 $45

Green, F. L. *Odd Man Out.* London: Michael Joseph ltd., 1945. First edition, very slight evidence of bookplate removal front flyleaf, else fine, bright copy in dust jacket. Buckingham Books   March 2015 - 17194   2015 $1250

Green, Gil *What's Happening to Labor.* New York: International, 1976. First edition, inscribed by author, wrappers, also issued in cloth, very good, lengthy inscription from Green.   Beasley Books   2013 - 2015 $45

Green, Henry *Back.* London: Hogarth Press, 1946. First edition, 8vo., near fine but for sunning to top edge, near fine dust jacket with art work by Vanessa Bell.   Beasley Books 2013 - 2015 $45

Green, Henry *Loving.* London: Hogarth Press, 1955. Later printing, inscribed to film producer John Sutro. Honey & Wax Booksellers   2 - 55   2015 $2800

Green, Mary McBurney *Everybody has a House.* New York: Young Scott, 1944. 4to., spiral backed pictorial boards, very good+, bold full page color illustrations by Jeanne Bendick.   Aleph-Bet Books, Inc.   108 - 413   2015 $200

Green, Richard Lancelyn *A Bibliography of A. Conan Doyle.* Oxford: Clarendon Press, 1983. First edition, very fine in dust jacket.   Mordida Books   March 2015 - 012712   2015 $450

Green, Thomas *Extracts from the Diary of a Lover of Literature.* Ipswich: printed and sold by John Raw, 1810. First edition, 4to., wanting half title, light foxing on titlepage and occasionally elsewhere, author's name in ink on titlepage, original cloth boards, generally boards little soiled and worn, rebacked, good, large copy with bookplates of Thomas Sanderson and Anne and F. G. Renier.   John Drury Rare Books   March 2015 - 25331   2015 $221

Green, Thomas J. *Journal of the Texian Expedition Against Mier; Subsequent Imprisonment of the Author...* Harper Bros., 1845. First edition, presentation copy inscribed in pencil to Col. M. M. Van Beuren by author, finely bound in 20th century half red morocco and cloth gold gilt, raised bands, titles stamped in gold gilt on spine, top edges gilt, 13 plates, 1 folding map, rare, some minor foxing throughout, yet still unusually nice, tight copy, exceptional copy.   Buckingham Books   March 2015 - 30510   2015 $2250

Greenaway, Kate   1846-1901   *Almanack for 1885.* London: Routledge, 1885. 16mo., cloth backed glazed pictorial board, light cover soil, near fine, color illustrations.   Aleph-bet Books, Inc.   109 - 209   2015 $200

Greenaway, Kate   1846-1901   *A Day in a Child's Life.* London: Routledge, n.d., 1881. First edition, first issue, 4to., cloth backed glazed pictorial boards, beveled edges, bottom edge and tips rubbed, else near fine in pictorial wrapper, wrapper lacking spine, chipped and frayed, beautiful color illustrations.   Aleph-bet Books, Inc.   109 - 208   2015 $850

Greenaway, Kate   1846-1901   *Kate Greenaway's Birthday Book for Children.* London: George Routledge, n.d. circa, 1881. New edition, 24mo., red cloth with beveled edges, stamped in black and gold, round glazed pictorial paste-on of 2 little girls on bottom left front cover, all edges gilt, near fine and unused, 12 beautiful color plates and hundreds of illustrations, this copy signed by Greenaway and has a stamp with her address on verso of presentation page.   Aleph-Bet Books, Inc.   108 - 222   2015 $1250

Greenaway, Kate   1846-1901   *Kate Greenaway Pictures from Originals Presented by Her to John Ruskin and Other Personal Friends.* London: Frederick Warne and Co., 1921. First edition, 4to., cloth, top edge gilt, other edges uncut, frontispiece, 20 mounted color illustrations on glazed paper, all tissue protected, title and owner/recipient on tissue protector, verso of illustration, foxing on some of tissue protectors and at edges of text.   Oak Knoll Books   306 - 21   2015 $150

Greenberg, Martin *Journey to Infinity.* New York: Gnome Press Incorporated Publ., 1951. First edition, octavo, cloth backed boards.   John W. Knott, Bookseller   Selected New Arrivals Jan. 2015 - 17037   2015 $75

Greenberg, Martin *Men Against the Stars.* New York: Gnome Press, 1950. First edition, octavo, cloth backed boards.   John W. Knott, Bookseller   Selected New Arrivals Jan. 2015 - 17036   2015 $250

Greenberg, Martin *The Robot and the Man.* New York: Gnome Press, 1953. First edition, octavo, cloth backed boards.   John W. Knott, Bookseller   Selected New Arrivals Jan. 2015 - 17039   2015 $250

Greenberg, Martin *Travelers of Space.* New York: Gnome Press Incorporated Pub., 1951. First edition, octavo, cloth backed boards, 16 full page color illustrations by Edd Cartier.   John W. Knott, Bookseller   Selected New Arrivals Jan. 2015 - 17038   2015 $150

Greenboathouse Press *Alphabetum Romanum.* Vernon: Greenboathouse Press, 2010. Limited to 115 copies, 1000 numbered, this copy is thus, 12mo., stiff paper wrappers, letters beautifully hand colored, prospectus loosely inserted.   Oak Knoll Books   Special Catalogue 24 - 19   2015 $400

Greene, Graham   1904-1991   *Brighton Rock.* New York: Viking, 1938. First edition, 8vo. original red cloth with black strip at head, separated by two horizontal silver rules on upper board, backstrip lettered silver and lightly faded with some faint spotting, top edge black, bookplate tipped in to flyleaf, dust jacket very bright with backstrip and rear panel very lightly toned, extremities only little rubbed, single short closed tear to front and rear panels, former with some associated creasing, couple of faint marks to rear panel and some light chipping to corners and foot of backstrip panel, very good.   Blackwell's Rare Books   B179 - 156   2015   £3000

Greene, Graham   1904-1991   *A Burnt-Out Case.* London: Heinemann, 1961. First edition, fine in price clipped dust jacket with short internal tape mend.   Mordida Books   March 2015 - 009050   2015 $150

Greene, Graham   1904-1991   *The End of the Affair.* London: Heinemann, 1951. First edition, first impression, publisher's gray cloth in original gray and white dust jacket, Raymond Chandler's copy stamped on front free endpaper with his La Jolla CA address and date JAN 7 1952, book pages toned, else near fine in very good dust jacket with few small chips to upper spine (not affecting lettering), spine toned and some light soiling.   B & B Rare Books, Ltd.   234 - 41   2015 $3500

Greene, Graham 1904-1991 *England Made Me.* London: Heinemann, 1947. Uniform edition (first edition 1935), publisher's black cloth in red and gray dust jacket, Raymond Chandler's copy stamped on front free endpaper with his LA Jolla CA address and date APR 22 1953, near fine in very good dust jacket. B & B Rare Books, Ltd. 234 - 42 2015 $1750

Greene, Graham 1904-1991 *The Heart of the Matter.* New York: Viking Press, 1948. First American edition, publisher's maroon and green cloth in matching dust jacket, Raymond Chandler's copy stamped on front free endpaper with his La Jolla CA address, near fine in very good dust jacket. B & B Rare Books, Ltd. 234 - 43 2015 $2500

Greene, Graham 1904-1991 *The Little Train.* London: Eyre & Spottiswoode, n.d., 1946. First edition, small oblong 4to., original yellow cloth, illustrated and lettered black and red on front cover, illustrations, very slight surface wear and slight marking, otherwise very good. Any Amount of Books 2015 - C5362 2015 £160

Greene, Graham 1904-1991 *The Ministry of Fear.* London: Heinemann, 1943. First edition, first impression, half maroon leather, marbled boards, 4 raised bands, lettered gilt on spine, fine. Any Amount of Books 2015 - A94612 2015 £225

Greene, Graham 1904-1991 *The Name of Action.* London: Heinemann, 1930. First edition, one or two faint foxspots to gutter of prelims, 8vo., original blue cloth with publisher's device and single fillet border blindstamped to lower and upper board respectively, backstrip lettered gilt and trifle rubbed, bookplate tipped in to flyleaf, dust jacket with small portions missing at tips of backstrip and heavily chipped at top corner of front panel, some lighter chipping elsewhere, backstrip panel darkened, very light speckling overall with brown spot at foot of rear panel, good. Blackwell's Rare Books B179 - 157 2015 £3000

Greene, Graham 1904-1991 *Our Man in Havana.* London: William Heinemann, 1958. First edition, inscribed by Greene to Alexander Frere (chairman of Heinemann), fine and unread in fine dust jacket, from the collection of Duke Collier. Royal Books 36 - 1 2015 $5500

Greene, Graham 1904-1991 *The Revenge.* London: privately printed at the Stellar Press for Bodley Head, 1963. First edition, one of 300 copies, 12mo., original green card sewn wrappers, printed in black, untrimmed, fine, inscribed by Max Reinhardt of Bodley Head to Cambridge University Press printer Brooke Crutchley. Blackwell's Rare Books B179 - 158 2015 £325

Greene, Graham 1904-1991 *Stamboul Train.* London: Heinemann, 1932. First edition, octavo, faint ownership signature, edges and prelims faintly spotted, very good. Peter Ellis, Bookseller 2014 - 018090 2015 £275

Greene, Graham 1904-1991 *The Third Man and the Fallen Idol.* London: Heinemann, 1950. First edition, tiny lightened spot on top edge and very slightly cocked, else near fine in near fine dust jacket with tiny nicks and tears at spine ends, scarce title, from the library of Kate Stettner Lobell and Carl D. Lobell. Between the Covers Rare Books 196 - 48 2015 $1600

Greene, Graham 1904-1991 *The 3rd Man.* New York: Viking Press, 1950. First edition and first separate edition after beng published jointly with The Fallen Idol by Heinemann earalier the same year, fine in stunning, about fine dust jacket, owner name on front endpaper, jacket shows absolutely none of the spine fading endemic to title, only a few pinhead size rubs and minute wear at extremities, from the collection of Duke Collier. Royal Books 36 - 179 2015 $950

Greene, Graham 1904-1991 *The Third Man and The Fallen Idol.* London: William Heinemann, 1950. First edition, fine in dust jacket with light wear to spine ends and extremities. Buckingham Books March 2015 - 23655 2015 $1500

Greene, Graham 1904-1991 *The Virtue of Disloyalty.* London: Bodley Head, 1972. First edition, privately printed in edition of 300 for distribution by author and publisher, ivory paper wrappers, inscribed in year of publication for Ragnar Svanstrom, Greene's Swedish publisher and his wife, Greta, Christmas 1972, fine. B & B Rare Books, Ltd. 234 - 44 2015 $2000

Greene, Graham 1904-1991 *A Visit to Morin.* London: Heinemann, 1959. First edition, limited to 250 copies, inscribed by author for Ian Fleming and his wife Anne, corners lightly bumped, else near fine in very good dust jacket with stray pen mark to front panel and some smudges, magnificent association. B & B Rare Books, Ltd. 234 - 4 2015 $30,000

Greene, Graham 1904-1991 *Yes and No.* Helsinki: Eurographica, 1984. 254/350 copies, signed by author, printed on Michelangelo paper, 8 pages manuscript facsimile printed rectos only, crown 8vo., original blue-grey wrappers, printed in black over stiff card, backstrip lettered in black and very slightly faded, touch of light fading at very head of flaps and few small water spots, very good. Blackwell's Rare Books B179 - 159 2015 £150

Greene, Robert *Twenty-Five Lessons in Rhyme.* Memphis: South Memphis Printing co., 1942. First edition, octavo, frontispiece, stapled printed green wrappers, fading around extremities of wrappers, else very good or better. Between the Covers Rare Books 197 - 22 2015 $1500

Greene, W. T. *Parrots in Captivity.* London: George Bell & Sons, 1884-1887. Tall octavo, 3 volumes, 81 color printed wood engraved plates, publisher's medium green blind-stamped cloth, very good, crisp set.   Andrew Isles   2015 - 26913   2015 $6000

Greene, W. T. *Parrots in Captivity.* London: George Bell Sons, 1884-1887. Octavo, 3 volumes, 402 pages, 81 color printed wood engraved plates by Benjamin Fawcett, drawn by A. F. Lydon, publisher's second issue green cloth (most common of the three variants) with printed macaw on upper boards, top edge gilt, some light wear and sunning, hinges lightly cracked, otherwise sound, clean copy.   Andrew Isles   2015 - 31855   2015 $4500

Greenleaf, Stephen *Grave Error.* New York: Dial Press, 1979. First edition, fine in dust jacket.   Buckingham Books   March 2015 - 20520   2015 $175

Greenshields, John *Reflections on the Administration of Civil Justice in Scotland; and on the Resolutions of the Committee of the House of Lords Relative to that Subject.* Edinburgh: William Blackwood and Longman, Hurst Rees & Orme, London, 1806. First edition, 8vo., titlepage just little dust soiled and marked, otherwise good, recently well bound in cloth lettered in gilt.   John Drury Rare Books   March 2015 - 19916   2015 $266

Greenwood, Christopher *Atlas of the Counties of England for Actual Surveys Made from the Years 1817 to 1833.* London: Greenwood & Co., 1st April, 1834. 46 engraved regional and county maps with vignettes, each hand colored in wash and outline mounted on 45 linen sheets with marbled paper covers and folding down to 245 x 165mm., housed in four contemporary green cloth boxed with paper labels, printed label on verso of most maps of J. W. Woolgar, Lewes, Sussex, a local historian.   Marlborough Rare Books   List 54 - 34   2015   £5500

Greenwood, James *Curiosities of Savage Life.* London: S. O. Beeton, 1865. Third edition, octavo, 2 volumes, numerous woodcuts after Harden Melville, 16 color lithograph plates, fine full calf with raised bands, gilt rules, leather title labels marbled edges and endpapers, contemporary Etonian gift inscription, bit of foxing here and there, very good in attractive binding.   Peter Ellis, Bookseller   2014 - 004334   2015   £300

Greenwood, James *The Philadelphia Vocabulary, English and Latin.* Philadelphia: Carey and Co., 1787. First American edition, 16mo., 8, 123 pages, contemporary calf, upper hinge cracked but sound, shaken, some foxing and soiling, two leaves repaired, without loss.   M & S Rare Books, Inc.   97 - 134   2015 $1500

Greg, Walter Wilson *The Editorial Problem in Shakespeare.* Oxford: Clarendon Press, 1942. Original dark blue cloth, faded, from the library of Geoffrey & Kathleen Tillotson, with her name in Geoffrey's hand and with ink note by Geoffrey, exchange of letters between Greg and Geoffrey preserved in envelope tipped on to following pastedown, with other notes.   Jarndyce Antiquarian Booksellers   CCVII - 462   2015   £25

Greg, William Rathbone *Essays on Political and Social Science, contributed Chiefly to the Edinburgh Review.* London: Longman, 1853. First collected edition, 2 volumes, 8vo., contemporary polished green calf, spines fully gilt with raised bands, contrasting labels, marbled edges and endpapers, fine, handsome binding.   John Drury Rare Books   March 2015 - 23449   2015   £306

Gregory, Herbert *Geology of the Navajo Country.* Washington: 1917. 161 pages, illustrations, many plates from photos, folding chart, 2 folding maps in back pocket, original printed wrappers, small reference number to spine, else good.   Dumont Maps & Books of the West   131 - 50   2015 $65

Gregory, Joseph W. *Gregory's Guide for California Travellers via the Isthmus of Panama.* San Francisco: Book Club of California, 1949. One of 300 copies, tinted frontispiece map and one full page illustration, facsimile of original titlepage, 2 other facsimiles tipped in, decorative yellow orange cloth, very fine.   Argonaut Book Shop   Holiday Season 2014 - 104   2015 $90

Gregory, W. D. *Little Men, The Press Enlightens the World.* Chicago: September & October, 1871. 2 issues, small folio, original printed wrappers, with illustrated ads, wrappers with light wear and soiling, internally clean and very good, rare.   M & S Rare Books, Inc.   97 - 53   2015 $350

Grendler, Paul F. *Encyclopedia of the Renaissance.* New York: Charles Scribner's Sons, 1999. First edition, 6 volumes, 4to., copiously illustrated in color and black and white, fine.   Any Amount of Books   2015 - A96976   2015   £260

Grenfell, Wilfred T. *The Harvest of the Sea: a Tale of Both Sides of the Atlantic.* New York: Toronto: Fleming H. Revell, 1905. Pictorial green cloth boards with fish and net illustrations on front board, half title, 8vo. frontispiece and 15 photo illustrations, small nick top of spine, otherwise good.   Schooner Books Ltd.   110 - 37   2015 $45

Grenville, William Wyndham *Substance of the Speech of the Right Hon. Lord Grenville in the House of Lords November 30 1819 on the Marquis Of Lansdowne's Motion that a Select Committee be Appointed to Inquire into the State of the Country...* London: John Murray, 1820. First edition, 8vo., half title, rather soiled, institutional library stamp (not lending library) on title and half title, well bound in linen backed marbled boards, lettered, very good.   John Drury Rare Books   2015 - 19053   2015 $89

Gresham, William Lindsay *Nightmare Alley.* Rinehart & Co., 1946. First edition, very lightly foxed on front and rear endpapers, else fine in dust jacket with light professional restoration to spine ends and top edge of rear panel, exceptional copy.   Buckingham Books   March 2015 - 27230   2015 $1250

Gresset *Oeuvres De Gresset.* Paris: Bleuet Jeune Libraire, 1803. New edition, 3 volumes, 12mo., half brown leather, marbled boards, gilt insignia, bookplate of Dr. H. J. Lundgren, sound, near very good with some rubbing at spine and corners, covers slightly marked and worn, tet and plates clean.   Any Amount of Books   2015 - A85830   2015   £180

Grey, Richard *The Encouragement to Works of Charity.* Northampton: printed and sold by William Dicey, 1744. First edition, 8vo., engraved frontispiece, possibly wanting half title, recent marbled boards lettered on spine, very good, crisp copy.   John Drury Rare Books   2015 - 25364   2015 $612

Grey, Zane 1872-1939 *The Arizona Clan.* New York: Harper, 1958. First edition, very fine in dust jacket.   Mordida Books   March 2015 - 006752   2015 $200

Grey, Zane 1872-1939 *Forlorn River.* New York: Harper & Bros., 1927. First edition (H-B), 8vo., title vignette, black and white decorations and color dust jacket by Robert Amick, near fine, tight copy in dust jacket with light wear to head and toe of spine and extremities, from Zane Grey's estate library with his blindstamp.   Buckingham Books   March 2015 - 12160   2015 $1275

Grey, Zane 1872-1939 *Horse Heaven Hill.* New York: Harper, 1959. First edition, very fine in dust jacket.   Mordida Books   March 2015 - 006751   2015 $200

Grey, Zane 1872-1939 *Tales of Fishing Virgin Seas.* New York: Harper & Bros., 1925. One of only a few deluxe leather bound first editions signed by author for exclusive use of author, not ever offered for sale, quarto, color frontispiece and 99 additional sepia photos and illustrations, , signed by Grey, publisher's three quarter red morocco over marbled paper boards, morocco ruled in gilt, spine lettered and stamped in gilt, marbled paper endpapers, top edge gilt, other pages uncut and partially unopened, bit of rubbing to boards and edges, overall about fine.   Heritage Book Shop   Holiday 2014 - 69   2015 $4000

Grey, Zane 1872-1939 *Tales of Swordfish and Tuna.* New York: Harper & Bros., 1927. First edition, first printing, 90 illustrations from photos taken by author and from drawings by Frank Phares, original publisher's blue cloth, spine and front cover lettered in gilt, spine end lightly rubbed and worn, few tiny tears to upper spine, else near fine, bright and clean.   B & B Rare Books, Ltd.   234 - 45   2015 $400

Grey, Zane 1872-1939 *Tales of Swordfish and Tuna.* London: Harper and Bros., 1927. First edition (so stated with correct "H-B" code), quarto, 90 photo plates, drawings by Frank Phares, publisher's dark blue cloth, gilt, tiny bump to lower edge of front cover, two leaves slightly rough at top of fore edge, but very fine, pictorial dust jacket, slight wear to jacket spine ends.   Argonaut Book Shop   Holiday Season 2014 - 105   2015 $1500

Grey, Zane 1872-1939 *Wanderer of the Wasteland.* New York: Harper & Bros., 1923. First edition (L-W), from Grey's estate with his blindstamp, illustrations by W. Herbert Dunton, near fine, bright copy in price clipped dust jacket lightly soiled on rear panel.   Buckingham Books   March 2015 - 12162   2015 $1150

Gribble, Leonard R. *The Stolen Statesman.* New York: Dodd Mead and Co., 1932. First US edition, fine, square, bright copy in dust jacket with professional restoration to spine ends, corners and extremities.   Buckingham Books   March 2015 - 37509   2015 $650

Grierson, Flora *Haunting Edinburgh.* London: John Lane, Bodley Head, 1929. First edition, quarto, 179 pages, 22 illustrations by Katharine Cameron, 16 color plates, plus 8 plates illustrating titlepages, blue cloth decorated in gilt, signed by artist on frontispiece, bottom corner front cover bumped, very good, uncommon dust jacket which is very good, bit tanned at spine with some mild rubbing.   Peter Ellis, Bookseller   2014 - 021592   2015   £300

Grieve, Symington *The Great Auk or Garefowl.* London: Thomas C. Jack, 1885. Quarto, 141 pages, 58 page appendix, (8) plates, including uncolored frontispiece and colored folding map, lacks plate 9, publisher's brown cloth and printed label, some wear top of spine and corners, few spots, otherwise sound.   Andrew Isles   2015 - 6396   2015 $500

Griffin, Julie *Someone's in the Kitchen with Dayton's, Marshall Fields, Hudson's.* Chicago: Contemporary Books, 1992. First edition, small 4to. hardcover, fine in fine dust jacket.   Beasley Books   2013 - 2015 $45

Griffin, W. E. B. *The Captains: Brotherhood of War Book 2.* London: Century, 1988. First hardcover edition, very fine in dust jacket.   Mordida Books   March 2015 - 009394   2015 $250

Griffin, W. E. B. *The Colonels: Brotherhood of War Book 4.* London: Century, 1989. First hardcover edition, page edges slightly darkened, otherwise fine in dust jacket. Mordida Books   March 2015 - 009396   2015 $250

Griffin, W. E. B. *The Generals: Brotherhood of War.* London: Century, 1990. First hardcover edition, pages slightly darkened, otherwise fine in dust jacket.   Mordida Books   March 2015 - 009398   2015 $250

Griffin, W. E. B. *The Lieutenants - Brotherhood of War - Book 1.* London: Century, 1988. First hardcover edition, fine in dust jacket.   Buckingham Books   March 2015 - 15209   2015 $225

Griffin, W. E. B. *The Majors: Brotherhood of War Book 3.* London: Century, 1989. First hardcover edition, very fine in dust jacket.   Mordida Books   March 2015 - 009395   2015 $250

Griffioen, Ruth van Baak   *Jacob Van Eyck's Der Fluyten Lust-Hof.*   The Hague: Nederlandse Muziekgeschiedenis, 1991. 8vo., cloth, dust jacket sunned on spine and spine edge of covers.   Oak Knoll Books   306 - 267   2015 $165

Griffis, William Elliot   *The Mikado's Empire....*   New York: Harper, 1890. Sixth edition, with supplementary chapters, octavo, 108 illustrations, 1 map, original brown cloth lettered gilt, presentation by author for Charles M. Dozy, Boston Jan. 31 1891, with 2 pictorial bookplates, covers little marked and little rubbed at edges, very good.   Peter Ellis, Bookseller   2014 - 01759   2015   £350

Griffiths, Anselm John   *Observations on Some Points of Seamanship; with Practical Hints on Naval Oeconomy.* Cheltenham: printed by J. J. Hadley Minerva Press Queen's Buildings, 1824. First edition, 8vo., contemporary sea green morocco over marbled boards, spine gilt and lettered, fine, uncommon.   John Drury Rare Books   2015 - 24050   2015 $1049

Griffiths, Arthur   *Ford's Folly, Ltd.*   London: MacQueen, 1900. First edition, near fine in brown pictorial cloth covered boards.   Mordida Books   March 2015 - 000986   2015 $180

Griffiths, Arthur   *Secrets of the Prison-House or Gaol Studies and Sketches.*   London: Chapman and Hall, 1894. First edition, 2 volumes, 8vo., half titles, frontispiece in each volume, good number of illustrations in text, contemporary dark red quarter roan over cloth boards, spines gilt and lettered, very good.   John Drury Rare Books   2015 - 21762   2015 $133

Griffiths, Philip Jones   *Vietnam Inc.*   New York: Macmillan, 1971. Rare hardcover issue, thought to number 200 copies, very scarce, ex-library, evidenced by bookplate, stamped 'withdrawn' and circulation list and card pocket on rear flyleaf, evidence of removal of previous jacket protector under flaps, binding only very good but in surprisingly fine dust jacket.   Ken Lopez, Bookseller   164 - 225   2015 $1250

Griffiths, William   *A Practical Treatise on Farriery: Deduced from the Experience of above Forty years in the Services of the late Sir Watkin Williams Wynn....*   Wrexham: privately published, 1784. First edition, 8vo., full leather lettered gilt and decorated on spine, frontispiece, slight splitting at spine but reasonable, sound, very good copy, neat contemporary names on front endpaper, slight wax marks on rear and front pastedowns, remains of bookplate.   Any Amount of Books   March 2015 - A87887   2015   £350

Griggs, Bob   *Elrae: the Littlest printer.*   Salem: Beaverdam Press, 1987. Limited to 225 numbered copies, signed by printer/binder, Earl H. Henness on colophon, 8.1 x 6.2cm., cloth, slipcase, illustrations in text by author, miniature bookplate of Kalman Levitan.   Oak Knoll Books   306 - 112   2015 $100

Grimaldi, Joseph   1779-1837   *Memoirs of Joseph Grimaldi.*   London: Richard Bentley, 1846. New edition, Frontispiece, plates slightly spotted or browned, illustrations by George Cruikshank, spotted or browned, original beige cloth, printed in red, spine little sunned, surface slightly rubbed, good, sound, from the library of Geoffrey & Kathleen Tillotson.   Jarndyce Antiquarian Booksellers   CCVII - 182   2015   £75

Grimaldi, Stacey   *A Suit of Armour for Youth.*   London: published by the Proprietor, 1824. First edition, small octavo, frontispiece, 11 engravings with moveable overlays, full contemporary decorated calf, gilt, raised bands, cover scuffed, hinges professionally repaired, rubber ownership stamp and initials in ink on front free endpaper, contemporary presentation inscription on first blank, ownership signature on titlepage, some offsetting from plates, good, scarce. Peter Ellis, Bookseller   2014 - 011398   2015   £350

Grimaud De Caux, Gabriel   *Des Eaux Publiques et de Leur Application aux Besoins des grandes Villes des Communes et des Habitations Rurales.*   Paris: Dezobry Fd. Tandou et Cie, 1803. First edition, 8vo., half title, occasional light foxing, later 19th century citron quarter morocco over marbled boards, spine fully gilt in compartments with art nouveau flowers and leaves, raised bands, contrasting red and green labels, top edge gilt, others uncut, fine.   John Drury Rare Books   March 2015 - 18016   2015   £306

Grimes, Martha   *The Anodyne Necklace.*   Boston: Little Brown, 1983. First edition, fine in dust jacket.   Mordida Books   March 2015 - 010822   2015 $100

Grimes, Martha *The Man with a Load of Mischief.* Boston: Little Brown, 1981. First appearance, page edges and gutters slightly darkened, otherwise fine in dust jacket with darkened spine. Mordida Books   March 2015 - 010870   2015 $200

Grimke, Sarah Moore *Joan of Arc. A Biography.* Boston: Adams, 1867. First edition, 12mo., green cloth stamped in blind and gilt, some internal staining, very good, portrait, scarce.   Second Life Books Inc.   189 - 105   2015 $325

Grimke, Thomas S. *Address.. at a Meeting in Charleston, South Carolina Held March 29 1831 to Consider the Resolution of the American Sunday School Union, Respecting Sunday Schools in the Valley of the Mississippi.* Philadelphia: American Sunday School Union, 1831. First edition, 8vo., removed, sheets toned, title foxed.   M & S Rare Books, Inc.   97 - 296   2015 $125

Grimm, Herman *Literature.* Boston: Cupples, Upham & Co., 1886. First American edition, 297 pages, with ANS from G. Grimm (?untranslated), also with publisher's inscription "With publisher's compliments and thanks for so kindly supervising the proof sheets while the book was in press Dec. 25 1885", uncommon, half leather and marbled boards and endpapers, raised bands, gilt spine decorations, leather labels, very good, little scuffing to boards, hinge professionally repaired, tight, clean text.   Stephen Lupack   March 2015 - 2015 $125

Grimm, The Brothers *Fairy Tales of the Brothers Grimm.* London: Constable, 1909. Limited to 750 copies signed by Rackham, large thick 4to., 325 pages, full vellum with gilt decorations, slight bit of rubbing and soil, else near fine with silk ties, 40 fabulous tipped in color plates with guards plus a profusion of full page and smaller black and whites, 5 inch pen drawing signed by Rackham on half title, extremely rare thus.   Aleph-bet Books, Inc.   109 - 397   2015 $15,000

Grimm, The Brothers *Fairy Tales by the Brothers Grimm.* New York: Limited Editions Club, 1931. Limited to 1500 numbered copies signed by artist, Fritz Kredel and designer, Rudolph Koch, square 8vo., full leather stamped in gilt, top edge stained red, all illustrations hand colored, slipcase shows minor rubbing along edges, well preserved.   Oak Knoll Books   25 - 4   2015 $385

Grimm, The Brothers *Faithful John.* Llandogo: Old Stile Press, 1998. 99/220 copies (from an edition of 246), signed by artist, Harry Brockway, printed on Zerkall mould made paper, imperial 8vo., original quarter maroon cloth with blue sides illustrated in gilt, backstrip lettered in gilt, top edge black, others untrimmed, matching slipcase with inset illustration, fine.   Blackwell's Rare Books   B179 - 206   2015   £80

Grimm, The Brothers *Gerlach's Jugendbucherei Kinder und Hausmarchen.* Wien Leipzig: Berlach & Wiedling, 1920. Square 12mo., cloth backed pictorial boards, 96 pages, very good+, illustrations by Otto Tauschek.   Aleph-Bet Books, Inc.   108 - 204   2015 $350

Grimm, The Brothers *Grimm's Fairy Tales.* London: Henry Frowde and Hodder & Stoughton, 1913. First edition, thick 8vo., green cloth with extensive gilt pictorial cover and spine, top edge gilt, foxing to first few and last few pages and fore edge, else near fine in dust jacket and publisher's pictorial box (mends on dust jacket and box), illustrations by Noel Pocock and 23 wonderful mounted color plates and pictorial endpapers, beautiful edition.   Aleph-bet Books, Inc.   109 - 210   2015 $1250

Grimm, The Brothers *Grimm's Fairy Tales.* New York: Limited Editions Club, 1962. Limited to 1500 copies, signed by artist, Lucille Corcos, tall 8vo., 4 volumes, patterned cloth, with Monthly Letter loosely inserted, well preserved, including original glassine wrappers.   Oak Knoll Books   25 - 40   2015 $250

Grimm, the Brothers *Hansel and Gretel and Other Stories.* New York: George H. Doran , n.d., 1925. 4to., red cloth, pictorial paste-on, cover plate bit rubbed and spine writing dull, else very good+, 12 magnificent tipped in color plates and 10 full page black and whites plus decorative initials by Kay Nielsen.   Aleph-Bet Books, Inc.   108 - 319   2015 $1250

Grimm, The Brothers *Hansel and Gretel and Other Stories.* London: Hodder & Stoughton, n.d., 1925. Limited to only 600 numbered copies signed by artist, large 4to., cloth and batiked paper over boards, fine in original plain paper slipcase (lacks a flap), 12 magnificent tipped-in color plates plus decorative endpapers, beautiful copy, scarce.   Aleph-Bet Books, Inc.   108 - 318   2015 $6000

Grimm, The Brothers *Hansel and Gretel.* New York: Grosset & Dunlap, 1944. Oblong 4to., pictorial boards, one tab extended, else near fine in dust jacket with tears and pieces missing, one of Julian Wehr's imaginative moveable books, with 4 intricate color moveable plates plus color illustrations in text.   Aleph-bet Books, Inc.   109 - 314   2015 $250

Grimm, The Brothers *Home Stories Collected by the Brothers Grimm.* London: Routledge & Co., 1855. First edition, frontispiece and plates, illustrations by George Thompson, slight tear to inner margin of front, not affecting image, binding cracking in places, but still firm, original blue decorated cloth, little rubbed and dulled, bookplate and signature of Vincent Starrett.   Jarndyce Antiquarian Booksellers   CCXI - 128   2015   £125

Grimm, The Brothers *The Juniper Tree and Other Tales from Grimm.* New York: Farrar, Straus and Giroux, 1973. First of this edition, 12mo., 2 volumes, 27 illustrations by Maurice Sendak, light brown cloth with gilt lettering and illustrations with dust jackets housed in original slipcase, very clean set, nearly fine with light sun to jacket spines, slipcase also near fine.   Ed Smith Books   82 - 23   2015 $250

Grimm, The Brothers *The Juniper Tree and Other Tales from Grimm.* New York: Farrar, Straus and Giroux, 1974. Limited edition, signed by Maurice Sendak and Lore Segal, #250 of 500 signed sets, the set consists of a copy of the first issue of the first edition of the two-volume text and extra suite of the illustrations by Sendak, printed exclusively for this edition on Beckett paper under supervision of the artist, near fine, sunning to jacket spines, cloth box, slipcase has sunning to edges.   Ed Smith Books   82 - 24   2015 $650

Grimm, The Brothers *Tales of the Brothers Grimm.* New York: Doubleday Page, 1909. Deluxe American large paper edition, signed by artist on half title and limited to 50 copies, printed on fine paper, 40 fabulous tipped-in color plates with guards and a profusion of full page and smaller black and whites, very rare in this edition in such nice condition, large thick 4to., full limp suede, with yapp edges, top edge gilt, others uncut, moire endpapers, gilt pictorial spine, repair to corner of rear endpaper, faint crease on corner of frontispiece, some wear to suede on edges as is inevitable with this type binding, else near fine and remarkably sound and clean.   Aleph-Bet Books, Inc.   108 - 381   2015 $6000

Grimston, Harbottle *The Speech Which the Speaker of the House of Commons Made unto the King in the House of Lords, at his Passing of the Bills Therein Mentioned, the 29 of August in the Year of Our Lord 1660.* London: Edward Husband and Tho. Newcomb, 1660. First edition, 4to, 8 pages, little age browned, recently well bound in quarter calf gilt, very good.   John Drury Rare Books   March 2015 - 9820   2015   £306

Grindle, Roger L. *Tombstones and Paving Blocks.* Rockland: Courier of Maine Book, 1977. First edition, nearly fine in very good+ dust jacket, minor age wear.   Stephen Lupack   March 2015 - 2015 $125

Grinstein, Alexander *The Index of Psychoanalytic Writings.* New York: IUP, 1956-1975. First edition, 11 (of 14) volumes, fine set, very good+ to fine dust jackets.   Beasley Books   2013 - 2015 $150

Grinstein, Alexander *Index of Psychoanalytic Writings.* New York: IUP, 1956-1975. First edition, 14 volumes, very good to near fine, 4 volumes lacks dust jackets, most jackets very good+ or better.   Beasley Books   2013 - 2015 $150

Griswold, P. R. *Colorado's Loneliest Railroad. The San Luis Southern.* Boulder: Pruett Pub., 1980. First edition, quarto, black and white photos, maps, line charts, blue cloth, fine with lightly soiled pictorial dust jacket, small tape repair to top edge.   Argonaut Book Shop   Holiday Season 2014 - 106   2015 $60

Griswold, Wayne *Kansas. Her Resources and Developments or the Kansas Pilot, Giving a Direct Road to Homes for Everybody.* Robert Clarke & Co., 1871. First edition, 8vo., original purple printed wrappers, illustrations, rare, very good, housed in 4 point cloth binder and slipcase, leather label on spine and titles stamped in gold.   Buckingham Books   March 2015 - 28497   2015 $1250

Grolier, Eric De *Le Portique 1-8.* Paris: Editions Rombaldi, 1945-1951. wrappers, issue 1-8, complete run, small 4to., near fine copies, although issues 3-4 have little spine wrinkling, amazingly well preserved as they were kept wrapped up tightly and hidden away.   Beasley Books   2013 - 2015 $250

Gross, Philip *The Abstract Garden.* Llandogo: Old Stile Press, 2006. 40/200 copies, signed by poet and engraver, 30 wood engravings, imperial 8vo., original quarter brown cloth with illustrated sides, backstrip lettered gilt, top edge black, others untrimmed, cloth slipcase with inset illustration, fine.   Blackwell's Rare Books   B179 - 207   2015   £160

Gross, Roni *the same... and yet.* New York: 1999. One of 22 copies, each signed and numbered by artist, all on Somerset and Hiromi papers, 20 copies for sale (2 reserved for the artist), page size 8 x 5 inches, 12 panel accordion, bound in tan Japanese cloth over boards, printed green and black with image of green apple 'the same' printed in black on tan label on front and 'and yet' printed in black on green label on back, in glassine plus green and yellow folding box designed by Peter Schell, text is letterpress from magnesium and polymer plates, designed on a Macintosh and printed in Gill Sans, photography by Yukan Hayashida and text by Ian Ganassi, drawings, printing and binding by Roni Gross.   Priscilla Juvelis - Rare Books   61 - 22   2015 $450

Grossmith, George *The Diary of a Nobody.* Bristol: J. W. Arrowsmith, London: Simpkin, Marshall Hamilton, Kent and Co., 1892. First edition, half title, frontispiece, illustrations, 3 pages ads, original orange, brown cloth, decorated and lettered in black and blue, spine lettered gilt, little marked and dulled.   Jarndyce Antiquarian Booksellers   CCXI - 129   2015   £350

Grossmith, George *The Diary of a Nobody.* Bristol: J. W. Arrowsmith; London: Simpkin Marshall, Hamilton, Kent and Co., 1910. Binding covered in brown decorated paper by Geoffrey Tillotson, from the library of Geoffrey & Kathleen Tillotson, paper label.   Jarndyce Antiquarian Booksellers   CCVII - 290   2015   £25

Grosz, George *Uber Alles Die Liebe.* Berlin: Bruno Cassirer, 1930. 4to., cloth, 60 illustrations, edges of covers and spine lightly sunned, gift inscription on front free endpaper.   Oak Knoll Books   306-22   2015 $125

Grote, George *Essentials of Parliamentary Reform.* London: Baldwin and Cradock, 1831. First edition, 8vo., titlepage and verso of final leaf little dust marked, early ownership name in ink at head of title, preserved in modern wrappers, printed title label on upper cover, entirely uncut, scarce, surprisingly scarce.   John Drury Rare Books   March 2015 - 19086   2015   £306

Grote, Harriet *Collected Papers (original and reprinted) in Prose and Verse 1842-1862.* London: John Murray, 1862. First edition, 8vo., lithographic frontispiece, wanting final ad leaves, contemporary tree calf gilt with arms in gilt of an English grammar school on upper cover (dated 1868), marbled edges, spine gilt with raised bands and label, very good.   John Drury Rare Books   March 2015 - 20630   2015 $221

Grotjahn, Martin *A Child Talks About Pictures.* 1941. First edition, paperback.   Beasley Books   2013 - 2015 $45

Grotjahn, Martin *Laughter in Psycho-analysis.* 1949. First edition, paperback, offprint from SAMIKSA 3:2 (1949), near fine with old folds, signed with his initials and short note.   Beasley Books   2013 - 2015 $45

Grotjahn, Martin *Notes on Reading the "Rundbriefe".* 1973. First edition, offprint, fine.   Beasley Books   2013 - 2015 $45

Grotjahn, Martin *Transvestite Fantasy Expressed in a Drawing.* 1948. First edition, offprint, about fine, signed by author with initials and short note.   Beasley Books   2013 - 2015 $45

Grover, Eulalie *Mother Goose.* Chicago: Volland, 1915. First edition, folio, blue gilt cloth, pictorial paste-on, oxidation spots on first few pages, else fine in original box (flaps strengthened), magnificently illustrated by Frederick Richardson with pictorial endpapers and a profusion of rich full page color illustrations.   Aleph-Bet Books, Inc.   108-306   2015 $950

Grove's Dictionary of Music and Musicians. New York: St. Martin's Press, 1962. Fifth edition, fifth printing, 10 volumes (10th is the 1961 supplement), very good set, personal owner name and black cross out on f.f.e.p.'s, some mild (unobtrusive) water marking to lower portions of the volumes which has not left any 'tide' marks in texts, little wear to dust jackets but no chipping, in all probably more appealing than description would suggest.   Stephen Lupack   March 2015 - 2015 $150

Growee, Leymah *Mighty Be Our Powers.* New York: Beast Books, 2011. Stated first edition, signed by author, 8vo., fine in fine dust jacket.   By the Book, L. C.   Special List 10-41   2015 $250

Grubb, Eugene H. *The Potato. A Compilation of Information from Every Available Source.* Doubleday Page & Co., 1912. First edition, inscribed by author for best friend E. Q. McCormick Christmas Day Dec. 25 1922, full leather, raised bands, gilt on spine, half title, frontispiece, numerous illustrations, charts, maps, beautiful copy, fine.   Buckingham Books   March 2015 - 15040   2015 $375

Gruber, Frank *The Gift Horse.* Farrar & Rinehart, 1942. First edition, near fine in dust jacket with light wear to spine ends and corners, tiny closed tear to top and bottom edge of rear cover.   Buckingham Books   March 2015 - 37522   2015 $250

Gruber, Frank *Johnny Vengeance.* New York: Rinehart, 1954. First edition, fine in dust jacket.   Mordida Books   March 2015 - 000997   2015 $75

Gruber, Frank *Outlaw.* Farrar & Rinehart Inc., 1941. First edition, bookplate of Ned Guymon, else fine, bright, square copy, dust jacket with one tiny closed tear to top edge of rear cover, sharp condition.   Buckingham Books   March 2015 - 37514   2015 $250

Gruber, Frank *Peace Marshall.* New York: William Morrow & Co., 1939. First edition, former owner's name but covered by dust jacket flap, words "A. W. Kuns rental Library" on front flyleaf and lightly stained along bottom edge of cloth, else good in dust jacket with moderate wear to extremities.   Buckingham Books   March 2015 - 2110   2015 $175

Gruber, Frank *Smoky Road.* New York: Rinehart, 1949. First edition, fine in dust jacket with slightly darkened spine.   Mordida Books   March 2015 - 000999   2015 $85

Gruelle, Johnny *All About Little Red Riding Hood retold and illustrated by Johnny Gruelle.* New York: Cupples & Leon, 1916. 16mo., boards, pictorial paste-on, fine in dust jacket (frayed), wonderful color plates and many black and whites.   Aleph-Bet Books, Inc.   108 - 229   2015 $300

Gruelle, Johnny *Friendly Fairies.* Chicago: Volland, 1919. First edition, no additional printings, 4to., pictorial boards, fine in box, illustrated with bright colors, especially beautiful, uncommon.   Aleph-bet Books, Inc.   109 - 213   2015 $850

Gruelle, Johnny *Little Brown Bear.* Joliet: Volland, 1920. Not a first edition but additional printings, 8vo., cloth backed pictorial boards, fine in box, rare, pictorial endpapers, full page and in text color illustrations, rare. Aleph-Bet Books, Inc. 108 - 228 2015 $350

Gruelle, Johnny *The Magical land of Noom.* Chicago: Volland, 1922. First edition, 2nd state, 4to., green cloth spine, pictorial boards, mint in box (only slightly rubbed), 12 color plates plus profusion of black and whites in text and pictorial endpapers, superb copy, rare in this condition with box. Aleph-bet Books, Inc. 109 - 214 2015 $1500

Gruelle, Johnny *Marcella Stories.* Joliet: Volland, 1929. First edition, 8vo. cloth backed pictorial boards, slight wear, else near fine, publisher's box (neat flap reapirs), bright color illustrations, great copy. Aleph-Bet Books, Inc. 108 - 223 2015 $600

Gruelle, Johnny *Raggedy Ann and Andy.* Akron: Saalfield, 1944. 8vo., spiral backed pictorial boards, tab extended on last page, else fine in slightly worn dust jacket, illustrations in color on every page and 6 fine color moveable plates by Julian Wehr. Aleph-Bet Books, Inc. 108 - 226 2015 $350

Gruelle, Johnny *Raggedy Ann and Andy and the Camel with the Wrinkled Knees.* Chicago: Volland, 1924. 8vo., pictorial boards, near fine, fine in publisher's pictorial box (flap repaired), wonderful illustrations in color. Aleph-Bet Books, Inc. 108 - 225 2015 $500

Gruelle, Johnny *Ragged Ann Stories.* Joliet: Volland, 1918. Later printing, pictorial boards, fine in original box very slightly worn, beautiful copy, color illustrations. Aleph-Bet Books, Inc. 108 - 224 2015 $400

Gruelle, Johnny *Raggedy Ann's Magical Wishes.* Joliet: Volland, 1928. 8vo., cloth backed pictorial boards, fine in publisher's pictorial box, pictorial endpapers, color illustrations, unusually fine. Aleph-bet Books, Inc. 109 - 212 2015 $600

Grunbaum, Adolf *Validation in the Clinical Theory of Psychoanalysis.* Madison: IUP, 1993. First edition, fine in fine dust jacket. Beasley Books 2013 - 2015 $150

Grundig, Christoph Gottlob *Historisch Kritisches Verzeichniss Alter und Neuer Schriftsteller von dem Erdboeben.* Schneeberg: Carl Wilhelm Fulden, 1756. First edition, 19th century German half calf over mottled boards, spine gilt labelled and lettered, fine. John Drury Rare Books 2015 - 25839 2015 $1049

Guarini, Battista 1538-1612 *Il Pastor Fido: Tragicomedia Pastorale.* Amsterdam: Lodovico Elzevier, 1640. 92 x 54mm. red morocco, covers gilt with french fillet border enlosing a field seme with rows of alternating ciphers "MM" and an interlaced double Phi used by Nicolas Fouquet (1615-1780), (Olivier 1398, fer 4), separated by an "S" ferme, raised bands, spine gilt compartments with double Phi cipher surrounded by small tools, delicately gilt turn-ins, marbled endpapers, all edges gilt (neat repairs to head and tail of spine), engraved vignette by C. C. Dusend on titlepage, one engraved plate and five full page engraved illustrations (blank on verso except for pagination and signature), front pastedown with part of an engraved armorial bookplate, rear pastedown with "HB" bookplate of Heribert Boeder, 9 blank leaves at end of work with ink notations in French in several hands, front joint cracked but still firm, spine slightly cocked, corners little rubbed, occasional mild foxing, final two quires with faint dampstain to upper corner, still very appealing, generally clean and fresh internally. Phillip J. Pirages 66 - 27 2015 $2800

Gudde, Erwin G. *California Gold Camps.* Berkeley and Los Angeles: University of California Press, 1975. First edition, numerous illustrations and maps, dark gray cloth, very fine with pictorial dust jacket. Argonaut Book Shop Holiday Season 2014 - 107 2015 $150

Gudde, Erwin G. *California Place Names.* Berkeley and Los Angeles: University of California Press, 1974. Third edition, 2nd printing, black cloth, very fine, dust jacket. Argonaut Book Shop Holiday Season 2014 - 108 2015 $60

Guerif, Francois *Les Amis Du Crime No. 3: Frederic Brown 1906-1972.* France: 1979. First edition, 30 mimeographed pages with illustrated paper covers and spiral binding, about fine. Mordida Books March 2015 - 07362 2015 $100

Guest, Barbara *The Altos.* San Francisco: Hine Editions/ Limestone Press, 1991. First edition, one of 40 Roman numeraled copies printed by hand on Somerset paper and signed by author and artist, from a total edition of 120 copies, folio, original full white calf stamped in blind on front cover, as new. James S. Jaffe Rare Books Modern American Poetry - 126 2015 $10,000

Guest, Barbara *Outside of This, That Is.* Calais: Z Press, 1999. First edition, one of only 26 copies with original 7-color engraving signed by artist and colophon signed by Ms. Guest out of a total edition of 226 copies printed on Bembo type on Zerkall & Fabriano paper by Grenfell Press, in the regular issue which is unsigned, frontispiece is reproduction, as new, 8vo., frontispiece, original wrappers with printed label. James S. Jaffe Rare Books Modern American Poetry - 127 2015 $450

Guest, Barbara *Poems: the Location of Things, Archaics, The Open Skies.* Garden City: Doubleday, 1962. First edition, 8vo., original boards, dust jacket, presentation copy inscribed by poet to Ted Berrigan, fine in slightly dust soiled dust jacket.   James S. Jaffe Rare Books   Many Happy Returns - 361   2015 $1250

Guest, Richard *The British Cotton Manufactures and a Reply to an Article on the Spinning Machinery Contained in a Recent Number of the Edinburgh Review.* Manchester: printed by Henry Smith sold by E. Thompson & sons and W. W. Clarke and Longman, Rees & Co., London, 1828. First edition, 8vo., errata at foot of final page, original boards rebacked, uncut, very good.   John Drury Rare Books   2015 - 14899   2015 $830

Guia de Forasteros de Siempre fiel Isla de Cuba Para el Ano Economico de 1880-81. Habana: Imprenta del Gobierno y Capitania General, 1880. Small 8vo., 12 in-text zodiac signs, red morocco embossed in blind, gilt ornamental borders, marbled endpapers, very good copy, minor rubbing, armorial bookplate from Biblioteca de Alberto Parreno.   Kaaterskill Books   19 - 45   2015 $750

Guichard, Edouard *L'Harmonie des Couleurs.* Paris: Ad Goubaud et Fils, Editeurs..., 1880. First edition, large 4to., 166 hand colored and lithograph plates, including 5 double page plates, some sporadic foxing and blotching to some plates as usual, original grey cloth, lettered in black, somewhat shaken with wear on spine, bookplate of Vincent Galloway (1894-1977) artist and curator Ferens Art Gallery, Hull.   Marlborough Rare Books   List 54 - 35   2015   £1850

Guichard, Edouard *Die Harmonie Der Farben 1300 Zusammenstellugen...* Frankfurt: Verlag on Wilhelm Rommel, 1882. First German edition, large 4to., 166 hand colored and lithograph plates, 5 double page plates, some sporadic foxing and blotching to some plates as usual, loose in original green cloth portfolio, upper cover panelled and lettered in gilt.   Marlborough Rare Books   List 54 - 36   2015   £1500

Guichenot, A. *Animaux Nouveaux ou Rares Recueillis Pendant...* Paris: A. Bertrand, 1855. Quarto, 96 pages, 18 chromolithographic plates, modern binder's cloth, fine, scarce.   Andrew Isles   2015 - 36045   2015 $6500

Guillaumin, Emile *La Vie d'un Simple.* Paris: les Editions Nationales, 1945. This number LXXXII of 100 copies, on velin d'Arches and with two extra suites of engravings (of an edition of 895), 4to., illustrations by Andre Jordan, unbound signatures laid into wrappers, fine in fine wrappers and glassine in handsome chemise and box.   Beasley Books   2013 - 2015 $350

Guillemin, Amedee Victor *La Lumiere et Les Couleurs: Ouvrage Illustre de 71 Figures Gravees sur Bois.* Paris: Librairie Hachette et cie 79 Boulevard Saint Germain, 1874. First edition, 8vo., wood engraved illustrations, original decorated wrappers, loose, upper cover with colour wheel illustration.   Marlborough Rare Books   List 54 - 37   2015   £85

Guitarman, Arthur *The School for Husbands.* New York: Samuel French, 1935. First edition, little light sunning to spine, else near fine, lacking dust jacket, bookplate of Garson Kanin and Ruth Gordon.   Between the Covers Rare Books, Inc.   187 - 130   2015 $200

Gulliver's Last Voyage. London: William Cole 10 Newgate Street, 1825. First edition, 8vo., original paper covered boards with printed spine label, spine label slightly chipped with slight loss, some minor marking to boards, some slight archival restoration at spine, overall pleasing sound, very good example with clean text, scarce, from the library of Allan Heywood Bright.   Any Amount of Books   March 2015 - C14930   2015   £450

Gunn, Thom *Fighting Terms: Poems.* Swinford: Fantasy Press, 1954. First edition, first issue, 8vo., original yellow cloth lettered red on cover, lower spine very slightly bumped, very faint cover wear, otherwise clean, very good+, decent copy.   Any Amount of Books   2015 - A92153   2015   £180

Gunn, Thom *Fighting Terms.* Swinford, Eynsham: Fantasy Press, 1954. First edition, first issue, lacking final g of the word 'thought' line 1 of poem "Tamer and Hawk" on page 38, octavo, 44 pages, spine very slightly faded, near fine.   Peter Ellis, Bookseller   2014 - 003064   2015   £350

Gunn, Thom *Mandrakes.* Cambridge: Rainbow Press/Ramapnt Lions Press, 1973. first edition, no. 124 of 150 signed copies on handmade paper (Barcham Green), 4to., original dark red cloth, quarter vellum lettered gilt on spine, fine in slightly used near very good slipcase.   Any Amount of Books   2015 - A99124   2015   £275

Gunn, Thom *Poems 1950-1966: a Selection.* London: Faber & Faber, 1969. First edition, uncorrected proof, 46 pages, fine in blue printed wrappers, signed by author, uncommon thus.   Jeff Hirsch Books   E-62 Holiday List 2014 - 14   2015 $125

Gunn, Thom *Poetry from Cambridge a Selection of Verse by Members of the University.* London: Fortune Press, 1952. 8vo., fore-edges very slightly spotted, otherwise fine in fine dust jacket, exceptional condition.   Any Amount of Books   2015 - A93097   2015   £225

Gunther, Albert *The Reptiles of British India.* London: Ray Society, 1864. Folio, 26 uncolored lithographic plates, publisher's quarter cloth and boards with label, some cracking and minor fraying of corners, few minor spots.   Andrew Isles   2015 - 6427   2015 $2250

Gunton, Symon *The History of the Church of Peterburgh.* London: printed for Richard Chiswell, 1686. First edition, 371 x 232mm., splendid honey brown diced russia by Roger Payne, covers with wide intricate and elegant dentelle frame composed of many small floral tools, raised bands, spine with gilt crest of Sir Richard Colt Hoare in top compartment, gilt titling in text two compartments and four elaborately tooled compartments below with gilt floral sprigs radiating from a central quatrefoil, interspersed with circlets and many small floral tools, turn-ins with simple gilt rules and delicate floral cornerpieces, endpapers of purple 'fine drawing paper' (Payne's words), all edges gilt, joints and very small portion at spine ends recently and expertly renewed by Courtland Benson, in a folding cloth box lined with felt (somewhat scuffed); 2 illustrations in text and 4 plates of views, large paper copy; front pastedown with armorial bookplate of Sir Henry Hope Edwardes and engraved bookplate of W. H. Corfield, front flyleaf with transcription in Hoare's hand of Payne's very detailed explanation of the work done and the bill for it; spine evenly darkened toward a chocolate brown, moderate foxing to half a dozen leaves, occasional rust spots, light stains or other trivial imperfections elsewhere in text, exceptionally desirable specimen in generally very fine condition, mostly clean and always fresh internally and very special binding entirely solid now, with virtually no wear and with all of the delicate gilt quite bright.   Phillip J. Pirages   66 - 57   2015 $15,000

Gurganus, Allan *Good Help.* Rocky Mount: North Carolina Wesleyan College, 1988. First edition, fine in wrappers, one of 1000 numbered copies, signed by author, this own of author's own copies, noted "Allan's Copy #3 out of series" additionally inscribed by author.   Between the Covers Rare Books, Inc.   187 - 114   2015 $200

Gurtler, Andre *Schrift und Kalligraefie im Experiment/ Experiments with Letterform and Calligraphy.* Basel: Schule fur Gestaltung Basel, Niggli, 1997. Small 4to., cloth, dust jacket, color and black and white illustrations throughout.   Oak Knoll Books   306 - 235   2015 $125

Gurwood, John *The General Orders of Field Marshal the Duke of Wellington, K.G. &c. in Portugal Spain and France from 1809 to 1814 and the Low Countries of France 1815.* London: published by William Clowes, 1832. First edition, 8vo., soundly rebound in modern red cloth, lettered gilt on spine, ex-British Foreign Office library with few library markings, slight foxing of prelims and fore edges, otherwise very good.   Any Amount of Books   2015 - A70523   2015   £160

Guth, Paul *Memoires D'Un Naif.* Lot-et garonne Editions Du Malih, 1967. Number 188 of 329 copies, 4to., softcover, unbound signatures laid into white wrappers printed in red, full page color illustrations by Yves Brayer, fine in red board chemise and white box matching wrappers.   Beasley Books   2013 - 2015 $250

Guthrie, A. B. *The Big Sky.* William Sloane Associates, 1947. First edition, 8vo., very fine in dust jacket.   Buckingham Books   March 2015 - 22080   2015 $375

Guthrie, A. B. *The Big Sky.* William Sloane Associates, 1947. First edition, 8vo., one of 500 numbered copies with extra leaf signed by Guthrie tipped in, fine, bright, tight copy in both regular grade pictorial dust jacket and the special plain grey printed in brown ink advance dust jacket which bears the limitation number at top of front panel, this copy number 179 some minor wear to top edge of trade jacket, the Norman Unger copy.   Buckingham Books   March 2015 - 25655   2015 $1000

Guthrie, A. B. *The Way West.* Pocket Books, 1951. First paperback edition, signed, fine in pictorial wrappers.   Buckingham Books   March 2015 - 7166   2015 $200

Guthrie, James Joshua *The Elf. A Sequence of the Seasons.* London: Old Bourne Press, 1902-1904. Limited editions, 81/250, 82/250, 35/250, 82/250 respectively, 4 volumes, small 4to., half titles, illustrations, parts II and III printed in red and black, part IV printed in blue and black, all uncut with volume partially unopened in original illustrated light blue paper boards, light brown hessian cloth spines, some minor worming to lower margin of following endpapers part III, very good.   Jarndyce Antiquarian Booksellers   CCXI - 130   2015   £650

Guthrie, Thomas *The City Its Sins and Sorrows Being a Series of Sermons from Luke XIX.41.* Edinburgh: Adam and Charles Black, 1857. First edition, including half title and final ad leaves, original maroon blind ruled cloth, spine simply lettered in gilt, fine, fresh copy.   John Drury Rare Books   March 2015 - 24287   2015 $266

Guthrie, Thomas Anstey *Mr. Punch's Pocket Ibsen: a Collection of Some of the Master's Best-Known Dramas, Condensed, revised and Slightly Re-arranged for the Benefit of the Earnest Student.* London: William Heinemann, March, 1893. First edition, partly unopened in original dark green cloth, very good, bookplate of Jessie Graham.   Jarndyce Antiquarian Booksellers   CCXI - 11   2015   £75

Guthrie, William B. *Socialism Before the French Revolution.* New York: Macmillan, 1907. First edition, hardcover, near fine.   Beasley Books   2013 - 2015 $45

Gutierrez Estrada, Jose Maria *Carta Dirigida al Escmo. sr. Presidente de la Republica, Sobre la Necesidad de buscar en una Convencion el Posible Remedio de los Males que Aquejan a la Republica.* Mexico: Impreso por Ignacio Cumplido, 1840. First edition, engraved pale, few tailpieces, 8vo., paper wrappers, spine reinforced with matching paper, dampstain on upper corner of some leaves, still very good.   Kaaterskill Books   19 - 69   2015 $350

Guziot, Elisabeth Charlotte Pauline Meulan *The Young Student or Ralph and Victor.* London: David Bogue, 1844. First English edition, half title, additional engraved title, 2 pages ads, original brown cloth, spine decorated and lettered gilt, boards blocked in blind, slightly rubbed, signed "Henry Wodehouse" on leading f.e.p.   Jarndyce Antiquarian Booksellers   CCXI - 201   2015   £85

Gwilym, Dafydd *Houses of Leaves.* Llandogo: Old Stile Press, 1993. 200/250 copies, signed by artist, printed on Zerkall cream mould made paper, 30 line drawings printed in grey, royal 8vo., original quarter green cloth with illustrated boards, backstrip lettered in grey, top edge grey, others untrimmed, cloth slipcase with inset illustration, fine.   Blackwell's Rare Books   B179 - 208   2015   £70

Gwynn, John *London and Westminster Improved Illustrated by Plans.* London: printed for the author, 1766. First edition, one of the rare copies with engraving hand colored, 4to., four engraved and contemporary hand colored folding plans, some browning to first few leaves, contemporary calf, skillfully rebacked, spine with red label lettered gilt.   Marlborough Rare Books   List 54 - 38   2015   £950

Gyoso, Sikota *Hirendi Porcelan.* Budapest: Musaki Konyvkiado, 1977. Limited to 500 copies, 7.2 x 5.3cm., leather, spine gilt stamped, porcelain ornament inlaid on front cover, housed in leather case, color plates.   Oak Knoll Books   306 - 113   2015 $250

H

H, A. C. *Tales for Thomas, Containing the Soldier, Little Harry, The Present, The Garden, The Return, Straweberries, The Mouse, The Kite, The Dog, The Black Man.* New York: printed and sold by Mahlon Day, 1833. 32mo., 17 pages, original printed wrappers with title woodcut, at head of front wrapper (no.) 17, publisher's catalog on rear wrapper, 4 1/4 2 3/4 inches, very good.   M & S Rare Books, Inc.   97 - 136   2015 $300

H. Harwood & Sons, Inc. *Base Ball and Soft Balls.* Boston: Herbert S. Porter, circa, 1936. 12mo., 16 pages, original stiff, blue printed wrappers, fine, illustrations, neat handstamp of Robert J. Stout, manuf. rep. 1760 Blenheim, Oakland, Ca.   M & S Rare Books, Inc.   97 - 21   2015 $250

Haas, Elise S. *Letters from Mexico.* San Francisco: 1937. One of 75 copies privately printed for the author and inscribed by her, 38 pages, original paper covered boards, extremities lightly rubbed, else near fine.   Dumont Maps & Books of the West   131 - 52   2015 $125

Haberly, Loyd *The Keeper of the Doves: a Tale of Notley Abbey.* Long Crendon, Bucks: Seven Acres Press, 1933. First edition, no. 70 of 100 copies, large 4to., original parchment backed lettered blue/grey boards, woodcuts by Haberly, fine, exceptional condition.   Any Amount of Books   2015 - A92554   2015   £225

Hackel, Sergei *Sobornost: the Journal of the Fellowship of St. Alban and St. Sergius...* London: The Fellowship of St. Alban and St. Sergius, 1979-1987. First editions, 17 volumes, 8vo., wrappers, very good+.   Any Amount of Books   2015 - A44130   2015   £175

Haddon, A. C. *Reports of the Cambridge Anthropological Expedition to Torres Straites.* New York: Johnson Reprint Corp., 1971. Reprint of 1904-1908 Cambridge University edition, 6 volumes, small 4to., original brown cloth lettered gilt at spine and covers, illustrations, tables, maps, plates, about fine in very good dust jacket, very slight edgewear and spine slightly sunned. Any Amount of Books   March 2015 - C3950   2015   £350

Haddon, Mark *The Curious Incident of the Dog in the Night-time.* London: Jonathan Cape, 2003. First edition, this copy signed by Haddon, is the adult edition, in both issued dust jacket and an unused trial dust jacket (white, with poodle photo on both front and back, the Ian McEwan blurb only, here on back rather than front panel; and without the Arthur Golden and Oliver Sacks blurbs), fine in fine dust jacket, scarce with trial jacket.   Ken Lopez, Bookseller   164 - 75   2015 $450

Hader, Berta *Mister Billy's Gun.* New York: Macmillan, 1960. Stated first edition, 4to., pictorial cloth, fine in fine dust jacket, , illustrations by the Haders in full color and black and white, publisher's file copy stamped not for resale.   Aleph-Bet Books, Inc.   108 - 230   2015 $150

Hader, Berta *Picture Book of Travel: the Story of Transportation.* New York: Macmillan, 1928. First printing, 4to., cloth, pictorial paste-on, fine and bright in attractive pictorial dust jacket (repaired on verso, backstrip toned), some soil, full color lithographs.   Aleph-bet Books, Inc.   109 - 218   2015 $325

Hadfield, John *Elizabethan Love Songs.* Barham Manor, 1955. 150/660 copies signed by artist and editor, 8vo., 8 chromolithographic plates by John Piper, titlepage border and numerous decorative fleuron borders, original quarter green cloth, mauve leather label, green and dark grey Cockerell boards, endpapers lightly foxed, top edge gilt, others untrimmed.   Blackwell's Rare Books   B179 - 142   2015   £100

Hafen, Leroy R. *Broken Hand. The Life Story of Thomas Fitzpatrick, Chief of the Mountain Men.* Old West Pub. Co., 1931. First edition, cloth, 316 pages, 8 plates, map, attractive copy.   Buckingham Books   March 2015 - 37395   2015 $450

Hafen, Leroy R. *Fort Laramie and the Pageant of the West.* Glendale: Arthur H. Clark Co., 1938. First edition, 8vo., cloth, frontispiece, plates, folding map, near fine.   Buckingham Books   March 2015 - 30844   2015 $300

Hafen, Leroy R. *The Overland Mail 1849-1869: Promoter of Settlement. Precursor of Rai.* Arthur H. Clark Co., 1926. First edition, cloth, 361 pages, illustrations, folding map, exceptionally fine, bright copy.   Buckingham Books   March 2015 - 34296   2015 $250

Hafiz, Shirazi *Poems form the Divan of Hafiz.* London: William Heinemann, 1897. First edition, 8vo., 14 pages ads dated 1897, original green buckram, lettered gilt at spine, some sun fading at spine, otherwise very good+ with clean text.   Any Amount of Books   2015 - C13674   2015   £170

Hager, Jean *Night Walker.* New York: St. Martin's, 1990. First edition, fine in dust jacket, signed by author.   Mordida Books   March 2015 - 001007   2015 $75

Hager, Jean *Yellow-Flower Moon.* Garden City: Doubleday, 1981. First edition, very fine in dust jacket, inscribed by author. Mordida Books March 2015 - 001009 2015 $90

Hague, Thomas *A Letter to His Royal Highness the Duke of York, or an Exposition of the Circumstances which Led to the Late Appointment of Sir Hew Dalrymple and an Inquiry into the Question Whether He, His Royal Highness, as Commander in Chief, or His Majesty's Ministers, be Most Responsible to the Country.* London: W. Horseman, 1808. First edition, 8vo., 42 pages, preserved in modern wrappers with printed title label on upper cover, very good. John Drury Rare Books 2015 - 16382 2015 $89

Hails, William Anthony *A Voice from the Ocean, the Ruins of Tyre, to the Inhabitants of Great Britain.* Gateshead: printed and sold by J. Marshall, 1807. First edition, 12mo., 24 pages, preserved in recent plain wrappers, good copy, very rare. John Drury Rare Books 2015 - 20142 2015 $133

Haines, Jennie Day *Sovereign Woman Versus Mere Man, a Medley of Quotations compiled and Arranged by.* San Francisco: Paul Elder, 1905. First edition, 8vo., stiff wrappers, Beardsley style frontispiece by Gordon Ross, good looking book, illustrated border, bound Japanese style, leaves little browned, very good. Second Life Books Inc. 189 - 106 2015 $125

Hakewill, William *The Libertie of the Subject; Against the Pretended Power of Impositions, Maintained by an Argument in Parliament Ano. 70 Jacob Regis.* London: printed by R. H. An. Dom., 1641. Only edition, final license leaf, fore-edge of title stained and neatly strengthened, one or two minute wormholes affecting several lower margins just touching the occasional letter but with virtually no loss, wide margined copy in contemporary ruled calf, rebacked and lettered, corners repaired, good, crisp copy. John Drury Rare Books 2015 - 25081 2015 $1049

Haldane, Henry *The Trial of Lieut. Col. Haldane on an Indictment for Perjury at Kingston in the County of Surrey on the 2d Day of April 1814.* London: J J. Stockdale, 1814. First edition, 8vo. recent marbled boards lettered on spine, very good, very rare. John Drury Rare Books March 2015 - 22894 2015 £306

Haldeman, Joe *The Forever War.* New York: St. Martin's Press, 1974. First edition, octavo, boards. John W. Knott, Bookseller Selected New Arrivals Jan. 2015 - 17041 2015 $1000

Hale, Christopher *Dead of Winter.* Garden City: Doubleday Doran & Co., 1941. First edition, fine, bright, tight copy, dust jacket, lightly rubbed at spine end and corners. Buckingham Books March 2015 - 29251 2015 $750

Hale, Christopher *Murder in Tow.* Garden City: Doubleday Doran and Co., 1943. First edition, near fine in dust jacket, lightly soiled on rear panel and tiny chip to top edge of rear panel. Buckingham Books March 2015 - 32180 2015 $675

Hale, E. E. *In His Name: a Story of the Waldeneses, Seven Hundred Years Ago.* Boston: Roberts Brothers, 1877. First edition, 12mo., publisher's green cloth, gilt, modest edgewear, one signature little sprung, very good, author Frances Parkinson Keyes' copy with her bookplate and later signature of her son, Henry W. Keyes, Jr. Between the Covers Rare Books, Inc. 187 - 115 2015 $400

Hale, George Ellery *The Study of Stellar Evolution, An Account of Some Recent Methods of Astrophysical Research.* Chicago: University of Chicago Press, 1908. First edition, frontispiece, 104 plates, including frontispiece, bound by Stikeman & Co. in half dark green crushed morocco, green cloth, gilt ruled and decorative spine, top edge gilt, marbled endleaves, inner hinge broken, extremities worn (with kozo repairs), bookplate of Katherine Duer Mackay (1880-1930), very good. Jeff Weber Rare Books 178 - 792 2015 $150

Hale, Kathleen *Orlando the Marmalade Cat Keeps a Dog.* London: Country Life, n.d. circa, 1944. First edition, folio, cloth backed pictorial boards, slightest of edge wear, else fine, frayed dust jacket, beautiful color lithographs. Alephbet Books, Inc. 109 - 219 2015 $350

Hale, Matthew *Why Women Should Not Vote. Remarks Made by....* Albany: 1894. First edition?, 8vo., 4 pages (two sheets, disbound). Second Life Books Inc. 189 - 107 2015 $65

Hale, Sara Josepha *Woman's Record; or Sketches of all Distinguished Women from the Creation to A.D. 1854.* New York: Harper, 1853. First edition, large 4to., rebound in brown cloth with original spine laid down, new endpapers, frontispiece stained and watermarked, some light foxing, good, scarce. Second Life Books Inc. 189 - 108 2015 $250

Haley, Alex *The Autobiography of Malcolm X with the Assistance of Alex Haley.* Secaucus: Castle Books, 1965. Reprint edition inscribed by Haley, near fine in brown boards, very good dust jacket with one small chip to top of rear panel, price clipped but "$" remains. Ed Smith Books 83 - 38 2015 $200

Haley, Alex *The Man Who Wouldn't Quit.* Pleasantville: Reader's Digest Assoc., 1963. First separate edition, offprint from Reader's Digest magazine, one leaf folded to make 6 pages, vertical crease, probably as mailed, one small snag on front page, else very good or better, sent by George Haley to senior law partner Leon J. Obermayer, Washington, signed by Alex Haley, rare.   Between the Covers Rare Books   197 - 24   2015 $3000

Haley, Alex *Roots.* New York: Doubleday, 1976. First edition, deluxe issue, being one of 500 numbered copies signed by author, fine in near fine slipcase, bound in leather.   Ed Smith Books   83 - 37   2015 $450

Haley, Charles Scott *Gold Placers of California.* Sacramento: California State Mining Haven, 1923. First edition, 36 photos, 7 plates and maps, including folding table and large folding map in rear pocket, folding table torn and damaged at one edge, large folding map with few breaks at fold junctions, else fine, ink name on end, fine, brown cloth stamped in black.   Argonaut Book Shop Holiday Season 2014 - 212   2015 $250

Haley, James Evetts *Earl Vandale on the trail of Texas books.* Palo Duro Press, 1965. First edition, limited to 500 copies, presentation inscription by author for Louise Evans, 8vo., cloth, title stamped in gilt on front cover and spine, frontispiece, illustrations, fine, bright, square copy.   Buckingham Books   March 2015 - 36842   2015 $175

Haley, James Evetts *George W. Littlefield, Texas.* Norman: University of Oklahoma, 1943. First edition, 8vo., cloth, fine, bright copy in fine dust jacket.   Buckingham Books   March 2015 - 19302   2015 $250

Haley, James Evetts *The Great Comanche War Trail.* Panhandle Plains Historical Review, 1950. First edition, signed by author, printed wrappers, very scarce, fine.   Buckingham Books   March 2015 - 36430   2015 $175

Haley, James Evetts *A Log of the Montana Trail as Kept by Ealy Moore.* Russell Stationery Co., 1932. First edition thus, 8vo., inscribed by Haley to C. C. Walsh, printed wrappers, fine, housed in quarter leather and cloth clamshell case with titles stamped in gold, gilt on spine.   Buckingham Books   March 2015 - 29752   2015 $2000

Haley, James Evetts *Lore of the Llano Estacado & Cowboy Songs Again.* Texas Folk Lore Society, 1927. First separate edition, 8vo., presentation inscription by author, printed wrappers, old evidence of label removal from top edge of front cover, else very good.   Buckingham Books   March 2015 - 3805   2015 $1250

Haley, James Evetts *Robbing Banks was My Business. The Story of J. Harvey Bailey America's Most Successful Bank Robber.* Palo Duro Press, 1973. First edition, black and white frontispiece, illustrations by Theda Rhea, fine in dust jacket, lightly rubbed at spine ends, corners and extremities.   Buckingham Books   March 2015 - 36898   2015 $300

Haley, James Evetts *Robbing Banks was My Business. The Story of J. Harvey Bailey, America's Most Successful Bank Robber.* Canyon: Palo Duro Press, 1973. First edition, signed by Bailey, and signed and inscribed by Haley to Tom and Hilda Lewis, cloth, black and white frontispiece, illustrations by Theda Rhea, fine in dust jacket, lightly rubbed along front spine channel and spine ends, housed in matching cloth slipcase with titles stamped in gold gilt on spine.   Buckingham Books   March 2015 - 31744   2015 $875

Haley, James Evetts *Story of the Shamrock.* Amarillo: Shamrock Oil and Gas, 1954. First edition, small quarto, original light green wrappers, illustrations, one of an undetermined number of copies issued with extended edges, tied with green leather at spine and enclosed in original two-tone cardboard slipcase, bookplate removed from inside cover, else fine in fine slipcase.   Buckingham Books   March 2015 - 24712   2015 $450

Haley, James Evetts *The XIT Ranch of Texas and the Early Days of the Llano Estacado.* Chicago: Lakeside Press, 1929. First edition, presentation inscription by author to R. G. Long, laid in is penned note on Prince George Hotel NYC stationery to Wright Howes, bookseller and author, decorated cloth, fine, bright copy, in protective transparent dust jacket, exceptional copy.   Buckingham Books   March 2015 - 28028   2015 $1875

Halhed, Nathaniel Brassey *Testimony of the Authenticity of the Prophecies of Richard Borthers, and of His Mission to Recall the Jews.* London: printed for R. Faulder, 1795. 4to., endpapers and title bit foxed, later half calf, marbled boards, spine ruled and decorated in gilt, red morocco label, red sprinkled edges, slight wear to hinges, Somerset armorial bookplate, very good.   Jarndyce Antiquarian Booksellers CCXI - 47   2015   £240

Hall, Anna Maria Fielding 1808-1881 *Sketches of Irish Character.* London: M. A. Nattall, 1844. First illustrated edition, small quarto, 5 full page tissue guarded plates, including frontispiece and many smaller wood engravings in text, original green cloth decorated in blind and in gilt on spine, all edges gilt, hinges starting, but tight, covers little marked and slightly rubbed at spine, prelims lightly spotted, very good.   Peter Ellis, Bookseller   2014 - 010323   2015   £325

Hall, Ansel F. *Handbook of Yosemite National Park.* G. P. Putnam's Sons, 1921. First edition, 8vo., presentation inscription by compiler written in pencil and signed 'Yosemite Valley August 22 1922", green pictorial cloth, frontispiece, illustrations, corners lightly rubbed, some light foxing to few page fore-edges, minor soiling to rear cover, else very good, clean copy. Buckingham Books   March 2015 - 3280   2015 $275

Hall, Carol D. *Bierce and the Poe Hoax.* San Francisco: Book Club of California, 1934. First edition, one of 250 numbered copies, small quarto, 2 photos, facsimiles, dark blue cloth, red labels on spine and front cover, overall fine. Argonaut Book Shop   Holiday Season 2014 - 110   2015 $175

Hall, Charles *An Enquiry into the Cause of the Present Distress of the People.* London: printed for the author and sold by J. Ridgway, 1820. First edition with this title, 8vo., final ad and errata leaves, contemporary half calf over marbled boards, spine simply gilt with label, very good from the early 19th century library of Bernard Edward,12th Duke of Norfolk (1765-1842) with his bookplate. John Drury Rare Books   2015 - 25943   2015 $6119

Hall, Covington *Battle of Hymns of Toil.* Oklahoma City: General Welfare Report, n.d., 1946. Wrappers, near fine, short tears at joints, 120 pages.   Beasley Books   2013 - 2015 $150

Hall, Donald *Ox-Cart Man.* New York: Viking Press, 1979. First edition, near fine, minimal foxing to edges, in very good++ dust jacket with minimal sun spine and edge wear, 8.5 x 10.5 inches, near fine, no Caldecott sticker or mention of award on book or jacket, illustrations by Barbara Cooney.   By the Book, L. C.   44 - 84   2015 $190

Hall, George Webb *The Origin and Proceedings of the Agricultural Associations in Great Britain, in Which their Claims to Protection Against Foreign Produce, Duty-Free, are Fully and Ably Set Forth.* London: printed at the office of the Farmers' Journal by Ruffy and Evans, nd., 1820. First edition, second issue, 8vo., 46 pages, one or two margins cut close by binder (no loss of text), modern boards, spine simply lettered, scarce.   John Drury Rare Books   2015 - 10637   2015 $177

Hall, James W. *Under Cover of Daylight.* New York: Norton, 1987. First edition, very fine in dust jacket, signed by author.   Mordida Books   March 2015 - 009053   2015 $90

Hall, Philip *The Collected Works of Philip Hall.* Oxford: Clarendon Press, 1988. First edition, large 8vo., (8) pages, original blue leather lettered gilt on spine and front cover, very slight marking to cloth, otherwise near fine.   Any Amount of Books   2015 - C14649   2015   £225

Hall, Robert *Modern Infidelity Considered with Respect to Its Influence on Society.* Cambridge: printed by M. Watson and sold by J. Deighton and O. Gregory, 1800. First edition, 8vo., one leaf with ragged margin, spotting and rust marks on title and few other leaves, modern ms. notes in ballpoint pen on blank verso of final leaf, recently well bound in linen backed marbled boards, lettered, scarce.   John Drury Rare Books   March 2015 - 19677   2015 $266

Hall, William Henry *The Death of Cain in Five Books after the Manner of The Death of Abel.* printed for B. Crosby, 1797. Unrecorded edition, 12mo., frontispiece almost detached, contemporary mottled calf, spine gilt and with red lettering piece, traces of red wax seals inside covers, sound.   Blackwell's Rare Books   B179 - 49   2015   £750

Hallahan, William H. *Catch Me: Kill Me.* Bobbs Merrill, 1977. First edition, fine in dust jacket.   Buckingham Books   March 2015 - 35853   2015 $175

Halle, J. N. *Report sur an Procede Mecanique ou Moyen Duquel M. Delaxroix a Supplee a l'Action des Tendons Extenseurs des Deux Mains, Paralyses chez un Musicien Pianiste Attache au Theatre Italien de Sa Majeste l'Imperatrice....* Paris: Migneret rue de Dragon, 1813. First separate edition?, folding engraved plate, 10 pages, disbound but now preserved in dark blue patterned card covers, very rare apparently, good copy.   John Drury Rare Books   2015 - 25553   2015 $1005

Hallett, Benjamin Franklin *The Right of the People to Establish Forms of Government. Mr. (Benjamin Franklin) Hallett's Argument in the Rhode Island Causes, Before the Supreme Court of the United States, January... 1848.* Boston: Beals & Greene, 1848. First edition, large 8vo., 71 pages, neatly bound in later? buckram and marbled boards, institutional bookplate marked 'withdrawn' on front pastedown.   M & S Rare Books, Inc.   97 - 268   2015 $275

Hallo, Neddy! London: Dean's Rag Book Co. Ltd. n.d. circa, 1935. 8vo., pictorial cloth, light cover soil, very good+, illustrations.   Aleph-Bet Books, Inc.   108 - 199   2015 $250

Halsted, Oliver *A Full and Accurate Account of the New Method of Curing Dyspepsia.* New York: 1831. Second edition, 4 plates, contemporary linen backed boards, printed paper label on cover, untrimmed, foxed, else very good.   Joseph J. Felcone Inc.   Science, Medicine and Technology - 33   2015 $100

Halvsa, Oldrich *A Book of Type and Design.* New York: Tudor Pub. Co., 1960. First US edition in English, square 8vo., two toned cloth, dust jacket, jacket chipped with tears and rubbing, especially along hinges, only slight jacket wear.   Oak Knoll Books   306 - 48   2015 $125

Hamada, Shoji *The Works of Shoji Hamada 1921-1969.* Tokyo: Asahi Shimbun, 1969. First edition, large 4to., plates, original brown cloth over handmade brown paper boards, lettered black on front cover, photos, 127 color plates, fine in original acetate wrapper and very good+, cloth slipcase. Any Amount of Books 2015 - C15569 2015 £325

Hamady, Walter *Interminable Gabberjabbs.* Mt. Horeb: Perishable Press, 1973. Limited to 120 numbered copies, small 4to., stiff paper wrappers, handset type on a variety of Shadwell papers of different sizes, handsewn into blue Fabriano wrappers with maps as inner wrappers. Oak Knoll Books 306 - 165 2015 $2000

Hamburger, Philip *Mayor Watching and Other Pleasures.* New York: Rinehart & Co., 1958. First edition, first printing, from the library of fellow writer at the New Yorker and friend, Joseph Mitchell, with his ownership stamp, presentation copy inscribed by author to Mitchell and his wife Therese, near fine, very lightly rubbed at extremities, jacket with some light wear rubbing and some light chipping to spine ends, some splitting and some chips along upper front flap, else very good, attractive copy, excellent. B & B Rare Books, Ltd. 234 - 46 2015 $600

Hamel, Felix John *The Laws of the Customs, Consolidated by Direction of the Lords Commissioners of Her Majesty's Treasury...* London: Butterworths, 1854. Royal 8vo., errata slip, little spotting at beginning, original cloth, gilt with royal arms on upper cover, university duplicate with label on foot of spine and occasional other marks. John Drury Rare Books 2015 - 8036 2015 $133

Hamerton, Philip Gilbert 1834-1894 *Drawing and Engraving: a Brief Exposition of Technical Principles and Practice.* London: & Edinburgh: Adam & Charles Black, 1892. First edition, large 8vo., 22 plates, original brown buckram, lettered gilt on spine and cover, illustrations, early dust jacket a remarkable survival, slight browning to endpapers, otherwise fine in complete about very good, printed red dust jacket, faded and slightly stained at spine with slightly worn ends. Any Amount of Books 2015 - C5080 2015 £160

Hamidi, Avigdor *Yeledim V'Hagim B'Israel. (Children and Holidays of Israel).* Tel Aviv: Sinai, n.d. circa, 1955. 4to., pictorial boards, slight edge rubbing, else fine, color linoleum block print by Miriam Bartov. Aleph-bet Books, Inc. 109 - 236 2015 $600

Hamill, Sam *Fatal Pleasure.* Portland: Breitenbusch Books, 1984. First edition, fine in near fine dust jacket (trifle rubbed), warmly inscribed by author to fellow poet Carolyn Kizer. Between the Covers Rare Books, Inc. 187 - 116 2015 $85

Hamilton, Bruce *Too Much of Water.* London: Cresset, 1958. First edition, fine in dust jacket. Mordida Books March 2015 - 001019 2015 $75

Hamilton, Charles *Collecting Autographs and Manuscripts.* Norman: University of Oklahoma Press, 1961. First edition, over 800 facsimiles and reproductions, beige cloth, lettered in metallic violet on spine, covers lightly soiled else fine, presentation inscription signed by author. Argonaut Book Shop Holiday Season 2014 - 111 2015 $75

Hamilton, Cicely *Modern Russia as Seen by an Englishwoman.* New York: Dutton, 1934. First edition, hardcover, many photos, little spotting to boards, otherwise fine and bright in chipped dust jacket. Beasley Books 2013 - 2015 $45

Hamilton, Elizabeth *Hints Addressed to the Patrons and Directors of Schools...* London: Longman, Hurst, Rees, Orme and Brown, 1815. First edition, 12mo., well bound in old style quarter calf over marbled boards, spine gilt and labelled with raised bands, fine. John Drury Rare Books 2015 - 25841 2015 $1049

Hamilton, Elizabeth *Letters, Addressed to a Daughter of a Nobleman on the Formation of Religious and Moral Principle.* London: T. Cadell and W. Davies, 1806. First edition, 2 volumes, 8vo., without half titles, contemporary calf, spines gilt in compartments and double labelled, just little rubbing of extremities, else near fine. John Drury Rare Books March 2015 - 24296 2015 $266

Hamilton, Elizabeth *Translation of the Letters of a Hindoo Rajah, Written Previous to and During the Period of His Residence in England.* London: G. and J. Robinson, 1801. Second edition, 2 volumes, uncut, contemporary brown boards imitating leather, later maroon labels, slight rubbing at tails of spines, very good. Jarndyce Antiquarian Booksellers CCXI - 131 2015 £280

Hamilton, Ian *The Review a Bi-Monthly Magazine of Poetry and Criticism No. 1 April/May 1962 to no. 29/30 (1972).* London: Oxford, 1962-1972. First edition, wrappers, 8vo., complete run of 30 issues including 3 individual three pamphlet series, no. 13 in original printed envelope, 19 and 21 and supplement to no. 25 by 'Backwaters' by Douglas Dunn, all clean, very good copies, some fine, issue 11/12 slightly stained at side. Any Amount of Books 2015 - A66949 2015 £175

Hamilton, Joseph *Some Short and Useful Reflections Upon Duelling, Which Should Be in the Hands of Every Person Who is Liable to Receive a Challenge, or an Offence.* Dublin: printed for the author by C. Bentham 19 Eustace Street..., 1823. First edition, 12mo., engraved frontispiece, half title, final ad leaf H12, original printed boards, these bit browned and spotted but still fine, crisp, uncut, with early 20th century armorial bookplate of William Walter Dowding, rare. John Drury Rare Books 2015 - 23065 2015 $2448

Hamilton, Patrick 1904-1962 *Hangover Square.* London: Constable, 1941. Second impression published September 1941 (first was August 1941), 8vo., from the library of Peter Haining (1940-2007) with his book label and brief ownership signature, covers tanned, slightly marked and mottled, sound, very good- with clean text, signed presentation from author to Ernest Borrow. Any Amount of Books 2015 - C1683 2015 £700

Hamilton, Patrick 1904-1962 *Mr. Stimpson and Mr. Gorse.* London: Constable, 1963. First edition, 8vo., original blue cloth, lettered silver at spine, slight browning at edges with neat Chelsea public library stamp on titlepage and first page, otherwise very good+ in clean, bright very good dust jacket with very faint edgewear and slight creasing, very slight chipping at spine end. Any Amount of Books 2015 - C13305 2015 £180

Hamilton, Patrick 1904-1962 *Unknown Assailant.* London: Constable, 1955. First edition, 8vo., original blue cloth, lettered silver at spine, slight rubbing, otherwise very good+, bright, clean, very good dust jacket with very slight edgewear and slight surface wear, decent copy. Any Amount of Books 2015 - C13304 2015 £300

Hamilton, Peter F. *The Reality Dysfunction.* London: Macmillan, 1996. First edition, signed by author, octavo, boards. John W. Knott, Bookseller Selected New Arrivals Jan. 2015 - 17045 2015 $450

Hamilton, Robert *Essays.* Aberdeen: printed by D. Chalmers and Co., 1831. First collected edition, 8vo., half title, original(?) cloth backed boards, minor staining on covers, little wear, uncut, very good. John Drury Rare Books March 2015 - 12776 2015 £306

Hamilton, Thomas *Men and Manners in America.* Edinburgh: William Blackwood, 1833. First edition, 12mo., 2 volumes, contemporary half brown calf by J. Seacome, Chester, gilt bands, black and maroon morocco labels, little rubbed, nice, crisp copy, armorial bookplate of James Tomkinson Willington. Jarndyce Antiquarian Booksellers CCXI - 132 2015 £280

Hammer, Martin *Graham Sutherland: Landscapes, War Scenes, Portraits 1924-1950.* London: Scala Pub. Ltd., 2005. First edition, wrappers, cloth, illustrated wrappers, copiously illustrated in color and black and white, fine. Any Amount of Books 2015 - !90767 2015 £160

Hammer, Victor *Those Visible Marks... The Visible Forms of Our Letters.* Lexington: Anvil Press, 1988. First edition, limited to 50 numbered copies, set Uncial and printed by Carolyn Hammer and Paul Holbrook on paper from Magnani Mills, Pescia, Italy, 8vo., paper covered boards, paper label, later cardboard slipcase, well preserved copy. Oak Knoll Books 306 - 123 2015 $350

Hammett, Dashiell *The Adventures of Sam Spade and other Stories.* New York: Lawrence E. Spivak, 1944. First edition, digest sized paperback original, little minor rubbing to spine, light wear to spine ends, else near fine in pictorial brown wrappers. Buckingham Books March 2015 - 27913 2015 $225

Hammett, Dashiell *The Battle of the Aleutians.* Adak: Field Force Hdqtrs, 1944. First edition, original blue black and white printed wrappers, illustrations, maps, light rubbing to spine and light creasing to bottom corner of front flap, else very good, scarce. Buckingham Books March 2015 - 25748 2015 $425

Hammett, Dashiell *"Bodies Piled Up." in Black Mask, December 1, 1923.* New York: Pro Distributors, 1923. First appearance, good in perfect bound wrappers, with corner chip at top right front panel, bruise at top left of same, light fray to outer edges, pages dry but still somewhat supple, some light chipping to edges of prelim leaves, from the collection of Duke Collier. Royal Books 36 - 181 2015 $750

Hammett, Dashiell *The Continental Op.* New York: Spivak, 1945. First edition, paperback original, spine darkened, otherwise near fine in wrappers. Mordida Books March 2015 - 012018 2015 $150

Hammett, Dashiell *The Continental OP.* Lawrence E. Spivak, 1945. First edition, digest size PBO, pages evenly tanned, lightly rubbed at spine ends and light wear to corners, else very good in pictorial wrappers with no fading at all to blue color on covers. Buckingham Books March 2015 - 36258 2015 $200

Hammett, Dashiell *The Creeping Siamese.* New York: Spivak, 1950. First edition, paperback original, near fine, spine slightly faded and light wear along spine fold, otherwise near fine in wrappers. Mordida Books March 2015 - 011701 2015 $125

Hammett, Dashiell *The Creeping Siamese.* New York: Spivak, 1950. First appearance, staining along bottom page edges, otherwise very good in wrappers. Mordida Books March 2015 - 009903 2015 $85

Hammett, Dashiell *The Dain Curse.* New York: Knopf, 1929. Second edition, stated "Second Printing August 1929", fine, with facsimile dust jacket, publisher's bookmark advertising Red Harvest laid in. Mordida Books March 2015 - 009399 2015 $650

Hammett, Dashiell *Dashiell Hammett: Crime Stories and Other Writings.* New York: Library of America, 2001. first edition thus, fine in near fine dust jacket, book is fine in near fine dust jacket, small 8vo. Beasley Books 2013 - 2015 $40

Hammett, Dashiell *The Dashiell Hammett Omnibus.* New York: Alfred A. Knopf, 1935. First edition, trace of shelfwear at base of spine, else fine, tight copy, bright dust jacket with very light wear to spine ends and closed tear at front hinge, from the collection of Duke Collier. Royal Books 36 - 180 2015 $2000

Hammett, Dashiell *Dead Yellow Women.* Lawrence E. Spivak, 1947. First edition, digest size PBO, page edges lightly tanned, else fine in pictorial wrappers with no fading of green color at all. Buckingham Books March 2015 - 36256 2015 $250

Hammett, Dashiell *The Glass Key.* New York: Grosset & Dunlap, Photoplay edition, pages darkened and covers slightly soiled, otherwise near fine in dust jacket with couple of closed tears, small chip at top corner of back panel and nicks at corners. Mordida Books March 2015 - 011387 2015 $150

Hammett, Dashiell *Hammett Homicides.* Lawrence Spivak, 1946. First edition, digest size PBO, pages evenly browned, light wear to spine ends and covers lightly rubbed and lightly soiled, else very good in pictorial wrappers. Buckingham Books March 2015 - 36260 2015 $175

Hammett, Dashiell *Hammett Homicides.* New York: Spivak, 1946. First edition, paperback original, very good, pages darkened, small nick on front cover and wear along spine folds, otherwise very good in wrappers. Mordida Books March 2015 - 006769 2015 $125

Hammett, Dashiell *Hammett Homicides.* New York: Lawrence E. Spivak, 1946. First edition, page edges uniformly tanned, light wear to spine ends, fine in pictorial wrappers. Buckingham Books March 2015 - 27912 2015 $225

Hammett, Dashiell *The Maltese Falcon.* New York: Otto Penzler Books Facsimile Edition, 1993. Facsimile of 1930 first edition, fine in dust jacket. Buckingham Books March 2015 - 30247 2015 $200

Hammett, Dashiell *A Man Named Thin.* Joseph W. Ferman, 1962. First edition, Digest size PBO, Mystery No. 233, pages evenly tanned, minor wear to fore edges, else near fine in printed wrappers. Buckingham Books March 2015 - 36259 2015 $175

Hammett, Dashiell *Modern Tales of Horror.* London: Victor Gollancz, 1932. First UK edition, fine, bright, tight copy in perfect rare dust jacket. Buckingham Books March 2015 - 24910 2015 $1650

Hammett, Dashiell *Modern Tales of Horror.* London: Gollancz, 1932. First English edition, pages slightly darkened, otherwise fine in very good darkened dust jacket with some internal tape reinforcing and repair, strip chipped from internal rear flap, couple of short closed tears. Mordida Books March 2015 - 002455 2015 $450

Hammett, Dashiell *Nightmare Town.* New York: Spivak, 1948. First edition, near fine, faint erasure on front cover, otherwise near fine, wrappers. Mordida Books March 2015 - 011700 2015 $150

Hammett, Dashiell *$106,000 Blood Money.* New York: Lawrence E. Spivak, 1943. First edition, wrappers digest size paperback, very good to near fine. Beasley Books 2013 - 2015 $40

Hammett, Dashiell *The Return of the Continental OP.* Lawrence E. Spivak, 1945. First edition, digest size PBO, pages evenly tanned, else fine in pictorial wrappers with no fading at all to red color on covers. Buckingham Books March 2015 - 36257 2015 $275

Hammett, Dashiell *The Thin Man.* New York: Grosset & Dunlap, Reprint edition, pages darkened, otherwise very good in dust jacket with quarter inch strip missing top of spine, heavy wear along folds and internal tape mends. Mordida Books March 2015 - 009901 2015 $85

Hammett, Dashiell *The Thin Man.* New York: Alfred A. Knopf, 1934. First edition, 8vo., cloth lightly mottled as is usually the case with this title, else near fine in dust jacket with light professional restoration to spine ends and corners, housed in two tone quarter leather and cloth clamshell case with titles stamped in gold on spine. Buckingham Books March 2015 - 26312 2015 $7500

Hammett, Dashiell *The Thin Man.* New York: Alfred A. Knopf, 1934. First edition, four jacket variants, of no established priority, this one is in red with no blurbs, cloth bit mottled as always found, else near fine in very good plus dust jacket, jacket has small chips at corners, one at crown which affects "DA" in author's name, the others much smaller, from the collection of Duke Collier.   Royal Books   36 - 182   2015 $4000

Hamnett, Nina *Is She a Lady? a Problem in Autobiography.* London: Allan Wingate, 1955. First edition, octavo, 161 pages, 6 photos, 4 pages of drawings, presentation from author for Lucy, she has also signed titlepage and made several corrections to text, edges bit spotted, corners slightly bumped, top of spine faded, good in remains of dust jacket.   Peter Ellis, Bookseller   2014 - 018778   2015   £275

Hancock, H. Irving *Japanese Physical Training.* New York and London: G. P. Putnam's Sons, 1905. First edition, 8vo., original orange cloth lettered black on spine and cover, 19 illustrations, about fine in dust jacket with slight wear and slight chip at head of spine and slight creasing and nick at front corner, from the library of Ronald Searle.   Any Amount of Books   2015 - A98969   2015   £180

Hancock, H. Irving *The Young Engineers in Arizona or Laying Tracks on the Man Killer Quicksand.* New York: Saalfield, 1912. First edition, illustrations, fine, bright copy in dust jacket, with light wear to extremities.   Buckingham Books   March 2015 - 13440   2015 $175

Handbook of North Carolina. Raleigh: Presses of Edwards & Broughton, 1893. First edition, 8vo., printed wrappers, large foldout map in rear, compliments slip tipped in photos, scarce.   Second Life Books Inc.   190 - 174   2015 $225

Hanft, Robert M. *Pine Across the Mountain. California's McCloud River Railroad.* San Marino: Golden West Books, 1971. First edition, over 295 photos and illustrations, wood grain beige cloth, fine with pictorial dust jacket.   Argonaut Book Shop   Holiday Season 2014 - 112   2015 $125

Hanke, Michael *Poems for Charles Causley.* Enitharmon Press, 1982. First edition, one of 200 copies (from an edition of 550), 8vo., original black cloth, backstrip lettered gilt, blue endpapers, dust jacket with lightest of fading to backstrip panel, near fine, unique copy, signed by 15 of the 25 contributors, George Barker, Kathleen Raine, Philip Larkin, George Mackay Brown, Christopher Fry, Chris Wallace-Crabbe, David Gascoyne, A. L. Rowse, Michael Hamburger, Seamus Heaney, Peter Redgrove, Lawrence Sail, D. M. Thomas, John Wain and Ted Hughes.   Blackwell's Rare Books   B179 - 183   2015   £1200

Hanmer, Karen *Big River.* Glenview: Karen Hanmer, 2004. Number 11 of 20 copies, like a child's pocket game, the viewer maneuvers the box to get each of the balls into a divot corresponding to a city mentioned in the Johnny Cash Song, Big River, where the lovesick narrator chases his woman down the Mississippi River, missing her at every port, text printed on back of box, issued in archival folding case 10.75 x 8.75 x 1.25 inches, fine.   The Kelmscott Bookshop   11 - 24   2015 $400

Hanmer, Karen *Celestial Navigation.* Glenview: 2008. Artist's proof, one of 30 copies, all on Somerset Velvet paper with hinges of Dover book cloth, signed by artist/author on hinged triangular hinges wrappers, page size 6 3/4 x 5 3/4 x 5 inches folded, 17 1/5 x 30 inches open, 16 pages, reading as traditional book, 6 of the 16 pages are double folds with another 4 pages each contained in folds, with another 4 pages each contained in folds, construct is of ink-jet printed, hinges triangles with text and images printed against a photo of the Milky Way.   Priscilla Juvelis - Rare Books   61 - 23   2015 $725

Hansberry, Lorraine *A Raisin in the Sun.* London: Methuen, 1960. First English edition, 8vo., paper over boards, edges spotted, otherwise very good, tight in scuffed and little soiled dust jacket.   Second Life Books Inc.   190 - 89   2015 $125

Hansen, Karen V. *Families in the U. S. Kinship and Domestic Politics.* Philadelphia: Temple University, 1998. First edition, large 8vo., green cloth, stamped in gilt, about as new.   Second Life Books Inc.   189 - 109   2015 $65

Hansen, Ron *Desperadoes.* New York: Knopf, 1979. First edition, signed by author, fine in fine dust jacket, from the estate of Beef Torrey.   Ed Smith Books   83 - 39   2015 $150

Hanson, E. R., Mrs. *Our Woman Workers.* Chicago: Star & Covenant, 1882. Second edition, 8vo., 14 engraved portraits, brown cloth stamped in black and gilt, rubbed along edges, hinges and couple of leaves loose, some foxed, just good.   Second Life Books Inc.   189 - 110   2015 $100

Hanson, Lawrence *The Four Brontes: the Lives and Works of Charlotte, Bramwell, Emily and Anne Bronte.* London: Oxford University Press, 1949. Half title, frontispiece and plates, original red cloth, signed by Kathleen Tillotson Nov.-Dec. 1949, with many notes in text and insertions.   Jarndyce Antiquarian Booksellers   CCVII - 100   2015   £35

Hanson, Mark *The Wizard of Berner's Abbey.* London: Melifont Press, n.d. circa 1950's, Reprint, 8vo., original illustrate wrappers, some marks and slight rubbing along spine, otherwise very good, front panel of jacket in good order.   Any Amount of Books   2015 - C3198   2015   £220

Hanson, Neil *Presences of Nature; Words and Images of the Lake District.* Carlisle: Carlisle Museum & Art Gallery, 1982. First edition, limited edition, unspecified but likely small, 4to., pages 223, black and white illustrations, signed by 41 contributors, hardback, faint handling wear, otherwise fine. Any Amount of Books March 2015 - A90707 2015 £350

Hanson, Warren *A is for Adult.* Minneapolis: Waldman House Press, 1993. Stated first printing, square 16mo., pictorial card covers, fine, illustrations by author. Aleph-bet Books, Inc. 109 - 2 2015 $60

Hanway, Jonas *Advice from the Farmer Trueman to His Daughter Mary Upon Her going to Service...* London: 1792. Reprint, 8vo., contemporary full calf rubbed with leather label, some foxing and toning but very good, tight copy. Second Life Books Inc. 189 - 111 2015 $450

Hanway, Jonas *The Defects of Police the Cause of Immorality, and the Continual Robberies Committed, Particularly in and about the Metropolis...* London: printed for J. Dodsley and Brotherton and Sewell, 1775. First edition, 4to., contemporary calf, gilt, neatly rebacked, spine fully gilt with labels, very good. John Drury Rare Books 2015 - 22679 2015 $3060

Hanway, Jonas *Three Letters on the Subject of the Marine Society, Let. I. On Occasion of their Clothing for the Sea 3097 Men and 2045 Boys to the End of Dec. 1757. II. Pointing Out Several Advantages Accruing to the Nation from this Institution. III. Being a Full Detail of the Rules and Forms of the Marine Society... (Bound with) Two Letters. Let. IV. Being thoughts on the Means of Augmenting the Number of Mariners in These Kingdoms, Upon Principles of Liberty. Let. V. To Robert Dingley, Esq...* London: printed in the year, 1758. Second edition, 4to., fine engraved frontispiece by Cipriani, general title printed in red and black, engraved frontispiece to Letter III, printed throughout on thick paper, contemporary calf, gilt ruled sides, neatly rebacked to match, spine gilt and labelled, fine, sometime in the library of Arnold Muirhead, with his bookplate on front pastedown; evidently bound for a contemporary owner. John Drury Rare Books 2015 - 25782 2015 $2185

Hapgood, Hutchins *The Spirit of Labor.* New York: Duffield, 1907. First edition, good, free endpapers excised, boards worn. Beasley Books 2013 - 2015 $40

Happersett, Susan *Box of Chaos.* New York: Purgatory Pie Press, 2012. No. 29 of 40 copies, signed by Happersett, designer, Esther Smith and printer Dikko Faust, box of 3 books, drawings, printed on Nepali Lokta paper in Future hand set type, housed in black cardstock box titled in gilt on spine panel, fine. The Kelmscott Bookshop 11 - 40 2015 $250

Happy Birthday, Kurt Vonnegut: a Festschrift for Kurt Vonnegut on His Sixtieth Birthday. New York: Delacorte, 1982. First and only edition, numerous photos, laid into this copy is mimeographed list of seating plan for the celebratory dinner at Michael's restaurant, fine in original slipcase. Ed Smith Books 83 - 112 2015 $350

Harcourt, John *John Harcourt's Original Jests.* London: Cowie and Strange, 1827. First edition, first issue, 12mo., frontispiece by George Cruikshank, contemporary or slightly later green half calf gilt over marbled boards, all edges gilt, original printed stiff grey wrappers preserved fine, scarce. John Drury Rare Books March 2015 - 23134 2015 £306

The Hard-Boiled Omnibus: Early Stories from Black Mask. New York: Simon & Schuster, 1946. First edition, fine in especially crisp, near fine dust jacket with some spotting on rear panel, very nice copy, from the library of Kate Stettner Lobell and Carl D. Lobell. Between the Covers Rare Books 196 - 49 2015 $275

Hardesty, H. H. *Hardesty's Historical and Geographical Encyclopedia...* Chicago: 1883. Folio, new backstrip and label, titlepage with age soil, balance unfoxed and solid (minor marginal marks), few ink family notes, all maps present, many double page, one loose. Bookworm & Silverfish 2015 - 6014992416 2015 $1250

Harding, Paul *The House of the Red Slayer.* Headline, 1992. First edition, signed twice by author, page edges uniformly tanned, else fine in dust jacket with light professional restoration to spine ends and corners. Buckingham Books March 2015 - 25525 2015 $175

Hardman, J. *The House of Labor. Internal Operations of American Unions.* New York: Prentice Hall, 1951. First edition, hardcover, very good+ in very good dust jacket with sunning and some soiling. Beasley Books 2013 - 2015 $45

Hardoin De La Reynnerie, Louis Eugene *Consultation Pour les Actionnaires de la Compagnie des Indes.* Paris: Lottin & Lottin, 1788. First edition, 4to., woodcut impression of arms of French East India Co. on titlepage, large folding table, well bound fairly recently in marbled boards with morocco spine label lettered in gilt, uncut, fine, large copy, rare. John Drury Rare Books 2015 - 21869 2015 $1486

Hardy, Thomas 1840-1928 *Jude the Obscure.* London: Osgood, McIlvaine and Co., 1896. First edition, 8vo., original dark green cloth lettered and decorated gilt on spine and cover, frontispiece, top edge gilt, excellent clean, very good+ copy. Any Amount of Books 2015 - A99126 2015 £240

Hardy, Thomas 1840-1928 *Jude the Obscure.* New York: Harper & Bros., 1896. First US edition, very good plus, just little shelfwear, bright gilt, tight and clean text.   Stephen Lupack   March 2015 - 2015 $125

Hardy, Thomas 1840-1928 *Late Lyrics and Earlier with many Other Verses.* London: Macmillan, 1922. First edition, small 8vo., near fine in near fine dust jacket.   Beasley Books   2013 - 2015 $125

Hardy, Thomas 1840-1928 *Time's Laughingstock.* London: Macmillan, 1909. First edition, hardcover, very good+.   Beasley Books   2013 - 2015 $125

Hardy, Thomas 1840-1928 *The Trumpet Major.* London: Smith, Elder & Co., 1880. First edition in book form, 3 volumes, octavo, without prelim blank, publisher's primary binding of volume 1 and secondary binding of volumes II and III, all of red diagonal fine ribbed cloth, only difference being back covers stamped in blind with double rule (volume 1) or triple rule (volumes II & III) border, front covers decoratively stamped in black with three panel design incorporating two vignettes, an encampment at top a mill at bottom and lettering in center panel, spines decoratively stamped in gilt and black with standard sword and bugle and lettered blind and gilt (with imprint at foot of Smith Elder & Co.), yellow coated endpapers, spines of all volumes, bit darkened, cloth of all spines with some wrinkling as well as cloth of back board of volume one, bit of soiling and rubbing to cloth, some light shelfwear to spines, previous owner's bookplate on front pastedown of each volume, occasional thumb soiling along fore-edges, volumes slightly skewed, overall good set housed in quarter morocco drop down clamshell and chemise.   Heritage Book Shop   Holiday 2014 - 71   2015 $7500

Hardy, Thomas 1840-1928 *The Works of....* London: Macmillan, 1924-1937. Pocket edition, 27 volumes, foolscap 8vo., printed on India paper, superior leather binding, plum colored leather, gilt, top edge gilt, dust jackets, some jackets slightly ragged, one defective on lower side, very good set.   Blackwell's Rare Books   B179 - 50   2015   £600

Hare, Cyril *With a Bare Bodkin.* London: Faber, 1946. First edition, fine in dust jacket.   Mordida Books   March 2015 - 007472   2015 $350

Hare, Cyril *With a Bare Bodkin.* London: Faber, 1946. First edition, name on front endpaper, light spotting on page edges, else very good in soiled dust jacket with nicks at spine ends and at corners and couple of tears.   Mordida Books   March 2015 - 001047   2015 $75

Harford, John Scandrett *Narrative of Conversations Held with Christopher Davis and Wm. Clarke, Who were Executed Jan. 27th 1832 for the Part They Took on the Bristol Riots...* Bristol: printed & Published by J. Chilcott, 1832. Recent brown cloth, spine uplettered in gilt, 31 pages.   Jarndyce Antiquarian Booksellers   CCXI - 133   2015   £180

Hargrave, Leonie *Clara Reeve.* New York: Alfred Knopf, 1975. First edition, fine in fine dust jacket, warmly inscribed by author to fellow sci-fi author Norman Spinrad, signed as both Hargrave and Disch.   Between the Covers Rare Books, Inc.   187 - 117   2015 $125

Harley, George *The Simplification of English Spelling, specially Adapted for the Rising Generation.* London: Trubner & Co., 1877. First edition, 8vo., frontispiece, errata slip, original cloth with title in gilt in central embossed shield on upper cover, very good, presentation copy, inscribed in ink from author for Sir George Denys, June 1877.   John Drury Rare Books   2015 - 22986   2015 $133

Harling, Robert *Alphabet and Image, a Quarterly Magazine of Typography.* New York: Arno Press, 1975. Numbers 1-8 complete set in 2 volumes, small 4to., cloth, many black and white illustrations.   Oak Knoll Books   306 - 45   2015 $125

Harlow, Alvin *Old Waybills: the Romance of the Express Companies.* New York: D. Appleton Century, 1934. First edition, profusely illustrated with early photos and engravings, red cloth gilt, very fine and bright copy with pictorial dust jacket chipped and lightly worn at edges.   Argonaut Book Shop   Holiday Season 2014 - 113   2015 $175

Harlow, Neal *Maps and Surveys of the Pueblo Lands of Los Angeles.* Los Angeles: Dawson's, 1976. First edition, one of 375 copies printed by Grant Dahlstrom on Curtis Rag paper, signed by author and printer, cloth backed decorated boards, gilt lettered spine, small bookplate of noted collector, very fine.   Argonaut Book Shop   Holiday Season 2014 - 114   2015 $350

Harlow, Neal *Maps of the Pueblo Lands of San Diego 1602-1874.* Los Angeles: Dawson's, 1987. First edition, limited to 375 numbered copies signed by author, small folio, numerous reproductions tinted or in color, cloth backed decorated boards, small oval bookplate.   Argonaut Book Shop   Holiday Season 2014 - 115   2015 $225

Harm, Ray *Ray Harm's African Sketchbook.* Louisville: 1973. 80 full page plates, fine in very good publisher box.   Bookworm & Silverfish   2015 - 6015032907   2015 $47

Harold, Childe *A Child's Book of Abridged Wisdom.* San Francisco: Paul Elder, 1905. First edition, 8vo., pictorial board arts and crafts binding, fine in dust jacket with pictorial 'Merry Christmas' add-on band, printed frenchfold paper, color illustrations on every page.   Aleph-Bet Books, Inc. 108 - 171   2015 $450

Harper, Ida Husted *The History of Woman Suffrage.* New York: National American Woman Suffrage Assoc., 1922. First edition, Volume V, 8vo., publisher's cloth, otherwise very good tight copy.   Second Life Books Inc.   189 - 115   2015 $375

Harper, Ida Husted *The History of Woman Suffrage.* New York: National American Suffrage Assoc., 1922. First edition, Volume VI 1900-1920, 8vo., publisher's cloth, very good tight copy, better than most.   Second Life Books Inc. 189 - 114   2015 $375

Harpsfield, Nicholas *The Life and Death of Sir Thomas Moore...* London: OUP, 1932. Half title, frontispiece and plates, 8 page catalog, handsome full white pigskin with elaborate pattern in blind and gilt, blind and gilt dentelles, marbled endpapers, fine in lined marbled slipcase, from the library of Geoffrey & Kathleen Tillotson, gilt lettered on front from GT, KMC 21XL 33 and with signed inscription from both editors to Tillotson's, with inserted p.c. from R. W. Chambers1933 and ALS from Gertrude Chambers and Edith Batho.   Jarndyce Antiquarian Booksellers   CCVII - 381   2015   £250

Harpur, Samuel *Can Typhoid Fever be Caused by the Use of the milk of Animals Fed Upon Produce Grown on Sewage Farms?* Merthyr-Tydfil: Farrant and Frost, 1873. First edition, 8vo., printed title just little dust marked, preserved in modern wrappers with printed title label on upper cover, very good, signed by editors, very rare.   John Drury Rare Books   2015 - 23491   2015 $89

Harraden, Beatrice *Ships that Pass in the Night.* London: George Bell & Sons, 1895. Half title, 16 page catalog, original pink mottled cloth, slightly marked and dulled, good plus.   Jarndyce Antiquarian Booksellers   CCXI - 134   2015   £35

Harrell, John M. *Proceedings of the National Railroad Convention at St. Louis Mo. November 23 and 24 1875 In Regard to the Construction of the Texas & Pacific Railway as a Southern Trans-Continental Line from the Mississippi Valley to the Pacific Ocean on the Thirty-Second Parallel of Latitude.* Woodward, Tiernan & Hale, 1875. First edition, 8vo., original printed wrappers, map in fine condition, spine panel reinforced with cellophane tape, tear to margin of page ix and 11, else very good.   Buckingham Books   March 2015 - 35967   2015 $875

Harrington, Alan *The Revelations of Dr. Modesto.* New York: Knopf, 1955. First edition, inscribed by author to another writer in year of publication, near fine in very good, spine sunned dust jacket.   Ken Lopez, Bookseller   164 - 79   2015 $350

Harrington, Kent *Dia De Los Muertos.* Tucson: Dennis McMillan, 1997. First edition, one of 200 numbered copies signed by author, very fine in dust jacket with slipcase.   Mordida Books   March 2015 - 001052   2015 $150

Harrington, Leicester Fitzgerald Charles Stanhope, 5th Earl of *Greece in 1823 and 1824; Being a Series of letters, and Other Documents on the Greek Revolution, Written during a Visit to that Country...* London: Sherwood Jones and Co., 1824. First edition, 8vo., hand colored frontispiece, 6 facsimiles of documents, contemporary calf, neatly rebacked and labelled to match, gilt lines and lettering, tips of boards worn, mid 19th century armorial bookplate of Anne Elinor Prevost, very good.   John Drury Rare Books   2015 - 23839   2015 $1136

Harrington, Ollie *Bootsie and Others.* New York: Dodd Mead, 1958. First edition, 4to., paper over boards, cover little scuffed at edges and corners, otherwise very good, tight in chipped and little soiled dust jacket.   Second Life Books Inc.   190 - 90   2015 $225

Harrington, R. E. *Souvenirs of the Palm Springs Area.* Simi Valley: by the author, printed by Peg Wilson, 1962. First edition, photos, maps, drawings, reproductions, folding map at rear, spiral bound, maroon pictorial semi-stiff boards, stamped in gold, very fine, very scarce.   Argonaut Book Shop   Holiday Season 2014 - 220   2015 $75

Harris-Lacewell, Melissa Victoria *Barbershops, Bibles and BET.* Princeton: Princeton University Press, 2004. First edition, inscribed by author, 8vo., fine in near fine dust jacket.   Beasley Books   2013 - 2015 $45

Harris, Elizabeth *The Art of Medal Engraving.* Newtown: Bird & Bull Press, 1991. First edition, limited to 230 numbered copies, printed on Johannot mouldmade paper, prospectus loosely inserted, 4to., Japanese cloth with leather spine label, 56 pages.   Oak Knoll Books   306 - 132   2015 $100

Harris, Elizabeth Furlong Skipton *From Oxford to Rome and How It Fared with Some Who Lately Made the Journey.* London: Longmans, 1847. Original dark brown cloth, worn at head and tail of spine, frontispiece, ownership inscription of JAS Southern? with long note by Geoffrey Tillotson, from the library of Geoffrey & Kathleen Tillotson.   Jarndyce Antiquarian Booksellers   CCVII - 294   2015   £150

Harris, Frank *Montes, the Matador and Other Stories.* London: Alexander Moring Ltd., 1906. First English edition, octavo, good plus with tanned spine, wear to extremities with chip at crown, foxing to pages, inscribed by author to Walter Lippmann.   Between the Covers Rare Books, Inc.   187 - 118   2015 $250

Harris, Joel Chandler   1848-1908 *A Little Union Scout.* New York: McClure Phillips, 1904. First edition, decorated green cloth, very slight cloth eruption to cover, otherwise very good, near fine and bright.   Stephen Lupack   March 2015 - 2015 $75

Harris, Joel Chandler   1848-1908 *Sister Jane: Her Friends and Acquaintances.* New York: Houghton Mifflin Co., 1899. Reprint, octavo, green cloth decorated in black and gilt, little spine cocked, small hole on edge of spine, overall very good, inscribed by author for friend Henry Rosenfeld.   Between the Covers Rare Books   196 - 78   2015 $950

Harris, Joel Chandler   1848-1908 *Uncle Remus His Songs and Sayings.* New York: D. Appleton Co., 1881. First edition, first issue with 'presumptive' mis-spelled on page 9 bottom line and without ads for this title, 8vo., olive green cloth stamped in gold and black, light wear to spine ends, else near fine and bright in custom box, illustrations by Frederick Church and James Moser, beautiful copy.   Aleph-Bet Books, Inc.   108 - 232   2015 $8500

Harris, John *Britannia; or the Moral Claims of Seamen, Stated and Enforced.* London: Thomas Ward and Co., 1837. First edition, 12mo., including half title and final 12 pages of Ward and Co.'s ads, original dark green blind-stamped cloth, spine simply lettered in gilt, inner hinges, cracked and some minor wear and straining of binding, else good copy, partially unopened.   John Drury Rare Books   2015 - 16810   2015 $89

Harris, John *The Life of the Rev. Francis Metherall and the History of the Bible Christian Church in Prince Edward Island.* London and Toronto: Bible Christian Book-Room, 1883. 12mo. light brown cloth with gilt titles and black line design to spine and front cover, half title, spine slightly darkened.   Schooner Books Ltd.   110 - 131   2015 $200

Harris, John *Navigation atque Itinerantium Bibliotheca...* London: printed for T. Osborne (and 17 others), 1764. Third edition, 2 volumes, folio, 61 engraved plates, including 15 folding maps, titlepages in red and black, beautifully bound in period style Cambridge paneled speckled calf with blind tooling, spine compartments densely gilt in a repeating leaf pattern, red and green morocco gilt lettering labels, marbled endpapers, scattered light foxing and small owner's stamp to purple red ink to outer margin of titlepage of volume II has been expertly repaired, overall very good, remarkably clean and bright.   Heritage Book Shop   Holiday 2014 - 72   2015 $15,000

Harris, Laura *Animated Noah's Ark.* New York: Grosset & Dunlap, 1945. Large oblong 4to., pictorial boards, fine in dust jacket (some small edge mends, else very good+), 4 fine color tab operated moveable papers by Wehr, very scarce in dust jacket.   Aleph-Bet Books, Inc.   108 - 310   2015 $300

Harris, Pixie O. *The "Pixie O. Harris Fairy Book." Stories and Verse...* Adelaide: Rigby Ltd., n.d., 1926. First edition, 4to., tipped-in colored plates including frontispiece, illustrations, original illustrated wrappers, highly uncommon, modestly worn condition with illustrated wrappers little soiled with some chips and wear at spine, gift inscription and name and address, plain rear wrapper little soiled and slightly marked, very good- with text and illustrations clean.   Any Amount of Books   2015 - A45446   2015   £225

Harris, Robert *Enigma.* London: Hutchinson, 1995. First edition, fine in dust jacket.   Mordida Books   March 2015 - 007929   2015 $100

Harris, Robert *Fatherland.* London: Hutchinson, 1992. First edition, uncorrected proofs, near fine in pictorial wrappers.   Buckingham Books   March 2015 - 14612   2015 $375

Harris, Robert *Samuels Funerall; or a Sermon Preached at the Funerall of Sir Anthonie Cope, Knight and Baronet.* London: printed by the assignes of Thomas Man, etc., 1630. Early, possibly second edition, 12mo., full plain leather (probably 19th century), very rare, titlepage professionally repaired at edges, page edges little chipped and rubbed, very good.   Peter Ellis, Bookseller   2014 - 020474   2015   £350

Harris, Thomas *Black Sunday.* New York: Putnam, 1975. First edition, fine in dust jacket with several short closed tears.   Mordida Books   March 2015 - 007930   2015 $200

Harris, Thomas *Black Sunday.* New York: G. P. Putnam's Sons, 1975. First edition, fine in dust jacket with light wear to extremities and three 2 inch light creases to back panel.   Buckingham Books   March 2015 - 20551   2015 $400

Harris, Timothy *Konski/McSmash.* Garden City: Doubleday, 1970. First edition, fine in dust jacket with small chip at base of spine.   Mordida Books   March 2015 - 008335   2015 $125

Harris, W. T. *Educational Theory. Second Series.* Bristol: Thoemmes, 2000. Reprint, 8vo., 10 volumes, fine.   Any Amount of Books   2015 - B22089   2015   £220

Harris, William Charles *Questions and Answers Framed for Instruction of Constables on Joining the Police.* London: printed and published by W. Clowes and Son, 1861. First edition, 8vo., 28 pages, original limp dark green cloth lettered gilt on upper cover, very good, apparently of some rarity.   John Drury Rare Books   March 2015 - 26139   2015   £306

Harrison, Benjamin S. *Fortune Favors the Brave. the Life and Times of Horace Bell Pioneer Californian.* Los Angeles: Ward Ritchie Press, 1953. First edition, illustrations, 4 photo plates, rust cloth, small, cut drawing on front end, tiny repair to inner hinge, else fine with pictorial dust jacket.   Argonaut Book Shop   Holiday Season 2014 - 28   2015 $50

Harrison, Florence *The Rhyme of a Run.* London & New York: Blackie & Caldwell, n.d. circa, 1907. Oblong 4to., green gilt pictorial cloth some of the usual creasing of the plates, else fine, extremely scarce, 20 very beautiful mounted color plates plus beautiful full page illustrations in brown, beautiful book.   Aleph-Bet Books, Inc.   108 - 233   2015 $900

Harrison, George *Education Respectfully Proposed and Recommended as the Surest Means Within the Power of Government to Diminish the Frequency of Crimes.* London: printed at the Royal Free School Press Borough Road Southwark by J. Lancaster for Longman and Co., 1810. Second edition, 8vo., without final ad leaf, old institutional inkstamp on title (not of lending library), label removed from last page of text, preserved in recent plain wrappers.   John Drury Rare Books   2015 - 20579   2015 $177

Harrison, George *Songs by George Harrison.* Guildford, Surrey: Genesis Publications Ltd., 1992. First edition, Number 1421 of 2500 copies signed in sepia ink by Harrison, also signed on colorful bookplate by artist, Keith West, large 8vo., illustrations in color by Keith West, original half black morocco, guitar blind pattern to front cover, keyboard to rear, lettered gilt at spine, all edges gilt, publisher's folding box with tray to enclosed limited edition, with audio CD.   Any Amount of Books   2015 - C11009   2015   £1300

Harrison, Jim *Braided Creek. A Conversation in Poetry.* Port Townsend: Copper Canyon, 2003. First edition, #117 of 250 numbered copies signed by both poets in two-tone cloth binding (green and black), from the estate of Beef Torrey, fine.   Ed Smith Books   83 - 43   2015 $200

Harrison, Jim *Brown Dog.* New York: Grove Press, 2013. First edition, light, very near fine with some bumping to spine ends, in very near fine dust jacket, signed by author on special tipped in page, unread.   Jeff Hirsch Books   E-62 Holiday List 2014 - 15   2015 $50

Harrison, Jim *Legends of the Fall, Revenge, The Man Who Gave Up His Name.* New York: Delacorte/Seymour Lawrence, 1979. First edition, 3 volumes, white cloth, each volume signed by author, slipcase with Russell Chatham illustration, from the estate of Beef Torrey, all fine in very good plus slipcase and some rubbing to extremities.   Ed Smith Books   83 - 41   2015 $450

Harrison, Jim *Plain Song. Poems.* New York: Norton, 1965. First edition, fine in green cloth, very good plus clean jacket, price clipped bottom, with price present on top of front flap, there is a tape pull that affects the N in Plain on top front panel, inscribed by author to friend Beef Torrey.   Ed Smith Books   83 - 42   2015 $500

Harrison, Jim *Sundog.* New York: E. P. Dutton/Seymour Lawrence, 1984. First edition, signed by author, fine in nearly fine dust jacket with two tiny closed tear to back panel.   Ed Smith Books   82 - 13   2015 $150

Harrison, Jim *The Theory and Practice of Rivers and New Poems.* Livingston: Clark City Press, 1989. First edition thus, inscribed by author with drawing added, wrappers, fine.   Beasley Books   2013 - 2015 $45

Harrison, Jim *Walking. A Long Poem.* Cambridge: Pym-Randall Press, 1967. First edition, oblong 8vo., one of 100 numbered copies signed by Harrison, out of a total of 126, this copy #14, heavy brown paper binding with black lettering, hand-sewn, near fine with some irregular sunning to rear wrapper.   Ed Smith Books   82 - 15   2015 $500

Harrison, Jim *Walking.* Cambridge: Pym Randall, 1967. First edition, one of 10 numbered copies, this being copy number 100, very near fine but for small blemish to front panel, signed by author.   Jeff Hirsch Books   E-62 Holiday List 2014 - 16   2015 $850

Harrison, Jim *Warlock.* New York: Delacorte, 1981. First edition, signed by author, fine in fine dust jacket.   Beasley Books   2013 - 2015 $125

Harrison, Michael *In the Footsteps of Sherlock Holmes.* London: Cassell, 1958. First edition, name on front endpaper, otherwise fine in dust jacket with internal tape reinforcing.   Mordida Books   March 2015 - 002632   2015 $75

Harrowby, Dudley Ryder, 1st Earl of *Substance of the Speech of the Right Honourable the Earl of Harrowby in the House of Lords Oct. 4th 1831 on the Motion that the Reform Bill be read a Second Time.* London: Rooke and Varly, 1831. First separate edition, 8vo., half title rather stained and marked, several near contemporary annotations and emphasis marks in ink, recent marbled boards lettered on spine, good copy, uncommon.   John Drury Rare Books   March 2015 - 23606   2015 $221

Hart, Ernest *The Protection of Infant Life. An Inquiry into the Practice of Baby Farming with Suggestions for the Protection of Infants.* London: published at the office of the British Medical Journal, n.d., 1871. First separate edition, 8vo., 36 pages, recent marbled boards lettered on spine, very good.   John Drury Rare Books   March 2015 - 25260   2015 $221

Hart, Frances Noyes *The Bellamy Trial.* Garden City: Doubleday Page & Co., 1927. First edition, former owner's name, else very good in dust jacket with light professional restoration to spine ends and extremities.   Buckingham Books   March 2015 - 6892   2015 $1750

Hart, Frances Noyes *Contact and Other Stories.* Garden City: Page & Co., 1923. First edition, fine in lightly soiled dust jacket, lightly sunned on spine.   Buckingham Books   March 2015 - 6891   2015 $225

Hart, Heber Leonidas *Woman Suffrage: a National Danger.* London: Murby, circa, 1909. First edition, 8vo., blue cloth stamped in white (little worn), former owner's pencil initials on endpaper, some light pencil marginal scoring, very good.   Second Life Books Inc.   191 - 38   2015 $150

Hart, James D. *John Steinbeck. His Language.* Aptos: Printed at the Grace Hoper Press for the Roxburghe and Zamorano Club, 1970. First edition, one of 150 copies, quarto, printed letterpress in black and white, 2 facsimiles, cream wrappers printed in red, very fine.   Argonaut Book Shop   Holiday Season 2014 - 279   2015 $150

Hart, Robert *On Appeal from Her Britannic Majesty's Supreme Court for China and Japan Between Robert Hart - Appellant and Johanes Von Bumpach, Respondent.* N.P. (London): n.p., 1872. First edition, 8vo., spine browned, edges slightly sunned, corners rubbed, very slight mottling at rear, front inner hinges cracked but holding, spine ends very slightly frayed, otherwise very good, spine label rubbed and slightly nicked.   Any Amount of Books   2015 - A9219   2015   £160

Harte, Bret   1838-1902   *The Adventure of Padre Vicentio: a Legend of San Francisco.* Berkeley: 1939. First edition, one of 450 copies, illustrations by Hans, bookplate, near fine.   Stephen Lupack   March 2015 - 2015 $60

Harte, Bret   1838-1902   *"The Outcasts of Poker Flat." in Oct. 7 1871 issue of Every Saturday.* 1871. Probably first illustrated edition, complete issue offered, double page illustration.   Bookworm & Silverfish   2015 - 3979590828   2015 $175

Harte, Bret   1838-1902   *The Right Eye of the Commander.* Berkeley: Wilder and Ellen Bentley, 1937. First edition, near fine, spine tanning.   Stephen Lupack   March 2015 - 2015 $60

Harte, Walter   1709-1774   *Essays on Husbandry.* London: W. Frederick W. Johnston, 1770. Second edition, 8vo., 5 engraved plates, several woodcuts in text, with final leaf of ads, contemporary calf, neatly rebacked, spine gilt, excellent crisp copy.   John Drury Rare Books   March 2015 - 6328   2015   £306

Hartenberg, Paul *Les Psychonevroses Anxieuses et Leur Traitement.* Paris: Librairie Felix Alcan, 1922. First edition, wrappers, tear at joint, library label on half title, but no other library marks, very good, large 8vo.   Beasley Books   2013 - 2015 $40

Harter, Pierre *Arts Anciens Du Cameroun.* Arnouville: Arts d'Afrique Noire, 1986. First edition, large 4to., original straw colored cloth, lettered in brown on spine and cover, copiously illustrated in color and black and white, fine in near fine dust jacket (very slightly used, bright, clean).   Any Amount of Books   2015 - C4789   2015   £950

Hartland, Michael *Down Among the Dead men.* London: Hodder and Stoughton, 1983. First edition, signed by author, fine in dust jacket.   Buckingham Books   March 2015 - 35384   2015 $185

Hartland, Michael *Frontier of Fear.* London: Hodder & Stoughton, 1988. First edition, very fine in dust jacket, signed by author.   Mordida Books   March 2015 - 01068   2015 $75

Hartland, Michael *The Third Betrayal.* London: Hodder and Stoughton, 1986. First edition, fine in dust jacket.   Buckingham Books   March 2015 - 36295   2015 $185

Hartland, Michael *The Year of the Scorpion.* Bristol: Scorpion, 1991. First edition, one of 75 numbered copies signed by author, very fine with acetate dust jacket.   Mordida Books   March 2015 - 009496   2015 $150

Hartshorne, Charles *Creative Synthesis and the Philosophic method.* London: SCM Press, 1970. First edition, signed by author, 8vo., very good++, minimal soil and foxing to edges, cover edge wear in very good dust jacket with mild chips, short closed tears, minimal sun spine.   By the Book, L. C.   44 - 55   2015 $350

Harvard University *Order of Performances for Exhibition Tuesday April 30 1822.* Cambridge: Hilliard and Metcalf, 1822. First edition, large 8vo., 4 pages, leaflet, folded in quarters horizontally, negligible separation at center fold, very good, generous margins.   M & S Rare Books, Inc.   97 - 98   2015 $85

Harvard, Stephen *Ornamental Initials, The Woodcut Initials of Christopher Plantin, a Complete Catalogue.* New York: American Friends of the Plantin-Moretus Musuem, 1974. 4to., cloth backed boards, dust jacket, plates, well preserved copy.   Oak Knoll Books   306 - 38   2015 $200

Harvey, Daniel Whittle *Documents Relating to the Application of Daniel Whittle Harvey, Esq. to be called to the Bar and His Rejection by the Benchers of the Inner Temple.* London: ordered by the House of Commons to be printed 3 June, 1834. First edition, folio, 182 pages, some intermittent but minor browning and foxing, contemporary half calf over marbled boards, spine gilt and labelled, extremities rubbed, good with armorial bookplate of John M. Traherne, apparently rare.   John Drury Rare Books   March 2015 - 25833   2015 $266

Harvey, Daniel Whittle *A Letter to the Burgesses of Colchester, Containing a Plain Statement of the Proceedings Before the Benches of the Inner Temple, Upon His Application to be Called to the Bar, and Upon His Appeal to the Judges.* London: printed by R. and A. Taylor and sold by Ridgway &c..., 1822. First edition, 8vo., first and last leaves with some edge chipping not touching printed surface, some browning, and dust marking, uncut, sewn as issued, good copy, inscribed "with the author's comts.", scarce.   John Drury Rare Books   2015 - 14145   2015 $133

Harvey, Jack *Blood Hunt.* London: Headline, 1995. First edition, front fore-edge lightly bumped, else fine in fine dust jacket.   Buckingham Books   March 2015 - 27707   2015 $850

Harvey, Jane *Travel Book: Peter and Peggy Go Round the World.* Racine: Whitman, 1931. Circular 12 inch diameter, pictorial wrappers, slightest bit of cover aoil, else near fine, illustrations in bright color on every page.   Aleph-bet Books, Inc.   109 - 445   2015 $300

Harvey, John *Lonely Hearts.* New York: Henry Holt & Co., 1989. First US edition, signed by author, fine in fine dust jacket.   Buckingham Books   March 2015 - 20564   2015 $225

Harvey, William Woodis *Sketches of Hayti: From the Expulsion of the French to the Death of Christophe.* London: L. B. Selley and Son, 1827. First edition, folding frontispiece, 8vo., original tan linen over brown paper covered boards, presentation copy inscribed by author, rebacked retaining original linen spine, paper label mostly gone, frontispiece foxed, title with bit of offsetting but still very good, untrimmed.   Kaaterskill Books   19 - 70   2015 $1000

Harwood, Anthony *Swan Song and Other Poems.* London: Favil Press, 1961. First edition, fine in near fine dust jacket with some soiling and tiny tears, Witter Bynner's copy with his bookplate.   Between the Covers Rare Books, Inc.   187 - 119   2015 $65

Harwood, Herbert H. *Blue Ridge Trolley. The Hagerstown & Frederick Railway.* San Marino: Golden West Books, 1970. First edition, first printing, quarto, black and white photos, map, black cloth, fine, lightly rubbed and chipped pictorial dust jacket.   Argonaut Book Shop   Holiday Season 2014 - 117   2015 $60

Harwood, Herbert H. *Blue Ridge Trolley. The Hagerstown & Frederick Railway.* San Marino: Golden West Books, 1970. First edition, 2nd printing, quarto, black and white photos, map, black cloth, fine with lightly rubbed pictorial dust jacket.   Argonaut Book Shop   Holiday Season 2014 - 118   2015 $45

Harwood's Illustrations of London.   London: J. Harwood issued circa, 1851. Oblong 8vo., 3 steel engraved views, mostly by J. Shury, plates with various dates from 1840-s up to 1850, original green cloth, large oval gilt cartouche 4 enclosing title on upper cover, gilt edges.   Marlborough Rare Books Ltd.   List 49 - 15   2015   £475

Haskell, Daniel C. *The United States Exploring Expedition 1838-1842 and Its Publications 1844-1874. A Bibliography.* New York: New York Public Library, 1942. First book edition, one of 400 copies, frontispiece, 2 plates, facsimile, portrait, navy blue cloth, gilt, very fine.   Argonaut Book Shop   Holiday Season 2014 - 317   2015 $325

Haskett, William J. *Shakerism Unmasked, or the History of the Shakers...* Pittsfield: Published by author, 1828. First edition, contemporary mottled calf, red leather spine label, ex-library, stamp at head of titlepage, bookplate, lacks front endpaper, some light toning to pages, very good, pages 232-233 were originally sealed.   Second Life Books Inc.   190 - 91   2015 $500

Hass, Robert *Field Guide.* New Haven & London: Yale University Press, 1973. First edition, 8vo., original cloth, dust jacket, fine.   James S. Jaffe Rare Books   Modern American Poetry - 128   2015 $750

Hass, Robert *Praise.* New York: Ecco Press, 1979. First edition, 8vo., original cloth, cloth bound issue, dust jacket, fine.   James S. Jaffe Rare Books   Modern American Poetry - 130   2015 $125

Hass, Robert *Praise.* New York: Ecco Press, 1979. First edition, 8vo., original cloth, clothbound issue, dust jacket, fine, presentation copy inscribed by author.   James S. Jaffe Rare Books   Modern American Poetry - 129   2015 $250

Hassell, John *Tour of the Grand Junction, Illustrated in a Series of Engravings with an Historical and Topographical Description of Those Parts of the Counties...* London: J. Hassall, 1819. First edition, 8vo., 24 colored aquatint plates (some occasional offsetting), uncut in modern red straight grained morocco with wide gilt tooled border, spine lettered and decorated in gilt, top edge gilt, by Bayntun, Bath. Marlborough Rare Books   List 54 - 39   2015   £1250

Hastings, Frank S. *A Ranchman's Recollections.* Breeder's Gazette, 1921. First edition, cloth, exceptionally fine, bright copy in original glassine dust jacket. Buckingham Books   March 2015 - 21863   2015 $400

Hastings, Frank S. *A Ranchman's Recollections.* Breeder's Gazette, 1921. First edition, cloth, 14 plates, near fine.   Buckingham Books   March 2015 - 26822   2015 $300

Hastings, Warren *The History of the Trial of Warren Hastings, esq. Late Governor-General of Benegal, Before the High Court of Parliament in Westminster-Hall on an Impeachment by the commons of Great Britain for High Crimes and Misdemeanours.* London: J. Debrett and Vernor and Hood, 1796. 8vo., folding plan, contemporary half calf over marbled boards, binding sound and good, but with wear to corners and some loss of marbled paper on boards, overall very good, complete in all respects.   John Drury Rare Books   2015 - 24792   2015 $787

Hathaway, Frederick *Statement of Facts Relating to the Dismissal by the Middlesex Visiting Justices of the Rev. Frederick Hathaway from Attending the Roman Catholic Prisoners at Tothill Fields Prison.* London: Burns, Lambert and Oates, 1866. First edition, with final blank leaf, modern wrappers with printed label on upper cover, good copy. John Drury Rare Books   2015 - 24780   2015 $133

Hathaway, Richard *The Tryal of Richard Hathaway, Upon an Information for Being a Cheat and Impostor for Endeavouring to Take Away the Life of Sarah Morduck for Being a Witch at Surry Assizes, Begun and Held in the Burrough of Southwark March the 24th 1702.* London: Isaac Cleave, 1702. First edition, folio, well bound in 19th or 20th century half calf over marbled boards, spine gilt lettered, slight wear to joints and head and foot of spine, from the Los Angeles Board of Law Library, bookplate but no other marks, very good, crisp copy, uncommon.   John Drury Rare Books   2015 - 25916   2015 $1661

Hauck, Cornelius W. *Colorado Rail Annual No. 15. A Journal of Railroad History in the Rocky Mountain West. Idaho-Montana Issue.* Golden: Colorado Railroad Museum, 1981. First edition, gold cloth, very fine with pictorial dust jacket.   Argonaut Book Shop   Holiday Season 2014 - 119   2015 $60

Hausam, L. H. *The Hausam System of Practical Writing.* Emporia: and Topeka: Eckdall & McCarty and the State of Kansas, 1917-1926. 32mo., stiff paper wrappers, 7 volumes, wrappers bent at edges, soiled and some stained, small tear at corner of volume for the fifth grade, light soiling and ink notations of previous owner in text of high school volume.   Oak Knoll Books   Special Catalogue 24 - 20   2015 $125

Have You Heard the News? An Address to the Freemen of all the Corporations of Great Britain Upon the Proposed Destruction of Their Rights by the Whig Ministry. London: C. F. Cock, 1835. Second edition, 12mo., 12 pages, preserved in modern wrappers, printed title label on upper cover, very good, apparently very rare.   John Drury Rare Books   2015 - 14903   2015 $177

Havins, T. R. *Camp Colorado: a Decade of Frontier Defense.* Brownwood: Brown Press, 1964. First edition, one of 25 copies specially bound in two-tone brown and tan cloth, inscribed to Texas bookseller, collector, historian - Fred White, Sr., original two-tone cloth, titles stamped in gilt on spine, maps on endpapers, fine, bright copy, in fine unprinted dust jacket.   Buckingham Books   March 2015 - 38094   2015 $1250

Havins, T. R. *Camp Colorado: a Decade of Frontier Defense.* Brownwood: Brown Press, 1964. First edition, 8vo., inscribed by author to historian Al Lowman by author, original green cloth, gold stamping on spine, maps on endpapers, fine, bright, square copy in fine, unprinted dust jacket.   Buckingham Books   March 2015 - 29545   2015 $750

Hawk, John *The House of Sudden Sleep.* New York: Mystery League Inc., 1930. First US edition, fine in fine dust jacket.   Buckingham Books   March 2015 - 25820   2015 $275

Hawk, John *The House of Sudden Sleep.* New York: Mystery League, 1930. First US edition,, very light offsetting to front and rear endpapers, light foxing to page edges, else near fine in fine dust jacket.   Buckingham Books   March 2015 - 29142   2015 $225

Hawke, Jonathan *Under the Street Lamp: Vignettes of Australian Bush Life.* London: Charles H. Kelly, 1910. First edition, original blue cloth, blocked in black and gilt, lettered in gilt, spine slightly faded, prize label on leading pastedown, very good.   Jarndyce Antiquarian Booksellers   CCXI - 135   2015   £50

Hawkes, John *The Cannibal.* New York: New Directions, 1949. First edition, small 8vo., original pale grey boards, fine in very good yellow and black dust jacket faintly marked and very slightly chipped at spine ends and with very slight edgewear, signed presentation from author for Dick and Mary (Richard and Mary Ellman.   Any Amount of Books   2015 - A75834   2015   £280

Hawkes, John *Las Cruces.* Madrid/Palma de Mallorca: Papeles de son Armandans, 1962. First separate edition, #7 of 500 numbered copies, 12mo., string-tied decorated wrappers, very slight age toning on wrappers, very near fine, inscribed by author for James Laughlin.   Between the Covers Rare Books, Inc.   187 - 121   2015 $2500

Hawley, James H. *History of Idaho. The Gem of the Mountains.* Chicago: S. J. Clarke Pub. Co., 1920. First edition, thick quarto, 3 volumes, green cloth, decorated endpapers, frontispieces, illustrations, portraits, all edges marbled, light bit of professional, cosmetic restoration to spine ends and corners, else near fine set, housed in cloth slipcase with leather label of spine and titles stamped in gold.   Buckingham Books   March 2015 - 26275   2015 $1775

Hawthorne, Julian *A Fool of Nature.* New York: Scribners, 1896. First edition, near fine in blue decorated cloth covered boards with gold stamped titles.   Mordida Books   March 2015 - 006780   2015 $85

Hawthorne, Nathaniel   1804-1864 *Doctor Grimshawe's Secret.* Boston: James R. Osgood, 1883. First edition, original grey pictorial cloth, very good or better with some wear and rubbing to edges, some spotting and few stains to endpapers.   B & B Rare Books, Ltd.   234 - 47   2015 $250

Hawthorne, Nathaniel   1804-1864 *The Scarlet Letter.* Boston: Ticknor, Reed and Fields, 1850. First edition, first issue, 2500 copies printed, original cloth with bright gilt lettered spine, publisher's catalog dated March 1 1850, spine ends and corners neatly repaired, small former owner signature at head of catalogue, hinges repaired, two mended tears to endpapers, internally very clean with few small spots, very attractive.   B & B Rare Books, Ltd.   234 - 48   2015 $3750

Hawthorne, Nathaniel   1804-1864 *The Scarlet Letter.* New York: privately printed, 1904. First of this illustrated edition, one of 150 copies on japanese imperial paper, 4to., contemporary navy morocco by the Doves Bindery, signed '19 C-S 10' gilt decorations and lettering, all edges gilt, each of the 15 plates in two states, color and black and white, tipped in to front free endpaper is letter for Cobden-Sanderson dated 23 March 1909 to Charles Walker Andrews, with Andrews bookplate, edges touched up and slightly repaired from wear, fine, handsome copy.   The Brick Row Book Shop   Miscellany 67 - 57   2015 $1750

Hawthorne, Nathaniel   1804-1864 *Septimus Felton.* Boston: James R. Osgood, 1872. First edition, first state, original publisher's green gilt stamped decorated cloth, excellent copy with bright gilt to spine, some rubbing to extremities, else near fine.   B & B Rare Books, Ltd.   234 - 49   2015 $225

Hawthorne, Nathaniel   1804-1864 *A Wonder-Book for Girls and Boys.* Boston: Ticknor Reed and Fields, 1852. First edition, first printing with misprint 'lifed' for 'lifted' on page 21, line 3, small octavo, frontispiece, 6 plates with tissue guards, one plate hand colored, publisher's gift binding in full purple cloth, covers paneled in blind with gilt central motif, spine stamped and lettered gilt, all edges gilt, original yellow endpapers, spine and adjacent covers bit sunned, some minor wear to spine edges, binding slightly skewed, occasional light spotting to text as usual, previous owner's old ink inscription dated 1852, overall very nice.   Heritage Book Shop   Holiday 2014 - 73   2015 $300

Hawthorne, Nathaniel   1804-1864 *A Wonder Book and Tanglewood Tales.* New York: Duffield, 1910. First edition, 4to., cloth, pictorial paste-on, slight cover rubbing, else near fine, 10 magnificent color plates with lettered tissue guards plus endpapers and cover plate by Maxfield Parrish.   Aleph-Bet Books, Inc.   108 - 337   2015 $550

Hawthorne, Nathaniel   1804-1864 *Hawthorne's Wonder Book.* London: Hodder & Stoughton, n.d., 1922. First Rackham edition, 4to., red gilt cloth, fine in dust jacket with mounted color plate, jacket margin mends and some soil, but very good+, 24 beautiful color plates with printed guards plus 8 color plate drawings, lovely text black and whites and pictorial endpapers.   Aleph-bet Books, Inc.   109 - 403   2015 $900

Hay, David Ramsay *The Laws of Harmonious Colouring, Adapted to Interior Decorations &c.* London: W. S. Orr and Co., Edinburgh: Fraser and Co., 1844. Fifth edition, 8vo., 5 hand colored plates and 3 line engravings, original brown cloth, border in blind, spine border.   Marlborough Rare Books   List 54 - 43   2015   £250

Hay, David Ramsay *A Nomenclature of Colours, Hues, Tints and Shades...* Edinburgh and London: William Blackwood and Sons, 1845. First edition, 8vo., 40 plates, each with 6 mounted painted paper triangles, spotting to text and some oxidization of color samples, as usual, original black cloth, rebacked and recased, spine lettered in gilt.   Marlborough Rare Books   List 54 - 42   2015   £850

Hay, David Ramsay *The Principles of Beauty in Colouring Systematized.* Edinburgh and London: William Blackwood and Sons, 1845. First edition, 8vo., 14 plates with mounted painted paper trapezoids, letterpress, plate XII is chromolithograph, original brown cloth, spine blocked with gilt lettering.   Marlborough Rare Books   List 54 - 41   2015   £500

Hay, John *A Narrative of Procedure Before the Court of Session and Circumstances Connected therewith in the trial of John Hay, Who was Prosecuted at the Instance of the Lord Advocate of Scotland...* Edinburgh: printed by D. Webster and Son for John Hay, 1822. First edition, 8vo., very good, untrimmed, original blue grey boards, tan paper spine (partly defective) and old printed label.   John Drury Rare Books   2015 - 26121   2015 $221

Hayburn, Robert F. *Papal Legislation on Sacred Music.* Collegeville: Liturgical Press, 1979. First edition, fine and bright in lightly worn and rubbed dust jacket with small chip on rear panel.   Beasley Books   2013 - 2015 $125

Haycraft, Howard *Murder for Pleasure; the Life and Times of the Detective Story.* New York: Appleton Century, 1941. First edition, fine in lightly rubbed dust jacket.   Mordida Books   March 2015 - 010777   2015 $200

Hayden, Jabez Haskell *Records of the Connecticut Line of the Hayden.* Windsor Locks: Jabez Haskelly Hayden, 1888. First edition, large octavo, 329 pages, green cloth with leather spine label gilt, corners worn, label quite rubbed, good or better, ownership signature of Mary E. Power Hayden, photos.   Between the Covers Rare Books, Inc.   187 - 122   2015 $300

Hayder, Mo *Birdman.* London: Bantam, 2000. First English edition, very fine in dust jacket with publisher's wraparound intact, signed by author.   Mordida Books   March 2015 - 006781   2015 $75

Hayek, F. A. *The Road to Serfdom.* London: George Routledge & Sons Ltd., 1944. Reprint, fourth impression (Oct. 1944), 8vo., original green boards, some sunning/fading and slight wear and small split at rear lower hinge, sound very good- with clean text, from the library of J. P. (Jacob Peter) Mayer with his neat blindstamp, Mayer has annotated the book with notes and questions and occasional marginal lining, all in pencil.   Any Amount of Books   2015 - C16178 2015   £160

Haygarth, William *Greece, a Poem in Three Parts..* London: W. Bulmer and Co. for G. and W. Nicol, 1814. First edition, 4to., inscribed by author for Henry Bright, very few pencilled notes, overall very good, contemporary half green morocco over matching buckram, gilt ruled decoration and lettering, marbled endpapers and marbled page edges, some foxing to few first and last pages, edges and joints somewhat scuffed and rubbed, bookplate of Henry Arthur Bright.   Any Amount of Books   March 2015 - C12295   2015   £450

Hayley, William *Ballads. Founded on Anecdotes Relating to Animals with Prints Designed and Engraved by William Blake.* Chichester: J. Seagrave for Richard Phillips, 1805. First edition, engraved plates in first state, small 8vo., original grey paper covered boards, sometime expertly rebacked preserving original backstrip and printed paper, endpapers renewed presumably at time of rebacking, 5 engraved plates by William Blake after his own designs, ink signature of Norman Davey dated Dec. 5th 1913, printed booklabel of Elaine Harwood Kenton, fine.   Henry Sotheran Ltd. William Blake Exhibition 17th Oct.-7th Nov. 2014 - 70   2015 £6595

Hayley, William *The Life and Posthumous Writings of William Cowper.* Chichester: printed by J. Seagrave for J. Johnson, 1803-1804. Second edition with final state of the 'Weatherhouse' plate designed by William Blake, 4to., 3 volumes, contemporary polished brown half calf over marbled boards, 2 black morocco and gilt labels to spine of each volume, 5 plates and engraving in text, one designed and engraved by Blake, others engraved by Blake after other artists, light spotting and foxing to edges of text blocks, occasionally within text.   Henry Sotheran Ltd.   William Blake Exhibition 17th Oct.-7th Nov. 2014 - 69   2015   £800

Hayley, William *The Triumphs of Temper. A Poem in six Cantos.* Chichester: printed by F. Seagrave for T. Cadell and W. Davies, 1803. Small 8vo., 19th century full calf gilt, sometime expertly rebacked preserving the original backstrip, preserved in brown cloth covered chemise and quarter brown morocco slipcase, 6 engraved plates by Blake after Maria Flaxman, some offsetting as usual, the copy of William Michael Rossetti, with his ink signature, dated 1868.   Henry Sotheran Ltd.   William Blake Exhibition 17th Oct.-7th Nov. 2014 - 67   2015   £625

Hayley, William *The Triumphs of Temper: a Poem in Six Cantos.* London: T. Cadell, 1788. Sixth edition, 165 x 102mm., once remarkably attractive and still very pleasing late 18th century citron morocco by Staggemeier & Welcher, covers with inlaid black and red morocco tooled in gilt to a diapered mosaic design, raised bands, spine compartments with central moire silk endleaves, all edges gilt, expertly rejointed, spine label with tiny repairs and some inlays artfully replicated and replaced by Courtland Benson, with 7 engraved plates, silk bookplate of R. M. Trench Chiswell, titlepage and ink ownership inscription of Augusta E. Vincent, inscription from A. Vincent to Blanche Cely-Trevilian, spine little darkened, minor soiling to boards, plates rather foxed, otherwise without any significant defect and, in all, an excellent (albeit restored) specimen, binding with much of its original dramatic appeal reclaimed.   Phillip J. Pirages   66 - 52   2015 $4500

Hayley, William *The Triumphs of Temper.* Chichester: printed by J. Seagrave for T. Cadell and W. Davies, strand, London, 1803. Royal 8vo., 20th century half green morocco over marbled paper covered boards, top edge gilt, all other edges untrimmed, 6 engraved plates by Blake after Maria Flaxman, particularly bright, fresh, large paper copy with fine impressions of the plates.   Henry Sotheran Ltd. William Blake Exhibition 17th Oct.-7th Nov. 2014 - 68   2015 £1750

Haynes, George Edmund *The Trend of the Races.* New York: Council of Women of ..., 1922. First edition, wrappers, 206 pages, very good, photos.   Beasley Books 2013 - 2015 $85

Hays, Mary *Female Biography: or Memoirs of Illustrious and Celebrated Women of all Ages and Countries.* London: Richard Phillips, 1803. First edition, 6 volumes, 12mo., bound without half titles in modern calf backed boards, little foxing, ex-library with ink numeral on titlepage, very good, scarce. Second Life Books Inc. 189 - 116 2015 $3500

Hayward, C. *The Courtesan.* London: Casanova Society, 1926. First edition, 1/138 copies, small 4to., red marbled paper boards and cloth back, printed on deckle edged antique laid rag paper, specially watermarked Zephyr, 8 illustrations, very good. Second Life Books Inc. 189 - 117 2015 $120

Haywood, Eliza 1693-1756 *The Female Spectator.* London: printed for T. Gardner, 1750. Third edition, i.e. fourth London edition, 4 volumes, 12mo., engraved frontispiece in each volume, contemporary calf, some rubbed, upper joint of volume on tender, generally very good. Second Life Books Inc. 189 - 118 2015 $950

Haywood, Gar Anthony *Fear of the Dark.* New York: St. Martin's, 1988. First edition, very fine in dust jacket. Mordida Books   March 2015 - 008337 2015 $175

Haywood, Gar Anthony *You Can Die Trying.* New York: St. Martin's, 1990. First edition, very fine in dust jacket signed by author. Mordida Books   March 2015 - 008338 2015 $90

Hazard, Benjamin *Argument in the Case (of) Rhode Island Against Massachusetts. Printed by order of the General Assembly.* Providence: Knowles, Vose & Co., 1838. First edition, 8vo., sewn as issued, outer leaves foxed and dust soiled, crimp to lower margin, still very good. M & S Rare Books, Inc. 97 - 269 2015 $325

Hazlitt, William *A Reply to the Essay on Population by the Rev. T. R. Malthus. In a Series of Letters.* London: Longman Hurst, Rees and Orme, 1807. First edition, 8vo., pages 41-42 absent as correct, old library stamp erased from title and another partially erased from page 55, otherwise very good in mid 19th century calf over marbled boards, spine gilt with raised bands and green gilt lettering piece, scarce. John Drury Rare Books   March 2015 - 24091 2015 $962

Hazzard, Mary *Idle and Disorderly Persons.* Seattle: Madrona, 1981. First edition, inscribed by author in year of publication with APS and ALS, each from 1982 from author, they have been stapled together in one corner and are near fine, book near fine in like dust jacket. Ken Lopez, Bookseller 164 - 80 2015 $100

Head Imports. Catalog Group (2). Aspen: Head Imports, circa, 1970. 4to., rare vintage catalog and catalog supplement, Skip Williamson covers, some age toning to both, staple bound in original illustrated wrappers, both very good plus to near fine.   Ed Smith Books   82 - 33   2015 $275

Head, Francis Bond *Rough Notes Taken During Some Rapid Journeys Across the Pampas and Among the Andes.* London: John Murray, 1826. Second edition, 12mo., rebacked in quarter navy cloth over marbled boards with morocco tips, morocco label, very good, chip to corner of front board, boards scuffed, owner's name and owner's bookplate, endpapers soiled, contents clean. Kaaterskill Books 19 - 72 2015 $100

Heads and Long Legs. London: Raphael Tuck, n.d., 1914. 4to., maroon cloth stamped in black and gold, color plate on cover, all edges gilt, margins of 2 plates neatly repaired, else very good+, illustrations by Hilda Cowham, 12 bright color plates, pictorial endpapers, and black and whites, scarce. Aleph-bet Books, Inc. 109 - 108 2015 $800

Heads for a Bill to Amend the Law, Concerning Tallies in the Part of Great Britain called Scotland. Edinburgh: printed in the year, 1765. First edition, 8vo., 16 pages, modern plain wrappers, very good, rare. John Drury Rare Books   2015 - 18281 2015 $133

Healey, Raymond J. *New Tales of Space and Time.* New York: Henry Holt and Co., 1951. First edition, octavo, cloth. L. W. Currey, Inc.   Featured Author: Ray Bradbury (Oct. 2014) - 94291 2015 $75

Heaney, Seamus 1939- *District and Circle.* London: Faber and Faber, 2006. First edition, 8vo., original green boards, backstrip lettered gilt, dust jacket, fine, signed by author. Blackwell's Rare Books B179 - 162 2015 £200

Heaney, Seamus 1939- *Door into the Dark.* London: Faber & Faber, 1969. First edition, 8vo., fine in near fine, bright, clean dust jacket with faint shelfwear, few tiny spots, faint rubbing, excellent condition. Any Amount of Books 2015 - C4955 2015 £225

Heaney, Seamus 1939- *Door into the Dark.* London: Faber and Faber, 1969. First edition, 56 pages, 8vo., original black cloth, backstrip lettered gilt, few tiny foxspots to top edge, dust jacket with one or two faint spots to rear panel, near fine. Blackwell's Rare Books B179 - 163 2015 £525

Heaney, Seamus 1939- *Electric Light.* London: Faber and Faber, 2001. First edition, 8vo., original navy boards, backstrips lettered in white, dust jacket, fine, signed by author on titlepage. Blackwell's Rare Books B179 - 164 2015 £200

Heaney, Seamus 1939- *Field Work.* London: Faber and Faber, 1979. First edition, 8vo., original brown boards, backstrip lettered gilt, dust jacket with merest hint of fading to backstrip panel, near fine, signed by author.   Blackwell's Rare Books   B179 - 165   2015   £550

Heaney, Seamus 1939- *The Haw Lantern.* London: Faber and Faber, 1987. First edition, light toning to textblock, crown 8vo., original red boards, backstrip lettered in silver, dust jacket, near fine, signed by author and dated '30vi87'.   Blackwell's Rare Books   B179 - 166   2015   £250

Heaney, Seamus 1939- *Human Chain.* London: Faber and Faber, 2010. 288/300 copies signed by author, (of an edition of 325), 8vo., original brown cloth backed cream boards, printed label, matching boards and cloth slipcase, unopened, fine.   Blackwell's Rare Books   B179 - 167   2015   £500

Heaney, Seamus 1939- *Human Chain.* London: Faber and Faber, 2010. First edition, signed by author, 8vo., original maroon boards, backstrip lettered gilt, dust jacket, fine.   Blackwell's Rare Books   B179 - 168   2015   £200

Heaney, Seamus 1939- *A Lough Neagh Sequence.* Manchester: Phoenix Pamphlet Poets Press, 1969. One of 950 copies from an edition of 1000 copies, crown 8vo., original white stapled wrappers printed in black, near fine.   Blackwell's Rare Books   B179 - 169   2015   £200

Heaney, Seamus 1939- *An Open Letter.* Derry: Field Day Theatre Co., 1983. First edition, printed in brown on cream paper, crown 8vo., original cream wrappers, printed in brown, fine.   Blackwell's Rare Books   B179 - 170   2015   £35

Heaney, Seamus 1939- *Poems and a Memoir.* New York: Limited Editions Club, 1982. Limited to 2000 numbered copies, signed by author, artist and Thomas Flanagan (provided preface), illustrations by Henry Pearson, small 4to., full lather stamped in blind, top edge gilt, slipcase, loosely inserted is printed slip indicating how to care for leather binding, with Monthly Letter.   Oak Knoll Books   25 - 47   2015 $475

Heaney, Seamus 1939- *Seeing Things.* London: Faber and Faber, 1991. First edition, 8vo., original blue-grey cloth, backstrip lettered gilt, dust jacket with little rubbing to corners and along folds, very good, signed by author on titlepage.   Blackwell's Rare Books   B179 - 172   2015   £175

Heaney, Seamus 1939- *Spelling It Out, in Honour of Brian Friel on his 80th Birthday.* Oldcastle: Gallery Press, 2009. First edition, frontispiece, titles and initials printed in brown, 8vo., original stitched wrappers printed in black, fine.   Blackwell's Rare Books   B179 - 173   2015   £30

Heaney, Seamus 1939- *The Spirit Level.* London: Faber and Faber, 1996. First edition, foolscap 8vo., original mid green boards, backstrip lettered gilt, dust jacket, fine, signed by author.   Blackwell's Rare Books   B179 - 174   2015   £250

Heaney, Seamus 1939- *Wintering Out.* London: Faber and Faber, 1972. First edition, crown 8vo. original wrappers. lightest of sunning to backstrip, near fine.   Blackwell's Rare Books   B179 - 175   2015   £600

Heard, Gerald *A Taste for Honey.* London: Cassell, 1924. First edition, 8vo., covers very slightly marked, otherwise clean, very good with clean text, presentation copy for Elizabeth from Eddie Marsh, Christmas 1942, probably Sir Edward Marsh.   Any Amount of Books   2015 - A96651   2015   £180

Hearn, Lafcadio 1850-1904 *Fairy Tales with Wraps in cloth Case.* Philadelphia: Macrae Smith Co. n.d. circa, 1915. 5 volumes, each 5 1/2 x 7 3/4 inches, bound with silk ties and printed on crepe paper, housed in publisher's folding cloth case with pictorial lining and ivory clasps, spine of case faded, and two joints on either side of backstrip are neatly reinforced, case is sound and complete with ivory clasps, without exception, each book fine, bright condition with delicate silk ties intact, original rice paper sleeves, color woodblock illustrations on crepe paper.   Aleph-bet Books, Inc.   109 - 222   2015 $2500

Hearn, Lafcadio 1850-1904 *Japanese Fairy Tales: the Boy Who Drew Cats.* Tokyo: Hasegawa, n.d., 1898. 8vo., crepe paper with silk ties, beautifully illustrated in color.   Aleph-Bet Books, Inc.   108 - 234   2015 $500

Hearn, Lafcadio 1850-1904 *Miscellanies.* London: Heinemann, 1924. First UK edition, octavo, 2 volumes, corners little bruised, free endpapers partially tanned, some spotting of prelims and fore-edges, very good in like dust jackets, litle chipped, nicked and creased at edges.   Peter Ellis, Bookseller   2014 - 007893   2015   £350

Heath, Charles *Descriptive Account of the Kymin Pavillion and Beaulieu Grove, with their Various Views...* Monmouth: Charles Heath, 1809. First edition, 8vo., one page with typographical diagram, recent marbled boards lettered on spine, very good, scarce.   John Drury Rare Books   2015 - 24926   2015 $787

Heath, Charles *Monmouthshire. Historical and Descriptive accounts of the Ancient and Present State of Tintern Abbey...* Monmouth: Charles Heath, 1806. 8vo., recent marbled boards lettered on spine, very good, scarce.   John Drury Rare Books   March 2015 - 24909   2015   £306

Heath, W. L. *Violent Saturday.* New York: Harper & Bros., 1955. First edition, fine in dust jacket with light wear to extremities. Buckingham Books   March 2015 - 12316   2015 $185

Heathfield, Richard *Elements of a Plan for the Liquidation of the Public Debt of the United Kingdom...* London: Longman, Hurst Rees Orme and Brown, J. M. Richardson and J. Hardin, 1819. Fourth edition, 8vo., without half title, with edition statement, blank verso of final leaf rather soiled, with large folding table bound in after page 26, bound fairly recently in red cloth, spine lettered in gilt, good copy.   John Drury Rare Books   2015 - 16302   2015 $221

Heathfield, Richard *Thoughts on the Liquidation of the Public Debt, and on the Relief of the Country from the Distress Incident to a Population Exceeding the Demand for Labour.* London: Longman, Rees, Orme Brown and Green, n.d.?, 1829. First edition, 8vo., small circular stamp of United Service Club, modern marbled boards with gilt spine label, very good.   John Drury Rare Books   2015 - 8408   2015 $177

Heaton, Rose Henniker *Chez James - The Wisdom and Foolishness of James...* London: Elkin Mathews & Marot, 1932. First edition, octavo, illustrations, cloth backed pictorial boards, silkscreened in vivid colors, text printed on different colored papers, bookplate of Bruce Arnold, flaps of dust jacket have offset onto free endpapers, near fine in very good, slightly nicked dust jacket slightly rubbed at head and tail of spine.   Peter Ellis, Bookseller   2014 - 006668   2015   £325

Heawood, Edward *Watermarks Mainly of the 17th and 18th Centuries.* Hilversum: The Paper Publications Society, 1950. Reprint of first edition, with addenda and corrigenda, thick 4to., cloth, 533 plates.   Oak Knoll Books   306 - 94   2015 $225

Heber, Reginald *Narrative of a Journey through the Upper Provinces of India from Calcutta to Bombay 1824-1825.* London: John Murray, 1826. First edition, 10 plates, 25 wood engravings in text, map at rear, this copy lacking plate of Pagoda facing page 47, but has an additional frontispiece plate of the Ghat between Calcutta and Barrackpoor, pencilled note says this in fact the plate that is supposed to be at page 47, but we have our doubts, quarto, original light red cloth, title labels on spine, presentation copy inscribed by author to friend Mrs. Leott, covers unevenly faded, rubbed at edges and bruised at corners, map repaired, labels rubbed but not affecting lettering, first gathering in volume I loose but not detached, some spotting of prelims, good.   Peter Ellis, Bookseller   2014 - 010377   2015   £300

Hecht, Anthony *Collected Earlier Poems.* New York: Knopf, 1990. First edition, 8vo., original cloth, dust jacket, signed by author, fine.   James S. Jaffe Rare Books   Modern American Poetry - 134   2015 $125

Hecht, Anthony *Obbligati Essays in Criticism.* New York: Atheneum, 1986. First edition, 8vo., original cloth backed paper over boards, dust jacket, fine, inscribed presentation by author.   James S. Jaffe Rare Books   Modern American Poetry - 133   2015 $100

Hecht, Anthony *A Summoning of Stones.* New York: Macmillan, 1954. First edition, 8vo., original cloth and paper over boards, dust jacket, fine in slightly rubbed dust jacket, scarce in this condition, inscribed by poet.   James S. Jaffe Rare Books   Modern American Poetry - 131   2015 $750

Hecht, Anthony *The Venetian Vespers.* Boston: David R. Godine, \1979. First edition, limited to 165 copies signed by author and artist, tall 8vo., quarter morocco and pictorial boards, glassine dust jacket, fine.   James S. Jaffe Rare Books   Modern American Poetry - 132   2015 $450

Hecht, Ben *The Cat That Jumped Out of the Story.* Philadelphia: Winston, 1947. Stated first edition, 8vo., boards, pictorial paste-on, fine in slightly worn dust jacket, illustrations by Peggy Bacon, with cover plate, pictorial endpapers, wonderful full page color illustrations plus smaller color illustrations in text as well as black and white.   Alephbet Books, Inc.   109 - 30   2015 $150

Hedgeland, John Pike *A Description, Accompanied by Sixteen Coloured Plates of the Splendid Decorations Recently made to the Church of St. Neot, in Cornwall...* London: printed for J. P. Hedgeland, 16 Claremont Place, Brunswick Square, 1830. First edition, 4to., 16 hand colored engraved plates, uncut in modern two tone cloth, spine lettered in gilt.   Marlborough Rare Books   List 54 - 44   2015   £950

Hedgepeth, Don *The Texas Breed. A Cowboy Anthology.* Flagstaff: Northland Press, 1978. First edition, 14 vintage photos, rust cloth, very fine with spine faded pictorial dust jacket.   Argonaut Book Shop   Holiday Season 2014 - 120   2015 $90

Hedin, Sven *History of the Expedition in Asia 1927-1935.* Stockholm: 1943. First edition, large 4to., 4 volumes, original printed paperbacks, plates, figures, folding maps, about fine, exceptional condition.   Any Amount of Books   2015 - C3130   2015   £800

Hegel, Georg Wilhelm Friedrich *Encyclopadie der Philosophischen Wissenschaften im Grundrisse...* Heidelberg: August Oswald, 1827. 8vo., paper throughout generally little browned and foxed, original boards with spine label lettered in gilt, wear to joints and extremities, red edges, good sound copy with several early ownership inscriptions, including I. F. C. Kampe (mid 19th century) Jonas Cohn (1931) and Selly Oake Colleges Library.   John Drury Rare Books   2015 - 24310   2015 $830

Hegel, Georg Wilhelm Friedrich *Wissenschafter der Logic. (The Science of Logic).* Nurnberg: Johann Leonhard Schrag, 1812. 1813. 1816. First editions, 3 volumes, bound in matching late 19th century three quarter leather with green and red (and blue on volume 1), marbled boards, spines have gilt decorations and title in gilt on red field, just bit of wear to exterior, overall a beautiful set for presentation on the shelf, text clean, bit tanned and lightly foxed at times, completely uncut and therefore preserving wide original margins, overall lovely copy. Athena Rare Books 15 - 7 2015 $12,000

Heidegger, Martin *Sein und Zeit. (Being and Time).* Halle: Max Niemeyer, 1927. First edition, octavo, stunningly preserved uncut copy in original wrappers that comes with custom clamshell box, just the lightest bit of wear on edges of cover, most noticeably to lower front corner, very slightly spotted on spine and on both covers, folded half sheet of paper inside front cover, one side is torn-in-half mimeographed sheet that clearly identifies it as coming from Gottingen with date June 15 1927 on upper corner, on reverse side there are five lines of handwritten German text (to date untranslated), interior uniformly bright and clean, uncut and unmarked, nothing less than spectacular. Athena Rare Books 15 - 8 2015 $12,500

Heidegger, Martin *Sein und Zeit. (Being and Time).* Halle: Max Niemeyer, 1929. Second edition, octavo, uncommon edition, original tan cloth with dark brown lettering to front cover and brown label with gilt lettering to spine, several scattered spots to front cover, book splitting, but completely firm, otherwise clean, solid, respectable. Athena Rare Books 15 - 9 2015 $600

Heinlein, Robert Anson 1907-1988 *Destination Moon.* Boston: Gregg Press, 1979. First edition, 13 full page stills, octavo, cloth. John W. Knott, Bookseller Selected New Arrivals Jan. 2015 - 17089 2015 $150

Heinlein, Robert Anson 1907-1988 *The Door Into Summer.* Garden City: Doubleday & Co., 1957. First edition, octavo, cloth. John W. Knott, Bookseller Selected New Arrivals Jan. 2015 - 17085 2015 $500

Heinlein, Robert Anson 1907-1988 *Double Star.* Garden City: Doubleday & Co., 1956. First edition, octavo boards. John W. Knott, Bookseller Selected New Arrivals Jan. 2015 - 17084 2015 $1250

Heinlein, Robert Anson 1907-1988 *Farmer in the Sky.* New York: Charles Scribner's Sons, 1950. First edition, Scribner 'A' on copyright page, 8vo., original blue cloth lettered yellow on spine and cover, inner flap of dust jacket has printed price of $2.50, slight lean otherwise about fine in near fine, clean, bright contemporary, slightly rubbed at spine and corner, no inscriptions, not price clipped. Any Amount of Books 2015 - C1727 2015 £300

Heinlein, Robert Anson 1907-1988 *Friday.* New York: Holt, Rinehart and Winston, 1982. First edition, number 189 of 500 numbered copies signed by author, octavo, cloth. John W. Knott, Bookseller Selected New Arrivals Jan. 2015 - 17091 2015 $500

Heinlein, Robert Anson 1907-1988 *Have Space Suit - Will Travel.* New York: Charles Scribner's Sons, 1958. First edition, octavo, titlepage and jacket by Ed Emshwiller, cloth. John W. Knott, Bookseller Selected New Arrivals Jan. 2015 - 17074 2015 $1750

Heinlein, Robert Anson 1907-1988 *I Will Fear No Evil.* New York: Putnam, 1970. First edition, nearly fine in fine dust jacket. Ed Smith Books 83 - 45 2015 $200

Heinlein, Robert Anson 1907-1988 *Orphans of the Sky.* New York: G. P. Putnam's Sons, 1964. First edition, octavo, cloth. John W. Knott, Bookseller Selected New Arrivals Jan. 2015 - 17080 2015 $500

Heinlein, Robert Anson 1907-1988 *Project Moonbase: and Others.* Burton: Subterranean Press, 2008. First edition, one of 750 numbered copies signed by John Scalzi, provided introduction, and by artist, Bob Eggleton, octavo, cloth,. John W. Knott, Bookseller Selected New Arrivals Jan. 2015 - 17094 2015 $125

Heinlein, Robert Anson 1907-1988 *The Puppet Masters.* Garden City: Doubleday and Co., 1951. First edition, octavo, cloth. John W. Knott, Bookseller Selected New Arrivals Jan. 2015 - 17081 2015 $2750

Heinlein, Robert Anson 1907-1988 *Red Planet.* New York: Charles Scribner's, 1949. First edition, octavo, illustration by Clifford Geary cloth, fine, previous owner's name and date to verso of front free endpaper and name stamp and string of numbers to facing page, in fine dust jacket, exceptional copy. John W. Knott, Bookseller Selected New Arrivals Jan. 2015 - 17065 2015 $3500

Heinlein, Robert Anson 1907-1988 *Revolt in 2100.* Chicago: Shasta Pub., 1953. First edition, octavo, illustrations by Hulbert Rogers, cloth backed boards, one of the signed subscriber copies on inserted blank leaf. John W. Knott, Bookseller Selected New Arrivals Jan. 2015 - 17078 2015 $2500

Heinlein, Robert Anson 1907-1988 *Rocket Ship Galileo.* New York: Charles Scribner's, 1947. First edition, illustrations by Thomas Voter, cloth, octavo. John W. Knott, Bookseller Selected New Arrivals Jan. 2015 - 17063 2015 $750

Heinlein, Robert Anson 1907-1988 *Space Cadet.* New York: Charles Scribner's Sons, 1948. First edition, octavo, cloth.   John W. Knott, Bookseller   Selected New Arrivals Jan. 2015 - 17064   2015 $2000

Heinlein, Robert Anson 1907-1988 *The Star Beast.* New York: Charles Scribners sons, 1954. First edition, illustrations by Clifford Geary, octavo, cloth.   John W. Knott, Bookseller   Selected New Arrivals Jan. 2015 - 17070   2015 $1000

Heinlein, Robert Anson 1907-1988 *Starship Troopers.* New York: G. P. Putnam's sons, 1959. First edition, octavo, cloth.   John W. Knott, Bookseller   Selected New Arrivals Jan. 2015 - 17221   2015 $4500

Heinlein, Robert Anson 1907-1988 *Stranger in a Strange Land.* New York: An Ace/Putnam Book Published by G. P. Putnam's Sons, 1991. First edition, octavo, boards.   John W. Knott, Bookseller   Selected New Arrivals Jan. 2015 - 17222   2015 $125

Heinlein, Robert Anson 1907-1988 *Time for the Stars.* New York: Charles Scribner's Sons, 1956. First edition, octavo, cloth.   John W. Knott, Bookseller   Selected New Arrivals Jan. 2015 - 17072   2015 $1750

Heinlein, Robert Anson 1907-1988 *Tunnel in the Sky.* New York: Charles Scribner's Sons, 1955. First edition, octavo, illustrations by P. A. Hutchison.   John W. Knott, Bookseller   Selected New Arrivals Jan. 2015 - 17071   2015 $1500

Heinlein, Robert Anson 1907-1988 *The Unpleasant Profession of Jonathan Hoag.* Hicksville: Gnome Press, 1959. First edition, octavo, cloth.   John W. Knott, Bookseller   Selected New Arrivals Jan. 2015 - 17082   2015 $450

Heinrigs, Johann *Musterbaltter fur Liebhaber der Hohem Kalligraphic.* Berlin: T. Trautwein, 1820. First edition, volumes one and two of 3, each stands on its own, large oblong 4to., later paper covered boards with original paper cover labels, foxing, covers discolored.   Oak Knoll Books Special Catalogue 24 - 21   2015 $400

Hejduk, John *Mask of Medusa: Works 1947-1983.* New York: Rizzoli International Publications, 1985. First edition, numerous color and black and white images, tight very good plus in wrappers with some minor wear and slight creasing to corners and small abrasion to verso front cover, still very nice.   Jeff Hirsch Books   E-62 Holiday List 2014 - 17   2015 $300

Held, Julius S. *The Oil Sketches of Peter Rubens: a Critical Catalogue.* Princeton: Princeton University Press/ National Gallery of Art, 1980. First edition, 4to, plates, original grey cloth, lettered gilt at spines and red on front covers, copiously illustrated, fine in very good+ dust jacket with very slight edgewear.   Any Amount of Books   March 2015 - C13573   2015   £400

Heller, Joseph *Catch-22.* New York: Simon & Schuster, 1961. Advance reading copy, bit of handling apparent to wrappers and light creasing to spine, overall crisp, clean, near fine copy.   Ken Lopez, Bookseller   164 - 81   2015 $2500

Heller, Joseph *God Knows.* New York: Alfred A. Knopf, 1984. First edition, fine in just about fine dust jacket with little rubbing at crown, inscribed by author to his daughter Erica 8/28/84.   Between the Covers Rare Books, Inc.   187 - 123   2015 $1000

Helms, Anne Adams *The Descendants of William James Adams and Cassandra Hills Adams.* Salinas: Anne Helms, 1999. First edition, quarto, photos, single page map, stiff red wrappers printed in black, very fine.   Argonaut Book Shop   Holiday Season 2014 - 4   2015 $150

Helms, Anthony Zachariah *Travels from Buenos Ayres, by Potsoi to Lima.* London: printed for Richard Phillips, 1806. First English language edition, 1 folding map, illustrations, 16mo., later half calf over marbled boards, red morocco lettering piece, spine decorated in gilt, near fine, from the Coleccion Monclau (bookplate), faint glue mark at hinge, minor foxing.   Kaaterskill Books   19 - 73   2015 $850

Helmut Salden: Lettrrontwerper en Boekverzorger. Rotterdam: 2003. 4to., cloth, dust jacket, Salden monogram on front cover, 192 pages, color illustrations.   Oak Knoll Books   306 - 236   2015 $150

Helps, Arthur *The Life of Hernando Cortes.* London: Bell and Daldy, 1871. First edition, small 8vo., black and white drawings and maps, 2 volumes, very good+ copies, boards lightly rubbed, owner's bookplate on front pastedowns, owner's notes tipped in to free rear endpaper in volume I, binder's ticket on rear pastedown, bookplate of James Torr Harmer.   Kaaterskill Books   19 - 74   2015 $100

Helu, Antonio *La Obligacion De Asesinar. (The Compulsion to Murder).* Mexico City: Albatros, 1946. First edition, fine in pictorial wrappers, very scarce.   Buckingham Books   March 2015 - 9587   2015 $375

Helvetius, Claude Adrien *Le Vrai Sens Du Systeme De La Nature, Ouvrage Posthume. (The True Meaning of the System of Nature).* London: (i.e. Durfour & Roux, Maastricht, 1774. First edition, first printing, original tan wrappers, octavo, 2 handwritten spine labels, all but unreadable because of minute size of text and cracking of labels, front cover separated from spine for bottom 2 inch and the spine just bit cocked, text bright and clean, completely uncut, really pretty copy, extremely rare condition for French book from this era.   Athena Rare Books   15 - 10   2015 $1200

Hemans, Felicia Dorothea Browne *Poems.* London: Liverpool; Printed by G. F. Harris for T. Cadell and W. Davies, 1808. First edition, frontispiece, vignette on titlepage, further vignettes in text, taped down portrait of author on front pastedown endpaper, original greenish blue boards, paper label on spine, black morocco slipcase, tipped in 'letter' from author to editor of the Literary Gazette Office, Strand, London postal stamp dated 1822 consisting of a three page handwritten poem entitled "England's Dead." initialled by her at end, a further two page handwritten poem entitled "To the Memory of Bishop Heber" tipped in and taped at front of 'letter' and signed by author St. Asaph Sept 1826, three holes to final page of "England's Dead" with list loss to text and address on verso, spine worn, upper joint partially torn, some slight wear to boards, occasional brown spotting, slipcase rubbed at extremities, covers little worn, otherwise very good.   Any Amount of Books   2015 - C13464   2015   £700

Hemingway, Ernest Millar   1899-1961 *Fact 16: The Spanish War.* London: Fact, 1938. Bright near fine copy, but for front cover starting to separate lower edge.   Ken Lopez, Bookseller   164 - 84   2015 $150

Hemingway, Ernest Millar   1899-1961 *For Whom the Bell Tolls.* New York: Charles Scribner's Sons, 1940. First edition, foxing to boards and endpapers, very good in very near fine (possibly supplied, but was with book when it came to us), second issue dust jacket, with little rubbing, author James Jones's copy with his ownership signature.   Between the Covers Rare Books, Inc.   187 - 124   2015 $2500

Hemingway, Ernest Millar   1899-1961 *For Whom the Bell Tolls.* New York: Charles Scribner's Sons, 1940. First edition, first printing, original cloth dust jacket, excellent copy in remarkably bright, crisp and unfaded, first state dust jacket, lacking photographer's credit to rear panel, with very few tiny tears to bottom along spine, touch of wear at corners of flap folds and without any of the usual chips, loss, fading or wear, rather common title, extremely difficult to find in nice jacket.   B & B Rare Books, Ltd.   234 - 50   2015 $2500

Hemingway, Ernest Millar   1899-1961 *Islands in the Stream.* New York: Scribners, 1970. First edition, fine in dust jacket with tiny wear at lower corner front panel.   Mordida Books   March 2015 - 012707   2015 $200

Hemingway, Ernest Millar   1899-1961 *The Old Man and the Sea.* New York: Charles Scribner's Sons, 1952. First edition, Honey & Wax Booksellers   2 - 32   2015 $2600

Hemingway, Ernest Millar   1899-1961 *The Old Man and the Sea.* New York: Scribners, 1952. First edition, lower front corner bumped, endpapers slightly darkened, few scattered spots on page edges, otherwise very good with Scribner A, light blue covers, price clipped dust jacket with darkened spine, chipping at spine ends and couple of scrapes on spine, probably later state of dust jacket with brown lettering on flaps, no mention of prizes but without production symbols.   Mordida Books   March 2015 - 012709   2015 $300

Hemingway, Ernest Millar   1899-1961 *The Spanish Earth.* Cleveland: Savage, 1938. Copy number 21 of 1000 numbered copies, despite low number, this is the second issue with plain endpapers and Hemingway disclaimer on rear pastedown, first edition exceptionally scarce, small stamp "H.B." on front pastedown, fine, without dust jacket, as issued.   Ken Lopez, Bookseller   164 - 83   2015 $1250

Hemingway, Ernest Millar   1899-1961 *The Sun Also Rises.* New York: Charles Scribner's Sons, 1926. First edition, first issue, original cloth, spine lightly faded, spine label little toned, extremities lightly rubbed, small tear to upper corner of spine, covers lightly scuffed, else very good, nicer copy than usually found.   B & B Rare Books, Ltd.   234 - 52   2015 $2250

Hemingway, Ernest Millar   1899-1961 *Three Stories and Ten Poems.* Paris: Contact Publishing, 1923. First edition, limited to 300 copies, original publisher's printed blue wrappers, attractive, unrestored copy, with some toning to spine, few minor spots to wrappers, spine slightly chipped, else very good to near fine, custom quarter leather case.   B & B Rare Books, Ltd.   234 - 53   2015 $40,000

Hemingway, Ernest Millar   1899-1961 *To Have and Have Not.* New York: Scribner, 1937. First edition, mild darkening to hinges, still fine in very good dust jacket with minor edge chipping.   Ken Lopez, Bookseller   164 - 82   2015 $2250

Hemingway, Ernest Millar   1899-1961 *To Have and Have Not.* New York: Charles Scribner's Sons, 1937. First edition, octavo, publisher's black cloth, spine stamped and lettered green and gilt, front board stamped with Hemingway's signature, dust jacket with $2.50 price, jacket edges with browning, some wear and light creasing, head and tail of jacket with few small chips, some very light rubbing to cloth and small amount of fraying to headcap, overall near fine, bright, unrestored dust jacket.   Heritage Book Shop   Holiday 2014 - 64   2015 $2000

Hemingway, Ernest Millar 1899-1961 *Today is Friday.* Englewood: The As Stable Publication, 1926. First edition, one of 300 numbered copies, original wrappers with front cover illustration by Jean Cocteau, original publisher's printed envelope, fine, bright copy, envelope flap detached and present, housed in custom folding case. B & B Rare Books, Ltd. 234 - 54 2015 $2250

Hemingway, Ernest Millar 1899-1961 *The Torrents of Spring.* New York: Charles Scribner's Sons, 1926. First edition, one of 1250 copies, original cloth, near fine with minor wear at spine tips, spine lettering bit dimmed, else fine, nice, bright copy. B & B Rare Books, Ltd. 234 - 55 2015 $1250

Hemming, George Wirgman *A Just Income Tax How Possible, Being a Review of the Evidence Reported by the Income Tax Committee and an Inquiry...* London: John Chapman, 1852. First edition, 8vo., 40 pages, modern wrappers, printed title label on upper cover, very good. John Drury Rare Books 2015 - 23724 2015 $133

Hemyng, Bracebridge *Jack Harkaway Among the Malay Pirates.* London: Hogarth House, circa, 1885. Bound without front wrapper in black binder's cloth, spine slightly faded, illustrations, few spots. Jarndyce Antiquarian Booksellers CCXI - 136 2015 £30

Henderson, David *Jim Hendrix: Voodoo Child of the Aquarian Age.* Garden City: Doubleday & Co., 1978. First edition, inscribed by author, well illustrated with several dozen black and white photos. Buckingham Books March 2015 - 11400 2015 $225

Henderson, G. W. *The Science and Art of Penmanship, a Text Book for Schools and the Home.* West Cairo: G. W. Henderson & Son, 1899. First edition, 8vo., original cloth, illustrations, very scarce, spine faded, back inside hinge cracked. Oak Knoll Books Special Catalogue 24 - 22 2015 $150

Henderson, Halton *Artistry in Single Action.* Chama Press, 1989. First edition, limited to 450 copies signed by designer and binder, this copy 181, also signed by J. Evetts Haley who provided introduction, quarto, quarter leather and brown cloth, gilt stamped leather label on front cover, illustrations, rare, fine, unread copy housed in matching brown cloth, slipcase. Buckingham Books March 2015 - 33729 2015 $750

Henderson, Louis T. *Ships. A Children's Picture Book of Ships and Stories about Them.* Chicago: Donohue, 1937. Folio, cloth backed pictorial boards, fine in frayed dust jacket, photos. Aleph-bet Books, Inc. 109 - 352 2015 $150

Henderson, Zenna *The People: No Different Flesh.* Garden City: Doubleday & Co., 1967. First US edition, octavo, cloth. John W. Knott, Bookseller Selected New Arrivals Jan. 2015 - 17095 2015 $350

Henderson's Sign Painter. Newark: Henderson, 1906. Oblong 8vo., quarter cloth, illustrated paper covered boards, illustrations, covers soiled, rubbed and scuffed at edges, front hinge repaired, back hinge cracked, two leaves text loose, inserted at back, front free endpaper chipped at edges, front free endpaper, title and four following leaves stained at edge, light soiling in text. Oak Knoll Books 306 - 237 2015 $350

Hendrickson, Richard H. *Furniture and Automobile Box Cars 1887-1997.* Highlands Ranch: Santa Fe Railway Historical & Modeling Society, 1997. First edition, oblong quarto, 157 pages, black and white photos, stiff pictorial wrappers, spiral bound, fine. Argonaut Book Shop Holiday Season 2014 - 121 2015 $40

Hendrickson, Richard H. *The Santa Fe Tank Cars.* Midwest City: Santa Fe Railway Historical & Modeling Society, 2004. First edition, black and white and color photos, detailed working plans, stiff pictorial wrappers, spiral bound, fine. Argonaut Book Shop Holiday Season 2014 - 122 2015 $75

Hening, William Waller *The Statutes at Large; Being a Collection of All the Laws of Virginia... first Session of the Legislature in 1619.* Richmond: 1823-1969. Mixed set in mixed bindings, volumes 1, 6, 8, 9 and 13 are the 1969 reprints, volume 1 is second edition, volumes 2-4, 7, 10-12 in full original calf, but have two internal library stamps, volume 2 has library # on backstrip, 13 volumes. Bookworm & Silverfish 2015 - 6016004691 2015 $325

Henriet, Frederic *Le Paysagiste Aux Champs.* Paris: A. Levy, 1876. Limited to 135 copies, 4to., original blue cloth with elaborate gilt design and black stamping, all edges gilt, fine, reproductions, beautiful copy of a beautiful book. Aleph-bet Books, Inc. 109 - 179 2015 $1850

Henriot, Emile *Mythologie Des Anciens Grecs et Romains.* Paris: Georges Guillot, 1955. From an edition of 550 copies, this copy XXI for friends of the presenters, 2 volumes, unbound signatures laid into wrappers, 66 superb copperplate engravings by Decaris, fine copies in fine wrappers in chemise and slipcase, chemise on volume II bit soiled, slipcase supplied by former owner, folio. Beasley Books 2013 - 2015 $300

Henry, Elisa Victorine *Le Charme, Suite de Compositions Gracienses.* London: Gambart Junin & Co. 25 Berners St. Oxf. St. Imp. Lemercier a Paris, 1845. Large folio, six hand colored lithograph plates, finished by hand in gum arabic, each plate enclosed in ornate blue and silver chromolithographic border with publisher's line below, original pale green glazed boards with title printed in gilt, brown and blue within elaborate copper lustre border, excellent copy. Marlborough Rare Books   List 54 - 45   2015   £1850

Henry, Sue *Murder on the Iditarod Trail.* New York: Atlantic Monthly Press, 1991. First edition, fine in fine dust jacket.   Buckingham Books   March 2015 - 29086   2015 $175

The Herald of Peace for the Year 1819-(1824). London: T. Hamilton, 1819-1824. First editions, 6 volumes, 8vo., short wormtrack in margins of first few leaves in volume I, else excellent crisp set in contemporary half calf over marbled boards, all volumes, rebacked to match with gilt lines and titles, very good set.   John Drury Rare Books   2015 - 24204   2015 $1311

Herbart, Johann Friedrich *Analytische Beleuchatung Des Naturrechts Und Der Moral: Zum Gebrauch Beym Vortrage der Praktischen Philosophie. (An Analytical Explanation of Natural Rights and Morality...).* Gottingen: Dieterichschen Buchhandlung, 1836. First edition, octavo, gorgeous little book in contemporary three quarter black leather with mottled blue boards, spine has gilt lettering and 6 decorative compartments, just bit of wear to boards and spine, overall bright, clean, tight and eminently collectible, extremely scarce.   Athena Rare Books   15 - 11   2015 $850

Herbert, Brian *Dune: The Battle of Corrin.* New York: Tor, 2004. First edition, octavo, full leather, limited to 51 copies, this one of 25 numbered copies signed by Herbert and Kevin Anderson.   John W. Knott, Bookseller   Selected New Arrivals Jan. 2015 - 17116   2015 $300

Herbert, Brian *Dune: the Butlerian Jihad.* New York: Tor, 2002. First edition, limited to 126 copies, this one of 100 numbered copies signed by Herbert and Kevin J. Anderson. John W. Knott, Bookseller   Selected New Arrivals Jan. 2015 - 17114   2015 $200

Herbert, Brian *Dune: the Machine Crusade.* New York: Tor, 2003. First edition, limited to 76 copies, this one of 50 copies signed by Herbert and Kevin J. Anderson, octavo, full leather.   John W. Knott, Bookseller   Selected New Arrivals Jan. 2015 - 17115   2015 $200

Herbert, Claude Jacques *Essai sur la Poliice general des grains seur leurs Prix & Sur les Effets de l'Agriculture.* Berlin: 1755. Fourth edition, small 8vo., contemporary mottled calf, spine fully gilt in compartments, marbled endpapers and edges, little wear to head and foot of spine, overall very good, crisp copy.   John Drury Rare Books   March 2015 - 19029   2015   £306

Herbert, Frank *Chapterhouse: Dune.* New York: G. P. Putnam's Sons, 1985. First US edition, one of 750 numbered copies signed by Herbert, octavo, cloth.   John W. Knott, Bookseller   Selected New Arrivals Jan. 2015 - 17102   2015 $250

Herbert, Frank *Children of Dune.* New York: Berkley Pub. Corp., 1976. First edition, octavo, cloth, signed by author.   John W. Knott, Bookseller   Selected New Arrivals Jan. 2015 - 17099   2015 $1500

Herbert, Frank *The Dragon in the Sea.* Garden City: Doubleday & Co., 1956. First edition, octavo, illustration by Mel Hunter, boards.   John W. Knott, Bookseller   Selected New Arrivals Jan. 2015 - 17096   2015 $750

Herbert, Frank *Dune Messiah.* New York: G. P. Putnam's Sons, 1969. First edition, octavo, boards.   John W. Knott, Bookseller   Selected New Arrivals Jan. 2015 - 17098   2015 $650

Herbert, Frank *God Emperor of Dune.* New York: G. P. Putnam's Sons, 1981. First edition, one of 750 numbered copies signed by author, octavo, cloth.   John W. Knott, Bookseller   Selected New Arrivals Jan. 2015 - 17100   2015 $750

Herbert, Frank *Heretics of Dune.* New York: G. P. Putnam's Sons, 1984. First US edition, one of 1500 numbered copies signed by author, octavo, cloth.   John W. Knott, Bookseller   Selected New Arrivals Jan. 2015 - 17101   2015 $200

Herbert, George *A Priest to the Temple or the County Parson, His Characer and Rule of Holy Life.* London: T. Roycroft for Tooke, 1671. Second edition, small 8vo., two neat signatures, one "Thomas Bean/his book 1676/price 0/.1.6", contemporary brown full leather little worn, backstrip very rubbed and chipped, internally very clean and crisp. Any Amount of Books   March 2015 - A98502   2015   £375

Herbert, George *The Works.* Oxford: Clarendon Press, 1941. Half title, frontispiece, facsimiles, uncut, original dark blue cloth, inner hinge cracking, from the library of Geoffrey & Kathleen Tillotson, signed by Geoffrey, ALs from editor, pencil notes, insertions.   Jarndyce Antiquarian Booksellers CCVII - 297   2015   £35

Herbert, Luke *The Engineer's and Mechanic's Encyclopaedia.* London: Thomas Kelly, 1837. 1836, 2 volumes, 8vo., original half leather, marbled paper covered boards, marbled endpapers, boards scuffed and rubbed, endpapers foxed and tanned, text lightly tanned.   Oak Knoll Books   306 - 268   2015 $750

Herbert, Thomas *A Relation of Some Yeares Travaile Begunne anno 1626.* London: printed by William Stansby & Jacob Blome, 1634. First edition, 4to., numerous well executed engraved illustrations and maps, contemporary full panelled calf, expertly rebacked raised bands, maroon leather label, from the Maxwell-Perceval Library, with signature of William Perceval, armorial bookplate of John Evans, very good. Jarndyce Antiquarian Booksellers CCXI - 137 2015 £1850

Herbst, Josephine *Nothing is Sacred.* New York: Coward McCann, 1928. First edition, spine lettering dulled, near very good, lacking dust jacket, nicely inscribed by author for Jean. Between the Covers Rare Books, Inc. 187 - 125 2015 $300

Hercules, Frank *Where the Hummingbird Flies.* New York: Harcourt Brace, 1961. First edition, 8vo., author's presentation to flyleaf for Bill Goodman Feb. 10 1970, rust cloth, cover little soiled, very good, tight copy in scuffed and slightly chipped dust jacket, scarce. Second Life Books Inc. 190 - 92 2015 $150

Herder, Johann Gottfreid *Ideen zur Philosophie der Geschichte der Menschheit. (Ideas of the Philosophy of the History of Mankind).* Riga und Leipzig: Johann Freidrich Hartsnoch, 1784. 1785. 1787. 1791. First edition, small quarto, 4 volumes, contemporary tan pasteboard bindings with lovely gilt titling to spines of first two volumes, titling has fallen off last two volumes, each book worn on covers, generally dented tips and overall signs of wear, still each volume solid and completely firm in bindings, each titlepage has small (quarter inch) black circular stamp with letters "H.R." inside, unsophisticated, but charming set. Athena Rare Books 15 - 12 2015 $1500

Hereford, Charles John *The History of France from the First Establishment of that Monarchy Brought Down to and Including a Complete Narrative of the Late Revolution.* London: C. & G. Kearsley, 1791. New edition, original 45 parts, 34 engraved portraits, some occasional minor creasing and marginal tears, otherwise largely crisp and clean, uncut in original blue gray wrappers, nos. *-XXVIII with printed title, nos. XXVIIII-XXXXV blank, spines of nos. I-XVI worn with wrappers to nos. I, X and XI rather more worn (back wrapper to no. 1 loose), some further slight wear to others with occasional slight tears and creasing, contemporary name of Mr. Beding on front wrapper of no. XLV, overall very good plus set in original wrappers with nos. XVII=XLV largely very good. Jarndyce Antiquarian Booksellers CCXI - 138 2015 £450

Hereford, Charles John *The History of Spain, from the Establishment of the Colony of Gades by the Phoenicians to the Death of Ferdinand...* London: printed for C. and G. Kearsley, 1793. 3 volumes, ads in volumes I and II, original blue boards, original paper labels on spines, edges untrimmed, volumes II and III entirely unopened, inevitable bending and wear to corners, slight soiling and chafing to covers, two leaves with lower corner torn away (text not affected), couple of trivial smudges internally, but remarkable survival in outstanding condition, original paper boards and spines with amazingly little wear, text showing almost no signs of use (two of the volumes, of course, not having been read). Phillip J. Pirages 66 - 78 2015 $1000

Hering, Ewald *Memory, Lectures on the Specific Energies of the Nervous System.* Chicago: Open Court, 1913. Fourth edition, very good+ with bit rubbed spine ends. Beasley Books 2013 - 2015 $45

Herman, Leonhard *Jazz Memories.* Paris: Filipacchi, 1995. First edition, folio, original dark grey boards lettered black at spine and cover, illustrations in black and white, boldly signed on half title, 8 page stapled English translation loosely inserted, fine in very good dust jacket with slight yellowing at spine. Any Amount of Books 2015 - A97141 2015 £180

Hermann, Jacques Dominique Armand De *De l"etat de l'Espagne et ses Colonies Considere Sous le Rapport des Interets Politiques et Commerciaux de la France...* Paris: C. J. Trouve Mars, 1824. First edition, 8vo., half title, original wrappers, entirely uncut, fine, rare. John Drury Rare Books 2015 - 17859 2015 $133

Herndon, Angelo *The Negro Quarterly. Volume I. No. 2 Summer 1942.* New York: Negro Publication Society of America, 1942. 8vo., paper wrappers, cover little soiled and rippled, small bit of corner missing on rear cover and two leaves, otherwise very good. Second Life Books Inc. 191 - 49 2015 $75

Hernu, Sandy *Q The Biography of Desmond Llewelyn.* London: S. B. Publications, 1999. First edition, limited to 1000 copies signed by author and Llewelyn, this #514, fine in fine dust jacket. Buckingham Books March 2015 - 14983 2015 $375

Herodianus *Herodian of Alexandria his History of the Twenty Roman Caesars and Emperors of His Time.* London: printed for Hugh Perry, 1629. Small quarto, cropping affects text of dedication page and list of emperors (sig. b), very light degree of marginal annotation throughout the book, some ink and some pencil, possibly in the hand of Thistlethwayte and or of Allan Heywood Bright (1862-1941) who owned the book in the 20th century, otherwise nice example in slightly faded and worn but very sound, attractive binding, ex-libris Alexandris Thistlthwayte, autograph note by Edmond Malone bound in and also bound in are couple of sheets of handwritten notes in later hand, binding by Haines of Liverpool, half red Levant morocco ruled gilt over marbled boards, spine with six compartments, with lettered gilt or bearing crescent and star device, marbled endpapers, top edge gilt,.   Any Amount of Books   2015 - C11789   2015   £2000

Hersch, Roger D. *Visual and Technical Aspects of Type.* Cambridge: Cambridge University Press, 1993. Small 4to., paper covered boards, 22 color illustrations, black and white illustrations.   Oak Knoll Books   306 - 217   2015 $100

Hersen, Michel *The Clinical Psychology Handbook.* New York: Pergamon, 1983. First edition, hardcover, fine, 850 pages.   Beasley Books   2013 - 2015 $45

Hersey, John *The Call.* Franklin Center: 1985. First edition, signed, gilt decorated leather with raised bands, all edges gilt, marbled endpapers, illustrations by Herbert Tauss, as new.   Stephen Lupack   March 2015 - 2015 $40

Hersey, John *Hiroshima.* New York: Limited Editions Club, 1983. Limited to 1500 numbered copies, oblong small 4to., full black aniline cowhide, slipcase, Monthly Newsletter loosely inserted, signed by author, Robert Penn Warren and artist, Jacob Lawrence, silk screens by Lawrence.   Oak Knoll Books   25 - 51   2015 $900

Hervey, John *The Reply of a Member of Parliament to the Mayor of His Corporation.* London: printed by J. Roberts, 1733. First edition, 8vo., modern calf backed boards, printed label on upper cover, very good.   John Drury Rare Books   2015 - 15910   2015 $221

Hervey, Maurice H. *Dean Man's Court.* New York: Stokes, 1895. First American edition, front hinge cracked and name on front endpaper, otherwise very good in pictorial cloth covered boards without dust jacket.   Mordida Books   March 2015 - 001082   2015 $90

Hervieu, Louise *Le Livre De Genevieve.* Paris: Bernheim Jeune, 1920. #129 of 150, with 20 illustrations by Hervieu, wrappers are near fine, slight running and one tear covered by publisher's glassine that has few tears and wrinkles, 4to.   Beasley Books   2013 - 2015 $300

Hess, Eckhard H. *The Tell-Tale Eye. How Your Eyes Reveal Hidden Thoughts and Emotions.* New York: Van Nostrand Reinhold, 1975. First edition, near fine but for owner's neat name, near fine dust jacket but for sunned spine, large 8vo.   Beasley Books   2013 - 2015 $40

Hess, Joseph F. *The Autobiography of Joseph F. Hess.* E. R. Andrews, Printer, 1886. 21cm., in orange pictorial wrappers, rare, minor chipping to wrapper edges, interior clean.   Buckingham Books   March 2015 - 35606   2015 $2100

Hesse Schwartzbourg, Princess *Queens & Kings and Other Things.* London: Chatto & Windus, n.d. circa, 1880. Folio, blue cloth stamped in black and gold, all edges gilt, light cover soil and spine expertly repaired, else tight and very good+, printed one side of paper, pictures highlighted in gold.   Aleph-Bet Books, Inc.   108 - 348   2015 $850

Hesse, Hermann *Feuerwerk. (Fireworks).* Olten: Privately printed by Vereinigung Olter Bucherfreunde, 1946. Limited to 350 numbered copies this is copy no 326, signed and inscribed by author, small 8vo., near fine, original printed wrappers, minimal cover edgewear.   By the Book, L. C. Special List 10 - 28   2015 $500

Hesse, Hermann *Steppenwolf.* Westport: Limited Editions Club, 1977. Limited to 1600 copies, signed and inscribed by author, signed by artist, Helmut Ackermann, illustrations, this copy not numbered, original glassine dust jacket with sun and chips to spine, 4to., original slipcase with spine lettering, mild sun.   By the Book, L. C.   Special List 10 - 27   2015 $200

Hesse, Raymond *Fleurs De France. Fables et Esquisses.* La Tradition, 1946. No. 87 of 100 copies, that include an extra suite of Hemard's color illustrations (in black and white) from an edition of 550 copies, unbound signatures laid into wrappers, contents fine, bit of foxing to blank spine of wrappers, titled board chemise and matching box bit sunned, small 4to.   Beasley Books   2013 - 2015 $400

Hesseltine, W. B. *Military Prisons of St. Louis.* privately printed, n.d. circa, 1929. First edition thus, 8vo., pages beginning to uniformly tan at edges, else fine.   Buckingham Books   March 2015 - 32658   2015 $200

Hester, T. I. *Names of the Committee of Subscribers, for the Relief of the Suffering French Clergy, Refugees in the British Dominions.* N.P.: London? n.d., 1793. John Drury Rare Books   2015 - 21847   2015 $787

Heward, Constance *Ameliaranne and the Green Umbrella.* Philadelphia: George W. Jacobs, 1920. First edition, 8vo., green cloth, pictorial paste-on, near fine in worn dust jacket with pieces off, edges and archival mends on verso, full page color illustrations and black and white pictorial borders by S. B. Pearse, printed on coated paper. Aleph-bet Books, Inc. 109 - 345 2015 $275

Heward, Constance *Mr. Pickles and the Party.* London: Frederick Warne, 1926. 12mo., green boards, pictorial paste-on, fine, printed on coated paper, illustrations by Anne Anderson with many beautiful full page and smaller color illustrations plus pictorial endpapers, few black and whites. Aleph-bet Books, Inc. 109 - 23 2015 $150

Hey, Richard *A Dissertation on the Pernicious Effects of Gaming.* Cambridge: printed by J. Archdeacon for J. & J. Merrill In Cambridge and for T. Cadell in the Strand, 1783. First edition, 8vo., tiny blank strip removed from upper margin of title (removing a signature?) but nowhere near printed surface, contemporary tree calf, gilt, little wear to spine and joints, but overall very good crisp copy, very scarce. John Drury Rare Books 2015 - 22685 2015 $1661

Hey, Richard *Observations on the Nature of Civil Liberty and the Principles of Government.* London: T. Cadell and T. and J. Merrill in Cambridge, 1776. First edition, 8vo., wanting half title, recent marbled boards, lettered on spine very good. John Drury Rare Books March 2015 - 25020 2015 $656

Heyer, Georgette *Beauvallet.* New York: Longmans, Green, 1930. First US edition, octavo, frontispiece, titlepage and endpapers by Henry Pitz, folding pedigree, bookplate on verso front free endpaper, covers little marked, very good in scarce, chipped and torn dust jacket darkened at spine and defective at head of spine. Peter Ellis, Bookseller 2014 - 012181 2015 £350

Heyer, Georgette *A Blunt Instrument.* Garden City: Doubleday Crime Club, 1938. First American edition, near fine in very good dust jacket with faded spine, chips at corners and several closed tears. Mordida Books March 2015 - 010210 2015 $200

Heyer, Georgette *Detection Unlimited.* London: Heinemann, 1953. First edition, fine in price clipped dust jacket. Mordida Books March 2015 - 010212 2015 $100

Heysham, John *An Account of the Jail Fever, or Thyphus Carecerum; as it appeared at Carlisle in the year 1781.* London: T. Cadell, J. Murray, R. Faulder and J. Milliken bookseller Carlilse, 1782. 8vo., large, unopened copy, stitched as issued, titlepage lightly soiled, final (blank) page browned and creased in lower margin, overall near fine, rare. John Drury Rare Books 2015 - 25711 2015 $1049

Heywood, Benjamin *An Address Delivered at the Opening of the new Building for the Manchester Mechanic's Institution on Monday 14th May 1827.* Robinson & Bent, 1827. Only separate edition, 8vo., 16 pages, spotted and generally rather soiled, old institutional inkstamp on title and related label on last leaf (pasted to upper margin with resulting loss of 4 or 5 words), disbound, spine crudely taped, rare. John Drury Rare Books March 2015 - 18532 2015 $266

Heywood, Samuel *The Right of Protestant Dissenter to a Compleat Toleration Asserted; Containing an Historical Account of the Text Laws...* London: J. Johnson and J. Debrett, 1789. Second edition, 8vo., light old waterstain, affecting upper part of few leaves, good copy, new boards, lettered. John Drury Rare Books 2015 - 24700 2015 $133

Hiaasen, Carl *Team Rodent.* New York: Ballantine, 1998. First edition, signed by author, very fine in soft covers. Mordida Books March 2015 - 07477 2015 $90

Hiaasen, Carl *Tourist Season.* New York: Putnam, 1986. First edition, very fine in dust jacket. Mordida Books March 2015 - 011415 2015 $250

Hickson, William Edward *Taxes on Knowledge. Reduction or Abolition of the Newspaper Stamp-Duty?* London: C. & W. Reynell Square, n.d. but, 1836. First separate edition, 8vo., 16 pages, contemporary signature of J. W. Mylne at head of title, recent plain wrappers, very good, rare. John Drury Rare Books 2015 - 19590 2015 $133

Hiebert, Helen *Alpha Beta.* Edwards: 2010. Artist's Book, abecedary and shadow lantern book, one of 25 copies, all on artist-made cotton paper, machine made gampi paper and balsa wood, each copy hand numbered by artist, page size 56 x 4 7/16 inches, 26 leaves plus folio colophon, bound in flexible Japanese hinge based on Shadow lantern featured in artist's book, paper illuminated, housed in custom made grey cloth over boards box by Claudia Cohen, lined with artist's own handmade wine colored paper and title, ALPHA, BETA is accomplished in white in wine colored paper as a pseudo-watermark paper and affixed to lid of box, flexible hinge allows book to be displayed in multiple ways, front of alphabet is Arts and Crafts, designed by Dard Hunter, dark, wine colored paper affixed to balsa wood over gampi paper is cut-out so light coming through gampi paper illuminates the letter with alphabet letter cutout casting a shadow onto second layer of handmade paper, paper made by artist has letters of alphabet engraved in it and was made by placing rubber letters on mould to form the letters using a watermarking technique. Priscilla Juvelis - Rare Books 63 - 8 2015 $750

Hiebert, Helen *Spring Theory.* Avon: 2010. One of 10 copies, all on handmade abaca paper with string drawings embedded into paper, each copy hand numbered and signed by artist, Helen Hiebert and poet, Carl Adamschick, page size 12 x 18 inches, 6 string drawings plus 1 page text with colophon, loose as issued in black cloth over boards clamshell box designed by Sandy Tilcock with Helen Heibert's string drawings are in red as well as white string and were inspired by knot illustrations in the Ashley Book of Knots, text printed letterpress by Sandy Tilcock, beautiful textured paper is the perfect backdrop for the drawings in string.   Priscilla Juvelis - Rare Books   62 - 7   2015 $1800

Higgens, Aileen *Dream Blocks.* New York: Duffield, 1908. First edition, 4to., tan cloth, large pictorial paste-on on cover, near fine, illustrations by Jessie Willcox Smith, with color pictorial endpapers, pictorial titlepage plus 14 beautiful color plates (printed on heavy coated stock), red and black illustrations in text, particularly nice, scarce.   Aleph-bet Books, Inc.   109 - 448   2015 $1200

Higgins, Anthony *New Castle Delaware 1651-1939.* Boston: Houghton Mifflin, 1939. First edition, limited to 765 copies, of which 750 are for sale, each numbered and signed by author, this copy 384 signed by author and Bayard Wootten, photographer, tall quarto, map sections on endpapers, section of plates, former owner's name and bookplate, else fine, housed in dark blue cloth slipcase, leather label on spine and titles stamped in gilt.   Buckingham Books   March 2015 - 20235   2015 $250

Higgins, George V. *The Friends of Eddie Coyle.* New York: Alfred A. Knopf, 1972. First edition, signed by author, variant with blue cloth and green topstain (no priority known), most uncommon to find signed, lightly faded spine and board edges, hint of fading to jacket spine, overall near fine in like dust jacket.   Royal Books   46 - 31   2015 $425

Higgins, George V. *The Friends of Eddie Coyle.* New York: Alfred A. Knopf, 1972. First edition, green cloth, top edge green, fine in dust jacket.   Buckingham Books   March 2015 - 37212   2015 $175

Higgins, Godfrey *The Celtic Druids or an Attempt to Shew that the Druids Were the Priests of Oriental Colonies Who Emigrated from India...* London: Rowland Hunter, 1829. Second edition, 4to., additional engraved titlepage on india paper, map and 45 numbered plates, 7 vignettes in text, 7 vignette tailpieces, occasional foxing and with some offsetting from folded plates, few pencil annotations, full contemporary diced tan calf, decorated gilt borders, raised gilt bands with elaborate gilt compartments, black morocco label, imperceptible expert repair to hinges, presentation inscription on titlepage "Sir Willm. Pilkington Baronet Chevet, Hull, Yorkshire with author's kindest regards, Oriental Club, Jan. 1833, Hanover Sq., London", handsome copy.   Jarndyce Antiquarian Booksellers   CCXI - 140   2015   £650

Higginson, Thomas Wentworth   1823-1911 *Ruling at Second-Hand (series title) Political Equality Series. Volume I no. 9 June 1905.* 12mo., single sheet, 5 1/2 x 3 1/4 inches folded to make 4 pages, little nicked, faded on last page.   Second Life Books Inc.   189 - 119   2015 $60

Highly Important to the Commercial World and to Persons in General who Keep Cash accounts with Bankers. the Interesting Trial (Lately tried Before Mr. Justice Burrough and a Special Jury of Price Versus Marsh, Stracey, Fauntleroy and Graham (Bankers of Berners Street). London: published by S. Chappell, n.d., 1823. 12mo., 32 pages, titlepage soiled, lower margins soiled throughout, stitched as issued, entirely uncut and partially unopened, now preserved in marbled wrappers, very rare.   John Drury Rare Books   2015 - 24408   2015 $787

Highmore, Anthony *Pietas Londinensis; the History, Design and Present State of the Various Public Charities in and Near London.* London: C. Cradock & W. Joy, Doig & Stirling, 1814. 8vo., half title, slight old dampstain in lower margin of first few leaves, one leaf with marginal tear (no loss), one page with corner text not printed, bound in handsome recent binding of tan morocco, raised bands, gilt lines and labels, bookplate of Royal Institution of Chartered Surveyors, good copy.   John Drury Rare Books   2015 - 24505   2015 $874

Highsmith, Patricia *Deep Water.* New York: Harper & Bros., 1957. First edition, fine in dust jacket with light wear to spine ends, small closed tear to top edge of rear panel, couple of small stains to back panel, brilliant copy.   Buckingham Books   March 2015 - 24571   2015 $2000

Highsmith, Patricia *A Game for the Living: a Novel of Suspense.* London: Heinemann, 1958. First edition, 8vo., signed by author, very good in like dust jacket.   Any Amount of Books   2015 - A90992   2015   £300

Highsmith, Patricia *The Glass Cell.* Garden City: Doubleday & Co., 1964. First edition, small date in ink on front flyleaf, else fine, bright, square copy in dust jacket with hint of wear to spine ends and corners, exceptional.   Buckingham Books   March 2015 - 27324   2015 $750

Highsmith, Patricia *Little Tales of Misogny.* New York: Penzler, 1986. First American edition, very fine, one of 250 numbered copies signed by author, very fine in slipcase, without dust jacket as issued.   Mordida Books   March 2015 - 001096   2015 $100

Highsmith, Patricia *Mermaids on the Golf Course.* New York: Penzler, 1988. First American edition, one of 250 numbered copies signed by author, very fine in slipcase.   Mordida Books   March 2015 - 010719   2015 $100

Highsmith, Patricia *Ripley Under Water.* London: Limited Editions Club, 1991. First edition, one of 150 specially bound numbered copies, signed by author, very fine in tissue dust jacket.   Mordida Books   March 2015 - 005256   2015 $300

Highsmith, Patricia *Where the Action Is and other Stories.* Helsinki: Eurographica, 1989. One of 350 numbered copies signed by author, very fine in plain stiff wrappers, with printed dust jacket.   Mordida Books   March 2015 - 005255   2015 $325

Hilary of Poitiers *Divi Hilarii Pictavorum Episcopi Lucubrationes...* Basel: Io. Frobenius, 1523. First edition, folio, 2 volumes, decorative initials and headpieces, contemporary full calf blindstamped on both sides with design of heraldic devices, rebacked (early) with red and gilt spine label, from the library of Allan Heywood Bright (1862-1941), loosely inserted is an ALS from fellow book collector E. Gordon Duff to Bright thanking him for the loan of the book, front board detached, rear joint and head and foot of spine well worn, armorial bookplate of Sir John Leveson Gower of Trentham, worming from titlepage on decreasing from about 60 holes throughout the first volume, few early ink annotations, ownership inscription of G(eorgius) Folberti(us), pencilled note identifies this book's provenance as "Sutherland Library".   Any Amount of Books   2015 - 12863   2015   £800

Hilbert, David *Grundzuge Der Theoretischen Logik. (Principles of Theoretical Logic).* Berlin: Julius Springer, 1928. First edition, 8vo., near fine, original printed yellow cloth covered boards mild sun spine, owner name.   By the Book, L. C.   44 - 56   2015 $185

Hill, Archibald V. *Living Machinery. Six Lectures Delivered Before a Juvenile Auditory at the Royal Institution Christmas 1926.* London: G. Bell, 1927. First edition, 8vo., very good++, foxing to endpapers and edges, in very good dust jacket with small piece missing, not affecting title, chips, short closed tears and mild soil.   By the Book, L. C. Special List 10 - 76   2015 $200

Hill, Edward Burlingame *Modern French Music.* Boston and New York: Houghton Mifflin Co., 1924. First edition, blue cloth gilt, embossed stamp of Virgil Thomson on titlepage, wear and small tears to cloth mostly along bottom extremities, else very good inscribed by author for Thomson, his assistant and friend.   Between the Covers Rare Books, Inc.   187 - 190   2015 $1250

Hill, Henry *Incidents In Chili, South America 1817-1821.* Weymouth: A. W. Blanchard, Printer, 1889. First edition, 8vo., red library buckram, gilt title on spine, very good ex-library, gilt accession numbers on spine, light soiling on title and last page, faint institutional stamp on rear pastedown.   Kaaterskill Books   19 - 75   2015 $500

Hill, Herbert *Anger and Beyond the Negro Writer in the United States.* New York: Harper and Row, 1966. First edition, inscribed by Hill, near fine in like dust jacket, but for one small internally mended tear at foot of front panel, 8vo.   Beasley Books   2013 - 2015 $40

Hill, James *Rita Hayworth: a memoir.* New York: Simon and Schuster, 1983. Uncorrected proof, moderately worn and read but tight, very good copy, Rex Harrison's copy with his ownership stamp.   Between the Covers Rare Books, Inc.   187 - 126   2015 $300

Hill, Jim Dan *The Texas Navy in Forgotten Battles and Shirt Sleeve Diplomacy.* Chicago: University of Chicago Press, 1937. (1950). First edition, cloth, 6 plates, very scarce, previous owners bookplate, else clean, bright, near fine, inscribed and numbered by author on half title.   Buckingham Books   March 2015 - 27930   2015 $275

Hill, Matthew Davenport *Plans for the Government and Liberal Instruction of Boys, in Large Numbers Drawn from Experience.* London: printed for G. and W. B. Whittaker, 1822. First edition, with half title, errata slip (tipped in before B1, with 1 errata), and prelim ad leaf dated July 1822, well bound recently in old style blue-grey boards with printed spine label, entirely uncut, very good.   John Drury Rare Books   March 2015 - 20394   2015 $874

Hill, Octavia *Homes of the London Poor...* New York: New York State Charities Aid Association 52 East 20th Street, 1875. True first edition, 8vo., 78 pages, dampstaining to several leaves at beginning and end of volume, contemporary dark green leather backed marbled boards, marbled paper sides, patches of wear, neatly rebacked, ownership inscriptions.   John Drury Rare Books   March 2015 - 18994   2015 $266

Hill, Reginald *Another Death in Venice.* London: Collins, 1976. First edition, small bump to bottom of spine, else very good in dust jacket with small crease to bottom of spine.   Buckingham Books   March 2015 - 28671   2015 $225

Hill, Reginald *Arms and the Women.* Harper Collins, 2000. First edition, 8vo., original black boards, backstrip lettered gilt, dust jacket, fine.   Blackwell's Rare Books   B179 - 177   2015   £20

Hill, Reginald *A Fairly Dangerous Thing.* London: Collins, 1972. First edition, fine in dust jacket.   Buckingham Books   March 2015 - 28670   2015 $300

Hill, Reginald *Fell of Dark.* London: Collins, 1971. First edition, signed, fine in dust jacket with light wear to foot of spine.   Buckingham Books   March 2015 - 9529   2015 $750

Hill, Reginald *Pascoe's Ghost and Other Brief chronicles of Crime.* London: Collins, 1979. First edition, fine in fine dust jacket.   Buckingham Books   March 2015 - 31378   2015 $250

Hill, Reginald *A Pinch of Snuff.* London: Collins, 1978. First edition, first impression, 8vo., slight rubbing at edges, fine in near fine dust jacket, excellent condition, from the Donald Rudd collection of detective fiction.   Any Amount of Books   2015 - A96965   2015   £260

Hill, Richard *Hard Measure, or a Real Statement of Facts, in a Letter to the Burgesses and Freemen Burgesses, of the Town of Shrewsbury.* London: printed for J. Stockdale and to be had of all the booksellers in Shrewsbury, 1796. (1795). Second edition, 8vo., trifling small stain on titlepage, fairly recent boards, spine lettered, very good.   John Drury Rare Books   March 2015 - 18266   2015 $266

Hill, S. S. *Travels on the Shores of the Baltic. Extended to Moscow.* London: Arthur Hall, Virtue & Co., 1854. Half title, 2 pages ads, 24 page catalog (May 1854), original green cloth, blocked in blind, lettered gilt, slightly rubbed, inner hinges slightly cracking, bookplate of John Percival Hill, inscribed "Mrs. Branford from her most attached friend Mary Ann Hill".   Jarndyce Antiquarian Booksellers   CCXI - 141   2015   £280

Hill, William *Jackie Boy in Rainbowland.* Chicago: Rand McNally, 1911. First edition, 4to., brick red cloth stamped in gold, pictorial paste-on, minimal shelfwear, else near fine, 8 color plates including plate on cover, 6 color illustrations in-text, scarce, beautiful copy.   Aleph-Bet Books, Inc.   108 - 108   2015 $300

Hillenbrand, Laura *Seabiscuit.* New York: Random House, 2001. First edition, fine in very near fine dust jacket with orange of spine lettering faded to yellow.   Ken Lopez, Bookseller   164 - 87   2015 $250

Hillerman, Tony *The Blessing Way.* New York: Harper and Row, 1970. First edition, fine in lovely, near fine dust jacket, bit of usual fading to jacket spine, but only to titling, some slight rubbing at spine ends and corners, else exceptionally sharp, unread copy, from the collection of Duke Collier.   Royal Books   36 - 189   2015 $3000

Hillerman, Tony *The Blessing Way.* New York: Harper & Row, 1972. Fifth printing, fine in price clipped dust jacket with slight spine fading, signed by author.   Mordida Books   March 2015 - 011452   2015 $200

Hillerman, Tony *The Boy Who Made Dragonfly.* New York: Harper and Row, 1972. First edition, nicely inscribed by author to fellow crime writer, John and Pat Ball, from the collection of Duke Collier.   Royal Books   36 - 192   2015 $1750

Hillerman, Tony *Coyote Waits.* New York: Harper and Row, 1990. First edition, uncorrected proof, fine in yellow printed soft covers, signed by author.   Mordida Books   March 2015 - 009597   2015 $100

Hillerman, Tony *Coyote Waits.* New York: Harper & Row, 1990. First edition, signed and numbered by author, limited to 500 copies, this #481, fine, fine decorated slipcase, as issued.   Buckingham Books   March 2015 - 20664   2015 $175

Hillerman, Tony *Dance Hall of the Dead.* New York: Harper & Row, 1973. First edition, signed by author, laid in is author's business card from University of New Mexico, exceptional copy.   Buckingham Books   March 2015 - 28626   2015 $2250

Hillerman, Tony *Dance Hall of the Dead.* New York: Harper & Row, 1973. First edition, signed by author, very fine in dust jacket with tiny scrape on front panel.   Mordida Books   March 2015 - 011449   2015 $1000

Hillerman, Tony *Dance Hall of the Dead.* New York: 1991. Limited edition of 126, numbered and signed by author, lightly rubbed and slight spotting to text block edges, else near fine in like slipcase.   Dumont Maps & Books of the West   131 - 53   2015 $150

Hillerman, Tony *The Dark Wind.* New York: Harper & Row, 1982. First edition, very fine in dust jacket.   Mordida Books   March 2015 - 009066   2015 $200

Hillerman, Tony *The Dark Wind.* New York: Harper Row, 1982. First edition, signed, fine in dust jacket with moderate wear to fore edges and tiny closed tear on back panel.   Buckingham Books   March 2015 - 20614   2015 $275

Hillerman, Tony *The Fly on the Wall.* New York: Harper and Row, 1971. First edition, review copy, publisher's slip laid in, fine in bright, very good plus dust jacket with light rubbing and shallow creasing on spine ends and soil to rear panel, from the collection of Duke Collier.   Royal Books   36 - 194   2015 $1000

Hillerman, Tony *The Ghostway.* San Diego: Dennis McMillan, 1984. First edition, one of 300 numbered copies of which this is no. 28 signed by author, very fine in dust jacket.   Mordida Books   March 2015 - 911475   2015 $600

Hillerman, Tony *The Ghostway.* San Diego: McMillan, 1984. First edition, limited to 300 numbered copies signed by author, this copy 286, fine in dust jacket.   Buckingham Books   March 2015 - 32983   2015 $750

Hillerman, Tony *The Ghostway.* London: Gollancz, 1985. First English edition, fine in dust jacket.   Mordida Books   March 2015 - 007480   2015 $100

Hillerman, Tony *The Ghostway.* New York: Harper & Row, 1985. First Harper and Row edition, signed, fine in fine dust jacket.   Buckingham Books   March 2015 - 20612   2015 $300

Hillerman, Tony *The Great Taos Bank Robbery and Other Indian Country Affairs.* Albuquerque: University of New Mexico Press, 1973. First edition, fine and unread in fine dust jacket, first issue jacket with only one image on rear panel, from the collection of Duke Collier.   Royal Books   36 - 196   2015 $650

Hillerman, Tony *The Great Taos Bank Robbery.* Albuquerque: University of New Mexico, 1973. First edition, small label moved from front endpaper, otherwise fine in dust jacket with tiny nick at top of spine, first state with grayish cloth covers boards and single picture of Shipwrock on back panel of jacket.   Mordida Books   March 2015 - 010901   2015 $350

Hillerman, Tony *Listening Woman.* New York: Harper and Row, 1978. Uncorrected proof, signed by Hillerman, small closed tear at fore edge of front wrapper, else fine in plain red wrappers as issued. From the collection of Duke Collier.   Royal Books   36 - 191   2015 $1750

Hillerman, Tony *Listening Woman.* New York: Harper & Row, 1978. First edition, fine, page edges slightly darkened, otherwise fine in dust jacket, signed by author.   Mordida Books   March 2015 - 011451   2015 $650

Hillerman, Tony *Listening Woman.* New York: Harper and Row, 1978. First edition, near fine in fine dust jacket, inscribed by author for Bruce Taylor, some loss to titling on backstrip (problem endemic to this title), else near fine in like dust jacket with none of the usual spine fading, attractive copy, from the collection of Duke Collier.   Royal Books   36 - 193   2015 $1250

Hillerman, Tony *People of Darkness.* New York: Harper, 1980. Uncorrected proof, signed by author, fine in plain red wrappers, from the collection of Duke Collier.   Royal Books   36 - 197   2015 $450

Hillerman, Tony *People of Darkness.* New York: Harper & Row, 1980. First edition, fine in dust jacket.   Mordida Books   March 2015 - 008349   2015 $400

Hillerman, Tony *People of Darkness.* New York: Harper & Row, 1980. First edition, tiny nick on bottom edge of back cover, otherwise fine in dust jacket, signed by author.   Mordida Books   March 2015 - 001450   2015 $500

Hillerman, Tony *Rio Grande.* Portland: Charles H. Beeding, 1975. First edition, fine in price clipped dust jacket with short crease on inner flap.   Mordida Books   March 2015 - 003107   2015 $175

Hillerman, Tony *Sacred Clowns.* New York: Harper Collins, 1993. First edition, fine in pale gray printed soft covers, uncorrected proof copy.   Mordida Books   March 2015 - 009598   2015 $85

Hillerman, Tony *Skinwalkers.* New York: Harper, 1986. First edition, very fine in dust jacket.   Mordida Books   March 2015 - 009907   2015 $85

Hillerman, Tony *Talking Mysteries.* Albuquerque: University of New Mexico, 1991. First edition, signed by author, very fine in dust jacket.   Mordida Books   March 2015 - 012055   2015 $85

Hillerman, Tony *A Thief of Time.* New York: Harper & Row, 1988. First edition, limited to 250 specially bound numbered copies signed by author, very fine in slipcase, without dust jacket as issued.   Buckingham Books   March 2015 - 20609   2015 $275

Hillerman, Tony *A Thief of Time.* New York: Harper & Row, 1988. One of 250 specially bound numbered copies, signed by author, very fine in slipcase.   Mordida Books   March 2015 - 007481   2015 $250

Hillerman, Tony *A Thief of Time.* New York: Harper & Row, 1988. First edition, fine in full color pictorial soft covers, uncorrected proof.   Mordida Books   March 2015 - 009596   2015 $85

Hillerman, Tony *Words, Weather and Wolfmen.* Gallup: Southwesterner Books, 1989. First edition, one of 26 lettered copies, this being a non-lettered presentation copy, with full color drawing by Franklin laid in, signed by author and artist, Ernie Franklin, and the publisher, fine in fine slipcase, from the collection of Duke Collier.   Royal Books   36 - 195   2015 $750

Hilliard, David *This Side of Glory: The Autobiography of David Hilliard and the Story of the Black Panther Party.* Boston: Little Brown and Co., 1993. Uncorrected proof, printed red wrappers, little light use, else very near fine, laid in is letter from publisher to Civil Rights pioneer Julian Bond, asking for comments on the book.   Between the Covers Rare Books   197 - 60   2015 $125

Hillyard, Susan *Before Oil: A Personal Memoir of Abu Dhabi 1954-1958.* Bakewell: Ashridge Press, 2002. First edition, large folio, original publisher's white cloth lettered at spine, black and white illustrations, including press cuttings, about fine, clean, very good+ dust jacket with very faint wear, excellent condition. Any Amount of Books 2015 - C16448 2015 £230

Hilton, George W. *The Cable Car in America.* Berkeley: Howell-North Books, 1971. First edition, frontispiece, 684 illustrations from photos and diagrams, text maps, map endpapers, brown cloth lettered black, owner's signature on end, very fine, pictorial dust jacket. Argonaut Book Shop Holiday Season 2014 - 123 2015 $60

Hilton, John Buxton *Death in Midwinter.* London: Cassell, 1969. First edition, fine in dust jacket with short closed tear, inscribed by author. Mordida Books March 2015 - 001107 2015 $75

Himes, Chester *Black on Black Baby Sister and Selected Writings.* Garden City: Doubleday, 1973. First edition, 8o., green cloth with black spine, cover little scuffed at edges, else very good, tight copy in little chipped and soiled dust jacket. Second Life Books Inc. 190 - 93 2015 $125

Himes, Chester *Blind Man with a Pistol.* William Morrow and Co., 1969. First edition, fine in bright, unfaded dust jacket, sharp copy. Buckingham Books March 2015 - 37744 2015 $175

Himes, Chester *Blind Man with a Pistol.* New York: Morrow, 1969. First edition, 8vo., paper over boards, Himes's obit laid in, cover slightly scuffed at edges, else very good, tight copy in scuffed and little browned dust jacket, some offsetting to front endpaper and half title. Second Life Books Inc. 190 - 94 2015 $150

Himes, Chester *Blind Man with Pistol.* New York: William Morrow, 1969. First edition, fine in near fine dust jacket with single crease at front panel and one faint stain. Between the Covers Rare Books 197 - 30 2015 $150

Himes, Chester *Une Affaire de Viol. (A Case of Rape).* Paris: Editions les Yeux Ouverts, 1963. First edition, text in French, small light stain to top of rear wrapper, else fine in glassine, dust jacket, signed by author, scarce thus. Between the Covers Rare Books 197 - 23 2015 $650

Himes, Chester *A Case of Rape.* New York: Targ, 1980. One of 350 signed copies, first edition in English, 8vo., author's signature, paper over boards with cloth spine, nice in chipped, original tissue dust jacket. Second Life Books Inc. 190 - 95 2015 $200

Himes, Chester *A Case of Rape.* New York: Targ Editions, 1980. First American edition, fine in quarter cloth and papercovered boards, near fine unprinted glassine dust jacket with small tears at extremities, one of 350 copies, signed by author, warmly inscribed by publisher William Targ to novelist Brad Morrow. Between the Covers Rare Books, Inc. 187 - 127 2015 $250

Himes, Chester *A Case of Rape.* Washington: Howard University, 1984. First trade edition, 8vo., red cloth, price stickers on dust jacket front and flap, otherwise as new. Second Life Books Inc. 190 - 96 2015 $50

Himes, Chester *Cast the First Stone.* New York: Coward McCann, 1952. First edition, 8vo., very good, tight copy in browned dust jacket, bookstore stamp on endpaper. Second Life Books Inc. 190 - 97 2015 $275

Himes, Chester *The Collected Stories of...* New York: Thunder's Mouth, 1991. First American edition, 8vo., purple cloth, nice, dust jacket. Second Life Books Inc. 190 - 98 2015 $45

Himes, Chester *Cotton Comes to Harlem.* New York: Putnam's, 1965. First American edition, 8vo., paper over boards, cloth spine, edges little soiled, otherwise very good, tight copy in scuffed and little chipped dust jacket. Second Life Books Inc. 190 - 99 2015 $165

Himes, Chester *Cotton Comes to Harlem.* New York: G. P. Putnam's, 1965. First American edition, fine in very near fine dust jacket with 3 short and nominally noticeable tears, less than usual amount of rubbing, nice. Between the Covers Rare Books 197 - 27 2015 $300

Himes, Chester *Cotton Comes to Harlem.* London: Frederick Miller, 1965. First edition, fine, unread in fine dust jacket, from the collection of Duke Collier. Royal Books 36 - 198 2015 $650

Himes, Chester *The Heat's On.* New York: G. P. Putnam's Sons, 1966. First edition, fine in near fine dust jacket with single closed tear on front panel. Between the Covers Rare Books 197 - 29 2015 $200

Himes, Chester *The Heat's On.* New York: Putnam's, 1966. 8vo., paper over boards with cloth spine, very good, tight copy in scuffed dust jacket. Second Life Books Inc. 190 - 100 2015 $135

Himes, Chester *If He Hollers Let Him Go.* New York: Doubleday Doran & Co., 1945. First edition, author's first book, fine in bright, unfaded dust jacket with some very minor paper loss at spine ends. Buckingham Books March 2015 - 35828 2015 $875

Himes, Chester *If He Hollars Let Him Go.* London: Falcon, 1947. First UK edition, 8vo., black cloth, very good, tight copy in little chipped dust jacket.   Second Life Books Inc.   190 - 191   2015 $325

Himes, Chester *Lonely Crusade.* Alfred A. Knopf, 1947. First edition, fine in dust jacket (lightly soiled on rear cover and light wear to spine ends).   Buckingham Books   March 2015 - 37745   2015 $300

Himes, Chester *Lonely Crusade.* New York: Knopf, 1947. First edition, 8vo., cover scuffed at edges and somewhat spotted, otherwise very good, tight copy.   Second Life Books Inc.   190 - 103   2015 $225

Himes, Chester *Lonely Crusade.* London: Falcon Press, 1950. First UK edition, 8vo., black cloth, nice in little scuffed dust jacket.   Second Life Books Inc.   190 - 102   2015 $250

Himes, Chester *My Life of Absurdity... volume II.* Garden City: Doubleday, 1976. First edition, 8vo., photos, edges of cover little rubbed, otherwise nice in little soiled dust jacket.   Second Life Books Inc.   190 - 104   2015 $45

Himes, Chester *Pinktoes.* London: Olympia Press, 1961. First edition, paperback original, fine and unread in green wrappers with black and white title, rule and design as issued, 'new price' stamp bottom right corner of rear wrapper, else pristine, most uncommon, from the collection of Duke Collier.   Royal Books   36 - 199   2015 $550

Himes, Chester *Pinktoes a novel.* New York: Putnam's, 1965. First American edition, 8vo., paper over boards with cloth spine, cover slightly faded at edges, otherwise very good tight in somewhat soiled and faded dust jacket.   Second Life Books Inc.   190 - 105   2015 $250

Himes, Chester *Plan B a Novel.* Jackson: University Press of Mississippi, 1993. First printing, small 8vo., about as new in dust jacket.   Second Life Books Inc.   190 - 106   2015 $125

Himes, Chester *The Primitive.* New York: Signet Books, 1956. 1955. First edition, Signet PBO 1264, light reader's crease, else fine in pictorial wrappers with terrific cover art by Tony Kokinas.   Buckingham Books   March 2015 - 29344   2015 $200

Himes, Chester *The Primitive.* New York: Signet, 1956. First printing, 12mo., cover little creased and soiled, else very good.   Second Life Books Inc.   190 - 107   2015 $150

Himes, Chester *The Quality of Hurt. The Autobiography of Volume I.* Garden City: Doubleday, 1972. First edition, 8vo., author's signature on blank, cover bumped at corners, otherwise very good in nicked and somewhat worn dust jacket, review copy with slip laid in.   Second Life Books Inc.   190 - 108   2015 $475

Himes, Chester *The Real Cool Killers.* London: Allison & Busby, 1985. First hardcover edition, pages slightly darkened otherwise fine in dust jacket.   Mordida Books   March 2015 - 008352   2015 $100

Himes, Chester *Run Man Run.* New York: Putnam's, 1966. First edition, 8vo., orange cloth, very good, tight copy, some chipping and soiling to dust jacket.   Second Life Books Inc.   190 - 109   2015 $150

Himes, Chester *Run Man Run.* New York: Putnam, 1966. First edition, owner name, small faint stain an little scrape, all on front fly, else fine in fine, price clipped dust jacket, with delicate pinkish orange spine lettering, which is usually found washed out, completely unfaded, nice, scarce.   Between the Covers Rare Books   197 - 28   2015 $375

Himes, Chester *The Third Generation.* Cleveland: World, 1954. First edition, 8vo., black cloth stamped in gilt and brown, cover stained, but very good, tight copy.   Second Life Books Inc.   190 - 110   2015 $40

Hinchcliffe, Henry Joyn *Thoughts on the repeal of the Usury laws Enclosed in a Letter to a Friend.* London: James Ridgway, 1828. First edition, 8vo., recently well bound in blue boards, lettered, very good.   John Drury Rare Books   March 2015 - 6622   2015 $266

Hinderwell, Thomas *History and Antiquities of Scarborough and the Vicinity with Views and Plans.* York: printed by William Blanchard for E. Bayley, successor to J. Schofield, Scarborough (and others), 1798. First edition, 4to., frontispiece, 4 engraved views, including frontispiece and 2 engraved maps, one folding, title and frontispiece foxed and occasional spotting throughout, early 19th century half rissai, joints worn, gilt edges.   Marlborough Rare Books   List 53 - 21   2015   £150

Hindley, Charles *The History of the Catnach Press at Berwick Upon Tweed, Alnwick Newcastle Upon Tyne and Seven Dials.* London: 1887. Second edition, 308 pages, many illustrations, many in color, tan buckram with printed titled labels, tipped in is excellent ALS in which author discusses Catnach, Bewick cuts for the book, very good, light wear, some spine tanning, small chip to spine label.   Stephen Lupack   March 2015 - 2015 $195

Hines, Gordon *Alfalfa Bill. an Intimate Biography.* Oklahoma City: Oklahoma Press, 1932. First trade edition, 8vo., inscribed by author, 14.2 x 22 cm., decorated cloth, frontispiece, fine, bright copy in internally reinforced dust jacket with moderate wear to spine ends and corner extremities.   Buckingham Books   March 2015 - 17218   2015 $175

Hines, Gordon *Alfalfa Bill. An Intimate Biography.* Oklahoma City: Oklahoma Press, 1932. First edition, limited to 375 copies set apart for private presentation, this #177 presented to R. H. Case and signed by R. H. Chase and Wm. H. Murray, Governor of Oklahoma and Gordon Hines, his biographer, two tone decorated cloth, frontispiece, illustrations, fine, bright copy.   Buckingham Books   March 2015 - 31793   2015 $675

Hines, J. W.   *Touching Incidents in the Life and Labours of a Pioneer on the Pacific Coast Since 1853.*   San Jose: Eaton & Co., 1911. First edition, small octavo, frontispiece, brown cloth stamped in dark brown on spine and front cover, some light spotting to lower front cover else very fine.   Argonaut Book Shop   Holiday Season 2014 - 124   2015 $90

Hinton, John Howard   *Letters Written During a Tour in Holland and North Germany in July and August 1851.* London: Houlston and Stoneman, 1851. First edition, 12mo., with final leaf of ads, original blindstamped cloth, spine lettered gilt, little worn and cracked at head and foot, very good, scarce.   John Drury Rare Books   2015 - 18217   2015 $168

Hinton, Milt   *Brass Line, The Stories and Photographs of Milt Hinton.*   Philadelphia: Temple University Press, 1988. First edition, oblong 4to., fine in fine dust jacket.   Beasley Books   2013 - 2015 $40

Hints to all Parties, by a man of No Party.   London: Bach and Co., 1834. First edition, rare, 8vo., very minor stiainng of last few leaves, else very good in original printed wrappers, entirely uncut and unopened.   John Drury Rare Books   March 2015 - 21688   2015   £266

Hinz, Evelyn J.   *The World of Anais Nin: Critical and Cultural Perspectives. A Special Issue of Mosaic: a Journal for the Comparative Study of Literature and Ideas Published by the University of Manitoba Press X1/2.* Winnipeg: University of Manitoba Press, 1978. First edition, 8vo., printed wrappers, very good, scarce.   Second Life Books Inc.   191 - 41   2015 $65

Hipkiss, James   *Unarmed Combat.*   London: F. W. Bridges, 1941. Third impression, frontispiece, folding plate, illustrations, original pictorial cream boards, little rubbed.   Jarndyce Antiquarian Booksellers   CCXI - 142   2015   £65

Hirschberg, Cornelius   *Florentine Finish.*   Harper & Row, 1963. First edition, small evidence of pencil erasure to top fore corner of half titlepage, else fine in lightly soiled, all white dust jacket.   Buckingham Books   March 2015 - 34682   2015 $250

Hirschfeld, Al   *Hirschfeld's Harlem.*   Milwaukee: Glenn Young Books, 2004. Revised and expanded, 4to., very good in near fine dust jacket, mildly ex-library but very nice.   Beasley Books   2013 - 2015 $45

Hirst, Damien   *I Want to Spend the Rest of My Life Everywhere with Everyone. One to One. Always, Forever. Now.* London: Booth-Clibborn Editions, 1997. First edition, large 4to., as new in publisher's cloth in like dust jacket (still in shrinkwrap), original faux leather board embossed and gilt decorated, fine jacket, illustrations in color including 7 pop-ups, die cuts, ephemera laid in, poster at rear, signed by Hirst.   Any Amount of Books   2015 - A22001   2015   £750

Hirst, Damien   *Theories, Models, Methods, Approaches Assumptions, Results and Findings.*   New York: Gagosian Gallery, 2000. First edition, quarto, many illustrations, full red leatherette, presentation copy from the artist, inscribed to another member of London's artworld, fine in glossy paper sleeve.   Peter Ellis, Bookseller   2014 - 003878   2015   £350

Historic Helena an Early-Day Photographic History 1864-1964. Helena: Home Bldg. & Loan Assoc., 1964. Limited edition, photos, small ink numeral and date on front pastedown, rear paste down has folded news article about publication of the book, top edge of the article taped to pastedown, else fine, no dust jacket as issued, good, scarce issue.   Baade Books of the West   2014 - 2015 $40

Historical Anecdotes of Old Prison Days.   privately printed, n.d. circa, 1948. First edition, 8vo., original grey pictorial wrappers, illustrations, fine.   Buckingham Books   March 2015 - 32362   2015 $250

History of Jackey Jingle and Sukey Single.   New York: McLoughlin Bros. 24 Beekman, circa, 1860. 12mo, pictorial wrappers, inconspicuous spine repair, slight soil, near fine, color cover plus 8 nice half page hand colored illustrations.   Aleph-bet Books, Inc.   109 - 150   2015 $300

The History of Jackson County, Missouri...   Kansas City: Union Historical Company, 1881. First edition, thick 8vo., full leather, frontispiece with tissue, large folding map, plates, portraits (with tissues), scarce, rebacked with original spine laid down, some cosmetic restoration to corners, lightly foxed throughout new front and rear endpapers, else very good, tight copy,.   Buckingham Books   March 2015 - 31136   2015 $1875

The History of King William the Third. London: printed for A. Roper, 1703. Second edition, 3 volumes, soundly rebound in modern green cloth lettered gilt at spine, 9 illustrations, ex-Foreign and Commonwealth Office library with their label and stamps lightly applied, very good. Any Amount of Books   2015 - A61250   2015   £180

History of Major Smalls and His Wooing. London: James Blackwood, 1860. Slightly dusted and damp marked, original orange cloth limp boards, faded and dulled, lacking following f.e.p., 63 pages, signature of S. Sewell on verso front cover.   Jarndyce Antiquarian Booksellers   CCXI - 8   2015   £85

History of the Anchor Line 1852-1911. Glasgow: John Horn Ltd., 1911. First edition, nicely illustrated in color (tissue guarded plates) and black and whites, very good+ (little soiling to white cloth, tight, clean text), scarce.   Stephen Lupack   March 2015 - 2015 $150

A History of the Isle of Anglesey from Its First Invasion by the Romans Until Finally Acceded to the Crown of England. London: Dodsley, 1775. First edition, 4to., half title present, recent navy blue half leather with marbled boards lettered gilt at spine with 5 raised bands, very good, few spots of foxing at prelims, otherwise text generally very clean.   Any Amount of Books   2015 - A69883   2015   £220

The History of the Wars, of His Present Majesty Charles XII King of Sweden... London: printed for A. Bell, T. Varnam & J. Osborn in Lombard Street and W. Taylor & J. Baker in Pater-Noster Row, 1715. 2 small paper shelf labels on spine "no. 995 Bx, 27', inscription for Michael (Foot), former labour leader, from wife Jill, contemporary unlettered panelled calf, raised bands, rubbed with slight loss to head of spine, joints cracked but firm, corners bumped.   Jarndyce Antiquarian Booksellers   CCXI - 9   2015   £350

The History of Tom Jones the Foundling, in His Married State. London: J. Robinson, 1750. (1749). Reissue of sheets of first edition with cancel title and added final chapter, 12mo., half title, small tears to blank fore margin on half title and titlepage, contemporary calf, some small expert repairs, most notably to head of spine, signature on title of W. Sleaford, 1749, very good. Jarndyce Antiquarian Booksellers   CCXI - 117   2015   £1100

The History of Tommy and Harry. York: Kendrew, n.d. circa, 1820. 16mo., green paper wrappers, (30) pages, fine, 8 nice woodcuts.   Aleph-bet Books, Inc.   109 - 155   2015 $250

A History of Will County, Illinois... Evansville: Unigraphic, 1973. Reprint of Chicago Le Baron edition, fine, hardcover, fine.   Beasley Books   2013 - 2015 $125

Hitchin Acrostic Club   *Acrostics. By the Hithcin Acrostic Club.*   London: Hodder and Stoughton, 1868. First edition, 8vo., title printed in red and black, few pencilled annotations, mainly marginal, old ms. notes including acrostic puzzle on verso of last leaf, original brown cloth gilt over bevelled boards, red edges just very little wear at extremities, very good, apparently very uncommon.   John Drury Rare Books   March 2015 - 20811   2015 $221

Hitschmann, Edward   *Great Men, Psychoanalytic Studies.*   New York: IUP, 1956. First edition, hardcover, fine.   Beasley Books   2013 - 2015 $45

Hittell, Theodore H.   *History of California.*   San Francisco: Stone and Co., 1897. Second printing, 2 volumes, publisher's brown cloth, gilt, overall rubbing, near fine, tight set.   Argonaut Book Shop   Holiday Season 2014 - 125   2015 $250

Hively, William   *Nine Classic California Photographers.*   Berkeley: Friends of the Bancroft Library, 1980. First edition, 10 plates, stiff printed black wrappers, spine very slightly faded, else very fine.   Argonaut Book Shop   Holiday Season 2014 - 126   2015 $45

Hoag, John D.   *Islamic Architecture.*   New York: Abrams, 1977. First edition, 4to., fine in fine dust jacket.   Beasley Books   2013 - 2015 $45

Hoagland, Tony   *A Change in Plans.*   Sierra Vista: San Pedro Press, 1985. First edition, 8vo., original tan printed wrappers, small stain in margin of first page of poetry, covers very slightly soiled, otherwise fine, very scarce, signed by poet.   James S. Jaffe Rare Books   Modern American Poetry - 136   2015 $850

Hoagland, Tony   *History of Desire. Poems.*   Tucson: Moon Pony Press, 1990. First edition, tall 8vo., original pictorial wrappers with linoleum cut by Heather Green, fine, very scarce.   James S. Jaffe Rare Books   Modern American Poetry - 137   2015 $500

Hoagland, Tony   *Moon Dog.*   N.P.: Plain Press, 1977. First edition, limited to 50 copies, 4to., illustrated an printed in 12 point Garamond type by Jane Miller, woodcuts by Miller, original decorated terra cotta wrappers, presentation copy inscribed by author on dedication page, with small drawing, laid in is broadside poem, broadside creased, and book lightly bumped at corners, otherwise fine.   James S. Jaffe Rare Books   Modern American Poetry - 135   2015 $2250

Hoban, Russell   *Letitia Rabbit's String Song.*   New York: Coward McCann & Geoghegan, 1973. First edition, square 8vo, pictorial cloth, slight spotting cover, else fine in dust jacket, beautiful full page and smaller watercolor drawings, nearly full page watercolor signed by artist, Mary Chalmers.   Aleph-Bet Books, Inc.   108 - 93   2015 $475

Hobart, Donald Bayne *Hunchback House.* Racine: Whitman, 1929. First edition, fine in lightly soiled dust jacket with very short internal tape repair. Mordida Books March 2015 - 001109   2015 $175

Hobbs, Robert *Milton Avery.* New York: Hudson Hills Press, 1990. First edition, oblong hardcover, 120 color plates and 38 black and white illustrations, very fine, slight bump to bottom of spine in very near fine dust jacket. Jeff Hirsch Books   E-62 Holiday List 2014 - 18   2015 $200

Hobhouse, John Cam *A Trifling Mistake on Thomas Lord Erskine's Recent Preface Shortly Noticed and Respectfully Corrected in a Letter to His Lordship by the author of the Defence of the People.* London: Robert Stodart, 1819. First edition, 8vo., slight paper browning and minor marginal staining at beginning and in recent plain wrappers. John Drury Rare Books   2015 - 19092   2015 $89

Hobson, G. D. *Maioli, Canevari and Others.* Boston: Little Brown and Co., 1926. First U S edition, 4to., cloth, top edge gilt, 64 full page plates, 6 in color, spine faded, bookplate of John Arnold Holland on front pastedown with Holland's signature in in below bookplate, endpapers toned, with small remnant of description mounted on front endpaper. Oak Knoll Books   306 - 2   2015 $145

Hocking, Anne *The Finishing Touch.* Doubleday & Co., 1948. First US edition, fine in dust jacket. Buckingham Books   March 2015 - 37125   2015 $185

Hockney, David *Hockney's Alphabet.* London: Faber and Faber for the Aids Crisis Trust, 1991. First edition, signed limited deluxe issue, number 133 of 300 copies signed by Hockney, Stephen Spender and 22 contributors, folio, original half vellum over original handmade Fabriano Roma boards, original decorated slipcase, beautiful production in fine condition. Manhattan Rare Book Company   Literature 2014 - 2015 $2600

Hockney, David *Hockney's Alphabet: Drawings by David Hockney.* London: Faber and Faber, 1991. Special edition, signed by Hockney and editor, Stephen Spender, color illustrated wrappers/paperback, fine in fine slipcase. Any Amount of Books   2015 - A90172   2015   £235

Hocquart De Courbron, M. *Nouvelles Vues sur l'Administration des Finances, et sur l'Allegement de l'Inpot, (bound with) Calculs sur la Circulation, Relativement aux Impts & L'Augmentation du Prix des Denrees et a la Dimuntion du Taux de L'Interet De l'Aragent.* La Haye: 1785. Londres: T. Payne & Fils, Pl. elmsley & T. Hookham, 1787. First edition, 8vo., half title, 4 statistical tables placed after p. 32 and final leaf; large folding table; bound in early 19th century half calf over marbled boards, neatly rebacked and labelled, excellent copy of the 19th century library of the Earls Harcourt with their armorial bookplate, very scarce, fine, crisp copy. John Drury Rare Books   2015 - 26285 2015 $787

Hodge, Charles *What is Darwinsim?* London: T. Nelson & Sons, 1874. First edition, 1 page initial ad, original brick red cloth, bevelled boards, some slight rubbing, very good, crisp copy. Jarndyce Antiquarian Booksellers   CCXI - 87 2015   £180

Hodges, Margaret *Saint George and the Dragon retold by...* Boston: Little Brown, 1984. Oblong 4to., 1/3 cloth, fine in very good+ dust jacket slightly worn at spine ends and one corner, magnificent illustrations by Trina Hyman. Aleph-Bet Books, Inc.   108 - 246   2015 $250

Hodgetts, Sheila *Toby Twirl in Pogland.* London: Sampson Low Marston, n.d. circa, 1947. Folio, pictorial wrappers, slightest bit of soil, else near fine, color lithographs on every page by E. Jeffrey. Aleph-Bet Books, Inc. 108 - 238   2015 $225

Hodgkinson, H. S., & Co. *Wokey Hole Mills.* Wells Somersetshire: H. S Hodgkinson & Co., 1870. 32mo., original stiff wrappers, price listed effect Jan. 1 1870, lightly worn around edges, covers lightly soiled, ink notations on front cover and throughout text. Oak Knoll Books   306 - 95 2015 $150

Hodgson, William *The Society of Friends in the Nineteenth Century.* Philadelphia: Smith English and Co., 1875-1876. First edition, 2 volumes, inscribed and signed 'from the author', very good set, some shelfwear to extremities, tight, clean text, inscribed by author. Stephen Lupack March 2015 - 2015 $250

Hodgson, William Hope *The House on the Borderland.* London: Holden & Hardingham, 1921. Cheap edition, 8vo., original beige cloth lettered black at spine, spine showing some slight wear, hinges at top and bottom have slight splitting but are holding well, some rubbing to spine and covers, 2 slight puncture marks in covers, else sound, very good- with clean text. Any Amount of Books   2015 - A94345 2015   £300

Hodnett, Edward *Five Centuries of English Book Illustration.* Aldershot: Scolar Press, 1988. First edition, 4to., cloth, dust jacket, well illustrated. Oak Knoll Books 306 - 23   2015 $100

Hodson, Arnold *Where Lion Reign.* London: Skeffington, 1928. First edition, burgundy leather, gold stamped on spine, frontispiece, lightly sunned on spine and lightly foxed along with light soiling and wear to extremities, else very good. Buckingham Books   March 2015 - 22710   2015 $1050

Hodson, Septimus *A Sermon, Delivered in the Parish Church of Thrapston in the County of Northampton...* Wellingborough: printed by T. March, 1800. Only edition, 8vo., titlepage and final leaf rather soiled, one leaf of prelims bound in verso first, rebound recently in boards with printed title label, very rare.   John Drury Rare Books   March 2015 - 24592   2015 $266

Hoffman-Donner, Heinrich   1809-1894 *Slovenly Peter.* Philadelphia: John C. Winston Co. n.d. circa early 20th century, Small 4to., profusely illustrated, red cloth stamped in black and gilt, buff printed dust jacket, faint red and yellow tinted highlights, very good+, cloth and gilt bright, gutter discoloration from binding glue, very good+ small stain to lower right rear panel/light edgewear, nice, uncommon dust jacket. Tavistock Books   Bah, Humbug? - 14   2015 $275

Hoffman-Donner, Heinrich   1809-1894 *Slovenly Peter.* New York: Limited Editions Club, 1935. Limited to 1500 numbered copies, large 4to., leather backed pictorial cloth, 34 ages, fine in original glassine housed in velvet chemise and slipcase with some rubbing at corners, pochoir illustrations redrawn from Hoffmann's originals by Fritz Kredel, printed on fine quality paper, frenchfold, increasingly scarce. Aleph-Bet Books, Inc.   108 - 239   2015 $600

Hoffman, Christian *Longevity: Being an Account of Various Persons Who Have Lived to an Extraordinary Age with Several Curious Particulars Respecting Their Lives....* New York: Jacob S. Mott, 1798. First edition, 120 pages, contemporary mottled sheep, covers worn and hinges glued, very good internally.   Joseph J. Felcone Inc.   Science, Medicine and Technology - 27   2015 $450

Hoffman, Conrad *The Prison Camps of Germany.* New York: Associated Press, 1920. First edition, 8o., original green cloth, black lettering, decoration with spine sunned, near fine dust jacket with mild sun spine, minimal edge wear, tipped on f.f.e.p. is TLS by Nobel Laureate, John Mott, discussing this book, scarce thus.   By the Book, L. C. Special List 10 - 42   2015 $350

Hoffman, Katherine *Collage. Critical Views.* Ann Arbor: Critical Views, 1989. First edition, fine in dust jacket. Beasley Books   2013 - 2015 $200

Hoffmann, Ernst Theodor Amadeus   1776-1822 *Nutcracker.* New York: Crown, 1984. Limited to 250 numbered copies, with signed limited etching by Maurice Sendak, square 4to., cloth, fine in slipcase, printed on paper especially made for this edition and beautifully illustrated in full color, with beautiful signed/ numbered hand drawn lithograph by Sendak, quite scarce.   Aleph-bet Books, Inc. 109 - 429   2015 $2000

Hoffmann, Frank *The Henry Red Allen & J. C. Higginbotham Collection.* Berlin: the author, 2000-2002. First edition, illustrations, wrappers, 4 volumes, near fine. Beasley Books   2013 - 2015 $200

Hoffmann, Herbert *Hoffmanns Schriftatlas Ausgewahlte Alphabete und Anwendungen aus Vergangenheit und Gegenwart Herausgebeben Von Alfred Finsterer.* Stuttgart: Julius Hoffmann, 1952. Revised from 1930 edition, tall 4to., cloth, dust jacket with piece missing at head of spine, slipcase.   Oak Knoll Books   306 - 238   2015 $125

Hofland, Barbara *A Descriptive Account of the Mansion and Gardens of White Knights.* London: printed for his Grace the Duke of Marlborough by W. Wilson, Greville-Street, Hatton Gardens, 1819. Folio, 23 engraved plates including 8 aquatints on India paper, all hand colored, uncut in original half vellum over buff boards, some repairs to spine.   Marlborough Rare Books List 54 - 46   2015 £2000

Hofmann, Coen *Shorty Rogers, a Discography.* Amsterdam: Micrography, 1983. First edition, wrappers, 2 volumes, near fine with little sunning.   Beasley Books 2013 - 2015 $40

Hofmann, Joseph E. *Michael Stifel (1487?-1567). Leben, Wiken and Bedeutung fur die Mathematik Seiner Zeit.* Wiesbaden: Franz Steiner Verlag, 1968. 8vo., 8 plates, 20 figrues, blue printed wrappers, bookplate of Barnabas Hughes, very good.   Jeff Weber Rare Books   178 - 1043 2015 $60

Hofmannsthal, Hugo Von   *Electra; a Tragedy in One Act.* New York: Brentano's, 1908. First American edition, ownership signature of noted journalist Walter Lippmann with his addresss and dated 1910.   Between the Covers Rare Books, Inc.   187 - 128   2015 $150

Hofstad, Mildred   *Mr. & Mrs. Peter Rabbit.* Willis Music Co., 1956. First edition, 8 full page black and white line drawings, numerous smaller illustrations, grey wrappers with dark green and red illustrated front cover, 8 1/2 x 11 inches, lower corner front cover and first few pages slightly creased, faint staining rear, ink notes and few page number circles, very good.   Ian Hodgkins & Co. Ltd.   134 - 233   2015 £38

Hofstadter, Douglas R.   *Godel, Escher, Bach: an Eternal Golden Braid.* New York: Vintage Books, 1989. Reprint, large 8vo., 16.5 x 23.5cm., large format paperback, copiously illustrated in black and white, signed presentation from author to Sir Malcolm Stanley Bradbury, about fine.   Any Amount of Books   2015 - C2866   2015   £160

Holbach, Paul Henri Thiry, Baron D'   *Systeme Social.* Londres: i.e. Amsterdam: M. M. Rey, 1773. First editions, 8vo., 3 volumes, half titles, faint old inkstamp of French Institute on lower margin of titlepages, uniformly bound in handsome French calf, spines ornately and beautiful gilt with double morocco labels gilt, all edges red, marbled endpaper, fine, crisp, set in choice 18th century French binding.   John Drury Rare Books   2015 - 24773   2015 $1311

Holbrook, Stewart H. *The Story of American Railroads.* Crown Pub., 1947. First edition, 8vo., illustrations, very good, tight copy in dust jacket with light wear to spine ends and extremities.   Buckingham Books   March 2015 - 30151   2015 $175

Holden, Raymond *Death on the Border.* New York: Holt, 1937. First edition, fine in dust jacket with tiny wear at spine ends and along edges.   Mordida Books   March 2015 - 010438   2015 $100

Holder, Charles Frederick *Living Lights: a Popular Account of Phosphorescent Animals and Vegetables.* London: Sampson Low, Marston Searle and Rivington, 1887. First edition, 8vo., original olive cloth lettered gilt on spine, lettered and decorated gilt and black on cover, 26 plates, slight edgewear, spine ends slightly bumped, corners rubbed, very slight scuffing, prize label pasted to endpaper, very lightly shaken, otherwise very good.   Any Amount of Books   2015 - A69402   2015   £220

Holdsworth, William *A History of English Law.* London: Methuen, 1922-1952. Mixed set, some first editions, mostly later printings, original blue cloth lettered gilt at spine, sound, very good set with some spines rebacked, occasional library stamps excised cut off at corners of titlepage not affecting text, some spine chipping, text clean.   Any Amount of Books   2015 - C8438   2015   £285

Holford, George *A Brief Warning Against the Measure Commonly called "Catholic Emancipation...".* London: C. J. G. & F. Rivington, 1829. First edition, 8vo., recent marbled boards lettered on spine, very good.   John Drury Rare Books   2015 - 26091   2015 $133

Holford, George *Third Vindication of the General Penitentiary, Shewing that There is no ground Whatever for Supposing that the Situation of that Prison had any Share in Producing the late Disease among the Prisoners Confined There.* London: C. & J. Rivington and J. Hatchard and Son, 1825. First edition, 8vo., bound recently in plain boards, spine lettered, margins of initial blank and titlepage just bit soiled, else good.   John Drury Rare Books   March 2015 - 25974   2015   £306

Holinshed, Raphael *The First and Second Volumes of Chronicles, Comprising the Description and Historie of England, Ireland and Scotland.* London: John Harrison, George Bishop et al, 1587. Revised second edition, two volumes bound as one, folio, 14.5 x 9.5 inches, 19th century blind tooled morocco gilt, gilt stag at base of spine, black letter, six woodcut titlepages, all cancels present, very handsome copy.   Honey & Wax Booksellers   3 - 22   2015 $10,000

Holland, Clive *Raymi; or the Children of the Sun.* London: Henry and Co., 1889. First edition, octavo, 4 inserted plates, illustrations by Percy Ebbutt, original red cloth, front and rear panels ruled in blind, spine panel stamped in gold.   L. W. Currey, Inc.   Boy's Adventure Fiction 2015 - 17   2015 $450

Holland, Marty *Fallen Angel.* E. P. Dutton Co., 1945. First edition, fine in dust jacket with light professional restoration to spine ends and fore-corners.   Buckingham Books   March 2015 - 38242   2015 $750

Hollander, John *Blue Wine an Other Poems.* Baltimore: Johns Hopkins University Press, 1979. First edition, corners little bumped, else fine in very slightly spine sunned dust jacket, presentation inscribed by author to his editor Harry (Ford) May 1979.   Between the Covers Rare Books, Inc.   187 - 129   2015 $350

Hollender, Marc *The Practice of Psychoanalytic Psychotherapy.* New York: Grune and Stratton, 1965. First edition, inscribed by author, fine in unprinted dust jacket.   Beasley Books 2013 - 2015 $45

Holley, Marietta *My Wayward Pardner or My Trials with Josiah, American, the Widow Bump...* Hartford: American Publishing Co., 1881. 8vo., 36 plates, in text engravings, frontispiece, green cloth, stamped in gilt, very good, well read condition.   Second Life Books Inc.   189 - 120   2015 $85

Holley, Marietta *Samantha on the Woman Question.* New York: Revell, 1913. First edition, 8vo., cover with some patchy fading, lacks some of the white stamping on spine, otherwise very good, scarce.   Second Life Books Inc.   191 - 42   2015 $75

Holling, Holling C. *Minn of the Mississippi.* Boston: Houghton Mifflin, 1951. First edition, 4to. cloth, fine in very good+ dust jacket with few closed tears, illustrations in rich color.   Aleph-Bet Books, Inc.   108 - 243   2015 $225

Hollinghurst, Alan *The Stranger's Child.* Dublin: Tuskar Rock Press, 2011. Limited edition, this copy 14 of an edition just 40 numbered copies, bound in full leather and sunned and dated by author, fine in slipcase.   Ken Lopez, Bookseller   164 - 88   2015 $550

Hollinghurst, Alan *The Swimming Pool Library.* London: Chatto & Windus, 1988. First edition, uncorrected proof, near fine in original perfect bound decorated wrappers, as issued.   Ed Smith Books   83 - 46   2015 $250

Hollingshead, John *Rubbing the Gilt Off. A West End Book for All Readers.*   London: John Camden Hotten, 1860. Reprinted, frontispiece, slightly foxed, 4 pages ads, original olive green embossed cloth, ownership inscription "Llewllyn Traherne, London, May 7 1860", very good.   Jarndyce Antiquarian Booksellers   CCXI - 143   2015   £110

Hollister, Horace A. *The Woman Citizen, a problem in education.*   New York: Appleton, 1919. First edition, 2nd printing, 8vo., cloth backed boards, very good.   Second Life Books Inc.   189 - 121   2015 $85

Hollister, John *Sunday-School Hymns and Tunes with Chants.*   New York: Dutton & Co., 1877. First edition, very good.   Stephen Lupack   March 2015 - 2015 $45

Hollo, Anselm *Ted. Time Flies by Like a Great Whale.*   New Orleans: Fell Swoop 64, 2003. First edition, one of 26 lettered copies signed by Hollo out of a total edition of 200 copies, 4to., illustrations in color, original pictorial cover stapled as issued, 2 original silkscreen prints of two Berrigan-Notley collages reproduced in bookplate, very fine.   James S. Jaffe Rare Books   Many Happy Returns - 79   2015 $450

Holloway, John *The Victorian Sage: Studies in Argument.*   London: Macmillan, 1953. Half title, original green cloth, very good in slightly torn dust jacket, from the library of Geoffrey & Kathleen Tillotson, Geoffrey's signed advance review copy with extensive notes, and some insertions.   Jarndyce Antiquarian Booksellers   CCVII - 301   2015   £20

Holman-Hunt, William *Pre-Raphaelitism and Pre-Raphaelite Brotherhood.*   London: Chapman & Hall, 1913. Second edition, 2 volumes, 8vo., original blue cloth lettered darker blue on spine and cover, illustrations, pages uncut, slight abrasion, scratches and marks to covers, some rubbing, otherwise very sound, near very good set with clean text.   Any Amount of Books   2015 - C3047   2015   £240

Holme, Edmond *An Account and Admeasurement of the Public Bridges, Within the Hundred of Salford, in the County of Palatine of Lancaster.*   Manchester: printed in the year, 1782. Only edition, 4to., interleaved contemporaneously with similar paper, occasional very minor soiling, mainly marginal, blindstamp of Wigan Free Public Library, mid 19th century maroon half roan oer marbled boards, top edge gilt, some minor wear to extremities, very good.   John Drury Rare Books   2015 - 25341   2015 $2622

Holmes, John *Some Correspondence on the Subject of the Grant of £1800 Made to the National School of the Hamlet of Highgate by the Committee of Privy Council for Education.*   London: Cox Brothers and Wyman, 1853. First edition, variant issue, 8vo., 30 pages, preserved in recent marbled wrappers with printed title, label to upper cover, good copy, uncommon.   John Drury Rare Books   2015 - 21705   2015 $89

Holmes, Norman W. *My Western Pacific Railroad.*   Reno: Steel Rails West, 1996. First edition, oblong quarto, color and black and white photos, maps, pictorial boards, spine faded, else very fine.   Argonaut Book Shop   Holiday Season 2014 - 127   2015 $60

Holmes, Richard R. *Queen Victoria.*   London: Boussod Valadon & Co., 1897. First edition, illustrations, folio, period deep maroon three quarter morocco with elaborate gilt decorated spine and red cloth boards, top edge gilt, marbled endpapers, professionally reinforced front joint, occasional foxing, pleasing, very good+ copy.   Tavistock Books   Bah, Humbug? - 25   2015 $750

Holmes, Ruth E. V. *Bibliographical and Historical Description of the Rarest Books in the Oliveira Lima Collection at the Catholic University of America.*   Washington: Catholic University of America, 1926. First edition, 12mo., later cloth with gilt titles, all edges marbled, marbled endpapers, very good, spine sunned, front endpapers scuffed.   Kaaterskill Books   19 - 76   2015 $100

Holt, Henry *The Midnight Mail.*   Garden City: Doubleday Doran & Co., 1931. first US edition, 8vo., near fine in dust jacket with wraparound promotional band.   Buckingham Books   March 2015 - 32178   2015 $675

Holt, O. H. *Dakota "Behold I Show You a Delightsome Land".*   Rand McNally & Co., 1885. First edition, 8vo., printed wrappers, 90 pages plus 6 pages of ads, illustrations, tiny library stamp and number on front cover, spine renewed with matching paper chips to cover filled in with matching paper wear, else very good.   Buckingham Books   March 2015 - 31407   2015 $1250

Holtan, Gene *Specimen Sheets Pulled from the Wood Type in Drawer Six. from the Cabinet at Green Gables and a Sheet or two of Type from Friends.*   Santa Cruz: Quad Press, 1983. Limited to 100 copies, printed on mouldmade Nideggen from Germany with handmade paper covered boards on over with paper made by Peter Papermaker, Santa Cruz, 4 page prospectus loosely inserted, oblong 16mo., cloth backed paper covered boards, spine sewn in Japanese manner, (36) pages printed French fold.   Oak Knoll Books   306 - 167   2015 $225

Holwell, John *A Sure Guide to the Practical Surveyor, in Two Parts.* London: printed by W. Godbid for Christopher Hassey at the Flower de Luce in Little Britain, 1678. First edition, 2 parts in one volume, 8vo., 12 engraved plates, many text figures, contemporary panelled calf with raised bands and blind lines, appropriately renewed, fine, scarce. John Drury Rare Books 2015 - 23959 2015 $2098

Holzschuher, August Freiherr Von *Die Materielle noth der Utnern Volksclassen und Ihre Uraschen Gekronte Preisschrift.* Augsburg: Matth. Rieger, 1850. First edition, 8vo., some light intermittent foxing, original printed wrappers, entirely uncut and partially unopened, very good. John Drury Rare Books March 2015 - 15166 2015 $266

Homage to the Book. N.P.: Westvaco, 1968. 4to., 16 folders loosely inserted in cloth, beautifully illustrated, box scuffed along top back cover. Oak Knoll Books 306 - 46 2015 $250

Homan, Johann Georg *Die Land-und Haus-Apotheke, Oder Getreuer und Grundlicher Unterricht fur den Bauer und Stadmann Enthaltend die Allerbesten Mittel...* Reading: Carl A. Bruckman, 1818. First American edition, 12mo., very nice, some stains and browning. M & S Rare Books, Inc. 97 - 278 2015 $2500

Home Kindness: a Picture Gift Book. New York: McLoughlin Bros. n.d. circa, 1875. 4to., pictorial wrappers, most minimal amount of cover soil, else fine, 6 fine full page chromolithographs. Aleph-bet Books, Inc. 109 - 283 2015 $350

The Home Knowledge Atlas. Toronto: Home Knowledge, 1888. Folio, original brown cloth, black design and gilt title to spine, folio, numerous colored maps, top and bottom of spine frayed and wear to edges, interior very good. Schooner Books Ltd. 110 - 176 2015 $25

Homer, Donald William *By Aeroplane to the Sun: Being the Adventures of a Daring Aviator and His Friends.* London: Century Press (Bennett & Co), 1910. First edition, octavo, inserted frontispiece with illustration by Mabel Spurrier, original green cloth, front panel stamped in gold and ruled in blind, spine panel stamped in gold, bottom edge untrimmed. L. W. Currey, Inc. Boy's Adventure Fiction 2015 - 14 2015 $550

Homer, Donald William *By Aeroplane to the Sun: Being the Adventures of a Daring Aviator and His Friends.* London: Century Press (Bennett & Co), 1910. First edition, octavo, inserted frontispiece with illustration by Mabel Spurrier, original green cloth, front panel stamped in gold and ruled in blind, spine panel stamped in gold, bottom edge untrimmed. L. W. Currey, Inc. Boy's Adventure Fiction 2015 - 18 2015 $450

Homer, Donald William *Their Winged Destiny Being a Tale of Two Planets.* London: Simpkin, Marshall, Hamilton, Kent & Co., 1912. First edition, octavo, inserted frontispiece, illustration by Mabel Spurrier, original blue cloth, front and spine panels stamped in black, pictorial paper onlay affixed to front cover. L. W. Currey, Inc. Boy's Adventure Fiction 2015 - 19 2015 $450

Homer, Donald William *The World's Double: Being a Tale of Two Planets.* London: Simpkin, Marshall, Hamilton, Kent & Co. Ltd., 1913. Second edition, octavo, inserted frontispiece with illustration by Mabel Spurrier, original red cloth, front and spine panels stamped inblack, pictorial paper onlay affixed to front cover. L. W. Currey, Inc. Boy's Adventure Fiction 2015 - 34 2015 $250

Homerus *Ilias. (The Iliad in Latin).* Parisiis: Apud Martinum Iuuenem Excvdebat Gvil. M., 1550. 121 x 89mm., beautiful and animated contemporary elaborately gilt and painted Parisian calf by Wooton's binder "B", covers with unusual frame of interlacing slender rectangular compartments formed by wide black painted fillets outlined in gilt, center panel with four foliate scrolls arched across frame in each quadrant and forming a centerpiece lozenge, azured curls at head and foot of panel and with stippled lobes, additional azured cornerpieces, stippled circles at top, bottom and either side of the panel, raised bands, spine compartments gilt with centered foliate tool or bull's eye, slightly later red morocco label, all edges gilt, spine ends and corners very artfully renewed, in fleece lined brown buckram clamshell case, with John Roland Abbey's morocco bookplate and large morocco title label on spine, front endpaper with morocco bookplate of Abbey, pastedowns with armorial bookplates of Scrope Berdmore, S.T.P. (dated 1790) at front and of Henry C. Compton esq. at rear, rear endpaper with modern bookplate of Philosophia Hermetica ruled in red throughout, half dozen light ink stains, two or three affecting a few words of text, quite clean and fresh internally, backstrip with minor flaking and few hairline cracks, one corner exposed, otherwise very decorative binding, pleasing and especially well preserved, boards still lustrous. Phillip J. Pirages 66 - 12 2015 $12,500

Homerus *The Iliads of Homer Prince of Poets.* London: Nathaniel Butter, 1611. First complete edition, first issue translated by George Chapman, folio modern full blind tooled morocco, engraved title by William Hale. Honey & Wax Booksellers 3 - 4 2015 $25,000

Homerus *(In Greek) Omerou Ilias Kai Odysseia. (and) Homeri Ilias & Odyssea et in Iandem Scholia & Interpretatio.* Lugduni Batavorum: Apud Franciscum Hackium, 1655-1656. First Schrevelius edited edition, 2 volumes, 248 x 171mm., handsome 18th century red straight grain moroccot, cover framed by lovely Neoclassical roll enclosed by double gilt rules, rosette cornerpieces, raised bands flanked by plain gilt rules, spine panels with central gilt medallion containing a narcissus, gilt titling, turn-in with gilt greek key roll purple endpapers, all edges, engraved allegorical title in volume I, woodcut printer's device on title in volume II, engraved armorial bookplate of Joannis Petri de Villeneuve, spines uniformly bit darkened (with slight dulling of some gilt), hint of rubbing to extremities, very minor spotting to covers, but original handsome unrestored bindings generally in fine condition, leather lustrous and with no significant wear, joints almost entirely unworn, vague browning in (ample) margins, isolated trivial rust or wax spots, other minor imperfections but text fresh, clean and generally quite pleasing. Phillip J. Pirages   66 - 37   2015 $2200

Homerus *The First Book of Homer's Iliad.* London: printed for J. Tonson, 1715. First edition, 4to., recent boards, engraved bust of Homer on titlepage, several engraved headpieces and tailpieces in text some browning, one lower blank, corner torn away, slight chipping to margins of last leaf, otherwise good.   C. R. Johnson   Foxon R-Z - 1011r-z   2015 $460

Homerus *The Iliad of Homer. (bound with) The Odyssey of Homer.* London: printed by T. Bensley, 1802. New edition, 5 volumes, 244 x 168mm., very attractive contemporary English red straight grain morocco extravagantly gilt, covers with frame containing alternating drawer handles and lozenges on stippled background with fleuron cornerpieces, central panel with intricate filigree fan cornerpieces, double raised bands, spine panels densely gilt in lacy pattern of small tools, inner gilt dentelles tooled in Oriental motif, turquoise endpapers, pastedowns framed by decorative gilt roll, all edges gilt; 7 engraved plates, including frontispiece in each volume, frontispieces moderately foxed, isolated foxing elsewhere (insignificant on half dozen leaves only, otherwise trivial), frontispiece of one volume with light dampstain affecting half engraved area (faint related discoloration at inner margin of next dozen leaves), otherwise very attractive internally, vast majority of text very clean, fresh and smooth, minor spotting to covers, spines uniformly faded to a pleasing maroon, insignificant rubbing to extremities, but lovely elaborately gilt contemporary bindings, very well preserved, lustrous leather, shining gilt, and only negligible wear. Phillip J. Pirages   66 - 64   2015 $3900

Homerus *The Odyssey of Homer and the Iliad of Homer.* Haarlem: Limited Editions Club, printed by Joh. Enschede en Zonen, 1931. Limited to 1500 numbered copies, signed by designer J. van Krimpen on colophon of both volumes, 2 volumes, 4to., cloth, top edge gilt, other edges uncut, title gilt stamped on spine and slipcase, in variant full leather slipcase issued by publisher to hold 2 volumes, (scuffed along edges, spines sunned),.   Oak Knoll Books   25 - 3   2015 $450

Homes, Geoffrey *And Then There were None.* New York: Morrow, 1938. First edition, fine in very good dust jacket with light wear at spine ends and wear along folds and edges.   Mordida Books   March 2015 - 1010213   2015 $185

Homes, Geoffrey *Forty Whacks.* New York: William Morrow and Co., 1941. First edition, 8vo., inscribed by author, front and rear free endpapers beginning to uniformly tan, else fine in dust jacket with light wear to spine ends and to extremities, also along top and bottom edges of inside of jacket are stains caused by removal of old fashioned protective book cover, none of the stain visible on front side of dust jacket.   Buckingham Books   March 2015 - 24899   2015 $2000

Homes, Geoffrey *The Man Who Didn't Exist.* New York: William & Morrow & Co., 1937. First edition, original black cloth, lettered red on spine and cover, 8vo., about fine in complete very good dust jacket with slight chips from edges and slightly soiled at rear, handsome copy in decent dust jacket.   Any Amount of Books   2015 - C5222   2015   £225

Honan, Park *Jane Austen: Her Life.* London: Weidenfeld & Nicholson, 1987. Half title, plates, original black cloth, very good in dust jacket, from the library of Geoffrey & Kathleen Tillotson, with inserted postcard from Kathleen. Jarndyce Antiquarian Booksellers   CCVII - 79   2015   £45

Honan, Park *Matthew Arnold: a Life.* New York: McGraw Hill, 1981. Half title, plates, original grey boards, white cloth spine, very good in creased, dust jacket, author's presentation to Kathleen Tillotson with letters from him and note by her inserted.   Jarndyce Antiquarian Booksellers   CCVII - 66   2015   £30

Honourable Artillery Company *List of the Chiefs, Officers, Courts of Assistants &c &c of the Honourable Artillery Company, for the Year 1798.* London: printed by Clark and Norris Moorfields, 1798. 8vo., 14 pages, first few leaves rather dampstained, contemporary perhaps original marbled wrappers, very rare.   John Drury Rare Books   March 2015 - 18862   2015   £306

Hood, Thomas 1799-1845 *The Letters.* Toronto: University of Toronto Press, 1973. Half title, frontispiece, original dark blue cloth, very good in creased and marked dust jacket, editor (Peter F. Morgan) presentation copy to Kathleen Tillotson, with 2 page ALS from him inserted and inserted notes by her.   Jarndyce Antiquarian Booksellers   CCVII - 303   2015   £35

Hood, Thomas 1799-1845 *Poems.* London: Edward Moxon, 1854. Seventh edition, 8 page catalog (March 1855), half title, frontispiece, original cloth covered with decorated paper by Geoffrey Tillotson, with ms. label, signed by same with few marginal marks.   Jarndyce Antiquarian Booksellers   CCVII - 302   2015   £20

Horgan, Paul *Peter Hurd. A Portrait Sketch from Life.* Austin: published for the Amon Carter Museum of Western Art by the University of Texas Press, 1965. First edition, two tone boards, 4to., 68 pages, color and black and white reproductions.　Argonaut Book Shop　Holiday Season 2014 - 128　2015　$125

Horgan, Paul *Peter Hurd A Portrait Sketch from Life.* Austin: University of Texas, 1965. First edition, 4to., 16 black and white illustrations, 5 color plates, author's presentation dated 1989, paper over boards with cloth spine, cover bumped at corners, slightly scuffed at ends of spine, otherwise very good, tight copy.　Second Life Books Inc.　190 - 112　2015　$125

Horler, Sydney *The Curse of Doone.* New York: Mystery League, 1930. First US edition, fine, bright, tight copy in fine dust jacket, sharp copy.　Buckingham Books　March 2015 - 25815　2015　$185

Horn, Calvin *Confederate Victories in the Southwest. (with) Union Army Operations in the Southwest.* Albuquerque: 1961. Facsimile reprints, 201 pages, maps; 152 pages, illustrations, large folding map, first work has some light soil to spine, but is near fine, second work has some fading to spine of dust jacket, else near fine. Dumont Maps & Books of the West　131 - 54　2015　$100

Horn, Georg *De Originibus Americanis.* Hemipoli (i.e. Nordhausen): Joannis Mulleri, 1669. Second edition, 12mo., engraved frontispiece in contemporary vellum, pastedown coming away from covers, fore edges of engraved frontispiece and titlepage chipped not affecting any letterpress, small hole in a4 which affects a couple of letters, contemporary ownership signature on endpaper, leaves toned but perfectly acceptable.　Second Life Books Inc.　190 - 113　2015　$1250

Horn, Tom *Life of Tom Horn.* Louthan Book Co., 1904. First edition, stiff pictorial wrappers, 317 pages, illustrations, very light wear to top edge of spine, two half inch closed tears and quarter inch chip to fore-edge of rear wrapper, else clean, tight, very good.　Buckingham Books　March 2015 - 37396　2015　$450

Hornaday, William T. *The Extermination of the American Bison.* N.P.: 1889. First separate printing, printed wrappers, large folding map, 21 plates, original wrappers very fragile as issued, fore-corners of front wrapper missing and chipping and short tears to edges of rear wrapper, very good, near fine.　Buckingham Books　March 2015 - 34482　2015　$400

Hornby, C. H. *A Descriptive Bibliography of the Books Printed at the Ashendene Press MDCCCXCV-MCMXXXV.* San Francisco: Alan Wofsy Fine Arts Press, 1976. Reprint of 1935 first edition, 4to., cloth, covers faded.　Oak Knoll Books　306 - 125　2015　$125

Horne, Henry *Essays Concerning Iron and Steel...* London: T. Cadell, 1773. First edition, 12mo., wanting half title, short tear to inner margin of title (no loss) inner margin (gutter) of following leaf stained, contemporary sheep, stamped in blind, some wear to joints, else sound, scarce. John Drury Rare Books　2015 - 21803　2015　$787

Horne, Richard Hengist *Cosmo de' Medici: an Historical Tragedy and Other Poems.* London: George Rivers, 1875. First edition, contemporary red polished half calf gilt and marbled paper covered boards, raised bands and floral decorations in compartments, front joint slightest bit tender, very good or better, inscribed by author to poet Charles Warren Stoddard, Aug. 21 1875.　Between the Covers Rare Books, Inc.　187 - 131　2015　$350

Horneck, Anthony *Delight and Judgment; or a Prospect of the Great Day of Judgment and Its Power to Damp and Imbitter Sensual Delights, Sports and Recreations.* London: printed by H. Hills Jun. for Mark Pardoe, 1684. First edition, contemporary ink annotations on endpapers and on a least two page margins, tiny hole in one text leaf affecting two or three letters on both recto and verso, contemporary blind ruled calf, very good, crisp copy.　John Drury Rare Books　2015 - 21542　2015　$2622

Hornung, E. W. *The Amateur Cracksman.* London: Methuen & Co., 1899. First edition, original red cloth, titles stamped in gilt on front cover and spines, affixed to front flyleaf is a label from author and publisher "With the compliments of the author" but label not signed, covers lightly soiled, else very good.　Buckingham Books　March 2015 - 34684　2015　$875

Horsbrugh, Boyd *The Game-Birds and Water-Fowl of South Africa.* London: Witherby & Co., 1912. Small quarto, 159 pages, colored plates by Sergeant C. G. Davies, handsome later half morocco with raised bands and decorative gilt spine, top edge gilt, few spots mainly confined to outer margins, very good.　Andrew Isles　2015 - 26251　2015　$500

Horsley, Samuel *The Speeches in Parliament of Samuel Horsley....* Dundee: printed by Robert Stephen Ritnoul for James Chalmers, 1813. 8vo., half title, prelim leaves lightly foxed, later 19th century polished calf gilt with raised bands, crimson label, top edge gilt, others uncut, fine, from the library of the Earl of Portsmouth, Hurstbourne Park Library. John Drury Rare Books　March 2015 - 17809　2015　$221

Horton, Robert John Wilmot *A Letter to the Duke of Norfolk, on the Catholic Question.* London: John Murray, 1826. 8vo., wanting half title, title and some other leaves little browned, in serviceable but not beautiful modern cloth, title on label on upper cover, good copy.　John Drury Rare Books　2015 - 13672　2015　$89

Horton, Robert John Wilmot *Protestant Securities Suggested in an Appeal to the Clerical Members of the University of Oxford.* London: John Murray, 1828. First edition, half title, with Murray's list of books published April 1928 at end, (16) pages, original boards, printed spine label, uncut, very good, perhaps fine. John Drury Rare Books 2015 - 16549 2015 $177

Horton, William Thomas *The Way of the Soul.* London: Rider & Son, 1910. First edition, 4to., 48 full page black and white illustrations, original blue illustrated cloth, slight iridescent sheen as published, lettered gilt at spine with cover illustration (gilt and black), cloth slightly tanned at spine and very slight wear at head, otherwise very good. Any Amount of Books 2015 - A83260 2015 £240

Hossack, David *The Most Noble the Marquis of Breadalbane's First Prize.* London: Partridge and Oakey, 1849. First separate edition, 8vo., recently bound in linen backed marbled boards, lettered, very good, inscribed by author. John Drury Rare Books 2015 - 16305 2015 $133

Hotel Ritz. Place Vendome 15 Paris. Paris: Edite par la Societe de Publications d'Art 59 rue de Provence Juin, 1899. Very deluxe production, large 4to., gravure plate in bistre and several full page facsimiles and half tone plates of the hotel facade ad rooms, original burgundy cloth, upper cover blocked in gilt spine lettered gilt. Marlborough Rare Books List 53 - 42 2015 £750

Hotman, Antoine *Traicte De La Dissolution Du Marriage...* Paris: Mamert Patisson for Rob. Estienne, 1581. First edition, 8vo., 30 leaves, woodcut Estienne device on titlepage, little light marginal waterstain, some page rippling, apparently inscribed by author, top margin trimmed so it is not possible to read name on donee, modern limp vellum, nice, clean copy, scarce. Second Life Books Inc. 189 - 123 2015 $4500

Hotman, Francois *Francogallia, Libellus Statum Verteris Rei Publica Gallicae...* Coloniae: Ex Officina Hieronymi Bertulphi, 1574. Second edition, small 8vo., light vertical stain on titlepage, engraved initial letters, bound in modern full calf, covers stamped in modest gilt and blind, very nice, clean. Second Life Books Inc. 189 - 124 2015 $4000

Houdin, Robert *The Sharper Detected and Exposed.* London: Chapman and Hall, 1863. First edition, 12mo., handsome modern three quarter calf, inscription, endpapers marbled and glued to front free marbled endpaper is small jack of clubs, on similar back endpaper is glued queen of diamonds, top of spine gilt, leaves crisp, unmarked. M & S Rare Books, Inc. 97 - 158 2015 $2750

Houdini, Harry *Elliott's Last Legacy...* New York: Adams Press Print, 1923. First edition, illustrations by Oscar Teale, binding lightly worn at extremities, tidemark from dampstain at top corner of pages throughout, front hinge tender but still sound, very good, Teale's copy, inscribed for him by Houdini, inscribed by Teale for Lester Grimes, Grimes then inscribed the book for friend Gertrude Elliott. Between the Covers Rare Books, Inc. 187 - 164 2015 $4000

Hough, Graham *The Last Romantics.* London: Gerald Duckworth & Co., 1949. Half title, original mauve cloth, very good in dusted dust jacket, Geoffrey Tillotson's signed copy with pencil notes, long inserted review from TLS. Jarndyce Antiquarian Booksellers CCVII - 310 2015 £20

Houghton, Claude *This Was Ivor Trent.* London: Heinemann, 1935. First edition, fine in very good dust jacket with chips at top of spine and at corners and several short closed tears, Book Society wraparound intact, inscribed by author. Mordida Books March 2015 - 001127 2015 $150

Houghton, Claude *Three Fantastic Tales.* London: Joiner, 1934. First edition, fine without dust jacket as issued. Mordida Books March 2015 - 003112 2015 $125

Houghton, Walter E. *The Art of Newman's Apologia.* New Haven: pub. for Wellesley College by Yale University Press, 1945. Frontispiece, original beige cloth, in slightly torn and dusted dust jacket, Geoffrey Tillotson's copy, signed, 25 viii 45, with few marginal notes and marks, with two ALS's from author, proof of Tillotson's review. Jarndyce Antiquarian Booksellers CCVII - 399 2015 £20

Houghton, Walter E. *The Victorian Frame of Mind 1830-1870.* New Haven: published for Wellesley College by Yale University Press, 1957. original black cloth, few pencil marginal marks and notes, signed by Geoffrey Tillotson with part of TLS from author 1938. Jarndyce Antiquarian Booksellers CCVII - 311 2015 £20

Houplain, Jacques *La Genese.* Paris: Chez Jean Porson, 1949. #32 of 75 copies, from an edition of 250, with extra set of illustrations + 13 planches inutilisees, a copper plate and an original drawing corresponding to the copper plate (constituting volume 2), 4to., 2 volumes, wrappers, unbound gatherings in chemise and slipcase. Beasley Books 2013 - 2015 $1200

House that Jack Built to Which is added Some Account of Jack Jingle... York: printed by J. Kendrew circa, 1820. 24mo., pictorial wrappers, 23 pages, fine, woodcuts on each page. Aleph-bet Books, Inc. 109 - 156 2015 $275

The House that Jack Built. New York: McLoughlin Bros. (24 Beekman) n.d. circa, 1860. 12mo., pictorial wrappers, near fine, 8 hand colored illustrations. Aleph-bet Books, Inc. 109 - 151 2015 $600

The House that Jack Built. New York: McLoughlin Bros., 1891. 4to., stiff pictorial wrappers, near fine, die cut in shape of Jack's house, fine chromolithographs on every page. Aleph-Bet Books, Inc. 108 - 289 2015 $400

House, Humphry *All in Due Time.* London: Rupert Hart-Davis, 1955. Half title, original red cloth, torn dust jacket, from the library of Geoffrey & Kathleen Tillotson, inscribed "Tillotson's 1955" with pencil notes, ALS from House's widow Madeline thanking Geoffrey for his review, with note and short review by Kathleen. Jarndyce Antiquarian Booksellers CCVII - 312 2015 £20

House, Humphry *Coleridge, the Clark Lectures 1951-1952.* London: Rupert Hart Davis, 1953. Half title, original decorated boards, very good in slightly dusted dust jacket, Geoffrey Tillotson's copy with TLS from Rupert Hart-Davis 1955 announcing House's sudden death, tipped in, pencil notes, obits, and two ALS's from Madeline House to Geoffrey. Jarndyce Antiquarian Booksellers CCVII - 153 2015 £30

Household, Geoffrey *The Brides of Solomon.* London: Michael Joseph, 1958. First edition, fine in dust jacket with darkened spine and faint stains on back panel. Mordida Books March 2015 - 008093 2015 $90

Household, Geoffrey *Rogue Male.* Boston: Little Brown and Co., 1939. First US edition, fine, tight, clean copy in especially bright dust jacket with just trace of rubbing at extremities. Buckingham Books March 2015 - 27318 2015 $2000

Household, Geoffrey *The Salvation of Pisco Gabar and Other Stories.* Boston: Little Brown and Co., 1940. First US edition, near fine in price clipped dust jacket with light wear to spine ends and extremities. Buckingham Books March 2015 - 17487 2015 $300

Household, Geoffrey *A Time to Kill.* Boston: Little Brown, 1951. First edition, fine in dust jacket with couple of short closed tears. Mordida Books March 2015 - 004256 2015 $85

Housewright, David *Penance.* Woodstock: Foul Play, 1995. First edition, very fine in dust jacket. Mordida Books March 2015 - 006811 2015 $80

Housman, Alfred Edward 1859-1936 *Last Poems.* London: Grant Richards, 1922. Half title, slight foxing, original dark blue cloth, Geoffrey Tillotson's copy 1926 with a number of inserted cuttings. Jarndyce Antiquarian Booksellers CCVII - 314 2015 £20

Housman, Laurence 1865-1959 *The Seven Goslings.* London: Blackie and Son, a1908. First edition, illustrations in color, 4to., cloth backed brown pictorial boards, occasional foxing, else very good+, 6 fabulous bold color plates by Mabel Dearmer. Aleph-bet Books, Inc. 109 - 228 2015 $750

Housman, Laurence 1865-1959 *Stories from the Arabian Nights.* New York & London: Charles Scribner's Sons & Hodder and Stoughton, 1907. First American edition, thick 4to., gilt decorated cloth, slight bit of rear cover soil and front endpaper rubbed at hinge (not weak), else near fine, 50 tipped in color plates mounted on dark paper at back of book as issued. Aleph-bet Books, Inc. 109 - 144 2015 $1500

Housman, Laurence 1865-1959 *Stories from the Arabian Nights retold by....* London: Hodder & Stoughton, 1907. Limited to 350 numbered copies, signed by artist, Edmund Dulac, 50 tipped in color plates at back of book, as issued, beautiful copy, very scarce, thick 4to., gilt pictorial vellum, top edge gilt, minimal soil, fine with original ties and with none of the warping that is usually found on this title. Aleph-Bet Books, Inc. 108 - 156 2015 $5500

Houston, Pam *Cowboys are My Weakness.* New York: Norton, 1992. First edition, signed, very fine in first state dust jacket. Buckingham Books March 2015 - 3055 2015 $175

How, Douglas *The 8th Hussars. A History of the Regiment.* Sussex: Maritime Pub., 1964. 8vo., frontispiece, 46 black and white photo illustrations, blue cloth, map decorated endpapers, dust jacket, very good. Schooner Books Ltd. 110 - 150 2015 $125

How, Harry *Illustrated Interviews.* London: George Newnes, 1893. First edition, 8vo., original pictorial green cloth, gilt lettering, all edges gilt, photos, sketches, facsimiles, hinges starting, edges slightly rubbed, very good. The Brick Row Book Shop Miscellany 67 - 59 2015 $150

Howard, Charles F. *Essays on the Age.* London: J. K. Chapman and Co., 1855. First edition, blind embossed brown cloth, gilt stamped spine lettering, small contemporary bookseller's label, very near fine, modest edgewear, corners lightly bumped, inscribed by author for Samuel Theobold, scarce. Between the Covers Rare Books 196 - 80 2015 $250

Howard, Edward *Sir Henry Morgan the Buccaneer.* London: Henry Colburn, 1842. First edition, 3 volumes, 12mo., half title, frontispiece in volume I, handsomely rebound in half tanned calf, gilt bands, dark green morocco labels.   Jarndyce Antiquarian Booksellers   CCXI - 145   2015   £380

Howard, George Bronson *God's Man.* Indianapolis: Bobbs Merrill, 1915. First edition, fine in dust jacket.   Mordida Books   March 2015 - 007493   2015 $100

Howard, H. R. *The History of Virgil a Stewart and His Adventure in Capturing and Exposing the Great Western Land Pirate and His Gang.* New York: Harper and Bros., 1836. First edition, 12mo., cloth, rare, moderate foxing, light wear to extremities, else very good, rare.   Buckingham Books   March 2015 - 25604   2015 $1250

Howard, John *An Account of the Principal Lazarettos in Europe: with Various Papers Relative to the Plague...* Warrington: printed by William Eyres and sold by T. Cadeel, J. Johnson, C. Dilly and J. Taylor in London, 1789. First edition, 4to., 22 engraved plates (of which 20 are folding), one very large engraved folding table, including half title, some marginal browning, original (probably) marbled boards with original (probably) printed spine label, entirely uncut, minor binding wear, excellent presentation copy, inscribed by author "Mr. Howard requests Mr. Sampson will be kind enough to accept this book from him, as a small mark of his esteem" with Margaret Sampson's ownership signature, later ownership signature of James Froud 1834 on titlepage, in all choice copy, largely in original state.   John Drury Rare Books   2015 - 25837   2015 $2622

Howard, Richard *Findings.* New York: Atheneum, 1971. First edition, fine, inscribed by author to Diana and Lionel Trilling, in 1971.   Between the Covers Rare Books, Inc.   187 - 132   2015 $200

Howard, Richard *Misgivings. Poems.* New York: Atheneum, 1979. First edition, paperback original, there was no hardcover issue, lightly foxed, spine and rear wrapper sunned, near fine, inscribed by author for Leon Edel.   Between the Covers Rare Books, Inc.   187 - 134   2015 $200

Howard, Richard *Two Part Inventions.* New York: Atheneum, 1974. First edition, paperback original, no hardcover issue, tall octavo, glossy wrappers, lightly foxed, inscribed by author for Leon Edel.   Between the Covers Rare Books, Inc.   187 - 133   2015 $150

Howard, Robert E. *The Coming of Conan.* New York: Gnome Press, 1953. First edition, octavo, jacket art by Frank Kelly Feas, boards.   John W. Knott, Bookseller   Selected New Arrivals Jan. 2015 - 17106   2015 $450

Howard, Robert E. *Conan the Barbarian.* New York: Gnome Press, 1954. First edition, jacket art by Ed Emshwiller, boards.   John W. Knott, Bookseller   Selected New Arrivals Jan. 2015 - 17107   2015 $450

Howard, Robert E. *Conan the Conqueror.* New York: Gnome Press, 1950. First edition, octavo, cloth.   John W. Knott, Bookseller   Selected New Arrivals Jan. 2015 - 17103   2015 $500

Howard, Robert E. *King Conan.* New York: Gnome Press Inc., 1953. First edition, octavo, cloth.   John W. Knott, Bookseller   Selected New Arrivals Jan. 2015 - 17105   2015 $450

Howard, Robert E. *The Sword of Conan.* New York: Gnome Press, 1952. First edition, octavo, jacket art by David Kyle, cloth.   John W. Knott, Bookseller   Selected New Arrivals Jan. 2015 - 17104   2015 $450

Howe, John *The Blessedness of the Righteous Opened and Further Recommended from the Consideration of the Vanity of this Moral Life in Two Treatises.* London: printed by A. Maxwell for Sa. Gellibrand, 1673. Second edition, small octavo, probably late 18th or early 19th century American full calf gilt, joints little tender but sound, tight, small strip cut from top of titlepage, presumably to remove a name, very good, ownership signature (twice) of Rev. Frederick T. Tiffany of Cooperstown NY with couple of ink notes in text, probably in his hand.   Between the Covers Rare Books, Inc.   187 - 135   2015 $800

Howe, Susan *Hinge Picture.* New York: Telephone Books, 1974. First edition, 4to., original photo glossy wrappers, stapled as issued, front wrapper lightly creased, near fine portion likely from reading, otherwise fine, uncommon.   James S. Jaffe Rare Books   Modern American Poetry - 138   2015 $750

Howe, Susan *The Nonconformist's Memorial.* New York: Grenfell Press, 1992. First edition, one of only 65 numbered copies signed by Howe and Mangold, out of a total edition of 83 copies, as new, 4to., 6 original woodcuts by Robert Mangold, original handmade hemp paper wrappers in publisher's folding cloth box, as new.   James S. Jaffe Rare Books   Modern American Poetry - 140   2015 $2000

Howe, Susan *The Nonconformist Memorial.* New York: Grenfell Press, 1993. First edition, one of 18 deluxe copies numbered in roman, specially bound and accompanied by separate original woodcut numbered and signed by artist, Robert Mangold, book signed by author and artist, from a total edition of 83 copies, as new, 6 original woodcuts by Robert Mangold, original full vellum with white leather ties by Claudia Cohen, in publisher's natural wood veneer folding box.   James S. Jaffe Rare Books   Modern American Poetry - 139   2015 $4500

Howel, Laurence *The Orthodox Communicant.* London: J. Sturt, 1721. Second edition, 165 x 102mm., attractive contemporary black morocco tooled in blind in somber style, covers with frame of scallops and floral tools, central panel with large cruciform fleuron surrounded by curving lines and small tools, raised bands, spine panels with small lozenge, marbled endpapers, all edges gilt, engraved throughout on silver, elaborate decorative and historiated initials, each page with fine pictorial frame, text pages with engraved biblical scenes, thick leaves of text apparently made up of two pieces of paper, printed on one side and glued together, front pastedown with engraved armorial bookplate, three flyleaves with obvious evidence of bookplate removal, very minor wear to joints and extremities, isolated faint stains or marginal smudges, really excellent copy of a book often otherwise, text clean and fresh, original binding especially bright and with only trivial signs of use.   Phillip J. Pirages   66 - 34   2015 $1500

Howell Books *Catalogue 50 California. The Library of Jennie Crocker Henderson with additions Parts I-V.* San Francisco: John Howell Books, 1979-1980. First edition, 5 volumes, photos, tan wrappers printed in dark brown and back, 2 volumes with date in ink on spine, else fine set.   Argonaut Book Shop   Holiday Season 2014 - 129   2015 $100

Howells, William Dean 1837-1920 *A Woman's Reason.* Toronto: Rose, First Canadian edition, 8vo., blue cloth, decorative stamping in black and gilt, hinges tender, cover somewhat scuffed, little worn at corners and ends of spine, else very good.   Second Life Books Inc.   189 - 125   2015 $65

Howes, Royce *Death on the Bridge.* Garden City: Doubleday Crime Club, 1935. First edition, near fine, scrape on spine, otherwise fine in near fine dust jacket with scrape on front and long narrow stain on front panel.   Mordida Books   March 2015 - 010215   2015 $250

Howland, Esther Allen *The American Economical Housekeeper and Family Receipt.* Cincinnati: Derby, 1845. Stereotype edition, 8vo., linen backed printed paper boards, spine well worn and held with tape, frontispiece, some stained internally.   Second Life Books Inc.   189 - 59   2015 $150

Howland, John *Address Delivered Before the Providence Association of Mechanicks and Manufacturers, on the Occasion of Opening Mechanick's Hall Jan. 10 A.D.1825.* Providence: H. H. Brown, 1830. First edition, 8vo., sewn as issued, old plain wrappers, chipped and detached, sheets uniformly toned, else fine, uncut and unopened.   M & S Rare Books, Inc.   97 - 270   2015 $85

Hoyle, Edmond 1672-1759 *Mr. Hoyle's Games of Whist, Quadrille, Piquet, Chess and Back-Gammon, Complete...* London: printed by assignment from T. Osborne for J. Rivington and J. Wilkie and 11 others, n.d. circa, 1772. 12mo., original blind ruled sheep, raised bands, some wear to extremities, very good.   John Drury Rare Books   March 2015 - 19134   2015 $221

Hubbard, John Gellibrand *Reform or Reject the Income Tax.* London: Longman Brown Green and Longmans, 1853. First edition, 8vo., modern wrappers, printed title label on upper cover, very good, uncommon.   John Drury Rare Books   March 2015 - 23723   2015 $266

Hubbard, L. R. *Final Blackout.* Providence: Hadley Publishing Co., 1948. First edition, octavo, cloth.   John W. Knott, Bookseller   Selected New Arrivals Jan. 2015 - 17110   2015 $200

Hubbard, Silas *John D. Rockefeller, His Career.* New York: the author, 1904. First edition, very good- soiling to boards, light pencil notes on titlepage.   Beasley Books   2013 - 2015 $45

Hubbell, Rose String *Quacky Doodles' and Danny Daddles' Book.* Chicago: Volland, 1916. First edition, No addition printings, 8vo., pictorial boards, covers dusty and minor spine mend, else fine in original pictorial box (flap repaired), illustrations on every page by Johnny Gruelle, including silhouette endpapers, amazing copy.   Aleph-bet Books, Inc.   109 - 211   2015 $1850

Hubin, Allen J. *Crime Fiction 1749-1980: a Comprehensive Bibliography.* New York: Garland, 1984. First edition, fine, without dust jacket as issued, without the supplement.   Mordida Books   March 2015 - 007596   2015 $100

Huch, Ricarda *Vita Somnium Breve: Eine Roman.* Leipzig: Insel Verlag, 1903. 12mo., cloth, spine and front cover gilt stamped, decorated endpapers, top edge gilt, frontispiece, decorative initials and tailpiece, covers rubbed at corners and scuffed.   Oak Knoll Books   306 - 270   2015 $250

Hudleston, William *A Daily Preparation for a Worthy Receiving of the Holy Sacrament.* London: printed for C. Rivington, 1734. First edition, few minor spots, 12mo., contemporary black morocco, boards bordered with triple gilt fillet, gilt centre and cornerpieces, spine gilt in compartments, marked endpapers, gilt edges, joints slightly rubbed, very good, remarkably attractive copy of a very rare book.   Blackwell's Rare Books   B179 - 51   2015   £600

Hudson's Bay Company *Minutes of the Hudson's Bay Company 1671-1674 and 179-1684.* London: Hudson's Bay Record Society, 1942. 1945. 1946. First edition, volumes V, VIII and IX, limited edition, 3 volumes, frontispiece, blue cloth, gilt, slight bumping to corners, fine set, mostly uncut.　　Argonaut Book Shop　　Holiday Season 2014 - 130　　2015　　$325

Hudson, Alma *The Peter Rabbit Box.* Cupples & Leon, 1921. 3 books, 12mo., boards, pictorial paste-on, fine in dust jackets, housed in original box with color plate on top (box lid edges reinforced), each book illustrated in color, very scarce, with 6 inch celluloid Peter Rabbit toy.　　Aleph-Bet Books, Inc.　　108 - 372　　2015　　$1500

Hudson, Guillermo Enrique *Alla Lejos Y Hace Tiemp. (Far Away and Long Ago. A History of My Early Life).* Buenos Aires: Ediciones Dos Amigos, 2004. One of 45 copies, all on cream Velin d'Arches paper, signed in pencil by artist, Alicia Scavino on page 119 of volume I, 11 full and half page etchings and aquatints by Alicia Scavino, page size 10 1/8 x 13 3/4 inches, loose as issued in original pale green paper wrappers, cork over boards clamshell box with title in green on spine, fine, set in 12 point Ronaldson and printed letterpress in three colors, by Ruben R. Lapolla under the direction of Samuel Cesar Palui and Ernesto Lowenstein.　　Priscilla Juvelis - Rare Books　　61 - 10　　2015　　$1500

Hudson, Thomson Jay *The Law of Mental Medicine.* Chicago: McClurg, 1903. hardcover.　　Beasley Books　　2013 - 2015　　$45

Huggler, Tom *A Fall of Woodcock.* Sunfield: Outdoor Images, 1996. First edition, one of 750 numbered and signed copies, signed by author and artist, Jim Foote, leather bound, fine.　　Beasley Books　　2013 - 2015　　$175

Hughes, Dorothy B. *The Fallen Sparrow.* New York: Duell Sloan and Pearce, 1942. First edition, fine in dust jacket with light professional restoration to spine ends and corners.　　Buckingham Books　　March 2015 - 30618　　2015　　$750

Hughes, Dorothy B. *Johnnie.* Duell, Sloan and Pearce, 1940. First edition, inscribed by author, fine in dust jacket with light professional restoration to spine ends and extremities.　　Buckingham Books　　March 2015 - 34683　　2015　　$750

Hughes, Dorothy B. *An Omnibus of Terror.* New York: Duell, Sloan and Pearce, 1842. First edition thus, fine in dust jacket with light professional restoration to spine ends corners and extremities, handsome copy.　　Buckingham Books　　March 2015 - 31230　　2015　　$750

Hughes, Jabez *An Ode on the Incarnation.* London: printed for and sold by H. Hills, 1709. Piracy, 8vo., disbound, very good.　　C. R. Johnson　　Foxon R-Z - 1222r-z　　2015　　$153

Hughes, Langston *Ask your Mama, 12 Moods for Jazz.* New York: Knopf, 1961. First edition, oblong 8vo., text block printed on pink paper with blue & brown lettering, near fine in dust jacket that is trifle rubbed at edges.　　Second Life Books Inc.　　190 - 114　　2015　　$250

Hughes, Langston *The Book of Rhythms.* New York: Franklin Watts, 1954. First edition, 8vo., near fine in fine dust jacket.　　Second Life Books Inc.　　190 - 115　　2015　　$300

Hughes, Langston *The Book of Negro Folklore.* New York: Dodd, Mead and Co., 1958. First edition, octavo, 624 pages, light wear and bit of soiling at extremities of cloth, else near fine in slightly spine and faded and rubbed, near fine, nicely inscribed by Hughes for radio personality Emily Kimbrough, NY Jan. 14 1959.　　Between the Covers Rare Books　　197 - 23　　2015　　$950

Hughes, Langston *"Don't You Want to Be Free?" in One Act Play Magazine Oct. 1938.* New York: Contemporary Play Publications, 1938. Large 8fo., paper wrappers, cover little browned and very slightly worn at edges, otherwise very good, scarce.　　Second Life Books Inc.　　191 - 43　　2015　　$65

Hughes, Langston *Fields of Wonder.* New York: Alfred Knopf, 1947. First edition, 8vo., fine in little nicked dust jacket, issued in an edition of 2500 copies only.　　Second Life Books Inc.　　190 - 118　　2015　　$165

Hughes, Langston *I Wonder as I Wander.* New York: Rinehart, 1956. First edition, 8vo., fine in price clipped dust jacket (lacks front upper corner, little nicked at extremities of spine).　　Second Life Books Inc.　　190 - 122　　2015　　$200

Hughes, Langston *Laughing to Keep from Crying.* New York: Holt, 1952. First edition, 8vo., 206 pages, paper over boards with cloth spine, owner's name on flyleaf, edges of cover little scuffed, otherwise very good, tight copy in somewhat chipped and soiled dust jacket.　　Second Life Books Inc.　　190 - 123　　2015　　$225

Hughes, Langston *A New Song.* New York: International Workers Order, 1938. First edition, 8vo., paper wrappers, cover drawing by Joe Jones, cover some soiled and scuffed, otherwise very good, rare.　　Second Life Books Inc.　　191 - 44　　2015　　$325

Hughes, Langston *The Panther and the Lash: Poems of Our Times.* New York: Knopf, 1967. First edition, 8vo., original cloth, dust jacket, fine in lightly rubbed dust jacket with publisher's label on front flap.   James S. Jaffe Rare Books   Modern American Poetry - 142   2015 $125

Hughes, Langston *"Slave on the Block." a story in Scribner's magazine Volume XCIV No. 3 September 1933.* New York: Scribner's, 1933. First edition, 4to., cover slightly worn, but very good.   Second Life Books Inc.   191 - 45   2015 $60

Hughes, Langston *Something in Common and Other stories.* New York: Hill & Wang, 1963. First Century Series edition, 8vo., yellow cloth very good, tight in scuffed and little chipped dust jacket.   Second Life Books Inc.   191 - 46   2015 $145

Hughes, Langston *The Sweet Flypaper of Life.* Washington: Howard University, 1988. Second printing, square 4to., photos by Roy De Carava, with presentation from De Carava on title to Andy Davis May 30 1992, olive cloth, nice in slightly scuffed dust jacket.   Second Life Books Inc.   190 - 54   2015 $325

Hughes, Langston *Troubled Island.* New York: Leeds Music, 1949. First edition, 8vo., light blue printed wrappers little soiled, near fine, inscribed by author for Richard M. Lourie.   Second Life Books Inc.   190 - 128   2015 $600

Hughes, Langston *The Weary Blues.* New York: Alfred A. Knopf, 1926. First edition, one of 1500 copies, small 8vo., original blue cloth backed decorated boards, inscribed presentation from author to George Gershwin, Jan. 31 1926, stellar association copy, covers lightly rubbed, lacking rare dust jacket as was the case with all of Gershwin's books, otherwise very good.   James S. Jaffe Rare Books   Modern American Poetry - 141   2015 $35,000

Hughes, Langston *The Weary Blues.* New York: Knopf, 1944. Ninth printing, 8vo., yellow cloth, dust jacket (lacks some paper at extremities of spine and small hole which affects two letters of author's name), very good, inscribed by author for Mrs. Lester Holt.   Second Life Books Inc.   190 - 131   2015 $450

Hughes, Langston *The Collected Works of.* Columbia: University of Missouri Press, 2001-2006. 6 volumes are first editions, 6 are second printings, 3 third printings, one is fourth printing, 16 volumes, fine, dust jacket.   Second Life Books Inc.   190 - 116   2015 $1500

Hughes, Ted   1930-1998 *The Burning of the Brothel.* London: Turret Books, 1966. First edition, number 6 of 75 copies signed by author, out of a total edition of 300, quarto, plain white wrappers with Japanese paper dust jacket, upper corner and text creased, frontispiece.   Peter Ellis, Bookseller   2014 - 019839   2015   £300

Hughes, Ted   1930-1998 *Meet My Folks!* London: Faber and Faber, 1961. Uncorrected proof, illustrations by George Adamson, tiny tear at crown of thin spine, little sunning at extremities of wrappers, else near fine, rare in this format.   Between the Covers Rare Books   196 - 161   2015 $800

Hughes, Ted   1930-1998 *Recklings.* London: Turret Books, 1966. First edition, octavo, number 88 of 150 copies signed by author, fine in fine dust jacket just little creased at upper corners.   Peter Ellis, Bookseller   2014 - 017325   2015   £325

Hughes, Thomas   1822-1896 *Mental Furniture; or the Adaptation of Knowledge for Man.* London: Hamilton Adams and Co., 1857. First edition, 8vo., original orange blindstamped cloth, title in gilt on upper cover and spine, cloth somewhat dust soiled, good copy, scarce.   John Drury Rare Books   2015 - 13803   2015 $133

Hughes, Thomas   1822-1896 *The Scouring of the White Horse; or the Long Vacation Ramble of a London Clerk.* Cambridge: Macmillan and Co., 1859. Small 4to., half title, double frontispiece, illustrations, 16 page catalog (Christmas 1858), slightly rubbed and dulled, library stamp and marks on leading endpapers, original royal blue morocco grained cloth, elaborately blocked in gilt, back board in blind, all edges gilt.   Jarndyce Antiquarian Booksellers   CCXI - 146   2015   £95

Hugo, Pieter *The Hyena & Other Men.* Munich: Prestel, 2008. Reprint, 4to., original binding lettered black at spine, copiously illustrated in color, gift inscription, very good in like dust jacket with slight dampstaining to top corner of cloth with faintly marked top fore-edge, not affecting images.   Any Amount of Books   2015 - C11068   2015   £225

Hugo, Richard *Death and the Good Life.* New York: St. Martin's, 1981. First edition, fine in price clipped dust jacket with some light rubbing along edges.   Mordida Books March 2015 - 006813   2015 $75

Hugo, Victor   1802-1865 *By Order of the King.* London: Bradbury, Evans and Co., 1870. First English edition, 3 volumes, half title, frontispiece, vignette title, illustrations, 2 page catalog volume 1, original green cloth, cloth slightly lifting from board volume I and splitting to back inner hinge, wear to tails of spines, slightly dulled and rubbed, good, sound copy, bookplates and ink signatures of Major Arthur Bott Cook, J.P. and W. H. Smith library labels, Greathead Manor (Lingfield Surrey), shelf numbers.   Jarndyce Antiquarian Booksellers   CCXI - 147   2015   £125

Hugo, Victor 1802-1865 *The History of a Crime.* London: Sampson Low, Marston, Searle and Rivington, 1878. First English edition volumes III and IV, second edition of volumes I and II, 4 volumes, half title volume I, original dark brown cloth, spines lettered in gilt, slightly rubbed, slight wear to heads and tails of spines volumes III and IV, good plus.   Jarndyce Antiquarian Booksellers   CCXI - 148   2015   £185

Hugo, Victor 1802-1865 *The Memoirs of Victor Hugo.* New York: G. W. Dillingham, 1899. First edition, 8vo., original olive green cloth, lettered gilt on spine and front cover, handsome copy, very slightly bumped at lower spine corner with front endpaper slightly creased and very slightly chipped, otherwise fine, printed dust jacket slightly chipped at spine ends.   Any Amount of Books   2015 - C13872   2015   £250

Hugo, Victor 1802-1865 *Les Miserables.* New York: Limited Editions Club, 1938. Limited to 1500 numbered copies signed by Ward, 5 volumes, small 4to., full black cloth with terra cotta spine labels in single slipcase, with monthly letter loosely inserted, slipcase with wear along edges.   Oak Knoll Books   25 - 23   2015 $325

Hugo, Victor 1802-1865 *Notre-Dame De Paris.* New York: Limited Editions Club, 1930. Limited to 1500 numbered copies signed by artist, Frans Masereel, 2 volumes, 4to., paper wrappers in chemise, slipcase, profusely illustrated, printed in Paris on Velin d'Arches paper, bound in French style in wrappers with publishing information and woodcut by Masereel on front cover of each volume, chemise and slipcase covered in matching cork patterned paper, with Monthly Letter/prospectus loosely inserted, unusually fine, rubbing to chemise and slipcase.   Oak Knoll Books   25 - 2   2015 $350

Hugo, Victor 1802-1865 *Things Seen.* Glasgow & New York: George Routledge & Sons, 1887. First English edition, ads preceding half titles, frontispiece volume I, 4 page catalog (unopened volume 2), original red cloth, spines slightly faded, very good.   Jarndyce Antiquarian Booksellers   CCXI - 149   2015   £150

Hugo, Victor 1802-1865 *Toilers of the Sea.* London: Sampson Low, Son & Marston, 1866. Second edition, 3 volumes, 16 page catalog (March 30 1866), volume III, original green pebble grained cloth, boards blocked in blind, spine lettered and decorated in gilt, small nick to leading hinge of volume I, slightly rubbed and dulled, very good.   Jarndyce Antiquarian Booksellers   CCXI - 150   2015   £225

Huie, William Bradford *The Klansman.* New York: Delacorte Press, 1967. First edition, signed by author, nearly fine in like dust jacket.   Ed Smith Books   83 - 48   2015 $150

Hujar, Peter *Peter Hujar: Night.* New York & San Francisco: Matthew Marks Gallery/Fraenkel Gallery, 2005. First edition, 43 black and white images, light near fine copy in very near fine dust jacket.   Jeff Hirsch Books   E-62 Holiday List 2014 - 19   2015 $125

Hulbert, Archer Butler *The Niagara River.* G. P. Putnam's sons, 1908. First edition, 8vo., blue cloth, picture affixed to front cover, gold stamping on front cover and spine, illustrations, maps, inscribed by author for Charles A. Dana.   Buckingham Books   March 2015 - 21290   2015 $300

Hull, Richard *And Death Came Too.* New York: Julian Messner, 1942. First US edition, fine, bright copy in dust jacket, sharp copy.   Buckingham Books   March 2015 - 27210   2015 $450

Hull, Richard *Invitation to an Inquest.* London: Collins/Crime Club, 1950. First edition, 8vo., original red cloth lettered black on spine, one pedigree chart, from the Donald Rudd collection of detective fiction, spine slightly faded, had of spine very slightly frayed, cover has faint ring, otherwise near very good, clean text.   Any Amount of Books   2015 - A96879   2015 £160

Hull, Richard *My Own Murderer.* New York: Julian Messner Inc., 1940. First US edition, minor rubbing to bottom edge of cloth and tiny red ink smear to rear flyleaf, else fine, bright copy, dust jacket, lightly soiled on rear panel with light wear to spine ends and extremities.   Buckingham Books   March 2015 - 23822   2015 $375

Humbert, Jean *Discours sur l'Utilite de la Langue arabe, Prononce le 16 Juin 1823 aux Promotions du College de Geneve.* Geneva: Guille Flick, 1823. First edition, small 8vo., half title inscribed 'Homamge de l'Auteur', recently well bound in cloth lettered in gilt, very good.   John Drury Rare Books   March 2015 - 17870   2015 $266

An Humble Remonstrance of the Batchelors, in and About London to the Honourable House in Answer to a (sic) Late Paper, Intituled a Petition of the Ladies for Husbands. London: printed for and sold by the book selling batchelors in St. Paul's Church Yard, 1693. First edition, very scarce, 4to., page numerals cropped, else fine, crisp, unbound, now preserved in marbled wrappers, very scarce.   John Drury Rare Books   2015 - 24746   2015 $2185

Hume, Allan C. *Stray Feathers: a Journal of Ornithology for India and Its Dependencies.* 1872-1878. Octavo, 8 volumes, hand colored plates, contemporary green half calf with red labels, some rubbing, set of the Royal Australasian Ornithologists' Union with library stamps.   Andrew Isles   2015 - 30873   2015 $1500

Hume, James Deacon *The Laws of the Customs, compiled by Direction of the Lords Commissioners of His Majesty's Treasury (bound with) Supplement for 1826.* London: J. Mawman, 1825. First editions, 8vo., contemporary calf gilt with raised bands, slight damage to head of spine, foot of spine stamped 'Pier Office', very good, scarce. John Drury Rare Books   2015 - 7851   2015 $177

Humphrey, Mabel *The Book of the Child.* New York: Frederick Stokes, October, 1903. First edition, large folio, cloth backed pictorial boards, except for slight general soil and tip wear, bright, clean, near fine copy, 3 exquisite full page color illustrations by Jessie Willcox Smith as well as color cover and smaller text illustrations, 4 magnificent full page color illustrations by Elizabeth Shippen Green, rarely found in such clean condition.   Aleph-bet Books, Inc.   109 - 447   2015 $3000

Humphrey, Mabel *Continentals.* New York: Frederick Stokes, 1900. Large 4to., cloth backed pictorial boards, slight bit of normal cover wear, near fine, 6 wonderful chromolithographed plates by Maud Humphrey.   Aleph-bet Books, Inc.   109 - 230   2015 $700

Humphrey, William *The Last Husband and Other Stories.* New York: William Morrow & Co., 1953. First edition, inscribed by author for Harry and Elizabeth Ford, very good in dust jacket lightly sunned on spine, short closed tear to top edge of front panel.   Buckingham Books   March 2015 - 14989   2015 $375

Hunt, Aurora *The Army of the Pacific: Its Operations in California, Texas, Arizona, New Mexico, Utah, Nevada, Oregon, Washington, Plains Region, Mexico, etc. 1860-1866.* A. H. Clark, 1951. First edition, cloth, fine, bright, signed copy, previous owners small name and address sticker on front free endpaper.   Buckingham Books   March 2015 - 34450   2015 $350

Hunt, Henry *Investigation at Ilchester Gaol in the County of Somerset into the Conduct of William Bridle, the Goaler, before the Commissioners Appointed by the Crown.* London: Thomas Dolby, 1821. First edition book form, 8vo., fine etched frontispiece by George Cruikshank, 5 other engraved plates, probably by Robert Cruikshank, with two supplementary addresses found in some copies, contemporary half calf gilt and marbled boards, some general wear to sides and extremities but nonetheless very good.   John Drury Rare Books   2015 - 18370   2015 $787

Hunt, John *The Ascent of Everest.* London: Hodder & Stoughton, 1953. First edition, first printing, from the library of British Army Lieutenant Colonel G. S. K. Maydon bearing his signature and dated "Nov. 53" to front pastedown near fine with slight rubbing to extremities and few minor stains to cloth along upper edge, unclipped jacket with light wear to spine ends, few small tears, else very good or better.   B & B Rare Books, Ltd.   234 - 56   2015 $175

Hunter, Dard 1883-1966 *Before Life Began 1883-1923.* Cleveland: The Rowfant Club, 1941. Limited to 219 numbered copies, signed by designer, Bruce Rogers, 8vo. quarter vellum, marbled paper covered boards, slipcase with label, top edge gilt, other edges uncut, presentation by Hunter to papermaker William Bond Wheelright, slipcase rubbed and scuffed at edges, pastedowns show foxing from material used to paste down binding.   Oak Knoll Books   306 - 96   2015 $550

Hunter, George *Reminiscences of an Old Timer.* Battle Creek: Review and Herald, 1889. Fourth edition, 8vo., illustrations, warmly inscribed on flyleaf "Compliments of author, Col. Geo. Hunter to J. T. Hunter as in other words Hunter to Hunter...Timus the chief to the Chief of Good Fellows July 8th '90", also signed with his Indian name, red cloth stamped in gilt, little worn, hinge tender, very good.   Second Life Books Inc.   191 - 49   2015 $75

Hunter, John 1728-1793 *A Treatise on the Blood, Inflammation and Gun-shot Wounds.* London: printed by John Richardson for George Nicol, 1794. First edition, frontispiece, 9 additional plates, 4to., modern quarter leather and marbled paper boards with raised bands spine, gilt lettering to spine, marbled endpapers, scattered foxing text and plates.   By the Book, L. C.   44 - 36   2015 $4500

Hunter, John Dunn *Memoirs of a Captivity Among the Indians of North America from Childhood to the Age of Nineteen...* London: Longman, Hurst, Rees, Orme, Brown and Green, 1824. Third edition, 8vo., frontispiece, later 19th century three quarter calf, rubbed and small piece missing leather on spine, very nice, clean copy.   Second Life Books Inc.   190 - 132   2015 $450

Hunter, John Marvin *The Trail Drivers of Texas.* Jackson Printing Co., 1920-1923. First editions, 2 volumes, pictorial cloth, frontispiece portraits, also included Revised Volume I San Antonio: Globe Publishing, 1924, revised second edition, original 2 volumes were very crudely printed and bound, making it difficult to find copies that aren't loose and heavily worn, first volume has the stamped name of former owner on front flyleaf, else very good, tight and housed in slipcase, volume II has name of former owner stamped on front flyleaf, else very good, tight copy, housed in slipcase, revised issue very good and housed in slipcase. Buckingham Books   March 2015 - 34392   2015 $2000

Hunter, John Marvin *The Trail Drivers of Texas.* San Antonio: Jackson Printing Co., 1920-1923. First editions, 2 volumes, pictorial cloth, frontispiece, rare, first volume with errata slip affixed to front pastedown sheet, else very good tight copy, volume II is also very good, tight copy. Buckingham Books   March 2015 - 29405   2015 $1250

Hunter, John Warren *Heel-Fly Time in Texas. A Story of the Civil War Period.* privately printed, circa, 1930. First edition, quarto, stapled self wrappers, chipped along edges and browned with age, housed in folding slipcase, handsome.   Buckingham Books   March 2015 - 21582   2015 $1000

Hunter, Lillie Mae *The Moving Finger.* Borger: Plains Printing Co., 1956. 1974. First edition, 8vo., signed by author, cloth, titles stamped in black ink on front cover and spine, light wear to spine ends and covers, 2 small stickers to bottom edges front pastedown ad front flyleaf, else good copy.   Buckingham Books   March 2015 - 32770   2015 $200

Hunter, Martin *A Century for the Century, Fine Printed Books from 1900 to 1999.* New York: Grolier Club, 1999. Special edition, printed at the Stinehour Press in an edition limited to 250 case bound copies set in Dante type of which are 50 bound thus and contain a section of five actual mounted specimen leaves from books in exhibition, these copies signed by authors on special colophon page, 4to., quarter red leather with wove cloth, slipcase, with 100 full page examples of titlepages, facsimiles and illustrations.   Oak Knoll Books   306 - 24   2015 $600

Hunter, Richard *Three Hundred Years of Psychiatry 1535-1860.* London: Oxford, 1963. First edition, Stout large 8vo., very good+ to near fine in very good dust jacket.   Beasley Books 2013 - 2015 $225

Hunter, Robert *The Preservation of Open Spaces and of Footpaths...* London: Eyre and Spottiswoode, 1898. First edition, half title, original green cloth lettered gilt, minor rubbing and signs of use to extremities, very good, internally fine.   John Drury Rare Books   March 2015 - 23662   2015 $266

Hunter, Robert *The Storming of the Mind.* Garden City: Doubleday, 1971. First edition, fine in near fine dust jacket with light wear at crown, complimentary copy with Doubleday stamp and compliments slip laid in, with handwritten name of Dick McCullough.   Ken Lopez, Bookseller   164 - 181   2015 $65

Hunter, Sam *Isamu Noguchi.* New York: Abbeville Press, 1978. First edition, fine book and dust jacket.   Stephen Lupack   March 2015 - 2015 $150

Hunter, Sara Hoagland *The Unbreakable Code.* Flagstaff: Rising Moon, 1996. First edition, oblong 4to., this copy signed by (6) original Navajo Code Talkers, fine in near fine dust jacket.   Ed Smith Books   83 - 70   2015 $350

Hunter, Stephen *The Day Before Midnight.* New York: Bantam, 1989. First edition, fine in dust jacket.   Mordida Books   March 2015 - 001135   2015 $85

Hunter, Stephen *The Master Sniper.* New York: Morrow, 1980. First edition, fine in dust jacket with two tiny closed tears to top edge of rear panel.   Buckingham Books   March 2015 - 30689   2015 $250

Hunter, Stephen *The Master Sniper.* New York: Morrow, 1980. First edition, near fine in like dust jacket, price clipped.   Beasley Books   2013 - 2015 $40

Huntington, George *Robber and Hero. The Story of the Raid on the First National Bank of Northfield, Minnesota.* Northfield: Christian Way Co., 1895. First edition, cloth, 119 pages, frontispiece, numerous illustrations, diagram of bank interior, very good in original cloth.   Buckingham Books   March 2015 - 37992   2015 $255

Huntington, Ida *Garden of Heart's Delight. A Fairy Tale.* Chicago: Rand McNally, 1911. First edition, 4to., green cloth, pictorial paste-on, occasional spot else, very good+, illustrations by Maginel Wright Enright with 15 beautiful color plates, quite uncommon.   Aleph-bet Books, Inc.   109 - 159   2015 $350

Huntington, William *Zion's Alarm, Not Without Cause...* London: printed by T. Bensley, sold at Providence Chapel on Monday and Wednesday evenings and at Monkwell street Meeting on Tuesay Evenings, 1798. First edition, 8vo., recent plain wrappers, very good, scarce.   John Drury Rare Books   2015 - 20697   2015 $133

Hurd, Peter *Peter Hurd Sketchbook.* Chicago: 1971. Limited edition, limitation reads "This special edition of two hundred fifty copies numbered and signed by artist published by Swallow Press in April 1971", phrase 'two hundred fifty' has been crossed out and 'twenty six' written in with letter "I" added, folio, three quarter leather with marbled boards and endsheets, binding little shaky, else clean and very good, with dust jacket from trade edition.   Dumont Maps & Books of the West   131 - 55   2015 $225

Hurlothrumbo *The Merry-Thought or The Glass Window and Bog-House Miscellany... (with) The Merry-Thought... Part II.* London: J. Roberts, 1731. First edition, octavo, full 19th century pebbled morocco gilt, scarce.   Honey & Wax Booksellers   3 - 18   2015 $4500

Hurst, A. E. *Show Card Writing, Application of Various Types of Letters from Mercantile Purposes...* New York: UPC Book Co., 1923. first edition, 2nd printing, many illustrations and plates, in stamp "Our Lady's Press Mart", small 8vo., cloth, well preserved copy.   Oak Knoll Books Special Catalogue 24 - 23   2015 $125

Hurst, Fannie *Imitation of Life.* New York: Harper & Brothers, 1933. First edition, fine in red cloth boards with especially fresh paper labels on spine an front board in very good dust jacket with few scattered spots on front wrapper, some sunning to spine, light wear at edges and few nicks, remarkably scarce.   Between the Covers Rare Books   196 - 81   2015 $5000

Hurston, Zora Neale *Dust Tracks on a Road.* Philadelphia: Lippincott, 1942. First edition, 8vo., tan cloth stamped in lilac, Donor's presentation on flyleaf, very good, tight in little scuffed and chipped first issue dust jacket ($3.00 on flap).   Second Life Books Inc.   189 - 128   2015 $750

Hurston, Zora Neale *I Love Myself When I am laughing...* Old Westbury: Feminist Press, 1979. First edition, 8vo., photos, dark gray cloth, edges of cover very slightly scuffed, otherwise nice in dust jacket (little soiled), plastic cover.   Second Life Books Inc.   190 - 133   2015 $350

Hurston, Zora Neale *Moses Man of the Mountain.* Philadelphia: Lippincott, 1939. First edition, 8vo., first state binding, brown cloth stamped in orange, cover little scuffed at edges, owner's name on flyleaf, otherwise tight copy.   Second Life Books Inc.   189 - 129   2015 $450

Hurston, Zora Neale *Mules and Men.* Philadelphia: Lippincott, 1935. First edition, 8vo., tan cloth stamped in black cover slightly worn at corners and ends of spine, otherwise very good, tight copy.   Second Life Books Inc.   189 - 130   2015 $450

Hurston, Zora Neale *Seraph on the Suwanee: a Novel.* New York: Scribner's, 1948. First edition, 8vo., gray cloth, cover slightly worn at corners and ends of spine, otherwise very good, tight in some worn dust jacket (marginal chipping, etc.).   Second Life Books Inc.   190 - 136   2015 $500

Hurston, Zora Neale *Tell My Horse.* Philadelphia: Lippincott, 1938. First edition, 8vo., photos, red and blue cloth, top edges spotted, cover scuffed, especially at corners and spine, very good tight copy.   Second Life Books Inc.   189 - 131   2015 $250

Hurtaut, Pierre Thomas *Coup D'Oeil Anglois Sur Les Ceremonies du Marriage...* Geneva: but Paris?, 1750. First French edition, 12mo., very nice, contemporary mottled calf, gilt.   Second Life Books Inc.   189 - 132   2015 $600

Huskisson, William *Navigation Laws, Speech of the right Hon. W. Huskisson in the House of Commons Friday the 12th of May 1826 on the Present State of the Shipping Interest.* London: J. Hatchard & Son, 1826. First edition, 8vo., 70 pages, well bound in moderately recent half calf over marbled boards, spine lettered in gilt, very good.   John Drury Rare Books   2015 - 17738   2015 $221

Huskisson, William *The Question Concerning the Depreciation of Our Currency Stated and Examined.* London: John Murray and J. Hatchard, W. Blackwood Edinburgh and M. N. Mahon, Dublin, 1810. Third edition, 8vo., recently well bound in linen backed marbled boards, lettered, very good.   John Drury Rare Books   2015 - 14298   2015 $177

Huskisson, William *The Speeches of the Right Honourable William Huskisson with a Biographical Memoir...* London: John Murray, 1831. First collected edition, 3 volumes, 8vo., frontispiece in volume I, half titles in volumes II and III, 19th century polished calf gilt with raised bands and contrasting labels, top edge gilt, others uncut, fine, from the 19th century library of the Earl of Portsmouth, with inscription.   John Drury Rare Books   March 2015 - 17808   2015   £306

Hutchins, Maude Phelps *Diagrammtics.* New York: Random House, 1932. First edition, one of only 250 numbered copies, this being copy no. 6, this copy also signed by Mortimer Adler, near fine with dulled spine.   Beasley Books 2013 - 2015 $45

Hutchinson, C. C. *Resources of Kansas. Fifteen Years Experience.* Topeka: Pub. by the author, 1871. First edition, 16mo., original maroon cloth, titles stamped in gold gilt on front panel, frontispiece, illustrations, map in fine condition, non authorial penciled presentation on front flyleaf, cloth covers bit faded, minor light foxing to fore-edges, else text clean, bright and tight, near fine.   Buckingham Books March 2015 - 31797   2015 $750

Hutchinson, Gilbert Linney *The Equalization of the Poor's Rate of the United Kingdom of Great Britain and Ireland, Proved to be Both Equitable and Practicable.* London: Robert Hardwicke, 1858. First edition, 8vo., recently well bound in cloth, spine lettered gilt, very good, rare.   John Drury Rare Books   March 2015 - 21179   2015   £266

Hutchinson, R. C. *Elephant and Castle.* London: Cassell, 1949. First edition, top of pages and endpapers foxed, otherwise fine in dust jacket with internal spotting, spotting on back panel and nicks and fraying at spine ends.   Mordida Books   March 2015 - 008354   2015 $90

Hutchinson, William *An Excursion to the Lakes in Westmoreland and Cumberland August 1773.* London: J. Wilkie and W. Goldsmith, a1774. First edition, 8vo., engraved vignette on titlepage, slight foxing, first few and final few leaves, contemporary half calf over marbled boards, corners worn, neatly rebacked reusing original label and spine, very good, contemporary armorial bookplate of Sir Ashton Lever and early ownership signature of Penelope Mosley, uncommon.   John Drury Rare Books   2015 - 25681   2015 $830

The Hutterian Brethren of Montana. Augusta: privately printed, 1963. First edition, printed wrappers, 41 pages, very slight fading, very scarce, fine, ink stamp of Rev. Joseph J. Kleinsasser, Milford Colony, Augusts, Montana. Baade Books of the West 2014 - 2015 $61

Huxley, Aldous Leonard 1894-1963 *Brave New World.* London: Chatto and Windus, 1932. First edition, first printing, blue cloth, spine lettered in gilt in original pictorial dark blue dust jacket with illustration of a globe and airplane to front panel, near fine with minor wear to spine ends, hint of long toning to spine, bright and fresh interior, unclipped dust jacket with minor wear and light creasing to spine ends, tiny nicks to corners, very faint toning to spine, bright and clean panels, exceptionally beautiful copy, rare in dust jacket, rare in fine condition. B & B Rare Books, Ltd. 2015 - 2015 $8000

Huxley, Aldous Leonard 1894-1963 *Ends and Means - an Enquiry into the nature of Ideals and into the methods Employed for Their Realization.* London: Chatto & Windus, 1937. First edition, one of 160 numbered copies signed by author, octavo, buckram backed patterned paper boards with bevelled edges, top edge gilt, very good in custom made quarter morocco folding box with raised bands, marbled paper sides and edges. Peter Ellis, Bookseller 2014 - 013024 2015 £295

Huysmans, J. K. *La Bas.* Paris: Le Livre Du Bibliophile/ Georges Briffaut, 1926. One of 500 numbered copies with woodcuts by Fernand Hertenberger, this copy unnumbered, but inscribed by publishers, Georges Briffaut to a colleague and designated collaborateur's copy, 4to., wrappers, fine but for some age wrinkling to spine. Beasley Books 2013 - 2015 $250

Hyde, Mark Powell *The Strange Inventor.* Garden City: Doubleday Page and Co., 1927. First edition, octavo, inserted frontispiece, color illustrations by John Whiting, original blue cloth, front and spine panels stamped in red. L. W. Currey, Inc. Boy's Adventure Fiction 2015 - 58 2015 $150

Hyde, Philip *A Glen Canyon Portfolio.* Flagstaff: Northland Press, 1979. First edition, folio, 20 high quality prints, all housed in printed and pictorial portfolio, very fine. Argonaut Book Shop Holiday Season 2014 - 131 2015 $250

Hymns Ancient and Modern for Use in the Services of the Church. London: William Clowes and Sons, n.d. but before, 1896. 5.5 x 4.8cm., original morocco, spine and front cover gilt stamped, rounded corners, all edges gilt, silver slipcase with attached chain, previous owner inscription, very light scuffing on bottom edge. Oak Knoll Books 306 - 115 2015 $450

I

I Wish I Were a Nurse. New York: Garden City, 1952. Oblong 8vo., 5 foot panorama with 3 sections of punch-out figures that the reader can use to play with and then replaced for storage, illustrations by Vivienne and replete with 50's gender stereotypes. Aleph-Bet Books, Inc. 108 - 332   2015 $350

Ibbetson, Julius Caesar *A Picturesque Guide to Bath, Bristol, Hot Wells, The River Avon and the Adjacent Country...* London: Hookham and Carpenter, 1793. Large paper copy, 4to., 16 aquatint plates with fine contemporary hand colouring, contemporary half russia with flat spine lettered in gilt, some minor chipping to extremities and upper hinge cracked with early ownership on title "Thos Howell" and unusually colorful heraldic bookplate of Edward Mash Browell.   Marlborough Rare Books   List 54 - 47   2015   £1750

Ibn Wahshiyah *Ancient Alphabets and Hieroglyphic Characters Explained...* London: W. Bulmer and Co., sold by G. and W. Nicol, 1806. First edition, small 4to., hieroglyphic illustrations in text, minor ex-library with 12 small oval library stamps at edge of text every 10 pages or so, no other markings, rebound in modern brown cloth with leather spine label lettered gilt at spine, vry good, clean text.   Any Amount of Books   March 2015 - A89008   2015   £375

Ibsen, Henrik *The Collected Works.* London: Heinemann, 1910-1914. Second impression, except for 12th volumes which was published as an afterthought in 1914 (often missing), 12 volumes, 8vo., original red cloth lettered and decorated gilt on spine, clean, very good set with slight sunning, slight rubbing and very slight marks.   Any Amount of Books   2015 - A85780   2015   £300

Ideals in Furnishing and Decoration Together with Some Suggestions as to the Means Whereby they May be Achieved Published 1925 by Trollope & Sons In London. London: Trollope & Sons, Eyre & Spottiswoode, 1925. First edition, 4to., wrappers, printed mostly recto only, 12 x 10 inches, many full page illustrations + 9 tipped in color plates by W. F. Burr (color frontispiece by Guy Lipscombe) with printed tissue guards, slight objectionable wear at edges as if yapped edges have been trimmed, spine ends slightly chipped, otherwise sound, very good with clean text.   Any Amount of Books   2015 - C15046   2015   £160

Ignatow, David *The One in the Many.* Middletown: Wesleyan University Press, 1988. First edition, signed by author on frontispiece, fine, 8vo., original cloth, dust jacket. James S. Jaffe Rare Books   Modern American Poetry - 143   2015 $100

Illiger, Johann Karl Wilhelm *Prodromus Systematis Mammalium et avium Additis Terminis Zoographicis Utriusque Classis, Eorunque Versione Germanica.* Berlin: Johann Karl Wilhelm, 1811. Octavo, later half calf and marbled boards, bookplate of H. M. Whittell.   Andrew Isles 2015 - 28084   2015 $7500

An Illustrated Sketch Book of Riley County, Kansas. "The Blue Ribbon County". Nationalist, 1881. 7 3/4 x 6 inches, blue printed wrappers, decorative type border, 142 pages, plates, spine cover missing, but all text still intact, light stamp of Anderson Memorial Library at bottom corner as well as small letters lightly printed top along with small area of sticker inside of front wrappers, light chipping to edges of front and rear wrappers.   Buckingham Books   March 2015 - 35615   2015 $1875

Illustration. September 2004-Spring 2009. St. Louis: Illustration Magazine, 2004-2009. 4to., stiff paper wrappers, 16 volumes, color illustrations.   Oak Knoll Books   306 - 25   2015 $150

Illustrirter London-Fuhrer. Leipzig: Brockhaus for J. J. Weber, 1851. First edition, small 8vo. tinted frontispiece and numerous wood engraved illustrations in text, cut-out newspaper article from about 1900 tipped in on page 37, resulting in even light toning of two leaves, one leaf with marginal tear, well preserved in original blindstamped cloth, gilt stamped logo of Great Exhibition on front cover, spine with gilt stamped illustration of monument and lettered gilt, yellow front endpapers are lithographic railway map of Central Europe including London, the yellow rear endpapers are a city map minimally rubbed.   Marlborough Rare Books Ltd.   List 49 - 13   2015   £350

Imaginative Book Illustration Society *Newsletter 1995-2005.* Working: Imaginative Book Illustration Society, 1995-2005. First edition, 31 issues, 8vo., stapled illustrated wrappers, nos. 1-29 (missing no. 27) with 3 extra issues, all issues fine or near fine, copiously illustrated in black and white.   Any Amount of Books   2015 - A970294   2015   £160

Imberdis, J. *Papyrus, or the Craft of Paper.* Hilversum: Paper Publications Society, 1952. First edition in English, limited to 20 numbered copies, 8vo., stiff handmade paper wrappers, marbled paper covered cardboard slipcase with paper cover and spine labels, slipcase rubbed along edges, uncommon.   Oak Knoll Books   306 - 97   2015 $450

Imitation de Jesus-Christ. Paris: Editions Rive Gauche, 1957. #40 of 51 copies, 8vo., with an extra suite, unbound signatures in fine condition in fine illustrated wrappers with extra set of prints, chemise fine but for sunned spine, lightly soiled box.   Beasley Books   2013 - 2015 $300

Imlay, Gilbert *A Topographical Description of the Western Territory of North America...* London: J. Debrett, 1793. Second edition, 8vo., 3 foldout maps and plan, contemporary calf, rebacked with calf spine and spine label, some light foxing, rear ad leaf partially loose, but very good, tight copy.   Second Life Books Inc.   189 - 133   2015 $3200

The Important Question Discussed; Whether Teaching the Art of Writing on the Lord's Day be Defensible on Christian Principles.   Sheffield: printed and sold by J. Blackwell, 1824. Only edition, 12mo., some old pencilled annotations, old inkstain on several margins but not affecting text, uncut in recent plain wrappers, good copy, apparently very scarce.   John Drury Rare Books   2015 - 19819   2015 $221

Imposture Unmasked; in a Letter to the Labourers & Working People of England, on the Schemes of the Church Robbers & Revolutionists with Regard to the Church. London: Roake & Varty, n.d., 1831. First edition, 12mo., large woodcut illustration on title, recent plain wrappers, very good, uncommon.   John Drury Rare Books   2015 - 19246   2015 $133

Imprint.   London: Imprint Pub. Co., 1913. Complete set of 9 issues, 4to., stiff paper wrappers, enclosed in two later cloth solander cases with cloth sleeves, covers detached and chipped along edge with tape repairs.   Oak Knoll Books   306 - 187   2015 $550

Ince Hall Coal Company   *1851. Rules to be Observed at the Ince Hall Coal & Cannel Company's Works, near Wigan.* Wigan: printed by H. B. Reckill Standishgate, 1851. 12mo., 12 pages, preserved in modern wrappers with printed label on upper cover, very good, probably very rare.   John Drury Rare Books   March 2015 - 25985   2015 $266

Indagine, Joannes   *Introductiones Apotelesmaticae in Physiognomiam, Complexiones Hominum Astrologiam Naturalem, Naturas Planetarum.*   Augusta Trebocorum: Simon Pauls, 1663. 16mo., 176 pages, title printed in red and black, numerous woodcuts and figures, contemporary limp vellum, some soiling or darkening to vellum, some browning, old ink signature on title has corroded, affecting text and staining next two leaves, lacking front free end, very good.   Argonaut Book Shop   Holiday Season 2014 - 135   2015 $350

India. Committee on Prison Discipline   *Report of the Committee on Prison-Discipline to the Governor General of India in Council, dated the eighth of January 1838.* Calcutta: printed at the Baptist Mission Press Circular Road, 1838. Large 4to., original card covers with printed title label on upper cover, covers rather dust marked, neatly rebacked, very good, rare.   John Drury Rare Books   2015 - 22602   2015 $830

Indian Basket Weaving by the Navajo School of Indian Basketry.   Los Angeles: Whedon and Spreng, 1903. First edition, stapled wrappers, under cord ties, unusually and interesting bound in ochre printed burlap, 103 pages, black and white photos, some drawings, former owner signature, laid in is large folded sheet, four inch tear archivally closed, very good.   Baade Books of the West   2014 - 2015 $131

Indian Students. The New Trail. A Book of Creative Writing by Indian Students.   Phoenix: Phoenix Indian School, 1941. Revised edition, large 8vo., brown printed wrappers, repaired closed tear on spine, illustrations, printed on different color papers, very good.   Second Life Books Inc.   190 - 139   2015 $200

Indian Students. The New Trail. A Book of Creative Writing by Indian Students.   Phoenix: Phoenix Indian School, 1953. Revised edition, large 8vo., brown printed wrappers, illustrations, printed on different color papers, very good. Second Life Books Inc.   190 - 140   2015 $125

International Motion Picture Almanac: Who, What, Where in Television and Radio.   New York: Quigley, 1943. First edition, 8vo., 15 volumes, slightly used, about very good copies, slightly marked at head of spines.   Any Amount of Books   2015 - A85524   2015   £225

Ingelow, Jean   *Mopsa the Fairy.*   London: Longmans, Green & Co., 1869. First edition, frontispiece + 7 plates, slight spotting, leading blank torn at upper corner and laid down on verso of leading f.e.p., contemporary half calf, gilt spine, red morocco label, rubbed, signed 'Albert Foot June 1879', extremely scarce first edition.   Jarndyce Antiquarian Booksellers   CCXI - 153 2015   £450

Ingersoll-Smouse, Florence   *Pater.*   Paris: Beaux Arts, 1928. First edition, wrappers, 4to., very good with small triangle 1 inch chip at head of spine, front joint starting. Beasley Books   2013 - 2015 $150

Ingpen, Roger   *One Thousand Poems for Children.* Philadelphia: Jacobs, 1923. 4to., green cloth, pictorial paste on, as new in dust jacket (box slightly worn), illustrations by Ethel Betts with cover plate, pictorial endpapers plus 8 color plates, incredible copy.   Aleph-bet Books, Inc.   109 - 50   2015 $500

Ingram, James   *Memorials of Oxford.*   Malvern: Cappella Archive, 2007. 9/100 copies, frontispiece, 300 further illustrations by John Le Keux from drawings by F. Mackenzie, 3 volumes, printed on 100 gm Five Seasons paper in letterpress spaced digital version of Fry's Baskerville of 1769, 8vo., original cream cloth stamped in blue to front and backstrips, blue-page markers, endpaper maps of contemporary Oxford, matching slipcase, fine.   Blackwell's Rare Books   B179 - 219   2015   £150

Ingram, John Kells *A History of Political Economy.* Edinburgh: Adam and Charles Black, 1893. Half title, original black cloth, booksellers ticket of B. H. Blackwell, Oxford, very good. Jarndyce Antiquarian Booksellers CCXI - 154 2015 £25

Ingram, Robert Acklom *A Sermon preached in the Parish-Church of St. James, Colchester on Sunday the 24th of August 1788...* Colchester: printed and sold by W. Keymer, sold also by G. G. and J. Robinson, London and J. and J. Merrill, Cambridge, 1788. First and only edition, 8vo., recent wrappers, very good, very rare. John Drury Rare Books March 2015 - 19051 2015 $266

Ingrams, Richard *The Tale of Driver Grope.* London: Dennis Dobson, 1969. First edition, 4to., illustrations in color, signed and dated by artist, Ralph Steadman, about fine in near very good+ slightly browned and slightly soiled and price clipped dust jacket. Any Amount of Books 2015 - A66647 2015 £150

Innes, Michael *The Bloody Word.* London: Gollancz, 1966. First edition, some darkening on endpapers, otherwise fine in price clipped dust jacket. Mordida Books March 2015 - 009915 2015 $85

Innes, Michael *A Private View.* London: Gollancz, 1952. First edition, pages slightly darkened, otherwise near fine in dust jacket with slightly darkened spine and few faint stains. Mordida Books March 2015 - 010015 2015 $100

Innes, Michael *Silence Observed.* London: Gollancz, 1961. First edition, fine in lightly soiled dust jacket with couple of tiny tears. Mordida Books March 2015 - 009914 2015 $85

An Inquiry into the State of the Currency of the Country, Its Defects and Remedy. London: Longman Rees Orme and Brown, 1818. First edition, 8vo., titlepage just little soiled, recent cloth backed marbled boards, morocco label on upper cover, lettered gilt, very good. John Drury Rare Books March 2015 - 25487 2015 $266

Instruction Sur La Maniere Dont Seront Ouverts Les Compte Courans En Banque... Paris: The Widow Saugrain & Pierre Prault, 1720. 4to., disbound, woodcut royal arms on title, woodcut head and tailpiece, woodcut initial, browned and spotted, small piece torn from fore margin of last leaf, paper flaw in another but without loss. Blackwell's Rare Books B179 - 8 2015 £900

International American Conference *Reports of Committees and Discussions thereon.* Washington: 1890. Volume 1 554 - Volume II -555-1203 - Volume III 343 - Volume IV - 375, 4to., 4 volumes, three quarter morocco, marbled boards, marbled endpapers, all edges marbled, one volume has leather hinges cracking, one cover loosening but intact, private library # on titlepage, no other marks. Bookworm & Silverfish 2015 - 5081715357 2015 $250

The Introductory Discourse and the Lectures Delivered Before the American Institute of Instruction in Boston August 1832, Including a Prize Essay on Penmanship... Boston: Carter, Hendee and Co., 1833. 8vo., original cloth, paper spine label, ex-library, spine label worn, covers soiled, rubbed, scuffed at edges and along spine, foxing on endpapers and throughout text. Oak Knoll Books Special Catalogue 24 - 24 2015 $325

Inwood, Jethro *Sermons: in Which are Explained and enforced the Religious, Moral and Poltical Virtues of Freemasonry, Preached Upon Several Occasions...* Deptford Kent: printed for the author by J. Del ahoy Deptford Bridge and to be had at the Rectory House Deptford as above and of Crosby and Letterman, London, n.d., 1799. First collected edition, with additional printed notice 'tipped in', contemporary tree calf, neatly rebacked preserving original label, very good, ownership signature of John Ward of new Road Lincoln, and on verso of first sectional titlepage, scarce. John Drury Rare Books 2015 - 24109 2015 $830

Ireland's Witness Fortified and Secured, in the Tower of Salvation and Chambers of Christ's Protection... Belfast?: printed in the year, 1728. Apparently of great rarity, 8vo., drophead title, 16 pages, early ink inscription 'Jean R' at head of title, general paper browning, margins cut close with loss of couple of catchwords and loss of final line of verse on page 13, preserved in modern marbled card covers. John Drury Rare Books March 2015 - 23999 2015 $874

Irrigated Lands on the Maxwell Grant New Mexico. Maxwell Irrigated Land Co., 1909. 20 pages, illustrations, 2 folding maps, insert, original printed wrappers soiled, else very good. Dumont Maps and Books of the West 130 - 24 2015 $500

Irvine, William *The Book, the Ring and the Poet: a Biography of Robert Browning.* London: Bodley Head, 1975. Half title, plates original blue cloth, spines slightly creased and in slightly creased dust jacket, with warm presentation to Kathleen Tillotson from Park Honan, ALS from Honan to Kathleen. Jarndyce Antiquarian Booksellers CCVII - 121 2015 £35

Irving, John 1942- *The Cider House Rules.* New York: Morrow, 1985. Uncorrected proof copy, from the library of author's friend, fellow National Book Award winner, Peter Mathiessen, well-read copy with inadvertent page turns and abrasions and wear to covers and spine, good copy only, but significant copy, letter of provenance available.   Ken Lopez, Bookseller   164 - 91   2015 $450

Irving, John 1942- *The Hotel New Hampshire.* New York: Dutton, 1981. First issue proof, with pages shot from typescript and Irving's holograph corrections evident (in photocopy), foxing to top edge, slight creasing to rear panel, near fine in wrappers (with promotional sheet and signed letter from publisher laid in), very uncommon.   Ken Lopez, Bookseller   164 - 90   2015 $1250

Irving, John 1942- *The Pension Grillparzer.* Logan Perfection Form Co., 1980. First edition, wrappers, first separate appearance, near fine but for little darkening to spine.   Beasley Books   2013 - 2015 $275

Irving, Washington 1783-1859 *Knickerbocker's History of New York.* New York: R. H. Russell, 1900. First edition, folio, cloth backed boards, pictorial paste-on, , except for some spine and cover soil and rubbing, near fine, 8 wonderful black and white plates and cover plate by Maxfield Parrish.   Aleph-Bet Books, Inc.   108 - 337   2015 $1850

Irving, Washington 1783-1859 *Legend of Sleepy Hollow.* Philadelphia: David McKay, 1928. Limited to only 125 numbered copies for the U.S. signed by Rackham, 4to., full gilt vellum, fine in publisher's box (flaps repaired), pictorial endpapers, 8 tipped in color plates and numerous black and whites, especially fine, scarce, not often found in box.   Aleph-bet Books, Inc.   109 - 402   2015 $5500

Irving, Washington 1783-1859 *The Legend of Sleepy Hollow.* Philadelphia: David McKay, n.d., 1928. First American edition, 4to., brown cloth, pictorial paste-on, top edge gilt, owner name (not offensive), dust jacket soiled, small piece off corner, some fraying, illustrations by Arthur Rackham with cover plate, pictorial endpapers plus 8 color plates, beautiful copy.   Aleph-bet Books, Inc.   109 - 398   2015 $550

Irving, Washington 1783-1859 *Rip Van Winkle.* Leipzig: E. A. Seemann, 1905. First German edition, fine, large 4to., bound in green wrappers, illustrations in line, by Arthur Rackham, each of the 50 incredible tipped-in color plates is mounted on separate sheet of heavy green paper (plates have white border), illustrations housed in original publisher's tan cloth portfolio that has lettering and illustration in brown on cover, printed in Leipzig on fine laid paper, beautiful copy, rare.   Aleph-Bet Books, Inc.   108 - 386   2015 $2750

Irving, Washington 1783-1859 *Voyage d'un Americain a Londres, ou Esquisses sur les Moeurs Anglaises et Americaines.* Paris: Chez Ponthieu, 1822. 2 volumes, 8vo., tan quarter calf, purple paper boards, red leather labels, gilt rules and lettering, half titles present, boards little stained and worn, very good.   The Brick Row Book Shop   Miscellany 67 - 61   2015 $500

Isherwood, B. F. *Experimental Researches in Steam Engineering, by Chief Engineer B. F. Isherwood, U. S. Navy Chief of the Bureau of Steam Engineering, Navy Department.* Philadelphia: 1865. Volume II only, 30 full page plates, 8 gate fold tables, text is soiled in half leather, top of backstrip splitting 4 inch on each side, bottom with same on one side, covers damped, rear with cloth loosening, preface with damp very light ghosting above text, preface and first 100 pages with same, last several pages with pronounced marginal dampness, last hundred pages, the same incremental towards end.   Bookworm & Silverfish   2015 - 6015842727   2015 $375

Isherwood, Christopher *Goodbye to Berlin.* London: Hogarth Press, 1939. First edition, 8vo., original pale grey textured cloth lettered red on spine, very slight discoloration to spine and corners, in badly distressed dust jacket, missing chunks from rear and along spine, otherwise very good, text clean and unmarked.   Any Amount of Books   2015 - C1970   2015   £260

Isherwood, Christopher *Mr. Norris Changes Trains.* London: Hogarth Press, 1935. First edition, first printing, one of only 1730 copies, fine with two minor spots to bottom edge, in superb dust jacket with only very mild soiling to rear panel and and slight nick to lower spine.   B & B Rare Books, Ltd.   234 - 57   2015 $8000

Ishiguro, Kazuo *When We Were Orphans.* London: Faber and Faber, 2000. First edition, 8vo., original black boards, backstrip lettered in white, fine, dust jacket, inscribed by author 4/4/00.   Blackwell's Rare Books   B179 - 179   2015   £60

Isocrates *Orationes et Epistolae.* Geneva: Excudebat Henricus Stephanus, 1593. Final blank discarded, lower blank margin of one index leaf trimmed, light toning and spotting, tiny dampmark in margin of first 20 leaves, title little creased, early ink note on title, folio, later boards and backstrip removed, exposing sewn bands, preserved in black cloth solander case, good.   Blackwell's Rare Books   Greek & Latin Classics VI - 56   2015   £600

Italix, the Calligraphic Quarterly. Fair Lawn: Haywood House, 1971. Small 4to., plastic slide covers on most volumes though some are bound in paper wrappers with four issues to a booklet, this run from Volume I No. 1 to Volume VI no. 4 complete and Volume XI No. 1 to Volume XIV No. 4 missing only one issue, a total of 39 issues.   Oak Knoll Books   Special Catalogue 24 - 25   2015 $200

Itten, Johannes *The Art of Color: the Subjective Experience and Objective Rationale of Color.* New York: Reinhold Publishing Corp., 1967. Fourth English printing, oblong 4to., cloth, dust jacket, tipped in color illustrations, dust jacket chipped and torn at edges, front cover stained along top edge, leaves of text bent at top edge.   Oak Knoll Books   306 - 188   2015 $125

Ivernois, Francis D'   *A Short Account of the Late Revolution in Geneva; and of the Conduct of France Towards that Republic from October 1792 to October 1794. In a Series of Letters to an American.*   London: printed by T. Spilsbury and Son for P. Elmsley and J. Debrett, 1795. First edition, 8vo., few blank outer corners damaged or stained, text unaffected, recently well bound in linen backed marbled boards lettered.   John Drury Rare Books   2015 - 21689   2015 $177

Ives, Joseph C.   *Report Upon the Colorado River of the West, Explored in 1857 and 1858 by Lieutenant Joseph C. Ives, Corps of Topographical Engineers...*   Washington: GPO, 1861. First edition, quarto, original gilt pictorial blind-stamped cloth, gold stamping to spine, 4 maps, 2 large folding map, color lithographs, lightly soiled on lower portion of front panel, rubbed along front edge, else very good. Buckingham Books   March 2015 - 25804   2015 $2000

Ivimey, Joseph   *John Milton His Life and Times.*   New York: D. Appleton, 1833. First edition, portrait frontispiece, full black calf with gilt spine and cover decorations, small owner label, very good+, little rubbing, some general foxing, tight, sound text and binding, uncommon in nice shape. Stephen Lupack   March 2015 - 2015 $125

J

Jack and the Beanstalk. New York: McLoughlin Bros., 1888. 4to., pictorial wrappers, faint name on upper cover, else near fine, illustrations by R. Andre with pictorial covers plus 6 fine full page chromolithographs.   Aleph-bet Books, Inc.   109 - 280   2015 $250

Jack and the Beanstalk. New York: Holiday House, 1935. 16mo., cloth backed pictorial boards, near fine, color and black and white woodcuts by Arvilla Parker.   Aleph-Bet Books, Inc.   108 - 176   2015 $200

Jack the Giant Killer and Other Tales. New York: Blue Ribbon, 1932. Thick 4to., pictorial boards, near fine, illustrations by Harold Lentz with color endpapers, many black and whites and 4 fabulous double page color pop-ups.   Aleph-bet Books, Inc.   109 - 368   2015 $600

Jackson County History. An Official Summary Resources and Opportunities. N.P.: Jackson County Court & Southern Pacific, 1914. First edition, printed stapled wrappers, 48 pages, illustrations, map, fair condition 2 x 1 1/2 inch piece torn from bottom corner of titlepage (slight loss of image on verso) rest of text block fine, tiny chip lower front cover, soiled, pencil numbers on back cover, slight vertical crease on front cover, rare, with this original booklet and 8 1/2 x 11 inch institutional photocopy with complete cover/verso and titlepage/verso fair.   Baade Books of the West   2014 - 2015 $150

Jackson, Arthur   *The World of Big Bands.* New York: Arco, 1977. First edition, fine in fine dust jacket.   Beasley Books   2013 - 2015 $45

Jackson, Helen Hunt 1830-1885 *Romona.* Los Angeles: Limited Editions Club, 1959. One of 1500 numbered copies, signed by artist and handsomely printed, color illustrations from drawings, multicolored buckram, printed paper label, very fine in slipcase.   Argonaut Book Shop Holiday Season 2014 - 136   2015 $175

Jackson, Jon A.   *The Blind Pig.* New York: Random House, 1978. First edition, review copy, fine in dust jacket.   Buckingham Books   March 2015 - 18726   2015 $225

Jackson, Jon A.   *The Blind Pig.* New York: Random House, 1978. First edition, very fine in dust jacket.   Mordida Books   March 2015 - 007496   2015 $200

Jackson, Jon A.   *Dead Folk.* Tucson: Dennis McMillan, 1995. First edition, one of 300 numbered copies signed by Jackson, very fine in dust jacket with slipcase.   Mordida Books   March 2015 - 008843   2015 $150

Jackson, Jon A.   *The Diehard.* New York: Random House, 1977. First edition, inscribed by author to former owner, also laid-in is post card written in longhand in which the author agrees to sign this book, fine in dust jacket.   Buckingham Books   March 2015 - 22960   2015 $350

Jackson, Jon A.   *Ridin' With Ray.* Santa Barbara: Neville, 1995. First edition, one of 300 numbered copies signed by Jackson, very fine without dust jacket as issued, illustrations by Barnaby Conrad.   Mordida Books   March 2015 - 005260   2015 $75

Jackson, K.   *Farm Stories.* New York: Simon & Schuster, 1946. One of 650 numbered copies, specially printed and bound, signed by K. and B. Jackson and artist, Gustaf Tenggren, folio, publisher's pictorial cloth, fine in very good+ dust jacket lightly worn at front fold and with small edge chip, 100 full color illustrations plus many black and whites.   Aleph-bet Books, Inc.   109 - 458   2015 $600

Jackson, Robert   *An Outline of the History and Cure of Fever, Endemic and Contagious; More Expressly the Contagious Fever of Jails, Ships and Hospitals...* Edinburgh: printed for Mundell & Son and for T. N. Longman and Murray & Highley, London, 1798. First edition, 8vo., wanting half title, Longman's booklet dated July 1800, inserted after text, contemporary tree sheep, sometime rebacked preserving original gilt spine, very good, sometime in library of Karolinska Institutet in Sweden, early 19th century stamp in red ink in title margin.   John Drury Rare Books   2015 - 26181   2015 $787

Jackson, Seguin Henry   *Cautions to Women, Respecting the State of Pregnancy, the Progress of Labour and Delivery...* London: J. Robson, 1801. Second edition, neatly rebound in brown buckram, handsome red leather spine label lettered gilt, uncut, top one inch of titlepage missing but with no loss of lettering and neatly replaced with a plain black paper, some odd marginal linings to text at beginning, otherwise pleasing, very good+ copy.   Any Amount of Books   2015 - A59934   2015   £180

Jackson, Shirley   *We Have Always Lived in the Castle.* New York: Viking, 1962. First edition, slightly bumped and soiled, else near fine in very good dust jacket with chip on rear panel and general modest wear at extremities, inscribed by author to her mother-in-law Lulu Hyman.   Between the Covers Rare Books, Inc.   187 - 136   2015 $2500

Jackson, W. H. *The Canon of Colorado.* Frank J. Thayer, n.d. circa 1890's, n.d. circa 1890's, Green cloth, 16 plates, accordion style portfolio of black and white photos by Jackson, cloth covers have some light edgewear, some occasional minor soiling and spotting and snap missing on front clasps, in all, very good, usually found in poor condition. Buckingham Books   March 2015 - 27642   2015 $225

Jackson, William   *A Lecture on Rail Roads Delivered Jan. 12 1829.* Boston: Henry Bowen, 1829. Second edition, 18mo., 37 pages, sewn and uncut, as issued.   M & S Rare Books, Inc.   97 - 253   2015 $450

Jackson, Zachariah   *Shakespeare's Genius Justified; Being Restorations and Illustrations of Seven Hundred Passages in Shakesepare's Plays...* London: printed by T. Johnson for John Major, 1819. 2 pages ads, odd spot, uncut in original green cloth, paper label, very good. Jarndyce Antiquarian Booksellers   CCXI - 252   2015   £75

Jacob, Giles   *The Compleat Court-Keeper; or Land-Steward's Assistant.* London: printed by John Nutt assignee of Edw. Sayer Esq. for Bernard Lintott and Thomas Ward, 1713. First edition, 8vo., contemporary rather worn calf, neatly rebacked and labelled, very good, very scarce. John Drury Rare Books   2015 - 22293   2015 $830

Jacob, Max   *Le Cornet a Des.* Paris: NRF, 1948. #278 of 422 copies, wrappers are fine in publisher's glassine, chemise fine but for slight sunning to spine in lightly soiled box, 113 full color gouaches by Jean Hugo, small 4to. Beasley Books   2013 - 2015 $500

Jacob, P. L.   *La Folle D'Orleans Histoire Du Temps De Louis XIV.* Paris: Eugene Renduel, 1830. First edition, 2 volumes, contemporary boards, reddish mauve color possibly thinly covered in leather, rare, sound, decent set with some marks and some rubbing, very good.   Any Amount of Books   2015 - A33499   2015   £180

Jacobi, Mary Putnam   *Life and Letters of...* New York: G. P. Putnam's Sons, 1925. First edition, 8vo., stain on pastedown offset from earlier insert, old paperclip stain on endpaper, very good, label on spine very worn, this copy belonged to Alice Thacher Post with her name and address.   Second Life Books Inc.   189 - 135   2015 $125

Jacobs, W. W.   *Sea Whispers.* New York: Scribners, 1926. First American edition, fine in dust jacket with slightly darkened spine.   Mordida Books   March 2015 - 005261   2015 $125

Jacobsen, Josephine   *The Sisters.* Columbia: Bench Press, 1987. First printing, 8vo., author's presentation on half title to poet and editor William Claire, paper wrappers, about as new.   Second Life Books Inc.   189 - 136   2015 $45

Jacobus De Varagine   *Legenda Aurea i.e Lombardica Historia que Plerisque Aureau Legenda Sanctorum Appletur.* Strassburg: Printer of the 1483 Jordanus de Quedlinburg George Husner, May, 1496. folio in 8's and 6's, 2 handsome decorated initials, rubrication in red throughout first half of book, edges of text block stained red, later full blind-stamped calf in Cambridge style, contemporary ink underlining and marginal notations embellish much of the text, paper repairs to margins and corners of 8 leaves, occasional dampstaining, mostly marginal but intruding to text of first 20 leaves, marginal wormhole to last 55 leaves, very good. Argonaut Book Shop   Holiday Season 2014 - 1341   2015 $3250

Jakubowski, Maxim   *No Alibi.* Blakeney: Scorpion Press, 1995. First edition, limited edition of 15 lettered copies, signed by 8 of the contributors, fine in quarter leather with raised bands and marbled boards, transparent dust jacket. Buckingham Books   March 2015 - 12439   2015 $375

Jakubowski, Maxim   *No Alibi.* Blakeney: Scorpion Press, 1995. First edition, 150 numbered copies signed by all contributors, fine in quarter leather and marbled boards, transparent dust jacket.   Buckingham Books   March 2015 - 29076   2015 $175

James Fisk, Jr. The Life of a Green Mountain Boy. Philadelphia: William Flint, 1872. 8vo., woodcuts, disbound, lacking covers, decent sound, clean text.   Any Amount of Books   2015 - A96356   2015   £175

James I, King of England   1566-1625   *Orders Appointed by His Maiestie to be straightly observed, for the preventing and remedying of the dearth of graine and other victuall.* London: by Bonham Norton and John bill printers to the Kings most Excellent Maiestie, 1622. Second printing, 4to., complete with initial leaf A1 (blank except for signature 'A' within floral woodblock on recto), with final blank D4, first and last leaves rather soiled, repaired hole in A1 (not touching printed surface), large woodcut of royal arms on verso of title, woodcut initial letter and headpiece on A3, general moderate paper discoloration else, good, large copy, entirely uncut, unbound as issued.   John Drury Rare Books   2015 - 23785   2015 $1311

James Pollock Sons & Co.   *Amazon Vessles of Various Types/Vapores de Varios Typos Para o Amazonas.* London: James Pollock Sons & co., 1911. First edition, 4to., text in English and Spanish, copiously illustrated in black and white with photos, original grey boards with color illustration front cover, rather splendid rare trade catalog, photos, sound clean very good copy with slight bump to top, faint rubbing and handling wear.   Any Amount of Books March 2015 - A74332   2015   £450

James, C. L.   *History of the French Revolution.* Chicago: Abe Isaak, 1902. First edition, very good, front hinge repaired.   Beasley Books   2013 - 2015 $150

James, Charles *A Correction of Abuses in Government, No Encroachment Upon the Constitution of the Country Nobility, although Proper, Not Only Superfluous...* London: printed for H. D. Symonds, 1792. Probably on early edition and certainly very rare, 8vo., emphasis marks in pencil and few annotations, also in pencil, contemporary calf, now neatly rebacked and labelled to match, very good with contemporary ownership signature of G. Ricketts and later armorial bookplate of Edwards Ricketts on pastedown. John Drury Rare Books   2015 - 24820   2015 $1311

James, Edward *The Next Volume.* London: James Press, 1939. #17 of an edition of 412 copies, second edition, 4to., grey cloth stamped in gold, top edge gilt, fine, illustrations by Rex Whistler with 3 full page and 23 large partial page engravings.   Aleph-bet Books, Inc.   109 - 484   2015 $500

James, Edward T. *Notable American Women 1607-1950.* Cambridge: Harvard University, 1982. Sixth printing, 3 volumes, 8vo., paper wrappers, covers somewhat faded, creased and scuffed otherwise very good, tight set.   Second Life Books Inc.   190 - 24   2015 $75

James, Eliot, Mrs. *A Guide to Indian Household Management.* London: Ward, Lock & Co., 1879. Half title, 6 pages ads, original brown decorated cloth, slight mark to lower board, otherwise very good, 90 pages.   Jarndyce Antiquarian Booksellers   CCXI - 156   2015   £200

James, George Wharton *Indian Blankets and Their Makers.* Chicago: McClurg, 1914. First edition, large 8vo., 95 plates, numerous photos by author, bound in slightly soiled tan cloth stamped in brown, very good, tight, clean copy.   Second Life Books Inc.   190 - 141   2015 $375

James, Henry   1843-1916 *The Ambassadors.* Boston: Harper & Bros., 1903. First American edition, first issue, in blue-gray boards, gilt spine titles and top edge "Published November 1913" on copyright page, near fine in near fine navy cloth dust jacket growing fragile at folds.   Ken Lopez, Bookseller   164 - 93   2015 $450

James, Henry   1843-1916 *The Bostonians.* New York: Modern Library, 1956. First edition thus, 8vo., very good in like dust jacket (price clipped), very clean, bright copy with marginal linings, underlinings and notes of page numbers and one pencil illustration by Ronald Searle, bought from the library of Searle.   Any Amount of Books   2015 - C10184   2015   £150

James, Henry   1843-1916 *Confidence.* Boston: Houghton Osgood, 1880. First American edition, first issue, with Houghton Osgood imprint at base of spine and errors on pages 171, 323 and 345, one of 1500 copies, bookplate of Margaret F. G. Whitney, with Whitney's ownership signature and date July 1880, light wear to boards, easily very good, without dust jacket.   Ken Lopez, Bookseller   164 - 92   2015 $650

James, Henry   1843-1916 *The Notebooks.* New York: Oxford University Press, 1947. Original blue cloth, spine faded, from the library of Geoffrey & Kathleen Tillotson, inscribed by Geoffrey for Kathleen, Harvard 20.II.45, inserted is tatty folded copy of dust jacket containing cuttings of significant reviews of book and about James.   Jarndyce Antiquarian Booksellers   CCVII - 324   2015   £20

James, Henry   1843-1916 *The Novels and Tales.* New York: Charles Scribner's Sons, 1907-1917. First edition, on handmade paper, 26 volumes, octavo, contemporary full morocco gilt, photogravures by Alvin Langdon Coburn, tipped into first volume is ANS and dated by James, fine presentation copy.   Honey & Wax Booksellers   2 - 9   2015 $30,000

James, Henry   1843-1916 *Sienna.* New York: Red Angel Press, 2000. One of 100 copies, printed on dampened Fabriano Ingres paper, all copies signed and numbered by artist/printer/publisher Ronald Keller on colophon, 4 page woodcut, rust cloth over boards, back board forms base of box, into which a woodcut image of Siena is nested (at a rounded slope deliberately reminiscent of the square's concave, shell-like shape), four surrounding woodcuts reproduce the vertiginous 360 degree medieval square, title printed in maroon on spine, handmade marbled paper on inside of front board, front board features inset papier mache sculpture, in cream handmade paper, on a Sienese column.   Priscilla Juvelis - Rare Books   61 - 45   2015 $750

James, Henry   1843-1916 *Stories Revived in Three Volumes.* London: Macmillan, 1885. First edition, 3 volumes, full red leather lettered gilt on spine, 5 raised bands, all edges gilt, bookplate of Margot Tennant in each volume, with 'Margot from Evan Charteris, the Glen 85', little scuffed at edges, covers slightly marked, hinges slightly tender with front board detached on volume 3, overall about very good.   Any Amount of Books   March 2015 - A79117   2015   £360

James, Henry   1843-1916 *Washington Square.* New York: Harper and Bros., 1881. (1880). First edition, octavo, 266 pages, 6 pages publisher's ads, illustrations by George Du Maurier, from the library of NY novelist Louis Auchincloss with his morocco gilt bookplate, excellent association copy.   Honey & Wax Booksellers   1 - 58   2015 $2000

James, Henry   1843-1916 *The Wings of the Dove.* Westminster: Archibald Constable & Co., 1902. First edition, 8vo., recently rebound in full navy blue leather with marbled endpapers, lettered gilt at spine with gilt decoration and five raised bands, slight dustiness at fore-edges, otherwise bright, clean, very good+.   Any Amount of Books   2015 - C15997   2015   £300

James, P. D. *The Black Tower.* London: Faber and Faber, 1975. First edition, fine in near fine dust jacket, jacket minutely rubbed at corners and at rear panel, attractive copy, from the collection of Duke Collier.   Royal Books   36 - 200   2015 $325

James, P. D. *Devices and Desires.* Franklin Center: Franklin Library, 1990. First American edition, very fine without dust jacket as issued, signed by author. Mordida Books   March 2015 - 009502   2015 $100

James, P. D. *Innocent Blood.* London: Faber and Faber, 1980. First edition, usual toning to pages, crown 8vo., original red boards, backstrip lettered in gilt, dust jacket, near fine, author's gift inscription on front free endpaper. Blackwell's Rare Books   B179 - 180   2015   £200

James, P. D. *Innocent Blood.* London: Faber and Faber, 1980. First edition, pages evenly browned, else fine in dust jacket.   Buckingham Books   March 2015 - 23619   2015 $250

James, P. D. *Murder in Triplicate.* London: Belmont Press, 2001. First edition, limited to 50 copies, bound with cloth spine and numbered 201 5 250, this copy 220, signed by author and artist, Eileen Hogan, as new in two-tone cloth and boards, decorated paper label on front cover, gold stamping on spine.   Buckingham Books   March 2015 - 17760   2015 $275

James, P. D. *Murder in Triplicate.* London: Belmont Press, 2001. First edition, limited to 150 copies bound with leather spine and with extra print enclosed in rear pocket, numbered 51 to 200, signed by author and by artist, Eileen Hogan, as new in two-tone leather and boards, decorated paper label on front cover and gold stamping on spine. Buckingham Books   March 2015 - 19260   2015 $375

James, P. D. *The Private Patient.* London: Faber & Faber, 2008. First edition, limited to 1000 numbered copies, signed by author, fine in dust jacket, slipcase. Buckingham Books   March 2015 - 27175   2015 $185

James, Paul Moon *A Summary Statement of the One Pound Note Question.* London: G. B. Whittaker, 1828. First edition, 8vo., later boards, with ms. little label on upper cover, good.   John Drury Rare Books   2015 - 25495   2015 $133

James, Will 1892-1942 *Smoky.* New York: Charles Scribner's Sons, 1926. First edition, 8vo., green cloth, slight soil and spine slightly faded, else near fine in pictorial dust jacket (slightly frayed at spine ends with few mends on verso), profusely illustrated in black and white by James, this copy signed by James with recipient's name followed by "From the Author" and dated 1926.   Aleph-bet Books, Inc.   109 - 232   2015 $4200

James, Will 1892-1942 *Young Cowboy.* New York: Charles Scribner's, 1935. A. First edition, oblong 4to., cloth, pictorial paste-on, fine in dust jacket with some soil and fraying but overall very good, 5 color plates plus many full page and smaller black and whites, rear in dust jacket. Aleph-Bet Books, Inc.   108 - 249   2015 $1200

James, William 1842-1910 *Essays in Psychology.* Cambridge: Harvard, 1984. First edition thus, advance review copy with slip laid in, fine in near fine dust jacket with short tear at foot of front panel.   Beasley Books   2013 - 2015 $175

James, William 1842-1910 *Essays in Radical Empiricism.* London: Longmans, Green and Co., 1912. First edition, octavo, original green covers with paper label to spine which is worn and (water?) stained, but almost completely readable, 1 1/2" scrape lower right front cover (showing as white) and very light wear to head and toe of spine with 4 1/2 x 7 inch tan discoloration offset to inside cover and front free endpaper from some earlier (but now missing) insert, with one line of handwritten text to top of rear blank leaf along with four handwritten additions to index on verso, overall clean, tight and bright.   Athena Rare Books   15 - 26   2015 $225

James, William 1842-1910 *The Meaning of Truth, a Sequel to 'Pragmatism'.* New York: Longmans, Green and Co., 1909. First edition, octavo, original greyish-green covers with green cloth spine, paper label lightly worn and still about 90 percent readable, publisher's loosely inserted ad for "A Pluralistic Universe" which is announced as being "Ready in April", only the lightest of wear to boards and spine, remarkably well preserved, bright and clean. Athena Rare Books   15 - 22   2015 $275

James, William 1842-1910 *Memories and Studies.* New York: Longmans, Green and Co., 1911. First edition, octavo, original green covers with almost no wear to board, spine has small quarter inch open tear to bottom left side, spine label has crack running vertically throughout which obliterates 1 letter and compromises another 3, but still completely readable, former owner's signature Alexander B. MacLeod and unfortunate presence of a (very) old bookseller's price in blue ink ($15) beside signature), with MacLeod's occasional pencil underlinings and vertical margin lines along with less frequent marginalia in the essays which most interest him, overall lovely, collectible copy. Athena Rare Books   15 - 26   2015 $225

James, William 1842-1910 *The Moral Equivalent of War.* Boston: Atlantic Monthly Press, Number 10, 1910, but really, 1918. Second offprint issue, octavo, publisher's original salmon wrappers with black lettering inside and out, stapled and with penciled inscription just above the words "Atlantic Readings" at top of front wrapper indicating prior ownership by some indecipherable library, with lightest of bumping to corners, otherwise beautifully preserved copy, rare. Athena Rare Books   15 - 23   2015 $150

James, William   1842-1910   *A Pluralistic Universe.*   New York: Longmans, Green and Co., 1909. First edition, octavo, original grayish-green covers with green cloth on spine, spine label with some light wear across top edge effecting early initial letter "A" in title of book, otherwise beautifully preserved and 90 preserved label, tips of boards lightly bumped with just bit of wear to top of spine, overall this is lovely and lovingly preserved first edition.   Athena Rare Books   15 - 21   2015 $275

James, William   1842-1910   *A Pluralistic Universe.*   New York: Longmans, Green and Co., 1909. First edition, octavo, gift presentation from author to F. C. S. Schiller, with preprinted "From the Author" slip loosely inserted before first half title and Schiller's ownership signature and notation C. Schiller/from W.J." written in upper right corner f.f.e.p., original grayish green covers with green cloth on spine, spine label with just lightest of wear along edges and crease down center, otherwise beautifully preserved and 100 per cent readable label, boards and spine particularly fresh for this book with just bit of white spotting to spine covering on front cover and two small white spots on rear cover, with 4 small pencil notations by Schiller along with occasional pencil lines in margin and even more occasionally underlining. Athena Rare Books   15 - 20   2015 $1800

James, William   1842-1910   *Pragmatism.*   New York: Longmans, Green and Co., 1907. First edition, octavo, presentation from author to F. C. S. Schiller, with preprinted "From the Author" slip loosely inserted before first half title and Schiller's ownership signature and notation, original brown boards with lighter colored cloth spine, spine label with just lightest of wear along right edge and light ding that has removed the letter 's' from "James", otherwise beautiful preserved and 100 per cent readable (rare thing the these books by James), boards and spine particularly fresh for this book, with just one small (3/8") white stain to front cover, gorgeous, well preserved and important presentation copy. Athena Rare Books   15 - 19   2015 $2200

James, William   1842-1910   *Pragmatism: a New Name for some Old Ways of Thinking.*   New York: Longmans, Green and Co., 1919. New impression, green publisher's cloth and printed paper spine label, label bit worn and little light fraying at spine ends, else near fine, American composer Virgil Thomson's copy with his pencil ownership signature.   Between the Covers Rare Books, Inc.   187 - 137   2015 $400

James, William   1842-1910   *The Principles of Psychology.*   New York: Henry Holt and Co., 1890. First edition, 2nd printing, octavo, this copy was owned by Simon Nelson Patten (1852-1922), with handwritten signature and date, Patten obviously donated these 2 volumes to University of PA library, although there is no indication of them being treated as library books, other than single blue ink withdrawal notice in each book, original publisher's dark green binding with gilt lettering on spine, covers fairly well preserved with just few hints of spotting and wear, both spines very lightly tattered and torn at top and bottom with one small (half inch) triangular chip missing from top rear volume I, inside front cover volume I is cracked but holding firm, somewhat unsophisticated but perfectly respectable copy. Athena Rare Books   15 - 15   2015 $1000

James, William   1842-1910   *Some Problems of Philosophy.*   New York: Longmans, Green and Co., 1911. First edition, octavo, gift from author's wife to F. C. S. Schiller, with Schiller's ownership signature, original green covers with perfectly legible paper spine label and just bit of wear to two top corners, half inch whitish discoloration to lower spine, with Schiller's ownership inscription and notation of presentation, with occasional vertical pencil lines and less frequent underlinings throughout text, some in black, some in blue and others in red, several notations in margins of book by Schiller and his list of relevant pages on inside rear cover, otherwise near fine.   Athena Rare Books   15 - 24   2015 $950

James, William   1842-1910   *Some Problems of Philosophy.*   New York: Longmans, Green and Co., 1911. First edition, octavo, original green covers with just bit of wear to surface of front cover and to spine tips, spine label has distinctive crack running vertically throughout, obliterating 10 of the 34 characters, inscribed "To Father with much love on his 55th birthday from J.T.A. sometime Asst. prof. of Metaphysics July 1911", overall well preserved, bright, tight copy.   Athena Rare Books   15 - 25   2015 $225

James, William   1842-1910   *Some Problems of Philosophy: a Beginning of an Introduction to Philosophy.*   London: Longman, Green and Co., 1911. First edition, 8vo., neat name on front endpaper, slight sunning at spine ends, slight browning to prelims, contents pages opened unevenly with large gap in page (one lettering missing of text), otherwise sound, clean, very good with bright covers in near very good- used dust jacket, chipped at spine ends, somewhat tanned.   Any Amount of Books   2015 - 189792   2015   £180

James, William 1842-1910 *The Varieties of Religious Experience.* London: Longmans, Green & Co., 1902. First edition, first issue, octavo, presentation gift from author to F. C. H. Schiller *1864-1937), with preprinted "From the Author" slip glued into inner front cover, this copy has Schiller's sketchy notes on prelim and blank blanks and pencil lines in margins with occasional written comments throughout, otherwise near fine, original green cloth (both boards and spine) unusually bright with just few signs of wear, most especially to rear cover, spine label very lightly worn around edges, with large section of ads which seem to appear in all English first-issues of this book, with enclosed letter attesting to provenance of presentation to Schiller, clean, tight, near fine. Athena Rare Books 15 - 17 2015 $3500

James, William 1842-1910 *The Varieties of Religious Experience.* London: Longmans Green & Co., 1902. First edition, first issue, octavo, original dark green covers with spine label worn around edges but perfectly readable except for final 's' in 'Varieties', original green cloth unusually bright with just few signs of use, with large section of ads at back which appear in all English issues, clean, tight very good copy. Athena Rare Books 15 - 18 2015 $1200

James, William 1842-1910 *The Will to Believe and Other Essays in Popular Philosophy.* New York: Longmans, Green & Co., 1897. First edition, octavo, original green cloth with 2 1/2 inch paper label to spine, which is darkened and very lightly chipped, still about 90 per cent readable (were effecting "James" more than anything else), most minimal of wear also to head and toe of spine, former owner's names in ink to rear of front cover (Hermine Gelering) and front free endpaper (Albert Gelering), otherwise amazingly well preserved. Athena Rare Books 15 - 16 2015 $900

Jameson, Anna Brownell Murphy 1794-1860 *The Communion of Labour.* London: Longman Brown, Green, Longmans & Roberts, 1856. First edition, small 8vo., small bookplate of Arthur Hoe, bound in flexible red cloth stamped in gilt, cover little soiled, very good, tight. Second Life Books Inc. 189 - 138 2015 $225

Jamieson, Alexander *A Celestial Atlas: Comprising a Systematic Display of the Heavens in a Series of Thirty Maps Illustrated by Scientific Descriptions of their Contents...* London: G. & W. B. Whittaker, 1822. First edition, oblong 4to., engraved title and dedication, 30 engraved plates, 28 are hand colored, original brown paper boards, expertly rebacked in black calf with some neat repair to cornerpieces, boards slightly rubbed and marked, presentation inscription from author for W. M. Wallis, with original recipient scratched away and replaced with W. M. Wallis, very nice, clean, without usual foxing and offsetting. Jarndyce Antiquarian Booksellers CCXI - 157 2015 £2000

Jamison, James Carson *With Walker in Nicaragua or Reminiscences of an Officer of the American Phalanx.* Columbia: E. W. Stephens Pub. Co., 1909. First edition, 8vo., original blue cloth, gold stamped front cover and spine, illustrations, former owner's neat bookplate and their ownership signature, lightly rubbed at spine ends and corners, else near fine, rare. Buckingham Books March 2015 - 24347 2015 $1250

Jammes, Paul *Collection de Specimens De Caracteres 1517-2004.* Paris: Librairie Paul Jammes Editions des Cendres, 2006. Limited to an edition of 1000, 4to., paper covered boards, dust jacket, 380 color illustrations, printed in Sabon Next type. Oak Knoll Books 306 - 218 2015 $320

Jance, J. A. *Kiss of the Bees.* New York: Avon, 1999. First edition, Special reader's edition, one of 300 specially bound numbered copies signed by Jance, very fine in slipcase without dust jacket as issued. Mordida Books March 2015 - 004380 2015 $75

Janes, J. Robert *Mannequin.* London: Constable, 1994. First edition, fine in dust jacket. Mordida Books March 2015 - 007500 2015 $85

Janet, Pierre *The Major Symptoms of Hysteria.* New York: Tryphon Press, 1993. Reprint of 1907 edition, fine in full leather with gilt smudging, raised bands, all edges gilt, ribbon marker. Beasley Books 2013 - 2015 $125

Janssen, Theodore *A Discourse Concerning Banks.* London: printed for James Knapton at the Crown in St. Paul's Church Yard, 1697. First edition, 4to., well bound in relatively modern but old style, green half morocco over marbled boards, spine lettered gilt, very good, crisp copy, scarce. John Drury Rare Books 2015 - 25588 2015 $1311

Janssen, Theodore *A Discourse Concerning Banks.* London: printed in the year and reprinted in the year, 1742. 8vo., titlepage just little soiled, else crisp copy, later boards with printed spine label. John Drury Rare Books March 2015 - 24333 2015 $656

Jansson, Tove *Sculptor's Daughter.* London: Ernest Benn, 1969. First Edition in English, 8vo., fine in very slightly sunned, slightly rubbed, near very good+ dust jacket with slight wear at corners and faint edgewear. Any Amount of Books 2015 - A63766 2015 £225

Janvier, Thomas Allibone *The Aztec Treasure-House: a Romance of Contemporaneous Antiquity.* New York: Harper & Bros., 1890. First edition, octavo, flyleaves at front and rear, 19 inserted plates, illustrations by Frederick Remington, original decorated gray green cloth, front and spine panels stamped in gold. L. W. Currey, Inc. Boy's Adventure Fiction 2015 - 10 2015 $750

Jardine, William *The Natural History of Gallinaeceous Birds. Volume One.* Edinburgh: W. H. Lizars, 1834. First edition, duodecimo, 232 pages, handcolored half title and 29 hand colored plates, contemporary full calf with new gilt decorated spine, lower corners of front pages and titlepage expertly repaired without loss, substantial inscription dated 1836.   Andrew Isles   2015 - 6817   2015 $500

Jarrell, Randall *Blood for a Stranger.* New York: Harcourt Brace & Co., 1942. First edition, one of 1700 copies, 8vo., original red cloth, dust jacket, fine, bright.   James S. Jaffe Rare Books   Modern American Poetry - 144   2015 $750

Jarrell, Randall *Little Friend, Little Friend.* New York: Dial Press, 1945. First edition, one of 2000 copies, 8vo., original cloth, dust jacket slightly dust soiled on back panel with one short closed tear on front panel, top front corner & heel of spine slightly worn, otherwise remarkably fine, extremely rare in collector's condition.   James S. Jaffe Rare Books   Modern American Poetry - 145   2015 $1500

Jarrell, Randall *Selected Poems.* New York: Knopf, 1955. First edition, one of 200 copies, 8vo., original cloth, dust jacket, covers slightly rubbed at extremities, top edge of back cover little bumped, otherwise fine in worn jacket, presentation copy from author.   James S. Jaffe Rare Books   Modern American Poetry - 148   2015 $1500

Jarrell, Randall *Poetry and The Age.* New York: Knopf, 1953. First edition, 8vo., original black cloth, dust jacket, presentation copy inscribed by author for Leonard and Maud Hurley, fine in dust jacket that is slightly faded and spotted along spine panel.   James S. Jaffe Rare Books   Modern American Poetry - 147   2015 $750

Jarrell, Randall *The Seven League Crutches.* New York: Harcourt Brace, 1951. First edition, one of 2000 copies, 8vo., original cloth, dust jacket, fine, presentation copy inscribed to Marc and Clara May from Randall and Mackie,.   James S. Jaffe Rare Books   Modern American Poetry - 146   2015 $1000

Jarrell, Randall *The Woman at the Washington Zoo Poems & Translations.* New York: Atheneum, 1960. First edition, 8vo., original cloth, dust jacket, fine in lightly worn dust jacket, presentation copy inscribed by author for David Posner.   James S. Jaffe Rare Books   Modern American Poetry - 149   2015 $2500

Jaspers, Karl *Von Ursprung und Ziel der Geschichte. (The Origin and Goal of History).* Munchen: R. Piper & Co. Verlag, 1949. and with a copy of another edition the Zurich: Artemis-Verlag, 1949. First edition, published simultaneously, octavo, Piper edition in original red cloth with gilt lettering on front cover and spine, original light tan dust jacket with dark brown and lettering on front and rear panel and spine, dust jacket has few very small nicks (most noticeably at top of spine), covers ever so slightly sprung, otherwise very pretty; the Artemis edition, original red cloth with gilt lettering and device on spine, original light tan dust jacket with dark brown and red lettering on front panel and spine, jacket has few small nicks and just bit of discoloration, else lovely copy.   Athena Rare Books   15 - 28   2015 $750

Jay, Ricky *Cards as Weapons.* New York: Darien House, 1977. First Scribner edition, very fine, soft covers without any creasing creases.   Mordida Books   March 2015 - 012745   2015 $300

Jebb, John *The Excellency of the Spirit of Benevolence, a Sermon Preached Before the University of Cambridge on Monday Dec.. 28 1772.* Cambridge: printed by J. Archdeacon printer to the University for T. and J. Merrill in Cambridge, 1773. First edition, 8vo., complete with final blank leaf (A8), rebound recently in maroon half morocco over marbled boards, spine lettered gilt, very good, very scarce.   John Drury Rare Books   March 2015 - 25310   2015   £266

Jecks, Michael *The Last Templar.* London: Headline, 1995. First edition, light wrinkling to head of spine, page edges just beginning to uniformly tan, else fine in dust jacket.   Buckingham Books   March 2015 - 24939   2015 $650

Jefferies, Richard   1848-1887 *After London; or Wild England.* London: Cassell and Co., 1885. First edition, half title, 8 pages ads (3.85), original grey cloth, bevelled boards, binding slightly loose, hinges slightly cracking, presentation inscription "John & Alice Brook from the author May 10th 1885", very good.   Jarndyce Antiquarian Booksellers   CCXI - 158   2015   £1500

Jefferies, Richard   1848-1887 *Jack Brass, Emperor of England.* London: T. Pettit & Co., 1873. Few small tears and creases to fore-edges with slight loss to lower corner of first 2 leaves, original light brown printed paper wrappers, sewn as issued, slightly dusted, some slight wear to head and tail of spine, corners slightly creased.   Jarndyce Antiquarian Booksellers   CCXI - 159 2015   £950

Jefferies, Richard   1848-1887 *The Scarlet Shawl.* London: Tinsley Bros., 1874. First edition, text slightly spotted, later half blue morocco by Bumpus, raised bands, compartments decorated in gilt, slightly rubbed, armorial bookplate of William Henry Radcliffe Saunders, top edge gilt, very good.   Jarndyce Antiquarian Booksellers   CCXI - 160   2015   £380

Jefferies, Richard 1848-1887 *Suez-Cide!! or, How Miss Britannia Bought a Dirty Puddle and Lost her Sugar-Plums.* London: John Snow & Co., 1876. (1893), Slight marking to fore-edge of page 7, original glazed printed pink paper wrappers, sewn as issued, slightly dulled, 20 pages, very good.   Jarndyce Antiquarian Booksellers   CCXI - 161   2015   £680

Jeffers, Robinson 1887-1962 *The Alpine Christ and Other Poems.* N.P.: Cayucos, 1973. First edition, one of 250 numbered copies signed by William Everson who provided introduction, preface and afterword, fine in cloth and boards.   Ed Smith Books   83 - 51   2015 $150

Jeffers, Robinson 1887-1962 *The Californians.* N.P.: Cayucos Books, 1971. First edition thus, one of 50 numbered copies, specially bound and signed by William Everson (provided introduction), quarter cloth and paper over boards, near fine in original acetate dust jacket.   Ed Smith Books   83 - 50   2015 $250

Jeffers, Robinson 1887-1962 *Flagons and Apples.* Los Angeles: Grafton Pub. Co., 1912. First edition, one of 500 copies of which 480 were sold by printer to a San Francisco used book store, 8vo., original cloth backed boards with paper labels on spine and front cover, spine sunned, spine label worn and some loss of text, otherwise very good.   James S. Jaffe Rare Books   Modern American Poetry - 152   2015 $750

Jeffers, Robinson 1887-1962 *Give Your Heart to the Hawks and other Poems.* New York: Random House, 1933. First trade edition, corners and spine ends worn and little frayed, good only, lacking dust jacket, inscribed by author to Mercedes de Acosta, writer and actress.   Between the Covers Rare Books   196 - 79   2015 $650

Jeffrey of Monmouth *The British History.* London: J. Bowyer, H. Clements and J. Innys, 1718. First edition, 8vo., errata leaf, recent half leather with marbled boards, lettered gilt at spine with 5 raised bands and gilt decoration, very good, very slight browning at beginning and end, text otherwise very clean, tight sound, bright copy.   Any Amount of Books   2015 - C15713   2015   £750

Jeffrey, Francis *Jeffrey's Criticism: a Selection.* Edinburgh: Scottish Academic Press, 1983. Frontispiece, original blue cloth, very good in slightly marked dust jacket, Kathleen Tillotson's dedication copy with inscription from editor, Peter Morgan with 2 page TLS from him 21 March 1983 at University College Toronto.   Jarndyce Antiquarian Booksellers   CCVII - 326   2015   £25

Jellett, Mainie *The Artist's Vision - Lectures and Essays on Art.* Dundalk: Dundalgan Press, 1958. First edition, 8 color plates of paintings by Jellett, others in black and white, small quarto, scarce, free endpapers partially browned, near fine in very good dust jacket rubbed at edges with enclosed two-inch tear at head of spine.   Peter Ellis, Bookseller   2014 - 010464   2015   £300

Jenkins, Dan *Semi-Tough.* New York: Antheneum, 1972. First edition, wrappers, advance reading copy, near fine.   Beasley Books   2013 - 2015 $45

Jenkins, John *Art of Writing Reduced to a Plain and Easy System on a Plan Entirely New in Seven Books ....* Cambridge: printed for the author, 1813. Revised from 1791 first edition, 8vo., original quarter calf over boards, frontispiece, with 10 unnumbered engraved plates, bottom of spine chipped away and worn spot on front hinge, front over partially detached, foxing.   Oak Knoll Books   Special Catalogue 24 - 26   2015 $450

Jennings, Al *Number 30664 by Number 31539. A Sketch in the Lives of William Sidney Porter and A. Jennings, The Bandit.* Hollywood: Pioneer Press, 1941. First edition, 8vo., inscribed by Jennings for Col. Tim McCoy, grey printed wrappers, 32 pages, frontispiece, illustrations, rare, fine.   Buckingham Books   March 2015 - 32237   2015 $1750

Jennings, Al *Through the Shadows with O. Henry.* H. K. Fly Co., 1921. First edition, 8vo., signed by author on extra leaf and bound in after titlepage, colorfully decorated dark blue cloth, frontispiece, illustrations, former owner's small name stamped on front flyleaf, else very good with gold gilt titles bright on front cover, but faded on spine, nice, especially signed.   Buckingham Books   March 2015 - 37582   2015 $450

Jennings, Linda Deziah *Washington Women's Cook Book.* Seattle: Trade Register print, 1909. First edition, 8vo., printed boards, little rubbed and soiled, hinges loose, inscription on endpaper, some recipes from "Rhodes Brothers Tea Room" tipped to rear blanks, some wrinkling to fore edge of titlepage, good, clean copy, rare.   Second Life Books Inc.   189 - 138   2015 $475

Jennings, Maureen *Except the Dying.* New York: St. Martin's, 1997. First edition, very fine in dust jacket.   Mordida Books   March 2015 - 001205   2015 $75

Jennings, Waylon *Waylon. An Autobiography.* Norwalk: Easton Press, 1996. First edition, one of 3000 numbered copies, signed by Jennings, fine in full black leather with gilt lettering and decorations, all edges gilt, ribbon marker.   Ed Smith Books   83 - 52   2015 $300

Jepsen, Jorgen Grunnet *Jazz Records 1942-1962.* Holte: Karl Emil Knudsen, 1963-1970. First edition, 11 volumes, good to very good set with some loosening pages, some volumes worse than others, notoriously fragile production, about average copy.   Beasley Books   2013 - 2015 $300

Jepsen, Jorgen Grunnet *Jazz Records 1942-1962.* Holte: Karl Emil Knudsen, 1963-1970. First edition, 11 volumes, complete, very good, original paper wrappers, some spines bit worn, several have loosening spine glue. Beasley Books   2013 - 2015 $350

Jepson, Edgar *Whitaker's Dukedom.* Bobbs Merrill Co. n.d., 1914. First US Edition, faintly stamped on dust jackets front cover "Review copy Oct. 2 1914", wear fine, bright, dust jacket with light professional restoration to spine ends, corners and extremities.   Buckingham Books   March 2015 - 37539   2015 $450

Jerrold, Walter *Bon-Mots of Sydney Smith and R. Brinsley Sheridan.* London: Dent, 1893. First edition, 12mo., illustrations by Aubrey Beardsley top edge gilt, ivory cloth stamped in maroon and gilt, cover darkened, otherwise very good, tight copy.   Second Life Books Inc.   190 - 10   2015 $175

Jerry and Jo Hop Off. Akron: Saalfield, 1928. Square 4to., pictorial wrappers, very good+, each illustration has piece cut-out through which one can see the next page and illustrations.   Aleph-bet Books, Inc.   109 - 332   2015 $100

Jesse James: the Life and Daring Adventures of This Bold Highwayman and Bank Robber... Barclay & Co., 1883. First edition, 2nd printing, 8vo., pictorial blue and black wrappers, illustrations, portraits on covers, good, solid copy housed in four point cloth and marbled paper folding case, titles stamped in gold on leather label affixed to spine. Buckingham Books   March 2015 - 33472   2015 $1375

Jesse, George Richard *Evidence Given Before the Royal Commission on Vivisection.* London: Basil Montagu Pickering, 1875. First edition thus, 8vo., with half title, original maroon cloth gilt, head and foot of spine, neatly restored, very good.   John Drury Rare Books   2015 - 22935   2015 $177

The "Jeweller & Metalworker" Annual... London: Allens, 1912. Issue for 1912, ads on endpapers, original dark brown cloth, 1 cm. chip to following hinge.   Jarndyce Antiquarian Booksellers   CCXI - 162   2015   £45

Jewett, Sarah Orne 1849-1909 *Betty Leicester, a Story for Girls.* Boston: Houghton Mifflin, 1890. First edition, 12mo., first printing consisted of 1500 copies, some soiling to cover, swear to spine, good copy, name on endpaper. Second Life Books Inc.   191 - 50   2015 $100

Jinman, John *All Things Bright. A Collection of Bird Paintings.* Charlury: Senecio Press, 1990. First edition, 81/250 copies (of an edition of 285) signed by author, printed on Zerkall mouldmade paper, 32 tipped-in color illustrations on Rivoli paper with descriptions on facing verso, crown 8vo., original quarter green leather with cloth sides, backstrip lettered in gilt, marbled endpapers, matching slipcase, fine.   Blackwell's Rare Books   B179 - 233   2015   £175

Joan, Natalie *Ameliaranne in Town.* London: Harrap, 1930. First edition, small 8vo., boards, pictorial paste-on, near fine, full page color illustrations by Susan Pearse, including pictorial endpapers.   Aleph-Bet Books, Inc.   108 - 339   2015 $250

Johannes Chrysotomus *Enarratio in Esaiam Prophetam. (bound with) Conciones in Celebrioribus Aliquot Anni Festivitatibus Habitae. (bound with) Homiliae in Aliquot Veteris Testamenti Loca.* Antverpiae: in Aedibus Ioan. Seelsii, 1555. 1553. 1553, 165 x 105mm., 3 separately published works bound in one volume, splendid armorial red Roman morocco done for Pope Pius V by Niccolo Franzese, covers gilt with papal arms in central cartouche, front cover with "Pivs V" above arms and initials "P.M." (Pontifex Maximus) below, back cover with "Io Chrys in Esa et Hom" in gilt above and "P.M." below, boards framed by a profusion of acanthus leaves emanating from the brass bosses at corners and with a background stamped with small floral and dot tools, raised bands, spine compartments with interwoven gilt vines and gilt titling, remnants of clasps, all edges gilt and gauffered in pink floral pattern and with Pius' name tooled into head and tail edges and his arms painted on the fore edge (apparently with very expert repairs at spine ends), titlepage with printer's device, bookplate of Carlo Ponzone di Casale and with ink inscription of Ch. Al. Ganora dated 1867, titlepage with ink inscription of a Capuchin convent, hinge separation at first titlepage, majority of the leaves with minor browning (a half dozen gatherings rather browned), other trivial defects but text unsoiled and consistently fresh, front joint with two-inch crack near bottom, leather on spine bit crackled, gilt lost in small area next to one box, but sumptuously decorated binding still quite lustrous showing little wear, and altogether pleasing.   Phillip J. Pirages   66 - 18   2015 $17,500

John, Augustus *Chiaroscuro: Fragments of Autobiography.* London: Cape, 1952. First edition, of two variants, this copy the variant with red topstain and "AJ" on front board, the Cape imprint on spine (no priority), trifle sunned at crown, corners little bumped, faint tape shadows where address label in John's hand had been affixed and now removed and laid in), this copy inscribed by painter to Hope Montgomery Scott.   Between the Covers Rare Books, Inc.   187 - 138   2015 $450

John, Juliet *Cult Criminals: the Newgate Novels (1830-1847).* London: Thoemmes Press, 2000. Reprint, 8vo., 6 volumes, about fine, hardback.   Any Amount of Books 2015 - A16321   2015   £320

Johns, Joseph *St. George and the Dragon; England and the Drink Traffic.* London: S. W. Partridge, 1907. First edition, half title, frontispiece, illustrations, paper browning, original blue cloth, spine slightly dulled with small mark at foot, booklabel of Eric Quayle on leading pastedown, bright copy. Jarndyce Antiquarian Booksellers CCXI - 163 2015 £45

Johns, W. E. *Biggles and The Deep Blue Sea.* Swanage: Norman Wright, 2007. Reprint, limited to 300 copies, this being designated 'comp', 8vo., original black cloth lettered gilt at spine, signed presentation from publisher, illustrations by Andrew Skilleter, including signed letter from Wright, fine in fine dust jacket. Any Amount of Books 2015 - C13308 2015 £240

Johnsen, Kenneth G. *Apple Country Interurban. A History of the Yakima Valley Transportation Company and the Yakima Interurban Trolley Lines.* San Marino: Golden West Books, 1979. First edition, 4to., photos, red cloth, gilt, very fine, pictorial dust jacket. Argonaut Book Shop Holiday Season 2014 - 138 2015 $60

Johnson, Anna C. *The Cottages of the Alps; or Life and Manners in Switzerland.* London: Sampson Low, 1860. First edition, 2 volumes in 1, half title, color frontispiece in volume 1, original red cloth, blocked and lettered in gilt, slightly dulled Belle Vue House prize label, 1864, all edges gilt, very good. Jarndyce Antiquarian Booksellers CCXI - 164 2015 £125

Johnson, Bruce L. *James Weld Towne Pioneer San Francisco Printer, Publisher and Paper Purveyor.* San Francisco: Book Club of California, 2008. First edition, one of 275 copies, small quarto, 31 photo illustrations, purple linen lettered in copper with acetate dust jacket, as new. Argonaut Book Shop Holiday Season 2014 - 289 2015 $200

Johnson, Burges *Pleasant Tragedies of Childhood.* New York: Harper, 1905. First edition, 4to., blue pictorial cloth, light cover soil, very good+, illustrations by Fanny Cory. Aleph-bet Books, Inc. 109 - 105 2015 $125

Johnson, Charles *Middle Passage.* New York: Atheneum, 1990. First printing, 8vo., paper over boards with cloth spine, nice, scuffed and little soiled dust jacket. Second Life Books Inc. 190 - 142 2015 $125

Johnson, Colonel *A Sketch of the Isle of Man: an Unrivalled Watering Place.* Liverpool: printed by Harris and Co., 1862. First edition, 16mo., engraved frontispiece, including final ad leaf, original printed blue wrappers, fine, fresh, apparently rare. John Drury Rare Books 2015 - 26273 2015 $133

Johnson, Crockett *Harold and the Purple Crayon.* New York: Harper and Bros., 1955. First edition, first printing, 16mo., cloth backed pictorial boards, spine stamped in white, slightest bit of edge rubbing, else fine in dust jacket with two quarter inch chips off spine ends and few tiny closed edge tears and with price intact, rare in any condition. Aleph-bet Books, Inc. 109 - 238 2015 $4750

Johnson, Crockett *Harold's Trip to the Sky.* New York: Harper Bros., 1957. First edition, tan cloth spine and pictorial boards, slight lean to binding, else fine in dust jacket with price intact, dust jacket has archival mends on verso. Aleph-bet Books, Inc. 109 - 239 2015 $2000

Johnson, Crockett *A Picture for Harold's Room.* New York: Harper & Bros., 1960. First edition, 8vo., cloth backed pictorial boards, slightest bit of edge rubbing, else fine in dust jacket, dust jacket very slightly frayed at spine ends, some shelf soil. Aleph-bet Books, Inc. 109 - 240 2015 $800

Johnson, Cuthbert, William *Observations on the Employment of Salt in Agriculture and Horticulture with Directions for This Application, founded on Practice.* London: Plummer and Brewin, 1826. First edition?, 8vo., 16 pages, stitched as issued, fine. John Drury Rare Books 2015 - 25200 2015 $151

Johnson, Edward *Life, Health and Disease.* London: Simpkin & Co., 1843. Seventh thousand, 4 pages ads and initial ad, slip for 'Nuces Philosophicae", uncut, original dark green cloth, blocked in blind with gilt title, very good, bright copy, large ownership inscription of William Jones, Glyn Castell, June 24th 1844. Jarndyce Antiquarian Booksellers CCXI - 165 2015 £45

Johnson, Fridolf *Rockwell Kent: an Anthology of His Works.* New York: Alfred A. Knopf, 1981. First edition, small folio, quarter cloth, paper covered boards, dust jacket, color and black and white illustrations, include lithographs. Oak Knoll Books 306 - 27 2015 $100

Johnson, George E. Q. *I Like America.* New York: privately printed (John C. Rogers Co.), 1939. First edition, one of 1000 numbered copies, 24mo., quarter rough cloth and textured and embossed cloth boards, corners rubbed, else fine, ownership signature of woodcut artist John De Pol. Between the Covers Rare Books, Inc. 187 - 139 2015 $50

Johnson, George William *A History of English Gardening, Chronological, Biographical, Literary and Critical.* London: Baldwin & Cradock and Longman & Co., H. & W. Wright..., 1829. First edition, uncommon, large 8vo., final leaf, near contemporary (original?) cloth with patches of fading and some wear to joints and corners, original printed label on spine, upper joint weakening, entirely uncut, very good, large copy uncommon. John Drury Rare Books 2015 - 21035 2015 $1486

Johnson, Hank *Railroads of the Yosemite Valley.* Trans-Anglo Books, 1975. Second edition, fourth print, 400 photos, illustrations, drawings, endpaper maps, brown cloth lettered white, very fine, spine faded pictorial dust jacket. Argonaut Book Shop   Holiday Season 2014 - 140   2015 $50

Johnson, Isaac *Slavery Days in Old Kentucky: a True Story of a Father who Sold His Wife and Four Children by One of the Children.* Ogdenburg: Republican & Journal Print, 1901. First edition, octavo, 40 pages, photo frontispiece, gray wrappers printed in black, substantial stains and small chips on front wrapper and spine, good, internally near fine, very scarce, especially in wrappers.   Between the Covers Rare Books   197 - 61   2015 $1750

Johnson, James Weldon *The Book of American Negro Spirituals.* New York: Viking, 1925. First edition, small 4to., tan cloth stamped in brown, edges somewhat soiled, cover scuffed at edges and corners, otherwise very good. Second Life Books Inc.   191 - 51   2015 $200

Johnson, James Weldon *The Second Book of American Negro Spirituals.* New York: Viking, 1925. First edition, small 8vo., tan cloth stamped in brown, edges somewhat soiled, cover scuffed at edges and corners, otherwise very good.   Second Life Books Inc.   191 - 52   2015 $165

Johnson, John 1777-1848 *Typographia, or the Printer's Instructor Including an Account of the Origin of Printing.* London: Longman, Hurst, Rees, Orme, Brown and Green, 1824. First edition, one of the large paper copies measuring 7.5 inches in height and with his designation printed on spine labels, 2 volumes, thick 8vo., original quarter blue cloth, paper spine labels, attractive frontispiece and titlepage decorations, covers soiled and rubbed, hinges split and back cover detached, inner hinge repaired on first volume, bookplate of Haley Hill Lending Library with their inkstamp. Oak Knoll Books   306 - 190   2015 $450

Johnson, Merle *Howard Pyle's Book of the American Spirit.* New York: Harper & Bros., 1923. b-x. Limited to 50 numbered copies signed by compiler, Johnson and editor Francis Dowd, stated first edition, 22 beautiful tipped in color plates plus a profusion of black and whites, this copy with special mounted illustration of a pirate by Pyle hitherto unpublished and made available by Frank Schoonover for this edition, great copy, rare, large thick 4to., cloth backed boards, pictorial paste-on, bottom margin of title wrinkled from bookplate on copyright page, else fine, bright copy with no edge wear and with white spine clean and bright. Aleph-Bet Books, Inc.   108 - 378   2015 $2250

Johnson, Michael *Masters of Crime. Lionel Davidson and Dick Francis.* Herefordshire: Scorpion Press, 2006. First edition, one of 250 numbered copies signed by Davison and Francis, very fine, leather bound copies in transparent dust jacket.   Buckingham Books   March 2015 - 24247   2015 $165

Johnson, Robert Wallace *The Nurse's Guide and Family Assistant...* Philadelphia: Published by Anthony Finley, A. Small, 1819. Second printing of the second US edition, 12mo., period full tree calf with maroon leather title label to spine, gilded decoration to board edges, some modest binding wear, boards bit splayed, personal owner signature, usual bit of browning and foxing, with old, unobtrusive stain to top half of first few leaves, very good.   Tavistock Books Bah, Humbug? - 15   2015 $495

Johnson, Samuel   1709-1784   *Diaries, Prayers and Annals.* New Haven: Yale University Press, 1958. Half title, plates, original blue cloth, very good in slightly torn dust jacket, from the library of Geoffrey & Kathleen Tillotson, signed by Kathleen for Geoffrey 25 De. 59, with inserted long review in TLS and correspondence between Geoffrey and others about revised edition.   Jarndyce Antiquarian Booksellers   CCVII - 327   2015   £45

Johnson, Samuel   1709-1784   *A Dictionary of the English language...* Philadelphia: Johnson & Warner, 1813. Thick 8vo., original two-toned boards, spine worn, uncut, front cover nearly detached, foxed and browned.   M & S Rare Books, Inc.   97 - 89   2015 $400

Johnson, Samuel   1709-1784   *Dr. Johnson's Table Talk.* London: printed for C. Dilly, 1798. First edition, 8vo., full brown leather, lettered and decorated in gilt at spine with five raised bands, prelim leaves including frontispiece, titlepage, ad leaf and contents leaf, boards little worn with some splitting at spine, chipped at top and looseness of front board, neat inscription dated 1826, frontispiece (often missing) present.   Any Amount of Books   2015 - C8117   2015 £280

Johnson, Samuel   1709-1784   *The Fountains...* London: Elkin Mathews & Marot, 1927. Number 433 of 500 copies of the first separate edition, uncut, original boards, slight rubbing at corners, signed by Geoffrey Tillotson with few pencil notes.   Jarndyce Antiquarian Booksellers CCVII - 328   2015   £35

Johnson, Samuel   1709-1784   *Rasselas, Priz Von Abyssinien.* Hamburg: Hartwig & Muller, 1826. First edition, 2 volumes in 1, 8vo., half brown leather, rare edition with text in English and German, frontispiece, uncommon, half brown leather rubbed at corners and slightly chipped at spine ends, slight splitting at upper spine hinge, otherwise very good with clean pages slightly stained at prelims and with slight 'waving' of pages, possibly from damp at some time.   Any Amount of Books   2015 - A64756   2015 £180

Johnson, Samuel   1709-1784   *The History of Rasselas, Prince of Abissinia.* London: Oxford University Press, 1971. Half title, original blue cloth, very good in dust jacket, with note at end by Kathleen Tillotson about distribution and some inserted correspondence.   Jarndyce Antiquarian Booksellers   CCVII - 329   2015   £18

Johnson, Samuel 1709-1784 *The Idler and the Adventurer.* New Haven: Yale University Press, 1963. Half title, plates, original blue cloth, very good in slightly torn dust jacket, W. J Bate's signed presentation copy to Geoffrey Tillotson, with review of "The Rambler" inserted. Jarndyce Antiquarian Booksellers CCVII - 330 2015 £45

Johnson, Samuel 1709-1784 *A Journey to the Western Islands of Scotland.* New Haven: Yale University Press, 1971. Half title, folding map, plates, original blue cloth, very good in slightly creased dust jacket, Mary Lascelles (editor) presentation copy to Kathleen Tillotson with one ink correction in Tillotson's hand and inserted reviews. Jarndyce Antiquarian Booksellers CCVII - 331 2015 £40

Johnson, Samuel 1709-1784 *The Letters, with Mrs. Thrale's Genuine Letters to Him.* Oxford: Clarendon Press, 1952. 3 volumes, half title, frontispiece, plate, few pencil notes, original maroon cloth in slightly worn dust jacket, with cuttings of review and obits of R. W. Chapman inserted, from the library of Geoffrey & Kathleen Tillotson. Jarndyce Antiquarian Booksellers CCVII - 335 2015 £45

Johnson, Samuel 1709-1784 *Lives of the English Poets.* Oxford: at the Clarendon Press, 1905. 3 volumes, original red cloth, hinges little rubbed, from the library of Geoffrey & Kathleen Tillotson, Kathleen's gift to Geoffrey Christmas 1937 with extensive notes and insertions including correspondence with R. W. Chapman and others. Jarndyce Antiquarian Booksellers CCVII - 332 2015 £75

Johnson, Samuel 1709-1784 *The Poems.* Oxford: Clarendon Press, 1941. Half title, original dark blue cloth, Geoffrey Tillotson's copy with notes in text and on following endpapers, much inserted material including reviews and note from R. W. Chapman. Jarndyce Antiquarian Booksellers CCVII - 334 2015 £60

Johnston, Alexander Keith *The Physical Atlas of Natural Phenomena.* Edinburgh & London: William Blackwood, 1850. Second edition, imperial folio issue, hand colored frontispiece, 24 hand colored plates, first few pages foxed including frontispiece, original half gilt stamped brown morocco over gilt stamped light brown cloth, all edges gilt, extremities rubbed, mild smoky aroma, rare, very good. Jeff Weber Rare Books 178 - 796 2015 $650

Johnston, Hank *The Whistles Blow No More Railroad Logging in the Sierre Nevada 1874-1942.* Glendale: Trans-Anglo Books, 1984. First edition, photos, map, green leatherette gilt, ink name and address to bottom edge of text block, else fine, spine faded pictorial dust jacket. Argonaut Book Shop Holiday Season 2014 - 139 2015 $50

Johnston, Samuel *The Advantage of Employing the Poor in Useful Labour and Mischief of Idleness or Ill-Judg'd Business, in a Sermon Preached at St. Mary's in Beverley Oct. 10 1725....* London: printed and sold by J. Downing, 1726. First London edition, 8vo., preserved in modern wrappers with printed title label on upper cover, very good. John Drury Rare Books March 2015 - 21635 2015 $266

Johnstone, David Lawson *The Paradise of the North.* London: Remington & Co., 1890. First edition, octavo, original decorated green cloth, front panel stamped in brown and gold, spine panel stamped in gold and blind, rear panel stamped in black, white endpapers with leaf pattern printed in green. L. W. Currey, Inc. Boy's Adventure Fiction 2015 - 3 2015 $1250

Johnstone, David Lawson *The Paradise of the North.* London and Edinburgh: W. & R. Chambers Ltd. n.d., 1893. Second (first illustrated) edition, octavo, undated 32 page catalog of Books Suitable for Prizes and Presentation inserted at rear, 15 full page illustrations by Boucher, plus several smaller uncredited illustrations in text, one map, original pictorial blue cloth, front and spine panels stamped in black, white, blue-gray and gold, white endpapers with floral pattern printed in purple. L. W. Currey, Inc. Boy's Adventure Fiction 2015 - 34 2015 $250

Johnstone, David Lawson *The White Princess of the Hidden City: Being the Record of Leslie Rutherford's Strange Adventures in Central Africa.* London and Edinburgh: W. & R. Chambers, 1898. First edition, octavo, 6 inserted plates with illustrations by W. Boucher, original pictorial salmon cloth, front and spine panels stamped in red, black, white and gold, rear panel plain, slate coated endpapers. L. W. Currey, Inc. Boy's Adventure Fiction 2015 - 43 2015 $200

Johnstone, David Lawson *The White Princess of the Hidden City: Being the Record of Leslie Rutherford's Strange Adventures in Central Africa.* London: and Edinburgh: W. R. Chambers ltd., 1898. First edition, octavo, 6 inserted plates, illustrations by W. Boucher, original pictorial blue cloth, front and spine panels stamped in red, brown, black, white and gold, rear panel stamped in black with publisher's floral device. L. W. Currey, Inc. Boy's Adventure Fiction 2015 - 25 2015 $350

Johnstone, George *Letters Which Passed Between Commodore Johnstone and Capt. Evelyn Sutton in 1781 with respect to the Bringing Captain Sutton to Trial.* n.p.: London, n.d.?, 1784. First edition, apparently very scarce, 8vo., modern wrappers with printed label on upper cover, very good. John Drury Rare Books March 2015 - 26284 2015 $266

Johnstone, James *An Historical Dissertation Concerning the Malignant Epidemical fever of 1756.* London: printed for W. Johnston, 1758. First edition, 8vo., without errata slip, titlepage little soiled and gutter stained by tape and now strengthened by archival tissue, bound in 1982 in rich blue calf gilt, spine lettered, very rare. John Drury Rare Books 2015 - 21526 2015 $787

Johnstone, John *An Address, Delivered at the Birmingham School of Medicine and Surgery on Monday October 6 1834 on the Occasion of the Passing of the Appended Laws and Regulations.* Birmingham: J. D. Barlow, 1834. First edition, 8vo., 22 pages, original cloth, bit faded, lettered gilt on upper cover, very good. John Drury Rare Books 2015 - 16269 2015 $177

Johnstone, John *An Address Delivered at the Birmingham School of Medicine and Surgery on Monday October 6 1834 on the Occasion of the Passing of the Appended Laws and Regulations.* Birmingham: J. C. Barlow, 1834. First edition, 8vo., 22 pages, final page rather foxed, preserved in modern wrappers with printed title label on upper cover, good. John Drury Rare Books 2015 - 22622 2015 $133

Johnstone, John *Medical Jurisprudence. On Madness.* Birmingham: printed at the office of J. Belcher and sold by J. Johnson St. Paul's Church Yard London, 1800. First edition, 8vo., contemporary calf, gilt, foot of spine chipped, else very good, from the 19th century library of John Scott, Earl of Eldon and Lord Chancellor with his circular armorial bookplate, uncommon. John Drury Rare Books 2015 - 25035 2015 $1136

Johnstone, John *A Statement of the Differences Subsisting Between the Proprietors and Performers of the Theatre Royal Covent Garden....* London: W. Miller, 1800. First edition, 8vo, half title, 3 page supplement, recent marbled boards lettered on spine, very good. John Drury Rare Books March 2015 - 24437 2015 $656

Johnstone, William *Paintings by William Johnstone.* Newcastle upon Tyne: Stone Gallery, 1963. Octavo, illustrated wrappers, fine, exhibition pamphlet, inscribed by Hugh MacDiarmid (provided foreword) for Jonathan Williams, 15/8/63. Between the Covers Rare Books, Inc. 187 - 162 2015 $250

Jolas, Eugene *Transition Number 19-20 June 1930.* Paris: Transition, 1930. Large 8vo., original illustrated wrappers, 21 plates, sound, slightly used, copy with slight soiling, slight wear at spine hinge and slight browning, ownership signature of British surrealist Roger Roughton. Any Amount of Books 2015 - C12882 2015 £160

Jonas, Lucien *Verdun, Mars-Avril 1916.* Paris: Librairie Dorbon-Aine, 1916. First edition, 18/50 copies "De Grande Luxe" with hand colored version of each plate preceding its monochrome equivalent and an original colored sketch by artist, little fraying at edges of some leaves, 4to., original beige canvas with loop to hold pencil and long strap to replicate sketchbook, lettered and signed by artist to front with original colored sketch of soldier, small amount of foxing to tail edge, light soiling to backstrip and few other small marks, limitation number in ink at bottom, corner of upper board splitting to front hinge with rear hinge starting to crack, endpapers with facsimile of holograph list of plates, little toned, good. Blackwell's Rare Books B179 - 181 2015 £750

Jones, A. H. M. *The Later Roman Empire 284-602: a Social Economic and Administrative Survey.* Oxford: Basil Blackwell, 1964. First edition, 4 volumes, 8vo., 7 maps in separate volume, clean very good+ set, neat name on front endpapers, corners slightly bumped but bright and clean text, excellent condition. Any Amount of Books 2015 - A89773 2015 £300

Jones, Charles Alfred *A History of the Jesus Lane Sunday School Cambridge (1827-1877) with Short Biographical Notices of Some Deceased Teachers, and Lists of Superintendents, Teachers, &c.* Cambridge: sold by Thomas Dixon n.d., 1877. 8vo., original brown cloth with title in gilt on spine and upper cover, very good. John Drury Rare Books 2015 - 25967 2015 $133

Jones, David *The Anathemata: Fragments of an Attempted Writing.* London: Faber and Faber, 1952. First edition, 8vo., cloth, title and author gilt stamped on spine, dust jacket, 9 black and white illustrations, top front corner bumped, news clippings, including Jones's obituary laid in. Oak Knoll Books 306 - 26 2015 $225

Jones, David *Epoch and Artist, Selected Writings by David Jones.* London: Faber and Faber, 1959. First edition, small tear along front hinge of jacket at head of spine, 8vo., cloth. Oak Knoll Books 306 - 271 2015 $250

Jones, David *On the Value of Annuities and Reversionary Payments with Numerous Tables.* London: Baldwin and Cradock, 1843. First edition, 2 volumes, 8vo., contemporary diced calf gilt, spines gilt with raised bands and labels, little wear to bindings and some old ink splashes on boards, marbled edges, good, well bound copies from 19th century library. John Drury Rare Books 2015 - 18757 2015 $177

Jones, Enid *Margery Fry: the Essential Amateur.* London: Oxford University Press, 1966. Half title, frontispiece and plates, mark at end of text, original blue cloth, slightly marked in slightly torn dust jacket, from the library of Geoffrey & Kathleen Tillotson with author's presentation inscription pasted to endpaper and ALS from her to Kathleen, and cuttings of 2 reviews inserted. Jarndyce Antiquarian Booksellers CCVII - 271 2015 £25

Jones, George *I Lived to tell It all.* Norwalk: Easton Press, 1996. First edition, one of 1500 numbered copies, inset color photo on front cover, fine in full brown leather with gilt lettering and decorations, all edges gilt, ribbon marker, all edges gilt. Ed Smith Books 83 - 53 2015 $300

Jones, Horatio Gates *Andrew Bradford, Founder of the Newspaper Press in the Middle States of America.* Philadelphia: King & Baird, 1869. First edition, 24.5cm., folded facsimile, 36 pages, printed wrappers, untrimmed, inscribed by author to Joseph Sabin Esq, neat ink on half titlepage, chipping to edges of wrappers, somewhat darkened and separate at spine, with age toning to text pages, else very good, very scarce. Between the Covers Rare Books, Inc. 187 - 140 2015 $650

Jones, J. Roy *Saddle Bags in Siskiyou.* Yreka: New Journal Print Shop, 1953. First edition, thick 8vo., presentation inscription from author, bookplate, cloth, illustrations, map, near fine in dust jacket with light wear to spine ends. Buckingham Books March 2015 - 31787 2015 $250

Jones, James *From Here to Eternity.* New York: Scribner's, 1951. First edition, first printing, fine in bright and crisp unclipped dust jacket, extremities slightly rubbed, spine lettering lightly faded, else fine, excellent copy. B & B Rare Books, Ltd. 234 - 58 2015 $325

Jones, James *The Pistol.* New York: Charles Scribner's Sons, 1958. First edition, modest smudge on front board, very good or better in very good dust jacket, with small scrape on spine, nicely inscribed by author for Terry Southern and his wife Carol. Between the Covers Rare Books, Inc. 187 - 141 2015 $1750

Jones, John Pike *Substance of the Speech of the Rev. J. P. Jones of North Bovey, Delivered at a county Meeting Held at the Castle of Exeter on Friday the16th day of March 1821...* Exeter: printed by R. Cullum, reprinted from the Exeter edition with additional note by Keating and Brown, London, 1821. First edition, 2nd issue, 8vo., 28 pages, some page browning, preserved in modern wrappers with printed title label on upper cover, good. John Drury Rare Books March 2015 - 20228 2015 $221

Jones, Nard *Swift Flows the River.* New York: Dodd Mead & Co., 1940. First edition, fine, bright copy in lightly rubbed dust jacket with tiny hole (about size of pencil eraser) on front panel, lightly sunned on spine and tiny scrape to lower rear panel. Buckingham Books March 2015 - 15198 2015 $175

Jones, Robert *An Inquiry into the State of Medicine on the Principles of Inductive Philosophy.* Edinburgh: for T. Longman and T. Cadell, London and C. Elliot, Edinburgh, 1781. First edition, 8vo., without half title, contemporary calf appropriately rebacked, spine now gilt and labelled, very good, uncommon. John Drury Rare Books 2015 - 24231 2015 $1180

Jones, Shirley *Scop Hwilum Sang (Sometimes a Poet Sang).* Llanhamlach: Red Hen Press, 1983. First edition, folio, terracotta morocco over black pictorial linen boards, 6 color etchings, typewritten statement by Jones describing the making of the book laid in, original box, fine. Honey & Wax Booksellers 2 - 48 2015 $2500

Jones, Tom *The Fantasticks.* New York: Drama Book Shop, 1967. Stated second printing, fine in slightly age toned, near fine dust jacket, inscribed by Jones and co-author Harvey Schmidt, also laid in is unsigned card engraved with initials 'J.F.B.". Between the Covers Rare Books 196 - 82 2015 $450

Jones, Tom *Miniature Scenic Souvenirs of Panama.* Scenic Souvenirs, 1906. First edition, 8vo., dark green cloth, gold stamping on front cover and spine, former owner's bookplate, light cosmetic restoration to the spine ends and lower corners, rebacked with original spine laid down, else very good, tight copy. Buckingham Books March 2015 - 29958 2015 $250

Jones, William *The Principles of Government in a Dialogue Between a Scholar and a Peasant.* London: printed and published by Richard Carlile, 1831. 8vo. very small inkstamp of Dutch academic institution on verso of title, title little dust marked, recent plain wrappers, good. John Drury Rare Books 2015 - 19553 2015 $89

Jones, William *A Prize Essay, in English and Welsh, on the Character of the Welsh as a Nation in the Present Age.* London: Simpkin and Marshall and Carnarvon, Potter and Co., 1841. First edition, 8vo., errata slip pasted on to foot of front leaf, original watered maroon cloth with printed paper spine label, very good. John Drury Rare Books March 2015 - 12425 2015 £306

Jonson, Ben *Plays.* Glasgow: printed by R(obert) Urie, 1752. 12mo., 3 parts in 1 volume, titlepage loose, contemporary calf, worn, loss of surface leather, a number of circular marks on both covers, upper joint split but cords holding, corners rather worn, lacking lettering piece, sound, rare edition. Blackwell's Rare Books B179 - 52 2015 £750

Jordan, Larry *Ivan the Terrible.* San Francisco: Larry Jordan, 1959. First edition, one of 100 copies hand bound by Jordan, printed on thick card stock with hand-tipped photo still images, oblong self wrappers, 5 x 4 inches, unbound, folded leaves as issued.   Royal Books   46 - 41   2015 $850

Jorgensen, S. J. *Thirty-Six Secret Knock-Out Blows Without the Use of Fists American Jij-Jitsu.* Seattle: S. J. Jorgensen, 1938. 24mo., illustrations, stapled illustrated wrappers, modest soiling, near fine.   Between the Covers Rare Books   196 - 176   2015 $125

Jorrocks, John *Jorrock's Jaunts and Jollities; or, The Hunting, Shooting, Racing, Driving, Sailing, Eating, Eccentric and Extravagant Exploits of that Renowned Sporting Citizen Jr. John Jorrocks.* London: Walter Speirs, 1838. First edition, 8vo., 12 black and white illustrations by Phiz, finely bound in full red leather with five raised bands, lettered and decorated gilt at spine and decorated along internal edge, two attractive bookplates on front pastedown and front endpaper with very slight marking at edges, not affecting text, slight rubbing and very slight dryness at hinge, very faint splitting at head of front hinge, otherwise clean, very good+ in superb, Riviere style binding.   Any Amount of Books   March 2015 - C7944   2015   £450

Joscelyn, Archie *The Golden Bowl.* Cleveland: World, 1931. First edition, pages darkened, otherwise very good in dust jacket with chips at top of spine, corners and along top back panel.   Mordida Books   March 2015 - 001210   2015 $75

Josephus, Flavius *Opera.* Basel: Froben, 1544. Editio princeps, titlepage printed in red and black, 3 small wormholes at beginning (one quickly shrinking away, the other two lasting until page 150 an often touching a letter but rarely affecting sense), one leaf with small patch of soiling over one word, little minor foxing, short closed tear and accompanying crease at foot of titlepage, several ownership inscriptions of a Jesuit college in Wurzburg (dated 1575), Arabic numerals and few short notes added to table of contents in later hand, folio, contemporary blindstamped pigskin, brass clasps and cornerpieces, two 19th century leather lettering pieces to spine, one defective and the other just chipped, bit darkened and soiled, endpapers renewed at same time as lettering pieces, small chip to head of rear joint, bookplate of W. T. Monson, good.   Blackwell's Rare Books   Greek & Latin Classics VI - 57   2015   £7000

Josephus, Flavius (in Greek) *Philabiou Josepou Hierosolymitou Heireos Ta Heuriskomena, Flavii Josephi Hierosolymitani Sacerdotis Opera Quae Extant. (Works in Greek and Latin).* Geneva: Petrus de la Rouviere, 1611. 362 x 222mm., sumptuous contemporary honey brown morocco richly gilt in modified fanfare design, covers with outer frame of multiple plain and decorative rules and rolls, frame surrounding a central panel formed by multiple plain rules and a filigree roll and featuring oblique fleurons pointing outward at corner, panel with very densely gilt and elaborate cornerpieces and a large central lozenge incorporating olive branch garlands and rosettes, an oval at center of lozenge with contemporary coat of arms of the Abbot of Potigny, either Claude Boucherat, or his cousin Charles, flat spine with a chain roll framing a single elongated panel tooled in a design similar to covers, all edges gilt, holes for ties (perhaps with small, very expert repairs at spine bottom); woodcut printer's device on titlepage, woodcut headpieces and decorative initials, Latin and Greek text printed in parallel columns, front pastedown with partially effaced 17th century ownership inscription of Henry (Becold?) Pembroke College, Oxford dated 1734 and 19th century inscription of D. C. Lewis, blank lower right corner of titlepage neatly replaced (in 19th century?), small, pale dampstain in bottom margin of a few leaves, branching marginal wormholes in half a dozen quires (but these always extremely thin and never intruding on text), minor soiling, browning and foxing here and there, still very good internally, leaves fresh, clean and with good margins; hint of wear to joints and extremities, spine uniformly little darkened (with gilt just slightly less bright tan on boards), covers with trivial discoloration and abrasions, but impressive binding in remarkable condition, entirely solid, only minor signs of use, and with once dazzling gilt nearly as good as it was 400 years ago.   Phillip J. Pirages   66 - 21   2015 $6500

Josh White Sings. Music of the New World. London: Granada TV, 1961. First edition, wrappers, photos, very uncommon.   Beasley Books   2013 - 2015 $45

Joslyn, R. Waite *History of Kane County III. Volume I.* Chicago: Pioneer Pub., 1908. First edition, stout 4to, upper and lower spine heavily taped thus good.   Beasley Books   2013 - 2015 $125

Joss, Morag *Funeral Music.* London: Hodder & Stoughton, 1998. First edition, fine in dust jacket.   Mordida Books   March 2015 - 007502   2015 $200

Jostes, Barbara Donohoe *John Parrot, Consul 1811-1884. Selected Papers of a Western Pioneer.* San Francisco: printed for the Compiler, 1972. First edition, frontispiece, 67 plates, 2 folding charts, 3 maps, dark green cloth, gilt, fine.   Argonaut Book Shop   Holiday Season 2014 - 141   2015 $175

Journal of Applied Econometrics. London: Wiley, 1986-2003. Volumes 1-18, 88 issues continuous, lacking one issue that of last quarter of 1990, 2 copies of the first issue, wrappers, very good.   Any Amount of Books   March 2015 - A73707   2015   £350

Journal of Negro History.   1927-1960. First edition, 10 volumes between 1927-1960.   Beasley Books   2013 - 2015 $150

Joyce, James   1882-1941   *Epiphanies.*   New York: Vincent FitzGerald & Co., 1987.   One of 65 copies only, 50 in an edition for sale and 15 Artist's Proofs, all on Moulin du Gue paper and Japanese papers with 62 etchings, employing over 150 plates, original watercolors, collage and hand cutting, collage by Vincent FitzGerald and Zahra Partovi, etchings printed by Marjorie Van Dyke assisted by Maria Luisa Rojo at the printmaking Workshop, lithographs editioned by Marjorie Van Dyke with Rhae Burden, calligraphy by Jerry Kelly, letterpress by Dan Keleher and Bruce Chandler at Wild Carrot Letterpress in 40 colors, type set by Dan Carr and Julia Ferrari at the Golgonooza Letter Foundry, page size 12 x 14 inches, 94 leaves, one printed page loose, two foldout images, loose as issued in original wrappers in handmade box by David Bourbeau at the Thistle Bindery in Japanese handmade silk woven for this box, incised line of Japanese tea paper showing profile of Joyce, spine of box slightly sunned, book fine.   Priscilla Juvelis - Rare Books   61 - 14   2015 $12,500

Joyce, James   1882-1941   *Exiles.*   New York: Viking, 1951. Limited to 1900 copies for sale and 75 for private circulation, fine in very good dust jacket (flap clip but price present), old tape mend to heaf and foot of spine.   Stephen Lupack   March 2015 - 2015 $65

Joyce, James   1882-1941   *Finnegans Wake.*   New York: Viking Press, 1939. First American edition, top corners well bumped, front hinge little tender, else about very good, lacking dust jacket, journalist Murray Kempton's copy with his bookplate.   Between the Covers Rare Books, Inc.   187 - 142   2015 $300

Joyce, James   1882-1941   *Finnegans Wake.*   London: Faber & Faber, 1939. First edition, original maroon cloth, near fine with some spotting to endpapers and stain to top edge in unclipped and completely unrestored jacket with minor wear to extremities, small chip to upper edge of rear panel, else much nicer copy than usual, often found heavily worn and price clipped.   B & B Rare Books, Ltd.   234 - 59   2015 $3750

Joyce, James   1882-1941   *Finnegans Wake.*   Mousehole: Houynhnm Press, 2010. First edition thus, 4to., fine in slipcase.   Any Amount of Books   2015 - A96683   2015   £300

Joyce, James   1882-1941   *Letters.*   New York: 1957. First edition, near fine in like dust jacket.   Stephen Lupack   March 2015 - 2015 $45

Joyce, James   1882-1941   *Pomes Penyeach.*   Paris: Shakespeare and Co., 1927. First edition, paper covered boards, errata slip bound in, near fine with just trace of wear at foot of spine, 32mo.   Beasley Books   2013 - 2015 $500

Joyce, James   1882-1941   *A Shorter Finnegans Wake.*   New York: Viking Press, 1967. First American edition edited by Anthony Burgess, octavo, original maroon cloth, original dust jacket, ownership stamps of novelist Jean Stafford and New Yorker writer Joseph Mitchell with his notes pencilled on envelope from his family's tobacco warehouse, laid in.   Honey & Wax Booksellers   2 - 50   2015 $1000

Joyce, James   1882-1941   *Stephen Hero.*   New York: New Directions, 1944. First American edition, one of only 3000 copies, frontispiece, near fine, near fine dust jacket (with map of Ireland in green).   Stephen Lupack   March 2015 - 2015 $75

Joyce, James   1882-1941   *Stephen Hero - Part of the First Draft of 'The Portrait of the artist as a Young Man".*   London: Jonathan Cape, 1944. First UK edition, octavo, hint of a bump to bottom edge of rear cover, near fine in very good dust jacket slightly darkened at spine, with few small nicks.   Peter Ellis, Bookseller   2014 - 012444   2015   £350

Joyce, James   1882-1941   *Ulysses.*   New York: Random House, 1934. First American edition, advance review copy with Berenice Abbot's portrait of Joyce and publisher's review slip tipped in, octavo, original ivory cloth, original dust jacket.   Honey & Wax Booksellers   2 - 52   2015 $3500

Joyce, James   1882-1941   *Ulysses.*   New York: Limited Editions Club, 1935. Limited to 1500 numbered copies, this is an early copy and signed by author and artist, 4to., brown cloth with abstract design including Matisse's "Nausicaa" stamped in gold on front cover, spine stamped in gold with miniature repeat of cover design, remnants of slipcase, printed in two colors, page numbers and title in margins in brown ink, etchings by Matisse, reproductions of prelim sketches by Matisse bound in, with Monthly Letter loosely inserted, slipcase rubbed around edges, some fading, book has some foxing along gutters.   Oak Knoll Books   25 - 14   2015 $20,000

Joyce, James   1882-1941   *The Works of Master Poldy.*   Dublin: Salvage Press, 2013. First edition, one of 120 copies, slim folio, original orange cloth over ivory boards, lettered in silver, original slipcases.   Honey & Wax Booksellers   2 - 51   2015 $600

Joyful Tales for Little Folks. New York: McLoughlin Bros., 1869. 8vo., pictorial wrappers, spine rubbed and scattered, light foxing, else very good+, 8 fine color lithographs by Cogger.   Aleph-Bet Books, Inc.   108 - 290   2015 $200

Judson, Boswell   *Observations on Two Epistles, Responsive of the Rev. Abner Kneeland of Philadelphia to My Letter Refuting His Inference of Universalism from the Benevolence of God.* Bridgeport: 1823. First edition, 12mo., 20 pages, removed, foxed.   M & S Rare Books, Inc.   97 - 141   2015 $200

Judy. Saint Valentine. Judy Office, Monday Jan. 30th, 1882. Judy's Comical Pennyworths No. 6, 12mo., illustrations, 24 pages, folded as issued, unopened, few small tears along folds.   Jarndyce Antiquarian Booksellers   CCXI - 167   2015   £85

Judy. Some Hints on Skating and Snowballing. London: Judy Office, Monday Feb. 13th, 1882. Judy's Comical Pennyworths no. 6, illustrations, 24 pages, folded as issued, unopened, few small tears along folds.   Jarndyce Antiquarian Booksellers   CCXI - 168   2015   £75

Jullien, Marc Antoine   *Essai General D'Education Physique, Morale et Intellectuelle...* Paris: Firmin Didot, 1808. First edition, half title, last few leaves little creased, final two leaves with very minor marginal staining, well bound in fine 20th century dark green quarter morocco over marbled boards, spine gilt and lettered with raised bands, handsome copy.   John Drury Rare Books   2015 - 25972   2015 $656

Jung, Carl Gustav   *Dream Symbols of the Individuation Process by....* N. P.: (but most likely NY), 1937-1938. First edition Multigraph copies, 2 volumes, original bound Multigraph copies with single sided pages, both books come in original green boards with darker green spines, both books have small vertical label to front cover, along with small blank white strip on spine, both covers have handwritten titles in green marker with additional title handwritten in black, with signature " V. de Laszlo" in green marker, lovely matched set.   Athena Rare Books   15 - 31   2015 $1200

Jung, Carl Gustav   *Fundamental Psychological Conceptions / a Report of Five Lectures by C. G. Jung...* London: privately printed, 1936. First edition numbered Multilith copy (number 196), 15 different line drawings, 7 1/2 x 9 3/4 inches, Mary Bancroft's (1903-1997) copy with her name written across top front free endpaper and address, single sided pages, bound using three large staples, covers are boards with brownish printed weave pattern and spine covered with green canvas, covers lightly worn, overall lovely copy, extremely scarce.   Athena Rare Books   15 - 30   2015 $1500

Jung, Carl Gustav   *Modern Psychology, Notes on Lectures....* Zurich: privately printed, 1933-1941. First edition Multigraph copies, 6 volumes, each volume with at least a few printed illustrations, each volume is original Multigraph copy with single sided text bound using large staples, covers are mottled light green and black boards with green canvas on spines (except for volume II which has black canvas, as issued), gilt lettering giving titles and years in which presentations were made, most minor bumps to exteriors of first five volumes, volume VI has suffered bit of warping to both covers and text from humidity, otherwise beautiful set.   Athena Rare Books   15 - 29   2015 $2800

Junius, Pseud.   *Stat Nominis Umbra.* London: T. Bensley, 1979. 2 volumes, 8vo., paper covered boards, gilt tooled spine with label, frontispiece, engraved vignettes, front joint of first volume cracked and almost detached, back cover detached on volume 2, rubbed and scuffed at edges, staining and foxing on endpapers and throughout text.   Oak Knoll Books   306 - 272   2015 $250

Jury, David   *Book Art Object 2: Second Catalogue of the Codex Foundation Biennial International Book Exhibition and Symposium.* Berkeley: Codex Foundation, 2013. 4to., cloth, dust jacket, decorated endpapers, over 1100 color illustrations.   Oak Knoll Books   306 - 49   2015 $150

Just for Fun. Chicago: Rand McNally, 1940. A. First edition, 4to., pictorial cloth, fine in dust jacket (frayed at spine ends and some other small edge chipping, overall bright and very good+), rare, illustrations by Robert Lawson.   Aleph-bet Books, Inc.   109 - 255   2015 $800

Juster, Norton   *The Phantom Tollbooth.* New York: Epstein & Carroll, 1961. First edition, 4to., blue cloth, fine in dust jacket (in very good condition, but with 2 small half inch chips off edge at front panel, few pinholes along fold, not price clipped), illustrations by Jules Feiffer, this copy signed by Feiffer, inscribed by him.   Aleph-bet Books, Inc.   109 - 243   2015 $2500

Justice, Donald   *Departures.* Iowa City: Penumbra Press/ Stone Wall Press, 1973. First edition, 8vo., original cloth with printed label on spine, signed by author, fine with erratum slip.   James S. Jaffe Rare Books   Modern American Poetry - 157   2015 $250

Justice, Donald   *From a Notebook.* Iowa City: Seamark Press, 1972. First edition, limited to 317 copies, 12mo., original green cloth with printed label on spine, fine, presentation copy from author for Mark Strand.   James S. Jaffe Rare Books   Modern American Poetry - 156   2015 $850

Justice, Donald *A Local Storm.* Iowa City: Stone Wall Press and the Finial Press, 1963. First edition, limited to 270 copies, tall 8vo., original wrappers, covers somewhat sunned along extremities, edges trifle nicked, two tiny pen marks on back cover, otherwise fine, presentation copy inscribed to poet Mark Strand and Antonia.   James S. Jaffe Rare Books   Modern American Poetry - 153   2015 $750

Justice, Donald *Night Light.* Middletown: Wesleyan University Press, 1967. First edition, square 8vo., original cloth, dust jacket, presentation copy inscribed by author to poet Mark Strand and Antonia, March 1967, with APCS from Justice to Strand laid in, fine in somewhat rubbed jacket with two short closed tears on back panel.   James S. Jaffe Rare Books   Modern American Poetry - 154   2015 $850

Justice, Donald *Sixteen Poems.* Iowa City: Stone Wall Press, 1970. First edition, limited to 250 copies, tall 8vo., original wrappers, presentation copy from author to Mark Strand and Antonia, May 1970, tall 8vo., original wrappers, top and bottom edge little nicked, covers trifle sunned, otherwise fine.   James S. Jaffe Rare Books   Modern American Poetry - 155   2015 $850

Justin Martyr *Tou Agiou Ioustinou Philosophou Kai Marturos.... (bound with) Opera Omnia, quae Adjue Inveniri Potuerunt...* Paris: Ex officinia Roberti Stephani, 1551. Paris: Iacobum Dupuys, 1554. Edition princeps of first work and first edition, first substantial translation of second work, ruled in red throughout, folio, first work titlepage lightly soiled an tiny dampstain to upper corner at beginning; bound together in early French biscuit calf, boards with central decorative oval gilt stamp, name "A Fournier' lettered in gilt above, circular gilt stamp in spine compartments, old paper label pasted in second, rebacked preserving original spine (now darkened), new endpapers, boards somewhat scratched and marked, still attractive, silk ties lost, good.   Blackwell's Rare Books   B179 - 53   2015   £1800

Justitia, Pseud. *Observations on the General Grand Jury Act 6 & 7 William IV. chapt. 116 with Reference to the Arrangements Thereby Provided...* Dublin: Hodges Smith and Co., 1857. First (only?) edition, 8vo., 30 pages, large folding chart tipped in, neatly disbound, good copy, apparently very scarce.   John Drury Rare Books   March 2015 - 18496   2015 $221

Jutson, Mary Carolyn Hollers *Alfred Giles: an English Architect in Texas and Mexico.* Trinity University Press, 1972. First edition, signed by author, quarto, gray cloth, titles stamped in gold gilt on front cover and spine, green endpapers, illustrations, fine, scarce today.   Buckingham Books   March 2015 - 36829   2015 $225

Juvenalis, Decimus Junius *(Satyrae).* Venice: per magistrum Antonium de Strata Cremonensem, 1486. First Valla edition, initial blank discarded, final blank present, occasional Greek text, capitals picked out in red or blue throughout, dedicatory letter and first satire with attractive decorative initials in red and blue, leaf a2 rather soiled and with repair to lower corner affecting a couple of letters on verso, occasional dust soiling and some staining elsewhere, few leaves browned, outer margin damp marked in places, few early manuscript notes to first few leaves, later ownership inscription (1651) to title, folio, modern dark brown calf, simple blind rules, unlettered spine with five raised bands, sound.   Blackwell's Rare Books   Greek & Latin Classics VI - 58   2015   £5000

Juvenalis, Decimus Junius *D. Junii Juvenalis et Auli Persii Flacci Satyrae.* Birmingham: John Baskerville, 1761. 4to., prize binding of full leather, gilt border on covers with gilt seal in center of front cover stamped "College of Fort William" and bears date Feby VI, MDCCCIII (1803), dentelles, gilt tooled spine with five raised bands, marbled endpapers, all edges gilt, with original leaves at E2, K4, U4 and Z3 uncancelled state, previous owner's inscription dated 1866, covers bumped and scuffed at edges, scratches on front and back, bookplates on front pastedown, spots on front free endpapers and title.   Oak Knoll Books   306 - 181   2015 $850

Juvenalis, Decimus Junius *Satirae XVI.* Oxford: Sumptibus J. Cooke et J. Parker, 1808. Early reprint, some foxing, little pencil marginalia, 8vo., contemporary biscuit calf, boards bordered with small gilt decorative roll, spine divided by raised bands between double gilt fillets, blue lettering piece, other compartments with small central gilt tool, joints cracking but strong, armorial bookplate of Capel Cure Esqr., good.   Blackwell's Rare Books   Greek & Latin Classics VI - 59   2015   £75

Juvenile Philosophy: Containing Amusing and Instructive Discourses on Hogarth's prints of the Industrious and Idle Apprentices, Analogy Between Plants and Animals &c. London: printed by Ruffy & Evans for Vernor and Hood, 1801. First edition, engraved frontispiece, first gathering (2 leaves), loosening, one gathering sprung with two tears in one of its leaves (without significant loss), 12mo., original green vellum backed boards, edges worn, short split in spine, ownership inscription inside back cover of Ann (next two names indecipherable) of Castle Cary, Somerset, 1821, sound, apparently only edition and scarce.   Blackwell's Rare Books   B179 - 55   2015   £250

K

Kaasbol, Hilarius Christophorus *Dissertatio Historico-Critca De Modis Salutandi...* Hafniae: Literis Wilhadi Jersini Universit. typogr., 1703. First and only edition, 8vo., original stiff paper boards, some waterstaining, heavier at end, very good.   Second Life Books Inc.   189 - 141   2015 $300

Kaberry, Phyllis M. *Aboriginal Woman. Sacred and Profane.* London: George Routledge & Sons, 1939. First edition, original orange cloth lettered gilt on spine, signed and dated presentation from author to H. Ian Hogbin, illustrations, little bumped, otherwise very good or better.   Any Amount of Books   2015 - C1988   2015   £175

Kafka, Franz   1883-1924 *The Great Wall of China and Other Pieces.* London: Martin Secker, 1933. First UK edition, octavo, black and white frontispiece, spine slightly faded, very good in very good dust jacket darkened at spine and with 1 cm. closed tear.   Peter Ellis, Bookseller   2014 - 017488   2015   £350

Kafka, Franz   1883-1924 *In the Penal Colony.* N.P.: Limited Editions Club, 1987. Limited to 800 numbered copies signed by artist, small 4to., limp paper wrappers, cord tied, folding box lined in velvet, paper spine label, text set in Monotype Walbaum at the Out of Sorts letter Foundry and printed on mould made Magnani paper at Shagbark Press, lithographs by Michael Hafftka were printed on handmade Japanese paper at Trestle Editions, bound by Carol Joyce.   Oak Knoll Books   25 - 56   2015 $250

Kafka, Franz   1883-1924 *The Metamorphosis.* London: Patron Press, 1937. First English edition, first printing, publisher's dark gray paper boards over blue cloth spine, light blue paper label lettered in black, publisher's original glassine dust jacket, near fine, hint of toning to spine, else fine, glassine with few small chips to spine, some rippling, overall, tight and pleasing copy.   B & B Rare Books, Ltd.   2015 - 2015 $4000

Kahn, Edgar M. *Bret Harte in California. A Character Study.* San Francisco: Privately printed and designed for author by Haywood H. Hunt, number 3 of a total edition of 200 copies, this copy signed by designer/printer Haywood H. Hunt, 1951. First book edition, number 3 of a total edition of 200 copies, frontispiece, tan cloth back, marbled boards, paper label on front cover, upper corners lightly rubbed, but fine, this copy signed by Hunt and by artist, William Wilke, also signed by Herbert McLean Evans.   Argonaut Book Shop   Holiday Season 2014 - 142   2015 $150

Kaikodo Journal. Kamakura: Kaikodo, 1996. First edition, wrappers, 24 volumes, issues 1-25 (lacks issue 24), 4to., original publisher's dark grey covers, each with small color illustrations inset on front, copiously illustrated in color and black and white, slight rubbing, otherwise very good.   Any Amount of Books   March 2015 - C8002   2015   £350

Kallman, Chester *Storm at Castelfranco.* New York: Grove Press, 1956. First edition, one of only 15 copies signed by author with original drawing and signed by Larry Rivers, tipped in as frontispiece, offsetting to titlepage from original drawing, otherwise very good, small 8vo., original cloth backed boards, glassine dust jacket,.   James S. Jaffe Rare Books   Modern American Poetry - 158   2015 $7500

Kalugin, David *The Leaves Still Talk.* London: Villiers, 1959. First edition, fine in lightly rubbed, near fine dust jacket, inscribed by Alfred Kreymborg to Kay Boyle, April 5, 1959.   Between the Covers Rare Books, Inc.   187 - 143   2015 $100

Kaminsky, Stuart M. *Rostinkov's Corpse.* London: Macmillan, 1981. First edition, fine in price clipped dust jacket.   Buckingham Books   March 2015 - 12458   2015 $275

Kaminsky, Stuart M. *Rostnikov's Corpse.* London: Macmillan, 1981. First hardcover edition, fine in price clipped dust jacket with publisher's price sticker.   Mordida Books   March 2015 - 012651   2015 $150

Kamph, Jamie *A Collector's Guide to Bookbinding.* New Castle: Oak Knoll Books, 1982. Limited to 250 numbered copies printed by Henry Morris, this copy no numbered and has following statement written by Henry Morris, "Binder's sample 8/7/82", 8vo., cloth backed boards.   Oak Knoll Books   306 - 134   2015 $250

Kandel, Eric R. *The Age of Insight. The Quest to Understand the Unconscious in Art, Mind and Brain from Vienna 1900 to the Present.* New York: Random House, 2012. First edition, signed and inscribed by author, 8vo., fine in fine dust jacket.   By the Book, L. C.   Special List 10 - 77   2015 $135

Kane, Elisha Kent *Arctic Explorations: the Second Grinnell Expedition in Search of Sir John Franklin 1853 '54 '55.* Philadelphia: Childs & Peterson, 1856. First edition, 2 volumes, steel engraved titles, 2 steel engraved frontispiece portraits, 18 steel engraved plates, hundreds of wood engraved text illustrations, 3 maps, lacking isothermal chart, newer gray cloth, gilt, contemporary owner's name on front end volume II, another early name on title volume I, some minor occasional spotting, but fine and clean set.   Argonaut Book Shop   Holiday Season 2014 - 143   2015 $600

Kansas State Historical Society *Kansas Historical Quarterly.* Topeka: 1956+, 10 volumes, each issue approximately 72 pages, wrappers, very good with very few ruffles to backstrip, color covers.   Bookworm & Silverfish   2015 - 4928335449   2015 $250

Kant, Immanuel *Metaphysische Anfangsgrunde der Tugendlehre. (The Metaphysical Foundations of the Theory of Virtue).* Konigsberg: Friedrich Nicolovius, 1797. First edition, octavo, contemporary mottled pasteboards (bit worn and rounded on corners), handwritten paper label on spine (which has noticeably peeled as shown in photo at right), blue stamped former owner's name (Oswald Weigel) to inside of front cover and contemporary three line inked inscription and short stamped line of Hebrew letters lower on same page, interior and text is lightly foxed, otherwise charmingly unsophisticated copy.   Athena Rare Books   15 - 32   2015 $500

Kanter, Frans De *Jo-Jot Grappige Javaantje.* Alkmaar: Kluitman, n.d., 1932. First edition, 4to., pictorial boards, light cover soil and wear, very good+, full page color lithographs.   Aleph-bet Books, Inc.   109 - 57   2015 $275

Kantor, Mackinlay *Andersonville.* Cleveland and New York: World Pub., 1955. First edition, very good plus with sunning around edges of blue cloth in very good, clean dust jacket with few closed tears and wear to extremities.   Ed Smith Books   82 - 16   2015 $100

Kantor, Mackinlay *Signal Thirty-Two.* New York: Random House, 1950. First edition, inscribed by author, also signed by author's wife, Irene Layne Kantor, some scattered light spotting on endpapers, otherwise fine in dust jacket with slightly faded spine and small nicks and tears at top of spine.   Mordida Books   March 2015 - 007510   2015 $200

Kapr, Albert *The Art of Lettering, the History, Anatomy and Aesthetics of the Roman Letter Forms.* Munchen: K. G. Saur, 1983. Third revised edition, small 4to., cloth, dust jacket, over 500 illustrations, well preserved copy.   Oak Knoll Books   306 - 219   2015 $150

Kapr, Albert *Schriftkunst, Geschichte, Anatomie Und Schonheit der Lateinischen Buch Staben.* Dresden: Verlag der Kunst, 1976. Second edition, thick small 4to., cloth, publisher's cardboards slipcase, over 500 illustrations, some of the lettering on spine of book partially rubbed away, name in ink in corner of front free endpaper.   Oak Knoll Books   306 - 220   2015 $100

Karabacek, Josef Ritter *Monumenta Palaeographica Vindobonensia.* Leipzig: Karl W. Hiersemann, 1910. 2 parts, folio, text and plates housed in portfolio, cloth spine and tips with paper covered boards and cloth edges with paper covered boards for the housing, with 26 loose plates and with plates 27-46, part one lightly soiled, corners and spine head lightly bumped, small tear at spine foot and small rubbed areas along left side of spine, cracks and tears in folds of portfolio, part two corners bumped, edges slightly dented, small tear at foot of right side of spine, large tear throughout left side of spine, light soiling, cracks and tears in folds of portfolio, soiling on inside of spine cloth.   Oak Knoll Books   Special Catalogue 24 - 27   2015 $250

Katz, Alex *Primus Inter Pares.* New York: Peter Blum Edition, 2003. First edition, no. 35 of 50 copies signed by artist, wrappers, folio, 16 pages with artwork by Katz, original buff wrappers, paper printed spine label, boards slipcase.   Any Amount of Books   2015 - A87343   2015   £650

Katz, Steve *Cheyenne River Wild Track.* Ithaca: Ithaca House, 1973. First edition, octavo, wrappers illustrated by George Schneeman, trifle rubbed, near fine, inscribed by author to Ted Berrigan and Alice Notley.   Between the Covers Rare Books, Inc.   187 - 144   2015 $125

Kauffman, Reginald Wright *Share and Share Alike: an Adventure Story.* New York: Chelsea House, 1925. First edition, very modest wear, just about fine in attractive example of scarce dust jacket, lacking rear flap and with some creases from being folded into book, author's own copy, initialed by him with note on titlepage, "First published in The Popular Magazine Dec. 20 1923 under pseudonym of George Parsons Broadfoot. R.K".   Between the Covers Rare Books, Inc.   187 - 193   2015 $350

Kaufman, George S. *Of Thee I Sing.* New York: Knopf, 1932. Third printing, very good with owner's stamp, R. Bloch's copy with pencilled ownership signature date 1939.   Beasley Books   2013 - 2015 $45

Kawakita, Michiaki *Craft Treasures of Okinawa.* London: Serindia Publications, 1978. Folio, cloth, dust jacket, 187 color plates, 99 black and white plates, map, slipcase lightly worn, especially around edges.   Oak Knoll Books   306 - 273   2015 $145

Kay-Shuttleworth, James *Letter to Earl Granville, K.G. on the Revised Code of Regulations Contained in the Minute of the Committee of Council on Education Dated July 29th 1861.* London: Smith, Elder & Co., 1861. First edition, uncommon, 8vo., title printed on original brown front wrapper, pamphlet now presented in modern plain wrappers, very good.   John Drury Rare Books   March 2015 - 15043   2015 $266

Kay, Gertrude *Adventures in Geography.* Joliet: Volland, 1930. First edition, illustrations by author with pictorial endpapers, plus a profusion of full and partial page color illustrations, fine in dust jacket (missing 2 pieces off rear panel). Aleph-bet Books, Inc.   109 - 477   2015 $250

Kay, Gertrude *Peter, Patter and Pixie.* New York: McBride, Sept., 1931. First edition, large 4to., cloth backed pictorial boards, tips rubbed and slight cover soil, else very good+, illustrations, very scarce.   Aleph-Bet Books, Inc.   108 - 256   2015 $225

Kay, Helen *Snow Birthday.* New York: Farrar, Straus & Cudahay, 1955. Stated first printing, Oblong 4to., cloth, fine in fine dust jacket, full page color and black and white illustrations by Barbara Cooney.   Aleph-Bet Books, Inc.   108 - 106   2015 $275

Kayser, Christian Gottlob *Index Locuppletissimus Librorum Bollstandiges Bucher Lexicon.* Leipzig: Ludwig Schumann and Others, 1834-1908. 37 volumes, variously paginated, 4to., quarter leather, marbled paper covered boards, ex-library with markings, some light wear, foxing, especially in earlier volumes.   Oak Knoll Books   306 - 77   2015 $750

Kazantazaki, Nikos *L'Odyssee.* Editions Richelieu and Librarie Plon, 1968-1969. 1 of 350 copies, first French edition, 2 volumes, 4to., full burgundy morocco with gilt and embossed stamping, without extra suite of lithographs, fine, previous owner's bookplate.   Beasley Books   2013 - 2015 $500

Kearney, Belle *A Slaveholder's Daughter.* New York: 1900. First edition, 269 pages, solid in green cloth, backstrip darkened, some cover spots.   Bookworm & Silverfish   2015 - 6016571565   2015 $75

Kearney, W. D. *An Epic Poem, Entitled the Open Hand.* Presque Isle: W. S. Gilman, 1864. Small 8vo., pressed cloth very worn and faded, titlepage has top part torn off, not affecting text some dampstaining, rear endpaper missing. Schooner Books Ltd.   110 - 16   2015 $275

Keate, Thomas *Observations on the Fifth Report of the Commissioners of Military Enquiry.* London: J. Hatchard, 1808. First edition, titlepage dust soiled and probably wanting half title, bound in mid 20th century cloth boards, spine lettered in gilt, good, rare.   John Drury Rare Books   2015 - 21046   2015 $787

Keate, Thomas *Observations on the Proceedings and Report of the Special Medical Board, Appointed by His Royal Highness the Commander in Chief and the Right Hon. the Secretary at War...* London: J. Hatchard, 1809. First edition, 8vo., half title, paper generally rather browned, half title and final page (errata) soiled, slightly cropped ms. presentation inscription from author for Captain Davis, good copy, recently bound in linen backed marbled boards, lettered, very rare.   John Drury Rare Books   2015 - 22501   2015 $787

Keaton, Eleanor *Buster Keaton Remembered.* New York: Harry N. Abrams Inc., 2001. First edition, 4to., copiously illustrated in black and white, fine in near fine dust jacket (very slightly creased), excellent condition.   Any Amount of Books   2015 - A87875   2015   £160

Keats, John   1795-1821 *La Belle Dame Sans Merci.* Eragny Press, 1906. One of 200 copies (of an edition of 210 copies) printed on Arches handmade paper in black, 2 large historiated initial letters, border to titlepage, fly title and one other page all printed in red, as is single line quarter border, paragraph mark, verso and pagination numbers to each page, no errata slip, 32mo., original quarter blue grey boards, printed front cover label, cream pale and dark green patterned boards, untrimmed and unopened, backstrip and fore-edge of front board toned, endpapers browned, very good.   Blackwell's Rare Books   B179 - 145   2015   £900

Keats, John   1795-1821 *Hyperion: a Facsimile of Keats's autograph manuscript.* Oxford: Clarendon Press, 1905. Folio, 27 pages facsimiles, colophon leaf, original green printed boards, beige buckram spine, corners rubbed, dusted, from the library of Geoffrey & Kathleen Tillotson, signed by Geoffrey 1942 with note by Kathleen.   Jarndyce Antiquarian Booksellers   CCVII - 345   2015   £85

Keats, John   1795-1821 *The Poems.* Hammersmith: William Morris at the Kelmscott Press, 1894. First edition, one of 300 copies, octavo, full 20th century russet morocco gilt, bound by Sangorski & Sutcliffe, gift inscription by English playwright Henry Arthur Jones.   Honey & Wax Booksellers   2 - 15   2015 $7000

Keats, John   1795-1821 *The Poetical Works.* London: Oxford University Press, 1922. Frontispiece, plate, original brown cloth, hinges repaired, signed Kathleen M. Constable (Tillotson) Sept. 1926 with ink and pencil notes, insertions and related cutting.   Jarndyce Antiquarian Booksellers   CCVII - 343   2015   £25

Keats, John   1795-1821 *The Poetical Works.* Oxford: Clarendon Press, 1958. Second edition, half title, frontispiece, original dark blue cloth, very good in slightly torn and dusty dustjacket, with review of Keats' 'Letters" 1959 inserted, from the library of Geoffrey & Kathleen Tillotson. Jarndyce Antiquarian Booksellers   CCVII - 344   2015   £35

Kebbell, William *The Climate of Brighton.* London: Longman, Green Longman and Roberts, 1859. First edition, 12mo., original blindstamped brown cloth, spine lettered, light wear to binding, else very good with old inkstamp of Brighton and Hove Archaeological Club, scarce. John Drury Rare Books March 2015 - 19276 2015 $266

Keeler, Harry Stephen *The Fourth King.* New York: E. P. Dutton & Co., 1930. First edition, spine panel bit darkened, else very good, fine, bright dust jacket. Buckingham Books March 2015 - 33111 2015 $750

Keeler, Harry Stephen *The Magic Ear-Drums.* London: Ward Lock & Co., 1939. First UK edition, light offsetting to front and rear flyleaves, else near fine in dust jacket with light professional restoration to the spine ends and corners. Buckingham Books March 2015 - 33039 2015 $750

Kees, Weldon *Poems 1947-1954.* San Francisco: Adrian Wilson, 1954. First edition, 8vo., original cloth backed pastepaper boards with printed label on spine, wraparound band, presentation copy inscribed by author to Jurgen (Ruesch) collaborator and friend of author, Jan. 1955, very fine. James S. Jaffe Rare Books Modern American Poetry - 160 2015 $2500

Kees, Weldon *Poems 1947-1954.* San Francisco: Adrian Wilson, 1954. First edition, limited to 25 copies with original abstract expressionist drawing/painting, signed and dated by Kees tipped in, tall 8vo., original cloth backed pastepaper boards, printed label on spine, printed wraparound band, bit of tape residue from previous dust jacket protector on endsheets, otherwise fine, beautiful book, in its rarest form, with publisher's prospectus laid in. James S. Jaffe Rare Books Modern American Poetry - 159 2015 $3500

Kees, Weldon *The Collected Poems of Weldon Kees.* Iowa City: Stone Wall Press, 1960. First edition, one of 20 copies on Rives Heavy, a French mould made paper and bound in full leather, 8vo., full black morocco with blindstamped slipcase, very fine, rare issue. James S. Jaffe Rare Books Modern American Poetry - 161 2015 $4500

Kees, Weldon *The Collected Poems of Weldon Kees.* Iowa City: Stone Wall Press, 1960. First edition, one of 200 numbered copies printed on Rives Light out of a total edition of 220 copies, tall 8vo., original quarter black morocco and Japanese paper covered boards, some fading to delicate paper boards, bottom fore-corner bumped, otherwise fine. James S. Jaffe Rare Books Modern American Poetry - 162 2015 $850

Keese, John *The Poets of America: Illustrated by One of Her Painters...* New York: S. Colman, 1840. First edition, 12mo., contemporary brown half morocco, black cloth boards, gilt lettering, frontispiece, engraved title and 36 wood engravings by John G. Chapman, family copy from one of the contributors, John Neal to his twin sister Rachel, Jan. 1 1840, beneath inscription is later signature in pencil of John Neal's daughter, Margaret Neal and her name gilt stamped at foot of spine, edges little rubbed, some light foxing, very good. The Brick Row Book Shop Miscellany 67 - 15 2015 $500

Keetley, Dawn *Public Women, Public Words a Documentary History of American Feminism.* Madison: Madison House, 1977. First edition, volume I only, large 8vo., orchid cloth, about as new in dust jacket. Second Life Books Inc. 189 - 145 2015 $95

Keith, Arthur *The Antiquity of Man.* Philadelphia: J. B. Lippincott, 1925. Sixth impression, 2 volumes, blue cloth, gilt, corners little bumped, else near fine, without dust jacket, each volume with attractive Theodore Roosevelt III (grandson of the president). Between the Covers Rare Books, Inc. 187 - 145 2015 $225

Kelland, Clarence Budington *The Cat's Paw.* New York: Harpers, 1934. First edition, fine in dust jacket with slightly darkened spine and nicks at spine ends and at corners. Mordida Books March 2015 - 009402 2015 $250

Kellerman, Jonathan *The Butcher's Theater.* New York: Bantam, 1988. First edition, review material laid in, very fine in wrappers with promotional knife/letter opener inserted in front cover, Advance Reading copy. Mordida Books March 2015 - 001234 2015 $100

Kellett, E. E. *Ex Libris: Confessions of a Constant Reader.* London: George Allen & Unwin, 1940. Half title, original dark blue cloth, library withdrawn stamps, Geoffrey Tilloton's signed copy with notes and correspondence from author. Jarndyce Antiquarian Booksellers CCVII - 349 2015 £20

Kelley, William Melvin *A Different Drummer.* Garden City: Doubleday, 1962. First edition, 8vo., author's presentation for William Raney, also author's correction on contents page, paper over boards, cloth spine, very good, tight copy in little scuffed and soiled dust jacket. Second Life Books Inc. 190 - 143 2015 $225

Kelly, A. Ashmun *The Expert Sign Painter.* West Chester: Press of the Horace F. Temple Printing and Stationery Co., 1910. corrected in ink to 1911, Small 8vo., cloth, wear at spine ends and corners. Oak Knoll Books Special Catalogue 24 - 28 2015 $150

Kelly, Jerry *About More Alphabets: the Types of Hermann Zapf.* New York: Typophiles, 2011. Deluxe edition signed by author and limited to 75 copies, 4.5 x 7 inches, hardcover, 112 pages, profusely illustrated with type specimens and drawings, includes four type specimens in a paper folder and slipcase for book and specimen folder. Oak Knoll Books   Special Catalogue 24 - 62   2015 $170

Kelly, Luther S. *"Yellowstone Kelly" The Memoirs of Luther S. Kelly.* New Haven: Yale University Press, 1926. First edition, frontispiece, 20 illustrations from photos, folding map, dark blue cloth gilt, light rubbing to spine ends and corners, almost imperceptible stain to upper front cover, else fine, frontispiece, scarce. Argonaut Book Shop   Holiday Season 2014 - 144   2015 $125

Kelly, Rob Roy *American Wood Type 1828-1900, Notes on the Evolution of Decorated and Large Types and Comments on Related Trades of the Period.* New York: Van Nostrand Reinhold Co., 1969. First edition, 4to., cloth, dust jacket, more than 600 types of wood type described and 100 specimens shown, clipped news paper obituary of author loosely inserted. Oak Knoll Books   306 - 221   2015 $135

Kelly, Thomas W. *Menana; a Romance of the Red Indians in ten Cantos with Notes...* London: printed for & published by the author, 33 Beaumont St., Portland Place, W, 1861. Largely unopened, original decorated blue cloth, signs of repair to leading inner hinge, otherwise very good. Jarndyce Antiquarian Booksellers   CCXI - 169   2015   £75

Kelsey, Sally *Gusta: a Story of the Virgin Islands.* New York: Island Press, 1944. First edition, 4to., 50 pages, cloth, pictorial paste-on, slight rubbing, very good+, very scarce first edition, black and white lithographs. Aleph-bet Books, Inc.   109 - 59   2015 $400

Kelton, Elmer *The Day the Cowboys Quit.* New York: Doubleday & Co. Inc., 1971. First edition, signed, boldly by author on front flyleaf, fine in dust jacket lightly soiled on white rear panel, lightly sunned on spine, light professional restoration to spine ends, handsome copy. Buckingham Books   March 2015 - 33688   2015 $400

Kemble, Edward W. *Kemble's Coons: a Collection of Southern Sketches by Edward W. Kemble.* New York: R. H. Russell, 1896. First edition, large oblong 4to., cloth backed pictorial boards, tips worn and some cover soil, clean and very good+, full page plates printed on glossy paper on rectos only. Aleph-bet Books, Inc.   109 - 55   2015 $850

Kemble, John Haskell *Gold Rush Steamers.* Grabhorn Press, 1958. One of 950 sets designed and printed by the Grabhorn Press, 12 parts, each containing tipped in reproductions, fine set in half leather blue cloth slipcase. Argonaut Book Shop   Holiday Season 2014 - 36   2015 $50

Kemelman, Harry *The Nine Mile Walk.* New York: Putnam, 1987. First edition, top front corner slightly bumped, otherwise fine in price clipped dust jacket. Mordida Books   March 2015 - 009947   2015 $100

Kempthorne, John *The Church's Self-Regulating Privilege, a National Safeguard in Respect of real Church-Reform...* London: J. Hatchard and Son, 1835. First edition, rare, 8vo., errata slip tipped in, contemporary half calf over marbled boards, spine labelled and gilt, very good, in ink "From the author's". John Drury Rare Books   March 2015 - 23303   2015 $221

Kendall, Maud *Woman's Welfare Volume II No. 1 March 1904.* 8vo., pages 36, photos, printed wrappers. Second Life Books Inc.   189 - 147   2015 $45

Kendall, May *Dreams to Sell.* London: Longmans, 1887. First edition, half title in red & black, uncut in original crimson cloth, bevelled boards, spine faded, top edge gilt, presentation inscription to Gilbert Redgrave, bibliographer and art historian from Frances and Evelyn Redgrave 12 may, 1889, note by former of short and apologetic AL from authoress dated Aug. 4th 1892 in another hand: Association books No. 67 and 1945 signature of John Gilman, from the library of Geoffrey & Kathleen Tillotson. Jarndyce Antiquarian Booksellers   CCVII - 350   2015   £50

Keneally, Thomas *Schindler's List.* New York: Simon and Schuster, 1982. First edition, photos, half tan cloth over gray boards, spine lettered black, very fine with spine faded dust jacket. Argonaut Book Shop   Holiday Season 2014 - 145   2015 $175

Kennedy, Elijah R. *The Contest for California in 1861: How Colonel E. D Baker Saved the Pacific States to the Union.* Boston and New York: Houghton Mifflin, 1912. First edition, 6 plates, maroon cloth, very minor rubbing to spine ends and corners, covers bit darkened, very good, signed by J. R. Knowland, owner of Oakland Tribune. Argonaut Book Shop   Holiday Season 2014 - 146   2015 $90

Kennedy, Grace *Anna Ross; a Story for Children.* New York: William Burgess Jr., 1828. Third American edition, 18mo., 156 pages, 4 colored plates, including frontispiece by Burgess, in excellent condition, red calf backed printed and pictorial boards (rubbed), very sound, light foxing. M & S Rare Books, Inc.   97 - 133   2015 $350

Kennedy, John *A Treatise Upon Planting, and the Management of the Hot-House.* York: printed by A. Ward for the author, 1776. First edition, 8vo., full brown leather, corner of prelims slightly stained, outer hinges slightly weak, corners bumped, spine ends very slightly worn, otherwise sound, clean, very good copy, bookplate of "Martin Brown Ffolkes, Bar.". Any Amount of Books   2015 - A47678   2015   £225

Kennedy, John Fitzgerald 1917-1963 *Profiles in Courage.* New York: Harper & Bros., 1956. First edition, first printing, presentation copy signed and inscribed by author for Tammany Hall boss and influential politician, Carmine DeSapio, near fine with light rubbing to extremities, unclipped dust jacket with some light wear and minor chipping to lower spine, housed in custom quarter leather case. B & B Rare Books, Ltd. 234 - 60 2015 $22,500

Kennedy, John Fitzgerald 1917-1963 *Profiles in Courage.* New York: Harper & Bros., 1956. First edition, octavo, original cloth, original dust jacket, book fine, jacket with only little fading to spine (much less than usual), some soiling to front panel, exceptional copy. Manhattan Rare Book Company Literature 2014 - 2015 $2300

Kennedy, Lewis *On the Necessity of Protection to the Agriculturists of the United Kingdom.* London: Messrs Ridgway, 1839. First edition?, 8vo., recently well bound in linen backed marbled boards lettered, very good, very rare. John Drury Rare Books 2015 - 12562 2015 $133

Kennedy, William 1928- *Ironweed.* New York: Viking, 1983. First edition, signed by author, mild sunning to upper board edges, else fine in fine dust jacket. Ken Lopez, Bookseller 164 - 95 2015 $450

Kennedy, William 1928- *Legs.* New York: Coward, McCann & Geoghegan, 1975. Uncorrected proof, couple of small smudges or spots on wrappers, else just about fine, ownership signature of Hunter S. Thompson on front blank, TLS from senior editor, Peggy Brooks to Thompson sending the proof and soliciting a blurb from him. Between the Covers Rare Books 196 - 83 2015 $2500

Kennedy, William 1928- *Legs.* New York: Coward McCann & Geoghegan, 1975. First edition, 8vo, paper over boards, cloth spine, edges very slightly spotted, otherwise tight copy in dust jacket. Second Life Books Inc. 190 - 144 2015 $150

Kennedy, William 1928- *Legs, Billy Phelan's Greatest Game, and Ironweed.* New York: Coward McCann/Viking, 1975-1983. Uncorrected proof copies,, publisher's slip, 2 page letter from publisher of Ironweed to reviewer at Chicago Tribune, 3 volumes, each near fine in wrappers or better, all three volumes signed by author, uncommon, especially signed. Ken Lopez, Bookseller 164 - 94 2015 $1500

Kenny, Maurice *Dancing Back Strong the Nation.* Marvin: Blue Cloud Quarterly Press, 1979. First edition, stapled wrappers, fine, inscribed by author to fellow author Gerald Vizenor, TLS from Kenny to Vizenor from 1979. Between the Covers Rare Books, Inc. 187 - 196 2015 $350

Kent Gaol, A Petition of Several Owners and Occupiers of lands and Hereditaments in the County of Kent, Has Been Presented to the House of Commons Praying for Leave to Bring in a "Bill for Building or Completing a Gaol and Bridewell and Court Houses for the County of Kent.... London: Luke Hansard & Sons Feb., 1813. Folio, 4 pages, folded for posting with docket title, minor soiling on verso of second leaf, unbound as issued, very good state of preservation, apparently rare. John Drury Rare Books March 2015 - 25735 2015 £306

Kent, Alexander *The Flag Captain.* London: Hutchinson, 1971. First edition, fine in dust jacket. Mordida Books March 2015 - 008451 2015 $85

Kent, Alexander *The Sioux Nation and the United States.* Published by the National Indian Defence Association, 1891. First edition, 8vo., printed wrappers, 32 pages, covers moderate chipped and soiled, internal contents clean and intact, else very good. Buckingham Books March 2015 - 33319 2015 $250

Kent, Charles *Charles Dickens as a Reader.* London: Chapman & Hall, 1872. First edition, plates, original green cloth, dulled, label removed from leading pastedown, stamps and pressmark of Malvern Public Library, from the library of Geoffrey & Kathleen Tillotson, with note by Kathleen. Jarndyce Antiquarian Booksellers CCVII - 216 2015 £50

Kent, James *Rules and Orders of the Court of Chancery of the State of New York.* Albany: E. F. Backus, 1815. First edition, 8vo., 67 pages, contemporary calf backed marbled boards, foxed, with signature of Archibald Smith, 1816, inserted at page 10 is page of contemporary letter, unsigned, to Smith. M & S Rare Books, Inc. 97 - 216 2015 $600

Kent, Kate Peck *Prehistoric Textiles of the Southwest.* Albuquerque: 1983. Stated first edition, bookplate, marker stain bottom edge, else near fine in like dust jacket. Dumont Maps & Books of the West 131 - 56 2015 $95

Kent, Nathaniel *Hints to Gentlemen of Landed Property.* London: J. Dodsley, 1775. First edition, 8vo., 10 engraved folding plates, contemporary polished calf, spine simply gilt with raised bands and crimson lettering piece, short crack in upper joint, still fine, crisp, sound, early ownership inscription on front pastedown "W. Honywood 1787. The gift of the Revd. J. H. Beckingham". John Drury Rare Books 2015 - 24036 2015 $612

Kenyon, George Kenyon, Baron *Observations on the Roman Catholic Question.* London: J. J. Stockdale, 1810. First edition, 8vo., final errata leaf, (15 errata), recent plan wrapper, good copy. John Drury Rare Books 2015 - 19816 2015 $133

Kernahan, Coulson *Captain Shannon.* London: Ward Lock, 1897. First edition, near fine, name on front endpaper, else near fine in black cloth covered boards.   Mordida Books   March 2015 - 001238   2015 $165

Kernfeld, Barry *The New Grove Dictionary of Jazz.* London: Macmillan/Grove, 2002. Second edition, 3 volumes, 4to., issued without dust jackets, fine copies.   Beasley Books   2013 - 2015 $250

Kerouac, Jack   1922-1969 *Big Sur.* New York: Farrar Straus & Cudahy, 1962. First edition, first printing, near fine in like dust jacket with small tears, extremities lightly rubbed, some minor spots.   B & B Rare Books, Ltd.   234 - 61   2015 $750

Kerouac, Jack   1922-1969 *Doctor Sax.* New York: Grove Press, 1959. First edition, first printing, original paper wrappers issued simultaneously with hardcover format, presentation copy signed and inscribed by author to NY Expressionist artist and close friend, Barbara Frost, very good or better copy, lightly soiled and rubbed, housed in custom quarter leather folding box.   B & B Rare Books, Ltd.   234 - 62   2015 $9500

Kerouac, Jack   1922-1969 *Doctor Sax: Faust Part Three.* New York: Grove Press, 1959. First edition, wrappered issue, Evergreen original E-160, modest rubbing but fresh, near fine, neat ownership signature of author Larry McMurtry dated by him in 1959, interesting association.   Between the Covers Rare Books   196 - 84   2015 $750

Kerouac, Jack   1922-1969 *Excerpts from Visions of Cody.* New York: New Directions, 1960. First edition, copy number 620 of 750 numbered copies, signed by author, owner's name front pastedown and his very faint embossed stamp, else about fine in fine example of the original acetate dust jacket, in custom quarter cloth and marbled paper covered clamshell case, scarce.   Between the Covers Rare Books   196 - 85   2015 $3200

Kerouac, Jack   1922-1969 *On the Road.* London: Andre Deutsch, 1958. First UK edition, inscribed by author to longtime friend Henri Cru, touching inscription, very good in very good, supplied second impression dust jacket.   Ken Lopez, Bookseller   164 - 251   2015 $85,000

Kerr, Philip *Dead Meat.* London: Chatto & Windus, 1993. First edition, very fine, dust jacket.   Mordida Books   March 2015 - 001241   2015 $75

Kersaint, Armand Guy, Comte De *The Speech of Kersaint to the French National Convention, with Resolutions of that Body Respecting a War with England.* London: printed for J. Ridgway, 1793. First edition in English, 8vo., 16 pages, green plain wrappers good copy with contemporary ownership signature of G. Lister, uncommon.   John Drury Rare Books   2015 - 16108   2015 $177

Kersh, Gerald *Night and the City.* New York: Simon & Schuster, 1946. First American edition, fine in very good dust jacket, chipped spine ends, wear at corners and several closed tears.   Mordida Books   March 2015 - 012655   2015 $85

Kesey, Ken   1935- *News that Stayed News 1974-1984: Ten Years of CoEvolution Quarterly.* North Point: 1986. This copy inscribed by Kesey, Gary Snyder and Stewart Brand, few tiny spots to top edge, else fine in fine dust jacket.   Ken Lopez, Bookseller   164 - 103   2015 $500

Kesey, Ken   1935- *The Sea Lion.* New York: Viking, 1991. Uncorrected proof copy, illustrations by Neil Waldman, with unbound signatures in trial dust jacket and actual dust jacket, with 8 1/2 x 11 pictorial poster announcing a Ken Kesey "Sea Lion story telling performance" presented at Naropa Inst. at Boulder Theater, fine, poster very good.   Ken Lopez, Bookseller   164 - 98   2015 $350

Kesey, Ken   1935- *Sometimes a Great Notion.* Universal City: Universal Studios, 1970. Gay's Second draft screenplay dated Feb. 10 1970, based on Kesey's novel, with name of legendary Hollywood editor Dede Allen written on front cover, bradbound in studio wrappers, bit dusty, near fine.   Ken Lopez, Bookseller   164 - 100   2015 $650

Kessler, Leo *Fire in the West.* London: Century, 1986. First edition, fine in dust jacket.   Mordida Books   March 2015 - 008357   2015 $90

Kessler, Stephen *Nostalgia of the Fortuneteller.* Santa Cruz: Kayak Books, 1975. First edition, octavo, one of 1000 copies, illustrated wrappers, inscribed by poet to fellow poet William Merwin 22 Nov. 1975.   Between the Covers Rare Books, Inc.   187 - 146   2015 $50

Kettering Building Society *Rules of the Kettering Permanent Benefit Building Society, Established Pursuant to act of Parliament 6 & & Wm. Iv. cap. 32 Commenced April 13th 1869.* Kettering: printed by Joseph Toller, 1869. 8vo., few minor stains, several clauses overstamped in ink, revised list of officer tipped in, recent ownership at head of title, recently well bound in linen backed marbled boards lettered, good, rare.   John Drury Rare Books   2015 - 14975   2015 $221

Ketton-Cremer, Robert Wyndham *Thomas Gray: a Biography.* Cambridge: at the University Press, 1955. Half title, frontispiece, marginal pencil marks, original maroon cloth, slightly torn dust jacket, author's signed presentation copy for Geoffrey and Kathleen Tillotson, with accompanying letter laid down and draft of Geoffrey's letter of thanks, other correspondence, typescript of Geoffrey's review and press cuttings. Jarndyce Antiquarian Booksellers CCVII - 289 2015 £40

Key, Francis Scott *"Star Spangled Banner." from National Music Series.* Boston: Oliver Ditson,, 1861. Early edition, part of a collection of national songs, cover sheet has lithograph illustration of crossed flags of US and France, good condition only, pages separated, tattered at edges and has light water stains not affecting readability, still nice, scarce. The Kelmscott Bookshop 11 - 27 2015 $475

Key, Thomas Hewitt *Invasion Invited by the Defenceless State of England.* London: Bell and Daldy, 1858. First edition, 8vo., preserved in recent plain wrappers, very good. John Drury Rare Books 2015 - 20747 2015 $89

Keyes, Daniel *Flowers for Algernon.* New York: Harcourt Brace & World Inc., 1966. First edition, octavo, cloth. John W. Knott, Bookseller Selected New Arrivals Jan. 2015 - 1716 2015 $2500

Keyes, Roger *The Art of Surimono: Privately Published Japanese Woodblock Prints and Books in Charles Beatty Library, Dublin.* London: Sotheby, 1985. 2 volumes, 4to., cloth, dust jacket, slipcase, color and black and white illustrations, slipcase shows wear around edges. Oak Knoll Books 306 - 29 2015 $175

Keynes, Geoffrey 1887-1982 *Blake's Pencil Drawings. Second Series.* London: Nonesuch Press, 1956. Limited to 1440 numbered copies, this number 68, 4to., original brick red cloth with bevelled edges, black paper dust jacket printed with gold stars, printed paper label to spine, one or two small closed tears in extremities of the jacket, 56 collotype plates, near fine in very good dust jacket. Henry Sotheran Ltd. William Blake Exhibition 17th Oct.-7th Nov. 2014 - 90 2015 £65

Keynes, Geoffrey 1887-1982 *Engravings by William Blake. The Separate Plates. A Catalogue Raisonne.* Dublin: Emery Walker (Ireland) Ltd., 1956. Limited to 500 copies, 4to., quarter blue buckram, lacking dust jacket?, 45 collotype plates, including 4 in color, each with leaf of brief descriptive text, near fine. Henry Sotheran Ltd. William Blake Exhibition 17th Oct.-7th Nov. 2014 - 91 2015 £145

Keynes, John Maynard, 1st Baron 1883-1946 *The General Theory of Employment, Interest and Money.* London: Macmillan and Co., 1936. First edition, crown 8vo., original dark blue cloth, backstrip gilt lettered, merest hint of fading to spine, very good. Blackwell's Rare Books B179 - 182 2015 £1250

Keynes, John Maynard, 1st Baron 1883-1946 *The General Theory of Employment Interest and Money.* London: Macmillan and Co., 1936. First edition, first issue, 8vo., original publishers' cloth lettered gilt, fine, bright copy without blemish, but without a dust jacket. John Drury Rare Books 2015 - 25840 2015 $2360

Keynes, John Maynard, 1st Baron 1883-1946 *How to Pay for the War.* New York: Harcourt Brace, 1940. First American edition, mild wear to spine tips in very good+ dust jacket with chips, jacket spine tip with mild wear, 8vo., particularly scarce in this condition in dust jacket. By the Book, L. C. 44 - 45 2015 $500

Keynes, John Maynard, 1st Baron 1883-1946 *A Revision of the Treaty.* London: Macmillan, 1922. First edition, signed by author on tipped in sheet, with second signature H. Latham beneath it, very good+, foxing to edges, darkening to endpapers as is common, mild cover edge wear, very good with usual darkening edges and spine, mild edgewear and mild chips, 8vo. By the Book, L. C. 44 - 46 2015 $2000

Keynes, John Maynard, 1st Baron 1883-1946 *A Treatise on Probability.* London: Macmillan and Co., 1921. First edition, 8vo., errata slip tipped in at page 423, original brown cloth, spine lettered gilt, fine. John Drury Rare Books March 2015 - 26291 2015 $1049

Keynes, John Maynard, 1st Baron 1883-1946 *A Treatise on Probability.* London: Macmillan and Co., 1921. First edition, 8vo., original brown cloth, lettered gilt at spine, sharp, clean, very good+ copy with small abrasion on top front cover with slightly bumped corners. Any Amount of Books 2015 - C14242 2015 £700

Keynes, John Maynard, 1st Baron 1883-1946 *A Treatise on Probability.* London: Macmillan and Co., 1921. First edition, errata slip tipped n at page 423 including first and final ad leaves, original brown cloth, spine lettered gilt, fine. John Drury Rare Books 2015 - 26291 2015 $1049

Khazin, E. *Neft. (Oil).* Moscow: Ogiz, 1931. 4to., pictorial wrappers, light cover soil, very good+, great color lithos. Aleph-bet Books, Inc. 109 - 422 2015 $975

Khlebnikov, Kiril Timofeevich *Notes on Russian America.* Kingston: and Fairbanks: Limestone Press, 1994. First edition in English, five parts in 2 volumes, illustrations, maps, black cloth, fine set. Argonaut Book Shop Holiday Season 2014 - 147 2015 $125

Kidd, Jas. H. *The Michigan Cavalry Brigade in the Wilderness.* Winn & Hammond, 1889. First edition, 8vo., stapled, printed wrappers, 17 pages, light wear to spine and extremities, uniformly tanned, else very good, clean copy. Buckingham Books March 2015 - 33968 2015 $300

Kidder, Alfred Vincent *The Pottery of Pecos Volume II.* New Haven: 1936. Previous owner's name on front pastedown, private library name stamp on titlepage, some rubbing to extremities, else clean and very good, many illustrations. Dumont Maps & Books of the West   131 - 57   2015 $175

Kiddie's Number Book. Springfield: McLoughlin Bros., 1927. Large 4to, printed on linen, light wear, from use, else very good++, bold color illustrations.   Aleph-Bet Books, Inc.   108 - 109   2015 $500

Kidgell, John *The Card.* London: printed for the maker and sold by J. Newbery, 1755. First edition, 2 volumes, hand colored engraved frontispiece in volume 1, the word 'Card' in fancy woodcut capitals on both titlepages, frontispiece repaired at inner corners and along fore-edge, loss of the final 'e' in frontispiece, first 2 gatherings in volume i semi-detached, slightly browned, 12mo., contemporary calf, sometime rebacked, tan lettering pieces, joints rubbed, spine of volume ii defective at foot, booklabel of James M. Osborn, sound.   Blackwell's Rare Books   B179 - 57   2015   £1500

Kijewski, Karen *Katapult.* New York: St. Martin's, 1990. First edition, fine in dust jacket.   Mordida Books   March 2015 - 006829   2015 $85

Killigrew, Thomas *Comedies and Tragedies.* London: printed for Henry Herringman, 1664. First edition, folio, red full morocco by Bedford, gilt rules, decorations, inner dentelles and lettering, all edges gilt, frontispiece, this copy agrees with Greg's second issue, fine, handsome copy. The Brick Row Book Shop   Miscellany 67 - 62   2015 $4500

Killip, Christopher *Isle of Man: a Book about the Manx.* London: Arts Council of Great Britain, 1980. First edition, 4to., copiously illustrated in black and white throughout, uncommon hardback issue in very good state, original white cloth, very slightly bumped at head of spine, otherwise fine in very good clean dust jacket slightly creased at spine ends, one very short closed nick at head of top rear hinge and slight creasing to top rear part of dust jacket near spine, slightly bumped at one corner, white corners slightly tanned, very good.   Any Amount of Books   March 2015 - A98810   2015   £375

Kilvert, Cory *The Kite Book.* New York: Dodd Mead, 1909. First edition, 4to., cloth, pictorial paste-on, cover plate finger soiled, else tight and fine, printed on heavy coated paper, full page color illustrations by author, rare.   Aleph-bet Books, Inc.   109 - 355   2015 $350

Kimball, John C. *Connecticut's Canterbury Tale, Its Heroine Prudence Crandall and Its Moral for To-Day.* Hartford: Plimpton Print, 1885. First edition, 16mo., two portrait illustrations, printed gray wrappers, light vertical crease, else very near fine, very uncommon.   Between the Covers Rare Books   197 - 121   2015 $450

Kimura, Shotaro *Poems from the Japanese.* Tokyo: Hasegawa, n.d. circa, 1910. 3 books, 5 x 7 inches, bound in pictorial creped covers, all in fine condition in repaired slipcase with ivory closures, printed on textured paper, each page beautifully illustrated in rich covers, beautiful set. Aleph-bet Books, Inc.   109 - 233   2015 $850

Kindersley, David *Variations on the Theme of Twenty-six Letters.* Northamptonshire: David Kindersley, n.d. circa, 1968-1970. Square 8vo., leather backed boards decorated in gilt, one of 50 signed and numbered copies, out of a total edition of 500 copies, issued thus and in this binding, each leaf printed French-fold on a different colored paper, shows alphabets with facing text.   Oak Knoll Books   Special Catalogue 24 - 29   2015 $225

The Kinema Comic No. 506-531 Jan.-June Volume 10. London: Amalgamated Press, 1930. First edition, large 4to., soundly bound in red cloth, lettered gilt at spine, illustrations throughout, 24 combined issues from 4/1/30-28/6/30, covers slightly used, worn and nicked, comics in excellent condition.   Any Amount of Books   2015 - C5681   2015   £240

King, C. Daly *Obelists Fly High.* New York: Smith, 1935. First American edition, bookplate, spine slightly faded, otherwise very good.   Mordida Books   March 2015 - 001245   2015 $75

King, Frank A. *Minnesota Logging Railroads.* Gold West Books, 1981. First edition, simulated leather, 205 pages, profusely illustrated, charts, tables, maps, illustrations, near fine, dust jacket has modest rubbing and light wear to top edge, three quarter inch closed tear.   Buckingham Books March 2015 - 27945   2015 $185

King, Jessie *Seven Happy Days.* London: International Studio Supp. New Year, 1914. 4to., wrappers, some cover soil and tears, very good, series of magnificent color illustrations heightened with gold and silver, with 7 smaller black and white illustrations, laid in is original water color plus handwritten letter with sketch housed in original mailing envelope, inscribed to A. J. Bennett.   Aleph-bet Books, Inc.   109 - 244   2015 $4250

King, Joseph L. *History of the San Francisco Stock and Exchange Board.* San Francisco: for L. King, 1910. First edition, facsimile, portraits, illustrations, publisher's gray cloth stamped in dark gray and gold, light rubbing to extremities, very good.   Argonaut Book Shop   Holiday Season 2014 - 148   2015 $150

King, Laurie R. *A Grave Talent.* New York: St. Martins, 1993. First edition, first state with upside down Hebrew dedication, very fine in dust jacket.   Mordida Books March 2015 - 012592   2015 $250

King, Laurie R. *A Grave Talent.* New York: St. Martin's Press, 1993. First edition, first issue, signed by author, fine and unread in fine dust jacket, from the collection of Duke Collier. Royal Books   36 - 201   2015 $325

King, Martin Luther *Daddy King: an autobiography.* New York: Morrow, 1980. First edition, fine in about fine dust jacket with very slight discoloration on rear panel inscribed by author.   Between the Covers Rare Books   197 - 62   2015 $250

King, Martin Luther *Daddy King. An Autobiography.* New York: Morrow, 1980. First edition, signed by author, hardcover, fine in very lightly used dust jacket.   Beasley Books   2013 - 2015 $125

King, Martin Luther *Stride Toward Freedom.* New York: Harper & Bros., 1958. First edition, faint dampstain tidemark in very upper margins of pages and jacket flaps, just touching few letters on rear flap, otherwise affecting no text, else very good in frontispiece dust jacket (spine faded with modest chips at spine ends), warmly inscribed by author for Dr. John Warren Davis.   Between the Covers Rare Books   197 - 74   2015 $10,000

King, Martin Luther *Where do We Go From Here Chaos or Community?* New York: Harper & Row, 1967. First edition, first printing, presentation copy signed and inscribed by author, additionally signed by his wife, Coretta Scott King to their close friends June & Kelvin Wall, about fine with only crease to one page (173), in excellent and extremely crisp unclipped dust jacket with few minor scuffs to rear panel, lovely copy.   B & B Rare Books, Ltd.   234 - 63   2015 $13,000

King, Rufus *Malice in Wonderland.* Garden City: Doubleday Crime Club, 1958. First edition, top corners slightly bumped, else fine in dust jacket with internal tape reinforcing and scrape and rubbing on front cover.   Mordida Books   March 2015 - 009968   2015 $85

King, Rufus *Murder by the Clock.* Garden City: Doubleday Doran & Co., 1929. First edition, professionally rebacked with original spine laid down, former owner's name on front flyleaf, else near fine in professionally restored dust jacket.   Buckingham Books   March 2015 - 25303   2015 $1350

King, Stephen 1947- *Carrie.* New York: Doubleday, 1974. First edition, first printing, (with "P6" first issue code) of author's first novel, about fine in like unclipped jacket with few tiny creases and some very minor signs of wear to extremities, excellent copy.   B & B Rare Books, Ltd.   234 - 64   2015 $2000

King, Stephen 1947- *The Green Mile.* Burton: Subterranean Press, 2006. First separate hardcover edition, octavo, 6 volumes, leather backed cloth, one of 148 numbered copies signed by author.   John W. Knott, Bookseller   Selected New Arrivals Jan. 2015 - 17118   2015 $2500

King, Stephen 1947- *The Stand: The Complete and Uncut Edition.* New York: London: Toronto: Sydney: Auckland: Doubleday, 1990. First printing, limited to 1302 copies, this one of 1250 numbered copies signed by author and artist, Berni Wrightson, this #1180, octavo, full leather.   John W. Knott, Bookseller   Selected New Arrivals Jan. 2015 - 1717   2015 $2500

Kinglake, John Alexander *The Invasion of the Crimea: its Origin and an Account of its Progress Down to the Death of Lord Raglan.* Edinburgh and London: William Blackwood & Sons, 1863. First editions, Volumes 1, 3, 4, 5, 6, 7, 8 , lacking volume 2 and 9, 8vo., original burgundy cloth decorated in blind, lettered gilt at spines, all plates present, excellent handwritten 4 page letter signed by author and written on House of Commons headed paper, decent, clean and slightly used set, occasional rubbing with slight fading and slight edgewear.   Any Amount of Books   March 2015 - C15639   2015   £350

Kingsbury, George W. *History of Dakota Territory/South Dakota Its History and Its People.* Chicago: S. J. Clarke Pub. Co., 1915. First edition, thick 8vo., 5 volumes, three quarter leather, gold stamping on spine, decorated editions, volume II spine internally reinforced, else near fine, volume III spine internally reinforced, minute waterstains to bottom edges of two-thirds of text, else very good, volume IV spine internally reinforced, else near fine, volume V spine internally reinforced, tiny portion clipped from bottom edge of front flyleaf, tiny waterstain to bottom edge of all pages, else very good, scarce, very attractive set.   Buckingham Books   March 2015 - 28010   2015 $1000

Kingsland, Gerald *Curious. the Sex Education Magazine for Men and Women. Issues 1 to 31.* London: Rosland Productions, 1969. 4to., wrappers, bright, clean copies, illustrations in color and black and white, very good+ set.   Any Amount of Books   2015 - A40219   2015   £225

Kingsley, Charles 1819-1875 *The Limits of Exact Science as Applied to History. An Inaugural Lecture, Delivered Before the University of Cambridge.* Cambridge & London: Macmillan and Co., 1860. 8vo., (4), 72 pages, without ads found in some copies, contemporary half calf lettered gilt, little wear to fore edges of boards, else very good, from the library of the Rathaspeck Parsonage Trust with its 19th century booklabel on front pastedown and neat gilt stamp.   John Drury Rare Books   2015 - 17955   2015 $89

Kingsley, Charles 1819-1875 *The Water Babies.* New York: Dodd, Mead, 1916. First edition, 2nd issue with plain endpapers, thick 4to., green gilt cloth, round pictorial paste-on, as new in original publisher's glassine and box with mounted color plate, box in very good condition, slightly rubbed and light soil, stunning copy, illustrations by Jessie Willcox Smith.   Aleph-bet Books, Inc.   109 - 449   2015 $1250

Kingston, Peter *A to Z.* Sydney: Peter Kingston, 1991. First edition, one of 20 copies, all on Rives paper, each signed by Kingston, page size 11 1/8 x 13 1/8 inches, 29 hand colored etchings, 26 images in letter form plus titlepage and two colophon etchings, endpapers, hand printed with potato-print letters in multi-colors, printed by Diana Davidson and James Whitington at Whaling Road Press, yellow buckram stamped in red and black after original design by artist/author.   Priscilla Juvelis - Rare Books   61 - 27   2015 $2500

Kingston, William H. G. *The Circassian Chief: a Romance of Russian.* London: David Bryce, 1854. New edition, small 8vo., full black blind patterned contemporary leather lettered gilt at spine, slight uneven gatherings although all edges gilt, some paper creasing at corners, slight wear at head else very good.   Any Amount of Books   2015 - A33909   2015   £150

Kinnaird, Charles, 8th Baron *A Letter to the Duke of Wellington on the Arrest of M. Marinet.* London: James Ridgway, 1818. First edition, 8vo., half title, recent marbled boards, lettered on spine, very good.   John Drury Rare Books   March 2015 - 24439   2015   £306

Kinnell, Galway *First Poems 1946-1954.* Mt. Horeb: Perishable Press, 1970. First edition, one of 150 press numbered copies, 8vo., original quarter leather and marbled boards by Douglas Cockerel, fine, although not called for, signed by author.   James S. Jaffe Rare Books   Modern American Poetry - 163   2015 $350

Kinnell, Galway *The Shoes of Wandering.* Mt Horeb: Perishable Press, 1971. First edition, one of 100 copies or less, printed on handmade paper, small 8vo., original decorated wrappers, fine.   James S. Jaffe Rare Books   Modern American Poetry - 164   2015 $350

Kino Eusebio Francisco 1644-1711 *Kino's Historical Memoir of Pimeria Alta. A Contemporary Account of the Beginnings of California, Sonora and Arizona.* Arthur H. Clark co., 1919. First edition, 2 volumes 8vo., original maroon cloth, titles stamped in gilt on spine, top edge gilt, frontispiece, illustrations, maps, both volumes lightly rubbed at spine ends, else fine, clean set.   Buckingham Books   March 2015 - 34343   2015 $850

Kinsey, Alfred C. *Sexual Behavior in the Human Female.* Philadelphia and London: Saunders, 1953. First edition, 8vo., maroon cloth, cover very slightly worn at corners and ends of spine, otherwise very good, tight copy.   Second Life Books Inc.   189 - 148   2015 $125

Kip, Leonard *Hannibal's Man and Other Tales.* Albany: Angus Co. Printers, 1878. First edition, octavo, original beveled edge decorated green cloth, little rubbed, near fine in good example of exceptionally rare dust jacket, jacket has moderate overall chipping and has been professionally reinforced internally at folds, but has no other restoration, signed note on stationary to bibliographer and sci-fi dealer L. W. Currey loosely inserted.   Between the Covers Rare Books   196 - 154   2015 $25,000

Kipling, John Lockwood *Beast and Man in India.* London: Macmillan and Co., 1891. First edition, with illustrations in text, some foxing as usual, bound without ads, 8vo., contemporary red straight grained morocco backed dark green cloth, top edge gilt, bookplate inside front cover of E. C., Edinburgh, good.   Blackwell's Rare Books   B179 - 58   2015   £175

Kipling, John Lockwood *Beast and Man in India...* London: Macmillan and Co., 1891. First edition, original reddish brown cloth lettered gilt and decorated in gilt and black, little bubbling to lower cover and small light stains to upper cover, little foxing, but nice, inscription by Neillie and/or Ernst Henrici, from the collection of Gavin H. Fryer.   Bertram Rota Ltd.   308 Part II - 150   2015   £200

Kipling, John Lockwood *Beast and Man in India...* London: Macmillan and Co., 1891. First edition, illustrations, later red half morocco gilt by Bayntun, spine in compartments with raised bands and animal decorations gilt, top edge gilt, upper cover with one small area sunned, some foxing, but nice, from the collection of Gavin H. Fryer.   Bertram Rota Ltd.   308 Part II - 152   2015   £200

Kipling, Rudyard 1865-1936 *Captains Courageous.* London: Macmillan and Co., 1897. First edition, first printing, original blue gilt decorated cloth, extremities lightly rubbed, former owner signature of that title, some scattered foxing, else sound, bright, very good.   B & B Rare Books, Ltd.   234 - 65   2015 $400

Kipling, Rudyard 1865-1936 *Captains Courageous.* London: Macmillan and co., 1897. First edition, illustrations by I. W. Tabor fine and bright.   Between the Covers Rare Books   196 - 162   2015 $500

Kipling, Rudyard 1865-1936 *The Jungle Book. (and) The Second Jungle Book.* London: Macmillan, 1894. 1895. First editions, 8vo., blue gilt pictorial cloth, all edges gilt, light foxing on prelim pages, light bubble on cover of Jungle Book, slight soil on cover of Second Jungle Book with light wear to spine ends, very good+ set, wonderfully illustrated with black and whites by J. Lockwood Kipling and others, laid in is 2 page handwritten letter from artist, J. L. Kipling.   Aleph-bet Books, Inc.   109 - 245   2015 $4500

Kipling, Rudyard 1865-1936 *The Jungle Book. (and) The Second Jungle Book.* London: Macmillan, 1894-1895. First editions, 8vo., 2 volumes, blue gilt pictorial cloth, all edges gilt, owner name on endpaper in one volume, else very fine with gilt shiny and bright and with none of the usual foxing, housed in handsome three quarter leather drop back box with raised bands and gilt designs on spines, wonderful illustrations by J. Lockwood Kipling and others.   Aleph-Bet Books, Inc.   108 - 257   2015 $7500

Kipling, Rudyard 1865-1936 *Poems 1886-1929.* Garden City: Doubleday Doran and Co., 1930. Limited to 537 numbered copies, 4to., 3 volumes, half leather, marbled vellum, title and volume gilt stamped on spine, covers gilt ruled, top edges gilt, other edges uncut, marbled endapers, first volume signed by author, news clipping laid in volume II, slight rubbing and scuffing along edges of spine.   Oak Knoll Books   306 - 784   2015 $1500

Kipling, Rudyard 1865-1936 *Rudyard Kipling's Letters from San Francisco.* San Francisco: Colt Press, 1949. One of 500 copies, 76 pages, line drawings by Otis Oldfield, printed with handset type in blue and black, cloth backed pictorial boards, paper spine label, upper corners slightly jammed, else fine.   Argonaut Book Shop   Holiday Season 2014 - 150   2015 $150

Kipling, Rudyard 1865-1936 *A Song of the English.* London: Hodder & Stoughton, n.d., 1909. Large 4to., blue gilt cloth with gilt pictorial decoration, nearly as new in publisher's box, pictorial label on cover box very good+ (slightly soiled and lightly faded), illustrations by W. Heath Robinson, including 30 magnificent tipped in color plates with illustrated/ lettered guards and with 59 line illustrations, spectacular copy, rarely found with box.   Aleph-bet Books, Inc.   109 - 415   2015 $1500

Kipling, Rudyard 1865-1936 *Verse.* London: Hodder & Stoughton, 1930. Fifth impression, half title creased, title in red and black, india paper, original red cloth, inner hinge splitting, top edge gilt, from the library of Geoffrey & Kathleen Tillotson.   Jarndyce Antiquarian Booksellers   CCVII - 352   2015   £30

Kippis, Andrew *A Sermon Preached at the Old Jewry on Wednesday the 26th of April 1786, on Occasion of a New Academical Institution Among the Protestant Dissenters...* London: printed by H. Goldney for T. Cadell and J. Johnson, 1786. First edition, 8vo., original wrappers, uncut, minor creasing, else fine copy, contemporary ownership signature of Nath(aniel) Barnardiston Esqr. Fenchurch Buildings 1786, rare variant issue.   John Drury Rare Books   March 2015 - 22815   2015   £266

Kirk, Edward N. *Great Men are God's Gift.* Boston: Tappan & Whittemore, 1852. First edition, 8vo., 24 pages, removed.   M & S Rare Books, Inc.   97 - 320   2015 $150

Kirk, Robert *Secret Commonwealth or a Treatise Displaying the Chiefe Curiosities as They are in Use Among Diverse of the People of the Scotland to this Day.* Llandogo: Old Stile Press, 2005. 29/150 copies, (from an edition of 160 copies), signed by artist, printed on Hahnemuhle Old Antique Laid paper, woodcut illustrations, 4to., original brown leather with section of woodcut illustrated green paper at foot, backstrip lettered in blind, top edge purple, others untrimmed, fine.   Blackwell's Rare Books   B179 - 209   2015   £200

Kirkland, Elithe H. *Divine Average.* Boston: Little Brown and Co., 1952. First edition, very good, bright copy in lightly rubbed dust jacket with light wear to extremities and lightly soiled on rear panel.   Buckingham Books   March 2015 - 11567   2015 $185

Kirkpatrick, Ernest E. *Dim Trails a Collection of Poems.* Brownwood: Ben H. Moore, 1938. First edition, 8vo., presentation inscription from author, text bound in wooden covers with copper hinges, light wear to fore edge of front wooden cover and text is fine.   Buckingham Books   March 2015 - 31383   2015 $275

Kirkpatrick, Robert J. *The Encyclopaedia of Boy's School Stories.* Aldershot: Ashgate, 2000. First edition, large 8vo., original navy cloth, lettered gilt at spine, signed presentation from author, fine in near fine dust jacket with very slight creasing to jacket, otherwise excellent.   Any Amount of Books   2015 - C6093   2015   £160

Kirkwood, Jim *There Must Be a Pony!* Boston: Little Brown, 1960. First edition, inscribed by author for Burt Britton, fine in rubbed, near fine dust jacket, quite uncommon, especially signed.   Ken Lopez, Bookseller   164 - 105   2015 $350

Kirst, Hans Hellmut *The Night of the Generals.* Collins, 1963. First English edition, fine, bright, tight copy in dust jacket lightly rubbed at head and toe of spine.   Buckingham Books   March 2015 - 36335   2015 $175

Kirti, B. P. *Eventide.* Calcutta: Subrata Kiriti, printed in English and Bengali, circa, 1965. Original pictorial wrappers, presentation inscription by author for Proft. Tillotson (Geoffrey or Kathleen), 6/9/65. Jarndyce Antiquarian Booksellers CCXI - 170 2015 £50

Kissinger, Henry A. *Does America Need a Foreign Policy.* First edition, near fine in like dust jacket, inscribed by author. Stephen Lupack March 2015 - 2015 $75

Kitcat, Dick *Grand Historical, Classical and Comical, Procession of Remarkable Personages Ancient Modern and Unknown.* London: T. McLean, 1842. First and only edition, 11 x 5 1/2 inches, later cloth with original covers laid-down, few captions trimmed else very good+, 60 pages of hand colored lithographs. Aleph-Bet Books, Inc. 108 - 149 2015 $1500

Kitchener, Henry Thomas *Letters on Marriage on the Causes of Matrimonial Infidelity and on the Reciprocal Relations of the Sexes in Two Volumes.* London: C. Chapple, 1812. First edition, 8vo., bound in plain boards, volume I with new spine and front cover, volume 2 with new spine, new printed spine labels, little toned, untrimmed, very good set, scarce. Second Life Books Inc. 189 - 149 2015 $750

Kitton, Fred G. *Phiz: a Memoir Including a Selection from His Correspondence and Notes on His Principal Works.* London: W. Satchell, 1882. First edition, 8vo., green quarter leather without original wrappers, pages 32, frontispiece and numerous illustrations, presentation copy by author his father, very good. Any Amount of Books 2015 - A92878 2015 £180

Kittredge, William *We Are Not In this Together.* Port Townsend: Graywolf, 1984. Wrapper issue of the simultaneous trade edition, signed by author, fine. Ken Lopez Bookseller E-list # 82 - 912365 2015 $100

Kjobenhavns Universitets *Journal Udgiven ved Professor Jac. Baden. Ferste Aagang. (- Niende Aagang).* Kjobenhavn: 1793-1801. 4to., 8 volumes, original printed wrappers, complete except for one defective index leaf and lack of some printed wrappers, entirely uncut, excellent set, now preserved in two purpose made boxes, each labelled appropriately, each separate issue has a very small discard stamp of Stockholm University Library, no other marks except for two early ownership signatures on upper wrapper. John Drury Rare Books 2015 - 23548 2015 $2185

Klee, Paul *Notebooks.* London: Lund Humphries, 1992. First edition, 2 volumes, 8vo., illustrations in black and white, few in color and couple folding, fine, dust jacket. Any Amount of Books 2015 - A94660 2015 £300

Klein, Lawrence *Economic Theory and Econometrics.* Philadelphia: University of Pennsylvania Press, 1985. First edition, 8vo., fine in fine dust jacket. By the Book, L. C. Special List 10 - 14 2015 $900

Kleinholz, Frank *A Self Portrait.* New York: Shorewood Publishers, 1964. First edition, fully bound in leather, stamped gilt and blind, slight wear to spine, very good+ in author's hand 'this one of twelve books bound in leather for those dear friends who have been of such help and encouragement to me. This one is for Senator and Mrs. William Benton March 7, 1964', 4to. Beasley Books 2013 - 2015 $250

Klemp, Egon *America in Maps Dating from 1500 to 1856.* New York: 1976. Large elephnat folio, 291 pages, maps, near fine in printed slipcase. Dumont Maps & Books of the West 131 - 58 2015 $275

Klimt, Gustav *Twenty-five Drawings (Gustav Klimt).* Graz-Wein: Vienna: Akademische Druck und Verlagsansalt...., 1964. First edition, large folio, 25 drawings, offset lithographs, some printed in colors, on wove paper, sheets loose in mounts with original black linen covered boards and slipcase, overall size 600 x 430mm., very good, with usual very slight waviness to some plates and mounts, slipcase sound with some use, very good, 26 plates present with 2 in duplicate. Any Amount of Books 2015 - C7688 2015 £1500

Kline, Milton V. *Clinical Correlations of Experimental Hypnosis.* Springfield: Charles C. Thomas, 1963. First edition, fine in very good dust jacket. Beasley Books 2013 - 2015 $45

Klinefelter, Walter *Sherlock Holmes, in Portrait and Profile.* Syracuse: Syracuse University, 1963. First edition, very good, fine in very good price clipped dust jacket with one inch piece missing at lower front corner, light wear at spine ends and at corner and short closed tear. Mordida Books March 2015 - 002699 2015 $75

Kling Klang Gloria. Wien and Leipzig: Tempsky & Freytag, 1907. First edition, large oblong 4to., cloth backed boards, paper chipped in areas long spine, light edge rubbing and scattered foxing, else very good+, illustrations by Heinrich Lefler with 16 beautiful color plates by Josef Urban, with lovely decorations. Aleph-bet Books, Inc. 109 - 197 2015 $650

Klingsberg, Harry *Doowinkle, D.A.* New York: Dial, 1940. First edition, pages darkened, otherwise fine in dust jacket with tiny wear at spine ends. Mordida Books March 2015 - 001257 2015 $135

Klopfenstein, Perry A. *Foundations Strong a History of Gridley Illinois 1856-1990.* Fort Scott: Sekan Publications n.d., First edition, fine in lightly rubbed, but fine dust jacket, 8vo.   Beasley Books   2013 - 2015 $45

Knapp, Moses L. *Address Delivered to the Graduating class of the Indiana Medical College at the Public Commencement Feb. 18, 1847.* Chicago: 1847. First edition, 8vo., removed.   M & S Rare Books, Inc.   97 - 52   2015 $500

Knapp, Samuel Lorenzo *The Picturesque Beauties of the Hudson River and Its Vicinity.* New York: J. Disturnell, 1836. First edition, square folio 16 pages, 3 full page engravings, original printed wrappers (soiled, frayed), foxed. M & S Rare Books, Inc.   97 - 121   2015 $750

Knapp, Samuel Lorenzo *Sketches of Public Characters.* New York: E. Bliss, 1830. First edition, 12mo., original brown quarter calf, marbled boards, gilt lettering, untrimmed, head and foot of spine slightly chipped, hinges just starting, but firm, some foxing, very good.   The Brick Row Book Shop   Miscellany 67 - 63   2015 $375

Kneale, Nigel *The Year of the Sex Olympics and Other TV Plays.* London: Ferret Fantasy, 1976. First edition, number 90 of special limited edition (100), 8vo., original black buckram lettered gilt on spine, signed by author, fine in fine dust jacket.   Any Amount of Books   2015 - A73443   2015   £250

Kneeland, Samuel *The Wonders of the Yosemite Valley and of California.* Boston: 1872. Third edition, 97 pages, 10 original photos tipped onto individual pages with tissue guards, original embossed boards with gilt title, all edges gilt, pages slightly browned, gift inscription on f.f.e.p, extremities slightly rubbed, else very good.   Dumont Maps & Books of the West   131 - 59   2015 $1250

Knight, Bob *Let's Get a Good Shot.* Walden: Robert M. Knight, 1969. First edition, 28 numbered pages, several scuffs to covers, owner name of high school basketball coach at the time, inside front and rear covers, very good in stapled wrappers, scarce.   Ken Lopez, Bookseller   164 - 10   2015 $500

Knight, Bob *Quickness, Reaction, Practice Planning.* Walden: Robert M. Knight, 1970. First edition, 23 numbered pages, owner name inside both front and rear covers, else fine in stapled wrappers.   Ken Lopez, Bookseller   164 - 11   2015 $500

Knight, Charles *Passages of a Working Life During Half a Century with a Prelude of Early Reminiscences.* London: Bradbury & Evans, 1865. 1864. First edition, 3 volumes, 8vo., contemporary uniform polished calf, gilt with raised bands, fully gilt in compartments with contrasting labels, all edges marbled by Hodgson of Liverpool, fine set, most attractive binding, with contemporary (unidentified) armorial bookplate.   John Drury Rare Books   March 2015 - 23109   2015 $266

Knight, Clifford *The Affair at Palm Springs.* New York: Dodd Mead & Co., 1938. First edition, fine, bright copy, dust jacket with professional restoration to spine ends and corners.   Buckingham Books   March 2015 - 28722   2015 $1250

Knight, George *Dust in the Balance.* London: Jarrold & Sons, 1896. First edition, 8vo. original green cloth, lettered gilt on spine and on front cover, uncommon book, neat inscription dated 1986 in hand of William Gher and pencilled on front endpaper, very slight rubbing with foxing to endpapers, otherwise very good+.   Any Amount of Books   2015 - C8102   2015   £275

Knight, George Wilson *The Burning Oracle.* London: Oxford University Press, 1939. Half title, uncut in original maroon cloth, slightly marked, from the library of Geoffrey & Kathleen Tillotson, Kathleen's review copy with ms. and penned review, with ALS from author to Geoffrey 1944 and long TLS article about him as critic.   Jarndyce Antiquarian Booksellers   CCVII - 353   2015   £30

Knight, George Wilson *The Imperial Theme.* London: Oxford University Press, 1931. Uncut, half title, original maroon cloth, Kathleen Tillotson's copy as Kathleen M. Constable with 2 pages notes.   Jarndyce Antiquarian Booksellers   CCVII - 463   2015   £20

Knight, James *A Review of the Private and Joint Stock Banks in the Metropolis; with Remarks Upon the Constitution of a New Chartered Joint Stock Bank Under the Provisions of the 7th and 8th Victoria....* London: Effingham, Wilson, 1847. Third edition, 8vo., titlepage with faint inkstamp in red ink of Jas. G. Bennett, recently well bound in cloth, spine gilt lettered, good copy.   John Drury Rare Books   March 2015 - 26024   2015 $266

Knights, L. C. *Scrutiny: a Quarterly Review, Reissued.* Cambridge: Cambridge University Press, 1963. 8vo., original black cloth lettered gilt in spine, very good in very good dust jackets slightly tanned at spine, 20 volumes with index and retrospect.   Any Amount of Books   2015 - A65136   2015   £200

Knipe, Alden Arthur *Red Magic Book.* New York: Doubleday Page, 1910. First edition, 8vo., cloth, pictorial paste-on, light shelfwear, near fine, full page illustrations in red with faint traces of blue done by Emily Benson Knipe, hinged into rear of book is large red translucent paper overlay, by placing overlay on top of each illustration red is masked out and a new illustration in blue appears, quite scarce.   Aleph-bet Books, Inc.   109 - 333   2015 $475

Knower, Daniel *The Adventures of a Forty-Niner.* Albany: Weed Parsons, 1894. First edition, frontispiece, 10 plates, newly bound in Victorian black moire cloth, gilt, very fine, clean throughout.   Argonaut Book Shop   Holiday Season 2014 - 151   2015 $175

Knowles, James Sheridan *The Love Chase. A comedy in Five Acts (bound with) Love. A Play.* London: Edward Moxon, 1837. 1839. First edition, and fifth edition respectively, half titles, initial ad leaf in 'Love', titlepage of 'Love Chase' detached and chipped at edges, 2 volumes in 1, early marbled boards, cloth spine rubbed and chipped, inner hinges weakening, 75th birthday gift to Kathleen Tillotson from friend Wendy Rintoul, each play inscribed by author to Mr. Norman.   Jarndyce Antiquarian Booksellers   CCVII - 354   2015   £35

Knowles, John *A Separate Peace.* London: Secker & Warburg, 1959. First edition, 8vo., ex-libris plain bookplate with ownership signature of Malcolm Bradbury (British novelist) pasted to front endpaper, clean slightly used copy with Boots label on lower part of front cover, about very good in original green cloth lettered in silver at spine.   Any Amount of Books   2015 - C2791   2015   £160

Knox, Vicesimus   1752-1821 *A Sermon Preached at the Opening of the Chapel of the Pilanthroplc Society Nov. 9 1806.* London: printed by the Philanthropic Society and sold at the Society's Manfuactory, 1807. First edition, 4to., half title, well rebound in modern grey boards, printed paper spine label, very good with presentation inscription "from the author", very rare.   John Drury Rare Books   March 2015 - 14446   2015   £306

Ko Won *Buddhist Elements in Dada...* New York: New York University Press, 1977. First edition, fine in fine dust jacket.   Beasley Books   2013 - 2015 $40

Koch, Kenneth *Ko or a Season on Earth.* New York and London: Grove Press/Evergreen Books, 1959. First edition, 8vo., original gray cloth dust jacket, inscribed by author for Ted Berrigan, few ink spots on fore-edge and rear free endpaper, otherwise very good.   James S. Jaffe Rare Books   Modern American Poetry - 167   2015 $1500

Koch, Kenneth *Ko or a Season on Earth.* New York: Grove Press, 1959. First edition, limited issue, one of only 4 copies, hors commerce and signed by Koch in black ink, 8vo., original cloth backed tan paper boards, this copy numbered '6' suggesting that this issue may have consisted of a few more copies than originally intended, very fine, without dust jacket as issued.   James S. Jaffe Rare Books   Modern American Poetry - 166   2015 $1000

Koch, Kenneth *Poems/Prints.* New York: Editions of the Tibor de Nagy Gallery, 1953. First edition, one of 300 numbered copies, scarce first book, 4to., original illustrated card wrappers, stapled, 4 original linoleum cuts by Nell Blaine who designed the cover typography and decorations for the book, this copy signed by Nell Blaine and has dated each of the three large mounted prints in bottom margin, in addition there is small linoleum cut and five black and white illustrations, very fine and rare in such beautiful condition, with none of the offsetting and staining that so often marks this book, in half morocco slipcase.   James S. Jaffe Rare Books   Modern American Poetry - 165   2015 $6500

Koch, Kenneth *When the Sun Tries to Go On.* Los Angeles: Black Sparrow Press, 1969. First edition, octavo, one of 200 numbered specially bound copies, out of a total edition of 1705, signed by author and artist, designed by Larry Rivers and with 4 color and 7 black and white full page designs, as well as upper cover design, which comprises collage of three pieces of cardboard over which are mounted reproductions of artist's designs, fine in original plain acetate wrapper.   Peter Ellis, Bookseller   2014 - 001177   2015   £350

Koella, W. P. *Sleep, Physiology, Biochemistry, Psychology, Pharmacology, Clinical Impress.* Basel: K. Karger, 1973. First edition, fairly clean ex-library, several bookplates, traces of pocket removal.   Beasley Books   2013 - 2015 $45

Koenig, Harry C. *A History of the Parishes of the Archdiocese of Chicago.* Archdiocese of Chicago, 1980. First edition, 2 volumes, fine in slipcase.   Beasley Books   2013 - 2015 $135

Kohl, J. G. *Kitchi-Gami: Wanderings Round Lake Superior.* London: 1860. First English edition, illustrations, half leather and marbled boards, light rubbing to externals, else very good.   Dumont Maps & Books of the West   131 - 60   2015 $475

Kohut, Heinz *The Curve of Life. Correspondence of Heinz Kohut 1923-1981.* Chicago: University of Chicago Press, 1994. First edition, 8vo., fine in fine dust jacket.   Beasley Books   2013 - 2015 $45

Kohut, Heinz *The Restoration of the Self.* New York: International Universities Press, 1977. First edition, inscribed by author to psychoanalyst Jerome Beigler, very good with some underlining, mostly in earlier pages, in very good+ dust jacket with few small tears and light edgewear, handsome copy, 8vo.   Beasley Books   2013 - 2015 $200

Komunyakaa, Yusef *Love in the Time of War.* Middletown: Robin Price, 2013. Number 36 of 70 copies, signed by author, bound in aluminum boards that are etched in a pattern based on camouflage fabric, spine and endpages are handmade Cave Paper, letterpress printed in silver ink in Adobe Jenson Pro type on hand dyed silk with small pieces of Moriki paper and glassine sewn inside folded sheets, designed, colored and printed by Price in collaboration with Brittney De Nigris, bound by Daniel Kelm of Easthampton MA, housed in archival folding case with printed title label to spine panel, prospectus and insert titled "Visual Backstory", fine.   The Kelmscott Bookshop   11 - 28   2015 $2400

Koolhaas, Rem *Delirious New York: A Retroactive Manifesto for Manhattan.* New York: Oxford University Press, 1978. First edition, 4to., original pink cloth, lettered black on spine and front cover, copiously illustrated in color and black and white, very slight wear at edges, otherwise very good+ in used, very good minus dust jacket, 2 cm. closed tear at head of spine and 6cm. closed tear at edge of rear panel, some edgewear and slight creasing, dust jacket reinforced with brown paper and complete.   Any Amount of Books   2015 - C16088   2015   £180

Koontz, Dean R. *The Bad Place.* New York: Putnam, 1990. First edition, very fine in printed wrappers, uncorrected proof.   Mordida Books   March 2015 - 001267   2015 $100

Koontz, Dean R. *Cold Fire.* New York: Putnam, 1991. First edition, one of 750 numbered copies signed by author, very fine in dust jacket, with slipcase.   Mordida Books   March 2015 - 002479   2015 $200

Koontz, Dean R. *The Door to December.* London: Inner Circle, 1987. First hardcover edition, pages slightly darkened, otherwise fine in dust jacket.   Mordida Books   March 2015 - 005269   2015 $100

Koontz, Dean R. *The Face of Four.* Indianapolis: Bobbs Merrill, 1977. First edition, fine in dust jacket with short crease on inner front flap.   Mordida Books   March 2015 - 009922   2015 $250

Koontz, Dean R. *Hanging On.* London: Barrie & Jenkins, 1974. First English edition, fine in dust jacket with nicks at top of spine and at corners, small chip at bottom edge of back panel.   Mordida Books   March 2015 - 008106   2015 $250

Koontz, Dean R. *The Mask.* London: Headline, 1989. First hardcover edition, very fine in dust jacket.   Mordida Books   March 2015 - 005270   2015 $100

Koontz, Dean R. *Strangers.* New York: Putnam, 1986. First edition, creases on spine, otherwise fine in glossy printed wrappers, advance reading copy.   Mordida Books   March 2015 - 001266   2015 $75

Koontz, Dean R. *Ticktock.* London: Headline, 1996. First edition, very fine in dust jacket.   Mordida Books   March 2015 - 005271   2015 $75

Kooser, Ted *Official Entry Blank. Poems.* Lincoln: University of Nebraska Press, 1969. First edition, this the rare hardcover issue, simultaneous paperback, signed by Kooser, fine in price clipped dust jacket, trifle sunned along spine.   James S. Jaffe Rare Books   Modern American Poetry - 168   2015 $1500

Kooser, Ted *Local Wonders. Seasons in the Bohemian Alps.* Lincoln/London: University of Nebraska, 2002. First edition, fine in fine dust jacket, this copy inscribed by author.   Ed Smith Books   83 - 56   2015 $75

Koran *The Koran, Commonly called the Alcoran of Mohammed.* London: printed by C. Ackers, 1734. First edition translated by George Sale, title printed in red and black, five engraved plates, variable moderate browning, contemporary panelled calf, blind tooling around the central mottled panel, spine gilt in compartments, red lettering piece, gilt Suffield crest in the 5th panel, rebacked preserving original compartments (raised bands showing lighter new calf), engraved armorial bookplate of Edward Lord Suffield, good, well above average copy.   Blackwell's Rare Books   B179 - 59   2015   £1800

Kornberg, Arthur *DNA Synthesis.* San Francisco: W. H. Freeman, 1974. First edition, signed by author, small 4to., very good++, spine tips and cover corners bumped.   By the Book, L. C.   Special List 10 - 78   2015 $500

Kornbluth, Cyril M. *Not This August.* Garden City: Doubleday & Co., 1955. First edition, octavo, boards.   John W. Knott, Bookseller   Selected New Arrivals Jan. 2015 - 17113   2015 $125

Kornitzer, Bela *The Great American Heritage.* New York: Farrar, Straus and Cudahy, 1955. First edition, 22cm., publisher's beige cloth with gilt title, very good with light spotting to endpapers and edges, else near fine in very good dust jacket with scattered spotting and few tiny tears, inscribed by author to Gene Tunney.   Between the Covers Rare Books, Inc.   187 - 148   2015 $150

Korthals-Altes, J. *Sir Cornelius Vermuyden; the Lifework of a Great Anglo-Dutchman in Land Reclamation and Drainage...* London: The Hague: Williams & Norgate/W. P. Van Stokum, 1925. First edition, 8vo., 15 illustrations, 6 maps, original blue cloth lettered gilt on spine and on front cover, pencilled ownership signature of F. R. Cowell, slight shelfwear, sound, very good+. Any Amount of Books 2015 - A49460   2015   £225

Kottaridi, Angeliki *Aigai: the Royal Metropolis of Macedonians.* Athens: John S. Latsis Public Benefit Foundation, 2013. First edition, large 4to., original black cloth lettered gilt at spine and front cover, copiously illustrated in color and black and white, excellent, fine in fine dust jacket.   Any Amount of Books   2015 - C13321   2015   £220

Kotzebue, Otto Von *A Voyage of Discovery into the South Sea and Beering's Straits from the Purpose of exploring a North-East Passage.* Amsterdam/New York: N. Israel/Da Capo Press, 1967. Facsmile of 1812 edition, cream laminated boards, boxed in blue and lettered gilt on spine and cover, issued without dust jackets, color plates with foldout maps and tables, fine.   Any Amount of Books   2015 - C2604   2015   £175

Kotzwinkle, William *E. T. The Extra-Terrestrial.* New York: Putnams, 1982. First edition, signed by three cast members, Dee Wallace Stone, Robert MacNaughton and C. Thomas Howell, near fine in near fine dust jacket.   Ed Smith Books   83 - 57   2015 $175

Koudelka, Josef *Gypsies.* New York: Aperture, 1975. First edition, oblong hardcover, tight close to near fine with some very faint foxing to top edge of pages in very near fine with small tear to top of front panel and some very slight wear to spine ends, very good.   Jeff Hirsch Books   E-62 Holiday List 2014 - 20   2015 $650

Kozakiewicz, Stefan *Bernardo Bellotto Volume I Text. Volume 2 Catalogue.* London: Paul Elek, 1972. First UK edition, 4to., original brown cloth, lettered gilt at spine and front cover, copiously illustrated in color and black and white throughout, 2 volumes, fine in fine dust jackets and slipcase.   Any Amount of Books   2015 - C12629   2015   £180

Krakel, Dean *The Saga of Tom Horn.* Laramie: Powder River, 1954. First unexpurgated edition, cloth, illustrations, rare, fine in fine dust jacket.   Buckingham Books   March 2015 - 32146   2015 $850

Kratville, William W. *Union Pacific Locomotives.* Omaha: Barnhart Press, 1960. First edition, 2 volumes, oblong quarto, photos, diagrams, stiff boards, spiral bound, some light wear or rubbing to extremities, few rings broken on plastic spiral spine, very good set, very scarce.   Argonaut Book Shop   Holiday Season 2014 - 152   2015 $200

Kratzig, Helene *A Collection of 40 Leaves of Ornamental Studies and Mostly Textile Design.* Tannwald and Morchenstern, 1910-1915. 36 leaves in water color, three stamped and one of cut-out pasted coloured paper, mostly in large folio, few in folio.   Marlborough Rare Books   List 54 - 2   2015   £750

Kraus, Joe W. *A History of Way & Williams with a Bibliography of their Publications.* Philadelphia: G. MacManus, 1984. First edition, one of 500 copies, fine hardcover, issued without dust jacket.   Beasley Books 2013 - 2015 $45

Kraus, Karl *Worte in Versen.* Leipzig: Verlag der Schriften Von Karl Kraus, 1916. First edition, volume 1 is 13 of 30 copies on Van Geldern Butten paper, volume 2 is no. 6 of 30 copies, 2 volumes, original blue leather covered boards lettered gilt on spine and cover, pages 72 and 75, German text, very rare, slight rubbing and slight scuffing, endpapers browned, otherwise very good.   Any Amount of Books   2015 - A82464   2015   £180

Krause, Dorothy Simpson *Rivers of Grass. An Homage to Marjory Stoneman Douglas.* Boca Raton: Minerva: the Press of Wimberly, 2012. One of 36 copies, on Yu Kou heavy for the images and text and interleaved with Yu Kou light paper, hand numbered and signed by artist, page size 9 7/8 x 6 7/8 inches, 10 pages, bound loose as issued housed in envelope made of terracotta Lokta oil paper fastened with tie (combination of terracotta and light orange string and tan leather cord) on lozenge shaped seed-pod from mahogany tree serves as fastener, printed letterpress (with small amount of ink) with words RIVER OF GRASS and Dorothy Simpson Krause on lower left front corner, artist tells us that the envelope.   Priscilla Juvelis - Rare Books   61 - 28   2015 $875

Krausel, Richard *Flore d'Europe I. Plantes Herbacees et Sous-Arbrisseaux.* Paris: Societe Francaise du Livre n.d. 1970's, 168 color plates taken from original prints by Caspari and Grossman, on back of each plate, in French, is detailed description of the flower, book in wrappers is very good, plates near fine, housed in turquoise linen covered clamshell box, few smudge marks, otherwise very good, near fine.   The Kelmscott Bookshop   11 - 29   2015 $150

Krauss, Ruth *I Want to Paint My Bathroom Blue.* New York: Harper and Brothers, 1956. First edition, 4to., cloth backed pictorial boards, slightest of edge rubbing, else fine in very good+ dust jacket with price intact, illustrations by Maurice Sendak.   Aleph-bet Books, Inc.   109 - 428   2015 $1200

Krauss, Ruth *Is This You?* New York: William Scott, 1955. First edition, pictorial boards, slight tip wear, else very good+ in dust jacket with light soil and few small edge mends, illustrations by Crockett Johnson.   Aleph-bet Books, Inc.   109 - 241   2015 $600

Krefft, Gerard *The Snakes of Australia.* Sydney: Thomas Richards, 1869. Quarto, 16 (four in duplicate) uncolored lithographic plates, cloth, plates crisp and free of foxing. Andrew Isles 2015 - 26971   2015 $2500

Kreymborg, Alfred *Our Singing Strength: an Outline of American Poetry.* New York: Coward McCann, 1929. First edition, spine lettering trifle rubbed, else fine, without dust jacket, inscribed by author for friend James A. McCann. Between the Covers Rare Books, Inc.   187 - 149   2015 $150

Krieger, J. L. *Valley Division Vignettes (Santa Fe).* Hanford: Valley Rail Press, 1988. Second edition, quarto, profusely illustrated with black and white photos, maps, 2 folding maps in rear envelope, slight rubbing to foot of spine and lower edge of board, else fine, pictorial dust jacket. Argonaut Book Shop   Holiday Season 2014 - 153   2015 $60

Kroeber, A. L. *Handbook of the Indians of California.* Washington: GPO, 1925. First edition, 83 plates and maps, 78 text figures, original gilt lettered olive cloth, spine bit dulled with light rubbing to ends and corners, fine. Argonaut Book Shop   Holiday Season 2014 - 154   2015 $250

Kroeber, Theodora *Ishi in Two Worlds.* Berkeley: University of California Press, 1961. First edition, numerous photos, beige cloth stamped in red, very fine. Argonaut Book Shop   Holiday Season 2014 - 155   2015 $90

Krugman, Paul *The Conscience of a Liberal.* New York: W. W. Norton, 2007. First edition, 8vo., signed by author, as new, in like dust jacket.   By the Book, L. C.   Special List 10 - 15   2015 $125

Krugman, Paul *Fuzzy Math.* New York: W. W. Norton, 2001. First edition, 8vo., fine in fine dust jacket, signed and inscribed by author.   By the Book, L. C.   Special List 10 - 16   2015 $100

Kubasta, Voitech *An American Indian Camp.* Bancroft & Co. Pub. Ltd., 1962. First edition, light wear to cover and extremities along with half inch corner bend, pop-up clean and in perfect working order, large 9 x 13 inch cloth hinged cardboard folder resembling game board in construction illustration front and back with portrait.   Buckingham Books   March 2015 - 38434   2015 $425

Kubler, George *Studies in Classic Maya Iconography.* New Haven: Hamden: Archon Books, 1969. First edition, very good dust jacket, mild foxing to boards, good plus dust jacket (staining), small closed tears, mild water bumping to top corners.   Stephen Lupack   March 2015 - 2015 $45

Kunhardt, Dorothy *Pat the Bunny.* New York: Simon & Schuster, 1940. First edition, first issue, 12mo., pink pictorial boards, fine in original box (ever so slightly worn, else fine), rare.   Aleph-Bet Books, Inc.   108 - 259   2015 $8500

Kunhardt, Dorothy *The Wise Old Aard-Vark.* New York: Viking Press, 1936. First edition, oblong 4to., pictorial boards, fine, dust jacket with small chip on rear corner of dust jacket and very slight fraying to spine ends, otherwise very good+ dust jacket, full page 3-color illustrations opposite very page of text, amazing copy, rare in any condition. Aleph-bet Books, Inc.   109 - 246   2015 $1500

Kunitz, Stanley *Intellectual Things.* New York: Doubleday Doran, 1930. First edition, 8vo., original cloth, dust jacket, very good, inscribed by author for Mrs. Hammond-Knowlton, 6/24/34.   James S. Jaffe Rare Books   Modern American Poetry - 169   2015 $1500

Kunitz, Stanley *Next-To-Last Things.* Boston: Atlantic Monthly Press, 1985. First edition, 8vo., original cloth, dust jacket, signed by Kunitz, fine.   James S. Jaffe Rare Books Modern American Poetry - 170   2015 $150

Kunitz, Stanley *Passing through the later Poems New and Selected.* New York: W. W. Norton, 1995. First edition, 8vo, original cloth, dust jacket, signed by author, very fine. James S. Jaffe Rare Books   Modern American Poetry - 171   2015 $150

Kurr, J. G. *The Mineral Kingdom.* Edinburgh: Edmonston & Douglas, 1859. Folio, 70 pages, 24 lithographed plates, publisher's (?) quarter brown morocco and morocco grained green cloth, gilt, top and bottom of spine badly worn, some slight rubbing, few spots throughout, otherwise handsome copy with plates generally fresh and crisp.   Andrew Isles 2015 - 36571   2015 $1200

Kuykendall, W. L. *Frontier Days.* J. J. & H. L. Kuykendall, 1917. First edition, 8vo., cloth, gold stamping on front cover and spine, illustrations, inked name on front pastedown, light evidence of bookplate removal on front pastedown, else very good.   Buckingham Books   March 2015 - 29959   2015 $350

Kyd, Joseph Clatyon Clark *Characters from Charles Dickens.* London: John Player & Sons, 1889. Set of 50 standard size coloured cigarette cards good clean set, in envelope possibly indicating purchase by Kathleen Tillotson from Dickens House.   Jarndyce Antiquarian Booksellers CCVII - 217   2015   £120

Kyle, David D. *Outline of a Proposed Plan for Building New Towns at Windsor and Eton; in Order Completely to Improve the Castle and Parks. Addressed to the Right Honourable the Commissioners of Her Majesty's Woods &c...* London: printed for private circulation only, 1847. First and only edition and apparently of some rarity, 8vo. 2 folding colored lithographic plates, each plate signed by the two authors, original plain dark green cloth.   John Drury Rare Books   2015 - 26172   2015 $2185

L

L'Anselme, Jean *L'Enfant Triste.* Paris: Pierre Seghers, 1955. First edition, printed wrappers, 2 small stains on front wrapper, else near fine in very good, original unprinted dust jacket, warmly inscribed by author for poet Michael Benedikt. Between the Covers Rare Books, Inc. 187 - 150 2015 $250

L'Estrange, Roger *Discovery Upon Discovery, in Defence of Doctor Oates Against B. W.'s Libellous Vindication of Him...* London: printed for Henry Brome at the Gun in St. Paul's church-yard, 1680. 4to., very good in recent plain wrappers. John Drury Rare Books 2015 - 18465 2015 $221

L'Estrange, Roger *A Further Discovery of the Plot: Dedicated to Dr. Titus Oates.* London: printed for Henry Brome at the Gun in St. Pauls Church-yard, 1680. First edition, 4to., including final ad leaf, neatly bound recently in cloth lettered gilt, very good. John Drury Rare Books March 2015 - 18463 2015 $266

L'Estrange, Roger *L'Estrange His Appeal Humbly Submitted to the Kings Most Excellent Majesty and the Three Estates Assembled in Parliament.* London: printed for Henry Brome at the Gun in S. Pauls Church-yard, 1681. First edition, 4to., some general light browning and paper discoloration, tiny old burn-hole in E3 without loss of lettering, but good copy neatly bound recently in cloth lettered in gilt. John Drury Rare Books March 2015 - 18462 2015 £306

L'Estrange, Roger *A Short Answer to a Whole Litter of Libels.* London: printed by J. B. for Hen. Brome at the Gun at the West End of St. Pauls, 1680. First edition, variant issue, 4to., good, well margined, neatly bound recently in cloth lettered in gilt. John Drury Rare Books March 2015 - 18454 2015 £306

L'Estrange, Roger *Sir Roger L'Estrange's Fables with Morals and Reflections in English Verse.* London: printed by M. Jenour for Thomas Harbin, 1717. First edition, engraved frontispiece, 8vo., contemporary panelled calf, rebacked, later brown morocco label (rubbed, corners worn, short crack in lower joint), wanting flyleaf at front, inner margin of plate crudely strengthened, very slightly affecting image, otherwise sound, ownership inscription of Henry White of Lichfield, dated Feb. 1 1722, later signature of Charles V. Green dated 1870. C. R. Johnson Foxon R-Z - 926r-z 2015 $2298

La Condamine, Charles Marie De 1701-1774 *Relation Abregee d'un Voyage Fait dans l'Interieur de l'Amerique Meridionale, Depuis la Cote de la mer du Sud...* Maestricht: Chez Jean Edme Dufour & Philippe Roux, imprimeurs libraires associes, 1778. Nouvelle edition, 2 folded leaves of plates, folding plate, folding map, reinforced contemporary cloth and paper wrappers, unopened (uncut) and untrimmed copy, bound in leaves from 1795 edition, covered in cloth, split to front cloth at joint, small tears to temporary binding, plates and first and last signatures detached, soiling along fore edge as expected. Kaaterskill Books 19 - 77 2015 $750

La Farge, Oliver *Long Pennant.* Boston: Houghton Mifflin Co., 1933. First edition, very good in dust jacket with some shallow chipping to spine ends and two inch closed tear ato edge of rear panel, scarce. Buckingham Books March 2015 - 15807 2015 $175

La Fayette, Marie Madeleine Ploche De La Vergne, Comtesse De *The Princess of Cleves.* London: R. Bentley and M. Magnes, 1679. First edition in English, octavo, period style full mottled calf. Honey & Wax Booksellers 3 - 13 2015 $5000

La Motte Fouque, Friedrich Heinrich Karl, Freiherr De 1777-1843 *Undine.* London & New York: W. Heinemann/Doubleday Page & Co., 1909. First edition, 4to., original blue cloth, lettered gilt on spine and front cover, 15 mounted plates by Arthur Rackham, with tissue guards, very slight rubbing and slightly sunned at spine, otherwise sound, very good, excellent condition, text and plates very clean. Any Amount of Books 2015 - C11998 2015 £220

La Motte Fouque, Friedrich Heinrich Karl, Freiherr De 1777-1843 *Undine.* London and New York: Heinemann & Doubleday, 1909. First American edition, 4to., cloth backed pictorial boards, edges slightly rubbed, else near fine in slightly worn dust jacket, 14 beautiful tipped in color plates mounted on heavy paper, pictorial endpapers and with lovely line illustrations in text by Arthur Rackham, nice. Aleph-bet Books, Inc. 109 - 406 2015 $600

La Presele, Jacques *Album D'Images.* Paris: Chez Alphonse Leduc, 1931. Numbered limited edition, folio, paper over boards, fine, illustrations by Andre Helle, rare. Aleph-Bet Books, Inc. 108 - 235 2015 $775

La Rive, Auguste De *Discours sur l'Instruction Publique de Geneve, Prononce le 13 Aout 1838 183 1840 a la Ceremonie des Promotions.* Geneva: imprimerie de Ferd. Ramboz 40, 1838. 3 reports in one volume, lower margins of texts cut close with perhaps 5 leaves cropped with loss or partial loss of last lines, well bound in recent cloth, lettered gilt. John Drury Rare Books March 2015 - 17871 2015 $266

La Roche De Maine, Jean Pierre Louis De, Marquis *Essai sur la Secte des Illumines.* Paris: 1789. First edition, variant issue, 8vo., old library blindstamped on few leaves (not title), contemporary calf backed marbled boards, some wear to sides but good copy, sometime neatly rebacked, formerly in the library of Herbert Somerton Foxwell (1849-1936) with his initialled note of purchase Dec. 1892 and initialled confirmation of authorship.   John Drury Rare Books   2015 - 17953   2015 $612

Labaume, Eugene   *Sketches of the Horrors of War, Chiefly Selected from Labaume's Narrative of the Campaign in Russia in 1812.*   London: printed by Bensely and Sons, 1818. First edition, 8vo., 24 pages, recent plain wrappers, good copy.   John Drury Rare Books   2015 - 16453   2015 $89

The Labor Student.   New York: Rand School of Social Science, 1925. Self wrappers, volume I no. I, very good, chipping and tearing near spine, printed subscription card laid in, 8vo.   Beasley Books   2013 - 2015 $45

Laborde, Guy   *Ecole De Patience, La Guerre Vue Par Chas. Laborde.*   Monaco: A La Voile Latine, 1951. No. 276 of 381 copies, unbound signatures laid into wrappers, illustrations by Charles Laborde, including 5 full page color illustrations, 4to., fine chemise and slipcase.   Beasley Books   2013 - 2015 $350

Labriola, A.   *Essays on the Materialistic conception of History.*   Chicago: Charles H. Kerr, n.d., First edition, very good, dark blue cloth.   Beasley Books   2013 - 2015 $45

Lacouture, Charles   *Repertoire Chromatique.*   Paris: Gauthier Villars et Fils Imprimeurs Libraires de Bureau des Longitudes de l'Ecole Polytechnique, 1890. First and only edition, large 4to., chromolithograph frontispiece, 28 chromolithograph plates, transparent printed overlay to each plate and separate accompanying printed card screen, uncut and partly unopened in modern red morocco backed cloth, spine lettered gilt, preserving original buff wrappers, head of spine cracked but holding, minor tears to edges, fine, inscribed by author to W. Berthold, scarce.   Marlborough Rare Books   List 54 - 48   2015   £650

Lacroix, Arda   *Billy the Kid. A Romantic Story Founded Upon the Play of the Same Name.*   New York: J. S. Ogilvie Pub. Co., 1907. First edition, 12mo., pictorial wrappers, frontispiece, pages uniformly browned, light wear to spine ends, else very good.   Buckingham Books   March 2015 - 31139   2015 $750

Lacroix, Georges   *Chacun Son Chat.*   Paris: Edition Fantome Diffusion Glenat, 1987. First edition, limited edition, no. 88 of 350, 4to. original grey cloth, lettered white on spine and cover in gray printed slipcase, Ronald Searle's copy, loosely inserted is card from publisher saying 'examplaire pour R. Searle".   Any Amount of Books   2015 - A99118   2015   £175

Lacroix, Jean Francois De   *Dictionnaire Historique Portatif des Femmes Celebres.*   Paris: Cellot, 1769. First edition, 12mo., contemporary calf, stamped in gilt, little light foxing and toning, very good set.   Second Life Books Inc.   190 - 25   2015 $2500

Lactantius   *Des Divines Institutions Contre Les Gentils & Idolatres.*   Lyon: Imprime par Balthazar Arnoullet (pour) Guillaume Gaseau, 1547. 127 x 89mm., without final blank, striking contemporary French calf in Entrelac style, covers with complex strapwork pattern tooled in gilt and painted black and white, design comprising borders, interlaced squares and complex scalloped and spade-like panels with green painted oval at center, original flat diapered spine with each lozenge enclosing a thick dot (covers and spine remounted in 19th century), all edges gilt, titlepage with large woodcut printer's device, historiated opening initial showing a scholar with book and a number of foliated initials throughout, early ink inscription "Bavet?) on titlepage, frequent underlinings and marginal annotations in neat contemporary hand; paint in strapwork decoration slightly eroded in spots, leaves with overall faint yellowing, isolated minor marginal stains or foxing, one page with ink blot obscuring one word, other trivial imperfections, still extremely appealing, splendid animated contemporary binding solid, bright and with only minor wear, nothing approaching significant problem internally.   Phillip J. Pirages   66 - 9   2015 $12,500

Ladies Floral Cabinet.   1882-1884. September 1882 - July 1884, wrappers, 16 issues, broken run, mostly very good or better, but one issue has split spine and final issue has fragile wrappers with piece missing from rear wrapper corner.   Beasley Books   2013 - 2015 $150

Ladies of California   *California Recipe Book.*   San Francisco: Cubery & Co. Steam Book and Job Printers, 1875. First edition thus and third edition overall, 8vo., buff paper wrappers printed in red, sewn, some modest wear, soiling and age toning to wrappers, half inch paper loss from spine bottom, occasional pencil check mark in margin, very good+, rare.   Tavistock Books   Bah, Humbug? - 11   2015 $1500

Ladies' Society Book for Promoting the Early Education of Negro Children.   London: printed by Edward Suter for the Ladies' Society for Promoting the Early Education of Negro Children, 1833. Folio, 6 aquatints, 20th century gray morocco, gilt title on front board, hand lettered titlepage, plus 12 leaves, tipped onto stubs and last leaf of text in facsimile, few spots on front board, else near fine, internally fine and bright.   Between the Covers Rare Books   197 - 67   2015 $65,000

Lafitau, Joseph Francois *Customs of the American Indians Compared with the Customs of Primitive Times.* Toronto: Champlain Society, 1974. 1977. Limited to 750 copies, this #498, 2 volumes, red cloth with gilt to spine, 8vo., frontispiece, 21 black and white plates, 1 map, both volumes fine.   Schooner Books Ltd.   110 - 177   2015 $150

Lafitau, Joseph Francois *Historie des Decouvertes et Conquestes des Portgais dans le Nouveau Monde...* Paris: chez Saugrain pere, quai des Augustins, au oin de la rue Pavee, a la Fleur de Ls Jean Baptiste Coignard fils, imprimeur du Roi, rue S. Jacques, a la Bible d'Or, 1733. First edition, 14 engraved plates, 1 folding map, 4to., modern full speckled calf to style, five raised bands, red morocco labels, gilt rules and titles, very good, small repair to titlepage on volume 1, some occasional browning, few tiny marginal wormholes, few small marginal chips, text and plates sharp, fine period style binding.   Kaaterskill Books   19 - 79   2015 $2950

Laforgue, Ren *The Relativity of Reality.* New York: NMD Pub., 1940. First edition, paper covered boards, fine.   Beasley Books   2013 - 2015 $45

Lake Superior Transit Company. Courier Co., 1881. pictorial wrappers, foldout map attached to front wrapper, illustrations, front wrapper lightly soiled, interior clean.   Buckingham Books   March 2015 - 35006   2015 $1025

Lama, G. De *Vita Del. Cavaliere Giambattista Bodoni, Tipografo Italiano E Catalogo Delle sur Edizioni.* Parma: Stamperia Ducale, 1816. First edition, tall 8vo., 20th century quarter parchment with parchment tips, 2 volumes bound as 1, frontispieces, some bowing of covers.   Oak Knoll Books   306 - 183   2015 $1250

Lamartine, Alphonse De *History of the French Revolution of 1848.* London: Henry G. Bohn, 1849. First English edition, half title, frontispiece, original dark green cloth, as on endpapers, bookplate of James Johnston, very good.   Jarndyce Antiquarian Booksellers   CCXI - 171   2015   £65

Lamartine, Alphonse De *The Wanderer and His Home.* London: Simms & McIntyre, 1851. Unopened in original green printed boards, ads on endpapers, very good, attractive copy.   Jarndyce Antiquarian Booksellers   CCXI - 172   2015   £180

Lamb, Martha J. *Magazine of American History with Notes and Queries.* New York: Historical Publication Co., 1885-1890. Volumes XIV to XXIV, together 11 consecutive volumes, well illustrated, three quarter dark brown morocco, black cloth sides, gilt decorated and lettered spines, some minor extremity rubbing, fine set.   Argonaut Book Shop   Holiday Season 2014 - 156   2015 $900

Lambert, Anne Therese De Marguenat De Courcelles, Marchioness De *Reflexions Nouvelles sur Les Femmes...* Londres: Paris or The Hague? Chez J. P. Coderc in Little New-port Street, 1730. First edition, 12mo., title printed in red and black engraved armorial bookplate "Sir William Purves-Hume-Campbell" (6th Baronet 1767-1833), early mottled calf, rubbed along extremities, very nice clean copy, with errata slip.   Second Life Books Inc.   189 - 150   2015 $2200

Lambert, Fred *Bunkhouse Tales of Wild Horse Charley and Other Epic Poems of the Cow Country.* Lambert & Brown, 1931. First edition, stiff printed wrappers, (58) pages, numerous illustrations, wrappers very good, internally fine, very scarce.   Buckingham Books   March 2015 - 37439   2015 $275

Lampden, Charles Dudley *O'Callaghan the Slave Trader.* London: Digby Long & Co., 1901. First edition, octavo, 4 inserted plates, illustrations by C. Dudley Tennant, original pictorial olive green bevel edged cloth, front and spine panels stamped in red, white and black, brown dark green and gold, publisher's monogram stamped in blind on rear panel, all edges untrimmed.   L. W. Currey, Inc.   Boy's Adventure Fiction 2015 - 29   2015 $275

Lamszus, Wilhelm *The Human Slaughter House: Scenes from the War that is Sure to Come.* New York: Frederick A. Stokes Co., 1913. First American edition, some modest sunning and slight erosion on paper covered boards, finger smudging on one leaf, very good in near very good dust jacket with several modest chips and tears and slight sunning on spine, scarce, especially in jacket.   Between the Covers Rare Books   196 - 155   2015 $300

The Lancashire Domesday Studies: The Lancashire Domesday: Folios and Maps, Domesday Book - Lancashire County Folio. London: Alecto Historical Editions, 1987. First edition, limited edition, 358 of 1000, 3 volumes, folios, maps and text, in slipcase, 3 large colored folding maps in front pocket, faint mark of map volume, else all very good+ in very good slipcase.   Any Amount of Books   2015 - A77233   2015   £160

Lancaster, Bill *The Thing.* Universal City: Universal Pictures, 1981. 2nd draft screenplay for the 1982 film, working copy belonging to uncredited crew member Jim Elkins with his name in holograph ink on front wrapper.   Royal Books   46 - 10   2015 $1250

Land. Llandogo: Old Stile Press, 1996. 133/240 copies, signed by artist Garrick Palmer, printed on Zerkall mould-made paper with text on cream and the 14 wood engravings on white, oblong 4to., original boards, additional engraving to front, backstrip lettered in terracotta, edges untrimmed, cloth slipcase with insert paper label, fine.   Blackwell's Rare Books   B179 - 200   2015   £150

Lander, Nicholas *Harry's Bar, London.* London: Harley Publishing, n.d., 2005. Member's edition, 4to., copiously illustrated in color and black and white, fine in fine dust jacket and box.   Any Amount of Books   2015 - A67393   2015   £160

Lander, Richard *Journal of an Expedition to explore the Course and Termination of the Niger...* London: John Murray, 1832. First edition, 3 volumes, 8vo., plates and maps, large folding map neat folded and intact, recent half brown morocco over marbled boards, spines lettered and decorated gilt, very occasional light blemish, generally very clean, lovely set.   Any Amount of Books   March 2015 - C6492   2015   £360

Landi, Gaetano *Architectural Decorations...* London: pub. Jan. 1 1810 by the proprietor G. Landi and sold by Thos. King..., 1810. Folio, engraved title, 24 hand colored enagraved and aquatint plates, on John Whatman paper, first 6 plates with edge chips and soiling and plate 16 with long tear, disbound.   Marlborough Rare Books   List 54 - 49   2015   £8500

Landon, Herman *The Room Under the Stairs.* New York: Watt, 1923. First edition, very good, fine in very good dust jacket with large closed tear and nicks at corners and along edges.   Mordida Books   March 2015 - 0001287   2015 $165

Lane-Poole, Stanley *Islam. A Prelection Delivered Before the University of Dublin March 10 1903.* Dublin: Hodges, Figgis & Co., 1903. First edition, 8vo., recently well bound in cloth lettered in gilt, very good.   John Drury Rare Books   2015 - 18362   2015 $133

Lane, Charles *Lane's Telescopic View of the Ceremony of Her Majesty Opening the Great Exhibition of all Nations.* London: published by C. A. Lane August 15th, 1851. 5 hand colored lithograph pierced panels and back-scene panel, hand colored vignette titled front panel with solo mica glazed peep-hole, measuring 15 x 18.6cm., mounted bellows-style with canvas sides, contained in original patterned slipcase, hand colored decorative label on upper cover, rubbed and faded, some light soiling to front panel of peepshow.   Marlborough Rare Books Ltd.   List 49 - 19   2015   £1650

Lane, Charles *Lane's Telescopic View of the Interior of the Exhibition.* London: published by C. Lane June 3rd, 1851. 8 hand colored lithographic panels and back-scene panel, front panel with hand colored title vignette with peep-hole, without mica lens which is usually missing, measuring 175 x 160mm., extending with paper bellows to c. 900mm., front panel bit soiled.   Marlborough Rare Books Ltd.   List 49 - 20   2015   £1000

Lang, Andrew *Ballads of Books.* London: Longmans, 1885. First edition, half title, title in red and black, uncut in original blue bevelled boards, spine slightly faded, cutting removed from endpaper, ticket of Slatter & Rose, Oxford, top edge gilt, signed by S. C. Rawlinson 1889 and with 3 related ms. insertions, from the library of Geoffrey & Kathleen Tillotson.   Jarndyce Antiquarian Booksellers   CCVII - 355   2015   £85

Lang, Andrew *The Blue Fairy Book.* London: Longmans, 1889. First edition of the first title in Fairy Book Series, 8vo., blue cloth, gilt pictorial cover, all edges gilt, light wear to spine ends and small repair to free endpaper, else near fine, illustrations, beautiful copy.   Aleph-Bet Books, Inc.   108 - 260   2015 $6000

Lang, Andrew *The Blue Poetry Book.* London: Longmans, Green, 1891. First edition, large paper copy, this being #61 of 150 numbered copies, royal 8vo., numerous black and white illustrations by H. J. Ford and Lancelot Speed, parchment backed grey boards, raised bands, lettered in blue, pages unopened, bookplate by Victorian artist Henry John Stock, spine slightly darkened, covers little marked and rubbed at corners, very good.   Peter Ellis, Bookseller   2014 - 016388   2015   £295

Lang, Andrew *The Gold of Fairnilee.* Bristol and London: Arrowsmith & Simpkin, Marshall, n.d. circa, 1880. Number 41 of an unstated limitation (150?), large paper copy, 4to., half parchment paper, brown gilt cloth, top edge gilt, general cover soil and offsetting on blank endpaper, else tight and internally fine, 15 chromolithographs, printed on handmade paper.   Aleph-bet Books, Inc.   109 - 248   2015 $600

Lang, Andrew *The Green Fairy Book.* London: Longmans, Green, 1892. First edition, royal octavo, large paper issue, this copy #41 of 150 numbered copies, numerous black and white illustrations by H. J. Ford, parchment backed grey boards, raised bands, lettered green, bookplate dated 1892 by Victorian Artist Henry John Stock, spine slightly darkened and spotted with snag at top band, covers little marked and rubbed at one corner, some light spotting, very good.   Peter Ellis, Bookseller   2014 - 016389   2015   £295

Lang, Andrew *The Princess Nobody: a Tale of Fairyland.* London: Longmans, Green and Co., n.d., 1884. First edition, 8vo, 286 color printed and 26 sepia illustrations, sound, clean, near very good with clean text, corners and edges little rubbed, cloth chipped at one corner, 2 pages with closed tears at side not affecting text, one sepia illustrations childlishly colored.   Any Amount of Books   2015 - A90263   2015   £280

Lang, John D. *Report of a Visit to some of the Tribes of Indians Located West of the Mississippi.* New York: Mahlon Day & Co., 1843. First edition, 8vo., original printed wrappers, little dusty, few small marginal chips, front wrapper and title creased, internally clean and crisp, very good. M & S Rare Books, Inc. 97 - 144 2015 $250

Lang, Leonora Blanche *The Book of Princes and Princesses.* London: Longmans, 1908. First edition, 8vo., blue cloth with extensive gilt pictorial binding, all edges gilt, few spots on endpaper, else mint in dust jacket (only slightly worn on edges), illustrations by H. J. Ford with 8 color plates plus black and whites and many lovely text illustrations, rare in pictorial wrapper. Aleph-bet Books, Inc. 109 - 247 2015 $900

Lange, Daniel Adolphus *The Isthmus of Suez Canal Question, Viewed in Its Political Bearings.* London: Richardson Brothers, 1859. First edition, 8vo., margins of titlepage and final blank bit soiled, one or two corners torn, minor marginal staining, preserved in recent plain wrappers. John Drury Rare Books 2015 - 18611 2015 $89

Langius, Josephus *Florilegii Magni Seu Polyantheae Floribus Novissimis Sparsae Libri XX.* Lugduni: Sumptibus Viduae Ant. De Harsy & Petri Ravaud, 1620. Editio optima, folio, red and black titlepage, contemporary full vellum with short title inked to spine, some wormholes visible on spine with little internal worming very rarely affecting text, some pages affected by toning, mottling, odd small ink or burn mark, occasional small chip or tear, but no inscriptions or defacements, occasional evidence of old water damage mainly in form of tidemarks and one late gathering (ZZZZZ) has been loosened possibly because of this, with resultant roughened fore-edge, vellum surface of one raised bands somewhat cracked, otherwise still very sturdy, handsome. Any Amount of Books 2015 - C14202 2015 £1050

Langley, Gilbert *The Life and Adventures of Gilbert Langley, Formerly of Serle Street near Lincoln's Inn, Goldsmith....* London: printed and sold by J. Applebee, 1740. First edition, 8vo., titlepage rather dust soiled, 19th century half calf over marbled boards, spine lettered gilt, joints worn or cracked, but good, crisp copy, sometime in the library of Los Angels board of Law (bookplate and faint inkstamp on covers), apparently rare. John Drury Rare Books 2015 - 25918 2015 $2622

Langton, Jane *The Transcendental Murder.* New York: Harper, 1964. First edition, fine with lightly soiled back panel. Mordida Books March 2015 - 001288 2015 $275

Langworthy, Franklin *Scenery of the Plains, Mountains and Mines.* Princeton: Princeton University Press, 1932. Reprinted from original 1855 edition, facsimile of original titlepage, 4 plates, brick cloth lettered and decorated gilt, spine very slightly faded, fine. Argonaut Book Shop Holiday Season 2014 - 158 2015 $75

Lanham, Edwin M. *Sailors Don't Care.* New York: Jonathan Cape and Harrison Smith, 1930. First American edition, contemporary owner name, light rubbing on spine, still easily fine in very attractive, near fine dust jacket with some modest fading to delicate blue on spine, couple of small tears and chips (largest on front panel). Between the Covers Rare Books 196 - 86 2015 $600

Lanier, Virginia *Death in Bloodhound Red.* Sarasota: Pineapple, 1995. First edition, very fine in dust jacket. Mordida Books March 2015 - 001291 2015 $200

Lansdale, Joe R. *Cold in July.* New York: Bantam Books, 1989. First edition, inscribed on titlepage and signed on dedication page by author, black back cover lightly rubbed, else near fine in pictorial wrappers. Buckingham Books March 2015 - 2466 2015 $225

Lansdale, Joe R. *God of the Razor.* Holyoke: Crossroads Press, 1992. Super limited edition, this copy "A-23/23" and is not only signed by Lansdale, but also signed by 8 artists, S. Clay Wilson, Elman Brown, A. C. Farley, Mark Masztal, Mark Nelson, Timothy Truman and Michael Zulli, stamp of another author inside front cover, fine, stapled wrappers, extremely rare edition. Ken Lopez, Bookseller 164 - 106 2015 $375

Lansdale, Joe R. *Jonah Hex: Riders of the Worm and Such.* New York: DC Comics, 1995. First edition, complete five part series, each issue signed by author, fine in stapled wrappers. Ken Lopez, Bookseller 164 - 109 2015 $150

Lansdale, Joe R. *Jonah Hex: Two-Gun Mojo.* New York: DC Comics August - December, 1993. Complete five part series in comic book form, signed by Lansdale in gold ink on front cover, fine in stapled wrappers, uncommon, scarce signed. Ken Lopez, Bookseller 164 - 107 2015 $150

Lansdale, Joe R. *The Long Ranger and Tonto: "It Crawls" Parts 1-4.* New York: Topps Comics, 1994. First edition, complete in 4 volumes, each signed by author, fine in stapled wrappers, scarce in original parts, especially signed. Ken Lopez, Bookseller 164 - 108 2015 $150

Lansdale, Joe R. *Mucho Mojo.* Baltimore: CD Publications, 1994. Limited numbered edition, one of 400 numbered copies, signed by author and artist, Mark Nelson, very fine in dust jacket. Mordida Books March 2015 - 00742 2015 $85

Lansdale, Joe R. *Texas Night Riders.* Burton: Subterranean, 1997. Copy 346 of 500 copies, signed by author as both Lansdale and Slater and signed by Mark Nelson who provided jacket art, fine in fine dust jacket. Ken Lopez, Bookseller 164 - 110 2015 $150

Larbaud, Valery *Ridasedirad les Dicmhypbdf.* New York: Adventures in Poetry, 1973. First edition, one of 250 copies, 4to., original wrappers with cover illustration by Lindsay Stamm Shapiro, inscribed by Padgett for Britton, fine. James S. Jaffe Rare Books   Many Happy Returns - 197   2015 $250

Lardner, Ring *Bib Ballads.* Chicago: Volland, 1915. 4to., brown cloth stamped in gold and white, fine, illustrations in color by Fontaine Fox, scarce, Ring Lardner's signature laid in.   Aleph-Bet Books, Inc.   108 - 261   2015 $750

Larguier, Leo *Les Ilots Insalubres et Glorieux De Paris.* Paris: Les Editions Du Laurier Noir, 1946. #216 of 300 copies, unbound signatures laid into wrappers, photos by Max Del and companion woodcuts by Louis Jou, fine in fine decorated wrappers, chemise and slightly soiled box.   Beasley Books   2013 - 2015 $375

Larmor, Joseph *Memoir and Scientific correspondence of the Late Sir George Gabriel Stokes Selected and Arranged by Joseph Larmor.* Cambridge: Cambridge University Press, 1907. First edition, volume I only of 2 volume set, 8vo., gravure frontispiece, 2 additional plates, some handwritten pen corrections, green cloth, gilt stamped spine title, extremities rubbed, front hinge bit cracked, still strong and tight, very good, quite scarce.   Jeff Weber Rare Books   178 - 1046   2015 $100

Larochejaquelein, Marie Louise Victoire *Memoirs of the Marchioness De Larochejaquelein.* Edinburgh: printed by George Ramsay and Co. for Archibald Constable and Co. and Longman, London, 1816. First edition in English, 8vo., folding partly colored engraved map, half title, well bound in old boards, newly rebacked with original printed label reused, entirely uncut, very good.   John Drury Rare Books   March 2015 - 22559   2015   £306

Larsson, Steig *The Girl with the Dragon Tattoo. The Girl Who Kicked the Hornet's Nest. The Girl Who Played with Fire.* London: Maclehose/Quercus, 2008. 2009. First UK editions, 3 volumes, each fine and unread in fine dust jacket, without trace of wear to spine bumping endemic to these titles, second volume signed by translator Reg Keeland on titlepage, incredible set, from the collection of Duke Collier.   Royal Books   36 - 4   2015 $5000

Larteguy, Jean *Presumed Dead.* Boston: Little Brown, 1976. Uncorrected proof of the first American edition, near fine in wrappers with short tear at upper front joint.   Ken Lopez, Bookseller   164 - 225   2015 $75

Lartigue, J. H. *Les Femmes.* New York: Dutton, 1974. First US edition, small 4to., fine in very good dust jacket with short tears at head of spine.   Beasley Books   2013 - 2015 $125

Lascelles, Mary Madge *Jane Austen and Her Art.* Oxford: Clarendon Press, 1939. Half title, original dark blue cloth, slightly marked, Kathleen Tillotson's signed copy with her friend's presentation slip.   Jarndyce Antiquarian Booksellers   CCVII - 80   2015   £40

Lashley, K. S. *Brain Mechanisms and Intelligence.* Chicago: University of Chicago Press, 1929. First edition, near fine with barely perceptible rubbing at extremities, owner's name on f.e.p. and remains of bookseller's label at foot of rear pastedown, large 8vo.   Beasley Books   2013 - 2015 $150

The Last Run. Kay County, Oklahoma 1893. Ponca City: Ponca City Chapter DAR, 1939. First edition, silver stamped pictorial cloth, 4to., illustrations, minor cover wear, first 50 pages in front of book with moderate to mild vertical crease (from bindery?) down middle but certainly very good, minor cover wear, scarce edition.   Baade Books of the West   2014 - 2015 $50

Lathen, Emma *When in Greece.* New York: Simon & Schuster, 1969. First edition, inscribed to Sam and Barbara Sebastiani of Sebastiani Vineyard and signed by Mary (Latsis) and Martha (Heinissard), actual names of Emma Lathem, fine in dust jacket.   Mordida Books   March 2015 - 010666   2015 $100

Latimer, Hugh, Bp. of Worcester *The Sermons of... Many of Which were Preached Before King Edward VI...* printed for J. Scott, 1758. First collected edition, 2 volumes, engraved frontispiece in each volume, 1 engraved plate, one gathering in volume i foxed, 8vo., contemporary polished calf panelled in gilt, spines gilt in compartments with dolphin within crowned circle, red lettering pieces numbered in gilt direct, 3 later inkstamps on flyleaves, very good, very attractive, fairly scarce.   Blackwell's Rare Books   B179 - 62   2015   £800

Latimer, Jonathan *The Mink-Lined Coffin.* London: Methuen, 1960. First edition, spotting on top of page edges, otherwise fine in dust jacket.   Mordida Books   March 2015 - 005275   2015 $135

Latimer, Jonathan *Red Gardenias.* New York: Doubleday Doran & Co., 1939. First edition, light offsetting to front and rear endpapers lightly soiled, else very good, tight copy, bright, unfaded dust jacket with some minor internal professional restoration.   Buckingham Books   March 2015 - 30951   2015 $650

Latimer, Jonathan *Solomon's Vineyard.* Santa Barbara: Neville, 1982. First American edition, one of 300 numbered copies signed by Latimer, very fine without dust jacket.   Mordida Books   March 2015 - 007427   2015 $100

Latimer, Jonathan *Solomon's Vineyard.* Santa Barbara: Neville, 1982. First American edition, one of 26 lettered leather bound numbered copies signed by author, very fine, without dust jacket.   Mordida Books   March 2015 - 010671   2015 $300

Latimore, Sarah Briggs *Arthur Rackham: a Bibliography.* Los Angeles: Suttonhouse, 1936. First edition, number 274 of 500 numbered copies for sale, color frontispiece, photo portrait, illustrations by Arthur Rackham, cloth backed decorated boards, spine slightly faded, else fine, publisher's slipcase, original printed announcement laid in.   Argonaut Book Shop   Holiday Season 2014 - 234   2015 $250

Lauderdale, James Maitland, 8th Earl of   1759-1839 *An Inquiry Into the Nature and Origin of Public Wealth and Into the means and Causes of Its Increase.* Edinburgh: Archibald Constable & Co., 1804. First edition, 8vo., without half title but with folding table, occasional minor foxing and few insignificant rust marks, contemporary half calf over marbled board, spine simply gilt with red morocco lettering piece, very good, binder's ticket of J. Tushingham of Chester.   John Drury Rare Books   2015 - 26228   2015 $1136

Laurie, David *A Treatise on Finance Under Which the General Interests of the British Empire are Illustrated.* Glasgow: printed by R. Chapman Trongate, 1815. 8vo., complete with half title, contemporary calf over marbled boards, sides rubbed, corners worn, neatly rebacked and lettered, very good, cancelled inkstamp of Chartered Accountants on blank margin of title, contemporary ink inscription ownership of His Royal Highness the Duke of Clarence.   John Drury Rare Books   2015 - 20100   2015 $1049

Laurie, J. S. *Sketches of Political Economy.* London: Thos. Murby and Simpkin Marshall & Co., 1864. First edition, small 8vo., original embossed cloth, very good.   John Drury Rare Books   2015 - 5679   2015 $89

Lauritzen, Jonreed *Arrows into the Sun.* New York: Alfred A. Knopf, 1943. First edition, fine in dust jacket with light wear to extremities.   Buckingham Books   March 2015 - 366   2015 $250

Lauterbach, Ann *A Clown, Some Colors, A Doll, Her Stories, A Song, A Moonlit Cove.* New York: Whitney Museum of American Art, 1995. One of 120 copies, printed by Leslie Miller at Grenfell Press, only 30 copies for sale, signed by poet and artist, 4to., accordion fold, 13 original photogravures by Ellen Phelan, original cloth and Japanese tea-chest paper, folding box, separate portfolio with additional signed hand colored print.   James S. Jaffe Rare Books   Modern American Poetry - 175   2015 $2750

Lauterbach, Ann *Later That Evening.* New York: Jordan Davies, 1981. First edition, one of 20 copies printed on Canterbury paper and bound in boards, out of a total edition of 230, signed by Lauterbach, thin 8vo., original cloth backed boards, fine.   James S. Jaffe Rare Books   Modern American Poetry - 173   2015 $250

Lauterbach, Ann *Sacred Weather.* New York: Grenfell Press, 1984. First edition, one of only 15 lettered copies printed on Chatham paper, especially bound, signed by poet and by artist, out of a total edition of 130 copies, small narrow 4to., titlepage drawing by Louisa Chase, original quarter morocco and decorated boards.   James S. Jaffe Rare Books   Modern American Poetry - 174   2015 $500

Lauterbach, Ann *Thripsis.* Calais: Z Press, 1998. First edition, one of 26 lettered copies signed by Lauterbach out of a total edition of 226 copies (only the lettered copies being signed), 8vo., original wrappers with printed label, as new.   James S. Jaffe Rare Books   Modern American Poetry - 176   2015 $350

Lautreamont, Comte De *Oeuvres Completes.* Paris: GLM, 1938. First edition thus, one of 1000 numbered copies on velin bibliophile, out of a total edition of 1120, octavo, wrappers, head of spine scuffed and defective, spine creased and darkened very good, illustrations.   Peter Ellis, Bookseller   2014 - 008141   2015   £300

Lavrentiev, Alexander *Alexander Rodchenko: Revolution in Photography.* Moscow: Pub. by Multimedia Complex of Actual Arts, 2008. First edition, 4to., copiously illustrated in color and black and white throughout, fine in fine dust jacket.   Any Amount of Books   2015 - A93152   2015   £160

Law, John *The Antient (Ancient) and Modern State of the Parish of Cramond...* Edinburgh: John Paterson, 1794. First edition, 4to., recently rebound in half green leather, marbled boards, lettered gilt on spine, map, 3 folding pedigree charts and 8 plates as called for, very good.   Any Amount of Books   March 2015 - A88255   2015   £350

Lawrance, Hannah *The History of Woman in England and Her Influence on Society and Literature from the Earliest Period Volume I. to the Year 1200.* London: Henry Colburn, 1843. First edition, frontispiece, slight foxing in prelims, uncut, original purple cloth by Orger & Meryon, blocked in blind, gilt vignette of flower centre panel of front board, spine and edges faded to brown, slight rubbing with small nick to leading edge, bibliographical pencil notes, nice.   Jarndyce Antiquarian Booksellers   CCXI - 173   2015   £250

Lawrence, David Herbert   1885-1930 *England, My England.* London: Martin Secker, 1924. First edition, nearly fine.   Stephen Lupack   March 2015 - 2015 $100

Lawrence, David Herbert 1885-1930 *Fig.* Octon: Verdigris Press, 2001. One of 48 copies, on Hahnemuhle paper each signed and numbered by artist, Judith Rothchild, page size 11 1/4 x 10 3/4 inches, 32 pages, bound loose in Somerset Velvet black paper wrappers with green silkscreens, title on front panel and on spine with author and artist's name, handset in Vendome and printed by Mark Lintott on an Albion Press and a Stanhope Press, slipcase and box by Claude Vallin with silkscreens by Rothchild, fine. Priscilla Juvelis - Rare Books   61 - 54   2015 $1100

Lawrence, David Herbert 1885-1930 *A Modern Lover.* London: Martin Secker, 1934. First edition, nearly fine. Stephen Lupack   March 2015 - 2015 $125

Lawrence, David Herbert 1885-1930 *New Poems.* London: Martin Secker, 1919. New edition (reset), paper covered boards with applied spine label, bit of wear to extremities of boards, else near fine, Roger Senhouse's copy with his tiny ownership signature and bookplate. Between the Covers Rare Books, Inc.   187 - 151   2015 $200

Lawrence, David Herbert 1885-1930 *The Paintings of D. H. Lawrence.* London: Mandrake Press, 1929. First edition, one of 500 numbered copies of a total edition of 510, 15 oil paintings and 11 watercolors reproduced, all in color, half leather buckram covers, letterpress and color work supervised by William Dieper, top edge gilt, laid in is publisher's prospectus for the book, spine just little scuffed, small mark at outer edge of upper cover, near fine.   Peter Ellis, Bookseller   2014 - 011348   2015   £325

Lawrence, David Herbert 1885-1930 *Pansies.* London: Martin Secker, 1929. First edition, no. 16 of 250 copies, signed, 8vo., one very short closed tear to edge of third contents page not affecting text, otherwise fine in fine dust jacket, exceptional copy.   Any Amount of Books   2015 - A93094   2015   £750

Lawrence, David Herbert 1885-1930 *Sex Literature and Censorship.* London: Heinemann, 1955. First edition, very good plus, some foxing to endpapers and fore edges, very good+ dust jacket (foxing on rear panel, price clipped). Stephen Lupack   March 2015 - 2015 $45

Lawrence, David Herbert 1885-1930 *Tortoises.* Williamsburg: Cheloniidae Press, 1983. One of 10 deluxe copies bound in full vellum with extra suite, original pencil drawing of "Tortoise Shout" all on Fabriano Perusia, from a total issue of 310 copies, signed by artist, Alan James Robinson, on colophon page and on the original etch portrait of Lawrence as well as on each of the seven individual wood engravings in extra suite and drawing, page size 11 x 8 inches, text was set by Winifred and Michael Bixler in Centaur and Arrighi and some additional hand composition by Art Larson and printed by Harold McGrath, bound by Gray Parrot, full vellum, housed in tan cloth clamshell box with vellum spine, extra suite of wood engravings and drawing in portfolio laid in to clamshell box with book, fine. Priscilla Juvelis - Rare Books   62 - 2   2015 $3500

Lawrence, David Herbert 1885-1930 *Women in Love.* New York: privately printed for subscribers, 1920. One of 1250 numbered copies, original blue cloth, lightly rubbed, minor toning to spine, front hinge cracked and secure, rear hinge slightly cracked, internally very clean and tight copy, without any of the usual repairs.   B & B Rare Books, Ltd.   234 - 66   2015 $1100

Lawrence, Miriam B. *Flowers & Plants on United States Postage Stamps.* East Greenwich: River's Edge Studio, 1970. Limited to 500 numbered copies, 200 bound in full leather with all edges gilt, of which this copy is one, 16 postage stamps with botanical themes tipped in with descriptive text, 6 x 8.5cm., full green leather, title gilt stamped on spine and front board, all edges gilt.   Oak Knoll Books   306 - 116   2015 $225

The Laws of Love. A Complete Code of Gallantry. New York: Dick & Fitzgerald 1870's, 12mo., original pale green glazed printed wrappers, with engraved vignette, wrappers bit worn and soiled, some light dampstains at edges throughout, still, good, above average copy.   M & S Rare Books, Inc.   97 - 161   2015 $350

Lawson, O. E. *The Canadian Provost Corps Silver Jubilee 1940-1965.* Ottawa: Director of Security Canadian Forces Headquarters, 1965. 8vo., blue cloth with silver titles and insignia to front, 8vo., photo illustrations, very good. Schooner Books Ltd.   110 - 151   2015 $50

Lawson, Robert *They Were Strong and Good.* New York: Viking, September, 1940. First edition, 4to., cloth, fine in dust jacket (not price clipped, no award medal, with dust soil, light fraying on top edge, overall very good dust jacket), full page black and whites.   Aleph-bet Books, Inc.   109 - 258   2015 $975

Laycock, Thomas *On the Principles and Method of a Practical Science of Mind. A Reply to a Criticism.* London: printed by J. E. Adlard, 1862. First separate edition, 8vo., recently well bound in linen backed marbled board, lettered, very good.   John Drury Rare Books   2015 - 16573   2015 $159

Laycock, Thomas *The Scientific Place.* Edinburgh: printed by Murray and Gibb, 1861. First edition, 8vo., recently well bound in linen backed marbled board, lettered, very good.   John Drury Rare Books   2015 - 16575   2015 $159

Laymon, Richard *Dreadful Tales.* London: Headline, 2000. First edition, inscribed by author to another horror writer Dec. 2 2000, with recipient's bookplate, faint foxing to top edge, else fine in fine dust jacket, very uncommon signed.   Ken Lopez, Bookseller   164 - 112   2015 $350

Laymon, Richard *A Writer's Tale.* Los Gatos: Deadline Press, 1998. Limited edition, copy 350 of 500 numbered copies, signed by author on tipped in half title, bookplate of another author, fine in fine dust jacket with 1999 unopened card from Laymon to recipient laid in.   Ken Lopez, Bookseller   164 - 111   2015 $300

Le Blanc, Maurice *The Eight Strokes of the Clock.* Macaulay Co., 1922. First edition, frontispiece by G. W. Gage, former owner's small stamp in ink on front and rear pastedown sheets, else fine in decorated brown cloth.   Buckingham Books   March 2015 - 37495   2015 $275

Le Carre, John 1931- *Absolute Friends.* London: Hodder & Stoughton, 2003. First edition, very fine in dust jacket, signed by author.   Mordida Books   March 2015 - 009408   2015 $125

Le Carre, John 1931- *Call for the Dead.* New York: Walker, 1962. First American edition, very good plus in like dust jacket, book very slightly cocked, hint of fading at edges, otherwise quite clean, jacket bright with closed tear starting at top of front flap fold and running into middle of front flap, author's uncommon first book, custom clamshell box, from the collection of Duke Collier.   Royal Books   36 - 206   2015 $950

Le Carre, John 1931- *A Delicate Truth.* Viking, 2013. First edition, 8vo., original black boards, backstrip gilt lettered, dust jacket, fine, signed by author on special tipped in leaf printed 'Exclusive Signed Edition, John Le Carre, May 2013".   Blackwell's Rare Books   B179 - 185   2015   £35

Le Carre, John 1931- *A Delicate Truth.* London: Viking, 2013. First edition, very fine in dust jacket, signed by author.   Mordida Books   March 2015 - 012620   2015 $100

Le Carre, John 1931- *The Honourable Schoolboy.* London: Hodder & Stoughton, 1977. First edition, fine in price clipped dust jacket with short crease on inner front flap, first printing with colored map endpapers.   Mordida Books   March 2015 - 001331   2015 $100

Le Carre, John 1931- *The Looking Glass War.* New York: Coward McCann, 1965. First American edition, fine in dust jacket.   Mordida Books   March 2015 - 012703   2015 $100

Le Carre, John 1931- *A Murder of Quality.* New York: Walker, 1963. First American edition, fine in dust jacket with slightly faded spine, exceptional copy, substantial fading to entire dust jacket.   Mordida Books   March 2015 - 008110   2015 $2300

Le Carre, John 1931- *A Murder of Quality.* New York: Walker, 1963. First American edition, signed by author, very good plus in very good plus dust jacket, moderately cocked with some light soil to cloth, jacket bright and unfaded with few tiny stresses at front flap folds, 2 inch closed tear top front panel and light rubbing at extremities, author's uncommon second book, from the collection of Duke Collier, signed by author Christmas 2004.   Royal Books   36 - 203   2015 $3500

Le Carre, John 1931- *The Naive and Sentimental Lover.* London: Hodder & Stoughton, 1971. First edition, fine in price clipped dust jacket.   Mordida Books   March 2015 - 012109   2015 $90

Le Carre, John 1931- *Nervous Times. An Address given at the Savoy at the Annual Dinner of the Anglo-Israel Association on 10 November 1997.* London: Anglo Israel Association, 1998. First edition, limited to 250 numbered copies signed by author, very fine, quarter leather and marbled boards, frontispiece.   Buckingham Books   March 2015 - 11886   2015 $275

Le Carre, John 1931- *Our Game.* London: Hodder & Stoughton, 1995. Correct first edition of about 1000 copies which was exported overseas and not available for sale in the Uk, very fine in dust jacket.   Mordida Books   March 2015 - 012113   2015 $250

Le Carre, John 1931- *Our Kind of Traitor.* Viking, 2010. First edition, 8vo., original black boards, stamped in gilt to upper board, backstrip lettered in gilt, yellow page marker, matching slipcase, fine, signed by author.   Blackwell's Rare Books   B179 - 186   2015   £45

Le Carre, John 1931- *A Perfect Spy.* London: Hodder & Stoughton, 1986. First edition, uncorrected proof, fine in printed wrappers with dust jacket,.   Mordida Books   March 2015 - 012112   2015 $175

Le Carre, John 1931- *A Perfect Spy.* New York: Knopf, 1986. First American edition, advance review copy with review slip and flyer laid in, very fine in dust jacket.   Mordida Books   March 2015 - 012115   2015 $85

Le Carre, John 1931- *Single and Single.* London: Hodder & Stoughton, 1999. First edition, very fine in printed wrappers, uncorrected proof copy.   Mordida Books March 2015 - 012111   2015 $100

Le Carre, John 1931- *The Spy Who Came in from the Cold.* London: Gollancz, 1963. First UK edition, very good plus in very good plus dust jacket, binding slightly cocked, backstrip and jacket spine, faded, strips of staining top and bottom edge of jacket verso from old jacket protector, with ALS by author discussing development of a new book "Carcass of the Lion" (which would eventually be published as The Spy Who Came in form the Cold), custom clamshell box designed to display book and letter when opened, from the collection of Duke Collier.   Royal Books   36 - 202   2015 $8500

Le Carre, John 1931- *The Spy Who Came in from the Cold.* New York: Coward McCann, 1964. Uncorrected proof, fine in publisher's wrappers, quarter leather clamshell box, from the collection of Duke Collier.   Royal Books   36 - 204   2015 $1500

Le Carre, John 1931- *The Spy Who Came in from the Cold.* Fyfield: Oak Tree Fine Press, 2008. 73/124 copies (from an edition of 150 copies), signed by author, titles, fly-titles and initial letters printed in red, frontispiece tipped-in and signed by artist Stephen Alcorn, 8vo., original quarter red cloth with marbled boards, printed paper label inset to upper board, backstrip lettered gilt, fine.   Blackwell's Rare Books   B179 - 187   2015   £115

Le Carre, John 1931- *The Tailor of Panama.* London: Hodder & Stoughton, 1996. First edition, signed by author, fine in fine dust jacket.   Buckingham Books   March 2015 - 33782   2015 $225

Le Carre, John 1931- *The Tailor of Panama.* New York: Knopf, 1996. First American edition, uncorrected proof copy, fine in slick wrappers,.   Mordida Books   March 2015 - 012117   2015 $100

Le Carre, John 1931- *Three Complete Novels: The Spy Who Came in From the Cold. A Small Town in Germany. The Looking Glass War.* New York: Avenel, 1983. First edition, fine in dust jacket.   Mordida Books   March 2015 - 001337   2015 $75

Le Clezio, J. M. G. *War.* London: Jonathan Cape, 1973. First English edition, 8vo., pages 300, groovy pink jacket by Bill Botten, fine in near fine dust jacket with very short closed tear and very slight rubbing at corners, from the working library of novelist Angela Carter (1940-1992) with her posthumous bookplate.   Any Amount of Books   2015 - C7841   2015   £175

Le Conte, Joseph N. *A Yosemite Camping trip 1889.* Berkeley: University of California, 1990. First edition, scarce, 13 photo reproductions, dark grey-green wrappers printed in black on light green background, very fine.   Argonaut Book Shop   Holiday Season 2014 - 163   2015 $90

Le Gallienne, Richard 1866-1947 *The Lonely Dancer.* New York: John Lane the Bodley Head, 1914. First American edition, near fine, Amita Fairgrieve's copy with her bookplate.   Between the Covers Rare Books, Inc.   187 - 152   2015 $75

Le Guin, Ursula K. *The Dispossessed.* New York: Harper & Row, 1974. First edition, octavo, quarter cloth with boards, signed by author.   John W. Knott, Bookseller Selected New Arrivals Jan. 2015 - 17127   2015 $750

Le Guin, Ursula K. *The Lathe of Heaven.* New York: Charles Scribner's Sons, 1971. First edition, octavo, quarter cloth with boards.   John W. Knott, Bookseller   Selected New Arrivals Jan. 2015 - 17130   2015 $850

Le Guin, Ursula K. *The Left Hand of Darkness.* New York: Walker and Co., 1969. First edition, octavo, title leaf from paperback copy signed by author.   John W. Knott, Bookseller   Selected New Arrivals Jan. 2015 - 17126   2015 $3500

Le May, Alan *The Searchers.* New York: Harper Bros., 1954. First edition, first printing dentoed by H-D on copyright page, very good, closed tear at spine top, in very good dust jacket (some chips, some general wear and tear).   Stephen Lupack   March 2015 - 2015 $75

Le Queux, William *Guilty Bonds.* New York: Collins, 1892. First American hardcover edition, very good in soft covers.   Mordida Books   March 2015 - 003118   2015 $100

Le Queux, William *The Lady in the Car.* London: Eveleigh Nash, 1908. First edition, 8vo., original blue cloth, titles in gold gilt on front cover and spine, moderate rubbing to cloth, vertical crease to spine panel, else good, very scarce.   Buckingham Books   March 2015 - 32073   2015 $175

Le Queux, William *Of Royal Blood.* London: Hutchinson, 1900. First edition, page edges lightly foxed, otherwise fine in pictorial cloth covered boards.   Mordida Books   March 2015 - 008118   2015 $100

Le Queux, William *Poison Shadows.* New York: Macaulay Co., 1927. First US edition, page edges lightly spotted, else very good in lovely bright dust jacket with small closed tear to bottom edge of front panel.   Buckingham Books   March 2015 - 11899   2015 $185

Le Queux, William *Rasputinism in London.* London: Cassell, 1919. First edition, very good, without dust jacket. Mordida Books   March 2015 - 001364   2015 $85

Le Queux, William *The Sting.* New York: Macaulay co., 1928. First US edition, short tear in cloth at head of spine, spine faded, else good copy in gorgeous dust jacket with wonderful pictorial front panel.   Buckingham Books   March 2015 - 10724   2015 $175

Le Sage, Alain Rene   1668-1747 *Les Avantures De Monsieur Robert Cheavlier De Beauchene...* Paris: Chez Etienne Ganeau, 1732. First edition, 2 volumes, 12mo., 6 full page engraved plates by Bonnard in contemporary full calf (hinge strengthened at an early date), spine gilt, one inch split to lower hinge calf of one volume, contemporary owner's notes at extremities of titlepage, some light foxing and staining, very good, signature of Pierre Paul David d'Angers, tear to lower margin of one leaf not affecting any text.   Second Life Books Inc.   190 - 146   2015 $1200

Le Vaillant, Francois *A New and Improved Edition of Histoire Naturelle des Perroquets.* Sydney: Imprime, 1989. Limited to 200 copies, elephant folio, 2 volumes, 144 loose plates, publisher's handsome green cloth solander boxes with colored label, fine set.   Andrew Isles   2015 - 13390   2015 $3500

Lea & Shepard *Trade Catalogue of Illustrated Juvenile Books Published by Lee & Shepard 41-43 franklin Street, Boston...* Boston: Lee & Shepard Pub. n.d., 8vo., original printed grey paper wrappers, sewn, minor wear and soiling, very good+, rare.   Tavistock Books   Bah, Humbug? - 19   2015 $195

Lea, Henry Charles *Materials Toward a History of Witchcraft.* Philadelphia: University of Pennsylvania Press, 1939. First edition, 3 volumes, 8vo., original maroon cloth, lettered gilt on spine, slight rubbing, else very good.   Any Amount of Books   2015 - C1724   2015   £175

Lea, Tom *The Brave Bulls.* Boston: Little Brown and Co., 1949. First edition, color title illustration, text illustrations, pictorial endpapers, all drawn by author, red cloth lettered and stamped in black, fine in pictorial dust jacket, just bit of minor rubbing to jacket, presentation inscription signed by author in his fine calligraphic hand.   Argonaut Book Shop   Holiday Season 2014 - 159   2015 $250

Lea, Tom *The King Ranch.* Boston: Little Brown and Co., 1957. First edition, first issue, 4to., 2 volumes, signed by Lea, fine set in publisher's binding, original publisher's decorated slipcase which shows some wear.   Ed Smith Books   83 - 58   2015 $250

Lea, Tom *Western Beef Cattle: a Series of Eleven Paintings by Tom Lea Depicting the Origin and Development of the Western Range Animal.* Encino Press, 1967. First edition, limited to 850 copies, quarto, cloth, very fine, unread copy in very fine original slipcase.   Buckingham Books   March 2015 - 20497   2015 $375

Leaf, Munro *The Story of Ferdinand.* New York: Viking, Sept., 1936. First edition, first printing, 8vo., cloth backed pictorial boards, near fine, dust jacket with usual sunning to spine, price clipped, with half inch triangular chip off bottom of spine, few archival mends on verso, price erasure, in reality a better than very good dust jacket, signed by Leaf on titlepage, exceedingly scarce signed and in such nice condition.   Aleph-bet Books, Inc.   109 - 254   2015 $10,500

Leaf, Munro *The Story of Ferdinand.* New York: Viking, 1936. First edition, illustrations by Robert Lawson.   Honey & Wax Booksellers   2 - 39   2015 $8500

Leaf, Munro *Wee Gillis.* New York: Viking, 1938. First edition, limited to 525 copies signed by Lawson and Leaf, 4to., burlap covered boards, fine in original slipcase (small pieces missing from endflaps and is rubbed), every page with full page illustration by Robert Lawson.   Aleph-bet Books, Inc.   109 - 257   2015 $600

Lean, Vincent Stuckey *Lean's Collectanea: Collections of Proverbs...* Bristol: J. W. Arrowsmith, 1902. First edition, large 8vo., original white buckram over red cloth boards, lettered gilt at spines, 4 volumes bound in 5, bright, clean, very good+ set, faint surface wear to white buckram at spines with endpapers browned.   Any Amount of Books   2015 - C13518   2015   £240

Leary, Timothy *Interpersonal Diagnosis of Personality.* New York: Ronald Press, 1957. First edition, inscribed by author to his longtime research assistant and later lover, Helen Lane, near fine in very good dust jacket with modest edge wear and few chips at corners, seldom found in jacket at all, equally seldom found signed, excellent association copy.   Ken Lopez, Bookseller   164 - 113   2015 $3500

Leavitt, Nancy Ruth *Puzzle 4.* Stillwater: 2008. Artist's book, one of a series of three, signed by artist, 10 x 3 3.4 x 1 1/8 inches, comprising box with collage puzzle of four pieces, each decorated with paste and found papers and postage stamps, puzzle housed in old pastel box decorated with paper and stamps.   Priscilla Juvelis - Rare Books   61 - 29   2015 $300

Leblanc, Maurice *Arsene Lupin.* London: Mills, 1909. First edition, very good, without dust jacket.   Mordida Books   March 2015 - 001320   2015 $100

Leblanc, Maurice *Arsene Lupin Versus Herlock Sholmes.* New York: Ogilvie, 1910. Reprint edition, very good in soiled pictorial wrappers with some chipping to page edges and scrape on front cover.   Mordida Books   March 2015 - 002666   2015 $100

Leblanc, Maurice *The Golden Triangle: the Return of Arsene Lupin.* New York: Macaulay, 1917. First American edition, near fine, spine slightly faded and name on front endpaper, otherwise near fine in pictorial cloth covered boards without dust jacket.   Mordida Books   March 2015 - 001322   2015 $85

Leckie, William H. *The Buffalo Soldiers.* University of Oklahoma Press, 1967. First edition, original yellow cloth, illustrations, maps, former owner's name stamped on front flyleaf, else fine in moderately rubbed, price clipped dust jacket with light wear to spine ends and extremities.   Buckingham Books   March 2015 - 23055   2015 $175

Lecky, E. *Letter from Old Father Christmas.* London: Raphael Tuck, n.d. circa, 1890. 4to., cloth backed pictorial card covers die-cut in shape of Santa, small corner repaired, else near fine, beautiful chromolithographs by Emily Harding with text inserted on page, very fine, rare.   Aleph-bet Books, Inc.   109 - 93   2015 $650

Lederberg, Joshua *The Excitement and Fascination of Science: Reflections by Eminent Scientists Volume 3 Part 2 (1990).* Palo Alto: Annual reviews, 1990. 8vo., fine hardback, gilt lettering spine and front cover, signed by author.   By the Book, L. C.   Special List 10 - 80   2015 $175

Lederman, Leon *The God Particle.* Boston: Houghton Mifflin, 1993. First edition, 8vo., fine in very good++ dust jacket with mild edge wear, remainder mark lower edge.   By the Book, L. C.   Special List 10 - 59   2015 $200

Leduc, Henri *Le Roman De Renard Tomes I Et II.* Paris: 1944. No. 113 of 1000 copies, 2 volumes, small 4to., wrappers, near fine in near fine wrappers, this copy has separate suite of the prints wrappered in publisher's glassine, all in somewhat soiled box.   Beasley Books   2013 - 2015 $400

Lee, Edwin *The State of the Medical Profession Further Exemplified.* London: W. J. Johnson, 1867. First edition, uncommon, titlepage slightly foxed, inner margin (gutter) repaired, recently well bound in cloth, spine gilt lettered.   John Drury Rare Books   March 2015 - 21410   2015 $266

Lee, Gypsy Rose *Mother Finds a Body.* New York: Simon and Schuster, 1942. First edition, near fine in dust jacket with tiny chipping at spine ends and two chips on front panel, inscribed by author.   Mordida Books   March 2015 - 012658   2015 $250

Lee, Hanna *Memoir of Pierre Toussaint, Born a Slave in St. Domingo.* Boston: Crosby, Nichols and Co., 1854. third edition, octavo, 124 pages, dark brown boards, gilt on spine, frontispiece, foxing to frontispiece, cloth on spine ends worn, tight and attractive, very good copy.   Between the Covers Rare Books   197 - 63   2015 $225

Lee, Harper *To Kill a Mockingbird.* London: Heinemann, 1960. Uncorrected proof of First English edition, printed buff wrappers, housed in custom quarter morocco clamshell case, couple of faint bends and penciled date ('3rd Oct') all on front wrapper, faint crease on rear wrapper, little age toning, but still near fine example of a fragile construction.   Between the Covers Rare Books   196 - 90   2015 $5000

Lee, Harper *To Kill a Mockingbird.* Philadelphia: J. B. Lippincott, 1960. First edition (stated), first printing, one of approximately 5000 copies, original cloth, dust jacket, about fine in very nice example of unclipped first issue dust jacket with Capote and Daniels quotes, jacket shows some light wear with few minor chips to spine ends, few tiny tears and minor creases, very attractive and bright, housed in custom quarter leather clamshell case.   B & B Rare Books, Ltd.   234 - 67   2015 $15,000

Lee, Harper *To Kill a Mockingbird.* Philadelphia: J. B. Lippincott, 1960. First edition, advance review copy with publicity photo laid in, fine in very good plus dust jacket with one tiny nick, some rubbing at spine folds and ends, but which is original with the book and completely unsophisticated.   Between the Covers Rare Books   196 - 89   2015 $26,000

Lee, Harper *To Kill a Mockingbird.* New York: Harper Collins, 1995. 35th Anniversary, first edition, later printing, signed by author, publisher's black cloth over black boards, original dust jacket with illustration after original first edition art to front panel, about fine with hint of wear to extremities, unclipped dust jacket with light wear to extremities, else fine, bright and attractive copy signed by author.   B & B Rare Books, Ltd.   2015 - 2015 $1500

Lee, Henry *Sea Monsters Unmasked.* London: William Clowes & Sons, 1884. Second edition, frontispiece, illustrations, original purple cloth, slightly dulled and marked, little rubbed, good plus.   Jarndyce Antiquarian Booksellers   CCXI - 174   2015   £180

Lee, John *The Man They Could Not Hand. The Life Story of John Lee.* Arthur Westbrook Co., 1908. First edition, 7 1/4 x 5 inches, color pictorial wrappers, 94 pages, near fine, scarce.   Buckingham Books   March 2015 - 35284   2015 $750

Lee, T. D. *Question of Parity Conservation in Weak Interactions. in The Physical Review Volume 104 Second Series No. 1 Oct. 1 1956.* Lancaster: American Institute of Physics, 1956. Entire issue offered, original printed wrappers, owner name front cover, mild sun spine, minimal cover edge wear, small 4to.   By the Book, L. C.   44 - 15   2015 $1100

Lee, Tom *Black Portrait of an African Journey.* Grand Rapids: Eerdmans, 1971. First edition, 4to., hardcover, signed by author, fine but for occasional soiling and owner's bookplate and name on blank part of 2 page titlepage, torn dust jacket (price clipped), laid in is newspaper interview with artist.   Beasley Books   2013 - 2015 $125

Lee, William *Les Etats Unis et L'Angleterre ou souvenirs et Reflexions d'un Citoyen Americain.* Bourdeaux: P. Coudert Dec., 1814. First edition, 8vo., errata, half title in modern boards, leather label, fine.   Second Life Books Inc.   191 - 55   2015 $750

Leek, Sybil *The Complete Art of Witchcraft.* New York & Cleveland: World, 1971. First edition, nearly fine book and dust jacket.   Stephen Lupack   March 2015 - 2015 $100

Leeke, William *A Few Suggestions for Increasing the Incomes of Many of the Smaller Livings for the Almost Total Abolition of Pluralitiees...* Derby: printed by William Bemrose and sold by Hatchard & Seeley, London, 1833. First edition, 8vo., misnumbered, uncut and unbound as issued, very good, presentation copy inscribed by author for Stephen Charles Hesketh, scarce.   John Drury Rare Books   2015 - 20224   2015 $106

Leeser, Isaac *The Jews and the Mosaic Law.* Philadelphia: printed for the author, 1834. First edition, 8vo., contemporary cloth, rebacked with later printed paper label, recent endpapers, very heavy foxing front and back and marginal foxing throughout, text leaves very sound.   M & S Rare Books, Inc.   97 - 129   2015 $750

Leet, Frank *Polka-Dot Cat.* Akron: Saalfield, 1930. Oblong 4to., die cut in shape of a toy gingham cat on wheels, wheels replaced, some light edge rubbing, else clean and very good+, front and back covers illustrate front and back of tiny cat sitting on wheeled base, rare, illustrations by Fern Bisel Peat.   Aleph-bet Books, Inc.   109 - 346   2015 $300

Lefranc, Jacques Francois, Abbe *Le Voile Leve Pour les Curieux ou le Secret de le Revolution Revele a l'aide de la Franc-Maconnerie.* N.P.: Paris, 1791. First edition, half title, well bound in early 20th century cloth backed marbled boards, spine labelled and lettered, excellent copy, apparently scarce outside European libraries.   John Drury Rare Books   2015 - 24122   2015 $787

Leger, Alexis Saint-Leger *Anabasis.* New York: Harcourt Brace and Co., 1949. Revised edition, modest wear, very good, lacking dust jacket, poet/critic Karl Shapiro's copy with his ownership signature and several ink notes in his hand.   Between the Covers Rare Books, Inc.   187 - 210   2015 $250

Leger, Alexis Saint-Leger *Winds (vents).* New York: Pantheon Books, 1953. First American edition, bilingual edition, quarto, little faint spotting on boards, else near fine in chipped, but good dust jacket, nicely inscribed by author to Inez Gallagher.   Between the Covers Rare Books   196 - 99   2015 $1500

Leggett, William *The Plaindealer.* New York: printed for the Proprietors by William Van Norden Dec. 3, 1836. - September 30 1837, all published, first edition, small folio, 44 issued, contemporary quarter calf neatly rebacked with original spine laid on, marbled paper boards, leather label, gilt rules and lettering, very good.   The Brick Row Book Shop   Miscellany 67 - 12   2015 $1250

Legrand, Edy *Pentatoli.* Paris: Librarie De France, 1931. First edition, number 93 of 150 copies, 2 volumes, folio, loose leaves in board chemise, fine, rubbing to edges of chemise, lithographs by Legrand, in cardboard box with one end panel detached (but present).   Beasley Books   2013 - 2015 $275

Legros, Lucien Alphonse *Note on the Legibility of Printed Matter Prepared for the Information of the Committee on Type Faces.* London: HMSO, 1922. Second edition, 4to., later quarter calf over red pebbled cloth, 17 pages, illustrations, leather spine worn and rubbed with small holes.   Oak Knoll Books   306 - 50   2015 $100

Legros, Lucien Alphonse *Typographical Printing Surfaces the Technology and Mechanism of their Production.* New York: Garland, 1980. Reprint of 1916 edition, 8vo., cloth.   Oak Knoll Books   306 - 192   2015 $350

Lehane, Dennis *Darkness, Take My Hand.* New York: Morrow, 1996. First edition, very fine in dust jacket, signed by author.   Mordida Books   March 2015 - 012582   2015 $125

Lehane, Dennis *The Given Day.* Gladestry: Scorpion Press, 2008. First edition, limited to 80 numbered copies, signed by author, very fine in quarter leather and marbled boards in transparent dust jacket.   Buckingham Books   March 2015 - 27370   2015 $165

Lehmann, Herman *Nine Years Along the Indians 1870-1879.* Von Boeckmann-Jones Co., 1927. First edition, 8vo., green cloth, gold stamping on front cover and spine, frontispiece, illustrations, the book appeared in five states, this is the second version edited by J. Marvin Hunter and published 28 years later, light offsetting to front and rear endpapers, else fine in original unprinted dust jacket with chips at spine ends.   Buckingham Books   March 2015 - 37609   2015 $350

Leiber, Fritz *Our Lady of Darkness.* New York: published by Berkeley Pub. Corporation..., 1977. First edition, octavo, cloth.   John W. Knott, Bookseller   Selected New Arrivals Jan. 2015 - 17133   2015 $150

Leigh, E. Chandos *Poems Now First Collected.* London: Edward Moxon, 1839. First edition, 8vo., original illustrated brown cloth, lettered gilt at spine, presentation from author, sound, clean, very good, slight splitting at spine hinges, but holding.   Any Amount of Books   2015 - C11837   2015   £285

Leigh, W. H. *Reconnoitering Voyages, Travels and Adventures in the New Colonies of South Australia.* London: Smith, Elder & Co., 1839. First edition, 8vo., original patterned mauve cloth, lettered gilt on spine, 8 very clear plates, uncommon in original state, not rebound, spine and edges showing very slight signs of discoloration and shelfwear, neat name written in ink on front pastedown, otherwise in excellent condition, very good.   Any Amount of Books   2015 - C1969   2015   £325

Leighton, Marie *Convict 99.* London: Richards, 1898. First edition, endpapers darkened, otherwise near fine in pictorial cloth covered boards.   Mordida Books   March 2015 - 001343   2015 $175

Leinster, Murray *Sidewise in Time and Other Scientific Adventures.* Chicago: Shasta Pub., 1950. First edition, one of an unknown number of signed subscriber copies, signed by author as William Jenkins, octavo, cloth.   John W. Knott, Bookseller   Selected New Arrivals Jan. 2015 - 17137   2015 $350

Leishman, James Blair *The Art of Marvell's Poetry.* Hutchinson University Library, 1968. Second edition, with proof copy of first edition, 1965, few ms. corrections and insertions, dust jacket, from the library of Geoffrey & Kathleen Tillotson.   Jarndyce Antiquarian Booksellers CCVII - 357   2015   £38

Leishman, James Blair *Milton's Minor Poems.* London: Hutchinson, 1969. First edition, half title, original dark green cloth, very good in torn dust jacket, from the library of Geoffrey & Kathleen Tillotson.   Jarndyce Antiquarian Booksellers CCVII - 377   2015   £38

Leishman, James Blair *Themes and Variations in Shakespeare's Sonnets.* London: Hutchinson, 1961. Half title, original pale maroon cloth slightly knocked, slightly marked dust jacket, this copy with creased Order of Service in Fleishman's memory at St. John's College, Cambridge in 1963 and offprint of his article on Wotton's 'you meaner beauties of the night', inscribed by Geoffrey Tillotson. Jarndyce Antiquarian Booksellers   CCVII - 464   2015 £20

Leishman, James Blair *The Three Paranssus Plays 1598-1601.* London: Ivor Nicholson & Watson, 1949. Half title, original black cloth, very good in torn dust jacket, editor's presentation to Geoffrey and Kathleen Tillotson. Jarndyce Antiquarian Booksellers   CCVII - 358   2015 £30

Leitch, Donovan *The Autobiography of Donovan the Hurdy Gurdy Man.* New York: St. Martin's, 2005. First edition, signed by author, fine in near fine dust jacket.   Ken Lopez, Bookseller   164 - 182   2015 $250

Lelille, Jacques *Les Jardins Poeme.* Paris: De L'Imprimerie de P. Didot l'aine, 1801. 152 x 124mm., extremely pretty contemporary green morocco gilt by Bozerian (stamp signed at foot of spine), covers with gilt frame entwined ribbon and leaf roll enclosed within double rules, daisy cornerpieces, flat spine densely gilt in compartments with inlaid red morocco dot at center radiating a profusion of small tools, turn-ins with gilt chain roll, pink watered silk endleaves, pastedowns with delicate gilt border, all edges gilt, 4 charming engraved plates, printed on Papier Velin, bit of fading to covers, but very fine inside and out, binding especially lustrous and entirely unworn, margins very ample and text unusually clean, fresh and bright. Phillip J. Pirages   66 - 63   2015 $4500

Lemay, Alan *Pelican Coast.* Garden City: Doubleday, Doran and Co. Inc., 1929. First edition, very good in dust jacket, lightly sunned on spine, light wear to head and foot of spine.   Buckingham Books   March 2015 - 10208   2015 $375

Lenehan, J. C. *The Tunnel Mystery.* New York: Mystery League Inc., 1931. First US edition, spine panel lightly faded and cover lightly soiled, else very good, internally clean in fine, bright crisp dust jacket.   Buckingham Books March 2015 - 31777   2015 $175

Lennox, William Pitt *Coaching with Anecdotes of the Road.* London: Hurst and Blackett, 1876. First edition, 8vo., original green cloth lettered gilt on spine with black bordering on cover, pages uncut, uncommon in original cloth, slight tear with slight loss to front endpaper, slightly rubbed, very slight shelfwear, very good+.   Any Amount of Books   2015 - A83681   2015   £160

Lenski, Lois *Little Farm.* New York: Oxford University Press, 1942. First edition, 7 1/4 inch square, pictorial cloth, fine in dust jacket slightly faded, else fine, full page color and grey-tone illustrations. Aleph-Bet Books, Inc. 108 - 270 2015 $425

Leon, Donna *Death and Judgment.* New York: Harper Collins, 1995. First edition, fine in dust jacket. Buckingham Books March 2015 - 26331 2015 $260

Leonard, Elmore *The Big Bounce.* London: Robert Hale, 1969. First UK edition, and first hardcover edition, signed by author on laid-in bookplate, fine in fine dust jacket, from the collection of Duke Collier. Royal Books 36 - 209 2015 $3500

Leonard, Elmore *Fifty-Two Pickup.* New York: Delacorte Press, 1974. Uncorrected proof, signed by author, near fine in tall plain mustard wrappers, some brief staining to top front wrapper, else bright copy, from the collection of Duke Collier. Royal Books 36 - 214 2015 $1250

Leonard, Elmore *Fifty-Two Pickup.* New York: Delacorte Press, 1974. First edition, near fine in fine dust jacket, sharp copy, from the collection of Duke Collier. Royal Books 36 - 212 2015 $500

Leonard, Elmore *Gold Coast.* London: W. H. Allen, 1982. First UK edition and first hardcover edition, signed by author, fine in fine price clipped dust jacket, from the collection of Duke Collier. Royal Books 36 - 211 2015 $1500

Leonard, Elmore *The Hardway in Branded West.* Boston: Houghton Mifflin, 1956. First hardcover appearance, fine in very good rubbed dust jacket with crease tear on front cover and light wear at spine ends. Mordida Books March 2015 - 006849 2015 $100

Leonard, Elmore *Hombre.* New York: Ballantine, 1961. First edition, paperback original, very good, scratch on front cover and first 38 pages separated but still attached otherwise very good in wrappers. Mordida Books March 2015 - 010388 2015 $95

Leonard, Elmore *La Brava.* New York: Arbor House, First edition, unbound full page proof stamped "Master Set 2nd Pass", near fine, signed by author. Mordida Books March 2015 - 012555 2015 $100

Leonard, Elmore *La Brava.* New York: Arbor House, 1983. First edition, uncorrected proof, very fine in printed wrappers. Mordida Books March 2015 - 001359 2015 $85

Leonard, Elmore *The Law at Randado.* Boston: Houghton Mifflin, 1955. First edition, signed by author on titlepage, fine in near fine example of scarce dust jacket, with only light wear at spine ends and corners, from the collection of Duke Collier. Royal Books 36 - 207 2015 $7500

Leonard, Elmore *Maximum Bob.* New York: Delacorte, 1991. First edition, one of 200 specially bound numbered copies, signed by author, very fine in slipcase. Mordida Books March 2015 - 008117 2015 $200

Leonard, Elmore *The Moonshine War.* Garden City: Doubleday, 1969. First edition, near fine in like dust jacket, inscribed by author to one of book's two dedicatees, Buck Beshear, 6-20-99, from the collection of Duke Collier. Royal Books 36 - 210 2015 $3250

Leonard, Elmore *Stick.* New York: Arbor House, 1983. First edition, fine in dust jacket, inscribed by author. Mordida Books March 2015 - 006851 2015 $75

Leonard, Elmore *Swag.* New York: Delacorte Press, 1976. Uncorrected proof, near fine in tall plain light green wrappers, front wrapper removed and substituted with page of early reviews for book tipped on to first leaf, clearly as issued, from the collection of Duke Collier. Royal Books 36 - 215 2015 $650

Leonard, Elmore *The Switch.* London: Secker & Warburg, 1979. First hardcover edition, fine in price clipped dust jacket with small tear at lower corner of internal rear flap. Mordida Books March 2015 - 010763 2015 $300

Leonard, Elmore *Unknown Man No. 89.* New York: Delacorte Press, 1977. Uncorrected proof, signed by author, near fine in tall plain blue wrappers small stain at top of front wrapper, from the collection of Duke Collier. Royal Books 36 - 213 2015 $1450

Leonard, Elmore *Valdez Is Coming.* London: Robert Hale, 1969. First UK edition and first hardcover edition, signed by author, fine in fine dust jacket, from the collection of Duke Collier. Royal Books 36 - 208 2015 $5000

Leonard, William Ellery *The Locomotive-God.* New York: Century, 1927. First edition, fine and bright in lightly tanned dust jacket with small chip at head of tanned spine, not affecting type. Beasley Books 2013 - 2015 $45

Leonardo Da Vinci 1452-1519 *Of Light and Shade from the Notebooks of Leonardo Da Vinci. Chapters 118 to 127...* Octon: Verdigris Press, 2009. One of 9 copies, from a total issue of 15 (6 with original copper plate), each only numbered and signed in pencil by artist on colophon as well as initialing each page, page size 9 x 11 3/4 inches, 20 pages, bound by Mark Lintott, loose in wrappers housed in slipcase covered with handmade papers, screen printed by Judith Rothchild in pink, blue and green showing Leonardo's larger sphere on front cover and smaller sphere on rear cover, black front wrapper embossed with circles, squares and triangle, with white label printed in black with title and author, translator and artist on front panel, 6 original full page intaglio prints, endsheets with embossed spheres along bottom edge by Judith Rothchild.   Priscilla Juvelis - Rare Books   62 - 18   2015 $1000

Leonowens, Anna *Memoirs of Anne C. L. Botta.* New York: J. Selwin Tait & Sons/De Vinne Press, 1894. First edition, octavo, yellow cloth, gilt, small tears and soiling on boards, tight, very good or better copy, laid in is handwritten card "With Mrs. Leonowens' compliments".   Between the Covers Rare Books, Inc.   187 - 30   2015 $400

Lepage-Medvey *National Costumes.* London: Hyperion Press, 1939. 4to., tan cloth covered portfolio of 40 (bound-in) pochoir color prints, ex-library book with some of the usual markings, thus good binding (cloth wear, call letters on spine, discard stamp and library stamps and numbers), plates near fine.   Stephen Lupack   March 2015 - 2015 $75

Lepper, Frank *Trajan's Column: a New edition of the Cichorius Plates.* Gloucester: Alan Sutton, 1988. Small 4to., cloth, dust jacket, 4 black and white illustrations in text, 3 maps, two foldout, 155 black and white plates follow text. Oak Knoll Books   306 - 239   2015 $150

Lesser, Isaac *Discourses on the Jewish Religion. Third Resources.* Philadelphia: printed for the author by Sherman & Co., 1867-1868. Volumes VI, VII, IX, X, 4 volumes, 8vo., half leather, volume VII rebacked and lacking front endpaper, endpapers renewed, spines worn, foxed. M & S Rare Books, Inc.   97 - 128   2015 $400

Lessing, Doris *The Grass is Singing.* London: Michael Joseph, 1950. First edition, signed by author, spine slightly cocked, mild sunning to spine and board edges, bookplate of Robert Lusty, Deputy chairman of Michael Joseph publishers, near fine in like dust jacket, complete with wrap-around band, laid in publishers' response card, nice, uncommon.   Ken Lopez, Bookseller   164 - 116   2015 $3000

Lesur, C. L. *Annuaire Historique Universel 1818-1833.* Paris: Fantin/A. Desplaces/A. Thosinier - Despalces/Alexis Pillot, 1818. First edition, 16 volumes, 8vo., half blue leather, blue cloth lettered gilt on spine, ex-British Foreign Office Library with library markings and label, corners slightly rubbed, splash marks on spines of few volumes, else very good.   Any Amount of Books   March 2015 - C966   2015   £400

Lesure, F. *Bibliographie Des Editions D'Adrian Le Roy et Robert Ballard (1551-1598).*   Paris: Societe Francaise de Musicologie, 1955. 8vo., stiff paper wrappers, wrappers tanned and separated at front hinge, previous owner's name on front free endpaper, supplement to bibliography published in Revue de Muscicologie 40 (December 1957) laid in.   Oak Knoll Books   306 - 78   2015 $100

Letchford, Frank *From the Inferno to Zos: Michelangelo in a Teacup: Austin Osman Spare.*   Thame, 1995. First edition, 4to., original black cloth lettered gilt on spine and cover, copiously illustrated in black and white, about fine.   Any Amount of Books   2015 - A64838   2015   £160

Leterman, Elmer G. *How Showmanship Sells.*   Evanston: 1965. 202 pages, fine in very good dust jacket.   Bookworm & Silverfish   2015 - 6013899159   2015 $50

Lethem, Jonathan *Dissident Gardens.* New York: Doubleday, 2013. First edition, as new, signed by author, as new jacket.   Stephen Lupack   March 2015 - 2015 $45

Lethem, Jonathan *Gun with Occasional Music.* New York: Harcourt, 1994. First edition, hardcover, fine in fine dust jacket.   Beasley Books   2013 - 2015 $40

A Letter Addressed to His Majesty's Ministers on the State of the County of Kent.   London: James Ridgway, 1830. First edition, wanting half title, preserved in modern wrappers with printed label on upper cover, 8vo., very good, apparently very rare.   John Drury Rare Books   March 2015 - 25854   2015 $266

A Letter Sent from a Private Gentleman to a friend in London, in Justification of his Owne Adhering to His Majestie in Times of Distraction...   London: for V.N. Anno. Dom., 1642. Small 4to., 8 pages, early 20th century quarter morocco, bookplate of Markree Library of the Cooper family at Markree Castle, Co. Sligo, Ireland, from the library of James Stevens Cox (1910-1997).   Maggs Bros. Ltd.   1447 - 90   2015   £120

A Letter Sent to the Right Honourable William Lenthall Esquire, Speaker to the Honourable House of Commons: Concerning the Routing of Col. Gorings Army near Bridgewater. London: for John Field, July 22, 1645. First edition, small 4to., 8 pages, uncut, upper edge unopened, verso of final leaf little soiled, disbound, from the library of James Stevens Cox (1910-1997). Maggs Bros. Ltd. 1447 - 97 2015 £150

A Letter to a Member of Parliament, Concerning the True Interest of Scotland, with Respect to the Succession. Edinburgh?: n.d.?, 1705. Only edition, 4to., some dust soiling, pinhole in first leaf touching a single letter, preserved in modern wrappers with printed label on upper cover, good, large copy, very scarce. John Drury Rare Books March 2015 - 24814 2015 £306

A Letter to a member of Parliament in the Country, from His Friend in London, Relative to the Case of Admiral Byng. London: J. Cooke, 1756. First edition, half title, paper generally rather browned, good, disbound, preserved in (expensive) cloth folder and half morocco slipcase, circa 1900. John Drury Rare Books March 2015 - 16413 2015 $221

A Letter to a New Member of the Honourable House of Commons Touching the Rise Of All the Imbezzlements and Mismanagements of the Kingdom's Treasure from the Beginning of the Revolution unto this Present Parliament. Amsterdam: printed in the year, 1710. First edition, 4to., later wrappers, very good. John Drury Rare Books 2015 - 14735 2015 $1093

A Letter to Ball Hughes Esq. on Club House and Private Gaming, His Dog Hector and Col. B-Y-K, Cribb's Dog and Lord H-R-H and Bet with Dean S. and Mr. Lloyd. London: printed and published by J. Evans 20 Wych Street Strand, 1824. Only edition, 8vo., possibly wanting a half title, preserved in modern wrappers with printed title label on upper cover, very good, only edition, exceptionally rare. John Drury Rare Books 2015 - 19432 2015 $1136

A Letter to His Majesty William IV. Paris?: 1830. Only edition, generally rather browned and foxed, original printed blue wrappers, contemporary ownership signature of Lord Visct. (John Charles Spencer) Althorpe, very rare. John Drury Rare Books March 2015 - 19079 2015 $221

A Letter to Sir John Phillips, Bart, Occasion'd by a Bill Brought into Parliament to Naturalize Foreign Protestants. London: M. Cooper, 1747. First edition, 8vo., 30 pages, recent plain wrappers, very good. John Drury Rare Books March 2015 - 19842 2015 $266

A Letter to the Clergy of the Agricultural Districts of the State and Prospects of Education in the Mining and Manufacturing Parts of England... Holt: printed by C. S. Ellis, 1843. First edition, 8vo., two old institutional stamps on title and related label on blank verso of last leaf, outer leaves little dust soiled, sewn as issued, rare. John Drury Rare Books March 2015 - 18540 2015 $266

A Letter to the Editor of the St. James's Chronicle, on the Price of Agricultural Labour, by a Magistrate of the County of Devon. Dartmouth: printed by J. Salter, 1831. Only edition, 12mo., 24 pages, old (19th century) library stamp on blank margin of title, ink inscription cropped, preserved in modern wrappers with printed label on upper cover, good copy, apparently rare. John Drury Rare Books March 2015 - 25624 2015 $266

A Letter to the Editor of the Times on the Question of the Bank Charter, Shewing the Inconsistency of Some of the Accounts Lately Furnished by the Bank to the Committee of the House of Commons. Camberwell: A. Vogel, 1833. Only edition, 8vo., very small inkstamp of Dutch academic institution on blank verso of title, title lightly dust marked, recently well bound in linen backed marbled boards lettered, good copy, apparently rare. John Drury Rare Books March 2015 - 19548 2015 $266

Letter to the Electors of the University of Cambridge from One of their Body. London: James Ridgway, 1827. First edition, 8vo., half title rather dust soiled, otherwise very good, preserved in plain wrappers with printed title label on upper cover. John Drury Rare Books 2015 - 22345 2015 $133

A Letter to the Free Thinkers. By a Lay-Man. London: B. Cowse, 1713. Only edition, 8vo., very good in later plain wrappers, very scarce. John Drury Rare Books 2015 - 14741 2015 $221

Letter to the Magistrates of Edinburgh, in Consequence of the Official Statement Lately Published in Justification of their conduct with Regard to the execution of Robert Johnston. Edinburgh: printed for the booksellers, 1819. First edition, 8vo., modern wrappers, printed title label on upper cover, very good. John Drury Rare Books March 2015 - 23044 2015 £306

A Letter to the Right Honourable Sir William Scott on His Clergy-Farmer's Bill. London: R. Faulder, 1803. First and only edition, 8vo., 16 pages, modern plain wrappers, very good, scarce. John Drury Rare Books 2015 - 14858 2015 $89

A Letter to the Right Honourable Viscount Cranborne, Lord-Lieutenant and Custos Rotulorum of the County of Hertford. London: J. Almon, 1780. First edition, 8vo., preserved in modern wrappers with printed title label on upper cover, very good, rare. John Drury Rare Books March 2015 - 19090 2015 $266

Lettice, John *Two Sermons. I. An Enquiry How Far the Knowledge and Manners of the World Can, With Safety or Propriety be Adopted in the Clerical Character.... II. The Present State of Discipline, Manners and Lettering In Our Universities...* Cambridge: printed by J. Archdeacon printer to the University for J. & J. Merrill &c, 1788. First edition, 4to., preserved in modern wrappers with printed title label on upper cover, very good, rare.   John Drury Rare Books   March 2015 - 23279   2015   £306

Levack, Daniel J. H. *PKD: a Philip K. Dick Bibliography.* San Francisco: Columbia: Underwood-Miller, 1981. First edition, octavo, pictorial cloth, illustrations, signed by Dick, Levack and Godersky.   John W. Knott, Bookseller   Selected New Arrivals Jan. 2015 - 17012   2015 $750

Levertov, Denise *Conversation in Moscow.* No Place: Hovey St. Press, 1973. First edition, one of 800 copies, inscribed by author for Alan (Helms), March 1975, thin octavo, printed wrappers, fine.   Between the Covers Rare Books, Inc.   187 - 153   2015 $150

Levertov, Denise *Three Poems.* Mt. Horeb: Perishable Press, 1968. One of 250 copies, all on handmade Shadwell paper, 8 1/2 x 5 1/4 inches, 38 pages, bound by printer, handsewn in grey Fabriano wrappers with title printed in pale brown and geological diagram by printer in ochre, handset in Palatino in black, white pink and cream and printed by Watler Hamady.   Priscilla Juvelis - Rare Books   61 - 41   2015 $200

Levin, Harry *Prospectives of Criticism.* Cambridge: Harvard University Press, 1950. Initial catalog, half title, frontispiece, original orange brown cloth, torn dust jacket, Geoffrey Tillotson's signed copy, with few notes by him, including TLS from editor.   Jarndyce Antiquarian Booksellers   CCVII - 359   2015   £20

Levin, Ira *A Kiss Before Dying.* New York: Simon & Schuster, 1953. First edition, pages uniformly browned throughout, else fine in dust jacket professionally restored at spine ends, corners and extremities, attractive copy of a scarce book.   Buckingham Books   March 2015 - 37527   2015 $875

Levin, Ira *Sliver.* New York: Bantam, 1991. First edition, very fine in dust jacket, inscribed by author.   Mordida Books   March 2015 - 001373   2015 $75

Levin, Meyer *The Obsession.* New York: Simon and Schuster, 1973. First edition, wrappers advance reading copy, fine, with the pamphlet by Meyer "Fifty Years in Writing".   Beasley Books   2013 - 2015 $45

Levine, David *Pens and Needles. Literary Caricatures.* Boston: Gambit, 1969. First edition, small 4to., fine in near fine dust jacket with slightly faded spine.   Beasley Books   2013 - 2015 $45

Levine, George *Mindful Pleasures: Essays on Thomas Pynchon.* Boston: Little Brown and Co., 1976. First edition, paperback issue, simultaneous with hardcover, fine in wrappers, Pynchon's editor, Ray Roberts's copy with his book label on front pastedown.   Between the Covers Rare Books, Inc.   187 - 227   2015 $125

Levine, Philip *Ashes, Poems New & Old.* Port Townsend: Graywolf Press, 1979. First edition, limited to 220 numbered copies, signed by author, 8vo., original cloth, printed spine label, very fine, presentation copy inscribed by author for Harry (Ford) and Kathleen.   James S. Jaffe Rare Books   Modern American Poetry - 181   2015 $1000

Levine, Philip *Naming. A Poem.* La Crosse: Sutton Hoo Press, 2004. First edition, Sutton Hoo Number four, one of 26 lettered and specially bound copies on Johannot paper and signed by Levine (out of a total edition of 200), 12mo., original quarter dark blue morocco and boards, morocco edges, black cloth folding box, very fine, calligraphic ornaments by Cheryl Jacobsen.   James S. Jaffe Rare Books   Modern American Poetry - 183   2015 $750

Levine, Philip *Not This Pig. Poems.* Middletown: Wesleyan University Press, 1968. First edition, 8vo., original cloth, dust jacket, presentation from author for poet Mark Strand, fine in lightly sunned, somewhat rubbed dust jacket with bit of wear to extremities.   James S. Jaffe Rare Books   Modern American Poetry - 176   2015 $1250

Levine, Philip *On the Edge.* Iowa City: Stone Wall Press, 1963. First edition, one of 220 copies printed from romanee type on Golden Hind paper by Kim Merker at Stone Wall Press, although not called for, this copy signed by poet, 8vo., original brown paper boards, printed label on spine, rare first book.   James S. Jaffe Rare Books   Modern American Poetry - 178   2015 $2000

Levine, Philip *Pili's Wall.* Santa Barbara: Unicorn Press, 1971. First edition, one of 750 copies, entire edition, fine in wrappers, and fine dust jacket, octavo, inscribed by author for Michael Waters.   Between the Covers Rare Books, Inc.   187 - 154   2015 $250

Levine, Philip *Selected Poems.* New York: Atheneum, 1984. First edition, 8vo., original black cloth, dust jacket, inscribed by author May 5 '84 for Harry (Ford) & Kathleen, fine.   James S. Jaffe Rare Books   Modern American Poetry - 180   2015 $1000

Levine, Philip *The Simple Truth. Poems.* New York: Knopf, 1994. First edition, 8vo., original cloth, dust jacket, presentation copy from author for Harry Ford (his editor) & Kathleen, as new.   James S. Jaffe Rare Books   Modern American Poetry - 182   2015 $1000

Levinson, Saul *Red-Hot Murder.* Phoenix Press, 1949. First edition, former owner's small stamp at top of front flyleaf, else fine in dust jacket with minor wear to spine ends. Buckingham Books   March 2015 - 37262   2015 $225

Levis, Larry *The Afterlife.* Iowa City: Windhover Press, 1977. First edition, one of 70 copies on Rives paper out of a total edition of 175 copies signed by Levis, 8vo., cloth backed boards with printed spine label, spine very slightly faded as often, otherwise fine, errata slip laid in.   James S. Jaffe Rare Books   Modern American Poetry - 184   2015 $375

Levitan, Kalma L. *Miniature Books Relating to Postage Stamps.* Skokie: Black Cat Press, 1983. Limited to 250 copies, 5.8 x 7.1cm., cloth, title gilt stamped on spine and front board, decorated endpapers, 2 volumes, frontispiece, first miniature US postage stamp issued, 13 cent stamp of 1976 depicting the Indian Head penny tipped-in.   Oak Knoll Books   306 - 117   2015 $100

Levy, D. A. *The Beginning of Sunny Dawn & Red Lady.* San Francisco: Open Skull, 1969. Second edition, one of 500 copies, wrappers, fine.   Beasley Books   2013 - 2015 $40

Levy, Deborah *An Amorous Discourse in the Suburbs of Hell.* London: Jonathan Cape, 1990. First edition, wrappers, 8vo., pages 77, illustrations by Polish artist Andrzej Borkowsk, large format paperback, very slight handling wear, but pretty much fine, from the working library of novelist Angela Carter (1940-1992) with her posthumous bookplate.   Any Amount of Books   2015 - A63695   2015   £180

Levy, Ferdinand *Flashes from the dark.* Dublin: printed at the Sign of the Three Candles, 1941. First edition, no. 7 of 12 copies on handmade paper, of this edition 162 copies numbered and signed by author, 8vo., original brown cloth lettered and illustrated gilt on spine and cover, signed presentation from author, spine slightly faded, rear cloth slightly wrinkled, slight rubbing at corners and cover otherwise very good.   Any Amount of Books   2015 - A76312   2015   £300

Lewallen, Constance M.   *Joe Brainard. A Retrospective.* 4to., original pictorial wrappers, illustrations, as new.   James S. Jaffe Rare Books   Many Happy Returns - 124   2015 $50

Lewes, G. H. *The Life of Maximilien Robespierre.* Philadelphia: Carey and Hart, 1849. First edition, very good-, rubbing and shelfwear to extremities, general random foxing.   Stephen Lupack   March 2015 - 2015 $45

Lewis, Alfred Henry *Confessions of a Detective.* New York: A. E. Barnes & Co., 1906. First edition, 8vo., illustrations by E. M. Ashe, moderate wear to spine ends, some ink loss on spine, else very good in decorated red cloth, handsome copy.   Buckingham Books   March 2015 - 26707   2015 $175

Lewis, Alfred Henry *Confessions of a Detective.* New York: A. E. Barnes & Co., 1906. First edition, 8vo., illustrations by E. M. Ashe, lettering on front cover is bright and clean, spine lettering lightly used, else near fine, bright, tight copy in decorated red cloth.   Buckingham Books   March 2015 - 37510   2015 $350

Lewis, Alfred Henry *Wolfville.* New York: Frederick A. Stokes Co., 1899. (1897). First paperback edition, red pictorial wrappers, illustrations by F. Remington, small crease lower corner of first 18 pages, light wear to spine ends and extremities, else very good, housed in 4 point binder and inserted into matching maroon colored slipcase with titles on paper label attached to spine, scarce.   Buckingham Books   March 2015 - 31134   2015 $250

Lewis, Angelo John 1839-1919 *Puzzles Old and New.* London and New York: Frederick Warne & Co., 1893. First edition, 8vo., original brown cloth lettered and decorated gilt and black on spine and cover, copiously illustrated in black and white, very slight puncture mark on spine, slight rubbing, minimal shelfwear, decent, very good.   Any Amount of Books   2015 - A98970   2015   £175

Lewis, Clive Staples 1898-1963 *The Allegory of Love: a Study in Medieval Tradition.* Oxford: Clarendon Press, 1936. from the library of Geoffrey & Kathleen Tillotson. original dark blue cloth, slightly marked, signed with initials and few pencil notes and marked proof of Kathleen's review.   Jarndyce Antiquarian Booksellers   CCVII - 362   2015   £25

Lewis, Clive Staples 1898-1963 *The Chronicles of Narnia...* London: Geoffrey Bles/Bodley Head, 1950-1956. First editions, 7 volumes, publisher's cloth, pictorial endpapers illustrated with maps to Narnia to volumes 2-5, original dust jackets with illustrations by Baynes, very good with some light wear and rubbing to extremities, minor toning to spines and board edges of volumes 1, and 3-5, slight lean to spines minor dampstaining to rear boards of volumes 6-7, few faint spots to endpapers, otherwise bright and clean pages, unclipped dust jacket with some wear and minor nicks to extremities, hint of toning to spines, few traces of minor soiling to panels and flaps, light stain to rear panel volume 6, minor chipping to spine ends volumes 1 and 3-6, short closed tears to top edges of volumes 2-3, slight loss to spine tail of volume 1, few small chips and discreet internal repairs to volume 4, else fine, overall tight and attractive set of complete Chronicles of Narnia.   B & B Rare Books, Ltd.   2015 - 2015 $15,000

Lewis, Clive Staples 1898-1963 *The Last Battle.* London: Bodley Head, 1956. First edition, 8vo., blue cloth, fine in dust jacket (slightly frayed at top of spine, else nice and free of tears), illustrations by Pauline Baynes.   Aleph-bet Books, Inc.   109 - 264   2015 $2400

Lewis, Clive Staples 1898-1963 *The Lion, the Witch and the Wardrobe.* New York: Macmillan, 1950. Stated first printing, 8vo., cloth, except for bit of inevitable fading that always occurs with this title, fine in near fine dust jacket with touch of fading on rear panel and ever so slightly rubbed, illustrations in black and white by Pauline Baynes, rare in this condition. Aleph-Bet Books, Inc.   108 - 272   2015 $3000

Lewis, Clive Staples 1898-1963 *The Witch and the Wardrobe.* London: Geoffrey Bles, 1950. First edition, first printing, 8vo., cloth very slightly faded on spine and bottom edge else, fine in attractive dust jacket with price present (dust jacket has slight soil on rear panel, one small chip, 3 small closed tears and few chips and tear at bottom of front fold, most of which are not obvious when handling the book), illustrations by Pauline Baynes, color plate frontispiece, numerous full page and smaller black and whites, lovely.   Aleph-bet Books, Inc.   109 - 263   2015 $6500

Lewis, Frank S. *The New Science Weaponless Defense.* Los Angeles: Frank S. Lewis 438 S. Spring St., 1906. First edition, frontispiece, many black and white photo images, 7 1/4 x 5 1/4 inches, red cloth with black lettering printed to spine and cover, light rubbing and wear to board and spine edges, light age toning to papers, in all very good+ copy.   Tavistock Books   Bah, Humbug? - 17   2015 $495

Lewis, H. H. *Road to Utterly.* Holt: B. C. Hagglund, 1935. First edition, wrappers, 32 pages, near fine, owner's unobtrusive stamp on front wrapper.   Beasley Books   2013 - 2015 $150

Lewis, Herbert Clyde *Season's Greetings.* New York: Dial, 1941. First edition, fine in dust jacket.   Mordida Books   March 2015 - 101055   2015 $85

Lewis, Jerry *The Total Film Maker.* London: Vision Press, 1974. First US edition, 8vo., plates, original yellow cloth, lettered black on spine, illustrations, handsome copy, scarce edition, fine in very good dust jacket with slight edgewear and faint wear to white rear panel.   Any Amount of Books   2015 - C14435   2015   £160

Lewis, Mary S. *Antonio Gardano, Venetian Music Printer 1538-1569. Volume I 1538-1549.* New York: Garland Publishing Co., 1988. Thick 8vo., cloth, 46 plates, bumped, name in ink on free endpaper.   Oak Knoll Books   306 - 74   2015 $135

Lewis, Meriwether 1774-1809 *Original Journals of Lewis and Clark Expeditions.* New York: Dodd Mead & Co., 1904. First edition, limited to 50 copies on Imperial Japan paper, this set no. 34 with all volumes so marked on colophons, edition deluxe with 33 of the plates in two states, black and white and hand tinted in color, unique to Imperial Japan edition, complete set with 7 volumes of text in 14 books plus atlas volume which is complete with all 54 maps as listed, near fine to fine volumes, tan buckram with gilt titling and ornamentation, as issued, inset tipped on color portraits of Lewis and Clark on all front covers, frontispieces in all volumes with tissue guards, mild toning to spines of few books, no writing, marking or bookplates, all bindings intact, tight, 4to.   By the Book, L. C.   44 - 6   2015 $14,000

Lewis, Meriwether 1774-1809 *Original Journals of the Lewis and Clark Expedition 1804-1806.* Antiquarian Press, 1959. First edition thus, limited to 750 copies, 700 for sale, 8vo., 7 volumes and atlas, this is an unnumbered set, red cloth, gilt stamping on cover and spine, illustrations, maps, fine set.   Buckingham Books   March 2015 - 29822   2015 $800

Lewis, Ramsey *Ramsey Lewis The Piano Player (Cadet Records Device).* Chicago: Cadet (Chess) Records, 1970. First edition, wrappers, 30 pieces of cover art from Lewis's 30 (up to 190) Cadet albums, this copy signed by Lewis on front wrapper (in 1998), rare and unusual piece, very good.   Beasley Books   2013 - 2015 $150

Lewis, Samella S. *Black Artists on Art I (and) II.* Los Angeles: Contemporary Crafts, 1969. 1971. First edition, 2 volumes, complete, very good ex-library in dust jackets.   Beasley Books   2013 - 2015 $150

Lewis, Sinclair 1885-1951 *Arrowsmith.* New York: Harcourt Brace, 1925. limited edition, number 327 of 500 numbered copies signed by author, little offsetting to hinges and horizontal crease to spine label, otherwise fine, in what appears to be original acetate dust jacket, in supplied slipcase.   Ken Lopez, Bookseller   164 - 118   2015 $2000

Lewis, Sinclair 1885-1951 *Arrowsmith.* New York: Harcourt Brace, 1925. First edition, 395/500 copies signed by author, titlepage printed in black and red, 8vo., original quarter cream cloth with blue boards, backstrip with printed paper label (spare label tipped in at rear), top edge gilt, others untrimmed, bookplate tipped in to flyleaf, protective acetate jacket, original slipcase, fine.   Blackwell's Rare Books   B179 - 189   2015   £1500

Lewis, Sinclair 1885-1951 *Dodsworth.* New York: Harcourt Brace, 1929. First edition, foxing to fore edge, spine dulled and front hinge cracked, very good with folded, thus very good, first issue dust jacket laid in (no reviews on front flap), jacket fragile where it has been folded, but it appears to have spent most of its life inside the book, color completely fresh and unfaded. Ken Lopez, Bookseller 164 - 120 2015 $250

Lewis, Sinclair 1885-1951 *The Job.* New York: Harper and Bros., 1917. First issue, offsetting to endpages from jacket flaps and slight wear to board edges, near fine in price clipped dust jacket, professionally restored to near fine, extremely scarce. Ken Lopez, Bookseller 164 - 115 2015 $9500

Lewis, Sinclair 1885-1951 *Main Street.* New York: Limited Editions Club, 1937. Limited to 1500 numbered copies, signed by artist, Grant Wood, small 4to., cloth, illustrations by Wood, lacks slipcase, spine age darkened, slight spotting. Oak Knoll Books 25 - 17 2015 $325

Lewis, Sinclair 1885-1951 *The Man Who Knew Coolidge.* New York: Harcourt Brace, 1928. First edition, fine in fine dust jacket, beautiful copy. Ken Lopez, Bookseller 164 - 119 2015 $1000

Lewis, Sinclair 1885-1951 *Our Mr. Wren.* New York: Harper & Bros., 1914. First edition, first printing "M-N" under published February 1914, very good+, spine somewhat darkened, tight, clean text. Stephen Lupack March 2015 - 2015 $100

Lewis, Sinclair 1885-1951 *The Prodigal Parents.* New York: Doubleday Doran & Co., 1938. First edition, 8vo., original red cloth lettered gilt on spine, 2 TLS's loosely inserted, one from Helen Clampitt of Scribner's about attaining Lewis's signature another form Lewis asking her to send over the book for inscription, signed presentation from author to Eleanor Crouse Barnum , very good+ in clean dust jacket, slight rubbing at edges, price intact, slight creasing at rear and repaired with no loss, overall very good. Any Amount of Books 2015 - C5042 2015 £300

Lewis, Virgil A. *Southern Historical Magazine.* Charleston: 1892. Volume I no. 1-3, 5, volume 2 no. 2 - ceased all publication, five issues, circa 300 pages, most wrappers present but loose, frayed or chipped. Bookworm & Silverfish 2015 - 5630469635 2015 $200

Lewis, William *Chess Problems.* London: Sampson Low, 1827. First edition, most uncommon, 8vo., 100 illustrations, original blindstamped cloth, spine joints neatly restored, gilt lettered, very good, perhaps fine. John Drury Rare Books March 2015 - 23647 2015 $656

Lewis, William S. *Reminiscences of Delia B. Sheffield.* University of Washington Press, 1924. Reprinted from Washington Historical Quarterly volume 15, number 1, 26.5cm., grey printed wrappers, 16 pages, neatly written on front panel "R.S. Ellison with cordial regards of Fred Sockley", along with lightly sunned panel edges, very good. Buckingham Books March 2015 - 35675 2015 $225

Lewis, William S. *The Story of Early Days in the Big Bend Country.* W. D. Allen, 1926. First edition, Big Bend edition, 8vo., issued in an edition limited to 105 copies and 100 autographed numbered copies, this copy 7, printed wrappers, frontispiece, illustrations, scarce, covers lightly soiled, small closed tear to bottom edge of spine, else very good. Buckingham Books March 2015 - 37012 2015 $450

Lewis, Wyndham 1882-1957 *The Apes of God.* London: Arthur Press, 1930. First edition, one of 750 copies numbered and signed by Lewis, very good+ in very good dust jacket with some rubbing and light soiling and browning from internal tape mends at edges of dust jacket. Beasley Books 2013 - 2015 $400

Lewis, Wyndham 1882-1957 *The Apes of God.* London: Nash and Grayson, 1931. First trade edition, fine in lightly sued dust jacket with little shallow chipping at spine head, 8vo., quite nice. Beasley Books 2013 - 2015 $200

Lewis, Wyndham 1882-1957 *The Apes of God.* London: Arco Pub. Ltd., 1955. One of 1000 numbered copies, small 4to., signed by author, 25th Anniversary edition, bound in first binding which is stamped in red and black rather than yellow, near fine in very good dust jacket by Michael Ayrton, with mild wear and spine sunning. Beasley Books 2013 - 2015 $150

Lewis, Wyndham 1882-1957 *The Apes of God.* Santa Barbara: Black Sparrow Press, 1981. New edition, one of 26 lettered copies, this being letter 'J', fine, although one hinge is bit overglued, in fine dust jacket, 8vo. Beasley Books 2013 - 2015 $150

Lewis, Wyndham 1882-1957 *Blast 1-3.* Santa Barbara: Black Sparrow Press, 1981. 1981. 1984. One of 26 lettered copies, first two volumes facsimile reprints of Lewis's Blast magazine, Volume I fine in near fine dust jacket, volume 2 fine in very good dust jacket which has dime size hole an inch down from top of (unprinted) spine), volume 3 fine in near fine dust jacket with bit faded (unprinted) spine, 4to. Beasley Books 2013 - 2015 $400

Lewis, Wyndham 1882-1957 *Blast 2. War Number.* London: John Lane, July, 1915. Wrappers, little wear to spine and tiny chip at top, otherwise nice, near fine, 4to. Beasley Books 2013 - 2015 $750

Lewis, Wyndham   1882-1957   *Blasting and Bombardiering. Autobiography (1914-1926).*   London: Eyre & Spottiswoode, 1937. First edition, advance review copy with slip tipped in, first state of binding, fine in near fine dust jacket bur for tiny tears at spine head and short clear tape reinforcement at head of spine on verso of dust jacket, 8vo.   Beasley Books   2013 - 2015 $200

Lewis, Wyndham   1882-1957   *Blasting and Bombardiering. Autobiography (1914-1926).*   London: Eyre & Spottiswoode, 1937. First edition, second state of binding, limp cloth, very slight dulling to spine, very good+ in very good dust jacket with fragile spine folds and small chip at head of front panel, 8vo.   Beasley Books   2013 - 2015 $125

Lewis, Wyndham   1882-1957   *The Caliph's Design. Architects! Where is Your Vortex?*   London: Egoist Ltd., 1919. First edition, 1000 copies printed, paper covered boards, paper covering spine partially chipped away, boards still holding fast, good+ spine on very good book, 8vo.   Beasley Books   2013 - 2015 $175

Lewis, Wyndham   1882-1957   *The Childermass Section I.*   London: Chatto & Windus, 1928. First edition, one of 225 numbered copies, signed by author, yellow cloth, near fine with slight sunning to spine, in very good dust jackets with small chips at spine ends and at foot of rear spine fold, 8vo.   Beasley Books   2013 - 2015 $450

Lewis, Wyndham   1882-1957   *The Childermass Section I.*   London: Chatto & Windus, 1928. First edition, 8vo. yellow cloth stamped in red, near fine (trace of spine faded) in near fine dust jacket but for small chip at head of front spine fold.   Beasley Books   2013 - 2015 $125

Lewis, Wyndham   1882-1957   *Creatures of Habit and Creatures of Change: Essays on Art, Literature and Society 1914-1956.*   Santa Rosa: Black Sparrow Press, 1989. First edition, one of 26 lettered copies, count of 126 numbered deluxe copies signed by editor, Paul Edwards on tipped-in leaf, fine in fine dust jacket, 8vo.   Beasley Books   2013 - 2015 $85

Lewis, Wyndham   1882-1957   *The Demon of Progress in the Arts.*   London: Methuen & Co., 1954. First edition, 8vo. fine in near fine dust jacket with few little tears.   Beasley Books   2013 - 2015 $40

Lewis, Wyndham   1882-1957   *The Enemy.*   London: Arthur Press, 1927-1929. First edition, small 4to. all three issues of Lewis's magazine Nos. 1 and 2 being signed and dated by Lewis, no. 1 has spine glued back down, perhaps reattaching rear wrapper, latter of which is chipped, tears starting at folds, good+, no. 2 in very good condition, no. 3 has also been re-glued, but is much better job than done with No. 1, thus very good.   Beasley Books   2013 - 2015 $350

Lewis, Wyndham   1882-1957   *The Hitler Cult.*   London: Dent, 1939. First edition, 2500 copies printed, but by 1949 only 1750 copies were sold, remaining copies were pulped, 8vo., near fine with light foxing to prelims, fine dust jacket, scarce.   Beasley Books   2013 - 2015 $800

Lewis, Wyndham   1882-1957   *The Human Age Book 2: Monstre Gal; Book 3: Malign Fiesta.*   London: Methuen & Co., 1955. First edition, near fine with little sunning to spine, very good++ dust jacket, 8vo.   Beasley Books   2013 - 2015 $45

Lewis, Wyndham   1882-1957   *The Ideal Giant.*   London: privately printed for the Little Review, 1917. First edition, one of 200 copies,, softcover, offprinted folded and gathered and string bound into paper covered boards with cloth backstrip, signed P. Wyndham Lewis, Dec. 1917, there are three small skinned area in lower right corner of front cover, pink card stock can be seen through these chips which are to the finish only, all edges age darkened, still very good, traces of very good- for the abraded areas, 8vo.   Beasley Books   2013 - 2015 $1500

Lewis, Wyndham   1882-1957   *The Jews, are they Human?*   London: George Allen & Unwin Ltd., 1939. First edition, near fine in very good+ dust jacket with few short tears, 12mo.   Beasley Books   2013 - 2015 $200

Lewis, Wyndham   1882-1957   *Journey into Barbary.*   Santa Barbara: Black Sparrow Press, 1983. Number 84 of 226 numbered and specially bound copies, signed by Fox on tipped in leaf, fine in fine acetate dust jacket, large 8vo.   Beasley Books   2013 - 2015 $40

Lewis, Wyndham   1882-1957   *The Roaring Queen.*   London: Secker & Warburg, 1973. First edition, one of 100 copies, original etching by Michael Ayrton, signed by Ayrton, Lewis and Walter Allen (provided introduction), 8vo., fine in fine slipcase.   Beasley Books   2013 - 2015 $200

Lewis, Wyndham   1882-1957   *Rude Assignment.*   London: Hutchinson, 1950. First edition, one of 2500 copies, fine in near fine dust jacket but for short tape reinforcements at each of the folds on verso only, 8vo.   Beasley Books   2013 - 2015 $125

Lewis, Wyndham   1882-1957   *Self Condemned.*   Santa Barbara: Black Sparrow Press, 1983. Number 77 of 226 specially bound copies, fine in fine acetate.   Beasley Books   2013 - 2015 $45

Lewis, Wyndham   1882-1957   *Sixteen Color Plates from Blast 3.*   N.P.: Black Sparrow press, n.d., First edition, 4to., wrappers, color plates.   Beasley Books   2013 - 2015 $40

Lewis, Wyndham 1882-1957 *Snooty Baronet.* Santa Barbara: Black Sparrow Press, 1984. First printing, no. 85 of 226 specially bound and numbered copies, signed by Lafourcase on tipped in leaf, fine in fine acetate dust jacket, large 8vo.   Beasley Books   2013 - 2015 $45

Lewis, Wyndham 1882-1957 *Tarr.* New York: Knopf, 1926. Second US edition, fine, bright copy, 8vo., nice bright red dust jacket with small chip at foot of rear panel and minor sunning to spine.   Beasley Books   2013 - 2015 $150

Lewis, Wyndham 1882-1957 *Tarr.* London: Methuen & Co., 1951. Second revised edition, inscribed by author, 12mo.   Beasley Books   2013 - 2015 $200

Lewis, Wyndham 1882-1957 *Thirty Personalities and a Self-Portrait.* London: Desmond Harmsworth, 1932. First edition, only 200 copies issued, this number 137, numbered and signed by author, folio, half bound in white cloth over glazed black paper covered boards, 31 plates, each with tissue guard printed with subject's name, protected by three wing flaps, both front and back board have skinned area top edge, half dollar size, otherwise very good+, one of the wing flaps have a few wrinkles but plates and text are fine throughout, string ties very good.   Beasley Books   2013 - 2015 $600

Lewis, Wyndham 1882-1957 *Time and Western Man.* London: Chatto & Windus, 1927. First edition, 8vo., very good, inscribed by author.   Beasley Books   2013 - 2015 $250

Lewis, Wyndham 1882-1957 *Time and Western Man.* London: Chatto & Windus, 1927. First edition, brick red cloth stamped in gilt and blind, fine in very good dust jacket on somewhat heavy paper, few shallow chips at top edge, 8vo.   Beasley Books   2013 - 2015 $500

Lewis, Wyndham 1882-1957 *Wyndham Lewis the Artist: from "Blast" to Burlington House.* London: Laidlaw & Laidlaw, 1939. First edition, 8vo., frontispiece, 12 plates, 6 black and and whites, three line drawings, 8vo., cloth dust jacket soiled, light foxing.   Oak Knoll Books   306 - 276   2015 $125

Leydet, Francois *Time and The River Flowing Grand Canyon.* San Francisco: Sierra Club, 1964. First edition, over 100 color photos, endpaper map, folio, rust cloth, gilt, very fine, pictorial dust jacket.   Argonaut Book Shop   Holiday Season 2014 - 166   2015 $75

Leys, John K. *At the Sign of the Golden Horn.* London: Newnes, 1898. First edition, very good, complimentary copy from publisher, George Newnes, spine faded, otherwise very good in pictorial red cloth covered boards.   Mordida Books   March 2015 - 001365   2015 $85

Leys, John K. *The Prisoner's Secret.* London: Ward Lock, 1904. First edition, very good in cloth covered boards with gold stamped titles.   Mordida Books   March 2015 - 001385   2015 $85

A Library of Fathers of the Holy Church. Oxford: J. H. Parker, 1839, circa, 1876. First edition, 8vo.,, 40 volumes (of 43), publisher's light blue cloth lettered gilt at spine, one volume lacks spine, one has detached boards, few slight covers chipped but overall reasonable sound good used set with clean text.   Any Amount of Books   March 2015 - A966641   2015   £425

Lichtenstein, Walter *Report to the President of Northwestern University on the Results of a Trip to South America.* Evanston: Northwestern University Press, 1915. Second edition, 43 pages, 4 black and white plates, small 4to., paper wrappers, very good, partially unopened (uncut) copy, edgeworn and lightly soiled wrappers, contents clean.   Kaaterskill Books   19 - 81 2015 $100

Liebknecht, Karl *The Future Belongs to the People.* New York: Macmillan, 1918. First edition, very good+ with spot on front board, stamp of Bulgarian S. L. Federation.   Beasley Books   2013 - 2015 $45

Life in Letters: American Autograph Journal. Merion Station: American Autograph Shop, 1939-1941. 12mo., stiff paper wrappers, 15 volumes, wrappers chipped along edges.   Oak Knoll Books   306 - 249   2015 $150

Lillingston, Charles *The Causes of the present Agricultural Distress Clearly Proved.* Warwick: sold by Merridew, Wightston and Webb, Birmingham; Tite Coleshill and Shalders, Ipswich, 1834. First edition, 8vo., well bound in linen backed marbled boards, lettered, very good.   John Drury Rare Books   March 2015 - 200929   2015   £266

Lilly, Joseph *Catalogue of a most Interesting Collection of Rare and Curious Books Especially Rich in English Literature, Including an Extensive Collection of Scarce and Curious Quarto Plays, Pageants and Masques...* London: Joseph Lilly n.d. circa, 1869. 8vo., disbound in original printed wrappers, very good.   John Drury Rare Books   2015 - 14911   2015 $89

Lilly, William *Supernatural Sights and Apparitions Seen in London June 30 1644, Interpreted.* London: printed for T. V and are to be sold by I. S. in Little Brittaine, 1644. First edition, 4to., 16 pages, 2 large zodiacal text figures, generally little spotted and browned, upper margin of title cut close, no loss of letters, errata slip pasted over blank foot of last page, bound in mid 19th century black half roan gilt, rather worn, pretty good copy, 19th century armorial bookplate of Sir William Grace, Baronet.   John Drury Rare Books   March 2015 - 18856   2015 $874

Limited Editions Club *Bibliography of the Fine Books Published by the Limited Editions Club 1929-1985.* New York: Limited Editions Club, 1985. Limited to 800 numbered copies, folio, half Oasis with hand marbled paper covered boards by Faith Harrison, cloth covered slipcase lined in ultrasuede, bound by Denis Gouey.   Oak Knoll Books   25 - 72   2015 $375

Limited Editions Club *Monthly Letters. The First Fifty Monthly Letters, The Limited Editions club 1929-1933.* New York: Limited Editions Club, 1987. Limited to 550 copies, 4to., half Oasis, slipcase, letterpress on Mohawk Superfine, bound by Denis Gouey in Nigerian Oasis goatskin with hand marbled sides.   Oak Knoll Books   25 - 73   2015 $250

Lincoln Lunatic Asylum *State of the Lincoln Lunatic Asylum 1829.* Lincoln: printed by Edward B. Drury next the Bank?, 1829. First edition, 8vo., 16 pages, large folding table, recent plain wrappers, good, rare.   John Drury Rare Books   2015 - 19003   2015 $133

Lincoln Motor Company *Lincoln Zephyr V12. the Modern 'Twelve' at Medium Price. "It Belongs to the Modern World".* Detroit: Lincoln Motor Co., 1937. First printing, unpaginated through 46 pages, double page art deco illustrated title by F. Chance, many color tinted photo plates, black and white photos, many color illustrations, with 2 mylar cell overlays, 9 5/8 x 12 5/8 inches, spiral bound color illustrated card stock paper covers, with front cover having beautiful art deco color lithograph image of car's front grill, tear drop headlights, rare, average wear, very good.   Tavistock Books   Bah, Humbug? - 4   2015 $595

Lincoln - Nebraska's Capital City 1867-1923.... Lincoln: Woodruff Printing, 1923. First edition, oblong 4to., pictorial wrappers with gilt embossing, approximately 193 pages, virtually fine, no chips, binding tight, clean and bright, scarce, fine.   Baade Books of the West   2014 - 2015 $85

Lincoln, Abraham   1809-1865 *Abraham Lincoln President of the United States 1861-1865: selections from His Writings.* Worcester: Achille J. St. Onge, 1950. Limited to 1500 copies, 8 x 5.3cm., leather, gilt stamped covers and spine, all edges gilt, frontispiece, miniature bookplate of Kathryn Rickard.   Oak Knoll Books   306 - 101   2015 $260

Lincoln, Abraham   1809-1865 *Lincoln: Speeches and Writings 1832-1858; Lincoln: Speeches and Writings 1859-1865.* New York: Library of America, 1989. First edition thus, small 8vo., 2 volumes, fine in near fine dust jackets, publisher's slipcase near fine.   Beasley Books   2013 - 2015 $45

Lincoln, Abraham   1809-1865 *The Works of Abraham Lincoln.* New York: G. P. Putnam's Sons, 1905. Limited to 1000 signed and numbered sets, 8vo., 8 volumes, very good, often with notes on front endpapers and pencil brackets scattered through text (here and there, not frequently), few separations between signatures, thus very good.   Beasley Books   2013 - 2015 $150

Lind, John *An Answer to the Declaration of the American Congress.* London: T. Cadell et al, 1776. Fifth edition, 8vo., 132 pages, including half title, modern marbled wrappers, tiny worm hole in blank margin of last leaf, otherwise clean and very good, inscription in contemporary hand.   M & S Rare Books, Inc.   97 - 258   2015 $1350

Lindberger, Herbert *Ulm Design, the Morality of Objects: Hochshuchle Fur Gestaltung Ulm 1952-1968.* Cambridge: MIT Press, 1990. 4to., cloth, dust jacket, color and black and white illustrations.   Oak Knoll Books   306 - 277   2015 $200

Lindbergh, Charles A. *The Spirit of St. Louis.* New York: Charles Scribner's Sons, 1953. First edition, first printing, near fine in like dust jacket with only minor wear at spine ends, else excellent, extremely bright.   B & B Rare Books, Ltd.   234 - 68   2015 $500

Lindbergh, Charles A. *We.* New York: G. P. Putnam's Sons, 1927. First edition, limited to 1000 copies signed by author, publisher note laid in, light wear to spine, else very bright and clean.   B & B Rare Books, Ltd.   234 - 69   2015 $1500

Lindegren, Erik *Vara Bokstaver.* Askim: Erik Lindegren Grafisk Studio, 1965. Oblong 12mo., paper covered boards, slipcase, text in Swedish, 3 volumes, covers lightly soiled, small stain on front cover of first volume.   Oak Knoll Books   Special Catalogue 24 - 30   2015 $225

Linden, Linden *Printers to the Club, a Portfolio.* San Francisco: Roxburghe Club, 1986. Limited to 100 numbered copies produced for the club and 30 copies produced for the participants, this one of the numbered copies, folio, paper wrappers in cloth clamshell box with paper cover label and spine label, 32 leaves, prospectus loosely inserted.   Oak Knoll Books   306 - 168   2015 $300

Lindenmaier, H. L. *25 Years of Fish Horn Recording. The Steve Lacy Discography 1954-1979.* Freiburg: Jazzrealities, 1982. First edition, 4to., wrappers, fine.   Beasley Books   2013 - 2015 $45

Lindgren, Astrid *Pippi Langstrump Gar Am Bord.* Stockholm: Raben & Sjogren, 1945. First edition, 12mo., cloth backed pictorial boards, tiny bit of wear on corners and 3 small inconspicuous margin mends, paper edges lightly toned as in all copies due to wartime restrictions, bright, clean and better than very good+ copy, illustrations by Ingrid Nyman with 8 full page black and whites, rare.   Aleph-bet Books, Inc.   109 - 267   2015 $1600

Lindley, John *Pomolgia Britannica; or Figures and Descriptions of the Most Important Varieties of Fruit Cultivated in Great Britain.*   London: Henry G. Bohn, 1841. First edition thus, 8vo., Volume 2 only, plates 49 to 96 with full text and titlepage, 49 plates complete + 5 plates from later volume inserted at rear, hand colored engraved plates, many heightened with gum arabic, tissue guards, plates exceptionally clean and bright, very good copy.   Any Amount of Books   2015 - C15328   2015   £900

Lindsay, Howard R.   *Fowl Murder.*   Boston: Little Brown, 1941. First edition, fine in dust jacket with couple of closed tears.   Mordida Books   March 2015 - 009409   2015 $200

Lindsay, Norman   *The Magic Pudding: Adventures of Bunyip Bluegum and His Friends...*   Sydney: L. Angus & Robertson, 1918. First edition, first issue with patterned endpapers, spine stamped in gold, 4to., cloth backed pictorial boards, slight bit of toning to edge of covers else, fine in dust jacket with mounted color plate (dust jacket is very good+ with old repairs on verso at folds), illustrations by Lindsay.   Aleph-Bet Books, Inc.   108 - 273   2015 $6250

Lindsay, Robert Bruce   *Lord Rayleigh - The Man and His Work.*   Oxford et al: Pergamon Press, 1970. First edition, pictorial cloth, bit rubbed, former library copy with usual markings and defects, including spine number and rear pocket removal, good, scarce.   Jeff Weber Rare Books   178 - 1051   2015 $45

Lindsay, Vachel   1879-1931   *The Art of the Moving Picture.*   New York: Macmillan Co., 1915. First edition, cloth professionally restored at spine ends, white painted backsground on front board, mostly rubbed away, corners rounded a bit, very good, lacking dust jacket, inscribed by author for Susan Willcox, author's high school English teacher.   Between the Covers Rare Books, Inc.   187 - 96   2015 $2500

Lindsay, Vachel   1879-1931   *Going to the Sun.*   New York: D. Appleton and Co., 1923. First edition, illustrations by author, cloth beautifully restored at spine, gilt lettering on spine dull, else near fine in attractive, internally repaired, good dust jacket with some loss to crown and has been supplied to this copy, inscribed by author for friend Marjorie Logan Dec. 25 1923.   Between the Covers Rare Books, Inc.   187 - 156   2015 $500

Lindsay, William Schow   *Confirmation of Admiralty Mismanagement Referred to at the Meeting in Favour of Administrative Reform at Drury Lane June 13 1855 with a Reply to the charges of Sir Charles Wood in the House of Commons June 22 and July 10 in a letter to Samuel Morley, Esq....*   London: Effingham Wilson, 1855. First edition, 8vo., recent marbled boards lettered on spine, very good, uncommon.   John Drury Rare Books   March 2015 - 23805   2015 $266

Linford, Velma   *Wyoming: Frontier State.*   Denver: Old West Publishing Co., 1947. First edition, profusely illustrated with photos and maps, drawings by Ramona Bowman, green cloth lettered in yellow, some light rubbing to extremities, very good.   Argonaut Book Shop   Holiday Season 2014 - 168   2015 $50

Lingard, Horace   *Hints & Ideas.*   N.P.: circa, 1910. Title on front wrapper, illustrations, original red printed paper wrappers, slightly dulled and creased, good copy.   Jarndyce Antiquarian Booksellers   CCXI - 175   2015   £40

Linguet, Simon Nicolas Henri   *Lettre de M. Linguet a l'Empereur Joseph second sur la Revolution du Brabant & du reste des Pays-Bas.*   Bruxelles: de l'imprimerie de l'auteur et se trouve chez Lemaire, 1790. First edition, 8vo., 32 pages, small stain at extreme foot of two or three lower margins, sewn as issued, entirely uncut, good, large copy, presumably scarce.   John Drury Rare Books   March 2015 - 19942   2015 $266

Linne, Carl Von   1707-1778   *Select Dissertations from the Amoenitates Academicae, a Supplement to Mr. Stillingfleet's Tracts Relating to Natural History.*   London: sold by G. Robinson and J. Robson, 1781. Only edition, 8vo., including half title and errata leaf, original boards and paper spine, boards rather soiled and spine worn, internally fine, uncut and partially unopened copy, very scarce.   John Drury Rare Books   2015 - 26114   2015 $1049

Linney, Romulus   *Heathen Valley.*   New York: Atheneum, 1962. First edition, fine, lacking dust jacket, inscribed by author for Reynolds Price.   Between the Covers Rare Books, Inc.   187 - 157   2015 $300

Linsley, Philip   *Baccalaureate Address, Pronounced on the Sixth Anniversary of Nashville, October 5 1831.*   Nashville: Herald Office, 1831. First edition, 8vo., removed, some staining, discreet library, withdrawal stamp.   M & S Rare Books, Inc.   97 - 300   2015 $175

Linton, Eliza Lynn   *My Literary Life...*   London: Hodder & Stoughton, 1899. Title in red and black, uncut in original yellow cloth, rather dulled, from the library of Geoffrey & Kathleen Tillotson.   Jarndyce Antiquarian Booksellers   CCVII - 363   2015   £20

Linton, William James *To the Future. The Dirge of the Nations.* London: privately printed W. J. Linton, 1848. Original wrappers, title and imprint on front wrapper only, four vignette cuts by Linton in text and another on front wrapper, very good, scarce.   Jarndyce Antiquarian Booksellers   CCXI - 176   2015   £250

Lionni, Leo *Frederick's Fables.* New York: Pantheon, 1985. First edition, limited to 500 copies, this no. 99, signed, 4to., very good++, green cloth with mild sun spine, original mildly worn green cloth covered slipcase, laid in at book is invitation from publisher to launch party for this book.   By the Book, L. C.   44 - 78   2015 $275

Lionni, Leo *Little Blue and Little Yellow.* New York: Ivan Obolensky an Astor Book, 1959. First edition, small square 4to., pictorial boards, fine in frayed and soiled dust jacket, very scarce.   Aleph-Bet Books, Inc.   108 - 274   2015 $325

Lippincott, Sara Jane *Greenwood Leaves: a Collection of Sketches and Letters.* Boston: Ticknor, Reed and Fields, 1850. First edition, 8vo., original blindstamped purple cloth, gilt decorations and lettering, all edges gilt, engraved title, scarce, probably a presentation binding with extra gilt decorations and all edges gilt, edges little faded, some light foxing, fine.   The Brick Row Book Shop   Miscellany 67 - 64   2015 $250

Lippmann, Walter *H. L. Mencken.* New York: Knopf, n.d., 2001. Reprint from Saturday Review, 8vo., wrappers, near fine.   Beasley Books   2013 - 2015 $45

Lipton, Lawrence *Rainbow at Midnight.* Francestown: Golden Quill, 1955. First edition, advance review copy with slip laid in, laid in is typed review of the book by Jacob Scher.   Beasley Books   2013 - 2015 $45

Lisbonne, M. Gaston *Legislation sur les Raisins Secs: Etude et Commentaire.* Montpelier: Paris: Camille Coulet/G. Masson, 1891. First edition, 12mo., contemporary cloth and paper covered boards with leather spine label, 2 small attractive bookplates of Arthur Christian, lightly rubbed, else near fine, scarce.   Between the Covers Rare Books   196 - 135   2015 $500

Lissauer, Robert *Lissauer's Encyclopedia of Popular Music in America 1888 to the Present.* New York: Facts on File, 1996. First edition, 3 volumes, near fine but for library marks on f.e.p.'s.   Beasley Books   2013 - 2015 $175

A List of the Flat Officers of His Majesty's Fleet with Dates of Their First Commissions....   London: privately printed, 1801. First edition, 8vo., full red leather gilt decorated binding, binding sound but little rubbed, scuffed and dull and slightly nicked at spine very good- clean bright text.   Any Amount of Books   2015 - A73483   2015   £300

Lister, Martin *Conchyliorum Bivalbvium Utriusque Aquae Exercitatio Anatomica Tertia.* London: Sumptibus authoris impressa, 1696. First edition, 4to., 10 engraved plates, with terminal blank Z4 in first work, contemporary sprinkled calf, very skillfully rebacked in period style, small early shelfmark in red ink on endpaper and on title, minor flaw in S2 just grazing catchword, very faint foxing in fore-edge, very lovely copy with text and plates clean and fresh, armorial bookplate of A. Gifford D. D. of the Museum", presentation from Lister inscribed for Mr. Dalone.   Joseph J. Felcone Inc.   Science, Medicine and Technology - 28   2015 $10,000

Little Deserter. New York: McLoughlin Bros. n.d. circa, 1880. 4to. pictorial wrappers, 12 pages, neat spine mend and one closed tear, very good+ bright and clean, 6 very fine full page chromolithographs on black backgrounds.   Aleph-bet Books, Inc.   109 - 284   2015 $475

Little Red Riding Hood and the Wicked Wolf.   London: George Routledge and Sons, n.d., 4to., owner inscription dated 1870, wrappers, spine rubbed, slight soil, very good+, full page chromolithographs.   Aleph-Bet Books, Inc.   108 - 177   2015 $300

Little Red Riding Hood. Hamburg: Gustav W. Seitz, circa, 1860. 16mo., pictorial wrappers die cut in shape of Little Red, fine, color lithographs on each page, rare.   Aleph-bet Books, Inc.   109 - 443   2015 $800

Little Red Riding Hood. New York: McLoughlin Bros., 1888. 4to., pictorial wrappers, small corner reinforced, else very good+, 6 magnificent full page chromolithographs and pictorial covers by R. Andre.   Aleph-Bet Books, Inc.   108 - 179   2015 $275

Little Red Riding Hood. London: Raphael Tuck, n.d. circa, 1890. 4to., pictorial wrappers, light soil, very good, 3 fine full page chromolithographs plus full page and smaller illustrations in brown.   Aleph-Bet Books, Inc.   108 - 178   2015 $200

The Little Red Hen. New York: Macmillan, 1928. First edition, 8vo., fine in dust jacket with some soil on rear panel, illustrations by Berta and Elmer Hader with full color lithos.   Aleph-bet Books, Inc.   109 - 217   2015 $275

Little Red Riding Hood. New York: Duenewald, 1944. 8vo., spiral backed boards, light edge wear, else fine in worn dust jacket with edge chips, 6 fine moveable plates and other color illustrations by Julian Wehr.   Aleph-bet Books, Inc.   109 - 315   2015 $200

Little Red Riding Hood. London: Folding Books, n.d. circa, 1947. 5 1/2 x 6 1/2 inches, pictorial boards, slight rubbing, near fine, charming book that opens to form six-sided book pop-up with each of the 6 panels revealing a different portion of Red Riding Hood, illustrations in color by Patricia Turner, 6 3-dimensional pop-up scenes.   Aleph-Bet Books, Inc.   108 - 364   2015 $175

Little Review IX: 4 Autumn and Winter 1923-1924. New York: 1923-1924. Wrappers, unfortunate scorch mark with small hole on front cover causing smaller hole on next page but also causing marginal stain on first few pages not affecting text, very uncommon, small 4to.   Beasley Books   2013 - 2015 $150

Little Review XII:I Spring-Summer 1926. New York: 1926. Small 4to., 64 pages, wrappers, very good, scarce issue, few tears to edges, including several mended tears, no browning of tape.   Beasley Books   2013 - 2015 $250

Liverpool Royal Institution   *Charter of Incorporation.* Liverpool: printed by G. F. Harris's Widow and Brothers, Water Street, 1822. First edition, 8vo., recent plain wrappers, very good, very rare.   John Drury Rare Books   March 2015 - 16479   2015 $266

Livingston, Armstrong   *The Guilty Accuser.* New York: Chelsea, 1928. First edition, very good in price clipped dust jacket with light wear to head and foot of spine.   Buckingham Books   March 2015 - 10907   2015 $250

Livingston, Robert R.   *Essay on Sheep: Their Varieties... account of the Merinoes...* Concord: Daniel Cooledge, 1813. Woodcut on title, sheep backed boards, foxed, else very nice, tight copy.   Joseph J. Felcone Inc.   Science, Medicine and Technology - 47   2015 $300

Livingston, William Farrand   *Israel Putnam Pioneer, Ranger and Major General.* New York: G. P. Putnam, 1901. First edition, burgundy cloth with gilt decoration and lettering, frontispiece, photos, drawings, facsimiles, bright, tight copy, nearly fine, uncommon.   Stephen Lupack   March 2015 - 2015 $95

Le Livre et Ses Amis. Paris: Revue mensuelle De L'Art Du Livre, 1945-1947. With mostly HC limitation of 200, though 3 issues are from the numbered 1700 limitation, all issues are gathered sheets in wrappers and are in at least near fine condition, though they all have sunning to wrappers, 4to., complete run.   Beasley Books   2013 - 2015 $250

Livy   *Historiarum ab Urbe Condita, Libri qui Extant, XXXV.* Venice: Apud Paulum Manutium, 1555. First edition by Sigonius, titlepage creased and pulling loose at foot, lightly dusty as well, first 20 or so gatherings evenly browned and bit spotted from having been lightly washed in an attempt to remove early marginal notes (these still mostly legible, albeit cropped), the rest of the book largely quite clean and bright, folio, 18th century vellum boards, boards with border and centre-piece in blind, spine lettered in ink, somewhat dusty and marked, front board bowing bit, small crack to head of front joint, sometime recased with endpapers renewed, bookplate removed from pastedown, good.   Blackwell's Rare Books   Greek & Latin Classics VI - 70   2015   £2000

Livy   *Historiarum ab Urbe Condita, Libri qui Extant, XXXV.* Venice: Apud Paulum Manutium, 1566. Second Signoio edition, tidy repairs to blank verso of titlepage and one or two other leaves, some staining to titlepage and occasionally elsewhere, few gatherings browned, occasional marginal notes in early hand, mostly numerals and manicules, few leaves with ink splashes, not obscuring text, old inscription rubbed out from margin of titlepage, folio, 18th century Italian vellum, brown morocco lettering piece to spine, slightly soiled, good.   Blackwell's Rare Books   Greek & Latin Classics VI - 71   2015   £1500

Lloyd Brothers & Co.   *Recollections of the Great Exhibition 1851.* London: published by Lloyd Brothers & Co., 22 Ludgate Hill & Simpkin Marshall & Co., Stationers Hall Court, Day & Son Lith. to the Queen, Sept. 1st, 1851. Large folio, one leaf of contents, hand colored lithograph, title and 24 plates, heightened in gum arabic, all trimmed and laid on thick card as issued, manuscript titles ink at foot of each mount, without imprint or titles, titlepage only with imprint, some spotting to title and few leaves with dust marks, leaf of contents laid down on Japanese paper with some loss to edges, not affecting text, loose as issued in original publisher's blue half morocco folio, cover blocked gilt, skillfully rebacked, corners repaired, rare.   Marlborough Rare Books Ltd.   List 49 - 21   2015   £5750

Lloyd, A.   *White Aster: a Japanese Epic Together with other Poems.* Tokyo: T. Hasegawa, 1897. 8vo., silk ties, light crease on first two leaves, else fine in pictorial case with ivory clasps, case is dusty, bound with Frenchfold pages, nearly every page completely illustrated with beautiful color woodblock prints by Mishima Yunosuke.   Aleph-bet Books, Inc.   109 - 234   2015 $650

Lloyd, L.   *Peasant Life in Sweden.* London: Tinsley Bros., printed by J. Childs & Son, 1870. First edition, 8vo., 9 plates, corners slightly bumped and rubbed, spine ends very slightly frayed, otherwise sound, about very good, clean decent above average copy.   Any Amount of Books   March 2015 - A88704   2015   £350

Lloyd, Nelson   *The Robberies Company Ltd.* New York: Scribners, 1906. First edition, fine in olive green cloth covered boards with gold stamped titles, fine.   Mordida Books   March 2015 - 001396   2015 $85

Lobeira, Vasco *Amadis of Gaul by Vasco Lobeira.* London: printed for T. N. Longman and Rees, 1803. First edition of Robert Southey's translation, 4 volumes, 12mo., later tan half calf, marbled paper boards, black leather labels, gilt rules and lettering, half title in volume one only, small bookplate of Grenville Kane, edges slightly rubbed, fine set. The Brick Row Book Shop Miscellany 67 - 84 2015 $450

Lobel, Arnold *On Market Street.* New York: Greenwillow, 1981. Stated first edition, with correct 1-10 number code, 4to., quarter cloth and boards, as new in dust jacket, full page color illustrations, this copy inscribed by the artist, Anita Lobel with sketch of a clown. Aleph-Bet Books, Inc. 108 - 275 2015 $450

Lobel, Arnold *Owl at Home.* New York: Harper & Row, 1975. Stated first edition, 8vo., pictorial boards, fine in dust jacket, illustrations by Lobel on very page. Aleph-bet Books, Inc. 109 - 268 2015 $100

Lochner, Louis P. *Mexico -- Whose War?* New York: Peoples Print, First edition, wrappers, good+, tall 8vo., tearing at spine and some fragility to browning wrappers. Beasley Books 2013 - 2015 $45

Locke, Alain *The New Negro.* New York: Albert and Charles Boni, 1925. First edition, very good with wear at edges as usual, owner's name. Beasley Books 2013 - 2015 $550

Locke, Alain *The New Negro.* New York: Albert & Charles Boni, 1925. First edition, very good- with staining to spine and rubbed boards, edges and corners, still quite tight, illustrations by Winold Reiss. Beasley Books 2013 - 2015 $500

Locke, John 1632-1704 *Essai Philosophique concernant l'Entendement Human ou l'on Montre Quelle est l'Etendue de Nos Connoissances Certaines, et la Maniere dont Nous y Parvenons. (A Philosophical Essay on Human Understanding...).* Amsterdam: Chez Henri Schelte, 1700. First edition in French, quarto, frontispiece, woodcut printer's device on titlepage, decorative woodcut head and tailpieces and initials, in this copy frontispiece bound after p. (iv) rather than opposite the titlepage, handsomely bound in 18th century calf, spine decoratively tooled in gilt compartments with red morocco gilt lettering label, both front and back boards each with single unobtrusive gouge, joints and head of spine expertly and unobtrusively repaired, some foxing and occasional browning, few small light stains on titlepage, excellent copy. Athena Rare Books 15 - 33 2015 $2500

Locke, John 1632-1704 *A Letter to the Right Reverend Edward Ld Bishop of Worcester Concerning Some Passages Relating to Mr. Locke's Essay of Humane Understanding... (bound with) Mr. Locke's Reply to the Right Reverend the Lord Bishop of Worcester's Answer to His Letter Concerning Some Passages Relating to Mr. Locke's Essay of Human Understanding.* London: printed by H. Clark for A. and J. Churchill and Edw. Castle, 1697. (Both titles). First editions, 8vo., 2 volumes i 1, contemporary black panelled morocco, brown morocco label, gilt decorations and lettering, all edges gilt, half titles present, edges rubbed, front hinge starting, but holding soundly, very good in original state. The Brick Row Book Shop Miscellany 67 - 65 2015 $3500

Locke, Samuel *A New Abstract of the Excise Statutes...* Sherborne: printed for and sold by the author and published in London by S. Smith, 1788. First and only edition, 8vo., contemporary sheep, recently rebound in old style half calf, gilt, very good, rare. John Drury Rare Books 2015 - 7852 2015 $1049

Lockridge, Frances *Death on the Aisle. A Mr. and Mrs. North Mystery.* Philadelphia and New York: J. B. Lippincott Co., 1942. First edition, fine with light professional restoration to foot of spine and fold flaps. Buckingham Books March 2015 - 30533 2015 $675

Lockridge, Frances *The Dishonest Murderer.* J. B. Lippincott, 1949. First edition, fine in dust jacket. Buckingham Books March 2015 - 37118 2015 $275

Lockridge, Frances *Murder Out of Turn.* London: Frederick A. Stokes, 1941. First edition, fine in dust jacket with minor edge wear, sharp copy. Buckingham Books March 2015 - 38445 2015 $875

Lockridge, Ross *Raintree County.* Boston: Houghton Mifflin, 1948. First edition, 8vo., fine in near fine, price clipped dust jacket. Beasley Books 2013 - 2015 $150

Lockwood, Frank C. *The Life of Edward E. Ayer.* Chicago: A. C. McClurg, 1929. First edition, 26 photo plates and portraits, one in color, two-tone dark and light brown cloth gilt, very fine, lightly worn slipcase. Argonaut Book Shop Holiday Season 2014 - 169 2015 $125

Lockwood, Ingersoll *Baron Trump's marvellous Underground.* Boston: Lee and Shepard, 1893. First edition, octavo,, 24 full page illustrations by Charles Howard Johnson original light brown cloth, front panel stamped in dark brown, spine panel stamped in dark brown and gold, floral patterned endpapers. L. W. Currey, Inc. Boy's Adventure Fiction 2015 - 59 2015 $150

Lockwood, Samuel *Temperance, Fortitude, Justice. An Address Delivered at the Eighth Anniversary of Chingarora Tent No. 204 I. O. of R.* New York: Published for Chingarora Tent by J. Moffet, 1855. First edition, original printed paper wrappers, very faint stain to bottom corner of first few leaves with tiny crease to top corner of final three, rear panel perished. Tavistock Books Temperance - 2015 $40

Lockyer, Nicholas *Baulme for Bleeding England and Ireland or Seasonable Instructions for Persecuted Christians.* London: printed by E. G. for John Rothwell and are to be sold at This Shop at the Signe of the Sun in Saint Paul's Church Yard, 1643. First edition, small 8vo., full leather unlettered, slight bowing, slight rubbing at corner and chipping at spine ends, otherwise very good. Any Amount of Books 2015 - A42245 2015 £220

Lodge, John *The Usage of Holding Parliaments and of Preparing and Passing Bills of Supply, in Ireland, Stated from Record.* Dublin printed: London reprinted for Robinson and Roberts, 1770. Reprint, 8vo., 76 pages, sewn into later wrappers, good copy. John Drury Rare Books March 2015 - 20220 2015 £266

Lofting, Hugh *Doctor Dolittle's Return.* New York: Stokes, 1933. First edition, 8vo. orange cloth, pictorial paste-on, 273 pages, fine in lightly worn dust jacket with chips, illustrations by Lofting with color frontispiece and numerous full page black and whites, nice, clean copy. Aleph-bet Books, Inc. 109 - 269 2015 $500

Lofting, Hugh *Story of Mrs. Tubbs.* New York: Frederick Stokes, 1923. Oblong 8vo., cloth, pictorial paste-on, repair on top margin of one page, else fine in slightly worn dust jacket, illustrations by author with full page color plates and full page line illustrations. Aleph-Bet Books, Inc. 108 - 277 2015 $250

Logan, Algernon Sydney *The Mirror of a Mind. A Poem.* New York: published for the author by G. P. Putnam's sons, 1875. First edition, 8vo., original green cloth, gilt lettered, all edges gilt, bookplate from the collection of Sidney Lanier (1842-1881), presented by his son Charles D. Lanier to Johns Hopkins University, very good. The Brick Row Book Shop Miscellany 67 - 16 2015 $325

Logan, James *Catalogue of the Books Belonging to the Loganian Library to Which is Prefixed a Short Account of the Institution with the Law for annexing the Said Library to that Belonging to the Library Company of Philadelphia and the Rules Regulating the Manner of Conducting the Same.* Philadelphia: n.p. Library Co. of Philadelphia?, 1837. 8vo., full contemporary calf with black leather spine label, frontispiece, frontispiece, covers rubbed and abrased in places, frontispiece engraving of James Logan, from the library of Henry Gilpin with his bookplate. Oak Knoll Books 306 - 79 2015 $175

Logan, Nick *The Face. May 1980 issue one.* London: Wagadon Ltd., 1980. First edition, 4to., scarce first issue, pages 62, copiously illustrated in color and black and white, slight wear at spine, used but pleasant, very good copy. Any Amount of Books 2015 - A35417 2015 £150

Lohser, Beate *Unorthodox Freud. the View from the Couch.* New York: Guilford Press, 1996. First edition, 8vo. fine in fine dust jacket. Beasley Books 2013 - 2015 $45

Loire, Gabriel *Une Nuit Fantastique.* Paris: Sesclee de Brouwer, 1929. Large 4to., cloth backed pictorial boards, sight cover soil, near fine, illustrations by author, full page and in-text color illustrations. Aleph-Bet Books, Inc. 108 - 194 2015 $600

Loiseau, Jean Simon *Traite des Enfans Naturels, Adulterins, Incesteueux et Abandonnes.* Paris: chez J. Antoine, 1811. First edition, 8vo., half title, lightly browned with minor sporadic foxing, contemporary sheep backed marbled boards, flat spine gilt with black morocco lettering piece, very good. John Drury Rare Books March 2015 - 16251 2015 $221

Lomax, John A. *Adventures of a Ballad Hunter.* New York: Macmillan, 1947. First edition, near fine with traces of wear to top edge, very good+ dust jacket with tiny chips at top edge, this copy signed by Lomax in year of publication. Beasley Books 2013 - 2015 $225

Lomax, John A. *Adventures of a Ballad Hunter.* New York: Macmillan Co., 1947. First edition, 8vo., decorated red cloth, blue ink stamping on front cover and spine, illustrations, fine in dust jacket with light wear to foot of spine and two tiny holes to edge of rear flap fold, handsome copy. Buckingham Books March 2015 - 30531 2015 $275

Lomax, John A. *Negro Folk Songs as Sung by Lead Belly.* Macmillan Co., 1936. First edition, 8vo., cloth, frontispiece, light offsetting to front and rear endpapers, few front endpages lighty foxed, else very good, internally clean copy in dust jacket with small chips to spine ends and extremities, scarce, elusive. Buckingham Books March 2015 - 37613 2015 $750

Lomberg, Einar *The Swedish Zoological Expedition to British East Africa 1911. Birds.* Upsala: Almqvist & Wiksells, 1911-1912. Quarto, 461 pages, 22 pales, single volume binder's cloth with 3 parts, marbled boards with some damage, sound. Andrew Isles 2015 - 11829 2015 $700

London and County Banking Co. Ltd. *London and County Joint Stock Bank 71 Lombard Street, Proceedings of the Annual Meeting of Proprietors Held at the Bank Premises on Thursday Feb. 3, 1842.* London: printed for the proprietors by Blaes and East, 1842. First edition, 8vo., 32 pages, preserved in modern wrappers with printed label on upper cover, very good.   John Drury Rare Books   March 2015 - 23796   2015 $266

London Cries for the Young. London: Darton and Co. circa, 1855. First edition, small 8vo., color frontispiece, 13 charming hand colored illustrations, vignette on titlepage, original green blindstamped cloth with gilt decorative design lettered green on spine and upper cover, very good, slight wear, very small nick at head of spine, corners little bowed.   Any Amount of Books   March 2015 - C13435   2015   £400

The London Fishery Laid Open; or the Arts of the Fishermen and Fishmongers Set in a True Light. London: printed by D. Henry and R. Cave, 1759. First and only edition, 4to., complete with half title, small hole and marginal tears in half title not affecting letters, otherwise very good, crisp, preserved in old style marbled wrappers with label, very scarce.   John Drury Rare Books   March 2015 - 25198   2015 $874

London Interiors: a Grand National Exhibition of the Religious, Regal and Civic Solemnities, Public Amusements, Scientific Meetings and Commercial Scenes of the British Capital. London: J. Mead, circa, 1851. First edition of this edition, 2 volumes in one, 4to., some light discoloration of text, additional engraved pictorial titlepage, frontispiece, 74 plates, publisher's original blue cloth blocked in gilt and blind.   Marlborough Rare Books Ltd.   List 49 - 31   2015   £450

The London Journal of Arts and Sciences... London: Sherwood, Neely and Jones and W. Newton, 1821-1822. 3 volumes, volumes II-IV only, 8vo., original paper covered boards, labels on spine, top edge gilt, other edges uncut, plates, from the library of Henry Morris who bought them for their information on papermaking, boards and endpapers of volume II separated, spines and labels thereon of all 3 volumes worn, boards of all volumes soiled, some light foxing in text. Oak Knoll Books   306 - 98   2015 $200

London Missionary Society *The London Missionary Society's Report of the Proceedings Against the Rev. J. Smith of Demerara Minister of the Gospel...* London: F. Westley, 1824. First edition, 8vo., original boards, corner of upper covers worn, neatly rebacked and labelled, entirely uncut very good.   John Drury Rare Books   2015 - 2015 $1136

London Survey Committee   *The Survey of London. Volume X. The Parish of St. Margaret, Westminster Part I.* London: B. T. Batsford, 1926. 4to., folding map and plates, uncut in original drab paper wrappers, very good.   Jarndyce Antiquarian Booksellers   CCXI - 178   2015   £65

London Survey Committee   *The Survey of London. Volume XIII. The Parish of St. Margaret Westminster. Part 2 volume Part one and Volume XIV. The Parish of St. Margaret Westminster, Part 3, volume 2.* London: B. T. Batsford, 1930-1931. Folding maps and plates, cloth, very good in dust jackets, card slipcase.   Jarndyce Antiquarian Booksellers   CCXI - 179   2015   £60

London Survey Committee   *The Survey of London. Volume XVII. The Village of Highgate.* London: London County Council, 1936. 4to., folding map and plates, cloth, very good in dust jacket.   Jarndyce Antiquarian Booksellers   CCXI - 180   2015   £70

London Survey Committee   *The Survey of London. Volume XVIII. The Strand.* London: London County Council, 1937. Folding map, plates, cloth, very good in slightly torn dust jacket.   Jarndyce Antiquarian Booksellers   CCXI - 181   2015   £70

London Survey Committee   *The Survey of London. Volume XXII. Barkside. The Parishes of St. Saviour and Christchurch Southwark.* London: London County Council, 1950. Folding map and plates, cloth, without dust jacket but with recent paper cover attached with sellotape, leaving few marks.   Jarndyce Antiquarian Booksellers   CCXI - 182   2015   £50

London Survey Committee   *The Survey of London. Volume XXVII. Spitalfields and Mile End New Town.* London: Athlone Press, 1957. 4to., folding map and plates, cloth, very good in torn dust jacket with sellotape repairs.   Jarndyce Antiquarian Booksellers   CCXI - 184   2015   £90

London Survey Committee   *The Survey of London. Volume XXVIII. Parish of Hackney, part I. Brooke House.* London: Athlone Press, 1960. 4to., folding map and plates, cloth, very good in dust jacket.   Jarndyce Antiquarian Booksellers   CCXI - 185   2015   £40

London, Jack   1876-1916   *Burning Daylight.* New York: Macmillan, 1910. First edition, 2nd state with 3 page blanks following rear ads, decorated cloth, illustrations, very good+ (little spotting and wear, clean, tight text).   Stephen Lupack   March 2015 - 2015 $100

London, Jack   1876-1916   *The Call of the Wild.* New York: Macmillan Co., 1903. First edition, first printing, publisher's olive green designed by CX, endpapers and titlepage by Charles Edward Hooper, illustrations by Goodwin and Bull, housed in custom quarter morocco slipcase, near fine, some light wear to extremities, light rubbing to front board and spine, otherwise bright and clean binding, fresh interior, slipcase with some light wear to extremities, hint of faint toning to spine, else fine, overall extremely bright and pleasing.   B & B Rare Books, Ltd.   2015 - 2015 $2000

London, Jack   1876-1916   *The Call of the Wild.*   New York: Macmillan, 1903. First edition, first printing, very good or better with some rubbing to extremities, in scarce and fragile jacket with some light wear, small tear to front panel, very minor toning to spine, some chipping to upper spine, spine folds tender and slightly cracked, else crisp and well preserved, housed in custom folding box, nice, completely unrestored copy.   B & B Rare Books, Ltd.   234 - 70   2015 $12,000

London, Jack   1876-1916   *The Game.*   New York: Macmillan, 1905. First edition, 2nd state with small Metropolitan stamp on copyright page, bright, near fine.   Stephen Lupack   March 2015 - 2015 $125

London, Jack   1876-1916   *The Night-Born. and also The Madness of John Harned. When the World was Young. The Benefit of the Doubt....*   Toronto: Bell & Cockburn, 1913. First Canadian edition, very good plus.   Stephen Lupack   March 2015 - 2015 $125

London, Jack   1876-1916   *White Fang.*   New York: The Macmillan Co., 1906. First edition, issue with tipped in titlepage on laid paper as usual, original pictorial grey-green vertically ribbed cloth, excellent copy, small former owner's signature to verso of front endpaper, slightest trace or rubbing at foot of spine, else very tight, clean, fine, without any of the usual wear.   B & B Rare Books, Ltd.   234 - 71   2015 $1000

The Long Vacation: a Satyr.   London: printed and sold by H. Hills, 1708. First of two pirated editions, 8vo., 16 pages, disbound, good.   C. R. Johnson   Foxon R-Z - 1206r-z   2015 $153

Long, Roger   *The Music Speech, Spoken at the Public Commencement in Cambridge July the 6th 1714.*   London: printed and sold by J. Morphew and C. Crownfield, 1714. First edition, 8vo., half title and final blank, minor browning and dust marking, old repairs in two blank corners, preserved in modern wrappers with printed title label on upper cover, good.   John Drury Rare Books   March 2015 - 21408   2015 $221

Longfellow, Henry Wadsworth   1807-1882   *Evangeline a Tale of Acadie Decorated with Leaves from the Acadian Forests.*   London: Belfast & New York: Marus Ward and Co., n.d., Inscription dated 1889, green cloth, gold titles and red and brown leaves to front cover and gilt to spine, all edges gilt, color drawings, wear to edges, interior very good.   Schooner Books Ltd.   110 - 3   2015 $45

Longfellow, Henry Wadsworth   1807-1882   *Evangeline.*   Boston and London: John W. Luce and Co., 1908. 8vo., (60) pages, each page has floral design to top and bottom margins, with illustrated capitals and few illustrations in outer margins, all in black and green, paper made to look like birch bark, slight waterstain to front cover and edge of spine has some light browning, decorative paper covered boards, Evangeline in black and white with forest in background in black and green, spine has four drilled holes for a silk ribbon.   Schooner Books Ltd.   110 - 2   2015 $45

Longfellow, Henry Wadsworth   1807-1882   *Poems on Slavery.*   Cambridge: John Owen, 1843. Third edition, 8vo., 31 pages, half title, folded, unbound and unopened sheets, uncut, some soiling on edges.   M & S Rare Books, Inc.   97 - 156   2015 $950

Longfellow, Henry Wadsworth   1807-1882   *The Song of Hiawatha.*   London: David Bogue, 1855. First edition, first issue, with 'dove' for 'dived' on page 96 line 7; original green cloth, blindstamped sides, spine lettered and decorated in gilt, 24 pages ads at end dated March 1855, sides little marked and slight wear at head and foot of spine, nice, poet Kenneth Hopkins' copy with his ownership signature, bibliographical notes in ink on front pastedown and another ownership signature on titlepage, from the collection of Gavin H. Fryer.   Bertram Rota Ltd.   308 Part II - 154   2015   £450

Longus   *Daphnis et Chloe.*   Jourde et Allard, 1949. No. 40, one of only 25 copies with two original drawings on one leaf and an extra suite of illustrations in single color, both fine, 4to., unbound signatures in wrappers, fine in fine wrappers, green velour chemise and striking cream box with bold leaf design, near fine.   Beasley Books   2013 - 2015 $500

Longwell, Dennis Steichen   *The Master Prints 1895-1914.*   Boston: New York: NYGS/MOMA, 1978. First edition, small 4to., fine in lightly rubbed dust jacket.   Beasley Books   2013 - 2015 $45

Lonsdale, John, Viscount   *Memoir of the Reign of James II.*   York: privately printed, 1808. First edition, 4to., half leather, marbled boards, signed presentation from author for Lord Camden, endpapers foxed, corners and spine slightly rubbed, otherwise very good, sound, clean copy with clean text.   Any Amount of Books   2015 - A77543   2015   £160

Look Here.   London: Dean's Rag Book Co. Ltd. n.d. circa, 1915. As new, charming color illustrations in color, 8vo, pictorial cloth.   Aleph-bet Books, Inc.   109 - 98   2015 $300

A Looking-Glasse for Sope-Patentees; or a Prospective Glasse, Making Discovery of New Projects Contrived and Propounded (by the Sope-projetors) to the Parliament... London: printed in the year, 1646. First edition, 4to., title printed within typographic border, 8 pages, final page rather soiled, else very good, untrimmed, bound in 20th century calf gilt and labelled.   John Drury Rare Books   2015 - 25672   2015 $1661

Loos, Anita   *Gentlemen Prefer Blondes.*   New York: Boni & Liveright, 1925. Later printing, published one month after first, inscribed by Loos for George Gershwin, octavo, 217 pages, later issue dust jacket.   Honey & Wax Booksellers   1 - 56   2015 $4800

Lopes Branco, Antonio   *Memoria dos Principaes actos e Trabalhos do Ministro e Secretario d'Estado dos Negocios da Fazenda.*   Lisboa: Imprensa Nacional, 1851. First edition, final leaf of errata, title lightly foxed with some slight dust soiling, otherwise clean, contemporary green morocco backed boards, boards and spine ruled in gilt, spine chipped at foot, else very good.   John Drury Rare Books   2015 - 20160   2015 $177

Lopez, Barry   *"The American Indian Mind".*   New York: Quest, 1978. Offprint, 8 1/2 x 11 inches, stapled sheet, 15 pages, slight rust near staples, otherwise fine.   Ken Lopez, Bookseller   164 - 122   2015 $250

Lopez, Barry   *Children in the Woods.*   Eugene: Lone Goose Press, 1992. First edition thus, one of 75 copies signed by author and artist, housed in original publishers' cloth clamshell box, with spine label, fine.   Ed Smith Books   83 - 59   2015 $400

Lopez, Barry   *Crossing Open Ground.*   New York: Vintage Books, 1989. First Vingate book edition, fine in wrappers, nicely inscribed by author for Nicholas Delbanco Oct. 7 1989.   Between the Covers Rare Books, Inc.   187 - 159   2015 $65

Lopez, Barry   *Desert Notes.*   Kansas City: Sheed Andrews McMeel, 1976. First edition, light splaying to boards, near fine in rubbed, near fine dust jacket with wear at spine tips, inscribed by author in month prior to publication.   Ken Lopez, Bookseller   164 - 121   2015 $450

Lopez, Barry   *The Near Woods. Images and Design by Charles Hobson.*   San Francisco: Pacific Editions, 2006. One of 26 lettered copies, each lettered (a to z) and signed in pencil by author and artist, Charles Hobson from a total of 26+ copies which includes few artist proof copies, page size 10 x 7 inches, 10 pages, double page foldout containing monotype image with pastel on German etching paper reproduced as a digital pigment print that has been hand colored with pastel and acrylic paint by the artist and another single page image on verso, the two images signed in pencil by Charles Hobson, bound by Hobson and Alice Shaw in original paper over boards bound in, paper a reproduction of a drawing used to establish land grants in California.   Priscilla Juvelis - Rare Books   61 - 40   2015 $850

Loraine and the Little People of the Ocean.   Chicago: Rand McNally, 1922. 8vo., pictorial boards, fine in dust jacket with small chip, illustrations by James McCracken with 8 lovely color plates plus many detailed black and whites, rarely found in dust jacket.   Aleph-bet Books, Inc.   109 - 163   2015 $275

Loraine, Nevison   *The Church and Liberties of England.*   London: Smith, Elder & Co., 1876. First edition, 8vo., original green cloth, spine lettered gilt, good copy, surprisingly rare.   John Drury Rare Books   March 2015 - 23010   2015 $221

Lord, Eliot   *Comstock Mining and Miners.*   Washington: 1883. 451 pages, illustrations, 3 maps, original cloth, ink notations, else clean and very good.   Dumont Maps and Books of the West   130 - 40   2015 $350

Lord, Myra B.   *History of the New England Woman's Press Association 1885-1931.*   Newton: Graphic Press, 1932. First edition, large 8vo., very good, illustrations.   Second Life Books Inc.   189 - 152   2015 $75

Lorde, Audre   *Coal.*   New York: Norton, 1976. First edition, hardcover, 8vo., fine in fine dust jacket.   Beasley Books   2013 - 2015 $40

Lorenz, Otto   *Catalogue General De La Librairie Francaise Pendant 25 Ans (1840-1865).*   Paris: O. Lorenz, 1867-1934. 8vo., 32 volumes variously bound, volumes 1-11 quarter leather, marbled paper covered boards, volumes 12-13 with later library binding, volumes 1-19 paper covered boards, volumes 20-32 half leather, marbled paper covered boards, rubbed and scuffed at edges, foxing, especially on endpapers, clipping attached to back endpaper of fourth volume, boards of volumes 14-19 worn, front board of volume 15 detached, small ink stamp indicates this was a duplicate from the Library of Congress.   Oak Knoll Books   306 - 80   2015 $2500

Lorenzini, Carlo 1829-1890 *"La Storia Di un Burattino."* (Pinocchio) in children's magazine Giornale Per I Bambini. 1881-1883. 4to., pictorial wrappers with few issues having some minor restoration, otherwise generally in very good condition housed in red cloth folder made from original cloth cover of old bound set of magazines. Aleph-bet Books, Inc. 109 - 99 2015 $25,000

Lorenzini, Carlo 1829-1890 *Story of a Puppet or the Adventures of Pinocchio.* New York: Cassell, 1892. First edition in English, 12mo., decorative cloth with designed repeated on edges, cloth age toned as usual, name erased from endpaper, tiny stain on edge of title, small inner hinge mend, else really very good+, marbled slipcase, the Bradley Martin copy with Mildred Greenhill's bookplate. Aleph-Bet Books, Inc. 108 - 103 2015 $9500

Lorenzini, Carlo 1829-1890 *Pinocchio.* Philadelphia: Lippincott, 1920. First edition, deluxe edition, 4to., blue and tan cloth, fine in original pictorial box, box rubbed and slightly soiled, 14 beautiful tipped in color plates by Maria Kirk, plus illustrations on text pages and pictorial endpapers, scarce in box. Aleph-bet Books, Inc. 109 - 100 2015 $500

Lorenzini, Carlo 1829-1890 *Pinocchio: Il Guardaroba Di Pinocchio.* Milano: Carroccio, n.d. circa, 1940. Folio, stiff pictorial wrappers, fine and unused, 6 leaves (plus rear cover), illustrations, rare. Aleph-Bet Books, Inc. 108 - 104 2015 $600

Lorioux, Felixe *Une Poule Sur un Mur.* Paris: Hachette, printed by Dean Rag Book co., n.d., 1924. 4to., printed on cloth, slight fading, else very good+, great color illustrations by Lorioux. Aleph-Bet Books, Inc. 108 - 278 2015 $425

Lorrain, Jean *Nightmares of an Ether-Drinker.* Leyburn: Tartarus Press, 2002. One of 350 copies, fine in fine dust jacket. Beasley Books 2013 - 2015 $150

Lotka, Alfred J. *Elements of Physical Biology.* Baltimore: Williams & Wilkins, 1925. First edition, 8vo., original blue cloth lettered gilt on spine, 72 illustrations, 36 tables, head of spine very slightly creased, otherwise very good+ in serviceable repaired tanned and slightly chipped very good- dust jacket. Any Amount of Books 2015 - A67975 2015 £240

Loudon, Jane *The Mummy!* London: Henry Colburn, 1828. Second edition, 3 volumes, 8vo., recent brown half morocco period style by Philip Dusel, marbled paper boards, gilt decorations and lettering, 2 pages of publisher's terminal ads in one volume, 2nd edition, some minor spots in text, fine, handsome copy. The Brick Row Book Shop Miscellany 67 - 66 2015 $8000

Louis, Adrian C. *Among the Dog Eaters.* Albuquerque: West End Press, 1992. First edition, paperback original, modest rubbing, else near fine, Advance review copy with promotional material laid in, inscribed by author for Larry McMurtry. Between the Covers Rare Books, Inc. 187 - 197 2015 $125

Louisville & Nashville Railroad *Gulf Coast. The American Riviera.* Poole Bros. Inc., 1935. 64 panels, 4 per page, doubled twice to 9 x 4 inches, bright color pictorial wrappers with golf scene, illustrations, beautiful 8 panel color panoramic map at center, bright brochure with minimal soiling to wrappers. Buckingham Books March 2015 - 34347 2015 $175

Louys, Pierre *Leda or in Praise of the Blessings of Darkness.* Easthampton: Cheloniidae Press, 1985. One of 60 copies, from a total edition of 75, each signed and numbered by artist, page size 11 x 8 inches, bound by Samuel Feinstein, full page green buffalo leather from Remy Carriat in France, covers tooled in 23K gold leaf and carbon in single fillets, gold gilt fillet connecting eggshell lacquer ovoid inlays on each of the panels, carbon fillet on back panel only, spine smooth with author and title in gold gilt, small circle surrounded by gold gilt separating them, 'sunken' grey suede doublures with black morocco border with tooled line between black and blue-green leathers, grey pig suede flyleaves, eggshell lacquer panels were inlaid in front and back panels in black and white, top edge gilt, blue and grey silk headbands signed "Samuel Feinstein" in blind on lower edge of back panel, housed in custom made grey cloth over boards clamshell box, with title LEDA a stamped in gold gilt on blue buffalo label affixed to spine of box, 5 drypoint etchings and 7 wood engravings by Alan James Robinson, all housed in custom made cloth and pigskin clamshell box, text printed by Dan Keleher at Wild Carrot Letterpress, wood engravings printed by Harold McGrath, drypoints printed by Alan James Robinson at Cheloniidae Press, type set by Mackenzie-Harris San Francisco. Priscilla Juvelis - Rare Books 61 - 4 2015 $2750

Louys, Pierre *Leda or In Praise of the Blessings of Darkness.* Easthampton: Cheloniidae Press, 1985. State proof edition, copy #1 of 15 deluxe copies, with designer binding by Daniel Kelm, with original drawing, three extra suites, all on Saunders hot press watercolor paper, etchings on hand made Gamp Torinoko paper, one of 15 copies from a total of 75, each signed and numbered by the artist, 60 regular copies and 15 deluxe copies (this copy), page size 8 x 11 inches, 46 pages, five drypoint etchings and 7 wood engravings by Alan James Robinson each signed and numbered, type set by MacKenzie-Harris and printed by Dan Keleher at Wild Carrot Letterpress, wood engravings printed by Harold McGrath and drypoints printed by Alan James Robinson, designed by Robinson and Arthur Larson, bound by Kelm in full white alum-tawed pigskin, front panel with inset bas relief paper casting, in white against blue paper ground with darker blue border, taken from an original wax sculpture by Robinson, torso of nude Leda with swan between her legs, housed in custom made tan cloth clamshell box with blue paper linings, three part foldout with inset in one to accommodate bas relief on binding cover, signed by Kelm on colophon, clamshell box housed original drawing by Robinson, 5 state proof etchings, 13 proofs of wood engravings and extra suite of the 5 etchings and 7 wood engravings as well as a copy of original prospectus, box has some soiling at edges, book and extra suites are fine. Priscilla Juvelis - Rare Books   61 - 3   2015 $2800

Love, W. De Loss *Thomas Short; the First Printer of Connecticut.* Hartford: Hartford Press, 1901. Limited to 102 numbered copies, 8vo., stiff paper wrappers.   Oak Knoll Books   306 - 201   2015 $175

Lovecraft, H. P. *Dreams and Fancies.* Sauk city: Arkham House, 1962. First edition, 8vo., signed by introducer, August Derleth, fine in about fine dust jacket with very slight edgewear, excellent condition.   Any Amount of Books   March 2015 - A74373   2015   £400

Lovecraft, H. P. *The Outsider and Others.* Sauk City: Arkham House, 1939. First edition, very good+ in about very good dust jacket, light bumps to top corners and slight lean, jacket rubbed, light toning to spine and rear panel with chips and tears overall, still mostly presentable.   Royal Books   46 - 30   2015 $2450

Lovejoy, Joseph C. *Memoir of the Rev. Elijah P. Lovejoy Who was Murdered in Defense of Liberty of the Press at Alton Illinois Nov. 7 1837...* New York: John S. Taylor, 1838. First edition, 8vo., publisher's cloth (rubbed through along some of the hinges, some foxed), good copy.   Second Life Books Inc.   190 - 147   2015 $150

Loveland, Cyrus C. *California Trail Herd: the 1850 Missouri to California Journal of...* Los Gatos: Talisman Press, 1961. First edition, one of 750 copies, signed by Richard Dillon, frontispiece, facsimile, engravings, map, red cloth, paper spine label, very fine with pictorial dust jacket, slight toning to jacket spine.   Argonaut Book Shop   Holiday Season 2014 - 170   2015 $125

Lovesey, Peter *The Last Detective.* London: Scorpion Press, 1991. First edition, limited to 99 numbered copies, signed by author, quarter leather and marbled boards, fine in transparent dust jacket.   Buckingham Books   March 2015 - 2716   2015 $175

Lovesey, Peter *The Last Detective.* Bristol: Scorpion, 1991. First edition, one of 99 numbered copies signed by author, very fine in acetate dust jacket.   Mordida Books   March 2015 - 001413   2015 $100

Lovesey, Peter *Swing, Swing Together.* London: Macmillan, 1976. First edition, signed, small letter "R" on front flyleaf, else fine in dust jacket.   Buckingham Books   March 2015 - 15402   2015 $375

Lovett, Richard *The English Bible in the John Rylands Library.* London: printed for private circulation, 1899. First edition, folio, crushed brown morocco, title gilt stamped on spine with five raised bands, top edge gilt, other edges uncut, 26 facsimile plates and 29 engravings, bound by Zaehnsdorf, richly gilt inner dentelles, printed in red and black, bookplate of Zion Research Library, light rubbing top and bottom of spine and at corners, extremely scarce.   Oak Knoll Books   306 - 68   2015 $3500

Low, Archibald Montgomery *Adrift in the Stratosphere.* London and Glasgow: Blackie & Son Ltd., 1937. First edition, octavo, 3 inserted plates signed "B", original decorated blue cloth, front and spine panels, stamped in white and black.   L. W. Currey, Inc.   Boy's Adventure Fiction 2015 - 93   2015 $100

Low, Sampson *A Handbook to the Charities of London comprising the Objects, Date, Address, Income and Expenditure, Treasurer and Secretary of above Eight Hundred Charitable Institutions and Funds, Corrected to March 1867...* London: Sampson Low Son and Marston, 1867. 8vo. errata slip, final 16 pages of Sampson Low ads, original red cloth lettered gilt, very good.   John Drury Rare Books   2015 - 21836   2015 $133

Lowe, Constance *What a Surprise.* London: Nister, n.d. circa, 1906. 4to., cloth backed pictorial boards, slight bit of soil and rubbing, else near fine, 6 fine chromolithographed leaves operated with a complicated mechanism that has the upper picture open on diagonal to reveal another below.   Aleph-bet Books, Inc.   109 - 308   2015 $1250

Lowe, Samuel E. *A New Story of Peter Rabbit.* Whitman Pub. Co., 1926. First edition thus, this copy in pale blue boards with brown titling on front cover, variant binding, 5 1/4 x 4 inches, fine in dust jacket, scarce, color illustrations by Allan Wright, black and white illustrations by Earnest Vetsch, color titlepage, 8 color plates and numerous black and white text illustrations.   Ian Hodgkins & Co. Ltd.   134 - 212   2015   £58

Lowe, W. R. L. *Illustrations to the Life of St. Alban in Trin. Coll. Dublin MS. E. i 40 Reproduced in Collotype Facsimile...* London: Oxford University Press, 1924. First edition, 8vo., three quarter leather, cloth, five raised bands, 54 full page black and white plates printed recto only on stiff paper, spine faded, small tear in leather at edge of first raised band, wear at tips. Oak Knoll Books Special Catalogue 24 - 31 2015 $450

Lowell, Percival *Mars.* Boston and New York: Houghton Mifflin and Co., 1895. First edition, 8vo., color frontispiece, 23 plates, illustrations, original gilt stamped red cloth, top edge gilt, spine bit sun faded, back cover with abrasion exposing boards, very good. Jeff Weber Rare Books 178 - 797 2015 $800

Lowell, Percival *Mars and Its Canals.* New York & London: Macmillan Co., 1906. First edition, frontispiece, 8 plates, 12 maps, 49 figures, original dark green gilt stamped cloth, top edge gilt, lightly rubbed, ownership signatures of Edwin M. Eckard and Russell Sullivan, Indianapolis, bookplate of LA lawyer Herbert Kraus, very good. Jeff Weber Rare Books 178 - 798 2015 $750

Lowell, Robert 1917-1977 *The Dolphin.* London: Faber and Faber, 1973. First US edition, inscribed by author to Sonia Orwell, widow of George Orwell. Ken Lopez, Bookseller 164 - 125 2015 $750

Lowell, Robert 1917-1977 *For the Union Dead.* London: Poetry Book Society, 1960. First edition, one of approximately 50 copies specially printed for Lowell, 12mo., single leaf folded, printed on four sides, issued without wrappers, custom made half morocco slipcase. James S. Jaffe Rare Books Modern American Poetry - 186 2015 $2250

Lowell, Robert 1917-1977 *History.* New York: Farrar, Straus & Giroux, 1973. First edition, fine in fine dust jacket, inscribed by author to his first wife Jean Stafford, with short typed letter by one of the proprietors of Argosy bookstore NY city confirming book's provenance. Between the Covers Rare Books 196 - 88 2015 $4000

Lowell, Robert 1917-1977 *Land of Unlikeness.* Cummington: Cummington Press, 1944. One of 224 copies, of a total edition of 250, inscribed by author to Anne Sweeney, daughter of James John Sweeney, longtime curator of MOMA, spine and cover edges little faded, tips of boards worn, some internal foxing up to titlepage, overall about very good, lacking plain tissue dust jacket, uncommon first book. Ken Lopez, Bookseller 164 - 123 2015 $4500

Lowell, Robert 1917-1977 *Land of Unlikeness. Poems.* Cummington: Cummington Press, 1944. First edition, one of 250 copies, 8vo., titlepage woodcuts by Gustav Wolf, original blue boards, without printed dust jacket as issued, very small spot of faint discoloration on back cover, otherwise very fine, book rarely seen without almost inevitable fading to spine in cloth folding box. James S. Jaffe Rare Books Modern American Poetry - 185 2015 $4500

Lowell, Robert 1917-1977 *Land of Unlikeness.* Cummington: The Cummington Press, 1944. First edition, one 224 copies of a total edition of 225, blue printed paper covered boards, lettered in red, light rubbing to crown, spine little faded, 2 very small spots small, light smudge on front board, lacking original unprinted glassine dust jacket, nice in very good copy of fragile volume, internally fine, inscribed by author to Stanley Hyman. Between the Covers Rare Books 196 - 87 2015 $7500

Lowell, Robert 1917-1977 *The Mills of the Kavanaughs.* New York: Harcourt Brace, 1951. First edition, inscribed by author to Edgar & Janice (McGuire), recipient's bookplate, nice, apparently contemporary inscription, near fine in like dust jacket, slightly spine faded. Ken Lopez, Bookseller 164 - 124 2015 $1000

Lowell, Robert 1917-1977 *Notebook 1967-1968.* New York: Farrar, Straus and Giroux, 1969. First edition, inscribed to dedicatee, poet Dwight MacDonald. Honey & Wax Booksellers 2 - 54 2015 $1350

Lowell, Robert 1917-1977 *The Voyage and Other Versions of Poems by Baudelaire.* London: Faber, 1968. First edition, one of 200 numbered copies, signed by author and artist, 10 additional copies out of series, illustrations by Sidney Nolan, small folio, original three piece cloth, acetate dust jacket, publisher's slipcase, very fine. James S. Jaffe Rare Books Modern American Poetry - 187 2015 $400

Lowell, Samuel *Early Piety Recommended from the Example of Josiah; a Sermon Occasioned by the Death of George Griffiths and Delivered at Bridge street Meeting House, Bristol on Lord's-Day Evening the 3rd October 1802.* Bath: printed by and for S. Hazard and sold also by Williams, London, James Bristol and all other booksellers, n.d., 1802. First edition, 8vo., 32 pages, original worn wrappers, inscribed in ink on upper cover by author for Mr. James Conder, fine, uncut, very rare. John Drury Rare Books 2015 - 18381 2015 $89

Lowenfels, Walter *Some Deaths.* Highlands: Jonathan Williams/Natahala Foundation, 1964. First edition, one of 1500 copies, ownership signature of poet Clayton Eshleman dated 1965, fore edge soiled, some edgewear, very good in pictorial wrappers. Between the Covers Rare Books, Inc. 187 - 160 2015 $65

Lowenstein, Frank L. *Clothed in Bark.* Kensington: Lion Stone Books, 2013. Number 37 of 650 copies, signed by book artist and author, binding, design and illustrations by Sallie Lowenstein, photos of tree bark transformed by drawing on top of each image to accentuate the lines and patterns formed by nature, each copy in unique binding, bound by hand in flexible dark brown leather wrappers decorated with an intricate pattern of circular punches, sewn with medieval long stitch, which is then woven in pattern resembling tree bark housed in cardboard box with velcro closures and plastic bag insert, which holds the book inside box, images from book decorate the exterior of the box, fine.   The Kelmscott Bookshop   11 - 31   2015 $195

Lower, Arthur R. M. *The North American Assault on the Canadian Forest. A History of the Lumber Trade Between Canada and the United States.* Toronto & New Haven: Ryerson Press & Yale University Press, 1938. 8vo., blue cloth, map endpapers in dust jacket, 5 maps, 11 diagrams, very good.   Schooner Books Ltd.   110 - 179   2015 $45

Lowery, Margaret Ruth *Windows of the Morning: a Critical Study of William Blake's Poetical Sketches 1783.* New Haven: Yale University Press, 1940. Half title plate, 3 pages ads, signed by Geoffrey Tillotson Oct. 1940 with few notes and inserted cuttings, original card wrappers in typical pasted covering made from printed map with blotched red and green coloring in 18th century style, ms. label.   Jarndyce Antiquarian Booksellers   CCVII - 88   2015   £30

Lowndes, Belloc, Mrs. *Motive.* London: Hutchinson, 1938. First edition, fine in lightly soiled dust jacket with nicks at spine ends and several short closed tears.   Mordida Books   March 2015 - 008378   2015 $200

Lowndes, Thomas *Four Letters on Lowndes's Bay Salt Published last Year in the morning Post.* Dover: printed at the Apollo Press by Gilbert and Rutley King's Street Market Place, 1822. First edition, 8vo., slight very minor foxing, preserved in modern wrappers, printed title label on upper cover, very rare.   John Drury Rare Books   March 2015 - 22045   2015   £266

Lowndes, Walter *The Quakers of Fritchley.* Fritchley: Fritchley Preparative Meeting, 1986. Revised reprint, illustrations, original blue illustrated wrappers, slightly marked, title roughly written on spine, Kathleen Tillotson's copy with few notes, inserted letter from Mary Lascelles and letter and notes by Kathleen about new edition, etc.   Jarndyce Antiquarian Booksellers   CCVII - 366   2015   £25

Lowndes, William   1652-1754 *A Report Containing an Essay for the Amendment of the Silver Coins.* London: printed by Charles Bill and the executrix of Thomas Newcomb deceas'd, printers to the Kings most excellent Majesty, 1695. First and only edition, 8vo., contemporary cottage style panelled calf, spine gilt in compartments, raised bands, worn at foot with minor general wear to binding, very good, crisp copy, with 19th century armorial bookplate of unidentified nobleman on front pastedown.   John Drury Rare Books   2015 - 26503   2015 $612

Lowndes, William Thomas *The Bibliographer's Manual of English Literature.* London: George Bell and Sons, 1864. Revised edition, 6 volumes, thick 8vo., later quarter cloth with marbled paper covered boards, thousands of pages, covers worn, leather spine labels missing, worn at spine ends.   Oak Knoll Books   306 - 81   2015 $125

Lowry, Lois *Number the Stars.* Boston: Houghton Mifflin, 1989. First edition (correct code), advance copy, 8vo., cloth, fine in dust jacket, inscribed by author.   Aleph-Bet Books, Inc.   108 - 279   2015 $275

Lowry, Malcolm   1909-1957 *Under the Volcano.* New York: Reynal Hitchcock, 1947. First edition, octavo, original cloth, original contemporary, fine, dust jacket expertly restored and reinforced at spine and flaps, quite attractive copy.   Manhattan Rare Book Company   Literature 2014 - 2015 $3500

The Loyal City of Bristol, Vindicated from Amsterdamism or Devil's Borough, Two Appelatives Occasioned by the Over Credulous Who Have Hitherto Taken it for Granted... London: or Bristol: for J. Davies, 1681. First edition, small 4to., very small stain just touching lower fore-corner of titlepage, minor marks on verso of final leaf but otherwise very clean, modern paper wrappers, from the library of James Stevens Cox (1910-1997).   Maggs Bros. Ltd.   1447 - 47   2015   £350

Loyd, Samuel Jones *Remarks on the Management of the Circulation and on the Condition and Conduct of the Bank of England and of the Country Issuers During the year 1839.* London: Pelham Richardson, 1840. Unopened, sewn as issued, title slightly dusted, very good.   Jarndyce Antiquarian Booksellers   CCXI - 186   2015   £120

Lucanus, Marcus Annaeus *Lucan's Pharsalia.* London: i.e. Hague, 1720. First Continental edition, small 8vo., 2 volumes in one as issued, contemporary calf, neatly rebacked, red morocco label, corners bit worn, one signature sprung at beginning, otherwise very good.   C. R. Johnson   Foxon R-Z - 848r-z   2015 $383

Lucanus, Marcus Annaeus *Pharsalia.* Parisiis: Apud Lefevre Bibliopolam, 1822. 2 volumes, 108 x 76mm., charming contemporary green straight grain morocco covers, panelled with fine gilt and blind raised bands, spine compartments outlined in blind, pretty quatrefoil gilt centerpiece ornament, gilt titling, turn-ins, decorative gilt roll, all edges gilt, each volume with lovely pastoral fore-edge painting, one depicting Featherstone Castle Northumberland, the other Lowther Castle, Westmorland, in later green cloth chemises and quarter morocco slipcase, spine decorated in much the same fashion as the volumes, front pastedown of both volumes with armorial bookplate of Sir James Stuart, Bart., front free endpaper of both volumes with oval morocco bookplate of R. B. Adam, front free endpaper of first volume with morocco bookplate of Mary Harriman Lecomte du Nouy; joints just slightly rubbed, spines faintly and uniformly darkened, touch of browning to edges of leaves, intermittent light foxing, else fine set, text generally clean and fresh, bindings lustrous and fore edge paintings particularly well preserved with rich colors.   Phillip J. Pirages   66 - 80   2015 $1500

Lucas, E. V. *Four and Twenty Toilers.* London: Grant Richards, n.d., 1900. First edition, large oblong 4to., cloth backed pictorial boards, cover scratched some with edge and corner wear, else tight and clean and very good, 24 full page color illustrations by F. D. Bedford.   Aleph-bet Books, Inc.   109 - 44   2015 $850

Lucas, John *Basic Jazz on Long Play. The Great Soloists ... and the Grand Bands...* Northfield: Carleton Jazz Club, 1954. First edition, wrappers, near fine but for sunning to spine and edges, inscribed by author.   Beasley Books 2013 - 2015 $40

Lucas, John *The Great Revival on Long Play.* Northfield: Carleton Jazz Club, 1957. First edition, inscribed by author, wrappers, near fine little darkening to edges.   Beasley Books   2013 - 2015 $45

Lucas, Margaret *An Account of the Convincement and Call to the Ministry of Margaret Lucas, Late of Leek in Staffordshire.* Printed and sold by Darton and Harvey, Gracechurch Street, 1797. First edition, 12mo., original sheep, joints cracked, cords holding, corners worn, sound.   Blackwell's Rare Books   B179 - 66   2015   £250

Lucas, Winifred *Poems.* London: Burns & Oates, 1919. First edition, 12mo., brown linen with title, author and ornament in gilt to front cover, slight bumping and fading, very good, interior pages also very good, gift inscription and annotation in red ink on page 17 noting that a line of verse could be a motto for a sundial, accompanied by five short ALS's from Lucas, very good.   The Kelmscott Bookshop   11 - 32   2015 $250

Luchetti, Cathy *Under God's Spell. Frontier Evangelists 1772-1915.* San Diego: Harcourt Brace Jovanovich, 1989. First edition, signed by author, photos, cloth backed boards, very fine, pictorial dust jacket.   Argonaut Book Shop Holiday Season 2014 - 171   2015 $50

Lucianus Samosatensis *Les Oeuvres...* Paris: Abel L'Angelier, 1582. First edition, 2nd issue, 3 parts in one, folio, L'Anglier device on titlepage, 8 large woodcuts in text, satyr headpieces and ram headpiece, arabesque tailpiece, arabesque, grotesque and foliated initials in several sizes, handsomely bound in early 17th century polished calf double gilt, fillet on covers, spine gilt in compartments with intricate unidentified monogram in six of them, other lettered with title, expert repairs headcaps and corners, covers with few small tears and scratches, little dampstained in upper margins more so towards end, some foxing here and there, generally fresh. Maggs Bros. Ltd.   Illustrated Books 2014 - 2015   £5500

Lucianus Samosatensis *Opera. (with) Index Verborum ac Phrasum Luciani, sive Lexicon Lucinaeum...* Amsterdam: sumptibus Jacobi Wetstenii, 1743. Utrecht: ex typographia Hermanni Besseling, 1746, Opera in 3 volumes, frontispiece in first volume, light toning and spotting index browned in places; 4to., uniformly bound in contemporary marbled sheep, spines with five raised bands, red and green morocco lettering pieces, other compartments infilled with gilt volute, flower and circle tools, marbled endpapers, edges red, rubbed, some surface damage to leather, good.   Blackwell's Rare Books   Greek & Latin Classics VI - 72   2015   £800

Lucretius Carus, Titus *Titi Lucretii Cari Der Rerum Natura Libri Sex.* Birminghamae: Typis Johannis Baskerville, 1772. First Baskerville edition, quarto, original full calf, spine with raised bands and decorated gilt, joints cracking, boards rather rubbed, corners bumped, spine somewhat faded and chipped top and bottom, bookplates of Rev. Edmund Maturin, clergyman and Henry Bright, English merchant, author and literary correspondent.   Any Amount of Books 2015 - C13208   2015   £280

Ludlow, William *Report of a Reconnaissance of the Black Hills of Dakota Made in the Summer of 1874.* Washington: 1875. 121 pages, illustrations, 3 folding maps, original front and back boards, recased with new spine and endpapers, internally clean and very good.   Dumont Maps and Books of the West   130 - 23   2015 $400

Ludlow, William *Report of a Reconnaissance from Carroll, Montana Territory on the Upper Missouri...* Washington: GPO, 1876. First edition, tall quarto, cloth, gold stamping on spine, plates, 3 large folding maps, some cosmetic restoration to spine, some repairs to one map, else very good, tight.   Buckingham Books   March 2015 - 26535   2015 $1250

Lytton, Edward George Earle Lytton Bulwer-Lytton, 1st Baron 1803-1873 *Rienzi the Last of the Tribunes.* London: Saunders & Otley, 1835. First edition, 3 volumes, 12mo., bound without half titles in contemporary half crimson calf, dark green morocco labels at head of spines, ruled in gilt with descending gilt motifs and gilt rules at tails of spines, slightly dulled, some slight marking to left margin of front board volume III, pencil note on leading f.e.p.'s 'shelf 62' of unknown private library, handsome copy.   Jarndyce Antiquarian Booksellers   CCXI - 51 2015   £280

M

M'Curdy, C. L. *A New and Choice Collection of Hymns, Designed to Aid in the Devotions of Prayer, Conference and Camp-Meetings.* Keene: printed by J. and J. W. Prentiss, 1840. 32mo., 96 pages, text only, no music, contemporary plain stiff wrappers backed with cloth, very good. M & S Rare Books, Inc. 97 - 50 2015 $150

M'Harry, Samuel *The Practical Distiller; or an Introduction to Making Whiskey, Gin, Brandy, Spirits &c of Better Quality and in Larger Quantities...* Harrisburg: John Wyeth, 1809. 184 pages, contemporary sheep, corner extremities uniformly clipped, front free endpaper wanting, some marginal staining but very good in very tight and attractive original binding, rare. Joseph J. Felcone Inc. Science, Medicine and Technology - 44 2015 $4000

M'William, James Ormiston *Some Account of the Yellow Fever Epidemy by Which Brazil was Invaded in the Latter Part of the Year 1849.* London: printed by William Tyler, 1851. First separate edition, 12mo., 32 pages, recently well bound in linen backed marbled boards lettered, very good, apparently rare. John Drury Rare Books March 2015 - 18618 2015 $266

Maas & Jungvogel *Monogramm Album.* Crefeld: Maas & Jungvogel, n.d. crica 1880's, 4to., original cloth stamped in gilt, all edges gilt, highly decorative titlepage followed by leaves showing combinations of different letters of the alphabet, from the reference library of Zaehnsdorf Company with commemorative booklabel loosely inserted, minor wear along edges. Oak Knoll Books Special Catalogue 24 - 34 2015 $650

Maathai, Wangari Muta *Unbowed. A Memoir.* New York: Alfred A. Knopf, 2006. First edition, signed and inscribed by Maathai, 8vo., fine in near to fine dust jacket with minimal soil and edge wear. By the Book, L. C. Special List 10 - 43 2015 $175

MacAllester, Oliver *A Series of Letters, Discovering the Scheme Projected by France in MDCCLIX for an Intended Invasion Upon England with Flat-Bottom'd Boats...* London: printed for the author and sold by Mr. Williams &c, 1767. First edition, 2 volumes in 1, 4to., contemporary half calf over marbled boards, spine with raised bands, gilt lines and label, minor rubbing to joints and little wear to head and foot of spine, very good, sound, from the 19th century library of first Marquis of Hastings with his armorial bookplate. John Drury Rare Books March 2015 - 25147 2015 $656

MacAskill, W. R. *Lure of the Sea: Leaves from My Pictorial Log.* Halifax: Eastern Photo Engravers, 1951. Quarto, white cloth with blue title and rope design to front cover, 73 blue tinted photo illustrations with captions and text, covers have light stain, interior good, signed by author. Schooner Books Ltd. 110 - 86 2015 $95

Macaulay, Catharine *Observations on a Pamphlet.* London: Dilly, 1770. Third edition, 8vo., removed, here with half title, very good, clean. Second Life Books Inc. 191 - 56 2015 $500

Macaulay, Catharine *Observations on a Pamphlet entitled Thoughts on the Cause of the Present Discontents.* London: Dilly, 1770. Third edition, 8vo., removed, here with half title, very good, clean copy. Second Life Books Inc. 190 - 229 2015 $500

Macaulay, Rose *Told by an Idiot.* London: Collins, 1923. First edition, octavo, prelims very slightly spotted, near fine in rare, very good dust jacket which is nicked and rubbed at edges and water stained at spine. Peter Ellis, Bookseller 2014 - 010012 2015 £350

Macaulay, Thomas Babington *Lays of Ancient Rome. with Jury and the Armada.* London: Longmans, Green and Co., 1897. 8vo., frontispiece, woodcut illustrations within text, some foxing, 8vo., contemporary tree calf, boards bordered with gilt roll, backstrip with five raised bands, green morocco label in second compartment, rest with central flower tools within oval borders and elaborate cornerpieces, marbled edges and endpapers, extremities just touch rubbed, very good. Blackwell's Rare Books Greek & Latin Classics VI - 92 2015 £120

MacBeth, George *Interview with Ted Berrigan.* N.P.: Ignu Publications, 1971. First edition, narrow 4to., original wrappers with holograph title, signed by MacBeth and inscribed by Berrigan to Burt (Britton), covers little dusty, otherwise fine. James S. Jaffe Rare Books Many Happy Returns - 81 2015 $650

MacBeth, R. G. *Policing the Plains.* London: 1922. 320 pages, illustrations cloth, some external wear and fading, internally clean and very good. Dumont Maps & Books of the West 131 - 62 2015 $50

Macclesfield, Thomas Parker, 1st Earl of *The Tryal of Thomas Earl of Macclesfield, in the House of Peers, for High Crimes and Misdemeanors Upon an Impeachment by the Knights, Citizens and Burgesses in Parliament....Begun the 6th Day of My 1725...* London: printed by Sam. Buckley, 1725. First edition, folio, initial license leaf, final leaf little creased and dust soiled, occasional other insignificant blemishes, stab holes in some margins, tiny hole in licence leaf just touching one letter, original panelled reversed calf with morocco spine label, wear to extremities and lower board which also has old burn hole, nonetheless good, sound copy.   John Drury Rare Books   March 2015 - 19085   2015 $221

MacCunn, John *Six Radical Thinkers: Bentham J.S. Mill, Cobden, Carlyle, Mazzini, T. H. Green.* New York: Arnold Press, 1979. Facsimile reprint of 1907 edition, facsimile, 8vo., original faux green leather boards, lettered silver on spine and front cover, from the library of J. P. Mayer (1903-1992) with his neat blindstamp.   Any Amount of Books 2015 - C16243   2015   £225

MacDonald, Clyde F. *More Murder Cases in Pictou County 1951-1978.* Pictou: 2008. Third edition, 8vo., black and white photos illustrations, very good.   Schooner Books Ltd.   110 - 88   2015 $45

MacDonald, George   1824-1905 *Alec Forbes of Howgden.* London: Hurst & Blackett, 1900. New edition, half title, 4 pages ads, original green cloth with blind design and gilt lettering, ownership signature, March 1909 on half title, very good.   Jarndyce Antiquarian Booksellers   CCXI - 187   2015   £35

MacDonald, George   1824-1905 *At the Back of the North Wind...* London: Strahan & Co., 1872? Early edition, half title, 87 original cloth, in same design as first edition, yellow endpapers, slightly marked and dulled, inner hinges slightly cracking.   Jarndyce Antiquarian Booksellers   CCXI - 188   2015   £450

MacDonald, George   1824-1905 *Dealings with Fairies.* London: Arthur Strahan, 1867. First edition, 12mo., green gilt cloth, all edges gilt, expertly rebacked with original spine laid down, few mends and light soil, very good+ in cloth slipcase, 12 fine full page illustrations by Arthur Hughes, very scarce.   Aleph-bet Books, Inc.   109 - 281   2015 $1750

MacDonald, George   1824-1905 *Dealings with the Fairies.* London: Alexander Strahan and Co., 1868. Second edition, 16mo., half title, frontispiece and plates by Arthur Hughes, 4 pages ads (Dec. 1867), few marks, original green cloth, blocked in black and gilt, slightly dulled, small split in leading hinge, all edges gilt, inscribed presentation from author for Mrs. Pulsford.   Jarndyce Antiquarian Booksellers   CCXI - 189   2015   £2250

MacDonald, George   1824-1905 *The Light Princess and other Fairy stories.* Blackie & Son, circa, 1893. Half title, frontispiece and plates by L. L. Brooke, 32 page catalog, original beige cloth blocked in black and white signature of Emma Loveluck, Christmas 1893 on half title, very good.   Jarndyce Antiquarian Booksellers   CCXI - 190   2015   £75

MacDonald, George   1824-1905 *Phantastes; a Faerie Romance for Men and Women.* London: Smith, Elder & Co., 1858. First edition, bound without half title, small corner torn form title, few marginal marks, contemporary half calf, rubbed, split in following hinge but sound, bookplate of Augustus Taylor Day, from the library of Geoffrey & Kathleen Tillotson.   Jarndyce Antiquarian Booksellers   CCVII - 368   2015   £520

MacDonald, George   1824-1905 *The Princess and Curdie.* London: Chatto & Windus, 1883. (1882). First edition, half title, frontispiece and plates, 32 page catalog (July 1882), few spots in text, original green cloth, blocked in gilt and brown, yellow edges, spine slightly rubbed, very good, scarce.   Jarndyce Antiquarian Booksellers   CCXI - 191   2015   £2200

MacDonald, George   1824-1905 *(Works of Fancy and Imagination). Phantastes; a Faerie romance.* London: Chatto & Windus, 1892. 1891. New edition, 2 volumes, 16mo., original grey green cloth blocked with Grolier pattern, armorial bookplates of Fanshaws, very good.   Jarndyce Antiquarian Booksellers   CCXI - 192   2015   £45

MacDonald, John D. *April Evil.* London: Robert Hale, 1957. First UK edition and first edition in hardcover, fine and unread in fine dust jacket, from the collection of Duke Collier.   Royal Books   36 - 52   2015 $2850

MacDonald, John D. *Barrier Island.* New York: Alfred A. Knopf, 1986. First edition, inscribed "For Captain Roo-Any, friend of T. Mcgee is a friend of mine! Best regards John D. MacDonald 19 Aug '86", scarce signed, fine in dust jacket.   Buckingham Books   March 2015 - 30688   2015 $750

MacDonald, John D. *Bright Orange for the Shroud.* Philadelphia: J. B. Lippincott, 1972. First hardcover edition, fine in fine dust jacket, none of the usual fading to sensitive jacket spine present, signed by author on bookplate tipped in at half title, bookplate of noted collected Duke Collier.   Royal Books   36 - 42   2015 $1250

MacDonald, John D. *A Bullet for Cinderella.* London: Robert Ale, 1960. First UK and first hardcover edition, near fine in fine dust jacket, from the collection of Duke Collier.   Royal Books   36 - 54   2015 $2500

MacDonald, John D. *The Damned.* New York: Fawcett, 1952. First edition, gold Medal no. 240, spine lamina slightly wrinkled, otherwise near fine, unread copy in wrappers.   Mordida Books   March 2015 - 010695   2015 $100

MacDonald, John D. *Darker than Amber.* Philadelphia: J. B. Lippincott, 1970. First American edition, very good plus in bright, near fine dust jacket, jacket is first issue with a price of $4.95 at bottom front flap and printer's code '470' at top front flap, book is very slightly cocked and bumped at crown, else clean, jacket bright lacking the spine fading that is found on nearly every copy, showing only small chip at one corner of crown, from the collection of Duke Collier. Royal Books   36 - 37   2015 $3500

MacDonald, John D. *A Deadly Shade of Gold.* Philadelphia: J. B. Lippincott, 1974. First edition in hardcover, near fine in about fine dust jacket, attractive copy, uncommon in this condition, from the collection of Duke Collier.   Royal Books   36 - 49   2015 $300

MacDonald, John D. *Death Trap.* London: Robert Hale, 1958. First UK and first hardcover edition, fine and unread in fine dust jacket, from the collection of Duke Collier. Royal Books   36 - 55   2015 $2500

MacDonald, John D. *The Deep Blue Good-by.* Philadelphia: J. B. Lippincott, 1975. First edition in hardcover, near fine in bright, near fine jacket, some fading to top edges of boards, jacket minutely rubbed at spine ends, from the collection of Duke Collier.   Royal Books   36 - 48   2015 $375

MacDonald, John D. *Dress Her in Indigo.* Philadelphia: J. B. Lippincott, 1971. First American edition, very good in like dust jacket, spine lean, bookplate of noted collector Duke Collier, jacket lightly rubbed with ink price notation front flap (offset very slightly to front endpaper), faint vertical crease running parallel to rear hinge fold, laid in is ard signed by author Nv. 18 1977.   Royal Books   36 - 45   2015 $650

MacDonald, John D. *The Empty Copper Sea.* Philadelphia and New York: J. B. Lippincott, 1978. First edition, signed by author on half titlepage, fine and unread in fine dust jacket, bookplate of noted collector Duke Collier. Royal Books   36 - 50   2015 $325

MacDonald, John D. *The Girl in the Plain Brown Wrapper.* New York: J. B. Lippincott, 1973. First printing of this edition and first American edition in hardcover, near fine in very good plus dust jacket, inscribed in year of publication to Denver Post book editor, Clarus Backus, laid in is sheet of Denver Post stationery, clipped article from Denver Post by Mr. Backus about MacDonald's death, and glossy Doubleday review photo from 1968, for the book 'Three for McGee', bookplate of noted collected Duke Collier, jacket lightly rubbed at extremities, touch of usual fading on spine, very nice, extremely scarce presentation copy.   Royal Books   36 - 38   2015 $2750

MacDonald, John D. *The Long Lavender Look.* Philadelphia: J. B. Lippincott, 1972. First hardcover edition, about fine in near fine dust jacket, minutely rubbed, from the collection of Duke Collier.   Royal Books   36 - 46   2015 $550

MacDonald, John D. *A Man of Affairs.* London: Robert Hale, 1959. First UK and first hardcover edition, fine and unread in fine dust jacket, from the collection of Duke Collier.   Royal Books   36 - 56   2015 $2500

MacDonald, John D. *Murder for the Bride.* New York: Fawcett, 1951. First edition, Gold medal no. 164, faint crease along spine, front cover edge, otherwise near fine in wrappers.   Mordida Books   March 2015 - 010699   2015 $100

MacDonald, John D. *The Neon Jungle.* London: Robert Hale, 1962. First UK edition and first edition in hardcover, fine and unread in fine dust jacket, from the collection of Duke Collier.   Royal Books   36 - 51   2015 $2850

MacDonald, John D. *Pale Gray for Guilt.* Philadelphia and New York: J. B. Lippincott, 1971. First American hardcover edition, trifle rubbed at foot of spine, else fine in modestly rubbed, near fine dust jacket with two tiny nicks, better than usual copy.   Between the Covers Rare Books   196 - 144   2015 $850

MacDonald, John D. *Pale Gray for Guilt.* Philadelphia: J. B. Lippincott, 1971. First American edition in hardcover, first issue jacket with code 971 top right corner of front flap and prie of $5.50 at bottom, inscribed by author on generic bookplate tipped in, bookplate of noted collector Duke Collier, fine and unread in about fine, minutely rubbed dust jacket, as sharp a copy of this series title as we have seen. Royal Books   36 - 40   2015 $2000

MacDonald, John D. *The Price of Murder.* London: Robert Hale, 1958. First UK and first hardcover edition, fine and unread in fine dust jacket, from the collection of Duke Collier.   Royal Books   36 - 57   2015 $2500

MacDonald, John D. *A Purple Place for Dying.* New York: J. B. Lippincott, 1976. First American edition, near fine in like dust jacket, inscribed by author for Patrick Hyman 4 June 1983, from the collection of Duke Collier.   Royal Books   36 - 43   2015 $950

MacDonald, John D. *The Quick Red Fox.* Philadelphia: J. B. Lippincott, 1973. First edition in hardcover, fine in about fine dust jacket, bookplate of noted collector, Duke Collier, just touch of rubbing in couple of spots, none of the usual fading to sensitive jacket spine, bright, fresh copy. Royal Books   36 - 44   2015 $950

MacDonald, John D. *The Scarlet Ruse.* New York: Lippincott & Crowell, 1973. First American edition, fine in near fine dust jacket with tiny tears to spine folds.   Ed Smith Books   83 - 61   2015 $200

MacDonald, John D. *The Scarlet Ruse.* New York: J. B. Lippincott and Thomas Y. Crowell, 1980. First American hardcover edition, near fine in like dust jacket, warmly inscribed by author for Louise and Joe, from the collection of Duke Collier.   Royal Books   36 - 41   2015 $1850

MacDonald, John D. *The Scarlet Ruse.* New York: Lippincott & Crowell, 1980. First US edition hardcover edition, fine in dust jacket, very lightly sunned on spine.   Buckingham Books March 2015 - 22563   2015 $185

MacDonald, John D. *Slam the Big Door.* London: Robert Hale, 1961. First UK and first hardcover edition, signed by author, fine in exceptionally bright, near fine dust jacket, from the collection of Duke Collier.   Royal Books   36 - 58   2015 $3250

MacDonald, John D. *Soft Touch.* London: Robert Hale, 1960. First UK edition and first edition in hardcover, fine and unread in fine dust jacket, from the collection of Duke Collier.   Royal Books   36 - 53   2015 $2000

MacDonald, John D. *A Tan and Sandy Silence.* London: Robert Hale, 1973. First edition, hint of foxing to page edges, else fine, unread in fine dust jacket, from the collection of Duke Collier.   Royal Books   36 - 47   2015 $450

MacDonald, John D. *A Tan and Sandy Silence.* London: Hale, 1973. First hardcover edition, fine in fine dust jacket.   Mordida Books   March 2015 - 011390   2015 $400

MacDonald, John D. *Three for McGee.* Garden City: Doubleday, 1967. Omnibus edition, fine in dust jacket with nicks at spine ends and corners.   Mordida Books   March 2015 - 001441 2015 $200

MacDonald, John D. *The Turquoise Lament.* Philadelphia: J. B. Lippincott, 1973. First edition, signed by author on titlepage and dated 21 Oct. 1983, very good plus in very good plus dust jacket, jacket is not price clipped and shows price of $5.95 on front flap, only the second such copy we have handled, bookplate of noted collector Duke Collier on front endpaper, jacket lightly rubbed at extremities with touch of fading to colors on spine.   Royal Books   36 - 39   2015 $2000

MacDonald, Marianne *Death's Autograph.* London: Hodder & Stoughton, 1996. First edition, pages edges beginning to uniformly tan, else fine in dust jacket.   Buckingham Books   March 2015 - 36283   2015 $300

MacDonald, Marianne *Smoke Screen.* London: Hodder & Stoughton, 1999. First edition, fine in dust jacket.   Mordida Books   March 2015 - 007545   2015 $100

MacDonald, Philip *The Crime Conductor.* New York: Doubleday Doran & Co., 1931. True first edition, near fine in fine, bright contemporary.   Buckingham Books   March 2015 - 37113   2015 $750

MacDonald, Philip *Death and Chicanery.* London: Jenkins, 1962. First English edition, fine in price clipped dust jacket with some spine fading.   Mordida Books   March 2015 - 007027   2015 $85

MacDonald, Philip *Guest in the House.* Garden City: Doubleday Crime Club, 1955. First edition, small blind-stamp of Mrs. Theodore Roosevelt Jr. with her Oyster Bay address, else fine in very good dust jacket with small nicks and tears.   Between the Covers Rare Books, Inc.   187 - 194   2015 $125

MacDonald, Philip *The Man Out of the Rain and Other Stories.* London: Jenkins, 1957. First English edition, fine in dust jacket with slightly faded spine and crease tear and chip to back panel.   Mordida Books   March 2015 - 001445   2015 $75

MacDonald, Philip *Persons Unknown.* Garden City: Doubleday Crime Club, 1931. First American edition, lower corners bumped, otherwise very good in dust jacket with darkened spine and nicks at top of spine and at corners.   Mordida Books   March 2015 - 009110   2015 $200

MacDonald, Philip *The Wraith.* Garden City: Doran & Co., 1931. First U.S. edition, 2 msall erasures to front pastedown, else very good in spectacular, bright price clipped dust jacket with minor restoration to tiny spot at head of spine.   Buckingham Books   March 2015 - 32160   2015 $675

Macdonald, Ross *Archer at Large.* New York: Knopf, 1970. First Omnibus edition, fine in dust jacket with slight spine fading.   Mordida Books   March 2015 - 001468   2015 $100

MacDonald, Ross *Archer in Hollywood.* New York: Knopf, 1967. First Omnibus edition, fine in price clipped dust jacket.   Mordida Books   March 2015 - 011382   2015 $100

MacDonald, Ross *The Barbarous Coast.* New York: Alfred A. Knopf, 1956. First edition, near fine in like dust jacket, price clipped, bright but with soil to rear panel, custom clamshell box, from the collection of Duke Collier.   Royal Books   36 - 74   2015 $1250

MacDonald, Ross *Black Money.* New York: Knopf, 1966. First edition, bookseller's small label on rear endpaper, name and date on front paper, otherwise fine in dust jacket with tiny closed tear at top of spine. Mordida Books March 2015 - 012714 2015 $300

MacDonald, Ross *Blue City.* New York: Alfred A. Knopf, 1947. First edition, fine, bright, tight copy, crisp dust jacket with light restoration to spine ends, beautiful copy, scarce. Buckingham Books March 2015 - 31348 2015 $1250

MacDonald, Ross *Blue City.* New York: Knopf, 1947. First edition, fine in dust jacket with tiny intrnal tape mend at top of spine and tiny wear at top of spine. Mordida Books March 2015 - 005286 2015 $750

MacDonald, Ross *Blue City.* London: Cassell, 1949. First edition, very good in like dust jacket, some brief soil to boards, jacket moderately worn and creased at extremities, uncommon, early Millar title, inscribed by author Xmas 1951 to Glenn Schiegel, from the collection of Duke Collier. Royal Books 36 - 79 2015 $1500

MacDonald, Ross *The Chill.* New York: Knopf, 1964. First edition, fine, top front corner slightly bumped and name and date on front endpaper, otherwise fine in dust jacket with tiny tears and tiny wear at spine ends. Mordida Books March 2015 - 0117764 2015 $200

MacDonald, Ross *A Collection of Reviews.* Northridge: Lord John, 1979. Galley proof, unbound uncorrected flat page proof with two pages to a sheet, very fine. Mordida Books March 2015 - 007957 2015 $250

MacDonald, Ross *The Dark Tunnel.* New York: Dodd, Mead, 1944. First edition, fine in bright, near fine dust jacket, lightly chipped at spine ends and lightly rubbed at hinges, rare, from the collection of Duke Collier. Royal Books 36 - 61 2015 $15,000

MacDonald, Ross *The Doomsters.* New York: Alfred A. Knopf, 1958. First edition, fine in dust jacket with just hint of spine fading to multicolors at base of spine, exceptional copy. Buckingham Books March 2015 - 25593 2015 $2000

MacDonald, Ross *The Drowning Pool.* New York: Alfred A. Knopf, 1950. First edition, near fine in bright, near fine dust jacket, dedication copy, doubly inscribed to legendary genre fiction editor and enthusiast Anthony Boucher, from the collection of Duke Collier. Royal Books 36 - 63 2015 $25,000

MacDonald, Ross *The Drowning Pool.* New York: Knopf, 1950. First edition, cover edges slightly darkened, otherwise very good, dust jacket with internal tape mends along inner flap folds, tears along folds, wear along spine folds and at corners. Mordida Books March 2015 - 011407 2015 $375

MacDonald, Ross *The Far Side of the Dollar.* New York: Alfred a. Knopf, 1965. First edition, fine and unread in fine dust jacket, vibrant yellow topstain, from the collection of Duke Collier. Royal Books 36 - 76 2015 $425

MacDonald, Ross *The Far Side of the Dollar.* New York: Knopf, 1965. First edition, bookseller's small label on rear pastedown, name and date on front endpaper, otherwise fine in dust jacket with short closed tear. Mordida Books March 2015 - 001462 2015 $300

MacDonald, Ross *The Ferguson Affair.* New York: Alfred A. Knopf, 1960. First edition, fine and unread, near fine dust jacket with touch of overall toning and light soil to rear panel, attractive copy, from the collection of Duke Collier. Royal Books 36 - 78 2015 $725

MacDonald, Ross *Find a Victim.* New York: Alfred A. Knopf, 1954. First edition, signed by author, laid in is 2 page letter in holograph pencil in author's hand, spelling out a variant version of the dust jacket's copy, that manifests author's direct involvement in marketing of his own book, fine and unread, spectacular copy, from the collection of Duke Collier. Royal Books 36 - 64 2015 $5000

MacDonald, Ross *The Galton Case.* New York: Alfred A. Knopf, 1959. First edition, signed by author, about near fine in bright, near fine dust jacket, from the collection of Duke Collier. Royal Books 36 - 70 2015 $2500

MacDonald, Ross *The Goodbye Look.* New York: Knopf, 1969. First edition, signed by author, fine, bright copy in price clipped dust jacket with light wear to spine ends, housed in cloth slipcase, leather labels on spine and titles stamped in gold. Buckingham Books March 2015 - 25594 2015 $1350

MacDonald, Ross *The Instant Enemy.* New York: Knopf, 1968. First edition, very fine in dust jacket. Mordida Books March 2015 - 012704 2015 $350

MacDonald, Ross *The Instant Enemy.* New York: Alfred A. Knopf, 1968. First edition, fine and unread in fine dust jacket, from the collection of Duke Collier. Royal Books 36 - 77 2015 $375

MacDonald, Ross *The Instant Enemy.* London: Collins Crime Club, 1968. First English edition, fine in price clipped dust jacket. Mordida Books March 2015 - 011384 2015 $85

MacDonald, Ross *Lew Archer: private Investigator.* New York: Mysterious Press, 1977. First edition, signed by author, fine pamphlet in printed wrappers.   Buckingham Books   March 2015 - 2777   2015 $275

MacDonald, Ross *The Moving Target.* New York: Alfred A. Knopf, 1949. First edition, first printing, fine in attractive jacket with few tiny chips to spine, few small tears and light fading to spine.   B & B Rare Books, Ltd.   234 - 72   2015 $4500

MacDonald, Ross *The Moving Target.* New York: Alfred A. Knopf, 1949. First edition, near fine in like dust jacket, merest trace of sunning to red band near bottom spine, otherwise bright and fresh as the day it was issued, extremely scarce in this condition, from the collection of Duke Collier.   Royal Books   36 - 62   2015 $12,500

MacDonald, Ross *The Moving Target.* London: Cassell, 1951. First edition, very good plus in very good dust jacket, mild soil to boards, some foxing to page edges, jacket moderately worn at extremities with few small chips and closed tears only signed copy of the UK edition we have encountered, inscribed by author to his in-laws Doogie and Clarence (Strum), from the collection of Duke Collier.   Royal Books   36 - 72   2015 $2000

MacDonald, Ross *Self-Portrait: Ceaselessly into the Past.* Santa Barbara: Capra Press, 1981. First edition, one of 26 lettered copies (this being letter 'J'), signed by author and Eudora Welty who provided introduction and additional inscription by book's publisher, Ralph Sipper, dated 1981, original photo of the two authors laid into pocket tipped on to front pastedown, as issued, fine in black leather, paper covered slipcase as issued, corners of slipcase lightly rubbed, from the collection of Duke Collier.   Royal Books   36 - 81   2015 $1500

MacDonald, Ross *The Three Roads.* New York: Alfred A. Knopf, 1948. First edition, fine in near fine dust jacket with small rubber stamp "Booth memorial Hospital, bump to heel, some minute rubbing at corners, from the collection of Duke Collier.   Royal Books   36 - 71   2015 $1750

MacDonald, Ross *Trouble Follows Me.* New York: Dodd Mead, 1946. First Edition, fine, tight copy in bright dust jacket with no tear or chips, wear at base of spine, exceptionally fine, fresh copy, from the collection of Duke Collier.   Royal Books   36 - 68   2015 $3500

MacDonald, Ross *The Way Some People Die.* New York: Alfred A. Knopf, 1951. First edition, fine in bright, near fine dust jacket with deep black topstain, jacket has touch of usual spine fading but much better than usual, tiny chip at top bottom front panel, from the collection of Duke Collier.   Royal Books   36 - 69   2015 $3500

MacDonald, Ross *The Zebra-striped Hearse.* New York: Alfred A. Knopf, 1962. First edition, fine and unread in fine, price clipped dust jacket, topstain brilliant, none of the usual fading to pink lettering, from the collection of Duke Collier.   Royal Books   36 - 75   2015 $950

MacDonald, Ross *The Zebra Striped Hearse.* New York: Knopf, 1962. First edition, fine, bright, tight copy in fine, unfaded dust jacket.   Buckingham Books   March 2015 - 25305   2015 $1250

MacDonald, Thomas *Thoughts on the Public Duties of Private Life; with Reference to Present Circumstances and Opinions.* London: T. Cadell Jun. and W. Davies, 1795. First and only edition, 8vo., bound fairly recently in boards with printed title label, very good, crisp copy, rather scarce.   John Drury Rare Books   2015 - 24681   2015 $133

MacDonald, William Colt *Blackguard.* London: Hodder and Stoughton, 1958. First UK edition, near fine in bright, near fine dust jacket with some rubbing to spine panel.   Royal Books   46 - 32   2015 $475

MacGill, Thomas *An Account of Tunis: of Its Government, Manners, Customs and Antiquities...* London: Longman Hurst Rees Orme and Brown, 1816. Second edition, 8vo., original boards with printed spine label, joints wearing, but good copy, entirely uncut, uncommon.   John Drury Rare Books   March 2015 - 16507   2015 $266

MacGrath, Harold *The Changing Road.* Doubleday Doran and Co., 1928. First edition, near fine in fine, bright dust jacket with light and minor tanning to front flap.   Buckingham Books   March 2015 - 3712   2015 $350

MacGrath, Harold *Deuces Wild.* Indianapolis: Bobbs Merrill, 1913. First edition, fine in lovely decorated green cloth covered boards with gold stamped titles, very good soiled dust jacket with nicks at base of spine and at corners.   Mordida Books   March 2015 - 005287   2015 $250

MacGrath, Harold *The Wolves of Chaos.* Garden City: Doubleday, 1929. First edition, light spotting on page edges, otherwise fine in very good dust jacket with internal tape mends and some color touch up at spine ends.   Mordida Books   March 2015 - 001609   2015 $85

Machen, Arthur 1863-1947 *The Three Impostors, or the Transmutations.* London: John Lane, 1895. First edition, 8vo., pages uncut, spine rubbed, spine ends slightly frayed, corners bumped, otherwise sound, very good- copy.   Any Amount of Books   2015 - A83679   2015   £160

Machiavelli, Niccolo 1469-1527 *The Prince.* New York: Limited Editions Club, 1954. Limited to 1500 numbered copies, 8vo., full morocco stamped in gilt, top edge gilt, slipcase with minor rubbing, well preserved, with Monthly Letter loosely inserted.   Oak Knoll Books   25 - 37   2015 $250

Mackail, John William *William Morris: an Address Delivered the XIth November MDCCCC at Kelmscott House Hammersmith Before the Hammersmith Socialist Society.* Hammersmith: Doves Press, 1901. First edition, one of 300 copies, small quarto, original full vellum, gilt lettering, vellum slightly worn at edges, fine.   The Brick Row Book Shop   Miscellany 67 - 37   2015 $425

MacKaness, George *Australian Historical Monographs.* Sydney: Dubbo, Review Publications, 1976. First edition thus, 44 volumes of facsimile reprint, 8vo., lime green printed card covers, edges very slightly rubbed, else clean, about fine set.   Any Amount of Books   2015 - A68484   2015   £200

MacKay, Magaret *The Poetic Parrot.* New York: John Day Co., 1951. First edition, illustrations by Kurt Wiese, top of thin spine little bumped and some creases on front fly, else near fine in very good dust jacket with little spine fading, small stain on rear panel and nicks at extremities, inscribed by author Sam McClerry (son of playwright William McCleery), laid in is Christmas card inscribed by McKay to McCleerys.   Between the Covers Rare Books, Inc.   187 - 50   2015 $200

MacKay, Robert *Songs and Poems, in the Gaelic Language...* Inverness: Kenneth Douglas, 1829. 8vo., half title, two titlepages (English and Gaelic) loose, original cloth backed boards, original printed label on spine, entirely uncut, very good.   John Drury Rare Books   2015 - 22610   2015 $612

MacKaye, Percy *Mater: an American Study in Comedy.* New York: Macmillan, 1908. First edition, spine tanned and boards bit soiled, very good, journalist Walter Lippmann's copy with his ownership signature and Cambridge address, nicely inscribed by author.   Between the Covers Rare Books, Inc.   187 - 163   2015 $200

MacKenzie, Alexander Muir *Letter to the Gentlemen of Landed Property of Scotland, Respecting the Late changes in the Local Militia.* Perth: printed by R. Morison for Messrs. Manners & Miller, Edinburgh, 1810. First edition, 8vo., 16 pages, some creases, else very good, uncut and unbound as issued, apparently very rare.   John Drury Rare Books   March 2015 - 25902   2015   £306

MacKenzie, Compton *April Fools: a Farce of Summer.* London: Cassell and Co., 1930. First edition, original binding, spine sunned and sides little marked, foxing to fore-edge, else nice, from the collection of Gavin H. Fryer.   Bertram Rota Ltd.   308 Part II - 165   2015   £20

MacKenzie, Compton *Ben Nevis Goes East.* London: Chatto & Windus, 1954. First edition, original binding, very nice in slightly chipped, creased and marked but still bright dust jacket, inscribed in red ink, from the collection of Gavin H. Fryer.   Bertram Rota Ltd.   308 Part II - 175   2015   £35

MacKenzie, Compton *Buttercups and Daisies.* London: Cassell, 1931. First edition, original binding, spine just little discolored and bumped at head, some foxing to first and last few leaves and fore-edge, but nice, from the collection of Gavin H. Fryer.   Bertram Rota Ltd.   308 Part II - 166   2015   £35

MacKenzie, Compton *Coral: a Sequel to 'Carnival'.* New York: George H. Doran Co., 1925. First American edition, original cloth, very good, from the collection of Gavin H. Fryer.   Bertram Rota Ltd.   308 Part II - 160   2015   £20

MacKenzie, Compton *The Early Life and Adventures of Sylvia Scarlett.* London: Martin Secker, 1918. First edition, original cloth binding little marked and worn, but very good, partly unopened, bookseller's small label, presentation copy inscribed by author for Doris Compton MacKenzie Oct. 13 32, from the collection of Gavin H. Fryer.   Bertram Rota Ltd.   308 Part II - 156   2015   £120

MacKenzie, Compton *Extraordinary Women.* London: Martin Secker, 1928. First edition, of an edition of 2000, this one of 100 special numbered copies, signed by author, original binding, some wear at edges and foxing to endpapers and prelims, otherwise nice, from the collection of Gavin H. Fryer.   Bertram Rota Ltd.   308 Part II - 163   2015   £30

MacKenzie, Compton *Extraordinary Women.* London: Martin Secker, 1928. First edition, of an edition of 2000, this one of 100 special numbered copies signed by author, original binding little cocked and some wear at edges, little foxing to endpapers and prelims, otherwise nice, somewhat soiled and frayed dust jacket little browned at spine panel, from the collection of Gavin H. Fryer.   Bertram Rota Ltd.   308 Part II - 162   2015   £100

MacKenzie, Compton *Extremes Meet.* London: Cassell and Co., 1928. First edition, 8vo., original binding, corners bumped and just little foxing, mostly at fore-edge, but nice, from the collection of Gavin H. Fryer.   Bertram Rota Ltd.   308 Part II - 164   2015   £20

MacKenzie, Compton *Fairy Gold.* London: Cassell & Co., 1926. First edition, very good, inscriptions, original binding, from the collection of Gavin H. Fryer.   Bertram Rota Ltd.   308 Part II - 161   2015   £20

MacKenzie, Compton *Figure of Eight.* London: Cassell and Co., 1936. First edition, original binding, spine creased and small mark, endpapers and prelims foxed, nice, from the collection of Gavin H. Fryer.   Bertram Rota Ltd.   308 Part II - 169   2015   £40

MacKenzie, Compton *Mezzotint.* London: Chatto & Windus, 1961. Advance proof copy, wrappers, just little wear to wrappers, upper portion of half title/contents page cut away, else nice, from the collection of Gavin H. Fryer. Bertram Rota Ltd.   308 Part II - 179   2015   £30

MacKenzie, Compton *Monarch of the Glen.* London: Chatto & Windus, 1941. First edition, original binding, endpapers little foxed, otherwise nice in slightly chipped little browned at spine panel, loosely inserted small embossed card inscribed by author, once held in place with paperclip which has left rust mark to card and dust jacket and indentation and mark to first few leaves, from the collection of Gavin H. Fryer.   Bertram Rota Ltd.   308 Part II - 172   2015   £180

MacKenzie, Compton *A Musical Chair.* London: Chatto & Windus, 1939. First edition, original binding, little foxing to prelims and fore-edge, otherwise very nice in foxed and frayed dust jacket which is little browned at spine panel, scarce, from the collection of Gavin H. Fryer.   Bertram Rota Ltd.   308 Part II - 171   2015   £40

MacKenzie, Compton *My Life and Times, Octave One.* London: Chatto & Windus, 1963. First edition, frontispiece, plates, original binding, very nice in dust jacket, from the collection of Gavin H. Fryer.   Bertram Rota Ltd.   308 Part II - 180   2015   £25

MacKenzie, Compton *Our Street.* London: Cassell and Co., 1931. Original binding, spine just little faded, endpapers slightly browned, rear free endpaper with small stain, label partly removed from front free endpaper, nice, bright copy, from the collection of Gavin H. Fryer, illustrations by Magdalen Fraser.   Bertram Rota Ltd.   308 Part II - 167   2015   £20

MacKenzie, Compton *Paper Lives: a Novel.* London: Chatto & Windus, 1966. First edition, original binding, fine in fine, bright dust jacket, from the collection of Gavin H. Fryer.   Bertram Rota Ltd.   308 Part II - 182   2015   £40

MacKenzie, Compton *Poems.* Oxford and London: B. H. Blackwell and Simpkin Marshall, Hamilton, Kent & Co., 1907. First edition, original grey printed wrappers, uncut, preserved in specially made chemise and blue quarter morocco bookform box, spine lettered gilt, wrappers little worn and soiled some chipping to edges, otherwise very nice, presentation copy inscribed by author for Elaise Tresent? and dated Aug. 1910, scarce, fragile first book, from the collection of Gavin H. Fryer.   Bertram Rota Ltd. 308 Part II - 155   2015   £250

MacKenzie, Compton *Rich Relatives.* New York and London: Harper & Bros., 1921. First American edition, original cloth, very good, from the collection of Gavin H. Fryer. Bertram Rota Ltd.   308 Part II - 158   2015   £20

MacKenzie, Compton *Rockets Galore.* London: Chatto & Windus, 1957. First edition, original binding, free endpapers browned and rather heavy foxing at fore edge, otherwise nice, nicked and partly foxed dust jacket, from the collection of Gavin H. Fryer.   Bertram Rota Ltd.   308 Part II - 177   2015   £30

MacKenzie, Compton *The Seven Ages of Woman.* London: Martin Secker, 1923. First edition, original cloth, fading spine and sides, endpapers browned and hinges, cracked, very good, ownership signature, from the collection of Gavin H. Fryer.   Bertram Rota Ltd.   308 Part II - 159   2015   £20

MacKenzie, Compton *Sublime Tobacco.* London: Chatto & Windus, 1957. First edition, original binding, endpapers just little browned, very nice in price clipped dust jacket, showing some tears and ear and one crude repair with adhesive tape, from the collection of Gavin H. Fryer. Bertram Rota Ltd.   308 Part II - 178   2015   £30

MacKenzie, Compton *Sylvia & Michael: the Later Adventures of Sylvia Scarlett.* London: Martin Secker, 1919. First edition, original cloth, very good only, ownership inscription, from the collection of Gavin H. Fryer.   Bertram Rota Ltd.   308 Part II - 157   2015   £20

MacKenzie, Compton *Thin Ice.* London: Chatto & Windus, 1956. First edition, original binding, very nice in very slightly nicked and marked dust jacket, from the collection of Gavin H. Fryer.   Bertram Rota Ltd.   308 Part II - 176   2015   £50

MacKenzie, Compton *Whiskey Galore.* London: Chatto & Windus, 1947. First edition, original binding, just little browning to endpapers, else very nice in chipped dust jacket, from the collection of Gavin H. Fryer.   Bertram Rota Ltd. 308 Part II - 174   2015   £60

MacKenzie, Compton *Wind of Freedom: the History of the Invasion of Greece...* London: Chatto & Windus, 1943. First edition, original binding, spine tad faded, otherwise very nice in slightly stained and nicked dust jacket, from the collection of Gavin H. Fryer.   Bertram Rota Ltd.   308 Part II - 173   2015   £30

MacKenzie, Compton *The Windsor Tapestry, Being a Study of the Life, Heritage and Abdication of H.R.H. the Duke of Windsor, K. G.* London: Rich & Cowan, 1938. First edition, original binding, corners bumped and some sunning to cloth as often, little spotting at fore edge, nice, from the collection of Gavin H. Fryer.   Bertram Rota Ltd. 308 Part II - 170   2015   £30

MacKenzie, Faith Compton *The Cardinal's Niece: the Story of Marie Mancini.* London: Martin Secker, 1935. First edition, frontispiece, plates, original binding somewhat marked and spine discolored, but very good, presentation copy inscribed by author for Joy Skinner, from the collection of Gavin H. Fryer.   Bertram Rota Ltd.   308 Part II - 183   2015   £60

MacKenzie, George *The Laws and Customs of Scotland, in Matters Criminal.* Edinburgh: printed by the heirs and successors of Andrew Anderson..., 1699. Folio, title printed in russet and black, fine and crisp Birmingham Law Society copy, BLS monogram on lower cover, name in gilt on upper, 19th century circular inkstamp n titlepage and occasionally elsewhere, bound in contemporary mottled calf, sympathetically rebacked, raised bands, gilt with crimson morocco label lettered gilt, excellent crisp copy, originally from the library of Jacob (or James) Winsam, with his signature and date of purchase 15 Nov. 1700.   John Drury Rare Books   March 2015 - 16208   2015 $874

MacKenzie, George *A Vindication of the Government in Scotland During the Reign of King Charles II.* London: printed for J. Hindmarsh at the Golden Ball in Cornhill, 1691. First edition, 4to., recent plain dark blue cloth, neatly lettered, fine, crisp copy.   John Drury Rare Books   March 2015 - 24381   2015   £306

MacKenzie, Henry *The Lounger.* Edinburgh: Published by William Creech, 1785-1787. First editions, Complete set, of 101 numbers, with a duplicate of number II in second edition bound in and of No. XCVII loosely inserted (latter frayed in inner and outer margins, pagination at head cropped), the usual fold marks, some of which little discolored, folio, contemporary calf backed marbled boards, vellum tips to corners, red lettering piece on spine, sides slightly rubbed, repairs to lower joint and foot of spine, good, contemporary signature of A. Erskine, bookplate Charles Cowie, noted Burns collector, late Earl of Perth (invoice from H. P. Kraus loosely inserted $750 in 1987).   Blackwell's Rare Books   B179 - 67   2015   £1500

MacKenzie, Kincaid *Statement In Answer to the protest, Published by a Small Minority of the Town-Council Against the Appointment of Mr. Thomas Henderson to be City Chamberlain....* Edinburgh: printed by George Ramsay and Co., 1810. First edition, 8vo., preserved in modern wrappers with printed title label on upper cover, very good, apparently rare outside Scotland.   John Drury Rare Books   2015 - 19261   2015 $89

MacKenzie, Seaforth *Chosen People.* London: Jonathan Cape, 1938. First edition, 8vo., original light blue cloth lettered gilt on spine, rare, very slight rubbing, slight fading to spine edges with small neat name on front pastedown, otherwise clean, very good.   Any Amount of Books   2015 - C2155   2015   £220

MacKenzie, William Bell *Married Life, Its Duties, Trials, Joys.* London: J. H. Jackson Islington Green, 1850. First edition, half title, catalog of J. H. Jackson publications, short closed tear in titlepage (but no loss), original green cloth embossed in blind, upper cover lettered gilt, within an ornamental cartouche, cloth little rubbed at extremities. bit good.   John Drury Rare Books   2015 - 26083   2015 $133

Mackey, Nathaniel *Four for Trane. Poems.* Los Angeles: Golenics, 1978. First edition, one of 250 copies, small 4to., illustrations, original printed wrappers, stapled as issued, very fine, scarce.   James S. Jaffe Rare Books   Modern American Poetry - 188   2015 $750

MacKinlay, John *An Account of Rothesay Castle.* Glasgow: James Hedderwick, 1818. Second edition, 8vo., 24 pages, engraved frontispiece, slightly offset, recent marbled boards lettered on spine.   John Drury Rare Books   March 2015 - 24920   2015   £306

Mackworth, Humphrey *A Vindication of the Rights of the Commons of England.* London: printed and are to be sold by J. Nutt, 1701. First edition, variant issue, folio, lower outer corners of several leaves rather frayed and stained, just affecting ruled border of titlepage, nowhere affecting text, recently well bound in cloth lettered gilt, good copy.   John Drury Rare Books   March 2015 - 18945   2015 $266

MacLaren, Charles *The Plain of Troy Described and the Identity of the Ilium of Homer with the New Ilium of Strabo Proved....* Edinburgh: Adam & Black, 1863. First edition thus, large 8vo., original burgundy cloth, lettered gilt on spine, now soundly rebound with new endpapers and attractively reinforced maps, spine slightly used, otherwise sound, very good.   Any Amount of Books   2015 - C5111   2015   £160

MacLean, Fitzroy *Eastern Approaches.* London: Jonathan Cape, 1949. First edition, 8vo., original red cloth, lettered gilt at spine, plates, portrait, foldout maps, very good+ in clean, very good dust jacket, slight surface wear and very slight closed tear with no loss at head of spine.   Any Amount of Books   2015 - C16447   2015   £160

MacLean, John *A Compendium of Kafir laws and Customs Including Genealogical Tables of Kafir Chiefs and Various Tribal Cenus Returns.* Mount Coke: Wesleyan Mission Press, printed for the government of British Kaffaria, 1858. 1st edition, 3 folding tables, original green cloth with printed spine label, label largely defective, old light stain on upper cover, very good, inscribed in ink by Maclean to Robert Vigne, with coy note in contemporary hand at head of title.   John Drury Rare Books   2015 - 26200   2015 $787

Maclean, Norman *A River Runs through it.* Chicago: University of Chicago, 1976. First edition, inscribed by author in Billings Montana April 1977, few small spots to top edge, else fine in near fine dust jacket (spine and edge sunned with slight rubbing to extremities).   Ken Lopez, Bookseller   164 - 126   2015 $6500

MacLeod, Allan *Lackington's Confessions, Rendered into Narrative.* London: B. Crosby and Co., 1804. First edition, 12mo., little very minor dampstaining, one leaf with closed tear (no loss of printed surface), recently well bound in linen backed marbled boards lettered, good copy.   John Drury Rare Books   March 2015 - 21809   2015 $266

MacLeod, Charlotte *Next Door to Danger.* New York: Avalon, 1965. First edition, very fine in dust jacket.   Mordida Books   March 2015 - 007958   2015 $300

MacMillan, John C. *The History of the Catholic Church in Prince Edward Island from 1835 till 1891.* Quebec: L'Evensment Prtg. Co., 1913. 8vo., blue pebbled cloth, frontispiece, photos, cloth with some staining, interior very good.   Schooner Books Ltd.   110 - 135   2015 $45

MacNab, Alexander M. *The Pioneers of Malagash.* Amherst: North Cumberland Historical Society, 1977. Reprint, 8vo., photo illustrations, card covers, very good.   Schooner Books Ltd.   110 - 96   2015 $45

MacNab, Henry Gray *Analysis and Analogy Recommended as the Means of rendering Experience and Observations Useful in Education.* Paris: printed by M. Nuzon, 1818. First edition, 4to., half title, explanatory 'errata leaf' at end, scattered foxing, signature of original owner Rich'd E. Wells Aug 4 1918, inkstamps of institutional library (not lending library) on titlepage, well bound in 19th century half calf over cloth boards, neatly rebacked with gilt lines and spine label, good, crisp copy, very rare.   John Drury Rare Books   2015 - 19968   2015 $1049

MacOrlan, Pierre *Le Chant De L'Equipage.* Paris: Les Arts Et Livre, 1926. #47 of 321, three quarter green leather over marbled paper covered boards, gilt stamped spine, raised bands, top edge gilt, fine and bright, although first two blanks have light foxing, wrappers retained, beautiful book, previous owner's slipcase, small 4to., illustrations by Dignimont.   Beasley Books   2013 - 2015 $400

MacOrlan, Pierre *Eloge De Daragnes avec Une Lettre De L'Editeur a L'Artiste.* Editions Manuel Bruker, 1956. Number 162 of 200 copies, 4to., unbound signatures laid into wrappers, fine in near fine, bit sunned wrappers with worn.   Beasley Books   2013 - 2015 $250

MacPherson, David *The History of the European Commerce with India.* London: Longman, Hurst Rees, Orme and Brown, 1812. First edition, 4to., half title, folding map as frontispiece, little offset, occasional very light spotting, contemporary red half morocco over marbled boards, spine gilt and lettered with raised bands, marbled edges, boards rubbed, wear at corners, still very good.   John Drury Rare Books   2015 - 25595   2015 $612

Macura, P. *Elsevier's Russian-English Dictionary.* Amsterdam: Oxford: New York Tokyo: Elsevier, 1990. Third impression, large 8vo., original burgundy boards, lettered white on spines and front cover, clean, very good+, excellent condition.   Any Amount of Books   2015 - C11540   2015   £150

MacVicar, Angus *The Canisbay Conspiracy.* London: Long, 1966. First edition, fine in dust jacket with slight spine fading and short closed tear, inscribed by author.   Mordida Books   March 2015 - 001841   2015 $75

MacVicar, Angus *Greybreek.* London: Paul, 1947. First edition, some tiny light spotting on page edges, otherwise fine in dust jacket with tiny wear at top of spine.   Mordida Books   March 2015 - 008680   2015 $100

Madan, Martin *Thelyphthora; or, a Treatise on Female Ruin...* London: printed for J. Dodsley, 1781. Second edition of volumes I an II, First edition of volume III, 3 volumes, 8vo., occasional very minor spotting, contemporary half calf over marbled boards, neatly and appropriately rebacked to match, spines fully gilt and labelled, very good set, scarce.   John Drury Rare Books   2015 - 23965   2015 $1311

Madan, Martin *Thelyphthora; or a treatise on Female Ruin in Its Causes, Effects, Consequences, prevention and Remedy...* London: Dodsley, 1781. Second edition of volumes 1 and 2, first edition of volume 3, top edge gilt, bound in later three quarter calf, stamped in gilt, first signature loose in volume 3, otherwise very good.   Second Life Books Inc.   189 - 154   2015 $750

Madden, Deirdre *Nothing is Black.* London: Faber & Faber, 1994. 8vo., original black cloth, lettered white on spine, signed presentation from author to Malcolm Stanley Bradbury, fine in near fine dust jacket.   Any Amount of Books   2015 - c3197   2015   £240

Madden, Samuel Molyneaux *Reflections and Resolutions Proper for the Gentlemen of Ireland as to Their Conduct for the Service of Their Country...* Dublin: printed by R. Reilly for George Ewing, 1738. First edition, 8vo., usual page misnumbering in two places, contemporary calf with raised bands, wanting title label on spine, very good, uncommon.   John Drury Rare Books   2015 - 24363   2015 $1136

Madison, Lucy Foster *Washington.* Philadelphia: Penn Publishing Co., 1925. First edition, 8vo., cloth, illustration inlaid on front cover, illustrated endpapers, this copy signed by illustrator, Frank Schoonover, cover inlaid, endpapers, frontispiece, chapter headers and 7 color plates in text by Schoonover.   Oak Knoll Books   306 - 41   2015 $100

Maeterlinck, Maurice *Tytyl.* New York: Dodd Mead, 1920. First edition, 4to., blue cloth, pictorial paste-on, 159 pages, as new in publisher's pictorial box, (some soil and flap repair but very good+ box), illustrations by Herbert Paus with 8 very lovely tipped in color plates with guards, pictorial endpapers.   Aleph-bet Books, Inc.   109 - 272   2015 $325

Magee, David *An Original Leaf from Francisco Palou's Life of the Venerable Father Junipero Serra 1787.* San Francisco: printed by the Grabhorn Press, 1958. First edition, one of 177 copies, tall folio, title in red and black, opening initial of text in red and gold, original tipped-in leaf and facsimile page within red rules, handset Janson type on English handmade paper, original cream wrappers, center sewn title in gold on red front cover label, very fine.   Argonaut Book Shop   Holiday Season 2014 - 162   2015 $450

Maggs Bros. Ltd. *Maggs 1075. Bookbinding in the British Isles Sixteenth to the Twentieth Century.* London: Maggs Bros., 1987. 2 volumes, 4to., stiff paper wrappers, 533 pages.   Oak Knoll Books   306 - 3   2015 $125

Maggs Bros. Ltd. *Maggs 1212. Bookbinding in the British Isles, Sixteenth to the Twentieth Century.* London: Maggs Bros., 1996. 4to., stiff paper wrappers, plates, many in color.   Oak Knoll Books   306 - 4   2015 $130

Maginnis, Arthur *The Atlantic Ferry, Its Ships, Men and Working, First Popular Edition.* Whitaker & Co., 1893. Half title, frontispiece, plates and illustrations, lacking following pastedown, 'yellowback', original printed yellow boards, following hinge slightly cracking, otherwise fine, ownership name of F. Brotherton, Gloucester.   Jarndyce Antiquarian Booksellers   CCXI - 193   2015   £150

Magnus, Olaus *Historia De Gentibus Septentrionalibus.* Antwerp: Jean Bellere, 1562. Woodcut printer's device on title and innumerable woodcuts in text, final leaf with corroded ink blot with loss of text to last 5 lines, rust spot in outer margin of another leaf touching initial letter of side note, 8vo., contemporary calf with 3 panels blind ruled on covers, connecting diagonals, central panels with gilt snowflake at each corner and a prancing reindeer at centre, 17th century paper manuscript lettering piece on spine and in superior compartment a similar shelf number, traces of later label at foot of spine, headcaps defective, old repair to head, few abrasions to lower cover, one early 17th century and one later ownership inscription of Jesuit College of Cordoba, with ink stamp of same provenance, part of the inscriptions unsuccessfully bleached, one or two early marginal annotations, printer's waste endpapers (two bifolia from a 1548 Lyons printing of the works of Horace), good.   Blackwell's Rare Books   B179 - 68   2015 £1400

Mahfouz, Naguib *Palace Walk.* Cairo: American University at Cairo Press, 1989. First edition, custom bound in gilt stamped red morocco with raised bands, fine.   Beasley Books   2013 - 2015 $150

Maier, Manfred *Basic Principles of Design.* New York: Van Nostrand Reinhold, 1980. First combined edition, small 4to., 384 pages, stiff paper wrappers, scarce.   Oak Knoll Books   306 - 51   2015 $200

Mailer, Norman   1923-2007 *The Executioner's Song. A True life Novel.* Boston: Little Brown and Co., 1979. First edition, near fine in like dust jacket.   Ed Smith Books   82 - 17   2015 $100

Mailer, Norman   1923-2007 *Existential Errands.* Boston: Little Brown and Co., 1972. First edition, very fine in very good plus dust jacket that is lightly soiled, signed by Mailer.   Jeff Hirsch Books   E-62 Holiday List 2014 - 21   2015 $150

Mailer, Norman   1923-2007 *Harlot's Ghost.* New York: Random House, 1991. First edition, fine book and dust jacket, inscribed and signed by author.   Stephen Lupack   March 2015 - 2015 $100

Mailer, Norman   1923-2007 *The Naked and the Dead.* New York: Rinehart & Co., 1948. First edition, first printing, very good or better with some light wear at corners and extremities, unclipped dust jacket with some wear and rubbing at corners and folds, small tears, else very good.   B & B Rare Books, Ltd.   234 - 73   2015 $600

Maimieux, Joseph De *Pasigraphie Premiers Elemens du Nouvel Art-Science d'ecrie et de'Imprimer et une Langue de Maniere...* Paris: au bureau de la Pasigraphie, 1797. First edition in French, 4to., blank strip cut away from lower margin of last leaf, titlepage bit dust soiled and with initials 'A.G.' ink stamped in margin, occasional light foxing, corners of some leaves curled, old, probably original marbled wrappers, entirely uncut, good copy.   John Drury Rare Books   2015 - 18331   2015 $699

Maitland, Barry *The Marx Sisters.* London: Hamish Hamilton, 1994. First edition, octavo, very small bump to bottom edge of upper cover, fine in fine dust jacket, very slightly creased at edges.   Peter Ellis, Bookseller   2014 - 004689   2015   £300

Maitland, Barry *The Marx Sisters.* London: Hamish Hamilton, 1994. First edition, tiny bump to lower front corner, else fine in dust jacket+.   Buckingham Books   March 2015 - 1786   2015 $850

Maitland, John *Observations on the Impolicy of Permitting the Exportation of British Wool and of Preventing the Free Importation of Foreign Wool.* London: William Phillips, 1818. First edition, 8vo., recently well bound in cloth, lettered on spine, entirely uncut, very good.   John Drury Rare Books   2015 - 6515   2015 $177

Major, Clarence *My Amputations.* New York: and Boulder: Fiction Collec., 1986. First edition, inscribed by author, fine in fine dust jacket with wraparound band.   Beasley Books   2013 - 2015 $45

Major, Harlan *Fishing Behind the Eight Ball.* Harrisburg: Stackpole Co., 1952. First edition, illustrations by Stephen Voorhies, corners bit bumped, else near fine in price clipped, near fine dust jacket, ownership signature of artist, Voorhies and inscribed by author to him April 1954.   Between the Covers Rare Books, Inc.   187 - 98   2015 $250

Majors, Alexander *Seventy Years on the Frontier. Alexander Majors Memoirs of a Lifetime.* Rand McNally & Co., 1893. First edition, cloth, numerous illustrations, handsome copy of true first edition, top edge gilt, beveled edges to boards, some occasional light rubbing, else exceptionally tight, bright, near fine, non-authorial presentation, neatly inscribed.   Buckingham Books   March 2015 - 37390   2015 $400

Makgill, George *Rent no robbery.* Edinburgh & London: William Blackwood & Sons, 1851. First edition, scarce, 8vo., wanting half title, minor stains on final leaf, well bound in linen backed marbled boards, lettered, very good, scarce.   John Drury Rare Books   2015 - 21827   2015 $115

Malamud, Bernard 1914-1986 *God's Grace.* New York: Farrar, Straus & Giroux, 1982. First edition, first printing, presentation copy signed and inscribed by author to close friend Nicholas Delbanco, near fine in like jacket,.   B & B Rare Books, Ltd.   234 - 74   2015 $500

Malamud, Bernard 1914-1986 *Idiots First.* New York: Farrar, Straus & Co., 1963. First edition, first printing, inscribed by Malamud to artist and close friend, Rosemarie Beck, very good, some staining to covers in like jacket with some wear and few small tear.   B & B Rare Books, Ltd.   234 - 75   2015 $650

Malcolm, John *The Godwin Sideboard.* London: Collins, 1984. First edition, fine in dust jacket.   Mordida Books   March 2015 - 001486   2015 $90

Malcolm, William *General View of the Agriculture of the county of Surrey, with Observations on the Means of Its Improvement.* London: printed by C. Macrae, 1794. First edition, 4to., 2 folding engraved plates, half title, well bound in early 20th century green cloth, partially faded, morocco spine label, bookplate removed from pastedown, but fine, usual generous margins.   John Drury Rare Books   March 2015 - 23371   2015   £306

Malkin, Benjamin Heath *A Father's Memoirs of His child.* London: printed for Longman, Hurst, Rees and Orme by T. Bentley, 1806. First edition, 8vo., recent half midnight blue morocco over marbled boards, spine divided into six compartments with raised bands, gilt title to second, remaining compartments attractively blocked in gilt, frontispiece, 3 plates, small closed lateral tear to margin of pages (i)/ii, expertly repaired, very occasional light spotting, otherwise bright, clean.   Henry Sotheran Ltd.   William Blake Exhibition 17th Oct.-7th Nov. 2014 - 71   2015   £1200

Mallarme, Stephane *Un Coup de Des Jamais N'Abolira le Hasard.* N.P.: Limited Editions Club, 1992. Folio, leather, title gilt stamped on spine, clamshell box, leather spine, lithographs by Ellsworth Kelly, Monthly letter loosely inserted.   Oak Knoll Books   25 - 60   2015 $3500

Mallet, David *The Works of Mr. Mallet: Consisting of Plays and Poems...* London: A. Millar, 1743. Presumed first edition, 8vo., full leather, probably 18th century, lacks f.e.p., some rubbing and scuffing to leather, slight splitting at lower hinge, but reasonably sound, near very good copy with clean text.   Any Amount of Books   2015 - A74742   2015   £225

Mallinson, Allan *A Close Run Thing, and His Nine Other Volumes.* London: Bantam Press, 1999-2008. First editions, 10 volumes, as new, unread condition, in as new dust jackets.   Buckingham Books   March 2015 - 13171   2015 $1250

Mallock, William Hurrell *Lucretius on Life and Death in the Metre of Omar Khayyam...* London: Adam & Charles Black, 1901. Original olive green cloth, embossed head, stab holes in endpapers, slightly marked and rubbed, from the library of Geoffrey & Kathleen Tillotson, undated presentation ANS from author and 2 page ALS from him to Williamson. Jarndyce Antiquarian Booksellers CCVII - 372 2015 £20

Malmgren, Ebby *Stone Dream and Other Poems by Ebby Malmgren.* Arnold: 2003. Artist's book, one of 18 copies, all on Nepalese Lokta paper and Hiromi Rayon Paper collaged on Indian handmade 'cork' paper, page size 6 1/4 x 10 1/4 inches, 24 pages, bound by Joan Machinchick, hand-sewn in brown paper over boards with title hand lettered and printed Gocco and collaged on front cover, housed in tan linen over boards clamshell box with title printed Gocco from hand lettering on spine and front panel. Priscilla Juvelis - Rare Books 62 - 09 2015 $750

Malory, Thomas *La Morte d'Arthur.* London: John Russell Smith, 1858. 3 volumes, bound in contemporary full black calf gilt. Honey & Wax Booksellers 2 - 37 2015 $1800

Malory, Thomas *Le Morte D'Arthur.* London: Philip Lee Warner, Pub. to the Medici Society Ltd., 1910-1911. One of 500 numbered copies printed on handmade Riccardi paper out of a total edition of 512, this number 257, 4 volumes, quarto, 48 mounted color plates after watercolor drawings by W. Russell Flint, descriptive tissue guards printed in blue and black, original quarter beige cloth over blue paper boards, paper labels on front covers and spines, top edge gilt, original blue printed dust jacket, jacket spines sunned, otherwise fine set in publisher's original cardboard slipcases. Heritage Book Shop Holiday 2014 - 55 2015 $1750

Malory, Thomas *The Noble and Joyous Boke Entytled Le Morte D'Arthur.* Oxford: Shakespeare Head Press, 1933. 2 volumes, printed on handmade paper, titles, chapter headings and initial letters printed in red, tissue guard to titlepage in first volume and further to later half of second, reproductions of 21 wood engravings from contemporary editions, royal 8vo., original full red hermitage calf, backstrips lettered gilt, touch of light rubbing to corners, marbled endpapers, top edge gilt on the rough, others untrimmed, very good, beautiful set. Blackwell's Rare Books B179 - 234 2015 £675

Malory, Thomas *Le Morte D'Arthur....* New York: Limited Editions Club, 1936. Limited to 1500 numbered copies signed by artist, Robert Gibbings, 3 volumes, wood engravings by Gibbings, 4to., cloth backed patterned paper covered boards, slipcase, monthly letter loosely inserted, edges of slipcase shows wear, well preserved set. Oak Knoll Books 25 - 15 2015 $450

Malory, Thomas *The Romance of King Arthur.* New York: Macmillan, 1917. Limited to 250 copies of American edition, large thick 4to., full kid binding, decorated in gold, light soil and rubbing, else very good in original publisher's box (worn), 16 mounted color plates with lettered tissue guards, 7 black and white plates plus a profusion of lovely text illustrations by Arthur Rackham. Aleph-Bet Books, Inc. 108 - 382 2015 $3200

Malthus, Thomas Robert 1766-1834 *Additions to the Fourth and Former Editions of an Essay on the Principle of Population &c &c.* London: John Murray, 1817. First and only edition, without ad leaves found in some copies, some intermittent foxing on titlepage and elsewhere, one leaf with long closed tear (repaired) but with no loss of printed surface, excellent early 20th century quarter calf over marbled boards, raised bands, spine label lettered gilt, entirely uncut, good copy. John Drury Rare Books March 2015 - 24860 2015 $656

Malthus, Thomas Robert 1766-1834 *An Essay on the principle of Population or a View of Its Past and Present Effects on Human Happiness...* London: J. Johnson, 1806. 2 volumes, 8vo., two half titles, intermittent very slight spotting and damp marking, contemporary sprinkled calf, professionally rebacked, spines gilt with labels lettered gilt, very good. John Drury Rare Books 2015 - 23206 2015 $1049

Malthus, Thomas Robert 1766-1834 *An Essay on the Principle of Population; or a View of Its Past and Present Effects on Human Happiness..* London: J. Johnson, 1807. Reprint of 1806 edition, 8vo., 2 volumes, with both half titles, short closed tear in titlepage to volume 1, original boards neatly rebacked, entirely uncut, near fine. John Drury Rare Books 2015 - 26146 2015 $787

Malthus, Thomas Robert 1766-1834 *An Essay on the Principle of Population or a View of Its Past and Present Effects on Human Happiness...* George Town: J. Milligan at J. March's Bookstore, 1809. Stated first American edition, 2 volumes, 8vo., half leather binding, marbled boards with raised bands spines, gilt lettering and decoration spines, minimal cover edge wear, scattered foxing, scuffs to covers, top corners of titlepage repaired. By the Book, L. C. 44 - 48 2015 $700

Malthus, Thomas Robert 1766-1834 *An Essay on the Principle of Population....* London: John Murray, 1826. 2 volumes, 8vo., well bound in relatively modern green quarter morocco over cloth boards, spine gilt with raised bands and contrasting labels, top edge gilt, very good, presentation copy inscribed in volume I to George Batten, from Mrs. Malthus. John Drury Rare Books 2015 - 25844 2015 $1049

Malthus, Thomas Robert 1766-1834 *The Grounds of an Opinion on the Policy of Restricting the Importation of Foreign Corn; Intended as an Appendix to "Observations on the Corn Laws".* London: John Murray and J. Johnson & Co., 1815. First edition, some minor staining to titlepage, otherwise fine, recent blue morocco backed marbled boards, gilt lettering to spine, ink note to pastedown 'Ex Libris Brent Gration-Maxfield", uncommon.   John Drury Rare Books 2015 - 25567   2015 $2185

Man, John *The History and Antiquities Ancient and Modern of the Borough of Reading, in the County of Berks.* Reading: printed for Snare and Man...., 1816. 4to., titlepage printed in red and black, some old damage to 3A2-3, 3B3 & 3C3, without loss, 21 aquatint and engraved maps, views and portraits, 19th century black morocco over marbled boards, somewhat rubbed, engraved armorial bookplate of Cyril Kendall Butler of Bourton House. Marlborough Rare Books   List 53 - 25   2015   £150

Mandal, Sant Ram *The Happy Flute.* New York: Stokes, 1939. First edition, 8vo., cloth, fine in slightly worn, very good dust jacket, illustrations by Dorothy Lathrop.   Aleph-bet Books, Inc.   109 - 252   2015 $125

Mandeville, Bernard De *The Fable of the Bees.* London: J. Tonson, 1729. Sixth edition, 8vo., half green leather, marbled boards, lettered gilt on spine, 5 raised bands, very slight spotting to text, otherwise near fine.   Any Amount of Books   2015 - A69898   2015   £240

Mangold, George B. *Problems of Child Welfare.* New York: Macmillan, 1914. First edition, fine an bright with homemade library tag at corner front pastedown and ownership signature of socialist historian Richard T. Ely.   Beasley Books   2013 - 2015 $85

Manilii, M. *Astronomicon, Liber Secundis.* London: Grant Richards, 1912. First edition, 8vo. original printed blue thick card paper covered boards, 11 illustrations, spine label missing with white remnants left, slight marking and slight scuffing at corners, otherwise sound, very good.   Any Amount of Books   2015 - A43329   2015   £200

Manley, Mary De La Riviere *Secret Memoirs and Manners of Several persons of Quality of both Sexes from the New Atlantis, an Island in the Mediterranean.* London: John Morphew, 1709. Second edition volume 1, first edition of volume 2, 8vo., frontispiece in volume 1, some worming to top margin of few leaves in volume 2 (not affecting any letterpress), some light foxing, very good, modern three quarter calf spine with heavy gilt stamping with new endpapers, bound in rear is scarce keys to both volumes. Second Life Books Inc.   189 - 155   2015 $1250

Mann, Heinrich *Small Town Tyrant.* New York: Creative Age, 1944. First American edition, fine in near fine dust jacket with few small tears, very scarce.   Between the Covers Rare Books   196 - 91   2015 $300

Mann, Leonard *A Murder in Sydney.* London: Cape, 1937. First edition, page edges spotted, otherwise very good in dust jacket with frayed spine ends, soiled back panel, wear along folds and couple of short closed tears. Mordida Books   March 2015 - 001490   2015 $100

Mann, Thomas *The Magic Mountain.* New York: Knopf, 1939. First one volume edition, very good+, foxing to endpapers, little disturbance to cloth's sizing, tight, clean text, in very good- dust jacket (some foxing to flaps, some chipping, light dampstain to rear panel).   Stephen Lupack   March 2015 - 2015 $95

Manners, John James Robert *A Plea for National Holy-Days.* London: Painter, 1843. First edition, 8vo., 34 pages, preserved in modern wrappers, printed title label on upper cover, very good, scarce.   John Drury Rare Books March 2015 - 19999   2015 $221

Manning, Hugo *The Secret Sea.* London: Trigram Press, 1968. One of 500 copies, tiny name inked over, else fine in fine dust jacket, warmly inscribed by author for poet Karl Shapiro. Between the Covers Rare Books, Inc.   187 - 165 2015 $150

Man's Only Affair or Reflections on the Four Last Things to be Remembered. New York: Seymour, 1813. First American edition, small 8vo., soundly bound in full brown leather, appears contemporary, lettering at spine illegible, reasonable, clean, near very good copy with some gatherings very slightly sprung, otherwise sound with some worming to titlepage and first 4 pages, not affecting legibility. Any Amount of Books   2015 - C7249   2015   £150

Mansel, Henry Longueville *Scenes from an Unfinished Drama Entitled Phronisterion or Oxford in the 19th Century.* Oxford: J. Vincent, 1852. Second edition, 12mo., 24 pages, recent plain wrapper, very good.   John Drury Rare Books 2015 - 16615   2015 $133

Mansion, Leon Larue *Lettres sur la Miniature...* Paris: chez Louis Janet, Libraire et chez l'Auteur...Londres: R. Ackermann... M. Mayaud, 1823. Second edition, 12mo., folding hand colored frontispiece, lightly foxed, due to paper stock, contemporary morocco backed mottled boards, spine ruled and lettered in gilt.   Marlborough Rare Books   List 54 - 51   2015   £285

Manso, Leo *Wild West.* Cleveland: World, 1950. Stated first edition, 4to., spiral backed boards, fine in dust jacket, brightly illustrated in color.   Aleph-Bet Books, Inc.   108 - 323   2015 $250

Mantel, Hilary *Beyond Black.* London: Fourth Estate, 2005. First edition, large 8vo., original red cloth, lettered silver at spine, boldly signed by author, fine in fine dust jacket. Any Amount of Books   2015 - C8072   2015   £160

Mantel, Hilary *Bring Up the Bodies.* 4th Estate, 2012. First edition, one of 1000 numbered copies signed by author, 8vo., original illustrated boards, lettered in gilt, slipcase, still in publisher's shrink wraps, fine. Blackwell's Rare Books B179 - 191 2015 £100

Manus, Willard *The Fighting Men.* Los Angeles: Panjandrum, 1981. Galley sheets, 8 1/2 x 14 inches, near fine. Ken Lopez, Bookseller 164 - 228 2015 $150

Manzarek, Ray *Light My Fire - My Life with the Doors.* G. P. Putnam's Sons, 1998. First edition, signed, very fine in dust jacket, illustrations. Buckingham Books March 2015 - 11952 2015 $250

Maracle, Lee *Bobbie Lee. Indian Rebel.* Toronto: Women's Press, 1990. First edition thus, signed by author, scarce signed, near fine in wrappers. Ken Lopez, Bookseller 164 - 157 2015 $125

Maran, Rene *Batouala, a Novel.* New York: Limited Editions Club, 1932. Limited to 1500 numbered copies, signed by artist, 4to., full leather, lavishly illustrated by Miguel Covarrubias in both color plates and line drawings, almost every page is decorated, with monthly letter loosely inserted, slipcase shows some rubbing and book spine has few scuff marks, much better preserved than most copies. Oak Knoll Books 25 - 6 2015 $385

Maran, Rene *Batoula, a Novel.* New York: Limited Editions Club, 1932. No. 1261 of 100 copies done for the LEC, illustrated and signed by Miguel Covarrubias, full morocco bit worn and scuffed but very good+ in very good slipcase, folio. Beasley Books 2013 - 2015 $200

Marble, Annie Russell *From Boston to Boston.* Boston: Lothrop, Lee & Shepard, 1930. First edition, decorated cloth, illustrations inscribed and signed by author in 1930, very good. Stephen Lupack March 2015 - 2015 $45

Marchen, Andere *Das Grosse Ding.* Oldenberg: Berhard Stalling, 1925. State first edition, 4to., cloth backed pictorial boards, slightest bit of edge rubbing, else fine in dust jacket (frayed), illustrations by Else Wenz-Vietor with 9 incredible full page color illustrations and 6 partial page color illustrations, beautiful copy. Aleph-bet Books, Inc. 109 - 188 2015 $450

Marcus, Greil *Double Trouble, Bill Clinton and Elvis Presley in a Land of No Alternatives.* New York: Henry Holt, 2000. First edition, inscribed by author, fine in dust jacket. Beasley Books 2013 - 2015 $45

Mardersteig, Giovanni *The Officina Bodoni, an Account of the Work of a Hand Press 1923-1977.* Verona: Edizioni Valonega, 1980. First edition, limited to 1500 copies, this one of 500 in English, 4to., cloth, cardboard slipcase. Oak Knoll Books 306 - 158 2015 $100

Mare, A. C. De La *Bartolomeo Sanvito: The Life and Work of a Renaissance Scribe.* London: Association Internationale de bibliophile, 2009. Large 4to., cloth, dust jacket, 196 images. Oak Knoll Books Special Catalogue 24 - 45 2015 $350

Marfield, Dwight *The Mandarin's Sapphire.* New York: E. P. Dutton and Co., 1938. First edition, very faint pencil name on front fly, modest 'surplus' stamp on rear fly, very slightly cocked, still near fine in slightly spine faded, very good or better dust jacket with small nicks and tears, handsome copy. Between the Covers Rare Books 196 - 145 2015 $150

Margaritha, Anthonius *Der Gantz Judisch Glaub mit Sampt Eyner Grundtlichenn und Warhafftigen Anzeygunge Aller Statzungen, Ceremonien Gebetten...* Augsburg: Heynrich Steyner, 1531. Early edition, small 4to., large woodcut on titlepage, five large text woodcuts, 19th century marbled boards, small label removed from fore-edge of titlepage, ff. A2/3 cropped close by binder at top edge, just touching top line of text, repaired tear to L3, otherwise good. Maggs Bros. Ltd. Illustrated Books 2014 - 2015 £3500

Maria Theresa, Empress of Austria *Constitutio Criminals Theresiana oder der Romisch Kaiserl zu Hungaran und Boheim..* Wien: Johann Thomas Edlen von Trattnern, 1769. First edition, folio, 27 engravings in text and 3 folding engraved plates, one of the plates misfolded and slightly frayed at lower edge, with old paper repair at fore edge, not affecting print area, woodcut and typographic ornaments and initials, bound in contemporary calf spine gilt, little rubbed and recently rebacked, red edges, woodblock printed endpapers, some toning to text, binding little rubbed, still very good, crisp and clean. Second Life Books Inc. 189 - 156 2015 $4500

Mariana *Journey of the Bangwell Putt.* New York: Lothrop Lee Shepard, 1965. First trade edition, 4to., cloth, fine in dust jacket, color illustrations, lovely book. Aleph-bet Books, Inc. 109 - 275 2015 $100

Marie, Queen of Roumania *The Lily of Life: a Fairy Tale.* London: Hodder & Stoughton, n.d. circa, 1914. 4to., white cloth with extensive gilt decoration and pictorial paste-on, top edge gilt, as new in publisher's pictorial box with some soil and flap mends, illustrations by Helen Stratton with 18 tipped in color plates. Aleph-bet Books, Inc. 109 - 170 2015 $750

Marie, Queen of Roumania *Magic Doll of Roumania.* New York: Stokes, 1929. First edition, 8vo., yellow cloth, pictorial paste-on, 319 pages, fine in frayed dust jacket, illustrations by Maud Petersham with 10 color plates plus many lovely black and whites, beautiful copy, rarely found with dust jacket. Aleph-bet Books, Inc. 109 - 350 2015 $400

Marie, Queen of Roumania *The Story of Naughty Kildeen.* London: Oxford University Press, 1922. First edition, folio, gilt pictorial cloth, fine in pictorial dust jacket (chipped with few tears, overall very good), magnificent hand colored illustrations plus detailed black and whites on almost every page. Aleph-Bet Books, Inc. 108 - 253 2015 $1950

Marine Society *The Bye-Laws and Regulations of the Marine Society Inc. in MDCCLXXII with the Several Instructions Forms of Indentures and Other Instruments Used by Them. Also a List of Subscribers from May 1769 to June 1772.* London: 1772. First edition, 12mo., engraved titlepage, contemporary calf, spine fully gilt in compartments with flower and leaf devices within raised bands, red morocco label, just smallest snag at foot of spine, still fine, from the library of Sir Timothy Waldo, one of the original subscribers, with his armorial bookplate on front pastedown, rare. John Drury Rare Books 2015 - 24856 2015 $1661

Marineau, Rene F. *Jacob Levy Moreno 1889-1974, Father of Psychodrama...* London: Tavistock/Routeldge, 1989. First edition, wrappers, uncommon, fine. Beasley Books 2013 - 2015 $150

Marinelli, Lucrezia *La Nobilta et Lieccellenza Delle Donne CoiDiffetti et Mancamenti de Gli Huomini.* Venezia: Giovanni Ciotti, 1601. Second edition, 8vo., small repair at bottom of titlepage with loss of few letters, some other tiny holes, skillfully repaired at page 237/238 which slightly affects text, minimal foxing but better than very good, clean copy with wide margins, later full calf with raised bands an modest gilt title,. Second Life Books Inc. 191 - 57 2015 $5000

Markham, Gervase *The Young Sportsman"s Instructor.* London: Apollo Press, 1820. 83 x 57mm., fine contemporary dark green morocco, elaborately gilt by Thomas Gosden, covers intricately gilt in Groliersque design of thick and thin fillets, interlinking strapwork, leafy flourishes and acorn tools, all of these forming a frame enclosing a central oval with gilt hunting horn, flat spine tooled with gilt vine forming 8 rounded compartments, 6 with sport equipment or an animal at center, one with initials "G.M." and one gilt, in excellent later custom made green morocco backed clamshell box by Aquarius of London, woodcut frontispiece, perhaps a breath of wear to leather, leaves shade less than bright with mild offsetting, last two gatherings with slight vertical crease, still very desirable example, text and beautiful binding both clean, fresh and generally well preserved. Phillip J. Pirages 66 - 75 2015 $4500

Markopoulos, Gregory J. *Quest for Serenity: Journal of a Filmmaker.* New York: Film-makers' Cinematheque, 1966. First edition, one of 1000 copies (this being no. 93), inscribed by author for actress Ruth Ford, very good in saddle stitched paper wrappers, lightly rubbed, minimal soiling, top right corner creased. Royal Books 46 - 26 2015 $850

Marks, Jeannette *Thirteen Days.* New York: Albert & Charles Boni, 1929. First edition, very good+ with sunned head of spine, good dust jacket with large chunk out of dust jacket top edge, 8vo. Beasley Books 2013 - 2015 $85

Markstein, George *Chance Awakening.* London: Souvenir Press, 1977. First edition, fine in dust jacket. Buckingham Books March 2015 - 30044 2015 $175

Markstein, George *The Man from Yesterday.* London: Souvenir Press, 1976. First edition, fine in dust jacket. Buckingham Books March 2015 - 30045 2015 $175

Marlow, Louis *Fool's Quarter Day.* London: Faber and Faber, 1935. First edition, staining to top of boards, good only in lightly chipped good plus dust jacket with staining not particularly noticeable, very scarce, especially in jacket. Between the Covers Rare Books 196 - 92 2015 $300

Marlow, Louis *Forth Beast!* London: Faber & Faber, 1946. First edition, 8vo., endpapers slightly foxed otherwise, very good+ in decent about very good dust jacket very slightly soiled and very slightly chipped at head of spine and corners with slight age toning. Any Amount of Books 2015 - A66207 2015 £150

Marlowe, Christopher 1564-1593 *Hero and Leander.* Edinburgh: Ballantyne Press, 1909. First edition thus, one of 500 copies, the poem was finished by George Chapman, extra illustrated with two portraits of Chapman, splendidly bound in crushed violet morocco, signed exhibition binding. Honey & Wax Booksellers 1 - 32 2015 $1750

Marlowe, G. S. *Pictures on the Pavement.* London: Collins, 1938. First edition, 8vo., original light brown cloth, some fox spotting at prelims, endpapers and fore-edges, otherwise near very good+ in near very good clipped jacket with slight wear at head of spine, slight edgewear and surface wear to lighter rear panel. Any Amount of Books 2015 - C14251 2015 £240

Marmaduke Multiply's Merry Method of Making Minor Mathematicians. London: 1816-1817. First edition, 16mo. bound from parts, period style red sheep gilt over marbled boards, 69 hand colored plates, printed on paper watermarked 1814 and 1815. Honey & Wax Booksellers 3 - 9 2015 $4500

Marmontel, Jean Francois 1723-1799 *Marmontel's Moral Tales.* London: George Allen, 1895. Octavo, 45 black and white illustrations by Chris Hammond, many pages still uncut, charming 'vellucent' binding by Cedric Chivers of Bath (stamp-signed in gilt), translucent vellum over painted boards, illustration on front cover with hand painted image, all in decorative border, lined and decorated with gilt, gilt turn-ins, top edge gilt, vellum beginning to separate on front cover slightly warped with small pink spot to bottom of rear cover, otherwise, fine example. Heritage Book Shop Holiday 2014 - 38 2015 $2000

Marolles, Michel De *Tableaux du Temple des Muses, Tirez du Cabinet de Feu Mr. Favereau avec les Descriptions, Remarques & Annotationis.* Paris: chez Antoine de Sommaville, 1655. First edition, folio, fine additional engraved title depicting the temple des Muses, engraved portrait of author, 58 stunning plates engraved by Cornelies Bloemart and others after designs by Abraham van Diepenbeek, 19th century calf backed marbled boards, armorial booklabel of Ducs de Luynes, Chateau de Dampierre with the 'DLP' (De Lynes Paris) stamp on titlepage. Maggs Bros. Ltd. Illustrated Books 2014 - 2015 £3000

Marquand, John *No Hero.* Boston: Little Brown, 1935. First edition, very good plus copy, light toning to yellow cloth, slight foxing at fore-edges, tight, clean text. Stephen Lupack March 2015 - 2015 $250

Marquet, Albert *Le Danube Voyage De Printemps.* Lausanne: Editions Mermod, 1954. First edition, 1/470 copies, this copy press numbered 223, 16 watercolors, paper covered boards in slipcase, spine chip expertly restored, joints professionally repaired, very good in very good slipcase. Beasley Books 2013 - 2015 $300

Marquis of Carabas' Picture Book. London: George Routledge, n.d., 1874. 4to., burgundy cloth pictorially stamped in gold and black, light fraying on spine ends and corners, some rubbing, very good+, magnificently printed in color by Edmund Evans and featuring 32 full page color illustrations one very leaf by Walter Crane, laid in is card from Scottish Widow's Fund with lovely 3 inch illustrations. Aleph-bet Books, Inc. 109 - 112 2015 $875

Marquis, Thomas B. *A Warrior who Fought Custer.* Midwest Co., 1931. First edition, 2 maps at rear, illustrations, fine, bright copy in near fine dust jacket, some minor edgewear and very light chipping to spine ends, very scarce in this condition. Buckingham Books March 2015 - 32814 2015 $250

Marriott, James *The Rights and Privileges of Both the Universities and of the University of Cambridge in Particular Defended in a Charge to the Grand Jury at the Quarter Sessions for the Peace Held in and for the Town of Cambridge the Tenth Day of October 1768.* Cambridge: printed by J. Archdeacon printer to the University sold by T. & J. Merrill &c, 1769. First edition, 8vo., 36 pages, recent marbled boards lettered on spine, very good. John Drury Rare Books 2015 - 24811 2015 $221

Marryat, Frederick 1792-1848 *A Diary in America, with Remarks on Its Institutions.* Paris: Baudry's European Library, 1839-1840. First Continental Edition, Series one and two, 8vo., uncut and unopened and bound in original printed wrappers with 2 folding maps, fine. Second Life Books Inc. 191 - 58 2015 $350

Marryat, Frederick 1792-1848 *Poor Jack.* London: Longmans, 1840. First edition, frontispiece, plates, illustrations by Clarkson Stanfield, some plates foxed, small portrait of author laid down on leading pastedown, uncut in original dark green cloth blocked in blind and gilt, at some time neatly recased, good, sound copy, from the library of Geoffrey & Kathleen Tillotson. Jarndyce Antiquarian Booksellers CCVII - 373 2015 £75

Marryat, Frederick 1792-1848 *The Privateer's Man One Hundred Years Ago.* London: Longman, Brown, Green and Longmans, 1846. First edition, 2 volumes, little cut down in contemporary half brown calf, brown morocco labels, little rubbed but nice, booklabels of Amy Wedgwood, booklabels of Francis Wedgwood. Jarndyce Antiquarian Booksellers CCXI - 197 2015 £180

Marryat, Joseph *A Reply to the Arguments Contained in Various Publications Recommending an Equalization of the Duties on East & West Indian Sugar.* London: J. M. Richardson and Ridgeways, 1823. First edition, 8vo., wanting half title, recently well bound in cloth backed boards lettered in gilt, very good. John Drury Rare Books 2015 - 8346 2015 $177

Marsh, James B. *Four Years in the Rockies; or the Adventures of Isaac P. Rose of Shenango Township, Lawrence County, Pennsylvania.* New Castle: W. B. Thomas, 1884. First edition, 12mo., rebound in full, tan morocco with raised bands on spine, with author and title in gilt on red and green morocco labels on spine, frontispiece, very good, offered in cloth clamshell box with leather label stamped gilt on spine. Buckingham Books March 2015 - 27770 2015 $1750

Marsh, Ngaio *The Nursing Home Murder.* New York: Sheridan House, 1941. First American edition, very good, some wear along cover edges, otherwise near fine in very good dust jacket with internal tape mends, external tape mend at base of spine, chipping at base of spine, chipped lower corner of front panel and wear along folds. Mordida Books March 2015 - 009451 2015 $250

Marsh, Ngaio *Overture to Death.* New York: Furman, 1939. First American edition, advance review copy with review slip tipped in on front endpaper, some slight darkening on pastedown, else fine in dust jacket with light soiling on spine and nicks at top of spine. Mordida Books March 2015 - 911442 2015 $600

Marsh, Ngaio *Singing in the Shrouds.* London: Collins, 1959. First edition, fine in dust jacket with some light spotting on back panel. Mordida Books March 2015 - 007037 2015 $90

Marsh, Ngaio *Surfeit of Lampreys.* London: Collins Crime Club, 1941. First edition, some staining on spine and spine slightly faded, otherwise very good in dust jacket with staining at base of spine, wear at corners and along spine ends, couple of short closed tears. Mordida Books March 2015 - 011444 2015 $650

Marsh, William *A Sermon Preached at the church of St. Lawrence, Jewry, near Guildhall on Sunday April 28th 1816 before the Society for the Support and Encouragement of Sunday schools throughout the British Dominions...* London: printed by H. Teape sold at the Society's Depository 19 Little Moorfields, 1816. First edition, 8vo., apparently rare, well bound fairly recently in plain grey boards, lettered on spine, very good. John Drury Rare Books March 2015 - 24601 2015 £306

Marshak, Sondra *Star Trek: The New Voyages 2.* New York: Bantam, 1978. First edition, near fine with few creases to wrappers, inscribed by Jesco Von Puttkamer (provided introduction) to Fred Durant with longer typed note from Von Puttkamer to Durant tipped-in. Between the Covers Rare Books, Inc. 187 - 251 2015 $275

Marshall, George *The Pleasures and Advantages of Literary Pursuit, Compared with Those which arise from the Excitement of Political Life. A Prize Essay read in the Sheldonian Theatre, Oxford June 15 1841.* Oxford: printed and published by J. Vincent, 1841. First edition, 8vo., 36 pages, recently well bound in linen backed marbled boards, lettered, very good, rare. John Drury Rare Books 2015 - 19998 2015 $133

Marshall, James *Four Little Troubles.* Boston: Houghton Mifflin, 1975. First printings with 1-10 number code, 5 x 4 inches, 4 books, pictorial wrappers, as new in slipcase, illustrations by Marshall with full page color illustrations. Aleph-Bet Books, Inc. 108 - 284 2015 $100

Marsten, Richard *Vanishing Ladies.* Permabooks, 1957. First edition, fine in pictorial wrappers. Buckingham Books March 2015 - 38258 2015 $200

Martel, Andre *Pages De Gloire De La Legion Etrangere.* Paris: Andre Martel, 1952. First edition, Wrappers, tall 8vo., 16 full page color plates, from an edition of 2900, this is number XV of XXX (15 of 30) 'hors commerce' on velin, faint wear at spine ends, otherwise bright, clean, very good+ on velin. Any Amount of Books 2015 - A40704 2015 £180

Martell, Dominic *Gitana.* London: Orion, 2001. First edition, very fine in dust jacket. Mordida Books March 2015 - 008123 2015 $85

Martens, Karl *Printed Matter/Druckwerk.* London: Hyphen Press, 1996. 8vo., stiff paper wrappers, color illustrations, pages french-fold. Oak Knoll Books 306 - 52 2015 $300

Martialis, Marcus Valerius *Epigrammata.* Venice: in Aedibus Aldi, 1501. First Aldine edition, some minor spotting, first two leaves lightly browned, last leaf mounted (obscured verso blank except for an old manuscript note just visible through the page) 8vo. 18th century sponge painted paper boards (probably Viennese), rubbed and worn at extremities and joints, backstrip darkened, bookplate of Robert Needham Cust (1821-1909), preserved in blue quarter morocco solander box, good. Blackwell's Rare Books Greek & Latin Classics VI - 73 2015 £2500

Martialis, Marcus Valerius *Epigrammaton Libri XIII.* Lugduni: Apud Haered Seb. Gryphius, 1559. 108 x 76mm., appealing contemporary olive brown morocco, covers bordered with fillets in gilt and in blind and with small gilt floral cornerpieces as well as central azured gilt arabesque, raised bands forming eight spine panels, each of these with small gilt cruciform sprigs flanking a central majuscule, the letters running vertically to spell out 'MARTIAL" all edges gilt; woodcut printer's device to titlepage, woodcut initials, from the library of Chatsworth House with modern bookplate "HB" (i.e collector Heribert Boeder); quarter inch chip at top of backstrip, half a dozen tiny wormholes near head or tail of spine, minor rubbing to corners and few abrasions on covers, but very appealing copy, unsophisticated contemporaneous binding completely solid with lustrous boards and virtually no wear to joints, text especially fresh and clean throughout. Phillip J. Pirages 66 - 16 2015 $1800

Martialis, Marcus Valerius *Epigrammata cum Notis Famabii et Variorum.* Leiden: Apud Franciscum Hackium, 1661. 8vo., some light spotting, few early ink annotations at beginning of text, contemporary vellum boards, spine lettered in ink, slightly soiled, armorial bookplate of Henry John Wollaston, gift inscription, very good. Blackwell's Rare Books Greek & Latin Classics VI - 74 2015 £250

Martialis, Marcus Valerius *Epigrammata. Ex museo Petri Scriverii.* Venice: Apud Benedictum Milochum, 1678. One leaf with original paper flaw causing loss to half a dozen words, some browning and spotting, two gatherings with dampmark to fore-edge, 12mo., contemporary vellum, spine lettered in ink, bit ruckled, spine darkened, sound, rare printing. Blackwell's Rare Books Greek & Latin Classics VI - 75 2015 £250

Martin, A. Richard *The Death of the Claimant.* New York: Robert M. McBride & Co., 1929. First US edition, near fine in dust jacket with some light internal restoration to spine ends and corners. Buckingham Books March 2015 - 24551 2015 $375

Martin, Cy *Gold Rush Narrow Gauge. The Story of the White Pass and Yukon Route.* Los Angeles: Trans-Anglo Books, 1974. Second edition, photos and map, brown cloth lettered in white, fine with very good, pictorial dust jacket. Argonaut Book Shop Holiday Season 2014 - 202 2015 $50

Martin, Francois *L'Ecole du Guerrier ou Instructions d'un Pere a Son Fils sur la Profession Militaire...* Paris: chez Lemarchand Libraire quai des Angustins no. 41..., 1811. First edition, 8vo., engraved titlepage with contemporary ms. note in ink at foot, lower margin folded by binder, contemporary French red quarter calf over marbled boards, spine gilt and lettered, marbled edges, silk marker, very good. John Drury Rare Books March 2015 - 24106 2015 £306

Martin, Frank *Drawn from Life.* Grove Park Press, 2004. IX/XVIII copies of an edition of 148 copies, signed by artist, numerous drawings by author throughout book, royal 8vo., original light grey wrappers, endpapers illustrated with numerous reproductions of author's sketches, untrimmed, fine, with 2 original signed drawings, both in white card mounts, two signed Artist's Drypoint Proofs and 16 plates of reproductions of Artist's Studies Drawn from Life, plates and book in folio protective drop-down back box, fine. Blackwell's Rare Books B179 - 161 2015 £450

Martin, George R. R. *Dying of the Light.* New York: Simon & Schuster, 1977. First edition, octavo, boards. John W. Knott, Bookseller Selected New Arrivals Jan. 2015 - 17141 2015 $250

Martin, George R. R. *Quartet: Four Tales from the Crossroads...* Framingham: NESFA Press, 2001. First edition, limited to 1200 numbered copies, this number 72 of 190 numbered copies signed by Martin and artist, Charles Vess, octavo, cloth. John W. Knott, Bookseller Selected New Arrivals Jan. 2015 - 17145 2015 $100

Martin, J. Wallis *A Likeness in Stone.* London: Hodder & Stoughton, 1997. First edition, fine in dust jacket. Buckingham Books March 2015 - 23157 2015 $300

Martin, J. Wallis *A Likeness in Stone.* London: Hodder & Stoughton, 1997. First edition, fine in dust jacket. Mordida Books March 2015 - 007552 2015 $250

Martin, J. Wallis *The Long Close Call.* Blakeney: Scorpion Press, 2000. First edition, limited to 85 numbered copies signed by author, fine in quarter leather and marbled boards. Buckingham Books March 2015 - 14575 2015 $175

Martin, Jack *Border Boss. Captain John R. Hughes - Texas Ranger.* San Antonio: Naylor Co., 1942. First edition, 238 pages, illustrations, very good in scarce dust jacket that has small chips at spine ends. Buckingham Books March 2015 - 31131 2015 $200

Martin, Robert Montgomery *The Past and Present State and of the Tea Trade of England and of the Continents of Europe and America...* London: Parbury Allen & Co., 1832. First edition, 8vo., large folding table (sale prices of teas) well bound relatively recently in quarter calf over marbled boards, spine lettered, very good, scarce. John Drury Rare Books 2015 - 22351 2015 $830

Martin, Ruth *Witchcraft and the Inquisition in Venice 1550-1650.* Oxford: Basil Blackwell, 1989. First edition, 8vo., original black cloth lettered gilt at spine, from the library of R. S. Walinski-Kiehl (1949-2013) with his ownership signature and some neat handwritten pencil notes and linings (all erasable), otherwise near fine in near fine dust jacket. Any Amount of Books 2015 - C12964 2015 £250

Martin, William E. *Catalogue of Flower and Vegetable Seeds, Seed Potatoes (sic) Bulbs for Spring Planting and Horticultural Sundries for 1890.* Hull: William E. Martin' Seed Establishment 20 Market Place, 1890. (1889), 4to., numerous woodcut illustrations, first couple of leaves with light red stain, original printed red wrappers, light general soiling and minor wear, overall good copy. John Drury Rare Books 2015 - 21347 2015 $133

Martinson, Harry *The Road.* London: Jonathan Cape, 1955. First edition in English, 8vo., very good+ in complete, very good- dust jacket with some soiling, age toning and slight marking and some slight creasing at edges. Any Amount of Books 2015 - A66204 2015 £150

Marvel, A., Junior, Psued. *Satirical and Panegyrical Instructions to Mr. William Hogarth, Painter, on Admiral Vernon's taking Porto Bello with Six Ships of War Only.* London: printed for H. Goreham, 1740. First edition, 20 pages, folio, recent half red morocco, fine, rare. C. R. Johnson Foxon R-Z - 857r-z 2015 $3065

Marvell, Andrew 1621-1678 *A Collection of Poems on Affairs of State. (bound with) The Second Part of the Collection of Poems on Affairs of State. (bound with) The Third Part of the Collection of Poems on Affairs of State.* London: printed in the year, 1689. Second edition of part one, first editions of parts two and three,, 3 parts, 4to., modern red morocco by Sangorski & Sutcliffe, gilt decorations, inner dentelles, rules and lettering, all edges gilt, fine, large copy.   The Brick Row Book Shop   Miscellany 67 - 67   2015 $4750

Le Merveilleuse de La Voyage Goutte De Vitamine - The Marvelous Voyage of a Drop of Vitamin. New York: published by the Coordinating council of French relief Societies, 1942. Oblong 8vo., spiral backed pictorial wrappers, very good+ 7 pages of handwritten text in French with English translation below, 7 full page hand colored illustrations. rare.   Aleph-bet Books, Inc.   109 - 492   2015 $1200

Marx, Karl 1818-1883 *Capital: a Critique of Political Economy....* London: George Allen & Unwin, 1928. First UK edition of this translation, 8vo., original dark brown cloth, lettered gilt at spine, sound, clean, near very good with bright clean spine but slight discoloration and mottling to boards and faint browning to half titlepage.   Any Amount of Books   2015 - C13526   2015   £175

Mary Goodchild. New York: McLoughlin Bros. n.d. circa, 1850. 8vo., pictorial wrappers, inconspicuous archival strengthening of spine, else very good+, hand colored woodcut on cover and with 7 fine three quarter page hand colored woodcuts in text.   Aleph-bet Books, Inc.   109 - 152   2015 $600

Masefield, John 1878-1967 *Odtaa.* London: Heinemann, 1926. Limited edition, number 157 of 295 copies signed by author, bookplate ex-libris of Henry Andrews Ingraham, noted angler and author, front hinge visible but solid, vellum spine, blue boards, mild darkening to boards, very good, lacking dust jacket but with folding map laid in, signed by E. Perman, the artist, map often missing.   Ken Lopez, Bookseller   164 - 127   2015 $200

Masefield, John 1878-1967 *Right Royal.* New York: Macmillan, 1922. First illustrated edition, fine with pictorial endpapers, front panel of dust jacket laid in, illustrations.   Beasley Books   2013 - 2015 $45

Masereel, Frans *Danse Macabre.* New York: Pantheon Books, 1942. Limited to 500 numbered copies, woodcut illustrations, 4to., covers scuffed and rubbed at top corners and along spine, pastedowns toned.   Oak Knoll Books   306 - 30   2015 $100

Masereel, Frans *Notre Temps.* Belves (Dordogne): Pierre Vorms, 1952. E189 of 300 copies, wrappers fine but for barely detectable crease on front cover, 16mo.   Beasley Books   2013 - 2015 $225

Maslow, A. H. *Motivation and Personality.* New York: Harper, 1954. First edition, 8vo., near fine in very good+ to near fine dust jacket with barely sunned spine and tiny tears at edges, superior copy.   Beasley Books   2013 - 2015 $150

Mason, Alfred Edward Woodley 1865-1948 *Fire Over England.* London: Hodder & Stoughton, 1936. First edition, pages lightly spotted, otherwise fine in very good dust jacket with soiled back panel, internal tape mends, chipping at spine ends and corners and creasing on front panel.   Mordida Books   March 2015 - 001533   2015 $75

Mason, Alfred Edward Woodley 1865-1948 *The Three Gentlemen.* Garden City: Doubleday, 1932. First American edition, fine in dust jacket with tiny wear at spine ends.   Mordida Books   March 2015 - 005290   2015 $125

Mason, George *An Essay on Design in Gardening First Published MDCCLXVIII Now greatly augmented.* London: printed by C. Roworth for Benjamin and John White, 1795. Second edition, half title, errata on verso of p. xi, closed tear in one leaf (no loss of surface), bound in early 20th century green half calf, neatly rebacked gilt lettered, top edge gilt, others uncut, excellent, crisp copy, early 20th century armorial bookplate of William Henry Mason.   John Drury Rare Books   2015 - 20997   2015 $1005

Mason, John Abraham *A Treatise on the Climate and Meteorology of Madeira by the late J. A. Mason, M.D.* London: John Churchill: Liverpool: Deighton and Laughton, 1850. First edition, 8vo., half title, wanting errata slip, 32 pages of Churchill ads dated Nov. 1849, 5 statistical charts on 3 plates, original blue cloth, upper cover and spine ornately gilt within borders of entwined grape vines and sugar cane, lower cover stamped in blind, slightest wear to head and foot of spine, still fine, bright copy, sometime in the library of Royal College of Surgeons in Ireland.   John Drury Rare Books   2015 - 26138   2015 $699

Mason, William 1725-1797 *Poems.* York: printed by W. Blanchard, 1796. 191 x 124mm., 2 volumes, handsome contemporary tree calf elaborately gilt by Kalthoeber (ticket on verso of front endpaper), covers bordered with gilt Greek key roll, flat spines ornately gilt in compartments featuring various repeated tools, each spine with black morocco label, gilt turn-ins, marbled endpapers, both volumes with early signature of Elizabeth Hervey; lower compartment of second volume with abrasion and moderate loss of gilt on corner, little rubbing, otherwise only trivial wear, bindings handsome and well preserved, blanks at back of each volume little soiled, otherwise fine and very pretty set, virtually pristine internally.   Phillip J. Pirages   66 - 59   2015 $1800

Massachusetts Emigrant Aid Co. *Nebraska and Kansas. Report of the Committee of the Massachusetts Emigrant Aid Co. With the Act of Incorporation and Other Documents.* Massachusetts Emigrant Aid Co., 1854. First edition, 12mo., original printed sewn wrappers, light wear to last page, internally clean, light vertical crease from having been folded at one time, else very good, very scarce. Buckingham Books March 2015 - 29139 2015 $750

Massachusetts Institute of Technology *Case Study on Arcturus IV (Product Design 2.734).* MIT (Dept. of Mechanical Engineering circa, 1952-1955. First edition, 4to., about 100 pages printed recto only, very scarce, very good. Any Amount of Books 2015 - C4372 2015 £1750

Massachusetts. Board of Railroad Commissioners *Special Report... to the Legislature in relation to the Disaster on Monday March 14 1887 on the Dedham Branch of the Boston and Providence Railroad at the Bridge Commonly Known as the Bussey Bridge...(in) West Roxbury.* Boston: Wright and Potter, 1887. First edition, 8vo., 420 pages, several heliotypes plus line drawn maps, original cloth, slight soiling, accompanied by four mounted photos, each 7.5 x 4.5 inches. M & S Rare Books, Inc. 97 - 251 2015 $750

Masserman, Jules H. *A Psychiatric Odyssey.* New York: Science House, 1971. First edition, inscribed by author, fine but for (additional, non-authorial gift inscription), in very good dust jacket. Beasley Books 2013 - 2015 $45

Masson, L. *Industrie Lainiere. Comparaison des conditions de Fabrication Entre la Belgique et l'Angleterre...Lettre Adresee a l'Economiste Beige.* Bruxelles et Leipzig: A. Lacroix Verboeckhoven & Cie, 1862. First edition, 8vo., half title and imprint leaf, unopened, original printed wrappers, fine. John Drury Rare Books 2015 - 17857 2015 $133

Masters, Priscilla *Winding Up the Serpent.* London: Macmillan, 1995. First edition, very fine in dust jacket, variant plain blue binding with no titles, signed by author. Mordida Books March 2015 - 001541 2015 $400

Masters, Priscilla *A Wreath for My Sister.* London: Macmillan, 1997. First edition, very fine, signed by author. Mordida Books March 2015 - 001543 2015 $75

Mastin, John *The Stolen Planet.* London: Charles Griffin & Co., 1909. First edition, 2nd issue, 8vo., original blue cloth lettered gilt on spine and cover and with gilt crest on cover, sound, clean, very good, some slight wear at front edges of boards. Any Amount of Books 2015 - A93676 2015 £160

Mateaux, Clara L. *Chats for Small Chatterers.* London: Cassell Petter & Galpin, circa, 1877. Frontispiece and plates 4 pages ads, sewing loose in places still firm, original maroon pictorial cloth, pictorial onlay on front board, some slight rubbed but very good, attractive, all edges gilt, inscription "Harold W. Smales from Father Christmas". Jarndyce Antiquarian Booksellers CCXI - 198 2015 £75

Mather, Cotton 1662-1727 *Ornaments for the Daughters of Zion and Happiness of a Virtuous Woman in a Discourse Which Directs the Female Sex How to Express the Fear of God in Every Age and State of their Life...* London: printed by Tho. Parkhurst at the Bible and Three Crowns, 1694. First English edition, 12mo., misbound after page 64, lacking first two leaves of Thomas Parkhurst ads at rear pages 141-42, contemporary blindstamped sheep worn, with loss to top third of spine, front hinge split loose in covers, text browned and edgeworn, with some horizontal tears at outer margin, inscription Sarah Pratt dated 1698, gift inscription Sarah Upton from her "Aunt Smith, March 15", 1873, gift inscription for Kelly from Sarah Upham August 30 1871, quite rare, housed in custom quarter morocco slipcase and chemise. Second Life Books Inc. 189 - 157 2015 $15,000

Mather, John C. *The Very First Light.* New York: Basic Books, 1996. First edition, 8vo., signed and inscribed by author, fine in like dust jacket. By the Book, L. C. Special List 10 - 60 2015 $250

Mathers, Edward Powys *Black Marigolds.* Llandogo: Old Stile Press, 2007. 29/200 copies signed by artist, printed in terracotta on special Zerkall paper, line-block collages printed in black, tall 8vo., original patterned boards with enfolding flap and magnetic closure, inside of flap stamped silver against black, top edge black, others untrimmed, illustration in terracotta to endpapers, fine. Blackwell's Rare Books B179 - 210 2015 £120

Matheson, Richard *Born of Man and Woman: Tales of Science Fiction and Fantasy.* Philadelphia: Chamberlain Press, 1954. First edition, octavo, cloth, signed by author. John W. Knott, Bookseller Selected New Arrivals Jan. 2015 - 17147 2015 $1500

Matheson, Richard *Nightmare at 20,000 Feet.* New York: TOR/Doherty, 2002. First edition, fine in fine dust jacket, inscribed by author. Ken Lopez, Bookseller 164 - 128 2015 $250

Mathews, Adrian *Vienna Blood.* London: Cape, 1999. First edition, very fine without dust jacket as issued. Mordida Books March 2015 - 007038 2015 $85

Mathews, Harry *Immeasurable Distances.* Venice: Lapis, 1991. First edition, inscribed by author, very good+, issued without dust jacket. Beasley Books 2013 - 2015 $45

Mathews, Shailer *The Woman Citizen's Library.* Chicago: Civics Society, 1913. 11 of 12 volumes, lacks volume 2, publisher's limp leather, most of leather missing from spine of volume one, other volumes show some wear, good set. Second Life Books Inc. 189 - 158 2015 $600

Mathews, Virginia *Stop Look Listen.* N.P.: Hampton Pub. Co., 1947. Oblong 4to., spiral backed boards, some cover and edge rubbing, very good, printed on thick board pages, every page has picture of different mode of transportation, illustrations by C. R. Schaare. Aleph-bet Books, Inc. 109 - 358 2015 $125

Matrix 07. Manor Farm: Whittington Press, 1987. Limited to 960 copies of which this is one of 110 special copies done in this manner, with tipped-in plates and other illustrations, small 4to., quarter bound in leather with pattern paper covered sides, accompanied by a separate case in which is mounted a cassette recording a talk by Stanley Morison on Eric Gill, both pieces inserted in slipcase. Oak Knoll Books 306 - 173 2015 $650

Matrix 10. Manor Farm: Whittington Press, 1990. Limited to 925 copies of which this is one of the 820 copies of the trade edition, bound thus, small 4to., stiff paper wrappers, filled with tipped in plates and other illustrations. Oak Knoll Books 306 - 174 2015 $200

Matrix 26. Lower Marston Farm, Risbury: Whittington Press, 2006. One of 680 copies bound thus, 4to., stiff paper wrappers, frontispiece, illustrated throughout with many tipped-in specimens on special paper, engravings, photos, color plates, etc., front corner bumped. Oak Knoll Books 306 - 175 2015 $300

Mattaire, Michael *Stephanorum Historia, Vitas Ipsorum ac Libros Complectens.* Typis Benj. Motte impensis Christoph Bateman, 1709. 8vo., engraved portrait frontispiece, 3 pages of woodcut devices (as is correct), variant issue without extra appendix, embossment of Earls of Macclesfield, 8vo., contemporary polished sprinkled calf, boards bordered with double gilt fillet, spine compartments similarly bordered, red morocco lettering piece in second compartment, rest with central gilt lozenge shaped decorative tools, all edges sprinkled red, small old paper labels at head and foot, just slightly rubbed, tiny chip at head of spine, bookplate of North Library (corrected by hand to South) of Shirburn castle, very good. Blackwell's Rare Books B179 - 71 2015 £500

Matthews, Brander *Tales of Fantasy and Fact.* New York: Harper, 1896. First edition, fine in rust covered boards with gold stamped titles and figures. Mordida Books March 2015 - 002517 2015 $100

Matthews, William *Modern Bookbinding Practically Considered a Lecture.* New York: Grolier Club, 1889. First edition, limited to 300 copies, small 4to., original gilt stamped cloth, top edge gilt, others uncut, 96 pages, 8 full page plates, 2 bookplates on front pastedown including that of the designer Lester Douglas. Oak Knoll Books 306 - 5 2015 $200

Matthiessen, Francis Otto *Sarah Orne Jewett.* Boston: Houghton Mifflin, 1929. Reprint, 8vo., illustrations, fine in dust jacket. Second Life Books Inc. 189 - 159 2015 $40

Matthiessen, Peter *In the Spirit of Crazy Horse.* New York: Viking, 1983. First edition, author's copy, little foxing in evidence, near fine in like dust jacket, letter of provenance available. Ken Lopez, Bookseller 164 - 130 2015 $150

Matthiessen, Peter *In the Spirit of Crazy Horse.* New York: Viking, 1983. First edition, wrappers, uncorrected advance proofs. Beasley Books 2013 - 2015 $150

Matthiessen, Peter *Partisans.* New York: Viking, 1955. First edition, author's copy with changes and corrections marked throughout, page notations in pencil on rear pastedown in author's hand, each referring to a notation in text top of front joint worn, otherwise very good in chipped, very good proof dust jacket with no text on flaps or rear panel, the only such copy we've ever seen. Ken Lopez, Bookseller 164 - 129 2015 $1500

Mattson, Morris *Family Guide Containing Anatomical Illustrations of the Stomach, Intestines, Uterus &c. with Directions for Using Mattson's family Syringe No. 1.* New York: Mattson's Mfg. circa, 1870. Twenty-second edition, 18mo., illustrations, original printed wrappers, slightly dust soiled, sewn as issued, tiny hole in back wrapper, small loss, very good. M & S Rare Books, Inc. 97 - 186 2015 $275

Mauclair, Camille *Louis Legrand. Les Artistes Du Livre.* Paris: Henry Babou, 1931. First edition, number 110 of 650 copies, unbound signatures laid into wrappers, fine but for offsetting to front and rear blanks, 17 plates, frontispiece, small 4to. Beasley Books 2013 - 2015 $125

Mauclair, Camille *Paul Jouve. Les Artistes Du Livre.* Paris: Henry Babou, 1931. First edition, number 657 of 700 copies, unbound signatures laid into wrappers, very good with inevitable wrinkling to gold foil wrappers, few tiny white flecks where gold has chipped away, 23 full page plates, frontispiece, small 4to. Beasley Books 2013 - 2015 $250

Maude, Clotilda Jennings *Linden Rhymes.* Halifax: Elbridge, Gerry Fuller, 1854. Small 8vo., original brown pressed cloth with gilt title to spine, prelim leaves and outer edges foxed, top and bottom of spine frayed and corners worn.   Schooner Books Ltd.   110 - 99   2015 $275

Maude, George Ashley *Letters from Turkey and the Crimea.* London: printed for private circulation, 1896. First edition, frontispiece laid down, original red cloth lettered gilt on upper cover, presentation from E. D. Baird to Mr. Bright (Allan Heywood Bright 1862-1941), slight foxing to fore-edge and prelims, otherwise very good, bright copy, slight foxing, otherwise very good.   Any Amount of Books   2015 - C13449   2015   £160

Maugham, William Somerset   1874-1965 *Of Human Bondage.* New York: Limited Editions Club, 1938. Limited to 1500 numbered copies signed by John Sloan, 16 etchings by Sloan, 2 volumes, tall 8vo., cloth, leather spine labels, slipcase, wear along back edge of slipcase, books fine.   Oak Knoll Books   25 - 20   2015 $300

Maugham, William Somerset   1874-1965 *The Razor's Edge.* Garden City: Doubleday Doran & Co., 1944. First edition, one of 750 numbered copies signed by author, very good plus, top edge gilt (sharp and bright), lacking original glassine, book's spine lightly sunned, covers bold so is the bright title label, few age spots to front cover, pages are fresh and clean, housed in original publisher's slipcase that shows wear and splits.   Ed Smith Books   82 - 18   2015 $2000

Maugham, William Somerset   1874-1965 *The Razor's Edge - a Novel.* London: Heinemann, 1944. First edition, octavo, head of spine and upper corners little bumped, very good in very good, marked, dusty and creased dust jacket frayed at head and tail of spine.   Peter Ellis, Bookseller   2014 - 019384   2015   £300

Maunder, Annie S. D. *The Heavens and Their Story.* London: Charles H. Kelly, 1910. Reprint, 8vo., 72 pages, occasional spotting, awarded by Walter Harris, Ph.D, Head Master, Dec. 1919 Longton High School, upper joint splitting bit, calf rubbed, very good.   Jeff Weber Rare Books   178 - 800   2015 $55

Maupassant, Guy De   1850-1893 *Bel Ami.* Paris: Editions de Cluny, 1947. From an edition of 1020 copies, this number 34 of 100 copies, small 4to., 2 volumes, wrappers, with extra suite of color lithographs by Jean Dennis Malcles, who has illustrated both volumes, fine in wrappers and glassine in nice chemise and matching box.   Beasley Books   2013 - 2015 $300

Maupassant, Guy De   1850-1893 *Bel-Ami.* New York: Limited Editions Club, 1968. Limited to 1500 numbered copies, signed by artist, Bernard Lamotte, artist's own copy with his initials on colophon under "copy number", small 4to., cloth, slipcase sunned at fore-edge and lightly soiled, lower front corner of spine scuffed.   Oak Knoll Books   25 - 44   2015 $4500

Maupassant, Guy De   1850-1893 *Sur L'Eau.* Paris: La Trireme, 1951. #181 of 200 copies, 4to., unbound signatures laid into wrapper, some foxing, fine wrappers, marbled paper covered clamshell box is sunned and soiled on one edge, still quite nice.   Beasley Books   2013 - 2015 $200

Maurel, Andre *Les Delices du Pays Des Doges.* Paris: J. Peyronnet, 1929. No. 202 of 210 copies, 4to., unbound signatures laid into wrappers, illustrations by Georges Loukomski, fine in fine wrappers, near fine glassine, chemise and box.   Beasley Books   2013 - 2015 $400

Maurer, David *The Big Con.* First edition, first printing, excellent copy with touch of rubbing to extremities, in bright unclipped jacket with some shallow chips and small tears, few small creases, otherwise bright, without any fading to spine.   B & B Rare Books, Ltd.   234 - 76   2015 $2000

Maurer, David *The Dying Place.* New York: Dell, 1986. Second printing, paperback original, near fine, from the library of author Peter Taylor and wife Eleanor Ross Taylor, inscribed by author for Taylor.   Between the Covers Rare Books, Inc.   187 - 166   2015 $50

Maurice, C. Edmund *Life of Octavia Hill as Told in Her Letters.* London: Macmillan, 1913. First edition, 8vo., portraits, untrimmed, partially unopened, very good, tight, clean copy, this the copy of founder of Hull House, Jane Addams with her ownership signature, from the library of consumer advocate Florence Kelley.   Second Life Books Inc.   189 - 160   2015 $250

Mauriceau, A. M. *The Married Woman's Private Medical Companion.* New York: 1847. First edition, 16mo., original cloth, fine, rare edition.   M & S Rare Books, Inc.   97 - 26   2015 $350

Mauriceau, Francis *The Diseases of Women with Child and In Child-Bed.* London: Cox, Clarke, Combes and Dove,, 1727. Sixth edition, 8vo., contemporary calf (some wear), good tight copy, 10 coper plates, five folding.   Second Life Books Inc.   189 - 291   2015 $1800

Maurois, Amdre *Fatapoufs & Thinifers.* New York: Henry Holt, 1940. First edition, 4to., cloth, fine in slightly worn dust jacket, publisher's file copy, illustrations by Jean Bruller with wonderfully bold color illustrations.   Aleph-bet Books, Inc.   109 - 277   2015 $600

Maw & Co. *Patterns Geometrical and Roman Mosaics Encaustic Tile Pavements and Enamelled Wall Decorations.* London: Leighton Bros. 1866, but this copy circa, 1880? Folio, 33 chromolithogaph plates, original brown cloth, upper cover overlaid with elaborately decorated chromolithograph sheet by Owen Jones, inscribed by architects "A & W Reid, Elgin". Marlborough Rare Books   List 54 - 53   2015   £2250

Mawe, J. *Wodrach's Introduction to the Study of Conchology, Describing the orders, Genera and Species of Shells...* London: Longman, Hurst, Rees, Orme, and Browne, 1822. Second edition, 12mo., contemporary plain cloth, 7 pages of colored figures, including frontispiece.   M & S Rare Books, Inc.   97 - 71   2015 $200

Mawson, Thomas H. *The Art and Craft of Garden Making.* London: B. T. Batsford, 1901. Second edition, photos, plans and drawings, green cloth, decorated in gilt, top edge gilt, covers bit faded at spine and edges, very good.   Peter Ellis, Bookseller   2014 - 003957   2015   £300

Maxon, P. B. *The Waltz of Death.* New York: Mystery House, 1941. First edition, former owner's inked name on front flyleaf, else very good in dust jacket with light restoration to spine ends and corners.   Buckingham Books   March 2015 - 33123   2015 $275

Maxwell, Robert *The Practical Husbandman: being a Collection of Miscellaneous Papers on Husbandry &c.* Edinburgh: printed by C. Wright and Co. for the author, 1757. First edition, 8vo., folding plate, contemporary calf gilt with raised bands and label, fine, crisp copy, signed by author on verso of title, authenticating this copy as genuine.   John Drury Rare Books   2015 - 13869   2015 $699

Maxwell, William *All the Days and Nights. The Collected Stories.* New York: Knopf, 1995. Advance reading copy, wrappers, fine, slipcase.   Gemini Fine Books & Arts, Ltd.   Art Reference & Illustrated Books: First Editions - 2015 $40

Maxwell, William *Ancestors.* New York: Alfred A. Knopf, 1971. First edition, fine in very good plus dust jacket with little rubbing and couple of tiny nicks, inscribed author to fellow editor at the New Yorker, Rachel MacKenzie.   Between the Covers Rare Books, Inc.   187 - 169   2015 $750

Maxwell, William *The Folded Leaf.* New York: Harper and Brothers, 1945. Second printing, stain at bottom of boards and label for out-of-print bookstore on front pastedown, fair copy, warmly inscribed by author to fellow editor at the New Yorker Rachel MacKenzie.   Between the Covers Rare Books, Inc.   187 - 167   2015 $750

Maxwell, William *The Old Man at the Railroad Crossing and Other Tales.* New York: Alfred A. Knopf, 1966. First edition, dampstain on front board, thus good in good plus dust jacket with corresponding stain on front panel, warmly inscribed by author to fellow editor Rachel MacKenzie.   Between the Covers Rare Books, Inc.   187 - 168   2015 $300

Maxwell, William *Over by the River.* New York: Alfred A. Knopf, 1977. First edition, just about fine in very near fine dust jacket, inscribed by author for Nicholas Delbanco.   Between the Covers Rare Books, Inc.   187 - 170   2015 $400

May, Julian *The Saga of Pliocene Exile...* Boston: Houghton Mifflin Co., 1981-1984. First editions, one of 500 numbered sets, each volume signed by May (#236), octavo, 5 volumes, cloth,.   John W. Knott, Bookseller   Selected New Arrivals Jan. 2015 - 17149   2015 $350

May, Robert *The Red-Nosed Reindeer.* N.P.: Montgomery Ward, 1939. True first edition, 4to., pictorial wrappers, some wear to spine, corner crease and light cover soil, else very good+, illustrations in color by Denver Gillen.   Aleph-bet Books, Inc.   109 - 92   2015 $1500

May, Walter *Geschichte Vom Rotkappchen. (Little Red Riding Hood).* Zurich: Albert Muller, 1940. First edition, 4to., cloth backed pictorial boards, fine, printed on heavy high quality paper on one side only, color linoleum cut illustrations with text arranged around pictures.   Aleph-bet Books, Inc.   109 - 167   2015 $975

Mayer, Bernadette *The Golden Book of Words.* Lenox: Angel Hair Books, 1978. First edition, limited to 750 copies, 4to., original pictorial wrappers with cover design by Joe Brainard and photo of author by Lewis Warsh on back cover, front cover trifle soiled, otherwise fine, inscribed by author.   James S. Jaffe Rare Books   Many Happy Returns - 268   2015 $150

Mayer, Henry *A Trip to Toyland.* London: Grant Richards, 1900. First edition, oblong folio, cloth backed pictorial boards, tips slightly rubbed and very slight cover soil, very good-, fine, full page color illustrations.   Aleph-bet Books, Inc.   109 - 360   2015 $1200

Mayer, Thomas *The Correspondence of Reginald Pole.* Aldershot: Ashgate Pub. Ltd., 2003. First edition, 3 volumes, 8vo., frontispiece to volume 3, fine in fine dust jackets.   Any Amount of Books   2015 - A98259   2015   £160

Mayer, Tom *The Weary Falcon.* Boston: Houghton Mifflin, 1971. Uncorrected proof copy, covers unevenly sunned, few small stains to rear cover, very good, spiralbound proof, printed from galley sheets, somewhat uncommon, proof is rare.   Ken Lopez, Bookseller   164 - 229   2015 $250

Mayeur *Specimen-Album De La Fonderie Gve, Mayeur Allainguillaume & Cie. Succrs. Labeurs & Journaux Initiales & Caracteres Varies de Fantaisie, Vignettes, Ornements, etc.* Paris: Mayeur, n.d. but circa, 1910. 4to., original quarter leather , cloth, (390) leaves including inserts, rubbed and scuffed along edges and along spine. Oak Knoll Books 306 - 222   2015 $1350

Mayhew, Experience *Indian Converts or Some Account of the Lives and Dying Speeches of a Considerable Number of the Christianized Indians of that Island.* London: printed for Samuel Gerrish, bookseller in Boston in New England, 1727. First edition, 8vo., 20th century calf backed marbled boards, spine gilt, front blank, titlepage and first three leaves professionally strengthened along edges, not affecting text, some toning and light staining throughout, 18th century ownership signature on front blank and cropped along top of titlepage. Second Life Books Inc.   189 - 161   2015 $500

Mayhew, Henry *Acting Charades or Deeds Not Words.* London: D. Bogue, 1850. Small 4to., color frontispiece and engraved title, silhouette illustrations, original red cloth, blocked in gilt and blind, slightly dulled, marked and rubbed, binding split but firm at pages 64/65, all edges gilt, signatures of Mrs. Lyson 1856 and John Howard, good plus. Jarndyce Antiquarian Booksellers   CCXI - 199   2015   £60

Maynwaring, Arthur *The Lives of the Two Illustrious Generals John, Duke of Marlborough and Francis Eugene, Prince of Savoy.* London: Andrew Bell & J. Phillips, 1713. First edition, 8vo., full brown leather with delicate surface decoration and fine raised bands along and lettered gilt on spine, separate titlepages (with portraits) for both generals, often they are missing, rubbed at edges, and along hinge, text and plates clean. Any Amount of Books   2015 - C5500   2015   £240

Mayo, Herbert *Letters on the Truths Contained in Popular Superstitions.* Frankfurt: John David Sauerlaender and Edinburgh: Blackwood, 1849. First edition in book form, 8vo., 152 pages, with at least 10 ms. corrections to text, perhaps in author's hand, original blindstamped cloth, recently rebacked with printed spine label, very good, presentation copy inscribed "From the author" with signatures of Tho. Watson and Wm. R. E. Smart on titlepage. John Drury Rare Books   March 2015 - 18412   2015 $221

Mayrocker, Friederike *Brancusi 'Der Kusz" (Klalkstein) Goethe Meine Rulh ist hin.* Unica T: 1991. One of 50 copies, each signed and numbered by the artist on colophon, on reverse of images and text, page size 15 7/16 x 5 5/8 inches, 40 pages, bound concertina (accordion) style book, 20 black and white photos, handset and three color letterpress images reproduced from polymer sheets, Mayrocker text in 14 point silver roman type forms a 90° angle to Goethe's lines and are distributed across the page. Priscilla Juvelis - Rare Books   61 - 51   2015 $500

Mazzei, Filippo *Recherches Historiques et Politiques sur les Etats Unis de l'Amerique Septentrionale.* Paris: Chez Froulle, 1788. First edition, 4 volumes, 8vo., contemporary tree calf, marbled endpapers, black leather labels, gilt rules, decorations and lettering, half titles present, edges little rubbed, few corners bumped, very good in fine contemporary binding. The Brick Row Book Shop   Miscellany 67 - 18   2015 $1500

McAleer, Neil *Arthur C. Clarke: the Authorized Biography.* Chicago: Contemporary Books, 1992. First edition, fine in fine dust jacket, ownership signature of Ian Macauley with few notes in text, else fine in fine dust jacket, signed by Clarke and McAleer on bookplate. Between the Covers Rare Books, Inc.   187 - 252   2015 $450

McAlmon, Robert *A Hasty Bunch.* Paris: Contact Editions, 1922. First edition, softcover, wrappers, with broadside laid in, 8vo., very good++ with bit of darkening to spine, otherwise fine. Beasley Books   2013 - 2015 $350

McAlmon, Robert *A Hasty Bunch.* Paris: Contact Editions, 1922. First edition, octavo, one of 300 copies, wrappers, laid in is flyer, from an English Printer to an English Publisher which was issued with book but is often missing, pages unopened, covers just little creased at edges, near fine. Peter Ellis, Bookseller   2014 - 017293   2015   £325

McAuley, Paul J. *Fairyland.* London: Victor Gollancz, 1995. First edition, octavo, boards. John W. Knott, Bookseller   Selected New Arrivals Jan. 2015 - 17150   2015 $100

McBain, Ed *Ax.* New York: Simon & Schuster, 1964. First edition, pages slightly darkened, otherwise fine in dust jacket. Mordida Books   March 2015 - 011028   2015 $250

McBain, Ed *The Con Man.* Permabooks, 1957. First edition, as new, unread copy in color, pictorial wrappers. Buckingham Books   March 2015 - 35890   2015 $225

McBain, Ed *Doll.* New York: Delacorte, 1965. First edition, small stains on couple of pages, otherwise fine in dust jacket with some tiny wear at corners and along folds. Mordida Books   March 2015 - 011029   2015 $150

McBain, Ed *Ed McBain's Mystery Book.* Pocket Books, 1960-1961. Complete run of three issues, each copy signed by author, scarce periodical and rare signed. Buckingham Books   March 2015 - 38265   2015 $400

McBain, Ed *The 87th Precinct.* New York: Simon & Schuster, 1959. First edition, signed on card-laid in, page edges evenly browned, else fine in dust jacket.   Buckingham Books   March 2015 - 6285   2015 $250

McBain, Ed *The 87th Precinct.* London: Boardman, 1966. Omnibus edition, fine in price clipped dust jacket.   Mordida Books   March 2015 - 007950   2015 $250

McBain, Ed *The Empty Hours.* New York: Simon and Schuster, 1962. First edition, fine in dust jacket with slightly darkened spine.   Mordida Books   March 2015 - 011026   2015 $350

McBain, Ed *Give the Boys a Great Big Hand.* New York: Simon and Schuster, 1960. First edition, signed by author, very faint die mark along bottom front endpaper, else book quite clean, jacket fine but for very slight fading to red titles, from the collection of Duke Collier.   Royal Books   36 - 186   2015 $450

McBain, Ed *Goldilocks.* New York: Arbor House, 1978. First edition, advance review copy with slip and photo laid in, very fine in dust jacket.   Mordida Books   March 2015 - 010765   2015 $85

McBain, Ed *Hail, Hail, The Gang's All Here.* Garden City: Doubleday, 1971. First edition, fine in dust jacket with tiny nick at top of spine.   Mordida Books   March 2015 - 011032   2015 $85

McBain, Ed *The Heckler.* New York: Simon and Schuster, 1960. First edition, signed by author, dated 8/25/90, fine and unread in fine dust jacket, from the collection of Duke Collier.   Royal Books   36 - 187   2015 $375

McBain, Ed *The Heckler.* New York: Simon and Schuster, 1960. First edition, pages slightly darkened, otherwise fine in dust jacket with small chip at top of spine and couple of closed tears along folds.   Mordida Books   March 2015 - 011023   2015 $150

McBain, Ed *Killer's Wedge.* New York: Simon and Schuster, 1959. First edition, fine and unread in fine dust jacket, single small sticker shadow to front panel, else pristine copy, from the collection of Duke Collier.   Royal Books   36 - 183   2015 $1500

McBain, Ed *King's Ransom.* Simon & Schuster, 1959. First edition, signed by author on a label and laid in, page edges uniformly tanned, else fine in fine dust jacket.   Buckingham Books   March 2015 - 36584   2015 $750

McBain, Ed *King's Ransom.* New York: Simon and Schuster, 1959. First edition, signed by author, pages darkened, otherwise very good in dust jacket with internal tape mends, small v-shaped chip on top edge of back panel, several closed tears and tiny wear at corners.   Mordida Books   March 2015 - 011020   2015 $400

McBain, Ed *King's Ransom.* New York: Simon and Schuster, 1959. First edition, near fine in very good plus dust jacket, touch of toning to edges of text block, jacket bright, some nick at spine ends and couple of corners, bright copy, from the collection of Duke Collier.   Royal Books   36 - 184   2015 $950

McBain, Ed *Lady, Lady, I Did It!* New York: Simon & Schuster, 1961. First edition, remainder mark on bottom of page edges and slight discoloring to purplish colored top page edges, otherwise fine in dust jacket with small scrape on front panel and short closed tear.   Mordida Books   March 2015 - 011024   2015 $200

McBain, Ed *Like Love.* New York: Simon and Schuster, 1962. First edition, fine in dust jacket with several short closed tears.   Mordida Books   March 2015 - 011025   2015 $200

McBain, Ed *Sadie When She Died.* Garden City: Doubleday, 1972. First edition, signed by author on titlepage, label of author's literary agent, Scott Meredith Literary agency in NY, fine and unread, fine dust jacket with tiniest pinpoint rubbing at spine ends, remarkable copy, from the collection of Duke Collier.   Royal Books   36 - 185   2015 $450

McBain, Ed *See Them Die.* New York: Simon and Schuster, 1960. First edition, signed by author, about near fine in fine dust jacket, some of the usual toning to text block edges, spine ends bumped, else book clean, from the collection of Duke Collier.   Royal Books   36 - 188   2015 $325

McBain, Ed *See them Die.* New York: Simon and Schuster, 1960. First edition, pages slightly darkened, otherwise fine in dust jacket.   Mordida Books   March 2015 - 011022   2015 $300

McBain, Ed *The Sentries.* Simon & Schuster, 1965. First edition, signed by author, fine in dust jacket, sharp copy.   Buckingham Books   March 2015 - 38262   2015 $175

McBain, Ed *Squad Room.* New York: Simon and Schuster, 1961. First edition, pages uniformly browned as usual, else fine in fine dust jacket with light wear to foot of spine, corners and extremities.   Buckingham Books   March 2015 - 23288   2015 $175

McBain, Ed *Ten Plus One.* New York: Simon and Schuster, 1964. First edition, fine in dust jacket.   Mordida Books   March 2015 - 011027   2015 $300

McCaffrey, Anne *Decision at Doona.* London: Rapp & Whiting, 1970. First UK edition, 8vo., original orange cloth, lettered silver on spine and cover, fine in very good+ dust jacket, very slightly rubbed at edges, no inscriptions, not price clipped.   Any Amount of Books   2015 - C4322   2015   £175

McCaffrey, Anne *Dragonsong.* New York: Atheneum, 1976. First edition, octavo, cloth.   John W. Knott, Bookseller   Selected New Arrivals Jan. 2015 - 17151   2015 $250

McCaleb, Charles S. *Tracks. Tires & Wires. Public Transportation in California's Santa Clara Valley.* Glendale: Interurban Press, 1981. First edition, quarto, profusely illustrated with photos, maps, facsimiles, color frontispiece, light rubbing to spine ends, else fine with pictorial dust jacket, spine ends lightly chipped.   Argonaut Book Shop   Holiday Season 2014 - 173   2015 $75

McCarry, Charles *The Better Angels.* E. P. Dutton, 1979. First edition, fine in fine dust jacket, exceptional copy.   Buckingham Books   March 2015 - 27423   2015 $200

McCarry, Charles *The Miernik Dossier.* Saturday Review Press, 1973. First edition, signed by author, fine in lightly rubbed dust jacket, complete with original wraparound promotional band, red top edges bright and unfaded.   Buckingham Books   March 2015 - 37171   2015 $750

McCarthy, Cormac *The Border Trilogy.* New York: Alfred A. Knopf, 1998. First edition, first impressions, 3 volumes, 8vo., fine in fine dust jacket.   Any Amount of Books   2015 - C1886   2015   £175

McCarthy, Cormac *Cities of the Plain.* New York: Knopf, 1998. First edition, one of 1000 copies signed by author, fine in fine dust jacket.   Ed Smith Books   83 - 62   2015 $500

McCarthy, Cormac *The Counselor.* New York: Vintage, 2013. Uncorrected proof copy, uncommon, fine in wrappers.   Ken Lopez, Bookseller   164 - 134   2015 $450

McCarthy, Cormac *The Crossing.* New York: Knopf, 1994. First edition, fine in fine dust jacket, this copy inscribed by author.   Ed Smith Books   83 - 63   2015 $1750

McCarthy, Cormac *No Country for Old Men.* New Orleans: B. E. Trice, 2005. First edition, copy 41 from a limited edition of only 325 numbered and specially bound copies, very fine, quarter leather with marbled boards, cloth slipcase, signed by McCarthy, still in original shrinkwrap.   Jeff Hirsch Books   E-62 Holiday List 2014 - 22   2015 $1250

McCarthy, Cormac *The Road.* New York: Alfred A. Knopf, 2006. First edition, octavo, boards.   John W. Knott, Bookseller   Selected New Arrivals Jan. 2015 - 17155   2015 $250

McCarthy, Mary *Winter Visitors.* New York: Harcourt Brace Jovanovich, 1970. First edition, 12mo., quarter cloth and paper covered boards, fine in near fine glassine dust jacket, published hors commerce, publisher's card laid in, inscribed by author for Burt Britton.   Between the Covers Rare Books, Inc.   187 - 171   2015 $375

McCarthy, Tom *Remainder.* Richmond: Alma, 2006. First edition, no. 2 of 15 copies, signed with doodle by author and quote from the book, 8vo., original blue cloth, lettered silver at spine, fine in fine dust jacket.   Any Amount of Books   2015 - C9124   2015   £160

McCauley, Kirby *Dark Forces: New Stories of Suspense and Supernatural Horror.* New York: Viking Press, 1980. First edition, octavo, cloth.   L. W. Currey, Inc.   Featured Author: Ray Bradbury (Oct. 2014) - 148670   2015 $150

McClintock, James *Arizona: Prehistoric-Aboriginal-Pioneer-Modern.* Chicago: S. J. Clarke Pub,. Co., 1916. First edition, small quarto, 3 volumes, two-tone black quarter leather and green cloth, gold stamping on spine, decorated endpapers, all edges decorated in green pattern, illustrations, very good, bright, some minor professional restoration to spine of volume II, else very good, bright attractive set.   Buckingham Books   March 2015 - 20933   2015 $875

McClintock, John S. *Pioneer Days in the Black Hills.* Deadwood: John S. McClintock, 1939. First edition, 8vo., very good, inscribed by D. M. Mcgahey, Curator of Adams Memorial Museum in Deadwood.   Buckingham Books   March 2015 - 24963   2015 $300

McCloskey, Michael *Destiny or Death.* N.P.: Michael McCloskey, 1971. First edition, 12mo., stapled printed yellow wrappers, near fine, without dust jacket, from the library of author Peter Taylor and wife Eleanor Ross Taylor, inscribed by author for Taylor.   Between the Covers Rare Books, Inc.   187 - 172   2015 $125

McCloskey, Robert *Blueberries for Sal.* New York: Viking, 1948. First edition, oblong 4to., pictorial cloth, fine in dust jacket (better than very good, slightly frayed on spine ends and corners with small closed tear), illustrations in blue line.   Aleph-bet Books, Inc.   109 - 278   2015 $4750

McCloskey, Robert *Make Way for Ducklings.* New York: Viking, 1941. First edition, 4to., cloth, fine in very good+ dust jacket (spine slightly faded and some fraying to spine ends, no tears), notoriously rare dust jacket. Aleph-bet Books, Inc. 109 - 279 2015 $18,500

McCloy, Helen *The Further side of Fear.* New York: Dodd Mead & Co., 1967. First edition, inscribed by author for former husband Brett Halliday and his parents Jan. 1967, fine in lightly rubbed dust jacket, lightly sunned on spine and with light wear to spine ends. Buckingham Books March 2015 - 6298 2015 $175

McCloy, Helen *The Man in the Moonlight.* New York: William Morrow & Co., 1940. First edition, cloth lightly soiled along bottom edge of spine and front panel, small rub mark to underside front panel, still near fine, tight copy in dust jacket lightly rubbed at bottom edge of spine and front panel, small rub mark to underside of front panel, else near fine, tight copy, lightly rubbed at bottom edge of spine with Light wear to two front corners. Buckingham Books March 2015 - 25913 2015 $450

McCloy, Helen *The Singing Diamonds and Other Stories.* Dodd Mead & Co., 1965. First edition, fine, bright, clean, unfaded dust jacket with minor wear to spine ends, very scarce. Buckingham Books March 2015 - 37498 2015 $350

McConaughy, J. W. *The Boss.* New York: Fly, 1911. First edition, spotting on top of page edges and name on front pastedown, otherwise very food in pictorial cloth covered boards. Mordida Books March 2015 - 008119 2015 $85

McCormick, Cyrus H. *McCormick's Self Raker Improved for 1867.* Chicago: 1867. Folio leaf, folded to 8 1/2 x 11 1/4 inches, (4) pages, 2 illustrations, couple of light edge chips, light dust and wear, very good. M & S Rare Books, Inc. 97 - 58 2015 $825

McCoy, Horace *Scalpel.* New York: Appleton, 1952. First edition, fine in dust jacket with tiny wear at corners. Mordida Books March 2015 - 005283 2015 $135

McCoy, Horace *Scalpel.* Appleton Century Drofts Inc., 1952. First edition, signed, lightly rubbed on bottom edges of cloth, else very good, tight, bright copy in price clipped dust jacket, lightly sunned on spine. Buckingham Books March 2015 - 9246 2015 $275

McCoy, Joseph G. *Historic Sketches of the Cattle Trade of the West and Southwest.* Glendale: Arthur H. Clark, 1940. First edition thus, cloth, 435 pages, illustrations, former owner ink signature and ink date (1940) owner's initials, text is not only trimmed but uncut, slight bump to one corner, fine hardcover. Baade Books of the West 2014 - 2015 $76

McCracken, Harold *George Catlin and the Old Frontier.* Dial Press, 1959. First edition, one of 250 numbered and signed copies by author, this copy 124, original full leather, gilt stamped picture on front cover and lettered gilt on spine, tan endpapers, frontispiece, 34 color illustrations and 120 black and white illustrations, fine, unread copy housed in original cloth slipcase. Buckingham Books March 2015 - 26481 2015 $375

McCrae, John *In Flanders Fields and Other Poems.* New York: G. P. Putnam's Sons, 1927. Seventh impression of American edition, ownership signature of editor and critic John S. Mayfield, lightly rubbed, very near fine in very good dust jacket, long inscription from poet and critic Carleton Noyes retelling how McCrae sent him the manuscript of title poem, tipped into back of original mailing envelope from Noyes and copies of correspondence leading up to Noyes signing the book. Between the Covers Rare Books, Inc. 187 - 174 2015 $500

McCready, T. L. *Adventures of a Beagle.* New York: Ariel/ Ferrar, Strauss, Cudahy, 1959. First edition, first printing, 8vo., green pictorial cloth, edges lightly faded, else fine in very good+ dust jacket with one small closed tear, color pictorial endpapers, plus a profusion of color and black and white illustrations by Tasha Tudor, very scarce. Aleph-bet Books, Inc. 109 - 465 2015 $850

McCready, T. L. *Increase Rabbit.* New York: Ariel/Farrar Strauss Cudahy, First edition, first printing, 8vo., yellow pictorial cloth, fine in dust jacket with 2 small closed edge tears, color and black and white illustrations. Aleph-bet Books, Inc. 109 - 466 2015 $700

McCullers, Carson 1917-1957 *The Ballad of the Sad Cafe: the Novels and Stories of Carson McCullers.* Boston: Houghton Mifflin Co., 1951. First edition, octavo, publisher's orange cloth, titled and decorated in red to spine and front board, slight bump at crown, else very near in scuffed and torn, about very good dust jacket with chipping at spine ends, inscribed by author for Monique and Valentin, uncommon thus. Between the Covers Rare Books 196 - 93 2015 $5500

McCullers, Carson 1917-1957 *Clock Without Hands.* Boston: Houghton Mifflin Co., 1961. First edition, octavo, publisher's red cloth titled and decorated in gilt and black to spine and front board, trifle bumped, near fine in price clipped, very good or better dust jacket with die-cut window as issued and little nicking around the die-cut window, with compliments of author slip with date of publication stamped on it laid in, as well as inscribed by author for Monique and Valentin. Between the Covers Rare Books 196 - 94 2015 $1200

McCullers, Carson 1917-1957 *The Mortgaged Heart.* Boston: Houghton Mifflin, 1971. First edition, about fine in price clipped, very good dust jacket with modest spine faded, nicely inscribed by editor, Margarita Smith (author's sister) to Clifford Milton and Julian Hayes. Between the Covers Rare Books, Inc. 187 - 175 2015 $450

McCulloch, John Ramsay 1789-1864 *Historical Sketch of the Rise and progress of the Science of Political Economy.* (bound with) *Outlines of Political Economy.* Edinburgh: printed by A. Balfour & Co., 1826. First edition, only 24 copies printed New York; Wilder and ampbell, 1825. First edition, privately printed, 8vo., well bound in later 19th century half calf, spine fully gilt with raised bands and label, marbled edges, fine, very rare,. John Drury Rare Books 2015 - 26322 2015 $3409

McCulloch, John Ramsay 1789-1864 *London in 1850-1851. From the Geographical Dictionary of J. R. McCulloch, Esq.* London: Longman, Brown, Green and Longmans, 1851. First edition, 8vo., 132 pages, occasional very light foxing, original printed wrappers, spine neatly repaired, good copy, early ownership signature of William Inge, very scarce. John Drury Rare Books 2015 - 14180 2015 $177

McCulloch, John Ramsay 1789-1864 *The Principles of Political Economy: with a Sketch of the Rise and Progress of the Science.* Edinburgh: printed for William and Charles Tait and Longman and Co., London, 1825. First edition, 8vo., wanting half title, else very good, contemporary half calf and marbled boards, rebacked in cloth, corners worn. John Drury Rare Books 2015 - 25896 2015 $1399

McCullough, Harrell *Selden Lindsey U.S. Deputy Marshal.* Oklahoma City: Paragon Pub., 1990. Limited numbered edition, one of 100 copies this #36, gilt stamped green cloth, 349 pages, frontispiece, map, fine, like new. Baade Books of the West 2014 - 2015 $73

McCully, Emily Arnold *Mirette on the High Wire.* New York: G. P. Putnam, 1992. First edition, signed by author, fine in fine, first state dust jacket, with no Caldecott Medal or mention of award, 4to. By the Book, L. C. 44 - 85 2015 $500

McCurdy, Edward B. *Dim Tracks Long the Trails.* Polon: privately printed, 1977. First edition, 4to., pictorial wrappers, 70 pages, few minor spots on covers, very good, quite scarce, very good. Baade Books of the West 2014 - 2015 $61

McCutcheon, George Barr *The Daughter of Anderson Crow.* New York: Dodd Mead, 1907. First edition, name and date on front endpaper and scrape on front cover, else very good in pictorial covers. Mordida Books March 2015 - 001602 2015 $75

McDermand, Charles *Waters of the Golden Trout Country.* New York: Putnam, 1946. Second edition, fine in very good dust jacket with closed tear along spine end and nicks at spine ends. Mordida Books March 2015 - 011426 2015 $85

McDermott, John Francis *Audubon in the West.* Norman: University of Oklahoma Press, 1965. First edition, 16 plates, 2 text facsimiles, gray cloth, very fine, pictorial dust jacket. Argonaut Book Shop Holiday Season 2014 - 174 2015 $45

McDermott, John Francis *Tixier's Travels on the Osage Prairies.* Norman: Oklahoma University Press, 1940. First edition, cloth, illustrations, maps, upper cover corner bumped, else near fine in complete dust jacket, now scarce. Baade Books of the West 2014 - 2015 $53

McDermott, Myra E. *Lariat Letters.* N.P.: 1907. First edition, 12mo., letter press paper wrappers, 42 pages, illustrations, rare, very good+. Baade Books of the West 2014 - 2015 $115

McDonald, Gregory *Flynn's In.* New York: Mysterious Press, 1984. First edition, one of 250 numbered copies signed by author and inscribed by same, very fine in dust jacket with slipcase. Mordida Books March 2015 - 012159 2015 $85

McDonald, Ian *Brasyl.* London: Victor Gollancz, 2007. First British edition, octavo, boards. John W. Knott, Bookseller Selected New Arrivals Jan. 2015 - 17159 2015 $100

McDonnell, Alexander *A Letter to Thos Fowell Buxton, Esq. M.P. in Refutation of His Allegations Respecting the Decrease of the Slaves in the British West India Colonies.* London: Effingham Wilson, 1833. First edition, 8vo., 80 pages, lightly foxed, recently well bound in cloth, spine lettered in gilt, very good. John Drury Rare Books March 2015 - 5820 2015 $266

McDowall, Nicolas *Latin Memories.* Llandogo: Old Stile Press, 2005. 28/45 copies signed by photographer, printed on Hahnemuhle Burga Butten paper, 14 tipped in photos, printed on handmade paper, 4to., original quarter leather with patterned boards, backstrip lettered gilt, rough trimmed, fine. Blackwell's Rare Books B179 - 211 2015 £130

McElroy, Joseph *Plus.* New York: Knopf, 1977. First edition, wrappers, advance, uncorrected proofs, tall narrow wrappers, publication date written at head of front wrapper, data sheet stapled on inside, very good++. Beasley Books 2013 - 2015 $125

McEwen, Inez Puckett *So This is Ranching.* Caldwell: 1948. Limited numbered edition, one of 1000 signed copies, cloth, illustrations, inscribed by author, gift inscription on half title, top of spine darkened, very good in chipped dust jacket with top bottom of spine missing. Baade Books of the West 2014 - 2015 $44

McFee, William *Sailors of Fortune.* London: Heinemann, 1930. First edition, name and date on titlepage, otherwise fine in dust jacket with couple of closed tears and slight wrinkling at base of spine. Mordida Books March 2015 - 009114 2015 $400

McGillycuddy, Julia B. *McGillycuddy Agent. A Biography of Dr. Valentine T. McGillycuddy.* Stanford: Stanford University Press, 1941. First edition, 8vo, cloth, frontispiece, numerous illustrations from old photos, fine, bright copy in scarce, price clipped dust jacket with light wear to spine ends, closed tear to top edge of front panel, two chips along front flap fold, moderate wear to corners, attractive copy. Buckingham Books March 2015 - 23647 2015 $325

McGillycuddy, Julia B. *McGillycuddy Agent. A Biography of Dr. Valentine T. McGillycuddy.* Stanford: Stanford University Press, 1941. First edition, 8vo., cloth, frontispiece, illustrations from old photos, fine, bright copy, scarce jacket lightly rubbed, very slightly sunned on spine with light wear to corners and spine ends, 2 inch closed tear to bottom of front panel along edges of spine and 5 inch closed tear to split to bottom of front panel, along fore-edge. Buckingham Books March 2015 - 37391 2015 $200

McGinty, Billy *The Old West.* Ripley: privately printed, 1937. First edition, printed wood grain decorated wrappers with stapled binding, 5 1/2 x 8 3/4 inches, pencil inscription by author to Hal Money(?), back cover has old triangular crease at bottom, else very good, very scarce. Baade Books of the West 2014 - 2015 $750

McGinty, Billy *The Old West.* Stillwater: Redlands Press, 1958. Reprint, printed wrappers, 96 pages, front cover pulled from staples with one tear to f.f.e.p repaired, else near fine, good+. Baade Books of the West 2014 - 2015 $85

McGown, Sonny *The Jump Records Story. A Discography.* Gross Pointe: Farms IAJRC, 2006. First edition, paperback, 4to., photo illustrations, wrappers, fine, signed by McGown. Beasley Books 2013 - 2015 $40

McGrandle, Leith *Europe: the Quest for Unity: Speeches and Writings.* London: Ranelagh Editions, 1975. One of 475 numbered copies, signed by artist, large folio, frontispiece by Pietro Annigoni, publisher's press-mark on titlepage from engraving by Reynolds Stone, designed by Giovanni and Martino Mardersteig, printed in Bembo on Cartiere Magnani paper, Pietro Annigoni frontispiece hand printed at Officina Bodoni, fine in full tan leather gilt at spine and cover and in plain wove beige cloth slipcase. Any Amount of Books 2015 - A48837 2015 £180

McGrew, Mac *American Metal Typefaces of the Twentieth Century.* New Castle: Oak Knoll Press, 1993. Second edition, cloth, dust jacket. Oak Knoll Books 306 - 223 2015 $125

McGuire, J. E. *Body and Void and Newton's De Mundi Systemate: Some New Sources.* New York: Springer, 1966. Offprint Archive for History of Exact Sciences Volume 3 No. 3 1966, 8vo., printed wrappers, inscribed by author for David C. Lindberg. Jeff Weber Rare Books 178 - 840 2015 $45

McGuire, Paul *Enter Three Witches.* New York: William Morrow & Co., 1940. First US edition, fine, bright copy in dust jacket very lightly rubbed along front flap fold. Buckingham Books March 2015 - 25047 2015 $375

McIlvanney, William *Laidlaw.* London: Hodder & Stoughton, 1977. First edition, fine in very good dust jacket with chips on front and back panels and at corners and several tears. Mordida Books March 2015 - 00161 2015 $75

McIntyre, A. A. *The Last Grand Roundup.* Sacramento: Chief Research Co., 1989. First edition thus, facsimile reprint, gilt stamped cloth, 88 pages, illustrations, very scarce, fine. Baade Books of the West 2014 - 2015 $61

McKay, Claude *Banjo a Story without a Plot.* New York: Harper, 1929. First edition, 8vo., paper over boards with cloth spine, cover somewhat worn at edges, otherwise very good in plastic dust jacket. Second Life Books Inc. 190 - 151 2015 $135

McKay, Claude *Harlem: Negro Metropolis.* New York: Dutton, 1940. First edition, 8vo., photos, brown cloth stamped gilt, cover spotted and little worn at edges, otherwise very good, tight copy in worn dust jacket. Second Life Books Inc. 190 - 152 2015 $425

McKay, Claude *Harlem shadows the Poems of.* New York: Harcourt Brace, 1922. First edition, 8vo., paper over boards with cloth spine, owner's sticker on flyleaf, cover little bumped and worn at edges, otherwise very good, tight copy. Second Life Books Inc. 190 - 153 2015 $350

McKay, Claude *A Long Way from Home.* New York: Lee Furman, 1937. First edition, first printing, in second issue green cloth, 8vo., cover faded and stained along for-edge, endpapers some browned, spotted and little worn at edges, otherwise very good, tight copy in worn dust jacket (nickle size piece missing from top of fore edge, some staining to rear boards, lacks piece between price and edge of front dust jacket flap). Second Life Books Inc. 190 - 153A 2015 $450

McKay, Claude *A Long Way from Home.* New York: Lee Furman, 1937. First edition, 2nd issue green cloth binding, light wear, near fine in very good, illustrated dust jacket with tape remnant at crown affecting title, still very nice, fragile. Between the Covers Rare Books 197 - 26 2015 $300

McKean, Hugh F. *The 'Lost' Treasures of Louis Comfort Tiffany.* Garden City: Doubleday, 1980. First edition, 2nd printing, small 4to., fine in very good+ dust jacket. Beasley Books 2013 - 2015 $45

McKee, Elizabeth *Entrance to the Greenhouse.* Moscow: 2006. Artist's book, one of a series of five all on Indian flowered paper, 2 of which are for sale, this copy with last two pages of window-sill gardens highlighted with colored pencils by artist, signed and dated by her on colophon, 6 3/4 x 7 1/2 inches, 38 pages, 4 of which are double-page fold-outs and one of which is a double page pop-up, bound by artist, hand sewn with exposed spine and tape, beige linen over boards, front panel with inlaid linen fabric, Indian flower paper overlay, housed in custom made tan cloth clamshell box with label printed on paper, fine, poem by Joan Finnigan. Priscilla Juvelis - Rare Books 62 - 13 2015 $1000

McKenney, Thomas Lorraine 1785-1859 *History of the Indian Tribes of North America with Biographical Sketches and Anecdotes of the Principal Chiefs.* Philadelphia: J. T. Bowen, 1848-1849-1850. First octavo edition, royal 8vo., contemporary ornate gilt stamped dark morocco, new spines, text and tissues with light foxing and occasional penciling, plates in excellent condition, binding with only slight wear, spines most appealing, done to match by Green Dragon Bindery. M & S Rare Books, Inc. 97 - 183 2015 $35,000

McKenney, Thomas Lorraine 1785-1859 *The Indian Tribes of North America with Biographical Sketches and Anecdotes of the Principal Chiefs.* John Grant, 1933-1934. First edition thus, 3 volumes, 123 full page plates in color, photogravure portraits and 2 maps, blue cloth, goldstamped on spine, pictorial embossment to front cover, top edge gilt, some light offsetting to front and rear free endpapers of all 3 volumes, else fine, bright, tight copies, handsome set. Buckingham Books March 2015 - 26082 2015 $1450

McKillop, Alan Dugald *Restoration and Eighteenth Century Literature...* Chicago: University of Chicago Press for William Marsh Rice University, 1963. Half title, original blue and grey cloth, very good in dust jacket, from the library of Geoffrey & Kathleen Tillotson. Jarndyce Antiquarian Booksellers CCVII - 370 2015 £20

McKinley, Robin *Hero and the Crown.* New York: Greenwillow, 1985. Stated first edition, with number code 1-10, 8vo., cloth, fine in dust jacket. Aleph-Bet Books, Inc. 108 - 285 2015 $200

McKinsey, John A. *The Lincoln Secret.* Dixon: Martin Pearl Pub., 2008. First edition, pictorial trade wrappers, signed by author. Baade Books of the West 2014 - 2015 $45

McKitterick, David *New Specimen Book of Curwen Pattern Papers.* Andoversford: Whittington Press, 1987. First edition, limited to 335 numbered copies, of which this is one of the 250 copies of the trade edition, small 4to., cloth backed patterned paper covered boards, 39 tipped-in examples of paper, beautifully produced book. Oak Knoll Books 306 - 176 2015 $300

McKitterick, David *Stanley Morison & D. B. Updike, Selected Correspondence.* New York: Moretus Press, 1979. First edition, one of 50 copies of Edition Deluxe, of which this is one of only five lettered copies, bound thus by Gray Parrot of Maine, signed by Parrot, McKitterick, Stinehour and Burton, the publisher, 8vo., full brown morocco, top edge gilt, folding cloth box with leather spine. Oak Knoll Books 306 - 53 2015 $295

McKitterick, David *Wallpapers by Edward Bawden Printed at the Curwen Press.* Andoversford: The Whittingon Press, 1989. limited to 120 numbered copies, printed by hand on Whittington Press on Oxford mould-made paper binding by Fine Bindery and half tone and color plates printed at Senecio Press, this one of the 40 copies to contain sheets or parts of sheets of seven original wallpapers, folio, quarter cloth with boards covered with a facsimile of a Bawden wall paper design, slipcase, 7 thick leaves on which are mounted foldout specimens of Bawden's wallpaper designs. Oak Knoll Books 306 - 177 2015 $1450

McLaren, Jack *A Diver Went Down.* London: Mandrake, 1929. First edition, fine in very good dust jacket with slightly darkened spine and small chips at spine ends and at corners. Mordida Books March 2015 - 005288 2015 $175

McLaughlin, James *My Friend the Indian.* Baltimore: The Proof Press, 1936. First edition thus, decorated wrappers, 30 pages, frontispiece, very good with a 1/2 inch tear at bottom of front cover closed, light stain in center of titlepage, very good, very scarce. Baade Books of the West 2014 - 2015 $150

McLoughlin, John *McLoughlin's Fort Vancouver Letters. Third Series 1844-1846.* N.P.: Champlain Society, 1944. Limited edition, blue cloth, 2 folding maps, former owner signature and date on f.f.e.p., fine.   Baade Books of the West 2014 - 2015 $82

McMahon, John R. *Toilers and Idlers.* New York: Wiltshire, 1907. First edition, hinges just starting, little rubbing to spine ends, thus very good- to very good.   Beasley Books 2013 - 2015 $300

McMillan, Joe *The Peoria Way.* N.P.: McMillan, 1984. First edition, quarto, profusely illustrated with color frontispiece and black and white photos, endpaper maps, black cloth, very fine, pictorial dust jacket.   Argonaut Book Shop Holiday Season 2014 - 178   2015 $50

McMillan, Joe *Route of the Warbonnets.* Arvada: McMillan Publications, 1998. Seventh printing, quarto, profusely illustrated with black and white photos, black cloth gilt, very fine, pictorial dust jacket.   Argonaut Book Shop Holiday Season 2014 - 176   2015 $40

McMillan, Joe *Warbonnets and Bluebonnets. Santa Fe in Color Series - Volume 3. Texas.* Arvanda: McMillan, 2004. First edition, quarto, color photos, map endpapers, blue cloth lettered in silver, very fine with pictorial dust jacket.   Argonaut Book Shop   Holiday Season 2014 - 177   2015 $90

McMillan, Terry *Breaking Ice.* New York: Viking, 1990. First printing, 8vo., editor's presentation on title, edges slightly soiled, otherwise fine in little scuffed dust jacket.   Second Life Books Inc.   190 - 154   2015 $125

McMurtry, Larry 1936 *Anything for Billy.* New York: Simon & Schuster, 1988. First edition, two-tone boards, very fine, pictorial dust jacket.   Argonaut Book Shop Holiday Season 2014 - 179   2015 $75

McMurtry, Larry 1936 *Buffalo Girls.* New York: Simon & Schuster, 1990. First edition, red cloth backed gray boards, gilt lettered spine, very fine, pictorial dust jacket.   Argonaut Book Shop Holiday Season 2014 - 181   2015 $90

McMurtry, Larry 1936 *By Sorrow's River.* New York: Simon & Schuster, 2003. First edition, green and beige boards, very fine with pictorial dust jacket.   Argonaut Book Shop   Holiday Season 2014 - 172   2015 $50

McMurtry, Larry 1936 *Comanche Moon.* New York: Simon & Schuster, 1997. First edition, dark blue and tan boards, very fine, pictorial dust jacket.   Argonaut Book Shop   Holiday Season 2014 - 183   2015 $75

McMurtry, Larry 1936 *Dead Man's Walk.* New York: Simon & Schuster, 1995. First edition, blue cloth backed boards, very fine, pictorial dust jacket.   Argonaut Book Shop   Holiday Season 2014 - 184   2015 $50

McMurtry, Larry 1936 *Desert Rose.* New York: Simon and Schuster, 1983. First edition, violet cloth backed grey boards, very fine with pictorial dust jacket.   Argonaut Book Shop   Holiday Season 2014 - 185   2015 $75

McMurtry, Larry 1936 *Duane's Depressed.* New York: Simon & Schuster, 1999. First edition, red and blue boards, very fine with dust jacket.   Argonaut Book Shop Holiday Season 2014 - 186   2015 $75

McMurtry, Larry 1936 *The Evening Star.* New York: Simon & Schuster, 1992. First edition, red cloth backed boards, slight dent to head of spine, else very fine with dust jacket.   Argonaut Book Shop   Holiday Season 2014 - 187   2015 $50

McMurtry, Larry 1936 *Folly and Glory.* New York: Simon & Schuster, 2004. First edition, tan cloth backed beige boards, spine lettered in metallic silver, very fine with pictorial dust jacket.   Argonaut Book Shop   Holiday Season 2014 - 188   2015 $60

McMurtry, Larry 1936- *In a Narrow Grave. Essays on Texas.* Austin: Encino Press, 1968. Fourth edition with "C" on copyright page, inscribed by author, fine in dust jacket.   Ed Smith Books   83 - 65   2015 $500

McMurtry, Larry 1936 *Lonesome Dove.* New York: Simon and Schuster, 1985. first edition, first issue with error 'he had none nothing' on page 621 and with $18.95 price on jacket flap unclipped, black cloth backed boards, gilt, small library bookplate, minor scar to upper edge of rear endpaper, else fine with perfect pictorial dust jacket.   Argonaut Book Shop   Holiday Season 2014 - 189   2015 $425

McMurtry, Larry 1936 *Loop Group.* New York: Simon & Schuster, 2004. First edition, gray cloth backed light gray boards, very fine with pictorial dust jacket, publisher's review copy with review slip and announcement laid in.   Argonaut Book Shop   Holiday Season 2014 - 190 2015 $60

McMurtry, Larry 1936- *Pretty Boy Floyd.* New York: Simon & Schuster, 1994. First edition, red cloth backed black boards, slight bumping to foot of spine, very fine with pictorial dust jacket.   Argonaut Book Shop   Holiday Season 2014 - 198   2015 $50

McMurtry, Larry 1936 *Roads. Driving America's Great Highways.* New York: Simon & Schuster, 2000. First edition, two-tone dark brown and beige boards, spine lettered in gold, very fine, pictorial dust jacket.   Argonaut Book Shop   Holiday Season 2014 - 191   2015 $50

McMurtry, Larry 1936 *Sacagawea's Nickname. Essays on the American West.* New York: New York Review of Books, Nov., 2001. First edition, scarce thus, gray and beige boards, very fine, pictorial dust jacket.   Argonaut Book Shop   Holiday Season 2014 - 192   2015 $75

McMurtry, Larry 1936 *Sin Killer.* New York: Simon & Schuster, 2002. First edition, brown and beige boards, very fine, pictorial dust jacket.   Argonaut Book Shop   Holiday Season 2014 - 193   2015 $50

McMurtry, Larry 1936 *Streets of Laredo.* New York: Simon & Schuster, 1993. First edition, dark blue cloth backed beige boards, gilt lettered spine, very fine, pictorial dust jacket.   Argonaut Book Shop   Holiday Season 2014 - 194   2015 $225

McMurtry, Larry 1936 *Terms of Endearment.* New York: 1975. First edition, nice, clean copy, pages very slightly browned, but less than usual, remainder mark, entirely fine dust jacket, overall excellent copy.   Gemini Fine Books & Arts, Ltd.   Art Reference & Illustrated Books: First Editions - 2015 $130

McMurtry, Larry 1936 *Texasville.* New York: Simon and Schuster, 1987. First edition, dark blue cloth backed rose boards, spine lettered white, very fine, pictorial dust jacket (price intact).   Argonaut Book Shop   Holiday Season 2014 - 195   2015 $75

McMurtry, Larry 1936- *Walter Benjamin at the Dairy Queen. Reflections at Sixty and Beyond.* Simon & Schuster, 1999. First edition, photos, photo endpapers, two-tone dark blue and tan boards, spine lettered in gold, remainder mark to bottom edge of text block, else very fine with pictorial dust jacket.   Argonaut Book Shop   Holiday Season 2014 - 196   2015 $60

McMurtry, Larry 1936- *The Wandering Hill.* New York: Simon & Schuster, 2003. First edition, two-tone beige and tan boards, spine lettered in metallic blue, very fine with pictorial dust jacket.   Argonaut Book Shop   Holiday Season 2014 - 197   2015 $60

McNeile, Hermann Cyril 1888-1937 *Bulldog Drummond at Bay.* London: Hodder & Stoughton, 1935. First edition, cloth lightly rubbed at spine, else very good in dust jacket with light professional restoration to spine ends, corners and extremities.   Buckingham Books   March 2015 - 33038   2015 $1250

McNeile, Hermann Cyril 1888-1937 *Uncle James' Golf Match.* London: Hodder & Stoughton, 1932. First separate edition, fine in lightly soiled dust jacket with small chip at top of spine.   Mordida Books   March 2015 - 009045   2015 $450

McNevin, John *Souvenir of the Great Exhibition Comprised in Six Authentic Coloured Interiors After Drawings by J. McNevin...* London: Ackermann and Co. 96 Strand (Day & Son Lithrs. to the Queen) December 31st, 1851. Folio, printed upper wrapper, 6 chromolithographs finished in colours by hand, preserved in modern blue cloth box, upper cover lettered in gilt.   Marlborough Rare Books   List 54 - 50   2015   £6500

McNevin, John *Souvenir of the Great Exhibition Comprised in Six Authentic coloured Interiors...* London: Ackermann and Co., 96 Strand Day & Son Lithographers to the Queen, December 31st, 1851. Folio, printed upper wrapper and 6 chromolithographs finished in colors by hand, preserved in modern blue cloth box, upper cover lettered gilt.   Marlborough Rare Books   List 53 - 24   2015   £6500

McPhee, John *The Deltoid Pumpkin Seed.* New York: FSG, 1973. First edition, inscribed by author, fine in very near fine dust jacket with just little edge toning.   Ken Lopez, Bookseller 164 - 136   2015 $150

McPhee, John *A Roomful of Hovings.* New York: FST, 1968. First edition, inscribed by author, fine in near fine, price clipped dust jacket.   Ken Lopez, Bookseller   164 - 135   2015 $175

McPhee, John *A Sense of Where You Are: a Profile of Princeton's Bill Bradley.* New York: Farrar, Straus and Giroux, 1965. First edition, hardcover, fine and tight copy in bright, about near fine dust jacket with some minor edge-wear and small tears, but none of the usual fading to spine.   Jeff Hirsch Books   E-62 Holiday List 2014 - 23   2015 $750

McPherson, Catriona *After the Armistice Ball.* London: Constable, 2005. First edition, 8vo. original black cloth lettered gilt at spine, signed presentation from author, fine in fine dust jacket.   Any Amount of Books   2015 - C8981   2015   £220

McRill, Albert *And Satan Also Came.* Oklahoma City: Britten, 1955. First edition, pictorial cloth, 264 pages, illustrations, Index, endpaper maps, minor wear to extremities, very good+.   Baade Books of the West   2014 - 2015 $431

McSorley, Harry J. *Luther: Right or Wrong?* New York & Minneapolis: Newman Press & Augsburg, 1969. First edition thus, moderate wear to extremities, very good hardcover, cloth, 2 dated presentations from author, personal library marks, spine call label, small person library label on front pastedown owner's library embossment on top of titlepage and his ink name stamp on lower top edge gilt as well as top and bottom text block edges.   Baade Books of the West   2014 - 2015 $74

McWhorter, L. V. *Hear Me, My Chiefs! Nez Perce History and Legend.* Caldwell: Caxton, 1952. First edition, cloth, very good+, owner's signature.   Baade Books of the West   2014 - 2015 $60

McWhorter, L. V. *Yellow Wolf - My Story.* Caldwell: Caxton, 1940. First edition, vintage photos, endpaper maps, missing half title leaf after f.f.e.p., worn at edges and corners, but without cloth wearing through, very scarce in first edition, with ownership name of Tom Sanger. Baade Books of the West   2014 - 2015 $75

McWilliams, Jane Wilson *Bay Ridge on the Chesapeake.* Annapolis: Brighton Editions, First edition, fine in near fine dust jacket (crease to front flap).   Stephen Lupack   March 2015 - 2015 $65

Mead, George Herbert *The Philosophy of the Act.* Chicago: University of Chicago Press, 1938. First edition, octavo, frontispiece, publisher's cloth with gilt spine, near fine, without dust jacket, signed and dated by John Nef, noted American historian.   Between the Covers Rare Books, Inc.   187 - 211   2015 $175

Mead, Henry *God's Goodness, the Joy and wonder of His People. A Sermon Preached April 23 1789, at St. Pancras' Church...* London: printed by J. Drew sold by Mr. Stratton, Mr. Matthews and Mr. Drew, 1789. Only edition, 8vo., title bit dust soiled and with some marginal tears (not touching printed surface), recent wrapper, rare.   John Drury Rare Books   2015 - 19154   2015 $133

Mead, Richard *De Imperio solis ac Lunae in Corpora Humana et Morbis Inde Oriundis.* Raphael Smith, 1704. First edition, title very slightly soiled, 8vo., crisp copy in contemporary Cambridge style calf, corners worn, rebacked, covers bowing, contemporary ownership inscription on title Wm. Dalzell, and on flyleaf of Sam. Caldwell, recording his purchase of the book in Dublin in 1754.   Blackwell's Rare Books   B179 - 72   2015   £750

Mead, Richard *Monita et Praecepta Medica.* Paris: G. Cavelier, 1757. Modern vellum backed boards, occasional light foxing, else fine.   Joseph J. Felcone Inc.   Science, Medicine and Technology - 34   2015 $300

Meade, George G. *Report of the Survey of the North and Northwest Lakes.* Daily Free Press Steam Printing House, 1861. 6 folding maps, original black leather boards, table, boards chipped and worn, spine chipped and loose with front board loose but attache, spine interior clean and uncut, stamp of Pacific Ry Co. Library.   Buckingham Books   March 2015 - 34984   2015 $1200

Meade, L. T. *The Sanctuary Club.* London: Ward, Lock & Co., 1900. First edition, 8vo., original blue cloth lettered gilt on spine and cover, illustrations by Sidney Paget, Spencer's select library label on front pastedown, covers slightly marked and rubbed, spine ends scuffed, inner hinge cracked and lacking frontispiece, otherwise near very good-. Any Amount of Books   2015 - C5258   2015   £150

Meade, L. T. *The Witch Maid.* London: Nisbet, 1903. First edition, near fine in green cloth covered boards, gold stamped titles.   Mordida Books   March 2015 - 001617   2015 $100

Meads, Gladys H. *At the Squaw and the Skunk.* Ames: privately published & Ames Daily Tribune, 1955. First edition thus, 4to., pictorial wrappers, vintage photos, light soiling, very good, very scarce.   Baade Books of the West   2014 - 2015 $101

Means, James *The Aeronautical Annual. Nos. 1-(23) 1895. (1896-1897). and Epitome of the Aeronautical Annual. 1910.* Boston: W. B. Clarke, 1895. 1896-1897. 1910. First editions, 8o., 69 plates, original printed and pictorial wrappers, fine, nearly original condition.   M & S Rare Books, Inc.   97 - 6   2015 $2750

Mease, James *Picture of Philadelphia, Giving an Account of Its Origin, Increase and Improvements in Arts, Sciences, Manufactures...* Philadelphia: B. & T. Kite, 1811. First edition, later cloth, 12mo., spine gilt stamped, small tears on foldout near edges foxing throughout does not obscure text. Oak Knoll Books   306 - 280   2015 $150

Mechi, John Joseph *A Series of Letters on Agricultural Improvement with an Appendix.* London: Longman, Brown Green and Longmans, 1845. First edition, 4to., engraved frontispiece, 3 other plates or plans (one loose), text figures, original embossed brown cloth, title gilt on upper cover, head of spine chipped, else very good.   John Drury Rare Books   2015 - 12475   2015 $177

The Mecklenburg Declaration of Independence May 20 1775. Chicago: Doris V. Welsh, 1954. Limited to 100 copies, frontispiece, 5.5 x 4.7 cm., half cloth, decorated paper covered boards, label on spine and front cover.   Oak Knoll Books   306 - 118   2015 $200

Mecklin, John *Mission in Torment: an Intimate account of the U. S. Role in Vietnam.* New York: Doubleday, 1965. First edition, inscribed by author to Osgood Caruthers, bureau chief at AP, Caruththers bookplate, cloth mottled, very good in like dust jacket. Ken Lopez, Bookseller 164 - 230   2015 $125

Medawar, Peter *On the Effecting of all Things Possible.* London: British Association for the Advancement of Science, 1969. Near fine, original green printed wrappers, owner marginal note page 1, signed and inscribed by author.   By the Book, L. C.   Special List 10 - 82   2015 $140

Medina, Jose T. *Los Aborijenes de Chile. (Aborigenes).* Santiago: Imprenta Gutenberg, 1882. First edition, small 4to., 232 illustrations on 40 lithographed plates, quarter brown morocco over marbled boards, gilt title and rules on spine, marbled endpapers, scarce in first edition, very good, spine and boards scuffed, small tears to few early leaves. Kaaterskill Books 19 - 90   2015 $350

Medina, Jose T. *La Araucana de Alonso de Ercilla y Zuniga. Edicion del Centenario...* Santiago de chile: Imprenta Elzeviriana, 1910-1918. Centennial edition, first edition thus, one of 600 copies, 5 volumes, black and white plates, photos, drawings, facsimiles and map, folio, quarter morocco over marbled boards, five raised bands, gilt titles, spines sunned and scuffed, leather corners of two rear boards lacking, most boards rubbed, small abrasions to front pastedowns, two leaves marginally torn, last volumes boards different color, printer pagination error, overall still very good. Kaaterskill Books 19 - 54 2015 $1850

Mee, Margaret Ursula *Flowers of the Brazilian Forests Collected and Painted by Margaret Mee.* London: L. van Leer & Vo. for the Tryon Gallery in association with George Rainbird, 1968. First and only edition, limited to 500 copies, this no. 27 of 100 deluxe copies signed by Mee with original gouache by Mee, folio, original full natural vellum by Zaehnsdorf, gilt facsimile of author's signature blocked on upper board, vignette of a teju-assu lizard after Mee blocked in gilt on lower board, spine lettered gilt, endpapers with printed vignettes of the etju-assu after Mee, top edge gilt, original green cloth slipcase, gilt lettering piece on upper panel, original shipping carton addressed to Richard Mitchell, Aldham, Essex with limitation numbers, title printed in green and black, original gouache over pencil painting on paper watermarked 'Raffaello Fabbriano' signed 'Margaret Mee' and titled 'Aristolochia' and further inscribed '48' mounted as an additional frontispiece, retaining tissue guard, 32 color lithographed plates, including frontispiece, all plates retaining tissue guards, text illustrations, double page map printed in red and black showing Mee's journey and locations where flowers depicted were collected, with loose original prospectus, fine.   Henry Sotheran Ltd. Natural History: Rarities 2015 - 2015   £7000

Meeks, Beth Thoma *Heck Thomas, My Papa.* Norman: Levite of Apache, 1988. Limited numbered edition, number 18 of an edition limited to 50 numbered and signed copies, hardbound, 79 pages, illustrations, signed by author and by collaborator, Bonnie Speer, very, very scarce, fine, like new. Baade Books of the West   2014 - 2015 $162

Meggendorfer, Lothar *Curious Creatures.* London: H. Grevel, n.d. circa, 1892. First English edition, folio, cloth backed pictorial boards, some soil, cover corners bit worn, metal pieces rust, really very good+ and fully operational, 8 fine hand colored tab operate hinged plates.   Aleph-Bet Books, Inc.   108 - 293   2015 $3250

Meggendorfer, Lothar *Lebende Thierbilder.* Munchen: Braun & Schneider, n.d. circa, 1890. Folio, cloth backed pictorial boards, some of the usual finger soil and wear to tabs and some of the usual rust offsetting, else bright, near fine, original glassine wrapper (chipped), moveable plate book, 8 fine hand colored plates, each with hinge moveable parts operated by tabs.   Aleph-Bet Books, Inc.   108 - 294   2015 $3750

Meggendorfer, Lothar *Prinz Liliput.* Esslingen: J. F. Schreiber, n.d. circa, 1895. Folio, cloth backed pictorial boards, slight bit of edge rubbing, near fine, 6 fabulous color mechanical plates, beautiful copy.   Aleph-Bet Books, Inc. 108 - 291   2015 $4000

Meier, August *Attorneys Black and White: a Case Study of Race Relations within the NAACP.* N.P.: Organization of American Historians, 1976. Reprinted from Journal of American History Volume LXII No. 4 March 1976, Stapled wrappers, light offsetting and small pinhole on front wrapper and short tear on top edge of rear wrapper, still very good, inscribed and signed by both authors on front wrapper, scarce.   Between the Covers Rare Books   197 - 80   2015 $250

Meigs, John *Peter Hurd. The Lithographs.* Lubbock: Baker Gallery Press, 1968. First edition, limited to 325 copies (25 not for sale), numbered and signed by Hurd and Meigs, each with original lithograph, quarto, green full leather, grey endpapers, 58 plates, this copy #146, this copy inscribed by Hurd for Goddard & Brigitta Lieberson, fine, bright, clean, housed in original cloth pictorial slipcase. Buckingham Books   March 2015 - 32552   2015 $1250

Meinig, D. W. *The Great Columbia Plain a Historical Geography 1805-1910.* Seattle: University of Washington, 1968. First edition, cloth, 576 pages, 52 maps, folding map, bookplate of Western historian John Caughey and wife Laree, fine in fine dust jacket.   Baade Books of the West 2014 - 2015 $40

Meldrum, Jeffrey *Sasquatch.* New York: Forge - Tom Doherty Associates, 2006. First edition, cloth, illustrations, tables, charts, presentation copy to bookseller signed twice and dated 2006 shortly after publication, near fine in like dust jacket, almost unnoticeable bump on bottom edge front cover.   Baade Books of the West   2014 - 2015 $90

Mellini, Domenico *Descrizione Della Entrata della Serenissima Regina Giovanna d'Austria et dell' Apparato fatto in Firenze.* Fiorenza: Appresso i Giunti, 1566. First edition, 4to., early 20th century brown half morocco, marbled paper sides and matching endpapers, gilt lettering, top edge gilt, others untrimmed, original stiff wrappers bound in, titlepage vignette with Medici coat-of-arms, text little foxed, fine, bookplate of American collector Charles Walker Andrews.   The Brick Row Book Shop   Miscellany 67 - 68   2015 $1250

Meloy, Maile *Both Ways Is the Only Way I Want It.* New York: Riverhead, 2009. Uncorrected proof, Ken Lopez, Bookseller   164 - 137   2015 $65

Meltzer, S. *Draw and Tell More - Fairy Tales. (Tsayer ve Sapir Od).* Palestine: circa, 1945. 12mo., pictorial wrappers, slight edge wear, else very good+, illustrations by Lev Dickstein with full page color linoleum cuts.   Aleph-Bet Books, Inc.   108 - 251-9   2015 $300

Meltzer, S. *Garden of Animals. (Gan Chaiyot).* Palestine: circa, 1945. 12mo., pictorial wrappers, slight edge wear, else very good+, illustrations by Lev Dickstein with full page color linoleum cuts.   Aleph-Bet Books, Inc.   108 - 251-10   2015 $300

Melville, Herman   1819-1891 *Bartleby the Scrivener, a Story of Wall-Street.* Minneapolis: Indulgence Press, 1995. One of 100 copies, all on Arches MBM mould made paper, each hand numbered and signed in pencil by Wilber Schilling, who designed, printed and bound the book, page size 12 x 6 inches, 56 pages, bound by printer 'sew-boards', debossed grey paper from deep etched plate then attached to a 20 pt. museum board using an etching press, grey stamped paper over boards, red cloth spine and tips, title printed in black on spine, handmade ochre colored end sheets by MacGregory & Vinzani, frontispiece, photo reproduced as a Kallitype print on Kitakata paper editioned by Mr. Shilling, in addition, noted book artist, Suzanne Moore, has lettered the phrase "I would prefer not to", printed in ochre from polymer plates in increasingly large size and in increasingly unreadable page position starting on page 16 and ending with faint ochre outline on colophon page, text composed in 12 point Bulmer using Monotype System with assistance of Kent Kasubodske at Carling Press.   Priscilla Juvelis - Rare Books   61 - 24   2015 $550

Melville, Herman   1819-1891 *Battle-Pieces and Aspects of War.* New York: Harper, 1866. First edition, printed in an edition of 1260 copies of which 471 were sold, 8vo., bound in blindstamped brown cloth, brown endpapers, edges beveled, contemporary bookplate, name written on top edge of leaves, little rubbed, very good plus, nice, tight, no foxing,.   Second Life Books Inc.   190 - 155   2015 $3000

Melville, Herman   1819-1891 *Benito Cereno.* Paris: Lafarge Editeur, 1946. No. VII of 11 copies with an extra suite of woodcuts on Japanese paper, from an edition of 380, loose gatherings laid into wrappers, 11 woodcuts by Patrick de Manceau, spine of chemise taped by former owner in somewhat damaged slipcase, 4to.   Beasley Books   2013 - 2015 $500

Melville, Herman   1819-1891 *Cetology. A Systematized Exhibition of the Whale on His Broad Genera.* Bremen: Red Angel Press, 1973. Artist's book, one of 100 copies, each signed and numbered by artist/printer/publisher, Ronald Keller, page size 9 5/8 x 10 3/4 inches, 48 pages, bound in brown paper over boards, brown kid spine, brown endpapers, woodcut printed in black of skeleton of whale, top of spine bit rubbed and touch sunned, book fine, laid in is original prospectus of book, as well as invoice from Red Angels Press to previous owner and ALS offering book, text hand set and printed letterpress in Plain and Times Roman on straw colored laid paper, original woodcuts by Keller printed on straw colored Nideggen paper, of these, two are triple gate fold pages with shaped text.   Priscilla Juvelis - Rare Books   61 - 46   2015 $800

Melville, Herman   1819-1891 *Encantadas. Two Sketches from Herman Melville's Enchanted Isles.* Northampton: Gehenna Press, 1963. First edition, large folio, book printed on 6 single folded sheets, unsewn, woodcuts printed on single sheets, gathered within a single folded sheet of Moriki, one of 150 copies, woodcuts drawn on cherry blocks by Rico Lebrun and cut by Leonard Baskin, paper used for text was copperplate and Shogun for woodcuts, this number 108 with single set of woodcuts signed by Lebrun and Baskin, placed in buckram covered portfolio and enclosed in buckram covered slipcase with leather label scratched and some wear to outer slipcase, internally fine.   Second Life Books Inc.   190 - 156   2015 $950

Melville, Herman   1819-1891 *Mardi and a Voyage Hither.* New York: Harper and Bros., 1849. First American edition, octavo, original brown blindstamped cloth, 2 volumes, cloth very clean and gilt exceptionally bright, beautiful copy, very light wear at spine ends, usual scattered occasional foxing, pastedowns toned and foxed, bookplates of Albert Henry Wiggin, noted book collector and famous Boston and NY banker, also with very attractive bookplates of Sydney Ansell Gimson and Flower Booksellers.   Manhattan Rare Book Company   Literature 2014 - 2015 $3800

Melville, Herman 1819-1891 *Mardi: and a Voyage Thither.* New York: Harper & Bros., 1849. First American edition, original blue green cloth, decorated in blind, spine in gilt, 2 volumes, excellent, unsophisticated copy with contemporary ownership inscription to front endpapers, volume II with signature of Richmond Enquirer editor, Thomas Ritchie, volume II corners lightly bumped and touch of wear to upper spine some light spotting and minor foxing to pages.   B & B Rare Books, Ltd.   234 - 77   2015 $2000

Melville, Herman 1819-1891 *Melville's Agatha Letter to Hawthorne.* Portland: Southworth Press, 1929. First separate printing, bound in green paper wrapper, spine little discolored, very good, signed on cover by Melville's granddaughter, Eleanor Melville Metcalf, rare.   Second Life Books Inc.   190 - 157   2015 $750

Melville, Herman 1819-1891 *Omoo...* London: John Murray, 1849. Early edition, small octavo, frontispiece map, contemporary full dark blue calf with raised bands, decorated compartments gilt, gilt rules, inner dentelles gilt, all edges gilt, marbled endpapers, from Stoke Rochford library of Christopher Turnor, with his armorial bookplate, slight rubbing to edges of covers, near fine.   Peter Ellis, Bookseller   2014 - 008839   2015   £285

Melville, Herman 1819-1891 *Piazza Tales.* New York: Dix and Edwards; London: Sampson Low, 1856. First edition, 12mo., blindstamped brown cloth stamped in gilt on spine, rubbed, wear to extremities of spine, bookplate on endpaper, yellow/tan endpapers, very good, tight copy.   Second Life Books Inc.   190 - 158   2015 $2500

Melville, Herman 1819-1891 *Pierre or the Ambiguities.* New York: Harper, 1852. First edition, 12mo., original blindstamped brown cloth, repaired at top of spine, some of the cloth replaced, brown coated endpapers, previous owner's bookplate, some light foxing, very good, tight, housed in cloth slipcase.   Second Life Books Inc.   190 - 159   2015 $3500

Melville, Herman 1819-1891 *Redburn: His First Voyage, Being the Sailor-Boy Confessions and Reminiscences of the Son-of-a-Gentleman in the Merchant Service.* New York: Harper, 1849. First edition, first issue, 12mo., purple blindstamped cloth, faded to brown on spine, yellow coated endpapers, except for some light foxing, some staining to endpapers, very good, tight copy.   Second Life Books Inc.   190 - 160   2015 $3000

Melville, Herman 1819-1891 *The Works of Herman Melville.* London: Constable & Co., 1922-1924. Standard edition, limited to 750 sets, large 8vo., 16 volumes, original blindstamped cloth with gilt lettering, top edge gilt, volume title 'Poems' lacks half inch traingle of cloth at top of spine, some intermittent pencil underlining 'Piazza Tales' has closed tear from one leaf having been carelessly opened, couple of dust jacket flaps laid in, couple of nicks at extremities of spine, otherwise nice, clean set, previous owner's bookplate, excellent, complete set.   Second Life Books Inc.   190 - 161   2015 $10,000

Melzo, Lodovico *Regole Militari sopra il governo e Servito Particolare Della Davalleria.* Antwerp: Gioachino Trognaesio, 1611. First edition, quarto, extra engraved title, 15 (of 16) copper engraved plates, many engraved headbands and initials, contemporary full vellum, lettered on spine in early brown ink, slight crack to upper hinge at page 1, minor bumping or slight wear to corners, fine, clean copy.   Argonaut Book Shop   Holiday Season 2014 - 205   2015 $2500

A Memento of the Quarter-Centenary Year of William Shakespeare 1564-1964 April 23. Worcester: Stanbrook Abbey Press, 1964. Limited to 200 copies, small 4to., printed in black and blue on dampened Millbourn Lexpar white wove handmade paper and containing two hand drawn initials by Margaret Adams, some age darkening along edges, parchment spine with white Japanese handmade paper covered boards with black and blue stencil dyed patterns by the Takumi artists of Tokyo, parchment cover label.   Oak Knoll Books   306 - 170   2015 $175

Memoirs of the Public Life and Administration of the Right Honourable the Earl of Liverpool, K.G. &c &c. London: Saunders and Otley, 1827. First edition, 8vo., frontispiece, half title and final ad leaf with 19th century armorial bookplate of Robert William Duff of Fetteresso Castle near Stonehaven, fine in original boards, uncut, boards little soiled, wear to head and foot of spine.   John Drury Rare Books   2015 - 26252   2015 $177

Memoirs of the Year Two Thousand Five Hundred. Liverpool: printed by and for W. Jones, 1802. New edition, small 4to., full brown leather, used, but near very good with splitting at spine hinges (holding) and some minor wear to leather, text clean with prelims slightly browned at edges.   Any Amount of Books   2015 - A66512   2015   £175

Menage, Gilles *Historia Mulierum Philosophorum...* Lugduni: Anissonios Joan Posuel & Claudium Rigaud, 1690. First edition, 12mo., lacks front blank, contemporary French calf, spine gilt with raised bands little wear, especially at top of spine, very good, clean copy.   Second Life Books Inc.   189 - 163   2015 $1200

Mencken, Henry L. *Christmas Story.* New York: Alfred Knopf, 1946. First state, first edition in first issue dust jacket, illustrations by Bill Crawford who also did the dust jacket and endpapers, near fine in very good minus dust jacket, inner seam repair, stain to verso, price clipped.   Stephen Lupack   March 2015 - 2015 $100

Mencken, Henry L. *In Defense of Women. the Free Lance Books VI.* New York: Knopf, 1925. Seventh printing, 8vo., covers bright and clean, little soiled dust jacket, very good.   Second Life Books Inc.   189 - 164   2015 $45

Mencken, Henry L. *The Philosophy of Friedrich Nietzsche.* Boston: Luce and Co., 1908. First edition, publisher's wine cloth, very good, some shelfwear, spine somewhat dulled, one page with mid fox like staining, early, uncommon.   Stephen Lupack   March 2015 - 2015 $150

Mencken, Henry L. *Supplement One: The American Language.* New York: Alfred A. Knopf, 1945. First edition, fine in moderately age toned, near fine dust jacket with short tear at one fold, nicely in inscribed by author to important literary editor, Bernard Smith.   Between the Covers Rare Books   196 - 95   2015 $750

Mendibil, Pablo De   *Resumen Historico de la Revolucion de Los Estados Unidos Mejicanos Sacado del 'Cudadro Historic' que en forma de cartas escribio el Lic. d. Carlos Maria Bustamente...* London: Lo Publica R. Ackermann, 1828. First edition, 5 black and white plates, 8vo., modern half red cloth over marbled boards, brown morocco gilt spine label, rules, marbled edges, very good or better in bright binding, title leaf soiled with old edge repair, expertly chip on corner, scattered foxing, minor damp marking to top edge of plates, small puncture on advertising leaves.   Kaaterskill Books   19 - 91   2015 $500

Menhart, Oldrich   *Menhart 1897-1962.* N.P.: Indiana University, 1966. First edition printed letterpress on Masa and Fabriano papers in an edition limited to 144 numbered copies, 4 volumes, folio, 4 paper wrapper fascicules, slipcase, unpaginated French fold pages, printed in various colors, this copy has loose slip inscribed "Phil, to recall our long years as colleagues & as fellow calligraphers, Paul (Standard) NY, Nov. 1966", some wear along edges of slipcase.   Oak Knoll Books   Special Catalogue 24 - 32   2015 $400

Menken, Adah Isaacs   *Infelicia.* Philadelphia: Lippincott, 1868. First American edition, 8vo., brown cloth, rubbed at extremities, very good, contemporary presentation on endpaper, scarce.   Second Life Books Inc.   190 - 152   2015 $250

Menotti, Gian-Carlo   *Amahl and the Night Visitors.* New York: McGraw Hill, 1952. First edition, illustrations by Roger Duvoisin, thin octavo, fine in price clipped, near fine dust jacket with slight overall age toning and few short tears.   Between the Covers Rare Books   196 - 163   2015 $100

Mera, H. P. *Pueblo Indian Embroidery.* Santa Fe: 1943. First edition, 4to., stiff printed wrappers and red/black printed dust jacket, black and white illustrations, three plates in color, fine, dust jacket very good or better.   Baade Books of the West   2014 - 2015 $49

Mercantile Library of Boston   *Catalogue of the Mercantile Library of Boston.* Boston: John Wilson and Son, 1854. 8vo., original stiff paper wrappers, text on back wrapper faded, wrappers soiled and stained, chipped at edges, largely worn, some pages of text chipped at corners, notations throughout text with tipped in explanatory note.   Oak Knoll Books   306 - 84 2015 $125

Mercer, Ian   *The Green Windmill.* London: John Crowther, 1945. First edition, 8vo., light foxing to few endpages, else very good in lightly soiled dust jacket with light wear to head of spine.   Buckingham Books   March 2015 - 22005   2015 $175

Merchant's Petitioners and Trustees for the Factory at Leghorn   *The Answer of the Merchants-Petitioners and Trustees for the Factory at Leghorn, to the Account of Damages, Laid to the Charge of the Great Duke of Toscany....* London: printed in the year, 1704. First edition, folio, bound in contemporary patterned pink boards with overall design of foliage and flowers with animals, birds and hunters, spine very worn, all edges gilt, crisp, rare.   John Drury Rare Books   2015 - 24543   2015 $2622

Meredith, William   *Hazard the Painter.* N.P.: Ironwood Press, 1972. First edition, 8vo., scarce printing, inscribed by author for William Claire.   Second Life Books Inc.   190 - 164   2015 $150

Meredith, William   *Hazard the Painter.* New York: Alfred A. Knopf, 1973. First edition, fine in fine dust jacket, inscribed by author to publisher Stuart Wright with two lines of verse.   Between the Covers Rare Books, Inc.   187 - 176   2015 $200

Merewether, Henry Alworth   *The Speech of Mr. Serjeant Merewether, in the Court of Chancery, Saturday, Dec. 8 1849 Upon the Claim of the Commissioners of Woods and Forests to the Sea-Shore and Soil and Bed of Tidal Harbours and Navigable Rivers....* London: Henry Butterworth, 1850. First edition, 8vo., 48 pages, recently well bound in linen backed marbled boards, lettered, very good.   John Drury Rare Books   2015 - 18192   2015 $133

Merimee, Prosper   *Carmen.* Paris: Editions Literaires de France, 1945. No. 99 of 330 copies with 20 copper plate engravings by D. Galanis, 12 full page illustrations, small 4to., unbound signatures in wrappers, fine in fine wrappers and glassine in fine chemise and near fine box with one sunned side.   Beasley Books   2013 - 2015 $350

Meriton, George *Land-Lords Law; a Treatise very Fit for the Perusal of all gentlemen and Others.* London: printed for Henry Twyford, Thomas Dring and John Place, 1665. First edition, variant issue, 12mo., wanting prelim blank, contemporary plain rule sheep, fine.   John Drury Rare Books   2015 - 26107   2015 $1311

Meritt, Paul *The Hidden Million: a Sensational Story.* New York: Georg Munro, 1883. First edition, quarto, scrape on front leaf, some soiling and small tears, mostly along spine, overall very good, rare.   Between the Covers Rare Books   196 - 146   2015 $450

Meriwether, Susan *Playbook of Robin Hood.* New York: Harper Bros., 1927. First edition, folio, stiff pictorial card covers, corner of one flap frayed bit, else fine and unused, bold color illustrations by Esther Peck, rare in unused condition.   Aleph-bet Books, Inc.   109 - 409   2015 $500

Merrall, Ann *Spotlight 1982/83 Edition: Agents & Production A-Z Actors A-Z.* London: Spotlight, n.d., circa, 1982. 4to., original pale green and lime wrappers, lettered black on spine and covers and illustrated throughout, slight creasing to volume 2, otherwise clean, very good or better.   Any Amount of Books   2015 - C6089   2015   £160

Merrick, George Byron *Old Times on the Upper Mississippi. The Recollections of a Steamboat Pilot from 1854 to 1863.* Cleveland: Arthur H. Clark Co., 1909. First edition, 8vo., original blue cloth, titles stamped in gold on the spine, frontispiece, top edge gilt, illustrations, maps, portraits, page edges untrimmed, many pages uncut, small bump to front and rear lower corners and some very light rubbing to cloth, else near fine without dust jacket, as issued.   Buckingham Books   March 2015 - 31914   2015 $225

Merrick, James *Annotations, Critical and Grammatical on Chap. I v. 1-14 of the Gospel According to St. John, Being Part of a Work, Particularly designed for the Use of Young Persons as an Introduction to the Study of the Greek Testament.* (bound with) *Second Part of Annotations....* Reading: printed and sold by J. Carnan and Co., sold also by Mr. Newbery; and by Mr. Fletcher and Mr. Prince in Oxford, 1764. 1767. First editions, 8vo., good, but quite recent blue cloth, lettered on spine, very good.   John Drury Rare Books   March 2015 - 24674   2015 $221

Merrie England: a Philatelic Celebration of Ancient Festivals. Berkeley: Poole Press, 1983. Limited to 101 copies, 81 numbered, signed by Maryline Poole Adams on colophon, 5.7 x 7.1 cm., quarter leather, marbled paper covered boards, title gilt stamped on spine, postage stamps tipped in as illustrations, pages french-fold.   Oak Knoll Books   306 - 119   2015 $225

Merrill, James *David Jackson: Scenes from His Life Today.* New York: Nadja, 1994. First edition of this 72nd birthday tribute to Merrill's lover, printed in an edition of 100 copies on Arches mouldmade paper, 4to., illustrated with tipped in color reproductions, loose sheets in bright blue linen portfolio with pictorial label on front cover, Japanese style clasp, as new.   James S. Jaffe Rare Books   Modern American Poetry - 194   2015 $7500

Merrill, James *Jim's Book. A Collection of Poems and Short Stories.* New York: privately printed, 1942. First edition of author's rare first book, 8vo., original cloth backed boards, tissue dust jacket, beautiful copy, seldom seen in this condition, preserved in linen folding box with leather label.   James S. Jaffe Rare Books   Modern American Poetry - 190   2015 $6500

Merrill, James *Mirabell: Books of Number.* New York: Atheneum, 1978. First edition, trifle foxed on fore edge, else fine in fine dust jacket with just touch of rubbing, inscribed by author to Judy Moffett.   Between the Covers Rare Books, Inc.   187 - 177   2015 $200

Merrill, James *The Seraglio.* New York: Knopf, 1957. First edition, 8vo., very good, tight in scuffed and chipped dust jacket inscribed by author to Bill Claire.   Second Life Books Inc.   190 - 165   2015 $175

Merrill, James *The Thousand and Second Night.* Athens: Christos Christou Press, 1963. First edition, privately printed for author, one of 20 copies, with 2 vignettes on titlepage and at end of text hand colored by Merrill, out of a total edition of 50 copies, small 8vo., original blue wrappers with printed paper label on front cover, fine, presentation from author for Harry Ford, Merrill's editor.   James S. Jaffe Rare Books   Modern American Poetry - 191   2015 $4500

Merrill, James *Volcanic Holiday.* New York: Nadja, 1992. First edition, one of 10 Roman numeraled copies with separate suite of the original prints, with margins, each signed by artist, Dorothea Tanning, out of a total edition of 110 copies printed on Rives BFK Paper and signed by Merrill and Tanning, this special issue includes a Revision of Stanza 5 typed on a small piece of cream paper and initialed by Merrill, which was not included with regular issue, 8vo., 8 original color etchings, loose signatures in handmade paper wrappers, with a suite of the 8 individually signed etchings enclosed in oblong gray cloth slipcase with printed spine label, mint, beautiful.   James S. Jaffe Rare Books   Modern American Poetry - 193   2015 $10,000

Merrill, James *The Yellow Pages 59 Poems.* Cambridge: Temple Bar Bookshop, 1974. First edition, one of only 50 copies specially bound and signed by Merrill, 8vo., original black cloth, very fine.   James S. Jaffe Rare Books   Modern American Poetry - 192   2015 $850

Merryman, Mildred *Daddy Domino.* Minneapolis: Volland Buzza, 1929. Stated first printing, 8vo., cloth backed pictorial boards, slight spine soil, else fine in original box (slightly worn), silhouettes by Janet Laura Scott.   Aleph-Bet Books, Inc.   108 - 411   2015 $450

Merton, Thomas *Thirty Poems.* Norfolk: New Directions, 1944. First edition, very uncommon hardcover edition, near fine, lacking dust jacket, 8vo.   Beasley Books   2013 - 2015 $150

Merwin, W. S. *The Dancing Bears.* New Haven: Yale University Press, 1954. First edition, small 8vo., original boards, dust jacket slightly faded at spine, otherwise fine, inscribed by author for Ted Wilentz.   James S. Jaffe Rare Books   Modern American Poetry - 195   2015 $850

Mesa Verde National Park. Mesa Verde Company, circa early 1940's, 9 x 12, plastic spiral boards, 16 black and white photos plus map, stain on lower back cover, else very good.   Baade Books of the West   2014 - 2015 $49

Mesens, E. L. T. *London Bulletin: Volume Two (Issues 10-20) with Newly Prepared Cumulative Index.* New York: Arno Press, 1969. Facsimile reprint, 4to., original blue cloth, lettered yellow on spine and on front cover, copiously illustrated in black and white, about fine.   Any Amount of Books   2015 - C6205   2015   £160

Metz, Leon C. *Robert E. McKee: Master Builder of Structures Beyond the Ordinary.* El Paso: Robert E. & Evelyn McKee Foundation, 1997. First edition, 4to., pictorial silver stamped cloth, illustrations, signed by Metz, Louis McKee (Typography, Design) and editor Nancy Hamilton, fine in fine, original silver stamped slipcase, very scarce, fine.   Baade Books of the West   2014 - 2015 $356

Metz, Leon C. *Turning Points in El Paso Texas.* El Paso: Mangan Books, 1985. Limited edition, #14 of the Conquistador edition, limited to 75 copies signed by Metz, cloth, 128 pages, photos, very scarce, fine in fine dust jacket, original custom black slipcase, silver stamped.   Baade Books of the West   2014 - 2015 $162

Mexico South. The Isthmus of Tehauntepec. New York: Alfred A. Knopf, 1946. First edition, one of 100 copies, octavo, original illustrations by Miguel Covarrubias, and additional inscription and illustration from Covarrubias for Natalia and John Drohojowski, original black cloth over pink paper boards, gilt stamped on spine, some light fading to top edge of book, otherwise fine, housed in black opened ended cloth slipcase.   Heritage Book Shop   Holiday 2014 - 44   2015 $3000

Meyer, Annie Nathan *The Dominant Sex a Play in Three Acts.* New York: Brandu's, 1911. First edition, 8vo., very good.   Second Life Books Inc.   189 - 166   2015 $75

Meyer, Carl *Bound for Sacramento.* Claremont: Saunders Studio Press, 1938. First English translation, scarce, limited to 450 numbered copies, facsimile insert, original cloth, very fine, pictorial dust jacket.   Argonaut Book Shop Holiday Season 2014 - 207   2015 $150

Meyer, Carl *Nach dem Sacramento. Resiebilder Eines Heimgekehrten von Carl Meyer.* Aarau: Druck und Verlag von H. R. Sauerlander, 1855. First edition, small octavo, yellow pictorial wrappers printed in black, just hint of occasional foxing, slight soiling to wrappers, very fine, uncut, unread copy, very rare in this original condition.   Argonaut Book Shop   Holiday Season 2014 - 206   2015 $1500

Meyer, Ernest *Hey! Yellowbacks!* New York: John Day, 1930. First edition, inscribed by author, very good, lacking dust jacket.   Beasley Books   2013 - 2015 $45

Meyer, Hans *Across East African Glaciers. An Account of the First Ascent of Kilimanjaro.* George Philip & Son, 1891. First edition, thick 8vo., full green pictorial cloth, light green endpapers, frontispiece, top edge gilt, illustrations, plates, maps, 40 illustrations and 3 maps, professionally recased with original spine laid down, lightly rubbed at spine ends, corners and extremities, former owner's neat inked name on half titlepage, else solid, very good, contents clean and attractive.   Buckingham Books   March 2015 - 33309 2015 $5000

Meyer, Russ *Vixen's Working copy.* Corona: Eve Productions circa, 1968. Shooting script for the 1968 film, Erica Gavin's shooting script, complete.   Royal Books   46 - 13   2015 $6500

Meyer, Thomas *Monotypes & Tracings. German Romantics. Sandra Fisher & Thomas Meyer.* London: Enitharmon Press, 1994. First edition of these translations, one of 50 deluxe copies signed by Meyer, Ashbery and Fisher, with original etching signed by Fisher laid into separate folder, 4to., original black and white monotypes by Sandra Fisher, original cloth with pictorial label, publisher's slipcase.   James S. Jaffe Rare Books   Modern American Poetry - 197   2015 $750

Meyer, Thomas *Sonnets & Tableaux.* London: Coracle Press, 1987. First edition, large 4to., tipped in reproductions of original oil paintings by Sandra Fisher, original cloth, glassine dust jacket, slipcase, as new.   James S. Jaffe Rare Books   Modern American Poetry - 196   2015 $650

Meyer, Tom *Poikilos.* Urbana: Finial Press/Stone Wall Press, 1971. First edition, one of 250 copies, 16mo., black leather grain cloth, gilt rules on front board, silk ribbon marker bound in, fine, inscribed by author in 1973 to Dorothy Neal,.   Between the Covers Rare Books, Inc.   187 - 178 2015 $300

Meyers, William H. *Journal of a Cruise to California and the Sandwich Islands in the United States Sloop-of-War Cyane 1841-1844.* San Francisco: Book Club of California, 1955. First edition, one of 400 copies, folio, frontispiece map, 10 full page color reproductions, gray linen, red morocco spine, slightest of rubbing to spine ends, fine. Argonaut Book Shop   Holiday Season 2014 - 297   2015 $350

Meynell, Laurence W. *Blue Feather.* D. Appleton and Co., 1928. First US edition, very good in fine, bright dust jacket. Buckingham Books   March 2015 - 33431   2015 $350

Meynert, Theodor *Psychiatry, a Clinical Treatise on Diseases of the Fore-Brain.* New York: Putnam, 1885. First edition in English, pale library numbers on spine, fraying at head of spine, very good+. Beasley Books   2013 - 2015 $250

Michaud, Jean Luc *Portrait de Helen Marre.* Editions Manuel Bruker, 1963. First edition, one of 150 copies, 4to., loose sheets in wrappers, 12 Helene Marre engravings, fine in torn glassine over fine wrappers. Beasley Books   2013 - 2015 $250

Micheaux, Oscar *The Forged Note. A Romance of the Darker Races.* Lincoln: Western Book Supply Co., 1915. First edition, gilt stamped cloth, 522 pages, 13 prelim drawings by Heller, endpaper photos and text, supremely rare, good+, hinges carefully and professionally repaired, spine speckled with small light spots and is slightly faded, front and back covers acceptably bright, rear joint has very narrow & broken band of light stain or bleach running along a limited assistance, occasional light prior crease to a few leaves, book is protected in newly made matching custom slipcase, good+. Baade Books of the West   2014 - 2015 $688

Michelet, Jules *La Genese De le Mer.* Paris: Les Bibliophiles Du Palais, 1937. No. II orf XX copies (from an edition of 200), numbered and signed by Daragnes, with his etchings and color woodcuts, 4to., unbound signatures laid into wrappers, fine in close to fine wrappers, very good+ glassine, chemise is green canvas over boards with gilt stained leather spine label, light green box. Beasley Books   2013 - 2015 $250

Michener, James *Iberia.* New York: Random House, 1968. First edition, hundreds of photos by Robert Vavra, fine in fine dust jacket, uncommon thus. Ken Lopez, Bookseller   164 - 146   2015 $200

Middendorp, Jan *Dutch Type.* Rotterdam: 2004. First edition, 4to., paper covered boards, illustrated endpapers, later cardboard slipcase, color and black and white illustrations. Oak Knoll Books   306 - 183   2015 $750

Middleton, Bernard C. *Recollections, My Life in Bookbinding.* Newtown: Bird & Bull Press, 1995. First edition, limited to 200 numbered copies, printed by hand on Arches mouldmade paper in Dante types composed by Golgonozza Letter Foundry, bound by Campbell-Logan Bindery, quarter leather, printed paper sides, leather spine label, slipcase, prospectus loosely inserted. Oak Knoll Books   306 - 135   2015 $350

Middleton, Stanley *Brazen Prison.* London: Hutchinson, 1971. First edition, 8vo., fine in near fine dust jacket very slightly creased at inner flap, signed presentation from author to Muriel Dumnachie Sept. 1971. Any Amount of Books   2015 - A38142   2015   £150

Middleton, Stanley *Terms of Reference.* London: Hutchinson, 1966. First edition, 8vo., near fine in near fine dust jacket with very slight creasing and rubbing at edges, no nicks or tears, no inscriptions. Any Amount of Books   2015 - A96491   2015   £175

Middleton, William D. *Smith Shore. The Last Interurban.* San Marino: Golden West Books, 1970. 4to. black and white photos and diagrams, index, map endpapers, gilt lettered maroon leatherette, circular embossed stamp to lower titlepage, else fine in lightly chipped pictorial dust jacket. Argonaut Book Shop   Holiday Season 2014 - 209   2015 $60

Midnight the Signal. London: sold by Dodsley, 1779. 2 volumes, 165 x 102mm., complete with usual pagination in volume II, pleasing contemporary crimson morocco bound for Jonas Hanway by his second binder, covers gilt with twining border enclosing a frame of roses with sunburst cornerpieces, upper cover with Greek cross at center encircled by motto "O save us from ourselves', lower cover with winged hourglass and motto 'Revere the appointment of nature', raised bands, spine compartments gilt in checkerboard pattern punctuated by daisies, one olive and one black morocco label, gilt turn-ins, marbled endpapers, all edges gilt, engraved titlepage with emblem depicting Death hovering over socializing persons, with a lutist in the background, large paper copy, verso of front free endpapers, with armorial bookplate from which the name has been excised, spines bit darkened with muted gilt leather on covers varying in color (from fading or soiling) but bindings entirely solid and with only trivial wear to joints, leaves with hint of offsetting and isolated soiling, faint dampstain to lower fore edge of one gathering, otherwise extremely pleasing internally, text clean, fresh and bright and with vast margins. Phillip J. Pirages   66 - 44   2015 $4800

Miege, Guy *The New State of England Under their Majesties K(ing) William and Q(ueen) Mary.* London: printed by H. C. for Jonathan Robinson at the Golden Lion, 1691. First edition, lovely copy, quite scarce thus, 12mo., 3 parts in one volume, frontispiece, contemporary polished calf, skillfully rebacked in antique style, slight rubbing or wear to corners, fine, complete, clean. Argonaut Book Shop   Holiday Season 2014 - 210   2015 $650

Miers, John *Travels in Chile and La Plata...* London: printed for Baldwin, Cradock and Joy, 1826. First edition, 16 plates, in text drawings, illustrations by Thomas Nann Baynes after John Miers, 8vo., modern half brown cloth over marbled boards, brown morocco title labels, tan volume labels, scattered foxing to plates, few leaves including titles, else near fine.   Kaaterskill Books   19 - 100   2015 $1500

Mieville, China *The Scar.* London: Macmillan, 2002. First edition, octavo, boards, signed by author.   John W. Knott, Bookseller   Selected New Arrivals Jan. 2015 - 17164   2015 $150

Mignot, M. *Histoire de l'Empire Ottoman.* Paris: Le Clerc, 1771. First edition, 4to., full brown tree calf lettered and decorated gilt on spine, map that can come loosely inserted is not present, uncommon large format one volume edition, slight edgewear, very good+.   Any Amount of Books   March 2015 - A85672   2015   £375

Mijatovi, Elodie Lawton *Kossovo: an Attempt to Bring Serbian National Songs about the Fall of the Serbian Empire into One Poem.* London: W. Isbister, 1881. First UK edition, 8vo., original decorative green cloth lettered gilt on spine, signed presentation from author July 1885 for Mrs. Benson, bright clean, very good+, very faint rubbing along spine edge.   Any Amount of Books   2015 - C5126   2015   £225

Miles, Keith *Bullet Hole.* London: Deutsch, 1986. First edition, signed by author, fine in dust jacket, inscribed by author.   Mordida Books   March 2015 - 006737   2015 $75

Miles, Nelson A. *Personal Recollections and Observations of General Nelson A. Miles...* Chicago: Werner, 1896. First edition, 2nd issue, royal 8vo., cloth pictorially and decoratively stamped in gilt and silver, 591 pages, paintings and engravings by Frederic Remington, et al, decorated endpapers, top and bottom of spine have just enough wear to cause a couple of very short splits at bottom and threatening to do so at top, trace of wear to extremities, another very minor flaw - hairline cracks to upper edges of hinges (front cover almost imperceptable, back cover slightly more visible), very good+.   Baade Books of the West   2014 - 2015 $213

Miles, Walter Loewenheim *Socialism's New Beginning a Manifesto from Underground Germany.* New York: 1934. First US edition, 148 pages, very good in paper covers.   Bookworm & Silverfish   2015 - 6016693038   2015 $50

Milhous, Katherine *Egg Tree.* New York: Charles Scribners sons, 1950. A, First edition, 4to., cloth, fine in dust jacket with no seal, small closed tear, else fine, illustrations in color by author.   Aleph-Bet Books, Inc.   108 - 295   2015 $500

The Militant Volume 1-57. New York: Communist League of America, 1933. 57 issues, bound in worn paper covered boards with cloth backstrip, moderately fragile issues browning, endpapers browning/torn, waterstain affecting lower half of all pages (quite legible), one page torn in half, 2-4 pages, trimmed at fore-edge slightly affecting of text, 21 x 16 inches, folio.   Beasley Books   2013 - 2015 $750

The Milkmaid. London: Routledge, n.d., 1882. 4to, pictorial wrappers of the slightest bit of cover soil, near fine, illustrations in color by Randolph Caldecott, nice copy.   Aleph-bet Books, Inc.   109 - 80   2015 $150

Mill, Harriet Taylor *Enfranchisement of Women Reprinted from Westminster Review for July 1851.* London: Trubner, 1868. First edition, 8vo., self wrappers, 1 x 2 inch strip darkened at top of titlepage and removal of some kind of label, remnants of label (1 x 1/2 icnh) at inner margin to left of imprint, tear wrapper with closed tear, very good, scarce edition.   Second Life Books Inc.   189 - 168   2015 $425

Mill, John Stuart   1806-1873 *Principles of Political Economy with Some of Their Applications to Social Philosophy.* London: John W. Parker and Son, 1857. Fourth edition, 2 volumes, 8vo., original green cloth with printed labels on sides, one of these with some loss, cloth just bit faded, else very good copies,.   John Drury Rare Books   March 2015 - 25373   2015   £266

Mill, John Stuart   1806-1873 *The Subjection of Women.* Philadelphia: Lippincott, 1869. First American edition, 8vo., brown cloth, owner's name and date on blank, cover faded and little spotted, worn at corners and edges of spine, otherwise very good.   Second Life Books Inc.   189 - 167   2015 $350

Mill, John Stuart   1806-1873 *A System of Logic, Ratiocinative and Inductive...* London: Parker Soun and Bourn, 1882. Fifth edition, 2 volumes, 8vo., original green cloth, printed spine labels, fine, fresh copy.   John Drury Rare Books   March 2015 - 25372   2015 $266

Mill, Stuart, Mrs. *Enfranchisement of Women.* London: Trubner and Co., 1868. First edition offprint, octavo, original self wrappers, front cover with 3/4 x 2 3/4" darkened area (from former label?) in upper right corner and remnants of partially removed label (1 x 1 3/4") in lower left corner, small (half inch) closed tear along upper right edge of spine and 4 inch closed tear running diagonally across back cover from left edge 3" down from top, sewn, as originally issued, in spite of cover defects already noted, this is delightful and charming copy, rare.   Athena Rare Books   15 - 34   2015 $1200

Millais, John Guille 1865-1931 *The Life and Letters of Sir John Everett Millais.* London: Methuen & Co., 1899. 2 volumes, photogravure frontispieces in each volume, 7 further photogravures elsewhere, numerous other illustrations within pagination, slight foxing to some plates, 8vo., original dark blue cloth, front board and backstrip blocked in gilt, little rubbed at extremities, slight bubbling to cloth, good. Blackwell's Rare Books   B179 - 73   2015   £150

Millais, John Guille 1865-1931 *The Life and Letters of John Everett Millais.* London: Methuen, 1899. First edition, cloth boards, number 46 of a special limited edition of 360 copies, mounted on laid-in card is 2 page ALS from author written when John Leech died, in answer to correspondent's request for a letter, mounted photo of Millais, dark blue cloth covers with gilt Art Nouveau style decorations on front and spine, spines faded and corners bumped, 7 photogravures and 410 black and white illustrations, interior is bright with light discoloration, typical foxing to photograuvres in volume I, bookplate of John Sparrow, very good.   The Kelmscott Bookshop   11 - 33   2015 $450

Millar, John *An Historical View of the English Government from the Settlement to the Saxons in Britain to the Revolution in 1688.* London: J. Mawman, 1803. Third edition, 4 volumes, 8vo., very occasional slight bit of foxing, contemporary uniform half calf over marbled boards, spines tooled in blind and gilt, gilt lettered morocco labels, fine set. John Drury Rare Books   2015 - 25540   2015 $1049

Millar, Margaret *The Cannibal Heart.* Random House, 1949. First edition, near fine in fine, bright dust jacket. Buckingham Books   March 2015 - 37168   2015 $225

Millard, E. C. *South America. The Neglected Continent.* New York: Fleming H. Revell, 1894. First edition, 1 color map, black and white photos, drawings, maps, square 12mo., illustrated paper wrappers, good+ copy, lacking spine, corner chips on soiled wrappers, title marginally chipped, offsetting on two pages.   Kaaterskill Books   19 - 101   2015 $75

Millard, Joseph *Mansion of Evil.* New York: Fawcett Publication, 1950. First edition, paperback original, Gold Medal 129, fine, unread copy in pictorial wrappers, spectacular copy.   Buckingham Books   March 2015 - 1800   2015 $375

Millay, Edna St. Vincent 1892-1950 *Fatal Interview.* New York: Harper and Brothers, 1931. First edition limited to 515 copies signed by author, original cloth backed paper boards, glassine and publisher's slipcase, about fine in close to fine glassine jacket, publisher's slipcase rather worn and rubbed to extremities with some minor loss to lower spine.   B & B Rare Books, Ltd.   234 - 78   2015 $500

Millay, Edna St. Vincent 1892-1950 *The King's Henchman.* New York and London: Harper & Bros., 1927. First trade edition, early printing, octavo, original black cloth over paper boards, ownership and presentation inscriptions of Aurelia Plath, her ownership inscription (Aurelia Schober, later Plath), inscribed by her for daughter, Sylvia Plath, bookplate of Sylvia Plath inscribed with her name and dated 1950, occasional underlining and marginal notes, no dust jacket, later ink annotations suggest that Aurelia Plath picked up this copy after her daughter's suicide in 1963, exceptional association.   Honey & Wax Booksellers   3 - 24   2015 $9500

Millay, Edna St. Vincent 1892-1950 *Wine from These Grapes.* New York: Harper & Bros., 1934. First edition, 8vo., original cloth backed boards, dust jacket, presentation inscribed by author to Natalie Clifford Barney, fine in lightly worn dust jacket.   James S. Jaffe Rare Books   Modern American Poetry - 198   2015 $1500

Mille, Pierre *Line En Nouvelle-Caledonie.* Paris: Callman Levy, 1934. 4to., cloth backed pictorial boards, boards slightly browned, else very good+ in nice dust jacket chipped on spine ends, illustrations on every page with beautiful color lithographs by Edy Legrand, quite uncommon.   Aleph-Bet Books, Inc.   108 - 268   2015 $275

Miller, Alden H. *The Lives of desert animals in Joshua Tree National Monument.* Berkeley: University of California Press, 1973. First edition, 2nd printing, small quarto, numerous plates, text drawings, photos, fine, two-tone cloth, pictorial dust jacket.   Argonaut Book Shop   Holiday Season 2014 - 211   2015 $90

Miller, Alice *Pictures of a Childhood.* New York: Farrar, 1986. First edition, hardcover, 65 watercolors, fine in close to fine dust jacket.   Beasley Books   2013 - 2015 $45

Miller, Arthur *Death of a Salesman.* New York: Limited Editions Club, 1949. limited to 150 copies signed by author and artist, illustrations by Leonard Baskin, 5 etchings, 4to., Nigerian goatskin, slipcase, with Monthly Letter prospectus loosely inserted, well preserved.   Oak Knoll Books   25 - 52   2015 $600

Miller, Arthur *Death of a Salesman.* New York: Viking Press, 1949. First edition, first printing, publisher's orange cloth in original first issue dust jacket, very good in like unclipped jacket with some wear to extremities, few minor creases, light soiling to rear jacket panel, spine lightly faded, very good and clean.   B & B Rare Books, Ltd.   234 - 79   2015 $1350

Miller, Arthur *Salesman in Beijing.* New York: Viking, 1984. First edition, signed by author, fine in near fine dust jacket.   Stephen Lupack   March 2015 - 2015 $100

Miller, Benjamin S. *Ranch Life in Southern Kansas and the Indian Territory.* Fless & Ridge Printing Co., 1896. First edition, signed by author, 8vo., original pictorial wrappers with title stamped in blue on spine and front cover, portrait, rare, two small old waterstains to fore-edges of front and rear covers, else near fine, bright, housed in quarter leather and cloth clamshell case, titles stamped in gold gilt on spine, choice copy, rare.   Buckingham Books   March 2015 - 37236   2015 $5000

Miller, David E. *Utah History Atlas.* N.P.: privately printed, 1964. First edition, 4to., plastic spiral stiff wrappers, 41 maps, spiral with couple short pieces missing, binding very good, lightly soiled, very scarce.   Baade Books of the West 2014 - 2015 $40

Miller, Eric *Passion for Murder. The Homicidal Deeds of Dr. Sigmund Freud.* San Diego: Future Directions, 1984. First edition, no. 31 hand numbered copies, signed by author, fine, hardcover.   Beasley Books   2013 - 2015 $125

Miller, George Frazier *Adventism Answered.* Brooklyn: Guide Printing & Publishing Co., 1905. First edition, octavo, 214 pages, light brown cloth stamped in black, very slight soiling on cloth, near fine or better, inscribed by author for Stephen T. Brooke, uncommon.   Between the Covers Rare Books   197 - 36   2015 $1500

Miller, George Noyes *The Strike of a Sex.* London: Reeves, circa, 1891. First UK edition?, small 8vo., red cloth, owner's bookplate, slightly faded on spine, otherwise nice, scarce.   Second Life Books Inc.   189 - 169   2015 $325

Miller, Helen Sullivan *The History of Chi Eta Phi Sorority Inc. 1932-1967.* Washington: Association for the Study of Negro Life and History Inc., 1968. First edition, small quarto, yellow cloth lettered in green, photos, fine in very near fine dust jacket with very light wear.   Between the Covers Rare Books   197 - 122   2015 $300

Miller, Henry   1891-1980   *The Air-Conditioned Nightmare.* New York: New Directions Book, 1945. First American edition, modest foxing on boards, very good or better in very good first issue dust jacket with shallow chips at crown, inscribed by author to his second wife June Mansfield, handsome copy and great association.   Between the Covers Rare Books   196 - 96   2015 $2750

Miller, Henry   1891-1980   *Black Spring.* Paris: Obelisk Press, June, 1936. First edition, one of 1000 copies, about 7.5 x 5.5 inches, 267 pages, original tan and red wrappers with front cover design by Maurice Kahane, 4 pages in back roughly opened at lower corners, causing very small chips, small collector's label, otherwise in excellent condition, unusually clean, bright and fresh.   Gemini Fine Books & Arts, Ltd.   Art Reference & Illustrated Books: First Editions - 2015 $1100

Miller, Henry   1891-1980   *Maurizius Forever.* San Francisco: Colt Press printed at the Grabhorn Press, 1946. First edition, 1/500 copies, color woodcuts after drawings by Henry Miller, fine in cloth, without plain brown paper dust jacket.   Gemini Fine Books & Arts, Ltd.   Art Reference & Illustrated Books: First Editions - 2015 $190

Miller, Henry   1891-1980   *The Mezzotints.* Ann Arbor: Roger Jackson, 1993. First edition "Library edition" issue, one of 400 copies, octavo, illustrated, printed wrapper in raspberry cloth portfolio, 8 loose broadsides laid in, fine, inscribed by publisher to Bertrand Mathieu, a Henry Miller scholar.   Between the Covers Rare Books, Inc.   187 - 179   2015 $150

Miller, Henry   1891-1980   *Scenario (A Film with Sound).* Paris: Obelisk Press, 1937. First edition, limited to 200 copies signed by author, additionally inscribed by author in 1938 to expat and friend, Bessie Breuer, original buff wrappers, gatherings loosely inserted and uncut as issued, wrappers browned with some wear and staining to front cover, light chipping to upper spine.   B & B Rare Books, Ltd. 234 - 80   2015 $2500

Miller, J. Hillis   *The Disappearance of God...* Cambridge: Belknap Press of Harvard University Press, 1963. Half title, original brown cloth, very good in marked dust jacket, Geoffrey Tillotson's copy with his notes and drafts for his review for TLS and cutting of printed reviews.   Jarndyce Antiquarian Booksellers   CCVII - 375   2015   £20

Miller, Joaquin   *Memorie and Rime.* Funk & Wagnalls, 1884. 12mo., color pictorial wrappers, moderate wear to spine ends, for edges and extremities to front and rear covers lightly chipped, else very good.   Buckingham Books March 2015 - 35715   2015 $275

Miller, Nyle H.   *Why the West was Wild.* Norman: Oklahoma University Press, 2003. Limited edition, one of 500 unnumbered copies, gilt stamped hardbound, all edges gilt, illustrations, map, as new.   Baade Books of the West 2014 - 2015 $95

Miller, Thomas C.   *West Virginia and Its People.* New York: 1913. First edition, 3 volumes, three quarter leather, very good, gilt backstrip lettering bright, all edges and endpapers marbled.   Bookworm & Silverfish   2015 - 6015802236   2015 $225

Miller, Walter   *A Canticle for Leibowitz.* Philadelphia and New York: J. B. Lippincott Co., 1960. First edition, octavo, cloth backed boards.   John W. Knott, Bookseller   Selected New Arrivals Jan. 2015 - 17164   2015 $4500

Millhauser, Steven   *Edwin Mullhouse.* New York: Alfred A. Knopf, 1972. First edition, fine in very near fine dust jacket, much nicer than usual copy.   Jeff Hirsch Books E-62 Holiday List 2014 - 24   2015 $75

Milligan, Spike *Puckoon.* London: Anthony Blond, 1963. First edition, 8vo., 5 illustrations, signed presentation from author, very good+ in very good dust jacket (very slightly soiled and slightly rubbed at corners), decent copy.   Any Amount of Books   2015 - C15664   2015   £240

Milling, Jane *Cambridge History: British Theatre.* Cambridge: Cambridge University Press, 2004. First edition, 3 volumes, 8vo., illustrations, fine in dust jacket.   Any Amount of Books   2015 - A98486   2015   £220

Mills, Bill *25 Years Behind Prison Bars.* privately printed, n.d., First edition or early reprint?, stiff printed wrappers, 56 pages, frontispiece, very good, very scarce.   Buckingham Books   March 2015 - 37448   2015 $225

Mills, C. Wright *The New Men of Power. America's Labor Leaders.* New York: Harcourt, 1948. First edition, lovely copy, near fine in close to fine dust jacket with tiny tear at rear panel.   Beasley Books   2013 - 2015 $85

Mills, George *The Beggar's Benison or a Hero without a Name...* London: & New York: Cassell, Petter and Galpin, 1866. First edition, 2 volumes, half titles, original brick red grained cloth, boards blocked in blind, spines decorated and lettered gilt, slight weakening to leading inner hinge volume I, otherwise very good, bright copy, signature of J. W. Arengo Cross.   Jarndyce Antiquarian Booksellers   CCXI - 202   2015   £250

Mills, William W. *Forty Years at El Paso 1858-1898.* Press of W. B. Conkey Co., 1901. First edition, 8vo., original decorated red cloth, frontispiece, very scarce, very good, clean copy. Buckingham Books   March 2015 - 34183   2015 $350

Mills, William W. *Forty Years at El Paso 1858-1898.* El Paso: Carl Hertzog, 1962. First edition thus, 8vo., signed by Hertzog, cloth, former owner's bookplate, else fine, bright in dust jacket.   Buckingham Books   March 2015 - 24980   2015 $250

Milne Edwards, M. A. *Recherches sur la Faune des Regions Australes.* Paris: Libraire de L'Academie De Medicine, 1879-1882. Octavo, erratically paginated, five lithographs, 6 folding maps, 4 parts bound in one volume, early plain wrappers, chipped, scarce.   Andrew Isles   2015 - 20077   2015 $1400

Milne, Alan Alexander   1882-1956 *The Christopher Robin Verses...* London: Methuen, 1932. First edition, octavo, 12 color plates and black and white decorations on almost every page by E. H. Shepard, original blue buckram decorated in gilt, edges lightly spotted. very good in good dust jacket with several chips, mainly to edges of rear panel, few short tears.   Peter Ellis, Bookseller   2014 - 111108   2015   £285

Milne, Alan Alexander   1882-1956 *The Christopher Robin Verses.* London: Methuen, 1932. First edition, 8vo., pictorial cloth, fine in dust jacket (few small closed tears, else very good+), 12 lovely new color plates by E. H. Shepard, color dust jacket plus original black and whites throughout text, beautiful copy.   Aleph-bet Books, Inc.   109 - 290   2015 $600

Milne, Alan Alexander   1882-1956 *Four Days Wonder.* London: Methuen, 1933. First edition, 8vo., orange cloth, binding slightly leaning, else fine in lightly frayed dust jacket, this copy has wonderful 10 line inscription from Milne. Aleph-Bet Books, Inc.   108 - 296   2015 $1600

Milne, Alan Alexander   1882-1956 *More Very Young Songs.* London: Methuen, 1928. Limited to 100 numbered copies, signed by author, E. H. Shepard and H. Fraser Simson, this copy has the number line crossed out and written in is a presentation copy for Children's Ward Hospital, 10 charming songs beautifully illustrated in black and white by E. H. Shepard, scarce, folio, cloth backed boards, tips rubbed, covers very slightly soiled, else very good-fine. Aleph-bet Books, Inc.   109 - 292   2015 $2500

Milne, Alan Alexander   1882-1956 *More Very Young Songs from When We Were Very Young and Now We are Six.* London: Methuen, 1928. First edition, 32/100 copies printed on Japense paper and signed by Milne, Fraser-Simon and E. H. Shepard and decorations by E. H. Shepard, large 4to., original quarter dark blue cloth, pale grey boards, front cover label, untrimmed and unopened, near fine.   Blackwell's Rare Books   B179 - 193   2015   £600

Milne, Alan Alexander   1882-1956 *Now We Are Six.* London: Methuen, 1927. First edition, first printing, light rubbing to extremities, spine slightly cocked, else fine.   B & B Rare Books, Ltd.   234 - 81   2015 $400

Milne, Alan Alexander   1882-1956 *Now We Are Six.* London: Methuen, 1927. First edition, deluxe edition, 8vo., full publisher's morocco, gilt pictorial cover with extensive gilt pictorial spine, all edges gilt, fine in original publisher's box with printed labels on cover and flap (box with some soil and flap mends), illustrations by E. H. Shepard.   Aleph-Bet Books, Inc.   108 - 297   2015 $2850

Milne, Alan Alexander   1882-1956 *Toad of Toad Hall.* New York: Scribners, 1929. First edition, decorated boards, very good+, minor shelfwear, tight, clean text.   Stephen Lupack   March 2015 - 2015 $100

Milne, Alan Alexander 1882-1956 *When We Were Very Young.* London: Methuen, 1924. Limited to 100 numbered copies, signed by Milne and Shepard, 4to., illustrations by E. H. Shepard, cloth backed boards, rear endpapers toned else fine in slightly soiled but very good dust jacket with old tape marks on verso, lightly visible on front, housed custom chemise and leather backed case. Aleph-bet Books, Inc. 109 - 291   2015 $16,000

Milne, Alan Alexander 1882-1956 *When We Were Very Young.* London: Macmillan, 1974. Limited numbered edition, one of 300 numbered copies, signed by Christopher Milne, author's son, fine in slightly faded blue morocco with gold stamped titles and decorations and gilt page edges. Mordida Books   March 2015 - 010881   2015 $400

Milne, Alan Alexander 1882-1956 *Winnie-the-Pooh.* London: Methuen & Co. Ltd., 1926. First edition, octavo, beautifully bound in full green morocco gilt, excellent copy. Manhattan Rare Book Company   Literature 2014 - 2015 $2500

Milne, Alan Alexander 1882-1956 *Winnie the Pooh.* London: Methuen, 1926. First edition, first printing, 8vo., green gilt cloth, top edge gilt, nearly as new in fine dust jacket, just touch of wear to top of spine, housed in custom chemise and leather backed case, illustrations by E. H. Shepard, unusually beautiful copy, as such quite rare. Aleph-bet Books, Inc. 109 - 288   2015 $8500

Milne, Alan Alexander 1882-1956 *Winnie the Pooh.* London: Methuen, 1926. First edition, deluxe issue, publisher's green calf stamped and decorated in gilt, all edges gilt, very good, minor rubbing to extremities, spine lightly faded, former owner gift inscription to first blank and small notation to dedication, else very clean and bright. B & B Rare Books, Ltd. 234 - 82   2015 $2000

Milne, Alan Alexander 1882-1956 *Winnie the Pooh.* London: Methuen, 1928. Large paper copy, limited to 350 numbered copies on handmade paper, signed by Milne and Shepard, 4to., illustrations by E. H. Shepard, 4to., cloth backed boards, small bump and rub on lower corner, some natural toning to paper, else fine in dust jacket (conserved on verso, some soil and wear), in custom slip case. Aleph-bet Books, Inc. 109 - 289   2015 $15,000

Milne, Alan Alexander 1882-1956 *Winnie-the-Pooh.* London: Methuen & Co., 1956. Reprint, 8vo., original red cloth, lettered gilt on spine and on front cover, signed by artist E. H. Shepard on titlepage, illustrations in black and white, slight lean and slightly faded at spine, otherwise very good. Any Amount of Books   2015 - C15688   2015   £220

Milner, Joe E. *California Joe Noted Scout and Indian Fighter.* Caldwell: Caxton, 1935. First edition, gilt stamped cloth, 396 pages, photos and portraits, tipped in nearly full page informative presentation in ink from Earle Forrest, laid in is TLS from Forrest to same recipient, near fine in very good dust jacket.   Baade Books of the West   2014 - 2015 $486

Milns, William *The Penman's Repository, Containing Twenty Correct Alphabets...* Heywood: n.d. circa 1860's, 19th Century reprint of earlier edition, Oblong 4to., original leather backed pebble cloth covered boards with leather tips, paper cover label, 35 plates, spine ends chipped away, leather worn spine and tips, cover faded, front cover detached.   Oak Knoll Books   Special Catalogue 24 - 33   2015 $450

Milosz, Czeslaw *Dolina Issy (The Issa Valley).* Paris: Instytut, 1955. First edition, printed wrappers, unopened, text in Polish, pages toned and darkened, wrappers slightly less so, slight erosion to paper spine at crown, very good, author's own copy, very scarce.   Between the Covers Rare Books   196 - 97   2015 $2000

Milosz, Czeslaw *The View.* New York: Library Fellows of Whitney Museum of American Art, 1985. First edition, small folio, printed in an edition of 120 copies, fine in paper covered boards with leather spine in very near fine slipcase, signed by author Milosz and Vija Celmins.   Jeff Hirsch Books   E-62 Holiday List 2014 - 25   2015 $12,500

Milton, John 1608-1674 *De Doctrina Christiana. The Complete Works of John Milton. Volume VIII.* Oxford: Oxford University Press, 2012. First edition, 2 volumes, 8vo., original black cloth, lettered gilt at spine, fine in fine dust jacket.   Any Amount of Books   2015 - C8958   2015   £150

Milton, John 1608-1674 *Paradise Lost.* London: printed by S. Simmons next door to the Golden Lion in Aldersgate St., 1678. Third edition, octavo, full period style crimson morocco gilt, elaborately tooled, fine, bound by Philip Dusel in the Restoration style of Queen's Binder B. Honey & Wax Booksellers   2 - 2   2015 $4200

Milton, John 1608-1674 *Paradise Lost. A Poem in Twelve Books.* London: J. and R. Tonson and S. Draper, 1750. Second edition, 2 volumes, 8vo., original leather, gilt framed covers, gilt stamped title and tooling on spine, five raised bands, red and green spine labels, front covers detached, covers spotted, scuffed and rubbed at edges, notes taped on front pastedown, endpapers and text tanned. Oak Knoll Books   306 - 291   2015 $200

Milton, John 1608-1674 *The Poetical Works. Volume I. Paradise Lost.* Oxford: Clarendon Press, 1952. Uncut in original dark blue cloth, very good in slightly creased dust jacket, with printed editor's presentation slip and ALS from editor, Helen Darbishire to Kathleen Tillotson, with review cutting, from the library of Geoffrey & Kathleen Tillotson, signed by both Nov. 8 1952.   Jarndyce Antiquarian Booksellers   CCVII - 376   2015   £20

Milward-Oliver, Edward *Len Deighton: an Annotated Bibliography 1954-1985.* Maidstone: Sammler Press, 1985. First edition, one of 375 copies, this number 81, signed and numbered by author with signed page proof from London Match laid in its special folder, fine in dust jacket. Buckingham Books   March 2015 - 15215   2015 $375

Milward-Oliver, Edward *Len Deighton: an Annotated Bibliography 1954-1985.* Maidstone: Sammler Press, 1985. First edition, one of 375 copies this one unnumbered, with signed page proof from London match laid in its special folder, inscribed on limitation page for Julian and Kathleen Symons, by author 16-09-1985, fine in dust jacket. Buckingham Books   March 2015 - 14532   2015 $750

Milwaukee. A Picturesque and Descriptive Account of the Present Mercantile and Industrial Interests and Advantages of the Metropolis of Wisconsin. Milwaukee: Merchants' and Manufacturers' Assn. of Milwaukee, 1903. First edition, very attractive, 4to., decorated and printed pictorial heavy wrappers, slight overlapping text block, covers grey, dark grey, orange and red with raised lettering and raised seal on back, (88) pages, illustrations, fine lithos and high quality photos, toned perhaps slightly, near fine, just couple of short tears at top bottom of binding, binding glued, not stapled and is sound, near fine, rare.   Baade Books of the West   2014 - 2015 $405

Miniature Book Society *Miniature Book Society Yearbooks.* N.P.: Miniature Book Society, 1991-1996. 1998-2004, 8vo., 1991 and 2001-04 in stiff paper wrappers, 1992-6 and 1998-2000 unbound, prepared for loose leaf binder.   Oak Knoll Books   306 - 282   2015 $100

Minnigerode, Meade *Some Personal Letters of Melville & Bibliography.* Princeton: E. B. Hackett/Brick Row Book Shop, 1922. Limited to 1500 copies, very good.   Stephen Lupack   March 2015 -   2015 $125

Minot, George Richards *The History of the Insurrections in Massachusetts in the Year Seventeen Hundred and Eighty-Six and the Rebellion Thereon.* Boston: Burditt, 1810. Second edition, tall 8vo. original linen backed paper boards, front hinge split, moderate to occasional heavy foxing and soiling, small hole at center front endpaper, untrimmed, scarce.   Second Life Books Inc.   191 - 60   2015 $450

Minto, Gilbert Eliot, 1st Earl of *The Speech of Lord Minto, in the House of Peers June 6th 1803 on Certain Resolutions of Censure on the conduct of His Majesty's Ministers Moved by earl Fitzwilliam, to which is added, His Lordship's Speech at a General Meeting of the County of Roxburgh, held at Jedburgh, 15th August 1803 on Moving an Address to His Majesty.* London: J. Budd, 1803. First edition, 8vo., small 19th century library inkstamp on one or two leaves (not title), later wrappers, very god, uncommon. John Drury Rare Books   2015 - 14753   2015 $89

Minucius Felix *Octavius. Cum Integris Observatonibus Nic. Rigaltii, et Selectis Aliorum.* Cambridge: Typis Academicis impensis Joan. Oweni, 1707. First edition, little minor spotting but generally quite bright, 8vo., contemporary Cambridge style panelled calf, frame with cats-paw staining, remnant of paper label to spine, rubbed, little wear to endcaps, joints just cracking at ends, good.   Blackwell's Rare Books   Greek & Latin Classics VI - 76   2015   £75

Mirbeau, Octave *Oeuvres Illustrees Le Calvaire, Sebastien Roch, Le Jardin des Supplices...* Paris: Les Editions Nationales, 1934-1936. #423 of 500 copies, 10 volumes, 8vo., all near fine or better wrappers, each volume illustrated by a single artist.   Beasley Books   2013 - 2015 $225

Mirror for Magistrates. London: printed for Lackington, Allen & Co. and Longman, Hurst, Rees, Orme & Brown, 1815. One of 150 copies, 248 x 191mm, 5 parts in 3 volumes, remarkably attractive contemporary chocolate brown morocco elaborately decorated in blind and gilt by Charles Lewis, covers with blind tooled frame enclosed by gilt fillets, wide raised bands with decorative gilt rolls, intricately blind tooled panels, gilt titling, turn-ins ruled with gilt, all edges gilt, large paper copy, verso of front free endpaper with pencilled notation, "3 volumes bound by Charles Lewis. £5.50/ Only 150 printed published at £10.10 in bds.", front free endpaper of volume I slightly creased at hinge, occasional light foxing, otherwise in beautiful condition with virtually no signs of use.   Phillip J. Pirages   66 - 69   2015 $3250

Mishima, Yukio *After the Banquet.* London: Secker & Warburg, 1963. First edition, 8vo. signed presentation from author to Angus (Wilson), very good in like dust jacket. Any Amount of Books   2015 - C14196   2015   £1400

Mishima, Yukio *Confessions of a Mask.* London: Peter Owen, 1964. Second impression, 8vo., pages 255, original cream cloth lettered gilt at spine, signed presentation from author to novelist Angus Wilson, 23 March 1965, very good+ in faintly used dust jacket, complete and very good with second, slightly chipped jacket underneath.   Any Amount of Books   2015 - C13524   2015   £1200

Mishima, Yukio *Thirst for Love.* New York: Alfred A. Knopf, 1969. First US edition, 8vo., original brown cloth, lettered gilt at spine, signed presentation from author on front endpaper to novelist Angus Wilson, very good+ in very good dust jacket, slight rubbing with slight surface wear and small nicks at top of spine. Any Amount of Books 2015 - C13525 2015 £1250

Missouri Pacific Railway Company *Statistics and Information Concerning the Indian Territory, Oklahoma and the Cherokee Strip.* Salem: MPRW Co., St. Louis: Woodward & Tiernan Printing Co.), 1893. Second edition, printed wrappers, 5 1/4 x 7 1/2 inches, 85 pages, several full page and smaller engravings, ads, folding map in facsimile, titlepage in facsimile and on paper virtually the same as text, rare promotional booklet, insect damage 2 3/4" diagonally, to upper corner of last four leaves and back cover, but very little loss of text, only few words, quarter coin size insect loss to upper right edge of front cover, no loss of text or even close to it as cover facsimile map, fair copy. Baade Books of the West 2014 - 2015 $750

Mr. Nobody's Cogitations or Dreamings Awake, about the Agricultural Report. London: 1821. Only edition, 8vo., title and last page dust soiled with partially erased pencillings on title recent plain wrappers, rare. John Drury Rare Books March 2015 - 17897 2015 $266

Mitchel, Ormsby McKnight *Popular Astronomy; a Concise Elementary Treatise on the Sun, Planets, Satellites and Comets.* New York: Phinney, Blakeman & Mason, 1860. First edition, 12mo., frontispiece, 8 plates, diagrams, original blind and gilt stamped brown publisher's cloth, extremities worn, corners showing, some fading, waterstained throughout, early ownership signature of I. Spottiswood on title, good. Jeff Weber Rare Books 178 - 801 2015 $50

Mitchell, George *Kernel, Cog and Little Miss Sweet Clover.* Chicago: Volland, 1918. First edition, no additional printings, 8vo., pictorial boards, slight fraying of spine ends, inconspicuous endpaper mend, else very good++, rare illustrations in full color by Tony Sarg. Aleph-Bet Books, Inc. 108 - 408 2015 $625

Mitchell, Gladys *Here Lies Gloria Mundy.* London: Michael Joseph, 1982. First edition, fine in dust jacket, signed by author. Mordida Books March 2015 - 005292 2015 $125

Mitchell, Gladys *Spotted Hemlock.* London: Michael Joseph, 1958. First edition, some light spotting on top of page edges and on endpapers, otherwise fine in dust jacket with tiny wear at spine ends. Mordida Books March 2015 - 008410 2015 $125

Mitchell, James L. *Colt. A Collection of Letters and Photographs about the Man - the Arms - the Company.* Harrisburg: Stackpole, 1959. First edition, 4to., gilt stamped cloth, 265 pages, fine in good+ dust jacket with edgewear, fine in good dust jacket. Baade Books of the West 2014 - 2015 $50

Mitchell, Silas Weir 1829-1914 *Clinical Lessons on Nervous Diseases.* Philadelphia: Lea Bros., 1897. First edition, very good, faded call numbers on spine, f.e.p. separated, owner's name at head of titlepage, library stamp at head of preface. Beasley Books 2013 - 2015 $200

Mitchell, Silas Weir 1829-1914 *Lectures on Diseases of the Nervous System, Especially in Women.* Philadelphia: Lea Brothers, 1885. Second edition, five plates, 1 folding table, near fine with slightest rubbing to edges, owner's name. Beasley Books 2013 - 2015 $125

Mitchell, Silas Weir 1829-1914 *The Wonderful Adventures of Fuz-Buz the Fly and Mother Grabem.* Philadelphia: J. B. Lippincott, 1867. (1866)., Large paper format with 6 more plates than small paper version, 4to., cloth backed boards, some edge rubbing and foxing, very good+, with handwritten letter from author on his printed stationery laid in. Aleph-Bet Books, Inc. 108 - 298 2015 $1500

Mitford, Nancy 1904-1973 *Christmas Pudding.* London: Thornton Butterworth, 1932. First edition, frontispiece and illustrations by Mark Ogilvie-Grant, 8vo., original textured woven pink cloth lettered blue on spine and on front cover, very slight abrasion at one corner, corners slightly bumped, else very good. Any Amount of Books 2015 - C16403 2015 £225

Mitford, Nancy 1904-1973 *Pigeon Pie: a Wartime Receipt.* London: Hamish Hamilton, 1940. First edition, 8vo., rebound in half blue leather with marbled boards, gilt lettered spine and 5 raised bands, excellent handsomely rebound copy, rare, about fine. Any Amount of Books 2015 - C3221 2015 £260

Moben *Squeaker's Long Legs.* London: Frederick Warne, 1941. First edition, 8vo., pictorial boards, dust jacket slightly soiled, full page color lithos. Aleph-bet Books, Inc. 109 - 357 2015 $125

The Model Book of Trains. London and New York: Nister & Dutton, n.d. circa, 1904. 4to., stiff pictorial card covers, some corner and edge wear, else near fine, complete and unused, 6 chromolithographed leaves printed on one side of the paper, with train related pieces that child is cut out and glue to make model train cars, coaches, coal carrier, goods, vans, station and more, illustrations in brown line, rare. Aleph-bet Books, Inc. 109 - 463 2015 $1250

Model, Lisette *Lisette Model.* Millerton: Aperture, 1979. First edition, folio, fine in very good+ dust jacket with several small tears at top edge.   Beasley Books   2013 - 2015 $185

Modern ABC Book. New York: John Day, 1930. First edition, 4to., pictorial boards, slight edge rubbing, else fine in dust jacket (frayed but really very good), illustrations by C. B. Falls.   Aleph-Bet Books, Inc.   108 - 181   2015 $2000

Modern Packaging (1944-1976).   New York: Breskins, Modern Packaging and Latterly McGraw Hill, 1944-1976. Sept. 1944-Dec. 1976, 4to., volumes 18-49 in 54 volumes, all issues illustrated and with tipped in examples, rebound in red cloth with library labels of ICI Plastics division and their accession numbers on spine and few stamps, sound, very good copies.   Any Amount of Books   March 2015 - B10210   2015   £400

Moffett, Cleveland   *Through the Wall.*   New York: D. Appleton and Co., 1909. First edition, illustrations, fine, tight and bright clean copy, original decorated blue cloth.   Buckingham Books   March 2015 - 37952   2015 $775

Moheau, Jean Baptiste   *Recherches et Considerations sur la Population de la France.*   Paris: Chez Montard, 1778. First edition, 2 parts in one volume, 8vo., with one extended folding table, numerous other tables in text, small piece torn away from one leaf margin but printed surface not affected, bound in contemporary French catspaw calf, spine fully gilt and labelled, red edges, marbled endpapers, slight wear to fore edges but sill fine and handsome copy.   John Drury Rare Books   2015 - 26314   2015 $1486

Molbach, Irving   *Last Dreams.*   San Francisco: Pompous Ass Press, 1974. First edition, decorated stapled wrappers, faint dampstain to top of most leaves, very good or better, inscribed by poet to Andrei Codrescu.   Between the Covers Rare Books, Inc.   187 - 180   2015 $100

Molina, Juan Ignacio   *Des Herr Abts Vidaure Kurzgefatzte Geographische Naturliche und Burgerliche Geschichte des Konigreichs Chile...*   Hamburg: Carl Ernst Bohn, 1782. First German edition, 12mo., large folding map, marbled boards, overall very good+, extremities rubbed, contents including map fine, uncommon.   Kaaterskill Books   19 - 102   2015 $750

Moline, Jon   *Plato's Theory of Understanding.*   Madison: University of Wisconsin Press, 1981. 8vo., cloth, dust jacket, ink ownership signature of David Lindberg, very good.   Jeff Weber Rare Books   178 - 892   2015 $50

Moll, Albert   *Perversions of the Sex Instinct.*   New York: Gargoyle Press, 1931. First edition, hardcover, very good, ex-library, mild library signs, including dot on spine, Julian Press imprint, apparent on copyright page is cancelled by sticker on titlepage.   Beasley Books   2013 - 2015 $45

Momaday, N. Scott   *House Made of Dawn.*   New York: Harper & Row, 1968. First edition, red cloth and boards, 212 pages, near fine, very slight spotting to red top edge, hardly worth mentioning, near fine price clipped dust jacket, first state dust jacket.   Baade Books of the West   2014 - 2015 $115

La Monaca Di Monza.   Pisa: Presso Nicclo Capurro, 1829. First edition, small 8vo., bookplate in each volume, few small ex-libris stamps, bookplate of Amelia Henry, otherwise very good+ in very attractive vellum binding decorated in gilt at spine with leather spine lettered gilt on spine.   Any Amount of Books   2015 - A68055   2015   £180

Monck, William Henry Stanley   *An Introduction to Stellar Astronomy.*   London: Hutchinson & Co., 1899. Small 8vo., 203 pages, frontispiece, 4 photo plates, original full blue cloth, gilt stamped spine, spine soiled or faded, lettering obscured, front hinge repaired (kozo), good.   Jeff Weber Rare Books   178 - 803   2015 $50

Monk, Samuel Holt   *Studies in Criticism and Aesthetics 1660-1800.*   Minneapolis: University of Minnesota Press, 1967. Original green cloth, half title, illustrations, very good in creased dust jacket, signed by Geoffrey Tillotson 22.iii.67 with correspondence with editors about his contribution and with TLS from Samuel Monk thanking him for essay in book.   Jarndyce Antiquarian Booksellers   CCVII - 380   2015   £30

Monnier, Henry   *Six Quartiers De Paris.*   Paris: Delpech, Que Voltaire No. 3 circa, 1827. Oblong 4to., 6 hand colored plates lithographed by Delpech after Monnier, light marginal spotting, otherwise fine, fresh coloring, lithographic front wrapper with pictorial vignette preserved, little browned, preserved in modern cloth portfolio.   Marlborough Rare Books   List 54 - 54   2015   £875

Montagu, Mary Wortley   *The Letters and Works of...*   London: Bohn, 1861. Third edition, 2 volumes, 8vo., portraits, covers worn, otherwise very good.   Second Life Books Inc.   189 - 170   2015 $150

Montalbano, William D.   *A Death in China.*   New York: Atheneum, 1984. First edition, fine in dust jacket with 1 inch closed tear to top of spine and light wear to extremities.   Buckingham Books   March 2015 - 28574   2015 $400

Montalbano, William D.   *Death in China.*   New York: Atheneum, 1984. First edition, very fine in dust jacket.   Mordida Books   March 2015 - 007476   2015 $500

Montalbano, William D.   *Powder Burn.*   New York: Atheneum, 1981. First edition, inscribed by Carl Hiaasen, some stains on covers, light spotting on page edges, otherwise fine in dust jacket.   Mordida Books   March 2015 - 008346   2015 $350

Montesquieu, Charles De Secondat, Baron De 1689-1755 *Lettres Persanes.* Cologne: Chez Pirre Marteau, 1744. Later edition, 12mo., contemporary full calf with gilt lettering and designs on spine which has five raised ribs, joints recently repaired, former owner's name (Ex Libris eg. Stephani Le Comu De Nailly), handsomely inscribed in faded ink beneath ornamental device in center of top edge gilt, handsome copy.   Athena Rare Books   15 - 35   2015 $550

Montesquieu, Charles De Secondat, Baron De 1689-1755 *Miscellaneous Pieces of M. De Secondat, Baron de Montesquieu.* London: printed by D. Wilson and T. Durham, 1759. First edition, 8vo., half title, but without final blank Y8, contemporary gilt ruled sprinkled calf with raised bands and gilt lines, spine generally rubbed and joints and head and foot of spine worn, still very good, sound contemporary binding.   John Drury Rare Books   2015 - 20945   2015 $612

Montesquieu, Charles De Secondat, Baron De 1689-1755 *Le Temple De Gnide, Suivi D; Arsace et Ismenie.* Paris: P. Didot l'Aine, 1796. One of 100 copies, 330 x 235mm., original? gray boards, flat spine, dark gray paper title label, two thirds of leaves unopened, engraved printer's device on titlepage and 7 fine and color printed engravings after Peyron by Chapuy and Lavallee, some finished by hand; couple of very small brown spots and just a hint of soiling as well as minor abrasions to covers, corners somewhat mashed (as expected), isolated trivial foxing to text, very fine, clean and bright internally , with vividly colored plates and in surprisingly sturdy and generally well preserved original temporary publisher's binding, from the oustanding library of American bibliophile Jacques Levy.   Phillip J. Pirages   66 - 60   2015 $7500

Monteverdi, Claudio *Tutte Le Opere Di Claudio Monteverdi Gia Maestro di Cappella. Della Serenissima Repubblica.* Asolo: G. Francesco Malipiero, 1926. Limited edition, no. 15 of 250, large 8vo., wrappers, 8 volumes, very good, slightly dusty, yapped edges slightly nicked, one has adhesive tape reinforcement at spine, 3 volumes have ownership signature of Maurice Jacobsen (1896-1976).   Any Amount of Books   March 2015 - C12757   2015   £350

Montgomery, John Warwick *Tillich's Philosophy of History the Bearing of His Historical Understanding on His Theological Commitments.* Deerfield: privately printed, 1966. First edition thus, printed with duplicator and stapled, few underlines in red ink by present owner, fine, very scarce, very good.   Baade Books of the West   2014 - 2015 $49

Montgomery, L. M. *Anne of Ingleside.* Toronto: McClelland & Stewart Ltd., 1939. First Canadian edition, 8vo., fine, color frontispiece by Charles John, this copy inscribed by author, rare thus.   Aleph-bet Books, Inc.   109 - 295   2015 $3500

Montgomery, L. M. *The Blue Castle.* Toronto: McLelland & Stewart, 1926. 8vo. grey cloth stamped in blue, castle illustration on half title, near fine in dust jacket with 1 inch piece off top of spine, otherwise nice, rare.   Aleph-bet Books, Inc.   109 - 296   2015 $3200

Montgomery, L. M. *Magic for Marigold.* Toronto: McLelland and Stewart, 1929. First Canadian edition (same year as US), 8vo., green cloth, pictorial paste-on, minor wear, near fine, illustrations by Edna Cooke Shoemaker, very scarce.   Aleph-bet Books, Inc.   109 - 297   2015 $275

Montgomery, L. M. *Magic for Marigold.* New York: Frederick Stokes, 1929. First edition, illustrations by Edna Cooke Shoemaker with color frontispiece, 8vo., green cloth, pictorial paste-on, fine in dust jacket, very scarce.   Aleph-Bet Books, Inc.   108 - 299   2015 $950

Montgomery, L. M. *Rilla of Ingleside.* New York: Frederick Stokes, 1921. First edition, 8vo., purple cloth, pictorial paste-on, slight foxing, else fine in dust jacket with 1 inch piece off top of spine, half inch off bottom of spine, illustrations by Maris Kirk with color frontispiece.   Aleph-Bet Books, Inc.   108 - 300   2015 $900

Montgomery, L. M. *The Spirit of Canada Dominion and Provinces 1939.* Queen Elizabeth Canadian Pacific Railway, 1939. Quarto, original color card covers bound in blue cloth with gilt title to front cover, 2 page color map, 1 printed color photo, 12 full page color and 12 color text illustrations by Charles Simpson, very good, enclosed is single sheet itinerary of the Royal visit.   Schooner Books Ltd.   110 - 137   2015 $45

Montifalchius, Petrus Iacobus *Petri Iacobi Montifalchi de cognominibus Deorum Opusculum.* Aedibus Hieronymi Francisci Chartulari Perugia, 1525. 91 leaves numbered recto only, small quarto, decorative woodcut border, woodcut initials in text, original full vellum lightly inked on spine, about three or four neat marginal annotations of 16th century date, two oval inkstamp marks, largely abraded from two page, few pages affected by mild tide mark in margins, otherwise very good, scarce.   Any Amount of Books   2015 - C14374   2015   £750

Montorguiel, G. *A L'Histoire!* Paris: Boivin, 1908. First edition, 4to., cloth backed pictorial boards, near fine, full page color illustrations by Job, pages hinged individually into book.   Aleph-bet Books, Inc.   109 - 237   2015 $800

Montufar Y Rivera Maestre, Lorenzo *Resena Historica de Centro-America.* Guatemala: tip. de El Progreso/La Union (v.6), 1878-1887. 6 volumes of 7, (7th volume not included here), 8vo., first five volumes uniformly bound in black morocco with red labels, marbled boards, volume 6 in quarter calf with gilt titles, overall very good or better, first five volumes very good plus, lightly rubbed, volume six spine sunned, extremities worn, few splits to joints. Kaaterskill Books   19 - 103   2015 $1000

Moody, Ralph *The Dry Divide.* New York: W. W. Norton, 1963. First edition, cloth, drawings, half page presentation to author's friend, Steve Taylor, fine in very good dust jacket. Baade Books of the West   2014 - 2015 $172

Moody, Ralph *The Fields of Home.* New York: W. W. Norton, 1953. First printing, drawings/illustrations, near fine in moderately worn dust jacket, uncommon now in first edition, near fine in very good dust jacket.   Baade Books of the West   2014 - 2015 $40

Moody, Ralph *Man of the Family.* New York: W. W. Norton, 1951. First edition, illustrations/drawings, cloth, presentation copy signed by Edna and Ralph Moody 10/25/51 for their friends the Hillaires, fine in chipped but good dust jacket, uncommon now in first edition.   Baade Books of the West   2014 - 2015 $172

Moon, Grace *Lost Indian Magic. A Mystery Story of the Red Man as He Lived Before the White Man Came.* New York: Stokes, 1918. First edition, pictorial cloth, color illustrations by Carl Moon, pencil signature of former owner, very good, rather scarce.   Baade Books of the West   2014 - 2015 $62

Moorcock, Michael *Breakfast in the Ruins: a Novel of Inhumanity.* London: New English Library, 1972. 8vo., original light blue and brown cloth lettered gilt at spine, signed presentation from author on dedication page, dedication for Angus Wilson, very good+ in very good dust jacket slightly rubbed at spine.   Any Amount of Books   2015 - C12515   2015   £225

Moore, Ben *Random Shots and Tales of Texas.* Seagraves: Pioneer, 1977. First edition, cloth, illustrations, index, inscribed and dated 1978 to friend of Moore's son, Elvin Roy Moore, who edited the book after his father's death, fine in lightly soiled dust jacket, latter has tape reinforcement around top of backstrip, scarce, fine in very good dust jacket.   Baade Books of the West   2014 - 2015 $54

Moore, Clement Clarke   1779-1863   *A Visit of St. Nicholas. (Night Before Christmas).* New York: McLoughlin Bros. n.d. circa, 1875. Printed on one side of paper, 4to., yellow pictorial wrappers, binding inconspicuously strengthened, some normal light cover soil, really nice and good+, 6 fabulous full page chromolithographs and black and white drawings by Thomas Nast, extremely scarce.   Aleph-Bet Books, Inc.   108 - 94   2015 $800

Moore, Clement Clarke   1779-1863   *A Visit from St. Nicholas. (Night Before Christmas).* London: F. Hildesheimer, n.d. circa, 1885. 12mo., cloth backed flexible pictorial covers, all edges gilt, rear corner repair and covers slightly darkened, else very good+, color lithographs by E. F. Manning, pictorial title, cloth illustrations on both covers. Aleph-bet Books, Inc.   109 - 91   2015 $600

Moore, Clement Clarke   1779-1863   *Denslow's Night Before Christmas.* New York: Dillingham, Sept., 1902. First edition, first issue, 4to., orange pictorial boards, usual edgewear and paper rubbing at joints, else clean and tight, very good++, full page color illustrations by Denslow. Aleph-Bet Books, Inc.   108 - 131   2015 $2000

Moore, Clement Clarke   1779-1863   *The Night Before Christmas.* New York: Holiday House, n.d., 1937. 16mo., cloth backed pictorial boards, fine, illustrations by Ilse Bischoff with charming color woodcuts.   Aleph-Bet Books, Inc.   108 - 95   2015 $250

Moore, Clement Clarke   1779-1863   *Visit from St. Nicholas. (Night Before Christmas).* New York: Privately printed in limited edition for friends of Aldus printers, 1945. 8vo., pictorial boards, corners toned and slight wear to spine ends, very good+, printed on fine paper, illustrations in color. Aleph-Bet Books, Inc.   108 - 85   2015 $100

Moore, Frank Frankfort *The Slaver of Zanzibar.* London: SPCK, 1889. First edition, frontispiece and plates by J. Nash, 16 page catalog, original red pictorial cloth, slightly dulled and rubbed, prize inscription "Lady Rothschild's Prize for regular attendance 1900-1901", nice copy.   Jarndyce Antiquarian Booksellers   CCXI - 204   2015   £45

Moore, Gloria *Margaret Sanger and the Birth Control Movement a Bibliography.* Metuchen: Scarecrow, 1986. First edition, 8vo., original cloth, fine.   Second Life Books Inc.   189 - 171   2015 $45

Moore, Jonas *A Mathematical Compendium or Useful Practices in Arithmetick, Geometry and Astronomy Geography and Navigation...* London: printed for J. Phillips, H. Rhodes and J. Tay, 1705. 12mo. 9 engraved plates, some on text leaves, (one folding, others free standing), contemporary panelled calf with raised bands, unlettered, slightly shaken, but fine, early signatures of William Dale and James Gilbert with old ms. notes, ink on endpapers and final blank leaf.   John Drury Rare Books   2015 - 24839 2015 $1049

Moore, Marianne   1887-1972   *Dress and Kindred Subjects.* New York: Ibex Press, 1965. First edition, one of 100 numbered copies, 8vo., original wrappers and illustration by Laurence Scott, although not called for signed by author, fine.   James S. Jaffe Rare Books   Modern American Poetry - 208   2015 $500

Moore, Marianne 1887-1972 *Eight Poems.* New York: Museum of Modern Art, 1962. First edition, number 98 of 195 copies signed by Marianne Moore and Robert Andrew Parker, 10 printed drawings colored by hand with original watercolors, boards in slipcase as new. Gemini Fine Books & Arts, Ltd.   Art Reference & Illustrated Books: First Editions - 2015 $800

Moore, Marianne 1887-1972 *A Face. A Poem.* Cummington: Cummington Press, 1949. First edition, one of about 2500 copies printed on Hand & Arrows paper, fine, folded in quarters, original unprinted gray-green wrappers, stitched as issued.   James S. Jaffe Rare Books   Modern American Poetry - 203   2015 $150

Moore, Marianne 1887-1972 *Letters from and to the Ford Motor Company.* New York: Pierpont Morgan Library, 1958. One of 550 copies, 8vo., engraving by Leonard Baskin, original cloth backed paper over boards, publisher's matching slipcase, very fine, preserved in custom cloth slipcase.   James S. Jaffe Rare Books   Modern American Poetry - 207   2015 $100

Moore, Marianne 1887-1972 *Marriage.* New York: Monroe Wheeler, 1923. First edition, small 8vo., original wrappers, with Glenway Wescott's essay "Miss Moore's Observations" printed as a four page leaflet, laid in as issued, spine slightly worn with small piece of wrapper detached from top of spine, otherwise remarkably fine, rare, preserved in cloth slipcase with leather label on spine.   James S. Jaffe Rare Books   Modern American Poetry - 299   2015 $1000

Moore, Marianne 1887-1972 *The Pangolin and Other Verse.* London: Brendin Publishing Co., 1936. First edition, limited to 120 copies printed at Curwen Press, 8o., illustrations by George Plank, original decorated paper boards with printed label on front cover, very fine, without dust jacket as issued.   James S. Jaffe Rare Books   Modern American Poetry - 201   2015 $2250

Moore, Marianne 1887-1972 *The Pangolin and Other Verse.* London: Brendin Pub. Co., 1936. First edition, 8vo., 25 pages, original Curwen patterned boards, illustrations, 120 copies printed, neat name, covers slightly bowed, faint shelfwear, very good.   Any Amount of Books   March 2015 - A89532   2015   £360

Moore, Marianne 1887-1972 *Poems.* London: Egoist Press, 1921. First edition, 8vo., original string tied decorated wrappers, printed paper label on front cover, few small faint spots on label, otherwise fine.   James S. Jaffe Rare Books   Modern American Poetry - 199   2015 $2000

Moore, Marianne 1887-1972 *Collected Poems.* New York: Macmillan, 1951. First American edition, 8vo., original cloth, dust jacket, fine, jacket spine slightly faded as usual, presentation copy inscribed by Moore to Winnefred Woods. James S. Jaffe Rare Books   Modern American Poetry - 204   2015 $1000

Moore, Marianne 1887-1972 *Collected Poems.* New York: Macmillan, 1952. 8vo., original cloth, dust jacket, inscribed by author in 1957 to Ida Hode, fine in dust jacket with spine slightly faded as usual.   James S. Jaffe Rare Books   Modern American Poetry - 205   2015 $750

Moore, Marianne 1887-1972 *Tell Me, Tell Me: Granite, Steel and Other Topics.* New York: Viking Press, 1966. First edition, octavo, 57 pages, original dust jacket, whimsically inscribed by Moore and signed and dated April 1967 for Brendan and Anne Gill.   Honey & Wax Booksellers   1 - 35   2015 $425

Moore, Marianne 1887-1972 *Tell Me, Tell Me.* New York: Viking, 1966. First edition, one of 7500 copies, 8vo., original cloth backed boards, dust jacket, mint, in custom cloth slipcase.   James S. Jaffe Rare Books   Modern American Poetry - 209   2015 $100

Moore, Marianne 1887-1972 *Tipoo's Tiger.* New York: Phoenix Book Shop, 1967. First edition, one of only 100 numbered copies signed by author (out of a total of 126 copies), with corrections in author's hand, thin oblong 12mo., original printed wrappers, very fine.   James S. Jaffe Rare Books   Modern American Poetry - 210   2015 $150

Moore, Robin *The Country Team.* New York: Crown, 1967. First edition, very good in like dust jacket, rubbed with moderate age wear, inscribed by author to film director Otto Preminger.   Ken Lopez, Bookseller   164 - 231   2015 $125

Moore, Roger *Bond on Bond. The Ultimate Book on 50 Years of Bond Movies.* Michael O'Mara, 2012. First edition, signed by author, special edition produced for Waterstones and limited to 1000 numbered copies, this no. 908, black cloth, titles and pictorial "James Bond" stamped in silver on front cover and spine, decorated front and rear endpapers, portraits.   Buckingham Books   March 2015 - 38102   2015 $275

Moore, Samuel *An Accurate System of Surveying... the Whole Performed Without the Use of Scale and Compasses, or a Table of Logarithms.* Litchfield: T. Collier, 1796. First edition, 8vo., contemporary unlettered sheep, spine rubbed, browned.   M & S Rare Books, Inc.   97 - 195   2015 $725

Moore, Suzanne *Zero: Cypher of Infinity.* Vashon Island: 2014. Artist's Book, one of a series of 50, first 5 of which are deluxe with additional hand lettered pages, each with variations, all on Arches text wove and BFK papers, with occasional Japanese paper interleaves, signed and dated by artist, page size 11 1/4 x 15 1/4 inches, 35 pages, bound by artist, custom dyed Cave paper, housed in custom made clamshell box, original painting, drawing, silkscreen, wood and metal type and polymer plate letterpress printing, embossing, gold foil and 23k gold leaf, all by Moore. Priscilla Juvelis - Rare Books   63 - 15   2015 $3500

Moorehead, Alan *Darwin and the Beagle.* New York: Harper & Row, 1969. First edition, 2nd impression, small quarto, profusely illus rated with color and black and white plates, portraits, maps, pictorial cloth, fine, pictorial dust jacket.   Argonaut Book Shop   Holiday Season 2014 - 214   2015 $75

Moorman, Mary *William Wordsworth: a biography.* Oxford: Oxford University Press, 1965. Half title, frontispiece, plates, original dark blue cloth, very good in slightly dusted dust jacket, Kathleen Tillotson's copy with inserted markers in text, cuttings of reviews and ALS form author. Jarndyce Antiquarian Booksellers   CCVII - 576   2015   £30

Mooso, Josiah *The Life and Travels of Josiah Mooso.* Telegram Print, 1888. First edition, cloth, frontispiece, minor professional reinforcement of spine ends and inner hinges, very good, exceptionally nice, rare.   Buckingham Books   March 2015 - 37945   2015 $1250

Mora, Jo *Trail Dust and Saddle Leather.* New York: Charles Scribners, 1946. First edition, wide octavo, pictorial cloth, 246 pages, illustrations, presentation from author inscribed, endpaper drawings by author tinted, very good copy, red tinted dust jacket is faded as typical, upper corner of jacket bumped, chipped at corners and head of spine, else good, uncommon with jacket and rare with Mora signature.   Baade Books of the West   2014 - 2015 $243

Moraes, Francisco De *Palmerin of England.* London: printed for Longman, Hurst, Rees and Orme, 1807. First edition translated and edited by Robert Southey, 4 volumes, 12mo., later tan half calf marbled paper boards, black leather labels, gilt rules and lettering, half titles present, small bookplate of Grenville Kane, edges slightly rubbed, fine set. The Brick Row Book Shop   Miscellany 67 - 85   2015 $500

The Morals of War; or, Ultra-Peace Principles Proved to be Unchristian and Unphilosophical. London: Simpkin Marshall and Co. and Ridgways, 1850. First edition, 8vo., 24 pages, recent plain wrappers, very good inscribed by author to editor of the Globe, scarce.   John Drury Rare Books   2015 - 19877   2015 $177

Morant, G. M. *A Bibliography of the Statistical and Other Writings of Karl Pearson.* Cambridge: Biometrika Office, University College, Cambridge University, 1939. 8vo., frontispiece, original gilt stamped rust cloth, fine.   Jeff Weber Rare Books   178 - 882   2015 $48

Morata, Olympia Fulvia *Opera Omnia quae hactenus Inveniri Potuerunt cum Eruditorum Testimoniis & Laudibus.* Basil: P. Perna, 1570. Third and final edition, 8vo., woodcut printer's device and elaborate woodcut border facing the beginning of text, contemporary green vellum with red fore-edges which are tooled in blind, 2 small old collection stamps on title and repaired at early time, in two blank places where an owner's name was removed, contemporary owner has supplied an index on back pastedown, later owner's inscription, some light toning of paper.   Second Life Books Inc.   189 - 172   2015 $6200

More Pleasant Surprises for Chicks of all Sizes. London: Nister, n.d., 1893. Folio, cloth backed pictorial boards, some edge rubbing and usual wear to tabs, else very good+, clean and bright copy, 8 fine chromolithographed tab-operated plates, when reader pulls tab, slatted illustration dissolves to reveal another picture below.   Aleph-bet Books, Inc.   109 - 307   2015 $1200

More, Hannah   1745-1833 *Sacred Dramas: Chiefly Intended for Young Persons.* Philadelphia: Edward Earle, 1818. 24mo., 172 pages, contemporary full mottled calf, wear to joints and corners, about very good, inscribed by Gen.. John M. McCalla, hero of the War of 1812 to wife Maria Frances, also inscribed in 1909 by Isabella McCalla, his granddaughter.   Between the Covers Rare Books, Inc. 187 - 181   2015 $250

More, Thomas   1478-1535 *De Optimo Republicae Statu, Deque Nova Insula Utopia...* Hanover: printed by Hans Jacob Henne for Peter Kopf, 1613. 12mo., woodcut printer's device on title, titlepage slightly soiled, occasional minor browning, contemporary ?English calf, double blind ruled borders on sides, blind ruled compartments on spine, spine slightly rubbed, lacking pastedowns, good.   Blackwell's Rare Books   B179 - 75   2015   £1200

More, Thomas   1478-1535 *A Frutefull Pleasaunt, and Wittie Worke of the Beste State of a Publique Weale & of the Newe Yle, Called Utopia.* Waltham St. Lawrence: Golden Cockerel Press, 1929. 173/500 copies, title printed in blue and black, woodcut decorations by Eric Gill, small folio, uncut in full navy (almost black) goatskin, full thickness blue and grey goatskin onlays applied to recessed panels edged in blue and grey acrylic, gold and blind tooling, spine lettered in gold doublures of grey goatskin, flyleaves of grey suede and Thai grass paper, edges airbrushed with acrylic by Glenn Bartley (signed inside back over and dated 2011), buckram box with felt lining, recessed navy goatskin label on spine lettered in gold, fine, most attractive binding. Blackwell's Rare Books   B179 - 132   2015   £1500

Moreau, Jacob Nicolas *Doutes Modestes sur la Richesse de l'Etat ou Lettre Ecrite a l'Auteur de ce systesme...* Paris: Bonaventure Buinart, n.d., 1763. First edition, 4to., 8 pages, occasional minor stains and rustmarks, else very good, uncut, unbound as issued.   John Drury Rare Books   2015 - 12747   2015 $177

Morfit, Campbell *Manures, Their Composition, Preparation and Action Upon Soils with the Quantities to be Applied Being a Field Companion to the Farmer.* Philadelphia: Lindsay & Blakiston, 1848. First edition, blindstamped hardbound (original paper over board) with gilt titles, 12mo., illustrations, tables, backstrip has some chips, light foxing, binding sound, good, very scarce.   Baade Books of the West   2014 - 2015 $95

Morgagni, Giovanni Battista 1682-1771 *The Seats and Causes of Diseases Investigated by Anatomy.* London: printed for A. Millar & T. Cadell and Johnson and Payne, 1769. 3 volumes, first edition in English, 3 volumes, contemporary marbled boards, modern half leather rebacking and corners, leather spine label, gilt lettered, cover edges with mild wear, scattered mild foxing, owner bookplate volume I, not ex-library copy, 4to., handsome set.   By the Book, L. C.   44 - 3   2015 $4500

Morgan, Clay *Shuttle-Mir.* Houston: NASA, 2001. First edition, wrappers, quarto, 208 pages plus CD ROM, fine, photos.   Beasley Books   2013 - 2015 $150

Morgan, Dale L. *Overland in 1846. Diaries and Letters of the California Oregon Trail.* Georgetown: Talisman Press, 1963. First edition, one of 1000 sets, folding map, large folding map in rear pocket, publisher's cloth backed decorated boards, fine set with pictorial dust jackets, somewhat darkened.   Argonaut Book Shop   Holiday Season 2014 - 215   2015 $250

Morgan, John Minter *Letters to a Clergyman on Institutions for Ameliorating the Condition of the People, Chiefly from Paris, in the Autumn of 1845 with an Account of Mettray and Petit Bourg.* London: Longman, Brown, Green and Longmans, 1851. 8vo, engraved lithographic view as frontispiece, 3 other lithographic plates, final ad leaf torn with loss of part of margin, frontispiece with little marginal soiling and creasing, endpapers foxed, rebound in cloth in 20th century by an amateur bookbinder, complete and reasonably good copy of a book that is scarce in any edition.   John Drury Rare Books   March 2015 - 24410   2015   £306

Morgan, Ruth Stemm *My Whirligig Fair Book.* Minneapolis: Gordon Volland Buzza, 1929. Folio, cloth backed pictorial boards, slight bit of cover fading, soil, else near fine, illustrations in color, 8 moveable pages operated with notched wheels with gear mechanisms so that turning one wheel causes another wheel to turn and 2 pieces move, rare.   Aleph-bet Books, Inc.   109 - 313   2015 $1250

Morgan, Sydney Owenson 1776-1859 *The Book of the Boudoir.* New York: Harper, 1829. First American edition?, 8vo., untrimmed and bound in linen backed boards, paper labels, rubbed along hinge of volume on, ex-library, some foxing and external wear, very good.   Second Life Books Inc.   189 - 174   2015 $325

Morgan, Sydney Owenson 1776-1859 *France in 1829-1830.* New York: Harper, 1830. First American edition, 8vo., untrimmed, bound in linen backed boards, paper labels, lacking some of the label on volume I, spine repaired, worn at extremities of spine, small hole to rear hinge volume 2 affecting margin of last few leaves, bookplate removed from pastedown, some light foxing and external wear, very good.   Second Life Books Inc.   189 - 175   2015 $325

Morgan, Sydney Owenson 1776-1859 *Woman and Her Master.* Paris: Baudry's European Library, 1840. First Continental edition, 8vo., contemporary three quarter calf with raised bands, spine gilt, contemporary former owner's signature "J. Colley", very good, clean, scarce.   Second Life Books Inc.   189 - 176   2015 $450

Morgan, Thomas Hunt *The Development of the Frog's Eggs.* New York: Macmillan, 1897. First edition, 8vo., original green cloth with gilt lettered spine, near fine, mild wear to spine tips, signed by author.   By the Book, L. C. Special List 10 - 83   2015 $2500

Morgan, William *Facts Addressed to the Serious Attention of the People of Great Britain Respecting the Expence of the War, and State of the National Debt.* London: J. Debrett and T. Cadell Jun. and W. Davies, 1796. First edition, 8vo., including half title and a final leaf of ads, bound in new marbled boards, lettered on upper cover, very good.   John Drury Rare Books   2015 - 21483   2015 $168

Morison, Stanley 1889-1957 *L'Art De L'Imprimeur, 250 Reproductions des Plus Beaux Specimens De La Typographie Depuis 1500 Jusqu'a 1900.* Paris: Dorbon-Aine, 1925. First French edition, 4to., cloth, dust jacket, 10 pages followed by plates, jacket has few spots on front cover and small chip out of bottom of spine.   Oak Knoll Books   306 - 56   2015 $125

Morison, Stanley 1889-1957 *The Fleuron a Journal of Typography.* London: at the Office of the Fleuron, 1923. 1924. 1924. 1925. 1926. 1928. 1930, Various limitations, but all about 1000 copies, 7 volumes, complete, 4to., cloth backed boards (first two volumes), cloth on others, dust jacket on 3 volumes, tipped-in plates and other illustrations, original dust jackets present on volumes one, three and seven (pieces missing from each of the jackets), bookplates in volume 1, faded spine in volume 2, bookplates in volume 3, faded spine in volume 4 and with prospectus to this volume loosely inserted, bookplate on half title in volume 5, rubbed with some wear along back hinge in volume 6 and with signature of Alfred Fairbank, original prospectus in volume 7.   Oak Knoll Books   306 - 55   2015 $2000

Morison, Stanley 1889-1957 *Fleuron, a Journal of Typography.* Westport: Greenwood Reprint Corporation, 1979. Reprint of first edition, cloth, 7 volumes bound as 5, illustrations, some foxing of edges and tops.   Oak Knoll Books   306 - 54   2015 $250

Morison, Stanley 1889-1957 *John Fell, the University Press and the "Fell" Types the Punches and Matrices Designed for Printing in the Greek, Latin and English and Oriental Lanuages Bequeathed in 1686 to the University of Oxford by John Fell.* Oxford: Clarendon Press, 1967. First edition, limited to 1000 copies, printed on rag paper, minor soiling and chipping of jacket, lengthy clipped news review of book from TLS loosely inserted.   Oak Knoll Books   306 - 194   2015 $450

Morison, Stanley 1889-1957 *The Typographic Book 1450-1935.* Chicago: University of Chicago Press, 1963. First US edition, small folio, cloth, dust jacket, slipcase, 377 plates, well perserved.   Oak Knoll Books   306 - 57   2015 $200

Morland, Nigel *The Case without a Clue.* New York: Farrar & Rinehart, 1938. First edition, fine in dust jacket with light wear to spine ends.   Buckingham Books   March 2015 - 18995   2015 $275

Morland, Nigel *A Rope for the Hanging.* New York: Farrar & Rinehart, 1939. First US edition, tiny bump to bottom edge of front panel of cloth, else near fine in fine dust jacket.   Buckingham Books   March 2015 - 27215   2015 $300

Morley, Christopher 1890-1957 *Mince Pie.* New York: George H. Doran, 1919. First edition, scarce first state with 'of' instead of 'on' on page vii, excellent inscription by author for Hank and Margaret Harris, very good (some general age wear, tight, clean text).   Stephen Lupack   March 2015 - 2015 $75

Morley, Christopher 1890-1957 *Where the Blue Begins.* London & New York: William Heinemann & Doubleday Page, 1922. 1925. Limited to 100 numbered copies (for America) signed by Rackham and Morley, 4to., cloth spine, patterned metallic paper boards, fine, publisher's slipcase (repaired and with wear), pictorial limitation label, that has the number inked on that matches number on limitation page, 4 beautiful and unusual color plates plus 16 fanciful line drawings in addition to a pictorial titlepage and pictorial endpapers, scarce, especially in original slipcase.   Alephbet Books, Inc.   109 - 405   2015 $2500

Morley, John *The Struggle for National Education.* London: Chapman & Hall, 1873. First edition in bookform, 8vo., half title, early 20th century maroon crushed half morocco, spine gilt with raised bands, top edge gilt, silk maker, by Hatchards, fine, from the library of Sir Weetman Dickinson Pearson, first Viscount Cowdray (1856-1927) with his armorial bookplate.   John Drury Rare Books   2015 - 17698   2015 $151

Morley, John Parker, 1st Earl of *Some Account of Lord Boringdon's Accident on 21st July 1817 and Its Consequences.* London: J. M'Creery printer Black Horse Court, n.d. but, 1818. 4to., 2 engraved plates, one of them rather foxed, contemporary probably original boards, neatly rebacked in cloth, very good, large copy with ALS from Earl of Morley tipped in, rare.   John Drury Rare Books   2015 - 23064   2015 $656

Mornington, William Pole Tylney Long Wellesley, 4th Earl of *Two letters to the Right Hon. Earl Eldon, Lord Chancellor &c &c with official and Other documents.* London: John Miller, 1827. First edition, uncommon, 8vo., wanting half title, recently well bound in linen backed marbled boards, lettered, very good, uncommon.   John Drury Rare Books   March 2015 - 22876   2015   £266

Moro, Cesar *Amour a Mort.* New York: TVRT Press, 1973. First edition, wrappers, fine.   Beasley Books   2013 - 2015 $45

Morpeth, Howard George, Viscount *Motion for a New Writ for the Borough of St. Mawes, in the Room of Francis Horner, Esq. Deceased on Monday, March 3 1817.* London: printed for Ridgways, 1817. First edition, 8vo., modern wrappers with printed label on upper cover, very good, scarce.   John Drury Rare Books   March 2015 - 24563   2015 $221

Morrell, David *Last Reveille.* New York: M. Evans, 1977. First edition, fine in fine dust jacket but for inked price change on jacket flap.   Beasley Books   2013 - 2015 $40

Morrell, John Daniel *An Historical and Critical View of the Speculative Philosophy of Europe in the Nineteenth Century.* London: William Pickering, 1846. First edition, 2 volumes, 8vo., original publisher's blindstamped cloth, short split at foot of volume II, spines lettered gilt, just little faded, overall fine, sound and uncut.   John Drury Rare Books   March 2015 - 25527   2015 $221

Morrell, John Daniel *On the Philosophical tendencies of the Age; Being Four Lectures Delivered at Edinburgh and Glasgow in Jan. 1848.* London and Edinburgh: John Johnstone, 1848. First edition, final ad leaf, original blindstamped cloth, just little faded, spine lettered gilt, fine. John Drury Rare Books   2015 - 25528   2015 $133

Morris, Alice Talwin *My Book About New Zealand.* London: Glasgow: Bombay: Blackie and Son, n.d. circa, 1912. 4to., cloth backed boards, pictorial paste-on, edges rubbed, else very good+, 4 full page color illustrations, cover, 1 double page color spread, 4 full page pen and inks and 9 partial page pen and inks, one 2-color picture by Charles Robinson.   Aleph-bet Books, Inc.   109 - 412   2015 $1200

Morris, Charles *Festival.* New York: George Braziller, 1966. First edition, fine in spine faded dust jacket, otherwise jacket very good or better, inscribed by author to noted philosopher and author Walter Kaufmann.   Between the Covers Rare Books, Inc.   187 - 182   2015 $75

Morris, Corbyn *A Letter from a By-stander to a member of Parliament....* London: J. Roberts i.e., 1742. (1741). First edition, 18vo., half title and final blank, recently bound in oversize cloth lettered gilt, good copy.   John Drury Rare Books   March 2015 - 8320   2015 $221

Morris, Edward *The History of the Temperance and Teetotal Societies in Glasgow from their Origin to the present Time...* Glasgow: City of Glasgow United Total Abstinence Association, 1855. First edition, 8vo., Hope Trust bookplate, original maroon cloth embossed in blind, title in gilt on upper cover, neatly rebacked, very good. John Drury Rare Books   March 2015 - 21060   2015 $221

Morris, Ernest *El Buckaroo.* Flagstaff: privately published, 1995. Limited edition, one of 100 numbered and signed copies, but this is not numbered and signed, nor does it have the CE items (original pen & ink, signed poster, slipcase), collector's edition, quarto, full gilt stamped leather, all edges gilt, photos, lithos, very very minor blemishes in gilt, fine.   Baade Books of the West   2014 - 2015 $304

Morris, Francis Orpen 1810-1893 *A History of English Birds.* London: John C. Nimmo, 1903. Fifth edition, 6 volumes, small 4to., cloth, gilt illustration stamped on front cover, top edge cut, other edges uncut, over 400 hand colored plates with frontispiece in each volume, cover scuffed and rubbed, volume 2 with cracked hinges.   Oak Knoll Books   306 - 283   2015 $250

Morris, Henry *Guilford & Green.* North Hills: Bird & Bull Press, 1970. Limited to 210 numbered copies, 8vo., quarter morocco over patterned paper covered boards, this copy lacks outer paper wrapper with pocket, containing a paper specimen that has to be used for cover of the book but found unsuitable, presentation from Morris dated 1970. Oak Knoll Books   306 - 136   2015 $325

Morris, Henry *Our Weekend With Oak Knoll, October 3-5 2008.* Newtown: Bird & Bull Press, 2008. Limited to 120 copies, printed on all cotton mouldmade Somerset Book paper in a variety of handset foundry type, 8vo., special woven cloth with paper cover label containing woodcut by Wesley Bates.   Oak Knoll Books   306 - 137   2015 $120

Morris, Lerona Rosamond *Oklahoma Land of Opportunity.* Guthrie: 1934. First edition, folio, gilt stamped cloth, 103 pages, illustrations, waterstaining to margins of text, good reading copy only, but very scarce, fair.   Baade Books of the West   2014 - 2015 $66

Morris, Mary *Vanishing Animals and Other Stories.* Boston: David R. Godine, 1979. First edition, fine in very good, spine sunned dust jacket, inscribed by author for Page, additionally signed on titlepage.   Between the Covers Rare Books, Inc.   187 - 183   2015 $125

Morris, R. A. V. *The Lyttleton Case. A Story of a Crime.* Detective Story Club Ltd. for William Collins Sons & Co. Ltd., n.d., 1922. First edition, 16mo., decorated cloth, 248 pages plus 4 pages of ads, very good, tight in dust jacket with light professional restoration to spine ends and to extremities.   Buckingham Books   March 2015 - 33388   2015 $400

Morris, William 1834-1896 *A Tale of the House of the Wolfings and all the Kindreds of the Mark Written in Prose and in Verse by William Morris.* London: Longmans, Green and Co., 1901. 4to., quarter cloth, paper covered boards, paper spine label, later cardboard slipcase, spine covering shows wear through in places, spine label chipped, boards rubbed and scuffed, especially at edges and soiled, endpapers tanned.   Oak Knoll Books   306 - 284   2015 $100

Morris, Wright *What a Way to Go.* New York: Atheneum, 1962. First edition, near fine in modestly worn, very good dust jacket with chips and small tears, African American author, Albert Murray's copy with his ownership signature. Between the Covers Rare Books, Inc.   187 - 184   2015 $100

Morrison, Arthur *Chronicles of Martin Hewitt.* New York: D. Appleton, 1896. First American edition, small label on front pastedown, page edges slightly darkened, otherwise fine in decorated blue cloth covered boards with some slight fading.   Mordida Books   March 2015 - 012253   2015 $150

Morrison, Arthur *The Green Diamond.* L. C. Page & Co., 1904. First US edition, illustrations by F. H. Townsend, fine in pictorial tan cloth with titles and decorations on front cover and spine. Buckingham Books   March 2015 - 38080   2015 $350

Morrison, Toni *Beloved.* New York: Knopf, 1987. First edition, 8vo., author's signature on half title, nice in dust jacket (little yellowed). Second Life Books Inc.   190 - 167   2015 $425

Morrison, Toni *The Bluest Eye.* London: Chatto & Windus, 1979. First British edition, signed by author, 8vo., fine in fine, striking dust jacket. By the Book, L. C. Special List 10 - 31   2015 $850

Morrison, Toni *The Dancing Mind.* New York: Alfred A. Knopf, 2003. Seventh printing, small 8vo., signed by author, as new in like dust jacket. By the Book, L. C. Special List 10 - 29   2015 $50

Morrison, Toni *Jazz.* Franklin Center: Franklin Library, 1992. Limited edition, 8vo., publisher's prospectus laid in, fine, full leather with raised bands spine, gilt lettering and decorationt to spine, gilt decoration to covers, all edges gilt marbled endpapers, silk ribbon bookmark. By the Book, L. C.   Special List 10 - 30   2015 $150

Morrison, Toni *Lecture and Speech of Acceptance Upon the Award of the Nobel Prize for Literature Delivered in Stockholm on the Seventh of December Nineteen Hundred and Ninety Three.* New York: Knopf, 1994. First edition, small 8vo., red cloth, stamped gilt with applied paper label in black, gilt and white, about as new. Second Life Books Inc.   190 - 168   2015 $300

Morrison, Toni *Love.* New York: Knopf, 2003. First edition, small 4to., hardcover, signed by author, fine in fine dust jacket. Beasley Books   2013 - 2015 $40

Morrison, Toni *Song of Solomon.* New York: Knopf, 1977. Third printing, 8vo., author's presentation on flyleaf, small stain on flyleaf, black cloth, very good, tight in somewhat chipped and faded dust jacket. Second Life Books Inc.   190 - 169   2015 $300

Morrison, Toni *Sula.* New York: Knopf, 1976. Fifth printing, 8vo., author's presentation on flyleaf, orange cloth stamped in gilt, nice in little worn dust jacket. Second Life Books Inc.   190 - 170   2015 $175

Morrison, Toni *Nobel Lecture 7 December 1993.* Fyfield: Oak Tree Fine Press, 2009. 571/150 copies (from an edition of 176 copies) signed by author, printed on Zerkall mould made paper, titlepage printed in black and purple with wood engraved portrait, wood engraved headpiece by same, tall 8vo., original quarter pink cloth with patterned cloth sides, backstrip lettered in gilt, edges untrimmed, slipcase, fine. Blackwell's Rare Books   B179 - 195   2015   £185

Morrow, Bradford *A Bibliography of the Writings of Wyndham Lewis / Crossing the Frontier.* Santa Barbara: Black Sparrow Press, 1978. First edition, "Y" of 26 lettered copies beyond an edition of 200 handbound copies, fine in fine acetate dust jacket, small 4to., housed in handsome slipcase, printed label, also near fine. Beasley Books 2013 - 2015 $125

Morrow, Bradford *The Forgers.* Mysterious Bookshop, 2014. First edition, limited to 60 numbered copies signed by author, very fine in quarter leather and marbled boards, transparent dust jacket. Buckingham Books   March 2015 - 37819   2015 $175

Morrow, Elizabeth *Beast, Bird and Fish.* New York: Alfred A. Knopf, 1933. Stated first edition, 4to., pictorial cloth, some cover soil, else very good+, no dust jacket, full page color illustrations by Rene D'Harnoncourt, this copy inscribed by Morrow, very scarce. Aleph-Bet Books, Inc. 108 - 301   2015 $400

Morrow, Elizabeth *The Painted Pig.* New York: Knopf, 1930. First edition, 4to., boards, fine in soiled and chipped dust jacket, illustrated in bold color by Rene D'Harnoncourt. Aleph-Bet Books, Inc.   108 - 302   2015 $300

Morse, Charles Fessenden *A Sketch of My Life.* Cambridge: 1927. First edition, cloth, 91 pages, portraits, signed and dated by Hugh Whitney Morse, top edge gilt, cover extremities lightly worn, near very good. Baade Books of the West   2014 - 2015 $197

Morse, William Inglis *Acadiensia Nova (1598-1779).* London: Bernard Quaritch, 1935. Limited to 375 numbered copies, 2 volumes, hardcovers, green buckram, gilt titles to spines with dust jackets, half title, 8vo., maps, charts and illustrations, both volumes very good. Schooner Books Ltd.   110 - 5   2015 $125

Morse, William Inglis *The Land of the New Adventure (The Georgian Era in Nova Scotia).* London: Bernard Quaritch, 1932. Limited to 350 numbered copies, 8vo., green cloth, gilt to spine, dust jacket, many pages of collotype plates in rear, many maps and illustrations, including folding map in rear pocket, frontispiece is folding map, very good to fine. Schooner Books Ltd.   110 - 101   2015 $55

Morse, William Inglis *Pierre Du Gua Sieur de Monts Records: Colonial and "Saintongeois".* London: Bernard Quaritch Ltd., 1939. limited edition 225, this #124, 8vo., frontispiece, map and 15 illustrations and 2 coats of arms plus three genealogical charts, light blue cloth, gilt to spine, very good.   Schooner Books Ltd.   110 - 4   2015 $55

Mortimer, John *Rumpole and the Angel of Death.* Viking, 1995. First edition, signed by author, fine in dust jacket. Buckingham Books   March 2015 - 38348   2015 $175

Mortimer, John *The Whole Art of Husbandry or the Way of Managing the Improving of Land.* London: printed by J. H. for H. Mortlock at the Phoenix and J. Robinson at the Golden Lion in St. Paul's Church Yard, 1707. First edition, 8vo. several woodcut text figures, contemporary panelled calf with gilt spine label, little wear to extremities and joints but very good in sound, original binding, signature and armorial bookplate of Ambrose Holbech, 18th century signature of Mr. Goodwyn, armorial bookplate 19th century of Archibald Philip (Primrose) Earl of Rosebery, uncommon. John Drury Rare Books   2015 - 25543   2015 $1311

Morton, George Highfield *The History of Paper Hangings with Review of Other Modes of Mural Decoration, Read before the Architectural and Archaeological Society of Liverpool, Feb. the 10th 1875.* Liverpool: published by G. H. Morton 122, London Road, printed at the Courier Works, Victoria Street, Liverpool, 1875. First edition, 8vo., original limp purple cloth, upper cover with title in gilt.   Marlborough Rare Books   List 54 - 55   2015   £150

Morton, Penny *Jane's Warm Welcome.* Hereford: The Academy Club, 1998. First (only?) edition, illustrations by Ashley Bristow, octavo, 108 pages, stapled illustrated wrappers, fine.   Between the Covers Rare Books   196 - 72   2015 $150

Morton, Sarah Wentworth *My Mind and Its Thoughts in Sketches, Fragments and Essays.* Boston: Wells and Lilly, 1823. First edition, 8vo., contemporary calf, red morocco label, gilt decorations and lettering, five page list of subscribers at end, uncommon, front hinge repaired, very good. The Brick Row Book Shop   Miscellany 67 - 70   2015 $650

Morton, Thomas *The Necessity of Christian Subjection Demonstrated and Proved by the Doctrine of Christ and the Apostles...* Oxford, i.e. London: printed in the yeere, 1643. 4to., modern boards, lettered, very good.   John Drury Rare Books   March 2015 - 24600   2015   £266

Morton, Thomas *The New English Canaan.* Boston: Prince Society, 1883. Reprint, one of 250 copies, three quarter leather over blue gray cloth, original wrappers bound in, near fine, handsomely bound copy for little sunning to spine, 8vo.   Beasley Books   2013 - 2015 $300

Mosel, Arlene *The Funny Little Woman retold by.* New York: E. P. Dutton, 1972. Stated first edition, 9 3/4 x 9 1/4 inches, cloth, fine in dust jacket, jacket very good with seal, (frayed at spine ends and corners), illustrations by Blair Lent, this copy inscribed by Lent.   Aleph-Bet Books, Inc. 108 - 271   2015 $400

Moses, Robert *Public Works: a Dangerous Trade.* New York: McGraw Hill, 1970. First edition, presumably deluxe binding of blue leatherette stamped gilt and red with four gilt devices on front board, marbled endpapers, publisher's unprinted acetate dust jacket, fine in very good+ acetate that show bit of rubbing and few tiny nicks, this copy inscribed to William Benton (10770-1973), large 8vo.   Beasley Books 2013 - 2015 $400

Mosley, Charles *Burke's Peerage: Baronetage & Knightage. Clan Chiefs. Scottish Feudal Barons.* Wilmington: 2003. First edition, 3 volumes, 4to., original red cloth lettered gilt on spine and cover and excellent printed slipcase, illustrated with family shields and crests.   Any Amount of Books   2015 - A89848   2015   £180

Mosley, Walter *Devil in a Blue Dress.* New York: W. W. Norton, 1990. First edition, signed by author, fine in price clipped, otherwise fine dust jacket with new publisher's price sticker, author's first book.   Between the Covers Rare Books   197 - 31   2015 $200

Mosley, Walter *A Red Death.* New York: W. W. Norton, 1991. First edition, fine in first issue dust jacket with price of $18.95, signed by author.   Between the Covers Rare Books   197 - 32   2015 $100

Mosley, Walter *White Butterfly.* New York: W. W. Norton, 1992. First edition, fine in fine dust jacket, signed by author, scarce.   Between the Covers Rare Books   197 - 33   2015 $125

Moss, Alfred *Pyramids for Gymnastic Displays and Competitions.* Athletic Publications, circa, 1910. Half title, illustrations, original brown illustrated printed paper wrappers, rebacked & with recent brown paper back wrapper, front wrapper slightly marked, 79 pages.   Jarndyce Antiquarian Booksellers   CCXI - 206   2015   £45

Moss, Robert F. *The Films of Carol Reed.* London: Macmillan, 1987. First UK edition, 8vo., 8 plates, original grey cloth, lettered gilt at spine, near fine in like dust jacket, faint creasing at edges, otherwise clean and bright, excellent condition.   Any Amount of Books   2015 - C14011   2015   £280

Moss, Stanley *Skull of Adam.* New York: Horizon, 1979. First edition, hardcover issue, fine in lightly rubbed, near fine dust jacket, warmly inscribed by author to fellow poet, William Meredith.   Between the Covers Rare Books, Inc. 187 - 185   2015 $75

Mossbauer, Rudlof Ludwig *Neutron Beam Research at the High Flux Reactor of the Institute max Von Laue-Paul Langevin.* N.P.: Europhyisics News, 1974. Offprint Volume 5 No. 6 June 1974, near fine. By the Book, L. C. Special List 10 - 61   2015 $90

Mota, Miranda *Contemporary International Ex-Libris Artists.* Portugal: privately printed, 2014. Limited to 150 numbered copies, 4to., illustrated paper covered boards, color illustrations. Oak Knoll Books   306 - 254   2015 $125

Mother Goose *Animated Mother Goose.* New York: Grosset & Dunlap, 1942. Oblong 4to., spiral backed pictorial boards, fine in dust jacket (slightly soiled), illustrations in color by Julian Wehr, including 4 fabulous tab operated moveable plates, great copy, scarce. Aleph-Bet Books, Inc.   108 - 309   2015 $325

Mother Goose *The Children's Mother Goose.* Chicago: Reilly & Lee, 1921. First edition, 4to., cloth, pictorial paste-on, fine, illustrations by William Donahey with over 100 illustrations, including pictorial endpapers, 12 great bright color plates, nice. Aleph-bet Books, Inc.   109 - 136   2015 $750

Mother Goose *The Indestructible Mother Goose.* Philadelphia: J. B. Lippincott & Co., 1881. Later printing, octavo, illustrated flexible linen, modest soiling, light foxing to extremities, most pronounced at base of spine, couple of tiny tears, sound and nice, very good, printed on flexible coated fabric, scarce. Between the Covers Rare Books   196 - 159   2015 $350

Mother Goose *Mother Goose.* New York: Century Co., 1913. First U.S. edition, thick 4to., cloth, pictorial paste-on, fine in dust jacket with piece off upper front corner, illustrations by Arthur Rackham with cover plate, 12 color plates, color titlepage and over 50 marvelous detailed black and whites in text, beautiful copy rarely found with dust jacket. Aleph-bet Books, Inc.   109 - 399   2015 $1100

Mother Goose *Mother Goose Collection of Six Limited Edition Prints.* New York: Serigrafia, 1990. Limited to 300 portfolios, this no. 70 with all 6 original prints pencil signed by artist, wonderful collections, each print is on museum quality Rives BFK Paper and measures 26.5 x 20.5, included is a single sheet of letterpress descriptive information concerning artists, prints in original paper covered printed portfolio which is mildly worn, portfolio measures 28.2 x 2.18 inches, each print in protective glassine folder and title and artist printed on front leaf of each folder, inside front of clamshell identifies each work and serves as the colophon. By the Book, L. C.   44 - 79   2015 $2000

Mother Goose *Old Mother Hubbard.* New York: Hurst, 1902. 4to., pictorial cloth, faint pink area on cover, else very good+, illustrations by Harry Otis Kennedy. Aleph-bet Books, Inc.   109 - 301   2015 $600

Mottram, Eric *Shelter Island the Remaining World.* London: Turret Books, 1971. First edition, one of 300 copies, 100 were intended to be numbered and signed by author, title and cover illustrations by Richard Moseley, quarto, corners slightly bumped, else fine in fine illustrated dust jacket, this copy not numbered but warmly inscribed by author to Gerard Malanga, Jan. 1972, additionally with Malanga's ownership signature. Between the Covers Rare Books, Inc.   187 - 186   2015 $125

Motyl, Alexander *Encyclopedia of Nationalism: Fundamental Themes.* San Diego: Academic Press, 2001. First edition, 2 volumes, ex-Foreign and Commonwealth Office Library with small label and two small stamps, otherwise fine, hardback. Any Amount of Books   2015 - A60713   2015   £175

Moulthrop, Samuel P. *Iroquois.* Rochester: Ernest Hart, 1901. First edition, pictorial cloth, 155 pages, drawings, map, hinges carefully reglued, sound, very scarce, very good. Baade Books of the West   2014 - 2015 $250

Moulton, Forest Ray *An Introduction to Celestial Mechanics.* New York: Macmillan, 1935. 8vo., xvi, 437 pages, figures, index, maroon blind and gilt stamped cloth, minor wear to spine ends, ink ownership signature of Harold Levine, very good. Jeff Weber Rare Books   178 - 808   2015 $60

Moulton, Gary F. *Atlas of the Lewis and Clark Expedition.* Lincoln and London: University of Nebraska, 1983. First edition, folio, 126 facsimile maps, dark blue cloth decorated in light blue and lettered gilt on spine and front cover, very fine, as new in original shipping box. Argonaut Book Shop Holiday Season 2014 - 165   2015 $2250

Moulton, Gary F. *Atlas of the Lewis & Clark Expedition.* Lincoln: University of Nebraska Press, 1983. First edition, folio, blue cloth, gilt stamped, 126 map plates, moderate fading and few minor spots and superficial scuffs on front cover, back cover has wide hand of band of fade running vertically 4 3/4" in from spine, and spine likewise moderately faded, minor scuffs to covers, internally fine, good copy. Baade Books of the West   2014 - 2015 $361

Mountford, Charles P. *Nomads of the Australian Desert.* Adelaide: Rigby, 1976. First edition, large 8vo., 628 page, original burgundy cloth lettered gilt on spine, copiously illustrated in black and white, fine in dust jacket. Any Amount of Books March 2015 - C2418   2015   £350

Mountford, Charles P. *The Tiwi: their Art Myth and Ceremony.* London: Phoenix House, 1958. First edition, large 8vo., original orange cloth lettered gilt on spine, color frontispiece and one other color plates including a further 64 plates and map, very good. Any Amount of Books 2015 - C2573   2015   £325

Mourey, Gabriel *Fetes Foraines De Paris.* Paris: Editions Droin-Labastie, 1947. No. 67 of 250 copies, folio, unbound signatures laid into brightly decorated wrappers, with color lithographs by Grau Sala, fine in wrappers. Beasley Books 2013 - 2015 $350

Mourning Dove, Pseud. *Co-Ge-We-A. the Half-Blood a Depiction of the Great Montana Cattle Range...* Boston: Four Seas Co., 1927. First edition, 8vo., frontispiece, red cloth, near fine. Second Life Books Inc. 189 - 127 2015 $900

Moxley, F. Wright *The Glassy Pond.* New York: Coward McCann, 1934. First edition, fine, without dust jacket. Mordida Books March 2015 - 010755 2015 $100

Moxon, Charles *The Grainer's Guide.* Edinburgh: 1842. First edition, folio, 21 mounted plates (of 22), including 16 hand grained sheets, one with adhering to blank divider due to bitumen, 3 lithograph sheets of graining patterns, one sheet with 16 samples of 'Grounds for Wood" and one plate with 3 smaller samples of grinning, original green ribbed cloth, upper cover with original, printed label, printed book label of Purdie, Bonnar and Carfrae decorators, 77 George street Edinburgh, rare. Marlborough Rare Books List 54 - 57 2015 £3250

Moynahan, J. M. *The Ace Powell Book.* J. M. Moynahan and Ace Powell Galleries, 1974. First edition, quarto, cloth, 184 pages, illustrations, dust jacket good with several small chips to edges and 3 inch closed tear, externally taped to front cover, original 2 x 4.5 signed drawing on front endpaper. Buckingham Books March 2015 - 28065 2015 $225

Moynahan, J. M. *The Fred Oldfield Book. The Man and His Art.* Cheney: Art of the Northwest, 1981. First edition, 4to., 192 pages, black and white plates, endpaper maps, front blank page has very nice, large pen and ink sketch by Oldfield, artist's signature and date and an additional presentation to Ethel with second signature and date, some moderate warping to covers, good+ thus in dust jacket with some light soiling and few minor spots on back panel, good+ in very good+ dust jacket. Baade Books of the West 2014 - 2015 $49

Mozart, Wolfgang Amaedus *Don Juan: a Grand Opera in Two Acts.* London: printed by W. Winchester and Son in the strand and sold at the Opera House...., 1817. Second edition in English, 8vo., Italian on verso of each leaf and English on facing recto, titlepage mounted, small blank corner of second leaf, later 19th century attractive straight grained red morocco, gilt spine, gilt edges, very good. Marlborough Rare Books List 53 - 29 2015 £1500

Muhyiddin Ibn Arabi Society *Journal of the Muhyiddin Ibn Arabi Society 1982-2006.* Oxford: Muhyiddin Ibn 'Arabi Society, 1982. First edition, 40 issues, 8vo., wrappers, from Volume I 1982 to Volume 40 2006, missing volume 21, 1996/97, circa 4000 pages in all, very good. Any Amount of Books 2015 - A47864 2015 £250

Muir, Augustus *The Shadow on the Left.* Indianapolis: Bobbs Merrill, 1928. First American edition, very good in dust jacket with date on front panel. Mordida Books March 2015 - 001658 2015 $85

Muir, John 1838-1914 *The Mountains of Colorado.* New York: 1911. Ninth printing, illustrations, maps, original decorated cloth, some wear visible to top and bottom of spine else handsome, near fine. Dumont Maps and Books of the West 130 - 43 2015 $175

Muir, John 1838-1914 *My First Summer in the Sierra.* Boston: 1911. First edition, original illustrated boards, extremities rubbed, spine faded with some insect damage, internally clean and very good. Dumont Maps & Books of the West 131 - 64 2015 $125

Muir, Percy H. *A. F. Johnson, Selected Essays on Books and Printing.* Amsterdam: Van Gendt & Co., 1970. First edition, thick 4to. cloth, dust jacket, facsimiles, two folding maps, 4 page prospectus loosely inserted, from the Frederic Melcher collection with his bookplate and spot on spine where label was removed. Oak Knoll Books 306 - 190 2015 $145

Muldrow, H. L. *Letter from the Acting Secretary of the Interior Transmitting in Pursuance of Law Report of the Surveyor-General of New Mexico on the Land Claim Called Salvador Gonzales No. 82.* Washington: GPO, 1886. 8vo., hard cover binder, titles stamped in gold gilt on front cover, maps. Buckingham Books March 2015 - 35796 2015 $350

Muller-Brockmann, Josef *Grid Systems in Graphic Design, A Visual Communication Manual for Graphic Designers, Typographers and Three Dimensional Designers.* New York: Hastings House, 1981. First US edition, 4to., cloth, dust jacket, head of spine bumped, scarce. Oak Knoll Books 306 - 33 2015 $195

Muller, C. *An Account of the Sacrifices Made, and the Sufferings Experienced by the Valiant Inhabitants of the Tyrol and Vorarlberg During the Last and Preceding Wars...* London: printed by R. Juigne, 1810. First edition, apparently rare, old dampstain rubbing through lower margins (never near text), recent marbled boards lettered on spine, apparently rare, good copy. John Drury Rare Books March 2015 - 24553 2015 £306

Muller, Fritz *Facts and Arguments for Darwin; with Additions by the Author.* London: John Murray, 1869. First edition, 8vo., original dark green cloth, lettered gilt at spine, ads at rear dated Sept. 1868, illustrations, slight wear at spine ends and corners, very slight fraying and chipping, covers rubbed and faintly marked, otherwise very good, clean text.   Any Amount of Books   March 2015 - C14280   2015   £400

Muller, Marcia *Ask the Cards a Question.* New York: St. Martins, 1982. First edition, fine in lightly worn dust jacket with one very small closed tear to top back panel.   Buckingham Books   March 2015 - 29238   2015 $175

Muller, Marcia *Edwin of the Iron Shoes.* New York: McKay Washburn, 1977. First edition, fine in dust jacket with some tiny wear at spine ends.   Mordida Books   March 2015 - 009122   2015 $200

Muller, Wilhelm *Mathematische Stromungslehre.* Berlin: Julius Springer, 1928. 8vo., pencil marginal page 3, ink marginalia pages 30, 52, by Louis Melville Milne-Thompson, original black gilt stamped cloth, some minor wear to extremities, very good.   Jeff Weber Rare Books   178 - 909   2015 $95

Mumford, Thomas Howland *Little Charley's Picture Alphabet.* Philadelphia: C. G. Henderson & Co., 1852. First edition, 24mo., woodcuts, brown cloth stamped in gilt and blind, contemporary Salem NJ bookstore label and pencil name, modest wear, very good or better, uncommon.   Between the Covers Rare Books   196 - 164   2015 $750

Munari, Bruno *Nella Nebbie di Milano.* Milan: Emma Edizioni, 1968. First edition, text in Italian.   Honey & Wax Booksellers   2 - 41   2015 $650

Munari, Bruno *Nella Notte Buia.* Milano: Giuseppe Muggiani, 1956. First edition, small 4to., pictorial boards, just touch of edge rubbing, else fine in original clear protective wrapper, hard to find in this condition.   Aleph-bet Books, Inc.   109 - 316   2015 $750

Munari, Bruno *What I'd Like to Be.* London: Harvill Press, 1945. First edition, folio, flexible card covers, slightly dusty, else near fine, bright full color illustrations.   Aleph-bet Books, Inc.   109 - 317   2015 $600

Munch, Caja *The Strange American Way. Letters from Wiota...* Carbondale: Southern Illinois University, 1970. First edition, cloth, 274 pages, signed by translators, Helene and Peter Munch, owner's label, fine in slightly chipped dust jacket, very good+ jacket.   Baade Books of the West   2014 - 2015 $53

Mundell, Alexander *The Influence of Interest and Prejudice Upon Proceedings in Parliament Stated, and Illustrated by What Has Been Done in Matters Relative to Education - Religion - the Poor...* London: John Murray, 1825. First edition, 8vo., probably wanting a half title, small circular inkstamp of National Liberal Club, few old discreet pencil markings and annotations, well bound in 20th century in quarter calf over marbled boards, raised bands, label lettered gilt, very good.   John Drury Rare Books   March 2015 - 25616   2015 $266

Munn, Irwin *Chickasha. A Journey Back in Time.* Chickasha: University of Arts and Sciences of Oklahoma, 1982. First edition, 4to., pictorial wrappers, 162 pages, illustrations, maps, very good, very scarce, very good.   Baade Books of the West   2014 - 2015 $67

Munroe, Kirk *Longfeather the Peacemaker.* London: George Newnes, 1901. First edition, pictorial cloth, all edges gilt, illustrations by Emlen McConnell, full color cover has some color loss, but remains quite attractive, former owner signature scribbled out on half title, good+, tight copy, very scarce.   Baade Books of the West   2014 - 2015 $61

Munsell, A. H. *Grammar of Color, Arrangements of Strathmore Papers in a Variety of Printed Color Combination According to the Munsell Color System.* Mittineague: Strathmore Paper Co., 1921. Tall 4to, 2 volumes, cloth backed boards, later cardboard slipcase, 19 paper samples and folded specimen sheets, accompanied by additional sample sheets numbered 20 to 46 which are loosely inserted, covers soiled and spotted, rubbing along edges, name in ink on front cover, back inside hinge cracked from inserted extra specimens.   Oak Knoll Books   306 - 58   2015 $750

Munthe, Axel *Letters from a Mourning City (Naples Autumn 1884).* London: John Murray, 1887. First edition, 8vo., original publisher's blue cloth, frontispiece, neat name on f.e.p., bookplate, cloth slightly worn at lower spine hinge, which has been briefly repaired, otherwise sound, clean copy, very good.   Any Amount of Books   2015 - A82453   2015   £175

Murakami, Haruki *1Q84. Books 1 and 2 Together with Book 3. Red Edge Limited Edition.* London: Harvill Secker, 2011. First edition, "Red Edged" limited edition with both books being limited to 1500 copies, with all edges stained red, fine in fine dust jackets.   Ed Smith Books   83 - 69   2015 $300

Murakami, Haruki *Blind Willow, Sleeping Woman.* Harvill Secker, 2006. 694/1000 copies, signed by author in English on tipped in bookplate, 8vo., original quarter black boards with willow tree design, backstrip lettered in silver, slipcase, stamped in silver with willow tree motif.   Blackwell's Rare Books   B179 - 196   2015   £180

Murakami, Haruki *Dance Dance Dance.* Tokyo: New York: Kodansha International, 1994. First English language edition, this copy with author's inscription to owner of Book Soup in Hollywood, Glenn Goldman, signed publisher's letter presenting the book laid in, fine in fine dust jacket.   Ed Smith Books   83 - 66   2015 $450

Murakami, Haruki *Hard-Boiled Wonderland and the End of the World.* Tokyo: Kodansha, 1991. First edition, review slip (in Japanese) laid in, fine, fresh, unread copy in fine dust jacket.   Ed Smith Books   83 - 67   2015 $175

Murakami, Haruki *Kafka on the Shore Kafka.* Harvill, 2005. 182/1000 copies signed by author, 8vo., original white boards, backstrip lettered in black, patterned endpapers, black slipcase stamped in silver, fine.   Blackwell's Rare Books   B179 - 197   2015   £250

Murakami, Haruki *A Wild Sheep Chase.* Tokyo and New York: Kodansha International, 1989. First American edition, laid into this copy is a folding color brochure announcing 'New! Japanese Fiction and Poetry", as well as large color postcard with dust jacket front cover art, for this book, reproduced on it, fine in dust jacket.   Ed Smith Books   83 - 68   2015 $200

Murdoch, James *Scenes from the Chiushingura and the Story of the Forty-Seven Ronin.* Tokyo: 1892. First edition, original string tied thin board colored printed wrappers with silver highlights, original silk spine present and intact, 17 collotype photo plates by Ogawa with intact tissue guards, front hinge renewed to style, beautiful production in excellent condition, folio.   By the Book, L. C.   44 - 71   2015 $900

Murdoch, John E. *Album of Science: Antiquity and the Middle Ages.* New York: Charles Scribner's Sons, 1984. Small 4to., frontispiece, 291 numbered illustrations, cloth, dust jacket extremities worn, torn, very good.   Jeff Weber Rare Books   178 - 813   2015 $40

Murdock, Dick *Port Costa 1879-1941. A Saga of Sails, Sacks and Rails.* Port Costa: Murdock Endom Publications, 1977. First edition, oblong quarto, 42 pages, including covers, designed and illustrated by Charles Endom, as well as 16 historical photos, 2 portraits and 2 maps, tan wrappers, very fine.   Argonaut Book Shop   Holiday Season 2014 - 57   2015 $50

Murger, Henri *Scenes De La Vie De Boheme.* Paris: Editions Athena, 1951. Number 529 of 996 copies on Rives rag paper, erotic dry-pints by Paul Emile Becat, unbound signatures laid into wrappers, fine in near fine board chemise and matching lightly soiled box, 8vo.   Beasley Books   2013 - 2015 $150

Murillo Verlarde, Pedro *Cursus Juris Canonici, Hispani, et Indici in quo Juxta Ordinem Titulorum Decretallium non Solum Canonicae Decisiones Asseruntur sed insuper additur, quod in Nostro Hispaniae Regno & Indiarum Provinciis...* Madrid: ex typographia Angelae De Apontes, 1763. 2 volumes, folio, 5 large folding tables in volume 1 with large emblematic on each titlepage, outer margin of volume I titlepage strengthened, both volumes bound in mid 18th century plain vellum with some general minor discoloration and insignificant wear, with two of the original string ties preserved, with early ms. notes in ink on volume II endpapers, signatures in two or three places of Dr. Yndabuxu (?), nice original set in very good state of preservation.   John Drury Rare Books   2015 - 25022   2015 $1661

Murphy, Antoin E. *John Law's Essay on a Land Bank.* Dublin: Aeon, 1894. Large 8vo., original publisher's green cloth lettered gilt on spine and front cover, fine in fine, green cloth slipcase.   Any Amount of Books   2015 - C7531   2015   £150

Murphy, Beatrice M. *Ebony Rhythm: an Anthology of Contemporary Negro Verse.* New York: Exposition Press, 1948. First edition, fine in about good dust jacket with stain and modest loss at foot of spine and modest erosion along edge of rear flap fold, scarce.   Between the Covers Rare Books   197 - 1   2015 $150

Murphy, Christopher *Bigfoot Film Journal.* Surrey & Blaine: Hancock House, 2008. First edition, pictorial glossy wrappers, color and black and white illustrations, map, signed by Murphy, fine, like new.   Baade Books of the West   2014 - 2015 $49

Murphy, Chuck *Jack and the Beanstalk Classic Collectible Pop-up.* New York: Simon & Schuster, 1998. First edition, fine, hardcover pop-up with all figures in excellent condition, 4to.   Beasley Books   2013 - 2015 $40

Murphy, Claire Rudolf *The Prince and the Salmon People.* New York: Rizzoli, 1993. First edition, 4to., cloth, 48 pages illustrations, map, signed by author, gift inscription of previous owner, fine in dust jacket, scarce signed, fine dust jacket.   Baade Books of the West   2014 - 2015 $40

Murphy, John Mortimer *Sporting Adventures in the Far West.* London: 1879. First edition, gilt and blindstamped cloth, silver dollar size splotch on front cover, but not on gilt illustration, new endpapers same color as original, wear to corners, moderate general wear, resewn, tight copy, scarce, good+.   Baade Books of the West   2014 - 2015 $131

Murphy, Richard *The Woman of the House - an Elegy.* Dublin: Dolmen Press, 1959. First edition, one of 250 copies, wrappers, presentation from author in month of publication inscribed for Colin Fenton, 20th May 1959, covers darkened at edges and little creased, very good, scarce.   Peter Ellis, Bookseller   2014 - 014029   2015   £295

Murphy, Robert *Murder in Waiting.* New York: Scribners, 1938. First edition, fine in dust jacket with some slight fading on spine. Mordida Books March 2015 - 008693 2015 $100

Murray, Albert *South to a Very Old Place.* New York: Modern Library, 1995. First Modern Library edition, fine in fine dust jacket, inscribed by author to writer Reynolds Price. Between the Covers Rare Books, Inc. 187 - 187 2015 $200

Murray, Amelia M. *Letters from the United States, Cuba and Canada.* New York: Putnam, 1856. First American edition, 8vo., 410 pages, very good in publisher's cloth, contemporary name on endpaper, rear hinge tender, some rubbed along extremities of cloth. Second Life Books Inc. 191 - 61 2015 $150

Murray, David *A Note on Some Glasgow and Other Provincial Coins and Tokens.* Glasgow: James Maclehose & sons, 1885. First separate edition, 4to., 4 collotype plates, contemporary half calf over marbled boards, spine lettered gilt, presentation copy inscribed in ink With author's compliments and with label on front pastedown recording this copy's gift to the library of the Faculty of Procurators in Glasgow Mach 1886, fine. John Drury Rare Books March 2015 - 23627 2015 $266

Murray, David Christie *In His Grip.* London: Long, 1907. First edition, name on copyright page and page edges soiled and lightly foxed, otherwise fine in pictorial blue cloth covered boards, gold stamped titles on spine. Mordida Books March 2015 - 001670 2015 $185

Murray, Eustace Clare Grenville *The Artful Vicar.* Leipzig: Bernhard Tauchnitz, 1879. Copyright edition, 2 volumes in 1, contemporary half dark blue calf, brown and maroon morocco labels, contemporary bookplate and ownership signature, very good. Jarndyce Antiquarian Booksellers CCXI - 208 2015 £50

Murray, John *The Round Up a Romance of Arizona.* New York: G. W. Dillingham Co., 1908. First edition, former owner's name and date, else fine, bright copy, neatly trimmed dust jacket. Buckingham Books March 2015 - 9287 2015 $250

Murray, Les A. *The Boys Who Stole the Funeral.* Sydney: Angus & Robertson Publishers, 1980. First edition, octavo, fine in very good or better dust jacket with moderate chip on rear panel, inscribed by author on titlepage to poet Mark Strand. Between the Covers Rare Books, Inc. 187 - 189 2015 $450

Murray, Les A. *Ethnic Radio. Poems.* Sydney: Angus & Robertson, 1977. First edition, some underscoring and marks in text in Mark Strand's hand, otherwise fine in rubbed and lightly chipped, very good dust jacket, inscribed by author for Mark Strand. Between the Covers Rare Books, Inc. 187 - 188 2015 $450

Murray, Max *The Voice of the Corpse.* New York: Farrar Straus and Co., 1947. First edition, cloth, light discolored at foot of spine, else fine in dust jacket. Buckingham Books March 2015 - 2447 2015 $300

Murray, William Henry Wood *Obi; or Three Fingered Jack.* London: John Dicks, 1883. Vignette title, sewn as issued. Jarndyce Antiquarian Booksellers CCXI - 209 2015 £40

Murry, John Middleton *The Blue Review Volume I Nos. 1-3 (all published).* London: Martin Secker, May-July, 1913. covers faded at spine and edges, spine of third issue splitting, very good set. Peter Ellis, Bookseller 2014 - 008306 2015 £300

Musaeus, J. K. A. *Die Nymphe Des Brunnens.* Wien & Leipzig: Gerlach, n.d. circa, 1920. Square 12mo., cloth backed pictorial boards, 48 pages, tips rubbed, else very good, illustrations by Ignatius Taschner with cover design, pictorial endpapers plus many beautiful full page color illustrations and many black and whites. Aleph-bet Books, Inc. 109 - 185 2015 $225

Muscatine, Doris *Old San Francisco. The Biography of a City from Early Days to the Earthquake.* New York: G. P. Putnam's Sons, 1975. First edition, 45 illustrations from photos, map endpapers, original champagne cloth, very fine, pictorial dust jacket, slightest of chipping to head of spine. Argonaut Book Shop Holiday Season 2014 - 216 2015 $45

Museum d'Histoire Naturelle *Bulletin du Museum d'Histoire Naturelle (Volumes 1-94).* Paris: Imprimerie Nationale, 1895-1996. Octavo, 92 volumes, mostly bound, 23 volumes unbound, in a mixture of publisher's boards and black half morocco and red label, very good set. Andrew Isles 2015 - 17045 2015 $5000

Musgrave, Thomas *Castaway on the Auckland Isles: a narrative of the Wreck of the 'Grafton' and of the Escape of the Crew After Twenty Months' Suffering.* London: Lockwood and Co., 1866. First London edition, 8vo., frontispiece, title vignette, folding map, occasional pencilled marks in text, original blue cloth gilt on upper cover, very good, from the library of the Cruising Association (bookplate and blindstamp). John Drury Rare Books March 2015 - 25864 2015 £306

Musick, L. W. *The Hermit of Siskiyou or Twice-Old Man.* Crescent City: Crescent City News, 1896. First edition, gilt stamped grey cloth, 12mo., 81 pages, professionally rebound in original covers, brittle endpapers replaced with appropriate and genuine antique papers representing the same period, rare, very good+.   Baade Books of the West   2014 - 2015 $800

Musset, Paul De *Mr. Wind and Madam Rain.* London: Sampson Low Son and Co., 1864. First English edition, frontispiece, vignette title, 27 woodcuts, original purple cloth, slightly rubbed and dulled, slight wear to head and tail of spine, all edges gilt.   Jarndyce Antiquarian Booksellers   CCXI - 211   2015   £55

Muter, Gladys Nelson *Mother Goose and Her Friends.* Volland, 1923. Oblong small folio, limp pictorial cloth, slight bit of cover fading and rubbing, else very good, rare.   Aleph-bet Books, Inc.   109 - 304   2015 $500

Mutwa, Vusamazulu Credo *Indaba, My Children.* Johannesburg: Blue Crane Books, circa, 1960. First edition, small quarto, 562 pages, black and white frontispiece, line drawings, small dampstain on top edge of rear board, still near fine in like dust jacket with small chip at base of spine.   Between the Covers Rare Books   197 - 20   2015 $75

My Honey ABC. London: Tuck, n.d. circa, 1900. Oblong 8vo., printed cloth, some soil and fraying and staining overall, very good, printed in full color on cloth, each page with grossly stereotypical Blacks for each letter of the alphabet, rare.   Aleph-bet Books, Inc.   109 - 3   2015 $1850

Mydans, Carl *Carl Mydans, Photojournalist.* New York: Harry N Abrams, 1985. Quarto, grey cloth with title in white to spine, pictorial dust jacket with photos of General Douglas MacArthur on front cover and Mydans on rear, near fine in like jacket.   The Kelmscott Bookshop   11 - 34   2015 $145

Myers, Walter *The Golden Serpent.* New York: Viking, 1980. First edition, fine, illustrations in color by Alice and Martin Provensen.   Aleph-bet Books, Inc.   109 - 387   2015 $125

Myrick, David F. *Railroads of Nevada and Eastern California.* Howell North Books, 1962-1963. 2 volumes, quarto, frontispieces, brown cloth, gold stamping on front cover and spine, decorated endpapers, near fine in dust jacket lightly rubbed at spine ends and to front flap fore-edge and tiny rub at mid spine panel, attractive set.   Buckingham Books   March 2015 - 22999   2015 $700

N

Nabokov, Vladimir 1899-1977 *The Eye.* New York: Phaedra, 1965. Advance copy, plain white wrappers laid into finished dust jacket which is slightly spine darkened and chipped at top edge around spine, fine in very good dust jacket, "compliments of the publisher" card laid in.   Ken Lopez, Bookseller   164 - 149   2015 $150

Nabokov, Vladimir 1899-1977 *The Gift.* New York: Putnam, 1963. First edition of first English translation, presentation copy inscribed on half title in pencil with chess imagery 'for the (two chess bishops) from Vladimir Nabokov April 2 1964 Ithaca NY" with two butterflies and their shadows and this annotation, corrected" two misprints on page 79/ one misprint on page 154', fine copy, near fine jacket, housed in custom quarter leather box with folding chemise, from the library of Morris Bishop (with his bookplate).   B & B Rare Books, Ltd.   234 - 83   2015 $17,500

Nabokov, Vladimir 1899-1977 *The Middle Passage.* London: Deutsch, 1962. First edition, inscribed by author to publisher, Andre Deutsch, London March 15 1963, minor browning to boards, near fine in good dust jacket with wear to edges and folds with foxing and heavy tape strengthening on verso, someone has written the number "2" at top of spine, protected in custom clamshell case.   Ken Lopez, Bookseller   164 - 150   2015 $7500

Nairn, Katharine *The Trial of Katharine Nairn and Patrick Ogilvie for the Crimes of Incest and Murder.* Edinburgh: printed: London: Reprinted for T. Becket and P. A. De Hondt, 1765. 8vo., wanting half title, foremargin of title creased and rather dust soiled, endpapers browned, bound in 19th century cloth backed boards, printed label on upper cover, corners and extremities worn, uncut.   John Drury Rare Books   March 2015 - 25315   2015   £306

Naismith, John *Thoughts on the Various Objects of Industry Pursued in Scotland..* Edinburgh: printed for the author, sold by Bell and Bradfute, 1790. First edition, 8vo., original blue boards, entirely uncut and largely unopened, later paper spine label, lettered in ink, binding generally lightly worn, else near fine.   John Drury Rare Books   2015 - 25574   2015 $1486

Nakabe, Kenkichi *My Report by Camera Eye Around the World (Watakushi No Kamera Hokoku).* Tokyo: Suisan Keizai Shinbunsha, 1956. First edition, attractive silver and black stamped cloth, black and white color photos, drawings, frontispiece, map, binding and text elegantly designed and printed, near fine.   Baade Books of the West   2014 - 2015 $1000

Nalson, John *Reflections Upon Coll. Sidney's Arcadia: the Old Cause, Being Some Observations Upon His Last Paper, Given to the Sheriffs at His Execution.* London: Thomas Dring, 1684. First edition, folio, 16 pages, recent plain wrappers, very good, large copy.   John Drury Rare Books   March 2015 - 17694   2015   £306

Nancarrow, Conlon *Study No. 3 for Player Piano.* Santa Fe: Soundings Press, 1983. First edition, wrappers, 4to., near fine.   Beasley Books   2013 - 2015 $45

Nance, R. Morton *Sailing-Ship Models.* London: Hatton and Truscott Smith, 1924. First edition, no. 958 of 1750 numbered copies, near fine in blue cloth covered boards, gold stamped titles, decoration and a ship on front cover, 126 plates.   Mordida Books   March 2015 - 010986   2015 $325

Napier, Charles James *Memoir on the Roads of Cefalonia.* London: James Ridgway, 1825. First edition, 8vo., 5 engraved lithographic plates, original boards, uncut, very good with Mountgarret (i.e. Butler family) armorial bookplate, unidentified early 19th century Book Society subscription list on pastedown, rare.   John Drury Rare Books   2015 - 24015   2015 $2185

Napora, Joseph *Scighte.* New York: Poote Press, 1987. One of 85 copies, on handmade paper by Ruth Lingen and Katherine Kuehn, hand set in Bodoni type, magnesium line cuts, printed by them damp on Vandercook proof press, bound by Tim Ely in coptic binding of paper over boards with original line cut hand colored and green and red morocco over spine stitching, pages pink printed in black, line cuts in yellow, black brown, red and other earth colors, beautiful book.   Priscilla Juvelis - Rare Books   61 - 13   2015 $3000

A Narration of the Great Victory (through Gods Providence) Obtained by the Parliamentary Forces Under Sir William Walker at Alton in Surrey the 13, of This Instant December 1643. London: for Edw. Husbands, Dec. 16, 1643. First edition, small 4to., 8 pages, very lightly browned and closely trimmed along upper margin, late 19th century half calf and marbled boards, from the library of James Stevens Cox (1910-1997).   Maggs Bros. Ltd.   1447 - 91   2015   £200

A Narrative of the late Riots at Edinburgh... London: printed in the year, 1779. First edition or first London edition, 4to., titlepage and page 28 both little dust soiled, preserved in later but old marbled card wrappers, good, crisp copy, rare.   John Drury Rare Books   2015 - 21637   2015 $743

A Narrative of What Passed at Killalla: in the County of Mayo and Parts Adjacent, During the French Invasion in the Summer of 1798. Dublin: Re-printed for J. Wright & J. Hatchard, 1800. Early reprint, 8vo., recently rebound in half color leather with marbled boards, lettered gilt at spine with gilt decoration and five raised bands, occasional very slight foxing, otherwise clean, bright, very good+.   Any Amount of Books   2015 - C15998   2015   £280

Nash, Claude W.   *Some Nashes of Virginia Two Hundred Years of an American Family 1774-1974.*   Radford: 1975. 188 pages, some tiny white spots to cover, gilt bright, corner sharp.   Bookworm & Silverfish   2015 - 6016450092   2015 $50

Nash, John   *Twenty One Wood Engravings.*   Netherton: Fleece Press, 1991. One of 100 copies (of an edition of 112 copies), printed on Zerkall mouldmade paper, frontispiece and 20 wood engravings, each printed on separate leaf, title printed in red, plates, small folio, original dark green morocco by Stephen Conway (president of the Designer Bookbinders), five horizontal gilt banded tan morocco onlays to backstrip and wrapping around onto front and rear covers, five holes exposing grained wood inlays to both of covers and with four small gilt rings and three tan morocco onlays, adjacent to each hole, rough trimmed, tan linen cloth box with printed back label, signed by binder "Bound by S. P. Conway 2009", fine.   Blackwell's Rare Books   B179 - 150   2015   £1500

Nash, Paul   *Aerial Flowers.*   Oxford: Counterpoint Publications, 1947. Limited to 1000 numbered copies, 4to., stiff paper wrappers, label on front wrapper, one color and four black and white illustrations, label on front wrapper and picture of Nash courtesy of Manchester Guardian, wrappers slightly soiled, front wrapper bent along fore-edge.   Oak Knoll Books   306 - 34   2015 $110

Nash, Paul   *Fertile Image.*   London: Faber and Faber, 1951. First edition, frontispiece, small 4to., cloth, dust jacket, 64 black and white plates, dust jacket chipped at top of spine and lightly soiled.   Oak Knoll Books   306 - 285   2015 $350

Nash, Paul   *Monster Field: a Discovery Recorded by Paul Nash.*   Oxford: Counterpoint Publications, 1946. Limited to 1000 numbered copies, 4to., stiff paper wrappers, label on front wrapper, color plate on front wrapper, wrappers lightly soiled and tanned around edges, ex-libris on inside front wrapper.   Oak Knoll Books   306 - 35   2015 $125

Nast, Elsa Ruth   *How to Have a Happy Birthday.*   New York: Simon & Schuster, 1952. A. First edition, LGB # 123, slight rubbing on upper corner, else near fine, unused, wonderfully illustrated by Retta Worcester including pages of party cut-outs, favors, games, invitations, place cards and cups, completely unused, quite scarce.   Aleph-bet Books, Inc.   109 - 203   2015 $350

Nathan, Maud   *Once Upon a Time and To-Day.*   New York: Putnam's, 1933. First edition, 8vo., 28 illustrations, cover somewhat faded, otherwise very good.   Second Life Books Inc.   189 - 178   2015 $60

Nathan, Maud   *The Story of an Epoch-Making Movement.*   Garden City: Doubleday Page, 1926. First edition, 8vo., maroon cloth, very good.   Second Life Books Inc.   189 - 179   2015 $65

Nathiri, N. Y.   *Zora! Zora Neale Hurston: a Woman and Her Community.*   Orlando: Orlando Sentinel/Sentinel Communications, 1991. First edition, 4to. this copy signed by Alice Walker, fine in fine dust jacket.   Beasley Books   2013 - 2015 $40

National American Woman Suffrage Association   *Victory how Women Won It.*   New York: Wilson, 1940. First edition, 8vo., illustrations, blue cloth, spine little faded, otherwise fine, one of 300 honor copies, inscribed by Carrie Chapman Catt.   Second Life Books Inc.   189 - 180   2015 $450

National Cheap-Freight Railway League   *Grand Rally in Behalf of the Producing Interests! Call for a National Convention.*   N.P.: 1868. First edition, 8vo., 16 pages, single sheet folded to form 8 leaves, self wrappers, outer leaves little dusty in margins, otherwise very good, small stamp of NY State Library on margin of first page with their small withdrawal stamp on last page.   M & S Rare Books, Inc.   97 - 143   2015 $100

National Live Stock Journal. Devoted to Improvement in Stock and the Interests of Stock-Raisers.   Stock Journal Co., 1876. First edition, 4to., color pictorial wrapper, illustrations, moderate wear to spine panel, light wear at corners of front cover, small chips and creases to bottom edge of rear cover, interior clean, else good+.   Buckingham Books   March 2015 - 38248   2015 $250

National Park Seminary (Incorporated) A Junior College for Young Women 1934-1935.   Forest Glen: 1935. First edition, 8vo., illustrated cloth, profusely illustrated with black and white photos, 6 color plates, cover title soiled, but very good.   Second Life Books Inc.   189 - 182   2015 $85

Natta, Giulio   *Dimensioni Degli Atomi E Degli Ioni Monovalenti Nei Reticoli Dei Cristalli...*   Rome: Reale Academica D'Italia, 1931. Small 4to., near fine offprint, original printed wrappers, mild age darkening to edges, partially uncut, signed and inscribed by author.   By the Book, L. C.   Special List 10 - 3   2015 $175

Naville, Francois Marc Louis *Memoire en reponse a la Question Sulvante, Proposee par La Societe Genevoise d'Utilite Publique quels Moyens Pourrait on Employer dans l'Enseignement Public Pour Developper dans les eleves l'amour de la Patrie Suisse?* Geneva: E. Pelletier, 1839. First edition, 8vo., traces of wrappers near spine, last few leaves slightly browned, recently well bound in cloth, lettered gilt, very good. John Drury Rare Books March 2015 - 17874 2015 $221

Naylor, Gloria *The Women of Brewster Place.* New York: Viking, 1982. First edition, author's signature on titlepage, paper over boards with cloth spine, fine in dust jacket. Second Life Books Inc. 190 - 172 2015 $500

Neal, Nathaniel *A Free and Serious Remonstrance to Protestant Dissenting Ministers; on Occasion of the Decay of Religion.* London: printed in the year MDCCXLVI, 1746. First edition, 8vo., new boards, printed title label, very good, very scarce. John Drury Rare Books March 2015 - 24683 2015 $266

Neale, Daniel *The History of New England.* London: Clark et al, 1720. First edition, titlepage printed in red and black, titlepage printed in red and black, titlepage some browned and stained along margins, inner margin strengthened, some toning to leaves, but not badly foxed, recent quarter calf with cloth boards and new endpapers, noted map has short tear but is excellent example. Second Life Books Inc. 190 - 227 2015 $3600

Nearing, Scott *Black America.* New York: Vanguard Press, 1929. First edition, very good+ to near fine in art deco boards, this copy signed by author, 8vo. Beasley Books 2013 - 2015 $200

Nearing, Scott *Dollar Diplomacy.* New York: B. W. Huebsch and the Viking Press, 1925. First edition, near fine, lacking rare dust jacket, attractive octagonal bookplate, small numeric ink notation to same, at top left corner, inscribed by co-author Joseph Freeman to Rex Stout and his wife Fay, from the collection of Duke Collier. Royal Books 36 - 125 2015 $1500

Nebel, Frederick *Fifty Roads to Town.* Boston: Little Brown and Co., 1936. First edition, presentation inscription by author for Bob and Gladys Ballard, cloth lightly soiled with few spots of light foxing, vertical crease to spine, else near fine in dust jacket with light professional restoration to spine ends and lightly toned on spine. Buckingham Books March 2015 - 29009 2015 $1275

Nebel, Frederick *Fifty Roads to Town.* Boston: Little Brown, 1936. First edition, very good plus in very good plus dust jacket, slightest lean, light toning and faint soil to backstrip and board edges, jacket is as nice as we have seen on this title, only small chip at crown and light edge rubbing to note, attractive copy, from the collection of Duke Collier, inscribed by author for Harry and Shirley Steeger Jan. 24 1936. Royal Books 36 - 216 2015 $1250

Nebel, Frederick *Six Deadly Dames.* New York: Avon Publishing, 1950. First edition thus, paperback original, pages uniformly browned, two tiny nicks to fore-edges of last two pages, else near fine, pictorial wrappers. Buckingham Books March 2015 - 29316 2015 $250

Nebraska. Legislature *State Journal of the State Legislature of Nebraska. First, Second and Third Sessions.* Omaha: published by author St. A. D. Balcombe State printer, 1867. First edition, brown printed wrappers, fragile covers chipped on front and one double thumb sized stain, rear cover torn and tattered with pieces missing, text very good, very scarce, good. Baade Books of the West 2014 - 2015 $62

The Necessity and Advantages of Closet Religion. London: printed for John Clark and Richard Hell, 1728. First edition, 12mo., 36 pages, few minor stains, but good, well margined copy in modern plain wrappers. John Drury Rare Books 2015 - 17784 2015 $89

Necker, Mr. *Of the Importance of Religious Opinions by Mr. Necker.* Boston: Thomas Hall, 1796. Second US edition, 12mo., lacks half of front blank, bound in contemporary chemical calf, excellent copy. Second Life Books Inc. 189 - 279 2015 $500

The Necklace. An Interesting tale for Youth. Newburyport: W. & J. Gilman, 1824. First edition?, 18mo., 36 pages, engravings, original printed and pictorial wrappers. M & S Rare Books, Inc. 97 - 132 2015 $250

Necrofile. The Review of Horrow Fiction. Issues #1-32. West Warwick: Necronomicon Press, 1991-1999. Complete run, 3 issues with little marginal staining to covers, some rust to staples common, overall fine run. Ken Lopez, Bookseller 164 - 89 2015 $650

Nedham, Marchamont *Digitus Dei; or God's Justice Upon Treachery and Treason, Exemplifyed in the Life and Death of the late James Duke of Hamilton.* London: 1649. First edition, variant issue, 4to., title printed within wide ornamental border, wanting A1 (blank or licence leaf?), 19th century half calf over marbled boards, some wear to joints, but good, firm copy with 19th century armorial bookplate of John George Home Drummond of Abbots Grange. John Drury Rare Books 2015 - 19478 2015 $874

Need of Law on the Indian Reservations. Sherman & Co., 1878. First edition, printed wrappers, 52 pages, one loose signature and rear wrapper missing, else very good. Buckingham Books   March 2015 - 37631   2015 $300

Needham, Violet   *The Great House of Estraville.* London: Collins, 1955. First edition, 8vo., original blue boards lettered gilt on spine, illustrations by Joyce Bruce, endpapers very slightly browned, otherwise clean, very good+ in very good dust jacket which is very slightly soiled and very slightly chipped at corners and with one very small chip at head of rear panel, well above average copy.   Any Amount of Books   2015 - A78346   2015   £300

Neel, Louis   *Magnetisme et Champ Molecualire.* Stockholm: Nobel Foundation, 1971. First separate edition, 8vo., fine in original orange printed wrappers, signed and inscribed by author.   By the Book, L. C.   Special List 10 - 62   2015 $450

Neet, George W.   *Studies in Psychology.* Valparaiso: M. E. Bogarte, 1917. hardcover, very good, possibly a first printing in spite of 1917 copyright date.   Beasley Books   2013 - 2015 $45

The Negro Forget-Me-Not-Songster. Philadelphia: Turner & Fisher, 1847. First edition, 16mo., incomplete, pages 243-249 (1) lacking), 16mo., frontispiece, illustrations, original brown cloth with Fisher & Brother Publishers blindstamped on boards, rebacked preserving little more than half of the original spine, new endpapers, stains on boards, modest foxing in text, good, sound, defective copy, very scarce. Between the Covers Rare Books   197 - 84   2015 $300

Nehru, Jawaharlal   *Jawaharlal Nehru: an Autobiography.* London: Bodley Head, 1941. Reprint, tiny Allahabad bookstore stamp, else near fine without dust jacket, inscribed by author to Eve Curie daughter of Madame Marie Curie. Between the Covers Rare Books   196 - 98   2015 $7500

Neil, Edward D.   *History of Washington County and the St. Croix Valley Including the Explorers and Pioneers of Minnesota.* Minneapolis: North Star, 1881. First edition, 4to., half leather and cloth with leather like pebble surface, marbled edges and endpapers, good, sound, well worn at cover corners and spine edges, some peeling scuffing to leather, not open fraying, scarce, good.   Baade Books of the West   2014 - 2015 $275

Neilson, Lloyd L.   *Gloria in Excelsis Deo.* San Francisco: Juniper Von Phitzer Press, 1994. Limited to 101 numbered copies signed by author, 7.3 x 5.9 cm., gilt leather, title stamped on front board, decorated endpapers, all edges gilt, illustrations.   Oak Knoll Books   306 - 120   2015 $150

Nellie's Christmas Eve. New York: McLoughlin Bros. n.d., 4to., wrappers, very good.   Beasley Books   2013 - 2015 $45

Nelson, Gilbert   *The Use of Human Reason in Religion. In Answer to the Methodists: the Doctrine of Free-Grace Being Explained in the Medium...* London: printed for the author and sold by Mr. Longman, Mr. Brotherton and Mr. Elliot, 1741. 8vo., 2 or 3 wormholes in lower (blank) margins throughout, very minor worming in text itself, occasionally affecting a letter or two, contemporary mottled calf double gilt fillets on sides, neatly rebacked with gilt titles, raised bands and label, good, crisp copy, very rare.   John Drury Rare Books   2015 - 23601   2015 $830

Nelson, Lawrence   *Pioneer Roads in Central Oregon.* Bend: Maverick, 1985. First edition, gilt stamped blue cloth, illustrations, maps, fine, very scarce hardbound.   Baade Books of the West   2014 - 2015 $100

Nelson, T., and Sons   *The Union Pacific Railroad: a trip Across the North American Continent from Omaha to Ogden.* New York: n.de., 1872. 46 pages, illustrations, map, slight wear to extremities, minor foxing, else near fine, 4 x 6 3/4 inches, 12 chromolithograph views.   Dumont Maps and Books of the West   130 - 32   2015 $200

Nelson, Thomas   *The Union Pacific Railroad.* T. Nelson and Sons, n.d. circa, 1870. 4 x 5 1/2 inches, maroon cloth with gold gilt and black stamping, few illustrations plus 12 lightly tinted plates, some light foxing, light wear to spine ends, front cover lightly soiled, else very good. Buckingham Books   March 2015 - 34556   2015 $275

Nelson, William   *The Laws Concerning Game. Of Hunting, Hawking, Fishing and Fowling &c.* London: in the Savoy: printed by Henry Lintot for T. Waller, 1751. Fourth edition, 8vo., very short closed marginal tear in titlepage, else near fine in contemporary plain ruled calf, early ownership inscription of Richard Neale, Callington, 1821 and of Charles Spraggs May 27 1871.   John Drury Rare Books   March 2015 - 25108   2015   £306

Nemerov, Howard   *War Stories: Poems About Long Ago and Now.* Chicago: University of Chicago Press, 1987. First edition, fine in fine dust jacket, inscribed by author to fellow poet John Hollander.   Between the Covers Rare Books, Inc.   187 - 201   2015 $450

Neruda, Pablo   *Canto General. A Song of the People.* St. Paul: College of St. Catherine, 1986. First edition, wrappers, fine.   Beasley Books   2013 - 2015 $45

Neruda, Pablo   *Epitialamio -una Carta e el Camino.* Buenos Aires: Ediciones Dos Amigos, 1989. Artist's book, one of 50 copies, all on Canson paper in several colors, signed by artist on each of the two etchings on pencil and dated "88", page size 9 1/3/16 x 6 1/2 inches, 32 pages, loose as issued in red wrappers printed in black with author and title, housed in custom made orange cloth over boards clamshell box with 'a sus amigo' printed in dark orange and names of press and paraph, a box bit rubbed, book fine,. Priscilla Juvelis - Rare Books   61 - 11   2015 $2500

Neruda, Pablo *El Habitante Y Su Espersanza.* Santiago di Chile: Editorial Nascimento, 1926. First edition, inscribed to American bookseller Maury Bromsen.   Honey & Wax Booksellers   2 - 53   2015 $3000

Neruda, Pablo *La Insepulta De Paita.* Buenos Aires: Editorial Losada, 1962. No. 217 of 400 copies, fine in fine dust jacket in very good cardboard slipcase, folio.   Beasley Books   2013 - 2015 $800

Nesbit, Edith *Fairies.* London, et al: Raphael Tuck n.d. circa, 1890. oblong 5 1/4 x 4 1/2 inches, pictorial card covers, die cut in shape of two large roses, 36 pages + covers, complete with silk cord, light edge wear, owner name else near fine, illustrations by Pauline Sunter with beautiful chromolithographs or in green line on every page, there is a full page color frontispiece, color pictorial titlepage and few others, lovely book, rare.   Aleph-bet Books, Inc.   109 - 162   2015 $400

Nesbit, Edith *Harding's Luck.* London: Hodder & Stoughton, 1909. First edition, 8vo., red gilt cloth, top edge gilt, slight darkening on bottom front cover and very occasional foxing, tight, near fine, illustrations by H. R. Millar with 16 plates, rare.   Aleph-bet Books, Inc.   109 - 321   2015 $750

Nesbo, Jo *The Leopard.* London: Harvill Secker, 2010. First English translation, fine in fine dust jacket.   Buckingham Books   March 2015 - 34713   2015 $225

Nesbo, Jo *The Snowman.* London: Harvill Secker, 2010-2011. First UK edition, signed by author, fine in dust jacket.   Buckingham Books   March 2015 - 31362   2015 $400

Ness, Evaline *Sam, Bangs and Moonshine.* New York: Holt Rinehart, Winston, 1966. Stated first edition, 4to., boards, fine in slightly worn dust jacket, no award seal on dust jacket, scarce.   Aleph-bet Books, Inc.   109 - 323   2015 $500

Nettleship, D N. *Voyage of Discovery Fifty Years of Marine Research at Canada's Bedford Institute of Oceanography.* Dartmouth: Bedford Institute of Oceanography Oceans Association, 2014. Quarto, profusely illustrated in color, graphs, maps and photos, as new.   Schooner Books Ltd.   110 - 181   2015 $45

Neugebauer, Otto *Mathematical Cuneiform Texts.* New Haven: American Oriental Society and the American Schools of Oriental Research, 1945. 4to., map, 23 monochrome plates, photographic reproductions, original dark green blind and gilt stamped cloth, bookplate of Barnabas Hughes, very good.   Jeff Weber Rare Books   178 - 822   2015 $55

Neuman, Henry *A Marine Pocket-Dictionary, of the Italian, Spanish, Portuguese and German Languages...* London: printed by J. Bonsor... and sold by Messrs. Vernor and Hood, 1800. Second edition, titlepage spotted and slightly browned, little dampstaining here and there, without blanks Y4 and S4, small 8vo., contemporary half red sheep, worn at extremities, spine devoid of color, good.   Blackwell's Rare Books   B179 - 77   2015   £450

Neumann, Robert Zaharoff *Zaharoff.* New York: Alfred A. Knopf, 1935. First American edition, spine little age toned, very good, without dust jacket, bookplate of film star Ricardo Cortez.   Between the Covers Rare Books, Inc.   187 - 202   2015 $45

Neuwirth, Waltraud *Wiener Keramik: Historismus Jugendstil art Deco.* Braunchweig: Klinkhardt & Biermann, 1974. Small 4to., cloth dust jacket, cardboard slipcase, 29 color plates and black and white illustrations, slipcase taped and worn at edges, dust jacket worn at edges.   Oak Knoll Books   306 - 86   2015 $135

Nevada County Promotion Committee *Nevada: the Banner Gold County of California.* Daily Miner Transcript Print, n.d. circa, 1904. 6 7/8 x 5 1/4 inches, gilt embossed purple wrappers, numerous black and white photographic illustrations, tiny stain in margin of last page which diminishes to nothing 8 pages later, on page 11 is stamped address of a real estate agent that is contained mostly in margin, portions of the covers lightly faded, else very good, internally clean.   Buckingham Books   March 2015 - 35049   2015 $875

Neve, Edward De, Pseud. *Barred.* London: Desmond Harmsworth, 8vo., a noted rarity, original black cloth lettered red at spine, covers slightly rubbed, slightly scuffed at spine ends, else very good, sound, from the library of Norman Douglas, with note in pencil by him.   Any Amount of Books   2015 - A40615   2015   £700

A New Collection of Enigmas, Charades, Transpositions &c. London: printed for T. Hookham and J. Carpenter, 1791. First editions of all 3 parts, 3 volumes in 1, 8vo., including errata slip in volume II, contemporary half calf over marbled boards, spine simply gilt and labelled, fine, rare.   John Drury Rare Books   2015 - 24849   2015 $2185

A New Conductor Generalis... of Justices of the Peace, Sheriffs Coroners, Constables, Jurymen, Overseers of the Poor... New York: D. & S. Whiting, 1803. First edition, 8vo., contemporary calf, leather label, front cover detached, browned, title leaf loose.   M & S Rare Books, Inc.   97 - 145   2015 $275

The New England Mercantile Union Business Directory. Boston: Pratt & Co., 1949. First edition thus, original gilt stamped cloth, maps, moderate wear, old silverfish spots on small portions of spine and lower front cover, soiled covers, bottom of spine reglued, good, tight copy, hardcover. Baade Books of the West   2014 - 2015 $85

The New Forget-Me-Not: a Calendar.   London: R. Cobden-Sanderson, 1929. First edition, one of 360 numbered copies signed by artist, Rex Whistler, with cover design and 4 color plates, numerous black and white headpieces and presentation page, all by Whistler, quarter blue vellum, decorated paper covers, vellum spine and corners faded (as usual), head and tail of spine slightly bumped, very good in very good, nicked and slightly rubbed dust jacket with couple of large chips to bottom edge of rear panel.   Peter Ellis, Bookseller   2014 - 016135   2015   £300

New Mexico   *Report of the Governor of New Mexico to the Secretary of the Interior 1893/1894/1895/1896/18971898.* Washington: 1893-1898. 6 volumes bound in one, folding geolgoical section, folding map, folding chart, plates. Dumont Maps & Books of the West   131 - 65   2015 $250

New Mexico: a Guide to the Colorful State.   Albuquerque: 1945. Stated second edition, map endpapers, 4 maps in text folding map in back pocket, extremities rubbed, previous owner's name on titlepage.   Dumont Maps & Books of the West   131 - 66   2015 $45

The New Orleans Riot: "My Policy" in Louisiana. Washington: Daily Morning Chronicle Print, 1863. First edition, 8vo., 16 pages, single sheet folded to form 8 leaves, couple of horizontal folds, else fine, uncut and untrimmed. M & S Rare Books, Inc.   97 - 254   2015 $125

The New Time VI: 2 (February 1898).   Chicago: Charles H. Kerr Co., 1898. Wrappers nearly separated, small 4to., very good-.   Beasley Books   2013 - 2015 $45

The New Time. (April 1898).   Chicago: Charles H. Kerr Co., 1898. Small 4to., wrappers, very good with some spine chipping and tearing.   Beasley Books   2013 - 2015 $45

New York Central & Hudson River Railroad   *Health and Pleasure on 'America's Greatest Railroad' Descriptive of Summer Resorts and Excursion Routes.*   New York: 1893. 350 pages, 2 folding maps, illustrations, original printed wrappers soiled and darkened, first leaf with illustration missing, else clean and very good.   Dumont Maps and Books of the West   130 - 28   2015 $150

New York Times   *The New York Times Theater Reviews 1920-1970.*   New York: New York Times and Arno Press, 1971. First edition, volumes 1-8 Reviews, 9-10 index, together 10 volmes, thick 4to., original cloth, lettered white and illustrated in black at spine and cover, clean, very good, neat bookplate.   Any Amount of Books   March 2015 - C12746   2015   £480

Newcastle, Margaret Lucas Cavendish, Duchess of 1693-1768   *Sociable Letters, written by the Thrice Noble, Illustrious and Excellent Princess, the Lady Marchioness of Newcastle.*   London: printed by William Wilson, 1664. First edition, large 4to., contemporary paneled calf, rebacked to style, brown morocco label, gilt lettering, endpapers little stained, fine, large copy.   The Brick Row Book Shop Miscellany 67 - 30   2015 $6000

Newcomb, Simon   *The Reminiscences of an Astronomer.* Cambridge: Riverside Press, 1903. 8vo., frontispiece, index browned due to offsetting of author's obit news notice from 1909, navy gilt stamped cloth, spine ends bit worn, bookplate of Elwyn B. Gould, good.   Jeff Weber Rare Books   178 - 824   2015 $45

Newcomb, W. W.   *The Indians of Texas from Prehistoric to Modern Times.*   Austin: University of Texas, 1961. First edition, cloth with gilt spine features, 404 pages, illustrations, portraits, superb drawings, maps, fine in slightly edgeworn dust jacket with small chip, very good dust jacket. Baade Books of the West   2014 - 2015 $77

Newcombe, Samuel Pourt   *Little Henry's Holiday at the Great Exhibition.*   London: Houlston & Stoneman, n.d., 1851. First edition, crown 8vo., engraved titlepage and frontispiece in sepia (foxed), 13 engraved plates (two in sepia and slightly foxed), 11 engraved illustrations within text, original pink cloth stamped in blind with gilt lettering on upper and lower covers, spine elaborately gilt repaired. Marlborough Rare Books Ltd.   List 49 - 12   2015   £150

Newdegate, Charles   *A Letter to the Right Hon. H. Labouchere, M.P., &c. On the Balance of trade, Ascertaiend from the market Value of all Articles Imported During the Last Four Years.*   London: Seeleys, 1849. First edition, 8vo., recent marbled boards lettered on spine, very good. John Drury Rare Books   2015 - 15306   2015 $177

Newdigate, Bernard H.   *Michael Drayton and His Circle.* Oxford: printed at Shakespeare Head Press, 1941. Half title, frontispiece, addenda & separate corrigenda slip, uncut in original dark blue cloth uniform with Drayton's Works, tipped in is charming presentation note from author to Kathleen Tillotson, inserted are some photos and unsigned account of visit to Polesworth in 1928.   Jarndyce Antiquarian Booksellers   CCVII - 242   2015   £35

Newell, Allen *Unified Theories of Cognition.* Cambridge: Harvard University Press, 1990. First edition, signed, inscribed and dated in year of publication by author, 8vo., fine in near fine dust jacket with sun spine. By the Book, L. C. 44 - 28 2015 $275

Newell, Davbid M. *If Nothin' Don't Happen.* New York: Knopf, 1975. First edition, very good plus, slight fading at perimeters, little foxing at fore-edges, very good dust jacket (mild chipping at extremities), inscribed. Stephen Lupack March 2015 - 2015 $150

Newell, Gordon *Totem Tales of Old Seattle. Legends and Anecdotes.* Seattle: Superior, 1956. Limited edition, limited to 2050 copies, this #37, royal 8vo., cloth, 176 pages, illustrations, maps, former owner's signature, fine in slightly edgeworn dust jacket with one quite small chip, fine in very good dust jacket. Baade Books of the West 2014 - 2015 $45

Newell, Peter *The Rocket Book.* New York: Harper & Bros. Oct., 1912. First edition, 8vo., cloth, pictorial paste-on, cover plate very slightly rubbed and very slightly rear cover soil, else clean and near fine, difficult to find in clean condition. Aleph-bet Books, Inc. 109 - 324 2015 $750

Newell, Peter *The Slant Book.* New York: Harper & Bros. Nov., 1910. First edition, 8vo., cloth backed pictorial boards, tips worn and edges rubbed, light finger soil on rear cover, really very good+, clean and tight copy, housed in custom cloth slipcase, full page illustrations. Aleph-bet Books, Inc. 109 - 325 2015 $750

Newell, Peter *Topsys & Turvys.* New York: Century, 1893. First edition, oblong small 4to., pictorial boards, less than usual flecking of paper and light edge wear, else beautiful, clean, very good++, 31 wonderful full page chromolithographed illustrations, scarce in such nice condition. Aleph-bet Books, Inc. 109 - 327 2015 $875

Newman, Harold *Genealogical Chart of Greek Mythology....* Chapel Hill: University of North Carolina Press, 2003. First edition, oblong folio, decorated paper over boards, 263 pages, fine, like new. Baade Books of the West 2014 - 2015 $93

Newman, John Henry 1801-1890 *Apologia Pro Vita Sua: The Two Versions of 1864 and 1865 Preceded by Newman's and Kingsley's Pamphlets...* London: Oxford University Press, 1931. Second impression, original blue cloth, crease on spine, Geoffrey Tillotson's copy 1 Jan. 1943 with notes, some inserts and marginal marks. Jarndyce Antiquarian Booksellers CCVII - 384 2015 £20

Newman, John Henry 1801-1890 *Certain Difficulties Felt by Anglicans in Catholic Teaching Considered...* London: Longmans Green, 1891. 2 volumes, half titles, initial request slip, 2 pages ads volume 2, original maroon cloth, spines slightly chipped at head and tail, annotated by Henry Tristram of Birmingham Oratory, presented to Geoffrey Tillotson, with his annotations. Jarndyce Antiquarian Booksellers CCVII - 385 2015 £25

Newman, John Henry 1801-1890 *Correspondence of John Henry Newman with John Keble and others 1839-1845.* London: Longmans, 1917. Half title, odd spot in prelims, original brown cloth, signed by Geoffrey Tillotson 16.xii47, with few notes. Jarndyce Antiquarian Booksellers CCVII - 386 2015 £25

Newman, John Henry 1801-1890 *Discussions and Arguments on Various Subjections.* London: Basil Montagu Pickering, 1872. Half title, final ad leaf, initial 8 page catalog, original dark blue cloth, spine faded and worn, hinges repaired, signature of Geoffrey Tillotson with notes. Jarndyce Antiquarian Booksellers CCVII - 387 2015 £20

Newman, John Henry 1801-1890 *An Essay on the Development of Christian Doctrine.* London: James Tovey, 1845. First edition, later half calf, slightly rubbed and chipped, light brown label, Geoffrey Tillotson's copy 20x43, with notes on leading pastedown and few in text. Jarndyce Antiquarian Booksellers CCVII - 388 2015 £110

Newman, John Henry 1801-1890 *Hymni Ecclesiae, Excerpti e Breviariis Romano, Salisburiensi, eboracensi...* Oxonii: J. H. Parker, 1838. 4 pages ads, original grey cloth, paper label, spine defective, scarce, inscribed Francis Palgrave from his affectionate NJ and EJJ Jan. 10 1839, from the library of Geoffrey & Kathleen Tillotson. Jarndyce Antiquarian Booksellers CCVII - 396 2015 £180

Newman, John Henry 1801-1890 *The Idea of a University Defined and Illustrated.* London: Longmans, Green, 1947. New edition, half title, title in red and black, original dark blue cloth in slightly torn dust jacket, signed by Geoffrey Tillotson Feb. 57. Jarndyce Antiquarian Booksellers CCVII - 389 2015 £20

Newman, John Henry 1801-1890 *John Henry Newman: Centenary Essays.* London: Burns, Oates & Washbourne, 1945. Half title, original green cloth, very good in torn dust jacket, Geoffrey Tillotson's copy, signed with extensive alterations in text of his essay. Jarndyce Antiquarian Booksellers CCVII - 397 2015 £22

Newman, John Henry 1801-1890 *Loss and Gain.* London: James Burns, 1848. First edition, original black cloth, slightly dulled and rubbed at corners, endpapers replaced, F. T. Palgrave's copy Mar 21:1848, with postcard photo of author inserted bearing birthday greetings to Geoffrey Tillotson. Jarndyce Antiquarian Booksellers CCVII - 390 2015 £180

Newman, John Henry 1801-1890 *Prose and Poetry.* London: Rupert Hart Davis, 1957. Half title, few pencil notes, original dark blue cloth, bevelled boards, very good in torn dust jacket, from the library of Geoffrey & Kathleen Tillotson, with his inscription to her 25.xii.56 with few inserted notes. Jarndyce Antiquarian Booksellers CCVII - 392 2015 £35

Newman, John Henry 1801-1890 *Prose and Poetry.* London: Rupert Hart Davis, 1957. Proof copy, half title, uncut in home-made rough paper wrappers, torn dust jacket, Geoffrey Tillotson's last proof 18 Jul 1956 with few notes in text, but with galley proof and few notes inserted. Jarndyce Antiquarian Booksellers CCVII - 393 2015 £30

Newman, John Henry 1801-1890 *Verses on Religious Subjects.* Dublin: James Duffy, 1853. First edition, contemporary calf, gilt borders and dentelles, spine chipped, boards detached, scarce, John Duke Coleridge's copy signed on original preserved endpaper, from the library of Geoffrey & Kathleen Tillotson. Jarndyce Antiquarian Booksellers CCVII - 394 2015 £220

Newman, John Henry 1801-1890 *Verses on Various Occasions.* London: Burns, Oates, 1880. Half title, erratum slip, final ad leaf, Geoffrey Tillotson's copy with signature 1942 indicating Hugh Walker's signature on preserved endpaper with numerous ink and pencil notes in text and inserted, Tillotson's decorated paper casing with ms. label. Jarndyce Antiquarian Booksellers CCVII - 395 2015 £45

Newmann, Alfred *Gitterwerk Des Lebens.* Los Angeles: Pazifischen Presse, 1943. Limited to 250 numbered copies, 150 signed by author on colophon, this copy thus, 8vo. quarter leather, paper covered boards fore edge uncut, spine gilt stamped, covers lightly soiled, some spotting of boards. Oak Knoll Books 306 - 162 2015 $300

Newsom, D. Earl *Drummright II: & Shamrock, Pemeta, Oilton & Olive a Thousand Memories.* Evans Perkins, 1987. First edition, royal 8vo., 275 pages, vintage photos, pictorial wrappers, fine in dust jacket. Baade Books of the West 2014 - 2015 $45

Newsom, D. Earl *The Life and Practice of the Wild and Modern Indian...* Oklahoma City: privately published, 1923. First edition, pictorial wrappers, illustrations, cover borders faded, last 2 leaves inside back cover near binding have pulled away from staples, but because binding is tight there is really no problem with them, small cosmetic issue, else very good, scarce. Baade Books of the West 2014 - 2015 $125

Newton, Alfred *Ootheca Wolleyana: an Illustrated Catalogue of the Collection of Birds.* London: 1864-1907. Large octavo, 2 volumes, 1289 pages, portrait, 37 lithographed plates, folding colored map, binder's cloth retaining two printed front wrappers, top edge gilt, others uncut, scarce. Andrew Isles 2015 - 26876 2015 $8500

Newton, Huey P. *Revolutionary Suicide.* New York: Harcourt Brace Jovanovich, 1973. First edition, tiny finger smudge on edge of half title, else fine in about fine dust jacket with tiny tear at foot and small dampstain inside of dust jacket, inscribed by author, especially uncommon inscribed. Between the Covers Rare Books 197 - 89 2015 $1000

Newton, Isaac 1642-1727 *Opticks; or a Treatise of the Reflexions, Refractions, Inflexions and Colours of Light. Also Two Treatises of the Species and Magnitude of Curvilinear Figures.* London: printed for Sam. Smith & Benj. Walford, printers to the Royal society, 1704. First edition, first issue, 2 parts in one volume, 4to., title printed in red and black, 19 folding engraved plates/diagrams, errata page, title lower margin trimmed (early signature on upper and lower edges of title faded and cannot be read without an infrared lamp, some light foxing, plates remarkably clean and free of tears, presentation binding of 19th century full vellum with covers gilt stamped with emblem of University of Edinburgh, calf gilt stamped spine label, edges red, small faint stamp inscribed for Thomas Smith, presented as a Prize in the Natural Philosophy Class University of Edinburgh, Session 1852-3, Philip Kelland, very small ink inscription at rear, titlepage with obscured signature of Charles Bernard (1650-1711). Jeff Weber Rare Books 178 - 830 2015 $55,000

Nguyen, Thi *The Little Shoeblack of Saigon.* South Vietnam: Giai Phong Pub. House, 1972. First edition, rubbing to covers otherwise near fine in wrappers. Ken Lopez, Bookseller 164 - 232 2015 $75

Niall, John *The Galloway Shepherd.* London: Heinemann, 1970. First edition, 8vo., frontispiece ad 4 full page illustrations, 21 smaller illustrations, signed presentation from Niall, sold with 25 of the original illustrations, very fine ink drawings by the late John Fleming, on art board with printers notes on rear and notes probably in artist's hand, drawings in excellent condition, book clean, tight, very good in slightly used but complete, about very good dust jacket. Any Amount of Books March 2015 - A40508 2015 £400

Nicely, Wilson S. *The Great Southwest.* St. Louis: 1867. Folding map, original stamped boards, spine slightly faded, two repaired tears to map with no loss, light very good copy. Dumont Maps and Books of the West   130 - 44   2015 $1450

Nicholas, Michael *Watermelons into Wine: Poems.* Honolulu: the author, 1968. First edition, small squarish quarto, stapled and self wrappers, collaged illustrations, very near fine, signed and dated in year of publication by author. Between the Covers Rare Books   197 - 34   2015 $275

Nicholl, John *The Judgement Delivered December 11th 1809 by the Right Honourable Sir John Nicholl Knt. LL.D. Official Principal of the Arches Court of Canterbury.* London: J. Butterworth and T. Conder, 1810. First separate edition, 8vo., titlepage rather dust marked with marginal tears and fraying (but no loss and printed surface not affected), with dust jacket ms. notes in ink on title verso, original lower wrapper, upper wrapper replaced, entirely uncut. John Drury Rare Books   March 2015 - 23613   2015 $221

Nichols, John *American Blood.* New York: Holt, 1987. First edition, inscribed by author, fine in fine dust jacket. Beasley Books   2013 - 2015 $45

Nichols, Madaline Wallis *El Gaucho. El Cazador De Ganado. El Jinete. Un Ideal De Novela.* Buenos Aires: Ediciones Peuser, 1963. First Spanish edition, limited to 5000 copies, quarter leather and marbled boards, numerous color plates, spine ends and fore-edges moderately worn, else very good.   Buckingham Books   March 2015 - 14201   2015 $375

Nicholson, Edward *Indian Snakes.* Madras: Higginbotham & Co., 1893. Second edition, octavo, 20 lithographic plates, many figures hand colored, publisher's brown cloth with gilt cobra titlepage and early leaves laid down, otherwise very good.   Andrew Isles   2015 - 35837   2015 $850

Nicholson, Henry John *Report of the Late Important Trial in the Court of King's Bench, in Which Sir Charles Merrik Burnell, Bart., was Plaintiff, and Henry John Nicholson, the Defendant, Respecting the Parochial Rates Claimed ...* London: J. B. Nichols & Son, 1834. First edition, 8vo., original maroon cloth, very faded, spine worn and rather shaken, internally good, very scarce.   John Drury Rare Books   March 2015 - 21891   2015 $266

Nicholson, James B. *A Manual of the Art of Bookbinding.* Limited to 300 numbered, signed copies, reprint of 1856 manual, 8vo., 18 hand marbled specimens, cloth with marbled paper specimen on front cover.   Oak Knoll Books   306 - 6   2015 $225

Nicholson, Michael Angelo *The Carpenter & Joiner's Companion in the Geometrical Construction of Working Drawings Required by Journeymen in the Progress of Building.* London: 1826. 8vo., portrait + 132 plates, text illustrations, contemporary calf backed boards, dampstain in lower margin of first few leaves, scattered spotting or browning or damp on some pages, some plates foxed, good, sound.   Joseph J. Felcone Inc.   Science, Medicine and Technology - 2   2015 $375

Nicholson, Peter *The Practical Cabinet Maker, Upholsterer and Complete Decorator.* London: H. Fischer and Son and Co. 38 Newgate Street, 1827. First edition, 4to., errata slip tipped in at page 11, additional engraved title with vignette and 23 engraved geometrical plates (irregularly numbered) and 81 decorative plates on 80 sheets, engraved title on stub, typographical title, little frayed at lower outer corners, occasional very light spotting or foxing, modern diced calf with gilt borders, green morocco label lettered gilt on spine, all edges blue, spine sunned.   Marlborough Rare Books   List 54 - 58   2015   £2650

Nicholson, Peter *Practical Carpentry, Joinery and Cabinet-Making; Being a New and Complete System of Lines for the Use of Workmen...* London: 1854. 4to., portrait, 110 plates, including engraved title, contemporary calf backed boards, neatly rebacked with original spine laid down several plates at rear dampstained, occasional spotting, most plates foxed at outer edges, good, tight copy. Joseph J. Felcone Inc.   Science, Medicine and Technology - 3   2015 $425

Nicholson, William   1753-1815 *A Dictionary of Chemistry.* London: printed for G. G. and J. Robinson, Paternoster Row, 1795. First edition, 2 volumes, 4 plates, clean, fresh copy throughout, handsomely bound in contemporary calf, spines gilt with morocco labels lettered and numbered in gilt, some surface wear wand rubbing to gilt, still very appealing copy.   Marlborough Rare Books   List 53 - 31   2015   £1250

Nicholson, William   1872-1949 *An Almanac of Twelve Sports.* London: William Heinemann, 1898. 4to., illustrations, 1 page ad verso final leaf, original illustrated paper boards, cloth spine repaired, some rubbing to edges and corners, inner hinges strengthened, from the library of Geoffrey & Kathleen Tillotson, with Kathleen's note recording joint purchase.   Jarndyce Antiquarian Booksellers   CCVII - 400   2015   £420

Nicholson, William   1872-1949 *The Pirate Twins.* London: Faber and Faber, 1929. Limited to only 60 numbered copies, special edition, signed by Nicholson, oblong 8vo., pictorial boards, covers very slightly dusty else fine, beautiful copy, very rare edition.   Aleph-Bet Books, Inc.   108 - 316   2015 $6500

Nicklin, Susan *Address to a Young Lady on Her Entrance into the World.* London: printed for Hookham and Carpenter, 1796. First editions, Volume I and II, contemporary uniform tree calf, spines gilt but worn with pretty, original, title label (red gilt) on volume II only, endpapers little marked, else very good copies, scarce. John Drury Rare Books 2015 - 25168 2015 $1049

Nicoll, Maurice *Psychological Commentaries on the Teaching of Gurdjieff & Ouspensky: Volumes 1-5.* London: published by Vincent Stuart, 1957. And 1955 reprint, First 3 volumes are third impressions published in 1957, volume 4 is first edition of 1955), decent about very good+ copies with used, near very good dust jackets (slightly chipped), last volume has neat ownership signature but decent set. Any Amount of Books 2015 - C7081 2015 £175

Nicolson, Dan H. *The Foresters and the Botany of the Second Cook Expedition (1772-1775).* A. R. G. Gantner Verlag, Ruggell, 2004. Second edition, 8vo., original yellow cloth lettered black at spine and over, endpaper maps, fine in fine. Any Amount of Books 2015 - A91764 2015 £180

Niedecker, Lorine *My Friend Tree. Poems.* Edinburgh: Wild Hawthorn Press, 1961. First edition, linocuts by Walter Miller, original wrappers, dust jacket, extremely rare, oblong 8vo., original wrappers, dust jacket, fine, inscribed by author for Jonathan Williams Sept. 3 69, extremely rare. James S. Jaffe Rare Books Modern American Poetry - 212 2015 $7500

Niedecker, Lorine *My Life by Water. Collected Poems 1936-1968.* London: Fulcrum Press, 1970. First edition, one of 100 copies printed on Glastonbury antique laid paper and signed by author, 8vo., original black cloth, actetate dust jacket, fine. James S. Jaffe Rare Books Modern American Poetry - 213 2015 $750

Niedecker, Lorine *North Central.* London: Fulcrum Press, 1968. First edition, one of 100 copies printed on mould made paper, deckled edged paper and signed by author, 4to., original cloth, dust jacket, head and foot of spine slightly bumped, otherwise fine. James S. Jaffe Rare Books Modern American Poetry - 214 2015 $750

Nietzsche, Friedrich *Ecce Homo. (Behold the Man).* Leipzig: Insel Verlag, 1908. First edition, one of 1250 copies, 150 on Japanese velum and 1100 on parchment, this copy is one of the 1250 printed on parchment with brown (rather than gold) ink throughout and numbered 964, square quarto. original half vellum and grey boards with embossed circular title on front cover in gilt and again in gilt on spine, front cover very slightly bowed outward (as usual with this book), some soiling to vellum on both front and back boards, otherwise well preserved, clean and bright copy. Athena Rare Books 15 - 48 2015 $1200

Nietzsche, Friedrich *Ecce Homo. (Behold the Man).* Leipzig: Insel-Verlag, 1908. First edition, one of 1250 copies, 150 on Japanese velin and 1,100 on parchment, this one of the premium copies on Japanese velin with gold (rather than brown) ink and with deluxe binding, numbered '93', original grey suede boards with embossed circular title on front cover in gilt and again in gilt on spine, small stain mark to bottom of spine from former owner's sticker and small library stamp (University of Jena) to verso of titlepage, letter of deaccession back to original owner enclosed, otherwise clean, tight and bright copy protected by modern slipcase. Athena Rare Books 15 - 47 2015 $3500

Nietzsche, Friedrich *Jenseits von gut and Bose. (Beyond Good and Evil).* Leipzig: Naumann, 1886. First edition, octavo, Richard Meyer's (1860-1914) copy, contemporary dark red pebbled boards with most minor wear, half leather spine has seven ribs and gilt titling on red field, Meyer's bookplate to inside front cover, lovely clean copy, remarkable association copy. Athena Rare Books 15 - 41 2015 $9000

Nietzsche, Friedrich *Jenseits von Gut and Bose. (Beyond Good and Evil).* Leipzig: Naumann, 1886. First edition, octavo, recent period style three quarter red morocco (with gilt lettering and decorations to spine) over contemporary red marbled boards and text block with marbled edges, tight, clean and beautiful copy. Athena Rare Books 15 - 42 2015 $6000

Nietzsche, Friedrich *Menschliches Allzumenschliches. Ein Buch fur Freie Geister. (Human All Too Human. A Book for Free Spirits).* Chemnitz: Schmeitzner, 1878. First edition, octavo, original front wrapper with some wear and reinforced corners along with partial remains of a bookseller's ticket in lower left hand corner, beautifully matched and lettered recent spine with similar rear cover, former owner's modern bookplate (Kristian Bathe) and handwritten ink inscription to first half title, custom clamshell box housing tight, clean and beautiful copy. Athena Rare Books 15 - 38 2015 $9500

Nietzsche, Friedrich *Menschliches, Allzumenschliches. Ein Buch fur Freie Geister. (Human All Too Human. A Book for free Spirits).* Chemnitz: Schmeitzner, 1878. First edition, first issue, octavo, recent period style three quarter red morocco with gilt lettering and decorations to spine, over contemporary green speckled boards and text block with marbled edges, boards show some light wear in spots, overall this is tight, clean, beautiful copy. Athena Rare Books 15 - 38 2015 $4500

Nietzsche, Friedrich *Menschliches Allzumenschliches, Anhang: Vermischte Meinungen und Spruche. (Human All Too Human. A Supplement: Mixed Opinions and Maxims).* Chemnitz: Schmeitzner, 1879. First edition, first issue, octavo, with publisher's penciled hand correction to page 35 correcting "Opefersims" to Opferthiers" as request by Nietzsche in his March 5 1879 letter to Schmeitzner, this copy lacks ads which are preserved in some copies, recent period style three quarter red morocco with gilt lettering ad decorations to spine, over contemporary green speckled boards and text block with marbled edges, boards show some light wear in spots, overall tight, clean, beautiful copy. Athena Rare Books   15 - 39   2015 $3800

Nietzsche, Friedrich *Zur Genealogie der Moral. (One the Geneaology of Morals).* Leipzig: C. G. Naumann, 1887. First edition, octavo, recent period style three quarter red morocco with gilt lettering and decorations to spine, over contemporary red marbled boards and text block with marbled edges, tight, clean, beautiful copy.   Athena Rare Books   15 - 43   2015 $5500

Nietzsche, Friedrich *Thus Spake Zarathustra.* New York: Macmillan Co., 1896. First Edition, American issue, octavo, original apple-green cloth boards with light edgewear and just bit of discoloration to front edges of boards, small 1 inch split at edge of lower rear spine, internally tight and clean, very presentable copy.   Athena Rare Books   15 - 45   2015 $3000

Nietzsche, Friedrich *Also Sprach Zarathustra. (Thus Spoke Zarathustra).* Leipzig: C. G. Naumann, 1899. Later edition, circular snake edition, small octavo, publisher's original pebbled tan covers with gilt lettering and designs on both front cover and spine in red, spine lettering bit faded, otherwise very good.   Athena Rare Books   15 - 46   2015 $150

Nietzsche, Friedrich *Also Sprach Zarathustra; Ein Buch fur Alle Und Keinen (Thus Spoke Zarathustra).* Leipzig: Insel-Verlag, 1908. Limited to 530 numbered copies, 430 parchment bound, of which copy is thus, small folio, full vellum with yapp edges, title gilt stamped on spine, gilt stamped vignette on front cover, top edge cut, other edges uncut, in later clamshell box, illustrations by Henry van de Velde, endpapers decorated around borders, double page ornamental title, printed title with vignette, all in purple and gold, text in black and gold, covers lightly soiled, light foxing to endpapers.   Oak Knoll Books   306 - 172   2015 $5500

Nietzsche, Friedrich *Unzeitgemasse Betrachtungen II: Vom Nutzen und Nachtheil. (Unconventional Observation II: The Use and Disadvanage of History for Life).* Leipzig: E. W Fritzsch, 1874. First edition, first issue, approximately 650 copies, octavo, recently rebound in three quarter green cloth, gilt lettering to spine, contemporary green marbled boards, text block with marbled edges, internally bright and clean, overall very good.   Athena Rare Books   15 - 36   2015 $1500

Nietzsche, Friedrich *Unzeitgemasse Betrachtungen. (Unconventional Observations I-IV).* Leipzig: C. G. Naumann, 1893. Second edition, octavo, 2 volumes, bound with original front wrappers and expertly matching (but recent) spines and rear covers, some scattered pencil underlinings and marginalia, otherwise really well preserved, excellent copy.   Athena Rare Books   15 - 44   2015 $850

Nietzsche, Friedrich *Der Wanderer und Sein Schatten. (The Wanderer and His Shadow).* Chemnitz: Schmeitzner, 1880. First edition, first issue, octavo, recent period style, three quarter red morocco with gilt lettering and decorations to spine, over contemporary green speckled boards and text block with marbled edges, boards show some light wear in spots, overall tight, clean and beautiful copy.   Athena Rare Books   15 - 40   2015 $3800

Nightingale, Florence 1820-1910 *Notes on Nursing: What It Is and Is Not.* London: Harrison, 1860. First edition, 2nd issue, 8vo., original pebbled limp cloth, some nicks to cloth, moderate foxing, former owner's name on titlepage.   Second Life Books Inc.   189 - 183   2015 $1200

Nightingale, Florence 1820-1910 *Notes on Nursing: What It Is and What It Is Not.* Boston: William Carter, 5 Water Street, 1860. First edition thus, 12mo., signed in 6s, original brown cloth with gilt stamping to front board, pale yellow endpapers, modest extremity wear to binding, period pencil owner signature to prelim blank, some age toning, foxing and browning to paper, still withal quite respectable copy, very good+.   Tavistock Books   Bah, Humbug? - 10   2015 $750

Nightingale, Joseph *A Portraiture of Methodism; Being an Impartial View of the Rise, Progress, Doctrines, Discipline and Manners of the Wesleyan Methodists.* London: Longman Hurst Rees and Orme, 1807. First edition, 8vo., endpapers with old dampstains, original boards, neatly rebacked and lettered, entirely uncut, excellent copy.   John Drury Rare Books   March 2015 - 16592   2015 $266

Nilsson, Martin P. *Primitive Time-Reckoning: a Study in the Origins and First Development of the Art of Counting Time Among the Primitive and Early Peoples.* Lund: C. W. K. Gleerup; London: Humphrey Milford; Oxford: Univerfsity Press, 1920. 8vo., original quarter vellum, plain boards, manuscript spine title, ink ownership signatures of Alexandri Phili (192), William Duane Stahlman and David C. Lindberg.   Jeff Weber Rare Books   178 - 846   2015 $45

Nin, Anais *Children of the Albatross.* New York: Dutton, 1947. First edition, fine, 8vo., inscribed by author, near fine dust jacket.   Second Life Books Inc.   191 - 62   2015 $400

Nin, Anais *Cities of the Interior.* Denver: Alan Swallow, 1959. First edition, hardcover issue, line engravings by Ian Hugo, illustrated white cloth, some foxing or light soiling, else near fine, beautifully inscribed to Caresse Crosby. Between the Covers Rare Books, Inc. 187 - 203 2015 $2500

Nin, Anais *Collages.* London: Peter Owen, 1964. First English edition, small 8vo., 170 pages, fine in price clipped dust jacket (rear cover little soiled). Second Life Books Inc. 191 - 63 2015 $65

Nin, Anais *D. H. Lawrence. An Unprofessional Study and Two Facsimile Manuscript Pages Out of Lady Chatterly's Lover.* Paris: Edward W. Titus, 1932. First edition, 8vo., fine in near fine dust jacket, one of 550 copies, this copy not numbered. Second Life Books Inc. 191 - 64 2015 $500

Nin, Anais *The Diary of Anais Nin. Volume Two. 1934-1939.* New York: Swallow Press/Harcourt Brace & World, 1967. First edition, 8vo., photos, very good, tight copy in dust jacket little scuffed and chipped, inscribed by author for Bill. Second Life Books Inc. 191 - 66 2015 $400

Nin, Anais *The Diary of .... 1944-1947.* New York: Harcourt Brace Jovanovich, 1971. First edition, photos, 8vo., photos, cover slightly stained, otherwise very good, tight copy in little scuffed and nicked price clipped dust jacket, laid in is advance complimentary slip with author's card, in addition author has inscribed the copy to poet and editor, Bill Claire. Second Life Books Inc. 191 - 65 2015 $600

Nin, Anais *The Four Chambered Heart.* New York: Duell Sloan and Pearce, 1950. First edition, 8vo. bound in gray cloth, no dust jacket, pages little toned, very good, inscribed by author for Bill. Second Life Books Inc. 191 - 67 2015 $300

Nin, Anais *Ladders to Fire.* New York: Dutton, 1496. First edition, 8vo., engravings by Ian Hugo, 8vo., very good in dust jacket little chipped and worn lacks some of the extremities of spine and on corners, inscribed by author for Bill (Claire). Second Life Books Inc. 191 - 68 2015 $450

Nin, Anais *Solar Barque.* N.P.: Edwards Brothers, 1958. First edition, inscribed to Norman Mailer and wife. Honey & Wax Booksellers 2 - 59 2015 $650

Nin, Anais *A Spy in the House of Love.* New York: British Book Center, 1954. First American edition, 8vo., excellent copy, variant blue cloth with black spine lettering, quarter inch wider than maroon cloth trade edition, slightly soiled dust jacket. Second Life Books Inc. 191 - 72 2015 $125

Ninetieth Anniversary of the Aberdeen Hospital School of Nursing, New Glasgow, Nova Scotia 1897-1987. New Glasgow: Aberdeen Hospital School of Nursing, 1987. 8vo., card covers, photo illustrations, very good. Schooner Books Ltd. 110 - 104 2015 $45

Nirenberg, Marshall W. *Dependence of Cell-Free Protein Synthesis in E. Coli Upon Naturally Occurring or Synthetic Polyribonucleotides.* National Academy of Sciences, 1961. Offprint from the Proceedings of the national Academy of Sciences volume 47 no. 10, Oct. 1961, first separate edition, near fine, 8vo., self wrappers as issued, mild horizontal crease, owner name, 4 figures, rare. By the Book, L. C. 44 - 23 2015 $1000

Nisbet, Hume *A Bush Girl's Romance.* London: F. V. White and Co., 1894. Illustrations by author, contemporary half maroon morocco, little rubbed, bookplate of J. Monro Walker. Jarndyce Antiquarian Booksellers CCXI - 217 2015 £50

Nisbet, Hume *The Bushranger's Sweetheart.* London: F. V. White & Co., 1892. First edition, frontispiece and title vignette by author, contemporary half maroon morocco, leading hinge slight worn, little rubbed, bookplate of J. Monro Walker. Jarndyce Antiquarian Booksellers CCXI - 218 2015 £60

Nisbet, Hume *A Colonial Tramp, Travels and Adventures through Australia and New Guinea.* London: Ward & Downey, 1891. First edition, 8vo., 2 volumes, original orange cloth, lettered gilt on spine with illustrated covers, 2 colored frontispieces and 41 plates with illustrated text, excellent condition, slight rubbing to spine ends and browning to free endpapers. Any Amount of Books 2015 - C1985 2015 £260

Nisbet, Hume *A Desert Bride.* London: F. V. White and Co., 1894. First edition, illustrations by author, contemporary half maroon morocco, little rubbed, bookplate of J. Monro Walker. Jarndyce Antiquarian Booksellers CCXI - 219 2015 £40

Nisbet, Hume *The Great Secret.* London: F.V. White & Co., 1895. First edition, half title, contemporary maroon morocco little rubbed, bookplate of J. Monro Walker. Jarndyce Antiquarian Booksellers CCXI - 220 2015 £125

Nisbet, Hume *Her Loving Slave.* London: Digby, Long & Co., 1894. Second edition, half title, frontispiece, bookplate of J. Monro Walker, contemporary half maroon roan, little rubbed,. Jarndyce Antiquarian Booksellers CCXI - 221 2015 £45

Nisbet, Hume *The "Jolly Roger".* London: Digby, Long & Co., 1891. First edition, frontispiece and title vignette by author, contemporary half maroon morocco, little rubbed, bookplate of J. Monro Walker,. Jarndyce Antiquarian Booksellers   CCXI - 222   2015   £125

Nisbet, Hume *My Love Noel.* London: F. V. White & Co., 1896. First edition, half title, contemporary half maroon morocco, little rubbed, bookplate of J. Monro Walker,. Jarndyce Antiquarian Booksellers   CCXI - 223   2015   £45

Nisbet, Hume *The Queen's Desire.* London: F. V. White & co., 1893. First edition, frontispiece and title vignette by author, contemporary half maroon morocco, little rubbed, bookplate of bookplate of J. Monro Walker,. Jarndyce Antiquarian Booksellers   CCXI - 224   2015   £50

Nisbet, Hume *The Savage Queen.* London: F. V. White & Co., 1891. First edition, contemporary half maroon morocco little rubbed, bookplate of bookplate of J. Monro Walker,. Jarndyce Antiquarian Booksellers   CCXI - 225   2015   £65

Niver, Joseph *Earth: a History Together with a Facsimile of Earth and Selected Letters of Romain Rolland and Leo Tolstoy.* Millwood: KTO Press, 1977. First edition thus, blue green cloth, slight sunning to spine, otherwise fine copy of this facsimile reprint, 4to.   Beasley Books   2013 - 2015 $125

Nix, Evett Dumas *Oklahombres Particularly the Wilder Ones.* St. Louis: Eden, 1929. First edition, gilt stamped pictorial cloth, 280 pages, vintage photos, chapter head drawings and pen and ink margin vignettes on all numbered pages, this copy near fine, bright, extreme top edge of front cover worn 5/8" near spine, hinge papers just barely cracked and book tight.   Baade Books of the West   2014 - 2015 $75

Nixon, Howard M. *Broxbourne Library, Styles and Designs of Bookbindings from the Twelfth to the Twentieth Century.* London: Maggs Bros., 1956. Limited to 300 copes, folio, quarter vellum over blue cloth, blue leather spine label, top edge gilt, later slipcase, old bookseller description mounted in corner of free endpaper.   Oak Knoll Books   306 - 7   2015 $1500

Nizer, Louis *Between You and Me.* New York: Beechhurst Press, 1948. First edition, very slightly rubbed at spinal extremities, inscribed by the lawyer to silent film star Harold Lloyd.   Between the Covers Rare Books, Inc.   187 - 204   2015 $130

Noah's Ark. New York: Grosset & Dunlap, 1943. 8vo., pictorial wrappers, fine in very good+ dust jacket with few creases, illustrations by Tibor Gergely with color lithos and in black and white.   Aleph-bet Books, Inc.   109 - 195   2015 $200

Noble, John *Fiscal Legislation 1842-1865, A Review of the Financial Changes of that Period and Their Effects Upon Revenue, Trade, Manufactures and Employment.* London: Longmans, Green Reader & Dyer, 1867. First edition, 8vo., half title, errata slip, original tan cloth, embossed in blind, spine lettered gilt, fine.   John Drury Rare Books   2015 - 8200   2015 $221

Noble, Samuel H. *Life and adventures of Buckskin Sam.* Rutherford Falls: Rutherford Falls Pub. Co., 1900. First edition, 8vo., signed by author on rear flyleaf, brown fabricoid, gold stamping on front cover, 185 pages, frontispiece, lightly rubbed at foot of spine and corners, else near fine.   Buckingham Books   March 2015 - 24134   2015 $175

Nodin, John *The British Duties of Customs, Excise &c. Containing an Account of the net Sums Payable on all Goods Imported, Exported or Carried Coastwise.* London: for J. Johnson and G. G. J. and J. Robinson, 1792. First edition, apparently rare, 3 folding table at end, original paper backed boards, uncut, contemporary or near, contemporary hand lettered lot ticket pasted on upper board, L3 torn without loss, boards very lightly soiled, neatly rebacked with printed label added, fine, uncut.   John Drury Rare Books   2015 - 8026   2015 $787

Nodin, John *The British Duties of Customs, Excise &c. containing an account of the New Sums Payable on all Goods Imported, Exported or carried Coastwise...* London: for J. Johnson and G. G. J. and J. Robinson, 1792. First edition, 8vo., 3 folding tables at end, contemporary mottled sheep, neatly rebacked to match, spine with gilt lines and old morocco label lettered gilt, very good, surprisingly uncommon.   John Drury Rare Books   March 2015 - 25263   2015 $656

Nolan, Frederick W. *The Lincoln County War: a Documentary History.* Norman: Oklahoma University Press, 1992. First edition, royal 8vo., cloth, illustrations, as new in fine dust jacket.   Baade Books of the West   2014 - 2015 $75

Norfleet, J. Frank *Norfleet. The Amazing Experiences of an Intrepid Texas Ranger with an International Swindling Ring.* Sugar land: Imperial Press, 1927. Revised edition, cloth, illustrations, signed by Norfleet and Gordon Hines and further inscribed by Hines to John C. Bennett, near very good.   Baade Books of the West   2014 - 2015 $49

Norman, George Warde *An Examination of Some Prevailing Opinions as to the Pressure of Taxation in this and Other Countries.* London: T. W. Boone, 1850. 8vo., recently well bound in cloth, spine gilt lettered, very good.   John Drury Rare Books   March 2015 - 25182   2015   £266

Norman, George Warde *An Examination of Some prevailing Opinions as the the Pressure of Taxation in this and other Countries.* London: T. & W. Boone, 1850. Third edition, 8vo., recent marbled boards lettered on spine, very good.   John Drury Rare Books   March 2015 - 23721   2015   £306

Norman, George Warde *Papers on Various Subjects.* London: printed for private circulation by T. & W. Boone, 1869. Only edition, 8vo., original green cloth lettered in gilt, covers rather faded, still good copy, inscribed in ink "from the author", scarce.   John Drury Rare Books   2015 - 21970   2015 $177

Norman, V. Garth *Izapa Sculpture Part 1 and 2.* Provo: New World Archaeological Foundation BYU, 1973-1976. First edition, quarto, printed wrappers, illustrations, volume I has nickel sized scuff on front cover in blank area, else fine, volume 2 has imperceptible small crease to corner of front cover and first couple of leaves but essentially fine, laid in order from the press 1973 1976, very good+.   Baade Books of the West   2014 - 2015 $77

Normanby, Constantine Henry Phipps, 1st Marquis of 1797-1853 *A Year of Revolution. From a Journal Kept in Paris in 1848.* London: Longman Brown, Green, Longmans & Roberts, 1857. First edition, 2 volumes, 8vo., contemporary uniform half calf gilt with raised bands and labels, speckled edges, very good.   John Drury Rare Books   March 2015 - 16412   2015 $221

Norris, P. W. *The Calumet of the Cocteau and Other Poetical Legends of the Border...* Philadelphia: J. B. Lippincott, 1884. Second edition, 8vo., illustrations and 2 maps, brown cloth stamped in gilt, frontispiece, waterstaining to front blanks, otherwise fine.   Second Life Books Inc.   190 - 173   2015 $300

North Country Anvil 1-13. Millville: June, 1972. through Oct. 1974. First edition, wrappers, first thirteen issues, very good+ to near fine.   Beasley Books   2013 - 2015 $200

North Dakota Historical Society *North Dakota Historical Quarterly.* Grand Forks: n.d., Volume VI #4 (Oct. 1926-Oct. 1932), 24 issues, above 1800 pages, original wrappers, very good to fine.   Bookworm & Silverfish   2015 - 3678580734   2015 $360

North, Alfred J. *Nests and Eggs of Birds Found Breeding in Australia and Tasmania.* Sydney: Australian Museum, 1901-1914. Quarto, 4 volumes, 25 egg plates, uncolored vignettes by Nevill Cayley, photos, near contemporary half black calf, all edges speckled, slight wear, otherwise excellent set.   Andrew Isles   2015 - 27134   2015 $2500

North, Alfred J. *Nests and Eggs of Birds Found Breeding in Australia and Tasmania.* Sydney: Australian Museum, 1901-1914. Quarto, 4 volumes, 25 egg plates, uncolored vignettes, binder's cloth showing signs of wear some pale foxing throughout, nonetheless sound set.   Andrew Isles   2015 - 13882   2015 $2250

Northcliffe, Counsellor *An Argument in Defence of the Right of Patrons to Advousons. and Incidently of the Right of Tythes in Generall.* London: printed for Edward Blackmore at the Angell in Pauls Church-Yard, 1653. First edition, 4to., 12 pages, generally dust soiled, very minor marginal fraying, ink library shelf number on blank verso of title with some through on recto, early 20th century roan backed cloth boards, lettered in gilt, very scarce.   John Drury Rare Books   March 2015 - 24632   2015 $266

Northern Pacific Railroad *The Wonderland Route to the Pacific Coast.* privately printed, 1885. 9.5 x 7 inches, pictorial wrappers with light green background, 64 pages, engraved illustrations, lightly colored map inside front cover, front and rear wrappers chipped and with wear to extremities along with much chipping to spine with penciling to both wrappers.   Buckingham Books   March 2015 - 36211   2015 $450

Northrup, John H. *Crystalline Enzymes.* New York: Columbia University Press, 1939. First edition, signed and inscribed by author, near fine, blue cloth, gilt lettered spine, 8vo.   By the Book, L. C.   Special List 10 - 4   2015 $600

Norton, Mary *The Borrowers.* London: J. M. Dent, 1952. First edition, 8vo., blue pictorial cloth, tiny imperfection in cloth, else fine in very good dust jacket with slight fraying restored, illustrations by Diane Stanley with pictorial endpapers, color frontispiece plus many nice text illustrations, excellent copy, quite hard to find.   Aleph-bet Books, Inc.   109 - 331   2015 $1450

Norwood, Hayden *Death Down East.* Phoenix Press, 1941. First edition, former owner's inked name on front flyleaf, else near fine in dust jacket with light professional restoration to head of spine.   Buckingham Books   March 2015 - 37543   2015 $400

Notes and Sketches of Lessons on Subjects Connected with the Great Exhibition. London: printed for the Society for Promoting Christian Knowledge, 1852. First edition, 12mo., few minor marks and pencilling in places, generally clean throughout, original brown blindstamped publisher's cloth, spine lettered gilt, some marking and rubbing to cloth, still near very good.   Marlborough Rare Books Ltd.   List 49 - 8   2015   £385

Nothing to Wear. London: T. Onwhyn Delt. Rock & Co. Nov. 30th, 1858. First edition, Engraved panorama, consisting of 10 hand colored illustrations, 14.5 x 148cm., original blue cloth backed glazed ochre covers, upper cover with illustrated title, lower cover affected by damp but illustrations, not affected. Marlborough Rare Books List 54 - 59 2015 £385

Notice sur l'Ecole Rurale pour les Orphelins. Geneve: Decembre, 1825. 8vo., 14 pages, lacking final blank (?), caption title, first word shaved and page numbers, patchy foxing, fold tears, recent plain wrappers. John Drury Rare Books 2015 - 17875 2015 $106

Nougaret, Pierre Jean Baptiste *Londres, la Cour et les Provinces d'Angleterre d'Ecosse et d'Irlande ou Esprit, Moeurs, Coutumes, Habitudes Privees des Habitans de la Grand Bretagne, Ouvrage dans Lequel on s'est Applique a Recueillir les Faits et les Anecdotes....* Paris: Briand, 1816. First edition, scattered foxing, 8vo., few marginal stains, uncut in original paper wrappers, upper wrapper volume II loose, with portion torn from upper outer corner, otherwise little worn, but good. Blackwell's Rare Books B179 - 78 2015 £300

Nouveau Recueil de Principes et de Modeles D'Ecritures a L'Usage des Pensionnats et Maisons d'Education. Bruxelles: Van Thielen, 1840. Oblong 32mo., contemporary leather backed marbled paper covered boards, label on front cover, modern slipcase, 22 plates, front cover separated, some spotting and foxing, ownership inscription dated 1844 on inside front cover, old ownership writing on front pastedown and title. Oak Knoll Books Special Catalogue 24 - 36 2015 $225

Nowell-Smith, Simon *Letters to Macmillan.* London: Macmillan, 1967. Half title, plates, facsimiles, original red cloth, very good in slightly marked dust jacket, editor's signed copy, from the library of Geoffrey & Kathleen Tillotson, presentation inscription to same with note by Kathleen inserted. Jarndyce Antiquarian Booksellers CCVII - 401 2015 £20

Noyes, A *In the Land of Chinook or the Story of Blaine County.* Helena: State Pub., 1917. First edition, 8vo., cloth, grey endpapers, illustrations, portrait, photos, scarce lightly rubbed at spine ends and bottom edges of two lower corners, else near fine, clean, tight, square copy, transparent dust jacket, handsome copy, very scarce. Buckingham Books March 2015 - 31672 2015 $750

Noyes, Alfred *Collected Poems.* Edinburgh and London: William Blackwood and Sons, 1919. Half title, uncut in original green buckram, spine faded, titlepage, signed by Geoffrey Tillotson 29/12/20 "Bought by Uncle Fred Sutcliffe in Bradford Market on Christmas eve 1920", with text of 'A Tale of Old Japan' written neatly in ink by Geoffrey throughout prelims, with few notes in text, 3 cuttings inserted. Jarndyce Antiquarian Booksellers CCVII - 402 2015 £20

Noyes, George Wallingford *The Religious Experience of John Humphrey Noyes.* New York: Macmillan, 1923. First edition, hardcover, lovely fine and bright in near fine dust jacket with few tiny tears, unusually bright copy. Beasley Books 2013 - 2015 $85

Nuckel, Otto *Schicksal. Eine Geschichte in Bildern.* Munich: Delphin Verlag, 1926. First edition, lead engraving to titlepage and then to each recto, square 8vo., original yellow cloth blocked in brown to front, backstrip lettered in brown, top edge brown, bookplate tipped in to pastedown, light dust soiling, overall very good. Blackwell's Rare Books B179 - 198 2015 £275

Nugent, Robert Craggs *Considerations Upon a Reduction of the Land-Tax.* London: R. Griffiths, 1749. First edition, 8vo. errata to page 67, large folding table following text table torn but with no loss, preserved in recent plain wrappers with label on upper cover, good, uncut. John Drury Rare Books 2015 - 21474 2015 $177

Nugent, Robert Craggs *Farther Considerations Upon a Reduction of the and Tax: Together with a State of the Annual Supplies of the Sinking-Fund and of the National Debt.* London: R. Griffiths, 1751. First edition, 8vo. half title, recently well bound in linen backed marbled boards, very good. John Drury Rare Books 2015 - 19260 2015 $177

Nunez, Ignacio Benito *Noticias Historicas, Politicas y Estadisticas de las Provincias Unidas del Rio de la Plata.* London: Publicado por R. Ackermann, 1825. First edition, 2 folding maps, 8vo., modern full black morocco ruled in gilt, four raised bands, gilt titles, marbled edges, silk book mark sewn in, overall very good or better copy, armorial bookplate, titlepage tender, rear blank with large chip, original contemporary rear wrapper bound in but worn, color map bound upside down, fine modern binding, from the Coleccion Monclau (bookplate). Kaaterskill Books 19 - 108 2015 $700

Nura's Children Go Visiting. New York & London: Studio, 1943. Large 4to., cloth, fine in dust jacket, illustrations by Nura with wonderful full page lithographs (16) done directly on stone. Aleph-Bet Books, Inc. 108 - 324 2015 $225

Nursery Nonsense. New York: Hurd & Houghton, n.d. circa, 1870. 5 x 7 1/4 inches, pictorial wrappers, neat spine repair very good, 8 fanciful color engravings by Charles Bennett.   Aleph-bet Books, Inc.   109 - 49   2015 $275

Nye, Wilbur Sturtevant   *Plains Indian Raiders. The Final Phases of Warfare from the Arkansas to the Red River.* Norman: Oklahoma University, 1968. First edition, royal 8vo., cloth, 418 pages, photo plates, signed by author, fine but dust jacket chipped and heavily creased, main chip is 1 1/2 x 1 inch triangle at top of front panel, signed copies scarce, fine in fine dust jacket.   Baade Books of the West   2014 - 2015 $53

O

O'Brien, Eoin *The Beckett Country: an Exhibition for Samuel Beckett's Eightieth Birthday.* Dublin: Black Cat Press, 1980. First edition, large 8vo., illustrated wrappers, illustrations, very slightly bumped, otherwise fine, excellent condition. Any Amount of Books 2015 - C1822 2015 £160

O'Brien, Tim *Going After Cacciato.* New York: Delacorte/Seymour Lawrence, 1978. First edition, near fine in nearly fine dust jacket, one tiny closed tear to top of front panel. Ed Smith Books 83 - 72 2015 $450

O'Brien, Tim *Going After Cacciato.* New York: Delacorte, 1978. First edition, 8vo., light blue cloth, very good+ in like dust jacket (department store price sticker remnant to dust jacket front flap), respectable copy. Tavistock Books Bah, Humbug? - 24 2015 $300

O'Bryen, Denis *The Prospect Before Us.* London: J. Almon, 1788. First collected edition, 8vo., short marginal tear in one leaf (no loss), well bound in linen backed marbled boards lettered, very good, crisp copy. John Drury Rare Books March 2015 - 22459 2015 $221

O'Bryen, Denis *Utrum Horum? The Government or the Country?* London: J. Debrett, 1796. First edition, 8vo., half title and final blank, very small old inkstamp of Dutch institution, well bound in 18th century style quarter calf gilt, very good. John Drury Rare Books March 2015 - 19555 2015 £306

O'Casey, Sean *The Story of the Irish Citizen Army.* Dublin and London: Maunsel & Co. Ltd., 1919. First edition, original printed wrappers little creased and slightly browned at edges, head of backstrip chipped and upper hinge professionaly repaired, else nice, from the collection of Gavin H. Fryer. Bertram Rota Ltd. 308 Part II - 184 2015 £225

O'Connell, Jack *My First Rifle and the Story of How I Became a Crack Shot.* Hopkins & Allen Arms, n.d. circa 1900. 6 1/4 x 3 1/2 inches, wrappers tied at spine, 3 full page photos photo of O'Connell on titlepage, lightly soiled, interior clean, very good. Buckingham Books March 2015 - 35290 2015 $225

O'Connor, Frank 1903-1966 *Guests of the Nation: Stories.* London: Macmillan & Co. Ltd., 1931. First edition, original binding, covers faded and marked, endpapers somewhat browned, very good, publisher's review slip tipped in and loosely inserted, V. S. Pritchett's copy, inscribed by him, from the collection of Gavin H. Fryer. Bertram Rota Ltd. 308 Part II - 185 2015 £120

O'Connor, Louise S. *Cryin' for Daylight. A ranching culture in the Texas Coastal bend.* Wexford Publishing, 1989. First edition, tall quarto, decorated green cloth, map, photos, fine in dust jacket lightly rubbed at spine ends. Buckingham Books March 2015 - 34181 2015 $275

O'Connor, Patricia Burns *Spectacular Hawaii.* N.P.: Beaux Arts Editions, 2005. New edition, oversize folio, fine in fine dust jacket. Beasley Books 2013 - 2015 $45

O'Connor, Sandra Day *The Majesty of the Law.* New York: Random House, First trade edition, 8vo., signed and inscribed by O'Connor, fine in near fine dust jacket with mild scuff. By the Book, L. C. 44 - 57 2015 $110

O'Conor, Andrew P. *Forty Years with Fighting Cocks.* Goshen: E. W. Rogers, 1929. First edition, 8vo., illustrations, publisher's cloth, front and rear hinges loose, inscribed by author to Henry Henkel Rlyue, March 11, 1931, also signed on front blank, scarce. Second Life Books Inc. 191 - 73 2015 $300

O'Dogherty, William *An Epitome of the History of Europe from the Reign of Charlemagne to the reign of George III.* London: printed for T. Hookham, 1788. First edition of this title, one leaf with portion torn out of fore-margin, not affecting text, occasional spots or stains, 8vo., contemporary calf backed marbled boards, vellum tips to corners, flat spine with gilt tooled compartments, slightly worn, childish and somewhat messy scribblings in pencil to endpapers and flyleaves, good. Blackwell's Rare Books B179 - 80 2015 £450

O'Donnell, Peter *Dragon's Claw.* London: Souvenir, 1978. First edition, fine in dust jacket. Mordida Books March 2015 - 010097 2015 $175

O'Donnell, Peter *Modesty Blaise.* London: Souvenir, 1965. First edition, fine, name and address on front endpaper and some light spotting on page edges, otherwise price clipped dust jacket. Mordida Books March 2015 - 009127 2015 $100

O'Donnell, Peter *Modesty Blaise.* London: Souvenir, 1965. First edition, couple of pages torn and creased and some tiny light spotting on page edges, otherwise fine in dust jacket with small stain on front panel and some tiny wear at spine ends. Mordida Books March 2015 - 010093 2015 $125

O'Donnell, Peter *Sabre Tooth.* London: Souvenir, 1966. First edition, fine in dust jacket with slightly darkened spine. Mordida Books   March 2015 - 010094   2015 $250

O'Donnell, Peter *The Silver Mistress.* London: Souvenir, 1973. First edition, fine in dust jacket.   Buckingham Books   March 2015 - 17535   2015 $175

O'Donnell, Peter *The Silver Mistress.* London: Souvenir, 1973. First edition, fine in dust jacket.   Mordida Books   March 2015 - 010096   2015 $200

O'Donnell, Peter *A Taste for Death.* London: Souvenir, 1969. First edition, fine in price clipped dust jacket with publisher's price sticker.   Mordida Books   March 2015 - 010095   2015 $250

O'Dowd, James Kylne *Customs' Administrators and Customs' Reformers or 'The Digest of the Proceedings of the Charlotte Row Committee' Examined.* London: Baily Brothers, 1853. 8vo., several marginal emphasis marks of previous reader, original green ribbed and blindstamped cloth, spine lettered gilt and trifle faded, very good, near fine.   John Drury Rare Books   March 2015 - 24033   2015   £306

O'Grady, Standish *Finn and His Companions.* London: T. Fisher Unwin, 1892. First edition, small 8vo., original white and blue floral illustrated cloth with similar fore-edges, illustrations by John Butler Yeats, attractive very good or better, sound copy with slight surface soiling and very slight fading, prize label on pastedown.   Any Amount of Books   2015 - A99831   2015   £160

O'Hara, Frank *A City Winter and Other Poems.* New York: Tibor De Nagy Gallery, 1951 i.e, 1952. First edition, tall 8vo., original signed frontispiece drawing & reproductions of 2 drawings by Larry Rivers, original cloth backed decorated boards, this copy number 13, tall 8vo., original signed frontispiece drawing & reproductions of two drawings by Larry Rivers, original cloth backed decorated boards, cover slightly worn along bottom edge and lower fore-corners, small stain to cloth near top of front panel, one page shows some faint indentations, otherwise very good, preserved in custom made half morocco slipcase, this the Thomas B. Hess - Elaine de Kooning copy, specially signed by O'Hara and signed by Hess and de Kooning's ownership stamp.   James S. Jaffe Rare Books   Modern American Poetry - 215   2015 $35,000

O'Hara, Frank *The End of the Far West.* N.P.: n.p., 1874. First edition, one of 220 copies of a mimeo publication of 11 poems of O'Hara, published after his death, 4to., 12 mimeograph sheets, original pictorial stapled wrappers by Alice Notley, wrappers faintly sunned, otherwise fine. James S. Jaffe Rare Books   Many Happy Returns - 357   2015 $250

O'Hara, Frank *Love Poems.* New York: Tibor De Nagy editions, 1965. First edition, limited to 500 copies, presentation from author for Ted (Berrigan), covers lightly soiled, but very good, enclosed in half leather and marbled board clamshell box.   James S. Jaffe Rare Books   Many Happy Returns - 363   2015 $5000

O'Hara, Frank *Love Poems (Tentative Title).* New York: Tibor De Nagy Editions, 1965. First edition, one of only 20 copies numbered and signed by O'Hara out of a total edition of 500 copies, square 8vo., original striped wrappers, usual offsetting to titlepage from striped wrappers, otherwise very fine.   James S. Jaffe Rare Books   Modern American Poetry - 219   2015 $4500

O'Hara, Frank *Lunch Poems.* San Francisco: City Lights Books, 1964. First edition, one of 1500 copies printed, small 8vo., original printed wrappers, very fine, virtually as new, extremely rare in this condition.   James S. Jaffe Rare Books   Modern American Poetry - 218   2015 $1000

O'Hara, Frank *Meditations in an Emergency.* New York: Grove Press, 1957. First edition, limited issue, one of 75 numbered hardbound copies, out of a total edition of 90 hardbound copies, with 15 copies containing original drawings by Grace Hartigan, inscribed by author for Mike Goldberg, fading along spine (as usual) and at finger-pull on front panel, otherwise very good in somewhat faded and marked slipcase.   James S. Jaffe Rare Books   Modern American Poetry - 216   2015 $4500

O'Hara, Frank *Meditations in an Emergency.* New York: Grove Press, 1957. First edition, this copy numbered '10' and signed by author on colophon page, 8vo., original green cloth, publisher's slipcase, some light foxing to endpapers, bit of foxing to cloth, otherwise fine.   James S. Jaffe Rare Books   Modern American Poetry - 216   2015 $2500

O'Hara, Frank *Poems.* New York: Limited Editions Club, 1988. Limited to 550 numbered copies, signed by artist, lithograph illustrations by Willem de Kooning, set in English Monotype Bodini by Jula Ferrari and Dan Carr at Golgonooza Letter Foundry, monthly letter loosely inserted, leather, cloth clamshell box with inlaid leather label on spine. Oak Knoll Books   25 - 59   2015 $5800

O'Hara, John *The Instrument.* New York: 1967. First edition, 1/300 copies signed by author, as new in acetate dust jacket and slipcase.   Gemini Fine Books & Arts, Ltd.   Art Reference & Illustrated Books: First Editions - 2015 $150

O'Hara, John *Lovey Childs.* New York: 1969. First edition, 1/200 copies signed by John O'Hara, as new in acetate dust jacket and slipcase.   Gemini Fine Books & Arts, Ltd. Art Reference & Illustrated Books: First Editions - 2015 $150

O'Hara, John *Waiting for Winter.* New York: 1966. First edition, 1/300 copies signed by author, cloth, acetate dust jacket and slipcase, as new.   Gemini Fine Books & Arts, Ltd.   Art Reference & Illustrated Books: First Editions - 2015 $150

O'Meara, James *The Vigilance Committee of 1856.* James H. Barry, 1887. First edition, 7 1/4 x 5 inches, tan printed wrappers, 57 pages, small closed tear to top of front panel and with light chipping to spine as well as 1 inch chip missing from top corner rear wrapper, very good.   Buckingham Books   March 2015 - 35716   2015 $175

O'Neal, Bill *The Arizona Rangers.* Austin: Eakin Press, 1987. First edition, simulated leather, 222 pages, illustrations, virtually fine in dust jacket, couple of dimples in dust jacket, almost unnoticeable superficial line mark on front cover, very scarce in first edition, fine in very good+ dust jacket.   Baade Books of the West   2014 - 2015 $61

O'Neal, Bill *Henry Brown the Outlaw-Marshall.* College Station: Early West, 1980. Limited edition, illustrations, presentation by author to a contemporary Western outlaw historian, fine in fine dust jacket.   Baade Books of the West   2014 - 2015 $53

O'Neil, Kerry *Mooney Moves Around.* New York: Reynal & Hitchcock, 1939. First edition, fine, bright, square copy in dust jacket lightly rubbed at corners and head of spine.   Buckingham Books   March 2015 - 32257   2015 $300

O'Neill, Brian *Easter Week.* New York: International, 1939. First edition, wrappers, near fine, Frederick Pohl's copy with his signature.   Beasley Books   2013 - 2015 $45

O'Neill, Eugene Gladstone 1888-1953 *The Emperor Jones, Diff'rent, The Straw.* New York: Boni & Liveright, 1921. Second printing, spine tanned, sticker shadow on rear boards, near very good, lacking dust jacket, actress Eva Le Gallienne's copy with her bookplate and initials.   Between the Covers Rare Books, Inc.   187 - 205   2015 $150

O'Neill, Rose *Kewpies and the Runaway Baby.* New York: Doubleday Doran, 1928. 8vo., cloth, spine ends rubbed, else very good+, inscribed by O'Neill with one page signed inscription in her fancy signature, illustrations in color on every page, uncommon.   Aleph-Bet Books, Inc.   108 - 325   2015 $1200

O'Neill, Rose *The Kewpies their Book.* New York: Stokes Nov., 1913. First edition, 4to., boards, pictorial paste-on, fine in tattered and worn dust jacket with some pieces off, pictorial endpapers, cover plate, numerous color illustrations on every page, beautiful copy, rare in dust jacket.   Aleph-bet Books, Inc.   109 - 337   2015 $1500

O'Neill, Timothy *Irish Hand: Scribes and Their Manuscripts from the Earliest Times to the Seventeenth Century with an Exemplar of Irish Scripts.* Porlaoise: The Dolmen Press, 1984. 4to., cloth, dust jacket, black and white illustrations, dust jacket slightly bent at top and bottom.   Oak Knoll Books   Special Catalogue 24 - 37   2015 $125

O'Neill, W. O. *Hoof and Horn: Official Organ of the Territorial Live Stock Association of Arizona. Issue Volume III No. 11, Oct. 27 1887.* Hoof and Horn, 1887. First edition, folio, printed wrappers, illustrations, few small closed tears to few pages at fore-edges, else very good.   Buckingham Books   March 2015 - 38426   2015 $250

O'Toole, Judith Hansen *Severin Roesen.* Lewisburg: London: & Toronto: Bucknell University Press/Associated University Presses, 1992. First edition, 4to., illustrations in color and black and white, very good in very good dust jacket with very slight marks to covers, dust jacket creased at edges.   Any Amount of Books   2015 - A73780   2015   £300

Oakeley, Frederick *The Subject of Tract XC, Historically Examined, with the View of Ascertaining the Object with Which the Articles of the Church of England Were Put Out, and the Sense in Which they are Allowed to be Subscribed.* London: James Toovey, 1845. 8vo., recently well bound in linen backed marbled boards lettered, frontispiece.   John Drury Rare Books   2015 - 19997   2015 $133

Oakes, William *Views of the Profile Mountain and the Profile Rock or the "Old Man of the Mountain" at Franconia, New Hampshire on Two Plates with Descriptive Letter Press.* Boston: S. N. Dickinson, printer, 1847. First edition, folio, 2 plates by Bufford from drawings by Isaac Sprague, original printed wrappers, fine, inscribed by Oakes, presentation for George B. Emerson.   M & S Rare Books, Inc.   97 - 209   2015 $2500

Oakley, Violet *The Law Triumphant: the Opening of the Book of Law and the Miracle of Geneva.* Published by Oakley, 1932. Limited to 300 numbered copies, signed by Oakley, large folio, full leather embossed and gilt stamped metallic endpapers, closed with 2 brass clasp, leather very slightly spotted in places, else fine in original plain box, pages are loose, laid into sections with printed covers, set in Garamond type and printed on high quality San Marco paper, 71 tipped in plates in color and black and white, rare.   Aleph-bet Books, Inc.   109 - 336   2015 $2250

Oastler, Richard *Vicarial Tithes, Halifax: a True statement of Facts and Incidents.* Halifax: printed and sold by P. K. Holden, 1827. First edition, 8vo., final errata leaf, well bound in mid 20th century dark green half morocco over cloth boards, spine lettered gilt, entirely uncut, original wrappers bound in, upper retaining its original printed title label, very good, from the library of John Clay at Raistrick House, with his signature and later form the library of his grandson, Sir Charles Travis Clay (1885-1978), very scarce. John Drury Rare Books   March 2015 - 24991   2015   £306

Oates, Eugene W. *The Fauna of British India Including Ceylon and Burma.* London: Taylor & Francis, 1889-1898. Octavo, 4 volumes, text illustrations, contemporary half morocco, slight wear and previous owner's notes, otherwise sound set.   Andrew Isles   2015 - 21235   2015 $600

Oates, Joyce Carol 1938- *Cybele.* Santa Barbara: Black Sparrow, 1979. First edition, number 64 of 300 copies signed by author, cloth in acetate dust jacket, as new. Gemini Fine Books & Arts, Ltd.   Art Reference & Illustrated Books: First Editions - 2015 $60

Obama, Barack *Dreams from my Father.* New York: Random House, 2004. First printing (with "1" in the number run) of the large print edition, near fine in close to fine dust jacket.   Stephen Lupack   March 2015 - 2015 $100

Oberman, Heiko Augustinus *Masters of the Reformation: The Emergence of a New Intellectual Climate in Europe.* Cambridge: Cambridge University Press, 1981. First English edition, 8vo., map, cloth, dust jacket, ink ownership signature of David Lindberg, fine.   Jeff Weber Rare Books 178 - 851   2015 $40

Observations on a Letter by John Eardley Eardley-Wilmot, Esq. One of His Majesty's Justices of Peace for the County of Warwick... London: T & G. Underwood..., 1820. First edition, 8vo., half title, fairly recent marbled wrappers, uncut, very good, rare.   John Drury Rare Books   2015 - 16380 2015 $177

Observations on Modern Gardening. London: T. Payne, 1771. Third edition, 8vo., full brown leather with decorated gilt at spine, raised bands and gilt title on red label, ornate armorial bookplate of Agneu (Baronet) of Lochnau, penciled ownership signature of F. R. Cowell, very handsome, very good, slightly rubbed at corner, slightly tender at hinges. Any Amount of Books   2015 - A47683   2015   £220

Observations on Mr. Gladstone's Denunciation of Certain Millowners of Lancashire, contained in a Speech Delivered by Him at Newcastle on the 7th of October 1862. London: James Ridgway, 1862. First edition, complete with half title, recently well bound in blue boards, printed label on spine, very good.   John Drury Rare Books   2015 - 4905   2015 $159

Observations on the Evidence Relating to the Duties on Leather, Taken Before the Committee of the House of Commons, Ordered to be printed 5th April 1813... London: printed by Joseph Hartnell, 1813. First edition, 8vo., with half title, 2 folding tables, one of which (the larger of the two) is torn (but with no loss of printed surface) and is loose, pamphlet was stitched as issued, uncut and unopened, apart from fault noted, very good, scarce.   John Drury Rare Books 2015 - 20057   2015 $177

Observations on that part of the Speaker's Speech, Which relates to trade. Dublin: printed by T. Burnside, 1799. First edition, 8vo., very good, recently well bound in linen backed marbled boards.   John Drury Rare Books   March 2015 - 19376   2015 $266

Observations on Various Publications Which Have Issued from the Press During the Last Twenty-Five Years on the Coronation Oath Taken by the Kings of England. London: Joseph Booker, 1825. First edition, 8vo., 8 pages, single printed sheet, folded and unbound as issued, fine, rare. John Drury Rare Books   2015 - 21714   2015 $89

Odets, Clifford *Paradise Lost.* New York: Random House, 1936. First edition, very good+, light shelfwear, spine somewhat dulled in very good dust jacket (chips at extremities), uncommon.   Stephen Lupack   March 2015 - 2015 $60

Oe, Kenzaburo *A Healing Family.* Tokyo: Kodansha, 1995. First American edition, signed by author, 8vo., fine in near fine dust jacket with minimal edge wear.   By the Book, L. C.   Special List 10 - 34   2015 $65

Oe, Kenzaburo *A Quiet Life.* New York: Grove Press, 1990. First edition in English, signed by author, 8vo., fine in fine dust jacket.   By the Book, L. C.   Special List 10 - 33 2015 $90

Oerter, John H. *The Social Question in the Light of History and the Word of Truth.* New York: E. Glaeser, 1887. First edition, green cloth stamped in gilt and blind, near fine. Beasley Books   2013 - 2015 $125

Office International Des Musees *Mouseion 1931-1937.* Paris: Office International Des Musees, 1931-1937. Volumes 13/14-39/40, only one missing, 15 volumes, wrappers, small 4to., black and white illustrations, reasonable copy, very good.   Any Amount of Books   2015 - B24082 2015   £175

The Official Railway Equipment Register of the United States, Canadian and Mexican Railroads. Volume LII No. 1. New York: Railway Equipment and Publication Co. July, 1936. Spine worn and taped, front cover edges badly chipped, very good.   Argonaut Book Shop   Holiday Season 2014 - 237   2015 $125

The Official Railway Equipment Register of the United States, Canadian and Mexican Railroads. Volume LVI. No. 1. New York: Railway Equipment and Publication Co., July, 1940. Spine worn and taped and detached, very good, complete. Argonaut Book Shop Holiday Season 2014 - 238 2015 $75

The Official Railway Equipment Register of the United States, Canadian and Mexican Railroads. Volume LXI. No. 3. New York: Railway Equipment and Publication Co. Jan., 1946. Spine taped, edge wear, very good complete copy. Argonaut Book Shop Holiday Season 2014 - 239 2015 $75

The Official Railway Equipment Register of the United States, Canadian and Mexican Railroads. Volume LXVI. No. 4. New York: Railway Equipment and Publication Co., April, 1951. Spine taped, very good, complete copy. Argonaut Book Shop Holiday Season 2014 - 240 2015 $75

The Offical Railway Equipment Register of the United States, Canadian and Mexican Railroads. Volume LXX. No. 4. New York: Railway Equipment and Publication Co. April, 1955. Spine taped, chipping, very good, complete copy. Argonaut Book Shop Holiday Season 2014 - 241 2015 $75

Offill, Jenny *Dept. of Speculation.* New York: Knopf, 2014. Advance reading copy, fine in wrappers, uncommon issue. Ken Lopez, Bookseller 164 - 160 2015 $125

Ogawa, Kazumasa *Illustrations of Japanese Life.* Tokyo: Sole agents Kelly and Walsh Ltd., Folio, title and 50 hand colored gravure plates, each with titles and captions, original decorated crepe paper boards with silk ties, fine. Marlborough Rare Books List 53 - 32 2015 £600

Ogden, C. K. *Psyche, Annual of General and Linguistic Psychology Volume XIII.* Cambridge: Orthological Institute, 1933. First edition, very good+, library marks inside numbers on spine, paper covered boards with red cloth backstrip. Beasley Books 2013 - 2015 $45

Ogden, C. K. *Psyche. an Annual of General and Linguistic Psychology. Volume XVII.* London: Orthological Institute, 1937. First edition, very good, paper covered boards with red cloth backstrip, library marks inside. Beasley Books 2013 - 2015 $45

Ogilvie-Grant, W. R. *Reports on the Collections made by the British Ornithologists' Union Expedition and the Wollaston expedition in Dutch New Guinea 1910-1913.* London: Francis Edwards, 1916. Limited to 150 numbered copies (this number 112), quarto, 2 volumes, 10 chromolithographs, 27 uncolored plates, publisher's blue wrappers, uncut, partly unopened, fine set with both volumes in matching blue cloth boxes, leather and gilt title labels. Andrew Isles 2015 - 15134 2015 $3250

Ohnet, Georges *The Battles of Life. The Ironmaster.* London: Wyman and Sons, 1884. First English edition, 3 volumes, half titles, original red cloth, front boards blocked in black, spines lettered gilt, spines slightly faded, boards little dulled, inner hinges slightly cracking, good plus. Jarndyce Antiquarian Booksellers CCXI - 226 2015 £180

Oklahoma Cattlemen's Association *The Oklahoma Cowman Volume 4.* Oklahoma City: Oklahoma Cattlemen's Association, 1964. Cloth with gilt stamped titles on spine, 12 issues, very scarce, fine, photos, maps. Baade Books of the West 2014 - 2015 $144

Oklahoma Cattlemen's Association *The Oklahoma Cowman Volume 8.* Oklahoma City: Oklahoma Cattlemen's Assoc., 1968. Bound volume in cloth with gilt stamped titles on spine, all 12 issues, cartoons, photos, maps, fine, very scarce. Baade Books of the West 2014 - 2015 $144

Oklahoma Cattlemen's Association *The Oklahoma Cowman. Volume 10.* Oklahoma City: Oklahoma Cattlemen's Association, 1970. Cloth with gilt stamped titles on spine, all 12 issues, printed on glossy stock, photos, maps, very scarce, fine. Baade Books of the West 2014 - 2015 $144

Old and New Ministry Compar'd as to These Three Grand Points. I. Bribery and Corruption from France. II. A Partition of the Spanish Monarchy. IIII. The Plea of the Prerogative of the Crown in Making Peace, War and Alliances. London: A. Baldwin, 1711. First edition, 8vo., half sheets, half title, new boards, lettered, very good. John Drury Rare Books 2015 - 24692 2015 $133

The Old B & M Railroad Ahead. Keep in the Right Latitude 750,000 Acres of the Best Lands for Sale. St. Louis: Gast & Co., 1878. First edition, 8vo, original yellow wrappers printed in black ink, plates, maps present on three of the four cover panels, full page views, lightly soiled along small portion of front page edge, else very good, tight. Buckingham Books March 2015 - 28298 2015 $850

Old Dame Trot and Her Pig. London: Blackie, circa, 1915. Large 4to., cloth backed pictorial boards, slight cover rubbing, very good+, 12 color plates, pictorial endpapers and line illustrations. Aleph-bet Books, Inc. 109 - 13 2015 $300

Old Dutch Nursery Rhymes. London: & Philadelphia: Augener & McKay, 1917. Large oblong 4to., blue cloth, pictorial paste-on, fine in dust jacket with some mends, illustrations by H. Willebeek Le Mair. Aleph-Bet Books, Inc. 108 - 267 2015 $425

Old Mother Bruin and Her Foolish Cubs. New York: McLoughlin Bros. n.d. circa, 1880. Oblong 4to., pictorial wrappers, spine slightly rough, owner stamp on rear cover, few faint spots on blank verso of a page, clean, bright and very good+ copy. printed on one side of the paper, 6 very fine full page chromolithographs, rare.   Aleph-Bet Books, Inc.   108 - 286   2015 $400

Old West Antiques & Collectables. Dallas: Great American Pub. co., 1979. First edition, quarto, pictorial cloth, 192 pages, frontispiece, illustrations, former owner's name, minor bumps to fore-edge, else near fine without dust jacket.   Buckingham Books   March 2015 - 20174   2015 $250

The Old Woman and Her Pig. Titty Mouse, Tatty Mouse. New York: Holiday House, n.d., 1936. 16mo., cloth backed pictorial boards, very good-fine, scarce, illustrations by Jack Tinker.   Aleph-Bet Books, Inc.   108 - 175   2015 $200

Oldenburg, Henry   *The Correspondence of Henry Oldenburg.* London: University of Wisconsin Press, 1965-1969. 6 volumes, nos. 1-6 (13 have been issued), large 8vo., each volume about 500 pages, illustrations, cloth, dust jackets worn, volume I lower corner bumped bookplates of H. L. Taylor, M.D., good set.   Jeff Weber Rare Books   178 - 858   2015 $150

Oldschool, Oliver   *Port Folio (A Monthly Magazine).* Philadelphia: 1822. Volume 1 #1-6, Volume 2 #1-6, 12 issues each had a copperplate engraving, text complete, very good, normal foxing, full calf with good labels, missing endpaper.   Bookworm & Silverfish   2015 - 4123698297   2015 $450

Oldum, Jerome   *The Morgue is Always Open.* New York: Charles Scribner's Sons, 1944. First edition, near fine in dust jacket with light restoration to lower portion of front panel.   Buckingham Books   March 2015 - 32258   2015 $750

Oldum, Jerome   *Nine Lives Are Not Enough.* New York: Sheridan House Publishers, 1940. First edition, fine in dust jacket with light wear to spine ends and corners.   Buckingham Books   March 2015 - 32341   2015 $850

Oliphant, Dave   *The Early Swing Era 1930 to 1941.* Westport: Greenwood Press, 2002. First edition, fine, issued without dust jacket.   Beasley Books   2013 - 2015 $40

Oliver, George   *An Apology for the Freemasons; Respectfully Submitted to the Consideration of Those Clergymen Who Doubt the Propriety of Allowing the Use of their Churches for Masonic Celebrations.* London: Richard Spencer, 1846. First edition, 8vo., titlepage little soiled with repair to upper margin, one short closed marginal tear, blindstamp foot of title of Wigan Free Library and with initials inkstamp verso, preserved in modern wrappers with printed label on upper cover, apparently rare.   John Drury Rare Books   March 2015 - 25730   2015 $221

Oliver, George   *History of Masonic Persecutions in Different Quarters of the Globe....* New York: Masonic Pub., 1867. 8vo., brown cloth, blindstamped with gilt lettering on spine, cover faded, spine little worn, few small holes, interior tight and very good.   Second Life Books Inc.   190 - 176   2015 $150

Ollyffe, George   *An Essay Humbly Offer'd for an Act of Parliament to Prevent Capital Crimes and the Loss of many Lives...* London: J. Downing, 1731. First edition, efficiently bound in mid 20th century in cloth backed boards, spine gilt lettered, bookplate of Los Angeles County Board of Law Library, pastedown and inkstamps on endpapers, very good, crisp, rare.   John Drury Rare Books   2015 - 26028   2015 $787

Ollyffe, George   *The Madness of Disaffection and Treason Against the Present Government.* London: Joseph Downing, 1724. First edition, 8vo., errata at foot of final text page, contemporary gilt ruled calf with raised bands, very good, crisp copy, contemporary armorial bookplate of Arthur St. Leger, 1st Viscount Doneraile of County Corks, scarce.   John Drury Rare Books   March 2015 - 25095   2015 $874

Olney, Peter J. S.   *The Wildfowl Paintings of Henry Jones.* London: Threshold/Harrap, 1987. Limited to 350 copies signed and numbered by author, Folio, oblong format, 272 pages, 60 color plates, publisher's quarter blue calf and blue cloth, blue cloth case, fine.   Andrew Isles   2015 - 3516   2015 $600

Olsen, D. B.   *Cats Don't Smile.* Garden City: Doubleday, 1945. First edition, fine in dust jacket, bookplate.   Mordida Books   March 2015 - 001725   2015 $75

Olsen, Theodore V.   *Summer of the Drums.* Garden City: Doubleday, 1972. First edition, fine in dust jacket with few short edge tears, fine in very good dust jacket, presentation copy signed by author.   Baade Books of the West   2014 - 2015 $73

Olson, Charles *Human Universe and Other Essays.* San Francisco: Auerhahn Society, 1965. First edition, one of 250 copies, 4to., original quarter vellum & pictorial boards, plain dust jacket, edges of covers trifle rubbed, otherwise fine, scarce, unprinted dust jacket, lightly chipped.   James S. Jaffe Rare Books   Modern American Poetry - 221   2015 $250

Olson, Charles *The Maximus Papers.* New York: Jargon/Corinth Books, 1960. Fifth printing, 8vo., original decorated wrappers, Ted Berrigan's copy with his ownership signature, stamped "Just Buffalo. Library Resource Center", wrappers somewhat sunned, otherwise very good.   James S. Jaffe Rare Books   Many Happy Returns - 358   2015 $350

Olson, Charles *The Maximus Poems. 1-10. (with) The Maximus Poems 11-22.* Stuggart: Jonathan Williams, 1953-1956. First editions, first volume one of 50 special copies signed by Olson, second volume one of 25 copies signed by Olson, subscriber's edition 2 volumes, 4to., original calligraphic covers by Jonathan Williams, original stiff wrappers, publisher's cloth tipped slipcases, fine set.   James S. Jaffe Rare Books   Modern American Poetry - 220   2015 $6500

Olson, Toby *Maps.* Mt. Horeb: Perishable Press, 1969. Limited to 132 numbered copies, signed by author, small 4to., quarter leather, marbled paper covered boards, title gilt stamped on spine, top edge gilt cut, other edges uncut, spine and edges of covers sunned.   Oak Knoll Books 306 - 164   2015 $100

Omar Khayyam *The Rubaiyat of Omar Khayyam.* London: Hodder & Stoughton, n.d., 1909. Limited to only 750 numbered copies signed by Dulac, large 4to., full vellum decorated in gold, top edge gilt, most minimal amount of cover soil, fine and bright with original ribbon ties, 20 magnificent tipped in color plates with tissue guards mounted on heavy stock with intricate gold decorative border plus decorative border on text pages as well, printed on handmade paper, beautifully produced book and on exceptionally nice copy, rarely found as clean as this copy.   Aleph-bet Books, Inc.   109 - 145   2015 $3000

Omar Khayyam *Rubaiyat.* Siegle: Hill, 1911. 155/550 copies, printed on handmade paper and signed by binders Francis Sangorski & George Sutcliffe, printed text and decorative borders all printed in black and red and several heightened in gold, to a caligraphic design by Alberto Sutcliffe, text interspersed with 12 plates printed on one side only, some plate edges trifle soiled (as usual?), plates carrying color printed illustrations by E. Geddes, large 4to., original full white vellum, backstrip with overall ornate gilt design, gilt lettered green leather label (sunned to brown and trifle chipped), front cover with overall gilt blocked peacock design, others untrimmed, very good.   Blackwell's Rare Books   B179 - 218   2015   £600

Omar Khayyam *The Rubaiyat of Omar Khayyam.* New York: Dodge Pub. Co., 1912. 4to., full leather binding with color embossed Craftsman style design on cover, top edge gilt, fine in publisher's plain felt lined box, 28 tipped in color photos (with tissue guards), text illustrations in black and white, exceptionally fine.   Aleph-bet Books, Inc.   109 - 420   2015 $950

Omar Khayyam *Rubaiyat of Omar Khayyam.* New York: Thomas Crowell, 1930. First of this edition, 4to., gilt decorated salmon colored cloth, top edge gilt, fine in dust jacket, 12 beautiful tipped in color plates plus 45 mounted gold and blak plates and black and whites in-text by Willy Pogany.   Aleph-Bet Books, Inc.   108 - 356   2015 $450

Omar Khayyam *Rubaiyat of.* New York: Heritage Press, 1940. First edition with Szyk illustrations, 4to., full padded blue leather stamped in gold, fine copy in publisher's pictorial box (box very good with some fading, flaps repaired), printed in England on heavy Frenchfold paper, 8 magnificent mounted color plates, rarely found in such nice condition with box.   Aleph-bet Books, Inc.   109 - 457   2015 $750

On the Laws and Liberties of Englishmen, Britons Ever Shall be Free! London: Roake & Varty, 1831. 12mo., preserved in plain wrappers with title label on upper cover.   John Drury Rare Books   2015 - 21674   2015 $89

On the Means of Retaining the Population within any Required Limits. London: 1820. First and only printing, 8vbo., recently well bound in linen backed marbled boards, lettered, very good.   John Drury Rare Books   2015 - 20817   2015 $151

On the Plains. Perry Mason Co., 1897. First edition, 64 pages, stiff printed wrappers, numerous illustrations, quite scarce, previous owners name written neatly at top of titlepage.   Buckingham Books   March 2015 - 37639   2015 $250

Ondaatje, Michael *Handwriting. Poems.* New York: Knopf, 1999. First edition, wrappers, advance, uncorrected proofs, fine with PR stapled to inside of front wrapper.   Beasley Books   2013 - 2015 $45

Onions, Oliver *Widdershins.* London: Martin Secker, 1911. First edition, 8vo., original red cloth lettered gilt on spine and cover, covers rather marked, scuffed and used, sound, worn, very good-, clean text.   Any Amount of Books   2015 - A92774   2015   £175

Onomatologia Curiosa Artificiosa et Magica, Oder, Ganz Naturliches Zauber-Lexicon. Ulm: Frankfurt und Leipzig: Auf Kosten der Gaumischen Handlung, 1759. First edition, 216 x 178mm., contemporary multi colored paste paper boards, flat spine, 3 engraved plates, and colophon with woodcut printer's device depicting a printed press, spine somewhat sunned, little chafing to boards and rubbing to extremities, but original fragile paper binding entirely sound and remarkably well preserved, occasional minor browning, foxing or offsetting, four leaves with small marginal inkstain, otherwise clean, fresh copy internally with few signs of use. Phillip J. Pirages   66 - 38   2015 $1500

Onwhyn, Thomas *Thirty-Two Plates to Illustrate the Cheap edition of Nicholas Nickleby...* London: J. Newman, 1848. 8 parts, plates slightly browned but not foxed, original green printed wrappers to each part, 1 split along spine and slightly chipped, 4 with some splitting, good set, scarce, in brown envelope with notes by Kathleen Tillotson indicating a gift from Simon Nowell-Smith.   Jarndyce Antiquarian Booksellers   CCVII - 219   2015   £180

The Official Railway Equipment Register of the United States, Canadian and Mexican Railroads. Volume XL No. 4. New York: Railway Equipment and Publication Co., September, 1924. Small quarto, maps, printed tan wrappers, spine worn and taped, cover edges with some chipping, very good, complete copy.   Argonaut Book Shop Holiday Season 2014 - 235   2015 $175

Oppenheim, E. Phillips *Advice Limited.* Boston: Little Brown, 1936. First American edition, top of page edges lightly soiled, otherwise fine in very good Bip Pares dust jacket with chipping at top of spine, wear at corners, several short closed tears.   Mordida Books   March 2015 - 0011336   2015 $125

Oppenheim, E. Phillips *The Curious Quest.* Boston: Little Brown, 1919. First American edition, very good in fine A, L. Burt reprint dust jacket.   Mordida Books   March 2015 - 011056   2015 $85

Oppenheim, E. Phillips *The Evil Shepherd.* Boston: Little Brown, 1922. First edition, spine slightly darkened, otherwise near fine in fine A. L. Burt reprint dust jacket with short crease tear on spine.   Mordida Books   March 2015 - 011428   2015 $85

Oppenheim, E. Phillips *The Fortunate Wayfarer.* Boston: Little Brown, 1928. First American edition, near fine, very good dust jacket with chipped and frayed spine ends and nicks along edges.   Mordida Books   March 2015 - 011052   2015 $85

Oppenheim, E. Phillips *General Besserley's Second Puzzle Box.* Boston: Little Brown, 1940. First American edition, fine in Bip Pares dust jacket with small chip and tear at top corner of front panel.   Mordida Books   March 2015 - 011335   2015 $125

Oppenheim, E. Phillips *The Great Impersonation.* Boston: Little Brown, 1920. First American edition, covers worn and page edges slightly darkened, otherwise very good in very fine A. L. Burt reprint dust jacket.   Mordida Books   March 2015 - 011332   2015 $85

Oppenheim, E. Phillips *The Kingdom of the Blind.* Boston: Little Brown, 1916. First edition, page edges spotted and slightly darkened, otherwise near fine in A. L. Burt reprint dust jacket.   Mordida Books   March 2015 - 011479   2015 $85

Oppenheim, E. Phillips *The Light Beyond.* Boston: Little Brown, 1928. First American edition, fine in very good dust jacket with long closed tars along spine/front flap fold and nicks at spine ends.   Mordida Books   March 2015 - 011061   2015 $85

Oppenheim, E. Phillips *The Lion and the Lamb.* Boston: Little Brown, 1930. First American edition, fine in very fine, as new dust jacket with publisher's wraparound intact.   Mordida Books   March 2015 - 010680   2015 $150

Oppenheim, E. Phillips *A Lost Leader.* Boston: Little Brown, 1907. First American edition, near fine, bookseller's small label on front endpaper, label removed from front endpaper, otherwise near fine in pictorial blue cloth covered boards with gold stamped titles on spine,.   Mordida Books   March 2015 - 011324   2015 $85

Oppenheim, E. Phillips *The Man without Nerves.* Boston: Little Brown, 1934. First American edition, some scattered light spotting on page edges, otherwise fine in very good dust jacket with chipped and frayed spine ends and wear at corners and along folds.   Mordida Books   March 2015 - 011337   2015 $250

Oppenheim, E. Phillips *Matomi's Vineyard.* Boston: Little Brown, 1928. First edition, very good in fine dust jacket.   Mordida Books   March 2015 - 011084   2015 $100

Oppenheim, E. Phillips *Michael's Evil Deeds.* Boston: Little Brown, 1923. First American edition, fine in very good dust jacket with three quarter inch piece missing top of spine, internal tape mends, wear and nicks along edges and folds.   Mordida Books   March 2015 - 010902   2015 $125

Oppenheim, E. Phillips *The Million Pound Deposit.* Little Brown and Co., 1930. First US edition, fine, bright, square copy in fine, bright dust jacket, exceptional copy.   Buckingham Books   March 2015 - 33504   2015 $300

Oppenheim, E. Phillips *The Million Pound Deposit.* Boston: Little Brown, 1930. First American edition, name and date on front endpaper, else fine in very fine as new, Bip Pares dust jacket. Mordida Books March 2015 - 010679 2015 $150

Oppenheim, E. Phillips *The Mystery Road.* Boston: Little Brown, 1923. First edition, fine in very fine A. L. Burt reprint dust jacket. Mordida Books March 2015 - 011420 2015 $85

Oppenheim, E. Phillips *The Pawns Court.* Boston: Little Brown, 1918. First American edition, name and date on front endpaper, else near fine in A. L. Burt reprint dust jacket. Mordida Books March 2015 - 011428 2015 $85

Oppenheim, E. Phillips *Peter Ruff and the Double-Four.* New York: A. L. Burt, Reprint edition, page edges darkened, otherwise fine in very fine, as new dust jacket. Mordida Books March 2015 - 008863 2015 $85

Oppenheim, E. Phillips *Simple Peter Cradd.* Boston: Little Brown, 1931. First American edition, pages darkened, otherwise very good in dust jacket with interal tape mends, fraying at top of spine and chips at corners. Mordida Books March 2015 - 012277 2015 $85

Oppenheim, E. Phillips *The Vanished Messenger.* New York: A. L. Burt, Reprint edition, very good in fine dust jacket. Mordida Books March 2015 - 011062 2015 $85

Oppenheim, James *American Types a Preface to Analytic Psychology.* New York: Knopf, 1931. First edition, fine in bit used dust jacket. Beasley Books 2013 - 2015 $45

Optic, Oliver *Boat Club; or the Bunkers of Rippleton.* Boston: Brown Bazin and Co., 1855. First edition, 12mo., brown pictorial cloth with front cover and spine stamped in gold, all edges gilt, spine ends frayed light oval stain on endpaper and next 2 leaves, tight, clean and overall very good+, presumably publisher's presentation binding, edges gilt, front cover has gilt vignette of 3 boys on a boat repaired on rear cover in blindstamping, 4 plates, rare. Aleph-Bet Books, Inc. 108 - 326 2015 $1200

Oranges and Lemons a Nursery Rhyme Picture Book. London: Frederick Warne & Co. n.d., 1913. First edition, 4to., pictorial wrappers, light cover soil, 8 fabulous color plates, numerous illustrations by L. Brooke Leslie. Alephbet Books, Inc. 109 - 70 2015 $250

Orationis Dominicae Versiones Ferme Centum. N.P: n.d., circa, 1670. Small 4to., recently bound in half brown calf over marbled paper, spine lettered gilt, silk page marker bound in, neat previous ownership signature on titlepage, text of one page slightly affected by cropping, other page edges slightly darkened and chipped but without loss of text, few ink marks in margins, occasional half page has been left blank. Any Amount of Books 2015 - C16378 2015 £1600

Orchard, Vance *The Walla Balla Bigfoot.* Prescott: Ox-Yoke Press, 2001. First edition, pictorial wrappers, 173 pages, fine. Baade Books of the West 2014 - 2015 $125

Orchard, William *Beads and Beadwork of the American Indians.* New York: 1929. 140 pages, illustrations, original stiff paper covers, binding starting to crack at titlepage, else bright and almost completely unopened. Dumont Maps & Books of the West 131 - 67 2015 $50

Orcutt, Samuel *History of the Town of Wolcott (Connecticut) from 1731 to 1874.* Waterbury: American Printing Co., 1874. First edition, original cloth with gilt to spine, very good, some shelfwear, tape to contents leaf, bright gilt. Stephen Lupack March 2015 - 2015 $150

Orczy, Baroness *The Old Man in the Corner.* Toronto: William Briggs, 1909. First Canadian edition, issued at the same time as the original UK edition, former owner's inked name on front pastedown sheet, else very good, tight copy, illustrations by H. M. Brock. rare. Buckingham Books March 2015 - 32071 2015 $875

An Ordinance of the Lords and Commons Assembled in Parliament, for Charging and taxing a Monthly Rate of 300 Pounds Upon the County of Essex... London: printed for Edward Husband, April 2, 1645. First edition, title printed within typographical border, date 'April 2' inked out, preserved in modern wrappers with printed label on upper cover, 8vo., very good. John Drury Rare Books March 2015 - 236035 2015 £306

Oregon Pioneer Association *Transactions of the Forty-Fifth Annual Reunion of the Oregon Pioneer Association Portland July 19 1917, containing the Proceedings of the Thirty-First Grand Encampment of Indian War Veterans of the North Pacific Coast and other matters of Historic Interest.* Chausse Prudhomme co., 1920. 21.5cm., tan printed wrappers, old dampstain to bottom 2 inches of pamphlet but not affecting text, otherwise clean. Buckingham Books March 2015 - 35678 2015 $175

The Oregonian's Handbook of the Pacific Northwest. Portland: Oregonian, 1894. First edition, cloth with lovely gilt stamped and decorated pictorial maroon leather label which comprises most of the front cover area, label of book binder, Meston-Dygert, signature F. R. Vautugel 1894, match head size spot on front label, very good+, tight copy, slight wear to extremities, very scarce, very good+.   Baade Books of the West   2014 - 2015 $243

Oresme, Nicole   *Nicole Oresme and the Kinematics of Circular Motion.*   Milwaukee & London: University of Wisconsin, 1971. 8vo., cloth, dust jacket with some edge tears, inscribed by author for David Lindberg.   Jeff Weber Rare Books   178 - 863   2015 $45

Orgone Institute   *Orgone Energy Bulletin. Volume I No. 1, 2, 3, 4. and Volume II No. 2.*   New York: Orgone Isntitute Press, 1949-1950. First edition, 8vo., original blue stapled wrappers, lettered black on front covers, scarce, illustrations in color and black and white, slight tanning at edges and faint rubbing, otherwise sound, very good copy.   Any Amount of Books   2015 - C15147   2015   £150

The Original Design, Progress and Present state of the Scots Corporation at London of the Foundation of K. Charles II....   London: printed in the year, 1714. First edition, 4to., general minor paper browning and little foxing, few page numerals just shaved where head margin cut close, bound in early/mid 20th century quarter leather over marbled boards, spine lettered gilt, generally pretty good, very rare.   John Drury Rare Books   2015 - 20466   2015 $787

The Original Posters of Barque, Chagall, Dufry, Le Er, Matisse, Miro, Picasso.   Monte Carlo & London: A Sauret/A. Zwemmer, 1959. First edition, 4to., copiously illustrated in color and black and white, light staining at lower spine, otherwise very good+, very slightly used, complete, very good dust jacket, very faint rubbing at spine ends.   Any Amount of Books   March 2015 - C11494   2015   £400

Orlovitz, Gil   *Concerning Man.*   New York: Banyan Press, 1947. First edition, copy 34 of 350 numbered copies, inscribed by author to artist Cornelia Tate, fine in fine dust jacket.   Between the Covers Rare Books, Inc.   187 - 206   2015 $175

Ormerod, Oliver   *O Full True en Pertikler Okeawnt a wat Me Un Maw Mistris Seede un Yerd wi' Gooin to the' Greyte Eggshibishun e' Lundun, e' Eyghtene Hunderth un Sixty two...*   Rochdale: printed by Wrigley un Son..., 1864. 8vo., engraved frontispiece, 7 other large woodcut illustrations, frontispiece just little soiled, few marks here and there, but good copy in near contemporary black half calf, title in gilt on upper cover, binder's ticket of Ormerod Bros. of Rochdale and later (1892) ownership inscription of Mrs. James Gartside of 301 Bury road, Rochdale.   John Drury Rare Books   March 2015 - 18991   2015 $221

Ornduff, Donald R.   *Aristocrats in the Cattle Country.*   Kansas City Posse of the Westerners, 1964. First edition, the Trial Guide volume IX No. 2 June 1964, printed wrappers, 18 pages, illustrations, with brief handwritten memo on Ornduff's personal stationary stating that he made corrections and few slight alterations, memo signed, original envelope for Trail Guide included.   Buckingham Books   March 2015 - 37478   2015 $350

Orpen, Mrs.   *Memories of the Old Emigrant Days in Kansas 1862-1865; Also of a Visit to Paris in 1867.*   Harper & Brothers, 1928. First edition, 8vo., maroon cloth, gold stamping on front cover and spine, frontispiece, illustrations, non-authorial inscription, few pages of front and rear of text foxed, else very good in dust jacket missing a 1 1/2 inch piece from foot of spine with moderate wear to head of spine, corners and extremities.   Buckingham Books   March 2015 - 26728   2015 $300

Ortega Y Gasset, Jose   *The Dehumanization of Art and Notes on the Novel.*   Princeton: Princeton Univ. Press, 1948. Half title, original brown cloth, very good in darkened dust jacket, from the library of Geoffrey & Kathleen Tillotson, his gift to her Xmas 1949, few pencil notes.   Jarndyce Antiquarian Booksellers   CCVII - 403   2015   £20

Orwell, George   1903-1950   *Animal Farm.*   London: Secker & Warburg, 1945. First edition, first printing, original publisher's green cloth in fragile dust jacket, about near fine with some light rubbing to extremities, touch of fading to spine ends, in jacket with some wear and rubbing to spine, spine ends chipped with minor loss, few small tears, else very good.   B & B Rare Books, Ltd.   234 - 84   2015 $3500

Orwell, George   1903-1950   *Burmese Days: a Novel.*   London: Victor Gollancz, 1935. First edition, 8vo., 318 pages, attractive half green leather with marbled boards, five raised bands, lettered gilt at spine, occasional light foxing to prelims, otherwise near fine.   Any Amount of Books   March 2015 - C14662   2015   £400

Orwell, George   1903-1950   *Nineteen Eighty-Four.*   London: Secker & Warburg, 1949. First edition, first printing, original light green cloth, top edge stained red, issued in both green and red dust jackets, without any priority, although red jackets are scarcer and preferred, near fine in unclipped red jacket with some light wear and minor chipping to spine ends and flap folds, usual fading to spine, very nice and clean example of book in jacket.   B & B Rare Books, Ltd.   234 - 85   2015 $5000

Orwell, George   1903-1950   *Shooting an Elephant and Other Essays.*   London: Secker & Warburg, 1950. First edition, first printing, near fine with some usual fading to cloth, former owner signature to verso of contents page, in jacket with some light wear and few minor chips to extremities, spine lightly faded, few tiny tears, very good overall.   B & B Rare Books, Ltd.   234 - 86   2015 $225

Osborn, Campbell *Let Freedom Ring.* Tokyo: The International Co., 1954. First edition, 12mo. orange cloth, 211 pages, map, fine in fine dust jacket. Baade Books of the West 2014 - 2015 $42

Osborn, Henry Fairfield *Fifty-Two Years of Research Observation and Publication 1877-1929: a Life Adventure in Breadth and Depth.* New York: Charles Scribner's Sons, 1930. 8vo., frontispiece, plates, burgundy cloth, gilt stamped cover and spine titles, dust jacket worn and stained with tape repair, very good, Dr. George Minot's copy with author's presentation. Jeff Weber Rare Books 178 - 865 2015 $300

Osborn, James M. *John Dryden: Some Biographical facts and Problems.* New York: Columbia University Press, 1940. Frontispiece, original brown cloth, very good in dusted dust jacket, signed by Geoffrey Tillotson Sept. 1941 with few marginal marks, notes on endpapers and proof and printed copy of this review and other items including typescript of a paper by Edwin Rhodes. Jarndyce Antiquarian Booksellers CCVII - 249 2015 £30

Osborne, John *A Patriot for Me.* London: Faber and Faber, 1966. First edition, fine in fine, price clipped dust jacket with just touch of rubbing, inscribed by author to NY literary figure Burt Britton, nicer than usual. Between the Covers Rare Books, Inc. 187 - 207 2015 $150

Osborne, Julia *John Piper and Stained Glass.* Stroud, Gloucestershire: Sutton Publishing, 1997. First edition, small 4to., cloth, dust jacket, illustrations in color and black and white. Oak Knoll Books 306 - 289 2015 $150

Osgood, Cornelius *Ingalik Social Culture.* New Haven: Yale University Press, 1958. First edition, 289 pages, illustrations, map, printed wrappers, near fine, very scarce. Baade Books of the West 2014 - 2015 $131

Osley, A. S. *Luminario and Introduction to the Italian Writing-Books of the Sixteenth and Seventeenth Centuries.* Nieuwkoop: Miland Pub., 1972. Limited to 800 copies, small folio, cloth, dust jacket, cardboard slipcase, illustrations and reproductions. Oak Knoll Books Special Catalogue 24 - 38 2015 $230

Ossoli, Sarah Margaret Fuller, Marchesa D' 1810-1850 *Summer on the Lakes in 1843.* Boston: Charles Little and James Brown; New York: Francis, 1844. First edition, 8vo., publisher's black cloth, rebacked with most of original spine laid down (affecting "S" in "Summer"), few stains to titlepage and couple of other ones as well, some foxed, gilt stamped spine title, sides blocked in blind, faded pink endpapers, this copy signed twice by Fuller with a 'signed' poem by E. A. Poe on endpaper, these signatures are probably in the hand of noted forger Joseph Cosey, with article about Cosey laid in, very good, tight copy. Second Life Books Inc. 189 - 187 2015 $4500

Ossoli, Sarah Margaret Fuller, Marchesa D' 1810-1850 *Woman in the Nineteenth Century and Kindred Papers...* Boston: Roberts Brothers, 1875. New and complete edition, 8th printing, 8vo., ownership bookplate, brown cloth, spine faded, hinge starting in front, good, tight, clean copy. Second Life Books Inc. 189 - 188 2015 $100

Osterberg, Richard *Betty Smith Silver Flatware Dictionary.* San Diego: A. S. Barnes, 1982. Second printing, small 4to., inscribed by author, fine in very good+ dust jacket with short tear at upper front spine fold. Beasley Books 2013 - 2015 $45

Osterhout, J. P. *Handbook of Songs & Rhymes.* Privately published, n.d., First edition or reprint?, fragile printed wrappers, very good. Buckingham Books March 2015 - 37619 2015 $200

Ostrander, Isabel *The Mathematics of Guilt.* New York: McBride, 1926. First edition, thin red mark on bottom page edges, otherwise fine in dust jacket with some internal staining. Mordida Books March 2015 - 005300 2015 $250

Oswald, John *Some Memorandums of matters of Fact Relating to the Original and preliminaries of a Suit in Doctors-Commons Between Sir Hugh Everard baronet..* London: printed in the year, 1702. First edition, lower margin of title rather soiled, contemporary ink signature of Dr. Jane in upper margin, bound in 19th century quarter calf over marbled card covers, good copy. John Drury Rare Books 2015 - 23521 2015 $787

Ot Moskevye Do Bukharye. Ogiz Molodaiya Gvardia, 1931. 8vo., pictorial wrappers, some cover soil and wear, very good+, illustrations by A. Petrovo with striking color lithographs. Aleph-bet Books, Inc. 109 - 425 2015 $975

Otis, Johnny *Listen to the Lambs.* New York: Norton, 1880. First edition, fine in near fine dust jacket but for light wear at spine head. Beasley Books 2013 - 2015 $450

Our Famous Women. Hartford: A. D. Worthington, 1884. Reprint, 8vo., drab cloth stamped in gilt, hinges little tender, very good. Second Life Books Inc. 189 - 189 2015 $50

Oury, Marcelle *Lettre a Mon Peintre Raoul Dufy.* Paris: Librairie Academique Perrin, 1965. First edition, no. 468 of 975 copies (from an edition of 6000), with an extra suite of lithographs, 27 full color lithographs, 8 of which are double page spreads, fine in close to fine wrappers with merest trace of wear at spine end corners, in board chemise with white leather spine stamped in gold, in decorated box, lovely copy. Beasley Books 2013 - 2015 $1200

Outcault, R. F. *Pore Lil Mose His Letters to His Mammy.* New York: Grand Union Tea Co./New York Herald, 1902. Oblong folio, cloth backed pictorial card covers, corners worn and slight cover soil, else near fine, printed rectos only, each leaf gloriously illustrated in color showing, very rare in complete condition, rarer still in such clean condition. Aleph-bet Books, Inc.   109 - 54   2015 $4000

Outland, Charles F. *Man-Made Disaster: the Story of the St. Francis Dame: Its Place in Southern California's Water System. Its Failure and the Tragedy of March 12 and 13 1928 in the Santa Clara River Valley.* Glendale: Arthur H. Clark Co., 1963. First edition, illustrations, maps, portraits, brown cloth, bookplate, very fine, pictorial dust jacket, presentation inscription signed by author to friend Harvey Starr, very scarce, especially in this condition, one of 2059 copies. Argonaut Book Shop   Holiday Season 2014 - 219   2015 $500

Outlaws of Amerika. Communiques from the Weather Underground. New York: Liberated Guardian, 1971. First edition, pages darkening, couple of small stains to covers, still near fine in stapled wrappers.   Ken Lopez, Bookseller   164 - 184   2015 $175

Overbury, Thomas *A True and Perfect Account of the Examination, Confession, Trial, condemnation and Execution of Joan Perry and Her Two Sons John and Richard Perry for the supposed Murder of Will. Harrison, gent.* London: printed for John Atkinson, n.d.?, 1750. 8vo., titlepage rather soiled, preserved in modern wrappers with printed label on upper cover.   John Drury Rare Books   March 2015 - 24775   2015   £306

An Overland Journey to the Great Exhibition showing a Few Extra Articles and Visitors. London: Chapman & Hall, n.d., 1851. 7 1/4 x 5 inches, printed green sage boards, archival and unobtrusive spine strengthening, very light spotting on blank side, very good-fine, 16 panels of hand colored wood engraved illustrations by Richard Doyle.   Aleph-Bet Books, Inc.   108 - 150 2015 $975

Overton, Robert *Naughty Children.* London and New York: Hagelberg, n.d. circa, 1880. Oblong 5 x 4 inches, stiff pictorial wrappers, near fine, scarce.   Aleph-bet Books, Inc.   109 - 225   2015 $450

Overton, Thomas Collins *The Temple Builder's Most Useful Companion.* London: I. Taylor, 1774. First edition, frontispiece and 50 engraved plates, modern quarter leather lettered gilt at spine with older marbled boards (slightly rubbed), very good, sound, clean, neat contemporary name on titlepage ('Ingilby') and small attractive drawings by same on front and rear endpapers of putative construction with measurements, also one plate at top are some neat handwritten notes in sepia ink in same hand, presumably to a builder or architect.   Any Amount of Books   2015 - a7473   2015   £900

Ovidius Naso, Publius *Heroidum Epistlae Et Auli Sabini Responsiones, cm Guidonis Morilonii Argumentis...* Venice: Apud Christophorum Gryphium, 1578. Rare printing, some light spotting and toning, 8vo., contemporary limp vellum, somewhat ruckled and soiled, one tie (of four) present, very good.   Blackwell's Rare Books   Greek & Latin Classics VI - 77   2015   £700

Ovidius Naso, Publius *Metamorphoseon.* Lugduni: Sebastianius Gryphius, 1553. 178 x 108mm. without final blank, contemporary calf by Jacob Bathen of Louvain with Bathen's elaborately blindstamped "Spes" binder's device and initials "I. B." in lower left, raised bands, spine with simple blind ruling, pastedowns removed exposing construction of the binding, first and last gatherings protected by strips from a 13th century vellum French or Southern Netherlandish Breviary (very expertly rebacked to style with restoration at corners), publisher's woodcut griffin device on titlepage, later (18th century?) ownership inscription of C. N. Cuvier on titlepage, rear flyleaf with early note in Latin, remnants of rear pastedown with signature of (Ro)bertus Camholt; little splaying to upper board, covers with slight crackling, but expertly restored binding entirely solid and details of panel stamps very sharp, faint dampstain cover small portion of many leaves at bottom (another dampstain sometimes at top with about half the page affected in four quires near end), minor soiling, here and there, two leaves with darker, though smaller areas of soiling, not without condition issues, internally but nothing fatal, text both fresh and with ample margins.   Phillip J. Pirages   66 - 13   2015 $4200

Ovidius Naso, Publius *Metamorphoses in Fifteen Book.* New York: Limited Editions Club, 1958. Limited to 1500 numbered copies signed by Givoanni Mardersteig, printer and Hans Erni, the artist, thick 8vo., cloth backed boards, dust jacket, slipcase, unusual to find so well preserved, with monthly Letter loosely inserted.   Oak Knoll Books   25 - 39   2015 $350

Ovington, John *The Labouring Man's Advocate; an Appeal to the Justice and Humanity of the British Public, Repsecting the Wages of Labour.* Clapham Common: printed and sold by J. Ovington, 1817. 12mo., final leaf of ads, titlepage rather soiled and with neat repair to one corner, paper in several of the gatherings rather browned, last few leaves stained, handsome but new binding of old style red morocco gilt lettered, all edges gilt.   John Drury Rare Books   March 2015 - 21834   2015 $874

Ovink, Gerritt Willem *Legibility, Atmosphere-Value and forms of Printing Types.* Leiden: A. W. Sijthoff's Uitgeversmaatschappij, 1938. First edition, English language version, 8vo., stiff paper wrappers, scarce, covers faded, especially spine.   Oak Knoll Books   306 - 224   2015 $175

Owen, David *Perswassion to Loyalty or the Subjects Dutie; Wherein is Proved that Resisting or Deposing of Kings....* London: printed, 1642. 4to., recently bound in boards with printed title label on spine, very good, crisp copy. John Drury Rare Books March 2015 - 24357 2015 £306

Owen, David Dale 1807-1860 *Report of a Geological Survey of Wisconsin, Iowa and Minnesota and Incidentally of a Portion of Nebraska Territory. (and) Illustrations to the Geological Report of Wisconsin, Iowa and Minnesota.* Philadelphia: Lippincott, Grambo & Co., 1852. First editions, 4to., 27 engraved plates, with captioned tissue guards, 21 maps, all but 3 folding, full elaborately stamped contemporary red morocco (some soiling, but very good), evidently lacks large folding geological map referred to end of volume I, near fine set, spectacular period binding. M & S Rare Books, Inc. 97 - 25 2015 $750

Owen, Ethel *Wish for Tomorrow.* New York: Robert Speller Publishing Corp., 1936. First edition, fine in lightly rubbed, near fine dust jacket with modest chip at crown, inscribed by author to her brother, Frank Owen. Between the Covers Rare Books, Inc. 187 - 208 2015 $675

Owen, Frank *Fireside Mystery Book.* New York: Lantern Press, 1947. First edition, very good in dust jacket with light wear to spine ends and small tear to front flap fold. Buckingham Books March 2015 - 1305 2015 $175

Owen, Harold *Woman Adrift. A Statement of the Case Against Suffragism.* New York: Dutton, 1912? First American edition?, 8vo., inscription on endpaper, bound in blue cloth stamped in gilt (front hinge repaired), very good, tight, scarce. Second Life Books Inc. 189 - 190 2015 $125

Owen, Mary Alicia *Voodoo Tales as Told Among the Negroes of the Southwest.* New York: G. P. Putnam's Sons, 1893. First edition, illustrations, very good with light soiling, spine bit darkened, tear to half tone, loosening of one page that lists illustrations and consequent fraying to the pages edges. Beasley Books 2013 - 2015 $200

Owen, R. Jones *The Chemists' and Druggists' Compendium.* London: printed for the author by H. J. Wicks, 1871. First edition, 8vo., title lightly spotted, original cloth lettered gilt on upper cover, slight wear to head and foot of spine, binding just little shaken, old ink splashes on covers, good, seemingly very rare. John Drury Rare Books March 2015 - 23607 2015 £306

Owen, Richard *A History of British Fossil Mammals and Birds.* London: John van Voorst, 1846. First edition, large 8vo., half title, folding table, woodcut illustrations, 4 page catalog Dec. 1845 in smaller format, bright clean copy, uncut in original olive green pebble grained cloth, spine slightly faded with faint mark to lower edge, near fine. Jarndyce Antiquarian Booksellers CCXI - 228 2015 £750

Owen, Richard *The Life of Richard Owen.* London: John Murray, 1894. First edition, 2 volumes, 8vo., frontispieces, plates, illustrations, dark green cloth, gilt ruled covers and spine titles, extremities very rubbed, inner hinge cracked, former library copy with usual markings and defects including library sticker on front cover both volumes, fair, rare. Jeff Weber Rare Books 178 - 867 2015 $300

Owen, Robert 1771-1858 *A New View of Society; or Essays on the Principle of the Formation of the Human Character...(bound with) A new View of Society; or Essays on the Principle of the Formation of the Human Character...* London: printed by Richard and Arthur Taylor, not published, 1814. First editions of both parts, 8vo. old library stamp on blank verso of title, well bound in later 19th century half morocco over marbled boards, spine gilt and lettered, top edge gilt, very good, crisp copy. John Drury Rare Books 2015 - 25148 2015 $6556

Owen, Robert 1771-1858 *A New View of Society; or Essays on the Formation of the Human Character Preparatory to the Development of a Plan.* London: printed for Longman Hurst Rees, Orme and Brown &c, 1817. First edition, large 8vo., endpapers rather foxed, occasional very minor foxing in text, original boards, rebacked and labelled, very good, large, entirely uncut, early 19th century armorial bookplate of John Henry Verinder. John Drury Rare Books 2015 - 22706 2015 $2185

Owen, Robert 1771-1858 *Observations on the Effect of the Manufacturing System with Hints for the Improvement of Those Parts of It Which are Most Injurious to Health and Morals.* London: printed by Richard and Arthur Taylor Shoe Lane sold by Messrs. Hatchard &c, 1815. First edition, 8vo., uncut, stitched as issued, fine. John Drury Rare Books 2015 - 26192 2015 $3060

Owen, Robert 1771-1858 *Observations on the Effect of the Manufacturing System with Hints for the Improvement of Those Parts of It Which are Most Injurious to Health and Morals.* London: Longman, Hurst, Rees, Orme and Brown and others, 1817. 8vo., recently well bound in old style quarter calf over marbled boards, spine lettered gilt, fine, large copy, entirely uncut. John Drury Rare Books 2015 - 22716 2015 $1486

Owen, Robert 1771-1858 *Registered for Foreign Transmission, Robert Owen's Millennial Gazette; Explanatory of the Principles and Practices by Which in Peace, with Truth, Honesty and Simplicity...* London: Effingham Wilson, n.d. but, 1857. 8vo., including two final blank leaves, some light paper browning, one or two edge nicks, recently well bound in cloth, spine lettered in gilt, entirely uncut, good copy. John Drury Rare Books 2015 - 20339 2015 $656

Owen, Robert 1771-1858 *The Revolution in the Mind and Practice of the Human Race; or the Coming Change from Irrationality to Rationality.* London: Effingham Wilson, 1849. First edition, 8vo., original green cloth, lettered gilt on upper cover and spine, small inkstamp of City of London library on blank field of titlepage and occasionally elsewhere and with small inkstamp of the Tate Library in few margins, but in all other respects a very good fresh copy with slight wear at head and foot of spine, presentation copy "With author's respects" on front endpaper. John Drury Rare Books 2015 - 25128 2015 $1486

Owen, Robert 1771-1858 *Robert Owen's Journal. Explanatory of the Mean to Well-Place and Well-Employ and Well-Educate the Population of the World. Volume I from November 2 to April 26. - Volume II from May 3 to October 25.* London: James Watson, 1851. 2 volumes in one, large 8vo., possibly wanting half title, contemporary half leather over marbled boards, neatly rebacked to match, spine with gilt letters and lines, very good. John Drury Rare Books March 2015 - 25776 2015 $874

Oxford & Sons Limited *Coach Builders & Harness Makers 67. George Street Portman Square 92 7 94 Gloucestershire Rd. South Kensington 30 Fulham Road Thurloe Square SW.* London: J. & C. Cooper, circa, 1890. Oblong folio, 40 colored plates, some marks, generally fine, original cloth, upper cover lettered in gilt. Marlborough Rare Books List 54 - 19 2015 £2400

Ozick, Cynthia *Trust.* New York: New American Library, 1966. First edition, inscribed by author, scarce, especially signed, fine in near fine dust jacket. Ed Smith Books 83 - 74 2015 $400

Ozick,, Cynthia *Trust.* New York: New American Library, 1966. Uncorrected proof copy, tall comb-bound galley sheets, laid in is a letter sent by editor, David Segal to author John Barth, with request for opinion, this copy signed by Barth, Ozick's name was left off cover and has been added in ink, mild sunning and curling to covers, small tear at upper spine, about near fine, very scarce proof. Ken Lopez, Bookseller 164 - 163 2015 $1500

P

P., J. *Oeconomica Sacra; or a Paraenetical Discourse of Marriage Together with some Particular Remarks on the Marriage of Isaac and Rebecca.* printed for John Salusbury, 1685. First edition, some browning, last leaf with old repair at foot, lacks initial and terminal blank leaves, 12mo., new calf in contemporary style by James Brockman, some contemporary annotations of interested and attentive reader, ex Wigan public library, blindstamps at beginning and end (that at end straddling repair to foot of page, meaning that the repair was done around or before 1900), good, very rare.   Blackwell's Rare Books   B179 - 70   2015   £2000

Packard, Alpheus S. *Address on the Life and Character of Thomas C. Upham, D. D. Delivered at the Interment Brunswick, Me. April 4 1872.* Brunswick: Joseph Griffin, 1873. First edition, 8vo., 24 pages, original printed wrappers, spine worn with small library stamp.   M & S Rare Books, Inc.   97 - 308   2015 $150

Packard, Frank L. *The Adventures of Jimmie Dale.* New York: A. L. Burt, Reprint edition, very good in fine dust jacket with tiny nicks at corners.   Mordida Books   March 2015 - 010904   2015 $150

Packard, Frank L. *Jimmie Dale and the Blue Envelope Murder.* Garden City: Doubleday Doran, 1930. First edition, near fine in fine, bright dust jacket with closed tear.   Mordida Books   March 2015 - 008699   2015 $150

Packer, Vin *The Damnation of Adam Blessing.* Greenwich: Gold Medal Books, 1961. First edition, GM s0174 PBO, inscribed, near fine in pictorial wrappers.   Buckingham Books   March 2015 - 9282   2015 $200

Packward, E. P. W., Mrs. *Marital Power Exemplified in Mrs. Packard's Trial and Self Defence from the Charge of Insanity or Three Years Imprisonment for Religious Belief by the Arbitrary Will of a Husband with an Appeal to the Government to So Change the Laws as to Afford Legal protection to Married Women.* Hartford: Case, Lockwood and Co., 1866. First edition, 8vo., 2 frontispieces, very rubbed and well worn midnight blue printed wrappers, old cloth spine, front inner hinge separated, text block intact, some foxing, stains, corners curled &c., sound and complete.   M & S Rare Books, Inc.   97 - 324   2015 $400

Paddy Hew; a Poem from the Brain of Timothy Tarpaulin. printed for (Charles) Whittingham (Senior) and (John) Arliss, 1815. First edition, hand colored wood engraved frontispiece, blank corner of B5 worn away, occasional light spotting, 8vo., contemporary half calf, spine gilt, extremities rubbed, armorial bookplate of George Maquay inside front cover, good.   Blackwell's Rare Books   B179 - 61   2015   £2200

Padgett, Ron   *The Adventures of Mr. and Mrs. Jim and Ron.* New York: Cape Goliard Press in Association with Grossman Pub., 1970. First edition, 4to., illustrations by Jim Dine, original boards, dust jacket slightly rubbed, fine.   James S. Jaffe Rare Books   Many Happy Returns - 279   2015 $150

Padgett, Ron   *The Adventures of Mr. and Mrs. Jim and Ron.* New York: Grossman Pub., 1970. First edition, simultaneous paperback issue, review copy with publisher's slip laid in, 4to., illustrations by Jim Dine, original wrappers, fine, inscribed by author, also signed by Dine.   James S. Jaffe Rare Books   Many Happy Returns - 280   2015 $250

Padgett, Ron   *The Adventures of Mr. and Mrs. Jim and Ron.* New York: Cape Goliard Press in Association with Grossman Publishers, 1970. First edition, review copy with publisher's slip laid in, signed by author and by artist, Jim Dine, with a drawing, 4to., illustrations by Jim Dine, original boards, dust jacket, fine dust jacket lightly soiled and sunned.   James S. Jaffe Rare Books   Many Happy Returns - 278   2015 $450

Padgett, Ron   *Albanian Diary.* Great Barrington: The Figures, 1999. First edition, one of 10 roman numeraled copies signed by author, as new.   James S. Jaffe Rare Books   Many Happy Returns - 175   2015 $350

Padgett, Ron   *Animals in Art.* New York and Paris: Bertrand Dorny, 2004. First edition, one of only 9 copies signed by Padgett & Dorny, square 8vo., 4 original collages, original printed wrappers, publisher's slipcase.   James S. Jaffe Rare Books   Many Happy Returns - 297   2015 $1000

Padgett, Ron   *An Anthology of New York Poets.* New York: Random House, 1970. First edition, 8vo., original cloth, fine in lightly tanned dust jacket, drawings by Joe Brainard.   James S. Jaffe Rare Books   Many Happy Returns - 389   2015 $50

Padgett, Ron   *Antlers in the Treetops.* Toronto: Coach House Press, 1973. First edition, one of 1000 copies, 8vo., glossy pictorial wrappers, signed by Padgett, covers lightly sunned, otherwise fine.   James S. Jaffe Rare Books   Many Happy Returns - 313   2015 $50

Padgett, Ron *Antlers in the Treetops.* Toronto: Coach House Press, 1973. First edition, one of 1000 copies, 8vo., glossy pictorial wrappers by George Schneeman, signed by Padgett and Tom Veitch, who continues the inscription, covers slightly sunned, otherwise fine.   James S. Jaffe Rare Books   Many Happy Returns - 314   2015 $125

Padgett, Ron *Ape Man.* Paris and New York: Bertrand Dorny, 1996. First edition, one of only 9 copies signed by Padgett and Dorny (entire edition), large 8vo., 3 original double page collages, original collage wrappers, publisher's plastic slipcase.   James S. Jaffe Rare Books   Many Happy Returns - 290   2015 $800

Padgett, Ron *Bang Goes the Literature.* New York and Paris: Bertrand Dorny, 1997. First edition, one of 10 numbered copies signed by author and artist (entire edition), seven of the 10 copies were issued in publisher's plastic slipcase, oblong 8vo., 3 original double page collages, original printed wrappers.   James S. Jaffe Rare Books   Many Happy Returns - 291   2015 $800

Padgett, Ron *The Big Something.* Great Barrington: The Figures, 1990. First edition, one of only 4 roman numeraled copies signed with self portrait by Padgett, this copy designated by author as roman numeral I, as new.   James S. Jaffe Rare Books   Many Happy Returns - 170   2015 $350

Padgett, Ron *The Big Something.* Great Barrington: The Figures, 1990. First edition, one of 26 lettered copies signed with self portrait by Padgett, as new, 12mo., original wrappers.   James S. Jaffe Rare Books   Many Happy Returns - 171   2015 $50

Padgett, Ron *Bun.* New York: Angel Hair Books, 1968. First edition, one of 19 numbered copies printed on Hosho paper with page of original ms. signed by Padgett and Tom Clark tipped in at back, 4to., original glossy wrappers by Jim Dine, bleed-through from glue used to affix manuscript page to inside back cover, otherwise, fine.   James S. Jaffe Rare Books   Many Happy Returns - 273   2015 $1250

Padgett, Ron *Bun.* New York: Angel Hair Books, 1968. First edition, one of 500 copies, 4to., had of spine and top corner bumped, covers slightly rubbed, else fine, bound in two sets of wrappers, cover by Jim Dine.   James S. Jaffe Rare Books   Many Happy Returns - 272   2015 $40

Padgett, Ron *Crazy Compositions.* Bolinas: Big Sky, 1974. First edition, 8vo., glossy wrappers, illustrations by George Scheeman, inscribed by author, covers lightly dusty soiled, otherwise fine.   James S. Jaffe Rare Books   Many Happy Returns - 157   2015 $50

Padgett, Ron *Crazy Compositions.*   Bolinas: Big Sky, 1974. First edition, original glossy wrappers, illustrations by George Scheeman, limited to 750 copies, inscribed by Padgett with self portrait for Burt Britton, fine.   James S. Jaffe Rare Books   Many Happy Returns - 156   2015 $125

Padgett, Ron *Crazy Compositions.*   Bolinas: Big Sky, 1974. First edition, one of 26 lettered copies signed by author and artist, George Scheeman, out of a total edition of 750 copies, this copy lettered G, 8vo., glossy wrappers, covers faintly foxed, otherwise fine.   James S. Jaffe Rare Books   Many Happy Returns - 155   2015 $125

Padgett, Ron *Esperluettes Imaginaires.*   Paris: Bertrand Dorny, 2004. First edition, one of only 4 numbered copies signed by author and artist, text in Padgett's hand, oblong 8vo., 3 original double page collages, original printed wrappers, publisher's plastic slipcase,.   James S. Jaffe Rare Books   Many Happy Returns - 298   2015 $800

Padgett, Ron *Feathers.*   New York and Paris: Bertrand Dorny, 1998. First edition, one of 13 numbered copies signed by author and artist, oblong 8vo., 5 original double page collages, original printed wrappers, publisher's plastic slipcase.   James S. Jaffe Rare Books   Many Happy Returns - 294   2015 $800

Padgett, Ron *From Dante.*   Colorado Springs: Press at Colorado College, 2009. First edition, limited to 60 copies printed by hand in Bulmer and Bodoni types on Rives Lightweight paper, numbered and signed by author, 8vo., illustrations, original grey wrappers, sewn as issued, as new.   James S. Jaffe Rare Books   Many Happy Returns - 185   2015 $125

Padgett, Ron *Great Balls of Fire.*   Chicago: Holt Rinehart & Winston, 1969. First edition, 8vo., decorated endpapers, original cloth, dust jacket by Joe Brainard, signed by Padgett and Brainard, publisher's material laid in, spine little cocked, covers slightly rubbed, otherwise fine in slightly rubbed jacket.   James S. Jaffe Rare Books   Many Happy Returns - 149   2015 $250

Padgett, Ron *Grosse Feuerballe Gedichte, Prosa, Bilder.*   Hamburg: Rowohlt, 1973. First German edition, 12mo., illustrations, original wrappers, inscribed from author for Burt Britton, fine.   James S. Jaffe Rare Books   Many Happy Returns - 154   2015 $150

Padgett, Ron *How to Be Modern Art.*   West Branch: Morning Coffee Chapbook Seven, 1984. First edition, one of 575 numbered copies signed by Padgett & Winkfield, oblong 16mo., original wrappers, fine.   James S. Jaffe Rare Books   Many Happy Returns - 315   2015 $50

Padgett, Ron *In Advance of the Broken Arm.* New York: Lorenz Gude, 1964. First edition, limited to 200 numbered copies signed by author, 4to., original wrappers, fine. James S. Jaffe Rare Books   Many Happy Returns - 141   2015 $125

Padgett, Ron *In Advance of the Broken Arm.* New York: C. Press, 1965. Second edition, 4to., original wrappers, limited to 200 numbered copies, covers slightly darkened, covers slight darkened and dust soiled, otherwise fine. James S. Jaffe Rare Books   Many Happy Returns - 143   2015 $100

Padgett, Ron *In the Future. Vol. 1.* Paris and New York: Bertrand Dorny, 1994. First edition, one of 9 numbered copies signed by author and artist (entire edition), 8vo., 5 original collages, original printed wrappers, publisher's plastic slipcase.   James S. Jaffe Rare Books   Many Happy Returns - 288   2015 $1750

Padgett, Ron *In the Future. Tome 2.* Paris and New York: Bertrand Dorny, 1995. First edition, one of 9 numbered copies signed by author and artist (entire edition). 8vo., original collages, original printed wrappers, publisher's plastic slipcase.   James S. Jaffe Rare Books   Many Happy Returns - 289   2015 $1500

Padgett, Ron *In the Future. Livre 3.* Paris and New York: Bertrand Dorny, 1997. First edition, one of 9 numbered copies signed by author and artist, 8vo., 5 original collages, original printed wrappers, publisher's plastic slipcase. James S. Jaffe Rare Books   Many Happy Returns - 292   2015 $1500

Padgett, Ron *In the Future. Album 4.* Paris and New York: Bertrand Dorny, 1997. First edition, one of 9 numbered copies signed by author and artist, 8vo., 5 original printed wrappers, publisher's plastic slipcase.   James S. Jaffe Rare Books   Many Happy Returns - 293   2015 $1500

Padgett, Ron *In the Future. Manual 5.* Paris and New York: Bertrand Dorny, 2001. First edition, one of 9 numbered copies signed by author and artist, 8vo., original double page collages, original collage wrappers, publisher's plastic slipcase.   James S. Jaffe Rare Books   Many Happy Returns - 296   2015 $1500

Padgett, Ron *In the Future. folio 6.* Paris and New York: Bertrand Dorny, 2006. First edition, one of 7 numbered copies signed by author and artist, 8vo., 5 original collages, original collage wrappers, publisher's plastic slipcase. James S. Jaffe Rare Books   Many Happy Returns - 299   2015 $1500

Padgett, Ron *In the Future. Opuscule 7.* Paris and New York: Bertrand Dorny, 2007. First edition, one of 9 numbered copies signed by author and artist, 8vo., 5 original collages, original printed wrappers, publisher's plastic slipcase.   James S. Jaffe Rare Books   Many Happy Returns - 300   2015 $1500

Padgett, Ron *In the Past. Vol. 1.* Paris and New York: Bertrand Dorny, 2007. First edition, one of only 9 numbered copies signed by author and artist, 8vo., 3 original double page collages, original printed wrappers, publisher's plastic slipcase.   James S. Jaffe Rare Books   Many Happy Returns - 301   2015 $1500

Padgett, Ron *In the Past. Livre 3.* Paris and New York: Bertrand Dorny, 2007. First edition, one of 9 numbered copies signed by author and artist, accompanied by a CD of the author reading the work, 8vo., 7 original double page collages, original printed wrappers, publisher's slipcase. James S. Jaffe Rare Books   Many Happy Returns - 303   2015 $1750

Padgett, Ron *In the Past. Album 4.* Paris and New York: Bertrand Dorny, 2010. First edition, one of 6 numbered copies signed by author and artist, 8vo., 9 original double page collages, original printed wrappers, publisher's slipcase, accompanied by a CD of author reading and commenting on the work.   James S. Jaffe Rare Books   Many Happy Returns - 304   2015 $2000

Padgett, Ron *Joe. A Memoir of Joe Brainard.* Minneapolis: Coffee House Press, 2004. First edition, original cloth, dust jacket, clothbound, fine, illustrations.   James S. Jaffe Rare Books   Many Happy Returns - 126   2015 $75

Padgett, Ron *Light as Air.* New York: Pace Editions, 1989. First edition, one of 30 numbered copies, signed by poet and artist, folio, portfolio box by Bernard Duval, aquatints by Alex Katz printed at the Atelier Aldo Commelnyck, Paris, on Hahnemuhle paper, sheet size is 17 34/ x 30 inches, text printed in 24 point Bodoni by Francois de Ros, copper plates were cancelled upon completion, as new. James S. Jaffe Rare Books   Many Happy Returns - 168   2015 $10,000

Padgett, Ron *Medieval Yawn.* Paris and New York: Bertrand Dorny, 1992. first edition of this synthetic book, one of only 7 numbered copies, signed by author and artist (entire edition) with Padgett's foreword in his holograph on tipped-in leaf, large 8vo., 4 original double page collages, original printed wrappers, one audio cassette and one small bottle of perfume, publisher's box.   James S. Jaffe Rare Books   Many Happy Returns - 286   2015 $2500

Padgett, Ron *New & Selected Poems.* Boston: David R. Godine, 1995. First edition, 8vo., original cloth backed boards, dust jacket, signed by author, as new.   James S. Jaffe Rare Books   Many Happy Returns - 173   2015 $75

Padgett, Ron *100,000 Fleeing Hilda.* Tulsa: Boke Press, 1967. Limited to 300 numbered copies, first edition, signed by Padgett & Brainard, 8vo., illustrations by Joe Brainard, wrappers, fine.   James S. Jaffe Rare Books   Many Happy Returns - 271   2015 $150

Padgett, Ron *100,000 Fleeing Hilda.* Tulsa: Boke Press, 1967. First edition, 8vo., limited to 300 numbered copies signed by author and artist, illustrations by Joe Brainard, original wrappers, white covers slightly darkened and dust soiled, otherwise fine, this copy inscribed by Padgett to Burt Britton.   James S. Jaffe Rare Books   Many Happy Returns - 270   2015 $250

Padgett, Ron *Oo La La.* London & New York: Petersburg Press, 1973. First edition, limited to 75 copies, 15 original collaborative lithographs by Jim Dine and Ron Padgett, loose in publisher's portfolio, lithographs printed on handmade paper and signed by Padgett and Dine, fine, rare.   James S. Jaffe Rare Books   Many Happy Returns - 282   2015 $17,500

Padgett, Ron *Ooo and Ahh.* Paris and New York: Bertrand Dorny, 1991. First edition, one of 5 numbered copies signed by author and artist, text in Padgett's holograph, oblong 8vo., original double page collages, original printed wrappers.   James S. Jaffe Rare Books   Many Happy Returns - 285   2015 $1250

Padgett, Ron *Quelques Poemes/Some Translations/Some Bombs.* N.P.: Ron Padgett, 1963. First edition, limited to 100 numbered copies, this number 43, small folio, with three full page illustrations and cover design by Joe Brainard, loose sheets measuring 8 1/2 x 11 inches, pictorial portfolio, although not issued signed, this copy signed by Padgett, spine of folder sunned and slightly rubbed, otherwise fine, rare.   James S. Jaffe Rare Books   Many Happy Returns - 140   2015 $5000

Padgett, Ron *Petite ode a Jean Francois Champollion.* Paris and New York: Bertrand Dorny, 1990. First edition, one of 24 numbered copies signed by author and artist (entire edition), triangular 8vo., 9 original collages, original velo-bound printed wrappers, book can be unfolded in such a way as to form a free-standing pyramid whose pages may then be turned.   James S. Jaffe Rare Books   Many Happy Returns - 284   2015 $650

Padgett, Ron *Phylactery.* Paris: Bertrand Dorny, 2007. First edition, one of only 5 numbered copies signed by Padgett and Dorny, large oblong 8vo., 7 original collages, publisher's plastic slipcase.   James S. Jaffe Rare Books   Many Happy Returns - 302   2015 $750

Padgett, Ron *Robert's Ball.* N.P.: Ron Padgett, 1966. Self published, holograph colophon reading "Limited Edition/This Copy is for Dick (Gallup)" fine, oblong 12mo., illustrated, accordion fold chapbook, hand lettered and colored by Padgett.   James S. Jaffe Rare Books   Many Happy Returns - 144   2015 $2500

Padgett, Ron *Self-Service Story. Conte Self-Service.* Paris and New York: Bertrand Dorny, 1992. First edition, one of 7 numbered copies, signed by author and artist, entire edition, text in Padgett's holograph, miniature book, 1 original collage, original printed wrappers.   James S. Jaffe Rare Books   Many Happy Returns - 287   2015 $500

Padgett, Ron *Song in G.* Paris and New York: Bertrand Dorny, 1999. First edition, one of 10 numbered copies signed by author and artist with text in Padgett's holograph, 4 double page collages, original decorated plastic covers, publisher's plastic slipcase.   James S. Jaffe Rare Books   Many Happy Returns - 295   2015 $800

Padgett, Ron *Strange Faces 3: Ron Padgett Issue.* London: Strange Faeces Press, 1971. Limited to 250 copies, signed by author, 4to., original wrappers, fine.   James S. Jaffe Rare Books   Many Happy Returns - 150   2015 $275

Padgett, Ron *Summer Balloons.* Tulsa: privately printed, 1960. First edition, inscribed presentation from author to poet Tony Towle, 12mo., original printed wrappers, fine in original envelope addressed by Padgett to Towle, rare.   James S. Jaffe Rare Books   Many Happy Returns - 138   2015 $3500

Padgett, Ron *Supernatural Overtones.* Great Barrington: The Figures, 1990. First edition, one of 26 lettered copies signed by Padgett and Clark Coolidge, out of total edition of 500 copies, as new.   James S. Jaffe Rare Books   Many Happy Returns - 275   2015 $250

Padgett, Ron *Supernatural Overtones.* Great Barrington: The Figures, 1990. First edition, one of 500 copies, square 8vo., white wrappers, as new, thought not called for, signed by Padgett and Clark Coolidge.   James S. Jaffe Rare Books   Many Happy Returns - 276   2015 $100

Padgett, Ron *Sweet Pea.* London: Aloes Books, 1971. First edition, limited to 200 copies, 16mo., original wrappers, inscribed by Padgett for Burt Britton, fine.   James S. Jaffe Rare Books   Many Happy Returns - 153   2015 $2500

Padgett, Ron *Sweet Pea.* London: Aloes Books, 1971. First edition, one of 25 numbered copies signed by Padgett & artist George Schneeman, out of a total edition of 200 copies, illustrations and cover by Schneeman, oblong 16mo., original wrappers, fine, inscribed by Padgett for Burt Britton.   James S. Jaffe Rare Books   Many Happy Returns - 152   2015 $600

Padgett, Ron *Tone Arm.* N.P.: A Once Book, 1967. First edition, one of only 10 copies signed and dated by author, Dec. 12 1966, small 4to., original pictorial wrappers, fine. James S. Jaffe Rare Books   Many Happy Returns - 147   2015 $350

Padgett, Ron *Tone Arm.* N.P.: Tone Arm, 1967. First edition, small 4to., original pictorial wrappers, inscribed by author, fine.   James S. Jaffe Rare Books   Many Happy Returns - 147   2015 $175

Padgett, Ron *Toujours l'Amour. Poems.* New York: Sun, 1976. First edition, one of 35 copies numbered and signed by author, 8vo., original cloth, dust jacket, fine in dust jacket with one short closed tear.   James S. Jaffe Rare Books   Many Happy Returns - 158   2015 $450

Padgett, Ron *Toujours l'Amour. Poems.* New York: Sun, 1976. First edition, 8vo., original cloth, dust jacket, fine. James S. Jaffe Rare Books   Many Happy Returns - 159   2015 $50

Padgett, Ron *Tulsa Kid.* Calais: Z Press, 1979. First edition, one of 100 numbered copies signed by Padgett out of a total edition of 1500 copies, fine.   James S. Jaffe Rare Books   Many Happy Returns - 166   2015 $350

Padgett, Ron *Tulsa Kid.* Calais: Z Press, 1979. First edition, one of 500 numbered hardcover copies, out of a total edition of 1500, 8vo., original cloth, fine.   James S. Jaffe Rare Books   Many Happy Returns - 165   2015 $100

Padgett, Ron *Tulsa Kid.* Calais: Z Press, 1979. First edition, one of 26 lettered copies, signed with original drawing by Padgett tipped-in, out of a total edition of 1500, 8vo., original cloth, dust jacket, fine.   James S. Jaffe Rare Books   Many Happy Returns - 167   2015 $750

Padgett, Ron *White Dove Review. Volume I no. 1 - Volume II no. 5.* Tulsa: White Dove Review, 1959-1960. Complete run, 5 volumes, no more than 5 sets bound thus for editor, inscribed by Padgett, very fine.   James S. Jaffe Rare Books   Many Happy Returns - 1   2015 $6500

Padgett, Ron *Wish Souhait.* Paris and New York: Bertrand Dorny, 1989. First edition, one of only 7 numbered copies signed by author and artist (entire edition), title in Padgett's holograph, 8vo., 5 original double page collages, original collage wrappers.   James S. Jaffe Rare Books   Many Happy Returns - 283   2015 $1250

Pafford, H. H. P. *W. P. Ker 1855-1923: a Bibliography.* London: University of London Press, 1950. Half title, frontispiece and plates, original brown cloth in slightly torn and browned dust jacket, signed by Geoffrey Tillotson 1953 with ms. anecdote of Ker.   Jarndyce Antiquarian Booksellers CCVII - 351   2015   £25

Page, John *Receipts for the Preparing and Compounding the Principal Medicines Made Used of by the Late Mr. Ward.* London: printed for and sold by Henry Whitridge, 1763. First edition, variant issue, 8vo., first and last leaves slightly soiled, preserved in modern wrappers with printed title label on upper cover, very good.   John Drury Rare Books March 2015 - 17707   2015   £306

Page, Myra *Southern Cotton Mills and Labor.* New York: Workers Library, 1929. First edition, wrappers, 96 pages, photos, very good.   Beasley Books   2013 - 2015 $125

Page, William *The Victoria History of the Country of Hertford.* London: Constable, 1902. First edition, 4 volumes, 4to., original half leather lettered gilt on spine, marbled endpapers, copiously illustrated in black and white with plates, maps and line drawings, handsome about very good with few ex-library stamps and labels, spine rubbed, some rubbing at corners, slight general shelfwear but decent sound set.   Any Amount of Books   2015 - A67794   2015 £300

Paget, Violet 1856-1935 *Baldwin: Being Dialogue on Views and Aspirations.* London: T. Fisher Unwin, 1886. First edition, 8vo., original dark green cloth lettered gilt on spine and on front cover, faint rubbing, slight scuffing, otherwise near fine, excellent condition.   Any Amount of Books 2015 - A66473   2015   £180

Pagnol, Marcel *Works/Oeuvres.* Monte Carlo: Editions Pastorelly, 1973. First edition thus, 8vo., 23 volumes, well illustrated, many color plates, richly gilt dark green (faux) leather (simili-cuir), top edge gilt, fine.   Any Amount of Books   2015 - A20384   2015   £160

Pain, Barry *Going Home: Being the Fantastic Romance of the Girl with Angel eyes and the Man Who Had Wings.* London: T. Werner Laurie, 1921. First edition, 8vo. original patterned green cloth lettered and decorated black at spine and cover, green covers have very slight marks and faint discoloration, otherwise clean, very good, bright copy, clean text.   Any Amount of Books   2015 - C649   2015   £160

Pain, Eva *Stories Barry Told Me.* London: Longmans, 1927. First edition, 8vo., cloth backed pictorial boards, 94 pages, near fine, full color illustrations.   Aleph-bet Books, Inc.   109 - 114   2015 $125

Paine, Bayard *Pioneers, Indians and Buffaloes.* Curtis Empire, 1935. First edition, 8vo., signed by author, cloth, titles stamped in gold, gilt on spine, 192 pages, frontispiece, illustrations, near fine, tight copy.   Buckingham Books   March 2015 - 37276   2015 $300

Paine, Thomas 1737-1809 *Letters to the Citizens of the United States of America After an Absence of Fifteen Years.* London: Sherwin, 1817. First edition, 8vo., 34 pages, sewn, removed, very nice, clean.   Second Life Books Inc.   191 - 74   2015 $250

Painter, William *The Palace of Pleasure.* London: reprinted for Robert Triphook by Harding and Wright, 1813. One of 150 copies, 3 volumes, 254 x 197mm., remarkably attractive contemporary chocolate brown morocco elaborately decorated in blind and gilt by Charles Lewis, covers with blind tooled frame enclosed by gilt fillets, wide raised bands, decorative gilt rolls, intricately blind tooled panels, gilt titling, turn-ins ruled in gilt, all edges gilt, large paper copy, verso of front free endpaper in volume I with pencilled notation, "3 volumes bound by Charles Lewis £5.50/Only 150 printed, published at £10.10 in bds.", hint of rubbing to head of one spine, occasional minor foxing and other trivial imperfections, but especially fine set, entirely clean and smooth internally, in lustrous unworn bindings.   Phillip J. Pirages   66 - 70   2015 $3250

The Painter's Primer; in Familiar Rhyme, without Notes. Oxford: printed by N. Bliss for Messrs. Macgivins, 1810. 8vo., frontispiece by Girtin, untrimmed in contemporary boards, rebacked contents slightly dusty, some pencillings. Marlborough Rare Books   List 54 - 61   2015   £275

Palade, George Emil *A Small Particulate Component of the Cytoplasm.* London: 1955. Offprint from Proceedings of International Conference on Electron Microscopy, July 1954, First separate edition, 8vo., near fine offprint in self wrappers, mild soil, 4 plates.   By the Book, L. C.   44 - 24   2015 $500

Palahniuk, Chuck *Fight Club.* New York: Norton, 1996. Advance reading copy, signed by author, very slight dustiness to rear white panel, else fine in wrappers.   Ken Lopez, Bookseller   164 - 164   2015 $1500

Palanti, Mario *Prima Esposizione Personale d'Architettura nella Republica Argentina.* Milano: Stabilmento di Arti Grafiche Rizzoli & Pizzio, 1917. First edition, illustrations with 137 color & black and white plates, folio, brown cloth decorated in blind, gilt titles, presentation copy from author to his fellow Italian painter, art critic and politician Cipriano Efisio Oppo (1891-1962), wear at spine ends and along joints, small tear to top front joint and at middle of spine, remnants of paper revenue stamps on spine, occasional offsetting or light soiling on few leaves, still very good.   Kaaterskill Books   19 - 198   2015 $500

Paley, William 1743-1805 *An Essay Upon the British Constitution: Being the seventh Chapter of the Sixth Book of the Principles of Moral and Political Philosophy.* London: R. Faulder, 1792. First edition thus, 8vo., half title, recent marbled boards lettered on spine, very good, apparently rare. John Drury Rare Books   March 2015 - 24138   2015   £306

Paley, William 1743-1805 *The Principles of Moral and Political Philosophy.* London: printed for R. Faulder, 1785. First edition, half title, contemporary dark green calf with ornately gilt borders, sometime neatly rebacked, gilt lines and lettered, very good, mid 19th century armorial bookplate of S. F. Steele Perkins Esq. and earlier signature of Shirley Perkins.   John Drury Rare Books   March 2015 - 25070   2015 $874

Palgrave, Francis Turner 1824-1897 *The Five Days Entertainments at Wentworth Garage.* London: Macmillan & Co., 1868. First edition, half title, plates and illustrations by Arthur Hughes, 2 pages ad, original blue cloth, inner hinges splitting, rubbed and dulled, top edge gilt, with slightly damaged half title and partly obscured presentation to Gwenllian Florence Palgrave 1866-1951, one of the dedicatees from her father 1873, overwritten in pencil with her childish signature, from the library of Geoffrey & Kathleen Tillotson.   Jarndyce Antiquarian Booksellers   CCVII - 404   2015   £60

Palgrave, Francis Turner 1824-1897 *The Golden Treasury of the Best Songs and Lyrical Poems in the English Language.* Cambridge: Macmillan and Co., 1861. First edition, second impression, lacking half title and leading f.e.p., original green glazed cloth by Burn, slightly rubbed, bookseller's ticket of Thomas Brady, York, Kathleen Tillotson's copy with pencil notes above variants, she had written on it sources, with copy of the Penguin Classics edition edited by Christopher Ricks 1991, with ink notes and containing drafts of letter from Kathleen to Ricks about Palgrave's annotationed copy of Nightingale Valley. Jarndyce Antiquarian Booksellers   CCVII - 405   2015   £30

Palgrave, Francis Turner 1824-1897 *The Visions of England. Second Part.* London: printed for F. T. Palgrave by Cousins & Co., 1881. First edition, one of 50 copies dated April 1881, marked by Palgrave 'To be returned' with faint address on wrapper and signed by him in pencil on top edge gilt 22 Ap 1881, from the library of Geoffrey & Kathleen Tillotson.   Jarndyce Antiquarian Booksellers   CCVII - 406   2015   £58

Palinurus *Familiar Letters, from Elder to a Younger Brother, Serving for His Freedom in the Trinity-House, Newcastle Upon Tyne.* Newcastle: printed for the author by L. Dinsdale, 1785. First edition, 8vo., half title and final leaf (errata on recto, ad verso), contemporary half calf over marbled boards with fairly recent unlettered reback, good copy, 19th century bookseller ticket Thomas Thorne on pastedown, very rare.   John Drury Rare Books   March 2015 - 23146   2015 $656

Paris, Matthew 1200-1259 *Flores Historiarum per Matthaeum Westmonasteriensem Collecti, Praecipue de Rebus Britannicis ab Exordio Usque ad Annum Domini 1307.* Ex officina Thomae Marshii, 1570. Second printed edition, titlepage trimmed close to woodcut border, final blank leaf discarded, index bound at front of text, one leaf with original paper law affecting few characters, first leaf of index with bottom margin folded over to preserve early manuscript note, verso of title also filled with text in early manuscript (trimmed at bottom), few short notes or marks later on, last dozen leaves showing faint but substantial dampmark, some soiling/minor staining elsewhere, touch of worming to blank fore-edge margin, two leaves remargined, gathering Ttt in earlier (?) state without (and not calling for) the additional unsigned singleton leaf, folio, 18th century mottled calf, spine with five raised bands, red morocco lettering pieces in second and third compartment, rubbed, front joint cracking (but strong), little peeling to leather, light wear to endcaps, marbled endpapers, bookplates of Robert Surtees and his Mainsforth Library, sound. Blackwell's Rare Books B179 - 81 2015 £1400

Paris. Chambre de Police *Sentence de Police qui Defend aux Maistres Rotisseurs de renvoyer aux Marchands Forains Aucunes Marchandises qu'ils Auront Achetees d'eux sur le Carreau de la Vallee...* Paris: P. J. Mariette, 1729. First separate edition, 4 pages, large woodcut headpiece, unbound, uncut and folded as issued, fine. John Drury Rare Books March 2015 - 21113 2015 £266

Parish, John C. *California Books and Manuscripts in the Huntington Library.* Cambridge: Harvard University Press, 1935. First book edition, presentation inscription signed by author to Samuel Farquhar (head of UC Press), light brown wrappers printed in black, minor crease to rear wrapper, fine. Argonaut Book Shop Holiday Season 2014 - 221 2015 $60

Park, Maud Wood *Front Door Lobby.* Boston: Beacon Press, 1960. First edition, 8vo., nice, repaired dust jacket. Second Life Books Inc. 189 - 193 2015 $125

Parker, B. *Arctic Orphans.* London & Edinburgh: W. & R. Chambers, n.d. circa, 1920. Oblong folio, pictorial boards, light edge and spine rubbing, else near fine, illustrations by N. Parker with 13 incredible full page color illustrations plus illustrations in text, pictorial endpapers and striking color covers, beautiful copy. Aleph-Bet Books, Inc. 108 - 333 2015 $1500

Parker, B. *The A's and K's or Twice Three is Six.* London & Edinburgh: W. & R. Chambers, n.d. circa, 1910. Oblong folio, pictorial boards, slightest bit of rubbing, else fine in original dust jacket (chipped at fold and spine ends), 24 full page chromolithographed plates plus illustrations in brown line, scarce. Aleph-bet Books, Inc. 109 - 341 2015 $1750

Parker, B. *The Hole and Corner Book.* London & Edinburgh: W. & R. Chambers, n.d. circa, 1910. Oblong folio, pictorial boards, fine in original dust jacket (some chipping), few mends, else very good dust jacket, full page color lithographed plates plus illustrations by Nancy Parker, very scarce. Aleph-Bet Books, Inc. 108 - 334 2015 $1750

Parker, Chan *To Bird With Love.* Poitiers: Editions Witzlov, 1981. First edition, folio, fine in very good box with rubbed edges and one internal joint mend, this copy inscribed by Parker, unusual thus. Beasley Books 2013 - 2015 $1200

Parker, G. M. N. *The Mountain Massacre: a True Story of the Massacre of the Court Officials at Hillsville, Virginia by the Allen Clan.* Bluefield: 1930. Fine in fine, unclipped dust jacket, inscribed and signed by author's wife. Bookworm & Silverfish 2015 - 6013858668 2015 $47

Parker, Gilbert *Round the Compass in Australia.* London: Hutchinson and Co., 1892. First edition, inscribed by author to Mrs. Andrew Chisholm, London 1892, original light blue cloth boards with gilt title to spine and front board illustration of sheep to spine and shovel with gold and pick axe to front cover, few splits to cloth along front joint and rear hinge cracked, binding little loose with few internal splits browning to spine fraying to spine ends and minor wear to corners, interior clean overall, just few spots of foxing, very good. The Kelmscott Bookshop 11 - 35 2015 $150

Parker, James Reid *Attorneys at Law: Forbes, Hathaway, Bryan and Devore.* Garden City: Doubleday Doran and Co., 1941. First edition, fine in fine dust jacket with tiny tear, beautiful copy. Between the Covers Rare Books 196 - 100 2015 $100

Parker, Joan H. *Three Weeks in Spring.* Boston: Houghton Mifflin Co., 1978. First edition, fine in lightly rubbed dust jacket with very light wear to toe of spine. Buckingham Books March 2015 - 20872 2015 $225

Parker, Robert *A Scholasticall Discourse Against Symbolizing with Antichrist in Ceremonies: Especially in the Signe of Crosse.* Middleburg: R. Schilders, 1607. First edition, First part only, quarto, brown buckram with calf spine ruled and lettered gilt, marbled endpapers, various early ownership signatures an ink blots on titlepage, some light ink staining and chipping to first and last few pages, otherwise very good, clean text block in very good later binding with partially faded spine. Any Amount of Books 2015 - C13207 2015 £240

Parker, Robert B. *Crimson Joy.* New York: Delacorte, 1988. First edition, one of 250 numbered copies signed by author, very fine in slipcase without dust jacket as issued, still in original shrinkwrap. Mordida Books March 2015 - 012607 2015 $150

Parker, Robert B. *Double Deuce.* New York: G. P. Putnam's Sons, 1992. First edition, limited to 135 numbered copies signed by author, as new in original cloth slipcase, wrapped in original plastic shrink wrap. Buckingham Books   March 2015 - 21250   2015 $225

Parker, Robert B. *Introduction to Raymond Chandler's Unknown Thriller: The Screenplay of Playback.* New York: Mysterious Press, 1985. First edition, one of a very few copies printed for copyright purposes, pamphlet, very fine in printed wrappers.   Mordida Books   March 2015 - 001773   2015 $200

Parker, Robert B. *The Judas Goat.* Boston: Houghton Mifflin, 1978. 1984. First edition, inscribed by author, fine in dust jacket.   Buckingham Books   March 2015 - 20871   2015 $175

Parker, Robert B. *Looking for Rachel Wallace.* New York: Delacorte, 1980. Uncorrected proof, fine in plain tall green wrappers as issued, from the collection of Duke Collier.   Royal Books   36 - 218   2015 $650

Parker, Robert B. *Looking for Rachel Wallace.* New York: Delacorte, 1980. First edition, fine and unread in fine dust jacket, from the collection of Duke Collier.   Royal Books   36 - 217 2015 $350

Parker, Robert B. *Pale Kings and Princes.* New York: Delacorte, 1987. First edition, one of 225 numbered copies signed by author, very fine in slipcase, still in original shrinkwrap.   Mordida Books   March 2015 - 012608   2015 $175

Parker, Robert B. *Pastime.* New York: G. P. Putnam's sons, 1991. first edition, limited to 150 numbered copies signed by author, as new in original cloth slipcase, packaged in original plastic shrinkwrap.   Buckingham Books   March 2015 - 21251   2015 $180

Parker, Robert B. *Playmates.* New York: G. P. Putnams Sons, 1980. First edition, limited to 250 numbered copies signed by author, this copy 197, fine, without dust jacket as issued, housed in cloth slipcase.   Buckingham Books   March 2015 - 21191   2015 $175

Parker, Robert B. *Poodle Springs.* New York: Putnam, 1989. First edition, very fine in pictorial wrappers, signed by author, advance reading copy.   Mordida Books   March 2015 - 001770   2015 $75

Parker, Robert B. *Spenser's Boston.* New York: Otto Penzler Books, 1994. First US edition, fine in dust jacket, signed by author, photos.   Buckingham Books   March 2015 - 31833   2015 $300

Parker, Robert B. *Surrogate.* Northridge: Lord John Press, 1982. First edition, one of 50 numbered (this being no. 7) signed by author, fine in red patterned paper covered boards and maroon quarter leather, near fine, black cloth slipcase, from the collection of Duke Collier.   Royal Books   36 - 219   2015 $2000

Parker, Robert B. *Walking Shadow.* New York: G. P. Putnam's Sons, 1994. First edition, limited to 100 copies, signed by author, as new in original cloth slipcase protected with original plastic shrinkwrap.   Buckingham Books   March 2015 - 21273   2015 $175

Parker, Thomas Lister *Description of Browsholme Hall, in the West Riding of the County of York and the Parish of Washington in the Same County...* London: printed by S. Gosnell Little Queen Street..., 1815. 4to., large folding pedigree, 20 etched plates, contemporary half calf, marbled boards, joints skillfully repaired, armorial bookplate of Sir Edmund Bacon.   Marlborough Rare Books   List 53 - 36   2015   £500

Parkinson, James *Organs Remains of a Former World: an Examination of the Mineralized Remains of the Vegetables and Animals of the Antediluvian World: Generally Termed Extraneous Fossils.* London: printed by C. Whittingham and published by J. Robson, J. White and J. Murray, H. D. Symonds, et al, 1804-1811. First edition, 3 volumes, 4to., 54 engraved plates, many hand colored, 2 errata leafs, titlepage vignettes, volume I prelims browned, occasional light foxing and offsetting throughout all volumes, contemporary full tan calf, gilt double ruled covers, 5 raised bands, gilt stamped spines and brown leather spine labels, volume I rebacked with original spine laid down, volume III front cover scratched, extremities rubbed all volumes, bookplate of Haskell Norman, bookplate and signature of J. Walton, 1952, near fine.   Jeff Weber Rare Books   178 - 875   2015 $5000

Parkman, Francis   1823-1893 *The California and Oregon Trail: Being Sketches of Prairie and Rocky Mountain Life.* New York: George P. Putnam, 1849. First edition, second printing, one of 500 copies, 8vo., original bluish gray blindstamped cloth, titles stamped in gold, gilt to spine, frontispiece, pictorial half title, former owner's inked name and date (1851), lightly foxed, rebound with original spine laid down, light domestic restoration to spine ends and corners, else very good.   Buckingham Books   March 2015 - 32539   2015 $2000

Parkman, Francis   1823-1893 *The Works of Francis Parkman.* Boston: Little Brown and Co., 1910. 8vo., 13 volumes, contemporary, top edge gilt, covers and spine ends and edges scuffed, some volumes rubbed at corners exposing tips of boards.   Oak Knoll Books   306 - 287   2015 $200

Parley's Magazine for 1840. New York & Boston: C. S. & J. H. Francis, 1840. Numerous engravings, half leather and marbled boards and endpapers, very good, usual shelfwear and rubbing, some random spotting. Stephen Lupack March 2015 - 2015 $75

Parnell, Edward Andrew *Dyeing and Calico Printing.* London: Taylor, Walton and Maberly, 1849. First edition, illustrations, 16 page catalog, some slight foxing and offsetting, original fine grained green cloth, blocked in blind, front board slightly marked, otherwise handsome copy, booksellers ticket R. Rowker, Accrington. Jarndyce Antiquarian Booksellers CCXI - 229 2015 £275

Parnell, Henry *A History of the Penal Laws Against the Irish Catholics from the Treaty of Limerick to the Union.* London: J. Harding, 1808. First edition?, 8vo., mid 20th century maroon quarter calf, spine lettered gilt, very good. John Drury Rare Books March 2015 - 15845 2015 £306

The Parallel; or a Collection of Extraordinary Cases, Relating to Concealed Births and Disputed Successions... London: J. Roberts, 1744. First edition, 8vo., titlepage little dust soiled in 19th century roan backed marbled boards, spine gilt lettered, good, scarce. John Drury Rare Books March 2015 - 21750 2015 $266

Parrish, Stephen Maxwell *A Concordance to the Poems of Matthew Arnold.* Ithaca: Cornell University Press, 1959. Original red cloth, half title, presentation to Geoffrey Tillotson with copies of his letters of thanks. Jarndyce Antiquarian Booksellers CCVII - 69 2015 £40

Parsons, Benjamin *A Letter to Richard Cobden, Esq. M.P. for the West Riding of Yorkshire on the Impolicy and Tyranny of any System of State Education.* London: John Snow, 1852. First edition, 8vo., title just little soiled and with old inkstamp of government department, sewn as issued, good, large copy. John Drury Rare Books 2015 - 25215 2015 $133

Parsons, Claudia *Vagabondage.* London: Chatto & Windus, 1941. First edition, 8vo., frontispiece, 15 plates, 3 maps, neat name "K. Coomaraswamy / Segennah Nov 11th 1941", covers heavily worn and soiled, spine slightly split, contents okay, good only, loosely inserted is long TLS from author to Dennis Collings discussing the book. Any Amount of Books 2015 - A36695 2015 £150

Parsons, Edward *A Letter to the Reverend author of a Candid Inquiry into the Democratic Schemes of the Dissenters.* Leeds: printed by Edward Baines, 1801. First and only edition, 8vo., 36 pages, recent marbled boards lettered on spine, very good. John Drury Rare Books March 2015 - 23443 2015 £306

Parsons, Edward *A Vindication of the Dissenters against the Charge of Democratic Scheming. Three Letters to the Rev. author of a Candid Inquiry into the Democratic Schemes of the Dissenters Vindication.* Leeds: printed by Edward Baines, 1802. Second edition, 8vo., recent marbled boards lettered on spine, very good, very scarce. John Drury Rare Books March 2015 - 23470 2015 £306

Parsons, George Whitwell *The Private Journal of George Whitwell Parsons.* Arizona Statewide Archival Records Project, 1939. First edition, quarto, stiff printed wrappers, all pages photolithographed, re-inforced along fore-edge of front panel and few prelim pages moderate vertical creases to front panel, else very good, tight copy of extremely difficult title, rare, housed in quarter leather and cloth folding case with raised bands and gold stamping on spine. Buckingham Books March 2015 - 20945 2015 $2500

Parsons, Philip *Six Letters to a Friend, on the Establishment of Sunday Schools.* London: T. Becket, 1786. First edition, 12mo., recently bound in marbled boards, spine lettered, very good, rare. John Drury Rare Books 2015 - 24248 2015 $1136

Partridge, William *A Practical Treatise on Dying of Woolen, Cotton and Skein silk.* New York: Wallis & Co., 1823. First edition, 8vo., includes single folding table and ad for Dye Stuffs being sold by Partridge at his store in NY, bound in full calf, chipped, front cover loose, some gnawing to lower fore edge of titlepage, but good copy. Second Life Books Inc. 191 - 75 2015 $400

Pascal, Blaise *Pensees de M. Pascal sur la religion et sur Quelques Autres Sujets qui ont Este Trouvees Apres sa Mort Parmy ses Papiers. (Thought of Mr. Pascal on Religion and Some Other Subjects...).* Paris: Guillaume Desprez, 1670. Counterfeit, True Second edition, gorgeous contemporary full leather, spine has five raised bands, gilt lettering and decorations in each compartment, with gilt embossed arms of William Paved Vendeuvre family to center of both front and back covers, lovely marbled endpapers, very handsome, clean, bright, tight copy. Athena Rare Books 15 - 49 2015 $3000

Pasero De Corneliano, Carlo Antonio, Comte *Considerations Politiques et Morales.* Paris: A La Librarie de Lacretelle..., 1820. First edition, stitched as issued, entirely uncut, fine, very scarce. John Drury Rare Books 2015 - 21411 2015 $177

Pasko, W. W. *American Dictionary of Printing and Bookmaking...* New York: Howard Lockwood & Co., 1894. First edition, thick 4to., later quarter leather over cloth pebbled cloth, illustrations, half of leather spine missing library bookplate and pocket in back. Oak Knoll Books 306 - 195 2015 $100

Pasley, Charles William *Observations on Limes, Calcareous Cements, Mortars, Stuccos and Concrete and on Puzzolanas Natural and Artificial.* London: John Weale Architectural Library, 1838. First edition, 8vo., several woodcut text figures, various neat emphasis marks and few marginal notes all in pencil by earlier reader, original blind-stamped cloth, rebacked and lettered gilt, very good, uncut. John Drury Rare Books   2015 - 25337   2015 $612

Pasmore, Victor *Burning Waters: Second Version: Visual and Poetic Images.* London: Enitharmon Press, 1995. First edition, 99 of 375 copies, initialled by author, 4to., original oatmeal cloth lettered in silver, very faint handling wear, about fine.   Any Amount of Books   2015 - A97425   2015   £225

Pasnau, Robert *Theories of Cognition in the Later Middle Ages.* Cambridge: Cambridge University Press, 1897. 8vo., cloth, dust jacket, ink ownership signature of David Lindberg, fine.   Jeff Weber Rare Books   178 - 874   2015 $110

Passeron, Roger *Michel Ciry: L'Oeuvre Grave.* Paris: La Bibliotheque des Arts, 1968. 1970. 1971. First edition, 3 volumes, 4to., each printed in an edition of 600 numbered copies, this set is no. 302, 245 and 431, fine in fine dust jackets, all three in cardboard slipcase, but volumes I and II are in custom slipcases.   Beasley Books   2013 - 2015 $175

The Passports Printed by Benjamin Franklin at His Passy Press, Washington's Farewell Address to the People of the United States; Benjamin Franklin in Oil and Bronze. Ann Arbor: Boston; New York: William L. Clements Library; Houghton Mifflin Co., William Edwin Rudge, 1913-1926. Limited to 505, 440, 1000 copies, 3 volumes, folio, 2 volumes in quarter cloth and paper covered boards, one in quarter leather and cloth, cloth slipcase,.   Oak Knoll Books   306 - 288   2015 $250

Passy, Hippolyte Philibert *On Large and Small Farms and Their Influence on the Social Economy: Including a View of the Progress of the Division of the Soil in France Since 1815.* London: Arthur Hall & Co., Edinburgh: Oliver & Boyd; Glasgow: F. Orr & Sons, Cupar-Fife: G. S. Tullis, 1848. First edition in English, including final two leaves of ads, occasional minor spotting and browning, original cloth, printed spine label, uncut, largely unopened, very good. John Drury Rare Books   2015 - 21065   2015 $177

Pasteur, Louis *Etudes sur la Vin. Ses Maladies Causes qui Les Provoquent Procedes Nouveau Pur le Conserver et Pour le Vieillir.* Paris: l'Imprimerie Imperiale, 1866. First edition, 8vo., 42 figures, original half morocco over moire black cloth, gilt stamped spine title, bookplate of Francis Reynolds Dickinson (1880-1974) and Alice May Dickinson (nee Stirling), ownership marks on half title and titlepage, fine.   Jeff Weber Rare Books   178 - 877   2015 $950

Pastor, Olive Prest *The Stories of Caribou.* Truro: Caribou District Two Heritage Society, 1992. Commemorative edition, 8vo., card covers, photos, very good.   Schooner Books Ltd.   110 - 108   2015 $45

Pastoret, Claude Emmanuel Joseph Pierre, Marquis De *Zoroastre. Confucius et Mahomet Compares Comme Sectaires, Legislateurs et Moralistes.* Paris: Chez Buisson, 1787. First edition, 8vo., contemporary quarter calf, spine gilt with citron label, paper boards rubbed, but excellent, crisp copy.   John Drury Rare Books   March 2015 - 14989   2015   £306

Patchett, Ann *Bel Canto.* New York: Harper Collins, 2001. First edition, warmly and lengthily inscribed by author to childhood friend, Patchett has signed her name in full above inscription, small label removal abrasion on front pastedown under flap, else fine in fine dust jacket.   Ken Lopez, Bookseller   164 - 165   2015 $250

Paternoster, Sidney *The Hand of the Spoiler.* London: Hodder & Stoughton, 1908. First English edition, very good in pictorial green cloth covered boards with gold stamped titles on spine.   Mordida Books   March 2015 - 001778   2015 $80

Paterson, Daniel   1739-1825 *A New and Accurate Description of all the Direct and Principal Cross Roads in Great Britain (bound with) A Travelling Dictionary.* London: T. N. Longman, Pater Noster Row, 1796. London: T. N. Longman, 1792. 11th edition and 6th edition, 8vo., recently rebound in half color leather with marbled boards, lettered gilt at spine with gilt decoration and five raised bands, 8vo., recently rebound in half color leather with marbled boards, lettered gilt at spine with gilt decoration and five raised bands, handsome, very good+, clean text.   Any Amount of Books   2015 - C15996   2015   £300

Paterson, David *Discourses on Subjects Chiefly Practical. (bound with) three Discourses on a Future State.* Alnwick: printed by and for J. Graham and sold by R. Baldwin and Williams and Son, London: D. Brown; Edinburgh: J. Finaly, Newcastle: and J. Reed Berwick, 1814. Alnwick: printed by J. Graham, 1819. Both first editions, 12mo., errata slip tipped in before B1, little general paper browning and foxing, titlepage of second work little soiled and now mounted, contemporary olive calf, sides panelled in blind and gilt, spine gilt with raised bands and label, very good.   John Drury Rare Books   2015 - 21342   2015 $177

Patmore, Coventry *Poems.* London: Edward Moxon, 1844. First edition, excellently rebound in half straight grained morocco, marbled boards, spine gilt, maroon label, all edges gilt, very good, pencil marginal lines and underlining in "Lilian the Tale".   Jarndyce Antiquarian Booksellers   CCXI - 230   2015   £450

Patrick, Chann *The House of Retrogression.* New York: Jacobsen, 1932. First edition, fine in dust jacket, author's solution present and seal is unbroken.   Mordida Books   March 2015 - 001779   2015 $300

Patten, Brian *The Early Poems of Brian Patten.* Leicester: Transican Books, 1971. First edition, number 33 of 100 copies signed by author, 8vo., interleaved with a variety of styles and colors of thing handmade papers, one full page colored illustration by Pamlar Kindred, other illustrations in text, original black textured faux leather boards, fine.   Any Amount of Books   2015 - A71941   2015   £250

Patten, William *Pioneering the Telephone in Canada.* Montreal: privately printed, 1926. Limited Pioneer's edition of 2000 copies, paper covered boards, black cloth spine, 8vo., illustrations, including frontispiece, previous owner's name on front endpaper, corners bumped, wear at endpapers.   Schooner Books Ltd.   110 - 183   2015 $45

Patterson, Harry *Cry of the Hunter.* London: Mystery Book Guild, 1960. Reprint edition, fine in very good dust jacket with lightly darkened spine, light wear at spine ends and nicks and tiny tears along top edge of back panel.   Mordida Books   March 2015 - 012650   2015 $90

Patterson, James *The Thomas Berryman Number.* Boston: Little Brown, 1976. First edition, fine in fine dust jacket, from the collection of Duke Collier.   Royal Books   36 - 220   2015 $1750

Patterson, James *Virgin.* New York: McGraw Hill, 1980. First edition, fine in dust jacket.   Mordida Books   March 2015 - 100227   2015 $150

Patterson, Richard North *The Outside Man.* Boston: Little Brown and Co., 1981. First edition, fine in dust jacket.   Buckingham Books   March 2015 - 3109   2015 $225

Paul, Elliot *Hugger-Mugger in the Louvre.* New York: Random House, 1940. First edition, some darkening on pastedown, otherwise fine in dust jacket.   Mordida Books   March 2015 - 008129   2015 $200

Paul, John R. *A History of Poliomyelitis.* New Haven: Yale University Press, 1971. First edition, signed and inscribed by author for Nobel Laureate Thomas Weller, near fine, in very good price clipped, edgeworn dust jacket with small chips, spine sunned.   By the Book, L. C.   44 - 38   2015 $1250

Pauline and the Matches and Envious Minnie. New York: McLoughlin Bros., 1896. 12mo., pictorial wrappers, printed on linen, color cover plus 6 color illustrations and line illustrations.   Aleph-bet Books, Inc.   109 - 226   2015 $250

Pauling, Linus *The Structure of Protein Molecules.* San Francisco: W. H. Freeman, 1954. Offprint from Scientific American July 1954, 4to., signed by author, fine offprint in original printed wrappers.   By the Book, L. C.   44 - 17   2015 $500

Paulsen, Martha *Toyland.* Akron: Saalfield, 1944. Oblong 4to., spiral backed boards, slight wear to spine, else very good-fine, 4 great moveable plates and many color and black and whites in text by Julian Wehr, scarce.   Aleph-Bet Books, Inc.   108 - 311   2015 $200

Pausanias *An Extract out of Pausanias, of the Statues, Pictures and Temples in Greece; which were Remaining There in his Time.* London: printed for W. Shropshire, 1758. First translation into English, some light spotting, small repair to titlepage verso, 8vo., contemporary calf, rebacked preserving old lettering piece, old leather darkened and crackled, corners repaired, bookplate of the Arts & Crafts movement artist Walter Crane, good copy, scarce.   Blackwell's Rare Books   Greek & Latin Classics VI - 78   2015   £1200

Pavlov, Ivan P. *Naturwissenschaft und Gehirn. (Science and the Brain).* Wiesbaden: J. F. Bergmann, 1910. First separate edition, offprint, 8vo., original printed wrappers with vertical crease down middle of paper, mild toning and wear to edges, ink numbers front cover, very good+, inscribed by author for John Leathes.   By the Book, L. C.   Special List 10 - 84   2015 $1000

Paxton, Joseph *Report from the Select Committee on Metropolitan Communications together with the Proceedings of the Committee, Minutes of Evidence and Appendix.* London: Ordered by the House of Commons to be printed 23 July, 1853. Folio, 35 folding maps and plates, many hand colored in outline, modern half calf, spine with red label lettered gilt.   Marlborough Rare Books Ltd.   List 49 - 23   2015   £1250

Payne, William *Maxims for Playing the Game of Whist; with all Necessary Calculations and Laws of the Game.* London: printed for T. Payne and Son next the Mews-Gate St. Martins, 1790. 8vo., contemporary ruled sheep, neatly rebacked and labelled to match, very good, crisp copy with early ownership note on free endpaper of Mary Williams 1792 the gift of Mr. Seaton, very scarce.   John Drury Rare Books   March 2015 - 24667   2015 $656

Paynter, John H. *Joining the Navy or Abroad with Uncle Sam.* Hartford: American Pub. Co., 1895. First edition, 298 pages, frontispiece, plates, tear on front fly near hinge with little offsetting at top of page and wear at ends of lightly toned spine, very good or better, this copy inscribed by author to President Wm. McKinley, Feb. 20/98.   Between the Covers Rare Books   197 - 93   2015 $4500

Payson, J. W. *Payson Dunton, & Scribner Manual of Penmanship.* New York: Potter, Ainsworth and Co., 1881. Revised edition, 8vo., original cloth, 13 plates, one plate detached, illustrations in text. Oak Knoll Books Special Catalogue 24 - 40 2015 $125

Paz, Octavio *Poemas (1935-1975).* Barcelona: Editorial Seix Barral, 1979. First edition, press copy numbered '075' and signed by author, owner's name, address at head of titlepage, otherwise near fine in fine dust jacket, very good, bit scarred slipcase. Beasley Books 2013 - 2015 $300

Paz, Octavio *Sight and Thought.* New York: Limited Editions Club, 1994. Limited to 300 numbered copies, signed by author and artist, folio, quarter leather, cloth with inlaid label with title on front cover, top edge gilt, other edges uncut, cloth clamshell box with leather label on front cover, 3 tipped in woodcut illustrations by Balthus with wood blocks cut and editioned by Keiji Shinhara, set in Monotype Luteria by Ferrari and Carr at Golgonooza Letter Foundry, monthly letter loosely inserted. Oak Knoll Books 25 - 63 2015 $1750

Paz, Octavio *Sunstone. Piedra Del sol.* New York: New Directions, 1991. First edition, limited to 250 copies, this no. 54, signed by Paz and Eliot Weinberger, 8vo., canvas covered boards with black lettering spine and front cover, fine in original matching canvas covered slipcase. By the Book, L. C. Special List 10 - 36 2015 $1000

Paz, Octavo *Three Poems (Tres Poemas).* N.P.: Limited Editions Club, 1988. Limited to 750 bound numbered copies and 70 portfolios, folio, cloth, illustrated label inlaid on front cover, author's names stamped on spine, cloth clamshell box with author and title stamped on spine. Oak Knoll Books 25 - 58 2015 $3500

Pazos Kanki, Vicente *An Expose Upon the Existing Dissensions Between Chile and the Peru-Bolivian Confederation.* London: printed by Cunningham and Salmon, 1837. First edition, 8vo., 44 pages, errata corrected by hand, titlepage rather soiled and with marginal damage but printed surface, unimpaired, preserved in modern wrappers with printed title label on upper cover, first edition, very rare. John Drury Rare Books March 2015 - 23011 2015 £266

Peabody, Elizabeth Palmer *Holiness; or the Legend of St. George: a Tale from Spencer's Faerie Queene by a Mother.* Boston: published by E. R. Broaders, 1836. First edition, 12mo., original embossed gray green cloth, gilt lettering, cloth slightly worn, some light foxing, very good. The Brick Row Book Shop Miscellany 67 - 70 2015 $500

Peabody, Elizabeth Palmer *Record of a School: Exemplifying the General Principles of a Spirutal Culture.* Boston: Russell, Shattuck, New York: Leavitt Lord, 1836. Second edition, 8vo., contemporary brown half calf, marbled paper boards, gilt rules and lettering, frontispiece and titlepage foxed, edges little worn, very good. The Brick Row Book Shop Miscellany 67 - 71 2015 $750

Peace Development Progress: Friendly Contacts of CPC with Political Parties of Other Countries. N.P. (Beijing): Contemporary World Publishing House, 2001. First edition, large 4to., copiously illustrated in color and black and white, fine in fine dust jacket, near fine slipcase. Any Amount of Books 2015 - A48844 2015 £220

Peace Principles Safe and Right. Boston: American Peace Society, circa, 1859-1865. First edition, small octavo, contemporary green cloth gilt, contemporary bookplate of Frank Batcheller, bit of rubbing on cloth, paper cracking over front hinge but tight and sound, inscribed by abolishionist Amasa Walker for Francis Batcheller. Between the Covers Rare Books 197 - 107 2015 $650

Peake, Mervyn *Slaughterboard Drops Anchor.* London: Eyre & Spottiswoode, 1945. First edition, color illustrations, cloth, 4to., fine in dust jacket. Aleph-bet Books, Inc. 109 - 344 2015 $700

Peake, Ora Brooks *The Colorado Range Cattle Industry.* Arthur H. Clark Co., 1937. First edition, cloth, top edge gilt, frontispiece, illustrations, 2 maps, as new, bright, uncut copy. Buckingham Books March 2015 - 16109 2015 $250

Pearce, Michael *The Mamur Zapt and the Men Behind.* London: Collins Crime Club, 1991. First edition, fine in dust jacket, signed by author. Mordida Books March 2015 - 007586 2015 $300

Pearce, Michael *The Mamur Zapt and the Return of the Carpet.* London: Collins Crime Club, 1988. First edition, pages slightly darkened, otherwise fine in price clipped dust jacket with publisher's price sticker, small nick at top and bottom of spine, couple of short closed tears and couple of internal tape mends removed from spine ends. Mordida Books March 2015 - 008562 2015 $200

Pearce, Michael *The Mamur Zapt and the Return of the Carpet.* London: Collins Crime Club, 1988. First edition, signed, fine in dust jacket with short closed tear, signed by author. Mordida Books March 2015 - 007572 2015 $500

Pears, Iain *The Bernini Bust.* London: Gollancz, 1992. First edition, very fine in dust jacket, signed by author. Mordida Books March 2015 - 009136 2015 $350

Pears, Iain *An Instance of the Fingerpost.* London: Cape, 1997. First edition, very fine in dust jacket.   Mordida Books   March 2015 - 003136   2015 $85

Pears, Iain *The Last Judgement.* London: Gollancz, 1993. First edition, very fine in dust jacket, signed by author.   Mordida Books   March 2015 - 009137   2015 $200

Pearson, Charles James *Italian Reminiscences and Scenes in North Wales....* Llanwst: printed by John Jones, 1841. First (only?) copy, 8vo., stitched as issued, uncut and unopened, very good, uncommon.   John Drury Rare Books   March 2015 - 25063   2015 $221

Pearson, Eliphalet *A Public Lecture Occasioned by the Death of the Rev. Joseph Willard...* Cambridge: printed at the University Press in Cambridge by William Hilliard, 1804. First edition, octavo, 21 pages, sewn unprinted blue wrappers, near fine, inscribed by Richard Henry Dana, poet and father of R.H. Dana, Jr., for William Ellery (Dana's grandfather and signer of the Declaration of Independence from RI).   Between the Covers Rare Books, Inc.   187 - 209   2015 $450

Pearson, Ridley *Blood of the Albatross.* New York: St. Martins, 1986. First edition, very fine in dust jacket.   Mordida Books   March 2015 - 010228   2015 $150

Peck, Mary Gray *Carrie Chapman Catt, a Biography.* New York: Wilson, 1944. First edition, 8vo., very good.   Second Life Books Inc.   189 - 195   2015 $75

Peck, William Dandridge *Natural History of the Slug Worm.* Boston: Young & Minns, 1799. First edition, 8vo., 14 pages, colored engraved frontispiece, removed, two part slipcase, paper stuck to few figures, unobtrusive.   M & S Rare Books, Inc.   97 - 234   2015 $600

Peepshow Pictures. London: Nister, n.d. circa, 1890. Small 4to., cloth backed pictorial boards, some normal edge rubbing, else very good, 4 magnificent chromolithographed pop-out scenes, nice copy.   Aleph-bet Books, Inc.   109 - 375   2015 $1350

Peirce, Benjamin *Physical and Celestial Mechanic's... Developed in Four Systems of Analytic Mechanics, Celestial Mechanics, Potential Physics and Analytic Morphology.* Boston: Little Brown, 1855. First edition, 4to., folding plate, original blindstamped pebbled brown cloth, spine replaced in quarter similarly grained black cloth, extremities lightly rubbed, front corners showing, presentation bookplate from Charles Anders Peirce, institutional holograph inscription to Harvard College, with matching rubber stamps (withdrawn stamp as duplicate), rare, very good.   Jeff Weber Rare Books   178 - 887   2015 $1600

Peirce, Charles Sanders *Description of a Notation for the Logic of Relatives. (with) On the Algebra of Logic. (with) Brief Description of the Algebra of Relatives.* Cambridge: Welch, Bigelow and Co., 1870. Cambridge: University Press, 1880. Baltimore: privately published, 1882. Extracted from Memoirs of the American Academy Volume IV, first edition offprints, quarto, item 1 - gathered and tied with original string utilizing three neat holes in center of left edge, with just bit of staining to front cover (just below bottom string hole) and in upper right corner throughout, but getting lighter as pages progress, excision was made on page 2, neatly removing Peirce's footnote in which he introduces his important 'copula symbol', excised text supplied in facsimile, other that these two unfortunate flaws, this is remarkably well preserved and handsome copy, extremely rare; item 2 - missing front cover which as noted above is uncommon, some minor remnants remain along left edge, neatly trimmed top and bottom but deckled along right edge, several small chips to preserved rear wrapper, overall excellent copy, rare offprint; item 3 - original privately printed light green cover with some browning and one minor chip to top center front cover and another to rear wrapper in lower left corner, otherwise fine.   Athena Rare Books   15 - 50   2015 $12,500

Pelecanos, George P. *The Big Blowdown.* New York: St. Martin's, 1996. First edition, very fine in dust jacket.   Mordida Books   March 2015 - 008434   2015 $85

Pelecanos, George P. *The Big Blowdown.* New York: St. Martin's, 1996. First edition, uncorrected proof, fine in printed wrappers.   Mordida Books   March 2015 - 007784   2015 $125

Pelecanos, George P. *Down by the River Where the Dead men Go.* New York: St. Martin's Press, 1995. First edition, fine in fine dust jacket.   Buckingham Books   March 2015 - 20195   2015 $250

Pelecanos, George P. *Hard Revolution. 1959 to 1968. A Crime Novel.* Tucson: Dennis McMillan, 2004. First edition, one of 300 numbered copies, signed by author, fine in fine dust jacket with publisher's slipcase.   Ed Smith Books   82 - 20   2015 $125

Pelecanos, George P. *Hard Revolution.* Tucson: Dennis McMillan, 2004. First edition, one of 300 numbered copies signed by author, very fine in dust jacket with slipcase.   Mordida Books   March 2015 - 009424   2015 $150

Pelecanos, George P. *Hell to Pay.* Tucson: Dennis McMillan, 2002. First edition, one of 350 numbered copies signed by author, fine in fine dust jacket with publisher's slipcase.   Ed Smith Books   82 - 19   2015 $100

Pelecanos, George P. *Nick's Trip.* New York: St. Martin's Press, 1993. First edition, signed by author, fine and unread in fine dust jacket, without trace of wear, name of usual bumping to spine ends superior example, from the collection of Duke Collier.   Royal Books   36 - 221   2015 $1250

Pelecanos, George P. *Nick's Trip.* New York: St. Martins, 1993. First edition, very fine in dust jacket with tiny nick at top of spine.   Mordida Books   March 2015 - 011016   2015 $500

Pelecanos, George P. *Shoedog.* New York: St. Martin's Press, 1994. First edition, signed by author on titlepage, review copy with publisher's announcement specific to this title laid in, fine and unread, fine dust jacket, from the collection of Duke Collier.   Royal Books   36 - 222   2015 $350

Pelecanos, George P. *Shoedog.* New York: St. Martin's, 1994. First edition, very fine in dust jacket.   Mordida Books   March 2015 - 008134   2015 $500

Pelecanos, George P. *Shoedog.* New York: St. Martin's Press, 1994. First edition, signed, fine in dust jacket.   Buckingham Books   March 2015 - 23770   2015 $650

Pelecanos, George P. *The Sweet Forever.* Boston: Little Brown, 1998. First edition, uncorrected proof, fine in printed wrappers, signed by author.   Mordida Books   March 2015 - 007785   2015 $125

Pellew, Mary Gray   *Carrie Chapman Catt, a Biography.* Boston: Houghton Mifflin, 1888. First edition, 8vo., later binder's cloth backed boards, portion of original printed wrapper used as a label, very good ex-library.   Second Life Books Inc.   189 - 196   2015 $75

Pelzer, Louis   *The Shifting Cow towns of Kansas.* Illinois Printing Co., 1926. First edition, 8vo., printed wrappers, very good.   Buckingham Books   March 2015 - 37376   2015 $225

Pemberton, Henry   *A View of Sir Isaac Newton's Philosophy.* London: S. Palmer, 1728. First edition, large 4to., engraved titlepage vignette by J. Pine, after original by J. Grison, T3 with neat repair at gutter, modern half calf over marbled paper backed boards, gilt stamped spine and black leather spine label, quarter gilt stamped morocco over red cloth, slipcase, from the Robert Honeyman collection, rebound in Honeyman commissioned slipcase.   Jeff Weber Rare Books   178 - 841   2015 $1000

Pemberton, Thomas   *A Letter to Lord Langdale on the Recent Proceedings in the House of Commons on the Subject of Privilege.*   London: Charles Hunter, 1837. First edition, 8vo. well bound in later cloth gilt, good copy, inscribed with author's respect, uncommon.   John Drury Rare Books   2015 - 12855   2015 $168

Pengelly, Hester   *A Memoir of William Pengelly of Torquay, F.R.S., Geologist with a Selection from His Correspondence.* London: John Murray, 1897. First edition, 8vo., gravure frontispiece, portrait and tissue guard, 10 plates, maroon cloth, gilt stamped spine title, cloth torn around spine ends, extremities bit rubbed and small waterstain to front cover, inner hinges cracked, good, signed presentation from editor (Pengelly's daughter).   Jeff Weber Rare Books   178 - 889   2015 $125

Peninou, Ernest   *History of the Sonoma Viticultural District. The Grape Growers, the Wine Makers and the Vineyards.* Santa Rosa: 1998. First edition, maps, cuts, portraits, facsimiles, maroon cloth, very fine, dust jacket.   Argonaut Book Shop   Holiday Season 2014 - 222   2015 $90

Pennell, Joseph   1857-1928   *Pen Drawing and Pen Draughtsmen, their Work and Their Methods.*   London and New York: Macmillan, 1889. First edition, 4to., original Japanese vellum over boards, 158 illustrations, including 15 separate plates printed on heavy paper stock and tissue guarded, light foxing.   Oak Knoll Books   306 - 37   2015 $225

Pennsylvania   *An Act Authorizing the Governor to Incorporate the Susquehanna and Delaware Canal and Rail Road Company.*   New York: William Mercein & Son, 1835. First edition, 8vo., 16 pages, stitching gone, held with later staples, else about fine.   M & S Rare Books, Inc.   97 - 252   2015 $200

Pennsylvania Anti-Slavery Society   *Declaration of Sentiments and Constitution of the American Anti-Slavery Society Adopted at the formation of said Society in Philadelphia on the 4th Day of December 1833.* Philadelphia: Anti-Slavery Society, 1861. Reprint, 8vo., printed wrappers, upper corner repaired, leaves toned, otherwise very good.   Second Life Books Inc.   190 - 180   2015 $75

Pennsylvania. Board of Commissioners for the Second Geological Survey   *Second Geological Survey of Pennsylvania: 1874-1878.* Harrisburg: Board of Commissioners for the Second Geological Survey, 1878. First edition, maps and plates, cuts, original cloth, very good, some shelfwear and spotting, scarce.   Stephen Lupack   March 2015 - 2015 $200

Penrose, Matt R. *Pots 'O Gold.* Reno: A Carlisle & Co. of Nevada, 1935. First edition, 8vo., original black cloth, gold stamping on front cover and spine, frontispiece, ink beginning to chip at bit, else very good, tight. Buckingham Books   March 2015 - 20621   2015 $375

Penton, Stephen *New Instructions to the Guardian: Shewing that the Last Remedy to Prevent the Ruin, Advance the Interest and Recover the Honour of This Nation...* London: printed for Walter Kettilby, 1694. First edition, 12mo., including initial imprimatur/ad leaf, bound in contemporary sheep, sides with simple blind ruled borders, raised bands, spine and corners worn, very good, internally crisp and fine.   John Drury Rare Books   2015 - 20389   2015 $1005

Penzler, Otto *Agents of Treachery.* New York: Mysterious Bookshop, 2010. First edition, limited to 26 lettered copies signed by author and Penzler, fine in quarter leather and marbled boards in transparent dust jacket.   Buckingham Books   March 2015 - 20371   2015 $275

The People's Manual or Notices Respecting the Majority of 197 Peers... London: James Ridgway, 1831. First edition, 8vo., 32 pages, recent marbled boards lettered on spine, fine.   John Drury Rare Books   March 2015 - 24519   2015   £266

Pepler, Hilary Douglas Clark *The Hand Press: an Essay Written and Printed by Hand for the Society of Typographic Arts, Chicago.* Ditchling Common, Sussex: St. Dominic's Press, 1934. First edition, limited to 250 numbered copies signed by author, index and errata, 6 facsimile pages and labels and 7 wood engravings and drawings, bibliographical notes on author laid in.   Oak Knoll Books   306 - 169   2015 $1200

Pepper, D. Stephen *Guido Reni: a Complete Catalogue of His Works with an Introductory Text.* Oxford: Phaidon, 1984. First edition, 4to., original pale green cloth letter gilt at spine, copiously in black and white, very slight rubbing, otherwise clean, bright very good+.   Any Amount of Books   2015 - C12008   2015   £180

Pepper, James *Letters. Raymond Chandler and James M. Fox.* Neville + Yellin, 1978.   Buckingham Books   March 2015 - 33619   2015 $300

Perceval, John *An Examination of the Principles and an Enquiry into the Conduct of the Two ... in Regard to the Establishment of Their Power and Their Prosecution of the War...* London: printed for A. Price, 1749. Second edition, half title, first few leaves little dust marked, else very good, crisp copy in recent wrappers.   John Drury Rare Books   2015 - 19401   2015 $168

Percy, Thomas, Bp. of Dromore 1729-1811 *Reliques of Ancient English Poetry.* London: J. Dodsley, 1765. First edition, 12mo., 3 volumes, engraved frontispiece, numerous engraved vignettes, leaf of music, with half title and final leaf of errata, but the rare "Advertisement" leaf, clean tear in one leaf (affecting text but without loss), contemporary mottled calf, rebacked, corners slightly worn, bookplate of Viscount Eversley each volume, clean tear in on leaf (affecting text without loss), corners slightly worn on all volumes.   Any Amount of Books   March 2015 - C5114   2015   £450

Percy, Thomas, Bp. of Dromore 1729-1811 *Reliques of Ancient English Poetry: consisting of Old Heroic Ballads, Songs and Other Pieces of Our Earlier Poets.* London: printed for J Dodsley, 1765. First edition, 12mo., 3 volumes, engraved frontispiece, illustrated titlepages, numerous engraved vignettes, leaf of music, final leaf of errata, binder's directions on verso, each volume bound in full brown leather with gilt ruled spine and gilt spine labels and volume number labels, some noticeable scuffing and chipping at spine and some worming to covers of first two volumes, sound, very good- with clean text and illustrations.   Any Amount of Books   March 2015 - C8789   2015   £450

Percy, Walker 1916-1990 *The Last Gentleman.* New York: FSG, 1966. First edition, inscribed by author, June 13 1966, slight sag to text block, some fading to spine cloth and top stain, very good in near fine, lightly rubbed dust jacket.   Ken Lopez, Bookseller   164 - 166   2015 $750

Percy, Walker 1916-1990 *The Moviegoer.* New York: Alfred A. Knopf, 1961. First edition, fine in lightly rubbed, near fine dust jacket with very light edgewear, inscribed by author to publisher and bibliographer Stuart Wright.   Between the Covers Rare Books   196 - 101   2015 $6000

Perdue, Virginia *The Case of the Foster Father.* Garden City: Doubleday, 1942. First edition, bookplate on front endpaper, page edges foxed, otherwise fine in dust jacket with light spotting on spine and scattered spotting on front panel.   Mordida Books   March 2015 - 003138   2015 $85

Pereire, Isaac *La Banque de France et l'Organisation de Credit en France.* Paris: Paul Dupont, 1864. First edition, 8vo., original printed wrappers, fine.   John Drury Rare Books   2015 - 22075   2015 $133

Perelman, S. J. *Dawn Ginsbergh's Revenge.* New York: Horace Liveright, 1929. Second printing, same month as the first, f.e.p. missing, half title bit over glued as a repair, good to very good, silver binding still fairly tight, some darkening to spine and rubbed at spine ends, 8vo., owner's name written neatly on pastedown.   Beasley Books   2013 - 2015 $150

Perez-Reverte, Arturo *The Fencing Master.* London: Harvill Press, 1999. First English translation, fine in dust jacket.   Buckingham Books   March 2015 - 12815   2015 $175

Perez-Reverte, Arturo *The Flanders Panel.* New York: Harcourt, 1994. First English language edition, very fine in dust jacket. Mordida Books   March 2015 - 007973   2015 $90

Perez-Reverte, Arturo *The Seville Communion.* London: Harvill, 1998. First English edition, very fine in dust jacket. Mordida Books   March 2015 - 009585   2015 $85

Periodico Oficial del Gobierno del Estado de Pueblo. Tomo Num I. Puebla de Zaragoza sabao 4 de enero de 1873 to Num. 104 mieroles 31 de Diciembre de 1873. Puebla: Gobienro del Estado de Puebla, Imp. del Hospicio, 1873. 104 issues bound in 1 volume, square folio, quarter cloth over marbled covered boards, uncommon on the market, bottom edges trimmed, else very good, spine scuffed and torn at ends, boards edge worn, about one third of issues with browned leaves, else quite bright, scattered foxing, occasional small tear to leaves at margin.   Kaaterskill Books   19 - 97   2015 $500

Perkins, Al *Ian Fleming's Story of Chitty Chitty Bang Bang!* New York: Beginner Books, Random House, 1968. First edition, near fine, illustrations by B. Toby, covers rubbed, some wear at corners and erasure on front endpaper otherwise near fine, without dust jacket.   Mordida Books   March 2015 - 006686   2015 $75

Perkins, Charles E. *The Phantom Bull.* Boston and New York: Houghton Mifflin Co., 1932. First edition, quarto, small pen and ink drawing on half titlepage and signed 'Ed Borein', original decorated red cloth, illustrations by Borein, very good tight copy, internally reinforced dust jacket. Buckingham Books   March 2015 - 27022   2015 $2000

Perkins, E. E. *A Treatise on Haberdashery and Hosiery; including the Manchester, Scotch, Silk, Linen and Woollen Departments...* London: Thomas Hurst, 1839. 12mo., little light foxing here and there, original green cloth embossed in blind, upper cover lettered gilt, very good.   John Drury Rare Books   March 2015 - 25427   2015   £306

Perkins, Frances *People at Work.* New York: Day, 1934. First edition, 8vo., very nice in little chipped and worn pictorial dust jacket.   Second Life Books Inc.   191 - 76   2015 $125

Perkins, Frances *The Roosevelt I Knew.* New York: Viking, 1946. First edition, 8vo. very good in chipped and worn dust jacket, front hinge loose, covers little faded, full page inscription by author to Pulitzer Prize winning journalist, Philip L. Geyelin.   Second Life Books Inc.   191 - 77   2015 $350

Perkins, Simeon *The Diary of Simeon Perkins 1766-1780.* Toronto: Champlain Society, 1948. #335 of a limited edition of 550 copies, 8vo., dark red cloth with Champlain crest on spine, half title, inner hinge starting to crack, otherwise very good.   Schooner Books Ltd.   110 - 111   2015 $225

Perkins, Simeon *The Diary of Simeon Perkins 1780-1789.* Toronto: Champlain Society, 1958. Limited to 650 numbered copies, this #335, 8vo., red cloth with gilt titles to spine and top edge gilt, illustrations and map, cloth slightly stained, otherwise very good.   Schooner Books Ltd.   110 - 112   2015 $100

Perkins, Simeon *The Diary of Simeon Perkins 1780-1789.* Toronto: Champlain Society, 1967. Limited to 725 numbered copies, this #728, 8vo., red cloth with gilt titles to spine and top edge gilt, spine lightly sunned, otherwise very good.   Schooner Books Ltd.   110 - 114   2015 $45

Perles, Anthony *The People's Railway. the History of the Municipal Railway of San Francisco.* Glendale: Interurban Press, 1981. First edition, first printing, profusely illustrated with old photos, charts, plans, color frontispiece, red cloth, gilt, very fine with pictorial dust jacket (head of jacket spine slightly rough).   Argonaut Book Shop   Holiday Season 2014 - 224   2015 $150

Perls, Frederick S. *Gestalt Therapy Verbatim.* Lafayette: Real People Press, 1969. First edition, near fine in like dust jacket with short tear at spine fold, large 8vo., 279 pages.   Beasley Books   2013 - 2015 $125

Peron, Juan *Por la Cooperacion Economica y la paz Mundial Declaracion del Excelentisimo Senor Presidente de la Nacion Argentina...* Buenos Aires: Subscretaria de Informaciones de la Presidencia de la Nacion, 1947. First edition, 12mo. black and white photos, cloth, very good+, interior detached at staples, leaves browned.   Kaaterskill Books   19 - 116   2015 $200

Perowne, Barry *All Exits Blocked.* New York: Mystery House, 1942. First US edition, near fine in dust jacket with light professional restoration to spine ends, corners and extremities.   Buckingham Books   March 2015 - 31426   2015 $400

Perrault, Charles 1628-1703 *Bluebeard.* London: Routledge, n.d., 1875. First edition, 4to., pictorial wrappers, light cover soil, few minor mends, else very good, 8 fine full page color illustrations by Walter Crane.   Aleph-Bet Books, Inc.   108 - 115   2015 $300

Perrault, Charles   1628-1703 *Cendrillon et Les Fees. La Barbe Bleue et La Belle au Bois Dormant. (Cinderella. The Fairies. Blue Beard and Sleeping Beauty).*   Paris: Boussod, Valadon, 1886-1887. 2 volumes, folio, top edge gilt, printed on heavy wove velin on one side of the paper only with each page individually hinged into binding, bound in beautiful contemporary full morocco with extensive gilt tooling, spines in compartments with raised bands, gilt dentelles, silk doublures and end leaves (instead of paste-down and free endpapers), housed in custom marbled slipcases, joint of Barbe Blue lightly worn and slipcases strengthened on edges, else fine condition, illustrations by Edouard De Beaumont with 73 magnificent aquarelles, color photogravure illustrations printed integrally with text.   Aleph-Bet Books, Inc.   108 - 172   2015 $5500

Perrault, Charles   1628-1703 *Cinderella or the Little Glass Slipper Freely Translated from Perrault.*   New York: Scribner, 1954. A, First edition, 4to., cloth, owner inscription on title, else fine in dust jacket with chip off bottom corner of front panel, no award seal, price clipped, illustrations in color by Marcia Brown.   Aleph-bet Books, Inc.   109 - 73   2015 $1200

Perrault, Charles   1628-1703 *Perrault's Fairy Tales.* Oxford: Clarendon Press, 1888. First edition, small 4to., vellum backed cloth, 153 pages, near fine, large paper copy, 2 engraved frontispieces, very scarce.   Aleph-bet Books, Inc.   109 - 349   2015 $750

Perrault, Charles   1628-1703 *Fairy Tales of Perrault.* New York: Dodge, 1922. First US edition, 4to., blue gilt cloth, pictorial paste-on, near fine and bright, 12 color plates and 12 black and whites plates and numerous text illustrations by Harry Clarke+.   Aleph-Bet Books, Inc.   108 - 99   2015 $1200

Perrault, Charles   1628-1703 *Puss in Boots.*   New York: Holiday House, 1936. 16mo. cloth backed pictorial boards, very good-fine, woodcuts by Fritz Eichenberg.   Aleph-Bet Books, Inc.   108 - 168   2015 $200

Perrin, John Jean Baptiste   *The Elements of French and English Conversation with New Familiar and Easy Dialogues.*   Paris: printed for F. Louis, 1804. Second edition, woodcut printer's device on title, some dampstaining, apparently lacking half title, 8vo., uncut in contemporary oddly crude half vellum, boards rubbed, sound.   Blackwell's Rare Books   B179 - 82   2015   £500

Perry, Anne   *Resurrection Row.*   New York: St. Martin's, 1981. First edition, very fine in dust jacket.   Mordida Books   March 2015 - 007974   2015 $250

Perry, E. A.   *American Authors and Their Homes.* Maiden: Perry Pictures, 1898. First edition, string tied wrappers, near fine with tiny corner chip on front cover, 8vo.   Beasley Books   2013 - 2015 $45

Perry, Matthew Calbraith   1794-1858   *Narrative of the Expedition of an American Squadron to the China Seas and Japan performed in the Years 1852, 1853 and 1854 Under the Command of....*   New York: D. Appleton and Co., 1856. Large 8vo., frontispiece, errata leaf, 11 folding charts & 75 further plates, internally very good and clean, original blue cloth, pictorially blocked in gilt with elaborate blind borders, little rubbed and dulled, wear to 1 inch of lower edge of front board with slight loss of cloth, signed by James Lawson, July 1856 in pencil on leading blank, overall good copy. Jarndyce Antiquarian Booksellers   CCXI - 233   2015   £580

Perry, Thomas   *The Butcher's Boy.*   New York: Scribners, 1982. First edition, very fine in dust jacket.   Mordida Books   March 2015 - 008702   2015 $800

Perry, Thomas   *Metzger's Dog.*   New York: Scribners, 1983. First edition, very fine in dust jacket.   Mordida Books   March 2015 - 012720   2015 $175

Pertinent & Profitable Meditation Upon the History of Pekah, His Invasion and great Victory Over Judah Recorded 2 Chron. 28 ver. 6 to the 16 Upon Occasion of the Thanksgiving Appointed Octob. 8 for the Late Successe in Scotland.   London: printed in the year, 1650. 4to., 24 pages, minor dust marking preserved in modern wrappers with printed label on upper cover, good only, uncommon.   John Drury Rare Books   March 2015 - 25139   2015   £306

Pervigilium Veneris.   Londres: et se trouve a Paris, Chez Barbou, 1766. Rare printing, some dust soiling and toning, piece of lower blank corner of final leaf torn away, slight damage to corner of previous three leaves, 8vo., later marbled boards, spine and edges rubbed, label chipped, good, rare.   Blackwell's Rare Books   Greek & Latin Classics VI - 79   2015   £300

Peter Rabbit and Chicken Little.   Whitman, 1948. First edition thus, title vignette and illustrations in 2 color, full color throughout, pages 40, 8 1/8 x 7 3/8 inches, blue glazed boards, color illustration on front with titling, pictorial endpapers, top/bottom backstrip slightly worn and some browning to edges of pages, very good.   Ian Hodgkins & Co. Ltd.   134 - 224   2015   £25

Peter Rabbit & The Three Bears Done in Poster Stamps. New York: United Art Pub. Co., 1915. First edition thus, 24 stamps, 28 pages, pictorial border in black and white surrounding each stamp, pale green boards with color stamp centre front cover, surrounded by yellow and black pictorial border and titling, 9 x 6 inches, covers dust soiled and small ink number rear cover, light thumbing and all stamps neatly stuck into place, very nice, uncommon.   Ian Hodgkins & Co. Ltd.   134 - 204   2015   £140

The Peter Rabbit Story Book. A Treasury of Sunshine Stories for Children. Philadelphia: John C. Winston Co., 1920. First edition thus, approximately 50 text illustrations in color, grey cloth with illustration and titling, front cover with color pictorial onlay pasted top front corner, blue and white illustrated endpapers, extremities little worn and some darkening around rear cover, inscription dated 1921, very good.　Ian Hodgkins & Co. Ltd.　134 - 234　2015　£58

Peters, Alan　*Who Killed the Doctors?*　New York: Loring & Mussey, 1924. First American edition, fine in very good dust jacket with chipped and frayed spine ends, wear along folds and at corners, several short closed tears.　Mordida Books　March 2015 - 001794　2015　$75

Peters, Ellis　*Black is the Colour of my True-Love's Heart.* London: Collins, 1967. First edition, light spotting on page edges, otherwise fine in dust jacket with short closed tear. Mordida Books　March 2015 - 001802　2015　$175

Peters, Ellis　*City of Gold and Shadows.*　London: Macmillan, 1973. First edition, fine in dust jacket. Mordida Books　March 2015 - 002520　2015　$250

Peters, Ellis　*Dead Man's Ransom.*　London: Macmillan, 1984. First edition, pages slightly darkened, otherwise fine in dust jacket.　Mordida Books　March 2015 - 010857　2015　$200

Peters, Ellis　*Death to the Landlords!*　London: 1972. First edition, very fine, dust jacket.　Mordida Books　March 2015 - 002519　2015　$350

Peters, Ellis　*The Devil's Novice.*　London: Macmillan, 1983. First edition, pages slightly darkened, otherwise fine in dust jacket, signed by author.　Mordida Books　March 2015 - 010858　2015　$375

Peters, Ellis　*The Devil's Novice.*　New York: Morrow, 1984. First American edition, fine in dust jacket.　Mordida Books　March 2015 - 010845　2015　$85

Peters, Ellis　*The Excellent Mystery.*　London: Macmillan, 1985. First edition, pages slightly darkened, else fine in dust jacket.　Mordida Books　March 2015 - 010856　2015 $200

Peters, Ellis　*The Heretic's Apprentice.*　London: Headline, 1989. First edition, pages slightly darkened, otherwise fine in dust jacket.　Mordida Books　March 2015 - 010834 2015　$85

Peters, Ellis　*The Hermit of Eyton Forest.*　London: Stoddart, 1987. First edition, pages slightly darkened, otherwise fine in dust jacket.　Mordida Books　March 2015 - 010837　2015　$85

Peters, Ellis　*The Horn or Roland.*　London: Macmillan, 1974. First edition, fine in dust jacket.　Mordida Books March 2015 - 002521　2015　$250

Peters, Ellis　*The Leper of Saint Giles.*　London: Macmillan, 1981. First edition, pages slightly darkened, otherwise fine in price clipped dust jacket.　Mordida Books March 2015 - 010864　2015　$350

Peters, Ellis　*The Leper of Saint Giles.*　New York: William Morrow and Co., 1982. First US edition, fine in dust jacket. Buckingham Books　March 2015 - 20639　2015　$175

Peters, Ellis　*The Leper of Saint Giles.*　New York: Morrow, 1982. first American edition, fine in dust jacket. Mordida Books　March 2015 - 010823　2015　$100

Peters, Ellis　*Monk's Hood.*　London: Macmillan, 1980. First edition, very fine in dust jacket.　Mordida Books March 2015 - 010862　2015　$500

Peters, Ellis　*Monk's-Hood.*　London: Macmillan, 1980. First edition, fine in dust jacket with scrape on spine and crease on back panel.　Mordida Books　March 2015 - 002525　2015　$250

Peters, Ellis　*Monk's Hood.*　New York: Morrow, 1981. First American edition, fine in dust jacket.　Mordida Books March 2015 - 010854　2015　$150

Peters, Ellis　*One Corpse Too Many a Medieval Whodunnit.*　London: Macmillan, 1979. First edition, first impression, 8vo., faint spotting to fore-edge, near fine in bright clean, complete dust jacket (very slightly creased at edges and very slightly toned at rear white area), excellent condition.　Any Amount of Books　2015 - A87291　2015 £220

Peters, Ellis　*One Corpse Too Many.*　London: Macmillan, 1979. First edition, fine in dust jacket.　Mordida Books March 2015 - 010860　2015　$650

Peters, Ellis　*One Corpse Too Many.*　New York: William Morrow and Co., 1980. First US edition, fine in dust jacket. Buckingham Books　March 2015 - 20635　2015　$275

Peters, Ellis　*The Pilgrim of Hate.*　London: Macmillan, 1984. First edition, fine in dust jacket.　Mordida Books March 2015 - 009142　2015　$200

Peters, Ellis　*The Rose Rent.*　London: Macmillan, 1986. First edition, pages slightly darkened, otherwise fine in dust jacket.　Mordida Books　March 2015 - 010831　2015 $85

Peters, Ellis *Saint Peter's Fair.* New York: Morrow, 1981. First American edition, very fine in dust jacket. Mordida Books   March 2015 - 007096   2015 $185

Peters, Ellis *Saint Peter's Fair.* London: Macmillan, 1981. First edition, fine in dust jacket. Mordida Books   March 2015 - 010859   2015 $400

Peters, Ellis *The Sanctuary Sparrow.* London: Macmillan, 1983. First edition, pages slightly darkened, otherwise fine in dust jacket. Mordida Books   March 2015 - 010861   2015 $250

Peters, Ellis *The Sanctuary Sparrow.* New York: Morrow, 1983. First American edition, fine in dust jacket. Mordida Books   March 2015 - 010844   2015 $85

Peters, Ellis *The Summer of the Danes.* London: Headline, 1981. First edition, pages slightly darkened, otherwise fine in dust jacket. Mordida Books   March 2015 - 010836   2015 $85

Peters, Ellis *The Virgin in the Ice.* London: Macmillan, 1982. First edition, pages slightly darkened, otherwise fine in dust jacket. Mordida Books   March 2015 - 010863   2015 $300

Peters, Harold S. *Birds of Newfoundland.* St. John's: Dept. of Natural Resources, 1951. 8vo., cloth, half title, illustrations by Roger Tory Peterson, very good. Schooner Books Ltd.   110 - 43   2015 $45

Peters, Harry T. *California on Stone.* New York: Doubleday, 1935. First edition, number 37 of 501 numbered copies, 112 plates on 99 leaves 12 in color, glazed linen stamped on front cover and spine in black and gold, beveled edges, bookplate tipped-in, very fine, printed dust jacket and slipcase, jacket spine faded, quarter inch tear to head. Argonaut Book Shop   Holiday Season 2014 - 225   2015 $425

Peters, Hugh *Gods Doings and Mans Duty Opened in a Sermon Preached Before Both Houses of Parliament, the Lord Major and Aldermen of the City of London...* London: M. S(immons) for G. Calvert, 1646. Second edition, small 4to., dark ink spot along upper margin of first few leaves, small rust spot to fore-margin of A2, slight foxing to B1-C1, several leaves uncut and with lower edge of d1 printed very close to edge (affecting the catchword on recto), mid 20th century half calf and marbled boards, from the library of James Stevens Cox (1910-1997), with bookplate and cipher and few pencil notes. Maggs Bros. Ltd.   1447 - 94   2015   £120

Petersham, Maud *An American ABC.* New York: Macmillan, Sept., 1941. First edition, 4to., cloth, fine in very slightly worn dust jacket, illustrations in color. Aleph-Bet Books, Inc.   108 - 344   2015 $350

Peterson, William S. *The Kelmscott Press, a History of William Morris's Typographical Adventure.* N.P.: University of California Press, 1991. First US edition, 4to., cloth, dust jacket, well illustrated, spine of jacket slightly faded. Oak Knoll Books   306 - 32   2015 $125

Petis De La Croix, Francois 1653-1713 *The Thousand and One Days: Persian Tales.* London: For J. & R. Tonson, 1765. Seventh edition, 2 volumes, 8vo., full light brown leather boards but attractively renewed leather spines, marbled endpapers, lettered gilt at spines, gilt decoration and five raised bands, engraved frontispiece in volume one, faint rubbing at edges, otherwise clean, very good+. Any Amount of Books   March 2015 - C15999   2015   £350

Le Petit Poucet. Paris: Hachette, 1926. First edition, large 4to., cloth backed pictorial boards, edges lightly rubbed, else very good+ magnificently illustrated in bright colors with 32 full page color illustrations and many smaller illustrations in text by Felix Lorioux. Aleph-bet Books, Inc.   109 - 270   2015 $650

Petry, Ann *Country Place.* London: Michael Joseph, 1948. First English edition, small 8vo., red cloth, top edges spotted, ends of slight slightly scuffed, otherwise nice, little soiled dust jacket. Second Life Books Inc.   190 - 181   2015 $250

Petry, Ann *The Street.* London: Michael Joseph, 1947. First English edition, 8vo., blue cloth with pictorial printed in red, owner's name on flyleaf, cover slightly faded and soiled at edges, otherwise very good, tight copy in chipped and soiled dust jacket. Second Life Books Inc.   190 - 184   2015 $225

Pettigrew, Richard Franklin *Imperial Washington. The Story of American Public Life from 1870 to 1920.* Chicago: Charles H. Kerr, 1922. First edition, 8vo., blue cloth stamped in black, very good. Second Life Books Inc.   190 - 185   2015 $75

Pettus, John *Volatiles from the History of Adam and Eve; containing Many Unquestioned Truths and Allowable Notions of Several Natures.* London: printed for T. Bassett at the George in Fleet-Street, 1674. Only edition, 8vo.,blank strip cut away from foot of titlepage but not near printed surface or ruled border, rather later calf backed boards, sympathetically rebacked, spine fully gilt in compartments with early 20th century bookplate of Leonard Lionel Bloomsfield. John Drury Rare Books   2015 - 24491   2015 $787

Peverelly, Charles A. *Book of American Pastimes, Containing a History of the Principal Base Ball, Cricket, Rowing and Yachting Clubs of United States.* New York: Published by the author, 1866. First edition, reddish brown cloth gilt, 556 pages, tiny early owner's name, corners little rubbed and bumped, very good or better with one signature slightly sprung, still unusually nice.   Between the Covers Rare Books   196 - 169   2015 $1750

Pfeffer, Wilhelm   *The Physiology of Plants: a Treatise Upon the Metabolism and Sources of Energy in Plants.* Oxford: Clarendon Press, 1900-1906. Second edition, 3 volumes, 70 figures, volume II free endpapers and pastedowns foxed, original quarter gilt stamped dark brown morocco over dark green, volume II in all gilt stamped dark green cloth over dark green, volume II in all gilt stamped dark green cloth, corners bumped, extremities lightly rubbed, volume I spine faded, ownership signature of J. R Furr, very good.   Jeff Weber Rare Books   178 - 893   2015 $180

Pfeifer, Jack A.   *West from Omaha. A Railroader's Odyssey.* Washington: Pacific Fast Mail, 1990. First edition, square quarto, profusely illustrated with color photos by author, red cloth, gilt very fine, pictorial dust jacket. Argonaut Book Shop   Holiday Season 2014 - 226   2015 $75

Pfister, Oskar   *Some Applications of Psycho-analysis.* London: George Allen & Unwin, 1923. First edition, hardcover, near fine.   Beasley Books   2013 - 2015 $45

Phelps, Amos Augustus   *Lectures on Slavery and its Remedy.* Boston: published by New England Anti-Slavery Society, 1834. First edition, 12mo., original rose line and printed paper label, cloth faded, little worn, some scattered foxing, very good in original state.   The Brick Row Book Shop   Miscellany 67 - 74   2015 $500

Philadelphia Prayer Meeting Convention. Philadelphia: 1860. 16mo., 56 pages, wrappers, front wrapper has a 2 inch tear, both wrappers with modest fray-chip to edges, scarce.   Bookworm & Silverfish   2015 - 248745322   2015 $165

Philip V, King of Spain   *His Catholick Majesty's Manifesto, Justifying His Conduct in Relation to the Late Convention.* London: printed for Robert Arney and A. Dodd, 1739. 8vo., uncut and stitched as issued, very good.   John Drury Rare Books   2015 - 20489   2015 $177

Philip V, King of Spain   *Observations Upon the Manifesto of His Catholick Majesty; with an Answer to His Reasons for Not Paying the Ninety-five Thousands Pounds. In Vindication of the Honour of Great Britain.* London: printed for T. Cooper, 1739. First edition, small 8vo., later stiff card wrappers, front card wrapper reattached, else very good. Kaaterskill Books   19 - 122 2015 $100

Philip, Alexander P. W.   *A Treatise on Indigestion and Its Consequences, Called Nervous and Bilious Complaints with Observations on the Organic Diseases.* New York: Evert Duyckinck and George Long, W. E. Dean, 1824. Fourth edition, untrimmed, neat modern cloth, leather label, spotting on few pages.   Joseph J. Felcone Inc.   Science, Medicine and Technology - 35   2015 $125

Philip, George, & Son   *Philips' Student's Atlas of Modern Geography, Constructed from the Most Recent Authorities.* London: George Philip & Son, 1853. 1 double page and 16 single page maps, all hand colored, tear to fore-edge of map 7 without loss (France), a little dusted with slight dampmarking to lower margin of final 6 plates reaching only slightly into map of final 3, original red-pink limp cloth boards, slightly dulled and marked.   Jarndyce Antiquarian Booksellers CCXI - 234   2015   £280

Philips, Francis   *An Exposure of the Calumnies Circulated by the Enemies of Social Order, and Reiterated by their Abettors...* London: Longman, Hurst Rees, Orme and Brown, Baldwin Cradock and Joy, W. and W. Clarke, Manchester, 1819. 8vo., words 'second edition' erased from title, else fine, crisp, uncut copy in original blue wrappers.   John Drury Rare Books   March 2015 - 21691   2015 $266

Philips, John   *Blenheim, a Poem.* London: printed by H. Hills and sold by booksellers of London and Westminster, 1709. First of two pirated editions by Hills, with page 5 wrongly numbered '4', 16 pages, 8vo., disbound, very good, outer edges untrimmed.   C. R. Johnson   Foxon R-Z - 1223r-z   2015 $115

Philips, John   *Blenheim, a Poem Inscrib'd to the Right Honourable Robert Harley, Esq.* London: printed by H. Hills and sold by booksellers of London and Westminster, 1709. 8vo., page 5 correctly numbered, 16 pages, wrappers, very good.   C. R. Johnson   Foxon R-Z - 1224r-z   2015 $115

Philips, John   *Cyder. A Poems in two books.. With the Splendid Shilling, Paradise Lost, and Two Songs.* London: printed and sold by H. Hills, 1708. First of three piracies by Hills, 8vo., very good, recent marble boards, printed paper side label, very good.   C. R. Johnson   Foxon R-Z - 1207r-z   2015 $192

Philips, John   *Cyder. A Poem, in two books... with Splendid Shilling; Paradise Lost and Two Songs.* London: printed and sold by H. Hills, 1709. Probably second of three piracies by Hills, 8vo., disbound, good.   C. R. Johnson   Foxon R-Z - 1225r-z   2015 $230

Phillippo, James *Jamaica: Its Past and Present State.* London: John Snow, 1843. First edition, 8vo., 16 full page woodcut illustrations and woodcut vignettes, inscribed "Sam. J. Wilkind/from Rev. Th. H. Clarke/Dry Harbor/Jamaica/ November 1843", original brown cloth, boards spine missing, otherwise very good with very clean text.   Any Amount of Books   2015 - A45552   2015   £150

Phillipps, Thomas *Index of Leases of Manors and Lands in England, Granted Since the Reformation...* London: printed by Gardiner and Son, 1832. First edition, original Middle Hill boards, paper spine neatly repaired, good, uncut.   John Drury Rare Books   2015 - 18351   2015 $168

Phillips, George M. *Two Millennia of Mathematics: from Archimedes to Gauss.* New York: Springer, 2000. 8vo., figures, index, pictorial boards, fine.   Jeff Weber Rare Books   178 - 894 2015 $70

Phillips, Harlan B. *Felix Frankfurter Reminiscences.* New York: Reynal, 1960. First edition, 8vo., very good++ with edge spotting, owner bookplate in very good+ supplied dust jacket with mild soil, edgewear, inscribed in year of publication by Frankfurter for Leonard Miall.   By the Book, L. C.   44 - 59   2015 $750

Phillips, J. Campbell *Plantation Sketches by..* New York: R. H. Russell, 1899. First edition, oblong folio, cloth backed pictorial boards, paper on tips worn, else tight and near fine, printed on glossy paper on rectos only, each leaf has fine, fully detailed illustration by Phillips, extremely scarce in such nice condition.   Aleph-bet Books, Inc.   109 - 62   2015 $900

Phillips, James M. *Nunchaku II: a Nunchaku Encyclopedia.* Camden: James M. Phillips, 1975. First edition, tall octavo, photos, charts and drawings, errata leaf laid in, slight foxing, very good or better in soiled, about very good dust jacket, self published.   Between the Covers Rare Books   196 - 17   2015 $275

Phillips, P. Lee *A List of Maps of America in the Library of Congress Preceded by a List of Works Relating to Cartography.* Washington: GPO, 1901. First edition, 8vo., leather, small stamp of McClelland Public Library, Pueblo, Colorado on titlepage, last page of text and top page of page 125, plus one inked number and date on introduction page, else fine, clean, tight copy in original full leather binding, handsome copy.   Buckingham Books   March 2015 - 17656   2015 $850

Phillips, Richard *The Sweepings of My Study.* London: J. Souter and G. and W. B. Whittaker, 1824. First edition, 12mo., 342 pages, few leaves misbound, contemporary half calf, spine simply gilt with label, very good.   John Drury Rare Books   2015 - 16558   2015 $133

Phillips, Robert *A Dissertation Concerning the Present State of the High Roads of England, Especially of Those Near London.* London: printed and sold by L. Gilliver and J. Clarke, J. Stephens and J. Roberts, 1737. 8vo., 8 engraved plates, wanting ad leaf, titlepage just little soiled, rebound in old style marbled boards with printed spine label, very good, scarce.   John Drury Rare Books   2015 - 24330   2015 $1049

Phillips, Samuel *Guide to the Crystal Palace and Park...* Sydenham: Crystal Library, Crystal Palace, 1859. 8vo., 3 folding map and plans, original printed wrappers.   Marlborough Rare Books Ltd.   List 49 - 28   2015   £150

Phillips, Scott *Cottonwood.* Tucson: Dennis McMillan, 2004. First edition, one of 300 numbered copies signed by author, very fine in dust jacket, slipcase.   Mordida Books March 2015 - 009426   2015 $125

Phillips, Scott *The Walkaway.* Tucson: Dennis McMillan, 2002. First edition, one of 400 numbered copies signed by author, very fine in dust jacket with slipcase.   Mordida Books   March 2015 - 008136   2015 $125

Phillips, Stephen *Dramatic Works: Ulysses, Herod, The Sin of David and Paolo and Francesca.* London and New York: John Lane, Macmillan and Co., 1901-1904. 4 volumes, atractive set in full leather bindings by The Adams Bindery, signed, bindings may be later, possibly 1910's or 1920's, full dark brown morocco with gilt titles and author to spines, each spine has six compartments with gilt rules and raised bands, marbled endpapers and top edge gilt, minor wear to hinges, edges and corners of boards, clean interiors overall, light foxing to few pages, very good.   The Kelmscott Bookshop   11 - 36   2015 $250

Phillips, Wendell *Speeches Lectures and Letters. Second Series.* Boston: Lee and Shepard, 1891. First edition, 8vo., frontispiece, brown cloth, lacks about an inch of cloth above gilt stamping, front hinge little tender, some underlining in text, good copy only.   Second Life Books Inc.   189 - 197   2015 $45

Phillpotts, Eden 1862-1960 *My Adventure in the Flying Scotsman: a Romance of London and North-Western Railway Shares.* London: James Hogg and Sons, 1888. First edition, rainbow colored cloth front cover and an rear cover, 63 pages, front cover moderately rubbed, else very good, rare, housed in clamshell case.   Buckingham Books March 2015 - 29326   2015 $5000

Philom, Ammah, Pseud. *The History of Defection in New-England... (and) Philom's Address to the People of New England....* New York: reprinted from the edition of 1817, 1832? First edition, 18mo., 92, 85 pages, contemporary calf backed plain boards, brown, front blank torn with loss.   M & S Rare Books, Inc.   97 - 244   2015 $350

Philosophical Society of Glasgow *Proceedings of the....* Published for the Society, circa, 1904. 1844., 35 volumes bound in 18, complete handsome, uniform mottled half calf over marbled boards, spines gilt and labelled, all in the finest state of preservation from the library of David Murray (1842-1928) Scottish lawyer, with his bookplate on each pastedown, with 3 ALS's to Murray from Alexander Gardner, Hon. Sec. of the Society. John Drury Rare Books 2015 - 25818 2015 $3147

Philp, J. M. *Places Worth Seeing in London.* London: Ward and Lock 158 Fleet Street, 1858. 8vo. second engraved illustrations by A. J. Mason, John Bastin and Dalziels, original decorative wood engraved orange covers, slightly chipped at head and tail of spine, generally good copy, binder's ticket and blindstamp "Gilbert Brothers 18 Gracechurch St. & 4 Copthall Buildings. Marlborough Rare Books List 53 - 39 2015 £175

Phinney, Mary Allen *Allen-Isham Genealogy. Jirah Isham Allen Montana Pioneer, Government Scout, Guide...* Tuttle Pub. Co. Inc., 1946. First edition, limited to 200 copies, this number 110, inscribed by author, original blue cloth, title in gilt on spine, illustrations. Buckingham Books March 2015 - 27282 2015 $1250

The Pic Nic Papers. By Various Hands. London: Henry Colburn, 1841. First edition, first state, without Bulmer imprint on (ii) and 'publisher young' on (iii) in volume I, 3 volumes, 12mo., 14 engraved plates, including 2 by Cruikshank, 6 by Phiz and 6 by Hammerton, original green fine diaper cloth stamped in blind on covers and spine and lettered gilt on spine, original pale yellow endpapers, spines sunned, corners bumped, overall very good, housed in custom quarter green morocco slipcase, gilt stamped. Heritage Book Shop Holiday 2014 - 58 2015 $1000

Pic, Francois Antoine *Code Des Imprimeurs, Libraires, Ecrivains et Artistes, ou Recueil et Concordance.* Paris: Corby, 1826. First edition, small 8vo. contemporary quarter leather, marbled paper covered boards, five false raised bands, foldout table, covers rubbed and scuffed, mostly at edges, light foxing, scattered throughout text. Oak Knoll Books 306 - 196 2015 $2250

Picabia, Francis *Francis Picabia 1999-2000.* Tokyo: Apt International Inc., 1999. First edition, large 8vo., color illustrated wrappers/paperbacks textured slipcase, copiously illustrated in color and black and white, about fine. Any Amount of Books 2015 - C2231 2015 £175

Picart, Bernard *A New Drawing Book of Modes.* London: Richard Ware, 1732. First edition, oblong octavo, early marbled boards, original red morocco label laid down, engraved titlepage, 12 engraved plates. Honey & Wax Booksellers 3 - 14 2015 $1100

Picasso, Pablo *Guernica. The 42 Sketches on Paper.* New York: Abrams, 1990. First English language, one of 1000 unnumbered copies edition, 42 color facsimiles on paper, each mounted within 31 folio-sized mats, some images matted singly, other mats containing two images, elephant folio, contents loose as issued within a clamshell box lettered in white with color facsimile, cover label of wailing woman, fine, still in original mailing box. Any Amount of Books 2015 - C8219 2015 £900

Piccolomini, Alessandro *Dialogo Dove Si Ragiona Della Bella Creanza Delle Donne.* Venice: Appresso Domenico Farri, n.d after, 1555. Fourth edition, 8bvo., lacking final blank leaf, large woodcut device and ornament on titlepage, leaves some toned, very good, early 19th century calf, gilt over marbled boards. Second Life Books Inc. 189 - 198 2015 $2250

Pichardo Y Tapia, Esteban *Diccionario Provincial Casi-Razonado de Vozes Cubanas.* Habana: Imprenta del Gobierno Capitania General y Real, 1861. Tercera edition, 8vo., modern half red morocco over red cloth boards, five raised bands, gilt titles and rules, very good+, occasional foxing and spotting, minor rubbing. Kaaterskill Books 19 - 124 2015 $400

Pichardo Y Tapia, Esteban *Geografia de la Isla de Cuba.* Habana: Establecimiento Tipografico de D. M. Soler, 1854-1855. First edition, 8vo., modern full brown calf, four raised bands, gilt title, rules and decorations, very good, chip to headband and minor scuff marks on spine, light foxing on title, leaves browned, first two parts with scattered pencil marginalia. Kaaterskill Books 19 - 125 2015 $1200

Pick-a-Hanky Every Day. H. H. Co., 1940. 4to., pictorial wrappers, some rubbing and margin mends, very good, every day of the week has different pictorial hanky inserted. Aleph-Bet Books, Inc. 108 - 231 2015 $275

Picture Writing. Helena: Montana Highway Dept., 1938. First edition thus, 4to., color pictorial wrappers, nice toned photos and pictographs, onion-skin/glassine endpapers, laid in "Key to Indian Pictographs" missing in most copies, wear to edges 2 1/2 inch split to top fold has been archivally mended, good+. Baade Books of the West 2014 - 2015 $50

Pictures in Color. New York: Scribner, 1910. First edition, large folio, cloth backed boards lettered in gold, pictorial paste-on, corners rubbed and cover slightly faded, else fine, 16 color plates done on heavy coated paper, printed on one side, by Harrison Fisher, beautiful copy. Aleph-Bet Books, Inc. 108 - 187 2015 $1850

The Picturesque Noyo River in the Redwood Forest of Mendocino County, Noyo River Tavern on the California Scenic Line Between Fort Bragg and Willits, Camping, Hunting, Fishing, Bathing, Perfect Climaste. Fort Bragg: privately printed for California Western Railroad and Navigation Co., 1915. 8vo., wrappers printed in red and black ink, 28 panels, illustrated, map, covers lightly rubbed, light wear to foot of spine, else very good, attractive copy. Buckingham Books   March 2015 - 30479   2015 $300

Pidgin, Charles Felton   *The Chronicles of Quincy Adams Sawyer, Detective.* Boston: L. C. Page, 1912. First edition, fine in decorated cloth, illustrations by Harold James Cue.   Buckingham Books   March 2015 - 12862   2015 $275

Pidgin, Charles Felton   *The Chronicles of Quincy Adams Sawyer.* Boston: Page, 1912. First edition, covers soiled, spine worn and faded, else very good in pictorial tan cloth covered boards.   Mordida Books   March 2015 - 001815   2015 $85

Pietro D'Ancarano   *Lectura Eximii Doctoris Domini Petri de Ancharano Super sexto Decreta Nouiter Edita...* (colophon): Venetiis: cura et industria Philippi Pincij Mantuani impressa 4 Idus Martias, 1501. First edition, title additionally printed in red on first page of text as well as two lines in red before the dedication woodcut printer's device at colophon, printed in double columns, guide spaces for initials, without terminal blank, titlepage dust soiled, short tear in inner margin and little frayed at fore edge , verso of last leaf also dust soiled and edges little more frayed (not affecting text or woodcut), some grey spotting in fore-edge margins of last few leaves, one or two leaves browned, folio, modern calf backed boards, good.   Blackwell's Rare Books   B179 - 83   2015   £5000

Pignoria, Lorenzo   *Laurentii Pignorii Patavini de Servis et Eorum apud Veteres Ministriss Commentarius.* Typis Petri Mariae Frambotti Patavii, 1694. Small 4to., attractively illustrated with woodcuts, contemporary full vellum, speckled page edges, little worming, three leaves of text slightly affected, small (blank) section of page replaced, otherwise excellent clean example in handsome vellum, without usual bowing, scarce.   Any Amount of Books   March 2015 - C14094   2015   £400

Pignoria, Lorenzo   *Der Servis & Eorum apud Veteres Ministeriis, Commentarius.* Augsburg: C. Daberholtzer for Marcus Welser, at the sign of the Pine, 1613. First edition, 4to., 6 full page and 21 text woodcuts, woodcut title device, contemporary vellum over thin soft boards, ms. spine title, fine, spot on two leaves, ownership signature of D. Attanzio Arcelli.   Second Life Books Inc.   189 - 199   2015 $4000

Pihan-Dufeillay, D. O.   *Etude sur la Mort Subite dans l'Infance Causee par les Troubels du Systeme Nerveux.* Paris: A. Coccoz, 1861. First edition, large 8vo., presentation inscription initialled by author, original printed blue wrappers, covers soiled, neatly rebacked, uncut.   John Drury Rare Books   2015 - 20995   2015 $177

Pijlman, Klaas   *Bli De Negerkoning.*   no publication information, published in Holland by Mulder and Zoon, n.d. circa, 1945. Large 4to., cloth backed flexible pictorial card covers, near fine, 6 fine, richly colored full page lithos and 8 pictorial text pages, scarce.   Aleph-bet Books, Inc.   109 - 60   2015 $400

Pilbeam, John   *Mammillaria: a Colour Supplement.* N.P.: n.p. Batsford?, 1987. 7 volumes, over 250 color prints of photos by Bill Weightman, 7 stationary volumes, black plastic covers containing 24 clear plastic sleeves with handwritten label on spine, one or two notes by a cactus scholar in margins, else very good+.   Any Amount of Books   2015 - A60235   2015   £175

Pim, Herbert Moore   *Unknown Immortals in the Northern City of Success.* Dublin and London: Talbot Press Ltd., T. Fisher Unwin Ltd., 1917. First collected edition, tall 8vo., frontispiece, 3 vignettes, decorative initials, quarter blue cloth, blue paper covered boards, titles and decorations in red on upper board, untrimmed fore and bottom edges, 'extra back title' printed label on back pastedown, very good, spine trifle worn, boards waterstained and little warped, uncommon.   Maggs Bros. Ltd.   Gathering of 26 Countercultural items Oct. 2013 - 2   2015   £100

Pinchard, Elizabeth   *The Blind Child or Anecdotes of the Wyndham Family, Written for the Use of Young People.* Hartford: Hale & Hosmer, 1814. 16mo., 90 pages, engraved frontispiece, contemporary calf backed marbled boards, text lightly foxed, very good.   M & S Rare Books, Inc.   97 - 137   2015 $275

Pindarus   *Odes of Pindar with several other pieces in prose and verse...* London: printed for R. Dodsely, 1749. First edition, 4to., contemporary mottled calf, spine ruled in gilt, some wear, upper joint cracked, but firm, lacks label, aside from slight binding wear, very good.   C. R. Johnson Foxon R-Z - 1120r-z   2015 $536

Pindarus   *Odes of Pindar.* Dublin: printed for P. Wilson, J. Exshaw, J. Esdall, R. James, S. Price and M. Williamson, 1751. First Dublin edition, very good, 12mo., contemporary calf, spine gilt (minor wear, lacks label), very good, with signature on a flyleaf of Thomas Vokes, dated 1758.   C. R. Johnson   Foxon R-Z - 1121r-z   2015 $230

Pindarus *Odes of Pindar, with Several Other Pieces in Prose and Verse.* London: printed for J. Dodsley, 1766. Third edition, engraved frontispiece, 3 volumes, contemporary half calf and marbled boards, spines gilt, rubbed, some wear to spines, several joints cracked, wanting labels, aside from binding wear, sound set, old booklabels of Rev. S. Jordan Lott.   C. R. Johnson   Foxon R-Z - 1122r-z   2015 $153

Pindarus *(Greek title) Olympia, Pythia, Nemea, Isthmia.* Rome: per Zachariam Calergi Cretensem, 1515. Second edition but editio princeps of the scholia, first leaf of text printed in red and black, that leaf with two small abrasions and one vertical hole, hole also reaching (though less so) the next leaf, with one or two letters lost from about 2 dozen words in total, intermittent dampmark in lower margin, some soiling and spotting, foliated in later hand, early annotations and manicules to last three leaves, 4to., 18th century calf, spine and corners skillfully repaired, new labels in impeccable period style, leather bit darkened and marked in places, sound.   Blackwell's Rare Books   Greek & Latin Classics VI - 80   2015   £9500

Pindarus *(Greek title) Olympia, Pythia, Nemea, Isthmia.* Glasgow: excudebant R. & A. Foulis, 1754-1758. 49 x 72mm., 4 volumes bound as three, some light spotting, 32mo., contemporary red turkey (possibly a Foulis binding), boards bordered with gilt fillet, spines divided by gilt fillet into five compartments, top and bottom blank apart from a dashed roll at spine ends, middle gilt lettered direct and other two with sunburst gilt tool containing a four spoked wheel, marbled endpapers, touch darkened and rubbed, very good attractive miniature edition.   Blackwell's Rare Books   Greek & Latin Classics VI - 81   2015   £600

Pinero, Arthur W. *A Wife Without a Smile: a comedy in Disguise in Three Acts.* Boston: Walter H. Baker & Co., 1905. First American edition, flowered cloth, original wrappers bound in, small repair to front wrapper, moderate wear to extremities of boards, good copy, Carl Van Vechten's copy with his ownership signature and bookplate. Between the Covers Rare Books, Inc.   187 - 215   2015 $150

Pinkerton, Robert *Russia; or Miscellaneous Observations on the Past and Present State of that Country and Its Inhabitants.* London: Seeley, 1833. First edition, royal octavo, 8 hand colored lithograph plates, original boards, rebacked with original title label relaid, endpapers bit spotted, boards rubbed at edges, very good.   Peter Ellis, Bookseller   2014 - 009382   2015   £325

Pinney, Charles *Trial of Charles Pinney, Esq. in the Court of King's Bench, on an Information Filed by His Majesty's Attorney General, Charging Him with Neglect of Duty in His Offce as Mayor of Bristol during the Riots...* Bristol: printed by Gutch and Martin... Blackwood, Edinbuurgh, 1833. First edition, 8vo., ad slip tipped in, original linen boards neatly rebacked with label to match, entirely uncut, very good. John Drury Rare Books   March 2015 - 21628   2015 $221

Pinter, Harold *Tea Party.* London: BBC, 1965. Draft script for 1965 BBC TV movie, inscribed by Pinter for Peter Colin Holder.   Royal Books   46 - 83   2015 $3000

Piper, John *The Complete Graphic Works - a Catalogue Raisonne 1923-1983....* London: Faber and Faber, 1987. First edition, quarto, 141 pages, profusely illustrated, 218 color and 194 black and white illustrations, spine slightly bruised at head, near fine in fine dust jacket.   Peter Ellis, Bookseller   2014 - 005726   2015   £275

Piper, John *The Prints of John Piper: Quality and Experiment: a Catalogue Raisonne 1923-1991.* Franham: Lund Humphries, 2010. first edition thus, one of 100 copies, 4to., original black cloth, lettered white on spine and in yellow on prints and photography volume, copiously illustrated in color and black and white, with 2 signed photos by Orde Levinson and 3 limited edition Piper photos, fine, sound, very good+ in slipcase.   Any Amount of Books March 2015 - C10018   2015   £385

Piran, T. *Intersection Between Elementary Particle Physics and Cosmology. volume I.* Singapore: World Scientific, 1986. First edition, signed by author, very good+, with minimal sun spine, owner name, 8vo.   By the Book, L. C. Special List 10 - 70   2015 $350

Piroli, Tommaso *Le Antichita Di Ercolano.* Rome: n.p., 1789-1807. First edition thus, 6 volumes including rare later published 6th volume, 308 engraved plates, contemporary white vellum lettered and decorated gilt at spine, some soiling, decent sound set, only fault being a patch of loss about 8 x 4 cm to front lower corner of fourth volume, printed on strong thick paper with plates, very clean.   Any Amount of Books   2015 - C13077   2015   £1800

Pirovano, Carlo *The Graphics of Emilio Greco.* N.P. (Venice): Electa Editrice, 1975. First English edition, folio, original green cloth lettered gilt on spine and cover with illustration in white on cover, signed presentation from artist to Australian art expert Robert Haines, slight rubbing, slight sun fading, otherwise sound clean, very good.   Any Amount of Books   2015 - A76883   2015   £300

Pitman, Isaac *The Reporter; or Phonography Adapted to Verbatim Reporting.* Bath and London: Isaac Pitman, 1846. Second edition, 8vo., old wax splashes on several leaves, few near contemporary annotations in ink, 19th century private stamp of J. Walker on title, contemporary cloth lettered gilt on upper cover, very good.   John Drury Rare Books   2015 - 13807   2015 $133

Pitois, Giuseppe Aureglio *Nuovo Libro di Caratteri Diversi De Scrittura Formata E Corsiva Perefetta.* Torino: Reycends & Guibert, circa, 1722. Oblong folio, contemporary blue wrappers, 26 engraved leaves (of 28), text in Italian, soiled, margins chipped, old fold at center, marks in ink throughout.   Oak Knoll Books   Special Catalogue 24 - 41   2015 $1500

Pitter, Ruth *The Rude Potato.* London: Cresset Press, 1941. First edition, illustrations by Roger Furse, old tape shadows on first and last two leaves, else very good in like dust jacket with short tear and some shallow chipping at crown, inscribed by author to fellow poet, John Gawsworth. Between the Covers Rare Books, Inc. 187 - 216 2015 $125

Pitts, J. Martin *Gymnopadiae.* Llandogo: Old Stile Press, 1989. 194/220 copies, signed by artist, printed on Saunders HP mould-made paper, linocut to titlepage printed in terracotta, further linocuts to each page printed in black, royal 8vo., original quarter black cloth with blue sides, illustration to upper board printed in terracotta, backstrip lettered in blind, top edge black, others untrimmed, beige cloth slipcase with multiple linocuts printed in terracotta, fine. Blackwell's Rare Books B179 - 212 2015 £100

Place, Francis *Illustrations and Proofs of the Principle of Population Including an Examination of Population...* London: Longman, Hurst, Rees, Orme and Brown, 1822. First edition, now in fine but recent old-style half russia gilt over marbled boards, spine fully gilt with raised bands by Trevor Lloyd, fine and handsome copy, uncommon. John Drury Rare Books 2015 - 25079 2015 $7867

Plachno, Larry *Sunset Lines. The Story of the Chicago Aurora & Elgin Railroad Volume I.* Polo: Transportation Trails, 1986. First edition, 8vo., wrappers, very good+, quite handsome and heavily illustrated. Beasley Books 2013 - 2015 $45

A Plain Statement with Respect to Wages Addressed Chiefly to Agricultural Labourers. London: Roake and Varty, n.d., 1831. 12mo., large woodcut vignette on title, recent plain wrappers, very good. John Drury Rare Books 2015 - 19248 2015 $168

A Plan for Raising the Supplies During the War, Humbly Submitted to the two Houses of Parliament, the Landed Monied Interest, and to all Ranks and conditions of the People, Capable of Contributing to the Expences of the State Plan. London: P. Elmsly and D. Bremmer, 1798. First edition, 8vo., half title and final blank, half title, just little soiled, well bound recently in linen backed marbled boards letter, very good. John Drury Rare Books 2015 - 21382 2015 $177

A Plan for the Establishing a Working-School for the Maintenance, Education and Employment of Poor Children, Especially Orphans. London: John Ward, 1758. First edition, 4to., margins little dusted in places, printed on heavy paper, early 19th century half calf over marbled boards, neatly rebacked and lettered with armorial bookplate of Ferguson of Raith, very good, rare. John Drury Rare Books 2015 - 24957 2015 $5245

The Plan of the Magdalen House for the Reception of Penitent Prostitutes. By Order of the Governors. London: printed by W. Faden, 1758. First edition, 4to., 28 pages, handsomely rebound recently in 18th century style calf backed marbled boards, with vellum tips, fine, rare. John Drury Rare Books 2015 - 24739 2015 $5245

Planche, J. R. *Lays and Legends of the Rhine.* London: Charles Tilt, 1832. Early edition, tall 8vo., soundly bound in green moire cloth, leather label on spine lettered gilt, complete plates with tissue guards, very slight staining at lower spine and very slight foxing to text, otherwise plates clean. Any Amount of Books 2015 - C5105 2015 £160

Plath, Sylvia **1932-1963** *Ariel.* London: Faber, 1965. First edition, 8vo., original cloth, fine in bright, unfaded dust jacket. James S. Jaffe Rare Books Modern American Poetry - 225 2015 $1500

Plath, Sylvia **1932-1963** *Ariel, Poems.* New York: Harper Row, 1966. First edition, 8vo., little toning to endpapers, fine in little marked dust jacket. Second Life Books Inc. 189 - 201 2015 $250

Plath, Sylvia **1932-1963** *The Colossus.* London: Heinemann, 1960. Uncorrected proof copy, 88 pages, crown 8vo., original printed wrappers, backstrip lettered in black and little creased, toned overall with few small spots, panel of exposed adhesive to front, expected publication date (3rd Oct. with actual publication date at end of the month) and price written in ink of front panel with a scribble in the same at foot of rear, good. Blackwell's Rare Books B179 - 220 2015 £1700

Plath, Sylvia **1932-1963** *The Colossus. Poems.* London: Heinemann, 1960. First edition, 8vo., original green cloth, dust jacket, inscribed by author for Luke (E. Lucas Myers) and Cynthia, signs of use but very good in worn, soiled dust jacket. James S. Jaffe Rare Books Modern American Poetry - 224 2015 $45,000

Plath, Sylvia **1932-1963** *Uncollected Poems.* London: Turret Books, 1965. First edition, one of 150 copies, wrappers, octavo, cover drawing by Plath, covers just trifle faded at edges, near fine. Peter Ellis, Bookseller 2014 - 020182 2015 £300

Plath, Sylvia **1932-1963** *A Winter Ship.* Edinburgh: Tragara Press, 1960. First edition, very fine in custom made half morocco slipcase, rare. James S. Jaffe Rare Books Modern American Poetry - 223 2015 $7500

Plath, Sylvia **1932-1963** *Winter Trees.* London: Faber & Faber, 1971. First edition, 8vo., original cloth, dust jacket, fine. James S. Jaffe Rare Books Modern American Poetry - 227 2015 $150

Plato *Crito, a Socratic Dialogue.* Paris: The Pleiad, 1926. Limited to 470 copies printed by Officina Bodoni at Montagnola, Switzerland, 8vo., marbled paper covered boards with parchment protective strip at spine extremities, paper spine label, printed in Arrighi-Vicenz italic 16 point on Binda handmade paper, paper chipped away at spine ends, bookplate removed.　Oak Knoll Books　306 - 159　2015 $150

Plato *I Dialoghi di Platone Intitolati 'l'Eugifrone Ouero Della Santita, l'Apologiae di Soccrate il Critone o Di quel che s'ha Affare il Fedone o Della Immortalita dell'anima. Il Timeo, Ouero Della Natura.* Venice: press Giovanni Varisco e Compagni, 1574. First Italian edition, some light foxing and browning, small rusthole in final leaf affecting three characters, 8vo., contemporary limp vellum spine lettered vertically in ink, yapp edges, bit ruckled, slightly marked, ties removed and front flyleaf lost, good.　Blackwell's Rare Books　Greek & Latin Classics VI - 83　2015　£1200

Plato (Greek text) *Omnia Platonis Opera.* Venice: in aedib. Aldi et Andreae Soceri, Sept, 1513. Editio princeps, 2 volumes, large Aldine anchor device on titlepage (volume i) and on verso of last leaf in volume ii, Greek text (apart from Aldus' dedicatory petition, contents and colophon), titlepage slightly soiled and with hole at inner margin repaired, minor stains on fore-edges, few wormholes in blank lower margin of opening leaves of volumes ii, volume, volume i in contemporary English quartered oak boards, resewn with spine uncovered, modern vellum endleaves, volume ii in contemporary German pigskin over wooden boards, blind tooled to panel design filled in with 'laus deo' and rosette stamps, brass catches and clasps, top of spine worn, inner hinge broken, cord intact, good, binding of the first volume of this copy is subject of 2 page report by Nicholas Pickwood (printout accompanies the volume), repairs carried out by James Brockman; first volume with signature of Thomas Colm of Oxford dated 1573, 17th century ownership inscription of Hendricus Ffeild, 19th century bookplate and stamp of King Edward's School, Birmingham, plus bookplate of Kenneth Rapoport, the second volume with early ownership inscriptions of Johannes (or Johann?) Lang of Erfurt and Philippus Kleissenius, few early marginalia, inscription 'de bibliotheca Johannis Langi Erphurdiensis. Blackwell's Rare Books　Greek & Latin Classics VI - 82　2015　£75,000

Plato *Opera Omnia: quae exstant. Marsilio Ficino Interprete.* Frankfurt: apud Claudium Marnium, 1602. Bound as 2 volumes, titlepage dusty and sometime laid down on matching paper, last leaf of index similarly laid down, first and last few leaves in each volume with corners little softened by damp and slightly frayed as a result, 20th century underlining and marginal annotations in pencil throughout, little worming in lower gutter (well clear of text), folio, late 18th century calf, red and green morocco lettering pieces somewhat scratched, touch of wear to extremities, spine of volume ii slightly defective at tail, front hinge volume i cracked after titlepage, repair to corner volume ii, endpapers renewed, good.　Blackwell's Rare Books　Greek & Latin Classics VI - 84　2015　£600

Platt, William *Love Triumphant.* London: Charles Hirsch, 1896. First edition, original green cloth, somewhat rubbed and bumped, interior pages have browning to margins, offsetting to free endpapers with chip to rear free endpaper, still nice, very good.　The Kelmscott Bookshop　11 - 37　2015　$200

Platt, William *Men, Women and Chance.* London: T. Fisher Unwin, 1898. First edition, rare, very nice in original grey cloth with gilt cover design attributed to Sidney Sime, very good plus, bookplate of Mark Samuels Lanser, very good+.　The Kelmscott Bookshop　11 - 38　2015　$200

Plaxton, George *The Yorkshire-Racers a Poem.* London: printed for the use of all sorts of jockeys...n.d., 1709. Pirated edition, 8vo., very good, disbound.　C. R. Johnson　Foxon R-Z - 1226r-z　2015　$230

Play and Learn ABC. New York: McLoughlin Bros., 1899. 4to., pictorial wrappers, slightest bit of soil and wear, near fine, illustrated with 6 fine full page chromolithographs and 3-color on other pages, nice.　Aleph-bet Books, Inc.　109 - 8　2015　$300

Playfair, I. S. O. *The Mediterranean and Middle East.* London: HMSO, 1966-1973. Fifth impression of volume 1, volume 2 is third impression, volume 3 is second impression, volume 4 is first edition, volume 5 is first impression, 5 volumes, 8vo., many folding maps, illustrations, very slight rubbing, otherwise sound, clean very good.　Any Amount of Books　2015 - A96725　2015　£220

Playfair, William *The Commercial and Political Atlas...* London: printed by T. Burton... for J. Wallis...., 1801. Third edition, 8vo., 26 colored engraved plates, two folding, although last plate of the "chart shewing variations in the price of the sack of flour at marks Lane for 10 years' is supplied in expert facsimile with engraved bookplate of Cheshunt College Library on front pastedown, their neat stamps on titlepage, contemporary marbled boards, expertly rebacked and recornered, spine ruled in gilt with red morocco lettered in gilt, some rubbing to boards, otherwise very appealing.　Marlborough Rare Books　List 54 - 65　2015　£1500

Plimpton, George Ames *Letters in Training.* privately printed, 1946. First edition, brownish red cloth with gray label on front board, fine.　Beasley Books　2013 - 2015　$600

Plimpton, Sarah *Doubling Back.* New York: 2005. One of 20 copies, all on Fabriano Tiepolopaper, signed and numbered by artist/author, page size 14 3/4 x 11 inches, 9 leaves, original aquatint by Peter Pettengill in Hinsdale, NH, plus titlepage with original aquatint plus colophon page, bound loose as issued in cloth, clamshell box by Claudia Cohen, aquatints in grays and blues, greens and tans, always with subtle shadings full of texture and often three dimensional in feel, color and texture work as one to form a frame and what splendid frames they are for the words. Priscilla Juvelis - Rare Books   61 - 43   2015 $1000

Plimpton, Sarah *For Now.* New York: 2008. Artist's book, one of 15 copies, all on Fabriano Tiepolo paper, each copy signed and misnumbered by poet/artist/printer, Plimpton, page size 8 3/4 x 11 3/4 inches, 20 pages, loose as issued in cinnamon colored wrappers, black label title printed in gold on spine housed in brick colored cloth, custom-made clamshell box, black leather label with title and author in gold gilt on spine, made by Claudia Cohen, text set in Dante and printed with help of Brad Ewing at Grenfell Press in NY, each page with original aquatint on ochre colored ground, with the exception of the middle double page spread on pale moss green ground with deeper green forms.   Priscilla Juvelis - Rare Books   62 - 15   2015 $750

Plimpton, Sarah *Noise of the rain.* New York: 2007. Artist's book, one of 15 copies, all on rives BFK paper, signed and numbered by artist/ author, page size 14 1/2 x 10 1/8 inches, 20 pages, each of the pages has original pochoir prints by artist/author in muted shades of orange, brown, plum, slate blue, yellow terracotta and green, text set in Bell Monotype and printed in black by artist with help of Brad Ewing at Grenfell Press, loose as issued in original plain gray wrapper with title debossed on front panel, housed in plum cloth clamshell box by Claudia Cohen, with title and artist's name debossed on Rives paper label on spine, fine.   Priscilla Juvelis - Rare Books   61 - 44   2015 $1200

Plimpton, Sarah *Storms.* New York: 2011. Artist's book, one of 15 copies only, all on Somerset black paper, each signed and numbered by author/artist, page size 11 34/ x 15 5/8 inches, 9 pages including titlepage and colophon, bound loose as issued in tan cloth over card stock of envelope printed with author and title in black on front panel, the 9 pages which are all original woodcuts, as well as text printed letterpress in Caslon, this is a jigsaw book, there are 9 'jigsaw' woodcuts printed in white on black paper, carved block is cut by jigsaw and then reassembled on letterpress bed and printed with white ink on black paper.   Priscilla Juvelis - Rare Books   63 - 16   2015 $950

Plowden, Francis *The Case Stated by Francis Plowden, Esq., Conveyancer of the Middle Temple. Occasioned by the Act of Parliament Lately Passed for the Relief of the English Roman Catholics.* London: printed for the author and sold by P. Keating, 1791. First edition, 8vo., wanting half title and errata leaf (as in most copies), titlepage lightly stained, else good copy, recently well bound in cloth, spine lettered gilt, uncommon outside Irish libraries.   John Drury Rare Books   March 2015 - 18410   2015   £306

Plunkett, William Conyngham *The Substance of the Speech of the Right Hon..... in the House of Commons on Tuesday the 23rd of November 1819.* Manchester: printed and sold by Bancks and Co., 1819. 8vo., 24 pages, modern wrappers with printed title label on upper cover, very good.   John Drury Rare Books   2015 - 19360   2015 $80

La Plus Vielle Histoire Du Monde. Paris: Jardin des Modes, n.d., 1931. Oblong 4to., accordion style folded linen pages, slight cover soil and faint stain on inner corner of 2 pages, else near fine, illustrations on every page, quite scarce. Aleph-Bet Books, Inc.   108 - 189   2015 $1200

Plutarchus *Vite di Plutarco Cheroneo de gil Huomini Illustri Greci et Romani.* Venetia: Marco Ginami, 1620. Later edition, 2 volumes, 229 x 149mm., extremely pleasing contemporary Italian calf lavishly gilt, covers framed by multiple plain and dotted rules and geometric roll diapered central panel with slender fleuron in each compartment, flat spines with elongated panel formed by multiple plain and dotted rules and floral filigree roll and containing three fleurons, holes for ties (now lacking), all edges gilt (apparently - though not certainly) - with some very expert repairs to spine ends and edges), with 54 ornate woodcut frames and tondo portraits to accompany each biography, printer's device on titlepage, woodcut decorative initials, titlepage of volume II with later ink inscription "A. Barbet/374i, indications of bookplate removal on front pastedowns, four leaves with short marginal tears, occasional faint dampstains to head margin, isolated minor smudges and foxing, otherwise clean, crisp and smooth, joints with minimal rubbing, couple of small stains to boards, other trivial defects, bindings in excellent condition, gilt still bright and generally with minor wear.   Phillip J. Pirages   66 - 24   2015 $4800

Plutarchus *Plutarch's Lives.* London: printed for Edward and Charles Dilly, 1760. 6 volumes, full brown leather with red leather title labels and gilt volume numbers to spines, raised bands, gilt rules to spines, splits to leather along hinges of volume one, short splot to front hinge volume 4, chipping to leather on spine ends of several volumes, cracking to leather on spines, minor wear to edges and corners of boards, minor rubbing to boards, bumping to corners of some volumes, frontispiece to each volume, offsetting to titlepages, bookplate of Charles Chauncey each volume, antiquated ownership signature top edge of each titlepage, occasional spots of foxing, few small ink stains to interiors, very good.   The Kelmscott Bookshop   11 - 39 2015 $500

Plutarchus *The Lives of the Noble Grecians and Romans Compared Together by the Grave Learned Philosopher and Historiographer Plutarch.* New York: Limited Editions Club, 1941. Limited to 1500 numbered copies, printed on Worthy paper by Southworth Anthoenson Press, designed by WAD and signed by him, decorative double page titlepages with designs in color by Dwiggins and headings printed in black and white, 8vo., cloth enclosed in two slipcases, each with paper spine label, the slipcases rubbed and cracking of some hinges, books well preserved.   Oak Knoll Books   25 - 28   2015 $250

Plutarchus *Les Ouvvres Morales & Meslees de Plutarque.* Paris: De l'Imprimerie de Michel de Vascosan, 1572. First edition of Jacques Amyot's translation, title creased and slightly frayed at edges, short closed tear reinforced with tissue, some light spotting elsewhere, few sections toned, folio, 18th century calf, scraped and worn at edges, rebacked, black morocco lettering piece, hinges relined, bookplate of drama critic Joseph Knight (1829-1920), sound.   Blackwell's Rare Books   Greek & Latin Classics VI - 85   2015   £2500

Poe, Edgar Allan   1809-1849 *The Bells & Other Poems.* London & New York: Hodder & Stoughton, n.d., 1912. Limited to 650 copies signed by artist, Edmund Dulac, with 28 magnificent color plates (with guards), plus many large pictorial headpieces as well, large 4to., full vellum binding extensively decorated in gold, top edge gilt, new silk ties, most minor cover soil, bump at head of spine, else fine with none of the bowing of covers that usually affects this book.   Aleph-Bet Books, Inc.   108 - 155   2015 $2500

Poe, Edgar Allan   1809-1849 *The Bells: a Numerical Exploration.* Vashon Island: 2014. Artist's book, one in a series of 10, on paper, polyester film, and metals, by noted book artist, Donald Glaister who has signed and numbered the book of colophon, page size 14 1/2 x 8 7/8 inches, bound by the artist, Glaister, painted paper over boards, hand sewn with each page on tabs to allow complete opening of each page spread, grey morocco spine, title written in dark grey on aluminum inset on front panel, edges of front and rear panel edges in orange, housed in clamshell box, designed, painted and bound by artist, this book uses paper, various metals and polyester, text printed by laser on mylar, mathematical formulas and equations are hand painted on metal inserts in each of the pages/boards.   Priscilla Juvelis - Rare Books   63 - 7   2015 $3900

Poe, Edgar Allan   1809-1849 *The Fall of the House of Usher.* N.P.: Limited Editions Club, 1985. Limited to 1500 numbered copies, this copy signed by Raphael Soyer and the artist, Alice Neel, folio, quarter morocco with marbled paper covered boards edged in leather, clamshell box with leather cover label, well illustrated with original etchings and lithographs by Neel, finely printed by Anthoensen Press on mould made paper by Cartiere Enrico Magnani, with monthly letter loosely inserted.   Oak Knoll Books   25 - 54   2015 $450

Poe, Edgar Allan   1809-1849 *The Literati: Some Honest Opinions about Authorial Merits and Demerits.* New York: J. S. Redfield, 1850. First edition, 8vo., original blind-stamped blue cloth, gilt lettering, edges slightly rubbed, light dampstain in margin of prelims and last several signatures, very good, binding bright and clean.   The Brick Row Book Shop   Miscellany 67 - 75   2015 $650

Poe, Edgar Allan   1809-1849 *The Poems of Edgar Allan Poe.* London: Kegan Paul, Trench & Co., 1881. First UK edition thus, one of 50 copies of the large paper edition, numbered and printed October 1881, this #38, signed by printers Ballantyne, Hanson & Co., 8vo., original full leather bound by Zaehnsdorf, raised bands on spine, titles stamped in gold on spine, decorated linen front and rear endpapers, frontispiece, former owner's neat attractive bookplate, bit of minor foxing to few pages, else near fine, bright copy.   Buckingham Books   March 2015 - 29431   2015 $750

Poe, Edgar Allan   1809-1849 *"The Raven." in The American Review: a Whig Journal of Politics, Literature, Art and Science.* New York: Wiley and Putnam, Jan.-June, 1845. First edition, first printing, octavo, contemporary three quarter morocco over marbled boards, the whole volume offered, occasional foxing and toning, as always, generally clean with only few spots of foxing, rubbing and general wear to contemporary binding, rare thus.   Manhattan Rare Book Company   Literature 2014 - 2015 $3800

Poe, Edgar Allan   1809-1849 *The Raven.* Easthampton: Cheloniidae Press, 1980. One of 100 copies, from a total of 125 copies all on arches paper, 100 regular issue, 25 deluxe issue, both long out of print, 5 etchings and 2 wood engravings, each of the plates signed and titled in pencil by artist, who printed the etchings as well, in addition, this copy has laid in artist proof of the 'Crow Quill' on titlepage and two proofs on colophon, text is 24 pages, Centaur hand set and printed by master pressman, Harold McGrath, book bound by David Bourbeau in specially painted cloth over boards and housed in black cloth clamshell box, black morocco spine, author, title and press paragraph in gilt, text handset by Harold McGrath in Bruce Rogers lovely 24pt. Centaur type in black and red ink, five full page original etchings and two original wood engravings.   Priscilla Juvelis - Rare Books   61 - 5   2015 $3200

Poe, Edgar Allan   1809-1849 *Tales.* New York: Wiley & Putnam, 1845. First edition, scarce first printing, octavo, period style full crushed morocco gilt, bound without half title and publisher's ads, fine copy.   Honey & Wax Booksellers   3 - 15   2015 $22,000

Poe, Edgar Allan 1809-1849 *Tales of Mystery and Imagination.* London: George Harrap, 1919. Limited to 170 numbered copies, signed by Clarke, thick 4to., full gilt vellum binding, top edge gilt, half tone toned and some foxing on free endpaper, else free from foxing, clean and bright and fine, this copy in original plain publisher's box lined with white fabric, printed label on top flap has number inked-in that matches limitation number in book (box has small repair to one edge and some soil, else very good), 24 full page plates and text illustrations by Harry Clarke, very rare. Aleph-bet Books, Inc.   109 - 95   2015 $9250

Poe, Edgar Allan 1809-1849 *Tales of Mystery and Imagination.* Tudor Pub. Co., 1933. First edition thus, quarto, black cloth, paper label on front cover gold stamping on spine, black endpapers, frontispiece, illustrations, fine, tight copy, transparent dust jacket, housed in original color pictorial box with bottom portion reinforced with cellophane tape, 8 color and 24 black and whites plates by Harry Clarke.   Buckingham Books   March 2015 - 33613   2015 $750

Poe, Edgar Allan 1809-1849 *Oeuvres Imaginatives Et Poetiques Completes De Edgar Poe.* Vialetay, 1966. #1637 of 2500 copies, wrappers, 6 volumes, 8vo., all fine in green cloth boxes showing very slight wear, also included prospectus for the set in wrappers slightly soiled.   Beasley Books   2013 - 2015 $300

Poe, John W. *The True Story of the Killing of Billy the Kid.* Los Angeles: Privately printed, n.d., 1923? Limited to 250 numbered copies, 15 pages, illustrations, original printed wrappers, light soil to wrappers, dampstain to portion of top edge, spine separating with tiny mend, else good.   Dumont Maps and Books of the West   130 - 29   2015 $150

Poems by a Lady. sold by Henry Payne, 1781. First edition, issue with printed titlepage instead of engraving, browned and soiled, few corrections in early ink, 4to., modern quarter blue calf, marbled boards, black morocco lettering piece, good, rare book.   Blackwell's Rare Books   B179 - 60   2015   £1500

Poems Fit for a Bishop; Which two Bishops Will Read. An American Prayer... London: printed for J. Almon, 1780. First edition, 4to., modern brown half calf, marbled paper boards, gilt lettered, without half title, small oval duplicate stamp of Theological Institute of Connecticut, lightly foxed, very good.   The Brick Row Book Shop   Miscellany 67 - 17   2015 $875

Poems on the Death of Her late majesty Queen Mary, of Blessed Memory. London: printed and sold by H. Hills, 1710. First edition, 8vo., recent wrappers, margins of titlepage bit browned, otherwise good.   C. R. Johnson   Foxon R-Z - 1236r-z   2015 $115

Poesie Per Le Felicissime Nozze Piovene. Vicenza: per Gio. Battista Vendramini Mosca, 1774. First edition, 305 x 216mm., original pastepaper boards covered in red and green block printed patterned paper, modern red cloth folding box, frontispiece, engraved allegorical vignettes on titlepage and at end, woodcut head and tailpieces and foliated initials, all done with considerable charm, spine and head edge just slightly faded, couple of very small snags in backstrip, one page with mild thumbing, but superb copy, exceptionally clean, fresh and bright, both text and original printed paper wrappers in almost unbelievable state of preservation.   Phillip J. Pirages   66 - 43   2015 $2900

A Poetry Book for National Schools. London: Bell & Daldy, 1857. New edition, frontispiece and numerous engravings, some marginal tears, original brown cloth, rebacked with back cloth, inner hinges strengthened, from the library of Geoffrey & Kathleen Tillotson.   Jarndyce Antiquarian Booksellers   CCVII - 9   2015   £300

Pogany, Nandor *Hungarian Fairy Book.* New York: Frederick Stokes, n.d. circa, 1913. 8vo., blue pictorial cloth, slightest bit of soil, else near fine, color frontispiece and a profusion of full and partial page black and whites by Willy Pogany.   Aleph-bet Books, Inc.   109 - 362   2015 $500

Pogany, Willy *Willy Pogany's Mother Goose.* New York: Nelson, 1928. Limited to 500 copies numbered and signed by Pogany, 4to., blue boards, fine, illustrations by Pogany, exceptionally rare limited edition.   Aleph-Bet Books, Inc.   108 - 352   2015 $2750

Pogany, Willy *Willy Pogany's Mother Goose.* New York: Nelson, 1928. First edition, first printing 'latch' mis-spelled as 'lalch' in "Crosspatch" rhyme, 4to., blue cloth with elaborate gilt pictorial cover and spine, top edge gilt, slightest bit of light wear, else near fine, many full page color illustrations and black and whites or color illustrations on each page of text, laid in is 8 x 10 black and white photo of Pogany discussing his 'new' book, Mother Goose at book store with crowd of admirers in audience.   Aleph-bet Books, Inc.   109 - 364   2015 $875

Poggendorff, Johann Christian *Biographisch Literarisches Handworterbuch zur Geschichte der exacten Wissenschaften Enthaltend Nachweisungen yuber Lebensverhalnissel....* Mansfield Centre: Martino, n.d., Facsimile reprint of 1863 first edition, 1898 third edition and 1904 fourth edition, 6 volumes, 8vo., green cloth, gilt stamped spine title, fine.   Jeff Weber Rare Books   178 - 905   2015 $300

Poggendorff, Johann Christian *J. C. Poggendorff's biographisch Literarisches Handworterbuch fur Mathematik, Astronomie, Physik, Chemie und Verwandte Wissenschaftsgebiete. Band V. 1940 bis 1922.* Garding: Cierco Presse, 1997. Facsimile reprint of 1925-1926 fifth edition, volume 5, large 8vo., blue cloth, gilt stamped spine title, near fine.   Jeff Weber Rare Books   178 - 906   2015 $235

Pohl, Frederik *Preferred Risk.* New York: Simon and Schuster, 1955. First edition, octavo, cloth backed boards, signed by Lester Del Rey and Pohl.   John W. Knott, Bookseller   Selected New Arrivals Jan. 2015 - 16994   2015 $150

Pointer, John *Oxoniensis Academia; or the Antiquities and Curiosities of the University of Oxford.* London: printed for S. Birt and J. Ward... sold also by J. Fletcher, and J. Barrett, at Oxford: and T. Merrill, at Cambridge, 1749. First edition, lower outer corner of D1 torn away (no loss of text), 12mo., contemporary calf, gilt rules on either side of raised bands, red lettering piece, very good.   Blackwell's Rare Books   B179 - 84   2015   £300

Poland *Constitutional Charter of the Kingdom of Poland, in the Year 1815, with Some Remarks on the Manner in Which Charter, and the Stipulations in the Treaties Relating to Poland...* London: James Ridgway et al, 1831. First edition, 8vo., recent marbled boards lettered on spine, very good.   John Drury Rare Books   2015 - 23565   2015 $177

Poland, Jefferson *Sex Marchers.* Los Angeles: Elysium Inc., 1968. First edition, fine in very near fine dust jacket with just touch of rubbing.   Between the Covers Rare Books   196 - 114   2015 $125

Polehampton, Edward *The Gallery of Nature and Art; or a Tour Through Creation and Science.* London: printed for R. N. Rose, 1821. New edition, 6 volumes, attractive contemporary brown polished calf, 216 x 133mm., covers with gilt fleur-de-lys and blindstamped palmette borders, large oblong octagonal panel at center of each board, all volumes with contemporary landscape paintings, three of these signed by R. Ashton, one dated 1821 (but all by the same hand), wide raised bands painted black and tooled gilt, spine panels with central arabesque surrounded by curling vines, gilt titling, marbled edges (very small and expert repairs apparently made to the ends of joints on two of the volumes); 7 illustrations within text and a total of 94 engraved plates, including a frontispiece for each volume one of which is foldout plate and of which two plates are comprised of two illustrations each, front flyleaves with inscription of Barbara Douglas Campbell dated 1st Jan. 1822 and with later indecipherable inscription below; just minor rubbing to joints and extremities (a portion of one joint with shallow damage from an insect), one landscape with small cluster of gouges, superficial scratches to some of the other scenes, variable (motly faint) offsetting from plates, other trivial imperfections, but still extremely attractive set, text fresh and clean, bindings lustrous with virtually all of the original appeal intact.   Phillip J. Pirages   66 - 79   2015 $7000

Polite, Carlene *Les Flagellants.* Paris: Christian Bourgois Editeur, 1966. First edition, copy #12 of 15 numbered special copies of the first edition, wrappers in original tissue dust jacket, pages unopened, fine in dust jacket with short tear, rare.   Between the Covers Rare Books   197 - 35   2015 $750

Politi, Leo *Bunker Hill Los Angeles.* Palm Desert: Desert Southwest Pub., 1964. First edition, large 4to., pictorial gilt cloth, fine in dust jacket, signed by Politi with watercolor embellishments, full page color illustrations.   Aleph-Bet Books, Inc.   108 - 357   2015 $400

Politi, Leo *Little Pancho.* New York: Viking, 1938. First edition, 12mo., pictorial boards, fine in dust jacket, pictorial endpapers and illustrations on every page.   Aleph-bet Books, Inc.   109 - 365   2015 $600

Politi, Leo *Mission Bell.* New York: Charles Scribner's Sons, 1953. A. First edition, oblong 4to., slight cover soil, else very good in frayed dust jacket with closed tears, illustrations in color, with full page inscription from Politi and watercolor decorations.   Aleph-bet Books, Inc.   109 - 366   2015 $600

The Political Prohibitionist for 1888: a Handbook for the Aggressive Temperance People of the United States. New York: Funk & Wagnalls, 1888. First edition, original printed wrappers, some general minor soiling and edgewear, else very good.   Tavistock Books   Temperance - 2015 $150

Polke, Sigmar *Sigmar Polke: Blunderstagswhal 1972 - Bizarre. Fotos Aufgenommen in Dusseldorf und Koln. (Election 1972 - Bizarre. Pictures Taken in Dusseldorf and Cologne).* Heidelberg: Edition Staeck 69, copyright, 1972. First signed limited edition, oblong 4to., unpaginated, 45 leaves, all but one printed on rectos, this printed on verso, offset photo lithography, block perfect bound with white plastic comb securing original transparent pvc wrappers, printed in black (uniform with 'Bizarre' records' font) signed and numbered '77/50' by artist on recto of last leaf, comb very lightly scratched, endemic light rippling of wrappers, first leaf slightly edgeworn, clean crisp copy, scarce, signed and limited copy.   Maggs Bros. Ltd.   Gathering of 26 Countercultural items Oct. 2013 - 3   2015   £2750

The Poll for the Election of Two Representatives in Parliament for the University of Cambridge on Thursday June 17, 1790, Candidates, Right Hon. William Pitt, Lord Euston, Lawrence Dundas, Esq. Cambridge: printed by John Archdeacon printer to the University, 1790. First edition, 8vo., title little dust soiled, fine, uncut and sewn as issued, rare outside various Cambridge libraries.   John Drury Rare Books   March 2015 - 19889   2015 $266

Pollard, G. *The Currency Question: a Republication of Three Letters Which Appeared in "The Times" in December 1848. Suggesting a Plan for a Domestic Currency to be made Independent to Foreign Exchanges and to be Measured in Standard Gold.* London: Letts Son & Steer, 1850. 8vo., 160 pages, preserved in modern wrappers with printed label on upper cover, very good.   John Drury Rare Books   2015 - 25414   2015 $89

Pollard, Josephine *Buds and Blossoms.* New York: Worthington, 1891. 4to., cloth backed pictorial boards, edges rubbed, else very good+, printed on heavy paper on one side of page only, 12 lovely full page chromolithographs by Lucie Villeplait, illustrations, inscribed by Pollard to her Niece dated Christmas 1891.   Aleph-bet Books, Inc.   109 - 472   2015 $250

Pollen, Richard *Spade Cultivation, Tried for Ten Years on an Estate in Wiltshire in a Letter to the Right Hon. W. Sturges Bourne.* Chelsea: Tilling for James Ridgway in London, 1831. Second edition, 8vo., 16 pages, preserved in modern wrappers, printed label on upper cover.   John Drury Rare Books   March 2015 - 24930   2015   £266

Pollock, Simon O. *The Russian Bastille.* Chicago: Kerr, 1908. First edition, inscribed by author, very good with wear at spine ends.   Beasley Books   2013 - 2015 $85

Pollux, Julius (in Greek) *Onomastikon. Onomasticum Graece & Latine.* Amsterdam: Ex Officina Wetsteniana, 1706. 318 x 203mm., 2 volumes, handsome contemporary Amsterdam Prize bindings, elaborately and handsomely gilt, covers with two elegant floral frames incorporating the arms of Amsterdam, inner frame with oblique armorial cornerpieces, large coat of arms at center framed by foliage and surmounted by an allegorical vignette, raised bands flanked by gilt floral rolls, spine panels with gilt coat of arms, two green silk ties, ornate engraved frontispiece and allegorical titlepage, one double page engraved plate, parallel Greek and Latin text, very lengthy annotations in both languages, with engraved certificate attesting to the scholarship of Jacob Johannes Ott, signed by the Rector of the public school of Amsterdam and dated 26, March 1830; centerpiece on front board volume I slightly abraded, minor loss of gilt here and there on covers and spines, otherwise very fine, bindings entirely tight, virtually unworn and almost without soiling and text unusually clean and fresh with no signs of use.   Phillip J. Pirages   66 - 31   2015 $2500

Polybius *Historiarum Libri Priores Quinque.* Lugduni: Seb. Gryphium, 1554. 178 x 108mm., pleasing contemporary (English?) calf, covers with single gilt fillet border and intricate arabesque centerpiece, raised bands, spine panels with central azured gilt fleur-de-lys or floral spring, apparently original morocco label (perhaps, but perhaps not - with very expert repairs at spine ends), publisher's woodcut griffin device on title and last page, 18th century? engraved armorial bookplate of Sir William Baird and modern bookplate of Kenneth Rapoport, titlepage with early ownership signature of Franciscus T.... (now washed away and consequently very faint), occasional contemporary underlinings and manicules, joints rubbed (and with thin cracks alongside top spine panel on upper and lower joint and along bottom two spine panels on upper joint), lower cover with minor discoloration (perhaps from damp), other trivial defects, binding entirely solid, still quite lustrous and with nothing approaching a major condition problem, without front free endpaper, n3 with branching tear (paper flaw?) from margin into text necessitating, (old) repair, but without loss, isolated faint browning, other small imperfections, but really consistently very fresh and clean, very well preserved, attractive mid 16th century binding.   Phillip J. Pirages   66 - 14   2015 $3200

Pomey, Francisco *Pantheum Mythicum seu Fabuloisa Decorum Historia.* Amsterdam: Antonium Schonenburg, 1730. Eighth edition, small 8vo., later vellum, title in manuscript on spine, frontispiece and 27 engraved plates by J. Van Vianen, vellum little dust soiled, fine, from the library of 20th century scholar Gershon Legman with his signature dated 1959.   The Brick Row Book Shop   Miscellany 67 - 77   2015 $450

Pona, Francesco *Cardiomorphoseos sive ex Corde Desumpta Smblemata Sacra.* Verona: Superiorum Permissu, 1645. First and only edition, allegorical title engraved by ?GG" with David and Petrus on both sides holding a heart with Trinity above, 101 numbered etchings of emblems, 4to., 17th/18th century marbled paper over pasteboards, spine faded, rare. Maggs Bros. Ltd. Illustrated Books 2014 - 2015   £4000

Pontoppidan, Erich *The Natural History of Norway...* London: A. Linde, 1755. First and only English edition, 2 parts in 1 volume, folio, large folding map, very slight repair at rear, 27 engraved copperplates and a plan, as called for, full contemporary leather with gilt lettered spine label and somewhat rubbed and sunned, raised bands, hinges weak but holding, some rubbing, wear at lower spine, else sound near very good.   Any Amount of Books   2015 - C11452   2015 £1450

The Pop-up Mickey Mouse. New York: Blue Ribbon, 1933. 8vo., pictorial boards, covers lightly soiled, else very good+, wonderful with 3 super double page pop-ups in perfect condition. Aleph-Bet Books, Inc.   108 - 351   2015 $900

Pop-Up Minnie Mouse. New York: Blue Ribbon, 1933. Small 4to., pictorial boards, fine and bright, 3 marvelous double page color pop-ups plus many black and whites in text, very scarce. Aleph-Bet Books, Inc.   108 - 352   2015 $1200

The "Pop-up" Pinocchio. New York: Blue Ribbon Books, 1932. First edition of a retelling of Collodi's story, thick 8vo., pictorial paper over boards, color Pinocchio on front and rear endpapers, 96 thick pages, illustrations, 4 pop-up illustrations in full color by Harold Lentz.   Buckingham Books March 2015 - 28153   2015 $650

Pope, Alexander 1688-1744 *The Correspondence.* Oxford: Clarendon Press, 1956. 5 volumes, half titles, frontispieces, original maroon cloth, very slightly torn dust jackets, good set, from the library of Geoffrey & Kathleen Tillotson, with TLS review copies with few pencil notes by Geoffrey, with insertions including letters from editor and offprints.   Jarndyce Antiquarian Booksellers   CCVII - 424   2015   £225

Pope, Alexander 1688-1744 *Imitations of Horace with an Epistle to Dr. Arbuthnot and The Epilogue to the Satires.* London: Methuen, 1939. Uncorrected page proofs, half title, from the library of Geoffrey & Kathleen Tillotson, with Geoffrey's pencil marks in introduction only, with Geoffrey's card and decorated paper wrappers with ms. label on spine, staples slightly rusting.   Jarndyce Antiquarian Booksellers CCVII - 410   2015   £20

Pope, Alexander 1688-1744 *Miscellaneous Poems and Translations. (Rape of the Lock).* London: printed for Bernard Lintott, 1712. First edition, containing the first appearance of Pope's Rape of the Lock, octavo, contemporary paneled calf, rebacked, frontispiece and half title, some light marginal worming, light occasional dampstaining (not affecting Pope's verses), handsome copy.   Manhattan Rare Book Company   Literature 2014 - 2015 $4300

Pope, Alexander 1688-1744 *The Poems.* London: Methuen & Co., 1963. One volume edition, Half title, original blue cloth, very good in slightly torn and dusted dust jacket, Geoffrey Tillotson's signed copy.   Jarndyce Antiquarian Booksellers   CCVII - 412   2015   £25

Pope, Alexander 1688-1744 *Pope's Own Miscellany being a reprint of Poems on Several Occasions 1717...* London: Nonesuch Press, 1935. One of 750 copies this out of series, Half title, uncut, original green cloth, very good in plain titled dust jacket, Geoffrey Tillotson's copy with 2 copies of his review inserted, with his notes on endpapers, marked by rusting clip.   Jarndyce Antiquarian Booksellers CCVII - 413   2015   £40

Pope, Alexander 1688-1744 *Poetical Works.* London: Oxford University Press, 1966. half title, frontispiece, original dark blue cloth, very good in dust jacket, review copy sent to Geoffrey Tillotson with cuttings of anonymous review. Jarndyce Antiquarian Booksellers   CCVII - 414   2015   £20

Pope, Alexander 1688-1744 *The Rape of the Lock.* London: John Lane, 1902. Small 4to., half title, frontispiece, plates, illustrations, 4 pages ads, original olive green cloth, spine dulled and rubbed, top edge gilt, Geoffrey Tillotson's signed copy.   Jarndyce Antiquarian Booksellers CCVII - 415   2015   £15

Pope, Alexander 1688-1744 *The Rape of the Lock and Other Poems.* London: Methuen and New Haven: Yale University Press, 1954. Twickenham edition, volume II, half title, frontispiece, original brick red cloth in slightly torn dust jacket, edited by Geoffrey Tillotson with insertions and few notes in text, and long note on leading f.e.p describing the method of production which by his standards did not amount to a revision, note on dust jacket describes it as 'working copy'.   Jarndyce Antiquarian Booksellers   CCVII - 419 2015   £50

Pope, Alexander 1688-1744 *The Rape of the Lock.* London: Methuen and New Haven: Yale University Press, 1962. Third Tillotson edition, Twickenham edition volume II, half title frontispiece, plates, original brick red cloth, following inner hinge cracking, slightly dusted, torn dust jacket, from the library of Geoffrey & Kathleen Tillotson, Geoffrey Tillotson's copy signed, with few pencil marks and note by Kathleen on dust jacket stating it was 'Work copy'. Jarndyce Antiquarian Booksellers   CCVII - 421   2015 £40

Pope, Simeon *Interesting Suggestions to Proprietors and Trustees of Estates Respecting the Land-Tax Sale and Redemption Act.* London: printed by Cooper and Graham and sold by W. and I. Richardson, 1798. 8vo., contemporary ms. annotations and emphasis marks in red ink, well bound in modern half calf gilt, very good.   John Drury Rare Books   2015 - 7980   2015 $221

Pope, Walter *The Memoires of Monsieur Du Vall.* London: printed for Henry Brome, 1670. First edition, variant issue, few early ink annotations, titlepage dusty, 19th century half calf over marbled boards, spine little rubbed, no label, good copy.   John Drury Rare Books   2015 - 21748   2015 $787

Popish Massacres and Plots for Destruction of Protestants, a Proper Caveat Against the Pretender. London: printed in the year, 1712. Only edition, 8vo., text generally little browned, lower margins generally cut close, cropping or shaving several catchwords and signatures, corner torn from one leaf with loss of single text letter, most of last line of text lost on page 65, well bound in 20th century in plain ruled sprinkled calf with raised bands.   John Drury Rare Books   2015 - 24316   2015 $1136

Popper, Karl R. *Birkhoff and Von Neumann's Interpretation of Quantum Mechanics.* Nature, Volume 219, August 17, 1968. Offprint, 4to., first separate edition, self wrappers, mild toning, edge wear, two horizontal creases, 4to., nice association copy, from Jacob Bronowski's library with his annotations.   By the Book, L. C.   44 - 18   2015 $600

Popper, Karl R. *The Logic of Scientific Discovery.* London: Hutchinson, 1959. First UK edition, 8vo., original gray cloth with red label on spine printed gilt, small neat name on front endpaper, otherwise fine in complete, very good dust jacket with closed tear at front and slight nicks at spine ends, superior copy.   Any Amount of Books   March 2015 - A85342   2015   £350

Popper, Karl R. *The Logic of Scientific Discovery.* London: Hutchinson, 1959. First edition in English, octavo, original publisher's grey pebble cloth with gilt lettering on red file dot spine, dust jacket lightly sunned on spine and has few small chips and closed tears, otherwise clean, tight and bright.   Athena Rare Books   15 - 52   2015 $500

Popper, Karl R. *Objective Knowledge. An Evolutionary Approach.* Oxford: Clarendon Press, 1972. First edition, octavo, inscribed by author to W. V. O. Quine, original dark grey cloth with gilt lettering to spine, bright blue dust jacket with white and black lettering, near fine with just most minor nicks and signs and very slight amount of sunning to spine, preserved in custom clamshell box.   Athena Rare Books   15 - 53   2015 $1800

Popper, Karl R. *The Poverty of Historicism.* London: Routledge & Kegan Paul, 1957. First edition, octavo, original black cloth with gilt lettering to spine, dust jacket lightly sunned on spine and has few small chips and closed tears, former owner's name and date (1957) to front free endpaper, otherwise clean, tight and bright copy.   Athena Rare Books   15 - 51   2015 $250

Popular Science Monthly *Index to the Popular Science Monthly for the Twenty Volumes from 1872-1882 and of the Three Volumes of the Supplement...* New York: D. Appleton, 1883. Green cloth, blindstamped cover title, gilt stamped spine title, slightly rubbed, former library copy with rubber stamps and embossed stamp on title, clean and tight copy, barely used, very good.   Jeff Weber Rare Books   178 - 0-0   2015 $85

Porter, Eliot *The Place No One Knew: Glen Canyon on the Colorado.* San Francisco: Sierra Club, 1966. First revised and expanded edition, signed by editor, David Brower, Folio, 80 exquisite color photos, cloth, very fine, pictorial dust jacket.   Argonaut Book Shop   Holiday Season 2014 - 231   2015 $200

Porter, Gene Stratton   1863-1924 *Keeper of the Bees.* Garden City: Doubleday Page, 1925. First edition, hardcover, very good+ to near fine.   Beasley Books   2013 - 2015 $45

Porter, George *Very Fast Chemical Reactions.* London: Royal Institution of Great Britain, 1960. Offprint, 8vo., fine, signed by Porter on sheet of paper with Royal Institution letterhead laid-in.   By the Book, L. C.   Special List 10 - 5   2015 $90

Porter, George Richardson *A Treatise on the Origin, Progressive Improvement and Present State of the Manufacture of Porcelain and Glass.* London: Longman Rees Orme Brown and Green, John Taylor, 1832. First edition, 8vo., 50 text figures, engraved and printed titles, original maroon cloth with printed spine label, spine faded, contemporary number '94' in ink below label, very good, 19th century armorial bookplate of Mary Napier Stuart.   John Drury Rare Books   2015 - 14838   2015 $89

Porter, Katherine Anne   1890-1980 *Hacienda.* New York: Harrison of Paris, 1934. First edition, hardcover, no. 145 of 895 numbered copies, fine in slipcase, with prospectus, signed by Porter although not called for, first state copy with page 51/52 integral and errata leaf laid in.   Beasley Books   2013 - 2015 $125

Porter, Katherine Anne   1890-1980 *A Note on the Author with the Key, One of Seventeen Stories from Miss Welty's Forthcoming "A Curtain of Green".* Garden City: Doubleday Doran, 1941. First edition, small octavo, saddle stitched wrappers as issued fine, this copy inscribed by Welty to her longtime friend, author Kenneth Millar (Ross MacDonald), laid in is a marvelous TLS from Welty to Millar dated May 11 1971 in which she recounts the history of the pamphlet and its cover photo, letter with one horizontal fold, fine in custom folding cloth chemise and full leather custom clamshell box, gilt titles, rule and decoration, rounded spine and raised bands, from the collection of Duke Collier.   Royal Books   36 - 67   2015 $12,500

Porter, Robert Ker *Letters from Portugal and Spain Written during the march of the British Troops Under Sir John Moore...*   London: Longman, Hurst, Rees and Orme, 1809. First edition, 8vo, original boards, printed spine label, pages uncut, 335 pages, engraved map, 6 tinted plates, 16 pages Longman's ads at rear dated 1808, boards almost loose, spine chipped and worn, text and plates in excellent state, bookplate of Annibal Fernandes Thomas.   Any Amount of Books   March 2015 - A92910   2015   £450

Porter, William Sidney   1862-1910 *Roads of Destiny.* New York: 1909. First edition, near fine.   Stephen Lupack   March 2015 - 2015 $40

Portland and the Pacific Northwest. Portland: Oregon Immigration Board & Union Pacific Railway, 1890. First edition, 5 x 6 1/2 inches, 64 pages, pictorial decorated wrappers, wood enravings, very fragile and rare, pages browning but flexible, stain to upper front and back covers and upper margins of some pages, quite rare.   Baade Books of the West   2014 - 2015 $230

Portrait and Biographical Album of Isabella County, Michigan. Chicago: 1884. Large heavy 4to., 589 pages, full brown morocco over beveled edges, cover gilt sharp and bright, backstrip leather reseated, with gilt lettering preserved, new endpapers bordered with gilt gardrooning, all edges gilt, portraits from photos, ex-library.   Bookworm & Silverfish   2015 - 4743170106   2015 $247

The Post Office London Directory for 1823. London: Critchett & Woods, 1823. First edition, small 8vo., soundly rebound in half red leather and marbled boards, 5 raised bands lettered gilt at spine, titlepage lightly chipped at edges, otherwise sound, clean, very good.   Any Amount of Books   2015 - A61718   2015   £240

Post, Melville Davisson *Monsieur Jonquelle, Perfect of Police of Paris.* New York: Appleton, 1923. Correct first edition, with pages 62 and 63 transposed, spine slight darkened and back cover lightly soiled, otherwise near fine, without dust jacket.   Mordida Books   March 2015 - 008878   2015 $90

Post, Melville Davisson *The Mystery of the Blue Villa.* New York: Appleton, 1919. First edition, spine slightly darkened, otherwise fine without dust jacket.   Mordida Books   March 2015 - 009945   2015 $100

Post, Melville Davisson *The Nameless Thing.* New York: Appleton, 1912. First edition, very good in reddish brown cloth covered boards with white titles on front cover and on spine.   Mordida Books   March 2015 - 009944   2015 $100

Post, Melville Davisson *The Nameless Thing.* New York: Appleton, 1912. First edition, couple of small spots on spine, otherwise fine in brown pictorial cloth covered boards.   Mordida Books   March 2015 - 009144   2015 $175

Post, Melville Davisson *The Revolt of the Birds.* New York: Appleton, 1927. First edition, fine in price clipped dust jacket.   Mordida Books   March 2015 - 003144   2015 $200

Post, Melville Davisson *The Silent Witness.* New York: Farrar, 1930. First edition, very good, faint stain on front cover, otherwise fine in very good signed by author with quarter inch piece missing at top of spine, small chips at base of spine, slight spine fading and several closed tears.   Mordida Books   March 2015 - 00946   2015 $250

Postgate, Raymond *Somebody at the Door.* Alfred A. Knopf, 1943. First US edition, fine in dust jacket, lightly rubbed at spine ends, excellent copy.   Buckingham Books   March 2015 - 33159   2015 $300

Postl, Karl *The Cabin Book; or National Characteristics by...*   London: Ingram Cooke, 1852. Second English edition, 8vo., frontispiece, title vignette and 5 (of 6) engraved illustrations, publisher's cloth (soiled), leaves toned, good copy.   Second Life Books Inc.   190 - 186   2015 $250

Postlethwayt, Malachy *Great Britain's True System: wherein is Clearly Shewn. I. That an Increase of the Public Debts and Taxes....*   London: printed for A. Millar in the Strand, J. Whiston and B. White and W. Sandby in Fleet Street, 1757. First edition, 8vo., edges of titlepage and final two leaves browned, contemporary speckled calf, rebacked preserving gilt morocco lettering piece, gilt outer dentelles, extremities little worn, outer dentelles rubbed, very good.   John Drury Rare Books   2015 - 25587   2015 $787

Pote, Joseph *The Foreigner's Guide or a necessary and Instructive Companion, both for the Foreigner and Native...* London: printed and sold by H. Kent, E. Comyns and Jo. Jolliffe, 1752. Third edition, 12mo., contemporary sheep, ownership signature of Ellis Iles dated 1760, front hinge repaired, edges little rubbed, small tear in one leaf with minor loss but not to sense, very good.   The Brick Row Book Shop   Miscellany 67 - 92   2015 $1200

Potter, Beatrix 1866-1943 *Appley Dapply's Nursery Rhymes.* London: Frederick Warne, and New York, n.d., 1917. First edition, 16mo., green boards stamped in red, some foxing on half title and verso of endpaper, else fine, charming color illustrations, lovely copy.   Aleph-Bet Books, Inc.   108 - 369   2015 $1200

Potter, Beatrix 1866-1943 *The Fairy Caravan.* Copyright of the author, 1929. Limited to 100 numbered copies, numbered 35 in Potter's hand, first edition, privately printed in Ambleside to secure the English copyright small 4to., cloth backed boards, tips worn, light cover soil, spine pasted down, tight, clean and very good, presentation copy inscribed by author for Eleanor Louise Choyce, rare.   Aleph-Bet Books, Inc.   108 - 368   2015 $12,500

Potter, Beatrix 1866-1943 *A Happy Pair.* London: Hildesheimer & Faulkner, 1890. First edition, illustrations by author, one of a handful of surviving copies, 16mo., original piecotrial wrappers, tasseled silk ties, all edges gilt, 6 color plates, bright, unmarked copy of a true rarity.   Honey & Wax Booksellers   2 - 10   2015 $24,000

Potter, Beatrix 1866-1943 *The Roly-Poly Pudding.* London: and New York: Frederick Warne and Co., 1908. First edition,, first issue, 8vo., red cloth stamped in green and gold, beveled edges, occasional finger soil, bookplate, very good+, 18 color plates, 38 black and white drawings by author.   Aleph-bet Books, Inc.   109 - 380   2015 $900

Potter, Beatrix 1866-1943 *Sister Anne.* Philadelphia: David McKay, 1932. First edition, second issue with frontispiece correctly placed, 8vo., blue gilt pictorial cloth, 154 pages, gilt on cover bright, slightly dulled on spine, fine in rare pictorial dust jacket (backstrip of jacket faded, square chip off top of backstrip with light fraying, old mend to fold), illustrations by Katharine Sturges with 13 full page black and whites, rare in dust jacket.   Aleph-bet Books, Inc.   109 - 382   2015 $1500

Potter, Beatrix 1866-1943 *The Tale of Little Pig Robinson.* Philadelphia: David McKay Co., 1930. First US edition, 8vo., blue cloth, pictorial paste-on, mint in near fine dust jacket (minor wear to spine ends), 6 fine color plates plus numerous line illustrations and pictorial endpapers, 12 drawings plus 13 head and tailpieces, rarely found in such condition, rare variant blue cloth binding.   Aleph-bet Books, Inc.   109 - 379   2015 $2000

Potter, Beatrix 1866-1943 *The Tale of Little Pig Robinson.* London: Frederick Warne, 1930. First edition, first printing, 8vo., blue gilt pictorial cloth, 141 pages, cloth, slightly faded in spots and faint spots on endpaper, else near fine in dust jacket (very good+, frayed on corners and spine ends), fine color plates plus numerous line illustrations in text, pictorial endpapers.   Aleph-Bet Books, Inc.   108 - 370   2015 $800

Potter, Beatrix 1866-1943 *The Story of Peter Rabbit.* printed in USA, n.p., n.d. circa 1940's, First edition thus, 10 pages with color illustrations, by Margot Voigt, wrapper with color illustrated covers, stapled, 6 1/4 x 4 3/4 inches, slight rubbing to rear cover, very good.   Ian Hodgkins & Co. Ltd.   134 - 242   2015   £25

Potter, Beatrix 1866-1943 *The Tale of Peter Rabbit. PreSchool Picture Play Book.* Saalfield, n.d., 10 color illustrations by Ethel Hays and story on thick card covers, gold paper backed card covers with color pictorial Peter walking up a path, watched by bird, rounded corners, 7 7/8 x 5 5/8 inches, slight rubbing to extremities, very good.   Ian Hodgkins & Co. Ltd.   134 - 195   2015   £25

Potter, Beatrix 1866-1943 *The Tale of Peter Rabbit.* Saalfield, n.d., 24 pages, black and white illustrations, red paper wrappers, color picture of Peter on covers, 6 3/4 x 5 inches, tear along top/bottom backstrip, small pieces torn from lower corner front cover, very good copy of fragile edition.   Ian Hodgkins & Co. Ltd.   134 - 196   2015   £45

Potter, Beatrix 1866-1943 *The Story of Peter Rabbit.* n.p. n.d., Color illustrations, color illustrated wrappers, stapled, 2 6/8 x 2 1/8 inches,.   Ian Hodgkins & Co. Ltd.   134 - 241   2015   £28

Potter, Beatrix 1866-1943 *Peter Rabbit.* no publisher, n.d., 12 full page black and white illustrations, 32 pages, black cloth backed card covers, illustrations in color, 3 x 12 1/4 inches, thin strip from top margin, very good, scarce.   Ian Hodgkins & Co. Ltd.   134 - 237   2015   £30

Potter, Beatrix 1866-1943 *The Story of Peter Rabbit.* Whitman, n.d., 6 black and white illustrations, cloth backed purple and white checked boards, large color pictorial front cover, 9 1/2 x 7 1/2 inches, light rubbing to extremities, rear endpapers cracked at hinge and pages browned, very good.   Ian Hodgkins & Co. Ltd.   134 - 230   2015   £45

Potter, Beatrix 1866-1943 *The Tale of Peter Rabbit.* Saalfield Pub. Co., (Muslin Book), 12 full page color illustrations + 12 black and white illustrations, pages 24, red printed cover with color illustrations and titling front, sewn with crimpled edges, 6 1/2 x 5 inches, few small marks and some discoloration and staining of some pages, very good.   Ian Hodgkins & Co. Ltd.   134 - 197   2015   £65

Potter, Beatrix 1866-1943 *The Tale of Peter Rabbit.* USA: no publisher, circa 1950's, 12 pages, 12 x 10 inches, fine, illustrations, pictorial page borders, color illustrated wrappers, fine.   Ian Hodgkins & Co. Ltd.   134 - 243   2015   £40

Potter, Beatrix 1866-1943 *The Tale of Peter Rabbit.* London: Frederick Warne, 1902. First trade edition, 12mo., dark grey green boards, instead of slightly earlier brown, this copy has white dot in the "o's" on cover, leaf patterned endpapers, word 'wept' on page 51 and all other points of first printing per Quinby 2, 97 pages, slightest of cover rubbing and slight finger soil, else bright, clean, fine in custom box, very rare in such fresh condition. Aleph-bet Books, Inc. 109 - 378   2015 $11,500

Potter, Beatrix 1866-1943 *The Tale of Peter Rabbit.* Philadelphia: Henry Altemus, 1904. Early (pirated) American edition, 16mo., tan cloth and pictorial boards, spine stamped in gold, cloth on cover printed in blue with floral design, tips worn, spine ends repaired, erasure mark on one page, tight and overall clean and very good, 31 color plates.   Aleph-Bet Books, Inc.   108 - 371   2015 $300

Potter, Beatrix 1866-1943 *The Tale of Peter Rabbit.* Saalfield, 1916. 7 1/2 x 5 inches, neat inscription dated 1932, color titlepage, 12 color illustrations, numerous blue line illustrations, initial letters in red and black, color pictorial boards, black titling both covers and backstrip, very nice in slightly worn dust jacket.   Ian Hodgkins & Co. Ltd.   134 - 188   2015   £58

Potter, Beatrix 1866-1943 *The Tale of Peter Rabbit.* Chicago: Saalfield Pub. Co., 1916. 7 3/4 x 5 inches, text illustrations and text printed in either brown or blue, color illustrations, thin card covers, wrappers shaped at top, covers little used with slight creases, very good.   Ian Hodgkins & Co. Ltd.   134 - 189   2015   £55

Potter, Beatrix 1866-1943 *The Tale of Peter Rabbit.* Saalfield Pub. Co., 1920. Saalfield Muslin Book 16, 16 text illustrations in color and 12 in black and white, printed on muslin, color pictorial covers, titling in black, red and green front cover, sewn, 11 3/4 x 8 1/2 inches, fold across centre, erased name top front cover, very good.   Ian Hodgkins & Co. Ltd.   134 - 190   2015   £95

Potter, Beatrix 1866-1943 *The Tale of Peter Rabbit.* Albert Whitman & Co., 1924. Frontispiece, titlepage and numerous illustrations in color and black and white, blue cloth with large color pictorial label pasted front cover, light brown endpapers with outline illustrations in dark brown thereon, 9 x 5 3/4 inches, slight soiling to onlay, inscription dated 1924, slight thumb creasing pages, very good.   Ian Hodgkins & Co. Ltd.   134 - 209   2015   £75

Potter, Beatrix 1866-1943 *The Tale of Peter Rabbit.* Albert Whitman & Co., 1926. Enlarged picture edition, 9 x 5 3/4 inches, pictorial titlepage, 20 full page color illustrations + several outline illustrations and color vignettes, color pictorial head and tailpieces, brown cloth with large color pictorial label pasted front cover, titling backstrip, grey endpapers with outline illustrations in blue thereon, titling dull on backstrip and some faint coloring of outlines on endpapers and outline text illustrations, very good.   Ian Hodgkins & Co. Ltd.   134 - 210   2015   £70

Potter, Beatrix 1866-1943 *The Story of Peter Rabbit.* Whitman, 1932. 6 x 4 3/4 inches, 10 full page illustrations in color and 13 in black and white, numerous smaller text illustrations in both color and black and white, purple boards with black printed backstrip, color illustration on covers, tiny bump lower rear corner tip, very nice.   Ian Hodgkins & Co. Ltd.   134 - 225   2015   £40

Potter, Beatrix 1866-1943 *The Story of Peter Rabbit.* Whitman, 1932. 7 3/4 x 6 1/2 inches, black and white and color illustrations, yellow mottled wrappers with color illustration, fore edge with very slight wear, small slight mark front cover and blue smudge on inside top corner wrapper, very nice.   Ian Hodgkins & Co. Ltd.   134 - 214   2015   £30

Potter, Beatrix 1866-1943 *The Story of Peter Rabbit.* Whitman, 1934. 8 full page illustrations in color and 9 in black and white, numerous smaller illustrations in both color and black and white by Nina Jordan, purple and white patterned boards with large color illustration to cover, bold color pictorial endpapers, top/bottom backstrip and corners, little worn, hinges cracked, odd small mark to contents, very good.   Ian Hodgkins & Co. Ltd.   134 - 226   2015   £38

Potter, Beatrix 1866-1943 *The Tale of Peter Rabbit.* Akron: Saalfield Pub. Co., 1934. First edition, 12 1/2 x 10 1/2 inches, stand-ups by Sidney Sage, with 6 pages of die-cut figures in color, illustrated card covers, very good unused copy.   Ian Hodgkins & Co. Ltd.   134 - 191   2015   £95

Potter, Beatrix 1866-1943 *The Story of Peter Rabbit.* Whitman Pub. Co., 1935. First edition thus, 15 black and white illustrations by Keith Ward, green boards with black and white titling and cover illustration, some general light rubbing to boards and slight crease rear cover, dated inscription on titlepage, very good, uncommon.   Ian Hodgkins & Co. Ltd.   134 - 228   2015   £48

Potter, Beatrix 1866-1943 *The Story of Peter Rabbit.* Whitman Pub., 1935. 8 5/8 x 6 4/8 inches, 4 color illustrations, 6 black and white illustrations by Maywill Dudley, on linen-like paper, some soiling and discoloration of covers, good copy.   Ian Hodgkins & Co. Ltd.   134 - 227   2015   £22

Potter, Beatrix 1866-1943 *The Tale of Peter Rabbit.* Whitman, 1936. 13 x 9 1/2 inches, pages 4, illustrations by Jo Musial, large color illustration each page, printed on linen-like finish, wrappers with color illustrations, covers very slightly used, very nice.   Ian Hodgkins & Co. Ltd. 134 - 215 2015 £38

Potter, Beatrix 1866-1943 *The Tale of Peter Rabbit.* Saalfield, 1938. 7 1/2 x 6 1/2 inches, 5 color and 6 black and white illustrations by Betty Bell Rea, color illustrated (linen like) wrappers with black titling, stapled, erased pencil name top front cover, rubbing along edge of backstrip, small split at top, staples rusted, very good, bold, bright cover illustration.   Ian Hodgkins & Co. Ltd.   134 - 192   2015   £35

Potter, Beatrix 1866-1943 *Peter Rabbit.* Whitman Pub. Co., 1938. First edition thus, color illustrations by Ruth Newton, printed on linen-like paper, color pictorial wrappers, backstrip little worn, covers little soiled, odd marginal mark, very good.   Ian Hodgkins & Co. Ltd.   134 - 216   2015   £35

Potter, Beatrix 1866-1943 *Peter Rabbit.* Whitman Pub. Co., 1940. 12 1/4 x 8 3/4 inches, 14 pages, large color illustration on each page by Ruth Newton, blue linson boards with red and white printed illustration of Peter, fine.   Ian Hodgkins & Co. Ltd.   134 - 217   2015   £35

Potter, Beatrix 1866-1943 *The Tale of Peter Rabbit.* Saalfield, 1942. First edition thus, pages 16 (including covers), printed on cloth like paper, illustrations in color by Ethel Hays, color illustrated covers, stapled, backstrip resewn, covers slightly used, very good.   Ian Hodgkins & Co. Ltd. 134 - 193 2015 £26

Potter, Beatrix 1866-1943 *The Tale of Peter Rabbit.* Saalfield, 1942. First edition thus, printed on cloth-like paper, illustrations in color by Ethel Hays, printed on cloth like paper, black cloth backed color pictorial covers with crimped top and bottom edges, 13 1/4 x 10 inches, backstrip with 2 staples, covers slightly used, very good.   Ian Hodgkins & Co. Ltd.   134 - 194   2015   £28

Potter, Beatrix 1866-1943 *The Tale of Peter Rabbit: Animated.* Saalfield pub,., 1949. First edition thus, 8 1/2 x 6 1/2 inches, animated color picture on inside covers, each with moveable tape and several other text illustrations, 16 pages, color pictorial paper, over boards with titling front, 2 small tears top edge front cover and small pencil note top rear cover, very good, uncommon.   Ian Hodgkins & Co. Ltd.   134 - 198   2015   £85

Potter, Beatrix 1866-1943 *Peter Rabbit.* Whitman, 1961. First edition thus, 28 illustrations in color by Carl and Mary Hague, color pictorial boards, extremities little worn, slight rub top titlepage, very good.   Ian Hodgkins & Co. Ltd.   134 - 221   2015   £24

Potter, Jack M. *Lead Steer and Other Tales.* Clayton: Leader Press, 1939. First edition, 8vo., signed by author, stiff pictorial wrappers, illustrated with drawings including front cover by H. D. Bugbee and from photos, scarce, inner hinges reinforced, tiny closed tear to fore-edge of front panel, else near fine.   Buckingham Books   March 2015 - 22383   2015 $1000

Potts, Ethelinda Margaretta *Moonshine.* London: printed for Longman, Hurst, Rees, Orme and Brown, 1814. First edition, 2 volumes bound in one, some occasional minor spotting, otherwise clean throughout, later green half calf over marbled boards, spine lettered gilt, lightly sunned, still very good, scarce edition.   Marlborough Rare Books   List 53 - 41   2015   £950

Potzl, Eduard *Beim Wolf in der Au.* Vienna: Weiner Werkstratte, 1924. First edition, limited edition, one of 150 copies, this copy unnumbered, 16mo., illustrations by Hans Schliessmann, near fine in marbled boards, some light spotting and one page repaired with archival tape, erotic silhouettes, very scarce.   Between the Covers Rare Books   196 - 73   2015 $2500

Poulin, A.   *The Widow's Taboo. Poems after the Catawba.* Tokyo: Mushinsha, 1977. First edition, hardcover issue, illustrations by Roy Nydorf, small quarto, fine in rubbed, very good dust jacket, inscribed by Poulin to translator and literary critic Bert Mathieu, hardcover issue scarce.   Between the Covers Rare Books, Inc.   187 - 219   2015 $125

Pound, Ezra Loomis 1885-1972 *A B C of Reading.* New Haven: Yale University Press, 1934. First American edition, one of 1016 copies, minor darkening at edges, otherwise fine in cloth and very good or better dust jacket with tiny edge chips and darkening of spine, unusually nice in dust jacket that is not price clipped.   Gemini Fine Books & Arts, Ltd.   Art Reference & Illustrated Books: First Editions -   2015 $200

Pound, Ezra Loomis 1885-1972 *Antheil and the Treatise on Harmony.* Paris: Mountains Press, 1924. First edition, 12mo., original printed salmon wrappers, price erased from front wrapper, spine slightly faded, otherwise fine, fragile book seldom found in collector's condition. James S. Jaffe Rare Books   Modern American Poetry - 232   2015 $1000

Pound, Ezra Loomis 1885-1972 *Cantos 110-116.* New York: printed & published by the Fuck You/Press at a secret location in the lower east side, New York City, 1967. First edition, limited to 300 copies, 4to., loose sheets, stapled as issued, fine, cover by Joe Brainard.   James S. Jaffe Rare Books   Many Happy Returns - 258   2015 $150

Pound, Ezra Loomis 1885-1972 *Canzoni.* London: Elkin Mathews, 1911. First edition, first issue, one of 1000 copies printed of which 'not more than 500' were later issued as part of the combined volume 'Canzoni & Ripostes' (1913), 12mo., original grey cloth, inscribed for Olivia Shakespeare, corners little bumped, spine lightly sunned, faint spot on back cover, otherwise fine. James S. Jaffe Rare Books   Modern American Poetry - 230   2015 $2000

Pound, Ezra Loomis 1885-1972 *Drafts & Fragments of Cantos CX-CXVII.* London: and Iowa City: Faber and Faber, 1968. First edition, no. 273 of 310 copies, the English issue, numbered and signed by Pound, fine in fine slipcase but for little mild sunning, errata slip laid in, printed on hand press by K. K. Merker on Umbria paper, 4to. Beasley Books   2013 - 2015 $900

Pound, Ezra Loomis 1885-1972 *Exultations.* London: Elkin Mathews, 1909. First edition, presumed first issue with 'of' in the title on front cover, of an edition of 1000 copies, approximately 500 sets of sheets were later bound together with sheets from 'Personae' in a single volume, 12mo., original printed boards, lightly rubbed at extremities, spine panel faintly sunned, otherwise fine. James S. Jaffe Rare Books   Modern American Poetry - 228   2015 $1000

Pound, Ezra Loomis 1885-1972 *Indiscretions or Une Revue de Deux Mondes.* Paris: Three Mountains Press, 1923. First edition, number 128 of 300 copies, this copy very good with some spotting to boards and mild rippling to various pages, not at all an unpleasant presentation, 4to. Beasley Books   2013 - 2015 $450

Pound, Ezra Loomis 1885-1972 *Personae of Ezra Pound.* London: Elkin Mathews, 1909. First edition in first issue binding, out of a total edition of 1000 copies, not more than 500 sets of sheets were subsequently bound up with left over sheets of 'Exultations' in a single volume in 1913, 12mo., original gilt lettered drab boards, news clipping tipped onto front free endpaper, fore-edge, bit foxed, boards rubbed, still near fine. James S. Jaffe Rare Books Modern American Poetry - 229   2015 $750

Pound, Ezra Loomis 1885-1972 *Quia Pauper Amavi.* London: The Egoist Ltd., 1919. First edition, number 30 of 100 copies signed by author with ink correction by author of misprint on line 24 of page 34, correcting 'Wherefore' to Wherefrom" (some copies were not corrected), printed on handmade paper, one short tear at margin of page 21, five pages have very minor fox marks, back endpapers with very minor waterstain at lower margin, binding with very slight discoloration, overall very crisp and very good.   Gemini Fine Books & Arts, Ltd.   Art Reference & Illustrated Books: First Editions - 2015 $2400

Pound, Ezra Loomis 1885-1972 *Ripostes of Ezra Pound.* London: Stephen Swift & Co., 1912. First edition, first issue, 8vo., original gray cloth, publisher's ads at end present in this copy, covers lightly soiled, spine darkened, some offsetting as usual to endpapers, otherwise very good, presentation copy inscribed by author for Allen Upward. James S. Jaffe Rare Books Modern American Poetry - 233 2015 $6500

Pound, Ezra Loomis 1885-1972 *Selected Poems.* New York: New Directions, 1949. First edition, one of 3400 copies printed, 8vo., frontispiece, original cloth, fine in dust jacket, inscribed by author for Norman Thomas Di Giovanni. James S. Jaffe Rare Books   Modern American Poetry - 234 2015 $1500

Pound, Ezra Loomis 1885-1972 *Umbra: the Early Poems of Ezra Pound.* London: Elkin Mathews, 1920. First edition, 8vo., original printed grey boards with cloth spine, slight soiling, slight marks but decent, very good copy, ownership signature of Humbert Wolfe Jan 18 1926.   Any Amount of Books   2015 - A45366   2015   £150

Powderly, T. V. *Thirty Years of Labor.* Columbus: Excelsior, 1889. First edition, hardcover, f.e.p. detached but present, some general wear, gilt stamping still bright. Beasley Books   2013 - 2015 $85

Powell, A. Clayton *Riots and Ruins.* New York: Richard R. Smith, 1945. First edition, contemporary gift inscription, lacking front endpaper, else near fine in very good plus dust jacket with small chip and tear at foot.   Between the Covers Rare Books   197 - 95   2015 $150

Powell, Alice *Characters Who tamed the West.* Ken Carlson & Paul Masa, 1973. Limited to 1000 copies, this number 192, 11 x 8 1/2 inches, tan pictorial folder with decorative border, portfolio of 15 color prints, each 10 x 8 inches, portfolio cover signed by artist, folder lightly soiled and with light wear to edges, prints fine.   Buckingham Books March 2015 - 37410   2015 $250

Powell, Colin *My American Journey.* New York: Random House, 1995. First edition, inscribed by author for George McGovern, near fine in near fine dust jacket.   Ed Smith Books   83 - 75   2015 $450

Powell, Dawn *Sunday, Monday and Always.* Boston: Houghton Mifflin Co., 1952. First edition, fair copy only, chipping at crown, lacking dust jacket, ownership signature of Powell's close friend and author Hannah, Green, scarce. Between the Covers Rare Books, Inc.   187 - 220   2015 $450

Powell, Dawn *The Wicked Pavilion.* Boston: Houghton Mifflin Co., 1954. Reprint, stain on front board, corners bumped, good only with substantial remnants of tattered dust jacket laid in, ownership signature of author's close friend, author, Hannah Green. Between the Covers Rare Books, Inc. 187 - 221 2015 $275

Powell, Frank *The Wolf-Men: a tale of Amazing Adventure in the Underworld.* London: Paris: New York: Melbourne: Cassell and Co., 1906. First edition, octavo, 8 inserted color plates, original pictorial red cloth, front and spine panels stamped in brown, green, black and gold. L. W. Currey, Inc. Boy's Adventure Fiction 2015 - 11 2015 $750

Powell, Lawrence Clark *Book Shops.* Los Angeles: Roy V. Boswell, 1965. No limitation given but obviously very small, 6 x 4.3cm., leather, bound by Bela Blau, miniature bookplate of Kathryn Pickard and Raymond A. Smith. Oak Knoll Books 306 - 121 2015 $200

Powell, Michael *A Life in Movies. An Autobiography.* London: Heinemann, 1986. First edition, wrappers, uncorrected proof copy, slight toning to spine area, scuff mark to rear cover, very slight wear, otherwise sound, very good. Any Amount of Books 2015 - A96881 2015 £300

Powell, Michael *A Life In the Movies: an Autobiography.* London: Heinemann, 1986. First edition, 8vo., original green boards lettered gilt on spine, signed by author, ownership signature of Stephen Wyatt, playwright and author of Doctor Who books, slight lean, slight bumping, otherwise near fine in near fine dust jacket with very slight creasing, spine somewhat faded as always. Any Amount of Books 2015 - A68824 2015 £225

Powell, Michael *200,000 Feet on Foula: the Edge of the World.* London: Faber and Faber, 1938. First edition, inscribed by Powell for Roy Plomley 1942, near fine in very good dust jacket. Royal Books 46 - 4 2015 $4250

Powers, Richard *The Gold Bug Variations.* New York: Morrow, 1991. First edition, signed by author, 8vo., mustard brown quarter cloth, aqua paper boards, lettered gilt at spine, deckled fore-edges, signed by author on looseley inserted publisher's card, fine in fine unclipped dust jacket. Any Amount of Books 2015 - A39561 2015 £300

Powers, Richard *Three Farmers on Their Way to a Dance.* New York: Beech Tree/Morrow, 1985. First edition, fine in fine dust jacket. Beasley Books 2013 - 2015 $150

Powers, Tom *Scotch Circus.* Boston: Houghton Mifflin, 1934. First edition, 8vo., patterned cloth, fine, 7 full page color illustrations plus black and whites by Lois Lenski, scarce. Aleph-bet Books, Inc. 109 - 272 2015 $200

Pownall, Thomas *The Administration of the Colonies.* London: J. Walter, 1768. Fourth edition, collated complete, contemporary full calf slight wear to head of spine and adjacent hinge area, corners mildly worn, light extremity rubbing beautiful copy, internally very fine, crisp and clean, contemporary owner's engraved armorial bookplate and ink signature "Rolle". Argonaut Book Shop Holiday Season 2014 - 11 2015 $3000

Powys, Thomas *To The Gentleman, Clergy and Freeholders of the County of Northampton April 1784.* N.P.: but presumably, London, n.d., 1784. 8vo., preserved in modern wrappers with printed label on upper cover, very good. John Drury Rare Books 2015 - 26278 2015 $133

Pozharskaya, N. N. *The Russian Seasons in Paris: Sketches of the Scenery and Costumes 1908-1929.* Moscow: Iskusstvo Art Publishers, 1988. First edition, oblong 4to., text in Russian and English, original blue cloth lettered gilt and purple and spine and cover, copiously illustrated in color and black and white, very good+ in printed very good slipcase, slightly used at corners. Any Amount of Books 2015 - A64843 2015 £150

Prairie Wool: a History of Climax and Surrounding School Districts. Climax: Stone Diggers Historical Society, 1980. First printing, 4to., pictorial cloth, illustrations, fine. Baade Books of the West 2014 - 2015 $85

Praktische Kostumkunde in 600 Bildern und Schnitten. Munchen: Bei F. Bruckmann A G, 1926. Near fine, 2 volumes, original full cloth with decorations to spine, attractive, nearly fine set, very good in slipcase. Stephen Lupack March 2015 - 2015 $125

Prang, Louis *Alphabets Plain, Ornamented and Illuminated a Selection from the Best Ancient and Modern Styles....* Boston: L. Prang and Co., n.d. before July, 1870. Oblong 8vo., original green cloth stamped in gilt, (16) leaves, former owner has added pencil addresses an comments on front pastedown, free endpaper and verso of free endpaper, shaken and pages detached, covers well preserved. Oak Knoll Books Special Catalogue 24 - 42 2015 $700

Prang, Louis *Prang's Standard Alphabets.* Boston: L. Prang and Co., 1886. Revised edition, oblong 8vo., publisher's blue cloth, decoratively embossed with gilt lettering, 36 plates, more than half the plates printed in color, rubbed at spine ends, ink ownership inscription, well preserved. Oak Knoll Books Special Catalogue 24 - 43 2015 $450

Pratchett, Terry *The Colour of Magic.* Smythe, Gerrards Cross, 1983. First edition, crown 8vo., original mid green boards, faint rubbing to backstrip head and tail, backstrip gilt lettered, dust jacket with publisher's overlay on front flap, carrying the revised text, near fine. Blackwell's Rare Books B179 - 222 2015 £6000

Pratt, Fletcher *Fleet Against Japan.* New York: Harper, 1946. First edition, owner name, spine gilt mostly rubbed away, very good lacking dust jacket, sci-fi author L. Sprague de Camp's copy with his bookplate. Between the Covers Rare Books, Inc. 187 - 222 2015 $350

Pratt, Samuel *The Regulating Silver Coin, Made Practicable and Easie to the Government and Subject.* London: printed for Henry Bonwick at the Red Lion in St Paul's Churchyard, 1696. First edition, 8vo., neat repair to lower margin of title (not affecting printed surface), occasional very minor marginal staining, overall good, crisp copy, rebound fairly recently in quarter calf and boards, spine lettered in gilt, near contemporary armorial bookplate of Sir John Anstruther of that Ilk Baronet. John Drury Rare Books 2015 - 23004 2015 $830

Prayer Society of Canada *Submission to the Book of Alternative Services Evaluation Commissioners.* Toronto: 1991. First edition, 107 pages, 4to., fine in spiral wire binder. Bookworm & Silverfish 2015 - 6015559290 2015 $45

Praz, Mario *The Hero in Eclipse in Victorian Fiction.* London: Oxford University Press, 1956. Original black cloth, split at tail of spine, half title plates, slightly worn dust jacket, Kathleen Tillotson's review copy with a letter form her to editor of Review of English Studies, with cuttings of her reviews. Jarndyce Antiquarian Booksellers CCVII - 441 2015 £35

Preaulx, Joseph Marthe Rene Gilbert, Marquis De *De la Charte Selon la Monarchie et du Droit d'Intervention Considere dans ses Rapports avec....* Paris: chez C. J. Trouve, 1823. First edition, 8vo., 116 pages, half title, recently well bound in cloth, spine gilt lettered, marbled edges, fine, apparently rare. John Drury Rare Books March 2015 - 18058 2015 $266

Preces Sancti Nersetis Clajensis Armeniorum Patriarchiae Viginti Quatu or Linguis Editae. Venetiis: In Insula L. Lazari, 1837. 12mo., later half leather, over old paper covered boards, leather spine label, frontispiece, engraved titlepage, stain at top of engraved titlepage. Oak Knoll Books 306 - 225 2015 $200

Premiere (2e, 3e, 4e, 5e) Lettre a un Membre du Conseil d'Instruction Publique sur l'Organisation Actuelle de l'Academie de Geneve. Geneva: Ch. Gruaz 40, 1839. First edition, 8vo., 5 parts in one volume, well bound recently in cloth, spine lettered gilt. John Drury Rare Books March 2015 - 17863 2015 £288

Prescott, H. F. M. *The Man on a Donkey.* London: Eyre & Spottiswoode, 1952. First edition, 2 volumes, both fine in near fine dust jackets with slight wear at spine head, very nice set, 8vo. Beasley Books 2013 - 2015 $175

The Present State of Sicily and Malta, Extracted From Mr. Brydone, Mr. Swinburne and other Modern Travellers. London: G. Kearsley, 1788. First edition, 12mo., with final errata leaf and with old blindstamp of Worcester Public Library on titlepage and occasionally elsewhere and with fine 19th century bookplate of the library, old, probably original, marbled boards, these rather rubbed, neatly rebacked and labelled, entirely uncut, good, rare. John Drury Rare Books March 2015 - 24081 2015 $874

Presnell, F. G. *No Mourners Present.* New York: William Morrow, 1940. First edition, few light scratches to front cover, else near fine in lightly rubbed dust jacket with minor wear to spine ends, small closed tear to bottom edge of rear panel. Buckingham Books March 2015 - 33112 2015 $250

Presnell, F. G. *Send Another Coffin.* New York: William Morrow and Co., 1939. First edition, fine, bright copy in dust jacket lightly soiled on rear panel. Buckingham Books March 2015 - 26927 2015 $250

Pressense, Edmond Dehault De *Speech of M. Ed. De Pressense Delivered in London, May 19th 1876 on the Occasion of the Annual Meeting of the British, Continental and General Federation for the Abolition of Government Regulation of Prostitution.* Liverpool: T. Brakell, printer Cook Street, 1876. First edition, apparently rare, 8vo., 16 pages, preserved in modern wrappers with printed title label on upper cover, good. John Drury Rare Books 2015 - 21721 2015 $133

Preston, Jack *Heil! Hollywood.* Chicago: Reilly & Lee, 1939. First edition, fine in very good dust jacket with small chips and tears, warmly inscribed by Preston for author/printer/publisher Ward Ritchie in 1942. Between the Covers Rare Books, Inc. 187 - 195 2015 $250

Preston, Jean F. *English Handwriting 1400-16130: an Introductory Manual.* Birmingham: Medieval & Renaissance Text & Studies, 1992. 4to., illustrations, printed wrappers, fine, ink ownership signature of David C. Lindberg, fine. Jeff Weber Rare Books 178 - 912 2015 $85

Preston, Tom *The Peek-a-Book Japs.* London: Henry Frowde/Hodder & Stoughton, n.d. circa, 1915. Square 4to., pictorial boards, cloth paste-on, some of the white lettering rubbed on cover, inner margin mend on one plate (not noticeable), else near fine, 12 exceptional color plates plus numerous black and whites, scarce. Aleph-Bet Books, Inc. 108 - 374 2015 $850

Prevost, Antoine Francois, called Prevost D'Exiles 1697-1763 *Histoire General des Voyages ou Nouvelle Collection de Toutes les Relations de Voyages par Mer et par Terre.* Amsterdam: E. Van Harrevelt and D. J. Changuion, 1774. Nouvelle edition, small quarto, title printed in red and black, engraved pictorial headband, 36 engraved maps and plates, contemporary calf, spine gilt, edges stained red, light wear to head of spine, light rubbing to extremities, fine, internally bright, fresh and clean. Argonaut Book Shop Holiday Season 2014 - 232 2015 $1750

Prevost, Louis *California Silk Grower's Manual.* San Francisco: 1867. 12mo., 246 pages, illustrations, 12mo., original flexible cloth, spine faded, some wear to extremities with minor loss at top and bottom of spine, else very good. Dumont Maps and Books of the West 130 - 45 2015 $250

Price, Anthony *Colonel Butler's Wolf.* London: Gollancz, 1972. First edition, presentation inscription on separate slip from publisher laid-in, fine in dust jacket. Buckingham Books March 2015 - 29749 2015 $250

Price, Anthony *The Labyrinth Makers.* London: Gollancz, 1970. First edition, some tiny staining on fore-edge, otherwise fine in very good soiled dust jacket with scrapping at lower part of spine, chipping at base of spine and at corners and some staining of front panel. Mordida Books March 2015 - 011462 2015 $200

Price, Con *Trails I Rode.* Pasadena: Trail's End Pub. Co., 1947. First trade edition, 8vo. signed by author, cloth, gold stamping on front cover and spine, endsheets decorated with brands, publisher's prologue, numerous illustrations, fine in price clipped dust jacket with light wear to spine ends and extremities. Buckingham Books March 2015 - 21962 2015 $175

Price, F. G. Hilton *A Handbook of London Bankers with Some Account of Their Predecessors the Early Goldsmiths Together with Lists of Bankers from 1670, Including the Earliest printed in 1677....* London: Leadenhall Press, 1890. Royal 8vo., sometime in the library of Bedford College for Women, with small inkstamp in lower margin of title and on front free endpaper, original brown cloth lettered gilt on upper cover and on spine, very good, bright. John Drury Rare Books March 2015 - 20934 2015 £306

Price, Howell *A Genuine Account of the Life and Transactions of Howell and David Price, Gentleman of Wales...* London: printed for T. Osborn in Gray's Inn, 1752. 12mo., flyleaf and endpapers stained, else very good in contemporary sheep, spine with raised bands and gilt lines. John Drury Rare Books 2015 - 23765 2015 $3234

Price, Reynolds 1933- *Clear Pictures.* New York: Atheneum, 1989. First edition, previous owner gift inscription, else fine in fine, price clipped dust jacket, inscribed by author to Virginia Spencer Carr. Ken Lopez, Bookseller 164 - 168 2015 $100

Price, Reynolds 1933- *Letter to a Godchild.* New York: Scribner, 2006. First edition, fine in fine dust jacket, inscribed by author in year of publication to Virginia Spencer Carr. Ken Lopez, Bookseller 164 - 171 2015 $100

Price, Reynolds 1933- *Noble Norfleet.* New York: Scribner, 2002. First edition, top stain faded, near fine in like dust jacket. Ken Lopez, Bookseller 164 - 169 2015 $100

Price, Reynolds 1933- *A Serious Way of Wondering.* New York: Scribner, 2003. First edition, fine in fine dust jacket, inscribed by author to Virginia Spencer Carr, with couple of Carr's notes to herself laid in, one with Price's e-mail address. Ken Lopez, Bookseller 164 - 170 2015 $150

Price, Richard 1723-1791 *Observations on the Nature of Civil Liberty, the Principles of Government and the Justice and Policy of the War with America.* London: for T. Cadell and J. Johnson, 1776. New edition, 12mo., title just little dust marked and inked 5 digit number in margin, preserved in modern wrappers with printed label on upper cover, good copy, entirely uncut. John Drury Rare Books March 2015 - 25019 2015 £306

Price, Richard 1723-1791 *Observations on the Nature of Civil Liberty, the Principles of Goverment and the Justice and Policy of the War with America.* London: T. Cadell, 1776. First edition, 8vo., wanting half title, early instruction in ink to binder on titlepage, recent cloth backed marbled boards, morocco label on upper cover lettered gilt, very good. John Drury Rare Books 2015 - 25450 2015 $2622

Prichard, Constantine Estlin *On the Principles and Objects of Human Punishments. An Essay Read in the Theatre Oxford June 20 1844.* Oxford: Francis Machperson, 1844. First edition, 8vo., very good, inscribed in ink by author. John Drury Rare Books 2015 - 13606 2015 $221

Prichard, G. W. *Bureau of Immigration of the Territory of New Mexico, Report of San Miguel County.* Santa Fe: 1882. 16 pages, original printed wrappers, light soil and name stamp to front wrapper, else very good, laid in custom folder and slipcase, rare. Dumont Maps and Books of the West 130 - 26 2015 $450

Prichard, Hesketh *November Joe.* Boston: Houghton Mifflin, 1913. First edition, very good, scrape on front cover, otherwise very good in brown pictorial cloth covered boards without dust jacket.   Mordida Books   March 2015 - 009957   2015 $135

Prichard, K. *The Chronicles of Don Q.* J. B. Lippincott, 1904. First edition, cloth lightly rubbed at spine ends and small inkstain near bottom of spine, else near fine, internally clean and square.   Buckingham Books   March 2015 - 38472   2015 $185

Prideaux, Sara T. *Bookbinders and Their Craft.* New York: Charles Scribner's Sons, 1903. First edition, limited to 500 numbered copies, 8vo., creme colored paper covered spine with gray paper covered boards, top edge gilt, many illustrations, jacket has small pieces chipped away and has been repaired along hinges, book is very fine except for small spot in corner of front cover where book was exposed to sunlight as jacket has chip missing.   Oak Knoll Books   306 - 8   2015 $350

Prideaux, Sara T. *An Historical Sketch of Bookbinding.* London: Lawrence & Bullen, 1893. First edition, one of 120 numbered copies printed on handmade paper, square 8vo., original cloth, chip out of bottom of spine, wear along front hinge at top and back hinge bookplate of Sarah Gilbert Wood who has added her ownership inscription dated 1898 on half title.   Oak Knoll Books   306 - 9   2015 $250

Priess, Richard *Funny Book of Bunny.* St. Louis: Louis Longe Pub. Co., 1923. 4to., pictorial boards, 48 pages, some spine wear, slight cover soil, tight and very good+ full page color lithograph by Ernst Kutzer with pictorial endpapers, rare.   Aleph-bet Books, Inc.   109 - 354   2015 $450

Priest, Cinthia *The Santa Fe Diesel Volume Two; 1960-1995.* Kansas City: Paired Rail Railroad Publications, 1998. First edition, profusely illustrated in full color, dark blue leatherette, gilt, very fine with pictorial dust jacket.   Argonaut Book Shop   Holiday Season 2014 - 233   2015 $175

Priest, Josiah *A Copy of the Grants to the Van Rensaelaer and Livingston Families Together with a History of the Settlement of Albany..* Albany: J. Munsell, 1844. First edition, 8vo., 34 pages, original printed wrappers, staining, but very good.   M & S Rare Books, Inc.   97 - 219   2015 $450

Priest, Josiah *The Low Dutch Boy a Prisoner Among the Indians: Being an Account of the Capture of Frederick Schermerhorn.*   E. Williams, Printer, 1839. 1939.First edition, 9 1/4 x 5 1/2 inches, missing pages 25-32 (of 32), full page woodcut verso of title, pages lightly soiled and evenly browned and with 6 inch closed tear to front panel beginning at center of spine and tearing upward and with wear to extremities, good.   Buckingham Books   March 2015 - 35961   2015 $450

Priestley, Joseph   1733-1804   *An Address to the Inhabitants of Birmingham, Upon the Necessity of Attending to the Philosophy of the Mind...*   Birmingham: printed by and for M. Swinney and G. G.J. and J. Robinson, London?, 1791. First edition, wanting half title, recently well bound in linen backed marbled lettered boards, good copy.   John Drury Rare Books   2015 - 21781   2015 $1005

Priestley, Joseph   1733-1804   *Disquisitions Relating to Matter and Spirit.* Birmingham: printed by Pearson and Rollason for J. Johnson, 1782. Second edition, 2 volumes, half titles, engraved frontispiece after Bartolozzi, bound without errata slip, slight foxing, recent red green speckled boards, red morocco labels, spines faded to red, contemporary signature of Samuel Wakefield on each prelimblank.   Jarndyce Antiquarian Booksellers   CCXI - 235   2015   £350

Priestley, Joseph   1733-1804   *A Free Address to Protestant Dissenters on the Subject of the Lord's Supper.* London: J. Johnson, 1768. 8vo., small inkstamp on blank verso of title, margins of title lightly dust soiled, old, perhaps original blue paper wrappers, neatly repaired, very good.   John Drury Rare Books   March 2015 - 19576   2015 $266

Priestley, Joseph   1733-1804   *Scientific Correspondence of Joseph Priestley.* New York: Kraus Reprint, 1969. Facsimile reprint of 1892 NY edition, 8vo., frontispiece, dark beige buckram, gilt stamped spine title, fine.   Jeff Weber Rare Books   178 - 913   2015 $50

Prince, F. T. *Afterword on Rupert Brooke.* London: Menard Press, 1976. First edition, octavo, fine in wrapper and fine dust jackets, inscribed by author to Raymond and Elisabeth Di Palma.   Between the Covers Rare Books, Inc.   187 - 224   2015 $150

Prince, F. T. *Drypoints of the Hasidim.* London: Menard Press, 1975. First edition, octavo, top corner bumped, else fine in wrappers, in near fine dust jacket with spine sunned, inscribed by author to Raymond and Elisabeth DiPalma.   Between the Covers Rare Books, Inc.   187 - 223   2015 $125

Prince, Thomas *A Sermon at the Publick Lecture in Boston July 25 1728 in the Audience of His Excellency the Govenour, His Honour the Lieut. Governour and the Honourable the Council and Representatives of the Province.* Boston: Samuel Gerrish, 1728. First edition, wanting half title, sewn as issued, fore and bottom margins untrimmed and little frayed with short tear at horizontal fold, tide-mark across pages throughout, owner's signature 1836. M & S Rare Books, Inc. 97 - 246 2015 $375

Le Printemps: Une Frise a Colorier. Paris: Flammarion, 1946. First edition, square 4to., pictorial wrappers, fine and unused, one long continuous sheet of paper folded, when opened up it measures nearly 3 feet long, illustrations by Pierre Belves in brown and white with ample white spaces for the child to color. Aleph-bet Books, Inc. 109 - 348 2015 $225

Prior, Matthew 1664-1771 *Poems on Several Occasions....* London: printed for R. Burough and J. Baker, 1707. Unauthorized edition, small 8vo., final page neatly repaired with missing words inked in, in old hand, sound, very good, neat name label pasted to verso of endpaper. Any Amount of Books 2015 - A78146 2015 £650

Pritchard, Ada *Charles Pritchard, D.D., F.R.S., F.R.A.S., F.R.G.S., Late Professor of Astronomy in the University of Oxford. Memoirs of His Life...* London: Seeley and Co., 1897. First edition, heliogravure frontispiece with facsimile inscription on tissue guard, navy cloth, gilt stamped cover and spine titles (with cover illustration), lightly rubbed, very good, rare. Jeff Weber Rare Books 178 - 916 2015 $200

Pritchard, Edward William *A Complete Report of the Trial of Dr. E. W. Pritchard for the Alleged Poisoning of His Wife and mother-in-law.* Edinburgh: William Kay, 1865. First edition thus, 8vo., frontispiece, rather later 19th century half calf over marbled boards, spine lettered gilt, original printed yellow upper wrapper bound in, slight wear to joints, else very good, from the library of Alfred Harmsworth, Lord Northcliffe (1865-1922) with his bookplate. John Drury Rare Books March 2015 - 21751 2015 $221

Pritchett, V. S. *Balzac.* London: Chatto & Windus, 1973. First edition, 4to., profusely illustrated in color and black and white, original binding, fine in dust jacket, dedication copy, inscribed by author for wife Dorothy, inscribed " I am so proud to have worked with Mr. Pritchett on this book. Joy Law', from author's library with posthumous VSP booklabel, from the collection of Gavin H. Fryer. Bertram Rota Ltd. 308 Part II - 213 2015 £160

Pritchett, V. S. *Blind Love and Other Stories.* London: Chatto & Windus, 1969. First edition, original binding, very nice in slightly browned and frayed dust jacket, from author's library with posthumous VSP booklabel, from the collection of Gavin H. Fryer. Bertram Rota Ltd. 308 Part II - 210 2015 £50

Pritchett, V. S. *A Cab at the Door: an Autobiography: Early Years.* London: Chatto & Windus, 1968. First edition, original binding, little fading at edges, else very nice in slightly browned and frayed dust jacket, from author's library with posthumous VSP booklabel, from the collection of Gavin H. Fryer. Bertram Rota Ltd. 308 Part II - 209 2015 £50

Pritchett, V. S. *A Cab at the Door and Midnight Oil.* Harmondsworth: Penguin Books, 1979. First paperback one volume edition, wrappers marked and lower two thirds of titlepage excised, else good, from author's library with posthumous VSP booklabel, from the collection of Gavin H. Fryer. Bertram Rota Ltd. 308 Part II - 218 2015 £30

Pritchett, V. S. *The Camberwell Beauty.* London: Chatto & Windus, 1974. First edition, original binding, small closed tear to title, otherwise very nice in dust jacket, from author's library with posthumous VSP booklabel, from the collection of Gavin H. Fryer. Bertram Rota Ltd. 308 Part II - 214 2015 £45

Pritchett, V. S. *A Careless Widow & Other Stories.* London: Chatto & Windus, 1989. First edition, fine in dust jacket, original binding, bookplate of J. E. Davies, inscribed by author on bookplate, with autograph card signed tipped-in agreeing to inscribe it and commenting on the dust jacket and further initialled by him "A Happy Christmas" on slip of paper mounted beneath bookplate, from the collection of Gavin H. Fryer. Bertram Rota Ltd. 308 Part II - 226 2015 £120

Pritchett, V. S. *Chekhov: a Spirit Set Free.* London: Hodder & Stoughton, 1988. First English edition, original binding, slightly browned, otherwise very nice in dust jacket, from author's library with posthumous VSP booklabel, from the collection of Gavin H. Fryer. Bertram Rota Ltd. 308 Part II - 225 2015 £40

Pritchett, V. S. *Christmas with the Cratchits: a Sketch.* Berkeley: Ruth and James D. Hart, Hart Press, 1964. First edition, illustrations by Victor Anderson, wrappers somewhat faded and soiled, internally nice, from author's library with posthumous VSP booklabel from the collection of Gavin H. Fryer. Bertram Rota Ltd. 308 Part II - 201 2015 £50

Pritchett, V. S. *Collected Stories.* London: Chatto & Windus, 1956. First edition, original binding, head and foot of spine little worn and covers slightly spotted, otherwise nice, author's copy with his autograph signature on front free endpaper and his inscription, with posthumous VSP booklabel, from the collection of Gavin H. Fryer. Bertram Rota Ltd. 308 Part II - 195 2015 £50

Pritchett, V. S. *Collected Stories.* London: Chatto & Windus, 1982. First edition of this collection, original binding, foot of spine and covers darkened and stained, otherwise very good in creased and soiled dust jacket, signed by author on titlepage, from author's library with posthumous VSP booklabel, from the collection of Gavin H. Fryer. Bertram Rota Ltd. 308 Part II - 223 2015 £40

Pritchett, V. S. *Dead Man Leading.* London: Oxford University Press, 1984. First edition with this introduction by Paul Theroux, wrappers, somewhat browned throughout and some leaves loose, otherwise nice, dedication copy, inscribed by author for wife Dorothy, from author's library with posthumous VSP booklabel, from the collection of Gavin H. Fryer. Bertram Rota Ltd. 308 Part II - 224 2015 £100

Pritchett, V. S. *Dublin: a Portrait.* London: Bodley Head, 1947. First edition, 4to., original binding, fine in creased and torn dust jacket with piece missing, photos in color and black and white by Evelyn Hofer, presentation copy inscribed by author to his wife, Dorothy, with posthumous VSP booklabel, from the collection of Gavin H. Fryer. Bertram Rota Ltd. 308 Part II - 192 2015 £140

Pritchett, V. S. *The Fly in the Ointment.* Cambridge University Press, 1977. First edition thus, wrappers, very nice, from author's library with posthumous VSP booklabel, from the collection of Gavin H. Fryer. Bertram Rota Ltd. 308 Part II - 215 2015 £30

Pritchett, V. S. *Foreign Faces.* London: Chatto & Windus, 1964. First edition, original binding, fine in slightly soiled dust jacket, from author's library with posthumous VSP booklabel, from the collection of Gavin H. Fryer. Bertram Rota Ltd. 308 Part II - 202 2015 £40

Pritchett, V. S. *The Gentle Barbarian.* New York: Random House, 1977. First American edition, very nice in dust jacket, little faded at spine panel, from author's library with posthumous VSP booklabel, from the collection of Gavin H. Fryer. Bertram Rota Ltd. 308 Part II - 217 2015 £35

Pritchett, V. S. *The Gentle Barbarian: The Life and Work of Turgenev.* London: Chatto & Windus Ltd., 1977. Advance proof copy, wrappers little creased and soiled, otherwise nice, publisher's label on upper wrapper explaining book does not contain illustrations; from author's library with posthumous VSP booklabel, from the collection of Gavin H. Fryer. Bertram Rota Ltd. 308 Part II - 216 2015 £60

Pritchett, V. S. *George Meredith and English Comedy: The Clark Lectures for 1969.* New York: Random House, 1969. First American edition, original binding, fine in dust jacket, from author's library with posthumous VSP booklabel, from the collection of Gavin H. Fryer. Bertram Rota Ltd. 308 Part II - 211 2015 £50

Pritchett, V. S. *In My Good Books.* London: Chatto & Windus, 1942. First edition, original binding, spine and covers somewhat marked and worn, hinges weak, otherwise very good, dedication copy inscribed to author's wife, with posthumous VSP booklabel, from the collection of Gavin H. Fryer. Bertram Rota Ltd. 308 Part II - 189 2015 £350

Pritchett, V. S. *It May Never Happen & Other Stories.* London: Chatto & Windus, 1946. First edition, original binding, covers marked, dedication copy, inscribed by author to his wife, posthumous VSP bookplate, from the collection of Gavin H. Fryer. Bertram Rota Ltd. 308 Part II - 190 2015 £350

Pritchett, V. S. *It May Never Happen & Other Stories.* London: Chatto & Windus, 1946. First edition, 2nd impression, original binding, fine in slightly darkened and soiled dust jacket, form author's library with VSP booklabel, from the collection of Gavin H. Fryer. Bertram Rota Ltd. 308 Part II - 191 2015 £25

Pritchett, V. S. *The Key to My Heart: a Comedy in Three Parts.* London: Chatto & Windus, 1963. First edition, full light green morocco, gilt, red morocco inlay lettering piece to upper cover, bearing author's name in style of visiting card, patterned endpapers, covers slightly sprung and somewhat soiled and marked, upper hinge showing signs of wear, otherwise very good, from the author's library with posthumous VSP booklabel, from the collection of Gavin H. Fryer. Bertram Rota Ltd. 308 Part II - 200 2015 £80

Pritchett, V. S. *The Key to My Heart: a comedy in Three Part.* New York: Random House, 1964. First American edition, illustrations by Paul Hogarth, original binding, fine in slightly darked and soiled dust jacket, from author's library with posthumous VSP booklabel, from the collection of Gavin H. Fryer. Bertram Rota Ltd. 308 Part II - 203 2015 £40

Pritchett, V. S. *The Living Novel and Later Appreciations.* New York: Random House, 1964. New edition, fine in fragmentary dust jacket, dedication copy inscribed by author to his wife, Dorothy, with posthumous VSP booklabel, from the collection of Gavin H. Fryer. Bertram Rota Ltd. 308 Part II - 204 2015 £150

Pritchett, V. S. *London Perceived.* London: Chatto & Windus and William Heinemann, 1962. First English edition, 4to., photos by Evelyn Hofer, original binding, dust jacket creased, worn, repaired dust jacket for the American edition and cardboard slipcase, presentation copy inscribed by author to his wife, Dorothy, from author's library with posthumous VSP booklabel, from the collection of Gavin H. Fryer. Bertram Rota Ltd. 308 Part II - 199 2015 £160

Pritchett, V. S. *Marching Spain.* London: J. M. Dent & Sons Ltd., 1933. New edition, contemporary three quarter pigskin, raised bands, gilt rules, green morocco lettering piece, gilt, maize colored cloth sides, top edge gilt, patterned endpapers, pigskin somewhat darkened and cloth sides soiled, otherwise very nice, some foxing of prelims, with posthumous VS Pritchett booklabel, from the collection of Gavin H. Fryer.   Bertram Rota Ltd.   308 Part II - 187   2015   £150

Pritchett, V. S. *Midnight Oil.* New York: Random House, 1972. First American edition, original binding, edges of covers faded, else very nice in creased and soiled dust jacket, dedication copy inscribed by author for wife Dorothy, from author's library with posthumous VSP booklabel, from the collection of Gavin H. Fryer.   Bertram Rota Ltd.   308 Part II - 212   2015   £200

Pritchett, V. S. *Mr. Beluncle.* London: Chatto & Windus, 1951. First edition, original binding, fine in repaired, slightly darkened and soiled dust jacket, slightly chipped and defective at head of spine panel and one corner, from author's library with posthumous VSP booklabel, from the collection of Gavin H. Fryer.   Bertram Rota Ltd.   308 Part II - 193   2015   £60

Pritchett, V. S. *The Myth Makers: Essays on European, Russian and South American Novelists.* London: Chatto & Windus, 1979. First edition, original binding, head and foot of spine slightly faded, otherwise very nice in soiled, faded and torn dust jacket, from author's library with posthumous VSP booklabel, from the collection of Gavin H. Fryer.   Bertram Rota Ltd.   308 Part II - 219   2015   £50

Pritchett, V. S. *New York Proclaimed.* New York: Harcourt, Brace & World, 1965. First American edition, photos in color and black and white by Evelyn Hofer, original binding, very nice in dust jacket just little rubbed at corners, from author's library with VSP booklabel, from the collection of Gavin H. Fryer.   Bertram Rota Ltd.   308 Part II - 206   2015   £70

Pritchett, V. S. *New York: Herz und Antlitz eienr Stadt (New York Proclaimed).* Munich: Dromer Knaur, 1966. First German edition, 4to., original binding, little browned, very nice in creased and torn, dust jacket, from author's library with posthumous VSP booklabel, from the collection of Gavin H. Fryer.   Bertram Rota Ltd.   308 Part II - 207   2015   £40

Pritchett, V. S. *The Offensive Traveller.* New York: Alfred A. Knopf, 1964. First edition, fine in dust jacket little rubbed and marked, slightly defective at top edge of lower panel, original binding, from author's library with posthumous VSP booklabel, from the collection of Gavin H. Fryer.   Bertram Rota Ltd.   308 Part II - 205   2015   £40

Pritchett, V. S. *On the Edge of the Cliff and Other Stories.* London: Chatto & Windus, 1980. First edition, original binding, fine in dust jacket, dedication copy inscribed by author to his wife, Dorothy, with his autograph signature on titlepage, from author's library with posthumous VSP booklabel, from the collection of Gavin H. Fryer.   Bertram Rota Ltd.   308 Part II - 220   2015   £150

Pritchett, V. S. *The Sailor, Sense of Humour and Other Stories.* New York: Alfred A. Knopf, 1956. First American edition of Collected Stories, original binding, spine and covers somewhat darkened and soiled, otherwise nice, author's copy with his autograph signature on front free endpaper, and posthoumous VSP booklabel, from the collection of Gavin H. Fryer.   Bertram Rota Ltd.   308 Part II - 196   2015   £70

Pritchett, V. S. *The Spanish Temper.* New York: Alfred A. Knopf, 1954. First edition, original binding, extremities of spine and boards just little faded, else very nice in fragmentary remains of dust jacket, from author's library with posthumous VSP booklabel, from the collection of Gavin H. Fryer. Bertram Rota Ltd.   308 Part II - 194   2015   £50

Pritchett, V. S. *The Tale Bearers: Literary Essays.* New York: Vintage Books, 1981. First American paperback edition, wrappers, little browned throughout, otherwise nice, from author's library with posthumous VSP booklabel, from the collection of Gavin H. Fryer.   Bertram Rota Ltd.   308 Part II - 221   2015   £40

Pritchett, V. S. *The Turn of the Years.* Wilton: Michael Russell, 1982. First edition in book form, one of 150 numbered copies, signed by author and Paul Theroux (provided introduction), original binding, fine, presentation copy inscribed by author for wife Dorothy, from author's library with posthumous VSP booklabel, from the collection of Gavin H. Fryer.   Bertram Rota Ltd.   308 Part II - 222   2015   £150

Pritchett, V. S. *When My Girl Comes Home.* London: Chatto & Windus, 1961. First edition, fine, original binding, slightly soiled and frayed dust jacket, with label of literary agent, A.D. Peters, and partly erased signature on front free endpaper, from author's library with posthumous VSP booklabel from the collection of Gavin H. Fryer.   Bertram Rota Ltd.   308 Part II - 198   2015   £40

Pritchett, V. S. *The Working Novelist.* London: Chatto & Windus, 1965. First edition, original binding, nice in somewhat soiled and slightly worn dust jacket, label of Intercontinental Literary Agency on flyleaf, from author's library with posthumous VSP booklabel, from the collection of Gavin H. Fryer.   Bertram Rota Ltd.   308 Part II - 208   2015   £35

Pritchett, V. S. *You Make Your Own Life: Short Stories.* London: Chatto and Windus, 1938. First edition, original binding, spine dulled, corners bumped, one little rubbed, half title browned, otherwise nice, small label and stamp to rear endpapers, presentation copy inscribed by author to James Hanley, from the collection of Gavin H. Fryer. Bertram Rota Ltd. 308 Part II - 188 2015 £175

Privas, Xavier *Petits Vacancies.* Paris: Dorbon Ainen, n.d. circa, 1915. Oblong 4to., cloth backed pictorial boards, rear cover rubbed, else very good+, pages individually hinged into book, lovely book, hand colored illustrations. Aleph-bet Books, Inc. 109 - 182 2015 $500

Proceedings at a Meeting of the British Inhabitants of Fort S. George Madras on Monday September 19 185 in Consequence of a Summons by the High Sheriff of the Said Town. London: J. Debrett, 1786. Only edition, 8vo., some minor staining of titlepage, recent marbled boards, lettered on spine, good, only edition, rare. John Drury Rare Books 2015 - 24021 2015 $656

Proclus *Proclus' Commentary on Plato's Parmenides.* Princeton: Princeton University Press, 1987. 8vo., brown cloth, ink ownership signature of David C. Lindberg, fine, scarce. Jeff Weber Rare Books 178 - 917 2015 $85

Procter, Adelaide A. *The Victoria Regia a Volume of Original Contributions in Poetry and Prose.* London: printed and published by Emily Faithfull & Co., Victoria Press for the Employment of Women, 1861. First edition, 8vo. full leather elaborately stamped in gilt, all edges gilt, gilt inner dentelles, designed by John Leighton, some foxing on endpapers, much less in text, some very light wear to boards, still near fine, inscribed by Emily Faithful for Blanche Resticaux, 1862, also inserted a few news clippings about Faithful, very small ALS from Henry Alford and small slip of paper signed yours faithfully Isa Craig. Second Life Books Inc. 191 - 78 2015 $1500

Procter, Maurice *Murder in Manhattan.* New York: Morrow, 1930. First edition, very good in fine dust jacket with couple of short closed tears, inscribed by author. Mordida Books March 2015 - 011081 2015 $300

Proctor, Mary *The Romance of Comets.* New York: and London: Harper Bros., 1926. First edition, small 8vo., frontispiece, 16 photographic plates, original pale blue stamped cloth, dust jacket, cover faded, jacket spotted and browned from exposure, scarce in jacket, very good, bookplate. Jeff Weber Rare Books 178 - 918 2015 $95

Proctor, Richard Anthony *Chance and Luck: a Discussion of the Laws of Luck, Coincidences, Wagers, Lotteries and the Fallacies of Gambling with Notes on Poker and Martingales...* London: Longmans, Green and Co., 1891. 8vo. half title, followed at end by 32 page Longmans catalog, original red cloth lettered in gilt (spine) and black (upper cover), covers just little soiled, still very good, uncut. John Drury Rare Books 2015 - 23608 2015 $89

Pronzini, Bill *Blue Lonesome.* New York: Walker, 1995. First edition, signed, very fine in dust jacket. Mordida Books March 2015 - 007109 2015 $75

Pronzini, Bill *Cat's Paw.* Richmond: Waves Press, 1983. First edition, limited to 50 unnumbered copies Bound into cloth over boards with titles on paper label affixed to front cloth cover, signed by author and John Field, binder, fine in maroon cloth covers. Buckingham Books March 2015 - 37665 2015 $175

Pronzini, Bill *Invitation to Murder.* Arlington Heights: Dark Harvest, 1991. First edition, one of 400 specially bound copies, numbered and signed by all contributors, fine in fine dust jacket in fine slipcase. Beasley Books 2013 - 2015 $125

A Proper Sonnet from a Gorgeous Gallery of Gallant Inventions. Printed in the Dept. of English at the University College, London, 1935. Small 4to., original orange brown printed wrappers, (2), 4, (2) pages, from the library of Geoffrey & Kathleen Tillotson. Jarndyce Antiquarian Booksellers CCVII - 8 2015 £45

Propper, Milton M. *The Strange Disappearance of Mary Young.* Harper & Bros., 1929. First edition, cloth little rubbed, else near fine in fine bright colorful dust jacket complete with promotional wraparound band. Buckingham Books March 2015 - 3716 2015 $750

Prose, Francine *Guided Tours of Hell.* New York: Henry Holt/Metropolitan Books, 1988. First edition, fine in slightly rubbed, still fine dust jacket, inscribed by author for Nicholas Delbanco and his wife Elena. Between the Covers Rare Books, Inc. 187 - 225 2015 $200

Prose, Francine *Women and Children First.* New York: Pantheon, 1988. First edition, fine in near fine, bit spine faded dust jacket, inscribed by author to author Nicholas Delbanco and family, laid in is invitation to a reading by Prose. Between the Covers Rare Books, Inc. 187 - 226 2015 $225

Protestant Episcopal Church in the United States of America. Book of Common Prayer *The Book of Common Prayer.* New York: published by R. Bartlett & S. Raynor, 1836. Illustrations, gilt decorated full calf with raised bands, blindstamping and all edges gilt, very good, some foxing, tight.   Stephen Lupack   March 2015 - 2015 $95

Proudhon, Pierre Joseph *Avertissement aux Proprietaires ou Lettre A M. Considerant, Redacteur de La Phalange, sur une Defense de la Propriete.* Paris: Garnier Freres, 1848. Deuxieme edition, 12mo., 100 pages, half title, original printed yellow wrappers, entirely uncut, few minor fox marks in text, fine, large copy.   John Drury Rare Books   2015 - 16741   2015 $177

Proulx, E. Annie *Brokeback Mountain.* London: Fourth Estate, 1998. First edition, wrappers, signed by author, fine.   Beasley Books   2013 - 2015 $200

Proulx, E. Annie *Heart Songs and Other Stories.* New York: Scribner's, 1988. First edition, fine in near fine dust jacket with sunned spine.   Beasley Books   2013 - 2015 $175

Proulx, E. Annie *Postcards.* New York: Scribner's, 1992. First edition, advance review copy with publisher's promotional leaf laid in, fine in fine dust jacket.   Beasley Books   2013 - 2015 $150

Proulx, E. Annie *Wyoming Stories. 3 Volumes: Close Range, Bad Dirt, and Fine Just the Way It Is.* London: Fourth Estate, 2008. First edition, 3 matching volumes, issued without jackets in original publisher's matching slipcase, fine in steel dark gray cloth with gilt lettering matching slipcase, "Fine Just the Way It Is" marked 1/250 and signed by author.   Ed Smith Books   83 - 76   2015 $250

Proust, Marcel   1871-1922 *A la Recherche du Temps Perdu.* Paris: Bernard Grasset (volume 1), 1913. Librairie Gallimard, Nouvelle revue Francaise (volumes II-XIII) 1918-1927, First edition, 13 volumes, octavo, original wrapper, original glassine, inscribed to fellow writer Marcel Prevost, dedicatee, extraordinary copy.   Honey & Wax Booksellers   2 - 25   2015 $65,000

Proust, Marcel   1871-1922 *A La Recherche Du Temps Perdu 7 Tomes.* Paris: Plasir Du Livre, 1963. #3811 of 5000 copies, red leather with printed publisher's plastic, all in fine condition, 7 volumes, publisher's leather prospectus is included, small 4to.   Beasley Books   2013 - 2015 $375

Proust, Marcel   1871-1922 *Remembrance of Things Past.* London: Chatto & Windus, 1971-1976. Lovely illustrated edition, 12 volumes, octavo, original dust jackets, remarkably clean and bright set, exceptional in this condition.   Honey & Wax Booksellers   1 - 62   2015 $500

Proust, Marcel   1871-1922 *Swann's Way: Part One.* London: Chatto & Windus, 1922. First edition in English, octavo, original blue cloth lettered gilt, no dust jacket, initialled in ink by novelist Joseph Conrad, inscribed to Conrad by Proust's translator Scott Moncrieff.   Honey & Wax Booksellers   2 - 62   2015 $3500

Provenson, Alice *Glorious Flight.* New York: Viking, 1983. First edition, oblong 4to., pictorial boards, as new in dust jacket with few small closed tears, illustrations in color.   Aleph-bet Books, Inc.   109 - 386   2015 $150

Providence Association of Mechanics and Manufacturers *The Charter, Constitution and Bye-Laws of the Providence Association of Mechanics and Manufacturers.* Providence: printed by Bennett Wheeler for the Association, 1789. First edition, of great rarity, half title, paper generally rather browned, several leaves affected by dampstains, bound in early 20th century blue half roan over marbled boards, spine lettered gilt, original plain wrappers bound in, these worn and very soiled, with early marks of ownership including Ephraim Arnold, contemporary and 19th and 20th century stamps of Rhode Island Historical Society.   John Drury Rare Books   2015 - 23319   2015 $4371

Provost, Charles Hope *How to Draw from the Nude.* N.P.: National Library Press, 1937. First edition, quarto, unpaginated, heavily illustrated, illustrated glossy wrappers, trifle rubbed, easily near fine.   Between the Covers Rare Books   196 - 102   2015 $75

Prynne, William   1600-1669 *A Declaration and Protestation Against the Illegal Detestable, Oft Condemned, New Tax and Extortion of Excise in General...* London: printed for the author and are to be sold by Edward Thomas in Green Arbor, 1654. First edition, 4to., title printed within typographical border, bound fairly recently in half calf over marbled boards, spine gilt lettered, stitching partially sprung, else very good, crisp, good margins.   John Drury Rare Books   March 2015 - 23900   2015 $874

Prynne, William   1600-1669 *The Signed Loyalty and Devotion of Gods True Saints and Pious Christians, Towards Their Kings.* London: T. C. and L. P. and are to be sold by Edward Thomas at the Adam and Eve in Little Britain, 1660. First edition, 4to., title printed within decorative typographical border, fine modern green half morocco with crimson spine label lettered gilt by Period Bookbinders, red edges, fine.   John Drury Rare Books   March 2015 - 24655   2015 $266

Prynne, William 1600-1669 *The Soveraigne Power of Parliaments and Kingdomes, Divided into Foure Parts...* London: printed for Michael Sparke Senior, 1643. First collected edition, 4to., title printed within border of typographical ornaments, including final errata leaf, two headlines cropped, paper flaw in one leaf affecting catchword on recto, small patch of wear on another leaf affecting letter or two, contemporary calf, spines ruled in blind, neatly rebacked with spine label and gilt lines, very good, crisp copy.   John Drury Rare Books   2015 - 22713   2015 $1049

Psychopathology and Pictorial Expression III.   Basel: S. Karger/Sandoz, n.d., First edition, folio, 2 inch thick, boxed portfolio containing color prints and text, fine, very good printed box with several abrasions on cover.   Beasley Books   2013 - 2015 $150

Ptolemy   *Ptolemy's Almagest.*   New York: Springer, 1984. First edition of this translation, 8vo., figures, index, cloth, dust jacket slightly worn at foot of spine, ownership ink signatures of David C. Lindberg, very good.   Jeff Weber Rare Books   178 - 919   2015 $150

The Publisher's Circular.   London: Sampson Low, 1837. First edition, 8vo., 30 issues from Oct. 2nd 1837 to December 15th 1838, disbound, lacking covers, otherwise decent sound condition, clean text, slight staining to prelims, red stamp on first page, otherwise sound, about very good. Any Amount of Books   2015 - A74018   2015   £160

Puckle, James   *England's Path to Wealth and Honour; in a Dialogue Between an English-Man and a Dutchman.* London: F. Cogan, 1750. 8vo., titlepage lightly dust soiled, bound in 19th century dark green half roan over marbled boards, general wear to joints and extremities, else good and sound.   John Drury Rare Books   March 2015 - 25411 2015   £306

Puffendorf, Samuel, Freiherr Von   1632-1694   *Of the Law of Nature and Nations.*   Oxford: printed by L. Lichfield for A. & J. Churchill...., 1703. First edition in English, folio, title printed within double ruled border, this copy with errata leaf at end of introduction, contemporary panelled calf, sometime sympathetically rebacked, spine gilt with raised bands and label, fine, crisp copy, from the mid 19th century library of William Hodges Tylden Pattenson (1857) with ownership inscription on front pastedown.   John Drury Rare Books   2015 - 24994   2015 $6119

Puffendorf, Samuel, Freiherr Von   1632-1694   *The Law of Nature and Nations; or a General System of the Most Important Principles of Morality, Jurisprudence and Politics in Eight Books.* London: for J. and J. Bonwicke, R. Ware, J. and P. Knapton, el al, 1749. Fifth edition, recently bound in half mocha calf over marbled paper with red burgundy title label lettered gilt and relief decorations to spine, new endpapers, light tidemark to margin of final pages, some foldng at some corner tips, otherwise very good in very handsome binding.   Any Amount of Books   March 2015 - C1540 2015   £425

Pullan, Matilda   *The Lady's Manual of Fancy-Work: a Complete Instructor in Every variety of Ornamental Needle-Work.*   New York: Dick & Fitzgerald, 1859. First edition, 8 monochrome foldout plates, near fine, scarce thus. Stephen Lupack   March 2015 - 2015 $175

Pullman, Philip   *The Golden Compass.*   New York: Alfred A. Knopf, 1995. (1-10 code) First U.S. edition, 8vo., cloth backed boards, as new in as new dust jacket, signed by author.   Aleph-bet Books, Inc.   109 - 389   2015 $750

Pullman, Philip   *His Dark Materials: Northern Lights.* London: Scholastic Children's Books, 1995. First edition, 8vo., original burgundy cloth, lettered gilt at spine, dust jacket has the word 'Point' at lower spine and address on rear flap reads "Scholastic Children's Books 7-9 Pratt Street London NW1 OAE", fine in about fine dust jacket with barely discernible edgewear, very faint creasing and one very minute nick, excellent condition.   Any Amount of Books   2015 - C13297   2015   £750

Pullman, Philip   *An Outrance.*   Fyfield: Oak Tree Fine Press, 2009. 121/250 copies, (from an edition of 315 copies) signed by author beneath his portrait on page 40, printed in red and black, woodcut illustrations and historiated initials, 4to., original half red cloth, gilt rules, marbled boards, backstrip lettered gilt, fine.   Blackwell's Rare Books   B179 - 223   2015   £150

Pulszky, Theresa   *Memoirs of a Hungarian Lady.*   London: Henry Colburn, 1850. 2 volumes, 16 page catalog volume 1, original blue cloth, slightly marked, very good, ownership inscription of Mary Ford 1850.   Jarndyce Antiquarian Booksellers   CCXI - 238   2015   £150

Pulteney, William   *The Effects to be Expected from the East India Bill, Upon the Constitution of Great Britain if Passed into Law.*   London: J. Stockdale, 1783. First edition, 8vo., recent marbled boards lettered on spine, very good.   John Drury Rare Books   March 2015 - 26282 2015 $266

Punch; or the Auckland Charivari. Volume I from November 14, 1868 to May 8 1869. Auckland: published by the proprietors Messrs Frank Varley & R. J. Morressey, 1868-1869. Collective titlepage, illustrations, tear to lower fold first leaf not affecting text, slight marking to lower corners, largely good and clean, few gatherings little proud, 24 8 page issues, contemporary full black morocco by T. Watters, Auckland, elaborately decorated in gilt with central royal arms on front board and crown on lower board, gilt dentelles, rubbed, still attractive copy, scarce, elaborate blue and gilt endpapers, armorial bookplate of Coburg Bibliothek. Jarndyce Antiquarian Booksellers   CCXI - 232   2015   £480

Punctuation; a Printer's Study. Stroud: Evergreen Press, 2001. 200/200 copies, printed in red and black, 515 x 175mm., original grey linen with irregular shaped grey label to upper board, fine.   Blackwell's Rare Books   B179 - 146   2015   £130

Punkin, Jonathan, Psued. *Downfall of Freemasonry, Being an Authentic History of the rise and Progress and Triumph of Antimasonry...* Harrisburg: published for the editor, 1838. First edition, 8vo., 2 full page etchings and 23 wood engravings, all in good condition, original cloth backed plain boards, lacking label, two leaves torn and frayed on outer edges, barely affecting text, two other leaves with lower outer corner lacking, affecting five lines of text on each page.   M & S Rare Books, Inc.   97 - 167   2015 $175

Punky Dunk's Friends. Chicago: Volland, 1912. 3 books original pictorial box, slight rubbing on Mamma Goose, else fine, illustrations in color and bound with card, very scarce, especially in box.   Aleph-bet Books, Inc.   109 - 475   2015 $600

Purdy, Richard Little *Thomas Hardy: a Bibliographical Study.* London: Oxford University Press, 1954. Half title, plates, original green cloth, inner hinge splitting, marked and slightly distorted by damp, Kathleen Tillotson's copy sent by Oxford press in payment for a report, with inserted correspondence.   Jarndyce Antiquarian Booksellers   CCVII - 293   2015   £25

Pushkin, Aleksandr Sergeevich   1799-1837 *Eugene Oneguine: a Romance of Russian Life.* London: Macmillan, 1881. First English translation, octavo, original pictorial green cloth, gilt, near fine.   Honey & Wax Booksellers   3 - 19   2015 $9500

Pushkin, Aleksandr Sergeevich   1799-1837 *The Golden Cockerel.* New York: Heritage Press, 1950. First edition, 4to., original blue cloth with cockerel printed in gilt in repeat pattern on covers, spine gilt lettered, copiously illustrated in color, signed by the artist, Edmund Dulac with inscription form Dulac to Isaac Jones, slight marks, head of spine slightly rubbed, slight soiling, very good+.   Any Amount of Books   2015 - A43024   2015   £175

Puss in Boots. New York: McLoughlin Bros., n.d. circa, 1885. 4to., pictorial wrappers, some wear to spine paper and some cover soil, very good, 6 stunning full page chromolithographs.   Aleph-Bet Books, Inc.   108 - 180   2015 $350

Puss in Boots. New York: McLoughlin Bros., 1897. 4to., pictorial wrappers, near fine, illustrations by R. Andre with 6 stunning full page chromolithographs with color cover as well.   Aleph-bet Books, Inc.   109 - 169   2015 $350

Putnam, Arthur Alwyn *Mysteries of Crime, as Shown in Remarkable Capital Trials.* Boston: Samuel Walker and Co., 1870. First edition, 8vo., original gilt stamped green cloth, very good, early stamp of Michael A Gimbrone, criminologist from Buffalo NY.   M & S Rare Books, Inc.   97 - 84   2015 $375

Putnam, Mabel Raef *The Winning of the First Wisconsin Bill of Rights for American Women.* Milwaukee: Frank Putnam, 1924. First edition, 8vo., covers little soiled, very good, scarce, inscribed by author Dec. 7 1923 for Mr. James Walker.   Second Life Books Inc.   189 - 204   2015 $450

Putnam, Samuel *The World in the Air, The Story of Flying in Pictures.* New York: Putnam, 1930. First edition, small 4to., 2 volumes, very good with little soiling to boards.   Beasley Books   2013 - 2015 $40

Puzo, Mario *The Godfather.* New York: Fawcett Crest, n.d., 1972-1974. First Movie edition and first TV edition, each with the same 36 page section of black and white photos, with signed bookplate, 2 volumes, small edge nick at bottom of front cover of movie version, otherwise both copies near fine and unread perfect-bound paperbacks.   Buckingham Books   March 2015 - 10990   2015 $250

Puzo, Mario *The Last Don.* New York: Random House, 1996. First edition, very fine in dust jacket, signed by author.   Mordida Books   March 2015 - 005504   2015 $100

Pye, Henry James *Sketches on Various Subjects; Moral, Literary and Political.* London: printed for J. Bell, 1797. Second edition, 8vo., half title, occasional minor foxing, paper generally lightly found throughout, contemporary sheep, neatly rebacked to match, flat spine gilt with morocco label lettered gilt, very good, from the 19th century library of Rev. William Long with his armorial bookplate.   John Drury Rare Books   March 2015 - 25402   2015 $656

Pyle, Howard *Howard Pyle's Book of Pirates.* New York: Harper & Bros., 1921. KV. First edition, early printing, folio, full brown morocco stamped in gold with gold decoration, top edge gilt, fine in original publisher's box with printed label stamped 'full morocco' (box flaps repaired), this copy boldly signed by Percival Hart, most likely the distinguished WWI hero.   Aleph-bet Books, Inc.   109 - 394   2015 $1800

Pyle, Howard *Pepper & Salt or Seasoning for Young Folk.* New York: Harper & Bros., 1885. First edition, 4to., cloth, decorated front cover, frontispiece, illustrations by author, covers soiled and rubbed, scuffed at edges.   Oak Knoll Books   306 - 39   2015 $125

Pynchon, Thomas   1937- *Bleeding Edge.* New York: Penguin Press, 2013. Advance reading copy,, fine in wrappers.   Ken Lopez, Bookseller   164 - 173   2015 $750

Pynchon, Thomas   1937- *Gravity's Rainbow.* New York: Viking Press, 1973. First edition, octavo, original orange cloth, original dust jacket, near fine with creasing to small section of text block, dust jacket price clipped and with small ink number (1049) written on front flap, otherwise dust jacket remarkably bright and fine with no edgewear, beautiful copy.   Manhattan Rare Book Company   Literature 2014 - 2015 $2300

Pyne, William Henry   1769-1843 *W. H. Pyne on Rustic Figures in Imitation of Chalk.* London: A. Ackermann, 1813. First edition, 4to., 36 engraved plates, all printed on heavy wove paper watermarked 1809, first two pages with thin streak of staining to foremargin, plates are all excellent impressions, 3 plates with imprints partially cropped, very few small spots or soil marks, original calf over boards, these rather soiled, corners and edges worn, rebacked, binding sound, internally very good state of preservation, very rare.   John Drury Rare Books   2015 - 25338   2015 $1311

Q

Quaife, M. M. *Yellowstone Kelly The Memoirs of Luther S. Kelly.* Yale University Press, 1926. First edition, 8vo., cloth, frontispiece, illustrations, fine, bright, tight copy in dust jacket with light wear to corners, small closed tear to bottom edge of front panel and small closed tear to top edge of rear panel. handsome copy.   Buckingham Books   March 2015 - 32329   2015 $250

Quaw, James E.   *The Cold Water Man; or a Pocket Companion for the Temperate.*   Albany: printed by Packard and Van Benthuysen, 1832. First edition, 12mo., original blue muslin binding, printed yellow paper spine label, some general foxing to contents, with printed yellow paper spine label, some general foxing to contents, period pencil inscription to front endpaper, only some occasional mild wear to board, else very nice.   Tavistock Books   Temperance - 2015 $250

Quayle, Eric   *The Collector's Book of Books.*   New York: Potter, 1971. First American edition, fine in dust jacket.   Mordida Books   March 2015 - 010984   2015 $100

Quayle, Eric   *The Collector's Book of Detective Fiction.*   London: Studio Vista, 1972. First edition, staining on top of covers, otherwise fine in price clipped dust jacket, inscribed by author.   Mordida Books   March 2015 - 007598   2015 $140

Queen, Ellery, Pseud.   *The Detective Short Story: a Bibliography.*   Boston: Little Brown, 1942. First edition, small stamp and inked numbers on front endpaper, else fine in dust jacket, one of 1060 copies.   Mordida Books   March 2015 - 012710   2015 $500

Queen, Ellery, Pseud.   *The Detective Short Story: a Bibliography.*   New York: Biblio and Tannen, 1969. Reprint edition, very fine in dust jacket.   Mordida Books   March 2015 - 011083   2015 $85

Queen, Ellery, Pseud.   *The Dragon's Teeth.*   New York: Stokes, 1939. First edition, staining on covers, otherwise very good in dust jacket with internal tape mends and external tape mend lower corner front panel, several closed tears, nicks at base of spine.   Mordida Books   March 2015 - 009151   2015 $200

Queen, Ellery, Pseud.   *The Female of the Species.*   Boston: Little Brown, 1943. First edition, small bookplate, fine in dust jacket with slightly faded spine and several short closed tears.   Mordida Books   March 2015 - 007118   2015 $85

Queen, Ellery, Pseud.   *Halfway House. A Problem in Deduction.*   Frederick A. Stokes, 1936. First edition, fine in dust jacket with some light professional restoration at spine ends and fore-corners, attractive copy.   Buckingham Books   March 2015 - 38266   2015 $875

Queen, Ellery, Pseud.   *The King is Dead.*   Boston: Little Brown, 1952. First edition, fine in price clipped dust jacket with internal tape mends and couple of crease tears on front panel.   Mordida Books   March 2015 - 009971   2015 $85

Queen, Ellery, Pseud.   *Queen's Quorum: a History of the Detective: Crime Short Story as Revealed by the 106 Most Important Books Published in this Field Since 1845.*   Boston: Little Brown, 1951. First edition, very fine in dust jacket.   Mordida Books   March 2015 - 012711   2015 $500

Quentin, Colonel   *The Trial of Colonel Quentin of the Tenth or Prince of Wales's Own Regiment of Hussars by a General Court Martial Held at Whitehall on Monday the 17th of October ...*   London: Gale Curtis and Fenner and Egerton, 1814. First edition, wanting half title, large folding chart bound in after page 218, slightly later black half calf gilt, over marbled boards, marbled edges, fine.   John Drury Rare Books   March 2015 - 19972   2015 $221

Quentin, Patrick   *Puzzle for Pilgrims.*   New York: Simon and Schuster, 1947. First edition, long inscription, fine in dust jacket.   Buckingham Books   March 2015 - 9667   2015 $275

Quercy De Fronsac, Blanche   *Metamorphoses.*   Paris: Les Editions Du Livre De Plantin, 1949. One of 100 numbered copies, this #87 signed by artist, unbound signatures laid into wrappers, folio, 10 engravings + a suite of the 10 engravings in brown, fine in fine wrappers and glassine, in blindstamped+ chemise in very good box bit soiled.   Beasley Books   2013 - 2015 $225

Querry, Ron   *The Death of Bernadette Lefthand.*   Santa Fe: Red Crane, 1993. First edition, very fine in dust jacket.   Mordida Books   March 2015 - 001874   2015 $100

Questions and Answers to American Trade Unionists.   New York: Workers Library, 1927. First edition, wrappers, very good+ to near fine.   Beasley Books   2013 - 2015 $45

Quick, Herbert *Double Trouble or Every Hero His Own Villain.* Indianapolis: Bobbs Merrill, 1906. First edition, single title dos-a-dos, advance promotional copy, illustrations by Orson Lowell, attractive decorated covers and spine, bright, very good, some little wear spots, here and there, but bright decorations.   Stephen Lupack   March 2015 - 2015 $60

Quiller Couch, Arthur Thomas   1863-1944 *In Powder and Crinoline.* London: Hodder & Stoughton, n.d., 1913. First trade edition, first issue, bound in pictorial boards instead of cloth, 4to., cloth backed pictorial boards, nearly as new in publisher's pictorial box with mounted color plate, light soil and wear to box, illustrations by Kay Nielsen with 24 tipped in color plates and pictorial tissue guards, pictorial endpapers, text decorations, incredible copy, magnificent book, rarely found with original box.   Aleph-bet Books, Inc.   109 - 330   2015 $2500

Quillet, Claude *Callipaedia or the Art of Getting Pretty Children.* London: printed for Bernard Lintott, 1710. First edition in English, small 8vo., five inserted copperplate engravings, bound in full blindstamped revent calf, gilt lettered red morocco spine label, small scrape to rear cover, some little foxing and staining, otherwise fine.   Second Life Books Inc.   189 - 205   2015 $750

Quillet, Claude *Callipaedia.* London: printed for E. Sanger and E. Curll, 1712. First edition of this translation by Nicholas Rowe, fair, 8vo., recent marbled boards, black leather label, engraved emblematic frontispiece by Martin Vander Gucht, 2 leaves containing 'arguments' of the 4 parts of title poem reversed in binding, otherwise sound.   C. R. Johnson   Foxon R-Z - 845r-z   2015 $383

Quillet, Claude *Callipaedia; or the Art of Getting Beautiful Children.* London: printed for A. Bell, J. Darby, A. Bettesworth, El Curll, J. Pemberton, C. Rivington, J. Hooke, R. Cruttenden, T. Cox, F. Clay, J. Battley and E. Symon, 1720. Reprint of translation by Nicholas Rowe and first published in 1712, 12mo., 4 engraved plates, 12mo., 19th century divinity calf, red morocco label, trifle rubbed, 4 plates by Gerard Vander Gucht, very scarce, very good.   C. R. Johnson   Foxon R-Z - 846r-z   2015 $230

Quinby, Henry Cole *Richard Harding Davis. A Bibliography.* New York: E. P. Dutton, 1924. First edition, one of 1000 copies, 32 photographic plates, dark green cloth, gilt, pages slightly toned, but fine with tattered and cellophane taped printed dust jacket.   Argonaut Book Shop   Holiday Season 2014 - 68   2015 $75

Quincy, Edmund *Where Will It End? a View of Slavery in the United States in Its Agressions and Results.* Providence: Knowles, Anthony & Co., 1863. First separate edition, 12mo., removed, lower blank corner chipped away, piece gone from top margin of title, fore-edge of last leaf frayed all with no loss of text, complete and sound.   M & S Rare Books, Inc.   97 - 285   2015 $125

Quine, Willard Van Orman *Set Theory and its Logic.* Cambridge: Belknap Press, Harvard University, 1963. First edition, inscribed by author, near fine with mild edge soil, minimal cover edgewear in near fine, price clipped dust jacket.   By the Book, L. C.   44 - 30   2015 $1000

Quine, Willard Van Orman *The Time of My Life.* Cambridge: MIT Press, 1985. First edition, signed and inscribed by author, fine in very good++ dust jacket with minimal sun spine, edge wear, 8vo.   By the Book, L. C.   44 - 29   2015 $650

Quint, Howard H. *The Forging of American Socialism, Origins of the Modern Movement.* Columbia: University of SC Press, 1953. First edition, fine in very good dust jacket with tears and darkened spine.   Beasley Books   2013 - 2015 $45

Quintilian *Epitome Fabii Quintiliani Nuper Summo & Ingenio & Diligentia Collecta...* Paris: apud Simonem Colinaeum, 1531. First edition, little minor spotting, early ownership inscription to foot of titlepage (dated 1609 but faded almoste beyond elgibility), 8vo., late 19th century burgundy straight grained morocco by Simier, boards bordered with gilt fillet enclosing blind roll, spine divided by raised bands ruled with double gilt fillets, second compartment and foot gilt lettered direct, rest with central tools, marbled endpapers, just touch rubbed at extremities, very good, very pleasant.   Blackwell's Rare Books   Greek & Latin Classics VI - 87   2015   £1500

Quintilian *Institutionum Oratioriarum Libri XII. Diligentius Recogniti MDXXII. Index capitum Totius Operis.* Venice: in aedibus Aldi et Andreae Soceri, 1521. Second Aldine edition, one small wormhole in text of first 30 and last 60 leaves (often touching a character but without loss of legibility), scattering of other small holes in margins of first and last 30 leaves, light browning at beginning and end, faint marginal dampmark to early leaves, some old marginal notes and underlining, inscriptions to title (one struck through, one dated 1630, slightly abraded, third a nineteenth century gift inscription - From James Heming to Rev. Dr. R. J. Bryce), 4to., 18th century calf, scratched and marked, corners worn, sometime serviceably rebacked, backstrip with five raised bands, red labels in second and last compartments, new endpapers, sound.   Blackwell's Rare Books   Greek & Latin Classics VI - 86   2015   £550

Raine, William MacLeod *The Black Tolts.* Boston: Houghton Mifflin Co., 1932. First edition, very good, bright, dust jacket with light wear to head and toe of spine and to extremities. Buckingham Books   March 2015 - 13431   2015 $250

Raines, C. W. *Six Decades in Texas or Memoirs of Francis Richard Lubbock, Governor of Texas in War time 1861-1863.* Ben C. Jones & Co., 1900. First edition, 8vo., two-tone red leather and black cloth, titles stamped in gilt on front cover and spine, Texas Star stamped in gold gilt on front cover, frontispiece, full page engravings and etchings, blue and green floral patterned endpaper is present at rear flyleaf but missing from front fly leaf, former owner's inked name on front flyleaf, moderate wear to cloth edges, spine panel lightly rubbed, else good, internally clean. Buckingham Books   March 2015 - 33805   2015 $405

Rainey, Lee *East Broad Top.* San Marion: Golden West Books, 1948. First edition 2nd printing, quarto, profusely illustrated with maps and many photos, black cloth, gilt, very fine, pictorial dust jacket.   Argonaut Book Shop   Holiday Season 2014 - 242   2015 $60

Rainsford, William Stephen *The Land of the Lion.* New York: Doubleday, Page and Co., 1909. First edition, green cloth, 8vo., gold stamping on spine, frontispiece, top edge gilt, numerous illustrations, folding map, light worn at fore-edges and wear to head and toe of spine, else very good. Buckingham Books   March 2015 - 22714   2015 $825

Raleigh, Walter   1552-1618 *The Poems.* London: Constable & Co., 1929. Half title, uncut, original red buckram, slightly dulled, top edge gilt, Kathleen Tillotson's copy signed Kathleen M. Constable, June 14 1929 with few pencil marks, review from Sat. rev. 1929 and article about new ms. 1925 inserted.   Jarndyce Antiquarian Booksellers   CCVII - 442   2015   £20

Ralph, James *Night: a Poem.* London: printed by C. Ackers for S. Billinglsey, 1728. First edition, 8vo., recent half dark green morocco and marbled boards, light stains to few leaves at beginning, but very good.   C. R. Johnson   Foxon R-Z - 817r-z   2015 $1149

Ralph, James *The Touch-Stone or Historical, Critical, Political, Philosophical and Theological Essays on the Reigning Diversions of the Town.* printed and sold by the booksellers of London and Westminster, 1728. First edition, woodcut initials, head and tailpieces, bit browned and spotted in places, apparently lacking a half title, 12mo., 19th century half calf, flat spine gilt in compartments, red lettering piece, skillfully rebacked, booklabel inside front cover of Mr. B. Warren, sound.   Blackwell's Rare Books   B179 - 85   2015   £950

Ramana, C. V. *On the Early History and Development of Psychoanalysis in India.* 1964. First separate appearance, 29 pages, printed rectos only, fine.   Beasley Books   2013 - 2015 $85

A Ramble thro'Hyde Park; or the Humours of the Camp, a Poem. London: printed for T. Payne, 1722. First edition, 8vo., disbound, outer margins trimmed trifle close, without loss, otherwise very good, rare.   C. R. Johnson   Foxon R-Z - 818r-z   2015 $2681

Rampazzo, Antonio Carlos *Cores Neutras.* Sao Paulo: Grafistyl Editora Grafica Ltd., 1977. First edition, 4to., wrappers, illustrations, Portuguese text, very slight edge-wear, otherwise very good.   Any Amount of Books   2015 - A76409   2015   £180

Rampersad, Arnold *The Life of Langston Hughes.* New York: Oxford, 1986-1988. First printing, 2 volumes, 8vo., author's presentation on title, paper over boards, cloth spines, nice set, dust jackets little scuffed.   Second Life Books Inc.   191 - 81   2015 $100

Ramsay, Alexander *The Scientific Roll and Magazine of Systematized Notes. Volume I. Climate. Parts I & II. Nos. 1-10.* London: Bradbury Agnew & Co., 1882. Single collected edition of magazine's first volume, 8vo., 308 pages, diagrams, navy cloth, gilt stamped spine title, spine chipped around hinges and ends, inner hinges cracked, f.f.ep. starting, former library copy with usual markings, good.   Jeff Weber Rare Books   178 - 924   2015 $50

Ramsay, Allan   1688-1758 *Poems by Allan Ramsay. (with) Poems by Allan Ramsay. Volume II.* Edinburgh: printed by Thomas Ruddiman, 1721. 1728. First edition, 2 volumes, 4to., contemporary tree calf, spines gilt, red morocco labels and circular numbering pieces (one upper joint cracked, but strong), subscriber's set with armorial bookplate of Earl of Moray in each volume, particularly attractive set, modern booklabels of Douglas Grant, old invoice laid in reveals he acquired the set from John Grant Booksellers, Ltd. of Edinburgh in 1956.   C. R. Johnson   Foxon R-Z - 819r-z   2015 $3831

Ramsay, Allan   1688-1758 *Poems.* London: printed for J. Clarke, A. Millar, F. Cogan, R. Willock and S. Palmer and J. Huggonson, 1731. First London edition, 2 volumes, small 8vo., contemporary calf, gilt, worn, one front cover loose, one red morocco label missing, fair.   C. R. Johnson   Foxon R-Z - 820r-z   2015 $153

Ramsay, Allan   1688-1758 *Robert, Richy and Sandy. A Pastoral on the Death of Matthew Prior, Esq.* London: printed by S. Palmer for Bernard Lintot and sold by J. Roberts, 1721. First edition, 19 pages, 8vo., disbound, very good, half title, variant with A4 signed "A2".   C. R. Johnson   Foxon R-Z - 821r-z   2015 $6129

Ramsden, Lewis *The Temple of Fire.* London and Glasgow: Collins Clear Type Press, n.d., 1905. First edition, octavo, 6 inserted plates, titlepage printed in orange and black, original pictorial bevel edged blue cloth, front and spine panels stamped in black green, brown, orange and gold, maroon coated endpapers.   L. W. Currey, Inc.   Boy's Adventure Fiction 2015 - 26   2015 $350

Rand, Ayn *Atlas Shrugged.* New York: Random House, 1957. First edition, first printing, publisher's green cloth with author's initials stamped to front board in gilt, original pictorial dust jacket lettered in white and pink, fine, unclipped dust jacket with some light wear and rubbing to extremities bright and unfaded spine, tiny nick to front hinge, fresh panels, superb copy.   B & B Rare Books, Ltd.   2015 - 2015 $3000

Rand, Ayn *The Fountainhead.* Indianapolis: Bobbs Merrill, 1943. First edition thus, movie edition, yellow label to front panel of dust jacket, near fine, blue boards with light soil to top edge in very good plus to near fine sharp clean dust jacket with $3.00 printed price, housed in custom sturdy cloth clamshell case with gilt lettering on front panel.   Ed Smith Books   82 - 21   2015 $375

Randall, Isabella *A Lady's Ranche Life in Montana.* London: W. H. Allen & Co., 1887. First edition, 16mo., original light blue cloth, titles stamped in gold on front cover and spine, black front and rear endpapers, laid in is a 2 page mimeographed poem that was published in the Bozeman Avant Carrier April 25, 1889, recased with original cloth laid down, spine panel darkened, light wear to spine ends, former owner's bookplate, former owner's inked name and date on verso of front fly leaf, else very good copy housed in cloth clamshell case with titles stamped in gilt on spine.   Buckingham Books   March 2015 - 33324   2015 $875

Randall, James *A Philosophical Inquiry on the Cause with directions to Cure the Dry Rot in Buildings.* London: printed for the author and sold by J. Taylor at the Architectural Library High Holborn, 1807. First edition, 8vo., half title and final ad leaf, original wrappers, spine neatly repaired, entirely uncut, fine, very rare.   John Drury Rare Books   2015 - 21912   2015 $787

Randall, W. *The State of the Hop Plantations, Including a Candid Review of the Disputes Between the Old and New Hop merchants...* London: printed by C. Whittingham for H. D. Symonds and J. Walker Maidstone, 1800. Only edition, of great rarity, 8vo., errata leaf, 2 extended folding tables of data, well bound in 20th century morocco backed boards, spine lettered gilt, very good.   John Drury Rare Books   2015 - 26302   2015 $3060

Randall, W. David *The Official Pullman Standard Library. Volume 2.* Godfrey: Railway Production Classics, 1987. First edition, number 609 of limited edition, oblong quarto, photos, detailed elevations and floor plans, internal metal-comb binding with publisher's red leatherette covers gilt, owner's ink name top border of titlepage, fine.   Argonaut Book Shop   Holiday Season 2014 - 245   2015 $150

Randall, W. David *The Official Pullman Standard Library. Volume 4: Pennsylvania Railroad.* Godfrey: Railway Production Classics, 1988. First edition, number 795 of limited edition, scarce, oblong quarto, 165 pages, photos, detailed elevations and floor plans, in ternal metal-comb binding with publisher's red leatherette covers, gilt, owner's ink name to top border of titlepage, fine.   Argonaut Book Shop   Holiday Season 2014 - 246   2015 $150

Randall, W. David *The Passenger Car Library. Volume 2: New York Central Northeast Railroads.* Alton: RPC Publications, 2000. First edition, limited edition, #920, photos, detailed elevations and floor plans, stiff red card stock covers, gilt, plastic spiral spine, owner's ink name top of titlepage, some minor rubbing, light crease to front cover, else fine.   Argonaut Book Shop   Holiday Season 2014 - 243   2015 $60

Rank, Otto *The Don Juan Legend.* Princeton: Princeton University, 1975. First edition, fine in fine dust jacket.   Beasley Books   2013 - 2015 $45

Rankin, Ian *Black and Blue.* London: Orion, 1997. First edition, signed by author on titlepage, fine and unread in fine dust jacket, from the collection of Duke Collier.   Royal Books 36 - 90   2015 $550

Rankin, Ian *Blood Hunt.* London: Headline, 1995. First edition, fine in fine dust jacket.   Mordida Books   March 2015 - 008443   2015 $750

Rankin, Ian *The Flood.* London: Polygon, 1986. First edition, signed by author on titlepage, fine in fine dust jacket, from the collection of Duke Collier.   Royal Books   36 - 88   2015 $2500

Rankin, Ian *The Flood.* Edinburgh: Polygon, 1986. First edition, signed by author, fine in dust jacket, author's first book.   Buckingham Books   March 2015 - 25118   2015 $2500

Rankin, Ian *A Good Hanging and Other Stories.* London: Century, 1992. First edition, fine in fine dust jacket.   Buckingham Books   March 2015 - 27704   2015 $200

Rankin, Ian *Hide and Seek.* London: Barrie and Jenkins, 1991. First edition, fine and unread in fine dust jacket, only hint of usual toning to page edges, inscribed by author for Duke Collier with drawing of hangman motif. Royal Books 36 - 94   2015 $450

Rankin, Ian *Hide and Seek.* London: Barrie & Jenkins, 1991. First edition, fine dust jacket. Mordida Books March 2015 - 007138   2015 $700

Rankin, Ian *Knots and Crosses.* Garden City: Doubleday, 1987. First American edition, signed by author along with his trademark 'knots-and-crosses' drawing, fine and unread in near fine dust jacket, just hint of fading to red titles on jacket spine, from the collection of Duke Collier. Royal Books 36 - 87   2015 $550

Rankin, Ian *Knots and Crosses.* London: Bodley Head, 1987. First edition, fine and unread in fine dust jacket, absolutely none of the usual fading at spine panel, inscribed by author for Duke (Collier). Royal Books 36 - 86   2015 $2750

Rankin, Ian *Let It Bleed.* London: Orion, 1995. First edition, signed by author on titlepage along with his trademark knots and crosses drawing, fine and unread in fine dust jacket, from the collection of Duke Collier. Royal Books 36 - 89   2015 $800

Rankin, Ian *The Naming of the Dead.* Gladestry: Scorpion Press, 2006. first edition, limited to 80 numbered copies signed by author, fine in quarter leather and marbled boards, transparent dust jacket. Buckingham Books March 2015 - 24524   2015 $165

Rankin, Ian *Strip Jack.* London: Orion, 1992. First edition, signed by author with his hangman motif, near fine in fine dust jacket, none of the usual to page edges present, jacket is export variant, with no price to front flap, from the collection of Duke Collier. Royal Books 36 - 93   2015 $450

Rankin, Ian *Watchman.* London: Bodley Head, 1988. First edition, fine and unread in fine dust jacket with none of the usual fading to red titling on jacket spine, from the collection of Duke Collier. Royal Books 36 - 92   2015 $450

Rankin, Ian *Westwind.* London: Barrie and Jenkins, 1990. First edition, fine and unread in about fine dust jacket, jacket fine but for tiniest crease to one corner of crown, from the collection of Duke Collier. Royal Books 36 - 95 2015 $325

Rankin, Ian *Wolfman.* London: Century, 1992. First edition, fine and unread in fine dust jacket, quite scarce, from the collection of Duke Collier. Royal Books 36 - 91 2015 $550

Rankin, J. E. *Hymns Pro Patria and Other Hymns, Christian and Humanitarian.* New York: John R. Alden, 1889. First edition, tall octavo, brown cloth decorated in black and gilt, bookplate of Byron N. Clark, second bookplate partly effaced, crease on two leaves, else tight, near fine copy, inscribed by author to NJ author Gen. Oliver O. Howard. Between the Covers Rare Books, Inc.   187 - 228 2015 $175

Ranney, Edward *Macchu Picchu Suite.* New York: Limited Editions Club, 1999. First edition, one of 60 number sets plus 14 proofs, 3 leaves of letterpress and 11 photogravures, each numbered and signed by photographer, leaves 43.5 x 36cm., publisher's velvet lined cloth clamshell box, inlaid brown morocco label titled in gilt on front board, box lightly rubbed, else fine. Kaaterskill Books   19 - 130 2015 $2250

Ransome, Arthur *Aladdin and His Wonderful Lamp in Rhyme by...* London: Nisbet, n.d., 1919. Limited to 250 numbered copies, signed by artist, large 4to., white cloth with elaborate gilt pictorial cover, top edge gilt, others uncut, some slight cover soil and fading, 2 tiny snags on cover, 12 magnificent tipped in color plates by Thomas MacKenzie with captioned tissue guards. Aleph-Bet Books, Inc.   108 - 280   2015 $5500

Ransome, Arthur *The Big Six.* London: Jonathan Cape, 1940. First edition, octavo, 400 pages, illustrations by author, endpaper maps, very good in very good marked dust jacket nicked, rubbed and creased and edges. Peter Ellis, Bookseller   2014 - 019392   2015   £300

Ranson, John Crowe *Selected Poems.* New York: Alfred A. Knopf, 1963. Second edition, fine in very near fine dust jacket with very slight wear, Lionel Trilling's copy with his ownership signature. Between the Covers Rare Books, Inc.   187 - 229   2015 $85

Rapaport, David *Diagnostic Psychological Testing.* New York: IUP, 1968. First edition, fine in close to fine dust jacket. Beasley Books   2013 - 2015 $45

Raposo, Jose *The Sesame Street Song Book.* New York: Simon & Schuster, 1971. First edition, near fine with few mild rubbed spots to rear board, very good+ dust jacket with some mild signs of wear, 4to., very nice. Beasley Books   2013 - 2015 $85

Rappaport, Philip *Looking Forward a Treatise on the Status of Woman and the Origin and Growth of the Family and the State.* Chicago: Kerr, 1908. First edition, 8vo., scarce. Second Life Books Inc.   189 - 207   2015 $65

Rasch, Rudolf *De Cantiones Natalitiae en Het Kerkelijke Muziekleven in de Zuidelijke Nederlanden Gedurende de Zeventiende Eeuw.* Utrecht: Vereniging voor Nederlandse Muziekgeschiedenis, 1985. 2 volumes, 8vo., stiff paper wrappers, black and white illustrations, spines sunned. Oak Knoll Books 306 - 290 2015 $125

Rashed, Roshdi *Histoire des Sciences Arabes.* Paris: editions du Seuil, 1997. 3 volumes, 8vo., illustrations, cloth, dust jackets bit rubbed, author's copy, very good, David C. Lindberg's copy. Jeff Weber Rare Books 178 - 935 2015 $100

Raskin, Ellen *The Westing Game.* New York: Dutton, 1978. Stated first edition, 8vo., quarter cloth and boards, fine in very good+ dust jacket (slight wear to spine ends, price clipped). Aleph-Bet Books, Inc. 108 - 387 2015 $350

Raspe, Rudolf Erich 1737-1794 *The Travels and Surprising Adventures of Baron Munchausen.* New York: World Pub., 1877. Near fine, tight copy, illustrations by Aflred Crowquill. Stephen Lupack March 2015 - 2015 $45

Ratcliffe, Stephen *Talking in Tranquility. Interviews with Ted Berrigan.* Bolinas: Avenue B/O Books, 1991. First edition, 8vo., original pictorial wrappers, fine. James S. Jaffe Rare Books Many Happy Returns - 67 2015 $75

Rathbone, Irene *We That Were Young.* London: Chatto & Windus, 1932. First edition, 8vo., signed by author and dated 1932, original brown cloth lettered gilt at spine, clean, very good with very slight marks and slight rubbing. Any Amount of Books 2015 - C8446 2015 £175

Rathman, Peggy *Officer Buckle and Gloria.* New York: Putnam, 1995. Stated first impression, 4to., pictorial boards, fine in dust jacket, bookplate signed by author laid in, illustrations by Rathman. Aleph-bet Books, Inc. 109 - 407 2015 $125

Rattray, David *A Red-Framed Print of the Summer Palace. Poems with Drawings by Peter Thompson.* New York: Vincent FitzGerald & Co., 1983. One of an edition of 150 on Hosho paper, signed in pencil by author and artist, printed at the Wild Carrot Letterpress employing Palatino type, titlepage calligraphy, printed on Moriki paper at Meriden Gravure Co., bound by Gerard Charriere and Carol Joyce, page size 6 x 8 1/2 inches, red linen with gray title label, title printed in silver, fine, titlepage printed in red and black with publisher's monogram VFG facsimiles of four drawings by Peter Thompson in pencil, pen and grey and green washes. Priscilla Juvelis - Rare Books 61 - 15 2015 $350

Rattray, David *To the Blue Wall.* New York: Vincent FitzGerald & Co., 1993. One of only 50 copies, all on Rives BFK and Dieu Donne' handmade paper, each signed and numbered by artist, page size 9 x 9 inches, bound by Zahra Partovi, wood maple covers by Dennis FitzGerald, Coptic style binding, opening to full circle, housed in custom box by BookLab, Inc., fine, etchings editioned by Marjorie Van Dyke and Vincent FitzGerald, very beautiful. Priscilla Juvelis - Rare Book 61 - 16 2015 $2500

Rau, Margaret *The Band of the Red Hand.* Alfred A. Knopf, 1938. First edition, fine, bright, square copy in fine dust jacket with light foxing and few tiny nicks to top edge of rear cover, illustrations by Joseph Low. Buckingham Books March 2015 - 38454 2015 $275

Raven, Simon *Brother Cain.* London: Blond, 1959. First edition, fine in dust jacket. Mordida Books March 2015 - 005546 2015 $100

Ravennes, Jean *La vie De Marie.* Paris: La Reue Francais, 1928. No. 203 of 300 copies, signed by Ravennes, 4to., unbound signatures laid into wrappers, watercolors by Vallieres and colored woodcuts by Gusman and Baudier, fine in fine wrappers, glassine has little wear at foot of spine, spine darkened chemise and box. Beasley Books 2013 - 2015 $500

Ravensclough, Arthur *The Journal of Commonwealth Literature. Volumes 1-8 September 1965-December 1969.* Leeds: Heinemann/University of Leeds, 1965-1969. First edition, 8vo., wrappers, decent, sound, very good copies with slight handling and shelfwear. Any Amount of Books 2015 - A35467 2015 £150

Ravizzotti, Gaetano *Viridarium Latinum; ou, Recuiel des Pensees et Bons-Mots le plus Remarquables, Tires des Plus Illustres Orateurs, Poetes, et Autres Ecrivains, tant Grecs que Latins.* L'Imprimerie de W. et C. Spilsbury, Snowhill, 1801. First edition, titlepage (a cancel) signed by author to prevent piracy, poor quality paper browned and foxed throughout, 8vo., contemporary brown cloth, black lettering piece to spine, cloth slightly bubbled, touch of wear to extremities, scarce. Blackwell's Rare Books Greek & Latin Classics VI - 67 2015 £400

Rawlings, Marjorie Kinnan *The Yearling.* New York: Charles Scribner's Sons, 1939. A. Limited to only 750 copies for sale, signed by Wyeth and Rawlings, 4to. bluish green cloth, top edge gilt, fine in matching chemise with leather label and publisher's blue slipcase (slightly rubbed on edges, else sound and very good+), only 520 copies were actually bound and sent out, with binding chemise and slipcase of this version, this copy with corrected pages, 14 full page color illustrations, titlepage decoration, plus 2 special charcoal and wash full page illustrations done for this limited edition, included is facsimile of 2 page letter by Wyeth discussing the book, very scarce. Aleph-bet Books, Inc. 109 - 493 2015 $4250

Rawnsley, Hardwicke Drummond *Reminiscences of Wordsworth Among the Peasantry of Westmoreland.* London: Dillon's, 1968. Frontispiece, original pink cloth, slightly marked, very good in slightly rubbed dust jacket, Kathleen Tillotson's copy with correspondence, reviews &c. inserted. Jarndyce Antiquarian Booksellers CCVII - 578 2015 £30

Rawson, Clayton *Death from a Top Hat.* New York: G. P. Putnam's Sons, 1938. First edition, spine lightly faded, else very good without dust jacket. Buckingham Books March 2015 - 30176 2015 $225

Ray, Gordon N. *Books as a Way of Life: Essays...* New York: Grolier Club, Pierpont Morgan Library, 1988. Frontispiece, original red cloth, from the library of Geoffrey & Kathleen Tillotson, very good in slightly marked dust jacket, with inserted ALS from editor thanking Kathleen for her generous appreciations. Jarndyce Antiquarian Booksellers CCVII - 443 2015 £20

Ray, Gordon N. *The Illustrator and the Book in England from 1790 to 1914.* New York: Pierpont Morgan Lib., 1976. 4to., color frontispiece, plates, illustrations, original dark wrappers, decorated gilt, spine slightly faded, Kathleen Tillotson's signed copy recording it as gift from author, with cutting of TLS review inserted. Jarndyce Antiquarian Booksellers CCVII - 444 2015 £25

Ray, Gordon N. *Nineteenth Century English Books...* Urbana: University of Illinois Press, 1952. Half title, title in red and black, original red and grey cloth, from the library of Geoffrey & Kathleen Tillotson, Geoffrey Tillotson's copy for Review of English Studies with pencil notes and copy of his review inserted, and other reviews, TLS from Gordon Ray to Tillotson's Jan. 1953 inserted. Jarndyce Antiquarian Booksellers CCVII - 445 2015 £25

Ray, Gordon N. *Thackeray: the Age of Wisdom 1847-1863.* New York: McGraw Hill, 1958. Half title, plates, original maroon cloth, very good in torn dust jacket, from the library of Geoffrey & Kathleen Tillotson, author's presentation for them. Jarndyce Antiquarian Booksellers CCVII - 501 2015 £20

Rayleigh, John William Strutt, 3rd Baron 1842-1919 *Scientific Papers.* Cambridge: University Press, 1899-1920. First collected edition, 6 volumes, tall 8vo., 6 plates, index, original maroon blind and gilt stamped cloth, lightly rubbed. Jeff Weber Rare Books 178 - 1050 2015 $450

Rayleigh, John William Strutt, 3rd Baron 1842-1919 *The Theory of Sound.* London and New York: Macmillan, 1894. Second edition, 8vo., original olive green blind and gilt stamped cloth, bottom corner bumped, near fine. Jeff Weber Rare Books 178 - 1048 2015 $175

Raymond, Clifford *Four Corners.* New York: Doran, 1921. First edition, covers spotted otherwise very good in dust jacket with light staining on back panel, nicks along edges and wear at corners and along folds. Mordida Books March 2015 - 001885 2015 $175

Raymond, Derek *He Died with His Eyes Open.* London: Secker & Warburg, 1984. First edition, 8vo., scarce, fine in near fine dust jacket with faint unobjectionable marking at edges of front inner flap. Any Amount of Books 2015 - A92441 2015 £220

Raymond, Dora Neill *Captain Lee Hall of Texas.* Norman: University of Oklahoma Press, 1940. First edition, 8vo., decorated cloth, illustrations by Louis Lundean and Frederic Remington, fine, tight copy in dust jacket with moderate wear to spine ends and extremities. Buckingham Books March 2015 - 30942 2015 $185

Read, Herbert *Collected Poems.* London: Faber & Faber Ltd., 1946. First edition, sunned at spine ends, else near fine in about very good dust jacket with corresponding chips at spine ends, inscribed, but not signed, by author to Huntington Cairns. Between the Covers Rare Books, Inc. 187 - 230 2015 $250

Read, Herbert *Surrealism.* New York: Harcourt n.d., First U.S. edition, orange cloth, lacking dust jacket, near fine. Beasley Books 2013 - 2015 $45

Reasons Against National Despondency: in Refutation of Mr. Erskine's View of the Causes and Consequences of the Present War. London: T. Cadell Jun and W. Davies successors to Mr. Cadell, 1797. First edition, 8vo., half title (dust soiled and frayed at fore-edge), contemporary sheep backed marbled card covers, generally bit worn, overall very good, ownership inscription of church library 1846. John Drury Rare Books March 2015 - 17903 2015 $221

Reasons Why They Should Not Grant Their Immediate Consent to the Petition of the Committee of the Union Canal from Leicester by Harborough to Northampton. London?: 1793. Only edition, 4to., large folding engraved map, small oval inkstamp of Hereford Public Library in several blank margins, nowhere touching printed surfaces, very good, crisp copy, printed on thick paper, original, but carefully repaired plain blue wrappers, rare. John Drury Rare Books 2015 - 21701 2015 $612

Rebello, Stephen *The Art of the Hunchback of Notre Dame.* New York: Hyperion, 1996. First edition, this copy signed by 10 members of the production company, including Gary Trousdale and Kirk Wise, artistic coordinator Randy Fullmer, writers Irene Meechi and Tab Murphy and five animators, numerous full color drawings and sketches in black and white, laid in is announcement for book signing party, fine in fine dust jacket. Ed Smith Books 83 - 15 2015 $250

Red Riding Hood. Boston: L. Prang & Co., 1863. Paperback, quite possibly the first shape book printed by American publisher, chromolithographic covers, cover separated from text block with smal tear near a sewing station, clean interior overall with minor dampstain and browning to bottom edges of most pages, minor soiling to some pages, 16 pages, very good.   The Kelmscott Bookshop   11 - 58   2015 $250

Red Riding Hood. New York: McLoughlin Bros., 1891. Large 4to., stiff pictorial card covers, minor rubbing on rear panel, else near fine, die cut in shape of theatre stage which opens from center to reveal full page chromolithographed scenes.   Aleph-bet Books, Inc.   109 - 168   2015 $650

Redgrave, Michael   *The Aspern Papers...*   London: Heinemann, 1959. First edition, fine in very good dust jacket with some rubbing and small chips and tears, famed literary agent Audrey Wood's ownership stamp on front fly, inscribed by Redgrave for Wood.   Between the Covers Rare Books, Inc.   187 - 231   2015 $275

Redmond, Patrick   *The Wishing Game.*   London: Hodder & Stoughton, 1999. First edition, very fine in dust jacket. Mordida Books   March 2015 - 001890   2015 $85

Redtenbacher, Ferdinand   *Geistige Bedeutung der Mechanik und Geschichtliche Skizze der Entdeckung ihrer Principien, Vortag Gehalten i Herbst 1859 von Ferdinand Redtenbacher.*   Munich: Fr. Bassermann, 1879. 8vo., original printed wrappers, extremities chipped, including spine ends, very good.   Jeff Weber Rare Books   178 - 938   2015 $200

Reed, Jeremy   *No Refuge Here.*   N.P. (London): Giels and Jonathan Leaman, 1981. First edition, no. 27 of 40 copies, 4to., original green wrappers, etching (tissue protected) by Giles Leaman, signed by Reed and Leaman, faint creasing otherwise clean, bright, very good+ copy.   Any Amount of Books   2015 - A64979   2015   £180

Reed, Nathaniel   *The Life of Texas Jack.*   Tulsa: Tulsa Printing Co. n.d. circa, 1936. First edition, pictorial wrappers 55 pages, frontispiece, portraits, portrait of author on front cover and titlepage, front and rear covers moderately chipped, words not affected, text tight, very good, rare, four point slipcase, with gilt stamped leather label on spine. Buckingham Books   March 2015 - 16104   2015 $1500

Reed, Peter Fishe   *Beyond the snow: being a History of Trim's Adventures in Nordlichtschein.*   Chicago: Lakeside Press, 1873. First edition, octavo, inserted chromolithograph half title, 12 full page illustrations in text, original pictorial plum cloth, front panel stamped in gold and ruled in blind, spine panel stamped in gold, rear panel stamped in blind, cream coated endpapers.   L. W. Currey, Inc.   Boy's Adventure Fiction 2015 - 27   2015 $350

Reed, Peter Fishe   *Beyond the Snow: Being a History of Trim's Adventures in Nordlichtschein.*   Chicago: Lakeside Press, 1873. First edition, octavo, inserted chromolithograph half title, 12 full page illustrations in text, original pictorial green cloth, front panel stamped in gold and ruled in blind, spine panel stamped in gold, rear panel stamped in blind, cream coated endpapers.   L. W. Currey, Inc.   Boy's Adventure Fiction 2015 - 15   2015 $550

Reed, Walt   *Harold Von Schmidt Draws and Paints the Old West.*   Flagstaff: Northland Press, 1972. First edition, special limited edition of 104 copies, tall quarto, leather and pictorial red cloth, grey endsheets, issued jointly with Von's first sculpture, the bronze is 7 inches high with handsome patina and mounted on light colored marbled base, book and bronze are numbered 96, very fine.   Buckingham Books   March 2015 - 22478   2015 $2000

Reeve, Arthur B.   *Craig Kennedy Listens In.*   New York: Harper, 1923. First edition, pages edges and endpapers darkened, otherwise very good in dust jacket with small chips at spine ends and at corners.   Mordida Books   March 2015 - 007128   2015 $100

Reeve, Clara   *The Old English Babon; a Gothick Story.*   London: Charles Dilly, 1780. Second edition, 12mo., frontispiece, modern calf backed boards, good.   Blackwell's Rare Books   B179 - 86   2015   £250

Reeve, Tapping   *The Law of Baron and Femme.*   New Haven: Oliver Steele, 1816. First US edition, 8vo., errata leaf, modern leather backed boards, some foxing and toning, name on front blank which is lacking lower corner, very good.   Second Life Books Inc.   189 - 108   2015 $600

Reeves, James   *Arcadian Ballads.*   Andoversford: Whittington Press, 1977. Limited to 200 cloth copies and 50 leather copies, numbered and signed by author and artist, this copy cloth copy, label on front cover, slipcase sunned and bumped at edges.   Oak Knoll Books   306 - 179   2015 $175

Reeves, Robert   *Dead and Done For.*   New York: Alfred A. Knopf, 1939. First edition, fine and unread in fine dust jacket, from the collection of Duke Collier.   Royal Books   36 - 224   2015 $400

Regild, Christoffer   *Intense Scotland.*   Copenhagen: Politisk Revy, 2001. First edition, quarto, brilliant color photos by Regild, very small bumps at lower board edges, else fine without dust jacket as issued, uncommon.   Ken Lopez, Bookseller   164 - 175   2015 $200

Reich, Jessie *They Called her Moses.* Aurora: Punky Press, 2013. Artist's book, one of 9 copies available for sale from a total issue of 20 copies, all on Polar white and Black Stonehenge print making paper, each signed and numbered by artist/author, page size 9 1/4 x 8 inches, 16 pages plus 5 inserted double sided leaves printed in grey on black paper on verso with image of location relevant to life of Harriet Tubman on recto, photos of silk-screen printed in grey tones, bound by artist/author - grey cloth over boards drum-leaf style binding with white label letterpress printed in grey on front panel, housed in grey paper envelope. Priscilla Juvelis - Rare Books   63 - 17   2015 $1250

Reichardt, Uwe *Like a Human Voice. The Eric Dolphy Discography.* Schmitten: Norbert Ruecket, 1986. First edition, wrappers, fine but for address on c.p., supplements laid in.   Beasley Books   2013 - 2015 $45

Reichenow, Anton *Vogelbilder aus Fernen zonen.* Kassel: Verlag Von Theodor Fischer, 1878-1883. Folio, 33 chromolithographic (finished by hand) plates, accompanying text leaves, publisher's green blindstamped and gilt cloth, some very minor shelf wear, otherwise fine, crisp copy, tipped in photographic print of author.   Andrew Isles   2015 - 38248   2015 $10,000

Reid, Elizabeth *Mayne Reid. A memoir of his life.* London: Ward and Downey, 1890. Original brown fine diaper cloth, front board with border and central device in black, spine and front board lettered gilt, back board with publisher's monogram in blind, half title, plate, very good. Jarndyce Antiquarian Booksellers   CCXI - 241   2015   £125

Reid, Forrest *The Gentle Lover: a Comedy of Middle Age.* London: Edward Arnold, 1913. First edition, 8vo., original publisher's cloth lettered black on spine and cover, 319 pages, signed presentation from author for Walter de la Mare, superb association, sound, near very good, spine appears to have been rebacked or repaired with consequent slight wear at hinges, endpapers original.   Any Amount of Books   March 2015 - A93277   2015   £450

Reid, Forrest *The Spring Song.* London: Edward Arnold, 1916. First edition, original green cloth lettered dark green on cover and spine, 8vo., bookplate of Warden of All Souls, Oxford the great collector John Sparrow, prelims very slightly foxed, else near fine in near complete, very good- pictorial dust jacket with some loss at middle of spine and some slight browning and slight chipping at edges, image on cover by H. Ryland.   Any Amount of Books   2015 - A91952   2015   £240

Reid, Mayne   1818-1883 *The Death Shot.* London: Ward Lock & Tyler, 1875. Plates, 32 page publisher's catalog, original green pictorial cloth, decorated gilt, spine slightly worn at head and tail, hinges little rubbed, leading inner hinge slightly cracking, signed presentation inscription to Mrs. R. G. Berford dated March 1875.   Jarndyce Antiquarian Booksellers   CCXI - 240   2015   £350

Reid, Peter *Letter addressed to the Right Honourable the Lord provost, Magistrates and Town Council of Edinburgh, Regarding the Institutions of Medicine.* Edinburgh: printed by John Pillans, 1821. First edition, 8vo., 16 pages, few minor spots, preserved in modern wrappers with printed title label, very good, apparently rare outside Scottish libraries. John Drury Rare Books   March 2015 - 24-74   2015   £306

Reik, Theodor *Ritual. Psycho-analytic Studies.* London: Hogarth Press/IPL No. 19, 1931. First edition, very good+ with gilt still bright on spine.   Beasley Books   2013 - 2015 $85

Reilly, James M. *Care and Identification of 19th Century Photographic Prints.* Rochester: Eastman Kodak Co., 1986. 4to., stiff paper wrappers, identification guide laid in, small bend to front wrapper at lower fore-edge corner, previous owner's name stamped on title.   Oak Knoll Books   306 - 291   2015 $100

Relation de ce qui s'est Passe Au Siege de Quebec, et de la Prise Du Canada. Quebec: Imprime au Bureau de Mercury Rue Boade, 1855. Second edition, 12mo., 24 pages, frontispiece, original pink printed wrappers, little wrinkled and soiled, starting at spine end, very scarce.   M & S Rare Books, Inc.   97 - 51   2015 $225

Relph, Josiah *A Miscellany of Poems, Consisting of Original Poems, Translations, Pastorals in the Cumberland Dialect, Familiar Epistles, Fables, Songs and Epigrams.* Glasgow: printed by Robert Foulis for Mr. Thomlinson (Wigton), 1747. First edition, 8vo., contemporary calf, gilt, rebacked, slight foxing, but very good, on front pastedown " E. C. ex dono Dom. Riccardi Hylton de Hylton Castle im. Cmt. Durham Bart" (Sir Richard Hilton sic) appears in list of subscribers for three copies, he sold Hylton Castle in 1749. C. R. Johnson   Foxon R-Z - 823r-z   2015 $460

Remarks on a Letter to Sir John Barnard; In Which the Proposals of the Worthy Patriot are Vindicated, and a Late Important Transaction set in a True Light. London: J. Hinton, 1746. First edition, 8vo. half title, bound fairly recently in overside cloth, spine lettered gilt, very good. John Drury Rare Books   2015 - 21479   2015 $168

Remarks Upon Mr. Webber's Scheme and the Draper's Pamphlet. London: Sold by J. Roberts, 1741. First edition, 8vo., 40 pages, well bound in 19th century dark blue half calf, spine lettered in gilt, very good.   John Drury Rare Books   2015 - 21469   2015 $168

Remarks Upon Mr. Webber's Scheme and the Draper's Pamphlet. London: sold by J. Roberts, 1741. First edition, 8vo., 40 pages, well bound in linen backed marbled boards, lettered, very good.   John Drury Rare Books   2015 - 21470   2015 $133

Remarque, Erich Maria   *All Quiet on the Western Front.* Boston: Little Brown and Company, 1929. First American edition, fine in just about fine dust jacket with two tiny nicks, beautiful copy, from the library of Kate Stettner Lobell and Carl D. Lobell.   Between the Covers Rare Books   196 - 30   2015 $1000

Rembaugh, Bertha   *The Political Status of Women in the United States.*   New York: Putnam, 1911. First edition, 8vo., green cloth, very good, frontispiece, scarce.   Second Life Books Inc.   189 - 209   2015 $300

Remembrances of the Great Exhibition. A Series of Views Beautifully Engraved on Steel from Drawings Made on the Spot.   London: Ackermann & Co., 1851. Oblong 4to., 10 pages, vignette title and 10 numbered engraved plates each measuring 230 x 160mm., occasional spotting, original publisher's elaborately decorated glazed boards printed in blue and gilt, cloth spine, somewhat rubbed.   Marlborough Rare Books Ltd.   List 49 - 16   2015   £950

Remington, Frederic   1861-1909   *Remington's Frontier Sketches.*   Chicago: Akron: New York: The Werner Co., 1898. First edition, oblong 8vo., cream colored, pictorial endpaper over beveled boards, all edges gilt, 15 plates with protective parchment title tissues, covers lightly soiled, text block and illustrated plates, clean and bright, else very good, tight square copy, housed in cloth slipcase with titles stamped in gold gilt on leather label that is affixed to spine. Buckingham Books   March 2015 - 32554   2015 $750

Remington, Frederic   1861-1909   *Remington's Frontier Sketches.*   Chicago: Akron: & New York: Werner Co., 1898. First edition, large oblong 4to., white pictorial boards, beveled edges, all edges gilt, as new in publisher's pictorial box (flaps repaired), most rare, 15 half tone plates with lettered guards, rare in this condition.   Aleph-Bet Books, Inc.   108 - 388   2015 $1500

Rendell, Ruth   *The Best Man to Die.*   London: John Long, 1969. First edition, 8vo., original brown cloth lettered gilt at spine, ex-library worn, lacking front endpaper, slight rubbing at edges and slight creasing with faint wear at spine ends, otherwise close to very good, in clean dust jacket, from the Donald Rudd collection of detective fiction.   Any Amount of Books   2015 - C11965   2015   £160

Rendell, Ruth   *The Face of Trespass.*   Garden City: Doubleday, 1974. First American edition, fine in dust jacket.   Mordida Books   March 2015 - 001923   2015 $75

Rendell, Ruth   *The Secret House of Death.*   Doubleday & Co., 1949. First US edition, fine in lightly soiled dust jacket lightly sunned on spine and minor wear to spine ends. Buckingham Books   March 2015 - 35651   2015 $275

Rennie, John   *Report Concerning the Different Lines Surveyed by Messrs. John Ainslie and Robert Whitworth, Jun. for a Canal, Proposed to be Made Between the cities of Edinburgh and Glasgow...(bound with) Report Concerning the Practicability and Expence of the Lines Surveyed by Messrs. John Ainslie & Robert Whitworth, Jun. for a Canal, Proposed to be Made Between the cities of Edinburgh and Glasgow and Intended to Communiate with the Firth of Fourth at Leith....*   Edinburgh?: 1797. First editions, 4to., 2 reports in one volume, large folding engraved and line colored map composed of two sheets cut close at lower margin, map repaired marginal tear, recent marbled boards, lettered on spine, very good.   John Drury Rare Books   2015 - 24895   2015 $1136

Renny, Robert   *A Demonstration of the Necessity and Advantages of a Free Trade to the East Indies. and of a Termination to the Present Monopoly of the East India Co.*   London: printed for and sold by C. Chapple, J. Ridgway and Others, n.d., 1807. Second edition, 8vo., half title, short closed tear to half title, well bound in modern red quarter morocco over cloth boards, spine gilt lettered, very good. John Drury Rare Books   2015 - 25750   2015 $656

Rentoul, Annie R.   *Fairyland.*   New York: Frederick Stokes, 1929. First American edition, folio, red gilt cloth, pictorial paste-on, slightest bit of soil on corner of cover, else fine, 19 magnificent large color plates, 32 large and incredibly detailed black and white plates plus drawings in text, scarce, particularly bright.   Aleph-Bet Books, Inc.   108 - 327   2015 $3750

Rentoul, Annie R.   *The Lady of the Blue Beads...* Melbourne, et al: George Robertson, 1908. First edition, cloth, near fine, illustrations by Ida Outhwaite, 4to., cloth, near fine, illustrations in black and white with 13 full page and several partial page black and whites.   Aleph-Bet Books, Inc.   108 - 329   2015 $1500

Rentoul, Annie R.   *Little Green Road to Fairyland.* London: A. & C. Black, 1922. 4to., floral patterned boards, pictorial label, slight foxing, else near fine, 8 black and white plates, 8 color plates plus pictorial endpapers by Ida Outhwaite, very scarce, especially in such nice condition. Aleph-Bet Books, Inc.   108 - 328   2015 $1875

Rentoul, Annie R.   *More Australian Songs for Young and Old.*   Melbourne; Sydney: and Adelaide: Allan & Co., n.d., Inscribed 1913? oblong 4to., pictorial wrappers, 36 pages, small margin mend on cover, first few leaves, else very good, pictorial cover and 8 wonderfully detailed full page black and whites and 9 smaller black and whites by Ida Rentoul, very scarce.   Aleph-bet Books, Inc.   109 - 338   2015 $600

Rentoul, Ida R. *Bush Songs of Australia for Young and Old.* Melbourne: Adelaide: Bendigo: Allan & Co., n.d., 1910. Imperial edition, #336, Oblong 4to., pictorial wrappers, 36 pages, covers slightly darkened, else very good+, fragile book, pictorial cover, 8 wonderfully detailed full page and 13 smaller black and whites by Ida Outhwaite.   Aleph-Bet Books, Inc.   108 - 330 2015 $600

Renwar *Illustrated Guide for Tourists in Search of Recreation, Health and Information...* London: Hackett and Rawlinson, 1877. 8vo., 4 woodburytypes, mounted with printed borders and titles and 5 folding railway maps, two with old tape repairs without loss, one has left a mark along inner margin, original decorative blue cloth, lettered in black and gilt.   Marlborough Rare Books   List 53 - 46   2015   £225

Renwick, Thomas   *A Narrative of the Case of Miss Margaret McAvoy: with an Account of Some Optical Experiments Connected With it.*   London: Baldwin Cradock and Joy, 1817. First edition, 4to., engraved plate (rather foxed and offset), contemporary dark blue half calf over marbled boards, spine fully gilt with raised bands and label (label chipped), marbled edges, very good presentation copy inscribed with author's compliments for Edinburgh Reviewers.   John Drury Rare Books   2015 - 22916   2015 $787

A Report of an Inquiry into the Present State of Warwick Corporation, as Given in Evidence before R. Whitcombe and A. E. Cockburn... Warwick: John Cooper, 1834. First edition, rare in this form, some minor intermittent foxing and one or two old ink splashes, well bound recently in calf backed marbled boards, spine lettered, good.   John Drury Rare Books   March 2015 - 21841   2015 $266

A Report of the Case of Homer Against Liddiard Upon the Question of What Consent is Necessary to the Marriage of Illegitimate Minors Determined on the 24th May 1799 in the Consistorial Court of London... London: printed by A. Strahan for J. Butterworth, 1800. First edition, 8vo., tiny hole in C8 just touching a couple of letters, recently well bound in cloth lettered in gilt, very good, sometime in the library of Dr. Peter Laslett of Trinity College, Cambridge, with his ownership label on blank margin of title, uncommon.   John Drury Rare Books   March 2015 - 20531   2015 $266

Reporting Vietnam: Part One: American Journalism 1959-1969 & Reporting Vietnam: Part Two: American Journalism 1969-1975. New York: Library of America, 1998. First edition thus, small 8vo., fine in good+ dust jacket, 2 volumes, books fine, first volume jacket near fine, second volume with tear at head of spine, else near fine.   Beasley Books   2013 - 2015 $40

The Reports of Sir Edward Coke, Kt. in Verse, Wherein the name of Each Case and the Principal Points are Contained in Two Lines...   In the Savoy: printed by Henry Lintot...., 1742. First edition, 8vo., recent wrappers, very good.   C. R. Johnson   Foxon R-Z - 824r-z   2015 $766

Representation of the Lords of the Committee of Council, Appointed for the Consideration of all Matters Relating to Trade and Foreign Plantations, Upon the Present State of the Laws for Regulating the Importation and Exportation of Corn...   London: John Stockdale, 1800. 8vo., many tables, titlepage lightly foxed, one leaf shaved at fore-edge with loss of final couple of figures on most lines of recto, preserved in recent plain wrappers with label to upper cover.   John Drury Rare Books   2015 - 21485   2015 $177

A Representation of the State of Christianity in England and of It's (sic) Decay and Danger from Sectaries Answel (sic) as Papists.   London: Benj. Tooke, 1674. First edition, 4to., bound fairly recently in red quarter morocco over marbled boards, spine gilt lettered, fine, well margined and crisp copy.   John Drury Rare Books   March 2015 - 23575   2015 $656

Residence in Bermuda. Bermuda: Bermuda Trade Development Board, 1936. First edition, number 1995 of 2000 numbered copies, large 4to., 52 illustrations including watercolors by Adolph Treidler and photos by David Knudsen, F. S. Lincoln, Thurman Rotan and Walter Rutherford, bright clean, near fine, faint shelf wear in original publisher's silver and turquoise cloth.   Any Amount of Books   2015 - A40933   2015   £180

Restif De La Bretonne, Nicolas Edme   1734-1806 *Les Dangers De La Ville, Ou Histoire Effrayante et Morale...* Paris: La Haie, 1784. First edition, 4 parts in 2 volumes, 8vo., parts 1to 4 of the 8 part Novel, volume II missing half title of part 3 and final page (xxi), half red morocco over marbled paper lettered and decorated gilt, top edge gilt, rather worn and well thumbed pair of volumes, each volume with bookplate of Mary Hunter (1856-1933).   Any Amount of Books   2015 - C7701   2015   £150

Restif De La Bretonne, Nicolas Edme   1734-1806 *Ou Le Coeur Humain Devoile.* Paris: Edition Du Cent Cinquantenaire, 1956-1957. No. 293 of 492 numbered copies, 4 volumes in wrappers, quite fine in board chemise and slipcases, small quarto.   Beasley Books   2013 - 2015 $275

Reumert, Ellen *Karen.* Copenhagen: Carl Lorsens Forlag, circa, 1905. 4to., cloth backed pictorial boards, tips rubbed, else very good-fine, 8 fine full page color illustrations and in line on very page of text in verse, lovely book.   Aleph-bet Books, Inc.   109 - 294   2015 $750

A Review of the Letter on Royal Fasts, Addressed to an Antiburgher, which Appeared in the Caledonian Mercury March 29th Last. Edinburgh: printed by D. Paterson for R. Inglis, bookseller, Potterrow and sold by him and by W. Gray bookseller, 1778. First edition, 16 pages, 8vo., preserved in modern wrappers with printed label on upper cover, very good, apparently very rare.   John Drury Rare Books   March 2015 - 24717   2015   £266

Review of the Quarterly Review; or an Exposure of the Erroneous Opinions Promulgated in that Work on the Subject of Colonial Slavery... London: J. Hatchard and Son, 1824. First edition, 8vo., ink 4 figure number on blank margin of title, old marbled wrappers, very good.   John Drury Rare Books   2015 - 15819   2015 $221

La Revolution Francaises Pot-Pourri. Paris: de l'Imprimerie de Crapart, 1791. 8vo., contemporary, probably original, mottled paper boards, one corner bruised, spine worn, very good, probably rather rare.   John Drury Rare Books   March 2015 - 23350   2015   £306

Rexroth, Kenneth   *The Signature of All Things, Poems Songs, Elegies, Translations and Epigrams.* New York: New Directions, 1949. Limited to 1500 copies, 50 are numbered, printed on Fabriano paper and signed by author on colophon, this copy thus, beautifully printed at Stamperia Valdonega by Hans Mardersteig, 8vo., quarter cloth, decorated paper covered boards, dust jacket lightly soiled.   Oak Knoll Books   306 - 292   2015 $750

Rey, H. A.   *Au Clair de la Lune and Other French Nursery Songs.* New York: Greystone Press, 1941. First edition,   Honey & Wax Booksellers   2 - 34   2015 $475

Rey, H. A.   *Cecily & the Monkeys.* Boston: Houghton Mifflin, 1942. First American edition, 4to., pictorial cloth, near fine in dust jacket very slightly frayed and slight soil, else very good+, great copy.   Aleph-Bet Books, Inc.   108 - 389   2015 $2000

Rey, Margaret   *Pretzel and the Puppies.* New York: Harper Bros., 1946. First edition (based on price and ads), 4to., cloth backed pictorial boards, slight edgewear, else near fine in worn dust jacket with tape mends on verso and 3 inch of spine paper off, marvelous color illustrations on every page by H. A. Rey.   Aleph-Bet Books, Inc.   108 - 390   2015 $300

Reynardson, Francis   *The Stage: a Poem. Inscrib'd to Joseph Addison, Esq. by Mr. Webster, (Pseud), of Christ Church, Oxon.* London: printed for E. Curll, 1713. First edition, 8vo., disbound, very good, complete with half title, very scarce.   C. R. Johnson   Foxon R-Z - 825r-z   2015 $2298

Reynolds, Henry   *The Tale of Narcissus.* Hull: J. R. Tutin, 1906. One of 666 copies, one page creased, uncut, original printed wrappers, dusted and slightly creased, inscribed on front wrapper from Tutin to Oliver Elton and by Elton to Kathleen Tillotson with compliments.   Jarndyce Antiquarian Booksellers   CCVII - 446   2015   £25

Reynolds, John   *Memoirs of the Life of the Late Pious and Learned Mr. Reynolds...* London: printed for R. Ford, R. Hett, J. Oswald and J. Gray, 1735. First edition, engraved frontispiece, 8vo., contemporary sheep, spine gilt, trifle worn, lacks title label, very good, signature of C. Valentine Senr. (1737) and Isabella Atkinson (August 10 1784).   C. R. Johnson   Foxon R-Z - 826r-z   2015 $306

Reynolds, Tim   *Slocum.* Santa Barbara: Unicorn Press, 1967. Second printing, limited to 1000 copies, perfect bound wrappers, fine, inscribed by author for Ted Berrigan.   Between the Covers Rare Books, Inc.   187 - 232   2015 $150

Rhode Island   *List of Income Earned in Rhode Island in 1864 and Taxed in 1865.* Providence: N. Bangs Williams, 1865. First edition, 12mo., original printed boards later(?) cloth shelf back, sheets lightly toned with several short marginal tears, not affecting text, small ink-blot on fore-edge, very sound, about very good.   M & S Rare Books, Inc.   97 - 261   2015 $175

Rhode, John   *Death Invades the Meeting.* London: Collins, 1944. First edition, fine in dust jacket with some tiny tears at spine ends.   Mordida Books   March 2015 - 007147   2015 $400

Rhode, John   *Open Verdict.* London: Bles, 1956. First edition, several pages stained and page edges darkened, otherwise very good in dust jacket with small chip on front panel, nicks and tears at spine ends, several tiny tears along edges.   Mordida Books   March 2015 - 008141   2015 $175

Rhode, John   *The Tower of Evil.* New York: Dodd Mead, 1938. First American edition, inscription, otherwise very good in lightly soiled dust jacket with light wear at spine ends.   Mordida Books   March 2015 - 007146   2015 $250

Rhode, John   *The Venner Crime.* London: Odhams, 1933. First edition, front cover mottled, otherwise fine in dust jacket with small chip at top corner of spine and top corner of front panel.   Mordida Books   March 2015 - 003145   2015 $75

Rhodes, Eugene Manlove   *Stepsons of Light.* Houghton Mifflin, 1921. First edition, pictorial brickish red cloth, former owner's name on front pastedown sheet, else very good in later state dust jacket, slipcase, sharp copy.   Buckingham Books   March 2015 - 11974   2015 $225

Rhodes, Henry T. *The Craft of Forgery.* London: John Murray, 1934. First edition, very good in fine, price clipped dust jacket.   Mordida Books   March 2015 - 010338   2015 $150

Ribot, T. *The Diseases of the Will.* Chicago: Open Court, 1894. First edition, very good+ with lightly faded spine.   Beasley Books   2013 - 2015 $250

Ribot, T. *Essay on the Creative Imagination.* Chicago: Open Court, 1906. First edition, very good+ to near fine, lightly rubbed spine ends.   Beasley Books   2013 - 2015 $250

Ribot, T. *The Evolution of General Ideas.* Chicago: Open Court, 1899. First edition, very good, wear at spine ends and slightly bumped and worn corners.   Beasley Books   2013 - 2015 $125

Ricardo, David   1772-1823   *On the Principles of Political Economy and Taxation.* London: John Murray, 1819. 8vo., without ads found in some copies, contemporary half calf over marbled boards, reback to match, spine gilt with raised bands, original label preserved, very good.   John Drury Rare Books   2015 - 26137   2015 $2622

Riccardi, Pietro   *Biblioteca Matematica Italiana.* Modenz: Coi Tipi della Societa Tipografica, Antica Tipografia Soliani, 1873-1928. First editions, 4 volumes, 4to., volumes I-III bound by Riviere & Son in half dark green leather with green cloth sides, gilt stamped spine title with raised bands, top edge gilt, some of the leather discolored to brown (as usual), volume IV bound by another binder, but to match originals very closely, fine, scarce.   Jeff Weber Rare Books   178 - 939   2015 $1000

Rice, Anne   *The Tale of the Body Thief.* New York: Knopf, 1992. First edition, inscribed and signed by author, as new in dust jacket.   Gemini Fine Books & Arts, Ltd.   Art Reference & Illustrated Books: First Editions - 2015 $60

Rice, Craig   *The April Robin Murders.* New York: Random House, 1958. First edition, signed on titlepage by Ed McBain, fine, bright, unread copy in spectacular price clipped dust jacket.   Buckingham Books   March 2015 - 38263   2015 $450

Rice, Craig   *The name is Malone.* New York: Pyramid, 1958. First edition, wear along folds and scrape on front cover, otherwise very good in wrappers.   Mordida Books   March 2015 - 009967   2015 $100

Rice, Craig   *The Sunday Pigeon Murders.* New York: Simon & Schuster, 1942. First edition, fine, tiny wear at spine ends and at corners, small slightly faded area at lower corner of front panel, closed tear.   Mordida Books   March 2015 - 010231   2015 $200

Rice, Craig   *The Thursday Turkey Murders.* New York: Simon & Schuster, 1943. First edition, fine in dust jacket lightly sunned on spine and with couple of tiny closed tears.   Buckingham Books   March 2015 - 32201   2015 $350

Rice, Craig   *Trial by Fury.* Simon & Schuster, 1941. First edition, signed by author, two-tone boards, lightly rubbed along bottom edges an corners, else near fine in bright, crisp dust jacket with few light rub to extremities.   Buckingham Books   March 2015 - 34402   2015 $2000

Rice, Elmer   *The Left Bank.* New York: Samuel French, 1931. First edition, hardcover, fine in torn dust jacket with small chips.   Beasley Books   2013 - 2015 $45

Rice, James L.   *Freud's Russia.* New Brunswick: Transaction, 1993. First edition, fine, owner's name in pencil, few pencilled notes, fine dust jacket.   Beasley Books   2013 - 2015 $45

Rich, Henry   *What is to Be Done? Or Past, Present and Future.* London: James Ridgway, 1844. First edition, 8vo., recent blue boards, lettered on upper cover, paper label on spine, very good, from the contemporary library of Lord William Russell with his signature, scarce.   John Drury Rare Books   2015 - 4916   2015 $177

Richards, Grant   *Bittersweet.* London: Grant Richards, 1915. First edition, original blue green cloth decorated an lettered gilt, positive review of the book from Punch affixed to front fly, corners little bumped, about very good, lacking dust jacket, inscribed by author for his wife Madeleine.   Between the Covers Rare Books   196 - 105   2015 $850

Richards, Grant   *Bittersweet.* London: Grant Richards, 1915. First edition, original blue green cloth decorated and lettered in gilt, modestly rubbed, near fine in handsome very good or better dust jacket with little soiling and light wear, author's own copy with his autograph monogram dated Oct. 31 1915.   Between the Covers Rare Books   196 - 106   2015 $650

Richards, Grant   *Vain Pursuit.* London: Grant Richards, 1931. First edition, slight foxing, very good or better with minimal wear in very good dust jacket with modest chipping at crown and some short tears, dedication copy inscribed by author to his daughter Helene, March 1931, scarce in dust jacket.   Between the Covers Rare Books   196 - 107   2015 $850

Richards, Grant   *Valentine.* London: Grant Richards, 1913. First edition, some foxing on fore edge, else ner fine in modestly chipped, very good dust jacket, scarce in jacket.   Between the Covers Rare Books   196 - 104   2015 $400

Richards, Ivor Armstrong *Practical Criticism: a Study of Literary Judgment.* London: Kegan Paul, 1929. Half title, folding tables, original red cloth, faded and marked, Geoffrey Tillotson's copy, inserted are 3 postcards to him, Christmas card insertion and note and typed and ms. letter from Richards and his wife Dorothy. Jarndyce Antiquarian Booksellers CCVII - 447 2015 £28

Richards, Mel *Peter Rabbit the Magician.* Aurora: Strathmore, 1942. 4to., spiral backed boards, fine in original pictorial box (rubbed), color illustrations, with 6 actual magic tricks and removable props incorporated into the illustrations, complete with all parts, rare in box. Aleph-Bet Books, Inc. 108 - 373 2015 $450

Richards, Mel *Peter Rabbit the Magician.* Illinois: Strathmore Co., 1942. First edition, 16 pages, illustrations in color, trick items inserted in pockets or holders on several pages with instructions for tricks at rear, spiralbound top/bottom with blue color illustrated boards with section cut away from front cover to reveal Peter on stage, 11 3/4 x 8 3/4 inches, very nice bright copy with 'wand' and Peter's magic carpet loosely inserted (both quite often missing). Ian Hodgkins & Co. Ltd. 134 - 201 2015 £155

Richards, Thomas *Cambriae Suspiria in Obitum Desideratissimae Reginae Carolinae...* Salopiae: excudit R. Lathrop, 1738. First edition, 8 pages, folio, original marbled wrappers, fine in original condition, very rare. C. R. Johnson Foxon R-Z - 828r-z 2015 $1915

Richardson, Charles *A New Dictionary of the English Language.* London: William Pickering, 1836-1837. First edition, 2 volumes, half titles, 4to., contemporary polished chestnut calf by H. Stamper, French fillets on sides with an outer roll tooled toothed border, spines richly gilt, gilt edges, spines very slightly faded, cracking to joints (but firm), slight wear to extremities, good. Blackwell's Rare Books B179 - 87 2015 £1100

Richardson, Robert *A State of the Evidence in the Cause Between His Grace the Duke of Hamilton and Others, Pursuers and Archibald Douglas of Douglas, Esquire, defender.* London: printed and sold by C. Bathurst and Mess. Kincaid and Bell in Edinburgh, 1769. First edition, 4to., long list of errata on verso of A4, including additional erratum on pasted-on slip, upper fore-corner of titlepage neatly repaired (no where near printed surface), minor soiling of first and last leaves, contemporary mottled calf, sympathetically rebacked to match with gilt lines and label, good copy, inscribed "From ye author". John Drury Rare Books 2015 - 20879 2015 $787

Richardson, Samuel *A New System of Short-Hand, by Which More May be Written in One Hour, than an Hour and a Half by any Other System Hitherto Published.* London: B. Crosby and Co., 1810. 8vo., 17 plates of which 14 are engraved and one (plate II) is in two parts, some light foxing, old 19th century black half roan, little rubbed, simple lettering on spine, good, uncommon. John Drury Rare Books 2015 - 15231 2015 $89

Richardson, Samuel 1689-1761 *The History of Sir Charles Grandison.* London: Oxford University Press, 1972. First edition, 8vo., original navy blue cloth, lettered gilt at spines, 3 volume set, very good+ in like slipcase. Any Amount of Books 2015 - C15694 2015 £180

Richter, Francis C. *Richter's History and Records of Base Ball: the American Nations's Chief Sport.* Philadelphia: Francis C. Richter, 1914. First edition, 306 pages, photos, front fly lacking, some erosion to cloth at spine ends and little foxing, well worn but sound, good copy, inscribed by author for son Francis C. jr., splendid association. Between the Covers Rare Books, Inc. 187 - 9 2015 $3500

Ricketts, Charles 1866-1931 *A Bibliography of the Books Issued by Hacon & Ricketts.* London: privately printed at the Ballantyne Press, 1904. First edition, octavo, one of 250 copies out of an edition of 260, cloth backed boards with title labels on spine and upper cover, frontispiece and titlepage designed by Ricketts, who also supervised the printing of the book, corners little rubbed, spine label bit chipped, very good. Peter Ellis, Bookseller 2014 - 010292 2015 £325

Ricketts, Ed *The Outer Shores.* Eureka: Mad River Press, 1978. First edition, little foxing at fore edge part 1, otherwise fine set. Stephen Lupack March 2015 - 2015 $150

Ricketts, W. P. *50 Years in the Saddle.* Sheridan: Star Publishing Co., 1942. First and only edition, 8vo., original green cloth with title stamped in black on front cover and spine, frontispiece, illustrations, map, very scarce to rare, lightly rubbed at spine ends and corners, else near fine, tight copy. Buckingham Books March 2015 - 28576 2015 $2250

Rico, Juan *Reales Exequias que por el Fallecimiento del Senor don Carlos III rey de Espana y de las Indias mando Celebrar en la Ciudad de Lima, Capital del Peru...* Lima: En la Imprenta Real de los Ninos Expositos, 1789. 4to., contemporary vellum, ms. title on spine, decorated edges, 1 folding plate. Kaaterskill Books 19 - 120 2015 $2500

Riddell, James *Animal Lore and Disorder.* New York: Harper Bros. circa, 1950. 4to., cloth backed pictorial boards, fine, each page sliced in half horizontally with pictures on top half and text on bottom pieces, enables reader to make over 200 combinations. Aleph-bet Books, Inc. 109 - 310   2015 $150

Riddle, Jeff C. *The Indian History of the Modoc War, and the Causes that led to It.* 1914. First edition, cloth, 288 pages, many illustrations, maps, near fine. Buckingham Books   March 2015 - 2686   2015 $300

Ridgway, Robert *Color Standards and Color Nomenclature.* Washington: published for the author, 1912. First edition, 8vo., colour title, 43 plates, each with 27 coloured samples, original green cloth, spine defective, some very old smoke damage to edge of cover and fore edge with light damp mark running along upper edge, nevertheless internally bright. Marlborough Rare Books   List 54 - 67   2015   £225

Ridho, Abu *The World's Great Collections: Oriental Ceramics Volume 3.* Tokyo: Kodansha International, 1982. Folio, cloth, slipcase, 95 color, 329 monochrome plates. Oak Knoll Books   306 - 293   2015 $150

Riding, Laura *It Has Taken Long, from the Writings of Laura (Riding) Jackson.* New York: Chelsea Inc., 1976. One of 200 numbered copies signed by author on special colophon leaf, 8vo., wrappers, near fine, 239 pages. Beasley Books   2013 - 2015 $40

Riding, Laura *The Life of the Dead.* London: Arthur Barker Ltd., 1933. First edition, signed by author, one of 200 copies, numbered and signed by artist and author, near fine, 4to., printed on Basingwerk parchment, brown card covers with yapped edges and printed label on front. Beasley Books   2013 - 2015 $400

Riding, Laura *Love as Love, Death as Death.* London: Seizin, 1928. First edition, one of 175 numbered copies, signed by author, near fine in tan cloth with publisher's shrunken and bit wrinkled, clear acetate dust jacket, 8vo., near fine cardboard slipcase. Beasley Books   2013 - 2015 $500

Riding, Laura *Poems, a Joking Word.* London: Jonathan Cape, 1930. First edition, near fine with little darkening to head of spine, very good dust jacket showing some soiling and shallow chipping, this copy signed by author, 8vo. Beasley Books   2013 - 2015 $750

Riding, Laura *Progress of Stories.* Deya Majorca: London: Seizin Press/Constable, 1935. First edition, near fine, little darkening to spine, 8vo., very good dust jacket with soil and darkening to spine. Beasley Books   2013 - 2015 $500

Riding, Laura *Some Communications of Broad Reference.* Northridge: Lord John Press, 1983. First edition, letter Z of 26 lettered copies (from a signed edition of 125), gilt stamped brown cloth over marbled paper covered boards, fine in acetate dust jacket. Beasley Books   2013 - 2015 $200

Riding, Laura *The Telling.* New York: Harper and Row, 1973. First US edition, number 48 of 100 hand numbered copies of the trade edition, 8vo., signed by author, copyright page carries here hand-correction of word 'essay' to word 'portion', fine in fine dust jacket, laid into this copy is a scolding letter to Peter Howard of Serendipity Books, for not using her authorially correct name in one of his catalogs, this is TLS sent April 11 1976. Beasley Books   2013 - 2015 $150

Riding, Laura *A Trojan Ending.* Deya Majorca: London: Seizin Press/Constable, 1937. First edition, 8vo., folding map, near fine in very good++ dust jacket with tiny nick at spine head. Beasley Books   2013 - 2015 $250

Riding, Laura *The World and Ourselves.* London: Chatto & Windus, 1938. First edition, 8vo., pencilled ownership signature of F. R. Cowell, very good+ in like dust jacket (faint edgewear). Any Amount of Books   2015 - A48862 2015   £150

Ridley, Matt *Francis Crick. Discoverer of the Genetic Code.* New York: Atlas Books/Harper Collins, 2006. First edition, small 8vo., signed and dated and inscribed by author, fine in fine dust jacket. By the Book, L. C.   Special List 10 - 74   2015 $200

Ridout, Thomas H. *Poems and Translations.* London: printed by W. Wilkins for W. Inchliffe, 1717. First edition, 4to., later half calf and marbled boards, gilt, spine gilt, very rare, titlepage neatly backed, blank inner margin of last leaf renewed, otherwise very good. C. R. Johnson   Foxon R-Z - 829r-z   2015 $1379

Rigby, Edward *Holkham, Its Agriculture &c.* Norwich: printed by Burks and Kinnebrook for R. Hunter, 1818. Third edition, 8vo., 16 page Sampson Low catalog at end, original blindstamped maroon cloth, spine lettered gilt, repairs to head and foot of spine, excellent, uncut copy. John Drury Rare Books   March 2015 - 24973   2015   £306

Riggs, Stephen Return *A Dakota-English Dictionary.* Washington: 1890. Rebound in red cloth, pages browned with minor chipping to few early leaves but no loss. Dumont Maps & Books of the West   131 - 69   2015 $125

Riggs, Thomas L. *The Last Buffalo Hunt.* Santee Normal Training School Press, 1935. First edition thus, 6 1/4 x 3 1/2 inches, tan pictorial wrappers, image of buffalo head to front wrapper, 20 pages including wrappers, very minor chipping to extremities and with a small blend to bottom corner of front wrapper, very good.   Buckingham Books   March 2015 - 35959   2015 $250

Rikhoff, Jim   *Hunting the African Elephant.*   Clinton: Amwell Press, 1985. First edition thus, limited to 1000 copies, signed by Jim Rikhoff, this #962, textured leather, gold stamping on spine, linen endpapers, frontispiece, original color plates and line drawings by Guy Coheleach, as new, unread copy housed in original lightly soiled cloth slipcase.   Buckingham Books   March 2015 - 22705   2015 $850

Riley, James Whitcomb   1849-1916   *While the Heart Beats Young.*   Indianapolis: Bobbs Merrill, various dates, 1906. First edition, small 4to., cloth, pictorial paste-on, mint in publisher's pictorial box, flaps repaired, else very good, illustrations by Ethel Betts with 15 beautiful color plates plus numerous smaller text illustrations, printed on heavy, glossy paper, amazing copy, rare in box.   Aleph-bet Books, Inc.   109 - 51   2015 $650

Rilke, Rainer Maria   1875-1926   *Mitsou: Quarante Images par Balthus.*   Erlenbach-Zurich & Leipzig: Rotapfel Verlag, 1921. First edition, quarto, original ivory boards, original glassine, clamshell box, stunning copy.   Honey & Wax Booksellers   2 - 64   2015 $6000

Rilke, Rainer Maria   1875-1926   *Stories of God.*   London: Sidgwick & Jackson, 1932. First English edition, penciled owner name of New Directions' publisher James Laughlin, else very near fine in good dust jacket with chips at crown and front panel.   Between the Covers Rare Books, Inc.   187 - 233   2015 $150

Rimbaud, Arthur   *A Season in Hell.*   Norfolk: New Directions, 1939. First edition, 8vo., original linen backed paper over boards, printed paper label on front cover, dust jacket, presentation copy inscribed by author for George Marion O'Donnell, small ownership signature, otherwise fine.   James S. Jaffe Rare Books   Modern American Poetry - 250   2015 $1500

Rinehart, Mary Roberts   *The Lipstick.*   New York: Farrar & Rinehart, 1941. First edition, former owner's name and date, else fine, tight, square copy in dust jacket with tiny closed tears to top edge front panel.   Buckingham Books   March 2015 - 31077   2015 $225

Rip, Pseud.   *Cocktails de Paris.*   Paris: Editions Demangel, 1929. First edition, copiously illustrated by famed poster artist Paul Colin, pages toned, two leaves roughly opened with resulting modest chips, barely touching text, modest rubbing on wrappers, handsome, very good copy, exceptionally uncommon, inscribed by RIP and by Paul Colin to Lieutenant Charles Comat.   Between the Covers Rare Books   196 - 136   2015 $1450

Rippe, Peter   *P. Buckley Moss, Painting the Joy of the Soul.*   Cumming: Landauer Books, 1997. First edition, signed by Moss, near fine.   Stephen Lupack   March 2015 - 2015 $100

Rist, John M.   *Platonism and Its Christian Heritage.*   London: Variorum Reprints, 1985. 8vo., blue cloth, ink ownership signature of David Lindberg, fine.   Jeff Weber Rare Books   178 - 943   2015 $150

Ritchie, Jack   *Little Boxes of Bewilderment.*   New York: St. Martins, 1989. First edition, fine in dust jacket.   Mordida Books   March 2015 - 012665   2015 $100

Ritson, Joseph   *An Essay on Abstinence from Animal Food, as a Moral Duty.*   London: Richard Phillips, 1802. First edition, 8vo., contemporary half calf over marbled boards, neatly rebacked spine gilt and labelled, good copy.   John Drury Rare Books   2015 - 18084   2015 $1136

Rittenhouse, David   *The Scientific Writings of David Rittenhouse.*   New York: Arno Press, 1980. Reprint, 8vo., 12 illustrations, gilt stamped green cloth, fine.   Jeff Weber Rare Books   178 - 944   2015 $60

Rittenhouse, Jack D.   *Disturnell's Treaty Map.*   Santa Fe: 1965. 20 pages, folding map, map is unfolded and both pieces are as new, new covers printed for unbound pamphlets, so not as issued, but text fine.   Dumont Maps & Books of the West   131 - 31   2015 $45

Rittenhouse, Jack D.   *The First Christmas Gifts.*   Houston: 1955. 8 pages, 3 small containers, boxed, box lightly rubbed, else very good, 3 tiny one inch square clear boxes pasted to labeled card contain minute quantities of the materials, all in 3 x 4 x 1 1/2 inch box.   Dumont Maps and Books of the West   130 - 33   2015 $85

Ritts, Herb   *Men and Woman.*   Santa Fe: Twin Palms, 1989. First edition, 2 volumes, original black cloth lettered gilt on spine with illustration onset to each cover, copiously illustrated in black and white, signed on front endpaper by author, fine in slipcase.   Any Amount of Books   2015 - A68262   2015   £200

Riva Aguero, Jose De La *Memorias y Documentos Para la Historia de la Independencia del Peru y Causas del mal exito que ha enido Esta. Obra Postuma.* Paris: Libreria de Garnier Hermanos, 1858. First edition, 2 volumes, 8vo., quarter morocco over green marbled boards, gilt rules and decorations, marbled endpapers, lacking headbands else very good, spines scuffed, boards worn, booksellers book description and Peruvian bookseller's small label on front pastedown of first volume, scattered foxing. Kaaterskill Books 19 - 129 2015 $700

The Rival Wives, or, the Greeting of Clarissa to Skirra in the Elysian Shades. London: printed for W. Lloyd an sold by booksellers of London and Westminster, 1738. First edition, 18 pages, folio, disbound, very good, very scarce. C. R. Johnson Foxon R-Z - 830r-z 2015 $1149

Rivers, George R. R. *Captain Shays, a Populist of 1786.* Boston: Little Brown, 1897. First edition, handsomely bound in gilt stamped green cloth, fine. Beasley Books 2013 - 2015 $125

Riviere, P. Louis *Poh-Deng Scenes De La Vie Siamoise.* Paris: L'Edition D'art, 1913. #183 of 288, original wrappers near fine with deep crease, 8vo., beautiful book with many of the 50 illustrations by Neziere enriched with gold. Beasley Books 2013 - 2015 $1700

Robb, Candace *The King's Bishop.* London: Heinemann, 1996. First edition, signed, fine in dust jacket, approximately 150 copies were printed for the true first edition of this book. Buckingham Books March 2015 - 18493 2015 $275

Robb, Candace *The Nun's Tale.* London: Heinemann, 1995. First edition, signed, fine in dust jacket, lightly sunned on spine. Buckingham Books March 2015 - 9418 2015 $175

Robbe-Grillet, Alain *Souvenirs du Triangle d'Or.* Paris: Les Editions de Minuit, 1978. First edition, inscribed in blue ink by author for novelist and film theorist William Van Wert, very good plus in wrappers, wrappers very lightly soiled, light foxing at spine, rear panel scuffed with single corner crease, slight spine lean. Royal Books 46 - 27 2015 $750

Robbins, C. A. *The Unholy Three.* New York: John Lane Co., 1917. First edition, fine in lovely near fine example of dust jacket with tear on rear panel, tiny nicks at extremities, with old tape repairs professionally removed leaving shadows only on inside of jacket, housed in attractive, loosely fitting clamshell case. Between the Covers Rare Books 196 - 148 2015 $8500

Robbins, Harold *A Stone for Danny Fisher.* New York: Alfred A. Knopf, 1952. First edition, fine in fine dust jacket with single tiny tear at foot, beautiful copy, from the library of Kate Stettner Lobell and Carl D. Lobell. Between the Covers Rare Books 196 - 29 2015 $200

Robbins, Louise S. *The Dismissal of Miss Ruth Brown. Civil Rights, Censorship and the American Library.* Norman: University of Oklahoma Press, 2000. First edition, inscribed by author, 8vo., fine in fine dust jacket. Beasley Books 2013 - 2015 $40

Robbins, Tom *Even Cowgirls Get the Blues.* Boston: Houghton Mifflin, 1976. First edition, signed by author, fine in fine dust jacket, closed tear at top of front panel. Ed Smith Books 83 - 77 2015 $850

Robert-Houdin, Jean Eugene *Card Sharping Exposed.* London: George Routledge & Sons, circa, 1890. Half title, illustrations, 4 pages ads, few fore edges slightly dusted, original blue cloth, decorated and lettered in red, black and gilt slightly dulled, corners slightly bumped, from the library of Frederick William Stephan, very good. Jarndyce Antiquarian Booksellers CCXI - 242 2015 £225

Robert Johnson, King of the Delta Blues. London: Immediate Music, 1969. First edition, 8vo., wrappers, 62 pages, very good with some age toning. Beasley Books 2013 - 2015 $125

Roberts, David *A Plan for Increasing the Incomes of Officers in the Army, after a Certain Period of Service on Being Disabled from Wounds, Diseases &c.* London: sold by Longman Hurst, Rees, Orme and Browne, J. Egerton, A. B. King, Dublin and W. Bulgin, Bristol, n.d., 1810. First edition, 8vo., wanting half title, recently well bound in linen backed marbled boards, lettered, very good, crisp, rare. John Drury Rare Books March 2015 - 19650 2015 £306

Roberts, Henry *The Dwellings of the Labouring Classes, Their Arrangement and Construction.* London: published by request and sold for the benefit of the Society for improving the Condition of the Labouring Classes at no. 21 Exeter Hall...n.d., 1850. First edition, royal 8vo., 12 unnumbered lithographic plates (each with closed and repaired tear but no loss), half title, numerous text figures, whole page illustrations, original blindstamped cloth with short title gilt on upper cover, neatly rebacked and recased with endpapers, very good. John Drury Rare Books 2015 - 23263 2015 $699

Roberts, Henry *The Dwellings of the Labouring Classes, their Arrangement and Construction....* London: published by request and sold for the Benefit of the Society for Improving the Condition of the labouring Classes at no. 21 Exeter Hall Strand but actually, 1855. (1853), Royal 8vo., 12 lithographic plates, half title, numerous text figures and whole page illustrations, occasional minor foxing, very good in original cloth, lettered gilt on upper cover, sometime in the library of Society of Medical Officers of Health (bookplate) and London School of Hygiene (bookplate).   John Drury Rare Books   2015 - 20821   2015 $656

Roberts, Kenneth *Lydia Bailey.* Garden City: Doubleday & Co., 1947. First edition, #6 of 10 specially bound copies, publisher's original full morocco presentation binding, signed by Roberts with page of working manuscript bound in, top edge gilt, fine.   Ed Smith Books   82 - 22   2015 $350

Roberts, Kenneth *Northwest Passage.* Garden City: Doubleday & Doran Co., 1937. First edition, presentation from author for Mel and Ethel Eaton, fine in dust jacket with hint of wear to spine ends.   Buckingham Books   March 2015 - 24507   2015 $1250

Roberts, Orlando *Narrative of Voyages and Excursions on the East Coast and in the Interior of Central America....* Edinburgh: Printed for Constable & Co., 1827. First edition, illustrations, extra engraved title and folding map, 24m., calf over marbled boards, rebacked in brown cloth, original spine label, very good, boards worn, scattered foxing and offsetting, tiny tear at inner margin of map, binding tight.   Kaaterskill Books   19 - 132   2015 $200

Robertson, Alexander *Poems on Various Subjects and Occasions...* Edinburgh: printed for Ch. Alexander and sold at his house in Geddes's Close....n.d., 1752? First edition, 8vo., contemporary sheep, spine gilt, little rubbed, sound, lacks label, very good, early signature on titlepage of W. Burgh, later armorial bookplate of H. F. Davies, Elmley Castle.   C. R. Johnson   Foxon R-Z - 831r-z   2015 $536

Robertson, Don *The Ideal Genuine Man.* Bangor: Philtrum, 1987. First edition, one of 500 numbered copies, signed by author and by Stephen King (provided introduction), very fine in dust jacket.   Mordida Books   March 2015 - 007514   2015 $200

Robertson, William *An Historical Disquisition Concerning the Knowledge, the Ancients Had of India...* London: A. Strahan, 1799. Third edition, octavo, 2 folding maps, contemporary full marbled calf with gilt decoration to spine, very good, some light foxing to prelims, very bright copy.   Peter Ellis, Bookseller   2014 - 019669   2015   £325

Robeson, Eslanda Goode *Paul Robeson, Negro.* New York: Harper and Bros., 1930. First edition, corners worn and spine has been professionally and neatly seamlessly rebacked, fair copy only, lacking dust jacket, Paul Robeson Jr.'s copy with his bold ownership signature, smaller ownership signature of Rev. Benjamin C. Robeson (Paul Robeson, Sr.'s brother).   Between the Covers Rare Books, Inc.   187 - 234   2015 $2500

The Robin. A Collection of Six Hundred and Eighty of the Most Celebrated English and Scotch Songs... London: printed for C. Hitch & I. Osborn & I Hodgson, 1749. First edition, 12mo., engraved frontispiece, contemporary sheep, gilt, neatly rebacked, spine gilt, red morocco label, wanting flyleaves, otherwise good copy.   C. R. Johnson   Foxon R-Z - 832r-z   2015 $460

Robin-Hood and the Duke of Lancaster. A Ballad to the Tune of The Abbot of Canterbury. London: printed for J. Roberts and sold by booksellers of London and Westminster, 1727. First edition, 6 pages, folio, disbound, titlepage bit dust soiled, otherwise very good, very uncommon.   C. R. Johnson   Foxon R-Z - 833r-z   2015 $766

Robin's Panegyrick. Or, the Norfolk Miscellany. London: printed for T. Time, n.d., 1729. First edition, 8vo., disbound, very good.   C. R. Johnson   Foxon R-Z - 834r-z   2015 $460

Robins, Benjamin *New Principles of Gunnery; Containing the Determination of the Force of Gun-Powder and an Investigation of the Difference in Resisting Power of the Air to Swift and Slow Motions.* London: J. Nourse, 1742. First edition, 8vo., folding engraved plates, 4 figures in text, bound in mid 20th century in oatmeal holland cloth with morocco label on spine lettered gilt, very good.   John Drury Rare Books   2015 - 23209   2015 $1136

Robinson, Alan James *Cetacea. The Great Whales.* Easthampton: Cheloniidae Press, 1981. One of 100 copies, this copy with original drawing by artist, signed by artist, binders David Bourbeau and Gray Parrot and printer, Harold McGrath, all on Arches Cover Buff from a total issue of 110 (100 copies plus 10 artist's proof copies), this copy with original prospectus laid in as well as separate copy of original wood engraving "Whale Flukes" that also appears on colophon, wood engraving is 5 1/2 x 8 1/2 inches, 27 leaves, page size 22 x 15 inches, bound loose as issued with sheets laid in, black Niger oasis goat over low relief sculpture of Right Whale head by Robinson, then cast in polyester resin and covered by David Bourbeau at the Thistle Bindery, rear panel is lack cloth over board, beautiful folder housed in quarter leather Moroccan goat drop back box by Gray Parrot, bit of wear to box, else fine, 7 bleed etchings by Robinson, tw two-color maps, printed in 12 point Garamond with 24 and 36 point Castellar for tilting, each etching protected by a sheet of Japanese tissue, Tomoe Blue, in a wave pattern, used as endsheets.   Priscilla Juvelis - Rare Books   63 - 3   2015 $4500

Robinson, Alan James *A Wildflower Alphabet.* Easthampton: Cheloniidae Press, 2014. One of 150 copies, all on Innova Smooth Cotton Hight White 110# paper, each copy signed and numbered by artist, page size 5 x 8 1/2 inches, 38 pages, bound by Peter Geraty at Praxis Bindery, accordion style with yellow cloth over boards, title stamped in gold gilt on front panel, housed in green cloth over boards slipcase, with title stamped on front cover of slipcase, designed by Robinson using lettering design by Suzanne Moore.   Priscilla Juvelis - Rare Books   63 - 18   2015 $750

Robinson, Alan James *A Wildflower Alphabet.* Easthampton: Cheloniidae Presss, 2014. One of 10 copies (+ 5 AP copies), all on Winsor Newton 908 watercolor paper Hotpress paper, all original watercolors, each copy signed and numbered by artist, Alan James Robinson, page size 5 x 8 1/2 inches, 38 pages, bound by Peter Geraty at Praxis Bindery, accordion style with yellow cloth over boards, title stamped in gold gilt on front panel, housed in custom made cloth over boards clamshell box, title stamped on front cover of slipcase, designed by Robinson using lettering design by Suzanne Moore, original watercolors of the 26 wildflowers and 2 butterflies done free hand.   Priscilla Juvelis - Rare Books   63 - 19   2015 $5500

Robinson, Bert *The Basket Weavers of Arizona.* Albuquerque: 1954. 73 plates, several in color, top edge little dust, dust jacket bright, particularly nice copy.   Dumont Maps & Books of the West   131 - 70   2015 $65

Robinson, Bryan *A Short Essay on Coin.* Dublin: printed in the year, 1737. First edition, 8vo., final blank B4, titlepage little foxed and browned, 19th century dark blue quarter calf over marbled boards, spine lettered gilt, good copy, without 8 page appendix published later in 1737, scarce.   John Drury Rare Books   March 2015 - 25610   2015   £306

Robinson, Bryan *Sir Isaac Newton's Account of the Aether with Some Additions by Way of Appendix.* Dublin: G. and A. Ewing and W. Smith, 1745. First edition, 8vo., very good+, full brown leather with spine repaired, mild scuffs, covers, soil and foxing to endpapers, housed in fine custom made black cloth covered chemise with gilt lettered spine.   By the Book, L. C.   44 - 14   2015 $750

Robinson, Herbert C. *The Birds of the Malay Peninsula...* London: H. F. & G. Witherby, 1927-1976. Small quarto, 5 volumes, 125 color plates, publisher's red cloth, volume five in dust jacket, fine set.   Andrew Isles   2015 - 25785   2015 $1850

Robinson, John *Letter to Sir John Sinclair, Bart. 5th April 1794.* London: printed by W. Bulmer and Co., 1794. First edition, 4to., 72 pages, wanting half title, recently well bound in cloth, spine lettered in gilt, very good large copy.   John Drury Rare Books   2015 - 5800   2015 $177

Robinson, Kim Stanley *The Mars Trilogy.* London: Harper Collins, 1992. 1993. 1996. First editions, all copies near fine with 1/16 of an inch corner creases in near fine dust jackets, Red Mars signed and inscribed by author in year of publication, Green Mars not signed, Blue Mars is signed.   Ed Smith Books   83 - 78   2015 $600

Robinson, Lelia Josephine *The Law of Husband and Wife.* Boston: Lee and Shephard, 1890. First edition, 8vo., brown cloth, stamped in gilt, rubbing to fore-edge, very good, scarce.   Second Life Books Inc.   189 - 210   2015 $225

Robinson, M. E. *The Wild Wreath.* London: Richard Philips, 1804. First edition, 8vo, quarter leather, marbled boards lettered gilt on spine, covers show rubbing and scuffing and some marks, leather spine slightly brittle with some chips and nicks, otherwise sound, very good, clean text.   Any Amount of Books   March 2015 - A98113   2015   £400

Robinson, Marilynne *Absence of Mind.* New Haven: Yale University Press, 2010. Advance reading copy, few nicks to front cover from label removal, small bit of staining to rear cover, very good in wrappers, scarce in advance issue.   Ken Lopez, Bookseller   164 - 176   2015 $125

Robinson, Mary Y. *The Songs of the Trees.* Indianapolis: Bobbs Merrill, Oct., 1903. First edition, pictorial boards, light rubbing, near fine, color illustrations, silhouettes, printed on coated paper.   Aleph-bet Books, Inc.   109 - 356   2015 $250

Robinson, W. W. *Los Angeles from the Days of the Pueblo. A Brief History and Guide to the Plaza Area.* San Francisco: California Historical Society, 1981. Revised edition, plates from photos, drawings, maps, rust cloth, color paste down on front, very fine with matching slipcase.   Argonaut Book Shop   Holiday Season 2014 - 248   2015 $45

Robinson, William 1838-1935 *The Parks and Gardens of Paris Considered in Relation to the Wants of Other Cities and of Public and Private Gardens.* London: John Murray, 1883. Third edition, 8vo., half dark brown leather, presentation from author to historian F. R. Cowell, endpapers slightly stained, corner and hinges rubbed, one signature slightly protruding, otherwise very good.   Any Amount of Books   2015 - A47680   2015   £175

Robinson, William Heath *The Adventures of Uncle Lubin.* New York: Brentanos, 1902. First US edition, 8vo., green pictorial cloth stamped in red, green and white, rear cover lightly soiled, binding tight, recased with paper at hinges neatly repaired, margin of tissue guard and frontispiece narrow light brown discoloration really clean and very good+ copy, color frontispiece, 55 full page black and whites and 72 vignettes plus pictorial endpapers, rare.   Aleph-Bet Books, Inc.   108 - 394   2015 $2850

Robinson, William Heath *Bill the Minder.* London: Constable, 1912. Limited to only 380 numbered copies signed by Robinson, this copy number 1 with full page pen and ink drawing signed and dated 1912 by Robinson, large thick 4to., full vellum binding embossed in gold, except for a modest amount of rubbing and soil on vellum and endpapers slightly foxed this is in near fine with ribbon ties, printed entirely on handmade paper, black and white illustrations. Aleph-Bet Books, Inc.   108 - 395   2015 $9000

Robison, John *Proofs of a Conspiracy Against all the Religions and Governments of Europe, Carried on in the Secret Meetings of Free Masons.* London & Edinburgh: T. Cadell Jun. and W. Davies, Strand and W. Creech, 1797. Second edition, 8vo., contemporary tree calf, rubbed at spine with spine lettering or label absent, very slight splitting at hinge ends, but sound, close to very good with clean text and heraldic (stag) bookplate of Archibald Campbell.   Any Amount of Books   March 2015 - A89311   2015   £350

Robson, William *Robson's London Directory and Street Key with British Court Guide for 1833.* London: William Robson, 1833. Thirteenth edition, 5 parts with ads on pages 41-116 of final section and 5 separate ads bound in, original full red calf, boards unevenly faded, spine faded and slightly chipped at tail, slight rubbing, good copy.   Jarndyce Antiquarian Booksellers CCXI - 243   2015   £250

Rocco, Francesco *A Manual of maritime Law, Consisting of a Treatise on Ships and Freight and a Treatise on Insurance.* Philadelphia: published by Hopkins and Earle, 1809. First edition in English, 8vo., half title, some paper discoloration and old waterstaining particularly in latter part of book, contemporary half calf, neatly rebacked and lettered, with early ownership signatures of J. Finnegan and John J. Van Allan, with Van Allan's signature at head of title, complete and generally pretty good.   John Drury Rare Books   2015 - 24312   2015 $830

Roch, Eugene *Insurrection de Strasbourg le 30 Octobre 1836 et proces des prevenus de Complicite avec le Prince Napoleon Louis, Devant la cour d'Assise du bas-Rhin.* Paris: au Bureau de l'Observateur des tribunaux, 1837. 8vo., half title, well bound in early 20th century dark green quarter morocco over marbled boards, raised bands, spine lettered gilt, original printed upper wrapper (repaired) bound in, very good, rare.   John Drury Rare Books   March 2015 - 25293   2015   £266

Rochat, Louis *Une Solutio du Probleme Socialiste... Salaires eleves - Vie a bon marche.* Paris: Guillaumin et Cie, 1851. First edition, 8vo., very good, sporadic and very minor spots and stains, original printed green wrappers, worn at fold, uncut, unopened, rare.   John Drury Rare Books   2015 - 16269   2015 $177

Roche, Arthur Somers *The Sport of Kings.* Indianapolis: Bobbs Merrill, 1917. First edition, near fine in pictorial green cloth covered boards.   Mordida Books   March 2015 - 007602   2015 $85

Rock & Co. *Rock's Illustrations of London.* London: Rock & Co. circa, 1851. Oblong 8vo., 30 engraved vignettes, publisher's blind and gilt blocked brown cloth, one plate with slight loss to imprint where trimmed in lower margin.   Marlborough Rare Books Ltd.   List 49 - 29   2015   £250

Rock, James L. *Southern and Western Texas Guide for 1878.* St. Louis: A. H. Granger, 1878. First edition, 8vo., original green decorated cloth, gilt on front cover and spine, frontispiece, 21 plates, tables, rare, still pictorial wrappers, lightly rubbed at spine ends and corners, spine rebacked with original spine laid down, covers lightly soiled, small stamp of Eastern Passenger Agent in NY and front prelim sheet lacks elusive map of Texas, else very good, bright and fresh overall.   Buckingham Books   March 2015 - 31670   2015 $400

Rock, Marion Tuttle *Illustrated History of Oklahoma.* C. B. Hamilton & Son, 1890. First edition, thick 8vo., maroon decorated cloth, gold stamping on front cover and spine, decorated endpapers, frontispiece, illustrations, plates, portraits, all edges red in color, some professional restoration to fore-edge of front fly-leaf, lightly sunned on spine, light wear to spine ends and corners, else very good, scarce, housed in maroon quarter leather and cloth slipcase with gold stamping on spine and raised bands.   Buckingham Books   March 2015 - 21004   2015 $2000

Rockhill, William Woodville *Diary of a Journey through Mongolia and Tibet in 1891 and 1892.* Washington: Smithsonian Institution, 1894. First edition, 8vo., 27 plates, folding map, 13 text illustrations, very good+, half red leather, marbled board binding, rebacked to style with gilt lettering to spine, marbled endpapers and edges, owner inscription, mild scuffs and edgewear covers.   By the Book, L. C.   44 - 63   2015 $1200

Rockwell, Donald S. *Women of Achievement Biographies and Portraits of Outstanding American Women.* New York: House of Field, 1940. First edition, press numbered edition, number 206, 4to., white cloth heavily embossed, stamped in gilt, cover worn at corners and ends of spine, spine split along part of its length, one hinge tender, some marginal chips to leaves, else very good, signed by author and artist, G. Maillard Kesslere.   Second Life Books Inc.   190 - 27   2015 $75

Rodgers, Jimmie, Mrs. *Jimmie Rodgers' Life Story.* Nashville: Ernest Tubb Pub., 1953. Second edition, printed from earlier edition, hardcover.   Beasley Books   2013 - 2015 $45

Roditi, Edouard *The Delights of Turkey: Twenty Tales.* New York: New Directions, 1979. First edition, foxing on fore edge, else very near fine in attractive, very good dust jacket with faint dampstains at lower corners, inscribed by author for Diane and Jerry Rothenberg.   Between the Covers Rare Books, Inc.   187 - 236   2015 $275

Roditi, Edouard *In a Lost World.* Santa Rosa: Black Sparrow Press Jan., 1978. First edition, stapled printed wrappers (16) pages, dampstain along edge of wrappers, inscribed by author for Jerome Rothenberg.   Between the Covers Rare Books, Inc.   187 - 235   2015 $250

Rodrigues, Eugene *Lettres sur la Religion et la Politique 1829.* Paris: au Bureau de l'Organisateur et chez A. Mesnier, 1831. First edition, 8vo., original printed blue wrappers, old repairs to spine and edges, entirely uncut, good copy.   John Drury Rare Books   2015 - 14994   2015 $177

Roe, Thomas *Sir Thomas Roe His Speech in Parliament. Wherein he Sheweth the Cause of the Decay of Coyne and trade in this Land, especially of Merchants Trade.* London: printed in the years, 1641. First edition, 4to., few old emphasis marks and amendments in ink in early hand, near contemporary parchment backed boards, board soiled, old small inkstamp of Royal Institution on blank margin of title, disposal stamp on lower pastedown, general light paper browning, still good, crisp copy, variant imprint.   John Drury Rare Books   2015 - 21967   2015 $830

Roeder, Adolph *Symbol-Psychology. A New Interpretation of Race-Traditions.* New York: Harper, 1903. First edition, hardcover, very good.   Beasley Books   2013 - 2015 $45

Roediger, Virginia More *Ceremonial Costumes of the Pueblo Indians.* Berkeley: 1941. First edition, 40 full page color plates, title on front board slightly faded, else clean and very good.   Dumont Maps & Books of the West   131 - 71   2015 $175

Roelands, David *T'Magazin of T' Pac-Huys der Loffelijcker Penn-Const.* Nieuwkoop: Miland Publishers, 1971. Facsimile reprint of 1616 edition, limited to 300 numbered copies.   Oak Knoll Books   306 - 240   2015 $165

Roethke, Theodore *Sequence Sometimes Metaphysical. Poems.* Iowa City: Stone Wall Press, 1963. First edition, one of 60 specially bound copies signed by author and artist, wood engravings by John Roy, small 4to., original quarter leather and pictorial boards, publisher's slipcase, very fine.   James S. Jaffe Rare Books   Modern American Poetry - 237   2015 $3500

Roger-Marx, Claude *Eloge De Maurice Brianchon.* Manuel Bruker, 1955. First edition, number 42 of 200 copies, 4to., unbound signatures laid into wrappers, beautiful lithographs by Brianchon, fine in near fine wrappers with tiniest signs of wear near spine ends and sunned edges.   Beasley Books   2013 - 2015 $250

Roger-Marx, Claude *Eloge De Roland Oudot.* Editions Manuel Bruker, 1956. First edition, unbound signatures laid into wrappers, number 167 of 200 copies, fine in near fine wrappers with lightly faded spine, original glassine, 8 original lithographs in color and in black and white, 8vo.   Beasley Books   2013 - 2015 $145

Roger-Marx, Claude *Portrait De Jacob Balgely.* Paris: Editions Manuel Bruker, 1959. #153 of 200 copies, unbound signatures, fine, 4to., wrappers very slightly soiled with sunned spine, otherwise fine, 9 engravings on separate sheets plus a 2 page engraving and full page frontispiece.   Beasley Books   2013 - 2015 $225

Roger-Marx, Claude *Portrait De Robert Lotiron.* Paris: Editions Manuel Bruker, 1955. #40 of 51 copies with an extra suite, unbound signatures in fine condition in fine, illustrated wrappers with extra set of prints, chemise fine but for sunned spine, in lightly soiled box, 8vo.   Beasley Books   2013 - 2015 $399

Rogers, Fred Blackburn *William Brown Ide, Bear Flagger.* San Francisco: John Howell Books, First edition, one of 750 copies, 101 pages, frontispiece, 6 plates, pictorial tan cloth stamped in white and red, gilt lettered spine, very fine.   Argonaut Book Shop   Holiday Season 2014 - 250   2015 $90

Rogers, J. R. *Chapters on Country Banking. Part I.* London: Effingham Wilson, 1847. Third edition, 8vo., 64 pages, little very light spotting, small blank corner torn from title, recent marbled boards, lettered on spine, good copy.   John Drury Rare Books   2015 - 25189   2015 $150

Rogers, Nathaniel P. *An Address Delivered Before the Concord Female Anti-Slavery Society at its Annual Meeting 25 Dec. 1837.* Concord: William White, 1838. First edition, 8vo., 32 pages, contemporary plain wrappers, sewn, wrappers becoming loose, last two leaves considerably foxed.   M & S Rare Books, Inc.   97 - 284   2015 $325

Rogers, Richard *Seuen Treatises, Containing Such Direction as Is Fathered Out of the Holie Scripture...* London: imprinted by Felix Kyngston, for Thomas Man and Robert Dexter, 1603. First edition, woodcut initials, one leaf with paper flaw removing most of one side-note, couple of other small paper flaws including 2 tiny holes in blank area of title leaf, titlepage and verso of last leaf very slightly soiled, few minor stains but in generally nice, clean crisp copy, folio, contemporary calf, triple blind fillets on sides, red lettering piece on spine, neat repair to head of spine, few scratches on covers, corners consolidated, early (probably 18th century) signature of Richard Newton on front free endpaper, very good. Blackwell's Rare Books B179 - 88 2015 £4000

Rogers, Robert W. *The Major Satires of Alexander Pope.* Urbana: University of Illinois Press, 1955. Half title, original brown printed paper wrappers, marked, spine creased, Geoffrey Tillotson's signed review copy with notes, with copy of his anonymous TLS. Jarndyce Antiquarian Booksellers CCVII - 426 2015 £30

Rogers, Samuel *Don't Look Behind You.* Harper & Bros., 1944. First edition, fine in fine, bright dust jacket. Buckingham Books March 2015 - 37182 2015 $250

Rogers, William Barton *Life and Letters of William Barton Rogers.* Boston & New York & Cambridge: Houghton Mifflin and Co. and The Riverside Press, 1896. 2 volumes, 8vo., frontispieces, plates, green cloth, gilt stamped spine title, dust jackets chipped with some stains (volume II only), else very good, rare in jackets. Jeff Weber Rare Books 178 - 952 2015 $95

Rogerson, Harry Summerfield *Modern Ornament.* Manchester: published by The Decorative Art Journals Co. Ltd. circa, 1901. First edition, 4 parts as issued, folio, 12 chromolithograph plates, including a number printed with gold and silver, original green and brown printed wrappers. Marlborough Rare Books List 54 - 69 2015 £850

Rohmer, Sax *The Bat Flies Low.* Doubleday, 1935. First edition, fine in near fine dust jacket with internal tape mends, some minor color restoration, some nicks along top edges and at top of spine. Mordida Books March 2015 - 007157 2015 $400

Rohmer, Sax *The Emperor of America.* New York: Doubleday Doran & Co., 1929. First edition, former owner's inked name, else very good in dust jacket with restoration to spine ends, corners and extremities. Buckingham Books March 2015 - 33711 2015 $1250

Rohmer, Sax *Little Tich.* London: Greening, 1911. First edition, 8vo., stiff color pictorial wrappers, photo frontispiece + 16 black and white plates and black and white line drawings in text, scarce, spine slightly worn and chipped, illustrated front has remnant of price label at corner, some rubbing and scuffing and slight edgewear, overall fairly sound very good- used copy with clean text. Any Amount of Books 2015 - A96088 2015 £225

Rohmer, Sax *She who Sleeps. A Romance of New York and the Nile.* New York: Doubleday Doran and Co. Inc., 1928. First US edition, fine, bright copy in fine, bright dust jacket, exceptional copy. Buckingham Books March 2015 - 35829 2015 $875

Rohmer, Sax *Sinister Madonna.* London: Jenkins, 1956. First edition, fine in price clipped dust jacket with price stamp and couple of tiny closed tears. Mordida Books March 2015 - 007604 2015 $275

Rohmer, Sax *The Slaves of Sumuru.* London: Jenkins, 1952. First edition, fine in dust jacket with light wear at corners. Mordida Books March 2015 - 00870 2015 $250

Rojas, Fernando De *La Ceslestina Tragicomedia De Claisto Y Melibeau.* Valencia: Del cid Editorial Castalia, 1946. 4to., number 276 of 300 copies on mould made paper, unbound signatures laid into chemise, original art work by Segrelles and etchings by Enriquez de Navarra, handsome production, fine in fine chemise in white box that shows wear. Beasley Books 2013 - 2015 $500

Rolfe, Frederick William 1880-1913 *A Letter to a Small Nephew Named Claud.* Iowa City: Typographic Library The University of Iowa School of Journalism, 1964. First edition, one of 150 copies, decorated paper wrappers, printed label. Any Amount of Books 2015 - C14204 2015 £180

Rolle, Samuel *Shilhavtiyah (Hebrew) or the Burning of London in the Year 1666.* London: printed by R. I. for Thomas Parkhurst at the Golden Bible on London-bridge, 1667. First edition, variant issue, 8vo., large folding engraved frontispiece, possibly wanting half title, skillfully rebound in old style half alf over marbled boards, flat spine with gilt lines and label, good, uncommon. John Drury Rare Books 2015 - 22926 2015 $2185

Rolleston, T. W. *The Tale of Lohengrin: Knight of the Swan after the Drama of Richard Wagner.* London: Harrup, n.d., 1913. First edition, 4to., brown gilt pictorial cloth, inconspicuous rub spot on endpaper, else fine in original pictorial slipcase (scuffed, neatly strengthened), 8 tipped in color plates, full page black and white lithographs and many full page color illustrations by Willy Pogany, all printed on heavy paper, beautiful copy, scarce in slipcase. Aleph-Bet Books, Inc. 108 - 351 2015 $1000

Rollins, Philip Ashton *The Discovery of the Oregon Trail.* New York: Charles Scribner's Sons, 1936. First edition, 8vo., cloth, 4 plates, 6 maps, top edge gilt, dust jacket. Buckingham Books   March 2015 - 24341   2015 $1250

Rollinson, John K. *Pony Trails in Wyoming.* Caxton Printers Ltd., 1941. First edition, 8vo., presentation inscription from E. A. Brininstool Xmas 1941 for L. H. Spragle, near fine, tight copy in dust jacket lightly chipped at spine ends, corners and extremities.   Buckingham Books   March 2015 - 29394   2015 $275

Rollinson, John K. *Pony Trails in Wyoming. Hoofprints of a cowboy and U.S. Ranger.*   Caldwell: Caxton Printers, 1941. First edition, presentation copy inscribed by author, promotional bookmark laid in, and original publication prospectus and order form, cloth, tan endpapers, photos, near fine, tight copy in dust jacket, lightly chipped at spine ends and extremities.   Buckingham Books   March 2015 - 28776   2015 $225

Rollinson, John K. *Wyoming Cattle Trails.* Caldwell: Caxton Printers Ltd., 1948. First trade edition, 8vo., cloth, illustrations, including 44 plates, 3 maps, frontispiece and pictorial dust jacket illustration by Frederic Remington, fine in dust jacket, beautiful copy.   Buckingham Books   March 2015 - 27759   2015 $250

Rolt-Wheeler, Francis William *The Monster-Hunters.* Boston: Lothrop, Lee & Shepard Co., 1916. First edition, 30 inserted plates, 53 illustrations, original pictorial green cloth, front and spine panels stamped in red, black and gold, pictorial paper onlay affixed to front panel.   L. W. Currey, Inc. Boy's Adventure Fiction 2015 - 94   2015 $100

Romains, Jules *Knock Ou le Triomphe De La Medecine.* Paris: Les Editions Du Valois, 1953. One of 350 copies from an edition of 2000, with extra suite of plates in black and white by Dubout, unbound signatures laid into wrappers, illustrations in color by artist, chemise and matching box, small quarto, chemise has water drop stain at foot of spine 2 x 3/4 inches, split to one joint.   Beasley Books 2013 - 2015 $300

Romano, Paul *The American Worker.* New York: 1947. First edition, very good, 8vo., wrappers, worn and chipped with water ring on front wrapper.   Beasley Books   2013 - 2015 $45

Ronchi, Vasco *Histoire de la Lumiere.* Paris: Librairie Armand Colin, 1956. 8vo., original printed wrappers, foot of spine bit worn, very good, ownership signature of Roger Hahn, scarce.   Jeff Weber Rare Books   178 - 958   2015 $50

Rong, Jiang *Wolf Totem.* New York: Penguin Press, 2008. 8vo., double page map, signed in ink by author, highly uncommon signature, fine in dust jacket very slightly used edges, complete, clean and near fine.   Any Amount of Books   2015 - C15228   2015   £750

Roos, Kelley *The Frightened Stiff.* New York: Dodd Mead & Co., 1942. First edition, former owner's name, date and stamp on front free flyleaf, covers lightly soiled, else very good in dust jacket with light professional restoration to spine ends and extremities.   Buckingham Books   March 2015 - 25752   2015 $400

Roosevelt, Eleanor *This Troubled World.* New York: Kinsey, 1938. First edition, 8vo., very good in slightly rubbed dust jacket.   Second Life Books Inc.   189 - 212   2015 $75

Roosevelt, Theodore 1858-1919 *Big Game Hunting in the Rockies and on the Great Plains Comprising "Hunting Trips of a Ranchman" and "The Wilderness Hunter".* New York and London: G. P. Putnam's Sons, 1899. Number 517 of 1000 copies, signed by author under frontispiece illustration. 55 original cloth, black leather title labels to spine and front cover, expertly rebacked with new material visible along head of spine and interior pages, gilt illustrations to front cover, black illustration to rear cover, covers and spine darkened and lightly soiled with scuff marks to leather labels, minor chipping to edges of endpapers, few spots of soiling verso colophon and few spots of foxing to first and last few pages, bookplate of Reginald Winans Hutton, very good, 2 books bound as one.   The Kelmscott Bookshop 11 - 42   2015 $5500

Roosevelt, Theodore 1858-1919 *Hunting Trips of a Ranchman.* G. P. Putnam's sons, 1885. First edition, Medora edition, #135 of an edition limited to 500 copies, pictorial cloth, 318 pages, 4 etchings by R. Swain Gifford, 7 drawings by J. C. Beard and full page plates by Frost, Sandham, et al, professionally rebacked with original spine laid down, previous owner's bookplate, else very good+. Buckingham Books   March 2015 - 34461   2015 $875

Root, Frank W. *The Overland Stage to California.* Topeka: Pub. by the authors, 1901. First edition, thick 8vo., original light brown pictorial cloth, illustrations, inked in author's hand on front cover "Author's Copy", else near fine. Buckingham Books   March 2015 - 25782   2015 $1275

Root, Henry *Personal History and Reminiscences with Personal Opinions on Contemporary Events 1845-1921.* San Francisco: Privately printed, 1921. First edition, presentation inscription signed and dated by author, portrait, original brown cloth lettered gilt on spine and front cover, spine ever so slightly faded, slight rubbing to spine ends, fine and clean copy.   Argonaut Book Shop   Holiday Season 2014 - 251   2015 $250

Roots, George *The Charters of the Town of Kingston Upon Thames Translated into English with Occasional Notes.* London: T. Cadell Jun and W. Davies, 1797. First edition, 8vo., half title little soiled, rebound fairly recently in good half calf over marbled boards, spine gilt and labelled with raised bands, very scarce. John Drury Rare Books March 2015 - 23531   2015   £266

Rose, George *A Brief Examination into the Increase of the Revenue, Commerce and Navigation of Great Britain During the Administration of the Rt. Hon. William Pitt...* London: J. Hatchard, 1806. First edition, half title, 4 folding tables, uncut and sewn as issued, original blue wrappers, fine. John Drury Rare Books   March 2015 - 9880   2015 $266

Rose, George *Cases in Bankruptcy.* London: Reed And Hunter, 1813. First edition, 2 volumes, 8vo., half leather lettered gilt on red and black spine labels, neat name and address on front endpaper, covers very slight mottled, very slight rubbing at corners and spine hinges, titlepage and first page of volume 1, slightly chipped at edge and creased not affecting text, otherwise sound, very good, handsome copies.   Any Amount of Books   2015 - A97538   2015   £240

Rose, George *The Proposed system of trade with Ireland explained.* London: John Nichols, 1785. First edition, 8vo., 58 pages, half title, recently well bound in linen backed marbled boards lettered, very good.   John Drury Rare Books   2015 - 17708   2015 $106

Rose, George *The Trial of George Rose Esq. Secretary to the Treasury...* London: J. Ridgway, 1791. First edition, 8vo., half title, contemporary half calf over marbled boards, neatly rebacked to match, spine lettered gilt, very good, uncommon.   John Drury Rare Books   2015 - 25317   2015 $787

Rose, Hugh James *The Gospel an Abiding System.* London: J. G. & F. Rivington, 1832. First edition, 8vo., recently well bound in linen backed marbled boards lettered, very good.   John Drury Rare Books   March 2015 - 20640   2015 $221

Rose, Hugh James *Untrodden Spain, and Her Black Country...* London: Samuel Tinsley, 1875. Second edition, 2 volumes, 8vo., original green cloth lettered gilt on spine and black on cover, slight foxing to prelims, slight rubbing to spine ends, else very good+ decent conditionA85208.   Any Amount of Books   2015 - A85208   2015   £225

Rose, Wendy *Academic Squaw: Report to the World from the Ivory Tower.* Marvin: Blue Cloud Quarterly, 1977. First edition, stapled illustrated wrappers, near fine, inscribed by author to Jerome Rothenberg.   Between the Covers Rare Books, Inc.   187 - 198   2015 $275

Rose, Wendy *Builder Kachina: a Home Going Cycle.* Marvin: Blue Cloud Quarterly, 1979. First edition, illustrations by author, stapled illustrated wrappers small stain on front wrapper, else near fine, inscribed by author to Jerome Rothenberg.   Between the Covers Rare Books, Inc.   187 - 199   2015 $250

Rose, Wendy *What Happened when the Hopi Hit New York.* New York: Contact II Publications, 1982. First edition, decorated blue self wrappers, some dampstains along spine and on very margins of leaves, else very good, inscribed by author for Jerome and Diane Rothenberg. Between the Covers Rare Books, Inc.   187 - 200   2015 $200

Rose, William *The History of Joseph.* London: printed for James Knapton, 1712. First edition, engraved frontispiece and 5 other plates, 8vo., half calf, rebacked, portions of original spine laid down (rubbed), uncommon, frontispiece mounted, some soiling and light stains, but sound.   C. R. Johnson   Foxon R-Z - 840r-z   2015 $230

Rose, William *The Radium Book.* Cleveland: Rose Pub. Co., 1905. First and probably only edition, 4to., cloth backed pictorial boards, edges worn, light cover soil, tight and very good+, illustrations by Harry Hornhorst, rare. Aleph-Bet Books, Inc.   108 - 322   2015 $875

Rose, William Ganson *The Rousing of Parkside.* New York: Duffield & Co., 1914. First edition, 12mo., decorated paper covered boards, spine toned and little worn, very good, bookplate of author Kenneth Roberts, full page poetic inscription from author to Roberts.   Between the Covers Rare Books, Inc.   187 - 237   2015 $150

Rosebery, Lord *The House of Lords and the Franchise Bill. A Speech Delivered in the House of Lords on the Second Reading of the Franchise Bill (8th July 1884).* Edinburgh: Andrew Elliot, 1884. First edition, 8vo., 24 pages, preserved in modern wrappers with printed label on upper cover, very good.   John Drury Rare Books   2015 - 25068   2015 $89

Rosebery, Lord *The Reform of the House of Lords. A Speech Delivered in that House June 20 1884 by Lord Rosebery.* Edinburgh: Andrew Elliot, 1884. First separate edition, 8vo., pencilled doodles on blank verso of last leaf, preserved in modern wrappers with printed label on upper cover, very good.   John Drury Rare Books   2015 - 25067   2015 $89

Rosen, R. D. *Strike Three You're Dead.* New York: Walker, 1984. First edition, very fine in dust jacket. Mordida Books   March 2015 - 00236   2015 $160

Rosenberg, Harold *Arshile Gorky, The Man, The Time, The Idea.* New York: Horizon, 1962. First edition, near fine in very good+ to near fine dust jacket with clean tear at head and front of spine fold. Beasley Books 2013 - 2015 $45

Rosenblatt, Julia Carlson *Dining with Sherlock Holmes.* Indianapolis: Bobbs Merrill, 1976. First edition, fine in dust jacket. Mordida Books March 2015 - 007877 2015 $100

Rosenstiehl, Auguste *Traite De la Couleur a Point De Vue Physique, Physiologique et Esthetique.* Paris: Dunod et Pinat editeurs 47 et 49 Quai des Grands Augustins, 1913. royal 8vo., 14 plates, including mounted paper and fabric samples, preserving original printed wrappers, red cloth, spine lettered in gilt. Marlborough Rare Books List 54 - 70 2015 £750

Rosenwald, Lessing J. *Vision of a Collector, the Lessing J. Rosenwald Collection the Library of Congress.* Washington: Library of Congress, 1991. One of 300 numbered copies bound thus and meant for subscribers, these special copies contain a signed and numbered etched portrait of Rosenwald by artist Tony Rosati, tall 8vo., quarter green morocco over patterned paper covered boards, this copy signed by William Matheson at end of his essay, illustrations, some in color, loosely inserted is exhibition catalogue dated 1992. Oak Knoll Books 306 - 294 2015 $215

Ross, Barnaby *Drury Lane's Last Case. The Tragedy of 1599.* New York: Viking Press, 1933. First edition, very good, clean lacking scarce dust jacket. Buckingham Books March 2015 - 31519 2015 $200

Ross, Diana *The Little Red Engine Gets a Name.* London: Faber & Faber, n.d., 1942. Oblong 8vo., pictorial boards, light soil, very good-fine in dust jacket, color illustrations by Lewitt and Him. Aleph-bet Books, Inc. 109 - 265 2015 $250

Ross, Edmund G. *Report of the Governor of New Mexico to the Secretary of the Interior.* Washington: GPO, 1885. First edition, printed wrappers, ex-DeGolyer Public Library copy with small imprint in front wrapper and label affixed to bottom edge of inside front wrapper, minor chipping to edges of fragile wrappers, else very good. Buckingham Books March 2015 - 376 2015 $200

Ross, George *Leading cases in the Commercial Law of England and Scotland.* London: W. G. Benning and Co.; Edinburgh: Thomas Constable and Co., 1857. 1853. First edition, fine set, 3 volumes, large 8vo., half titles in volumes II and III, contemporary uniform calf, raised bands and gilt lettered, uncut, fine set. John Drury Rare Books 2015 - 24852 2015 $787

Ross, Marvin C. *The West of Alfred Jacob Miller.* Norman: Oklahoma University Press, 1951. First edition, 4to., cloth, black and white illustrations, frontispiece in color, fine in edgeworn, but complete dust jacket which is good. Baade Books of the West 2014 - 2015 $112

Ross, Ronald *In Exile.* Liverpool: privately printed, 1906. First edition, pencil and occasional ink notes and corrections, original maroon printed paper wrappers, slightly creased with slight loss to upper corner front wrapper, presentation inscription "With Sir Ronald Ross's compliments. Author's working copy see page 6, 22, see especially page 81", from the collection of Kathleen and Geoffrey Tillotson. Jarndyce Antiquarian Booksellers CCXI - 245 2015 £250

Ross, Thomas *The Procane Chronicle.* New York: William Morrow & Co., 1972. First edition, page edges uniformly tanned, else fine in price clipped dust jacket, scarce. Buckingham Books March 2015 - 21485 2015 $200

Rosse, William Parsons, 3rd Earl of *The Scientific Papers of William Parsons, Third Earl of Rosse 1800-1867.* London: Collected and republished by the Hon. Sir Charles Parsons, 1926. 4to., plates, charts, some minor foxing, rebound professionally in handsome black cloth, gilt stamped spine title, near fine. Jeff Weber Rare Books 178 - 873 2015 $625

Rossetti, Christina 1830-1894 *A Pageant and Other poems.* London: Macmillan, 1881. First edition, half title, occasional pencil annotations in text, uncut in original dark blue cloth, blocked and lettered gilt, slightly marked, armorial bookplate of Marcia Dalyrmple and also her signature dated Aug 25 81, very good, bright copy. Jarndyce Antiquarian Booksellers CCXI - 246 2015 £150

Rossetti, Christina 1830-1894 *Poems.* London: Blackie and Son, 1906. Red Letter Library edition, green cloth with Mackintosh style gilt design, inscribed by author for Anita Battle Brackenbury. Between the Covers Rare Books, Inc. 187 - 238 2015 $250

Rossetti, Christina 1830-1894 *Poems by Christina Rossetti.* London: Blackie & Son, n.d., 1910. Thick 4to., white cloth with extensive gilt decoration, top edge gilt, very fine in original pictorial dust jacket, 36 magnificent mounted color plates, 34 full page black and white illustrations plus many black and whites by Florence Harrison, magnificent copy, rare in dust jacket. Aleph-bet Books, Inc. 109 - 221 2015 $1800

Rossetti, Christina 1830-1894 *Verses.* London: SPCK, 1893. Sixth edition, printed on thick paper, rubricated text, uncut in original dark blue buckram, bevelled boards, lettered gilt, top edge gilt, very good, inscribed to "Mackenzie Bell Esq. 1894". Jarndyce Antiquarian Booksellers CCXI - 247 2015 £750

Rossetti, Dante Gabriel 1828-1882 *Hand and Soul.* Hammersmith: Kelmscott Press, 1895. Printed in an edition limited to 546 copies, this one of 225 copies printed on paper for Way and Williams of Chicago, 12mo., original stiff vellum, woodcut borders on facing titlepage and first page of text, ornamented with numerous six line and smaller initial letters throughout text, two small spots along front hinge, bookplate of Anna H. Wilmarth, few foxed spots along outer edge of pages.   Oak Knoll Books   306 - 155   2015 $1500

Rossetti, Dante Gabriel 1828-1882 *The House of Life.* Boston: Copeland and Day, 1894. Limited to 550 copies, 8vo., quarter cloth, paper covered boards, top edge cut, other edges uncut, dust jacket torn at spine and chipped at edges, joints and hinges cracking, 3 borders and 114 initials by Bertram Grosvenor Goodhue, bookplate of Mary Hawes Wilmarth (1837-1919).   Oak Knoll Books   306 - 147   2015 $250

Rossetti, Michael *Notes on the Royal Academy Exhibition 1868.* London: John Camden Hutton, Piccadilly, 1868. First edition, scarce, very good in original cream paper wrappers with black title to front panel, covers darkened along edges, minor soiling and few spots of foxing, few chips to spine panel and to rear corner, interior clean overall, with few splits to binding and few small spots to foxing on first and last few pages, housed in modern green cloth covered slipcase with black leather title label to spine and pull out chemise.   The Kelmscott Bookshop   11 - 43   2015 $750

Rossi, Nicola Giuseppe *Della Garanzia nel Commercio Degli Animali Domestici Utili. Secondo le Consuetudini Gli Statuti ed I Codici Nella Plu Parte Degli Statj Esteri si d'Italia che d'Oltramonte...* Vicenze: G. Longo, 1856. First edition, with final errata leaf, original printed wrappers, upper wrapper embellished with ornate design incorporating images of farm animals, tools and agricultural machinery, etc., lower wrapper neatly repaired, very good, uncut, partially unopened.   John Drury Rare Books   2015 - 18004   2015 $159

Rostaing, Jules *Voyage dans les Deux Ameriques ou les neveus de L'Oncle Tom.* Paris: Louis Janet, 1854. First edition, 8vo., original blindstamped red cloth, gilt lettering, 12 color lithographed plates by C. Lemercier, lightly foxed throughout, text little shaken, very good.   The Brick Row Book Shop   Miscellany 67 - 87   2015 $850

Rostand, Edmond *Cyrano de Bergerac.* Paris: Librairie Charpentier et Fasquelle, 1898. First edition, original printed pale green wrappers, bit smudged and soiled on wrappers, else near fine, housed in chemise and quarter morocco slipcase.   Between the Covers Rare Books   196 - 103   2015 $4500

Rota, Gian-Carlo *Gian-Carlo Rota on Combintorics.* Boston: Birkhauser, 1995. First edition, signed and inscribed by author, small 4to., fine in near fine dust jacket.   By the Book, L. C.   44 - 31   2015 $500

Roth, Philip *Goodbye, Columbus.* Boston: Houghton Mifflin Co., 1959. First edition, fine in fine dust jacket with slightest of toning at spine, author's very scarce first book, almost always found quite worn, lovely copy, from the library of Kate Stettner Lobell and Carl D. Lobell.   Between the Covers Rare Books   196 - 31   2015 $2500

Roth, Philip *My Life as a Man.* New York: Holt, Rinehart & Winston, 1974. First edition, first printing, inscribed by Roth and signed, very good with some wear to lower edge in like jacket with some minor rubbing to extremities, else fine.   B & B Rare Books, Ltd.   234 - 87   2015 $500

Roth, Philip *Operation Shylock: a Confession.* New York: 1993. Advance Reading copy, printed from proof plates and preceding first edition, hardcover, new condition, not issued in dust jacket.   Gemini Fine Books & Arts, Ltd.   Art Reference & Illustrated Books: First Editions - 2015 $50

Rothstein, Arnold *Psychoanalytic Technique and the Creation of Analytic Patients.* Maidson: International Universities Press, 1995. First edition, fine in fine dust jacket, 8vo.   Beasley Books   2013 - 2015 $45

Roualt, Georges *Stella Vespertina Avant Propos De M. L'Abbe maurice Morel.* Paris: Rene Drouin, 1947. #1793 of 2000 copies, gathered sheets, folio, all pages over printed with gray watercolor like printing, 12 plates, fine pages laid into paper covered boards of matching gray, chemise showing one small stain to spine and box that is soiled and sunned.   Beasley Books   2013 - 2015 $175

Rouget De Lisle, Amedee *Chromagraphie Ou L'Art De Composer Un Dessin a l'Aide de Lignes et De Figures Geometriques....* Paris: Chez l'Auteur Rue Du Faubourg Poissonniere * Chez Pitoois Levrault et Compagnie, Rue de la Harpe, 81 chez les Principaux Libraires et Fabricants de Coleurs, 1839. First edition, 4to., 9 double page hand colored lithograph plates, after Chevreul and 6 double page engraved plates, original decorative printed wrappers, preserved in early 20th century green art vellum backed marbled boards.   Marlborough Rare Books   List 54 - 71   2015   £2850

Rouille D'Orefeuil, Augustin *L'Alambic des Loix ou l'Ami des Francois sur l'Homme et sur les Loix.* Paris: 1773. First edition, 8vo., half title with rare preface, contemporary calf, spine fully gilt with raised bands, marbled endpapers, edges red, foot of upper cover little stained, still fine, crisp, rare.   John Drury Rare Books   2015 - 25143   2015 $1661

Rourke, Thomas *The Scarlet Flower.* London: Nicholson & Watson, 1934. First English edition, fine in dust jacket. Mordida Books March 2015 - 008449 2015 $375

Rousseau, Jean Jacques 1712-1778 *The Confessions of Jean Jacques Rousseau.* London: Nonesuch Press, 1938. First edition thus, number 105 of 800 copies, 2 volumes, octavo, ornamental wood engravings by Reynolds Stone, full tan morocco, top edge gilt, spines slightly tanned, otherwise fine set in slightly rubbed card slipcase. Peter Ellis, Bookseller 2014 - 014263 2015 £285

Rousseau, Jean Jacques 1712-1778 *Original Letters of J. J. Rousseau, to M. De Malesherbes, M. D'Alembert Madame La M. De Luxeembourg &c.* London: H. D. Symonds, 1799. Original panel stamped calf, spine decorated and lettered gilt, marbled page edges, some cracking to joints, spine slightly faded, foldout facsimile sheet of Rousseau's hand-writing slightly creased and chipped at bottom right quarter with slight loss of text, small printed cameo portrait of author pasted to front pastedown, some offsetting to titlepage from frontispiece which is quite foxed, similarly with engraved music sheets and enclosing pages, some pages have light crease at top forecorner, otherwise very good. Any Amount of Books 2015 - C13209 2015 £250

Routh, Edward John *A Treatise on Analytical Statics with Numerous Examples.* Cambridge: University Press, 1896. 1902. Second edition, volume II revised, 2 volumes, 8vo., later blue cloth, preserving original black leather gilt stamped spine labels, title ink signature of Harold Levine, 1941, 3 red ink underlining marks on page 131 volume II, very good. Jeff Weber Rare Books 178 - 968 2015 $45

Routh, Edward John *A Treatise on the Stability of a Given State of Motion, Paricularly Steady Motion.* London: Macmillan, 1877. 8vo., titlepage ink inscription of St. John Stephen, Caius Coll(ege) Camb. 16th Oct. 1877, early half plain calf, brick red cloth, red and black gilt stamped spine labels, head spine worn, otherwise rubbed, St. J. S." in gilt foot of spine, very good. Jeff Weber Rare Books 178 - 966 2015 $250

Rouzet, Anne *Dictionnaire Des Imprimeurs, Libraires et Editeurs des XVe et XVIe Siecles dans les Limites Geographiques de la Belgique Actuelle.* Nieuwkoop: B. de Graaf, 1975. First edition, small 4to., cloth , tables at end of volume. Oak Knoll Books 306 - 199 2015 $165

Rowan, Richard W. *Spy and County-Spy: the Development of Modern Espionage.* New York: Viking, 1928. First edition, very good, spine and page edges darkened, otherwise very good in fine dust jacket. Mordida Books March 2015 - 010039 2015 $135

Rowe, Elizabeth *The History of Joseph.* London: printed for T. Worrall, 1736. First edition, 8vo., engraved frontispiece, recent boards, fine. C. R. Johnson Foxon R-Z - 843r-z 2015 $1149

Rowe, Elizabeth *Philomela; or, Poems.* (bound with) *The History of Joseph a poem in ten books.* London: printed for E. Curll, 1737. London: printed for B. D. and sold by S. Birt, S. Harding and T. Worrall, 1738. Second edition, engraved frontispiece, 8vo, 2 volumes in 1, contemporary calf, gilt, spine gilt, joints slightly cracked, lacks label, very good. C. R. Johnson Foxon R-Z - 841r-z 2015 $1149

Rowe, Henry *Fables in Verse.* London: printed for J. J. Stockdale, 1810. Bookplate of Gustaf Berndtsson, illustrations, contemporary half dark brown calf, elaborate gilt spine, very good. Jarndyce Antiquarian Booksellers CCXI - 248 2015 £120

Rowe, Nicholas *Ode for the New Year MDCCXVI.* London: printed for J. Tonson, 1716. First edition, folio, disbound, slight signs of prior folding, half title trifle dusty, but very good, uncommon. C. R. Johnson Foxon R-Z - 849r-z 2015 $1149

Rowe, Nicholas *A Poem Upon the Late Glorious Successes of Her Majesty's Arms &c, inscribed to Rt. on. Earl of Godolphin, Lord High-Treasurer of England.* London: printed for Jacob Tonson, 1707. First edition, folio, wanting half title, some light browning, otherwise good, disbound. C. R. Johnson Foxon R-Z - 8504r-z 2015 $306

Rowe, Nicholas *Poems on Several Occasions and Translations.* Glasgow: printed by Robert Urie, 1751. First Glasgow edition, small 8vo., contemporary stiff marbled wrappers, fine, rare. C. R. Johnson Foxon R-Z - 844r-z 2015 $460

Rowland, Henry Augustus *The Physical Papers of Henry August Rowland, Ph.D., LL.D.* Baltimore: Johns Hopkins Press, 1902. First collected edition, 8vo., gravure frontispiece portrait with tissue guard, 10 plates, figures, tables, burgundy cloth, gilt stamped cover and spine titles, inner hinge cracked, former library copy with usual marking and defects, some plates blindstamped, good. Jeff Weber Rare Books 178 - 967 2015 $90

Rowland, John *The Glorious Mission of the American People. A Thanksgiving Discourse.* Circleville: printed at the Religious Telescope Office, 1850. First edition, 12mo., 24 pages, original printed wrappers lightly soiled and worn, text foxed, with signature on title (smudged) and on following leaf of Mrs. Deborah G. Rowland, Windsor, Ct. M & S Rare Books, Inc. 97 - 232 2015 $175

Rowlandson, Thomas *The High Mettled Racer.* London: Pub... by S. W. Fores, N. 3 Piccadilly, July 20, 1789. A set of four hand colored engravings with aquatint by J. Hassell (305 x 445mm), each print with double fillet order in wash containing engraved lines of verse and title imprint at foot of two plates shaved also minor nicks to blank edges and some skillful restoration, overall very fine set, preserved in custom made cloth portfolio. Marlborough Rare Books List 54 - 72   2015   £2000

Rowlandson, Thomas *Rowlandson's Characteristic Sketches of the Lower Orders Intended as a Companion to the new Picture of London, consisting of Fifty-Four Plates, Neatly Coloured.* London: printed for Samuel Leigh 18 Strand, 1820. First edition, first issue, 12mo., 54 hand colored plates, including frontispiece, later straight ribbed morocco, spine decorated in six compartments, two lettered in gilt, gilt top, silk endpapers, bound by Zaehnsdorf 1902. Marlborough Rare Books   List 54 - 73   2015   £2500

Rowling, J. K. *Complete set of Seven Harry Potter Deluxe Editions.* London: Bloomsbury, 1999. First collector's edition, as new, bound in decorated red cloth with all edges gilt,. Buckingham Books   March 2015 - 26387   2015 $8000

Rowling, J. K. *Harry Potter and the Prisoner of Azkaban.* London: Bloomsbury, 1999. First edition, evening browning to pages along with foxing to front and rear flyleaf, else fine in dust jacket. Buckingham Books   March 2015 - 26393   2015 $450

Rowson, Susanna Haswell *Lucy Temple: One of the Three Orphans. A Sequel to Charlotte Temple.* New York: Richard Marsh; Philadelphia: Wm. A. Leary, 1852. Later printing of second or third edition, 12mo., original printed yellow boards, scarce, boards somewhat soiled and worn, text little shaken, good, sound.   The Brick Row Book Shop Miscellany 67 - 79   2015 $175

Royal Astronomical Society *Supplementary Catalogue of the Library of the Royal Astronomical Society June 1898 to June 1925.* London: Royal Astronomical Society, 1926. 8vo., quarter red cloth with printed paper boards, edges slightly worn, very good, rare.   Jeff Weber Rare Books 178 - 968   2015 $45

Royal College of Art: Births, Marriages and Deaths. London: Lion and Unicorn Press, 1954. First edition, 4to., original maroon cloth lettered gilt on spine with gilt insignia on cover, color and black and white illustrations, very slight rubbing, faint wear at extremities, very good+.   Any Amount of Books   2015 - A89406   2015   £160

Royal College of Physicians of London *Report... on Vaccination.* London: by Luke Hansard & Sons, 1807. 15 pages, removed, very good.   Joseph J. Felcone Inc. Science, Medicine and Technology - 36   2015 $175

The Royal Fortune Teller; or the Art of Fortune-Telling by Cards, the Signs of the Zodiac, a Number of Charms and Spells... London: circa, 1850. 24 pages, one color plate, plate has had bookplate removed, with staining to verso and one small hole professionally mended, front wrapper with attic soil.   Bookworm & Silverfish   2015 - 5451114750 2015 $400

The Royal Martyrs; or a List of the Lords, Knights, Officers and Gentlemen, That Were Slain (by the Rebels) in the Late Wars in Defence of Their King and Country. London: by Henry Lloyd and are to be sold by H. Marsh,, 1663. mall 4to. without final blank leaf, very lightly browned throughout and with small damp spot on (A)2(touching one line of text), mid 20th century red morocco, from the library of James Stevens Cox (1910-1997).   Maggs Bros. Ltd.   1447 - 95 2015   £150

Royce, Josiah *William James and Other Essays in Philosophy of Life.* New York: Macmillan Co., 1911. First edition, octavo, original green cloth, gilt lettering on front board and spine, some wear to spine edges and tips, spine not noticeably discolored by sun but with gilt lettering that has faded significantly, this one darkened stain to upper left corner of front board, former owner's bookplate to inside front cover and pencil signature, overall nice.   Athena Rare Books   15 - 55   2015 $75

Royce, Josiah *The World and the Individual.* New York: Macmillan Co., 1900. First edition, octavo, gorgeous inscription by author Nov. 5 1900, original green binding with gilt lettering on spine, just lightest of wear to spine edges and tips, final four leaves uncut, occasional horizontal and vertical small pencil lines (typically 1/4" or so) in margins, overall, beautiful copy with fine inscription.   Athena Rare Books   15 - 54   2015 $2200

Rubeanus, Johannes Crotus *Epistolae Obscuroru Virorum ...* Francofurti: Ad Maenum, 1643. Nova edition, 12mo., original full calf, dark brown somewhat rubbed with handwritten paper spine label faded, lacks endpapers, otherwise very good.   Any Amount of Books   2015 - C13396 2015   £160

Rubinow, I. M. *Social Insurance.* New York: Henry Holt, 1916. Second edition, very scarce early printing, very good in original cloth, little staining at bottom, neat repair to paper hinges.   Stephen Lupack   March 2015 - 2015 $250

Rubottom, Sibyl *The Water Book: Lanes of Thought.* San Diego: Bay Park Press, 2010. Number 4 of 10 copies, 6 etchings and 3 unique oil paintings on mylar, printed on Fabriano Rosapina Bianco paper using letterpress and intaglio prints, some with chine colle, set in Bernhard modern, oblong folio, housed in blue clamshell box, fine.   The Kelmscott Bookshop   11 - 3   2015 $1500

Ruskin, John 1819-1900 *The Queen of the Air: Being a Study of the Greek Myths of Cloud and Storm.* London: Smith, Elder, 1869. Second edition, 8vo., presentation from author for Mrs. A. J. Scott, April 1870, decent clean very good copy in original green cloth lettered gilt at spine, top of titlepage has been cut out to reveal presentation at top of next page, (not affecting text), slight rubbing at spine ends, else very good.   Any Amount of Books   2015 - A63060 2015   £200

Ruskin, John 1819-1900 *The Complete Works of...* London: George Allen & Unwin, 1903-1912. 8vo., 39 volumes, original burgundy cloth, gilt illustration on upper cover, lettered gilt on spine, deckled edges, excellent, clean, very good set with some fading at spines and some differential fading to few volumes.   Any Amount of Books   2015 - C13615   2015   £1600

Russell, Bertrand 1872-1970 *Bolshevism: Practice and Theory.* New York: Harcourt Brace and Howe, 1920. First American edition, spine little toned, very good, without dust jacket, American poet Melville Cane's copy with his ownership signature.   Between the Covers Rare Books, Inc. 187 - 239   2015 $100

Russell, Carl Parcher *One Hundred Years in Yosemite. The Story a a Great Park and Its Friends.* Berkeley and Los Angeles: University of California Press, 1947. Second edition, 242 pages, photos, map, light green cloth, fine. Argonaut Book Shop   Holiday Season 2014 - 252   2015 $60

Russell, Charles Marion 1864-1926 *A Bibliography of the Published Works of Charles M. Russell.* Lincoln: 1971. Limited to 600 copies, #41 signed by Frederic Renner, 4to., full leather, illustrations, light wear to cover edges, couple of minor abrasions, very good in dust jacket with corners slipped, near fine dust jacket.   Baade Books of the West 2014 - 2015 $89

Russell, Charles Marion 1864-1926 *Rawhide Rollins Stories. (with) More Rawhides.* Pasadena: Trail's End Publishing Co., 1946. First revised edition, 2 volumes, small quarto, 60 pages each, illustrations by author/artist, gray and terra cotta pictorial cloth, fine set with elusive pictorial dust jackets (slight chipping or rubbing to extremities). Argonaut Book Shop   Holiday Season 2014 - 253   2015 $325

Russell, Charles Marion 1864-1926 *Reproductions of Original Russell Sketches - 15 Famous Sketches.* Leader Co., 1962. Folio, printed decorated yellow colored envelope, 11 1/2 x 17 inches, with 15 black and white prints, 11 x 16 1'2 inches, each print has small explanatory slip attached, all prints fine, envelope with some moderate wear to extremities and tear along bottom edge of front panel, else very good.   Buckingham Books   March 2015 - 18426 2015 $275

Russell, Don *One Hundred and Three Fights and Scrimmages. The Story of General Reuben F. Bernard.* Washington: United States Cavalry Assoc., 1936. First edition, real printed grey wrappers, 173 pages, illustrations, maps, front cover upper fore corner has triangular ship 1/2 inch deep, else very good+, scarce.   Baade Books of the West   2014 - 2015 $82

Russell, James *A Letter Addressed to the Treasurer of the Royal Infirmary of Edinburgh.* Edinburgh: Neill & Co., 1818. First edition, 8vo., 15 pages, title inscribed "With Author's compliments", preserved in modern wrappers with printed label on upper cover, presentation copy, scarce. John Drury Rare Books   March 2015 - 24934   2015   £266

Russell, Osborne *Journal of a Trapper or Nine Years in the Rocky Mountains 1834-1943.* Boise: Symes-York Co., 1921. Second edition, cloth, gilt titles on spine, 149 pages, ink gift inscription from someone, ink stamped 1937 date, front pastedown has 1961 bookplate and small booksellers' label, near fine with bit of fading to spine, very scarce, near fine.   Baade Books of the West   2014 - 2015 $201

Russell, Richard *The Impeachment; or, the Church Triumphant. a poem.* London: printed in the year, 1712. First edition, 8vo., disbound, trimmed trifle close at top, touching couple of page numbers, otherwise good, uncommon.   C. R. Johnson   Foxon R-Z - 851r-z   2015 $613

Russell, Ross *Bird Lives! The High Life and Hard Times of Charles (Yardbird) Parker.* New York: Charterhouse, 1973. First edition, fine in fine dust jacket.   Beasley Books 2013 - 2015 $45

Rust, Art *Recollections of a Baseball Junkie.* New York: William Morrow, 1985. First edition, fine in fine dust jacket, inscribed by author to Joe DiMaggio, with letter of provenance signed by DiMaggio's two granddaughters. Between the Covers Rare Books, Inc.   187 - 10   2015 $850

Rust, Brian *Jazz Records 1932 to 1942.* Hatch End: the author, 1962. First edition, hardcover, very good+. Beasley Books   2013 - 2015 $150

Rust, Brian *Jazz Records 1897 to 1942.* New Rochelle: Arlington House, 1978. First printing, good to very good set, rippling and warping of pages throughout, boards bit worn, still tightly bound, good bargain set, stout 8vo. Beasley Books   2013 - 2015 $45

Rust, Brian *Jazz Records 1897 to 1942.* New Rochelle: Arlington House, 1978. Fourth edition, very good+ in very good- dust jackets with some wear and short tears. Beasley Books   2013 - 2015 $125

Rust, Brian *The Victor Master Book. Volume 2.* Stanhope: Walter C. Allen, 1970. Second printing, hardcover.   Beasley Books   2013 - 2015 $150

Rusticus, Junicus, Pseud. *Enumeration of the Contributions, Confiscations, and Requisitions of the French Nation.* London: W. Clarke, 1798. First edition, 8vo., recently well bound in linen backed marbled boards lettered, very good, scarce.   John Drury Rare Books   March 2015 - 19375   2015   £306

Ruthenberg, C. E. *The Workers (Communist) Party. What It Stands For, Why Workers Should Join.* Chicago: Workers (Communist) Party, 1925. First edition, fine, wrappers.   Beasley Books   2013 - 2015 $45

Rutherford, Constance *Double Entry.* London: Heinemann, 1939. First edition, 8vo., original red cloth lettered gilt on spine, very good+ in clean, about very good dust jacket with very slight edgewear, slight marks and closed tears, excellent condition.   Any Amount of Books   2015 - A00412   2015   £175

Rutherford, Ernest *Radioactive Substances and their Radiations.* Cambridge: University Press, 1913. First edition, 8vo., diagrams, original gilt stamped dark green cloth, tail rubbed, hinge repaired, short spine end tear, ex-library, multiple rubber stamps, very good.   Jeff Weber Rare Books   178 - 977   2015 $125

Ruthin Friendly Society *Rules to be Observed by the members of the Friendly Society Held at the Sign of The Red Lion, in Ruthin, Established May 3 1823.* Ruthin: printed by R. Jones, 1832. 8vo., 26 pages, printed throughout in parallel English and Welsh, bound in fairly recent cloth boards, spine gilt lettered, very good, apparently rare.   John Drury Rare Books   March 2015 - 25137   2015 $221

Rutledge, Maryse *The Silver Peril.* New York: Fiction League, 1931. First edition, name and address on front endpaper, otherwise fine in dust jacket with slightly faded spine and few nicks.   Mordida Books   March 2015 - 007160   2015 $125

Rutter, John *Modern Eden; or the Gardener's Universal Guide...* London: printed by J. Cooke, 1767. First edition, 8vo., very small piece chipped from fore edge of titlepage (nowhere near printed surface), contemporary calf recently rebacked with labels and gilt lettering, corners rather worn, else good, sound copy, very scarce, ownership inscription "Thos Croucher his book Septr 6th 1835 a gift from his well wisher P. Stedman bricklayer Dorking Surrey".   John Drury Rare Books   2015 - 26290   2015 $1049

Ruxton, George Frederic *Life in the Far West.* New York: Harper & Bros., 1849. First edition thus, blind-stamped decorative cloth, signature of owner Robert A. Bacon, three times, also ink stamp of Frederick Thompson, Mill Valley, good.   Baade Books of the West   2014 - 2015 $93

Ruzicka, Rudolph *Studies in Type Design, Alphabets with Random Quotations.* Hanover: Friends of Dartmouth Library, 1968. First edition, folio, cloth, slipcase, 4 page folder with titlepage, description and index, followed by 10 folders, each with plate on which is printed quotation from a famous author, 10 plates printed by Meriden Gravure company in different shades, bookplate on front pastedown.   Oak Knoll Books   306 - 59   2015 $100

Ryan, Cheli Duran *Hildilid's Night.* New York: Macmillan, 1971. First printing in such nice condition are scarce, oblong 4to., pictorial boards, fine in fine dust jacket, pen and ink drawings with yellow overlays.   Aleph-Bet Books, Inc.   108 - 276   2015 $275

Ryerson, Egerton *The Loyalists of America and their Times from 1620 to 1816.* New York: Haskell House, 1970. Facsimile reprint of 2nd edition, 2 volumes, 8vo., frontispiece, pink cloth, front board scuffed, generally both volumes in very good condition.   Schooner Books Ltd.   110 - 187   2015 $55

Ryle, Gilbert *Plato's Progress.* Cambridge: Cambridge University press, 1966. First edition, 8vo., signed, and inscribed by author, with two TLS's by Ryle laid in as well, fine in near fine dust jacket.   By the Book, L. C.   44 - 58   2015 $700

Rymer, Thomas   1641-1713 *A Short View of Tragedy...* printed and are to be sold by Richard Baldwin, 1693. First edition, initial blank, name erased from titlepage with resulting thinness of paper and small holes, just touching ascender of the "l" in the printer's name, 8vo., contemporary mottled calf, double blind fillets on sides with corner ornaments, manuscript paper label on spine placed upside down in lowest compartment, trifle rubbed at extremities, a number of marginal notes in neat contemporary hand, very good.   Blackwell's Rare Books   B179 - 89   2015   £700

Rynning, Thomas H. *Gun Notches. the Life Story of a Cowboy Soldier.* Frederick A. Stokes Co., 1931. First edition, 8vo., cloth, former owner's bookplate removed from front flyleaf, else near fine in elusive which has light wear to head of spine and extremities, rare wrap around promotional band.   Buckingham Books   March 2015 - 38422   2015 $450

Ryser, Fred *Birds of the Great Basin. A Natural History.* Reno: University of Nevada Press, 1985. First edition, drawings by Jennifer Dewey, 60 color photos, dark blue cloth gilt, very fine with pictorial dust jacket.   Argonaut Book Shop   Holiday Season 2014 - 255   2015 $75

S

Sabra, A. I. *Theories of Light from Descartes to Newton.* Cambridge: Cambridge University Press, 1981. 8vo., 365 pages, cloth, dust jacket, very good.   Jeff Weber Rare Books   178 - 980   2015 $50

Sabretache *Shires and Provinces.* London: Eyre & Spottiswoode, 1926. First edition, signed limited numbered edition, 43 of 100 copies signed in pencil by Lionel Edwards and Sabretache, large 4to., original gold embossed cream vellum, fine, 16 full page color illustrations by Lionel Edwards with tissue guards, fine, clean, bright in remnants of plain jacket in original box (also numbered (43), amazing survivial, as new.   Any Amount of Books   2015 - C8440   2015   £750

Sackett, Susan *Letters to Star-Trek.* New York: Ballantine, 1977. First edition, paperback original small scrape to top of front cover, else near fine in wrappers, inscribed by author to noted scientist Fred Durant.   Between the Covers Rare Books, Inc.   187 - 253   2015 $275

Sackheim, Eric *The Blues Line. A Collection of Blues Lyrics.* New York: Grossman, 1969. First edition, signed by Sackheim, lovely copy, fine in fine dust jacket.   Beasley Books   2013 - 2015 $300

Sacks, Oliver *The Man Who Mistook His Wife for a Hat.* New York: Summit Books, 1985. First edition, 8vo., inscribed by author, fine in close to fine dust jacket but for tiny tear at head of slightly sunned spine.   Beasley Books   2013 - 2015 $250

Sackville-West, Victoria Mary   1892-1952 *The Garden.* London: Michael Joseph, 1946. First edition, number 193 of 750 numbered copies signed by author, decorations by Broom Lynne, decorated gilt buckram, top edge gilt, printed on handmade paper, pages unopened, edges slightly spotted, fine in scarce plain, unprinted dust jacket which is torn and chipped, darkened at spine and defective at head and tail of spine.   Peter Ellis, Bookseller   2014 - 007748   2015   £325

Sade, Donatien Alphonse Francois, Comte, Called Marquis De   1740-1814 *De Sade on Virtue and Vice.* Girard: Haldeman Julius, 1946. First edition, wrappers, 8vo., 32 pages, near fine.   Beasley Books   2013 - 2015 $45

Sadler, Francis *The Exactions and Impositions of Parish Fees Discovered.* London: printed for the author and sold by D. Farmer, A. Dodd, Mrs. Nutt and by the author of Stangate Stairs near Lambeth, 1738. Second edition, 8vo., titlepage somewhat dust soiled and with couple of edge tears (not touching printed surface), recently well bound in linen backed marbled boards lettered, good copy, signed by author at end of preface.   John Drury Rare Books   March 2015 - 19136   2015 $266

Sage, Elizabeth *Occupations for Little Fingers.* New York: Scribner's Sons, 1905. First edition, 8vo., little rubbed, red cloth, stamped in black, very good, illustrations by author.   Second Life Books Inc.   189 - 215   2015 $75

Sage, Rufus B. *Rocky Mountain Life or Startling and Perilous Adventures in the Far West.* Omaha: W. T. Seman, n.d.1860 or 1870's, Enlarged edition, later printing, gilt stamped and decorative blindstamped original cloth with title gilt on spine and also blindstamped "New Adventure Library" on spine, 363 pages, well executed woodcuts, notes by owner, this edition apparently rare, very good, remarkable condition with minor wear to corners and upper corners ever so slightly bumped, apparently rare.   Baade Books of the West   2014 - 2015 $164

Sailaja, P. *Experimental Studies of the Differential Effect in Life Setting.* New York: Parapsychology Foundation, 1973. First edition, 8vo., original grey wrappers, lettered red on covers, blindstamp of writer M. H. Coleman, faint shelfwear, otherwise very good.   Any Amount of Books   2015 - C6750   2015   £160

The St. James's Beauties; or the Real Toast. A Poem. London: printed for J. Robinson, 1744 altered in MS. to, 1747. First edition, folio, disbound, fine, very scarce.   C. R. Johnson   Foxon R-Z - 853r-z   2015 $2298

Saint-Exupery, Antoine De *The Little Prince.* New York: Reynal & Hitchcock, 1943. Limited to 525 copies signed by author, illustrations in color by author, 8vo., cloth, fine in dust jacket with limitation number inked on spine that matched limitation number of both, housed in custom cloth box.   Aleph-Bet Books, Inc.   108 - 404   2015 $22,000

Saint-Exupery, Antoine De *The Little Prince.* New York: Reynal & Hitchcock, 1943. First edition, first printing, first issue dust jacket with publisher's 4th Ave. address to front flap, near fine, hint of light wear to extremities, very light offsetting to endpapers, bright and clean interior, unclipped dust jacket with very light toning to spine and panel edges, few chips to bottom edges of panels, short closed tears and minor creasing to edges, few faint spots of light soiling, overall pleasing.   B & B Rare Books, Ltd.   2015 - 2015 $2500

Saint-Exupery, Antoine De *Night Flight.* New York: Century Co., First edition, very good, spine faded, bright cover, tight clean text, with facsimile of original dust jacket. Stephen Lupack   March 2015 - 2015 $45

Saint-Real, L'Abbe Cesar Vicarhd De *Histoire De La Conjuration des Espagnols Contre la Republique de Venise.* A. Dulau et Co., 1800. printed on fine paper, which however has a tendency to spotting, 8vo., contemporary tree style calf, gilt roll tooled borders on sides, spine gilt in compartments, red lettering piece, gilt edges, slightly worn, chip missing from foot of upper joint, good.   Blackwell's Rare Books   B179 - 90   2015   £400

Saint-Simon, Claude Henri, Comte De *Opinions Litteraires Philosophiques et Industrielles.* Paris: Galerie de Bossange Pere, 1825. First edition, 8vo., with half title, near contemporary ownership inscriptions on half title, one inscription cropped at head of leaf, contemporary red cloth boards, spine simply lettered in gilt, excellent, crisp copy. John Drury Rare Books   2015 - 18222   2015 $656

Sainte-Croix, Guillaue Emmanuel Joseph Guilhem de Clermont Lodeve, Baron De *Historie Des Progres De La Puissance Navale De L'Angleterre Suivie d'Observations dur l'Acte de Navigation et des Pieces Justicatives.* Yverdon: 1783. First edition, 2 volumes, half titles, contemporary calf, volume I worn at top of spine, very good, clean copy. Second Life Books Inc.   190 - 189   2015 $1100

Saintsbury, George *Specimens of English Prose Style from Malory to Macaulay.* London: Kegan Paul Trench and Co., 1885. First edition, no 1 of 50 copies signed "Charles Whittingham & Co. " (of Chiswick Press), 8vo., green cloth with spine label and marbled boards, uncut, signed in pencil on titlepage dated Xmas 1887 to Dorothy Cornish, presumably the educationalist, spine label browned and marked (legible), edges rubbed, boards quite scuffed at rear, pages uncut with clean text.   Any Amount of Books   2015 - A47686   2015   £180

Sakevich, A. *Tsyiplta. (Chickens).* Detizat: 1938. 4to., pictorial wrappers, slight edge fraying, very good+, illustrations by Olga Bontch-Osmolovskaia with terrific color lithographs.   Aleph-Bet Books, Inc.   108 - 399   2015 $300

Saladin, Charles *Coup d'Oeil Politique sur le Continent.* Londres: de l'Imprimerie de W. et C. Spilsbury et se trouve chez, J. Deboffe, T. Wright; A. Dulau et Co. et T. Boosey, 1800. First edition, one of two issues, both rare, 8vo., contemporary English half calf gilt over marbled boards, raised bands, labels, marbled edges, some wear to joints but very good, from the 19th century library of Archibald Speirs esq. of Elerslee with his armorial bookplate,.   John Drury Rare Books   March 2015 - 18051   2015   £306

Salaman, Nina Davis *Songs of Exile by Hebrew Poets.* Philadelphia and London: The Jewish Publication Society of America and Jewish Historical Publication Society of England, 1901. First edition, fine in slightly age toned, near fine dust jacket with shallow nicking at spine ends. Between the Covers Rare Books   196 - 110   2015 $1500

Saliga, Pauline *The Architecture of Bruce Goff 1904-1982: Design for the Continuous Present.* Munich and New York: Prestel and Art Institute of Chicago, 1995. First edition, 4to., copiously illustrated in color and black and white, decent copy, scarce, fine in very good dust jacket with slight wear.   Any Amount of Books   2015 - A48241   2015   £180

Salinger, Jerome David *The Catcher in the Rye.* Boston: Little Brown and Co., 1951. First edition, publisher's black cloth in unrestored first issue dust jacket with 43.00 price correctly positioned and photo by Lotte Jacobi to rear panel, Raymond Chandler's copy stamped on front free endpaper with his La Jolla CA address and date AUG 4 1951, book with offsetting to endpapers from printer's glue, edges of text block very minimally foxed, small creases to top corner of first few pages, else clean and square with bright gilt to spine, bright and clean dust jacket with few nicks and creases to corners, spine very slightly toned, light rubbing to extremities, housed in custom quarter leather case, beautiful copy.   B & B Rare Books, Ltd.   234 - 88   2015 $22,500

Salinger, Jerome David *Franny and Zooey.* Boston: Little Brown and Co., 1961. First edition, first printing, excellent copy in unclipped dust jacket with very minor wear to spine ends and some fading to spine.   B & B Rare Books, Ltd.   234 - 89   2015 $375

Salisbury, Robert Cecil *The Copie of a Letter to the Right Honourable the Earle of Leycester, Lieutenant General of all Her Majesties Forces in the United Provinces of the Low Countreys.* London: Christopher Barker, 1586. 4to., without final blank leaf, woodcut arms on A, verso facing titlepage, large woodcut initials, this copy is the variant with A, recto starting, bound by Pratt in 19th century brown crushed morocco with gilt arms on covers, all edges gilt, bookplate of 'Fairfax of Cameron', fine.   Second Life Books Inc.   190 - 226   2015 $4000

Sallustius Crispus, C. *Belli Catilinarii et Jugurthini Historiae Secundum Exempla Emendatissima.* Ayr: Excudebant J. & P. Wilson, 1808. 12mo., contemporary mottled sheep, spine divided by gilt fillets, red morocco lettering piece, other compartments with gilt floral tools, boards with central gilt stamp of arms of Edinburgh, bit of insect damage to arms on rear board and foot of spine, touch of wear to headcap, very good, rare.   Blackwell's Rare Books Greek & Latin Classics VI - 94   2015   £500

Sallustius Crispus, C. *La Conjuracion de Catilina y la Guerra de Jugurta Del Alfabeto y Lengua de los Fenices y de sus Colonias...* Madrid: J. Ibarra, 1772. 120 copies of this edition issued, all on large paper and printed on rich cream paper, hot press by Ibarra himself, some copies have a half title, not found here, Folio, engraved titlepage by Montfort, four engraved plates and numerous smaller engravings by Montefort and Carmona after Maella, three engraved plates by Fabregat and Ballester, two plates of scrips and one of coins, contemporary Spanish red morocco covers decorated with gilt Greek key border, having gilt suns at corners, enclosing inner roll border of foliate design, flat spine gilt at either end, central neo-classical motif built of various tools, green morocco label, green silk doublures and marker, edges gilt head of spine chipped, extremities rubbed, excellent copy, bookplate by Reynolds Stone of Jonathan and Phillida Gili. Maggs Bros. Ltd. Illustrated Books 2014 - 2015   £8000

Sallustius Crispus, C. *Caius Crispus Salustius ab Ascensio Familiariter Explanatus.* Paris: Jean Petit, 1504. First Badius edition, some light foxing and staining (heavier o titlepage), first leaf of text bound slightly askew and 3 sidenotes copped as a result, 4to., 18th century calf, worn and crackled, rebacked (somewhat crudely), black lettering piece, hinges relined with black cloth tape, bookplates of Wigan public Library, Rev. T. H. Passmore, Sir Robert Shafto Adair and Augustus Frederick, Duke of Sussex, sound. Blackwell's Rare Books   Greek & Latin Classics VI - 93   2015   £2000

Salmon, Andre *Les Artistes Du Livre.* Paris: Henry Babou, 1930. First edition, one of 650 copies, this one unnumbered, unbound signatures laid into wrappers, small 4to., fine in very good+ to near fine glassine (few tears), 22 full page plates. Beasley Books   2013 - 2015 $85

Salmony, Alfred *Sino-Siberian Art in the Collection of C. T. Loo.* Paris: C. T. Loo, 1933. First edition, large 8vo., 44 black and white plates, soundly rebound in mustard-yellow cloth lettered gilt on spine, original printed front wrapper (chipped at edges) bound in, last three pages of plates slightly chipped at edges but not affecting images, few faint marks to boards, otherwise very good. Any Amount of Books   2015 - C2304   2015   £160

Salomon, Julian Harris *The Book of Indian Crafts & Indian Lore.* New York: Harper & Bros., 1928. First edition, pictorial cloth, illustrations, endpaper maps, near fine in very slightly chipped dust jacket, scarce printing, very good dust jacket. Baade Books of the West   2014 - 2015 $67

Salt, H. S. *Percy Bysshe Shelley.* London: 1888. First edition, frontispiece, very good+, some spotting to boards and endpapers, but no chipping and nice, tight copy, thick mylar wrapper, scarce. Stephen Lupack   March 2015 - 2015 $75

Salvadori, Tommaso *Ornitologia della Papuasia e Delle Molucche (with 3 supplements).* Torino: Ermanno Loeschuer, 1881-1891. Quarto 4 volumes, 2690 pages, modern quarter morocco, marbled boards, some minor marginal staining in volume one, publisher's blue wrappers retained, very scarce. Andrew Isles   2015 - 13685   2015 $4250

Salzmann, Christian Gotthilf *Elements of Morality for the Use of Children...* Providence: Carter & Wilkinson, 1795. First American edition, 12mo., contemporary calf (chipped and worn, front cover and flyleaf separate, one signature pulled, some foxing and stain), frontispiece. Second Life Books Inc.   189 - 278   2015 $1250

Salzmann, Christian Gotthilf *Elements of Morality for the Use of Children...* London: printed for J Crowder for J. Johnson, 1799. Fourth edition translated by Mary Wollstonecraft, 3 volumes, 12mo., 51 engraved plates, most by William Blake, lacking half titles but with leaves of directions to the binder which are often missing, one plate amateurishly hand colored, generally lightly soiled throughout and with other signs of use including a few marginal tears, early 19th century black half roan, sides rubbed, slight chipping at foot of two spines, cloth slipcase. Second Life Books Inc.   189 - 277   2015 $3000

Samaritani, G. L. Da *Raccolta Di Costumi Napoletani.* Naples: 1846. 4to., 20 hand colored lithograph costume plate, including title, contemporary roan backed decorative cloth. Marlborough Rare Books   List 54 - 75   2015   £1350

Sampson, Emma Speed *Miss Minerva's Scallywagg.* Chicago: Reilly & Lee, 1927. First edition, 8vo., red pictorial cloth, fine in slightly worn dust jacket, illustrations by William Donahey in black and white, beautiful copy. Alephbet Books, Inc.   109 - 64   2015 $150

Samuelson, Nancy B. *Shoot from the Lip: the Lives, Legends & Lives of the Three Guardsmen of Oklahoma & U.S. Marshal Nix.* Eastford: Shooting star, 1998. First edition, quarto, pictorial hardbound, 188 pages, maps, illustrations, fine, scarce now. Baade Books of the West   2014 - 2015 $85

Sancho, Ignatius *Letters of the Late Ignatius Sancho...* London: printed by J. Nichols and sold by J. Dodsley...., 1782. First edition, 2 volumes in one, 8vo., fine, engraved portrait of Sancho by F. Bartolozzi, after painting by Gainsborough in volume I and engraved allegorical frontispiece in volume II also by Bartolozzi, complete with both half titles, with additional leaf C4 in volume 1, contemporary calf, neatly and appropriately rebacked, spine gilt and labelled, very good, owned by one of the subscribers with her signature "M. Bouchery". John Drury Rare Books   2015 - 24962   2015 $4371

Sandburg, Carl 1878-1967 *Lincoln Collector. The Story of Oliver R. Barrett's Great Private Collection.* New York: Harcourt Brace and Co., 1949. First edition, limited to 2425, this number 1208, signed by author on special limitation page bound in front, illustrations, near fine, neat bookplate, publisher's black cloth over beveled boards, lettered gilt, original decorated slipcase (very good).   Ed Smith Books 83 - 79 2015 $300

Sandburg, Carl 1878-1967 *The Sandburg Range.* New York: Harcourt, 1957. Inscribed by author, very good, tape offsetting on endpapers, probably from dust jacket protector, lightly used dust jacket has shallow chipping at spine ends.   Beasley Books 2013 - 2015 $225

Sandby, George *Mesmerism and Its Opponents.* New York: Longman, Brown, Green &, 1848. Second edition, very good with little fraying to spine ends.   Beasley Books 2013 - 2015 $150

Sanders, Alvin H. *At the Sign of the Stock Yard Inn the Same Being a True account of How Certain Great Achievements of the Past Have Been Commemorated and Cleverly Linked with the Present.* Chicago: Breeder's Gazette Print, 1915. First edition, half leather and cloth, 322 pages, photos, very good+.   Baade Books of the West 2014 - 2015 $48

Sanders, Alvin H. *Short-Horn Cattle.* Chicago: Sanders Pub. Co., 1901. Second edition, half leather professionally rebound in gilt stamped leather with original boards, 872 pages, illustrations, back cover scraped in few spots, still very good.   Baade Books of the West 2014 - 2015 $75

Sanders, Gwendolline *The Harper County Story.* North Newton: privately printed Mennonite Press, 1968. First edition, cloth, illustrations, folding map, fine in dust jacket with some staining on back panel and couple of edge tears, fine in good dust jacket.   Baade Books of the West 2014 - 2015 $40

Sandford, John *Winter Prey.* New York: Putnam, 1993. First edition, signed by author, fine in fine dust jacket.   Beasley Books 2013 - 2015 $40

Sandoe, James *The Hard Boiled Dicks.* Chicago: Lovell, 1952. First edition, 10 page stamped pamphlet, fine in printed wrappers.   Mordida Books March 2015 - 010051 2015 $100

Sandoz, Mari *Old Jules.* New York: Blue Ribbon, 1938. Reprint, possibly first thus, dated 1938 from gift inscription, full page presentation (not by author) 12 12 38, long superficial scratch on back cover, very good, very scarce thus.   Baade Books of the West 2014 - 2015 $75

Sands, Diane *Women of Montana Essays 1981-1985.* Kalispell: American Association of University Women - Montana Division, 1986. First edition, 4to., pictorial wrappers, 44 pages, photos and drawings, with typical slight fading to spine edge of blue covers, very scarce, near fine.   Baade Books of the West 2014 - 2015 $61

Sands, Frank *A Pastoral Prince. The History and Reminiscences of J. W. Cooper.* Privately printed, 1893. First edition, 8vo. pictorial cloth, marbled endpapers, frontispiece, illustrations, rare, lightly rubbed at spine ends and front corners, else very good, tight copy.   Buckingham Books March 2015 - 23186 2015 $800

Sandweiss, Martha A. *Eyewitness to War: Prints and Daguerreotypes of the Mexican War 1846-1848.* Fort Worth: 1989. Maps and illustrations, light rubbing to dust jacket and shelfwear, else near fine.   Dumont Maps & Books of the West 131 - 72 2015 $75

Sanger, Margaret *An Autobiography.* New York: Norton, 1938. First edition, 8vo, bookseller bookplate, very good in little worn dust jacket.   Second Life Books Inc. 189 - 217 2015 $150

Sanger, Margaret *The Pivot of Civilization.* New York: Brentano's, 1922. First edition, red cloth, bookplate of Gilbert Beaver Conference Farm, very good+, spine gilt darkened tight, clean text, scarce.   Stephen Lupack March 2015 - 2015 $150

Sanger, Margaret *Woman and the New Race.* New York: Brentano's, 1923. Sixth printing, 8vo., author's presentation on half title under scotch tape, red cloth stamped in black, ex-library with bookplate and stamps, rear hinge near tender, very good.   Second Life Books Inc. 189 - 218 2015 $50

Santayana, George 1863-1952 *The Works of George Santayana.* New York: Charles Scribner's Sons, 1936. Limited to 950 numbered copies signed by author on colophon, Triton edition, 14 volumes, 8vo., quarter cloth, paper covered boards, label on spine, publisher's logo gilt stamped on front cover, top edge gilt, other edges uncut, slipcases, with publisher's prospectus, laid in news clipping with review, slipcases rubbed and scuffed, especially at corners, labels tanned.   Oak Knoll Books 306 - 296 2015 $450

Santlofer, Jonathan *The Dark End of the Street.* New York: Mysterious Bookshop, 2010. First edition, one of 26 lettered copies, signed by each author and editors, fine in quarter leather and marbled boards and transparent dust jacket,.   Buckingham Books March 2015 - 29518 2015 $275

Sanzenbacher, Dorothea A. *A Trail Creek Ranch, Park County Wyoming.* Privately printed, 1957. First edition, boards, illustrations, very scarce, exceptional fine copy. Buckingham Books   March 2015 - 37437   2015 $175

Sappho *Poesies De Sappho.* Chez Jean Porson, 1952. #246 of 275 copies, unbound signatures laid into wrappers, some light foxing throughout, etchings by J. Houplain, quite nice but for foxing, in nice chemise and matching box, 4to. Beasley Books   2013 - 2015 $200

The Sarah-ad; or a Flight for Fame. London: printed for T. Cooper, 1742. First edition, 32 pages, 8vo., disbound, very good.   C. R. Johnson   Foxon R-Z - 855r-z   2015 $766

Sarg, Tony *Sarg's Sayings Book.* Cleveland: World, 1946. First edition, oblong large 4to., spiral backed boards, slight foxing, else fine in slightly frayed dust jacket, each illustration has several slots into which the owner can insert coins, illustrations.   Aleph-Bet Books, Inc.   108 - 407   2015 $225

Sargant, William Lucas *Apology for Sinking-Funds.* London: Williams and Norgate, 1868. First edition, 8vo., sometime in the Library of the Institute of Actuaries, bookplate, cancelled on pastedown, small inkstamp in title margin, front free endpaper with corner torn away, original blind-stamped cloth with bevelled boards, just little wear at head and foot of spine, else good to very good.   John Drury Rare Books   March 2015 - 25793   2015 $266

Sargent, Lucius M. *Dealings with the Dead.* Boston: Dutton & Wentworth/Ticknor & Fields, 1856. First book edition, 2 volumes, lacks frontispiece in volume 1, otherwise near fine set in protective thick mylar.   Stephen Lupack   March 2015 - 2015 $125

Sargeson, Frank *Memoirs of a Peon.* London: MacGibbon & Kee, 1965. First edition, foxing, else near fine in about fine dust jacket with light foxing on rear panel, Advance Review copy with slip tipped onto front pastedown, bookplate of D. M. Davin.   Between the Covers Rare Books, Inc.   187 - 241   2015 $150

Saroyan, Aram *Lines.* New York: 1964-1965. First edition, whole numbers 1-6 (all published), Sept 1964 - Nov. 1965, some occasional light dusting, otherwise complete run in fine condition.   James S. Jaffe Rare Books   Many Happy Returns - 390   2015 $1500

Saroyan, William *Inhale and Exhale.* New York: Random House, 1936. First edition, 2 small tears at crown, modest soiling, very good, lacking dust jacket, inscribed by author for William Meredith, signed again on titlepage.   Between the Covers Rare Books, Inc.   187 - 243   2015 $500

Sarton, George *Introduction to the History of Science.* Baltimore: Carnegie Inst. of Washington, Williams & Wilkins, 1953. 1963., 3 volumes in , 8vo., plates, blue cloth, gilt spines, bookplate of David Lindberg with his signatures, near fine.   Jeff Weber Rare Books   178 - 989   2015 $275

Sartre, Jean Paul *Being and Nothingness, an Essay on Phenomenological Ontology.* New York: Philosophical Library, 1956. First US edition, small clean tear at head of spine in very good+ dust jacket with short tears at head of rear panel.   Beasley Books   2013 - 2015 $40

Sartre, Jean Paul *Explicaion de l'Etranger.* Paris: Aux depens de Palimugre, 1946. First edition, 12mo., wrappers, pages unopened, fine.   Peter Ellis, Bookseller   2014 - 002697   2015   £350

Sartre, Jean Paul *Oeuvre Romanesque.* Paris: Editions Lidis, 1964-1965. One of 4000 sets on velin Vercors paper, 5 volumes, wrappers, 4to., fine set in original acetate dust jackets with few tears to latter and one small mend, lithographs by Walter Spitzer, including double page spread, elaborate prospectus included, also fine, previous owner's mini chemise and slipcase.   Beasley Books   2013 - 2015 $250

Satterthwait, Walter *At Ease with the Dead.* New York: St. Martin's, 1990. First edition, very fine in dust jacket. Mordida Books   March 2015 - 009158   2015 $1990

Satterthwait, Walter *The Gold of Mayani.* Gallup: Buffalo Medicine, 1995. First edition, one of 250 numbered copies signed by author, artist and author of introduction, Sarah Caudwell, illustrations by Ernest Franklin, very fine, in dust jacket with extra dust jacket suitable for framing.   Mordida Books   March 2015 - 001984   2015 $125

Satterthwait, Walter *Wall of Glass.* New York: St. Martins, 1988. First edition, very fine in dust jacket. Mordida Books   March 2015 - 012593   2015 $250

A Satyr Upon the Present Times. London: printed and sold by John Morphew, 1717. First edition, 8vo., disbound, fine, very rare.   C. R. Johnson   Foxon R-Z - 856r-z   2015 $3831

Saubidet, Tito *Vocabulario y Refranero Griollo, Con Textos Y Dibujos Originales.* Buenos Aires: Guillermo Kraft Ltd, 1952. Curata edition, large quarto, original pictorial stiff wrappers, numerous color plates, very good.   Buckingham Books   March 2015 - 15468   2015 $375

Saunders, Louise *Knave of Hearts.* New York: Scribner, 1925. First edition, folio, black cloth, pictorial paste-on, some rubbing to cover plate and cloth, very good+ in custom facsimile box, glorious pictorial endpapers plus really magnificent full page color illustrations (printed on rectos only) and numerous rich color illustrations in text, by Maxfield Parrish, all printed on thick, heavy coated paper, laid in is handwritten letter from Parrish to His editor, J. H. Chapin Discussing His Progress on the Knave, written on both sides of 3 1/2 x 5 inch card, dated January 26 1922. Aleph-Bet Books, Inc.   108 - 335   2015 $6000

Savage, C. R. *Views of Utah and the Tourist's Guide.* Salt Lake City: C. R. Savage, 1887. 32mo., dark maroon cloth, blindstamped and gold gilt title, accordion style viewstrip with 16 panels of glossy views of Utah, accompanied by the Guide which consists of 30 pages of text, spine ends and lightly rubbed, else very good.   Buckingham Books March 2015 - 31006   2015 $300

Savage, John *Horace to Scaeva. Epistle XVII. Book I. Imitated.* London: printed for John Brindley, 1730. First edition, 8vo., disbound, very good, complete with half title.   C. R. Johnson   Foxon R-Z - 858r-z   2015 $383

Savage, Richard *The Authors of the Town; a Satire inscribed to the author of The Universal Passion.* London: printed for J. Roberts, 1725. First edition, folio, disbound, very scarce, very good, complete with half title.   C. R. Johnson   Foxon R-Z - 861r-z   2015 $2298

Savage, Richard *The Bastard. A Poem. Inscribed with all due reverence to Mrs. Bret, Once Countess of Macclesfield.* London: printed for T. Worrall, 1728. Second edition, folio, sewn as issue, very fine, entirely uncut as issued.   C. R. Johnson   Foxon R-Z - 862r-z   2015 $2681

Savage, Richard *Various Poems. The Wanderer, a Moral Poem. The Triumph of Mirth and Health. And The Bastard...* London: printed for J. Turner, 1761. First edition, small 8vo., contemporary sheep, rebacked, brown morocco label (corners rubbed), titlepage just trifle soiled, but very good, uncommon, early signature on titlepage of Susanna Williams, later signature of H. F. House.   C. R. Johnson   Foxon R-Z - 859r-z   2015 $460

Savage, Richard *The Wanderer; a Poem in five cantos.* London: printed for J. Walthoe, 1729. First edition, 8vo., modern calf, gilt, spine gilt, contrasting red and black labels, some repair to last leaf of dedication (without loss), otherwise very good, complete with three pages of ads at end.   C. R. Johnson   Foxon R-Z - 865r-z   2015 $2298

Savage, Richard *The Works of Richard Savage, Esq. son of the Earl Rivers...* Dublin: printed for William Whitestone, 1777. First Dublin edition, 2 volumes, recent half calf and marbled boards, spines gilt, maroon morocco labels, some stains to last two leaves of first volume, otherwise good copy, complete with half titles, early signature on titlepages of Isabelle Robinson and Ellen Waite, good copy.   C. R. Johnson   Foxon R-Z - 860r-z   2015 $383

Savage, William *A Dictionary of the Art of Printing.* London: Longman, Brown, Green and Longmans, 1841. First edition, thick 8vo., modern quarter leather over cloth, five raised bands, red leather spine label, titlepage partially detached and has piece missing which has been replaced with later paper, number in ink at top of preface, lacks half title, old stains along edge of first few leaves.   Oak Knoll Books   306 - 200   2015 $250

Say, Benjamin *An Annual Oration Pronounced Before the Humane Society of Philadelphia on the Objects and Benefits of Said Institution.* Whitehall: William Young, Bookseller, Philadelphia, 1799. First edition, 8vo., possibly lacking half title, removed, sheets toned, foxed, presentation from author for Dr. (Henry) Disborough.   M & S Rare Books, Inc.   97 - 188   2015 $275

Say, Jean Baptiste *Catechisme d'Economie Politique ou Instruction Familiere qui monte de Quelle Facon les Richesses Sont Produites, Distribuees et Consommees dans la Societe.* Bruxelles: Societe Beige de Librairie, 1939. 12mo., half title, some pencilled emphasis marks and annotations, contemporary quarter morocco and marbled boards, spine gilt with raised bands, sides rubbed, corners worn, very good.   John Drury Rare Books   2015 - 15240   2015 $89

Say, Samuel *Poems on Several Occasions; and Two Critical Essays...* London: printed by John Hughs, 1745. First edition, 4to., contemporary calf, panelled gilt, spine gilt, lacks label, ends of spine bit worn, very good, binding has been padded with a number of blank leaves at beginning and end.   C. R. Johnson   Foxon R-Z - 866r-z   2015 $919

Sayers, Dorothy L. *Busman's Honeymoon.* London: Victor Gollancz, 1938. First UK edition, very good plus in very good plus, price clipped example of scarce dust jacket, owner name, slight lean, touch of foxing to front endpapers, else book is quite clean, jacket has only slightest fray at crown, with some toning to spine and at extremities, from the collection of Duke Collier.   Royal Books   36 - 231   2015 $375

Sayers, Dorothy L. *Dorothy L. Sayers Omnibus.* New York: Harcourt Brace, 1934. First edition, review copy with publisher's slip affixed to lower portion of front flap, fine in near fine dust jacket that has minor professional restoration at spine ends, remarkably scarce, from the collection of Duke Collier.   Royal Books   36 - 230   2015 $750

Sayers, Dorothy L. *The Five Red Herrings.* London: Victor Gollancz, 1931. First edition, 8vo., soundly rebound in red leather with marbled boards, gilt lettering at spine with five raised bands, neat name on front endpaper, otherwise near fine.   Any Amount of Books   2015 - C3220   2015   £175

Sayers, Dorothy L. *Gaudy Night.* London: Victor Gollancz, 1935. First edition, very good plus in poor example of scarce dust jacket, jacket is basically in pieces, lacking a significant portion at top and bottom of spine, detached at folds, rare, custom quarter leather clamshell box, inscribed by author to her husband (Oswald Atherton) Mac (Fleming), from the collection of Duke Collier.   Royal Books   36 - 225   2015 $6500

Sayers, Dorothy L. *Gaudy Night.* London: Victor Gollancz, 1935. First edition, very good plus, very good example of scarce dust jacket, neat contemporary gift inscription dated Christmas 1935, spine gilt bright, jacket has no loss whatsoever, but is lightly faded ad spine, shows moderate uniform soil, from the collection of Duke Collier.   Royal Books   36 - 228   2015 $1500

Sayers, Dorothy L. *In the Teeth of Evidence.* New York: Harcourt Brace, 1940. First American edition, fine and unread, in fine dust jacket, from the collection of Duke Collier.   Royal Books   36 - 229   2015 $1500

Sayers, Dorothy L. *The Nine Tailors.* New York: Harcourt Brace, 1934. First American edition, very good plus in fine dust jacket, with some professional restoration at extremities, binding very slightly cocked, from the collection of Duke Collier.   Royal Books   36 - 227   2015 $1750

Sayers, Dorothy L. *OP, 1.* Oxford: Basil Blackwell, 1916. First edition, 8vo., original dun wrappers with spine label and title label on cover, pages uncut, sound, clean about very good with yapped edges, very slightly creased, slight wrinkling at spine and slight wear at head of spine, small nick and slight rubbing.   Any Amount of Books   2015 - A93098   2015   £300

Sayers, Dorothy L. *Papers Relating to the Family of Wimsey.* London: privately printed for the Family by Humphrey Milford, 1936. First edition, one of 500 copies, frontispiece, 1 further plate, 8vo., original blue wrappers printed in black with fading to borders, couple of waterspots at head of front and chipping to edges, 2 cm. loss at head of backstrip, few foxspots to inside front cover and flyleaf, good, inscribed by Matthew Wimsey and Peter Death Bredon Wimsey to Gerard Hopkins, nephew of Gerard Manley Hopkins, with 2 photocopies TLS's from Sayers to Basil Blackwell loosely inserted.   Blackwell's Rare Books   B179 - 231   2015   £750

Sayers, Dorothy L. *The Unpleasantness at the Bellona Club.* New York: Payson & Clarke, 1928. First American edition, slightly faded spine, otherwise fine in very near fine dust jacket, exceptional copy.   Mordida Books   March 2015 - 010684   2015 $3500

Sayers, Dorothy L. *The Unpleasantness at the Bellona Club.* New York: Payson and Clarke Ltd., 1928. First American edition, very good to fine, supplied dust jacket, book has slight lean and is faded at spine and board edges with small stain on backstrip, jacket is impeccable, quite fresh with no wear to note, from the collection of Duke Collier.   Royal Books   36 - 226   2015 $2250

Sayers, Dorothy L. *Unpopular Opinions.* London: Gollancz, 1946. First edition, very good in lightly faded and soiled dust jacket, with small piece missing lower corner front panel and several short closed tears.   Mordida Books   March 2015 - 009844   2015 $85

Sayler, Harry Lincoln   *The Airship Boys Adrift or Saved by an Aeroplane.* Chicago: Reilly & Britton, 1909. First edition, 8vo., 4 inserted plates, illustrations by J. O. Smith, pictorial blue gray cloth, front panel stamped in white and black, spine and rear panels stamped in white.   L. W. Currey, Inc.   Boy's Adventure Fiction 2015 - 95   2015 $100

Sayler, Harry Lincoln   *The Airship Boys or the Quest of the Aztec Treasure.* Chicago: Reilly & Britton, 1909. First edition, 4 inserted plates, illustrations by F. R. Harper, full page map, pictorial blue gray cloth, front panel stamped in white and black, spine and rear panels stamped in white.   L. W. Currey, Inc.   Boy's Adventure Fiction 2015 - 96   2015 $100

Sayre, John W.   *Ghost Railroads of Central Arizona: a Journey through Yesteryear.* Phoenix: Red Rock Pub., 1985. First edition, 4to., pictorial wrappers, illustrations, maps, top corner of covers and text block bumped, good reading copy.   Baade Books of the West   2014 - 2015 $59

Scarlett, James   *Opinions of Sir James Scarlett, Sir Edward B. Sugden and Mr. Richards, on the Privilege of the bank of England. Read at a General Court of Proprietors 16th August 1833.* London: 1833. First edition, 8vo., titlepage soiled, recent cloth backed marbled boards with morocco label on upper cover, lettered in gilt, rare.   John Drury Rare Books   March 2015 - 25497   2015 $266

Scarrow, Simon   *Under the Eagle.* Headline, 2000. First edition, signed by author and dated in year of publication, fine in dust jacket, exceptional copy.   Buckingham Books   March 2015 - 33145   2015 $750

Scelter & Giesecke *Allerlei Zierat.* Leipzig: J. G. Schelter & Giesecke, n.d. circa, 1902. Small 4to., 384 pages followed by 9 additional leaves, cloth, cover shows minor rubbing with small split at bottom of back hinge, loosely inserted in this copy is 28 page listing of "Vignetten".   Oak Knoll Books   306 - 226   2015 $1900

Scenes in Florida. Chicago: W. H. Parish Pub. Co., 1894. First edition, folio, 112 photogravures on 75 plates, contemporary three quarter morocco, light wear to spine ends, scattered foxing, near fine.   M & S Rare Books, Inc.   97 - 105   2015 $750

The Scenic Way Across America through the Colorado Rockies, Burlington Route, Missouri Pacific Lines. privately printed, n.d. circa, 1931. 9 x 15 inches folded to 32 panels, each 9 x 3.5 inches, beautiful bright colorful brochure, light wear to folds and light soiling, very good, very attractive brochure with lots of good information.   Buckingham Books   March 2015 - 36118   2015 $225

Schaff, Philip *The Ante-Nicene Fathers.* Edinburgh and Michigan, T. & T. Clark/Wm. B. Eerdmans, 1989-1996. Reprint, Complete in 38 volumes, large 8vo., original cloth lettered gilt at spine, handsome facsimile reprint, fine.   Any Amount of Books   March 2015 - C16609   2015   £450

Scheme for the Management and Regulation of the Chairty of Seckford Hospital and the Grammar School at Woodbridge, in the County of Suffolk and for the Application of the Incomes Thereof, Directed by the High Court of Chancery by Order dated June 14th 1861. London: printed by C. Roworth and Sons, 1861. First edition, 8vo., original blindstamped brown cloth with printed paper label on upper cover, nice, rare.   John Drury Rare Books   2015 - 14142   2015 $221

Schenkman, David E. *A Survey of American Trade Tokens.* Lawrence: Quarterman, 1975. First edition, silver stamped cloth, 493 pages, illustrations, binding cocked, else very good in slightly worn dust jacket.   Baade Books of the West   2014 - 2015 $88

Schevill, James *The Black President and Other Plays.* Denver: Alan Swallow, 1965. First edition, wrappered issue, near fine in wrappers, nicely inscribed by poet to Karl Shapiro.   Between the Covers Rare Books, Inc.   187 - 243   2015 $150

Schevill, James *The Mayan Poems.* Providence: Copper Beech Press, 1978. First edition, printed wrappers, light soiling on front wrapper, else fine, warmly inscribed to author James Norman Hall.   Between the Covers Rare Books, Inc.   187 - 244   2015 $125

Schier, Norma *The Anagram Detectives.* New York: Mysterious Press, 1979. First edition, one of 250 numbered copies signed by Scheir and author of introduction, Stanley Ellin, very fine in dust jacket with slipcase. Mordida Books   March 2015 - 009975   2015 $85

Schiff, James A. *Updike's Version: Rewriting the Scarlet Letter.* Columbia: University of Missouri Press, 1992. First edition, fine in fine dust jacket, inscribed by author to Reynolds Price.   Between the Covers Rare Books, Inc. 187 - 245   2015 $125

Schiller, Johann Christoph Friedrich Von   1759-1805 *Schiller's Fammtliche Werke in Zwolf Banden.* Stuttgart und Tubingen: 1847. 12 volumes in 6, attractive set, half leather and marbled boards, highly decorated gilt spines (angel holding a band with author's name, above which is a cameo portrait above which is another angel with lyre), very good set, mild scuffing/wear to leather, one volume with paper worn away from about 40 per cent of the surface, light damp staining to upper portion of volume 5.6, tight clean texts.   Stephen Lupack   March 2015 - 2015 $150

Schlegel, Friedrich *Ueber Die Sprache und Weisheit der Indier: ein Beitrag Zur Begrundung der Alterthumskunde.* Heidelberg: Mohr Und Zimmer, 1808. 8vo., attractively bound in half green leather with marbled boards, lettered gilt at spine, five raised bands, including frontispiece, titlepage and titlepage vignette, slight creasing to first 15 pages but not affecting text, otherwise clean, very good+.   Any Amount of Books   2015 - C12219   2015   £180

Schlegel, Gustave *Uranographie Chinoise ou Preuves Directs que L'Astronomie Primitive est Originaire de la Chine et qu'elle a ete Empruntee par les Anciens Peuples Occidentaux a la Spehre Chinoise...* La Haye: Librairie de Martinus Nijhoff; Leyde: Imprimerie de E. J. Brill Relie, 1875. First edition, 2 volumes, mismatched, with separate atlas volume, large 8vo., atlas with 7 large plates, volume on in 19th century quarter calf with original printed cover mounted over marbled boards, volume two with original wrappers, volume II disbound (spine lacking), both volumes worn with extensive internal pencil notes, atlas wrapper is remnant, but printed cover present, good, very rare.   Jeff Weber Rare Books   178 - 990   2015 $750

Schlegel, Jorgen U. *The Luger.* Independence: International University Press, 1989. First edition, pictorial wrappers, slight vertical crease to back cover, else fine, very scarce.   Baade Books of the West   2014 - 2015 $81

Schlossberg, Joseph *The Workers and Their World.* New York: A. L. P. Committee, 1935. First edition, hardcover, fine in fine dust jacket.   Beasley Books   2013 - 2015 $45

Schmitt, Charles R. *The Cambridge History of Renaissance Philosophy.* Cambridge: Cambridge University Press, 1988. Thick 8vo., cloth, dust jacket, ink ownership, signature of David Lindberg, very good+. Jeff Weber Rare Books 178 - 993 2015 $75

Schnabel, Julian *C.V.J. Nicknames of Maitre D's & Other Exceprts from Life.* New York: Unicorn Publishing Studio, 1987. 4to., original orange cloth, lettered black on acetate dust jacket, illustrations in color and black and white, signed presentation from author to John Reid (rock manger to Queen & Elton John), fine in acetate dust jacket. Any Amount of Books 2015 - C11092 2015 £320

Schnitzler, Arthur *Casanovas Heimfahrt.* Berlin: S. Fischer, 1921. 8vo., quarter cloth, marbled paper covered boards, covers rubbed and scuffed at edges, endpapers foxed. Oak Knoll Books 306 - 297 2015 $150

Schnitzler, Arthur *Die Hirtenflote.* Wien: Vienna: Deutsch-Ostereichischer Verlag, 1912. First edition, number 261 of 400 copies, small 8vo., original Wiener Werkstatte binding, green full crushed leather gilt patterned and decorated, designed by Josef Hoffmann, clean, tight and unmarked in excellent clean, very good condition, slight rubbing at extremities, 9 original etchings by Ferdinand Schmutzer with tissue guards. Any Amount of Books 2015 - C9490 2015 £700

Schnitzler, Arthur *The Lonely Way: Intermezzo: Countless Mizzie.* New York: Mitchell Kennerley, 1915. First American edition, spine lettering dull and little foxing in text, very good without dust jacket, Walter Lippmann's copy with his ownership signature and address "From Mitchell Kennerley, May 1915". Between the Covers Rare Books, Inc. 187 - 246 2015 $400

Schoenbaum, S. *William Shakespeare: a Documentary Life.* New York: Oxford University Press in Association with the Scholar Press, 1975. First edition, trade issue, folio, slightly musty, else near fine in price clipped, near fine dust jacket, inscribed by author to author Peter Taylor, laid in is TLS for executive director to Pen/Faulkner Award for Fiction presenting the book to Taylor. Between the Covers Rare Books, Inc. 187 - 247 2015 $125

Schofield, A. T. *Functional Nerve Diseases.* London: Methuen, 1908. First edition, hardcover, very good+. Beasley Books 2013 - 2015 $45

Schofield, Lily *Tom Catapus and Potiphar: a Tale of Ancient Egypt.* London: Frederick Warne, 1903. 12mo., pictorial cloth, fine, printed on one side of the paper, almost every page of text faces full page color illustration by author. Aleph-Bet Books, Inc. 108 - 409 2015 $200

Scholarlau, Wolfgang *Down at Theresa's Chicago Blues.* Munich: Prestel Verlag, 2000. First edition, inscribed by photographer and uncommon thus, fine in fine dust jacket, 4to., 95 pages. Beasley Books 2013 - 2015 $200

Schomburgk, Robert Hermann *Robert Hermann Schomburgk's Reisen in Guiana und am Orinoko, Wahrend der jahre 1835-1839.* Leipzig: Herausgegeben O. A. Schomburgk, Verland Vo Georg Wigand, 1841. First edition, 6 hand colored lithographic plates with tissue guards, 1 folding map, and one in text drawing, small 4to., original quarter brown morocco over pebble cloth boards, gilt decorated spine, silk bookmark, sewn in, the copy of Gustav Blass dated 1852 (The firm of F. Blass & Schomburgk was involved in the Caribbean trade), contemporary owner's name, extremities worn especially at tips, few splits at joints, contemporary owner's name on first blank, small tear at fore edge of title not affecting text, leaves foxed, plates brilliant, map offset in one section with fore edge bit worn, uncommon title. Kaaterskill Books 19 - 138 2015 $1500

Schoolcraft, Henry Rowe 1793-1864 *The Indian in His Wigwam.* Dewitt & Davenport, 1848. Black cloth, titles stamped in gilt on spine, illustrations, some foxing, else very good. Buckingham Books March 2015 - 37960 2015 $450

Schoolcraft, Henry Rowe 1793-1864 *The Personal memoirs of a residence of Thirty Years with the Indian Tribes on the American Frontiers...* Philadelphia: Lippincott, Grambo and Co., 1851. First edition, 703 pages, no portrait in this copy, library rebacked, typed label, library marks/plates, hinges broken after first signature, but intact with library's repair at front hinge, back hinge cracked. Baade Books of the West 2014 - 2015 $225

Schoolcraft, Henry Rowe 1793-1864 *Summary Narrative of an Exploratory Expedition to the Sources of the Mississippi River in 1820...* Philadelphia: Lippincott, Grambo and Co., 1855. Reprint without maps, decorated cloth, cracked hinges reglued, nearly very good, scarce. Baade Books of the West 2014 - 2015 $98

Schopper, Hartmann *De Omnibus Illiberalibus Sive Mechanicis Artibus.* Frankfurt: Georg Rabe (Corvinus) for Sigismund Carl Feyerabend, 1574. Second edition in Latin, small 8vo., woodcut printer's device on title ruled in red, another on final recto with colophon on verso, 132 woodcut illustrations by Jost Amman, all but one printed on rectos only, full straight grain red morocco by Roger Payne, spine lettered in gilt, gilt edges with armorial bookplate of Richard Bull of Ongar and signature Roger Payne, Delt on small piece pasted to front free endpaper, fine. Marlborough Rare Books List 53 - 1 2015 £7850

Schreiben Eines Bayern an Seinen Freund Uber die Moglichkeit der Ganzlichen Abstellung des Betteins und der Versorgung der Armen in Einem Land. Nuremberg: Wolfgang Schwarzkopf, 1774. 8vo., margins of title soiled, some mostly marginal foxing, minor stain on last few leaves, original wrappers, uncut, good copy, from Schloss Diepenbrock Library with old armorial stamp, rare outside German libraries. John Drury Rare Books   March 2015 - 21112   2015   £306

Schroder, Severin   *Die Farbenharmonie in Der Damen-Toilette.*   Vienna: Verlag von Emil Berte & Cie und S. Czeiger, I. Lothringerstrasse 3, 1897. First edition, 8vo., six colored plates with pocket at back of work containing a color wheel chart an accompanying pierced sheet "Harmonie des Contrastes and Harmone des Verwandten Analogen", original white cloth, upper cover of a fashionable lady within a grey palette border gilt, red edges, slightly soiled. Marlborough Rare Books   List 54 - 76   2015   £875

Schrodinger, Erwin   *What is Life? The Physical Aspect of the Living Cell.*   Cambridge: Cambridge University Press, 1944. First edition, 8vo., original green cloth, lettered gilt at spine, clean, bright, about fine in clean, very good, price clipped dust jacket, slightly rubbed at spine, slightly chipped at lower edge, faint wear at spine ends.   Any Amount of Books   2015 - C14190   2015   £700

Schubarth, Ernst Ludwig   *Repertorium der Technischen Literatur die Jahre 1828 bis Einschl. 1853 Umfassend.*   Berlin: Deckerschen Geheimen Ober-Hofbuchdruckerei, 1856. 8vo., quarter brown leather with marbled paper sides, gilt stamped spine, title with raised spine bands, extremities worn, spine corners chipped, some marginal waterstains, former library copy with usual markings, very good, rare. Jeff Weber Rare Books   178 - 996   2015 $180

Schuch, Werner   *Der Schwarze Kasper...*   Frankfurt: n.p. (Kreuzkam), n.d., 1897. 4to., cloth backed pictorial boards, some strengthening, else very good, every page illustrated by author in color or in brown, quite scarce.   Aleph-Bet Books, Inc.   108 - 242   2015 $600

Schultz, James Willard   *My Life as an Indian...*   New York: Doubleday Page & Co., 1907. Pictorial cloth, 426 pages, photos, nine-line presentation signed and dated by Schulz in 1943, covers generally rubbed from use, with loss of sharpness of front cover illustration and lettering, but no fraying of cloth, moisture tide-lines throughout text, but faintly so for the most part, mainly resulting in waviness of paper.   Baade Books of the West   2014 - 2015 $486

Schultz, Theodore W.   *Economic Crises in World Agriculture.*   Ann Arbor: University of Michigan, 1965. First edition, signed and inscribed to noted Illinois Attorney Walter T. Fisher, by author, 8vo., near fine in very good+ dust jacket, with minimal edgewear and scuffs.   By the Book, L. C. Special List 10 - 17   2015 $300

Schuman, William   *New England Triptych.*   Bryn Mawr: Merion Music, 1957. First edition, signed by author, scarce, near fine, softcover.   Stephen Lupack   March 2015 - 2015 $250

Schurman, Anna Maria Von   *Opuscula Hebraea, Graeca, Latina, Gallica.*   Ludg. Batador: Ex Officina Elseviriorum, 1648. First edition, 8vo., titlepage printed in black and red with engraving of Elzevir logo of a sage under a tree, some ink writing in old hand on leaf opposite titlepage, with few words at top of titlepage (seems to have been issued with and without portrait, none here), later three quarter morocco and marbled paper, paper little toned but very good, rare. Second Life Books Inc.   189 - 223   2015 $1500

Schuyler, George S.   *Black No More Being an Account of the Strange and Wonderful Workings of Science in the Land of the Free A.D. 1933-1940.*   New York: Macaulay, 1931. 8vo., ivory cloth, cover soiled an darkened, flaps of dust jacket glued on pastedowns, rest of dust jacket missing, hinges tender, otherwise very good.   Second Life Books Inc.   190 - 190   2015 $300

Schuyler, George S.   *Ethiopian Stories.*   Boston: Northeastern University, 1994. Advance uncorrected proof, 8vo., paper wrappers, very good, tight copy.   Second Life Books Inc.   190 - 192   2015 $75

Schuyler, James   *Broadway: a Poets and Painters Anthology.*   New York: Swollen Magpie Press, 1979. First edition, 4to., illustrations, original wrappers with front cover illustration by Paula North, covers slightly dust soiled, one tiny short closed tear, presentation copy inscribed by Schuyler for Tom (Carey).   James S. Jaffe Rare Books Many Happy Returns - 392   2015 $750

Schuyler, James   *Collabs.*   New York: Misty Terrace Press, 1980. First edition, one of 200 copies, 4to., original wrappers with cover design by George Schneeman, stapled as issued, presentation from all contributors, Helena Hughes, Michael Scholnick and signed by small pen and ink self-portrait by Schneeman for Ted Berrigan, fine.   James S. Jaffe Rare Books   Modern American Poetry - 244   2015 $1750

Schuyler, James   *The Fireproof Floors of Witley Court.*   Newark, West Burke: Janus Press, 1976. First edition, limited to 150 numbered copies, torn, cut and bound by Claire Van Vliet on Kozu, Fabriano and Canon paper, although not issued signed, this copy signed by author, 8vo., architectural cut-out endpapers, original orange decorated wrappers, narrow three quarter inch strip of light fading along top of front cover, otherwise fine.   James S. Jaffe Rare Books Modern American Poetry - 240   2015 $2500

Schuyler, James *49 South.* Southampton: privately printed, 1972. First edition, 4to., drawings, mimeographed sheets in stiff paper wrappers with front cover illustration by Robert Dash, stapled, covers slightly sunned, dust soiled and foxed, otherwise fine.   James S. Jaffe Rare Books   Many Happy Returns - 391   2015 $850

Schuyler, James *The Home Book: Prose and Poems 1951-1970.* Calais: Z Press, 1977. First edition, one of 26 lettered copies signed by Schuyler, out of a total edition of 100 copies, although not called for, this copy signed by Darrah Park who designed covers, 8vo., original wrappers, cover illustration by Darrah Park, spine slightly cocked, otherwise fine.   James S. Jaffe Rare Books   Modern American Poetry - 241   2015 $750

Schuyler, James *Hymn to Life. Poems.* New York: Random House, 1974. First edition, 8vo., original cloth backed boards, dust jacket, fine, presentation copy inscribed by author for Barbara Guest March 12 1974.   James S. Jaffe Rare Books   Modern American Poetry - 239   2015 $2500

Schuyler, James *Locus Solus I - Winter 1961.* Locus Solus Press, 1960. First issue, small octavo, printed wrappers, boxed, Frank O'Hara's personal copy with his ownership signature in ink on first page, he has marked each of his ten included poems with dates of composition.   Honey & Wax Booksellers   1 - 54   2015 $2500

Schuyler, James *May 24th or So.* New York: Tibor De Nagy Editions, 1966. First edition, one of only 20 copies signed by author, out of a total edition of 300 copies, this copy #1, square small 8vo., original decorated wrappers, very fine.   James S. Jaffe Rare Books   Modern American Poetry - 238   2015 $2500

Schuyler, James *The Morning of the Poem.* New York: Farrar Straus & Giroux, 1980. First edition, 8vo., cloth backed boards, dust jacket, fine in slightly sunned jacket, presentation copy inscribed by author for Barbara Guest, Feb. 1980.   James S. Jaffe Rare Books   Modern American Poetry - 245   2015 $2500

Schuyler, James *The Morning of the Poems.* New York: Farrar Straus & Giroux, 1980. First edition, presentation copy inscribed by author for Ted (Berrigan Aug. '80), fine.   James S. Jaffe Rare Books   Many Happy Returns - 364   2015 $3500

Schuyler, James *Selected Poems.* New York: Farrar Straus & Giroux, 1988. First edition, original cloth, dust jacket, signed by author, top edge of inner flaps sunned, otherwise fine.   James S. Jaffe Rare Books   Modern American Poetry - 246   2015 $375

Schuyler, James *A Sun Cab.* New York: Adventures in Poetry, 1972. First edition, one of 26 lettered copies signed by author and artist, out of a total edition of 300 copies, cover and illustrations by Fairfield Porter, 4to., mimeographed sheets in original stiff paper covers, fine.   James S. Jaffe Rare Books   Modern American Poetry - 242   2015 $1000

Schuyler, James *What's for Dinner?* Santa Barbara: Black Sparrow Press, 1978. First edition, one of 26 lettered copies signed by author, out of a total edition of 226 copies, handbound in boards by Earle Gray, 8vo., original quarter patterned cloth and boards with printed label on spine and front cover, illustrations by Jane Freilicher, acetate dust jacket, fine.   James S. Jaffe Rare Books   Modern American Poetry - 243   2015 $350

Schwartz, Delmore *In Dreams Begin Responsibilities.* Norfolk: New Directions, 1938. First edition, one of 1000 copies, 8vo., original black cloth, very fine, dust jacket. James S. Jaffe Rare Books   Modern American Poetry - 247   2015 $1500

Schwartz, Delmore *Vaudeville for a Princess.* New York: New Directions, 1950. First edition, 8vo., original cloth, dust jacket, fine in fine jacket, presentation copy inscribed by author for friend Anatole Broyard.   James S. Jaffe Rare Books   Modern American Poetry - 249   2015 $1250

Schwartz, Delmore *The World is a Wedding.* Norfolk: New Directions, 1948. First edition, 8vo., original cloth, dust jacket, inscribed by author to S. A. Jacobs, head of spine rubbed, otherwise very good in slightly dust soiled jacket.   James S. Jaffe Rare Books   Modern American Poetry - 248   2015 $1250

Schwartzberg, Joseph E. *A Historical Atlas of South Asia.* Chicago & London: University of Chicago Press, 1978. First edition, large folio, original red cloth, lettered gilt on spine, copiously illustrated in color and black and white, fine.   Any Amount of Books   March 2015 - C3231   2015   £400

Schwob, Marcel *Vies Imaginaires.* Paris: Les Editions Lumiere, 1946. First edition, no. 953 of 1500 copies, 8vo., original illustrated self wrappers, French text, 22 illustrations by Felix Labisse, signed presentation from artist, Felix Labisse, spine ends slightly worn, otherwise clean, very good.   Any Amount of Books   2015 - C3446   2015   £150

Scieszka, Jon *The Stinky Cheese Man and Other Fairly Stupid Tales.* New York: Viking Press, 1992. Stated first edition, 4to., signed and inscribed by Scieszka and Lane Smith with small drawing by Smith, fine in fine dust jacket, uncommon.   By the Book, L. C.   44 - 86   2015 $120

Sclauzero, Mariarosa *Narcissism and Death.* Barrytown: Station Hill Press, 1984. First edition, small 4to., wrappers, 10 illustrations by Sue Coe, signed presentation from author to Angela Carter, novelist, with posthumous bookplate, loosely inserted flier for Stamperia Valdonega limited edition, very slight rubbing, faint edgewear, very good+. Any Amount of Books 2015 - A64551 2015 £150

Scott, Hugh Stowell 1862-1903 *From One Generation to Another.* London: Smith, Elder & Co., 1892. First edition, 2 volumes, half titles, 2 pages ads volume II, original pea green cloth, lettered black on front covers within double black borders, spines lettered gilt, fine, Carter's variant B binding. Jarndyce Antiquarian Booksellers CCXI - 200 2015 £225

Scott, Manda *Boudica: Dreaming the Eagle.* London: Bantam Press, 2003. First edition, signed by author, fine in dust jacket. Buckingham Books March 2015 - 31693 2015 $200

Scott, Peter Dale *Coming to Jakarta;. A Poem About Terror.* New York: New Directions, 1989. First edition, 150 pages, fine in wrappers, gift inscription by author to Clayton (Eshleman). Ken Lopez, Bookseller 164 - 192 2015 $125

Scott, Robert *An Antidote for Deism, or, Scripture Prophecy Fulfilled.* Pittsfield: Phinehas Allen, 1816. First edition, 8vo., 145 pages, contemporary calf backed boards, foxed. M & S Rare Books, Inc. 97 - 4 2015 $275

Scott, Robert Eden *Elements of Intellectual Philosophy: or an Analysis of the Powers of the Human Understanding...* Edinburgh and London: Archibald Constable & Co. and T. Cadell & W. Davies, 1805. First edition, 8vo., disbound, ownership inscription, some foxing, most prominent on prelims and final leaves, disbound, (i.e. lacking covers), otherwise in decent sound condition with clean text, suitable for rebinding or reading. Any Amount of Books 2015 - C7447 2015 £160

Scott, T. *Verses in Honour of their Present Majesties.* London: printed for J. Walthoe, 1727. First edition, 8vo., recent wrappers, very rare, small piece chipped from blank inner margin of titlepage, at top some soiling of titlepage and last two leaves, otherwise good copy. C. R. Johnson Foxon R-Z - 868r-z 2015 $1915

Scott, Thomas *A Father's Instructions to His Son.* London: printed for R. Dodsley and M. Cooper, 1748. First edition, 4to., 19th century half calf and marbled boards (bit scuffed), on front flyleaf is ownership inscription dated 1907 of Hardinge F. Giffard, contemporary signature on half title of George Notcutt, nonconformist minister in Ipswich,. C. R. Johnson Foxon R-Z - 869r-z 2015 $1302

Scott, Thomas *Observations on the Sign and Duties of the Present Times...* London: printed by D. Jacques, sold by Mathews &c, 1799. First and only edition, rare outside UK libraries, 8vo., recently bound in plain boards with printed title label, fine, crisp copy. John Drury Rare Books March 2015 - 24679 2015 £306

Scott, Walter 1771-1832 *The Abbot.* Edinburgh: printed for Longman, Hurst, Rees, Orme and Brown; London and for Archibald Constable and Co. and John Ballantyne, Edinburgh, 1820. First edition, 3 volumes, contemporary calf and marbled paper covered boards, black morocco spine label, titled and spine decorations in gilt, bookplate of Coleman O. Parsons in volume one, moderate rubbing and wear to extremities, half titles lacking in volume one, very good. Between the Covers Rare Books, Inc. 187 - 254 2015 $250

Scott, Walter 1771-1832 *Quentin Durward.* New York: Charles Scribners Sons, 1923. First edition, 4to., black cloth, pictorial paste-on, slight cover rubbing, very good+, illustrations by C. Rosseron Chambers. Aleph-bet Books, Inc. 109 - 426 2015 $125

Scott, Walter 1771-1832 *Rob Roy.* Edinburgh: printed by James Ballantyne & Co. for Archibald Constable and Co., 1818. First edition, half titles, 3 volumes, contemporary full brown speckled calf very good some wear and rubbing to extremities, rubbing and minor scratches to boards, former owner's bookplates to front pastedown, some light spotting and minor toning to first and last pages of text, volume 2 with some spotting to page edges, few minor creases to otherwise bright and clean pages, clean set in contemporary binding, free of any repairs or restoration. B & B Rare Books, Ltd. 2015 - 2015 $800

Scott, Winfield Townley *The Sword on the Table Thomas Dorr's Rebellion.* Norfolk: New Directions, 1842. First edition, 8vo., 16 leaves, plain wrappers, stiff printed dust jacket, rust stain from paper clip on first several leaves, otherwise about very good, laid in is small rust stained card of a Mr. Green, with presentation to member of the Burges family. M & S Rare Books, Inc. 97 - 92 2015 $125

Scowrers and Molly Maguires of San Francisco *West by One and By One.* San Francisco: privately published, 1965. First edition, laid in is program for 20th Anniversary Dinner for the Scowers and Molly Maguires at the Leopard Cafe in San Francisco in May 1964, fine in dust jacket. Mordida Books March 2015 - 007879 2015 $200

Scriblerus Club *Memoirs of the Extraordinary Life, Works and Discoveries of Martinus Scriblerus...* New Haven: for Wellesley College by Yale Univ. Press, 1950. Half title, illustrations, original dark blue cloth, very good in torn dust jacket, Geoffrey Tillotson's signed copy. Jarndyce Antiquarian Booksellers CCVII - 454 2015 £20

Scriptural Epitaphs. London: Smith Elder and Co., 1947. 12mo., contemporary calf gilt, spine fully gilt with raised bands, red edges, inner gilt dentelles by Riviere, fine, rare. John Drury Rare Books   March 2015 - 15838   2015 $266

Scrivener, Matthew   *A Treatise Against Drunkenesse...* London: printed for Charles Brown, bookseller in Cambridge, 1685. First edition, 12mo., errata leaf (with short closed tear, no loss), contemporary calf gilt, neatly rebacked, very good, crisp copy, scarce.   John Drury Rare Books   2015 - 21821   2015 $2185

Scrope, George Poulett   *A Letter to the Magistrates of the South of England, on the Urgent Necessity of Putting a Stop to the Illegal Practice of making Up Wages Out of Rates...* London: James Ridgway, 1831. First edition, recent marbled boards lettered on spine, very good.   John Drury Rare Books   March 2015 - 24942   2015   £306

Scudder, Horace Elisha   *The Game of Croquet: It's Appointment and Laws.* New York: Abercrombie & Fitch, 1968. First edition, fine in very good dust jacket with nicks at spine ends, several closed tears and light wear along folds and at corners.   Mordida Books   March 2015 - 008184   2015 $125

Seago, Edward   *With Capricorn to Paris.* London: Published by Collins, 1956. First edition, 8vo., frontispiece and 7 plates, several illustrations in text, signed presentation from author to Mollie (Mary Montagu Douglas Scott, Duchess of Buccleuch 1900-1968), very good in near very good, used dust jacket little chipped and nicked at edges but with only minor loss and still presentable.   Any Amount of Books   2015 - A72902   2015   £160

Seagrave, Robert   *The Peace of Europe. A Congratulatory Poem. inscribed to Rt. Hon. Robert Walpole.* London: printed for J. Roberts, 1732. First edition, recent marbled boards, fine, large copy with outer edges uncut, rare.   C. R. Johnson   Foxon R-Z - 871r-z   2015 $1149

Seasonable Considerations Relative to the Smugglers. London: printed by W. Strahan, 1746. First edition, 4to., titlepage with wear at old central fold, leaf now lined with paper but without compromising the prefatory note, well bound in 19th century half calf gilt over marbled boards, very good, old bookplate of Los Angeles board of Law Library on pastedown, but no other marks of ownership. John Drury Rare Books   2015 - 26018   2015 $1705

A Seasonable Recapitulation of Enormous National Crimes and Grievances to Help the Memory for the Use and Consideration of all Honest men and True Britons. London: printed for M. Cooper at the Globe in Paternoster Row, 1749. First edition, variant issue, 8vo., without half title, well bound in early 20th century half sheep over cloth boards, spine lettered gilt, very good, very scarce.   John Drury Rare Books   March 2015 - 22804   2015   £266

Seasonable Reflections on the Late Convention Concluded the 3d of May Last Between the Courts of Vienna and Turin for Partitioning Between them the Territories Belonging to the Republic of Genoa... London: M. Cooper, n.d., 1747. First and only edition, 8vo., titlepage rather soiled and with several old ownership inscriptions, some further soiling of first few leaves, preserved in recent plain wrappers with label on upper cover, scarce.   John Drury Rare Books   2015 - 20777   2015 $177

Seaton, Elizabeth   *WPA Federal Art Project - Printmaking in California 1935-1943.* San Francisco: Book Club of California, 2005. First edition, one of 450 copies, quarto, 86 color and doutone photos and other illustrations, printed in red and black, titlepage printed letterpress in black, red, yellow and blue, blue silk cloth spine lettered in gilt, blue cloth sides with decoration in black, very fine, as new, original announcement, identification guide and errata laid in. Argonaut Book Shop   Holiday Season 2014 - 259   2015 $300

The Secret History of an Old Shoe. First edition, folio, disbound, fine, titlepage mounted on stub and appears to be a cancel, very scarce.   C. R. Johnson   Foxon R-Z - 872r-z   2015 $1379

Secretary Janus, a Dialogue between Simon Lord Frazer of Lovat and J. M--r--y, Secretary to the Late Pretender. London: printed and sold by G. Foster, 1747. First edition, 6 pages, folio, disbound, blue cloth folding case, very good, rare.   C. R. Johnson   Foxon R-Z - 873r-z   2015 $1302

Seddon, John   *The Penman's Paradise, Both Pleasant & Profitable.* Stuttgart: Dr. Cantz'sche Druckerei, 1966. Limited to 250 copies, oblong small 4to., paper spine with Cockerel paper covered boards, paper spine label, later cardboard slipcase, 34 page facsimile of original edition. Oak Knoll Books   Special Catalogue 24 - 46   2015 $150

Sedgwick, Adam   *A Discourse on the Studies of the University...* Cambridge: J. & J. J. Deighton and John W. Parker, London, 1835. Fourth edition, 8vo., original patterned blue cloth, spine simply lettered in gilt, very good, uncut and partially unopened.   John Drury Rare Books   2015 - 16540   2015 $168

Sedgwick, Anne Douglas   *The Old Countess.* Boston and New York: Houghton Mifflin, 1927. First US edition, 8vo., original blue cloth lettered gilt on spine and cover sepia photo of author pasted in at rear, signed presentation to Lady Ottoline Morrell from author, spine slightly dusty and very slightly frayed at top, otherwise sound, near very good copy.   Any Amount of Books   2015 - C3445   2015   £280

Sedley, Charles *Asmodeus; or the Devil's in London: a Sketch.* London: printed by J. Dean, Wardourt Street, Soho for F. F. Hughes 15 Paternoster Row, 1808. First edition, 3 volumes, 12mo., without half titles, apart from few minor marks in places, clean copy, contemporary green half calf over marbled boards, spines ruled and numbered in gilt, labels missing, chipped at head and rubbed at extremities, still appealing copy, armorial of Felix Booth and Renier booklabels.   Marlborough Rare Books   List 53 - 43   2015   £900

Sedley, Charles *The Miscellaneous Works of the Honourable Sir Charles Sedley, Bart.* London: printed and sold by J. Nutt, 1702. First edition, 8vo., contemporary panelled calf, cracked hinges, but good, light foxing but very good, bookplate of Oliver Brett, Viscount Esher.   C. R. Johnson   Foxon R-Z - 875r-z   2015 $306

Sedley, Charles *The Poetical Works of the Honourable Sir Charles Sedley Bar. and His Speeches in Parliament...* London: printed for Sam. Briscoe an sold by James Woodward and John Morphew, 1710. Second edition, in fact reissue of sheets of 1707 edition with cancel titlepage, 8vo., contemporary panelled calf, joints rubbed, spine bit worn, label defective, good condition, early armorial Jolliffe bookplate.   C. R. Johnson   Foxon R-Z - 877r-z   2015 $230

Seebohm, Henry *The Geographical Distribution of the Family Charadriidae or the Plovers, Sandpipers, Snipes and their Allies.* London: Henry Sotheran & Co., 1887-1888. Quarto, 21 hand colored lithographs by Keulemans, publisher's green panelled cloth, hinges expertly strengthened, all edges uncut, very good.   Andrew Isles   2015 - 35668   2015 $5000

Seeger, Laura Vaccaro *First the Egg.* New Milford: Roaring Brook Press, 2007. First edition, signed and dated in year of publication by author, 8vo., fine in fine dust jacket.   By the Book, L. C.   44 - 87   2015 $125

Seeger, Peter *American Favorite Ballads.* New York: Oak Publications, 1969. 20th printing, scarce cloth bound edition, large 8vo., fine.   Beasley Books   2013 - 2015 $40

Segal, Erich *Love Story.* New York: Harper, 1970. First edition, boards very slightly soiled, still fine in near fine dust jacket with small, very faint stain and two short tears, signed by author, nice, uncommon signed, from the library of Kate Stettner Lobell and Carl D. Lobell.   Between the Covers Rare Books   196 - 32   2015 $350

Segal, Hyman R. *They Called Him Champ: the Story of Champ Segal.* New York: Citadel Press, 1959. First edition, fine in very good plus dust jacket with tiny nicks and tears, small coffee stain on front panel, inscribed by subject of book to Joe DiMaggio, with letter of provenance signed by Di Maggio's two granddaughters.   Between the Covers Rare Books, Inc.   187 - 31   2015 $850

Segrave, Kerry *Payola in the Music Industry a History 1880-1991.* Jefferson: McFarland & Co. Inc., 1994. First edition, 8vo., uncommon, near fine.   Beasley Books   2013 - 2015 $45

Seguin, Armand *Reve d'Ameliorations Administratives et Financieres.* Paris: Lecointe & Durey Janvier, 1828. First edition, 8vo., lacking half title, very good in plain wrappers.   John Drury Rare Books   2015 - 17858   2015 $133

Segur, Sophie Rostopchine, Comtesse De 1799-1874 *Old French Fairy Tales.* Philadelphia: Penn, 1920. First edition, large thick 4to., blue cloth, pictorial paste-on, as new in original publisher's box with colorplate on cover (box flaps strengthened, some rubbing), 8 truly magnificent color plates (tissue guards) and many lovely black and whites as well as yellow pictorial endpapers.   Aleph-bet Books, Inc.   109 - 451   2015 $975

Selden, Ambrose *Love and Folly. A Poem in four Cantos.* London: printed for W. Johnston, 1749. First edition, 8vo., contemporary speckled calf, neatly rebacked, spine gilt, red morocco label, , as in many copies, list of errata at end of prelims is a paste-on cancel, expanding the corrections from four lines to twelve, very good complete with half title, early signature of Charles Barnwell of Melcham, uncommon.   C. R. Johnson   Foxon R-Z - 878r-z   2015 $689

A Select Collection of Modern Poems. By Several Hands. Dublin: printed by John Henly, 1713. First edition, 12mo., contemporary calf, joints bit rubbed, fine, signature of William Worth dated Feb. 12 1714 with acquisition price of one shilling, small neat signature of Anne Worth on titlepage dated 1725.   C. R. Johnson   Foxon R-Z - 879r-z   2015 $5363

Select Poems from Ireland... (bound with) Selected Poems from Ireland. Part II. Printed Dublin,: London: Reprinted and sold by T. Warner, 1730. First edition, each printed in an edition of 500 copies, 2 parts, 8vo., disbound, very good.   C. R. Johnson   Foxon R-Z - 880r-z   2015 $4597

Selfridge, Thomas O. *Trial of Thomas O. Selfridge, Attorney at Law, Before the Hon. Isaac Parker, Esquire for Killing Charles Austin on the Public Exchange, in Boston August 4th 1806.* Boston: Russell & Cutler Belcher and Armstrong and Oliver and Munroe, 1807. First edition, 8vo., errata leaf, table of contents and street plan, some paper browning and dust soiling, recently well bound in old style quarter calf, gilt, good.   John Drury Rare Books   2015 - 15220   2015 $133

Selkirk, Thomas Douglas, 5th Earl of 1771-1820 *A Letter Addressed to John Cartwright, Eaq. Chairman of the Committee at the Crown and Anchor, on the Subject of Parliamentary Reform.* London: Constable Hunter Park and Hunter and A. Constable, & Co., Edinburgh, 1809. First edition, 8vo., well bound in modern quarter morocco over cloth boards, spine lettered gilt, very good, scarce. John Drury Rare Books March 2015 - 25767 2015 $266

Selkirk, Thomas Douglas, 5th Earl of 1771-1820 *A Letter Addressed to John Cartwright esq. Chairman of the Committee of the Crown and Anchor on the Subject of Parliamentary reform.* London: printed by J. M'Creery for Constable Hutner Park & Hutner and A. Constable & Co., Edinburgh, 1809. Second edition, 8vo., preserved in modern wrappers with printed label on upper cover, very good, uncommon. John Drury Rare Books March 2015 - 25516 2015 $221

Sellon, Priscilla Lydia *Reply to a Tract by the Rev. J. Spurrell, Vicar of Great Shelford, Containing Charges Concerning the Society of the Sisters of Mercy of Devonport and Plymouth.* London: Joseph Masters, Plymouth: Roger Listone,

1852. Fifth edition, 8vo., 28 pages, recently bound in cloth backed marbled boards with printed title label on upper cover, titlepage just slightly marked but very good copy. John Drury Rare Books 2015 - 24389 2015 $150

Semple, James *Representative Women of Colorado.* Denver: James Alexander Semple..., 1911. Deluxe edition limited to 620 numbered copies, Large 8vo., photos, title within floral border printed in two colors, original rough leather printed in blind and gilt, all edges gilt, inscribed by Semple, recipient's name stamped gilt on front cover, very nice. Second Life Books Inc. 189 - 225 2015 $400

Semple, Robert *Sketch of the Present State of Caracas: Including a Journey from Caracas through La Victoria and Valencia to Puerto Cabello.* London: printed for Robert Baldwin, 1812. First edition, 12mo., modern quarter brown cloth over marbled boards, red morocco spine label titled in gilt, near fine with only very occasional foxing. Kaaterskill Books 19 - 139 2015 $900

Sen, Amartya K. *Poor, Relatively Speaking.* Economic and Social Research Institute, 1983. First edition, 8vo., original staple bound printed wrappers with minimal creases spine, scuffs and edgewear to covers, paper clip rust stain verso front cover and top of titlepage, signed and inscribed by author for Dorothy (Weddenburn). By the Book, L. C. Special List 10 - l18 2015 $175

Senault, Louis *Heures Nouvelles Dediees a Madame La Dauphine.* Paris: chez l'Autheur n.d. circa 1680's, 8vo., full 19th century polished calf with gilt panels, red morocco label, (signed binding by de Haas with his label), joints repaired at head and foot, paper repair to head of titlepage not affecting text, worn at joints, book is printed form engraved plates. Oak Knoll Books Special Catalogue 24 - 47 2015 $2250

Senault, Louis *Petit Office De la Sainte Vierge.* Paris: Chez Senault, circa, 1680. 181 x 127mm., remarkably beautiful black straight grain morocco elegantly and lavishly gilt by Thouvenin (signed at base of spine), covers with elaborate broad frame featuring repeated palmettes, central panel with complex cornerpieces of massed antique tools, raised bands, spine compartments with red cruciform inlay at center and with stylized tulips and multiple stippled leaves emanating from central ornament, very lovely broad inner gilt dentelles featuring 52 additional red morocco inlays (26 inside each cover), these within large 'semis' rectangles with concave sides, dentelles surrounding pink watered silk pastedowns bordered with a neoclassical foliate and floral roll (facing a free endpaper of the same material and with the same decoration), all edges gilt, small and very expert repair, just top of joints, marbled paper slipcase; engraved throughout with a great variety of immensely charming calligraphic initials, headpieces, tailpieces, borders, flourishes and other decorative elements; bookplate of Hans Furstenberg; just the faintest hint of wear to joints, two minor blemishes on rear cover, discoloration at gutter of free endpapers (apparently from binder's glue), but fine, with extraordinarily handsome binding with glistening and with text nearly pristine. Phillip J. Pirages 66 - 77 2015 $7500

Sendak, Maurice *Kenny's Window.* New York: Harper Bros, 1956. First edition, 4to., dark brown spine, tan pictorial cloth, fine in bright fine dust jacket with price intact, review copy with slip laid-in, beautiful full page and in-text color illustrations by author, scarce. Aleph-Bet Books, Inc. 108 - 416 2015 $1275

Sendak, Maurice *Nutshell Library.* New York: Harper & Row, 1962. 4 volumes, pictorial slipcase with original $2.95 price sticker intact, slipcase very slightly scuffed, books fine in lightly frayed dust jacket with some small chips, rare with sticker. Aleph-bet Books, Inc. 109 - 432 2015 $1200

Sendak, Maurice *Very Far Away.* New York: Harper & Bros., 1957. 8vo., blue pictorial cloth, fine in very good dust jacket with price intact, some general soil on dust jacket, full page color illustrations by author. Aleph-bet Books, Inc. 109 - 431 2015 $1200

Sendak, Maurice *Where the Wild Things Are.* New York: Harper Row, 1963. First edition, oblong 4to., cloth backed pictorial boards, fine in slightly toned dust jacket with small amount of rubbing to top of spine with price intact, this copy inscribed by Sendak and dated 1964 with charming ink drawing of a dog. Aleph-bet Books, Inc. 109 - 427 2015 $20,500

Sendak, Maurice *Where the Wild Things Are.* New York: Harper Row, 1963. First edition, oblong 4to., cloth backed pictorial boards, fine, very lightly soiled and slightly frayed, price clipped dust jacket, with correct $3.50 issue price. Aleph-Bet Books, Inc. 108 - 414 2015 $13,500

Sendak, Maurice *Where the Wild Things Are.* N.P.: Harper Collins, 1988. 25th Anniversary edition, color illustrations by author, signed by author on half title, oblong 8vo., quarter cloth, illustrated paper covered boards. Oak Knoll Books 306 - 298 2015 $125

Seneca, Lucius Annaeus *Seneca's Morals by way of Abstract...* Edinburgh: printed for Gilb. Martin and Sons, 1776. New edition, small hole in blank area of half title, somewhat browned and foxed, old ownership inscriptions of M. Doyle and Joshua Marsden, 8vo., contemporary mottled calf, crackled and pitted, rebacked, endpapers renewed, sound, scarce. Blackwell's Rare Books Greek & Latin Classics VI - 95 2015 £300

Seneca, Lucius Annaeus *Tragoediae.* Florence: Studio et Impensa Philippi di Guinta, 1506. 8vo., final blank discarded, rather foxed in places, some soiling, intermittent stain in gutter, few early ink marks, early ownership inscription to second leaf, 8vo., later vellum, spine with four raised bands lettered in ink, somewhat soiled and splayed, bookplates of Biblioteca Senequiana and the Prince of Liechtenstein, sound. Blackwell's Rare Books Greek & Latin Classics VI - 96 2015 £750

Seneca, Lucius Annaeus *Tragoediae.* Excudebat Felx Kingstonius impensis Gulielmi Welby, 1613. First Farnaby edition, last leaf dusty, cut down slightly and with blank verso mounted, penultimate leaf with small area torn from blank corner, some spotting and soiling elsewhere, initial blank discarded, 8vo., 19th century sheep in antique style, bordered with blind rolls, darkened and bit rubbed, label lost from spine, signature excised from front pastedown, short crack to upper joint, sound. Blackwell's Rare Books B179 - 93 2015 £750

Senex, John *Itineraire de Toutes les Routes de l'Angleterre, Revues, Corrigees, Augmentees et Reduites.* Paris: Le Rouge, 1759. First edition in French, 181 x 127mm., maps, contemporary limp calf, lower cover extending into a flap, tiny hole (for some kind of closure) in flap, manuscript title "Itineraire du Royaume d'Anglterre' on lower cover, rear pastedown (including flap), composed of printing scraps, engraved title, engraved map, 101 plates with maps, titlepage with parallel text in French and English, armorial bookplate of Dampierre, the grand library of the Dukes de Luynes at Chateau Dampierre begun in 17th century, slight wear to leather, small waterstain to flap, titlepage detached, couple of openings faintly browned, otherwise fine, insubstantial binding very well preserved and text unusually bright, fresh and clean with especially strong impressions of the maps. Phillip J. Pirages 66 - 39 2015 $3750

Senghor, Leopold Sedar *Poems.* N.P.: Limited Editions Club, 1996. Limited to 300 numbered copies, signed by author and artist, Lois Mailou Jones, folio, frontispiece and paintings in text by Jones, folio, cloth, cloth clamshell box with inlaid leather label on spine, with Monthly Letter loosely inserted. Oak Knoll Books 25 - 66 2015 $1250

Senior, Nassau William 1790-1864 *Statement of the Provision for the Poor, and of the Condition of the Labouring Classes in a Considerable Portion of America and Europe.* London: B. Fellowes, 1835. First edition, 8vo., modern red half leather lettered gilt at spine with raised bands and marbled boards, half title and first blank not present, prelims slightly creased at corners, otherwise very good. Any Amount of Books 2015 - B26989 2015 £250

Senn, Edward L. *Deadwood Dick and Calamity Jane a Thorough Sifting of Facts from fiction.* Deadwood: South Dakota, 1939. First edition, 12mo., printed wrappers, scarce, from the library of Clint and Dot Josey, very scarce to rare today, fine. Buckingham Books March 2015 - 36711 2015 $250

Sepp, Jakob *Schrift + Symbol in Stein Holz Und metal.* Munchen: Callwey, 1984. Second edition, 4to., cloth, dust jacket, slipcase, drawings and black and white illustrations, Callwey brochure laid in, signature of previous owner in pencil on front free endpaper. Oak Knoll Books 306 - 241 2015 $225

Sequence: Film Quarterly. London: Oxford University Film Society, 1946-1952. First edition, 4to., all 14 issues, copiously illustrated in black and white, clean, very good with some minor edge wear (slight repairs to issue 7). Any Amount of Books 2015 - C8218 2015 £225

Serious Reflections on the Manifold Dangers Attending the Use of Copper Vessels and Other Utensils of Copper and Brass... London: printed and sold by M. Cooper, 1755. First and only edition, complete with half title, preserved in old plain card covers, fine, rare. John Drury Rare Books 2015 - 22828 2015 $2622

Serling, Rod *As Timeless as Infinity.* Colorado Springs: Gauntlet Press, 2004-2006. Volumes 1, 2 and 3, each is the numbered limited edition, volume 1 is copy 314 of 750; volume 2 is copy 86 of 750; and volume 3 is copy 266 of 750, each volume signed by Carol Serling and has bookplate of another author on front flyleaf, apart from couple of small corner bumps, set is fine in fine dust jackets, scarce. Ken Lopez, Bookseller   164 - 179   2015 $1500

Serling, Rod *"I am the Night - Color me Black.".* Colorado Springs: Gauntlet, 2005. Printed in an edition of 500 copies, fine in stapled wrappers.   Ken Lopez, Bookseller   164 - 180   2015 $150

Serrano, Andres *The Morgue.* Reims: Palais du Tau, 1993. First edition, quarto, 36 color photos, card wrappers, fine, scarce.   Peter Ellis, Bookseller   2014 - 018744   2015   £325

Serviss, Garrett Putnam *Pleasures of the Telescope an Illustrated Guide for Amateur Astronomers and a Popular Description of the Chief Wonders of the Heavens for General Readers.* New York: D. Appleton and Co., 1901. 8vo., illustrations, 26 star maps, original navy blue black and gilt stamped cloth, extremities rubbed, both pastedowns damaged by adhesive tape pulled away, even so binding handsomely preserved, bookplate, very good.   Jeff Weber Rare Books   178 - 1004   2015 $125

The Servitour: a Poem. London: printed and sold by H. Hills, 1709. First edition, 16 pages, 8vo., disbound, bit dust soiled at beginning and end, otherwise good.   C. R. Johnson   Foxon R-Z - 1227r-z   2015 $383

The Session of Musicians. In Imitation of the Session of Poets. London: printed for M. Smith, 1724. First edition, 12 pages, folio, disbound, fine, very rare.   C. R. Johnson   Foxon R-Z - 861r-z   2015 $3831

Seto, William *The Chinese Experience in New Brunswick a Historic Perspective.* Fredericton: Chinese Cultural Association of New Brunswick, 1985. Card covers, 8vo. photo illustrations, very good.   Schooner Books Ltd.   110 - 25   2015 $45

Settle, Elkanah *Eusebia Triumphanis.* London: printed for John Nutt, 1702. Changed in ms. to 1703. First edition, fair copy, small folio, old half calf and wooden boards, rubbed and worn, joints cracked, inner margins strengthened at front and back, some marginal stains an soiling, old repair to blank corner of last leaf, single word on page 10 ("suprema") corrected by manuscript paste-on cancel.   C. R. Johnson   Foxon R-Z - 883r-z   2015 $306

Settle, Elkanah *Threnodia Apollonaris. A Funeral Poem to the Memory of the Right Honourable William Earl Cowper &c.* London: printed for the author, 1723. First edition, 12 pages, folio, contemporary calf by Elkanah Settle's binder, covers panelled in gilt, with thistles at corners and angels' heads at center of each side of inner panel with Cowper coat of arms in middle (spine and sides rubbed), titlepage printed within mourning border with comparable black rules above and below the headlines throughout,.   C. R. Johnson   Foxon R-Z - 885r-z   2015 $6895

Settle, Mary Lee *The Killing Ground.* New York: Farrar Straus, 1982. First edition, number 90 of 150 copies signed by author, cloth, slipcase, as new.   Gemini Fine Books & Arts, Ltd.   Art Reference & Illustrated Books: First Editions - 2015 $50

Settle, Raymond W. *The March of the Mounted Riflemen. First United States Military Expedition to Travel the Full Length of the Oregon Trail from Fort Leavenworth to Fort Vancouver May to October 1849...* Arthur H. Clark, 1940. First edition, 8vo., blue cloth, frontispiece, plates, fine, bright copy.   Buckingham Books   March 2015 - 34299   2015 $225

Seventeen Hundred and Thirty-Nine; or the Modern P----s. A Satire. London: printed for T. Reynolds and sold by booksellers of London and Westminster, 1739. First edition, 8 pages, folio, disbound, trifle dusty at beginning and end, slight signs of prior folding, with small unobtrusive library number at top of titlepage, otherwise good.   C. R. Johnson   Foxon R-Z - 887r-z   2015 $689

70 Pocket Penguins. Penguin, 2005. First edition, all are fine in printed cardboard slipcase, two of the books signed. Beasley Books   2013 - 2015 $500

Several Arguments Against Bowing at the Name of Jesus. London: printed in the year, 1660. Only edition, 4to., wanting A1*, preserved in modern wrappers with printed title label on upper cover, good copy.   John Drury Rare Books   2015 - 20482   2015 $89

Seward, Samuel *Specification of the Patent Granted to Samuel Seaward of the Parish of All Saints, Poplar in the County of Middlesex, Engineer for Certain Improvements in the Construction of Steam Engines sealed Oct. 17 1834.* London: printed by J. S. Hodson, 1835. First (and only?) edition, apparently very rare, engraved plate little foxed, sewn as issued in plain card covers, very good.   John Drury Rare Books   March 2015 - 14233   2015   £306

Sewell, George *A New Collection of Original Poems, Never Printed in Any Miscellany.* London: printed for J. Pemberton and J. Peele, 1720. First edition, one of 750 copies printed, 8vo., recent calf antique, spine gilt, brown morocco label, fine, scarce.   C. R. Johnson   Foxon R-Z - 889r-z   2015 $2298

Sewell, George *Poems on Several Occasions.* London: printed for E. Curll and J. Pemberton, 1719. First edition, 8vo., polished mottled calf, gilt spine and inner dentelles, gilt, by Root & Son, excellent copy, complete with two final leaves of index, sometimes missing, very scarce, bookplate of Oliver Brett, Viscount Esher.   C. R. Johnson   Foxon R-Z - 888r-z   2015 $2298

Sexton, Anne *To Bedlam and Part Way Back.* Boston: Houghton Mifflin, 1960. First edition, 8vo., original cloth backed boards, fine in dust jacket, inscribed by author April 1961.   James S. Jaffe Rare Books   Modern American Poetry - 251   2015 $1000

Seymour, Mary F. *Report of the International Council of Women, Assembled by the National Woman Suffrage Association, Washington ....* Washington: Darby, 1888. First edition, 8vo., rust cloth, spine rubbed and faded, stamped in gilt, frontispiece, ex-library, bookplate and numeral on spine, otherwise very good.   Second Life Books Inc.   189 - 226   2015 $750

Shaara, Michael *The Killer Angels.* New York: David McKay, 1974. First edition, original blue cloth, original dust jacket, superb copy, rare in this condition.   Manhattan Rare Book Company   Literature 2014 - 2015 $3000

Shacter, James D. *Loose Shoes. The Story of Ralph Sutton.* Chicago: Jaynar, 1994. Updated version, hardcover, quite uncommon signed by author with signed inscription from Sutton tipped in, fine in fine dust jacket.   Beasley Books   2013 - 2015 $85

Shadegg, Stephen *Barry Goldwater: Freedom Is His Flight Plan.* New York: Fleet Pub. Corp., 1962. First edition, fine in fine dust jacket with couple of tiny tears, inscribed by Goldwater to the Gene Tunneys.   Between the Covers Rare Books, Inc.   187 - 217   2015 $550

Shaffer, Peter *Equus.* Llandogo: Old Stile Press, 2009. 22/200 copies (from an edition of 210 copies), signed by artist with signed and numbered slip signed by author laid in at colophon page, 4to., original illustrated boards, backstrip lettered gilt, top edge blue, endpapers blue, folding slipcase, illustrated inside and out, fine.   Blackwell's Rare Books B179 - 213   2015   £250

Shaftesbury, Anthony Ashley Cooper, 3rd Earl of   1671-1713 *Characteristicks of Men, Manners, Opinions, Times.* Birmingham: printed by John Baskerville, 1773. Fifth edition, various copperplate vignettes on titlepages and Treatise sectional titles or as headpieces, without errata leaf, some offsetting from vignettes, occasional minor browning or spotting, royal 8vo., contemporary red Turkey, gilt roll tooled borders on sides, incorporating a distinctive bee, flat spines richly gilt with a seme of drawer handles, dots and pyramids, twin green lettering pieces, very minor shelfwear, very good, binding of the highest quality, with contemporary cost notes in volume 1 that at front partially erased, these notes suggest that the binding was specially comissioned.   Blackwell's Rare Books   B179 - 33   2015   £2500

Shaftesbury, Anthony Ashley Cooper, 3rd Earl of   1671-1713 *Moral and Religious Education of the Working Classes. The Speech of Lord Ashley, M.P. in the House of Commons on Tuesday Feb. 28 1843.* London: John Ollivier, 1843. First separate edition, titlepage rather soiled, 2 old institutional library stamps stitched but now disbound retaining lower plain wrapper, inscribed in ink 'from the author'.   John Drury Rare Books   March 2015 - 18539   2015 $266

Shahn, Ben *Ben Shahn, Photographer.* New York: Da Capo Press, First edition, near fine, light sunning in very good dust jacket with few tiny chips, 8vo.   Beasley Books 2013 - 2015 $45

Shakespeare, William   1564-1616 *The Dramatic Works of William Shakespeare.* London: J. Walker et al, 1821. 6 volumes, 12mo., contemporary full straight grained morocco gilt, beautifully bound miniature set.   Honey & Wax Booksellers   3 - 21   2015 $1800

Shakespeare, William   1564-1616 *The Tragedy of Hamlet, Prince of Denmark.* New York: Limited Editions Club, 1933. Limited to 1500 numbered copies signed by Eric Gill, printed by Hague and Gill on Barcham green handmade paper in Gill's Johanna, wood engraved initial letters and illustrations by Gill, small 8vo., full English pigskin blindstamped with design by Gill, slipcase shows only minor rubbing, leather spine of book only slightly darkened, well preserved.   Oak Knoll Books   25 - 10   2015 $600

Shakespeare, William   1564-1616 *Julius Caesar. A Tragedy.* Gottingen: widow of A. Vandenhoek, 1777. 8vo. some foxing, especially of outer leaves, little dampstainng in upper margins towards end, red oval Hungarian library stamp, original blue paper wrappers, spine partly defective, traces of paper label on upper cover, sound, rare Continental edition.   Blackwell's Rare Books   B179 - 94 2015   £1200

Shakespeare, William 1564-1616 *The Tragedie of Ivlivs Caesar...* San Francisco: Grabhorn Press, 1954. First edition thus, one of 180 copies, folio, red French morocco backed decorated black boards, gilt lettered spine, 56 leaves printed on both sides, 7 pictures by Mary Grabhorn, composed in Inkvnabvla type founded by the Society of Nebiolo of Turin, Italy, printed on handmade paper, printed in red and black, minor rubbing to extremities of spine, otherwise fine. Second Life Books Inc. 190 - 194 2015 $350

Shakespeare, William 1564-1616 *The Tragedie of King Lear.* San Francisco: Grabhorn Press, 1959. One of 180 copies, handset type on English handmade paper, red patterned cloth, linen spine, gilt stamped red leather spine label scuffed, spine darkened, edges of boards with light soiling, else very nice. Argonaut Book Shop Holiday Season 2014 - 260 2015 $250

Shakespeare, William 1564-1616 *A Mid-Summer Night's Dream.* New York: Henry Holt, 1914. First US edition, 12 beautiful tipped-in color plates, 32 full page black and whites and other line drawings by W. Heath Robinson, 4to., blue cloth, pictorially stamped in green and gold, top edge gilt, covers very slightly dulled, else near fine. Aleph-Bet Books, Inc. 108 - 396 2015 $850

Shakespeare, William 1564-1616 *The Plays of William Shakespeare.* London: 1723. Volumes 1, 5 and 8 of 8 volumes, full original leather, volume I missing front cover, f.f.e.p. chipped, affecting owner name, first 100 pages damped, volume 5 with both covers loose, f.f.e.p. gone, volume 8 top cover three quarter loose, all 3 volumes with signature of Nathaniel Pendleton (first volume signature missing letters after second "l"). Bookworm & Silverfish 2015 - 60159644200 2015 $250

Shakespeare, William 1564-1616 *The Poems and Sonnets of William Shakespeare.* London: Golden Cockerel Press, 1960. One of 370 numbered copies (of an edition of 470), bound in gilt stamped red cloth, 4to., near fine but for small dampstain at lower left corner of front board, titlepage in yellow, black and red. Beasley Books 2013 - 2015 $200

Shakespeare, William 1564-1616 *Stockdale's Edition of Shakespeare: Including in One Volume, The Whole of His Dramatic Works.* London: John Stockdale, First single volume, thick octavo, full contemporary mottled calf, gilt, black spine label. Honey & Wax Booksellers 2 - 21 2015 $2800

Shakespeare, William 1564-1616 *The Handy-Volume Shakespeare.* London: Bradbury Agnew and Co., circa, 1866? 13 volumes, half titles, original limp purple morocco, lettered gilt, all edges gilt, very good, original purple leather box, largely faded to brown. Jarndyce Antiquarian Booksellers CCXI - 250 2015 £350

Shakespeare, William 1564-1616 *The Works of William Shakespeare.* London: Swan Sonnenschein & Co., 1891. Half titles, contemporary half dark green crushed morocco, raised gilt bands and compartments, some occasional slight rubbed, very good. Jarndyce Antiquarian Booksellers CCXI - 251 2015 £1450

Shakespeare, William 1564-1616 *The Complete Works of William Shakespeare.* Garden City: Doubleday, Doran and Co., 1936. Limited to 750 numbered copies, signed by artist, Rockwell Kent, 4to., cloth, gilt stamped labels on spine, top edge gilt, other edges uncut, slipcase has some wear at bottom edge, rubbed and scuffed. Oak Knoll Books 306 - 28 2015 $750

Sharp, James A. *On the Establishment of Navigation Institutions at the Outports; a Letter to the Right Hon. the Viscount Sandon, M.P.* London: R. B. Bate, 1845. First edition, 8vo., recently well bound in linen backed marbled boards, lettered, inscribed in ink "with the author's compts" at head of title, very good, uncommon. John Drury Rare Books March 2015 - 21058 2015 $221

Sharpe, James Birch *The Gregorian Oration Delivered Before the Literary, Scientific and Mechanics' Institution of Windsor and Eton, September 1841.* London: Shaw and Sons, 1841. First edition, 8vo.,4 2 pages, sometime in Norwich City library (bookplate and small inkstamp on flyleaf and lower margin of couple of leaves), contemporary green calf, spine fully gilt with raised bands, slight wear to extremities, very good, presentation copy inscribed in ink by author to Mr. J. W. S. Potter, apparently rare. John Drury Rare Books 2015 - 25557 2015 $168

Shaver, J. R. *Little Shavers: Sketches from Real Life.* New York: Century Co., 1913. First edition, small octavo, grey cloth with applied illustration, corners bumped and rubbed, nice and tight, very good, inscribed by editor of Vanity Fair Frank Crowninshield for Mrs. Buel Xmas 1913. Between the Covers Rare Books, Inc. 187 - 51 2015 $200

Shaw, Artie *I Love You, I Hate You, Drop Dead!: Variations on a Theme.* New York: Fleet Pub. Corp., 1965. First edition, couple of stains on boards, good or better in supplied, near fine dust jacket, inscribed by musician to Carol Southern, wife of Terry. Between the Covers Rare Books, Inc. 187 - 255 2015 $1500

Shaw, Artie *The Trouble with Cinderella.* New York: Farrar, 1952. Later printing, near fine in dust jacket with 2 inch tear at foot of front spine fold. Beasley Books 2013 - 2015 $150

Shaw, Barnabus *A Missionary Sermon, Preached at Flambro', June 14 and 15 Kilham June 26 and published at Request.* Hull: printed for the author by Topping and Dawson Low-Gate, 1815. First edition, 8vo., 28 pages, title and following leaf, little foxed, preserved in modern wrappers with printed title label on upper cover, good, rare. John Drury Rare Books   2015 - 22571   2015 $133

Shaw, Frederic *Casey Jones' Locker.* San Francisco: Hesperian House, 1959. First edition, small quarto, black and white photos, portraits, maps and line drawings, green cloth, lettered in black, fine, lightly rubbed dust jacket. Argonaut Book Shop   Holiday Season 2014 - 263   2015 $45

Shaw, George Bernard   1856-1950 *Fabian Essays in Socialism.* London: Walter Scott, n.d., First edition, owner's name, occasional pencil mark, very good or better. Beasley Books   2013 - 2015 $125

Shaw, George Bernard   1856-1950 *The Intelligent Woman's Guide to Socialism and Capitalism.* London: Constable, 1928. First edition, 8vo., original olive green cloth, bump to top edge and light rubbing at corners, Celtic design in green and gilt to front and backstrip lettered in gilt, top edge gilt, tail edge rough trimmed, green endpapers with few small adhesive marks, dust jacket with light chipping at corners and ends of backstrip panel, light dustsoiling to backstrip and rear panel, rubbing to edges, few nicks, very good, with ALS from author tipped in to half title, to the treasurer of the Fabian Society, Emil Davies.   Blackwell's Rare Books   B179 - 235   2015   £750

Shaw, George Bernard   1856-1950 *Saint Joan.* London: Constable and Co., 1924. First illustrated edition, one of 750 copies, folio, very good, top edge gilt, fore edge little wavy in very good dust jacket with few chips and browned spine.   Ed Smith Books   83 - 80   2015 $400

Shaw, George Bernard   1856-1950 *Saint Joan.* London: Constable, 1925. Ninth impression, 8vo., very good+ in slightly browned about very good, complete jacket, inscribed presentation from author for Mrs. Diplock, Morrison Davidson's daughter.   Any Amount of Books   2015 - A74375   2015   £250

Shaw, George Bernard   1856-1950 *Socialism the Fabian Essays.* Boston: Charles F. Brown, 1894. First Authorized US edition, 8vo., little rubbed on top of spine which is little darkened, near fine, red cloth stamped in black and gilt. Second Life Books Inc.   191 - 11   2015 $250

Shaw, George Bernard   1856-1950 *Ayot St. Lawrence Edition of the Collected Works of Bernard Shaw.* New York: Wm. H. Wise and Co., 1930. Limited to 1750 numbered sets, 8vo., cloth backed boards, cloth spine label, dust jackets, top edges gilt, others uncut, some illustrations, some creasing, chipping and tears in fragile dust jackets, very unusual to find in jackets, well preserved set.   Oak Knoll Books   306 - 299   2015 $750

Shaw, Joseph T. *Out of the Rough.* New York: Winward House, 1934. First edition, USGA library on label on front pastedown, front hinge cracked, otherwise very good in dust jacket with chipped and frayed spine ends, several closed tears, small library label on spine and wear along edges. Mordida Books   March 2015 - 009745   2015 $240

Shaw, Samuel *A New Grammar, Composed out of the Classick writers.* London: printed for William Innys, 1730. First edition, 4 leaves of folding tables, 8vo., several woodcut head and tailpieces, contemporary calf with double gilt fillets, sympathetically rebacked, spine gilt with raised bands, very good, crisp copy, apparently rare.   John Drury Rare Books   March 2015 - 24865   2015 $874

Shaw, Samuel *The Voice of One Crying in a Wilderness.* Boston: printed by Rogers and Fowle for J. Edwards, 1746. First American edition, 16mo., lacking covers, very sound. M & S Rare Books, Inc.   97 - 255   2015 $350

Shaw, T. E. *More Letters from T. E. Shaw to Bruce Rogers.* N.P.: Bruce Rogers, 1936. First edition, one of 300 copies printed by Rogers, rebound in library style buckram, wavieness to pages from dampness but no actual staining, good copy, complimentary slip inscribed by Rogers to Selden Rodman.   Between the Covers Rare Books, Inc. 187 - 256   2015 $350

Shaw, William *Aspects of Malaysian Magic.* Kuala Lumpur: Muzium Negara, 1975. First edition, fine in near fine dust jacket.   Stephen Lupack   March 2015 - 2015 $150

Shea & Patten *The "Soapy" Smith Tragedy.* Shea & Patten, 1907. First edition, oblong 16mo., red pictorial wrappers, (24 pages), illustrations, 13 plates, exceedingly rare, housed in clamshell case with titles stamped in gold on spine, original covers slightly worn at fore-edges and extremities, however all text is fine.   Buckingham Books March 2015 - 26286   2015 $2250

Shearer, Thomas *Percy's Relations with Cadell and Davies..* London: Bibliographical Society, 1934. Reprinted from Transactions of the Bibliographical Society Sept. 1934, Original grey printed wrappers, slightly dusted, from the library of Geoffrey & Kathleen Tillotson.   Jarndyce Antiquarian Booksellers   CCVII - 408   2015   £30

Shearing, Joseph *Moss Rose.* London: William Heinemann Ltd., 1934. First edition, light foxing to few prelim pages, else near fine, professionally restored dust jacket at spine end, corners and top edge of rear panel. Buckingham Books   March 2015 - 26116   2015 $2250

Shearing, Joseph *Moss Rose.* New York: Harrison Smith and Robert Haas, 1935. First US edition, fine, bright, square copy in dust jacket with light wear to spine ends and corners, complete with original wraparound promotional band, exceptional copy.   Buckingham Books   March 2015 - 30373   2015 $750

Shee, William *Papers, Letters and Speeches in the House of Commons on the Irish Land Question with a Summary of Its Parliamentary History...* London: Thomas Richardson and Son, 1863. First edition, half title, errata slip, original green cloth over heavy bevelled boards, spine slightly dulled, very good.   Jarndyce Antiquarian Booksellers   CCXI - 155   2015   £90

Sheey, Shawn *A Pop-Up Culinary Herbal. Volume Two of the Plant Lore of the 21st Century Series.* Chicago: Paperboy Press, 2013. Artist's book, one of 30 copies, all on commercial cover paper in various weights from various manufacturers, each copy signed and numbered by artist, page size 6 1/2 x 4 1/2 x 1 1/4 inches, 30 pages, including 12 double page spread pop-up vegetables, drab boards with red paper spine, small collaged decoration of maize on front panel, brightly colored papers serve as base for double page pop-ups, each with small green printed folded note held closed with matching tab, these folio cards mounted in corner of each double page spread.   Priscilla Juvelis - Rare Books   63 - 21   2015 $1050

Sheffauer, Herman *A Survey of the Woman Problem from the German of...* New York: Doran, 1913. First American edition, 8vo. couple of pages roughly opened, nice tight copy.   Second Life Books Inc.   189 - 162   2015 $125

Sheffield, John Baker Holroyd, 1st Earl of   1735-1821 *Observations on the Impolicy, Abuses and False Interpretation of the Poor Laws and on the Reports of the two Houses of Parliament.* London: J. Hatchard, 1818. First edition, 8vo., recent cloth backed marbled boards with morocco label on upper cover lettered gilt, very good. John Drury Rare Books   March 2015 - 25601   2015   £306

Sheil, Richard Lalor *The Speeches of the Right Honourable Richard Lalor Sheil, M.P., with Memoir &c.* Dublin: James Duffy, 1845. First collected edition, 8vo., later 19th century full polished calf, gilt, with raised bands and crimson label, top edge gilt, others uncut, slight wear to upper joint, else fine, form the 19th century library of Earl of Portsmouth with his armorial bookplate and inscription "Earl of Portsmouth Hurstbourne Park Library 1880" on flyleaf. John Drury Rare Books   2015 - 17816   2015 $221

Shelley, John Villiers *Mr. John Ellman's Examination and Criticism of Calculations as to the Comparative results on a Two-Hundred Acre Farm at the Present Time (1850) and 12, 13 or 14 years back.* Lewes: presented by George P. Bacon, Sussex Advertiser Office, 1850. First edition, 8vo., 16 pages, very small Dutch inkstamp on blank verso of titlepage, entirely uncut and unbound as issued, some minor edge fraying and dust marking of outer leaves, good, large copy, rare.   John Drury Rare Books   2015 - 19546   2015 $133

Shelley, Mary Wollstonecraft Godwin   1797-1851 *The Choice.* London: printed for the editor for Private distribution, 1876. First edition, 8vo., unbound sheets laid into printed wrapper, little soiled, otherwise fine, printed on Whatman laid paper, laid in is engraved portrait of Shelly that is called for.   Second Life Books Inc.   189 - 228   2015 $1500

Shelley, Mary Wollstonecraft Godwin   1797-1851 *Essays, Letters from Abroad.* London: Moxon, 1840. First edition, 2 volumes, 8vo., untrimmed, later three quarter calf, covers, small waterstain to prelim matter, including titlepage of volume 1, more significant waterstain to first pages of volume 2, mostly clean copy, except for waterstained leaves. Second Life Books Inc.   189 - 231   2015 $150

Shelley, Mary Wollstonecraft Godwin   1797-1851 *Frankenstein or the Modern Prometheus.* New York: Limited Editions Club, 1934. Limited to 1500 numbered copies, signed by artist, Everett Henry, 8vo., quarter leather with multicolor woven cloth covered boards, slipcase rubbed with some abraded spots, book fine.   Oak Knoll Books   25 - 12   2015 $350

Shelley, Mary Wollstonecraft Godwin   1797-1851 *The Letters of Mary W. Shelley.* Norman: University of Oklahoma, 1944. First edition, 2 volumes, 8vo., illustrations, very good in little chipped dust jacket.   Second Life Books Inc.   189 - 229   2015 $150

Shelley, Mary Wollstonecraft Godwin   1797-1851 *Monsieur Nongtongpaw.* London: Alfred Miller, 1830. First illustrated edition, 12mo., 6 engraved plates, contemporary hand coloring, bound in later three quarter morocco and marbled boards by Root, front cover very loose, very clean. Second Life Books Inc.   189 - 230   2015 $600

Shelley, Percy Bysshe   1792-1822 *An Address to the People on the Death of Princess Charlotte.* London: reprinted for Thomas Rodd, 1843. First edition, 8vo., self wrappers, stitched as issued, 16 pages, paper little browned in top of margin, wrappers just splitting at spine, very good. The Brick Row Book Shop   Miscellany 67 - 81   2015 $2250

Shelley, Percy Bysshe 1792-1822 *The Cenci.* London: C. and J. Ollier, 1821. Second edition, 8vo., bound as usual without the first or last blanks, new endpapers in plain navy buckram, lettered gilt to front board, pages edges untrimmed, few pages trifle spotted, some slight chipping, overall very good.   Any Amount of Books   March 2015 - A99648   2015   £350

Shelley, Percy Bysshe 1792-1822 *The Sensitive Plant.* London & Philadelphia: Heinemann & Lippincott, n.d., 1911. Printed in England, first edition, 4to., full publisher's vellum with elaborate gilt pictorial design on cover and spine, top edge gilt, fine in pictorial dust jacket chipped at spine ends, illustrations by Charles Robinson, pictorial endpapers, 18 tipped in color plates with tissue guards, plus illustrations on each page of text, printed on heavy coated stock, magnificent copy, vellum edition scarce.   Aleph-bet Books, Inc. 109 - 413   2015 $1200

Shelton, Richard *Desert Water a Poem.* New York: Monument Press, 1972. First edition, one of 150 copies on Mould Made Rives paper, 12mo., unpaginated in little loose original wrappers, composed in Hunt roman type, lino cuts were printed direction from blocks, this one of 50 copies signed by poet and artist, this is a presentation copy from printer Tom Pears and each of the images signed in pencil. Second Life Books Inc.   190 - 196   2015 $75

The Scheme for the Management and Regulation of Christ's Hospital in Sherburn, near Durham in the County of Durham and for the Application of the Income Thereof, as Approved by the Court of Chancery 21st Dec. 1857. London: printed by C. Roworth & Sons, 1857. First edition, 8vo., very good, recent marbled boards lettered on spine, apparently very rare.   John Drury Rare Books   2015 - 24786   2015 $221

Shenstone, William 1714-1763 *The Judgment of Hercules, a Poem. Inscrib'd to George Lyttleton, Esq.* London: printed for R. Dodsley and sold by T. Cooper, 1741. First edition, 8vo., full rose morocco, gilt, spine gilt, all edges gilt, by Riviere & Son, bookplate of Oliver Brett, later Viscount Esher.   C. R. Johnson   Foxon R-Z - 893r-z   2015 $2298

Shenstone, William 1714-1763 *The School-Mistress, a Poem in Imitation of Spenser.* London: printed for R. Dodsley and sold by T. Cooper, 1742. First edition, 8vo., recent wrappers in dark blue cloth folding case, very good, complete with half title, half title missing from many of the surviving copies.   C. R. Johnson   Foxon R-Z - 894f-z   2015 $4214

Shenstone, William 1714-1763 *The Works in Verse and Prose of William Shenstone, Esq.* London: printed for R. and J. Dodsley, 1764. First edition, 8vo., 2 volumes, 8vo., dust jacket calf, red morocco labels rubbed, one lower joint cracked, spines restored, (foot of one spine chipped), frontispiece in volume and plate, engraved vignette, presumably later issue, on verso of each frontispiece is calligraphic signature of Bazil Heron dated 1764.   C. R. Johnson   Foxon R-Z - 892r-z   2015 $115

Shepherd, Eric *Murder in a Nunnery.* New York: Sheed & Ward, 1940. First edition, fine in darkened dust jacket. Mordida Books   March 2015 - 002015   2015 $75

Shepherd, Sandra Brubaker *California Heartland. A Pictorial History and Tour Guide of Eight Northern Calfiornia Counties.* San Francisco: Scottwall Associates, 1993. First edition, quarto, blue cloth, gilt, very fine, pictorial dust jacket.   Argonaut Book Shop   Holiday Season 2014 - 261   2015 $40

Shepherd, Thomas H. *London and Its Environs in the Nineteenth Century, Illustrated by a Series of Views...* London: published by Jones & Co., 1827-1830. 42 original parts, engraved vignette title, 82 engraved plates, uncut in original printed brown wrappers.   Marlborough Rare Books List 53 - 44   2015   £585

Sheppard, James *Hints to the Landlord and Tenant; Being a Review of the Present Averages and Showing their Fallacy....* Doncaster: G. Brooke, 1833. First edition, 8vo., recently well bound in cloth lettered, very good, rare.   John Drury Rare Books   March 2015 - 7846   2015 $266

Sheppard, Sam *Endure and Conqueor.* Cleveland: World, 1966. First edition, inscribed by author, fine in very good dust jacket with chips and tears.   Beasley Books   2013 - 2015 $125

Sherburn, George *The Early Career of Alexander Pope.* Oxford: at the Clarendon Press, 1934. Half title, frontispiece, original dark blue cloth, slightly dulled, Geoffrey Tillotson's copy with few pencil notes and inserted letter from author thanking him for favorable review and inserted note thanking him for loan.   Jarndyce Antiquarian Booksellers   CCVII - 428   2015   £25

Sherburn, George *Pope and His Contemporaries: Essays Presented to George Sherburn.* Oxford: at the Clarendon Press, 1949. Half title, portrait, printed presentation slip, original dark blue cloth in slightly torn and dusted dust jacket, from the library of Geoffrey & Kathleen Tillotson. Jarndyce Antiquarian Booksellers   CCVII - 429   2015 £40

Sheridan, Charles L. *State of Montana Highway Patrol Driver's Manual.* Helena?: circa, 1946. First edition thus, 4to., printed wrappers, 65 pages, illustrations, very scarce, general soiling, else very good. Baade Books of the West 2014 - 2015 $75

Sheridan, Richard Brinsley Butler   1751-1816 *The Camp.* London: 1795. 8vo., sewn original publisher's plain wrappers (little worn, old catalog entry laid in), housed in cloth chemise and full morocco slipcase by Riviere & Son, former owner's bookplate on inside flap of chemise, fine. Second Life Books Inc.   190 - 197   2015 $325

Sheridan, Richard Brinsley Butler   1751-1816 *The Critic or a Tragedy Rehearsed.* London: T. Becket, 1781. First edition, 8vo., lacks terminal ad, bound with half title in later wrappers, housed in soiled folding chemise, former owner's bookplate on inside of case.   Second Life Books Inc.   190 - 198   2015 $325

Sheridan, Richard Brinsley Butler   1751-1816 *The Governess. A comic opera.* Dublin: 1777. First edition, small 8vo., sewn into later marbled wrappers (half circle missing on front cover, former owner's bookplate inside front cover).   Second Life Books Inc.   190 - 199   2015 $350

Sheridan, Thomas *A Complete Dictionary of the English Language, Both with Regard to Sound and Meaning...* Philadelphia: W. Young, Mills & Son, 1796. Sixth edition, 12mo., contemporary calf, title gilt stamped on spine with five gilt stamped bands, worn at joints and edges, front hinge cracked, light stains and foxing, previous owner's name on titlepage, title page trimmed at bottom above date. Oak Knoll Books   306 - 300   2015 $400

Sherman, John *Selected Speeches and Reports of Finance and Taxation from 1859 to 1878.* New York: D. Appleton and Co., 1879. First edition, half morocco and marbled paper covered boards, rubbed at extremities and small piece of leather peeled on rear board, else near fine copy, inscribed by John Sherman to leading American banker, financier and philanthropist, George Baker, ALS by Sherman to Baker.   Between the Covers Rare Books, Inc. 187 - 39   2015 $1250

Sherwin, Elizabeth *Poems.* Wolverhampton: Printed and published by Joseph Bridges and London: Simpkin Marshall and Co., 1851. Only edition, 8vo., original blindstamped green cloth with title in gilt on upper cover, all edges gilt, endpapers naturally discolored, spine faded, but very good, apparently rare.   John Drury Rare Books   March 2015 - 22700   2015   £266

Shiel, M. P. *Prinze Zaleski.* London: John Lane, 1895. First edition, spine panel sunned, lettering plainly visible, else very good, uncommon.   Buckingham Books   March 2015 - 33538   2015 $1250

Shiller, Robert J. *Irrational Exuberance.* Princeton: Princeton University, 2000. Second printing, 8vo., fine in fine dust jacket, signed by author.   By the Book, L. C. Special List 10 - 19   2015 $100

Shillitoe, Thoma *An Address to the Rulers of this Nation and all those in Power.* London: printed by Darton and Harvey, 1808. First edition, 8vo., very scarce, preserved in modern wrappers with printed title label on upper cover, very good.   John Drury Rare Books   March 2015 - 22991 2015 $221

Shinn, Charles Howard *The Story of the Mine as Illustrated by the Great Comstock Lode of Nevada.* New York: 1896. illustrations, original printed boards, some wear to extremities, faint stain across top of spine, endpapers stained, else clean and very good.   Dumont Maps & Books of the West   131 - 73   2015 $50

Shinton, William Edward *Lectures on an Improved System of Teaching the Art of Writing to Which are Added Practical Hints to Young Penmen.* London: Longman, Hurst, Rees, Orme, Brown & Co., 1823. First edition, tall 8vo., modern cloth back with pebbled cloth sides, 13 engraved plates.   Oak Knoll Books   Special Catalogue 24 - 49   2015 $250

Ship Registers and Enrollments. Port of Eureka California 1859-1920. San Francisco: WPA, 1941. First edition, quarto, text illustrations, map, 4 tables, printed rectos only, printed and pictorial stiff wrappers, fine.   Argonaut Book Shop   Holiday Season 2014 - 87   2015 $250

Shipman, O. L., Mrs. *Taming the Big Bend. A History of the Extreme Western Portion of Texas From Fort Clark to El Paso.* N.P.: privately printed, 1926. First edition, 8vo., signed and dated by author on 4/5//27, from the library of Captain and Mrs. R. L. George, Camp Marfa, Texas April 5 1927, purple cloth, gold stamping on front cover and spine, frontispiece, illustrations, plates, portraits, folding map, bound in at rear of book, exceptional copy, near fine, bright, square copy.   Buckingham Books   March 2015 - 31770 2015 $1750

Shippen, William *Faction Display'd. a poem.* London: printed in the year, 1704. First edition, 4to., full polished calf, gilt, spine and inner dentelles gilt, red morocco label by Riviere and Son, some pale waterstains to lower corners, but very good, large copy, outer edges untrimmed, early owner has identified a passage on page 15 as referring to the bookseller Jacob Tonson.   C. R. Johnson   Foxon R-Z - 896r-z   2015 $383

Shippen, William *Faction Display'd. A Poem.* London: printed and sold by H. Hills, 1709. First of two Hills editions, this printing with phrase 'near the water-side' imprint positioned to left of page, 8vo., recent stiff wrappers, very good.   C. R. Johnson   Foxon R-Z - 1230r-z   2015 $77

Shippen, William *Moderation Display'd: a Poem.* London: printed in the Year, 1704. First edition, 4to., recent boards, good copy.   C. R. Johnson   Foxon R-Z - 898r-z   2015 $230

Shippen, William *Moderation Display'd A Poem...* London: printed and sold by H. Hills, 1709. Pirated edition, 8vo., recent boards, very good.   C. R. Johnson   Foxon R-Z - 1231r-z   2015 $77

Shippen, William *Three Speeches Against Continuing the Army &c. as They Were Spoken in the House of Commons the Last Session of Parliament.* London: John Morphew, 1718. First edition, variant issue, 8vo., 46 pages, small stain affecting last three leaves, well bound recently in grey boards, printed label on upper cover, perhaps wanting final blank.   John Drury Rare Books   March 2015 - 18298   2015 $266

Shirley, Evelyn Philip *Lower Ettington: its Manor House and Church.* London: Pickering and Co., 1880. Second edition, small 4to., vignettes, decorative headpieces and capitals, all colored by hand, original blue boards, parchment spine, slightly discolored, corners rubbed.   Marlborough Rare Books   List 54 - 77   2015   £200

Shirley, Glenn *Guardian of the Law: the Life and Times of William Matthew Tilghman.* Eakin Press, 1988. First edition, Special collector's edition, limited to 106 signed and numbered copies, this no. 90, 8vo., quarter leather and cloth, gilt stamping on spine, chapter head decorations, photos, illustrations, as new, slipcase.   Buckingham Books   March 2015 - 18855   2015 $175

Shirley, Glenn *Guardian of the Law: the Life and times of William Matthew Tilghman.* Eakin Press, 1988. First edition, 8vo., inscribed by author, brown cloth, gold stamping on spine, brown endpapers.   Buckingham Books   March 2015 - 24102   2015 $225

Shirley, John *The Golden Gleanings: Being Sketches of Female Character from Bible History.* London: Emily Faithfull printer and publisher in ordinary to Her Majesty, 1863. First edition, 8vo., maroon cloth, stamped gilt and blind, water stain to paste downs, but very good, tight, clean copy, scarce.   Second Life Books Inc.   189 - 77   2015 $250

Shoji, Hamada *Okinawan Pottery.* Plomwa: Ryukyu Telegraph & Telephone Co., 1872. First edition, 4to., 126 plates, original pale brown cloth over handmade paper boards, lettered gilt on spine and illustrated in red on front cover, copiously illustrated in color and black and white, fine in beige cloth, clamshell box and cardboard shipping box with attractive label.   Any Amount of Books   March 2015 - C15700   2015   £400

A Short Account of the Late Application to Parliament Made by the merchants of London Upon the Neglect of their Trade... London: T. Cooper, 1742. First edition, 8vo., recent plain wrappers with label on upper cover, very good.   John Drury Rare Books   2015 - 20491   2015 $177

A Short and True Relation Concerning the Soap-Business. London: printed for Nicholas Bourne at the South Entrance of the Royal Exchange, 1641. First and only edition, 4to., without final blank, inksplash to title, no pages numbered after page, late 19th century half calf with label, good copy.   John Drury Rare Books   2015 - 8083   2015 $1486

A Short Treatise in Support of National Religion; containing a Slight Comparative Survey of the Roman Catholic and Protestant Institutions. London: printed for J. Tindal, 1791. First edition, 8vo., half title with repaired tear but no loss, bound in late 19th century dark blue half calf, neatly rebacked with original label and gilt lines, entirely uncut, very good, uncut, 19th century armorial bookplate of Earl Fitzwilliam.   John Drury Rare Books   2015 - 21584   2015 $787

Short Verses in Imitation of Long Verses; in an Epistle to W-----m P--tt, Esq. London: printed for M. More, 1746. First edition, 7 pages, folio, disbound, fine, very scarce.   C. R. Johnson   Foxon R-Z - 899r-z   2015 $919

A Short View of the Inconveniencies of War; with Some Observations on the Expediency of Peace in a Letter to a Friend. London: printed for J. S. Jordan, 1796. First edition, slightly browned, 8vo., disbound, becoming loose, pencil attribution to one Wilson via pencil inscription on titlepage.   Blackwell's Rare Books   B179 - 120   2015   £800

Short, Thomas *A Rational Discourse of the Inward Uses of Water.* London: for Samuel Chandler, 1725. First edition, removed, foxing on title.   Joseph J. Felcone Inc.   Science, Medicine and Technology - 37   2015 $350

Shorthouse, H. J. *Sir Percival: a Story of the Past and Present.* London: Macmillan and Co., 1886. First edition, presentation copy inscribed "Edward Shorthouse from his affectionate brother and sister J. Henry & Sarah Shorthouse", original dark blue cloth, gilt strips with embossed design on front over and spine, fine, housed in fine custom half red morocco slipcase, octavo, fine, bookplate of Ohio book collector Paul Lemperly with his inscription stating he received the book as a gift from Morris L. Parrish, with Parrish's letter of presentation inserted.   The Kelmscott Bookshop   11 - 46   2015 $600

Shreve, Robert F. *The Wanton Wedge.* New York: Carlton, 1993. First edition, fine in dust jacket with some light creasing at lower part of front panel, signed by author.   Mordida Books   March 2015 - 011345   2015 $125

Shulman, Irving *The Amboy Dukes.* Garden City: Doubleday, 1947. First edition, fine in just about fine, prie clipped dust jacket with some very slight rubbing, superb copy, seldom found thus, from the library of Kate Stettner Lobell and Carl D. Lobell.   Between the Covers Rare Books   196 - 33   2015 $1500

Shuster, George N. *The English Ode from Milton to Keats.* New York: Columbia Univ. Press, 1940. Half title, original blue cloth, very good in slightly torn dust jacket, from the library of Geoffrey & Kathleen Tillotson with inserted notes by Geoffrey.   Jarndyce Antiquarian Booksellers   CCVII - 468   2015   £20

Shuster, Philip *C & O Power Steam and Disel Locomotives of the Chesapeake and Ohio Railway 190-1965.* Carrollton: Alvin F. Staufer, 1965. First edition, signed by Shuster, quarto, color frontispiece and multitude of black and white photos, maps, rosters, black cloth, very good copy with pictorial dust jacket.   Argonaut Book Shop Holiday Season 2014 - 264   2015 $75

Shute, James *A Scared Poem of the Glory & Happiness of Heaven.* London: printed and sold by Jose Downing, 1712. Second edition, 8vo., sewn as issued, half title and titlepage bit wrinkled, paper flaw at top of ad leaf, affecting a couple of letters, generally very good in original condition, entirely uncut, rare.   C. R. Johnson   Foxon R-Z - 900r-z   2015 $766

Shute, Michael N. *The Scientific Work of John Winthrop.* New York: Arno Press, 1980. 8vo., illustrations, including fold-out, green cloth gilt stamped cover and spine titles, purple library stamps on title and copyright, else fine.   Jeff Weber Rare Books   178 - 1166   2015 $62

Sibly, Ebenezer *The Medical Mirror, or Treatise on the Impregnation of the Human Female.* printed for the author and sold by Champante and Whitrow and at the British Directory Office, 1796. First edition, printed on blue paper with colored stipple engraved portrait frontispiece and 4 plates, each with original tissue guard, 1 gathering and with it 2 plates sprung, tissue guards (and to much lesser extent the plates) foxed, 8vo., contemporary tree calf, spine gilt in compartments, red lettering piece good.   Blackwell's Rare Books   B179 - 96   2015   £1800

Sickles, Daniel *The General Ahiman Rezon and Freemason's Guide.* New York: Masonic Pub., 1867. First edition, 12mo., very good with owner's name on blank prelim, some rubbing and general wear, solid, very good copy.   Beasley Books   2013 - 2015 $150

Sidney, John Apsley *A Scheme for Improving Small Sums of Money Showing that Great Part of the National Specie which Now Lies Hidden and Unimproved.* Rochester: printed by W. Epps Troy Town, 1801. First and only edition, 8vo., half title, original boards, gilt morocco lettering piece on upper cover (lettered 'for improving money'), fine, excessively rare.   John Drury Rare Books   2015 - 25585   2015 $657

Sidney, Philip *The Defence of Poesie.* Cambridge: Cambridge University, 1904. Limited edition, one of 250 copies, Honey & Wax Booksellers   2 - 31   2015 $95

Sidney, Philip *The Lad Philisides, being a Selection of Songs, Pastoral, Eclogues & Elegies from the Countess of Pembroke's Arcadia.* Llandogo: Old Stile Press, 1988. 192.225 copies (of an edition of 251) signed by artist, printed on Zerkall Halbmatt mould-mad paper, titlepage printed in black and blue, 19 wood engravings and two small engravings by Harry Brockway, tall 8vo., original quarter Japanese raw silk with red patterned sides, backstrip with red leather label, lettered gilt, top edge gilt, others untrimmed, cloth slipcase with inset illustration, fine.   Blackwell's Rare Books   B179 - 214   2015   £70

Siegelman, Steve *The Marshall Field's Cookbook.* San Francisco: Book Kitchen, 2006. First edition, fine in very good+ dust jacket with short tears at spine fold, small 4to., 231 pages.   Beasley Books   2013 - 2015 $45

Siegmeister, Elie *Work and Sing a collection of the Songs that Built America.* William R. Scott, 1944. First edition, cloth backstrip over decorated paper covered boards, near fine but for owner's name, very good dust jacket, small 4to.   Beasley Books   2013 - 2015 $40

Sienkiewicz, Henryk *Quo Vadis.* Boston: Little Brown, 1896. First edition, first printing of the Aemrican edition with 1896 on titlepage (uncommon thus), small owner label of Herbert Boyce Satcher (book collector, bibliographer), very good, some shelfwear at extremities, green cloth shows little toning, fairly nice, gilt, tight, clean text.   Stephen Lupack March 2015 - 2015 $95

Sienkiewicz, Henryk *Quo Vadis: a Narrative of the Time of Nero.* Boston: Little Brown, 1897. Limited to 250 numbered copies printed on handmade paper, 2 volumes, 8vo., full vellum with applied gilt designs on covers, top edge gilt, fine, 6 photogravures by Howard Pyle and other illustrations, beautiful set, scarce.   Aleph-bet Books, Inc.   109 - 392   2015 $750

Sigdwick, Arthur *Henry Sidgwick a memoir.* London: Macmillan & Co., 1906. Half title, frontispiece, plates, final ad leaf, original brown cloth, small split at head of spine, Geoffrey Tillotson's copy Harvard 31.1.48 with pencil notes on leading endpapers and textual marks.   Jarndyce Antiquarian Booksellers   CCVII - 469   2015   £35

Sigourney, Lydia Huntley *Whisper to a Bride.* Hartford: H. S. Parsons, 1850. First edition, 12mo., original blind and gilt decorated brown cloth, all edges gilt, in variant binding not recorded, binding worn, text little waterstained, sound, good copy, scarce. The Brick Row Book Shop Miscellany 67 - 82 2015 $200

Sigsby, William *The Life and Adventures of Timothy Murphy, the Benefactor and Adventures of Timothy Murphy...* New York: A. B. F. Pond, Schoharie Republican Job Printing Office July, 1863. Second printing, tall 8vo., original dark tan printed wrappers, some discoloration and light wear. M & S Rare Books, Inc. 97 - 220 2015 $250

Sike, Henricus *Evangeliu Infantiae. Vel Liber Apocryphus de Infantia Servatoris Ex Manuscripto Edidit Ac Latina Versione et Notis Illustravit Henricus sike.* Utrecht: Franciscu Halman - Guillaume Vande Water, 1697. First edition, small 8vo., full leather rather rubbed and scuffed, lacking spine leather with loose detached boards, text block sound and clean and complete. Any Amount of Books March 2015 - A774870 2015 £375

Sikorsky, Igor I. *Invisible Encounter.* New York: Scribners, 1947. First edition, inscribed by author to Col. Truman Smith Nov. 7 1947, very good in good dust jacket, tears, chip at spine top. Stephen Lupack March 2015 - 2015 $125

Silverstein, Shel *A Light in the Attic.* New York: Harper & Row, 1981. First edition, 8vo, signed by author, fine in near fine dust jacket. By the Book, L. C. 44 - 5 2015 $1400

Silvester, Tipping *Original Poems and Translations. Consisting of the Microscope, Piscatio, or Angling, the Beau and Academic...* London: printed for J. Wilford, 1733. First edition, 8vo., later brown wrappers (loose) in brown cloth folding case, bookplate of Samuel W. Lambert very scarce, very good. C. R. Johnson Foxon R-Z - 902r-z 2015 $1149

Simenon, Georges *Maigret Loses His Temper.* London: Hamilton, 1965. First English edition, bookplate of actor/director Fletcher Markle, very fine in dust jacket. Mordida Books March 2015 - 002043 2015 $85

Simenon, Georges *Maigret Travels South.* New York: Harcourt Brace, 1940. First edition, bookplate, fine in dust jacket with nicks at base of spine and couple of tiny closed tears. Mordida Books March 2015 - 011006 2015 $350

Simenon, Georges *The Patience of Maigret.* Harcourt Brace and Co., 1940. First US. edition, fine, bright copy in fine bright dust jacket. Buckingham Books March 2015 - 34400 2015 $1250

Simenon, Georges *The Shadow Falls.* London: Routledge, 1945. First English edition, some light spotting on endpapers and few scattered light spots on page edges, otherwise fine in dust jacket with some very unobtrusive internal tape reinforcing and small scrape on spine. Mordida Books March 2015 - 009161 2015 $165

Simenon, Georges *The Son.* London: Hamilton, 1958. First English edition, fine in dust jacket. Mordida Books March 2015 - 002033 2015 $75

Simenon, Georges *Tropic Moon.* New York: Harcourt, 1943. First American edition, some darkening on endpapers, otherwise fine in dust jacket, internal tape reinforcing and some color restoration at spine ends. Mordida Books March 2015 - 007607 2015 $85

Simic, Charles *Displaced Person.* New York: New Directions, 1995. First edition, limited to 150 copies printed on Arches, total edition signed by author, 4to., original quarter vellum and patterned Japanese paper cover boards, glassine dust jacket, new. James S. Jaffe Rare Books Modern American Poetry - 254 2015 $250

Simic, Charles *Nine Poems. A Childhood.* Cambridge: Exact Change, 1989. First edition, one of 25 copies signed by author, out of a total edition of 500 copies, folio, decorated wrappers, glassine dust jacket, mint. James S. Jaffe Rare Books Modern American Poetry - 253 2015 $450

Simic, Charles *On the Music of the Spheres.* New York: Library Fellows of the Whitney Museum of American Art, 1996. First edition, one of 350 numbered copies signed by author and Linda Connor, square 4to., 15 tipped in illustrations with photos by Linda Connor, dark blue cloth, as new. James S. Jaffe Rare Books Modern American Poetry - 256 2015 $350

Simic, Charles *On the Music of the Spheres.* New York: Library Fellows of the Whitney Museum of American Art, 1996. First edition, deluxe issue,, one of 100 numbered copies signed by author and artist, 15 tipped in photo plates by Linda Connor, original navy cloth, black morocco labels lettered gilt, publisher's slipcase, specially bound and with original signed planinum palladium print by the artist, as new. James S. Jaffe Rare Books Modern American Poetry - 257 2015 $1500

Simic, Charles *Three Poems.* Syracuse: Clockworks Press, 1998. First edition, one of 12 numbered copies, 4to., 3 loose signatures in blue Japanese book cloth folding clam-shell box with title printed in silver on front, as issued, with 8 original etchings printed on Arches Cover paper and signed and editioned by artist, Holly Brown, as new, prospectus laid in. James S. Jaffe Rare Books Modern American Poetry - 258 2015 $1750

Simic, Charles *Wendy's Pinball Poems.* East Hampton: Horowitz, 1996. First edition, one of 15 specially bound copies, there were also 135 regular copies in wrappers, images by Wendy Mark, printed on Rives mould made paper at the Stinehour Press, with original monotype by Mark and signed by author, 8vo., original cloth, acetate dust jacket, as new. James S. Jaffe Rare Books Modern American Poetry - 255 2015 $1750

Simic, Charles *What the Grass Says.* San Francisco: Kayak, 1967. First edition, 8vo., illustrations, original illustrated wrappers, stapled as issued, signed by author. James S. Jaffe Rare Books Modern American Poetry - 252 2015 $150

Simmons, Dan *Song of Kali.* New York: Bluejay Books, 1985. First edition, fine book and dust jacket. Stephen Lupack March 2015 - 2015 $125

Simmons, William J. *Men of Mark: Eminent, Progressive and Rising.* Cleveland: Geo. M. Rewell & Co., 1887. First edition, thick octavo, 104 of 106 plate portraits present (with no evidence the two lacking were ever present), publisher's dark green or black cloth stamped in black and gilt, paper over front hinge cracked, modest edgewear at extremities, near very good, uncommon. Between the Covers Rare Books 197 - 64 2015 $850

Simms, Eric *Larks, Pipits and Wagtails.* London: Collins, 1992. First edition, 8vo., original green cloth lettered gilt on spine, illustrations, tables, maps, fine in fine dust jacket. Any Amount of Books 2015 - C3506 2015 £320

Simms, Frederick Walter 1803-1865 *Rules for Making and Repairing Roads as laid Down by the Late Thomas Telford, Esq., Civil Engineer.* London: John Weale Architectural Library, n.d. circa, 1837. First edition, 8vo., 2 large folding plates, 2 text figures, tiny 4 digit number in red crayon on titlepage with long (32 page) John Weale book catalog bound in at end, recently well bound in linen backed marbled boards, lettered, very good, rare. John Drury Rare Books March 2015 - 21295 2015 $221

Simms, William Gilmore 1806-1870 *The Partisan: a Tale of the Revolution.* New York: Harper and Bros., 1835. First edition, 2 volumes, 12mo., original brown embossed cloth, printed paper labels, contemporary ink signatures on pastedowns and titlepages, labels worn, cloth little spotted and faded, very good. The Brick Row Book Shop Miscellany 67 - 83 2015 $650

Simon, John *English Sanitary Institutions, Reviewed in Their Course of Development and in Some of their Political and Social Relations.* London: Cassell & Co., 1890. First edition, original rich brown cloth, lettered gilt, fine, bright copy. John Drury Rare Books March 2015 - 20417 2015 $266

Simon, Neil *Laughter on the 23rd Floor.* New York: Random House, 1995. First edition, fine in fine dust jacket, inscribed by author. Stephen Lupack March 2015 - 2015 $95

Simon, Oliver *The Curwen Press Miscellany.* London: The Curwen Press by The Soncino Press, 1931. Limited to 275 numbered copies, small 4to. cloth, slipcase, paper spine label, initial letters, borders', printers' flowers, Curwen Press ornaments, headpieces and vignettes, slipcase shows wear around edges and is bumped at head of spine, upper corners show slight bump, unusual to find in original slipcase. Oak Knoll Books 306 - 149 2015 $1500

Simonds, John C. *The Story of Manual Labor in all Lands and Ages.* Chicago: R. S. Peale, 1886. First edition, three quarter bound in gilt stamped leather over brown pebbled cloth, very good. Beasley Books 2013 - 2015 $125

Simons, Lao Genevra *Bibliography of Early American Textbooks on Algebra.* New York: Scripta Mathematica, Yeshiva College, 1936. 8vo., navy cloth, gilt stamped cover and spine titles, very lightly rubbed, near fine. Jeff Weber Rare Books 178 - 1011 2015 $45

Simpson-Lawrence Ltd. *Marine Equipment. Catalogue Q.* Glasgow: Sampson Lawrence, 1961. Original decorated gray paper boards, illustrations, blue cloth spine, very good. Jarndyce Antiquarian Booksellers CCXI - 256 2015 £30

Simpson, James *The Philosophy of Education, with Its Practical Application to a System and Plan of Popular Education as a National Object.* Edinburgh: Adam and Charles Black, 1836. Second edition, 8vo., one prelim leaf bound out of order, occasional light spotting, original cloth backed boards with printed spine label with some minor wear and soiling, good, untrimmed copy. John Drury Rare Books March 2015 - 17966 2015 $221

Simpson, James H. *Report of the Secretary of War, Communicating in Compliance with a Resolution of the Senate, Captain Simpson's Report and Map of Wagon road Routes in Utah Territory.* Senate Executive Document 40, 1859. First edition, 84 pages, large folding map, newly bound in cloth, map in protective pocket at rear, map has splitting at several corners of folds and 2" closed tear to left edge, professionally repaired on verso, else clean copy of fragile map. Buckingham Books March 2015 - 37648 2015 $1250

Simpson, John *The Wild Rabbit in a New Aspect, or Rabbit-Warrens that Pay...* Edinburgh & London: William Blackwood & Sons, 1895. Second edition, half title, 2 pages reviews, 30 page catalog, colophon leaf, original dark green cloth, bevelled boards, armorial bookplate of W. R. M. Wynne, very good. Jarndyce Antiquarian Booksellers CCXI - 255 2015 £48

Simpson, John Palgrave *Letters from the Danube.* London: Richard Bentley, 1847. First edition, 2 volumes, 12mo., half titles, finely bound in contemporary full tan calf, gilt borders, raised gilt bands, gilt compartments, dark green and brown morocco labels, presentation inscription "Robert Peel from his sincere friend Henry James Vansittart Neale on his leaving Eton, Election 1860', fine, (grandson of Conservative statesman, Sir Robert Peel.   Jarndyce Antiquarian Booksellers   CCXI - 254   2015   £350

Simpson, Louis *The Best Hour of the Night.* New Haven and New York: Ticknor & Fields, 1983. First edition, fine in lightly rubbed, very good dust jacket with bit of wear at head of spine and puncture on front panel, inscribed by poet to his son Tony, Christmas 83.   Between the Covers Rare Books, Inc.   187 - 257   2015 $250

Simpson, Louis *Collected Poems.* New York: Paragon House, 1988. First edition, fine in fine dust jacket, inscribed by author for son Tony, Oct. '88.   Between the Covers Rare Books, Inc.   187 - 258   2015 $750

Simpson, Louis *Searching for the Ox.* New York: Morrow, 1976. First printing, 8vo., author's presentation on title to poet and editor William Claire, paper over boards with cloth spine, top edges slightly spotted, otherwise nice, little chipped and soiled dust jacket.   Second Life Books Inc.   190 - 201   2015 $275

Simpson, Mona *Anywhere but Here.* New York: Alfred A. Knopf, 1987. Third printing, fine in very good or better dust jacket (spine faded), inscribed by author to Nicholas Delbanco.   Between the Covers Rare Books, Inc.   187 - 259   2015 $50

Simpson, Percy *Proof-Reading in the Sixteenth, Seventeenth and Eighteenth Centuries.* London: Oxford University Press, 1970. Reprint of first edition, 17 plates, 4 facsimiles in text, 4to., cloth, dust jacket, well preserved. Oak Knoll Books   306 - 301   2015 $100

Sims, Judge Orland L. *Cowpokes, Nesters & So Forth.* Austin: Encino Press, 1970. First edition, limited to 250 numbered and signed copies this copy 234, quarter leather and cloth, leather corners, fine in fine slipcase. Buckingham Books   March 2015 - 19457   2015 $300

Sinclair, John *Work/3.* Detroit: Artist's Workshop Press, 1966. 4to., side stapled softcover, very good+ copy. Beasley Books   2013 - 2015 $85

Sinclair, John   1754-1835 *Address to the Society for the Improvement of British Wool; Constituted at Edinburgh on Monday Jan. 31 1791.* London: T. Cadell, 1791. Second edition, 8vo., well bound in old-style quarter calf, gilt, fine. John Drury Rare Books   March 2015 - 14059   2015 $266

Sinclair, John   1754-1835 *The History of the Public Revenue of the British Empire.* London: by W. and A. Strahan for T. Cadell, 1785. First edition, but without third part published in 1790, 2 parts in one volume, 4to., light spotting throughout but heavier, good copy.   John Drury Rare Books   2015 - 8062   2015 $699

Sinclair, Upton   1878-1968 *The Cry for Justice, an Anthology of Social Protest.* Philadelphia: Winston, 1915. First edition, nearly 900 pages, very good, sunned spine. Beasley Books   2013 - 2015 $45

Sinclair, Upton   1878-1968 *The Jungle.* New York: Limited Editions Club, 1965. Limited to 1500 numbered copies signed by author and artist, thick 8vo., illustrations by Fletcher Martin, quarter leather, slipcase, with Monthly letter loosely inserted, well preserved.   Oak Knoll Books   25 - 42   2015 $350

Singer, Isaac Bashevis *The Collected Stories of Isaac Bashevis Singer.* New York: Farrar, Straus and Giroux, 1982. First edition, one of 450 copies, numbered and signed by author, this is the trade issue in blue cloth and gray slipcase, fine in lightly soiled slipcase with mild sticker stain to one corner, 8vo.   Beasley Books   2013 - 2015 $125

Singer, Isaac Bashevis *The Magician of Lublin.* New York: Limited Editions Club, 1984-1985. First edition with these illustrations, one of 1500 copies signed by Singer and Larry Rivers, 3 original color lithographs by Larry Rivers, hand-bound in quarter blue goatskin stamped in gold with linen sides, 236 pages, slipcase, as new.   Gemini Fine Books & Arts, Ltd. Art Reference & Illustrated Books: First Editions - 2015 $250

Singer, Isaac Bashevis *A Young Man in Search of Love.* Garden City: Doubleday, 1978. First edition, this number 42 of 300 copies, illustrations by Raphael Soyer with limited edition color print, signed by artist, very good, sunned spine and tiny spot on half title, near fine slipcase.   Beasley Books   2013 - 2015 $250

Siringo, Charles Angelo   1855-1928 *Riata and Spurs. The Story of a Lifetime Spent in the Saddle as Cowboy and Detective.* Boston: Houghton Mifflin, 1927. Revised edition, inscairbed by author for friend L. H. Spragle, Jan. 14th 1928, cloth, illustrations, scarce, some underlining throughout, else very good.   Buckingham Books   March 2015 - 29398   2015 $750

Siskind, Aaron *Harlem Document Photographs 1932-1940.* Providence: Matrix, 1981. First edition, horizontal 8vo., blue cloth, nice in very good dust jacket.   Second Life Books Inc.   190 - 202   2015 $250

Sitwell, Edith 1887-1964 *The Canticle of the Rose: Poems 1917-1949.* New York: Vanguard Press, 1949. First American edition, inscribed to James Laughlin, founder of New directions. Honey & Wax Booksellers 2 - 56 2015 $275

Sitwell, Osbert 1892-1969 *Out of the Flame.* London: Grant Richards, 1923. First edition, frontispiece, 8vo., original green cloth with few light spots, backstrip with orange paper label little chipped to border, top edge lightly dust soiled, endpapers faintly browned, good, with holograph manuscript of 'Superstition', from the library of baron Emile D'Erlanger. Blackwell's Rare Books B179 - 236 2015 £130

Sitwell, Sacheverell *Fine Bird Books 1700-1900.* London: 1953. Trade edition of 2000 copies, elephant folio, 38 color plates, 36 black and white, extremities rubbed, interior clean and very good. Dumont Maps & Books of the West 131 - 74 2015 $200

Sitwell, Sacheverell *The People's Palace.* Oxford: Blackwell, 1918. First edition, one of two faint foxspots, crown 8vo., original orange wrappers, usual creasing to edges, few nicks with light handling marks, printed backstrip and front cover labels, little toned, edges untrimmed and lightly foxed, very good. Blackwell's Rare Books B179 - 238 2015 £45

Six Essays on Commons Preservation: Written in Competition for Prizes Offered by Henry W. Peek, Esq. of Wimbledon House. London: Sampson Low Son and Marston, 1887. First edition, 8vo., 16 page Sampson Low catalog at end, original blindstamped maroon cloth, spine lettered tilt, repairs to head and foot of spine, excellent, uncut copy. John Drury Rare Books March 2015 - 24973 2015 £306

Six Letters Addressed to a congregation of Indepdenent Dissenters, Upon Separating from their Communion. London: printed for R. Hunter and W. Harwood, 1817. First edition, 8vo., fairly recently bound in plain boards with printed spine label, very good, apparently rare. John Drury Rare Books March 2015 - 24707 2015 $221

Six Questions Stated and Answered Upon Which the Whole Force of the Arguments for and Against the Peerage Bill Depends. London: printed for J. Roberts, 1719. First edition, 8vo., wanting half title, recent plain wrappers, very good. John Drury Rare Books 2015 - 17723 2015 $177

The Sixteenth Epode of Horace, Imitated and Addressed to the People of England. London: printed for J. Standen, 1739. First edition, 12 pages, folio, disbound, rare, some light foxing and dampstains, otherwise very good, rare. C. R. Johnson Foxon R-Z - 903r-z 2015 $1149

Sjowall, Maj *The Laughing Policeman.* Pantheon Books, 1970. First US edition, from the library of mystery author Thomas Gifford with his neat inked signature and date, fine in dust jacket with light wear to head of spine. Buckingham Books March 2015 - 35108 2015 $175

Skeel, Adelaide *My Three Legged Story Teller.* Philadelphia: Rufus C. Hartranft, 1892. First edition, 8vo., original paper covered boards, covers soiled and rubbed, inside front hinge cracked. Oak Knoll Books 306 - 302 2015 $250

Skelton, Christopher *The Engravings of Eric Gill.* Wellingborough: Christopher Skelton, 1983. First edition, limited to 1350 copies, thick 4to. two-toned cloth with Gill engraving stamped in blind on front cover, slipcase, over 1000 engravings described and illustrated, book review from TLS, prospectus and order form laid in, well preserved. Oak Knoll Books 306 - 20 2015 $475

Skelton, John 1460-1529 *Pithy Pleasaunt and Profitable Workes of Maister Skelton.* London: C. Davis, 1736. First edition thus, small blindstamp on titlepage, 2 small round stamps on verso of same library and note 'Welsh Fund', slight repair to edge of titlepage, otherwise clean, very good+ in recent half dark blue leather and marbled boards lettered gilt at spine. Any Amount of Books 2015 - A44877 2015 £170

A Sketch of the Political History of the Past Three Years, In Connexion with the Press newspaper... London: Press Office 110 Strand, 1856. First edition, 8vo., 16 pages, last page rather dusty in recent plain wrappers, good. John Drury Rare Books 2015 - 18273 2015 $89

Sketchley, William *The Cocker.* Burton-on-Trent: J. Croft, 1814. Second edition, 8vo., rebacked contemporary boards with foldout frontispiece of cock fight, contemporary ownership signature and later bookplate. Second Life Books Inc. 191 - 83 2015 $400

Skidmore, Thomas *The Rights of man to Property!* New York: printed for the author by Alexander Ming Jr., 1829. First edition, 12mo., original calf, sides stamped, binding rubbed and slightly worn, some foxing, very good, early bookplate of Eli West of Carthage, Jefferson County (NY?). M & S Rare Books, Inc. 97 - 279 2015 $6000

Skirving, John *A Comparative View of the Situation of Great Britain, from the Conclusion of the Amerian War in 1783 to the year 1832...* Elgin: printed by A. C. Brander, 1833. First edition, 4 folding tables, stitching strained and one gathering loose, original cloth, original printed spine label, spine faded, entirely uncut, very good, crisp copy, scarce. John Drury Rare Books March 2015 - 21654 2015 $266

Skutsch, Otto *Alfred Edward Housman 1859-1936.* London: University of London Athlone Press, 1960. Half title, original blue printed wrappers, presentation copy to Geoffrey Tillotson from librarian Joseph Scott, with TLS mentioning omissions from the lecture.   Jarndyce Antiquarian Booksellers   CCVII - 317   2015   £30

Slack, Samuel *Considerations on the nature and tendency of classical literature...* London: printed for the author, 1822. First edition, 8vo., half title, rather dust soiled, recently well bound in linen backed marbled boards lettered, very good, rare.   John Drury Rare Books   March 2015 - 22425   2015   £306

Sladek, Jon *Black Aura.* London: Cape, 1974. First edition, fine in dust jacket.   Mordida Books   March 2015 - 002701   2015 $100

Slaney, Robert Aglionby *Essay on the Beneficial Direction of Rural Expenditure.* London: Longman Hurst Rees Orme Brown and Green, 1824. First edition, 12mo., contemporary green calf gilt, marbled edges, head of spine snagged else very good with 19th century armorial bookplate of J. G Barclay.   John Drury Rare Books   March 2015 - 20665   2015   £306

Slaney, Robert Aglionby *Speech of R. A. Slaney, Esq. M.P. in the House of Commons on Thursday Nov. 30 1837....* London: J. Hatchard and Son, 1837. 12mo., 24 pages, old wrappers, old inkstamp of British Government Library on wrapper and titlepage, label to lower wrapper, good copy, rare.   John Drury Rare Books   2015 - 20946   2015 $177

Slate Pencil Drawings for the Self Instruction of Children. London: R. Ganton, n.d. circa, 1850. 12mo., pictorial wrappers, cover rubbed, else very good.   Aleph-Bet Books, Inc.   108 - 165   2015 $350

Slavitt, David R. *Dozens.* Baton Rouge: Lousiana State University Press, 1981. First edition, fine in slightly spine faded, near fine dust jacket, nicely inscribed to poet Karl (and Teri) Shapiro 4/3081.   Between the Covers Rare Books, Inc.   187 - 260   2015 $125

Slavson, S. R. *The Practice of Group Psychotherapy.* New York: IUP, 1947. First edition, fine in very good dust jacket.   Beasley Books   2013 - 2015 $45

Sleator, William *The Angry Moon.* Boston: Little Brown and Co., 1970. First edition, fine in near fine dust jacket with price intact, 8vo., scarce.   By the Book, L. C.   44 - 88   2015 $400

Sleigh, William Campbell *The Grand Jury System Subversive of the Moral Interests of Society: a Letter to the Rt. Hon. Spencer H. Walpole, M.P., Secretary of State for the Home Department.* London: S. Sweet and Hodges and Smith, Dublin, 1852. First edition, 8vo., some spotting and pencillings, recently well bound in linen backed marbled boards, lettered, good copy, inscribed by author for Hon P. J. Locke King M.P.   John Drury Rare Books   2015 - 16761   2015 $168

Slick, Grace *Somebody to Love - a Rock and Roll Memoir.* New York: Warner Books, 1998. First edition, fine in dust jacket, signed, dust jacket.   Buckingham Books   March 2015 - 12014   2015 $200

Sloan, John *Introduction to American Indian Art.* New York: 1931. 2 volumes, 22 black and white and 9 color half and full page photos; 67 black and white and full page photos, original decorative paper wrappers, wrappers on part I trimmed to text block, part II soiled with stain, very good.   Dumont Maps & Books of the West   131 - 75   2015 $100

Sloan, Samuel *Sloan's Constructive Architecture, a Guide to the Practical Builder and Mechanic...* Philadelphia: 1866. 4to., 148 pages, 66 lithographed plates, neat modern cloth, leather spine label, very nice.   Joseph J. Felcone Inc.   Science, Medicine and Technology - 4   2015 $700

Sloane, Eric *A Reverence for Wood.* New York: Wilfred Funk Inc., 1965. First edition, quarto, fine in fine dust jacket with perhaps slightest of sunning at spine, promotional brochure for Sloane's works laid in, inscribed by Sloane to boxing champion Gene Tunney.   Between the Covers Rare Books, Inc.   187 - 3   2015 $650

Sloane, Hans *An Account of a Most Efficacious Medicine for Soreness, Weakness and Several Other Distempers of the Eyes.* London: for Dan Browne, circa, 1750. Second edition, neat modern cloth backed boards, fine.   Joseph J. Felcone Inc.   Science, Medicine and Technology - 38   2015 $475

Slocum, John J. *A Bibliography of James Joyce 1882-1941.* New Haven: Yale University Press, 1953. First edition, fine in near fine, price clipped dust jackets with tiny nicks at ends of barely darkened spine.   Beasley Books   2013 - 2015 $125

Slugg, J. T. *Reminiscences of Manchester Fifty Years Ago.* London: J. E. Cornish & Simpkin, Marshall, 1881. Foldout frontispiece map, tiny hole on title, rebound preserving original green cloth with black and gilt stamped cover and spine titles, extremities rubbed, scarce original printing.   Jeff Weber Rare Books   178 - 1014   2015 $50

Smail, David Cameron *Prestwick Golf Club: Birthplace of the Open: The Club, The Members and Championships 1851 to 1989.* Prestwick: Prestwick Golf Club, 1989. First edition, no. 28 of 250 leather bound copies, large 4to., original green leather boards, lettered gilt on spine and on front cover, copiously illustrated in color and black and white, fine in fine slipcase. Any Amount of Books 2015 - C7648 2015 £300

Small, Albion W. *Between Eras from Capitalism to Democracy.* Kansas City: Intercollegiate Press, 1913. First edition, very good hardcovers, some spotting to boards (not ostentatious). Beasley Books 2013 - 2015 $45

Smalley, Janet *Rice to Rice Pudding and Other Picture Tales.* New York: Morrow, 1928. First edition, signed by author, very good in chipped and separated dust jacket with all panels present. Beasley Books 2013 - 2015 $40

Smallwood, Charles A. *The White Front Cars of San Francisco. Interurbans Special 44.* First revised edition, quarto, 482 pages, frontispiece, photos, 4 folding diagrams, folding map, gilt lettered green cloth, very fine, lightly worn and rubbed pictorial dust jacket, very scarce. Argonaut Book Shop Holiday Season 2014 - 267 2015 $175

Smallwood, Charles A. *The White Front Cars of San Francisco.* South Gate: Interurbans, 1970. First edition, quarto, 478 pages, frontispiece, photos, folding map, 4 folding diagrams, dark green cloth, gilt, very fine, pictorial dust jacket bit rubbed at spine ends and corners, very scarce. Argonaut Book Shop Holiday Season 2014 - 266 2015 $175

Smart, Christopher 1722-1771 *Jubilate Agno.* Cambridge: Harvard University Press, 1954. Half title, original green cloth, very good, repaired dust jacket, inscribed by George Sherburn Sept. 1954 for Geoffrey Tilltoson, with inserted postcard. Jarndyce Antiquarian Booksellers CCVII - 472 2015 £25

Smart, Christopher 1722-1771 *The Collected Poems.* London: Routledge & Kegan Paul, 1949. 2 volumes, half titles, frontispiece volume I, original dark blue cloth, very good in slightly dusted dust jacket, signed by Geoffrey Tillotson with few notes and 2 inserted letters from publisher. Jarndyce Antiquarian Booksellers CCVII - 471 2015 £20

Smart, Christopher 1722-1771 *Poems.* Princeton: Princeton Univ.. Press, 1950. Half title, frontispiece, plates, original green cloth, very good in slightly dusted dust jacket, Geoffrey's Tillotson's signed review copy with few notes. Jarndyce Antiquarian Booksellers CCVII - 473 2015 £35

Smedley, Francis *Frank Fairliegh; or Scenes from the Life of a Private Pupil.* London: A. Hall Virtue, 1850. First edition, 30 steel engravings by George Cruikshank, bound by Sangorski & Sutcliffe in three quarter navy leather with fancy gilt decorations to spine, raised bands, top edge gilt, ribbon marker housed in plain slipcase, very good plus, some minor scuffing and scratches to boards, offsetting to endpapers, very solid handsome copy. Ed Smith Books 82 - 25 2015 $350

Smedley, Frank *Last Leaves from Beechwood.* Enfield: printed by J. H. Meyers, 1867. Photographic portrait of author as frontispiece and one other small photo laid down on page 7, errata slip with two additional corrections in ms., original green cloth blocked in blind, lettered gilt, slightly dulled with small ink mark on front board, presentation inscription "Frances Sarah Smedley 1867 in affectionate remembrance of her beloved son". Jarndyce Antiquarian Booksellers CCXI - 257 2015 £180

Smelt, Leonard *The Speech of Leonard Smelt, Esq. Delivered by Him at the Meeting of the County of York December 30 1779.* York: printed by A. Ward and sold by all the booksellers in York and sold by R. Faulder, London, 1780. First edition, 4to., preserved in modern wrappers with printed title label on upper cover, very good, very scarce. John Drury Rare Books March 2015 - 22964 2015 $656

Smelt, Leonard *The System Occasioned by the Speech of Leonard Smelt, Esq. Late Sub-Governor to their Royal Highnesses the Prince of Wales and Bishop of Osnabrugh at the Meeting at York, Dec. 30 1779.* London: J. Almon, 1780. 8vo., preserved in modern wrappers with printed title label on upper cover, very good, crisp copy, very scarce. John Drury Rare Books March 2015 - 190091 2015 $221

Smet, Pierre Jean De 1801-1873 *Missions de l'Oregon et Voyages Dans les Montagnes Rocheuses en 1845 et 18456.* Paris: 1848. 408 pages, illustrations, leather, externally quite worn, gilt title still legible, binding sound with little foxing, 14 tinted lithographic plates, all present. Dumont Maps & Books of the West 131 - 49 2015 $400

Smethurst, Gamaliel *Tables of Time; Whereby the Day of the month, Either new or Old Style; Day of the Week, Rising of the Sun, time of the Sun's Solstices...* Manchester: printed by R. Whitworth, bookseller and sold by R. Dodsely at Tully's Head in Pall Mall, London, n.d, 1749. 12mo., 48 engraved plates, one gathering of 6 leaves bound out of order, titlepage just little foxed and with old blindstamp of Wigan Free Public Library, bound in 19th century half morocco over marbled boards, spine gilt and lettered with raised bands, head of spine chipped, marbled edges, very good with Wigan Library bookplate, very scarce. John Drury Rare Books 2015 - 25347 2015 $612

Smiles, Samuel *Self-Help: with Illustrations of Character and Conduct.* London: John Murray, 1859. First edition, 8vo., light marking or spotting of first few leaves, original maroon blindstamped cloth, spine and gilt lettered, very slight rubbing to extremities, uncut, else very good.   John Drury Rare Books   2015 - 26080   2015 $2185

Smith, Adam   1723-1790   *An Enquiry into the Nature and Causes of the Wealth of Nations.* London: printed for A. Strahan and T. Cadell in the Strand, 1786. Fourth edition, 3 volumes, 8vo., errata at end of volumes I and II, with two contents leaves in both volume II and III present but misbound, wormtrack affecting top portion of several leaves the end of volume I, occasionally affecting letters, contemporary uniform calf with minor restoration to spine of volume I, morocco label lettered in gilt, in spine of minor faults, very good, crisp set in original binding.   John Drury Rare Books   2015 - 24406   2015 $2622

Smith, Adam   1723-1790   *An Inquiry into the Nature and Causes of the Wealth of Nations...* London: T. Cadell and W. Davies, 1805. 3 volumes, 8vo., one gathering in volume II and one gathering in volume III foxed, else very good set in contemporary tree calf with minor restoration to edges, all volumes skillfully rebacked recently, spines fully gilt and labelled.   John Drury Rare Books   2015 - 23736   2015 $1661

Smith, Albert   *The English Hotel Nuisance.* London: Bradbury & Evans, 1858. Second edition, small 4to., frontispiece and illustrations, some slight spotting and marking, original illustrated printed paper wrappers, dusted, slightly marked, spine worn.   Jarndyce Antiquarian Booksellers   CCXI - 258   2015   £45

Smith, Amanda   *An Autobiography.* Chicago: Meyer and Brother, 1893. First edition, 8vo., frontispiece, 25 illustrations, former owner's signature on endpaper, hinges loose, rubbed at extremities, good copy, few pencil scores in margins, scarce.   Second Life Books Inc.   189 - 234   2015 $250

Smith, Arthur Dougals Howden   *Swain's Saga.* New York: Macmillan, 1931. First edition, octavo, original purple pebbled cloth.   L. W. Currey, Inc.   Boy's Adventure Fiction 2015 - 97   2015 $100

Smith, Betty   *A Tree Grows in Brooklyn.* New York: Harper & Brothers, 1943. First edition, first printing, original cloth, first issue unclipped dust jacket (price intact and 'No. 5538"), signed and inscribed by author on day of publication August 18 1943 to Miss Ruth M. Batrau, about very good with some fading and smudges to cloth, rear hinge cracked in like dust jacket with some chipping to spine ends, splitting to upper front flap, few small tears and rubbing, else very good, housed in custom box.   B & B Rare Books, Ltd.   234 - 90   2015 $7500

Smith, Boyd   *Boyd Smith Mother Goose.* New York: G. P. Putnam, 1919. 4to., red cloth stamped in black, occasional margin soil, else near fine in pictorial dust jacket, frayed but very good, 20 color plates by E. Boyd Smith, rare in dust jacket.   Aleph-bet Books, Inc.   109 - 446   2015 $1250

Smith, Charles A.   *A Comprehensive History of Minnehaha County, South Dakota.* Educator Supply company, 1949. First edition, inscribed by author, additionally signed by author, maroon fabricoid, frontispiece, portraits, plates, near fine, tight.   Buckingham Books   March 2015 - 27663 2015 $200

Smith, Charles John   *Common Words with Curious Derivations.* London: Bell & Daldy, 1865. First edition, errata, original purple cloth, slightly rubbed.   Jarndyce Antiquarian Booksellers   CCXI - 259   2015   £45

Smith, Charlotte   *Rural Walks; in Dialogues.* Philadelphia: Thomas Stephens, 1795. Two volumes in 1, engraved allegorical frontispiece by James Thackara, little browning and foxing, 2 leaves (including frontispiece) with small pieces detached from margin (without loss), 12mo., original tree sheep, rebacked, contemporary ownership inscription inside front cover of Miss Yates (ink has bled and something below signature is inked out), recto of frontispiece inscribed to "The Misses Taylor from their Mother 1893", good.   Blackwell's Rare Books   B179 - 97   2015   £500

Smith, Dave   *In the House of the Judge.* New York: Harper and Row, 1983. First edition, hardcover issue, fine in spine faded, very good or better dust jacket, warmly inscribed to author Nicholas Delbanco, scarce.   Between the Covers Rare Books, Inc.   187 - 261   2015 $75

Smith, David Eugene   *Rara Arthmetica: a Catalogue of the Arithmetics Written Before the Year MDCI with a Description of Those in the Library of George Arthur Plimpton of New York.* New York: Chelsea, 1970. Fourth edition, 8vo., 8 plates, illustrations, navy cloth, gilt stamped spine title, fine. Jeff Weber Rare Books   178 - 1018   2015 $45

Smith, David Nichol   *Some Observations on Eighteenth Century Poetry.* London: Oxford University Press, printed in Canada by the University of Toronto Press, 1937. Half title, original light brown cloth, slightly dusted in dusted dust jacket, Geoffrey Tillotson's signed copy with initial note, inserted publisher's slip and 2 copies of short review. Jarndyce Antiquarian Booksellers   CCVII - 474   2015 £20

Smith, Dodie   *The Girl from the Candle-Lit Bath.* London: W. H. Allen, 1978. First edition, 8vo., fine in clean, very good dust jacket with very slight shelfwear, signed presentation from author for Murray MacDonald, director.   Any Amount of Books   2015 - A89369   2015   £180

Smith, Duane A. *The Mesa Verde Centennial Series.* Durango: Durango Herald Small Press, 2005. 2006. One of 150 sets, 7 volumes, each booklet signed by author(s) and housed in decorated slipcase with limitation label affixed to top, 8vo., pictorial wrappers, illustrations, maps. Buckingham Books   March 2015 - 26644   2015 $185

Smith, Eaglesfield *Sir John Butt: a Farce. In Two acts.* Edinburgh: 1798. First edition, outer leaves variously remargined or mounted, other paper repairs, 8vo, uncut in modern hard grained red morocco backed board.   Blackwell's Rare Books   B179 - 98   2015   £800

Smith, Edgar *Letters from Baker Street.* New York: Pamphlet House, 1942. First edition, one of 200 copies bound in blue printed wrappers of which this is copy number 270, fine in printed wrappers.   Buckingham Books   March 2015 - 17860   2015 $235

Smith, Edmund *A Poem on the Death of Mr. John Phillips...* London: printed for Bernard Lintott, n.d., 1710. First edition, disbound, lacks last page of text but is otherwise in good condition.   C. R. Johnson   Foxon R-Z - 906r-z   2015 $689

Smith, Edmund *The Works of Mr. Edmund Smith, Late of Christ Church Oxford.* London: printed for Bernard Lintot, 1719. Third edition, 12mo., recent unlettered calf, engraved frontispiece, little foxed, few stains, otherwise good copy, outer edges uncut, on a flyleaf preserved at front is old signature of Jane Taylor.   C. R. Johnson   Foxon R-Z - 905r-z   2015 $192

Smith, Elias *The History of Anti-Christ: in Three Books Written in Scripture Stile in Chapter and Verse, for the Use of Schools.* Portland: Herald printers Office and Book Store, John P. Colcord printers, 1811. 32mo., 120 pages, contemporary boards, worn, crudely backed with buckram, spine lettered in white, ex-library with bookplate, title with old blindstamp, front hinge reinforced with tape, paper starting to crack along hinge, complete, but fair copy only.   M & S Rare Books, Inc.   97 - 287   2015 $125

Smith, Elizabeth Oakes *Bertha and Lily; or the Parsonage of Beech Glen.* New York: Boston: Cincinnati: Derby, 1854. First edition, 8vo., illustrations, frontispiece, brown cloth stamped in blind and gilt, little worn, some staining to pastedowns, very good copy.   Second Life Books Inc.   189 - 236   2015 $400

Smith, Elizabeth Oakes *The Lover's Gift; or Tributes to the Beautiful American Series.* Hartford: Henry S. Parsons, 1848. First edition, 12mo., frontispiece, all edges gilt, gilt stamped publisher's cloth, faded, with one inch tear to spine, some foxed, very good.   Second Life Books Inc.   189 - 235   2015 $400

Smith, Elizabeth Oakes *Riches without Wings or the Cleveland Family.* Boston: George W. Lights, 1838. First edition, 12mo., original blind and gilt stamped blue green cloth, gilt lettering, two pages of publisher's terminal ads, cloth little rubbed, lacking front free endpaper and blank, very good.   The Brick Row Book Shop   Miscellany 67 - 9   2015 $375

Smith, Frederick W. *"Confound that Boy!".* London: George Newnes, 1898. Original red pictorial cloth, spine slightly faded and rubbed at head, illustrations, 2 pages ads, embossed W. H. Smith stamp on title, signature of W. Hood.   Jarndyce Antiquarian Booksellers   CCXI - 260 2015   £40

Smith, George *A Collection of Designs for Household Furniture and Interior Decoration...* London: published for J. Taylor at the architectural Library no. 49, High Holborn, 1808. 4to., 158 plates, plates 23 and 26 cut to plate mark and mounted plate 146 with repair to margin, some occasional spotting, still unusually bright copy, contemporary vellum, upper cover lettered in gilt, Marquis of Downshire, Hillsborough Castle, some marks on lower board, inscribed on title for the Use of James McBlaine, Hillsborough, bookplate of Donald & Mary Hyde.   Marlborough Rare Books List 54 - 78   2015   £9500

Smith, George *Essay on the Construction of Cottages Suited for the Labouring Classes...* Glasgow: 1834. First edition, text illustrations, 11 folding plates, original ribbed cloth, printed paper label on cover, engraved title foxed and very light foxing on some plates, else very attractive, pencilled note on pastedown states this is the first architecture book published in Glasgow.   Joseph J. Felcone Inc. Science, Medicine and Technology - 5   2015 $400

Smith, Gyles, Pseud. *Serious Reflections on the Dangerous Tendency of the Common Practice of Card-Playing, Especially of the Game of All Fours...* London: W. Owen, 1754. First edition, 8vo., well bound in modern boards with morocco labels on both upper cover and spine lettered gilt, scarce.   John Drury Rare Books   2015 - 25228   2015 $874

Smith, H. Maynard *Inspector Frost in Crevenna Cove.* New York: Minton Balch, 1933. First US edition, fine in dust jacket with closed rear and small crease to lower portion of back panel, light wear to corners.   Buckingham Books March 2015 - 25819   2015 $350

Smith, Hannah Whitall *Every-Day Religion or the Common-Sense Teaching of the Bible.* New York: Chicago: Toronto: Revell, 1893. First edition, 8vo., little worn drab green cloth stamped in gilt, previous owner endpaper, little pencil marginalia, good, tight copy.   Second Life Books Inc.   191 - 84   2015 $120

Smith, Horace *The Runaway; or the Seat of Benevolence.* printed by T. Davison for Crosby and Letterman, 1800. First edition, 4 volumes, printed on blue-ish paper (tone varying), apart from titlepages, 12mo., contemporary half green roan, gilt ruled compartments on spine, lettered and numbered direct, spines darkened, slightly worn at extremities, labels of some description removed from upper covers leaving traces of gilt at edges (hence perhaps an armorial bookplate or something decorative, rather than a library label), contemporary signature inside front covers erased (except in volume iv) of Harriet Holland, mid 20th century ownership inscription, contemporary tiny ticket of E. Upham, bookseller, good.   Blackwell's Rare Books   B179 - 99   2015   £4000

Smith, Hugh *Letters to Married Women.* London: printed for the author and sold by G. Kearsly, 1774. Third edition, 12mo., contemporary armorial bookplate of Grant Mitchell on front pastedown and near contemporary signature of Charlotta Amelia Mitchell on titlepage, contemporary plain sheep worn at joints, very good crisp copy.   John Drury Rare Books   2015 - 20556   2015 $1311

Smith, J. P. *The North Sydney Flight.* North Sydney: Personnel of the US Naval Air Station, Dec. 1st, 1918. Farewell issue, quarto, illustrated card covers, covers and first page dirtied and chipped along edges, interior good.   Schooner Books Ltd.   110 - 117   2015 $75

Smith, J. V. C. *The Ways of Women in Their Physical, Moral and Intellectual Relations.* New York: Jewett, 1873. First edition, large 8vo., brown cloth stamped in black, very good, tight copy.   Second Life Books Inc.   189 - 233   2015 $150

Smith, James Edward   1759-1828 *English Botany.* London: 1790-1814. First editions, 254 x 162mm., 36 volumes, (without the four supplements published over a period of 35 years after 1814), in original publisher's temporary muslin-back paper boards, entirely untrimmed, flat spines with titling in gilt (one volume expertly rebacked using original backstrip), 2592 hand colored botanical plates as called for, with four of the plates inserted from other copies, light fading to a number of spines, minor fraying and losses to cloth at spine ends and tiny losses in a few joints, original fragile binding in remarkably fine state, covers and spines very clean, smooth and altogether surprisingly well preserved, minor foxing and faint offsetting here and there, few text leaves and perhaps two or three plates per volume, more noticeably foxed, though never severely so, some of the text printed on paper of a lesser quality than used for the plates and consequently with overall mild browning, still very nearly fine internally, text apparently unread and plates very clean and fresh with rich coloring.   Phillip J. Pirages   66 - 54   2015 $25,000

Smith, James H. *Vital Facts Concerning the African Methodist Episcopal Church Its Origins, Doctrines, Government, Usages....* N.P.: James H. Smith, 1941. Revised edition, near fine in very good dust jacket with spine fading and chipping at spine ends, small pamphlet supplement "A Supplement to Vital Facts Concerning the AME Church" laid in, scarce, especially in dust jacket.   Between the Covers Rare Books   197 - 37   2015 $225

Smith, John *England's Improvement Reviv'd: in a Treatise of all Manner of Husbandry & Trade by Land and Sea...* London: printed by Tho. Newcomb for Benjamin Southwood at the Star next to Sergeants-Inn...., 1673. Second edition, 4to., wanting initial blank, Bookseller to the reader leaf & titlepage laid down, titlepage with critique of book around margins in ink, cut close at head very occasionally touching running title, some paper browning, well bound in late 19th/early 20th century in dark blue crushed morocco, spine gilt and lettered with raised bands, all edges gilt, very good.   John Drury Rare Books   2015 - 24364   2015 $2185

Smith, John *The General Historie of Virginia, New England and the Summer Isles...* London: printed by J(ohn) D(awson) and J(ohn) H(aviland) for Michael Sparkes, 1626. Second edition, quarto, elaborate engraved titlepage, portrait (in facsimile), 4 folding maps (in facsimile), full contemporary calf, covers and corners lightly worn, upper cover detached, housed in folding cloth chemise and slipcase with leather spine label, exceptions noted, a very nice, clean copy with elaborate engraved titlepage in lovely condition.   Argonaut Book Shop   Holiday Season 2014 - 279   2015 $4250

Smith, John *General View of the Agriculture of the County of Argyll...* Edinburgh: printed by Mundell & Sons sold by G. Nicoll, London &c, 1798. First edition, 8vo., 3 engraved plates, folding table, contemporary tree calf, spine gilt with gilt bit worn, later replacement labels, very good.   John Drury Rare Books   March 2015 - 23189   2015   £306

Smith, John *Memoirs of Wool, Woolen Manufacture and Trade (Particularly in England) from the Earliest to the Present Times...* London: printed for the author, 1756-1757. 2 volumes, 4to., little worm damage in blank upper margin of a few leaves in volume II (nowhere near text), marginal dampstain in final few leaves also of volume II, recently bound by Trevor Lloyd in old style half calf, gilt and labelled, very good.   John Drury Rare Books   2015 - 22878   2015 $2185

Smith, John *Poems on Several Occasions.* London: printed for H. Clements, 1713. First edition, 8vo., contemporary panelled calf, spine gilt red morocco label, neatly rebacked, original spine laid down, fine, scarce, early armorial bookplate of Viscount Tamworth.   C. R. Johnson   Foxon R-Z - 907r-z   2015 $1915

Smith, John *Substance of the Work Entitled Fruits and Farinacea the Proper Food of Man.* Manchester: John Heywood, London: The Vegetarian Society's Depot, n.d. circa, 1875. 8vo., original brown cloth, lettered gilt on upper cover, very good. John Drury Rare Books 2015 - 18061 2015 $168

Smith, John Thomas 1766-1833 *Nollekens and His Times: Comprehending a Life of that Celebrated Sculptor and Memoirs of Several Contemporary Artists.* London: Henry Colburn, 1828. First edition, 8vo., 2 volumes, bound in recent royal blue morocco, top edge gilt, marbled endpapers, engraved frontispiece to volume I, fresh, clean set. Henry Sotheran Ltd. William Blake Exhibition 17th Oct.-7th Nov. 2014 - 73 2015 £165

Smith, Marshall *An Entire Set of the Monitors, Intended for the Promoting of Religion and Virtue and Supressing of Vice and Immorality.* London: printed for the author, 1714. Reprint, 8vo., old blue wrappers, very scarce, very good. C. R. Johnson Foxon R-Z - 908r-z 2015 $1149

Smith, Marshall *The Vision or a Prospect of Death, Heav'n and Hell.* London: printed for Andrew Bell, 1702. First edition, engraved frontispiece, 8vo., panelled calf antique, spine gilt, rare, some offsetting from insufficient drying of sheets, but generally very good. C. R. Johnson Foxon R-Z - 909r-z 2015 $1226

Smith, Martin *Canto for a Gypsy.* New York: G. P. Putnam's Sons, 1972. First edition, fine and unread in about fine dust jacket, uncommon, exceptionally bright, fresh copy, from the collection of Duke Collier. Royal Books 36 - 232 2015 $325

Smith, Philip *New Directions in Bookbinding.* London: Studio Vista, 1974. First edition, 4to., cloth, dust jacket, many illustrations, photos, some of the binding plates in full color. Oak Knoll Books 306 - 10 2015 $135

Smith, Sheila M. *The Other Nation: the Poor in English Novels of the 1840s and 1850s.* Oxford: Clarendon Press, 1980. Half title, plates, original dark blue cloth, very good in dust jacket, ALS from author inserted thanking her for her review, Kathleen Tillotson's signed copy. Jarndyce Antiquarian Booksellers CCVII - 475 2015 £20

Smith, Vivienne *The Birman Cat: the Sacred Cat of Burma.* Riseley: published by the author, First UK edition, author's small address label on inner front cover inked title on spine, otherwise fine in soft covers. Mordida Books March 2015 - 012708 2015 $100

Smith, W. Anderson *"According to Cocker." the Progress of Penmanship.* London: Alexander Gardner, 1887. First edition, oblong 8vo., cloth, later cardboard slipcase, facsimile plates, former owner has added calligraphic writing to a number of pages, covers soiled, inside hinges cracked, bookplate. Oak Knoll Books Special Catalogue 24 - 50 2015 $125

Smith, W. Eugene *Minamata.* New York: Alskog-Sosorium/Holt, 1975. First edition, 4to., fine in very good+ dust jacket with 3 inch clean tear on rear spine, else near fine. Beasley Books 2013 - 2015 $125

Smith, W. Robertson *Kinship and Marriage in Early Arabia.* Cambridge: Cambridge University Press, 1885. First edition, original brown cloth lettered gilt on spine, 16 page publisher's catalog at rear, small ink mark on back and front, spine very slightly rubbed and very slightly nicked, otherwise clean, very good copy with clean text, above average copy of scarce book. Any Amount of Books 2015 - A91462 2015 £300

Smith, William Cusack *Review of a Publication Entitled. The Speech of the Right Honourable John Foster, Speaker of the House of Commons of Ireland.* Dublin: printed and sold by Marchbank, 1799. First edition, 8vo., very good, recently bound in linen backed marbled boards, lettered. John Drury Rare Books 2015 - 19379 2015 $177

Smith, William H. *Early days in Seward County, Nebraska.* Seward: Seward Independent, 1937. Pictorial wrappers, frontispiece, illustrations, covers lightly soiled, else very good. Buckingham Books March 2015 - 30954 2015 $250

Smith, William Jay *New and Selected Poems.* New York: Delacorte Press, 1970. First edition, fine in price clipped and rubbed, about very good dust jacket, nicely inscribed by author for J. D. McClatchy. Between the Covers Rare Books, Inc. 187 - 262 2015 $100

Smith, Worthington G. *Mushrooms and Toadstools: How to Distinguish Easily the Differences Between Edible and Poisonous Fungi...* London: Robert Hardwicke, 192 Piccadilly, 1867. First edition, 8vo., original printed blue wrappers, small loss at margins, skillfully repaired, two large folding chromolithographs, segmented and mounted on linen, folding plate into original green cloth slipcase, upper cover with printed orange label. Marlborough Rare Books List 54 - 79 2015 £950

Smithsonian Institution *Catalogue of Publications of Societies and Periodical Works...* Washington: Smithsonian Institution, 1866. 8vo., half tan morocco with corners and marbled paper sides, gilt stamped spine title with raised spine bands, all edges gilt marbled, spine rubbed, inner hinges cracked, former library copy with usual markings, very good. Jeff Weber Rare Books 178 - 1025 2015 $40

Smollett, Tobias George 1721-1771 *Smollett's Novels.* Boston: Houghton Mifflin Co., 1926. Limited to 500 numbered copies, 8vo., half morocco, cloth gilt spine with five raised bands, top edge gilt, other edges uncut, tissue protected black and white plates, light rubbing and scuffing, especially at bottom edge.   Oak Knoll Books   306 - 303   2015 $1850

Smollett, Tobias George 1721-1771 *The Works of Tobias Smollett.* New York: Jenson Society, 1905. Limited edition one of 1000 sets, 12 volumes, very good plus set, some shelfwear, little spotting, tight clean texts.   Stephen Lupack   March 2015 - 2015 $200

Smyth, Henry De Wolf *A General Account of the Development of methods of Using Atomic Energy for Military Purposes Under the Auspices of the United States Government 1940-1945.* Washington: Adjutant General's Office August, 1945. 10 1/38 x 7 7/8 inches, diagrams, printed by lithoprint from stencils made by multiple typewriters, stapled in cream textured stiff paper covers, pristine, signed by him on titlepage.   Joseph J. Felcone Inc.   Science, Medicine and Technology - 51   2015 $4200

Smyth, James Carmichael *A Description of the Jail Distemper, as it Appeared Amongst the Spanish Prisoners at Winchester in the year 1780....* London: J. Johnson, 1795. First edition, 8vo., rebound recently in fine 18th century style quarter calf gilt over marbled boards, raised bands, crimson label by Trevor Lloyd, most attractive, uncommon.   John Drury Rare Books   2015 - 22272   2015 $1136

Smythies, Harriet Maria *The Prince and the People: a Poem.* London: William Skeffington, 1854. First edition, royal 8vo., minor stain to prelims in gutter, not affecting text, contemporary presentation binding, upper board with central red morocco inlay lettered gilt, spine tooled gilt, expertly repaired at foot, minor stain visible to boards, not detracting from this being handsome and appealing copy.   Marlborough Rare Books Ltd.   List 49 - 32   2015   £485

Snap Shots of Cloudcroft, New Mexico. N.P.: n.d., 3 x 5 inches, limp suede covers with a string tie and 12 photos on individual sheets.   Dumont Maps and Books of the West   130 - 27   2015 $95

Snell, Charles *The Art of Writing In Its Theory and Practice.* London: Henry Overton, 1712. Oblong 8vo., half leather, marbled paper covered boards, cover scrubbed and scuffed, bookplate on front pastedown, front free endpapers creased, lacks title, one plate and 6 leaves of text (all supplied in Xerox), one leaf torn near center, other leaves with small tears near corners, few ink notations by Wm. Parrish in text.   Oak Knoll Books   Special Catalogue 24 - 51   2015 $500

Snell, George D. *Search for Rational Ethics.* New York: Springer, 1988. First edition, 8vo., fine in fine dust jacket.   By the Book, L. C.   Special List 10 - 86   2015 $325

Snodgrass, W. D. *After Experience: Poems and Translations.* New York: Harper & Row, 1968. First edition, signed by author, 8vo., original cloth, fine in dust jacket.   James S. Jaffe Rare Books   Modern American Poetry - 260   2015 $100

Snodgrass, W. D. *Heart's Needle.* New York: Knopf, 1959. First edition, limited to 1500 copies, 8vo., original red cloth, dust jacket, inscribed by author for William Targ on titlepage.   James S. Jaffe Rare Books   Modern American Poetry - 259   2015 $450

Snow, Edgar *The Other Side of the River/Red China Today.* New York: Random House, 1962. First edition, large 8vo., 810 pages, near fine in very good dust jacket with short tears and small chip at bottom of rear spine fold.   Beasley Books   2013 - 2015 $125

Snyder, Gary *Mountains and Rivers Without End.* Washington: Counterpoint, 1996. Uncorrected proof, hint of sunning, else fine in wrappers, from the library of Clayton Eshleman with his notes in text.   Ken Lopez, Bookseller   164 - 189   2015 $85

Snyder, Gary *Montagnes et Rivieres Sans Fin. (Mountains and Rivers Without End).* Monaco: Editions du Rocher, 2002. Uncorrected proof, fine wrappers, with a snapshot of Snyder, inscribed by author for Clayton (Eshleman).   Ken Lopez, Bookseller   164 - 190   2015 $125

Snyder, Gary *A Range of Poems.* London: Fulcrum Press, 1966. First edition, special issue, one of only 50 copies signed by author, out of a total edition of 100 numbered copies printed on Glastonbury antique laid paper, frontispiece, illustrations by Will Peterson, original brown cloth, white dust jacket, very fine.   James S. Jaffe Rare Books   Modern American Poetry - 261   2015 $2250

Snyder, Gary *Regarding Wave.* Iowa City: Windhover Press, 1969. First edition, one of 280 numbered copies, printed on Shogun paper and signed by author, few spots of discoloration on back cover, otherwise fine, 8vo., original cloth.   James S. Jaffe Rare Books   Modern American Poetry - 262   2015 $450

Snyder, Gary *Smokey the Bear Sutra.* Oakland: RatArt Press, 1993. First edition in book form, one of only 25 numbered copies, (entire edition) signed by author and printer, Michael Henninger, large 8vo., illustrations, original pictorial plywood covers tied with cord, very fine.   James S. Jaffe Rare Books   Modern American Poetry - 263   2015 $2500

Snyder, Gary *Turtle Island.* New York: New Directions, 1974. First edition, inscribed by author for fellow author Peter Matthiessen, moderate rubbing and staining to covers, very good in wrappers, wonderful inscription and excellent association.   Ken Lopez, Bookseller   164 - 186   2015 $1000

Soaring. Wilmington: 1946-1962. Volumes 10-26, 120 issues, all in excellent condition.   Bookworm & Silverfish 2015 - 2279425985   2015 $450

Societe Oeconomique De Berne *Essays on the Spirit of Legislation in the Encouragement of Agriculture, Population, Manufactures and Commerce.* London: W. Nicoll and G. Robinson, 1772. First edition in English, 8vo., occasional browning and light spotting, contemporary calf backed marbled boards, raised bands, crimson label lettered in gilt, little wear to joints but very good.   John Drury Rare Books 2015 - 14891   2015 $656

Societe Pou L'Avancement De L'Instruction Religieuse de la Jeunesse *Rapport fait a la Societe, sur els deux Ecoles Lancastriennes etablier par cette Societe..* J. J. Padshoud, 1820. 8vo., few browned patches, mostly on outer leaves, inscription at head of title "Monsieur le Prof. de la Rive" (cropped?), well bound in cloth, lettered gilt, very good.   John Drury Rare Books   March 2015 - 17878 2015 $266

Society for Bettering the Condition and Increasing the Comforts of the Poor *The Reports of the Society.... Volume I-Volume V.* London: printed for th Society by W. Bulmer and Co., 1808. (1798), Reports 1-30 in 5 volumes, contemporary marbled boards, uniformly rebacked fairly recently in calf, gilt lettered and lines, in very good state of preservation.   John Drury Rare Books   2015 - 22421 2015 $3234

Society for Italic Handwriting *Bulletin of the Society for Italic Handwriting.* London: Figaro Press, 1955-1958. Issues 3-15, tall 12mo., stiff paper wrappers, pagination varies between 20 and 30 pages, 13 issues in quarter cloth portfolio, ribbon ties.   Oak Knoll Books   Special Catalogue 24 - 6   2015 $120

Society for the Acclimatisation of Animals *First Annual Report of the Society for the Acclimatisation of Animals, Birds, Fishes, Insects and Vegetables Within the United Kingdom.* London: printed for the Society, Temporary offices, 346 Strand, 1861. Little dusted with old vertical fold, bound in functional library red cloth binding with blindstamp of British Library of Political and Economic Science on front board, library stamps on title.   Jarndyce Antiquarian Booksellers   CCXI - 261   2015   £50

Society for the Diffusion of Useful Knowledge *An Address to the Labourers on the Subject of Destroying Machinery.* London: Charles Knight, 1830. First edition, 8vo., 8 pages, unbound and unopened as issued, very good.   John Drury Rare Books   March 2015 - 20833 2015   £266

Society for the Encouragement of Arts, Manufactures & Commerce *Report addressed to the Council by the Special Committee on the Statistics of Dwellings Improvement in the Metropolis.* London: printed by Simpkins, 1864. First edition, 8vo., 48 pages, inner margin of title and final leaf stained by tape (not affecting printed surface), light dust soiling, recently well bound in linen backed marbled boards, lettered, good, scarce.   John Drury Rare Books   March 2015 - 18609   2015 $221

Society of Arts *Report of the Committee of the Society of Arts, &c. Together with the Approved Communications and evidence Upon the Same....* London: sold by the housekeeper at the Society's house in the Adelphi, 1819. First and only edition, royal 8vo., 6 engraved plates, one folding, complete with half title, small 19th century stamp of London Institution on blank margin of title, fine old style half calf over marbled boards, spine gilt with raised bands and label, fine, unusually for this book, completely free of foxing, scarce. John Drury Rare Books   2015 - 20820   2015 $1311

Society of British Artists *The Exhibition of the Society of British Artists, Suffolk Street, Pall Mall East MDCCCXXIV. The First.* London: Davidson and Son, 1824. First edition, 4to., page 4 cropped at lower margin affecting two words which are still legible, recent marbled boards lettered on spine, rare.   John Drury Rare Books   2015 - 24946   2015 $878

Society of California Pioneers *Quarterly of the Society of California Pioneers Volume I. No. 1 - Volume IX No. 4.* San Francisco: 1924-1932. Together the first 36 consecutive issues, illustrations, portraits, maps, facsimiles, original light blue printed wrappers, spines faded to white, else very fine set, housed in custom slipcase.   Argonaut Book Shop Holiday Season 2014 - 269   2015 $750

Society of California Pioneers *The Society of California Pioneers Centennial Roster.* San Francisco: Society of California Pioneers May 1, 1948. Commemorative edition, frontispiece, publisher's blue suede wrappers, front cover and spine bit faded, else fine.   Argonaut Book Shop Holiday Season 2014 - 270   2015 $75

Society of Friends *Some Account of the Conduct of the Religious Society of Friends Towards the Indian Tribes in the Settlement of the Colonies of East and West Jersey and Pennsylvania.* London: The Aborigines' Committee of the Meeting for Sufferings, 1844. Color frontispiece map, occasional slight waterstaining to upper margin, partially unopened in handsome half calf, marbled boards, raised bands, spine decorated gilt, green label.   Jarndyce Antiquarian Booksellers   CCXI - 262   2015   £225

Society of Lincoln's Inn *Records of the Honorable Society of Lincoln's Inn, The Black Books Volumes 1-5 (1422 to 1914).* London: Lincoln's Inn, 1897-1968. First edition, 5 volumes, large stout octavo, original dark green buckram, handsome, very good+ set with slight fading and slight rubbing and some differential fading to rear board of first volume, folding plates, plans.   Any Amount of Books 2015 - A36276   2015   £150

Society of the Framers of the Constitution of the State of Montana *Third and Fourth Renunion of the.... 1911 and 1916.* Butte: 1916. or 1917. First edition thus, pictorial stapled wrappers, 40 pages, illustrations, laid in TLS from Walter Bickford, Asst. sec. & letter of receipt from Peter Schmidt, son of member of constitutional convention, one page creased and section bracketed in pencil, back cover almost detached and tear repaired, unusual, scarce, fair. Baade Books of the West   2014 - 2015 $91

Soddy, Frederick *The Interpretation of the Atom.* London: John Murray, 1932. First edition, 8vo., 2 foldout tables, rare in original printed dust jacket, book and jacket very good++, foxing, owner bookplate.   By the Book, L. C. 44 - 19   2015 $800

Sohncke, L. A. *Bibliotheca Mathematica.* Leipzig: Wilhelm Engelmann, 1854. 4to., foxed, later green buckram, gilt stamped spine title with original front wrapper preserved, cloth faded, former library copy, very good, rare. Jeff Weber Rare Books   178 - 1028   2015 $85

Soldans *Specimen Book of Bauer Types.* London: Soldans, n.d. but circa, 1935-1937. Second edition, 3 volumes, 4to., cloth spine and front covers stamped, corners of first volume bumped, spines of first two volumes lightly sunned.   Oak Knoll Books   306 - 227   2015 $450

Soliday, George W. *A Descriptive Checklist, Together with Short Title Index Describing Almost 7500 Items of Western Americana.* New York: Antiquarian Press Ltd., 1960. First combined edition, reprint, one of 550 copies of which 500 were for sale, 4 parts plus index bound in one volume, frontispiece, dark green cloth, gilt, very fine.   Argonaut Book Shop   Holiday Season 2014 - 271   2015 $125

Solis Y Rivadeneira, Antonio De   1610-1686 *Histoire de la Conqueste du Mexique ou de la Nouvelle Espagne par Fernand Cortez.* Paris: Chez Henry Charpentier, 1704. Third French edition, 2 maps and 12 further plates, most folding, head and tailpieces, 12mo., contemporary mottled calf, five raised bands, spine labels, compartments decorated in gilt, armorial gilt emboss on boards, very good, spines quite rubbed, few small splits at upper joints, closed tear to i5, one plate slightly worn at top edge, minor marginal foxing, few owner's marks, bookseller's label on pastedowns. Kaaterskill Books   19 - 142   2015 $750

Solity, Jonathan *The Learning Revolution.* London: Hodder Education/Hachette Livre, 2008. First edition, 8vo., original publisher's black cloth lettered silver on spine, fine in fine dust jacket.   Any Amount of Books   2015 - C821 2015   £180

Sollid, Roberta Beed *Calamity Jane. A Study in Historical Criticism.* Montana: The Western Press Historical Society of Montana, 1958. First edition, number 942 of 2000 copies, numerous plates from photos, tan cloth, lettered in red, owner's small address sticker, fine, worn and spine faded dust jacket.   Argonaut Book Shop   Holiday Season 2014 - 272   2015 $90

Solly, Henry *Our Sunday Schools: Six months among them.* London: E. T. Whitfield, 1858. First edition, 12mo., including final ad leaf, light dust marked, recently well bound in linen backed marbled boards, lettered, good copy, apparently very rare.   John Drury Rare Books   2015 - 18610 2015 $177

Solomon, Charles *The Prince of Egypt.* New York: Abrams, 1998. First edition, 4to., signed by author and 10 of the animation supervisors, one of whom has added a pen drawing of the young Moses, numerous full color drawings as well as sketches in black and white, fine in fine dust jacket.   Ed Smith Books   83 - 16   2015 $250

Solow, Robert M. *Growth Theory and After.* Sweden: Nobel Foundation, 1988. First separate edition, offprint, original printed wrappers, fine.   By the Book, L. C.   44 - 49 2015 $150

Solt, Andrew *Imagine: John Lennon.* New York: Macmillan, 1989. First edition, large 4to., 255 pages, original black cloth over grey boards, lettered silver at spine, copiously illustrated in color and black and white throughout, signed presentation from Yoko Ono for Victor Spinetti (1929-2012) actor, poet, author.   Any Amount of Books   March 2015 - C12727   2015   £450

Solzhenitsyn, Aleksandr *Bodalsja Telenok s Dubom.* Paris: YMCA Press, 1975. First Russian language edition, printed on India paper, 8vo., original grey plastic wrappers stamped in black to front, backstrip lettered in black, very good.   Blackwell's Rare Books   B179 - 239   2015   £100

Some Papers Hand Made by John Mason. London: Maggs, 1959. First edition, limited to 100 numbered copies, 8vo., parchment backed paper covered boards with actual leafs inlaid in both covers, enclosed in cardboard box with paper over label, 32 leaves, very fine, illustrations. Oak Knoll Books 306 - 99 2015 $655

Some Verses on the Death of Our Late Sovereign King William of Blessed Memory with an Epitaph... N.P.: London? printed in the year, 1702. First edition, small 8vo., disbound, bit dust soiled, old stab holes from prior binding, generally very good. C. R. Johnson Foxon R-Z - 912r-z 2015 $1149

Somervile, William 1675-1742 *The Chace. A Poem.* London: printed for G. Hawkins and sold by T. Cooper, 1735. First octavo edition, recent half calf and marbled boards, some spotting at beginning and end, otherwise good copy, entirely uncut, binding bit amateurish. C. R. Johnson Foxon R-Z - 916r-z 2015 $115

Somervile, William 1675-1742 *The Chace.* London: printed for G. Hawkins and sold by T. Cooper, 1735. Third edition, 8vo., contemporary calf, gilt, spine gilt, remains of old manuscript title label, fine. C. R. Johnson Foxon R-Z - 917r-z 2015 $153

Somervile, William 1675-1742 *The Chace, a Poem.* London: printed for J. Stagg, G. Hawkins and sold by M. Cooper, 1743. Fourth edition, 8vo., disbound, very good. C. R. Johnson Foxon R-Z - 918r-z 2015 $77

Somervile, William 1675-1742 *Hobbinol, or the Rural Games.* London: printed for J. Stagg, 1740. First edition, 4to., later board, red morocco label (trifle rubbed), very good. C. R. Johnson Foxon R-Z - 920r-z 2015 $613

Somervile, William 1675-1742 *Hobbinol, or the Rural Games.* London: printed for J. Stagg, 1740. Second edition, 4to., disbound, excellent condition. C. R. Johnson Foxon R-Z - 921r-z 2015 $115

Somervile, William 1675-1742 *Hobbinol, or the Rural Games.* London: printed for J. Stagg, 1740. Third edition, 8vo., disbound, very good. C. R. Johnson Foxon R-Z - 022r-z 2015 $77

Somervile, William 1675-1742 *Occasional Poems, Translations, Tales &c.* London: printed for Bernard Lintot, 1727. First edition, 8vo., contemporary calf, gilt, rebacked, much of original spine preserved, later brown morocco label, very good inscription "Mr. Thos. D. Llewelyn's book bought of Mr. Wm. Davies bookseller Aberdeen Dec. 30th 1863", later bookplate of Oliver Brett, Viscount Esher. C. R. Johnson Foxon R-Z - 913r-z 2015 $460

Somervile, William 1675-1742 *Occasional Poems, Translations, Fables, Tales, &c.* London: printed for Bernard Lintot, 1727. First edition, 8vo., contemporary speckled calf, spine gilt, red morocco label, joints repaired, top of spine little chipped, presentation copy inscribed "Eliz. Mason her book. Given by the Author" presumably in hand of recipient, very good, later bookplate of Sir Humphrey Edmund de Trafford, Bart. C. R. Johnson Foxon R-Z - 914r-z 2015 $1149

Something for Every Body; or the Last Will and Testament of a Welch Man, Lately Deceased. London: printed for W. Rayner and sold by the booksellers of London and Westminster, 1729. First edition thus, 4to., recent wrappers, very good. C. R. Johnson Foxon R-Z - 1106r-z 2015 $2298

Sommerfeld, Arnold *Atomic Structure and Special Lines.* New York: Dutton, n.d., 1923. First US edition, 8vo., original olive green cloth, lettered gilt on spine and on front cover, illustrations, ex-library with inked number at spine and chipped at spine ends, somewhat sound, near very good with clean text. Any Amount of Books 2015 - C14642 2015 £175

Sommerville, Duncan M. Y. *Bibliography of Non-Euclidean Geometry...* London: Harrison & Sons for the University of St. Andrews, 1911. 8vo., printed wrappers, front cover starting, covers bit chipped at extremities, good+. Jeff Weber Rare Books 178 - 1031 2015 $50

The Song of the Robin-Redbreast Turn'd Canary-Bird. London: printed and sold by J. Roberts, 1715. First edition, 8vo., 23 pages, disbound, fine, rare. C. R. Johnson Foxon R-Z - 923r-z 2015 $1149

Songs the Gang Will Sing Printed Especially for the Boys of the Second Montana. Helena: Helena Independent, 1917. Printed pictorial wrappers, (16) pages, vignette drawings, fair copy with long tear along binding edge of front cover, now archivally closed, chip on back corner, scarce, fair. Baade Books of the West 2014 - 2015 $45

Sonnichsen,, C. L. *Colonel Green and the Copper Skyrocket.* Tucson: University of Arizona Press, 1974. First edition, 67 photos, few maps, green cloth, gilt lettering, very fine in lightly rubbed and wrinkled pictorial dust jacket, presentation inscription signed by author. Argonaut Book Shop Holiday Season 2014 - 273 2015 $150

Sons of the Copper Beeches *Leaves from the Copper Beeches.* Philadelphia: Baker Street Irregulars, 1959. First edition, fine, short tear along bottom edge of back cover, otherwise fine without dust jacket as issued. Mordida Books March 2015 - 007880 2015 $125

Sontag, Susan *Women.* New York: Random House, 1999. First edition, small folio, Annie Leibovitz presentation inscription for Lena Horne, very good plus, small abrasion to rear pastedown in very good plus dust jacket.   Ed Smith Books   83 - 47   2015 $1500

Soos, Troy *Murder at Fenway Park.* New York: Kensington, 1994. First edition, fine in dust jacket.   Mordida Books   March 2015 - 002361   2015 $135

Sophia *Woman Not Inferior to Man; or a Short and Modest Vindication of the Natural Right of the Fair-Sex to a Perfect Equality of Power, Dignity and Esteem with Men.* London: printed for John Hawkins at the Falcon in St. Paul's Church Yard, 1739. First edition, 8vo., half title, without final leaf of ads, half title little soiled, few leaves creased, well bound recently by Trevor Lloyd in contemporary style half calf over marbled boards, spine gilt and lettered with raised bands, very good, uncut.   John Drury Rare Books   2015 - 26113   2015 $6906

Sophocles *Oedipe Roi.* Paris: Romagnol Librairie De La Collection Des Dix, 1922. Limited to 300 copies, this copy marked HC, wrappers are some soiled and spine lightly creased, small 4to., illustrations by Raphael Freide.   Beasley Books   2013 - 2015 $500

Sophocles *Quae Exstant Omnia cum Veterum Grammaticorum Scholiis.* Strasbourg: Apud Joannem Georgium Treuttel, 1786. First Brunck edition, bound without final leaf in volume ii (blank except for colophon on verso, often missing), few minor spots, early ms. date to volume i title, 4to., contemporary russia, boards bordered with gilt roll with torch tools at corners, spines divided by double gilt fillet, second and fourth compartments gilt lettered direct, rest with central gilt tool of mask and instruments, all edges gilt, marbled endpapers, front board of volume I with prize inscription lettered direct in gilt and enclosed on top and sides by gilt flower and pearl tools, old repair to spine ends in slightly different color, some cracking to front joint of volume i, few old scratches and marks, bookplate of author Nevil Shute and lending label of Sandford Press, good.   Blackwell's Rare Books   Greek & Latin Classics VI - 97   2015   £750

Sorbin, Arnaud De *Tractatus de Monstris, que a Temporibus Constantini Bucusque Ortum Babuerunt ac ies Quae Circa Eorum te(m)pora Misere Acciderunt, ex Historiarum...* Paris: apud Hieronimum de Marnet & Gulielmum Cavellat sub Pelicano, 1570. First edition, 12mo., 14 woodcut illustrations, woodcut printer's device on titlepage, contemporary limp vellum, bold contemporary mss. title in ink on spine, lower edge with fine contemporary mss. of author and abbreviated title, ties perished, neat 17th century mss. ownership inscription on titlepage P. Marie Boschetti, 18th century unreadable ecclesiastical library stamp on verso of titlepage and verso of final leaf, minute neat mss. ownership inscription, engraved bookplate of Docteur Francois Mouteir, c. 1920, some light browning, but very good.   Maggs Bros. Ltd.   Illustrated Books 2014 - 2015   £2500

Soren, John *The Narrative of Mr John Soren a Native of the United States of America, Piratically Captured on the High Seas...* London: printed at the Oriental press by Wilson & Co. wild Court, Lincoln's Inn Fields, 1800. Bound without initial ad leaf, for J. Hatchard in 19th century half calf, spine lettered gilt, plain paper boards.   Jarndyce Antiquarian Booksellers   CCXI - 263   2015   £380

Sorenson, Alfred *Early History of Omaha.* Omaha: printed at the office of the Daily Bee, 1876. First edition, 8vo., original orange cloth, brown endpapers, frontispiece, illustrations, bookplate of Ames Free Library, library stamp on frontispiece and titlepage, removal of library cards rear pastedown and flyleaf, rear spine starting to loosen, light wear to spine ends, else good, tight.   Buckingham Books   March 2015 - 31024   2015 $175

Sorrentino, Gilbert *Steelwork.* New York: Pantheon, 1970. Uncorrected proof, inscribed by author to well known bookseller and book collector, padbound proof, front cover detached but present, thus only good copy, scarce, especially signed.   Ken Lopez, Bookseller   164 - 194   2015 $150

Sotheby, Wilkinson & Hodge *The J. E. Hodgkin Collections. Catalogue of The Works of Art Including Porcelain and Pottery, Glass, Fans, Furniture, Pewter, Netsuke, Gems...* London: Sotheby Wilkinson & Hodge, 1914. 8vo., cloth, variously paginated, 5 catalogs, rubbed and scuffed at edges, light foxing.   Oak Knoll Books   306 - 76   2015 $125

Sotheby, William *A Tour Through Parts of Wales.* London: printed by J. Smeeton for R. Blamire, 1794. First edition, 295 x 229mm, extremely handsome dark blue straight grain morocco, elaborately decorated in gilt and blind by Lubbock of Newcastle (their ticket on front free endpaper), covers with intricate frame in gilt and blind (featuring stippling, fleurons, drawer handles, wreaths, etc.), large central panel of an unusual design with blind stamped lozenge at center and horizontal blindstamped boards above and below, all enclosed by double gilt fillets (to form a large "I" with a convex vertical element) raised bands, space panels with gilt or blind tooled fleurons, wide densely gilt turn-ins with inlaid red morocco cornerpieces, marbled endpapers, all edges gilt, with modern fore-edge painting showing three landscape vignettes, castle ruins, an arched bridge, and a castle by the sea, surrounded by colored volutes, fruits and cornucopia, 13 sepia tone engravings of Welsh castles and scenery after J. Smith, front pastedown with engraved armorial bookplate of Ravensworth Castle, titlepage with ink ownership inscription of T. H. Liddell, this the copy of (and most likely bound for) Thomas Henry Liddell, 1st Baron Ravensworth; corners and extremities little rubbed joints slightly flaked, but well masked with dye, faint offsetting from engravings, otherwise fine copy, binding lustrous and without significant wear and text and plates with only most trivial imperfections. Phillip J. Pirages 66 - 56 2015 $6500

Sous La Colline. Paris: H. Floury, 1908. First French edition, small 4to., one of 1000 copies, frontispiece photos, several Beardsley illustrations and bookplate, top edge gilt, gray paper over boards, stamped with gilt and red lettering, cover slightly worn at corners and at ends of spine, else very good. Second Life Books Inc. 190 - 12 2015 $350

Soutar, Andrew *Secret Ways.* New York: Kendall, 1934. First American edition, name and date on front endpaper, otherwise near fine in dust jacket with chipped and frayed top of spine, faded spine and closed tear. Mordida Books March 2015 - 009163 2015 $100

South Carolina. Legislature *Reports and Resolutions of the General Assembly of the State of South Carolina, Passed at the Annual Session of 1863. (and) Journal of the House of Representatives of the State of South Carolina. Being the session of 1863. (and) Journal of the Senate of South Carolina. Being the Session of 1863.* Columbia: Charles P. Pelham, State printer, 1863. First editions, tall 8vo., late cloth, very sound and clean, fore and lower edges uncut, soiling to lower edges, first title leaf very soiled, small fraying, scattered foxing. M & S Rare Books, Inc. 97 - 74 2015 $600

South Kensington Museum *Conferences Held in Connection with the Special Loan Collection of Scientific Apparatus 1876. Chemistry, Biology, Physical Geography, Geology, Mineralogy and Meteorology.* London: Chapman and Hall, 1876. 8vo., original dark green black lined cloth, gilt spine, presentation bookplate from the Committee, South Kensington Museum, presentation copy, very good+, scarce. Jeff Weber Rare Books 178 - 1036 2015 $85

South Kensington Museum *Conferences Held in Connection with the Special Loan Collection of Scientific Apparatus 1876. Physics and Mechanics.* London: Chapman and Hall, 1876. 8vo,. original dark green black lined cloth, gilt spine, rubbed, bottom of spine worn, presentation bookplate from Committee, South Kensington Museum, presentation copy, scarce. Jeff Weber Rare Books 178 - 1035 2015 $95

South, Robert *Musica Incantans sive Poema Experimens Musicae Vires, Juvenem in Insaniam Adigentis...* London: typis & impensis H. Hills, n.d., 1709. 8vo., disbound, every good, 14 pages + final leaf of bookseller's ads, very good copy. C. R. Johnson Foxon R-Z - 1232r-z 2015 $77

Southcott, Joanna *An Answer to Thomas Paine's Third Part of the Age of Reason..* London: printed by Marchant and Galabin, 1812. First edition, 8vo., attractively bound in old style quarter calf gilt, very good, scarce. John Drury Rare Books 2015 - 15701 2015 $656

Southcott, Joanna *Copies of Letters Sent to the Clergy of Exeter, from 1796 to 1800 with Communications and Prophecies Put in the Newspapers in 1813.* London: Marchant and Galabin, 1813. 8vo., 64 pages, disbound, bit dusty, good copy. John Drury Rare Books 2015 - 21243 2015 $89

Southcott, Joanna *Joanna Southcott's Answer to Five Charges in the Leeds Mercury, four of Which are Absolutely False, but as in the first Charge, Her Accuser Might Have Some Room for Cavilling, She Wishes to Make Every Allowance; and Give a clear Answer, How that Was Misunderstood and Not only to Answer the Four False Charges Against Her Adversaries, which Will be Seen in the Following Pages.* London: printed by A. Seale, Sold by E. J. Field &c., 1805. First edition, 8vo., 24 pages, outer leaves rather dust marked, recent marbled boards lettered on spine, good copy. John Drury Rare Books 2015 - 21255 2015 $177

Southcott, Joanna *Letters and Communications of Joanna Southcott, the Prophetess of Exeter; lately written to Jane Townley... June 1804.* Stourbridge: printed by J. Heming, 1804. First edition, 8vo., 128 pages, recently well bound in linen backed marbled boards lettered, fine. John Drury Rare Books March 2015 - 21241 2015 $221

Southcott, Joanna *Sound an Alarm in My Holy Mountain.* Leeds: E. Baines, 1804. 8vo., 76 pages, disbound, very good. John Drury Rare Books 2015 - 21263 2015 $133

Southern Pacific Passenger Cars. Volume 3: Head End Equipment. Pasadena: Southern Pacific Historical and Technical Society, 2007. First edition, oblong quarto, color and black and white photos, car diagrams, rosters, etc., gray cloth, very fine, as new with pictorial dust jacket. Argonaut Book Shop Holiday Season 2014 - 274 2015 $150

Southern Workman. Hampton: Hampton Normal and Agricultural Institute, 1918-1919. Wrappers, a run of 24 consecutive issues, very good+ to near fine copies, small 4to.   Beasley Books   2013 - 2015 $500

Southey, Robert   1774-1843   *The Life of Nelson.* London: printed for Joh Murray, 1813. First edition, 8vo., full leather lettered gilt on red leather labels, frontispiece of volume on depicts a portrait of Nelson and frontispiece of volume two shows gradual decline of Nelson's handwriting, from the library of playwright John Osborne, some rubbing and slight cracking along spine hinges but holding fast, few missing chips at foot of spines, slight edge wear and rubbing at corner tips, otherwise clean, very good.   Any Amount of Books   2015 - C7943   2015   £300

Southey, Thomas   *Chronological History of the West Indies.* London: Longman, Rees, Orme, Brown and Green, 1827. First edition, scarce, 8vo., 3 volumes, original paper covered boards, rebacked, three quarter morocco over marbled boards, marbled endpapers, gilt titles and decoration, very good, unmatched set, chips to tail of spine in volume II, all boards scuffed, spine ends rubbed, front hinge starting in volume III, occasional marginalia, extensive notes on endpapers in volume 1, few leaves with creased corners. Kaaterskill Books   19 - 143   2015 $750

Souvenir of Galveston Texas 90 Views.   Galveston: 1897. 12 accordion leaves with multiple images on each, larger than usual at 9 1/2 x 6 1/4 inches original printed boards, rubbed with loss of color to spine and extremities, binding reinforced internally minor loss to top and bottom of some of the leaves at folds, previous owner's name on first leaf. Dumont Maps and Books of the West   130 - 34   2015 $125

Souvenir of Newport. "The City By the Sea".   Newport: Pub. by Walter Sherman for J. F. Murphy, O. C. Depot, circa, 1885. First edition, square 16mo, embossed boards with title gilt on upper cover, binding worn at extremities, single sheet of glazed stock accordion folded to form 16 leaves, tipped to front board with map printed on rear pastedown. M & S Rare Books, Inc.   97 - 273   2015 $85

Sowerby, James   1757-1822   *A New Elucidation of Colours Showing Their Concordance in Three Primitives...* London: Printed by Richard Taylor and Co. Shoe Lane, 1809. 4to., 7 engraved plates, including 5 hand colored original boards, spine defective, upper cover with original printed label, armorial bookplate of Captain Sir Christopher Cole KB, the Honeyman copy.   Marlborough Rare Books List 54 - 80   2015   £2500

Sowerby, John Edward   1825-1870   *The Ferns of Great Britain. (with) The Fern Allies: a supplement.*   London: Henry G. Bohn, 1859. Octavo, 80 hand colored plates, publisher's (?) handsome blindstamped and decorated cloth, all edges gilt, few occasional spots and signature on front endpaper, fine.   Andrew Isles   2015 - 15220   2015 $1650

Spackman, William Frederick   *An Analysis of the Occupations of the People.*   London: Reynell and Weight, 1847. First edition, 8vo., unopened folding chart at rear, full brown leather lettered gilt at spine on red label, 5 raised bands, sound, very good copy with some rubbing at spine and some scuffing to leather at front corners, some text slightly browned, overall decent copy, rare.   Any Amount of Books   2015 - A47674   2015   £260

Spafford, Horatio Gates   *The Mother-in-Law or Memoirs of Madam de Morville.*   Boston: published by A. Bowan and sold by Cummings and Hilliard, 1817. First edition, 12mo., recent gray paper boards with original printed upper board laid on, untrimmed, frontispiece and one plate, one leaf of publisher's terminal ads, some minor stains to prelims and titlepage, very good.   The Brick Row Book Shop   Miscellany 67 - 10   2015 $650

Spalding, John   *A Few Reasons for Leaving the National Established Mode of Worship, Addressed principally to Those who Attend at the Place Called St. Giles's Church, Reading.*   London: printed and sold by James Phillips, 1794. First edition, 12mo., without ad leaf, but including half title, preserved in original blue wrappers, entirely uncut, very good with contemporary ink note "For James Pemberton", very scarce.   John Drury Rare Books   2015 - 25132   2015 $177

Spangenberg, Johannes *Postilla. Das Ist: Auslegung Der Episteln Und Evangelien...* Luneburg: Sternische Buchdruckerey, 1794. 219 x 137mm., 3 parts in 1 volume, striking engraved Repousse Silver Binding (probably 18th century German), covers with a beaded border surrounding a broad ornate frame featuring flowers, volutes and cherubs, this frame enclosing a central medallion portraying a scene from the Old Testament, spine divided into three compartments by beaded frames, top with grotesque face surrounded by flowers and arabesques, middle featuring Moses with the Ten Commandments, and the bottom with device for Faith, Hope and Charity framed by volutes, silver head and tail guards (in the form of a winged cherub) extending from the backstrip over a short portion of top and bottom of text block, two silver clasps depicting a male and female saint, presumably recased perhaps in the 19th century; with printer's device on titlepages and 64 woodcut illustrations (measuring approximately 80 x 11mm); titlepage backed, front hinge cracked (causing little looseness, though everything still intact), leaves rather soiled from use, two leaves with tears from fore-edge into text (affecting two lines of text, tears secured at fore edge with transparent tape), third part of the volume bit dampstained, final leaf reattached, its verse with loss of approximately half a column of text along gutter, not without condition problems, but text fresh, and original splendid binding still well preserved, silver lustrous and altogether pleasing. Phillip J. Pirages 66 - 55 2015 $9500

Spankie, Robert *A second Letter from Mr. Sergeant Spankie to His Constituents of the Metropolitan Borough of Finsbury.* London: Roake and Varty, 1834. First edition, 8vo., 16 pages, preserved in modern wrappers with printed title label on upper cover, some carelessly opened leaves, else good, large copy, rare. John Drury Rare Books 2015 - 19094 2015 $89

Spark, Muriel *Emily Bronte: Her Life and Work.* London: Peter Owen Ltd., 1960. Octavo, original orange cloth, original dust jacket. Honey & Wax Booksellers 2 - 11 2015 $750

Spark, Muriel *The Prime of Miss Jean Brodie.* Philadelphia: New York: Lippincott, 1962. First American edition, fine in fine, price clipped dust jacket, aside from clipped dust jacket, immaculate copy, from the library of Kate Stettner Lobell and Carl D. Lobell. Between the Covers Rare Books 196 - 34 2015 $500

Spatz, H. Donald *Murder with Long Hair.* New York: Phoenix Press, 1940. First edition, former owner's name on front flyleaf, covers little soiled, else very good in dust jacket with light professional restoration to spine ends and fore-corners. Buckingham Books March 2015 - 22449 2015 $375

Speaking Picture Book. New York: FAO Schwartz, n.d. circa, 1893. 16th edition, large 4to., red cloth with pictorial paste-on, carved wood edges painted gold, some soil and rubbing on covers, edge repairs on some pages, else very good+. Aleph-bet Books, Inc. 109 - 309 2015 $1800

Spear, Charles *An Appeal to the Friends of Humanity.* Boston: Prisoners' Friend Office, 1854. First edition, 8vo., text illustrations, sewn as issued, sheets browned, stitching loosened. M & S Rare Books, Inc. 97 - 247 2015 $175

Specimens of Heraldic Painting, Illuminating &c... Great Yarmouth: 1905. Small 4to., 8 illuminations in gold and colors, 8 photographic reproductions, 6 binding samples, 6 endpaper samples, decorating binding sample and crest interleaved in calligraphic manuscript bound in straight grained red roan by C. A. Campling Ltd. binders Gt. Yarmouth, rebacked, lettered gilt on upper cover. Marlborough Rare Books List 53 - 22 2015 £850

A Speech in Behalf of the Constitution, Against the Suspending and Dispensing Prerogative &c. London: J. Almon, 1767. First edition, first edition, 8vo., little dampstaining at beginning and end, recently well bound in linen backed marled boards, lettered, good. John Drury Rare Books March 2015 - 19836 2015 $266

A Speech Without Doors. London: printed for A. Baldwin, 1710. First edition, early signature in ink on title, 8vo., last two or three leaves rather browned and foxed, recent plain wrappers, good. John Drury Rare Books March 2015 - 18330 2015 £306

Speed, Robert *The Counter Scuffle. a Poem.* London: printed and sold by booksellers of London and Westminster, 1710. 8vo., very good, recent stiff marbled wrappers, very good. C. R. Johnson Foxon R-Z - 1237r-z 2015 $115

Speke, John Hanning *What led to the Discovery of the Source of the Nile.* William Blackwood and Sons, 1864. First edition, 8vo., modern full leather, titles stamped in gold gilt on spine, raised bands, new front and rear endpapers, map, frontispiece, foldout map has some cellophane tape repairs on verso of few fold points, double page sketch map has old small cellophane tape repair verso to reinforce tiny closed tear, titlepage has small faint stamp of private library, minor wear to few internal pages, else near fine, tight copy. Buckingham Books March 2015 - 33305 2015 $2250

Spence, William *The Objections Against the Corn Bill Refuted...* London: Longman, Hurst Rees Orme and Brown, 1815. Second edition, 8vo., tiny hole in one text leaf just affecting couple of letters on recto and verso, recent marbled boards, lettered on spine, very good. John Drury Rare Books March 2015 - 24482 2015 $656

Spence, William *Tracts on Political Economy.* London: printed for Longman Hurst Rees, Orme and Brown, 1822. First collected edition, 8vo., half title, with individual titlepage for each part, original boards, sometime rebacked, label on spine defective, some wear to extremities, entirely uncut, very good.   John Drury Rare Books   2015 - 25370   2015 $1136

Spencer-Churchill, H. *Classic English Interiors.* New York: Rizzoli, 1992. First edition, 4to., fine in fine dust jacket, inscribed by author.   Beasley Books   2013 - 2015 $45

Spencer, Baldwin *Report on the Work of the Horn Expedition to Central Australia: Part three.* London: Dulau & Co., 1896. Quarto, 204 pages, uncolored plates, publisher's printed wrappers, very fragile with missing pieces, but all text present, scarce.   Andrew Isles   2015 - 18220   2015 $600

Spencer, Baldwin *Report on the Work of the Horn Expedition to Central Australia Part One.* London: Dulau & Co., 1896. Small quarto, 220 pages, folding map, publisher's handsome blue cloth, uncut, partly unopened, folded map at rear with tears, owner's signature on front pastedown, very good.   Andrew Isles   2015 - 15054   2015 $950

Spencer, Herbert *An Autobiography.* London: Williams & Norgate, 1904. First edition, 2 volumes, thick octavo, brown cloth gilt, very short tear crown volume one, slight foxing on titlepages, modest bumping at extremities, near fine set, signature "Thomas Hardy, Max Gate, Dorchester", one small note in pencil in index in unknown hand, possibly Hardy's.   Between the Covers Rare Books, Inc.   187 - 264   2015 $950

Spencer, Herbert *The Visible Word.* New York: Visual Communication Books, 1969. Second US edition, small 4to., cloth, 107 pages, dust jacket, very scarce, well preserved.   Oak Knoll Books   306 - 60   2015 $400

Spender, Stephen *Engaged in Writing: and the Fool and the Princess.* London: Hamish Hamilton, 1958. First edition, 8vo., original grey cloth lettered gilt at spine, signed presentation from author to writer Angus Wilson, Jan. 1958, very good+ in very slightly discolored but decent, very good dust jacket.   Any Amount of Books   2015 - C12512   2015   £160

Spender, Stephen *Poems.* New York: Random House, 1934. First American edition, rebound, top corner scorched or smoke damaged, good copy, warmly inscribed, ink has feathered a bit, probably from exposure to dampness, although no staining present, inscribed by author to Selden Rodman.   Between the Covers Rare Books, Inc.   187 - 265   2015 $300

Spender, Stephen *Poems for Spain.* London: Hogarth Press, 1939. First edition, slightly soiled, very good without dust jacket, inscribed by John Lehmann to his sister Beatrix.   Between the Covers Rare Books, Inc.   187 - 257   2015 $350

Spender, Stephen *Returning to Vienna 1947: Nine Sketches.* New York: Banyan Press, 1947. First edition, one of 350 numbered copies for sale (out of total edition of 500), tied decorated paper wrappers with printed label, small nicks and splitting along spine, otherwise handsome, very good copy, signed by author, Carl van Vechten's copy with his bookplate, inscribed by him to Milton Saul and Claude Fredericks, publishers at Banyan Press.   Between the Covers Rare Books, Inc.   187 - 266   2015 $250

Spender, Stephen *Returning to Vienna 1947: Nine Sketches.* New York: Banyan Press, 1947. First edition , one of 150 numbered copies for friends of author (out of total of 500), rebound in library style buckram, scorch marks at edges of few pages, clearly the book has been through a fire, else good or better, signed by author inscription by author of Selden Rodman.   Between the Covers Rare Books, Inc.   187 - 267   2015 $150

Spenser, Edmund   1552-1599 *Spenser's Faerie Queen.* London: George Allen Ruskin House, 1897. Limited to 1000 copies on handmade paper, 6 volumes, 4to., white clott, gilt pictorial panels, top edge gilt, very fine with original wrappers bound in as issued, housed in original cloth box (edges reinforced), 88 full page plates plus numerous partial page illustrations by Walter Crane, printed on fine handmade paper, magnificent set.   Aleph-bet Books, Inc.   109 - 111   2015 $5000

Spenser, Edmund   1552-1599 *Spenser's Minor Poems...* Chelsea: Ashendene Press, 1925. Limited to 200 copies, printed on paper of which 175 are for sale, large folio, printed in red, blue and black, numerous large and small Roman style initials, quarter brown calf over vellum boards, gilt stamped spine with seven raised bands, some natural vellum discoloration, near fine.   Heritage Book Shop   Holiday 2014 - 5   2015 $3000

Spenser, Edmund   1552-1599 *The Works.* London: printed for Jacob Tonson, 1715. First printing of this edition prepared by John Hughes, 191 x 121mm., exceptionally fine contemporary red morocco, covers bordered by plain gilt rule and dogtooth roll, raised bands, spines heavily gilt in compartments, with large central fleuron, feather cornerpieces, each spine with green morocco label, gilt turn-ins, marbled endpapers, all edges gilt, woodcut headpieces, tailpieces and initials and 19 engraved plates, intermittent neat pencil marks in margin, tiny dent to one board, light offsetting from engraved material, one opening with stain, couple of dozen leaves moderately browned, but all of these imperfections minor, the set being otherwise in outstanding contemporary condition, text especially fresh and clean, bindings lustrous and showing no significant signs of use.
Phillip J. Pirages   66 - 33   2015 $4800

Spicer, Jack *After Lorca.* San Francisco: White Rabbit Press, 1957. First edition, one of 26 lettered copies signed by Spicer and with drawing by poet on colophon page (out of a total edition of 500 copies on Olivetti Lexikon 80 by Robert Duncan, with cover design by Jess), although not noted, this copy came from the library of poet Jack Gilbert, Spicer has inscribed the colophon page, original drawing above printed colophon, 8vo., original pictorial wrappers, covers lightly soiled, otherwise very good, rare. James S. Jaffe Rare Books   Modern American Poetry - 264   2015 $5000

Spielmann, M. H., Mrs. *Love Family.* London: George Allen & sons, 1908. First edition, 8vo., cloth backed pictorial boards, 63 pages, some edge wear, very good, illustrations by Carlton Moore Park, 12 color plates, 38 black and white drawings, this copy inscribed by artist to the Chelsea Art Club with signed presentation slip laid in and with artist's own bookplate, special copy.   Aleph-bet Books, Inc.   109 - 340   2015 $250

Spies, Werner *Max Ernst Collages The Invention of the Surrealist Universe.* New York: Abrams, 1991. First edition, 4to., very good+ dust jacket with small tear on rear panel and slight lacking in freshness.   Beasley Books   2013 - 2015 $175

Spillane, Mickey *The Big Kill.* E. P. Dutton, 1951. First edition, inked inscription by author, four inked numbers on front pastedown sheet partially covered by dust jacket flap, else near fine in lightly rubbed dust jacket with minor wear to foot of spine and front corners, sharp copy.   Buckingham Books   March 2015 - 38471   2015 $2000

Spillane, Mickey *The Erection Set.* London: W. H. Allen, 1972. First edition, inscribed by author for Graham Lindsay, near fine in like dust jacket, from the collection of Duke Collier.   Royal Books   36 - 233   2015 $650

Spillane, Mickey *I the Jury.* London: Arthur Barker, 1952. First edition, very good plus in very good plus jacket, some light soil to boards, jacket has chip at crown (titling not affected) and couple of smaller chips at corners, light rubbing overall, from the collection of Duke Collier.   Royal Books   36 - 234   2015 $950

Spillane, Mickey *I the Jury. Vengeance is Mine. The Big Kill. My Gun is Quick. Kiss Me, Deadly.* New York: Avenel Books, 1987. First edition thus, signed by author, pages edges uniformly tanned, else fine in dust jacket, excellent one volume collection.   Buckingham Books March 2015 - 30170   2015 $300

Spillane, Mickey *I, the Jury.* Norwalk: Easton Press, 2003. Collector's edition, signed by author, laid in is certificate of authenticity by Spillane authenticating his signature in the book, very fine in leather bound boards with gilt page edges.   Mordida Books   March 2015 - 012616   2015 $250

Spillane, Mickey *The Long Wait.* London: Arthur Barker, 1953. First edition, fine in very good plus dust jacket, jacket has no loss, only some light fray at crown and light wear at few extremities, from the collection of Duke Collier.   Royal Books   36 - 237   2015 $300

Spillane, Mickey *My Gun is Quick.* New York: Dutton, 1950. First edition, some light spotting on endpapers and small stain to back cover, otherwise fine in dust jacket with couple of short closed tears, tiny wear at spine ends.   Mordida Books   March 2015 - 919573   2015 $2000

Spillane, Mickey *My Gun is Quick.* New York: Dutton, 1956. Second edition, fine in very good dust jacket with chipped spine ends, slightly darkened back panel, crease tear on front panel and wear at corners.   Mordida Books   March 2015 - 010341   2015 $250

Spillane, Mickey *One Lonely Night.* London: Arthur Barker, 1952. First edition, fine in very good plus jacket (no loss, only some light wear at extremities, and light rubbing), from the collection of Duke Collier.   Royal Books   36 - 236   2015 $450

Spillane, Mickey *Vengeance is Mine.* London: Arthur Barker, 1941. First edition, near fine in very good dust jacket, light foxing to prelim leaves, page edges and jacket verso, jacket lightly rubbed overall, some fading to spine and light wear at corners and spine ends, from the collection of Duke Collier.   Royal Books   36 - 235   2015 $550

Spiltimber, George *The Weather-Menders: a Tale. A Proper Answer to Are These Things So?* London: printed for J. Roberts, 1740. First edition, 8 pages, folio, disbound, blank inner margins bit chipped, titlepage slightly dusty, but sound, very uncommon.   C. R. Johnson   Foxon R-Z - 925r-z   2015 $613

Spinoza, Benedict De *Tractatus Theologico-Politicus: a Critical Inquiry into the History, Purpose an Authenticity of the Hebrew Scriptures...* London: Trubner, 1862. First edition thus, 8vo., original brown blindstamped cloth lettered gilt on spine, 32 page publisher's catalog at rear, slight rubbing, slight marks, very slight splitting at spine, otherwise very good, bookplate of Robert Howell Perks and 2 labels of the Order of the Cross and accession number label on spine.   Any Amount of Books   2015 - A83265   2015   £180

The Spirit of Humanity, and Essence of Morality... Albany: O. Steele and by D. M'Kercher, 1835. 16mo., extensively illustrated, covers detached, sound, foxed.   M & S Rare Books, Inc.   97 - 12   2015 $275

Spisak, David *Psychoanalysis of Culture and History.* Knoxville: the author, 1999. First edition, wrappers, quite scarce, fine.   Beasley Books   2013 - 2015 $45

Spizelius, Theophilus *Vetus Academia Jesu Christi in Qua XXII Priscae Sinceraesque Pietatis Professorum Icones Exhibentur.* Augsburg: Apud Gottlieb Goebelium Augustae Vindelic, 1671. First edition, full page copperplate portraits, engraved titlepage plus engraved frontispiece, recently bound in brown half calf gilt with new endpapers, few light property stamps of Norfolk & Norwich Archaeological society, neat previous owner inscription dated 1778, facing second top edge gilt, otherwise excellent, clean condition. Any Amount of Books   March 2015 - A75897   2015   £350

Spooner, Alden *The Cultivation of American Grape Vines and Making of Wine.* Brooklyn: A. Spooner & Co., 1846. First edition, 12mo., 96 pages, illustrations, original cloth, small blank pieces from several corners torn away, medium foxing throughout.   M & S Rare Books, Inc.   97 - 313   2015 $400

Sprague, Henry H. *Women Under the Law of Massachusetts their Rights, Privileges and Disabilities.* Boston: Clarke & Carruth, 1884. First edition, 8vo., news clipping pinned to rear endpaper, near fine.   Second Life Books Inc.   189 - 238   2015 $225

Spring-Rice, Thomas *Speech of the Right Honourable Thomas Spring Rice, Joint Secretary of the Treasury, M.P. for Cambridge...* London: printed for the proprietor of the Mirror of Parliament and sold by J. Ridgway, 1834. First edition, 8vo., recent marbled boards lettered on spine, very good, scarce.   John Drury Rare Books   March 2015 - 24561   2015   £306

Spurgeon, Caroline *Shakespeare's Imagery and What It Tells Us.* Cambridge: University Press, 1935. Half title, frontispiece, color folding table, original brown cloth, from the library of Geoffrey & Kathleen Tillotson, with press cutting of review.   Jarndyce Antiquarian Booksellers   CCVII - 466   2015   £35

Spurling, Laurence *Sigmund Freud, Critical Assessments.* London: Routledge, 1989. First edition, 4 volumes, slipcase, issued without dust jackets.   Beasley Books   2013 - 2015 $450

Spurrell, James *Miss Sellon and the 'Sisters of Mercy.' An Exposure of the Constitution, Rules, Religious Views and Practical Working of Their Society...* London: Thomas Hatchard, 1852. First edition, ninth thousand, 8vo., bound recently in plain grey boards with printed title label on spine, very good,.   John Drury Rare Books   2015 - 24390   2015 $221

Spurzheim, Johann Gaspar   1776-1832   *Observations sur la Phraenologie ou la Connoisassance de l'Homme Moral et Intellectuel, Fondee sur les Fonctions du Systeme Nerveux.* Paris: chez Treuttel et Wurtz, 1818. First edition, 8vo., 7 engraved plates, half title, some general paper browning and occasional minor foxing, half title with old institutional stamp and release mark, one corner of half title chipped and edges frayed, sympathetically recased in marbled paper wrappers with printed spine label, entirely uncut, good copy.   John Drury Rare Books   March 2015 - 18284   2015   £306

Spyri, Johanna *Cornell: a Story of the Swiss Alps.* Philadelphia: Lippincott, 1921. First edition of the beautiful gift edition, illustrations by Maria Kirk with 14 color plates plus pictorial boards and pictorial endpapers, 4to., red and tan cloth, pictorial paste-on, top edge gilt, fine in frayed dust jacket.   Aleph-Bet Books, Inc.   108 - 258   2015 $225

Squier, Ephraim George *Honduras: Descriptive, Historical and Statistical.* London: Trubner & Co., 1870. First separate edition, 1 partly colored folding map, small 8vo., reddish brown pebbled cloth, beveled edges, very good, lower spine neatly renewed, boards rubbed, new endpapers, titlepage remounted, binding tight, map near fine with just small marginal tear at one fold.   Kaaterskill Books   19 - 144   2015 $175

The Seafarer. Llandogo: Old Stile Press, 1988. 8/240 copies signed by translator and artist, printed on Zerkall irregular laid silurian paper, 42 woodcuts of which 9 have additional blocking in gold, oblong 8vo., original stab-bound wrappers with woodcut repeated to each panel, tail edge untrimmed, enclosed in portfolio of limp jute, lined with blue buckram and laced with ties of bookbinder's tape, fine.   Blackwell's Rare Books   B179 - 201   2015   £120

St. Aubyn, Edward *Some Hope.* London: Heinemann, 1994. First edition, 8vo., original blue cloth lettered black on spine, fine in near fine dust jacket, very slight rubbing at edges.   Any Amount of Books   2015 - C13091   2015   £220

St. Dunstan's Alumni Association *Centenniel Booklet and Directory of all Students Registered Since January 17, 1855.* Charlottetown: St. Dunstan's Alumni Association, 1954. 8vo., photo illustrations, card covers, very good.   Schooner Books Ltd.   110 - 144   2015 $45

St. German, Christian *Doctor and Student; or Dialogues Between a Doctor in Divinity and a Student in the Laws of England.* London: printed by Henry Lintot for J. Worall, 1751. Fifteenth edition, contemporary full calf, raised bands, contemporary ownership signature of Henry Duxley on titlepage, leather label missing from spine and result that the lettering "Doctor and Student" is only barely visible, cover edges rubbed and little defective at head of spine, surface of lower cover grazed, very good, internally bright copy.   Peter Ellis, Bookseller   2014 - 015530   2015   £350

St. John, David *Terraces of Rain: an Italian Sketchbook Poems.* Santa Fe: Santa Fe Literary Center Books/ Recursos, 1991. First edition, paperback original drawings by Antoine Predock, oblong octavo, wrappers, tiny crease on rear wrapper, else fine, inscribed by author for his editor, Harry Ford, additionally laid in is ALS from St. John to Ford. Between the Covers Rare Books, Inc.   187 - 258   2015 $275

St. John, Oliver *The Speech or Declaration of Mr. St. John, His Majesties Solicitor Generall. Delivered at a Conference of Both Houses of Parliament held 16o Caroll. 1640. Concerning Ship-Money.* London: by J. N. for Henry Seyle, 1641. First edition, variant issue, 4to., title within rules with head device as central ornament, uninked blindstamp of institutional library on titlepage and library inkstamp on blank verso, final leaf rather dust soiled, bound in early 20th century cloth, spine labelled but worn, even so a good, crisp copy, sometime in the Wigan Free Library having been presented to it by the Earl of Crawford.   John Drury Rare Books   March 2015 - 21454   2015   £266

Stables, William Gordon *The Cruise of the Snowbird: a Story of Arctic Adventure.* New York: A. C. Armstrong & Son, 1884. First US edition, octavo, flyleaves at front and rear, 8 inserted illustrations, full page plan, original pictorial blue cloth, front and spine panels stamped in black, gold and silver, rear panel stamped in blind, yellow endpapers.   L. W. Currey, Inc.   Boy's Adventure Fiction 2015 - 61   2015 $150

Stables, William Gordon *From Pole to Pole: a tale of the Sea.* London: Hodder and Stoughton, 1886. First edition, 12 inserted plates, original blue cloth, front and spine panels stamped in black, white, red and gold, publisher's monogram on rear panel stamped in black, floral endpapers, all edges gilt.   L. W. Currey, Inc.   Boy's Adventure Fiction 2015 - 44   2015 $200

Stables, William Gordon *Wild Adventures Round the Pole...* London: Hodder and Stoughton, 1883. First edition, octavo, 8 inserted illustrations, original pictorial red cloth, front and spine panels stamped in black, white and gold, peach coated endpapers, all edges gilt.   L. W. Currey, Inc.   Boy's Adventure Fiction 2015 - 63   2015 $150

Stables, William Gordon *Wild Adventures Round the Pole...* New York: A. C. Armstrong & Son, 1885. First US edition, octavo, flyleaves at front and rear, 8 inserted illustrations, original pictorial sea green cloth, front and spine panels stamped in black, gold and silver, rear panel stamped in blind, all edges stained brown, yellow endpapers.   L. W. Currey, Inc.   Boy's Adventure Fiction 2015 - 62   2015 $150

Stacy, Edmund *The Blackbird's Song.* London: printed for J. More, 1715. First edition, 8vo., 24 pages, disbound, fine, scarce.   C. R. Johnson   Foxon R-Z - 927r-z   2015 $689

Stacy, Edmund *The Black-Bird's Tale. A Poem.* London: printed in the year, 1710. First edition, 8vo., disbound, fine.   C. R. Johnson   Foxon R-Z - 928r-z   2015 $536

Stacy, Edmund *The Parliament of Birds.* London: printed for John Morphew, 1712. First edition, 8vo., 24 pages, disbound, fine, uncommon.   C. R. Johnson   Foxon R-Z - 929r-z   2015 $613

Stael-Holstein, Anne Louise Germaine Necker, Baronne De 1766-1817 *Reflections on Suicide.* London: Longmans Hurst, Rees, Orme and Brown, 1813. First edition, 8vo., leather boards, loose rubbed, no spine, bookplate of Alfred Fagge, endpapers slightly browned, covers somewhat used, text clean and very good with slight browning.   Any Amount of Books   2015 - A97755   2015   £225

Stafford, P. *Poems on several occasions.* London: printed for Tho. Atkins and sold by booksellers of London and Westminster, 1721. First edition, 8vo., recent boards, little dusty at beginning and end, but very good, entirely uncut, from the library of Ralph Edward Gathorne-Hardy with his bookplate, later in the collection of John Brett-Smith.   C. R. Johnson   Foxon R-Z - 931r-z   2015 $2298

Stafford, William *Traveling through the Dark.* New York: Harper & Row, 1962. First edition, 8vo., author's presentation on flyleaf to poet and editor William Claire, paper boards, fine in dust jacket.   Second Life Books Inc.   190 - 203   2015 $275

Stagg, Amos Alonzo *A Scientific and Practical Treatise on American Football for Schools and Colleges.* Hartford: Press of the Case, Lockwood & Brainard Co., 1893. First edition, 12mo., diagrams, blue cloth gilt, illustrations front board, two small contemporary owner's name stamps, modest rubbing and tiny tears at spine ends, handsome, near fine, scarce, signed by Stagg and co-author Henry L. Williams, very scarce, especially signed.   Between the Covers Rare Books   196 - 175   2015 $4800

Stahl, P. J. *Scenes De La Vie Privee et Publique des Animaux.* Paris: J. Hetzel, 1842. First edition, 2 volumes, 4to., contemporary leather backed red cloth with elaborate gilt spine designs, slight bit of cover rubbing, else clean and near fine with no foxing, 323 illustrations, full page engraved plates plus numerous vignettes,.   Aleph-bet Books, Inc.   109 - 207   2015 $3000

A Stake in the West Carnduff and District. Carnduff & Altona: Carnduff & District Historical Society, 1979. First edition, 4to., pictorial cloth, illustrations, fore-edge water stain and couple of margins affected, lightly soiled covers, good+.   Baade Books of the West   2014 - 2015 $53

Stampkraft. Six Favorite Stories. Peter Rabbit. The Three Bears. Cinderella. Puss in Boots. Robinson Crusoe. Jack and the Beanstalk.   New York: United Art. Pub. Co., 1916. 12 picture poster stamps on 5 pages for each story, black and white decorated vignettes and initial letters, green cloth backed grey boards, color illustrations, titling on front, 8 x 10 1/2 inches, few minor marks to boards, some browning and rubbing to extremities, very good, fragile book with stamps all carefully pasted-in.   Ian Hodgkins & Co. Ltd.   134 - 206   2015   £85

Stang, Richard   *The Theory of the Novel in England 1850-1870.*   London: Routledge & Kegan Paul, 1959.   Half title, original red cloth, torn dust jacket, signed by Kathleen Tillotson in 1959 with pencil notes referring the book to Nina Burgis, typescript, proof and printed text inserted.   Jarndyce Antiquarian Booksellers   CCVII - 476   2015   £25

Stange, Maren   *Bronzeville Black Chicago in Pictures 1941-1943.*   New York: New Press, 2003.   First edition, oblong small 4to., fine in fine dust jacket.   Beasley Books   2013 - 2015 $40

Stanhope, Eugenia   *The Deportment of a Married Life Laid Down in a Series of Letters Written by...*   London: printed for Mr. Hodges, Pall Mall and sold by C. Mason, 1798. Second edition, 8vo., all edges gilt, bound in full 19th century polished calf, couple of minor spots but very nice, rare.   Second Life Books Inc.   189 - 241   2015 $1000

Stanhope, Hugh   *An Epistle to His Royal Highness the Prince of Wales; Occasion'd by the State of the Nation...*   London: printed for E. Curll, 1720.   First edition, 8vo., disbound, old signature deleted on half title, but very good.   C. R. Johnson   Foxon R-Z - 932r-z   2015 $919

Stanke, Julian   *The Saviours and Liberators.*   N.P.: privately printed, 1950.   First edition, small oblong 4to., mimeographed text, mounted photos, soundly rebound, couple of ex-Foreign and Commonwealth Office library stamps, otherwise very good.   Any Amount of Books   2015 - A65219   2015   £150

Stanley, George F. G.   *The War of 1812 Land Operations.*   Toronto: Macmillan of Canada, 1983.   8vo. red cloth with gilt to spine and map endpapers, dust jacket, very good.   Schooner Books Ltd.   110 - 154   2015 $55

Stanley, Henry Morton   1841-1904   *How I Found Livingstone.*   London: Sampson Low, Marston, Low and Searle, 1872.   Second English edition, exceptional association copy, inscribed at time of publication to friend John Goodenow from Henry M. Stanley, London Nov. 5 1872, original brown cloth with embossed design on spine and front cover, gilt illustration, boards chipped, bumped and spine has chip to top left edge, rear cover watermarked, but binding nicer than it sounds, hinges weak but text block tight, endpapers chipped and folding map is entirely intact but cleanly split along fold, later ownership signature on half title, frontispiece is original mounted photo of Stanley, full and partial page illustrations, 4 folding maps, overall very good.   The Kelmscott Bookshop   11 - 47   2015 $3500

Stanley, Maude Alethea   *Clubs for Working Girls.* London: Macmillan and Co., 1890.   First edition, 8vo., including half title and 4 pages of Macmillan ads, original dark blue cloth, spine gilt lettered, lower cover just trifle marked, else very good, presentation copy with long autograph inscription in ink by author.   John Drury Rare Books   2015 - 25945   2015 $830

Stansberry, Domenic   *The Spoiler.*   New York: Atlantic Monthly, 1987.   First edition, very fine in dust jacket, signed by author.   Mordida Books   March 2015 - 008459   2015 $80

Stansbery, Lon   *The Passing of the 3D Ranch.*   Tulsa: printed for the author by Geo. W. Henry Printing Co. n.d. circa, 1930.   First edition, pictorial cloth, 92 pages, illustrations with plates and portraits, rare, non-authorial inscription, else near fine in pictorial cloth.   Buckingham Books   March 2015 - 25073   2015 $650

Stansfeld, Hamer   *Reasons for thinking Trade with Raise the Rent of Land, as Well as the Profit of Capital and the Wages of labour, and that it Would be Foolish in the Landlords to incur the Odium of Enacting a Corn Law to Protect the Value of Their Property...*   London: Henry Hooper, n.d." (1822) or later,   First edition, folding table, 8vo., sewn as issued, fine, very rare.   John Drury Rare Books   2015 - 22386   2015 $177

Stanton, Elizabeth Cady   *History of Woman Suffrage.* New York: Fowler & Wells, 1881.   First edition, volume I only, 8vo., steel engravings, with editor, Matilda Joslyn Gage's presentation dated 1888, maroon cloth, cover quite scuffed and somewhat worn at spine and corners, little foxing, otherwise very good.   Second Life Books Inc.   189 - 244   2015 $350

Stanton, Elizabeth Cady   *History of Woman Suffrage.* New York: Susan B. Anthony, 1887.   First edition, volume III only, 8vo., steel engravings, maroon cloth, cover quite scuffed and spotted, slightly worn at spine and corners, little foxing, front hinge tender and blank leaf partly detached, otherwise very good.   Second Life Books Inc.   189 - 245   2015 $300

Stanton, Elizabeth Cady *Solitude of Self, an Address Delivered by Elizabeth Cady Stanton Before the United Sates Congressional Committee on Judiciary Monday Jan. 18 1892.* N.P.: n.d. circa, 1920? 8vo., pages 20, bound in brown printed wrappers, name written in ink on endpaper, some light spotting, very nice, scarce.   Second Life Books Inc.   191 - 86   2015 $325

Stanton, William *The Great United States Exploring Expedition of 1838-1842.* Berkeley: University of California Press, 1975. First edition, illustrations, gray cloth lettered on spine in blue and gold, fine, chipped pictorial dust jacket.   Argonaut Book Shop   Holiday Season 2014 - 318   2015 $60

Stark, Richard *The Damsel.* New York: Macmillan, 1967. First edition, fine in dust jacket.   Mordida Books   March 2015 - 008577   2015 $125

Starke, Mariana *Travels on the Continent.* London: John Murray, 1820. First edition, spotting to title and first few leaves, slightly later half black calf gilt spine, maroon morocco label, very good.   Jarndyce Antiquarian Booksellers   CCXI - 264   2015   £420

Starkey, William *The Divine Obligation of Humane Ordinances Delivered in a Sermon Upon the 26th of February...* Cambridge: printed by John Field printer to the University..., 1668. First edition, 4to., well bound recently in half pigskin over marbled boards, spine lettered in gilt, very good, crisp copy.   John Drury Rare Books   2015 - 19338   2015 $177

Starr, Frederick *Fujiyama. The Sacred Mountain of Japan (Mount Fuji).* Chicago: Covici McGee, 1924. First edition, 8vo., near fine in like dust jacket with minimal chips and sun spine, color pictorial endpapers, signed and inscribed by author, rare.   By the Book, L. C.   44 - 72   2015 $1500

Starrett, Vincent *Bookman's Holiday.* New York: Random House, 1942. First edition, fine in dust jacket with tiny wear at spine ends and short closed tear.   Mordida Books   March 2015 - 009977   2015 $125

Starrett, Vincent *Facsimile of Scribner's 1925 Catalogue of Vincent Starrett's Collection.* Starrett Memorial Library 1976, Fine facsimile edition, one of 300 numbered copies in stapled unbound printed covers, fine.   Mordida Books   March 2015 - 012468   2015 $100

Starrett, Vincent *The End of Mr. Garment.* New York: Crime Club/Doubleday Doran, 1932. First edition, near fine in very good dust jacket (some chipping, wear and crease), uncommon.   Stephen Lupack   March 2015 - 2015 $150

Starrett, Vincent *Persons from Porlock.* Chicago: Bookfellows, 1923. First separate edition, back page darkened, otherwise fine in string tied printed wrappers.   Mordida Books   March 2015 - 003157   2015 $85

State of Ireland. Letters from Ireland on the Present Political, Religious & Moral State of that Country. London: J. Hatchard & Son & R. Milliken, Dublin, 1825. First edition, 8vo., half title, appendix leaf, original green cloth backed boards, little rubbed, entirely uncut, very good, presentation copy to Lord Eldon with Eldon's circular armorial bookplate and his usual signature in ink with half title inscribed for Earl of Eldon.   John Drury Rare Books   March 2015 - 25044   2015 $656

The State of Justice Impartially Considered. London: printed by E. Rayner for the author and sold by the booksellers of London and Westminster, n.d., 1732. Only edition, 8vo., well bound recently in fine 18th century quarter calf, gilt, excellent copy, apparently rare.   John Drury Rare Books   2015 - 25249   2015 $1311

The State of Rome, Under Nero and Domitian; a Satire. London: printed for C. Corbett, 1729. First edition, folio, disbound, 17 pages, some dust soiling at beginning and end, few short marginal tears, without loss, otherwise good.   C. R. Johnson   Foxon R-Z - 933r-z   2015 $689

The State of Rome Under Nero and Domitian; a Satire. London: i.e.: Edinburgh: printed for C. Corbett, 1739. Scottish piracy, 24 pages, 8vo., green buckram cloth, fair, ex-library with Harvard bookplate and release stamp, uncommon.   C. R. Johnson   Foxon R-Z - 934r-z   2015 $230

The State of the Nation with a General Balance of the Publick Accounts. London: M. Cooper, 1748. First edition, 8vo., large folding table printed on recto and verso, half title dusty and inner margin of title strengthened, else good, uncut, modern cloth, gilt.   John Drury Rare Books   2015 - 8271   2015 $177

The State of the Nation with a General Balance of the Publick Accounts. London: M. Cooper, 1748. Second edition, half title (with marginal tears), large folding table printed on recto and verso, paper generally rather browned throughout, few leaves lightly dampstained, preserved in recent wrappers with label on upper cover.   John Drury Rare Books   2015 - 21476   2015 $89

State Papers and Documents of the United States from the Accession of George Washington to the Presidency... Boston: T. E. Wait, 1817. Second edition, 10 volumes, 8vo., soundly rebound in beige buckram with red leather spine labels, lettered gilt, ex-British Foreign Office library with few library markings, covers have occasional marks, text has some foxing, sound, clean set.   Any Amount of Books   2015 - A93607   2015   £750

Staufer, Alvin F. *New York Central's Early Power 1831 to 1916.* Medina: Alvin F. Staufer, 1967. First edition, quarto, 2 color plates, black and white photos, drawings, facsimiles, green cloth, fine with pictorial dust jacket. Argonaut Book Shop Holiday Season 2014 - 277 2015 $60

Stauffer, Serge *Marcel Duchamp: Die Schriften.* Zurich: Theo Ruff Edition, 1994. First edition thus, 4to., one of 1000 copies, copiously illustrated in color and black and white, minimal handling wear, otherwise fine. Any Amount of Books 2015 - A94248 2015 £220

Steadman, Ralph *Ralph Steadman's Jelly Book.* London: Dennis Dobson, 1967. First edition, small oblong 4to., bright and clean original orange cloth, illustrations in color, boldly signed by Steadman, very good+ in very good complete dust jacket, browned and tanned largely at edges and rear cover. Any Amount of Books 2015 - A66644 2015 £220

Stealingworth, Slim *Tom Wesselmann.* New York: Abbeville, 1980. First edition, folio, fine in very good- acetate dust jacket with serious tears on rear panel and spine. Beasley Books 2013 - 2015 $125

Stearne, John *The Death and Burial of John Asgill, Esq...* Dublin: printed in the year, 1702. First edition, small 4to., disbound, titlepage bit abraded, with few small holes, affecting several leaves, some light browning, otherwise good, outer margins untrimmed, scarce. C. R. Johnson Foxon R-Z - 935r-z 2015 $919

Stearns, Charles *The Ladies' Philosophy of Love.* Leonminster: printed by John Prentiss for the author, 1797. First edition, small 4to., self wrappers, stitched as issued, untrimmed, 76 pages, unopened, first and final leaves slightly dust soiled and lightly foxed, fine. The Brick Row Book Shop Miscellany 67 - 13 2015 $500

Steel, Kurt *Madman's Buff.* Boston: Little Brown, 1941. First edition, fine in dust jacket. Mordida Books March 2015 - 008899 2015 $200

Steel, Kurt *Madman's Buff.* Boston: Little Brown and Co., 1941. First edition, fine in dust jacket. Buckingham Books March 2015 - 24898 2015 $275

Steele, Chester K. *The Golf Course Mystery.* Cleveland: International Fiction Library, Later edition, front hinge slightly cracked and dampstain on bottom of page edges, otherwise very good in darkened dust jacket with several closed tears and chips at corners. Mordida Books March 2015 - 009600 2015 $85

Steele, Chester K. *The Golf Course Mystery.* New York: George Sully, 1919. First edition, very good, endpapers stained and staining on pages, otherwise very good, illustrations by A. O. Scott. Mordida Books March 2015 - 010678 2015 $175

Steele, James *Conveyor.* New York: International, 1935. First edition, fine in near fine dust jacket. Beasley Books 2013 - 2015 $300

Steele, James W. *West of the Missouri. Sketches and Stories of Frontier Life in the Old Times.* Rand McNally & Co., 1885. 7 3/8 x 5 inches, printed wrappers, front cover and half titlepage detached but present, spine and extremities chipped and worn, on half titlepage "Geo. E. Bradnock 35 Blatchley Ave., New Haven, Conn". Buckingham Books March 2015 - 37986 2015 $250

Steffen, Randy *The Horse Soldier - Volume I.* Norman: 1977. First edition, illustrations, dust jacket rubbed, else clean, very good, dozens of line drawings and 9 color plates. Dumont Maps & Books of the West 131 - 76 2015 $45

Stegner, Wallace *Beyond the Hundredth Meridian: John Wesley Powell and the Second Opening of the West.* Boston: 1954. First edition, illustrations, folding frontispiece, dust jacket with slight edgewear and minor loss at top corner of spine, folding frontispiece is wrinkled as often seen, else book is clean and tight. Dumont Maps & Books of the West 131 - 66 2015 $275

Stegner, Wallace *California. The Dynamic State.* Santa Barbara: McNally and Loftin, 1966. First edition, 16mo., signed by Stegner on titlepage, illustrations, fine in fine dust jacket. Ed Smith Books 82 - 27 2015 $300

Stein, Gertrude 1874-1946 *In Savoy, or Yes Is for a Very Young Man.* London: Pushkin Press, 1946. First edition, small 8vo., fine in wrappers and illustrated dust jacket with slight soiling, word 'Savoy' stamped on front fly, as usual, scarce in this condition. Gemini Fine Books & Arts, Ltd. Art Reference & Illustrated Books: First Editions - 2015 $80

Stein, Gertrude 1874-1946 *The Making of Americans, Being a History of a Family's Progress Part I.* Paris: Contact Editions, Three Mountains Press, 1925. First printing, disbound, inscribed to critic Henry McBride. Honey & Wax Booksellers 2 - 60 2015 $2200

Stein, Gertrude 1874-1946 *Tender Buttons, tenderly.* Boston: 2006. Artist's book, one of 24 copies, each on Frankfurt paper, each copy signed and numbered by artist, Laura Davidson, page size - double sized pages are each 1 3/4 inches in diameter, 28 pages, each double side page is hinged with pink silk ribbon forming an accordion style binding bound in brass box, measuring 2 x 2 x 5/8 inches, 7 buttons of various colors and shapes and sizes are 'sewn' onto top of brass box lid, box lined with paper containing additional text, new.   Priscilla Juvelis - Rare Books   61 - 8   2015 $1000

Stein, Gertrude 1874-1946 *The World is Round.* New York: William Scott, 1939. Stated first edition, 4to., cloth backed pictorial boards, fine in slightly worn, frayed dust jacket, printed on rose colored paper, increasingly scarce, illustrations by Clement Hurd.   Aleph-bet Books, Inc.   109 - 450   2015 $850

Steinbeck, John Ernst 1902-1968 *Bombs Away.* New York: Viking Press, 1942. First edition, presentation copy signed and inscribed by author for Lunt (?) and Col. Merecutti, very good plus in very good dust jacket.   Ed Smith Books   83 - 91   2015 $4500

Steinbeck, John Ernst 1902-1968 *Burning Bright.* New York: Viking Press, 1950. First edition, about fine in very good, unclipped dust jacket with spine ends, bit rubbed and lightly nicked, spine lightly faded, crease and small closed tear to upper edge of front panel, nice copy.   B & B Rare Books, Ltd.   234 - 91   2015 $275

Steinbeck, John Ernst 1902-1968 *Burning Bright.* New York: Viking Press, 1950. First edition, fine in near fine dust jacket (light shelfwear, but neither chipped nor clipped).   Stephen Lupack   March 2015 - 2015 $125

Steinbeck, John Ernst 1902-1968 *Cannery Row.* New York: Viking Press, 1945. First edition, inscribed by author for Tom Work, irregular sunning to cloth, very good price clipped dust jacket with soiling to rear panel.   Ed Smith Books   83 - 89   2015 $4500

Steinbeck, John Ernst 1902-1968 *Cannery Row.* New York: Viking Press, 1945. First edition, advance issue in publisher's blue wrappers, excellent copy with some minor fading to spine, else fine.   B & B Rare Books, Ltd.   234 - 92   2015 $1750

Steinbeck, John Ernst 1902-1968 *Cup of Gold.* New York: McBride, 1929. First edition, first issue, this special copy from author's sister's collection, Esther (Steinbeck) Rodgers and includes bookplates from the library of the Steinbeck Family and "Josephine Rodgers", signed by author, additionally inscribed to Josie, from Emily, near fine with bold lettering to yellow cloth, very good dust jacket with usual spine fading and some slight wear along edges.   Ed Smith Books   83 - 101   2015 $45,000

Steinbeck, John Ernst 1902-1968 *East of Eden.* New York: Viking Press, 1952. First edition, one of 1500 signed copies, laid in slip "with the Compliments of/the Viking Press", signed by editor in chief Marshall Best, fine with original glassine in publisher's original slipcase (very good).   Ed Smith Books   83 - 84   2015 $4500

Steinbeck, John Ernst 1902-1968 *East of Eden.* New York: Viking Press, 1952. First edition, limited to 1500 copies signed by author, original cloth, slipcase and acetate jacket, fine, extremely bright copy, very slightly rubbed at spine in rubbed slipcase with some wear to fore-edge and corners, acetate chipped with some loss to lower spine, else very good.   B & B Rare Books, Ltd.   234 - 93   2015 $4000

Steinbeck, John Ernst 1902-1968 *The Grapes of Wrath.* New York: Viking Press, 1939. First edition, nearly fine in very good plus dust jacket with closed tear to rear panel lower spine fold and some sunning to spine.   Ed Smith Books   83 - 94   2015 $4750

Steinbeck, John Ernst 1902-1968 *The Grapes of Wrath.* New York: Viking Press, 1939. Fifth printing, 8vo., signed, inscribed and dated in year of publication by author, near fine, 8vo., very good dust jacket with small pieces missing, edge wear and scuffs, price intact on jacket flap.   By the Book, L. C.   Special List 10 - 38   2015 $5000

Steinbeck, John Ernst 1902-1968 *The Grapes of Wrath.* Norwalk: Easton Press, 1968. Special edition, illustrations by Thomas Hart Benton, full leather with raised bands and gilt decorations on covers and spine, all edges gilt, silk moire endpapers, matching sewn-in ribbon bookmark, as new.   Stephen Lupack   March 2015 - 2015 $75

Steinbeck, John Ernst 1902-1968 *In Dubious Battle.* New York: Covici Friede, 1936. First edition, Rare limited edition, 'Printer's copy B", as indicated below Steinbeck's signature, fine in fine slipcase, both housed in custom beige folding box with black spine label.   Ed Smith Books   83 - 97   2015 $17,500

Steinbeck, John Ernst 1902-1968 *In Dubious Battle.* New York: Covici Friede, 1936. First edition, limited edition, one of 99 copies signed by author, copy # 4, original slipcase with orange paper label printed in black, fine in very good to near fine slipcase with little flaking around opening.   Ed Smith Books   83 - 96   2015 $7500

Steinbeck, John Ernst 1902-1968 *The Log from the Sea of Cortez.* New York: Viking Press, 1951. Second edition, signed by author with Steinbeck Family bookplate, fine in dust jacket that only shows the lightest of use (light spine sunning).   Ed Smith Books   83 - 85   2015 $4500

Steinbeck, John Ernst   1902-1968   *The Moon is Down.* New York: Viking Press, 1942. First edition, second state, special copy signed by author in blue felt tip pen with Steinbeck family bookplate, very good in blue cloth with light spine sunning, nearly fine dust jacket.   Ed Smith Books   83 - 92   2015 $4500

Steinbeck, John Ernst   1902-1968   *The Moon is Down.* New York: Viking Press, 1942. First edition, first state with period on page 112 line 11 between 'talk. This", 8vo., near fine with minimal sun and wear cover edges, in near fine, price clipped dust jacket with minimal edge wear, from the library of Carol and John Steinbeck.   By the Book, L. C. Special List 10 - 37   2015 $4000

Steinbeck, John Ernst   1902-1968   *The Moon is Down.* New York: Viking, 1942. First edition, first printing with large period on pae 112 between words 'talk' and 'this', very good, little shelfwear, little spine faded, very good+ dust jacket (little rubbing, little toning to rear panel).   Stephen Lupack   March 2015 - 2015 $95

Steinbeck, John Ernst   1902-1968   *Of Mice and Men.* New York: Covici Friede, 1937. First edition, first issue, with dot between numbers on page 88, little surface adhesion to gutter of half title, foolscap 8vo., original beige cloth stamped in orange and black to upper board and backstrip edges of cloth, just little darkened, dust jacket very lightly toned with touch of chipping at corners, lightest of rubbing to extremities and couple of very small nicks, light dust soiling to rear panel, near fine, top edge of this copy is not stained blue, as Goldstone and Payne call for, but the other first issue points on page 9 and 88 are present.   Blackwell's Rare Books   B179 - 242   2015   £3000

Steinbeck, John Ernst   1902-1968   *Of Mice and Men.* New York: Covici Friede, 1937. First edition, first issue, signed by author, two inch closed tear to bottom of front flap, sunning at spine and few internal tape repaired small tears, fine in very good dust jacket.   Ed Smith Books   83 - 95   2015 $5000

Steinbeck, John Ernst   1902-1968   *The Pastures of Heaven.* New York: Brewer, Warren & Putnam, 1932. First edition, first issue, one of about 650 printed, near fine, clean copy in nearly fine dust jacket that has been expertly restored.   Ed Smith Books   83 - 100   2015 $17,500

Steinbeck, John Ernst   1902-1968   *The Pearl.* New York: Viking Press, 1947. First edition, first printing in first issue jacket, about fine in unclipped dust jacket with some wear and light chipping to spine ends, few tiny tears, light spotting to rear panel, else very good, housed in custom folding box.   B & B Rare Books, Ltd.   234 - 94   2015 $350

Steinbeck, John Ernst   1902-1968   *The Red Pony.* New York: Viking Press, 1945. First illustrated edition, first printing with gilt lettered spine, paste-on color illustration of red pony front cover, signed by author, from the library of John and Carol Steinbeck, 8vo, near fine, original very good+ cardboard slipcase, slipcase with mild stains and wear.   By the Book, L. C. Special List 10 - 39   2015 $400

Steinbeck, John Ernst   1902-1968   *A Russian Journal.* New York: Viking Press, 1948. First edition, pictures by Robert Capa, into this copy is tipped large review slip with three paragraphs of text on publishers' letterhead, very good plus in very good dust jacket with some chipping at spine crown and foot.   Ed Smith Books   83 - 86   2015 $1000

Steinbeck, John Ernst   1902-1968   *A Russian Journal.* New York: Viking Press, 1948. First edition, special copy inscribed to author's cousin and his wife, Bea and Stanford Steinbeck, very good with some soiling to cloth in very good bright dust jacket.   Ed Smith Books   83 - 87 2015 $4500

Steinbeck, John Ernst   1902-1968   *Sea of Cortez.* New York: Viking Press, 1941. First edition, near fine, clean with darkening from glue interaction at joints, nearly fine dust jacket, sharp copy, seldom found in such condition.   Ed Smith Books   83 - 93   2015 $1750

Steinbeck, John Ernst   1902-1968   *The Short Reign of Pippin IV: a Fabrication.* New York: Viking Press, 1957. First edition, special copy signed by author, with Steinbeck family bookplate, fine in near fine dust jacket with only light use.   Ed Smith Books   83 - 83   2015 $4500

Steinbeck, John Ernst   1902-1968   *To a God Unknown.* New York: Ballou, 1933. first edition, first issue, one of only 598 issued, very good, tight, clean copy, light sunning at spine in very good dust jacket with archival restoration at both ends of spine and front flap folds.   Ed Smith Books   83 - 99   2015 $4500

Steinbeck, John Ernst   1902-1968   *Tortilla Flat.* New York: Covici Friede, 1935. First edition, first issue, one of 4000 copies, this copy briefly inscribed by author, very good but for uniform foxing of covers and intermittent foxing to pages and fore-edge, small bookplate of the person the book is inscribed to, dust jacket very good with full width eighth of an inch chip to spine crown and sunning (darkening) to spine, some interior tape marks.   Ed Smith Books   83 - 98   2015 $10,500

Steinbeck, John Ernst   1902-1968   *Travels with Charley.* New York: Viking Press, 1962. First edition, first printing, about fine in very good, unclipped, slightly worn dust jacket with light toning to spine, small chip to upper spine and upper corner of front flap fold.   B & B Rare Books, Ltd.   234 - 95   2015 $325

Steinbeck, John Ernst 1902-1968 *The Viking Portable Library Steinbeck.* New York: Viking Press, 1943. First edition, 16mo., special copy signed by author, near fine with bookplate, near fine, bright dust jacket.   Ed Smith Books   83 - 90   2015 $3750

Steinbeck, John Ernst 1902-1968 *The Wayward Bus.* New York: Viking Press, 1947. First edition, inscribed by author, near fine in very good dust jacket with light sunning to spine and some darkening around edges of rear panel.   Ed Smith Books   83 - 88   2015 $4750

Steinbeck, John Ernst 1902-1968 *The Winter of Our Discontent.* New York: Viking Press, 1961. First edition, one of 500 copies, nearly fine, printed glassine wrapper.   Ed Smith Books   83 - 82   2015 $1250

Steinbeck, John Ernst 1902-1968 *Zapata.* Covelo: Yolla Bolla Press, 1991. First and limited edition, 4to., one of 257 copies signed by Karin Wikstrom who illustrated the book with woodcuts, laid into this copy is original prospectus and associated publisher literature, housed in original publisher's slipcase, fine.   Ed Smith Books   83 - 119   2015 $750

Steinberg, Saul *The Passport.* New York: Harper and Bros., 1954. First edition, folio, touch of wear to bottom of spine, else fine in slightly chipped very good dust jacket with wear at edges, nicely inscribed by author with large drawing of a cat playing the guitar, inscribed to Leo, signed by author 1954.   Between the Covers Rare Books   196 - 131   2015 $2500

Steinbrunner, Chris *Detectionary.* Lock Haven: Hammermill, 1972. Later edition, some faint creasing on covers otherwise fine in soft covers.   Mordida Books   March 2015 - 007314   2015 $100

Steiner, George *Tolstoy or Dostoevesky: an Essay in Contrast.* London: Faber, 1959. First edition, bit of foxing on endpapers, near fine, price clipped dust jacket very good or better, inscribed to Peter and Eleanor Ross Taylor, by literary critic E. D. Hirsch and his wife Polly.   Between the Covers Rare Books, Inc.   187 - 270   2015 $175

Steiner, Rudolf *Occult Seals and Columns.* N.P.: n.p., n.d. circa, 1910. First edition, large portfolio, 7 pages of text with 6 single sided black and white lithographic plates, reproduced on card, rare, text leaves little dusty and creased, plates clean, cloth backed purple covers little soiled and bumped, spine worn, frayed and slightly split, original printed folder with spine recently and skillfully renewed boards show slight even discoloration, slight rub, near very good, new ties supplied.   Any Amount of Books   2015 - A97433   2015   £750

Steiner, Rudolf *Photogravure and Half-Tone Reproductions of Occult Seals and Columns...* London: Anthroposophical Pub. Co., 1924. First edition, large portfolio, 7 pages of text with 6 black and white lithographic plates on 3 folded sheets, and 7 plates on single sheets (each showing a seal) reproduced on card, rare, original printed folder with spine recently and skillfully renewed in red leather with new gray pastedowns and new cloth ties, boards show slight discoloration, slight wear, rubbing, near very good.   Any Amount of Books   2015 - C12655   2015   £750

Stekel, Wilhelm *Compulsion and Doubt.* New York: Liveright, 1949. First edition in English, fine in lightly used dust jacket although spine of volume I is very slightly cocked.   Beasley Books   2013 - 2015 $45

Stekel, Wilhelm *Impotence in the Male.* New York: Liveright, 1939. Library edition, 2 volumes, ex-library, slightly worn dust jackets.   Beasley Books   2013 - 2015 $45

Stephen, James *Lectures on the History of France.* London: Longman, Brown, Green & Longmans, 1851. First edition, 8vo., original light brown cloth, lettered gilt at spine, signed letter to George Melly 20 August 1830-27 Feb. 1894, Liverpool politician, from the library of Henry A. Bright with attractive armorial bookplate, some rubbing and fraying at spine ends and light scuffing to boards, otherwise sound, close very good or better, clean text and clean boards.   Any Amount of Books   2015 - C11844   2015   £180

Stephen, Leslie *Selected Letters of Leslie Stephen. Volume 2 1882-1904.* Basingstoke: Palgrave/Macmillan, 1996. First edition, 8vo., color illustrated dust jacket, original publisher's blue cloth with lettered gilt at spine, 7 black and white figures, very good in like dust jacket.   Any Amount of Books   2015 - A95651   2015   £180

Stephen, Leslie *The "Times" on the American War: a Historical Study.* London: William Ridgway, 1865. Disbound and loose in slightly dusted and torn cream paper wrappers, with letter of presentation from Norma Hodgson to Geoffrey Tillotson.   Jarndyce Antiquarian Booksellers   CCVII - 477   2015   £65

Stephenson, Neal *The Big U.* New York: Vintage Books/Random House, 1984. First edition, wrappers as issued, fine with just slightest of toning at edges of pages.   Between the Covers Rare Books   196 - 157   2015 $200

Stephenson, Shirley E. *John J. Baumgartner Jr.; Reflections of a Scion of the Rancho Santa Margarita.* Fullerton: 1982. Gift inscription, else near fine, illustrations.   Dumont Maps and Books of the West   130 - 46   2015 $125

Stephenson, Terry E. *Caminos Viejos. Tales Found in the History of California of Especial Interest to Those Who Love the Valleys, The Hills and the Canyons of Orange County, Its Traditions and Its Landmarks.* Santa Ana: Press of the Santa Ana High School and Junior College, 1930. First edition, limited to 250 copies, this #239, signed by printer and author, 8vo., decorated covers and spine, decorated endpapers, frontispiece, photos, woodcut drawings, former owner's brief inscription, lightly rubbed along edges and spine ends, else very good, tight copy.   Buckingham Books   March 2015 - 18550   2015 $675

Sterling, George   *A Wine of Wizardry and Other Poems.* San Francisco: A. M. Robertson, 1909. First edition, 8vo., signed presentation from author for Frank McConnors, original burgundy red cloth lettered gilt on spine and gilt illustration on front cover, slight fading at spine, otherwise bright, very good+.   Any Amount of Books   2015 - A39601   2015   £220

Sterling, William Warren   *Trails and Trials of a Texas Ranger.* N.P.: privately printed, 1959. First edition, two-tone quarter leather and decorated cloth, decorated endpapers, illustrations, fine in lightly rubbed dust jacket with one tiny chip to bottom edge of front panel.   Buckingham Books   March 2015 - 31783   2015 $185

Stern, Gerald   *Bread without Sugar.* N.P.: Sutton Hoo Press, 1991. First edition, one of 30 'special copies, covered in Tim Barrett's handmade UICB pc4 flax paper', numbered and signed by Stern, (out of a total edition of 250), Press's first book, tall 8vo., illustrations by Nadya Brown, wrappers with printed label on front cover, fine.   James S. Jaffe Rare Books   Modern American Poetry - 265   2015 $350

Stern, Meredith   *Mine.* Providence: n.d., One of an unsigned edition of 72, silkscreened and hand stamped, and then machine and handsewn into a stuff cat, cloth book 'inside' the stomach starts with words 'is his mine', multi-colored animal stamped all over with words "This Space is Mine", very good, 18 x 4 inches x 2.5 inches plus 10 inch tail, comes with wooden doll stand (not originally issued with book), very good.   The Kelmscott Bookshop   11 - 48   2015 $400

Sterne, Laurence   1713-1768   *Letters of the Late Rev. Mr. Laurence Sterne to His Most Intimate Friends.* London: printed for T. Becket, 1776. New edition, i.e. second edition, 165 x 102mm., extraordinarily pretty contemporary red straight grain morocco, elaborately gilt in style of Roger Payne (though not definitely attributable to him), covers with frame of alternating long stemmed tulips and daisies, corners with floral spring surrounded by dots and stars inside a laurel wreath, flat spines densely gilt in compartments with central lily on a stippled ground, framed by 8 pointed stars and with sunbursts at corners, gilt tiling and turn-ins, marbled endpapers, all edges gilt; with (usually missing) frontispiece in volume I, bookplate of Louis Auchincloss, presentation inscription from Bronson Winthrop dated 23 Feb. 1932, verso of titlepage with pictorial library stamp of Schlossbibliothek Dessau; volume 1 with slight browning, offsetting and foxing (other two volumes only very moderately affected), leaves generally a shade less than bright, uniform faint fading to spines (scarcely noticeable because of abundance of gilt), corners with minor wear but beautiful set, text fresh and clean, bindings lustrous, glittering and so little used as to resist opening.   Phillip J. Pirages   66 - 58   2015 $4500

Sternheim, Carl   *Fairfax.* 1968. Reprint of 1922 edition, 4to., quarter cloth, paper covered boards, covers tanned, bumped at top corners, 10 lithographs by Frans Masereel, front cover illustrated, ex-library with markings.   Oak Knoll Books   306 - 31   2015 $750

Sterrett, Cliff   *The Complete Color Polly and Her Pals.* Princeton: Kitchen Sink/Remco, 1990. First edition, folio, fine in fine dust jacket.   Beasley Books   2013 - 2015 $45

Steuart, James   *Dirleton's Doubts and Questions in the Law of Scotland, Resolved and Answered.* Edinburgh: printed by James Watson, 1715. Folio, fine engraved portrait frontispiece, title printed in red and black within ruled borders and with large woodcut device, contemporary panelled calf, neatly rebacked to match raised bands and label, fine, crisp copy.   John Drury Rare Books   2015 - 24193   2015 $656

Stevens, Errol Wayne   *Incidents of a Voyage to California 1849. A Diary of Travel Abroad the Bark Hersilia and In Sacramento 1850.* Los Angeles: Western History Association, 1987. First edition, 44 pages, 3 full page plates, light blue cloth, very fine.   Argonaut Book Shop   Holiday Season 2014 - 280   2015 $45

Stevens, Isaac N. *An American Suffragette.* New York: William Rickey, 1911. First edition, 8vo., very good, scarce.   Second Life Books Inc.   189 - 246   2015 $150

Stevens, Joanne Darsey *Santos by Twentieth Century Santeras: Continuation of a Traditional Art Form.* Dallas: 1986. Quarto, illustrations, boards issued without a dust jacket, presentation inscription by author, else near fine, 12 photos plates. Dumont Maps & Books of the West 131 - 78 2015 $125

Stevens, John H. *The Early History of Hennepin County; Embodied in an address Delivered Before the Minneapolis Lyceum.* Minneapolis: North-western Democrat Office, 1856. First edition, 8vo., later binder's cloth with earlier green morocco gilt title label, laid on spine, text complete but lacking cover title, rare. M & S Rare Books, Inc. 97 - 192 2015 $100

Stevens, Shane *Way Uptown in Another World.* New York: G. P. Putnam's Sons, 1971. First edition, fine in lightly rubbed dust jacket. Buckingham Books March 2015 - 16249 2015 $275

Stevens, W. Bertrand *Victorious Mountaineer. A Memoir of Harry Peirce Nichols.* Louisville: Cloister Press, 1943. First edition, small 8vo., cloth, 78 pages, drawings, frontispiece, inscribed by Stevens, lightly soiled, very good, very scarce, original black and white photos of Nichols, signed by him. Baade Books of the West 2014 - 2015 $230

Stevens, Wallace 1879-1955 *The Auroras of Autumn.* New York: Knopf, 1950. First edition, 8vo., original cloth, dust jacket, fine, presentation copy inscribed by poet. James S. Jaffe Rare Books Modern American Poetry - 274 2015 $5000

Stevens, Wallace 1879-1955 *Esthetique du Mal.* Cummington: Cummington Press, 1945. First edition, one of 300 copies printed on Pace paper, one of only a few copies in rose Natsume straw paper covered boards, 8vo., original quarter black morocco and rose natsume paper covered boards, original? glassine dust jacket, pen and ink drawings by Wightman Williams, very fine, preserved in cloth folding box. James S. Jaffe Rare Books Modern American Poetry - 271 2015 $7500

Stevens, Wallace 1879-1955 *Esthetique du Mal.* Cummington: Cummington Press, 1945. First edition, one of 300 copies printed in Centaur type on Italian Pace paper, 8vo., original quarter black morocco and green Natsume paper covered boards, glassine dust jacket, unusually fine, pen and ink drawings by Wightman Williams. James S. Jaffe Rare Books Modern American Poetry - 270 2015 $2250

Stevens, Wallace 1879-1955 *Harmonium.* New York: Knopf, 1923. First edition, first issue, first binding, octavo, 140 pages, no dust jacket, boxed, this copy belonged to Connecticut writer Annie Eliot Trumbull, this copy partially unopened. Honey & Wax Booksellers 1 - 36 2015 $6200

Stevens, Wallace 1879-1955 *Ideas of Order.* New York: Alfred A. Knopf, 1936. First trade edition, first binding, small 8vo., original vertically striped parti-colored cloth, printed label on spine, dust jacket, one of approximately 500 bound thus, very fine. James S. Jaffe Rare Books Modern American Poetry - 267 2015 $1500

Stevens, Wallace 1879-1955 *Letters of Wallace Stevens.* New York: Knopf, 1966. First edition, one of 6000 copies, thick 8vo., decorated endpapers, original cloth, fine in dust jacket. James S. Jaffe Rare Books Modern American Poetry - 277 2015 $250

Stevens, Wallace 1879-1955 *The Man with the Blue Guitar & Other Poems.* New York: Knopf, 1937. First edition, one of 1000 copies, this in second issue dust jacket with word 'conjunctions' (rather than misprinting 'conjunctioning') on front inner flap, 8vo., original yellow cloth, dust jacket, signed by author, offsetting from clipping on titlepage and facing page measuring approximately 3 1/2 x 4 inches, endpapers discolored at gutters, as usual, covers lightly dust soiled with some mottling of spine, otherwise very good. James S. Jaffe Rare Books Modern American Poetry - 268 2015 $6500

Stevens, Wallace 1879-1955 *The Necessary Angel. Essays on Reality and the Imagination.* New York: Knopf, 1951. First edition, one of 3000 copies, 8vo., original cloth, signed by author, fine, dust jacket. James S. Jaffe Rare Books Modern American Poetry - 285 2015 $6500

Stevens, Wallace 1879-1955 *Notes Toward a Supreme Fiction.* Cummington: Cummington Press, 1942. Limited first edition, octavo, 45 pages, this copy out of series and marked as a reviewer's copy, this copy belonged to Fugitive poet John Crowe Ransom, then editor of Kenyon Review. Honey & Wax Booksellers 1 - 37 2015 $1500

Stevens, Wallace 1879-1955 *Notes Toward a Supreme Fiction.* Cummington: Cummington Press, 1943. Second edition, limited to 330 hand printed copies, 8vo. original cloth backed boards plain unprinted dust jacket, although not called for, this copy signed by author, endpapers little discolored at gutters, small tape stain to upper edge of back board, otherwise fine, jacket missing piece a base of spine. James S. Jaffe Rare Books Modern American Poetry - 269 2015 $4500

Stevens, Wallace 1879-1955 *The Palm at the End of the Mind.* New York: Alfred A. Knopf, 1971. First edition, 4000 copies printed, tall 8vo., original cloth, dust jacket, fine. James S. Jaffe Rare Books Modern American Poetry - 278 2015 $100

Stevens, Wallace   1879-1955   *A Primitive Like an Orb.* New York: Banyan Press, 1948. First edition, limited to 500 copies, 8vo., original printed orange wrappers, although not called for, this copy signed by author, very fine.   James S. Jaffe Rare Books   Modern American Poetry - 273   2015 $4500

Stevens, Wallace   1879-1955   *Raoul Dufy.* New York: Pierre Beres, 1953. First edition, one of 200 numbered copies on handmade Arnold paper printed by Ram Press, oblong large 4to., original printed blue wrappers as issued, no copyright stamp on inside front wrapper and colophon page is not numbered in holograph, very fine.   James S. Jaffe Rare Books   Modern American Poetry - 276   2015 $1500

Stevens, Wallace   1879-1955   *Transport to Summer.* New York: Knopf, 1947. First edition, one of 1750 copies, small 8vo., original cloth backed boards, printed spine label, dust jacket, signed by author, endpapers discolored at gutters as often, otherwise near fine in dust jacket which is lightly faded at spine.   James S. Jaffe Rare Books   Modern American Poetry - 272   2015 $6500

Stevenson, Edward Luther   *Terrestrial and Celestial Globes: Their History and Construction, Including a Consideration of their Value as Aids in the Study of Geography and Astronomy.*   Mansfield Centre: Martino, n.d., Facsimile reprint of 1921 edition, one of 150 copies, 2 volumes bound as one, 8vo., numerous half tone plates and illustrations, dark blue cloth, gilt stamped red spine label, fine.   Jeff Weber Rare Books   178 - 1041   2015 $90

Stevenson, Robert Louis Balfour   1850-1894   *A Child's Garden of Verses.* London: Longmans, Green and Co., 1885. First edition, first printing of 1000 copies, with apostrophe on spine shaped like the number 7, the word "OF' in smaller type on spine and with no mention of "Two Series" in list of other works by author, small 8vo., blue cloth stamped in gilt, top edge gilt except for usual offsetting on endpaper, bright and fine, beautiful custom half leather box, printed on fine quality paper.   Aleph-bet Books, Inc.   109 - 452   2015 $6000

Stevenson, Robert Louis Balfour   1850-1894   *A Child's Garden of Verses.* London: Longman's Green and Co., 1885. First edition, first issue, publisher's presentation copy with their blindstamp on title "Presented by the Publisher", few very minor stains on last leaves at either end, 16mo., original blue cloth with bevelled edges, publisher's logo in gilt on upper cover, spine lettered gilt, spine very slightly faded, extremities trifle worn, top edge gilt, others untrimmed, preserved in cloth covered card chemise, blue cloth slip-in case with red lettering piece on spine, very good.   Blackwell's Rare Books   B179 - 100   2015   £2000

Stevenson, Robert Louis Balfour   1850-1894   *A Child's Garden of Verses.* London: Collins, n.d. circa, 1925. 4to., full leather with round gilt pictorial vignette on cover, top edge gilt, fine in publisher's box with color plate on cover, some fading to box, illustrations by Kate Elizabeth Oliver with color pictorial endpapers, 4 color plates plus numerous full and partial page black and whites, very scarce, rare in box.   Aleph-bet Books, Inc.   109 - 453   2015 $675

Stevenson, Robert Louis Balfour   1850-1894   *A Child's Garden of Verses.* Philadelphia: McKay, 1926. First edition with Le Mair illustrations, oblong 4to., green cloth, pictorial paste-on, fine in somewhat worn dust jacket, pictorial endpapers and 12 magnificent color plates by Le Mair, beautiful copy.   Aleph-bet Books, Inc.   109 - 259   2015 $875

Stevenson, Robert Louis Balfour   1850-1894   *The Dynamiter.* London: Longmans, Green & Co., 1885. First edition, original wrappers, very good, spine rebacked with green linen, very slight shelfwear, tight, clean copy.   Stephen Lupack   March 2015 - 2015 $195

Stevenson, Robert Louis Balfour   1850-1894   *Hitherto Unpublished Prose Writings.* Boston: Bibliophile Society, 1921. First edition, vellum backstrip and corners over maroon paper covered boards, near fine.   Beasley Books   2013 - 2015 $45

Stevenson, Robert Louis Balfour   1850-1894   *Island Nights Entertainments.* New York: Scribners, 1893. First edition, illustrations, very good+, spine trifle darkened, light surface soiling.   Stephen Lupack   March 2015 - 2015 $75

Stevenson, Robert Louis Balfour   1850-1894   *The Letters of Robert Louis Stevenson 1854-1894.* New Haven: Yale University Press, 1994. 8 volumes, large 8vo., still shrink wrapped, mint.   Any Amount of Books   2015 - C13578   2015   £240

Stevenson, Robert Louis Balfour   1850-1894   *Strange Case of Dr. Jekyll and Mr. Hyde.* London: Longmans Green and Co., 1886. First English edition, first issue and state, octavo, original printed wrappers with publication date corrected in ink as called for.   Honey & Wax Booksellers   3 - 17   2015 $7500

Stevenson, Robert Louis Balfour   1850-1894   *Strange Case of Dr. Jekyll and Mr. Hyde.* London: Longmans, Green and Co., 1886. First UK and first hardcover edition, fine, bright, square copy, housed in green quarter leather and cloth clamshell case with raised bands on spine and titles stamped in gold gilt, exceptional copy.   Buckingham Books   March 2015 - 22471   2015 $6000

Stevenson, Robert Louis Balfour 1850-1894 *Treasure Island.* London: Cassell, 1883. First edition, first issue, original red cloth, very attractive, tight copy with trivial rubbing to spine ends and corners, cloth tear to upper corner of front cover, spine gilt bright and unfaded, '1929' news clipping to front pastedown, former owner signatures to half title and name noted at head of page 1, front hinge cracked and holding, rear hinge starting, some scattered foxing, much nicer than usually found and without any repair or restoration, housed in custom folding box. B & B Rare Books, Ltd. 234 - 96 2015 $15,000

Stevenson, Robert Louis Balfour 1850-1894 *Treasure Island.* London: Ernest Benn, 1927. Limited to only 50 numbered copies, printed on handmade paper and signed by Edmund Dulac, 4to., full vellum with leather label on spine, 12 tipped in color plates and many detailed illustrations in black and white, beautiful copy, rare limited edition. Aleph-bet Books, Inc. 109 - 140 2015 $10,500

Stewart, Eliza Daniel *Memories of the Crusade: a Thrilling Account of the Great Uprising of the Women of Ohio in 1873, Against the Liquor Crime.* Columbus: William B. Hubbard & Co., 1889. Second edition, octavo, original red cloth with pictorial black and gilt stamping, negligible foxing to prefatory and concluding pages and along edges, some general dust staining to top edge, spine touch faded, minor wear to corners and tips, else very good. Tavistock Books Temperance - 2015 $50

Stewart, George R. *John Phoenix, Esq. The Veritable Squailbob. A Life of Captain George H. Derby U.S.A.* New York: Henry Holt and Co., 1937. First edition, frontispiece, 19 plates and illustrations, maroon cloth, gilt, fixed ends bit darkened from publisher's binding glue, else fine with pictorial dust jacket. Argonaut Book Shop Holiday Season 2014 - 281 2015 $75

Stewart, John *A New Practical System of Human Reason, Divested of all Supernatural and Metaphysical Relations and Founded on its Only True Basis...* Philadelphia?: Thomas Dobson?, 1796? First American edition?, 12mo., removed, severe browning spot on title affecting one or two letters, other browning spots toward front, much less severe. M & S Rare Books, Inc. 97 - 106 2015 $3750

Stewart, John *The Revelation of Nature, with the Prophesy of reason.* New York: Mott & Lyon, 1796. First edition, 12mo., contemporary two-toned boards, detached, uncut. M & S Rare Books, Inc. 97 - 293 2015 $2000

Stewart, John *The Revelation of Nature with the Prophesy of Reason.* New York: Mott & Lyon, 1796. First edition, 16mo., contemporary calf, leather label, spine worn. M & S Rare Books, Inc. 97 - 294 2015 $1750

Stewart, Rick *Charles M. Russell, Sculptor.* Amon Carter Museum, 1994. First edition, one of the special edition limited to 350 copies, bound in leather, signed by editor, this #151, dark green full leather, titles stamped in silver gilt on spine, tan endpapers, rare, fine in original cloth slipcase. Buckingham Books March 2015 - 36785 2015 $695

Stiglitz, Joseph E. *Freefall. America, Free Markets and the Sinking World Economy.* New York: W. W. Norton, 2010. Stated first edition, signed and inscribed by author, 8vo., fine in fine dust jacket. By the Book, L. C. Special List 10 - 22 2015 $175

Stiglitz, Joseph E. *Making Globalization Work.* New York: W. W. Norton, 2006. First edition, 8vo., signed by author, fine hardback in fine dust jacket. By the Book, L. C. Special List 10 - 20 2015 $110

Stiglitz, Joseph E. *The Three Trillion Dollar War.* New York: W. W. Norton, 2008. First edition, 8vo., signed by author, as new in like dust jacket. By the Book, L. C. Special List 10 - 21 2015 $150

Stiles, Percy Goldthwait *Dreams.* Cambridge: Harvard University Press, 1927. First edition, very good, sticker removal traces in lower corner front board. Beasley Books 2013 - 2015 $45

Stillingfleet, Benjamin 1702-1771 *An Essay on Conversation.* London: printed for L. Gilliver and J. Clarke, 1737. First edition, folio, recent marbled wrappers, very good, fine. C. R. Johnson Foxon R-Z - 1197r-z 2015 $536

Stillingfleet, Edward *A Discourse Concerning Bonds of resignation of Benefices in Point of law and Conscience.* London: printed by J. H. for Henry Mortlok, 1695. First edition, 8vo., complete with final leaf of ads, contemporary panelled calf rather worn, but very good, crisp copy with original label, early ownership signature on front free endpaper of John Willis of Lymington. John Drury Rare Books 2015 - 15119 2015 $221

The Stilton Hero: a Poem. London: printed for M. Cooper, 1745. First edition, 4to., 14 pages, disbound, wanting half title as are two of the five copies listed in ESTC, otherwise excellent condition. C. R. Johnson Foxon R-Z - 937r-z 2015 $1379

Stilwell, Hart *Uncovered Wagon.* Garden City: Doubleday, 1947. First edition, 8vo., near fine in lightly rubbed dust jacket, scarce. Buckingham Books March 2015 - 19324 2015 $250

Stindt, Fred A. *The Northwestern Pacific Railroad 1964-1985.* Kelseyville: Fred A. Stindt, 1988. Second printing, quarto, 177 pages, photos, maps, charts, dark green cloth, gilt, very fine, pictorial dust jacket (slight chipping to head of jacket spine).   Argonaut Book Shop   Holiday Season 2014 - 282   2015 $125

Stindt, Fred A. *San Francisco's Century of Street Cars.* Kelseyville: Fred A. Stindt, 1990. first edition, first printing, quarto, profusely illustrated with photos, double page color map, green pictorial cloth, gilt, very fine with pictorial dust jacket (short repaired tear to top edge).   Argonaut Book Shop   Holiday Season 2014 - 283   2015 $90

Stockdale, John *The Whole Proceedings on the Trial of an Information Exhibited ex Officio, by the King's Attorney General, Against John Stockdale for a Libel on the House of Commons Tried in the Court of King's Bench Westminster on Wednesday the 9th of December 1789...* London: John Stockdale, 1790. First edition, 8vo., large copy with generous margins, contemporary marbled boards, now rebacked in plain calf with printed spine label, entirely uncut, very good, sometime in subscription library with borrowing slip (complete with names and dates of borrowing).   John Drury Rare Books   2015 - 24414   2015 $656

Stockdale, Robert L. *Tommy Dorsey on the Side.* Institute Jazz Studies/Scare, 1995. First edition, very good+ with sticker and residue on rear board, glossy photo section.   Beasley Books   2013 - 2015 $40

Stocks, Michael *Report of the Trial of Michael Stocks, Esq. for Willful and Corrupt Perjury at the Yorkshire lent Assizes 1815 before the Hon. Sir Alexander Thompson...* Huddersfield: printed for the editor by J. Lancashire and sold by Longman, Hurst, Rees and Co., London..., 1815. 8vo., contemporary half calf over marbled boards, neatly rebacked and gilt lettered, very good, only edition, very scarce.   John Drury Rare Books   2015 - 23453   2015 $787

Stoddard, William O. *Little Smoke.* New York: D. Appleton & Co., 1891. First edition, 8vo., illustrations by Fred Dellenbaugh with 14 full page illustrations plus many head and tailpieces, exceptional copy, red gilt cloth, light cover soil, owner name and bookplate, tight and clean, very good+.   Aleph-bet Books, Inc.   109 - 454   2015 $150

Stoddard, William O. *Ned, Son of Webb; What He Did.* Boston: Dana Estes & Co., 1900. First edition, octavo, 8 inserted plates with illustrations by Victor Searles, original pictorial red cloth, front cover stamped in blue, black and white, spine panel stamped in white and black.   L. W. Currey, Inc.   Boy's Adventure Fiction 2015 - 74   2015 $125

Stoker, Bram 1847-1912 *Dracula.* New York: Limited Editions Club, 1965. Limited to 1500 numbered copies, signed by artist, wood engravings by Felix Hoffmann, 4to., cloth, slipcase, well preserved, Monthly letter loosely inserted.   Oak Knoll Books   25 - 43   2015 $285

Stoker, Bram 1847-1912 *Dracula's Guest and Other Weird Stories.* London: Routledge, 1914. First edition, 8vo., original scarlet cloth blind patterned, endpapers very slightly browned, prelims and fore edges very slightly foxed, cloth, very clean and bright, near fine.   Any Amount of Books   March 2015 - C1303   2015   £375

Stoker, Bram 1847-1912 *The Jewel of Seven Stars.* New York: Harpers, 1904. First American edition, very good in pictorial black cloth covered boards in later (1920's) jacket with internal tape mends and wear along folds.   Mordida Books   March 2015 - 002117   2015 $350

Stokes, G. Vernon *A Town Dog in the Country.* London & Edinburgh: W. & R. Chambers, 1924. First edition, large 4to., original illustrated boards, lettering slightly rubbed and slightly chipped at spine, corners slightly rubbed, inner hinge slightly broken, overall bright, very good- copy, neat non-authorial inscription to half title.   Any Amount of Books   2015 - A69335   2015   £160

Stokes, J. *The Complete Cabinet Maker and Upholsterer's Guide...* London: A. K. Newman & Co., circa, 1829. First edition?, small 8vo., lacking half titles, 16 engraved plates, original pictorial boards, skillfully rebacked and preserved in neat calf backed slipcase, rare issue with Newman imprint.   Marlborough Rare Books   List 54 - 81   2015   £1100

Stokes, W. Royal *The Jazz Scene an Informal History from New Orleans to 1990.* New York: Oxford, 1991. First printing, 8vo., author's presentation for Vance Allen, photos, paper over boards with cloth spine, very good in dust jacket.   Second Life Books Inc.   190 - 204   2015 $150

Stokowski, Olga Saaroff *The Magic World of Music.* New York: Norton, 1936. First edition, inscribed by author to Edward Specter (helped organize the Pittsburgh Symphony orchestra), illustrations by Emil Preetorius, very good, some wear to extremities, clean, tight text.   Stephen Lupack   March 2015 - 2015 $125

Stone, L. Joseph *The Competent Infant.* New York: Basic Books, 1973. First edition, near fine with sunned spine in like dust jacket.   Beasley Books   2013 - 2015 $45

Stone, Mary *Children's Stories that Never Grow Old.* Chicago: Reilly & Britton, 1908. First edition, 8vo., yellow pictorial cloth, near fine, illustrations by John R. Neill with over 70 full page color illustrations plus several black and whites.   Aleph-bet Books, Inc.   109 - 320   2015 $750

Stone, Oliver *The Platoon.* Los Angeles: 1985. Typescript schooting script, very good, black and white clear thermal binding. Any Amount of Books 2015 - C11788 2015 £180

Stone, Peter F. *The Oriental Rug Lexicon.* Seattle: University of Washington Press, 1997. First edition, 4to., wrappers, fine. Beasley Books 2013 - 2015 $45

Stone, Robert *Children of Light.* New York: 1986. First edition, signed by author, as new in dust jacket. Gemini Fine Books & Arts, Ltd. Art Reference & Illustrated Books: First Editions - 2015 $50

Stone, Robert *A Hall of Mirrors.* Boston: Houghton Mifflin, 1967. First edition, inscribed by author, near fine in very good, lightly foxed dust jacket with creased tear to lower rear panel. Ken Lopez, Bookseller 164 - 195 2015 $950

Stone, Robert *Outerbridge Reach.* Boston: 1992. First edition, 1/300 copies numbered and signed by author, as new in slipcase. Gemini Fine Books & Arts, Ltd. Art Reference & Illustrated Books: First Editions - 2015 $95

Stone, Thomas *An Essay on Agriculture with a View to Inform Gentlemen of Landed Property...* Lynn: printed by W. Whittingham and sold by J. Robson and R. Baldwin, 1785. First edition, scarce, 8vo., original boards, covers with minor stains and wear to spine, entirely uncut, good, scarce. John Drury Rare Books 2015 - 20178 2015 $699

Stone, William *Pepe was the Saddest Bird.* New York: Alfred Knopf, 1944. Stated first edition, 8vo., pictorial boards, very good+ in dust jacket with few big chips, illustrations by Nicolas Mordvinoff. Aleph-bet Books, Inc. 109 - 300 2015 $125

Stoneham, Charles *The Birds of the British Islands.* London: E. Grant Richards, 1906. First edition, 5 volumes, 2 color foldout maps, double page black and red anatomical diagram and 318 black and white plates, all with captioned tissue guards, list of subscribers at rear, errata slip tipped into volume 1, original red buckram cloth lettered gilt, first 3 volumes in original red dust jackets lettered gilt, occasional light foxing or browning to pages, plates generally very clean, boards and spines partially sunned, slightly rubbed, slight fraying to some dust jacket edges, some sunning, overall very decent and sound. Any Amount of Books 2015 - A85628 2015 £650

Stones, A. W. *A Complete System of Shorthand, Adapted to the Pulpit and Courts of Law, and to every Purpose of Neat and Expeditious Writing.* Whitby: printed by and for Clark and Medd, sold also by Rest Fenner & T. Banshard London, 1818. First edition, very rare, 12mo., engraved titlepage and 9 other engraved plates, recently well bound in cloth lettered in gilt, very good. John Drury Rare Books March 2015 - 19298 2015 £306

Stonham, Charles *The Birds of the British Islands.* London: E. Grant Richards, 1906-1911. Large quarto, 5 volumes, 318 uncolored plates by Lillian Medland, publisher's cloth, top edge gilt, few flecks, internally some light spotting. Andrew Isles 2015 - 32428 2015 $2000

Stopar, Ivan *Goldenstein's National Costumes of Carniola.* Arterika: Goldenstein's National Costumes of Carniola, 1993. number 59 of 299?, nicely illustrated, black silken binding, in silken clamshell box, fine copy in fine box. Stephen Lupack March 2015 - 2015 $150

Stopes, Marie Carmichael *Contraception (Birth Control). Its Theory, History and Practice a*

Manual for the Medical and Legal Professions. London: John Bale, Sons & Danielson, 1923. First edition, 8vo., 4 plates, fern green cloth with remnant of dust jacket laid in, endpaper browned, else near fine, scarce. Second Life Books Inc. 191 - 87 2015 $450

Stoppard, Tom *The Coast of Utopia: a Trilogy.* London: Faber & Faber, 2002. First edition, 8vo., 3 volumes, fine copies in fine dust jackets (third volume faintly bumped at foot of spine, else as new), each signed by author. Any Amount of Books March 2015 - A08110 2015 £450

Stops, Mrs. *Punctuation Personified; or Painting Made Easy.* London: 1824. First edition, 12mo., 16 hand colored plates, original grey printed wrappers,. Honey & Wax Booksellers 3 - 7 2015 $3000

Stories for Little People. J. H. Shears & Co., 1926. 9 1/2 x 7 1/4 inches, color frontispiece, each page text with red pictorial wide borders, red cloth with color illustrated onlay front cover, gilt titling front cover and backstrip, black and white pictorial endpapers, gilt tarnished on backstrips, inscription dated 1926, very good. Ian Hodgkins & Co. Ltd. 134 - 199 2015 £85

The Story of Peter Rabbit. Done in Poster Stamps. New York: United Art Pub. Co., 1915. 28 pages, pictorial border facing each page text, centre of which owner has affixed corresponding color stamp, blue/grey boards with color stamp front cover, surrounded by dark blue and brown pictorial border and titling, 4 3.4 x 4 inches, name on pastedown, very good. Ian Hodgkins & Co. Ltd. 134 - 205 2015 £95

The Story of Peter Rabbit and Other Stories. L. W. Walter Co., 1910. 35 full page color illustrations, frontispiece, pictorial borders, red cloth backed boards with color pictorial and titling on front cover, 7 3/4 x 7 1/4 inches, light soiling to boards and little wear to extremities, very good.   Ian Hodgkins & Co. Ltd.   134 - 207   2015   £68

The Story of Peter Rabbit. (And Other Stories).   Whitman, 1928. 9 1/8 x 7 inches, frontispiece, titlepage illustration, numerous text illustrations by Marion Frederick, yellow cloth backed color boards, front cover with color illustration and titling on yellow ground, 9 1/8 x 7 inches, pages browned as usual, very nice.   Ian Hodgkins & Co. Ltd.   134 - 229   2015   £45

Story of the Three Little Pigs.   London: Frederick Warne, n.d. circa, 1908. First Book illustrated edition, featuring 8 fine and fabulous full page color illustrations plus many line illustrations in text by L. Leslie Brooke, quite scarce.   Aleph-bet Books, Inc.   109 - 71   2015 $200

Stout, G. F.   *Analytic, Psychology.*   London: Swan Sonnenschein, 1909. Third edition, 2 volumes, very good+.   Beasley Books   2013 - 2015 $85

Stout, Hosea   *On the Mormon Frontier. The Diary of Hosea Stout 1844-1861.*   Salt Lake City: University of Utah Press, 1964. First edition, 8vo., 2 volumes, green cloth, titles stamped gilt on front cover and spine, maps on endpapers, volume I fine, bright, clean in dust jacket with light wear to head of spine and corners and lightly rubbed on rear panel, volume II fine, bright, clean in dust jacket with light wear to head of spine, corners and extremities.   Buckingham Books   March 2015 - 32818   2015 $250

Stout, Rex   *And Be a Villan.*   New York: Viking Press, 1948. First edition, fine in near fine, very lightly rubbed dust jacket, from the collection of Duke Collier.   Royal Books   36 - 120   2015 $450

Stout, Rex   *Before Midnight.*   New York: Viking, 1955. First edition, fine in dust jacket with nicks at top of spine.   Mordida Books   March 2015 - 010239   2015 $200

Stout, Rex   *Before Midnight.*   New York: Viking Press, 1955. First edition, fine in near fine dust jacket, very lightly corner rubbed, from the collection of Duke Collier.   Royal Books   36 - 121   2015 $350

Stout, Rex   *Black Orchids.*   New York: Farrar and Rinehart, 1942. First edition, fine in near fine dust jacket, jacket extremely fresh and colorful, only touch of rubbing to couple of corners, stunning copy, from the collection of Duke Collier.   Royal Books   36 - 105   2015 $4500

Stout, Rex   *The Broken Vase.*   New York: Farrar & Rinehart Inc., 1941. First edition, fine in near fine, clean dust jacket with light sunning to spine and light wear at spine crown, superior copy.   Ed Smith Books   82 - 28   2015 $750

Stout, Rex   *The Broken Vase.*   New York: Farrar and Rinehart, 1941. First edition, fine in exceptionally bright, near fine dust jacket, spectacular copy, from the collection of Duke Collier.   Royal Books   36 - 109   2015 $2000

Stout, Rex   *Death of a Doxy.*   New York: Viking Press, 1966. First edition, fine in near fine dust jacket, some faint rubbing to rear jacket panel, tiny closed tear at bottom front hinge fold (with associated small, neat cello tape repair at verso), from the collection of Duke Collier.   Royal Books   36 - 122   2015 $325

Stout, Rex   *Death of a Doxy.*   New York: Viking, 1966. First edition, fine in dust jacket.   Mordida Books   March 2015 - 010424   2015 $150

Stout, Rex   *Double for Death.*   New York: Farrar Rinehart, 1939. First edition, slightly cocked, else near fine in bright, about near fine dust jacket with some very shallow creasing at crown and top front panel, from the collection of Duke Collier.   Royal Books   36 - 119   2015 $450

Stout, Rex   *The Father Hunt.*   New York: Viking, 1968. First edition, fine, inscription, otherwise fine in price clipped dust jacket with some tiny wear and couple of short closed tears.   Mordida Books   March 2015 - 0009981   2015 $95

Stout, Rex   *Fer-De-Lance.*   New York: Farrar & Rinehart, 1934. First edition, lettering on spine faded, otherwise very good.   Mordida Books   March 2015 - 011423   2015 $400

Stout, Rex   *Fer-de-Lance.*   New York: Farrar and Rinehart, 1934. First edition, near fine in like dust jacket, jacket rare, with Farrar and Rinehart circular 'recommendation' sticker on front panel, pink topstain very bright gilt bright and complete, jacket with only couple of tiny chips and some expert repairs (not restoration) at upper spine panel, from the collection of Duke Collier.   Royal Books   36 - 97   2015 $25,000

Stout, Rex   *Fer-de-Lance.*   New York: Otto Penzler Books, 1996. First facsimile edition, as new, unread copy in dust jacket.   Buckingham Books   March 2015 - 30605   2015 $300

Stout, Rex   *Fer-De-Lance.*   New York: Otto Penzler, 1996. First edition, exact facsimile of Farrar & Rinehart first edition, very fine in dust jacket.   Mordida Books   March 2015 - 010237 2015 $200

Stout, Rex *Forest Fire.* London: Faber and Faber, 1934. Uncorrected proof, very good in plain brown wrappers, title label on spine, square and tight with few crease to spine panel, custom quarter leather clamshell box, from the collection of Duke Collier.   Royal Books   36 - 104   2015 $4500

Stout, Rex *Gambit.* New York: Viking Press, 1962. First edition, fine and unread in fine dust jacket pristine copy, only hint of rubbing at a couple of spine corners to note, absolutely none of the color fading usually found, from the collection of Duke Collier.   Royal Books   36 - 118   2015 $475

Stout, Rex *Golden Remedy.* New York: Vanguard, 1931. First edition, fine in about fine dust jacket, only minute traces on rear panel, from the collection of Duke Collier.   Royal Books 36 - 103   2015 $4750

Stout, Rex *The Hand in the Glove.* New York: Farrar and Rinehart, 1937. First edition, fine in very good example of rare dust jacket, jacket with some chipping at spine ends and corners, though no titling affected, custom clamshell box, from the collection of Duke Collier.   Royal Books   36 - 101   2015 $7500

Stout, Rex *Homicide Trinity.* New York: Viking, 1962. First edition, fine in dust jacket with crease tear at lower edge of front panel and tiny wear at spine ends.   Mordida Books   March 2015 - 010240   2015 $200

Stout, Rex *The League of Frightened Men.* Farrar & Rinehart Inc., 1935. First edition, gold gilt on spine bit faded, gilt on front cover sharp and bright, pages 301-304 carelessly penned at bottom edge, green top color is bright and unfaded, else near fine, tight, square in dust jacket which has been internally restored, extremely handsome, very scarce.   Buckingham Books   March 2015 - 35185   2015 $10,750

Stout, Rex *The League of Frightened Men.* Farrar & Rinehart, 1935. First edition, spine lettering slightly faded, otherwise fine.   Mordida Books   March 2015 - 011424   2015 $500

Stout, Rex *The League of Frightened Men.* New York: Farrar and Rinehart, 1935. First edition, review copy with publisher's slip with rubber stamped date of publication, along with slip containing quote by William Lyons regarding Stout's first book, Fer-de-lance, fine in near fine dust jacket, absolutely stunning copy, from the collection of Duke Collier.   Royal Books   36 - 98   2015 $20,000

Stout, Rex *Not Quite Dead Enough.* New York: Farrar & Rinehart, 1944. First edition, fine in near fine dust jacket, attractive bookplate, tiny date notation on front endpaper, else book quite clean, jacket has single very tiny chip at crown (no titling affected), else fine, from the collection of Duke Collier.   Royal Books   36 - 114   2015 $1500

Stout, Rex *O Careless Love.* New York: Farrar & Rinehart, 1935. First edition, very good in like dust jacket, binding slightly cocked, touch of soil to front endpaper, jacket has few small chips at spine ends and extremities and bit of rubbing to front flap fold, uncommon in jacket, from the collection of Duke Collier.   Royal Books   36 - 108   2015 $2000

Stout, Rex *Over My Dead body.* New York: Farrar and Rinehart, 1940. First edition, very good in like dust jacket, slight lean, very light soil to book, single lending library stamp at top of front endpaper, jacket complete but with archival tape mends on verso and one mend to recto at crown, from the collection of Duke Collier.   Royal Books 36 - 110   2015 $1850

Stout, Rex *Plot It Yourself.* New York: Viking Press, 1959. First edition, near fine in fine dust jacket, faintest bit of toning at edge of rear jacket flap, else superb, fresh copy, without trace of usual fading to jacket spine, from the collection of Duke Collier.   Royal Books   36 - 117   2015 $550

Stout, Rex *The President Vanishes.* New York: Farrar and Rinehart, 1934. First edition, fine in near fine dust jacket, lightly worn at top of spine and toned at spine and edges of front panel, from the collection of Duke Collier.   Royal Books   36 - 113   2015 $1500

Stout, Rex *The Red Box.* New York: Farrar and Rinehart, 1937. First edition, very good in like dust jacket, spine lean and some wear along joints, else book bright and clean, jacket complete with touch of fading to red titling on spine, small chips at couple of corners, split along front flap fold running about halfway down, bright, presentable copy, from the collection of Duke Collier.   Royal Books   36 - 99   2015 $9500

Stout, Rex *A Right to Die.* New York: Viking Press, 1964. First edition, inscribed by author Dec. 26 1964 to Elizabeth Boyne, fine in fine dust jacket, from the collection of Duke Collier.   Royal Books   36 - 107   2015 $2500

Stout, Rex *The Second Confession.* New York: Viking Press, 1949. First edition, signed and dated in year of publication by author 10/3/49, spine bit cocked, else near fine in very good, price clipped dust jacket with moderate shelfwear, slight fading to spine, rubbing at spine ends and extremities, from the collection of Duke Collier.   Royal Books   36 - 115   2015 $1250

Stout, Rex *The Second Confession.* New York: Viking, 1949. First edition, very good in dust jacket with internal tape mends, chips at base of spine and at corners, slightly faded spine, several short closed tears, scrape on spine and wear along folds.   Mordida Books   March 2015 - 011437   2015 $90

Stout, Rex *Seed on the Wind.* New York: Vanguard Press, 1930. First edition, fine, no soiling to fragile yellow cloth and top edge still richly colored, rare dust jacket, near fine, remarkably clean and bright with no tears, chips or rubbed spots, from the collection of Duke Collier.   Royal Books   36 - 102   2015 $6000

Stout, Rex *The Silent Speaker.* New York: Viking, 1946. First edition, very good in dust jacket with label removed from base of spine chipping at top of spine, darkened spine, wear along front flap fold.   Mordida Books   March 2015 - 011432   2015 $150

Stout, Rex *Some Buried Caesar.* New York: Viking Press, 1939. First edition, binding very slightly cocked, else near fine in bright, very good dust jacket, with small chips and some shallow creasing at corners, but quite colorful overall, from the collection of Duke Collier.   Royal Books   36 - 106   2015 $2750

Stout, Rex *Some Buried Caesar.* New York: Farrar & Rinehart, 1939. First edition, staining along front cover, hinge and along internal hinges, spine slightly darkened, stamp on front endpaper, otherwise very good.   Mordida Books   March 2015 - 011426   2015 $100

Stout, Rex *Three Doors to Death.* New York: Viking, 1950. First edition, very good in dust jacket with faded spine, large chips at spine ends and at corners, several closed tears along folds and along edges.   Mordida Books   March 2015 - 011438   2015 $80

Stout, Rex *Too Many Clients.* New York: Viking Press, 1960. First edition, fine in fine dust jacket, inscribed by author Nov. 17 1960 for Ed, from the collection of Duke Collier.   Royal Books   36 - 111   2015 $1750

Stout, Rex *Too Many Cooks.* London: Collins, 1938. First edition, very good in good dust jacket, foxing to prelim leaves, binding bit cocked, some discoloration to cloth at heel, jacket is moderately worn, chipping at spine ends, chip at heel affects portion of publisher's device, scarce in any condition, from the collection of Duke Collier.   Royal Books 36 - 112   2015 $1750

Stout, Rex *Too Many Women.* New York: Viking Press, 1947. First edition, fine and unread in fine dust jacket, touch of foxing to endpapers, else nice, unworn, from the collection of Duke Collier.   Royal Books   36 - 116   2015 $650

Stout, Rex *Triple Jeopardy.* New York: Viking, 1952. First edition, inscription, spotting on fore edge and some darkening on endpapers, else very good in dust jacket with some short internal tape mends and some tiny wear along edges.   Mordida Books   March 2015 - 010422   2015 $85

Stout, Rex *Trouble in Triplicate.* New York: Viking, 1949. First edition, fine in very good price clipped dust jacket, few nicks along edges, couple of short closed tears, some slight spine fading.   Mordida Books   March 2015 - 011433   2015 $150

Stout, Rex *Where There's a Will.* New York: Farrar & Rinehart, 1940. Near fine in like dust jacket, usual slight fading to jacket's red spine title, attractive owner bookplate on front pastedown, else superior copy, couple of tiny closed tears and corner rubs to note, from the collection of Duke Collier.   Royal Books   36 - 100   2015 $6500

Stowe, Harriet Elizabeth Beecher 1811-1896 *Alone with Thee.* London: Raphael Tuck and Sons, n.d. circa, 1900. 3 3/4 x 4 1/2 inches, due cut in shape of star surrounded by flowers, string bound, fine, 5 very beautiful full page chromolithographs, 1 smaller chromo plus delicate line illustrations on other pages.   Aleph-bet Books, Inc.   109 - 455   2015 $750

Stowe, Harriet Elizabeth Beecher 1811-1896 *House and Home Papers.* Boston: Ticknor & Fields, 1865. First edition, very good+, light shelfwear, little light random foxing, cloth wrinkle to upper rear cover, spine gilt solid, nice, tight text.   Stephen Lupack   March 2015 - 2015 $100

Stowe, Harriet Elizabeth Beecher 1811-1896 *Uncle Tom's Cabin; or Life Among the Lowly.* New York: Limited Editions Club, 1938. Limited to 1500 numbered copies signed by artist, Miguel Covarrubias, tall 8vo., quarter leather over marbled paper covered boards, all edges marbled, slipcase (minor wear), well preserved, 16 lithographs.   Oak Knoll Books   25 - 19   2015 $350

Strachey, John *The Finances and Public Works of India From 1869-1881.* London: Kegan Paul, Trench & co., 1882. First edition, appealing presentation copy, inscribed by authors, John and Richard Strachey for Sir Edward Strachey, 3rd Baronet, bound in original red cloth with corners slightly bumped and spine faded, text pages clean and binding tight, very good.   The Kelmscott Bookshop   11 - 49   2015 $450

Strack, Don *Diesels of the Union Pacific 1934 to 1982. The Classic Era - volume I.* Halifax: Withers Pub., 1999. First edition, 4to., black and white photos, black cloth, gilt, very fine with pictorial dust jacket.   Argonaut Book Shop Holiday Season 2014 - 284   2015 $60

Strada, Famiano *Famiani Stradae Romani e Societate Iesu De Bello Belgico Decades Duae Ab Excess Caroli V...* Mainz: Impensis Johann Godfrid Schonwetter Mogutiae, 1651. 30 folding battle scenes and 25 portraits, few misbound as usual, titlepage preceded by decorative titlepage featuring a map, later half morocco over brown buckram, red title label lettered and ruled gilt, later endpapers, pencilled note to f.f.e.p states "rebound Sheffield 1949", very mild chipping to decorative titlepage, mild to moderate brown spotting/toning to certain sections of text block, very occasional tear, overall very good.   Any Amount of Books   2015 - C5774   2015   £750

Strahan, Kay Cleaver *Footprints.* Garden City: Doubleday, 1929. First edition, fine in very good dust jacket with chipped spine ends and corners, wear along folds and several short closed tears.   Mordida Books   March 2015 - 002128   2015 $75

Strain, Isaac G. *Cordillera and Pampa, Mountain and Plain. Sketches of a Journey in Chili, and the Argentine Provinces in 1849.* New York: Horace H. Moore, 1853. First edition, inscribed by author, small 8vo., brown cloth stamped in blind and gilt, gilt medallion, very good+, spine sunned to medium brown, minor wear at tips.   Kaaterskill Books   19 - 145   2015 $250

Straker, C. *Instructions in the Art of Lithography.* London: published by Straker and Sons, 80 Bishopsgate Street, 1867. Royal 8vo., price list of lithographic presses inks and materials 6 color plates, original green cloth, upper cover blocked in blind and gilt lettered.   Marlborough Rare Books List 53 - 45   2015   £485

Strand, Mark *& Clouds.* New York: ACA Galleries, 1999. First edition, square 8vo., illustrations by Wendy Mark, boards, dust jacket, signed by author and artist, fine.   James S. Jaffe Rare Books   Modern American Poetry - 287   2015 $1750

Strand, Mark *The Continuous Life. Eighteen Poems.* Iowa City: Windhover Press, 1990. First edition, folio, 2 woodcuts by Neil Welliver, original Japanese style handmade paper wrappers, poet Phil Levine's own copy with his ownership signature, fine.   James S. Jaffe Rare Books   Modern American Poetry - 288   2015 $450

Strang, Herbert *The Flying Boat: a Story of Adventure and Misadventure.* London: Henry Frowde and Stoughton, 1912. First edition, octavo, 6 inserted plates with color illustrations by T. C. Dugdale, original pictorial blue cloth, front and spine panels stamped in black, red, yellow, white and gold, all edges stained black.   L. W. Currey, Inc.   Boy's Adventure Fiction 2015 - 38 2015 $225

Strange Tales of Peril and Adventure. London: Religious Tract Society, n.d., 1901? First edition, octavo, 23 inserted plates, including frontispiece, original pictorial brown cloth, front and spine panels stamped in gray, black and gold.   L. W. Currey, Inc.   Boy's Adventure Fiction 2015 - 79   2015 $100

Strasbourg, Thomas De *Thoma Ab Argentina. Eremitarum Diui Augustini Prioris Generalis Qui Floruit Anno Christi 1345 Commentaria in IIII...* Ridgewood: Greg Press, 1965. Facsimile, 2 parts bound together, tall 4to., red cloth, very good+.   Jeff Weber Rare Books   178 - 1057   2015 $200

Straub, Peter *Ghost Story.* New York: Coward McCann & Geoghegan, 1979. First edition, fine in about fine dust jacket with small bump at bottom of spine, this copy signed by author and annotated + deformed, as he calls it, on approximately 40 of the first 100 pages.   Between the Covers Rare Books   196 - 156   2015 $650

Straub, Peter *Open Air.* Shannon: Irish University Press, 1972. First edition, inscribed by author, fine in wrappers, near fine dust jacket, scarce.   Ken Lopez, Bookseller   164 - 199   2015 $250

Streeter, Floyd B. *The Kaw: the Heart of a nation.* New York: Farrar & Rinehart, 1941. First edition, 8vo., grey cloth, blindstamped front cover, titles stamped in gold on spine, pictorial endpapers, illustrations, map, fine in price clipped dust jacket.   Buckingham Books   March 2015 - 27936   2015 $175

Streeter, Floyd B. *Prairie Trails & Cow Towns.* Boston: Chapman & Grimes, 1936. First edition, 8vo., signed and dated by author, laid in is type letter dated May 9 1946 on Kansas State College stationery and signed in ink by Streeter, fine, tight and bright copy in internally reinforced with archival tape dust jacket with light wear to spine end and corners, lightly soiled at head of spine, sharp, rare in dust jacket.   Buckingham Books   March 2015 - 31789   2015 $2250

Strevell, Charles Nettleton *As I Recall Them.* N.P.: privately printed, n.d. circa, 1943. First edition, cloth, illustrations, spine ends and corners lightly rubbed, else near fine.   Buckingham Books   March 2015 - 28202   2015 $275

Strickland, George *A Discourse on the Poor Laws of England and Scotland on the state of the Poor of Ireland and On Emigration.* London: James Ridgway, 1827. First edition, 8vo., early 19th century half calf over marbled boards, neatly rebacked and lettered, armorial bookplate of Ferguson of Raith, very good, uncommon.   John Drury Rare Books   2015 - 24455   2015 $612

Strickland, George *Sobriety. A Letter to the Rate Payers of England on Asylums, Their Management and Expenses.* York: J. Sampson; London: Whittaker and Co., 1861. 8vo., 52 pages, 4 colored lithographic plates, original yellow glazed pictorial card covers, paper of spine worn, short tear, no loss, affecting inner margin of covers and first few leaves, nonetheless reasonably good copy. John Drury Rare Books 2015 - 18088 2015 $177

Stringer, Arthur *The Shadow.* New York: Century, 1913. First edition, hinges repaired, otherwise near fine in tan pictorial cloth covered boards in good fragment dust jacket which has numerous pieces missing and internal tape repairs. Mordida Books March 2015 - 002135 2015 $75

Stringer, Arthur *The Wire Tappers.* Boston: Little Brown, 1906. First edition, fine in pictorial gray cloth covered boards, fine, illustrations by Arthur William Brown. Mordida Books March 2015 - 002133 2015 $75

Stringham, Paul H. *Illinois Terminal. The Electric Years.* Glendale: Interurban Press, 1989. First edition, 4to., fine in fine dust jacket. Beasley Books 2013 - 2015 $45

Strong, Leonard Alfred George *The Big Man.* London: William Jackson, 1931. First edition, slip tipped-in announcing that Joiner & Steele published Furnival Books, but the original Jackson imprint is retained for typographical uniformly, printed at the Chiswick Press in an edition limited to 550 numbered copies signed by author, of which 500 only were for sale, frontispiece by Tirzah Garwood, near fine, scarce paper and glassine dust jacket with small chips. Stephen Lupack March 2015 - 2015 $60

Strouse, Norman *The Passionate Pirate.* North Hills: Bird & Bull Press, 1964. First edition, limited to 200 numbered copies, this written on colophon "No. 1, H.M. copy Bound by myself - I decided binding was not for me - M.M.", printed and bound by Bird and Bull Press, and printed on Mosher handmade paper, loosely inserted is xerox of small review in NY Times Book Review for this book, two TLS's from Stouse to Morris dated 1967 and 1981, handmade paper has foxed along edges, 8vo., quarter brown morocco, decorated paper over boards. Oak Knoll Books 306 - 138 2015 $450

Strunk, William *The Elements of Style.* New York: Harcourt, Brace and Co., 1920. First published edition, octavo, original blue cloth cover printed paper boards. Honey & Wax Booksellers 2 - 20 2015 $1500

Struthers, John *How to Improve the Teaching in the Scottish Universities.* Edinburgh: Sutherland and Knox, 1859. First edition, 8vo., 36 pages, original printed card covers, minor edge chips, very good, inscribed by author for Dr. Handyside. John Drury Rare Books 2015 - 13968 2015 $89

Strutt, Robert John *John William Strutt, Third Baron Rayleigh by his son Robert John Strutt.* London: Edward Arnold, 1924. 8vo., frontispiece, 4 plates, original maroon blind and gilt stamped cloth, very good. Jeff Weber Rare Books 178 - 1049 2015 $40

Struve, Friedrich Georg Wilhelm *Expediton Chronometrique Executee par Ordre de Sa Majeste l'Empereur Nicolas 1er entre Poulkova et Altona pour la Determination de la Longitude Geographique Relative de l'Observatoire Central de Russie.* St. Petersburg: 1844. First edition, folio, half title, some foxing beginning and end, original boards, paper spine labels, labels and extremities of boards with areas of wear, very good, sometime in the Bibliotheck der Koniglichen Sternwarte, Berling-Babelsberg with its 19th century inkstamp on half title and early 20th century stamp on titlepage, scarce. John Drury Rare Books 2015 - 17893 2015 $699

Stuart, Gilbert *A View of Society in Europe.* London: J. Murray, 1782. 4to., half title, final leaf of corrections, contemporary half calf over marbled boards, sometime skillfully rebacked with raised bands and gilt lines and with original morocco label retained, very good crisp copy. John Drury Rare Books 2015 - 23925 2015 $699

Stuart, Granville *Forty Years on the Frontier.* Cleveland: Arthur H. Clark Co., 1925. First edition, 2 volumes, cloth, 10 plates, fine, bright set, very scarce. Buckingham Books March 2015 - 28818 2015 $850

Stuart, William L. *Night Cry.* Dial Press, 1948. First edition, page edges uniformly browned, else fine, in superb dust jacket with absolutely no fading to spine. Buckingham Books March 2015 - 36581 2015 $1250

Stuck, Hudson *The Alaskan Missions of the Episcopal Church.* New York: 1920. First edition, near fine in paper wrappers, folding map not present in all copies. Bookworm & Silverfish 2015 - 6014425542 2015 $75

The Studio. London: The Studio Limited, 1947-1959. Volumes 133-157, large 8vo., 26 volumes bound in 13, rebound with wrapper covers bound in, Curwen Press style patterned boards and various color uniform cloth spines lettered gilt, copiously illustrated in color and black and white, clean, sound, very good set. Any Amount of Books March 2015 - A866007 2015 £350

Stuhlmann, Gunther *Anais An International Journal. Volume 9 1991 - Volume 18 2000.* Los Angeles: 1999-2000. 8vo., printed wrappers, pages 136, laid in TLS from Stuhlmann to editor and poet William Claire, 6 issues, 9, 10, 11, 14, 15, 18. Second Life Books Inc. 191 - 88 2015 $125

Sturge, Helen Winifred *The Mount School, York, 1785 to 1814, 1831 to 1931.* London: J. M. Dent & Sons, 1931. Half title, frontispiece, plates, illustrations, few spots, original blue cloth, faded and slightly rubbed and marked, Kathleen Tillotson's signed copy with ALS asking her for information with typescript copy of her reply.   Jarndyce Antiquarian Booksellers   CCVII - 479   2015   £25

Sturge, Mary Charlotte *Some Little Quakers in their Nursery.* London: Simpkin Marshall, 1906. Half title, illustrations, original yellow cloth, mark on spine, else very good, signed presentation inscription to Nurse Gertrude from author, the Constable family copy, with pencil notes by Kathleen Tillotson inserted.   Jarndyce Antiquarian Booksellers   CCVII - 480   2015   £30

Style 1900: The Magazine of Turn-of-the-Century Design. Lambertville: Style, 1900. 2002-2010, 24 volumes, 4to., stiff paper wrappers, set includes May, August, November 2002, February, May, Summer/Fall, Fall/Winter 2003; Winter/Spring, Spring/Summer, Summer/Fall, Fall/Winter 2004; Summer/Fall 2005, Winter/Spring, Summer/Fall 2006; Spring, Summer, Fall 2009, Spring, Fall 2010, color illustrations.   Oak Knoll Books   306 - 304   2015 $150

Styles, John *Strictures on two Critiques in the Edinburgh Review on the Subject of Methodism and Missions...* London: sold by Williams and Smith, 1808. First edition, 8vo., half title, little general browning and foxing, recently well bound in cloth lettered gilt, good copy, rare.   John Drury Rare Books   March 2015 - 18229   2015   £306

Styron, William *Admiral Robert Penn Warren and Snows of Winter.* Palaemon, 1977. First edition, one of 26 copies signed by author, as new in wrappers.   Gemini Fine Books & Arts, Ltd.   Art Reference & Illustrated Books: First Editions - 2015 $170

Styron, William *Against Fear.* Palaemon, 1981. First edition, 1/50 copies signed by author, as new in wrappers.   Gemini Fine Books & Arts, Ltd.   Art Reference & Illustrated Books: First Editions - 2015 $150

Styron, William *This Quiet Dust and Other Writings.* New York: 1982. First edition, 1/250 signed copies, fine in slipcase.   Gemini Fine Books & Arts, Ltd.   Art Reference & Illustrated Books: First Editions - 2015 $100

Styron, William *A Tidewater Morning.* New York: Random House, 1993. First edition, limited to 200 copies, specially bound, signed, fine in like slipcase, number slip and (opened) shrink-wrap are still present.   Stephen Lupack   March 2015 - 2015 $125

Styron, William *A Tidewater Morning.* New York: Random House, 1993. First edition, signed on half title, fine in fine dust jacket.   Stephen Lupack   March 2015 - 2015 $125

Suarez, Raoul Quintano *Libertad O' Meurte! Episodios de la revolution.* Habana: Dibujas Publicitorious Luque circa, 1960. 4to., pictorial wrappers, 40 pages, spine cover soil, very good+ and complete, 325 numbered picture cards, each mounted in numbered space with printed caption.   Aleph-bet Books, Inc.   109 - 385   2015 $3250

Sub Rosa *Drifting, or the Romances of an Octopus.* Chicago: Elysian Fields, 1904. First edition, hardcover, very good with little spotting and fading of lettering.   Beasley Books   2013 - 2015 $45

Sucquet, Antoine S. *Via Vitae Aeternae Iconibus Illustrata per Boetium a Bolswert.* Antwerp: typis Martini Nutti, 1620. First edition, 8vo., engraved frontispiece title and 32 engraved emblematic plates by Boetius a Bolswert, contemporary vellum, later endpapers, few minor marks, fine presentation copy from author to unidentified fellow Jesuit, presentation inscription of Pater J. de Beare 1912 to Mount St. Mary's Jesuit College.   Maggs Bros. Ltd.   Illustrated Books 2014 - 2015   £2200

Suetonius *Caesarum XII Libri.* Basel: per Henricum Petrum, 1537. First Gallus edition, touch of soiling to titlepage, institutional stamp and small paper shelfmark label at foot, earlier inscription at head, 8vo., contemporary wooden boards backed in blindstamped pigskin, spine dyed black with 3 raised bands, later paper labels in second and fourth compartments, two clasps (both lost), little bit rubbed, old inscriptions, one of purchase note of Jonas Christian Weber, very good.   Blackwell's Rare Books   Greek & Latin Classics VI - 98   2015   £1200

Suggestions for a Domestic Currency founded Upon Philosophic and Unerring Principles... London: Wiley and Putnam, 1847. First edition, 8vo., well bound in early 20th century blue cloth, spine gilt lettered, excellent copy.   John Drury Rare Books   March 2015 - 26244   2015 $266

Suicide, Selections of Pamphlets. London: Printed by J. Read, 1708. First or early editions, wrappers but O'Dea pamphlet disbound, occasional browning, light wear, otherwise sound, very good.   Any Amount of Books   2015 - A58622   2015   £250

A Suite of 30 Typographic Prints Shaped Poetry Chronicling this Literary Form From 300 BC to the Present. San Francisco: Arion Press, 1981. One of 300 copies, 30 prints are all on different handmade papers, different types, with "Companion volume" that is commentary on the 30 poems/plates, page size: most 12 x 16 inches, housed in black cloth and plastic clamshell box issued by publisher, bit of rubbing to black cloth of box with Lucite frame that was issued with book, book itself fine as is fragile frame, each page contains a poem shaped through typographical arrangement on page to reflect visual image of meaning of the subject matter of text.   Priscilla Juvelis - Rare Books 62 - 1   2015 $2500

Sull, Michael R. *Spencerian Script and Ornamental Penmanship.* Prairie Village: LDG Pub., 1989. First edition, small 4to., stiff paper wrappers, plastic spiral binding, presentation from author on first leaf, protected by later cardboard slipcase.   Oak Knoll Books   Special Catalogue 24 - 52   2015 $350

Sullivan, Edward Dean *This Labor Union Racket.* New York: Hillman Curl, 1936. First edition, fine with handsomely printed boards, lightly used dust jacket with fading to spine.   Beasley Books   2013 - 2015 $45

Sullivan, J. H. *Broncho John Writes a Letter of His First Trip up the Trail and Sends Copies of War Credentials to Theodore Roosevelt, President...*   J. H. Sullivan, 1905. First edition, portrait, printed wrappers, 8vo., small old waterstain to bottom edge of front cover, moderate wear to front and rear covers with interior clean and few pages exhibiting old corner crease to top fore corners of 3 pages, else very good.   Buckingham Books   March 2015 - 37234   2015 $1250

Sullivan, Maurice S. *The Travels of Jedediah Smith...* Fine Arts Press, 1934. First edition, 1985 pages, illustrations, folding map, usual yellowing to white cloth, rubbed with light soiling to back panel and moderate wear and general soiling to front panel, internally clean, tight and fine, good to very good due to soiling and rubbing to cloth and priced accordingly, very scarce.   Buckingham Books March 2015 - 34146   2015 $450

Sullivan, Richard Joseph *A View of Nature, In Letters to a Traveller Among the Alps.* London: T. Becket, 1794. First edition, 6 volumes, 8vo., errata leaf in each volume and half titles as required in volumes I and VI, one leaf in volume I with closed tear (no loss), few gatherings bit foxed, couple of leaves soiled, contemporary calf backed marbled boards, spines with raised bands, gilt lines and green labels, foot of two volumes worn with loss of leather, entirely uncut, very good set, very scarce.   John Drury Rare Books   2015 - 22928   2015 $1486

Sullivan, T. D. *Speeches from the Dock; or Protests of Irish Patriotism. The Manchester Tragedy and the Cruise of the Packet Jackmel...*   New York: P. J. Kennedy & Sons, 1885. Later printing, good+ with 1 inch tear at head of front joint, free endpapers excised some signatures removed, 8vo.   Beasley Books   2013 - 2015 $200

A Summer Miscellany; or a Present for the Country. London: printed for T. Cooper, 1742. Second edition, 8vo., disbound, slight foxing, but very good, early signature of John Tucker on titlepage.   C. R. Johnson   Foxon R-Z - 939r-z   2015 $536

Sumner, Charles *Slavery and the Rebellion One and Inseparable Speech... Before the New Your Young Men's Republican Union at Cooper Institute, NY on the Afternoon of Nov. 5 1864.*   Boston: Wright and Potter, 1864. First edition, 8vo., 30 pages, plus blank leaf, removed.   M & S Rare Books, Inc.   97 - 286   2015 $125

Sumner, Helen *Equal Suffrage, the Results of an Investigation in Colorado made for the Collegiate Equal Suffrage League of NY & State.*   New York: Harper & Bros., 1909. First edition, 8vo., label removed from spine, very good, tight copy.   Second Life Books Inc.   189 - 247 2015 $125

Sumner, J. B. *The Evidence of Christianity, Derived from Its Nature and Reception.*   London: printed for J. Hatchard and Son, 1824. First edition, tall octavo, contemporary brown calf with gilt armorial device of Lewis Richard Ashurst on front board, joints split and neatly repaired, corners rounded, sound, good only, William Wilberforce's copy with his bookplate an ownership signature thrice on titlepage and once at beginning of preface.   Between the Covers Rare Books   197 - 106   2015 $3500

Sumner, James *The Mysterious Marbler with an Historical Introduction, Notes and 11 Original Marbled Samples by Richard J. Wolfe.*   North Hills: Bird & Bull Press, 1976. First edition, one of about 250 numbered copies, 8vo., quarter blue leather over marbled paper covered boards, prospectus loosely inserted.   Oak Knoll Books   306 - 139 2015 $425

Sunderland, La Roy *The Testimony of God.*   American Anti-Slavery Society, 1839. Third edition, x 3 3/4 inches, blue leather boards and title printed in gold on spine, corners of book lightly bent with rubbing to tops and bottoms, spine sunned and foxing.   Buckingham Books   March 2015 - 36379   2015 $325

Superman "The Magic Ring" in Song and Adventure with the Original Radio Cast.   National Comics Pub. Inc. (DC comics), 1947. First edition color pictorial illustrated stiff wrappers, front inside pocket contains two 45 rpm vinyl phono records, 12 pages illustrated in color, wrappers lightly toned and soiled and lightly rubbed at corners, spine ends and extremities, else very good.   Buckingham Books   March 2015 - 31804   2015 $300

Supervielle, Jules *L'Enfant De La Haute Mer.*   Paris: NRF, 1946. No. 152 of 431 copies on velin de Rives, 27 lithographs by Pierre Roy, near fine, light sunning at fore-edge, in lightly worn chemise with paper label bearing title, bit worn box, 4to.   Beasley Books   2013 - 2015 $350

Sutcliffe, Joseph *A Check to Infidelity; or a Demonstration that the Christian Religion is as Worthy of the Wisdom, Power and Goodness of God as the Works of Creation and Providence.* Doncaster: printed at the Gazette Office by W. Sheardown, 1798. First edition, 12mo., 24 pages, minor dust soiling, preserved in modern wrappers with printed label on upper cover, good copy, very scarce. John Drury Rare Books 2015 - 24989 2015 $159

Sutcliffe, Joseph *A Treatise on the Universal Spread of the Gospel, the Glorious Millenium and the Second Coming of Christ.* Doncaster: printed at the Gazette Office by W. Sheardown, 1798. First edition, 12mo., 24 pages, titlepage lightly soiled and with couple of short edge nicks, nowhere near printed surface, preserved in modern wrappers with printed label on upper cover, good copy, very scarce. John Drury Rare Books 2015 - 24990 2015 $159

Sutherland, C. H. V. *The Roman Imperial Coinage: Volume I from 31 BC to AD 69.* London: Spink & Son, 1984. Revised edition, large 8vo, 32 plates, original green cloth, lettered gilt at spine, fine in fine dust jacket. Any Amount of Books 2015 - C15975 2015 £180

Sutherland, James *Defoe.* London: Methuen, 1937. Half title, plates, original maroon buckram, very good in slightly torn dust jacket, signed by Geoffrey Tillotson 1937, with inserted ink and pencil notes and his printed review. Jarndyce Antiquarian Booksellers CCVII - 167 2015 £20

Sutherland, William *Four Marble Panels.* Manchester: Decorative Art Journals Co., 1898. Small folio, 4 loosely inserted chromolithograph plates probably printed by Kleinertz, Law and Co., of Manchester, stitched as issued. Marlborough Rare Books List 54 - 83 2015 £120

Sutherland, William *Marbles and Marbling.* Manchester: Decorative Art Journals Co. Ltd. circa, 1890. Small folio, 8 loosely inserted chromolithograph plates, stitched as issued, title with 5 cm. tear. Marlborough Rare Books List 54 - 82 2015 £120

Sutherland, William *The Sign Writer and Glass Embosser.* Manchester: Decorative Art Journals Co., 1896. Folio, numerous half tone text illustrations, 32 chromolithograph plates by Kleinertz, Law and Co., of Manchester loosely inserted in pocket at end, original decorated brown cloth, portfolio printed in black, unusually clean copy. Marlborough Rare Books List 54 - 84 2015 £650

Sutton, Allan *Montgomery Ward Records. A Discography.* Denver: Mainspring Press Digital, 2008. First edition, hardcover, CD-ROM edition. Beasley Books 2013 - 2015 $45

Sutton, James *An Atlas of Typeforms.* London: Lund Humphries, 1968. First edition, folio, cloth, foldout specimen. Oak Knoll Books 306 - 202 2015 $125

Suzuki, Daisetz Teitaro *Manual of Zen Buddhism.* Kyoto: Eastern Buddhist Society, 1935. First edition, long gift inscription, 8vo., very good+, foxing to edges and first and last few pages with age darkening endpapers in very good+ dust jacket with tape spine, short closed tears spine, mild sun spine, edge wear. By the Book, L. C. 44 - 74 2015 $1500

Swaine, Agnes *A Flower Garland and Alphabet.* London: Selwyn & Blount, 1926. First edition, 4 5/8 x 6 7/8 inches, boards, pictorial paste-on, near fine, printed on rectos only, 26 charming color lithographs by author, scarce. Aleph-bet Books, Inc. 109 - 4 2015 $275

The Swan Tripe-Club; a Satyr, on the High-Flyers: in the year 1705. London: printed and sold by the booksellers of London and Westminster, 1710. Piracy, 8vo., disbound, very good. C. R. Johnson Foxon R-Z - 1239r-z 2015 $268

Swan, Oliver *Deep Water Days.* Philadelphia: Macrae Smith, 1929. Stated first edition, 4to., green pictorial cloth, top edge blue, mint in original pictorial box, box slightly rubbed but very good+, illustrations, extraordinary copy, rare in this condition. Aleph-bet Books, Inc. 109 - 499 2015 $600

Swanston, Clement *An Essay on "The Conditions Which Much Exist Among a People to Admit of the Successful Working of Constitutional Monarchy".* Cambridge: Metcalfe & Palmer printers?, 1853. 8vo., iv, 92 pages, recent linen black marbled boards, very good inscribed in ink by author, rare. John Drury Rare Books 2015 - 18037 2015 $133

Sweet, Alex E. *On a Mexican Mustang.* Hartford: 1883. First edition, 672 pages, illustrations, pictorial gilt cloth, expertly recased retaining original boards and spine, several early pages with tissue repairs to edges, gilt spine and pictorial front cover bright and binding tight, uncommonly sound and attractive. Dumont Maps & Books of the West 131 - 79 2015 $175

Swendeborg, Emanuel *De Nova Hierosolyma et Ejus Doctrina Coelesti...* London: 1758. First edition, 4to., including final leaf with errata on recto, excellent, crisp copy in contemporary gilt ruled calf, extremities and joints worn, binding still sound, large impressive armorial bookplate of Washington Sewaliis Shirley, 9th Earl Ferrers (1822-1859). John Drury Rare Books 2015 - 25868 2015 $1244

Swift, Graham *Shuttlecock.* London: Allen Lane, 1981. First edition, 8vo., fine in fine dust jacket. Any Amount of Books 2015 - A92920 2015 £220

Swift, Jonathan   1667-1745   *Irish Tracts 1702-1723 and Sermons...*   Oxford: Basil Blackwell, 1948. Half title, frontispiece, facsimiles, original green cloth, very good in slightly torn dust jacket, Geoffrey Tillotson's copy signed with few notes.   Jarndyce Antiquarian Booksellers   CCVII - 483   2015   £30

Swift, Jonathan   1667-1745   *The Lady's Dressing Room...*   London: printed for J. Roberts, 1732. First edition, 4to., disbound, very good.   C. R. Johnson   Foxon R-Z - 955r-2015 $11,492

Swift, Jonathan   1667-1745   *A Libel on D----- D----- and a Certain Great Lord.*   N.P.: Dublin: printed in the year, 1730. Probably first octavo edition, 8 pages, small 8vo., disbound, two press-variant of this edition known, this one has rectangular ornament at head of tet, as opposed to a group of type flowers, very good.   C. R. Johnson   Foxon R-Z - 956r-z   2015 $3831

Swift, Jonathan   1667-1745   *The Life and Genuine Character of...written by himself.*   London: (i.e. Dublin): printed for J. Roberts, 1733. One of two Dublin editions, the other Dublin printing has the genuine imprint of Edward Waters, the imprint here is clearly false, small 8vo., very good, disbound, rare.   C. R. Johnson   Foxon R-Z - 958r-z   2015 $1915

Swift, Jonathan   1667-1745   *The Life and Genuine Character of Doctor Swift, written by Himself.*   London: printed for J. Roberts and sold at the pamphlet shops, 1733. First edition, 19 pages, folio, later stiff wrappers in brown cloth slipcase (label of case chipped), fine, large copy, outer edges uncut.   C. R. Johnson   Foxon R-Z - 957r-z   2015 $1915

Swift, Jonathan   1667-1745   *Miscellaneous Pieces, in prose and Verse...*   London: printed for C. Dilly, 1789. First edition, 8vo., contemporary tree calf, gilt, spine gilt, red morocco label, fine.   C. R. Johnson   Foxon R-Z - 949r-z   2015 $536

Swift, Jonathan   1667-1745   *Miscellanies Consisting Chiefly of Original Pieces in Prose and Verse.*   London: reprinted for A. Moore, 1734. First edition, 8vo., disbound, very good.   C. R. Johnson   Foxon R-Z - 944r-z   2015 $3064

Swift, Jonathan   1667-1745   *Miscellanies....*   London: printed in the Year, 1736. Pirated edition, 12mo., modern brown cloth, gilt lettering, frontispiece, very good.   The Brick Row Book Shop   Miscellany 67 - 88   2015 $600

Swift, Jonathan   1667-1745   *On Poetry; a Rapsody.*   printed at Dublin: London: reprinted and sold by J. Huggonson and at the booksellers and pamphlet shops, 1733. First edition, 28 pages, folio, half dark green morocco and marbled boards, very large armorial bookplate of Earl of Iveagh, very good.   C. R. Johnson   Foxon R-Z - 959r-z   2015 $1149

Swift, Jonathan   1667-1745   *On poetry: a rapsody.*   Dublin: reprinted at London: (.e. Edinburgh): sold by J. Huggonson, n.d., 1734. First Edinburgh edition, 8vo., disbound, fine, uncommon piracy.   C. R. Johnson   Foxon R-Z - 960r-z   2015 $613

Swift, Jonathan   1667-1745   *The Poems of.*   Oxford: at the Clarendon Press, 1937. 3 volumes, half titles, frontispieces, original blue cloth slightly torn and dusted dust jackets, Kathleen Tillotson's presentation copies for Geoffrey Tillotson, with few notes and insertions.   Jarndyce Antiquarian Booksellers   CCVII - 484   2015   £120

Swift, Jonathan   1667-1745   *The Poetical Works of Jonathan Swift, Dean of St. Patrick's, Dublin.*   London: i.e. Edinburgh: sold by A. Manson, R. Dilton, J. Thomson, H. Gray, T. Nelson and P. Bland, n.d., 1753? 2 volumes, 12mo., contemporary sheep, spines gilt, contrasting red and black morocco labels (spines trifle rubbed), very scarce collected edition of Scottish origin, attractive set, very good.   C. R. Johnson   Foxon R-Z - 948r-z   2015 $460

Swift, Jonathan   1667-1745   *The Story of the Injured Lady.*   London: printed for M. Cooper, 1746. First edition, 8vo., recent marbled wrappers, rare, fine.   C. R. Johnson   Foxon R-Z - 947r-z   2015 $2681

Swift, Jonathan   1667-1745   *A Tale of a Tub to which is added the Battle of the Books and The Mechanical Operation of the Spirit.*   Oxford: at the Clarendon Press, 1920. Half title, facsimiles, original dark blue cloth, worn, following inner hinge strengthened, Geoffrey Tillotson's signed copy with marginalia and inserted notes, notes on endpapers.   Jarndyce Antiquarian Booksellers   CCVII - 485   2015   £35

Swift, Jonathan   1667-1745   *To Doctor D-l----y, on the Libels Writ Against Him.*   London: printed: Dublin: reprinted in the year, 1730. First edition, 16 pages, small 8vo., disbound, slight spotting, but very good, rare.   C. R. Johnson   Foxon R-Z - 962r-z   2015 $9193

Swift, Jonathan 1667-1745 *Travels into Several Remote Nations of the World.* London: printed for Benj. Motte, 1726. First edition, Teerink's "B" with engraved frontispiece in second state, as usual, volume II is second edition, as stated on titlepage, bound without ad leaf, bound in contemporary full polished brown calf, spines attractively rebacked early with floral decorations in blind, gilt bands, red lettered labels, dates in gilt to lower spines, spines lightly worn and rubbed, some scattered foxing and toning to pages, small stain to upper corner of leaves of volume II, very good set. B & B Rare Books, Ltd.   234 - 97   2015 $4500

Swift, Jonathan 1667-1745 *The Travels of Lemuel Gulliver.* N.P.: Limited Editions Club, 1929. Limited to 1500 numbered copies, signed by artist, Alexander King, tall 8vo., half leather over cloth, slipcase, with Monthly Letter/prospectus loosely inserted, slipcase soiled, wear along edges, leather spine of book shows some age darkening, name in ink along top of front pastedown, better preserved than most copies.   Oak Knoll Books   25 - 1   2015 $275

Swift, Jonathan 1667-1745 *A Voyage to Lilliput by Dr. Lemuel Gulliver MDCIC. (with) A Voyage to Brobdingnag made by Lemuel Gulliver in the Year MDCCII.* New York: Limited Editions Club, 1950. Limited to 1500 copies, initialled by designer, Bruce Rogers, 16mo. and folio, 2 volumes, half cloth, pictorial paper covered boards, spines stamped in gilt, specially made slipcase which holds the two different sized books, some toning to large specially built slipcase.   Oak Knoll Books   25 - 34   2015 $450

Swift, Jonathan 1667-1745 *Verses on the Death of Doctor Swift.* London: printed for C. Bathurst, 1739. First edition, 18 pages, folio, recent brown cloth, dark brown morocco side label, very good, bookplate of E. M. Cox.   C. R. Johnson   Foxon R-Z - 963r-z   2015 $1379

Swift, Jonathan 1667-1745 *The Virtues of Sid Hamet the Magician's Rod.* Colophon: London: printed for John Morphew, 1710. 2 pages, folio, single sheet printed on both sides, folding case, fine.   C. R. Johnson   Foxon R-Z - 966r-z   2015 $7661

Swinburne, Algernon Charles 1837-1909 *Bothwell.* London: Chatto & Windus, 1874. First edition, very good, light shelfwear at extremities.   Stephen Lupack   March 2015 - 2015 $125

Swinburne, Algernon Charles 1837-1909 *Poems and Ballads: Second Series.* London: Chatto and Windus, 1878. First edition, ownership signature of Havelock Ellis, original dark blue green cloth with title, author and publisher device on spine, some bumping to corners, very good, front hinge slightly split and rear hinge weak, interior pages clean and bright, very good, marginal annotations and few lines of French by unidentified hand on pages 196-198.   The Kelmscott Bookshop   11 - 51   2015 $250

Swinburne, Algernon Charles 1837-1909 *The Queen Mother. Rosamund. Two Plays.* London: Basil Montagu Pickering, 1860. First edition, first issue in second state with cancel titlepage and addition of half titles to each play, lovely copy, rebound in contemporary three quarter green morocco with red marbled paper boards and endpapers, all edges marbled, slightly rubbed and bumped but very good, interior pages very good with occasional light pencil checks of lines in margins to highlight line or phrase, interesting association copy, very good, inscribed by author for W. M. Rossetti, this is the copy of author and critic John Skelton with his pencil note "Given to me by D. G. Rossetti for review in Fraser's magazine".   The Kelmscott Bookshop   11 - 52   2015 $4500

Swinburne, Algernon Charles 1837-1909 *Studies in Prose and Poetry.* London: Chatto & Windus, 1894. First edition, 8vo., original dark blue cloth, extraordinary association copy, inscribed by author for cousin Mary C. J. Leith, Nov. 8 1894, original dark blue cloth with gilt rule to front cover borders and title and author in gilt to spine, light offsetting to free endpapers, otherwise near fine.   The Kelmscott Bookshop   11 - 53   2015 $1500

Swinburne, Algernon Charles 1837-1909 *A Study of Shakespeare.* London: Chatto & Windus, 1880. First edition, original green cloth, gilt title and author to spine and gilt ruling to front cover, slightly bumped corners and light fraying, but near fine, interior pristine, near fine, presentation copy inscribed by author for sister Alice Swinburne.   The Kelmscott Bookshop   11 - 54   2015 $2250

Swinburne, Algernon Charles 1837-1909 *Tristram of Lyonesse.* Portland: Thomas B. Mosher, 1904. Limited edition of 450 copies, original paper spine and blue boards, erasure of a name at top of titlepage has resulted in some thinning and tiny holes, otherwise fine, fresh copy. Stephen Lupack   March 2015 - 2015 $125

Swinburne, Henry *A Treatise of Spousals, or Matrimonial Contracts: Wherein all the Questions Relating to that Subject are Ingeniously Debated and Resolved.* London: printed by S. Roycroft for Robert Clavell, 1686. First edition, 4to., contemporary panelled calf with some wear to joints and extremities, still sound, text crisp with good margins, very good with near contemporary signature of J. Agar and late 18th early 19th century armorial bookplate of Rev. L. W. Hepenstal, uncommon.   John Drury Rare Books   2015 - 23326   2015 $3147

Swineford, A. P. *Annual Review of the Iron Mining and Other Industries of the Upper Peninsula for the Year Ending Dec. 31 1880.* Mining Journal, 1881. 7.5 x 5.5 inches, pink printed wrappers, 170 pages, 30 pages ads, folded Reed & Breese plat map of the Lake Superior Iron Mines, front cover faded, extremities and spine considerably chipped as well as the title being written in pen on spine, rear cover chipped and with tear that has been repaired with cellophane tape.   Buckingham Books   March 2015 - 34989   2015 $750

Swing, P. *The Profile of the Absorption Lines in Rotating Stars, Taking Into Account the Variation of Ionization Due to Centrifugal Force.* Royal Astronomical Society, 1936. First Separate edition, 8vo., original printed wrappers, near fine, supplement with minimal dampstain to rear cover not affecting text. By the Book, L. C. Special List 10 - 56 2015 $300

Swinton, Archibald *Digest of Decisions in the Registration Appeal Court at Glasgow, in the Years 1835 1836, 1837 and 1838 with Notes of Decisions in Other Districts.* Edinburgh: Thomas Clark, 1839. First edition, 8vo., original cloth backed boards, inkstain on upper cover neatly rebacked and labelled, good, uncut copy. John Drury Rare Books 2015 - 19320 2015 $159

Swinton, John *A Momentous Question.* Philadelphia: A. R. Keller, 1895. First edition, hardcover, very nice, bright gilt stamping, handsome edition. Beasley Books 2013 - 2015 $85

Swire, Herbert *The Voyage of the Challenger.* Golden Cockerel Press, 1938. 142/300 copies printed on Van Gelder mouldmade paper, color frontispiece, 90 reproductions of sketches by author, those in color being specially painted for the edition by hand, these latter with tissue guards present, few faint foxspots to prelims one or two elsewhere, small folio, original quarter white buckram and blue cloth, backstrip trifle darkened, lettered and decorated in gilt, small amount of rubbing to corners, edges untrimmed, endpaper maps at front of first volume, endpapers faintly foxed, matching slipcase, some rubbing and soiling, very good. Blackwell's Rare Books B179 - 154 2015 £800

Swisshelm, Jane Grey *Crusader and feminist Letters of 1858-1865.* St. Paul: Minnesota Historical Society, 1934. First edition, some fading to spine, very good. Second Life Books Inc. 189 - 249 2015 $55

Sydenham, Thomas *The Whole Works of that Excellent Practical Physician, Dr. Thomas Sydenham...* London: by J. Darby for M. Wellington, 1717. Seventh edition, contemporary panelled calf, extremities worn, two gatherings trifle pulled, numerous contemporary marginal annotations, from the library of Sir John Rodes, with his signature on titlepage. Joseph J. Felcone Inc. Science, Medicine and Technology - 40 2015 $500

Sydenham, Thomas *The Whole Works of that Excellent Practical Physician.* London: For W. Feales, R. Wellington &c, 1734. Seventh edition, Early 19th century calf, neatly rebacked to style, bookplates, very clean, attractive copy. Joseph J. Felcone Inc. Science, Medicine and Technology - 39 2015 $475

Symington, Andrew *The Duty of stated and select private Christian fellowship briefly inculcated and directed.* Paisley: printed by Stephen Young 210 High Street, 1823. First edition, 8vo., 44 pages, couple of short closed marginal tears, near contemporary ink inscription on upper margin of titlepage, rebound recently in cloth, spine lettered gilt, original blue upper wrapper preserved, 19th century ownership inscription Rev. Gilbert McMaster of Duanesburgh. John Drury Rare Books March 2015 - 23502 2015 £306

Symons, Jelinger *The Excise Laws Abridged and Digested Under their Proper Heads in alphabetical Order.* London: J. Nourse, 1775. Second edition, 8vo., title bit spotted, contemporary calf, neatly rebacked, very good, from the Ripley Castle Library and with signature of J. Ingilby on title. John Drury Rare Books 2015 - 976 2015 $656

Symson, David *A True and Impartial Account of the Life of the most Reverend Father in God, R. James Sharp Archbishop of St. Andrews, Primate of all Scotland.* Edinburgh: printed in the year, 1723. 8vo., tear in gutter of one leaf, pages 137-8, touching letters but with no discerible loss, contemporary sheep backed marbled boards, spine worn, rare outside British libraries. John Drury Rare Books March 2015 - 23284 2015 £306

Synge, Edward *An Account of the Erection, Government and Number of Charity Schools in Ireland...* Dublin: printed for J. Pepyat bookseller in Skinner Row, 1717. First edition, 4to., title printed within double ruled border, 44 pages, contemporary ink erasures and a marginal note, bound fairly recently in old style quarter calf over marbled boards, vellum corners, simple gilt and labelled, fine, crisp, rare. John Drury Rare Books 2015 - 24740 2015 $3324

Syracuse Poems and Stories 1980. Syracuse: Syracuse University, 1980. Limited to 300 copies, this copy unnumbered, previous owner name on titlepage, covers mildly dusty, near fine in stapled wrappers, scarce, foreword by Raymond Carver. Ken Lopez Bookseller E-list # 82 - 013443 2015 $175

Szarkowski, John *Ansel Adams at 100.* Boston: Little Brown, 2001. First edition, oblong folio, 114 tritone photo plates and 23 duotone text photos, reproduction in original envelope laid in, as issued, 2 sheet prospectus laid in, natural linen cloth lettered in white on spine, printed label mounted to front cover, housed in matching slipcase lettered on cover, very fine. Argonaut Book Shop Holiday Season 2014 - 5 2015 $250

Szekely, Al *Illustrations to Andersen.* London: 1963. Housed in portfolio are 8 fine watercolor illustrations for Andersen's fairy tales, on art paper, 10 x 12 1/2 inches and each signed. Aleph-bet Books, Inc. 109 - 22 2015 $500

Szent-Gyorgyi, Albert *Chemistry of Muscular Contraction.* New York: Academic Press, 1951. Second edition, signed and inscribed by author, 8vo., very good++ with scattered foxing in very good dust jacket with small pieces missing, soil and foxing, 8vo.   By the Book, L. C.   Special List 10 - 87   2015 $275

T

Tabor, J. A. *Ode, Delivered on the Occasion of the Opening (by the Mechanics' Institution) of the Public Hall, Colchester on Tuesday, October 14 1851.* Colchester: J. B. Harvey, 1851. Probably only edition, 8vo., 10 pages, original printed wrappers, lower cover bit soiled but good copy, presentation copy inscribed "With the author's compts", very rare.   John Drury Rare Books   2015 - 14144   2015 $133

Tacitus, Cornelius *Cornelii Taciti de Vita et Moribus Iulii Agricolae Lbier.* Hammersmith: The Doves Press, 1900. First Doves Press edition, one of 225 copies, fine, small quarto, original full vellum, gilt lettered, bookplate of Charles Walker Andrews.   The Brick Row Book Shop   Miscellany 67 - 38   2015 $750

Taffrail *Fred Travis, A. B.* London: Hodder & Stoughton, 1930. First edition, name on titlepage and some scattered light foxing on page edges, else fine in dust jacket and tiny wear at corners.   Mordida Books   March 2015 - 008467   2015 $200

Taft, Michael *Blues Lyric Poetry. A Concordance.* New York: Garland, 1984. First edition, 4to., 3 hefty volumes, fine.   Beasley Books   2013 - 2015 $400

Tagereav, V. *Discovrs sur L'Impvissance De L'Homme et de La Femme...* Paris: Edme Pepingue, 1655. Second edition, 8vo., contemporary vellum little worn, some light waterstaining on lower margin, but excellent copy.   Second Life Books Inc.   189 - 250   2015 $750

Tait, George *A Summary of the Powers and Duties of a Constable in Scotland, in Public and in Private.* Edinburgh: printed by Michael Anderson for John Anderson and Co. and Longman &c., 1815. 8vo., final ad leaf, paper just little browned and titlepage, little soiled, but good, uncut copy, recent cloth backed marbled boards, morocco label on upper cover lettered gilt, relatively uncommon.   John Drury Rare Books   2015 - 25586   2015 $177

Takakusu, Junjiro *The New Japanism and the Buddhist View Nationality.* Tokyo: Hokuseido Press, 1938. First edition, fine in wrappers, presentation copy, signed by in English and Japanese.   Beasley Books   2013 - 2015 $45

Take Over. Madison: 1973-1979. First edition, 57 issues, year/number - 73/17, 74/13, 75/13, 76/4, 77/7, 78/8 and 79/2, very good copies.   Beasley Books   2013 - 2015 $250

Talbot, William Henry Fox *Improvements in coating or Covering Metals with other Metals and in colouring Metallic Surfaces (and) Improvements in Photography Contained in The Chemical Gazette or Journal of Practical Chemistry...* London: Richard and John E. Taylor, 1842-1844. First edition, 2 volumes, 8vo., half brown calf over marbled boards, gilt stamped spine titles, joints rubbed, bookplates and signatures of George Dawson Coleman, very good.   Jeff Weber Rare Books   178 - 1053   2015 $800

The Tale of Tsarevich Ivan, the Fire Bird and Grey Wolf. Moscow: 1901. Folio, pictorial wrappers, near fine, illustrations by Ivan Bilibin with cover design plus 3 full page and 5 smaller magnificent chromolithographs.   Aleph-bet Books, Inc.   109 - 53   2015 $1200

A Tale of Two Tubs... London: i.e. Dublin, printed in the year, 1749. first Dublin edition, fair, 48 pages, engraved folding frontispiece, 8vo., disbound, frontispiece somewhat dust soiled and creased, titlepage bit dusty, trimmed bit close at top, touching 'A' in title, occasional page numbers.   C. R. Johnson   Foxon R-Z - 967r-z   2015 $613

Tales of the Wars; or, Naval and Military Chronicle. Nos. 1 (Jan. 2 1836) - 156 (Dec. 22, 1838). London: William Mark Clark, 1836-1838. 3 volumes, frontispieces in volumes I and II, vignette illustrations to each issue, additional woodcut illustrations, some dusting and foxing, prelims to volume II spotted, tear to pages 103/4 volume II without loss, contemporary half black calf, little rubbed.   Jarndyce Antiquarian Booksellers   CCXI - 212   2015   £280

Tallent, Annie D. *The Black Hills or the Last Hunting Ground of the Dakotahs.* St. Louis: Nixon Jones Printing Co., 1899. First edition, thick 8vo., decorate blindstamped full leather, gold stamping on front cover and spine, raised bands, marbled endpapers, illustrations, fine, tight, bright copy, housed in cloth slipcase, exceptional copy.   Buckingham Books   March 2015 - 28739   2015 $1000

Tallent, Elizabeth *Time With Children.* New York: Alfred A. Knopf, 1987. First edition, fine in dust jacket which is spine faded, else near fine, warmly inscribed to author Nicholas Delbanco.   Between the Covers Rare Books, Inc.   187 - 271   2015 $65

Tan, Amy *The Bonesetter's Daughter.* New York: Putnam's, 2001. First edition, signed by author, fine in fine dust jacket.   Stephen Lupack   March 2015 - 2015 $45

Tapply, William G. *Death at Charity's Point.* New York: Scribners, 1984. First edition, very fine in dust jacket.   Mordida Books   March 2015 - 011469   2015 $185

Tapply, William G. *Death at Charity's Point.* New York: Scribners, 1984. First edition, very fine in dust jacket, signed by author. Mordida Books March 2015 - 009173 2015 $200

Tapply, William G. *The Dutch Blue Error.* New York: Charles Scribner's, 1984. First edition, fine in dust jacket, scarce. Buckingham Books March 2015 - 21398 2015 $175

Taraval, Sigismundo *The Indian Uprising in Lower California 1734-1737 as Described by Father Sigismundo Taraval.* Los Angeles: 1931. Numbered edition of 665, illustrations, spine slightly darkened, previous owner's name on f.f.e.p. and one internal page, else clean and almost unopened. Dumont Maps & Books of the West 131 - 80 2015 $100

Tarrant, John *A Premonitary Address to the Catholics of the United Kingdom.* London: printed and published by T. Davison, 1819. First edition, 8vo., 16 pages, preserved in modern wrappers with printed label on upper cover, very good, apparently rare. John Drury Rare Books March 2015 - 24999 2015 £306

Tasso, Torquato 1544-1595 *L'Aminte du Tasse: Pastorale en Cinq Actes....* Londres: chez Mr. Elmsley et chez l'auteur (de l'imprimerie de T. Spilsbury), 1784. First edition, errata slip pasted onto blank space on last page, some waterstaining in middle of fore margins, mostly light but more severe on 20 leaves, 8vo., contemporary calf, gilt ruled compartments on spine, red lettering piece, rubbed and worn, armorial bookplates of George Steuart, sound. Blackwell's Rare Books B179 - 102 2015 £400

Taswell, Edward *Miscellanea Sacra, Consisting of Three Divine Poems: Viz The Song of Deborah and Barak. The Lamentation of David over Saul and Jonathan, The Prayer of Solomon at the Dedication of the Temple.* London: printed for the author and sold by J. Morphew, 1716. First edition, 8vo., disbound, very good, rare. C. R. Johnson Foxon R-Z - 971r-z 2015 $1379

Tate, Allen *Mr. Pope and Other Poems.* New York: Minton, Balch & Co, 1928. First edition, small 8vo., original black cloth, printed labels, dust jacket, fine, presentation copy with correction and few holograph revisions by Tate. James S. Jaffe Rare Books Modern American Poetry - 289 2015 $750

Tate, Allen *Mr. Pope and Other Poems.* New York: Minton, Balch & Co., 1928. First edition, first state with his poem 'Ode to the Confederate Dead' tipped-in, octavo, cloth with applied printed label, housed in custom clamshell case with morocco label gilt, boards very slightly splayed and rubbed, short tear on one leaf, else near fine, inscribed by author to Peggy and Malcom Cowley, Aug. 14 1928. Between the Covers Rare Books 196 - 116 2015 $3750

Tate, James *Bewitched.* Llangynog: Embers Handpress, 1989. First edition, limited to 100 numbered copies, signed by Tate, of which this is one of approximately 40 copies printed on rough Saunders mould made pure rag paper and cloth bound, there were an additional 40 copies printed on Smooth Saunders paper bound in stiff paper wrappers and 20 on handmade Barcham Green paper, specially bound, very fine, 4to., drawings by Laurie Smith, original loden green cloth and decorated boards. James S. Jaffe Rare Books Modern American Poetry - 295 2015 $250

Tate, James *Hottentot Ossuary.* Cambridge: Temple Bar Bookshop, 1974. First edition, one of 50 specially bound (hardbound) copies numbered and signed by author out of a total edition of 1500 copies, this copy number 1, a presentation copy inscribed on front free endpaper to publisher's James and Eugene O'Neil, with holograph note of provenance from Eugene O'Neil laid in, small 8vo., original black cloth, fine in dust jacket which is slightly rubbed alone one fold. James S. Jaffe Rare Books Modern American Poetry - 293 2015 $850

Tate, James *If It Would All Please Hurry. A Poem.* Amherst: Shanachie Press, 1980. First edition, one of only 10 lettered copies reserved for author and artist, this being copy "J" out of a total edition of 35 copies, folio, 10 original etchings and engravings, on Arches Cover white paper, loose sheets in folding box, portfolio lightly soiled, otherwise very fine, rare, presentation from Tale and the artist, Stephen Riley for Stanley Wiater. James S. Jaffe Rare Books Modern American Poetry - 294 2015 $4000

Tate, James *Notes of Woe. Poems.* Iowa City: Stone Wall Press, 1968. First edition, limited to 230 copies on Hayle paper, small 8vo., original salmon boards, very fine. James S. Jaffe Rare Books Modern American Poetry - 290 2015 $350

Tate, James *Return to the City of White Donkeys.* New York: Ecco, 2004. First edition, signed by author, 8vo., original boards, dust jacket, fine. James S. Jaffe Rare Books Modern American Poetry - 296 2015 $75

Tate, James *The Torches.* Santa Barbara: Unicorn Press, 1968. First edition, one of only 30 numbered copies, specially bound in original fabric by Joe and Anna Burgess and signed by Tate, only 1030 copies bound in wrappers and 250 in boards, very fine copy of this rare issue, 8vo., original linen. James S. Jaffe Rare Books Modern American Poetry - 291 2015 $350

Tate, James *Viper Jazz.* Middletown: Wesleyan University Press, 1976. First edition, 8vo., original cloth, dust jacket, presentation copy inscribed by Tate. James S. Jaffe Rare Books Modern American Poetry - 292 2015 $150

Tate, Nahum *A Congratulatory Poem to His Royal Highness Prince George of Denmark, Lord High Admiral of Great Britain...* London: printed by Herny Hills, 1708. Piracy, 16 pages, 8vo., disbound, very good.   C. R. Johnson   Foxon R-Z - 1208r-z   2015 $153

Tatham, William *National Irrigation, or the Various Methods of Watering Meadows...* London: J. and T. Carpenter, 1801. First edition, 8vo., engraved plates and two text figures, plates rather stained, wanting half title, few emphasis marks in pencil and early annotations in ink, old, probably original boards, rebacked in cloth, printed paper label, uncut, good, large copy.   John Drury Rare Books   March 2015 - 14248   2015   £306

Taverner, H. T. *Charles Dickens. The Story of His Life.* New York: Harper & Bros., 1870. First American edition, 8vo., original printed and pictorial wrappers, repeating title vignette, including frontispiece portrait with facsimile on recto, title vignette, text illustrations, 2 pages of publisher's ads at end dated Sept. 1870, corners front wrapper chipped away, few small edge chips, internally very good, scarce.   M & S Rare Books, Inc.   97 - 88   2015 $650

Taylor, Alison G. *Simeon's Bride.* London: Hale, 1995. First edition, fine in price clipped dust jacket.   Mordida Books   March 2015 - 008183   2015 $250

Taylor, Andrew *Waiting for the End of the World.* London: Gollancz, 1984. First edition, very fine in dust jacket.   Mordida Books   March 2015 - 005996   2015 $75

Taylor, Bayard   1825-1878 *Eldorado, or, Adventures in the Path of Empire: Comprising a Voyage to California via Panama Life in San Francisco and Monterey...* London: George Routledge and Co., 1850. Early pirated edition, 2 volumes, 16mo., rebound in half dark green leather, marbled boards, large red leather spine labels, gilt, contemporary owner's name A. J. Landon to top blank portion of titlepages (one erased), fine set, clean.   Argonaut Book Shop   Holiday Season 2014 - 285   2015 $250

Taylor, Elmer E. *George Sanders Bickerstaff 1893-1954 'Painter of Pictures".* Glendale: Los Angeles Westerners, 1988. First edition, one of 500 copies, frontispiece 9 photo reproductions, 11 color reproductions, gray leatherette gilt, fine.   Argonaut Book Shop   Holiday Season 2014 - 286   2015 $60

Taylor, Graham *Chicago Commons through Forty Years.* Chicago: Chicago Commons Assn., 1936. First edition, very good, hardcover.   Beasley Books   2013 - 2015 $40

Taylor, Herbert *Remarks on an Article in the Edinburgh Review, No. 135 On the Times of the George the Third and George the Fourth.* London: John Murray, 1836. First edition, 8vo., 40 pages, including half title, but without ads, contemporary half calf over marbled boards, spine lettered gilt, very good, very scarce.   John Drury Rare Books   March 2015 - 23978   2015 $266

Taylor, John *Currency Explained; in Refutation of the Last Fallacy of "The Times." 8 Nov. 1843.* London: Samuel Clarke, 1843. First separate edition, half title and final leaf (imprint recto, ads verso), first and last leaves soiled, small library inkstamp on verso of title, recent cloth, uncommon.   John Drury Rare Books   2015 - 19591   2015 $133

Taylor, John *The Minister Mistaken; or the Question of Depreciation Erroneously stated by Mr. Huskisson.* London: Samuel Clarke, 1843. First edition, 8vo., 40 pages, recently well bound in linen backed marbled boards, lettered, good copy, rare.   John Drury Rare Books   March 2015 - 21180   2015 $221

Taylor, John *The Music Speech at the Public Commencement in Cambridge July 6 MDCCXXX.* London: printed by William Bowyer, Jun. and sold by W. Thurlbourn (Cambridge, R. Clements (Oxford): and the booksellers of London and Westminster, 1730. First edition, 8vo., disbound, presentation copy inscribed for Danieli Wray (1701-1766), half title present, very good.   C. R. Johnson   Foxon R-Z - 972r-z   2015 $613

Taylor, Peter Alfred *Payment of Members; Speech of Mr. P. A. Taylor, M.P., in the House of Commons, on Tuesday the 5th of April 1870.* London: Trubner & Co., 1870. First separate edition, 8vo. 48 pages, margins of title slightly soiled, preserved in modern wrappers with printed label on upper cover, good copy, ownership signature of A. Cook Dune 22 1871.   John Drury Rare Books   2015 - 25806   2015 $133

Taylor, Phoebe Atwood *Banbury Bog.* New York: W. W. Norton & Co., 1938. First edition, spine slightly faded, else very good in internally reinforce, moderately soiled dust jacket with moderate wear to spine ends and corners.   Buckingham Books   March 2015 - 16506   2015 $185

Taylor, Phoebe Atwood *Proof of the Pudding.* New York: Norton, 1945. First edition, fine in dust jacket with nicks at top of spine and along top edge and light wear along folds.   Mordida Books   March 2015 - 002151   2015 $75

Taylor, Phoebe Atwood *Punch with Care.* New York: Farrar Straus, 1946. First edition, near fine in dust jacket with several closed tear and chips and nicks at spine ends.   Mordida Books   March 2015 - 002152   2015 $85

Taylor, Samuel W. *The Grinning Gismo.* A. A. Wyn, 1951. First edition, fine in dust jacket with light professional restoration to spine ends and extremities. Buckingham Books   March 2015 - 33069   2015 $300

Taylor, Thomas F. *The Golf Murders. A Readers' and Collectors' Guide to Golf Mystery Fiction...* Westland: Golf Mystery Press, 1997. First edition, limited to 400 numbered copies signed by author, this copy #103, fine, bound in Imperial Bonded leather and protected by fine slipcase, 144 color photos, dust jackets. Buckingham Books   March 2015 - 27536   2015 $200

Taylor, William *Seven Years Street Preaching in San Francisco.* New York: Carlton & Porter, 1856. First edition, 8th thousand, decorated blue cloth, very good, foxing to text old name on titlepage, tight, nice, protected in thick mylar wrapper. Stephen Lupack   March 2015 - 2015 $45

Teasdale, Sara 1884-1933 *Helen of Troy and Other Poems.* New York: G. P. Putnam's Sons, 1912. Second edition, corners little bumped, photo of author tipped-in, very good, lacking presumed dust jacket, nicely inscribed by author for Anita Bartle-Brackenbury, anthologist. Between the Covers Rare Books, Inc.   187 - 272   2015 $275

Teasdale, Sara 1884-1933 *Rivers of the Sea.* New York: Macmillan, 1915. First edition, moderate edgewear, very good or better, lacking presumed dust jacket, nicely inscribed by author for Anita Bartle-Brackenbury. Between the Covers Rare Books, Inc.   187 - 273   2015 $450

Tegner, Elias *Frithiof a Norwegian Story from the Swedish.* London: T. Hookham, 1838. First English edition, unopened in contemporary pink glazed cloth, paper spine label, spine faded to brown, very good. Jarndyce Antiquarian Booksellers   CCXI - 267   2015   £125

Tehuantepec Railway Company *Proceedings of a Public Meeting Held in the Gentlemen's Parlor of the Southern Hotel (St. Louis) on the Evening of November 4 1885 to Consider the Subject of Building a Ship Railway Across the Isthmus of Tehuantepec.* St. Louis: Great Western Printing Co., 1885. First edition, 28 pages, 1 black and white map, 8vo., paper wrappers, very good, small tape repair to spine head, minor soiling on wrappers. Kaaterskill Books   19 - 146   2015 $100

The Temperance Almanac, for the Year of Our Lord 1837. Albany: from the Steam Press of Packard and Van Benthuysen, 1836. Original printed paper wrappers, woodcut on front, faint stain to fore-edge, some general foxing and toning to prefatory and concluding leaves and wrappers. Tavistock Books   Temperance - 2015 $50

Le Temple De Gnide. Paris: Imprimerie et Fonderie de J. Pinard, 1824. Limited to 140 copies, large folio, contemporary paper covered boards, leather spine label, covers and spine soiled, rubbed and scuffed at edges, pencilled notes on front free endpaper, some foxing throughout. Oak Knoll Books   306 - 228   2015 $1750

Temple, Edmond *Travels in Various parts of Peru, Including a Year's Residence in Potosi.* London: Henry Colburn and Richard Bentley, 1830. First edition, 2 volumes, 8 uncolored aquatint plates, 1 map, 17 wood engraved vignettes, 8vo., red buckram, gilt titles, from the NY Historical Society, very good, accession numbers on spines, recolored, faint institutional rubber stamp on rear pastedowns, scattered foxing, one plate heavily spotted, else most quite clean and bright. Kaaterskill Books   19 - 147   2015 $600

Ten Little Mulligan Guards. New York: McLoughlin Bros., 1874. Oblong 4to., pictorial wrappers, 12 leaves including covers, spine neatly repaired with few margin mends, else fine and bright, chromolithographs. Aleph-bet Books, Inc.   109 - 58   2015 $675

Tench, Watkin *Letters Written in France to a Friend in London, Between the Month of November 1794 and the Month of May 1795.* London: J. Johnson, 1796. First edition, 8vo., front free endpaper creased, some foxing at foot of title, occasional old marginal emphasis marks, contemporary half calf over marbled boards, flat spine gilt and labelled, very good, really quite rare. John Drury Rare Books   2015 - 23905   2015 $1311

Tenfold. Poems for Frances Horovitz. Marin Booth for the Frances Horovitz Benefit, 1983. First edition, one of 500 copies (from an edition of 550), 8vo., original grey stapled wrappers, printed in red, fine. Blackwell's Rare Books   B179 - 176   2015   £35

Tenison, Thomas *An Argument for Union Taken from True Interest of Those Dissenters in England, Who Profess and Call Themselves Protestants.* London: printed for Tho. Basset; Benj. Toke and F. Gardiner, 1683. First edition, 4to., very faint dampstain at foot of first few leaves, preserved in modern wrappers with printed label on upper cover, nice, crisp copy. John Drury Rare Books   2015 - 25679   2015 $133

Tenney, Caleb J. *A Summary View of God's Gracious Covenant with Abraham and His Seed, of the Right and Design of the Baptism of Infants...* Newport: Office of the Newport Mercury, 1808. First edition, 8vo., 96 pages, contemporary drab wrappers, sewn as issued, spine mostly perished, light dampstain upper corner several leaves at beginning and end, not affecting text, small shelf label at corner of upper wrapper, old oval blindstamp on title. M & S Rare Books, Inc.   97 - 274   2015 $400

Tennyson, Alfred Tennyson, 1st Baron 1809-1892 *In Memoriam.* London: Edward Moxon, 1850. First edition, half title, without initial catalog, brown morocco presentation binding by Budden, Cambridge, little rubbed with small split in leading hinge, all edges gilt, lettered on front board, inscribed to Julain Fane from HAJ, with very poor copy of the 10th edition 1861 in original cloth, heavily annotated with insertions by Geoffrey Tillotson, from the library of Geoffrey & Kathleen Tillotson.   Jarndyce Antiquarian Booksellers   CCVII - 486   2015   £350

Tennyson, Alfred Tennyson, 1st Baron 1809-1892 *The Lady of Shalott.* New York: Dodd Mead, 1881. First edition, 4to., gilt pictorial cloth with beveled edges, some light soil and rubbing, else clean and very good+, lush color lithographs with calligraphic text, beautiful book.   Aleph-bet Books, Inc.   109 - 393   2015 $600

Tennyson, Alfred Tennyson, 1st Baron 1809-1892 *The Letters.* Oxford: Clarendon Press, 1987-1990. 3 volumes, half titles, original dark blue cloth, very good, in creased dust jacket, Kathleen Tillotson's copy with few notes, 4 ALS's from Cecil Lang to Kathleen, inserts.   Jarndyce Antiquarian Booksellers   CCVII - 490   2015   £125

Tennyson, Alfred Tennyson, 1st Baron 1809-1892 *Lyrical Poems.* London: Maxmillan, 1885. First edition, half title, 6 pages ads, pages 119-20 torn through without loss, uncut in remains of original blue boards, lacking spine strip, last gathering detached, possibly a proof copy, selected and annotated by Francis T. Palgrave, his copy, signed Mch 9 1885, but with no internal marks, from the library of Geoffrey & Kathleen Tillotson, inscribed by them.   Jarndyce Antiquarian Booksellers   CCVII - 487   2015   £45

Tennyson, Alfred Tennyson, 1st Baron 1809-1892 *Poems, Chiefly Lyrical.* London: Effingham Wilson, 1830. Uncut, recased in stiff paper with paper label, signature of Whitley Stokes 14/6/55, from the library of Geoffrey & Kathleen Tillotson.   Jarndyce Antiquarian Booksellers   CCVII - 488   2015   £450

Tennyson, Alfred Tennyson, 1st Baron 1809-1892 *The Princess; a Medley.* London: Edward Moxon, 1847. First edition, inscribed by author for fellow poet Mary Howitt, little light spotting, 8vo., original green cloth, boards with decorative border blocked in blind, spine lettered in gilt direct, sunned, corners bumped some wear to spine ends, hinges just cracking, sound.   Blackwell's Rare Books   B179 - 104   2015   £750

Tennyson, Alfred Tennyson, 1st Baron 1809-1892 *The Princess, a Medley.* London: Edward Moxon, 1866. Original dark blue cloth, bevelled boards, embossed in gilt and blind, spine slightly faded, bookseller's ticket of Wm. Mullan, Belfast, all edges gilt, 26 illustrations engraved on wood, attractive larger format edition, Kathleen Tillotson's copy as K. Constable with earlier signature 1867 of great great aunt Anna Waring.   Jarndyce Antiquarian Booksellers   CCVII - 489   2015   £85

Tennyson, Alfred Tennyson, 1st Baron 1809-1892 *Seven Poems and Two Translations.* Hammersmith: Doves Press, 1902. First Doves Press edition, one of 325, small quarto, original full vellum, gilt, bookplate of Charles Walker Andrews, fine.   The Brick Row Book Shop   Miscellany 67 - 39   2015 $500

Tennyson, Alfred Tennyson, 1st Baron 1809-1892 *Timbuctoo. A Poem...* Cambridge: John Smith, 1829. First edition, few tiny spots, 8vo., stab-sewn, original plain wrappers discarded, title and rear blank somewhat dusty, cornertips slightly creased, good.   Blackwell's Rare Books   B179 - 103   2015   £350

Tennyson, Alfred Tennyson, 1st Baron 1809-1892 *Works.* London: Strahan, 1870. 10 pocket volumes, bound in contemporary full polished black calf, gilt.   Honey & Wax Booksellers   2 - 46   2015 $750

Tennyson, Hallan Tennyson *Materials for a Life of A. T. Collected for My Children.* N.P.: privately printed, 1895? 4 volumes, original blue card wrappers, slight rubbing, from the library of Geoffrey & Kathleen Tillotson, volume I signed by Geoffrey 30 xi 42 with few marginal marks and few pencil notes in each volume, volume I in Geoffrey's paper covers with his notes.   Jarndyce Antiquarian Booksellers   CCVII - 493   2015   £750

Terentius Afer, Publius *Comoediae Sex.* The Hague: Apud Petrum Gosse, 1726. 2 volumes, one engraved frontispiece in each volume and one further engraved portrait, some significant browning in prelims and index, just few leaves browned elsewhere, bit of light spotting, one blank corner trimmed, 4to., modern period style vellum, boards panelled in blind with central decorative blindstamped lozenge, unlettered spines with five raised bands, marbled endpapers, very good.   Blackwell's Rare Books   Greek & Latin Classics VI - 99   2015   £300

Terentius Afer, Publius *The Comedies of Terence.* Dublin: Printed by Boulter Grierson, 1766. First or Second Dublin edition, engraved frontispiece, some light browning, ownership inscription of H. Davies, rector of Llandegfan (177*) to titlepage, 8vo., contemporary calf speckled black and green, green morocco lettering piece, touch rubbed at extremities, front joint just cracking at foot, very good.   Blackwell's Rare Books   Greek & Latin Classics VI - 100   2015   £200

Terhune, Albert Payson *The Luck of the Laird.* New York: Harper and Bros., 1927. Later printing, blue cloth, gilt, spine lettering worn away, else very good, lacking dust jacket, author's own copy with his Riverside Drive NY address stamped on front fly.   Between the Covers Rare Books, Inc.   187 - 274   2015 $650

Terhune, Albert Payson *The Runway Bag.* New York: Burt, Reprint edition, some staining on page edges, otherwise very good in fine dust jacket with closed tear. Mordida Books   March 2015 - 010042   2015 $90

Terpereau, Jules Alphonse *Societe Philomatique De Bordeaux... XIIE Exposition Generale.* Bordeaux: Photographie Terpereau 29 cour de l'Intendance, 1882. Oblong folio, title printed in red on buff coated paper, 20 woodbury plates and one albumen print each mounted on card with titles and decorative border printed in red, original red cloth, upper cover with title blocked in gilt, somewhat worn and soiled.   Marlborough Rare Books   List 53 - 14   2015   £1350

Terrasse, Charles *Elogue de Henri Manguin.* Manuel Bruker, 1954. First edition, number 69 of 200 copies, 4to., fine in wrappers with lightly faded spine, 9 original engravings by artist.   Beasley Books   2013 - 2015 $300

Territory of Orleans *Territory of the Civil Laws Now in Force in Territory of Orleans.* New Orleans: 1868. Ex-library, Supreme court, some cover soil, scarce. Bookworm & Silverfish   2015 - 4761269583   2015 $250

Tevis, Walter *The Hustler.* New York: Harper, 1959. First edition, slight sunning to board edges and shallow push to spine, near fine in like dust jacket, unfaded with shallow unobtrusive repair to crown.   Ken Lopez, Bookseller   164 - 202   2015 $2500

Texas Conference for Education *Bulletin 3, 4 and 5, Proceedings, Second Annual Conference.* Austin: 1908. 87 pages, tipped in are six folding broadsides, scarce. Bookworm & Silverfish   2015 - 33586333111   2015 $250

Tey, Josephine *The Singing Sands.* London: Davies, 1952. First edition, fine in dust jacket with some tiny wear at spine ends and along folds.   Mordida Books   March 2015 - 005305   2015 $275

Thacher, James   1754-1844 *Observations on Hydrophobia, Produced by the Bite of a Mad Dog, or Other Rabid Animal...* Plymouth: Joseph Avery, 1812. hand colored plate, contemporary mottled sheep, foxed as this book always is, very attractive copy, binding being particularly nice.   Joseph J. Felcone Inc.   Science, Medicine and Technology - 41   2015 $500

Thackeray, Franciscus St. John *Anthologia Latina.* London: A. M. Bell et Daldy, 1865. First edition, presentation copy, paper lightly toned throughout, few fox spots to first and last leaves, small 8vo., contemporary dark brown morocco by Holloway, boards bordered with double gilt fillet, spine divided by raised bands with gilt fillet borders to compartments, second compartment gilt lettered direct, rest with central fleuron tools and fleur-de-lis cornerpieces, turn-ins decoratively gilt, all edges gilt, marbled endpapers, bookplate of William Thirlwall Bayne, near fine, inscribed by editor for Thirlwall.   Blackwell's Rare Books   Greek & Latin Classics VI - 64   2015   £200

Thackeray, William Makepeace   1811-1863 *The Letters and Private Papers of William Makepeace Thackeray.* London: Oxford University Press, 1945-1946. First edition, 4 volumes, half titles, plates, illustrations, original pink cloth, spines slightly faded, from the library of Geoffrey & Kathleen Tillotson, signed, some notes and markings by both. Jarndyce Antiquarian Booksellers   CCVII - 499   2015   £75

Thackeray, William Makepeace   1811-1863 *Mr. Thackeray's Writings in the "The National Standard" and "Constitutional".* London: W. T. Spencer, 1899. First edition, half title, frontispiece, illustrations, contemporary quarter red morocco, blue cloth boards, pictorial blocked gilt, some wear to head and tail of spine, otherwise very nice, crisp copy, scarce.   Jarndyce Antiquarian Booksellers   CCXI - 270   2015   £220

Thackeray, William Makepeace   1811-1863 *Vanity Fair.* Boston: Houghton Mifflin Co., 1963. Riverside edition, half title, illustrations, original printed boards, Kathleen Tillotson's copy with few alterations indicated to text and appendices, she notes this is first edition.   Jarndyce Antiquarian Booksellers   CCVII - 498   2015   £20

Thanet, Octave *The Lion's Share.* Indianapolis: Bobbs Merrill, 1907. First edition, fine in dar red pictorial cloth covered boards with gold stamped titles, fine.   Mordida Books   March 2015 - 002163   2015 $100

Thanet, Octave *The Missionary Sheriff.* New York: Harper, 1897. First edition, fine in blue decorated cloth covered boards with gold stamped titles, fine.   Mordida Books   March 2015 - 002162   2015 $125

Tharaud, J. *La Fete Arabe.* Paris: Aux Editions Lupina, 1926. Number 177 of 400 copies, small 4to., wrappers, with 32 color woodcuts by Sureda, spine shows considerable vertical wrinkling from shrinking glue or amateur re-gluing, otherwise fine in original labeled slipcase.   Beasley Books   2013 - 2015 $800

Tharaud, J. *Un Royaume De Dieu.* Paris: Aux Editions Lapina, 1925. No. 172 of 400 copies, wrappers, 86 etchings by Lucien Madrassi, fine, spine wrinkles from glue aging not wear, previous owner's slipcase, small quarto. Beasley Books   2013 - 2015 $375

Tharaud, J. *La Semaine Sainte a Seville.* Paris: Editions Lapina, 1927. #X of 50 copies marked HC, with extra suite of etchings by Polat, 8vo., wrappers near fine with slight soil and sunning to spine in slightly worn marbled box. Beasley Books   2013 - 2015 $300

That Unknown Country or What Living Men Believe Concerning Punishment After Death etc. Springfield & Dayton: 1888. Apparent first edition, gilt stamped and decorated full leather, portrait, minor wear to extremities, few scratches to spine, very good, very scarce.   Baade Books of the West   2014 - 2015 $162

Thayer, Evelyn *Catalogue of a Collection of Books on Ornithology in the Library of John E. Thayer.* Boston: privately printed, 1913. First printing, 8vo., early half dark blue morocco with marbled paper sides, gilt stamped spine title with raised bands, top edge gilt, outer front spine hinge badly gnawed, still tightly bound, good.   Jeff Weber Rare Books   178 - 864   2015 $75

Theal, George McCall *Records of South Eastern Africa.* N.P.: London? Government of the Cape Colony, 1964. Reprint of 1898-1903 edition, 9 volumes, 8vo., about fine, endpapers slightly browned, hardback.   Any Amount of Books   March 2015 - A67795   2015   £370

Theobald, John *Every Man His Own Physician.* London: printed and sold by W. Griffin, R. Withy and G. Kearsly, 1764. Fourth edition, 8vo., paper rather browned throughout, little foxing on titlepage and elsewhere, stitched as issued in blue paper wrappers (upper wrapper wanting), entirely uncut with some marginal fraying but overall good, large copy, near contemporary inscription "To Mrs. Strutt at Mrs. Bagots Harwich".   John Drury Rare Books   2015 - 17782   2015 $177

Theobald, John *Miscellaneous Poems and Translations.* London: printed and sold by J. Roberts, 1734. First edition, 8vo., full dark blue morocco antique, spine and inner dentelles gilt, all edges gilt, wanting half title, otherwise nice, very rare title.   C. R. Johnson   Foxon R-Z - 975r-z   2015 $2298

Theobald, John *Poems on Several Occasions.* London: printed for John Morphew, 1719. First edition, 8vo., disbound, some pale waterstains but very good, very rare.   C. R. Johnson   Foxon R-Z - 974r-z   2015 $3831

Theobald, Lewis *The Cave of Poverty, a Poem.* London: printed for Jonas Browne and sold by J. Roberts, 1715. First edition, 8vo., sewn as issued, in folding case, half title somewhat dust soiled with small piece chipped from blank upper corner, otherwise very good in original condition, entirely uncut.   C. R. Johnson   Foxon R-Z - 976r-z   2015 $1379

Theobald, Lewis *The Cave of Poverty a Poem.* London: printed for Jonas Browne and sold by J. Roberts, n.d., 1715. First edition, 8vo., disbound, half title little soiled, otherwise good, early ownership inscription on title 'Liber Joh(ann)is Thom's" dated 1716.   C. R. Johnson   Foxon R-Z - 977r-z   2015 $919

Theobald, William *A Practical Treatise on the Poor Laws, As Altered by the Poor Law Amendment act and Other Recent Statutes.* London: S. Sweet, Stevens and Sons, 1836. First edition, 8vo., near contemporary stamp of Poor Law commission, contemporary black half calf over marbled boards, binding evidently restored and recased, spine with faded gilt lettering and generally worn, nevertheless very good, tightly bound.   John Drury Rare Books   March 2015 - 25936   2015 $221

Theroux, Paul   1941- *The Mosquito Coast.* Boston: Houghton Mifflin, 1982. First American edition, number 328 of 350 copies signed by author, cloth in slipcase, fine. Gemini Fine Books & Arts, Ltd.   Art Reference & Illustrated Books: First Editions - 2015 $90

Theroux, Paul   1941- *Travelling the World: the Illustrated Travels of Paul Theroux.* London: Sinclair Stevenson, 1990. First edition, quarto, fine in fine dust jacket, inscribed by author to brother-in-law and sister Jack and Mary. Between the Covers Rare Books   196 - 117 2015 $650

Thesiger, Wilfred *The Life of My Choice.* London: Collins, 1987. First edition, 8vo., 32 plates, original black cloth lettered gilt at spine, illustrations, signed presentation from author, near fine in like dust jacket.   Any Amount of Books   2015 - C14004   2015   £220

Thevenot, Melchisedech *The Swimmer' and Skater's Guide...* Derby: Published by Thomas Richardson circa, 1838. 12mo., hand colored wood engraved folding frontispiece, partly unopened, original printed pink wrappers. Marlborough Rare Books   List 54 - 85   2015   £850

Thiebaut, C. A. *Newport 1875.* New York: J. Bien, 1875. First edition, folio, 20 black and white photo lithographic views, unbound as issued, image size 10.25 x 6.75 inches on thick paper 22 x 16.5 inches, images clear but title leaf soiled, occasional foxing, dampstaining and soiling, overall very good.   M & S Rare Books, Inc.   97 - 276   2015 $2500

The Third Chapter of Accidents and Remarkable events Containing Caution and Instruction for Children. Philadelphia: J. Johnson, 1807. Marbled wrappers, 24 leaves, fine, 12 engravings.   Aleph-Bet Books, Inc.   108 - 161   2015 $850

30 Years of Indonesia's Independence 1945-1975. Republic of Indonesia: State Secretariat, 1975. First edition, wrappers, 3 volumes, 4to., stiff illustrated covers, copiously illustrated in black and white, very slight rubbing, otherwise sound, very good in used and worn, very good- slipcase with edges cracking and laminate peeling.   Any Amount of Books   2015 - A85879   2015   £220

Thoinot, L.   *Medicolegal Aspects of Moral Offenses.* Philadelphia: Davis, 1913. First edition, 8vo., original cloth, very good, 17 engravings.   Second Life Books Inc.   189 - 253   2015 $75

Thomas A Kempis   1380-1471   *The Christian's Pattern; or a Treatise of the Imitation of Jesus Christ...*   London: printed for Barker (and others), 1742. 203 x 127mm., animated contemporary black morocco, lavishly gilt, covers with central cottage-roof design enclosed by ornate floral rolls and small tools, the 'roof' frame containing a large and elaborate fleuron within a lozenge of small tools, raised bands, spine gilt in compartments bordered by plain rules and dogtooth rolls, each compartment divided into quarters by gilt diagonal lines, each quarter with a delicate stippled floral tool, red morocco label, gilt turn-ins, marbled endpapers, all edges gilt, engraved frontispiece of Crucifixion, plus engravings of the nativity, Adoration of the Magi, Christ in the Wilderness and the Last Supper; 18th century bookplate of Fane William Sharpe, 18th or 19th century armorial bookplate of W. Combes, spine faded to pleasing hazel brown, little rubbing to joints and extremities, minor chafing to boards, occasional faint foxing, isolated dust soiling to head edge, other trivial imperfections, but fine, nevertheless, leaves clean and fresh and intricately tooled unsophisticated binding very lustrous and showing no significant wear, splendid copy. Phillip J. Pirages   66 - 35   2015 $3200

Thomas A Kempis   1380-1471   *The Christian's Pattern or a Treatise of the Imitation of Jesus Christ.*   London: printed by T. C. Hansard, 1831. First edition thus, 8vo., full brown leather with gilt lettered spine label, long handwritten note on tips to verso front endpaper from printer, T. C. Hansard, signed with a flourish by TCH, head of spine chipped, front outer hinges cracked but holding, very good.   Any Amount of Books   2015 - A36006   2015   £175

Thomas A Kempis   1380-1471   *Opera.*   Paris: Iodocus Badius Ascensius, 1523. Second collected edition, first edition printed in France, 330 x 216mm., lacking final blank, fine contemporary London blindstamped calf, covers tooled in panels, outer frame of a roll of Renaissance designs including fountain topped by three heads, central panel composed mainly of five vertical rows of foliage and flowers, raised bands, spine very expertly rebacked to style, two original brass clasps and catches with leather thongs (perhaps later but perhaps not), original vellum tabs marking important textual sections, rear board with contemporaneous inscription (perhaps author and title), rear pastedown comprising a portion of a proclamation dealing with beggars and vagabonds, in recent clamshell box backed with calf, titlepage with woodcut device dated 1520 depicting printer's workshop, large and small woodcut initials in text (few artlessly colored), titlepage with signature of Johannes Person above woodcut vignette and of another member of Person family at top of page, (this inscription dated 1566 with purchase details for the volume), also signature of A. Fletcher, inside cover of box and front pastedown with modern morocco bookplate of Michael Sharpe, lower board with small abraded area, other trivial marks and very small wormholes in leather, thongs bit dried and deteriorating, but expertly restored binding entirely solid and blindstamping still quite sharp, titlepage little dust soiled and with small shadow of turn-in glue at bottom, last three gatherings with minor stains along gutter, final gathering with similar stain at fore-edge, short tears and other trivial imperfections in text, generally quite fine internally, text mostly quite clean, especially fresh and unusually bright.   Phillip J. Pirages   66 - 7   2015 $12,500

Thomas Aquinas, Saint   *Institutiones Philosophicae Ad mentem Angelici Doctoris S. Thomae Aquinatis.*   Ex typis Abbatiae Montis Casini, 1875. First edition, 5 volumes, 8vo., black cloth lettered gilt on spine, some volumes slightly mottled and slightly worn and slightly chipped, very good with slight staining (no loss of legibility) to few prelim pages in some volumes.   Any Amount of Books   2015 - A853054   2015   £225

Thomas Aquinas, Saint *Summa Theologica Pars Secunda; Prima Pars.* Venice: Theodorus de Ragazonibus 31 March, 1490. 324 x 222mm., 200 unnumbered leaves (complete) with first last, and leaf 194 blank, 60 lines, gothic type, excellent contemporary blindstamped Northern Italian calf (perhaps from Venice or Milan), outer border of blind fillets with mitered corners, inner frame formed by chain roll within triple fillets, frame enclosing large central panel dominated by a cross formed by repeated impressions of a diamond tool and with four small crosses composed of same tool in quadrants formed by large cross, background punctuated with small rosettes, raised bands, spine compartments with saltire of blind fillets, the same diamond and rosette tools decorating the quandrants, old paper label with ink year of publication, four original brass catches on lower cover (two along fore edge, one each at top and bottom), top clasp and rawhide thong intact (remnants of the other thongs present), 4 particularly fine 12th century vellum manuscript flyleaves from liturgical ms. in fine Carolingian hand; 8 large decorated initials (most five to seven line, one 14-line) in elaborate vinestem designs in red infilled with yellow, blue and green, one of the initials containing a charming deer, small patch of leather missing from head of front board, exposing wood beneath, upper inner corner of cover solid, without serious wear, still very attractive as an unrestored period artifact, flyleaves with inch or so of discoloration around edges (from binder's glue), vellum slightly rumpled, otherwise manuscript leaves especially fine and well preserved, first four gatherings with small dampstain to upper gutter (quite minor dampstaining and foxing elsewhere), half dozen leaves slightly browned, but really excellent copy internally, mostly very clean and fresh, especially ample margins.   Phillip J. Pirages   66 - 1   2015 $95,000

Thomas, Adah B. *Pathfinders: the Progress of Colored Graduate Nurses with Biographies of Many Prominent Nurses.* New York: Kay Printing House, 1929. First edition, 24 pages, photos, modest wear to corners and spine ends, very good or better, almost certainly issued without dust jacket, exceptionally scarce.   Between the Covers Rare Books   197 - 65   2015 $1200

Thomas, Alan G. *Great Books and Book Collectors.* London: Weidenfeld & Nicolson, 1975. First edition, large volume, fine in dust jacket (crease on inner front flap). Mordida Books   March 2015 - 010988   2015 $85

Thomas, Craig *Firefox.* New York: Holt, Rinehart & Winston, 1977. First American edition, fine in dust jacket. Mordida Books   March 2015 - 002167   2015 $100

Thomas, Dorothy *Hi-Po the Hippo.* New York: Random House, 1942. Stated first edition, folio, cloth backed pictorial boards, fine in dust jacket with closed tear and semi-circular piece off top edge which is not offensive because dust jacket matches the pictorial cover, full page and partial page color and black and white lithographs.   Aleph-bet Books, Inc.   109 - 190   2015 $500

Thomas, Dylan Marlais 1914-1953 *Poemas.* Madrid: Ediciones Rialp, 1955. First Catalan edition, 16mo., wrappers, near fine.   Beasley Books   2013 - 2015 $125

Thomas, Dylan Marlais 1914-1953 *Collected Poems 1934-1952.* London: Dent, 1952. First edition, frontispiece, 8vo., original mid blue cloth, gilt lettered backstrip, price clipped dust jacket, trifle chipped and wine stained on rear panel, short tear to front fold, very good, inscribed by author to his American agent John Malcolm Brinnin. Blackwell's Rare Books   B179 - 243   2015   £2000

Thomas, Dylan Marlais 1914-1953 *Twenty-Six Poems.* printed at the Offficina Bodoni for James Laughlin and J. M. Dent, 1949. First English edition, 37/60 copies (of an edition of 150 copies), signed by author, printed in black on Fabriano handmade paper with the pressmark printed in red, small folio, original quarter cream canvas, printed label on backstrip which is just touch browned, white boards closely patterned overall in black and green, untrimmed, some wear to board slipcase, near fine.   Blackwell's Rare Books   B179 - 199   2015   £2500

Thomas, Dylan Marlais 1914-1953 *Under Milk Wood, a Play for Voices. A Reproduction of the Illuminated Manuscript...* Santa Ana: International Letter Arts Network, 1989. 4to., quarter cloth, paper covered boards, blindstamped titling and cover designs, later cardboard slipcase, full page color reproduction of the illuminated manuscript handwritten and illustrated by Sheila Waters.   Oak Knoll Books   Special Catalogue 24 - 53   2015 $250

Thomas, Edith *Babes of the Nations.* New York: Stokes, 1889. Small 4to., 12 magnificent full page chromolithographs by Maud Humphrey.   Aleph-bet Books, Inc.   109 - 228   2015 $950

Thomas, Edward *Selected Poems of Edward Thomas.* Newtown: Gregynog Press, 1927. First edition, no. 53 of 275 copies, 8vo., original yellow buckram lettered gilt on spine, slight general even dust soiling, slight abrasion at lower spine, sound, clean, very good with clean text.   Any Amount of Books   2015 - A69337   2015   £180

Thomas, Edward *Words into Wood. Eight Poems, Eighteen Wood-Engravings.* St. Lawrence: Edward Thomas Fellowship, 2010. 44/50 copies (of an edition of 250), titlepage printed in black and copper, crown 4to.,original quarter brown leather and green cloth, backstrip lettered gilt, tail edge rough trimmed, matching slipcase, new.   Blackwell's Rare Books   B179 - 244   2015   £135

Thomas, Henry *Andres Brun, Calligrapher of Saragossa, Some Account of His Life and Work...* Paris: Officina Bodoni for the Pegasus Press, 1928. Limited to an edition of 175 numbered copies, 4to., decorate cloth, plain cardboard slipcase, printed by Mardersteig for the Pegasus Press, Paris, in Janson type on Fabriano paper, with facsimile in collotype of the surviving text and plates, plain cardboard slipcase is worn with pieces missing. Oak Knoll Books   Special Catalogue 24 - 54   2015 $2500

Thomas, Rex *No Questions Asked.* New York: Morrow, 1976. First edition, signed by author "Oliver Bleeck a.k.a. Ross Thomas Oct. 7 1987", fine in lightly soiled dust jacket with tiny staining at top of spine. Mordida Books   March 2015 - 011459   2015 $150

Thomas, Ross *The Backup Men.* New York: William Morrow, 1971. First edition, fine in dust jacket. Buckingham Books   March 2015 - 21484   2015 $175

Thomas, Ross *The Backup Men.* New York: Morrow, 1971. First edition, very fine in dust jacket. Mordida Books   March 2015 - 012692   2015 $250

Thomas, Ross *The Backup Men.* New York: Morrow, 1971. First edition, name on front pastedown, fine in dust jacket with several short closed tears. Mordida Books   March 2015 - 008476   2015 $100

Thomas, Ross *The Brass Go-Between.* New York: William Morrow, 1969. First edition, fine in fine dust jacket, from the collection of Duke Collier. Royal Books   36 - 131   2015 $400

Thomas, Ross *Briarpatch.* New York: Simon & Schuster, 1984. First edition, fine, wrappers, uncorrected proof. Mordida Books   March 2015 - 002175   2015 $75

Thomas, Ross *Brown Paper and Some String.* San Rafael: California Mystery and Suspense Writers Conference, 1987. First edition, 8vo., wrappers, fine, signed by Thomas. Beasley Books   2013 - 2015 $45

Thomas, Ross *Cast a Yellow Shadow.* New York: William Morrow, 1967. First edition, signed by author, fine in dust jacket with light wear to spine. Buckingham Books   March 2015 - 21431   2015 $225

Thomas, Ross *Cast a Yellow Shadow.* New York: Morrow, 1967. First edition, fine, top corner slightly bumped, otherwise fine in dust jacket. Mordida Books   March 2015 - 007251   2015 $250

Thomas, Ross *The Cold War Swap.* First edition, fine in near fine dust jacket with light wear at spine ends and one corner, mild sunning to spine, from the collection of Duke Collier. Royal Books   36 - 127   2015 $1000

Thomas, Ross *The Cold War Swap.* New York: Morrow, 1966. First edition, erasures on front endpaper, otherwise fine in very good dust jacket with slightly faded spine, chipped and frayed spine ends, closed crease tear on front panel, wear at corners. Mordida Books   March 2015 - 012691   2015 $350

Thomas, Ross *The Cold War Swap.* New York: William Morrow & Co., 1966. First edition, 8vo., lightly rubbed at spine ends, else near fine, tight copy, dust jacket lightly sunned on spine, light professional restoration to spine ends. Buckingham Books   March 2015 - 28282   2015 $675

Thomas, Ross *The Fools in Town are on Our Side.* London: Hodder and Stoughton, 1970. First edition, near fine in like dust jacket, quite uncommon thus, from the collection of Duke Collier. Royal Books   36 - 132   2015 $375

Thomas, Ross *The Fools in Town are on Our Side.* New York: Morrow, 1971. First American edition, fine in dust jacket. Mordida Books   March 2015 - 009184   2015 $250

Thomas, Ross *The Highbinders.* New York: William Morrow, 1974. First edition, inscribed by author to a collection and signed as Thomas and Bleeck, fine in dust jacket. Buckingham Books   March 2015 - 21481   2015 $200

Thomas, Ross *The Highbinders.* New York: Morrow, 1974. First edition, fine in dust jacket, inscribed by author. Mordida Books   March 2015 - 011458   2015 $175

Thomas, Ross *If You Can't Be Good.* New York: Morrow, 1973. First edition, fine in dust jacket with short crease on inner front flap. Mordida Books   March 2015 - 010673   2015 $150

Thomas, Ross *The Money Harvest.* New York: William Morrow, 1975. Uncorrected proof, inscribed by author, fine and unread in green wrappers, from the collection of Duke Collier. Royal Books   36 - 129   2015 $450

Thomas, Ross *The Money Harvest.* New York: Morrow, 1975. First edition, small spot bottom of page edges, otherwise fine in dust jacket with short closed tear. Mordida Books   March 2015 - 011393   2015 $90

Thomas, Ross *The Mordida Man.* New York: Simon & Schuster, 1981. First edition, fine in dust jacket. Mordida Books   March 2015 - 010437   2015 $90

Thomas, Ross *No Questions Asked.* New York: William Morrow and Co. Inc., 1978. First edition, fine in dust jacket with 1" closed tear to bottom edge of front panel. Buckingham Books   March 2015 - 21478   2015 $175

Thomas, Ross *Protocol for a Kidnapping.* New York: William Morrow, 1971. First edition, moderate staining to top and bottom edges of boards, else near fine in dust jacket, very lightly sunned on spine. Buckingham Books March 2015 - 21486   2015 $175

Thomas, Ross *Protocol for a Kidnapping.* New York: William Morrow, 1971. First edition, fine in fine dust jacket, from the collection of Duke Collier. Royal Books 36 - 130 2015 $450

Thomas, Ross *The Seersucker Whipsaw.* New York: William Morrow & Co., 1967. First edition, fine in lightly soiled dust jacket with light wear to head of spine and two 1 inch closed tears to back panel. Buckingham Books March 2015 - 21491   2015 $175

Thomas, Ross *The Seersucker Whipsaw.* New York: William Morrow, 1967. First edition, signed by author, fine in fine dust jacket, none of the usual yellowing to white background, from the collection of Duke Collier. Royal Books 36 - 128   2015 $650

Thomas, Ross *The Seersucker Whipsaw.* New York: Morrow, 1967. First edition, small label removed from front endpaper and name on same, otherwise fine in dust jacket, exceptional copy. Mordida Books March 2015 - 011334 2015 $400

Thomas, Ross *Signal the Instructions, Please.* Frank Perry Films Inc., 1973. First edition, inscribed, original screenplay, 133 pages bound in red leather binder, very scarce. Buckingham Books March 2015 - 21496   2015 $1000

Thomas, Ross *The Singapore Wink.* New York: Morrow, 1969. First edition, glue reside under jacket flaps, otherwise fine in dust jacket with crease on inner front flap. Mordida Books March 2015 - 010436   2015 $85

Thomas, Ross *The Singapore Wink.* New York: William Morrow & Co., 1969. First edition, fine in price clipped dust jacket. Buckingham Books March 2015 - 21490   2015 $200

Thomas, Ross *Spies, Thumbsuckers etc.* Northridge: Lord John Press, 1989. First edition, one of 50 deluxe copies, especially bound in leather and marbled boards, signed by author, as new. Buckingham Books March 2015 - 21488   2015 $250

Thomas, Ross *Twilight at Mac's Place.* New York: Mysterious Press, 1990. First edition, one of 26 lettered copies signed by author, very fine in slipcase without dust jacket. Mordida Books March 2015 - 000002   2015 $150

Thomas, Ross *Yellow-Dog Contract.* New York: Morrow, 1977. First edition, very fine in dust jacket, signed by author. Mordida Books March 2015 - 007250   2015 $150

Thomas, Simon *Hanes y Byd a'r Amseroedd, er Hyfforddiad Rhai o'r Cymru.* printed by J. Batly, 1721. First London edition, some browning and staining, small 8vo., original sheep, crudely rebacked, new endpapers, sound. Blackwell's Rare Books   B179 - 105   2015 £400

Thompson, Charles *Rules for Bad Horsemen: Addressed to the Society for the Encouragement of Arts.* London: J. Robson, 1762. First edition, small 8vo., half red leather lettered gilt on spine with five raised bands, slightly rubbed with weak, complete front hinge, very good, text very clean, bookplate of Sir William A. H. Bass, Baronet. Any Amount of Books   2015 - C4845   2015   £275

Thompson, Edward Maunde *An Introduction to Greek and Latin Paleography.* Oxford: at Clarendon Press, 1912. First edition, small 4to., cloth, dust jacket, from the library of J. R. Abbey with his bookplate, over half of the jacket spine is missing inside hinges cracked scarce. Oak Knoll Books Special Catalogue 24 - 55   2015 $250

Thompson, Hunter S. *Fear and Loathing in Las Vegas.* New York: Random House, 1971. First edition, illustrations by Ralph Steadman, nearly fine with inevitable sunning around edges of black boards, nearly fine dust jacket with few creases to rear flap. Ed Smith Books   82 - 29 2015 $1250

Thompson, Hunter S. *Fear and Loathing in Las Vegas. A Savage Journey to the Heart of the American Dream.* New York: Random House, 1971. First edition, first printing, fine in bright, fine dust jacket without any of the usual fading to red lettering, very crisp and sharp. B & B Rare Books, Ltd. 234 - 98   2015 $1250

Thompson, Hunter S. *Fear and Loathing in America.* New York: Simon & Schuster, 2000. Review copy, 3 volumes, signed by author on bookplate on front flyleaf fine in fine dust jacket, with form letter serving as a review slip announcing Dec. 13 publication of this title as well as simultaneous publication of a trade edition of Screwjack, with "Gonzo" drink coaster laid in. Ken Lopez, Bookseller   164 - 204   2015 $500

Thompson, Hunter S. *The Great Shark Hunt; Strange Tales from a Strange Time.* London: Picador/Pan Books, 1981. Third UK paperback printing, 8vo., wrappers, illustrations, signed for Jeremy Beadle by author, very good. Any Amount of Books   March 2015 - A99130   2015 £400

Thompson, Hunter S. *Hell's Angels.* New York: Random House, 1967. First edition, laid in loose is bookplate signed by author, near fine in very good dust jacket with spine sunning and some nicks and old one inch dampstain to spine foot, visible on jacket verso only. Ed Smith Books 83 - 106 2015 $600

Thompson, Hunter S. *The Proud Highway.* New York: Villard, 1997. Advance copy, first issue proof, 8 1/2 x 11 inch sheets, tapebound in cardstock covers, spotting/handling to covers, near fine, date 3/19 on front cover. Ken Lopez, Bookseller 164 - 203 2015 $450

Thompson, Hunter S. *Screwjack.* Santa Barbara: Neville, 1991. First edition, one of 300 numbered copies signed in full by author, bright red cloth with gilt decoration, issued without dust jacket, fine. Ed Smith Books 83 - 105 2015 $1250

Thompson, Hunter S. *Screwjack.* New York: Simon & Schuster, 2000. First trade edition, signed in full by Thompson on large bookplate mounted to front endpaper, fine in black cloth with silver spine stamping, fine dust jacket, from the estate of Beef Torrey. Ed Smith Books 83 - 102 2015 $400

Thompson, Hunter S. *Songs of the Doomed.* New York: Summit, 1990. First edition, remarkable presentation copy with full page inscription from author to friend, Senator George McGovern, near fine in like dust jacket. Ed Smith Books 83 - 108 2015 $6500

Thompson, Isaac *A Collection of Poems, Occasionally writ on Several Subjects.* Newcastle upon Tyne: printed by John White for the author and sold by booksellers, 1731. First edition, 8vo., contemporary calf, spine gilt, red morocco label, some rubbing ends of spine neatly restored, slightly later signature of Miss Humphrey is at front, volume printed on thick paper and embellished with unusually wide range of woodcut ornaments, some light marginal inkstains to first few leaves, very good, scarce. C. R. Johnson Foxon R-Z - 980r-z 2015 $1149

Thompson, Isaac *Poetic Essays, on Nature, Men and Morals.* Newcastle upon Tyne: printed for R. Akenhead, Jun. and C. Hitch, 1750. First edition, 4to., sewn, recent stitching, half title present, very good. C. R. Johnson Foxon R-Z - 981r-z 2015 $1149

Thompson, Jane Smeal *Silvanus Phillips Thompson....His Life and Letters.* New York: E. P. Dutton, 1920. First edition, 8vo., 12 plates including frontispiece portrait with tissue guard, red cloth, blindstamped cover signature and gilt stamped spine title, tiny hole punch on front cover, else very good. Jeff Weber Rare Books 178 - 1063 2015 $45

Thompson, Jim *"The End of the Book." in American Stuff.* New York: Viking, 1937. First appearance of this story, spotting on top of page edges, otherwise fine in dust jacket with short closed tear and faint crease on inner front flap. Mordida Books March 2015 - 007981 2015 $650

Thompson, Jim *4 Novels.* London: Zomba, 1983. First edition, very fine in dust jacket. Mordida Books March 2015 - 008477 2015 $100

Thompson, Jim *The Getaway.* New York: NAL, 1959. First edition, Signet no. 1584, very good in wrappers. Mordida Books March 2015 - 007623 2015 $135

Thompson, Jim *The Killer Inside Me.* New York: Lion No. 99, 1952. First edition, paperback original, very good plus, tight and square, couple of very faint vertical creases (paper not broken) on front and rear panel, touch of wrinkle to spine, superior copy, from the collection of Duke Collier. Royal Books 36 - 238 2015 $1850

Thompson, Jim *The Killer Inside Me.* Cedar Rapids: Fedora, 1983. First edition, fine in soft covers with some slight rubbing. Mordida Books March 2015 - 007621 2015 $85

Thompson, Jim *The Killer Inside Me.* Los Angeles: Blood and Guts Press, 1991. First edition in hardcover, one of 26 lettered copies, this being letter U, signed by Stephen King who contributes introduction, fine , leather bound slipcase, from the collection of Duke Collier. Royal Books 36 - 239 2015 $650

Thompson, Jim *King Blood.* London: Sphere, 1973. First edition, paperback original, Sphere 7221-8480, light reading crease, lightly foxed on few prelim pages, yet still one of the nicest copies we've seen, very scarce. Buckingham Books March 2015 - 29366 2015 $385

Thompson, Jim *King Blood.* London: Sphere, 1973. First edition, short faint crease on back cover and on front cover, some light wear along edges, otherwise very good, no reading creases, wrappers, paperback original. Mordida Books March 2015 - 012600 2015 $85

Thompson, Jim *King Blood.* New York: Armchair Detective, 1993. First hardcover edition, one of 26 lettered copies, signed by author of introduction, James Ellroy, very fine in slipcase without dust jacket, as issued. Mordida Books March 2015 - 000001 2015 $100

Thompson, Jim *Nothing but a Man.* New York: Popular Library, 1970. First edition, fine, unread copy in pictorial wrappers, exceptional copy. Buckingham Books March 2015 - 37042 2015 $300

Thompson, Jim *Nothing More than Murder.* New York: Harper & Bros., 1949. First edition, fine in dust jacket with light professional internal restoration to spine ends and corners and some minor light rubbing to front fore-edge, attractive copy with no loss.   Buckingham Books   March 2015 - 23289   2015 $2500

Thompson, Jim *Wild Town.* New York: NAL, 1957. Paperback original, Signet no. 1461, faint crease along front cover spine edge, otherwise fine in wrappers.   Mordida Books   March 2015 - 009682   2015 $200

Thompson, John N. *Coevolutionary Process.* Chicago and London: University of Chicago Press, 1994. First printing, 8vo., photos, illustrations, figures, navy cloth, gilt stamped spine title, fine, rare in cloth.   Jeff Weber Rare Books   178 - 1062   2015 $90

Thompson, Kay *Eloise.* New York: Simon & Schuster, 1955. First edition, first printing, very good with light wear to extremities, minor toning to spine and board edges, foldout page (13-16), slightly loose at head, still firmly bound into text block, bright and clean pages, price clipped dust jacket with some wear and minor chipping to extremities, small chip to spine head, some rubbing to hinges, light toning to spine and rear panel, few light spots of minor soiling to otherwise bright panels.   B & B Rare Books, Ltd.   2015 - 2015 $1500

Thompson, Sydney *Lost April.* New York: Thomas Y. Crowell Co., 1938. First edition, octavo, 335 pages, lightly cocked with wear at spine ends abut near fine in scarce dust jacket with scattered swear, tape repaired tear and tiny chips at folds, very good, inscribed by author for Bertha, laid in is promotional flyer for book along with 3 pamphlets for Thomson's dramatic costumed recitals.   Between the Covers Rare Books, Inc.   187 - 275   2015 $350

Thompson, William *An Hymn to May.* London: printed and sold by R. Dodsley, T. Waller and M. Cooper, n.d., 1746. First edition, 33 pages, 4to., recent marbled boards, wanting half title, otherwise very good, from the library of H. Bradley Martin, uncommon.   C. R. Johnson   Foxon R-Z - 983r-z   2015 $230

Thompson, William *Poems on Several Occasions to which is added Gondibert and Birtha, a tragedy.* Oxford: printed at the Theatre, 1757. First edition, 8vo., contemporary calf, spine gilt, red morocco label, slight wear to spine, very good, bookplate of Oliver Brett, Viscount Esher.   C. R. Johnson   Foxon R-Z - 982r-z   2015 $383

Thompson, William *Sickness. A Poem in Three Books.* London: printed for R. Dodsley and sold by M. Cooper, 1745. First editions, parts 1 and 2 (part 3 missing, as frequently the case), very good, disbound, part I complete with half title.   C. R. Johnson   Foxon R-Z - 984r-z   2015 $192

Thomson, Andrew Mitchell *A Letter to the R-v-r-nd Pr-nc-p-l H-ll on Some of the Proceedings of the Lst G-en-r-al Assmbly of the Ch-rch of Sc-tl-nd.* Edinburgh: J. Pillans & Son for Guthrie & Tait, 1803. First edition, 8vo., 40 pages, recent marbled boards lettered on spine, scarce.   John Drury Rare Books   March 2015 - 24947   2015 $221

Thomson, Charles Poulett *Speech of C. P(oulett) Thomson, Esq. in the House of Commons on the 26th of March 1830 on Moving the Appointment of a Select committee to Inquire into the state of Taxation of the United Kigndom.* London: James Ridgway 169 Picadilly, 1830. First edition, 8vo., recent marbled boards lettered on spine, very good.   John Drury Rare Books   March 2015 - 24948   2015   £266

Thomson, Don W. *Men and Meridians the History of Surveying and Mapping in Canada.* Ottawa: Dept. of Mines and Technical Survey, 1966. 1967. 1969, 8vo., 3 volumes, black cloth, dust jackets, many maps, numerous photo illustrations, all volumes very good.   Schooner Books Ltd.   110 - 191   2015 $95

Thomson, H. Douglas *Masters of Mystery: a Study of the Detective Story.* London: Collins, 1931. First edition, 8vo., pages uncut, slight mottling and slight bumps at lower edge, covers very slightly bumped, spine slightly mottled, otherwise sound, near very good in very good- tape reinforced dust jacket, slightly creased and with some chip and nicks, short closed tears, front panel of jacket in good order showing a photo collage mixing.   Any Amount of Books   2015 - A99134   2015   £225

Thomson, H. Douglas *Sherlock Holmes.* London: Collins, 1931. First hardcover appearance in Masters of Mystery, covers soiled and lightly tattered, otherwise very good in fine later state dust jacket.   Mordida Books   March 2015 - 008056   2015 $85

Thomson, James 1700-1748 *Antient and Modern Italy Compared: being the First Part of Liberty a Poem. (bound with) Greece; being the second part of Liberty. A Poem. (bound with) Rome: being the third part of Liberty. A Poem. (bound with) Britain: being the fourth part of Liberty. A Poem. (bound with) The Prospect being the Fifth Part of Liberty. A Poem.* London: printed for A. Millar, 1735. 1735. 1735. 1736. 1736. First editions, 5 volumes in one, 4to., early 20th century half brown morocco and old marbled boards (some rubbing), complete set on fine paper, without price on titlepage, first part is reissue of the sheets of first edition with titlepage cancelled, not only removing price but adding as well a page of contents on verso, very good.   C. R. Johnson   Foxon R-Z - 991r-z   2015 $2298

Thomson, James 1700-1748 *Autumn.* London: printed by N. Blandford for J. Millan, 1730. Second edition, 8vo., disbound, very good.   C. R. Johnson   Foxon R-Z - 1001r-z   2015 $115

Thomson, James 1700-1748 *Britannia. A Poem.* London: printed for T. Warner, 1720. First edition, folio, 16 pages, recent boards, printed paper side label, uncommon folio, very good.   C. R. Johnson   Foxon R-Z - 987r-z   2015 $1149

Thomson, James 1700-1748 *Britannia.* London: printed for John Millan, 1730. Second edition, 16 pages, 4to., disbound, very good, large margins.   C. R. Johnson   Foxon R-Z - 988r-z   2015 $192

Thomson, James 1700-1748 *The Castle of Indolence; an Allegorical Poem.* London: printed for A. Millar, 1748. First edition, 4to., contemporary red morocco, wide gilt borders, spine and inner dentelles, gilt, all edges gilt, slight cracking of joints, in red cloth slipcase, fine, apparently a presentation copy to a member of the royal family, at front is armorial bookplate of William Henry, Duke of Gloucester, brother of George III, at back is armorial bookplate of William R. Frederick second Duke of Gloucester, later in the Britwell Court Library with shelfmark, bookplate of H. Bradley Martin.   C. R. Johnson   Foxon R-Z - 989r-z   2015 $2298

Thomson, James 1700-1748 *The Castle of Indolence; an Allegorical Poem.* London: printed for A. Millar, 1748. First edition, 4to., original pale blue wrappers, rather worn along spine, some fraying, short clean tear in margin of first two leaves, piece torn from blank upper margins of B2.   C. R. Johnson   Foxon R-Z - 990r-z   2015 $536

Thomson, James 1700-1748 *A Poem Sacred to the Memory of Sir Isaac Newton.* London: printed for J Millan, 1727. First edition, 15 pages, folio, old wrappers, faint stain to upper inner corners, slight signs of use, generally very good.   C. R. Johnson   Foxon R-Z - 994r-z   2015 $3831

Thomson, James 1700-1748 *A Poem Sacred to the Memory of Sir Isaac Newton.* London: printed for J. Millan, 1727. First edition, 15 pages, folio, full marbled calf gilt, spine and inner dentelles gilt, green morocco label, top edge gilt, copy on fine paper, with Strasburg bend watermark, as opposed to a circular snake in copies on ordinary paper, fine, 20th century bookplate designed by A. Airy lettered 'Newton' but otherwise unidentified.   C. R. Johnson   Foxon R-Z - 995r-z   2015 $5363

Thomson, James 1700-1748 *Poems on Several Occasions.* London: printed for A. Millar, 1750. First edition, 8vo., half calf, spine gilt, very uncommon, fine, complete with half title.   C. R. Johnson   Foxon R-Z - 985r-z   2015 $1379

Thomson, James 1700-1748 *The Seasons, a Hymn, a Poem to the Memory of Sir Isaac Newton and Britannia, a Poem.* London: printed for J. Millan and A. Millar, 1730. First collected edition, engraved frontispiece, 3 plates, 8vo., contemporary panelled calf, red morocco label (upper joint very slightly cracked but firm), signature on titlepage of J. Gibbon dated 1786.   C. R. Johnson   Foxon R-Z - 1002r-z   2015 $383

Thomson, James 1700-1748 *The Seasons.* London: printed for A. Millar, 1752. Second edition, 4 engraved plates and 2 leaves bookseller's ads at end, 12mo., contemporary speckled calf, spine gilt, red morocco label (slight wear to tip of spine), signature of J. Mordant dated 1752, who has inscribed an ode by Shenstone on front flyleaves, armorial bookplate of Sir John Mordaunt, Bart. of Walton in Warwickshire.   C. R. Johnson   Foxon R-Z - 1003r-z   2015 $153

Thomson, James 1700-1748 *Spring. A Poem.* London: printed and sold by A. Millar and G. Strahan, 1728. First edition, 8vo., recent marbled boards, fine, printed on heavy stock and without price on titlepage, copies on ordinary paper have price of 1s6d, very good, complete with half title and final leaf of proposals.   C. R. Johnson   Foxon R-Z - 1000r-z   2015 $919

Thomson, James 1700-1748 *Spring. A Poem.* London: printed and sold by A. Miller, G. Strahan, 1728. First edition, 8vo., recent unlettered half calf, signature of William Vaughan, dated March 18 1730, he has added a crude sketch of author.   C. R. Johnson   Foxon R-Z - 998r-z   2015 $383

Thomson, James 1834-1882 *Vane's Story, Weddah and Om-El-Bonain and Other Poems.* London: Reeves and Turner, 1881. First edition, large paper issue, original dark blue cloth with title and author gilt to spine, small stamp to half title "Dominican Fathers Edinburgh", near fine, scarce.   The Kelmscott Bookshop   11 - 55   2015 $275

Thomson, Joseph John *Recollections and Reflections.* London: G. Bell & Sons, 1936. First edition, 8vo., signed and dated by author Dec. 1936, laid in is short note from his wife, Rose Elisabeth Thomson on Trinity Lodge stationery dated Dec. 7 1936, also laid in is review of the book from the Sunday Times Dec. 6 1936, very good+ in very good dust jacket with edge chips and wear, foxing, soil, sun spine, scarce.   By the Book, L. C.   Special List 10 - 65   2015 $1000

Thomson, June *The Secret Files of Sherlock Holmes.* London: Constable, 1990. First edition, pages slightly darkened, otherwise fine in dust jacket.   Mordida Books   March 2015 - 007438   2015 $100

Thomson, Roddy *When I'm on the Table Saw at Work, I Grieve for You My Love.* London: Sadie Coles HQ, 1997. Number 29 of 50 copies, signed by Thomson and co-author Colin Lowe, printed in black ink on fine paper and housed in black paper covered box, titled in silver on front panel, fine. The Kelmscott Bookshop   11 - 56   2015 $350

Thomson, Ruth Plumly *Giant Horse of Oz.* Chicago: Reilly & Lee, 1928. First edition, first issue (H/G xxii), this copy has the 'r' in 'morning' page 116, line 1 in perfect type which H/G says may indicate the earliest copies, 12 color plates by J. R. Neill, nice, 8vo., rust cloth, pictorial paste-on, cover plate very slightly rubbed, else fine.   Aleph-bet Books, Inc.   109 - 41   2015 $800

Thomson, Thomas *The Case of the Right Honourable Thomas Winnington, Esq.* London: printed by T. Gardner and sold at his printing office, 1746. First and only edition, 8vo., 24 pages, half title, but without final errata leaf, recent plain wrappers, very good.   John Drury Rare Books   2015 - 19980   2015 $177

Thomson, Virgil *A Virgil Thomson Reader.* New York: Alfred A. Knopf, 1948. First edition, about very good without dust jacket, inscribed by author to critic Tim Page and Vanessa Page, 1986.   Between the Covers Rare Books, Inc.   187 - 191   2015 $450

Thomson, William Thomas *The Bank of England and the Bank Acts & the Currency.* Edinburgh and London: William Blackwood & Son, 1866. First edition, 8vo., 74 pages, 6 folding graphic charts highlighted in colors, contemporary half calf over marbled boards, spine gilt and labelled with raised bands, spine chipped at foot, upper joint worn and split but binding still sound, good, clean.   John Drury Rare Books   March 2015 - 25500   2015 $266

Thorburn, Grant *Forty Years' Residence in America or the Doctrine of a Particular Providence Exemplified in the Life of Grant Thorburn, Seedsman, NY.* Boston: Russell Odiorne & Metcalf, 1834. First edition, publisher's green pebble grain cloth with leather spine label gilt, 264 pages, ownership signature on titlepage of children's book author Susan Anne Livingston Ridley Sedgewick, light scattered foxing, nice, near fine, inscribed by author for Sedgewick.   Between the Covers Rare Books, Inc.   187 - 276   2015 $400

Thoreau, Henry David 1817-1862 *Men of Concord.* Boston: Houghton Mifflin, 1936. First edition, 4to., green cloth, very fine in dust jacket and pictorial box, box flaps faded, illustrations by N. C. Wyeth and Andrew Wyeth, exceptionally fine, rare in box.   Aleph-bet Books, Inc.   109 - 498   2015 $875

Thoreau, Henry David 1817-1862 *Some Unpublished Letters of Henry D. and Sophie E. Thoreau.* New York: Marion Press, 1899. First edition, number 78 of 150 numbered copies, uncommon, 8vo., contemporary red half morocco by Stikeman, marbled paper boards and matching endpapers, gilt rules and lettering, top edge gilt, others untrimmed, frontispiece and five plates, wear at edges neatly repaired, fine.   The Brick Row Book Shop   Miscellany 67 - 90   2015 $450

Thoreau, Henry David 1817-1862 *Walden or Life in the Wood.* Boston: Limited Editions Club, 1936. Limited to 1500 numbered copies signed by Edward Steichen, small 4to., quarter black cloth, paste paper covered boards, slipcase, paper spine label, fine photos by Steichen, Monthly Letter prospectus loosely inserted, slipcase shows light rubbing, much better preserved than most copies.   Oak Knoll Books   25 - 15   2015 $750

Thoreau, Henry David 1817-1862 *The Winged Life. The Poetic Voice of Henry David Thoreau.* Covelo: Yolla Bolly Press, 1986. One of 85 copies, all on Arches 88 paper, each hand numbered and signed by Robert Bly and Michael McCurdy, page size 10 x 14 inches, set in monotype Van Dijck and Caslon 471 at Mackenzie Harris Corp and at Yolla Bolly Press, handsewn oatmeal colored cloth over boards, with wood engraving by Michael McCurdy on front panel and title printed in black on spine, housed in publisher' slipcase, laid in is original subscriber's invoice, 7 wood engravings by Michael McCurdy, fine in slightly used slipcase.   Priscilla Juvelis - Rare Books   61 - 56   2015 $1250

Thornbury, George Walter *The Monarchs of the Main; or Adventures of the Buccaneers.* London: Hurst & Blackett, 1855. First edition, 3 volumes, final ad leaf volume III, uncut in early 20th century half red crushed morocco by P. B. Sanford, raised gilt bands, gilt compartments, slight wear to hinges, some slight marking, booklabels of J. B. Troy, Library labels and stamps from St. Charles College Library, Catonsville, attractive copy.   Jarndyce Antiquarian Booksellers   CCXI - 271   2015   £320

Thorndike, Lynn *The Sphere of Sacrobosco and Its Commentators.* Chicago: University of Chicago Press, 1949. First edition, 8vo., cloth, dust jacket quite worn, ink ownership signature of David Lindberg, fine.   Jeff Weber Rare Books   178 - 983   2015 $65

Thornton, George B. *Best Poems.* Orangeburg: the author, 1937. First edition, wrappers, 28 pages, fine but for fading library stamp on front wrapper.   Beasley Books   2013 - 2015 $300

Thorogood, Augustine H. *The Globe & Laurel. The Journal of the Royal Marines (Volume 37).* Great Britain: Royal Marines, 1929. 12 issues bound in one volume (Volume 37 Numbers 1-12, Jan. - Dec. 1929), photos, full blue cloth, gilt, spine titles, with gilt seal on front board, moderate rubbing to boards and light fading to spine, else fine, presented Sept. 21 1950 by US Marine Commander Augustine Thorogood to boxing champion Gene Tunney. Between the Covers Rare Books, Inc.   187 - 277   2015 $300

Thorp, William   *England's Liberties Undefended.*   Bristol: printed and published by J. M. Gutch, 1829. First edition, 8vo., 36 pages, title and final page bit dust soiled, stitched as issued, uncut, good, rare.   John Drury Rare Books   2015 - 19815   2015 $133

Thorpe, Joseph   *Early Days in the West, along the Missouri One Hundred Years Ago.*   Irving Gilmore, 1924. First edition thus, 9 x 6 inches, tan printed covers, 98 pages, including covers, lightly soiled and with bumps to corners of wrappers with rubbing and small splits to top and bottom of spine, very good.   Buckingham Books   March 2015 - 35965   2015 $250

Thoth: a Romance.   Edinburgh and London: William Blackwood & Sons, 1888. First edition, 8vo., original orange cloth, lettered gilt at spine, gilt decoration on front cover, lacks front endpaper with library label on front pastedown and abrasion from label removal, neat stamp on verso titlepage with ex-library attributes, slight rubbing and tanning at spine, slight wear to covers and spine ends, very good. Any Amount of Books   March 2015 - C6433   2015   £375

Three Erfurt Tales 1497-1498.   North Hills: Birds & Bull Press, 1962. Limited to 310 numbered copies, Small 8vo., cloth, woodblock cuts throughout, printed and bound by Morris using handmade Bird & Bull Paper.   Oak Knoll Books   306 - 140   2015 $325

Three Letters Addressed to a Friend in India by a Proprietor, Principally on the Subject of Importing Bengal Sugars into England.   printed for J. Debrett, 1793. First edition, folding table, first few leaves little spotted with slight damp stain in upper margins, 8vo, disbound, good.   Blackwell's Rare Books   B179 - 41   2015   £400

The Three Little Kittens.   New York: McLoughlin Bros., 1892. 4to., pictorial wrappers, fine, 6 full page chromolithographs and color covers plus 6 half page and one double page 2 color illustrations, most attractive.   Aleph-Bet Books, Inc.   108 - 298   2015 $300

Through Wonderland Yellowstone National Park.   N.P.: Northern Pacific RR, 1920. First edition thus, 4to., color wrappers, embossed frames, 69 pages, illustrations, good+ with moderate wear, bump to lower corner, bottom of spine worn, good+.   Baade Books of the West 2014 - 2015 $48

Thucydides   *Bellum Peloponnesiacum.*   Glasgow: in aedibus Academicis excudebant Robertus et Andreas Foulis, 1759. First Foulis edition, variant issue with Latin text at end, 5 of 8 blank leaves discarded, two gatherings in volume iii swopped, some light browning and occasional spotting, small ownership inscription of P. Francis in volume i, some light browning an occasional ownership inscription. Blackwell's Rare Books   B179 - 106   2015   £1800

Thucydides   *The History of the Peloponnesian War.* Oxford: printed by S. Collingwood, 1830. 1832. 1835. First Arnold edition, 11 engraved maps, half title of volume ii (the only one called for) present, frequent pencilled underlining and marginalia (mostly ticks but some more substantial notes, some erased), 3 volumes, 8vo., contemporary half navy blue calf, marbled boards, spines with five raised band, second and fourth compartments gilt lettered direct, rest infilled with pattern of rolls comprising swashes, leaves and dots, boards little scuffed, bookplate of Henry Stuttard over that of Richard Fort, very good.   Blackwell's Rare Books Greek & Latin Classics VI - 104   2015   £350

Thucydides   *History of the Peloponnesian War.*   Chelsea: printed at the Ashendene Press, 1930. One of 260 copies on paper (240 for sale) of a total edition of 280, folio, printed in black in Ptolemy type with three-line initials at beginning of each chapter and larger initials and opening line of each of the 8 books, designed by Graily Hewitt and printed in red, marginal chapter summaries also in red in Blado Italic type, printer's mark D printed in black, publisher's white pigskin by W. H. Smith Son, Ltd., spine lettered gilt with raised bands, all edges uncut, bit of light spotting to boards and endpapers, else excellent, housed in custom brown cloth slipcase.   Heritage Book Shop   Holiday 2014 - 4   2015 $4000

Thucydides   *Lexicon Thucydidaeum: a Dictionary in Greek and English...*   printed for G. B. Whittaker, 1824. Some light spotting, occasional marginal pencil marks and few terms added in same hand, 8vo., contemporary reversed calf, black morocco lettering piece, little bit soiled and rubbed, later ownership inscription, very good.   Blackwell's Rare Books   Greek & Latin Classics VI - 103   2015   £60

Thudichum, J. L. W.   *A Treatise on the Origin, Nature and Varities of Wine: Being a Complete Manual of Viticulture ...*   London: Macmillan, 1872. First edition, 8vo., original green cloth lettered gilt on spine and illustrated black on cover, spine toned and rubbed at hinges with some damp mottling at rear board, covers slightly soiled, corners rubbed, slight chips and nicks at spine ends, slight edgewear at endpapers, inner hinges slightly cracked, very slight foxing, otherwise sound, near very good with clean text.   Any Amount of Books   2015 - A97533   2015   £300

Thurber, James 1894-1961 *Many Moons.* St. Joseph: A. M. & R. W. Roe, 1958. 8vo., blue cloth with elaborate gold stamping in moon motif, fine in original acetate wrapper, illustrations by Philip Reed with 3 full page, 13 half page and 3 smaller beautiful color woodcuts.   Aleph-bet Books, Inc.   109 - 461   2015 $100

Thurber, James 1894-1961 *The Wonderful O.* New York: Simon & Schuster, 1957. Stated first edition, 8vo., cloth backed boards, minimal wear, very good+ in slightly worn dust jacket, illustrations by Simont.   Aleph-bet Books, Inc.   109 - 462   2015 $100

Thurman, Wallace *The Blacker the Berry.* New York: Macaulay, 1929. First edition, 8vo., some remnants of bookplate removal from rear endpaper, otherwise near fine, publisher's brown cloth stamped in black.   Second Life Books Inc.   190 - 205   2015 $900

Thurston, Joseph *Poems on Several Occasions.* London: printed by W. P. for Benj. Motte, 1729. First edition, 8vo., panelled calf antique, spine and inner dentelles gilt, brown morocco label, fine, rare title, bookplate of Oliver Brett, Viscount Esher.   C. R. Johnson   Foxon R-Z - 1006r-z   2015 $1915

Thurston, Joseph *The Toilette. In Three Books.* London: printed for Benj. Motte, 1730. First edition, engraved frontispiece, 8vo., disbound, frontispiece by Andrew Motte, very good.   C. R. Johnson   Foxon R-Z - 1008r-z   2015 $460

Thynne, Molly *The Case of Sir Adam Braid.* London: Thomas Nelson and Sons, 1930. First edition, near fine in beautiful art deco internally reinforced dust jacket.   Buckingham Books   March 2015 - 13330   2015 $275

Tickell, Thomas *An Epistle from a Lady in England to a Gentleman at Avignon.* London: printed for J. Tonson, 1717. First edition, folio, disbound, on fine paper, watermarked with a star, copies on ordinary paper have a TH watermark, very light dampstaining in part of lower margins, but very good, uncommon.   C. R. Johnson   Foxon R-Z - 1109r-z   2015 $1149

Tickell, Thomas *An Epistle from a Lady in England to a Gentleman at Avignon.* London: printed for J. Tonson, third edition, folio, recent boards, slight worming in the blank outer margins towards the end, otherwise very good.   C. R. Johnson   Foxon R-Z - 1010r-z   2015 $230

Tickell, Thomas *An Ode Inscrib'd to the right Honourable the Earl of Sunderland at Windsor.* London: printed for Jacob Tonson, 1720. First edition, folio, this copy on fine paper with fleur-de-lys watermark, copies on ordinary paper watermarked with script 'J', very good, complete with half title, very scarce.   C. R. Johnson   Foxon R-Z - 1013r-z   2015 $1149

Tickell, Thomas *An Ode on His Excellency the Earl Stanhope's Voyage to France.* London: engraved and sold by Clark & Pine; M. Henneking; G. Wildey and J. Garret, 1718. Folio, very good, engraved print neatly mounted on slightly larger sheet, one of two prints, presumably more or less simultaneous, in this format the verses have been engraved in double columns beneath large rectangular illustration containing, within an emblematic border, two views of Stanhope, one standing, the other on horseback.   C. R. Johnson   Foxon R-Z - 1014r-z   2015 $2298

Tickell, Thomas *On Her Majesty's re-building the Lodgings of the Black Prince and Henry V. at Queen's College Oxford.* London: printed for T. Tonson, 1733. First edition, 7 pages, folio, original marbled wrappers, (rectangular piece clipped from corner and back wrapper), scarce, slight soiling, very good.   C. R. Johnson   Foxon R-Z - 1015r-z   2015 $1379

Tickell, Thomas *A Poem to His Excellency the Lord Privy-Seal on the Prospect of Peace.* London: printed for J. Tonson, 1713. First edition, folio, recent wrappers, very good, scarce title.   C. R. Johnson   Foxon R-Z - 1017r-z   2015 $1149

Tickell, Thomas *The Scotch Prophecy, Being and Imitation of the Prophecy of Nereus From Horace Book I. Ode XV.* Dublin: printed and sold by Thomas Humes, 1716. First Dublin edition, good, 4to. 4 pages, all editions are rare.   C. R. Johnson   Foxon R-Z - 1012r-z   2015 $996

The Tickler; or Monthly Compendium of Good Things in Prose and Verse. London: printed by J. White, 1818-1819. First edition, issues 1-13, lacking no. 4, wrappers, generally very good, original printed brown wrappers, although volume 1 no. 1 is somewhat worn at edges and slightly soiled.   Any Amount of Books   2015 - A47495   2015   £180

Tickner, Lisa *The Spectacle of Women. Imagery of the Suffrage Campaign 1907-1914.* Chicago: University of Chicago Press, 1988. First edition, large 8vo., illustrations, some in color, fine copy, dust jacket.   Second Life Books Inc.   189 - 254   2015 $85

Tidcombe, Marianne *Bookbinding of T. J. Cobden-Sanderson a Study of His work 1884-1893 Based on His Time Book.* London: British Library, 1984. First edition, 4to., cloth, spine slightly faded, slipcase, some minor wear along edges of slipcase, 200 black and white photos, color frontispiece.   Oak Knoll Books   306 - 12   2015 $125

Tidcombe, Marianne *Twenty-Five Gold-Tooled Bookbindings. An International Tribute to Bernard C. Middleton's Recollections.* New Castle: Oak Knoll Press, 1997. Limited to 200 copies, 8vo., cloth, paper cover label.   Oak Knoll Books   306 - 11   2015 $150

Tiercy, Georges *"Un Astronome Artiste-Opticien: Emile Schaer 1862-1931."* in Publications de l'Obswervatoire de Geneve, Serie A. Astronome, Chronomente Geophysique. Geneve: Albert Kundig, 1928-1933. One of 24 issues bound in one volume, 8vo., plates, tables, dark blue green library buckram, gilt stamped spine title, very good. Jeff Weber Rare Books   178 - 987   2015 $125

Tierney, George *Two Letters addressed to the right Hon. Henry Dundas and the Hon. Henry Hobart on the conduct Adopted Respecting the Colchester Petition.* London: J. Debrett, 1791. Only edition, 4to., half title and final blank, outer leaves dust marked, good, uncut, sewn as issued, very rare.   John Drury Rare Books   March 2015 - 14146   2015   £306

Tileston, Mary W. *The Children's Book of Ballads.* Boston: Little Brown, 1883. Early 20th century reprint, very good, spine wear, red cloth stamped in gilt, gray and tan. Beasley Books   2013 - 2015 $45

Tillotson, F. H. *How to Be a Detective.* Hailman Printing Co., 1909. First edition, 16mo., original maroon cloth, titles in white on front cover, decorated endpapers, numerous illustrations from photos, scarce, very good, clean, square copy.   Buckingham Books   March 2015 - 34211   2015 $450

Tillotson, Geoffrey *Augustan Studies.* London: University of London, Athlone Press, 1961. Half title, original black cloth, paper label, very good in slightly torn and creased dust jacket, author's initialled working copy with few notes, insertions.   Jarndyce Antiquarian Booksellers   CCVII - 509   2015   £35

Tillotson, Geoffrey *Criticism and the Nineteenth Century.* London: University of London, Athlone Press, 1951. Half title, original red cloth, spine slightly faded, slightly torn dust jacket, author's copy with photo portrait, few notes, large amount of inserted correspondence.   Jarndyce Antiquarian Booksellers   CCVII - 516   2015   £85

Tillotson, Geoffrey *Criticism and the Nineteenth Century.* Hamden: Archon Books, 1967. Half title, original dark blue cloth, very good in slightly marked dust jacket, author's signed copy.   Jarndyce Antiquarian Booksellers   CCVII - 518   2015   £20

Tillotson, Geoffrey *Essays in Criticism and Research.* Cambridge: University Press, 1942. Half title, original red cloth, paper label, dulled and marked, author's inscription for wife Kathleen, dedication copy, ink corrections, insertions, few ink notes, ALS to Kathleen from Mary Lascelles 1937. Jarndyce Antiquarian Booksellers   CCVII - 520   2015   £50

Tillotson, Geoffrey *Essays in Criticism and Research.* Hamden: Archon Books, 1967. Half title, original dark blue cloth, very good in slightly torn dust jacket, author's signed copy with inserted correspondence about permission to repair, with TLS.   Jarndyce Antiquarian Booksellers   CCVII - 522   2015   £35

Tillotson, Geoffrey *Mid-Victorian Studies.* London: Clarendon Press, 1965. Half title, original black cloth, pink paper label, very good in torn and dusted dust jacket, author's signed copy with few notes and insertions, note by co-author Kathleen on wrapper.   Jarndyce Antiquarian Booksellers   CCVII - 529   2015   £20

Tillotson, Geoffrey *On the Poetry of Pope.* Oxford: Clarendon Press, 1938. First edition, half title, original dark blue cloth, paper label slightly marked, inscribed by author for Kathleen Tillotson, with note by Kathleen?, preserved with this is copy made up of page proofs stamped 3 Sep. 1937 with typical GT colored paper casing.   Jarndyce Antiquarian Booksellers   CCVII - 433   2015   £120

Tillotson, Geoffrey *On the Poetry of Pope.* Oxford: Clarendon Press, 1950. Second edition, half title, original dark blue cloth paper label, 2 copies of dust jacket, signed by author, with publisher history by Kathleen on endpaper, inserted related correspondence and notes, from the library of Geoffrey & Kathleen Tillotson.   Jarndyce Antiquarian Booksellers   CCVII - 434   2015   £20

Tillotson, Geoffrey *Pope and Human Nature.* Oxford: Clarendon Press, 1958. Half title, original dark blue cloth, paper label, very good in dust jacket, inscribed to wife Kathleen.   Jarndyce Antiquarian Booksellers   CCVII - 436   2015   £20

Tillotson, Geoffrey *Pope and Human Nature.* Oxford: Clarendon Press, 1958. Half title, original dark blue cloth, paper label, author's signed copy with few notes and insertions.   Jarndyce Antiquarian Booksellers   CCVII - 437   2015   £25

Tillotson, Geoffrey *Pope and Human Nature.* Oxford: Clarendon Press, 1966. Reprint, half title, original dark blue cloth, paper label, very good in dusted dust jacket, author's signed copy with inserted note.   Jarndyce Antiquarian Booksellers   CCVII - 438   2015   £25

Tillotson, Geoffrey *Thackeray: the Critical Heritage.* London: Routledge and Kegan Paul, 1968. Half title, original blue cloth, very good in slightly torn dust jacket, author's copy with notes and correspondence inserted and review cuttings.   Jarndyce Antiquarian Booksellers   CCVII - 507   2015   £40

Tillotson, Geoffrey *Thackeray the Novelist.* Cambridge: at the University Press, 1954. Unbound copy in Geoffrey's decorated paper wrappers, his working copy for new edition with marginal notes and inserted notes and correspondence. Jarndyce Antiquarian Booksellers   CCVII - 503   2015   £30

Tillotson, Geoffrey *Thackeray the Novelist.* Cambridge: at the University Press, 1954. Half title, plate, original yellow cloth in slightly torn and dusted dust jacket, from the library of Geoffrey & Kathleen Tillotson, his presentation to her with page of her notes inserted.   Jarndyce Antiquarian Booksellers   CCVII - 502   2015   £20

Tillotson, Geoffrey   *A View of Victorian Literature.* Oxford: Clarendon Press, 1978. Half title, original red cloth, very good in dust jacket, complimentary copy.   Jarndyce Antiquarian Booksellers   CCVII - 528   2015   £20

Tillotson, Kathleen   *'Haworth Churchyard" the Making of Arnold's Elegy.* N.P.: 1967. 20 pages, stabbed as issued, little discolored, marked and creased, two corrections by author.   Jarndyce Antiquarian Booksellers   CCVII - 74   2015   £20

Tillotson, Kathleen   *Matthew Arnold and Carlyle.* Oxford University Press, 1956. Original grey wrappers, slightly dusted and creased, ms. notes by author.   Jarndyce Antiquarian Booksellers   CCVII - 75   2015   £25

Tillotson, Kathleen   *Novels of the Eighteen-Forties.* Oxford: Clarendon Press, 1971. Reprint, half title, original blue cloth, near mint, dust jacket.   Jarndyce Antiquarian Booksellers CCVII - 537   2015   £20

Tillyard, E. M. W.   *The Personal Heresy: a Controversy.* London: Oxford University Press, 1939. Half title, from the library of Geoffrey & Kathleen Tillotson, very good in slightly torn dust jacket, Geoffrey Tillotson's signed copy with few notes, and proof of his review, Kathleen' special marker.   Jarndyce Antiquarian Booksellers   CCVII - 538   2015   £30

Tilton, Alice   *The Hollow Chest.* New York: Norton, 1941. First edition, name on front endpaper, else near fine in dust jacket with lightly frayed spine ends and wear along folds.   Mordida Books   March 2015 - 007255   2015 $165

Timkowski, George   *Travels of the Russian Mission through Mongolia to China: and Residence in Peking in the Years 1820-1821.* London: Longman, Rees Orme, Brown and Green, 1827. First English edition, 2 volumes, large 8vo., 2 engraved plates, folding map, soundly bound in half red leather, lettered gilt at spine and five raised bands, bookplate, some light spotting to maps, plates and adjacent leaves, few edges dust soiled to prelims of second volume, else very good, large copy, uncommon.   Any Amount of Books   2015 - 7950   2015   £1050

Timmins, Henry Thornhill   *Nooks and Corners of Shropshire.* London: Elliot Stock, 62 Paternoster Row, 1899. First edition, royal 8vo., frontispiece, 25 plates, numerous text illustrations, original burgundy cloth, upper cover with inlaid illustration on linen, spine and upper cover lettered in gilt.   Marlborough Rare Books   List 53 - 47   2015   £35

Timmons, Wilbert H.   *Morelos of Mexico: Priest, Soldier, Statesman.* Texas Western College Press, 1963. First edition, limited to 500 copies, Peso edition, presentation inscription dated 2 28 92 from author, two-tone cloth, maps on front and rear endpapers, illustrations, fine in lightly rubbed dust jacket with light edge wear, housed in matching cloth slipcase.   Buckingham Books   March 2015 - 33453   2015 $300

Timner, W. E.   *Ellingtonia. The Recorded Music of Duke Ellington.* Metuchen: Inst. Jazz St./Scarecrow, 1988. First edition, 4to., fine, hardcover, issued without dust jacket.   Beasley Books   2013 - 2015 $45

Tindall, William York   *James Joyce: His Way of Interpreting the Modern World.* New York: Charles Scribner's Sons, 1950. First edition, octavo, original blue cloth, original dust jacket, warmly inscribed to Dylan Thomas.   Honey & Wax Booksellers   2 - 49   2015 $450

Ting, Joseph   *The Art of Xu Beihong.* Hong Kong: Urban Council, 1988. First edition, 4to., original brown boards lettered black on spine and cover with color portrait onset to cover, copiously illustrated in color and black and white, covers very slightly bumped, otherwise fine, exceptional condition.   Any Amount of Books   2015 - C612   2015   £160

Tinker, Edward Larocque   *The Horsemen of the Americas and the Literature they Inspired.* Hastings House Publishers, 1953. First US edition, limited to 1575 numbered copies, however this copy unnumbered, quarto, decorated boards, color frontispiece, fine, bright, tight copy in fine dust jacket.   Buckingham Books   March 2015 - 23886   2015 $175

Tinling, Christine I.   *About Our Country: Lessons on Prohibiton for the Loyal Temperance Legion.* Evanston: National Woman's Christian Temerpance Union, 1914. Original printed paper wrappers, very good, this the copy of Etta Sadler Shaw of Grand Rapids Michigan with her pencil signature.   Tavistock Books   Temperance - 2015 $60

Tinney, John Pern   *A Letter to the Viscount Folkestone; on the Unlawfulness of the Votes of Thanks to Mr. Wardle and the Late Minority.* London: C. and R. Baldwin and for Brodie and Co. Salisbury, 1809. First edition, apparently very scarce, 8vo., later marbled card covers, very good.   John Drury Rare Books   2015 - 14751   2015 $80

Tip and Top on the Farm. London: Bancroft, 1961. Large square 4to., flexible pictorial card covers, light tip and edge rubbing, else near fine, 6 double page pop-up pages which also have moveable tab operated parts, illustrations in color by Kubasta.   Aleph-bet Books, Inc.   109 - 374   2015 $450

Tiphaigne De La Roche, Charles Francois *Giphantia: or a view of what has passed, what is now passing, and during the present century will pass, in the world.* London: Robert Horsfield, 1761. First edition in English, 2 parts in one volume, 8vo., first title printed in red and black, including final ad leaf, contemporary calf, neatly rebacked, gilt in compartments, raised bands and label, very good, crisp copy.   John Drury Rare Books   2015 - 25544   2015 $2622

Tiraboschi, Girolamo *Storia della Letteratura Italiana.* Roma: Luigi Perego Salvioni, 1782. 4to., full leather, gilt decorated spine, five raised bands, all edges stained red, covers rubbed and scuffed, damage to lower right corner of front cover, insect damage to front free endpaper with foxing.   Oak Knoll Books   306 - 306   2015 $200

The Tit-Bit. A Tale. London: printed for T. Cooper, 1738. First edition, folio, recent boards, rare, lower portion of titlepage bit dust soiled, lower margins in trimmed just trifle short, otherwise good.   C. R. Johnson   Foxon R-Z - 1018r-z   2015 $2298

Tit for Tat. Or an Answer to the Epistle to a Nobleman. London: printed for T. Cooper, 1734. First edition, 8 pages, folio, disbound, very good, very scarce.   C. R. Johnson   Foxon R-Z - 1019r-z   2015 $1149

Titon, Jeff *Early Downhome Blues.* Urbana: University of Illinois Press, 1977. First edition, small 4to., fine in very lightly used dust jacket, with flexible disc laid in at rear, as issued.   Beasley Books   2013 - 2015 $45

Titon, Jeff *From Blues to Pop. The Autobiography of Leonard 'Baby Doo' Caston.* Los Angeles: JEMF, 1974. First edition, wrappers, photos, near fine.   Beasley Books   2013 - 2015 $45

To Mr. S-------- M-----, on his Turning Evidence. London: i.e. Edinburgh: printed for T. Cooper, 1747. First edition, 8vo., 4 pages, disbound, very good, uncommon.   C. R. Johnson   Foxon R-Z - 1020r-z   2015 $766

To the Inhabitants of Scotland. The Following Resolutions Which Appeared in the name of a Very Respectable Body of Citizens, the merchants of Leith, Have Received Much Apporbation in Different Parts of the Country. Edinburgh: 1791. Only printing, apparently very rare, 8vo., large uncut copy, two minute holes in second leaf, some marginal fraying and closed tear at head but with no loss of text, unbound and folded as issued, very rare.   John Drury Rare Books   March 2015 - 18957   2015 $266

To the Praise and Glory of R W. N.P.: London, n.d., 1732. First edition, 4to., very good.   C. R. Johnson   Foxon R-Z - 1021r-z   2015 $689

The Toasts of the Rump-Steak Club. London: printed and sold by booksellers of London and Westminster, 1734. First edition, 8 pages, folio, titlepage trifle dusty where once folded, but very good.   C. R. Johnson   Foxon R-Z - 1023r-z   2015 $689

Tobacco a Poem. N.P.: London, n.d., 1733. First edition, 2 pages, folio, single sheet printed on both sides, cloth folding case, blank side margins largely clipped away not affecting text, some dust soiling and signs of prior folding, otherwise sound.   C. R. Johnson   Foxon R-Z - 1024r-z   2015 $7661

Tobin, Agnes *Love's Crucifix: Nine Sonnets and a Canzone from Petrarch.* London: Heinemann, 1902. First edition, 8vo., original illustrated parchment covers, pages 32 (unpaginated) 10 plates and 10 pictorial initials by Graham Robertson, ties mostly lacking spine chipped with loss at head (2 inches) and tail (one inch), covers slightly browned, very good- with clean text.   Any Amount of Books   2015 - A02--1   2015   £180

Tocqueville, Alexis Charles Henri Maurice Clerel De 1805-1859 *Democracy in America.* London: 1835. First edition in English, 2 volumes, folding map, rebound in serviceable cloth and paper over boards, map and four inch tear but no loss, text block with slight edge browning, else clean and very good.   Dumont Maps and Books of the West   130 - 47   2015 $2750

Tocqueville, Alexis Charles Henri Maurice Clerel De 1805-1859 *De La Democratie en Amerique... Tome Premier (-Cinquieme).* Bruxelles: Meline, Cans et Compagnie, 1840. 16mo., with all five half titles, contemporary cloth backed green boards (scuffed), very sound, folding hand colored lithographic map bound in at end of fifth volume, title with European library stamps, spine with old orange and blue paper reinforcements, sound.   M & S Rare Books, Inc.   97 - 301   2015 $6500

Todd, Charles *A Test of Wills.* New York: St. Martin's, 1996. First edition, fine in dust jacket with closed tear on back panel.   Mordida Books   March 2015 - 007256   2015 $100

Todhunter, Isaac *A History of the Mathematical Theories of Attraction and the Figure of the Earth from the Time Of Newton to that of La Place.* New York: Dover, 1962. Reprint of 1873 Macmillan edition, 8vo., 2 volumes in 1, blue cloth, gilt stamped spine title, dust jacket rubbed, else fine, Dirk Bromer's copy (recipient of Bruce Medal in 1966).   Jeff Weber Rare Books   178 - 1072   2015 $135

Toibin, Colm *The Street.* Dublin: Tuskar Rock Press, 2010. Limited edition, copy 17 of 50 roman-numeraled copies bound in full leather and signed by author, fine in fine cloth slipcase. Ken Lopez, Bookseller 164 - 209 2015 $500

Tolbert, Mildred *Patroncinio Barela Taos Wood Carver.* Taos: 1955. True first edition, 65 pages, illustrations, comb binding, card stock illustrated covers, wear and soil to covers, internally very good, scarce. Dumont Maps and Books of the West 130 - 48 2015 $100

Tolkien, John Ronald Reuel 1892-1973 *The Hobbit or There and Back Again.* London: George Allen and Unwin, 1976. Deluxe edition, first printing, publisher's cloth, with illustrations in gilt, silver and red to front board, spine lettered and ruled in gilt, light blue spotted edges, black and white marbled endpapers, book fine with only faint hint of light rubbing to front board, otherwise bright binding, fresh interior, beautiful copy, housed in publisher's black clamshell box, white paper label lettered in red and black to top panel with some wear to extremities, bottom corners somewhat split but sturdy, few light spots of minor soiling, else fine. B & B Rare Books, Ltd. 2015 - 2015 $400

Tolkien, John Ronald Reuel 1892-1973 *The Hobbit or There and Back Again.* New York: Abrams, 1997. First edition, illustrations, oblong 4to., near fine in fine printed acetate dust jacket. Beasley Books 2013 - 2015 $125

Tolkien, John Ronald Reuel 1892-1973 *The Lord of the Rings: The Fellowship of the Ring, The Two Towers, The Return of the King.* London: George Allen and Unwin, 1954-1955. First editions, first printings, with terminal fold-out maps, near fine, unclipped dust jacket, with some light wear and few nicks to extremities, few faint spots to panels, light rubbing to hinges, Fellowship with some discreet internal archival repairs to spine ends and heads of flap folds and some rubbing to spine, Two Towers with short clip to spine tail and hint of toning, Return with some rubbing to spine, overall a tight and pleasing set, housed in custom clamshell box. B & B Rare Books, Ltd. 2015 - 2015 $17,500

Tolkien, John Ronald Reuel 1892-1973 *The Lord of the Rings.* London: George Allen and Unwin, 1969. Deluxe one volume edition, first printing, publisher's black cloth, with illustrations to front board, spine lettered gilt, light blue speckled edges, marbled endpapers with both of Tolkien's fold-out pictorial maps bound in, printed on India paper, about near fine with light wear to extremities, bright gilt minor nick to spine tail, light rubbing to board edges, bright interior, clean and pleasing, housed in publisher's black slipcase with some light wear to extremities, else fine. B & B Rare Books, Ltd. 2015 - 2015 $800

Toller, Ernest *Masse mensch. Ein Stock Aus Der Sozialen Revolution Des 20 Jahrhunderts.* Potsdam: Gustav Kiepenheuer Ver, 1921. First edition, red paper covered boards with vellum backstrip, very good+. Beasley Books 2013 - 2015 $45

Tolson, Francis *Hermathenae, or Moral Emblems and Ethnick Tales.* N.P.: (London), n.d., 1740. First edition, 8vo., full speckled calf antique, gilt, gilt spine, red morocco label, with 6 page list of subscribers, fine. C. R. Johnson Foxon R-Z - 1025r-z 2015 $1149

Tolstoi, Lev Nikolaevich 1828-1910 *Anna Karenina.* New York: Limited Editions Club, 1933. Limited to 1500 numbered copies, signed by artist, Nikolas Piskariov, 2 volumes, wood engravings, small 4to., light brown cloth stamped in gilt brown leather spine labels, tops stained yellow, slipcase worn with hinge at top cracked and part of spine of slipcase missing at ends, spines of books show some toning and rubbing at bottoms, with monthly letter loosely inserted. Oak Knoll Books 25 - 11 2015 $250

Tolstoi, Lev Nikolaevich 1828-1910 *War and Peace.* New York: Limited Editions Club, 1938. Limited to 1500 numbered copies, signed and finger printed by artist, Barnett Freedman, 8vo. 6 volumes, pictorial cloth, enclosed in two slipcases, this is number 1500, color illustrations, spine labels of slipcases foxed, minor rubbing of spine ends of books. Oak Knoll Books 25 - 22 2015 $400

Tolstoi, Lev Nikolaevich 1828-1910 *Works of Leo Tolstoy.* London: William Heinemann, 1901-1904. Library edition, 6 octavo volumes, original green cloth gilt, 2 frontispiece portraits of Tolstoy, bright, near fine. Honey & Wax Booksellers 3 - 20 2015 $2200

Tom Mix Western Songs. M. M. Cole, 1935. First edition, quarto, pictorial wrappers, 64 pages, photos, former owner name inked top edge front inside cover, spine reinforced with cloth by former owner, tiny bit of minor rubbing to front cover fore-edge, else well preserved, very good. Buckingham Books March 2015 - 372686 2015 $200

Tom Tearabout. New York: McLoughlin Bros. circa, 1880. 5 x 6 inches, pictorial wrappers, fine, 8 half page full color lithos. Aleph-bet Books, Inc. 109 - 227 2015 $200

Tom Thumb. New York: McLoughlin Bros., 1888. 8vo., pictorial wrappers, fine, 6 full page chromolithographs and pictorial covers by R. Andre. Aleph-Bet Books, Inc. 108 - 288 2015 $275

Tombaugh, Clyde W. *Out of the Darkness: the Planet Pluto.* Harrisburg: Stackpole Books, 1980. First edition, signed by Tombaugh, fine, blue cloth effect boards lettered silver. Any Amount of Books 2015 - C13998 2015 £250

Townsend, Charles Wendell *A Labrador Spring.* Boston: Dana Estes Co., 1910. 8vo., pictorial cloth, white and green illustration on front cover, frontispiece and 55 black and white illustrations, edges worn and spine lightly soiled, corners bumped and inner spine cracks. Schooner Books Ltd. 110 - 48 2015 $40

Townsend, H. C. *Statistics and Information Concerning the State of Nebraska, Taken from State and National Reports...* St. Louis: Woodward & Tiernan Printing Co., n.d. circa, 1892. Second edition, 12mo., stiff printed wrappers, bound into quarter cloth and boards binder, 64 pages, illustrations, map, rare, large folded map of Nebraska affixed to rear cover in fine condition. Buckingham Books March 2015 - 2829 2015 $675

Townsend, William C. *Modern State Trials.* London: Longman, Brown, Green and Longmans, 1850. 2 volumes, 8vo., numerous ad leaves bound in, one or two signatures beginning to spring, original blindstamped maroon cloth, spines gilt lettered, slight wear to headband volume II, good, untrimmed copy. John Drury Rare Books 2015 - 24119 2015 $89

Toy Boats 1870-1955. A Pictorial History. New York: Scribner's, 1979. First edition, oblong small 4to., fine in fine dust jacket. Beasley Books 2013 - 2015 $45

Tracy, Clarence *Browning's Mind and Art...* Edinburgh: Oliver & Boyd, 1968. Half title, original dark blue cloth, very good in slightly spotted dust jacket, Geoffrey Tillotson's signed copy with TLS from editor, Tracy and 3 notes from Park Honan inserted. Jarndyce Antiquarian Booksellers CCVII - 122 2015 £20

Tracy, Louis *The Albert Gate Mystery.* New York: Fenno, 1904. First American edition, name stamp and address on front pastedown, otherwise near fine in red pictorial cloth covered boards with gold stamped titles. Mordida Books March 2015 - 002194 2015 $100

Tracy, Louis *The Manning-Burke Murder.* New York: Clode, 1930. First edition, covers and spine heavily spotted, otherwise very good in very fine, as new dust jacket. Mordida Books March 2015 - 003169 2015 $90

Trade to the East Indies. Please to read This Paper Through. Manchester: Henry Smith, printer but circa, 1823. 4to., (4) pages, final page blank, very minor dust-marking, two contemporary pen amendments in ink, folded, presumably for posting, unbound as issued, possibly rare. John Drury Rare Books March 2015 - 18956 2015 $221

The Trade with France, Italy, Spain and Portugal Considered with Some Observations on the Treaty of Commerce Between Great Britain and France. London: J. Baker, 1713. 8vo., fine, crisp copy, rebound in linen backed marbled boards, spine lettered on paper label. John Drury Rare Books 2015 - 14633 2015 $221

Traherne, Thomas *Joys. Passages from the Works.* Llandogo: Old Stile Press, 2003. 92/200 copies (from an edition of 226 copies), signed by artist, 9 wood engravings printed in dark blue, 5 woodcuts printed in burnt sienna with linocut borders in sage, text printed in brown, small 4to., original quarter terracotta cloth with patterned boards, backstrip lettered in silver, beige cloth slipcase with large inset illustration in sage, fine. Blackwell's Rare Books B179 - 215 2015 £120

Train, Arthur *Tut, Tut! Mr. Tutt.* New York: Scribner, 1923. First edition, near fine in very good heavily chipped and internally mended dust jacket with 2 inch piece missing at base of spine, inscribed by author. Mordida Books March 2015 - 009989 2015 $175

Transatlantic Review 16. London: Transatlantic Review, 1964. Signed by Paul Bowles at his contribution (translation of "The Oven" by Charhadi), titlepage detached and laid in, sunning to spine, good in wrappers. Ken Lopez, Bookseller 164 - 17 2015 $125

Transon, Abel *Religion Saint-Simonienne. Predication du 11 Decembre vue Generale sur la Nouveau Caractere du l'Apostolat Saint-Simonnien. Morale Individuelle. Allocution Prononcee Arpes la Predication.* Paris: au Bureau du Globe, 1832. First edition, 8vo., 20 pages, with final conjugate blank, stitched as issued, uncut and unopened, very good, rare. John Drury Rare Books March 2015 - 13614 2015 £306

Transportation. Tel Aviv: B(inyamin) Barlevy, n. d. circa, 1945. 8vo., pictorial boards, some toning, very good+, each panel features a different type of transportation, text in Hebrew under each picture, color lithographs, scarce. Aleph-Bet Books, Inc. 108 - 252 2015 $400

Trapp, Joseph *Peace a Poem. inscribed to Rt. Hon. Lord Viscount Bolingbroke.* London: printed for John Barber and Henry Clements, 1713. First edition, folio, recent stiff wrappers, very good. C. R. Johnson Foxon R-Z - 1032r-z 2015 $766

Trapp, Joseph *Peace. A Poem. inscribed to Rt. Hon. Lord Viscount Bolingbroke.* London: printed for J. Barber and H. Clements, 1713. Second edition, 8vo., disbound, fine, complete with half title. C. R. Johnson Foxon R-Z - 1033r-z 2015 $306

Trapp, Joseph *Thoughts Upon the Four Last Things; Death; Judgment; Heaven; Hell.* London: printed by J. Wright, 1735. First edition of parts II-IV, folio, recent unlettered half calf and marbled boards, lower margins trimmed trifle close, affecting two type ornaments and few catchwords, otherwise good.   C. R. Johnson   Foxon R-Z - 1034r-z   2015 $613

Trapp, Joseph *Thoughts Upon the Four Last Things: Death, Judgment, Heaven, Hell.* London: printed by J. Wright for Lawton Gilliver, 1735. First edition of parts II-IV, folio, disbound, very good.   C. R. Johnson   Foxon R-Z - 1035r-z   2015 $766

Trapp, Joseph *Thoughts Upon the Four Last Things: Death: Judgment: Heaven and Hell.* London: printed for W. Russel, 1745. Second edition, small 8vo., contemporary calf, gilt, rebacked, covers rubbed, rare, very good.   C. R. Johnson   Foxon R-Z - 1036r-z   2015 $306

Trask, George *Letters on Tobacco for American Lads; or Uncle Toby's Anti-Tobacco advice to His Nephew Billy Bruce.* Fitchburg: Published by author, 1860. 12mo., original printed yellow paper wrappers, bit of wear to corners, some mild loss to bottom corner of final leaf, wrappers bit toned, faint stain to front panel and closed tear to bottom rear joint, else very good. Tavistock Books   Temperance -   2015 $40

Trask, George *Letters on Tobacco for American Lads...* Geo. Trask, 1860. First edition, 12mo., original cloth, gold stamping on front cover, frontispiece, illustrations, former owner's name on front flyleaf, few pages lightly soiled, else very good, clean copy.   Buckingham Books March 2015 - 29741   2015 $250

Travaglia, Pinella *Magic, Causality and Intentionality.* Sismel: Edizioni del Galluzzo, 1990. Small 8vo., printed wrappers, fine, very scarce, ink ownership signature of David Lindberg.   Jeff Weber Rare Books   178 - 1074   2015 $45

Traver, Robert *Anatomy of a Murder.* New York: St. Martins, 1958. First edition, couple of tiny spots on foreedge, still fine in near fine dust jacket with few short tears, uncommon in this condition from the library of Kate Stettner Lobell and Carl D. Lobell.   Between the Covers Rare Books   196 - 50   2015 $750

Travers, Henry *Miscellaneous Poems and Translations.* London: printed for Benj. Motte, 1731. First edition, 8vo., contemporary mottled calf, gilt, spine gilt, some wear, very good.   C. R. Johnson   Foxon R-Z - 1037r-z   2015 $919

Travers, Henry *Miscellaneous Poems and Translations.* York: printed by C. Ward and R. Chandler, 1740. Second edition, 8vo., contemporary panelled calf, rubbed, some wear to corners, wanting a flyleaf at front, some soiling and signs of use throughout but sound copy, scarce, complete with half title.   C. R. Johnson   Foxon R-Z - 1038r-z   2015 $689

Travers, P. L. *Ah Wong.* New York: High Grade Press, 1943. First edition, 12mo., 23 pages, stapled and printed pale blue wrappers, copy #386 of 500 numbered copies signed by author, modest offsetting on limitation page from a clipping of Travers with young children, little soiling on wrappers, very good or better.   Between the Covers Rare Books   196 - 118   2015 $150

Treat, Lawrence *Pictorial Mysteries.* New York: Beach, n.d. but apparently early 1930's, with 5 pads of different solve them yourself picture mysteries, pads slightly darkened, otherwise fine, descriptive wraparound band present. Mordida Books   March 2015 - 009188   2015 $250

Tredgold, Thomas *Elementary Principles of Carpentry; a Treatise on the Pressure and Equilibrium of Timber Framing the Resistence of Timber and Construction of Floors, Roofs, Centres, Bridges.* London: J. Taylor, 1828. Second edition, 4to., 22 engraved plates, contemporary calf backed boards, rubbed at extremities, front hinge beginning to crack, plates moderate foxed, good, signature of Isaac Trimble, Maryland engineer and Civil War general.   Joseph J. Felcone Inc.   Science, Medicine and Technology - 6   2015 $400

Tree, Gregory *The Case Against Butterfly.* New York: Scribners, 1951. First edition, slight darkening on endpapers, small date on rear pastedown, otherwise fine in dust jacket.   Mordida Books   March 2015 - 003011   2015 $85

Trehern, Gaspard *The Old Ecstasies: a Story of To-Day.* London: Bellairs & Co., 1897. First edition, octavo, blue cloth decorated in green and titled in gilt, bookplate of Paul Creswick and another small rubbed stamp, bit cocked and rubbed, about very good, Advance Review Copy with perforated stamp and pair of ALS's laid in, to fellow author Creswick.   Between the Covers Rare Books, Inc.   187 - 278   2015 $300

Tremayne, Peter *Suffer the Little Children.* London: Headline, 1995. First edition, fine in fine dust jacket. Buckingham Books   March 2015 - 22752   2015 $275

Trench, Frederick William *Royal Palaces and Hints for other Improvements in the Metropolis.* N.P.: n.d. but certainly privately printed, London, 1852. 4to., 24 plates and plans, many folding, one colored in outline, two with moveable overlays, original blindstamped cloth, spine neatly repaired, very good, very rare.   John Drury Rare Books   2015 - 18332   2015 $1661

Trenhalie, John *Kyril.* London: Severn House, 1981. First edition, fine in dust jacket.   Mordida Books   March 2015 - 002200   2015 $75

Tresselt, Alvin *Snow Bright Snow.* New York: Lothrop Lee & Shepard, 1947. First edition, 4to., pictorial boards, fine in very good+ dust jacket with few small closed tears and faded area on corner, color illustrations on every page by Duvoisin, beautiful copy.   Aleph-bet Books, Inc. 109 - 147   2015 $1200

Trevelyan, Julian *A Place, a State - A Suite of Drawings.* London: Enitharmon Press, 1974. First edition, of 200 copies, this one of only 20 signed by artist and author, folio, 18 black and white plates by Julian Trevelyan, cloth backed marbled paper boards, fine in near fine dust jacket, slightly creased at edges.   Peter Ellis, Bookseller   2014 - 015538   2015   £350

Treves, Frederick *The Elephant Man and Other Reminiscences.* London: Cassell, 1923. First edition, octavo, two-tone cloth, small stain to top edge, some foxing to endpapers, very good, uncommon.   Peter Ellis, Bookseller   2014 - 016948   2015   £350

Trevnain *The Eiger Sanction.* New York: Crown, 1972. First edition, fine in dust jacket with small scrape on spine and closed tear on front and back panels.   Mordida Books   March 2015 - 010585   2015 $85

Trevor, William *The Old Boys.* London: Bodley Head, 1964. First edition, 8vo., original brown cloth lettered gilt at spine, fine in very good+, clean dust jacket with slight edgewear with two short closed tears, no loss, excellent condition.   Any Amount of Books   2015 - C5783   2015   £160

The Trial in the Supreme Court... on the Relations of Coles Bashford vs. Wm. A. Barstow, Contesting the Right to the Office of Governor of Wisconsin. Madison: Calkins & Proudfit and Atwood & Rublee, 1856. First edition, 8vo., 368 pages, original dark green printed wrappers chipped and torn with loss but mostly intact, small blindstamp on title, else internally fine.   M & S Rare Books, Inc.   97 - 322   2015 $250

The Trial of Thomas Hunter, Peter Hacket, Richard M'niel, James Gibb and William M'Lean the Glasgow Cotton-Spinners, before the High Court of Justiciary at Edinburgh on Charges of Murder... Edinburgh: William Tait, 1838. 8vo., frontispiece, foxed and browned, well bound recently in watered cloth, spine lettered gilt.   John Drury Rare Books   March 2015 - 25393   2015   £306

The Trials on the Informations Which in Pursuance of an Order of the House of Commons were filed by His Majesty's Attorney General Against Richard Smith, Esq. for having been guilty of notorious bribery.... London: sold by G. Kearsley and M. Gurney, n.d., 1776. First edition, 4to., small old inkstamp on lower blank margin of title, repeated on one other leaf margin, well bound in late 19th century half calf over marbled boards, gilt lettered, very good, very scarce.   John Drury Rare Books   2015 - 24053   2015 $612

Trier, Johann Wolfgang *Einleitung Zur der Wapen Kunts. Nebst Einem Vorbericht von der Gesammten Hrolds Wissenschaft.* Leipzig: Carl Ludwig, 1744. Reprint of 1714 edition, frontispiece, titlepage printed in red and black, 132 plates of coats of arms, numerous additional text vignettes, unnumbered section at rear of 44 pages 'Register' + 10 pages further plates, soundly bound in unlettered black boards, slight chipping and slight marks at spine, overal near very good, clean text and plates.   Any Amount of Books   2015 - A33623   2015   £175

Trigueros, Ignacio *Memoria de los Ramos Municipales Correspondiente al Semestre de Julio a Diciembre de 1866 Presentada a S. M. el Emperador.* Mexico: Imprenta Economica, 1867. First edition, rare, 2 black and white folding charts, 8vo., quarter green morocco over marbled boards, spine decorated in gilt, marbled endpapers, very good, boards worn at corners, few letters inked to verso free front endpaper, two tiny holes near top of free rear endpaper, otherwise contents near fine.   Kaaterskill Books   19 - 151   2015 $500

Trimmer, Sarah *The Oeconomy of Charity; or an Address to Ladies Concerning Sunday Schools...* London: printed by T. Bensley for T. Longman, G. G. J. and J. Robinson and J. Johnson, 1787. First edition, 12mo., full sheep period style by Philip Dusel, red morocco label, gilt rules, decorations and lettering, 2 folding plates, fine.   The Brick Row Book Shop   Miscellany 67 - 93   2015 $2250

Trinity House *The Royal Charter of Confirmation Granted by His Most Excellent Majesty King James II to the Trinity House of Deptford-Stroud; for the Government and Encrease of the Navigation of England...* London: printed anno, 1685. First edition, 8vo., frontispiece, titlepage and A2 printed in red and black, divisional titlepage on N54, early ownership name on title, wanting blank leaf H8, contemporary calf, gilt, sides generally rather worn, neatly rebacked, spine gilt and labelled, very good, crisp copy, surprisingly scarce.   John Drury Rare Books   2015 - 23897   2015 $1049

Triolet, Elsa *L'Age de Nylon - Roses a Credit, Luna-Park (et) L'Ame.* Paris: Librairie Gallimard, 1959-1963. First editions, 3 volumes, octavo, wrappers, slight nick at top of front free endpaper of first volume, spine rubbed at tail of second volume, very good.   Peter Ellis, Bookseller   2014 - 004958   2015   £300

Trocheck, Kathy Hogan *Every Crooked Nanny.* New York: Harper Collins, 1992. First edition, very fine in dust jacket.   Mordida Books   March 2015 - 002204   2015 $100

Troil, Magnus *Orkney & Shetland Election. A Letter to Eric Hoy from Magnus Troil.* London: printed for J. Unwin, 1847. First edition, 8vo., 8 pages, modern plain wrappers, good copy, rare.   John Drury Rare Books   2015 - 16387   2015 $177

Troil, Magnus *A Third Letter to the Earl of Zetland from Magnus Troil.* Kirkwall: printed by J. V. Anderson Victoria Street, 1847. First edition, 8vo., modern plain wrappers, very good, rare.   John Drury Rare Books   March 2015 - 16388   2015 $266

Trojan, J. *Struwwepleter Junior.* London: Jarrolds, 1893. First English edition, 4to., color illustrated boards, illustrations, mostly in color, boards little soiled, chipped a corners, text slightly loose, used and slightly worn otherwise, very good, of considerable rarity.   Any Amount of Books   2015 - A62579   2015   £220

Trolle, Frank H. *James P. Johnson Father of the Stride Piano.* Alphen an de Rijn Micrography, 1981. First edition, wrappers, 2 volumes, near fine.   Beasley Books   2013 - 2015 $40

Trollope, Anthony 1815-1882 *Framley Parsonage.* London: Smith, Elder & Co., 1861. First edition, 8vo., half dark red leather with marbled boards, lettered and decorated gilt at spines, five raised bands, including 6 illustrations by J. E. Millais, clean, very good, very clean plates (very slight staining to frontispiece of volume 3), excellent condition.   Any Amount of Books   2015 - C8105   2015   £700

Trollope, Anthony 1815-1882 *Lotta Schmidt and Other Stories.* London: Strahan & Co., 1870. Original maroon cloth, blocked in black, dulled and slightly rubbed.   Jarndyce Antiquarian Booksellers   CCXI - 273   2015   £120

Trollope, Anthony 1815-1882 *North America.* London: Chapman & Hall, 1862. First edition, 2 volumes, original blind patterned pink/red cloth gilt at spine, very early issue with publisher's ad rear of volume one dated May 1862, complete very good- copies somewhat worn and shaken but with clean text, folding map slightly torn at side with map itself complete.   Any Amount of Books   2015 - A45822   2015   £200

Trollope, Anthony 1815-1882 *Phineas Redux.* London: Chapman and Hall, 1874. First edition, 8vo., uncommon, 2 volumes in one edition in original decorated green cloth lettered gilt on spine and on front cover, frontispiece and 23 plates, slightly chipped at head of spine, slightly larger chip at bottom of spine, slight edgewear, otherwise very good, with slight foxing to prelims.   Any Amount of Books   2015 - a45761   2015   £180

Trollope, Anthony 1815-1882 *Tales of all Countries. Second Series.* London: Chapman & Hall, 1863. Original green glazed smooth linen cloth, front board with triple borders and centrepiece in gilt, back board with triple borders in blind, spine blocked heavily gilt with two stars at tail, lettered in gilt, very slight rubbing, inscription.   Jarndyce Antiquarian Booksellers   CCXI - 274   2015   £650

Trollope, Anthony 1815-1882 *The Three Clerks.* London: Richard Bentley, 1858. First edition, 3 volumes, 8vo., half grained red leather, red cloth and lettered gilt at spines with five raised bands, very slight rubbing to boards, very slight sunning to spines, otherwise fine.   Any Amount of Books   2015 - C8132   2015   £700

Trollope, Frances Milton 1780-1863 *Domestic Manners of the Americans.* London: Whittaker, Treacher & Co., 1832. Second edition, 2 volumes, half titles, frontispieces and plates after A. Herrieu, odd spot, contemporary half calf, spines attractively blocked in gilt, dark green labels, head of leading hinge splitting volume I, good plus.   Jarndyce Antiquarian Booksellers   CCXI - 275   2015   £380

Trollope, Frances Milton 1780-1863 *The Life and Adventures of a Clever Woman.* London: Chapman and Hall, 1864. Second edition, contemporary half tan calf, spine gilt in compartments, dark green leather label, very good.   Jarndyce Antiquarian Booksellers   CCXI - 276   2015   £150

Troncoso, Francisco P. *Las Guerras con las Tribus Yaqui Mayo del Estado de Sonora.* Mexico: Tip. del Departmento de Estado Mayor, 1905. First edition, map, illustrations with 1 black and white folding map, 4to., quarter morocco over marbled boards, 4 raised bands, gilt title, bookplate of Joseph M. Gleason, very good, wear to spine head, extremely faint accession numbers at foot of spine, scuffed boards, owner's bookplate, owner's stamp on half title, few small repairs to map on verso, contents clean and bright.   Kaaterskill Books   19 - 6   2015 $500

Trotskii, Lev 1879-1940 *From October to Brest Litovak.* Brooklyn: Socialist Publication Society, 1919. First US edition, 8vo., softcover, wrappers, very good+ with neat rubber stamp at head of front wrapper an Clarion Book Shop (Chicago) rubber stamp at foot of titlepage.   Beasley Books   2013 - 2015 $45

Trotter, Alexander *A Plan of Communication Between the New and Old Town of Edinburgh, in the Line of the Earthen Mound...* Edinburgh: Oliver & Boyd & Simpkin & Marshall, London and Robertson & Atkinson, Glasgow, 1929. 4to., 6 large folding lithographic plates, fine later binding of half calf gilt over marbled boards, fine, sometime in the library of Charles Sebag-Montefiore with his armorial bookplate. John Drury Rare Books   2015 - 24351   2015 $787

Trotter, James M. *Music and Some Highly Musical People... (with) Sketches of the Lives of Remarkable Musicians of the Colored Race....* Boston: 1883. Sixth thousand, cover edges damped, backstrip with very few modest scrapes, all gilt bright.   Bookworm & Silverfish   2015 - 6016976475   2015 $150

Trotter, John Bernard *Memoirs of the latter Years of the Right Honourable Charles James Fox.* London: Richard Phillips, 1811. Third edition, 8vo., contemporary half russia, spine gilt, fine.   John Drury Rare Books   March 2015 - 25376   2015 $221

Trow, M. J. *The Adventures of Inspector Lestrade.* London: Macmillan, 1985. First edition, fine in dust jacket, signed by author.   Mordida Books   March 2015 - 008287   2015 $135

Trow, M. J. *Lestrade and the Brother of Death.* London: Macmillan, 1988. First edition, pages slightly darkened, otherwise fine in dust jacket, signed by author.   Mordida Books   March 2015 - 008289   2015 $85

Trow, M. J. *Lestrade and the Leviathan.* London: MacMillan, 1987. First edition, fine in dust jacket.   Mordida Books   March 2015 - 008288   2015 $85

Trow, M. J. *Lestrade and the Ripper.* London: Macmillan, 1988. First edition, pages slightly darkened, otherwise fine in dust jacket.   Mordida Books   March 2015 - 008290   2015 $125

Trow, M. J. *Lestrade and the Ripper.* London: Macmillan, 1988. First edition, fine in dust jacket.   Buckingham Books   March 2015 - 15674   2015 $175

Trowbridge, John *The Electrical Boy, or the Career of Great Man and Great Things.* Boston: Roberts Bros., 1891. First edition, octavo, 4 inserted plates with illustrations by Bridgman, other illustrations in text, original pictorial blue cloth, front panel stamped in brown, spine panel stamped in gold, decorated white endpapers with floral pattern printed in brown.   L. W. Currey, Inc.   Boy's Adventure Fiction 2015 - 75   2015 $125

Trowbridge, John *The Resolute Mr. Pansy: an Electrical Story for boys.* Boston: Roberts Bros., 1897. First edition, flyleaves at front and rear, 6 inserted plates with illustrations by Victor Searles, original red pictorial cloth, front and spine panels stamped in black, gold with floral patterned endpapers.   L. W. Currey, Inc.   Boy's Adventure Fiction 2015 - 98   2015 $100

Trowbridge, John *Three Boys on an Electrical Boat.* Boston and New York: Houghton Mifflin, 1894. First edition, octavo, original blue-gray cloth, front and spine panels stamped in dark blue, gray coated endpapers.   L. W. Currey, Inc.   Boy's Adventure Fiction 2015 - 76   2015 $125

A True and Impartial Collection of Pieces, in Prose and Verse Which Have Been Written and Published on Both Sides of the Question During the Contest for the Westminster Election. London: printed for W. Owen, 1749. First edition, 8vo., sewn as issued, couple of minor marginal tears, but very fine, entirely uncut, very uncommon.   C. R. Johnson   Foxon R-Z - 1041r-z   2015 $1379

True Causes of Riot and Rebellion. Petition to the King on Behalf of the Prisoners Convicted Under the Late Special Commissions at Bristol and Nottingham. London?: 1832. 8vo., 16 pages, modern wrappers, printed label on upper cover, very good, scarce.   John Drury Rare Books   2015 - 25395   2015 $133

A True Relation of the Great and Glorious Victory through Gods Providence, Obtained by Sir William Waller, Sir Arthur Haslerig and Others of the Parliament Forces... London: for Edward Husbands July 14, 1643. First edition, small 4to., some catchwords and final line of text trimmed, early 20th century half maroon morocco and cloth boards (covers dampstained), from the library of James Stevens Cox (1910-1997).   Maggs Bros. Ltd.   1447 - 98   2015   £150

True, Louise *Number Men.* Chicago: Children's Press, 1948. Oblong 4to., pictorial boards, slightest of cover soil, else near fine in dust jacket, illustrations by Lillian Owens. Aleph-bet Books, Inc.   109 - 107   2015 $200

Truel, Madeleine *L'Enfant Du Metro.* Paris: Editions du Chene, 1943. 4to., cloth backed pictorial boards, light cover soil, near fine, illustrations by Lucha Truel with full page color illustrations.   Aleph-bet Books, Inc.   109 - 181   2015 $450

Truman, Benjamin C. *Occidental Sketches.* San Francisco: San Francisco News, 1881. First edition, blind and gilt stamped red cloth, minor extremity rubbing, fine, owner's dated signature "Homer S. King 1881".   Argonaut Book Shop   Holiday Season 2014 - 290   2015 $150

Trumbo, Dalton *Johnny Got His Gun.* Philadelphia: J. B. Lippincott, 1939. First edition, light pencilled name, easily erasable (but we think it is of the important author's agent Harold Ober), else fine in handsome very good plus dust jacket with nicks at crown and little light edgewear, from the library of Kate Stettner Lobell and Carl D. Lobell. Between the Covers Rare Books 196 - 35 2015 $2500

Trusler, John *The London Adviser and Guide...* London: printed for the author no. 14 Red Lion St. Clerkenwell, 1786. First edition, 12mo., recent half calf over marbled boards with raised bands and gilt lettered label, scarce. John Drury Rare Books 2015 - 25968 2015 $1661

Truth, Sojourner *Narrative of Sojourner Truth. A Bondswoman of Olden Time.* Boston: the author, 1875. Third edition, 8vo., joints and spine ends bit rubbed, rear free endpaper adhering to pastedown and showing a tear otherwise very nice copy, quite bright. Beasley Books 2013 - 2015 $1000

Tryon, George W. *List of American Writers on Recent Conchology; with the Titles of their Memoirs and Dates of Publication.* New York, et al: Balliere Brothers, 1861. 8vo., black cloth, gilt stamped cover title with blindstamped decorative borders, extremities worn, spine nearly chipped off (still tightly bound), generally very good. Jeff Weber Rare Books 178 - 1075 2015 $40

Tschichold, Jan *Gute Schriftformen, Eine Beispielsammlung fur Zeichner, Maler und Bild Hauser, Herausegeben Von der Allg....* Basel: Lehrmittelverlag des Erziehungs-Departments, 1946. Third edition, small 4to. board portfolio, cord ties containing 6 fascicles, outer portfolio soiled with some toning. Oak Knoll Books 306 - 203 2015 $175

Tschichold, Jan *Schatzkammer Der Schreibkunst, Meisterwerke der Kalligraphie aus Vier Jahrhunderten auf Zweihundert Tafelin.* Basel: Verlag Birkhauser, 1945. First edition, oblong small 4to., cloth backed decorated boards, 16 pages, followed by 200 plates, covers show wear along edges, bookseller's booklabel in corner of front pastedown, first three leaves including titlepage have crease marks in them from being folded at one time, lacks dust jacket. Oak Knoll Books Special Catalogue 24 - 56 2015 $125

Tschichold, Jan *Typographische Gestaltung.* Basel: Benno Schwabe & Co., 1935. First edition, 8vo., cloth, paper spine label, dust jacket with small piece missing along top edge of front cover. Oak Knoll Books 306 - 61 2015 $450

Tubbs, Stephenie Ambrose *The Lewis and Clark Companion. An Encyclopedic Guide to the Voyage of Discovery.* New York: Henry Holt and Co., 2003. First edition, illustrations, map, portraits, two-tone boards, very fine with pictorial dust jacket. Argonaut Book Shop Holiday Season 2014 - 166 2015 $35

Tucker, Abraham *Vocal Sounds by Edward Search, Esq.* London: printed by T. Jones and sold by T. Payne, 1773. First edition, small 8vo., 19th century half maroon morocco by E. Riley & Son, very good,. Blackwell's Rare Books B179 - 108 2015 £900

Tucker, Beverley R. *The Gift of Genius.* Boston: Stratford, 1930. First edition, hardcover, fine but for sunned spine, lightly used dust jacket. Beasley Books 2013 - 2015 $45

Tucker, Elizabeth *Old Youngsters.* New York: Stokes, 1897. 4to., cloth backed pictorial boards, edges rubbed, else tight, very good+, very scarce, text illustrations by Tucker and chromolithograph illustrations by Maud Humphrey. Aleph-Bet Books, Inc. 108 - 245 2015 $950

Tucker, Josiah *An Earnest and Affectionate Address to the Common People of England, Concerning the Usual Recreations on Shrove Tuesday.* London: F. and C. Rivington..., 1800. New edition, small 8vo., 8 pages, well bound recently in boards, spine lettered on paper label, very good. John Drury Rare Books March 2015 - 24616 2015 $266

Tucker, St. George *Blackstone's Commentaries; with Notes of Reference to the Constitution and Laws of the Federal Government of the United States and of the Commonwealth of Virginia.* Philadelphia: published by William Young Birch and Abraham Small, 1803. First edition, 8vo., folding charts & facsimiles, contemporary calf, leather labels, hinges cracking but sound, scuffed, Bushrod Washington's set with his ink signature at Mount Vernon, in each volume. M & S Rare Books, Inc. 97 - 77 2015 $30,000

Tucker, St. George *Woman's Suffrage by Constitutional Amendment.* New Haven: Yale University, 1916. First edition, small 8vo., inscribed by author, very nice. Second Life Books Inc. 189 - 255 2015 $150

Tucker, Susie I. *Portean Shape: a Study in Eighteenth Century Vocabulary and Usage.* London: University Of London, Athlone Press, 1967. Half title, original olive green cloth, very good, Geoffrey Tillotson's copy with ALs from author. Jarndyce Antiquarian Booksellers CCVII - 544 2015 £20

Tuckerman, Henry T. *A Memorial of Horatio Grennough Consisting of a Memoir, Selections from His Writings and Tributes to His Genius.* New York: 1853. First edition, cloth, top of spine slightly chipped, faint glue reside at base of spine, occasional light marginal foxing, light stain on front endpaper, generally very good, inscribed "Russell Smith from the Author". Joseph J. Felcone Inc. Science, Medicine and Technology - 52 2015 $100

Tudor, Tasha *The County Fair.* New York: Oxford University Press, 1940. First edition, 32mo., fine in mostly age toned near fine dust jacket, lovely copy. Between the Covers Rare Books 196 - 165 2015 $1500

Tudor, Tasha *Linsey Woolsey.* New York: Oxford University Press, `946. First edition, 32mo., fine in very near fine dust jacket, lovely copy. Between the Covers Rare Books 196 - 166 2015 $800

Tuel, J. E. *The Moral for Authors as Contained in the Autobiography of Eureka.* New York: Stringer & Townsend, 1849. First edition, 8vo., contemporary black quarter calf, marbled paper boards, gilt rules, edges little rubbed, very good, inscribed by author for Hon. Millard Fillmore, President, Washington Oct. 9 1850. The Brick Row Book Shop Miscellany 67 - 76 2015 $875

Tufnell, Ben *Mythologies.* London: Haunch of Venison, 2009. First edition, 8vo., wrappers, copiously illustrated in color and black and white, faint rubbing, very slightly bumped, otherwise fine. Any Amount of Books 2015 - A94291 2015 £180

Tufnell, Edward Carlton *Character, Object and Effects of Trades' Unions: with some Remarks on the Law Concerning Them.* London: James Ridgway and Sons, 1834. First and only edition, very scarce, recent marbled boards lettered on spine, very good. John Drury Rare Books March 2015 - 24483 2015 $656

Les Tuileries. Paris: n.d. circa, 1830. 7 1/4 x 5 inches, front cover and old linen repair, very good+ in original marbled slipcase with label, opening to 19 inches, this a 6 panel peepshow, including cover and backdrop, nice set. Aleph-Bet Books, Inc. 108 - 342 2015 $2850

Tuit, J. E. *The Tower Bridge: its History and Construction from the Date of the Earliest Project to the Present Time.* London: Office of "The Engineer", 1894. First edition, 4to., frontispiece, 6 folding plates at rear, 62 figures, original publisher's green cloth lettered gilt on spine and on front cover, spine slightly rubbed with slight wear at spine ends, covers very slightly marked, otherwise sound, very good or better. Any Amount of Books 2015 - A67468 2015 £150

Tuke, Margaret J. *A History of Bedford College for Women 1849-1937.* London: Oxford University Press, 1939. Half title, frontispiece and plates, folding tables, original purple cloth, slightly marked with split at head of spine, Kathleen Tillotson's copy with inserted material about Tuke. Jarndyce Antiquarian Booksellers CCVII - 545 2015 £35

Tuke, Samuel *Description of the Retreat, an Institution Near York, for Insane Persons of the Society of Friends.* York: printed for W. Alexander and sold by him, 1813. First edition, 8vo. issue, engraved double page plate, two double page engraved plates, plates with some dampstaining and foxing, mainly marginal, intermittent slight foxing throughout, old (19th century) ink stamp in title margin "Medical Staff Library", stamp repeated on frontispiece, contemporary half calf over marbled boards, fairly recently rebacked, sound but not beautiful copy. John Drury Rare Books 2015 - 22371 2015 $1311

Tull, Jethro *The Horse-Hoing Husbandry; or an Essay on the Principles of Tillage and Vegetation.* London: printed for the author and sold by G. Strahan, T. Woodward, A. Millar, J. Stagg and J. Brindley, 1733. Second edition. (bound with) Supplement, London: 1740, folio, 6 folding engraved plates, printed on heavy paper, initial license leaf, one prelim leaf, bound out of order, contemporary mottled calf, gilt, skillfully rebacked to match, raised bands, gilt devices in compartments, label, red edge, fine, crisp, supplement fine. John Drury Rare Books 2015 - 24782 2015 $1661

Tullie, George *An Answer to a Discourse concerning the Celibacy of the Clergy printed at Oxford.* London: printed at the Theater for Richard Chiswell at the Rose and Crown in S. Pauls Church Yard London, 1688. First edition, 4to., imprimatur leaf and final 2 ad leaves, bound fairly recently in grey boards with printed title label, closed marginal tear in one leaf (N1) but with no loss, else very good. John Drury Rare Books March 2015 - 25099 2015 £306

Tunbelly, Tim, Pseud. *The Letters of Tim. Tunbelly, Gent. Free Brugess Newcastle Upon Tyne, on the Tyne, the Newcastle Corporation...Volume I.* Newcastle upon Tyne: printed and published by W. A. Mitchell, 1823. 8vo., frontispiece, errata on verso of final leaf fairly recently in boards with printed spine label, entirely uncut, very good. John Drury Rare Books March 2015 - 23535 2015 £306

The Tunbridge-Miscellany; Consisting of Poems &c Written at Tunbridge-Wells this Summer. London: printed for E. Curll, 1712. First edition, 8vo., disbound, fine, complete with half title, which was printed as part of the last gathering, final leaf of text has inadvertently been left in place to follow half title, very scarce. C. R. Johnson Foxon R-Z - 1043r-z 2015 $2681

Tunbrigialia; or, Tunbridge Miscellanies for the Year 1733. London: printed for J. Penn, 1733. First edition, 24 pages, 8vo., disboun, fine, very rare. C. R. Johnson Foxon R-Z - 1044r-z 2015 $3831

Tunstall, William *Ballads and Some Other Occasional Poems by W----- T----- in the Marshalsea.* London: printed by E. Berington for the benefit of the author, 1716. First edition, old boards, 8vo., red morocco label bit rubbed, top of spine chipped, one leaf shaved in outer margin, touching first letter of each line, but text is completely clear, otherwise very good, uncommon.   C. R. Johnson   Foxon R-Z - 1045r-z   2015 $1149

Tunstall, William *St. Cyprian's Discourse to Donatus.* London: printed for the author by E. Berington, 1716. First edition, final blank leaf with paste-on errata slip, 8vo., recent half red morocco and flowered boards, some browning, titlepage dusty with very slight chipping of blank margins, but sound.   C. R. Johnson   Foxon R-Z - 1047r-z   2015 $1379

Tupper, John Lucas *Hiatus: the Void in Modern Education its Cause and Antidote.* London: Macmillan, 1869. 8vo., disbound, 51 page publisher's catalog at rear, presentation copy from author for William Michael Rossetti, last page has a note about errata on 3 pages, possibly in the hand of Rossetti, or Tupper, disbound, otherwise in decent condition with clean text, suitable for rebinding.   Any Amount of Books   2015 - A62731   2015   £220

Turbyfill, Mark *A Marriage with Space and Other Poems.* Chicago: Pascal Covici, 1927. First edition, fine in slightly rubbed, very near fine dust jacket.   Between the Covers Rare Books   196 - 119   2015 $100

Turenne, Henri De La Tour D'Auvergne *Military Memoirs and Maxims of Marshal Turenne...* London: J. & P. Knapton, 1740. First edition, 8vo., full brown calf leather, raised bands and lettered gilt on spine, leather slightly pitted and mottled, hinge somewhat weak but still holding well, bookplate of James Glafsford, otherwise text clean, overall very good.   Any Amount of Books   2015 - C35499   2015   £220

Turgenev, Ivan Sergeevich 1818-1883 *Fathers and Sons.* New York: Leypoldt & Holt, 1867. First edition in English, octavo, contemporary red morocco over marbled boards, translator Eugene Schuyler's copy with his bookplate.   Honey & Wax Booksellers   2 - 63   2015 $6000

Turgenev, Ivan Sergeevich 1818-1883 *The Novels and Stories of...* New York: Charles Scribner's Sons, 1903. First edition thus, 16 volumes, original maroon cloth with ornate gilt decoration to spine and to front covers, top edges gilt, each volume with tissue protected frontispiece, bookplates of Brand Whitlock (municipal reformer, diplomat, author), some mild wear to extremities, some random damp stains at corners, small owner stamps.   Stephen Lupack   March 2015 -   2015 $150

Turgenev, Ivan Sergeevich 1818-1883 *The Torrents of Spring.* London: Hamish Hamilton, 1960. New edition, imperial 8vo., illustrations in color and black and white by Robin Jacques, original binding, top edge gilt, others uncut, fine in original glassine dust jacket and pictorial slipcase, from the library of V. S. Pritchett, with posthumous VSP booklabel, from the collection of Gavin H. Fryer.   Bertram Rota Ltd.   308 Part II - 227   2015   £40

Turkin, Hy *The Official Encyclopedia of Baseball.* New York: A. S. Barnes, 1951. Jubilee edition, fine in modestly worn, very good or better dust jacket, inscribed by Turkin for Joe DiMaggio, with letter of provenance signed by DiMaggio's two granddaughters.   Between the Covers Rare Books, Inc.   187 - 11   2015 $850

Turnbull, Peter Evan *Austria.* London: John Murray, 1840. First edition, 2 volumes, handsome, tall 8vo., half brown leather lettered gilt at spine, raised bands, marbled boards, highly uncommon, slight foxing to prelims, bookplate of Sir Norton Joseph Knatchbull, minor rubbing and scuffing, else close to very good+.   Any Amount of Books   2015 - A65104   2015   £200

Turner, Bryan S. *Social Theories of the City.* London: Thoemmes Press, 1998. Reprint, 10 volumes, illustrations, diagrams, hardback, about fine.   Any Amount of Books   March 2015 - B16277   2015   £400

Turner, George *Narrow Gauge Nostalgia. A Compendium of California Short Lines.* Harbo City: J-H Publications, 1965. First edition, photos, maps, illustrations, light green boards, slight rubbing to spine ends, but fine, very lightly chipped dust jacket.   Argonaut Book Shop   Holiday Season 2014 - 292   2015 $45

Turner, John *A Catalogue of Goods to be sold by Auction in Lots Upon the Premises on Monday the 6th of March 1786...the property of the Late John Turner of Derby...* Derby: printed by J. Drewry, 1786. 8vo., titlepage lightly soiled, but very good, uncut, preserved in recent marbled wrappers, apparently exceptionally rare.   John Drury Rare Books   2015 - 26269   2015 $1311

Turner, Samuel *A Letter Addressed to the Right Hon. Robert Peel, &c &c Late Chairman of the Committee of secrecy, Appointed to Consider the state of the Bank of England.* London: printed for the author and sold by J. Asperne and J. M. Richardson and J. Hatchard, 1819. First edition, 8vo., presentation copy inscribed in ink by author for Mr. Ferguson, recent marbled boards, lettered on spine, very good.   John Drury Rare Books   2015 - 24484   2015 $612

Turnor, Thomas *The Case of the Bankers and Creditors More Fully Stated and Examined and a Second Time Printed with More than a Third Part Added...* London: printed for the year, 1675. 4to., many pages misnumbered as always, large, uncut copy in old, perhaps original wrappers, fine state of preservation. John Drury Rare Books 2015 - 20480 2015 $1049

Turow, Scott *One L.* New York: G. P. Putnam's Sons, 1977. First edition, fine in fine dust jacket with two tiny tears and touch of rubbing, signed by author, from the library of Kate Stettner Lobell and Carl D. Lobell. Between the Covers Rare Books 196 - 36 2015 $400

Turri, Raphaele de *Dissidentis Desciscentis Receptaeque Neapolis Libri VI.* N.P.: Insula, 1651. 8vo., contemporary vellum, leather label on spine, list of errata, label on spine chipped at edges, damage spot on lower front cover, covers lightly soiled and scuffed, pastedowns and endpapers stained, back pastedown torn. Oak Knoll Books 306 - 307 2015 $1100

Turton, Godfrey *The Emperor Arthur.* New York: 1967. First edition, fine in bright, near fine dust jacket. Stephen Lupack March 2015 - 2015 $40

Turton, Thomas *The Text of the Englisn Bible as Now Printed by the Universities Considered with Reference to a Report by a Sub-Committee of Dissenting Ministers.* Cambridge & London: John W. Parker and Rivingtons, 1833. First edition, 8vo., errata slip bound in after text (3 errata), preserved in modern wrappers with printed title label on upper cover, very good. John Drury Rare Books 2015 - 21706 2015 $89

Tussaud, Frank B. *The Great Exhibition Polka 1851 for the Piano forte composed and Dedicated to His Royal Highness Prince Albert.* London: Duff & Hodgson 65 Oxford St., 1851. Folio, upper wrapper only with lithograph, old tear "printed in Colors by Stannard & Dixon 7 Poland St. Marlborough Rare Books Ltd. List 49 - 36 2015 £30

Tuttle, W. C. *The Silver Bar Mystery.* Boston: Houghton Mifflin, 1933. First US edition, fine, bright, tight copy in lightly rubbed dust jacket. Buckingham Books March 2015 - 14218 2015 $225

Tutu, Desmond Mpilo *Hope and Suffering. Sermons and Speeches.* Grand Rapids: William B. Eerdmans, 1986. Later printing, very good+, original printed wrappers, crease to front cover, cover edge wear, minimal soil and foxing to edges, 8vo., signed and inscribed by author. By the Book, L. C. Special List 10 - 46 2015 $125

Tutu, Desmond Mpilo *The Rainbow People of God.* London: Doubleday, 1994. First edition, signed and dated by author, 8vo., fine, usual toning to edges, near fine price clipped dust jacket. By the Book, L. C. Special List 10 - 45 2015 $400

Tutu, Desmond Mpilo *The Words of Desmond Tutu.* New York: Newmarket Press, 1989. First edition, signed and inscribed by author to daughter Naomi Tutu, 8vo., fine in near fine dust jacket with mild sun spine. By the Book, L. C. Special List 10 - 47 2015 $650

Tuve, Rosamond *Elizabethan and Metaphysical Imagery.* Chicago: University of Chicago Press, 1947. Half title, from the library of Geoffrey & Kathleen Tillotson, original red cloth, inscribed by author of Kathleen Tillotson, signed by Kathleen and Geoffrey, inserted review by Maynard Mack and review by Cleanth Brooks. Jarndyce Antiquarian Booksellers CCVII - 546 2015 £25

Tuve, Rosamond *Images and Themes in Five Poems by Milton.* Cambridge: Harvard University Press, 1957. Half title, original green cloth, very good in slightly torn dust jacket, author's signed presentation for Geoffrey and Kathleen Tillotson, with 4 TLS from author. Jarndyce Antiquarian Booksellers CCVII - 379 2015 £25

Tweeddale, Arthur *The Ornithological Works...* London: the author, 1881. Large quarto, 760 pages, 11 hand colored plates, one colored map, contemporary half olive morocco and marbled boards, two library stamps of Royal Australasian Ornithologist Union, note "Captain Legge with Lord Tweeddale's kind regards April 1882. Andrew Isles 2015 - 28036 2015 $3500

Twelve Hawks, John *The Traveler.* New York: Doubleday, 2005. First edition, one of 777 numbered copies, signed by author, fine in fine dust jacket. Beasley Books 2013 - 2015 $300

XXV Queries: Modestly and Humbly and Yet Sadly and Seriously Propounded to the People of England and their Representatives and Likewise to the Army in this Juncture of Affairs. London: printed for L. Chapman at the Crown in Popes-head Ally, 1659, i.e., 1660. First edition, 4to., interleaved with blanks, some inner margins strengthened, bound in early 20th century parchment backed boards, spine lettered, very good from the early 20th century library of Fairfax of Cameron, with armorial bookplate. John Drury Rare Books 2015 - 26085 2015 $656

Twining, Richard *Observations on the Tea and Window Act and on the Tea Trade.* London: T. Cadell, 1785. 8vo., half title, final ad leaf, recent marbled boards lettered on spine, very good. John Drury Rare Books 2015 - 24016 2015 $656

Twiss, Travers *The Law of Nations Considered as Independent Political Communities.* London: Oxford University Press/Longman, Green, Longman and Roberts, 1863. 1861. First edition, 2 volumes, 8vo., including both titles, handsomely bound in uniform contemporary Exeter College, Oxford prize binding of plum calf gilt, raised bands and contrasting labels with fully gilt spines, gilt armorial Exeter College on each cover, marbled edges, extremities lightly rubbed, else fine.   John Drury Rare Books   March 2015 - 25754   2015 $874

Two Nursery Favourites: Three Tiny Pigs/Great Bear and Little Bear. London: Dean & Sons, n.d. circa, 1910. Folio, cloth, pictorial paste-on, some cover soil, else very good+, printed with each page mounted on cloth, illustrations by Helen Jacobs and by E. Berkeley, quite scarce.   Aleph-Bet Books, Inc.   108 - 248   2015 $450

Tyler, Alice Jaynes *I Who Should Command All.* New Haven: The Framamat Co., 1937. First edition, purple cloth, gilt, bit of rubbing, near fine, inscribed by author for mother.   Between the Covers Rare Books, Inc.   187 - 279   2015 $125

Tyler, Anne   18941- *Breathing Lessons.* Franklin Center: Franklin Library, 1988. First edition, precedes trade edition, signed by author, publisher's letter laid in, gilt decorated full leather, raised bands, all edges gilt, satin bookmark.   Stephen Lupack   March 2015 - 2015 $100

Tyler, Anne   18941- *The Clock Winder.* London: Chatto & Windus, 1973. First English edition, near fine in very good dust jacket (wrinkle at bottom of rear panel, neither chipped nor clipped), scarce.   Stephen Lupack   March 2015 - 2015 $175

Tyler, Anne   18941- *Dinner at the Homesick Restaurant.* New York: Knopf, 1982. First edition, inscribed by author in year of publication, recipient's name on front flyleaf, fading to top stain, corners bit rounded and shallow reading crease to spine, very good in like dust jacket, spine and edge tanned dust jacket with modest edgewear.   Ken Lopez, Bookseller   164 - 210   2015 $175

Tyler, Anne   18941- *A Patchwork Planet.* New York: 1998. First edition, near fine, dust jacket.   Stephen Lupack   March 2015 - 2015 $40

Tyler, Anne   18941- *Saint Maybe.* Franklin Center: Franklin Library, 1991. First edition, signed by author, frontispiece by Joannie Schwarz, gilt decorated full leather, raised bands, all edges gilt, satin bookmark.   Stephen Lupack   March 2015 - 2015 $100

Tyler, George W. *The History of Bell County.* San Antonio: Naylor Co., 1936. First edition, 8vo., red cloth, gold stamping on front cover and spine, frontispiece, illustrations, maps, lightly foxed along top edge and fore-edge, staining to front and rear pastedown to sheets due to binder's glue discoloration, else near fine in moderately rubbed and lightly foxed dust jacket with light wear to extremities.   Buckingham Books   March 2015 - 23656   2015 $250

Tyler, Lee *The Clue of the Clever Canine.* New York: Vantage, 1994. First edition, very fine in dust jacket, 3 notes signed by Tyler, golf Christmas card with signed note and 3 reviews of the book, inscribed by author.   Mordida Books   March 2015 - 010757   2015 $85

Tyrrell, James *A Brief Disquisition of the Law of Nature, According to the Principles and Method Laid Down ...* London: printed and are to be sold by Richard Baldwin near the Oxford Arms in Warwick Lane, 1692. First edition, 8vo., with imprimatur leaf (with repair but with no loss of printed surface) and 2 ads leaves, minor general paper toning, early signature of D. Campbell, another old signature crossed through in upper margin, contemporary calf, most appropriately rebacked to match, raised bands and red morocco label gilt, very good, rather scarce.   John Drury Rare Books   2015 - 24385   2015 $1311

Tyson, Job Roberts *A Brief Survey of the Great Extent and Evil Tendencies of the Lottery System as Existing in the United States.* Philadelphia: William Brown, 1833. First edition, 8vo., 48 pages, generally little browned and foxed, just little soiled, original printed blue wrappers, worn at spine, still good copy, seemingly rare in libraries.   John Drury Rare Books   March 2015 - 20016   2015 $266

Tyssot De Patot, Simon *Voyages et Avantures de Jaques Masse.* Bordeaux (i. e. The Hague): James L'Aveugle 1710, i.e., 1714. First edition, 12mo., contemporary calf, neatly rebacked in antique style, little rubbed, some minor foxing, soiling, very good, tight copy.   Second Life Books Inc.   190 - 225   2015 $2500

U

Udden, Johan August *An Old Indian Village.* Rock Island: Lutheran Augustana Book Concern, 1900. First edition, printed boards, quarto, cloth spine, gold stamping on spine, 80 pages, illustrations, covers moderately rubbed, light wear to corners, else very good. Buckingham Books March 2015 - 25591   2015 $375

Udry, Janice May *Let's Be Enemies.* New York: Harper and Bros., 1961. First edition, 8vo., pictorial boards, owner name on endpaper, else fine in dust jacket with small closed tear, not price clipped, grey color illustration on every page by Maurice Sendak. Aleph-bet Books, Inc. 109 - 430   2015 $600

Ueda, Shoji *Polaroid 35-mm Photo Album.* Tokyo: Self Published, 1986. First edition, one of 1000 numbered copies signed by Ueda, 3 soft-cover folios with 20 sheets each (loose) with lithograph on each page (60) presented in original corrugated sleeve, uncommon, fine. Ed Smith Books 83 - 110   2015 $1350

Ulanov, Barry *Duke Ellington.* New York: Creative Age, 1946. First edition, very good+ in good dust jacket, lacking lower third of rear panel. Beasley Books 2013 - 2015 $45

Ullathorne, William Bernard *A Plea for the Rights and Liberties of Religious Women...* London: Thomas Richardson and Son, 1851. First edition, 8vo. 24 pages, recently well bound in linen backed marbled boards lettered, very good. John Drury Rare Books   March 2015 - 19885   2015 $266

Ullman, James Ramsey *The Age of Mountaineering.* Philadelphia: J. B. Lippincott, 1954. First edition, 24 photos, 6 maps, endpaper map, addendum tipped in at rear, two tone cloth, very fine, spine faded pictorial dust jacket. Argonaut Book Shop   Holiday Season 2014 - 293   2015 $90

Ullmann, Anne *The Wood-Engravings of Tirzah Ravilious.* London: Gordon Fraser, 1987. Limited to 1000 numbered copies, 4to., stiff paper wrappers, 43 black and white illustrations, frontispiece, spine shows some fading. Oak Knoll Books 306 - 40   2015 $225

Ulloa, Antonio De *Noticias Americanas; Entretenimientos Phisicos-Historicus Sobre la America Meridional...* Madrid: FranciscoManuel de Mena, 1772. First edition, 4to., 18th century mottled sheep, five raised bands, five compartments decorated in gilt, red morocco lettering, edges stained red, marbled endpapers, very good, boards rubbed, inconspicuous groove to front board, wear to head of spine with tiny split at joint, occasional foxing, mostly marginal, handsome example. Kaaterskill Books   19 - 154   2015 $4000

Ulloa, Antonio De *Noticias Americanas; Entretenimientos Fisico-Historicos Sobre la America Meridional y la Septentrional Oriental.* Madrid: Imprenta Real, 1792. Second edition, 4to., contemporary marbled sheep, red morocco lettering piece, spine ruled in gilt, marbled endpapers, very good, minor wear to boards and spine, upper fore corner of free endpaper and first three leaves with small marginal worn hole. Kaaterskill Books   19 - 155   2015 $600

Unamuno, Miguel De *Del Diario Poetico De Miguel De Unamuno.* Buenos Aires: Editorial Losada, 1961. Number 284 of 400 copies, folio, cloth in dust jacket, both fine with tiniest bit of darkening to spine, very good- cardboard slipcase. Beasley Books   2013 - 2015 $350

Unamuno, Miguel De *The Selected Works of Unamuno.* Princeton: Princeton University Press, 1983. First edition, 7 volumes, 8vo., sound, very good set, volume I has slight chipping at spine label, second volume has neat names and one volume has some browning at front endpapers. Any Amount of Books   2015 - A86234   2015   £175

The Unbeliever Convinced: in a Dialogue Between David Doubtful and His Neighbour Christian. London: F. C. and J. Rivington for the SPCK, 1819. First edition, 12mo., 12 pages, last three leaves cut close just touching few final letters on several lines and cropping last letter of three words, sense unimpaired, recent plain wrappers,. John Drury Rare Books   2015 - 18347   2015 $177

The Uncle's Present. a New Battledoor. Philadelphia: Jacob Johnson (147 Market St.) (on flap), Philadelphia: sold by Benjamin Arner (on rear cover), n.d., circa, 1810. 3 3/4 x 6 1/2 inches, brown pictorial wrappers, some darkening of covers, else fine, front and back covers have woodcuts attributed to W. Mason on front and A. Anderson on rear, woodcuts. Aleph-bet Books, Inc.   109 - 37   2015 $1200

Underwood, Bert *The Grand Canon of Arizona through the Stereoscope.* New York: and London: Underwood & Underwood, 1908. 18 stereo-photographic views on stiff cardboard with printed captions, printed explanations on versos, together with cloth bound volume (18cm), consisting of pages 64 and 2 'Grand Tour maps", one folding and bound in original brown cloth, upper cover gilt, views contained in original black cloth box in form of book, spine lettered gilt. Marlborough Rare Books   List 53 - 40   2015   £650

Underwood, Michael *A Party to Murder.* London: Macmillan, 1983. First edition, pages slightly darkened, else fine in dust jacket. Mordida Books March 2015 - 011342 2015 $85

The Union, a Poem. Humbly inscrib'd to her Royal Highness the Princess Ann. London: printed for J. Roberts, 1733. First edition, folio, 9 pages, recent stiff marbled wrappers, rare, very good. C. R. Johnson Foxon R-Z - 1048r-z 2015 $3831

Union Pacific and Southern Pacific Passenger Departments *The Overland Route to the Road of a Thousand Wonders. The Route of the Union Pacific and Southern Pacific...* Union Pacific and Southern Pacific Passenger Depts., 1908. 9 1/4 x 11 3/4 inches, colored pictorial stiff wrappers, embossed color scene on front cover and embossed color scene, color illustrations, map, oversized wrappers chipped and with wear to spine, interior clean. Buckingham Books March 2015 - 34840 2015 $425

Union Pacific Railroad *Over the Overland Route to California.* Rand McNally & Co., 1915. 9 x 4 inches, color pictorial wrappers, illustrations, wear to extremities, else very good. Buckingham Books March 2015 - 33903 2015 $275

United Nations. Economic Commission for Latin America *El Descarrollo Economico de la Argentina Parte I. Los Problemas y Perspectivas del Crecimiento Economico Argentino...* Mexico: Naciones Unidas Departmento de Asuntos Economicos y Sociales, 1959. First edition, small 4to., cloth, very good or better, light soiling, owner's name on original wrapper, leaves clean. Kaaterskill Books 19 - 156 2015 $175

United Radical Industrial Provident Loan & Investment Society Limited *Rules.* London: Co-operative Printing Society Ltd., 1888. 8vo., original printed wrappers, tiny inkstamp on blank verso of title of Int. Institut Soc. Geschiedenis Amsterdam, very good, apparently rare. John Drury Rare Books 2015 - 21613 2015 $89

United States. Congress. House of Representatives - 1811 *Report of the Select Committee to Who was Referred...the Petition of John Brumback and Others of... Virginia. January 19, 1811.* Washington: A. and G. Way, 1810, i.e., 1811. 7 pages, unbound as issued, two horizontal fold marks, trifle dusty, else very good. Joseph J. Felcone Inc. Science, Medicine and Technology - 45 2015 $150

United States. Congress. Senate - 1794 *In Senate May 12th 1794,. On Motion, Ordered that the Memorial of Mr. Pinckney, the answer of Mr. Hammond and the letter of the Secretary of State on the 1st of May to Mr. Hammond, Relative to the British Instructions of the 8th of June last, be printed for use of the members of the Senate.* Philadelphia: printed by John Fenno!, 1794. Printed area bit browned, pages 32, 8vo., modern marbled boards, good. Blackwell's Rare Books B179 - 107 2015 £450

United States. Interior Department - 1867 *Letter from the Secretary of the Interior Communicating, in Obedience to a Resolution of the Senate of the 30th of January, Information in Relation to the Late Massacre of the United States Troops by Indians at or Near Fort Phil. Kearney in Dakota Territory.* Washington: GPO, 1867. First edition, 8vo., printed wrappers, very good in custom slipcase with title stamped in gold on spine. Buckingham Books March 2015 - 26053 2015 $650

United States. Interior Department - 1883 *Letter from the Secretary of the Interior in Response to a Resolution of the House of Representatives Transmitting a Report on the Commissioner of the General Land Office in Relation to the Leavenworth, Pawnee and Western Railroad Company.* Washington: GPO, 1883. First edition, 8vo., quarter cloth and boards binder, titles stamped in gold gilt on front cover, 19 pages, 2 foldout maps, fine copy. Buckingham Books March 2015 - 31841 2015 $300

United States. Laws, Statutes, etc. - 1823 *Acts of the 17th Congress (Second Session) 1823.* Washington: 1823. First edition, plain contemporary wrappers, stitched, scare, good plus, mild dampstaining, upper corner, quarter size darker stain for several leaves at inner margin, some random chipping to wrappers. Stephen Lupack March 2015 - 2015 $100

United States. Laws, Statutes, etc. - 1832 *Acts of the 22nd Congress (First Session) 1832.* Washington: 1832. First edition, plain wrappers, stitched, very good plus, mild dampstaining to several leaves, solid copy. Stephen Lupack March 2015 - 2015 $125

United States. Laws, Statutes, etc. - 1835 *Acts of the 23rd Congress Second Session 1835.* Washington: 1835. First edition, plain contemporary wrappers, stitched, this copy is in very good plus condition, mild dampstaining to several leaves, minor chipping at spine, solid copy. Stephen Lupack March 2015 - 2015 $125

United States. Laws, Statutes, etc. - 1837 *Acts of the 24th Congress Second Session 1837.* Washington: 1837. First edition, plain contemporary wrappers, stitched, scarce, very good, some mild tanning, chipping along front edge of paper wrapper, solid copy. Stephen Lupack March 2015 - 2015 $125

United States. Patent Office - 1878 *Catalogue of the Library of the United States Patent Office.* Washington: GPO, 1878-1889. 3 volumes, includes two supplements, ex-library, with markings, 4to., cloth, spine of first volume torn off at top, 3 volumes scuffed and rubbed, back inside hinge of first volume cracked.   Oak Knoll Books   306 - 89   2015 $125

United States. War Department - 1855 *Report of Explorations and Surveys to Ascertain the Most Practicable and Economical Route for a Railroad from the Mississippi River to the Pacific Ocean Made Under the Direction of the Secretary of War 1853-1854.* Washington: A. O. P. Nicholson printer, 1855-1861. each volume rebound in black buckram and signatures resewn, titles stamped in gold on spine panel, each volume stamped with word "Senate" on spine, five of the volumes are actually for the House of Representatives, Volume I with small stamp of Library of Washington and Jefferson College with word 'withdrawn' stamped in light blue ink at bottom of titlepage and "contents of volume I" page, else very good, tight copy; volume IV presentation inscription to Irving Holcomb from Hon. F. E. Sprimer (?) dated Nov. 1857; small waterstain to bottom edges front flyleaf which continues lightly to page 3, else very good, tight, volume X with light foxing to first 8 pages in front of volume and to last 8 pages in rear of volume else very good, tight copy; volume XI with moderate foxing and two small waterstains that dimish over first 16 pages, else very good, tight, volume XI with maps and plates, plates and maps uncommonly fine, very handsome, completely rebound set that is in very good to fine condition.   Buckingham Books   March 2015 - 26611   2015 $15,000

United States. War Department - 1867 *Letter of the Secretary of War, Communicating, in Compliance with a Resolution of the Senate of the 30th Ultimo, the Official Reports, Papers and other Facts in Relation to the Causes and Extent of the Late Massacre of the United States Troops by Indians at fort Phil. Kearney.* Washington: GPO, 1867. First edition, 8vo., very good.   Buckingham Books   March 2015 - 26052   2015 $650

United States. War Department - 1880 *Letter from the Secretary of War transmitting estimates of Appropriation Required, with Tracings of Plans, for the Construction of Officers' Quarters at Omaha, Nebraska.* Washington: GPO, 1880. First edition, 8vo., quarter cloth and boards, titles stamped in gold gilt on front cover, plus 8 foldout sets of drawings, fine.   Buckingham Books   March 2015 - 31839   2015 $250

The University Miscellany; or, More Burning Work for the Oxford Convocation. London: printed for A. Baldwin, 1713. Second edition, 8vo., recent half calf and marbled boards, spine gilt, fine, scarce.   C. R. Johnson   Foxon R-Z - 1049r-z   2015 $1149

University of California - Office of the Registrar *Summary of Degrees and Certificates Awarded by the University of California 1864 to 1933-1934.* Berkeley: University of California, Office of the Registrar, 1934. First edition, oblong octavo, 3 prelim leaves, 82 leaves printed rectos only, all leaves are actual photos, black cloth, gilt lettered spine, bookplate on inner cover of Hobart M. Lovett, very fine.   Argonaut Book Shop   Holiday Season 2014 - 294   2015 $250

University of Edinburgh *Catalogue of the Printed Books in the Library of the University of Edinburgh.* Edinburgh: at the University Press, T. and A. Constable, 1918-1923. 3 volumes, oversize 8vo., navy cloth, gilt stamped cover emblem and spine title, extremities rubbed, title of volume I repaired using archival tape, inner hinge volume II bit cracked, ex-library with usual markings and defects including remainder marks and blindstamp on each title, very good.   Jeff Weber Rare Books   178 - 1082   2015 $75

Updike, Daniel Berkeley   1860-1941 *Printing Types, Their History, Forms, and Use a Study in Survival.* Cambridge: Harvard University Press, 1937. Second edition, 8vo., 2 volumes, cloth, dust jackets, original slipcase worn and hinges broken, jacket spines darkened, profusely illustrated.   Oak Knoll Books   306 - 62   2015 $125

Updike, John   1932-2009 *Bath After Sailing.* Stevenson: Country Squire, 1968. Limited edition, #43 of 125 numbered copies signed by author, slightest hint of edge sunning, else fine in saddle stitched cardstock covers.   Ken Lopez, Bookseller   164 - 211   2015 $450

Updike, John   1932-2009 *Bech: a Book.* New York: Alfred A. Knopf, 1970. First edition, ine in fine dust jacket, inscribed by author for Susan Sheehan.   Between the Covers Rare Books, Inc.   187 - 283   2015 $950

Updike, John   1932-2009 *"A Conversation with John Updike." in The Idol.* Schenecdaty: Union College, 1971. Printed as a special issue of "The Idol", fine in glossy stapled wrappers with pencil sketch of author on cover, this copy inscribed by Updike, uncommon, scarce signed.   Ken Lopez, Bookseller   164 - 212   2015 $375

Updike, John   1932-2009 *Couples: a Short Story.* Cambridge: Halty Ferguson, 1976. Of a total edition of 276, this #16 of 250 numbered copies, signed by author, fine in wrappers, inscribed by author, with brief signed note by Updike on prospectus, what hand addressed mailing envelope.   Ken Lopez, Bookseller   164 - 214   2015 $500

Updike, John   1932-2009 *Ego and Art in Walt Whitman.* New York: Targ Editions, 1980. First edition, fine in fine, unprinted dust jacket, one of 350 copies, signed by author, inscribed by author to publisher William Targ.   Between the Covers Rare Books, Inc.   187 - 284   2015 $150

Updike, John 1932-2009 *A Good Place.* N.P.: Aloe, 1973. Lettered issue, early limited edition, this copy W of 26 lettered copies, signed by author, fine in saddle stitched wrappers.   Ken Lopez, Bookseller   164 - 213   2015 $550

Updike, John 1932-2009 *Hoping for a Hoopoe.* London: Victor Gollancz, 1959. First English edition, fine in fine dust jacket with very light wear, inscribed by author to Alfred A. Knopf.   Between the Covers Rare Books, Inc.   187 - 280   2015 $5000

Updike, John 1932-2009 *January.* Concord: W. B. Ewert, 1997. First edition, 1 of 10 ad personam 'gold thread' copies, signed by author, printed on special paper at Firefly Press, with reproduction of Thomas Bewick engraving, as new in wrappers.   Gemini Fine Books & Arts, Ltd. Art Reference & Illustrated Books: First Editions - 2015 $250

Updike, John 1932-2009 *January.* Concord: W. B. Ewert, 1997. First edition, number 11 of 40 'red thread' copies signed by author, printed on special paper at Firefly Press and illustrated with reproduction from Thomas Bewick engraving, as new in wrappers.   Gemini Fine Books & Arts, Ltd.   Art Reference & Illustrated Books: First Editions - 2015 $140

Updike, John 1932-2009 *The John Updike Newsletter.* Northridge: Herb Yellin/Lord John Press, 1977-1980. 1992, 16 consecutive issues (with 11 year hiatus between Number 14 and Number 15), complete run, issue 1 has tiny edge crease, issue 16 has annotation in hand of bookseller, double issue number 11 and 12 does have 3 page insert "The Coup" laid in, issue number 2 does not contain laid in broadside 'Raining at Magens Bay', otherwise lot is fine.   Ken Lopez, Bookseller   164 - 218   2015 $1000

Updike, John 1932-2009 *The Music School.* New York: Alfred A. Knopf, 1966. First edition, 2nd state with pages 45-46 as a cancel, slight printer's paper flaw, else fine in dust jacket with offsetting on front panel, otherwise fine, inscribed by author to Susan and Neil Sheehan.   Between the Covers Rare Books, Inc.   187 - 282   2015 $1500

Updike, John 1932-2009 *The Poorhouse Fair.* New York: Alfred A. Knopf, 1959. First edition, one corner slightly bumped, else fine in fine dust jacket, inscribed by author for Susan Sheehan.   Between the Covers Rare Books, Inc.   187 - 271   2015 $3000

Updike, John 1932-2009 *Rabbit, Run.* New York: Fawcett, Fifth edition or later edition, signed 11/7/91, very good+ (repaired upper corner break), signed by author.   Stephen Lupack   March 2015 - 2015 $60

Updike, John 1932-2009 *Radiators.* Concord: W. B/ Ewert, 1998. One of 15 ad personam copies, first edition, signed by author, printed on special paper at Firefly Press, as new in wrappers.   Gemini Fine Books & Arts, Ltd.   Art Reference & Illustrated Books: First Editions - 2015 $275

Updike, John 1932-2009 *Roger's Version.* Franklin Center: Franklin Library, 1986. First edition, limited edition, signed by author, full leather, raised bands, gilt spine titles, elaborate gilt designs to front and rear covers, all edges gilt, ribbon place marker sewn in, marbled endpapers with the FL letter laid in, very fine.   Stephen Lupack   March 2015 - 2015 $100

Updike, John 1932-2009 *S.* New York: Knopf, 1988. First edition, 338 of 350 copies signed by author, fine in acetate and slipcase.   Gemini Fine Books & Arts, Ltd.   Art Reference & Illustrated Books: First Editions - 2015 $125

Upfield, Arthur W. *The Battling Prophet.* London: Heinemann, 1956. First edition, fine in price clipped dust jacket with short closed tear.   Mordida Books   March 2015 - 009991   2015 $150

Upfield, Arthur W. *The Battling Prospect.* London: William Heinemann, 1956. First edition, former owner's inked name on front flyleaf, else fine in dust jacket with light wear to corners.   Buckingham Books   March 2015 - 36324   2015 $185

Upfield, Arthur W. *The Body at Madman's Bend.* London: Heinemann, 1963. First US edition, light foxing to fore-edges and few front and rear end pages, else very good in price clipped dust jacket.   Buckingham Books   March 2015 - 33714   2015 $200

Upfield, Arthur W. *Bony and the Black Virgin.* London: Heinemann, 1959. First edition, name on front endpaper and top of page edges lightly spotted, otherwise fine in dust jacket with lightly soiled back panel and couple of short closed tears.   Mordida Books   March 2015 - 009994   2015 $100

Upfield, Arthur W. *The Murchison Murders.* Miami Beach: Dennis McMillan, 1987. First US edition, limited to 600 copies, reprint of very scarce paperback original, fine in dust jacket.   Buckingham Books   March 2015 - 36173   2015 $250

Upfield, Arthur W. *The Mystery of Swordfish Reef.* Garden City: Doubleday Crime Club, 1943. First American edition, very good in dust jacket with half inch piece missing top of spine, chipping at base of spine, at corners and along edges, internal tape, numerous short close tears, wear along folds.   Mordida Books   March 2015 - 011488   2015 $80

Upfield, Arthur W. *The Mystery of the Swordfish Reef.* London: Heinemann, 1960. First UK edition, fine in price clipped dust jacket with very minor wear to foot of spine. Buckingham Books   March 2015 - 36314   2015 $250

Upfield, Arthur W. *Wings Above the Claypan.* Garden City: Doubleday Crime Club, 1943. First American edition, very good, page edges slightly darkened, otherwise fine in very good dust jacket with internal tape, slightly faded spine, chipping at top of spine and atop edge of front panel, several short closed tears.   Mordida Books   March 2015 - 011493   2015 $250

Upham, Charles Wentworth *Life Explorations and Public Services of John Charles Fremont.* Boston: Ticknor & Fields, 1856. First edition, 14 wood engravings, including frontispiece and Kit Carson plate which is not bound in all copies, original blindstamped cloth, plain, early private owner bookplate on pastedown, very good, little light spotting to boards, little shelfwear, clean, tight text, nice gilt titles.   Stephen Lupack   March 2015 - 2015 $125

Upham, Thomas C. *Elements of Mental Philosophy.* Boston: 1833. Second edition, 2 volumes in 1, original linen, paper spine label, neatly rebacked with original spine laid down, modern (but appropriate) endpapers, scattered foxing, else nice.   Joseph J. Felcone Inc.   Science, Medicine and Technology - 53   2015 $250

Upham, Thomas C. *Outlines of Imperfect and Disordered mental Action.* New York: Harper & Brothers, 1840. First edition, 12mo., original cloth some spine wear, with Haskell Norman bookplate.   M & S Rare Books, Inc.   97 - 307   2015 $600

Upritchard, Francis *Human Problems.* London: Veenman Pub./Gijs Stork, 2006. First edition, small 4to., 51 color plates, original dusky pink cloth lettered brown on spine, illustrations, fine in fine dust jacket.   Any Amount of Books   2015 - C4961   2015   £150

Upton, Bertha *Little Hearts.* London: George Routledge, 1897. First edition, 4to., cloth backed pictorial boards, some edge wear and slight bit of cover soil, very good+, illustrations in color by Florence Upton.   Aleph-bet Books, Inc.   109 - 469   2015 $1500

Upton, George P. *Woman in Music. An essay.* Chicago: McClurg, 1895. Fifth edition, 8vo., endpapers browned from newspaper previously laid in, very good, tight. Second Life Books Inc.   189 - 257   2015 $45

Urban, Sylvanus *The Gentleman's Magazine and Historical Chronicle.* London: Printed by Edward Cave At St. John's Gate, 1749. First edition, Volume XIX ofr the Year MDCCXLIX, 8vo., half leather with marbled boards, foldout plan, very used copy, rubbed and scuffed boards with cracked and split leather and neat inscription dated 1959, otherwise sound with complete text and plates.   Any Amount of Books   2015 - C15496   2015   £180

The Ursuline Manual or a Collection of Prayers, Spiritual Exercises etc. New York: Edward Dunigan, 1840. First American edition, thick 16mo., 520 pages, original gilt stamped calf with gilt stamped cross on front cover, all edges gilt.   M & S Rare Books, Inc.   97 - 309   2015 $275

Usher, James Ward *An Art Collector's Treasures, Illustrated and Described by Himself...* London: privately printed at the Chiswick Press, 1916. folio, one of 300 copies, original sumptuous burgundy leather lettered gilt on spine and on front cover with gilt decoration, faint mottling, otherwise about fine in original box now somewhat worn, exceptionally handsome, 80 illustrations in color.   Any Amount of Books   2015 - C14053   2015   £300

Utamaro *Songs of the Garden.* New York: Metropolitan Museum of Art, 1984. Fine, accordion binding, fine slipcase, beautiful book.   Stephen Lupack   March 2015 - 2015 $45

Utley, Robert M. *Billy the Kid. A Short and Violent Life.* Lincoln: University of Nebraska, 1989. First edition, 39 photo illustrations, 5 maps, gilt lettered cloth, very fine, as new, pictorial dust jacket.   Argonaut Book Shop   Holiday Season 2014 - 295   2015 $60

Utley, Robert M. *Cavalier in Buckskin. George Armstrong Custer and the Western Military Frontier.* Norman: University of Oklahoma Press, 1988. First edition, 45 illustrations, 8 maps, blue cloth, very fine with dust jacket. Argonaut Book Shop   Holiday Season 2014 - 296   2015 $45

Utley, Robert M. *Custer and Me.* Norman: University of Oklahoma Press, 2004. First edition, numerous photos, brown cloth, lettered in copper, paper label to front cover, very fine, pictorial dust jacket.   Argonaut Book Shop   Holiday Season 2014 - 297   2015 $50

Utley, Robert M. *High Noon in Lincoln, Violence on the Western Frontier.* Albuquerque: University of New Mexico Press, 1987. First edition, maps, portraits, cloth backed tan boards, very fine as new, pictorial dust jacket.   Argonaut Book Shop   Holiday Season 2014 - 298   2015 $90

Utley, Robert M. *The Indian Frontier of the American West 1846-1890.* Albuquerque: University of New Mexico Press, 1984. First edition, maps, black and white photos and illustrations, blue cloth backed boards, very fine, dust jacket. Argonaut Book Shop   Holiday Season 2014 - 299   2015 $45

Utley, Robert M. *The Lance and the Shield. The Life and Times of Sitting Bull.* New York: Henry Holt, 1993. First edition, 51 photo illustrations, cloth backed boards, very fine, as new with pictorial dust jacket, presentation inscription signed by author.   Argonaut Book Shop   Holiday Season 2014 - 300   2015 $75

Utley, Robert M. *The Last Days of the Sioux Nation.* New Haven and London: Yale University Press, 1963. First edition, scarce thus, review copy with review slip laid in, 24 photos, 5 maps, text illustrations, tan cloth printed in red, very fine, pictorial dust jacket, scarce thus.   Argonaut Book Shop   Holiday Season 2014 - 301   2015 $125

Utley, Robert M. *Lone Star Justice. The First Century of the Texas Rangers.* Oxford: Oxford University Press, 2002. First edition, cloth backed beige boards, very fine (as new), with pictorial dust jacket, photos, maps.   Argonaut Book Shop   Holiday Season 2014 - 302   2015 $60

Uttley, Alison *The Great Adventure of Hare.* London: William Heinemann, 1931. 8vo., boards, pictorial paste-on, fine, printed in blue on coated paper, 24 wonderful full page color illustrations and pictorial endpapers by Margaret Tempest, extremely rare in this condition.   Aleph-bet Books, Inc.   109 - 471   2015 $1200

V

Vache, Warren W. *Jazz Gentry. Aristocrats of the Music World.* Lanham: Rutgers: Scarecrow Press/Institute of Jazz Studies, 1999. First edition, inscribed by author, fine in fine dust jacket, 8vo.   Beasley Books   2013 - 2015 $45

Vachss, Andrew *Strega.* New York: Knopf, 1987. First edition, very fine in dust jacket, inscribed by author.   Mordida Books   March 2015 - 002213   2015 $90

Vail, R. W. G. *The Voice of the Old Frontier.* Philadelphia: University of Pennsylvania Press, 1949. First edition, dark green cloth gilt, fine.   Argonaut Book Shop   Holiday Season 2014 - 304   2015 $90

Vaillant-Couturier, Paul *The French Boy.* Philadelphia: J. B. Lippincott, 1931. First American edition, decorated cloth, near fine in near fine, very scarce dust jacket, illustrations, very scarce, jacket not price clipped but price is inked out.   Stephen Lupack   March 2015 - 2015 $125

Valdes, Mario J. *Literary Cultures of Latin America: a Comparative History.* Oxford: Oxford University Press, 2004. First edition, 3 volumes, 4to. original orange/red cloth, lettered blue and decorated gilt on spine and cover, illustrations.   Any Amount of Books   2015 - A96835   2015   £160

Valenti Angelo. the Man and the Artist. Concord: Heron House, 2010. First edition, quarto, 159 pages, profusely illustrated with photos, plates, facsimiles, line drawings, light blue blindstamped cloth, very fine.   Argonaut Book Shop   Holiday Season 2014 - 13   2015 $250

Valentine, Laura *Aunt Louisa's Gift Books. The Zoological Gardens.* Frederick Warne and Co., circa, 1882. 24 color plates, some foxing, 4to., original royal blue pictorial cloth gilt, spine lettered in black, front fly-leaf loosening, good.   Blackwell's Rare Books   B179 - 109   2015   £400

Valentiner, W. *Handwortebuch der Astronomie Unter Mitwurkung von Prof. Dr. E. Becker-Strassburg, et al...* Breslau: Eduard Trewendt, 1901. 8vo., illustrations, tables, charts, glossy green paper boards, gilt stamped spine title, extremities severely chipped, former library copy with usual markings and defects, good+.   Jeff Weber Rare Books   178 - 1084   2015 $85

Valeriano, Giovanni Pierio *Hieroglyphica Sive de Sacris Aegyptiorvm Literis Commentarii... A Caelio Augustino Curione Duobus Libris Aucti et Multis Imaginibus Illustrati.* Basileae: Per Thomam Guarinum, 1567. Second edition, 362 x 235mm., excellent contemporary blindstamped pigskin, covers with multiple frames of palmettes, rosettes, floral rolls, and an allegorical roll depicting Fides, Justitia, Caritas and Spes, raised bands, traces of ink titling to spine, intact original brass clasps, small hole at head of rear board where a chain was once attached; woodcut printer's device on title and last page, frontispiece, 12 charts in text, 265 mostly emblematic illustrations, (18th century?) engraved armorial bookplate and 19th century woodcut bookplate of William Schott, titlepage with two early (probably 17th century) inscriptions from monastery library at Kaisersheim; very minor soiling to pigskin, small area of discoloration at top of back board (where chain hasp had been located), front hinge beginning to open at top, final few leaves with minor traces of mildew, barely perceptible diagonal dampstain at upper corner on a number of text leaves, other trivial imperfections, nearly fine contemporary copy, unrestored binding showing almost no signs of use, text bright, clean and fresh with spacious margins.   Phillip J. Pirages   66 - 19   2015 $7500

Valeriano, Giovanni Pierio *Hieroglyphica sive de Sacris Aegyptorum Aliarumque Gentium Literis Commentariorum libri LVIII.* Frankfurt: C. Kirkchner, 1678. Excellent late edition, 2 parts in 1 volume, 4to., fine engraved portrait frontispiece, printers devices, 286 text woodcuts.   Maggs Bros. Ltd.   Illustrated Books 2014 - 2015   £1800

Valin, Jonathan *Final Notice.* New York: Dodd Mead, 1980. First edition, very fine in dust jacket.   Mordida Books   March 2015 - 009190   2015 $125

Vallotton, Felix *Crimes et Chatiments.* Paris: Mars, 1902. First edition, numero special, cover and 22 full page lithographs printed rectos only by Vallotton, quarto, wrappers, with the Sotheby's catalog of the Vallotton Collection sold in Zurich on 4 June 1997 and which included original trial proofs of Crimes, covers chipped and soiled at edges, small marginal tears not affecting images, very good, very fragile, very scarce.   Peter Ellis, Bookseller   2014 - 998812   2015   £350

Valmont, Victor *The Prussian Spy.* London: Tinsley Bros., 1871. First edition, 2 volumes, half titles, much of text block of vclume I has been heavily creased at some time, original blue cloth, boards and spines blocked in black, spines lettered gilt, apart from slight signs of removal of small labels to spines, nice, bright copy.   Jarndyce Antiquarian Booksellers   CCXI - 277   2015   £280

Valotaire, Marcel *Carlegle. Les Artistes Du Livre.* Paris: Henry Babou, 1928. First edition, number 133 of 650 copies, unbound signatures laid into wrappers, fine in near fine glassine, folds of the glassine have been reinforced on inside corners (without offsetting) but rear wrapper shows small strip of sunning at fore-edge, still lovely copy, color and black and white illustrations, vignettes and devices, type fonts by Carlegle and more, small 4to.   Beasley Books   2013 - 2015 $150

Valpey, F. B. *The Art of Lettering for the Use of Architects, Civil Engineers, Draughtsmen, Designers, Illuminators, Marble Workers and the Decorative Artist.* Lynn: F. B. Valpey, circa, 1890. Oblong small 8vo., original quarter cloth, paper covered boards, unpaginated, boards soiled and worn at edges, free endpapers detached, hinges cracked.   Oak Knoll Books   Special Catalogue 24 - 58   2015 $295

Van Buren, Martin *Plan of a Standing Army of 200,000 Men Submitted to Congress by the Secretary of War and Recommended by the President of the United States, Washington May 26, 1840.* Washington: D. C. Gideon, 1850. First edition, 8vo, 16 pages, sewn as issued, later thread, old folds and few spots of foxing, overall fairly crisp copy.   M & S Rare Books, Inc.   97 - 310   2015 $225

Van De Wetering, Jan Willem *Robert Van Gulik. His Life His work.* Miami Beach: Dennis Macmillan Publications, 1987. First edition, limited to 350 copies, each signed and numbered by author, this #173, fine in dust jacket.   Buckingham Books   March 2015 - 36284   2015 $450

Van Denburgh, John *The Reptiles of Western North America...* San Francisco: California Academy of Sciences, 1922. Quarto, 2 volumes, 1028 pages, photo, publisher's printed wrappers, uncut, partly unopened, all housed in two matching fleece lined quarter green morocco folding solander boxes, superb set.   Andrew Isles   2015 - 8370   2015 $1500

Van Denburgh, Mary T. *Ye On's Ten Hundred Sorrows and Other Stories.* San Francisco: Murdock Press, 1907. First edition, 8vo., original decorated yellow wrappers with silk ties, vignettes in text, wrappers little worn, some slight foxing, very good.   The Brick Row Book Shop   Miscellany 67 - 32   2015 $425

Van Deusen, Delia *Murder Bicarb.* Indianapolis: Bobbs Merrill, 1940. First edition, pages slightly darkened, otherwise fine in dust jacket, nicks at spine ends, several short closed tears and tiny wear at corners.   Mordida Books   March 2015 - 002223   2015 $75

Van Dyck, Leonard B. *Remarks on Liberty of Conscience, Human Creeds, and Theological Schools, Suggested by the Facts in Recent Case.* New York: printed by J. & J. Harper, 1828. First edition, 8vo. 102 pages, later wrappers, very good.   John Drury Rare Books   2015 - 14722   2015 $133

Van Dyke, Henry *The Tragedy of Little Red Tom: a Contribution to the Fight About Nature Books.* San Diego: Ash Ranch Press, 1988. Limited to 26 numbered copies and 26 lettered and signed by printer, 5.1 x 6.6cm., leather, title and author gilt stamped on spine, edges uncut, cloth slipcase, title and author gilt stamped on spine, miniature bookplate of Kathryn Rickard on front pastedown.   Oak Knoll Books   306 - 122   2015 $150

Van Engelen, Piet *Where's the Music. A Discography of Kai Winding.* Amsterdam: Micrography, 1985. First edition, paperback, wrappers, 2 volumes, near fine.   Beasley Books   2013 - 2015 $40

Van Gieson, Judith *The Other Side of Death.* New York: Harper Collins, 1991. First edition, very fine in dust jacket, signed by author.   Mordida Books   March 2015 - 002232   2015 $75

Van Gulik, Robert *The Chinese Maze Murders.* W. Van Hoeve, 1956. True first edition, fine, bright copy, dust jacket very slightly tanned at spine panel.   Buckingham Books   March 2015 - 34200   2015 $1250

Van Gulik, Robert *Chinese Pictorial Art as Viewed by the Connoisseur...* Rome: Instituto Itaiano per Il Mediio Ed Estremo Oriente, 1958. First edition, one of 950 numbered copies, 160 illustrations, 42 paper samples mounted in separate booklet housed in rear pocket, spine slightly foxed, else fine, from the collection of Duke Collier.   Royal Books   36 - 241   2015 $1500

Van Gulik, Robert *The Emperor's Pearl.* London: Heinemann, 1963. First edition, fine in dust jacket, lightly sunned on spine.   Buckingham Books   March 2015 - 34199   2015 $275

Van Gulik, Robert *Vier Vingers. (Four Fingers).* Amsterdam: Netherlands Society, 1964. First edition, fine in soft covers with short crease at corner and tiny wear at corners.   Mordida Books   March 2015 - 009556   2015 $100

Van Gulik, Robert *The Monkey and the Tiger.* London: Heinemann, 1965. First English edition, name and address stamped on front endpaper, otherwise near fine in dust jacket with some tiny tears and wear.   Mordida Books   March 2015 - 001487   2015 $90

Van Gulik, Robert *Necklace and Calabash.* London: Heinemann, 1967. First English edition, fine in dust jacket. Mordida Books   March 2015 - 009557   2015 $125

Van Gulik, Robert *Necklace and Calabash.* London: Heinemann, 1967. First edition, fine in dust jacket, minor professional restoration to head of spine.   Buckingham Books   March 2015 - 26979   2015 $275

Van Gulik, Robert *Poets and Murder.* London: Heinemann, 1968. First English edition, name and date on verso of front endpaper, otherwise fine in dust jacket, lightly rubbed jacket with tiny wear at corners.   Mordida Books   March 2015 - 002236   2015 $90

Van Gulik, Robert *Sexual Life in Ancient China.* Leiden: E. J. Brill, 1961. First edition, nearly 400 over-sized pages, heavily illustrated with plates and drawings, small rubber stamp front endpaper, waterstains to covers, else very good in chipped, about very good dust jacket with some staining to verso, from the collection of Duke Collier.   Royal Books   36 - 242   2015 $650

Van Gundy, John C. *Reminiscences of Frontier Life on the Upper Neosho in 1855 and 1856.* Topeka: 1925. First issue with no place of publication stated, 41 pages, illustrations, original printed wrappers, near fine.   Dumont Maps & Books of the West   131 - 32   2015 $100

Van Lier, J. *Verhandeling Over de Slangen en Adders Die in Het Landschap Drenthe.* Amsterdam: Erven Houtuin, 1781. Quarto, uncolored engraved half title, 3 hand colored engraved plates, contemporary boards and red calf spine with all edges uncut and colored, superb copy, modern Solander box, rare.   Andrew Isles   2015 - 32211   2015 $6000

Van Rensselaer, Marianna Griswold *Henry Hobson Richardson and His Works.* Park Forest: Prairie School Press, 1967. Reprint of 1888 edition, folio, illustrations, plates, cloth, fine.   Joseph J. Felcone Inc.   Science, Medicine and Technology - 7   2015 $100

Van Vechten, Carl 1880-1964 *Nigger Heaven.* New York: Avon, 1951. First paperback edition, lamination starting to peel, little wear on rear wrapper, else bright and fresh, near fine.   Between the Covers Rare Books   197 - 49   2015 $75

Van Waters, George *The Poetical Geography.* Cincinnati: 1852. 80 pages, unusually nice copy, yellow wrappers intact save for chip to lower free corner (ditto 1st five leaves), old staining lower free corner, diminishing through the first 35 pages, ditto upper bound corner of rear, half page map, 2 woodcuts half page each.   Bookworm & Silverfish   2015 - 3318954228   2015 $175

Vance, Jack *The Dying Earth.* Hillman Periodicals, 1950. First edition, 16mo., signed by author, scarce paperback original, pictorial wrappers, light creasing to front panel, else near fine.   Buckingham Books   March 2015 - 34056   2015 $275

Vance, Joel *Fats Waller. His Life and Times.* Chicago: CBI, 1977. First edition, fine in very slightly soiled dust jacket.   Beasley Books   2013 - 2015 $45

Vance, John Holbrook *The Deadly Isles.* Bobbs Merrill Co., 1969. First edition, fine in dust jacket with black ink panel bottom front panel, lightly rubbed.   Buckingham Books   March 2015 - 29884   2015 $200

Vance, Louis Joseph *The Lone Wolf Returns.* New York: Dutton, 1923. First edition, small bump on front edge of front cover, otherwise fine in very good dust jacket (chipped spine ends, several closed tears, nicks along spine fold and at corners).   Mordida Books   March 2015 - 008906   2015 $175

Vance, Louis Joseph *Sheep's Clothing.* Boston: Little Brown and Co., 1915. First edition, former owner's bookplate, else fine, bright copy, dust jacket with light professional restoration to spine ends, corners and extremities, illustrations by James Montgomery Flagg.   Buckingham Books   March 2015 - 33037   2015 $750

Vance, Louis Joseph *The Street of Strange Faces.* Philadelphia: Lippincott, 1934. First edition, file copy stamps front endpaper and bottom of pages, fine in very good dust jacket with slightly darkened spine and chipping top of spine on back panel and at corners.   Mordida Books   March 2015 - 002221   2015 $75

Vanishing Pictures: a Novel Picture Book wih Diaramic Effects. London: Nister, n.d. circa, 1890. 4to., cloth backed pictorial boards, very good-fine, 6 round chromolithographed pages with ribbon ties, upper illustration revolves to reveal a new illustration below, also illustrated in brown line.   Aleph-Bet Books, Inc.   108 - 308   2015 $900

Vargas, Alberto *Vargas.* New York: Harmony Books, 1978. First edition, 4to., signed on half title by Vargas, fine in near fine dust jacket, 200 illustrations.   Ed Smith Books   83 - 111   2015 $175

Varin, Amedee *Les Papillons.* Paris: Gabriel de Gonet, 1852. 2 volumes, 4to., 35 hand colored engraved plates, some spotting as usual, tissue guards, more heavily foxed in places, contemporary red morocco backed cloth, spine in compartments, lettered and decorated in gilt, gilt edges. Marlborough Rare Books   List 54 - 88   2015   £1950

Varmus, Harold *The Art and Politics of Science.* New York: W. W. Norton, 2009. First edition, signed, inscribed and dated by author, 8vo., fine in near fine dust jacket.   By the Book, L. C.   Special List 10 - 88   2015 $250

Vaucher, J. B. *Apologie Des Dames de France au Dix-Neuvieme Siecle.* Paris: Desloges, 1855. First edition, 8vo., original printed wrappers, untrimmed, rare.   Second Life Books Inc.   189 - 259   2015 $250

Vegetarian Society England *The Vegetist's Dietary and Manual of Vegetable Cookery.* Manchester: Vegetarian Society, 1888. Eighth edition, 16th thousand, final ad, original green cloth, dulled and marked, contemporary signature on title.   Jarndyce Antiquarian Booksellers   CCXI - 278   2015   £55

Veillard, Regens *Du College de Geneve.* Geneva: Manget et Cherbuliez, 1821. 8vo., few minor tears and and patches of light browning, recent plain wrappers, good copy.   John Drury Rare Books   2015 - 17867   2015 $115

Veitch, Tom *Literary Days.* New York: "C" Press, 1964. First edition, 4to., mimeographed and stapled in wrappers, some very light dust soil, fine, presentation copy from author to publisher Lorenz Gude.   James S. Jaffe Rare Books   Many Happy Returns - 367   2015 $850

Veitch, Tom *Literary Days.* New York: Lorenz & Ellen Gude, 1964. First edition, one of 200 numbered copies signed by Veitch, 4to, original printed wrappers, stapled as issued, lightly dust soiled, otherwise fine.   James S. Jaffe Rare Books   Many Happy Returns - 366   2015 $250

Velde, Jan Van Den *Spieghel der Schrijfkonste in den Welcken Ghesien Worden Veelderhande Gheschirften emt Hare Fondementen Ende Onderrichtinghe.* Nieuwkoop: Miland, 1969. Facsimile reprint of 1605 edition, limited to 300 numbered copies, oblong 4to., paper wrappers, slipcase tape repaired along edges, 75 plates.   Oak Knoll Books   306 - 243   2015 $195

Venn, John *Symbolic Logic.* London: Macmillan and Co., 1881. First edition, octavo, original burgundy cloth, gilt lettered spine, front board is discolored with lighter spots around edges and similarly but much less so on the rear board, former owner's names to top right corner of half title and one owner's name (Harold Sprague) at top of titlepage, otherwise clean and tight copy.   Athena Rare Books   15 - 56   2015 $700

Vercel, Roger *Jean Villemeur.* Paris: Editions du Trefle, 1946. Number 687 of 750 copies, unbound signatures laid into wrappers, near fine with tiny bit of waviness to plates, in board chemise with barely sunned spine, very good+ box, small 4to., 12 plates and 33 in text illustrations by D. Charles Fouqueray.   Beasley Books   2013 - 2015 $150

Vercors *Tapiesseries De Jean Lurcat.* Belves: Pierre Vorms, 1957. Deluxe edition, limited to 100 copies signed on colophon and with original signed color lithograph, our copy has signed lithograph and is signed on colophon and marked HC, book near fine with small stain at foot of spine in near fine box, 4to.   Beasley Books   2013 - 2015 $400

Vergilius Maro, Publius *The Aeneis of Virgil.* London: printed in the year, 1718. First edition translated by Joseph Trapp, 2 volumes, 4to., contemporary calf, spines gilt, contrasting red and black morocco labels, spines bit worn, joints slightly cracked, frontispiece in volume 1 was engraved by B. Baron after design by Joseph Goupy, plate in second volume unsigned, engraved headpieces, tailpieces and initial letters, good copy.   C. R. Johnson   Foxon R-Z - 1031r-z   2015 $613

Vergilius Maro, Publius *Antiquissimi Virgilliani Codicis Fragmenta et Picturae ex Bibliotheca Vaticana.* Rome: ex Chalcographia R. C. A. Apud Pedem Marmoreum, 1741. First printed edition of Verglilius Vaticanus, engraved titlepage, bit dusty, 61 further engravings within letterpress, some spotting and staining (mostly marginal), few corners touched by damp, contemporary half calf, marbled boards, red morocco lettering piece, rubbed, some wear to extremities and particularly to marbled paper, edges untrimmed, bookplate of William Markham of Becca Lodge.   Blackwell's Rare Books   Greek & Latin Classics VI - 108   2015   £1500

Vergilius Maro, Publius *Publii Virgilii Maronis Bucolica et Georgica tabulis Aeneis olim a Johanne Pine...* n.p., 1774. 2 volumes bound as one, 80 plates on 59 sheets, 6 engraved dedications, frequent further engravings within text, ad leaf discarded, 8vo., contemporary marbled calf, spine divided by gilt fillet, red morocco lettering piece, other compartments with central sunburst gilt tools, bit rubbed, spine creased, gutters cracking towards middle of textblock but binding perfectly sound, bookplates of Magdalen College, Oxford and Sir Richard Paul Jodrell with inscription indicating gift of the volume from former to latter, dated 1802, good.   Blackwell's Rare Books   Greek & Latin Classics VI - 109   2015   £800

Vergilius Maro, Publius *Bucolica, Georgica, et Aeneis...* Oxford: Impensis N. Bliss, 1812. 32mo., foxed in places, 2 volumes, untrimmed in original terra cotta paper boards backed in light green paper, printed paper spine labels, backstrips darkened and creased, little rubbed, very good, rare.   Blackwell's Rare Books   Greek & Latin Classics VI - 111   2015   £200

Vergilius Maro, Publius *Les Bucoliques.* Paris: Editions Galatea, 1946. No. 19 of 20 copies with two extra suites and 2 original drawings, from an edition of 220, 3 volumes, 2 of which are extra suites, one in black and one in red, illustrations by Rene Dumeurisse, fine in wrappers and glassine, with little spine darkening and mild wear to glassines, board chemise 4 inches thick, in slipcase that shows some soiling and staining, folio.   Beasley Books   2013 - 2015 $750

Vergilius Maro, Publius *Georgica et Aeneis.* A. Dulau & Co. Printed by T. Bensley, 1800. 15 engravings, occasional light foxmark, bit more so to plates, large 8vo., contemporary diced russia, boards bordered with gilt roll, spine divided by decorative gilt roll, second and fifth compartments gilt lettered direct, rest with elaborate gilt tools, extremities little rubbed, three small patches of surface abrasion to lower corners of boards, few marks, armorial bookplate of Richard Mann, very good.   Blackwell's Rare Books   Greek & Latin Classics VI - 110   2015   £300

Vergilius Maro, Publius *Georgica Publii Virgilii Maronis Hexaglotta.* E Typographeo Gulielmi Nicol, 1827. Presentation copy from English translator & printer, inscribed "for the library of the Royal Institution from William Sotheby 12 Grosvenor Street, Feby. 19 1833". a letter from the printer presenting the volume tipped in, text in six languages, some light dust soiling, imperial 4to., contemporary half purple roan over marbled boards, edges untrimmed, spine divided by triple gilt fillets, second compartment gilt lettered direct, rubbed, extremities worn, front hinge cracking after title, rare flyleaf removed, 'withdrawn' stamp on front pastedown, good.   Blackwell's Rare Books   Greek & Latin Classics VI - 113   2015   £1000

Vergilius Maro, Publius *The Works of Virgil.* London: printed for Jacob Tonson, 1697. First edition, first issue, large paper copy, engraved frontispiece and 102 engraved plates, light dampmark to fore-edge throughout with some resultant purple spotting to lower corner, frontispiece and couple of other plates with short tears and old repairs in that corner, one plate just shaved at fore-edge, some spotting and soiling, folio, 18th century reversed calf, red morocco lettering piece, rubbed, worn at extremities, front joint cracked, gutter cracking in few places, sound.   Blackwell's Rare Books   Greek & Latin Classics VI - 107   2015   £2000

Vergilius, Polydorus *Proverbiorum Libellus.* colophon: Venice: per Ioannem de Cereto de Tridino alias Tacunum, 1503. Rare and early edition, roughly half the gatherings browned, some light spotting, frequent marginal notes and underlinings in early hand (some shaved), recto of final leaf dusty, 4to., modern boards covered with incunable leaf, lightly soiled and spotted, good.   Blackwell's Rare Books   B179 - 110   2015   £2000

Verini, Giovam Baptista *Luminario or the Third Chapter of the Liber Elementorum Litterarum on the Construction of Roman Capitals.* Cambridge and Chicago: Harvard College Library and The Newberry Library, 1947. First edition thus, limited to 500 copies, this one of the 360 on wove paper, 4to, cloth, slipcase shows some wear around edges, book is very fine with most of glassine wrapper preserved, beautifully illustrated.   Oak Knoll Books   306 - 244   2015 $125

Verlaine, Paul 1844-1896 *Parallelement.* Paris: Leon Vanier, 1889. First edition, one of 600 copies, 8vo., modern dark green leather and marbled boards, lettered gilt at spine, excellent condition with clean text.   Any Amount of Books   2015 - A76718   2015   £280

Vermont, Marquis De *London and Paris; or Comparative Sketches.* London: Printed for Longman, Hurst, Rees Orme, Brown and Green, 1823. First edition, 8vo., 19th century red half morocco, marbled paper sides with matching endpapers and edges, black labels, gilt decorations and lettering, edges somewhat rubbed, very good.   The Brick Row Book Shop   Miscellany 67 - 94   2015 $400

Verne, Jules 1828-1905 *The Archipelago on Fire.* London: Sampson Low Marston and Co., n.d., about, 1910. New edition, 8vo., original red pictorial cloth, covers faintly tanned, otherwise very good+.   Any Amount of Books   2015 - A67385   2015   £240

Verne, Jules 1828-1905 *The Castaways of the Flag.* London: Sampson Low, Marston & Co., 1923. First UK edition, 8vo., pages 242, original publisher's pictorial cloth, lettered black on spine and cover, illustrations, including frontispiece, neat name & school stamp on front endpaper, slight rubbing at spine ends, hinges & edges, otherwise clean, very good.   Any Amount of Books   2015 - C3516   2015   £700

Verne, Jules 1828-1905 *For the Flag.* London: Sampson Low Marston and Co., 1897. First edition, original printed brown cloth lettered gilt on spine and cover, exceptional bright clean fresh, very good copy, but lacks 6 plates.   Any Amount of Books   2015 - A67381   2015   £240

Verne, Jules 1828-1905 *Martin Paz.* London: Sampson Low Marston, Searle & Rivington, 1876. Yellowback edition, binder's cloth, half title, frontispiece.   Jarndyce Antiquarian Booksellers   CCXI - 279   2015   £65

Verne, Jules 1828-1905 *The Master of the World: a Tale of Mystery and Marvel.* London: Sampson Low Marston & Co., n.d. but known to be, 1914. First edition, 8vo., original pictorial green cloth, lettered gilt on spine and light blue on front cover, illustrations complete, including frontispiece, white paint spots on spine and top of hinge area, neat purple inkstamp "Thacker Spink & Co.", rubbing and slight scuffing at edges, otherwise about sound, clean, very good.   Any Amount of Books   2015 - C3517   2015   £750

Verne, Jules 1828-1905 *Michael Strogoff.* New York: Charles Scribners Sons, 1927. First edition, 4to., black cloth, pictorial paste-on, fine in publisher's box with pictorial label pasted on (box slightly rubbed, else near fine), illustrations by N. C. Wyeth, magnificent copy, rarely found in box. Aleph-bet Books, Inc.   109 - 497   2015 $1350

Verne, Jules 1828-1905 *Tempete et Calme. Poeme de Jules Verne.* Octon: Verdigris Press, 2004. One of 38 copies only, all on Hahnemuhle paper, each copy hand numbered and signed by artist, Judith Rothchild, the artist and Mark Lintott, the printer, page size 11 3/4 x 5 15/16 inches, 4 leaves + colophon printed on gray paper mounted on inside rear cover, bound by Lintott Leporello style, but on vertical, original screen prints by Judith Rohchild in subtle shades of gray on front and back boards with gray silk ribbon pull at bottom of front board, housed in publisher's clamshell box of gray paper title printed in black on front panel, lined with screen prints by Rothchild in shades of gray, fine.   Priscilla Juvelis - Rare Books   61 - 55   2015 $750

Verne, Jules 1828-1905 *Works of Jules Verne.* New York: London: Vincent Parke & Co., 1911. Prince Edward of Wales Edition, Large octavo, 15 volumes, numerous inserted plates, each with printed tissue guard, additional hand colored frontispiece in volume 1, original red cloth, spine panels stamped in gold, top edge gilt, fore-edges untrimmed, bottom edges rough trimmed.   L. W. Currey, Inc. Boy's Adventure Fiction 2015 - 1   2015 $2500

Verrill, Alpheus Hyatt *The Golden City: a tale of adventure in Unknown Guiana.* New York: Duffield & Co., 1916. First edition, frontispiece, original brown cloth, front and spine panels stamped in yellow.   L. W. Currey, Inc. Boy's Adventure Fiction 2015 - 65   2015 $150

Vertue, George *Anecdotes of Painting in England: with Some Account of the Principal Artists: and Incidental Notes on Other Arts.* London: Printed for J. Dodsley, 1782. Third editions, volume 4 is second edition, 4 volumes, full tree calf decorated gilt at spine, text clean and complete, boards somewhat worn and loose, good, bookplate of Sir Claude Alexander and his neat ownership signature dated 1828. Any Amount of Books   2015 - A62201   2015   £180

Vertue, George *Prints. King Charles I and the Heads of the Noble Earls, Lords and Others who Suffered for Their Loyalty in the... Civil Wars of England.* printed for J. Ryall and R. Withy, 1757. Folio, frontispiece, 1 engraved plates, Hull City Libraries accession stamp to verso of title and their blindstamp in the upper blank margins of all leaves, two small (?worm) holes in first four leaves not affecting text but with slight loss to the hair of James I, titlepage a little dust soiled, modern (not new) morocco backed boards, lettered gilt on spine including library shelf mark, spine faded and little rubbed, good.   Blackwell's Rare Books   B179 - 111   2015   £600

Vervliet, Hendrik *Cyrillic & Oriental Typography in Rome at The End of the Sixteenth Century: an Inquiry into the Later Work of Robert Granjon (1578-1590).* Berkeley: Poltroom Press, 1981. Limited to 500 copies, half cloth over decorated paper covered boards, paper spine label, 31 illustrations in text.   Oak Knoll Books   306 - 309   2015 $250

Vesper, Will *Des Wiesenm'a'nnchens Brautfahrt.* Oldenburg: Stalling, 1932. First edition, 4to., cloth backed pictorial boards, slightest bit of edge rubbing, else near fine, beautiful color illustrations.   Aleph-bet Books, Inc.   109 - 299   2015 $300

Vestal, Stanley *Dobe Walls. A Story of Kit Carson's Southwest.* Houghton Mifflin, 1929. First edition, 8vo., cloth, titles in light blue ink on front cover and spine, some page edges carelessly opened, else very good, tight, square copy in dust jacket with chips to spine ends and corners and a closed tear to rear cover panel, uncommon title and especially so in elusive dust jacket.   Buckingham Books   March 2015 - 37994   2015 $875

Vetch, Thomas, Pseud. *The Amber City.* London: Biggs & Debenham, n.d., 1888. First edition, octavo, 8 inserted plates, full page map, original bevel edged purple cloth, front and spine panels stamped in gold, yellow coated endpapers. L. W. Currey, Inc.   Boy's Adventure Fiction 2015 - 20   2015 $450

Vicaire, Georges *Manuel de L'Amateur de Livres Du Xixe Siecle 1801-1893...* Teaneck: Somerset House, 1973. Reprint of first edition, 8 volumes in 1, folio, cloth, not paginated, duplicate from the Library of Congress, with small ink stamp stating this on free endpaper, head of spine bumped, some toning along edges of pages.   Oak Knoll Books   306 - 90   2015 $350

Vicars, John *Former Ages Never Heard Of, and After Ages Will Admire.* London: by M. S(immons) for Thomas Jenner, 1656. Third edition, small 4to., 13 engraved illustrations in text, fore-margin of title renewed and upper blank corner of A2 repaired, little soiled throughout, stain to centre of C3-4, lower inner margin browned and with heavy foxing to H3-4, late 19th century calf, gilt edges, joints rubbed, from the library of James Stevens Cox (1910-1997).   Maggs Bros. Ltd.   1447 - 99   2015   £375

Vickers, Roy *The Department of Dead Ends.* New York: Lawrence E. Spivak, 1947. First edition, digest sized PBO, ink mark to front cover, else very good in pictorial wrappers. Buckingham Books   March 2015 - 24390   2015 $175

Vickers, Roy *The Department of Dead Ends.* New York: Lawrence E. Spivak, 1947. First edition, digest sized PO, very good in pictorial wrappers.   Buckingham Books March 2015 - 36168   2015 $225

Vickers, Roy *The Department of Dead Ends.* London: Faber and Faber, 1949. second of the two editions listed by Queen as Queen's Quorum 104, former owner's signature, lightly faded at spine ends, else very good in dust jacket with internal cellophane tape repairs, moderate wear to spine ends, chip to top edge of rear panel and to corner points.   Buckingham Books   March 2015 - 36167   2015 $300

Vicq, Enea *Augustarum Imagines...* Vinegia: 1558. Small 4to., engraved titlepage and 61 full page engravings (closed tear to one illustrations+, 103 medallion portraits, contemporary vellum, front hinge just little loose, with bookplate of Victor Albert George Villiers, Earl of Jersey, some light waterstain on upper inner margin, closed tear to one engraving, lacks five leaves of prelim matter (index and two leaves of errata in rear), but good, clear impression of engravings.   Second Life Books Inc.   189 - 260   2015 $1250

Victor Hammer, an Artist's Testament. Lexington: Anvil Press, 1988. First edition, limited to 200 copies, 4to., cloth, cardboard slipcase, printed in Dante types by Martino Mardersteig of Stamperia Valdonega.   Oak Knoll Books 306 - 153   2015 $200

Victoria Permanent Benefit Building Society *Rules of the Victoria Permanent Benefit Building Society. Established December 1855 Incorporated August 1882. Chief Office - 43 Piccadilly, Manchester.* Manchester: Charlton and Knowles, 1883. 8vo., 44 pages, intermittent minor foxing and rust marks, original printed wrappers, good copy.   John Drury Rare Books   2015 - 25346   2015 $89

Vidal, Gore *Death Likes it Hot.* London: Heinemann, 1955. First English edition, fine in dust jacket, lightly soiled back panel, tiny wear at spine ends and at corners, small chip on spine, signed by author.   Mordida Books   March 2015 - 008216   2015 $200

Vievar, Alexander *What is man?* London: printed for J. Buckland and sold by W. Meadows and R. Dodsley, 1738. First edition, 18 pages, folio, old dark grey paper wrappers (rather worn), scarce, half title present, but rather covered in pen trials, scribbles and ink splashes, small amount of scribbling elsewhere as well, including two ownership inscriptions of W. Parson, one of them dated 1742, somewhat dog eared, otherwise sound.   C. R. Johnson   Foxon R-Z - 1052r-z   2015 $536

A View of the Penal Laws Concerning Trade and Trafick, Alphabetically Disposed Under Proper Heads... London: printed by the assigns of Rich. and Edw. Atkins Esq. for John Walthoe at his shop in Middle Temple Cloysters, 1697. First edition, 12mo, very small piece torn from lower margin of pages 325/6 with loss of part of one word on verso, titlepage and few subsequent leaves stained at head, else very good, crisp copy, contemporary calf, sometime inelegantly rebacked and recornered, bookplate and ink stamps of Los Angeles board of Law Library, uncommon.   John Drury Rare Books   2015 - 26019   2015 $2622

Vigne, Jacques *Sure and Honest Means for the Conversion of All Hereticks; and Wholesome Advice and Expedients for the Reformation of the Church.* London: Randal Taylor, 1688. First edition, small 4to., imperfect printing with jump from page 72 to 81 with interruption of text, but no hiatus in sequence of signatures, recently bound in full tan buckram with spine lettered gilt, 20 century ownership tamp to front blank, very good.   Any Amount of Books 2015 - C7524   2015   £160

The Village Orphan; a tale for Youth. London: printed by C. Whittingham for Longman and Rees, 1797. 12mo., 25 woodcut vignettes and tailpieces, little bit of browning around edges, sporadic very minor staining, uncut in original pink boards, plain paper spine renewed, edges slightly worn, inscription at head of title 'J. St. J., Chelsea 1818', good, scarce.   Blackwell's Rare Books   B179 - 54   2015   £600

Villars, Nicolas Pierre Henri De Monfaucon, Abbe De *The Count of Gabalis of the Extravagant Mysteries of the Cabalists, Exposed in Five Pleasant Discourses on the Secret Sciences, done into English....* printed for B. M. Printer to the Cabalistical Society of the Sages, at the Sign of the Rosy-Crusian, 1680. First edition in English, few small stains, several leaves with short tear to blank margin, others with little white fungicide powder residue to fore-edge (but no mould or worming visible inside), 12mo., contemporary red morocco, boards, elaborately decorated with circle, flower and drawer handle tools, expertly rebacked to style, near invisibly, except that the colour has faded from newer leather, later marbled endpapers, hinges neatly relined, edges gilt, bookplate and ownership inscription of Hugh Morrison Davies to endpapers (dated 1900), very good. Blackwell's Rare Books   B179 - 112   2015   £1500

Viller, Frederick *The Black Tortoise.* London: Heinemann, 1901. First English edition, front endpaper replaced, otherwise very good in tan pictorial cloth covered boards with black titles.   Mordida Books   March 2015 - 002252   2015 $85

Villon, Francois *The Poems of.* Boston: Houghton Mifflin, 1977. First edition, fine in trifle dust soiled, otherwise fine dust jacket, inscribed by Galway Kinnell to fellow poet Jane (Cooper).   Between the Covers Rare Books, Inc. 187 - 147   2015 $250

Vincent, Francis *A History of the State of Delaware from Its First Settlement Until the Present Time...* Philadelphia: John Campbell, 1870. First edition, rebound in cloth with gold stamping on spine and pages uncut, else fine. Buckingham Books   March 2015 - 19993   2015 $225

Vincent, William *A Defence of Public Education, Addressed to the Most Reverend the Lord Bishop of Meath...in Answer to a Charge Annexed to His Lordship's Discourse Preached at St. Paul's...* London: printed by A. Grahan for T. Cadell Jun. and W. Davies, 1802. 8vo., 48 pages, preserved in recent plain wrappers, good, crisp copy. John Drury Rare Books   2015 - 20574   2015 $106

Viollet Le Duc, Eugene *Encyclopedie Medievale I & II.* Inter-Livres, n.d., First edition, volumes I and II in single volume, bit shaken, very good+ in very good+ dust jacket with few short tears. Beasley Books   2013 - 2015 $250

Vipont, Elfrida *Bless This Day: a Book of Prayer for Children.* London: Collins, 1958. First US edition, 4to., cloth, fine in dust jacket, beautifully illustrated in color by Harold Jones. Aleph-bet Books, Inc.   109 - 242   2015 $95

The Virgin Muse. Being a Collection of Poems from the Most Celebrated English Poets, Designed for the Use of Young Gentlemen and Ladies, at Schools. London: printed and are to be sold by T. Varnam and J. Osborne, R. Halsey, J. Brotherton and Jonas Brown, 1717. First edition, engraved frontispiece, 12mo., contemporary calf, spine gilt, trifle worn, engraved frontispiece, plate rather crudely backed, otherwise good, scarce.   C. R. Johnson   Foxon R-Z - 1053r-z   2015 $1915

Virginia *Constitution of the State of Virginia and Ordinances Adopted by the Convention Which Assembled at Alexandria on the 13th Day of February 1864.* Alexandria: D. Turner, printer to the State, 1864. First edition, 8vo., neatly removed, retaining original tan front printed wrapper only.   M & S Rare Books, Inc.   97 - 67   2015 $450

Virginia. General Assembly *The Code of Virginia.* Richmond: 1887. Full leather, backstrip repaired with red tape, two interior cancelled library stamps.   Bookworm & Silverfish   2015 - 6014020632   2015 $47

The Visit of Humpty. London: Siegle & Hill, 1910. 12mo., cloth, pictorial paste-on, spine bit darkened, else very good+, color plates by May Seton.   Aleph-bet Books, Inc.   109 - 231   2015 $125

The Visions of Dom Francisco de Quevedo Villegas, Knight of the Order of St. James. London: printed and sold by B. Harris, 1702. First edition, 8vo., contemporary mottled calf, spine gilt, some wear to spine, back cover detached), aside from binding wear, very good, uncommon.   C. R. Johnson   Foxon R-Z - 1054r-z   2015 $689

Visscher, William Lightfoot *A Thrilling and Truthful History of the Pony Express; or Blazing the Westward Way and Other Sketches and Incidents of Those Stirring Times.* Chicago: Charles T. Powner Co., 1946. 98 pages, photo illustrations, publisher's brown cloth gilt, spine gilt slightly dulled, but very fine.   Argonaut Book Shop   Holiday Season 2014 - 230   2015 $90

Visser-Hooft, Jenny *Among the Kara-Korum Glaciers in 1925.* London: Edward Arnold, 1926. First edition, 8vo., original blue cloth lettered gilt on spine and cover, pages uncut, frontispiece, 24 plates, 2 maps, neat name on half title "Gilbert Satterthwaite and H. Spencer Jones, stamp on titlepage "Presentation copy",.   Any Amount of Books   2015 - A91390   2015   £220

Vitali, Robert *The Kingdoms of Gu.Gepu.Hrang: According to Mgna - Ris Rgyal Rabs...* Dharamsala: Tho - Li Dpal Dpe Med Lhun Gyis Grub Pa..., 1996. First edition, large 8vo., original light brown paper wrappers, lettered dark brown on spine and front cover, slight abrasion at spine, otherwise very good.   Any Amount of Books   2015 - C7831   2015   £150

Volland Book Catalogue: Books Good for Children. n.d. circa, 1929. 3.5 x 6 inches, pictorial wrappers, 35 pages, fine, illustrations, rare.   Aleph-bet Books, Inc.   109 - 474   2015 $400

Vollmann, William T. *Norse Wood Block Prints. A Portfolio of Woodblock Prints and Stanza 1 of Voluspa.* Sacramento: Co-Tangent Press, 2013. Artist's book, one of a series of five, all on handmade Nideggen paper, signed and dated by artist/author, William T. Vollmann page size 19 x 25 1/2 inches, 10 leaves, bound by artist/author, loose in portfolio made of boards, each portfolio unique, gessoed and then painted in acrylics, then covered in Thai paper, PVA applied, then waxed with two labels on front panel, upper is gray paper lettered 'Freil" in red and the lower is white paper lettered "Nore Wood Block prints" in brown and black inks with rune design, portfolio bound in tan leather with tan ties, boards bound in grey cloth, turn-ins painted grey, front turn-in with two hand painted labels, first on black paper with abstract design in white, second on blue with artist/author's signature and hand numbered, back turn-in with black Burgra paper envelope on lower half of board to house the 15 leaves, label on exterior of envelope on painted tan ground with yellow and red design, envelope with intentional rough tears at edges, intentional cut slash at center, fine, 7 original woodblock prints hand colored by artist and printed with wood spoon.   Priscilla Juvelis - Rare Books   63 - 22   2015 $5000

Vollmann, William T. *Rising Up and Rising Down. Some Thoughts on Violence, Freedom and Urgent Means.* San Francisco: McSweeney's, 2003. First edition, 7 volumes, one of 3500, bound in black cloth with gilt lettering, housed in original publisher's red slipcase with gilt lettering, mild rubbing and bumping to slipcase, fine set.   Ed Smith Books   82 - 30   2015 $750

Voltaire, Francois Marie Arouet De   1694-1778   *Le Brutus, avec un Discours sur la Tragedie.*   Paris: Chez Je. Fr. Josse Libr. Impr. Ordinaire de S. M. C. la Reine d'Espagne (but actually London: Henry Woodfalll), 1731. First London edition, 8vo., woodcut ornament on titlepage, woodcut headpieces and woodcut ornaments between scenes, few sidenotes shaved, with loss of few letters, bound (stab holes visible) with 4 other English plays of the period, contemporary calf, double gilt fillets on sides and on either side of raised bands on spine, lettering piece mostly defective and what remains slid down a bit, good, rare. Blackwell's Rare Books   B179 - 113   2015   £650

Voltaire, Francois Marie Arouet De   1694-1778   *Le Caffee ou L'Ecosssaise: Comedie.*   London (Geneva?): N.P., 1760. Early pirated edition translated by John Hume, 8vo., handsomely bound in later quarter light brown leather and marbled boards, half title little soiled, prelims very slightly edgeworn, overall very good,.   Any Amount of Books   2015 - A39615   2015   £150

Voltaire, Francois Marie Arouet De   1694-1778   *La Henriade.*   Londres: 1728. First edition, 4to., frontispiece, 10 engraved plates, 10 engraved vignettes, 10 engraved tailpieces, 19th century half red hard grained morocco and marbled boards, top edge gilt, some foxing and few stains, but very good.   C. R. Johnson   Foxon R-Z - 1056r-z   2015 $1149

Voltaire, Francois Marie Arouet De   1694-1778   *The History of the Russian Empire Under Peter the Great.*   New York: George Dearborn, 1835. First American edition, 8vo., 126 pages, removed.   M & S Rare Books, Inc.   97 - 314   2015 $225

Voltaire, Francois Marie Arouet De   1694-1778   *Letters Concerning the English Nation.*   London: C. David and A. Lyon, 1733. First edition, octavo, contemporary full paneled leather, five raised bands on spine and author/title in gilt lettering, joints have been professionally reinforced, front and rear flyleaves darkened on edges, very good.   Athena Rare Books   15 - 56 2015 $3500

Volunteer for Liberty.   New York: Veterans of the Abraham Lincoln Brigade, 1949. Reprint, one of 100 numbered copies, this no. 583, very good with nicely repaired front hinge and fraying to spine ends + 1 inch tear at head of rear joint, 4to.   Beasley Books   2013 - 2015 $150

Von Perckhammer, Heinz   *the Culture of the nude in China.*   Berlin: Eigenbrodler Verlag, 1928. First edition, near fine, small 4to., 32 photogravures plates, very good++ dust jacket with mild soil and edgewear.   By the Book, L. C.   44 - 64   2015 $2750

Von Wullerstor-Urbair, B.   *Reise der Osterreichischen Fregatte Novara um Die Erde in den Jahren 1857, 1858, 1859. Zoologischer theil.*   Vienna: Kaiserlich-Konigliche, 1869. Quarto, 33 lithographed plates, 8 chromolithographs, binder cloth, few spots, otherwise very good.   Andrew Isles   2015 - 27149   2015 $2650

Vonnegut, Kurt   *Breakfast of Champions.*   New York: Delacorte Press, 1973. Uncorrected proof, tall sheets, bound in green wrappers, few strips of sunning and corner crease on rear cover, near fine.   Ken Lopez, Bookseller   164 - 235   2015 $600

Vonnegut, Kurt   *Cat's Cradle.*   London: Gollancz, 1963. First English edition, crown 8vo., original orange boards, backstrip gilt lettered, rear panel crease at head, dust jacket, wraparound band little foxed in part, very good.   Blackwell's Rare Books   B179 - 245   2015   £500

Vonnegut, Kurt   *Consider It Among Friends.*   Vancouver: Poppin Publications, 1970. First edition, bit of sunning, small chip threatening at base of spine, near fine in wrappers, quite scarce.   Ken Lopez, Bookseller   164 - 183   2015 $175

Vonnegut, Kurt   *If This Isn't Nice, What Is?*   New York: Seven Stories Press, 2014. Advance copy in the form of comb-bound 8 1/2 x 11 inch sheets, fine.   Ken Lopez, Bookseller   164 - 236   2015 $250

Voss, Walter C.   *Architectural Construction.*   New York: 1925. First edition, volumes I and II in 3 parts, 4to., expected wear, backstrips of both parts of volume 2 dull, volume 1 with corner wear, nearly 2000 pages.   Bookworm & Silverfish   2015 - 6015761745   2015 $225

Voth, H. R.   *The Traditions of the Hopi.*   Chicago: 1905. Original printed wrappers, name stamp on titlepage, minor edge chipping, title inked on spine, else near fine.   Dumont Maps & Books of the West   131 - 81   2015 $95

A Voyage to the Court of Neptune.   London: printed for J. Roberts, 1714. First edition, 8vo., disbound.   C. R. Johnson   Foxon R-Z - 1058r-z   2015 $3064

Vredeman De Vriese, J.   *Recueil De Cartouches.*   Bruxelles: G. A. Van Trigt, 1870. Facsimile reproduction of original edition, folio, quarter cloth, paper covered boards, 24 loose plates, ads on back cover, tie damaged, binding foxed and worn at edges, previous owner's bookplate.   Oak Knoll Books   306 - 204   2015 $450

Vreede, Max   *Paramount 12000 13000.*   Chigwell: Storyville, 1971. First edition, very good.   Beasley Books   2013 - 2015 $150

Vreeland, Frank *Dishonoured.* London: Readers Library Pub. Co., 1931. First British edition, small 8vo., patterned boards slightly rubbed, faintly marked, otherwise very good in like dust jacket with few small closed tears, excellent condition.   Any Amount of Books   2015 - A44801   2015
£150

W

W. Richardson & Co. *Horticultural Builders and Heating Engineers, North of England Horticultural Works, Darlington.* Wexford: printed at the Liberty Press, circa, 1890. 4to., 78 profusely illustrated, within red border, 29 additional fliers, illustrations in catalog, original cloth backed glazed boards upper cover lettered and printed in black, red and gold. Marlborough Rare Books   List 53 - 18   2015   £850

W. W. Woodward *Gogebic Range Directory 1938.* Ironwood: W. W. Woodward, 1938. First edition thus, red and black cloth, 721 pages, few photos, index page has cear tape on it top to bottom but recto shows only short tear, some white stain on top-bottom of black spine, else very good, very, very scarce.   Baade Books of the West   2014 - 2015 $180

Waddington, Samuel *Arthur Hugh Clough: a Monograph.* London: George Bell & Sons, 1883. Half title, final ad leaf, original blue cloth, signed by Robert Menzies 1883 and Geoffrey Tillotson.   Jarndyce Antiquarian Booksellers CCVII - 145   2015   £50

Wade, John   1788-1875 *The Black Book; or corruption Unmasked!* London: John Fairburn, 1820. First edition, 8vo., some signatures bit foxed, contemporary calf, sometime rebacked with most of original spine preserved, good copy.   John Drury Rare Books   March 2015 - 8486   2015 $266

Wade, John   1788-1875 *The Black Book: an Exposition of Abuses in Church and State...* London: Effingham Wilson, 1835. 8vo., engraved frontispiece, engraved plate, original watered cloth with printed spine label, some wear to joints, else very good, uncut and unopened.   John Drury Rare Books   March 2015 - 21632   2015   £266

Wade, John   1788-1875 *The Extraordinary Black Book: an Exposition of Abuses in Church and State, Courts of Law Representation, Municipal and Corporate Bodies...* London: published by Effingham Wilson, 1832. 8vo., engraved frontispiece, contemporary dark blue half calf, spine gilt with raised bands and labels, fine.   John Drury Rare Books 2015 - 21630   2015 $177

Wade, John   1788-1875 *Unreformed Abuses in Church and state with Preliminary Tractate on the Continental Revolutions.* London: Effingham Wilson, 1849. Second edition, 12mo., short tear in one text leaf but no loss of surface, efficently rebound recently in cloth, spine gilt lettered, very good, scarce.   John Drury Rare Books   March 2015 - 23267   2015   £306

Wade, Mary Hazelton *Our Little Brown Cousin.* Boston: L. C. Page, 1901. Edition unknown, octavo, decorated cloth, front board little rubbed, still about fine in near fine example of dust jacket with small chips and few small stains on rear panel, very scarce, especially in jacket.   Between the Covers Rare Books   197 - 10   2015 $150

Wagner, Henry Raup   1862-1957 *Commercial Printers of San Francisco from 1851 to 1880.* Portland: Southworth Anthoensen Press, 1939. First separate edition, thin octavo, tan wrappers printed in black, very fine.   Argonaut Book Shop   Holiday Season 2014 - 304   2015 $150

Wagner, Henry Raup   1862-1957 *Juan Rodriguez Cabrillo, Discoverer of the Coast of California.* San Francisco: California Historical Society, 1941. First edition, one of 750 copies, printed in red and black, cloth backed decorated boards, paper spine label, very fine.   Argonaut Book Shop   Holiday Season 2014 - 307   2015 $125

Wagner, Henry Raup   1862-1957 *The Plains and the Rockies a Critical Bibliography of Exploration, Adventure and Travel in the American West 1800-1865.* San Francisco: John Howell Books, 1982. Fourth edition, frontispiece, illustrations, very fine.   Argonaut Book Shop Holiday Season 2014 - 310   2015 $150

Wagner, Henry Raup   1862-1957 *The Spanish Southwest 1542-1794.* Albuquerque: The Quivira Society, 1937. Second edition, frontispiece, folding map, white cloth spines, tan boards, gilt, four minor spots to inner over of each volume from removed bookplate, else fine and clean set. Argonaut Book Shop   Holiday Season 2014 - 308   2015 $600

Wagner, Henry Raup   1862-1957 *Spanish Voyages to the Northwest Coast of America on the Sixteenth Century.* Amsterdam: Nico Israel, 1966. Reprint very rare first edition of 1929, quarto, text maps and plans, 16 map plates, facsimiles, gilt lettered blue cloth, fine.   Argonaut Book Shop   Holiday Season 2014 - 309   2015 $225

Wagner, Richard   1813-1883 *The Flying Dutchman.* London: Corvinus Press, 1938. First edition, one of 130 copies, quarto, printed in black and red on handmade paper, full vellum with gilt device on rear and gilt rules, top edge gilt, covers bowed as always, near fine.   Peter Ellis, Bookseller   2014 - 020093   2015   £325

Wagner, Richard   1813-1883 *The Rhinegold & The Valkyrie.* London & New York: Heinemann & Doubleday, 1910. Limited to 1150 numbered copies (150 for U.S.), signed by artist, 34 magnificent tipped-in color plates and 14 black and whites by Arthur Rackham, 4to., full vellum, some rubbing on spine, else beautiful copy with silk ties renewed. Aleph-Bet Books, Inc.   108 - 383   2015 $1950

Wagner, Robert R. *The Cartography of the Northwest Coast of America to the Year 1800.* Mansfield Centre: Maurizio Martino, 1999. Second reprint edition, 40 maps, quarto, 2 volumes in one, original cloth, mint.   Argonaut Book Shop   Holiday Season 2014 - 306   2015 $125

Wagoner, David *Dry Sun, Dry Wind.* Bloomington: Indiana University, 1953. First edition, 8vo., black cloth, nice in soiled and chipped dust jacket, author's presentation on title to poet and editor William Claire.   Second Life Books Inc.   190 - 207   2015 $125

Wahba, Magdi *Bicentenary Essays on Rasselas.* Cairo: S. O. P. Press, 1959. Plates, original cream printed wrappers marked, signed by Geoffrey Tillotson July 59, with TLS & cards from editor.   Jarndyce Antiquarian Booksellers CCVII - 342   2015   £20

Wahloo, Per   *The Thirty-First Floor.* New York: Knopf, 1967. First American edition, very fine in dust jacket. Mordida Books   March 2015 - 007281   2015 $80

Wain, Louis   *Daddy Cat.* New York: Dodge, 1925. 8vo., cloth backed boards, pictorial paste-on, slight edgewear, near fine, 32 rich full page color illustrations plus few illustrations in line and pictorial endpapers, scarce.   Aleph-bet Books, Inc.   109 - 479   2015 $2000

Wain, Louis   *Louis Wain's Cats and Dogs.* London: Raphael Tuck, n.d., 1902. Folio, cloth backed pictorial boards, edges and covers rubbed, closed tear on first leaf, tight and very good+, pages mounted on linen which has prevented deterioration, 20 full page and 2 glorious double page chromolithographs plus 3 illustrations in blue, every page illustrated and text printed in blue, scarce.   Aleph-bet Books, Inc.   109 - 480   2015 $2250

Wain, Louis   *Pa Cats Ma Cats and Their Kittens.* London: Raphael Tuck, n.d., 1902. Folio, cloth backed pictorial boards, edges rubbed, closed tear on first leaf, edge of paper toned with fraying on one page, tight and very good+, 10 full page and one glorious double page chromolithograph, plus 22 full and partial page illustrations in blue, every page illustrated and text is printed in blue, scarce. Aleph-bet Books, Inc.   109 - 481   2015 $2250

Waite, Edgar R.   *A Popular Account of Australian Snakes with Complete List of the Species and an Introduction to their Habits and Organizations.* Sydney: Thomas Shine, 1898. Small octavo, 72 pages, 16 chromolithograph plates, publisher's blindstamped cloth, lightly cracked and few flecks, otherwise very good.   Andrew Isles   2015 - 8444 2015 $950

Waite, Peter   *Law in a Colonial Society: the Nova Scotia Experience.* Toronto: Carswell, 1984. 8vo., blue cloth, very good.   Schooner Books Ltd.   110 - 124   2015 $75

Wake, Robert   *Southwold and Its Vicinity, Ancient and Modern.* Yarmouth: F. Skill, 1839. First edition, 8vo., half red leather, marbled boards, attractively bound with gilt decoration at spine and 5 raised bands, 5 folding illustrations, cover sound and clean, very good+, endpapers slightly spotted, occasional tape repair to charts, overall excellent condition.   Any Amount of Books   2015 - A61720   2015   £180

Wake, William   *A Practical Discourse Concerning Swearing; Especially in the two Great Points of Perjury and Common-Swearing.* London: Richard Sare, 1696. First edition, 8vo., contemporary panelled calf with raised bands, unlettered, short split at head of upper joint but nonetheless, fine, crisp copy.   John Drury Rare Books   2015 - 25652 2015 $1049

Wakefield, Edward Gibbon   1796-1862   *The Trial of Edward Gibbon Wakefield, William Wakefield and Frances Wakefield Indicted with One Edward Thevenot a Servant for a Conspiracy and for the Abduction of Miss Ellen Turner, the Only Child and Heiress of William Turner Esq. of Shrigley Park in the County of Chester.* London: John Murray, 1827. First edition, 8vo, complete with half title and appendix, half title rather soiled, rebound relatively recently in cloth with leather gilt lettered spine label, solid, very appealing binding, good copy.   John Drury Rare Books   2015 - 23988   2015 $1049

Wakefield, Priscilla   *Reflections on the Present Condition of the Female Sex; with Suggestions for its Improvement.* London: printed for J. Johnson and Darton and Harvey, 1798. First edition, small 8vo., lacking half title, outer leaves lightly browned, repair to blank inner corner of penultimate leaf, last leaf misbound in reverse order, rebound in paneled calf very uncommon.   Second Life Books Inc.   190 - 208 2015 $4200

Wakeman, Geoffrey   *Nineteenth Century Trade Binding.* Oxford: Plough Press, 1983. Limited to 152 numbered copies, 2 volumes, small 4to., cloth, top edge gilt, paper spine labels, slipcase, second volume is cloth folder containing one sheet with seven specimens of different types of leather pasted on, another sheet with 9 specimens of cloth pasted on, four page section with 71 reproductions of cloth rubbings being the Winterbottom designs and a specimen of brass type that would be used by a bookbinder, book printed by Jonathan Stephenson at his Rocket Press in two colors on mould made paper.   Oak Knoll Books   306 - 166   2015 $650

Wakoski, Diane   *Saturn's Rings.* New York: Targ Editions, 1982. First edition, signed by author, quarter cloth, photographic paper covered boards, fine in slightly age-toned, near fine, unprinted tissue dust jacket, signed by author and inscribed by Wakoski and by Robert Tunney (who took the photo of Wakoski) to author Brad Morrow.   Between the Covers Rare Books, Inc.   187 - 285   2015 $225

Walcott, Derek *The Caribbean Poetry of Derek Walcott and The Art of Romare Bearden.* New York: Limited Editions Club, 1983. Limited to 2000 numbered copies signed by author and artist, Romare Bearden, 4to., illustrated cloth, slipcase, binding designed by Bearden, print by Bearden limited to 275 numbered copies loosely inserted, with Monthly letter loosely inserted. Oak Knoll Books 25 - 50 2015 $450

Walcott, Derek *In a Green Night. Poems 1948-1960.* London: Jonathan Cape, 1962. First edition, 8vo., fine in near fine dust jacket, faintly rubbed at edges (possibly price clipped). Any Amount of Books 2015 - A75548 2015 £175

Walcott, Derek *The Poet in the Theatre.* London: Poetry Book Society, 1990. First edition, crown 8vo., original printed pale cream stapled wrappers, near fine. Blackwell's Rare Books B179 - 246 2015 £40

Walcott, Thomas *A True Copy of a Paper written by Capt. Tho. Walcott in Newgate, After His Condemnation and Delivered to His Son...* London: printed for Timothy Goodwin at the Maiden-head..., 1683. First and only edition, folio, unbound as issued, very good. John Drury Rare Books March 2015 - 24184 2015 $266

Walden, Arthur *A List of Birds Known to Inhabit the Island of Celebes.* London: Transactions of the Zoological Society of London, 1872. Quarto, 23-118 pages, colored map and 10 hand colored plates, contemporary brown half morocco and marbled boards, upper corner of drop title restored without affecting text, very good. Andrew Isles 2015 - 26603 2015 $850

Waldman, Anne *Baby Breakdown.* New York & Indianapolis: Bobbs Merrill Co., 1970. First edition, 8vo., original cloth, dust jacket, cover photos by Joe Brainard, fine in slightly rubbed dust jacket. James S. Jaffe Rare Books Many Happy Returns - 368 2015 $50

Waldman, Anne *First Baby Poems.* Rocky Ledge: Cottage Editions, 1982. Limited to 526 copies, original decorated glossy white wrappers, covers slightly soiled, but very good, presentation copy from author June 30 1982 for Ted Berrigan. James S. Jaffe Rare Books Many Happy Returns - 369 2015 $750

Waldman, Anne *Giant Night. Poems.* New York: Corinth Books, 1970. First edition, review copy with publisher's slip laid in, 8vo., pictorial wrappers by Joe Brainard, signed by Waldman and Brainard in 1973, spine slightly darkened, otherwise fine. James S. Jaffe Rare Books Many Happy Returns - 259 2015 $250

Waldman, Anne *Life Notes.* Indianapolis: Bobbs Merrill, 1973. First edition, 8vo., review copy with publisher's slip laid in, illustrations by Joe Brainard, George Schneeman and author, original cloth, pictorial dust jacket by Brainard, fine, inscribed by author for Burt (Britton), also signed by Brainard. James S. Jaffe Rare Books Many Happy Returns - 265 2015 $200

Waldman, Anne *Life Notes.* Indianapolis: Bobbs Merrill, 1973. First edition, review copy with publisher's slip laid in, 8vo., illustrations by George Scheeman and author, wrappers by Joe Brainard, fine, signed by Waldman and Brainard. James S. Jaffe Rare Books Many Happy Returns - 266 2015 $450

Waldman, Anne *Makeup on Empty Space.* West Branch: Toothpaste Press, 1984. First edition, 8vo., one of 100 numbered and signed copies, deluxe edition printed on Frankfurt White, quarterbound in cloth and Tokutairei Tanahata, a handmade paper at the Campbell-Logan Bindery, fine in acetate dust jacket. Second Life Books Inc. 190 - 209 2015 $125

Waldman, Anne *Nice to See You: Homage to Ted Berrigan.* Minneapolis: Coffee House Press, 1991. First edition, hardcover issue, small 4to., illustrations, original cloth, dust jacket, as new. James S. Jaffe Rare Books Many Happy Returns - 84 2015 $100

Waldman, Anne *On the Wing/Highjacking.* New York: Boke Press, 1968. First edition, 4to., original pictorial wrappers designed by Joe Brainard, published in dos-a-dos format, lightly soiled, otherwise very good. James S. Jaffe Rare Books Many Happy Returns - Addendum 2015 $100

Waldman, Anne *On the Wing/Highjacking.* New York: Boke Press, 1968. First edition, published in a dos-a-dos format, one of 25 numbered copies signed by Waldman, Lewis Warsh and Joe Brainard, lightly soiled, otherwise near fine. James S. Jaffe Rare Books Many Happy Returns - Addendum 2015 $750

Waldman, Anne *Up Thru the Years.* New York: Angel Hair, 1970. First edition, one of 100 copies, 4to., original xerographic wrappers designed by Joe Brainard, trace of dusting to white cover wrappers, otherwise fine. James S. Jaffe Rare Books Many Happy Returns - Addendum 2015 $150

Waldman, Anne *West Indies Poems.* New York: Adventures in Poetry, 1972. First edition, one of 26 lettered copies, 4to., illustrations and original wrappers by Joe Brainard, signed by Brainard and Waldman, fine. James S. Jaffe Rare Books Many Happy Returns - 264 2015 $750

Waldman, Anne *West Indies Poems.* New York: Adventures in Poetry, 1972. First edition, limited to 300 copies, 4to., illustrations and original wrappers by Joe Brainard, signed by Brainard and Waldman, fine. James S. Jaffe Rare Books   Many Happy Returns - 263   2015 $350

Waldman, Anne *The World Anthology.* Indianapolis & New York: Bobbs Merrill, 1969. First edition, 8vo., illustrations, original cloth, dust jacket, fine, jacket lightly tanned and dust soiled.   James S. Jaffe Rare Books   Many Happy Returns - 393   2015 $125

Waldo, Edna Lamoore *Dakota. An Informal Study of Territorial Days Gleaned from Contemporary Newspapers.* Capital Publishing Co., 1932. First edition, 8vo., black cloth, silver stamping on front cover and spine, non authorial presentation inscription on front flyleaf, else very good, tight copy, scarce book.   Buckingham Books   March 2015 - 23701   2015 $400

Wales, Hubert *The Brocklebank Riddle.* New York: Century, 1914. First edition, near fine, page edges slightly darkened and top of front cover slightly bumped, otherwise near fine in blue cloth covered boards with gold stamped titles on spine and on front cover.   Mordida Books   March 2015 - 011339   2015 $150

Wales, Hubert *The Brocklebank Riddle.* Century Co., 1914. First edition, Rules of Maine Charitable Mechanic Assoc. Lib., small library stamp on front flyleaf and titlepage, small inked library number on front flyleaf and spine panel professionally reinforced internally, else near fine, bright. Buckingham Books   March 2015 - 35882   2015 $175

Walesby, Francis Pearson *Is England's Safety or Admiralty Interest to be Considered?* London: William Edward Painter, 1841. First edition, 8vo., 48 pages, titlepage with some foxing, recent marbled boards lettered on spine, presentation copy inscribed for Rt. Hon. Earl of Ashburnham, apparently very rare.   John Drury Rare Books   March 2015 - 23828   2015   £306

Walk, Charles E. *The Silver Blade.* Chicago: McClurg, 1908. First edition, fine in picotiral orange cloth covered boards.   Mordida Books   March 2015 - 008592   2015 $100

Walker, A. Earl *A History of Neurological Surgery.* Baltimore: William & Wilkins, 1951. First edition, signed, dated and inscribed by author, near fine in very good dust jacket with mild soil, sun spine, edgewear, 1 inch chip at dust jacket panel, 8vo.   By the Book, L. C.   44 - 40   2015 $500

Walker, Alice   1944- *Once.* New York: Harcourt, 1968. First edition, signed by author and date 1991, fine in very good+ dust jacket with small spot on lower front spine-fold where the blue finish has been rubbed away.   Beasley Books   2013 - 2015 $750

Walker, Alice   1944- *Revolutionary Petunias & Other Poems.* New York: Harcourt Brace Jovanovich, 1973. First edition, trifle rubbed at base of spine, else fine in very near fine dust jacket with minimal soiling, warmly inscribed by author to Howard Zinn and his wife Roz, scarce. Between the Covers Rare Books, Inc.   187 - 286   2015 $600

Walker, D. P. *Spiritual and Demonic Magic from Ficino to Campanaella.* Nendeln/Liechtenstein: 1969. Reprint of 1958 printing, 8vo., linen cloth, ink ownership signature of David Lindberg, very good, scarce in cloth.   Jeff Weber Rare Books   178 - 1109   2015 $45

Walker, Dale L. *Death Was the Black Horse. The Story of Rough Rider Buckey O'Neill.* Madrona Press, 1975. First edition, 8vo., limited to 200 copies, each signed by author, Carl Hertzog, designer and Robert Weddle, publisher, two-tone black quarter leather and blue cloth, decorated front and rar endpapers, frontispiece, fine in fine original slipcase. Buckingham Books   March 2015 - 38419   2015 $175

Walker, Dugald Stewart *Sally's A B C.* New York: Harcourt Brace, 1929. First edition, 4to., cloth, fine in dust jacket, illustrations, pictorial endpapers and in 3-color on every page, most lovely book.   Aleph-bet Books, Inc.   109 - 12   2015 $600

Walker, Frederick *English Rustic Pictures.* London: George Routledge, 1882. First 'India Proof' edition, small folio, one of 300 numbered copies, 15 proof wood engravings by Walker, and 17 by G. J. Pinwell, decorated gilt parchment, covers with bevelled edges, wood engravings printed from original blocks by Brothers Dalziel on India Proof paper and mounted on rectos, with Agincourt bookplate of Pickford Waller, covers marked and rubbed at corners, very good, engravings in excellent state.   Peter Ellis, Bookseller   2014 - 005239   2015   £350

Walker, Jim *Key System Album.* Glendale: Interurbans, 1978. First edition, oblong 4to., photos, gilt decorated and lettered orange cloth, fine, lightly rubbed pictorial dust jacket chipped at head of spine.   Argonaut Book Shop   Holiday Season 2014 - 311   2015 $95

Walker, Margaret *For My People (Poems).* New Haven: Yale University Press, 1943. Fourth printing, 8vo., author's presentation on half title, yellow cloth, cover little soiled at edges, otherwise tight in some worn dust jacket.   Second Life Books Inc.   190 - 210   2015 $650

Walker, Margaret *Jubilee.* Boston: Houghton Mifflin, 1966. First printing, 8vo., green cloth, map on endpapers, very good, tight in chipped and stained dust jacket. Second Life Books Inc. 190 - 211 2015 $135

Walker, Mary Willis *The Red Scream.* New York: Doubleday, 1994. First edition, very fine in dust jacket. Mordida Books March 2015 - 00886 2015 $100

Walker, Thomas *The Original.* London: Henry Renshaw, 1836. Reprint in one volume of complete collection of weekly issues nos. 1-29 for 20 May 1835 - 2 Dec. 1835, 8vo., contemporary dark blue half calf, spine gilt, raised bands, crimson label, very good. John Drury Rare Books March 2015 - 19163 2015 £306

Walker, Thomas *A Treatise on the Art of Flying, by Mechanical Means with a Full Explanation of the Natural Principles by Which Birds are Enabled to Fly..* New York: printed and sold by Samuel Wood & Sons at the Juvenile Book Store no. 357 Pearl Street, 1816. Second American edition, 12mo., two whole page illustrations, paper generally rather discolored (i.e. browned) and with light old waterstain rubbing throughout, original printed card covers with woodcut emblematic vignettes on both covers, old dampstain affecting lower part of upper cover, in spite of minor faults just described, this is in fact a complete and pretty good copy. John Drury Rare Books 2015 - 22881 2015 $2622

Walker, William *The War in Nicaragua.* Mobile: S. H. Goetzel & Co., 1860. First edition, 8vo., 431 pages, frontispiece, original cloth, ex-library, fine. M & S Rare Books, Inc. 97 - 315 2015 $550

Wall, Alexander J. *A List of New York Almanacs 1694-1850.* New York: New York Public Library, 1921. First edition, cloth bound with wrappers bound in, slight foxing to text, else fine, signature of Wilberforce Eames, inscribed by author to Eames, Eames has corrected a few entries, laid in are few pages of additional notes in his hand. Between the Covers Rare Books, Inc. 187 - 287 2015 $275

Wall, Bernhardt *Roosevelt.* New Preston: n.p., 1924. Limited to 100 numbered copies signed by author on half title and on etching itself, 4to., etching of the President, quarter leather, paper covered boards, edges uncut, covers rubbed at corners and along spine, previous owner's bookplate. Oak Knoll Books 306 - 42 2015 $950

Wall, Dorothy *Blinky Bill.* Racine: Whitman, 1935. Square 8vo., pictorial wrappers, spine lightly worn and slight soil, else very good, 3 colorful pop-ups and black and white illustrations. Aleph-Bet Books, Inc. 108 - 365 2015 $250

Wallace, Alfred Russel 1823-1913 *Australasia.* London: Edward Stanford, 1879. First edition, 8vo., 14 plages, 20 maps, original illustrated green cloth lettered gilt at spine and cover, color maps and many illustrations, faint rubbing at spine and hinges, otherwise near fine, exceptional condition. Any Amount of Books March 2015 - C14243 2015 £450

Wallace, Alfred Russel 1823-1913 *Darwinism: an Exposition of the Theory of Natural Selection with Some of Its Applications.* London: Macmillan, 1912. Third edition, 8vo., frontispiece, 37 illustrations, first signature loose, pastedown and free endpapers foxed, original gilt stamped green cloth, extremities rubbed, front hinge repaired (Kozo), top right front edge dented, floral paper residue affixed to pastedowns, ownership signature of Edwin Shroeder, Lost Nation, Iowa, titlepage ownership signature of Jane Camerini, with date of first edition '1889' inked next to publishing date. Jeff Weber Rare Books 178 - 785 2015 $50

Wallace, Alfred Russel 1823-1913 *The Geographical Distribution of Animals.* New York: Harper & Bros., 1876. First US edition, 2 volumes, 20 full pa wood engravings, 7 colored maps, 8vo., original green cloth bindings with gilt stamped title lettering to spine lettering and elaborate gilt front cover design of animals & birds in a forest setting, beveled boards, brown coated endpapers, gilt bright, light shelfwear, volume I front hinge paper starting, prior owner label and bookseller ticket, fore-edge chip to volume 1 f.f.ep, withal a pleasing, very good+ set. Tavistock Books Bah, Humbug? - 12 2015 $750

Wallace, Alfred Russel 1823-1913 *The Geographical Distribution of Animals; with Study of the Relations of Living and Extinct Faunas as Elucidating the Past Changes of the Earth's Surface.* London: Macmillan & Co., 1876. First edition, 8vo., 20 plates 7 maps, soundly rebound in red cloth, lettered gilt on spines, 2 volumes, illustrations, ex-library, label with gilt number on spine, some folding to large map, some fading and marking to boards, otherwise sound, very good minus, clean text. Any Amount of Books March 2015 - C14403 2015 £450

Wallace, Alfred Russel 1823-1913 *Island Life; or the Phenomena and Causes of Insular Faunas and Floras, Including a Revision and Attempted Solution of the Problem of Geological Climates.* London: Macmillan, 1880. First edition, 8vo., hand colored frontispiece map, 25 additional maps, index, few maps lightly foxed, original black and gilt stamped pebbled green cloth, top edge gilt, new pastedowns and endpapers, neatly restored preserving original spine, very good. Jeff Weber Rare Books 178 - 1112 2015 $600

Wallace, Alfred Russel 1823-1913 *My Life: a Record of Events and Opinions.* New York: Dodd Mead, 1905. First American edition, 2 volumes, 8vo., frontispieces, plates, original gilt stamped red cloth, top edge gilt, extremities worn especially at spine ends, volume I hinges repaired, titlepage University Lake School, Hartland, W1 rubber stamps, additional withdrawn stamps, good.   Jeff Weber Rare Books   178 - 1114   2015 $75

Wallace, Alfred Russel 1823-1913 *Studies Scientific & Social.* London: Macmillan, 1900. First edition, 2 volumes, 8vo., illustrations, 1 folding color map, errata slips tipped in, pastedowns as well as first and last few pages foxed, original gilt stamped green pebbled cloth, lightly rubbed corners bumped, volume I spine head slightly torn, presentation copy titlepage with embossed stamps, very good.   Jeff Weber Rare Books   178 - 1115   2015 $350

Wallace, Alfred Russel 1823-1913 *Tropical Nature and Other Essays.* London: Macmillan, 1878. First edition, 8vo., cords split at pages 160-1 and 288-289 (reinforced with kozo), original black stamped green cloth, gilt stamped spine, corners heavily repaired with Kozo paper, armorial bookplate of Francis Reynolds Dickinson and Alice May Dickinson, bookseller label of Philip, Son & Nephew, Liverpool, as is.   Jeff Weber Rare Books   178 - 1116   2015 $300

Wallace, David Foster *Infinite Jest.* Boston: Little Brown, 1996. Advance reading copy, signed by author, nearly 1100 pages, shallow corner creasing to cover and some pages, small nick and scratch to lower covers, near fine in wrappers with reader response card laid in.   Ken Lopez, Bookseller   164 - 238   2015 $750

Wallace, David Foster *A Supposedly Fun Thing I'll Never Do Again.* Boston: Little Brown, 1997. Uncorrected proof, tiny spine tap, else fine in wrappers.   Ken Lopez, Bookseller   164 - 239   2015 $750

Wallace, Edgar *Again Sanders.* Doubleday Doran & Co., 1929. First US edition, fine, bright, tight, clean copy in dust jacket with minor wear to spine ends, closed tear to top rear flap fold and lightly foxed at top rear panel.   Buckingham Books   March 2015 - 33675   2015 $250

Wallace, Edgar *The Green Ribbon.* Garden City: Doubleday, 1930. First American edition, fine in very fine, as new dust jacket.   Mordida Books   March 2015 - 010793   2015 $200

Wallace, Edgar *The Law of the Three Just Men.* Garden City: Doubleday Crime Club, 1931. First American edition, lower corner bumped, otherwise fine in dust jacket with tiny scrape on spine and small scrape on back panel.   Mordida Books   March 2015 - 1931   2015 $200

Wallace, Edgar *The Ringer Returns.* Garden City: Doubleday Crime Club, 1931. First American edition, near fine in very fine as new dust jacket with some tiny rubbing on spine.   Mordida Books   March 2015 - 010796   2015 $200

Wallace, Edgar *Sanders of the River.* Garden City: Doubleday Doran, 1930. first American edition, fine in very fine, as new dust jacket with publisher's wraparound intact.   Mordida Books   March 2015 - 010792   2015 $200

Wallace, Edgar *Sanders of the River.* Doubleday, Doran & Co., 1930. First edition, fine in fine bright dust jacket with fine wraparound promotional band.   Buckingham Books   March 2015 - 33392   2015 $300

Wallace, Edgar *The Traitor's Gate.* Doubleday Page & Co., 1927. First US edition, near fine in dust jacket lightly rubbed along front flap fold, minor wear to spine ends and corners.   Buckingham Books   March 2015 - 33423   2015 $300

Wallace, Ernest *Ranald S. MacKenzie on The Texas Frontier.* West Texas Museum Association, 1964. First edition, cloth, titles and decoration stamped in silver gilt on front cover and spine, 2 photos, 2 maps, fine, bright dust jacket.   Buckingham Books   March 2015 - 38093 2015 $350

Wallace, Robert *Characteristics of the Present Political State of Great Britain.* London: A. Millar, 1758. First edition, 8vo., wanting half title, contemporary calf, double ruled gilt borders to sides, ruled gilt spine with raised bands and gilt red morocco lettering piece, fine.   John Drury Rare Books   2015 - 25591   2015 $699

Wallace, W. H. *Speeches of Wm. H. Wallace, Democratic Nominee for Congress Fifth Congressional District of Missouri.* Press of Frank T. Riley, n.d. circa, 1907. Later edition, 22cm., light green pictorial wrappers, 96 pages, very light tanning to edges of both wrappers, else fine copy.   Buckingham Books   March 2015 - 35688   2015 $200

Walmsley, David *The Lions. The Complete History of the British and Irish Rugby Union Team 1888-2005.* Surrey: Genesis, 2005. First edition, one of 100 Classic leather copies, deluxe issue, signed by 8 team members, folio, signed photo in original envelope, fine in full red leather, housed in clamshell case, original string tied bag.   Ed Smith Books   83 - 114   2015 $500

Walpole, Horace *The Letters of Horace Walpole, Earl of Oxford.* London: Richard Bentley, 1858. First edition, 9 volumes, 8vo., modern red cloth lettered gilt on spine, 40 plates, ex-Foreign and Commonwealth Office library with usual attributes, otherwise very good.   Any Amount of Books   2015 - A60910   2015   £220

Walpole, Horace 1719-1797 *A Catalogue of the Royal and Noble Authors of England.* Twickenham: printed at Strawberry Hill, 1758. First edition, second state (A2 verso line 3 reads 'to have a bias' rather than 'to be partial'), 2 volumes, 8vo., vignette titlepage and Grignion frontispiece, very slightly browned, otherwise clean but disbound copies with wide margins, rubbed, leather spines preserved. Any Amount of Books 2015 - A72899 2015 £220

Walpole, Horace 1719-1797 *Horace Walpole's Description of the Villa at Strawberry Hill.* London: Roxburghe Club, 2010. Facsimile edition, limited to 200 copies, large 4to., quarter red leather and red cloth boards, lettered gilt on spine, copiously illustrated, presentation in hand of Nicolas Barker for Norman Routledge, very slight rubbing, else very good+. Any Amount of Books March 2015 - C9634 2015 £400

Walpole, Robert 1784-1859 *Some Considerations Concerning the Publick Funds, the Publick Revenues and the Annual Supplies Granted by Parliament.* London: J. Roberts, 1735. First edition, 8vo., preserved in recent plain wrappers with label on upper cover. John Drury Rare Books 2015 - 21464 2015 $89

Walrond, Eric *Tropic Death.* New York: Boni & Liveright, 1926. First edition, 8vo., black cloth, slightly cocked, hinge tender, very good, inscribed by author for Philitus Joyce. Second Life Books Inc. 190 - 212 2015 $750

Walsh, J. M. *Spies in Spain.* London: Odhams Press Ltd., n.d., 1937. First edition, 8vo., near fine in lightly soiled dust jacket with light wear to spine ends, small chip bottom edge of front panel and few tiny closed tears to rear panel. Buckingham Books March 2015 - 21947 2015 $275

Walsh, J. M. *Spies in Spain.* London: Odhams, 1937. First edition, some scattered foxing on page edges, otherwise fine in dust jacket. Mordida Books March 2015 - 008489 2015 $85

Walsh, John *Bill Viola: The Passions.* Los Angeles: London: The J. Paul Getty Museum/The National Gallery, 2003. First edition, 4to., copiously illustrated in color black and white, fine in fine dust jacket. Any Amount of Books 2015 - A93129 2015 £180

Walsh, John *Popular Opinions on Parliamentary reform Considered.* London: James Ridgway, 1831. 8vo., modern wrappers with printed title label on upper cover, very good. John Drury Rare Books 2015 - 20047 2015 $133

Walsh, M. *Chemical and Geological Observations Relating to Brick-Making in Western India.* London: E. & F. N. Spon, 1869. First edition, apparently rare, occasional and minor spots and other marks, preserved in later wrappers with printed label on upper cover. John Drury Rare Books 2015 - 22599 2015 $150

Walsh, Maurice *The Man in Brown.* Edinburgh: Chambers, 1945. First edition, inscription, otherwise fine in dust jacket with couple of closed tears at base of spine, two internal tape mends. Mordida Books March 2015 - 011341 2015 $85

Walsh, William *A Dialogue Concerning woman, Being a Defence of the Sex...* London: R. Bentley and J. Tonson, 1691. First edition, 8vo. contemporary neatly speckled calf (worn along hinge, spine stamping worn off). Second Life Books Inc. 189 - 262 2015 $7500

Walsh, William *Ode for the Thanksgiving Day.* London: printed for Jacob Tonson, 1706. First edition, folio, recent marbled wrappers, titlepage dust soiled, tiny chip at lower corner touching outer rule, some foxing, otherwise good. C. R. Johnson Foxon R-Z - 1062r-z 2015 $613

Walter, William W. *The Great Understander Truelife Story of the Last of the Wells Fargo Shotgun Express Messengers.* William W. Walter, 1931. First edition, inscribed by compiler for Doctor Hart, fine. Buckingham Books March 2015 - 23898 2015 $275

Walter, William W. *The Great Understander: True Life Story of the last of the Wells Fargo Shotgun Express Messengers.* William W. Walter, 1931. First edition, 8vo., original decorated grey cloth, near fine without dust jacket as issued. Buckingham Books March 2015 - 20530 2015 $225

Walters, Minette *The Dark Room.* London: Macmillan, 1995. First edition, very fine in dust jacket, signed by author. Mordida Books March 2015 - 008718 2015 $85

Walters, Minette *The Echo.* London: Macmillan, 1997. First edition, very fine in dust jacket, signed by author. Mordida Books March 2015 - 008719 2015 $85

Walters, Minette *The Ice House.* London: Macmillan, 1992. First edition, fine in dust jacket. Buckingham Books March 2015 - 21450 2015 $1000

Walters, Minette *The Ice House.* New York: St. Martin's Press, 1992. First US edition, fine in fine dust jacket. Buckingham Books March 2015 - 23554 2015 $300

Walters, Minette *The Scold's Bridle.* Bristol: Scorpion, 1994. First edition, one of 75 specially bound numbered copies, signed by Walters, very fine in acetate dust jacket. Mordida Books   March 2015 - 007627   2015 $200

Walters, Minette *The Scold's Bridle.* London: Macmillan, 1994. First edition, very fine in dust jacket, signed by author.   Mordida Books   March 2015 - 008717   2015 $90

Walters, Minette *The Sculptress.* London: Macmillan, 1993. First edition, signed by author, page edges uniformly tanned, else fine in dust jacket.   Buckingham Books   March 2015 - 28623   2015 $175

Walters, Minette *The Sculptress.* London: Macmillan, 1993. First edition, fine in fine dust jacket.   Buckingham Books   March 2015 - 21432   2015 $225

Walther, Richard *A Voyage Round the world in the Years MDCCXL I II III IV.* London: printed for the author by John and Paul Knapton, 1749. Fifth edition, 43 large folding engraved plates, maps, plans and charts with extra folding frontispiece map, full recent brown calf, lettered gilt at spine with 5 raised bands, handsome, clean bright copy with plates in fresh state (one plate has short closed tear with no loss), there is an additional fine portrait engraving of Anson from on the blank page opposite titlepage, presumably bound in former owner, very good.   Any Amount of Books 2015 - A75274   2015   £1050

Waltmire, W. E. *The Red Baiter's Patriotism!* Chicago: the author circa, 1938. First edition, wrappers, very good, 8vo., 16 pages.   Beasley Books   2013 - 2015 $45

Walton, A. *A Tour on the Banks of the Thames from London to Oxford in the Autumn of 1829.* London: printed for the author by T. W. Hord, 1834. First and only edition, 8vo., wanting front free endpaper, original maroon cloth, rather faded and slightly soiled, with original but rather worn printed label on spine, good copy, very scarce.   John Drury Rare Books   2015 - 26006   2015 $133

Walton, Izaak   1593-1683 *The Complete Angler of Izaak Walton and Charles Cotton...* printed at the Shakespeare Press by W. Nicol for) John Major, 1823. First Major edition, large paper copy, 14 engraved plates, printed upon India paper and mounted, numerous woodcuts in text, some foxing, emanating from leaves upon which plates are mounted and from the binder's endleaves, 8vo. half brown morocco, circa 1920 by Tout, top edge gilt, others uncut, good. Blackwell's Rare Books   B179 - 115   2015   £600

Walton, Izaak   1593-1683 *The Lives of Dr. John Donne, Sir Henry Wotton, Mr. Richard Hooker, Mr. George Herbert...* printed by Tho. Newcombe for Richard Marriott, 1670. First collected edition, without 4 portraits (as often) and 2 blanks A1 & 8 (as often) with some errata, other corrections in Walton's hand, 8vo., contemporary mottled calf, rebacked, good.   Blackwell's Rare Books   B179 - 114   2015   £1500

War Songs for Anniversaries and Gatherings of Soldiers. New York: Oliver Ditson, 1890. First edition, wrappers in taped spine, some pages starting to loosen, just very good. Beasley Books   2013 - 2015 $45

War with Priestcraft; or the Free-Thinker's Iliad. London: printed for J. Roberts, 1732. First edition, 8vo., half calf and marbled boards, black morocco label, half title is present, bit dust soiled, very good, scarce.   C. R. Johnson Foxon R-Z - 1063r-z   2015 $1149

The Warbling Muses, or Treasure of Lyric Poetry.. London: printed for G. Woodfall, 1749. First edition, 12mo., 19th century half calf and marbled boards, very scarce, very good, signature of Henry Robertson Jr. on titlepage (partly rubbed out), repeated at back.   C. R. Johnson   Foxon R-Z - 1064r-z   2015 $1302

Warburg, Sandol Stoddard *The Thinking Book.* Boston: Little Brown, 1960. Stated first edition, oblong 4to., cloth, slight fraying at base of spine ends, else near fine in dust jacket with few chips and soil, inscribed by author, illustrations by Ivan Chermayeff.   Aleph-bet Books, Inc.   109 - 88 2015 $450

Ward, Artemus *Artemus Ward, His book... (with) Letters to Punch...* London: Ward, Lock & Tyler, circa, 1870. Half title, frontispiece, 2 volumes in 1, rebound in green binder's cloth, red leather label, very good.   Jarndyce Antiquarian Booksellers   CCXI - 280   2015   £35

Ward, Edward   1667-1731 *The Dancing Devils; or the Roaring Dragon.* London: printed and sold by A. Bettesworth, J. Bately and J. Brotherton, 1724. First edition, 80 pages, 8vo., panelled calf antique, spine gilt, red morocco label, fine, uncommon, this copy has leaf C4 in its uncancelled state, with reading "King Hector" on page 24 with "Hector" changed to "Paris" in early hand, in most copies the leaf has been cancelled, and reading is "Young Paris".   C. R. Johnson   Foxon R-Z - 1068r-z   2015 $1915

Ward, Edward   1667-1731 *The Dutch Riddle; or a Character of a H--ry Monster, often found in Holland.* London: printed in the year, 1708. Second in two early printings, 8vo., old marbled boards, maroon morocco label (label bit worn), very good.   C. R. Johnson   Foxon R-Z - 1086r-z   2015 $7661

Ward, Edward 1667-1731 *The History of the Grand Rebellion; Containing the Most Remark-able Transactions from the Beginning of the Reign of King Charles I to the Happy Restoration....* London: printed for J. Morphew, 1713. First edition, 3 volumes, 84 (of 85) engraved portraits, otherwise fine, 3 folding maps, 8vo., full polished calf panelled in gilt, spines and inner dentelles gilt, red morocco labels, all edges gilt by Bedford, attractive collector's binding.   C. R. Johnson   Foxon R-Z - 1072r-z   2015 $2298

Ward, Edward 1667-1731 *Honesty in Distress...* London: printed and sold by H. Hills, 1708. Pirated edition, 8vo., recent blue cloth, price of 1d on titlepage, some browning, few page numbers slightly shaved, otherwise good.   C. R. Johnson   Foxon R-Z - 1209r-z   2015 $192

Ward, Edward 1667-1731 *Hudibras Redivivus; or a Burlesque Poem. Part 1-12 and volume II Part 1-12.* London: printed and sold by B. Bragge, 1705-1707. First edition, together 24 parts in one volume, small 4to., contemporary calf, spine gilt, some wear, upper joint slightly cracked, complete set of first editions, flyleaves removed, some light browning and soiling, quite sound and complete, full sets of first editions very uncommon, this set seems to have been assembled by a certain "D.E." who has signed many of the parts with initials.   C. R. Johnson   Foxon R-Z - 1073r-z   2015 $3064

Ward, Edward 1667-1731 *The Merry Travellers; or a Trip Upon Ten-Toes from Moorfields to Bromley. .. Part I. (bound with) The Wand'ring Spy or the Merry Travellers Part II.* London: printed for the author and sold by A. Bettesworth, 1724. 1722. Second edition of part 1, first edition of part II, 2 volumes in 1, 8vo, later marbled boards, red morocco label, scarce, very good.   C. R. Johnson   Foxon R-Z - 1074r-z   2015 $2298

Ward, Edward 1667-1731 *The Modern Courtier; or the Ambitious Statesman's Advice to his Son.* London: printed and sold by J. Torbuck and by the booksellers and publishers in town and country, n.d., 1741. First edition, 8vo., disbound, very good, complete with half title.   C. R. Johnson   Foxon R-Z - 1066r-z   2015 $1149

Ward, Edward 1667-1731 *The Northern Cuckold; or the Gardenhouse Intrigue.* London: printed in the year, 1721. First edition, 8vo., recent marbled boards, red morocco label, very good, scarce.   C. R. Johnson   Foxon R-Z - 10754-r-z   2015 $1915

Ward, Edward 1667-1731 *Nuptial Dialogues and Debates; or an Useful Prospect of the Felicities and Discomforts of a Marry'd Life...* London: printed by H. Meere for T. Norris and A. Bettesworth and sold by J. Woodward, 1710. 2 volumes, 8vo., full marbled calf, gilt, spines gilt, brown morocco labels, red edges, traces of rubbing, fine, bookplates of Walter E. Shirley.   C. R. Johnson   Foxon R-Z - 1076r-z   2015 $1915

Ward, Edward 1667-1731 *Nuptial Dialogues and Debates; or an Useful Prospect of the Felicities and the Discomforts of a Marry'd Life, Incident to all Degrees, from the Throne to the Cottage.* London: printed for C. Hitch and L. Hawes, R. Baldwin, S. Crowder and Co., J. Wren, P. Davey and B. Law, C. Ware and J. Hope, 1759. Fourth edition, 2 volumes, 12mo., 19th century half maroon morocco, gilt, some wear, joints rubbed, early signatures on titlepages of John Adamson and Eliza D. Good.   C. R. Johnson   Foxon R-Z - 1078r-z   2015 $383

Ward, Edward 1667-1731 *The Parish Gutt'lers; or the Humours of a Select Vestry.* London: printed in the year, 1722. First edition, 64 pages, 8vo., recent half calf and marbled boards, red morocco label, very good.   C. R. Johnson   Foxon R-Z - 1079r-z   2015 $996

Ward, Edward 1667-1731 *The Parish Gutt'lers; or the Humours of a Select Vestry.* London: printed for Sam. Briscoe, 1722. First edition, very rare issue with bookseller's name in imprint, 8vo., disbound, fine.   C. R. Johnson   Foxon R-Z - 1080r-z   2015 $1379

Ward, Edward 1667-1731 *The Poet's Ramble after Riches; with Reflections Upon a Country Corporation.* London: printed and sold by J. How, 1701. Third edition, folio, 19th century half calf, gilt, red morocco label, crude tape repair to top of spine, slight browning, but very good. C. R. Johnson   Foxon R-Z - 1081r-z   2015 $1302

Ward, Edward 1667-1731 *The Republican Procession; or, the Tumultuous Cavalcade. A Merry Poem.* N.P.: London: printed in the year, 1714. Second edition, 8vo., disbound, several leaves loose at beginning, old tape residue along blank inner margin of titlepage, otherwise good, contemporary owner has noted Ward's authorship on title and has added the word 'Read', he has also identified many of the 'characters' who appear in text.   C. R. Johnson   Foxon R-Z - 1084r-z   2015 $613

Ward, Edward 1667-1731 *The Republican Procession or the Tumultuous Cavalcade.* London: printed and are to be sold by the booksellers of London and Westminster, 1727. 8vo., disbound, very good.   C. R. Johnson   Foxon R-Z - 1085r-z   2015 $613

Ward, Edward 1667-1731 *The Republican Procession; or the Tumulltuous Calavacade.* N.P.: London: printed in the year, 1741. First edition, 8vo., recent marbled boards, little dusty at beginning and end, but very good.   C. R. Johnson   Foxon R-Z - 1083r-z   2015 $766

Ward, H. *A Short but Clear System of English Grammar with Exercises of Bad English, Designed for the Use of Schools and for Those Gentlemen and Ladies Who May want the Assistance of a Master...* Whitehaven: printed in the year, 1777. Only edition, 12mo., small adhesion fault to titlepage, touching but not obscuring 3 or 4 letters, contemporary plain calf, raised bands with old torn paper title label on spine, very good, early ownership signature of Ann or Annie Welsh dated 1785, apparently of great rarity. John Drury Rare Books   2015 - 25529   2015 $1661

Ward, Herbert Dickinson *A Dash to the People.* New York: Lovell Coryell & Co., 1895. First edition, first issue with Lovell, Coryell imprint, first binding with airship flying above Arctic landscape, frontispiece, illustrations, original pictorial gray cloth, front and spine panels stamped in brown, silver and gold.   L. W. Currey, Inc.   Boy's Adventure Fiction 2015 - 99   2015 $100

Ward, James *Ueber die Auslosung von Reflexbewegungen Durch eine Summe Schwacher Reize. (On the Triggering of Reflex Movements by a Sum of Weak Stimuli).* Leipzig: Veit & Comp, 1880. First edition, offprint, octavo, from the library of William James, with his signature top of front wrapper in pencil and 4 citations in his hand to rear wrapper in black ink, , original tan wrappers printed with black type on front cover only with original(?) spine tape, old tape repairs (in well matched color) to small chips on both front and rear wrappers.   Athena Rare Books   15 - 13   2015 $1000

Ward, John *Happiness; a Poem.* London: printed for J. Wilford, 1737. First edition, 8vo., pale blue wrappers, some foxing, margins of last few leaves browned, otherwise good, complete with half title, rare.   C. R. Johnson   Foxon R-Z - 1093r-z   2015 $1916

Ward, Joseph *An Epitome of Scripture History or a Brief Narration of the Principal Facts and Events Recorded in the Scriptures of the Old Testament...* Newport-Pagnell: printed and sold by S. Manning sold also by W. Baynes, London, 1819. First edition, 12mo., folding map, final errata leaf, both free endpapers removed, original tree sheep, joints worn, still pretty good copy, very rare.   John Drury Rare Books   2015 - 20670   2015 $133

Ward, Sarah F. *The White Ribbon Story: 125 Years of Service to Humanity.* Evanston: Signal Press, 1999. First edition, small octavo, original blue buckram binding, gilt titles, fine.   Tavistock Books   Temperance - 2015 $50

Ward, Thomas *England's Reformation; from the Time of King Henry VIII, to the End of Oates's Plot a Poem.* London: printed for W(illiam) B(ray) and sold by Thomas Bickerton, 1716. Third edition, 8vo., contemporary panelled calf, plainly rebacked, good, early signature on titlepage of Fran McNaghtan.   C. R. Johnson   Foxon R-Z - 1094r-z   2015 $115

Ward, William *An Essay on Grammar as It May Be Applied to the English Language.* printed for Robert Horsfield, 1765. First edition, dampstained, foxed and browned in places, 4to., contemporary tree calf, red lettering piece on spine, surface affected by damp, obscuring 'tree' on upper cover, signature of John Dalton, (not that of the great chemist).   Blackwell's Rare Books   B179 - 116   2015   £650

Warde, Frederick *Bruce Rogers, Designer of Book.* Cambridge: Harvard University Press, 1925. First book edition, 15 full page illustrations, type and ornament designs, publisher's blue gray cloth, printed paper label on spine, bookplate on inner cover label bit darkened, offsetting to rear ends, else fine.   Argonaut Book Shop   Holiday Season 2014 - 249   2015 $75

Warden, R. *C. M. Russell Boyhood Sketchbook.* Bozeman: Treasure Products, 1972. First edition, limited to 300 copies numbered and signed by author, this copy 164, quarto, full leather with 6 inch vignette in gold of Russell on front cover, illustrations, as new in original mailing carton. Buckingham Books   March 2015 - 20096   2015 $325

Warden, R. *C. M. Russell Boyhood Sketchbook.* Treasure Products Bozeman, 1972. First edition, quarto, simulated leather with gold foil picture in strong relief of Russell, illustrations, errata slip, very good+, upper cover corners slightly bumped, else fine, very good+.   Baade Books of the West   2014 - 2015 $49

Wardlaw, Elizabeth *Hardyknute; a Fragment.* London: printed for R. Dodsley, 1740. First London edition, 36 pages, 4to., disbound very scarce, very good.   C. R. Johnson   Foxon R-Z - 1095r-z   2015 $1302

Wardle, Thomas *Select Works of the British Poets from Falconer to Sir Walter Scott.* Philadelphia: Thomas Wardle, 1838. First edition, half leather and marbled boards, gilt lines to spine, very good, light shelfwear, some foxing to endpapers and prelims, nice, tight copy.   Stephen Lupack March 2015 - 2015 $100

Ware, John *Remarks on the History and Treatment of Delirium Tremens.* Boston: N. Hale's Steam Power Press, 1831. First separate edition, 8vo., sewn as issued, title uniformly browned, light foxing throughout, upper corner gnawed without loss of text, otherwise very good, exceptionally wide margined copy with fore and bottom margins untrimmed.   M & S Rare Books, Inc.   97 - 189   2015 $275

Ware, Thomas E. *Wesley's Family Physician, Revised and Ware's medical Adviser: a Book of Receipts...* Salem: S. Prior, 1839. Sheep backed marbled paper covered boards (considerably worn at extremities with pastepaper boards exposed), piece torn from fore-edge of margin of pages 49/50, costing several letters, usual foxing, but good, tight with sheep spine in very good state. Joseph J. Felcone Inc. Science, Medicine and Technology - 54 2015 $450

Warhol, Andy *Warhol. The Tate Gallery 17 February - 28 March 1971.* London: Tate Gallery, 1971. First edition, 4to., endpaper, frontispiece, grey cloth, titles in silver on upper board and spine, dust jacket, signed by Warhol, very good, jacket dampstained, worn and torn. Maggs Bros. Ltd. Gathering of 26 Countercultural items Oct. 2013 - 20 2015 £375

Waring, Henry *Miscellanies; or a Variety of Notion and Thought...* N.P.: Edinburgh? printed for the author, 1708. First edition, small 4to., contemporary calf, panelled in gilt with fleurons at corners, rubbed, some wear to spine, joints cracked, small quarto is very rare, very good. C. R. Johnson Foxon R-Z - 1096r-z 2015 $2298

Warmington, Eric Herbert *A History of Birkbeck College, University of London During the Second World War 1939-1945.* 1955. Half title, frontispiece and plates, folding plan, original dark green cloth, presentation by author for Geoffrey Tillotson. Jarndyce Antiquarian Booksellers CCVII - 548 2015 £20

Warner, F. *Memoirs of the Life of Thomas More. To Which is Added His History of Utopia.* London: L. Davis and C. Reymers, 1758. First edition, 8vo., half leather, lettered gilt, 5 raised bands, frontispiece, front board starting to detach but holding, slight rubbing, otherwise used, very good- with clean text, modern bookplate. Any Amount of Books March 2015 - A99-53 2015 £360

Warner, George F. *Facsimiles of Royal Historical, Literary and Other Autographs in the Department of Manuscripts, British Museum.* London: British Museum, 1899. Folio, later cloth, spine gilt stamped, top edge gilt, other edges uncut, series I-V, 150 facsimiles in all, covers and spine lightly soiled and lightly rubbed at edges. Oak Knoll Books 306 - 250 2015 $350

Warner, Oliver *A Secret of the Marsh.* London: Chatto & Windus, 1927. First edition, review slip inscribed by author laid in, fine in near fine, lightly soiled dust jacket with wear at corners and tiny tears. Mordida Books March 2015 - 008722 2015 $600

Warner, Rex *Men and Gods.* New York: Random House, 1959. First edition thus, illustrated and signed by Gorey. Honey & Wax Booksellers 2 - 30 2015 $375

Warner, Samuel *Authentic and Impartial Narrative of the Tragical Scene Which was Witnessed in Southampton County (Virginia) on Monday the 22d of August Last, When Fifty-Five of Its Inhabitants (mostly women and children) were Inhumanly Massacred by the Blacks!* New York: printed for Warner & West, 1831. First edition, 8vo., 38 pages, contemporary plain wrappers, uncut, lacks pages 35-38 and folding frontispiece, all supplied in facsimile. M & S Rare Books, Inc. 97 - 305 2015 $1250

Warnes, John *Flax Versus Cotton or the Two-edged Sword Against Pauperism and Slavery.... No. 1.* London: James Ridgway, 1850. First edition, 8vo., few emphasis marks and occasional annotations in pencil and pen, original printed wrappers, rather dust soiled but good. John Drury Rare Books 2015 - 14112 2015 $142

Warnod, Andre *Dignimont. Les Artistes Du Livre.* Paris: Henry Babou, 1929. First edition, number 657 of 700 copies, unbound signatures laid into wrappers, fine and bright, illustrations, small 4to. Beasley Books 2013 - 2015 $150

Warren, Alba H. *English Poetic Theory 1825-1865.* Princeton: Princeton University Press, 1950. Half title, original brown cloth, corner knocked, otherwise very good in dust jacket, Geoffrey Tillotson's signed copy with few notes and cutting of TLS review. Jarndyce Antiquarian Booksellers CCVII - 549 2015 £20

Warren, Ed *Graveyard. True Hauntings from an Old New England Cemetery.* New York: St. Martin's, 1992. Special collector's edition, inscribed by Ed and Lorraine Warren in 1994, flyer for a program featuring the Warrens laid in, along with recipient's notes on the Evening, recipient's stamp inside front cover, fine in stapled wrappers, from the library of horror writer Stanley Wiater. Ken Lopez, Bookseller 164 - 242 2015 $150

Warren, Edward *Some Account of the Letheon; or Who Is the Discoverer.* Boston: Dutton and Wentworth, 1847. First edition, 88 pages, original printed wrappers, ex-library stamps, text foxed, inscribed by author to Prof. G(eorge) Ticknor. M & S Rare Books, Inc. 97 - 10 2015 $1250

Warren, G. K. *Explorations in the Dacota Country in the Year 1855.* A. O. P. Nicholson, Senate Printer, 1856. First edition, red quarter leather and red and black marbled paper over boards, titles stamped in gold on spine, raised bands, 3 folded maps, illustrations, text and maps very good in fine binding. Buckingham Books March 2015 - 28009 2015 $1875

Warren, Henry *Cripple Creek and Colorado Springs Illustrated.* Warren & Stride, 1895. Second edition, 12 x 9 1/2 inches, rebound in blue cloth boards, front wrapper missing, folding map, illustrations, maps, some soiling along with moderate chipping and closed tears throughout, rare. Buckingham Books March 2015 - 37443 2015 $1250

Warren, Henry *Cripple Creek and Colorado Springs Illustrated.* Warren & Stride, 1896. First edition, 12 x 91 1/2 inches, copper embossed wrappers, 104 pages, illustrations, maps, folding map, red stamp of Pikes Peak Tunnel Mining Railway on front and rear covers and with blueprint map of their line laid in, covers lightly soiled, 3 inch section at top of spine removed, interior clean, all maps in fine condition, overall very good.   Buckingham Books   March 2015 - 34608   2015 $2000

Warren, John *A Sermon Preached before the Governor of Addenbrooke's Hospital on Thursday June 27 1776 in Great St. Mary's Church, Cambridge.* Cambridge: printed by J. Archdeacon printer to the University, 1776. First edition, 4to., fine, crisp copy, later blue wrappers, very scarce.   John Drury Rare Books   March 2015 - 19269   2015   £306

Warren, Mary Bowers *Little Journeys Abroad.* Boston: Joseph Knight Co., 1895. First edition, half title, frontispiece, plates and illustrations, original dark green cloth, attractively blocked and lettered gilt, all edges gilt, very good, bright copy.   Jarndyce Antiquarian Booksellers   CCXI - 281   2015   £40

Warren, Robert Penn   1905-1989 *All the King's Men.* New York: Harcourt Brace & Co., 1946. First edition, top corner of the front board little bumped, else fine in bright, near fine, first issue dust jacket with short tear, little rubbing at spinal extremities and some subtle fading at spine, unusually nice, seldom found in this condition, and often with later dust jacket, from the library of Kate Stettner Lobell and Carl D. Lobell.   Between the Covers Rare Books   196 - 37   2015 $6500

Warren, Robert Penn   1905-1989 *Audubon: a Vision.* New York: Random House, 1969. First edition, number 212 of 250 copies signed by author, book fine, dust jacket very crisp and bright, very slight corner of crease, slipcase very close to fine.   Gemini Fine Books & Arts, Ltd. Art Reference & Illustrated Books: First Editions - 2015 $125

Warren, Robert Penn   1905-1989 *Eleven Poems on the Same Theme.* Norfolk: New Directions, 1942. First edition, wrapper issue, wrappers fine and fine dust jacket (very slightly soiled), housed in custom cloth clamshell case with morocco label gilt, inscribed by author to poet Isabella Gardner.   Between the Covers Rare Books   196 - 120   2015 $1750

Warren, Robert Penn   1905-1989 *New and Selected Poems 1923-1985.* New York: Random House, 1985. First edition, number 279 of 350 copies signed by author, fine in slipcase.   Gemini Fine Books & Arts, Ltd.   Art Reference & Illustrated Books: First Editions - 2015 $70

Warren, Robert Penn   1905-1989 *Selected Poems 1923-1975.* New York: Random House, 1975. First edition, number 23 of 250 copies, signed by author, fine in slipcase.   Gemini Fine Books & Arts, Ltd.   Art Reference & Illustrated Books: First Editions - 2015 $75

Warren, Rosanna *Stained Glass.* New York: W. W. Norton & Co., 1993. First edition, 8vo., original cloth, dust jacket, presentation copy inscribed by author to fellow author Peter Taylor and his wife, poet Eleanor Taylor, Warren has corrected one word and supplied a comma in text of poem 'The Broken Pot', very fine.   James S. Jaffe Rare Books   Modern American Poetry - 298   2015 $250

Warsh, Lewis *Moving through Air.* New York: Angel Hair Books, 1968. First edition, limited to 500 copies, this one of 25 copies with manuscript poem tipped onto inside of rear cover, this copy with the poem 'The Eye', the poem has become detached (as usual) and has left glue shadows on inside of rear wrapper, according to limitation page, these issued thus also signed by artist, but this copy does not bear her signature, quarto, stapled wrappers, slight age toning, else near fine.   Between the Covers Rare Books   196 - 121   2015 $300

Warsh, Lewis *Moving through Air.* New York: Angel Hair Books, 1968. First edition, one of 25 numbered copies signed by Warsh, one of the publishers and Donna Dennis (cover design), folio, original pictorial wrappers, glue residue (as usual) where manuscript sheet is pasted in, otherwise fine, Ted Berrigan's copy with his ownership signature ("one of the 25 special copies given to me by Anne Waldman").   James S. Jaffe Rare Books   Many Happy Returns - 370   2015 $1500

Warton, Thomas *The Triumph of Isis, a Poem. Occasioned by Isis an Elegy.* London: printed for W. Owen and sold by J. Barrett (Oxford), 1750. Second edition, very good, 4to., 16 pages.   C. R. Johnson   Foxon R-Z - 1101r-z   2015 $345

Warwick, Frances Evelyn *A Woman and the War.* London: Chapman & Hall, 1916. First edition, 8vo., frontispiece, red cloth little foxed, very good, tight copy, inscribed by author for Clifford Carver Oct. 1916.   Second Life Books Inc.   189 - 263   2015 $325

Wascher-James, Sande *What Every Woman Needs.* Whidbey Island: 2013. Artist's book, four separate fascicles (books) housed together, one of 5 copies only, each on fine cotton lawn fabric, signed and numbered on colophon by artist, page size 6 1/4 x 8 inches closed, opening when hung to 40 1/2 x 8 inches, bound by artist accordion style for each of the four books, unfolding to make a piece of wall art, housed in box of Red Rose Iris bookcloth, box 17 1/2 x 7 x 1 7/8 inches, box with two storage spaces for books in base and two trays on top to hold the other two books, box with cyanotype of the author, Sophie Tucker, printed on fine lawn cotton on front cover, printed with cyanotype photo on front of each of the four 6-panel books which is bound in Red Rose Iris bookcloth, the six panels contain vintage photos of women.   Priscilla Juvelis - Rare Books   62 - 19   2015 $2500

Wase, Christopher *Considerations Concerning Free-Schools, as Settled in England.* Oxford: printed at the Theater..., 1678. First edition, 8vo., large engraved vignette on titlepage, well bound in mid 20th century maroon morocco gilt, armorial bookplate of a ducal member of the Order of the Garter (presumably transferred from an earlier binding), very good.   John Drury Rare Books   2015 - 22389   2015 $874

Washburn, Robert Collyer *The Life and Times of Lydia E. Pinkham.* New York: Putnam, 1931. First edition, 8vo., very good, tight, clean copy, chipped and nicked dust jacket.   Second Life Books Inc.   189 - 264   2015 $85

Washington, Booker T. *Up from Slavery: an Autobiography.* New York: Doubleday Page, 1901. First edition, octavo, red cloth, little rubbing at extremities couple of leaves little roughly opened resulting in small nicks at page edges, else very near fine, gilt bright, inscribed by author shortly after publication for Joel Chandler Harris, Washington April 14 1901.   Between the Covers Rare Books   197 - 66   2015 $65,000

Waterhouse, Benjamin *Cautions to Young Persons Concerning Health in a Public Lecture Delivered at the Close of the Medical Course in ... Cambridge Nov. 20 1804.* Cambridge: University Press by W. Hilliard, 1805. 32 pages, contemporary marbled paper covers, printed paper label on upper cover, neatly bound in later cloth, light, mostly marginal foxing, some spotting on label, else very good wide margined copy.   Joseph J. Felcone Inc.   Science, Medicine and Technology - 55   2015 $650

Waters, Frank *Oo-oonah Art.* Taos: Taos Pueblo Governor's Office, 1970. First printing was 1200 copies, scarce, inscribed by Waters, oblong hardcover, tops of two pages unevenly opened, else fine, without dust jacket, as issued.   Ken Lopez, Bookseller   164 - 158   2015 $150

Waters, Reuben D. *A Treatise... on the Town of Calais and Vicinity, With Some Sketches of Jewish, Pagan, Mahometan and Other Religions, Character of Bonaparte, Columbus and Notaries!* Calais?: published by the author, 1852. First edition, 8vo., 31, sewn as issued, margins, bit browned otherwise very nice.   M & S Rare Books, Inc.   97 - 312   2015 $125

Waterton, Charles *Wanderings in South America, The North-West of the United States and the Antilles in the Years 1812, 1816, 1820 and 1824.* London: for J. Mawman, 1825. First edition, frontispiece, early half leather over marbled boards, spine restored and later label lettered gilt, some light spotting including to frontispiece with mild offsetting to titlepage, vestige of small bookplate, otherwise sound and clean.   Any Amount of Books   2015 - A94586 2015   £300

Watkin, David *Why is There Only One Word for Thesaurus.* Brighton: Trouser Press, 1998. First edition, large 8vo., original green cloth, letters gilt on spine, signed by author, fine in near fine dust jacket (couple of faint spots).   Any Amount of Books   2015 - C5088   2015   £220

Watkins, Charles *Sonnets and Poems.* Tewkesbury: printed by W. Dyde and sold by W. Wester Paternoster Row, London, 1799. First (and only?) edition, seemingly of great rarity, contemporary green half roan over marbled boards, very slight wear to extremities, fine, crisp copy, with mid 19th century inscription "C. W. Merrifield with his grand mothers love May 13th 1863".   John Drury Rare Books   2015 - 24245   2015 $2185

Watkins, W. H. *The South, Her Position and Dusty. A Discourse Delivered at the Methodist Church, Natchez, Miss., Jan. 4 1861.* Natchez: Natchez Daily Courier Book and Job Office, 1861. First edition, 8vo., original dark green printed wrappers, edges with few chips, starting along spine, crease vertically for mailing, address in ms. on back wrapper, with 1 cent stamp and Natchez cancel to Revd. Silas McKeen/Bradford/Vermont.   M & S Rare Books, Inc.   97 - 73   2015 $475

Watson, Douglas S. *The Spanish Occupation of California...* San Francisco: Grabhorn Press, 1934. First edition, one of 550 copies, small quarto, 2 woodcut portraits, folding facsimile map, decorative boards, light green cloth spine, printed spine label, very fine.   Argonaut Book Shop Holiday Season 2014 - 312   2015 $175

Watson, Elizabeth L. *Houses for Science.* Plainview: Cold Spring Harbor Laboratory Press, 1991. First edition, 4to., fine in fine dust jacket, signed by Elizabeth and James Watson.   By the Book, L. C.   Special List 10 - 89   2015 $175

Watson, G. Gilchrist *The Methodism of the Future.* London: Partridge and Oakey, 1852. First edition, 8vo., recently well bound in cloth lettered in gilt, very good. John Drury Rare Books   2015 - 19823   2015 $177

Watson, Henry William *Cambridge Senate-House Problems and Readers for the Year 1860; with Solutions.* Cambridge: Macmillan, 1860. Small 8vo., 3 folding plates, original olive green blind and gilt stamped cloth, f.f.e.p. clipped (large section missing), 2 manuscript sheets with mathematical problems explored (laid-in), very good.   Jeff Weber Rare Books   178 - 1122   2015 $60

Watson, James D. *The Double Helix: a Personal Account of the Discovery of the Structure of DNA.* Norwalk: Easton Press, 2009. Collector's edition, 8vo., photos, gilt stamped leather, five raised bands, all edges gilt, silk endleaves and place keeping ribbon, signed by author, mint deluxe copy. Jeff Weber Rare Books   178 - 1124   2015 $250

Watson, James D. *Genes, Girls and Gamow. After the Double Helix.* New York: Alfred A. Knopf, 2002. First American edition, 8vo., signed by James Watson, Walter Gilbert and dedicatee, Cecilia Gilbert, 8vo., fine in fine dust jacket.   By the Book, L. C.   Special List 10 - 90   2015 $250

Watson, James D. *Molecular Biology of the Gene.* Menlo Park: Benjamin Cummings, 1977. Third edition, 4to., signed and dated by Marshall Nirenberg, 4to., near fine, few pages dog eared, original color illustrated cloth.   By the Book, L. C.   Special List 10 - 91   2015 $200

Watson, John *The Universal Gazetteer or Modern Geographical Index.* London: C. and G. Kearsley, 1794. Reprint, 8vo., folding frontispiece map, 5 folding maps, some colored, contemporary full calf, rebacked preserving original leather label lettered gilt pastedown over new label, raised bands, new endpapers, some ink marks and light wear to boards, handsome, solid copy, light wear, otherwise very good.   Any Amount of Books   March 2015 - C16199   2015   £400

Watson, Richard *A Letter to His Grace the Archbishop of Canterbury....* London: T. Evans, 1783. First edition, 4to., half title and final ad leaf, stitched as issued, entirely uncut, fine, large copy.   John Drury Rare Books   March 2015 - 16336   2015   £306

Watson, Richard *A Sermon Preached at Albion-Street Chapel, Leeds, at the Formation of the Methodist Missionary Society for the Leeds District, Oct. 6th 1813 and Published by Request, The Profits Will be Paid into the Missionary Fund.* Liverpool: printed by Thos. Kaye, sold by Blanshard City Road London, Nichols Leeds and Smith Wakefield, 1813. First edition, 8vo., 20 pages, wanting half title, preserved in modern wrappers with printed title label on upper cover, very good, scarce.   John Drury Rare Books   2015 - 22783   2015 $168

Watt, Robert *A Summary Practical Elucidation of national Economy.* Edinburgh: printed for the author by R. Marshall, 1848. First edition, 12mo., original blind stamped cloth with title in gilt on spine and both covers, fine copy inscribed by a member of author's family.   John Drury Rare Books   March 2015 - 21535   2015   £266

Watterston, George *A Course of Study, Preparatory to the Bar or the Senate to which is Annexed a Memoir of the Private or Domestic Lives of the Romans.* Washington: Davis and Force, 1823. First edition, 12mo., 240 pages, somewhat later three quarter calf and marbled boards, ex-library, front endleaves loose.   M & S Rare Books, Inc.   97 - 148   2015 $150

Watts, Alan *The Book: on the Taboo against Knowing Who You Are.* New York: Pantheon, 1966. First edition, inscribed by author, large but light stains to boards, very good in very good dust jacket, spine and edge sunned, with couple of closed tears.   Ken Lopez, Bookseller   164 - 243   2015 $650

Watts, Isaac *Divine Songs Attempted in an Easy Language for the Use of Children.* London: printed for J. Buckland, J. and F. and C. Rivington, T. Longman, T. Field, and C. Dilly, 1790. 12mo., few spots and stains, original linen, joints cracked but boards held firm by cords, corners worn, spine defective, ownership inscription inside front cover 'Richard Booker His Book April 17th 1794', sound. Blackwell's Rare Books   B179 - 117   2015   £250

Watts, Isaac *Divine and Moral Songs for Children.* Boston: L. C. Page, n.d., 1896. First US edition, 8vo., blue cloth, pictorial paste-on, 92 pages, covers slightly faded, else near fine, 14 color plates by Mrs. Gaskin.   Aleph-bet Books, Inc.   109 - 193   2015 $350

Watts, Isaac *Horae Lyricae. Poems, Chiefly of the Lyrical Kind.* London: printed by S. and D. Bridge for John Lawrence, 1706. First edition, 8vo., full dark blue morocco, covers decorated with arabesque borders, gilt turn-ins, all edges gilt, very slight rubbing at top of spine, fine, very uncommon edition.   C. R. Johnson   Foxon R-Z - 1102r-z   2015 $2298

Watts, Isaac *Logick; or the Right Use of Reason in the Enquiry after Truth with a Variety of Rules to Guard Against Terror in the affairs of Religion and Human Life as Well as in the Sciences.* London: printed for Buckland, Strahan, Rivington, Caslon, Longman, Field, Dilly, Robinson, Flexney and Goldsmith, 1782. Later edition, contemporary calf with gilt rules to outside borders of each board, red morocco label with gilt lettering to spine which is also richly decorated with floral tools and edges in gilt, just bit of wear to binding with one noticeable bump to top middle of rear board, otherwise clean, bright and tight contemporary copy.   Athena Rare Books   15 - 58   2015 $375

Watts, Isaac *A Paraphrase on the... Celebrated Distich on the Study of Languages. Addressed to the Young Gentlemen of the English Grammar School.* London?: 1795? Small 8vo., short tear in upper margins, pages 4, contemporary drab paper to spine, good.   Blackwell's Rare Books   B179 - 118   2015   £400

Watts, Isaac *Reliquiae Juveniles: Miscellaneous Thoughts in Prose and Verse, on Natural, Moral and Divine Subjects.* London: printed for Richard Ford, and Richard Hett, 1734. First edition, 12mo., late 19th century full polished calf, gilt, spine gilt, dark brown morocco labels, very good.   C. R. Johnson   Foxon R-Z - 1103r-z   2015 $421

Wauchope, Robert *Handbook of Middle American Indians.* Austin: University of Texas Press, First editions, Set (volumes 1-16), hardback, all volumes but 5 and 6 have jackets, clean very good+ copies in mostly very good dust jackets with some slight rubbing and toning and occasional light wear, illustrations, maps, plans, diagrams, from the library of Prof. G. H. Bushnell (103-1978) Curator of Cambridge Univ. Museum.   Any Amount of Books   2015 - A49503   2015   £300

Waugh, Evelyn 1903-1966 *Black Mischief.* London: Chapman & Hall, 1932. First edition first printing, about fine book, jacket with some light wear and few small nicks and toning to spine, very good or better, free of any repairs or restoration.   B & B Rare Books, Ltd.   234 - 100   2015 $1500

Waugh, Evelyn 1903-1966 *The Loved One.* Boston: Little Brown, 1948. First US edition, advance review copy with slip/card laid in, little sunning to spine, thus blind-stamped+ in very good+ dust jacket with darkening spine and tiny tears at spine head, 8vo.   Beasley Books   2013 - 2015 $45

Waugh, Frederick J. *The Clan of Munes.* New York: Scribner, Nov., 1916. Large oblong 4to., fine in dust jacket (missing some pieces, repaired on verso), printed on heavy coated paper, fabulous full page plates (8 color and 20 black and white) plus decorative initials and illustrations in text, beautiful copy, rare in pictorial dust jacket.   Aleph-Bet Books, Inc.   108 - 182   2015 $1750

Wayland, Francis *The Affairs of Rhode-Island. A Discourse Delivered at the Meeting House of the First Baptist Church, Providence May 22, 1842.* Providence: B. Cranston & Co. and H. H. Brown, 1842. 8vo., original salmon color printed wrappers, bit faded and shelf worn, spine reinforced with later staples, scattered foxing, about good, complete and sound.   M & S Rare Books, Inc.   97 - 265   2015 $125

Waylett, Richard *Puppy Tales.* New York: E. P. Dutton, n.d., Owner inscription dated 1915, 4to., cloth backed pictorial boards, slightest bit of rubbing on tips and edges, near fine, 16 full page color illustrations by Cecil Aldin and 16 large pen and inks on text pages.   Aleph-bet Books, Inc.   109 - 20   2015 $950

The Wealth of Great Britain in the Ocean, Exemplified from Materials laid Before the Committee of the House of Commons, Appointed Last Sessions of Parliament... London: printed for M. Cooper and W. Owen, 1749. First edition, 8vo., titlepage just little dustmarked, preserved in recent marbled card wrappers, printed label o upper cover.   John Drury Rare Books   2015 - 21498   2015 $133

Weatherley, F. E. *Sweet Dreams.* No publication information, probably published by Nister or Tuck, circa, 1900. Conical, almost triangular, shaped book, 2 3/4" at its widest point and 4 1/4" at its height, stiff pictorial card covers with ribbon tie, as new in original publisher's decorative slipcase (chip and light wear), cover picture plus 4 beautiful chromolithographs, extremely charming.   Aleph-bet Books, Inc.   109 - 441   2015 $275

Weaver, Lawrence *Houses & Gardens by Sir Edwin Lutyens, R.A.* London: 1925. Third impression, illustrations, cloth, spine bit faded, extremities worn, else very good.   Joseph J. Felcone Inc.   Science, Medicine and Technology - 8   2015 $250

Webb, Arthur, Mrs. *The Doctor in the Kitchen.* London: Newnes, 1935. First edition, photo frontispiece and 4 inserted photo plates, intratextual drawings, crown 8vo., original cloth linen cloth binding with black stamped title lettering to spine, dust jacket bit of foxing to edges, otherwise very good+ in very good jacket which has slightly sun tanned spine panel.   Tavistock Books   Bah, Humbug? - 6   2015 $145

Webb, John *Memorials of the Civil War Between King Charles I and the Parliament of England As It Affected Herfordshire and the Adjacent Counties.* London: Longmans, Green and Co., 1879. First edition, 2 volumes, 8vo., original light brown cloth, lettered gilt at spine, illustrations throughout, from the library of Allan Heywood Bright (1862-1941), slight scuffing and marking to covers, some rubbing at spine ends with slight nicks at head of spine, with no loss and faint foxing to prelims, otherwise near very good, clean text.   Any Amount of Books   2015 - C11839   2015   £175

Webb, Mary *The Chinese Lion: a Story.* London: Bertram Rota, 1937. First edition, one of 350 numbered copies, original batik paper covered boards, red cloth spine and lettering label to upper cover, little foxing to endpapers and spine trifle sunned, but very nice, slightly marked slipcase, from the collection of Gavin H. Fryer.   Bertram Rota Ltd.   308 Part II - 228   2015   £80

Webb, Timothy *Keats-Shelley Review.* Messington, York: Keats-Shelley Memorial Association, 1986. First edition, volumes 1-8, wrappers, 8vo., illustrations, clean, very good, from the library of Ian Gilmour with his ownership signatures and occasional erasable marginal linings and neat notes in pencil.   Any Amount of Books   2015 - A83550   2015   £225

Webb, W. L. *Battles and Biographies of Missourians or the Civil War Period of Our State.* Hudson Kimberly Pub. co., 1900. First edition, 19 portrait plates at end, occasional neat, brief erasable lightly penciled margin notes, else clean, tight.   Buckingham Books   March 2015 - 28356   2015 $275

Webber, Samuel *War, a Poem.* Cambridge: Hilliard & Metcalf, 1823. First edition, 16mo., original printed wrappers, light wear and soiling, nice, internally fresh, fore and bottom margins untrimmed, contemporary signature (Taylor). M & S Rare Books, Inc.   97 - 233   2015 $125

Weber, J. C. *Die Alpen-Pflanzen Deutschlands und der Schweiz in 400 nach der Natur Coloriten Abbildungen...* Munchen: Christian Kaiser, 1879. 12mo., 4 volumes, each containing 100 hand colored plates, green buckram covers, decorated in gilt and black, some foxing to endpapers but not to any of the plates.   Peter Ellis, Bookseller   2014 - 005114   2015   £350

Weber, John Langdon *A Modern Miracle: the Remarkable Conversion of Former Governor Patterson of Tennessee.* Westerville: American Issue Pub. Co., 1914. First edition, 3 1/2 x 6 inches, 8 pages, light toning, mild soiling to titlepage, else very good.   Tavistock Books   Temperance - 2015 $40

Webster, Daniel 1782-1852 *Speech... In Reply to Mr. Hayne, of South Carolina. The Resolution of Mr. Foot, of Connecticut, Relative to the Public Lands, Being Under Consideration Delivered in the Senate Jan. 26 1830.* Washington: Gales & Seaton, 1830. 8vo., 96 pages, removed, very good.   Second Life Books Inc.   190 - 213   2015 $200

Webster, George *Santa Claus and His Works.* New York: McLoughlin Bros. n.d., 1869 (based on listing on rear cover), 4to., decorative wrappers, slight cover soil and front small soil in upper corners, else very good+ and a remarkably clean and tight copy, printed on one side of paper, 6 fine full page chromolithographs and 6 black and whites on text pages by Thomas Nast, rare early copy.   Aleph-Bet Books, Inc.   108 - 313   2015 $750

Webster, George *Van Winkle.* New York: McLoughlin Bros. n.d. circa, 1870. 4to., pictorial wrappers, slightest of spine wear, near fine, illustrations by Thomas Nast with 6 wonderful full page chromolithographs (printed on one side of paper) and with 9 very detailed illustrations in text. Aleph-Bet Books, Inc.   108 - 312   2015 $500

Webster, J. Provand *The Oracle of Baal: a Narrative of some Curious events in the Life of Professor Horatio Carmichael.* London: Hutchinson & Co., 1896. First edition, probably first binding, octavo, 13 inserted plates with illustrations by Warwick Goble, one inserted facsimile, titlepage printed in orange and black, original pictorial dark green vertically ribbed cloth, front and panels stamped in brown and gold, all edges untrimmed, black coated endpapers. L. W. Currey, Inc.   Boy's Adventure Fiction 2015 - 22   2015 $375

Weddington, Sarah *A Question of Choice.* New York: Grosset/Putnam, 1992. First edition, 8vo., fine in dust jacket, signed by author.   Second Life Books Inc.   189 - 265   2015 $45

Weeks, William Rawle *Knock and Wait A While.* Boston: Houghton Mifflin, 1957. First edition, fine, bright, tight, price clipped dust jacket lightly rubbed and with some light professional restoration to spine ends and corners, exceptional copy.   Buckingham Books   March 2015 - 27373   2015 $1000

Wehr, Julian *The Animated Picture Book of Alice in Wonderland.* New York: Grosset & Dunlap, 1945. Oblong 4to., spiral bound, pictorial boards, light edge rubbing, else near fine in frayed dust jacket, illustrations in color by Wehr, plus 4 full page color moveable plates as well, beautiful copy, scarce.   Aleph-bet Books, Inc.   109 - 83   2015 $500

Weichelt, August *Buntpapier-Fabrikation.* Berlin: Papier-Zeitung/Carol Hoffmann, 1927. Third and final edition, 8vo., half green cloth with patterned paper covered boards, leather spine label, specimens illustrations, covers very worn with spine covering attached to back cover only, ex-library markings, all specimens present.   Oak Knoll Books   306 - 100   2015 $400

Weidler, Johann Friedrich *Institutiones Mathematicae Decem et sex Purae Mixtaeque Matheseos Disciplinas Complexae.* Wittenberg: Sam. Hanauer, 1718. First edition, title printed in red and black, 44 engraved plates, some browning, small 8vo., contemporary calf, double gilt fillets on sides, inner roll tooled border, spine gilt in compartments, slightly rubbed, Macclesfield copy with blindstamps and bookplate, very good.   Blackwell's Rare Books   B179 - 110   2015   £750

Weidman, Jerome *I, and I Alone.* New York: Pocket Books, 1972. First separate edition, very good, 12mo., pictorial wrappers.   Buckingham Books   March 2015 - 14866   2015 $225

Weil, James L. *Uses and Other Selected Poems.* New Rochelle: The Elizabeth Press, 1974. First edition, one of 200 copies, 24mo., printed paper covered boards, fine in custom quarter morocco clamshell case, inscribed by author for his father.   Between the Covers Rare Books, Inc.   187 - 288   2015 $200

Weinberg, H. B. *American Impressionism and Realism.* New York: Metropolitan Museum of Art (Abrams), 1994. First edition, fine, fine book and dust jacket.   Stephen Lupack   March 2015 - 2015 $60

Weinberg, Steven *Dreams of a Final Theory.* New York: Pantheon, 1992. First edition, 8vo., signed by author, near fine, in like dust jacket.   By the Book, L. C.   Special List 10 - 68   2015 $200

Weinberg, Steven *The First three Minutes.* London: Andre Deutsch, 1977. First British edition, 8vo., signed by author, fine in fine dust jacket.   By the Book, L. C.   Special List 10 - 69   2015 $400

Weiner, Irving B. *Psychodiagnosis in Schizophrenia.* New York: Wiley, 1966. Fourth printing, near fine, owner's name erased on top edge and bookplate.   Beasley Books 2013 - 2015 $45

Weir, Andy *The Martian.* N.P.: Del Rey, 2014. Advance reading copy, marked "uncorrected proof" of first British edition, scarce, near fine in wrappers.   Ken Lopez, Bookseller 164 - 244   2015 $250

Weis, Helmut *Ernst Fuchs. Das Graphische Werk.* Vienna and Munich: Verlag Fur Jugend Und volk, 1967. First edition, 4to., fine with triptych etched folded and bound in at rear, as issued, signed on each panel by artist, fine in near fine dust jacket with just little waviness, fine cloth box but for mild stain in one corner.   Beasley Books   2013 - 2015 $300

Weisbord, Albert *The Conquest of Power.* New York: Covici Friede, 1937. First edition, hardcover, 2 volumes, fine but for slightly sunned spines in lightly used dust jackets, uncommon set, especially in jackets.   Beasley Books 2013 - 2015 $150

Weisheipi, James Athanasius *Nature and Gravitation.* River Forest: Albertus Magnus Lyceum, 1955. 8vo., printed wrappers, ink ownership signature of David Lindberg, fine, scarce.   Jeff Weber Rare Books   178 - 1128   2015 $50

Weisheipi, James Athanasius *Philosophy and the God of Abraham; Essays in Memory of James Athansius Weisheipl.* Toronto: Pontifical Institute of Mediaeval Studies, 1991. 8vo., frontispiece, printed wrappers, ink ownership signature of David Lindberg, fine.   Jeff Weber Rare Books   178 - 1129   2015 $40

Weismann, August *The Evolution Theory.* New York: AMS Press, 1983. Reprint of 1904 edition, 8vo., 2 volumes, plates, illustrations, figures, index, black cloth, gilt stamped spine title, fine, scarce.   Jeff Weber Rare Books 178 - 1130   2015 $100

Weismann, August *The Germ-Plasm: a Theory of Heredity.* London: Walter Scott, 1893. 8vo., 24 illustrations, burgundy cloth, gilt stamped cover and spine titles, extremities bit rubbed, inner hinge cracked, rubber stamp of East London Natural History and Microscopical Society on title, very good.   Jeff Weber Rare Books   178 - 1131 2015 $40

Weismann, August *Studies in the Theory of Descent.* London: Sampson Low, Marston, Searle & Rivington, 1882. First edition, 8vo., original green cloth, lettered gilt at spine, 8 color plates, slight rubbing at hinges, spine ends with neat Glasgow University library stamps on verso titlepages, otherwise decent, clean, very good.   Any Amount of Books March 2015 - C14254   2015   £375

Weissl, August *The Mystery of the Green Car.* London: Nelson, 1913. First edition, very good without dust jacket. Mordida Books   March 2015 - 002276   2015 $85

Welby, T. Earle *The Victorian Romantics 1850-1870.* London: Gerald Howe Ltd., 1929. 1 of 750 copies, 'Presentation Copy' stamped on limitation page, inserted is 1 and 1/4 page TLS in ink from author to a Mr. Church, also inserted is printed card from publisher requesting a review of the book, recipient has written several notes in pencil about book on both sides, lovely frontispiece by Simeon Solomon and many illustrations throughout, brown cloth boards with gilt title to spine, slight bump to corners, minor wear to spine ends and bump to spine near head, laid paper interior is overall very clean save for offsetting to endpapers, few pencil markings to interior, very good.   The Kelmscott Bookshop   11 - 61   2015 $150

Welch, James *Killing Custer.* New York: W. W. Norton and Co., 1994. First edition, cloth backed boards, one lower corner very slightly jammed, else very fine, pictorial dust jacket.   Argonaut Book Shop   Holiday Season 2014 - 313   2015 $50

Welch, Naomi *The Complete Works of Harrison Fisher.* La Selva Beach: Images of Past, 1999. First edition, 4to., hardcover, issued without dust jacket.   Beasley Books 2013 - 2015 $150

The Welchman's Last Will and Testament. London: printed and sold by Tho. Bickerton, 1719. Second edition, 24 pages, 8vo., half dark green morocco and marbled boards, spine gilt, top edge gilt, woodcut on titlepage, very good. C. R. Johnson   Foxon R-Z - 1105r-z   2015 $2681

Wellington, Arthur Wellesley, 1st Duke of *The Principles of War, Exhibited in the Practice of the Camp and as Developed in a Series of General Orders of Field-Marshal the Duke of Wellington..* London: William Clowes, 1815. First edition, 8vo., occasional very minor rust mark or stain, with relevant, old ms. annotations on two pages, bookplate removed from front pastedown, contemporary half calf over marbled boards, extremities and joints rather worn, spine gilt and lettered but with some wear, generally good, sound really quite uncommon.   John Drury Rare Books   2015 - 26104   2015 $1049

Wells, Carolyn *The Black Night Murders.* Philadelphia: J. B. Lippincott, 1941. First edition, fine in dust jacket with light professional restoration to spine ends, corners and extremities, top edges color bright and unfaded.   Buckingham Books   March 2015 - 36525   2015 $650

Wells, Carolyn *The Happychaps.* New York: Century, Oct., 1908. First edition, brown pictorial cloth, near fine, full page and in text drawings, rare in such nice condition.   Aleph-bet Books, Inc.   109 - 79   2015 $600

Wells, Carolyn *The Technique of the Mystery Story.* Springfield: Home Correspondence School Publisher's, 1913. First edition, crown 8vo., red cloth, gilt stamped lettering, printed grey paper dust jacket, very good+ square and tight, jacket very good+ with spine and edges age toned, some modest extremity wear, nice in uncommon jacket.   Tavistock Books   Bah, Humbug? - 22   2015 $250

Wells, Herbert George   1866-1946 *Boon, the Mind of the Race, The Wild Asses of the Devil and The Last Trump.* London: T. Fisher Unwin, 1915. First edition, half title, illustrations, occasional light spotting, original illustrated dark green cloth, slightly dulled with some slight wear to head of spine, embossed presentation stamp on title, tipped in on leading pastedown is a manuscript note signed "HG" by Wells, on headed card.   Jarndyce Antiquarian Booksellers CCXI - 282   2015   £250

Wells, Herbert George   1866-1946 *The Bulpington of Blup.* New York: Macmillan, 1933. Early reprint, couple of ink numbers, else about fine in very good supplied Grosset & Dunlap dust jacket with some light chips and tears, inscribed by author to screenwriter Anita Loos.   Between the Covers Rare Books, Inc.   187 - 289   2015 $850

Wells, Herbert George   1866-1946 *The First Men in the Moon.* London: George Newnes, 1901. First UK edition, octavo, 12 illustrations, including frontispiece, original front and rear blue cloth as issued with professionally restored quarter leather to spine and fore edges, gold gilt stamping to front and spine, raised bands.   Buckingham Books   March 2015 - 19605   2015 $425

Wells, Herbert George   1866-1946 *The Food of the Gods.* New York: Scribner's Sons, 1904. First edition, near fine, bright gilt, clean, tight text, titlepage.   Stephen Lupack   March 2015 - 2015 $97

Wells, Herbert George   1866-1946 *The Passionate Friends, a Novel.* London: Macmillan, 1913. Crown 8vo., original sage green fine ribbed cloth, backstrip and front cover gilt lettered, with decoration, overall, stamped in blind, browned endpapers, top edge gilt, very good, inscribed by author to poet W. E. Henley.   Blackwell's Rare Books   B179 - 247   2015   £650

Wells, Herbert George   1866-1946 *The Stolen Bacillus and Other Incidents.* London: Methuen, 1895. First edition, Colonial issue, 8vo., original bottle green cloth, lettered gilt on spine, ads dated March 1897, 40 page publisher's catalog at rear, sound very good+ (cover slightly marked, very slight discoloration at spine, 2 small stamps (MJS) (Mervyn Jas Stewart).   Any Amount of Books   2015 - A89058   2015   £160

Wells, Herbert George   1866-1946 *The Stolen Bacillus.* London: Methuen, 1895. First edition, crown 8vo., original dark blue cloth, backstrip and front cover lettered and decorated gilt, endpapers lightly browned, bookplate, untrimmed, very good.   Blackwell's Rare Books   B179 - 248   2015   £1000

Wells, Herbert George   1866-1946 *The Story of a Great School Master: Being a Plain Account of the Life and Ideas of Sanderson of Oundle.* London: Chatto & Windus, 1924. First edition, 8vo., original green cloth, lettered lime green on spine and front cover, illustrations, review copy with publisher's printed review slip loosely inserted and dated Jan. 17th 1924, one corner slightly bumped, otherwise very good+ in slightly creased, very good dust jacket with faint wear at edges with no loss and closed tear at head of spine.   Any Amount of Books   2015 - C13469   2015   £160

Wells, Herbert George   1866-1946 *Tono-Bungay.* London: Macmillan, 1909. First edition, first issue, housed in custom cloth chemise and leather and cloth slipcase, very good plus to near fine with some offsetting to endpapers, top edge gilt, gilt spine lettering and decorations.   Ed Smith Books   83 - 115   2015 $350

Wells, Herbert George   1866-1946 *The War of the Worlds.* New York: and London: Harper & Bros. date code marks this as July, 1915. Near fine, decorated maroon boards, near fine.   Stephen Lupack   March 2015 - 2015 $200

Wells, Herbert George 1866-1946 *Codagh na Reann. (The War of the Worlds).* Baile Atha Cliath:: Oifig Diolta Foillseachain Rialtais, 1934. First Gaelic edition, small octavo, text in Gaelic, trifle rubbed, near fine in lightly chipped, good or better pictorial dust jacket with price inked over on front flap, attractive volume.   Between the Covers Rare Books   196 - 158   2015 $450

Wells, Samuel *The Revenue and the Expenditure of the United Kingdom.* London: James Ridgway, 1835. First edition, 8vo., original green boards, printed spine label, uncut, unopened, ink stain to front cover, boards slightly bumped at edges, slight mottling to covers, corners bumped, spine ends slightly worn and nicked, otherwise about very good with slight foxing to endpapers.   Any Amount of Books   2015 - A47676   2015   £180

Wells, William *Some Particulars of the Life, Trial, Behaviour and Execution of William Wells, Who was Executed on Nottingham Gallows on Monday April 2 1827 for Highway Robbery.* Nottingham: printed by Sutton and Son at the Review Office, n.d., 1827. First separate edition, 12mo., sewn as issued, entirely uncut and partially unopened, fine, apparently very rare.   John Drury Rare Books   March 2015 - 25520   2015 $266

The Welsh-Monster; or the Rise and Downfall of the Late Upstart... London: printed in the year of grace and sold by the booksellers, n.d., 1708. First edition, 8vo., recent marbled wrappers, some foxing, especially towards end, otherwise very good, rare.   C. R. Johnson   Foxon R-Z - 1104r-z   2015 $2298

Welsh, Herbert *Four Weeks Among Some of the Sioux Tribes of Dakota and Nebraska...* Horace F. McCann, Steam Power Printer, 1882. First edition, 8vo., original printed wrappers, 31 pages, spine reinforced with cellophane tape, light wear to corners and extremities, else good, housed in cloth four point case and inserted into matching slipcase with leather label on spine and titles stamped in gold gilt.   Buckingham Books   March 2015 - 35018   2015 $750

Welsh, William *Report of a Visit to the Sioux and Ponka Indians on the Missouri River Made by Wm. Welsh July 1872.* M'Calla & Stavely, 1872. First edition, 8vo., light blue printed wrappers lightly soiled, interior clean, very nice.   Buckingham Books   March 2015 - 36425   2015 $425

Welsted, Leonard *Epistles, Odes, &c.* London: printed for J. Walthoe & J. Peele, 1724. First edition, 8vo., contemporary panelled calf, very slight wear to tips of spine, fine copy, early armorial bookplate of John Orlebar (1697-1765) of the Middle Temple.   C. R. Johnson   Foxon R-Z - 1107r-z   2015 $1149

Welsted, Leonard *Epistles, Odes &c.* London: printed for J. Walthoe and J. Peeple, 1725. Second edition, 12mo., contemporary sheep, rebacked, corners worn, bound without prelim leaf of bookseller's ads, titlepage bit foxed, otherwise good copy, early signature of Charles Walmesley.   C. R. Johnson   Foxon R-Z - 1108r-z   2015 $153

Welsted, Leonard *Of False Fame. An Epistle to the Right Honourable the Earl of Pembroke.* London: printed for T. Cooper, 1732. First edition, 8vo., disbound, fine, rare, complete with half title and final leaf listing other titles by Welsted.   C. R. Johnson   Foxon R-Z - 1109r-z   2015 $2298

Welsted, Leonard *Oikographia; a Poem to His Grace the Duke of Dorset.* London: printed for T. Woodward, J. Walthoe and J. Peele, 1725. First edition, folio, 16 pages, disbound, fine, scarce.   C. R. Johnson   Foxon R-Z - 1110r-z   2015 $1379

Welty, Eudora *The Collected Stories of Eudora Welty.* New York: Harcourt Brace Jovanovich, 1980. First edition, 8vo., signed by author, fine in fine dust jacket.   Beasley Books   2013 - 2015 $350

Welty, Eudora *The Eye of the Story: Selected Essays and Reviews.* New York: Random House, 1978. First edition, fine in very near fine dust jacket with slight sunning at crown, inscribed by Welty to her editor and close friend Mary Lou Aswell.   Between the Covers Rare Books, Inc.   187 - 290   2015 $950

Welty, Eudora *The Golden Apples.* New York: Harcourt Brace and Co., 1949. First edition, signed by author, nearly fine in very good dust jacket with two snags to middle of spine.   Ed Smith Books   82 - 32   2015 $300

Welty, Eudora *Retreat.* Winston Salem: Palaemon Press, 1981. First edition, one of 40 copies numbered with Roman numerals intended for distribution by author and publisher, signed by author, card laid in stating 'Sent at the request of Miss E. Welty" although not indicated, this copy from the collection of close friend, editor and co-dedicatee of The Ponder Heart, Mary Lou Aswell.   Between the Covers Rare Books, Inc.   187 - 291   2015 $850

Welty, Eudora *The Shoe Bird.* New York: Harcourt Brace, 1954. First edition, 4to., presentation from author to friend Willie Spann, near fine in fine dust jacket, with author's characteristic insertion of missing musical stave and lyrics on page 72 (in blue ink).   Ed Smith Books   82 - 31   2015 $500

Wemys, Thomas *Beth-Hak-Kodesh, or the Separation and Conservation of Places in God's Public Service and Worship and the Reverence due unto them Vindicated.* London: printed for Thomas Dring at the Harrow over against the inner Temple gate in Fleet Street, 1674. First and only edition, 12mo., with initial imprimatur leaf (A1), wormtracks affect lower margins throughout occasionally with loss of single letter of text, small tear in margin of leaf F4 with loss of single letter on recto, contemporary sheep, unlettered, spine and corners rather worn but sound from the 17th century library of John Rawlett with his signature, scarce. John Drury Rare Books 2015 - 23670 2015 $1136

Wenger, Lisa *Hut Isch Wider Fasenacht Wo-n-is D'Muetter Cheuchli Bacht.* Bern: Francke, n.d. circa, 1910. Narrow oblong 4to., cloth backed pictorial boards, near fine, 15 richly colored full page illustrations. Aleph-bet Books, Inc. 109 - 187 2015 $600

Wentworth, Edward N. *Progressive Sheep Raising.* Armour's Livestock Bureau, 1925. First edition, pictorial wrappers, frontispiece, illustrations, maps and charts, minor corner crease to few early pages, else near fine. Buckingham Books March 2015 - 34375 2015 $175

Wentworth, Patricia *Beggar's Choice.* Philadelphia: J. B. Lippincott, 1931. First US edition, fine, bright, tight copy in fine dust jacket, exceptional copy. Buckingham Books March 2015 - 31380 2015 $750

Wentworth, Patricia *The Coldstone.* Philadelphia: J. B. Lippincott, 1930. First edition, fine in fine dust jacket. Buckingham Books March 2015 - 36582 2015 $750

Wentworth, T. H. *Views of Niagara.* Oswego: 1821. First edition, 8vo., title, ad leaf, five etched views, not bound, title leaf with 8 paragraphs of text surrounded by typographical border on slate blue paper, cut close to border (with more affected than height), narrower than the views which seem untrimmed, but have several marginal repairs, one small margin replacement and one backed, overall very nice, etchings bright and appealing, images 6.25 x 4.25 inches on sheets two inches larger in both height and width. M & S Rare Books, Inc. 97 - 218 2015 $3500

Werfel, Franz *Die Wahre Geschichte Vom Viederhergestelten Kreux.* Los Angeles: Pazifischen Presse, 1942. Limited to 250 numbered copies, first 1550 bound quarter leather and signed by author on colophon, this copy thus, 8vo., quarter leather, paper covered boards, fore-edge uncut, spine gilt stamped, lightly sunned at top of front cover, light scuffing to spine. Oak Knoll Books 306 - 163 2015 $450

Wesley, Charles *The International Library of Negro Life and History.* New York: Publisher's Co., 1967-1968. Mixed firsts, 10 volumes, very good ex-library. Beasley Books 2013 - 2015 $450

Wesley, John 1703-1791 *Primative (sic) Physic or an Easy and Natural method of Curing Most Diseases.* Trenton: Quequelle and Wilson, 1788. 12mo., modern full sheep, superbly executed in period style, title leaf washed and very skillfully laid down, lower corner neatly replaced, random dampstaining and few chipped corners, correctly restored copy, very scarce. Joseph J. Felcone Inc. Science, Medicine and Technology - 56 2015 $1800

Wesley, Samuel *The Battle of the Sexes: a Poem.* London: printed by J. Brotherton and sold by J. Roberts, 1724. Second edition, 8vo., recent half calf, black morocco label, early signature on titlepage of P. Carter, piece torn from one blank margin, one other clean tear without affecting text, otherwise good, bound in at back is half title of unrelated Neo-Latin poem by Nicholas Rowe. C. R. Johnson Foxon R-Z - 1114r-z 2015 $613

Wesley, Samuel *The Battle of the Sexes: a Poem.* Dublin: printed by George Faulkner, 1740. Third edition, 8vo., disbound, very good, scarce. C. R. Johnson Foxon R-Z - 1115r-z 2015 $613

Wesley, Samuel *The Battles of the Sexes.* Dublin: printed by Edward Waters, 1740. 8vo., disbound, very rare Dublin printing, slight foxing, several stamps of old lending library, otherwise good. C. R. Johnson Foxon R-Z - 1116r-z 2015 $919

Wesley, Samuel *The History of the New Testament, Representing the Actions and Miracles of Our Blessed Saviour and His Apostles....* London: printed for Benj. Cowse and John Hooke, 1715. First edition, 2nd issue, 12mo., engraved frontispiece and titlepage, 19th century half calf and green cloth boards, gilt, spine gilt, later brown morocco label, top edge gilt, little rubbed, upper joint weak, very good. C. R. Johnson Foxon R-Z - 1111r-z 2015 $613

Wesley, Samuel *The Iliad in a Nutshell or Homers Battle of the Frogs and Mice.* London: printed for R. Barker and sold by J. Roberts, 1726. First edition, 8vo., disbound, very good, scarce. C. R. Johnson Foxon R-Z - 1117r-z 2015 $1149

Wesley, Samuel *Letters to ... Mr. Jacobs Relating to the Introduction into this Country of the Works of John Sebastian Bach.* London: S. W. Partridge & Co., 1875. Blue boards, vellum spine, ink title, armorial bookplate of Charles Buller Heberden, very good, Geoffrey Tillotson's inscription 17.5.1926. Jarndyce Antiquarian Booksellers CCVII - 554 2015 £20

Wesley, Samuel *Neck or Nothing; A Consolatory Letter from Mr. D-ent-n to Mr. C-url upon his being tost in a blanket &c.* London: sold by Charles King, 1716. First edition, 16 pages, 8vo., disbound, fine with duty stamp on verso of titlepage as usual. C. R. Johnson Foxon R-Z - 1118r-z 2015 $2298

Wesley, Samuel *The Parish Priest. A Poem Upon a Clergyman Lately Deceas'd.* London: printed for J. Roberts, 1732. First edition, 4to., disbound, pale waterstain in lower portion, but very good, rare. C. R. Johnson Foxon R-Z - 1119r-z 2015 $2298

Wesley, Samuel *Poems on Several Occasions.* London: printed for the author by E. Say and sold by S. Birt, 1736. First edition, 4to., contemporary calf, gilt, spine gilt, red morocco label, just trifle rubbed, fine copy. C. R. Johnson Foxon R-Z - 1112r-z 2015 $919

Wesley, Samuel *Poems on Several Occasions.* Cambridge: printed by J. Bentham for J. Brotherton and S. Birt., London, 1743. Second edition, 12mo., contemporary sheep, spine gilt, red morocco label (some rubbing), early signature of T. Chas. Clark and T. Clarke (sic) twice on titlepage, fair. C. R. Johnson Foxon R-Z - 1113r-z 2015 $61

Wesson, Marianne *Render Up the Body.* London: Headline, 1997. First edition, very fine in dust jacket. Mordida Books March 2015 - 002279 2015 $75

The West, thru the Columns of the Denver Daily Record Stockman. Denver Daily Record Stockman, 1925. First edition, 4to., pictorial newsprint, illustrations, light corner creases to front cover and with few fore-edge small closed tears, else good. Buckingham Books March 2015 - 38245 2015 $200

West, Arthur Graeme *The Diary of a Dead Officer.* Llandogo: Old Stile Press, 2014. 11/140 copies (from an edition of 150 copies), signed by artist, John Abell, printed on Velin Arches paper, linocuts throughout printed directly from block, many full page and double spread, titlepage printed in red and gray, oblong 4to., original quarter beige cloth with linocut illustrated boards, cloth to both boards stamped in red, backstrip lettered in red, top edge speckled black, other edges untrimmed, green cloth slipcase with red 'velvet' lining, fine. Blackwell's Rare Books B179 - 216 2015 £295

West, Dorothy *The Living is Easy.* Old Westbury: Feminist Press, 1982. First Feminist Press edition, 8vo., author's presentation on title, paper wrappers, cover scuffed, otherwise very good, tight copy. Second Life Books Inc. 190 - 214 2015 $150

West, Gilbert *A Canto of the Fairy Queen.* London: printed for G. Hawkins, 1739. First edition, sewn as issued, few minor spots, but very fine copy in original condition entirely uncut. C. R. Johnson Foxon R-Z - 1123r-z 2015 $536

West, Gilbert *Stowe, the Gardens of the Right Honourable Richard Lord Viscount Cobham....* London: printed for L. Gilliver, 1732. First edition, folio, disbound, this copy printed on fine paper, watermark of fleur-de-lys on shield, only other copies as yet identified as printed on fine paper are two at the British Library, fine. C. R. Johnson Foxon R-Z - 1124r-z 2015 $1302

West, Jane *A Tale of the Times.* London: printed for T. N. Longman and O. Rees, 1799. Second edition, 3 volumes, 12mo., 7 pages ads at end volume 3, some foxing, contemporary quarter calf, marbled paper boards, vellum tips, neatly rebacked, spines ruled in gilt, red morocco labels, numbered direct, grey sprinkled edges, bit rubbed, early armorial bookplates of Delapre Abbey, name repeated on each title, lager labels of Anne and F. G. Renier, very good. Jarndyce Antiquarian Booksellers CCXI - 283 2015 £280

West, Jessamyn *The Friendly Persuasion.* New York: Harcourt Brace and Co., 1945. Fifth printing, extremities rubbed, very good, tattered remnants of dust jacket, author's complimentary slip laid in, inscribed by author to Rachel MacKenzie. Between the Covers Rare Books, Inc. 187 - 292 2015 $150

West, Paul *Gala: a Fictional Sequel to Words for a Deaf Daughter.* New York: Harper & Row, 1976. First edition, fine in fine dust jacket with light wear to crown and corners, inscribed by author to novelist Monica Dickens (granddaughter of Charles Dickens). Between the Covers Rare Books, Inc. 187 - 293 2015 $250

West, Paul *Pearl and the Pumpkin.* New York: Dillingham, 1904. First edition, probably earlier issue (priority uncertain) with blue endpapers, 4to., green cloth stamped in dark green, pictorial paste-on, spine slightly faded, else very clean, bright, near fine copy, illustrations by W. W. Denslow with 16 bold color plates and a profusion of color illustrations in text, particularly bright copy. Aleph-Bet Books, Inc. 108 - 132 2015 $850

West, Paul *Wyandotte Soda and Bell Starch Rhymes; or Father Gander's Sequel to Mother Goose.* New York: Knopf, 1930. 3 1/2 x 5 1/2 inches, pictorial wrappers, very good, chromolithographs on almost every page. Aleph-Bet Books, Inc. 108 - 303 2015 $225

West, Philip *Una Mirada Hacia Philip West/Menu.* Cuenca MENA/Taller de Ediciones, 2000. First edition, hardcover, folio, boxed presentation of two spiral bound books: MENU (serigraphs) and Poemas, Escritos, Collages. Beasley Books 2013 - 2015 $750

West, Richard *An Inquiry into the Manner of Creating Peers.* London: printed for J. Roberts, 1719. First edition, 8vo., recent plain wrappers, very good. John Drury Rare Books 2015 - 17730 2015 $177

West, Richard Samuel *Target: The Political Cartoon Quarterly Volume 1-6 (Complete).* Warminster: Richard Samuel West and Kendall B. Mattern Jr., 1981-1987. one of only 36 copies (26 lettered and 10 numbered), this letter 'O', signed by West, the complete 24 issue run, illustrations by Bill Watterson, quarto, approximately 750 pages, presentation binding, contemporary full cloth stamped gilt on spine, fine, rare.   Between the Covers Rare Books   196 - 132   2015 $3500

Westall, William *The Old Bank.* London: Chatto & Windus, 1902. First edition, light cosmetic restoration to spine and corners, moderately foxed, former owner's inked name on front flyleaf, else very good, tight copy.   Buckingham Books   March 2015 - 30175   2015 $300

Westall, William *Picturesque Tour of the River Thames.* London: R. Ackerman, 96 Strand, 1828. First edition, 4to., 24 finely hand colored aquatint plates, colored aquatint vignette on title and another to final leaf, contemporary full green crushed morocco, spine decorated and lettered gilt within raised bands, spine faded to brown by Riviere and Son, preserving original cloth at end of work, armorial bookplate of Fairfax Rhodes and C. Robert Bagnold and bookseller tickets of Thomas Thorp and R. D. Steadman, fine.   Marlborough Rare Books   List 54 - 89   2015   £4500

Westall, William Bury *Nigel Fortescue; or the Hunted Man.* London: Ward and Downey, 1888. First edition, octavo, original pictorial red cloth, front panel stamped in black, spine panel stamped in black and gold, publisher's monogram stamped in blind on rear cover, top edge untrimmed, floral patterned endpapers.   L. W. Currey, Inc.   Boy's Adventure Fiction 2015 - 28   2015 $300

Westcott, Kenneth E. *The Pacific Coast Railway.* Los Altos: Benchmark Publications, 1998. First edition, quarto, profusely illustrated with photos, maps, schedules and diagrams, blue cloth, gilt, very fine with pictorial dust jacket.   Argonaut Book Shop   Holiday Season 2014 - 314   2015 $175

Westerberg, Hans *Boy from New Orleans. Louis Satchmo Armstrong On Records, Films, Radio.* Copenhagen: Jazz Media, 1981. First edition, wrappers, fine.   Beasley Books   2013 - 2015 $40

Westerman, Percy Francis *The Dreadnought of the Air.* London: S. W. Partridge & Co. Ltd. n.d., 1914. First edition, octavo, 6 inserted plates with color illustrations by C. Williams, original pictorial gray-green cloth, front panel stamped in blue, black and tan, spine panel stamped in blue, black, tan and gold, all edges stained green.   L. W. Currey, Inc.   Boy's Adventure Fiction 2015 - 100   2015 $100

Westerman, Percy Francis *The Secret of the Plateau.* London and Glasgow: Blackie & Son, n.d., 1931. First edition, 4 inserted plates and illustrations by W. Edward Wigfull, original pictorial grey cloth, front and spine panels stamped in black and yellow.   L. W. Currey, Inc.   Boy's Adventure Fiction 2015 - 66   2015 $150

The Western Agriculturist; a Farmer's Magazine containing a Course of Lectures on Agricultural Chemistry. London: J. Crockford Axminster, G. P. Putnam, 1845. First edition, 8vo., folding table, occasional slight foxing, wanting lower free endpaper, original maroon cloth, printed title label on upper cover, spine faded but very good, very rare.   John Drury Rare Books March 2015 - 21845   2015   £266

Western, Charles Callis *A Letter to the President and Members of the Chelmsford Agricultural Society Upon the Causes of the Distressed State of the Agricultural Classes of the United Kingdom of Great Britain and Ireland.* London: James Ridgway, 1835. Third edition, 8vo., half title, final leaf and ads in recent plain wrappers, very good.   John Drury Rare Books   2015 - 18078   2015 $89

Westlake, Donald E. *Adios, Scherazade.* New York: Simon and Schuster, 1970. First edition, fine but for remainder dot on bottom edge, mild erasure in corner of f.e.p., in very close to fine dust jacket with one short, clean tear.   Beasley Books   2013 - 2015 $125

Westlake, Donald E. *Bank Shot.* New York: Simon & Schuster, 1972. First edition, presentation inscription from author, fine in dust jacket lightly soiled on rear panel.   Buckingham Books   March 2015 - 32282   2015 $250

Westlake, Donald E. *Drowned Hopes.* New York: Mysterious Press, 1900. First edition, one of 100 specially bound numbered copies signed by Westlake, very fine in slipcase, without dust jacket as issued.   Mordida Books   March 2015 - 006299   2015 $75

Westlake, Donald E. *God Save the Mark.* New York: Random House, 1967. First edition, fine with top stain bright red, in fine dust jacket.   Buckingham Books   March 2015 - 35159   2015 $275

Westlake, Donald E. *Help I Am Being Held Prisoner.* M. Evans and Co., 1974. First edition, signed by author on titlepage, fine in cloth dust jacket.   Buckingham Books   March 2015 - 34193   2015 $200

Westlake, Donald E. *The Hot Rock.* New York: Simon & Schuster, 1970. First edition, fine in dust jacket, signed by author.   Buckingham Books   March 2015 - 34096   2015 $750

Westlake, Donald E. *Killy.* 1963. First edition, fine, bright, square copy in dust jacket with one tiny restoration to bottom front corner, inscribed by author.   Buckingham Books   March 2015 - 35192   2015 $425

Westlake, Donald E. *Levine.* New York: Mysterious Press, 1984. First edition, one of 250 numbered copies signed by author, very fine in like slipcase.   Mordida Books   March 2015 - 006304   2015 $85

Westlake, Donald E. *Murder Among Children.* New York: Random House, 1967. First edition, presentation from author for Sam Sorowitz, tiny stamped letter to top edge of front flyleaf and small brown mark (about size of pencil eraser), to top edge of front leaf, else near fine, tight square copy in very lightly soiled dust jacket.   Buckingham Books   March 2015 - 32283   2015 $300

Westlake, Donald E. *The Spy in the Ointment.* New York: Random House, 1966. First edition, bookseller's small label on rear endpaper, fine in dust jacket with small light stain on spine.   Mordida Books   March 2015 - 012705   2015 $90

Westlake, Donald E. *361.* New York: Random House, 1962. First edition, fine and unread in about fine dust jacket, exceptional copy, from the collection of Duke Collier.   Royal Books   36 - 243   2015 $350

Weston, Brett *Photographs from Five Decades.* Millerton: Aperture, 1980. First edition, folio, fine in fine dust jacket.   Beasley Books   2013 - 2015 $135

Weston, Charles *Remarks on the Poor Laws and on the State of the Poor.* Brentford: printed by P. Norbury sold by Payne and Mackinlay London and J. Martin Kensington, 1802. First edition, 8vo., contemporary half calf over marbled boards, rebacked spine lettered gilt, very good, 19th century armorial bookplate of Thomas Hammond Foxcroft with his signature, rare.   John Drury Rare Books   2015 - 22656   2015 $656

Weston, Charles Wilson *California and the West.* New York: Duell Sloan and Pearce, 1940. First edition, 96 photographic plates and 1 map, black cloth lettered in silver, upper corners very slightly jammed, contemporary owner's signature on front free endpaper, else fine and clean, lacking dust jacket.   Argonaut Book Shop   Holiday Season 2014 - 315   2015 $225

Weston, Edward *My Camera At Point Lobos.* Yosemite/Boston: V. Adams/Houghton Mifflin, 1950. First edition, spiral bound folio, stiff card covers, without dust jacket, very good with few spots where glossy black finish as come away, leaving dark gray.   Beasley Books   2013 - 2015 $250

Westwood, Vivienne *Vivienne Westwood Opus.* London: Opus Media (Kraken), 2008. First edition, large folio, 97 exclusive photos taken by Zenon Texeira, all copies personally signed by Westwood,.   Any Amount of Books   2015 - A94196   2015   £750

Weyer, Johann *Witches, Devils and Doctors in the Renaissance: Johann Weyer, De Praestigiis Daemonum.* Binghamton: Medieval & Renaissance Texts & Studies, 1991. First English translation, large 8vo., original publisher's black cloth, lettered gilt on spine and front cover, clean, sound, very good+.   Any Amount of Books   2015 - C12966   2015   £225

Weyl, Hermann *Gruppentheorie and Quatenmechanik.* Leipzig: S. Hirzel, 1931. Second edition, large 8vo., original maroon reddish gilt stamped cloth, bookplate and signature of G(eorge) Polya (1887-1985), near fine.   Jeff Weber Rare Books   178 - 1139   2015 $175

Weyland, John *A Short Inquiry into the Policy, Humanity and Past Effects of the Poor Laws...* London: printed for J. Hatchard, Mess. F. C. and J. Rivington and J. Asperne, 1807. First edition, 8vo., half title and errata leaf, old tear in on text leaf (but no loss of surface), well bound fairly recently in cloth backed marbled boards, black spine label, gilt lettered, entirely uncut, very good, surprisingly uncommon.   John Drury Rare Books   2015 - 25582   2015 $1049

Whaley, John *A Collection of Poems.* London: printed for the author by John Willis and Joseph Boddington and sold by Messieurs Innys and Manby...., 1732. First edition, 8vo., contemporary panelled calf, rebacked at early date, red morocco label (some wear to spine and corners, joints cracked), aside from binding wear, very good, signed on titlepage by Spark Molesworth whose name appears in subscriber's list as student at Trinity Hall, Cambridge, later bookplate of Oliver Brett, Viscount Esher.   C. R. Johnson   Foxon R-Z - 1128r-z   2015 $460

Whaley, John *A Collection of Original Poems and Translations.* London: printed for the author and sold by R. Manby and H. S. cox, 1745. First edition, 8vo., contemporary marbled calf, gilt, spine gilt, red morocco label, just trifle rubbed, wanting flyleaf, else fine, with early armorial bookplate of Sir William Beauchamp Proctor (1722-1773) of Langley Park in Norfolk, recent signature of Margaret Morgan.   C. R. Johnson   Foxon R-Z - 1129-r-z   2015 $613

Wharton, Edith 1862-1937 *The Age of Innocence.* New York: D. Appleton and Co., 1920. First edition, first printing with "1" at end of last page of text, original red cloth, very good, some rubbing and light wear to extremities, spine and lower part of front board lightly faded, two small tears to upper spine, former owner bookplate to front pastedown, some offsetting to endpapers, nice, fragile.   B & B Rare Books, Ltd.   234 - 191   2015 $2750

Wharton, Edith 1862-1937 *A Backward Glance.* New York: D. Appleton Co., 1934. First edition, first printing, photos, about fine with some glue residue from former owner bookplate to front pastedown in near fine, lightly toned and unclipped jacket with very minor wear. B & B Rare Books, Ltd. 234 - 102 2015 $300

Wharton, Edith 1862-1937 *Certain People.* D. Appleton and Co., 1930. First edition, half title, original brown cloth, lettered gilt, small repaired tear in cloth on front board. Jarndyce Antiquarian Booksellers CCXI - 284 2015 £50

Wharton, Edith 1862-1937 *Ethan Frome.* New York: Charles Scribner's Sons, 1911. First edition, first issue with 'wearily' unbattered on page 135, one of 6000 copies, publisher's red cloth, about near fine, some light wear to extremities, faint soiling to front board, slight lean to spine, former owner name erased from front free endpaper, otherwise clean interior, overall bright and attractive. B & B Rare Books, Ltd. 2015 - 2015 $600

Wharton, Edith 1862-1937 *The Glimpses of the Moon.* D. Appleton and Co., 1922. First edition, half title, 4 pages ads, original orange cloth lettered black, small light stain in lower margin front board, spine little faded, small nick at head, good plus. Jarndyce Antiquarian Booksellers CCXI - 285 2015 £35

Wharton, Edith 1862-1937 *Italian Villas and Their Gardens.* New York: Century, 1904. First edition, 4to., gilt pictorial cloth, top edge gilt, except for light corner bump and very few fox spots on tissue guards, fine, bright copy, cover by Maxfield Parrish plus 26 stunning full page color and black and whites by him as well, lovely copy. Aleph-Bet Books, Inc. 108 - 336 2015 $2500

Wharton, Edith 1862-1937 *Twelve Poems.* London: Riccardi Press for the Medici Society, 1926. First edition, limited to 130 numbered copies, presentation copy inscribed by Wharton, Dec. 1926, blue paper covered boards, blue gray cloth spine lettered gilt, top edge gilt, minor rubbing to extremities, slight browning to edge, lower corners lightly worn with small tears, light offsetting and some foxing to front endpaper, especially scarce with personal inscription. B & B Rare Books, Ltd. 234 - 103 2015 $9500

Wharton, Francis *A Treatise on Criminal Law.* Philadelphia: 1880. Eighth edition, full law calf, some rubbing. Bookworm & Silverfish 2015 - 5623606410 2015 $158

What is a Geisha? Tokyo: Foreign Auxiliary of the WCTU, 1920. Presumed first and only edition with Japanese imprint on final leaf, 16 pages, original printed paper wrappers, front panel somewhat faded and dust soiled, otherwise very good. Tavistock Books Temperance - 2015 $250

What is Luxury? To Which is Added a Manipulus of Etymological and Other Nugae. London: Samuel Maunder, 1829. First and only edition, 8vo., uncut, partly unopened, half title and final leaf with publisher's notice, some very light occasional foxing, original cloth, printed spine label, short tear to head of spine, very good, near contemporary signature of George Grantham of Barcombe Place, scarce. John Drury Rare Books March 2015 - 14835 2015 $266

Whately, Elizabeth *English Life, social and Domestic, in the Middle of the Nineteenth Century...* London: John W. Parker, 1847. 4 pages ads, uncut, original green cloth, borders and central ornaments blocked in blind, spine lettered gilt, very good, clean. Jarndyce Antiquarian Booksellers CCXI - 286 2015 £125

Whately, Richard *Historic Certainties Respecting the Early History of America, Developed in a Critical Examination of the Book of the Chronicles of the land of Ecnarf...* London: John W. Parker, 1851. First edition, 8vo., half title, recently well bound in linen backed marbled boards, lettered, very good, very scarce. John Drury Rare Books March 2015 - 19891 2015 $221

Whately, Thomas *Observations on Modern Gardening.* London: printed for T. Payne & Son, 1777. Fourth edition, full contemporary speckled calf, gilt ruled border and bands, red morocco label, little rubbed, corners slightly bumped, very good. Jarndyce Antiquarian Booksellers CCXI - 287 2015 £650

Whatley, Robert *A Letter to the Right Honourable the Lord-Chief-Justice King on His Lordship's Being Design'd a Peer.* London: J. Roberts, 1725. First edition, 4to., preserved in later plain wrappers with printed title label on upper cover, very good, rare. John Drury Rare Books 2015 - 22426 2015 $133

Wheat, Carl Irving *The Maps of the California Gold Region 1848-1857. A Biblio-Cartography and an Important Decade.* Storrs-Mansfield: Maurizio Martino, 1995. Reprinted from rare first edition, small folio, 27 facsimile maps, original tan cloth printed in red on white background on spine, very fine. Argonaut Book Shop Holiday Season 2014 - 316 2015 $150

Wheatley, Dennis *The Irish Witch.* London: Hurchinson, 1973. First edition, some light spotting on page edges, otherwise fine in dust jacket with internal tape mend, inscribed by author. Mordida Books March 2015 - 009559 2015 $100

Wheatley, Dennis *The Prisoner of the Mask.* London: Hutchinson, 1957. First edition, some light spotting on page edges, otherwise fine in dust jacket with couple of internal tape mends and tiny wear at corners, inscribed by author. Mordida Books March 2015 - 009556 2015 $100

Wheeler, George M. *Report Upon Geographical and Geological Explorations and Surveys West of the One Hundredth Meridian Volume V - Zoology.* Washington: 1875. 1021 pages, illustrations, original cloth, boards rubbed, dampstain to a corner of last 180 or so pages at no point touching text or illustrations, recased with new endpapers and spine laid down, thus a tight, mostly clean copy of a huge volume, excellent copy.   Dumont Maps and Books of the West   130 - 49   2015 $650

Wheeler, John Archibald *Geons, Black Holes and Quantum Foam: a Life in Physics.* New York: W. W. Norton, 1998. 8vo., photos, quarter gilt stamped black cloth over similar black cloth dust jacket, signed and inscribed by author to Dr. Carson Todd in ink at half title, signed and inscribed black and white photo portrait of Wheeler laid in, TLS from Wheeler to Todd, near fine.   Jeff Weber Rare Books   178 - 1140   2015 $450

Wheeler, John Archibald *A Journey into Gravity and Spacetime.* New York: Scientific American Library, 1999. Square 8vo., illustrations, original printed wrappers, signed and inscribed by author to Dr. Carson Todd, very good.   Jeff Weber Rare Books   178 - 1141   2015 $125

Wheeler, Olin D. *Wonderland 1901.* privately printed, 1901. 9 1/2 x 7 inches, color pictorial wrappers, 108 pages, numerous black and white illustrations with some in color, two maps, one with some color.   Buckingham Books March 2015 - 35172   2015 $450

Wheeler, Zenas *Quartz Operator's Handbook.* San Francisco: Mingin and Scientific Press Job Printing Office, 1865. First edition, 12mo., 2 plates, text drawings and calculations, errata page, blindstamped lavender cloth, gilt lettered front cover, scattered light foxing, spine faded to brown, very good, very scarce.   Argonaut Book Shop Holiday Season 2014 - 213   2015 $450

When the Cat's Away the Mice May Play. Colophon: (London): printed for A. Baldwin, n.d., 1712. First edition, 4 pages, folio, 2 leaves, folded as issued in light brown cloth folding case (cover detached), very good, from the library of Jerome Kern with his booklabel.   C. R. Johnson   Foxon R-Z - 1130r-z   2015 $2681

Whewell, William 1794-1866 *Additional Remarks on Some Parts of Mr. Thirlwall's Two Letters on the admission of Dissenters to Academical Degrees.* Cambridge: J. & J. J. Deighton and Rivington, 1834. First edition, 8vo., preserved in recent plain wrappers with printed title label on upper cover, very good.   John Drury Rare Books   2015 - 21504   2015 $133

Whewell, William 1794-1866 *The Doctrine of Limits with its Applications: namely Conic Sections, the First Three Sections of Newton, The Differential Calculus.* Cambridge: printed at the University Press for J. and J. J. Deighton and John W. Parker, 1838. 8vo., diagrams, errata sheet, additional errata tipped in slip, contemporary quarter blue library cloth over paper boards, extremities worn, spine repaired with Kozo paper, armorial bookplate and ownership signature of Joseph William Dunning, very scarce.   Jeff Weber Rare Books   178 - 1142   2015 $75

Whewell, William 1794-1866 *Of a Liberal Education in General and with Particular Reference to the Leading Studies of the University of Cambridge.* London: John W. Parker, 1845. First edition, 8vo, original paper covered boards with green linen spine and spine label (now somewhat faded and hard to read), corners scuffed and worn, front inner hinge cracked by holding well, slight soiling but otherwise sound, near very good, pencilled ownership signature of historian F. R. Cowell.   Any Amount of Books 2015 - A46028   2015   £150

Whibley, Charles *Studies in Frankness.* London: William Heinemann, 1898. First edition, presentation copy inscribed by author for friend Marcel Schwob Nov.. 1897, original black cloth with rubbing to front cover, bumping to corners and edge of front board, spotting to prelims, otherwise very good.   The Kelmscott Bookshop   11 - 62   2015 $250

Whig and Tory; or Wit on both Sides. London: printed and sold by booksellers, 1712. First edition under this title, 8vo., contemporary panelled calf, slight cracks in joints, very good, uncommon.   C. R. Johnson   Foxon R-Z - 1131r-z 2015 $919

Whishaw, Fred *The Diamond of Evil.* London: Long, 1902. First edition, endpapers darkened and page edges spotted, otherwise fine in red pictorial cloth covered boards, gold stamped titles on spine.   Mordida Books   March 2015 - 002290   2015 $175

Whistler, James McNeil *The Gentle Art of Making Enemies.* London: William Heinemann, 1904. Third edition, half title, 4to., unopened in original brown boards, blocked and lettered gilt, mustard cloth spine, library label of Easton Neston, near fine.   Jarndyce Antiquarian Booksellers   CCXI - 288   2015   £45

Whiston, William *Reflexions on an Anonymous Pamphlet Entituled, a Discourse of free Thinking.* London: printed for the author and sold by A. Baldwin, 1713. First edition, 8vo. very good, later plain wrappers.   John Drury Rare Books 2015 - 14743   2015 $221

Whitaker, John *The Real Origin of Government.* London: printed for John Stockdale, 1795. First edition, titlepage rather soiled and stabbed in inner margin, ads on verso of final leaf preserved in recent blue card covers, with printed title label on upper cover, scarce.   John Drury Rare Books 2015 - 21634   2015 $177

Whitcombe, Samuel *Considerations Addressed to the Legislature Upon the Expediency and Policy of Authorising the Alienation of Estates Belonging to Corporate Bodies, Particularly Bishops and Deans and Chapters...* London: G. and W. Nicol, 1810. First edition, half title, well bound recently in cloth backed boards, spine gilt lettered, very good presented and inscribed by author to Lord Castlereagh, first scarce.   John Drury Rare Books   March 2015 - 19533   2015 $266

White Cycle Co. *Catalogue of the Best Makes of Bicycles 1893.* Trenton: White Cycle Co., 1893. 40 pages, plus illustrations, wrappers, front wrapper with two small dark spots inpper margin and one short tear, else very good, 4 page insert laid in.   Joseph J. Felcone Inc.   Science, Medicine and Technology - 11   2015 $225

White, Clarence W. *The Story of a Reformed Desperado.* Privately printed circa, 1924. First edition, 8 1/4 x 5 1/5 inches, printed wrappers, 42 pages, spine reinforced with tape, few pin holes and with light wear to extremities.   Buckingham Books   March 2015 - 35301   2015 $275

White, Daniel Appleton *Eulogy on John Pickering, LL.D., President of the American Academy of Arts and Sciences.* Cambridge: Metcalf, 1847. Original first printing, small 4to., original printed wrappers bottom spine end chipped, ownership signature of Henry W. Pickering, very good.   Jeff Weber Rare Books   178 - 900   2015 $45

White, Elwyn Brooks *Charlotte's Web.* New York: Harper Bros., 1952. First edition, 8vo., tan cloth, fine in dust jacket (nice and clean with small archival mends at spine ends and on one edge), inscribed by White, illustrations by Garth Williams with more than 40 black and whites plus color dust jacket, extremely scarce, particularly beautiful.   Aleph-bet Books, Inc.   109 - 485   2015 $10,000

White, Elwyn Brooks *Charlotte's Web.* New York: Harper and Bros., 1952. First edition, first printing, very good, light wear to spine ends, former owner signature erased from front endpaper, unclipped jacket with few tears, some creasing along upper edge, wear to spine and few small nicks, else very bright jacket without usual toning.   B & B Rare Books, Ltd.   234 - 104   2015 $1500

White, Elwyn Brooks *The Essays of E. B. White.* New York: Harper & Row, 1977. First edition, inscribed by Helen Thurber (wife of James) to Mary (Mian) and her husband Aristide, near fine in very good, moderately edgeworn dust jacket with one small tape repair.   Ken Lopez, Bookseller 164 - 159   2015 $150

White, Michael G. *A Brother's Blood.* New York: Harper Collins, 1996. First edition, very fine in dust jacket.   Mordida Books   March 2015 - 002292   2015 $85

White, Randy Way *The Man Who Invented Florida.* New York: St. Martin's, 1993. First edition, light foxing to endpages and page edges, near fine in like dust jacket with bit of wear to crown, dedication copy inscribed by author for Peter Matthiessen, dedicatee.   Ken Lopez, Bookseller   164 - 245   2015 $1000

White, Stewart Edward *On Tiptoe. A Romance of the Redwoods.* New York: George H. Doran Co., 1922. First edition, inscribed by author for J. C. Dykes, very good in dust jacket with moderate wear to extremities.   Buckingham Books   March 2015 - 13515   2015 $300

White, Terence Hanbury   1906-1964 *Loved Helen and Other Poems.* London: Chatto & Windus, 1929. First edition, octavo, signed by author, cloth slightly rubbed at head and tail of spine, very good in good dust jacket rubbed and frayed at edges with 2 cm. closed tear at upper hinge.   Peter Ellis, Bookseller   2014 - 016811   2015   £325

White, Terence Hanbury   1906-1964 *They Winter Abroad - a Novel.* London: Chatto & Windus, 1932. First edition, octavo, two pages of ads at rear, edges very faintly spotted, covers slightly dusty, head and tail of spine slightly bumped, very good in like dust jacket, chipped, rubbed and creased defective at top edge.   Peter Ellis, Bookseller   2014 - 012219   2015   £285

White, Terence Hanbury   1906-1964 *The Witch in the Wood.* London: Collins, 1940. First printing, near fine in very good+ dust jacket with tiny chips at folds, 8vo.   Beasley Books   2013 - 2015 $150

Whitefield, Theodore M. *Slavery Agitation in Virginia 1829-1832.* Baltimore: 1930. Issued in wrappers, bound in library cloth, very good.   Bookworm & Silverfish   2015 - 4897197870   2015 $50

Whitehead, Alfred North   1861-1947 *Process and Reality, an Essay in Cosmology.* New York: Macmillan Co., 1929. First American edition, octavo, former owner's name 'Clifton C. Winn' in ink and typed note crudely taped to inside front cover, given by him to Dr. Donald Kleckner, original navy blue cloth, gilt lettering on slightly sunned spine, inside tight, bright, clean copy.   Athena Rare Books   15 - 59   2015 $4000

Whitehead, Colson *The Intuitionist.* New York: Anchor Books, 1999. First edition, 8vo., inscribed by author, fine in fine dust jacket.   Beasley Books   2013 - 2015 $45

Whitehead, Paul *The Gymnasiad; or Boxing-Match, an Epic Poem.* Dublin: printed for Thomas Butler, 1744. First Dublin edition, small 8vo., disbound, stamp on titlepage and one leaf of very early lending library, otherwise very good, rare.   C. R. Johnson   Foxon R-Z - 1135r-z   2015 $1149

Whitehead, Paul *Honour a Satire.* London: printed for M. Cooper, 1747. First edition, 4to., disbound, wanting half title, last page little dusty, otherwise good.   C. R. Johnson   Foxon R-Z - 1136r-z   2015 $153

Whitehead, Paul *Manners: a Satire.* London: printed for R. Dodsley, 1739. First edition, folio, disbound, few minor marginal tears, otherwise good.   C. R. Johnson   Foxon R-Z - 1137r-z   2015 $153

Whitehead, Paul *The Poems and Miscellaneous Compositions of Paul Whithead.* London: printed for G. Kearsely and J. Ridley, 1777. Second edition, 4to., frontispiece, contemporary calf, neatly rebacked, spine gilt, old red morocco label, very good, scarce, portrait retouched and erratum added at end.   C. R. Johnson   Foxon R-Z - 1134r-z   2015 $536

Whitehead, Paul *Satires Written by Mr. Whithead...* London: printed in the year, 1739. Inexpensive printing, 8vo., later marbled wrappers, very good, outer edges uncut.   C. R. Johnson   Foxon R-Z - 1132r-z   2015 $460

Whitehead, Paul *Satires Written by Mr. Whithead...* Islington: printer near the Three Pumps in the year, 1748. 8vo., 52 pages, recent green cloth, very scarce, small piece torn from blank upper corner of titlepage, otherwise very good.   C. R. Johnson   Foxon R-Z - 1133r-z   2015 $460

Whitehead, W. B. *A Letter to the Right Honorable the Lord Viscount Sidmouth, His Majesty's Principal Secretary of State for the Home Department...* London: A. J. Valpy, 1820. First edition, 8vo., recent wrappers, very good.   John Drury Rare Books   2015 - 15000   2015 $89

Whitehead, William *Atys and Adrastus, a Tale in the Manner of Dryden's Fables.* London: printed for R. Manby and sold by M. Cooper, 1744. First edition, fine large copy, scarce, folio, disbound.   C. R. Johnson   Foxon R-Z - 1144r-z   2015 $689

Whitehead, William *Atys and Adrastus, a Tale in the Manner of Dryden's Fables.* London: printed for R. Manby and sold by M. Cooper, 1744. Second edition, folio disbound, very good. C. R. Johnson   Foxon R-Z - 1145r-z   2015 $306

Whitehead, William *Atys and Adrastus, a Tale.* London: i.e. Edinburgh: printed for R. Manby and sold by M. Cooper, 1749. Fourth edition, fair, 8vo., disbound, very scarce, titlepage loose and bit dust soiled, otherwise sound.   C. R. Johnson   Foxon R-Z - 1146r-z   2015 $153

Whitehead, William *The Danger of Writing Verse: an Epistle.* London: printed for R. Dodsley and sold by T. Cooper, 1741. First edition, folio, disbound, very good.   C. R. Johnson Foxon R-Z - 1147r-z   2015 $306

Whitehead, William *An Essay on Ridicule.* London: printed for R. Dodsely and sold by M. Cooper, 1743. First edition, folio, 20 pages, disbound, very good.   C. R. Johnson   Foxon R-Z - 1148r-z   2015 $192

Whitehead, William *On the Nobility: an Epistle to the Right Hon. the Earl of ****.* London: printed for D. Dodsley and sold by M. Cooper, 1744. First edition, folio, disbound, titlepage loose, little soiled at beginning and end, otherwise good.   C. R. Johnson   Foxon R-Z - 1149r-z   2015 $383

Whitehead, William *Poems on Several Occasions, with the Roman Father.* London: printed for R. and J. Dodsley, 1754. First edition, 8vo., contemporary calf, red morocco label (some rubbing of spine), very good, complete with half title, list of errata on verso, early signature of 'Tighe' of St. John's College, Cambridge dated Dec. 1755, later bookplate of Olivier Brett, Viscount Esher,.   C. R. Johnson   Foxon R-Z - 1142r-z   2015 $230

Whitehead, William *Ann Boleyn to Henry the Eighth.* London: printed for R. Dodsley and sold by M. Cooper, 1743. First edition, 16 pages, folio, disbound, fair condition, titlepage little browned, clean tear in outer margin and small piece clipped from blank upper corner.   C. R. Johnson   Foxon R-Z - 1143r-z   2015 $153

Whiteman, Paul *As Paul Whiteman Sees the Stars of the Kraft Music Hall.* N.P.: Kraft Phenix Cheese Corp., 1934. First edition, wrappers, very good+ to near fine, photos, 8vo.   Beasley Books   2013 - 2015 $45

Whiteside, Derek Thomas *Patterns of Mathematical Thought in the Later Seventeenth Century.* Berlin: Gottingen: Heidelberg: Springer, 1961. Offprint, 8vo., 123 figures, printed wrappers, minor manuscript on spine, very good, scarce.   Jeff Weber Rare Books   178 - 1149   2015 $45

Whitfield, Christopher *Together and Alone. Two Short Novels.* Golden Cockerel Press, First edition, 251/400 copies (of an edition of 500 copies), printed on Arnold mouldmade paper, 10 wood engravings by John O'Connor, one small and light spot on title, 8vo., uncut in full black goatskin, full thickness crimson goatskin onlays applied to recessed panels edges in olive green acrylic, doublures of crimson goatskin with black onlays, flyleaves of crimson suede and Thai grass paper, edges airbrushed with acrylic, gold, palladium and blind tooling, by Glen Bartley (signed inside back cover and dated 2011), buckram box with felt lining, recessed label on spine tooled in palladium, fine. Blackwell's Rare Books   B179 - 133   2015   £1500

Whitin, James *The Abingdon Letter Now Published Entire for the Satisfaction of the Society of Friends...* Cambridge: printed by James Hodson, 1814. First edition, 8vo., preserved in modern wrappers, printed title label on upper cover, very good.   John Drury Rare Books   2015 - 16345   2015 $133

Whiting, William B. *The First Queen of Canary and Her... coup D'etat.* New York: Edward O. Jenkins, 1875. First edition, 16mo., gilt stamped brown cloth, inked note on one page, otherwise near fine.   Beasley Books   2013 - 2015 $45

Whitman, Walt   1819-1892 *Specimen Days & Collect.* Philadelphia: David McKay, 1882-1883. First edition, 2nd printing, 8vo., original mustard yellow cloth, gilt decorations and lettering, photo portrait, remarkable to have survived in such fine, bright condition, almost like new.   The Brick Row Book Shop   Miscellany 67 - 95   2015 $500

Whitman, Walt   1819-1892 *Specimen Days in America.* Walter Scott, Camelot Series, 1887. First English edition, original green cloth, spine with (rubbed) printed label, uncut, covers with some soiling and slight wear to extremities, tears at foot of spine, endpapers somewhat foxed, very good, ownership inscription, ownership stamp and bookseller's small labels on front endpapers, from the collection of Gavin H. Fryer.   Bertram Rota Ltd.   308 Part II - 229   2015   £80

Whitmore, George *The Duty of Not Running in Debt: Considered in a Discourse preached before the University of Cambridge Jan. 1800.* London: printed at the Philanthropic Reform by J. Richardson, n.d.?, 1800. First (only) edition, 8vo., wanting half title well bound recently in cloth spine lettered in gilt, good.   John Drury Rare Books   March 2015 - 15086   2015 $266

Whitney, A. *Memorial of A. Whitney. Praying a Grant of Public Land to Enable Him to Construct a Railroad from Lake Michigan to the Pacific Ocean.* Ritchie & Heiss, 1846. First edition, 8vo., hardcover binder, titles stamped in gold gilt on cover, 10 pages, large folding map, both map and text are fine.   Buckingham Books   March 2015 - 35788   2015 $750

Whitten, Leslie H. *Moon of the Wolf.* Garden City: Doubleday, 1967. First edition, name on front endpaper, otherwise fine in dust jacket with slightly darkened back panel.   Mordida Books   March 2015 - 003186   2015 $85

Whittington Press *Nine Artists & a Press. An Exhibition of the Work of Nine Artists Working for the Whittington Press, Held at the Fiery Beacon Gallery, 2-17 December '89.* Manor Farm: Whittington, 1989. First edition, limited to 950 copies, this being one of the 50 special copies, signed by seven of the artists, this copy not numbered but designated as the Press Copy & dated 1-12-89, 8vo., quarter leather, marbled paper over boards, slipcase, wood engravings, presentation inscription.   Oak Knoll Books   306 - 178   2015 $400

Whitworth, Robert *A Report and Survey of the Canal Proposed to be made on One Level from Waltham-Abbey to Moorfields.* London: 1773. First edition, folio, 2 large folding plans on thick paper, inner blank margins of text, leaves strengthened for binding, outer margins of two of the text leaves also strengthened with archival tape, rebound recently in maroon cloth, title lettered gilt on upper cover, good copy, maps (plans) themselves in fine state of preservation.   John Drury Rare Books   2015 - 21012   2015 $787

Who Killed Cock Robin. London: Tuck, n.d. circa, 1890. 4to., pictorial wrappers, fine, 6 fine full page chromolithographs plus many brown illustrations.   Aleph-Bet Books, Inc.   108 - 102   2015 $275

Who Was Who. London: Adam and Charles Black, 1972-2006. 12 volumes, including cumulated index (1897-2005), large 8vo., handsome, clean, very good+ set in very good+ jackets.   Any Amount of Books   March 2015 - A86831   2015   £400

Who Was Who. London: Adam & Charles Black, 1966. Mostly reprints, 8vo., 9 volumes, first 6 volumes presented from Roy Jenkins to Ian Gilmour, all clean, very good or better.   Any Amount of Books   2015 - A70295   2015   £225

The Whole Book of Psalms Collected in English Metre by Thomas Sternhold, John Hopkins and Others Conferred with the Hebrew. London: printed by J. Roberts for the Company of Staioenrs, 1749. Fine, crisp copy, contemporary panelled reverse unlettered calf, raised bands, two slips pasted on to prelim blank with name Thos. Smith and Wakefield 21 April 1753, very good.   Jarndyce Antiquarian Booksellers   CCXI - 237   2015   £125

Who's Who in Richmond Hill and Vicinity. A Classified Advertising and Telephone Directory. Richmond Hill: Men's Club of the Union Congregational Church, 1946. Twenty eighth edition, printed wrappers with binding, 162 pages, very good, moderate wear, very scarce.   Baade Books of the West   2014 - 2015 $100

Whyte Melville, George John *The Gladiators: a tale of Rome and Judea.* London: Longmans, 1878. New edition, 2 pages ads, 32 page catalog (March 1877), yellowback, original printed paper boards, rubbed and little worn, contemporary signature of A. A. Litten on leading f.e.p., modern booklabel of Ronald George Taylor, good plus copy. Jarndyce Antiquarian Booksellers CCXI - 289 2015 £65

Wiater, Stanley *Mysteries of the Word.* Holyoke: Crossroads Press, 1994. Copy 247 of 250 numbered copies, signed by author, artist Gahan Wilson and Jack Ketchum (provided introduction), pamphlet, fine in stapled wrappers, with 9 x 12 inch prints of three Wilson illustrations on heavy cardstock, fine. Ken Lopez, Bookseller 164 - 246 2015 $200

Wicks, Mark *To Mars Via the Moon: an Astronomical Story.* Philadelphia: J. B. Lippincott Co., 1911. First edition, US issue, Octavo, sixteen inserted plates, original pictorial blue cloth, front and spine panels stamped in gold. L. W. Currey, Inc. Boy's Adventure Fiction 2015 - 16 2015 $500

Wicks, Mark *To Mars via the Moon: an Astronomical Story.* London: Seeley and Co., 1911. First edition, octavo, 16 inserted plates, illustrations and maps mostly drawn by author, original pictorial blue cloth, front and spine panels stamped in gilt. L. W. Currey, Inc. Boy's Adventure Fiction 2015 - 67 2015 $150

Wicksell, Knut *Interest and Prices (Geldzins und Guterpreise) a Study on the Causes Regulating the Value of Money.* London: Macmillan, 1936. First edition in English, very good+, dampstain to rear tip rear board and adjacent dust jacket, page edges, text not affected, foxing to edges, 8vo., owner inscription front pastedown, very good+ sunned dust jacket with small label residue spine, mild edge wear. By the Book, L. C. 44 - 50 2015 $650

Wiedemann, Gustav Heirnich *De Lehre von Galvanismus und Elektromagnetismus.* Braunschweig: Friedrich Vieweg und Sohn, 1863. 2 volumes, 8vo., 395 figures, 1 folding color plate, early black half calf over marbled boards, worn, hinges cracked (holding at cords), 'cancelled' bookplates of Dr. Atkinson, Royal Military College, titlepage rubberstamps of Finbury Technical College, good. Jeff Weber Rare Books 178 - 1152 2015 $225

Wiederseim, Grace *Tiny Tots: Their Adventures.* New York: Stokes, Sept., 1909. 4to., cloth backed pictorial boards, edges worn and light cover soil, else tight and internally fine, 12 wonderful color plates and black and whites by Grace Drayton. Aleph-Bet Books, Inc. 108 - 151 2015 $375

Wien, Wilhelm *Lehrbuch der Hydrodynamik.* Leipzig: S. Hirzel, 1900. 8vo., 18 figures, original half black gilt stamped cloth, patterned paper over boards, rubbed, ink titlepage ownership signature of Harold Levine, very good. Jeff Weber Rare Books 178 - 1153 2015 $70

Wiesel, Elie *Night.* London: MacGibbon & Kee, 1960. First English edition, bit of foxing to top edge, fine in almost imperceptibly age toned, else fine dust jacket, very scarce title, beautiful copy, from the library of Kate Stettner Lobell and Carl D. Lobell. Between the Covers Rare Books 196 - 39 2015 $2000

Wiggin, Kate Douglas *The Birds' Christmas Carol.* San Francisco: C. A. Murdock, 1887. First edition, fewer than copies of this first printing are thought to exist and probably fewer than that in such beautiful condition, laid in is printed photo of Wiggin signed by her plus 2 page handwritten letter, outstanding copy, rare, pictorial wrappers, minute wear to tail of spine, else very fine in original dust jacket. Aleph-bet Books, Inc. 109 - 486 2015 $4800

Wigton Controversy: containing a Complete Exposure of the literary Dishonesty and Evasive Conduct of a Romish Priest. London: 8 Exeter Hall; Nottingham Dearden Wigton Hoodless?, 1846. First edition, 8vo., contemporary cloth spine lettered gilt, very good with Hope trust bookplate on front pastedown, very scarce. John Drury Rare Books March 2015 - 18227 2015 $221

Wilberforce, William *An Appeal to the Religion, Justice and Humanity of the Inhabitants of the British Empire.* London: J. Hatchard, 1823. First edition, paper in prelims slightly brittle and top outer margin of title and pages half repaired, attractively rebound in quarter calf, marbled boards, vellum tips, gilt bands, red label, lettered gilt, scarce. Jarndyce Antiquarian Booksellers CCXI - 290 2015 £420

Wilbur, Richard *The 1996 Frost Medal Lecture.* New York: Poetry Society of America, 1997. First edition, one of100 numbered copies signed by author and Stanley Kunitz provided introduction, out of a total of 120 (20 copies reserved for participants), 8vo., original cloth, patterned endpapers, printed paper spine label, fine, without dust jacket as issued. James S. Jaffe Rare Books Modern American Poetry - 300 2015 $350

Wilbur, Richard *Seed Leaves Homage to R. F.* Boston: Godine, 1972. First edition, limited to 160 copies signed by author and artist, 8vo., original colored etchings, marbled wrappers with printed label, folding cloth and marbled case, fine, lovely book. James S. Jaffe Rare Books Modern American Poetry - 299 2015 $450

Wilbur, Richard *The Writer.* San Francisco: Pacific Editions, 2004. One of 54 copies, two part limited edition, the larger book printed on BFK Rives paper and second volume - a flip book, or rather a 'flutter book' is printed on card stock, each copy hand numbered and signed by artist/printer/designer, Charles Hobson on colophon page, page size 11 1/8 x 7 15/16 inches, 16 pages, plus 8 pages of images interleaved for large book, flutter book is 3 3/8 x 5 1/8 inches, 50 pages, bound with blue cloth spine with yellow and blue paste paper over boards, white label pasted to front panel for larger book, flutter book laid into oblong slipcase of blue linen with papers made from artist's striking bird images, both books housed in clamshell box designed to hold both books and to act as a platform from which to read the two volumes in conjunction with one another, box measures 12 x 12 x 1 /4 inches.   Priscilla Juvelis - Rare Books   62 - 14   2015 $1600

Wilcock, Donald E. *Damn Right I've Got the Blues.* San Francisco: Woodford, 1993. First printing, 8vo., signed by Wilcock and Buddy Guy, copiously illustrated with photos, paper wrappers, cover slightly scuffed, otherwise very good, tight copy.   Second Life Books Inc.   190 - 215   2015 $150

Wilde, Oscar   1854-1900 *The Happy Prince.* London: Duckworth, 1913. First edition with illustrations by Charles Robinson, 4to., gilt pictorial purple cloth, top edge gilt, offsetting on endpaper, else near fine, 12 magnificent tipped in color plates with lettered tissue guards plus numerous text drawings as well as pictorial endpapers and titlepage, nice copy.   Aleph-bet Books, Inc.   109 - 411   2015 $1250

Wilde, Oscar   1854-1900 *The Happy Prince.* London: Duckworth, 1913. First edition, first issue with these illustrations, 4to., gilt pictorial purple cloth, top edge gilt, fore edge foxed and offset on endpaper from dust jacket flap else near fine in pictorial dust jacket and publisher's box, box flaps repaired, illustrations by Charles Robinson with 12 tipped in color plates and lettered tissue guards plus numerous text drawings as well as with pictorial endpapers and titlepage, beautiful copy, rare in pictorial dust jacket and box. Aleph-Bet Books, Inc.   108 - 392   2015 $2000

Wilde, Oscar   1854-1900 *Salome, a Tragedy in One Act.* (accompanied by) *Salome, Drame en Un Acte.* Paris: Limited Editions Club, 1938. Limited to 1500 numbered copies with the second volume signed by artist, Andre Derain, 4to., cloth and stiff paper wrappers, both inserted in slipcase, color illustrations in second volume done in gouache on black paper in color using pochoir process by Saude of Paris, cloth volume contains English translation by Lord Alfred Douglas with illustrations by Aubrey Beardsely, including 4 omitted from original, with Monthly letter loosely inserted, slipcase shows wear along edges, spine of book faded.   Oak Knoll Books   25 - 21   2015 $365

Wilde, Oscar   1854-1900 *A Woman of No Importance.* London: John Lane at the Sign of The Bodley Head, 1894. First edition, one of 50 large paper copies printed on handmade paper, original publisher's yellow buckram boards with gilt decorations to covers and spine, spine toned, only slightest trace of rubbing to extremities, former owner bookplate to front pastedown, light offsetting to endpapers, very good, tight and clean, extremely scarce.   B & B Rare Books, Ltd.   234 - 105   2015 $7500

Wilde, Percival *Rogues in Clover.* D. Appleton and Co., 1929. First edition, spine rebacked and resewn with original spine laid down, new front and rear endpapers, library stamp to top margin of page 1, else bright, squre, clean, very good, very scarce.   Buckingham Books   March 2015 - 37499   2015 $450

Wilden, Theodore *The Exchange.* London: Collins, 1981. First edition, warmly inscribed by author in year of publication, fine in dust jacket.   Mordida Books   March 2015 - 001984   2015 $125

Wilder, Laura Ingalls *Farmer Boy.* New York: Harper Bros., 1933. 8vo., pictorial cloth, fine with front flap and part of front panel of dust jacket, color frontispiece and black and white illustrations by Helen Sewell, this copy signed by author, rare thus.   Aleph-bet Books, Inc.   109 - 487   2015 $4000

Wilder, Laura Ingalls *Little Town on the Prairie.* New York: Harper, 1941. Stated first edition, 8vo., very good+, mild foxing to cover, edges, in very good+ dust jacket with minimal foxing, chips, short closed tear.   By the Book, L. C.   44 - 8   2015 $2250

Wilder, Laura Ingalls *These Happy Golden Years.* New York: Harper & Bros., 1943. Stated first edition, 8vo., pictorial cloth, slight cover soil, near fine in slightly frayed and soiled dust jacket, illustrations by Helen Sewell and Mildred Boyle with color dust jacket, color frontispiece plus full page black and whites.   Aleph-bet Books, Inc.   109 - 488   2015 $1750

Wilder, Thornton   1897-1976 *The Bridge of San Luis Ray.* New York: Albert & Charles Boni, 1927. First American edition, signed and inscribed by author to Ida Freedman, octavo, original cloth, original dust jacket, text block with few splits (as often) but holding, cloth clean, rare jacket with few small chips to head of spine and light spine toning, overall extraordinary copy.   Manhattan Rare Book Company   Literature 2014 - 2015 $5000

Wildman, Tommaso *Trattato Sopra la Cura Delle Api contenente l'istoria Naturale di Quest' Insetti Co' Vari Metodi si Antichi...* Torino: presso in Fratelli Reycends, 1771. First edition in Italian, 8vo., 3 folding engraved copper plates, including half title, occasional insignificant marks but very good, uncut, preserved in later marbled wrappers with printed title label.   John Drury Rare Books   2015 - 22683   2015 $699

Wiley, William *Godot. An Imaginary Staging.* San Francisco: Arion Press, 2006. Limited to 300 copies, this being no. 168, signed by artist, folio, 50 color illustrations by Wiley, publisher's quarter blue cloth over printed pictorial yellow paper boards, yellow paper spine label, lettered in black, housed in cloth and paper pictorial slipcase, mint with prospectus laid in.   Heritage Book Shop   Holiday 2014 - 3   2015 $850

Wilkes, Thomas *The Golden Farmer a Poem. inscribed to Rt. Hon. Wliam (sic) Lord Craven.* London: printed for T. Payne, 1723. First edition, folio, original pale blue wrappers worn, portion of back wrapper missing, card folding case, some signs of prior folding, otherwise very good, uncut, with half title.   C. R. Johnson   Foxon R-Z - 1150r-z   2015 $766

Wilkes, Wetenhall *Hounslow-Heath, a Poem.* London: printed for C. Corbett and sold at the booksellers in London and Westminster, 1748. First edition, reissue of 1747 printing with date in imprint reset, 4to., 19th century half Roxburghe, purple boards, green morocco spine (rubbed), later bookplates of the celebrated Schwerdt collection and of the Duke of Gloucester, fine.   C. R. Johnson   Foxon R-Z - 1151r-z   2015 $3831

Wilkins, Mary E. *The Jamesons.* New York: Doubleday and McClure, 1899. First edition, small octavo, color plates, decorated green cloth, small booklabel, slight wear, spine little toned, else near fine, bears ownership signatures of Meta Neilson dated in 1899 and also of artist, Helen Neilson Armstrong, sister of Margaret Armstrong, dated 1805.   Between the Covers Rare Books   196 - 122   2015 $350

Wilkins, W. Henri *Three Glasses a Day; or the Broken Home: a Moral and Temperance Drama in Three Acts.* Clyde: A. D. Ames, 1878. Original printed paper wrappers, few mild stains to top edge, bit of toning and wear to extremities of wrappers, else very good.   Tavistock Books   Temperance - 2015 $125

Willard, Frances E. *A Wheel within a Wheel: How I Learned to Ride the Bicycle with Some Reflections by the Way.* Chicago: Woman's Temperance Pub. Association, 1895. First edition, 12mo., original green cloth, pictorial silver and dark green stamping, spine lightly faded, few faint spots to boards, else very good or better.   Tavistock Books   Temperance - 2015 $250

Willard, Nancy *A Visit to William Blank's Inn: Poems for Innocent and Experienced Travelers.* New York and London: Harcort Brace Jovanovich, 1981. First edition, slim quarto, original beige cloth over paper boards, original dust jacket, illustrations by Alice and Martin Provensen.   Honey & Wax Booksellers   2 - 6   2015 $100

Willder, Jim *Elisabeth Frink: Sculpture: Catalogue Raisonne.* Salisbury: Harpvale, 1984. First edition, 4to., copiously illustrated in color and black and white, signed presentation from artist, fine in fine dust jacket in slipcase.   Any Amount of Books   2015 - C15536   2015   £175

Wille, Lois *Forever Open Clear and Free.* Chicago: Regnery, 1972. First edition, one of 100 copies numbered and signed by author, fine in fine slipcase.   Beasley Books   2013 - 2015 $150

Willeford, Charles *Cockfighter.* Chicago: Chicago Paperback House, 1962. First edition, paperback original, fine and unread, from the collection of Duke Collier.   Royal Books   36 - 248   2015 $325

Willeford, Charles *Cockfighter.* Chicago: Chicago Paperback House, 1962. Correct first edition, bright, tight, fine, unread copy.   Buckingham Books   March 2015 - 25699   2015 $375

Willeford, Charles *Cockfighter.* New York: Crown, 1972. First edition, fine in very good dust jacket with wear at spine ends and at corners, several short closed tears, small label removed from front panel.   Mordida Books   March 2015 - 010798   2015 $185

Willeford, Charles *Cockfighter.* New York: Crown Publishers Inc, 1972. First hardcover edition, review copy with review slip laid in, yellow cloth lightly soiled, else fine in dust jacket with light wear to spine ends and lightly rubbed along fore-edge, review copies uncommon for this title. Buckingham Books   March 2015 - 23819   2015 $650

Willeford, Charles *Cockfighter.* New York: Avon, 1974. first edition thus, scarce edition, paperback.   Buckingham Books   March 2015 - 11658   2015 $185

Willeford, Charles *Everybody's Metamorphosis.* Missoula: Dennis McMillan, 1968. First edition, one of 400 numbered copies signed by author, very fine in dust jacket. Mordida Books March 2015 - 008207   2015 $300

Willeford, Charles *High Priest of California.* New York: Universal Publishing, 1953. Oversized Royal Giant paperback, internally fine in very good pictorial wrappers with some wear to 1 inch thick spine and back cover, scarce. Buckingham Books   March 2015 - 15349   2015 $375

Willeford, Charles *High Priest of California and Wild Wives.* New York: Beacon, 1953. First edition, short scratch and light soiling on back cover, otherwise fine, unread copy in wrappers. Mordida Books March 2015 - 010709 2015 $300

Willeford, Charles *High Priest of California/Wild Wives.* New York: Beacon No. B13, 1956. First edition, paperback original, fine, from the collection of Duke Collier. Royal Books 36 - 250 2015 $375

Willeford, Charles *High Priest of California & Wild Wives.* New York: Beacon, 1956. First edition, paperback original, fine, unread copy in wrappers, with Willeford misspelled "Willliford' on front cover. Mordida Books March 2015 - 007986 2015 $400

Willeford, Charles *Honey Gal.* New York: Beacon No. B160, 1958. First edition, fine and unread, touch of production wrinkle to spine panel, from the collection of Duke Collier. Royal Books 36 - 247 2015 $475

Willeford, Charles *Lust is a Woman.* New York: Beacon No. B175, 1958. First edition, paperback original, fine and unread, tiniest bit of rubbing at spine ends, superb cover art by Micarelli, from the collection of Duke Collier. Royal Books 36 - 245 2015 $650

Willeford, Charles *The Machine in Ward Eleven.* New York: Belmont Books, 1963. First edition, fine, bright, unread copy in pictorial wrappers. Buckingham Books March 2015 - 25700 2015 $225

Willeford, Charles *The Machine in Ward Eleven.* New York: Belmont, 1963. First edition, fine in wrappers. Mordida Books March 2015 - 012609 2015 $100

Willeford, Charles *Miami Blues.* New York: St. Martin's Press, 1984. First edition, fine in dust jacket lightly rubbed at spine ends and fore edge along with two quarter closed tears on back panel. Buckingham Books March 2015 - 18723 2015 $300

Willeford, Charles *Miami Blues.* New York: St. Martins, 1984. First edition, fine in dust jacket with some slight fading on front panel. Mordida Books March 2015 - 009204 2015 $275

Willeford, Charles *New Hope for the Dead.* New York: St. Martins, 1985. First edition, fine in dust jacket with slightly faded spine. Mordida Books March 2015 - 010429 2015 $150

Willeford, Charles *Off the Wall.* Montclair: Pegasus Rex Press, 1980. First edition, fine in dust jacket with very light wear to extremities. Buckingham Books March 2015 - 8233 2015 $325

Willeford, Charles *Poontang and Other Poems.* Crescent City: New Athenaeum Press, 1966. First edition, as new in printed green wrappers, scarce, this green binding scarcer of the two bindings. Buckingham Books March 2015 - 12934 2015 $1500

Willeford, Charles *Poontang and Other Poems.* Crescent City: New Athenaeum Press, 1966. First edition, as new in printed gray wrappers, scarce, the book was issued in green wrappers as well. Buckingham Books March 2015 - 18718 2015 $1500

Willeford, Charles *Proletarian Laughter.* Yonkers: Alicat Bookshop, 1948. First edition, fine in stapled soft covers. Mordida Books March 2015 - 007985 2015 $250

Willeford, Charles *Sideswipe.* New York: St. Martins, 1987. First edition, signed, fine in dust jacket. Buckingham Books March 2015 - 23817 2015 $325

Willeford, Charles *Understudy for Love.* Chicago: Newstand Library No. &170, 1961. First edition, paperback original, fine and unread, scarce, from the collection of Duke Collier. Royal Books 36 - 246 2015 $450

Willeford, Charles *Whip Hand.* New York: Gold Medal Books No. S1087, 1961. First edition, paperback original, fine and unread, from the collection of Duke Collier. Royal Books 36 - 249 2015 $325

Willeford, Charles *The Woman Chaser.* Chicago: Newsstand Library Book, 1960. First edition, fine, bright, unread copy in pictorial wrappers, beautiful copy. Buckingham Books March 2015 - 35698 2015 $325

Willement, Thomas *Heraldic Notices of Canterbury Cathedral...* London: Harding, Lepard & Co., 1827. First edition, large 8vo., soundly rebound in brown cloth with marbled boards, lettered gilt on spine, frontispiece, typographic bookplate 'TFM, very good+ bright copy, clean. Any Amount of Books 2015 - C2425 2015 £150

William of Conches *Philosophia Mundi: Ausgabe des I. Buchs von Wilhelm von Conches 'Philosophia' mit Anhang.* Pretoria: University of South Africa, 1974. 8vo., figures, original printed wrappers, ink ownership signature of David Lindberg, very good, rare. Jeff Weber Rare Books 178 - 1158 2015 $45

William, R. F. *Shakespeare and His Friends: or the Golden Age of Merrie England.* London: 1838. 3 volumes, volume III backstrip worn, original paper. Bookworm & Silverfish 2015 - 360282273 2015 $245

Williams, Archibald *Petrol Peter.* London: Methuen, n.d., 1906. First edition, 4to., cloth backed pictorial boards, owner name and 1906, date on endpaper, 24 pages, near fine in pictorial dust jacket, illustrations by A. Wallis Mills after Hoffmann's originals, printed in color on one side of paper only, with color illustrations on every page by A. Wallis Mills, very scarce in dust jacket. Aleph-bet Books, Inc. 109 - 224   2015 $1875

Williams, Aubrey L. *Pope's Dunciad: a Study of Its Meaning.* London: Methuen, 1955. Half title, map, original brick red cloth, boards, slightly bowed, slightly rubbed, dust jacket marked 'Keep', Geoffrey Tillotson's signed copy. Jarndyce Antiquarian Booksellers   CCVII - 439   2015   £20

Williams, Brock *The Earl of Chicago.* Indianapolis: New York: Bobbs Merrill, 1937. First edition, light wear at crown, else near fine in very good dust jacket, attractively illustrated by Paul Laune with light chipping at crown and few tears, small nicks. Between the Covers Rare Books   196 - 123   2015 $650

Williams, C. K. *Creatures.* Haverford: Green Shade, 2006. First edition, deluxe issue, one of 26 lettered copies printed on Twinrocker handmade paper, specially bound and signed by author, small 4to., original quarter black morocco & handmade pastepaper over boards, paper slipcase by Claudia Cohen, as new. James S. Jaffe Rare Books Modern American Poetry - 305   2015 $850

Williams, C. K. *Creatures.* Haverford: Green Shade, 2006. First edition, one of 150 numbered copies printed by hand, signed by poet, small 4to., original hand made pastepaper wrappers by Claudia Cohen, as new. James S. Jaffe Rare Books   Modern American Poetry - 304   2015 $150

Williams, C. K. *A Day for Anne Frank.* Philadelphia: Falcon Press, 1968. First edition, 4to., illustrations, original pictorial wrappers, although not called for, this copy signed by poet, fine, rare. James S. Jaffe Rare Books   Modern American Poetry - 301   2015 $1500

Williams, C. K. *I Am the Bitter Name.* Boston: Houghton Mifflin, 1972. First edition, 8vo., original cloth, dust jacket, review copy with publisher's promotional material, including photo laid in, signed by author, fine. James S. Jaffe Rare Books   Modern American Poetry - 303   2015 $225

Williams, C. K. *Lies.* Boston: Houghton Mifflin, 1969. First edition, signed by author, 8vo., cloth backed boards, dust jacket, fine, jacket slightly rubbed. James S. Jaffe Rare Books   Modern American Poetry - 302   2015 $225

Williams, Charles *Aground.* New York: Viking, 1960. First edition, fine in very good dust jacket with internal staining, several short closed tears, wear at spine ends, corners and along folds. Mordida Books   March 2015 - oo7299   2015 $100

Williams, Charles *Big City Girl.* New York: Fawcett, 1951. First edition, fine, Gold Medal no. 163, unread copy in wrappers. Mordida Books   March 2015 - 010710   2015 $85

Williams, Charles *The Catfish Tangle.* London: Cassell, 1963. First hardcover edition, fine in dust jacket. Mordida Books   March 2015 - 012307   2015 $200

Williams, Charles *Scorpion Reef.* New York: Macmillan, 1955. First edition, very good plus in like dust jacket, board edges lightly faded, only minor rubbing and nicking to jacket extremities, very nice, scarce title, extremely uncommon signature, from the collection of Duke Collier. Royal Books   36 - 251   2015 $1850

Williams, Charles *The Wrong Venus.* New York: New American Library, 1966. First edition, inscribed by author for fellow mystery writer John D. MacDonald, near fine in like dust jacket, from the collection of Duke Collier. Royal Books   36 - 3   2015 $3500

Williams, Charles Hanbury *A Dialogue Between G--s E---3 and B--b D---n.* London: sold by T. Taylor, 1741. One of two editions, of uncertain sequence, one may be partly a reimpression of the other, in this printing signature "B" is under the space between 'cloth to' in the other, it is under 'Green', the two variants are of equal scarcity, very good. C. R. Johnson   Foxon R-Z - 1152r-z   2015 $421

Williams, Charles Hanbury *Esq: S--ys's Budget Open'd; or, Drink and be D---'d.* London: printed for W. Webb, 1743. First edition, folio, disbound, very good, half title present, this copy has page vi correctly numbered (presumably a press variant), very scarce. C. R. Johnson   Foxon R-Z - 1153r-z   2015 $613

Williams, Charles Hanbury *An Ode Addressed to the author of the Conquered Duchess.* London: printed for A. Moore, 1746. First edition, 8 pages, folio, recent cloth boards, parchment spine, this copy has no punctuation after "rul'd" in the third line of stanza IX, with Fairfax of Cameron bookplate, very good. C. R. Johnson   Foxon R-Z - 1154r-z   2015 $613

Williams, Charles Hanbury *An Ode from the E----- of B----- to Ambition.* London: printed for A. Moore, n.d., 1746. First edition, folio, disbound, fine, uncommon. C. R. Johnson   Foxon R-Z - 1155r-z   2015 $613

Williams, Charles Hanbury *An Ode to the Honourable H---y F--x on the Marriage of the Du---s of M-----r to H---s----v, Esq.* London: printed for A. Moore, 1746. First edition, folio, recent cloth boards, parchment spine, very good, Fairfax of Cameron bookplate, very scarce.   C. R. Johnson   Foxon R-Z - 1156r-z   2015 $689

Williams, Charles Hanbury *An Ode to the Right Honourable Stephen Poyntz, Esq.* London: printed for R. Dodsley and sold by M. Cooper, 1746. First edition, folio, recent wrappers, first impression with misprint 'fond virtue' in penultimate line on page 5, few inconspicuous stamps of Cardiff Public Libraries, otherwise good copy, scarce.   C. R. Johnson   Foxon R-Z - 1157r-z   2015 $766

Williams, Charles Hanbury *Plain Thoughts in Plain Language.* London: printed for W. Webb, 1742. First edition, 8 pages, folio, disbound, uncommon.   C. R. Johnson   Foxon R-Z - 1159r-z   2015 $536

Williams, Charles Hanbury *S----s and J----l. A New Ballad.* London: printed for W. Webb, 1743. Second edition, 8 pages, folio disbound, very good, very scarce.   C. R. Johnson   Foxon R-Z - 1160r-z   2015 $230

Williams, Charles Hanbury *The Wife and the Nurse: a New Ballad.* London: printed for W. Webb, 1743. First edition, 8 pages, folio, disbound, very good, in this copy the ornament on titlepage points just to the left of the D" in "London" below.   C. R. Johnson   Foxon R-Z - 1161r-z   2015 $460

Williams, Chauncey Pratt *Lone Elk. The Life Story of Bill Williams: Trapper and Guide of the Far West.* John Van Male, 1935-1936. First editions, quarto, 2 volumes, limited to 500 copies, stiff wrappers, 50, 35 pages, volume one has small ding to top edge of rear cover panel, else both are fine copies.   Buckingham Books   March 2015 - 34407   2015 $275

Williams, Chauncey Pratt *Lone Elk. the Life Story of Bill Williams: Trapper and Guide of the Far West.* John VanMale, 1935-1936. First editions, limited to 500 copies, 2 volumes, quarto, stiff wrappers, fine.   Buckingham Books   March 2015 - 34405   2015 $350

Williams, David *A Letter to the Right Rev. Dr. Warren on His conduct as Bishop of Bangor.* N.P.:: London?, n.d., 1796. First and only edition, 8vo., contemporary ms. notes in ink on first leaf of text, bound in early 20th century cloth backed boards, spine lettered, boards faded, very good, really quite rare.   John Drury Rare Books   2015 - 25141   2015 $1136

Williams, Gomer *History of the Liverpool Privateers and Letters of Marque: with an Account of the Liverpool Slave Trade.* London: Liverpool: Heinemann/Edward Howell, 1897. First edition, large 8vo., original red cloth lettered gilt on spine, illustrations, from the library of Allan Heywood Bright, clean, bright, very good+, exceptional condition.   Any Amount of Books   March 2015 - C12161   2015   £350

Williams, Helen Maria *A Narrative of the Events Which Have Taken Place in France from the Landing of Napoleon Bonaparte on the 1st of March 1815 till the Restoration of Louis XVIII.* London: John Murray, 1815. First edition, 8vo., half title, contemporary three quarter morocco by Zaehnsdorf stamped in gilt, little scuffed, very nice, untrimmed.   Second Life Books Inc.   189 - 268   2015 $950

Williams, Jody *My Name is Jody Williams.* Berkeley: University of California Press, 2013. First edition, signed by author, fine in fine dust jacket, 8vo.   By the Book, L. C. Special List 10 - 48   2015 $200

Williams, John *Speeches in the House of Commons on Friday the 24th of February 1826... on the Motion that a Select Committee be Appointed to Consider of the Petition Presented from persons Connected with the Silk Trade.* London: John Hatchard and Son, 1826. First separate edition, 8vo., 100 pages, recently well bound in linen backed marbled boards, lettered, very good.   John Drury Rare Books   2015 - 14066   2015 $177

Williams, John A. *Sissie.* New York: Farrar Straus and Cudahy, 1963. First printing, 8vo., paper over boards with cloth spine, pages toned, otherwise very good, tight copy in scuffed and very slightly dust jacket.   Second Life Books Inc.   190 - 216   2015 $125

Williams, John D. *Williams & Packard's Original Gems of Penmanship Respectfully Dedicated to Bryant, Stratton and Co's International Chain of Business Colleges.* New York: D. Appleton & Co., 1867. First edition, oblong small 4to., original leather backed boards, spine covering missing, engraved titlepage, 47 engraved plates, covers detached with leather spine covering lacking, internally very good, old calligraphic inscription on front free endpaper " John R. Campbell's Book.   Oak Knoll Books   306 - 245   2015 $350

Williams, John D. *Williams & Packard's Original Gems of Penmanship Respectfully Dedicated to Bryant, Stratton and Co.'s Chain of Business Colleges.* New York: D. Appleton & Co., 1867. First edition, 4 pages of text followed by many excellent plates, oblong 4to., original quarter leather, engraved titlepage, 4 pages followed by 47 plates, wear at spine ends and rubbing along hinges, occasional foxing, old ink ownership inscription on front endpapers, abrased spots on front cover.   Oak Knoll Books   Special Catalogue 24 - 59   2015 $450

Williams, Jonathan *Gay BCs.* Champaign: Finial Press, 1976. First edition, one of 1000 copies on Strathmore grandee paper and designed by Alvin Doyle Moore, this copy out of series, signed by Williams, oblong 8vo., original wrappers fine, drawings by Joe Brainard.   James S. Jaffe Rare Books   Many Happy Returns - 269   2015 $150

Williams, Kit *Masquerade.* London: Jonathan Cape, 1979. First edition, 4to., illustrated laminated boards, issued without dust jacket, copiously illustrated in color, signed presentation from author, loosely inserted article from the Times revealing solution to riddle contained within book, fine.   Any Amount of Books   2015 - A92292   2015   £180

Williams, Margery *The Velveteen Rabbit.* New York & London: George H. Doran & Heinemann, 1922. First US edition, 4to., pictorial boards, except for very slight bit of rubbing to head of spine, super fine condition in bright, clean, pictorial dust jacket (1 inch piece off bottom backstrip and some mild fraying at folds, 2 1/4" closed tears on back panel), housed in custom full leather clamshell box, illustrations by William Nicolson with pictorial endpapers, 7 richly colored full page lithographs, several are double page spreads, rare.   Aleph-bet Books, Inc.   109 - 328   2015 $26,000

Williams, Mary Floyd *Papers of the San Francisco Committee of Vigilance of 1851. Minutes and Miscellaneous Papers, Financial Accounts and Vouchers.* Berkeley: University of California Press, 1919. First edition, thick 8vo., folding map, folding table, 11 photo plates, publisher's gilt lettered dark blue cloth, fine.   Argonaut Book Shop   Holiday Season 2014 - 258 2015 $225

Williams, Moses *The Cracked Jug or Five Answers to My neighbor Parley's Five Letters, Cracking His 'Fifteen Gallon Jug".* Boston: printed for the author, 1838. Second edition, 8vo., 24 pages, removed with traces of original wrapper on spine, foxed, bound with an unidentified defective copy, lacking title.   M & S Rare Books, Inc.   97 - 299   2015 $175

Williams, Philip *Report of the Proceedings in the Case of an Appeal Preferred by the Provost and Scholars of King's College, Cambridge, Against the Provost and fellows of Eton College, to the lord Bishop of Lincoln the Visitor of Both Societies Determined August 15th 1815.* London: J. Butterworth and Son, 1816. First edition, 8vo., early 20th century green half calf, top edge gilt, spine lettered, silk marker by Hatchards very good.   John Drury Rare Books   March 2015 - 12371   2015 $266

Williams, R. H. *With the Border Ruffians. Memories of the Far West 1852-1868.* London: John Murray, 1907. First edition, 8vo., light blue cloth, frontispiece, illustrations, lightly foxed along fore-edges, light offsetting to front and rear endpapers, very light foxing, lightly rubbed at spine ends and corners, else very good.   Buckingham Books   March 2015 - 31026   2015 $225

Williams, Samuel Cole *History of the Lost State of Franklin.* New York: 1933. 318 pages, very good and solid, backstrip faded, private owner embossed stamp, not ex-library.   Bookworm & Silverfish   2015 - 6016490583   2015 $75

Williams, Sidney Herbert *Some Rare Carrolliana.* London: printed for Private Circulation only, 1924. Number 41 of only 79 copies signed by author, 4to., cloth backed boards, slight soil on few pages, near fine, frontispiece, rare.   Aleph-bet Books, Inc.   109 - 87   2015 $500

Williams, Tennessee   1911-1983 *Androgyne, mon Amour.* New York: New Directions, 1977. First edition, uncorrected galley proofs, narrow, unbound folio sheets, folded once and stapled at corner, publisher's review slip, 6 1/4 x 9 1/2 inch photo of the mock-up dust jacket cover, with hard crease and some chipping to top corners, housed in elegant red cloth chemise and slipcase of same cloth but with gilt stamped red morocco spine with raised bands, some chipping along fold and at bottom corner of first sheet, very good set, rare.   Ed Smith Books   83 - 117   2015 $750

Williams, Tennessee   1911-1983 *Cat on a Hat Tin Roof.* New York: New Directions, 1955. First edition, first issue, publisher's light brown orange cloth in original pictorial dust jacket, beautiful copy with only hint of wear to spine ends, else fine with bright and fresh pages, unclipped dust jacket with hint of light wear to extremities, bright spine, without usual toning, bright and clean panels, fine, rare in such excellent condition.   B & B Rare Books, Ltd.   2015 - 2015 $800

Williams, Tennessee   1911-1983 *A Streetcar Named Desire.* New York: New Directions, 1947. First edition, first printing, original lavender boards, about fine with very slight rubbing to extremities in crisp, unclipped dust jacket, only slightly faded to spine, spine ends very lightly chipped, early tape reinforcement to jacket verso, else near fine, very bright and crisp.   B & B Rare Books, Ltd.   234 - 106   2015 $2250

Williams, Tennessee   1911-1983 *A Streetcar Named Desire.* New York: Limited Editions Club, 1982. Limited to 2000 numbered copies, signed by artist, Al Hirshfeld, 4to., quarter leather, decorated cloth boards, slipcase, illustrations, frontispiece, with Monthly Letter, prospectus loosely inserted, slipcase very lightly soiled.   Oak Knoll Books   25 - 48   2015 $350

Williams, Tennessee   1911-1983 *You Touched Me! A Romantic comedy in three acts.* New York: Samuel French, 1947. First edition, small 8vo., rare hardcover edition, being one of only 506 copies, 4 photo plates inserted throughout, fine in dark green cloth with front cover and spine lettered gilt, only mild rubbing to cloth in near fine dust jacket.   Ed Smith Books   83 - 116   2015 $450

Williams, Thomas *The Age of Infidelity: in Answer to Thomas Paine's Age of Reason. (bound with) Part II.* London: printed for W. Button n.d., 1794. First editions, 8vo., half titles, contemporary half calf over marbled boards, spine rubbed and joints worn and cracked at foot, wanting label, very good, quite rare.   John Drury Rare Books   2015 - 22924   2015 $656

Williams, Valentine *The Crouching Beast.* Boston: Houghton Mifflin, 1928. First American edition, very good in soiled and rubbed dust jacket with nicks at spine ends. Mordida Books   March 2015 - 002303   2015 $85

Williams, Valentine *Dead Man Manor.* Boston: Houghton Mifflin, 1936. First American edition, some darkening along gutters, otherwise very good, internal tape reinforcing with chips at corners.   Mordida Books   March 2015 - 010799   2015 $85

Williams, Valentine *The Key Man.* Houghton Mifflin Co., 1926. First US edition, near fine in like dust jacket. Buckingham Books   March 2015 - 33456   2015 $300

Williams, Valentine *The Knife Behind the Curtain. Tales of Crime and The Secret Service.* Boston and New York: Houghton Mifflin, 1930. First US edition, fine in fine bright dust jacket, exceptional copy.   Buckingham Books   March 2015 - 25821   2015 $375

Williams, Valentine *The Knife Behind the Curtain. Tales of Crime and the Secret Service.* Boston & New York: Houghton Mifflin, 1930. First US edition, stain to red cloth panel, else near fine in fine in bright dust jacket. Buckingham Books   March 2015 - 25085   2015 $250

Williams, Valentine *The Man with the Clubfoot.* Boston: Houghton Mifflin, 1931. Later American edition, fine in near fine, lightly soiled dust jacket with internal tape mends and nicks at spine ends.   Mordida Books   March 2015 - 002308   2015 $85

Williams, Valentine *The Spider's Touch.* Houghton Mifflin Co., 1936. First US edition, fine, tight bright copy in bright dust jacket with light wear to spine ends, corners and extremities.   Buckingham Books   March 2015 - 33455   2015 $300

Williams, William Carlos 1883-1963 *Al Que Quiere!* Boston: Four Seas, 1917. First edition, very good, little spine wear and owner's name on titlepage margin, variant with tan boards and "Williams' on spine.   Beasley Books   2013 - 2015 $200

Williams, William Carlos 1883-1963 *Al Que Quiere! A Book of Poems.* Boston: Four Seas Co., 1917. First edition, one of 1000 copies, small 8vo., original buff printed boards, slightly rubbed, else fine, not commonly found signed, inscribed to Waldo Frank by the poet in May 1919.   James S. Jaffe Rare Books   Modern American Poetry - 307   2015 $7500

Williams, William Carlos 1883-1963 *The Clouds, Aigeltinger, Russia.* Wells College & Cummington Press, 1948. First edition, one of 60 roman numeraled copies on handmade paper signed by author, out of a total edition of 310 copies 8vo., original cloth, printed spine label, slipcase, signed issue is rare.   James S. Jaffe Rare Books   Modern American Poetry - 320   2015 $5000

Williams, William Carlos 1883-1963 *Collected Poems 1921-1931.* New York: Objectivist Press, 1934. First edition, 8vo., original cloth, printed label on spine, dust jacket, bookplate, otherwise fine.   James S. Jaffe Rare Books   Modern American Poetry - 315   2015 $850

Williams, William Carlos 1883-1963 *The Collected later Poems of William Carlos Williams.* Norfolk: New Directions, 1950. First edition, limited to 100 copies signed by author, 8vo., original red cloth, slipcase, printed label, fine.   James S. Jaffe Rare Books   Modern American Poetry - 321   2015 $1500

Williams, William Carlos 1883-1963 *The Collected Poems of William Carlos Williams.* New York: New Directions, 1986-1988. First edition, 2 volumes, 8vo., fine in fine dust jackets. Beasley Books   2013 - 2015 $175

Williams, William Carlos 1883-1963 *The Desert Music and Other Poems.* New York: Random House, 1954. First trade edition, 8vo., original cloth, very good, inscribed by author to Harold Norse, with Norse's ownership signature. James S. Jaffe Rare Books   Modern American Poetry - 324   2015 $2500

Williams, William Carlos 1883-1963 *The Desert Music and Other Poems.* New York: Random House, 1954. First edition, 8vo., original cloth backed green boards, glassine dust jacket, slipcase, very fine in slightly torn glassine, signed by author.   James S. Jaffe Rare Books Modern American Poetry - 323   2015 $1500

Williams, William Carlos 1883-1963 *An Early Martyr and Other Poems.* New York: Alcestis Press, 1935. First edition, limited to 165 copies of which this is one of 135 on Strathmore rag paper signed by author, 8vo., original printed wrappers, outer glassine wrapper, shallow dampstain at bottom edge of one leaf, otherwise very fine.   James S. Jaffe Rare Books   Modern American Poetry - 316   2015 $1500

Williams, William Carlos 1883-1963 *The Great American Novel.* Paris: Three Mountains Press, 1923. First edition, one of 300 copies, tall 8vo., original cloth backed boards, printed spine label, fine.   James S. Jaffe Rare Books   Modern American Poetry - 310   2015 $1250

Williams, William Carlos 1883-1963 *In the American Grain.* New York: Albert & Charles Boni, 1925. First edition, tall 8vo., aside from some faint darkening and very slight rubbing to rare jacket, fine.   James S. Jaffe Rare Books   Modern American Poetry - 311   2015 $2500

Williams, William Carlos 1883-1963 *In the Money White Mule - Part II.* Norfolk: New Directions, 1940. First edition, 8vo., original cloth, dust jacket, signed by poet, good.   James S. Jaffe Rare Books   Modern American Poetry - 319   2015 $1500

Williams, William Carlos 1883-1963 *The Knife of the Times and Other Stories.* Ithaca: Dargon Press, 1932. First edition, one of 500 copies, 8vo., original blue cloth, glassine dust jacket with outer printed dust jacket, fine.   James S. Jaffe Rare Books   Modern American Poetry - 313   2015 $850

Williams, William Carlos 1883-1963 *Make Light of it.* New York: Random House, 1950. First edition, first printing, 8vo., original cloth, fine in custom made slipcase, dust jacket, Marianne Moore's copy with her notes on review slip.   James S. Jaffe Rare Books   Modern American Poetry - 322   2015 $2500

Williams, William Carlos 1883-1963 *A Novelette and other Prose (1921-1931).* Toulon: To Publishers, 1932. First edition, one of approximately 500 copies, signed by author, 8vo., original printed wrappers, marginal browning to wrappers as usual with verly slight wear to extremities, otherwise very good.   James S. Jaffe Rare Books   Modern American Poetry - 314   2015 $850

Williams, William Carlos 1883-1963 *Paterson.* New York: New Directions, 1946. 1948. 1949. 1951. 1958. First editions, first four volumes limited to 1000 copies, the fifth to 3000, 5 volumes, touch of wear on jacket of Book Two, else fine in fine dust jackets, superior set, this set virtually free of soiling, from the library of Kate Stettner Lobell and Carl D. Lobell.   Between the Covers Rare Books   196 - 38   2015 $4500

Williams, William Carlos 1883-1963 *Paterson: Books I-V.* New York: New Directions, 1946-1958. First editions, tall octavo, original cloth, original dust jackets, fine set with only slightest wear, rare in this condition.   Manhattan Rare Book Company   Literature 2014 - 2015 $2400

Williams, William Carlos 1883-1963 *Paterson (Books 1-5).* New York: New Directions, 1946-1958. First editions, first four parts limited to 1000 copies, fifth to 3000, 5 volumes, 8vo., original cloth, dust jackets, inscribed by poet to Laurence Scott, fine set.   James S. Jaffe Rare Books   Modern American Poetry - 325   2015 $8500

Williams, William Carlos 1883-1963 *Paterson.* New York: New Directions, 1951. First collected edition of Books 1-4, one of 200 copies, 8vo., original cloth, dust jacket, fine, jacket very slightly rubbed at top of spine panel, presentation copy inscribed by author for Norman Thomas Di Giovanni, 12/24/51.   James S. Jaffe Rare Books   Modern American Poetry - 326   2015 $1250

Williams, William Carlos 1883-1963 *The Selected Letters of William Carlos Williams.* New York: McDowell Obolensky, 1957. First edition, one of 75 copies siged by author, 8vo., original cloth, glassine dust jacket, very fine, virtually as new, preserved in half morocco slipcase.   James S. Jaffe Rare Books   Modern American Poetry - 327   2015 $950

Williams, William Carlos 1883-1963 *Sour Grapes. A Book of Poems.* Boston: Four Seas Co., 1921. First edition, one of 1000 copies, small 8vo., original green boards, printed label on spine, dust jacket, boards lightly rubbed at extremities, inch long and 3/8 inch at its widest marginal chip in fore-edge of one leaf, not affecting text, otherwise fine in rare dust jacket, which is slightly chipped in few places, with 1 1/2 inch closed tear to top edge back panel, signed by poet.   James S. Jaffe Rare Books   Modern American Poetry - 308   2015 $2500

Williams, William Carlos 1883-1963 *Spring and All.* Paris: Contact Pub. Co., 1923. First edition, one of 300 copies, small 8vo., original printed wrappers, ownership signature on front inner wrapper, spine panel chipped, internally very good, very scarce.   James S. Jaffe Rare Books   Modern American Poetry - 309   2015 $2250

Williams, William Carlos 1883-1963 *The Tempers.* London: Elkin Mathews, Cork St., 1913. First edition, probably 1000 copies printed, 12mo., original pale yellow boards, spine ends trifle rubbed, otherwise fine, fragile book, inscribed by author in April 1919.   James S. Jaffe Rare Books   Modern American Poetry - 306   2015 $5000

Williams, William Carlos 1883-1963 *Two Poems.* N.P.: Stovepipe Press, 1937. First edition, limited to 500 copies, 8vo., original green wrappers, printed label, fine, 2 drawings by William Zorach.   James S. Jaffe Rare Books   Modern American Poetry - 318   2015 $250

Williams, William Carlos 1883-1963 *A Voyage to Pagany.* New York: Macaulay Co., 1928. First edition, 8vo., original cloth, pictorial dust jacket, fine in very slightly frayed dust jacket.   James S. Jaffe Rare Books   Modern American Poetry - 312   2015 $2500

Williams, William Carlos 1883-1963 *White Mule.* Norfolk: New Directions, 1937. First edition, one of 1100 copies, 8vo., original cloth, signed by author. James S. Jaffe Rare Books Modern American Poetry - 317 2015 $1500

Williamson, Thomas *The East India Vade-Mecum; or Complete guide to Gentlemen Intended for the Civil, Military of Naval Service of the Hon. East India Company.* London: printed for Black Parry and Kingsbury..., 1810. First edition, 8vo., 2 volumes, short closed tear leaf Y1 (pages 321-2) of first volume but with no loss, bound uniformly in contemporary half sheep over marbled boards, flat spines with labels, labels rather rubbed and faded, slightest wear to extremities but overall very good, 19th century armorial bookplate of Roberth Smith (Smyth) of Gaybrook, County Estmeath. John Drury Rare Books 2015 - 25962 2015 $4983

Willingham, Calder *Geraldine Bradshaw.* New York: Vanguard Press, 1950. First edition, boards little smudged, very good in about very good dust jacket, inscribed by author to fellow author James Jones. Between the Covers Rare Books, Inc. 187 - 294 2015 $375

Willis, Robert Darling *Philosophical Sketches of the Principles of Society and Government.* London: printed by W. Bulmer and Co. for P. Elmsly, 1795. First edition, 8vo., half title, contemporary diced russia gilt, fine, from the library of Lord Eldon with his armorial bookplate and ownership signature, uncommon. John Drury Rare Books March 2015 - 25034 2015 $656

Willis, W. S. *A Story of the Big Western ranches.* privately printed, 1955. First edition, limited to 400 copies, 8vo., pictorial wrappers, illustrations, light wear to spine ends, else very good. Buckingham Books March 2015 - 37307 2015 $225

Willocks, Tim *Bad City Blues.* London: MacDonald, 1991. First edition, fine in dust jacket. Buckingham Books March 2015 - 15183 2015 $425

Willson, Dixie *Clown Town.* New York: Doubleday Page, 1924. Stated first edition, 4to., pictorial boards, near fine in original box (flaps repaired), full color and line illustrations by Erick Berry. Aleph-Bet Books, Inc. 108 - 98 2015 $300

Willson, Harry *The Use of a Box of Colours in a Practical Demonstration.* London: Published by Tilt and Bogue..., 1842. Royal 8vo., 12 lithograph plates including frontispiece of which 6 hand colored and three tinted, some plates containing several views, original green cloth, upper cover with gilt blocked title vignette, spine lettered in gilt, somewhat shaken with some foxing to half title and frontispiece. Marlborough Rare Books List 54 - 90 2015 £350

Wilshire, William Hughes *A Descriptive Catalogue of Playing the Other Cars in the British Museum.* London: British Museum, 1975. Reprint of 1876 edition, very fine in dust jacket. Mordida Books March 2015 - 012623 2015 $150

Wilson, Augustus, Mrs. *Parsons' Memorial and Historical Library Magazine.* St. Louis: Beckfold & Co., 1885. First edition thus, quarto, presentation inscription form author, pictorial decorated cloth, gold stamping on front cover and spine, frontispiece, illustrations, plates, portraits, very good, tight copy. Buckingham Books March 2015 - 27376 2015 $1750

Wilson, Colin *Ritual in the Dark.* London: Victor Gollancz Ltd., 1960. First edition, fine in bright dust jacket, lightly rubbed at head of spine and top front corner. Buckingham Books March 2015 - 27640 2015 $250

Wilson, Colin *Ritual in the Dark.* London: Victor Gollancz, 1960. First edition, fine in bright dust jacket with original promotional wraparound band. Buckingham Books March 2015 - 33978 2015 $350

Wilson, Colin *Ritual in the Dark.* London: Gollancz, 1960. First edition, page edges darkened, otherwise fine in lightly soiled dust jacket with nicks at corners and publisher's wraparound intact. Mordida Books March 2015 - 002313 2015 $100

Wilson, Edmund *Poets, Farewell!* New York: Charles Scribner's sons, 1929. First edition, inscribed to Malcolm Cowley. Honey & Wax Booksellers 2 - 57 2015 $3000

Wilson, Elijah Nicholas *Among the Shoshones.* Salt Lake City: Skelton Pub. Co., 1910. First edition, first issue, 8vo., original dark green cloth, handwritten titles on orange labels affixed to front cover and spine, 222 pages, frontispiece, illustrations, portraits, plates, variant binding when compared in a side-by-side comparison with actual trade edition, this copy 23cm. in height compared to 21cm. for trade edition, bound in at end following a typewritten leaf is a set of altered sheets pages 185-247 of the second issue (222 pages plus 25 additional pages), excluding some objectionable sentences, light wear to spine ends an corners, some pages carelessly opened, few pages repaired or lightly soiled, binding lightly shaken, else very good, rare. Buckingham Books March 2015 - 28498 2015 $2500

Wilson, Elijah Nicholas *Among the Shoshones.* Salt Lake City: Skelton Publishing, 1910. First edition, first issue, 8vo., presentation inscription by publisher, signed by him, signature of publisher is rare, original dark green decorated cloth, titles on front cover and spine stamped in black ink, frontispiece, illustrations, portraits, plates, some light professional restoration to spine ends and corners, else near fine, bright, tight copy, housed in decorated cloth clamshell case with title stamped in black, rare. Buckingham Books March 2015 - 24796 2015 $7500

Wilson, Frank Percy *Elizabethan and Jacobean Studies Presented to Frank Percy Wilson in Honour of His Seventieth Birthday.* Oxford: Clarendon Press, 1959. Half title, frontispiece, plates, original dark blue cloth, very good in creased and slightly marked dust jacket, from the library of Geoffrey & Kathleen Tillotson.   Jarndyce Antiquarian Booksellers   CCVII - 555   2015   £35

Wilson, George *Researches on Colour-Blindness with a Supplement.* Edinburgh: London: Sutherland & Knox/Simpkin Marshall, 1855. First edition, 8vo., inscribed by author to Alexander Gordon, very good+, original burgundy cloth with mild edge wear, paper label on spine scuffed, label and spine sunned, mild scattered soil, bookplate of Alexander Gordon.   By the Book, L. C.   44 - 41   2015 $500

Wilson, Harry Leon *The Spenders: a Tale of the Third Generation.* Boston: Lothrop Pub. Co., 1902. Stated 'Twenty-six Thousand", illustrations, front hinge little tender, else near fine with light wear at spine ends, this copy inscribed by author for Robert House Mackey, additionally inscribed by the illustrator, the author's wife, Rose O'Neill Wilson.   Between the Covers Rare Books   196 - 125   2015 $650

Wilson, Joseph T. *The Black Phalanx: a History of the Negro Soldiers of the United States in the Wars of 1775-1812, 1861-1865.* Hartford: American Pub. Co., 1891. Reprint, 56 illustrations, page edges little browned at extremities, little scuffing on rear board, beautiful and bright, just about fine.   Between the Covers Rare Books   197 - 104   2015 $400

Wilson, Joshua L. *Four Propositions Sustained Against the Claims of the American Home Missionary Society.* Cincinnati: Pub. for the author, 1831. First edition, 8vo., neatly removed, tide mark lower corner of title, affecting imprint and on follow leaf, spotty foxing.   M & S Rare Books, Inc.   97 - 321   2015 $85

Wilson, L. S. *Memoirs of John Frederic Oberlin, Pastor of Waldbach, in the Ban de la Roche.* London: Holdsworth and Ball, 1829. First edition, 8vo., engraved silhouette frontispiece, 4 other plates, 3 fine lithographic views, contemporary diced lilac russia, spine gilt and lettered, marbled edges, fine, from the early 19th century library of John Gladstone, the Liverpool merchant and father of W.E. Gladstone, with Fasque bookplate.   John Drury Rare Books   March 2015 - 26115   2015   £306

Wilson, Patrick *'Biographical Account of Alexander Wilson M.D. late Professor of Practical Astronomy in the University of Glasgow....' (read Feb. 2, 1793) in Transactions of the Royal Society of Edinburgh Volume X.* Edinburgh and London: William Tait and Charles Tait, 1826. 4to., engraved title illustration, 22 plate sin rear, original blue paper wrappers, printed paper spine label, extremities worn, soiled, substantially unopened, entire issue is complete, very good.   Jeff Weber Rare Books   178 - 1163   2015 $100

Wilson, R. R. *History of Grant County, Kansas.* Wichita: Eagle Press, 1950. First edition, cloth, numerous illustrations, 2 maps, charts, very good signed by Wilson.   Buckingham Books March 2015 - 28356   2015 $275

Wilson, Robert *The Company of Strangers.* London: Harer Collins, 2001. First edition, very fine in dust jacket with torn publisher's wraparound intact.   Mordida Books March 2015 - 007651   2015 $85

Wilson, Robert *The Correspondence Between Sir Robert Wilson, His Royal Highness, the Duke of York and the Electors of Southwark...* London: James Ridgway, 1821. First edition, 8vo., recent marbled boards lettered on spine, very good, scarce.   John Drury Rare Books   March 2015 - 24460   2015   £266

Wilson, Robert *A Darkening Stain.* London: Harper Collins, 1998. First edition, very fine in dust jacket.   Mordida Books   March 2015 - 007649   2015 $90

Wilson, S. Clay *Wilson's Grimm.* San Francisco: Cottage Classics, 1999. Of a total edition of 1250 copies, this one of 1250 copies of trade edition, fine in wrappers, illustrations.   Ken Lopez, Bookseller   164 - 248   2015 $45

Wilson, Samuel *The Solemn Declaration of Richard Coleman Who was Executed at Kennington-Common the County of Surry on Wednesday April 12 1749 for the Murder of Sarah Green Widow with Behaviour Confession and Dying Words of the Four Other Malefactors, Who were Executed at the Same Time and Place....* London: printed for J. Nicholson near the Sessions House in the Old Baily and sold at the pamphlet shops in London and Westminster, 1749. Only edition of great rarity, 4to., 12 pages, titlepage soiled with tiny hole but no loss, final leaf at little soiled, all margins trimmed close occasionally touching letters, one catchword lost, preserved in modern wrappers with printed label on upper cover.   John Drury Rare Books   March 2015 - 25890   2015 $874

Wilson, Thomas *A Description of the Correct Method of Waltzing the Truly Fashionable Species of Dancing, that from the Graceful and Pleasing Beauty of Its Movements, Has Obtained an Ascendancy Over Every Department of that Public Branch of Education.* London: printed for the author 2 Greville Street Halton Garden, published by Sherwood Neely and Jones, 1816. First edition, 8vo., fine folding colored frontispiece, 6 other uncolored engraved plates, original pink boards with green glazed paper spine, printed title label, some wear to head and foot of spine entirely uncut, fine, scarce.   John Drury Rare Books   2015 - 24646   2015 $4371

Wimsatt, William Kurtz *Hateful Contraries: Studies in Literature and Criticism.* Lexington: University of Kentucky Press, Half title, original dark brown cloth, very good in slightly rubbed dust jacket, from the library of Geoffrey & Kathleen Tillotson, with Geoffrey's letter of thanks ofr the book.   Jarndyce Antiquarian Booksellers   CCVII - 556   2015   £20

Wimsatt, William Kurtz *The Portraits of Alexander Pope.* New Haven: Yale University Press, 1965. 4to., half title, frontispiece, original brown buckram, very good in slightly torn dust jacket, author's presentation copy for Geoffrey Tillotson, with 2 TLS's from him, Geoffrey's typewritten review and cutting from TLS, related material, ALS from R. Kenton Cremer, photos of Pope's annotations to an edition of "The Pastorals" in worn folder.   Jarndyce Antiquarian Booksellers   CCVII - 440   2015   £60

Wimsatt, William Kurtz *The Verbal Icon: Studies in the meaning of Poetry...* Lexington: University of Kentucky Press, 1954. Original green cloth, slightly faded in torn dust jacket, half title, Geoffrey Tillotson's copy signed 19.ii 53, with copy of his letter of thanks for the book.   Jarndyce Antiquarian Booksellers   CCVII - 557   2015   £20

Winch, Terence *The Beautiful Indifference.* New York: O Press, 1976. First edition, 4to., 6 pages, stapled stiff wrappers, little soiled, very good, inscription on titlepage by author.   Second Life Books Inc.   191 - 92   2015 $75

Windeler, B. C. *Elimus.* Paris: Three Mountains Press, 1923. First edition, Bryher's copy with her bookplate, wonderful association as Bryher financed McAlmon's Contact Press, small 4to., hardcover, illustrations by D. Shakespeare and Robert Dill.   Beasley Books   2013 - 2015 $400

Windham, Donald *Stone in the Hourglass.* Verona: printed on magnani paper by Stamperia Voldonega under the supervision of Martino Mardersteig, 1981. First edition, number 24 of 50 copies signed by author (total edition 750), cover art after Fritz Bultman, 8vo., stiff wrappers in slipcase, as new, original Scribner price label affixed to slipcase.   Gemini Fine Books & Arts, Ltd.   Art Reference & Illustrated Books: First Editions - 2015 $155

Windham, William *Speech of the Rt. Hon. William Windham in the House of Commons May the 26th 1809 on Mr. Curwen's Bill 'for better securing the Independence and Purity of Parliament by Preventing the Procuring or Obtaining of Seats by Corrupt Practices'.* London: printed for J. Budd, 1810. First separate edition, 8vo., modern wrappers with printed title label on upper cover, very good, uncommon.   John Drury Rare Books   2015 - 20829   2015 $89

Windsor Castle, a Poem... London: printed and sold by H. Hills, the Black-Fryars near Waterside, for the poor, 1708. Pirated edition, 16 pages, 8vo., disbound, very good.   C. R. Johnson   Foxon R-Z - 1210r-z   2015 $153

Wingfield, Lewis *Abigel Rowe.* London: Richard Bentley & Son, 1883. First edition, 3 volumes, slightly later half crimson calf by Maclehose, Glasgow, raised gilt bands, black and maroon morocco labels, slight rubbing, but very good, ownership signature of Charles F. Grant.   Jarndyce Antiquarian Booksellers   CCXI - 292   2015   £280

Wingfield, R. D. *Frost at Christmas.* London: Constable, 1889. First UK edition, as new, unread copy in as new dust jacket.   Buckingham Books   March 2015 - 36121   2015 $750

Wingfield, R. D. *Night Frost.* London: Constable, 1992. First edition, signed, fine in dust jacket.   Buckingham Books   March 2015 - 8555   2015 $850

Winner, Anthony *Studies in Joseph Conrad's Major Novels.* Charlottesville: University Press of Virginia, 1988. First edition, slight foxing of endpapers, else fine in fine dust jacket, from the library of author Peter Taylor and wife Eleanor Ross Taylor, inscribed to same by author.   Between the Covers Rare Books, Inc.   187 - 295   2015 $85

Winner, Fred *Surgeons Blue Coal.* Garden City: Murphy Pub., 1968. First edition, slight price sticker shadow on front fly, corners trifle bumped, near fine in very good dust jacket with chip and tar on spine, corresponding price sticker on front flap.   Between the Covers Rare Books   196 - 126   2015 $250

Winship, George Parker   1871-1952 *Early Mexican Printers: A.* Cambridge: Club of Odd Volumes, 1899. First separate edition, one of 50 copies printed on special paper for members of the Club, 8vo., paper wrappers, very good, front wrapper darkened at edges, few minor stains, tear to top edge, contents fine.   Kaaterskill Books   19 - 162   2015 $150

Winsor, Justin *Narrative and Critical History of America.* Boston: Houghton Mifflin, 1889. Riverside Press edition, 8 volumes, small thick quarto, approximately 500-600 pages per volume, well illustrated with hundreds of portraits, facsimiles engravings, maps, facsimile signatures, publisher's three quarter dark brown morocco, spines gilt and blind-stamped, dark brown pebbled cloth sides, light extremity rubbing, bookplate in each volume, fine set.   Argonaut Book Shop   Holiday Season 2014 - 319   2015 $1250

Winstanley, John *Poems written Occasionally by John Winstanley... (with) Poems written Occasionally by John Winstanley....Volume II.* Dublin: printed by S. Powell for the editor, 1751. First editions, 2 volumes, frontispiece mezzotint portrait, 8vo., contemporary calf, brown morocco label, fine, volume I with early bookplate bearing arms of the Tisdall family of Charlesfort Co., Meath.   C. R. Johnson   Foxon R-Z - 1165r-z   2015 $4597

Winstone, Benjamin *Extracts from the Minutes of the Epping and Ongar Highway Trust from Its Commencement in 1769 to its Termination in 1870.* London: Harrison, 1891. First edition, royal octavo, plates and maps, some folding, original green buckram with gilt rules and inner dentelles, top edge gilt, author's presentation copy inscribed with author's compliments for Gaynes Park Library, bit of foxing to prelims, very good, scarce.   Peter Ellis, Bookseller   2014 - 006084   2015   £350

Winter, John *A Sermon on the Settlement of the Rev. Archibald Douglas, as Minister of the Congregation of Protestant Dissenters, Lately under the Charge of The Rev. Thomas Noon, Reading, Bers. on February the 24th 1796.* Newbury: printed and sold by B. Fuller, n.d., 1796. First and only edition, fine, 8vo., sewn as issued in original blue wrappers, uncut and unopened, fine, very rare.   John Drury Rare Books   2015 - 20065   2015 $177

Winters, E. A. *De Princes en die Drie Verborgern Schatten. (The Princess and the Three Hidden Treasures).* St. Augustinus: R. K. Boekhandel, 1944. First edition, 8vo., cloth backed pictorial boards, near fine in dust jacket with small closed tear and slight fraying, but very good, double page and 3 full page vibrant color lithographs, 4 full page black and whites, 2 half page black and whites, plus 21 lovely large pictorial initials, printed on good quality paper.   Aleph-bet Books, Inc.   109 - 166   2015 $125

Winterson, Jeanette *Oranges are Not the Only Fruit.* London: Pandora Press, 1985. First edition, wrappers, octavo, cheap paper bit tanned as always, otherwise fine.   Peter Ellis, Bookseller   2014 - 015964   2015   £325

Winterson, Jeannette *Oranges are Not the Only Fruit.* London: Boston: Pandora Press, 1985. First edition, illustrated wrappers, clean bright, near fine copy, little browned at page edges as is almost invisible.   Any Amount of Books   2015 - A47346   2015   £175

Winwar, Frances *The Haunted Palace: a Life of Edgar Allan Poe.* New York: Harper and Bros., 1959. First edition, author Kenneth Millar/Ross MacDonald's review copy annotated by him in holograph pencil, laid in is 5 page ms. letter signed of his review for the book, book near fine in like dust jacket, letter fine and approximately quarter quarto leaves, lined three-hole notebook paper, rectos only, in blue holograph ink with exception of the last few sentences and corrections in same blue ink, folded horizontally at center, else near fine, from the collection of Duke Collier.   Royal Books   36 - 65   2015 $4500

Wire, H. C. *Marked Man.* D. Appleton Century Co., 1934. First edition, small chip missing from bottom of spine, else very good in dust jacket with light wear to extremities.   Buckingham Books   March 2015 - 1380   2015 $185

Wisconsin Labor 1937. Milwaukee: Wisconsin State Fed. of Labor, 1937. First edition, 4to., wrappers, about fine.   Beasley Books   2013 - 2015 $45

Wisconsin Prohibition Party *Badger Hot Shot: Issued by the State Central Committee of the Wisconsin Prohibition Party No. 2 - May 1896.* Madison: Wisconsin Prohibition Party, 1896. Original printed yellow paper wrappers, light vertical crease down middle, mild toning to contents, faint stain to fore edge, wrappers bit soiled and faded, some minor splitting to spine heel.   Tavistock Books   Temperance - 2015 $95

Wisdom in Miniature or the Young Gentleman and Lady's Pleasing Instructor. Worcester: Thomas Son & Thomas, Oct., 1796. Second Worcester, 24mo., 192 pages, somewhat later half calf, marbled boards, library label inside front cover.   M & S Rare Books, Inc.   97 - 139   2015 $600

Wiseman, Richard *Eight Chirurgical Treatises on These Following Heads, viz. 1. Of Tumours. II. Of Ulcers. III. Of Diseases of the Anus. Iv. Of the King's Evil. V. Of Wounds. VI. Of Gun-Shot Wounds. VII. Of Fractures and Luxations. VIII. Of the Lues Venerea.* London: for B. T. and L. M. and sold by W. Keblewhite and J. Jones, 1697. Third edition, folio, including half title, 18th century paneled calf, very skilfully rebacked retaining original gilt spine, period-style label, tiny (half inch) repaired tear in lower margin of third leaf, else remarkably fine, fresh copy, contemporary ownership signature of Stewart Sparkes on half title.   Joseph J. Felcone Inc.   Science, Medicine and Technology - 42   2015 $3200

Wisilzenus, A. *Memoirs of a Tour to Northern Mexico Connected with Col. Doniphan's Expedition in 1846 and 1847.* Albuquerque: 1969. Facsimile reprint of rare 1848 first edition, 2 folding maps, folding chart, book near fine in lightly worn dust jacket.   Dumont Maps & Books of the West   131 - 82   2015 $75

Wismer, F. D. *The Life of Harry Tracy. The Convict Outlaw.* Dacotah Pub. Co., 1990. First edition thus, 8vo., reprint of 1902 edition, limited to 250 leather bound copies, signed by editor, Douglas Ellison, leather, gold stamping on front cover and spine, illustrations, as new, unread.   Buckingham Books   March 2015 - 39124   2015 $175

Wisniewski, David *Golem.* New York: Clarion, 1996. First edition, 4to., fine in fine dust jacket, signed by author.   By the Book, L. C.   44 - 89   2015 $400

Wister, Owen   1860-1938 *A Journey In Search of Christmas.* New York: Harper & Bros., 1904. First edition, 9 x 6 inches, illustrations by Frederic Remington, 3 plates including frontispiece, decorative endpapers and borders, 9 x 6 inches, red cloth with gilt lettering, decorative front board imprinted with mountain scene, wreath and small black trees, top edge gilt, spine bit sunned, slight lean.   Tavistock Books   Bah, Humbug? - 18   2015 $150

Wister, Owen   1860-1938 *The Virginian: a Horseman of the Plains.* New York: 1902. First edition, first printing with no additional printings listed after 'Set up and electrotyped April 1902', illustrations, original tan pictorial cloth, slight soil externally little dusty on top, internally clean and no writing or marks, binding sound, very good, scarce.   Dumont Maps and Books of the West   130 - 50   2015 $750

Wister, Owen   1860-1938 *The Virginian. A Horseman of the Plains.* Cody: Buffalo Bill Historical Center, 2002. First edition thus, 100th Anniversary edition, limited to 200 numbered signed copies, illustrations by Thom Ross, embossed quarter leather and cloth, black endpapers, frontispiece, 9 full color plates, several block prints, signed by editor Nathan Bender, as new in black cloth slipcase with colored pictorial label affixed to front cover and gilt stamping on spine. Buckingham Books   March 2015 - 19573   2015 $375

Witham, Henry   *The Internal Structure of Fossil Vegetables Found in the Carboniferous and Oolitc Deposits of Great Britain.* Edinburgh: Adam & Charles Black, 1833. Quarto, 884 pages, 16 engraved plates, contemporary full calf, expertly rebacked, prize binding with contemporary written inscription pasted in.   Andrew Isles   2015 - 3672   2015 $1200

Witherby, H. F. *British Birds an Illustrated Magazine Devoted chiefly to the Birds on the British List.* London: Witherby & Co., 1907-1996. Octavo, 89 volumes, photos, first 42 volumes in publisher's brown cloth, remaining volumes in brown binder's cloth, fine set.   Andrew Isles   2015 - 30204   2015 $4500

Withers, John   *The Dutch Better Friends than the French to the Monarchy, Church and Trade of England.* London: for John Clark, 1713. 8vo., 36 pages, margins trimmed, just shaving a couple of foot notes, otherwise good, crisp copy in modern plain wrappers.   John Drury Rare Books   2015 - 16102   2015 $106

Withers, John   *An Epistle to the Right Honourable Robert Walpole, Esq. Upon His Majesty's Arrival.* London: printed for Jacob Tonson, 1723. First edition, folio, disbound, fine, complete with half title.   C. R. Johnson   Foxon R-Z - 1166r-z   2015 $1916

Withers, Paul K. *Connail - The Final Years 1992-1997.* Halifax: Withers Publishing, 1997. First edition, quarto, black and white and color photos, blue cloth lettered in silver, very fine with pictorial dust jacket.   Argonaut Book Shop   Holiday Season 2014 - 320   2015 $60

Withers, Philip   *Alfred or a Narrative of the Daring and Illegal Measures to Suppress a Pamphlet Intituled Strictures on the Declaration of Horne Tooke, esq....* London: printed for the author, 1789. 8vo., 48 pages, title lightly spotted and soiled, well bound recently in cloth, spine lettered in gilt, very good.   John Drury Rare Books   2015 - 16201   2015 $133

Withnall, S. E. *Diary of Motor-Car Tour. Easter 1903.* Oxford: n.p, 1903. First edition, 8vo., 31 pages, recto only, red buckram, lettered in gilt on cover, top edge gilt, text mimeographed, probably a unique example of one of very few copies, good, handwritten signed letter loosely inserted written on headed notepaper from Magdalen College, Oxford dated 22.7.03 and consisting of approximately 70 words addressed to a Mr. Leslie from the author, minor marks to covers, spine darkened, very good.   Any Amount of Books   2015 - C6944   2015   £175

Wittgenstein, Ludwig   *Last Writings on Philosophy of Psychology. Volume I.* Oxford: Basil Blackwell, 1982. True first edition, 8vo., near fine with mild soil and stains to edges, in very good++ dust jacket with sun spine, edge wear.   By the Book, L. C.   44 - 60   2015 $200

Wittgenstein, Ludwig   *Philosophical Investigations.* Oxford: Basil Blackwell, 1953. First edition, 8vo., original publisher's navy blue lettered gilt at spine, neat name on front pastedown, slight fading at spine ends, otherwise very good in slightly used and faded, very good- dust jacket with nicks and chips.   Any Amount of Books   2015 - C1425   2015   £225

Wittgenstein, Ludwig *Tractatus Logico-Philosophicus.* London: Kegan Paul, Trench, Trubner & Co., 1933. Second corrected printing, octavo, with 8 page catalog at end dated 1944, original green cloth, bright gilt lettering to spine lower corner front board has been bumped, otherwise binding near fine, new address for publisher carefully pasted over former address on titlepage, overall gorgeous copy. Athena Rare Books 15 - 60 2015 $600

Wittington, Harry *A Ticket to Hell.* Greenwich: Fawcett, 1959. First edition, signed, near fine in pictorial wrappers. Buckingham Books March 2015 - 11425 2015 $175

Wittke, Carl *Against the Current. The Life of Carl Heinzen.* Chicago: University of Chicago Press, 1945. First edition, fine in lightly worn dust jacket with small chip. Beasley Books 2013 - 2015 $45

Witzel, Morgan *Foundations of Modern Management: Human Resource Management.* Bristol: Thoemmes Press with Kyokuto of Tokyo, 2000. First edition thus, 8vo., 8 volumes, hardbacks, about fine. Any Amount of Books 2015 - B16280 2015 £240

Wodehouse, Pelham Grenville 1881-1975 *The Luck of Bodkins.* Herbert Jenkins, 1935. First edition, little light foxing at head of initial blank, half title and to ads at rear, crown 8vo., original variant binding of orange cloth stamped in black, backstrip lettered black, slight lean to spine, very good. Blackwell's Rare Books B179 - 249 2015 £200

Wodehouse, Pelham Grenville 1881-1975 *Performing Flea: a Self-Portrait in Letters.* London: Herbert Jenkins, 1954. Reprint, from the library of Geoffrey & Kathleen Tillotson, half title, frontispiece, original blue cloth, slightly torn dust jacket, few margin markers and number of press cuttings inserted by Kathleen, press cuttings. Jarndyce Antiquarian Booksellers CCVII - 558 2015 £20

Wodehouse, Pelham Grenville 1881-1975 *Summer Moonshine.* Doubleday, Doran and Co., Inc., 1937. First edition, fine, bright copy in dust jacket lightly sunned on spine, light wear to spine ends, lightly rubbed along front flap fold, closed to top edge of front panel and light wear to extremities. Buckingham Books March 2015 - 33677 2015 $300

Wolf, Gary K. *Who Censored Roger Rabbit?* New York: St. Martin's, 1981. First edition, fine in printed wrappers, uncorrected proof. Mordida Books March 2015 - 001314 2015 $75

Wolf, Johann Rudoloph *Handbuch der Astronomie, Ihrer Geschichte und Litteranar mit Zahlreichen in den text Eingedruckten Holzstichen.* Amsterdam: Merdian, 1973. Facsimile reprint of 1890, 8vo., diagrams, index, green cloth, gilt stamped dark blue cover and spine labels, near fine. Jeff Weber Rare Books 178 - 1169 2015 $150

Wolfe, Thomas Clayton *Look Homeward, Angel.* New York: Charles Scribner's, 1929. First edition, spine lettering worn but readable, very good in worn, good only first issue dust jacket (with Wolfe portrait on rear panel), lacking bottom couple of inches of spine and several other modest chips and tears, several internal tape repairs, this copy inscribed by author for Fidelia E. Stark, Oct. 30 1929, laid in 4 page carbon manuscript (folded, small breaks at folds, else near fine), unsigned but almost certainly by Maxwell Perkins dated April 17, 1929. Between the Covers Rare Books 196 - 127 2015 $12,000

Wolfe, Tom *The Electric Kool-Aid Acid Test.* New York: FSG, 1968. First edition, fading to and foxing to top edge, couple of faint fore edge smudges, else fine in fine dust jacket, beautiful copy. Ken Lopez, Bookseller 164 - 249 2015 $850

Wolff, Christian *Elementa Matheseos Universae. Tomus III qui Opticam, Perspectivan, Catopriticam, Dioptricam, Sphaerica et Trigonometriam Sphaericam Atque Astronomiam tam Sphaericam Quam Theoricam Complectiur.* Halle: Prostat in Officina Rengeriana, 1735. 5 parts in 1, volume III only, small 4to., engraved head and tailpieces, each section with numbered folding plates, 6, 7, 12, 4, 15, (14) respectively, plates 4-6 with marginal tears, third section plates 2-12 with small holes, occasional light scattered foxing, contemporary full calf, gilt stamped spine, worn, hinges cracked, corners showing, spine ends missing large pieces, armorial bookplate, ownership signature of Berthold Hinkle(?), ownership signature C. de Kelilerl?, good, as is. Jeff Weber Rare Books 178 - 1171 2015 $1000

Wolff, Geoffrey *Black Sun: the Brief Transit and Violent Eclipse of Harry Crosby.* New York: Random House, 1976. First edition, fine in very good dust jacket with wear at spine ends, very warmly inscribed by author for author Nicholas Delbanco. Between the Covers Rare Books, Inc. 187 - 296 2015 $150

Wolff, Geoffrey *Inklings.* New York: Random House, 1977. First edition, fine in spine faded, very good dust jacket with some short tears, warmly inscribed by author for Nicholas Delbanco. Between the Covers Rare Books, Inc. 187 - 297 2015 $150

Wolff, Tobias *This Boy's Life.* New York: Atlantic Monthly Press, 1989. First edition, inscribed and signed by author in year of publication, publisher postcard laid in, fine in fine dust jacket. Ed Smith Books 82 - 34 2015 $150

Wolfrum, C. *Aussig (Usti nad Labem).* Czechoslovakia: C. Wolfrum, circa, 1930. First editions, tall 8vo., 12, 11 and 7 leaves each, original green thick buckram portfolios, handwritten labels on front cover of each, very slightly shelfworn, exceptional set, 3 pattern books with 100 samples for Halbwood Popeline. Marlborough Rare Books List 54 - 87 2015 £525

Wolfson, Harry Austryn *Philo: Foundations of Religious Philosophy in Judaism, Christianity and Islam.* Cambridge & London: Harvard University Press, 1982. Fifth printing, 2 volumes, 8vo., navy cloth, ink ownership signature of David Lindberg, very good. Jeff Weber Rare Books 178 - 1172 2015 $40

Wollstonecraft, Mary 1759-1797 *Bref Skrifna Under et Kort Wistande I Sverige. Norrige och Danmark. Ofwersatte fran Engelskan.* Stockholm: Holmberg, 1798. First edition in Swedish, 8vo., title a cancel tipped on to a sub, contemporary half sheep over marbled boards, spine gilt but worn and wanting label, good, sound copy. John Drury Rare Books 2015 - 22682 2015 $787

Wollstonecraft, Mary 1759-1797 *Letters Written During a Short Residence in Sweden, Norway and Denmark.* London: J. Johnson, 1802. Second edition, small 8vo., contemporary calf with later rebacking, worn along extremities of covers and along hinges, scarce. Second Life Books Inc. 191 - 94 2015 $750

Wollstonecraft, Mary 1759-1797 *The Love Letters of... to Gilbert Imlay...* London: Hutchinson, 1908. First edition, 8vo., 3 sepia portraits, stamped maroon cloth, front hinge tender, very good, scarce. Second Life Books Inc. 191 - 95 2015 $200

Wollstonecraft, Mary 1759-1797 *Original Stories from Real Life...* London: Johnson, 1791. Second edition, contemporary calf, hinges tender, spine chipped and worn at extremities, good copy, this was issued with and without plates, this has no illustrations, 8vo., some foxing and staining to titlepage and prelim leaf, with ads in rear, with ownership bookplate of Author Joseph Strutt 1749-1802, issued without half title. Second Life Books Inc. 189 - 271 2015 $2000

Wollstonecraft, Mary 1759-1797 *Original Stories from Real Life...* London: Chiswick Press, printed by C. Whittingham for Charles Tilt, 1832. Second edition, 12mo., engraved vignettes on titlepage and at edge of each of the 25 stories, bound with half title in contemporary calf backed boards, spine rubbed and worn at extremities, front hinge tender, good copy, scarce. Second Life Books Inc. 189 - 272 2015 $400

Wollstonecraft, Mary 1759-1797 *A Vindication of the Rights of Woman...* London: Johnson, 1792. Second edition, 8vo., modern calf backed marbled boards, morocco label, some light toning to titlepage, very nice. Second Life Books Inc. 189 - 275 2015 $3500

Wollstonecraft, Mary 1759-1797 *A Vindication of the Rights of Woman.* Dublin: James Moore, 1793. First Irish edition, 8vo., modern calf backed marbled boards, morocco label, some toning to leaves, contemporary ownership signature (M. Lloyd), very nice. Second Life Books Inc. 189 - 274 2015 $3200

Wollstonecraft, Mary 1759-1797 *A Vindication of the Rights of Woman..* London: Johnson, 1796. Third edition, 8vo., modern full calf, new endpapers, last leaf tipped in, all edges stained yellow, very nice, clean copy. Second Life Books Inc. 189 - 276 2015 $2750

Wollstonecraft, Mary 1759-1797 *A Vindication of the Rights of Woman; with Strictures on Political and Moral Subjects.* London: J. Johnson, 1796. 8vo., recently bound in 18th century style half calf gilt by Trevor Lloyd of Ludlow, fine. John Drury Rare Books 2015 - 24574 2015 $2185

Wollstonecraft, Mary 1759-1797 *Posthumous Works.* London: J. Johnson, 1798. First edition, bound with errata leaves and half titles in 4 volumes, original boards, new paper spine, pastedowns and spine labels, ownership signature of John Flather, St. Johns coll(ege) Cambridge in each volume, with library stamp on titlepage of each volume and library stamp on verso of each titlepage, nice clean set, scarce. Second Life Books Inc. 191 - 93 2015 $7500

Wolman, Benjamin B. *Clinical Diagnosis of Mental Disorders.* New York: Plenum, 1978. First edition, small 4to., 922 pages, fine in lightly used dust jacket. Beasley Books 2013 - 2015 $45

Wolpe, Berthold *A Newe Booke of Copies 1574, a Facsimile of a Unique Elizabethan Writing.* London: Lion and Unicorn Press, 1959. Limited to 200 numbered copies printed and bound at the press, facsimile reprint, small 4to., cloth, 100 pages. Oak Knoll Books Special Catalogue 24 - 60 2015 $100

Wolstenholme, Joseph *Mathematical Problems on the Subjects fot the Cambridge Mathematical Tirpos Examination.* London: Macmillan, 1891. third edition, 8vo., ink ownership inscription of T. W. Chaundy, Balliol College Dec. 1905,. Jeff Weber Rare Books 178 - 1173 2015 $70

Woman in Miniature. A Satire. London: printed for John Huggonson, 1742. First edition, 8vo., 32 pages, disbound, one tiny wormhole catching odd letter, otherwise fine, very scarce. C. R. Johnson Foxon R-Z - 1167r-z 2015 $1302

Wood, Ann *The Trial of Mrs. Ann Wood, Wife of William Wood, Esq. Commissary and Pay-Master of Artillery for Adultery with Quintin Dick, Esq. Merchant of King Street, Cheapside, London...* London: printed for G. Lister no. 46 Old Bailey, 1786. First edition, 8vo., engraved frontispiece, most leaves with largely marginal foxing, ads on verso of titlepage but no additional ad leaf, well bound in 19th/20th century half calf over marbled boards, spine lettered in gilt, minor wear to extremities, bookplate on front pastedown of Los Angeles Board of Law Library, apparently of great rarity. John Drury Rare Books 2015 - 25917 2015 $3234

Wood, Edward J. *Giants and Dwarfs.* London: Richard Bentley, 1868. First edition, title in red and black, slight spotted, original dark blue cloth, bevelled boards, slight rubbing, inner hinge weakening, very good.   Jarndyce Antiquarian Booksellers   CCXI - 298   2015   £180

Wood, F. M. *Catalogue of Short Horns to be sold by W. H. Bayliss, Highland, Kan. and B. O. Cowan, New Point, Mo. at the Bohanan Barn, Lincoln Neb. Thursday May 19 1892. Col. F. M. Wood Auctioneer.* Times Print, 1892. 8 1/4 x 5 3/4 inches in grey/green printed wrappers, light soiling and light staining to front wrapper with closed tear to lower edge and tiny chip missing from corner of rear wrapper and light chipping to bottom of spine, very good.   Buckingham Books   March 2015 - 35972   2015 $325

Wood, John *Letter to the Rev. George m. Musgrave, A. M., Chaplain to the Downham Union, Norfolk.* N.P.: Edinburgh? n.d.?, 1838. First edition, 8vo., 40 pages, few minor spots on titlepage, recent marbled boards lettered on, very good, apparently rare.   John Drury Rare Books   March 2015 - 21072   2015 $221

Wood, R. E. *Life and Confessions of James Gilbert Jenkins; The Murderer of Eighteen Men...* C. H. Allen and R. E. Wood, 1864. First edition, 8vo., pictorial wrappers, frontispiece, exceedingly rare, small water stain to first page that gradually becomes smaller as the text progresses, minor edge wear to bottom edge of first 38 pages, else very good, tight copy, housed in full leather four point folding case, gold stamped front cover and spine.   Buckingham Books   March 2015 - 2792   2015 $1500

Wood, Stanley *Six Aquarelles from the Rockies.* Denver: Great Divide Pub. Co., 1891. First edition, oblong 4to., original gold and silver textured wrappers bound with string, 6 chromolithographs, each with page of descriptive text, very light staining to decorative wrappers, otherwise very good+, all plates clean and bright.   Any Amount of Books   2015 - C11877   2015   £750

Wood, Thomas *The Youth's Biblical and Theological Companion...* London: printed for the author and sold by Ricahrd Baynes & Others, 1827. First edition, 12mo., inoffensive light dampstain affecting text throughout, contemporary half calf gilt over marbled boards, some wear to lower cover, else acceptable copy.   John Drury Rare Books   2015 - 17713   2015 $133

Wood, William, & Son *1836 & 1837. A Catalogue of Roses, Grown by Willia Wood & Son Nursery Seedsmen and Florists Woodlands' Nursery, Maresfield..* N.P.: n.d. but evidently, 1837. (1836), 8vo., paper generally rather browned, uncut, preserved in modern wrappers, printed title label on upper cover, very rare.   John Drury Rare Books   March 2015 - 23306   2015   £306

Woodbridge Volunteer Fire Brigade *Rules and Regulations of the Woodbridge Volunteer Fire Brigade.* Woodbridge: printed by G. Booth Church Street, n.d., 187-. First edition, 8vo., engraving on titlepage, original printed red card covers, fine, almost certainly rare.   John Drury Rare Books   March 2015 - 21648   2015 $221

Woodhouse, F. C. *A Manual for Holy Days: a Few Thoughts for Those Week Days for Which the Church Provides Special Services.* London: Wells Gardner Darton & Co., 1889. First edition, small octavo, publisher's green cloth gilt, old pencil ownership signature as well as 1945 signature of novelist Peter Taylor, very scarce.   Between the Covers Rare Books, Inc.   187 - 298   2015 $350

Woodhouse, S. C. *Two Cats At Large.* London: New York and Toronto: George Routledge, E. P. Dutton and Musson, n.d., 1910. 4to., cloth backed pictorial boards, edges lightly rubbed and slight cover soil, else near fine, printed on rectos only, each leaf has marvelous full color illustration of Wain's cats, rare.   Aleph-bet Books, Inc.   109 - 483   2015 $2250

Woodhull, Victoria *The Human Body the Temple of God.* London: 1890. First edition, 8vo., maroon cloth stamped in gilt, 2 frontispiece portraits, several engravings, hinges tender, half title and flyleaf loose, cover little worn at edges and ends of spine, else very good, very scarce.   Second Life Books Inc.   189 - 282   2015 $1200

Woodhull, Victoria *The Origin, Tendencies and Principles of Government...* New York: Woodhull, Claflin, 1871. First edition, tall 8vo. 247 pages, brown cloth stamped in gilt, steel engraved frontispiece, some rubbing on spine and wear to extremities, otherwise very good, very scarce. Second Life Books Inc.   189 - 283   2015 $900

Woodman, John *The Rat-Catcher at Chelsea College.* London: printed for the author and sold by booksellers of London and Westminster, 1740. First edition, 8vo., later blue wrappers, titlepage bit dust soiled, otherwise very good, rare.   C. R. Johnson   Foxon R-Z - 1168r-z   2015 $2298

Woodruff, Elizabeth *Dickey Byrd.* Springfield: Milton Bradley, 1928. First edition, folio, black imitation leather stamped in yellow, 6 large and magnificent tipped-in color plates, full page and text illustrations, pictorial endpapers. Aleph-bet Books, Inc.   109 - 459   2015 $875

Woods, Robert Archey *English Social Movements.* New York: Scribners, 1891. First edition, hardcover, inscribed by author, fine but for slightly marked spine.   Beasley Books   2013 - 2015 $150

Woodson, Carter Godwin *African Myths: Together with Proverbs.* Washington: Associated Pub. Inc., 1928. First edition, octavo, 184 pages, illustrations, illustrated tan cloth, slight age toning on boards, very modest rubbing at base of spine, near fine, lacking presumed dust jacket. Between the Covers Rare Books   197 - 11   2015 $300

Woodthorpe, R. C. *Death in Little Town.* New York: Crime Club/Doubleday Doran, 1935. Second edition, stated "First edition", this is the (trade edition) in black cloth with yellow decorations not the special Crime Club edition in red cloth, near fine in very good-dust jacket (some age wear and tear chipping to head and foot of spine).   Stephen Lupack   March 2015 - 2015 $75

Woodward, Henry *A Letter from Henry Woodward, Comedian, the Meanest of all Characters... to Dr. John Hill, Inspector General of Great Britain...* London: printed for M. Cooper, 1752. Second edition, final blank present, handsomely rebound in quarter calf, marbled boards, red label, very good.   Jarndyce Antiquarian Booksellers   CCXI - 297   2015   £280

Woodward, Woody *Jazz Americana.* Los Angeles: Trend Books, 1956. First edition, wrappers, very good, owner's name, inscribed by author, heavily illustrated.   Beasley Books   2013 - 2015 $85

Woolf, Virginia   1882-1941 *Beau Brummell.* New York: Rimmington & Hooper, 1930. First edition, limited to 550 copies, signed by author, finely bound in three quarter calf over marbled boards, excellent copy, few minor spots, else fine.   B & B Rare Books, Ltd.   234 - 108 2015 $1500

Woolf, Virginia   1882-1941 *Between the Acts.* London: Hogarth Press, 1941. First edition, first printing, one of 6358 copies, personal copy of author's sister Vanessa Bell with her ownership initials, publisher's bright blue cloth boards lettered gilt, very good with slight lean, rubbing to extremities, toning and light spotting to endpapers, pencil marks to list of works by author, bright and clean pages, housed in custom quarter leather clamshell box.   B & B Rare Books, Ltd.   239 - 2   2015 $7500

Woolf, Virginia   1882-1941 *The Captain's Death Bed and their Essays.* London: Hogarth Press, 1950. First UK edition (preceded by US edition by 7 days), publisher's cedar-brown cloth in original Vanessa Bell dust jacket, near fine book with light fading to spine, jacket with light soiling and few spots of foxing.   B & B Rare Books, Ltd.   234 - 109   2015 $275

Woolf, Virginia   1882-1941 *The Captain's Death Bed and Other Essays.* London: Hogarth Press, 1950. First English edition, one of 10,000 copies, personal copy of author's sister Vanessa Bell with her ownership inscription, publisher's cedar brown cloth boards, lettered gilt, dark brown topstain, original white dust jacket designed by Bell with flower illustrations and decorations, very good with slight lean, toning to spine, small dent to top edge of front board with some light spotting to top edge, some light offsetting to endpapers, otherwise bright and clean interior, dust jacket is good only, unclipped, 1 inch loss to spine head affecting the title lettering, tears and loss to center of spine, toning and stains to spine and panels, chips to corners and rubbing to extremities, housed in custom quarter leather clamshell box.   B & B Rare Books, Ltd.   239 - 6   2015 $4000

Woolf, Virginia   1882-1941 *The Death of the Moth and Other Essays.* New York: Harcourt, 1942. First American edition, 8vo., spine faded, very good, tight, little browned dust jacket that shows wear at extremities of spine.   Second Life Books Inc.   189 - 284   2015 $150

Woolf, Virginia   1882-1941 *Granite and Rainbow.* London: Hogarth Press, 1958. First edition, personal copy of author's sister, Vanessa Bell with her ownership signature, with front panel of dust jacket designed by Bell adhered to front pastedown and dust jacket spine adhered to front free endpaper, publisher's royal blue cloth, lettered gilt, white dust jacket with decorations in light blue and black, very good, some wear and rubbing to edges, hint of toning to spine, faint hint of foxing to page edges, otherwise bright, clean pages, custom quarter leather clamshell box.   B & B Rare Books, Ltd.   239 - 10   2015 $4000

Woolf, Virginia   1882-1941 *A Haunted House and Other Short Stories.* London: Hogarth Press, 1943. First edition, first printing, one of 6000 copies, copy of author's sister Vanessa Bell with her ownership signature, publisher's dull crimson cloth boards lettered in gilt, good, with toning and staining to spine and boards, small nick to left edge of front board, bright gilt, some faint toning to pages, pencil correction to page 90, laid in is photocopy of a broadside featuring Woolf's text from "The Mark on the Wall", woodblocks by Bell, housed in custom quarter leather clamshell box.   B & B Rare Books, Ltd.   239 - 3   2015 $5000

Woolf, Virginia   1882-1941 *Hours in a Library.* New York: Harcourt Brace and Co., 1957. One of 1800 copies, personal copy of author's sister, Vanessa Bell, with presentation from Leonard Woolf Christmas 1957, publisher's royal blue cloth spine over black paper boards, with author's initials stamped in blind to front board, lettered gilt in original publisher's glassine jacket, near fine with hint of wear to extremities, slightest toning to spine, faint hint of light soiling to board edges, glassine tipped in to frontispiece as protective sheet, bright and fresh interior, light toning to glassine with chipping to extremities and some loss to spine ends, light creasing to front panel, rare in any condition, complete copy, custom quarter clamshell box.   B & B Rare Books, Ltd.   239 - 9   2015 $6500

Woolf, Virginia 1882-1941 *A Letter to a Young Poet.* London: Hogarth Press, 1932. First edition, Honey & Wax Booksellers 2 - 33 2015 $125

Woolf, Virginia 1882-1941 *The Moment and Other Essays.* London: Hogarth Press, 1947. First edition, first printing, one of 10,000 copies, the copy of author's sister Vanessa Bell, with her ownership signature, with front panel of dust jacket designed by Bell adhered to front pastedown, pale ruby red cloth boards, lettered in gilt, pink dust jacket with vase of flowers illustration printed in black, good, with toning to spine, fading to edges of boards, light soiling, bright gilt, hint of light spotting to free endpapers, clean pages, housed in custom quarter leather clamshell box. B & B Rare Books, Ltd. 239 - 4 2015 $4500

Woolf, Virginia 1882-1941 *The Moment and Other Essays.* London: Hogarth Press, 1947. First edition, first impression, publisher's pale ruby red cloth in pink Vanessa Bell dust jacket, fine book with bookplate, near fine dust jacket with tiny nicks to crown of spine, fading to spine and vertical crease to rear panel, without any chips, nicer than usually found. B & B Rare Books, Ltd. 234 - 110 2015 $450

Woolf, Virginia 1882-1941 *A Room of One's Own.* London: Hogarth Press, 1929. First English edition, small crown 8vo., bound in cinnamon cloth, couple of bumps, endpapers stained from old offsetting, very good, tight clean copy. Second Life Books Inc. 189 - 287 2015 $475

Woolf, Virginia 1882-1941 *A Room of One's Own.* New York: Harcourt Brace, 1929. First American edition, one of 4000 copies, 8vo. edges little spotted cover slightly bumped and worn at corners and ends of spine, otherwise very good, tight copy. Second Life Books Inc. 189 - 285 2015 $350

Woolf, Virginia 1882-1941 *A Room of One's Own.* New York: London: Fountain/Hogarth Press, 1929. First edition, limited issue, one of 492 copies signed by Woolf, original cinnamon cloth, spine very lightly faded, touch of rubbing to upper spine, otherwise excellent. B & B Rare Books, Ltd. 234 - 107 2015 $7500

Woolf, Virginia 1882-1941 *A Room of One's Own.* London: Hogarth, 1931. Second edition, 8vo., green cloth, owner's bookplate, name on flyleaf, edges slightly spotted, few pencil notations in margins, cover slightly spotted, otherwise very good, tight copy, poet Barbara Howes' copy with her bookplate and signature. Second Life Books Inc. 189 - 286 2015 $135

Woolf, Virginia 1882-1941 *Street Haunting.* San Francisco: Westgate Press, 1930. First edition, small octavo, quarter blue morocco gilt and paper covered boards, thin spine toned to rich brown and touch bumped, else near fine lacking cardstock slipcase, copy number 329 of 500 numbered copies, signed by author. Between the Covers Rare Books 196 - 12u 2015 $1450

Woolf, Virginia 1882-1941 *Virginia Woolf and Lytton Strachey: Letters.* London: Hogarth Press/Chatto & Windus, 1956. First edition, one of 4000 copies, personal copy of author's sister Vanessa Bell, with her ownership signature, publisher's pale tan cloth boards lettered gilt, cream dust jacket, near fine, hint of wear to extremities, very slight lean, unfaded spine, gilt lightly dimmed, few scattered spots to cloth, otherwise clean covers bright and fresh, housed in custom quarter leather clamshell box. B & B Rare Books, Ltd. 239 - 8 2015 $4000

Woolf, Virginia 1882-1941 *The Voyage Out.* New York: George Doran, 1920. First US edition, 8vo., green cloth, bookplate, inscription. Second Life Books Inc. 189 - 288 2015 $250

Woolf, Virginia 1882-1941 *The Waves.* London: published by Leonard and Virginia Woolf at Hogarth Press, 1931. Review copy, octavo, 325 pages, original dust jacket, very good copy of a fragile book. Honey & Wax Booksellers 1 - 58 2015 $3200

Woolf, Virginia 1882-1941 *The Waves.* London: published by Leonard and Virginia Woolf at the Hogarth Press, 1931. First edition, first printing, one of 7113 copies, publisher's purple cloth lettered gilt, printed on laid paper, good with slight lean, two short tears to spine head, rubbing to spine ends, toning and light soiling to spine ends, toning and light soiling to spine, boards slightly bowed, minor soiling and some fading, very light spotting to first few and last pages of text block, pencil correction to page 47, bright and clean pages, housed in custom quarter leather clamshell box, personal copy of author's sister Vanessa Bell, with her ownership signature by descent to her daughter Angelica Garnett, thence to her two surviving daughters Henrietta Coupe and Frances Partridge. B & B Rare Books, Ltd. 239 - 1 2015 $9500

Woolf, Virginia 1882-1941 *The Waves - Two Holograph Drafts.* London: Hogarth Press, 1976. First edition, facsimiles, patterned cloth, fine in near fine price clipped dust jacket, little rubbed at edges, very scarce. Peter Ellis, Bookseller 2014 - 018719 2015 £275

Woolf, Virginia 1882-1941 *A Writer's Diary.* London: Hogarth Press, 1953. First edition, octavo, fragmentary original dust jacket, this the copy of author's sister Vanessa Bell, signed in ink by Bell, well used copy with extraordinary association. Honey & Wax Booksellers 3 - 10 2015 $6000

Woolf, Virginia 1882-1941 *A Writer's Diary.* London: Hogarth Press, 1953. First edition, first printing, one of 9000 copies, personal copy of author's sister, Vanessa Bell, with her signature, publisher's orange cloth boards, lettered gilt, orange topstain to original white dust jacket designed by Bell with flower illustrations and decorations printed in orange and black, very good with slight lean, some rubbing to extremities, minor toning to spine, light spotting to top edge and endpapers, bright and fresh pages, unclipped dust jacket lacking rear panel and flap and left half of bottom of spine, half inch loss to spine head, toning to spine, some minor soiling and small chips to front panel, housed in custom quarter leather clamshell box.   B & B Rare Books, Ltd.   239 - 7   2015 $5000

Woolf, Virginia 1882-1941 *The Years.* London: Hogarth Press, 1937. First edition, octavo, original green cloth, fine in very clean, attractive dust jacket with few spots to spine and few internal, unobtrusive tape repairs, overall excellent copy.   Manhattan Rare Book Company   Literature 2014 - 2015 $2500

Woolf, Virginia 1882-1941 *The Years.* London: Hogarth Press, 1937. First edition, jade green cloth in original Vanessa Bell dust jacket, fine book in exceptionally fine dust jacket, bright and clean without any fading, toning or tears, absolutely spectacular copy as jacket is notoriously fragile and prone to toning.   B & B Rare Books, Ltd.   234 - 111   2015 $4500

Woolley, Milton *Science of the Bible.* Printed for the author by Knight & Leonard, 1877. First edition, illustrations, very good, shelfwear at extremities, tight, essentially clean text, nice gilt, Zodiac chart with spinner on rear pastedown.   Stephen Lupack   March 2015 -   2015 $200

Woolly West. Judge's Library. A Monthly Magazine of Fun. Judge Publishing Co., 1893. First edition, no. 48, March 1893 of Judge's Library magazine, quarto, color pictorial wrappers, illustrations, spine ends lightly worn, else very good, solid copy.   Buckingham Books   March 2015 - 32425   2015 $175

Woolrich, Cornell *After Dinner.* Philadelphia: J. B. Lippincott, 1944. First edition, former owner's neat small name stamp bottom of copyright page, else fine, bright, square copy, in dust jacket with minor professional restoration to head of spine.   Buckingham Books   March 2015 - 36819   2015 $875

Woolrich, Cornell *Beyond the Night.* New York: Avon, 1959. First edition, very fine, unread copy in wrappers.   Mordida Books   March 2015 - 009564   2015 $100

Woolrich, Cornell *The Black Angel.* Doubleday Doran and Co., 1943. First edition, fine in dust jacket with some minor professional restoration to spine ends and corners.   Buckingham Books   March 2015 - 29809   2015 $2250

Woolrich, Cornell *The Black Angel.* New York: Doubleday Doran Co. Inc., 1943. First edition, some offsetting to front and rear endpapers, former owner's neat small name stamp at bottom of copyright page, binder's flaw to bottom of titlepage and two other pages, else fine in dust jacket with some professional restoration to spine ends and corners.   Buckingham Books   March 2015 - 36816   2015 $2000

Woolrich, Cornell *Borrowed Crime and Other Stories.* New York: Avon Book Co., 1946. First edition, Murder Mystery Monthly 42, digest sized paperback, fine in pictorial wrappers.   Buckingham Books   March 2015 - 36807   2015 $175

Woolrich, Cornell *The Bride Wore Black.* New York: Simon & Schuster, 1940. First edition, spine bit sunned, else near fine internally clean in price clipped dust jacket with minor wear to foot of spine, attractive copy.   Buckingham Books   March 2015 - 35313   2015 $8500

Woolrich, Cornell *Cover Charge.* New York: Boni & Liveright, 1926. First edition, near fine in superb, about near fine dust jacket, jacket has no loss and no toning, only few nicks and tiny closed tears, custom clamshell box, from the collection of Duke Collier.   Royal Books   36 - 252   2015 $7500

Woolrich, Cornell *Deadline at Dawn.* Philadelphia: J. B. Lippincott, 1944. First edition, fine, tight copy in dust jacket with light foxing to reverse side.   Buckingham Books   March 2015 - 36817   2015 $650

Woolrich, Cornell *Hotel Room.* New York: Random House, 1958. First edition, fine in price clipped dust jacket.   Mordida Books   March 2015 - 008601   2015 $150

Woolrich, Cornell *If I Should Die Before I Wake and Other Stories.* New York: Avon Book Co., 1945. First edition, page edges uniformly tanned, else fine in pictorial wrappers.   Buckingham Books   March 2015 - 36806   2015 $200

Woolrich, Cornell *If I Should Die Before I Wake.* New York: Avon, 1945. First edition, paperback original, pages darkened and faint crease on front cover, otherwise near fine wrappers.   Mordida Books   March 2015 - 010004   2015 $135

Woolrich, Cornell *Nightwebs.* New York: Harper, 1971. First edition, fine in dust jacket.   Mordida Books   March 2015 - 010008   2015 $100

Woolrich, Cornell *Phantom Lady.* Philadelphia: Lippincott, 1942. First edition, fine in very good dust jacket with chipping at top of spine, nicks at base of spine, wear along folds and at corners, couple of closed tears. Mordida Books   March 2015 - 0101246   2015 $1000

Woolrich, Cornell *Savage Bride.* New York: Fawcett, 1950. First edition, short closed tear on top edge, front cover otherwise fine, paperback original in wrappers. Mordida Books   March 2015 - 010006   2015 $100

Woolrich, Cornell *Strangler's Serenade.* New York: Rinehart & Co., 1951. First edition, (letter 'R' in circle) on copyright page, fine in dust jacket with professional restoration to spine ends.   Buckingham Books   March 2015 - 33011   2015 $750

Woolrich, Cornell *Strangler's Serenade.* New York: Rinehart, 1951. First edition, some faint darkening on endpapers, otherwise fine in dust jacket with tape mark on front and rear flap and three quarter inch strip missing at top of inner front flap.   Mordida Books   March 2015 - 010007   2015 $150

Woolrich, Cornell *The Ten Faces of Cornell Woolrich.* New York: Simon & Schuster, 1965. First edition, fine in dust jacket with several short closed tears.   Mordida Books   March 2015 - 009589   2015 $200

Woolrich, Cornell *The Ten Faces of Cornell Woolrich.* London: Boardman, 1966. First English edition, fine in dust jacket.   Mordida Books   March 2015 - 008506   2015 $85

Woolsey, Georgeanna Murison *Three Weeks at Gettysburg.* New York: Anson D. F. Randolph, 1863. First trade edition, square 12mo., 24 pages, self wrappers, sewn as issued, lightly dust soiled, fine.   M & S Rare Books, Inc.   97 - 110   2015 $1000

Worcester, G. R. G. *The Junks and Sampans of the Yangtze.* Shanghai: Statistical Department of the Impectorate General of Customs, 1947. First edition, signed, inscribed and dated by author with author's chop in volume I, 2 volumes, near fine, original green cloth with gilt lettering spines and covers, minimal cover edge wear, toning endpapers and page edges, 4to., prospectus for volume I laid in, rare thus.   By the Book, L. C.   44 - 65   2015 $1500

Worcester, G. R. G. *Sail and Sweep in China.* London: Her Majesty's Stationery Office, 1966. First edition, signed and inscribed to Captain Erik Bush (1899-1985) and dated in year of publication by author, small 4to., very good++, foxing and cover edge wear in very good dust jacket with foxing, mild chips and scuffs, scarce.   By the Book, L. C.   44 - 66   2015 $250

Wordsworth, William   1770-1850 *The Early Letters of William and Dorothy Wordsworth. (1787-1805). The Letters of William and Dorothy Wordsworth. The Middle Years. (1806-1820). and (The Later Years (1821-1850).* Oxford: Clarendon Press, 1935-1939. First edition, octavo, 6 volumes, full red cloth, lettered gilt, spines of first 3 volumes little faded and cloth at heads of volumes 4 and 5 just little nicked, volume 6 has mark on upper cover, free endpapers tanned, handsome set.   Peter Ellis, Bookseller   2014 - 019326   2015   £300

Wordsworth, William   1770-1850 *Lines Composed a Few Miles Above Tintern Abbey, on Revisiting the Banks of the Wye During a Tour July 13th 1798.* Llandogo: Old Stile Press, 2002. 112/150 copies signed by artist, printed on handmade paper, frontispiece, 5 further images by Nicolas McDowall printed in blue, 3 of them full page, 4to., original quarter blue leather with illustrated boards, backstrip lettered in silver, untrimmed, fine.   Blackwell's Rare Books   B179 - 217   2015   £100

Wordsworth, William   1770-1850 *Lyrical Ballads 1798.* London: Oxford University Press, 1927. Original olive green cloth, signed KMC with ink and pencil notes, from the library of Geoffrey & Kathleen Tillotson.   Jarndyce Antiquarian Booksellers   CCVII - 150   2015   £20

Wordsworth, William   1770-1850 *Lyrical Ballads 1798-1805.* London: Methuen, 1944. Tenth edition, from the library of Geoffrey & Kathleen Tillotson, color paper wrappers by Geoffrey, with some notes and various inserts. Jarndyce Antiquarian Booksellers   CCVII - 573   2015   £50

Wordsworth, William   1770-1850 *Lyrical Ballads.* London: Methuen, 1963. Half title, original green cloth, very good in dust jacket, Geoffrey Tillotson's copy with 2 TLS's from Raymond Brett, Geoffrey adds pencil notes to presentation letter.   Jarndyce Antiquarian Booksellers   CCVII - 151   2015   £20

Wordsworth, William   1770-1850 *Poems in Two volumes 1807.* Oxford: Clarendon Press, 1942. Original green printed cloth, 2 volumes, spine faded, inner hinges splitting, from the library of Geoffrey & Kathleen Tillotson, signed by them Oxford 26.iv.44 with copious notes and insertions. Jarndyce Antiquarian Booksellers   CCVII - 563   2015   £30

Wordsworth, William   1770-1850 *The Poetical Works of William Wordsworth.* London: Edward Moxon, 1846. 7 volumes, octavo, full 19th century polished calf gilt, near fine set bound by Hayday, warmly inscribed to Louisa Fenwick from her friend, the author.   Honey & Wax Booksellers   2 - 17   2015 $16,000

Wordsworth, William   1770-1850   *The Poetical Works.* Oxford: Oxford University Press, 1923. Half title, frontispiece, original blue cloth, battered copy, lacking spine strip, signed by Kathleen Tillotson as Constable and as Tillotson, further note records the gift from E. A. Constable.   Jarndyce Antiquarian Booksellers   CCVII - 565   2015   £30

Wordsworth, William   1770-1850   *The Poetical Works.* Oxford: Clarendon Press, 1940-1949. Volumes I, III-V, half titles, original dark blue cloth, volume 1 slightly worn, signed by Geoffrey Tillotson with few pencil notes, text and cuttings of reviews and various insertions.   Jarndyce Antiquarian Booksellers   CCVII - 566   2015   £60

Wordsworth, William   1770-1850   *The Prelude, or Growth of a Poet's Mind.*   London: Edward Moxon, 1850. First edition, octavo, original brown cloth, rebacked, from the library of writer Charles Dickens with his bookplates.   Honey & Wax Booksellers   2 - 18   2015 $6000

Wordsworth, William   1770-1850   *The Prelude; or Growth of a Poet's Mind.*   London: Edward Moxon, 1850. First edition, half title, notes page slightly chipped at tail, bust ticket marker causing browning, Geoffrey Tillotson's copy, disbound in Tillotson's characteristic thick paper wrappers, original leather label placed upside down on spine,.   Jarndyce Antiquarian Booksellers   CCVII - 567   2015   £40

Wordsworth, William   1770-1850   *The Prelude.*   Oxford: Clarendon Press, 1926. Half title, frontispiece, plates, original brown buckram, paper label browned and chipped, inner hinge cracking, Kathleen Tillotson's copy as Kathleen Constable, and name Eric Constable, many pencil notes by Tillotson.   Jarndyce Antiquarian Booksellers   CCVII - 568   2015   £35

Wordsworth, William   1770-1850   *The Prelude.* Darbishire: Clarendon Press, 1959. Second edition, half title, frontispiece, plates, original dark blue cloth, very good in slightly worn dust jacket, from the library of Geoffrey & Kathleen Tillotson, with few marginal and inserted notes.   Jarndyce Antiquarian Booksellers   CCVII - 569   2015   £30

Wordsworth, William   1770-1850   *Yarrow Revisited and Other Poems.*   London: Longman, Rees, Orme, Brown, Green & Longman, 1835. First edition, presentation copy "From the author, written on half title by publisher's clerk, erratum slip absent, slightly browned around edges, frequent longitudinal pencil markings in margins, 12mo., early 20th century half dark brown morocco, spine gilt, top edges gilt, others uncut, good.   Blackwell's Rare Books   B179 - 122   2015   £1200

Wordsworth, William   1770-1850   *Yarrow Revisited and Other Poems.*   London: Longman, Rees, Orme, Brown, Green & Longman, 1835. First edition, presentation copy inscribed by author for fellow poet Eliz M. Hamilton on a slip of paper pasted on to verso of title and with "From the Author" written on half title by publisher's clerk, erratum slip tipped in, ads discarded, 12mo., slightly later 19th century olive pebble grain morocco by Tuckett ('binder to the Queen'), backstrip panelled and ruled in gilt and infilled with volutes and other tools, lettered gilt in second compartment, sides with triple gilt borders, inner panel with gilt cornerpieces and central panels of curing lines, all edges gilt, marbled endpapers, bookplate of J. O. Edwards, small scrape to upper board, extremities slightly rubbed, good.   Blackwell's Rare Books   B179 - 121   2015   £2500

Work Among Women.   London: CP of Great Britain, 1924. First edition, wrappers, front wrapper detaching, thus very good-.   Beasley Books   2013 - 2015 $45

The Works of Celebrated Author of Whose Writings There are but Small Remains. Volume the First... Volume the Second.   London: printed for J. and R. Tonson, 1750. First edition, 12mo., 2 volumes, contemporary marbled calf, spines gilt, contrasting orange and brown morocco labels, good.   C. R. Johnson   Foxon R-Z - 1170r-z   2015 $613

The Works of the Most Celebrated Poets; Namley Wentworth, Earl of Roscommon; Charles, Earl of Dorset; Charles, Earl of Halifax; Sir Samuel Garth, George Stephney, Esq., William Walsh, Esq., Thomas Tickell, Esq.... (with) A supplement to the Works of the Most Celebrated Minor Poets...   London: printed for F. Cogan, 1750. First edition, 8vo., 3 volumes, contemporary calf, gilt, spines gilt, spines rather rubbed but sound, very good, armorial bookplates of Arthur Gregory, Esq.   C. R. Johnson   Foxon R-Z - 1172r-z   2015 $613

The World of Gilbert & George: the Storyboard.   London: Enitharmon Press, 2001. First edition, limited to 1000 copies, oblong 4to., original blue cloth lettered gilt on spine with printed title label onset to cover, issued without dust jacket, this with signed presentation from Gilbert and George.   Any Amount of Books   2015 - C273   2015   £180

The World's Great Collections: Oriental Ceramics. Volume 7.   Tokyo: Kodansha International, 1981. Folio, cloth, 242 monochrome plates.   Oak Knoll Books   306 - 275   2015 $150

Worlidge, John   *Systema Agriculturae; the Mystery of Husbandry Discovered.*   London: Tho. Dring, 1681. Third edition, one whole section added, frontispiece and engraved plate, 3 parts in 1 volume, folio, old calf, rebacked, lacks corner of one leaf without affecting text, leaf opposite engraved frontispiece, explanation of frontispiece expertly remargined, little wrinkled.   Second Life Books Inc.   191 - 97   2015 $1500

Worsley, Henry *Juvenile Depravity £100 Prize Essay.* London: Charles Gilpin, 1849. First edition, 8vo., original blindstamped charcoal cloth, spine gilt lettered, neat repair at foot, very good, uncut. John Drury Rare Books   March 2015 - 26105   2015 $266

Worsley, Robert *A Plain Enquiry Into the nature, Values and Operation of Coin and Paper Money.* London: printed for the author, 1811. First edition, 8vo., with half title and postscript, early 19th century half calf over marbled boards, neatly rebacked and labelled, armorial bookplate of Ferguson of Raith, fine, scarce.   John Drury Rare Books   2015 - 24461   2015 $787

Worthington's Annual 1889. New York: Worthington Co., 1889. First edition, upwards of 500 engravings, decorated pictorial boards, lovely color frontispiece, hundreds of full page monochrome illustrations, very good, some wear, mostly to corners.   Stephen Lupack   March 2015 - 2015 $60

Wotton, Henry *Reliquiae Wottonianae; or a Collection of Lives, Letters, Poems...* London: By T. Roycroft for R. Marriott, 1672. Third edition, portraits, 19th century red morocco, early signatures of J. Grien? 1725, Thomas Price and John Francis Cole 1828, bookplates of J. J. Chapman and Molly Flagg Gibb, very good.   Joseph J. Felcone Inc. Science, Medicine and Technology - 57   2015 $900

Wouk, Herman *The Caine Mutiny.* Garden City: Doubleday, 1951. First edition in first issue dust jacket, fine in just about fine, first issue jacket with tiny tear and little rubbing at spine, from the library of Kate Stettner Lobell and Carl D. Lobell.   Between the Covers Rare Books   196 - 40   2015 $2500

Wouk, Herman *Marjorie Morningstar.* Garden City: Doubleday, 1955. First edition, near fine in near fine, unfaded, clean dust jacket (one tiny closed tear).   Ed Smith Books   82 - 35   2015 $275

Wouk, Herman *Marjorie Morningstar.* Garden City: Doubleday, 1955. First edition, fine in fine dust jacket with just touch of toning on spine lettering, rarely found in this condition, beautiful copy, from the library of Kate Stettner Lobell and Carl D. Lobell.   Between the Covers Rare Books   196 - 41   2015 $350

Wrangham, Francis *Sermons, Practical and Occasional; Dissertations....* London: Baldwin, Cradock and Joy, 1816. First edition, 3 volumes, octavo, contemporary half red leather, gilt scroll decoration on spine, olive green leather title labels lettered in gilt, marbled paper boards, engraved armorial bookplate of Elizabeth Thorold, cover edges just little rubbed, very good.   Peter Ellis, Bookseller   2014 - 919298   2015   £325

Wraxall, Nathaniel William   1751-1831 *An Answer to the Calumnious Misrepresentations of the Quaterly Review, The British Critic, and the Edinburgh Review...* London: T. Cadell and W. Davies, 1815. First edition, 8vo., two leaves rather creased, recently well bound in cloth, spine gilt lettered, very good.   John Drury Rare Books   March 2015 - 25695   2015 $266

Wraxall, Nathaniel William   1751-1831 *A Short Review of the Political State of Great Britain at the Commencement of the Year 1787.* London: for J. Debrett, 1787. First edition, 8vo., 72 pages, closed tear in one leaf (but no loss of surface), good copy in recent plain wrappers.   John Drury Rare Books   2015 - 19262   2015 $106

Wren, Percival Christopher *Mysterious Ways.* New York: Frederick A. Stokes, 1930. First American edition, fine in fine dust jacket, beautiful copy.   Between the Covers Rare Books   196 - 149   2015 $350

Wren, Percival Christopher *Mysterious Ways.* New York: Stokes, 1930. First American edition, fine in dust jacket with short closed tear.   Mordida Books   March 2015 - 002338   2015 $200

Wretmark, Gerdt *The Peptic Ulcer Individual.* Copenhagen: Munksgaard, 1953. First edition, signed by author, wrappers, near fine.   Beasley Books   2013 - 2015 $45

Wright & Butler, Ltd. *Wright & Butler's Patent. Oil Cooking Stoves Supersede all Others, Complete Illustrated Catalogue.* Devonport: J. Gould & Son 25 Marlborough Street, n.d. circa, 1880. 8vo., illustrations, original pictorial wrappers, just little dust soiling of outer leaves, still very good.   John Drury Rare Books   2015 - 22637   2015 $133

Wright, Charles *The Venice Notebook.* Boston: Barn Dream Press, 1971. First edition, one of 26 specially bound lettered copies, signed by author, out of a total edition of 526 copies, 500 of which were bound in paper wrappers, 8vo., original red cloth, fine.   James S. Jaffe Rare Books   Modern American Poetry - 328   2015 $750

Wright, Ernest Vincent *Gadsby: a Story of Over 50,000 Words withou Using the Letter "E".* Los Angeles: Wetzel Pub. Co., 1939. First edition, 8vo., 267 pages, rarity due to L.A. warehouse fire, original red cloth lettered black at spine and on cover, clean sound very good copy with slight creasing at head of spine and two slight marks to covers, decent copy, scarce.   Any Amount of Books   2015 - A68218   2015   £650

Wright, Frances 1795-1852 *Course of Popular Lectures.* Philadelphia: published by the author, 1836. First edition, Volume II, 8vo., original blue printed wrappers, some soiled, rear wrapper soiled with closed tear, rear endpaper soiled. Second Life Books Inc. 189 - 289 2015 $750

Wright, Frank Lloyd 1869-1959 *Modern Architecture. Being the Kahn Lectures for 1930.* Princeton: 1931. 4to., plates, cloth, occasional light underlining in red pencil, otherwise very good, clean copy. Joseph J. Felcone Inc. Science, Medicine and Technology - 9 2015 $200

Wright, Franz *The One Whose Eyes Open When You Close Your Eyes.* Roslindale: Pym Randall Press, 1982. First edition, one of 400 hardcover copies of total edition of 1000, of which 50 ere numbered and signed by author, slight rubbing to boards, trifle foxed on fore-edge, still just about fine in very lightly rubbed, near fine dust jacket, although this copy is unnumbered it bears warm and long inscription from Wright in year of publication to another poet and close personal friend. Between the Covers Rare Books, Inc. 187 - 299 2015 $1000

Wright, Ichabod Charles *Thoughts on the currency.* London: Pelham Richardson and Dearden Nottingham, 1841. First edition, 8vo., recent marbled boards, lettered on spine, very good. John Drury Rare Books March 2015 - 24578 2015 £306

Wright, Irene Aloha *The Early History of Cuba 1492-1586.* New York: Macmillan, 1916. First edition, black and white plan and description of Havana, 8vo., cloth with gilt titles, very good+ copy with minor shelf wear. Kaaterskill Books 19 - 164 2015 $100

Wright, James *The Green Wall.* New Haven: Yale University Press, 1957. First edition, 8vo., original boards, dust jacket. James S. Jaffe Rare Books Modern American Poetry - 329 2015 $450

Wright, James *Observations Upon the Important Object of Preserving Wheat and Other Grain from Vermin, with a Safe and Efficacious method to Prevent the Great Depredations that are made on Those Valuable Articles.* London: printed by Cooper and Graham Bow Street Covent Garden..., 1796. First edition, half title, contemporary mottled sheep, sometime neatly rebacked, very good, very scarce. John Drury Rare Books March 2015 - 22311 2015 $874

Wright, John Martin Frederick *A Collection of Cambridge Mathematical Examination Papers; as given at the several colleges...* Cambridge: W. P. Grant, 1830-1831. 2 parts in 1 volume, 8vo., original half brown calf, marbled boards, joints broken, mended with kozo. Jeff Weber Rare Books 178 - 1177 2015 $50

Wright, L. R. *The Suspect.* Toronto: Doubleday, 1985. First Canadian edition, fine in dust jacket. Mordida Books March 2015 - 008729 2015 $150

Wright, L. R. *The Suspect.* Doubleday Canada, 1985. First edition, true first, fine in dust jacket. Buckingham Books March 2015 - 35852 2015 $200

Wright, Laurie *King Joe Oliver.* Chigwell: Storyville, 1987. First edition, illustrations, fine, hardcover. Beasley Books 2013 - 2015 $125

Wright, Laurie *Okeh Race Records. The 8000 Race Series.* Chigwell: Storyville, 2001. First edition, illustrated with reproductions, fine. Beasley Books 2013 - 2015 $200

Wright, Richard 1908-1960 *Jeunesse Noire. (Black Boy).* Paris: Gallimard, 1947. First French edition, wrappers in glassine dust jacket, pages browned, small chip on last leaf affecting no text, else near fine, inscribed by author to Jean Paul Sartre, magnificent association. Between the Covers Rare Books 197 - 47 2015 $12,500

Wright, Richard 1908-1960 *Bright and Morning Star.* New York: International, 1941. First separate American edition, 8vo., pages 48, paper wrappers, very good, tight copy in plastic dust jacket. Second Life Books Inc. 191 - 98 2015 $85

Wright, Richard 1908-1960 *The Long Dream.* New York: Doubleday, 1958. Advance mimeograph, 2 volumes, 4to., original printed stiff card stock covers, bound with brass brads, front cover volume I worn at edges and detached, housed in two cardboard clamshell style boxes, rare. Second Life Books Inc. 190 - 22 2015 $2200

Wright, Richard 1908-1960 *Native Son.* New York: Harpers, 1940. First edition, fine in fine dust jacket with one small internal repair, beautiful, fresh copy of true first edition, superior copy, from the library of Kate Stettner Lobell and Carl D. Lobell. Between the Covers Rare Books 196 - 42 2015 $7500

Wright, Richard 1908-1960 *12 Million Black Voices.* New York: Viking, 1941. First edition, large 8vo., photo direction by Edwin Rosskam, ivory cloth, cover somewhat browned, slightly worn at corners, but very good, tight copy. Second Life Books Inc. 190 - 218 2015 $125

Wright, Richard 1908-1960 *Uncle Tom's Children.* New York: Harper, 1938. First edition, 8vo., 317 pages, author's greetings and signature March 24 1938, red cloth stamped in blue and light gray, nice in plastic dust jacket, rare early presentation. Second Life Books Inc. 190 - 220 2015 $1250

Wright, S. Flower *The Hidden Tribe.* London: Robert Hale, 1938. First edition, 8vo., original green (teal) cloth lettered black on spine, front panel of jacket in good order but showing chips at spine ends, some slight discoloration to spine with neat ownership signature and impression on front endpaper, otherwise content clean an unmarked, very good. Any Amount of Books   2015 - C1971   2015   £300

Wright, Thomas *The History and Topography of the County of Essex, Comprising its Ancient and Modern History.* London: George Virtue, 1831. First edition, 2 volumes, 4to., half black leather lettered and decorated gilt over marbled boards, folding map present (slight tear and creasing), volume 2 lacks one plate but volume 1 has extra plate not called for, front board of first volume detached but present, slight rubbing and wear to covers, occasional slight foxing to plates, near very good apart from loose board. Any Amount of Books   2015 - C6697   2015   £240

Wright, Willard Huntington   1888-1939 *The 'Canary" Murder Case.* New York: Charles Scribner's Sons, 1927. First edition, first state dust jacket with "The Taxicab Murder Case" listed as the forthcoming third book in the series on back flap, former owner's small stamped name at top of front flyleaf, else fine, bright copy in attractive, colorful, lightly rubbed dust jacket with light wear to spine ends and corners and tiny closed tear to top edge of front cover and bottom edge of rear cover, housed in four point protective cloth case that is inserted into a cloth clamshell case with red leather labels on spine and titles stamped in gold gilt. Buckingham Books   March 2015 - 38203   2015 $5500

Wright, Willard Huntington   1888-1939 *The Canary Murder Case.* New York: Charles Scribner's Sons, 1927. First edition, near fine, with lettering on front cover and spine bright and unfaded, in second state dust jacket professionally restored at spine ends, corners and extremities; the second state jacket has "The Greene Murder Case" for the forthcoming third book of series listed on rear flap. Buckingham Books   March 2015 - 27346   2015 $1000

Wright, Willard Huntington   1888-1939 *The 'Canary' Murder Case.* New York: Charles Scribner's, 1927. First edition, blindstamp on titlepage, else fine in lightly rubbed, near fine dust jacket with professional and virtually invisible restoration to spine ends, from the collection of Duke Collier. Royal Books   36 - 240   2015 $1500

Wright, Willard Huntington   1888-1939 *The Canary Murder Case.* New York: Scribners, 1927. First edition, page edges darkened and lightly spotted and name on front endpaper, otherwise very good without dust jacket. Mordida Books   March 2015 - 002229   2015 $75

Wright, Willard Huntington   1888-1939 *The Dragon Murder Case.* New York: Scribner's, 1933. First edition, bookplate on flyleaf and crease on following flyleaf, otherwise fine in dust jacket with nicks at spine ends ad small chips at corners.   Mordida Books   March 2015 - 002536   2015 $475

Wright, Willard Huntington   1888-1939 *The Gracie Allen Murder Case.* New York: Scribner's, 1938. First edition, very near fine in near fine, price clipped dust jacket with touch of rubbing, very attractive copy.   Ken Lopez, Bookseller   164 - 221   2015 $450

Wright, Willard Huntington   1888-1939 *The Kennel Murder Case.* New York: Scribner, 1933. First edition, very good, some flaking to lettering on front cover and name on front endpaper, otherwise fine in very good dust jacket with rubbed streak on front cover, small chip at top corner of spine and light wear at spine ends and at corners. Mordida Books   March 2015 - 00997   2015 $275

Wright, Willard Huntington   1888-1939 *The Scarab Murder Case.* New York: Charles Scribner's Sons, 1930. First edition, so called 'First issue' with only a single date (1930) on copyright page, with capital letter "A" on copyright page, fine, bright, tight, all lettering on cloth bright and unchipped, fine dust jacket with two tiny closed tears at head of spine, exceptional copy.   Buckingham Books   March 2015 - 33470   2015 $1250

Wright, William   1829-1898 *A History of the Comstock Silver Lode & Mines. Nevada and the Great Basin Region: Lake Tahoe and the High Sierras.* F. Boegle, 1889. First edition, 16mo., original printed grey wrappers, three quarter leather with marbled endpapers, stain on front wrapper, rubbing to edges of three quarter leather, internally fine, considerably rare today.   Buckingham Books   March 2015 - 37388   2015 $250

Wright, William   1829-1898 *A History of the Comstock Silver Lode & Mines.* F. Boegle, 1889. First edition, 16mo., original printed grey wrappers, rare, front and rear covers chipped at fore-corners, light wear to spine ends, closed tear top edge, next to spine that extends to mid point of front cover, internally clean, overall good to very good. Buckingham Books   March 2015 - 34414   2015 $350

Wright, William   1829-1898 *A History of the Comstock Silver Lode & Mines.* F. Boegle Bookseller & Stationer, 1889. First edition, 16mo., original printed grey wrappers, tiny closed tear to fore edge of front cover and bit of light pencil markings in margins, text easily erasable, else near fine, tight, clean copy, housed in clamshell case, titles stamped in silver on spine, rare today.   Buckingham Books March 2015 - 33824   2015 $750

Wrighte, William *Grotesque Architecture or Rural Amusement Consisting of Plans, Elevations and Sections for Huts, Retreats, Summer and Winter Hermitages...* London: printed for Henry Webley, 1767. First edition, 8vo., 14 pages (2) page publisher's list, with engraved frontispiece, 28 pages of engraved plates, older marbled boards, leather corners, newer leather spine and leather spine label, text slightly browned, plates als faintly browned but in very good order, sound, uncommon.   Any Amount of Books   2015 - C70271   2015   £650

Wundt, Wilhelm *Outlines of Psychology.* Leipzig: London: New York: Englemann, 1907. Third revised English edition, boards quite rubbed, especially at spine, author and title still visible, fairly tight, very good-.   Beasley Books   2013 - 2015 $125

Wurm, E. *Erwin Wurm: One Minute Sculptures 1988-1998.* Bregenz: pub. by Hatje Cantz, 1999. First edition, 4to., wrappers, copiously illustrated in black and white, very good.   Any Amount of Books   2015 - A85205   2015   £160

Wurm, Ted *The Crookedest Railroad in the World.* Berkeley: Howell North, 1960. Second edition, photos, facsimiles, diagrams, gray cloth lettered and illustrated in black, very fine with pictorial dust jacket.   Argonaut Book Shop   Holiday Season 2014 - 323   2015 $60

Wurm, Ted *Hetch Hetchy and Its Dam Railroad.* Berkeley: Howell North, 1973. First edition, quarto, color frontispiece, 480 illustrations, mostly photos, yellow cloth lettered in black, fine with lightly chipped and dampstained pictorial dust jacket not intruding onto covers, quite scarce.   Argonaut Book Shop   Holiday Season 2014 - 480   2015 $90

Wurm, Ted *Mallets on the Mendocino Coast Casper Lumber Company Railroads and Steamships.* Glendale: Trans-Anglo Books, 1986. First edition, quite scarce thus, frontispiece in color, numerous photos, drawings, plans, folding map, black leatherette, gilt, very fine, pictorial dust jacket.   Argonaut Book Shop   Holiday Season 2014 - 322   2015 $150

Wyatt, Harvey *An Address to the Owners and Occupiers of Land on the Importance of an Adequate Protection to Agriculture.* London: John Hatchard, 1827. 8vo., 52 pages, recent plain wrappers, very good.   John Drury Rare Books   2015 - 17778   2015 $133

Wyatt, Harvey *Considerations on the Present State of the Different Classes of the landed Interest, on the Causes of the Distress which exists Among the Farmers and Labourers...* London: James Ridgway & Sons, 1834. First edition, 8vo., occasional pencilled emphasis marks and with several errata on verso of final leaf followed by 24 page publisher's list dated April 1834, later calf backed marbled boards, spine labelled and lettered, very good, uncut.   John Drury Rare Books   March 2015 - 26147   2015   £306

Wycherley, William *The Idleness of Businnes; a Satyr.* London: printed for Benj. Bragg, 1705. First edition, 2nd issue, folio, half red morocco, slight browning, but fine.   C. R. Johnson   Foxon R-Z - 1174r-z   2015 $5363

Wyeth, John *Wyeth's Repository of Sacred Music. Part Second.* Harrisburg: John Wyeth, 1813. First edition, oblong 8vo, contemporary calf backed boards (very worn), front cover becoming loose (and cracked), corners of text bent & browned with some light staining, limp, complete and unsophisticated, very are.   M & S Rare Books, Inc.   97 - 198   2015 $2000

Wykes, Alan *The Pen Friend.* London: Gerald Duckworth & Co. Ltd., 1950. First edition, presentation inscription by author, fine in price clipped dust jacket with few light waterstains to spine.   Buckingham Books   March 2015 - 25946   2015 $175

Wylie, Alexander *Labour Leisure and Luxury.* London: Longmans, Green, 1887. New edition, full calf, little rubbed, maroon label, signed presentation in presentation binding to Miss Christina Glen from Wylie.   Jarndyce Antiquarian Booksellers   CCXI - 298   2015   £65

Wylie, Alexander *Labour, Leisure and Luxury. A contribution to present practical political economy.* London: Longmans Green and Co., 1887. New edition, 8vo., contemporary calf, gilt, very good, presentation copy from author for Samuel Smith M.P. (1836-1906), in 1902.   John Drury Rare Books   2015 - 12404   2015 $133

Wyman, W. J. *Catalogue. English Saddlery. Saddles, Bridles, Etc. and riding Equipment, bits, Spurs, Stirrups, Specialities.* Privately printed, 1921. 9 x 6 inches, blue printed wrappers, illustrations, tanning to edges of both covers, very good.   Buckingham Books   March 2015 - 36117   2015 $275

Wyndham, John *Planet Plane.* London: Newnes, 1936. First edition, 8vo., pages 248, original mustard yellow cloth, titles to spine in black, sound, very good, faintly marked at rear board and with very slight tape ghost mark on endpapers, decent copy.   Any Amount of Books   2015 - C1923   2015   £175

Wyndham, John *The Secret People.* London: George Newnes, 1935. First edition, 8vo., original green cloth lettered black on spine, sound, very good-, used copy, slightly rubbed and slightly marked.   Any Amount of Books   2015 - C1998   2015   £160

Wyoming. A guide to Its History, Highways and People. Oxford University Press, 1941. First edition, cloth, 490 pages, numerous illustrations, 9 maps, large folding map in pocket at rear, previous owner's name and address on small sticker affixed to upper extremity of front pastedown, else near fine, clean, tight copy, price clipped dust jacket is very good with light general soiling and three half inch chips to corners and top edge of rear panel.   Buckingham Books   March 2015 - 34977   2015 $300

Wyvill, Christopher *A Letter to the Right Hon. William Pitt, by the Rev. Christopher Wyvill...* York: printed by W. Blanchard for J. Johnson and J. Stockdale, Lond and J. Todd York, n.d., 1793. First edition, 8vo., three numerals written in ink in modern hand in upper margin of title, modern plain wrappers, entirely uncut, very good.   John Drury Rare Books   March 2015 - 16591   2015   £306

Association Copies

Association – Abbey, John Roland

Homerus *Ilias. (The Iliad in Latin).* Parisiis: Apud Martinum Iuuenem Excvdebat Gvil. M., 1550. 121 x 89mm., beautiful and animated contemporary elaborately gilt and painted Parisian calf by Wooton's binder "B", covers with unusual frame of interlacing slender rectangular compartments formed by wide black painted fillets outlined in gilt, center panel with four foliate scrolls arched across frame in each quadrant and forming a centerpiece lozenge, azured curls at head and foot of panel and with stippled lobes, additional azured cornerpieces, stippled circles at top, bottom and either side of the panel, raised bands, spine compartments gilt with centered foliate tool or bull's eye, slightly later red morocco label, all edges gilt, spine ends and corners very artfully renewed, in fleece lined brown buckram clamshell case, with John Roland Abbey's morocco bookplate and large morocco title label on spine, front endpaper with morocco bookplate of Abbey, pastedowns with armorial bookplates of Scrope Berdmore, S.T.P. (dated 1790) at front and of Henry C. Compton esq. at rear, rear endpaper with modern bookplate of Philosophia Hermetica ruled in red throughout, half dozen light ink stains, two or three affecting a few words of text, quite clean and fresh internally, backstrip with minor flaking and few hairline cracks, one corner exposed, otherwise very decorative binding, pleasing and especially well preserved, boards still lustrous.   Phillip J. Pirages   66 - 12   2015 $12,500

Thompson, Edward Maunde *An Introduction to Greek and Latin Paleography.* Oxford: at Clarendon Press, 1912. First edition, small 4to., cloth, dust jacket, from the library of J. R. Abbey with his bookplate, over half of the jacket spine is missing inside hinges cracked scarce.   Oak Knoll Books Special Catalogue 24 - 55   2015 $250

Association – Abbott, Keith

Berrigan, Ted *Clear the Range.* New York: Adventures in Poetry, 1977. First edition, one of 750 copies, 8vo., original wrappers, top right corner bumped, else fine, presentation copy inscribed by author for Keith Abbott.   James S. Jaffe Rare Books   Many Happy Returns - 40   2015 $375

Berrigan, Ted *The Sonnets.* New York: Grove Press, 1964. First trade edition, paperback original, one page smudged, otherwise very good, inscribed by author for Keith Abbott, with Abbott's ownership signature.   James S. Jaffe Rare Books   Many Happy Returns - 7   2015 $1000

Berrigan, Ted *Train Ride (February 18th 1971) for Joe.* New York: Vehicle Editions, 1978. First edition, simultaneous paperback issue, limited to 1500 copies, 12mo., original illustrated wrappers by Joe Brainard, presentation copy inscribed by author for Keith Abbott, fine.   James S. Jaffe Rare Books   Many Happy Returns - 47   2015 $450

Association – Abner, William

Bonomo, Joe *The Strongman: a True Life, Pictorial Autobiography of the Hercules of the Screen, Joe Bonomo.* New York: Bonomo Studios, 1968. First edition, quarto, red cloth gilt, some posting to boards, small stain on page edges, good copy, without dust jacket, inscribed by author 12-2-67 for friend William Abner.   Between the Covers Rare Books, Inc.   187 - 28   2015 $85

Association – Adair, Robert Shafto

Sallustius Crispus, C. *Caius Crispus Salustius ab Ascensio Familiariter Explanatus.* Paris: Jean Petit, 1504. First Badius edition, some light foxing and staining (heavier o titlepage), first leaf of text bound slightly askew and 3 sidenotes copped as a result, 4to., 18th century calf, worn and crackled, rebacked (somewhat crudely), black lettering piece, hinges relined with black cloth tape, bookplates of Wigan public Library, Rev. T. H. Passmore, Sir Robert Shafto Adair and Augustus Frederick, Duke of Sussex, sound.   Blackwell's Rare Books   Greek & Latin Classics VI - 93   2015   £2000

Association – Adam, Robert B.

Lucanus, Marcus Annaeus *Pharsalia.* Parisiis: Apud Lefevre Bibliopolam, 1822. 2 volumes, 108 x 76mm., charming contemporary green straight grain morocco covers, panelled with fine gilt and blind raised bands, spine compartments outlined in blind, pretty quatrefoil gilt centerpiece ornament, gilt titling, turn-ins, decorative gilt roll, all edges gilt, each volume with lovely pastoral fore-edge painting, one depicting Fetherstone Castle Northumberland, the other Lowther Castle, Westmorland, in later green cloth chemises and quarter morocco slipcase, spine decorated in much the same fashion as the volumes, front pastedown of both volumes with armorial bookplate of Sir James Stuart, Bart., front free endpaper of both volumes with oval morocco bookplate of R. B. Adam, front free endpaper of first volume with morocco bookplate of Mary Harriman Lecomte du Nouy; joints just slightly rubbed, spines faintly and uniformly darkened, touch of browning to edges of leaves, intermittent light foxing, else fine set, text generally clean and fresh, bindings lustrous and fore edge paintings particularly well preserved with rich colors.   Phillip J. Pirages   66 - 80   2015 $1500

Association – Adams, Leonie

Carruth, Hayden *Journey to a Known Place.* Norfolk: New Directions, 1961. First edition, one of 300 numbered copies, small quarto, printed on Hayle paper by Harry Duncan and Kim Merker, prospectus laid in, this copy inscribed by Carolyn Kizer to fellow poet Leonie Adams, Christmas 1962.   Between the Covers Rare Books, Inc. 187 - 43   2015 $450

Association – Addams, Jane

Maurice, C. Edmund *Life of Octavia Hill as Told in Her Letters.* London: Macmillan, 1913. First edition, 8vo., portraits, untrimmed, partially unopened, very good, tight, clean copy, this the copy of founder of Hull House, Jane Addams with her ownership signature, from the library of consumer advocate Florence Kelley.   Second Life Books Inc.   189 - 160   2015 $250

Association – Adler, Mortimer

Hutchins, Maude Phelps *Diagrammatics.* New York: Random House, 1932. First edition, one of only 250 numbered copies, this being copy no. 6, this copy also signed by Mortimer Adler, near fine with dulled spine.   Beasley Books 2013 - 2015 $45

Association – Agar, J.

Swinburne, Henry *A Treatise of Spousals, or Matrimonial Contracts: Wherein all the Questions Relating to that Subject are Ingeniously Debated and Resolved.* London: printed by S. Roycroft for Robert Clavell, 1686. First edition, 4to., contemporary panelled calf with some wear to joints and extremities, still sound, text crisp with good margins, very good with near contemporary signature of J. Agar and late 18th early 19th century armorial bookplate of Rev. L. W. Hepenstal, uncommon.   John Drury Rare Books 2015 - 23326   2015 $3147

Association – Agneu

Observations on Modern Gardening. London: T. Payne, 1771. Third edition, 8vo., full brown leather with decorated gilt at spine, raised bands and gilt title on red label, ornate armorial bookplate of Agneu (Baronet) of Lochnau, penciled ownership signature of F. R. Cowell, very handsome, very good, slightly rubbed at corner, slightly tender at hinges. Any Amount of Books   2015 - A47683   2015   £220

Association – Aiken, Conrad

Berrigan, Ted *The Sonnets.* New York: Lorenz & Ellen Gude, 1964. First edition, limited to 300 numbered copies plus an unspecified number of unnumbered copies, this copy (as with most copies) unnumbered, laid in is 1 page TLS from Ted Berrigan to Conrad Aiken sending him the book, unlike the majority of copies seen, this copy has the back wrapper, letter is creased, otherwise fine, book exceptionally fine.   James S. Jaffe Rare Books   Many Happy Returns - 2   2015 $4500

Association – Aldan, Daisy

Ashbery, John *The Double Dream of Spring.* New York: E. P. Dutton & Co., 1970. First edition, first issue, 8vo., original cloth backed boards, dust jacket, fine, jacket slightly rubbed, two short closed tears and some minor wear to top edge, presentation copy inscribed by author for Daisy Aldan, editor of "Folder", with original invitation to book's publication party at Gotham Book Mart on Feb. 9 1970 laid in.   James S. Jaffe Rare Books   Modern American Poetry - 13   2015 $1500

Association – Alexander, Claude

Vertue, George *Anecdotes of Painting in England: with Some Account of the Principal Artists: and Incidental Notes on Other Arts.* London: Printed for J. Dodsley, 1782. Third editions, volume 4 is second edition, 4 volumes, full tree calf decorated gilt at spine, text clean and complete, boards somewhat worn and loose, good, bookplate of Sir Claude Alexander and his neat ownership signature dated 1828. Any Amount of Books   2015 - A62201   2015   £180

Association – Alexandridi, S.

Bosschere, Jean De   1878-1953 *Arabesques.* Paris: Bibliothque de L'Occident, 1909. First edition, one of 250 numbered copies out of a total edition of 260, quarto, 27 illustrations, decorations and initials, contemporary three quarter morocco, raised bands, marbled endpapers, preserving original wrappers, presentation copy from author, inscribed on second blank in black and red for S. Alexandridi, head of spine splitting, leather partially faded at upper cover, very good.   Peter Ellis, Bookseller   2014 - 014048   2015   £235

Association – Alford, Henry

Procter, Adelaide A. *The Victoria Regia a Volume of Original Contributions in Poetry and Prose.* London: printed and published by Emily Faithfull & Co., Victoria Press for the Employment of Women, 1861. First edition, 8vo. full leather elaborately stamped in gilt, all edges gilt, gilt inner dentelles, designed by John Leighton, some foxing on endpapers, much less in text, some very light wear to boards, still near fine, inscribed by Emily Faithful for Blanche Resticaux, 1862, also inserted a few news clippings about Faithful, very small ALS from Henry Alford and small slip of paper signed yours faithfully Isa Craig.   Second Life Books Inc.   191 - 78   2015 $1500

Association – Algood, Jill

Daniels, Bebe *282 Ways of Making a Salad...* London: Cassell and Co., 1950. First edition, slightly cocked, else near fine in attractive, very good dust jacket with little bit of chipping at crown and extremities, signed by Daniels and Jill Algood, as well as 2 others.   Between the Covers Rare Books   196 - 137   2015 $450

Association – Alhadeff, Joan

Furst, Alan *Your Day in the Barrel.* New York: Atheneum, 1976. First edition, fine in fine dust jacket, lengthily inscribed to Joan and Morris Alhadeff, from the collection of Duke Collier. Royal Books 36 - 172 2015 $1500

Association – Alhadeff, Morris

Furst, Alan *Your Day in the Barrel.* New York: Atheneum, 1976. First edition, fine in fine dust jacket, lengthily inscribed to Joan and Morris Alhadeff, from the collection of Duke Collier. Royal Books 36 - 172 2015 $1500

Association – Allabon, John

Balmford, William *The Seaman's Spiritual Companion or Navigation Spiritualized.* London: for Benj. Harris, 1678. First edition, small 8vo., variant state of title with double rule border and price on titlepage, A2 shaved at foot affecting signature and catchword on recto, minor worming in upper outer corner of D4-K8 (affecting end of text in places), stain to B3-E2 affecting three lines, occasional foxing, small hole from paper flaw in lower margin of E2, short tear at foot of F3 slightly affecting last line on recto and catchword on verso, small hole from paper flaw in centre of I2 touching two lines, actually reasonable and much loved copy, contemporary sheep (rubbed, covers scuffed, fore edge of lower cover worn exposing board, corners worn), several pen trials, scribbles, ownership inscriptions John Allab(on) His Booke October ye 24th 16, Charles Canning his book 1679, James Purnell His Booke Anno Domini (deleted), "Thomas Nichols His Book May ye 10 1718", "James Croome His Book March ye 9th 1757" "Jane Hanley", from the library of James Stevens Cox (1910-1997). Maggs Bros. Ltd. 1447 - 21 2015 £2800

Association – Allen, Dede

Kesey, Ken 1935- *Sometimes a Great Notion.* Universal City: Universal Studios, 1970. Gay's Second draft screenplay dated Feb. 10 1970, based on Kesey's novel, with name of legendary Hollywood editor Dede Allen written on front cover, bradbound in studio wrappers, bit dusty, near fine. Ken Lopez, Bookseller 164 - 100 2015 $650

Association – Allen, Vance

Stokes, W. Royal *The Jazz Scene an Informal History from New Orleans to 1990.* New York: Oxford, 1991. First printing, 8vo., author's presentation for Vance Allen, photos, paper over boards with cloth spine, very good in dust jacket. Second Life Books Inc. 190 - 204 2015 $150

Association – Allingham, Helen

Allingham, William *Life and Phantasy.* London: Longmans Green and Co., 1893. 8vo., white vellum under light green paper boards, lettered gilt at spine, signed presentation by Allingham's widow, Helen, very slight soiling and very slight spotting to endpapers, otherwise clean, very good. Any Amount of Books 2015 - C8507 2015 £240

Association – Althorpe, John Charles Spencer, Viscount

A Letter to His Majesty William IV. Paris?: 1830. Only edition, generally rather browned and foxed, original printed blue wrappers, contemporary ownership signature of Lord Visct. (John Charles Spencer) Althorpe, very rare. John Drury Rare Books March 2015 - 19079 2015 $221

Association – Andrew, Abram Piatt

Cannan, Edwin *A History of the Theories of Production and Distribution in English Political Economy from 1776 to 1848.* London: Rivington Percival & Co., 1894. 8vo., half title and Rivington's lengthy book catalog of 1893, original dark blue cloth, spine lettered gilt, uncut, very good, from the library of Abram Piatt Andrew, with his signature. John Drury Rare Books 2015 - 24402 2015 $177

Association – Andrews, Charles Walker

Cobden-Sanderson, Thomas James 1840-1922 *The Ideal Book or Book Beautiful: a Tract of Calligraphy printing and Illustration and On the Book Beautiful as a Whole.* Hammersmith: Doves Press, 1900. First edition, one of 300 copies, small quarto, original full vellum, gilt lettering, bookplate of American collector Charles Walker Andrews, with his notation in pencil that this was purchased from Slocum Hyde's library in 1924, fine. The Brick Row Book Shop Miscellany 67 - 36 2015 $1250

Du Bois, Henri Pene *American Bookbindings in the Library of Henry William Poor...* Jamaica: printed at the Marion Press, published by George D. Smith, 1903. First edition, number 164 of 200 numbered copies on Dutch handmade paper, 8vo., original grey green cloth, gilt lettering, frontispiece and 39 chromolithographed plates, striking color plates, bookplate of American book collector Charles Walker Andrews, binding slight worn and soiled, some offsetting from plates, very good. The Brick Row Book Shop Miscellany 67 - 4 2015 $450

Gay, John 1685-1732 *Polly. An Opera.* London: printed for the author, 1729. First edition, 4to., contemporary quarter calf marbled paper boards, red leather label, gilt rules and lettering, 31 pages of engraved sheet music, contemporary armorial bookplate of Henry Streatfield, his library was later sold by W. H. Robinson Ltd., bookplate of American collector Charles Walker Andrews, noted in pencil above bookplate that he purchased this from Robinson in 1935, binding bit worn and stained, some light dampstains in text, very good, large copy. The Brick Row Book Shop Miscellany 67 - 49 2015 $500

Goldsmith, Oliver 1730-1774 *The Miscellaneous Works.* London: printed for W. Griffin, 1775. First collected edition, 8vo., contemporary sheep, rebacked with original spine retained, red morocco label, gilt rules and lettering, half title present, uncommon first collected edition, bookplate of collector Charles Walker Andrews, edges little rubbed, outer margins of endpapers browned, very good. The Brick Row Book Shop Miscellany 67 - 51 2015 $500

Gray, Thomas 1716-1771 *Designs by Mr. R. Bentley for Six Poems by Mr. T. Gray.* London: printed for R. Dodsley, 1753. Second edition, folio, brown quarter contemporary calf, marbled paper boards, gilt rules, 6 engraved plates and 13 vignettes by Richard Bentley, bookplate of collector Charles Walker Andrews, edges little rubbed, some light foxing, very good. The Brick Row Book Shop Miscellany 67 - 52 2015 $1250

Gray, Thomas 1716-1771 *Elegia Inglese di Tommaso Gray Sopra un Cimietero Campestre Trasportata in Verso Italiano da Giuseppi Torello Veronese.* Parma: Nel regel Palazzo Co' tipi Bodoniani, 1793. First Bodoni edition, 4to., 19th century black quarter morocco, marbled paper boards, gilt decorations and lettering, text interleaves with blank paper and ruled by hand in red throughout, bookplate of Charles Walker Andrews, notations in ink about edition by another previous owner on front blank, edges bit rubbed, some foxing, very good. The Brick Row Book Shop Miscellany 67 - 53 2015 $750

Hawthorne, Nathaniel 1804-1864 *The Scarlet Letter.* New York: privately printed, 1904. First of this illustrated edition, one of 150 copies on japanese imperial paper, 4to., contemporary navy morocco by the Doves Bindery, signed '19 C-S 10' gilt decorations and lettering, all edges gilt, each of the 15 plates in two states, color and black and white, tipped in to front free endpaper is letter for Cobden-Sanderson dated 23 March 1909 to Charles Walker Andrews, with Andrews bookplate, edges touched up and slightly repaired from wear, fine, handsome copy. The Brick Row Book Shop Miscellany 67 - 57 2015 $1750

Mellini, Domenico *Descrizione Della Entrata della Serenissima Regina Giovanna d'Austria et dell' Apparato fatto in Firenze.* Fiorenza: Appresso i Giunti, 1566. First edition, 4to., early 20th century brown half morocco, marbled paper sides and matching endpapers, gilt lettering, top edge gilt, others untrimmed, original stiff wrappers bound in, titlepage vignette with Medici coat-of-arms, text little foxed, fine, bookplate of American collector Charles Walker Andrews. The Brick Row Book Shop Miscellany 67 - 68 2015 $1250

Tacitus, Cornelius *Cornelii Taciti de Vita et Moribus Iulii Agricolae Lbier.* Hammersmith: The Doves Press, 1900. First Doves Press edition, one of 225 copies, fine, small quarto, original full vellum, gilt lettered, bookplate of Charles Walker Andrews. The Brick Row Book Shop Miscellany 67 - 38 2015 $750

Tennyson, Alfred Tennyson, 1st Baron 1809-1892 *Seven Poems and Two Translations.* Hammersmith: Doves Press, 1902. First Doves Press edition, one of 325, small quarto, original full vellum, gilt, bookplate of Charles Walker Andrews, fine. The Brick Row Book Shop Miscellany 67 - 39 2015 $500

Association – Anstruther, John

Pratt, Samuel *The Regulating Silver Coin, Made Practicable and Easie to the Government and Subject.* London: printed for Henry Bonwick at the Red Lion in St Paul's Churchyard, 1696. First edition, 8vo., neat repair to lower margin of title (not affecting printed surface), occasional very minor marginal staining, overall good, crisp copy, rebound fairly recently in quarter calf and boards, spine lettered in gilt, near contemporary armorial bookplate of Sir John Anstruther of that Ilk Baronet. John Drury Rare Books 2015 - 23004 2015 $830

Association – Arcelli, A. Attanzio

Pignoria, Lorenzo *Der Servis & Eorum apud Veteres Ministeriis, Commentarius.* Augsburg: C. Daberholtzer for Marcus Welser, at the sign of the Pine, 1613. First edition, 4to., 6 full page and 21 text woodcuts, woodcut title device, contemporary vellum over thin soft boards, ms. spine title, fine, spot on two leaves, ownership signature of D. Attanzio Arcelli. Second Life Books Inc. 189 - 199 2015 $4000

Association – Armstrong, Helen Neilson

Wilkins, Mary E. *The Jamesons.* New York: Doubleday and McClure, 1899. First edition, small octavo, color plates, decorated green cloth, small booklabel, slight wear, spine little toned, else near fine, bears ownership signatures of Meta Neilson dated in 1899 and also of artist, Helen Neilson Armstrong, sister of Margaret Armstrong, dated 1805. Between the Covers Rare Books 196 - 122 2015 $350

Association – Armstrong, Phyllis

Bishop, Elizabeth *North & South - a Cold Spring.* Boston: Houghton Mifflin, 1955. First edition, one 2000 copies, 8vo., original cloth, dust jacket, inscribed by author for Phyllis Armstrong, faint offsetting to endpapers, covers little spotted, otherwise fine in trifle rubbed and dust soiled dust jacket.   James S. Jaffe Rare Books   Modern American Poetry - 37   2015 $7500

Association – Arnold, Bruce

Heaton, Rose Henniker *Chez James - The Wisdom and Foolishness of James...* London: Elkin Mathews & Marot, 1932. First edition, octavo, illustrations, cloth backed pictorial boards, silkscreened in vivid colors, text printed on different colored papers, bookplate of Bruce Arnold, flaps of dust jacket have offset onto free endpapers, near fine in very good, slightly nicked dust jacket slightly rubbed at head and tail of spine.   Peter Ellis, Bookseller   2014 - 006668   2015   £325

Association – Ashbee, Charles Robert

Andersen, Hans Christian 1805-1875 *Wonderful Stories for Children.* New York: Wiley and Putnam, 1847. Early U.S. edition, 12mo, frontispiece and one other illustration, original green cloth, lettered and decorated gilt on spine and on front cover, small bookplate with arts and crafts style lettering reading "From the Library of Janet Ashbee and C. R. Ashbee", and pictorial bookplate of Janet designed by her husband C.R., sound, clean, very good, slight wear at head of spine, slight foxing, very slight shelfwear and some family note, press cutting about author's chair on blank prelims.   Any Amount of Books   2015 - A466337   2015   £160

Association – Ashbee, Janet

Andersen, Hans Christian 1805-1875 *Wonderful Stories for Children.* New York: Wiley and Putnam, 1847. Early U.S. edition, 12mo, frontispiece and one other illustration, original green cloth, lettered and decorated gilt on spine and on front cover, small bookplate with arts and crafts style lettering reading "From the Library of Janet Ashbee and C. R. Ashbee", and pictorial bookplate of Janet designed by her husband C.R., sound, clean, very good, slight wear at head of spine, slight foxing, very slight shelfwear and some family note, press cutting about author's chair on blank prelims.   Any Amount of Books   2015 - A466337   2015   £160

Association – Ashburnham, Earl of

Walesby, Francis Pearson *Is England's Safety or Admiralty Interest to be Considered?* London: William Edward Painter, 1841. First edition, 8vo., 48 pages, titlepage with some foxing, recent marbled boards lettered on spine, presentation copy inscribed for Rt. Hon. Earl of Ashburnham, apparently very rare.   John Drury Rare Books   March 2015 - 23828   2015   £306

Association – Aston, Lord

Anthropologie Abstracted; or the Idea of Humane Nature Reflected in Briefe Philosophicall and Anatomicall Collections. London: for Henry Herringman, 1655. First edition, 8vo., small chip from blank corner of A2, minor rust spot in blank fore-margin of A3, light stain at head in first part, text lightly browned, large (5mm) rust hole in lower blank inner margin of I1, closely trimmed along upper edge in places, contemporary sheep, rebacked, corners repaired, lower cover scuffed, new endleaves, from the library of James Stevens Cox (1910-1997), "Lo. Aston" contemporary ink signature, probably Walter Aston, 2nd Baron Aston of Exeter.   Maggs Bros. Ltd.   1447 - 9   2015   £700

Association – Aswell, Mary Lou

Welty, Eudora *The Eye of the Story: Selected Essays and Reviews.* New York: Random House, 1978. First edition, fine in very near fine dust jacket with slight sunning at crown, inscribed by Welty to her editor and close friend Mary Lou Aswell.   Between the Covers Rare Books, Inc.   187 - 290   2015 $950

Welty, Eudora *Retreat.* Winston Salem: Palaemon Press, 1981. First edition, one of 40 copies numbered with Roman numerals intended for distribution by author and publisher, signed by author, card laid in stating 'Sent at the request of Miss E. Welty" although not indicated, this copy from the collection of close friend, editor and co-dedicatee of The Ponder Heart, Mary Lou Aswell.   Between the Covers Rare Books, Inc.   187 - 291   2015 $850

Association – Atherstone, Edwin

Buckingham, James Silk *An Earnest Plea for the Reign of Temperance and Peace as Conducive to the Prosperity of Nations; submitted to the Visitors of the Great Exhibition...* London: Peter Jackson, Late Fisher Son & Co. Angel Street, St. Martin's-le-Grand, n.d., 1851. First edition, presentation copy, 8vo., lithographed frontispiece and folding colored chart on taxation at rear, strangely paginated, as noted in an apology at end of work, but would appear to be complete, apart from few minor marks and cancelled library stamp at foot of title (not touching text), clean throughout, original blindstamped cloth, upper cover lettered and tooled gilt, spine lettered in white, lightly sunned, still very good, inscribed by author to poet and writer Edwin Atherstone, dated July 26 1851.   Marlborough Rare Books Ltd.   List 49 - 3   2015   £300

Association – Auchincloss, Louis

Flaubert, Gustave 1821-1880 *Madame Bovary Moeurs De Province.* Paris: Michel Levy, 1857. First edition, first issue with dedicatee's name misspelled 'Senart for Senard, 2 volumes, original green cloth, covers paneled in blind, spines lettered in gilt, yellow coated endpapers, extremities lightly worn and rubbed, hinges of volume 1 cracked and rear hinge tender, former owner bookplate of novelist Louis Auchincloss, cracked at front hinge, very good and unsophisticated set and extremely scarce in cloth, housed in custom folding case.   B & B Rare Books, Ltd.   234 - 31   2015 $12,500

James, Henry 1843-1916 *Washington Square.* New York: Harper and Bros., 1881. (1880). First edition, octavo, 266 pages, 6 pages publisher's ads, illustrations by George Du Maurier, from the library of NY novelist Louis Auchincloss with his morocco gilt bookplate, excellent association copy.   Honey & Wax Booksellers   1 - 58   2015 $2000

Sterne, Laurence 1713-1768 *Letters of the Late Rev. Mr. Laurence Sterne to His Most Intimate Friends.* London: printed for T. Becket, 1776. New edition, i.e. second edition, 165 x 102mm., extraordinarily pretty contemporary red straight grain morocco, elaborately gilt in style of Roger Payne (though not definitely attributable to him), covers with frame of alternating long stemmed tulips and daisies, corners with floral spring surrounded by dots and stars inside a laurel wreath, flat spines densely gilt in compartments with central lily on a stippled ground, framed by 8 pointed stars and with sunbursts at corners, gilt tiling and turn-ins, marbled endpapers, all edges gilt; with (usually missing) frontispiece in volume I, bookplate of Louis Auchincloss, presentation inscription from Bronson Winthrop dated 23 Feb. 1932, verso of titlepage with pictorial library stamp of Schlossbibliothek Dessau; volume 1 with slight browning, offsetting and foxing (other two volumes only very moderately affected), leaves generally a shade less than bright, uniform faint fading to spines (scarcely noticeable because of abundance of gilt), corners with minor wear but beautiful set, text fresh and clean, bindings lustrous, glittering and so little used as to resist opening.   Phillip J. Pirages   66 - 58   2015 $4500

Association – Auckland, Lord

Bowles, John *A View of the Moral State of Society at the Close of the Eighteenth Century....* London: F. and C. Rivington, J. Hatchard, J.Asperne and J. Spragg, 1804. Third edition, 8vo., half title, rebound fairly recently in plain boards, spine lettered, very good inscribed in ink on half title, Right Hon. Lord Aucklan(d) from the author.   John Drury Rare Books   March 2015 - 23137   2015   £266

Association – Ayres, Philip

Anacreon *Anacreon Done into English out of the Original Greek.* Oxford: by L. Litchfield, Printer to the University, for Anthony Stephens, 1683. First edition of this translation, 8vo., leaf (c)1 is duplicated; (c)2 was also duplicated, but the second leaf has been torn away, lightly browned, dampstaining along lower edge of a1-4, corners of K2-L2 and fore margin of P1-2 and in top half of last few leaves, small rust hole in D2 (affecting one letter on each side), marginal rust spot on H1, contemporary calf, spine gilt and lettered (headcap damaged and with upper joint slightly split at head), from the library of James Stevens Cox (1910-1997), inscribed "Sum Philippi Ayresij 1683" on titlepage (Philip Aryes (1638-1712), signature of Madam. Mary Redman, ink signature under bookplate of John Holmes (1702/03-1760) of Holt, Norfolk, Master of Gresham School and writer on education, with his signature, early 19th century circular label with manuscript lot number 12/4 pasted to foot of front flyleaf, the pencil mark of Christie-Miller Britwell Court with pencil shelf mark.   Maggs Bros. Ltd.   1447 - 7   2015   £1500

Association – Backus, Clarus

MacDonald, John D. *The Girl in the Plain Brown Wrapper.* New York: J. B. Lippincott, 1973. First printing of this edition and first American edition in hardcover, near fine in very good plus dust jacket, inscribed in year of publication to Denver Post book editor, Clarus Backus, laid in is sheet of Denver Post stationery, clipped article from Denver Post by Mr. Backus about MacDonald's death, and glossy Doubleday review photo from 1968, for the book 'Three for McGee', bookplate of noted collected Duke Collier, jacket lightly rubbed at extremities, touch of usual fading on spine, very nice, extremely scarce presentation copy.   Royal Books   36 - 38   2015 $2750

Association – Bacon, Edmund

Parker, Thomas Lister *Description of Browsholme Hall, in the West Riding of the County of York and the Parish of Washington in the Same County...* London: printed by S. Gosnell Little Queen Street..., 1815. 4to., large folding pedigree, 20 etched plates, contemporary half calf, marbled boards, joints skillfully repaired, armorial bookplate of Sir Edmund Bacon.   Marlborough Rare Books   List 53 - 36   2015   £500

Association – Bagley, Nancy Reynolds

Conrad, Joseph 1857-1924 *Lord Jim.* Edinburgh and London: William Blackwood and Sons, 1900. First edition, octavo, original green cloth slightly cocked, cloth clean with only light toning to spine and little rubbing at joints, browning to endpapers as usual, few spots of scattered foxing, text generally very clean, exceptionally nice copy, from the library of Nancy Reynolds Bagley, daughter of R. J. Reynolds and her husband, Henry Walker Bagley, with bookplate on front pastedown.   Manhattan Rare Book Company   Literature 2014 - 2015 $4200

Association – Bagnold, C. Robert

Westall, William *Picturesque Tour of the River Thames.* London: R. Ackerman, 96 Strand, 1828. First edition, 4to., 24 finely hand colored aquatint plates, colored aquatint vignette on title and another to final leaf, contemporary full green crushed morocco, spine decorated and lettered gilt within raised bands, spine faded to brown by Riviere and Son, preserving original cloth at end of work, armorial bookplate of Fairfax Rhodes and C. Robert Bagnold and bookseller tickets of Thomas Thorp and R. D. Steadman, fine.   Marlborough Rare Books   List 54 - 89   2015   £4500

Association – Bailey, J. Harvey

Haley, James Evetts *Robbing Banks was My Business. The Story of J. Harvey Bailey, America's Most Successful Bank Robber.* Canyon: Palo Duro Press, 1973. First edition, signed by Bailey, and signed and inscribed by Haley to Tom and Hilda Lewis, cloth, black and white frontispiece, illustrations by Theda Rhea, fine in dust jacket, lightly rubbed along front spine channel and spine ends, housed in matching cloth slipcase with titles stamped in gold gilt on spine.   Buckingham Books   March 2015 - 31744   2015 $875

Association – Baird, E. D.

Maude, George Ashley *Letters from Turkey and the Crimea.* London: printed for private circulation, 1896. First edition, frontispiece laid down, original red cloth lettered gilt on upper cover, presentation from E. D. Baird to Mr. Bright (Allan Heywood Bright 1862-1941), slight foxing to fore-edge and prelims, otherwise very good, bright copy, slight foxing, otherwise very good.   Any Amount of Books   2015 - C13449   2015   £160

Association – Baird, John

Dinsdale, Alfred *Television.* London: Television Press ltd., 1928. Second edition, signed presentation inscribed by John Baird, inventor of TV to G. G. Mulligan 12th April 1929, frontispiece also inscribed "J. H. Baird", octavo, original blue cloth, lightly sunned on spine, title and author embossed in black on front cover and spine, first few leaves bit foxed, lovely copy.   Athena Rare Books   15 - 6   2015 $3800

Association – Baird, William

Polybius *Historiarum Libri Priores Quinque.* Lugduni: Seb. Gryphium, 1554. 178 x 108mm., pleasing contemporary (English?) calf, covers with single gilt fillet border and intricate arabesque centerpiece, raised bands, spine panels with central azured gilt fleur-de-lys or floral spring, apparently original morocco label (perhaps, but perhaps not - with very expert repairs at spine ends), publisher's woodcut griffin device on title and last page, 18th century? engraved armorial bookplate of Sir William Baird and modern bookplate of Kenneth Rapoport, titlepage with early ownership signature of Franciscus T.... (now washed away and consequently very faint), occasional contemporary underlinings and manicules, joints rubbed (and with thin cracks alongside top spine panel on upper and lower joint and along bottom two spine panels on upper joint), lower cover with minor discoloration (perhaps from damp), other trivial defects, binding entirely solid, still quite lustrous and with nothing approaching a major condition problem, without front free endpaper, n3 with branching tear (paper flaw?) from margin into text necessitating, (old) repair, but without loss, isolated faint browning, other small imperfections, but really consistently very fresh and clean, very well preserved, attractive mid 16th century binding.   Phillip J. Pirages   66 - 14   2015 $3200

Association – Baker, Edward

Bysshe, Edward *The Art of English Poetry.* London: printed for Sam. Buckley at the Dolphin in Little Britain, 1710. Fourth edition, top corner of front endpaper clipped, otherwise internally very good, clean and crisp, contemporary unlettered panelled calf, blindstamped floral cornerpieces, raised bands, very slight chip to base of spine, bottom 2cm. of upper joint cracked, very good, attractive, E. Libris Chris Clitherow March 21 1709, later armorial bookplate of Sir Edward B. Baker, Bart.   Jarndyce Antiquarian Booksellers   CCXI - 56   2015   £280

Association – Baker, George

Doyle, Arthur Conan 1859-1930 *The Adventures of Sherlock Holmes.* (with) *The Memoirs of Sherlock Holmes.* Newnes, 1892-1894. First editions, 104 and 90 text illustrations by Signey Paget, royal 8vo., original blue (Adventures dark, Memoirs pale), bevel edged cloth backstrips and boards blocked in gilt and black (street name absent on 'Adventures' but present on 'Memoirs'), both volumes recased with backstrips reinforced (hinges notoriously fragile), rear flyleaf of 'Adventures' replaced, spine gilt rubbed, 'Adventures' with two lines of staining to front board matching gift inscription to front flyleaves, gift inscriptions dated 1892 and 1894 from George Baker to his father Thomas.   Blackwell's Rare Books   B179 - 143   2015   £2000

Sherman, John *Selected Speeches and Reports of Finance and Taxation from 1859 to 1878.* New York: D. Appleton and Co., 1879. First edition, half morocco and marbled paper covered boards, rubbed at extremities and small piece of leather peeled on rear board, else near fine copy, inscribed by John Sherman to leading American banker, financier and philanthropist, George Baker, ALS by Sherman to Baker. Between the Covers Rare Books, Inc. 187 - 39 2015 $1250

Association – Baker, Robert

Gorey, Edward *Amphigorey: Fifteen Books.* New York: Putnam, 1972. First edition, 4to., original cream illustrated boards, lettered black and red on spine and covers, copiously illustrated in color and black and white, signed presentation from author for Robert Baker, edgewear, lower spine very slightly creased, otherwise near fine in near very good dust jacket nicked with slight edge wear. Any Amount of Books March 2015 - C6715 2015 £375

Association – Baker, Robert Buckingham

Yourcenar, Marguerite *Memoirs of Hadrian.* London: Secker & Warburg, 1955. First English edition, 8vo., half red morocco, red buckram sides, spine lettered gilt, original endpaper map preserved at end, bookplate of Robert Buckingham Baker, very good. Blackwell's Rare Books B179 - 250 2015 £50

Association – Baker, Thomas

Doyle, Arthur Conan 1859-1930 *The Adventures of Sherlock Holmes.* (with) *The Memoirs of Sherlock Holmes.* Newnes, 1892-1894. First editions, 104 and 90 text illustrations by Signey Paget, royal 8vo., original blue (Adventures dark, Memoirs pale), bevel edged cloth backstrips and boards blocked in gilt and black (street name absent on 'Adventures' but present on 'Memoirs'), both volumes recased with backstrips reinforced (hinges notoriously fragile), rear flyleaf of 'Adventures' replaced, spine gilt rubbed, 'Adventures' with two lines of staining to front board matching gift inscription to front flyleaves, gift inscriptions dated 1892 and 1894 from George Baker to his father Thomas. Blackwell's Rare Books B179 - 143 2015 £2000

Association – Ball, John

Hillerman, Tony *The Boy Who Made Dragonfly.* New York: Harper and Row, 1972. First edition, nicely inscribed by author to fellow crime writer, John and Pat Ball, from the collection of Duke Collier. Royal Books 36 - 192 2015 $1750

Association – Ball, Pat

Hillerman, Tony *The Boy Who Made Dragonfly.* New York: Harper and Row, 1972. First edition, nicely inscribed by author to fellow crime writer, John and Pat Ball, from the collection of Duke Collier. Royal Books 36 - 192 2015 $1750

Association – Ballard, Bob

Nebel, Frederick *Fifty Roads to Town.* Boston: Little Brown and Co., 1936. First edition, presentation inscription by author for Bob and Gladys Ballard, cloth lightly soiled with few spots of light foxing, vertical crease to spine, else near fine in dust jacket with light professional restoration to spine ends and lightly toned on spine. Buckingham Books March 2015 - 29009 2015 $1275

Association – Ballard, Gladys

Nebel, Frederick *Fifty Roads to Town.* Boston: Little Brown and Co., 1936. First edition, presentation inscription by author for Bob and Gladys Ballard, cloth lightly soiled with few spots of light foxing, vertical crease to spine, else near fine in dust jacket with light professional restoration to spine ends and lightly toned on spine. Buckingham Books March 2015 - 29009 2015 $1275

Association – Bancroft, Mary

Jung, Carl Gustav *Fundamental Psychological Conceptions / a Report of Five Lectures by C. G. Jung...* London: privately printed, 1936. First edition numbered Multilith copy (number 196), 15 different line drawings, 7 1/2 x 9 3/4 inches, Mary Bancroft's (1903-1997) copy with her name written across top front free endpaper and address, single sided pages, bound using three large staples, covers are boards with brownish printed weave pattern and spine covered with green canvas, covers lightly worn, overall lovely copy, extremely scarce. Athena Rare Books 15 - 30 2015 $1500

Association – Baraka, Amiri

The Black Nation: Position of the Revolutionary Communist League (MLM) on the Afro-American National Question. Newark: n.p., 1978. Quarto, 57 pages, photomechanically reproduced sheets with stapled printed wrappers, about very good with wear at extremities, price sticker and heavy staining to front and rear wrapper affecting few interior pages, Amiri Baraka's personal copy, signed on first page, numerous comments, deletions and additions in his hand. Between the Covers Rare Books 197 - 55 2015 $4500

Association – Barbet, A.

Plutarchus *Vite di Plutarco Cheroneo de gil Huomini Illustri Greci et Romani.* Venetia: Marco Ginami, 1620. Later edition, 2 volumes, 229 x 149mm., extremely pleasing contemporary Italian calf lavishly gilt, covers framed by multiple plain and dotted rules and geometric roll diapered central panel with slender fleuron in each compartment, flat spines with elongated panel formed by multiple plain and dotted rules and floral filigree roll and containing three fleurons, holes for ties (now lacking), all edges gilt (apparently - though not certainly) - with some very expert repairs to spine ends and edges), with 54 ornate woodcut frames and tondo portraits to accompany each biography, printer's device on titlepage, woodcut decorative initials, titlepage of volume II with later ink inscription "A. Barbet/374i, indications of bookplate removal on front pastedowns, four leaves with short marginal tears, occasional faint dampstains to head margin, isolated minor smudges and foxing, otherwise clean, crisp and smooth, joints with minimal rubbing, couple of small stains to boards, other trivial defects, bindings in excellent condition, gilt still bright and generally with minor wear.   Phillip J. Pirages   66 - 24   2015 $4800

Association – Barker, Elsa

Clymer, R. Swinburne *The Rosicrusians Their Teachings.* Allentown: Philosophical Pub. Co., 1910. Second edition, tall octavo, red cloth stamped in gilt and blind, ownership signature (twice) of Elsa Barker (American novelist and poet), extensive pencil notes and several pencil markings in text, bottom corners rubbed through, still very good, bright copy.   Between the Covers Rare Books, Inc.   187 - 56   2015 $225l

Association – Barker, Nicolas

Walpole, Horace   1719-1797 *Horace Walpole's Description of the Villa at Strawberry Hill.* London: Roxburghe Club, 2010. Facsimile edition, limited to 200 copies, large 4to., quarter red leather and red cloth boards, lettered gilt on spine, copiously illustrated, presentation in hand of Nicolas Barker for Norman Routledge, very slight rubbing, else very good+.   Any Amount of Books   March 2015 - C9634   2015   £400

Association – Barnard, Robert

Cody, Liza *Culprit: a Crime Writer's Annual.* London: Chatto & Windus, 1992. First edition, 3 annual volumes, first volume signed by Robert Barnard, Liza Cody, Michael Lewin, Susan Moody and H. R. F. Keating, fine in soft covers and pictorial dust jackets.   Mordida Books   March 2015 - 008749   2015 $150

Association – Barneby, Richard

Denham, John *Poems and Translations with the Sophy.* London: for H. Herringman, 1668. First collected edition, first issue, 8vo., small ink stain to lower margin of titlepage and fore-edges of D1-D7, small rust spots to 2E5 and 2E8, with small piece torn away from lower blank margin of I1, contemporary polished mottled calf, covers with double gilt fillet and gilt floral tool in each corner, smooth spine ruled in gilt, gilt edges joints rubbed, three small wormholes in upper joint, slight surface crazing to covers, from mottling acid, one corner slightly worn, bottom corner of front flyleaf torn away, errata has been corrected by hand, signature of Edmund Smith (16)88, inscription of Jenks Lutley Esquire 1729, early 18th century armorial bookplate of Richard Barneby of Brockhampton, Herefordshire, from the library of James Stevens Cox (1910-1997).   Maggs Bros. Ltd.   1447 - 136   2015   £600

Association – Barney, Nathalie Clifford

Millay, Edna St. Vincent   1892-1950 *Wine from These Grapes.* New York: Harper & Bros., 1934. First edition, 8vo., original cloth backed boards, dust jacket, presentation inscribed by author to Natalie Clifford Barney, fine in lightly worn dust jacket.   James S. Jaffe Rare Books   Modern American Poetry - 198   2015 $1500

Association – Barney, Nora Stanton

Blatch, Harriot Stanton *Challenging Years: the memoirs of...* New York: Putnams, 1940. First edition, 8vo., very nice in dust jacket, inscribed by Nora Stanton Barney (author's daughter) to Winifred A. Tyler.   Second Life Books Inc.   189 - 26   2015 $150

Association – Barrington, Shute

Cotton, Charles *Scarronnides; or, Virgile Travestie.* London: by E. Cotes for Henry Brome, 1666. 1665. Reprint of Book 1, first edition of book 4, 8vo., first and last leaves blank except for bookseller's woodcut device of a crowned cannon, long closed tear from paper flaw down D5 (touching seven lines of text), small spot at head of E1, contemporary sheep ruled in blind, smooth spine with red morocco and gilt label, no pastedowns, parts of two printed leaves from 17th century English 8vo. Bible as binder's waste (lower headcap torn, joints little rubbed), armorial bookplate of Hon. Shute Barrington, Bp. of Salisbury, from the library of James Stevens Cox (1910-1997).   Maggs Bros. Ltd.   1447 - 118   2015   £700

Association – Bartel, Paul

Crews, Harry *This Thing Don't Lead to Heaven.* New York: William Morrow, 1970. First edition, inscribed by author to Paul Bartel, fine in dust jacket.   Ed Smith Books   83 - 13   2015 $350

Association – Bartelot, Richard Grosvenor

Cook, John *Redintegratio Amoris, or a Union of Hearts...* London: for Giles Calvert, 1647. First edition, small 4to., without first and final blank leafs, dark circular dampstain (45 x 25mm) in upper fore-corner of titlepage (from deleted signature), some spotting and browning throughout and with small (15mm) closed tear to margin of F2, some minor worming in inner margin dampstain in top margin at end, late 19th century calf, covers panelled blind, red edges, spine defective at head and tail, corners bumped, signature of Rev. Richard Grosvenor Bartelot, FSA, earlier signature deleted from titlepage, from the library of James Stevens Cox (1910-1997). Maggs Bros. Ltd. 1447 - 113 2015 £350

Association – Barth, John

Ozick,, Cynthia *Trust.* New York: New American Library, 1966. Uncorrected proof copy, tall comb-bound galley sheets, laid in is letter sent by editor, David Segal to author John Barth, with request for opinion, this copy signed by Barth, Ozick's name was left off cover and has been added in ink, mild sunning and curling to covers, small tear at upper spine, about near fine, very scarce proof. Ken Lopez, Bookseller 164 - 163 2015 $1500

Association – Bartle-Brackenbury, Anita

Teasdale, Sara 1884-1933 *Helen of Troy and Other Poems.* New York: G. P. Putnam's Sons, 1912. Second edition, corners little bumped, photo of author tipped-in, very good, lacking presumed dust jacket, nicely inscribed by author for Anita Bartle-Brackenbury, anthologist. Between the Covers Rare Books, Inc. 187 - 272 2015 $275

Teasdale, Sara 1884-1933 *Rivers of the Sea.* New York: Macmillan, 1915. First edition, moderate edgewear, very good or better, lacking presumed dust jacket, nicely inscribed by author for Anita Bartle-Brackenbury. Between the Covers Rare Books, Inc. 187 - 273 2015 $450

Association – Bartlett, R. E.

Arnold, Matthew 1822-1888 *The Strayed Reveller and Other Poems.* London: B. Fellowes, 1849. First edition, original green blindstamped cloth, spine lettered gilt, half title, cloth little marked and rubbed, else very nice, armorial bookplate of R. E. Bartlett, scarce, from the collection of Gavin H. Fryer. Bertram Rota Ltd. 308 Part II - 126 2015 £500

Association – Bass, William

Thompson, Charles *Rules for Bad Horsemen: Addressed to the Society for the Encouragement of Arts.* London: J. Robson, 1762. First edition, small 8vo., half red leather lettered gilt on spine with five raised bands, slightly rubbed with weak, complete front hinge, very good, text very clean, bookplate of Sir William A. H. Bass, Baronet. Any Amount of Books 2015 - C4845 2015 £275

Association – Batcheller, Francis

Peace Principles Safe and Right. Boston: American Peace Society, circa, 1859-1865. First edition, small octavo, contemporary green cloth gilt, contemporary bookplate of Frank Batcheller, bit of rubbing on cloth, paper cracking over front hinge but tight and sound, inscribed by abolishionist Amasa Walker for Francis Batcheller. Between the Covers Rare Books 197 - 107 2015 $650

Association – Bate, W. J.

Johnson, Samuel 1709-1784 *The Idler and the Adventurer.* New Haven: Yale University Press, 1963. Half title, plates, original blue cloth, very good in slightly torn dust jacket, W. J Bate's signed presentation copy to Geoffrey Tillotson, with review of "The Rambler" inserted. Jarndyce Antiquarian Booksellers CCVII - 330 2015 £45

Association – Bathe, Kristian

Nietzsche, Friedrich *Menschliches Allzumenschliches. Ein Buch fur Freie Geister. (Human All Too Human. A Book for Free Spirits).* Chemnitz: Schmeitzner, 1878. First edition, octavo, original front wrapper with some wear and reinforced corners along with partial remains of a bookseller's ticket in lower left hand corner, beautifully matched and lettered recent spine with similar rear cover, former owner's modern bookplate (Kristian Bathe) and handwritten ink inscription to first half title, custom clamshell box housing tight, clean and beautiful copy. Athena Rare Books 15 - 38 2015 $9500

Association – Batho, Edith

Harpsfield, Nicholas *The Life and Death of Sir Thomas Moore...* London: OUP, 1932. Half title, frontispiece and plates, 8 page catalog, handsome full white pigskin with elaborate pattern in blind and gilt, blind and gilt dentelles, marbled endpapers, fine in lined marbled slipcase, from the library of Geoffrey & Kathleen Tillotson, gilt lettered on front from GT, KMC 21XL 33 and with signed inscription from both editors to Tillotson's, with inserted p.c. from R. W. Chambers1933 and ALS from Gertrude Chambers and Edith Batho. Jarndyce Antiquarian Booksellers CCVII - 381 2015 £250

Association – Batrau, Ruth

Smith, Betty *A Tree Grows in Brooklyn.* New York: Harper & Brothers, 1943. First edition, first printing, original cloth, first issue unclipped dust jacket (price intact and 'No. 5538"), signed and inscribed by author on day of publication August 18 1943 to Miss Ruth M. Batrau, about very good with some fading and smudges to cloth, rear hinge cracked in like dust jacket with some chipping to spine ends, splitting to upper front flap, few small tears and rubbing, else very good, housed in custom box. B & B Rare Books, Ltd. 234 - 90   2015 $7500

Association – Batten, George

Malthus, Thomas Robert   1766-1834 *An Essay on the Principle of Population....* London: John Murray, 1826. 2 volumes, 8vo., well bound in relatively modern green quarter morocco over cloth boards, spine gilt with raised bands and contrasting labels, top edge gilt, very good, presentation copy inscribed in volume I to George Batten, from Mrs. Malthus.   John Drury Rare Books   2015 - 25844   2015 $1049

Association – Bayne, William Thirlwall

Thackeray, Franciscus St. John *Anthologia Latina.* London: A. M. Bell et Daldy, 1865. First edition, presentation copy, paper lightly toned throughout, few fox spots to first and last leaves, small 8vo., contemporary dark brown morocco by Holloway, boards bordered with double gilt fillet, spine divided by raised bands with gilt fillet borders to compartments, second compartment gilt lettered direct, rest with central fleuron tools and fleur-de-lis cornerpieces, turn-ins decoratively gilt, all edges gilt, marbled endpapers, bookplate of William Thirlwall Bayne, near fine, inscribed by editor for Thirlwall.   Blackwell's Rare Books   Greek & Latin Classics VI - 64   2015   £200

Association – Beadle, Jeremy

Thompson, Hunter S. *The Great Shark Hunt; Strange Tales from a Strange Time.* London: Picador/Pan Books, 1981. Third UK paperback printing, 8vo., wrappers, illustrations, signed for Jeremy Beadle by author, very good.   Any Amount of Books   March 2015 - A99130   2015 £400

Association – Beaufort, Henry

An Essay on the Polity of England with a View to Discover the True Principles of the Government. London: printed by T. Cadell, 1785. First edition, 8vo., half leather, marbled boards, 4 raised bands at spine, corners rubbed, spine ends rubbed, very slight fraying at top of spine, spine rubbed, gilt lettering faded, bookplate of Henry Beaufort on pastedown, inner spine hinges slightly cracked, otherwise sound, very good with clean text.   Any Amount of Books   2015 - A97612   2015   £180

Association – Becher, Hilla

Becher, B. *Anonyme Skulpturen.* New York: Wittenborn and Co., 1970. First edition, fine in near fine dust jacket with short closed tear and few small nicks, signed by Hilla and Bernhard Becher, very uncommon thus.   Jeff Hirsch Books   E-62 Holiday List 2014 - 1   2015 $5500

Association – Bechofer Roberts, C. E.

Forester, Cecil Scott   1899-1966 *Love Lies Dreaming.* London: John Lane, The Bodley Head, 1927. First edition, 8vo., signed presentation from author for Peggy, penciled note in hand of respected dealer Peter Jolliffe to wife of C. E. Bechofer Roberts, endpapers slightly browned, original jade green cloth lettered gilt on spine and on front cover, slight tanning at spine, slight sunning, else very good or better.   Any Amount of Books   2015 - A63488   2015   £220

Association – Beck, Rosemarie

Malamud, Bernard   1914-1986 *Idiots First.* New York: Farrar, Straus & Co., 1963. First edition, first printing, inscribed by Malamud to artist and close friend, Rosemarie Beck, very good, some staining to covers in like jacket with some wear and few small tear.   B & B Rare Books, Ltd. 234 - 75   2015 $650

Association – Beckham, Barry

Davis, George *Black Life in Corporate America: Swimming in the Mainstream.* Garden City: Anchor/Doubleday, 1982. First edition, fine in near fine dust jacket with usual rubbing, inscribed by Davis and co-author, Glegg Watson for novelist Barry Beckham.   Between the Covers Rare Books, Inc. 187 - 68   2015 $250

Fuentes, Carlos *Terra Nostra.* New York: Farrar Straus and Giroux, 1976. First American edition, fine in very good dust jacket with some rubbing and light wear to spinal extremities and edges of panel, inscribed by author fellow author Barry Beckham.   Between the Covers Rare Books, Inc.   187 - 104   2015 $175

Association – Beckingham, J. H.

Kent, Nathaniel *Hints to Gentlemen of Landed Property.* London: J. Dodsley, 1775. First edition, 8vo., 10 engraved folding plates, contemporary polished calf, spine simply gilt with raised bands and crimson lettering piece, short crack in upper joint, still fine, crisp, sound, early ownership inscription on front pastedown "W. Honywood 1787. The gift of the Revd. J. H. Beckingham".   John Drury Rare Books   2015 - 24036   2015 $612

Association – Becold, Henry

Josephus, Flavius *(in Greek) Philabiou Josepou Hierosolymitou Heireos Ta Heuriskomena, Flavii Josephi Hierosolymitani Sacerdotis Opera Quae Extant. (Works in Greek and Latin).* Geneva: Petrus de la Rouviere, 1611. 362 x 222mm., sumptuous contemporary honey brown morocco richly gilt in modified fanfare design, covers with outer frame of multiple plain and decorative rules and rolls, frame surrounding a central panel formed by multiple plain rules and a filigree roll and featuring oblique fleurons pointing outward at corner, panel with very densely gilt and elaborate cornerpieces and a large central lozenge incorporating olive branch garlands and rosettes, an oval at center of lozenge with contemporary coat of arms of the Abbot of Potigny, either Claude Boucherat, or his cousin Charles, flat spine with a chain roll framing a single elongated panel tooled in a design similar to covers, all edges gilt, holes for ties (perhaps with small, very expert repairs at spine bottom); woodcut printer's device on titlepage, woodcut headpieces and decorative initials, Latin and Greek text printed in parallel columns, front pastedown with partially effaced 17th century ownership inscription of Henry (Becold?) Pembroke College, Oxford dated 1734 and 19th century inscription of D. C. Lewis, blank lower right corner of titlepage neatly replaced (in 19th century?) small, pale dampstain in bottom margin of a few leaves, branching marginal wormholes in half a dozen quires (but these always extremely thin and never intruding on text), minor soiling, browning and foxing here and there, still very good internally, leaves fresh, clean and with good margins; hint of wear to joints and extremities, spine uniformly little darkened (with gilt just slightly less bright tan on boards), covers with trivial discoloration and abrasions, but impressive binding in remarkable condition, entirely solid, only minor signs of use, and with once dazzling gilt nearly as good as it was 400 years ago.   Phillip J. Pirages   66 - 21   2015 $6500

Association – Bedford, Duke of

Adam, William *A Treatise and Observations on Trial by Jury in Civil Causes as Now Incorporated with the Jurisdiction of the Court of Session.* Edinburgh: Thoms Clark, 1836. First edition, 8vo., recently rebound in half leather, marbled boards, lettered gilt on spine, 5 raised bands, all edges gilt, from the library of the Dukes of Bedford with 2 page signed letter dated 1836 to the then Duke from William Adam tipped in, slight foxing to prelims, otherwise sound, clean, near fine.   Any Amount of Books   March 2015 - A71748   2015   £325

Epstein, M. *The Annual Register: a review of Public Events at Home and Abroad 1931-1938.* London: Longmans, Green and Co., 1932. First edition, 8 volumes, 8vo., original purple cloth lettered gilt on spine, new series, all clean, very good copies, slightly sunned at spine, bookplates of 11th Duke of Bedford, Woburn Abbey.   Any Amount of Books   2015 - A70517   2015   £180

Association – Beigler, Jerome

Kohut, Heinz *The Restoration of the Self.* New York: International Universities Press, 1977. First edition, inscribed by author to psychoanalyst Jerome Beigler, very good with some underlining, mostly in earlier pages, in very good+ dust jacket with few small tears and light edgewear, handsome copy, 8vo.   Beasley Books   2013 - 2015 $200

Association – Bell, Elizabeth

Cooper, James Fenimore 1789-1851 *The Deerslayer; a Tale.* London: Richard Bentley, 1841. Second edition, 3 volumes, half titles, original drab boards, brown horizontally ribbed cloth spines, paper labels, slightly chipped, signatures of J. and Elizabeth Bell, recent labels of Ronald George Taylor.   Jarndyce Antiquarian Booksellers   CCXI - 72   2015   £125

Association – Bell, J.

Cooper, James Fenimore 1789-1851 *The Deerslayer; a Tale.* London: Richard Bentley, 1841. Second edition, 3 volumes, half titles, original drab boards, brown horizontally ribbed cloth spines, paper labels, slightly chipped, signatures of J. and Elizabeth Bell, recent labels of Ronald George Taylor.   Jarndyce Antiquarian Booksellers   CCXI - 72   2015   £125

Association – Bell, James

The Conspiracy of Aeneas & Antenor Against the State of Troy. London: for John Spicer, 1682. First edition, small 4to., 20 pages, titlepage and recto of B3 lightly soiled, lower margins uncut, late 19th century half calf and marbled boards (foot of spine lightly chipped, one or two bumps to top edge of both boards), 20th century signature of James Bell, from the library of James Stevens Cox (1910-1997). Maggs Bros. Ltd.   1447 - 112   2015   £450

Darwin, Charles Robert 1809-1882 *On the Origin of Species by Means of Natural Selection.* London: John Murray, 1891. 41st thousand, half title, folding plate, final ad leaf, original green cloth, slightly rubbed at head and tail of spine, contemporary signature of James Bell, very good. Jarndyce Antiquarian Booksellers   CCXI - 85   2015   £380

Association – Bell, MacKenzie

Rossetti, Christina 1830-1894 *Verses.* London: SPCK, 1893. Sixth edition, printed on thick paper, rubricated text, uncut in original dark blue buckram, beveled boards, lettered gilt, top edge gilt, very good, inscribed to "Mackenzie Bell Esq. 1894".   Jarndyce Antiquarian Booksellers   CCXI - 247   2015   £750

Association – Bell, Thomas

Ansell, Charles *A Treatise on Friendly Societies, in Which the Doctrine of Interest of Money and the Doctrine of Probability are Practically Applied to the Affairs of Such Societies...* London: Baldwin and Cradock, 1835. First edition, with errata, 2 folding statistical charts, contemporary half calf over marbled boards, spine simply gilt and lettered, some general but minor wear, very good, sound copy with later 19th century booklabel of Mr. Thomas Bell.   John Drury Rare Books   2015 - 26253   2015 $221

Boruwlaski, Joseph *Memoirs of the Celebrated Dwarf, Joseph Boruwlaski. A Polish Gentleman.* Kelso: James Ballantyne at the Kelso Mail Printing Office, 1801. First edition thus, 8vo., inscribed by author for Christ. Ebdon (1744-1824), full contemporary calf, front board detached, bears 1797 Thomas Bell bookplate, spine rather chipped and faded, small chip at top of f.f.e.p., otherwise very good.   Any Amount of Books   March 2015 - C13206   2015   £450

Association – Bell, Vanessa

Woolf, Virginia   1882-1941 *Between the Acts.* London: Hogarth Press, 1941. First edition, first printing, one of 6358 copies, personal copy of author's sister Vanessa Bell with her ownership initials, publisher's bright blue cloth boards lettered gilt, very good with slight lean, rubbing to extremities, toning and light spotting to endpapers, pencil marks to list of works by author, bright and clean pages, housed in custom quarter leather clamshell box.   B & B Rare Books, Ltd.   239 - 2   2015 $7500

Woolf, Virginia   1882-1941 *The Captain's Death Bed and Other Essays.* London: Hogarth Press, 1950. First English edition, one of 10,000 copies, personal copy of author's sister Vanessa Bell with her ownership inscription, publisher's cedar brown cloth boards, lettered gilt, dark brown topstain, original white dust jacket designed by Bell with flower illustrations and decorations, very good with slight lean, toning to spine, small dent to top edge of front board with some light spotting to top edge, some light offsetting to endpapers, otherwise bright and clean interior, dust jacket is good only, unclipped, 1 inch loss to spine head affecting the title lettering, tears and loss to center of spine, toning and stains to spine and panels, chips to corners and rubbing to extremities, housed in custom quarter leather clamshell box.   B & B Rare Books, Ltd.   239 - 6   2015 $4000

Woolf, Virginia   1882-1941 *Granite and Rainbow.* London: Hogarth Press, 1958. First edition, personal copy of author's sister, Vanessa Bell with her ownership signature, with front panel of dust jacket designed by Bell adhered to front pastedown and dust jacket spine adhered to front free endpaper, publisher's royal blue cloth, lettered gilt, white dust jacket with decorations in light blue and black, very good, some wear and rubbing to edges, hint of toning to spine, faint hint of foxing to page edges, otherwise bright, clean pages, custom quarter leather clamshell box.   B & B Rare Books, Ltd.   239 - 10   2015 $4000

Woolf, Virginia   1882-1941 *A Haunted House and Other Short Stories.* London: Hogarth Press, 1943. First edition, first printing, one of 6000 copies, copy of author's sister Vanessa Bell with her ownership signature, publisher's dull crimson cloth boards lettered in gilt, good, with toning and staining to spine and boards, small nick to left edge of front board, bright gilt, some faint toning to pages, pencil correction to page 90, laid in is photocopy of a broadside featuring Woolf's text from "The Mark on the Wall", woodblocks by Bell, housed in custom quarter leather clamshell box.   B & B Rare Books, Ltd.   239 - 3   2015 $5000

Woolf, Virginia   1882-1941 *Hours in a Library.* New York: Harcourt Brace and Co., 1957. One of 1800 copies, personal copy of author's sister, Vanessa Bell, with presentation from Leonard Woolf Christmas 1957, publisher's royal blue cloth spine over black paper boards, with author's initials stamped in blind to front board, lettered gilt in original publisher's glassine jacket, near fine with hint of wear to extremities, slightest toning to spine, faint hint of light soiling to board edges, glassine tipped in to frontispiece as protective sheet, bright and fresh interior, light toning to glassine with chipping to extremities and some loss to spine ends, light creasing to front panel, rare in any condition, complete copy, custom quarter clamshell box.   B & B Rare Books, Ltd.   239 - 9   2015 $6500

Woolf, Virginia   1882-1941 *The Moment and Other Essays.* London: Hogarth Press, 1947. First edition, first printing, one of 10,000 copies, the copy of author's sister Vanessa Bell, with her ownership signature, with front panel of dust jacket designed by Bell adhered to front pastedown, pale ruby red cloth boards, lettered in gilt, pink dust jacket with vase of flowers illustration printed in black, good, with toning to spine, fading to edges of boards, light soiling, bright gilt, hint of light spotting to free endpapers, clean pages, housed in custom quarter leather clamshell box.   B & B Rare Books, Ltd.   239 - 4   2015 $4500

Woolf, Virginia   1882-1941 *Virginia Woolf and Lytton Strachey: Letters.* London: Hogarth Press/Chatto & Windus, 1956. First edition, one of 4000 copies, personal copy of author's sister Vanessa Bell, with her ownership signature, publisher's pale tan cloth boards lettered gilt, cream dust jacket, near fine, hint of wear to extremities, very slight lean, unfaded spine, gilt lightly dimmed, few scattered spots to cloth, otherwise clean covers bright and fresh, housed in custom quarter leather clamshell box.   B & B Rare Books, Ltd.   239 - 8   2015 $4000

Woolf, Virginia   1882-1941 *A Writer's Diary.* London: Hogarth Press, 1953. First edition, first printing, one of 9000 copies, personal copy of author's sister, Vanessa Bell, with her signature, publisher's orange cloth boards, lettered gilt, orange topstain to original white dust jacket designed by Bell with flower illustrations and decorations printed in orange and black, very good with slight lean, some rubbing to extremities, minor toning to spine, light spotting to top edge and endpapers, bright and fresh pages, unclipped dust jacket lacking rear panel and flap and left half of bottom of spine, half inch loss to spine head, toning to spine, some minor soiling and small chips to front panel, housed in custom quarter leather clamshell box.   B & B Rare Books, Ltd.   239 - 7   2015 $5000

Woolf, Virginia   1882-1941 *A Writer's Diary.* London: Hogarth Press, 1953. First edition, octavo, fragmentary original dust jacket, this the copy of author's sister Vanessa Bell, signed in ink by Bell, well used copy with extraordinary association.   Honey & Wax Booksellers   3 - 10   2015 $6000

Woolf, Virginia   1882-1941 *The Waves.* London: published by Leonard and Virginia Woolf at the Hogarth Press, 1931. First edition, first printing, one of 7113 copies, publisher's purple cloth lettered gilt, printed on laid paper, good with slight lean, two short tears to spine head, rubbing to spine ends, toning and light soiling to spine ends, toning and light soiling to spine, boards slightly bowed, minor soiling and some fading, very light spotting to first few and last pages of text block, pencil correction to page 47, bright and clean pages, housed in custom quarter leather clamshell box, personal copy of author's sister Vanessa Bell, with her ownership signature by descent to her daughter Angelica Garnett, thence to her two surviving daughters Henrietta Coupe and Frances Partridge.   B & B Rare Books, Ltd.   239 - 1   2015 $9500

Association – Bellamy, John Haley

Bellamy, Edward *Looking Backward 2000-1887.* Boston and New York: Houghton Mifflin, 1889. First edition, later printing, with "One Hundred and Second Thousand" on titlepage, 8vo., original brown cloth, gilt lettering, top edge of upper board and first few signatures bumped, fine, signed "With compliments of / Edward Bellamy", heraldic bookplate with names John Haley Bellamy and John W. P. Frost typed in lower margin.   The Brick Row Book Shop   Miscellany 67 - 24   2015 $500

Association – Belper, Edward Strutt

Bass, Michael Thomas *Street Music in the Metropolis. Correspondence and Observations on the Existing Law and Proposed Amendments.* London: John Murray, 1864. First edition, 8vo. half title, original maroon cloth, fine presentation copy from 19th century library of Edward Strutt, Lord Belper, with author's compliments, scarce.   John Drury Rare Books   2015 - 25788   2015 $1049

Association – Benedikt, Michael

L'Anselme, Jean *L'Enfant Triste.* Paris: Pierre Seghers, 1955. First edition, printed wrappers, 2 small stains on front wrapper, else near fine in very good, original unprinted dust jacket, warmly inscribed by author for poet Michael Benedikt.   Between the Covers Rare Books, Inc.   187 - 150   2015 $250

Doty, M. R. *An Alphabet.* Ithaca: Alembic Press, 1979. First edition, one of 600 copies, initials by Teresa McNeil, wrappers as issued, modest age toning, at least near fine, very warmly inscribed by co-author, Ruth Doty for Michael Benedikt.   Between the Covers Rare Books, Inc. 187 - 79   2015 $450

Association – Benet, Stephen Vincent

Agee, James   1909-1955 *Permit Me Voyage.* New Haven: Yale University Press, 1934. First edition, scarce first book, tipped to front free endpaper is slip of paper inscribed note from Stephen Vincent Benet for Miss Locke, spine little faded, inch deep strip at top of back cover faded as well, otherwise near fine.   James S. Jaffe Rare Books   Modern American Poetry - 1   2015 $1,250

Association – Bennett, A. J.

King, Jessie *Seven Happy Days.* London: International Studio Supp. New Year, 1914. 4to., wrappers, some cover soil and tears, very good, series of magnificent color illustrations heightened with gold and silver, with 7 smaller black and white illustrations, laid in is original water color plus handwritten letter with sketch housed in original mailing envelope, inscribed to A. J. Bennett.   Aleph-bet Books, Inc. 109 - 244   2015 $4250

Association – Bennett, John

Norfleet, J. Frank *Norfleet. The Amazing Experiences of an Intrepid Texas Ranger with an International Swindling Ring.* Sugar land: Imperial Press, 1927. Revised edition, cloth, illustrations, signed by Norfleet and Gordon Hines and further inscribed by Hines to John C. Bennett, near very good.   Baade Books of the West   2014 - 2015 $49

Association – Benson, A.

D'Israeli, Isaac   1776-1843 *Curiosities of Literature.* London: printed for J. Murray, 1793. Third edition, volume II second edition, 2 volumes, folding facsimile, large uncut and unpressed copy with corner of Hh3 in volume I torn with loss not affecting text, contemporary quarter calf, marbled boards, slight wear to head of one spine and corners, boards rubbed, ownership label of A. Benson, Reading, who has also created manuscript half titles on endpapers, the first with naive roundel portrait, he has also neatly added calligraphic subject headings to few pages.   Jarndyce Antiquarian Booksellers   CCXI - 92   2015   £125

Association – Benton

Breeskin, Adelyn Dohme *Mary Cassatt, a Catalogue Raisonne of the Oils, Pastels, Watercolors and Drawings.* Washington: Smithsonian Institution, 1970. First edition, very good, few small chips and tears, dust jacket slightly shorter than book as issued, previous owner's gift inscription to "The Bentons" (either the family of William Benton (1900-1973) or that of his son Charles (1949-1953).   Beasley Books   2013 - 2015 $200

Association – Benton, William

Kleinholz, Frank *A Self Portrait.* New York: Shorewood Publishers, 1964. First edition, fully bound in leather, stamped gilt and blind, slight wear to spine, very good+ in author's hand 'this one of twelve books bound in leather for those dear friends who have been of such help and encouragement to me. This one is for Senator and Mrs. William Benton March 7, 1964', 4to.   Beasley Books   2013 - 2015 $250

Moses, Robert *Public Works: a Dangerous Trade.* New York: McGraw Hill, 1970. First edition, presumably deluxe binding of blue leatherette stamped gilt and red with four gilt devices on front board, marbled endpapers, publisher's unprinted acteate dust jacket, fine in very good+ acetate that show bit of rubbing and few tiny nicks, this copy inscribed to William Benton (10770-1973), large 8vo.   Beasley Books   2013 - 2015 $400

Association – Berdmore, Scrope

Homerus *Ilias. (The Iliad in Latin).*   Parisiis: Apud Martinum Iuuenem Excvdebat Gvil. M., 1550. 121 x 89mm., beautiful and animated contemporary elaborately gilt and painted Parisian calf by Wooton's binder "B", covers with unusual frame of interlacing slender rectangular compartments formed by wide black painted fillets outlined in gilt, center panel with four foliate scrolls arched across frame in each quadrant and forming a centerpiece lozenge, azured curls at head and foot of panel and with stippled lobes, additional azured cornerpieces, stippled circles at top, bottom and either side of the panel, raised bands, spine compartments gilt with centered foliate tool or bull's eye, slightly later red morocco label, all edges gilt, spine ends and corners very artfully renewed, in fleece lined brown buckram clamshell case, with John Roland Abbey's morocco bookplate and large morocco title label on spine, front endpaper with morocco bookplate of Abbey, pastedowns with armorial bookplates of Scrope Berdmore, S.T.P. (dated 1790) at front and of Henry C. Compton esq. at rear, rear endpaper with modern bookplate of Philosophia Hermetica ruled in red throughout, half dozen light ink stains, two or three affecting a few words of text, quite clean and fresh internally, backstrip with minor flaking and few hairline cracks, one corner exposed, otherwise very decorative binding, pleasing and especially well preserved, boards still lustrous.   Phillip J. Pirages   66 - 12   2015 $12,500

Association – Bere, John

Busby, Richard *Rudimentum Grammaticae Latinae Metricum.* London: Ex Officina Eliz Redmayne, 1699. Early edition, 8vo., interleaved with blanks, woodcut Westminster School arms on title, small circular stain just touching titlepage coat of arms and minor spotting throughout, errata page has been misprinted with some loss to text, top corners beginning to fold between gatherings B-D but generally clean copy, contemporary sprinkled calf, covers panelled in blind (worn, corners bumped, pastedowns unstruck), signed by John and Robert Bere, annotations on only two of the blank interleaves, from the library of James Stevens Cox (1910-1997).   Maggs Bros. Ltd.   1447 - 60   2015   £240

Association – Bere, Robert

Busby, Richard *Rudimentum Grammaticae Latinae Metricum.* London: Ex Officina Eliz Redmayne, 1699. Early edition, 8vo., interleaved with blanks, woodcut Westminster School arms on title, small circular stain just touching titlepage coat of arms and minor spotting throughout, errata page has been misprinted with some loss to text, top corners beginning to fold between gatherings B-D but generally clean copy, contemporary sprinkled calf, covers panelled in blind (worn, corners bumped, pastedowns unstruck), signed by John and Robert Bere, annotations on only two of the blank interleaves, from the library of James Stevens Cox (1910-1997).   Maggs Bros. Ltd.   1447 - 60   2015   £240

Association – Berford, R. G., Mrs.

Reid, Mayne 1818-1883 *The Death Shot.* London: Ward Lock & Tyler, 1875. Plates, 32 page publisher's catalog, original green pictorial cloth, decorated gilt, spine slightly worn at head and tail, hinges little rubbed, leading inner hinge slightly cracking, signed presentation inscription to Mrs. R. G. Berford dated March 1875. Jarndyce Antiquarian Booksellers CCXI - 240 2015 £350

Association – Berkenhead, J.

Beaumont, Francis *Comedies and Tragedies written by Francis Beaumont and John Fletcher.* London: for Humphrey Robinson and Humphrey Moseley, 1647. First edition, small folio, lacking final leaf of text, engraved portrait, second state with "Vates Duplex" in fourth line of the inscription and "J. Berkenhead' in smaller letters (backed with old paper, at time of rebinding, slightly cropped at foot, ink blot in inscription) titlepage stained and slightly dusty, loose at upper inner margin, margins bit frayed, small hole in blank area near outer edge, lower outer corner of F3 torn away with loss to five lines, few words on 7 lines on Dd1v have adhered to blank page opposite upper corner 3U4 torn away affecting pagination, loss at foot of 7A1 from paper flaw affecting a few letters, closed vertical tears, minor spots and stains throughout, some ink blots, upper inner margin of first few leaves and lower outer corner of last few leaves dampstained, late 17th/early 18th century sheep, covers ruled in blind (headcaps and top and bottom of spine torn away, covers somewhat scuffed, cup ring on lower cover, upper corner of lower cover chewed and dampstained), from the library of James Stevens Cox (1910-1997), name Wyndham Harbin, 2nd son of William and Elizabeth Harbin of Newton Surmaville, Somerset with his signature, name Elizabeth (probably Harbin). Maggs Bros. Ltd. 1447 - 25 2015 £600

Association – Bernard, Charles

Newton, Isaac 1642-1727 *Opticks; or a Treatise of the Reflexions, Refractions, Inflexions and Colours of Light. Also Two Treatises of the Species and Magnitude of Curvilinear Figures.* London: printed for Sam. Smith & Benj. Walford, printers to the Royal society, 1704. First edition, first issue, 2 parts in one volume, 4to., title printed in red and black, 19 folding engraved plates/diagrams, errata page, title lower margin trimmed (early signature on upper and lower edges of title faded and cannot be read without an infrared lamp, some light foxing, plates remarkably clean and free of tears, presentation binding of 19th century full vellum with covers gilt stamped with emblem of University of Edinburgh, calf gilt stamped spine label, edges red, small faint stamp inscribed for Thomas Smith, presented as a Prize in the Natural Philosophy Class University of Edinburgh, Session 1852-3, Philip Kelland, very small ink inscription at rear, titlepage with obscured signature of Charles Bernard (1650-1711). Jeff Weber Rare Books 178 - 830 2015 $55,000

Association – Berndtsson, Gustaf

Rowe, Henry *Fables in Verse.* London: printed for J. J. Stockdale, 1810. Bookplate of Gustaf Berndtsson, illustrations, contemporary half dark brown calf, elaborate gilt spine, very good. Jarndyce Antiquarian Booksellers CCXI - 248 2015 £120

Association – Bernheiemr, Earle

Frost, Robert Lee 1874-1963 *North of Boston.* London: David Nutt, 1914. First edition, binding A, one of 350 copies in original coarse green linen, out of a total edition of 1000 copies, 8vo., fine, preserved in black cloth slipcase with chemise, presentation copy inscribed by author for Earle Bernheimer. James S. Jaffe Rare Books Modern American Poetry - 88 2015 $12,500

Association – Berrigan, Ted

Ashbery, John *Houseboat Days. Poems.* New York: Viking, 1977. First edition, erratum slip laid in, 8vo., original cloth backed boards, contemporary, presentation copy inscribed by Ashbery for Ted Berrigan and wife Alice Notley, 9/20/77, fine. James S. Jaffe Rare Books Many Happy Returns - 352 2015 $3500

Carroll, Jim *4 Ups and 1 Down.* New York: Angel Hair Books, 1970. First edition, one of 13 numbered copies signed by Caroll and Dona Dennis (cover art), with strands of their hair tipped in, out of a total edition of 313 copies, 4to., pictorial wrappers, inscribed by Carroll to Ted Berrigan, very fine. James S. Jaffe Rare Books Many Happy Returns - 354 2015 $3500

Ceravolo, Joseph *Fits of Dawn.* New York: "C" Press, 1965. First edition, 4to., original cloth over boards, gilt title on front cover, original illustrated wrappers (with cover design by Rosemary Ceravolo) bound in, this copy 1 of 1 Hor Commerce, publisher Ted Berrigan's copy annotated by him, signed by Berrigan, laid in is ALS from Ceravolo to Berrigan, letter folded from mailing, otherwise it and original mailing envelope fine, gutters and margins of pastedowns in book are variably darkened from binding adhesive, otherwise fine, rare. James S. Jaffe Rare Books Modern American Poetry - 48 2015 $500

Ceravolo, Joseph *Fits of Dawn.* New York: "C" Press, 1965. First edition, 4to., original cloth over boards, gilt title on front cover, original illustrated wrappers bound in, publisher Ted Berrigan's copy, specially bound for Berrigan and annotated by him, signed by Berrigan, laid in is ALS 4to., from Ceravolo to Berrigan, letter folded from mailing, otherwise it and envelope fine, gutters and margins of pastedowns in book variably darkened from binding adhesive, otherwise fine. James S. Jaffe Rare Books Many Happy Returns - 360 2015 $5000

Duncan, Robert *The Opening of the Field.* New York: Grove Press, 1960. First edition, Ted Berrigan's copy with his ownership signature in pencil, 1962, fine copy, presentation from author to Berrigan.   James S. Jaffe Rare Books   Modern American Poetry - 78   2015 $1500

Friedman, Richard *15 Chicago Poets.* Chicago: Yellow Press, 1976. First edition, 8vo., illustrations, original boards, fine in lightly rubbed dust jacket with one short closed tear, review copy with publisher's slip laid in, signed by Ted Berrigan on page 3 and dated "London 1973".   James S. Jaffe Rare Books   Many Happy Returns - 387   2015 $150

Guest, Barbara *Poems: the Location of Things, Archaics, The Open Skies.* Garden City: Doubleday, 1962. First edition, 8vo., original boards, dust jacket, presentation copy inscribed by poet to Ted Berrigan, fine in slightly dust soiled dust jacket.   James S. Jaffe Rare Books   Many Happy Returns - 361   2015 $1250

Katz, Steve *Cheyenne River Wild Track.* Ithaca: Ithaca House, 1973. First edition, octavo, wrappers illustrated by George Schneeman, trifle rubbed, near fine, inscribed by author to Ted Berrigan and Alice Notley.   Between the Covers Rare Books, Inc.   187 - 144   2015 $125

Koch, Kenneth *Ko or a Season on Earth.* New York and London: Grove Press/Evergreen Books, 1959. First edition, 8vo., original gray cloth dust jacket, inscribed by author for Ted Berrigan, few ink spots on fore-edge and rear free endpaper, otherwise very good.   James S. Jaffe Rare Books   Modern American Poetry - 167   2015 $1500

MacBeth, George *Interview with Ted Berrigan.* N.P.: Ignu Publications, 1971. First edition, narrow 4to., original wrappers with holograph title, signed by MacBeth and inscribed by Berrigan to Burt (Britton), covers little dusty, otherwise fine.   James S. Jaffe Rare Books   Many Happy Returns - 81   2015 $650

O'Hara, Frank *Love Poems.* New York: Tibor De Nagy editions, 1965. First edition, limited to 500 copies, presentation from author for Ted (Berrigan), covers lightly soiled, but very good, enclosed in half leather and marbled board clamshell box.   James S. Jaffe Rare Books   Many Happy Returns - 363   2015 $5000

Olson, Charles *The Maximus Papers.* New York: Jargon/Corinth Books, 1960. Fifth printing, 8vo., original decorated wrappers, Ted Berrigan's copy with his ownership signature, stamped "Just Buffalo. Library Resource Center", wrappers somewhat sunned, otherwise very good.   James S. Jaffe Rare Books   Many Happy Returns - 358   2015 $350

Reynolds, Tim *Slocum.* Santa Barbara: Unicorn Press, 1967. Second printing, limited to 1000 copies, perfect bound wrappers, fine, inscribed by author for Ted Berrigan.   Between the Covers Rare Books, Inc.   187 - 232   2015 $150

Schuyler, James *Collabs.* New York: Misty Terrace Press, 1980. First edition, one of 200 copies, 4to., original wrappers with cover design by George Schneeman, stapled as issued, presentation from all contributors, Helena Hughes, Michael Scholnick and signed by small pen and ink self-portrait by Schneeman for Ted Berrigan, fine.   James S. Jaffe Rare Books   Modern American Poetry - 244   2015 $1750

Schuyler, James *The Morning of the Poems.* New York: Farrar Straus & Giroux, 1980. First edition, presentation copy inscribed by author for Ted (Berrigan Aug. '80), fine.   James S. Jaffe Rare Books   Many Happy Returns - 364   2015 $3500

Waldman, Anne *First Baby Poems.* Rocky Ledge: Cottage Editions, 1982. Limited to 526 copies, original decorated glossy white wrappers, covers slightly soiled, but very good, presentation copy from author June 30 1982 for Ted Berrigan.   James S. Jaffe Rare Books   Many Happy Returns - 369   2015 $750

Warsh, Lewis *Moving through Air.* New York: Angel Hair Books, 1968. First edition, one of 25 numbered copies signed by Warsh, one of the publishers and Donna Dennis (cover design), folio, original pictorial wrappers, glue residue (as usual) where manuscript sheet is pasted in, otherwise fine, Ted Berrigan's copy with his ownership signature ("one of the 25 special copies given to me by Anne Waldman").   James S. Jaffe Rare Books   Many Happy Returns - 370   2015 $1500

Association – Berthold, W.

Lacouture, Charles *Repertoire Chromatique.* Paris: Gauthier Villars et Fils Imprimeurus Libraires de Bureau des Longitudes de l'Ecole Polytechnique, 1890. First and only edition, large 4to., chromolithograph frontispiece, 28 chromolithograph plates, transparent printed overlay to each plate and separate accompanying printed card screen, uncut and partly unopened in modern red morocco backed cloth, spine lettered gilt, preserving original buff wrappers, head of spine cracked but holding, minor tears to edges, fine, inscribed by author to W. Berthold, scarce.   Marlborough Rare Books   List 54 - 48   2015   £650

Association – Beshear, Buck

Leonard, Elmore *The Moonshine War.* Garden City: Doubleday, 1969. First edition, near fine in like dust jacket, inscribed by author to one of book's two dedicatees, Buck Beshear, 6-20-99, from the collection of Duke Collier. Royal Books   36 - 210   2015 $3250

Association – Best, Mary

Allestree, Richard *The Ladies Calling.* Oxford: printed at the Theater, 1673. First edition, 8vo., 2 parts in 1, early 18th century panelled calf with marbled endpapers, frontispiece, the copy of Barbara Dobell with her signature, and below is "Sally Harrison/June 11th 1797" with note about her marriage and on facing blank is 19th century inscription "the gift of S. Mitchell to her niece Mary Best December 1855, in lower margin of final page of text is note in Dobell's hand about binding and cost charged by a Mr. Double on March 30 1706, edges little rubbed, marbled endpapers have cleanly lifted from boards, firmly held in place by sewing, fine.   The Brick Row Book Shop   Miscellany 67 - 3   2015 $500

Association – Betjeman, John

Drayton, Michael 1563-1631 *England's Heroical Epistles.* London: printed for J. Johnson, 1788. Some leaves slightly browned, 19th century half dark green morocco, slightly rubbed with scars on marbled boards, with early note on page 308, with names of Geoffrey and Kathleen Tillotson, inserted correspondence shows Kathleen offered this to British Library which in fact had acquired a copy, ALS from John Betjeman probably to Bernard Newdigate. Jarndyce Antiquarian Booksellers   CCVII - 233   2015   £280

Association – Betts, R.

Coles, Elisha *Christologia or a Metrical paraphrase on the History of Our Lord and Saviour Jesus Christ.* London: for Peter Parker, 1671. First edition, 8vo., without first blank leaf, light browning particularly in margins, words "OR A" on title deleted with ink and replaced with "a" in later manuscript, closely shaved, mid 20th century blue quarter morocco and marbled boards, from the library of James Stevens Cox (1910-1997), inscribed by Lewis Caesar Hill, 19th century signature George R. Hales, signature R. Betts dated "Silverhill 15.1 (18)90", booklabel of Gerald P Mander (d. 1951) of Tettenhall Wood, Staffordshire.   Maggs Bros. Ltd.   1447 - 105   2015   £240

Association – Bibler, Noni

Gardner, Erle Stanley *The Case of the Baited Hook.* New York: William Morrow, 1940. First edition, bit of staining at lower edges of cover, else near fine in near fine dust jacket with light wear along edges, inscribed by author to early assistant, Noni (Bibler), from the collection of Duke Collier.   Royal Books   36 - 21   2015 $3000

Gardner, Erle Stanley *The Case of the Caretaker's Cat.* New York: William Morrow, 1935. First edition, fine in near fine, lightly rubbed dust jacket with light wear to top of spine and corners and tiny closed tear on front panel, inscribed by author for Noni (Bibler), one of author's early assistants, from the collection of Duke Collier.   Royal Books   36 - 14   2015 $3500

Gardner, Erle Stanley *The Case of the Curious Bride.* New York: William Morrow, 1934. First edition, fine in bright, very good dust jacket with several modest chips, largest being at top of spine, affecting word 'The', inscribed by author for Noni Bibler, one of author's early assistants, from the collection of Duke Collier.   Royal Books   36 - 12   2015 $3000

Gardner, Erle Stanley *The Case of the Dangerous Dowager.* New York: William Morrow, 1937. First edition, very good plus in good dust jacket, 1 3/4 inch loss to top portion of jacket spine, else very good in couple of droplet stains on rear panel and light rubbing overall, warmly inscribed by author to early assistant, Noni (Bibler), from the collection of Duke Collier.   Royal Books   36 - 17   2015 $1250

Gardner, Erle Stanley *The Case of the Howling Dog.* New York: William Morrow, 1934. First edition, near fine in very good and scarce dust jacket (couple of neat repairs along two of the folds, fading to reds on spine panel, chipping at spine ends affecting a portion of word 'The' in title, warmly inscribed by author for Noni Bibler, one of author's early assistants, from the collection of Duke Collier.   Royal Books   36 - 11   2015 $3250

Gardner, Erle Stanley *The Case of the Lame Canary.* New York: William Morrow, 1937. First edition, very good in like dust jacket, dampstain along fore-edges of boards (and conversely along flap folds of jacket at verso) and top right corner of text block, jacket has two chips, one at the crown and one at bottom rear panel, neither affecting any titling, despite noted flaws, bright copy, warmly inscribed by author to early assistant Noni (Bibler), from the collection of Duke Collier.   Royal Books   36 - 18   2015 $2250

Gardner, Erle Stanley *The Case of the Rolling Bones.* New York: William Morrow, 1939. First edition, about fine in bright, near fine dust jacket, which is lightly worn at top of spine and corners, with fingernail sized chip at base of spine, affecting publisher's logo, inscribed by author to early assistant Noni (Bibler), from the collection of Duke Collier. Royal Books   36 - 20   2015 $3000

Gardner, Erle Stanley *The Case of the Silent Partner.* New York: William Morrow, 1940. First edition, fine in bright, unrubbed dust jacket, jacket lightly worn at spine tips, small chip top of front hinge, inscribed by author for early assistant, Noni (Bibler), from the collection of Duke Collier. Royal Books   36 - 22   2015 $3000

Gardner, Erle Stanley *The Case of the Sleepwalker's Niece.* New York: William Morrow, 1936. First edition, fine in near fine dust jacket, very lightly rubbed, lightly chipped at top of spine, inscribed by author to early assistant Noni (Bibler), from the collection of Duke Collier.   Royal Books   36 - 15   2015 $3500

Gardner, Erle Stanley *The Case of the Substitute Face.* New York: William Morrow, 1938. First edition, fine in bright, unrubbed dust jacket with trivial rubbing to spine tips, inscribed by author for early assistant, Noni (Bibler), from the collection of Duke Collier.   Royal Books   36 - 19   2015 $3500

Gardner, Erle Stanley *The Case of the Velvet Claws.* New York: William Morrow, 1936. Second printing, near fine in very good dust jacket (both clearly state 'Second Printing'), jacket lightly rumpled along spine panel, with small bit of loss at crown and heel in (not titling affected), shallow rectangular chip at top rear panel, light general overall rubbing and nicking, very presentable copy, inscribed by author for early assistant Noni (Bibler), from the collection of Duke Collier.   Royal Books   36 - 24   2015 $2500

Gardner, Erle Stanley *The D. A. Draws a Circle.* New York: William Morrow, 1939. First printing of this edition, near fine in very good or better dust jacket, dampstain bottom right corner of front board, affecting jacket verso in same spot, otherwise only lightly rubbed overall, inscribed by author to early assistant, Noni (Bibler), from the collection of Duke Collier.   Royal Books   36 - 30   2015 $1850

Gardner, Erle Stanley *The D. A. Goes to Trial.* New York: William Morrow, 1940. First edition, dampstain bottom right corner of front board, endpapers toned, else near fine in about very good dust jacket with small chips at extremities and some of the usual color-fading to pink spine title, warmly inscribed by author to early assistant, Noni (Bibler), from the collection of Duke Collier.   Royal Books   36 - 31   2015 $1850

Gardner, Erle Stanley *The D. A. Holds a Candle.* New York: William Morrow, 1938. First edition, very slightly cocked, else very good plus in very good dust jacket with small chips at extremities and some of the usual color fading to pink spine title, warmly inscribed by author to early assistant, Noni (Bibler), from the collection of Duke Collier. Royal Books   36 - 29   2015 $2250

Association – Bickford, Walter

Society of the Framers of the Constitution of the State of Montana   *Third and Fourth Reunion of the.... 1911 and 1916.*   Butte: 1916. or 1917. First edition thus, pictorial stapled wrappers, 40 pages, illustrations, laid in TLS from Walter Bickford, Asst. sec. & letter of receipt from Peter Schmidt, son of member of constitutional convention, one page creased and section bracketed in pencil, back cover almost detached and tear repaired, unusual, scarce, fair. Baade Books of the West   2014 - 2015 $91

Association – Billson, George

Clerke, Agnes Mary   *The Concise Knowledge: Astronomy.* London: Hutchinson & Co., 1896. 4 plates, 99 figures, frontispiece, prelims and rear endpapers showing offsetting, original quarter red calf, maroon gilt stamped cloth, leather heavily damaged, fragmented, with circa 1970's plastic covering applied over original binding - if removed will further damage the leather (though cloth with not be affected), bookplate of George H. Billson (Times Book Club, London). Jeff Weber Rare Books   178 - 782   2015 $75

Association – Birrell, Augustine

Beerbohm, Max   1872-1956   *A Christmas Garland.* London: William Heinemann, 1912. First edition, blue cloth gilt, boards quite stained, particularly rear board, which extends to final leaf, fair copy only, bookplate of Beerbohm's contemporary, author and politician, Augustine Birrell. Between the Covers Rare Books, Inc.   187 - 12   2015 $150

Association – Bishop, Morris

Nabokov, Vladimir   1899-1977   *The Gift.* New York: Putnam, 1963. First edition of first English translation, presentation copy inscribed on half title in pencil with chess imagery 'for the (two chess bishops) from Vladimir Nabokov April 2 1964 Ithaca NY" with two butterflies and their shadows and this annotation, corrected" two misprints on page 79/ one misprint on page 154', fine copy, near fine jacket, housed in custom quarter leather box with folding chemise, from the library of Morris Bishop (with his bookplate).   B & B Rare Books, Ltd.   234 - 83   2015 $17,500

Martialis, Marcus Valerius *Epigrammaton Libri XIII.* Lugduni: Apud Haered Seb. Gryphius, 1559. 108 x 76mm., appealing contemporary olive brown morocco, covers bordered with fillets in gilt and in blind and with small gilt floral cornerpieces as well as central azured gilt arabesque, raised bands forming eight spine panels, each of these with small gilt cruciform sprigs flanking a central majuscule, the letters running vertically to spell out 'MARTIAL" all edges gilt; woodcut printer's device to titlepage, woodcut initials, from the library of Chatsworth House with modern bookplate "HB" (i.e collector Heribert Boeder); quarter inch chip at top of backstrip, half a dozen tiny wormholes near head or tail of spine, minor rubbing to corners and few abrasions on covers, but very appealing copy, unsophisticated contemporaneous binding completely solid with lustrous boards and virtually no wear to joints, text especially fresh and clean throughout.   Phillip J. Pirages   66 - 16   2015 $1800

Association – Boethiah, W. E.

Rae, Edward *The White Sea Peninsula: a Journey in Russian Lapland and Karelia.* London: John Murray, 1881. First edition, 8vo., original blue cloth with bevelled edges, lettered gilt on spine and decorated in gilt on front cover, plates, including facsimile maps in pocket at rear, presentation from author to W. E. Boethiah, clean, very good.   Any Amount of Books   2015 - C11705   2015   £220

Association – Bond, Julian

Hilliard, David *This Side of Glory: The Autobiography of David Hilliard and the Story of the Black Panther Party.* Boston: Little Brown and Co., 1993. Uncorrected proof, printed red wrappers, little light use, else very near fine, laid in is letter from publisher to Civil Rights pioneer Julian Bond, asking for comments on the book.   Between the Covers Rare Books   197 - 60   2015 $125

Association – Bonde, Gustav

Deveria, Laure *Fleurs Dessinees D'Apres Nature et Lithographiees.* Paris: Jeannin, 1833-1838. First and only edition, folio, contemporary dark green half morocco, cloth boards with blind floral pattern, gilt spine with raised bands, titlepage and 24 hand colored lithographs after Deveria printed by Lemercier, some with original publisher's blindstamp, no text, rubbing to spine, repair to front hinge, occasional faint spots, very good, ink stamp of Ohrhybus Castle to front pastedown with pencil inscription attribution ownership to Gustav Bonde, exceptionally rare.   Henry Sotheran Ltd.   Natural History: Rarities 2015 - 2015   £17,500

Association – Booth, Felix

Sedley, Charles *Asmodeus; or the Devil's in London: a Sketch.* London: printed by J. Dean, Wardourt Street, Soho for F. F. Hughes 15 Paternsoter Row, 1808. First edition, 3 volumes, 12mo., without half titles, apart from few minor marks in places, clean copy, contemporary green half calf over marbled boards, spines ruled and numbered in gilt, labels missing, chipped at head and rubbed at extremities, still appealing copy, armorial of Felix Booth and Renier booklabels.   Marlborough Rare Books   List 53 - 43   2015   £900

Association – Boothby, William

Camoens, Luis De *The Lusiad or Portugals Historicall Poem.* London: by Thomas Newcombe for Humphrey Moseley, 1655. Folio, A5 with paper repair top corner and loss of about a dozen letters in total, few minor stains, 2 small wormholes in lower blank margin throughout, contemporary panelled calf, covers with gilt arms block of Sir William Boothby, rebacked lower right corner of cover repaired, covers rather worn and faded, front flyleaf repaired, from the library of James Stevens Cox (1910-1997).   Maggs Bros. Ltd.   1447 - 62   2015   £4000

Association – Borein, Ed

Perkins, Charles E. *The Phantom Bull.* Boston and New York: Houghton Mifflin Co., 1932. First edition, quarto, small pen and ink drawing on half titlepage and signed 'Ed Borein', original decorated red cloth, illustrations by Borein, very good tight copy, internally reinforced dust jacket. Buckingham Books   March 2015 - 27022   2015 $2000

Association – Borrow, Ernest

Hamilton, Patrick   1904-1962 *Hangover Square.* London: Constable, 1941. Second impression published September 1941 (first was August 1941), 8vo., from the library of Peter Haining (1940-2007) with his book label and brief ownership signature, covers tanned, slightly marked and mottled, sound, very good- with clean text, signed presentation from author to Ernest Borrow.   Any Amount of Books   2015 - C1683   2015   £700

Association – Borrow, Isaac

Bonnefons, Nicolas De *The French Gardiner...* London: by T. B. for B. Took and are to be sold by J. Taylor, 1691. Fourth (i.e. fifth edition) translated by John Evelyn, 12mo., engraved frontispiece, 4 engraved plates, browned throughout, except plates which are on different paper, slight worming in lower margin at front, mid 20th century blue buckram, armorial bookplate of Isaac Borrow (1673-1745), from the library of James Stevens Cox (1910-1997).   Maggs Bros. Ltd.   1447 - 34   2015   £750

Association – Bosanquet, George Jacob

Dickens, Charles 1812-1870 *Hard Times.* London: Bradbury and Evans, 1854. First edition, half title, few spots, original olive green horizontal ribbed cloth, sunned, spine torn and worn at tail, slight damp marking at fore-edge, inner hinges cracking, armorial bookplate of George Jacob Bosanquet, Kathleen Tillotson's copy, signed 1949 with pencil notes , in Kathleen's brown paper wrappers. Jarndyce Antiquarian Booksellers CCVII - 178 2015 £350

Association – Bosari, Giovanni

Gazzadi, Domenico *Zoologia Morale Esposta in Cento Venti Discorsi in Versi o in Prosa.* Florence: Vincenzo Batelli e Compagni, 1843-1846. First and only edition, 2 volumes, contemporary quarter brown morocco, marbled boards, elaborate gilt tools and lettering to spines, 93 hand colored engraved plates, binding little rubbed to edges, browning to 3 plates on volume II, closed tear not affecting image to bottom margin of plate of St. Bernard's in volume I, occasional marking elsewhere, generally very clean and bright indeed, very good, with ownership stamps of Giovanni Bosari, Bosari's stamp and two censors' stamps to half title volume I. Henry Sotheran Ltd. Natural History: Rarities 2015 - 2015 £20,000

Association – Boschetti, P. Marie

Sorbin, Arnaud De *Tractatus de Monstris, que a Temporibus Constantini Bucusque Ortum Babuerunt ac ies Quae Circa Eorum te(m)pora Misere Acciderunt, ex Historiarum...* Paris: apud Hieronimum de Marnet & Gulielmum Cavellat sub Pelicano, 1570. First edition, 12mo., 14 woodcut illustrations, woodcut printer's device on titlepage, contemporary limp vellum, bold contemporary mss. title in ink on spine, lower edge with fine contemporary mss. of author and abbreviated title, ties perished, neat 17th century mss. ownership inscription on titlepage P. Marie Boschetti, 18th century unreadable ecclesiastical library stamp on verso of titlepage and verso of final leaf, minute neat mss. ownership inscription, engraved bookplate of Docteur Francois Mouteir, c. 1920, some light browning, but very good. Maggs Bros. Ltd. Illustrated Books 2014 - 2015 £2500

Association – Boucher, Anthony

MacDonald, Ross *The Drowning Pool.* New York: Alfred A. Knopf, 1950. First edition, near fine in bright, near fine dust jacket, dedication copy, doubly inscribed to legendary genre fiction editor and enthusiast Anthony Boucher, from the collection of Duke Collier. Royal Books 36 - 63 2015 $25,000

Association – Boucherat, C.

Josephus, Flavius *(in Greek) Philabiou Josepou Hierosolymitou Heireos Ta Heuriskomena, Flavii Josephi Hierosolymitani Sacerdotis Opera Quae Extant. (Works in Greek and Latin).* Geneva: Petrus de la Rouviere, 1611. 362 x 222mm., sumptuous contemporary honey brown morocco richly gilt in modified fanfare design, covers with outer frame of multiple plain and decorative rules and rolls, frame surrounding a central panel formed by multiple plain rules and a filigree roll and featuring oblique fleurons pointing outward at corner, panel with very densely gilt and elaborate cornerpieces and a large central lozenge incorporating olive branch garlands and rosettes, an oval at center of lozenge with contemporary coat of arms of the Abbot of Potigny, either Claude Boucherat, or his cousin Charles, flat spine with a chain roll framing a single elongated panel tooled in a design similar to covers, all edges gilt, holes for ties (perhaps with small, very expert repairs at spine bottom); woodcut printer's device on titlepage, woodcut headpieces and decorative initials, Latin and Greek text printed in parallel columns, front pastedown with partially effaced 17th century ownership inscription of Henry (Becold?) Pembroke College, Oxford dated 1734 and 19th century inscription of D. C. Lewis, blank lower right corner of titlepage neatly replaced (in 19th century?) small, pale dampstain in bottom margin of a few leaves, branching marginal wormholes in half a dozen quires (but these always extremely thin and never intruding on text), minor soiling, browning and foxing here and there, still very good internally, leaves fresh, clean and with good margins; hint of wear to joints and extremities, spine uniformly little darkened (with gilt just slightly less bright tan on boards), covers with trivial discoloration and abrasions, but impressive binding in remarkable condition, entirely solid, only minor signs of use, and with once dazzling gilt nearly as good as it was 400 years ago. Phillip J. Pirages 66 - 21 2015 $6500

Association – Bowles, Paul

Transatlantic Review 16. London: Transatlantic Review, 1964. Signed by Paul Bowles at his contribution (translation of "The Oven" by Charhadi), titlepage detached and laid in, sunning to spine, good in wrappers. Ken Lopez, Bookseller 164 - 17 2015 $125

Association – Boyle, Kay

Kalugin, David *The Leaves Still Talk.* London: Villiers, 1959. First edition, fine in lightly rubbed, near fine dust jacket, inscribed by Alfred Kreymborg to Kay Boyle, April 5, 1959. Between the Covers Rare Books, Inc. 187 - 143 2015 $100

Association – Boyne, Elizabeth

Stout, Rex *A Right to Die.* New York: Viking Press, 1964. First edition, inscribed by author Dec. 26 1964 to Elizabeth Boyne, fine in fine dust jacket, from the collection of Duke Collier. Royal Books 36 - 107 2015 $2500

Association – Brackenbury, Anita Battle

Rossetti, Christina 1830-1894 *Poems.* London: Blackie and Son, 1906. Red Letter Library edition, green cloth with Mackintosh style gilt design, inscribed by author for Anita Battle Brackenbury. Between the Covers Rare Books, Inc. 187 - 238 2015 $250

Association – Bradbury, Malcolm Stanley

Hofstadter, Douglas R. *Godel, Escher, Bach: an Eternal Golden Braid.* New York: Vintage Books, 1989. Reprint, large 8vo., 16.5 x 23.5cm., large format paperback, copiously illustrated in black and white, signed presentation from author to Sir Malcolm Stanley Bradbury, about fine. Any Amount of Books 2015 - C2866 2015 £160

Knowles, John *A Separate Peace.* London: Secker & Warburg, 1959. First edition, 8vo., ex-libris plain bookplate with ownership signature of Malcolm Bradbury (British novelist) pasted to front endpaper, clean slightly used copy with Boots label on lower part of front cover, about very good in original green cloth lettered in silver at spine. Any Amount of Books 2015 - C2791 2015 £160

Madden, Deirdre *Nothing is Black.* London: Faber & Faber, 1994. 8vo., original black cloth, lettered white on spine, signed presentation from author to Malcolm Stanley Bradbury, fine in near fine dust jacket. Any Amount of Books 2015 - c3197 2015 £240

Association – Brainard, Joe

Berrigan, Ted *Bean Spasms.* New York: Kulchur Press, 1967. First edition, paperback issue, signed by all three (Berrigan, Ron Padgett and artist, Joe Brainard with a note by Berrigan for Burt Britton), fine. James S. Jaffe Rare Books Many Happy Returns - 212 2015 $1250

Berrigan, Ted *The Drunken Boat.* New York: Adventures in Poetry, 1974. First edition, inscribed by author and artist, Joe Brainard for Burt (Britton), fine. James S. Jaffe Rare Books Many Happy Returns - 29 2015 $350

Berrigan, Ted *Living with Chris.* N.P. but New York: A Boke Press Publication, n.d. but, 1968. First edition, mimeographed, inscribed by Berrigan and Joe Brainard to Burt (Britton), 4to., original stapled wrappers, cover slightly dust soiled, otherwise fine. James S. Jaffe Rare Books Many Happy Returns - 13 2015 $1250

Berrigan, Ted *Many Happy Returns.* New York: Corinth Books, 1969. First edition, one of 1500 copies, review copy with publisher's slip laid in, 12mo., original illustrated wrappers by Joe Brainard, inscribed by author for Burt Britton, titlepage also signed by Brainard, mint. James S. Jaffe Rare Books Many Happy Returns - 17 2015 $350

Berrigan, Ted *Some Things.* New York: n.p. late 1963 or 1964, First edition, drawings by Joe Brainard, one of probably fewer than 100 copies printed, signed by all authors (presumably) as issued, on this copy the artist, Joe Brainard signed two times. James S. Jaffe Rare Books Many Happy Returns - 208 2015 $1250

Elmslie, Kenward *Album.* New York: Kulchur Press, 1969. First edition, 4to., original decorated wrappers, cover and drawings by Joe Brainard, covers little sunned, otherwise fine, although not called for, this copy signed by author and artist. James S. Jaffe Rare Books Many Happy Returns - 246 2015 $350

Elmslie, Kenward *The Baby Book.* N.P.: n.p., 1965. First edition, one of 40 numbered copies signed by author and artist, out of a total edition of 500 copies, 4to., illustrations by Joe Brainard, original wrappers, fine, this copy inscribed by auhor and artist for Burt Britton. James S. Jaffe Rare Books Many Happy Returns - 236 2015 $375

Elmslie, Kenward *The 1967 Game Calendar.* N.P.: n.p., 1967. First edition, 4to., original wrappers, drawings by Joe Brainard, fine, signed by Elmslie and Brainard. James S. Jaffe Rare Books Many Happy Returns - 239 2015 $500

Elmslie, Kenward *The Orchid Stories.* Garden City: Doubleday & Co., 1973. First edition, review copy with publisher's materials laid in, 8vo., original cloth, dust jacket by Joe Brainard, fine in lightly dust soiled jacket, signed by author and artist. James S. Jaffe Rare Books Many Happy Returns - 253 2015 $250

Elmslie, Kenward *Pay Dirt.* Flint: Bamberger Books, 1992. First edition, one of 26 lettered copies signed by author and artist, 4to., illustrations by Joe Brainard, original glossy wrappers, price label on back cover, otherwise very fine. James S. Jaffe Rare Books Many Happy Returns - 254 2015 $650

Padgett, Ron *Great Balls of Fire.* Chicago: Holt Rinehart & Winston, 1969. First edition, 8vo., decorated endpapers, original cloth, dust jacket by Joe Brainard, signed by Padgett and Brainard, publisher's material laid in, spine little cocked, covers slightly rubbed, otherwise fine in slightly rubbed jacket.   James S. Jaffe Rare Books   Many Happy Returns - 149   2015 $250

Waldman, Anne *Giant Night. Poems.* New York: Corinth Books, 1970. First edition, review copy with publisher's slip laid in, 8vo., pictorial wrappers by Joe Brainard, signed by Waldman and Brainard in 1973, spine slightly darkened, otherwise fine.   James S. Jaffe Rare Books   Many Happy Returns - 259   2015 $250

Waldman, Anne *Life Notes.* Indianapolis: Bobbs Merrill, 1973. First edition, review copy with publisher's slip laid in, 8vo., illustrations by George Scheeman and author, wrappers by Joe Brainard, fine, signed by Waldman and Brainard.   James S. Jaffe Rare Books   Many Happy Returns - 266   2015 $450

Waldman, Anne *Life Notes.* Indianapolis: Bobbs Merrill, 1973. First edition, 8vo., review copy with publisher's slip laid in, illustrations by Joe Brainard, George Schneeman and author, original cloth, pictorial dust jacket by Brainard, fine, inscribed by author for Burt (Britton), also signed by Brainard.   James S. Jaffe Rare Books   Many Happy Returns - 265   2015 $200

Association – Bralove, Bob

Brandelius, Jerilyn Lee *Grateful Dead Family Album.* New York: Warner Books, 1989. First edition, 'Grateful Dead All Area Acess sticker laid down to jacket, this copy signed by band members Jerry Garcia, Mickey Hart and Bob Bralove as well as long time road crew members Ram Rod Shurtliff, Bill 'Kid' Candelario, Steve Parish and Robbie Taylor among others, hundreds of intimate photos and stories, very good plus to near fine with little soil and handling marks, in very good plus to near fine dust jacket with short closed tear to bottom of front flap.   Ed Smith Books   83 - 34   2015 $950

Association – Brand, Stewart

Kesey, Ken 1935- *News that Stayed News 1974-1984: Ten Years of CoEvolution Quarterly.* North Point: 1986. This copy inscribed by Kesey, Gary Snyder and Stewart Brand, few tiny spots to top edge, else fine in fine dust jacket.   Ken Lopez, Bookseller   164 - 103   2015 $500

Association – Branford, Mrs.

Hill, S. S. *Travels on the Shores of the Baltic. Extended to Moscow.* London: Arthur Hall, Virtue & Co., 1854. Half title, 2 pages ads, 24 page catalog (May 1854), original green cloth, blocked in blind, lettered gilt, slightly rubbed, inner hinges slightly cracking, bookplate of John Percival Hill, inscribed "Mrs. Branford from her most attached friend Mary Ann Hill".   Jarndyce Antiquarian Booksellers   CCXI - 141   2015   £280

Association – Brayer, Herbert

Graff, Everett D. *Fifty Texas Rarities. Selected from the Library of Mr. Everett D. Graff for an Exhibition to Commemorate the Hundredth Anniversary of the Annexation of Texas by the United States.* Ann Arbor: William L. Clements Library, 1946. First edition, limited to 50 copies, inscribed by Graff for Herbert Brayer, laid in is TLS by Graff for Brayer, light wear to head of spine and minor wear to extremities, else very good.   Buckingham Books   March 2015 - 31539   2015 $300

Association – Brenchley, Julius Lucius

De Lolme, John Louis *The Constitution of England, or an Account of the English Government....* London: printed by T. Spilsbury and sold by G. Kearsley, 1775. First edition in English, small blindstamp on title and cancelled inkstamp on verso of title of Maidstone Museum, first and final leaves just bit spotted or browned, contemporary half calf gilt over marbled boards, little wear to spine, but very good, 19th century armorial bookplate of Julius Lucius Brenchley.   John Drury Rare Books   2015 - 22812   2015 $787

Association – Brett, Raymond

Wordsworth, William 1770-1850 *Lyrical Ballads.* London: Methuen, 1963. Half title, original green cloth, very good in dust jacket, Geoffrey Tillotson's copy with 2 TLS's from Raymond Brett, Geoffrey adds pencil notes to presentation letter.   Jarndyce Antiquarian Booksellers   CCVII - 151   2015   £20

Association – Breuer, Bessie

Miller, Henry 1891-1980 *Scenario (A Film with Sound).* Paris: Obelisk Press, 1937. First edition, limited to 200 copies signed by author, additionally inscribed by author in 1938 to expat and friend, Bessie Breuer, original buff wrappers, gatherings loosely inserted and uncut as issued, wrappers browned with some wear and staining to front cover, light chipping to upper spine.   B & B Rare Books, Ltd.   234 - 80   2015 $2500

Association – Bright, Allan Heywood

Bonaparte, Napoleon III, Emperor of the French   1808-1873 *Fragmens Historiques 1688 et 1830.* Paris: Administration De Librairie, 1841. Inscribed on slip pasted to half title "Baron Le Crespy-Le Prince", the dedicatee is presumably the artist Charles Edouard Le Prince, Baron de Crespy (1784-1850), note pasted to front endpaper states that the inscription is the autograph of Napoleon III, but is more likely that of an amanuensis, red buckram quarter bound with red calf spine ruled and lettered gilt, from the library of Allan Heywood Bright, with his calling card loosely inserted, neat 19th century ownership inscription to titlepage, some light foxing, especially to first few pages, binding little rubbed and scuffed, otherwise very good.   Any Amount of Books   2015 - C11782   2015   £240

Bourchier, John *The History of Valiant Knight Arthur of Little Britain: a Romance of Chivalry.* London: printed for White, Cochrane & Co., 1814. Limited to 200 copies, 25 on large paper with plates in two states, this one of 175 regular copies, from the library of Allan Heywood Bright (1862-1941), with his attractive bookplate (by Downey), 4to., 25 leaves of plates, green paper covered boards with darker green cloth spine and red leather spine label, lettered gilt, possibly original publisher's binding, slight rubbing to covers and marking with foxing to prelims an slight foxing to plates, otherwise pleasing, sound, very good, copy, scarce.   Any Amount of Books   2015 - C11873   2015   £900

Digby, Kenelm   1603-1665 *Castrations from the Private Memoirs of Sir Kenelm Digby.* London: not published, 1828. First edition, 8vo., later grey buckram beveled edges, spine gilt ruled, from the library of Allan Heywood Bright (1862-1941), Liberal politician and book collector, pictorial bookplate (by Downey) on front pastedown showing coats of arms and motto "Post Tenebras Lucem" and view of the valley with hills beyond, a church and rising sun, printed as a supplement to "Private memoirs of Sir Kenelm Digby..." London Saunders and Otley 1827, text bound with additional leaves, near fine.   Any Amount of Books   2015 - C13447   2015   £180

Gibbs, John Arthur *The History of Anthony and Dorothea Gibbs and of their Contemporary Relatives...* London: Saint Catherine Press, 1922. 4to., original publisher's dark blue cloth, lettered gilt on spine and on front cover, excellent condition, slight browning to endpapers, otherwise very good+, from the library of Allan Heywood Bright (1862-1941).   Any Amount of Books   2015 - C11662   2015   £285

Gulliver's Last Voyage. London: William Cole 10 Newgate Street, 1825. First edition, 8vo., original paper covered boards with printed spine label, spine label slightly chipped with slight loss, some minor marking to boards, some slight archival restoration at spine, overall pleasing sound, very good example with clean text, scarce, from the library of Allan Heywood Bright.   Any Amount of Books   March 2015 - C14930   2015   £450

Herodianus *Herodian of Alexandria his History of the Twenty Roman Caesars and Emperors of His Time.* London: printed for Hugh Perry, 1629. Small quarto, cropping affects text of dedication page and list of emperors (sig. b), very light degree of marginal annotation throughout the book, some ink and some pencil, possibly in the hand of Thistlethwayte and or of Allan Heywood Bright (1862-1941) who owned the book in the 20th century, otherwise nice example in slightly faded and worn but very sound, attractive binding, ex-libris Alexandris Thistlthwayte, autograph note by Edmond Malone bound in and also bound in are couple of sheets of handwritten notes in later hand, binding by Haines of Liverpool, half red Levant morocco ruled gilt over marbled boards, spine with six compartments, with lettered gilt or bearing crescent and star device, marbled endpapers, top edge gilt,.   Any Amount of Books   2015 - C11789   2015   £2000

Hilary of Poitiers *Divi Hilarii Pictavorum Episcopi Lucubrationes...* Basel: Io. Frobenius, 1523. First edition, folio, 2 volumes, decorative initials and headpieces, contemporary full calf blindstamped on both sides with design of heraldic devices, rebacked (early) with red and gilt spine label, from the library of Allan Heywood Bright (1862-1941), loosely inserted is an ALS from fellow book collector E. Gordon Duff to Bright thanking him for the loan of the book, front board detached, rear joint and head and foot of spine well worn, armorial bookplate of Sir John Leveson Gower of Trentham, worming from titlepage on decreasing from about 60 holes throughout the first volume, few early ink annotations, ownership inscription of G(eorgius) Folberti(us), pencilled note identifies this book's provenance as "Sutherland Library".   Any Amount of Books   2015 - 12863   2015   £800

Maude, George Ashley *Letters from Turkey and the Crimea.* London: printed for private circulation, 1896. First edition, frontispiece laid down, original red cloth lettered gilt on upper cover, presentation from E. D. Baird to Mr. Bright (Allan Heywood Bright 1862-1941), slight foxing to fore-edge and prelims, otherwise very good, bright copy, slight foxing, otherwise very good.   Any Amount of Books   2015 - C13449   2015   £160

Yates, James *Textrinum Antiquorum: an Account of the Art of Weaving Among the Ancients. Part I.* London: Taylor and Walton, 1843. First edition, 8vo., sound, clean, very good in original green cloth lettered gilt on spine and on front cover, soundly rebacked, with new printed spine made to match and reinforcement at inner hinges, sympathetically done, cloth very faintly marked, new endpapers but old endpapers preserved, from the library of Allan Heywood Bright. Any Amount of Books   2015 - C11587   2015   £275

Association – Bright, Henry Arthur

Cruikshank, George 1792-1878 *Sir John Falstaff Knight.* London: Longman & Co., 1857. First edition, small oblong 4to., 20 leaves of plates drawn and etched by Cruikshank, contemporary half green morocco green cloth boards lettered gilt on upper cover and spine, all edges gilt by Webb & Hunt, Liverpool, marbled endpapers, extremities little rubbed, some occasional scattered foxing, very good, slight rubbing, some occasional foxing, otherwise very good, tipped in handwritten signed letter from Cruikshank to H. A. Bright.   Any Amount of Books   March 2015 - C16212   2015   £375

Haygarth, William *Greece, a Poem in Three Parts..* London: W. Bulmer and Co. for G. and W. Nicol, 1814. First edition, 4to., inscribed by author for Henry Bright, very few pencilled notes, overall very good, contemporary half green morocco over matching buckram, gilt ruled decoration and lettering, marbled endpapers and marbled page edges, some foxing to few first and last pages, edges and joints somewhat scuffed and rubbed, bookplate of Henry Arthur Bright.   Any Amount of Books   March 2015 - C12295   2015   £450

Lucretius Carus, Titus *Titi Lucretii Cari Der Rerum Natura Libri Sex.* Birminghamae: Typis Johannis Baskerville, 1772. First Baskerville edition, quarto, original full calf, spine with raised bands and decorated gilt, joints cracking, boards rather rubbed, corners bumped, spine somewhat faded and chipped top and bottom, bookplates of Rev. Edmund Maturin, clergyman and Henry Bright, English merchant, author and literary correspondent.   Any Amount of Books 2015 - C13208   2015   £280

Stephen, James *Lectures on the History of France.* London: Longman, Brown, Green & Longmans, 1851. First edition, 8vo., original light brown cloth, lettered gilt at spine, signed letter to George Melly 20 August 1830-27 Feb. 1894, Liverpool politician, from the library of Henry A. Bright with attractive armorial bookplate, some rubbing and fraying at spine ends and light scuffing to boards, otherwise sound, close very good or better, clean text and clean boards.   Any Amount of Books   2015 - C11844   2015   £180

Association – Brininstool, E. A.

Rollinson, John K. *Pony Trails in Wyoming.* Caxton Printers Ltd., 1941. First edition, 8vo., presentation inscription from E. A. Brininstool Xmas 1941 for L. H. Spragle, near fine, tight copy in dust jacket lightly chipped at spine ends, corners and extremities.   Buckingham Books   March 2015 - 29394   2015 $275

Association – Brinnin, John Malcolm

Thomas, Dylan Marlais 1914-1953 *Collected Poems 1934-1952.* London: Dent, 1952. First edition, frontispiece, 8vo., original mid blue cloth, gilt lettered backstrip, price clipped dust jacket, trifle chipped and wine stained on rear panel, short tear to front fold, very good, inscribed by author to his American agent John Malcolm Brinnin.   Blackwell's Rare Books   B179 - 243   2015   £2000

Association – Britton, Burt

Apollinaire, Guillaume *The Poet Assassinated.* New York: Holt Rinehart Winston, 1968. First American edition translated by Ron Padgett, small 4to., original pictorial boards, dust jacket, fine in slightly sunned dust jacket, inscribed by artist, Jim Dine for Burt (Britton) 1978, also inscribed with drawing by Ron Padgett (translator) to same.   James S. Jaffe Rare Books   Many Happy Returns - 192   2015 $50

Berrigan, Ted *A Feeling for Leaving.* New York: Frontward Books, 1975. First edition, limited to 400 copies, 4to., wrappers, hand colored front cover by Rochelle Kraut, very fine, inscribed by author for Burt (Britton).   James S. Jaffe Rare Books   Many Happy Returns - 32   2015 $300

Berrigan, Ted *Clear the Range.* New York: Adventures in Poetry, 1977. First edition, one of 750 copies, 8vo., original wrappers, fine, inscribed by author for Burt (Britton).   James S. Jaffe Rare Books   Many Happy Returns - 41   2015 $225

Berrigan, Ted *Guillaume Apollinaire Ist Tot. Tedichte, Prosa, Kollaborationen Mit Notizen von Tom Clark, Allen Kaplan und Rod Padgett.* Frankfurt: Marz Verlag, 1970. First edition, 8vo., photos of Berrigan and friends, original yellow printed wrappers, inscribed by author for Burt, fine.   James S. Jaffe Rare Books   Many Happy Returns - 18   2015 $400

Berrigan, Ted *In the Early Morning Rain.* New York: Cape Goliard Press in association with Grossman Pub., 1970. First American edition, review copy with publisher's slip laid in, 8vo., original boards, inscribed by author for Burt Britton, fine, cover and drawings by George Schneeman.   James S. Jaffe Rare Books   Many Happy Returns - 20   2015 $200

Berrigan, Ted *In the Early Morning Rain.* New York: Cape Goliard Press in Association with Grossman Publishers, 1970. First American edition, simultaneous paperback issue, review copy with publisher's slip laid in, inscribed by author for Burt Britton, cover and drawings by George Schneeman, fine.   James S. Jaffe Rare Books   Many Happy Returns - 25   2015 $150

Berrigan, Ted *Living with Chris.* N.P. but New York: A Boke Press Publication, n.d. but, 1968. First edition, mimeographed, inscribed by Berrigan and Joe Brainard to Burt (Britton), 4to., original stapled wrappers, cover slightly dust soiled, otherwise fine.   James S. Jaffe Rare Books   Many Happy Returns - 13   2015 $1250

Berrigan, Ted *Many Happy Returns.* New York: Corinth Books, 1969. First edition, one of 1500 copies, review copy with publisher's slip laid in, 12mo., original illustrated wrappers by Joe Brainard, inscribed by author for Burt Britton, titlepage also signed by Brainard, mint.   James S. Jaffe Rare Books   Many Happy Returns - 17   2015 $350

Berrigan, Ted *Memorial Day. A Collaboration by Anne Waldman & Ted Berrigan.* New York: The Poetry Project, 1971. First edition, mimeographed, 4to., original stapled pictorial wrappers by Donna Dennis, fine, inscribed by author for Burt (Britton).   James S. Jaffe Rare Books   Many Happy Returns - 223   2015 $450

Berrigan, Ted *Nothing for You.* Lenox: Angel Hair Books, 1977. First edition, one of 1000 copies, 8vo., illustrations, original wrappers, covers slightly dust soiled, else fine, inscribed by author for Burt (Britton).   James S. Jaffe Rare Books   Many Happy Returns - 46   2015 $250

Berrigan, Ted *Red Wagon.* Chicago: Yellow Press, 1976. First edition, simultaneous paperback issue, 8vo., original wrappers, fine, inscribed by author with small self portrait for Burt (Britton).   James S. Jaffe Rare Books   Many Happy Returns - 34   2015 $150

Berrigan, Ted *Red Wagon.* Chicago: Yellow Press, 1976. First edition, review copy with publisher's materials laid in, 8vo., original boards, dust jacket, fine, inscribed by author for Burt Britton.   James S. Jaffe Rare Books   Many Happy Returns - 37   2015 $450

Berrigan, Ted *The Drunken Boat.* New York: Adventures in Poetry, 1974. First edition, inscribed by author and artist, Joe Brainard for Burt (Britton), fine.   James S. Jaffe Rare Books   Many Happy Returns - 29   2015 $350

Brainard, Joe *29 Mini-Essays.* Calais: Z Press, 1978. First edition, one of 500 numbered copies, oblong 16mo., original wrappers, inscribed by author for Burt (Britton), covers slightly sunned, otherwise fine.   James S. Jaffe Rare Books   Many Happy Returns - 115   2015 $250

Brainard, Joe *Bolinas Journal.* Bolinas: Big Sky Books, 1971. First edition, one of 300 copies, 4to., illustrations by author, original patterned wrappers stapled as issued, fine, inscribed by author to Burt Britton.   James S. Jaffe Rare Books   Many Happy Returns - 88   2015 $250

Brainard, Joe *I Remember Christmas.* New York: Museum of Modern Art, 1973. First edition, 8vo., illustrations and original pictorial wrappers by Brainard, inscribed by author for Burt Britton, fine.   James S. Jaffe Rare Books   Many Happy Returns - 104   2015 $650

Brainard, Joe *I Remember Joe.* New York: Full Court Press, 1975. First edition, 8vo., original cloth, fine, dust jacket, inscribed by author for Burt (Britton).   James S. Jaffe Rare Books   Many Happy Returns - 110   2015 $250

Brainard, Joe *I Remember More.* New York: Angel Hair Books, 1972. First edition, one of 800 copies, small 4to., original wrappers, inscribed by author for Burt Britton, covers little age darkened, otherwise fine.   James S. Jaffe Rare Books   Many Happy Returns - 98   2015 $450

Brainard, Joe *I Remember.* New York: Angel Hair Books, 1970. First edition, limited to 700 copies, small 4to., original wrappers, fine, inscribed by author for Burt Britton.   James S. Jaffe Rare Books   Many Happy Returns - 86   2015 $450

Brainard, Joe *More I Remember More.* New York: Angel Hair Books, 1973. First edition, one of 700 copies, small 4to., original wrappers, spine little tanned, otherwise fine, inscribed by author for Burt Britton.   James S. Jaffe Rare Books   Many Happy Returns - 105   2015 $450

Brainard, Joe *New Work.* Los Angeles: Black Sparrow Press, 1973. First edition, 8vo., original wrappers, review copy with publisher's slip laid in, fine, inscribed for Burt (Britton).   James S. Jaffe Rare Books   Many Happy Returns - 106   2015 $250

Brainard, Joe *Selected Writings 1962-1971.* New York: Kulchur Foundation, 1971. First edition, small 4to., original wrappers, review copy with publisher's slip laid in, inscribed by author for Burt Britton, fine.   James S. Jaffe Rare Books   Many Happy Returns - 90   2015 $350

Brainard, Joe *Self Portrait.* New York: Siamese Banana Press, 1972. First edition, 4to., original wrappers, fine, signed by Anne Waldman and inscribed by Brainard for Burt Britton.   James S. Jaffe Rare Books   Many Happy Returns - 262   2015 $350

Brainard, Joe *The Banana Book.* New York: Siamese Banana Press, 1972. First edition, 4to., illustrations by author, original wrappers, covers little darkened, otherwise fine, inscribed by author for Burt Britton.   James S. Jaffe Rare Books   Many Happy Returns - 95   2015 $500

Brainard, Joe *The Cigarette Book.* New York: Siamese Banana Press, 1972. First edition, 4to., illustrations by author, original illustrated wrappers by author, stapled as issued, inscribed by author for Burt Britton, fine.   James S. Jaffe Rare Books   Many Happy Returns - 96   2015 $450

Cendrars, Blaise *Kodak.* New York: Adventures in Poetry, 1976. First edition translated by Ron Padgett, 4to., original black wrappers, inscribed by Padgett for Burt, mint.   James S. Jaffe Rare Books   Many Happy Returns - 195   2015 $150

Elmslie, Kenward *The Baby Book.* N.P.: n.p., 1965. First edition, one of 40 numbered copies signed by author and artist, out of a total edition of 500 copies, 4to., illustrations by Joe Brainard, original wrappers, fine, this copy inscribed by auhor and artist for Burt Britton.   James S. Jaffe Rare Books   Many Happy Returns - 236   2015 $375

Kirkwood, Jim *There Must Be a Pony!* Boston: Little Brown, 1960. First edition, inscribed by author for Burt Britton, fine in rubbed, near fine dust jacket, quite uncommon, especially signed.   Ken Lopez, Bookseller   164 - 105   2015 $350

Larbaud, Valery *Ridasedirad les Dicmhypbdf.* New York: Adventures in Poetry, 1973. First edition, one of 250 copies, 4to., original wrappers with cover illustration by Lindsay Stamm Shapiro, inscribed by Padgett for Britton, fine.   James S. Jaffe Rare Books   Many Happy Returns - 197   2015 $250

MacBeth, George *Interview with Ted Berrigan.* N.P.: Ignu Publications, 1971. First edition, narrow 4to., original wrappers with holograph title, signed by MacBeth and inscribed by Berrigan to Burt (Britton), covers little dusty, otherwise fine.   James S. Jaffe Rare Books   Many Happy Returns - 81   2015 $650

McCarthy, Mary *Winter Visitors.* New York: Harcourt Brace Jovanovich, 1970. First edition, 12mo., quarter cloth and papercovered boards, fine in near fine glassine dust jacket, published hors commerce , publisher's card laid in, inscribed by author for Burt Britton.   Between the Covers Rare Books, Inc.   187 - 171   2015 $375

Osborne, John *A Patriot for Me.* London: Faber and Faber, 1966. First edition, fine in fine, price clipped dust jacket with just touch of rubbing, inscribed by author to NY literary figure Burt Britton, nicer than usual.   Between the Covers Rare Books, Inc.   187 - 207   2015 $150

Padgett, Ron *100,000 Fleeing Hilda.* Tulsa: Boke Press, 1967. First edition, 8vo., limited to 300 numbered copies signed by author and artist, illustrations by Joe Brainard, original wrappers, white covers slightly darkened and dust soiled, otherwise fine, this copy inscribed by Padgett to Burt Britton.   James S. Jaffe Rare Books   Many Happy Returns - 270   2015 $250

Padgett, Ron *Crazy Compositions.* Bolinas: Big Sky, 1974. First edition, original glossy wrappers, illustrations by George Scheeman, limited to 750 copies, inscribed by Padgett with self portrait for Burt Britton, fine.   James S. Jaffe Rare Books   Many Happy Returns - 156   2015 $125

Padgett, Ron *Grosse Feuerballe Gedichte, Prosa, Bilder.* Hamburg: Rowholt, 1973. First German edition, 12mo., illustrations, original wrappers, inscribed from author for Burt Britton, fine.   James S. Jaffe Rare Books   Many Happy Returns - 154   2015 $150

Padgett, Ron *Sweet Pea.* London: Aloes Books, 1971. First edition, limited to 200 copies, 16mo., original wrappers, inscribed by Padgett for Burt Britton, fine.   James S. Jaffe Rare Books   Many Happy Returns - 153   2015 $2500

Padgett, Ron *Sweet Pea.* London: Aloes Books, 1971. First edition, one of 25 numbered copies signed by Padgett & artist George Schneeman, out of a total edition of 200 copies, illustrations and cover by Schneeman, oblong 16mo., original wrappers, fine, inscribed by Padgett for Burt Britton.   James S. Jaffe Rare Books   Many Happy Returns - 152   2015 $600

Waldman, Anne *Life Notes.* Indianapolis: Bobbs Merrill, 1973. First edition, 8vo., review copy with publisher's slip laid in, illustrations by Joe Brainard, George Schneeman and author, original cloth, pictorial dust jacket by Brainard, fine, inscribed by author for Burt (Britton), also signed by Brainard.   James S. Jaffe Rare Books   Many Happy Returns - 265   2015 $200

Association – Broca, Pierre Paul

Barbette, Paul *Opera Chirurgico-Anatomica ad circularem Sanguinis Motum...* Lugd. Batav. (Leiden): Ex Officina Hackiana, 1672. First Latin edition, 12mo., engraved titlepage, letterpress titlepage with woodcut vignette, and one full page engraving, contemporary full vellum, title in manuscript on spine, edges sprinkled brown, Bookplate of Dr. Pierre Broca, small contemporary owner's name in ink on titlepage, two later ownership signatures on front pastedown, vellum moderately darkened with light bowing to front board, very good, scarce, true first Latin edition, 2 fine copperplate engravings.   Between the Covers Rare Books   196 - 112   2015 $2000

Association – Bromer, Dirk

Todhunter, Isaac *A History of the Mathematical Theories of Attraction and the Figure of the Earth from the Time Of Newton to that of La Place.* New York: Dover, 1962. Reprint of 1873 Macmillan edition, 8vo., 2 volumes in 1, blue cloth, gilt stamped spine title, dust jacket rubbed, else fine, Dirk Bromer's copy (recipient of Bruce Medal in 1966). Jeff Weber Rare Books 178 - 1072 2015 $135

Association – Bromsen, Maury

Neruda, Pablo *El Habitante Y Su Espersanza.* Santiago di Chile: Editorial Nascimento, 1926. First edition, inscribed to American bookseller Maury Bromsen. Honey & Wax Booksellers 2 - 53 2015 $3000

Association – Bronowski, Jacob

Popper, Karl R. *Birkhoff and Von Neumann's Interpretation of Quantum Mechanics.* Nature, Volume 219, August 17, 1968. Offprint, 4to., first separate edition, self wrappers, mild toning, edge wear, two horizontal creases, 4to., nice association copy, from Jacob Bronowski's library with his annotations. By the Book, L. C. 44 - 18 2015 $600

Association – Brook, Alice

Jefferies, Richard 1848-1887 *After London; or Wild England.* London: Cassell and Co., 1885. First edition, half title, 8 pages ads (3.85), original grey cloth, bevelled boards, binding slightly loose, hinges slightly cracking, presentation inscription "John & Alice Brook from the author May 10th 1885", very good. Jarndyce Antiquarian Booksellers CCXI - 158 2015 £1500

Association – Brook, John

Jefferies, Richard 1848-1887 *After London; or Wild England.* London: Cassell and Co., 1885. First edition, half title, 8 pages ads (3.85), original grey cloth, bevelled boards, binding slightly loose, hinges slightly cracking, presentation inscription "John & Alice Brook from the author May 10th 1885", very good. Jarndyce Antiquarian Booksellers CCXI - 158 2015 £1500

Association – Brooke, Stephen

Miller, George Frazier *Adventism Answered.* Brooklyn: Guide Printing & Publishing Co., 1905. First edition, octavo, 214 pages, light brown cloth stamped in black, very slight soiling on cloth, near fine or better, inscribed by author for Stephen T. Brooke, uncommon. Between the Covers Rare Books 197 - 36 2015 $1500

Association – Brooks, Peggy

Kennedy, William 1928- *Legs.* New York: Coward, McCann & Geoghegan, 1975. Uncorrected proof, couple of small smudges or spots on wrappers, else just about fine, ownership signature of Hunter S. Thompson on front blank, TLS from senior editor, Peggy Brooks to Thompson sending the proof and soliciting a blurb from him. Between the Covers Rare Books 196 - 83 2015 $2500

Association – Brooks, Van Wyck

Zapf, Hermann *Manuale Typographicum 100 Typographical Arrangements.* Frankfurt am main: D. Stempel, 1954. First edition, Limited to 1000 copies, oblong 8vo., publisher's parchment backed cloth with "MT" in gilt on front cover, later cardboard slipcase, typographic displays, printed in red and black, prospectus for Museum Books loosely inserted, parchment spine age darkened, presentation from Zapf to Van Wyck Brooks. Oak Knoll Books Special Catalogue 24 - 63 2015 $425

Association – Brotherton, F.

Maginnis, Arthur *The Atlantic Ferry, Its Ships, Men and Working, First Popular Edition.* Whitaker & Co., 1893. Half title, frontispiece, plates and illustrations, lacking following pastedown, 'yellowback', original printed yellow boards, following hinge slightly cracking, otherwise fine, ownership name of F. Brotherton, Gloucester. Jarndyce Antiquarian Booksellers CCXI - 193 2015 £150

Association – Browell, Edward Mash

Ibbetson, Julius Caesar *A Picturesque Guide to Bath, Bristol, Hot Wells, The River Avon and the Adjacent Country...* London: Hookham and Carpenter, 1793. Large paper copy, 4to., 16 aquatint plates with fine contemporary hand colouring, contemporary half russia with flat spine lettered in gilt, some minor chipping to extremities and upper hinge cracked with early ownership on title "Thos Howell" and unusually colorful heraldic bookplate of Edward Mash Browell. Marlborough Rare Books List 54 - 47 2015 £1750

Association – Brower, David

Porter, Eliot *The Place No One Knew: Glen Canyon on the Colorado.* San Francisco: Sierra Club, 1966. First revised and expanded edition, signed by editor, David Brower, Folio, 80 exquisite color photos, cloth, very fine, pictorial dust jacket. Argonaut Book Shop Holiday Season 2014 - 231 2015 $200

Association – Browne, Thomas

Cleveland, John *The Idol of the Clownes or Insurrection of Wat the Tyler with His Priests Baal and Straw...* London: in the Year, 1654. Second edition, small 8vo., without engraved portrait found in some copies and without final blank, light dampstaining to first few leaves, closely shaved at head (just touching pagination in places), early 19th century calf, covers ruled in gilt, spine tooled in gilt and blind, marbled edges and endpapers, small stain on front cover and minor repair on rear, old front flyleaf preserved, from the library of James Stevens Cox (1910-1997), with late 17th/early 18th century inscription "Thomas Browne/His booke", not that of Sir Thomas Browne (1605-1682), with bookplate of Albert M. Cohn, posthumous sale, Christie 26/2/1934 lot 176 (as Sir Thomas Browne's copy), £5 to Charles H. Stonehill.   Maggs Bros. Ltd.   1447 - 102   2015   £200

Association – Broyard, Anatole

Schwartz, Delmore *Vaudeville for a Princess.* New York: New Directions, 1950. First edition, 8vo., original cloth, dust jacket, fine in fine jacket, presentation copy inscribed by author for friend Anatole Broyard.   James S. Jaffe Rare Books   Modern American Poetry - 249   2015 $1250

Association – Brunner, John

Glass, I. I. *Shock Waves and Man.* Toronto: University of Toronto, Institute for Aerospace Studies, 1974. First edition, 8vo., signed presentation from author for John Brunner, attractive Brunner bookplate, very good+ in like jacket.   Any Amount of Books   2015 - A66971   2015   £150

Association – Bruschwig, Silvain S.

Congreve, William 1670-1729 *The Way of the World.* London: printed for Jacob Tonson, 1700. First edition, half title, ad verso of last leaf, variant with catchword 'Enter' on page 80, small hole in E3 with loss of two letters on either side of leaf and three more touched on verso (sense recoverable), trifle browned, light staining to upper margin, 4to., half blue morocco (presumably for Rosenbach), spine gilt lettered longitudinally between gilt panels at either end, small leather booklabel on front pastedown, monogram SSB (Silvain S. Bruschwig), offset onto foot of label "From the Rosenbach Collections" with a summary description, later Quaritch collation note inside back cover, good. Blackwell's Rare Books   B179 - 32   2015   £1750

Association – Bryce, R. J.

Quintilian *Institutionum Oratioriarum Libri XII. Diligentius Recogniti MDXXII. Index capitum Totius Operis.* Venice: in aedibus Aldi et Andreae Soceri, 1521. Second Aldine edition, one small wormhole in text of first 30 and last 60 leaves (often touching a character but without loss of legibility), scattering of other small holes in margins of first and last 30 leaves, light browning at beginning and end, faint marginal dampmark to early leaves, some old marginal notes and underlining, inscriptions to title (one struck through, one dated 1630, slightly abraded, third a nineteenth century gift inscription - From James Heming to Rev. Dr. R. J. Bryce), 4to., 18th century calf, scratched and marked, corners worn, sometime serviceably rebacked, backstrip with five raised bands, red labels in second and last compartments, new endpapers, sound.   Blackwell's Rare Books   Greek & Latin Classics VI - 86   2015   £550

Association – Bryher

Windeler, B. C. *Elimus.* Paris: Three Mountains Press, 1923. First edition, Bryher's copy with her bookplate, wonderful association as Bryher financed McAlmon's Contact Press, small 4to., hardcover, illustrations by D. Shakespeare and Robert Dill.   Beasley Books   2013 - 2015 $400

Association – Buccleuch, Mary Montagu Douglas Scott, Duchess of

Seago, Edward *With Capricorn to Paris.* London: Published by Collins, 1956. First edition, 8vo., frontispiece and 7 plates, several illustrations in text, signed presentation from author to Mollie (Mary Montagu Douglas Scott, Duchess of Buccleuch 1900-1968), very good in near very good, used dust jacket little chipped and nicked at edges but with only minor loss and still presentable.   Any Amount of Books   2015 - A72902   2015   £160

Association – Buckingham, Lew

Ellroy, James *Blood on the Moon.* New York: Mysterious Press, 1984. First edition, presentation inscription on front endpaper to Lew Buckingham, by author, fine, unread copy in dust jacket.   Buckingham Books   March 2015 - 32057   2015 $275

Association – Buel, Mrs.

Shaver, J. R. *Little Shavers: Sketches from Real Life.* New York: Century Co., 1913. First edition, small octavo, grey cloth with applied illustration, corners bumped and rubbed, nice and tight, very good, inscribed by editor of Vanity Fair Frank Crowninshield for Mrs. Buel Xmas 1913.   Between the Covers Rare Books, Inc.   187 - 51   2015 $200

Association – Bukowski, Charles

Amidei, Sergio *Tales of Ordinary Madness.* Rome: Nuova Stampa, 1981. Screenplay by Amidei and Ferreri, this copy signed by Charles Bukowski on front cover, velobound with gray cardstock covers and typed label on front cover, near fine, scarce, signed by Charles Bukowski on front cover.   Ken Lopez, Bookseller   164 - 23   2015 $3500

Association – Bull, Richard

Schopper, Hartmann *De Omnibus Illiberalibus Sive Mechanicis Artibus.* Frankfurt: Georg Rabe (Corvinus) for Sigismund Carl Feyerabend, 1574. Second edition in Latin, small 8vo., woodcut printer's device on title ruled in red, another on final recto with colophon on verso, 132 woodcut illustrations by Jost Amman, all but one printed on rectos only, full straight grain red morocco by Roger Payne, spine lettered in gilt, gilt edges with armorial bookplate of Richard Bull of Ongar and signature Roger Payne, Delt on small piece pasted to front free endpaper, fine.   Marlborough Rare Books   List 53 - 1   2015   £7850

Association – Bunbury, Henry Edward, 7th Baronet

Blount, Thomas Pope   1649-1697 *De Re Poetica; or Remarks Upon Poetry with Characters and Censures of the Most Considerable Poets, Whether Ancient or Modern.* London: for Ric(hard) Everingham, 1694. First edition, small 4to., occasional spotting and browning, small marginal tear to L1, contemporary calf, covers panelled in blind, spine with late 18th century elaborate gilt tooling with armorial crest of Bunbury (Sir Henry Edward Bunbury, 7th Baronet 1778-1860) in top panel (joints and corners rubbed), bookplate and gilt crest, from the library of James Stevens Cox (1910-1997).   Maggs Bros. Ltd.   1447 - 32   2015   £220

Association – Burchell, Ruth

Burchell, William John *Travels in the Interior of Southern Africa.* London: printed for Longman, Hurst, Rees, Orme and Brown, 1822-1824. First edition, 2 volumes, quarto, bound without half titles and final blank in first volume but with the 4 page "Hints on Emigration to the Cape of Good Hope" (which was printed separately in 1824 and not found in all copies), with half page errata slip to beginning of volume 1, largely folding engraved map, 20 hand colored aquatint plates, 96 wood engraved vignettes, inscribed by author for niece Ruth Burchell, contemporary purple morocco, expertly rabacked to style over blue morocco, covers with elaborate gilt panels, spines with gilt on compartments and lettering, all edges gilt, some offsetting from plates, map with some minor fold tears, ZZ4 volume two with one inch tear to upper blank margin (not affecting any lettering), hinges starting, previous owner's bookplate of each volume, overall very good, tight and clean.   Heritage Book Shop Holiday 2014 - 23   2015 $12,500

Association – Burgh, W.

Robertson, Alexander *Poems on Various Subjects and Occasions...* Edinburgh: printed for Ch. Alexander and sold at his house in Geddes's Close....n.d., 1752? First edition, 8vo., contemporary sheep, spine gilt, little rubbed, sound, lacks label, very good, early signature on titlepage of W. Burgh, later armorial bookplate of H. F. Davies, Elmley Castle.   C. R. Johnson   Foxon R-Z - 831r-z   2015 $536

Association – Burt, Henry

Ayres, Philip *Cupids address to the Ladies.* London: sold by R. Bently, 5 Tidmarsh, 1683. First edition, small 8vo., engraved throughout, 44 engraved emblem plates, without final blank leaf, small chip torn from fore-margin of titlepage, titlepage lightly soiled, small unobtrusive waterstaining to upper blank margin of first third of the work, short tear to foot of L1, contemporary calf, gilt spine with brown morocco label, corners, head and foot of spine repaired, this copy includes, presumably autograph, 20 line commendatory poem by poet and playwright Nahum Tate addressed "To My Honb. Friend Philip Ayres esq on his book of Emblems in four Languages", 18th century signature Henry Burt, large bookplate removed, from the library of James Stevens Cox (1910-1997).   Maggs Bros. Ltd.   1447 - 15   2015   £3500

Association – Bush, Erik

Worcester, G. R. G. *Sail and Sweep in China.* London: Her Majesty's Stationery Office, 1966. First edition, signed and inscribed to Captain Erik Bush (1899-1985) and dated in year of publication by author, small 4to., very good++, foxing and cover edge wear in very good dust jacket with foxing, mild chips and scuffs, scarce.   By the Book, L. C. 44 - 66   2015 $250

Association – Bushnell, G. H.

Wauchope, Robert *Handbook of Middle American Indians.* Austin: University of Texas Press, First editions, Set (volumes 1-16), hardback, all volumes but 5 and 6 have jackets, clean very good+ copies in mostly very good dust jackets with some slight rubbing and toning and occasional light wear, illustrations, maps, plans, diagrams, from the library of Prof. G. H. Bushnell (103-1978) Curator of Cambridge Univ. Museum.   Any Amount of Books   2015 - A49503   2015   £300

Association – Butler

Napier, Charles James *Memoir on the Roads of Cefalonia.* London: James Ridgway, 1825. First edition, 8vo., 5 engraved lithographic plates, original boards, uncut, very good with Mountgarret (i.e. Butler family) armorial bookplate, unidentified early 19th century Book Society subscription list on pastedown, rare.   John Drury Rare Books 2015 - 24015   2015 $2185

Association – Butler, Cyril Kendall

Man, John *The History and Antiquities Ancient and Modern of the Borough of Reading, in the County of Berks.* Reading: printed for Snare and Man...., 1816. 4to., titlepage printed in red and black, some old damage to 3A2-3, 3B3 & 3C3, without loss, 21 aquatint and engraved maps, views and portraits, 19th century black morocco over marbled boards, somewhat rubbed, engraved armorial bookplate of Cyril Kendall Butler of Bourton House. Marlborough Rare Books   List 53 - 25   2015   £150

Association – Butt, John

Dyson, H. V. D. *Augustans and Romantics 1689-1830.* London: Cresset Press, 1940. Half title, original grey green cloth, inscribed to Geoffrey and Kathleen Tillotson by John Butt.   Jarndyce Antiquarian Booksellers   CCVII - 253   2015   £20

Association – Buxton, A. F.

Butler, Arthur Gray *The Three Friends: a Story of Rugby in the Forties.* London: Henry Frowde, 1900. Original maroon cloth, spine slightly faded, signed by A. F. Buxton, Christmas 1900 and Kathleen Tillotson Oct. 1594, ALS from Dorothy Ward to Kathleen.   Jarndyce Antiquarian Booksellers   CCVII - 124   2015   £40

Association – Byers, J. Frederic

Dodgson, Charles Lutwidge   1832-1898 *Alice's Adventures in Wonderland. (with) Through the Looking-Glass and What Alice Found There.* London: Macmillan, 1870-1873. Later printings, illustrations by John Tenniel, finely bound in full red calf by Root and Son, boards stamped after original cloth bindings with illustrations of Alice and Cheshire Cat and the Red and White Queens, with the original cloth bound into rear of texts, very good with some light wear and rubbing to extremities, minor toning to spine and board edges, light rubbing to spines and hinges, Looking Glass with shallow chip to spine head, bookplates of noted art collector and art historian, J. Frederic Byers, bright and clean pages, overall lovely, finely bound copy.   B & B Rare Books, Ltd.   2015 - 2015 $1500

Association – Bygott, James

Fraser, Alexander *The Account of the Proceedings at the Festival of the Society of Freemasons at their Hall on Wednesday the 27th of Jan. 1813...* London: printed for Brother James Asperne, 1813. First edition, 8vo., 2 engraved portraits, engraved plate, double page engraved facsimile of ticket of admission to the festival, minor foxing and slight paper browning, contemporary half calf over marbled boards, general light wear to binding, good, sound with early 19th century ownership signature of James Bygott and later ms. note that this copy was presented in 1868 to the Witham Lodge, very rare.   John Drury Rare Books   March 2015 - 21853   2015 $874

Association – Bynner, Witter

Ford, Julia Ellsworth *Snickerty Nick and the Giant.* New York: Moffat Yard, 1919. First edition, 4to., blue pictorial cloth, near fine, illustrations by Arthur Rackham with 3 color plates, 10 full page black and whites, lovely inscription from Julia Ford Ellsworth and signed by Witter Bynner. Aleph-bet Books, Inc.   109 - 404   2015 $850

Harwood, Anthony *Swan Song and Other Poems.* London: Favil Press, 1961. First edition, fine in near fine dust jacket with some soiling and tiny tears, Witter Bynner's copy with his bookplate.   Between the Covers Rare Books, Inc.   187 - 119   2015 $65

Association – Byshopp, Cecil

Cooper, W. D. *The History of South America, Containing the Discoveries of Columbus, the Conquest of Mexico and Peru...* London: E. Newbery, 1789. First edition, 16mo., 14 x 9cm., frontispiece, 5 engraved plates, full brown tree calf with plain leather gilt lettered spine with 7 gold bands, sound clean, very good copy with few marks to leather, front endpaper excised, bookplate of one Cecil Byshopp and note dated 1791 in neat sepia ink about the gifting of the book from Katherine Byshopp, first blank has modern neat name, plates and text noticeably clean and bright.   Any Amount of Books   2015 - A66548   2015   £320

Association – Byshopp, Katherine

Cooper, W. D. *The History of South America, Containing the Discoveries of Columbus, the Conquest of Mexico and Peru...* London: E. Newbery, 1789. First edition, 16mo., 14 x 9cm., frontispiece, 5 engraved plates, full brown tree calf with plain leather gilt lettered spine with 7 gold bands, sound clean, very good copy with few marks to leather, front endpaper excised, bookplate of one Cecil Byshopp and note dated 1791 in neat sepia ink about the gifting of the book from Katherine Byshopp, first blank has modern neat name, plates and text noticeably clean and bright.   Any Amount of Books   2015 - A66548   2015   £320

Association – Cairns, Huntington

Read, Herbert *Collected Poems.* London: Faber & Faber Ltd., 1946. First edition, sunned at spine ends, else near fine in about very good dust jacket with corresponding chips at spine ends, inscribed, but not signed, by author to Huntington Cairns.   Between the Covers Rare Books, Inc.   187 - 230   2015 $250

Association – Caldwell, Sam

Mead, Richard *De Imperio solis ac Lunae in Corpora Humana et Morbis Inde Oriundis.* Raphael Smtih, 1704. First edition, title very slightly soiled, 8vo., crisp copy in contemporary Cambridge style calf, corners worn, rebacked, covers bowing, contemporary ownership inscription on title Wm. Dalzell, and on flyleaf of Sam. Caldwell, recording his purchase of the book in Dublin in 1754.   Blackwell's Rare Books   B179 - 72   2015   £750

Association – Cambridge, George, Duke of

Fry, Elizabeth *Observations on the Visiting, Superintendence, and Government of Female Prisoners.* London: John and Arthur Arch and W. Wilkin Norwich, 1827. First edition, 12mo., contemporary red straight grain morocco, sides panelled gilt, spine fully gilt with raised bands, joints and extremities rubbed, else handsome copy, all edges gilt, from the library of Prince George, Duke of Cambridge, Earl of Tipperary, Baron Culloden (1850-1904) with his posthumous bookplate Dec. 1904, and subsequent armorial bookplate of Wigan Free Public Library with blindstamp at foot of titlepage, ink stamp on blank verso and further blindstamp on final leaf, uncommon, particularly pleasing copy.   John Drury Rare Books   2015 - 25151   2015 $1136

Association – Camden, Lord

Lonsdale, John, Viscount *Memoir of the Reign of James II.* York: privately printed, 1808. First edition, 4to., half leather, marbled boards, signed presentation from author for Lord Camden, endpapers foxed, corners and spine slightly rubbed, otherwise very good, sound, clean copy with clean text.   Any Amount of Books   2015 - A77543   2015   £160

Association – Camholt, Robertus

Ovidius Naso, Publius *Metamorphoseon.* Lugduni: Sebastianius Gryphius, 1553. 178 x 108mm. without final blank, contemporary calf by Jacob Bathen of Louvain with Bathen's elaborately blindstamped "Spes" binder's device and initials "I. B." in lower left, raised bands, spine with simple blind ruling, pastedowns removed exposing construction of the binding, first and last gatherings protected by strips from a 13th century vellum French or Southern Netherlandish Breviary (very expertly rebacked to style with restoration at corners), publisher's woodcut griffin device on titlepage, later (18th century?) ownership inscription of C. N. Cuvier on titlepage, rear flyleaf with early note in Latin, remnants of rear pastedown with signature of (Ro)bertus Camholt; little splaying to upper board, covers with slight crackling, but expertly restored binding entirely solid and details of panel stamps very sharp, faint dampstain cover small portion of many leaves at bottom (another dampstain sometimes at top with about half the page affected in four quires near end), minor soiling, here and there, two leaves with darker, though smaller areas of soiling, not without condition issues, internally but nothing fatal, text both fresh and with ample margins.   Phillip J. Pirages   66 - 13   2015 $4200

Association – Campbell, Archibald

Robison, John *Proofs of a Conspiracy Against all the Religions and Governments of Europe, Carried on in the Secret Meetings of Free Masons.* London & Edinburgh: T. Cadell Jun. and W. Davies, Strand and W. Creech, 1797. Second edition, 8vo., contemporary tree calf, rubbed at spine with spine lettering or label absent, very slight splitting at hinge ends, but sound, close to very good with clean text and heraldic (stag) bookplate of Archibald Campbell.   Any Amount of Books   March 2015 - A89311   2015   £350

Association – Campbell, Barbara Douglas

Polehampton, Edward *The Gallery of Nature and Art; or a Tour Through Creation and Science.* London: printed for R. N. Rose, 1821. New edition, 6 volumes, attractive contemporary brown polished calf, 216 x 133mm., covers with gilt fleur-de-lys and blindstamped palmette borders, large oblong octagonal panel at center of each board, all volumes with contemporary landscape paintings, three of these signed by R. Ashton, one dated 1821 (but all by the same hand), wide raised bands painted black and tooled gilt, spine panels with central arabesque surrounded by curling vines, gilt titling, marbled edges (very small and expert repairs apparently made to the ends of joints on two of the volumes); 7 illustrations within text and a total of 94 engraved plates, including a frontispiece for each volume one of which is foldout plate and of which two plates are comprised of two illustrations each, front flyleaves with inscription of Barbara Douglas Campbell dated 1st Jan. 1822 and with later indecipherable inscription below; just minor rubbing to joints and extremities (a portion of one joint with shallow damage from an insect), one landscape with small cluster of gouges, superficial scratches to some of the other scenes, variable (mostly faint) offsetting from plates, other trivial imperfections, but still extremely attractive set, text fresh and clean, bindings lustrous with virtually all of the original appeal intact.   Phillip J. Pirages   66 - 79   2015 $7000

Association – Campbell, John

Williams, John D. *Williams & Packard's Original Gems of Penmanship Respectfully Dedicated to Bryant, Stratton and Co's International Chain of Business Colleges.* New York: D. Appleton & Co., 1867. First edition, oblong small 4to., original leather backed boards, spine covering missing, engraved titlepage, 47 engraved plates, covers detached with leather spine covering lacking, internally very good, old calligraphic inscription on front free endpaper " John R. Campbell's Book.   Oak Knoll Books   306 - 245   2015 $350

Association – Candealrio, Bill

Brandelius, Jerilyn Lee *Grateful Dead Family Album.* New York: Warner Books, 1989. First edition, 'Grateful Dead All Area Access sticker laid down to jacket, this copy signed by band members Jerry Garcia, Mickey Hart and Bob Bralove as well as long time road crew members Ram Rod Shurtliff, Bill 'Kid' Candelario, Steve Parish and Robbie Taylor among others, hundreds of intimate photos and stories, very good plus to near fine with little soil and handling marks, in very good plus to near fine dust jacket with short closed tear to bottom of front flap.   Ed Smith Books   83 - 34   2015 $950

Association – Cane, Melville

Russell, Bertrand   1872-1970 *Bolshevism: Practice and Theory.* New York: Harcourt Brace and Howe, 1920. First American edition, spine little toned, very good, without dust jacket, American poet Melville Cane's copy with his ownership signature.   Between the Covers Rare Books, Inc.   187 - 239   2015 $100

Association – Canning, Charles

Balmford, William *The Seaman's Spiritual Companion or Navigation Spiritualized.* London: for Benj. Harris, 1678. First edition, small 8vo., variant state of title with double rule border and price on titlepage, A2 shaved at foot affecting signature and catchword on recto, minor worming in upper outer corner of D4-K8 (affecting end of text in places), stain to B3-E2 affecting three lines, occasional foxing, small hole from paper flaw in lower margin of E2, short tear at foot of F3 slightly affecting last line on recto and catchword on verso, small hole from paper flaw in centre of I2 touching two lines, actually reasonable and much loved copy, contemporary sheep (rubbed, covers scuffed, fore edge of lower cover worn exposing board, corners worn), several pen trials, scribbles, ownership inscriptions John Allab(on) His Booke October ye 24th 16, Charles Canning his book 1679, James Purnell His Booke Anno Domini (deleted), "Thomas Nichols His Book May ye 10 1718", "James Croome His Book March ye 9th 1757" "Jane Hanley", from the library of James Stevens Cox (1910-1997).   Maggs Bros. Ltd.   1447 - 21   2015   £2800

Association – Canning, Edward J.

Cable, George Washington   1844-1925 *Bonaventure. A Prose Pastoral of Acadian Louisiana.* New York: Charles Scribner's Sons, 1899. 8vo., 314 pages, original cloth, very good ex-library, fine ink presentation inscription from Cable to Edward J. Canning, head gardener at Smith College, Mass.   M & S Rare Books, Inc.   97 - 46   2015 $225

Association – Carey, M. L.

Church of England. Book of Common Prayer *The Book of Common Prayer... together with The Psalter or Psalms of David.* Oxford: Clarendon Press, 1783. 1784, 140 x 83mm., very appealing contemporary vellum over boards, almost certainly by Edwards of Halifax, covers bordered by a neoclassical pentaglyph and metope roll against a blue wash, center of each board with large gilt bordered medallion containing gilt monogram "M L C" on a blue background, flat spine divided into panels by gilt pentaglyph and metope border (the one at bottom over blue wash), panels with classical urn centerpiece and volute cornerpieces, second panel with gilt titling on blue background, turn-ins with gilt chain roll, marbled endpapers, all edges gilt, with fine fore-edge painting, very probably by Edwards, depicting Fountains Abbey In Yorkshire, in original (rubbed and soiled but quite intact) soft green leather slipcase, titlepage with ink ownership inscription of M. L. Carey, spine gilt slightly dulled in places, rear turn-in lifting a little at one corner, title and couple of gatherings with moderate foxing, still quite excellent copy binding showing no wear, text clean and fresh and painting well preserved. Phillip J. Pirages 66 - 46 2015 $5500

Association – Carey, Tom

Schuyler, James *Broadway: a Poets and Painters Anthology.* New York: Swollen Magpie Press, 1979. First edition, 4to., illustrations, original wrappers with front cover illustration by Paula North, covers slightly dust soiled, one tiny short closed tear, presentation copy inscribed by Schuyler for Tom (Carey). James S. Jaffe Rare Books Many Happy Returns - 392 2015 $750

Association – Carman, Harry James

Ernst, Robert *Immigrant Life in New York City 1825-1863.* New York: King's Crown Press, Columbia University, 1949. First edition, octavo, blue cloth, little spotting on boards, else fine without dust jacket, dedication copy inscribed for Harry James Carman, Dean of Columbia College. Between the Covers Rare Books, Inc. 187 - 90 2015 $300

Association – Carnall, Geoffrey

Butt, John *Pope, Dickens and Others: Essays and Addresses.* Edinburgh: University Press, 1969. First edition, half title, original pink cloth, very good, with correspondence between editor, Geoffrey Carnall and Kathleen Tillotson. Jarndyce Antiquarian Booksellers CCVII - 127 2015 £25

Association – Carr, Virginia Spencer

Price, Reynolds 1933- *Clear Pictures.* New York: Atheneum, 1989. First edition, previous owner gift inscription, else fine in fine, price clipped dust jacket, inscribed by author to Virginia Spencer Carr. Ken Lopez, Bookseller 164 - 168 2015 $100

Price, Reynolds 1933- *Letter to a Godchild.* New York: Scribner, 2006. First edition, fine in fine dust jacket, inscribed by author in year of publication to Virginia Spencer Carr. Ken Lopez, Bookseller 164 - 171 2015 $100

Price, Reynolds 1933- *A Serious Way of Wondering.* New York: Scribner, 2003. First edition, fine in fine dust jacket, inscribed by author to Virginia Spencer Carr, with couple of Carr's notes to herself laid in, one with Price's e-mail address. Ken Lopez, Bookseller 164 - 170 2015 $150

Association – Carrington, Solomon

Du Bois, William Edward Burghardt 1868-1963 *The Souls of Black Folk.* Chicago: McClurg, 1903. First edition, front hinge repaired, moderate loss to the corners and spinal extremities, contemporary owner's signature (Solomon Carrington of Walden, Massachusetts) and later embossed stamp of well-known collector, both on front fly, very good with spine and front board lettering legible and clear, very uncommon. Between the Covers Rare Books 197 - 16 2015 $4000

Association – Carroll, Jim

Berrigan, Ted *Red Wagon.* Chicago: Yellow Press, 1976. First edition, simultaneous paperback issue, 8vo., original wrappers, Jim Carroll's copy with his ownership signature and date 1977, inscribed to him by author, with Carroll's notations throughout and with fragment of poem in Carroll's hand on separate folded sheet of paper laid in, covers bit rubbed and sunned, otherwise fine. James S. Jaffe Rare Books Many Happy Returns - 35 2015 $1750

Berrigan, Ted *Sonnets.* New York: Grove Press, 1964. First trade edition, paperback original, inscribed by author for Jim Carroll, pen scribbles, covers somewhat rubbed, upper corner of front wrapper dampstained, still good. James S. Jaffe Rare Books Many Happy Returns - 6 2015 $1500

Association – Carter, Angela

Le Clezio, J. M. G. *War.* London: Jonathan Cape, 1973. First English edition, 8vo., pages 300, groovy pink jacket by Bill Botten, fine in near fine dust jacket with very short closed tear and very slight rubbing at corners, from the working library of novelist Angela Carter (1940-1992) with her posthumous bookplate.   Any Amount of Books   2015 - C7841   2015   £175

Levy, Deborah *An Amorous Discourse in the Suburbs of Hell.* London: Jonathan Cape, 1990. First edition, wrappers, 8vo., pages 77, illustrations by Polish artist Andrzej Borkowsk, large format paperback, very slight handling wear, but pretty much fine, from the working library of novelist Angela Carter (1940-1992) with her posthumous bookplate.   Any Amount of Books   2015 - A63695   2015   £180

Sclauzero, Mariarosa *Narcissism and Death.* Barrytown: Station Hill Press, 1984. First edition, small 4to., wrappers, 10 illustrations by Sue Coe, signed presentation from author to Angela Carter, novelist, with posthumous bookplate, loosely inserted flier for Stamperia Valdonega limited edition, very slight rubbing, faint edgewear, very good+.   Any Amount of Books   2015 - A64551   2015   £150

Association – Carter, P.

Wesley, Samuel *The Battle of the Sexes: a Poem.* London: printed by J. Brotherton and sold by J. Roberts, 1724. Second edition, 8vo., recent half calf, black morocco label, early signature on titlepage of P. Carter, piece torn from one blank margin, one other clean tear without affecting text, otherwise good, bound in at back is half title of unrelated Neo-Latin poem by Nicholas Rowe.   C. R. Johnson   Foxon R-Z - 1114r-z   2015 $613

Association – Caruthers, Osgood

Mecklin, John *Mission in Torment: an Intimate account of the U. S. Role in Vietnam.* New York: Doubleday, 1965. First edition, inscribed by author to Osgood Caruthers, bureau chief at AP, Caruthers bookplate, cloth mottled, very good in like dust jacket.   Ken Lopez, Bookseller 164 - 230   2015 $125

Association – Carver, Clifford

Warwick, Frances Evelyn *A Woman and the War.* London: Chapman & Hall, 1916. First edition, 8vo., frontispiece, red cloth little foxed, very good, tight copy, inscribed by author for Clifford Carver Oct. 1916.   Second Life Books Inc.   189 - 263   2015 $325

Association – Carver, Raymond

Burke, Bill *Portraits.* New York: Ecco Press, 1987. First edition, signed by Ray Carver and inscribed by Carver, photos by Burke, fine in near fine dust jacket.   Ed Smith Books   83 - 8   2015 $500

Association – Castlereagh, Viscount

Whitcombe, Samuel *Considerations Addressed to the Legislature Upon the Expediency and Policy of Authorising the Alienation of Estates Belonging to Corporate Bodies, Particularly Bishops and Deans and Chapters...* London: G. and W. Nicol, 1810. First edition, half title, well bound recently in cloth backed boards, spine gilt lettered, very good presented and inscribed by author to Lord Castlereagh, first scarce.   John Drury Rare Books   March 2015 - 19533   2015 $266

Association – Cator, John

Young, Arthur 1741-1820 *Political Arithmetic.* London: W. Nicoll, 1774. First edition, complete with final leaf of ads, mottled calf, spine fully gilt with raised bands and gilt label, joints with some wear and cracking, still good, sound, very good in late 18th century library of John Cator with his armorial bookplate.   John Drury Rare Books   2015 - 26306   2015 $1136

Association – Catt, Carrie Chapman

National American Woman Suffrage Association *Victory how Women Won It.* New York: Wilson, 1940. First edition, 8vo., illustrations, blue cloth, spine little faded, otherwise fine, one of 300 honor copies, inscribed by Carrie Chapman Catt.   Second Life Books Inc.   189 - 180   2015 $450

Young, Rose *The Record of the Leslie Woman Suffrage Commission Inc. 1917-1929.* Leslie Commission, 1929. First edition, small 8vo., 94 pages, little soiled, very good inscribed by Carrie Chapman Catt for Josephine Fowler Post.   Second Life Books Inc.   189 - 52   2015 $600

Association – Caughey, John

Meinig, D. W. *The Great Columbia Plain a Historical Geography 1805-1910.* Seattle: University of Washington, 1968. First edition, cloth, 576 pages, 52 maps, folding map, bookplate of Western historian John Caughey and wife Laree, fine in fine dust jacket.   Baade Books of the West   2014 - 2015 $40

Association – Caughey, Laree

Meinig, D. W. *The Great Columbia Plain a Historical Geography 1805-1910.* Seattle: University of Washington, 1968. First edition, cloth, 576 pages, 52 maps, folding map, bookplate of Western historian John Caughey and wife Laree, fine in fine dust jacket. Baade Books of the West 2014 - 2015 $40

Association – Cely-Trevilian, Cely

Hayley, William *The Triumphs of Temper: a Poem in Six Cantos.* London: T. Cadell, 1788. Sixth edition, 165 x 102mm., once remarkably attractive and still very pleasing late 18th century citron morocco by Staggemeier & Welcher, covers with inlaid black and red morocco tooled in gilt to a diapered mosaic design, raised bands, spine compartments with central moire silk endleaves, all edges gilt, expertly rejointed, spine label with tiny repairs and some inlays artfully replicated and replaced by Courtland Benson, with 7 engraved plates, silk bookplate of R. M. Trench Chiswell, titlepage and ink ownership inscription of Augusta E. Vincent, inscription from A. Vincent to Blanche Cely-Trevilian, spine little darkened, minor soiling to boards, plates rather foxed, otherwise without any significant defect and, in all, an excellent (albeit restored) specimen, binding with much of its original dramatic appeal reclaimed. Phillip J. Pirages 66 - 52   2015 $4500

Association – Chagall, Marc

Chagall, Bella *Burning Lights. Thirty Six Drawings by Marc Chagall.* New York: Schocken Books, 1946. First edition, inscribed by Marc Chagall 1946 along with original drawing by him, publisher's full blue cloth, front board stamped gilt with drawing by Chagall, spine lettered gilt, original unclipped dust jacket, jacket spine bit darkened and bit toned overall, some small chips to head and tail of jacket spine as well as top edge, book with some very light shelf-wear to corners, otherwise about fine in very good jacket. Heritage Book Shop   Holiday 2014 - 34   2015 $6500

Association – Chalmers, Mary

Hoban, Russell *Letitia Rabbit's String Song.* New York: Coward McCann & Geoghegan, 1973. First edition, square 8vo, pictorial cloth, slight spotting cover, else fine in dust jacket, beautiful full page and smaller watercolor drawings, nearly full page watercolor signed by artist, Mary Chalmers. Aleph-Bet Books, Inc.   108 - 93   2015 $475

Association – Chambers, Gertrude

Harpsfield, Nicholas *The Life and Death of Sir Thomas Moore...* London: OUP, 1932. Half title, frontispiece and plates, 8 page catalog, handsome full white pigskin with elaborate pattern in blind and gilt, blind and gilt dentelles, marbled endpapers, fine in lined marbled slipcase, from the library of Geoffrey & Kathleen Tillotson, gilt lettered on front from GT, KMC 21XL 33 and with signed inscription from both editors to Tillotson's, with inserted p.c. from R. W. Chambers1933 and ALS from Gertrude Chambers and Edith Batho.   Jarndyce Antiquarian Booksellers   CCVII - 381   2015   £250

Association – Chambers, R. W.

Harpsfield, Nicholas *The Life and Death of Sir Thomas Moore...* London: OUP, 1932. Half title, frontispiece and plates, 8 page catalog, handsome full white pigskin with elaborate pattern in blind and gilt, blind and gilt dentelles, marbled endpapers, fine in lined marbled slipcase, from the library of Geoffrey & Kathleen Tillotson, gilt lettered on front from GT, KMC 21XL 33 and with signed inscription from both editors to Tillotson's, with inserted p.c. from R. W. Chambers1933 and ALS from Gertrude Chambers and Edith Batho.   Jarndyce Antiquarian Booksellers   CCVII - 381   2015   £250

Association – Chambers, Raymond

Chambers, R. W. *Man's Unconquerable Mind: Studies of English Writers from Bede to A. E. Housman and W. P. Ker.* London: Jonathan Cape, 1939. Half title, plates, author's presentation copy to Geoffrey Tillotson and wife, with 2 ALS's from Raymond Wilson Chambers to Geoffrey. Jarndyce Antiquarian Booksellers   CCVII - 132   2015   £20

Association – Chandler, Raymond

Gardner, Erle Stanley *The Case of the Backward Mule.* New York: William Morrow, 1946. First edition, fine in fine, price clipped dust jacket, inscribed by author for Raymond Chandler, from the collection of Duke Collier.   Royal Books   36 - 10   2015 $20,000

Greene, Graham   1904-1991 *The End of the Affair.* London: Heinemann, 1951. First edition, first impression, publisher's gray cloth in original gray and white dust jacket, Raymond Chandler's copy stamped on front free endpaper with his La Jolla CA address and date JAN 7 1952, book pages toned, else near fine in very good dust jacket with few small chips to upper spine (not affecting lettering), spine toned and some light soiling.   B & B Rare Books, Ltd.   234 - 41   2015 $3500

Greene, Graham 1904-1991 *England Made Me.* London: Heinemann, 1947. Uniform edition (first edition 1935), publisher's black cloth in red and gray dust jacket, Raymond Chandler's copy stamped on front free endpaper with his LA Jolla CA address and date APR 22 1953, near fine in very good dust jacket.   B & B Rare Books, Ltd.   234 - 42   2015 $1750

Salinger, Jerome David   *The Catcher in the Rye.*   Boston: Little Brown and Co., 1951. First edition, publisher's black cloth in unrestored first issue dust jacket with 43.00 price correctly positioned and photo by Lotte Jacobi to rear panel, Raymond Chandler's copy stamped on front free endpaper with his La Jolla CA address and date AUG 4 1951, book with offsetting to endpapers from printer's glue, edges of text block very minimally foxed, small creases to top corner of first few pages, else clean and square with bright gilt to spine, bright and clean dust jacket with few nicks and creases to corners, spine very slightly toned, light rubbing to extremities, housed in custom quarter leather case, beautiful copy.   B & B Rare Books, Ltd.   234 - 88   2015 $22,500

Association – Chapman, J. J.

Wotton, Henry   *Reliquiae Wottonianae; or a Collection of Lives, Letters, Poems...*   London: By T. Roycroft for R. Marriott, 1672. Third edition, portraits, 19th century red morocco, early signatures of J. Grien? 1725, Thomas Price and John Francis Cole 1828, bookplates of J. J. Chapman and Molly Flagg Gibb, very good.   Joseph J. Felcone Inc.   Science, Medicine and Technology - 57   2015 $900

Association – Chapman, R. W.

Johnson, Samuel 1709-1784   *The Poems.*   Oxford: Clarendon Press, 1941. Half title, original dark blue cloth, Geoffrey Tillotson's copy with notes in text and on following endpapers, much inserted material including reviews and note from R. W. Chapman.   Jarndyce Antiquarian Booksellers   CCVII - 334   2015   £60

Johnson, Samuel 1709-1784   *Lives of the English Poets.* Oxford: at the Clarendon Press, 1905. 3 volumes, original red cloth, hinges little rubbed, from the library of Geoffrey & Kathleen Tillotson, Kathleen's gift to Geoffrey Christmas 1937 with extensive notes and insertions including correspondence with R. W. Chapman and others.   Jarndyce Antiquarian Booksellers   CCVII - 332   2015   £75

Association – Charteris, Evan

James, Henry 1843-1916   *Stories Revived in Three Volumes.*   London: Macmillan, 1885. First edition, 3 volumes, full red leather lettered gilt on spine, 5 raised bands, all edges gilt, bookplate of Margot Tennant in each volume, with 'Margot from Evan Charteris, the Glen 85', little scuffed at edges, covers slightly marked, hinges slightly tender with front board detached on volume 3, overall about very good. Any Amount of Books   March 2015 - A79117   2015   £360

Association – Chatsworth House

Martialis, Marcus Valerius   *Epigrammaton Libri XIII.* Lugduni: Apud Haered Seb. Gryphius, 1559. 108 x 76mm., appealing contemporary olive brown morocco, covers bordered with fillets in gilt and in blind and with small gilt floral cornerpieces as well as central azured gilt arabesque, raised bands forming eight spine panels, each of these with small gilt cruciform sprigs flanking a central majuscule, the letters running vertically to spell out 'MARTIAL" all edges gilt; woodcut printer's device to titlepage, woodcut initials, from the library of Chatsworth House with modern bookplate "HB" (i.e collector Heribert Boeder); quarter inch chip at top of backstrip, half a dozen tiny wormholes near head or tail of spine, minor rubbing to corners and few abrasions on covers, but very appealing copy, unsophisticated contemporaneous binding completely solid with lustrous boards and virtually no wear to joints, text especially fresh and clean throughout.   Phillip J. Pirages   66 - 16   2015 $1800

Association – Chauncey, Charles

Gibbon, Edward 1737-1794   *The History of the Decline and Fall of the Roman Empire.*   Dublin: William Hallhead, 1777. Pirated Dublin edition, 10 Volumes, Volume 1 states that it is the Fourth edition, it was printed in Dublin for Hallhead in 1777, Volumes 2- were also printed in Dublin for Hallhead and are dated 1781, Volumes 7-10 were printed in Dublin for Luke White in 1788, lacks volumes 11 and 12, Volume 2 has folding map, bookplate of Charles Chauncey to front pastedown of each volume, bound in full leather with title and volumes labels to spines, however, one volume lacks volume label, volumes 1-6 have matching full calf and volumes 7-10 are bound in matching mottled calf bindings, very good.   The Kelmscott Bookshop   11 - 21   2015 $1200

Plutarchus *Plutarch's Lives.* London: printed for Edward and Charles Dilly, 1760. 6 volumes, full brown leather with red leather title labels and gilt volume numbers to spines, raised bands, gilt rules to spines, splits to leather along hinges of volume one, short spot to front hinge volume 4, chipping to leather on spine ends of several volumes, cracking to leather on spines, minor wear to edges and corners of boards, minor rubbing to boards, bumping to corners of some volumes, frontispiece to each volume, offsetting to titlepages, bookplate of Charles Chauncey each volume, antiquated ownership signature top edge of each titlepage, occasional spots of foxing, few small ink stains to interiors, very good. The Kelmscott Bookshop 11 - 39 2015 $500

Association – Chester, Alida

Chester, George Randolph *Get-Rich-Quick Wallingford.* Henry Artemus Co., 1908. First edition, inscribed by author's daughter, Alida for Mr. and Mrs. Geo. R. Chester, College Hill, Cincinnati May 21 -09, spine letters faded out, else very good, elusive title. Buckingham Books March 2015 - 37310 2015 $750

Association – Chester, G. R.

Chester, George Randolph *Get-Rich-Quick Wallingford.* Henry Artemus Co., 1908. First edition, inscribed by author's daughter, Alida for Mr. and Mrs. Geo. R. Chester, College Hill, Cincinnati May 21 -09, spine letters faded out, else very good, elusive title. Buckingham Books March 2015 - 37310 2015 $750

Association – Cheyney, William

Coles, Elisha *An English Dictionary Explaining the Difficult terms that are Used in Divinity, Husbandry, Physick, Philosophy, Law, Navigation, Mathematicks and Other Arts and Sciences.* London: for Peter Parker, 1696. Sixth edition, titlepage lightly soiled and with margins browned by turn-ins, single wormhole to A1-B1, H1-L1 and short worm trail to Z6-2A3, minor ink staining to Q6 and 2C2-4, lower edge of H1 little ragged, with small spider neatly pressed between R3-4, cut fairly close at head, contemporary calf, ruled in blind, spine creased, upper headcap split and short crack at head of upper joint, small hole in foot of spine, corners and edges worn, no pastedowns, rear flyleaf only, ink inscription of William Cheyney, from the library of James Stevens Cox (1910-1997). Maggs Bros. Ltd. 1447 - 104 2015 £500

Association – Chisholm, Andrew, Mrs.

Parker, Gilbert *Round the Compass in Australia.* London: Hutchinson and Co., 1892. First edition, inscribed by author to Mrs. Andrew Chisholm, London 1892, original light blue cloth boards with gilt title to spine and front board illustration of sheep to spine and shovel with gold and pick axe to front cover, few splits to cloth along front joint and rear hinge cracked, binding little loose with few internal splits browning to spine fraying to spine ends and minor wear to corners, interior clean overall, just few spots of foxing, very good. The Kelmscott Bookshop 11 - 35 2015 $150

Association – Chiswell, Richard Muilman Trench

Hayley, William *The Triumphs of Temper: a Poem in Six Cantos.* London: T. Cadell, 1788. Sixth edition, 165 x 102mm., once remarkably attractive and still very pleasing late 18th century citron morocco by Staggemeier & Welcher, covers with inlaid black and red morocco tooled in gilt to a diapered mosaic design, raised bands, spine compartments with central moire silk endleaves, all edges gilt, expertly rejointed, spine label with tiny repairs and some inlays artfully replicated and replaced by Courtland Benson, with 7 engraved plates, silk bookplate of R. M. Trench Chiswell, titlepage and ink ownership inscription of Augusta E. Vincent, inscription from A. Vincent to Blanche Cely-Trevilian, spine little darkened, minor soiling to boards, plates rather foxed, otherwise without any significant defect and, in all, an excellent (albeit restored) specimen, binding with much of its original dramatic appeal reclaimed. Phillip J. Pirages 66 - 52 2015 $4500

Association – Cholmondeley

Estienne, Charles 1504-1564 *Praedium Rusticum.* Lutetiae: Apud Carolum Stephanum, 1554. First edition of this collection, 178 x 114mm., fine period French calf, covers with blind ruled borders and attractive gilt chain roll frame with fleuron cornerpieces pointing obliquely outward, ornate central arabesque, raised bands flanked by plain gilt rules, spine panels with small gilt fleuron apparently original green morocco label, titlepage with printer's device, front pastedown with bookplate of Cholmondeley Library, little wear to joints and extremities (three corners rubbed, one of them with loss of its leather tip), half inch cracks at head of joints, shallow chip out of top of backstrip, titlepage with hint of soiling, isolated minor marginal spots or smudges, elsewhere in text but still excellent, contemporary copy with ample margins, binding solid and without any serious condition problems, very fine internally, unusually fresh, clean, smooth and bright. Phillip J. Pirages 66 - 15 2015 $8000

Association – Choyce, Eleanor Louise

Potter, Beatrix 1866-1943 *The Fairy Caravan.* copyright of the author, 1929. Limited to 100 numbered copies, numbered 35 in Potter's hand, first edition, privately printed in Ambleside to secure the English copyright small 4to., cloth backed boards, tips worn, light cover soil, spine pasted down, tight, clean and very good, presentation copy inscribed by author for Eleanor Louise Choyce, rare. Aleph-Bet Books, Inc.   108 - 368   2015 $12,500

Association – Christian, Arthur

Lisbonne, M. Gaston *Legislation sur les Raisins Secs: Etude et Commentaire.*   Montpelier: Paris: Camille Coulet/G. Masson, 1891. First edition, 12mo., contemporary cloth and paper covered boards with leather spine label, 2 small attractive bookplates of Arthur Christian, lightly rubbed, else near fine, scarce.   Between the Covers Rare Books   196 - 135   2015 $500

Association – Christie-Miller

Anacreon *Anacreon Done into English out of the Original Greek.* Oxford: by L. Litchfield, Printer to the University, for Anthony Stephens, 1683. First edition of this translation, 8vo., leaf (c)1 is duplicated; (c)2 was also duplicated, but the second leaf has been torn away, lightly browned, dampstaining along lower edge of a1-4, corners of K2-L2 and fore margin of P1-2 and in top half of last few leaves, small rust hole in D2 (affecting one letter on each side), marginal rust spot on H1, contemporary calf, spine gilt and lettered (headcap damaged and with upper joint slightly split at head), from the library of James Stevens Cox (1910-1997), inscribed "Sum Philippi Ayresij 1683" on titlepage (Philip Aryes (1638-1712), signature of Madam. Mary Redman, ink signature under bookplate of John Holmes (1702/03-1760) of Holt, Norfolk, Master of Gresham School and writer on education, with his signature, early 19th century circular label with manuscript lot number 12/4 pasted to foot of front flyleaf, the pencil mark of Christie-Miller Britwell Court with pencil shelf mark.   Maggs Bros. Ltd.   1447 - 7   2015   £1500

Association – Ciardi, John

Corman, Cid *For Good.* Kyoto: Origin Press, 1964. First edition, 16mo., string-tied wrappers, fine, nicely inscribed by author to poet John Ciardi, and his wife, Judith.   Between the Covers Rare Books, Inc.   187 - 62   2015 $150

Corman, Cid *In Good Time.* Kyoto: Origin Press, 1964. First edition, one of 300 copies, small octavo, fine in wrappers, sunned, else near fine dust jacket, this copy inscribed by author to poet John Ciardi and wife Judith.   Between the Covers Rare Books, Inc.   187 - 63   2015 $250

Association – Ciardi, Judith

Corman, Cid *For Good.* Kyoto: Origin Press, 1964. First edition, 16mo., string-tied wrappers, fine, nicely inscribed by author to poet John Ciardi, and his wife, Judith.   Between the Covers Rare Books, Inc.   187 - 62   2015 $150

Corman, Cid *In Good Time.* Kyoto: Origin Press, 1964. First edition, one of 300 copies, small octavo, fine in wrappers, sunned, else near fine dust jacket, this copy inscribed by author to poet John Ciardi and wife Judith.   Between the Covers Rare Books, Inc.   187 - 63   2015 $250

Association – Claire Helen

Dillard, Annie *Tickets for a Prayer Wheel.* Columbia: University of Missouri, 1974. First edition, 8vo., author's presentation to poet and editor William Claire and his wife Helen, orchid cloth over flexible boards, top edges little spotted, otherwise very good, tight copy in somewhat toned dust jacket.   Second Life Books Inc.   190 - 56   2015 $350

Association – Claire, William

Conover, Anne *Caresse Crosby from Black Sun to Roccasinibalda.* Santa Barbara: Capra Press, 1989. First edition, 8vo., fine in dust jacket, inscribed to William Claire, with 10 typed letters and autograph post cards from author to Claire as well as invitation to autograph party, announcement of lecture and copy of Claire's interview of Conover in Horizon Magazine.   Second Life Books Inc.   189 - 24   2015 $750

Dillard, Annie *Tickets for a Prayer Wheel.* Columbia: University of Missouri, 1974. First edition, 8vo., author's presentation to poet and editor William Claire and his wife Helen, orchid cloth over flexible boards, top edges little spotted, otherwise very good, tight copy in somewhat toned dust jacket.   Second Life Books Inc.   190 - 56   2015 $350

Jacobsen, Josephine *The Sisters.* Columbia: Bench Press, 1987. First printing, 8vo., author's presentation on half title to poet and editor William Claire, paper wrappers, about as new.   Second Life Books Inc.   189 - 136   2015 $45

Meredith, William *Hazard the Painter.* N.P.: Ironwood Press, 1972. First edition, 8vo., scarce printing, inscribed by author for William Claire.   Second Life Books Inc.   190 - 164   2015 $150

Merrill, James *The Seraglio.* New York: Knopf, 1957. First edition, 8vo., very good, tight in scuffed and chipped dust jacket inscribed by author to Bill Claire.   Second Life Books Inc.   190 - 165   2015 $175

Nin, Anais *The Diary of .... 1944-1947.* New York: Harcourt Brace Jovanovich, 1971. First edition, photos, 8vo., photos, cover slightly stained, otherwise very good, tight copy in little scuffed and nicked price clipped dust jacket, laid in is advance complimentary slip with author's card, in addition author has inscribed the copy to poet and editor, Bill Claire.   Second Life Books Inc.   191 - 65   2015 $600

Nin, Anais *Ladders to Fire.* New York: Dutton, 1496. First edition, 8vo., engravings by Ian Hugo, 8vo., very good in dust jacket little chipped and worn lacks some of the extremities of spine and on corners, inscribed by author for Bill (Claire).   Second Life Books Inc.   191 - 68   2015 $450

Simpson, Louis *Searching for the Ox.* New York: Morrow, 1976. First printing, 8vo., author's presentation on title to poet and editor William Claire, paper over boards with cloth spine, top edges slightly spotted, otherwise nice, little chipped and soiled dust jacket.   Second Life Books Inc.   190 - 201   2015 $275

Stafford, William *Traveling through the Dark.* New York: Harper & Row, 1962. First edition, 8vo., author's presentation on flyleaf to poet and editor William Claire, paper boards, fine in dust jacket.   Second Life Books Inc.   190 - 203   2015 $275

Stuhlmann, Gunther *Anais An International Journal. Volume 9 1991 - Volume 18 2000.* Los Angeles: 1999-2000. 8vo., printed wrappers, pages 136, laid in TLS from Stuhlmann to editor and poet William Claire, 6 issues, 9, 10, 11, 14, 15, 18.   Second Life Books Inc.   191 - 88   2015 $125

Wagoner, David *Dry Sun, Dry Wind.* Bloomington: Indiana University, 1953. First edition, 8vo., black cloth, nice in soiled and chipped dust jacket, author's presentation on title to poet and editor William Claire.   Second Life Books Inc.   190 - 207   2015 $125

Association – Clare, John FitzGibbon, 1st Earl of

Ariosto, Lodovico *Orlando Furioso.* Birmingham: Da' Torch di G. Baskerville per P. Molini, 1773. One of 100 large paper copies, 4 volumes, with subscriber list at end of volume IV, contemporary red morocco by Derome Le Jeune (his ticket on titlepage of volume I), covers gilt with French fillet borders and with FitzGibbon family arms of Earl of Clare at Center, raised bands, spines gilt in double ruled compartments with simple lozenge centerpiece, gilt titling, densely gilt turn-ins, marbled endpapers, all edges gilt, frontispiece by Eisen after Titian and 46 fine engraved plates, large paper copy, vellum bookplate of Burnham Abbey and engraved armorial bookplate of Charles Tennant, The Glen, spines slightly and evenly sunned, hint of rubbing to extremities, titles faintly browned and with an inch of slightly darker browning to edges from binder's glue), a dozen other leaves with pale browning or spotting, occasional very faint offsetting from plates, isolated light spots of foxing, small marginal smudges or other trivial imperfections with just handful of plates affected, still an elegant set in fine condition, impressive bindings lustrous and scarcely worn, leaves clean and smooth, margins enormous and with strong impressions of the engravings.   Phillip J. Pirages   66 - 49   2015 $19,500

Association – Clarence, Duke of

Laurie, David *A Treatise on Finance Under Which the General Interests of the British Empire are Illustrated.* Glasgow: printed by R. Chapman Trongate, 1815. 8vo., complete with half title, contemporary calf over marbled boards, sides rubbed, corners worn, neatly rebacked and lettered, very good, cancelled inkstamp of Chartered Accountants on blank margin of title, contemporary ink inscription ownership of His Royal Highness the Duke of Clarence.   John Drury Rare Books   2015 - 20100   2015 $1049

Association – Clark-Jervaise, Miss

Ayer, A. J. *The Foundations of Empirical Knowledge.* London: Macmillan, 1940. First edition, 8vo., original blue cloth lettered gilt on spine, signed presentation from author, for his nurse Miss Clark-Jervaise, endpapers very slightly browned, otherwise very good+ in like dust jacket, complete with faint shelfwear, excellent condition.   Any Amount of Books   2015 - A92758   2015   £675

Association – Clark, Byron N.

Rankin, J. E. *Hymns Pro Patria and Other Hymns, Christian and Humanitarian.* New York: John R. Alden, 1889. First edition, tall octavo, brown cloth decorated in black and gilt, bookplate of Byron N. Clark, second bookplate partly effaced, crease on two leaves, else tight, near fine copy, inscribed by author to NJ author Gen. Oliver O. Howard.   Between the Covers Rare Books, Inc.   187 - 228   2015 $175

Association – Clark, John

Berrigan, Ted *The Sonnets.* New York: Grove Press, 1964. First trade edition, paperback original inscribed by author with elaborate pen and ink self portrait for John Clark, fine.   James S. Jaffe Rare Books   Many Happy Returns - 8   2015 $450

Association – Clark, Leonard

Clare, John *Madrigals & Chronicles: Being Newly Found Poems Written by John Clare.* London: Beaumont Press, 1924. First edition, one of 310 numbered copies on handmade paper of a total of 400, octavo, quarter cloth and decorated paper covered boards, bookplate of Leonard Clark, corners rubbed, very good, this copy inscribed by Edmund Blunden for editor Leonard Clark.   Between the Covers Rare Books, Inc.   187 - 54   2015 $250

Association – Clark, Richard

Charles I, King of England *The King's Maiesties Declaration to His Subjects Concerning Lawfull Sports to Bee Used.* London: Richard Barker and by the Assignes of John Bill, 1633. First edition, 4to., woodcut device on titlepage, large woodcut royal arms on verso, woodcut head and tailpieces, wanting final blank, few minor stains and rust marks, near contemporary ms. annotation in ink, ownership signature of 'Sam. Ware" with 19th century armorial bookplates of Richard Clark Esq. Chamberlain of London (1739-1831) and of William Henry Drummond, 9th Viscount Strathallan (1810-1886), bound, presumably for Richard Clark in late 18th or early 19th century half russia gilt, good copy, wanting only final blank.   John Drury Rare Books   2015 - 25124   2015 $2185

Association – Clarke, Arthur

McAleer, Neil *Arthur C. Clarke: the Authorized Biography.* Chicago: Contemporary Books, 1992. First edition, fine in fine dust jacket, ownership signature of Ian Macauley with few notes in text, else fine in fine dust jacket, signed by Clarke and McAleer on bookplate.   Between the Covers Rare Books, Inc.   187 - 252   2015 $450

Association – Clarke, T. H.

Phillippo, James *Jamaica: Its Past and Present State.* London: John Snow, 1843. First edition, 8vo., 16 full page woodcut illustrations and woodcut vignettes, inscribed "Sam. J. Wilkind/from Rev. Th. H. Clarke/Dry Harbor/Jamaica/November 1843", original brown cloth, boards spine missing, otherwise very good with very clean text.   Any Amount of Books   2015 - A45552   2015   £150

Association – Clay, Charles Travis

Oastler, Richard *Vicarial Tithes, Halifax: a True statement of Facts and Incidents.* Halifax: printed and sold by P. K. Holden, 1827. First edition, 8vo., final errata leaf, well bound in mid 20th century dark green half morocco over cloth boards, spine lettered gilt, entirely uncut, original wrappers bound in, upper retaining its original printed title label, very good, from the library of John Clay at Rastrick House, with his signature and later form the library of his grandson, Sir Charles Travis Clay (1885-1978), very scarce.   John Drury Rare Books   March 2015 - 24991   2015   £306

Association – Clay, John

Oastler, Richard *Vicarial Tithes, Halifax: a True statement of Facts and Incidents.* Halifax: printed and sold by P. K. Holden, 1827. First edition, 8vo., final errata leaf, well bound in mid 20th century dark green half morocco over cloth boards, spine lettered gilt, entirely uncut, original wrappers bound in, upper retaining its original printed title label, very good, from the library of John Clay at Rastrick House, with his signature and later form the library of his grandson, Sir Charles Travis Clay (1885-1978), very scarce.   John Drury Rare Books   March 2015 - 24991   2015   £306

Association – Clement, Emile Louis Bruno

Buckland, Francis Trevelyan *Log-Book of a Fisherman and Zoologist.* London: Chapman & Hall, 1875. First edition, wood engraved frontispiece, 3 plates, illustrations in text, endpapers through-set on to outside of flyleaves, 8vo., original cloth, slightly darkened an worn, neat repair to front inner hinge and spine ends, inscribed by author on inside front cover, good, presentation from author to friend Henry Lee Aug. 12 1875, the copy of Dr. Emile Louis Bruno Clement (1844-1928).   Blackwell's Rare Books   B179 - 23   2015   £225

Association – Clitherow, Christopher

Bysshe, Edward *The Art of English Poetry.* London: printed for Sam. Buckley at the Dolphin in Little Britain, 1710. Fourth edition, top corner of front endpaper clipped, otherwise internally very good, clean and crisp, contemporary unlettered panelled calf, blindstamped floral cornerpieces, raised bands, very slight chip to base of spine, bottom 2cm. of upper joint cracked, very good, attractive, E. Libris Chris Clitherow March 21 1709, later armorial bookplate of Sir Edward B. Baker, Bart.   Jarndyce Antiquarian Booksellers   CCXI - 56   2015   £280

Association – Clive, Edward Herbert, Viscount

Horatius Flaccus, Quintus *Opera, cum variis lectionibs notis varorium et indice locupletissimo.* Excudebant Gul. Browne, et Joh. Warren, 1792-1793. Regular paper issue, engraved portrait frontispiece (foxed), titlepage toned and showing some offsetting from frontispiece, little light spotting elsewhere, contemporary straight grained red morocco., boards bordered with trio of decorative gilt rolls, spines divided by double raised bands between and containing gilt fillets, second compartments gilt lettered direct, all edges gilt, 4to., touch of rubbing to joints, slight darkening to leather in parts, armorial bookplate of Edward Herbert, Viscount Clive, very good. Blackwell's Rare Books Greek & Latin Classics VI - 54 2015 £500

Association – Cloetta, Yvonne

Connell, Mary *Help is on the Way. (Poems).* Reinhardt, 1986. First edition, line drawings by author, pages 48, crown 8vo., original light blue card wrappers printed in black, red and white, fine, touching an extremely revealing inscription illustrating Greene's love for Yvonne Cloetta, "for Yvonne (Cloetta) the love of my life....". Blackwell's Rare Books B179 - 160 2015 £120

Association – Clutterbuck, Nesta

Byrne, Muriel St. Clair *Somerville College 1879-1921.* London: Oxford University Press, 1922. Frontispiece, illustrations, music, original dark blue cloth, slightly rubbed, Kathleen Tillotson's copy with note 'Helen Darbishire's copy given me by Nesta Clutterbuck, May 1878". Jarndyce Antiquarian Booksellers CCVII - 128 2015 £22

Association – Codrescu, Andrei

Molbach, Irving *Last Dreams.* San Francisco: Pompous Ass Press, 1974. First edition, decorated stapled wrappers, faint dampstain to top of most leaves, very good or better, inscribed by poet to Andrei Codrescu. Between the Covers Rare Books, Inc. 187 - 180 2015 $100

Association – Cohn, Albert

Cleveland, John *The Idol of the Clownes or Insurrection of Wat the Tyler with His Priests Baal and Straw...* London: in the Year, 1654. Second edition, small 8vo., without engraved portrait found in some copies and without final blank, light dampstaining to first few leaves, closely shaved at head (just touching pagination in places), early 19th century calf, covers ruled in gilt, spine tooled in gilt and blind, marbled edges and endpapers, small stain on front cover and minor repair on rear, old front flyleaf preserved, from the library of James Stevens Cox (1910-1997), with late 17th/early 18th century inscription "Thomas Browne/His booke", not that of Sir Thomas Browne (1605-1682), with bookplate of Albert M. Cohn, posthumous sale, Christie 26/2/1934 lot 176 (as Sir Thomas Browne's copy), £5 to Charles H. Stonehill. Maggs Bros. Ltd. 1447 - 102 2015 £200

Association – Cohn, Jonas

Hegel, Georg Wilhelm Friedrich *Encyclopadie der Philosophischen Wissenschaften im Grundrisse...* Heidelberg: August Oswald, 1827. 8vo., paper throughout generally little browned and foxed, original boards with spine label lettered in gilt, wear to joints and extremities, red edges, good sound copy with several early ownership inscriptions, including I. F. C. Kampe (mid 19th century) Jonas Cohn (1931) and Selly Oak Colleges Library. John Drury Rare Books 2015 - 24310 2015 $830

Association – Cole, Christopher

Sowerby, James 1757-1822 *A New Elucidation of Colours Showing Their Concordance in Three Primitives...* London: Printed by Richard Taylor and Co. Shoe Lane, 1809. 4to., 7 engraved plates, including 5 hand colored original boards, spine defective, upper cover with original printed label, armorial bookplate of Captain Sir Christopher Cole KB, the Honeyman copy. Marlborough Rare Books List 54 - 80 2015 £2500

Association – Cole, John Francis

Wotton, Henry *Reliquiae Wottonianae; or a Collection of Lives, Letters, Poems...* London: By T. Roycroft for R. Marriott, 1672. Third edition, portraits, 19th century red morocco, early signatures of J. Grien? 1725, Thomas Price and John Francis Cole 1828, bookplates of J. J. Chapman and Molly Flagg Gibb, very good. Joseph J. Felcone Inc. Science, Medicine and Technology - 57 2015 $900

Association – Coleby, John

Rack, Edmund *Essays, Letters and Poems.* Bath: printed by C. Crutwell for the author, 1781. First edition, 8vo., wanting half title and final leaf of ads, some minor browning and foxing, defect to blank margin of one leaf, contemporary calf backed marbled boards, flat spine gilt, with label, usual wear to boards and extremities but good, firm copy, early ownership signature of John Coleby 1791.   John Drury Rare Books   March 2015 - 16808   2015   £306

Association – Coleman, George Dawson

Talbot, William Henry Fox *Improvements in coating or Covering Metals with other Metals and in colouring Metallic Surfaces (and) Improvements in Photography Contained in The Chemical Gazette or Journal of Practical Chemistry...* London: Richard and John E. Taylor, 1842-1844. First edition, 2 volumes, 8vo., half brown calf over marbled boards, gilt stamped spine titles, joints rubbed, bookplates and signatures of George Dawson Coleman, very good.   Jeff Weber Rare Books   178 - 1053   2015 $800

Association – Coleman, M. H.

Sailaja, P. *Experimental Studies of the Differential Effect in Life Setting.* New York: Parapsychology Foundation, 1973. First edition, 8vo., original grey wrappers, lettered red on covers, blindstamp of writer M. H. Coleman, faint shelfwear, otherwise very good.   Any Amount of Books   2015 - C6750   2015   £160

Association – Coleridge, Bernard

Young, Edward   1683-1765 *The Complaint and the Consolation or Night Thoughts.* R. Noble, 1797. First edition, large 4to., bound by Aquarius in late 20th century full midnight blue straight grain morocco, period style, boards richly decorated gilt and blind, gilt lettered and decorated backstrip, gilt ruled edges, marbled endpapers, 43 full page engravings by William Blake, very tall, well margined copy, the Coleridge family, with bookplate of Bernard Lord Coleridge and family signatures of J. T., Mary and Jane Coleridge.   Henry Sotheran Ltd.   William Blake Exhibition 17th Oct.-7th Nov. 2014 - 64   2015   £11,150

Association – Coleridge, J. T.

Young, Edward   1683-1765 *The Complaint and the Consolation or Night Thoughts.* R. Noble, 1797. First edition, large 4to., bound by Aquarius in late 20th century full midnight blue straight grain morocco, period style, boards richly decorated gilt and blind, gilt lettered and decorated backstrip, gilt ruled edges, marbled endpapers, 43 full page engravings by William Blake, very tall, well margined copy, the Coleridge family, with bookplate of Bernard Lord Coleridge and family signatures of J. T., Mary and Jane Coleridge.   Henry Sotheran Ltd.   William Blake Exhibition 17th Oct.-7th Nov. 2014 - 64   2015   £11,150

Association – Coleridge, Jane

Young, Edward   1683-1765 *The Complaint and the Consolation or Night Thoughts.* R. Noble, 1797. First edition, large 4to., bound by Aquarius in late 20th century full midnight blue straight grain morocco, period style, boards richly decorated gilt and blind, gilt lettered and decorated backstrip, gilt ruled edges, marbled endpapers, 43 full page engravings by William Blake, very tall, well margined copy, the Coleridge family, with bookplate of Bernard Lord Coleridge and family signatures of J. T., Mary and Jane Coleridge.   Henry Sotheran Ltd.   William Blake Exhibition 17th Oct.-7th Nov. 2014 - 64   2015   £11,150

Association – Coleridge, John Duke

Newman, John Henry   1801-1890 *Verses on Religious Subjects.* Dublin: James Duffy, 1853. First edition, contemporary calf, gilt borders and dentelles, spine chipped, boards detached, scarce, John Duke Coleridge's copy signed on original preserved endpaper, from the library of Geoffrey & Kathleen Tillotson.   Jarndyce Antiquarian Booksellers   CCVII - 394   2015   £220

Association – Coleridge, John Taylor

Coleridge, Sarah *Phantasmion, a Fairy Tale.* Henry S. King & Co., 1874. 8vo., first titlepage spotted, 8vo., original grass green sand grain cloth blocked in silver and gold and lettered in gold on front, ruled and lettered in gold on spine, bevelled boards, some loss to silver on front cover, slight wear to extremities, inner hinges strained, ownership inscription of Sir J(ohn) T(aylor) Coleridge, of Heath's Court, Ottery St. Mary Aril 8 1874 and below this an inscription 'Amy ?Metson with the affectionate regards of her cousin ?Coleridge, Heath's Court, September 1876", good. Blackwell's Rare Books   B179 - 31   2015   £750

Association – Coleridge, Mary

Young, Edward   1683-1765 *The Complaint and the Consolation or Night Thoughts.* R. Noble, 1797. First edition, large 4to., bound by Aquarius in late 20th century full midnight blue straight grain morocco, period style, boards richly decorated gilt and blind, gilt lettered and decorated backstrip, gilt ruled edges, marbled endpapers, 43 full page engravings by William Blake, very tall, well margined copy, the Coleridge family, with bookplate of Bernard Lord Coleridge and family signatures of J. T., Mary and Jane Coleridge.   Henry Sotheran Ltd.   William Blake Exhibition 17th Oct.-7th Nov. 2014 - 64   2015   £11,150

Association – Colin, Paul

Rip, Pseud. *Cocktails de Paris.* Paris: Editions Demangel, 1929. First edition, copiously illustrated by famed poster artist Paul Colin, pages toned, two leaves roughly opened with resulting modest chips, barely touching text, modest rubbing on wrappers, handsome, very good copy, exceptionally uncommon, inscribed by RIP and by Paul Colin to Lieutenant Charles Comat.   Between the Covers Rare Books   196 - 136   2015 $1450

Association – Colley, J.

Morgan, Sydney Owenson 1776-1859 *Woman and Her Master.* Paris: Baudry's European Library, 1840. First Continental edition, 8vo., contemporary three quarter calf with raised bands, spine gilt, contemporary former owner's signature "J. Colley", very good, clean, scarce.   Second Life Books Inc.   189 - 176   2015 $450

Association – Collier, Duke

Ambler, Eric *Background to Danger.* New York: Alfred A. Knopf, 1937. First American edition, fine in exceptionally fresh, about fine dust jacket with only tiny bit of rubbing to couple of corners to note, from the collection of Duke Collier.   Royal Books   36 - 135   2015 $2500

Bailey, H. C. *The Red Castle Mystery.* New York: Doubleday Crime Club, 1932. First American edition, red topstain mottled, else near fine in like, price clipped dust jacket with professional restoration to spine ends, and extremities, from the collection of Duke Collier.   Royal Books   36 - 136   2015 $750

Block, Lawrence *A Week as Andrea Benstock.* New York: Arbor House, 1975. First edition, fine and unread in fine dust jacket, signed by author as Jill Emerson, executed with his left hand, from the collection of Duke Collier.   Royal Books   36 - 141   2015 $675

Block, Lawrence *Eight Million Ways to Die.* New York: Arbor House, 1982. First edition, slight lean, else near fine in fine dust jacket, bright, clean copy, from the collection of Duke Collier.   Royal Books   36 - 140   2015 $325

Block, Lawrence *Ronald Rabbit is a Dirty Old Man.* New York: Bernard Geis Assoc., 1971. First edition, fine and unread in fine dust jacket, from the collection of Duke Collier.   Royal Books   36 - 138   2015 $400

Block, Lawrence *Such Men are Dangerous: a Novel of Violence.* New York: Macmillan, 1969. First edition, signed by author as Block, fine and unread, in very good plus dust jacket with couple of closed tears, from the collection of Duke Collier.   Royal Books   36 - 142   2015 $325

Block, Lawrence *The Burglar in the Closet.* New York: Random House, 1978. First edition, fine and unread, very lightly rubbed, near fine dust jacket, from the collection of Duke Collier.   Royal Books   36 - 139   2015 $450

Bruen, Ken *The Dead Room.* Mission Viejo: ASAP Press, 2005. First edition, one of 150 numbered copies signed by Bruen, Jason Starr (provided introduction) and Phil Parks (the artist), fine in publisher's green linen covered boards, from the collection of Duke Collier.   Royal Books   36 - 143   2015 $750

Bruen, Ken *The Dead Room.* Mission Viejo: ASAP Press, 2005. First edition, one of 26 lettered copies signed by Bruen, Jason Starr (provided introduction and Phil Parks (artist), fine in publisher's green linen covered boards and matching clamshell box, wooden cross and printed bronze plate affixed to inside front panel, from the collection of Duke Collier.   Royal Books   36 - 144   2015 $1500

Burke, James Lee *Lay Down My Sword and Shield.* New York: Thomas Y Crowell, 1971. First edition, inscribed by author, review copy with publisher's slip and promotional letter laid in, fine in fine dust jacket, from the collection of Duke Collier.   Royal Books   36 - 145   2015 $2000

Burke, James Lee *The Convict.* Baton Rouge: Louisiana University Press, 1985. First edition, signed by author, fine in fine dust jacket, from the collection of Duke Collier.   Royal Books   36 - 146   2015 $4000

Cain, James M. *Mildred Pierce.* New York: Alfred A. Knopf, 1941. First edition, near fine in about near fine, lightly rubbed dust jacket, much brighter than usually found, from the collection of Duke Collier.   Royal Books   36 - 147   2015 $1500

Carr, John Dickson *The Problem of the Wire Cage.* New York: Harper and Bros., 1939. First edition, very good in very good plus dust jacket with light wear at spine ends and corners and edges, from the collection of Duke Collier.   Royal Books   36 - 150   2015 $500

Chandler, Raymond 1886-1959 *The Big Sleep.* New York: Alfred A. Knopf, 1939. First edition, near fine in very good plus dust jacket, jacket uniformly toned, but quite nice with couple of corner nicks and few small closed tears, attractive, unrestored example, from the collection of Duke Collier.   Royal Books   36 - 5   2015 $12,500

Chandler, Raymond 1886-1959 *The Big Sleep.* San Francisco: Arion Press, 1986. First printing of this edition, one of 425 non-numbered copies signed by photographer, fine in cream lucite boards with beveled edges, blue silk-screened titles and design, 10 x 8 inches, 40 duotone photo illustrations, printed in Monotype scotch Roman and handset Futura Black by letterpress on Mohawk Superfine paper, from the collection of Duke Collier.   Royal Books   36 - 8   2015 $950

Chandler, Raymond 1886-1959 *The Lady in the Lake.* New York: Alfred A. Knopf, 1943. First edition, near fine in like dust jacket with miniscule wear at spine extremities, scarce in such outstanding condition, from the collection of Duke Collier.   Royal Books   36 - 6   2015 $8500

Chandler, Raymond 1886-1959 *The Little Sister.* Boston: Houghton Mifflin, 1949. First American edition, first issue with correct date on titlepage and in the orange first issue binding, fine in fine, crisp dust jacket that shows only trace of usual sunning to spine and has couple of tiny dings at edges, far superior to most copies one encounters, from the collection of Duke Collier.   Royal Books   36 - 7   2015 $2000

Chesterton, Gilbert Keith 1874-1936 *The Poet and the Lunatics.* London: Cassell, 1929. First edition, fine in near fine dust jacket, very light wear at base of spine and both corners of front panel, from the collection of Duke Collier.   Royal Books   36 - 151   2015 $1500

Christie, Agatha 1891-1975 *The Mystery of the Blue Train.* New York: Dodd Mead, 1928. First American edition, near fine in fine dust jacket, backstrip very slightly toned, else book quite clean and bright, jacket is exceptional, without wear, bright and colorful, from the collection of Duke Collier.   Royal Books   36 - 152   2015 $2000

Crais, Robert *Lullaby Town.* New York: Bantam Books, 1992. First edition, signed by author, fine and unread in fine dust jacket, from the collection of Duke Collier.   Royal Books   36 - 153   2015 $450

Creasey, John *Blue Mask Strikes Again.* Philadelphia: J. B. Lippincott, 1940. First American edition, very good pus in like (scarce) dust jacket, jacket bright and complete, minor rubbing and nicking at extremities, from the collection of Duke Collier.   Royal Books   36 - 154   2015 $325

Crumley, James *The Muddy Fork and Other Things.* Northridge: Lord John Press, 1984. First edition, preceding trade edition by 7 years, one of 200 numbered copies signed by Crumley, this is designated an unnumbered 'Presentation Copy' and additionally inscribed to his friend, writer Andre Dubus, fine, with no dust jacket, as issued, from the collection of Duke Collier.   Royal Books   36 - 156   2015 $850

Crumley, James *The Wrong Case.* New York: Random House, 1975. First edition, about very good in very good plus dust jacket, spine lean and with light shelfwear and edge toning, jacket bright with little toning at extremities, crease to rear flap, small dampstain at bottom of front flap fold, inscribed by author June 16th '76 for Steve, from the collection of Duke Collier.   Royal Books   36 - 155   2015 $1250

Davis, Lindsey *Shadows in Bronze.* London: Sidgwick and Jackson, 1990. First edition, signed by author, fine in fine dust jacket, from the collection of Duke Collier.   Royal Books   36 - 157   2015 $500

Deighton, Len *Billion Dollar Brain.* London: Jonathan Cape, 1966. First edition, laid in are a facsimile of Deighton notebook and a facsimile of a TLS from Deighton describing the notebook, fine in near fine example of the fragile foil dust jacket, exceptional copy, from the collection of Duke Collier.   Royal Books   36 - 158   2015 $1850

Dexter, Colin *Last Bus to Woodstock.* London: Macmillan, 1975. Uncorrected proof, good to very good in publisher's plain green wrappers with black titles, spine lean, some vertical creasing to spine panel, light soil, lengthily inscribed by author for Staffan, from the collection of Duke Collier.   Royal Books   36 - 159   2015 $6500

Dexter, Colin *Last Bus to Woodstock.* London: Macmillan, 1975. First UK edition, very good in like dust jacket, slight spine lean, bumped at corners with mild shelfwear, jacket shows some fading along left edge of front panel, with 2 inch closed tear top of same and light soil overall, inscribed by author for Joan Spencer (colleague of author at Oxford), from the collection of Duke Collier.   Royal Books   36 - 160   2015 $3500

Dunning, John *Booked to Die.* New York: Charles Scribner's Sons, 1992. First edition, fine in fine dust jacket, from the collection of Duke Collier.   Royal Books   36 - 161   2015 $850

Fearing, Kenneth *The Big Clock.* New York: Harcourt Brace, 1946. First edition, near fine in strong, very good plus dust jacket, jacket bright and lovely, none of the spine fading nearly always found on this title, only short closed tear and associated crease at top front panel and some rubbing to crown, from the collection of Duke Collier. Royal Books 36 - 162 2015 $1500

Fish, Robert L. *Mute Witness.* New York: Doubleday, 1963. First edition, incredibly scarce, fine in near fine dust jacket with trace of rubbing to corners and some sunning to small bit of orange coloring on spine, from the collection of Duke Collier. Royal Books 36 - 223 2015 $1750

Fisher, Rudolph *The Conjure-Man Dies.* New York: Covici Friede, 1932. First edition, few small stains to cloth, else near fine in dust jacket that has been restored at extremities and presents as fine, from the collection of Duke Collier. Royal Books 36 - 2 2015 $7500

Francis, Dick 1920- *Blood Sport.* London: Michael Joseph, 1967. Uncorrected proof, very good plus in plain brown wrappers as issued, very slightly cocked, small stray red pen mark near fore edge of front wrapper, vertical wrinkling at spine, from the collection of Duke Collier. Royal Books 36 - 170 2015 $300

Francis, Dick 1920- *Dead Cert.* London: Michael Joseph, 1962. First edition, boards very slightly bowned, else book clean and bright, near fine in about near fine dust jacket, jacket shows none of the usual fading, nor any chips or tears, just a bit of uniform rubbing, inscribed by author for Elaine and Michael, from the collection of Duke Collier. Royal Books 36 - 163 2015 $8500

Francis, Dick 1920- *For Kicks.* New York: Harper and Row, 1965. First American edition, signed by author on half titlepage, near fine in near fine dust jacket with only touch of usual fading to jacket spine, diagonal crease fold at top of front flap, from the collection of Duke Collier. Royal Books 36 - 167 2015 $425

Francis, Dick 1920- *In the Frame.* London: Michael Joseph, 1976. Uncorrected proof, very good in plain brown wrappers as issued, spine roll and associated vertical wrinkling to spine, from the collection of Duke Collier. Royal Books 36 - 171 2015 $300

Francis, Dick 1920- *Nerve.* London: Michael Joseph, 1965. Uncorrected proof, very good in plain brown wrappers as issued, spine lean, some vertical wrinkling to same, generic bookplate signed by author laid in, earliest state of this title, from the collection of Duke Collier. Royal Books 36 - 168 2015 $1850

Francis, Dick 1920- *Nerve.* London: Michael Joseph, 1965. First edition, signed by author, near fine in like dust jacket, price clipped, touch of foxing to page edges, else book bright and clean, jacket exceptionally nice, only small amount of toning usually found, from the collection of Duke Collier. Royal Books 36 - 154 2015 $1500

Francis, Dick 1920- *Odds Against.* London: Michael Joseph, 1965. Uncorrected proof, very good in plain brown wrappers as issued, spine roll and associated vertical wrinkling to same, generic bookplate signed by author laid in, from the collection of Duke Collier. Royal Books 36 - 169 2015 $425

Francis, Dick 1920- *Odds Against.* London: Michael Joseph, 1965. First edition, near fine in bright, easily very near fine dust jacket, inscribed by author, from the collection of Duke Collier. Royal Books 36 - 166 2015 $825

Francis, Dick 1920- *The Sport of Queens.* London: Michael Joseph, 1957. First edition, signed by author, fine in fine dust jacket, truly superior copy, scarce first book, from the collection of Duke Collier. Royal Books 36 - 165 2015 $850

Freeman, R. Austin *The Red Thumb Mark.* New York: Dodd, Mead, 1924. First printing of this edition, fine, bight copy in equally fine dust jacket, from the collection of Duke Collier. Royal Books 36 - 178 2015 $1500

Furst, Alan *Dark Star.* Boston: Houghton Mifflin, 1991. First edition, fine and unread in fine dust jacket, from the collection of Duke Collier. Royal Books 36 - 177 2015 $400

Furst, Alan *Night Soldiers.* Boston: Houghton Mifflin, 1988. First edition, fine and unread in fine dust jacket, from the collection of Duke Collier. Royal Books 36 - 174 2015 $500

Furst, Alan *Shadow Trade.* New York: Delacorte, 1983. First edition, signed by author, fine in near fine dust jacket, touch of rubbing to jacket corners, one of the usual fading, from the collection of Duke Collier. Royal Books 36 - 175 2015 $500

Furst, Alan *The Caribbean Account.* New York: Delacorte Press, 1981. First edition, spine ends tapped, else fine in fine dust jacket, from the collection of Duke Collier. Royal Books 36 - 176 2015 $500

Furst, Alan *The Paris Drop.* Garden City: Doubleday, 1980. First edition, fine in about fine dust jacket, jacket has faintest crease at heel, else lovely, uncommon second book, from the collection of Duke Collier.   Royal Books   36 - 173   2015 $850

Furst, Alan *Your Day in the Barrel.* New York: Atheneum, 1976. First edition, fine in fine dust jacket, lengthily inscribed to Joan and Morris Alhadeff, from the collection of Duke Collier. Royal Books   36 - 172   2015 $1500

Gardner, Erle Stanley *Murder Up My Sleeve.* New York: William Morrow, 1937. First Canadian edition, fine in bright, price clipped dust jacket, lightly worn at spine ends and with three small chips on back panel, exceptional copy, very scarce in jacket, from the collection of Duke Collier.   Royal Books   36 - 32   2015 $2000

Gardner, Erle Stanley *Over the Hump.* London: Gordon Martin Publishing, 1945. First UK edition, and first separate edition, near fine in very good example of scarce dust jacket, jacket has light rubbing and few small cellophane repairs at verso, attractive copy, most uncommon, from the collection of Duke Collier.   Royal Books   36 - 33   2015 $1250

Gardner, Erle Stanley *The Case of the Backward Mule.* New York: William Morrow, 1946. First edition, fine in fine, price clipped dust jacket, inscribed by author for Raymond Chandler, from the collection of Duke Collier.   Royal Books   36 - 10   2015 $20,000

Gardner, Erle Stanley *The Case of the Baited Hook.* New York: William Morrow, 1940. First edition, bit of staining at lower edges of cover, else near fine in near fine dust jacket with light wear along edges, inscribed by author to early assistant, Noni (Bibler), from the collection of Duke Collier.   Royal Books   36 - 21   2015 $3000

Gardner, Erle Stanley *The Case of the Caretaker's Cat.* New York: William Morrow, 1935. First edition, fine in near fine, lightly rubbed dust jacket with light wear to top of spine and corners and tiny closed tear on front panel, inscribed by author for Noni (Bibler), one of author's early assistants, from the collection of Duke Collier.   Royal Books   36 - 14   2015 $3500

Gardner, Erle Stanley *The Case of the Counterfeit Eye.* New York: William Morrow, 1935. First edition, publisher's file copy with 'OFFICE FILE COPY' stamped on rear panel of jacket and several pencilled notations and deletions on front flap and front endpaper, near fine in very good or better dust jacket, evidence of removal on front pastedown, else book quire clean, jacket has no significant loss, only some rubbing at folds, light fading to spine panel, small chips at corners, very presentatble copy, from the collection of Duke Collier.   Royal Books   36 - 13   2015 $3500

Gardner, Erle Stanley *The Case of the Curious Bride.* New York: William Morrow, 1934. First edition, fine in bright, very good dust jacket with several modest chips, largest being at top of spine, affecting word 'The', inscribed by author for Noni Bibler, one of author's early assistants, from the collection of Duke Collier.   Royal Books   36 - 12   2015 $3000

Gardner, Erle Stanley *The Case of the Dangerous Dowager.* New York: William Morrow, 1937. First edition, very good plus in good dust jacket, 1 3/4 inch loss to top portion of jacket spine, else very good in couple of droplet stains on rear panel and light rubbing overall, warmly inscribed by author to early assistant, Noni (Bibler), from the collection of Duke Collier.   Royal Books   36 - 17   2015 $1250

Gardner, Erle Stanley *The Case of the Empty Tin.* New York: William Morrow, 1941. First edition, fine in bright, unrubbed dust jacket, lightly chipped at top of spine and corners, from the collection of Duke Collier.   Royal Books   36 - 23   2015 $1750

Gardner, Erle Stanley *The Case of the Haunted Husband.* New York: William Morrow, 1941. First edition, near fine in about very good scarce dust jacket, jacket rubbed with small chips at spine ends and folds one triangular chip at bottom right corner front panel, affecting part of author's name, from the collection of Duke Collier.   Royal Books   36 - 25   2015 $450

Gardner, Erle Stanley *The Case of the Howling Dog.* New York: William Morrow, 1934. First edition, near fine in very good and scarce dust jacket (couple of neat repairs along two of the folds, fading to reds on spine panel, chipping at spine ends affecting a portion of word 'The' in title, warmly inscribed by author for Noni Bibler, one of author's early assistants, from the collection of Duke Collier.   Royal Books   36 - 11   2015 $3250

Gardner, Erle Stanley *The Case of the Lame Canary.* New York: William Morrow, 1937. First edition, very good in like dust jacket, dampstain along fore-edges of boards (and conversely along flap folds of jacket at verso) and top right corner of text block, jacket has two chips, one at the crown and one at bottom rear panel, neither affecting any titling, despite noted flaws, bright copy, warmly inscribed by author to early assistant Noni (Bibler), from the collection of Duke Collier.   Royal Books   36 - 18   2015 $2250

Gardner, Erle Stanley *The Case of the Rolling Bones.* New York: William Morrow, 1939. First edition, about fine in bright, near fine dust jacket, which is lightly worn at top of spine and corners, with fingernail sized chip at base of spine, affecting publisher's logo, inscribed by author to early assistant Noni (Bibler), from the collection of Duke Collier.   Royal Books   36 - 20   2015 $3000

Gardner, Erle Stanley *The Case of the Silent Partner.* New York: William Morrow, 1940. First edition, fine in bright, unrubbed dust jacket, jacket lightly worn at spine tips, small chip top of front hinge, inscribed by author for early assistant, Noni (Bibler), from the collection of Duke Collier. Royal Books   36 - 22   2015 $3000

Gardner, Erle Stanley *The Case of the Sleepwalker's Niece.* New York: William Morrow, 1936. First edition, fine in near fine dust jacket, very lightly rubbed, lightly chipped at top of spine, inscribed by author to early assistant Noni (Bibler), from the collection of Duke Collier.   Royal Books   36 - 15   2015 $3500

Gardner, Erle Stanley *The Case of the Smoking Chimney.* New York: William Morrow, 1942. Uncorrected proof, about very good in publisher's self wrappers with publication date of Jan. 6 1942 and projected price of $2.00 rubber stamped on front endpaper, slight lean, vertical creasing to spine panel, some splitting to front flap fold, from the collection of Duke Collier.   Royal Books   36 - 28   2015 $950

Gardner, Erle Stanley *The Case of the Stuttering Bishop.* First edition, small mark on front cover, else about fine in bright, unrubbed, price clipped dust jacket, gorgeous copy, inscribed by author for Louise Weisberger, Aug. 1936, from the collection of Duke Collier.   Royal Books   36 - 16   2015 $3000

Gardner, Erle Stanley *The Case of the Substitute Face.* New York: William Morrow, 1938. First edition, fine in bright, unrubbed dust jacket with trivial rubbing to spine tips, inscribed by author for early assistant, Noni (Bibler), from the collection of Duke Collier.   Royal Books   36 - 19   2015 $3500

Gardner, Erle Stanley *The Case of the Velvet Claws.* First edition, near fine in very good plus example of rare dust jacket, jacket is quite nice with slight loss at crown, just barely touching word 'The' in title, light wear at heel, corners and top of back panel and couple of closed tears, otherwise bright and clean, inscribed by author for Capt. Joe Shaw, editor, from the collection of Duke Collier.   Royal Books   36 - 9   2015 $37,500

Gardner, Erle Stanley *The Case of the Velvet Claws.* New York: William Morrow, 1936. Second printing, near fine in very good dust jacket (both clearly state 'Second Printing'), jacket lightly rumpled along spine panel, with small bit of loss at crown and heel in (not titling affected), shallow rectangular chip at top rear panel, light general overall rubbing and nicking, very presentable copy, inscribed by author for early assistant Noni (Bibler), from the collection of Duke Collier.   Royal Books   36 - 24   2015 $2500

Gardner, Erle Stanley *The D. A. Draws a Circle.* New York: William Morrow, 1939. First printing of this edition, near fine in very good or better dust jacket, dampstain bottom right corner of front board, affecting jacket verso in same spot, otherwise only lightly rubbed overall, inscribed by author to early assistant, Noni (Bibler), from the collection of Duke Collier.   Royal Books   36 - 30   2015 $1850

Gardner, Erle Stanley *The D. A. Goes to Trial.* New York: William Morrow, 1940. First edition, dampstain bottom right corner of front board, endpapers toned, else near fine in about very good dust jacket with small chips at extremities and some of the usual color-fading to pink spine title, warmly inscribed by author to early assistant, Noni (Bibler), from the collection of Duke Collier.   Royal Books   36 - 31   2015 $1850

Gardner, Erle Stanley *The D. A. Holds a Candle.* New York: William Morrow, 1938. First edition, very slightly cocked, else very good plus in very good dust jacket with small chips at extremities and some of the usual color fading to pink spine title, warmly inscribed by author to early assistant, Noni (Bibler), from the collection of Duke Collier. Royal Books   36 - 29   2015 $2250

Greene, Graham   1904-1991 *Our Man in Havana.* London: William Heinemann, 1958. First edition, inscribed by Greene to Alexander Frere (chairman of Heinemann), fine and unread in fine dust jacket, from the collection of Duke Collier.   Royal Books   36 - 1   2015 $5500

Greene, Graham   1904-1991 *The 3rd Man.* New York: Viking Press, 1950. First edition and first separate edition after beng published jointly with The Fallen Idol by Heinemann earlier the same year, fine in stunning, about fine dust jacket, owner name on front endpaper, jacket shows absolutely none of the spine fading endemic to title, only a few pinhead size rubs and minute wear at extremities, from the collection of Duke Collier.   Royal Books   36 - 179   2015 $950

Hammett, Dashiell *"Bodies Piled Up." in Black Mask, December 1, 1923.* New York: Pro Distributors, 1923. First appearance, good in perfect bound wrappers, with corner chip at top right front panel, bruise at top left of same, light fray to outer edges, pages dry but still somewhat supple, some light chipping to edges of prelim leaves, from the collection of Duke Collier.   Royal Books   36 - 181   2015 $750

Hammett, Dashiell *The Dashiell Hammett Omnibus.* New York: Alfred A. Knopf, 1935. First edition, trace of shelfwear at base of spine, else fine, tight copy, bright dust jacket with very light wear to spine ends and closed tear at front hinge, from the collection of Duke Collier.   Royal Books   36 - 180   2015 $2000

Hammett, Dashiell *The Thin Man.* New York: Alfred A. Knopf, 1934. First edition, four jacket variants, of no established priority, this one is in red with no blurbs, cloth bit mottled as always found, else near fine in very good plus dust jacket, jacket has small chips at corners, one at crown which affects "DA" in author's name, the others much smaller, from the collection of Duke Collier. Royal Books 36 - 182 2015 $4000

Hillerman, Tony *Listening Woman.* New York: Harper and Row, 1978. Uncorrected proof, signed by Hillerman, small closed tear at fore edge of front wrapper, else fine in plain red wrappers as issued. from the collection of Duke Collier. Royal Books 36 - 191 2015 $1750

Hillerman, Tony *Listening Woman.* New York: Harper and Row, 1978. First edition, near fine in fine dust jacket, inscribed by author for Bruce Taylor, some loss to titling on backstrip (problem endemic to this title), else near fine in like dust jacket with none of the usual spine fading, attractive copy, from the collection of Duke Collier. Royal Books 36 - 193 2015 $1250

Hillerman, Tony *People of Darkness.* New York: Harper, 1980. Uncorrected proof, signed by author, fine in plain red wrappers, from the collection of Duke Collier. Royal Books 36 - 197 2015 $450

Hillerman, Tony *The Blessing Way.* New York: Harper and Row, 1970. First edition, fine in lovely, near fine dust jacket, bit of usual fading to jacket spine, but only to titling, some slight rubbing at spine ends and corners, else exceptionally sharp, unread copy, from the collection of Duke Collier. Royal Books 36 - 189 2015 $3000

Hillerman, Tony *The Boy Who Made Dragonfly.* New York: Harper and Row, 1972. First edition, nicely inscribed by author to fellow crime writer, John and Pat Ball, from the collection of Duke Collier. Royal Books 36 - 192 2015 $1750

Hillerman, Tony *The Fly on the Wall.* New York: Harper and Row, 1971. First edition, review copy, publisher's slip laid in, fine in bright, very good plus dust jacket with light rubbing and shallow creasing on spine ends and soil to rear panel, from the collection of Duke Collier. Royal Books 36 - 194 2015 $1000

Hillerman, Tony *The Great Taos Bank Robbery and Other Indian Country Affairs.* Albuquerque: University of New Mexico Press, 1973. First edition, fine and unread in fine dust jacket, first issue jacket with only one image on rear panel, from the collection of Duke Collier. Royal Books 36 - 196 2015 $650

Hillerman, Tony *Words, Weather and Wolfmen.* Gallup: Southwesterner Books, 1989. First edition, one of 26 lettered copies, this being a non-lettered presentation copy, with full color drawing by Franklin laid in, signed by author and artist, Ernie Franklin, and the publisher, fine in fine slipcase, from the collection of Duke Collier. Royal Books 36 - 195 2015 $750

Himes, Chester *Cotton Comes to Harlem.* London: Frederick Miller, 1965. First edition, fine, unread in fine dust jacket, from the collection of Duke Collier. Royal Books 36 - 198 2015 $650

Himes, Chester *Pinktoes.* London: Olympia Press, 1961. First edition, paperback original, fine and unread in green wrappers with black and white title, rule and design as issued, 'new price' stamp bottom right corner of rear wrapper, else pristine, most uncommon, from the collection of Duke Collier. Royal Books 36 - 199 2015 $550

James, P. D. *The Black Tower.* London: Faber and Faber, 1975. First edition, fine in near fine dust jacket, jacket minutely rubbed at corners and at rear panel, attractive copy, from the collection of Duke Collier. Royal Books 36 - 200 2015 $325

King, Laurie R. *A Grave Talent.* New York: St. Martin's Press, 1993. First edition, first issue, signed by author, fine and unread in fine dust jacket, from the collection of Duke Collier. Royal Books 36 - 201 2015 $325

Larsson, Steig *The Girl with the Dragon Tattoo. The Girl Who Kicked the Hornet's Nest. The Girl Who Played with Fire.* London: Maclehose/Quercus, 2008. 2009. First UK editions, 3 volumes, each fine and unread in fine dust jacket, without trace of wear to spine bumping endemic to these titles, second volume signed by translator Reg Keeland on titlepage, incredible set, from the collection of Duke Collier. Royal Books 36 - 4 2015 $5000

Le Carre, John 1931- *A Murder of Quality.* New York: Walker, 1963. First American edition, signed by author, very good plus in very good plus dust jacket, moderately cocked with some light soil to cloth, jacket bright and unfaded with few tiny stresses at front flap folds, 2 inch closed tear top front panel and light rubbing at extremities, author's uncommon second book, from the collection of Duke Collier, signed by author Christmas 2004. Royal Books 36 - 203 2015 $3500

Le Carre, John 1931- *Call for the Dead.* New York: Walker, 1962. First American edition, very good plus in like dust jacket, book very slightly cocked, hint of fading at edges, otherwise quite clean, jacket bright with closed tear starting at top of front flap fold and running into middle of front flap, author's uncommon first book, custom clamshell box, from the collection of Duke Collier.   Royal Books   36 - 206   2015 $950

Le Carre, John 1931- *The Spy Who Came in from the Cold.* London: Gollancz, 1963. First UK edition, very good plus in very good plus dust jacket, binding slightly cocked, backstrip and jacket spine, faded, strips of staining top and bottom edge of jacket verso from old jacket protector, with ALS by author discussing development of a new book "Carcass of the Lion" (which would eventually be published as The Spy Who Came in form the Cold), custom clamshell box designed to display book and letter when opened, from the collection of Duke Collier.   Royal Books   36 - 202   2015 $8500

Le Carre, John 1931- *The Spy Who Came in from the Cold.* New York: Coward McCann, 1964. Uncorrected proof, fine in publisher's wrappers, quarter leather clamshell box, from the collection of Duke Collier.   Royal Books   36 - 204   2015 $1500

Leonard, Elmore *Fifty-Two Pickup.* New York: Delacorte Press, 1974. First edition, near fine in fine dust jacket, sharp copy, from the collection of Duke Collier.   Royal Books   36 - 212   2015 $500

Leonard, Elmore *Fifty-Two Pickup.* New York: Delacorte Press, 1974. Uncorrected proof, signed by author, near fine in tall plain mustard wrappers, some brief staining to top front wrapper, else bright copy, from the collection of Duke Collier.   Royal Books   36 - 214   2015 $1250

Leonard, Elmore *Gold Coast.* London: W. H. Allen, 1982. First UK edition and first hardcover edition, signed by author, fine in fine price clipped dust jacket, from the collection of Duke Collier.   Royal Books   36 - 211   2015 $1500

Leonard, Elmore *Swag.* New York: Delacorte Press, 1976. Uncorrected proof, near fine in tall plain light green wrappers, front wrapper removed and substituted with page of early reviews for book tipped on to first leaf, clearly as issued, from the collection of Duke Collier.   Royal Books   36 - 215   2015 $650

Leonard, Elmore *The Big Bounce.* London: Robert Hale, 1969. First UK edition, and first hardcover edition, signed by author on laid-in bookplate, fine in fine dust jacket, from the collection of Duke Collier.   Royal Books   36 - 209   2015 $3500

Leonard, Elmore *The Law at Randado.* Boston: Houghton Mifflin, 1955. First edition, signed by author on titlepage, fine in near fine example of scarce dust jacket, with only light wear at spine ends and corners, from the collection of Duke Collier.   Royal Books   36 - 207   2015 $7500

Leonard, Elmore *The Moonshine War.* Garden City: Doubleday, 1969. First edition, near fine in like dust jacket, inscribed by author to one of book's two dedicatees, Buck Beshear, 6-20-99, from the collection of Duke Collier.   Royal Books   36 - 210   2015 $3250

Leonard, Elmore *Unknown Man No. 89.* New York: Delacorte Press, 1977. Uncorrected proof, signed by author, near fine in tall plain blue wrappers small stain at top of front wrapper, from the collection of Duke Collier.   Royal Books   36 - 213   2015 $1450

Leonard, Elmore *Valdez Is Coming.* London: Robert Hale, 1969. First UK edition and first hardcover edition, signed by author, fine in fine dust jacket, from the collection of Duke Collier.   Royal Books   36 - 208   2015 $5000

MacDonald, John D. *A Bullet for Cinderella.* London: Robert Ale, 1960. First UK and first hardcover edition, near fine in fine dust jacket, from the collection of Duke Collier.   Royal Books   36 - 54   2015 $2500

MacDonald, John D. *A Deadly Shade of Gold.* Philadelphia: J. B. Lippincott, 1974. First edition in hardcover, near fine in about fine dust jacket, attractive copy, uncommon in this condition, from the collection of Duke Collier.   Royal Books   36 - 49   2015 $300

MacDonald, John D. *A Man of Affairs.* London: Robert Hale, 1959. First UK and first hardcover edition, fine and unread in fine dust jacket, from the collection of Duke Collier.   Royal Books   36 - 56   2015 $2500

MacDonald, John D. *A Purple Place for Dying.* New York: J. B. Lippincott, 1976. First American edition, near fine in like dust jacket, inscribed by author for Patrick Hyman 4 June 1983, from the collection of Duke Collier.   Royal Books   36 - 43   2015 $950

MacDonald, John D. *A Tan and Sandy Silence.* London: Robert Hale, 1973. First edition, hint of foxing to page edges, else fine, unread in fine dust jacket, from the collection of Duke Collier.   Royal Books   36 - 47   2015 $450

MacDonald, John D. *April Evil.* London: Robert Hale, 1957. First UK edition and first edition in hardcover, fine and unread in fine dust jacket, from the collection of Duke Collier.   Royal Books   36 - 52   2015 $2850

MacDonald, John D. *Bright Orange for the Shroud.* Philadelphia: J. B. Lippincott, 1972. First hardcover edition, fine in fine dust jacket, none of the usual fading to sensitive jacket spine present, signed by author on bookplate tipped in at half title, bookplate of noted collected Duke Collier. Royal Books   36 - 42   2015 $1250

MacDonald, John D. *Darker than Amber.* Philadelphia: J. B. Lippincott, 1970. First American edition, very good plus in bright, near fine dust jacket, jacket is first issue with a price of $4.95 at bottom front flap and printer's code '470' at top front flap, book is very slightly cocked and bumped at crown, else clean, jacket bright lacking the spine fading that is found on nearly every copy, showing only small chip at one corner of crown, from the collection of Duke Collier. Royal Books   36 - 37   2015 $3500

MacDonald, John D. *Death Trap.* London: Robert Hale, 1958. First UK and first hardcover edition, fine and unread in fine dust jacket, from the collection of Duke Collier. Royal Books   36 - 55   2015 $2500

MacDonald, John D. *Dress Her in Indigo.* Philadelphia: J. B. Lippincott, 1971. First American edition, very good in like dust jacket, spine lean, bookplate of noted collector Duke Collier, jacket lightly rubbed with ink price notation front flap (offset very slightly to front endpaper), faint vertical crease running parallel to rear hinge fold, laid in is card signed by author Nv. 18 1977.   Royal Books   36 - 45   2015 $650

MacDonald, John D. *Pale Gray for Guilt.* Philadelphia: J. B. Lippincott, 1971. First American edition in hardcover, first issue jacket with code 971 top right corner of front flap and price of $5.50 at bottom, inscribed by author on generic bookplate tipped in, bookplate of noted collector Duke Collier, fine and unread in about fine, minutely rubbed dust jacket, as sharp a copy of this series title as we have seen. Royal Books   36 - 40   2015 $2000

MacDonald, John D. *Slam the Big Door.* London: Robert Hale, 1961. First UK and first hardcover edition, signed by uthor, fine in exceptionally bright, near fine dust jacket, from the collection of Duke Collier.   Royal Books   36 - 58   2015 $3250

MacDonald, John D. *Soft Touch.* London: Robert Hale, 1960. First UK edition and first edition in hardcover, fine and unread in fine dust jacket, from the collection of Duke Collier.   Royal Books   36 - 53   2015 $2000

MacDonald, John D. *The Deep Blue Good-by.* Philadelphia: J. B. Lippincott, 1975. First edition in hardcover, near fine in bright, near fine jacket, some fading to top edges of boards, jacket minutely rubbed at spine ends, from the collection of Duke Collier.   Royal Books   36 - 48   2015 $375

MacDonald, John D. *The Empty Copper Sea.* Philadelphia and New York: J. B. Lippincott, 1978. First edition, signed by author on half titlepage, fine and unread in fine dust jacket, bookplate of noted collector Duke Collier. Royal Books   36 - 50   2015 $325

MacDonald, John D. *The Girl in the Plain Brown Wrapper.* New York: J. B. Lippincott, 1973. First printing of this edition and first American edition in hardcover, near fine in very good plus dust jacket, inscribed in year of publication to Denver Post book editor, Clarus Backus, laid in is sheet of Denver Post stationery, clipped article from Denver Post by Mr. Backus about MacDonald's death, and glossy Doubleday review photo from 1968, for the book 'Three for McGee', bookplate of noted collected Duke Collier, jacket lightly rubbed at extremities, touch of usual fading on spine, very nice, extremely scarce presentation copy.   Royal Books   36 - 38   2015 $2750

MacDonald, John D. *The Long Lavender Look.* Philadelphia: J. B. Lippincott, 1972. First hardcover edition, about fine in near fine dust jacket, minutely rubbed, from the collection of Duke Collier.   Royal Books   36 - 46   2015 $550

MacDonald, John D. *The Neon Jungle.* London: Robert Hale, 1962. First UK edition and first edition in hardcover, fine and unread in fine dust jacket, from the collection of Duke Collier.   Royal Books   36 - 51   2015 $2850

MacDonald, John D. *The Price of Murder.* London: Robert Hale, 1958. First UK and first hardcover edition, fine and unread in fine dust jacket, from the collection of Duke Collier.   Royal Books   36 - 57   2015 $2500

MacDonald, John D. *The Quick Red Fox.* Philadelphia: J. B. Lippincott, 1973. First edition in hardcover, fine in about fine dust jacket, bookplate of noted collector, Duke Collier, just touch of rubbing in couple of spots, none of the usual fading to sensitive jacket spine, bright, fresh copy. Royal Books   36 - 44   2015 $950

MacDonald, John D. *The Scarlet Ruse.* New York: J. B. Lippincott and Thomas Y. Crowell, 1980. First American hardcover edition, near fine in like dust jacket, warmly inscribed by author for Louise and Joe, from the collection of Duke Collier.   Royal Books   36 - 41   2015 $1850

MacDonald, John D. *The Turquoise Lament.* Philadelphia: J. B. Lippincott, 1973. First edition, signed by author on titlepage and dated 21 Oct. 1983, very good plus in very good plus dust jacket, jacket is not price clipped and shows price of $5.95 on front flap, only the second such copy we have handled, bookplate of noted collector Duke Collier on front endpaper, jacket lightly rubbed at extremities with touch of fading to colors on spine. Royal Books 36 - 39 2015 $2000

MacDonald, Ross *Blue City.* London: Cassell, 1949. First edition, very good in like dust jacket, some brief soil to boards, jacket moderately worn and creased at extremities, uncommon, early Millar title, inscribed by author Xmas 1951 to Glenn Schiegel, from the collection of Duke Collier. Royal Books 36 - 79 2015 $1500

MacDonald, Ross *Find a Victim.* New York: Alfred A. Knopf, 1954. First edition, signed by author, laid in is 2 page letter in holograph pencil in author's hand, spelling out a variant version of the dust jacket's copy, that manifests author's direct involvement in marketing of his own book, fine and unread, spectacular copy, from the collection of Duke Collier. Royal Books 36 - 64 2015 $5000

MacDonald, Ross *Self-Portrait: Ceaselessly into the Past.* Santa Barbara: Capra Press, 1981. First edition, one of 26 lettered copies (this being letter 'J'), signed by author and Eudora Welty who provided introduction and additional inscription by book's publisher, Ralph Sipper, dated 1981, original photo of the two authors laid into pocket tipped on to front pastedown, as issued, fine in black leather, paper covered slipcase as issued, corners of slipcase lightly rubbed, from the collection of Duke Collier. Royal Books 36 - 81 2015 $1500

MacDonald, Ross *The Barbarous Coast.* New York: Alfred A. Knopf, 1956. First edition, near fine in like dust jacket, price clipped, bright but with soil to rear panel, custom clamshell box, from the collection of Duke Collier. Royal Books 36 - 74 2015 $1250

MacDonald, Ross *The Dark Tunnel.* New York: Dodd, Mead, 1944. First edition, fine in bright, near fine dust jacket, lightly chipped at spine ends and lightly rubbed at hinges, rare, from the collection of Duke Collier. Royal Books 36 - 61 2015 $15,000

MacDonald, Ross *The Drowning Pool.* New York: Alfred A. Knopf, 1950. First edition, near fine in bright, near fine dust jacket, dedication copy, doubly inscribed to legendary genre fiction editor and enthusiast Anthony Boucher, from the collection of Duke Collier. Royal Books 36 - 63 2015 $25,000

MacDonald, Ross *The Far Side of the Dollar.* New York: Alfred a. Knopf, 1965. First edition, fine and unread in fine dust jacket, vibrant yellow topstain, from the collection of Duke Collier. Royal Books 36 - 76 2015 $425

MacDonald, Ross *The Ferguson Affair.* New York: Alfred A. Knopf, 1960. First edition, fine and unread, near fine dust jacket with touch of overall toning and light soil to rear panel, attractive copy, from the collection of Duke Collier. Royal Books 36 - 78 2015 $725

MacDonald, Ross *The Galton Case.* New York: Alfred A. Knopf, 1959. First edition, signed by author, about near fine in bright, near fine dust jacket, from the collection of Duke Collier. Royal Books 36 - 70 2015 $2500

MacDonald, Ross *The Instant Enemy.* New York: Alfred A. Knopf, 1968. First edition, fine and unread in fine dust jacket, from the collection of Duke Collier. Royal Books 36 - 77 2015 $375

MacDonald, Ross *The Moving Target.* London: Cassell, 1951. First edition, very good plus in very good dust jacket, mild soil to boards, some foxing to page edges, jacket moderately worn at extremities with few small chips and closed tears only signed copy of the UK edition we have encountered, inscribed by author to his in-laws Doogie and Clarence (Strum), from the collection of Duke Collier. Royal Books 36 - 72 2015 $2000

MacDonald, Ross *The Moving Target.* New York: Alfred A. Knopf, 1949. First edition, near fine in like dust jacket, merest trace of sunning to red band near bottom spine, otherwise bright and fresh as the day it was issued, extremely scarce in this condition, from the collection of Duke Collier. Royal Books 36 - 62 2015 $12,500

MacDonald, Ross *The Three Roads.* New York: Alfred A. Knopf, 1948. First edition, fine in near fine dust jacket with small rubber stamp "Booth memorial Hospital, bump to heel, some minute rubbing at corners, from the collection of Duke Collier. Royal Books 36 - 71 2015 $1750

MacDonald, Ross *The Way Some People Die.* New York: Alfred A. Knopf, 1951. First edition, fine in bright, near fine dust jacket with deep black topstain, jacket has touch of usual spine fading but much better than usual, tiny chip at top bottom front panel, from the collection of Duke Collier. Royal Books 36 - 69 2015 $3500

MacDonald, Ross *The Zebra-striped Hearse.* New York: Alfred A. Knopf, 1962. First edition, fine and unread in fine, price clipped dust jacket, topstain brilliant, none of the usual fading to pink lettering, from the collection of Duke Collier. Royal Books 36 - 75 2015 $950

MacDonald, Ross *Trouble Follows Me.* New York: Dodd Mead, 1946. First Edition, fine, tight copy in bright dust jacket with no tear or chips, minor wear at base of spine, exceptionally fine, fresh copy, from the collection of Duke Collier.   Royal Books   36 - 68   2015 $3500

McBain, Ed *Give the Boys a Great Big Hand.* New York: Simon and Schuster, 1960. First edition, signed by author, very faint die mark along bottom front endpaper, else book quite clean, jacket fine but for very slight fading to red titles, from the collection of Duke Collier.   Royal Books   36 - 186   2015 $450

McBain, Ed *Killer's Wedge.* New York: Simon and Schuster, 1959. First edition, fine and unread in fine dust jacket, single small sticker shadow to front panel, else pristine copy, from the collection of Duke Collier.   Royal Books   36 - 183   2015 $1500

McBain, Ed *King's Ransom.* New York: Simon and Schuster, 1959. First edition, near fine in very good plus dust jacket, touch of toning to edges of text block, jacket bright, some nick at spine ends and couple of corners, bright copy, from the collection of Duke Collier.   Royal Books   36 - 184   2015 $950

McBain, Ed *Sadie When She Died.* Garden City: Doubleday, 1972. First edition, signed by author on titlepage, label of author's literary agent, Scott Meredith Literary agency in NY, fine and unread, fine dust jacket with tiniest pinpoint rubbing at spine ends, remarkable copy, from the collection of Duke Collier.   Royal Books   36 - 185   2015 $450

McBain, Ed *See Them Die.* New York: Simon and Schuster, 1960. First edition, signed by author, about near fine in fine dust jacket, some of the usual toning to text block edges, spine ends bumped, else book clean, from the collection of Duke Collier.   Royal Books   36 - 188   2015 $325

McBain, Ed *The Heckler.* New York: Simon and Schuster, 1960. First edition, signed by author, dated 8/25/90, fine and unread in fine dust jacket, from the collection of Duke Collier.   Royal Books   36 - 187   2015 $375

Nearing, Scott *Dollar Diplomacy.* New York: B. W. Huebsch and the Viking Press, 1925. First edition, near fine, lacking rare dust jacket, attractive octagonal bookplate, small numeric ink notation to same, at top left corner, inscribed by co-author Joseph Freeman to Rex Stout and his wife Fay, from the collection of Duke Collier.   Royal Books   36 - 125   2015 $1500

Nebel, Frederick *Fifty Roads to Town.* Boston: Little Brown, 1936. First edition, very good plus in very good plus dust jacket, slightest lean, light toning and faint soil to backstrip and board edges, jacket is as nice as we have seen on this title, only small chip at crown and light edge rubbing to note, attractive copy, from the collection of Duke Collier, inscribed by author for Harry and Shirley Steeger Jan. 24 1936.   Royal Books   36 - 216   2015 $1250

Parker, Robert B. *Looking for Rachel Wallace.* New York: Delacorte, 1980. First edition, fine and unread in fine dust jacket, from the collection of Duke Collier.   Royal Books   36 - 217 2015 $350

Parker, Robert B. *Looking for Rachel Wallace.* New York: Delacorte, 1980. Uncorrected proof, fine in plain tall green wrappers as issued, from the collection of Duke Collier.   Royal Books   36 - 218   2015 $650

Parker, Robert B. *Surrogate.* Northridge: Lord John Press, 1982. First edition, one of 50 numbered (this being no. 7) signed by author, fine in red patterned paper covered boards and maroon quarter leather, near fine, black cloth slipcase, from the collection of Duke Collier.   Royal Books 36 - 219   2015 $2000

Patterson, James *The Thomas Berryman Number.* Boston: Little Brown, 1976. First edition, fine in fine dust jacket, from the collection of Duke Collier.   Royal Books 36 - 220   2015 $1750

Pelecanos, George P. *Nick's Trip.* New York: St. Martin's Press, 1993. First edition, signed by author, fine and unread in fine dust jacket, without trace of wear, name of usual bumping to spine ends superior example, from the collection of Duke Collier.   Royal Books   36 - 221   2015 $1250

Pelecanos, George P. *Shoedog.* New York: St. Martin's Press, 1994. First edition, signed by author on titlepage, review copy with publisher's announcement specific to this title laid in, fine and unread, fine dust jacket, from the collection of Duke Collier.   Royal Books   36 - 222   2015 $350

ASSOCIATION COPIES

Porter, Katherine Anne 1890-1980 *A Note on the Author with the Key, One of Seventeen Stories from Miss Welty's Forthcoming "A Curtain of Green".* Garden City: Doubleday Doran, 1941. First edition, small octavo, saddle stitched wrappers as issued fine, this copy inscribed by Welty to her longtime friend, author Kenneth Millar (Ross MacDonald), laid in is a marvelous TLS from Welty to Millar dated May 11 1971 in which she recounts the history of the pamphlet and its cover photo, letter with one horizontal fold, fine in custom folding cloth chemise and full leather custom clamshell box, gilt titles, rule and decoration, rounded spine and raised bands, from the collection of Duke Collier.   Royal Books 36 - 67   2015 $12,500

Rankin, Ian *Black and Blue.* London: Orion, 1997. First edition, signed by author on titlepage, fine and unread in fine dust jacket, from the collection of Duke Collier.   Royal Books 36 - 90   2015 $550

Rankin, Ian *Hide and Seek.* London: Barrie and Jenkins, 1991. First edition, fine and unread in fine dust jacket, only hint of usual toning to page edges, inscribed by author for Duke Collier with drawing of hangman motif.   Royal Books 36 - 94   2015 $450

Rankin, Ian *Knots and Crosses.* Garden City: Doubleday, 1987. First American edition, signed by author along with his trademark 'knots-and-crosses' drawing, fine and unread in near fine dust jacket, just hint of fading to red titles on jacket spine, from the collection of Duke Collier.   Royal Books 36 - 87   2015 $550

Rankin, Ian *Knots and Crosses.* London: Bodley Head, 1987. First edition, fine and unread in fine dust jacket, absolutely none of the usual fading at spine panel, inscribed by author for Duke (Collier).   Royal Books   36 - 86   2015 $2750

Rankin, Ian *Let It Bleed.* London: Orion, 1995. First edition, signed by author on titlepage along with his trademark knots and crosses drawing, fine and unread in fine dust jacket, from the collection of Duke Collier.   Royal Books 36 - 89   2015 $800

Rankin, Ian *Strip Jack.* London: Orion, 1992. First edition, signed by author with his hangman motif, near fine in fine dust jacket, none of the usual to page edges present, jacket is export variant, with no price to front flap, from the collection of Duke Collier.   Royal Books   36 - 93   2015 $450

Rankin, Ian *The Flood.* London: Polygon, 1986. First edition, signed by author on titlepage, fine in fine dust jacket, from the collection of Duke Collier.   Royal Books   36 - 88   2015 $2500

Rankin, Ian *Watchman.* London: Bodley Head, 1988. First edition, fine and unread in fine dust jacket with none of the usual fading to red titling on jacket spine, from the collection of Duke Collier.   Royal Books   36 - 92   2015 $450

Rankin, Ian *Westwind.* London: Barrie and Jenkins, 1990. First edition, fine and unread in about fine dust jacket, jacket fine but for tiniest crease to one corner of crown, from the collection of Duke Collier.   Royal Books   36 - 95   2015 $325

Rankin, Ian *Wolfman.* London: Century, 1992. First edition, fine and unread in fine dust jacket, quite scarce, from the collection of Duke Collier.   Royal Books   36 - 91   2015 $550

Reeves, Robert *Dead and Done For.* New York: Alfred A. Knopf, 1939. First edition, fine and unread in fine dust jacket, from the collection of Duke Collier.   Royal Books 36 - 224   2015 $400

Sayers, Dorothy L. *Busman's Honeymoon.* London: Victor Gollancz, 1938. First UK edition, very good plus in very good plus, price clipped example of scarce dust jacket, owner name, slight lean, touch of foxing to front endpapers, else book is quite clean, jacket has only slightest fray at crown, with some toning to spine and at extremities, from the collection of Duke Collier.   Royal Books   36 - 231   2015 $375

Sayers, Dorothy L. *Dorothy L. Sayers Omnibus.* New York: Harcourt Brace, 1934. First edition, review copy with publisher's slip affixed to lower portion of front flap, fine in near fine dust jacket that has minor professional restoration at spine ends, remarkably scarce, from the collection of Duke Collier.   Royal Books   36 - 230   2015 $750

Sayers, Dorothy L. *Gaudy Night.* London: Victor Gollancz, 1935. First edition, very good plus, very good example of scarce dust jacket, neat contemporary gift inscription dated Christmas 1935, spine gilt bright, jacket has no loss whatsoever, but is lightly faded ad spine, shows moderate uniform soil, from the collection of Duke Collier. Royal Books   36 - 228   2015 $1500

Sayers, Dorothy L. *Gaudy Night.* London: Victor Gollancz, 1935. First edition, very good plus in poor example of scarce dust jacket, jacket is basically in pieces, lacking a significant portion at top and bottom of spine, detached at folds, rare, custom quarter leather clamshell box, inscribed by author to her husband (Oswald Atherton) Mac (Fleming), from the collection of Duke Collier.   Royal Books 36 - 225   2015 $6500

Sayers, Dorothy L. *In the Teeth of Evidence.* New York: Harcourt Brace, 1940. First American edition, fine and unread, in fine dust jacket, from the collection of Duke Collier.   Royal Books   36 - 229   2015 $1500

Sayers, Dorothy L. *The Nine Tailors.* New York: Harcourt Brace, 1934. First American edition, very good plus in fine dust jacket, with some professional restoration at extremities, binding very slightly cocked, from the collection of Duke Collier.   Royal Books   36 - 227   2015 $1750

Sayers, Dorothy L. *The Unpleasantness at the Bellona Club.* New York: Payson and Clarke Ltd., 1928. First American edition, very good to fine, supplied dust jacket, book has slight lean and is faded at spine and board edges with small stain on backstrip, jacket is impeccable, quite fresh with no wear to note, from the collection of Duke Collier.   Royal Books   36 - 226   2015 $2250

Smith, Martin *Canto for a Gypsy.* New York: G. P. Putnam's Sons, 1972. First edition, fine and unread in about fine dust jacket, uncommon, exceptionally bright, fresh copy, from the collection of Duke Collier.   Royal Books   36 - 232   2015 $325

Spillane, Mickey *I the Jury.* London: Arthur Barker, 1952. First edition, very good plus in very good plus jacket, some light soil to boards, jacket has chip at crown (titling not affected) and couple of smaller chips at corners, light rubbing overall, from the collection of Duke Collier.   Royal Books   36 - 234   2015 $950

Spillane, Mickey *One Lonely Night.* London: Arthur Barker, 1952. First edition, fine in very good plus jacket (no loss, only some light wear at extremities, and light rubbing), from the collection of Duke Collier.   Royal Books   36 - 236   2015 $450

Spillane, Mickey *The Erection Set.* London: W. H. Allen, 1972. First edition, inscribed by author for Graham Lindsay, near fine in like dust jacket, from the collection of Duke Collier.   Royal Books   36 - 233   2015 $650

Spillane, Mickey *The Long Wait.* London: Arthur Barker, 1953. First edition, fine in very good plus dust jacket, jacket has no loss, only some light fray at crown and light wear at few extremities, from the collection of Duke Collier.   Royal Books   36 - 237   2015 $300

Spillane, Mickey *Vengeance is Mine.* London: Arthur Barker, 1941. First edition, near fine in very good dust jacket, light foxing to prelim leaves, page edges and jacket verso, jacket lightly rubbed overall, some fading to spine and light wear at corners and spine ends, from the collection of Duke Collier.   Royal Books   36 - 235   2015 $550

Stout, Rex *A Right to Die.* New York: Viking Press, 1964. First edition, inscribed by author Dec. 26 1964 to Elizabeth Boyne, fine in fine dust jacket, from the collection of Duke Collier.   Royal Books   36 - 107   2015 $2500

Stout, Rex *And Be a Villain.* New York: Viking Press, 1948. First edition, fine in near fine, very lightly rubbed dust jacket, from the collection of Duke Collier.   Royal Books   36 - 120   2015 $450

Stout, Rex *Before Midnight.* New York: Viking Press, 1955. First edition, fine in near fine dust jacket, very lightly corner rubbed, from the collection of Duke Collier.   Royal Books   36 - 121   2015 $350

Stout, Rex *Black Orchids.* New York: Farrar and Rinehart, 1942. First edition, fine in near fine dust jacket, jacket extremely fresh and colorful, only touch of rubbing to couple of corners, stunning copy, from the collection of Duke Collier.   Royal Books   36 - 105   2015 $4500

Stout, Rex *Death of a Doxy.* New York: Viking Press, 1966. First edition, fine in near fine dust jacket, some faint rubbing to rear jacket panel, tiny closed tear at bottom front hinge fold (with associated small, neat cello tape repair at verso), from the collection of Duke Collier.   Royal Books   36 - 122   2015 $325

Stout, Rex *Double for Death.* New York: Farrar Rinehart, 1939. First edition, slightly cocked, else near fine in bright, about near fine dust jacket with some very shallow creasing at crown and top front panel, from the collection of Duke Collier.   Royal Books   36 - 119   2015 $450

Stout, Rex *Fer-de-Lance.* New York: Farrar and Rinehart, 1934. First edition, near fine in like dust jacket, jacket rare, with Farrar and Rinehart circular 'recommendation' sticker on front panel, pink topstain very bright gilt bright and complete, jacket with only couple of tiny chips and some expert repairs (not restoration) at upper spine panel, from the collection of Duke Collier.   Royal Books   36 - 97   2015 $25,000

Stout, Rex *Forest Fire.* London: Faber and Faber, 1934. Uncorrected proof, very good in plain brown wrappers, title label on spine, square and tight with few crease to spine panel, custom quarter leather clamshell box, from the collection of Duke Collier.   Royal Books   36 - 104   2015 $4500

Stout, Rex *Gambit.* New York: Viking Press, 1962. First edition, fine and unread in fine dust jacket pristine copy, only hint of rubbing at a couple of spine corners to note, absolutely none of the color fading usually found, from the collection of Duke Collier.   Royal Books   36 - 118   2015 $475

Stout, Rex *Golden Remedy.* New York: Vanguard, 1931. First edition, fine in about fine dust jacket, only minute traces on rear panel, from the collection of Duke Collier. Royal Books 36 - 103   2015 $4750

Stout, Rex *Not Quite Dead Enough.* New York: Farrar & Rinehart, 1944. First edition, fine in near fine dust jacket, attractive bookplate, tiny date notation on front endpaper, else book quite clean, jacket has single very tiny chip at crown (no titling affected), else fine, from the collection of Duke Collier.   Royal Books   36 - 114   2015 $1500

Stout, Rex *O Careless Love.* New York: Farrar & Rinehart, 1935. First edition, very good in like dust jacket, binding slightly cocked, touch of soil to front endpaper, jacket has few small chips at spine ends and extremities and bit of rubbing to front flap fold, uncommon in jacket, from the collection of Duke Collier.   Royal Books   36 - 108   2015 $2000

Stout, Rex *Over My Dead body.* New York: Farrar and Rinehart, 1940. First edition, very good in like dust jacket, slight lean, very light soil to book, single lending library stamp at top of front endpaper, jacket complete but with archival tape mends on verso and one mend to recto at crown, from the collection of Duke Collier.   Royal Books 36 - 110   2015 $1850

Stout, Rex *Plot It Yourself.* New York: Viking Press, 1959. First edition, near fine in fine dust jacket, faintest bit of toning at edge of rear jacket flap, else superb, fresh copy, without trace of usual fading to jacket spine, from the collection of Duke Collier.   Royal Books   36 - 117   2015 $550

Stout, Rex *Seed on the Wind.* New York: Vanguard Press, 1930. First edition, fine, no soiling to fragile yellow cloth and top edge still richly colored, rare dust jacket, near fine, remarkably clean and bright with no tears, chips or rubbed spots, from the collection of Duke Collier.   Royal Books   36 - 102   2015 $6000

Stout, Rex *Some Buried Caesar.* New York: Viking Press, 1939. First edition, binding very slightly cocked, else near fine in bright, very good dust jacket, with small chips and some shallow creasing at corners, but quite colorful overall, from the collection of Duke Collier.   Royal Books 36 - 106   2015 $2750

Stout, Rex *The Broken Vase.* New York: Farrar and Rinehart, 1941. First edition, fine in exceptionally bright, near fine dust jacket, spectacular copy, from the collection of Duke Collier.   Royal Books   36 - 109   2015 $2000

Stout, Rex *The Hand in the Glove.* New York: Farrar and Rinehart, 1937. First edition, fine in very good example of rare dust jacket, jacket with some chipping at spine ends and corners, though no titling affected, custom clamshell box, from the collection of Duke Collier.   Royal Books   36 - 101   2015 $7500

Stout, Rex *The League of Frightened Men.* New York: Farrar and Rinehart, 1935. First edition, review copy with publisher's slip with rubber stamped date of publication, along with slip containing quote by William Lyons regarding Stout's first book, Fer-de-lance, fine in near fine dust jacket, absolutely stunning copy, from the collection of Duke Collier. Royal Books   36 - 98   2015 $20,000

Stout, Rex *The President Vanishes.* New York: Farrar and Rinehart, 1934. First edition, fine in near fine dust jacket, lightly worn at top of spine and toned at spine and edges of front panel, from the collection of Duke Collier. Royal Books   36 - 113   2015 $1500

Stout, Rex *The Red Box.* New York: Farrar and Rinehart, 1937. First edition, very good in like dust jacket, spine lean and some wear along joints, else book bright and clean, jacket complete with touch of fading to red titling on spine, small chips at couple of corners, split along front flap fold running about halfway down, bright, presentable copy, from the collection of Duke Collier.   Royal Books   36 - 99   2015 $9500

Stout, Rex *The Second Confession.* New York: Viking Press, 1949. First edition, signed and dated in year of publication by author 10/3/49, spine bit cocked, else near fine in very good, price clipped dust jacket with moderate shelfwear, slight fading to spine, rubbing at spine ends and extremities, from the collection of Duke Collier.   Royal Books   36 - 115   2015 $1250

Stout, Rex *Too Many Clients.* New York: Viking Press, 1960. First edition, fine in fine dust jacket, inscribed by author Nov. 17 1960 for Ed, from the collection of Duke Collier.   Royal Books   36 - 111   2015 $1750

Stout, Rex *Too Many Cooks.* London: Collins, 1938. First edition, very good in good dust jacket, foxing to prelim leaves, binding bit cocked, some discoloration to cloth at heel, jacket is moderately worn, chipping at spine ends, chip at heel affects portion of publisher's device, scarce in any condition, from the collection of Duke Collier.   Royal Books 36 - 112   2015 $1750

Stout, Rex *Too Many Women.* New York: Viking Press, 1947. First edition, fine and unread in fine dust jacket, touch of foxing to endpapers, else nice, unworn, from the collection of Duke Collier.   Royal Books   36 - 116   2015 $650

Stout, Rex *Where There's a Will.* New York: Farrar & Rinehart, 1940. Near fine in like dust jacket, usual slight fading to jacket's red spine title, attractive owner bookplate on front pastedown, else superior copy, couple of tiny closed tears and corner rubs to note, from the collection of Duke Collier.   Royal Books   36 - 100   2015 $6500

Thomas, Ross *Protocol for a Kidnapping.* New York: William Morrow, 1971. First edition, fine in fine dust jacket, from the collection of Duke Collier.   Royal Books   36 - 130   2015 $450

Thomas, Ross *The Brass Go-Between.* New York: William Morrow, 1969. First edition, fine in fine dust jacket, from the collection of Duke Collier.   Royal Books   36 - 131   2015 $400

Thomas, Ross *The Cold War Swap.* First edition, fine in near fine dust jacket with light wear at spine ends and one corner, mild sunning to spine, from the collection of Duke Collier.   Royal Books   36 - 127   2015 $1000

Thomas, Ross *The Fools in Town are on Our Side.* London: Hodder and Stoughton, 1970. First edition, near fine in like dust jacket, quite uncommon thus, from the collection of Duke Collier.   Royal Books   36 - 132   2015 $375

Thomas, Ross *The Money Harvest.* New York: William Morrow, 1975. Uncorrected proof, inscribed by author, fine and unread in green wrappers, from the collection of Duke Collier.   Royal Books   36 - 129   2015 $450

Thomas, Ross *The Seersucker Whipsaw.* New York: William Morrow, 1967. First edition, signed by author, fine in fine dust jacket, none of the usual yellowing to white background, from the collection of Duke Collier.   Royal Books   36 - 128   2015 $650

Thompson, Jim *The Killer Inside Me.* Los Angeles: Blood and Guts Press, 1991. First edition in hardcover, one of 26 lettered copies, this being letter U, signed by Stephen King who contributes introduction, fine , leather bound slipcase, from the collection of Duke Collier.   Royal Books   36 - 239   2015 $650

Thompson, Jim *The Killer Inside Me.* New York: Lion No. 99, 1952. First edition, paperback original, very good plus, tight and square, couple of very faint vertical creases (paper not broken) on front and rear panel, touch of wrinkle to spine, superior copy, from the collection of Duke Collier. Royal Books   36 - 238   2015 $1850

Van Gulik, Robert *Chinese Pictorial Art as Viewed by the Connoisseur...* Rome: Instituto Itaiano per Il Mediio Ed Estremo Oriente, 1958. First edition, one of 950 numbered copies, 160 illustrations, 42 paper samples mounted in separate booklet housed in rear pocket, spine slightly foxed, else fine, from the collection of Duke Collier.   Royal Books   36 - 241   2015 $1500

Van Gulik, Robert *Sexual Life in Ancient China.* Leiden: E. J. Brill, 1961. First edition, nearly 400 over-sized pages, heavily illustrated with plates and drawings, small rubber stamp front endpaper, waterstains to covers, else very good in chipped, about very good dust jacket with some staining to verso, from the collection of Duke Collier.   Royal Books   36 - 242   2015 $650

Westlake, Donald E. *361.* New York: Random House, 1962. First edition, fine and unread in about fine dust jacket, exceptional copy, from the collection of Duke Collier. Royal Books   36 - 243   2015 $350

Willeford, Charles *Cockfighter.* Chicago: Chicago Paperback House, 1962. First edition, paperback original, fine and unread, from the collection of Duke Collier.   Royal Books   36 - 248   2015 $325

Willeford, Charles *High Priest of California/Wild Wives.* New York: Beacon No. B13, 1956. First edition, paperback original, fine, from the collection of Duke Collier.   Royal Books 36 - 250   2015 $375

Willeford, Charles *Honey Gal.* New York: Beacon No. B160, 1958. First edition, fine and unread, touch of production wrinkle to spine panel, from the collection of Duke Collier.   Royal Books   36 - 247   2015 $475

Willeford, Charles *Lust is a Woman.* New York: Beacon No. B175, 1958. First edition, paperback original, fine and unread, tiniest bit of rubbing at spine ends, superb cover art by Micarelli, from the collection of Duke Collier.   Royal Books   36 - 245   2015 $650

Willeford, Charles *Understudy for Love.* Chicago: Newstand Library No. &170, 1961. First edition, paperback original, fine and unread, scarce, from the collection of Duke Collier.   Royal Books   36 - 246   2015 $450

Willeford, Charles *Whip Hand.* New York: Gold Medal Books No. S1087, 1961. First edition, paperback original, fine and unread, from the collection of Duke Collier.   Royal Books   36 - 249   2015 $325

Williams, Charles *Scorpion Reef.* New York: Macmillan, 1955. First edition, very good plus in like dust jacket, board edges lightly faded, only minor rubbing and nicking to jacket extremities, very nice, scarce title, extremely uncommon signature, from the collection of Duke Collier. Royal Books 36 - 251   2015 $1850

Williams, Charles *The Wrong Venus.* New York: New American Library, 1966. First edition, inscribed by author for fellow mystery writer John D. MacDonald, near fine in like dust jacket, from the collection of Duke Collier. Royal Books   36 - 3   2015 $3500

Winwar, Frances *The Haunted Palace: a Life of Edgar Allan Poe.* New York: Harper and Bros., 1959. First edition, author Kenneth Millar/Ross MacDonald's review copy annotated by him in holograph pencil, laid in is 5 page ms. letter signed of his review for the book, book near fine in like dust jacket, letter fine and approximately quarter quarto leaves, lined three-hole notebook paper, rectos only, in blue holograph ink with exception of the last few sentences and corrections in same blue ink, folded horizontally at center, else near fine, from the collection of Duke Collier. Royal Books   36 - 65   2015 $4500

Woolrich, Cornell *Cover Charge.* New York: Boni & Liveright, 1926. First edition, near fine in superb, about near fine dust jacket, jacket has no loss and no toning, only few nicks and tiny closed tears, custom clamshell box, from the collection of Duke Collier. Royal Books   36 - 252   2015 $7500

Wright, Willard Huntington   1888-1939 *The 'Canary' Murder Case.* New York: Charles Scribner's, 1927. First edition, blindstamp on titlepage, else fine in lightly rubbed, near fine dust jacket with professional and virtually invisible restoration to spine ends, from the collection of Duke Collier. Royal Books   36 - 240   2015 $1500

Association – Collings, Dennis

Parsons, Claudia *Vagabondage.* London: Chatto & Windus, 1941. First edition, 8vo., frontispiece, 15 plates, 3 maps, neat name "K. Coomaraswamy / Segennah Nov 11th 1941", covers heavily worn and soiled, spine slightly split, contents okay, good only, loosely inserted is long TLS from author to Dennis Collings discussing the book. Any Amount of Books   2015 - A36695   2015   £150

Association – Colm, Thomas

Plato *(Greek text) Omnia Platonis Opera.* Venice: in aedib. Aldi et Andreae Soceri, Sept, 1513. Editio princeps, 2 volumes, large Aldine anchor device on titlepage (volume i) and on verso of last leaf in volume ii, Greek text (apart from Aldus' dedicatory petition, contents and colophon), titlepage slightly soiled and with hole at inner margin repaired, minor stains on fore-edges, few wormholes in blank lower margin of opening leaves of volumes ii, volume, volume i in contemporary English quartered oak boards, resewn with spine uncovered, modern vellum endleaves, volume ii in contemporary German pigskin over wooden boards, blind tooled to panel design filled in with 'laus deo' and rosette stamps, brass catches and clasps, top of spine worn, inner hinge broken, cord intact, good, binding of the first volume of this copy is subject of 2 page report by Nicholas Pickwood (printout accompanies the volume), repairs carried out by James Brockman; first volume with signature of Thomas Colm of Oxford dated 1573, 17th century ownership inscription of Hendricus Ffeild, 19th century bookplate and stamp of King Edward's School, Birmingham, plus bookplate of Kenneth Rapoport, the second volume with early ownership inscriptions of Johannes (or Johann?) Lang of Erfurt and Philippus Kleissenius, few early marginalia, inscription 'de bibliotheca Johannis Langi Erphurdiensis. Blackwell's Rare Books   Greek & Latin Classics VI - 82   2015   £75,000

Association – Colvin, Sidney

Elton, Oliver *Michael Drayton: a Critical Study with Bibliography.* London: Constable & Co., 1905. Half title, frontispiece and plates, original brown cloth, dulled and ink marked, Kathleen Tillotson's copy, signed Kathleen M. Constable Nov. 12 1927, with few notes, bookplate of Sidney Colvin. Jarndyce Antiquarian Booksellers   CCVII - 241   2015   £20

Association – Comat, Charles

Rip, Pseud. *Cocktails de Paris.* Paris: Editions Demangel, 1929. First edition, copiously illustrated by famed poster artist Paul Colin, pages toned, two leaves roughly opened with resulting modest chips, barely touchng text, modest rubbing on wrappers, handsome, very good copy, exceptionally uncommon, inscribed by RIP and by Paul Colin to Lieutenant Charles Comat. Between the Covers Rare Books   196 - 136   2015 $1450

Association – Combes W.

Thomas A Kempis 1380-1471 *The Christian's Pattern; or a Treatise of the Imitation of Jesus Christ...* London: printed for Barker (and others), 1742. 203 x 127mm., animated contemporary black morocco, lavishly gilt, covers with central cottage-roof design enclosed by ornate floral rolls and small tools, the 'roof' frame containing a large and elaborate fleuron within a lozenge of small tools, raised bands, spine gilt in compartments bordered by plain rules and dogtooth rolls, each compartment divided into quarters by gilt diagonal lines, each quarter with a delicate stippled floral tool, red morocco label, gilt turn-ins, marbled endpapers, all edges gilt, engraved frontispiece of Crucifixion, plus engravings of the nativity, Adoration of the Magi, Christ in the Wilderness and the Last Supper; 18th century bookplate of Fane William Sharpe, 18th or 19th century armorial bookplate of W. Combes, spine faded to pleasing hazel brown, little rubbing to joints and extremities, minor chafing to boards, occasional faint foxing, isolated dust soiling to head edge, other trivial imperfections, but fine, nevertheless, leaves clean and fresh and intricately tooled unsophisticated binding very lustrous and showing no significant wear, splendid copy. Phillip J. Pirages   66 - 35   2015 $3200

Association – Comerford, James

A Description of Stonehenge, Abiry & c. In Wiltshire. Salisbury: printed and sold by Collins and Johnson, sold also by J. Wilkie, London, 1776. First edition, 6 woodcut plates (on leaves which form part of the gatherings, but are not included in pagination), 12mo., original mottled sheep, double gilt fillet borders on sides, rebacked preserving most of original red lettering piece, armorial bookplate of James Comerford placed over another, good.   Blackwell's Rare Books   B179 - 101   2015   £600

Association – Compton, Frances

Bloomfield, Robert *Wild Flowers; or Pastoral and Local Poetry.* London: printed for Vernor Hood and Sharpe, Poultry and Longman, Hurst Rees and Orme, 1806. First edition, contemporary speckled calf, ruled and spine heavily gilt, spine rubbed, some loss of leather at corners, handsome, very good, engraved bookplate of Lady Frances Compton.   Between the Covers Rare Books, Inc.   187 - 25   2015 $375

Association – Compton, Henry

Homerus *Ilias. (The Iliad in Latin).* Parisiis: Apud Martinum Iuuenem Excvdebat Gvil. M., 1550. 121 x 89mm., beautiful and animated contemporary elaborately gilt and painted Parisian calf by Wooton's binder "B", covers with unusual frame of interlacing slender rectangular compartments formed by wide black painted fillets outlined in gilt, center panel with four foliate scrolls arched across frame in each quadrant and forming a centerpiece lozenge, azured curls at head and foot of panel and with stippled lobes, additional azured cornerpieces, stippled circles at top, bottom and either side of the panel, raised bands, spine compartments gilt with centered foliate tool or bull's eye, slightly later red morocco label, all edges gilt, spine ends and corners very artfully renewed, in fleece lined brown buckram clamshell case, with John Roland Abbey's morocco bookplate and large morocco title label on spine, front endpaper with morocco bookplate of Abbey, pastedowns with armorial bookplates of Scrope Berdmore, S.T.P. (dated 1790) at front and of Henry C. Compton esq. at rear, rear endpaper with modern bookplate of Philosophia Hermetica ruled in red throughout, half dozen light ink stains, two or three affecting a few words of text, quite clean and fresh internally, backstrip with minor flaking and few hairline cracks, one corner exposed, otherwise very decorative binding, pleasing and especially well preserved, boards still lustrous.   Phillip J. Pirages   66 - 12   2015 $12,500

Association – Conder, James

Lowell, Samuel *Early Piety Recommended from the Example of Josiah; a Sermon Occasioned by the Death of George Griffiths and Delivered at Bridge street Meeting House, Bristol on Lord's-Day Evening the 3rd October 1802.* Bath: printed by and for S. Hazard and sold also by Williams, London, James Bristol and all other booksellers, n.d., 1802. First edition, 8vo., 32 pages, original worn wrappers, inscribed in ink on upper cover by author for Mr. James Conder, fine, uncut, very rare.   John Drury Rare Books   2015 - 18381   2015 $89

Association – Conrad, Joseph

Proust, Marcel 1871-1922 *Swann's Way: Part One.* London: Chatto & Windus, 1922. First edition in English, octavo, original blue cloth lettered gilt, no dust jacket, initialled in ink by novelist Joseph Conrad, inscribed to Conrad by Proust's translator Scott Moncrieff.   Honey & Wax Booksellers   2 - 62   2015 $3500

Association – Constable

Sturge, Mary Charlotte *Some Little Quakers in their Nursery.* London: Simpkin Marshall, 1906. Half title, illustrations, original yellow cloth, mark on spine, else very good, signed presentation inscription to Nurse Gertrude from author, the Constable family copy, with pencil notes by Kathleen Tillotson inserted.   Jarndyce Antiquarian Booksellers   CCVII - 480   2015   £30

Association – Constable, A. J.

Ainsworth, William Harrison 1805-1882 *Hilary St. Ives.* London: George Routledge & Sons, 1881. Illustrations by Frederick Gilbert, contemporary half red roan, spine faded and slightly rubbed, bookplate with crest of A. J. Constable over another, from the library of Geoffrey & Kathleen Tillotson.   Jarndyce Antiquarian Booksellers   CCVII - 2   2015   £20

Association – Constable, E. A.

Wordsworth, William 1770-1850 *The Poetical Works.* Oxford: Oxford University Press, 1923. Half title, frontispiece, original blue cloth, battered copy, lacking spine strip, signed by Kathleen Tillotson as Constable and as Tillotson, further note records the gift from E. A. Constable.   Jarndyce Antiquarian Booksellers   CCVII - 565   2015   £30

Association – Constable, Eric

Ambulance Train in the Great War: Selections from the Pages of La Vie Sanitaire August 1916 to February 1919. No. 5. Blackburn: Geo. Toulmin & Sons, 1919? frontispiece, illustrations, original black boards with paper label, cream cloth spine, inner hinges cracking, Kathleen Tillotson's copy with signature and 'my father Eric Constable's copy'.   Jarndyce Antiquarian Booksellers CCVII - 4   2015   £125

Wordsworth, William 1770-1850 *The Prelude.* Oxford: Clarendon Press, 1926. Half title, frontispiece, plates, original brown buckram, paper label browned and chipped, inner hinge cracking, Kathleen Tillotson's copy as Kathleen Constable, and name Eric Constable, many pencil notes by Tillotson.   Jarndyce Antiquarian Booksellers   CCVII - 568   2015   £35

Association – Coolidge, Clark

Padgett, Ron *Supernatural Overtones.* Great Barrington: The Figures, 1990. First edition, one of 500 copies, square 8vo., white wrappers, as new, though not called for, signed by Padgett and Clark Coolidge.   James S. Jaffe Rare Books   Many Happy Returns - 276   2015 $100

Association – Coomaraswamy, K.

Parsons, Claudia *Vagabondage.* London: Chatto & Windus, 1941. First edition, 8vo., frontispiece, 15 plates, 3 maps, neat name "K. Coomaraswamy / Segennah Nov 11th 1941", covers heavily worn and soiled, spine slightly split, contents okay, good only, loosely inserted is long TLS from author to Dennis Collings discussing the book.   Any Amount of Books   2015 - A36695   2015   £150

Association – Cooper

A Letter Sent from a Private Gentleman to a friend in London, in Justification of his Owne Adhering to His Majestie in Times of Distraction...   London: for V.N. Anno. Dom., 1642. Small 4to., 8 pages, early 20th century quarter morocco, bookplate of Markree Library of the Cooper family at Markree Castle, Co. Sligo, Ireland, from the library of James Stevens Cox (1910-1997).   Maggs Bros. Ltd.   1447 - 90   2015   £120

Association – Cooper, Jane

Villon, Francois *The Poems of.* Boston: Houghton Mifflin, 1977. First edition, fine in trifle dust soiled, otherwise fine dust jacket, inscribed by Galway Kinnell to fellow poet Jane (Cooper).   Between the Covers Rare Books, Inc. 187 - 147   2015 $250

Association – Cope, Henry

Brome, James *An Historical Account of Mr. Rogers's Three Years Travels over England and Wales.* London: by J. Moxon and B. Bearwell, 1694. First (unauthorized) edition, 8vo., large folding map of England and Wales (closely trimmed), light dampstain to fore edge of first few leaves, occasional minor worming to blank fore margin, final four leaves browned, early 19th century russia, extremities rubbed, signature of Henry Cope with inscription "given me by Sr. Richard Middleton 1697 H. Cope", (Sir Richard Middleton, 3rd Bart - 1655-1716) of Chirk Castle Co. Denbigh, Wales, label of R. Beckley bookseller, JSC's signature, from the library of James Stevens Cox (1910-1997).   Maggs Bros. Ltd.   1447 - 48   2015   £1200

Association – Corey, Steven

Antoninus, Brother 1912-1994 *Tendril in the Mesh.* N.P.: Cayucos Books, 1973. printed in an edition limited to 250 numbered copies, signed by author, tall 4to., quarter leather with decorated paper covered boards, printed in Goudy thirty on handmade paper from English Wookey Hole Mill, titles and section numbers finely printed in tan and brown, bookplate of Steven Corey on front pastedown. Oak Knoll Books   306 - 148   2015 $125

Association – Corfield, William Henry

Gunton, Symon *The History of the Church of Peterburgh.* London: printed for Richard Chiswell, 1686. First edition, 371 x 232mm., splendid honey brown diced russia by Roger Payne, covers with wide intricate and elegant dentelle frame composed of many small floral tools, raised bands, spine with gilt crest of Sir Richard Colt Hoare in top compartment, gilt titling in text two compartments and four elaborately tooled compartments below with gilt floral sprigs radiating from a central quatrefoil, interspersed with circlets and many small floral tools, turn-ins with simple gilt rules and delicate floral cornerpieces, endpapers of purple 'fine drawing paper' (Payne's words), all edges gilt, joints and very small portion at spine ends recently and expertly renewed by Courtland Benson, in a folding cloth box lined with felt (somewhat scuffed); 2 illustrations in text and 4 plates of views, large paper copy; front pastedown with armorial bookplate of Sir Henry Hope Edwardes and engraved bookplate of W. H. Corfield, front flyleaf with transcription in Hoare's hand of Payne's very detailed explanation of the work done and the bill for it; spine evenly darkened toward a chocolate brown, moderate foxing to half a dozen leaves, occasional rust spots, light stains or other trivial imperfections elsewhere in text, exceptionally desirable specimen in generally very fine condition, mostly clean and always fresh internally and very special binding entirely solid now, with virtually no wear and with all of the delicate gilt quite bright. Phillip J. Pirages 66 - 57   2015 $15,000

Association – Cornerford, James

Cole, John *Bookselling Spiritualised. Books and Articles of Stationery Rendered Monitors of Religion.* Scarborough: imprinted by John Cole Newborough St., 1826. First edition, limited impression of only 60 copies, printed on thick paper extended with many blank leaves, contemporary dark red morocco by gilt extra by J. MacKenzie, gilt edges with gilt cypher on each cover and 19th century armorial bookplate of James Cornerford on pastedown, extremities lightly rubbed, fine, handsome. John Drury Rare Books   2015 - 25207   2015 $830

Association – Cornish, Dorothy

Saintsbury, George *Specimens of English Prose Style from Malory to Macaulay.* London: Kegan Paul Trench and Co., 1885. First edition, no 1 of 50 copies signed "Charles Whittingham & Co. " (of Chiswick Press), 8vo., green cloth with spine label and marbled boards, uncut, signed in pencil on titlepage dated Xmas 1887 to Dorothy Cornish, presumably the educationalist, spine label browned and marked (legible), edges rubbed, boards quite scuffed at rear, pages uncut with clean text. Any Amount of Books   2015 - A47686   2015   £180

Association – Cortez, Ricardo

Curtiss, Thomas Quinn *Von Stroheim.* New York: Farrar, Straus and Giroux, 1971. First edition, fine in very near fine dust jacket, inscribed by author to film actor, Ricardo Cortez. Between the Covers Rare Books, Inc.   187 - 65   2015 $250

Grapewin, Charley *The Bronze Bull.* Boston: Christopher Pub. House, 1930. First edition, front fly lacking, else near fine, lacking dust jacket, inscribed by author on dedication page to film actor, Ricardo Cortez. Between the Covers Rare Books, Inc.   187 - 113   2015 $350

Neumann, Robert Zaharoff *Zaharoff.* New York: Alfred A. Knopf, 1935. First American edition, spine little age toned, very good, without dust jacket, bookplate of film star Ricardo Cortez. Between the Covers Rare Books, Inc.   187 - 202   2015 $45

Association – Coupe, Henrietta

Woolf, Virginia 1882-1941 *The Waves.* London: published by Leonard and Virginia Woolf at the Hogarth Press, 1931. First edition, first printing, one of 7113 copies, publisher's purple cloth lettered gilt, printed on laid paper, good with slight lean, two short tears to spine head, rubbing to spine ends, toning and light soiling to spine ends, toning and light soiling to spine, boards slightly bowed, minor soiling and some fading, very light spotting to first few and last pages of text block, pencil correction to page 47, bright and clean pages, housed in custom quarter leather clamshell box, personal copy of author's sister Vanessa Bell, with her ownership signature by descent to her daughter Angelica Garnett, thence to her two surviving daughters Henrietta Coupe and Frances Partridge. B & B Rare Books, Ltd.   239 - 1   2015 $9500

Association – Courtney, Leonard

Arnold, Matthew 1822-1888 *Friendship's Garland; Being the Conversations, Letters and Opinions of the Late Arminius, Baron von Thunder-Ten-Tronckh.* London: Smith Elder, 1871. First edition, 2 pages ads, half title removed, original white cloth by Hanbury & Simpson, spine sunned, slightly discolored, attractive bookplate of Leonard Courtney, 15 Cheyne Walk, with inserted letters and cuttings including exchange between R. H. Super and Geoffrey Tillotson. Jarndyce Antiquarian Booksellers   CCVII - 22   2015   £35

Association – Coventry, Anne

Cotton, Charles *The Wonders of the Peake.* London: W. Everingham and Tho. Whitledge, 1694. Third edition, 8vo., engraved vignette of cannon on title, first sheet browned, rest less so with some spotting, A6 with two holes from paper flaw (affecting a few letters), red sprinkled edges have occasionally spread onto leaf and a number of lower edges uncut, contemporary sheep (small wormtrail to front board and large scuff on rear board), lower joint split at head, pastedowns unstuck, Lady Anne Coventry's signature, from the library of James Stevens Cox (1910-1997). Maggs Bros. Ltd. 1447 - 117 2015 £300

Association – Covici, Allan

Berryman, John 1914-1972 *Poems.* Norfolk: New Directions, 1942. First edition, one of 1500 copies in wrappers out of a total edition of 2000 copies, 8vo., original unprinted wrappers, dust jacket, spine portion faintly sunned, otherwise fine, presentation copy inscribed by author for Allan Covici. James S. Jaffe Rare Books Modern American Poetry - 29 2015 $1000

Association – Cowdray, Weetman Dickinson Pearson, 1st Viscount

Morley, John *The Struggle for National Education.* London: Chapman & Hall, 1873. First edition in bookform, 8vo., half title, early 20th century maroon crushed half morocco, spine gilt with raised bands, top edge gilt, silk maker, by Hatchards, fine, from the library of Sir Weetman Dickinson Pearson, first Viscount Cowdray (1856-1927) with his armorial bookplate. John Drury Rare Books 2015 - 17698 2015 $151

Association – Cowell, F. R.

Korthals-Altes, J. *Sir Cornelius Vermuyden; the Lifework of a Great Anglo-Dutchman in Land Reclamation and Drainage...* London: The Hague: Williams & Norgate/W. P. Van Stokum, 1925. First edition, 8vo., 15 illustrations, 6 maps, original blue cloth lettered gilt on spine and on front cover, penciled ownership signature of F. R. Cowell, slight shelfwear, sound, very good+. Any Amount of Books 2015 - A49460 2015 £225

Observations on Modern Gardening. London: T. Payne, 1771. Third edition, 8vo., full brown leather with decorated gilt at spine, raised bands and gilt title on red label, ornate armorial bookplate of Agneu (Baronet) of Lochnau, penciled ownership signature of F. R. Cowell, very handsome, very good, slightly rubbed at corner, slightly tender at hinges. Any Amount of Books 2015 - A47683 2015 £220

Riding, Laura *The World and Ourselves.* London: Chatto & Windus, 1938. First edition, 8vo., penciled ownership signature of F. R. Cowell, very good+ in like dust jacket (faint edgewear). Any Amount of Books 2015 - A48862 2015 £150

Robinson, William 1838-1935 *The Parks and Gardens of Paris Considered in Relation to the Wants of Other Cities and of Public and Private Gardens.* London: John Murray, 1883. Third edition, 8vo., half dark brown leather, presentation from author to historian F. R. Cowell, endpapers slightly stained, corner and hinges rubbed, one signature slightly protruding, otherwise very good. Any Amount of Books 2015 - A47680 2015 £175

Whewell, William 1794-1866 *Of a Liberal Education in General and with Particular Reference to the Leading Studies of the University of Cambridge.* London: John W. Parker, 1845. First edition, 8vo, original paper covered boards with green linen spine and spine label (now somewhat faded and hard to read), corners scuffed and worn, front inner hinge cracked by holding well, slight soiling but otherwise sound, near very good, penciled ownership signature of historian F. R. Cowell. Any Amount of Books 2015 - A46028 2015 £150

Association – Cowley, Malcolm

Tate, Allen *Mr. Pope and Other Poems.* New York: Minton, Balch & Co., 1928. First edition, first state with his poem 'Ode to the Confederate Dead' tipped-in, octavo, cloth with applied printed label, housed in custom clamshell case with morocco label gilt, boards very slightly splayed and rubbed, short tear on one leaf, else near fine, inscribed by author to Peggy and Malcom Cowley, Aug. 14 1928. Between the Covers Rare Books 196 - 116 2015 $3750

Wilson, Edmund *Poets, Farewell!* New York: Charles Scribner's sons, 1929. First edition, inscribed to Malcolm Cowley. Honey & Wax Booksellers 2 - 57 2015 $3000

Association – Cowley, Peggy

Tate, Allen *Mr. Pope and Other Poems.* New York: Minton, Balch & Co., 1928. First edition, first state with his poem 'Ode to the Confederate Dead' tipped-in, octavo, cloth with applied printed label, housed in custom clamshell case with morocco label gilt, boards very slightly splayed and rubbed, short tear on one leaf, else near fine, inscribed by author to Peggy and Malcom Cowley, Aug. 14 1928. Between the Covers Rare Books 196 - 116 2015 $3750

Association – Cowper, Francis Thomas De Grey, 7th Earl of

Chaucer, Geoffrey 1340-1400   *The Works of Our Ancient and Learned and Excellent English Poet...*   London: 1687. Folio, frontispiece, Black Letter, some browning and light foxing throughout and with small ink blot on Yy3, touching two lines of text, fore margin rather narrow, early 19th century calf, rebacked. large armorial bookplate of Francis Thomas de Grey Cowper, 7th and last Earl Cowper (1834-1905), from the library of James Stevens Cox (1910-1997). Maggs Bros. Ltd.   1447 - 80   2015   £1100

Association – Cox, E. M.

Swift, Jonathan 1667-1745   *Verses on the Death of Doctor Swift.*   London: printed for C. Bathurst, 1739. First edition, 18 pages, folio, recent brown cloth, dark brown morocco side label, very good, bookplate of E. M. Cox.   C. R. Johnson   Foxon R-Z - 963r-z   2015 $1379

Association – Cox, James Stevens

A., T.   *Religio Clerici.*   London: for Henry Brome, 1681. 12mo., frontispiece, small piece 55 x 5mm. neatly sliced away from lower margin of I2, minor ink spots just touching fore-edge of G3, G4, E5 and E6, small rust spot to C10 and I7, early 19th century calf, gilt spine, upper joint cracked, lower joint rubbed, corners worn, from the library of James Stevens Cox (1910-1997).   Maggs Bros. Ltd.   1447 - 1   2015   £240

Abell, William   *A True Discovery of the Proiectors of the Wine Project, Out of the Vintners Owne orders made at Their Common Hall Whereby it Clearley Appeares that This Project was Contrived at Vintners Hall by the drawing Vintners of London...*   London: Thomas Walkley, 1641. First edition, small 4to., titlepage shaved at head and some loss to first line dampstaining to lower corners of C3-4 and D1-2, early 20th century half calf and marbled boards, boards slightly faded, from the library of James Stevens Cox (1910-1997).   Maggs Bros. Ltd.   1447 - 2   2015   £750

Allestree, Richard   *The Ladies Calling in Two Parts.*   Oxford: at the Theater, 1676. Fourth impression, 8vo., engraved frontispiece, vignette on title, some minor rust spotting to B2, I3 and S4 (forming small hole), occasional marginal dampstaining and small (30mm) closed tear to blank fore-margin of Z1, contemporary brown morocco, covers gilt panelled with floral tool at each corner, spine divided into six gilt tool panels, joints lightly worn, attractive copy, from the library of James Stevens Cox (1910-1997). Maggs Bros. Ltd.   1447 - 3   2015   £450

Allestree, Richard   *The Ladies Calling. In Two Parts.*   Oxford: at the Theater, 1677. Fifth impression, 8vo., engraved frontispiece, vignette of the Sheldonian theatre on the title, light marginal browning and occasional spotting, very small paper flaw in lower blank margin of B2, contemporary black morocco, covers with fillet border, gilt panel with small floral tool at corners, spine with five raised bands, panels tooled in gilt, marbled endleaves and gilt edges (corners lightly bumped, few minor bumps and scuffs), from the library of James Stevens Cox (1910-1997), with ink signature (J(ane) Dymoke (of Scriveldaby, Yorkshire).   Maggs Bros. Ltd.   1447 - 4   2015   £500

Alsted, Johann Heinrich   *Templum Musicum; oro the Musical Synopsis of the Learned and Famous Johannes Henricus Alstedius, Being a Compendium of the Rudiments both of the Mathematical and Practical part of Musick...*   London: by Will. Godbid for Peter Dring, 1664. First edition in English, 8vo., without final blank leaf, emblematic engraved frontispiece (inner margin torn at head and an ink blot on lyre of Orpheus), without final blank leaf, some light soiling to titlepage, margins browned throughout and with some marginal staining, small piece torn away from upper blank margin of G7, contemporary sheep (old rebacking, now very worn again and with joints split and upper cover detached), corners worn, 19th century endleaves, from the library of James Stevens Cox (1910-1997).   Maggs Bros. Ltd.   1447 - 5   2015   £450

Ames, Richard   *Fatal Friendship; or the Drunkards Misery; Being a Satyr Against Hard Drinking.*   London: for and sold by Randal Taylor, 1693. First edition, small 4to., final ad leaf, final two leaves uncut at tail, penultimate leaf closely shaved along upper edge, touching pagination, disbound, from the library of James Stevens Cox (1910-1997). Maggs Bros. Ltd.   1447 - 6   2015   £400

Anacreon   *Anacreon Done into English out of the Original Greek.*   Oxford: by L. Litchfield, Printer to the University, for Anthony Stephens, 1683. First edition of this translation, 8vo., leaf (c)1 is duplicated; (c)2 was also duplicated, but the second leaf has been torn away, lightly browned, dampstaining along lower edge of a1-4, corners of K2-L2 and fore margin of P1-2 and in top half of last few leaves, small rust hole in D2 (affecting one letter on each side), marginal rust spot on H1, contemporary calf, spine gilt and lettered (headcap damaged and with upper joint slightly split at head), from the library of James Stevens Cox (1910-1997), inscribed "Sum Philippi Ayresij 1683" on titlepage (Philip Aryes (1638-1712), signature of Madam. Mary Redman, ink signature under bookplate of John Holmes (1702/03-1760) of Holt, Norfolk, Master of Gresham School and writer on education, with his signature, early 19th century circular label with manuscript lot number 12/4 pasted to foot of front flyleaf, the pencil mark of Christie-Miller Britwell Court with pencil shelf mark.   Maggs Bros. Ltd.   1447 - 7   2015   £1500

ASSOCIATION COPIES

Anthropologie Abstracted; or the Idea of Humane Nature Reflected in Briefe Philosophicall and Anatomicall Collections. London: for Henry Herringman, 1655. First edition, 8vo., small chip from blank corner of A2, minor rust spot in blank fore-margin of A3, light stain at head in first part, text lightly browned, large (5mm) rust hole in lower blank inner margin of I1, closely trimmed along upper edge in places, contemporary sheep, rebacked, corners repaired, lower cover scuffed, new endleaves, from the library of James Stevens Cox (1910-1997), "Lo. Aston" contemporary ink signature, probably Walter Aston, 2nd Baron Aston of Exeter. Maggs Bros. Ltd. 1447 - 9 2015 £700

Argences, Tanneguy Joseph Cauvin, Sieur D' *The Countess of Salisbury; or the Most Noble Order of the garter.* London: R. Bentley and S. Magnes, 1683. 1682. First edition, 12mo., small piece torn away from upper edge of titlepage, blank lower fore-corner of D1-2 torn, a number of slightly short uncut lower edges, long closed tear across centre of F10, paper flaw corner of I1, contemporary blind ruled sheep (leather torn away from upper cover exposing the board, headcaps torn away, all edges heavily worn), rare, from the library of James Stevens Cox (1910-1997), contemporary signature of Anne Whyte. Maggs Bros. Ltd. 1447 - 10 2015 £750

Aristotle, Pseud. *Aristoteles Master-Piece, or the secrets of Generation Displayed in all Parts Thereof.* London: for J. How and are to be sold next to the Anchor Tavern in Sweeting Rents in Cornhill, 1684. First or second edition, 12mo., woodcut frontispiece (3rd line of text beneath slightly shaved and with catchword 'Jovia' cropped off), 6 woodcuts at end, initial engravings slightly chipped, torn in lower gutter margin and trimmed along lower edge (just touching caption), very light staining to A9-B8, D1-D2, E6v, E12, G4 and H11, 3mm. hole through blank fore-margin of d4, small (20mm.) closed tear to fore-margin of final leaf I6 (just missing text and woodcut) and with a number of edges and corners lightly bumped, otherwise good unsophisticated copy, contemporary sheep (slightly worn), inscriptions "Charles Roane His Booke January ye 15 1697", from the library of James Stevens Cox (1910-1997). Maggs Bros. Ltd. 1447 - 11 2015 £7500

The Armies Remembrancer. London: for Stephen Bowtell, 1649. First edition, small 4to., titlepage slightly soiled and with remnants of small circular sticker to upper inner margin (affecting type ornament frame), closely trimmed long lower edge throughout (touching catchwords and signatures in places), some occasional light foxing, early 19th century half green morocco and marbled boards, covers rubbed and corners bumped, from the library of James Stevens Cox (1910-1997). Maggs Bros. Ltd. 1447 - 96 2015 £100

Atkins, Maurice *Cataplus or, Aeneas His Descent to Hell. A Mock Poem...* London: for Maurice Atkins, 1672. First edition, small 8vo., number of small discreet repairs and some light staining to cancel titlepage, titlepage little browned and some light dampstaining to edges, mid 20th century red morocco, small hole in upper joint, this copy preserved an additional unique cancel title at front with imprint "London, printed for Abisha Brocas, Bookseller in Exiter (sic) 1672", from the library of James Stevens Cox (1910-1997). Maggs Bros. Ltd. 1447 - 12 2015 £1100

Atkinson, James *Epitome of the Whole Art of Navigation.* London: by J. D. for James Atkinson and R. Mount, 1695. Second edition?, 12mo., 8 (of 10) folding engraved diagram plates (Plates 1-6, a fragment of 7, 8, 9 torn and loose, 10 lower third missing and volvelle missing, plates generally bit tatty and frayed at fore-edges), titlepage dusty, edges occasionally ragged and torn throughout, closely shaved along fore-edge throughout (occasionally touching text), final gathering M detached from book block and M1 damaged in inner margin, last page dusty), contemporary sheep, panelled in blind, very worn, heavily rubbed and bumped, corners scuffed and holed, headcaps torn, marks of two catches/ties?), 18th century signature "Thos. Gandin" and "Geo. Matthew", from the library of James Stevens Cox (1910-1997). Maggs Bros. Ltd. 1447 - 13 2015 £950

Austen, Ralph *A Treatise of Fruit-Trees Shewing the Manner of Grafting, Setting, Pruning and Ordering of Them in all Respects.* Oxford: for Tho. Robinson, 1653. First edition, small 4to., engraved title with image of ornamental walled garden, small wormtrail in inner margin L4-T4 (partially repaired M2-R1), contemporary calf, spine stamped with gilt shelf mark '393', spine rubbed and scuffed, boards slightly warped, pastedowns unstuck, with "Robert Stone his book/ Anne Coombar 1677" and various pen trials of his name on front flyleaf and on last blank page, signature John Stone, from the library of James Stevens Cox (1910-1997). Maggs Bros. Ltd. 1447 - 14 2015 £600

Ayres, Philip *Cupids addresse to the Ladies.* London: sold by R. Bently, 5 Tidmarsh, 1683. First edition, small 8vo., engraved throughout, 44 engraved emblem plates, without final blank leaf, small chip torn from fore-margin of titlepage, titlepage lightly soiled, small unobtrusive waterstaining to upper blank margin of first third of the work, short tear to foot of L1, contemporary calf, gilt spine with brown morocco label, corners, head and foot of spine repaired, this copy includes, presumably autograph, 20 line commendatory poem by poet and playwright Nahum Tate addressed "To My Honb. Friend Philip Ayres esqe on his book of Emblems in four Languages", 18th century signature Henry Burt, large bookplate removed, from the library of James Stevens Cox (1910-1997). Maggs Bros. Ltd. 1447 - 15 2015 £3500

Ayres, Philip *Lyric Poems, Made in Imitation of the Italians.* London: by J. M. for Jos. Knight and F. Saunders, 1687. First edition, 8vo., single wormhole to upper right blank, corner throughout touching an occasional letter and small tear to lower blank margin of D3, contemporary calf over thin, wooden boards, (usually characteristic of American bindings), gilt tooled spine, printed waste pastedowns, lacking label, top half of front joint split, cords holding, lower corners worn), from the library of James Stevens Cox (1910-1997). Maggs Bros. Ltd. 1447 - 16 2015 £1500

Bacon, Francis, Viscount St. Albans 1561-1626 *Historia Vitae et Mortis.* Amsterdam: Joannem Ravesteinium, 1663. Fifth separate edition, 12mo., contemporary mottled calf covers ruled in gilt, rebacked, new endleaves, old flyleaves perserved, inscription "Guil Rayner Aedis Ch. Alummus 1683" (William Rayner of London 1664-1730), signature of W. Leigh, from the library of James Stevens Cox (1910-1997). Maggs Bros. Ltd. 1447 - 17 2015 £120

Bacon, Francis, Viscount St. Albans 1561-1626 *Opera Omnia.* Frankfurt: Impensis Joannis Baptistae Schonwetteri typis Matthaei Kempfferi, 1665. One of only two issues with variant titles printed in 1665, folio, browned throughout, heavily in many places, due to poor paper quality, contemporary English calf, covers with floral cornerpieces in blind, joints split, wear to head and foot of spine, edges rubbed, from the library of James Stevens Cox (1910-1997). Maggs Bros. Ltd. 1447 - 19 2015 £200

Bacon, Francis, Viscount St. Albans 1561-1626 *Sermones Fideles, Ethici, Politici, Oeconomici...* Leiden: F. Hackium, 1644. Second Latin edition, 12mo., engraved allegorical frontispiece, small rust spot to inner margin of H9 and with some light occasional foxing in places (F1-G1), contemporary French or Low Countries calf, ruled in gilt, gilt spine (lightly worn, edges bumped, upper and lower headcaps damaged), signature "A M J J Dupin" (Andre Marie Jean Jacques Dupin 1783-1865), from the library of James Stevens Cox (1910-1997). Maggs Bros. Ltd. 1447 - 18 2015 £200

Bacon, Roger *The Cure of Old Age and Preservation of Youth.* London: for Tho. Flesher and Edward Evets, 1683. First edition in English, 8vo., early 19th century half russia, drab boards, gilt edges, ribbon marker (joints cracked), bookplate of George Field (1777-1854), with occasional pencil notes, from the library of James Stevens Cox (1910-1997). Maggs Bros. Ltd. 1447 - 20 2015 £300

Baker, Thomas *The Geometrical Key or the Gate of Equations Unlock'd.* London: by J. Playford for R. Clavel, 1684. First edition, small 4to., 10 leaves of folding engraved diagrams, very occasional light spotting, paper flaw in blank corner of K2, a number of leaves uncut in tail, minor dampstaining to lower fore-corner of folded plates, mid 18th century polished calf, gilt spine (joints split but held by cords, boards little scuffed, label half missing, lower corners bumped), from the library of James Stevens Cox (1910-1997). Maggs Bros. Ltd. 1447 - 21 2015 £400

Balmford, William *The Seaman's Spiritual Companion or Navigation Spiritualized.* London: for Benj. Harris, 1678. First edition, small 8vo., variant state of title with double rule border and price on titlepage, A2 shaved at foot affecting signature and catchword on recto, minor worming in upper outer corner of D4-K8 (affecting end of text in places), stain to B3-E2 affecting three lines, occasional foxing, small hole from paper flaw in lower margin of E2, short tear at foot of F3 slightly affecting last line on recto and catchword on verso, small hole from paper flaw in centre of I2 touching two lines, actually reasonable and much loved copy, contemporary sheep (rubbed, covers scuffed, fore edge of lower cover worn exposing board, corners worn), several pen trials, scribbles, ownership inscriptions John Allab(on) His Booke October ye 24th 16, Charles Canning his book 1679, James Purnell His Booke Anno Domini (deleted), "Thomas Nichols His Book May ye 10 1718", "James Croome His Book March ye 9th 1757" "Jane Hanley", from the library of James Stevens Cox (1910-1997). Maggs Bros. Ltd. 1447 - 21 2015 £2800

Banks, John *The Destruction of Troy, a Tragedy Acted at His Royal Highness the Duke's Theatre.* London: by A. G. and J. P. are to be sold by Charles Blount, 1679. First edition, small 4to., lightly dampstained throughout, shaved close at head with occasional cropping of headlines, light ink staining to recto of final and verso penultimate leaves, holes from early stitched in gutter throughout, 19th century half morocco and marbled boards, from the library of James Stevens Cox (1910-1997). Maggs Bros. Ltd. 1447 - 23 2015 £150

Bayly, Thomas *Witty Apophthegms Delivered at several Times and Upon Several Occasions by King James King Charls (sic) the Marquess of Worcester, Francis Lord Bacon and Sir Thomas Moor.* London: printed by W(illiam) R(awlins) for Matthew Smelt, 1669. Second edition, 12mo., engraved frontispiece, browned throughout, staining to C2 and c6, closed tear to fore margin of #12 and with small piece missing from corner of B6 and blank fore margin of F3, contemporary sheep, ruled in gilt, gilt lettered spine, rubbed, corners bumped, from the library of James Stevens Cox (1910-1997). Maggs Bros. Ltd. 1447 - 24 2015 £550

Beaumont, Francis *Comedies and Tragedies written by Francis Beaumont and John Fletcher.* London: for Humphrey Robinson and Humphrey Moseley, 1647. First edition, small folio, lacking final leaf of text, engraved portrait, second state with "Vates Duplex" in fourth line of the inscription and "J. Berkenhead' in smaller letters (backed with old paper, at time of rebinding, slightly cropped at foot, ink blot in inscription) titlepage stained and slightly dusty, loose at upper inner margin, margins bit frayed, small hole in blank area near outer edge, lower outer corner of F3 torn away with loss to five lines, few words on 7 lines on Dd1v have adhered to blank page opposite upper corner 3U4 torn away affecting pagination, loss at foot of 7A1 from paper flaw affecting a few letters, closed vertical tears, minor spots and stains throughout, some ink blots, upper inner margin of first few leaves and lower outer corner of last few leaves dampstained, late 17th/early 18th century sheep, covers ruled in blind (headcaps and top and bottom of spine torn away, covers somewhat scuffed, cup ring on lower cover, upper corner of lower cover chewed and dampstained), from the library of James Stevens Cox (1910-1997), name Wyndham Harbin, 2nd son of William and Elizabeth Harbin of Newton Surmaville, Somerset with his signature, name Elizabeth (probably Harbin). Maggs Bros. Ltd. 1447 - 25 2015 £600

Beaumont, John *the Present State of the Universe...* London: for William Whitwood, 1696. First edition, 2nd issue, small 4to., browned, dampstained and with some worming (particularly severe near centre) in inner margin, edges dusty, uncut, stitched as issued, Maggs catalog note tipped onto inside front cover with price of £8 and old Maggs cost code pencilled verso final leaf, from the library of James Stevens Cox (1910-1997). Maggs Bros. Ltd. 1447 - 26 2015 £380

Behn, Aphra 1640-1689 *Miscellany, Being a Collection of Poems by Several Hands.* London: for J. Hindmarsh, 1685. Only edition, 8vo., corner of Y4 torn away with loss of catchword and two or three letters of text, blank corner D8 torn away (no loss of text), light dampstain lower right corner of last half of work, some light soiling, later calf rebacked, new endleaves, from the library of James Stevens Cox (1910-1997), 'with "J.W." contemporary initials to titlepage. Maggs Bros. Ltd. 1447 - 27 2015 £1800

Behn, Aphra 1640-1689 *The Widdow Ranter, or the History of Bacon in Virginia.* London: printed for James Knapton, 1690. First edition, small 4to., titlepage lightly soiled, light dampstain to blank fore margins throughout, odd page number just touched by binder, late 19th century brown morocco by Pratt, gilt edges, joints and corners shipped, fore edge of front cover slightly bowed, good copy, inkstamp "J. W. Bouton, Bookseller NY", from the library of James Stevens Cox (1910-1997). Maggs Bros. Ltd. 1447 - 28 2015 £4500

Beveridge, William *De Linguarum Orientalium...(bound with) Grammatica Linguae Domini Nostri Jesu Christi...* London: Thomas Roycroft, 1664. London: Thomas Roycroft for Humphrey Robinson, 1664., First edition 2nd issue, 8vo., show-through of print on B2-6 in first work, contemporary mottled calf panelled in blind, joints split, lower cover almost detached, rubbed, spine label missing, from the library of James Stevens Cox (1910-1997). Maggs Bros. Ltd. 1447 - 29 2015 £220

Blackmore, Richard 1654-1729 *King Arthur. An Heroick Poem.* London: for Awnsham and John Churchil at the Black Swan in Pater Noster-Row and Jacob Tonson at Judges Head in Fleet-Street, 1697. Third edition, 4to., small hole close to inner margin of A2, large piece torn away from blank margin of Nn2, otherwise very clean, contemporary speckled calf, spine divided into 6 panels tooled in gilt and with red morocco label in second (joints split - upper board held by one cord - covers little scuffed), early signature effaced from front pastedown leaving only date 1758, from the library of James Stevens Cox (1910-1997). Maggs Bros. Ltd. 1447 - 31 2015 £300

Blount, Thomas Pope 1649-1697 *De Re Poetica; or Remarks Upon Poetry with Characters and Censures of the Most Considerable Poets, Whether Ancient or Modern.* London: for Ric(hard) Everingham, 1694. First edition, small 4to., occasional spotting and browning, small marginal tear to L1, contemporary calf, covers panelled in blind, spine with late 18th century elaborate gilt tooling with armorial crest of Bunbury (Sir Henry Edward Bunbury, 7th Baronet 1778-1860) in top panel (joints and corners rubbed), bookplate and gilt crest, from the library of James Stevens Cox (1910-1997). Maggs Bros. Ltd. 1447 - 32 2015 £220

Blount, Thomas Pope 1649-1697 *Essays on Several Subjects.* London: for Richard Bentley, 1691. First edition, F8vo., lacking A4, blank, intermittently foxed, more pronounced in gatherings M and N, contemporary calf, rebacked, corners repaired, from the library of James Stevens Cox (1910-1997). Maggs Bros. Ltd. 1447 - 33 2015 £300

Bonnefons, Nicolas De *The French Gardiner...* London: by T. B. for B. Took and are to be sold by J. Taylor, 1691. Fourth (i.e. fifth edition) translated by John Evelyn, 12mo., engraved frontispiece, 4 engraved plates, browned throughout, except plates which are on different paper, slight worming in lower margin at front, mid 20th century blue buckram, armorial bookplate of Isaac Borrow (1673-1745), from the library of James Stevens Cox (1910-1997). Maggs Bros. Ltd. 1447 - 34 2015 £750

Boyle, Robert 1627-1691 *Certain Physiological Essays and Other Tracts.* London: Henry Herringman, 1669. Second edition, 4to., without final blank leaf, small wormhole through upper blank margin, long wormtrail in inner margin and into text around line 14 of Pp1(3)E2, leaf B1 dusty at head, small piece torn away from blank corner of T2 and with tear to foot of O3, contemporary sprinkled calf, covers panelled in blind, paper label in second panel of spine, covers affected by worm damage, in particular they have chewed out corner ornaments of panels, early inscription of George Sampson, 18th century signature J. W. Hawker, from the library of James Stevens Cox (1910-1997). Maggs Bros. Ltd.   1447 - 35   2015   £950

Boyle, Robert 1627-1691 *Essays of the Strange Subtilty, Great Efficacy, Determinate Nature of Effluviums.* London: by W(illiam) G(odbid) for M. Pitt, 1673. First edition, first issue, 8vo., lightly browned in places, mostly in margins, rust mark of head of E1-3, contemporary calf, covers ruled in blind, marbled edges (rebacked, new endpapers), from the library of James Stevens Cox (1910-1997).   Maggs Bros. Ltd.   1447 - 36   2015   £1200

Boyle, Robert 1627-1691 *Experiments, Notes, &c. about the Mechnical Origine or Proudction of Divers Particular Qualities...* London: by E. Flesher for R. Davis bookseller in Oxford, 1675. First edition, 8vo., without leaf of 'Directions to Binder' and errata, general title dusty, light browning stronger in margins throughout, small chip at head of title, contemporary calf, covers panelled in blind, rebacked, new endleaves, contemporary signature of Thos. Smith, few marginal ink notes, some with chemical signs, from the library of James Stevens Cox (1910-1997). Maggs Bros. Ltd.   1447 - 38   2015   £1100

Boyle, Robert 1627-1691 *Hydrostatical Paradoxes made Out by New Experiments.* Oxford: by William Hall for Richard Davis, 1666. First edition, with all 3 folding engraved plates, but lacking contents and imprimatur leaves, some very light dampstaining to edges throughout, late 19th century tree calf, rebacked, later endleaves, from the library of James Stevens Cox (1910-1997).   Maggs Bros. Ltd.   1447 - 39   2015   £600

Boyle, Robert 1627-1691 *Medicinal Experiments or a Collection of Choice Remedies for the most Part Simple, and Easily Prepared...* London: for Sam. Smith, 1692. First edition, 12mo., very lightly foxed, contemporary sheep (worn, edges rubbed and bumped, text block split down centre and loose in case), from the library of James Stevens Cox (1910-1997). Maggs Bros. Ltd.   1447 - 40 2015   £500

Boyle, Robert 1627-1691 *New Experiments and Observations Touching Cold, or an Experimental History of Cold, Begun.* London: for John Crook, 1665. First edition, 8vo., without final blank leaf, two folding plates, bound at end, tightly bound, text-block starting to split in places, title little stained very small piece torn away from blank corner of d4, contemporary calf (rebacked, corners worn, 19th century endleaves), old front flyleaf (stained), preserved, late 18th/early 19th century signature Edward Kendall, from the library of James Stevens Cox (1910-1997).   Maggs Bros. Ltd.   1447 - 41   2015   £3500

Boyle, Robert 1627-1691 *Some considerations Touching the Style of the H. Scriptures.* London: for Henry Herringman, 1663. Second edition, 8vo. in 4's, light marginal browning with some occasional spotting, contemporary sheep ruled in blind, front cover detached, worn, scuffed, bumped and with small pieces missing from upper and lower headcaps, contemporary signature "Dan(ie)l Williams, ex-libris J. Kembler Anno 1755, from the library of James Stevens Cox (1910-1997).   Maggs Bros. Ltd.   1447 - 42   2015   £180

Boyle, Robert 1627-1691 *Some considerations Touching the Usefulnesse of Experimental naturall Philosophy...* Oxford: by Henry Hall printer to the University for Ric. Davis, 1664. Second edition, London issue A, 4to., some minor intermittent light dampstaining to blank margins, verso of g2 and recto of G3 lightly soiled, closed, vertical paper flaw near gutter at edge of printed text on L2, small closed paper flaw to blank corner of H4, verso of K2 and recto of k3 soiled, small rusthole to lower blank margin of Mm4-Nn2, contemporary calf, covers with double gilt fillet border and small floral tool at corners, worn edges and corners chipped, turn-ins coming unglued, spine chipped at head and foot, from the library of James Stevens Cox (1910-1997). Maggs Bros. Ltd.   1447 - 43   2015   £600

Boyle, Robert 1627-1691 *Some Motives and Incentives to the love of God, pathetically Discorus'd of in a Letter to a friend.* London: for Henry Herringman, 1665. Fourth edition, title browned by turn-ins, one or two wormholes in lower margin, extending to a short trail from C4 to D3 each leaf throughout, H2 trimmed along lower edge, small piece torn away and a close tear I3 (touching text), 8vo., contemporary sheep (heavily worn and scuffed, upper joint split but holding, headcaps missing, pastedowns unstuck torn and stained by turn-ins), from the library of James Stevens Cox (1910-1997), 19th century bookplate William Warren, Bristol, signature A. S. Quick 17 may 1883, number of pencil markings by him.   Maggs Bros. Ltd.   1447 - 44   2015   £150

Boyle, Robert 1627-1691 *The Excellency of Theology.* London: by T. N. for Henry Herringmann, 1674. 8vo., titlepage badly defective having been affected by damp and stuck to front pasteboard (where some of it still remains) and has large (145 x35mm) piece torn away and two (approximately 50mm) closed tears caused by leaf being torn away from pastedown, first sheet dampstained, continuing less severely in places throughout, final blank and binders blank little ragged and stained by turn-ins, contemporary sheep, large piece torn away from leather exposing book block, covers almost detached, holes and scuffs to both boards, no pastedowns, late 20th century brown cloth folding box, the duplicate copy of John Evelyn (1630-1706), from the library of James Stevens Cox (1910-1997). Maggs Bros. Ltd. 1447 - 37 2015 £550

Breton, Nicholas 1545-1626 *A Poste with a Packet of mad letters.* London: for George Badger, 1653. Small 4to., lacking title to part 2, lacking final leaf of text, woodcut on title (block much wormed), inner margin of title and first few leaves and final leaf of part 1 dampstained, dampstain in lower margin of pages 31-42 and 59-68, short wormtrail (breaking into holes in places) in inner margin of first part (old patch over worming on final leaf of part 1), final leaf somewhat soiled and slightly short at lower margin, late 19th century half maroon morocco, marbled boards slightly rubbed, signature, J. S. Hasted, bookplate of Allan D. MacDonald, from the library of James Stevens Cox (1910-1997). Maggs Bros. Ltd. 1447 - 46 2015 £950

Brome, Alexander *Rump: or an Exact Collection of the Choycest Poems and Songs Relating to the late Times.* London: for Henry Brome and Henry Marsh, 1662. First edition, 8vo., lacking longitudinal half title final blank, Oo4 with added etched titlepage by Wenceslaus Hollar and additional engraved plate, circa 1850, of the Rump bound at front, small burn-hole to gutter of K2 affecting one letter to verso, light discoloration to K3 from burn-hole on preceding leaf, light spotting to O2-O4, small burn-hole to O6 affecting a letter of text on recto, very light dampstain to lower blank margin of gatherings S-X, repaired burn-hole to gutter of X3 affecting three letters on recto, some occasional discoloration, lightly pressed, late 19th century emerald morocco by Bedford, spine lightly sunned, lower edges lightly chipped, couple of minor scrapes to front cover, good copy, from the library of James Stevens Cox (1910-1997). Maggs Bros. Ltd. 1447 - 50 2015 £575

Brome, James *An Historical Acccount of Mr. Rogers's Three Years Travels over England and Wales.* London: by J. Moxon and B. Bearwell, 1694. First (unauthorized) edition, 8vo., large folding map of England and Wales (closely trimmed), light dampstain to fore edge of first few leaves, occasional minor worming to blank fore margin, final four leaves browned, early 19th century russia, extremities rubbed, signature of Henry Cope with inscription "given me by Sr. Richard Middleton 1697 H. Cope", (Sir Richard Middleton, 3rd Bart - 1655-1716) of Chirk Castle Co. Denbigh, Wales, label of R. Beckley bookseller, JSC's signature, from the library of James Stevens Cox (1910-1997). Maggs Bros. Ltd. 1447 - 48 2015 £1200

Brome, Richard *Five New Plays, Viz. The English Moor, or The Mock-Marriage. The Love Sick Court, or The Ambitious Politique. Covent Garden Weeded. The New Academy or the New Exchange. The Queen and Concubine.* London: A. Crook and for H. Brome, 1659. First edition, lacking A1, paper flaw to lower right corner of C4 affecting a letter or two of text on recto and verso, blank corner of K1 torn away without loss, occasional headline cropped and lightly browned throughout, old rembottage binding of early 17th century vellum with early manuscript title written vertically to spine partly recoverable, vellum lightly soiled, later endpapers, label removed from foot of spine, lacking ties, from the library of James Stevens Cox (1910-1997). Maggs Bros. Ltd. 1447 - 49 2015 £450

Brown, Thomas *Amusements Serious and Comical, Calculated for the Meridian of London.* London: for John Nutt, 1700. First edition, 8vo., some light dampstaining (Particularly to sheet B), contemporary sprinkled calf, joints split at head and foot of spine, corners bumped and with front flyleaves coming loose), from the library of James Stevens Cox (1910-1997), signature of Russell Robartes, with armorial bookplate, another signature roughly deleted. Maggs Bros. Ltd. 1447 - 51 2015 £220

Browne, Thomas 1605-1682 *Hyrdriotaphia, Urne Buriall or a Discourse of the Sepulchral Urnes Lately found in Norfolk...* London: printed for Hen(rey) Brome, 1658. First edition, 8vo., lacking errata leaf found in some copies, titlepage lightly soiled, spotted, some occasional light foxing, 19th century olive morocco by Ramage, gilt edges, few minor chips to spine, 19th century pencil notes in margins, early 20th century signature S. A. Pope, from the library of James Stevens Cox (1910-1997). Maggs Bros. Ltd. 1447 - 54 2015 £1200

Browne, Thomas 1605-1682 *Pseudeodoxia Epidemica...* London: Edward Dod, and are to be sold by Andrew Crook, 1658. Fourth edition of Pseudodoxia, second edition of Hydriotaphia and the Garden of Cyrus, 4to., longitudinal half title before second section, titlepage very lightly browned small dampstain in lower margin of sheet 'a' and with occasional spotting, pastedown and endleaves stained by turn-ins, contemporary calf ruled in blind, early manuscript paper label on spine, endleaves from printed sheets from an edition of Aristotle and another work in Latin, joints rubbed, handsome copy, probably an Oxford binding with diagonal blind hatching at head and tail of spine, from the library of James Stevens Cox (1910-1997). Maggs Bros. Ltd. 1447 - 53   2015   £450

Buchanan, George 1506-1582 *Octupla; hoc est Octo Paraphrases Poeticae Psalmi CIV.* Edinburgh: Excudebant Haeredes & Successores Andreae Anderson, 1696. One of two reissues, 8vo., contemporary sprinkled panelled calf, spine with gilt crowned orange device of the Earl of Marchmont (joints cracking, spine rubbed), bound for Patrick Hume, 1st Earl of Marchmont, 1641-1724, signature of Lord Polwarth, from the library of James Stevens Cox (1910-1997). Maggs Bros. Ltd. 1447 - 55   2015   £280

Bulteel, John *The Apophthegms of the Ancients...* London: for William Cademan, 1683. First edition, 8vo., first blank leaf, small paper flaw to lower blank margin of N6, light browning and some light spotting, contemporary sheep, joints rubbed, wormhole to top joint, tiny chip to headcap, pastedowns unstuck, from the library of James Stevens Cox (1910-1997). Maggs Bros. Ltd. 1447 - 56   2015   £360

Burnet, Thomas *The Theory of the Earth...* London: R. Norton for Walter Kettilby, 1684. First edition, folio, engraved frontispiece, 12 engraved plates in text and 2 double page engraved plates, 80mm. tear along fold of second plate from lower margin, occasional spotting and light browning, contemporary sprinkled calf, covers panelled in blind, front joint split but firm, covers little scuffed, headcaps broken, lower corner on front cover damaged, other corners and edges rubbed, from the library of James Stevens Cox (1910-1997). Maggs Bros. Ltd. 1447 - 58   2015   £750

Burton, William *A Commentary on Antoninus His Itinerary or Journies of the Roman Empire...* London: Tho. Roycroft and are to be sold by Henry Twyford and T. Wyford, 1658. First edition in English, folio, etched portrait of Burton by Hollar, double page etched map by Hollar, few woodcut illustrations in text, small stain on titlepage, very lightly spotted in places, contemporary sheep, old reback, corners repaired, area of loss to leather at head of lower cover, new endleaves, from the library of James Stevens Cox (1910-1997). Maggs Bros. Ltd. 1447 - 59   2015   £350

Busby, Richard *Rudimentum Grammaticae Latinae Metricum.* London: Ex Officina Eliz Redmayne, 1699. Early edition, 8vo., interleaved with blanks, woodcut Westminster School arms on title, small circular stain just touching titlepage coat of arms and minor spotting throughout, errata page has been misprinted with some loss to text, top corners beginning to fold between gatherings B-D but generally clean copy, contemporary sprinkled calf, covers panelled in blind (worn, corners bumped, pastedowns unstruck), signed by John and Robert Bere, annotations on only two of the blank interleaves, from the library of James Stevens Cox (1910-1997). Maggs Bros. Ltd. 1447 - 60   2015   £240

Butler, Samuel 1612-1680 *Hudibras.* (bound with) *Hudibras, the second part.* London: printed in the year, 1663. London: T(homas) R(oycrofts) for John Martyn and James Allestry, 1664. Fourth pirated edition and second authorized edition of second part, small 8vo., imprimatur verso of title lacking final blank H8, some minor repairs to margins of titlepage of first work, first work lightly soiled and foxed, second work with minor dampstain to lower right corner of first three or four gatherings, 19th century half calf and marbled boards, spine rubbed and chipped, corners chipped, boards rubbed, from the library of James Stevens Cox (1910-1997). Maggs Bros. Ltd. 1447 - 61   2015   £150

Camoens, Luis De *The Lusiad or Portugals Historicall Poem.* London: by Thomas Newcombe for Humphrey Moseley, 1655. Folio, A5 with paper repair top corner and loss of about a dozen letters in total, few minor stains, 2 small wormholes in lower blank margin throughout, contemporary panelled calf, covers with gilt arms block of Sir William Boothby, rebacked lower right corner of cover repaired, covers rather worn and faded, front flyleaf repaired, from the library of James Stevens Cox (1910-1997). Maggs Bros. Ltd. 1447 - 62   2015   £4000

Capel, Arthur *Excellent Contemplations, Divine and Moral.* London: for Nath(aniel) Crouch, 1683. First edition, 12mo., engraved portrait of Capel (mounted and repaired along inner margin), small piece torn from blank lower margin of F1, small hole (paper flaw?) to blank corner of F6, 19th century sprinkled calf by Bedford, William Twopenny late 19th/early 20th century label, from the library of James Stevens Cox (1910-1997). Maggs Bros. Ltd. 1447 - 63   2015   £350

Carew, Thomas 1595-1639 *Poems, Songs and Sonnets, Together with a Masque.* London: Henry Herringman, 1670. Fourth edition, 8vo., foxed and browned, heaviest in margins, occasional repairs to fore and upper edge, closely shaved along lower edge, touching catchwords and signatures on a number of leaves, early 20th century half calf and cloth boards, with W(illia)m Gates 18th century signature, pencil signature of H. F. B. Brett Smith (1896-1942), ink inscription March 20th 1922 of Francis K. W. Needham, signature John (?Harr)ison dated 1926, from the library of James Stevens Cox (1910-1997).   Maggs Bros. Ltd.   1447 - 64   2015   £180

Carleton, George *Astrologomania; the Madnesse of Astrologers.* London: by R. C. for John Hammond, 1651. Second edition, 8vo., first blank leaf (inner margin with old guard), closely shave date head, contemporary sheep ruled in blind, rebacked, corners chewed, upper edge front cover slightly wormed, signature of Ni(cholas?) Saunderson, from the library of James Stevens Cox (1910-1997).   Maggs Bros. Ltd.   1447 - 65   2015   £400

Carter, Matthew *Honor Rediviuus (sic) or an Analysis of Honor and Armory.* London: for Henry Herringman, 1660. Second edition, engraved frontispiece, 7 etched plates, numerous woodcut coats of arms in text, very minor foxing to blank margins of B1-2 and with some early inked hash markings in margins, 19th century calf, covers with gilt tooled border, rebacked, corners repaired, new endleaves, 19th century manuscript family tree from Thomas Carter (d. 1603) (family of author) to children of Mary Toke d. 1875 and Charles Frederick Jarvis d. 1903, from the library of James Stevens Cox (1910-1997).   Maggs Bros. Ltd.   1447 - 67   2015   £200

Carter, Matthew *Honor Rediviuus (sic) or an Analysis of Honor and Armory.* London: by E(llen) Coates, 1655. First edition, one of two issues, 8vo., engraved frontispiece, 7 etched portraits, numerous armorial woodcuts with four in contemporary hand color, possibly a thick paper copy, some light foxing and occasional staining, contemporary calf, covers ruled in gilt, expertly rebacked, covers worn, chipped especially at corners and edges, mid 19th century endleaves, presentation by author to William Dugdale (1605-1686), the copy of James Robinson Planche (17696-1880) with bookplate, from the library of James Stevens Cox (1910-1997).   Maggs Bros. Ltd.   1447 - 66   2015   £3200

Cartwright, William *Comedies, Tragi-Comedies with other Poems.* London: for Humphrey Mosely, 1651. First edition, 8vo., engraved portrait by Lombart (small rust hole at foot of image repaired), G8v stained, otherwise occasional small stains, early 19th century calf, covers ruled in gilt, gilt spine, armorial bookplate of Sir Frances Freeling, 1st Bart. 1764-1836, 19th century armorial bookplate of Francis Darby, from the library of James Stevens Cox (1910-1997). Maggs Bros. Ltd.   1447 - 68   2015   £600

Cary, John *A Discourse Concerning the East India Trade.* London: for E. Baldwin, 1699. Small 4to., lightly browned and with small faint ink splash on titlepage, disbound, from the library of James Stevens Cox (1910-1997).   Maggs Bros. Ltd.   1447 - 70   2015   £750

Cary, John *A Discourse Concerning the Trade of Ireland and Scotland as they Stand in Competition with the Trade of England...* Reprinted at London, 1695. First separate edition, small 4to., small hole through titlepage and second leaf, A2-3 heavily soiled and with some dampstaining to upper fore-corner throughout, stitched as issued, edges trimmed, light pencil notes on blank verso of final leaf, from the library of James Stevens Cox (1910-1997).   Maggs Bros. Ltd.   1447 - 71   2015   £750

Cary, John *A Vindication of the Parliament of England...* London: Freeman Collins and to be sold by Sam. Crouch and Eliz. Whitlock, 1698. First edition, 8vo., lightly browned, mid 19th century half calf and marbled boards, one corner scuffed, early 20th century label Charles Wells, from the library of James Stevens Cox (1910-1997). Maggs Bros. Ltd.   1447 - 73   2015   £250

Cary, John *An Account of the Proceedings of the Corporation of Bristol in Execution of the Act of Parliament for the Better Employing and maintaining the Poor of that City.* London: by F. Collins and are to be sold by John Nutt, 1700. Scarcer of two editions, 8vo., light spotting, small wormhole and short tear (not touching text) to titlepage, mid 20th century quarter morocco and cloth boards, from the library of James Stevens Cox (1910-1997).   Maggs Bros. Ltd.   1447 - 69   2015   £750

Cary, John *An Essay on the Coyn and credit of England.* Bristol: by Will. Bonny and sold by bookseller sof London and Bristo., October 22d, 1696. First edition, small 8vo. half title, light staining to inner margin on verso of half title and with final leaf slightly foxed, mid 20th century half brown pigskin and marbled boards, from the library of James Stevens Cox (1910-1997), JSC's pencil signature.   Maggs Bros. Ltd.   1447 - 72   2015   £2000

Caryll, John *Naboth's Vinyard; or the Innocent Traytor...* London: for C. R., 1679. Second edition, small 4to., 20 pages, title lightly browned with two small (55 20mm) circular dampstains at foot of B1 and b2, 19th century marbled wrappers, from the library of James Stevens Cox (1910-1997).   Maggs Bros. Ltd.   1447 - 74   2015   £100

Certain Observations Upon the new League or Covenant as It Was Explained by a Divine of the New Assembly in a Congregation at London. Bristol: for Rich. Harsell, 1643. First edition, small 4to., without final blank, first gathering loose, C3-D4 dampstained and with a number of uncut leaves, disbound, from the library of James Stevens Cox (1910-1997).   Maggs Bros. Ltd.   1447 - 87   2015   £100

Chalkhill, John *Thealma and Clarchus. A Pastoral History in Smooth and Easie Verse.* London: for Benj. Tooke, 1683. First edition, second issue with corrected state of title with Edward Spencer corrected to Edmund Spencer, 8vo., small chip from paper flaw at foot of C3 with small piece from lower blank corner of C4 torn away, A3 very closely trimmed along fore-edge, not touching text, 30mm. closed tear from a paper flaw to corner of D3 (touching catchword on recto) and with small stain on H6v, contemporary sheep, worn, covers heavily scuffed and bumped, spine very rubbed and with some worm damage at foot, upper headcap torn away, rear flyleaf torn and beginning to come loose, signature of Hon. Edward Monckton (1744-1823) and armorial bookplate, from the library of James Stevens Cox (1910-1997). Maggs Bros. Ltd. 1447 - 76 2015 £600

Charles I, King of England *Eikon Basilike.* London: by W(illiam) D(u-gard) (for Francis Eglesfield) in R.M., Anno dom, 1649. 8vo., lacking final blank, 2 engraved plates laid down and mounted on stub opposite the title, small piece torn away from upper corner of titlepage (not touching text but removing in ink name or price), inscription cut from head of first leaf, light browning to margin throughout, dampstain to inner margin of (2)A1-(2)B4, book-block split at page 160, contemporary black morocco, covers elaborately tooled gilt with border and panel, inside corners filled with flower and scroll tools and small hearts and central lozenge with crown and initials 'CR' in middle, smooth spine (once handsome binding, covers still bright, spine badly worn and defective at head and tail, corners worn, some rubbing on lower cover), late 19th century marbled endleaves, from the library of James Stevens Cox (1910-1997). Maggs Bros. Ltd. 1447 - 78 2015 £200

Chaucer, Geoffrey 1340-1400 *The Works of Our Ancient and Learned and Excellent English Poet...* London: 1687. Folio, frontispiece, Black Letter, some browning and light foxing throughout and with small ink blot on Yy3, touching two lines of text, fore margin rather narrow, early 19th century calf, rebacked. large armorial bookplate of Francis Thomas de Grey Cowper, 7th and last Earl Cowper (1834-1905), from the library of James Stevens Cox (1910-1997). Maggs Bros. Ltd. 1447 - 80 2015 £1100

Child, Josiah 1630-1699 *A New Discourse about Trade, Wherein the Reduction of Interest of Money to 4 1. per Centrum is Recommended.* London: printed by A. Sowle, 1690. First edition, small 8vo., with initial license leaf A1 but lacking errata leaf P8, some occasional light soiling and ink markings to blank margins throughout the occasional headline shaved by the binder, lower fore-corners of first few leaves chipped away, modern quarter blue morocco and marbled boards, from the library of James Stevens Cox (1910-1997). Maggs Bros. Ltd. 1447 - 81 2015 £1100

Child, Josiah 1630-1699 *A New Discourse of Trade, Wherein is recommended Several Weighty Points Relating to Companies of Merchants.* London: printed and sold by T. Sowle, 1698. Fourth edition, 8vo., final blank titlepage heavily browned, following seven leaves less severely marked, contemporary sheep ruled in blind, rebacked, corners repaired, corners worn and leather affected by damp, (new endleaves), from the library of James Stevens Cox (1910-1997). Maggs Bros. Ltd. 1447 - 82 2015 £280

Clarke, Samuel 1599-1683 *A True and Faithful Account of the Four Chiefest Plantations of the English in America.* London: for Robert Clavel, Thomas Passenger, William Cadman, William Whitwood, Thomas Saiwbridge and William Birch, 1670. Small folio, occasional light browning and soiling, blank fore-margin of 7A2 stained, contemporary calf, rebacked, recornered and with new endpapers, from the library of James Stevens Cox (1910-1997). Maggs Bros. Ltd. 1447 - 100 2015 £250

Cleveland, John *Clievlandi Vindiciae or Cleveland's Genuine Poems, Orations, Epistles &c.* London: for Obadiah Blagrave, 1677. 8vo., engraved portrait (small piece missing from lower margin), tear to lower inner margin of L2, light worming to lower fore-corner between a1-N1 and with minor spotting and dampstaining in places, late 19th century mottled calf, rebacked, corners repaired, new endpapers, from the library of James Stevens Cox (1910-1997). Maggs Bros. Ltd. 1447 - 101 2015 £150

Cleveland, John *The Idol of the Clownes or Insurrection of Wat the Tyler with His Priests Baal and Straw...* London: in the Year, 1654. Second edition, small 8vo., without engraved portrait found in some copies and without final blank, light dampstaining to first few leaves, closely shaved at head (just touching pagination in places), early 19th century calf, covers ruled in gilt, spine tooled in gilt and blind, marbled edges and endpapers, small stain on front cover and minor repair on rear, old front flyleaf preserved, from the library of James Stevens Cox (1910-1997), with late 17th/early 18th century inscription "Thomas Browne/His booke", not that of Sir Thomas Browne (1605-1682), with bookplate of Albert M. Cohn, posthumous sale, Christie 26/2/1934 lot 176 (as Sir Thomas Browne's copy), £5 to Charles H. Stonehill. Maggs Bros. Ltd. 1447 - 102 2015 £200

Coke, Roger *A Treatise Wherein is Demonstrated that the Church and state of England are in Equal Danger with the Trade of It.* London: by J. C. for Henry Brome, 1671. First edition, small 4to., two small wormholes in blank corner of A1-3 reducing to a single hole A4-B2, occasionally closely shaved along upper edge, large ink blot in centre of A2v-A34, contemporary sprinkled sheep, rebacked, lower corner of board heavily bumped, from the library of James Stevens Cox (1910-1997). Maggs Bros. Ltd. 1447 - 103 2015 £700

Coles, Elisha *An English Dictionary Explaining the Difficult terms that are Used in Divinity, Husbandry, Physick, Philosophy, Law, Navigation, Mathematicks and Other Arts and Sciences.* London: for Peter Parker, 1696. Sixth edition, titlepage lightly soiled and with margins browned by turn-ins, single wormhole to A1-B1, H1-L1 and short worm trail to Z6-2A3, minor ink staining to Q6 and 2C2-4, lower edge of H1 little ragged, with small spider neatly pressed between R3-4, cut fairly close at head, contemporary calf, ruled in blind, spine creased, upper headcap split and short crack at head of upper joint, small hole in foot of spine, corners and edges worn, no pastedowns, rear flyleaf only, ink inscription of William Cheyney, from the library of James Stevens Cox (1910-1997).   Maggs Bros. Ltd.   1447 - 104   2015   £500

Coles, Elisha *Christologia or a Metrical paraphrase on the History of Our Lord and Saviour Jesus Christ.* London: for Peter Parker, 1671. First edition, 8vo., without first blank leaf, light browning particularly in margins, words "OR A" on title deleted with ink and replaced with "a" in later manuscript, closely shaved, mid 20th century blue quarter morocco and marbled boards, from the library of James Stevens Cox (1910-1997), inscribed by Lewis Caesar Hill, 19th century signature George R. Hales, signature R. Betts dated "Silverhill 15.1 (18)90", booklabel of Gerald P Mander (d. 1951) of Tettenhall Wood, Staffordshire.   Maggs Bros. Ltd. 1447 - 105   2015   £240

Collier, Jeremy *A Short View of the Immorality and Profaneness of the English Stage together with the Sense of Antiquity Upon the Argument.* London: for S. Keble, R. Sare and H. Hindmarch, 1698. Second edition, 8vo., light dampstain to blank fore-margin of sheet #, two tears to blank margins of E7 and E8 (just touching a sidenote or two), light worming to blank lower right corner of G4-T8, some discoloration due to poor paper quality, contemporary calf, covers panelled in blind, spine tooled in gilt and with red morocco label, covers slightly scuffed, from the library of James Stevens Cox (1910-1997) with bookplate.   Maggs Bros. Ltd.   1447 - 107   2015   £350

Collier, Jeremy *Essays Upon Several Moral Subjects.* London: for R. Sare and H. Hindmarsh, 1697. Second edition, 8vo., small piece torn from B8 with loss to 3 words, small hole to C8 with loss of letter or two, some occasional light foxing and staining, contemporary calf, rebacked, corners repaired, from the library of James Stevens Cox (1910-1997).   Maggs Bros. Ltd.   1447 - 106   2015   £120

Colvil, Samuel *Whiggs Supplication.* Edinburgh: by Jo. Reid for Alexander Ogston, 1687. Second edition, 8vo., very small chip from upper fore corner with four minor circular stains on titlepage, some occasional staining throughout, dampstaining just touching corners of F4-F6, some heavy modern pencil markings in a number of margins, and with a number of gatherings beginning to come loose from book block, signed by author sheep (worn, large piece torn away from foot of spine and with upper headcap damaged, boards heavily rubbed and corners bumped, early signature of Geo(rge) Dundas, bookplate of Frederick Locker-Lampson (1821-1895), given by him to Lytton Strachey (1880-1932), from the library of James Stevens Cox (1910-1997). Maggs Bros. Ltd.   1447 - 108   2015   £150

Comber, Thomas *The Occasional Offices of Matrimony, Visitation to the Sick, Burial of the Dead, Churching of Women...* London: by M. C. for Henry Brome and Robert Clavel, 1679. 8vo., dampstaining to fore-margin of Q2-Z-4 and lower fore corner Ff1-Kk8, contemporary black morocco 'semi sombre' binding, covers finely tooled with double gilt fillet containing blind tooled fronds, sequins and daisies, central gilt panel with vase and flower tool at each corner and containing further blind tooling and central lozenge, spine in six panels, tooled in gilt with red morocco label in second panel, gilt edges and marbled endleaves, early 20th century marbled slipcase (slight worm damage at foot of spine, slightly rubbed, corners very lightly bumped), from the library of James Stevens Cox (1910-1997).   Maggs Bros. Ltd.   1447 - 110   2015   £550

Compton, Henry *The Jesuites Intrigues...* London: for Benjamin Tooke, 1669. First edition, small 4to., titlepage browned and frayed at head, few ink spots, inner margin dampstained throughout (not affecting text), with occasional spotting to B1, E2 and F1, small piece missing from upper margin of D2 with soiling and damage to corners of I1-2, mid 20th century quarter mauve morocco and marbled boards (boards sunned and with slight worm damage to foot of spine), from the library of James Stevens Cox (1910-1997).   Maggs Bros. Ltd.   1447 - 111   2015   £120

The Conspiracy of Aeneas & Antenor Against the State of Troy. London: for John Spicer, 1682. First edition, small 4to., 20 pages, titlepage and recto of B3 lightly soiled, lower margins uncut, late 19th century half calf and marbled boards (foot of spine lightly chipped, one or two bumps to top edge of both boards), 20th century signature of James Bell, from the library of James Stevens Cox (1910-1997). Maggs Bros. Ltd.   1447 - 112   2015   £450

Cook, John *Redintegratio Amoris, or a Union of Hearts...* London: for Giles Calvert, 1647. First edition, small 4to., without first and final blank leafs, dark circular dampstain (45 x 25mm) in upper fore-corner of titlepage (from deleted signature), some spotting and browning throughout and with small (15mm) closed tear to margin of F2, some minor worming in inner margin dampstain in top margin at end, late 19th century calf, covers panelled blind, red edges, spine defective at head and tail, corners bumped, signature of Rev. Richard Grosvenor Bartelot, FSA, earlier signature deleted from titlepage, from the library of James Stevens Cox (1910-1997).   Maggs Bros. Ltd.   1447 - 113   2015   £350

Cooke, James *Mellificium Chirurgiae or the Marrow of Many Good Authors.* London: for Samuel Cartwright, 1648. First edition, 12mo., upper fore corners of B6-7 and P5 torn from paper flaws (affecting rule border not touching text), some worming in inner margin (heavily between Q5-R11), contemporary sheep ruled in blind (rubbed, 30mm piece torn at head of spine, a number of loose gatherings, bumped and rubbed, pastedowns unstuck), early ink initials "E K", late 18th century signature Isaac Webster/Hull, signature Isaac Raines 1802, by descent to Rev. George Francis Twycross-Raines, vicar and antiquary of Hull, with ink inscription, of "H. Page from his old friend G. F. Twycross-Raines Sept. 11, 1911", from the library of James Stevens Cox (1910-1997).   Maggs Bros. Ltd.   1447 - 114   2015   £750

Coole, Benjamin *Honesty the Truest Policy, Shewing the Sophistry, Envy and Perversion of George Keith, in His Three Books...* Bristol?: by W. Bonny for the author, 1700. First edition, small 8vo., very small stain in inner margin of A8-B4, 19th century half red calf and marbled boards, early 20th century label of K. G. Pittard, inkstamp of George's bookshop in Bristol, from the library of James Stevens Cox (1910-1997).   Maggs Bros. Ltd.   1447 - 115   2015   £200

Corbet, Richard *Poems.* London: by J. C for William Crook, 1672. Third edition, 12mo., without first blank leaf, woodcut publisher's device of a dragon on title, some spotting on titlepage, wormed at head up to page 28 then declining to a single tiny pinhole, affecting headlines (repaired on first six leaves), closely shaved (touching some headlines and catchwords), fore margin of A6 (The Table) unevenly trimmed with slight loss on recto), early 20th century brown morocco, tooled in blind, by Riviere, from the library of James Stevens Cox (1910-1997).   Maggs Bros. Ltd.   1447 - 116   2015   £240

Cotton, Charles *Scarronnides; or, Virgile Travestie.* London: by E. Cotes for Henry Brome, 1666. 1665. Reprint of Book 1, first edition of book 4, 8vo., first and last leaves blank except for bookseller's woodcut device of a crowned cannon, long closed tear from paper flaw down D5 (touching seven lines of text), small spot at head of E1, contemporary sheep ruled in blind, smooth spine with red morocco and gilt label, no pastedowns, parts of two printed leaves from 17th century English 8vo. Bible as binder's waste (lower headcap torn, joints little rubbed), armorial bookplate of Hon. Shute Barrington, Bp. of Salisbury, from the library of James Stevens Cox (1910-1997).   Maggs Bros. Ltd.   1447 - 118   2015   £700

Cotton, Charles *The Wonders of the Peake.* London: W. Everingham and Tho. Whitledge, 1694. Third edition, 8vo., engraved vignette of cannon on title, first sheet browned, rest less so with some spotting, A6 with two holes from paper flaw (affecting a few letters), red sprinkled edges have occasionally spread onto leaf and a number of lower edges uncut, contemporary sheep (small wormtrail to front board and large scuff on rear board), lower joint split at head, pastedowns unstuck, Lady Anne Coventry's signature, from the library of James Stevens Cox (1910-1997).   Maggs Bros. Ltd.   1447 - 117   2015   £300

Cowley, Abraham   1618-1667 *Poemata Latina.* London: T. Roycroft, Impensis Jo. Martyn, 1668. First collected edition, 8vo., engraved frontispiece by Faithorne, small hole to blank inner gutter of O1-O4 some occasional light soiling, contemporary blind ruled calf, red morocco label to spine (half of label has perished), from the library of James Stevens Cox (1910-1997), contemporary signature of Benjamin Spann, a contemporary signature of Richard Inett, contemporary signature of John Leslie, early 18th century auction or fixed price lot number, acquisition note of John Loveday, by descent to Loveday family library at Willamscote, Banbury, Oxfordshire dispersed in the 1960's.   Maggs Bros. Ltd.   1447 - 119   2015   £240

Cowley, Abraham   1618-1667 *The Works of Mr. Abraham Cowley.* London: by J(ohn) M(acock) for Henry Herringman, 1668. First edition, small folio, engraved portrait by William Faithorne, stain along lower margin of A1, inksplash on H1, margins of H1-H4 creased (by binder?), uncut corner of (2)Q4 folded, contemporary calf, spine with partial remains of red morocco label (heavily rubbed, covers scuffed and worn, corners worn, endleaves dusty, lower front third of front flyleaf torn away, pastedowns coming loose), ink initials A B H on front flyleaf, handsome engraved bookplate of Dominick Trant has come detached from pastedown and loosely inserted, from the library of James Stevens Cox (1910-1997).   Maggs Bros. Ltd.   1447 - 120   2015   £200

Denham, John *Poems and Translations with the Sophy.* London: for H. Herringman, 1668. First collected edition, first issue, 8vo., small ink stain to lower margin of titlepage and fore-edges of D1-D7, small rust spots to 2E5 and 2E8, with small piece torn away from lower blank margin of I1, contemporary polished mottled calf, covers with double gilt fillet and gilt floral tool in each corner, smooth spine ruled in gilt, gilt edges joints rubbed, three small wormholes in upper joint, slight surface crazing to covers, from mottling acid, one corner slightly worn, bottom corner of front flyleaf torn away, errata has been corrected by hand, signature of Edmund Smith (16)88, inscription of Jenks Lutley Esquire 1729, early 18th century armorial bookplate of Richard Barneby of Brockhampton, Herefordshire, from the library of James Stevens Cox (1910-1997). Maggs Bros. Ltd. 1447 - 136   2015   £600

Dennis, John *Rinaldo and Armida; a Tragedy...* London: Jacob Tonson, 1699. First edition, small 4to., lacking half title and without errata slip pasted below 'Dramatis Personae' in some copies, heavily browned and stained throughout, repair to upper corner of B4 touching first letter on verso, large repair to upper blank corner of d4 and with a number of leaves mounted on stubs, early 20th century full black morocco, signature of Dr. Thomas Loveday (d. 1968), from the library of James Stevens Cox (1910-1997). Maggs Bros. Ltd.   1447 - 138   2015   £220

Descartes, Rene *Renati Descartes Epistolae...* London: Joh(n) Dunmore & Octavian Pulleyn, 1668. First London edition, small 4to., 14 folding plates and numerous illustrations, endpapers little stained by original turn-ins, some light dampstaining to first three leaves of sheet O, contemporary calf, covers panelled in blind, rebacked new endpapers, John Wheeler with inscription, 18th century armorial bookplate of Johnstone family of Westerhall, Dumfries, from the library of James Stevens Cox (1910-1997). Maggs Bros. Ltd.   1447 - 141   2015   £750

Descartes, Rene *Renatus Descartes Excellent Compendium of Musick.* London: by Thomas Harper for Humphrey Moseley and Thomas Heath, 1653. First edition in English, small 4to., later engraved portrait, dampstaining to lower margins throughout, dark ink stain to upper margins of a1-b1- (not touching text), worming to lower margin of I4-M4 and with small piece torn away from margins of B3, G3 and L3 (not touching text), contemporary sheep, covers ruled in blind, spine worn and with some worm damage, edges and corners worn and chewed, 18th century inscription William Wilsons, 19th century signature G. U. Hart, Killderry, from the library of James Stevens Cox (1910-1997). Maggs Bros. Ltd.   1447 - 139   2015   £1500

Descartes, Rene *Six Metaphysical Meditations, Wherein It is proved that There is a Gold.* London: by B G. for Benj. Tooke, 1680. First edition in English, 12mo., titlepage soiled in margins and with small piece torn away from blank upper margin (to delete signature), soiling and dampstaining to margins throughout, small closed tear to lower blank margin of C1 (not touching text), some minor rust spots, mid 19th century calf, gilt ruled, rebacked, corners repaired, new endleaves, old signature torn away from upper margin of titlepage, from the library of James Stevens Cox (1910-1997). Maggs Bros. Ltd.   1447 - 140   2015   £1500

Digby, George *A Choice Collection of Rare Chymical Secrets and Experiments in Philosophy.* London: for the publisher (George Hartman), 1682. First edition, second issue, 8vo., 4 engraved plates, lower edge of titlepage shaved, just touching border, very slight browning to final few leaves, contemporary calf, ruled in blind, 19th century reback and endpapers, corners bumped and headcaps torn, inscription R. Sydney Marsden University of Edin. 1882, later pencil note, from the library of James Stevens Cox (1910-1997), with his pencil notes "Bought 1930 (Douglas) Cleverdon. Maggs Bros. Ltd.   1447 - 43   2015   £350

Digby, George *Letters Between the Ld. George Digby and Sr Kenelm Digby, Kt. Concerning Religion.* London: for Humphrey Moseley, 1651. First edition, small 8vo., printer's crease across top corner to final leaf disturbing top four lines, small semi circular ink spot touching upper edge of A1-B8, page numbers occasionally shaved at upper edge, contemporary calf, rebacked, new endpapers, boards little scuffed, some occasional underlinings, from the library of James Stevens Cox (1910-1997). Maggs Bros. Ltd.   1447 - 142   2015   £220

Digby, Kenelm   1603-1665   *A Late Discourse made in a Solemne Assembly of nobles and Learned Men at Montpellier in France.* London: R. Lownes and (T) Davies, 1658. First edition in English, 12mo., inner margin of title little stained with some loss of imprint due to adhesion of flyleaf, contemporary sheep tightly rebacked, large repair to front cover and corners repaired, from the library of James Stevens Cox (1910-1997). Maggs Bros. Ltd.   1447 - 144   2015   £240

Digby, Kenelm   1603-1665   *A Late Discourse made in a Solemne assembly of Nobles and Learned Men at Montpellier in France.* London: for R. Lowndes and T. Davies, 1658. Second edition in English, 12mo., browned and spotted throughout, a number of leaves faintly printed, small burn-hole to blank margin of F1, early 19th century russia, ruled in gilt, upper head cap damaged and joints rubbed and just starting to crack, marbled endleaves stained by turn-ins, bookplate of Henry Montagu Digby, 1874-1934, from the library of James Stevens Cox (1910-1997). Maggs Bros. Ltd.   1447 - 145   2015   £180

Digby, Kenelm 1603-1665 *Of Bodies and of Mans Soul.* London: by S(arah) G(riffin) and B(ennet) G(riffin) for John Williams, 1669. First collected edition, 4to., some light dampstaining and spotting throughout, small closed tear to upper edge of L8 (just touching pagination), 2 minor chips to fore margin of 2F1-2, contemporary calf, covers ruled in blind, later spine label and small gilt ornament in each panel (surface of leather on covers crazed by damp, some surface rubbing and slight insect damage on lower cover chipped and rubbed), bookplate of Helyar family of Coker Court, Somerset, from the library of James Stevens Cox (1910-1997). Maggs Bros. Ltd. 1447 - 147 2015 £400

Diodorus Siculus *The History of Diodorus Siculus.* London: by John Macock for Giles Calvert, 1653. First edition in English, small folio, longitudinal half title has been cut-out leaving a stub, 271 pages, small circular stain in inner margins of first few leaves and Kk4-L12, rust spot on Kk4, contemporary sheep, smooth spine ruled in blind and with red morocco and gilt label, covers heavily scuffed, piece missing from top corner of lower cover, upper headcap torn, front pastedown torn away at head, early inscription on flyleaf heavily deleted, early signature Nic. Hare, signature on title Edm. Sex. Pery, 1st and last Viscount Pery (1719-1806) by descent to his elder daughter Diana Jane, Countess of Ranfurly to Earls of Ranfurly, with 19th century bookplate, from the library of James Stevens Cox (1910-1997). Maggs Bros. Ltd. 1447 - 148 2015 £380

Drake, Judith *An Essay in Defence of the female Sex.* London: for A. Roper and R. Clavel, 1697. Third edition, large 8vo., frontispiece, light waterstaining to lower right corner of second half of work, section cut from top of titlepage (62 x 25mm) removing 'An' from title, contemporary panelled calf, corners and edges slightly chipped, joints cracked, pencil inscription Frances Cotton Anne Fleming Aug 14 1715, H. Hall 18th century red ink stamp, from the library of James Stevens Cox (1910-1997). Maggs Bros. Ltd. 1447 - 150 2015 £1500

England and Wales. Parliament - 1642 *A Declaration of the Lords and Commons Assembled in Parliament, with their Resolution, That if Captaine Catesby, Captaine Lilborne, Captaine Vivers or any Others Which are or shall be Taken Prisoners, by His Majesties Army Shall be Put to Death...* London: Decemb. 19 printed for John Wright, 1642. First edition, small 4to, 8 pages, nasty marks along inner margin of title where a cloth backing has been removed, last leaf stained with white blob obscuring parts of two words, type ornament border at foot of title shaved, disbound, the copy of Sidney Russell, of Fairway, Gorway Rad, Walsall, circa 1936, from the library of James Stevens Cox (1910-1997). Maggs Bros. Ltd. 1447 - 92 2015 £150

England and Wales. Parliament - 1643 *An Ordinance of the Lords and Commons Assembled in Parliament for the Better Raising, Leavying and Impresting of Mariners Saylers and Others...* London: for L. Blaiklock, Jan. 15, 1643-1644. Small 4to., browned, early 20th century half blue roan and marbled boards, slightly rubbed, from the library of James Stevens Cox (1910-1997). Maggs Bros. Ltd. 1447 - 93 2015 £180

A Letter Sent from a Private Gentleman to a friend in London, in Justification of his Owne Adhering to His Majestie in Times of Distraction... London: for V.N. Anno. Dom., 1642. Small 4to., 8 pages, early 20th century quarter morocco, bookplate of Markree Library of the Cooper family at Markree Castle, Co. Sligo, Ireland, from the library of James Stevens Cox (1910-1997). Maggs Bros. Ltd. 1447 - 90 2015 £120

A Letter Sent to the Right Honourable William Lenthall Esquire, Speaker to the Honourable House of Commons: Concerning the Routing of Col. Gorings Army near Bridgewater. London: for John Field, July 22, 1645. First edition, small 4to., 8 pages, uncut, upper edge unopened, verso of final leaf little soiled, disbound, from the library of James Stevens Cox (1910-1997). Maggs Bros. Ltd. 1447 - 97 2015 £150

The Loyal City of Bristol, Vindicated from Amsterdamism or Devil's Borough, Two Appelatives Occasioned by the Over Credulous Who Have Hitherto Taken it for Granted... London: or Bristol: for J. Davies, 1681. First edition, small 4to., very small stain just touching lower fore-corner of titlepage, minor marks on verso of final leaf but otherwise very clean, modern paper wrappers, from the library of James Stevens Cox (1910-1997). Maggs Bros. Ltd. 1447 - 47 2015 £350

A Narration of the Great Victory (through Gods Providence) Obtained by the Parliamentary Forces Under Sir William Walker at Alton in Surrey the 13, of This Instant December 1643. London: for Edw. Husbands, Dec. 16, 1643. First edition, small 4to., 8 pages, very lightly browned and closely trimmed along upper margin, late 19th century half calf and marbled boards, from the library of James Stevens Cox (1910-1997). Maggs Bros. Ltd. 1447 - 91 2015 £200

Peters, Hugh *Gods Doings and Mans Duty Opened in a Sermon Preached Before Both Houses of Parliament, the Lord Major and Aldermen of the City of London...* London: M. S(immons) for G. Calvert, 1646. Second edition, small 4to., dark ink spot along upper margin of first few leaves, small rust spot to fore-margin of A2, slight foxing to B1-C1, several leaves uncut and with lower edge of d1 printed very close to edge (affecting the catchword on recto), mid 20th century half calf and marbled boards, from the library of James Stevens Cox (1910-1997), with bookplate and cipher and few pencil notes. Maggs Bros. Ltd. 1447 - 94 2015 £120

The Royal Martyrs; or a List of the Lords, Knights, Officers and Gentlemen, That Were Slain (by the Rebels) in the Late Wars in Defence of Their King and Country. London: by Henry Lloyd and are to be sold by H. Marsh,, 1663. mall 4to. without final blank leaf, very lightly browned throughout and with small damp spot on (A)2(touching one line of text), mid 20th century red morocco, from the library of James Stevens Cox (1910-1997). Maggs Bros. Ltd. 1447 - 95 2015 £150

Rupert, Prince, Count Palatine 1619-1682 *A Declaration of His Hignesse Prince Rupert.* London: Edward Griffin, 1645. 4to. uncut at fore-edge and tail, title browned, edges dusty, small rust spot on E3v and with fore margin of E4 stained, late 20th century calf, ruled in gilt by Salisbury Bookbinders, very light white scuff marks on front board and foot of spine, from the library of James Stevens Cox (1910-1997). Maggs Bros. Ltd. 1447 - 85 2015 £200

Rushworth, John *A True Relation of the Storming of Bristoll, and the taking the Town, Castle, Forts, Ordnance, Ammunition and Arms by Sir Thomas Fairfax's army on Thursday the 11 of this instant Septemb. 1645.* London: Edward Husband, 1645. First edition, small 4to., titlepage browned and foxed, some light spotting, closely trimmed in places but with no loss of text, late 19th century calf by Kerr & Richardson, Glasgow, joints and edges rubbed, covers discolored, signature of James Reilly, from the library of James Stevens Cox (1910-1997). Maggs Bros. Ltd. 1447 - 86 2015 £120

A True Relation of the Great and Glorious Victory through Gods Providence, Obtained by Sir William Waller, Sir Arthur Haslerig and Others of the Parliament Forces... London: for Edward Husbands July 14, 1643. First edition, small 4to., some catchwords and final line of text trimmed, early 20th century half maroon morocco and cloth boards (covers dampstained), from the library of James Stevens Cox (1910-1997). Maggs Bros. Ltd. 1447 - 98 2015 £150

Vicars, John *Former Ages Never Heard Of, and After Ages Will Admire.* London: by M. S(immons) for Thomas Jenner, 1656. Third edition, small 4to., 13 engraved illustrations in text, fore-margin of title renewed and upper blank corner of A2 repaired, little soiled throughout, stain to centre of C3-4, lower inner margin browned and with heavy foxing to H3-4, late 19th century calf, gilt edges, joints rubbed, from the library of James Stevens Cox (1910-1997). Maggs Bros. Ltd. 1447 - 99 2015 £375

Association – Coxe, George Harmon

Coxe, George Harmon *The Reluctant Heiress.* New York: Knopf, 1965. First edition, advance review copy with review slip laid in, also laid in is Typed personal note from the desk of George Harmon Coxe dated 2 29 68 and signed by Coxe requesting addressee send his copy of this book to author for him to sign, fine in dust jacket. Mordida Books March 2015 - 010442 2015 $100

Association – Craig, Isa

Procter, Adelaide A. *The Victoria Regia a Volume of Original Contributions in Poetry and Prose.* London: printed and published by Emily Faithfull & Co., Victoria Press for the Employment of Women, 1861. First edition, 8vo. full leather elaborately stamped in gilt, all edges gilt, gilt inner dentelles, designed by John Leighton, some foxing on endpapers, much less in text, some very light wear to boards, still near fine, inscribed by Emily Faithful for Blanche Resticaux, 1862, also inserted a few news clippings about Faithful, very small ALS from Henry Alford and small slip of paper signed yours faithfully Isa Craig. Second Life Books Inc. 191 - 78 2015 $1500

Association – Crane, Walter

Pausanias *An Extract out of Pausanias, of the Statues, Pictures and Temples in Greece; which were Remaining There in his Time.* London: printed for W. Shropshire, 1758. First translation into English, some light spotting, small repair to titlepage verso, 8vo., contemporary calf, rebacked preserving old lettering piece, old leather darkened and crackled, corners repaired, bookplate of the Arts & Crafts movement artist Walter Crane, good copy, scarce. Blackwell's Rare Books Greek & Latin Classics VI - 78 2015 £1200

Association – Crawford, Earl of

St. John, Oliver *The Speech or Declaration of Mr. St. John, His Majesties Solicitor Generall. Delivered at a Conference of Both Houses of Parliament held 16o Caroll. 1640. Concerning Ship-Money.* London: by J. N. for Henry Seyle, 1641. First edition, variant issue, 4to., title within rules with head device as central ornament, uninked blindstamp of institutional library on titlepage and library inkstamp on blank verso, final leaf rather dust soiled, bound in early 20th century cloth, spine labelled but worn, even so a good, crisp copy, sometime in the Wigan Free Library having been presented to it by the Earl of Crawford. John Drury Rare Books March 2015 - 21454 2015 £266

Association – Creeley, Genevieve Jules

Creeley, Robert *The Island.* New York: Charles Scribner's Sons, 1963. First edition, 8vo., original cloth, dust jacket, spine discolored, top edge faintly foxed, otherwise fine in slightly rubbed dust jacket with bit of wear to head and heel of spine, presentation copy inscribed by author to his mother.   James S. Jaffe Rare Books   Modern American Poetry - 53   2015 $1500

Creeley, Robert *Words. Poems.* New York: Scribner's, 1967. First edition, 8vo., original cloth, top corner bit bumped, horizontal crease on front cover, otherwise fine, dust jacket trifle rubbed, presentation copy inscribed by author for his mother.   James S. Jaffe Rare Books   Modern American Poetry - 54   2015 $1500

Association – Creeley, Robert

Dorn, Edward *The Newly Fallen.* New York: Totem Press, 1961. First edition, drawings by Fielding Dawson, illustrated wrappers, bit of age-toning to wrappers, thus near fine, poet Robert Creeley's copy with his ownership signature.   Between the Covers Rare Books, Inc.   187 - 78   2015 $150

Association – Cremer, R. Kenton

Wimsatt, William Kurtz *The Portraits of Alexander Pope.* New Haven: Yale University Press, 1965. 4to., half title, frontispiece, original brown buckram, very good in slightly torn dust jacket, author's presentation copy for Geoffrey Tillotson, with 2 TLS's from him, Geoffrey's typewritten review and cutting from TLS, related material, ALS from R. Kenton Cremer, photos of Pope's annotations to an edition of "The Pastorals" in worn folder.   Jarndyce Antiquarian Booksellers   CCVII - 440   2015   £60

Association – Crespy, Charles Edouard, Baron De

Bonaparte, Napoleon III, Emperor of the French 1808-1873 *Fragmens Historiques 1688 et 1830.* Paris: Administration De Librairie, 1841. Inscribed on slip pasted to half title "Baron Le Crespy-Le Prince", the dedicatee is presumably the artist Charles Edouard Le Prince, Baron de Crespy (1784-1850), note pasted to front endpaper states that the inscription is the autograph of Napoleon III, but is more likely that of an amanuensis, red buckram quarter bound with red calf spine ruled and lettered gilt, from the library of Allan Heywood Bright, with his calling card loosely inserted, neat 19th century ownership inscription to titlepage, some light foxing, especially to first few pages, binding little rubbed and scuffed, otherwise very good.   Any Amount of Books   2015 - C11782   2015   £240

Association – Cressey, E. H.

Blackwell, Elizabeth *The Laws of Life, with Special Reference to the Physical Education of Girls.* New York: George P. Putnam, 1852. First edition, slate-gray cloth, edges stained red, spine bit faded, few very tiny spots, else remarkably fresh, tight copy, as close to fine as one could hope for, contemporary signature of E. H. Cressey on front endpaper.   Joseph J. Felcone Inc.   Science, Medicine and Technology - 12   2015 $12,000

Association – Creswick, Paul

Trehern, Gaspard *The Old Ecstasies: a Story of To-Day.* London: Bellairs & Co., 1897. First edition, octavo, blue cloth decorated in green and titled in gilt, bookplate of Paul Creswick and another small rubbed stamp, bit cocked and rubbed, about very good, Advance Review Copy with perforated stamp and pair of ALS's laid in, to fellow author Creswick.   Between the Covers Rare Books, Inc.   187 - 278   2015 $300

Association – Crockett, S. R.

Arnold, Matthew 1822-1888 *Poems.* London: Longmans, 1853. New edition, half title, 32 page catalog (March 31 1853), unexplained erasure of edition statement, original green cloth by Westleys, yellow endpapers with printed ads, spine quite worn at head and tail, trace of lending library label, novelist S. R. Crockett's copy, signed by him, H. J. Macrory and Geoffrey Tillotson.   Jarndyce Antiquarian Booksellers   CCVII - 45   2015   £35

Association – Croft, Addison

Cudworth, William *Life and Correspondence of Abraham Sharp, the Yorkshire Mathematician and Astronomer and Assistant of Flamsteed...* London & Bradford: Sampson Low, Marston, Searle & Rivington & Thos. Brear, 1889. Tall 8vo., frontispiece with tissue guard, 9 unnumbered plates, 19 figures, half vellum with marbled paper sides, gilt stamped black morocco spine labels, top edge gilt, soiled, extremities worn, author's presentation for Rev. Addison Croft.   Jeff Weber Rare Books   178 - 1006   2015 $300

Association – Crookshank

Butler, Samuel 1835-1902 *Luck or Cunning as the Main means of Organic Modification?* London: Longmans, 1890. Half title, final ad leaf, original brick brown cloth, bevelled boards, slightly rubbed, presentation from author to Mr. and Mrs. Crookshank with author's very kind regards Jul 11 1898.   Jarndyce Antiquarian Booksellers   CCXI - 86   2015   £280

Association – Croome, James

Balmford, William *The Seaman's Spiritual Companion or Navigation Spiritualized.* London: for Benj. Harris, 1678. First edition, small 8vo., variant state of title with double rule border and price on titlepage, A2 shaved at foot affecting signature and catchword on recto, minor worming in upper outer corner of D4-K8 (affecting end of text in places), stain to B3-E2 affecting three lines, occasional foxing, small hole from paper flaw in lower margin of E2, short tear at foot of F3 slightly affecting last line on recto and catchword on verso, small hole from paper flaw in centre of I2 touching two lines, actually reasonable and much loved copy, contemporary sheep (rubbed, covers scuffed, fore edge of lower cover worn exposing board, corners worn), several pen trials, scribbles, ownership inscriptions John Allab(on) His Booke October ye 24th 16, Charles Canning his book 1679, James Purnell His Booke Anno Domini (deleted), "Thomas Nichols His Book May ye 10 1718", "James Croome His Book March ye 9th 1757" "Jane Hanley", from the library of James Stevens Cox (1910-1997). Maggs Bros. Ltd. 1447 - 21 2015 £2800

Association – Crosby, Caresse

Nin, Anais *Cities of the Interior.* Denver: Alan Swallow, 1959. First edition, hardcover issue, line engravings by Ian Hugo, illustrated white cloth, some foxing or light soiling, else near fine, beautifully inscribed to Caresse Crosby. Between the Covers Rare Books, Inc. 187 - 203 2015 $2500

Association – Cross, J. W. Arengo

Mills, George *The Beggar's Benison or a Hero without a Name...* London: & New York: Cassell, Petter and Galpin, 1866. First edition, 2 volumes, half titles, original brick red grained cloth, boards blocked in blind, spines decorated and lettered gilt, slight weakening to leading inner hinge volume I, otherwise very good, bright copy, signature of J. W. Arengo Cross. Jarndyce Antiquarian Booksellers CCXI - 202 2015 £250

Association – Crossley, H.

Arnold, Matthew 1822-1888 *Merope.* London: Longmans, 1858. First edition, half title, 2 pages ads, 32 pages partly unopened catalog (Jan. 1877), plain grey endpapers, original deep blue green wavy grained cloth, ownership inscription "H. Crossley 1878", fine, bright, in Carter's C binding. Jarndyce Antiquarian Booksellers CCXI - 15 2015 £150

Association – Crowninshield, Frank

Shaver, J. R. *Little Shavers: Sketches from Real Life.* New York: Century Co., 1913. First edition, small octavo, grey cloth with applied illustration, corners bumped and rubbed, nice and tight, very good, inscribed by editor of Vanity Fair Frank Crowninshield for Mrs. Buel Xmas 1913. Between the Covers Rare Books, Inc. 187 - 51 2015 $200

Association – Crownshield, F. A.

Burgoyne, John *A State of the Expedition from Canada, As laid before the House of Commons by Lieutenant General Burgoyne and Versified by Evidence...* London: printed for J. Almon, 1780. First edition, quarto, 6 folding maps, including frontispiece, all maps have some contemporary hand coloring in outline, two of the maps with overslips all maps engraved by William Faden, 19th century half black morocco over marbled boards, spine stamped and lettered gilt, all edges speckled brown, green silk place holder, edges bit rubbed, bit of light offsetting to maps, generally very clean, previous owner F. A. Crownshield's bookplate, overall very good. Heritage Book Shop Holiday 2014 - 24 2015 $8500

Association – Cru, Henri

Kerouac, Jack 1922-1969 *On the Road.* London: Andre Deutsch, 1958. First UK edition, inscribed by author to longtime friend Henri Cru, touching inscription, very good in very good, supplied second impression dust jacket. Ken Lopez, Bookseller 164 - 251 2015 $85,000

Association – Crutchley, Brooke

Greene, Graham 1904-1991 *The Revenge.* London: privately printed at the Stellar Press for Bodley Head, 1963. First edition, one of 300 copies, 12mo., original green card sewn wrappers, printed in black, untrimmed, fine, inscribed by Max Reinhardt of Bodley Head to Cambridge University Press printer Brooke Crutchley. Blackwell's Rare Books B179 - 158 2015 £325

Association – Cunliffe, Henry

Blake, William 1757-1827 *Illustrations of the Book of Job.* Limited to 100 sets on wove paper with word 'Proof' removed and one hundred and fifty sets on India paper and 65 on "French paper' were also lettered at the same time, latter two having word "Proof" on every plate except title,, 1825. folio, late 19th century full red morocco, boards panelled gilt with gilt fleurons at corners, spine in seven compartments with raised bands, olive green morocco lettering piece to second compartment, remainder panelled gilt and tooled with gilt floral motifs, decorated gilt turn-ins, all edges gilt, marbled endpapers, engraved title and 21 engraved plates printed on handmade paper, five of which are watermarked 'J. Whatman Turkey Mill 1825', the copy of Henry Cunliffe with his engraved bookplate, exceptionally fine set with sparkling impressions of the plates,. Henry Sotheran Ltd. William Blake Exhibition 17th Oct.-7th Nov. 2014 - 51 2015 £57,000

Association – Cunninghame-Graham, Robert Bontine

Conrad, Joseph 1857-1924 *Nostromo. A Tale of the Seaboard.* London: and New York: Harper and Bros., 1904. First edition, crown 8vo., bright blue cloth boards, stamped gilt to spine and white front cover, inscribed by author in month of publication to his close friend R. B. Cunninghame-Graham, Oct. 1904, book with very slight lean top of spine little bumped and frayed, rubbing to edges, some foxing to edges and few internal leaves, housed in custom quarter leather box, sturdy, fresh copy with outstanding association. B & B Rare Books, Ltd. 234 - 15 2015 $30,000

Association – Cure, Capel

Juvenalis, Decimus Junius *Satirae XVI.* Oxford: Sumptibus J. Cooke et J. Parker, 1808. Early reprint, some foxing, little pencil marginalia, 8vo., contemporary biscuit calf, boards bordered with small gilt decorative roll, spine divided by raised bands between double gilt fillets, blue lettering piece, other compartments with small central gilt tool, joints cracking but strong, armorial bookplate of Capel Cure Esqr., good. Blackwell's Rare Books Greek & Latin Classics VI - 59 2015 £75

Association – Curie, Eve

Nehru, Jawaharlal *Jawaharlal Nehru: an Autobiography.* London: Bodley Head, 1941. Reprint, tiny Allahabad bookstore stamp, else near fine without dust jacket, inscribed by author to Eve Curie daughter of Madame Marie Curie. Between the Covers Rare Books 196 - 98 2015 $7500

Association – Currey, L. W.

Kip, Leonard *Hannibal's Man and Other Tales.* Albany: Angus Co. Printers, 1878. First edition, octavo, original beveled edge decorated green cloth, little rubbed, near fine in good example of exceptionally rare dust jacket, jacket has moderate overall chipping and has been professionally reinforced internally at folds, but has no other restoration, signed note on stationary to bibliographer and sci-fi dealer L. W. Currey loosely inserted. Between the Covers Rare Books 196 - 154 2015 $25,000

Association – Curtis, John

Elkins, Aaron J. *Fellowship of Fear.* New York: Walker and Co., 1982. First edition, inscribed by author for John Curtis, review copy with slip laid-in, fine in dust jacket with very small professional restoration spot to top edge of front panel,. Buckingham Books March 2015 - 28627 2015 $1275

Association – Cust, Robert Needham

Martialis, Marcus Valerius *Epigrammata.* Venice: in Aedibus Aldi, 1501. First Aldine edition, some minor spotting, first two leaves lightly browned, last leaf mounted (obscured verso blank except for an old manuscript note just visible through the page) 8vo. 18th century sponge painted paper boards (probably Viennese), rubbed and worn at extremities and joints, backstrip darkened, bookplate of Robert Needham Cust (1821-1909), preserved in blue quarter morocco solander box, good. Blackwell's Rare Books Greek & Latin Classics VI - 73 2015 £2500

Association – Cuvier, C. N.

Ovidius Naso, Publius *Metamorphoseon.* Lugduni: Sebastianius Gryphius, 1553. 178 x 108mm. without final blank, contemporary calf by Jacob Bathen of Louvain with Bathen's elaborately blindstamped "Spes" binder's device and initials "I. B." in lower left, raised bands, spine with simple blind ruling, pastedowns removed exposing construction of the binding, first and last gatherings protected by strips from a 13th century vellum French or Southern Netherlandish Breviary (very expertly rebacked to style with restoration at corners), publisher's woodcut griffin device on titlepage, later (18th century?) ownership inscription of C. N. Cuvier on titlepage, rear flyleaf with early note in Latin, remnants of rear pastedown with signature of (Ro)bertus Camholt; little splaying to upper board, covers with slight crackling, but expertly restored binding entirely solid and details of panel stamps very sharp, faint dampstain cover small portion of many leaves at bottom (another dampstain sometimes at top with about half the page affected in four quires near end), minor soiling, here and there, two leaves with darker, though smaller areas of soiling, not without condition issues, internally but nothing fatal, text both fresh and with ample margins. Phillip J. Pirages 66 - 13 2015 $4200

Association – D'Angers, Pierre Paul David

Le Sage, Alain Rene 1668-1747 *Les Avantures De Monsieur Robert Cheavlier De Beauchene...* Paris: Chez Etienne Ganeau, 1732. First edition, 2 volumes, 12mo., 6 full page engraved plates by Bonnard in contemporary full calf (hinge strengthened at an early date), spine gilt, one inch split to lower hinge calf of one volume, contemporary owner's notes at extremities of titlepage, some light foxing and staining, very good, signature of Pierre Paul David d'Angers, tear to lower margin of one leaf not affecting any text.   Second Life Books Inc.   190 - 146   2015 $1200

Association – D'Arch Smith, Tim

Audry, Andre *Arcadie: revue Litt Raire et Scientifique.* Paris: Arcadie, 1954-1972. First edition, circa 210 issues, bound volumes are 1957-1961 and 1963-1972, loose issues 2-5 from the library of Tim D'Arch Smith (the first bound volume has pencilled instructions with his name), 15 bound volumes slightly rubbed, top edge gilt, all bound volumes have front wrappers bound in, loose issues 2-5, 10, 17-24, 25 to 31/32, 229-240, 241-250, 252, odd issue of 311, very good.   Any Amount of Books   2015 - A98793   2015   £650

Association – D'Erlanger, Emile, Baron

Sitwell, Osbert 1892-1969 *Out of the Flame.* London: Grant Richards, 1923. First edition, frontispiece, 8vo., original green cloth with few light spots, backstrip with orange paper label little chipped to border, top edge lightly dust soiled, endpapers faintly browned, good, with holograph manuscript of 'Superstition', from the library of baron Emile D'Erlanger.   Blackwell's Rare Books   B179 - 236   2015   £130

Association – Dale, William

Moore, Jonas *A Mathematical Compendium or Useful Practices in Arithmetick, Geometry and Astronomy Geography and Navigation...* London: printed for J. Phillips, H. Rhodes and J. Tay, 1705. 12mo. 9 engraved plates, some on text leaves, (one folding, others free standing), contemporary panelled calf with raised bands, unlettered, slightly shaken, but fine, early signatures of William Dale and James Gilbert with old ms. notes, ink on endpapers and final blank leaf.   John Drury Rare Books   2015 - 24839   2015 $1049

Association – Dallas, James

Dallas, W. S. *A Natural History of the Animal Kingdom...* London: Houlston & Stoneman, 1856. First edition, 8vo., recently rebound in green half leather, marbled boards, gilt on spine, illustrations, color frontispiece and titlepage, inscription presumably by author's son James Dallas 8 March 1898, very slight foxing to prelims, very good+.   Any Amount of Books   2015 - A88401   2015   £300

Association – Dalone, Mr.

Lister, Martin *Conchyliorum Bivalbvium Utriusque Aquae Exercitatio Anatomica Tertia.* London: Sumptibus authoris impressa, 1696. First edition, 4to., 10 engraved plates, with terminal blank Z4 in first work, contemporary sprinkled calf, very skillfully rebacked in period style, small early shelfmark in red ink on endpaper and on title, minor flaw in S2 just grazing catchword, very faint foxing in fore-edge, very lovely copy with text and plates clean and fresh, armorial bookplate of A. Gifford D. D. of the Museum", presentation from Lister inscribed for Mr. Dalone.   Joseph J. Felcone Inc. Science, Medicine and Technology - 28   2015 $10,000

Association – Dalrymple, Marcia

Rossetti, Christina 1830-1894 *A Pageant and Other poems.* London: Macmillan, 1881. First edition, half title, occasional pencil annotations in text, uncut in original dark blue cloth, blocked and lettered gilt, slightly marked, armorial bookplate of Marcia Dalyrmple and also her signature dated Aug 25 81, very good, bright copy.   Jarndyce Antiquarian Booksellers   CCXI - 246   2015   £150

Association – Dalton, John

Ward, William *An Essay on Grammar as It May Be Applied to the English Language.* printed for Robert Horsfield, 1765. First edition, dampstained, foxed and browned in places, 4to., contemporary tree calf, red lettering piece on spine, surface affected by damp, obscuring 'tree' on upper cover, signature of John Dalton, (not that of the great chemist).   Blackwell's Rare Books   B179 - 116   2015   £650

Association – Dalzell, William

Mead, Richard *De Imperio solis ac Lunae in Corpora Humana et Morbis Inde Oriundis.* Raphael Smith, 1704. First edition, title very slightly soiled, 8vo., crisp copy in contemporary Cambridge style calf, corners worn, rebacked, covers bowing, contemporary ownership inscription on title Wm. Dalzell, and on flyleaf of Sam. Caldwell, recording his purchase of the book in Dublin in 1754.   Blackwell's Rare Books   B179 - 72   2015   £750

Association – Dana, Charles A.

Hulbert, Archer Butler *The Niagara River.* G. P. Putnam's sons, 1908. First edition, 8vo., blue cloth, picture affixed to front cover, gold stamping on front cover and spine, illustrations, maps, inscribed by author for Charles A. Dana.   Buckingham Books   March 2015 - 21290   2015 $300

Association – Dana, Richard Henry

Pearson, Eliphalet *A Public Lecture Occasioned by the Death of the Rev. Joseph Willard...* Cambridge: printed at the University Press in Cambridge by William Hilliard, 1804. First edition, octavo, 21 pages, sewn unprinted blue wrappers, near fine, inscribed by Richard Henry Dana, poet and father of R.H. Dana, Jr., for William Ellery (Dana's grandfather and signer of the Declaration of Independence from RI). Between the Covers Rare Books, Inc.   187 - 209   2015 $450

Association – Darbishire, Helen

Byrne, Muriel St. Clair *Somerville College 1879-1921.* London: Oxford University Press, 1922. Frontispiece, illustrations, music, original dark blue cloth, slightly rubbed, Kathleen Tillotson's copy with note 'Helen Darbishire's copy given me by Nesta Clutterbuck, May 1878".   Jarndyce Antiquarian Booksellers   CCVII - 128   2015   £22

Milton, John   1608-1674 *The Poetical Works. Volume I. Paradise Lost.* Oxford: Clarendon Press, 1952. Uncut in original dark blue cloth, very good in slightly creased dust jacket, with printed editor's presentation slip and ALS from editor, Helen Darbishire to Kathleen Tillotson, with review cutting, from the library of Geoffrey & Kathleen Tillotson, signed by both Nov. 8 1952.   Jarndyce Antiquarian Booksellers   CCVII - 376   2015   £20

Association – Darby, Francis

Cartwright, William *Comedies, Tragi-Comedies with other Poems.* London: for Humphrey Mosely, 1651. First edition, 8vo., engraved portrait by Lombart (small rust hole at foot of image repaired), G8v stained, otherwise occasional small stains, early 19th century calf, covers ruled in gilt, gilt spine, armorial bookplate of Sir Frances Freeling, 1st Bart. 1764-1836, 19th century armorial bookplate of Francis Darby, from the library of James Stevens Cox (1910-1997). Maggs Bros. Ltd.   1447 - 68   2015   £600

Association – Davey, Norman

Hayley, William *Ballads. Founded on Anecdotes Relating to Animals with Prints Designed and Engraved by William Blake.* Chichester: J. Seagrave for Richard Phillips, 1805. First edition, engraved plates in first state, small 8vo., original grey paper covered boards, sometime expertly rebacked preserving original backstrip and printed paper, endpapers renewed presumably at time of rebacking, 5 engraved plates by William Blake after his own designs, ink signature of Norman Davey dated Dec. 5th 1913, printed booklabel of Elaine Harwood Kenton, fine.   Henry Sotheran Ltd. William Blake Exhibition 17th Oct.-7th Nov. 2014 - 70   2015   £6595

Association – Davidson, George

Garnett, Louis A. *For Private Circulation. the Paris Monetary Conference of 1881 and Bi-Metallism.* San Francisco: May 28, 1881. First edition, large 8vo., original printed wrappers, fine presentation copy inscribed by author to professor George Davidson in August 1881.   John Drury Rare Books   2015 - 26236   2015 $177

Association – Davidson, Thomas

Church of England. Book of Common Prayer *The Book of Common Prayer...* Cambridge: printed by C. J. Clay for SPCK, circa, 1880. small 4to., original full black morocco with embossed device, slight rubbing, stamp of Thomas Davidson, Fritchley Nr. Derby and Kathleen Tillotson's note that he was her grandfather, ink and pencil notes. Jarndyce Antiquarian Booksellers   CCVII - 156   2015   £35

Association – Davies, Emil

Shaw, George Bernard   1856-1950 *The Intelligent Woman's Guide to Socialism and Capitalism.* London: Constable, 1928. First edition, 8vo., original olive green cloth, bump to top edge and light rubbing at corners, Celtic design in green and gilt to front and backstrip lettered in gilt, top edge gilt, tail edge rough trimmed, green endpapers with few small adhesive marks, dust jacket with light chipping at corners and ends of backstrip panel, light dustsoiling to backstrip and rear panel, rubbing to edges, few nicks, very good, with ALS from author tipped in to half title, to the treasurer of the Fabian Society, Emil Davies.   Blackwell's Rare Books   B179 - 235   2015   £750

Association – Davies, H. F.

Robertson, Alexander *Poems on Various Subjects and Occasions...* Edinburgh: printed for Ch. Alexander and sold at his house in Geddes's Close....n.d., 1752? First edition, 8vo., contemporary sheep, spine gilt, little rubbed, sound, lacks label, very good, early signature on titlepage of W. Burgh, later armorial bookplate of H. F. Davies, Elmley Castle.   C. R. Johnson   Foxon R-Z - 831r-z   2015 $536

ASSOCIATION COPIES

Association – Davies, Hugh Morrison

Villars, Nicolas Pierre Henri De Monfaucon, Abbe De *The Count of Gabalis of the Extravagant Mysteries of the Cabalists, Exposed in Five Pleasant Discourses on the Secret Sciences, done into English....* printed for B. M. Printer to the Cabalistical Society of the Sages, at the Sign of the Rosy-Crusian, 1680. First edition in English, few small stains, several leaves with short tear to blank margin, others with little white fungicide powder residue to fore-edge (but no mould or worming visible inside), 12mo., contemporary red morocco, boards, elaborately decorated with circle, flower and drawer handle tools, expertly rebacked to style, near invisibly, except that the colour has faded from newer leather, later marbled endpapers, hinges neatly relined, edges gilt, bookplate and ownership inscription of Hugh Morrison Davies to endpapers (dated 1900), very good. Blackwell's Rare Books   B179 - 112   2015   £1500

Association – Davies, J. E.

Pritchett, V. S. *A Careless Widow & Other Stories.* London: Chatto & Windus, 1989. First edition, fine in dust jacket, original binding, bookplate of J. E. Davies, inscribed by author on bookplate, with autograph card signed tipped-in agreeing to inscribe it and commenting on the dust jacket and further initialled by him "A Happy Christmas" on slip of paper mounted beneath bookplate, from the collection of Gavin H. Fryer.   Bertram Rota Ltd.   308 Part II - 226   2015   £120

Association – Davin, D. M.

Sargeson, Frank *Memoirs of a Peon.* London: MacGibbon & Kee, 1965. First edition, foxing, else near fine in about fine dust jacket with light foxing on rear panel, Advance Review copy with slip tipped onto front pastedown, bookplate of D. M. Davin.   Between the Covers Rare Books, Inc.   187 - 241   2015 $150

Association – Davis, Angela

Brown, H. Rap *Die Nigger Die!* New York: Dial Press, 1969. First edition, near fine with slight soiling on boards, little foxing and stamp of the Liberation Book Store of Harlem on front blank, slightly rubbed, near fine dust jacket, very warmly inscribed by author to Angela Davis using most of the blank page facing half title.   Between the Covers Rare Books   197 - 52   2015 $8000

Association – Davis, Captain

Keate, Thomas *Observations on the Proceedings and Report of the Special Medical Board, Appointed by His Royal Highness the Commander in Chief and the Right Hon. the Secretary at War...* London: J. Hatchard, 1809. First edition, 8vo., half title, paper generally rather browned, half title and final page (errata) soiled, slightly cropped ms. presentation inscription from author for Captain Davis, good copy, recently bound in linen backed marbled boards, lettered, very rare.   John Drury Rare Books   2015 - 22501   2015 $787

Association – Davis, Hallie Flanagan

Davis, Herbert *Stella: a Gentlewoman of the Eighteenth Century.* New York: Macmillan Co., 1942. First edition, boards trifle soiled near fine, bookplate of Hallie Flanagan Davis, with bookplate.   Between the Covers Rare Books, Inc.   187 - 69   2015 $125

Association – Davis, John Warren

King, Martin Luther *Stride Toward Freedom.* New York: Harper & Bros., 1958. First edition, faint dampstain tidemark in very upper margins of pages and jacket flaps, just touching few letters on rear flap, otherwise affecting no text, else very good in frontispiece dust jacket (spine faded with modest chips at spine ends), warmly inscribed by author for Dr. John Warren Davis.   Between the Covers Rare Books   197 - 74   2015 $10,000

Association – Day, Augustus Taylor

MacDonald, George   1824-1905 *Phantastes; a Faerie Romance for Men and Women.* London: Smith, Elder & Co., 1858. First edition, bound without half title, small corner torn form title, few marginal marks, contemporary half calf, rubbed, split in following hinge but sound, bookplate of Augustus Taylor Day, from the library of Geoffrey & Kathleen Tillotson.   Jarndyce Antiquarian Booksellers   CCVII - 368   2015   £520

Association – De Acosta, Mercedes

Jeffers, Robinson   1887-1962 *Give Your Heart to the Hawks and other Poems.* New York: Random House, 1933. First trade edition, corners and spine ends worn and little frayed, good only, lacking dust jacket, inscribed by author to Mercedes de Acosta, writer and actress.   Between the Covers Rare Books   196 - 79   2015 $650

Association – De Beare, J.

Sucquet, Antoine S. *Via Vitae Aeternae Iconibus Illustrata per Boetium a Bolswert.* Antwerp: typis Martini Nutti, 1620. First edition, 8vo., engraved frontispiece title and 32 engraved emblematic plates by Boetius a Bolswert, contemporary vellum, later endpapers, few minor marks, fine presentation copy from author to unidentified fellow Jesuit, presentation inscription of Pater J. de Beare 1912 to Mount St. Mary's Jesuit College. Maggs Bros. Ltd. Illustrated Books 2014 - 2015   £2200

Association – De Camp, L. Sprague

Pratt, Fletcher *Fleet Against Japan.* New York: Harper, 1946. First edition, owner name, spine gilt mostly rubbed away, very good lacking dust jacket, sc-fi author L. Sprague de Camp"s copy with his bookplate. Between the Covers Rare Books, Inc.   187 - 222   2015 $350

Association – De Carava, Roy

Hughes, Langston *The Sweet Flypaper of Life.* Washington: Howard University, 1988. Second printing, square 4to., photos by Roy De Carava, with presentation from De Carava on title to Andy Davis May 30 1992, olive cloth, nice in slightly scuffed dust jacket.   Second Life Books Inc.   190 - 54   2015 $325

Association – De Kay, J. E.

Rafinesque, C. S. *Principes Fondamentaux de Somiologie ou les Loix de la Nomenclature et de la Classification de l'Empire Orangique ou des Animaux et des Vegetabux....* Palermo: De l'Imprimerie de Franc. Abate uax depens de l'Auteur, 1814. First edition, 8vo., modern half calf, leather label, top blank portion of title cut away, affecting first line of title, clipping top half of last four letters, otherwise very fine, rare, inscribed in ink by American botanist, J(ohn) Torrey to naturalist & J. E. De Kay.   M & S Rare Books, Inc.   97 - 250   2015 $3250

Association – De Kooning, Elaine

O'Hara, Frank *A City Winter and Other Poems.* New York: Tibor De Nagy Gallery, 1951 i.e, 1952. First edition, tall 8vo., original signed frontispiece drawing & reproductions of 2 drawings by Larry Rivers, original cloth backed decorated boards, this copy number 13, tall 8vo., original signed frontispiece drawing & reproductions of two drawings by Larry Rivers, original cloth backed decorated boards, cover slightly worn along bottom edge and lower fore-corners, small stain to cloth near top of front panel, one page shows some faint indentations, otherwise very good, preserved in custom made half morocco slipcase, this the Thomas B. Hess - Elaine de Kooning copy, specially signed by O'Hara and signed by Hess and de Kooning's ownership stamp.   James S. Jaffe Rare Books   Modern American Poetry - 215   2015 $35,000

Association – De La Mare, Walter

Reid, Forrest *The Gentle Lover: a Comedy of Middle Age.* London: Edward Arnold, 1913. First edition, 8vo., original publisher's cloth lettered black on spine and cover, 319 pages, signed presentation from author for Walter de la Mare, superb association, sound, near very good, spine appears to have been rebacked or repaired with consequent slight wear at hinges, endpapers original.   Any Amount of Books   March 2015 - A93277   2015   £450

Association – De La Rive, Professor

Societe Pou L'Avancement De L'Instruction Religieuse de la Jeunesse *Rapport fait a la Societe, sur els deux Ecoles Lancastriennes etablier par cette Societe..* J. J. Padshoud, 1820. 8vo., few browned patches, mostly on outer leaves, inscription at head of title "Monsieur le Prof. de la Rive" (cropped?), well bound in cloth, lettered gilt, very good.   John Drury Rare Books   March 2015 - 17878 2015 $266

Association – De Luynes, Duc

Marolles, Michel De *Tableaux du Temple des Muses, Tirez du Cabinet de Feu Mr. Favereau avec les Descriptions, Remarques & Annotationis.* Paris: chez Antoine de Sommaville, 1655. First edition, folio, fine additional engraved title depicting the temple des Muses, engraved portrait of author, 58 stunning plates engraved by Cornelies Bloemart and others after designs by Abraham van Diepenbeek, 19th century calf backed marbled boards, armorial booklabel of Ducs de Luynes, Chateau de Dampierre with the 'DLP' (De Lynes Paris) stamp on titlepage.   Maggs Bros. Ltd.   Illustrated Books 2014 - 2015 £3000

Senex, John *Itineraire de Toutes les Routes de l'Angleterre, Revues, Corrigees, Augmentees et Reduites.* Paris: Le Rouge, 1759. First edition in French, 181 x 127mm., maps, contemporary limp calf, lower cover extending into a flap, tiny hole (for some kind of closure) in flap, manuscript title "Itineraire du Royaume d'Anglterre' on lower cover, rear pastedown (including flap), composed of printing scraps, engraved title, engraved map, 101 plates with maps, titlepage with parallel text in French and English, armorial bookplate of Dampierre, the grand library of the Dukes de Luynes at Chateau Dampierre begun in 17th century, slight wear to leather, small waterstain to flap, titlepage detached, couple of openings faintly browned, otherwise fine, insubstantial binding very well preserved and text unusually bright, fresh and clean with especially strong impressions of the maps.   Phillip J. Pirages   66 - 39   2015 $3750

Association – De Nailly, Stephani

Montesquieu, Charles De Secondat, Baron De   1689-1755 *Lettres Persanes.* Cologne: Chez Pirre Marteau, 1744. Later edition, 12mo., contemporary full calf with gilt lettering and designs on spine which has five raised ribs, joints recently repaired, former owner's name (Ex Libris eg. Stephani Le Comu De Nailly), handsomely inscribed in faded ink beneath ornamental device in center of top edge gilt, handsome copy.   Athena Rare Books   15 - 35   2015 $550

Association – De Pol, John

Bly, Robert *In the Month of May.* New York: Red Ozier Press, 1985. First edition, copy 23 of 140 numbered copies, signed, 12mo., printed self wrappers, neat ownership signature of woodcut artist John DePol, wrappers trifle soiled, else fine.   Between the Covers Rare Books, Inc.   187 - 26   2015 $75

Causley, Monroe S. *Arthur W. Rushmore and the Golden Hind Press.* Madison: Madison Public Library, 1994. First edition, one of 500 copies, stapled pastepaper style wrappers, with applied printed label, fine, Artist John DePol's copy with his ownership signature and notations on pages his woodcuts appear.   Between the Covers Rare Books, Inc.   187 - 45   2015 $150

Copley, Heather *Drawings of the Katydid.* Bainbridge: Katydid Press, 1958. First edition, 24mo., printed paper covered boards, fine in near fine, unprinted dust jacket, ownership signature of wood engraved John De Pol, with ALS from publisher John Lehmann to De Pol presenting the book.   Between the Covers Rare Books, Inc.   187 - 61   2015 $450

Digby, John *Incantations: Poems and Collages.* Roslyn: Stone House Press, 1987. First edition, ownership signature of noted engraver John De Pol, fine copy, inscribed to De Pol by publisher Morris Gelfand with complimentary slip, signed by Gelfand.   Between the Covers Rare Books, Inc.   187 - 74   2015 $150

Johnson, George E. Q. *I Like America.* New York: privately printed (John C. Rogers Co.), 1939. First edition, one of 1000 numbered copies, 24mo., quarter rough cloth and textured and embossed cloth boards, corners rubbed, else fine, ownership signature of woodcut artist John De Pol.   Between the Covers Rare Books, Inc.   187 - 139   2015 $50

Association – De Rothesay, Stuart

Cumming, Alexander *A Sketch of the Properties of the Machine Organ, Invented, Constructed and Made by Mr. Cumming for the Earl of Bute...* London: printed by E. and H. Hudson Cross Street Hatton Garden, 1812. First edition, printed rectos only, contemporary red half roan gilt, neatly rebacked, original backstrip retained, very good, of great rarity, from the library of Lord Stuart de Rothesay at Highcliffe Castle with his coat of arms stamped in blind on covers, signature (1952) and one amendment by him in red ink of American composer Bernard Herrmann and NY Public Library.   John Drury Rare Books   2015 - 22640   2015 $8741

Association – De Sapio, Carmine

Kennedy, John Fitzgerald   1917-1963 *Profiles in Courage.* New York: Harper & Bros., 1956. First edition, first printing, presentation copy signed and inscribed by author for Tammany Hall boss and influential politician, Carmine DeSapio, near fine with light rubbing to extremities, unclipped dust jacket with some light wear and minor chipping to lower spine, housed in custom quarter leather case.   B & B Rare Books, Ltd.   234 - 60   2015 $22,500

Association – De Trafford, Humphrey Edmund

Somervile, William   1675-1742 *Occasional Poems, Translations, Fables, Tales, &c.* London: printed for Bernard Lintot, 1727. First edition, 8vo., contemporary speckled calf, spine gilt, red morocco label, joints repaired, top of spine little chipped, presentation copy inscribed "Eliz. Mason her book. Given by the Author" presumably in hand of recipient, very good, later bookplate of Sir Humphrey Edmund de Trafford, Bart.   C. R. Johnson   Foxon R-Z - 914r-z   2015 $1149

Association – Delbanco, Elena

Prose, Francine *Guided Tours of Hell.* New York: Henry Holt/Metropolitan Books, 1988. First edition, fine in slightly rubbed, still fine dust jacket, inscribed by author for Nicholas Delbanco and his wife Elena.   Between the Covers Rare Books, Inc.   187 - 225   2015 $200

Elkin, Stanley *George Mills.* New York: E. P. Dutton, 1982. First edition, fine in fine dust jacket with tiny tear at crown, inscribed by author to fellow author Nicholas Delbanco and his wife, Elena.   Between the Covers Rare Books, Inc.   187 - 88   2015 $350

Association – Delbanco, Nicholas

Bell, Madison Smartt *Doctor Sleep.* New York: Harcourt Brace Jovanovich, 1991. First edition, fine in fine dust jacket, inscribed by author for Nicholas Delbanco and his wife. Between the Covers Rare Books, Inc. 187 - 13 2015 $100

Buck, Frank *Wild Cargo.* New York: Simon and Schuster, 1932. First edition, nicely inscribed by author for Nicholas Delbanco, fine in slightly soiled but fine dust jacket. Between the Covers Rare Books, Inc. 187 - 36 2015 $225

Busch, Frederick *Harry and Catherine.* New York: Alfred A. Knopf, 1990. First edition, top corner little bumped, near fine in slightly spine sunned, thus near fine, warmly inscribed by author for Nicholas Delbanco. Between the Covers Rare Books, Inc. 187 - 38 2015 $150

Dew, Robb Forman *Dale Loves Sophie to Death.* New York: Farrar Straus and Giroux, 1981. First edition, fine in fine dust jacket with very slight sunning to spine, with ALS sending the book to Nicholas Delbanco Dec. 1989. Between the Covers Rare Books, Inc. 187 - 72 2015 $350

Dybek, Stuart *The Coast of Chicago.* New York: Alfred A. Knopf, 1990. First edition, fine in fine dust jacket, in nicely inscribed by author for Nicholas Delbanco, signed in full. Between the Covers Rare Books, Inc. 187 - 84 2015 $225

Dybek, Stuart *I Sailed with Magellan.* New York: Farrar, Straus & Giroux, 2003. First edition, fine in fine dust jacket, nicely inscribed by author for Nicholas Delbanco, additionally signed in full. Between the Covers Rare Books, Inc. 187 - 85 2015 $225

Elkin, Stanley *George Mills.* New York: E. P. Dutton, 1982. First edition, fine in fine dust jacket with tiny tear at crown, inscribed by author to fellow author Nicholas Delbanco and his wife, Elena. Between the Covers Rare Books, Inc. 187 - 88 2015 $350

Lopez, Barry *Crossing Open Ground.* New York: Vintage Books, 1989. First Vingate book edition, fine in wrappers, nicely inscribed by author for Nicholas Delbanco Oct. 7 1989. Between the Covers Rare Books, Inc. 187 - 159 2015 $65

Malamud, Bernard 1914-1986 *God's Grace.* New York: Farrar, Straus & Giroux, 1982. First edition, first printing, presentation copy signed and inscribed by author to close friend Nicholas Delbanco, near fine in like jacket,. B & B Rare Books, Ltd. 234 - 74 2015 $500

Maxwell, William *Over by the River.* New York: Alfred A. Knopf, 1977. First edition, just about fine in very near fine dust jacket, inscribed by author for Nicholas Delbanco. Between the Covers Rare Books, Inc. 187 - 170 2015 $400

Prose, Francine *Guided Tours of Hell.* New York: Henry Holt/Metropolitan Books, 1988. First edition, fine in slightly rubbed, still fine dust jacket, inscribed by author for Nicholas Delbanco and his wife Elena. Between the Covers Rare Books, Inc. 187 - 225 2015 $200

Prose, Francine *Women and Children First.* New York: Pantheon, 1988. First edition, fine in near fine, bit spine faded dust jacket, inscribed by author to author Nicholas Delbanco and family, laid in is invitation to a reading by Prose. Between the Covers Rare Books, Inc. 187 - 226 2015 $225

Simpson, Mona *Anywhere but Here.* New York: Alfred A. Knopf, 1987. Third printing, fine in very good or better dust jacket (spine faded), inscribed by author to Nicholas Delbanco. Between the Covers Rare Books, Inc. 187 - 259 2015 $50

Smith, Dave *In the House of the Judge.* New York: Harper and Row, 1983. First edition, hardcover issue, fine in spine faded, very good or better dust jacket, warmly inscribed to author Nicholas Delbanco, scarce. Between the Covers Rare Books, Inc. 187 - 261 2015 $75

Tallent, Elizabeth *Time With Children.* New York: Alfred A. Knopf, 1987. First edition, fine in dust jacket which is spine faded, else near fine, warmly inscribed to author Nicholas Delbanco. Between the Covers Rare Books, Inc. 187 - 271 2015 $65

Wolff, Geoffrey *Black Sun: the Brief Transit and Violent Eclipse of Harry Crosby.* New York: Random House, 1976. First edition, fine in very good dust jacket with wear at spine ends, very warmly inscribed by author for author Nicholas Delbanco. Between the Covers Rare Books, Inc. 187 - 296 2015 $150

Wolff, Geoffrey *Inklings.* New York: Random House, 1977. First edition, fine in spine faded, very good dust jacket with some short tears, warmly inscribed by author for Nicholas Delbanco. Between the Covers Rare Books, Inc. 187 - 297 2015 $150

Association – Denton, Frank William

Capern, Edward *Sungleams and Shadows.* London: Kent & Co.; Birmingham: Cornish Bros. &c, 1881. First edition, title browned by endpapers, 12 pages ads, original green cloth, inscription on title for Frank Denton, Esq. from friend the author May 10th 1881, signed by Denton. Jarndyce Antiquarian Booksellers   CCXI - 59   2015   £50

Association – Denys, George

Harley, George *The Simplification of English Spelling, specially Adapted for the Rising Generation.* London: Trubner & Co., 1877. First edition, 8vo., frontispiece, errata slip, original cloth with title in gilt in central embossed shield on upper cover, very good, presentation copy, inscribed in ink from author for Sir George Denys, June 1877.   John Drury Rare Books   2015 - 22986   2015 $133

Association – Derleth, August

Lovecraft, H. P. *Dreams and Fancies.* Sauk city: Arkham House, 1962. First edition, 8vo., signed by introducer, August Derleth, fine in about fine dust jacket with very slight edgewear, excellent condition.   Any Amount of Books March 2015 - A74373   2015   £400

Association – Di Giovanni, Norman Thomas

Dugan, Alan *Poems.* New Haven: Yale University Press, 1961. First edition, 8vo., original cloth, dust jacket, presentation copy inscribed by author for Norman Thomas DiGiovanni, top and fore edges of text block lightly foxed, otherwise fine.   James S. Jaffe Rare Books   Modern American Poetry - 65   2015 $1500

Pound, Ezra Loomis   1885-1972 *Selected Poems.* New York: New Directions, 1949. First edition, one of 3400 copies printed, 8vo., frontispiece, original cloth, fine in dust jacket, inscribed by author for Norman Thomas Di Giovanni. James S. Jaffe Rare Books   Modern American Poetry - 234 2015 $1500

Williams, William Carlos   1883-1963 *Paterson.* New York: New Directions, 1951. First collected edition of Books 1-4, one of 200 copies, 8vo., original cloth, dust jacket, fine, jacket very slightly rubbed at top of spine panel, presentation copy inscribed by author for Norman Thomas Di Giovanni, 12/24/51.   James S. Jaffe Rare Books   Modern American Poetry - 326   2015 $1250

Association – Di Maggio, Joe

Rust, Art *Recollections of a Baseball Junkie.* New York: William Morrow, 1985. First edition, fine in fine dust jacket, inscribed by author to Joe DiMaggio, with letter of provenance signed by DiMaggio's two granddaughters. Between the Covers Rare Books, Inc.   187 - 10   2015 $850

Segal, Hyman R. *They Called Him Champ: the Story of Champ Segal.* New York: Citadel Press, 1959. First edition, fine in very good plus dust jacket with tiny nicks and tears, small coffee stain on front panel, inscribed by subject of book to Joe DiMaggio, with letter of provenance signed by Di Maggio's two granddaughters.   Between the Covers Rare Books, Inc.   187 - 31   2015 $850

Turkin, Hy *The Official Encyclopedia of Baseball.* New York: A. S. Barnes, 1951. Jubilee edition, fine in modestly worn, very good or better dust jacket, inscribed by Turkin for Joe DiMaggio, with letter of provenance signed by DiMaggio's two granddaughters.   Between the Covers Rare Books, Inc.   187 - 11   2015 $850

Association – Di Palma, Elisabeth

Prince, F. T. *Afterword on Rupert Brooke.* London: Menard Press, 1976. First edition, octavo, fine in wrapper and fine dust jackets, inscribed by author to Raymond and Elisabeth Di Palma.   Between the Covers Rare Books, Inc. 187 - 224   2015 $150

Prince, F. T. *Drypoints of the Hasidim.* London: Menard Press, 1975. First edition, octavo, top corner bumped, else fine in wrappers, in near fine dust jacket with spine sunned, inscribed by author to Raymond and Elisabeth DiPalma. Between the Covers Rare Books, Inc.   187 - 223   2015 $125

Association – Di Palma, Ray

Bernstein, Charles *Rough Trades.* Los Angeles: Sun & Moon Press, 1991. First edition, paperback original, small octavo, glossy wrappers, fine, inscribed by author to Ray DiPalma.   Between the Covers Rare Books, Inc.   187 - 19 2015 $50

Berssenbrugge, Mei-Mei *Four Year Old Girl.* Berkeley: Kelsey St. Press, 1998. First edition, oblong octavo, decorated wrappers, very near fine, inscribed by poet to Ray DiPalma.   Between the Covers Rare Books, Inc.   187 - 20 2015 $85

Prince, F. T. *Afterword on Rupert Brooke.* London: Menard Press, 1976. First edition, octavo, fine in wrapper and fine dust jackets, inscribed by author to Raymond and Elisabeth Di Palma.   Between the Covers Rare Books, Inc.   187 - 224   2015 $150

Prince, F. T. *Drypoints of the Hasidim.* London: Menard Press, 1975. First edition, octavo, top corner bumped, else fine in wrappers, in near fine dust jacket with spine sunned, inscribed by author to Raymond and Elisabeth DiPalma.   Between the Covers Rare Books, Inc.   187 - 223   2015 $125

Association – Dickens Charles

Wordsworth, William   1770-1850 *The Prelude, or Growth of a Poet's Mind.* London: Edward Moxon, 1850. First edition, octavo, original brown cloth, rebacked, from the library of writer Charles Dickens with his bookplates.   Honey & Wax Booksellers   2 - 18   2015 $6000

Association – Dickens, Monica

West, Paul   *Gala: a Fictional Sequel to Words for a Deaf Daughter.* New York: Harper & Row, 1976. First edition, fine in fine dust jacket with light wear to crown and corners, inscribed by author to novelist Monica Dickens (granddaughter of Charles Dickens).   Between the Covers Rare Books, Inc.   187 - 293   2015 $250

Association – Dickerson, Earl

Graham, Margaret   *Swing Shift.* New York: Citadel Press, 1951. First edition, fine in slightly spine toned, near fine dust jacket, tipped in to fly is TLS by author to Earl Dickerson using her real name (Grace McDonald) about the pattern of violence in labor struggles.   Between the Covers Rare Books, Inc.   187 - 112   2015 $200

Association – Dickinson, Alice May

Pasteur, Louis   *Etudes sur la Vin. Ses Maladies Causes qui Les Provoquent Procedes Nouveau Pur le Conserver et Pour le Vieillir.* Paris: l'Imprimerie Imperiale, 1866. First edition, 8vo., 42 figures, original half morocco over moire black cloth, gilt stamped spine title, bookplate of Francis Reynolds Dickinson (1880-1974) and Alice May Dickinson (nee Stirling), ownership marks on half title and titlepage, fine.   Jeff Weber Rare Books   178 - 877   2015 $950

Wallace, Alfred Russel   1823-1913   *Tropical Nature and Other Essays.* London: Macmillan, 1878. First edition, 8vo., cords split at pages 160-1 and 288-289 (reinforced with kozo), original black stamped green cloth, gilt stamped spine, corners heavily repaired with Kozo paper, armorial bookplate of Francis Reynolds Dickinson and Alice May Dickinson, bookseller label of Philip, Son & Nephew, Liverpool, as is.   Jeff Weber Rare Books   178 - 1116   2015 $300

Association – Dickinson, Francis Reynolds

Pasteur, Louis   *Etudes sur la Vin. Ses Maladies Causes qui Les Provoquent Procedes Nouveau Pur le Conserver et Pour le Vieillir.* Paris: l'Imprimerie Imperiale, 1866. First edition, 8vo., 42 figures, original half morocco over moire black cloth, gilt stamped spine title, bookplate of Francis Reynolds Dickinson (1880-1974) and Alice May Dickinson (nee Stirling), ownership marks on half title and titlepage, fine.   Jeff Weber Rare Books   178 - 877   2015 $950

Wallace, Alfred Russel   1823-1913   *Tropical Nature and Other Essays.* London: Macmillan, 1878. First edition, 8vo., cords split at pages 160-1 and 288-289 (reinforced with kozo), original black stamped green cloth, gilt stamped spine, corners heavily repaired with Kozo paper, armorial bookplate of Francis Reynolds Dickinson and Alice May Dickinson, bookseller label of Philip, Son & Nephew, Liverpool, as is.   Jeff Weber Rare Books   178 - 1116   2015 $300

Association – Digby, Henry Montagu

Digby, Kenelm   1603-1665   *A Late Discourse made in a Solemne assembly of Nobles and Learned Men at Montpellier in France.* London: for R. Lowndes and T. Davies, 1658. Second edition in English, 12mo., browned and spotted throughout, a number of leaves faintly printed, small burn-hole to blank margin of F1, early 19th century russia, ruled in gilt, upper head cap damaged and joints rubbed and just starting to crack, marbled endleaves stained by turn-ins, bookplate of Henry Montagu Digby, 1874-1934, from the library of James Stevens Cox (1910-1997).   Maggs Bros. Ltd.   1447 - 145   2015   £180

Association – Diller, Phyllis

Davis, Ronald L.   *Phyllis Diller's Oral History Interview Transcript.* Dallas: Southern Methodist University, 1982. First edition, 4to., near fine, attractively bound in blue cloth, from the estate of Phyllis Diller.   Ed Smith Books   83 - 14   2015 $200

Association – Dine, Jim

Apollinaire, Guillaume *The Poet Assassinated.* New York: Holt Rinehart Winston, 1968. First American edition translated by Ron Padgett, small 4to., original pictorial boards, dust jacket, fine in slightly sunned dust jacket, inscribed by artist, Jim Dine for Burt (Britton) 1978, also inscribed with drawing by Ron Padgett (translator) to same. James S. Jaffe Rare Books   Many Happy Returns - 192   2015 $50

Apollinaire, Guillaume *The Poet Assassinated.* New York: Holt Rinehart & Winston, 1968. First American edition, translated by Ron Padgett, small 4to., original pictorial boards, dust jacket, fine in slightly sunned and dust soiled jacket, illustrations by Jim Dine, inscribed by Dine with drawing for Burt Britton, also inscribed with drawing by Padgett. James S. Jaffe Rare Books   Many Happy Returns - 191   2015 $350

Padgett, Ron *The Adventures of Mr. and Mrs. Jim and Ron.* New York: Grossman Pub., 1970. First edition, simultaneous paperback issue, review copy with publisher's slip laid in, 4to., illustrations by Jim Dine, original wrappers, fine, inscribed by author, also signed by Dine.   James S. Jaffe Rare Books   Many Happy Returns - 280   2015 $250

Padgett, Ron *The Adventures of Mr. and Mrs. Jim and Ron.* New York: Cape Goliard Press in Association with Grossman Publishers, 1970. First edition, review copy with publisher's slip laid in, signed by author and by artist, Jim Dine, with a drawing, 4to., illustrations by Jim Dine, original boards, dust jacket, fine dust jacket lightly soiled and sunned.   James S. Jaffe Rare Books   Many Happy Returns - 278   2015 $450

Association – Diplock, Mrs.

Shaw, George Bernard 1856-1950 *Saint Joan.* London: Constable, 1925. Ninth impression, 8vo., very good+ in slightly browned about very good, complete jacket, inscribed presentation from author for Mrs. Diplock, Morrison Davidson's daughter.   Any Amount of Books   2015 - A74375   2015   £250

Association – Disborough, Henry

Say, Benjamin *An Annual Oration Pronounced Before the Humane Society of Philadelphia on the Objects and Benefits of Said Institution.* Whitehall: William Young, Bookseller, Philadelphia, 1799. First edition, 8vo., possibly lacking half title, removed, sheets toned, foxed, presentation from author for Dr. (Henry) Disborough.   M & S Rare Books, Inc.   97 - 188   2015 $275

Association – Dix, F. H. R.

Drayton, Michael 1563-1631 *Nimphidia the Court of Fayrie.* Stratford-upon-Avon: printed at the Shakespeare Head Press, 1924. 4to., half title, original decorated paper wrappers, spine slightly browned with small chips, with Christmas greetings from F. H. R. Dix, Hemingford or Stratford-on-Avon sending this poem, from the library of Geoffrey & Kathleen Tillotson.   Jarndyce Antiquarian Booksellers   CCVII - 237   2015   £50

Association – Dobell, Barbara

Allestree, Richard *The Ladies Calling.* Oxford: printed at the Theater, 1673. First edition, 8vo., 2 parts in 1, early 18th century panelled calf with marbled endpapers, frontispiece, the copy of Barbara Dobell with her signature, and below is "Sally Harrison/June 11th 1797" with note about her marriage and on facing blank is 19th century inscription "the gift of S. Mitchell to her niece Mary Best December 1855, in lower margin of final page of text is note in Dobell's hand about binding and cost charged by a Mr. Double on March 30 1706, edges little rubbed, marbled endpapers have cleanly lifted from boards, firmly held in place by sewing, fine.   The Brick Row Book Shop   Miscellany 67 - 3   2015 $500

Association – Dobell, Emily

Dobell, Sydney *The Poetical Works of Sydney Dobell.* London: Smith Elder & Co., 1875. First edition thus, 2 volumes, 8vo., original black cloth lettered gilt on spine, ownership signature of author's wife, Emily Dobell dated Jan. 1st 1901, with good signed letter in plain envelope which is pasted to front endpaper, sound, clean, very good set with very slight shelfwear and slight nick at spine of one volume. Any Amount of Books   2015 - A88049   2015   £160

Association – Doheny, Estelle

Bacheller, Irving *Vergilius: a Tale of the Coming of Christ.* New York: Harper & Bros., 1904. First edition, lightly edgeworn, near fine, without dust jacket, bookplate of collector Frederick W. Skiff and later book label of Estelle Doheny collection, inscribed by Bacheller to Skiff Dec. 22 1916. Between the Covers Rare Books, Inc.   187 - 5   2015 $125

Association – Domenach, Jean Marie

Camus, Albert *Le Minotaure ou La Halte d'Oran.* Paris: Charlot, 1950. Limited edition, edition was 1343 copies, this one of 120 copies reserved for use of author, this copy inscribed by author for Nicole et Jean, most certainly Nicole & Jean-Marie Domenach, French intellectuals and friends of author, this issue in vellum on rives paper, remarkable rarity.   Ken Lopez, Bookseller   164 - 28   2015 $4500

Association – Domenach, Nicole

Camus, Albert *Le Minotaure ou La Halte d'Oran.* Paris: Charlot, 1950. Limited edition, edition was 1343 copies, this one of 120 copies reserved for use of author, this copy inscribed by author for Nicole et Jean, most certainly Nicole & Jean-Marie Domenach, French intellectuals and friends of author, this issue in vellum on rives paper, remarkable rarity.   Ken Lopez, Bookseller   164 - 28   2015 $4500

Association – Doneraile, Arthur St. Leger, 1st Viscount

Ollyffe, George *The Madness of Disaffection and Treason Against the Present Government.* London: Joseph Downing, 1724. First edition, 8vo., errata at foot of final text page, contemporary gilt ruled calf with raised bands, very good, crisp copy, contemporary armorial bookplate of Arthur St. Leger, 1st Viscount Doneraile of County Corks, scarce.   John Drury Rare Books   March 2015 - 25095   2015 $874

Association – Doty, Charlotte

Goodrich, Samuel Griswold   1793-1860 *The Story of the Trapper: One of (Peter) Parley's Winter Evening Tales.* Boston: S. G. Goodrich, 1830. First edition, 16mo., 16 pages, including frontispiece and 1 other full page illustration, both crude, original printed and pictorial wrappers, imprint on printed slip pasted down on title, wrapper imprint also on slip pasted down, worn and little soiled but still sound, whip-stitched, titlepage bit grubby, scattered stains in text &c, fair to good only, but intact and complete, youthful ownership signature of one Charlotte M. Doty.   M & S Rare Books, Inc.   97 - 135   2015 $250

Association – Doty, Ruth

Doty, M. R. *An Alphabet.* Ithaca: Alembic Press, 1979. First edition, one of 600 copies, initials by Teresa McNeil, wrappers as issued, modest age toning, at least near fine, very warmly inscribed by co-author, Ruth Doty for Michael Benedikt.   Between the Covers Rare Books, Inc.   187 - 79   2015 $450

Association – Douglas, Lester

Matthews, William *Modern Bookbinding Practically Considered a Lecture.* New York: Grolier Club, 1889. First edition, limited to 300 copies, small 4to., original gilt stamped cloth, top edge gilt, others uncut, 96 pages, 8 full page plates, 2 bookplates on front pastedown including that of the designer Lester Douglas.   Oak Knoll Books   306 - 5   2015 $200

Association – Douglas, Norman

Neve, Edward De, Pseud. *Barred.* London: Desmond Harmsworth, 8vo., a noted rarity, original black cloth lettered red at spine, covers slightly rubbed, slightly scuffed at spine ends, else very good, sound, from the library of Norman Douglas, with note in pencil by him.   Any Amount of Books   2015 - A40615   2015   £700

Association – Dowd, Anthony

Bible. English - 1995 *The Song of Songs Which is Solomon's.* Alton: Clarion Press, 1995. 38/199 copies of an edition of 499 copies, this for Anthony Dowd, signed by artist Henry Fuller and designer Trevor Weston and with folder containing a set of color illustrations, each numbered and signed by artist Henry Fuller and designer Trevor Weston and with a folder containing a set of color illustrations each numbered and signed by artist, line drawings throughout with occasional splashes of gold, 8 panel foldout color illustrations tipped-in to inside read cover, original illustrated wrappers, slight bump at head of upper joint, slipcase, near fine.   Blackwell's Rare Books   B179 - 139   2015   £140

Association – Dowding, William Walter

Hamilton, Joseph *Some Short and Useful Reflections Upon Duelling, Which Should Be in the Hands of Every Person Who is Liable to Receive a Challenge, or an Offence.* Dublin: printed for the author by C. Bentham 19 Eustace Street..., 1823. First edition, 12mo., engraved frontispiece, half title, final ad leaf H12, original printed boards, these bit browned and spotted but still fine, crisp, uncut, with early 20th century armorial bookplate of William Walter Dowding, rare.   John Drury Rare Books   2015 - 23065   2015 $2448

Association – Downshire, Marquis of

Smith, George *A Collection of Designs for Household Furniture and Interior Decoration...* London: published for J. Taylor at the architectural Library no. 49, High Holborn, 1808. 4to., 158 plates, plates 23 and 26 cut to plate mark and mounted plate 146 with repair to margin, some occasional spotting, still unusually bright copy, contemporary vellum, upper cover lettered in gilt, Marquis of Downshire, Hillsborough Castle, some marks on lower board, inscribed on title for the Use of James McBlaine, Hillsborough, bookplate of Donald & Mary Hyde.   Marlborough Rare Books   List 54 - 78   2015   £9500

Association – Dowson, Ernest

Aristophanes *The Comedies of...* London: John Murray, 1820. First edition thus, 8vo., 2 volumes bound as one, neat name on endpaper of poet Ernest Downson, disbound, i.e. lacking covers, otherwise in decent, sound condition with clean text, very good. Any Amount of Books 2015 - A96146 2015 £225

Association – Dozier, Mary Dudley

Girvin, Ernest Alexander *Domestic Duels or Evening talks on the Woman Question.* San Francisco: Bronson, 1898. First edition, 8vo., grey cloth stamped in green and gilt, hinge little tender, but very good, tipped in slip "Compliments of E. E. Washburn personal friend of author", contemporary ownership signature "Mary Dudley Dozier Nov. 23rd 1898", scarce. Second Life Books Inc. 189 - 92 2015 $300

Association – Dozy, Charles

Griffis, William Elliot *The Mikado's Empire....* New York: Harper, 1890. Sixth edition, with supplementary chapters, octavo, 108 illustrations, 1 map, original brown cloth lettered gilt, presentation by author for Charles M. Dozy, Boston Jan. 31 1891, with 2 pictorial bookplates, covers little marked and little rubbed at edges, very good. Peter Ellis, Bookseller 2014 - 01759 2015 £350

Association – Drohojowski, John

Mexico South. The Isthmus of Tehauntepec. New York: Alfred A. Knopf, 1946. First edition, one of 100 copies, octavo, original illustrations by Miguel Covarrubias, and additional inscription and illustration from Covarrubias for Natalia and John Drohojowski, original black cloth over pink paper boards, gilt stamped on spine, some light fading to top edge of book, otherwise fine, housed in black opened ended cloth slipcase. Heritage Book Shop Holiday 2014 - 44 2015 $3000

Association – Drohojowski, Natalia

Mexico South. The Isthmus of Tehauntepec. New York: Alfred A. Knopf, 1946. First edition, one of 100 copies, octavo, original illustrations by Miguel Covarrubias, and additional inscription and illustration from Covarrubias for Natalia and John Drohojowski, original black cloth over pink paper boards, gilt stamped on spine, some light fading to top edge of book, otherwise fine, housed in black opened ended cloth slipcase. Heritage Book Shop Holiday 2014 - 44 2015 $3000

Association – Drummond, John George Home

Nedham, Marchamont *Digitus Dei; or God's Justice Upon Treachery and Treason, Exemplified in the Life and Death of the late James Duke of Hamilton.* London: 1649. First edition, variant issue, 4to., title printed within wide ornamental border, wanting A1 (blank or licence leaf?), 19th century half calf over marbled boards, some wear to joints, but good, firm copy with 19th century armorial bookplate of John George Home Drummond of Abbots Grange. John Drury Rare Books 2015 - 19478 2015 $874

Association – Dubus, Andre

Crumley, James *The Muddy Fork and Other Things.* Northridge: Lord John Press, 1984. First edition, preceding trade edition by 7 years, one of 200 numbered copies signed by Crumley, this is designated an unnumbered 'Presentation Copy' and additionally inscribed to his friend, writer Andre Dubus, fine, with no dust jacket, as issued, from the collection of Duke Collier. Royal Books 36 - 156 2015 $850

Association – Duff, E. Gordon

Hilary of Poitiers *Divi Hilarii Pictavorum Episcopi Lucubrationes...* Basel: Io. Frobenius, 1523. First edition, folio, 2 volumes, decorative initials and headpieces, contemporary full calf blindstamped on both sides with design of heraldic devices, rebacked (early) with red and gilt spine label, from the library of Allan Heywood Bright (1862-1941), loosely inserted is an ALS from fellow book collector E. Gordon Duff to Bright thanking him for the loan of the book, front board detached, rear joint and head and foot of spine well worn, armorial bookplate of Sir John Leveson Gower of Trentham, worming from titlepage on decreasing from about 60 holes throughout the first volume, few early ink annotations, ownership inscription of G(eorgius) Folberti(us), pencilled note identifies this book's provenance as "Sutherland Library". Any Amount of Books 2015 - 12863 2015 £800

Association – Duff, Richard Thornton

Bridges, Thomas *A Burlesque Translation of Homer.* London: printed for G. G. & J. Robinson, Paternoster Row, 1797. Fourth edition, 2 volumes, frontispiece, titlepage devices, 23 engraved plates, fine contemporary calf with double gilt banded spine, red morocco title labels, small circular dark green volume labels, pencil signature of Richard Thornton Duff, 1807. Jarndyce Antiquarian Booksellers CCXI - 38 2015 £280

Association – Duff, Robert William

Memoirs of the Public Life and Administration of the Right Honourable the Earl of Liverpool, K.G. &c &c. London: Saunders and Otley, 1827. First edition, 8vo., frontispiece, half title and final ad leaf with 19th century armorial bookplate of Robert William Duff of Fetteresso Castle near Stonehaven, fine in original boards, uncut, boards little soiled, wear to head and foot of spine. John Drury Rare Books 2015 - 26252 2015 $177

Association – Dugdale, William

Carter, Matthew *Honor Rediviuus (sic) or an Analysis of Honor and Armory.* London: by E(llen) Coates, 1655. First edition, one of two issues, 8vo., engraved frontispiece, 7 etched portraits, numerous armorial woodcuts with four in contemporary hand color, possibly a thick paper copy, some light foxing and occasional staining, contemporary calf, covers ruled in gilt, expertly rebacked, covers worn, chipped especially at corners and edges, mid 19th century endleaves, presentation by author to William Dugdale (1605-1686), the copy of James Robinson Planche (17696-1880) with bookplate, from the library of James Stevens Cox (1910-1997). Maggs Bros. Ltd. 1447 - 66 2015 £3200

Association – Duggan, W. T.

Doyle, Arthur Conan 1859-1930 *The Exploits of Brigadier Gerard.* New York: D. Appleton and Co., 1896. First American edition, decorated maroon cloth, contemporary owner's name on front of Capt. W. T. Duggan 10th Inty, bookplate of noted Sherlockian Edgar W. Smith with his pencil notation. Between the Covers Rare Books, Inc. 187 - 192 2015 $450

Association – Dulac, Edmund

Pushkin, Aleksandr Sergeevich 1799-1837 *The Golden Cockerel.* New York: Heritage Press, 1950. First edition, 4to., original blue cloth with cockerel printed in gilt in repeat pattern on covers, spine gilt lettered, copiously illustrated in color, signed by the artist, Edmund Dulac with inscription form Dulac to Isaac Jones, slight marks, head of spine slightly rubbed, slight soiling, very good+. Any Amount of Books 2015 - A43024 2015 £175

Association – Dumnachie, Muriel

Middleton, Stanley *Brazen Prison.* London: Hutchinson, 1971. First edition, 8vo., fine in near fine dust jacket very slightly creased at inner flap, signed presentation from author to Muriel Dumnachie Sept. 1971. Any Amount of Books 2015 - A38142 2015 £150

Association – Dundas, George

Colvil, Samuel *Whiggs Supplication.* Edinburgh: by Jo. Reid for Alexander Ogston, 1687. Second edition, 8vo., very small chip from upper fore corner with four minor circular stains on titlepage, some occasional staining throughout, dampstaining just touching corners of F4-F6, some heavy modern pencil markings in a number of margins, and with a number of gatherings beginning to come loose from book block, signed by author sheep (worn, large piece torn away from foot of spine and with upper headcap damaged, boards heavily rubbed and corners bumped, early signature of Geo(rge) Dundas, bookplate of Frederick Locker-Lampson (1821-1895), given by him to Lytton Strachey (1880-1932), from the library of James Stevens Cox (1910-1997). Maggs Bros. Ltd. 1447 - 108 2015 £150

Association – Dune, A. Cook

Taylor, Peter Alfred *Payment of Members; Speech of Mr. P. A. Taylor, M.P., in the House of Commons, on Tuesday the 5th of April 1870.* London: Trubner & Co., 1870. First separate edition, 8vo. 48 pages, margins of title slightly soiled, preserved in modern wrappers with printed label on upper cover, good copy, ownership signature of A. Cook Dune 22 1871. John Drury Rare Books 2015 - 25806 2015 $133

Association – Dunning, Joseph William

Whewell, William 1794-1866 *The Doctrine of Limits with its Applications: namely Conic Sections, the First Three Sections of Newton, The Differential Calculus.* Cambridge: printed at the University Press for J. and J. J. Deighton and John W. Parker, 1838. 8vo., diagrams, errata sheet, additional errata tipped in slip, contemporary quarter blue library cloth over paper boards, extremities worn, spine repaired with Kozo paper, armorial bookplate and ownership signature of Joseph William Dunning, very scarce. Jeff Weber Rare Books 178 - 1142 2015 $75

Association – Dupee, Fred

Bogan, Louise *Poems and New Poems.* New York: Charles Scribner's Sons, 1941. First edition, sunned at spine ends, else very good in about very good dust jacket with internal repairs and chips that correspond to the sunning on spine, presentation copy inscribed by author for friend Fred Dupee, May 13 1942, with autograph postcard dated Sept. 18 1944 from Botang to Dupee laid in. Between the Covers Rare Books, Inc. 187 - 27 2015 $475

Association – Dupin, Andre Marie Jean Jacques

Bacon, Francis, Viscount St. Albans 1561-1626 *Sermones Fideles, Ethici, Politici, Oeconomici...* Leiden: F. Hackium, 1644. Second Latin edition, 12mo., engraved allegorical frontispiece, small rust spot to inner margin of H9 and with some light occasional foxing in places (F1-G1), contemporary French or Low Countries calf, ruled in gilt, gilt spine (lightly worn, edges bumped, upper and lower headcaps damaged), signature "A M J J Dupin" (Andre Marie Jean Jacques Dupin 1783-1865), from the library of James Stevens Cox (1910-1997). Maggs Bros. Ltd. 1447 - 18 2015 £200

Association – Durant, Donald

Hoole, Henry *The Science and Art of Training a Handbook for Athletes.* London: Horace Cox, The "Field" Office, 1895. Third edition, finely bound in full green crushed morocco by Pfister, double ruled gilt borders, raised bands, illustrations, compartments, gilt dentelles, spine faded to brown, front board slightly marked, little rubbed, armorial bookplate of Donald Durant, top edge gilt, attractive copy. Jarndyce Antiquarian Booksellers CCXI - 144 2015 £150

Association – Durant, Fred

Marshak, Sondra *Star Trek: The New Voyages 2.* New York: Bantam, 1978. First edition, near fine with few creases to wrappers, inscribed by Jesco Von Puttkamer (provided introduction) to Fred Durant with longer typed note from Von Puttkamer to Durant tipped-in. Between the Covers Rare Books, Inc. 187 - 251 2015 $275

Sackett, Susan *Letters to Star-Trek.* New York: Ballantine, 1977. First edition, paperback original small scrape to top of front cover, else near fine in wrappers, inscribed by author to noted scientist Fred Durant. Between the Covers Rare Books, Inc. 187 - 253 2015 $275

Association – Duxley, Henry

St. German, Christian *Doctor and Student; or Dialogues Between a Doctor in Divinity and a Student in the Laws of England.* London: printed by Henry Lintot for J. Worall, 1751. Fifteenth edition, contemporary full calf, raised bands, contemporary ownership signature of Henry Duxley on titlepage, leather label missing from spine and result that the lettering "Doctor and Student" is only barely visible, cover edges rubbed and little defective at head of spine, surface of lower cover grazed, very good, internally bright copy. Peter Ellis, Bookseller 2014 - 015530 2015 £350

Association – Dwiggins

Catich, Edward M. *Letters Redrawn from the Trajan Inscription in Rome.* Davenport: Catfish Press, 1961. 8vo., cloth, with 93 4to. broadside plates, two sections enclosed in cloth bound case specially constructed to hold the two different sized parts, presentation "Dr. J. C. McMillan, E. Catich", preface signed and dated by Dwiggins. Oak Knoll Books 306 - 145 2015 $410

Association – Dykes, J. C.

White, Stewart Edward *On Tiptoe. A Romance of the Redwoods.* New York: George H. Doran Co., 1922. First edition, inscribed by author for J. C. Dykes, very good in dust jacket with moderate wear to extremities. Buckingham Books March 2015 - 13515 2015 $300

Association – Dymoke, Jane

Allestree, Richard *The Ladies Calling. In Two Parts.* Oxford: at the Theater, 1677. Fifth impression, 8vo., engraved frontispiece, vignette of the Sheldonian theatre on the title, light marginal browning and occasional spotting, very small paper flaw in lower blank margin of B2, contemporary black morocco, covers with fillet border, gilt panel with small floral tool at corners, spine with five raised bands, panels tooled in gilt, marbled endleaves and gilt edges (corners lightly bumped, few minor bumps and scuffs), from the library of James Stevens Cox (1910-1997), with ink signature (J(ane) Dymoke (of Scriveldaby, Yorkshire). Maggs Bros. Ltd. 1447 - 4 2015 £500

Association – Dyson Perrins, C. W.

Chaucer, Geoffrey 1340-1400 *The Workes of Geffrey Chaucer.* London: imprinted by John Kyngston for Jhon Wight, 1561. First collected edition, first issue, 22 woodcuts in The Prologues, folio, title within woodcut border, 22 woodcuts of Pilgrims in "The Prologues" and woodcut of knight on horse at head of "The Knightes Tale", large and small historiated and decorative initials and other ornaments, Black letter, fifty-six lines, double columns; late 19th century crimson morocco by Riviere, covers with gilt fillet and roll tool border enclosing central olive wreath and elaborate cornerpieces composed of scroll-work and spreading olive branches, remaining field same with cinquefoils, spine in 7 compartments with six raised bands, lettered gilt in two compartments, rest decoratively tooled gilt with repeated olive leaf motif, board edges and turn-ins decoratively tooled in gilt, all edges gilt, marbled endpapers (pastedowns with decorative gilt tooling), title creased and lightly soiled, small repair to outer blank margin, lower corner of second leaf renewed, affecting catchword on recto and two letters on verso, closed tear through lower half of divisional title to "The Caunterburie Tales", closed tear to A2 of "The Prologues" affecting 8 lines of text to first column and another closed tear at lower margin, F2 with small paper repair to margin and closed tear just touching text, 2U2 with paper fault affecting one word in bottom line of text on recto and verso, few additional small marginal tears or repairs not affecting text, occasional early ink underlining and markings, early signature of James Rea (faded) on title, wonderful copy, from the libraries of C. W. Dyson Perrins and William Foyle, with bookplates. Heritage Book Shop   Holiday 2014 - 36   2015 $65,000

Association – Eales, Mr.

Cruikshank, George 1792-1878 *George Cruikshank's Omnibus.* London: Tilt and Bogue, 1841-1842. First edition, 100 engravings on steel and wood, half title, frontispiece, plates and illustrations, some plates slightly browned and spotted, illustrations, front wrappers numbers I-IX bound in at front of volume, slightly dusted, some expert paper repair, uncut in later full light brown crushed morocco by Zaehnsdorf, very good, handsome copy, 11 line ALS from Cruikshank to Mr. Eales tipped in.   Jarndyce Antiquarian Booksellers   CCXI - 80   2015   £850

Association – Eames, Wilberforce

Wall, Alexander J. *A List of New York Almanacs 1694-1850.* New York: New York Public Library, 1921. First edition, cloth bound with wrappers bound in, slight foxing to text, else fine, signature of Wilberforce Eames, inscribed by author to Eames, Eames has corrected a few entries, laid in are few pages of additional notes in his hand.   Between the Covers Rare Books, Inc.   187 - 287   2015 $275

Association – Eaton, Ethel

Roberts, Kenneth *Northwest Passage.* Garden City: Doubleday & Doran Co., 1937. First edition, presentation from author for Mel and Ethel Eaton, fine in dust jacket with hint of wear to spine ends.   Buckingham Books   March 2015 - 24507   2015 $1250

Association – Eaton, Mel

Roberts, Kenneth *Northwest Passage.* Garden City: Doubleday & Doran Co., 1937. First edition, presentation from author for Mel and Ethel Eaton, fine in dust jacket with hint of wear to spine ends.   Buckingham Books   March 2015 - 24507   2015 $1250

Association – Ebdon, Christopher

Boruwlaski, Joseph *Memoirs of the Celebrated Dwarf, Joseph Boruwlaski. A Polish Gentleman.* Kelso: James Ballantyne at the Kelso Mail Printing Office, 1801. First edition thus, 8vo., inscribed by author for Christ. Ebdon (1744-1824), full contemporary calf, front board detached, bears 1797 Thomas Bell bookplate, spine rather chipped and faded, small chip at top of f.f.e.p., otherwise very good.   Any Amount of Books   March 2015 - C13206   2015   £450

Association – Ebourne, Ann

De Grey, William *The Compleat Horse-Man and Expert Ferrier.* London: by J. and R. and R. H. for Samuel Lowndes, 1684. Fifth edition, small 4to., some minor staining and spotting throughout, small piece torn away from fore-corner of I2, minor tearing to edges of some, small hole through centre of M3 affecting 4 words, contemporary sheep (covers rubbed, corners worn, large piece torn away from lower headcap, flyleaves bit torn and stained, pastedowns unstuck, signatures of William Ebourne and Ann Ebourne 1689, from the library of James Stevens Cox (1910-1997).   Maggs Bros. Ltd.   1447 - 134   2015   £300

Association – Ebourne, William

De Grey, William *The Compleat Horse-Man and Expert Ferrier.* London: by J. and R. and R. H. for Samuel Lowndes, 1684. Fifth edition, small 4to., some minor staining and spotting throughout, small piece torn away from fore-corner of I2, minor tearing to edges of some, small hole through centre of M3 affecting 4 words, contemporary sheep (covers rubbed, corners worn, large piece torn away from lower headcap, flyleaves bit torn and stained, pastedowns unstuck, signatures of William Ebourne and Ann Ebourne 1689, from the library of James Stevens Cox (1910-1997).   Maggs Bros. Ltd.   1447 - 134   2015   £300

Association – Eckard, Edwin M.

Lowell, Percival *Mars and Its Canals.* New York & London: Macmillan Co., 1906. First edition, frontispiece, 8 plates, 12 maps, 49 figures, original dark green gilt stamped cloth, top edge gilt, lightly rubbed, ownership signatures of Edwin M. Eckard and Russell Sullivan, Indianapolis, bookplate of LA lawyer Herbert Kraus, very good.   Jeff Weber Rare Books   178 - 798   2015 $750

Association – Edel, Leon

Howard, Richard *Misgivings. Poems.* New York: Atheneum, 1979. First edition, paperback original, there was no hardcover issue, lightly foxed, spine and rear wrapper sunned, near fine, inscribed by author for Leon Edel. Between the Covers Rare Books, Inc.   187 - 134   2015 $200

Howard, Richard *Two Part Inventions.* New York: Atheneum, 1974. First edition, paperback original, no hardcover issue, tall octavo, glossy wrappers, lightly foxed, inscribed by author for Leon Edel.   Between the Covers Rare Books, Inc.   187 - 133   2015 $150

Association – Eden, John

Cumberland, Richard *Arundel.* printed for C. Dilly, 1791. Second edition, 2 volumes, scorch mark to first age of text volume ii, no loss, very minor browning and spotting here and there, contemporary calf, spines gilt in compartments, contrasting labels on spines, those for the volume nos. circular, numbering piece on volume ii lacking, that on volume i slightly defective, without flyleaf in volume i, slight wear to extremities, engraved armorial bookplate of Sir John Eden inside front covers, attractive copy, rare edition. Blackwell's Rare Books   B179 - 34   2015   £500

Graham, Catharine Macaulay *The History of England from the Revolution to the Present Time in a Series of letters to a Friend.* Bath: printed by R. Cruttwell and sold by E. & C. Dilly, T. Cadell and J. Walter, London, 1778. First edition, 4to., engraved portrait and additional engraved titlepage (foxed as usual), contemporary speckled calf, spine gilt, contrasting labels, spine numbered "Volume 6), spine rather rubbed and eroded, joints cracked, despite wear to spine, an excellent copy, with wide margins, bookplate of Sir John Eden, Bart of West Auckland Co. Durham. Second Life Books Inc.   189 - 103   2015 $2500

Association – Eden, Robert Johnson

Great Britian. Board of Agriculture - 1816 *Agricultural State of the Kingdom, in February March and April 1816 Being the Substance of the Replies to a Circular letter Sent by the Board of Agriculture to Every Part of the Kingdom.* London: printed by Sherwood Neely and Jones, 1816. First edition, 8vo., evidence of erasure on verso of title and foot of final leaf, contemporary half calf gilt, neatly rebacked, good copy, 19th century armorial bookplate of Sir Robert Johnson Eden, Bart.   John Drury Rare Books   March 2015 - 16526   2015 $266

Association – Edge, A. A.

Dury, Andrew *A Collection of Plans of the Principal Cities of Great Britain and Ireland...* London: printed and sold by A. Drury in Dukes Court, St. Martin's Lane, 1764. 12mo., engraved title, dedication and index with 41 hand colored maps and city plans, all mounted on guards, each measuring 115 x 140mm. but London and Edinburgh folding out to 115 x 220mm and 115 x 200mm., upper margin of one plan scorched, contemporary vellum, slightly soiled with 19th century armorial bookplate of A. A. Edge.   Marlborough Rare Books   List 54 - 25   2015   £3800

Association – Edwardes, Henry Hope

Gunton, Symon *The History of the Church of Peterburgh.* London: printed for Richard Chiswell, 1686. First edition, 371 x 232mm., splendid honey brown diced russia by Roger Payne, covers with wide intricate and elegant dentelle frame composed of many small floral tools, raised bands, spine with gilt crest of Sir Richard Colt Hoare in top compartment, gilt titling in text two compartments and four elaborately tooled compartments below with gilt floral sprigs radiating from a central quatrefoil, interspersed with circlets and many small floral tools, turn-ins with simple gilt rules and delicate floral cornerpieces, endpapers of purple 'fine drawing paper' (Payne's words), all edges gilt, joints and very small portion at spine ends recently and expertly renewed by Courtland Benson, in a folding cloth box lined with felt (somewhat scuffed); 2 illustrations in text and 4 plates of views, large paper copy; front pastedown with armorial bookplate of Sir Henry Hope Edwardes and engraved bookplate of W. H. Corfield, front flyleaf with transcription in Hoare's hand of Payne's very detailed explanation of the work done and the bill for it; spine evenly darkened toward a chocolate brown, moderate foxing to half a dozen leaves, occasional rust spots, light stains or other trivial imperfections elsewhere in text, exceptionally desirable specimen in generally very fine condition, mostly clean and always fresh internally and very special binding entirely solid now, with virtually no wear and with all of the delicate gilt quite bright.   Phillip J. Pirages 66 - 57   2015 $15,000

Association – Edwards, J. O.

Wordsworth, William   1770-1850 *Yarrow Revisited and Other Poems.*   London: Longman, Rees, Orme, Brown, Green & Longman, 1835. First edition, presentation copy inscribed by author for fellow poet Eliz M. Hamilton on a slip of paper pasted on to verso of title and with "From the Author" written on half title by publisher's clerk, erratum slip tipped in, ads discarded, 12mo., slightly later 19th century olive pebble grain morocco by Tuckett ('binder to the Queen'), backstrip panelled and ruled in gilt and infilled with volutes and other tools, lettered gilt in second compartment, sides with triple gilt borders, inner panel with gilt cornerpieces and central panels of curing lines, all edges gilt, marbled endpapers, bookplate of J. O. Edwards, small scrape to upper board, extremities slightly rubbed, good.   Blackwell's Rare Books   B179 - 121   2015   £2500

Association – Eldon, John Scott, Earl of

Bath Penitentiary and Lock Hospital   *The Collective Reports of the Bath Penitentiary and Lock Hospital from 1816 to 1824...*   Bath: printed by Wood, Cunningham and Smith, 1824. First edition, 8vo., contemporary dark blue calf, gilt borders, spine gilt in compartments, fine presentation copy inscribed by chairman of the Penitentiary to Lord Eldon with his armorial bookplate and signature, apparently rare.   John Drury Rare Books   2015 - 25027   2015 $1136

Comber, William Turner   *An Inquiry into the State of National Subsistence, as Connected with the Progress of Wealth and Population...*   London: printed for the author and sold by J. M. Richardson, 1822. 8vo., half title and appendix original boards, printed spine label (slightly chipped), entirely uncut, fine, from the library of Lord Eldon with his circular armorial bookplate and signature in ink.   John Drury Rare Books   2015 - 25037   2015 $1049

Great Britain. Parliament - 1789   *The History and Proceedings of the Lords and Commons of Great Britain, in Parliament, with Regard to the Regency, Containing a full Account of all Their Speeches on the Proposed Regency Bill from Nov. 20 1788 to March 10 1789...*   London: John Stockdale, 1789. 8vo., very occasional minor spotting, generally little just bit foxed, contemporary tree calf, sympathetically rebacked, flat spine gilt and labelled, excellent copy, 19th century library of John Scott, Lord Eldon with his circular armorial bookplate and signature.   John Drury Rare Books   2015 - 25069   2015 $1136

Johnstone, John   *Medical Jurisprudence. On Madness.*   Birmingham: printed at the office of J. Belcher and sold by J. Johnson St. Paul's Church Yard London, 1800. First edition, 8vo., contemporary calf, gilt, foot of spine chipped, else very good, from the 19th century library of John Scott, Earl of Eldon and Lord Chancellor with his circular armorial bookplate, uncommon.   John Drury Rare Books   2015 - 25035   2015 $1136

State of Ireland. Letters from Ireland on the Present Political, Religious & Moral State of that Country.   London: J. Hatchard & Son & R. Milliken, Dublin, 1825. First edition, 8vo., half title, appendix leaf, original green cloth backed boards, little rubbed, entirely uncut, very good, presentation copy to Lord Eldon with Eldon's circular armorial bookplate and his usual signature in ink with half title inscribed for Earl of Eldon.   John Drury Rare Books   March 2015 - 25044   2015 $656

Willis, Robert Darling   *Philosophical Sketches of the Principles of Society and Government.*   London: printed by W. Bulmer and Co. for P. Elmsly, 1795. First edition, 8vo., half title, contemporary diced russia gilt, fine, from the library of Lord Eldon with his armorial bookplate and ownership signature, uncommon.   John Drury Rare Books   March 2015 - 25034   2015 $656

Association – Elkins, Jim

Lancaster, Bill   *The Thing.*   Universal City: Universal Pictures, 1981. 2nd draft screenplay for the 1982 film, working copy belonging to uncredited crew member Jim Elkins with his name in holograph ink on front wrapper.   Royal Books   46 - 10   2015 $1250

Association – Ellery, William

Pearson, Eliphalet   *A Public Lecture Occasioned by the Death of the Rev. Joseph Willard...*   Cambridge: printed at the University Press in Cambridge by William Hilliard, 1804. First edition, octavo, 21 pages, sewn unprinted blue wrappers, near fine, inscribed by Richard Henry Dana, poet and father of R.H. Dana, Jr., for William Ellery (Dana's grandfather and signer of the Declaration of Independence from RI).   Between the Covers Rare Books, Inc.   187 - 209   2015 $450

Association – Elliott, E.

Four Satires. Viz. 1. On National Vices... II. On Writers.... III. On Waucks... IV. O Religious Disputes.   London: printed for T. Cooper, 1737. First edition, woodcut headpieces, initials and ornaments, small hole at head of A4 and B1 without loss, tear at head of B4, entering text but without loss, bit stained and soiled, 8vo., modern half calf, contemporary signature of Edw. Elliott, sound.   Blackwell's Rare Books   B179 - 4   2015   £450

Association – Elliott, Gertrude

Houdini, Harry *Elliott's Last Legacy...* New York: Adams Press Print, 1923. First edition, illustrations by Oscar Teale, binding lightly worn at extremities, tidemark from dampstain at top corner of pages throughout, front hinge tender but still sound, very good, Teale's copy, inscribed for him by Houdini, inscribed by Teale for Lester Grimes, Grimes then inscribed the book for friend Gertrude Elliott. Between the Covers Rare Books, Inc. 187 - 164 2015 $4000

Association – Elliott, Isaac

Art Work of Delaware. N.P.: Charles Madison Co., 1898. First edition, quarto, contemporary leather, 22 pages of text, 70 pages of photos, with ink binding stamp indicating that this copy was bound by R.T. Stuart 615 Shipley Street, Wilmington, Del." and with name "Isaac C. Elliott" stamped in gilt on lower portion of front cover, spine replaced and stamped with author's name and title, professional restoration to original front and rear covers, new front and rear endpapers, some tissues replaced, else near fine, housed in cloth slipcase with leather label on spine and titles stamped in gilt. Buckingham Books March 2015 - 23961 2015 $1250

Association – Ellis, Havelock

Swinburne, Algernon Charles 1837-1909 *Poems and Ballads: Second Series.* London: Chatto and Windus, 1878. First edition, ownership signature of Havelock Ellis, original dark blue green cloth with title, author and publisher device on spine, some bumping to corners, very good, front hinge slightly split and rear hinge weak, interior pages clean and bright, very good, marginal annotations and few lines of French by unidentified hand on pages 196-198. The Kelmscott Bookshop 11 - 51 2015 $250

Association – Ellis, Jessie

Duniway, Abigail Scott *Path Breaking an Autobiographical History of the Equal Suffrage Movement in Pacific Coast States.* Portland: by the author, 1914. Second edition, 8vo., covers little browned, near fine, contemporary name Jessie M. Ellis, scarce. Second Life Books Inc. 189 - 66 2015 $250

Association – Ellis, Mary Fergusson

Fergusson, B. Menzies *Through Holland and Belgium on Wheels.* Stirling: Messrs James Hogg and Co., 1904. First edition, octavo, pale red cloth, (penciled ownership "Mary Fergusson Ellis") volume appears to lack front fly, corners little bumped, near fine. Between the Covers Rare Books 196 - 172 2015 $350

Association – Ellman, Mary

Hawkes, John *The Cannibal.* New York: New Directions, 1949. First edition, small 8vo., original pale grey boards, fine in very good yellow and black dust jacket faintly marked and very slightly chipped at spine ends and with very slight edgewear, signed presentation from author for Dick and Mary (Richard and Mary Ellman. Any Amount of Books 2015 - A75834 2015 £280

Association – Ellman, Richard

Hawkes, John *The Cannibal.* New York: New Directions, 1949. First edition, small 8vo., original pale grey boards, fine in very good yellow and black dust jacket faintly marked and very slightly chipped at spine ends and with very slight edgewear, signed presentation from author for Dick and Mary (Richard and Mary Ellman. Any Amount of Books 2015 - A75834 2015 £280

Association – Elton, Oliver

Reynolds, Henry *The Tale of Narcissus.* Hull: J. R. Tutin, 1906. One of 666 copies, one page creased, uncut, original printed wrappers, dusted and slightly creased, inscribed on front wrapper from Tutin to Oliver Elton and by Elton to Kathleen Tillotson with compliments. Jarndyce Antiquarian Booksellers CCVII - 446 2015 £25

Association – Elwell, Henry

Beste, John Richard *Alcazar; or the Dark Ages.* London: Hurst & Blackett, 1857. 3 volumes, original dark green horizontal fine ribbed moire cloth by Edmonds & Remnants, boards blocked in blind, spine decorated and lettered in gilt, fine, half titles, ownership inscription of Henry Elwell. Jarndyce Antiquarian Booksellers CCXI - 25 2015 £480

Association – Ely, Richard

Mangold, George B. *Problems of Child Welfare.* New York: Macmillan, 1914. First edition, fine an bright with homemade library tag at corner front pastedown and ownership signature of socialist historian Richard T. Ely. Beasley Books 2013 - 2015 $85

Association – Emerson, George

Oakes, William *Views of the Profile Mountain and the Profile Rock or the "Old Man of the Mountain" at Franconia, New Hampshire on Two Plates with Descriptive Letter Press.* Boston: S. N. Dickinson, printer, 1847. First edition, folio, 2 plates by Bufford from drawings by Isaac Sprague, original printed wrappers, fine, inscribed by Oakes, presentation for George B. Emerson. M & S Rare Books, Inc. 97 - 209 2015 $2500

Association – Engle, Paul

Young, Marguerite *Moderate Fable and Other Poems.* New York: Reynal & Hitchcock, 1944. First edition, slight offsetting to endpapers and slight foxing to boards, else fine in very good plus dust jacket with some faint offsetting along edge of front panel, poet Paul Engle's copy with his ownership signature.   Between the Covers Rare Books, Inc.   187 - 300   2015 $150

Association – Erbe, Ned

Dahlberg, Edward *Can These Bones Live.* New York: New Directions, 1960. First revised edition, illustrations by James Kearns, fine in like dust jacket, nicely inscribed by author for Ned Erbe, head of publicity at New Directions.   Between the Covers Rare Books, Inc.   187 - 67   2015 $150

Association – Ernst, Paul

Ernst, Donna B. *Sundance, My Unle.* Early West Creative Pub. Co., 1992. First edition, 8vo., limited to 1500 copies, signed by author and by her husband, Paul Ernst, a descendant of the Longabaugh family, red cloth titles stamped in black on spine, red pictorial endpapers, illustrations, as new, unread in like dust jacket.   Buckingham Books   March 2015 - 34087   2015 $175

Association – Erval, Francois

Cesaire, Aime *Toussaint Louverture - La Revolution.* Paris: Presence Africaine, 1962. New edition, octavo, 312 pages, 2 full page maps at rear, wrappers, presentation from author inscribed for Francois Erval, very scarce thus, covers little creased and slightly bruised at spine, very good in very good dust jacket, little creased and rubbed at edges, small internal repair at head of spine.   Peter Ellis, Bookseller   2014 - 019786   2015   £350

Association – Esher, Oliver Brett, Viscount

Sedley, Charles *The Miscellaneous Works of the Honourable Sir Charles Sedley, Bart.* London: printed and sold by J. Nutt, 1702. First edition, 8vo., contemporary panelled calf, cracked hinges, but good, light foxing but very good, bookplate of Oliver Brett, Viscount Esher.   C. R. Johnson   Foxon R-Z - 875r-z   2015 $306

Sewell, George *Poems on Several Occasions.* London: printed for E. Curll and J. Pemberton, 1719. First edition, 8vo., polished mottled calf, gilt spine and inner dentelles, gilt, by Root & Son, excellent copy, complete with two final leaves of index, sometimes missing, very scarce, bookplate of Oliver Brett, Viscount Esher.   C. R. Johnson   Foxon R-Z - 888r-z   2015 $2298

Shenstone, William   1714-1763 *The Judgment of Hercules, a Poem. Inscrib'd to George Lyttleton, Esq.* London: printed for R. Dodsley and sold by T. Cooper, 1741. First edition, 8vo., full rose morocco, gilt, spine gilt, all edges gilt, by Riviere & Son, bookplate of Oliver Brett, later Viscount Esher.   C. R. Johnson   Foxon R-Z - 893r-z   2015 $2298

Somervile, William   1675-1742 *Occasional Poems, Translations, Tales &c.* London: printed for Bernard Lintot, 1727. First edition, 8vo., contemporary calf, gilt, rebacked, much of original spine preserved, later brown morocco label, very good inscription "Mr. Thos. D. Llewelyn's book bought of Mr. Wm. Davies bookseller Aberdeen Dec. 30th 1863", later bookplate of Oliver Brett, Viscount Esher.   C. R. Johnson   Foxon R-Z - 913r-z   2015 $460

Thompson, William *Poems on Several Occasions to which is added Gondibert and Birtha, a tragedy.* Oxford: printed at the Theatre, 1757. First edition, 8vo., contemporary calf, spine gilt, red morocco label, slight wear to spine, very good, bookplate of Oliver Brett, Viscount Esher.   C. R. Johnson   Foxon R-Z - 982r-z   2015 $383

Thurston, Joseph *Poems on Several Occasions.* London: printed by W. P. for Benj. Motte, 1729. First edition, 8vo., panelled calf antique, spine and inner dentelles gilt, brown morocco label, fine, rare title, bookplate of Oliver Brett, Viscount Esher.   C. R. Johnson   Foxon R-Z - 1006r-z   2015 $1915

Whitehead, William *Poems on Several Occasions, with the Roman Father.* London: printed for R. and J. Dodsley, 1754. First edition, 8vo., contemporary calf, red morocco label (some rubbing of spine), very good, complete with half title, list of errata on verso, early signature of 'Tighe' of St. John's College, Cambridge dated Dec. 1755, later bookplate of Olvier Brett, Viscount Esher,.   C. R. Johnson   Foxon R-Z - 1142r-z   2015 $230

Whaley, John *A Collection of Poems.* London: printed for the author by John Willis and Joseph Boddington and sold by Messieurs Innys and Manby...., 1732. First edition, 8vo., contemporary panelled calf, rebacked at early date, red morocco label (some wear to spine and corners, joints cracked), aside from binding wear, very good, signed on titlepage by Spark Molesworth whose name appears in subscriber's list as student at Trinity Hall, Cambridge, later bookplate of Oliver Brett, Viscount Esher.   C. R. Johnson   Foxon R-Z - 1128r-z   2015 $460

Young, Edward 1683-1765 *The Force of Religion; or, Vanquish'd Love.* London: printed for E. Curll and J. Pemberton, 1714. First edition, engraved frontispiece, 8vo., half blue morocco, gilt, spine gilt, top edge gilt by Roger de Coverly & sons (traces of rubbing), copy on fine paper, remarkable presentation copy inscribed to Revd. Doct. Pa(rnell) from the author, margins trimmed somewhat close, but not touching text, otherwise very good, bookplate of Oliver Brett, Viscount Esher. C. R. Johnson Foxon R-Z - 1187r-z 2015 $1915

Association – Eshleman, Clayton

Enslin, Theodore *Agreement and Back: Sequences.* New York: Elizabeth Press, 1969. First edition, fine in slightly spine faded, else very near fine dust jacket, inscribed by author to Clayton Eshleman. Between the Covers Rare Books, Inc. 187 - 89 2015 $250

Lowenfels, Walter *Some Deaths.* Highlands: Jonathan Williams/Natahala Foundation, 1964. First edition, one of 1500 copies, ownership signature of poet Clayton Eshleman dated 1965, fore edge soiled, some edgewear, very good in pictorial wrappers. Between the Covers Rare Books, Inc. 187 - 160 2015 $65

Scott, Peter Dale *Coming to Jakarta;. A Poem About Terror.* New York: New Directions, 1989. First edition, 150 pages, fine in wrappers, gift inscription by author to Clayton (Eshleman). Ken Lopez, Bookseller 164 - 192 2015 $125

Snyder, Gary *Mountains and Rivers Without End.* Washington: Counterpoint, 1996. Uncorrected proof, hint of sunning, else fine in wrappers, from the library of Clayton Eshleman with his notes in text. Ken Lopez, Bookseller 164 - 189 2015 $85

Snyder, Gary *Montagnes et Rivieres Sans Fin. (Mountains and Rivers Without End).* Monaco: Editions du Rocher, 2002. Uncorrected proof, fine wrappers, with a snapshot of Snyder, inscribed by author for Clayton (Eshleman). Ken Lopez, Bookseller 164 - 190 2015 $125

Association – Euston, Dr.

Chalmers, Thomas *On Political Economy: in Connexion with the Moral State and Moral Prospects of Society.* Glasgow: Printed for William Collins, 1832. First edition, 8vo., contemporary polished calf, sides embossed in blind, spine gilt with raised bands an label, all edges gilt, fine presentation copy inscribed in ink in author's hand for Revd. Dr. Euston (?). John Drury Rare Books March 2015 - 25454 2015 $874

Association – Evans, Frederick

Evans, Frederick H. *William Blake's Illustrations to Thornton's Pastorals of Virgil in Ambrose Phillips' Imitation of Vergil's First Eclogue. 1821.* Privately printed, 1912. Enlarged facsimiles in Platinotype from scarce original edition, limited to two copies, from a total of 25, this copy inscribed by Evans as one of two 'unnumbered presentation copies' and was his own copy, letter from Cecil Smith of the V & A accepting the other presentation copy tipped-in to front of volume, tipped in rear is review of the present volume from The Athenaeum dated Jan. 25th 1903, large 4to., original half midnight blue morocco gilt, spine lettered gilt and stamped with Evans's initials, 38ff., 17 woodcuts by Blake enlarged and mounted, frontispiece by John Linnell, photo of the life marks of Blake by Deville, Frederick Evans copy with his engraved bookplate. Henry Sotheran Ltd. William Blake Exhibition 17th Oct.-7th Nov. 2014 - 74 2015 £3500

Association – Evans, John

Herbert, Thomas *A Relation of Some Yeares Travaile Begunne anno 1626.* London: printed by William Stansby & Jacob Blome, 1634. First edition, 4to., numerous well executed engraved illustrations and maps, contemporary full panelled calf, expertly rebacked raised bands, maroon leather label, from the Maxwell-Perceval Library, with signature of William Perceval, armorial bookplate of John Evans, very good. Jarndyce Antiquarian Booksellers CCXI - 137 2015 £1850

Association – Evans, Louise

Haley, James Evetts *Earl Vandale on the trail of Texas books.* Palo Duro Press, 1965. First edition, limited to 500 copies, presentation inscription by author for Louise Evans, 8vo., cloth, title stamped in gilt on front cover and spine, frontispiece, illustrations, fine, bright, square copy. Buckingham Books March 2015 - 36842 2015 $175

Association – Evans, Montgomery

Cummings, Edward Estlin 1894-1962 *Is 5.* New York: Liveright, 1926. First edition deluxe issue, one of 77 copies on special paper, specially bound and signed by author, 8vo., original cloth backed decorated paper over boards, publisher's matching slipcase with paper label, presentation copy inscribed by author, Montgomery Evans bookplate, otherwise fine in slipcase with two short cracks. James S. Jaffe Rare Books Modern American Poetry - 57 2015 $1500

Association – Evans, Walker

Eliot, Thomas Stearns 1888-1965 *The Waste Land.* New York: Boni & Liveright, 1923. First edition, 2nd impression, octavo, 64 pages, no dust jacket, boxed, ownership signature of American photographer Walker Evans with note "New York/March, 1926" in his hand.   Honey & Wax Booksellers   1 - 34   2015 $7000

Association – Evelyn, John

Boyle, Robert 1627-1691 *The Excellency of Theology.* London: by T. N. for Henry Herringmann, 1674. 8vo., titlepage badly defective having been affected by damp and stuck to front pasteboard (where some of it still remains) and has large (145 x35mm) piece torn away and two (approximately 50mm) closed tears caused by leaf being torn away from pastedown, first sheet dampstained, continuing less severely in places throughout, final blank and binders blank little ragged and stained by turn-ins, contemporary sheep, large piece torn away from leather exposing book block, covers almost detached, holes and scuffs to both boards, no pastedowns, late 20th century brown cloth folding box, the duplicate copy of John Evelyn (1630-1706), from the library of James Stevens Cox (1910-1997). Maggs Bros. Ltd.   1447 - 37   2015   £550

Association – Eversley, Viscount

Percy, Thomas, Bp. of Dromore 1729-1811 *Reliques of Ancient English Poetry.* London: J. Dodsley, 1765. First edition, 12mo., 3 volumes, engraved frontispiece, numerous engraved vignettes, leaf of music, with half title and final leaf of errata, but the rare "Advertisement" leaf, clean tear in one leaf (affecting text but without loss), contemporary mottled calf, rebacked, corners slightly worn, bookplate of Viscount Eversley each volume, clean tear in on leaf (affecting text without loss), corners slightly worn on all volumes.   Any Amount of Books   March 2015 - C5114   2015   £450

Association – Fagge, Alfred

Stael-Holstein, Anne Louise Germaine Necker, Baronne De 1766-1817 *Reflections on Suicide.* London: Longmans Hurst, Rees, Orme and Brown, 1813. First edition, 8vo., leather boards, loose rubbed, no spine, bookplate of Alfred Fagge, endpapers slightly browned, covers somewhat used, text clean and very good with slight browning.   Any Amount of Books   2015 - A97755   2015   £225

Association – Fairbank, Alfred

Morison, Stanley 1889-1957 *The Fleuron a Journal of Typography.* London: at the Office of the Fleuron, 1923. 1924. 1924. 1925. 1926. 1928. 1930, Various limitations, but all about 1000 copies, 7 volumes, complete, 4to., cloth backed boards (first two volumes), cloth on others, dust jacket on 3 volumes, tipped-in plates and other illustrations, original dust jackets present on volumes one, three and seven (pieces missing from each of the jackets), bookplates in volume 1, faded spine in volume 2, bookplates in volume 3, faded spine in volume 4 and with prospectus to this volume loosely inserted, bookplate on half title in volume 5, rubbed with some wear along back hinge in volume 6 and with signature of Alfred Fairbank, original prospectus in volume 7.   Oak Knoll Books   306 - 55   2015 $2000

Association – Fairfax

England and Wales. Parliament - 1642 *A Declaration of the Lords and Commons Assembled in Parliament that all such Persons Who Shall Advance Present Moneyes Upon the Credit of their Late Ordinance for the Carrying on the Great Affaires of this Kingdome...* London: Dec. 3 printed by John Wright in the Old Bailey, 1642. First edition, 4to., title printed within typographical border, very good, crisp copy with good margins, rebound in early 20th century in cloth backed boards, spine lettered, from the Fairfax of Cameron Library with armorial bookplate.   John Drury Rare Books   2015 - 24358   2015 $612

Salisbury, Robert Cecil *The Copie of a Letter to the Right Honourable the Earle of Leycester, Lieutenant General of all Her Majesties Forces in the United Provinces of the Low Countreys.* London: Christopher Barker, 1586. 4to., without final blank leaf, woodcut arms on A, verso facing titlepage, large woodcut initials, this copy is the variant with A, recto starting, bound by Pratt in 19th century brown crushed morocco with gilt arms on covers, all edges gilt, bookplate of 'Fairfax of Cameron', fine.   Second Life Books Inc.   190 - 226   2015 $4000

XXV Queries: Modestly and Humbly and Yet Sadly and Seriously Propounded to the People of England and their Representatives and Likewise to the Army in this Juncture of Affairs. London: printed for L. Chapman at the Crown in Popes-head Ally, 1659, i.e., 1660. First edition, 4to., interleaved with blanks, some inner margins strengthened, bound in early 20th century parchment backed boards, spine lettered, very good from the early 20th century library of Fairfax of Cameron, with armorial bookplate.   John Drury Rare Books   2015 - 26085   2015 $656

Williams, Charles Hanbury *An Ode Addressed to the author of the Conquered Duchess.* London: printed for A. Moore, 1746. First edition, 8 pages, folio, recent cloth boards, parchment spine, this copy has no punctuation after "rul'd" in the third line of stanza IX, with Fairfax of Cameron bookplate, very good.   C. R. Johnson   Foxon R-Z - 1154r-z   2015 $613

Williams, Charles Hanbury *An Ode to the Honourable H---y F--x on the Marriage of the Du---s of M-----r to H---s-----v, Esq.* London: printed for A. Moore, 1746. First edition, folio, recent cloth boards, parchment spine, very good, Fairfax of Cameron bookplate, very scarce.   C. R. Johnson Foxon R-Z - 1156r-z   2015 $689

Association – Fairgrieve, Amita

Le Gallienne, Richard   1866-1947   *The Lonely Dancer.* New York: John Lane the Bodley Head, 1914. First American edition, near fine, Amita Fairgrieve's copy with her bookplate.   Between the Covers Rare Books, Inc.   187 - 152   2015 $75

Association – Faithful, Emily

Procter, Adelaide A.   *The Victoria Regia a Volume of Original Contributions in Poetry and Prose.* London: printed and published by Emily Faithfull & Co., Victoria Press for the Employment of Women, 1861. First edition, 8vo. full leather elaborately stamped in gilt, all edges gilt, gilt inner dentelles, designed by John Leighton, some foxing on endpapers, much less in text, some very light wear to boards, still near fine, inscribed by Emily Faithful for Blanche Resticaux, 1862, also inserted a few news clippings about Faithful, very small ALS from Henry Alford and small slip of paper signed yours faithfully Isa Craig.   Second Life Books Inc.   191 - 78   2015 $1500

Association – Fane, Julian

Tennyson, Alfred Tennyson, 1st Baron   1809-1892   *In Memoriam.* London: Edward Moxon, 1850. First edition, half title, without initial catalog, brown morocco presentation binding by Budden, Cambridge, little rubbed with small split in leading hinge, all edges gilt, lettered on front board, inscribed to Julain Fane from HAJ, with very poor copy of the 10th edition 1861 in original cloth, heavily annotated with insertions by Geoffrey Tillotson, from the library of Geoffrey & Kathleen Tillotson.   Jarndyce Antiquarian Booksellers CCVII - 486   2015   £350

Association – Farquhar, Samuel

Parish, John C.   *California Books and Manuscripts in the Huntington Library.* Cambridge: Harvard University Press, 1935. First book edition, presentation inscription signed by author to Samuel Farquhar (head of UC Press), light brown wrappers printed in black, minor crease to rear wrapper, fine.   Argonaut Book Shop   Holiday Season 2014 - 221   2015 $60

Association – Farrer, Reginald

Blackwood, Algernon   *John Silence, Physician Extraordinary.* London: Eveleigh Nash, 1908. First edition, 8vo., original red cloth, lettered gilt on spine and on front cover, ownership signature of gardener Reginald Farrer, slight browning to endpapers, some fading at spine with rubbing at corners and spine ends, else sound, very good- with clean text.   Any Amount of Books   2015 - C16278   2015   £280

Association – Fawcus, Arnold

Graves, Robert   1895-1985   *Adam's Rib and Other Anomalous Elements in the Hebrew Creation Myth.* Jura: Trianon Press, 1955. First edition, copy "R" of 26 lettered copies signed by Graves and Metcalf, large 8vo., original red cloth lettered gilt at spine, wood engravings by James Metcalf, signed presentation from book's designer Arnold Fawcus, fine in slightly browned but very good plani slipcase.   Any Amount of Books   2015 - A49568   2015   £280

Association – Feather, Leonard

Charters, Sam   *Jazz: a History of the New York Scene.* Garden City: Doubleday, 1962. First edition, very good, few little bumps, tall 8vo., very good dust jacket with wear and tiny chips at top edge, somewhat ornately inscribed by Leonard Feather in 1964, nice association.   Beasley Books 2013 - 2015 $200

Association – Federman, Raymond

Dixon, Stephen   *Time to Go.* Baltimore: Johns Hopkins University Press, 1984. Second edition, fine in fine dust jacket, very warmly inscribed by author to Raymond Federman.   Between the Covers Rare Books, Inc.   187 - 75   2015 $125

Association – Feiffer, Jules

Juster, Norton *The Phantom Tollbooth.* New York: Epstein & Carroll, 1961. First edition, 4to., blue cloth, fine in dust jacket (in very good condition, but with 2 small half inch chips off edge at front panel, few pinholes along fold, not price clipped), illustrations by Jules Feiffer, this copy signed by Feiffer, inscribed by him. Aleph-bet Books, Inc. 109 - 243 2015 $2500

Association – Fenwick, Louisa

Wordsworth, William 1770-1850 *The Poetical Works of William Wordsworth.* London: Edward Moxon, 1846. 7 volumes, octavo, full 19th century polished calf gilt, near fine set bound by Hayday, warmly inscribed to Louisa Fenwick from her friend, the author. Honey & Wax Booksellers 2 - 17 2015 $16,000

Association – Ferguson

Beaumont, Charles *A Treatise on the Coal Trade.* London: J. Crowder for G. G. J. and J. Robinson, 1789. First edition, 4to., blank final page attached to original rear wrapper, early 19th century half calf over marbled boards, neatly rebacked and lettered, with armorial bookplate of Ferguson of Raith, very good, inscribed by author for William Ferguson Esqr. John Drury Rare Books 2015 - 24872 2015 $1311

Berkeley, George, Bp. of Cloyne 1685-1753 *Bishop Berkeley's Querist Republished with Notes, showing How Many of the Same Questions Still remain to be Asked, Respecting Ireland.* London: T. Bretell for James Ridgway, 1829. First edition thus, 8vo., wanting half title, early 19th century half calf over marbled boards, neatly rebacked and lettered, armorial bookplate of Ferguson of Raith, seemingly rare. John Drury Rare Books 2015 - 24874 2015 $787

Dupin, Charles *Institut Royal der France, Influence des Sciences sur l'Humanite des Peuples. Discours Prononce dans la Seance Publique des Quatre Academies le 24 Avril 1819.* Paris: Firmin Didot, 1819. First separate edition, apparently rare, 8vo., half title and final blank, early 19th century half calf over marbled boards, neatly rebacked and labelled with armorial bookplate of Ferguson of Raith, fine presentation copy inscribed and signed in ink, apparently rare. John Drury Rare Books 2015 - 24467 2015 $787

Edinburgh School of Arts *First Report of the Directors of the School of Arts of Edinburgh for the education of Mechanics in Such Branches of Physical Science as are of Practical Application in their Several Trades.* Edinburgh: printed by George Ramsay and Co., May, 1822. First edition, 8vo., early 19th century half calf over marbled boards, neatly rebacked and labelled, armorial bookplate of Ferguson of Raith, fine. John Drury Rare Books 2015 - 24514 2015 $787

Gilbert, Thomas *A Plan for the Better Relief and Employment of the Poor...* London: G. Wilkie, 1781. First edition, including half title, early 19th century half calf over marbled boards, neatly rebacked and label, armorial bookplate of Ferguson of Raith, fine, large, crisp copy, partially unopened. John Drury Rare Books 2015 - 24432 2015 $1311

A Plan for the Establishing a Working-School for the Maintenance, Education and Employment of Poor Children, Especially Orphans. London: John Ward, 1758. First edition, 4to., margins little dusted in places, printed on heavy paper, early 19th century half calf over marbled boards, neatly rebacked and lettered with armorial bookplate of Ferguson of Raith, very good, rare. John Drury Rare Books 2015 - 24957 2015 $5245

Strickland, George *A Discourse on the Poor Laws of England and Scotland on the state of the Poor of Ireland and On Emigration.* London: James Ridgway, 1827. First edition, 8vo., early 19th century half calf over marbled boards, neatly rebacked and lettered, armorial bookplate of Ferguson of Raith, very good, uncommon. John Drury Rare Books 2015 - 24455 2015 $612

Turner, Samuel *A Letter Addressed to the Right Hon. Robert Peel, &c &c Late Chairman of the Committee of secrecy, Appointed to Consider the state of the Bank of England.* London: printed for the author and sold by J. Asperne and J. M. Richardson and J. Hatchard, 1819. First edition, 8vo., presentation copy inscribed in ink by author for Mr. Ferguson, recent marbled boards, lettered on spine, very good. John Drury Rare Books 2015 - 24484 2015 $612

Worsley, Robert *A Plain Enquiry Into the nature, Values and Operation of Coin and Paper Money.* London: printed for the author, 1811. First edition, 8vo., with half title and postscript, early 19th century half calf over marbled boards, neatly rebacked and labelled, armorial bookplate of Ferguson of Raith, fine, scarce. John Drury Rare Books 2015 - 24461 2015 $787

Association – Ferrers, Washington Sewallis Shirley, 9th Earl

Swendeborg, Emanuel *De Nova Hierosolyma et Ejus Doctrina Coelesti...* London: 1758. First edition, 4to., including final leaf with errata on recto, excellent, crisp copy in contemporary gilt ruled calf, extremenities and joints worn, binding still sound, large impressive armorial bookplate of Washington Sewallis Shirley, 9th Earl Ferrers (1822-1859). John Drury Rare Books 2015 - 25868 2015 $1244

Association – Ffeild, Hendricus

Plato *(Greek text) Omnia Platonis Opera.* Venice: in aedib. Aldi et Andreae Soceri, Sept, 1513. Editio princeps, 2 volumes, large Aldine anchor device on titlepage (volume i) and on verso of last leaf in volume ii, Greek text (apart from Aldus' dedicatory petition, contents and colophon), titlepage slightly soiled and with hole at inner margin repaired, minor stains on fore-edges, few wormholes in blank lower margin of opening leaves of volumes ii, volume, volume i in contemporary English quartered oak boards, resewn with spine uncovered, modern vellum endleaves, volume ii in contemporary German pigskin over wooden boards, blind tooled to panel design filled in with 'laus deo' and rosette stamps, brass catches and clasps, top of spine worn, inner hinge broken, cord intact, good, binding of the first volume of this copy is subject of 2 page report by Nicholas Pickwood (printout accompanies the volume), repairs carried out by James Brockman; first volume with signature of Thomas Colm of Oxford dated 1573, 17th century ownership inscription of Hendricus Ffeild, 19th century bookplate and stamp of King Edward's School, Birmingham, plus bookplate of Kenneth Rapoport, the second volume with early ownership inscriptions of Johannes (or Johann?) Lang of Erfurt and Philippus Kleissenius, few early marginalia, inscription 'de bibliotheca Johannis Langi Erphurdiensis. Blackwell's Rare Books Greek & Latin Classics VI - 82 2015 £75,000

Association – Ffolkes, Martin Brown

Kennedy, John *A Treatise Upon Planting, and the Management of the Hot-House.* York: printed by A. Ward for the author, 1776. First edition, 8vo., full brown leather, corner of prelims slightly stained, outer hinges slightly weak, corners bumped, spine ends very slightly worn, otherwise sound, clean, very good copy, bookplate of "Martin Brown Ffolkes, Bar.". Any Amount of Books 2015 - A47678 2015 £225

Association – Field, George

Bacon, Roger *The Cure of Old Age and Preservation of Youth.* London: for Tho. Flesher and Edward Evets, 1683. First edition in English, 8vo., early 19th century half russia, drab boards, gilt edges, ribbon marker (joints cracked), bookplate of George Field (1777-1854), with occasional pencil notes, from the library of James Stevens Cox (1910-1997). Maggs Bros. Ltd. 1447 - 20 2015 £300

Association – Fillmore, Millard

Tuel, J. E. *The Moral for Authors as Contained in the Autobiography of Eureka.* New York: Stringer & Townsend, 1849. First edition, 8vo., contemporary black quarter calf, marbled paper boards, gilt rules, edges little rubbed, very good, inscribed by author for Hon. Millard Fillmore, President, Washington Oct. 9 1850. The Brick Row Book Shop Miscellany 67 - 76 2015 $875

Association – Findlay, J. N.

Aristoelian Society *Proceedings.* London: Methuen/Compton Press/Aristotelian Society, 1969-1987. First edition, Run from 1969-1987, lacking volumes 72, 75-78, 81, together 13 volumes, most about 300 pages, 8vo., from the library of philosophy professor J. N. Findlay (1903-187), with no sign of his ownership apart from train times written in his hand on front endpaper, all volumes complete and good. Any Amount of Books 2015 - B26238 2015 £175

Association – Fisher, Walter

Schultz, Theodore W. *Economic Crises in World Agriculture.* Ann Arbor: University of Michigan, 1965. First edition, signed and inscribed to noted Illinois Attorney Walter T. Fisher, by author, 8vo., near fine in very good+ dust jacket, with minimal edgewear and scuffs. By the Book, L. C. Special List 10 - 17 2015 $300

Association – Fitzwilliam, Earl

A Short Treatise in Support of National Religion; containing a Slight Comparative Survey of the Roman Catholic and Protestant Institutions. London: printed for J. Tindal, 1791. First edition, 8vo., half title with repaired tear but no loss, bound in late 19th century dark blue half calf, neatly rebacked with original label and gilt lines, entirely uncut, very good, uncut, 19th century armorial bookplate of Earl Fitzwilliam. John Drury Rare Books 2015 - 21584 2015 $787

Association – Flather, John

Wollstonecraft, Mary 1759-1797 *Posthumous Works.* London: J. Johnson, 1798. First edition, bound with errata leaves and half titles in 4 volumes, original boards, new paper spine, pastedowns and spine labels, ownership signature of John Flather, St. Johns coll(ege) Cambridge in each volume, with library stamp on titlepage of each volume and library stamp on verso of each titlepage, nice clean set, scarce.   Second Life Books Inc.   191 - 93   2015 $7500

Association – Fleming, Anne

Greene, Graham   1904-1991   *A Visit to Morin.*   London: Heinemann, 1959. First edition, limited to 250 copies, inscribed by author for Ian Fleming and his wife Anne, corners lightly bumped, else near fine in very good dust jacket with stray pen mark to front panel and some smudges, magnificent association.   B & B Rare Books, Ltd.   234 - 4   2015 $30,000

Association – Fleming, Frances Cotton Anne

Drake, Judith   *An Essay in Defence of the female Sex.* London: for A. Roper and R. Clavel, 1697. Third edition, large 8vo., frontispiece, light waterstaining to lower right corner of second half of work, section cut from top of titlepage (62 x 25mm) removing 'An' from title, contemporary panelled calf, corners and edges slightly chipped, joints cracked, pencil inscription Frances Cotton Anne Fleming Aug 14 1715, H. Hall 18th century red ink stamp, from the library of James Stevens Cox (1910-1997).   Maggs Bros. Ltd.   1447 - 150   2015   £1500

Association – Fleming, Ian Lancaster

Greene, Graham   1904-1991   *A Visit to Morin.*   London: Heinemann, 1959. First edition, limited to 250 copies, inscribed by author for Ian Fleming and his wife Anne, corners lightly bumped, else near fine in very good dust jacket with stray pen mark to front panel and some smudges, magnificent association.   B & B Rare Books, Ltd.   234 - 4   2015 $30,000

Association – Fleming, Oswald Atherton

Sayers, Dorothy L.   *Gaudy Night.*   London: Victor Gollancz, 1935. First edition, very good plus in poor example of scarce dust jacket, jacket is basically in pieces, lacking a significant portion at top and bottom of spine, detached at folds, rare, custom quarter leather clamshell box, inscribed by author to her husband (Oswald Atherton) Mac (Fleming), from the collection of Duke Collier.   Royal Books   36 - 225   2015 $6500

Association – Fletcher, Andrew

Boccaccio, Giovanni   1313-1375   *Amorosa Visione.* (bound with) *Urbano.* Milan: Zanottie Castiglione per Andrea Calvo 10 Feb., 1521. Bologna: Franciscus Plato de Benedictis circa, 1492-1493. First printing of both works, 210 x 133mm., 2 separately published works in one volume; handsome Renaissance intricately decorated blindstamped calf by Claes Van Doermaele, covers with outer frame of medallion and foliate roll, inner frame of long stemmed lilies and scrolling vines, large central panel containing a medallion with three quarter portrait of Holy Roman Emperor of Charles V, binder's small 'CvD' escutcheon stamp below central panel, raised bands, early ink titled paper label, small paper shelf number of private library at foot of spine, unobtrusive repairs to head of front joint, tail of both joints and upper corners, lacking ties, in (slightly worn) linen clamshell box, 16th century ink ownership inscription of Johannes Hoyel, inscription of A(ndrew) Fletcher (of Saltoun), titlepage just slightly soiled, two leaves with minor browning to lower corners, two tiny marginal stains, otherwise fine, fresh copy in very well preserved binding, leather lustrous and blindstamped details remarkably sharp. Phillip J. Pirages   66 - 6   2015 $35,000

Thomas A Kempis   1380-1471   *Opera.*   Paris: Iodocus Badius Ascensius, 1523. Second collected edition, first edition printed in France, 330 x 216mm., lacking final blank, fine contemporary London blindstamped calf, covers tooled in panels, outer frame of a roll of Rennaisance designs including fountain topped by three heads, central panel composed mainly of five vertical rows of foliage and flowers, raised bands, spine very expertly rebacked to style, two original brass clasps and catches with leather thongs (perhaps later but perhaps not), original vellum tabs marking important textual sections, rear board with contemporaneous inscription (perhaps author and title), rear pastedown comprising a portion of a proclamation dealing with beggars and vagabonds, in recent clamshell box backed with calf, titlepage with woodcut device dated 1520 depicting printer's workshop, large and small woodcut initials in text (few artlessly colored), titlepage with signature of Johannes Person above woodcut vignette and of another member of Person family at top of page, (this inscription dated 1566 with purchase details for the volume), also signature of A. Fletcher, inside cover of box and front pastedown with modern morocco bookplate of Michael Sharpe, lower board with small abraded area, other trivial marks and very small wormholes in leather, thongs bit dried and deteriorating, but expertly restored binding entirely solid and blindstamping still quite sharp, titlepage little dust soiled and with small shadow of turn-in glue at bottom, last three gatherings with minor stains along gutter, final gathering with similar stain at fore-edge, short tears and other trivial imperfections in text, generally quite fine internally, text mostly quite clean, especially fresh and unusually bright.   Phillip J. Pirages   66 - 7   2015 $12,500

Association – Fletcher, S.

Zayas Y Sotomayor, Maria De *Nouvelles Amoureuses et Exemplaires.* Paris: G. Quinet, 1680. First complete edition in French, 16mo., printed with woodcut initials and headpieces, bound in contemporary calf with modern rebacking, blank marginal tears to three leaves in volume 1 (without any loss of text), includes stamp of Netherby Library on titlepages, with ownership signature of one of the baronets Graham of Netherby, Cumberland, 2 volumes have ownership signatures 'Su Fletchers Book" and same hand as copied two speeches from tragedy Roland by Quinault, this first complete translation quite rare.   Second Life Books Inc.   191 - 100   2015 $4500

Association – Folbertius, Georgius

Hilary of Poitiers *Divi Hilarii Pictavorum Episcopi Lucubrationes...* Basel: Io. Frobenius, 1523. First edition, folio, 2 volumes, decorative initials and headpieces, contemporary full calf blindstamped on both sides with design of heraldic devices, rebacked (early) with red and gilt spine label, from the library of Allan Heywood Bright (1862-1941), loosely inserted is an ALS from fellow book collector E. Gordon Duff to Bright thanking him for the loan of the book, front board detached, rear joint and head and foot of spine well worn, armorial bookplate of Sir John Leveson Gower of Trentham, worming from titlepage on decreasing from about 60 holes throughout the first volume, few early ink annotations, ownership inscription of G(eorgius) Folberti(us), pencilled note identifies this book's provenance as "Sutherland Library".   Any Amount of Books   2015 - 12863   2015   £800

Association – Foot, Albert

Ingelow, Jean *Mopsa the Fairy.* London: Longmans, Green & Co., 1869. First edition, frontispiece + 7 plates, slight spotting, leading blank torn at upper corner and laid down on verso of leading f.e.p., contemporary half calf, gilt spine, red morocco label, rubbed, signed 'Albert Foot June 1879', extremely scarce first edition.   Jarndyce Antiquarian Booksellers   CCXI - 153 2015   £450

Association – Foot, Jill

The History of the Wars, of His Present Majesty Charles XII King of Sweden... London: printed for A. Bell, T. Varnam & J. Osborn in Lombard Street and W. Taylor & J. Baker in Pater-Noster Row, 1715. 2 small paper shelf labels on spine "no. 995 Bx, 27', inscription for Michael (Foot), former labour leader, from wife Jill, contemporary unlettered panelled calf, raised bands, rubbed with slight loss to head of spine, joints cracked but firm, corners bumped.   Jarndyce Antiquarian Booksellers   CCXI - 9   2015   £350

Association – Foot, Michael

The History of the Wars, of His Present Majesty Charles XII King of Sweden... London: printed for A. Bell, T. Varnam & J. Osborn in Lombard Street and W. Taylor & J. Baker in Pater-Noster Row, 1715. 2 small paper shelf labels on spine "no. 995 Bx, 27', inscription for Michael (Foot), former labour leader, from wife Jill, contemporary unlettered panelled calf, raised bands, rubbed with slight loss to head of spine, joints cracked but firm, corners bumped.   Jarndyce Antiquarian Booksellers   CCXI - 9   2015   £350

Association – Ford, Elizabeth

Humphrey, William *The Last Husband and Other Stories.* New York: William Morrow & Co., 1953. First edition, inscribed by author for Harry and Elizabeth Ford, very good in dust jacket lightly sunned on spine, short closed tear to top edge of front panel.   Buckingham Books   March 2015 - 14989   2015 $375

Association – Ford, Harry

Hollander, John *Blue Wine an Other Poems.* Baltimore: Johns Hopkins University Press, 1979. First edition, corners little bumped, else fine in very slightly spine sunned dust jacket, presentation inscribed by author to his editor Harry (Ford) May 1979.   Between the Covers Rare Books, Inc.   187 - 129   2015 $350

Humphrey, William *The Last Husband and Other Stories.* New York: William Morrow & Co., 1953. First edition, inscribed by author for Harry and Elizabeth Ford, very good in dust jacket lightly sunned on spine, short closed tear to top edge of front panel.   Buckingham Books   March 2015 - 14989   2015 $375

Levine, Philip *Ashes, Poems New & Old.* Port Townsend: Graywolf Press, 1979. First edition, limited to 220 numbered copies, signed by author, 8vo., original cloth, printed spine label, very fine, presentation copy inscribed by author for Harry (Ford) and Kathleen.   James S. Jaffe Rare Books   Modern American Poetry - 181   2015 $1000

Levine, Philip *Selected Poems.* New York: Atheneum, 1984. First edition, 8vo., original black cloth, dust jacket, inscribed by author May 5 '84 for Harry (Ford) & Kathleen, fine.   James S. Jaffe Rare Books   Modern American Poetry - 180   2015 $1000

Levine, Philip *The Simple Truth. Poems.* New York: Knopf, 1994. First edition, 8vo., original cloth, dust jacket, presentation copy from author for Harry Ford (his editor) & Kathleen, as new.   James S. Jaffe Rare Books   Modern American Poetry - 182   2015 $1000

Merrill, James *The Thousand and Second Night.* Athens: Christos Christou Press, 1963. First edition, privately printed for author, one of 20 copies, with 2 vignettes on titlepage and at end of text hand colored by Merrill, out of a total edition of 50 copies, small 8vo., original blue wrappers with printed paper label on front cover, fine, presentation from author for Harry Ford, Merrill's editor.   James S. Jaffe Rare Books   Modern American Poetry - 191   2015 $4500

St. John, David *Terraces of Rain: an Italian Sketchbook Poems.* Santa Fe: Santa Fe Literary Center Books/Recursos, 1991. First edition, paperback original drawings by Antoine Predock, oblong octavo, wrappers, tiny crease on rear wrapper, else fine, inscribed by author for his editor, Harry Ford, additionally laid in is ALS from St. John to Ford.   Between the Covers Rare Books, Inc.   187 - 258   2015 $275

Association – Ford, James

Young, Edward   1683-1765 *The Complaint; or Night-Thoughts on Life, Death & Immortality. Nights I-VI. (bound with) Nights VII-IX.* London: printed for J. Dodsley, 1749. 2 volumes in 1, 8vo., contemporary calf, gilt, spine gilt, red morocco label (rather rubbed, some wear to joints and top of spine), aside from binding wear, in very good condition, early signature of Ann Sanders, later signature of James Ford of Heavitree, dated 1837.   C. R. Johnson   Foxon R-Z - 1186r-z   2015 $230

Association – Ford, Kathleen

Levine, Philip *Ashes, Poems New & Old.* Port Townsend: Graywolf Press, 1979. First edition, limited to 220 numbered copies, signed by author, 8vo., original cloth, printed spine label, very fine, presentation copy inscribed by author for Harry (Ford) and Kathleen.   James S. Jaffe Rare Books   Modern American Poetry - 181   2015 $1000

Levine, Philip *Selected Poems.* New York: Atheneum, 1984. First edition, 8vo., original black cloth, dust jacket, inscribed by author May 5 '84 for Harry (Ford) & Kathleen, fine.   James S. Jaffe Rare Books   Modern American Poetry - 180   2015 $1000

Levine, Philip *The Simple Truth. Poems.* New York: Knopf, 1994. First edition, 8vo., original cloth, dust jacket, presentation copy from author for Harry Ford (his editor) & Kathleen, as new.   James S. Jaffe Rare Books   Modern American Poetry - 182   2015 $1000

Association – Ford, Lady

Ford, St. Clair *Scraps from Indian and Other Journals.* Cheltenham: printed by R. Edwards circa, 1858. (1857), 8vo., headings printed in red, contemporary crushed red morocco, fully gilt, sides with extravagant gilt panelling, spine fully gilt with raised bands, all edges gilt, cream silk doublures, superb but unsigned binding, lettered in gilt "Lady Ford" on upper cover.   John Drury Rare Books   2015 - 25666   2015 $1049

Association – Ford, Ruth

Markopoulos, Gregory J. *Quest for Serenity: Journal of a Filmmaker.* New York: Film-makers' Cinematheque, 1966. First edition, one of 1000 copies (this being no. 93), inscribed by author for actress Ruth Ford, very good in saddle stitched paper wrappers, lightly rubbed, minimal soiling, top right corner creased.   Royal Books   46 - 26   2015 $850

Association – Forrest, Earle

Milner, Joe E. *California Joe Noted Scout and Indian Fighter.* Caldwell: Caxton, 1935. First edition, gilt stamped cloth, 396 pages, photos and portraits, tipped in nearly full page informative presentation in ink from Earle Forrest, laid in is TLS from Forrest to same recipient, near fine in very good dust jacket.   Baade Books of the West   2014 - 2015 $486

Association – Fouquet, Nicolas

Guarini, Battista   1538-1612 *Il Pastor Fido: Tragicomedia Pastorale.* Amsterdam: Lodovico Elzevier, 1640. 92 x 54mm. red morocco, covers gilt with french fillet border enclosing a field seme with rows of alternating ciphers "MM" and an interlaced double Phi used by Nicolas Fouquet (1615-1780), (Olivier 1398, fer 4), separated by an "S" ferme, raised bands, spine gilt compartments with double Phi cipher surrounded by small tools, delicately gilt turn-ins, marbled endpapers, all edges gilt (neat repairs to head and tail of spine), engraved vignette by C. C. Dusend on titlepage, one engraved plate and five full page engraved illustrations (blank on verso except for pagination and signature), front pastedown with part of an engraved armorial bookplate, rear pastedown with "HB" bookplate of Heribert Boeder, 9 blank leaves at end of work with ink notations in French in several hands, front joint cracked but still firm, spine slightly cocked, corners little rubbed, occasional mild foxing, final two quires with faint dampstain to upper corner, still very appealing, generally clean and fresh internally.   Phillip J. Pirages   66 - 27   2015 $2800

Association – Fowler, Mary Blackford

Dow, Arthur Wesley *Composition: a Series of Exercises in Art Structure for the Use of Students and Teachers.* Garden City: Doubleday Page and Co., 1923. Ninth edition, quarto, illustrations, quarter cloth and decorated paper over boards, ownership signature of artist Mary Blackford Fowler, corners rubbed, small tear on spine, else near fine in edgeworn, good dust jacket with several tears and modest chipping at and near crown, scarce in jacket.   Between the Covers Rare Books, Inc.   187 - 81   2015 $250

Association – Fowles, John

Bellow, Saul *Herzog.* London: Weidenfeld & Nicolson, 1964. First British edition, foxing to page edges, very good in very good dust jacket, John Fowles copy with his bookplate.   Ken Lopez, Bookseller   164 - 13   2015 $300

Association – Fox, Francis Frederick

The Bridgewater Treatises: on the Power, Wisdom and Goodness of God as Manifested in the Creation. London: William Pickering, 1833-1839. London: John Murray 1838. Mixed set, Treatises I-IX in 13 volumes, 8vo., all plates and engravings present, occasional light foxing to first and last few pages, contemporary half black calf over marbled paper backed boards, gilt stamped spines and brown leather spine labels, extremities rubbed, some spine labels missing, corners showing, armorial bookplates of Francis Frederick Fox, signature of John Usborne (volume II), very good.   Jeff Weber Rare Books   178 - 779   2015 $1850

Association – Foxcroft, Thomas Hammond

Weston, Charles *Remarks on the Poor Laws and on the State of the Poor.* Brentford: printed by P. Norbury sold by Payne and Mackinlay London and J. Martin Kensington, 1802. First edition, 8vo., contemporary half calf over marbled boards, rebacked spine lettered gilt, very good, 19th century armorial bookplate of Thomas Hammond Foxcroft with his signature, rare.   John Drury Rare Books   2015 - 22656   2015 $656

Association – Foxwell, Herbert Somerton

La Roche De Maine, Jean Pierre Louis De, Marquis *Essai sur la Secte des Illumines.* Paris: 1789. First edition, variant issue, 8vo., old library blindstamped on few leaves (not title), contemporary calf backed marbled boards, some wear to sides but good copy, sometime neatly rebacked, formerly in the library of Herbert Somerton Foxwell (1849-1936) with his initialled note of purchase Dec. 1892 and initialled confirmation of authorship.   John Drury Rare Books   2015 - 17953   2015 $612

Association – Foyle, William

Chaucer, Geoffrey   1340-1400 *The Workes of Geffrey Chaucer.* London: imprinted by Jhon Kyngston for Jhon Wight, 1561. First collected edition, first issue, 22 woodcuts in The Prologues, folio, title within woodcut border, 22 woodcuts of Pilgrims in "The Prologues" and woodcut of knight on horse at head of "The Knightes Tale", large and small historiated and decorative initials and other ornaments, Black letter, fifty-six lines, double columns; late 19th century crimson morocco by Riviere, covers with gilt fillet and roll tool border enclosing central olive wreath and elaborate cornerpieces composed of scroll-work and spreading olive branches, remaining field seme with cinquefoils, spine in 7 compartments with six raised bands, lettered gilt in two compartments, rest decoratively tooled gilt with repeated olive leaf motif, board edges and turn-ins decoratively tooled in gilt, all edges gilt, marbled endpapers (pastedowns with decorative gilt tooling), title creased and lightly soiled, small repair to outer blank margin, lower corner of second leaf renewed, affecting catchword on recto and two letters on verso, closed tear through lower half of divisional title to "The Caunterburie Tales", closed tear to A2 of "The Prologues" affecting 8 lines of text to first column and another closed tear at lower margin, F2 with small paper repair to margin and closed tear just touching text, 2U2 with paper fault affecting one word in bottom line of text on recto and verso, few additional small marginal tears or repairs not affecting text, occasional early ink underlining and markings, early signature of James Rea (faded) on title, wonderful copy, from the libraries of C. W. Dyson Perrins and William Foyle, with bookplates.   Heritage Book Shop   Holiday 2014 - 36   2015 $65,000

Association – Francis, P.

Thucydides *Bellum Peloponnesiacum.* Glasgow: in aedibus Academicis excudebant Robertus et Andreas Foulis, 1759. First Foulis edition, variant issue with Latin text at end, 5 of 8 blank leaves discarded, two gatherings in volume iii swopped, some light browning and occasional spotting, small ownership inscription of P. Francis in volume i, some light browning an occasional ownership inscription.   Blackwell's Rare Books   B179 - 106   2015   £1800

Association – Frank, Waldo

Williams, William Carlos   1883-1963 *Al Que Quiere! A Book of Poems.* Boston: Four Seas Co., 1917. First edition, one of 1000 copies, small 8vo., original buff printed boards, slightly rubbed, else fine, not commonly found signed, inscribed to Waldo Frank by the poet in May 1919.   James S. Jaffe Rare Books   Modern American Poetry - 307   2015 $7500

Association – Frankenberg, Lloyd

Bishop, Elizabeth *Poem.* New York: Phoenix Book Shop, 1973. First edition, one of author's copies from the lettered issue, copy "L" (presumably chosen for Loren) of 26 lettered copies from a total edition of 126, signed by author, this copy with presentation from author for Loren MacIver & Lloyd Frankenberg, housed in custom green cloth clamshell box with black morocco spine label, superb association copy.   James S. Jaffe Rare Books   Modern American Poetry - 41   2015 $10,000

Association – Frankfurter, Felix

Phillips, Harlan B. *Felix Frankfurter Reminiscences.* New York: Reynal, 1960. First edition, 8vo., very good++ with edge spotting, owner bookplate in very good+ supplied dust jacket with mild soil, edgewear, inscribed in year of publication by Frankfurter for Leonard Miall.   By the Book, L. C.   44 - 59   2015 $750

Association – Fredericks, Claude

Spender, Stephen *Returning to Vienna 1947: Nine Sketches.* New York: Banyan Press, 1947. First edition, one of 350 numbered copies for sale (out of total edition of 500), tied decorated paper wrappers with printed label, small nicks and splitting along spine, otherwise handsome, very good copy, signed by author, Carl van Vechten's copy with his bookplate, inscribed by him to Milton Saul and Claude Fredericks, publishers at Banyan Press.   Between the Covers Rare Books, Inc.   187 - 266   2015 $250

Association – Freedman, Ida

Wilder, Thornton   1897-1976 *The Bridge of San Luis Ray.* New York: Albert & Charles Boni, 1927. First American edition, signed and inscribed by author to Ida Freedman, octavo, original cloth, original dust jacket, text block with few splits (as often) but holding, cloth clean, rare jacket with few small chips to head of spine and light spine toning, overall extraordinary copy.   Manhattan Rare Book Company   Literature 2014 - 2015 $5000

Association – Freeling, Frances

Cartwright, William *Comedies, Tragi-Comedies with other Poems.* London: for Humphrey Mosely, 1651. First edition, 8vo., engraved portrait by Lombart (small rust hole at foot of image repaired), G8v stained, otherwise occasional small stains, early 19th century calf, covers ruled in gilt, gilt spine, armorial bookplate of Sir Frances Freeling, 1st Bart. 1764-1836, 19th century armorial bookplate of Francis Darby, from the library of James Stevens Cox (1910-1997). Maggs Bros. Ltd.   1447 - 68   2015   £600

Association – Freeman, Joseph

Nearing, Scott *Dollar Diplomacy.* New York: B. W. Huebsch and the Viking Press, 1925. First edition, near fine, lacking rare dust jacket, attractive octagonal bookplate, small numeric ink notation to same, at top left corner, inscribed by co-author Joseph Freeman to Rex Stout and his wife Fay, from the collection of Duke Collier.   Royal Books   36 - 125   2015 $1500

Association – Frere, Alexander

Greene, Graham   1904-1991 *Our Man in Havana.* London: William Heinemann, 1958. First edition, inscribed by Greene to Alexander Frere (chairman of Heinemann), fine and unread in fine dust jacket, from the collection of Duke Collier.   Royal Books   36 - 1   2015 $5500

Association – Frink, Elisabeth

Willder, Jim *Elisabeth Frink: Sculpture: Catalogue Raisonne.* Salisbury: Harpvale, 1984. First edition, 4to., copiously illustrated in color and black and white, signed presentation from artist, fine in fine dust jacket in slipcase. Any Amount of Books   2015 - C15536   2015   £175

Association – Frost, Barbara

Kerouac, Jack   1922-1969 *Doctor Sax.* New York: Grove Press, 1959. First edition, first printing, original paper wrappers issued simultaneously with hardcover format, presentation copy signed and inscribed by author to NY Expressionist artist and close friend, Barbara Frost, very good or better copy, lightly soiled and rubbed, housed in custom quarter leather folding box.   B & B Rare Books, Ltd.   234 - 62   2015 $9500

Association – Frost, John W. P.

Bellamy, Edward *Looking Backward 2000-1887.* Boston and New York: Houghton Mifflin, 1889. First edition, later printing, with "One Hundred and Second Thousand" on titlepage, 8vo., original brown cloth, gilt lettering, top edge of upper board and first few signatures bumped, fine, signed "With compliments of / Edward Bellamy", heraldic bookplate with names John Haley Bellamy and John W. P. Frost typed in lower margin.   The Brick Row Book Shop   Miscellany 67 - 24   2015 $500

Association – Froud, James

Howard, John *An Account of the Principal Lazarettos in Europe: with Various Papers Relative to the Plague...* Warrington: printed by William Eyres and sold by T. Cadeel, J. Johnson, C. Dilly and J. Taylor in Londonn, 1789. First edition, 4to., 22 engraved plates (of which 20 are folding), one very large engraved folding table, including half title, some marginal browning, original (probably) marbled boards with original (probably) printed spine label, entirely uncut, minor binding wear, excellent presentation copy, inscribed by author "Mr. Howard requests Mr. Sampson will be kind enough to accept this book from him, as a small mark of his esteem" with Margaret Sampson's ownership signature, later ownership signature of James Froud 1834 on titlepage, in all choice copy, largely in original state. John Drury Rare Books 2015 - 25837 2015 $2622

Association – Fryer, Gavin

Aldington, Richard *Love and the Luxembourg.* New York: Covici Friede, 1930. First edition, one of 475 numbered copies signed by author and designer, Frederic Warde, title vignette printed in green, original red cloth gilt, top edge gilt, others uncut, spine trifle dulled, very nice in marked and somewhat worn slipcase, from the collection of Gavin H. Fryer. Bertram Rota Ltd. 308 Part II - 124 2015 £30

Aldington, Richard *Soft Answers: Stories.* London: Chatto & Windus, 1932. First edition, cloth little marked and bumped, spine faded, otherwise nice, inscription on front free endpaper and bookseller's small label on front pastedown, from the collection of Gavin H. Fryer. Bertram Rota Ltd. 308 Part II - 125 2015 £20

Arnold, Matthew 1822-1888 *The Strayed Reveller and Other Poems.* London: B. Fellowes, 1849. First edition, original green blindstamped cloth, spine lettered gilt, half title, cloth little marked and rubbed, else very nice, armorial bookplate of R. E. Bartlett, scarce, from the collection of Gavin H. Fryer. Bertram Rota Ltd. 308 Part II - 126 2015 £500

Bridges, Robert 1844-1930 *Poems.* London: Basil Montagu Pickering, 1873. First edition, original blue cloth, uncut, spine with printed label (rubbed), cloth somewhat soiled, endpapers severely browned as always, otherwise nice, Logan Pearsall's copy, with his ownership signature, from the collection of Gavin H. Fryer. Bertram Rota Ltd. 308 Part II - 127 2015 £280

Compton-Burnett, Ivy 1892-1962 *Brothers and Sisters.* Heath Cranton Ltd., 1929. First edition, sides little marked, spine creased and somewhat faded, little worn at head and foot, just little foxing to bottom edge, nevertheless nice copy, ownership signature, scarce, from the collection of Gavin H. Fryer. Bertram Rota Ltd. 308 Part II - 129 2015 £60

Compton-Burnett, Ivy 1892-1962 *Dolores.* Edinburgh and London: William Blackwood and Sons, 1911. First edition, original blue cloth lettered gilt and decorated in black, spine very slightly darkened and worn, covers just little marked, but very nice, bright copy, in specially made book-form box with printed label gilt, from the collection of Gavin H. Fryer. Bertram Rota Ltd. 308 Part II - 128 2015 £650

Conrad, Joseph 1857-1924 *A Set of Six.* London: Methuen & Co., 1908. First edition, domestic issue, published state with corrected text verso half title and publisher's ads dated June 1908, original dark blue cloth lettered and decorated gilt and dark red, spine little faded, covers slightly marked, very nice, from the collection of Gavin H. Fryer. Bertram Rota Ltd. 308 Part II - 139 2015 £250

Conrad, Joseph 1857-1924 *Almayer's Folly.* London: T. Fisher Unwin, 1895. First edition, with page 110 in first state with dropped 'e' and 'of', original dark green cloth, spine gilt, top edge gilt, others uncut, upper hinge partly cracked and just little foxing and light bumping to corners, otherwise exceptionally nice, bright in slightly worn book-form folding box, spine lettered gilt to match book, rare first book, from the collection of Gavin H. Fryer. Bertram Rota Ltd. 308 Part II - 130 2015 £2500

Conrad, Joseph 1857-1924 *An Outcast of the Islands.* London: T. Fisher Unwin, 1896. First edition, first issue with errors uncorrected, with very good copy of the Eveleigh Nash and Grayson reprint of 1922, original dark green cloth, spine gilt, top edge gilt, others uncut, corners bumped and spine little cocked, sides just little marked, free endpapers slightly browned, else very nice, from the collection of Gavin H. Fryer. Bertram Rota Ltd. 308 Part II - 131 2015 £1500

Conrad, Joseph 1857-1924 *Chance: a Tale in Two Parts.* London: Methuen & Co., 1914. First impression, domestic issue, published state, state with cancel title dated 1914, with 'METHUEN" binding and missing the second quotes around "Narcissus" in list of books facing titlepage, original dark green cloth, gilt, binding just little faded, very nice, from the collection of Gavin H. Fryer. Bertram Rota Ltd. 308 Part II - 141 2015 £300

Conrad, Joseph 1857-1924 *Falk: Amy Foster; To-Morrow; Three Stories.* New York: McClure, Phillips & Co., 1903. First edition, original dark blue blindstamped cloth, gilt, bookplate removed to half title and somewhat unsightly inscription, cloth very lightly rubbed, otherwise very nice, particularly bright, from the collection of Gavin H. Fryer. Bertram Rota Ltd. 308 Part II - 135 2015 £250

ASSOCIATION COPIES

Conrad, Joseph 1857-1924 *Nostromo; a Tale of the Seaboard.* London: and New York: Harper Bros., 1904. First edition, page 187 misnumbered, original dark blue cloth lettered and decorated in light blue and gilt, corners trifle rubbed and sides little marked, else very nice, scarce, from the collection of Gavin H. Fryer.   Bertram Rota Ltd.   308 Part II - 137   2015   £700

Conrad, Joseph 1857-1924 *Notes by Joseph Conrad Written in a Set of His First Editions in the Possession of Richard Curle....* London: privately printed, 1925. First edition, one of 100 numbered copies signed by Richard Curle, original cloth, top edge gilt, others uncut, paper spine label little rubbed and browned, book-label remove from front pastedown to free endpaper, else very nice, from the collection of Gavin H. Fryer.   Bertram Rota Ltd.   308 Part II - 145   2015   £225

Conrad, Joseph 1857-1924 *Tales of Unrest.* London: T. Fisher Unwin, 1898. First English edition, first issue, original dark green cloth, spine gilt, top edge gilt (some copies have top edge plain), others uncut, ads at end, cloth just little marked and bumped and some slight foxing, else very nice, bright copy, from the collection of Gavin H. Fryer. Bertram Rota Ltd.   308 Part II - 132   2015   £850

Conrad, Joseph 1857-1924 *The Mirror of the Sea.* London: Methuen & Co., 1906. First edition, original green cloth, spine and top edge gilt, others uncut, 40 pages ads dated August 1906, extremities little bumped, otherwise very nice, bright cop, from the collection of Gavin H. Fryer. Bertram Rota Ltd.   308 Part II - 138   2015   £500

Conrad, Joseph 1857-1924 *The Shadow-Line: a Confession.* London: J. M. Dent & Sons Ltd., 1917. First edition, original green cloth, lettered and decorated in gilt and black, gilt lettering to spine little dull and light foxing to endpapers, but very nice, this copy on laid paper, from the collection of Gavin H. Fryer.   Bertram Rota Ltd.   308 Part II - 144   2015   £350

Conrad, Joseph 1857-1924 *Typhoon and Other Stories.* London: William Heinemann, 1903. First English edition, first binding, original grey cloth gilt, ad leaf beginning and 32 pages at end, corners bumped and light browning to endpaper, otherwise very nice, from the collection of Gavin H. Fryer.   Bertram Rota Ltd.   308 Part II - 136   2015   £500

Conrad, Joseph 1857-1924 *Under Western Eyes.* London: Methuen & Co., 1911. First edition, original red cloth, spine gilt, spine touch faded and with minor damage at foot, sides little marked, endpapers browned and little foxing, otherwise very nice, from the collection of Gavin H. Fryer.   Bertram Rota Ltd.   308 Part II - 139   2015   £250

Conrad, Joseph 1857-1924 *Victory; an Island Tale.* London: Methuen & Co., 1915. First English edition, original red cloth, spine gilt, spine little faded and upper cover marked, prelims foxed, but nice, ownership inscription, from the collection of Gavin H. Fryer.   Bertram Rota Ltd.   308 Part II - 142   2015   £150

Conrad, Joseph 1857-1924 *Within the Tides.* London: J. M. Dent & Sons, 1915. First edition, original green cloth, spine gilt, sides faded as usual, spine bright and fresh, browning to free endpapers and little foxing, but very nice in dust jacket, professionally restored at hinges and little browned at spine panel, from the collection of Gavin H. Fryer.   Bertram Rota Ltd.   308 Part II - 143   2015 £1750

Conrad, Joseph 1857-1924 *Youth: a Narrative and Two Other Stories.* Edinburgh and London: William Blackwood and Sons, 1902. First edition, publisher's catalog at end dated "11/02 ("10/02" first state), original green cloth lettered and decorated black and gilt, spine little dulled, damage to head and foot, minor tears to margin of final ad leaf, corners little rubbed, hinges cracked and endpapers little foxed, still nice, ownership inscription, from the collection of Gavin H. Fryer.   Bertram Rota Ltd.   308 Part II - 133   2015 £1200

Conrad, Joseph 1857-1924 *Youth: a Narrative and two other stories.* London: J. M. Dent & Sons Ltd., 1917. Second English edition, original green cloth lettered and decorated in gilt and black, corners bumped and gilt lettering to spine somewhat dulled, sides very slightly marked and light browning to free endpapers, else very nice, inscription and ownership stamp, bookseller's small label, from the collection of Gavin H. Fryer.   Bertram Rota Ltd.   308 Part II - 134   2015   £250

Crane, Stephen 1871-1900 *The Black Riders and Other Lines.* Boston: Copeland and Day, 1895. First edition, small 8vo., original boards printed in black with floral design, exceptional copy, in specially made cloth dust jacket and slipcase, spine lettered gilt, from the collection of Gavin H. Fryer.   Bertram Rota Ltd.   308 Part II - 146   2015   £700

De La Mare, Walter 1873-1956 *Songs of Childhood.* London: Longmans, Green and Co., 1902. First edition, frontispiece by Richard Doyle, original quarter parchment, spine lettered and decorated gilt, gilt ruled pale blue linen sides with gilt publisher's device stamped on upper cover, top edge gilt, spine little rubbed and browned, sides slightly soiled and light spotting to endpapers, label removed from front pastedown, otherwise nice in worn and partly defective slipcase, bookplate, scarce, from the collection of Gavin H. Fryer.   Bertram Rota Ltd.   308 Part II - 148   2015   £400

Dickens, Charles 1812-1870 *Bleak House.* London: Bradbury and Evans, 1853. First edition with all points and date in Roman numerals at foot of spine, original olive blindstamped cloth, rebacked with new endpapers preserving original spine gilt, spine somewhat browned, some soiling to cloth, one plate oddly trimmed, only affecting blank margin and plates, some foxing, but nice, from the collection of Gavin H. Fryer. Bertram Rota Ltd. 308 Part II - 149 2015 £850

Graham, Robert Bontine Cunninghame 1852-1936 *Economic Evolution.* Aberdeen: James Leatham and London: William Reeves, 1891. First edition, 16mo., original grey wrappers, ad leaf at end, upper wrapper with small brown mark, some foxing, nice, fragile, rare, from the collection of Gavin H. Fryer. Bertram Rota Ltd. 308 Part II - 147 2015 £250

Kipling, John Lockwood *Beast and Man in India...* London: Macmillan and Co., 1891. First edition, illustrations, later red half morocco gilt by Bayntun, spine in compartments with raised bands and animal decorations gilt, top edge gilt, upper cover with one small area sunned, some foxing, but nice, from the collection of Gavin H. Fryer. Bertram Rota Ltd. 308 Part II - 152 2015 £200

Kipling, John Lockwood *Beast and Man in India...* London: Macmillan and Co., 1891. First edition, original reddish brown cloth lettered gilt and decorated in gilt and black, little bubbling to lower cover and small light stains to upper cover, little foxing, but nice, inscription by Neillie and/or Ernst Henrici, from the collection of Gavin H. Fryer. Bertram Rota Ltd. 308 Part II - 150 2015 £200

Longfellow, Henry Wadsworth 1807-1882 *The Song of Hiawatha.* London: David Bogue, 1855. First edition, first issue, with 'dove' for 'dived' on page 96 line 7; original green cloth, blindstamped sides, spine lettered and decorated in gilt, 24 pages ads at end dated March 1855, sides little marked and slight wear at head and foot of spine, nice, poet Kenneth Hopkins' copy with his ownership signature, bibliographical notes in ink on front pastedown and another ownership signature on titlepage, from the collection of Gavin H. Fryer. Bertram Rota Ltd. 308 Part II - 154 2015 £450

MacKenzie, Compton *A Musical Chair.* London: Chatto & Windus, 1939. First edition, original binding, little foxing to prelims and fore-edge, otherwise very nice in foxed and frayed dust jacket which is little browned at spine panel, scarce, from the collection of Gavin H. Fryer. Bertram Rota Ltd. 308 Part II - 171 2015 £40

MacKenzie, Compton *April Fools: a Farce of Summer.* London: Cassell and Co., 1930. First edition, original binding, spine sunned and sides little marked, foxing to fore-edge, else nice, from the collection of Gavin H. Fryer. Bertram Rota Ltd. 308 Part II - 165 2015 £20

MacKenzie, Compton *Ben Nevis Goes East.* London: Chatto & Windus, 1954. First edition, original binding, very nice in slightly chipped, creased and marked but still bright dust jacket, inscribed in red ink, from the collection of Gavin H. Fryer. Bertram Rota Ltd. 308 Part II - 175 2015 £35

MacKenzie, Compton *Buttercups and Daisies.* London: Cassell, 1931. First edition, original binding, spine just little discolored and bumped at head, some foxing to first and last few leaves and fore-edge, but nice, from the collection of Gavin H. Fryer. Bertram Rota Ltd. 308 Part II - 166 2015 £35

MacKenzie, Compton *Coral: a Sequel to 'Carnival'.* New York: George H. Doran Co., 1925. First American edition, original cloth, very good, from the collection of Gavin H. Fryer. Bertram Rota Ltd. 308 Part II - 160 2015 £20

MacKenzie, Compton *Extraordianry Women.* London: Martin Secker, 1928. First edition, of an edition of 2000, this one of 100 special numbered copies signed by author, original binding little cocked and some wear at edges, little foxing to endpapers and prelims, otherwise nice, somewhat soiled and frayed dust jacket little browned at spine panel, from the collection of Gavin H. Fryer. Bertram Rota Ltd. 308 Part II - 162 2015 £100

MacKenzie, Compton *Extraordinary Women.* London: Martin Secker, 1928. First edition, of an edition of 2000, this one of 100 special numbered copies, signed by author, original binding, some wear at edges and foxing to endpapers and prelims, otherwis nice, from the collection of Gavin H. Fryer. Bertram Rota Ltd. 308 Part II - 163 2015 £30

MacKenzie, Compton *Extremes Meet.* London: Cassell and Co., 1928. First edition, 8vo., original binding, corners bumped and just little foxing, mostly at fore-edge, but nice, from the collection of Gavin H. Fryer. Bertram Rota Ltd. 308 Part II - 164 2015 £20

MacKenzie, Compton *Fairy Gold.* London: Cassell & Co., 1926. First edition, very good, inscriptions, original binding, from the collection of Gavin H. Fryer. Bertram Rota Ltd. 308 Part II - 161 2015 £20

MacKenzie, Compton *Figure of Eight.* London: Cassell and Co., 1936. First edition, original binding, spine creased and small mark, endpapers and prelims foxed, nice, from the collection of Gavin H. Fryer. Bertram Rota Ltd. 308 Part II - 169 2015 £40

MacKenzie, Compton *Mezzotint.* London: Chatto & Windus, 1961. Advance proof copy, wrappers, just little wear to wrappers, upper portion of half title/contents page cut away, else nice, from the collection of Gavin H. Fryer. Bertram Rota Ltd.   308 Part II - 179   2015   £30

MacKenzie, Compton *Monarch of the Glen.* London: Chatto & Windus, 1941. First edition, original binding, endpapers little foxed, otherwise nice in slightly chipped little browned at spine panel, loosely inserted small embossed card inscribed by author, once held in place with paperclip which has left rust mark to card and dust jacket and indentation and mark to first few leaves, from the collection of Gavin H. Fryer.   Bertram Rota Ltd.   308 Part II - 172   2015   £180

MacKenzie, Compton *My Life and Times, Octave One.* London: Chatto & Windus, 1963. First edition, frontispiece, plates, original binding, very nice in dust jacket, from the collection of Gavin H. Fryer.   Bertram Rota Ltd.   308 Part II - 180   2015   £25

MacKenzie, Compton *Our Street.* London: Cassell and Co., 1931. Original binding, spine just little faded, endpapers slightly browned, rear free endpaper with small stain, label partly removed from front free endpaper, nice, bright copy, from the collection of Gavin H. Fryer, illustrations by Magdalen Fraser.   Bertram Rota Ltd.   308 Part II - 167   2015   £20

MacKenzie, Compton *Paper Lives: a Novel.* London: Chatto & Windus, 1966. First edition, original binding, fine in fine, bright dust jacket, from the collection of Gavin H. Fryer.   Bertram Rota Ltd.   308 Part II - 182   2015   £40

MacKenzie, Compton *Poems.* Oxford and London: B. H. Blackwell and Simpkin Marshall, Hamilton, Kent & Co., 1907. First edition, original grey printed wrappers, uncut, preserved in specially made chemise and blue quarter morocco bookform box, spine lettered gilt, wrappers little worn and soiled some chipping to edges, otherwise very nice, presentation copy inscribed by author for Elaise Tresent? and dated Aug. 1910, scarce, fragile first book, from the collection of Gavin H. Fryer.   Bertram Rota Ltd. 308 Part II - 155   2015   £250

MacKenzie, Compton *Rich Relatives.* New York and London: Harper & Bros., 1921. First American edition, original cloth, very good, from the collection of Gavin H. Fryer. Bertram Rota Ltd.   308 Part II - 158   2015   £20

MacKenzie, Compton *Rockets Galore.* London: Chatto & Windus, 1957. First edition, original binding, free endpapers browned and rather heavy foxing at fore edge, otherwise nice, nicked and partly foxed dust jacket, from the collection of Gavin H. Fryer.   Bertram Rota Ltd.   308 Part II - 177   2015   £30

MacKenzie, Compton *Sublime Tobacco.* London: Chatto & Windus, 1957. First edition, original binding, endpapers just little browned, very nice in price clipped dust jacket, showing some tears and ear and one crude repair with adhesive tape, from the collection of Gavin H. Fryer. Bertram Rota Ltd.   308 Part II - 178   2015   £30

MacKenzie, Compton *Sylvia & Michael: the Later Adventures of Sylvia Scarlett.* London: Martin Secker, 1919. First edition, original cloth, very good only, ownership inscription, from the collection of Gavin H. Fryer.   Bertram Rota Ltd.   308 Part II - 157   2015   £20

MacKenzie, Compton *The Early Life and Adventures of Sylvia Scarlett.* London: Martin Secker, 1918. First edition, original cloth binding little marked and worn, but very good, partly unopened, bookseller's small label, presentation copy inscribed by author for Doris Compton MacKenzie Oct. 13 32, from the collection of Gavin H. Fryer.   Bertram Rota Ltd.   308 Part II - 156   2015   £120

MacKenzie, Compton *The Seven Ages of Woman.* London: Martin Secker, 1923. First edition, original cloth, fading spine and sides, endpapers browned and hinges, cracked, very good, ownership signature, from the collection of Gavin H. Fryer.   Bertram Rota Ltd.   308 Part II - 159 2015   £20

MacKenzie, Compton *The Windsor Tapestry, Being a Study of the Life, Heritage and Abdication of H.R.H. the Duke of Windsor, K. G.* London: Rich & Cowan, 1938. First edition, original binding, corners bumped and some sunning to cloth as often, little spotting at fore edge, nice, from the collection of Gavin H. Fryer.   Bertram Rota Ltd. 308 Part II - 170   2015   £30

MacKenzie, Compton *Thin Ice.* London: Chatto & Windus, 1956. First edition, original binding, very nice in very slightly nicked and marked dust jacket, from the collection of Gavin H. Fryer.   Bertram Rota Ltd.   308 Part II - 176   2015   £50

MacKenzie, Compton *Whiskey Galore.* London: Chatto & Windus, 1947. First edition, original binding, just little browning to endpapers, else very nice in chipped dust jacket, from the collection of Gavin H. Fryer.   Bertram Rota Ltd. 308 Part II - 174   2015   £60

MacKenzie, Compton *Wind of Freedom: the History of the Invasion of Greece...* London: Chatto & Windus, 1943. First edition, original binding, spine tad faded, otherwise very nice in slightly stained and nicked dust jacket, from the collection of Gavin H. Fryer.   Bertram Rota Ltd.   308 Part II - 173   2015   £30

MacKenzie, Faith Compton *The Cardinal's Niece: the Story of Marie Mancini.* London: Martin Secker, 1935. First edition, frontispiece, plates, original binding somewhat marked and spine discolored, but very good, presentation copy inscribed by author for Joy Skinner, from the collection of Gavin H. Fryer.   Bertram Rota Ltd.   308 Part II - 183   2015   £60

O'Casey, Sean *The Story of the Irish Citizen Army.* Dublin and London: Maunsel & Co. Ltd., 1919. First edition, original printed wrappers little creased and slightly browned at edges, head of backstrip chipped and upper hinge professionaly repaired, else nice, from the collection of Gavin H. Fryer.   Bertram Rota Ltd.   308 Part II - 184   2015   £225

O'Connor, Frank   1903-1966 *Guests of the Nation: Stories.* London: Macmillan & Co. Ltd., 1931. First edition, original binding, covers faded and marked, endpapers somewhat browned, very good, publisher's review slip tipped in and loosely inserted, V. S. Pritchett's copy, inscribed by him, from the collection of Gavin H. Fryer.   Bertram Rota Ltd.   308 Part II - 185   2015   £120

Pritchett, V. S. *A Cab at the Door and Midnight Oil.* Harmondsworth: Penguin Books, 1979. First paperback one volume edition, wrappers marked and lower two thirds of titlepage excised, else good, from author's library with posthumous VSP booklabel, from the collection of Gavin H. Fryer.   Bertram Rota Ltd.   308 Part II - 218   2015   £30

Pritchett, V. S. *A Cab at the Door: an Autobiography: Early Years.* London: Chatto & Windus, 1968. First edition, original binding, little fading at edges, else very nice in slightly browned and frayed dust jacket, from author's library with posthumous VSP booklabel, from the collection of Gavin H. Fryer.   Bertram Rota Ltd.   308 Part II - 209   2015   £50

Pritchett, V. S. *A Careless Widow & Other Stories.* London: Chatto & Windus, 1989. First edition, fine in dust jacket, original binding, bookplate of J. E. Davies, inscribed by author on bookplate, with autograph card signed tipped-in agreeing to inscribe it and commenting on the dust jacket and further initialled by him "A Happy Christmas" on slip of paper mounted beneath bookplate, from the collection of Gavin H. Fryer.   Bertram Rota Ltd.   308 Part II - 226   2015   £120

Pritchett, V. S. *Balzac.* London: Chatto & Windus, 1973. First edition, 4to., profusely illustrated in color and black and white, original binding, fine in dust jacket, dedication copy, inscribed by author for wife Dorothy, inscribed " I am so proud to have worked with Mr. Pritchett on this book. Joy Law', from author's library with posthumous VSP booklabel, from the collection of Gavin H. Fryer.   Bertram Rota Ltd.   308 Part II - 213   2015   £160

Pritchett, V. S. *Blind Love and Other Stories.* London: Chatto & Windus, 1969. First edition, original binding, very nice in slightly browned and frayed dust jacket, from author's library with posthumous VSP booklabel, from the collection of Gavin H. Fryer.   Bertram Rota Ltd.   308 Part II - 210   2015   £50

Pritchett, V. S. *Chekhov: a Spirit Set Free.* London: Hodder & Stoughton, 1988. First English edition, original binding, slightly browned, otherwise very nice in dust jacket, from author's library with posthumous VSP booklabel, from the collection of Gavin H. Fryer.   Bertram Rota Ltd.   308 Part II - 225   2015   £40

Pritchett, V. S. *Christmas with the Cratchits: a Sketch.* Berkeley: Ruth and James D. Hart, Hart Press, 1964. First edition, illustrations by Victor Anderson, wrappers somewhat faded and soiled, internally nice, from author's library with posthumous VSP booklabel from the collection of Gavin H. Fryer.   Bertram Rota Ltd.   308 Part II - 201   2015   £50

Pritchett, V. S. *Collected Stories.* London: Chatto & Windus, 1956. First edition, original binding, head and foot of spine little worn and covers slightly spotted, otherwise nice, author's copy with his autograph signature on front free endpaper and his inscription, with posthumous VSP booklabel, from the collection of Gavin H. Fryer.   Bertram Rota Ltd.   308 Part II - 195   2015   £50

Pritchett, V. S. *Collected Stories.* London: Chatto & Windus, 1982. First edition of this collection, original binding, foot of spine and covers darkened and stained, otherwise very good in creased and soiled dust jacket, signed by author on titlepage, from author's library with posthumous VSP booklabel, from the collection of Gavin H. Fryer.   Bertram Rota Ltd.   308 Part II - 223   2015   £40

Pritchett, V. S. *Dead Man Leading.* London: Oxford University Press, 1984. First edition with this introduction by Paul Theroux, wrappers, somewhat browned throughout and some leaves loose, otherwise nice, dedication copy, inscribed by author for wife Dorothy, from author's library with posthumous VSP booklabel, from the collection of Gavin H. Fryer.   Bertram Rota Ltd.   308 Part II - 224   2015   £100

Pritchett, V. S. *Dublin: a Portrait.* London: Bodley Head, 1947. First edition, 4to., original binding, fine in creased and torn dust jacket with piece missing, photos in color and black and white by Evelyn Hofer, presentation copy inscribed by author to his wife, Dorothy, with posthumous VSP booklabel, from the collection of Gavin H. Fryer. Bertram Rota Ltd.   308 Part II - 192   2015   £140

Pritchett, V. S. *Foreign Faces.* London: Chatto & Windus, 1964. First edition, original binding, fine in slightly soiled dust jacket, from author's library with posthumous VSP booklabel, from the collection of Gavin H. Fryer.   Bertram Rota Ltd.   308 Part II - 202   2015   £40

Pritchett, V. S. *George Meredith and English Comedy: The Clark Lectures for 1969.* New York: Random House, 1969. First American edition, original binding, fine in dust jacket, from author's library with posthumous VSP bookalbel, from the collection of Gavin H. Fryer.   Bertram Rota Ltd.   308 Part II - 211   2015   £50

Pritchett, V. S. *In My Good Books.* London: Chatto & Windus, 1942. First edition, original binding, spine and covers somewhat marked and worn, hinges weak, otherwise very good, dedication copy inscribed to author's wife, with posthumous VSP booklabel, from the collection of Gavin H. Fryer.   Bertram Rota Ltd.   308 Part II - 189   2015   £350

Pritchett, V. S. *It May Never Happen & Other Stories.* London: Chatto & Windus, 1946. First edition, 2nd impression, original binding, fine in slightly darkened and soiled dust jacket, form author's library with VSP booklabel, from the collection of Gavin H. Fryer.   Bertram Rota Ltd.   308 Part II - 191   2015   £25

Pritchett, V. S. *It May Never Happen & Other Stories.* London: Chatto & Windus, 1946. First edition, original binding, covers marked, dedication copy, inscribed by author to his wife, posthumous VSP bookplate, from the collection of Gavin H. Fryer.   Bertram Rota Ltd.   308 Part II - 190   2015   £350

Pritchett, V. S. *London Perceived.* London: Chatto & Windus and William Heinemann, 1962. First English edition, 4to., photos by Evelyn Hofer, original binding, dust jacket creased, worn, repaired dust jacket for the American edition and cardboard slipcase, presentation copy inscribed by author to his wife, Dorothy, from author's library with posthumous VSP booklabel, from the collection of Gavin H. Fryer.   Bertram Rota Ltd.   308 Part II - 199   2015   £160

Pritchett, V. S. *Marching Spain.* London: J. M. Dent & Sons Ltd., 1933. New edition, contemporary three quarter pigskin, raised bands, gilt rules, green morocco lettering piece, gilt, maize colored cloth sides, top edge gilt, patterned endpapers, pigskin somewhat darkened and cloth sides soiled, otherwise very nice, some foxing of prelims, with posthumous VS Pritchett bookabel, from the collection of Gavin H. Fryer.   Bertram Rota Ltd.   308 Part II - 187   2015   £150

Pritchett, V. S. *Midnight Oil.* New York: Random House, 1972. First American edition, original binding, edges of covers faded, else very nice in creased and soiled dust jacket, dedication copy inscribed by author for wife Dorothy, from author's library with posthumous VSP booklabel, from the collection of Gavin H. Fryer.   Bertram Rota Ltd.   308 Part II - 212   2015   £200

Pritchett, V. S. *Mr. Beluncle.* London: Chatto & Windus, 1951. First edition, original binding, fine in repaired, slightly darkened and soiled dust jacket, slightly chipped and defective at head of spine panel and one corner, from author's library with posthumous VSP booklabel, from the collection of Gavin H. Fryer.   Bertram Rota Ltd.   308 Part II - 193   2015   £60

Pritchett, V. S. *New York Proclaimed.* New York: Harcourt, Brace & World, 1965. First American edition, photos in color and black and white by Evelyn Hofer, original binding, very nice in dust jacket just little rubbed at corners, from author's library with VSP booklabel, from the collection of Gavin H. Fryer.   Bertram Rota Ltd.   308 Part II - 206   2015   £70

Pritchett, V. S. *New York: Herz und Antlitz eienr Stadt (New York Proclaimed).* Munich: Dromer Knaur, 1966. First German edition, 4to., original binding, little browned, very nice in creased and torn, dust jacket, from author's library with posthumous VSP booklabel, from the collection of Gavin H. Fryer.   Bertram Rota Ltd.   308 Part II - 207   2015   £40

Pritchett, V. S. *On the Edge of the Cliff and Other Stories.* London: Chatto & Windus, 1980. First edition, original binding, fine in dust jacket, dedication copy inscribed by author to his wife, Dorothy, with his autograph signature on titlepage, from author's library with posthumous VSP booklabel, from the collection of Gavin H. Fryer.   Bertram Rota Ltd. 308 Part II - 220   2015   £150

Pritchett, V. S. *The Camberwell Beauty.* London: Chatto & Windus, 1974. First edition, original binding, small closed tear to title, otherwise very nice in dust jacket, from author's library with posthumous VSP booklabel, from the collection of Gavin H. Fryer.   Bertram Rota Ltd.   308 Part II - 214   2015   £45

Pritchett, V. S. *The Fly in the Ointment.* Cambridge University Press, 1977. First edition thus, wrappers, very nice, from author's library with posthumous VSP booklabel, from the collection of Gavin H. Fryer.   Bertram Rota Ltd.   308 Part II - 215   2015   £30

Pritchett, V. S. *The Gentle Barbarian.* New York: Random House, 1977. First American edition, very nice in dust jacket, little faded at spine panel, from author's library with posthumous VSP booklabel, from the collection of Gavin H. Fryer.   Bertram Rota Ltd.   308 Part II - 217   2015   £35

Pritchett, V. S. *The Gentle Barbarian: The Life and Work of Turgenev.* London: Chatto & Windus Ltd., 1977. Advance proof copy, wrappers little creased and soiled, otherwise nice, publisher's label on upper wrapper explaining book does not contain illustrations; from author's library with posthumous VSP booklabel, from the collection of Gavin H. Fryer.   Bertram Rota Ltd.   308 Part II - 216   2015   £60

Pritchett, V. S. *The Key to My Heart: a comedy in Three Part.* New York: Random House, 1964. First American edition, illustrations by Paul Hogarth, original binding, fine in slightly darkened and soiled dust jacket, from author's library with posthumous VSP booklabel, from the collection of Gavin H. Fryer.   Bertram Rota Ltd.   308 Part II - 203   2015   £40

Pritchett, V. S. *The Key to My Heart: a Comedy in Three Parts.* London: Chatto & Windus, 1963. First edition, full light green morocco, gilt, red morocco inlay lettering piece to upper cover, bearing author's name in style of visiting card, patterned endpapers, covers slightly sprung and somewhat soiled and marked, upper hinge showing signs of wear, otherwise very good, from the author's library with posthumous VSP booklabel, from the collection of Gavin H. Fryer.   Bertram Rota Ltd.   308 Part II - 200   2015   £80

Pritchett, V. S. *The Living Novel and Later Appreciations.* New York: Random House, 1964. New edition, fine in fragmentary dust jacket, dedication copy inscribed by author to his wife, Dorothy, with posthumous VSP booklabel, from the collection of Gavin H. Fryer.   Bertram Rota Ltd.   308 Part II - 204   2015   £150

Pritchett, V. S. *The Myth Makers: Essays on European, Russian and South American Novelists.* London: Chatto & Windus, 1979. First edition, original binding, head and foot of spine slightly faded, otherwise very nice in soiled, faded and torn dust jacket, from author's library with posthumous VSP booklabel, from the collection of Gavin H. Fryer.   Bertram Rota Ltd.   308 Part II - 219   2015   £50

Pritchett, V. S. *The Offensive Traveller.* New York: Alfred A. Knopf, 1964. First edition, fine in dust jacket little rubbed and marked, slightly defective at top edge of lower panel, original binding, from author's library with posthumous VSP booklabel, from the collection of Gavin H. Fryer.   Bertram Rota Ltd.   308 Part II - 205   2015   £40

Pritchett, V. S. *The Sailor, Sense of Humour and Other Stories.* New York: Alfred A. Knopf, 1956. First American edition of Collected Stories, original binding, spine and covers somewhat darkened and soiled, otherwise nice, author's copy with his autograph signature on front free endpaper, and posthumous VSP booklabel, from the collection of Gavin H. Fryer.   Bertram Rota Ltd.   308 Part II - 196   2015   £70

Pritchett, V. S. *The Spanish Temper.* New York: Alfred A. Knopf, 1954. First edition, original binding, extremities of spine and boards just little faded, else very nice in fragmentary remains of dust jacket, from author's library with posthumous VSP booklabel, from the collection of Gavin H. Fryer.   Bertram Rota Ltd.   308 Part II - 194   2015   £50

Pritchett, V. S. *The Tale Bearers: Literary Essays.* New York: Vintage Books, 1981. First American paperback edition, wrappers, little browned throughout, otherwise nice, from author's library with posthumous VSP booklabel, from the collection of Gavin H. Fryer.   Bertram Rota Ltd.   308 Part II - 221   2015   £40

Pritchett, V. S. *The Turn of the Years.* Wilton: Michael Russell, 1982. First edition in book form, one of 150 numbered copies, signed by author and Paul Theroux (provided introduction), original binding, fine, presentation copy inscribed by author for wife Dorothy, from author's library with posthumous VSP booklabel, from the collection of Gavin H. Fryer.   Bertram Rota Ltd.   308 Part II - 222   2015   £150

Pritchett, V. S. *The Working Novelist.* London: Chatto & Windus, 1965. First edition, original binding, nice in somewhat soiled and slightly worn dust jacket, label of Intercontinental Literary Agency on flyleaf, from author's library with posthumous VSP booklabel, from the collection of Gavin H. Fryer.   Bertram Rota Ltd.   308 Part II - 208   2015   £35

Pritchett, V. S. *When My Girl Comes Home.* London: Chatto & Windus, 1961. First edition, fine, original binding, slightly soiled and frayed dust jacket, with label of literary agent, A.D. Peters, and partly erased signature on front free endpaper, from author's library with posthumous VSP booklabel from the collection of Gavin H. Fryer.   Bertram Rota Ltd.   308 Part II - 198   2015   £40

Pritchett, V. S. *You Make Your Own Life: Short Stories.* London: Chatto and Windus, 1938. First edition, original binding, spine dulled, corners bumped, one little rubbed, half title browned, otherwise nice, small label and stamp to rear endpapers, presentation copy inscribed by author to James Hanley, from the collection of Gavin H. Fryer. Bertram Rota Ltd. 308 Part II - 188 2015 £175

Turgenev, Ivan Sergeevich 1818-1883 *The Torrents of Spring.* London: Hamish Hamilton, 1960. New edition, imperial 8vo., illustrations in color and black and white by Robin Jacques, original binding, top edge gilt, others uncut, fine in original glassine dust jacket and pictorial slipcase, from the library of V. S. Pritchett, with posthumous VSP booklabel, from the collection of Gavin H. Fryer. Bertram Rota Ltd. 308 Part II - 227 2015 £40

Webb, Mary *The Chinese Lion: a Story.* London: Bertram Rota, 1937. First edition, one of 350 numbered copies, original batik paper covered boards, red cloth spine and lettering label to upper cover, little foxing to endpapers and spine trifle sunned, but very nice, slightly marked slipcase, from the collection of Gavin H. Fryer. Bertram Rota Ltd. 308 Part II - 228 2015 £80

Whitman, Walt 1819-1892 *Specimen Days in America.* Walter Scott, Camelot Series, 1887. First English edition, original green cloth, spine with (rubbed) printed label, uncut, covers with some soiling and slight wear to extremities, tears at foot of spine, endpapers somewhat foxed, very good, ownership inscription, ownership stamp and bookseller's small labels on front endpapers, from the collection of Gavin H. Fryer. Bertram Rota Ltd. 308 Part II - 229 2015 £80

Zangwill, Israel *Ghetto Tragedies.* London: McClure & Co., 1893. First edition, bound in full light blue calf by Zaehnsdorf, spine dated with red leather label lettered gilt, inner dentelles gilt, original wrappers somewhat crudely cut down, but preserved, spine little darkened and worn, nice, from the library of Neville Lynn, bearing his autograph signature and notes about Zangwill, presentation copy with author's signed autograph presentation inscription to Lynn, neatly bound in at end, APS signed by Zangwill to Lynn and mounted on front and rear endpapers various press cuttings concerning author, label of package addressed by Zangwill to Lynn, with news paper photos of author, loosely inserted is photo postcard portrait of author, shown seated at his study desk, from the collection of Gavin H. Fryer. Bertram Rota Ltd. 308 Part II - 230 2015 £250

Association – Fullmer, Randy

Rebello, Stephen *The Art of the Hunchback of Notre Dame.* New York: Hyperion, 1996. First edition, this copy signed by 10 members of the production company, including Gary Trousdale and Kirk Wise, artistic coordinator Randy Fullmer, writers Irene Meechi and Tab Murphy and five animators, numerous full color drawings and sketches in black and white, laid in is announcement for book signing party, fine in fine dust jacket. Ed Smith Books 83 - 15 2015 $250

Association – Furstenberg, Hans

Bible. English - 1736 *The Holy Bible Containing the Old and New Testaments.* Edinburgh: Robert Freebairn, 1736. 178 x 144m., animated contemporary red morocco, heavily gilt in characteristically Scottish design, covers framed by dogtooth rolls and densely tooled with gilt flowers, foliage turnips, swirls and dots, central panel with vaguely herringbone design formed by interlocking full and half circles accented by floral tools, fleurons and dots, panel framed by very prominent densely cross-hatched pear shaped ornaments, each containing a stylized thistle within it, raised bands, spine intricately gilt in compartments with scrolling cornerpieces and large fleuron centerpiece incorporating a saltire, patterned paper pastedowns (lacking free endpapers), all edges gilt (boards with shallow, thin blind rules as part of the design or else added later demarcating central panel as well as extending from top to bottom and side to side along exact center of the cover, very expert repairs to head of joints, tiny restoration to corners, bookplate of Hans Furstenberg, hint of splaying to front board, joints and extremities little rubbed (though carefully refurbished), gilt bit muted in places, but once spectacular binding still extremely appealing with nothing approaching a major condition issue, mild browning throughout, occasional trivial foxing, marginal stains, or other trivial imperfections, still excellent copy, internally few signs of use, fresh, clean leaves with comfortable margins. Phillip J. Pirages 66 - 41 2015 $13,000

Senault, Louis *Petit Office De la Sainte Vierge.* Paris: Chez Senault, circa, 1680. 181 x 127mm., remarkably beautiful black straight grain morocco elegantly and lavishly gilt by Thouvenin (signed at base of spine), covers with elaborate broad frame featuring repeated palmettes, central panel with complex cornerpieces of massed antique tools, raised bands, spine compartments with red cruciform inlay at center and with stylized tulips and multiple stippled leaves emanating from central ornament, very lovely broad inner gilt dentelles featuring 52 additional red morocco inlays (26 inside each cover), these within large 'semis' rectangles with concave sides, dentelles surrounding pink watered silk pastedowns bordered with a neoclassical foliate and floral roll (facing a free endpaper of the same material and with the same decoration), all edges gilt, small and very expert repair, just top of joints, marbled paper slipcase; engraved throughout with a great variety of immensely charming calligraphic initials, headpieces, tailpieces, borders, flourishes and other decorative elements; bookplate of Hans Furstenberg; just the faintest hint of wear to joints, two minor blemishes on rear cover, discoloration at gutter of free endpapers (apparently from binder's glue), but fine, with extraordinarily handsome binding with glistening and with text nearly pristine.   Phillip J. Pirages   66 - 77   2015 $7500

Association – Furstenberg, Jean

Bible. German - 1784 *Biblia das ist; Die Ganze Heilige Schrift Alten Und Neuen Testamentes.* Basel: Johann Rudolf Im-Hof und Sohn, 1784. 197 x 121mm., 2 volumes bound 'dos-a-dos', very appealing contemporary red morocco Dos-a-Dos binding, covers gilt with delicate roll border featuring calligraphic flourishes at corners, at center a pineapple like oval ornament flanked by curling acanthus leaves from which a floral garland is draped, flap spines divided into compartments by multiple plain and decorative gilt rules, floral spring centerpiece and small tools at corners and sides, gilt turn-ins, all edges gilt, original (somewhat rubbed) marbled paper pull-off case, front pastedowns with booklabel of Jean Furstenberg, isolated trivial spots of foxing, really excellent specimen and virtually no internal signs of use in very bright binding with only very superficial wear.   Phillip J. Pirages   66 - 47   2015 $6500

Association – Gage, Matilda Joslyn

Stanton, Elizabeth Cady *History of Woman Suffrage.* New York: Fowler & Wells, 1881. First edition, volume I only, 8vo., steel engravings, with editor, Matilda Joslyn Gage's presentation dated 1888, maroon cloth, cover quite scuffed and somewhat worn at spine and corners, little foxing, otherwise very good.   Second Life Books Inc.   189 - 244   2015 $350

Association – Gall, Jane

Cruden, William *Nature Spiritualised in a Variety of Poems.* London: printed by J. and W. Oliver for the author, 1766. First edition, 12mo., general intermittent soiling and finger marking, some minor dampstaining, contemporary calf, unlettered, ms. ownership inscription on lower free endpaper of Jane Gall her book 1802.   John Drury Rare Books March 2015 - 23201 2015   £306

Association – Gallagher, Inez

Leger, Alexis Saint-Leger *Winds (vents).* New York: Pantheon Books, 1953. First American edition, bilingual edition, quarto, little faint spotting on boards, else near fine in chipped, but good dust jacket, nicely inscribed by author to Inez Gallagher.   Between the Covers Rare Books   196 - 99   2015 $1500

Association – Galloway, Vincent

Guichard, Edouard *L'Harmonie des Couleurs.* Paris: Ad Goubaud et Fils, Editeurs..., 1880. First edition, large 4to., 166 hand colored and lithograph plates, including 5 double page plates, some sporadic foxing and blotching to some plates as usual, original grey cloth, lettered in black, somewhat shaken with wear on spine, bookplate of Vincent Galloway (1894-1977) artist and curator Ferens Art Gallery, Hull.   Marlborough Rare Books   List 54 - 35   2015 £1850

Association – Gallup, Dick

Padgett, Ron *Robert's Ball.* N.P.: Ron Padgett, 1966. Self published, holograph colophon reading "Limited Edition/ This Copy is for Dick (Gallup)" fine, oblong 12mo., illustrated, accordion fold chapbook, hand lettered and colored by Padgett.   James S. Jaffe Rare Books   Many Happy Returns - 144   2015 $2500

Association – Gandin, Thomas

Atkinson, James *Epitome of the Whole Art of Navigation.* London: by J. D. for James Atkinson and R. Mount, 1695. Second edition?, 12mo., 8 (of 10) folding engraved diagram plates (Plates 1-6, a fragment of 7, 8, 9 torn and loose, 10 lower third missing and volvelle missing, plates generally bit tatty and frayed at fore-edges), titlepage dusty, edges occasionally ragged and torn throughout, closely shaved along fore-edge throughout (occasionally touching text), final gathering M detached from book block and M1 damaged in inner margin, last page dusty), contemporary sheep, panelled in blind, very worn, heavily rubbed and bumped, corners scuffed and holed, headcaps torn, marks of two catches/ ties?), 18th century signature "Thos. Gandin" and "Geo. Matthew", from the library of James Stevens Cox (1910-1997).   Maggs Bros. Ltd.   1447 - 13   2015   £950

Association – Gannon, Patricio

Gray, John *The Person in Question.* Buenos Aires: F. A. Colombo, 1958. Number 22 of 50 copies of which 10 were reserved for the press, presentation copy inscribed by Patricio Gannon to bookseller (librarian and collector) Herbert Faulkner West, fine in white paper wrappers with black title and illustration to front cover, clean, bright interior printed on handmade paper in black with red initials, loose and unopened as issued, fine in original slipcase, fine. The Kelmscott Bookshop   11 - 5   2015 $450

Association – Ganora, C. A.

Johannes Chrysotomus *Enarratio in Esaiam Prophetam. (bound with) Conciones in Celebrioribus Aliquot Anni Festivitatibus Habitae. (bound with) Homiliae in Aliquot Veteris Testamenti Loca.* Antverpiae: in Aedibus Ioan. Seelsii, 1555. 1553. 1553, 165 x 105mm., 3 separately published works bound in one volume, splendid armorial red Roman morocco done for Pope Pius V by Niccolo Franzese, covers gilt with papal arms in central cartouche, front cover with "Pivs V" above arms and initials "P.M." (Pontifex Maximus) below, back cover with "Io Chrys in Esa et Hom" in gilt above and "P.M." below, boards framed by a profusion of acanthus leaves emanating from the brass bosses at corners and with a background stamped with small floral and dot tools, raised bands, spine compartments with interwoven gilt vines and gilt titling, remnants of clasps, all edges gilt and gauffered in pink floral pattern and with Pius' name tooled into head and tail edges and his arms painted on the fore edge (apparently with very expert repairs at spine ends), titlepage with printer's device, bookplate of Carlo Ponzone di Casale and with ink inscription of Ch. Al. Ganora dated 1867, titlepage with ink inscription of a Capuchin convent, hinge separation at first titlepage, majority of the leaves with minor browning (a half dozen gatherings rather browned), other trivial defects but text unsoiled and consistently fresh, front joint with two-inch crack near bottom, leather on spine bit crackled, gilt lost in small area next to one box, but sumptuously decorated binding still quite lustrous showing little wear, and altogether pleasing.   Phillip J. Pirages   66 - 18   2015 $17,500

Association – Garcia, Jerry

Brandelius, Jerilyn Lee *Grateful Dead Family Album.* New York: Warner Books, 1989. First edition, 'Grateful Dead All Area Access sticker laid down to jacket, this copy signed by band members Jerry Garcia, Mickey Hart and Bob Bralove as well as long time road crew members Ram Rod Shurtliff, Bill 'Kid' Candelario, Steve Parish and Robbie Taylor among others, hundreds of intimate photos and stories, very good plus to near fine with little soil and handling marks, in very good plus to near fine dust jacket with short closed tear to bottom of front flap.   Ed Smith Books   83 - 34   2015 $950

Association – Gardner, Alexander

Philosophical Society of Glasgow *Proceedings of the....* Published for the Society, circa, 1904. 1844., 35 volumes bound in 18, complete handsome, uniform mottled half calf over marbled boards, spines gilt and labelled, all in the finest state of preservation from the library of David Murray (1842-1928) Scottish lawyer, with his bookplate on each pastedown, with 3 ALS's to Murray from Alexander Gardner, Hon. Sec. of the Society.   John Drury Rare Books   2015 - 25818   2015 $3147

Association – Gardner, Erle Stanley

Fair, A. A. *Traps Need Fresh Bait.* New York: Morrow, 1967. First edition, inscribed "To Helen Moore, my Hollywood Della Street. With love from 'Uncle Erle' Erle Stanley Gardner, fine in dust jacket with short closed tear on front panel.   Mordida Books   March 2015 - 011705 2015 $300

Association – Gardner, Isabella

Warren, Robert Penn 1905-1989 *Eleven Poems on the Same Theme.* Norfolk: New Directions, 1942. First edition, wrapper issue, wrappers fine and fine dust jacket (very slightly soiled), housed in custom cloth clamshell case with morocco label gilt, inscribed by author to poet Isabella Gardner.   Between the Covers Rare Books   196 - 120   2015 $1750

Association – Garnett, Angelica

Woolf, Virginia 1882-1941 *The Waves.* London: published by Leonard and Virginia Woolf at the Hogarth Press, 1931. First edition, first printing, one of 7113 copies, publisher's purple cloth lettered gilt, printed on laid paper, good with slight lean, two short tears to spine head, rubbing to spine ends, toning and light soiling to spine ends, toning and light soiling to spine, boards slightly bowed, minor soiling and some fading, very light spotting to first few and last pages of text block, pencil correction to page 47, bright and clean pages, housed in custom quarter leather clamshell box, personal copy of author's sister Vanessa Bell, with her ownership signature by descent to her daughter Angelica Garnett, thence to her two surviving daughters Henrietta Coupe and Frances Partridge.   B & B Rare Books, Ltd.   239 - 1   2015 $9500

Association – Garrett, Frank

Gay, John   1685-1732   *The Fables of.*   published and sold by the booksellers and (printed) by T. Wilson and R. Spence... York, 1806. 12mo., woodcut vignette on title and numerous 'cuts' in text by T. Bewick, minor spotting and staining, red crushed morocco, elaborate gilt tooled borders on sides of leafy tendrils punctuated with flowers, spine gilt with leaf sprays in 6 compartments between raised bands, wide gilt turn-ins, gilt edges signed F. G. and dated 1906, booklabel of Peter Summers inside front cover, very good in early Arts & Crafts binding by Frank Garrett.   Blackwell's Rare Books   B179 - 45   2015   £750

Association – Garrett, George

Davis, Paxton   *Two Soldiers.*   New York: Simon & Schuster, 1956. First edition, pages age toned, else near fine in very good or better dust jacket with two small chips at crown and some rubbing, inscribed by author for fellow author George Garrett 12 Dec. 1962, typed slip laid-in with request to send the book to Garrett.   Between the Covers Rare Books, Inc.   187 - 70   2015 $125

Botsford, Keith   *Benvenuto.*   London: Hutchinson of London, 1961. First edition, endpapers foxed, corners trifle bumped, very good in very good dust jacket (rubbed with small chip on front panel), stamp of Helga Greene Literary Agency fof London, beneath which is Botsford's inscription to author George Garrett and Susan.   Between the Covers Rare Books, Inc.   187 - 29   2015 $200

Association – Garrett, Susan

Botsford, Keith   *Benvenuto.*   London: Hutchinson of London, 1961. First edition, endpapers foxed, corners trifle bumped, very good in very good dust jacket (rubbed with small chip on front panel), stamp of Helga Greene Literary Agency fof London, beneath which is Botsford's inscription to author George Garrett and Susan.   Between the Covers Rare Books, Inc.   187 - 29   2015 $200

Association – Gartside, James, Mrs.

Ormerod, Oliver   *O Full True en Pertikler Okeawnt a wat Me Un Maw Mistris Seede un Yerd wi' Gooin to the' Greyte Eggshibishun e' Lundun, e' Eyghtene Hunderth un Sixty two...*   Rochdale: printed by Wrigley un Son..., 1864. 8vo., engraved frontispiece, 7 other large woodcut illustrations, frontispiece just little soiled, few marks here and there, but good copy in near contemporary black half calf, title in gilt on upper cover, binder's ticket of Ormerod Bros. of Rochdale and later (1892) ownership inscription of Mrs. James Gartside of 301 Bury road, Rochdale.   John Drury Rare Books   March 2015 - 18991   2015 $221

Association – Gates, William

Carew, Thomas   1595-1639   *Poems, Songs and Sonnets, Together with a Masque.*   London: Henry Herringman, 1670. Fourth edition, 8vo., foxed and browned, heaviest in margins, occasional repairs to fore and upper edge, closely shaved along lower edge, touching catchwords and signatures on a number of leaves, early 20th century half calf and cloth boards, with W(illia)m Gates 18th century signature, pencil signature of H. F. B. Brett Smith (1896-1942), ink inscription March 20th 1922 of Francis K. W. Needham, signature John (?Harr)ison dated 1926, from the library of James Stevens Cox (1910-1997).   Maggs Bros. Ltd.   1447 - 64   2015   £180

Association – Gathorne-Hardy, Ralph Edward

Stafford, P.   *Poems on several occasions.*   London: printed for Tho. Atkins and sold by booksellers of London and Westminster, 1721. First edition, 8vo., recent boards, little dusty at beginning and end, but very good, entirely uncut, from the library of Ralph Edward Gathorne-Hardy with his bookplate, later in the collection of John Brett-Smith.   C. R. Johnson   Foxon R-Z - 931r-z   2015 $2298

Association – Gavin, Erica

Meyer, Russ   *Vixen's Working copy.*   Corona: Eve Productions circa, 1968. Shooting script for the 1968 film, Erica Gavin's shooting script, complete.   Royal Books   46 - 13   2015 $6500

Association – Gawsworth, John

Pitter, Ruth   *The Rude Potato.*   London: Cresset Press, 1941. First edition, illustrations by Roger Furse, old tape shadows on first and last two leaves, else very good in like dust jacket with short tear and some shallow chipping at crown, inscribed by author to fellow poet, John Gawsworth.   Between the Covers Rare Books, Inc.   187 - 216   2015 $125

Association – Geest, Christopher Clark

Doyle, Arthur Conan   1859-1930   *Micah Clarke: His Statement as Made to His Three Grandchildren Joseph, Gervas & Robert during the hard winter of 1734...*   London: Longmans, 1889. Half title, final ad leaf, few leaves roughly opened, original navy blue cloth, bevelled boards, little rubbed, booklabel of Christopher Clark Geest on leading pastedown, signature on half title of Vincent Starrett, 1886-1974.   Jarndyce Antiquarian Booksellers   CCXI - 93   2015   £220

Association – Gelering, Albert

James, William 1842-1910 *The Will to Believe and Other Essays in Popular Philosophy.* New York: Longmans, Green & Co., 1897. First edition, octavo, original green cloth with 2 1/2 inch paper label to spine, which is darkened and very lightly chipped, still about 90 per cent readable (were effecting "James" more than anything else), most minimal of wear also to head and toe of spine, former owner's names in ink to rear of front cover (Hermine Gelering) and front free endpaper (Albert Gelering), otherwise amazingly well preserved. Athena Rare Books 15 - 16 2015 $900

Association – Gelering, Hermine

James, William 1842-1910 *The Will to Believe and Other Essays in Popular Philosophy.* New York: Longmans, Green & Co., 1897. First edition, octavo, original green cloth with 2 1/2 inch paper label to spine, which is darkened and very lightly chipped, still about 90 per cent readable (were effecting "James" more than anything else), most minimal of wear also to head and toe of spine, former owner's names in ink to rear of front cover (Hermine Gelering) and front free endpaper (Albert Gelering), otherwise amazingly well preserved. Athena Rare Books 15 - 16 2015 $900

Association – Gelfand, Morris

Digby, John *Incantations: Poems and Collages.* Roslyn: Stone House Press, 1987. First edition, ownership signature of noted engraver John De Pol, fine copy, inscribed to De Pol by publisher Morris Gelfand with complimentary slip, signed by Gelfand. Between the Covers Rare Books, Inc. 187 - 74 2015 $150

Association – Gensmer, Margaret Wadsworth

Beard, Mary R. *On Understanding Women.* New York: Longmans Green, 1931. First edition, 8vo., very good, laid in is TLS about the book from author to Mrs. Margaret Wadsworth Gensmer. Second Life Books Inc. 189 - 18 2015 $275

Association – George, R. L.

Shipman, O. L., Mrs. *Taming the Big Bend. A History of the Extreme Western Portion of Texas From Fort Clark to El Paso.* N.P.: privately printed, 1926. First edition, 8vo., signed and dated by author on 4/5//27, from the library of Captain and Mrs. R. L. George, Camp Marfa, Texas April 5 1927, purple cloth, gold stamping on front cover and spine, frontispiece, illustrations, plates, portraits, folding map, bound in at rear of book, exceptional copy, near fine, bright, square copy. Buckingham Books March 2015 - 31770 2015 $1750

Association – Georges, John

Brooke, Henry *The History of a Reprobate; being the Life of David Doubtful.* Printed for the Booksellers, 1784. First edition, bit browned and spotted, first few leaves brittle at fore-edge, small hole in one leaf with loss of part of a word on recto and touching four letters on verso, small 8vo., original sheep, worn, spine defective at head, lower cover nearly detached, ownership inscription of John Georges (25 July 1793 price 1/3) and some annotations in text, sound. Blackwell's Rare Books B179 - 22 2015 £1100

Association – Geough, Elizabeth

Disraeli, Benjamin 1804-1881 *Vivian Grey.* London: Henry Colburn, 1826-1827. First edition of volumes III-V, new edition, i.e. second edition of volumes I & II, complete with half titles and ads, as called for, 8vo., 5 volumes, untrimmed in original boards, volumes iii-v with pink paper backstrips, small puncture to front board of volume v resulting in tiny hole to first 1- leaves and a dent detectable as far as page 50, otherwise just little worn overall, modern bookplate to volume i, very good, scarce first novel, each volume with contemporary inscription of E(lizabeth) M. Geough. Blackwell's Rare Books B179 - 35 2015 £600

Association – Gerhard, William

Blanchard, Jean Pierre *An Exact and Authentic Narrative of M. Blanchard's Third Aerial Voyage.* London: C. Heydigner, 1784. First edition, small folio, frontispiece, early dark brown paper wrappers, housed in dark blue cloth folder by Sangorski & Sutcliffe for E. P. Dutton, gilt lettering on outside of folder, balloon themed bookplate of pervious owner William G. Gerhard =, lacking half title, slight offsetting to titlepage from frontispiece and some light foxing to final leaf, very good. Heritage Book Shop Holiday 2014 - 18 2015 $2750

Association – Gershwin, George

Hughes, Langston *The Weary Blues.* New York: Alfred A. Knopf, 1926. First edition, one of 1500 copies, small 8vo., original blue cloth backed decorated boards, inscribed presentation from author to George Gershwin, Jan. 31 1926, stellar association copy, covers lightly rubbed, lacking rare dust jacket as was the case with all of Gershwin's books, otherwise very good. James S. Jaffe Rare Books Modern American Poetry - 141 2015 $35,000

Loos, Anita *Gentlemen Prefer Blondes.* New York: Boni & Liveright, 1925. Later printing, published one month after first, inscribed by Loos for George Gershwin, octavo, 217 pages, later issue dust jacket. Honey & Wax Booksellers 1 - 56 2015 $4800

Association – Geyelin, Philip

Perkins, Frances *The Roosevelt I Knew.* New York: Viking, 1946. First edition, 8vo. very good in chipped and worn dust jacket, front hinge loose, covers little faded, full page inscription by author to Pulitzer Prize winning journalist, Philip L. Geyelin.   Second Life Books Inc.   191 - 77   2015 $350

Association – Gher, William

Knight, George *Dust in the Balance.* London: Jarrold & Sons, 1896. First edition, 8vo. original green cloth, lettered gilt on spine and on front cover, uncommon book, neat inscription dated 1986 in hand of William Gher and pencilled on front endpaper, very slight rubbing with foxing to endpapers, otherwise very good+.   Any Amount of Books   2015 - C8102   2015   £275

Association – Gibb, Molly Flagg

Wotton, Henry *Reliquiae Wottonianae; or a Collection of Lives, Letters, Poems...* London: By T. Roycroft for R. Marriott, 1672. Third edition, portraits, 19th century red morocco, early signatures of J. Grien? 1725, Thomas Price and John Francis Cole 1828, bookplates of J. J. Chapman and Molly Flagg Gibb, very good.   Joseph J. Felcone Inc.   Science, Medicine and Technology - 57   2015 $900

Association – Gibbon, J.

Thomson, James 1700-1748 *The Seasons, a Hymn, a Poem to the Memory of Sir Isaac Newton and Britannia, a Poem.* London: printed for J. Millan and A. Millar, 1730. First collected edition, engraved frontispiece, 3 plates, 8vo., contemporary panelled calf, red morocco label (upper joint very slightly cracked but firm), signature on titlepage of J. Gibbon dated 1786.   C. R. Johnson   Foxon R-Z - 1002r-z   2015 $383

Association – Gibson, G. M.

Darwin, Charles Robert 1809-1882 *Journal of Researches into the Natural History and Geology of the Countries Visited During the Voyage of the HMS Beagle Round the Wold Under the Command of Capt. Fitz Roy.* London: John Murray, 1860. 10th thousand, illustrations, 32 page catalog (Jan. 1863), original green cloth, by Edmonds & Remnant, neatly recased, little dulled, contemporary signature of G. M. Gibson.   Jarndyce Antiquarian Booksellers   CCXI - 84   2015   £580

Association – Gifford, A.

Lister, Martin *Conchyliorum Bivalbvium Utriusque Aquae Exercitatio Anatomica Tertia.* London: Sumptibus authoris impressa, 1696. First edition, 4to., 10 engraved plates, with terminal blank Z4 in first work, contemporary sprinkled calf, very skillfully rebacked in period style, small early shelfmark in red ink on endpaper and on title, minor flaw in S2 just grazing catchword, very faint foxing in fore-edge, very lovely copy with text and plates clean and fresh, armorial bookplate of A. Gifford D. D. of the Museum", presentation from Lister inscribed for Mr. Dalone.   Joseph J. Felcone Inc.   Science, Medicine and Technology - 28   2015 $10,000

Association – Gifford, Thomas

Sjowall, Maj *The Laughing Policeman.* Pantheon Books, 1970. First US edition, from the library of mystery author Thomas Gifford with his neat inked signature and date, fine in dust jacket with light wear to head of spine.   Buckingham Books   March 2015 - 35108   2015 $175

Association – Gilbert, Cecilia

Watson, James D. *Genes, Girls and Gamow. After the Double Helix.* New York: Alfred A. Knopf, 2002. First American edition, 8vo., signed by James Watson, Walter Gilbert and dedicatee, Cecilia Gilbert, 8vo., fine in fine dust jacket.   By the Book, L. C.   Special List 10 - 90   2015 $250

Association – Gilbert, Jack

Ginsberg, Allen *Howl and Other Poems.* San Francisco: City Lights Pocket Bookshop, 1956. First edition, one of 1000 copies printed letterpress at Villiers Publications Ltd. in England, 12mo., printed wrappers, presentation copy inscribed by author for poet Jack Gilbert, printed cover label lightly soiled, otherwise fine.   James S. Jaffe Rare Books   Modern American Poetry - 108   2015 $15,000

Ginsberg, Allen *Siesta in Xbalba and Return to the States.* Near Icy Cape, Alaska: At the Sign of the Midnight Sun as published by the author July, 1956. First edition, small 4to., original mimeographed self wrappers stapled as issued, trifle soiled, but fine, rare, Jack Gilbert's copy signed by Ginsberg, with Gilbert's ownership signature dated 5ix1956 in upper left hand corner of same page.   James S. Jaffe Rare Books   Modern American Poetry - 109   2015 $25,000

Spicer, Jack *After Lorca.* San Francisco: White Rabbit Press, 1957. First edition, one of 26 lettered copies signed by Spicer and with drawing by poet on colophon page (out of a total edition of 500 copies on Olivetti Lexikon 80 by Robert Duncan, with cover design by Jess), although not noted, this copy came from the library of poet Jack Gilbert, Spicer has inscribed the colophon page, original drawing above printed colophon, 8vo., original pictorial wrappers, covers lightly soiled, otherwise very good, rare.   James S. Jaffe Rare Books   Modern American Poetry - 264   2015 $5000

Association – Gilbert, James

Moore, Jonas *A Mathematical Compendium or Useful Practices in Arithmetick, Geometry and Attronomy Geography and Navigation...* London: printed for J. Phillips, H. Rhodes and J. Tay, 1705. 12mo. 9 engraved plates, some on text leaves, (one folding, others free standing), contemporary panelled calf with raised bands, unlettered, slightly shaken, but fine, early signatures of William Dale and James Gilbert with old ms. notes, ink on endpapers and final blank leaf.   John Drury Rare Books   2015 - 24839   2015 $1049

Association – Gilbert, Walter

Watson, James D. *Genes, Girls and Gamow. After the Double Helix.* New York: Alfred A. Knopf, 2002. First American edition, 8vo., signed by James Watson, Walter Gilbert and dedicatee, Cecilia Gilbert, 8vo., fine in fine dust jacket.   By the Book, L. C.   Special List 10 - 90   2015 $250

Association – Gilbertson, George

Code, Henry Brereton *The Insurrection of the Twenty-Third July 1803.* Dublin: printed by Grassberry and Campbell 10 Black lane, 1803. First edition, 8vo., few leaves little creased, recent marbled boards, lettered on spine, very good, from the 20th century library of George Gilbertson (1915) with his signature, uncommon.   John Drury Rare Books   2015 - 24817   2015 $1049

Association – Gilchriese, John

Clum, John P. *It All Happened in Tombstone.* Flagstaff: Northland Press, 1965. First edition, signed by John Gilchriese, two-toned decorated cloth, fine, unread copy in unused dust jacket, exceptional copy.   Buckingham Books   March 2015 - 26743   2015 $175

Association – Gili, Jonathan

Cervantes Saavedra, Miguel De   1547-1616 *El Ingenioso Hidalgo Don Quixote de la Mancha.* Madrid: J. Ibarra, 1780. Deluxe edition, 4 volumes, 4to., frontispieces, portrait of Cervantes, 31 plates, 14 ornamental capital letters, 22 vignettes, 20 culs-de-lampe and folding engraved map, contemporary Spanish binding of green stained calf, covers 'marbled' with octagonal panel of pale brown calf set in gilt tooled border, spines gilt in compartments, red morocco labels, marbled endpapers, gilt edges, slight worm damage to foot of spine volume 1, head of volume 4 slightly chipped, armorial bookplate of Sarah Sophia Child (Villiers), Countess of Jersey (1785-1867) with old pressmarks of Osterley Park Library, bookplate of Jonathan and Phillida Gili (by Reynolds Stone).   Maggs Bros. Ltd.   Illustrated Books 2014 - 2015   £12,000

Goya Y Lucientes, Francisco *Los Caprichos.* Madrid: 1881-1886? Fifth edition, limited to 210 copies, this one of those printed on thick paper measuring 365 x 260mm and probably cut down by binder, folio, 80 etched and aquatint plates on which thick paper, bound without original grey cover in modern brown morocco, gilt spine, slipcase, printed in sepia ink and with plates bevelled they are numbered 1-80, first being portrait of Goya, which was also printed on upper cover not found here, some plates show signs of wear, most very well preserved, margins somewhat foxed in places, bookplate of Jonathan and Phillida Gili by Reynolds Stone.   Maggs Bros. Ltd.   Illustrated Books 2014 - 2015   £10,000

Sallustius Crispus, C. *La Conjuracion de Catilina y la Guerra de Jugurta Del Alfabeto y Lengua de los Fenices y de sus Colonias...* Madrid: J. Ibarra, 1772. 120 copies of this edition issued, all on large paper and printed on rich cream paper, hot press by Ibarra himself, some copies have a half title, not found here, Folio, engraved titlepage by Montfort, four engraved plates and numerous smaller engravings by Montefort and Carmona after Maella, three engraved plates by Fabregat and Ballester, two plates of scrips and one of coins, contemporary Spanish red morocco covers decorated with gilt Greek key border, having gilt suns at corners, enclosing inner roll border of foliate design, flat spine gilt at either end, central neo-classical motif built of various tools, green morocco label, green silk doublures and marker, edges gilt head of spine chipped, extremities rubbed, excellent copy, bookplate by Reynolds Stone of Jonathan and Phillida Gili.   Maggs Bros. Ltd.   Illustrated Books 2014 - 2015   £8000

Association – Gili, Phillida

Cervantes Saavedra, Miguel De 1547-1616 *El Ingenioso Hidalgo Don Quixote de la Mancha.* Madrid: J. Ibarra, 1780. Deluxe edition, 4 volumes, 4to., frontispieces, portrait of Cervantes, 31 plates, 14 ornamental capital letters, 22 vignettes, 20 culs-de-lampe and folding engraved map, contemporary Spanish binding of green stained calf, covers 'marbled' with octagonal panel of pale brown calf set in gilt tooled border, spines gilt in compartments, red morocco labels, marbled endpapers, gilt edges, slight worm damage to foot of spine volume 1, head of volume 4 slightly chipped, armorial bookplate of Sarah Sophia Child (Villiers), Countess of Jersey (1785-1867) with old pressmarks of Osterley Park Library, bookplate of Jonathan and Phillida Gili (by Reynolds Stone). Maggs Bros. Ltd. Illustrated Books 2014 - 2015 £12,000

Goya Y Lucientes, Francisco *Los Caprichos.* Madrid: 1881-1886? Fifth edition, limited to 210 copies, this one of those printed on thick paper measuring 365 x 260mm and probably cut down by binder, folio, 80 etched and aquatint plates on which thick paper, bound without original grey cover in modern brown morocco, gilt spine, slipcase, printed in sepia ink and with plates bevelled they are numbered 1-80, first being portrait of Goya, which was also printed on upper cover not found here, some plates show signs of wear, most very well preserved, margins somewhat foxed in places, bookplate of Jonathan and Phillida Gili by Reynolds Stone. Maggs Bros. Ltd. Illustrated Books 2014 - 2015 £10,000

Sallustius Crispus, C. *La Conjuracion de Catilina y la Guerra de Jugurta Del Alfabeto y Lengua de los Fenices y de sus Colonias...* Madrid: J. Ibarra, 1772. 120 copies of this edition issued, all on large paper and printed on rich cream paper, hot press by Ibarra himself, some copies have a half title, not found here, Folio, engraved titlepage by Montfort, four engraved plates and numerous smaller engravings by Montefort and Carmona after Maella, three engraved plates by Fabregat and Ballester, two plates of scrips and one of coins, contemporary Spanish red morocco covers decorated with gilt Greek key border, having gilt suns at corners, enclosing inner roll border of foliate design, flat spine gilt at either end, central neo-classical motif built of various tools, green morocco label, green silk doublures and marker, edges gilt head of spine chipped, extremities rubbed, excellent copy, bookplate by Reynolds Stone of Jonathan and Phillida Gili. Maggs Bros. Ltd. Illustrated Books 2014 - 2015 £8000

Association – Gill, Anne

Moore, Marianne 1887-1972 *Tell Me, Tell Me: Granite, Steel and Other Topics.* New York: Viking Press, 1966. First edition, octavo, 57 pages, original dust jacket, whimsically inscribed by Moore and signed and dated April 1967 for Brendan and Anne Gill. Honey & Wax Booksellers 1 - 35 2015 $425

Association – Gill, Brendan

Moore, Marianne 1887-1972 *Tell Me, Tell Me: Granite, Steel and Other Topics.* New York: Viking Press, 1966. First edition, octavo, 57 pages, original dust jacket, whimsically inscribed by Moore and signed and dated April 1967 for Brendan and Anne Gill. Honey & Wax Booksellers 1 - 35 2015 $425

Association – Gillmore, Margalo

Anderson, Maxwell *Valley Forge.* Washington: Anderson House, 1934. First edition, limited issue, one of 200 numbered copies, full leather gilt as issued, signed by Anderson and inscribed by him to actress Margalo Gillmore thanking her for performing beautifully in the Play. Between the Covers Rare Books, Inc. 187 - 1 2015 $275

Association – Gilman, John

Kendall, May *Dreams to Sell.* London: Longmans, 1887. First edition, half title in red & black, uncut in original crimson cloth, bevelled boards, spine faded, top edge gilt, presentation inscription to Gilbert Redgrave, bibliographer and art historian from Frances and Evelyn Redgrave 12 may, 1889, note by former of short and apologetic AL from authoress dated Aug. 4th 1892 in another hand: Association books No. 67 and 1945 signature of John Gilman, from the library of Geoffrey & Kathleen Tillotson. Jarndyce Antiquarian Booksellers CCVII - 350 2015 £50

Association – Gilmour, Caroline

Ayer, A. J. *Part of My Life.* London: Collins, 1977. First edition, 8vo., illustrations, signed presentation from author to Lady Caroline Gilmour, Nov. 3rd 1977, in price clipped dust jacket with slight edgewear. Any Amount of Books 2015 - A74370 2015 £175

Association – Gilmour, Ian

Webb, Timothy *Keats-Shelley Review.* Messington, York: Keats-Shelley Memorial Association, 1986. First edition, volumes 1-8, wrappers, 8vo., illustrations, clean, very good, from the library of Ian Gilmour with his ownership signatures and occasional erasable marginal linings and neat notes in pencil. Any Amount of Books 2015 - A83550 2015 £225

Who Was Who. London: Adam & Charles Black, 1966. Mostly reprints, 8vo., 9 volumes, first 6 volumes presented from Roy Jenkins to Ian Gilmour, all clean, very good or better. Any Amount of Books 2015 - A70295 2015 £225

Association – Grand, Archibald

Chesterfield, Philip Dormer Stanhope, 4th Earl of 1694-1773 *Letters written by the Late Right Honourable Philip Dormer Stanhope, Earl of Chesterfield to his Son Philip Stanhope...* London: J. Dodsley, 1774. First edition, 2 volumes, frontispiece volume I, contemporary boards, calf backs and tips, rubbed, worn at joints and edges, some foxing, soiling and minor stains, generally very good, tight copy, first issue with half title, errata leaf at end of volume 2, first issue with 'quia uroit' line 16 page 55 in volume I, contemporary ownership inscription and bookplates of Sir Archibald Grant of Monymoske, housed in custom cloth slipcase. Second Life Books Inc. 189 - 54 2015 $2000

Association – Grant, Douglas

Graves, Robert 1895-1985 *Mockbeggar Hall.* London: Hogarth Press, 1924. First edition, small quarto, original paper boards, pictorial bookplate of W. MacDonald MacKay, Scottish historian and bookman and name plate of Douglas Grant, Prof. of American Lit. at Leeds University, spine little bruised at foot, lower corners slightly bumped, very good. Peter Ellis, Bookseller 2014 - 006488 2015 £325

Ramsay, Allan 1688-1758 *Poems by Allan Ramsay. (with) Poems by Allan Ramsay. Volume II.* Edinburgh: printed by Thomas Ruddiman, 1721. 1728. First edition, 2 volumes, 4to., contemporary tree calf, spines gilt, red morocco labels and circular numbering pieces (one upper joint cracked, but strong), subscriber's set with armorial bookplate of Earl of Moray in each volume, particularly attractive set, modern booklabels of Douglas Grant, old invoice laid in reveals he acquired the set from John Grant Booksellers, Ltd. of Edinburgh in 1956. C. R. Johnson Foxon R-Z - 819r-z 2015 $3831

Association – Grantham, George

What is Luxury? To Which is Added a Manipulus of Etymological and Other Nugae. London: Samuel Maunder, 1829. First and only edition, 8vo., uncut, partly unopened, half title and final leaf with publisher's notice, some very light occasional foxing, original cloth, printed spine label, short tear to head of spine, very good, near contemporary signature of George Grantham of Barcombe Place, scarce. John Drury Rare Books March 2015 - 14835 2015 $266

Association – Granville, Wilfred

Cory, William *Ionica with Biographical Introduction...* London: George Allen, 1905. Third edition, half title, final colophon leaf, original light blue cloth, marked, top edge gilt, Geoffrey Tillotson's copy May 46 which had belonged to Wilfred Granville. Jarndyce Antiquarian Booksellers CCVII - 159 2015 £120

Association – Gration-Maxfield, Brent

Malthus, Thomas Robert 1766-1834 *The Grounds of an Opinion on the Policy of Restricting the Importation of Foreign Corn; Intended as an Appendix to "Observations on the Corn Laws".* London: John Murray and J. Johnson & Co., 1815. First edition, some minor staining to titlepage, otherwise fine, recent blue morocco backed marbled boards, gilt lettering to spine, ink note to pastedown 'Ex Libris Brent Gration-Maxfield", uncommon. John Drury Rare Books 2015 - 25567 2015 $2185

Association – Green, Charles

L'Estrange, Roger *Sir Roger L'Estrange's Fables with Morals and Reflections in English Verse.* London: printed by M. Jenour for Thomas Harbin, 1717. First edition, engraved frontispiece, 8vo., contemporary panelled calf, rebacked, later brown morocco label (rubbed, corners worn, short crack in lower joint), wanting flyleaf at front, inner margin of plate crudely strengthened, very slightly affecting image, otherwise sound, ownership inscription of Henry White of Lichfield, dated Feb. 1 1722, later signature of Charles V. Green dated 1870. C. R. Johnson Foxon R-Z - 926r-z 2015 $2298

Association – Green, Hannah

Powell, Dawn *Sunday, Monday and Always.* Boston: Houghton Mifflin Co., 1952. First edition, fair copy only, chipping at crown, lacking dust jacket, ownership signature of Powell's close friend and author Hannah, Green, scarce. Between the Covers Rare Books, Inc. 187 - 220 2015 $450

Powell, Dawn *The Wicked Pavilion.* Boston: Houghton Mifflin Co., 1954. Reprint, stain on front board, corners bumped, good only with substantial remnants of tattered dust jacket laid in, ownership signature of author's close friend, author, Hannah Green. Between the Covers Rare Books, Inc. 187 - 221 2015 $275

Association – Greene, Graham

Eliot, George, Pseud. 1819-1880 *The George Eliot Letters.* New Haven: Yale University Press, 1954-1955. First American edition, 7 volumes, large octavo, no dust jackets, this set belonged to novelist Graham Greene who has signed the front free endpaper of each volume and scrupulously marked text throughout. Honey & Wax Booksellers 1 - 57 2015 $5200

Gough, J. W. *John Locke's Political Philosophy: Eight Studies.* Oxford: Clarendon Press, 1950. First edition, small label from London bookseller Blackwell's, near fine without dust jacket, Graham Greene's ownership signature, which has been lightly struck through with another name beneath it.   Between the Covers Rare Books, Inc.   187 - 158   2015 $350

Association – Greenhill, Henry

Donne, John   1571-1631 *Biathanatos (First word in Greek).* printed by John Dawson, circa, 1647. First edition, first issue, with undated titlepage, woodcut initials, woodcut and typographic headpieces, initial blank, last 4 leaves with few short marginal tears, light browning at edges of titlepage (offset from binding turn-ins), 4to., contemporary blind ruled calf with corner ornaments, spine gilt, rebacked preserving original spine, lacking lettering piece, preserved in full brown morocco pull-off case, early signature of Wm. Vernon at head of initial blank, engraved bookplate of Henry Greenhill dated 1911, inside front cover, bookplate of H. Bradley Martin inside rear cover, modern bookplate recto of initial blank very good.   Blackwell's Rare Books   B179 - 37   2015   £5000

Association – Greenhill, Mildred

Lorenzini, Carlo   1829-1890 *Story of a Puppet or the Adventures of Pinocchio.* New York: Cassell, 1892. First edition in English, 12mo., decorative cloth with designed repeated on edges, cloth age toned as usual, name erased from endpaper, tiny stain on edge of title, small inner hinge mend, else really very good+, marbled slipcase, the Bradley Martin copy with Mildred Greenhill's bookplate.   Aleph-Bet Books, Inc.   108 - 103   2015 $9500

Association – Gregory, Arthur

The Works of the Most Celebrated Poets; Namley Wentworth, Earl of Roscommon; Charles, Earl of Dorset; Charles, Earl of Halifax; Sir Samuel Garth, George Stephney, Esq., William Walsh, Esq., Thomas Tickell, Esq.... (with) A supplement to the Works of the Most Celebrated Minor Poets... London: printed for F. Cogan, 1750. First edition, 8vo., 3 volumes, contemporary calf, gilt, spines gilt, spines rather rubbed but sound, very good, armorial bookplates of Arthur Gregory, Esq.   C. R. Johnson   Foxon R-Z - 1172r-z   2015 $613

Association – Gretton, John

Blackwell, John   *A Compendium of Military Discipline, As It Is Practised by the Honourable the Artillery Company of the City of London, for the Initiating and Instructing the Officers of the Trained-Bands of the Said City.* London: printed for the author and are to be sold at his house in Well Court in Queen Street near Cheapside, 1726. First and only edition, 8vo., 3 large double folding engraved plates, old name inked out on titlepage and later ownership signature in upper margin, 20th century armorial bookplate of John Gretton of Stapleford, contemporary calf, gilt, appropriately rebacked with raised bands, gilt lines and label, very good, crisp, quite rare.   John Drury Rare Books   2015 - 25303   2015 $3324

Association – Gretton, Lord

Bloemaert, Abraham   *Oorpronkelyk En Vermaard Konstryk Tekenboek.* Amsterdam: Reiner & Josua Ottens, 1740. Engraved title added, engraved dedication plate, portrait of author and plates numbered 1 (engraved title) to 166; engraved title, portrait and duplicates of plates 80, 94, 95, 108, 137, 144 & 145 overprinted with chiaroscuro blacks to ochre, making a total of 175 plates by Frederick Bloemaert after Abraham Bloemaert; folio, contemporary half calf, speckled boards, remains of label on upper cover, rubbed, from the library of Lord Gretton.   Maggs Bros. Ltd. Illustrated Books 2014 - 2015   £7500

Gorton, John   *A General Biographical Dictionary.* London: Whittaker and Co., 1833. 3 substantial volumes, 8vo., original maroon/pink pebbled dash cloth, spines lettered gilt but cloth color little faded, fine, uncut, from the library of Lord Gretton of Stapleford (1867-1947).   John Drury Rare Books   2015 - 26214   2015 $106

Association – Grey, Zane

Grey, Zane   1872-1939 *Forlorn River.* New York: Harper & Bros., 1927. First edition (H-B), 8vo., title vignette, black and white decorations and color dust jacket by Robert Amick, near fine, tight copy in dust jacket with light wear to head and toe of spine and extremities, from Zane Grey's estate library with his blindstamp.   Buckingham Books March 2015 - 12160   2015 $1275

Association – Grien, J.

Wotton, Henry   *Reliquiae Wottonianae; or a Collection of Lives, Letters, Poems...* London: By T. Roycroft for R. Marriott, 1672. Third edition, portraits, 19th century red morocco, early signatures of J. Grien? 1725, Thomas Price and John Francis Cole 1828, bookplates of J. J. Chapman and Molly Flagg Gibb, very good.   Joseph J. Felcone Inc. Science, Medicine and Technology - 57   2015 $900

Association – Grigson, Geoffrey

Coleridge, Samuel Taylor 1772-1834 *Biographia Literaria; or Biographical Sketches...* London: Rest Fenner, 1817. First edition, 2 volumes, half titles, without final ad leaf volume II, some spotting, few leaves rather browned, half red calf, spines chipped, hinges weak, signed S. Palmer and with his pencil notes at end of Chapter I, inserted is ALS of inquiry to Geoffrey Tillotson from Geoffrey Grigson. Jarndyce Antiquarian Booksellers   CCVII - 147   2015   £850

Association – Grimes, Lester

Houdini, Harry *Elliott's Last Legacy...* New York: Adams Press Print, 1923. First edition, illustrations by Oscar Teale, binding lightly worn at extremities, tidemark from dampstain at top corner of pages throughout, front hinge tender but still sound, very good, Teale's copy, inscribed for him by Houdini, inscribed by Teale for Lester Grimes, Grimes then inscribed the book for friend Gertrude Elliott.   Between the Covers Rare Books, Inc.   187 - 164   2015 $4000

Association – Grimm, G.

Grimm, Herman *Literature.* Boston: Cupples, Upham & Co., 1886. First American edition, 297 pages, with ANS from G. Grimm (?untranslated), also with publisher's inscription "With publisher's compliments and thanks for so kindly supervising the proof sheets while the book was in press Dec. 25 1885", uncommon, half leather and marbled boards and endpapers, raised bands, gilt spine decorations, leather labels, very good, little scuffing to boards, hinge professionally repaired, tight, clean text.   Stephen Lupack   March 2015 - 2015 $125

Association – Gruen, Bob

Buckland, Gail *Who Shot Rock & Roll: a Photographic History 1955-the Present.* New York: Knopf, 2009. First edition, more than 200 photos, this copy signed by Buckland and by photographers Bob Gruen and Godlis, fine in fine dust jacket, uncommon with signatures.   Ken Lopez, Bookseller   164 - 167   2015 $300

Association – Gude, Lorenz

Veitch, Tom *Literary Days.* New York: "C" Press, 1964. First edition, 4to., mimeographed and stapled in wrappers, some very light dust soil, fine, presentation copy from author to publisher Lorenz Gude.   James S. Jaffe Rare Books Many Happy Returns - 367   2015 $850

Association – Guerrero, Agustin

Colombia. Laws, Statutes, etc. *Coleccion de las Leyes Dadas por el Congreso Constitucional de la Republica de Combia en las sesiones de los anos 1825 i 1836.* Bogota: Imp. de P. Cubiddes, 1827. First edition, signed by Agustin Guerrero (1817-1902) President of the Provisional government of the Republic of Ecuador, very good, two tiny wormholes in spine, scuffing to boards, partial label on spine, minor dampstaining to rear leaves, last leaf soiled.   Kaaterskill Books   19 - 39   2015 $1250

Association – Guest, Barbara

Ashbery, John *Some Trees.* New Haven: Yale University Press, 1956. First edition, one of only 817 copies, small 8vo., original black cloth, dust jacket, presentation copy inscribed to poet Barbara Guest, covers slightly soiled, otherwise fine in dust jacket.   James S. Jaffe Rare Books Modern American Poetry - 10   2015 $2500

Berrigan, Ted *Red Wagon.* Chicago: Yellow Press, 1976. First edition, 8vo, original boards, dust jacket, very fine, presentation copy inscribed by author for poet Barbara Guest.   James S. Jaffe Rare Books   Many Happy Returns - 39   2015 $1000

Eberhart, Richard *Collected Poems 1930-1960.* New York: Oxford University Press, 1960. First edition, fine in spine faded, otherwise very good dust jacket, inscribed by author for Barbara Guest and her husband, military historian Trumbull Higgins.   Between the Covers Rare Books, Inc.   187 - 86   2015 $225

Schuyler, James *Hymn to Life. Poems.* New York: Random House, 1974. First edition, 8vo., original cloth backed boards, dust jacket, fine, presentation copy inscribed by author for Barbara Guest March 12 1974.   James S. Jaffe Rare Books   Modern American Poetry - 239   2015 $2500

Schuyler, James *The Morning of the Poem.* New York: Farrar Straus & Giroux, 1980. First edition, 8vo., cloth backed boards, dust jacket, fine in slightly sunned jacket, presentation copy inscribed by author for Barbara Guest, Feb. 1980.   James S. Jaffe Rare Books   Modern American Poetry - 245   2015 $2500

Association – Gunkle, William

Burke, B. W. *A Compendium of the Anatomy, Physiology and Pathology of the Horse...* Philadelphia: James Humphreys, 1806. First American edition, 12mo., 2 plates, contemporary mottled sheep, plates moderately foxed, upper spine cap partly chipped, small chip from spine label, else very attractive in handsome period binding, ownership signature of Wm. Gunkle 1818. Joseph J. Felcone Inc. Science, Medicine and Technology - 15   2015 $1000

Association – Guy, Buddy

Wilcock, Donald E. *Damn Right I've Got the Blues.* San Francisco: Woodford, 1993. First printing, 8vo., signed by Wilcock and Buddy Guy, copiously illustrated with photos, paper wrappers, cover slighty scuffed, otherwise very good, tight copy.   Second Life Books Inc.   190 - 215   2015 $150

Association – Guymon, Ned

Gruber, Frank *Outlaw.* Farrar & Rinehart Inc., 1941. First edition, bookplate of Ned Guymon, else fine, bright, square copy, dust jacket with one tiny closed tear to top edge of rear cover, sharp condition.   Buckingham Books March 2015 - 37514   2015 $250

Association – Haight, Gordon

Eliot, George, Pseud. 1819-1880 *Daniel Deronda.* Oxford: Clarendon Press, 1984. Half title, original black cloth, very good in slightly marked dust jacket, Kathleen Tillotson's copy from the editor, Graham Handley, with TLS of explanation from him inserted 1985, with draft copy of the introduction and notes in response to criticism by General editor, Gordon Haight.   Jarndyce Antiquarian Booksellers CCVII - 254   2015   £60

Eliot, George, Pseud. 1819-1880 *Selections from George Eliot's Letters.* New Haven: Yale University Press, 1985. Original olive green cloth, very good in dust jacket, presentation for Kathleen Tillotson, TLS from Gordon Haight for Kathleen.   Jarndyce Antiquarian Booksellers   CCVII - 258   2015   £30

Association – Haines, Robert

Pirovano, Carlo *The Graphics of Emilio Greco.* N.P. (Venice): Electa Editrice, 1975. First English edition, folio, orginal green cloth lettered gilt on spine and cover with illustration in white on cover, signed presentation from artist to Australian art expert Robert Haines, slight rubbing, slight sun fading, otherwise sound clean, very good.   Any Amount of Books   2015 - A76883   2015   £300

Association – Haining, Peter

Hamilton, Patrick 1904-1962 *Hangover Square.* London: Constable, 1941. Second impression publsihed September 1941 (first was August 1941), 8vo., from the library of Peter Haining (1940-2007) with his book label and brief ownership signature, covers tanned, slightly marked and mottled, sound, very good- with clean text, signed presentation from author to Ernest Borrow.   Any Amount of Books   2015 - C1683   2015   £700

Association – Hale, George Ellery

Anniversary Volume Dedicated to Professor Hantaro Nagaoka by His Friends and Pupils on the Completion of Twenty-Five Years of His Professorship. Tokyo: privately published, 1925. One of 1280 copies, 4to., 19 half tone plates, tissue guards (few with tissue overlays), figures, tables, maroon cloth, gilt stamped cover and spine titles, spine ends frayed, covers lightly faded, former library copy with usual markings and defects, signature of George Ellery Hale, fair, scarce with 4 page errata sheet loosely placed in. Jeff Weber Rare Books   178 - 816   2015 $200

Association – Hales, George

Coles, Elisha *Christologia or a Metrical paraphrase on the History of Our Lord and Saviour Jesus Christ.* London: for Peter Parker, 1671. First edition, 8vo., without first blank leaf, light browning particularly in margins, words "OR A" on title deleted with ink and replaced with "a" in later manuscript, closely shaved, mid 20th century blue quarter morocco and marbled boards, from the library of James Stevens Cox (1910-1997), inscribed by Lewis Caesar Hill, 19th century signature George R. Hales, signature R. Betts dated "Silverhill 15.1 (18)90", booklabel of Gerald P Mander (d. 1951) of Tettenhall Wood, Staffordshire.   Maggs Bros. Ltd. 1447 - 105   2015   £240

Association – Haley, James Evetts

Bell, James G. *A Log of the Texas-California Cattle Trail 1854.* Reprinted from the Southwestern Historical Quarterly, 1932. first book edition of only 100 copies, 8vo., original blue printed wrappers, minor wear to extended edges of front and rear covers, else near fine, clean, inscribed by James Evetts Haley for Mr. John Thomas Lee, June 29 1934.   Buckingham Books   March 2015 - 37237 2015 $1750

Association – Hall, James Norman

Schevill, James *The Mayan Poems.* Providence: Copper Beech Press, 1978. First edition, printed wrappers, light soiling on front wrapper, else fine, warmly inscribed to author James Norman Hall.   Between the Covers Rare Books, Inc.   187 - 244   2015 $125

Association – Halliday, Brett

McCloy, Helen *The Further side of Fear.* New York: Dodd Mead & Co., 1967. First edition, inscribed by author for former husband Brett Halliday and his parents Jan. 1967, fine in lightly rubbed dust jacket, lightly sunned on spine and with light wear to spine ends. Buckingham Books March 2015 - 6298   2015 $175

Association – Hamilton, E.

Wordsworth, William 1770-1850 *Yarrow Revisited and Other Poems.* London: Longman, Rees, Orme, Brown, Green & Longman, 1835. First edition, presentation copy inscribed by author for fellow poet Eliz M. Hamilton on a slip of paper pasted on to verso of title and with "From the Author" written on half title by publisher's clerk, erratum slip tipped in, ads discarded, 12mo., slightly later 19th century olive pebble grain morocco by Tuckett ('binder to the Queen'), backstrip panelled and ruled in gilt and infilled with volutes and other tools, lettered gilt in second compartment, sides with triple gilt borders, inner panel with gilt cornerpieces and central panels of curing lines, all edges gilt, marbled endpapers, bookplate of J. O. Edwards, small scrape to upper board, extremities slightly rubbed, good. Blackwell's Rare Books   B179 - 121   2015   £2500

Association – Hamilton, Nancy

Metz, Leon C. *Robert E. McKee: Master Builder of Structures Beyond the Ordinary.* El Paso: Robert E. & Evelyn McKee Foundation, 1997. First edition, 4to., pictorial silver stamped cloth, illustrations, signed by Metz, Louis McKee (Typography, Design) and editor Nancy Hamilton, fine in fine, original silver stamped slipcase, very scarce, fine. Baade Books of the West   2014 - 2015 $356

Association – Hammond-Knowlton, Mrs.

Kunitz, Stanley *Intellectual Things.* New York: Doubleday Doran, 1930. First edition, 8vo., original cloth, dust jacket, very good, inscribed by author for Mrs. Hammond-Knowlton, 6/24/34. James S. Jaffe Rare Books Modern American Poetry - 169   2015 $1500

Association – Handley, Graham

Eliot, George, Pseud. 1819-1880 *Daniel Deronda.* Oxford: Clarendon Press, 1984. Half title, original black cloth, very good in slightly marked dust jacket, Kathleen Tillotson's copy from the editor, Graham Handley, with TLS of explanation from him inserted 1985, with draft copy of the introduction and notes in response to criticism by General editor, Gordon Haight. Jarndyce Antiquarian Booksellers CCVII - 254   2015   £60

Eliot, George, Pseud. 1819-1880 *Romola.* Leipzig: Bernhard Tauchnitz, 1863. Copyright edition, extra illustrated with numerous photos, elaborate gilt binding, contemporary full vellum, bevelled boards, embossed in maroon, finely tooled gilt, gilt endpapers, small bookseller's ticket, G. Giannini, Florence, very good, handsome copy in red cloth jacket now broken red cloth box, presentation by Graham Handley for Kathleen Tillotson, with his inscription, his appreciation, occasional ink marginal notes and accompanying letter and copy of Kathleen's reply. Jarndyce Antiquarian Booksellers   CCVII - 256   2015   £65

Association – Handyside, Dr.

Struthers, John *How to Improve the Teaching in the Scottish Universities.* Edinburgh: Sutherland and Knox, 1859. First edition, 8vo., 36 pages, original printed card covers, minor edge chips, very good, inscribed by author for Dr. Handyside. John Drury Rare Books   2015 - 13968   2015 $89

Association – Hanley, James

Pritchett, V. S. *You Make Your Own Life: Short Stories.* London: Chatto and Windus, 1938. First edition, original binding, spine dulled, corners bumped, one little rubbed, half title browned, otherwise nice, small label and stamp to rear endpapers, presentation copy inscribed by author to James Hanley, from the collection of Gavin H. Fryer. Bertram Rota Ltd.   308 Part II - 188   2015   £175

Association – Hanley, Jane

Balmford, William *The Seaman's Spiritual Companion or Navigation Spirituallized.* London: for Benj. Harris, 1678. First edition, small 8vo., variant state of title with double rule border and price on titlepage, A2 shaved at foot affecting signature and catchword on recto, minor worming in upper outer corner of D4-K8 (affecting end of text in places), stain to B3-E2 affecting three lines, occasional foxing, small hole from paper flaw in lower margin of E2, short tear at foot of F3 slightly affecting last line on recto and catchword on verso, small hole from paper flaw in centre of I2 touching two lines, actually reasonable and much loved copy, contemporary sheep (rubbed, covers scuffed, fore edge of lower cover worn exposing board, corners worn), several pen trials, scribbles, ownership inscriptions John Allab(on) His Booke October ye 24th 16, Charles Canning his book 1679, James Purnell His Booke Anno Domini (deleted), "Thomas Nichols His Book May ye 10 1718", "James Croome His Book March ye 9th 1757" "Jane Hanley", from the library of James Stevens Cox (1910-1997). Maggs Bros. Ltd. 1447 - 21   2015   £2800

Association – Hans, Lenz

Antiquelades Mexicanas. Mexico: Officina Tiografico de la Secretaria de Fomento, 1892. Large folio, half red morocco over marbled paper boards, gilt stamped at spine with five raised bands, 80 pages of text bound in front, chromolithograph title and 149 plates, some double page, some in color, bit of dampstaining to few pages, small location sticker on bottom of spine and two small location stickers on top right corners of front free endpapers, previous owner's bookplate on front pastedown of Hans Lenz (German politician), few spots on spine, otherwise fine.   Heritage Book Shop   Holiday 2014 - 41   2015 $2500

Association – Hansard, T. C.

Thomas A Kempis 1380-1471 *The Christian's Pattern or a Treatise of the Imitation of Jesus Christ.* London: printed by T. C. Hansard, 1831. First edition thus, 8vo., full brown leather with gilt lettered spine label, long handwritten note on tips to verso front endpaper from printer, T. C. Hansard, signed with a flourish by TCH, head of spine chipped, front outer hinges cracked but holding, very good.   Any Amount of Books   2015 - A36006   2015   £175

Association – Hanway, Jonas

Midnight the Signal. London: sold by Dodsley, 1779. 2 volumes, 165 x 102mm., complete with usual pagination in volume II, pleasing contemporary crimson morocco bound for Jonas Hanway by his second binder, covers gilt with twining border enclosing a frame of roses with sunburst cornerpieces, upper cover with Greek cross at center encircled by motto "O save us from ourselves', lower cover with winged hourglass and motto 'Revere the appointment of nature', raised bands, spine compartments gilt in checkerboard pattern punctuated by daisies, one olive and one black morocco label, gilt turn-ins, marbled endpapers, all edges gilt, engraved titlepage with emblem depicting Death hovering over socializing persons, with a lutist in the background, large paper copy, verso of front free endpapers, with armorial bookplate from which the name has been excised, spines bit darkened with muted gilt leather on covers varying in color (from fading or soiling) but bindings entirely solid and with only trivial wear to joints, leaves with hint of offsetting and isolated soiling, faint dampstain to lower fore edge of one gathering, otherwise extremely pleasing internally, text clean, fresh and bright and with vast margins.   Phillip J. Pirages   66 - 44   2015 $4800

Association – Harbin

Gracian y Morales, Baltasar 1601-1658 *The Art of Prudence, or a Companion for a Man of Sense.* printed for D. Browne... J. Walthoe... and W. Mears and Jonas Browne, 1714. 8vo., contemporary panelled calf, lettered gilt on front cover 'I. Phelipps Y', (Rev. John Phelipps), red lettering piece, cracks at head of spine, very good, delightful copy, this copy from Newton Surmaville, in Somerset, the home of Robert Harbin, it remained in the library which remained untouched for hundreds of years (until it was sold in 2007), when the last member of the family, Sophia Wyndham died.   Blackwell's Rare Books   B179 - 48   2015   £600

Association – Harbin, Wyndham

Beaumont, Francis *Comedies and Tragedies written by Francis Beaumont and John Fletcher.* London: for Humphrey Robinson and Humphrey Moseley, 1647. First edition, small folio, lacking final leaf of text, engraved portrait, second state with "Vates Duplex" in fourth line of the inscription and "J. Berkenhead' in smaller letters (backed with old paper, at time of rebinding, slightly cropped at foot, ink bot in inscription) titlepage stained and slightly dusty, loose at upper inner margin, margins bit frayed, small hole in blank area near outer edge, lower outer corner of F3 torn away with loss to five lines, few words on 7 lines on Dd1v have adhered to blank page opposite upper corner 3U4 torn away affecting pagination, loss at foot of 7A1 from paper flaw affecting a few letters, closed vertical tears, minor spots and stains throughout, some ink blots, upper inner margin of first few leaves and lower outer corner of last few leaves dampstained, late 17th/early 18th century sheep, covers ruled in blind (headcaps and top and bottom of spine torn away, covers somewhat scuffed, cup ring on lower cover, upper corner of lower cover chewed and dampstained), from the library of James Stevens Cox (1910-1997), name Wyndham Harbin, 2nd son of William and Elizabeth Harbin of Newton Surmaville, Somerset with his signature, name Elizabeth (probably Harbin).   Maggs Bros. Ltd.   1447 - 25   2015   £600

Association – Harcourt, Earl of

Hocquart De Courbron, M. *Nouvelles Vues sur l'Administration des Finances, et sur l'Allegement de l'Inpot, (bound with) Calculs sur la Circulation, Relativement aux Impts & L'Augmentation du Prix des Denrees et a la Dimuntion du Taux de L'Interet De l'Aragent.* La Haye: 1785. Londres: T. Payne & Fils, Pl. elmsley & T. Hookham, 1787. First edition, 8vo., half title, 4 statistical tables placed after p. 32 and final leaf; large folding table; bound in early 19th century half calf over marbled boards, neatly rebacked and labelled, excellent copy of the 19th century library of the Earls Harcourt with their armorial bookplate, very scarce, fine, crisp copy.   John Drury Rare Books   2015 - 26285   2015 $787

Association – Hardy, Thomas

Spencer, Herbert *An Autobiography.* London: Williams & Norgate, 1904. First edition, 2 volumes, thick octavo, brown cloth gilt, very short tear crown volume one, slight foxing on titlepages, modest bumping at extremities, near fine set, signature "Thomas Hardy, Max Gate, Dorchester", one small note in pencil in index in unknown hand, possibly Hardy's.   Between the Covers Rare Books, Inc.   187 - 264   2015 $950

Association – Hare, N.

Diodorus Siculus *The History of Diodorus Siculus.* London: by John Macock for Giles Calvert, 1653. First edition in English, small folio, longitudinal half title has been cut-out leaving a stub, 271 pages, small circular stain in inner margins of first few leaves and Kk4-L12, rust spot on Kk4, contemporary sheep, smooth spine ruled in blind and with red morocco and gilt label, covers heavily scuffed, piece missing from top corner of lower cover, upper head-cap torn, front pastedown torn away at head, early inscription on flyleaf heavily deleted, early signature Nic. Hare, signature on title Edm. Sex. Pery, 1st and last Viscount Pery (1719-1806) by descent to his elder daughter Diana Jane, Countess of Ranfurly to Earls of Ranfurly, with 19th century bookplate, from the library of James Stevens Cox (1910-1997).   Maggs Bros. Ltd.   1447 - 148   2015   £380

Association – Hargraves, Alice

Dodgson, Charles Lutwidge   1832-1898 *Alice's Adventures in Wonderland. (with) Through the Looking Glasss and What Alice Found There.* New York: Limited Editions Club, 1912. 1935. Both limited to 1500 numbered copies, signed by the original Alice, Alice Hargraves, signed by Frederic Warde, this copy of of the few signed by the 'original Alice', octavo, original text illustrations by Tenniel re-engraved on wood by Bruno Rollitz, printed by members of the LEC by the Printing House of William Edwin Rudge, typography and binding design by Frederic Warde, publisher's full red morocco by George McKibbin & Son, NY. covers decoratively bordered in gilt, smooth spine decoratively tooled and lettered gilt in compartments, some rubbing to spine, near fine, housed in original blue cloth slipcase (some browning and light wear); Looking Glass with original text illustrations by Tenniel, Re-engraved (in metal) by Frederick Warde, publisher's full blue morocco by McKibbin, covers decoratively bordered gilt, smooth spine decoratively tooled and lettered in gilt in compartments, all edges gilt some rubbing, some scuffing to spine, near fine copy, housed in original red cloth slipcase, fine.   Heritage Book Shop   Holiday 2014 - 30   2015 $4000

Association – Harris, Hank

Morley, Christopher   1890-1957 *Mince Pie.* New York: George H. Doran, 1919. First edition, scarce first state with 'of' instead of 'on' on page vii, excellent inscription by author for Hank and Margaret Harris, very good (some general age wear, tight, clean text).   Stephen Lupack   March 2015 - 2015 $75

Association – Harris, Joel Chandler

Washington, Booker T. *Up from Slavery: an Autobiography.* New York: Doubleday Page, 1901. First edition, octavo, red cloth, little rubbing at extremities couple of leaves little roughly opened resulting in small nicks at page edges, else very near fine, gilt bright, inscribed by author shortly after publication for Joel Chandler Harris, Washington April 14 1901.   Between the Covers Rare Books   197 - 66   2015 $65,000

Association – Harris, Margaret

Morley, Christopher   1890-1957 *Mince Pie.* New York: George H. Doran, 1919. First edition, scarce first state with 'of' instead of 'on' on page vii, excellent inscription by author for Hank and Margaret Harris, very good (some general age wear, tight, clean text).   Stephen Lupack   March 2015 - 2015 $75

Association – Harrison, John

Carew, Thomas   1595-1639 *Poems, Songs and Sonnets, Together with a Masque.* London: Henry Herringman, 1670. Fourth edition, 8vo., foxed and browned, heaviest in margins, occasional repairs to fore and upper edge, closely shaved along lower edge, touching catchwords and signatures on a number of leaves, early 20th century half calf and cloth boards, with W(illia)m Gates 18th century signature, pencil signature of H. F. B. Brett Smith (1896-1942), ink inscription March 20th 1922 of Francis K. W. Needham, signature John (?Harr)ison dated 1926, from the library of James Stevens Cox (1910-1997).   Maggs Bros. Ltd.   1447 - 64   2015   £180

Association – Harrison, Rex

Hill, James *Rita Hayworth: a memoir.* New York: Simon and Schuster, 1983. Uncorrected proof, moderatley worn and read but tight, very good copy, Rex Harrison's copy with his ownership stamp.   Between the Covers Rare Books, Inc.   187 - 126   2015 $300

Association – Harrison, Sally

Allestree, Richard *The Ladies Calling.* Oxford: printed at the Theater, 1673. First edition, 8vo., 2 parts in 1, early 18th century panelled calf with marbled endpapers, frontispiece, the copy of Barbara Dobell with her signature, and below is "Sally Harrison/June 11th 1797" with note about her marriage and on facing blank is 19th century inscription "the gift of S. Mitchell to her niece Mary Best December 1855, in lower margin of final page of text is note in Dobell's hand about binding and cost charged by a Mr. Double on March 30 1706, edges little rubbed, marbled endpapers have cleanly lifted from boards, firmly held in place by sewing, fine.   The Brick Row Book Shop   Miscellany 67 - 3   2015 $500

Association – Hart-Davis, Rupert

House, Humphry *Coleridge, the Clark Lectures 1951-1952.* London: Rupert Hart Davis, 1953. Half title, original decorated boards, very good in slightly dusted dust jacket, Geoffrey Tillotson's copy with TLS from Rupert Hart-Davis 1955 announcing House's sudden death, tipped in, pencil notes, obits, and two ALS's from Madeline House to Geoffrey.   Jarndyce Antiquarian Booksellers   CCVII - 153   2015   £30

Association – Hart, Doctor

Walter, William W. *The Great Understander Truelife Story of the Last of the Wells Fargo Shotgun Express Messengers.* William W. Walter, 1931. First edition, inscribed by compiler for Doctor Hart, fine.   Buckingham Books   March 2015 - 23898   2015 $275

Association – Hart, G. U.

Descartes, Rene *Renatus Descartes Excellent Compendium of Musick.* London: by Thomas Harper for Humphrey Moseley and Thomas Heath, 1653. First edition in English, small 4to., later engraved portrait, dampstaining to lower margins throughout, dark ink stain to upper margins of a1-b1- (not touching text), worming to lower margin of I4-M4 and with small piece torn away from margins of B3, G3 and L3 (not touching text), contemporary sheep, covers ruled in blind, spine worn and with some worm damage, edges and corners worn and chewed, 18th century inscription William Wilsons, 19th century signature G. U. Hart, Killderry, from the library of James Stevens Cox (1910-1997).   Maggs Bros. Ltd.   1447 - 139   2015   £1500

Association – Hart, Mickey

Brandelius, Jerilyn Lee *Grateful Dead Family Album.* New York: Warner Books, 1989. First edition, 'Grateful Dead All Area Access sticker laid down to jacket, this copy signed by band members Jerry Garcia, Mickey Hart and Bob Bralove as well as long time road crew members Ram Rod Shurtliff, Bill 'Kid' Candelario, Steve Parish and Robbie Taylor among others, hundreds of intimate photos and stories, very good plus to near fine with little soil and handling marks, in very good plus to near fine dust jacket with short closed tear to bottom of front flap.   Ed Smith Books   83 - 34   2015 $950

Association – Hart, Percival

Pyle, Howard *Howard Pyle's Book of Pirates.* New York: Harper & Bros., 1921. KV. First edition, early printing, folio, full brown morocco stamped in gold with gold decoration, top edge gilt, fine in original publisher's box with printed label stamped 'full morocco' (box flaps repaired), this copy boldly signed by Percival Hart, most likely the distinguished WWI hero.   Aleph-bet Books, Inc.   109 - 394   2015 $1800

Association – Harvey, J. R.

Fortescue, J. W. *A History of the British Army.* London: Macmillan, 1899-1930. First edition, 20 volumes complete, 6 map volumes with colored maps, original red cloth, lettered gilt at spine, very good or better, sound copies with some slight fading, some volumes have mottling to covers/and or edges, contents text and maps clean and sound, bookplate of Lieut. Colonel. J. R. Harvey in many volumes, occasional label of Officer's Mess 5th Battalion of S. Staffordshire Regiment or small oval stamp of 2nd Battalion.   Any Amount of Books   2015 - C5522   2015   £750

Association – Hasse, Doctor

Blochman, Lawrence G. *Diagnosis: Homicide the Casebook of Dr. Coffee.* Philadelphia: J. B. Lippincott, 1950. First edition, signed by author on titlepage, presentation from author for Doc. Hasse, lightly rubbed at spine ends, else near fine in dust jacket lightly rubbed at spine ends and corners.   Buckingham Books   March 2015 - 27777   2015 $2500

Association – Hasted J. S.

Breton, Nicholas 1545-1626 *A Poste with a Packet of mad letters.* London: for George Badger, 1653. Small 4to., lacking title to part 2, lacking final leaf of text, woodcut on title (block much wormed), inner margin of title and first few leaves and final leaf of part 1 dampstained, dampstain in lower margin of pages 31-42 and 59-68, short wormtrail (breaking into holes in places) in inner margin of first part (old patch over worming on final leaf of part 1), final leaf somewhat soiled and slightly short at lower margin, late 19th century half maroon morocco, marbled boards slightly rubbed, signature, J. S. Hasted, bookplate of Allan D. MacDonald, from the library of James Stevens Cox (1910-1997).   Maggs Bros. Ltd.   1447 - 46   2015   £950

Association – Hastings, 1st Marquis of

MacAllester, Oliver   *A Series of Letters, Discovering the Scheme Projected by France in MDCCLIX for an Intended Invasion Upon England with Flat-Bottom'd Boats...* London: printed for the author and sold by Mr. Williams &c, 1767. First edition, 2 volumes in 1, 4to., contemporary half calf over marbled boards, spine with raised bands, gilt lines and label, minor rubbing to joints and little wear to head and foot of spine, very good, sound, from the 19th century library of first Marquis of Hastings with his armorial bookplate.   John Drury Rare Books   March 2015 - 25147   2015 $656

Association – Hathway, J.

Crouch, Nathaniel   *Admirable Curiosities Rarities and Wonders in England Scotland and Ireland.* London: for Nath. Crouch, 1697. Fifth edition, 12mo., engraved frontispiece, 6 woodcut illustrations lightly browned, printer's crease across B10 (touching three lines of text) and F2 (touching to lines), fore-margin of G2 little frayed, small piece torn away from corner of G4 and G6 (with loss to ends of four lines), fore margin of C1 creased and with some light staining to E11 and G9, mid 19th century half calf and marbled boards, label of Upham and Beet, 46 New Bond Street, rebacked with original spine laid down, covers faded, early signature of J. Hathway, from the library of James Stevens Cox (1910-1997).   Maggs Bros. Ltd.   1447 - 123   2015   £250

Association – Hawker, J. W.

Boyle, Robert 1627-1691   *Certain Physiological Essays and Other Tracts.* London: Henry Herringman, 1669. Second edition, 4to., without final blank leaf, small wormhole through upper blank margin, long wormtrail in inner margin and into text around line 14 of Pp1(3)E2, leaf B1 dusty at head, small piece torn away from blank corner of T2 and with tear to foot of O3, contemporary sprinkled calf, covers panelled in blind, paper label in second panel of spine, covers affected by worm damage, in particular they have chewed out corner ornaments of panels, early inscription of George Sampson, 18th century signature J. W. Hawker, from the library of James Stevens Cox (1910-1997).   Maggs Bros. Ltd.   1447 - 35   2015   £950

Association – Hayden, Mary E. Power

Hayden, Jabez Haskell   *Records of the Connecticut Line of the Hayden.* Windsor Locks: Jabez Haskelly Hayden, 1888. First edition, large octavo, 329 pages, green cloth with leather spine label gilt, corners worn, label quite rubbed, good or better, ownership signature of Mary E. Power Hayden, photos.   Between the Covers Rare Books, Inc.   187 - 122   2015 $300

Association – Hayes, Julian

McCullers, Carson 1917-1957   *The Mortgaged Heart.* Boston: Houghton Mifflin, 1971. First edition, about fine in price clipped, very good dust jacket with modest spine faded, nicely inscribed by editor, Margarita Smith (author's sister) to Clifford Milton and Julian Hayes.   Between the Covers Rare Books, Inc.   187 - 175   2015 $450

Association – Hayward, John

Auden, Wystan Hugh 1907-1973   *The Old Man's Road.* New York: Voyage Press, 1956. First edition, octavo, one of 750 copies (of which 50 had been numbered and signed by author), signed by author, presentation copy from publisher, inscribed to Mr. John Hayward, fine in near fine dust jacket with hint of darkening to spine.   Peter Ellis, Bookseller   2014 - 012140   2015   £350

Association – Hazo, Sam

Bowles, Jane   *The Collected Works of Jane Bowles.* New York: Noonday Press, 1966. First edition, inscribed to Arab-American poet, Sam Hazo.   Honey & Wax Booksellers   2 - 58   2015 $1000

Association – Heath, Thomas

Dreyer, John Louis Emil *Tycho Brahe; a Picture of Scientific Life and Work in the Sixteenth Century.* Edinburgh: Adam and Charles Black, 1890. First edition, 8vo., frontispiece, 4 plates, original navy blue gilt stamped cloth, somewhat rubbed, still very good, color added to endleaves, inscribed by author to Thomas Heath, bookplate of Herbert Kraus.   Jeff Weber Rare Books   178 - 787   2015 $450

Association – Heberden, Charles Buller

Wesley, Samuel *Letters to ... Mr. Jacobs Relating to the Introduction into this Country of the Works of John Sebastian Bach.* London: S. W. Partridge & Co., 1875. Blue boards, vellum spine, ink title, armorial bookplate of Charles Buller Heberden, very good, Geoffrey Tillotson's inscription 17.5.1926.   Jarndyce Antiquarian Booksellers   CCVII - 554   2015   £20

Association – Heflin, Van

Benefield, Barry *Short Turns.* New York: Century Co., 1926. First edition, spine lettering bit worn, faint dampstain on fore edge, very good plus in very good example of scarce dust jacket with some shallow chipping at spinal extremities, not affecting any lettering, Gloria Swanson's copy with her ownership signature and stamp, this copy was given by Swanson to Van Heflin who later gave it to a friend.   Between the Covers Rare Books, Inc.   187 - 17   2015 $475

Association – Heinrich, Helen

Dahl, Roald *Danny the Champion of the World.* London: Puffin Books, 1979. Reprint, paperback, fine in wrappers, inscribed by author to children's book reviewer Helen Heinrich.   Between the Covers Rare Books, Inc.   187 - 49   2015 $350

Association – Heller, Erica

Heller, Joseph *God Knows.* New York: Alfred A. Knopf, 1984. First edition, fine in just about fine dust jacket with little rubbing at crown, inscribed by author to his daughter Erica 8/28/84.   Between the Covers Rare Books, Inc.   187 - 123   2015 $1000

Association – Heller, Joshua

Dreyfus, John *A History of the Nonesuch Press.* London: Nonesuch Press, 1981. Limited to 950 numbered copies, 4to., cloth, dust jacket, printed on specially made paper from Dalmore Mill of William Sommerville, Edinburgh, many illustrations, some black and white, few with color, various news reviews laid in, presentation from Dreyfus for Joshua Heller, toning to inside flaps of jacket.   Oak Knoll Books   306 - 157   2015 $350

Association – Helms, Alan

Bidart, Frank *The Book of the Body.* New York: Farrar, Straus and Giroux, 1977. First edition, tiny spot on front fly, else fine in fine dust jacket, very warmly inscribed to Alan Helms in year of publication.   Between the Covers Rare Books, Inc.   187 - 22   2015 $250

Bidart, Frank *Golden State.* New York: George Braziller, 1973. First edition, one of 500 copies, fine in fine dust jacket with bit of age toning at extremities, inscribed by aauthor for essayist, author and academic Alan Helms, June 23 1973.   Between the Covers Rare Books, Inc.   187 - 21   2015 $375

Levertov, Denise *Conversation in Moscow.* No Place: Hovey St. Press, 1973. First edition, one of 800 copies, inscribed by author for Alan (Helms), March 1975, thin octavo, printed wrappers, fine.   Between the Covers Rare Books, Inc.   187 - 153   2015 $150

Association – Helyar

Digby, Kenelm 1603-1665 *Of Bodies and of Mans Soul.* London: by S(arah) G(riffin) and B(ennet) G(riffin) for John Williams, 1669. First collected edition, 4to., some light dampstaining and spotting throughout, small closed tear to upper edge of L8 (just touching pagination), 2 minor chips to fore margin of 2F1-2, contemporary calf, covers ruled in blind, later spine label and small gilt ornament in each panel (surface of leather on covers crazed by damp, some surface rubbing and slight insect damage on lower cover chipped and rubbed), bookplate of Helyar family of Coker Court, Somerset, from the library of James Stevens Cox (1910-1997).   Maggs Bros. Ltd.   1447 - 147   2015   £400

Association – Heming, James;

Quintilian *Institutionum Oratioriarum Libri XII. Diligentius Recogniti MDXXII. Index capitum Totius Operis.* Venice: in aedibus Aldi et Andreae Soceri, 1521. Second Aldine edition, one small wormhole in text of first 30 and last 60 leaves (often touching a character but without loss of legibility), scattering of other small holes in margins of first and last 30 leaves, light browning at beginning and end, faint marginal dampmark to early leaves, some old marginal notes and underlining, inscriptions to title (one struck through, one dated 1630, slightly abraded, third a nineteenth century gift inscription - From James Heming to Rev. Dr. R. J. Bryce), 4to., 18th century calf, scratched and marked, corners worn, sometime serviceably rebacked, backstrip with five raised bands, red labels in second and last compartments, new endpapers, sound.   Blackwell's Rare Books   Greek & Latin Classics VI - 86   2015   £550

Association – Hemingway, Grace Hall

Cronin, A. J. *The Keys to the Kingdom.* Boston: Little Brown, 1941. Fourth printing, 8vo., very good, lacking dust jacket, this the copy of Grace Hall Hemingway (Ernest's mother) with her name and address in her hand.   Beasley Books   2013 - 2015 $45

Association – Henderson, Alex

Denham, John *Poems and Translations with the Sophy.* London: for H. Herringman, 1668. First collected edition, 2nd issue, 8vo., small dampstain and some very minor worming to lower inner margin of A1-K6, 2 small holes in lower part margin of Hh6, with paper flaw in lower corner of M3, 2B1 and lower edge of I2, stain on Aa8, slight rust spotting to Cc3, small slip of paper glued to lower corner of cc4 covering old neat repair, contemporary sheep (20mm. piece torn away from foot of spine, lower corners worn and boards lightly rubbed, old label missing, pastedowns unstuck), Alex Henderson 16?84 signature, early 19th century bookplate of Morough O'Bryen, purple ink oval library stamp of George Stawell, solicitor Torrington, from the library of James Stevens Cox (1910-1997).   Maggs Bros. Ltd.   1447 - 137   2015   £500

Association – Henderson, Thomas

Bell, James *Influence of Physical Research on Mental Philosophy.* Edinburgh: Adam and Charles Black, 1839. First edition, 12mo., few very small minor spots and rustmarks, original cloth, original printed spine label, uncut, very good, presentation inscription by author for Mr. Thomas Henderson, Haddington Dec. 1843, rare.   John Drury Rare Books   2015 - 19901   2015 $177

Association – Henley, W. E.

Wells, Herbert George   1866-1946   *The Passionate Friends, a Novel.* London: Macmillan, 1913. Crown 8vo., original sage green fine ribbed cloth, backstrip and front cover gilt lettered, with decoration, overall, stamped in blind, browned endpapers, top edge gilt, very good, inscribed by author to poet W. E. Henley.   Blackwell's Rare Books   B179 - 247   2015   £650

Association – Henry, Amelia

La Monaca Di Monza. Pisa: Presso Nicclo Capurro, 1829. First edition, small 8vo., bookplate in each volume, few small ex-libris stamps, bookplate of Amelia Henry, otherwise very good+ in very attractive vellum binding decorated in gilt at spine with leather spine lettered gilt on spine.   Any Amount of Books   2015 - A68055   2015   £180

Association – Hepenstal, L. W.

Swinburne, Henry *A Treatise of Spousals, or Matrimonial Contracts: Wherein all the Questions Relating to that Subject are Ingeniously Debated and Resolved.* London: printed by S. Roycroft for Robert Clavell, 1686. First edition, 4to., contemporary panelled calf with some wear to joints and extremities, still sound, text crisp with good margins, very good with near contemporary signature of J. Agar and late 18th early 19th century armorial bookplate of Rev. L. W. Hepenstal, uncommon.   John Drury Rare Books   2015 - 23326   2015 $3147

Association – Heron, Bazil

Shenstone, William   1714-1763   *The Works in Verse and Prose of William Shenstone, Esq.* London: printed for R. and J. Dodsley, 1764. First edition, 8vo., 2 volumes, 8vo., dust jacket calf, red morocco labels rubbed, one lower joint cracked, spines restored, (foot of one spine chipped), frontispiece in volume and plate, engraved vignette, presumably later issue, on verso of each frontispiece is calligraphic signature of Bazil Heron dated 1764.   C. R. Johnson   Foxon R-Z - 892r-z   2015 $115

Association – Herrmann, Bernard

Cumming, Alexander *A Sketch of the Properties of the Machine Organ, Invented, Constructed and Made by Mr. Cumming for the Earl of Bute...* London: printed by E. and H. Hudson Cross Street Hatton Garden, 1812. First edition, printed rectos only, contemporary red half roan gilt, neatly rebacked, original backstrip retained, very good, of great rarity, from the library of Lord Stuart de Rothesay at Highcliffe Castle with his coat of arms stamped in blind on covers, signature (1952) and one amendement by him in red ink of American composer Bernard Herrmann and NY Public Library.   John Drury Rare Books   2015 - 22640   2015 $8741

Association – Hersholt, Jean

Luhan, Mabel Dodge *Lorenzo in Taos.* New York: Harcourt Brace and Co., 1932. First edition, photos by Edward Weston and others, bookplate of actor and collector Jean Hersholt, fine in near fine dust jacket with little sunning on spine.   Between the Covers Rare Books, Inc.   187 - 161   2015 $275

Association – Hertzog, Carl

De Baca, Manuel C. *Vicente Silva and his 40 Bandits.* Edward McLean, Libros Escogidos, 1947. First edition, 4to., limited of 500 copies, signed by Lane Kauffmann, the translator and Fanita Lanier, who did the illustrations, further inscribed to Carl Hertzog by Edward McLean, the publisher, two-tone cloth, titles in red on front cover, bookplate of Carl Hertzog, illustrations, fine, clean, bright copy in original dust jacket with chips at spine ends and light wear to extremities. Buckingham Books   March 2015 - 35962   2015 $200

Association – Hervey, Elizabeth

Mason, William 1725-1797 *Poems.* York: printed by W. Blanchard, 1796. 191 x 124mm., 2 volumes, handsome contemporary tree calf elaborately gilt by Kalthoeber (ticket on verso of front endpaper), covers bordered with gilt Greek key roll, flat spines ornately gilt in compartments featuring various repeated tools, each spine with black morocco label, gilt turn-ins, marbled endpapers, both volumes with early signature of Elizabeth Hervey; lower compartment of second volume with abrasion and moderate loss of gilt on corner, little rubbing, otherwise only trivial wear, bindings handsome and well preserved, blanks at back of each volume little soiled, otherwise fine and very pretty set, virtually pristine internally.   Phillip J. Pirages   66 - 59   2015 $1800

Association – Hesketh, Stephen Charles

Leeke, William *A Few Suggestions for Increasing the Incomes of Many of the Smaller Livings for the Almost Total Abolition of Pluralitiees...* Derby: printed by William Bemrose and sold by Hatchard & Seeley, London, 1833. First edition, 8vo., misnumbered, uncut and unbound as issued, very good, presentation copy inscribed by author for Stephen Charles Hesketh, scarce.   John Drury Rare Books   2015 - 20224   2015 $106

Association – Hess, Thomas

O'Hara, Frank *A City Winter and Other Poems.* New York: Tibor De Nagy Gallery, 1951 i.e, 1952. First edition, tall 8vo., original signed frontispiece drawing & reproductions of 2 drawings by Larry Rivers, original cloth backed decorated boards, this copy number 13, tall 8vo., original signed frontispiece drawing & reproductions of two drawings by Larry Rivers, original cloth backed decorated boards, cover slightly worn along bottom edge and lower fore-corners, small stain to cloth near top of front panel, one page shows some faint indentations, otherwise very good, preserved in custom made half morocco slipcase, this the Thomas B. Hess - Elaine de Kooning copy, specially signed by O'Hara and signed by Hess and de Kooning's ownership stamp.   James S. Jaffe Rare Books   Modern American Poetry - 215   2015 $35,000

Association – Heyward, Dorothy

Erskine, John *Collected Poems 1907-1922.* New York: Duffield and Co., 1922. First edition, lacks front free endpaper, else very good, without dust jacket, Du Bose and Dorothy Heyward's copy with their joint bookplate. Between the Covers Rare Books, Inc.   187 - 91   2015 $45

Association – Heyward, Du Bose

Erskine, John *Collected Poems 1907-1922.* New York: Duffield and Co., 1922. First edition, lacks front free endpaper, else very good, without dust jacket, Du Bose and Dorothy Heyward's copy with their joint bookplate. Between the Covers Rare Books, Inc.   187 - 91   2015 $45

Association – Hiassen, Carl

Montalbano, William D. *Powder Burn.* New York: Atheneum, 1981. First edition, inscribed by Carl Hiaasen, some stains on covers, light spotting on page edges, otherwise fine in dust jacket.   Mordida Books   March 2015 - 008346   2015 $350

Association – Higgins, Trumbull

Eberhart, Richard *Collected Poems 1930-1960.* New York: Oxford University Press, 1960. First edition, fine in spine faded, otherwise very good dust jacket, inscribed by author for Barbara Guest and her husband, military historian Trumbull Higgins.   Between the Covers Rare Books, Inc.   187 - 86   2015 $225

Association – Hilder, Arthur

Cherke, John *De Pronuntiatione Graecae Potissimum Linguae Disputationes cum Stephano Vuintoniensi Episcopo, Septem Contrariss Epistolis Comprehensae, Magna Quadam Elegantia & Eruditionere Sertae.* Basel: per Nicol. Episcopium iuniorem, 1555. First edition, few minor creases and small splashmarks, blindstamp of Earls of Macclesfield to first few leaves, early ownership inscription of Arthur Hilder, 8vo., contemporary English blind-stamped dark calf, boards with decorative frame inside set of blind rules, vellum pastedowns, from an older manuscript with music and red and blue initials, ties removed, joints little rubbed, spine ends slightly defective, front hinge cracking and flyleaf lost, bookplate of Shirburn Castle, good. Blackwell's Rare Books   B179 - 19   2015   £1500

Association – Hill, John Percival

Hill, S. S. *Travels on the Shores of the Baltic. Extended to Moscow.* London: Arthur Hall, Virtue & Co., 1854. Half title, 2 pages ads, 24 page catalog (May 1854), original green cloth, blocked in blind, lettered gilt, slightly rubbed, inner hinges slightly cracking, bookplate of John Percival Hill, inscribed "Mrs. Branford from her most attached friend Mary Ann Hill".   Jarndyce Antiquarian Booksellers   CCXI - 141   2015   £280

Association – Hill, Lewis Caesar

Coles, Elisha *Christologia or a Metrical paraphrase on the History of Our Lord and Saviour Jesus Christ.* London: for Peter Parker, 1671. First edition, 8vo., without first blank leaf, light browning particularly in margins, words "OR A" on title deleted with ink and replaced with "a" in later manuscript, closely shaved, mid 20th century blue quarter morocco and marbled boards, from the library of James Stevens Cox (1910-1997), inscribed by Lewis Caesar Hill, 19th century signature George R. Hales, signature R. Betts dated "Silverhill 15.1 (18)90", booklabel of Gerald P Mander (d. 1951) of Tettenhall Wood, Staffordshire.   Maggs Bros. Ltd.   1447 - 105   2015   £240

Association – Hill, Mary Ann

Hill, S. S. *Travels on the Shores of the Baltic. Extended to Moscow.* London: Arthur Hall, Virtue & Co., 1854. Half title, 2 pages ads, 24 page catalog (May 1854), original green cloth, blocked in blind, lettered gilt, slightly rubbed, inner hinges slightly cracking, bookplate of John Percival Hill, inscribed "Mrs. Branford from her most attached friend Mary Ann Hill".   Jarndyce Antiquarian Booksellers   CCXI - 141   2015   £280

Association – Hill, Roy

Bontemps, Arna *The Harlem Renaissance Remembered.* New York: Dodd, Mead, 1972. First edition, portraits, signed on flyleaves Roy L. Hill, poet and professor, fairly extensive underlining and marking, edges little stained, otherwise very good, tight copy in worn dust jacket.   Second Life Books Inc.   190 - 34   2015 $100

Association – Hillaires

Moody, Ralph *Man of the Family.* New York: W. W. Norton, 1951. First edition, illustrations/drawings, cloth, presentation copy signed by Edna and Ralph Moody 10/25/51 for their friends the Hillaires, fine in chipped but good dust jacket, uncommon now in first edition.   Baade Books of the West   2014 - 2015 $172

Association – Hines, Gordon

Norfleet, J. Frank *Norfleet. The Amazing Experiences of an Intrepid Texas Ranger with an International Swindling Ring.* Sugar land: Imperial Press, 1927. Revised edition, cloth, illustrations, signed by Norfleet and Gordon Hines and further inscribed by Hines to John C. Bennett, near very good.   Baade Books of the West   2014 - 2015 $49

Association – Hirsch, E. D.

Steiner, George *Tolstoy or Dostoevesky: an Essay in Contrast.* London: Faber, 1959. First edition, bit of foxing on endpapers, near fine, price clipped dust jacket very good or better, inscribed to Peter and Eleanor Ross Taylor, by literary critic E. D. Hirsch and his wife Polly.   Between the Covers Rare Books, Inc.   187 - 270   2015 $175

Association – Hirsch, Polly

Steiner, George *Tolstoy or Dostoevesky: an Essay in Contrast.* London: Faber, 1959. First edition, bit of foxing on endpapers, near fine, price clipped dust jacket very good or better, inscribed to Peter and Eleanor Ross Taylor, by literary critic E. D. Hirsch and his wife Polly.   Between the Covers Rare Books, Inc.   187 - 270   2015 $175

Association – Hirsch, Rudolf

Benzing, Josef *Buchdrucker des 16 und 17 Jahrhunderts Im Deutschen Sprachgebiet.* Wiesbaden: Otto Harrassowitz, 1963. Thick 8vo., cloth, leather spine and cover labels, spine label rubbed and small piece chipped off edge, from the library of Rudolf Hirsch with his name and comment.   Oak Knoll Books   306 - 182   2015 $125

Association – Hoare, Richard Colt

Gunton, Symon *The History of the Church of Peterburgh.* London: printed for Richard Chiswell, 1686. First edition, 371 x 232mm., splendid honey brown diced russia by Roger Payne, covers with wide intricate and elegant dentelle frame composed of many small floral tools, raised bands, spine with gilt crest of Sir Richard Colt Hoare in top compartment, gilt titling in text two compartments and four elaborately tooled compartments below with gilt floral sprigs radiating from a central quatrefoil, interspersed with circlets and many small floral tools, turn-ins with simple gilt rules and delicate floral cornerpieces, endpapers of purple 'fine drawing paper' (Payne's words), all edges gilt, joints and very small portion at spine ends recently and expertly renewed by Courtland Benson, in a folding cloth box lined with felt (somewhat scuffed); 2 illustrations in text and 4 plates of views, large paper copy; front pastedown with armorial bookplate of Sir Henry Hope Edwardes and engraved bookplate of W. H. Corfield, front flyleaf with transcription in Hoare's hand of Payne's very detailed explanation of the work done and the bill for it; spine eevely darkened toward a chocolate brown, moderate foxing to half a dozen leaves, occasional rust spots, light stains or other trivial imperfections elsewhere in text, exceptionally desirable specimen in generally very fine condition, mostly clean and always fresh internally and very special binding entirely solid now, with virtually no wear and with all of the delicate gilt quite bright.   Phillip J. Pirages   66 - 57   2015 $15,000

Association – Hobgin, H. Ian

Kaberry, Phyllis M. *Aboriginal Woman. Sacred and Profane.* London: George Routledge & Sons, 1939. First edition, original orange cloth lettered gilt on spine, signed and dated presentation from author to H. Ian Hogbin, illustrations, little bumped, otherwise very good or better.   Any Amount of Books   2015 - C1988   2015   £175

Association – Hode, Ida

Moore, Marianne   1887-1972 *Collected Poems.* New York: Macmillan, 1952. 8vo., original cloth, dust jacket, inscribed by author in 1957 to Ida Hode, fine in dust jacket with spine slightly faded as usual.   James S. Jaffe Rare Books   Modern American Poetry - 205   2015 $750

Association – Hodgson, Norma

Stephen, Leslie *The "Times" on the American War: a Historical Study.* London: William Ridgway, 1865. Disbound and loose in slightly dusted and torn cream paper wrappers, with letter of presentation from Norma Hodgson to Geoffrey Tillotson.   Jarndyce Antiquarian Booksellers   CCVII - 477   2015   £65

Association – Hodgson, Ralph

Baker, Silvia *Journey to Yesterday.* London: Peter Davies, 1950. First edition, top corner little bumped, near fine in near fine dust jacket, author Ralph Hodgson's copy, unsigned but with Baker's London address with date in 1953 on front fly annotated on (p. 138) and supplied the book with further handmade and hand lettered brown paper dust jacket.   Between the Covers Rare Books, Inc.   187 - 6   2015 $125

Association – Hoe, Arthur

Jameson, Anna Brownell Murphy   1794-1860 *The Communion of Labour.* London: Longman Brown, Green, Longmans & Roberts, 1856. First edition, small 8vo., small bookplate of Arthur Hoe, bound in flexible red cloth stamped in gilt, cover little soiled, very good, tight.   Second Life Books Inc.   189 - 138   2015 $225

Association – Holbech, Ambrose

Mortimer, John *The Whole Art of Husbandry or the Way of Managing the Improving of Land.* London: printed by J. H. for H. Mortlock at the Phoenix and J. Robinson at the Golden Lion in St. Paul's Church Yard, 1707. First edition, 8vo. several woodcut text figures, contemporary panelled calf with gilt spine label, little wear to extremities and joints but very good in sound, original binding, signature and armorial bookplate of Ambrose Holbech, 18th century signature of Mr. Goodwyn, armorial bookplate 19th century of Archibald Philip (Primrose) Earl of Rosebery, uncommon. John Drury Rare Books   2015 - 25543   2015 $1311

Association – Holcolmb, Irving

United States. War Department - 1855 *Report of Explorations and Surveys to Ascertain the Most Practicable and Economical Route for a Railroad from the Mississippi River to the Pacific Ocean Made Under the Direction of the Secretary of War 1853-1854.* Washington: A. O. P. Nicholson printer, 1855-1861. each volume rebound in black buckram and signatures resewn, titles stamped in gold on spine panel, each volume stamped with word "Senate" on spine, five of the volumes are actually for the House of Representatives, Volume I with small stamp of Library of Washington and Jefferson College with word 'withdrawn' stamped in light blue ink at bottom of titlepage and "contents of volume I" page, else very good, tight copy; volume IV presentation inscription to Irving Holcomb from Hon. F. E. Sprimer (?) dated Nov. 1857; small waterstain to bottom edges front flyleaf which continues lightly to page 3, else very good, tight, volume X with light foxing to first 8 pages in front of volume and to last 8 pages in rear of volume else very good, tight copy; volume XI with moderate foxing and two small waterstains that diminish over first 16 pages, else very good, tight, volume XI with maps and plates, plates and maps uncommonly fine, very handsome, completely rebound set that is in very good to fine condition. Buckingham Books   March 2015 - 26611   2015 $15,000

Association – Holder, Peter Colin

Pinter, Harold *Tea Party.* London: BBC, 1965. Draft script for 1965 BBC TV movie, inscribed by Pinter for Peter Colin Holder.   Royal Books   46 - 83   2015 $3000

Association – Holland, Harriet

Smith, Horace *The Runaway; or the Seat of Benevolence.* printed by T. Davison for Crosby and Letterman, 1800. First edition, 4 volumes, printed on blue-ish paper (tone varying), apart from titlepages, 12mo., contemporary half green roan, gilt ruled compartments on spine, lettered and numbered direct, spines darkened, slightly worn at extremities, labels of some description removed from upper covers leaving traces of gilt at edges (hence perhaps an armorial bookplate or something decorative, rather than a library label), contemporary signature inside front covers erased (except in volume iv) of Harriet Holland, mid 20th century ownership inscription, contemporary tiny ticket of E. Upham, bookseller, good.   Blackwell's Rare Books   B179 - 99   2015   £4000

Association – Holland, John Arnold

Hobson, G. D. *Maioli, Canevari and Others.* Boston: Little Brown and Co., 1926. First U S edition, 4to., cloth, top edge gilt, 64 full page plates, 6 in color, spine faded, bookplate of John Arnold Holland on front pastedown with Holland's signature in in below bookplate, endpapers toned, with small remnant of description mounted on front endpaper.   Oak Knoll Books   306 - 2   2015 $145

Association – Hollander, John

Nemerov, Howard *War Stories: Poems About Long Ago and Now.* Chicago: University of Chicago Press, 1987. First edition, fine in fine dust jacket, inscribed by author to fellow poet John Hollander.   Between the Covers Rare Books, Inc.   187 - 201   2015 $450

Association – Hollo, Anselm

Berrigan, Ted *Doubletalk.* Iowa City: Miller, 1969. First edition, limited to 240 copies signed by Berrigan and Anselm Hollo, tall narrow 8vo., portraits, wrappers, very fine.   James S. Jaffe Rare Books   Many Happy Returns - 207   2015 $250

Association – Holme, Hilda

Examiner, Pseud. *Some Thoughts on Examinations, by an Examiner.* London: privately printed in the Department of English at University College, London, 1936. 4to., original blue printed wrappers, slightly creased, 7 pages, inscribed to Geoffrey Tillotson by Hilda Holme and L. Paulin, with quotation inserted by Tillotson.   Jarndyce Antiquarian Booksellers   CCVII - 268   2015   £60

Association – Holmes, J. T.

Connolly, James B. *The Book of Gloucester Fisherman.* New York: John Day Co., 1927. First edition, illustrations by Henry O'Connor, publisher's orange cloth, very good or better with light scattered spotting, without dust jacket, with ALS and TLS and one news clipping laid in, the ALS addressed boxer Gene Tunney, from J. T. Holmes.   Between the Covers Rare Books, Inc.   187 - 60   2015 $400

Association – Holmes, John

Anacreon *Anacreon Done into English out of the Original Greek.* Oxford: by L. Litchfield, Printer to the University, for Anthony Stephens, 1683. First edition of this translation, 8vo., leaf (c)1 is duplicated; (c)2 was also duplicated, but the second leaf has been torn away, lightly browned, dampstaining along lower edge of a1-4, corners of K2-L2 and fore margin of P1-2 and in top half of last few leaves, small rust hole in D2 (affecting one letter on each side), marginal rust spot on H1, contemporary calf, spine gilt and lettered (headcap damaged and with upper joint slightly split at head), from the library of James Stevens Cox (1910-1997), inscribed "Sum Philippi Ayresij 1683" on titlepage (Philip Aryes (1638-1712), signature of Madam. Mary Redman, ink signature under bookplate of John Holmes (1702/03-1760) of Holt, Norfolk, Master of Gresham School and writer on education, with his signature, early 19th century circular label with manuscript lot number 12/4 pasted to foot of front flyleaf, the pencil mark of Christie-Miller Britwell Court with pencil shelf mark.   Maggs Bros. Ltd.   1447 - 7   2015   £1500

Association – Holt, Lester, Mrs.

Hughes, Langston *The Weary Blues.* New York: Knopf, 1944. Ninth printing, 8vo., yellow cloth, dust jacket (lacks some paper at extremities of spine and small hole which affects two letters of author's name), very good, inscribed by author for Mrs. Lester Holt.   Second Life Books Inc.   190 - 131   2015 $450

Association – Honan, Park

Irvine, William *The Book, the Ring and the Poet: a Biography of Robert Browning.* London: Bodley Head, 1975. Half title, plates original blue cloth, spines slightly creased and in slightly creased dust jacket, with warm presentation to Kathleen Tillotson from Park Honan, ALS from Honan to Kathleen.   Jarndyce Antiquarian Booksellers   CCVII - 121   2015   £35

Association – Honeyman

Sowerby, James 1757-1822 *A New Elucidation of Colours Showing Their Concordance in Three Primitives...* London: Printed by Richard Taylor and Co. Shoe Lane, 1809. 4to., 7 engraved plates, including 5 hand colored original boards, spine defective, upper cover with original printed label, armorial bookplate of Captain Sir Christopher Cole KB, the Honeyman copy.   Marlborough Rare Books   List 54 - 80   2015   £2500

Association – Honeyman, Robert

Pemberton, Henry *A View of Sir Isaac Newton's Philosophy.* London: S. Palmer, 1728. First edition, large 4to., engraved titlepage vignette by J. Pine, after original by J. Grison, T3 with neat repair at gutter, modern half calf over marbled paper backed boards, gilt stamped spine and black leather spine label, quarter gilt stamped morocco over red cloth, slipcase, from the Robert Honeyman collection, rebound in Honyeman commissioned slipcase.   Jeff Weber Rare Books   178 - 841   2015 $1000

Association – Honywood, W.

Kent, Nathaniel *Hints to Gentlemen of Landed Property.* London: J. Dodsley, 1775. First edition, 8vo., 10 engraved folding plates, contemporary polished calf, spine simply gilt with raised bands and crimson lettering piece, short crack in upper joint, still fine, crisp, sound, early ownership inscription on front pastedown "W. Honywood 1787. The gift of the Revd. J. H. Beckingham".   John Drury Rare Books   2015 - 24036   2015 $612

Association – Hooks, Bell

Cortez Cruz, Ricardo *Straight Outta Compton.* Boulder: Fiction Collective 2, 1992. First edition, octavo, fine in near fine dust jacket with minor rubbing, inscribed by Cortez Cruz to feminist/philosopher/critic Bell Hooks.   Between the Covers Rare Books   197 - 6   2015 $375

Association – Hopkins, Gerard

Sayers, Dorothy L. *Papers Relating to the Family of Wimsey.* London: privately printed for the Family by Humphrey Milford, 1936. First edition, one of 500 copies, frontispiece, 1 further plate, 8vo., original blue wrappers printed in black with fading to borders, couple of waterspots at head of front and chipping to edges, 2 cm. loss at head of backstrip, few foxspots to inside front cover and flyleaf, good, inscribed by Matthew Wimsey and Peter Death Bredon Wimsey to Gerard Hopkins, nephew of Gerard Manley Hopkins, with 2 photocopies TLS's from Sayers to Basil Blackwell loosely inserted.   Blackwell's Rare Books   B179 - 231   2015   £750

Association – Hopkins, Kenneth

Longfellow, Henry Wadsworth 1807-1882 *The Song of Hiawatha.* London: David Bogue, 1855. First edition, first issue, with 'dove' for 'dived' on page 96 line 7; original green cloth, blindstamped sides, spine lettered and decorated in gilt, 24 pages ads at end dated March 1855, sides little marked and slight wear at head and foot of spine, nice, poet Kenneth Hopkins' copy with his ownership signature, bibliographical notes in ink on front pastedown and another ownership signature on titlepage, from the collection of Gavin H. Fryer.   Bertram Rota Ltd.   308 Part II - 154   2015   £450

Association – Hopton, John

Gifford, William *The Anti-Jacobin; or Weekly Examiner.* London: printed for J. Wright, 1799. Fourth edition, 8vo., half brown leather with dark orange boards lettered gilt on black spine label, 2 volumes, no. 1-36 dated 20 Nov. 1797-9 July 1798, with index, clean, very good, neat name on first blank page and bookplate of John Hopton.   Any Amount of Books   2015 - C11845   2015   £220

Association – Hornby, C. H. St. John

Ashendene Press *A Chronological List, With Prices of the Forty Books printed at the Ashendene Press MDCCCXCV-MCMXXXV.* Ashendene Press, 1935. Sole separate edition, printed in red and black, 4to. original stitched blue wrappers, upper stitching, loose from centre, discolored at edges, edges untrimmed, good, with ALS by C. H. St. John Hornby loosely inserted, written in black ink on headed paper and dated 13 Feb. 1939.   Blackwell's Rare Books   B179 - 125   2015   £150

Association – Horne, Lena

Sontag, Susan *Women.* New York: Random House, 1999. First edition, small folio, Annie Leibovitz presentation inscription for Lena Horne, very good plus, small abrasion to rear pastedown in very good plus dust jacket.   Ed Smith Books   83 - 47   2015 $1500

Association – Horton, Edward Everett

Dixon, William Hepworth *Her Majesty's Tower.* New York: Thomas Y. Crowell and Co., n.d. circa, 1900. Reprint, green cloth, gilt, 2 volumes in 1, small nick at crown, some staining to rear board, tight, about very good copy, Edward Everett Horton's copy with bookplate, pencil note indicating it was purchased at Dawson's in LA in 1913.   Between the Covers Rare Books, Inc.   187 - 77   2015 $150

Association – House, Madeline

House, Humphry *All in Due Time.* London: Rupert Hart-Davis, 1955. Half title, original red cloth, torn dust jacket, from the library of Geoffrey & Kathleen Tillotson, inscribed "Tillotson's 1955" with pencil notes, ALS from House's widow Madeline thanking Geoffrey for his review, with note and short review by Kathleen.   Jarndyce Antiquarian Booksellers   CCVII - 312   2015   £20

House, Humphry *Coleridge, the Clark Lectures 1951-1952.* London: Rupert Hart Davis, 1953. Half title, original decorated boards, very good in slightly dusted dust jacket, Geoffrey Tillotson's copy with TLS from Rupert Hart-Davis 1955 announcing House's sudden death, tipped in, pencil notes, obits, and two ALS's from Madeline House to Geoffrey.   Jarndyce Antiquarian Booksellers   CCVII - 153   2015   £30

Association – Howard, Oliver O.

Rankin, J. E. *Hymns Pro Patria and Other Hymns, Christian and Humanitarian.* New York: John R. Alden, 1889. First edition, tall octavo, brown cloth decorated in black and gilt, bookplate of Byron N. Clark, second bookplate partly effaced, crease on two leaves, else tight, near fine copy, inscribed by author to NJ author Gen. Oliver O. Howard.   Between the Covers Rare Books, Inc.   187 - 228   2015 $175

Association – Howard, Peter

Riding, Laura *The Telling.* New York: Harper and Row, 1973. First US edition, number 48 of 100 hand numbered copies of the trade edition, 8vo., signed by author, copyright page carries here hand-correction of word 'essay' to word 'portion', fine in fine dust jacket, laid into this copy is a scolding letter to Peter Howard of Serendipity Books, for not using her authorially correct name in one of his catalogs, this is TLS sent April 11 1976.   Beasley Books   2013 - 2015 $150

Association – Howard, Sidney

Brown, John Mason *George Pierce Baker - a Memorial.* New York: Dramatists Play Service, 1939. First edition, octavo, 46 pages, frontispiece, marbled paper boards, title label on front cover, signed on front free endpaper by all authors, John Mason Brown, Eugene O'Neill, Sidney Howard, Allardyce Nicoll, Stanley R. McCandless, drawing by Gluyas Williams, frontispiece, marbled paper boards, title on label on front cover, covers rubbed at head and tail of spine, corners bruised, very good in chipped and torn original tissue jacket, largely defective at bottom edge.   Peter Ellis, Bookseller   2014 - 018199   2015   £300

Association – Howe, Ellic

Bible. Latin - 1785 *Bibliorum Sacorum Vulgatae Versionis Editio.* Parisiis: Excudebat Fr. Amb. Didot, 1785. 2 volumes, 318 x 235mm, superb crimson straight grain morocco by Bozerian, covers with distinctive wide frame incoporating arches, Grecian urns, floral garlands and sunburst cornerpieces, the outer and inner edge of the frame flanked by thick and thin gilt rules and cresting and floral rolls, double raised bands separated by a gilt tooled inlaid strip of black morocco, spines densely gilt in compartments filled with much foliage and many flowers against a stippled background, turn-ins with interlacing flame roll, light green glazed endpapers, all edges gilt, wood engraved bookplate of Ellic Howe (1910-1991) with faint evidence of earlier bookplate removal, verso of rear flyleaf with small engraved heraldic book label; half a dozen or so faint scratches or small spots to boards, occasional mild browning or small marginal spots, couple of gatherings in second volume with faint overall browning, otherwise an excellent copy internally, clean and smooth with generous margins, elegant bindings in fine condition, especially lustrous and with only insignificant wear.   Phillip J. Pirages   66 - 62   2015 $6500

Association – Howell, C. Thomas

Kotzwinkle, William *E. T. The Extra-Terrestrial.* New York: Putnams, 1982. First edition, signed by three cast members, Dee Wallace Stone, Robert MacNaughton and C. Thomas Howell, near fine in near fine dust jacket.   Ed Smith Books   83 - 57   2015 $175

Association – Howell, Thomas

Ibbetson, Julius Caesar *A Picturesque Guide to Bath, Bristol, Hot Wells, The River Avon and the Adjacent Country...* London: Hookham and Carpenter, 1793. Large paper copy, 4to., 16 aquatint plates with fine contemporary hand colouring, contemporary half russia with flat spine lettered in gilt, some minor chipping to extremities and upper hinge cracked with early ownership on title "Thos Howell" and unusually colorful heraldic bookplate of Edward Mash Browell.   Marlborough Rare Books   List 54 - 47   2015   £1750

Association – Howes, Barbara

Woolf, Virginia 1882-1941 *A Room of One's Own.* London: Hogarth, 1931. Second edition, 8vo., green cloth, owner's bookplate, name on flyleaf, edges slightly spotted, few pencil notations in margins, cover slightly spotted, otherwise very good, tight copy, poet Barbara Howes' copy with her bookplate and signature.   Second Life Books Inc.   189 - 286   2015 $135

Association – Howes, Wright

Haley, James Evetts *The XIT Ranch of Texas and the Early Days of the Llano Estacado.* Chicago: Lakeside Press, 1929. First edition, presentation inscription by author to R. G. Long, laid in is penned note on Prince George Hotel NYC stationery to Wright Howes, bookseller and author, decorated cloth, fine, bright copy, in protective transparent dust jacket, exceptional copy. Buckingham Books   March 2015 - 28028   2015 $1875

Association – Howitt, Mary

Tennyson, Alfred Tennyson, 1st Baron 1809-1892 *The Princess; a Medley.* London: Edward Moxon, 1847. First edition, inscribed by author for fellow poet Mary Howitt, little light spotting, 8vo., original green cloth, boards with decorative border blocked in blind, spine lettered in gilt direct, sunned, corners bumped some wear to spine ends, hinges just cracking, sound.   Blackwell's Rare Books   B179 - 104   2015   £750

Association – Hoyel, Johannes

Boccaccio, Giovanni 1313-1375 *Amorosa Visione. (bound with) Urbano.* Milan: Zanottie Castiglione per Andrea Calvo 10 Feb., 1521. Bologna: Franciscus Plato de Benedictis circa, 1492-1493. First printing of both works, 210 x 133mm., 2 separately published works in one volume; handsome Renaissance intricately decorated blindstamped calf by Claes Van Doermaele, covers with outer frame of medallion and foliate roll, inner frame of long stemmed lilies and scrolling vines, large central panel containing a medallion with three quarter portrait of Holy Roman Emperor of Charles V, binder's small 'CvD' escutcheon stamp below central panel, raised bands, early ink titled paper label, small paper shelf number of private library at foot of spine, unobtrusive repairs to head of front joint, tail of both joints and upper corners, lacking ties, in (slightly worn) linen clamshell box, 16th century ink ownership inscription of Johannes Hoyel, inscription of A(ndrew) Fletcher (of Saltoun), titlepage just slightly soiled, two leaves with minor browning to lower corners, two tiny marginal stains, otherwise fine, fresh copy in very well preserved binding, leather lustrous and blindstamped details remarkably sharp. Phillip J. Pirages   66 - 6   2015 $35,000

Association – Hughes, Barnabas

Hofmann, Joseph E. *Michael Stifel (1487?-1567). Leben, Wiken and Bedeutung fur die Mathematik Seiner Zeit.* Wiesbaden: Franz Steiner Verlag, 1968. 8vo., 8 plates, 20 figrues, blue printed wrappers, bookplate of Barnabas Hughes, very good.   Jeff Weber Rare Books   178 - 1043   2015 $60

Neugebauer, Otto *Mathematical Cuneiform Texts.* New Haven: American Oriental Society and the American Schools of Oriental Research, 1945. 4to., map, 23 monochrome plates, photographic reproductions, original dark green blind and gilt stamped cloth, bookplate of Barnabas Hughes, very good.   Jeff Weber Rare Books   178 - 822   2015 $55

Association – Hughes, Dorothy

Gardner, Erle Stanley *The Case of the Worried Waitress.* New York: William Morrow and Co., 1966. First edition, review slip tipped in, signature of American crime writer and literary critic Dorothy B. Hughes on front blank in red ink, near fine in red cloth with black spine lettering in very good plus to near fine dust jacket with wear to spine crown.   Ed Smith Books   83 - 28   2015 $250

Association – Hughes, Helena

Schuyler, James *Collabs.* New York: Misty Terrace Press, 1980. First edition, one of 200 copies, 4to., original wrappers with cover design by George Schneeman, stapled as issued, presentation from all contributors, Helena Hughes, Michael Scholnick and signed by small pen and ink self-portrait by Schneeman for Ted Berrigan, fine.   James S. Jaffe Rare Books   Modern American Poetry - 244   2015 $1750

Association – Hughes, Langston

Bontemps, Arna *Popo and Fifina.* New York: Macmillan Co., 1949. Sixth printing, illustrations by E. Simms Campbell, cloth, considerable edge wear to cloth at extremities, presentable and sound copy, inscribed by Langston Hughes for the Second Grade Class of Alexander Street School, Charlotte, Nov. 15, 1950.   Between the Covers Rare Books   197 - 7   2015 $450

Association – Hume, Abraham

Gee, Joshua *The Trade and Navigation of Great Britain Considered.* London: J. Almon and S. Bladon, 1767. 12mo., contemporary calf, spine gilt with raised bands and label, joints and head and foot of spine worn, otherwise very good, crisp copy, early 19th century armorial bookplate of Sir Abraham Hume bart, with later 19th century ink stamp of the board of Trade Library with a government withdrawn stamp on blank flyleaf.   John Drury Rare Books   March 2015 - 16811   2015   £306

Association – Humphrey, Miss

Thompson, Isaac *A Collection of Poems, Occasionally writ on Several Subjects.* Newcastle upon Tyne: printed by John White for the author and sold by booksellers, 1731. First edition, 8vo., contemporary calf, spine gilt, red morocco label, some rubbing ends of spine neatly restored, slightly later signature of Miss Humphrey is at front, volume printed on thick paper and embellished with unusually wide range of woodcut ornaments, some light marginal inkstains to first few leaves, very good, scarce.   C. R. Johnson   Foxon R-Z - 980r-z   2015 $1149

Association – Hunter, J. T.

Hunter, George *Reminiscences of an Old Timer.* Battle Creek: Review and Herald, 1889. Fourth edition, 8vo., illustrations, warmly inscribed on flyleaf "Compliments of author, Col. Geo. Hunter to J. T. Hunter as in other words Hunter to Hunter...Timus the chief to the Chief of Good Fellows July 8th '90", also signed with his Indian name, red cloth stamped in gilt, little worn, hinge tender, very good.   Second Life Books Inc.   191 - 49   2015 $75

Association – Hunter, Mary

Restif De La Bretonne, Nicolas Edme   1734-1806 *Les Dangers De La Ville, Ou Histoire Effrayante et Morale...* Paris: La Haie, 1784. First edition, 4 parts in 2 volumes, 8vo., parts 1 to 4 of the 8 part Novel, volume II missing half title of part 3 and final page (xxi), half red morocco over marbled paper lettered and decorated gilt, top edge gilt, rather worn and well thumbed pair of volumes, each volume with bookplate of Mary Hunter (1856-1933).   Any Amount of Books   2015 - C7701   2015   £150

Association – Hurley, Leonard

Jarrell, Randall *Poetry and The Age.* New York: Knopf, 1953. First edition, 8vo., original black cloth, dust jacket, presentation copy inscribed by author for Leonard and Maud Hurley, fine in dust jacket that is slightly faded and spotted along spine panel.   James S. Jaffe Rare Books   Modern American Poetry - 147   2015 $750

Association – Hurley, Maud

Jarrell, Randall *Poetry and The Age.* New York: Knopf, 1953. First edition, 8vo., original black cloth, dust jacket, presentation copy inscribed by author for Leonard and Maud Hurley, fine in dust jacket that is slightly faded and spotted along spine panel.   James S. Jaffe Rare Books   Modern American Poetry - 147   2015 $750

Association – Hussey, J. C.

Alger, John Goldworth *Englishmen in the French Revolution.* London: Sampson Low, 1889. First edition, half title, 4 pages ads, 32 page catalog (Sept. 1888), few leaves roughly opened, original olive green cloth, spine slightly dulled, little rubbed, contemporary signature of J. C. Hussey on half title.   Jarndyce Antiquarian Booksellers   CCXI - 5   2015   £50

Association – Hutton, Joseph

Clough, Arthur Hugh *Letters and Remains.* London: Spottiswoode & Co., 1865. Half title, original green patterned cloth, inner hinges rather crudely strengthened, presented to Miss Rankin, sent by her to Joseph Hutton 1888, signed by Geoffrey Tillotson 12.v.47.   Jarndyce Antiquarian Booksellers   CCVII - 141   2015   £40

Association – Hutton, Reginald Winans

Roosevelt, Theodore   1858-1919 *Big Game Hunting in the Rockies and on the Great Plains Comprising "Hunting Trips of a Ranchman" and "The Wilderness Hunter".* New York and London: G. P. Putnam's Sons, 1899. Number 517 of 1000 copies, signed by author under frontispiece illustration. 55 original cloth, black leather title labels to spine and front cover, expertly rebacked with new material visible along head of spine and interior pages, gilt illustrations to front cover, black illustration to rear cover, covers and spine darkened and lightly soiled with scuff marks to leather labels, minor chipping to edges of endpapers, few spots of soling verso colophon and few spots of foxing to first and last few pages, bookplate of Reginald Winans Hutton, very good, 2 books bound as one.   The Kelmscott Bookshop   11 - 42   2015 $5500

Association – Hyde, Donald

Smith, George *A Collection of Designs for Household Furniture and Interior Decoration...* xyz London: published for J. Taylor at the architectural Library no. 49, High Holborn, 1808. 4to., 158 plates, plates 23 and 26 cut to plate mark and mounted plate 146 with repair to margin, some occasional spotting, still unusually bright copy, contemporary vellum, upper cover lettered in gilt, Marquis of Downshire, Hillsborough Castle, some marks on lower board, inscribed on title for the Use of James McBlaine, Hillsborough, bookplate of Donald & Mary Hyde.   Marlborough Rare Books   List 54 - 78   2015   £9500

Association – Hyde, Mary

Smith, George *A Collection of Designs for Household Furniture and Interior Decoration...* London: published for J. Taylor at the architectural Library no. 49, High Holborn, 1808. 4to., 158 plates, plates 23 and 26 cut to plate mark and mounted plate 146 with repair to margin, some occasional spotting, still unusually bright copy, contemporary vellum, upper cover lettered in gilt, Marquis of Downshire, Hillsborough Castle, some marks on lower board, inscribed on title for the Use of James McBlaine, Hillsborough, bookplate of Donald & Mary Hyde. Marlborough Rare Books List 54 - 78 2015 £9500

Association – Hyde, Slocum

Cobden-Sanderson, Thomas James 1840-1922 *The Ideal Book or Book Beautiful: a Tract of Calligraphy printing and Illustration and On the Book Beautiful as a Whole.* Hammersmith: Doves Press, 1900. First edition, one of 300 copies, small quarto, original full vellum, gilt lettering, bookplate of American collector Charles Walker Andrews, with his notation in pencil that this was purchased from Slocum Hyde's library in 1924, fine. The Brick Row Book Shop Miscellany 67 - 36 2015 $1250

Association – Hylton, Richard

Relph, Josiah *A Miscellany of Poems, Consisting of Original Poems, Translations, Pastorals in the Cumberland Dialect, Familiar Epistles, Fables, Songs and Epigrams.* Glasgow: printed by Robert Foulis for Mr. Thomlinson (Wigton), 1747. First edition, 8vo., contemporary calf, gilt, rebacked, slight foxing, but very good, on front pastedown " E. C. ex dono Dom. Riccardi Hylton de Hylton Castle im. Cmt. Durham Bart" (Sir Richard Hilton sic) appears in list of subscribers for three copies, he sold Hylton Castle in 1749. C. R. Johnson Foxon R-Z - 823r-z 2015 $460

Association – Hyman, Lulu

Jackson, Shirley *We Have Always Lived in the Castle.* New York: Viking, 1962. First edition, slightly bumped and soiled, else near fine in very good dust jacket with chip on rear panel and general modest wear at extremities, inscribed by author to her mother-in-law Lulu Hyman. Between the Covers Rare Books, Inc. 187 - 136 2015 $2500

Association – Hyman, Patrick

MacDonald, John D. *A Purple Place for Dying.* New York: J. B. Lippincott, 1976. First American edition, near fine in like dust jacket, inscribed by author for Patrick Hyman 4 June 1983, from the collection of Duke Collier. Royal Books 36 - 43 2015 $950

Association – Hyman, Stanley

Lowell, Robert 1917-1977 *Land of Unlikeness.* Cummington: The Cummington Press, 1944. First edition, one 224 copies of a total edition of 225, blue printed paper covered boards, lettered in red, light rubbing to crown, spine little faded, 2 very small spots small, light smudge on front board, lacking original unprinted glassine dust jacket, nice in very good copy of fragile volume, internally fine, inscribed by author to Stanley Hyman. Between the Covers Rare Books 196 - 87 2015 $7500

Association – Iles, Ellis

Pote, Joseph *The Foreigner's Guide or a necessary and Instructive Companion, both for the Foreigner and Native...* London: printed and sold by H. Kent, E. Comyns and Jo. Jolliffe, 1752. Third edition, 12mo., contemporary sheep, ownership signature of Ellis Iles dated 1760, front hinge repaired, edges little rubbed, small tear in one leaf with minor loss but not to sense, very good. The Brick Row Book Shop Miscellany 67 - 92 2015 $1200

Association – Ingalls, Mary Ann

Child, Lydia Maria 1802-1880 *An Appeal in Favor of the Class of Americans Called Africans.* Boston: Allen and Ticknor, 1833. First edition, 8vo., frontispiece inserted with two full page plates in text, light stain to flyleaves, some foxing to margins of frontispiece, otherwise text good and clean, contemporary ownership of Mary Ann Ingalls on top of titlepage, bound in original cloth, little rubbed and couple of nicks to cloth and edge of spine label, which is complete, better than average copy of a book usually found in tough condition, with errata slip noted by BAL, scarce. Second Life Books Inc. 190 - 40 2015 $2500

Association – Inge, William

McCulloch, John Ramsay 1789-1864 *London in 1850-1851. From the Geographical Dictionary of J. R. McCulloch, Esq.* London: Longman, Brown, Green and Longmans, 1851. First edition, 8vo., 132 pages, occasional very light foxing, original printed wrappers, spine neatly repaired, good copy, early ownership signature of William Inge, very scarce. John Drury Rare Books 2015 - 14180 2015 $177

Association – Ingraham, Henry Andrews

Masefield, John 1878-1967 *Odtaa.* London: Heinemann, 1926. Limited edition, number 157 of 295 copies signed by author, bookplate ex-libris of Henry Andrews Ingraham, noted angler and author, front hinge visible but solid, vellum spine, blue boards, mild darkening to boards, very good, lacking dust jacket but with folding map laid in, signed by E. Perman, the artist, map often missing. Ken Lopez, Bookseller 164 - 127 2015 $200

Association – Isham, Ralph

Bible. Latin - 1726 *Biblia Scacra ex Sebastiani Castellionis Interpretatione Ejusque Postrema Recognitione (Volume I).* Londoni: Excudebat Jacob Bettenham, Impensis J. Knapton, R. Knaplock..., 1726. First edition, volume one only, 12mo., text in Latin, from the library of American book collector Ralph Isham with his engraved bookplate, dust jacket inscription to Mrs. Hester Lynch Thrale from Dr. Samuel Johnson, contemporary full sheep, dark red morocco spine label, gilt edges light cracking to joints, very good, housed in dark red full morocco box, gold silk interior and gold edges, presumably commissioned by Isham, with the Johnston presentation "Bible presented to Mrs. Thrale by Dr. Johnson" in gilt on front cover, front joint of box professionally repaired, very good.   Between the Covers Rare Books, Inc.   187 - 44   2015 $3000

Association – Iveagh, Earl of

Swift, Jonathan 1667-1745 *On Poetry; a Rhapsody.* printed at Dublin: London: reprinted and sold by J. Huggonson and at the booksellers and pamphlet shops, 1733. First edition, 28 pages, folio, half dark green morocco and marbled boards, very large armorial bookplate of Earl of Iveagh, very good.   C. R. Johnson   Foxon R-Z - 959r-z   2015 $1149

Association – Jack, Ian

Ruffhead, James *The Passions Man.* London: printed for the author, 1746. First edition, 8vo., engraved frontispiece and 3 other plates, contemporary calf, gilt, neatly rebacked, corners worn, very good, scarce, comparatively recent bookplate of William Roughead and booklabel of Ian Jack.   C. R. Johnson   Foxon R-Z - 850r-z   2015 $1302

Association – Jackson, Roger

Miller, Henry 1891-1980 *The Mezzotints.* Ann Arbor: Roger Jackson, 1993. First edition "Library edition" issue, one of 400 copies, octavo, illustrated, printed wrapper in raspberry cloth portfolio, 8 loose broadsides laid in, fine, inscribed by publisher to Bertrand Mathieu, a Henry Miller scholar.   Between the Covers Rare Books, Inc.   187 - 179   2015 $150

Association – Jacobs, Joe

Barbash, Jack *Labour Unions in Action.* New York: Harper, 1948. First edition, inscribed by author, fine and bright in lightly chipped dust jacket (one chip retained), inscribed to labor lawyer Joe Jacobs.   Beasley Books   2013 - 2015 $45

Association – Jacobs, S. A.

Schwartz, Delmore *The World is a Wedding.* Norfolk: New Directions, 1948. First edition, 8vo., original cloth, dust jacket, inscribed by author to S. A. Jacobs, head of spine rubbed, otherwise very good in slightly dust soiled jacket.   James S. Jaffe Rare Books   Modern American Poetry - 248   2015 $1250

Association – Jacobsen, Maurice

Monteverdi, Claudio *Tutte Le Opere Di Claudio Monteverdi Gia Maestro di Cappella. Della Serenissima Repubblica.* Asolo: G. Francesco Malipiero, 1926. Limited edition, no. 15 of 250, large 8vo., wrappers, 8 volumes, very good, slightly dusty, yapped edges slightly nicked, one has adhesive tape reinforcement at spine, 3 volumes have ownership signature of Maurice Jacobsen (1896-1976).   Any Amount of Books   March 2015 - C12757   2015   £350

Association – James, William

Ward, James *Ueber die Auslosung von Reflexbewegungen Durch eine Summe Schwacher Reize. (On the Triggering of Reflex Movements by a Sum of Weak Stimuli).* Leipzig: Veit & Comp, 1880. First edition, offprint, octavo, from the library of William James, with his signature top of front wrapper in pencil and 4 citations in his hand to rear wrapper in black ink, original tan wrappers printed with black type on front cover only with original(?) spine tape, old tape repairs (in well matched color) to small chips on both front and rear wrappers.   Athena Rare Books   15 - 13   2015 $1000

Association – Jeffrey, Francis

Campbell, Hector *The Impending Ruin of the British Empire; Its Cause and Remedy Considered.* London: E. Wilson, 1813. First edition, 8vo., fairly modern paper wrappers, title on upper cover, good presentation copy inscribed by author for Francis Jeffrey.   John Drury Rare Books   March 2015 - 25606   2015   £306

Association – Jenkins, Roy

Who Was Who. London: Adam & Charles Black, 1966. Mostly reprints, 8vo., 9 volumes, first 6 volumes presented from Roy Jenkins to Ian Gilmour, all clean, very good or better.   Any Amount of Books   2015 - A70295   2015   £225

Association – Jerome, Aaron Brainard

Brewster, David *A Treatise on Optics.* Philadelphia: Carey, Lea & Blanchard, 1833. First American edition, text diagrams, contemporary linen backed paper covered boards, printed paper spine label, text untrimmed, scattered foxing, spine bit faded, book was owned by Aaron Brainard Jerome (1813-1839) who has dated his signature "Nassau Hall March 2 1835", and several pencil drawings and a poem poking fun at Jerome.   Joseph J. Felcone Inc.   Science, Medicine and Technology - 14   2015 $300

Association – Jersey, Sarah Sophia Child Villers, Countess of

Cervantes Saavedra, Miguel De   1547-1616 *El Ingenioso Hidalgo Don Quixote de la Mancha.* Madrid: J. Ibarra, 1780. Deluxe edition, 4 volumes, 4to., frontispieces, portrait of Cervantes, 31 plates, 14 ornamental capital letters, 22 vignettes, 20 culs-de-lampe and folding engraved map, contemporary Spanish binding of green stained calf, covers 'marbled' with octagonal panel of pale brown calf set in gilt tooled border, spines gilt in compartments, red morocco labels, marbled endpapers, gilt edges, slight worm damage to foot of spine volume 1, head of volume 4 slightly chipped, armorial bookplate of Sarah Sophia Child (Villiers), Countess of Jersey (1785-1867) with old pressmarks of Osterley Park Library, bookplate of Jonathan and Phillida Gili (by Reynolds Stone).   Maggs Bros. Ltd.   Illustrated Books 2014 - 2015   £12,000

Association – Jersey, Victor Albert George Villiers, Earl of

Vicq, Enea *Augustarum Imagines...* Vinegia: 1558. Small 4to., engraved titlepage and 61 full page engravings (closed tear to one illustrations+, 103 medallion portraits, contemporary vellum, front hinge just little loose, with bookplate of Victor Albert George Villiers, Earl of Jersey, some light waterstain on upper inner margin, closed tear to one engraving, lacks five leaves of prelim matter (index and two leaves of errata in rear), but good, clear impression of engravings.   Second Life Books Inc.   189 - 260   2015 $1250

Association – Jodrell, Richard Paul

Vergilius Maro, Publius *Publii Virgilii Maronis Bucolica et Georgica tabulis Aeneis olim a Johanne Pine...* n.p., 1774. 2 volumes bound as one, 80 plates on 59 sheets, 6 engraved dedications, frequent further engravings within text, ad leaf discarded, 8vo., contemporary marbled calf, spine divided by gilt fillet, red morocco lettering piece, other compartments with central sunburst gilt tools, bit rubbed, spine creased, gutters cracking towards middle of textblock but binding perfectly sound, bookplates of Magdalen College, Oxford and Sir Richard Paul Jodrell with inscription indicating gift of the volume from former to latter, dated 1802, good.   Blackwell's Rare Books   Greek & Latin Classics VI - 109   2015   £800

Association – Johnson, Oliver

Garrison, William Lloyd *Sonnets and Other Poems.* Boston: Oliver Johnson, 1843. First edition, 16mo., 96 pages, original cloth, some browning, near fine, inscribed in ink by publisher, O(liver) Johnson to his sister.   M & S Rare Books, Inc.   97 - 108   2015 $600

Association – Johnson, Samuel

Bible. Latin - 1726 *Biblia Scacra ex Sebastiani Castellionis Interpretatione Ejusque Postrema Recognitione (Volume I).* Londoni: Excudebat Jacob Bettenham, Impensis J. Knapton, R. Knaplock..., 1726. First edition, volume one only, 12mo., text in Latin, from the library of American book collector Ralph Isham with his engraved bookplate, dust jacket inscription to Mrs. Hester Lynch Thrale from Dr. Samuel Johnson, contemporary full sheep, dark red morocco spine label, gilt edges light cracking to joints, very good, housed in dark red full morocco box, gold silk interior and gold edges, presumably commissioned by Isham, with the Johnston presentation "Bible presented to Mrs. Thrale by Dr. Johnson" in gilt on front cover, front joint of box professionally repaired, very good.   Between the Covers Rare Books, Inc.   187 - 44   2015 $3000

Association – Johnston, James

Lamartine, Alphonse De *History of the French Revolution of 1848.* London: Henry G. Bohn, 1849. First English edition, half title, frontispiece, original dark green cloth, as on endpapers, bookplate of James Johnston, very good.   Jarndyce Antiquarian Booksellers   CCXI - 171   2015   £65

Association – Johnstone

Descartes, Rene *Renati Descartes Epistolae...* London: Joh(n) Dunmore & Octavian Pulleyn, 1668. First London edition, small 4to., 14 folding plates and numerous illustrations, endpapers little stained by original turn-ins, some light dampstaining to first three leaves of sheet O, contemporary calf, covers panelled in blind, rebacked new endpapers, John Wheeler with inscription, 18th century armorial bookplate of Johnstone family of Westerhall, Dumfries, from the library of James Stevens Cox (1910-1997).   Maggs Bros. Ltd.   1447 - 141   2015   £750

Association – Joliot, F.

Biquard, P. *Deux Heures de Physique.* Paris: Editions KRA, 1930. First edition, signed and inscribed by P. Biquard and F. Joliot, very good++, original printed wrappers, 8vo., mild cover edge wear, spotting to covers, 247 pages.   By the Book, L. C.   Special List 10 - 1   2015 $200

Association – Jolliffe

Sedley, Charles *The Poetical Works of the Honourable Sir Charles Sedley Bar. and His Speeches in Parliament...* London: printed for Sam. Briscoe an sold by James Woodward and John Morphew, 1710. Second edition, in fact reissue of sheets of 1707 edition with cancel titlepage, 8vo., contemporary panelled calf, joints rubbed, spine bit worn, label defective, good condition, early armorial Jolliffe bookplate.   C. R. Johnson   Foxon R-Z - 877r-z   2015 $230

Association – Jolliffe, William

Gardiner, Robert William *Considerations on the Military Organization of the British Army; Respectfully addressed to the Honourable the Members of the House of Commons.* London: Byfield Hawksworth and Co., 1858. First edition, large 8vo., original red cloth, embossed in blind and lettered in gilt on upper cover, gilt edges, fine, presentation inscription by author for Sir William Jolliffe, Bart.   John Drury Rare Books   March 2015 - 16415   2015 $266

Association – Jones, H. Spencer

Visser-Hooft, Jenny *Among the Kara-Korum Glaciers in 1925.* London: Edward Arnold, 1926. First edition, 8vo., original blue cloth lettered gilt on spine and cover, pages uncut, frontispiece, 24 plates, 2 maps, neat name on half title "Gilbert Satterthwaite and H. Spencer Jones, stamp on titlepage "Presentation copy",.   Any Amount of Books 2015 - A91390   2015   £220

Association – Jones, Henry Arthur

Keats, John 1795-1821 *The Poems.* Hammersmith: William Morris at the Kelmscott Press, 1894. First edition, one of 300 copies, octavo, full 20th century russet morocco gilt, bound by Sangorski & Sutcliffe, gift inscription by English playwright Henry Arthur Jones.   Honey & Wax Booksellers   2 - 15   2015 $7000

Association – Jones, Isaac

Pushkin, Aleksandr Sergeevich 1799-1837 *The Golden Cockerel.* New York: Heritage Press, 1950. First edition, 4to., original blue cloth with cockerel printed in gilt in repeat pattern on covers, spine gilt lettered, copiously illustrated in color, signed by the artist, Edmund Dulac with inscription form Dulac to Isaac Jones, slight marks, head of spine slightly rubbed, slight soiling, very good+.   Any Amount of Books   2015 - A43024   2015   £175

Association – Jones, James

Duncan, David Douglas *Picasso's Picassos.* New York: Harper & Brothers, 1961. First edition, folio, endpapers little foxed, little cocked, very good in chipped, fair only dust jacket, inscribed by author to author James Jones 19 May 63, Paris.   Between the Covers Rare Books, Inc.   187 - 213   2015 $600

Hemingway, Ernest Millar 1899-1961 *For Whom the Bell Tolls.* New York: Charles Scribner's Sons, 1940. First edition, foxing to boards and endpapers, very good in very near fine (possibly supplied, but was with book when it came to us), second issue dust jacket, with little rubbing, author James Jones's copy with his ownership signature. Between the Covers Rare Books, Inc.   187 - 124   2015 $2500

Willingham, Calder *Geraldine Bradshaw.* New York: Vanguard Press, 1950. First edition, boards little smudged, very good in about very good dust jacket, inscribed by author to fellow author James Jones.   Between the Covers Rare Books, Inc.   187 - 294   2015 $375

Association – Jones, Llewellyn

Frost, Robert Lee 1874-1963 *Selected Poems.* New York: Henry Holt, 1923. First edition, one of 1025 copies, 8vo., dark green cloth backed patterned boards, dust jacket, presentation copy inscribed by author for friend Llewellyn Jones, beautiful copy, virtually as new in rare dust jacket which is splitting at one of the folds, in half morocco slipcase.   James S. Jaffe Rare Books   Modern American Poetry - 92   2015 $4500

Association – Jones, William

Johnson, Edward *Life, Health and Disease.* London: Simpkin & Co., 1843. Seventh thousand, 4 pages ads and initial ad, slip for 'Nuces Philosophicae", uncut, original dark green cloth, blocked in blind with gilt title, very good, bright copy, large ownership inscription of William Jones, Glyn Castell, June 24th 1844.   Jarndyce Antiquarian Booksellers CCXI - 165   2015   £45

Association – Joyce, Philitus

Walrond, Eric *Tropic Death.* New York: Boni & Liveright, 1926. First edition, 8vo., black cloth, slightly cocked, hinge tender, very good, inscribed by author for Philitus Joyce. Second Life Books Inc.   190 - 212   2015 $750

Association – Kachline, Cliff

Getz, Mike *Baseball's 3000-Hit Men: a Book of Stats, Facts and Trivia.* Brooklyn: Gemmeg Press, 1982. First edition, fine in fine dust jacket, inscribed by author to Cliff Kachline.   Between the Covers Rare Books, Inc.   187 - 8   2015 $550

Association – Kahn, Bruce

Burroughs, William S. *The Naked Lunch, The Soft Machine, The Ticket that Exploded.* Paris: Olympia Press, 1959. 1961. 1962. First editions, with Naked Lunch in first state, 3 volumes, each fine in fine dust jacket, price of Soft Machine neatly crossed out in black pen, beautiful copies, all 3 housed in very nice cloth clamshell case with morocco spine label gilt, Soft Machine inscribed, although not marked in any way, this copy from distinguished modern first collection of Bruce Kahn.   Between the Covers Rare Books   196 - 67   2015 $5500

Carver, Raymond *Will You Please Be Quiet, Please?* New York: McGraw Hill, 1976. First edition, signed by author, trifle spotting to top stain, still fine in fine dust jacket, beautiful copy from the Bruce Kahn collection.   Ken Lopez Bookseller   E-list # 82 - 911022   2015 $5000

Association – Kamenetz, Herman

Da Vaz, Jurg *Psychospheres 1975-1978.* Washington: The Artist, 1978. First edition, copy #4 of 300 numbered and handbound copies, monogrammed and dated by Da Vaz, nicely inscribed by Da Vaz to co-editor, Herman Kamenetz and his wife, very large oblong folio,.   Between the Covers Rare Books, Inc.   187 - 2   2015 $1500

Association – Kampe, I. F. C.

Hegel, Georg Wilhelm Friedrich *Encyclopadie der Philosophischen Wissenschaften im Grundrisse...* Heidelberg: August Oswald, 1827. 8vo., paper throughout generally little browned and foxed, original boards with spine label lettered in gilt, wear to joints and extremities, red edges, good sound copy with several early ownership inscriptions, including I. F. C. Kampe (mid 19th century) Jonas Cohn (1931) and Selly Oake Colleges Library.   John Drury Rare Books   2015 - 24310   2015 $830

Association – Kane, Grenville

Lobeira, Vasco *Amadis of Gaul by Vasco Lobeira.* London: printed for T. N. Longman and Rees, 1803. First edition of Robert Southey's translation, 4 volumes, 12mo., later tan half calf, marbled paper boards, black leather labels, gilt rules and lettering, half title in volume one only, small bookplate of Grenville Kane, edges slightly rubbed, fine set.   The Brick Row Book Shop   Miscellany 67 - 84   2015 $450

Moraes, Francisco De *Palmerin of England.* London: printed for Longman, Hurst, Rees and Orme, 1807. First edition translated and edited by Robert Southey, 4 volumes, 12mo., later tan half calf marbled paper boards, black leather labels, gilt rules and lettering, half titles present, small bookplate of Grenville Kane, edges slightly rubbed, fine set.   The Brick Row Book Shop   Miscellany 67 - 85   2015 $500

Association – Kanin, Garson

Guitarman, Arthur *The School for Husbands.* New York: Samuel French, 1935. First edition, little light sunning to spine, else near fine, lacking dust jacket, bookplate of Garson Kanin and Ruth Gordon.   Between the Covers Rare Books, Inc.   187 - 130   2015 $200

Association – Kantor, Irene Layne

Kantor, Mackinlay *Signal Thirty-Two.* New York: Random House, 1950. First edition, inscribed by author, also signed by author's wife, Irene Layne Kantor, some scattered light spotting on endpapers, otherwise fine in dust jacket with slightly faded spine and small nicks and tears at top of spine.   Mordida Books   March 2015 - 007510   2015 $200

Association – Karmiole, Kenneth

Bliss, Carey S. *Julius Firmicus Maternus and the Aldine Edition of the Scriptores Astronomici Veteres.* Los Angeles: Kenneth Karmiole, 1981. First edition, number 56 of 164 copies printed by Parick Reagh, small folio, decorated titlepage plus 6 illustrations, gray cloth, paper spine label, very fine, presentation inscription by publisher.   Argonaut Book Shop   Holiday Season 2014 - 160   2015 $800

Association – Kaufmann, Walter

Morris, Charles *Festival.* New York: George Braziller, 1966. First edition, fine in spine faded dust jacket, otherwise jacket very good or better, inscribed by author to noted philosopher and author Walter Kaufmann.   Between the Covers Rare Books, Inc.   187 - 182   2015 $75

Association – Kearney, Michael

Ferguson, Adam *An Essay on the History of Civil Society.* Dublin: printed by Boutler Grierson, 1767. First Irish edition, 8vo., intermittent worming in many lower margins (but nowhere touching letters), sometimes a single perforation, at others a worm track, contemporary catspaw calf, raised bands and morocco spine label, very good, well bound and crisp copy from contemporary library of Michael Kearney 1734-1814, with his armorial bookplate, very scarce.   John Drury Rare Books   2015 - 21158   2015 $1005

Association – Keating, H. R. F.

Cody, Liza *Culprit: a Crime Writer's Annual.* London: Chatto & Windus, 1992. First edition, 3 annual volumes, first volume signed by Robert Barnard, Liza Cody, Michael Lewin, Susan Moody and H. R. F. Keating, fine in soft covers and pictorial dust jackets. Mordida Books March 2015 - 008749 2015 $150

Association – Keeland, Reg

Larsson, Steig *The Girl with the Dragon Tattoo. The Girl Who Kicked the Hornet's Nest. The Girl Who Played with Fire.* London: Maclehose/Quercus, 2008. 2009. First UK editions, 3 volumes, each fine and unread in fine dust jacket, without trace of wear to spine bumping endemic to these titles, second volume signed by translator Reg Keeland on titlepage, incredible set, from the collection of Duke Collier. Royal Books 36 - 4 2015 $5000

Association – Kelley, Florence

Maurice, C. Edmund *Life of Octavia Hill as Told in Her Letters.* London: Macmillan, 1913. First edition, 8vo., portraits, untrimmed, partially unopened, very good, tight, clean copy, this the copy of founder of Hull House, Jane Addams with her ownership signature, from the library of consumer advocate Florence Kelley. Second Life Books Inc. 189 - 160 2015 $250

Association – Kembler, J.

Boyle, Robert 1627-1691 *Some considerations Touching the Style of the H. Scriptures.* London: for Henry Herringman, 1663. Second edition, 8vo. in 4's, light marginal browning with some occasional spotting, contemporary sheep ruled in blind, front cover detached, worn, scuffed, bumped and with small pieces missing from upper and lower headcaps, contemporary signature "Dan(ie)l Williams, ex-libris J. Kembler Anno 1755, from the library of James Stevens Cox (1910-1997). Maggs Bros. Ltd. 1447 - 42 2015 £180

Association – Kempton, Murray

Joyce, James 1882-1941 *Finnegans Wake.* New York: Viking Press, 1939. First American edition, top corners well bumped, front hinge little tender, else about very good, lacking dust jacket, journalist Murray Kempton's copy with his bookplate. Between the Covers Rare Books, Inc. 187 - 142 2015 $300

Association – Kendall, Alice Tyldesley

Gogarty, Oliver St. John 1878-1957 *It Isn't This Time of Year at All! An Unpremeditated Autobiography.* New York: Doubleday and Co., 1964. First U. S. edition, 8vo., prelims very slightly marked (from press cuttings?), otherwise very good+ in bright, clean, slightly edgeworn (otherwise very good) dust jacket, signed presentation from author to Alice Tyldesley Kendall, a Canadian artist, loosely inserted are 2 good short TLS's from author to Kendall. Any Amount of Books 2015 - A84548 2015 £160

Association – Kendall, Edward

Boyle, Robert 1627-1691 *New Experiments and Observations Touching Cold, or an Experimental History of Cold, Begun.* London: for John Crook, 1665. First edition, 8vo., without final blank leaf, two folding plates, bound at end, tightly bound, text-block starting to split in places, title little stained very small piece torn away from blank corner of d4, contemporary calf (rebacked, corners worn, 19th century endleaves), old front flyleaf (stained), preserved, late 18th/early 19th century signature Edward Kendall, from the library of James Stevens Cox (1910-1997). Maggs Bros. Ltd. 1447 - 41 2015 £3500

Association – Kennedy, Charles William

Boswell, James 1740-1795 *The Journal of a Tour to the Hebrides, with Samuel Johnson...* London: printed by Henry Baldwin for Charles Dilly, 1785. Second edition, half title, final leaf advertising Boswell's Life of Johnson, occasional light spotting, light marginal stain to last few leaves, early 19th century quarter calf, marbled paper boards, spine decorated and lettered gilt, slightly rubbed, marbled endpapers, red sprinkled edges, bookplate of Charles William Kennedy, University College, Oxford, attractive copy. Jarndyce Antiquarian Booksellers CCXI - 34 2015 £420

Association – Kennerley, Mitchell

Schnitzler, Arthur *The Lonely Way: Intermezzo: Countess Mizzie.* New York: Mitchell Kennerley, 1915. First American edition, spine lettering dull and little foxing in text, very good without dust jacket, Walter Lippmann's copy with his ownership signature and address "From Mitchell Kennerley, May 1915". Between the Covers Rare Books, Inc. 187 - 246 2015 $400

Association – Kent, Victoira Mary Louisa, Duchess of

Grandineau, Francois *Conversations Familieres or Conversational Lessons for the use of Young Ladies from Nine to Twelve Years of Age.* Kensington: 1832. First edition, 12mo., contemporary full straight grained morocco gilt, this copy inscribed from Kensington Palace by Victoria's mother to her young grandson by her first marriage. Honey & Wax Booksellers 3 - 5 2015 $2500

Association – Kenton, Elaine Harwood

Hayley, William *Ballads. Founded on Anecdotes Relating to Animals with Prints Designed and Engraved by William Blake.* Chichester: J. Seagrave for Richard Phillips, 1805. First edition, engraved plates in first state, small 8vo., original grey paper covered boards, sometime expertly rebacked preserving original backstrip and printed paper, endpapers renewed presumably at time of rebacking, 5 engraved plates by William Blake after his own designs, ink signature of Norman Davey dated Dec. 5th 1913, printed booklabel of Elaine Harwood Kenton, fine.   Henry Sotheran Ltd. William Blake Exhibition 17th Oct.-7th Nov. 2014 - 70   2015   £6595

Association – Kern, Jerome

When the Cat's Away the Mice May Play. Colophon: (London): printed for A. Baldwin, n.d., 1712. First edition, 4 pages, folio, 2 leaves, folded as issued in light brown cloth folding case (cover detached), very good, from the library of Jerome Kern with his booklabel.   C. R. Johnson   Foxon R-Z - 1130r-z   2015 $2681

Association – Ketchum, Ralph

Tomlins, Thomas Edlyne *The Law-Dictionary; Retaining the Rise, Progress and Present state of the British Law...* London: 1820. Third edition, full brown calf, quarto, 2 volumes, both repaired with modern brown calf spine with black and red spine labels, new calf corners, front and rear endpapers have been replaced and half title to volume I missing, this is Andrew Rainsford Wetmore's copy with his signature to inner margins of titlepage of both volumes, presented to him by his uncle Charles P. Wetmore with his signature stating that they were presented to him from Ralph Ketchum July 1853, it appears the original owner was Charles Putnam.   Schooner Books Ltd.   110 - 28   2015 $275

Association – Keyden, James

Cruden, Alexander *A Complete Concordance to the Holy Scriptures of the Old and New Testament or a Dictionary and alphabetical Index to the Bible.* London: Longman, T. Cadell, 1838. 4to., frontispiece, silk doublures, contemporary full brown morocco decorated in gilt, elaborate gilt dentelles, gilt inscription on leading pastedown "Presented to Mr. James Keyden...Glasgow 15 February 1839", booklabel of James Keyden, all edges gilt, handsome copy.   Jarndyce Antiquarian Booksellers   CCXI - 79   2015   £150

Association – Keyes, Frances Parkinson

Hale, E. E. *In His Name: a Story of the Waldeneses, Seven Hundred Years Ago.* Boston: Roberts Brothers, 1877. First edition, 12mo., publisher's green cloth, gilt, modest edgewear, one signature little sprung, very good, author Frances Parkinson Keyes' copy with her bookplate and later signature of her son, Henry W. Keyes, Jr. Between the Covers Rare Books, Inc.   187 - 115   2015 $400

Association – Keynes, Quentin

Bannister, Saxe *Humane Policy; or Justice to the Aborigines of New Settlements Essential to a Due Expenditure of British Money...* London: Thomas and George Underwood, 1830. First edition, 8vo., fine folding lithographic map, colored by hand, with half title but without ads found in some copies, mid 19th century half calf gilt with raised bands, red morocco label, very minor wear to extremities, very good, recently from the library of the late Quentin Keynes, originally belonging to the Aborigines Protection Society (name in ink at head of title).   John Drury Rare Books   2015 - 19428   2015 $2185

Association – Kimbrough, Emily

Hughes, Langston *The Book of Negro Folklore.* New York: Dodd, Mead and Co., 1958. First edition, octavo, 624 pages, light wear and bit of soiling at extremities of cloth, else near fine in slightly spine and faded and rubbed, near fine, nicely inscribed by Hughes for radio personality Emily Kimbrough, NY Jan. 14 1959.   Between the Covers Rare Books   197 - 23   2015 $950

Association – King, Coretta Scott

King, Martin Luther *Where do We Go From Here Chaos or Community?* New York: Harper & Row, 1967. First edition, first printing, presentation copy signed and inscribed by author, additionally signed by his wife, Coretta Scott King to their close friends June & Kelvin Wall, about fine with only crease to one page (173), in excellent and extremely crisp unclipped dust jacket with few minor scuffs to rear panel, lovely copy.   B & B Rare Books, Ltd.   234 - 63   2015 $13,000

Association – King, Frances

Horatius Flaccus, Quintus *A Translation of the Odes and Epodes of Horace into English Verse/ attempted by T. Hare, A. B. Master of Blandford School.* London: printed for the author in the year, 1737. First edition, 8vo., bookplate of novelist Frances King, titlepage professionally repaired at inner edge and complete, original brown leather lettered gilt at spine with rubbed marbled boards, very good, not common.   Any Amount of Books   2015 - A87245   2015   £160

Association – King, H. S.

Arnold, Matthew 1822-1888 *On The Study of Celtic Literature.* London: Smith, Elder & Co., 1867. First edition, half title, without ads, original brown cloth, bevelled boards, brick red endpapers, inner hinges noticeably strengthened with blue paper, presentation from H. S. King to the Hon. Mrs. Gordon, with Kathleen Tillotson's booklabel. Jarndyce Antiquarian Booksellers CCVII - 41 2015 £35

Association – King, Martha

Broonzy, William *Big Bill Blues.* London: Cassell, 1955. First edition, 8vo., in Grove Press dust jacket, (is this the US edition or a made up copy?), photos and drawings by Paul Olliver, donor's presentation on flyleaf, author's presentation under his frontispiece for Mrs. Martha King, black cloth, top edges slightly soiled, otherwise very good, tight copy in little chipped and somewhat soiled dust jacket, scarce signature. Second Life Books Inc. 190 - 38 2015 $2500

Association – King, P. J. Locke

Fane, Robert George Cecil *Ministry of Justice: Its Necessity as an Instrument of Law Reform.* London: Spottiswoode and Shaw, 1848. First separate edition, 8vo., half title, recent plain wrappers, very good presentation copy inscribed by author for P. J. Locke King 38 Dover St. John Drury Rare Books 2015 - 16769 2015 $133

Sleigh, William Campbell *The Grand Jury System Subversive of the Moral Interests of Society: a Letter to the Rt. Hon. Spencer H. Walpole, M.P., Secretary of State for the Home Department.* London: S. Sweet and Hodges and Smith, Dublin, 1852. First edition, 8vo., some spotting and pencillings, recently well bound in linen backed marbled boards, lettered, good copy, inscribed by author for Hon P. J. Locke King M.P. John Drury Rare Books 2015 - 16761 2015 $168

Association – Kington, Thomas

Aiken, P. F. *A Comparative View of the Constitutions of Great Britain and the United States of America in Six Lectures.* London: Longman and Co., Hamilton Adams and Co., 1842. First edition, 8vo., original green cloth lettered gilt on spine, few scattered white marks to covers, otherwise very good with some light wear, presentation copy from Thomas Kington to Alexis de Tocqueville, very good with some light wear. Any Amount of Books 2015 - C16194 2015 £160

Association – Kinnell, Galway

Villon, Francois *The Poems of.* Boston: Houghton Mifflin, 1977. First edition, fine in trifle dust soiled, otherwise fine dust jacket, inscribed by Galway Kinnell to fellow poet Jane (Cooper). Between the Covers Rare Books, Inc. 187 - 147 2015 $250

Association – Kipling, John Lockwood

Kipling, Rudyard 1865-1936 *The Jungle Book. (and) The Second Jungle Book.* London: Macmillan, 1894. 1895. First editions, 8vo., blue gilt pictorial cloth, all edges gilt, light foxing on prelim pages, light bubble on cover of Jungle Book, slight soil on cover of Second Jungle Book with light wear to spine ends, very good+ set, wonderfully illustrated with black and whites by J. Lockwood Kipling and others, laid in is 2 page handwritten letter from artist, J. L. Kipling. Aleph-bet Books, Inc. 109 - 245 2015 $4500

Association – Kizer, Carolyn

Carruth, Hayden *Journey to a Known Place.* Norfolk: New Directions, 1961. First edition, one of 300 numbered copies, small quarto, printed on Hayle paper by Harry Duncan and Kim Merker, prospectus laid in, this copy inscribed by Carolyn Kizer to fellow poet Leonie Adams, Christmas 1962. Between the Covers Rare Books, Inc. 187 - 43 2015 $450

Hamill, Sam *Fatal Pleasure.* Portland: Breitenbusch Books, 1984. First edition, fine in near fine dust jacket (trifle rubbed), warmly inscribed by author to fellow poet Carolyn Kizer. Between the Covers Rare Books, Inc. 187 - 116 2015 $85

Association – Kleckner, Donald

Whitehead, Alfred North 1861-1947 *Process and Reality, an Essay in Cosmology.* New York: Macmillan Co., 1929. First American edition, octavo, former owner's name 'Clifton C. Winn' in ink and typed note crudely taped to inside front cover, given by him to Dr. Donald Kleckner, original navy blue cloth, gilt lettering on slightly sunned spine, inside tight, bright, clean copy. Athena Rare Books 15 - 59 2015 $4000

Association – Kleinsasser, Joseph

The Hutterian Brethren of Montana. Augusta: privately printed, 1963. First edition, printed wrappers, 41 pages, very slight fading, very scarce, fine, ink stamp of Rev. Joseph J. Kleinsasser, Milford Colony, Augusts, Montana. Baade Books of the West 2014 - 2015 $61

Association – Kleissenius, Philippus

Plato *(Greek text) Omnia Platonis Opera.* Venice: in aedib. Aldi et Andreae Soceri, Sept, 1513. Editio princeps, 2 volumes, large Aldine anchor device on titlepage (volume i) and on verso of last leaf in volume ii, Greek text (apart from Aldus' dedicatory petition, contents and colophon), titlepage slightly soiled and with hole at inner margin repaired, minor stains on fore-edges, few wormholes in blank lower margin of opening leaves of volumes ii, volume, volume i in contemporary English quartered oak boards, resewn with spine uncovered, modern vellum endleaves, volume ii in contemporary German pigskin over wooden boards, blind tooled to panel design filled in with 'laus deo' and rosette stamps, brass catches and clasps, top of spine worn, inner hinge broken, cord intact, good, binding of the first volume of this copy is subject of 2 page report by Nicholas Pickwood (printout accompanies the volume), repairs carried out by James Brockman; first volume with signature of Thomas Colm of Oxford dated 1573, 17th century ownership inscription of Hendricus Ffeild, 19th century bookplate and stamp of King Edward's School, Birmingham, plus bookplate of Kenneth Rapoport, the second volume with early ownership inscriptions of Johannes (or Johann?) Lang of Erfurt and Philippus Kleissenius, few early marginalia, inscription 'de bibliotheca Johannis Langi Erphurdiensis. Blackwell's Rare Books   Greek & Latin Classics VI - 82   2015   £75,000

Association – Klinger, Lee

Blochman, Lawrence G. *See You at the Morgue.* New York: Duell, Sloan and Pearce, 1941. First edition, signed by author on titlepage, presentation inscription from author to Lee & Mike Klinger, cloth little faded on spine, light offsetting to front and rear pastedown sheets, else very good, tight, price clipped dust jacket with light professional restoration to spine ends and corners.   Buckingham Books March 2015 - 29112   2015 $875

Association – Klinger, Mike

Blochman, Lawrence G. *See You at the Morgue.* New York: Duell, Sloan and Pearce, 1941. First edition, signed by author on titlepage, presentation inscription from author to Lee & Mike Klinger, cloth little faded on spine, light offsetting to front and rear pastedown sheets, else very good, tight, price clipped dust jacket with light professional restoration to spine ends and corners.   Buckingham Books March 2015 - 29112   2015 $875

Association – Knatchbull, Norton Joseph

Turnbull, Peter Evan *Austria.* London: John Murray, 1840. First edition, 2 volumes, handsome, tall 8vo., half brown leather lettered gilt at spine, raised bands, marbled boards, highly uncommon, slight foxing to prelims, bookplate of Sir Norton Joseph Knatchbull, minor rubbing and scuffing, else close to very good+.   Any Amount of Books   2015 - A65104   2015   £200

Association – Knight, Joseph

Plutarchus *Les Ouvvres Morales & Meslees de Plutarque.* Paris: De l'Imprimerie de Michel de Vascosan, 1572. First edition of Jacques Amyot's translation, title creased and slightly frayed at edges, short closed tear reinforced with tissue, some light spotting elsewhere, few sections toned, folio, 18th century calf, scraped and worn at edges, rebacked, black morocco lettering piece, hinges relined, bookplate of drama critic Joseph Knight (1829-1920), sound.   Blackwell's Rare Books   Greek & Latin Classics VI - 85   2015   £2500

Association – Knopf, Alfred

Updike, John **1932-2009** *Hoping for a Hoopoe.* London: Victor Gollancz, 1959. First English edition, fine in fine dust jacket with very light wear, inscribed by author to Alfred A. Knopf.   Between the Covers Rare Books, Inc.   187 - 280   2015 $5000

Association – Knowland, J. R.

Kennedy, Elijah R. *The Contest for California in 1861: How Colonel E. D Baker Saved the Pacific States to the Union.* Boston and New York: Houghton Mifflin, 1912. First edition, 6 plates, maroon cloth, very minor rubbing to spine ends and corners, covers bit darkened, very good, signed by J. R. Knowland, owner of Oakland Tribune.   Argonaut Book Shop   Holiday Season 2014 - 146   2015 $90

Association – Koteliansky, S. S.

Dostoevskii, Fyodor Mikhailovich **1821-1881** *The Grand Inquisitor.* London: Elkin Matthews, 1930. First edition, limited to 300 numbered copies, this no. 267, 4to., original ultra modernist decorated pigskin, lettered black on spine and front cover, signed presentation from S. S. Koteliansky for Raphael Salaman (1906-1993 and wife Miriam Polianovsky, very faint surface soiling, otherwise fine in sound, used slipcases, excellent copy.   Any Amount of Books 2015 - C11380   2015   £225

Association – Kraus, Herbert

Lowell, Percival *Mars and Its Canals.* New York & London: Macmillan Co., 1906. First edition, frontispiece, 8 plates, 12 maps, 49 figures, original dark green gilt stamped cloth, top edge gilt, lightly rubbed, ownership signatures of Edwin M. Eckard and Russell Sullivan, Indianapolis, bookplate of LA lawyer Herbert Kraus, very good.   Jeff Weber Rare Books   178 - 798   2015 $750

Association – Lehmann, Beatrix

Spender, Stephen *Poems for Spain.* London: Hogarth Press, 1939. First edition, slightly soiled, very good without dust jacket, inscribed by John Lehmann to his sister Beatrix. Between the Covers Rare Books, Inc.   187 - 257   2015 $350

Association – Lehmann, John

Copley, Heather *Drawings of the Katydid.* Bainbridge: Katydid Press, 1958. First edition, 24mo., printed paper covered boards, fine in near fine, unprinted dust jacket, ownership signature of wood engraver John De Pol, with ALS from publisher John Lehmann to De Pol presenting the book.   Between the Covers Rare Books, Inc.   187 - 61   2015 $450

Spender, Stephen *Poems for Spain.* London: Hogarth Press, 1939. First edition, slightly soiled, very good without dust jacket, inscribed by John Lehmann to his sister Beatrix. Between the Covers Rare Books, Inc.   187 - 257   2015 $350

Association – Leibovitz, Annie

Sontag, Susan *Women.* New York: Random House, 1999. First edition, small folio, Annie Leibovitz presentation inscription for Lena Horne, very good plus, small abrasion to rear pastedown in very good plus dust jacket.   Ed Smith Books   83 - 47   2015 $1500

Association – Leigh, W.

Bacon, Francis, Viscount St. Albans   1561-1626 *Historia Vitae et Mortis.* Amsterdam: Joannem Ravesteinium, 1663. Fifth separate edition, 12mo., contemporary mottled calf covers ruled in gilt, rebacked, new endleaves, old flyleaves preserved, inscription "Guil Rayner Aedis Ch. Alummus 1683" (William Rayner of London 1664-1730), signature of W. Leigh, from the library of James Stevens Cox (1910-1997).   Maggs Bros. Ltd.   1447 - 17   2015   £120

Association – Leinster, Duke of

Dale, Samuel *The History and Antiquities of Harwich and Dovercourt, Topographical, Dynastical, and Political.* London: C. Davis and T. Green, 1730. First edition, large paper copy, 4to., large paper copy, 14 engraved plates, printed on thick paper, contemporary panelled calf, some wear to extremities, neatly rebacked retaining original labels (although one label worn), very good, sometime in the library of the Dukes of Leinster at their country house Carton or Carten House with their armorial bookplate and shelf number and arms in gilt at head of spine, of great rarity. John Drury Rare Books   2015 - 24774   2015 $787

Association – Leishman, J. B.

Donne, John   1571-1631 *The Poems.* Oxford: Clarendon Press, 1912. 2 volumes, original brown buckram, paper labels slightly split at edges, with inserted, notes, probably by J. B. Leishman, the editor to whom correspondence is addressed, from the library of Geoffrey & Kathleen Tillotson.   Jarndyce Antiquarian Booksellers   CCVII - 227   2015   £60

Hopkins, Gerard Manley *The Sermons and Devotional Writings.* London: Oxford University Press, 1959. Half title, frontispiece, map, original brown buckram, very good in slightly torn dust jacket, Geoffrey Tillotson's signed copy, containing notes by J. B. Leishman, former owner. Jarndyce Antiquarian Booksellers   CCVII - 305   2015   £25

Horatius Flaccus, Quintus *Translating Homer: Thirty Odes Translated...* Oxford: Bruno Cassirer, 1956. Half title, parallel English & Latin text, original light brown cloth, very good in slightly dusted and chipped dust jacket, from the library of Geoffrey & Kathleen Tillotson, signed by both, with signed presentation slip from J. B. Leishman laid in, with ALS's from him to Tillotson's.   Jarndyce Antiquarian Booksellers   CCVII - 309   2015   £20

Association – Leistikow, Gurmar

Bendix, Hans *The Lady Who Kept Her Promise.* New York: American Artists Group, 1941. First edition, 12mo., illustrated paper covered boards, slight edgewear, else near fine, inscribed by author for Gurmar Leistikow(?).   Between the Covers Rare Books, Inc.   187 - 15   2015 $75

Association – Leith, Mary

Swinburne, Algernon Charles   1837-1909 *Studies in Prose and Poetry.* London: Chatto & Windus, 1894. First edition, 8vo., original dark blue cloth, extraordinary association copy, inscribed by author for cousin Mary C. J. Leith, Nov. 8 1894, original dark blue cloth with gilt rule to front cover borders and title and author in gilt to spine, light offsetting to free endpapers, otherwise near fine.   The Kelmscott Bookshop   11 - 53   2015 $1500

Association – Lemperly, Paul

Shorthouse, H. J. *Sir Percival: a Story of the Past and Present.* London: Macmillan and Co., 1886. First edition, presentation copy inscribed "Edward Shorthouse from his affectionate brother and sister J. Henry & Sarah Shorthouse", original dark blue cloth, gilt strips with embossed design on front over and spine, fine, housed in fine custom half red morocco slipcase, octavo, fine, bookplate of Ohio book collector Paul Lemperly with his inscription stating he received the book as a gift from Morris L. Parrish, with Parrish's letter of presentation inserted. The Kelmscott Bookshop   11 - 46   2015 $600

Association – Lent, Blair

Mosel, Arlene *The Funny Little Woman retold by.* New York: E. P. Dutton, 1972. Stated first edition, 9 3/4 x 9 1/4 inches, cloth, fine in dust jacket, jacket very good with seal, (frayed at spine ends and corners), illustrations by Blair Lent, this copy inscribed by Lent.   Aleph-Bet Books, Inc.   108 - 271   2015 $400

Association – Leott, Mrs.

Heber, Reginald *Narrative of a Journey through the Upper Provinces of India from Calcutta to Bombay 1824-1825.* London: John Murray, 1826. First edition, 10 plates, 25 wood engravings in text, map at rear, this copy lacking plate of Pagoda facing page 47, but has an additional frontispiece plate of the Ghat between Calcutta and Barrackpoor, pencilled note says this in fact the plate that is supposed to be at page 47, but we have our doubts, quarto, original light red cloth, title labels on spine, presentation copy inscribed by author to friend Mrs. Leott, covers unevenly faded, rubbed at edges and bruised at corners, map repaired, labels rubbed but not affecting lettering, first gathering in volume I loose but not detached, some spotting of prelims, good. Peter Ellis, Bookseller   2014 - 010377   2015   £300

Association – Lessing, Friedrich

Duhring, E. *Die Uberschatzung Lessing's und Dessen Anwaltschaft fur die Juden. (The Overevaluation of Lessing and His Advocacy of the Jews).* Karlsruhe und Leipzig: Verleg von H. Reuther, 1881. First edition, octavo, green cloth gilt, spine bit faded and little foxing in text, very good or better, signed by Duhring at conclusion of introduction, bookplate of Friedrich Lessing (presumably a descendant of the subject), with much pencil marginalia.   Between the Covers Rare Books, Inc.   187 - 82   2015 $950

Association – Lethem, Jonathan

Eggers, Dave *Timothy McSweeny's Trying, Trying, Trying, Trying, Trying. Issue IIII.* Brooklyn: McSweeney's, 2000. Issue 4, With individually bound works, all 14 along with extremely entertaining subscriber agreement laid into fine folding pictorial box, signed by Jonathan Lethem at his contribution and signed by Eggers on front of box.   Ken Lopez, Bookseller   164 - 61   2015 $200

Association – Levenson-Gower, John

Cox, Nicholas *The Gentleman's Recreation.* London: by Jos. Phillips and Hen. Rodes (part 4 Oxford by L. Lichfield for Nicholas Cox), 1685-1686. Third edition, 4 engraved plates, engraved frontispiece by W. Sherwin, large folding engraved plate (old repair to a long tear), double page plate of hawking and double page plate of fish, both by Dolle, lightly browned, light marginal dampstaining throughout, minor worming to top of gatherings C-G that touches the headlines and occasionally the first line of text, contemporary calf, front cover with 19th century arms of Duke of Sutherland and blindstamped to front cover, covers worn, front cover detached, spine split at head and tail; armorial bookplate of Sir John Levenson-Gower (1675-1609) 1st Baron Gower by descent to John Levenson-Gower (1694-1754, 1st Earl Gower with early 19th century armorial bookplate, by descent to George Granville Levenson-Gower, 1st Duke of Sutherland with his arms stamped in blind on front cover, from the library of James Stevens Cox (1910-1997). Maggs Bros. Ltd.   1447 - 121   2015   £1500

Association – Lever, Ashton

Hutchinson, William *An Excursion to the Lakes in Westmoreland and Cumberland August 1773.* London: J. Wilkie and W. Goldsmith, 1774. First edition, 8vo., engraved vignette on titlepage, slight foxing, first few and final few leaves, contemporary half calf over marbled boards, corners worn, neatly rebacked reusing original label and spine, very good, contemporary armorial bookplate of Sir Ashton Lever and early ownership signature of Penelope Mosley, uncommon.   John Drury Rare Books   2015 - 25681   2015 $830

Association – Levertov, Denise

Gilchrist, Ellen *The Land Surveyor's Daughter.* Fayetteville: Lost Road, 1979. First edition, first book, paperback original, 8vo., original wrappers, presentation copy inscribed by author for Denise Levertov.   James S. Jaffe Rare Books   Modern American Poetry - 107   2015 $1500

Association – Levine, Harold

Moulton, Forest Ray *An Introduction to Celestial Mechanics.* New York: Macmillan, 1935. 8vo., xvi, 437 pages, figures, index, maroon blind and gilt stamped cloth, minor wear to spine ends, ink ownership signature of Harold Levine, very good.   Jeff Weber Rare Books   178 - 808   2015 $60

Routh, Edward John *A Treatise on Analytical Statics with Numerous Examples.*   Cambridge: University Press, 1896. 1902. Second edition, volume II revised, 2 volumes, 8vo., later blue cloth, preserving original black leather gilt stamped spine labels, title ink signature of Harold Levine, 1941, 3 red ink underlining marks on page 131 volume II, very good.   Jeff Weber Rare Books   178 - 968   2015 $45

Wien, Wilhelm *Lehrbuch der Hydrodynamik.* Leipzig: S. Hirzel, 1900. 8vo., 18 figures, original half black gilt stamped cloth, patterned paper over boards, rubbed, ink titlepage ownership signature of Harold Levine, very good.   Jeff Weber Rare Books   178 - 1153   2015 $70

Association – Levine, Phil

Strand, Mark   *The Continuous Life. Eighteen Poems.* Iowa City: Windhover Press, 1990. First edition, folio, 2 woodcuts by Neil Welliver, original Japanese style handmade paper wrappers, poet Phil Levine's own copy with his ownership signature, fine.   James S. Jaffe Rare Books   Modern American Poetry - 288   2015 $450

Association – Levitan, Kalman

Griggs, Bob   *Elrae: the Littlest printer.*   Salem: Beaverdam Press, 1987. Limited to 225 numbered copies, signed by printer/binder, Earl H. Henness on colophon, 8.1 x 6.2cm., cloth, slipcase, illustrations in text by author, miniature bookplate of Kalman Levitan.   Oak Knoll Books   306 - 112   2015 $100

Association – Levy, Hermann

Bible. English - 1875   *Isaiah XL-LXVI with the shorter prophecies ... edited with notes by Matthew Arnold.* London: Macmillan, 1875. First edition, original brown cloth, signed by Geoffrey Tillotson 30.iii.42 with note that it was given to him by Prof. Hermann Levy.   Jarndyce Antiquarian Booksellers   CCVII - 58   2015   £38

Association – Levy, Jacques

Montesquieu, Charles De Secondat, Baron De   1689-1755   *Le Temple De Gnide, Suivi D; Arsace et Ismenie.* Paris: P. Didot l'Aine, 1796. One of 100 copies, 330 x 235mm., original? gray boards, flat spine, dark gray paper title label, two thirds of leaves unopened, engraved printer's device on titlepage and 7 fine and color printed engravings after Peyron by Chapuy and Lavallee, some finished by hand; couple of very small brown spots and just a hint of soiling as well as minor abrasions to covers, corners somewhat mashed (as expected), isolated trivial foxing to text, very fine, clean and bright internally , with vividly colored plates and in surprisingly sturdy and generally well preserved original temporary publisher's binding, from the outstanding library of American bibliophile Jacques Levy. Phillip J. Pirages   66 - 60   2015 $7500

Association – Levy, Pauline

Caspary, Vera   *Thicker than Water.*   New York: Liveright, 1932. First edition, 8vo., original textured beige cloth under mauve paper covered board, lettered black on spine, signed and dated presentation from author to Pauline Levy, slight fading and rubbing to boards, otherwise very good.   Any Amount of Books   2015 - C2223   2015   £850

Association – Lewin, Michael

Cody, Liza   *Culprit: a Crime Writer's Annual.*   London: Chatto & Windus, 1992. First edition, 3 annual volumes, first volume signed by Robert Barnard, Liza Cody, Michael Lewin, Susan Moody and H. R. F. Keating, fine in soft covers and pictorial dust jackets.   Mordida Books   March 2015 - 008749   2015 $150

Association – Lewis, D. C.

Josephus, Flavius *(in Greek) Philabiou Josepou Hierosolymitou Heireos Ta Heuriskomena, Flavii Josephi Hierosolymitani Sacerdotis Opera Quae Extant. (Works in Greek and Latin).* Geneva: Petrus de la Rouviere, 1611. 362 x 222mm., sumptuous contemporary honey brown morocco richly gilt in modified fanfare design, covers with outer frame of multiple plain and decorative rules and rolls, frame surrounding a central panel formed by multiple plain rules and a filigree roll and featuring oblique fleurons pointing outward at corner, panel with very densely gilt and elaborate cornerpieces and a large central lozenge incorporating olive branch garlands and rosettes, an oval at center of lozenge with contemporary coat of arms of the Abbot of Potigny, either Claude Boucherat, or his cousin Charles, flat spine with a chain roll framing a single elongated panel tooled in a design similar to covers, all edges gilt, holes for ties (perhaps with small, very expert repairs at spine bottom); woodcut printer's device on titlepage, woodcut headpieces and decorative initials, Latin and Greek text printed in parallel columns, front pastedown with partially effaced 17th century ownership inscription of Henry (Becold?) Pembroke College, Oxford dated 1734 and 19th century inscription of D. C. Lewis, blank lower right corner of titlepage neatly replaced (in 19th century?) small, pale dampstain in bottom margin of a few leaves, branching marginal wormholes in half a dozen quires (but these always extremely thin and never intruding on text), minor soiling, browning and foxing here and there, still very good internally, leaves fresh, clean and with good margins; hint of wear to joints and extremities, spine uniformly little darkened (with gilt just slightly less bright tan on boards), covers with trivial discoloration and abrasions, but impressive binding in remarkable condition, entirely solid, only minor signs of use, and with once dazzling gilt nearly as good as it was 400 years ago. Phillip J. Pirages 66 - 21 2015 $6500

Association – Lewis, Hilda

Haley, James Evetts *Robbing Banks was My Business. The Story of J. Harvey Bailey, America's Most Successful Bank Robber.* Canyon: Palo Duro Press, 1973. First edition, signed by Bailey, and signed and inscribed by Haley to Tom and Hilda Lewis, cloth, black and white frontispiece, illustrations by Theda Rhea, fine in dust jacket, lightly rubbed along front spine channel and spine ends, housed in matching cloth slipcase with titles stamped in gold gilt on spine. Buckingham Books March 2015 - 31744 2015 $875

Association – Lewis, Tom

Haley, James Evetts *Robbing Banks was My Business. The Story of J. Harvey Bailey, America's Most Successful Bank Robber.* Canyon: Palo Duro Press, 1973. First edition, signed by Bailey, and signed and inscribed by Haley to Tom and Hilda Lewis, cloth, black and white frontispiece, illustrations by Theda Rhea, fine in dust jacket, lightly rubbed along front spine channel and spine ends, housed in matching cloth slipcase with titles stamped in gold gilt on spine. Buckingham Books March 2015 - 31744 2015 $875

Association – Lieberson, Brigitta

Behrman, S. N. *The Burning Glass.* Boston: Little Brown, 1968. First edition, fine in very good dust jacket that has been trimmed along bottom edge, dedication copy, nicely inscribed by author to Brigitta and Goddard Lieberson on dedication page. Between the Covers Rare Books 196 - 66 2015 $650

Meigs, John *Peter Hurd. The Lithographs.* Lubbock: Baker Gallery Press, 1968. First edition, limited to 325 copies (25 not for sale), numbered and signed by Hurd and Meigs, each with original lithograph, quarto, green full leather, grey endpapers, 58 plates, this copy #146, this copy inscribed by Hurd for Goddard & Brigitta Lieberson, fine, bright, clean, housed in original cloth pictorial slipcase. Buckingham Books March 2015 - 32552 2015 $1250

Association – Lieberson, Goddard

Behrman, S. N. *The Burning Glass.* Boston: Little Brown, 1968. First edition, fine in very good dust jacket that has been trimmed along bottom edge, dedication copy, nicely inscribed by author to Brigitta and Goddard Lieberson on dedication page. Between the Covers Rare Books 196 - 66 2015 $650

Meigs, John *Peter Hurd. The Lithographs.* Lubbock: Baker Gallery Press, 1968. First edition, limited to 325 copies (25 not for sale), numbered and signed by Hurd and Meigs, each with original lithograph, quarto, green full leather, grey endpapers, 58 plates, this copy #146, this copy inscribed by Hurd for Goddard & Brigitta Lieberson, fine, bright, clean, housed in original cloth pictorial slipcase. Buckingham Books March 2015 - 32552 2015 $1250

Association – Liechtenstein, Prince

Seneca, Lucius Annaeus *Tragoediae.* Florence: Studio et Impensa Philippi di Guinta, 1506. 8vo., final blank discarded, rather foxed in places, some soiling, intermittent stain in gutter, few early ink marks, early ownership inscription to second leaf, 8vo., later vellum, spine with four raised bands lettered in ink, somewhat soiled and splayed, bookplates of Biblioteca Senequiana and the Prince of Liechtenstein, sound.   Blackwell's Rare Books   Greek & Latin Classics VI - 96   2015   £750

Association – Lima, Frank

Ceravolo, Joseph *Fits of Dawn.* New York: "C" Press, 1965. First edition, 4to., original illustrated wrappers wrappers lightly to moderately soiled, otherwise fine, presentation copy inscribed by author to Frank and Sheyla Lima.   James S. Jaffe Rare Books   Modern American Poetry - 49   2015 $2250

Association – Lima, Sheyla

Ceravolo, Joseph *Fits of Dawn.* New York: "C" Press, 1965. First edition, 4to., original illustrated wrappers wrappers lightly to moderately soiled, otherwise fine, presentation copy inscribed by author to Frank and Sheyla Lima.   James S. Jaffe Rare Books   Modern American Poetry - 49   2015 $2250

Association – Lindberg, David

McGuire, J. E. *Body and Void and Newton's De Mundi Systemate: Some New Sources.* New York: Springer, 1966. Offprint Archive for History of Exact Sciences Volume 3 No. 3 1966, 8vo., printed wrappers, inscribed by author for David C. Lindberg.   Jeff Weber Rare Books   178 - 840   2015 $45

Moline, Jon *Plato's Theory of Understanding.* Madison: University of Wisconsin Press, 1981. 8vo., cloth, dust jacket, ink ownership signature of David Lindberg, very good.   Jeff Weber Rare Books   178 - 892   2015 $50

Nilsson, Martin P. *Primitive Time-Reckoning: a Study in the Origins and First Development of the Art of Counting Time Among the Primitive and Early Peoples.* Lund: C. W. K. Gleerup; London: Humphrey Milford; Oxford: University Press, 1920. 8vo., original quarter vellum, plain boards, manuscript spine title, ink ownership signatures of Alexandri Phili (192), William Duane Stahlman and David C. Lindberg. Jeff Weber Rare Books   178 - 846   2015 $45

Oberman, Heiko Augustinus *Masters of the Reformation: The Emergence of a New Intellectual Climate in Europe.* Cambridge: Cambridge University Press, 1981. First English edition, 8vo., map, cloth, dust jacket, ink ownership signature of David Lindberg, fine.   Jeff Weber Rare Books   178 - 851   2015 $40

Oresme, Nicole *Nicole Oresme and the Kinematics of Circular Motion.* Milwaukee & London: University of Wisconsin, 1971. 8vo., cloth, dust jacket with some edge tears, inscribed by author for David Lindberg.   Jeff Weber Rare Books   178 - 863   2015 $45

Pasnau, Robert *Theories of Cognition in the Later Middle Ages.* Cambridge: Cambridge University Press, 1897. 8vo., cloth, dust jacket, ink ownership signature of David Lindberg, fine.   Jeff Weber Rare Books   178 - 874   2015 $110

Preston, Jean F. *English Handwriting 1400-16130: an Introductory Manual.* Birmingham: Medieval & Renaissance Text & Studies, 1992. 4to., illustrations, printed wrappers, fine, ink ownership signature of David C. Lindberg, fine.   Jeff Weber Rare Books   178 - 912   2015 $85

Proclus *Proclus' Commentary on Plato's Parmenides.* Princeton: Princeton University Press, 1987. 8vo., brown cloth, ink ownership signature of David C. Lindberg, fine, scarce.   Jeff Weber Rare Books   178 - 917   2015 $85

Ptolemy *Ptolemy's Almagest.* New York: Springer, 1984. First edition of this translation, 8vo., figures, index, cloth, dust jacket slightly worn at foot of spine, ownership ink signatures of David C. Lindberg, very good.   Jeff Weber Rare Books   178 - 919   2015 $150

Rashed, Roshdi *Histoire des Sciences Arabes.* Paris: editions du Seuil, 1997. 3 volumes, 8vo., illustrations, cloth, dust jackets bit rubbed, author's copy, very good, David C. Lindberg's copy.   Jeff Weber Rare Books   178 - 935   2015 $100

Rist, John M. *Platonism and Its Christian Heritage.* London: Variorum Reprints, 1985. 8vo., blue cloth, ink ownership signature of David Lindberg, fine.   Jeff Weber Rare Books   178 - 943   2015 $150

Sarton, George *Introduction to the History of Science.* Baltimore: Carnegie Inst. of Washington, Williams & Wilkins, 1953. 1963., 3 volumes in , 8vo., plates, blue cloth, gilt spines, bookplate of of David Lindberg with his signatures, near fine.   Jeff Weber Rare Books   178 - 989   2015 $275

Schmitt, Charles R. *The Cambridge History of Renaissance Philosophy.* Cambridge: Cambridge University Press, 1988. Thick 8vo., cloth, dust jacket, ink ownership, signature of David Lindberg, very good+. Jeff Weber Rare Books   178 - 993   2015 $75

Thorndike, Lynn *The Sphere of Sacrobosco and Its Commentators.* Chicago: University of Chicago Press, 1949. First edition, 8vo., cloth, dust jacket quite worn, ink ownership signature of David Lindberg, fine.   Jeff Weber Rare Books   178 - 983   2015 $65

Travaglia, Pinella *Magic, Causality and Intentionality.* Sismel: Edizioni del Galluzzo, 1990. Small 8vo., printed wrappers, fine, very scarce, ink ownership signature of David Lindberg.   Jeff Weber Rare Books   178 - 1074   2015 $45

Walker, D. P. *Spiritual and Demonic Magic from Ficino to Campanaella.* Nendeln/Liechtenstein: 1969. Reprint of 1958 printing, 8vo., linen cloth, ink ownership signature of David Lindberg, very good, scarce in cloth.   Jeff Weber Rare Books   178 - 1109   2015 $45

Weisheipi, James Athanasius *Nature and Gravitation.* River Forest: Albertus Magnus Lyceum, 1955. 8vo., printed wrappers, ink ownership signature of David Lindberg, fine, scarce.   Jeff Weber Rare Books   178 - 1128   2015 $50

Weisheipi, James Athanasius *Philosophy and the God of Abraham; Essays in Memory of James Athansius Weisheipl.* Toronto: Pontifical Institute of Mediaeval Studies, 1991. 8vo., frontispiece, printed wrappers, ink ownership signature of David Lindberg, fine.   Jeff Weber Rare Books   178 - 1129   2015 $40

William of Conches *Philosophia Mundi: Ausgabe des I. Buchs von Wilhelm von Conches 'Philosophia' mit Anhang.* Pretoria: University of South Africa, 1974. 8vo., figures, original printed wrappers, ink ownership signature of David Lindberg, very good, rare.   Jeff Weber Rare Books   178 - 1158   2015 $45

Wolfson, Harry Austryn *Philo: Foundations of Religious Philosophy in Judaism, Christianity and Islam.* Cambridge & London: Harvard University Press, 1982. Fifth printing, 2 volumes, 8vo., navy cloth, ink ownership signature of David Lindberg, very good.   Jeff Weber Rare Books   178 - 1172   2015 $40

Association – Lindsay, Graham

Spillane, Mickey *The Erection Set.* London: W. H. Allen, 1972. First edition, inscribed by author for Graham Lindsay, near fine in like dust jacket, from the collection of Duke Collier.   Royal Books   36 - 233   2015 $650

Association – Lingom, Joseph

Crouch, Nathaniel *The English Empire in America.* London: Nath(aniel) Crouch, 1692. Second edition, 12mo., engraved frontispiece map of New England, engraved map of the Caribbean and one of two engraved plates of "Strange Creatures in America", lacking one plate and text leaves D6-7, wormed in gutter throughout, fore-edges chipped and bumped, piece torn away from corner of d4 (touching four lines of text), large stain in inner margin of D4-D5, pencil markings on rear pastedown, contemporary sheep, garment from unidentifiable broadside showing royal arms and "by the Queen (Anne) has been used as front pastedown, 20mm. piece torn away from top of spine, hole lower down spine, covers and spine rubbed, chipped and corners heavily bumped, signature 'John Topping his booke 1710', early 18th century signature Joseph A. Lingom, from the library of James Stevens Cox (1910-1997).   Maggs Bros. Ltd.   1447 - 124   2015   £500

Association – Lippmann, Walter

Clark, Barrett H. *Eugene O'Neill.* New York: Robert M. McBride & Co., 1926. First edition, slight wear at crown and spine lettering little dull, very good or better without dust jacket, inscribed by author in year of publication to journalist Walter Lippmann, 8 Sept. 1926.   Between the Covers Rare Books, Inc.   187 - 55   2015 $275

Harris, Frank *Montes, the Matador and Other Stories.* London: Alexander Moring Ltd., 1906. First English edition, octavo, good plus with tanned spine, wear to extremities with chip at crown, foxing to pages, inscribed by author to Walter Lippmann.   Between the Covers Rare Books, Inc.   187 - 118   2015 $250

Hofmannsthal, Hugo Von *Electra; a Tragedy in One Act.* New York: Brentano's, 1908. First American edition, ownership signature of noted journalist Walter Lippmann with his address and dated 1910.   Between the Covers Rare Books, Inc.   187 - 128   2015 $150

MacKaye, Percy *Mater: an American Study in Comedy.* New York: Macmillan, 1908. First edition, spine tanned and boards bit soiled, very good, journalist Walter Lippmann's copy with his ownership signature and Cambridge address, nicely inscribed by author.   Between the Covers Rare Books, Inc.   187 - 163   2015 $200

Schnitzler, Arthur *The Lonely Way: Intermezzo: Countless Mizzie.* New York: Mitchell Kennerley, 1915. First American edition, spine lettering dull and little foxing in text, very good without dust jacket, Walter Lippmann's copy with his ownership signature and address "From Mitchell Kennerley, May 1915".   Between the Covers Rare Books, Inc.   187 - 246   2015 $400

Association – Lister, G.

Kersaint, Armand Guy, Comte De *The Speech of Kersaint to the French National Convention, with Resolutions of that Body Respecting a War with England.* London: printed for J. Ridgway, 1793. First edition in English, 8vo., 16 pages, green plain wrappers good copy with contemporary ownership signature of G. Lister, uncommon.   John Drury Rare Books   2015 - 16108   2015 $177

Association – Littell, Guy

Blair, Robert *The Grave.* R. H. Cromek, 1808. First quarto edition, 4to., later half calf over contemporary marbled paper covered boards, spine divided into seven compartments with raised bands, frontispiece, etched titlepage, plates engraved by Luigi Schiavonetti after Blake's designs, with ticket of Liverpool bookseller, W. Robinson to front pastedown, Neva and Guy Littell copy with their gilt and red morocco book label to upper edge, of considerable rarity in early boards.   Henry Sotheran Ltd.   William Blake Exhibition 17th Oct.-7th Nov. 2014 - 72   2015   £3000

Association – Littell, Neva

Blair, Robert *The Grave.* R. H. Cromek, 1808. First quarto edition, 4to., later half calf over contemporary marbled paper covered boards, spine divided into seven compartments with raised bands, frontispiece, etched titlepage, plates engraved by Luigi Schiavonetti after Blake's designs, with ticket of Liverpool bookseller, W. Robinson to front pastedown, Neva and Guy Littell copy with their gilt and red morocco book label to upper edge, of considerable rarity in early boards.   Henry Sotheran Ltd.   William Blake Exhibition 17th Oct.-7th Nov. 2014 - 72   2015   £3000

Association – Litten, A. A.

Whyte Melville, George John *The Gladiators: a tale of Rome and Judea.* London: Longmans, 1878. New edition, 2 pages ads, 32 page catalog (March 1877), yellowback, original printed paper boards, rubbed and little worn, contemporary signature of A. A. Litten on leading f.e.p., modern booklabel of Ronald George Taylor, good plus copy. Jarndyce Antiquarian Booksellers   CCXI - 289   2015   £65

Association – Llewelyn, Thomas D.

Somervile, William 1675-1742 *Occasional Poems, Translations, Tales &c.* London: printed for Bernard Lintot, 1727. First edition, 8vo., contemporary calf, gilt, rebacked, much of original spine preserved, later brown morocco label, very good inscription "Mr. Thos. D. Llewelyn's book bought of Mr. Wm. Davies bookseller Aberdeen Dec. 30th 1863", later bookplate of Oliver Brett, Viscount Esher.   C. R. Johnson   Foxon R-Z - 913r-z   2015 $460

Association – Lloyd, Harold

Nizer, Louis *Between You and Me.* New York: Beechhurst Press, 1948. First edition, very slightly rubbed at spinal extremities, inscribed by the lawyer to silent film star Harold Lloyd.   Between the Covers Rare Books, Inc.   187 - 204   2015 $130

Association – Lloyd, Mary

Cobbe, Frances Power *Essays on the Pursuits of Women.* London: Emily Faithfull, printer ad publisher in Ordinary to Her Majesty, 1863. First edition, 8vo., 239 pages, bound in brown buckram with gilt title, new endpapers with cutting from The Spectator dated 16 June 1866 of a letter written by Cobbe to editor of Women's petition for votes attached to rear pastedown, ownership signature of her partner Mary Lloyd on pastedown, with 11 lines of holograph written by Cobbe or Lloyd on endpaper.   Second Life Books Inc.   191 - 24   2015 $350

Association – Lobel, Anita

Lobel, Arnold *On Market Street.* New York: Greenwillow, 1981. Stated first edition, with correct 1-10 number code, 4to., quarter cloth and boards, as new in dust jacket, full page color illustrations, this copy inscribed by the artist, Anita Lobel with sketch of a clown.   Aleph-Bet Books, Inc.   108 - 275   2015 $450

Association – Lobell, Carl

Ball, John *In the Heat of the Night.* New York: Harper & Row, 1965. First edition, fine in price clipped, otherwise fine dust jacket, superb copy, scarce especially in this condition, from the library of Kate Stettner Lobell and Carl D. Lobell.   Between the Covers Rare Books   196 - 43   2015 $1200

Bronson, F. W. *Nice People Don't Kill.* New York: Farrar & Rinehart, 1933. First edition, fine in handsome, very good dust jacket with some modest chips at crown and few tears, very scarce, from the library of Kate Stettner Lobell and Carl D. Lobell.   Between the Covers Rare Books   196 - 44   2015 $650

Brown, Fredric *The Murderers.* New York: E. P. Dutton, 1961. First edition, fine, fresh dust jacket with slightest bit of rubbing, beautiful copy, from the library of Kate Stettner Lobell and Carl D. Lobell.   Between the Covers Rare Books   196 - 45   2015 $350

Dunning, John *Booked to Die.* New York: Charles Scribner's Sons, 1992. First edition, fine in fine dust jacket, from the library of Kate Stettner Lobell and Carl D. Lobell.   Between the Covers Rare Books   196 - 46   2015 $600

Finnegan, Robert *The Bandaged Nude.* New York: Simon & Schuster, 1946. First edition, fine in fine dust jacket with touch of rubbing, lovely copy, from the library of Kate Stettner Lobell and Carl D. Lobell.   Between the Covers Rare Books   196 - 47   2015 $250

Fleming, Ian Lancaster   1908-1964 *Diamonds are Forever.* London: Jonathan Cape, 1956. First edition, binding A, fine in just about fine price clipped dust jacket with small tear on front panel, seldom found in this condition, from the library of Kate Stettner Lobell and Carl D. Lobell.   Between the Covers Rare Books   196 - 52   2015 $5000

Fleming, Ian Lancaster   1908-1964 *For Your Eyes Only.* London: Jonathan Cape, 1960. First edition, binding A, top corners little bumped, else fine in very attractive, near fine dust jacket with small rubbed spot at crown and very slight age toning, exceptional copy, from the library of Kate Stettner Lobell and Carl D. Lobell.   Between the Covers Rare Books   196 - 55   2015 $2500

Fleming, Ian Lancaster   1908-1964 *From Russia, with Love.* London: Jonathan Cape, 1957. First edition, binding A, fine in very near fine dust jacket with very slight age toning at spine, very nice, from the library of Kate Stettner Lobell and Carl D. Lobell.   Between the Covers Rare Books   196 - 53   2015 $8500

Fleming, Ian Lancaster   1908-1964 *Goldfinger.* London: Jonathan Cape, 1959. First edition, first issue, second state (with 'skull' design on front board), small London bookseller's label front pastedown, corners slightly bumped, small rubbed spot bottom of front board, still near fine, attractive good plus only dust jacket that has been trimmed along edge of titlepage, attractive copy, from the library of Kate Stettner Lobell and Carl D. Lobell.   Between the Covers Rare Books   196 - 54   2015 $1000

Fleming, Ian Lancaster   1908-1964 *Live and Let Die.* London: Jonathan Cape, 1954. First edition, first issue, 2nd state, fore edge and top edge trifle toned, slight tarnish on gilt lettering, very near fine in attractive, near fine, second state dust jacket (with artist's name centered between bottom of blurb and bottom of front flap), price clipped and with some modest age-toning to rear panel, from the library of Kate Stettner Lobell and Carl D. Lobell.   Between the Covers Rare Books   196 - 51   2015 $12,000

Fleming, Ian Lancaster   1908-1964 *On Her Majesty's Secret Service.* London: Jonathan Cape, 1963. First edition, binding A, fine in fine, price clipped dust jacket, beautiful copy, from the library of Kate Stettner Lobell and Carl D. Lobell.   Between the Covers Rare Books   196 - 58   2015 $1250

Fleming, Ian Lancaster   1908-1964 *The Spy Who Loved Me.* London: Jonathan Cape, 1962. First edition, very faint foxing on fore-edge, still easily fine in fine dust jacket with just touch of toning on rear panel, from the library of Kate Stettner Lobell and Carl D. Lobell.   Between the Covers Rare Books   196 - 57   2015 $1500

Greene, Graham   1904-1991 *The Third Man and the Fallen Idol.* London: Heinemann, 1950. First edition, tiny lightened spot on top edge and very slightly cocked, else near fine in near fine dust jacket with tiny nicks and tears at spine ends, scarce title, from the library of Kate Stettner Lobell and Carl D. Lobell.   Between the Covers Rare Books   196 - 48   2015 $1600

The Hard-Boiled Omnibus: Early Stories from Black Mask. New York: Simon & Schuster, 1946. First edition, fine in especially crisp, near fine dust jacket with some spotting on rear panel, very nice copy, from the library of Kate Stettner Lobell and Carl D. Lobell.   Between the Covers Rare Books   196 - 49   2015 $275

Remarque, Erich Maria *All Quiet on the Western Front.* Boston: Little Brown and Company, 1929. First American edition, fine in just about fine dust jacket with two tiny nicks, beautiful copy, from the library of Kate Stettner Lobell and Carl D. Lobell.   Between the Covers Rare Books   196 - 30   2015 $1000

Robbins, Harold *A Stone for Danny Fisher.* New York: Alfred A. Knopf, 1952. First edition, fine in fine dust jacket with single tiny tear at foot, beautiful copy, from the library of Kate Stettner Lobell and Carl D. Lobell.   Between the Covers Rare Books   196 - 29   2015 $200

Roth, Philip *Goodbye, Columbus.* Boston: Houghton Mifflin Co., 1959. First edition, fine in fine dust jacket with slightest of toning at spine, author's very scarce first book, almost always found quite worn, lovely copy, from the library of Kate Stettner Lobell and Carl D. Lobell.   Between the Covers Rare Books   196 - 31   2015 $2500

Segal, Erich *Love Story.* New York: Harper, 1970. First edition, boards very slightly soiled, still fine in near fine dust jacket with small, very faint stain and two short tears, signed by author, nice, uncommon signed, from the library of Kate Stettner Lobell and Carl D. Lobell.   Between the Covers Rare Books   196 - 32   2015 $350

Shulman, Irving *The Amboy Dukes.* Garden City: Doubleday, 1947. First edition, fine in just about fine, prie clipped dust jacket with some very slight rubbing, superb copy, seldom found thus, from the library of Kate Stettner Lobell and Carl D. Lobell.   Between the Covers Rare Books   196 - 33   2015 $1500

Spark, Muriel *The Prime of Miss Jean Brodie.* Philadelphia: New York: Lippincott, 1962. First American edition, fine in fine, price clipped dust jacket, aside from clipped dust jacket, immaculate copy, from the library of Kate Stettner Lobell and Carl D. Lobell.   Between the Covers Rare Books   196 - 34   2015 $500

Traver, Robert *Anatomy of a Murder.* New York: St. Martins, 1958. First edition, couple of tiny spots on fore-edge, still fine in near fine dust jacket with few short tears, uncommon in this condition from the library of Kate Stettner Lobell and Carl D. Lobell.   Between the Covers Rare Books   196 - 50   2015 $750

Trumbo, Dalton *Johnny Got His Gun.* Philadelphia: J. B. Lippincott, 1939. First edition, light pencilled name, easily erasable (but we think it is of the important author's agent Harold Ober), else fine in handsome very good plus dust jacket with nicks at crown and little light edgewear, from the library of Kate Stettner Lobell and Carl D. Lobell.   Between the Covers Rare Books   196 - 35   2015 $2500

Turow, Scott *One L.* New York: G. P. Putnam's Sons, 1977. First edition, fine in fine dust jacket with two tiny tears and touch of rubbing, signed by author, from the library of Kate Stettner Lobell and Carl D. Lobell.   Between the Covers Rare Books   196 - 36   2015 $400

Warren, Robert Penn   1905-1989 *All the King's Men.* New York: Harcourt Brace & Co., 1946. First edition, top corner of the front board little bumped, else fine in bright, near fine, first issue dust jacket with short tear, little rubbing at spinal extremities and some subtle fading at spine, unusually nice, seldom found in this condition, and often with later dust jacket, from the library of Kate Stettner Lobell and Carl D. Lobell.   Between the Covers Rare Books   196 - 37   2015 $6500

Wiesel, Elie *Night.* London: MacGibbon & Kee, 1960. First English edition, bit of foxing to top edge, fine in almost imperceptibly age toned, else fine dust jacket, very scarce title, beautiful copy, from the library of Kate Stettner Lobell and Carl D. Lobell.   Between the Covers Rare Books   196 - 39   2015 $2000

Williams, William Carlos   1883-1963   *Paterson.* New York: New Directions, 1946. 1948. 1949. 1951. 1958. First editions, first four volumes limited to 1000 copies, the fifth to 3000, 5 volumes, touch of wear on jacket of Book Two, else fine in fine dust jackets, superior set, this set virtually free of soiling, from the library of Kate Stettner Lobell and Carl D. Lobell.   Between the Covers Rare Books   196 - 38   2015 $4500

Wouk, Herman *The Caine Mutiny.* Garden City: Doubleday, 1951. First edition in first issue dust jacket, fine in just about fine, first issue jacket with tiny tear and little rubbing at spine, from the library of Kate Stettner Lobell and Carl D. Lobell.   Between the Covers Rare Books   196 - 40   2015 $2500

Wouk, Herman *Marjorie Morningstar.* Garden City: Doubleday, 1955. First edition, fine in fine dust jacket with just touch of toning on spine lettering, rarely found in this condition, beautiful copy, from the library of Kate Stettner Lobell and Carl D. Lobell.   Between the Covers Rare Books   196 - 41   2015 $350

Wright, Richard   1908-1960 *Native Son.* New York: Harpers, 1940. First edition, fine in fine dust jacket with one small internal repair, beautiful, fresh copy of true first edition, superior copy, from the library of Kate Stettner Lobell and Carl D. Lobell.   Between the Covers Rare Books   196 - 42   2015 $7500

Association – Lobell, Kate Stettner

Ball, John *In the Heat of the Night.* New York: Harper & Row, 1965. First edition, fine in price clipped, otherwise fine dust jacket, superb copy, scarce especially in this condition, from the library of Kate Stettner Lobell and Carl D. Lobell.   Between the Covers Rare Books   196 - 43   2015 $1200

Bronson, F. W. *Nice People Don't Kill.* New York: Farrar & Rinehart, 1933. First edition, fine in handsome, very good dust jacket with some modest chips at crown and few tears, very scarce, from the library of Kate Stettner Lobell and Carl D. Lobell. Between the Covers Rare Books 196 - 44 2015 $650

Brown, Fredric *The Murderers.* New York: E. P. Dutton, 1961. First edition, fine, fresh dust jacket with slightest bit of rubbing, beautiful copy, from the library of Kate Stettner Lobell and Carl D. Lobell. Between the Covers Rare Books 196 - 45 2015 $350

Dunning, John *Booked to Die.* New York: Charles Scribner's Sons, 1992. First edition, fine in fine dust jacket, from the library of Kate Stettner Lobell and Carl D. Lobell. Between the Covers Rare Books 196 - 46 2015 $600

Finnegan, Robert *The Bandaged Nude.* New York: Simon & Schuster, 1946. First edition, fine in fine dust jacket with touch of rubbing, lovely copy, from the library of Kate Stettner Lobell and Carl D. Lobell. Between the Covers Rare Books 196 - 47 2015 $250

Fleming, Ian Lancaster 1908-1964 *Diamonds are Forever.* London: Jonathan Cape, 1956. First edition, binding A, fine in just about fine price clipped dust jacket with small tear on front panel, seldom found in this condition, from the library of Kate Stettner Lobell and Carl D. Lobell. Between the Covers Rare Books 196 - 52 2015 $5000

Fleming, Ian Lancaster 1908-1964 *For Your Eyes Only.* London: Jonathan Cape, 1960. First edition, binding A, top corners little bumped, else fine in very attractive, near fine dust jacket with small rubbed spot at crown and very slight age toning, exceptional copy, from the library of Kate Stettner Lobell and Carl D. Lobell. Between the Covers Rare Books 196 - 55 2015 $2500

Fleming, Ian Lancaster 1908-1964 *From Russia, with Love.* London: Jonathan Cape, 1957. First edition, binding A, fine in very near fine dust jacket with very slight age toning at spine, very nice, from the library of Kate Stettner Lobell and Carl D. Lobell. Between the Covers Rare Books 196 - 53 2015 $8500

Fleming, Ian Lancaster 1908-1964 *Goldfinger.* London: Jonathan Cape, 1959. First edition, first issue, second state (with 'skull' design on front board), small London bookseller's label front pastedown, corners slighltly bumped, small rubbed spot bottom of front board, still near fine, attractive good plus only dust jacket that has been trimmed along edge of titlepage, attractive copy, from the library of Kate Stettner Lobell and Carl D. Lobell. Between the Covers Rare Books 196 - 54 2015 $1000

Fleming, Ian Lancaster 1908-1964 *Live and Let Die.* London: Jonathan Cape, 1954. First edition, first issue, 2nd state, fore edge and top edge trifle toned, slight tarnish on gilt lettering, very near fine in attractive, near fine, second state dust jacket (with artist's name centered between bottom of blurb and bottom of front flap), price clipped and with some modest age-toning to rear panel, from the library of Kate Stettner Lobell and Carl D. Lobell. Between the Covers Rare Books 196 - 51 2015 $12,000

Fleming, Ian Lancaster 1908-1964 *On Her Majesty's Secret Service.* London: Jonathan Cape, 1963. First edition, binding A, fine in fine, price clipped dust jacket, beautiful copy, from the library of Kate Stettner Lobell and Carl D. Lobell. Between the Covers Rare Books 196 - 58 2015 $1250

Fleming, Ian Lancaster 1908-1964 *The Spy Who Loved Me.* London: Jonathan Cape, 1962. First edition, very faint foxing on fore-edge, still easily fine in fine dust jacket with just touch of toning on rear panel, from the library of Kate Stettner Lobell and Carl D. Lobell. Between the Covers Rare Books 196 - 57 2015 $1500

Greene, Graham 1904-1991 *The Third Man and the Fallen Idol.* London: Heinemann, 1950. First edition, tiny lightened spot on top edge and very slightly cocked, else near fine in near fine dust jacket with tiny nicks and tears at spine ends, scarce title, from the library of Kate Stettner Lobell and Carl D. Lobell. Between the Covers Rare Books 196 - 48 2015 $1600

The Hard-Boiled Omnibus: Early Stories from Black Mask. New York: Simon & Schuster, 1946. First edition, fine in especially crisp, near fine dust jacket with some spotting on rear panel, very nice copy, from the library of Kate Stettner Lobell and Carl D. Lobell. Between the Covers Rare Books 196 - 49 2015 $275

Remarque, Erich Maria *All Quiet on the Western Front.* Boston: Little Brown and Company, 1929. First American edition, fine in just about fine dust jacket with two tiny nicks, beautiful copy, from the library of Kate Stettner Lobell and Carl D. Lobell. Between the Covers Rare Books 196 - 30 2015 $1000

Robbins, Harold *A Stone for Danny Fisher.* New York: Alfred A. Knopf, 1952. First edition, fine in fine dust jacket with single tiny tear at foot, beautiful copy, from the library of Kate Stettner Lobell and Carl D. Lobell. Between the Covers Rare Books 196 - 29 2015 $200

Roth, Philip *Goodbye, Columbus.* Boston: Houghton Mifflin Co., 1959. First edition, fine in fine dust jacket with slightest of toning at spine, author's very scarce first book, almost always found quite worn, lovely copy, from the library of Kate Stettner Lobell and Carl D. Lobell.   Between the Covers Rare Books   196 - 31   2015 $2500

Segal, Erich *Love Story.* New York: Harper, 1970. First edition, boards very slightly soiled, still fine in near fine dust jacket with small, very faint stain and two short tears, signed by author, nice, uncommon signed, from the library of Kate Stettner Lobell and Carl D. Lobell.   Between the Covers Rare Books   196 - 32   2015 $350

Shulman, Irving *The Amboy Dukes.* Garden City: Doubleday, 1947. First edition, fine in just about fine, prie clipped dust jacket with some very slight rubbing, superb copy, seldom found thus, from the library of Kate Stettner Lobell and Carl D. Lobell.   Between the Covers Rare Books   196 - 33   2015 $1500

Spark, Muriel *The Prime of Miss Jean Brodie.* Philadelphia: New York: Lippincott, 1962. First American edition, fine in fine, price clipped dust jacket, aside from clipped dust jacket, immaculate copy, from the library of Kate Stettner Lobell and Carl D. Lobell.   Between the Covers Rare Books   196 - 34   2015 $500

Traver, Robert *Anatomy of a Murder.* New York: St. Martins, 1958. First edition, couple of tiny spots on fore-edge, still fine in near fine dust jacket with few short tears, uncommon in this condition from the library of Kate Stettner Lobell and Carl D. Lobell.   Between the Covers Rare Books   196 - 50   2015 $750

Trumbo, Dalton *Johnny Got His Gun.* Philadelphia: J. B. Lippincott, 1939. First edition, light pencilled name, easily erasable (but we think it is of the important author's agent Harold Ober), else fine in handsome very good plus dust jacket with nicks at crown and little light edgewear, from the library of Kate Stettner Lobell and Carl D. Lobell.   Between the Covers Rare Books   196 - 35   2015 $2500

Turow, Scott *One L.* New York: G. P. Putnam's Sons, 1977. First edition, fine in fine dust jacket with two tiny tears and touch of rubbing, signed by author, from the library of Kate Stettner Lobell and Carl D. Lobell.   Between the Covers Rare Books   196 - 36   2015 $400

Warren, Robert Penn 1905-1989 *All the King's Men.* New York: Harcourt Brace & Co., 1946. First edition, top corner of the front board little bumped, else fine in bright, near fine, first issue dust jacket with short tear, little rubbing at spinal extremities and some subtle fading at spine, unusually nice, seldom found in this condition, and often with later dust jacket, from the library of Kate Stettner Lobell and Carl D. Lobell.   Between the Covers Rare Books   196 - 37   2015 $6500

Wiesel, Elie *Night.* London: MacGibbon & Kee, 1960. First English edition, bit of foxing to top edge, fine in almost imperceptibly age toned, else fine dust jacket, very scarce title, beautiful copy, from the library of Kate Stettner Lobell and Carl D. Lobell.   Between the Covers Rare Books   196 - 39   2015 $2000

Williams, William Carlos 1883-1963 *Paterson.* New York: New Directions, 1946. 1948. 1949. 1951. 1958. First editions, first four volumes limited to 1000 copies, the fifth to 3000, 5 volumes, touch of wear on jacket of Book Two, else fine in fine dust jackets, superior set, this set virtually free of soiling, from the library of Kate Stettner Lobell and Carl D. Lobell.   Between the Covers Rare Books   196 - 38   2015 $4500

Wouk, Herman *The Caine Mutiny.* Garden City: Doubleday, 1951. First edition in first issue dust jacket, fine in just about fine, first issue jacket with tiny tear and little rubbing at spine, from the library of Kate Stettner Lobell and Carl D. Lobell.   Between the Covers Rare Books   196 - 40   2015 $2500

Wouk, Herman *Marjorie Morningstar.* Garden City: Doubleday, 1955. First edition, fine in fine dust jacket with just touch of toning on spine lettering, rarely found in this condition, beautiful copy, from the library of Kate Stettner Lobell and Carl D. Lobell.   Between the Covers Rare Books   196 - 41   2015 $350

Wright, Richard 1908-1960 *Native Son.* New York: Harpers, 1940. First edition, fine in fine dust jacket with one small internal repair, beautiful, fresh copy of true first edition, superior copy, from the library of Kate Stettner Lobell and Carl D. Lobell.   Between the Covers Rare Books   196 - 42   2015 $7500

Association – Locke, Miss

Agee, James 1909-1955 *Permit Me Voyage.* New Haven: Yale University Press, 1934. First edition, scarce first book, tipped to front free endpaper is slip of paper inscribed note from Stephen Vincent Benet for Miss Locke, spine little faded, inch deep strip at top of back cover faded as well, otherwise near fine.   James S. Jaffe Rare Books Modern American Poetry - 1   2015 $1,250

Association – Locker-Lampson, Frederick

Colvil, Samuel *Whiggs Supplication.* Edinburgh: by Jo. Reid for Alexander Ogston, 1687. Second edition, 8vo., very small chip from upper fore corner with four minor circular stains on titlepage, some occasional staining throughout, dampstaining just touching corners of F4-F6, some heavy modern pencil markings in a number of margins, and with a number of gatherings beginning to come loose from book block, signed by author sheep (worn, large piece torn away from foot of spine and with upper headcap damaged, boards heavily rubbed and corners bumped, early signature of Geo(rge) Dundas, bookplate of Frederick Locker-Lampson (1821-1895), given by him to Lytton Strachey (1880-1932), from the library of James Stevens Cox (1910-1997). Maggs Bros. Ltd.   1447 - 108   2015   £150

Association – Logan, Marjorie

Lindsay, Vachel   1879-1931   *Going to the Sun.*   New York: D. Appleton and Co., 1923. First edition, illustrations by author, cloth beautifully restored at spine, gilt lettering on spine dull, else near fine in attractive, internally repaired, good dust jacket with some loss to crown and has been supplied to this copy, inscribed by author for friend Marjorie Logan Dec. 25 1923.   Between the Covers Rare Books, Inc.   187 - 156   2015 $500

Association – Long, R. G.

Haley, James Evetts   *The XIT Ranch of Texas and the Early Days of the Llano Estacado.*   Chicago: Lakeside Press, 1929. First edition, presentation inscription by author to R. G. Long, laid in is penned note on Prince George Hotel NYC stationery to Wright Howes, bookseller and author, decorated cloth, fine, bright copy, in protective transparent dust jacket, exceptional copy.   Buckingham Books   March 2015 - 28028   2015 $1,875

Association – Long, William

Pye, Henry James   *Sketches on Various Subjects; Moral, Literary and Political.*   London: printed for J. Bell, 1797. Second edition, 8vo., half title, occasional minor foxing, paper generally lightly found throughout, contemporary sheep, neatly rebacked to match, flat spine gilt with morocco label lettered gilt, very good, from the 19th century library of Rev. William Long with his armorial bookplate.   John Drury Rare Books   March 2015 - 25402   2015 $656

Association – Loos, Anita

Wells, Herbert George   1866-1946   *The Bulpington of Blup.*   New York: Macmillan, 1933. Early reprint, couple of ink numbers, else about fine in very good supplied Grosset & Dunlap dust jacket with some light chips and tears, inscribed by author to screenwriter Anita Loos.   Between the Covers Rare Books, Inc.   187 - 289   2015 $850

Association – Lott, S. Jordan

Pindarus   *Odes of Pindar, with Several Other Pieces in Prose and Verse.*   London: printed for J. Dodsley, 1766. Third edition, engraved frontispiece, 3 volumes, contemporary half calf and marbled boards, spines gilt, rubbed, some wear to spines, several joints cracked, wanting labels, aside from binding wear, sound set, old booklabels of Rev. S. Jordan Lott.   C. R. Johnson   Foxon R-Z - 1122r-z   2015 $153

Association – Lourie, Richard

Hughes, Langston   *Troubled Island.*   New York: Leeds Music, 1949. First edition, 8vo., light blue printed wrappers little soiled, near fine, inscribed by author for Richard M. Lourie.   Second Life Books Inc.   190 - 128   2015 $600

Association – Loveday, Thomas

Dennis, John   *Rinaldo and Armida; a Tragedy...*   London: Jacob Tonson, 1699. First edition, small 4to., lacking half title and without errata slip pasted below 'Dramatis Personae' in some copies, heavily browned and stained throughout, repair to upper corner of B4 touching first letter on verso, large repair to upper blank corner of d4 and with a number of leaves mounted on stubs, early 20th century full black morocco, signature of Dr. Thomas Loveday (d. 1968), from the library of James Stevens Cox (1910-1997). Maggs Bros. Ltd.   1447 - 138   2015   £220

Association – Lovett, Hobart

University of California - Office of the Registrar   *Summary of Degrees and Certificates Awarded by the University of California 1864 to 1933-1934.*   Berkeley: University of California, Office of the Registrar, 1934. First edition, oblong octavo, 3 prelim leaves, 82 leaves printed rectos only, all leaves are actual photos, black cloth, gilt lettered spine, bookplate on inner cover of Hobart M. Lovett, very fine.   Argonaut Book Shop   Holiday Season 2014 - 294   2015 $250

Association – Lowe, William Somerton

Brannon, George   *Brannon's Picture of the Isle of Wight: or, The Expeditious Traveller's Index to Its Prominent Beauties and Objects of Interest.*   Wooton, Isle of Wight: George Brannon, 1844. First edition, 8vo., half red leather lettered gilt at spine, frontispiece, 20 engravings, spine and marbled little rubbed, endpapers slightly marked, neat name on front endpaper "Wm. Somerton Lowe, Grenoble House Nelson St. Ryde", plates slightly foxed, folding map dated 1844 in good shape, overall sound, very good.   Any Amount of Books   2015 - A35754   2015   £150

Association – Lowenfels Walter

Beach, Marion *Come Ride with Me.* Chicago: DMAAH, 1970. First edition, warmly inscribed by author to well-known writer and activist Walter Lowenfels, with two page signed manuscript poem "The Theft of Two Continents" folded and tipped inside front cover, light staining to covers, very good in stapled wrappers.   Ken Lopez, Bookseller   164 - 12   2015 $125

Association – Lowman, Al

Bell, James G. *A Log of the Texas California Cattle Trail 1854.* Austin: Southwestern Historical Quarterly, 1932. First edition, in Southwestern Historical Quarterly, Volume XXXV No. 3 Jan. 1932, Volume XXXV No. 4 April 1932, Volume XXXVI No. 1 July 1932, 8vo., original tan printed wrappers, near fine, from the collection of Al Lowman.   Buckingham Books   March 2015 - 29639   2015 $750

Association – Lusty, Robert

Lessing, Doris *The Grass is Singing.* London: Michael Joseph, 1950. First edition, signed by author, spine slightly cocked, mild sunning to spine and board edges, bookplate of Robert Lusty, Deputy chairman of Michael Joseph publishers, near fine in like dust jacket, complete with wraparound band, laid in publishers' response card, nice, uncommon.   Ken Lopez, Bookseller   164 - 116   2015 $3000

Association – Lutley, Jenks

Denham, John *Poems and Translations with the Sophy.* London: for H. Herringman, 1668. First collected edition, first issue, 8vo., small ink stain to lower margin of titlepage and fore-edges of D1-D7, small rust spots to 2E5 and 2E8, with small piece torn away from lower blank margin of I1, contemporary polished mottled calf, covers with double gilt fillet and gilt floral tool in each corner, smooth spine ruled in gilt, gilt edges joints rubbed, three small wormholes in upper joint, slight surface crazing to covers, from mottling acid, one corner slightly worn, bottom corner of front flyleaf torn away, errata has been corrected by hand, signature of Edmund Smith (16)88, inscription of Jenks Lutley Esquire 1729, early 18th century armorial bookplate of Richard Barneby of Brockhampton, Herefordshire, from the library of James Stevens Cox (1910-1997).   Maggs Bros. Ltd.   1447 - 136   2015   £600

Association – Lynn, Neville

Zangwill, Israel *Ghetto Tragedies.* London: McClure & Co., 1893. First edition, bound in full light blue calf by Zaehnsdorf, spine dated with red leather label lettered gilt, inner dentelles gilt, original wrappers somewhat crudely cut down, but preserved, spine little darkened and worn, nice, from the library of Neville Lynn, bearing his autograph signature and notes about Zangwill, presentation copy with author's signed autograph presentation inscription to Lynn, neatly bound in at end, APS signed by Zangwill to Lynn and mounted on front and rear endpapers various press cuttings concerning author, label of package addressed by Zangwill to Lynn, with news paper photos of author, loosely inserted is photo postcard portrait of author, shown seated at his study desk, from the collection of Gavin H. Fryer.   Bertram Rota Ltd.   308 Part II - 230   2015   £250

Association – Macauley, Ian

Clarke, Arthur C. *Astounding Days: a Science Fictional Autobiography.* London: Victor Gollancz, 1989. First edition, ownership signature of Ian Macauley who made a few notations in text, on front fly, else fine in near fine dust jacket, with faint crease on spine, signed by Clarke on his own bookplate.   Between the Covers Rare Books, Inc.   187 - 250   2015 $750

Clarke, Arthur C. *Greetings, Carbon-Based Bipeds" Collected Essays 1934-1998.* New York: St. Martin's Press, 1999. First edition, fine in fine dust jacket with touch of rubbing, editor Ian Macauley's copy with his ownership signature, Macauley was Clarke's protege and one-time secretary and longtime friend.   Between the Covers Rare Books, Inc.   187 - 248   2015 $400

Clarke, Arthur C. *2010: Odyssey Two.* New York: Ballantine Books/Del Rey, 1982. First edition, fine in fine dust jacket, inscribed by Arthur C. Clarke to his protege and one time secretary and longtime friend Ian Macauley.   Between the Covers Rare Books, Inc.   187 - 249   2015 $950

McAleer, Neil *Arthur C. Clarke: the Authorized Biography.* Chicago: Contemporary Books, 1992. First edition, fine in fine dust jacket, ownership signature of Ian Macauley with few notes in text, else fine in fine dust jacket, signed by Clarke and McAleer on bookplate.   Between the Covers Rare Books, Inc.   187 - 252   2015 $450

Association – Macclesfield, Earl of

Cherke, John *De Pronuntiatione Graecae Potissimum Linguae Disputationes cum Stephano Vuintoniensi Episcopo, Septem Contrariss Epistolis Comprehensae, Magna Quadam Elegantia & Eruditionere Sertae.* Basel: per Nicol. Episcopium iuniorem, 1555. First edition, few minor creases and small splashmarks, blindstamp of Earls of Macclesfield to first few leaves, early ownership inscription of Arthur Hilder, 8vo., contemporary English blindstamped dark calf, boards with decorative frame inside set of blind rules, vellum pastedowns, from an older manuscript with music and red and blue initials, ties removed, joints little rubbed, spine ends slightly defective, front hinge cracking and flyleaf lost, bookplate of Shirburn Castle, good. Blackwell's Rare Books   B179 - 19   2015   £1500

Mattaire, Michael *Stephanorum Historia, Vitas Ipsorum ac Libros Complectens.* Typis Benj. Motte impensis Christoph Bateman, 1709. 8vo., engraved portrait frontispiece, 3 pages of woodcut devices (as is correct), variant issue without extra appendix, embossment of Earls of Macclesfield, 8vo., contemporary polished sprinkled calf, boards bordered with double gilt fillet, spine compartments similarly bordered, red morocco lettering piece in second compartment, rest with central gilt lozenge shaped decorative tools, all edges sprinkled red, small old paper labels at head and foot, just slightly rubbed, tiny chip at head of spine, bookplate of North Library (corrected by hand to South) of Shirburn castle, very good.   Blackwell's Rare Books   B179 - 71 2015   £500

Papacino D'Antoni, Alessandro Vittorio *A Treatise on Gun-Powder; a Treatise on Fire-Arms and a treatise on the Service of Artillery in Time of War.* London: sold by T. and J. Egerton, 1789. First English translation, 8vo., errata, 24 folding engraved plates, lacking half title, contemporary tree calf, spine heavily gilt tooled, exceptionally handsome volume, very fine condition, contemporary bookplate of Lt. Gen. George Lane Parker, later bookplate of Earls of Macclesfield.   Marlborough Rare Books   List 53 - 35   2015   £1850

Ruscelli, Giorlamo *Kriegs Und Archeley Kunst.* Frankfurt: Lukas Jennis (second part Jakob de Zetter), 1620. First edition in German, 292 x 191mm, 2 parts in one volume, very fine late 18th century tree calf, flat spine handsomely gilt in compartments filled with closely spaced horizontal rows of alternating strapwork and flowing floral and foliate stamps, reddish orange morocco label, historiated headpieces and tailpieces, both titlepages attractively framed with design of military implements, with 24 double page engraved Military Plates, 15 accompanying the first section and 9 in the second; armorial bookplate of Lt. Gen. G. L. Parker, 4th Earl of Macclesfield and similar armorial bookplate of Macclesfield Library, first three leaves with small embossed Macclesfield stamp, bottom of second titlepage just barely touched by binder's knife, 3 gatherings with inoffensive dampstain at lower inner margin, light offsetting on some of the plates, handful of leaves (including first title) with light overall browning, additional trivial defects, otherwise really fine, lovely binding lustrous and scarcely worn, text very clean and exceptionally fresh.   Phillip J. Pirages   66 - 53   2015 $5500

Weidler, Johann Friedrich *Institutiones Mathematicae Decem et sex Purae Mixtaeque Matheseos Disciplinas Complexae.* Wittenberg: Sam. Hanauer, 1718. First edition, title printed in red and black, 44 engraved plates, some browning, small 8vo., contemporary calf, double gilt fillets on sides, inner roll tooled border, spine gilt in compartments, slightly rubbed, Macclesfield copy with blindstamps and bookplate, very good.   Blackwell's Rare Books   B179 - 110   2015   £750

Association – MacDiarmid, Hugh

Johnstone, William *Paintings by William Johnstone.* Newcastle upon Tyne: Stone Gallery, 1963. Octavo, illustrated wrappers, fine, exhibition pamphlet, inscribed by Hugh MacDiarmid (provided foreword) for Jonathan Williams, 15/8/63.   Between the Covers Rare Books, Inc.   187 - 162   2015 $250

Association – MacDonald, Allan

Breton, Nicholas 1545-1626 *A Poste with a Packet of mad letters.* London: for George Badger, 1653. Small 4to., lacking title to part 2, lacking final leaf of text, woodcut on title (block much wormed), inner margin of title and first few leaves and final leaf of part 1 dampstained, dampstain in lower margin of pages 31-42 and 59-68, short wormtrail (breaking into holes in places) in inner margin of first part (old patch over worming on final leaf of part 1), final leaf somewhat soiled and slightly short at lower margin, late 19th century half maroon morocco, marbled boards slightly rubbed, signature, J. S. Hasted, bookplate of Allan D. MacDonald, from the library of James Stevens Cox (1910-1997).   Maggs Bros. Ltd.   1447 - 46 2015   £950

Association – MacDonald, Dwight

Lowell, Robert 1917-1977 *Notebook 1967-1968.* New York: Farrar, Straus and Giroux, 1969. First edition, inscribed to dedicatee, poet Dwight MacDonald. Honey & Wax Booksellers 2 - 54 2015 $1350

Association – MacDonald, John

Williams, Charles *The Wrong Venus.* New York: New American Library, 1966. First edition, inscribed by author for fellow mystery writer John D. MacDonald, near fine in like dust jacket, from the collection of Duke Collier. Royal Books 36 - 3 2015 $3500

Association – MacDonald, Murray

Smith, Dodie *The Girl from the Candle-Lit Bath.* London: W. H. Allen, 1978. First edition, 8vo., fine in clean, very good dust jacket with very slight shelfwear, signed presentation from author for Murray MacDonald, director. Any Amount of Books 2015 - A89369 2015 £180

Association – MacDonald, Ross

Porter, Katherine Anne 1890-1980 *A Note on the Author with the Key, One of Seventeen Stories from Miss Welty's Forthcoming "A Curtain of Green".* Garden City: Doubleday Doran, 1941. First edition, small octavo, saddle stitched wrappers as issued fine, this copy inscribed by Welty to her longtime friend, author Kenneth Millar (Ross MacDonald), laid in is a marvelous TLS from Welty to Millar dated May 11 1971 in which she recounts the history of the pamphlet and its cover photo, letter with one horizontal fold, fine in custom folding cloth chemise and full leather custom clamshell box, gilt titles, rule and decoration, rounded spine and raised bands, from the collection of Duke Collier. Royal Books 36 - 67 2015 $12,500

Winwar, Frances *The Haunted Palace: a Life of Edgar Allan Poe.* New York: Harper and Bros., 1959. First edition, author Kenneth Millar/Ross MacDonald's review copy annotated by him in holograph pencil, laid in is 5 page ms. letter signed of his review for the book, book near fine in like dust jacket, letter fine and approximately quarter quarto leaves, lined three-hole notebook paper, rectos only, in blue holograph ink with exception of the last few sentences and corrections in same blue ink, folded horizontally at center, else near fine, from the collection of Duke Collier. Royal Books 36 - 65 2015 $4500

Association – MacFarlane, Gordon

Evans-Wentz, Walter *The Tibetan Book of the Dead or the After Death Experiences...* London: Oxford University Press, 1957. Third edition, octavo, green cloth, gilt, bookplate of Gordon MacFarlane, some foxing on fore edge and first and last few leaves, some light spotting on front board, very good or better in price clipped, about very good, second edition dust jacket (presumably married to the book or a publisher's extra), with some spotting on spine and some misfolding, inscribed by author to MacFarlane. Between the Covers Rare Books, Inc. 187 - 94 2015 $1500

Evans-Wentz, Walter *The Tibetan Book of the Great Liberation or the method of Realizing Nirvana through Knowing the Mind.* London: Oxford University Press, 1954. First edition, octavo, green cloth, gilt, bookplate of Gordon B. MacFarlane, some foxing on fore edge and first and last few leaves, some light foxing on fore edge and first and last few leaves with some light spotting on front board, very good or better in price clipped, very good dust jacket, inscribed by author for MacFarlane. Between the Covers Rare Books, Inc. 187 - 93 2015 $1750

Association – MacIver, Loren

Bishop, Elizabeth *Poem.* New York: Phoenix Book Shop, 1973. First edition, one of author's copies from the lettered issue, copy "L" (presumably chosen for Loren) of 26 lettered copies from a total edition of 126, signed by author, this copy with presentation from author for Loren MacIver & Lloyd Frankenberg, housed in custom green cloth clamshell box with black morocco spine label, superb association copy. James S. Jaffe Rare Books Modern American Poetry - 41 2015 $10,000

Association – MacKay, Katherine Duer

Hale, George Ellery *The Study of Stellar Evolution, An Account of Some Recent Methods of Astrophysical Research.* Chicago: University of Chicago Press, 1908. First edition, frontispiece, 104 plates, including frontispiece, bound by Stikeman & Co. in half dark green crushed morocco, green cloth, gilt ruled and decorative spine, top edge gilt, marbled endleaves, inner hinge broken, extremities worn (with kozo repairs), bookplate of Katherine Duer Mackay (1880-1930), very good. Jeff Weber Rare Books 178 - 792 2015 $150

Association – MacKay, W. MacDonald

Graves, Robert 1895-1985 *Mockbeggar Hall.* London: Hogarth Press, 1924. First edition, small quarto, original paper boards, pictorial bookplate of W. MacDonald MacKay, Scottish historian and bookman and name plate of Douglas Grant, Prof. of American Lit. at Leeds University, spine little bruised at foot, lower corners slightly bumped, very good. Peter Ellis, Bookseller 2014 - 006488 2015 £325

Association – Mackenzie, Doris Compton

MacKenzie, Compton *The Early Life and Adventures of Sylvia Scarlett.* London: Martin Secker, 1918. First edition, original cloth binding little marked and worn, but very good, partly unopened, bookseller's small label, presentation copy inscribed by author for Doris Compton MacKenzie Oct. 13 32, from the collection of Gavin H. Fryer.   Bertram Rota Ltd.   308 Part II - 156   2015   £120

Association – MacKenzie, John Whiteford

F., W. *An Account of Some Strange Apparitions Had by a Godly Man in Kintyre, who hath been blind six years...* Edinburgh?: printed in the year, 1730. First edition, 8vo., 8 pages, paper just little soiled, bound in 19th century half calf over marbled boards, spine gilt lettered "Predictions", very good with 19th century armorial bookplate of John Whiteford Mackenzie, of some rarity.   John Drury Rare Books   2015 - 25872   2015 $2622

Association – MacKenzie, Rachel

Cullinan, Elizabeth *Yellow Roses.* New York: Viking Press, 1977. First edition, fine in fine dust jacket, this copy inscribed by author to her editor at the New Yorker, Rachel MacKenzie.   Between the Covers Rare Books, Inc.   187 - 64   2015 $125

Flanner, Hildegarde *In Native Light.* Calistoga: n.p., 1970. First edition, engravings by Frederick Monhoff, cloth with printed paper spine label toned and rubbed, touch of edgewear to cloth, else near fine, inscribed by Flanner and Monhoff to their editor at the New Yorker, Rachel MacKenzie.   Between the Covers Rare Books, Inc.   187 - 99   2015 $100

Maxwell, William *Ancestors.* New York: Alfred A. Knopf, 1971. First edition, fine in very good plus dust jacket with little rubbing and couple of tiny nicks, inscribed author to fellow editor at the New Yorker, Rachel MacKenzie.   Between the Covers Rare Books, Inc.   187 - 169   2015 $750

Maxwell, William *The Folded Leaf.* New York: Harper and Brothers, 1945. Second printing, stain at bottom of boards and label for out-of-print bookstore on front pastedown, fair copy, warmly inscribed by author to fellow editor at the New Yorker Rachel MacKenzie.   Between the Covers Rare Books, Inc.   187 - 167   2015 $750

Maxwell, William *The Old Man at the Railroad Crossing and Other Tales.* New York: Alfred A. Knopf, 1966. First edition, dampstain on front board, thus good in good plus dust jacket with corresponding stain on front panel, warmly inscribed by author to fellow editor Rachel MacKenzie. Between the Covers Rare Books, Inc.   187 - 168   2015 $300

West, Jessamyn *The Friendly Persuasion.* New York: Harcourt Brace and Co., 1945. Fifth printing, extremities rubbed, very good, tattered remnants of dust jacket, author's complimentary slip laid in, inscribed by author to Rachel MacKenzie.   Between the Covers Rare Books, Inc.   187 - 292   2015 $150

Association – MacKenzie, Simon

Bruce, Alexander *The Tutor's Guide...* Edinburgh: printed by M. Robert Freebairn..., 1714. First edition, 8vo., title printed in red and black, errata on verso of final leaf, contemporary panelled calf, raised bands, dark red spine label lettered gilt, very good, crisp copy with 18th century armorial bookplate of Simon Mackenzie of Scotsburn.   John Drury Rare Books   2015 - 23128   2015 $787

Association – Mackey, Robert House

Wilson, Harry Leon *The Spenders: a Tale of the Third Generation.* Boston: Lothrop Pub. Co., 1902. Stated 'Twenty-six Thousand", illustrations, front hinge little tender, else near fine with light wear at spine ends, this copy inscribed by author for Robert House Mackey, additionally inscribed by the illustrator, the author's wife, Rose O'Neill Wilson.   Between the Covers Rare Books   196 - 125   2015 $650

Association – Mackintosh, Graham

Duncan, Robert *Medea at Kolchis. The Maiden Head.* Berkeley: Oyez, 1965. First edition, hardbound issue, one of 28 numbered copies signed by Duncan (out of a total edition of 500), 8vo., original unprinted linen over boards, dust jacket, although not called for, this copy signed by Graham Mackintosh, book's designer and printer, this copy also with second dust jacket with same design (as first) but printed on white enameled stock with design of first jacket embossed on front cover, covers slightly splayed, otherwise fine. James S. Jaffe Rare Books   Modern American Poetry - 71   2015 $1250

Association – MacLeod, Alexander

James, William   1842-1910 *Memories and Studies.* New York: Longmans, Green and Co., 1911. First edition, octavo, original green covers with almost no wear to board, spine has small quarter inch open tear to bottom left side, spine label has crack running vertically throughout which obliterates 1 letter and compromises another 3, but still completely readable, former owner's signature Alexander B. MacLeod and unfortunate presence of a (very) old bookseller's price in blue ink ($15) beside signature), with MacLeod's occasional pencil underlinings and vertical margin lines along with less frequent marginalia in the essays which most interest him, overall lovely, collectible copy. Athena Rare Books   15 - 26   2015 $225

Association – MacNaughton, Robert

Kotzwinkle, William *E. T. The Extra-Terrestrial.* New York: Putnams, 1982. First edition, signed by three cast members, Dee Wallace Stone, Robert MacNaughton and C. Thomas Howell, near fine in near fine dust jacket.   Ed Smith Books   83 - 57   2015 $175

Association – Macrory, H. J.

Arnold, Matthew 1822-1888 *Poems.* London: Longmans, 1853. New edition, half title, 32 page catalog (March 31 1853), unexplained erasure of edition statement, original green cloth by Westleys, yellow endpapers with printed ads, spine quite worn at head and tail, trace of lending library label, novelist S. R. Crockett's copy, signed by him, H. J. Macrory and Geoffrey Tillotson.   Jarndyce Antiquarian Booksellers   CCVII - 45   2015   £35

Association – Magruder, William

Carlisle, Anthony *An Essay on the Disorders of Old Age and on the Means of Prolonging Human Life.* Philadelphia: by Edward Earle, W. Myer, printer, New Brunswick, 1819. First American edition, original paper covered boards, paper covered spine and printed spine label, covers moderately worn and soiled, particularly along spine, faint dampstain on first few leaves, but withal very good copy in fragile original boards, signature of Wm. B. Magruder 1824.   Joseph J. Felcone Inc.   Science, Medicine and Technology - 16   2015 $300

Association – Mailer, Norman

Nin, Anais *Solar Barque.* N.P.: Edwards Brothers, 1958. First edition, inscribed to Norman Mailer and wife.   Honey & Wax Booksellers   2 - 59   2015 $650

Association – Malanga, Gerard

Mottram, Eric *Shelter Island the Remaining World.* London: Turret Books, 1971. First edition, one of 300 copies, 100 were intended to be numbered and signed by author, title and cover illustrations by Richard Moseley, quarto, corners slightly bumped, else fine in fine illustrated dust jacket, this copy not numbered but warmly inscribed by author to Gerard Malanga, Jan. 1972, additionally with Malanga's ownership signature.   Between the Covers Rare Books, Inc.   187 - 186   2015 $125

Association – Malone, Edmond

Herodianus *Herodian of Alexandria his History of the Twenty Roman Caesars and Emperors of His Time.* London: printed for Hugh Perry, 1629. Small quarto, cropping affects text of dedication page and list of emperors (sig. b), very light degree of marginal annotation throughout the book, some ink and some pencil, possibly in the hand of Thistlethwayte and or of Allan Heywood Bright (1862-1941) who owned the book in the 20th century, otherwise nice example in slightly faded and worn but very sound, attractive binding, ex-libris Alexandris Thistlthwayte, autograph note by Edmond Malone bound in and also bound in are couple of sheets of handwritten notes in later hand, binding by Haines of Liverpool, half red Levant morocco ruled gilt over marbled boards, spine with six compartments, with lettered gilt or bearing crescent and star device, marbled endpapers, top edge gilt,.   Any Amount of Books   2015 - C11789   2015   £2000

Association – Malthus, Mrs.

Malthus, Thomas Robert 1766-1834 *An Essay on the Principle of Population....* London: John Murray, 1826. 2 volumes, 8vo., well bound in relatively modern green quarter morocco over cloth boards, spine gilt with raised bands and contrasting labels, top edge gilt, very good, presentation copy inscribed in volume I to George Batten, from Mrs. Malthus.   John Drury Rare Books   2015 - 25844   2015 $1049

Association – Man, Robert

Church of England. Book of Common Prayer *The Book of Common Prayer. (bound with) The Whole Book of Psalms Collected into English Metre.* London: John Bill and Christopher Barker, 1676. 184 x 127mm., very animated contemporary black morocco, elaborately gilt and with many inlays and onlays, covers with large central panel framed by citron morocco in a modified cottage-roof design, (including a peaked roof and protruding eaves under vertical supports but with scalloped interruptions on all four sides), vertical sidepieces entwined with gilt and black morocco vines bearing gilt leaves and acorns, panel within filled with lowers and geometrical designs accented with and surrounded by delicate gilt tooling, raised bands, spine compartments gilt and inlaid and either geometric shapes or a rosette, marbled endpapers, all edges gilt and gauffered, with floral vine painted in pinks and blues, fine modern black morocco clamshell box, extra illustrated with 55 hand colored engravings, rear flyleaf with handwritten list of five children born into the Man family between 1745 and 1752 verso of same with pencilled inscription of the eldest child, Robert Man, front flyleaf with pencilled note identifying the family as relatives of Admiral Man, hint of rubbing to joints, very small stain to foot of titlepage, edges of leaves slightly browned, trimmed close at top, isolated minor foxing, other trivial imperfections, but extremely pleasing copy, immensely appealing binding with only insignificant wear and text smooth and clean.   Phillip J. Pirages   66 - 28   2015 $22,500

Association – Mander, Gerald

Coles, Elisha *Christologia or a Metrical paraphrase on the History of Our Lord and Saviour Jesus Christ.* London: for Peter Parker, 1671. First edition, 8vo., without first blank leaf, light browning particularly in margins, words "OR A" on title deleted with ink and replaced with "a" in later manuscript, closely shaved, mid 20th century blue quarter morocco and marbled boards, from the library of James Stevens Cox (1910-1997), inscribed by Lewis Caesar Hill, 19th century signature George R. Hales, signature R. Betts dated "Silverhill 15.1 (18)90", booklabel of Gerald P Mander (d. 1951) of Tettenhall Wood, Staffordshire. Maggs Bros. Ltd. 1447 - 105   2015   £240

Association – Mann, Richard

Vergilius Maro, Publius *Georgica et Aeneis.* A. Dulau & Co. Printed by T. Bensley, 1800. 15 engravings, occasional light foxmark, bit more so to plates, large 8vo., contemporary diced russia, boards bordered with gilt roll, spine divided by decorative gilt roll, second and fifth compartments gilt lettered direct, rest with elaborate gilt tools, extremities little rubbed, three small patches of surface abrasion to lower corners of boards, few marks, armorial bookplate of Richard Mann, very good. Blackwell's Rare Books   Greek & Latin Classics VI - 110   2015   £300

Association – Mansfield, June

Miller, Henry 1891-1980 *The Air-Conditioned Nightmare.* New York: New Directions Book, 1945. First American edition, modest foxing on boards, very good or better in very good first issue dust jacket with shallow chips at crown, inscribed by author to his second wife June Mansfield, handsome copy and great association. Between the Covers Rare Books   196 - 96   2015 $2750

Association – Maquay, George

Paddy Hew; a Poem from the Brain of Timothy Tarpaulin. printed for (Charles) Whittingham (Senior) and (John) Arliss, 1815. First edition, hand colored wood engraved frontispiece, blank corner of B5 worn away, occasional light spotting, 8vo., contemporary half calf, spine gilt, extremities rubbed, armorial bookplate of George Maquay inside front cover, good. Blackwell's Rare Books   B179 - 61   2015   £2200

Association – Marchant, Stephen

Chapin, James P. *The Birds of the Belgian Congo.* New York: American Museum of Natural History, 1932-1954. Octavo, 4 volumes, 3054 pages, 3 color plates, photos, illustrations, binder's red cloth, all edges specked, bookplate and signatures of Stephen Marchant, very good, scarce. Andrew Isles   2015 - 12104   2015 $1200

Association – Marchmont, Patrick Hume, 1st Earl of

Buchanan, George 1506-1582 *Octupla; hoc est Octo Paraphrases Poeticae Psalmi CIV.* Edinburgh: Excudebant Haeredes & Successores Andreae Anderson, 1696. One of two reissues, 8vo., contemporary sprinkled panelled calf, spine with gilt crowned orange device of the Earl of Marchmont (joints cracking, spine rubbed), bound for Patrick Hume, 1st Earl of Marchmont, 1641-1724, signature of Lord Polwarth, from the library of James Stevens Cox (1910-1997). Maggs Bros. Ltd.   1447 - 55   2015   £280

Association – Markham, William

Vergilius Maro, Publius *Antiquissimi Virgilliani Codicis Fragmenta et Picturae ex Bibliotheca Vaticana.* Rome: ex Chalcographia R. C. A. Apud Pedem Marmoreum, 1741. First printed edition of Vergilius Vaticanus, engraved titlepage, bit dusty, 61 further engravings within letterpress, some spotting and staining (mostly marginal), few corners touched by damp, contemporary half calf, marbled boards, red morocco lettering piece, rubbed, some wear to extremities and particularly to marbled paper, edges untrimmed, bookplate of William Markham of Becca Lodge. Blackwell's Rare Books   Greek & Latin Classics VI - 108   2015   £1500

Association – Markle, Fletcher

Simenon, Georges *Maigret Loses His Temper.* London: Hamilton, 1965. First English edition, bookplate of actor/director Fletcher Markle, very fine in dust jacket. Mordida Books   March 2015 - 002043   2015 $85

Association – Marsden, R. Sydney

Digby, George *A Choice Collection of Rare Chymical Secrets and Experiments in Philosophy.* London: for the publisher (George Hartman), 1682. First edition, second issue, 8vo., 4 engraved plates, lower edge of titlepage shaved, just touching border, very slight browning to final few leaves, contemporary calf, ruled in blind, 19th century reback and endpapers, corners bumped and headcaps torn, inscription R. Sydney Marsden University of Edin. 1882, later pencil note, from the library of James Stevens Cox (1910-1997), with his pencil notes "Bought 1930 (Douglas) Cleverdon. Maggs Bros. Ltd.   1447 - 43   2015   £350

Association – Marshall, James

Allen, Jeffrey *Nursery Mrs. Rat.* New York: Viking Kestrel, 1985. First edition, first printing, with correct number code, 4to., glazed pictorial boards, as new in as new dust jacket, illustrations by artist, illustrations in color on every page by James Marshall, this copy has large and detailed full page drawing of Mrs. Rat, inscribed by Marshall and dated Oct. 1985. Aleph-Bet Books, Inc.   108 - 283   2015 $600

Association – Martin, H. Bradley

Donne, John 1571-1631 *Biathanatos (First word in Greek).* printed by John Dawson, circa, 1647. First edition, first issue, with undated titlepage, woodcut initials, woodcut and typographic headpieces, initial blank, last 4 leaves with few short marginal tears, light browning at edges of titlepage (offset from binding turn-ins), 4to., contemporary blind ruled calf with corner ornaments, spine gilt, rebacked preserving original spine, lacking lettering piece, preserved in full brown morocco pull-off case, early signature of Wm. Vernon at head of initial blank, engraved bookplate of Henry Greenhill dated 1911, inside front cover, bookplate of H. Bradley Martin inside rear cover, modern bookplate recto of initial blank very good.   Blackwell's Rare Books   B179 - 37   2015   £5000

Lorenzini, Carlo 1829-1890 *Story of a Puppet or the Adventures of Pinocchio.* New York: Cassell, 1892. First edition in English, 12mo., decorative cloth with designed repeated on edges, cloth age toned as usual, name erased from endpaper, tiny stain on edge of title, small inner hinge mend, else really very good+, marbled slipcase, the Bradley Martin copy with Mildred Greenhill's bookplate.   Aleph-Bet Books, Inc.   108 - 103   2015 $9500

Thompson, William *An Hymn to May.* London: printed and sold by R. Dodsley, T. Waller and M. Cooper, n.d., 1746. First edition, 33 pages, 4to., recent marbled boards, wanting half title, otherwise very good, from the library of H. Bradley Martin, uncommon.   C. R. Johnson   Foxon R-Z - 983r-z   2015 $230

Thomson, James 1700-1748 *The Castle of Indolence; an Allegorical Poem.* London: printed for A. Millar, 1748. First edition, 4to., contemporary red morocco, wide gilt borders, spine and inner dentelles, gilt, all edges gilt, slight cracking of joints, in red cloth slipcase, fine, apparently a presentation copy to a member of the royal family, at front is armorial bookplate of William Henry, Duke of Gloucester, brother of George III, at back is armorial bookplate of William R. Frederick second Duke of Gloucester, later in the Britwell Court Library with shelfmark, bookplate of H. Bradley Martin.   C. R. Johnson   Foxon R-Z - 989r-z   2015 $2298

Association – Masias, Felipe

Fuentes, Manual *Memorias de los Vireyes que han Gobernado el Peru Duranate el Tiempo del Coloniaje Espanol.* Lima: Libreria Central de Feilipe Bailly, 1859. First edition, 6 volumes one folding map, 12 plates, 4to., original dark brown pebbled cloth, ruled in blind, gilt titles on spine, and front board with armorial device, gift copy with note on official letterhead dated 1867 tipped in from Felipe Masias, Director of Administration of the Ministerio de Hacienda and later Finance Minister of Peru, good or better, boards rubbed, few joints split but quite solid, corners heavily worn, spines chipped, especially at heads with repairs, cloth separating from boards on one volume, free endpapers heavily offset, pencil notations in last volume, otherwise contents clean and very good, plates sharp and map fine but for tiny marginal tear along crease line.   Kaaterskill Books   19 - 117   2015 $600

Association – Mason, C. F.

Arnold, Matthew 1822-1888 *Friendship's Garland.* London: Smith, Elder, 1897. Second edition, half title, 4 pages ads, original white cloth, spine slightly dulled, few spots, bookplate of C. F. Mason, presented to Geoffrey Tillotson by WEB.   Jarndyce Antiquarian Booksellers   CCVII - 23   2015   £30

Association – Mason, E.

Somervile, William 1675-1742 *Occasional Poems, Translations, Fables, Tales, &c.* London: printed for Bernard Lintot, 1727. First edition, 8vo., contemporary speckled calf, spine gilt, red morocco label, joints repaired, top of spine little chipped, presentation copy inscribed "Eliz. Mason her book. Given by the Author" presumably in hand of recipient, very good, later bookplate of Sir Humphrey Edmund de Trafford, Bart.   C. R. Johnson   Foxon R-Z - 914r-z   2015 $1149

Association – Mason, W. M.

Fry, Elizabeth *Memoir of the Life of Elizabeth Fry with Extracts from her Journal and Letters.* London: John Hatchard and Son, 1848. Second edition, 2 volumes, half titles, frontispieces, errata slip volume II, some slight foxing in prelims, uncut in original purple cloth, borders in blind, spines little faded, bookplates of W. M. Mason, very good.   Jarndyce Antiquarian Booksellers   CCXI - 120   2015   £125

Association – Mason, William Henry

Mason, George *An Essay on Design in Gardening First Published MDCCLXVIII Now greatly augmented.* London: printed by C. Roworth for Benjamin and John White, 1795. Second edition, half title, errata on verso of p. xi, closed tear in one leaf (no loss of surface), bound in early 20th century green half calf, neatly rebacked gilt lettered, top edge gilt, others uncut, excellent, crisp copy, early 20th century armorial bookplate of William Henry Mason.   John Drury Rare Books   2015 - 20997   2015 $1005

Association – Matheson, William

Rosenwald, Lessing J. *Vision of a Collector, the Lessing J. Rosenwald Collection the Library of Congress.* Washington: Library of Congress, 1991. One of 300 numbered copies bound thus and meant for subscribers, these special copies contain a signed and numbered etched portrait of Rosenwald by artist Tony Rosati, tall 8vo., quarter green morocco over patterned paper covered boards, this copy signed by William Matheson at end of his essay, illustrations, some in color, loosely inserted is exhibition catalogue dated 1992.   Oak Knoll Books   306 - 294   2015 $215

Association – Mathieu, Bertrand

Berg, Stephen *With Akhmatova at the Black Gates.* Urbana: University of Illinois Press, 1981. First edition, fine in fine dust jacket but for tiny tear at top of front flap fold, inscribed by Berg to author and translator Bertrand Mathieu, scarce hardcover issue.   Between the Covers Rare Books, Inc.   187 - 18   2015 $200

Dunbar, Margaret *Bern! Porter! Interview! Conducted by Margaret Dunbar.* N.P.: Dog Ear Press, n.d., First edition, octavo, illustrations, stiff wrappers, front wrapper with one interior tape mend, covers lightly rubbed, else near fine, inscribed by Porter, but unsigned to noted scholar Bertrand Mathieu, Belfast 6.24.90, few annotations by Mathieu in text, five APS's from Porter to Mathieu dated from May 29 1990 to June 25 1991 laid in.   Between the Covers Rare Books, Inc.   187 - 218   2015 $375

Miller, Henry 1891-1980 *The Mezzotints.* Ann Arbor: Roger Jackson, 1993. First edition "Library edition" issue, one of 400 copies, octavo, illustrated, printed wrapper in raspberry cloth portfolio, 8 loose broadsides laid in, fine, inscribed by publisher to Bertrand Mathieu, a Henry Miller scholar.   Between the Covers Rare Books, Inc.   187 - 179   2015 $150

Poulin, A. *The Widow's Taboo. Poems after the Catawba.* Tokyo: Mushinsha, 1977. First edition, hardcover issue, illustrations by Roy Nydorf, small quarto, fine in rubbed, very good dust jacket, inscribed by Poulin to translator and literary critic Bert Mathieu, hardcover issue scarce.   Between the Covers Rare Books, Inc.   187 - 219   2015 $125

Association – Matthew, G.

Atkinson, James *Epitome of the Whole Art of Navigation.* London: by J. D. for James Atkinson and R. Mount, 1695. Second edition?, 12mo., 8 (of 10) folding engraved diagram plates (Plates 1-6, a fragment of 7, 8, 9 torn and loose, 10 lower third missing and volvelle missing, plates generally bit tatty and frayed at fore-edges), titlepage dusty, edges occasionally ragged and torn throughout, closely shaved along fore-edge throughout (occasionally touching text), final gathering M detached from book block and M1 damaged in inner margin, last page dusty), contemporary sheep, panelled in blind, very worn, heavily rubbed and bumped, corners scuffed and holed, headcaps torn, marks of two catches/ties?), 18th century signature "Thos. Gandin" and "Geo. Matthew", from the library of James Stevens Cox (1910-1997).   Maggs Bros. Ltd.   1447 - 13   2015   £950

Association – Matthiessen, Peter

Burroughs, William S. *Naked Lunch.* Paris: Olympia, 1959. First edition, 5000 copies, this the copy of Peter Matthiessen with his ownership signature, slight fore-edge foxing and minor sunning to spine and rear panel, near fine in very dust jacket with just few small edge chips.   Ken Lopez, Bookseller   164 - 25   2015 $3000

Delillo, Don *White Noise.* N.P.: Viking, 1985. Advance reading copy, light foxing to rear cover and edges of text block, near fine in wrappers, from the library of National Book Award-winning author Peter Matthiessen.   Ken Lopez, Bookseller   164 - 46   2015 $250

Irving, John 1942- *The Cider House Rules.* New York: Morrow, 1985. Uncorrected proof copy, from the library of author's friend, fellow National Book Award winner, Peter Mathiessen, well-read copy with inadvertent page turns and abrasions and wear to covers and spine, good copy only, but significant copy, letter of provenance available.   Ken Lopez, Bookseller   164 - 91   2015 $450

Snyder, Gary *Turtle Island.* New York: New Directions, 1974. First edition, inscribed by author for fellow author Peter Matthiessen, moderate rubbing and staining to covers, very good in wrappers, wonderful inscription and excellent association.   Ken Lopez, Bookseller   164 - 186   2015 $1000

White, Randy Way *The Man Who Invented Florida.* New York: St. Martin's, 1993. First edition, light foxing to endpages and page edges, near fine in like dust jacket with bit of wear to crown, dedication copy inscribed by author for Peter Matthiessen, dedicatee.　Ken Lopez, Bookseller 164 - 245　2015　$1000

Association – Mattingly, Dr.

Green, Ben K. *Horse Conformation as to Soundness Performance-Ability. (and) Hoss Trades of Yesteryear.* privately printed by the author, 1963. One of 1000 copies, of which 944 were offered for sale, 8vo., presentation to Dr. Mattingly from author, illustrations, lightly foxed along edges, else very good in lightly rubbed black dust jacket with light wear to spine ends and corners.　Buckingham Books March 2015 - 30902　2015　$400

Association – Maturin, Edmund

Lucretius Carus, Titus *Titi Lucretii Cari Der Rerum Natura Libri Sex.* Birminghamae: Typis Johannis Baskerville, 1772. First Baskerville edition, quarto, original full calf, spine with raised bands and decorated gilt, joints cracking, boards rather rubbed, corners bumped, spine somewhat faded and chipped top and bottom, bookplates of Rev. Edmund Maturin, clergyman and Henry Bright, English merchant, author and literary correspondent.　Any Amount of Books 2015 - C13208　2015　£280

Association – Maxwell, William

Beaumont, Cyril W. *The Wonderful Journey a Fairy Tale.* London: C. W. Beaumont, 1927. Special edition, #46 of 110 copies signed by author and artist, white vellum boards with gold stamped figures are sunned on spine and lightly on front edges, else close to fine, previous owner's slipcase and half chemise, William Maxwell bookplate was designed by John Fairleigh, 8vo.　Beasley Books　2013 - 2015　$150

Association – May, Clara

Jarrell, Randall *The Seven League Crutches.* New York: Harcourt Brace, 1951. First edition, one of 2000 copies, 8vo., original cloth, dust jacket, fine, presentation copy inscribed to Marc and Clara May from Randall and Mackie,.　James S. Jaffe Rare Books　Modern American Poetry - 146　2015　$1000

Association – May, Marc

Jarrell, Randall *The Seven League Crutches.* New York: Harcourt Brace, 1951. First edition, one of 2000 copies, 8vo., original cloth, dust jacket, fine, presentation copy inscribed to Marc and Clara May from Randall and Mackie,.　James S. Jaffe Rare Books　Modern American Poetry - 146　2015　$1000

Association – Maydon, G. S. K.

Hunt, John *The Ascent of Everest.* London: Hodder & Stoughton, 1953. First edition, first printing, from the library of British Army Lieutenant Colonel G. S. K. Maydon bearing his signature and dated "Nov. 53" to front pastedown near fine with slight rubbing to extremities and few minor stains to cloth along upper edge, unclipped jacket with light wear to spine ends, few small tears, else very good or better.　B & B Rare Books, Ltd.　234 - 56　2015　$175

Association – Mayer, Bernadette

Berrigan, Ted *The Sonnets.* New York: United Artists Books, 1982. First of this edition, inscribed by author to one of the publisher's Lewis (Warsh) and wife Bernadette Mayer.　James S. Jaffe Rare Books　Many Happy Returns - 62　2015　$1250

Association – Mayer, Jacob P.

Hayek, F. A. *The Road to Serfdom.* London: George Routledge & Sons Ltd., 1944. Reprint, fourth impression (Oct. 1944), 8vo., original green boards, some sunning/fading and slight wear and small split at rear lower hinge, sound very good- with clean text, from the library of J. P. (Jacob Peter) Mayer with his neat blindstamp, Mayer has annotated the book with notes and questions and occasional marginal lining, all in pencil.　Any Amount of Books　2015 - C16178　2015　£160

MacCunn, John *Six Radical Thinkers: Bentham J.S. Mill, Cobden, Carlyle, Mazzini, T. H. Green.* New York: Arnold Press, 1979. Facsimile reprint of 1907 edition, facsimile, 8vo., original faux green leather boards, lettered silver on spine and front cover, from the library of J. P. Mayer (1903-1992) with his neat blindstamp.　Any Amount of Books 2015 - C16243　2015　£225

Association – Mayes, D. L.

Rupp, Israel Daniel *Early History of Western Pennsylvania and the West and of Western Expeditions and Campaigns from 1754-1833.* Pittsburgh: Daniel W. Kauffman, 1846. First edition, scarce thus, especially in this condition, author's inscription to D. L. Mayes by the writer, 2 folding maps, full leather, gilt lettered maroon spine label, original endpapers, one leaf (publisher's notice) in facsimile, else very fine, clean.　Argonaut Book Shop　Holiday Season 2014 - 223　2015　$525

Association – Mayfield, John

McCrae, John *In Flanders Fields and Other Poems.* New York: G. P. Putnam's Sons, 1927. Seventh impression of American edition, ownership signature of editor and critic John S. Mayfield, lightly rubbed, very near fine in very good dust jacket, long inscription from poet and critic Carleton Noyes retelling how McCrae sent him the manuscript of title poem, tipped into back of original mailing envelope from Noyes and copies of correspondence leading up to Noyes signing the book. Between the Covers Rare Books, Inc. 187 - 174   2015 $500

Association – McBlaine, James

Smith, George *A Collection of Designs for Household Furniture and Interior Decoration...* London: published for J. Taylor at the architectural Library no. 49, High Holborn, 1808. 4to., 158 plates, plates 23 and 26 cut to plate mark and mounted plate 146 with repair to margin, some occasional spotting, still unusually bright copy, contemporary vellum, upper cover lettered in gilt, Marquis of Downshire, Hillsborough Castle, some marks on lower board, inscribed on title for the Use of James McBlaine, Hillsborough, bookplate of Donald & Mary Hyde.   Marlborough Rare Books List 54 - 78   2015   £9500

Association – McBride, Henry

Stein, Gertrude   1874-1946 *The Making of Americans, Being a History of a Family's Progress Part I.* Paris: Contact Editions, Three Mountains Press, 1925. First printing, disbound, inscribed to critic Henry McBride.   Honey & Wax Booksellers   2 - 60   2015 $2200

Association – McCalla, Isabella

More, Hannah   1745-1833 *Sacred Dramas: Chiefly Intended for Young Persons.* Philadelphia: Edward Earle, 1818. 24mo., 172 pages, contemporary full mottled calf, wear to joints and corners, about very good, inscribed by Gen.. John M. McCalla, hero of the War of 1812 to wife Maria Frances, also inscribed in 1909 by Isabella McCalla, his granddaughter.   Between the Covers Rare Books, Inc. 187 - 181   2015 $250

Association – McCalla, John

More, Hannah   1745-1833 *Sacred Dramas: Chiefly Intended for Young Persons.* Philadelphia: Edward Earle, 1818. 24mo., 172 pages, contemporary full mottled calf, wear to joints and corners, about very good, inscribed by Gen.. John M. McCalla, hero of the War of 1812 to wife Maria Frances, also inscribed in 1909 by Isabella McCalla, his granddaughter.   Between the Covers Rare Books, Inc. 187 - 181   2015 $250

Association – McCalla, Maria Frances

More, Hannah   1745-1833 *Sacred Dramas: Chiefly Intended for Young Persons.* Philadelphia: Edward Earle, 1818. 24mo., 172 pages, contemporary full mottled calf, wear to joints and corners, about very good, inscribed by Gen.. John M. McCalla, hero of the War of 1812 to wife Maria Frances, also inscribed in 1909 by Isabella McCalla, his granddaughter.   Between the Covers Rare Books, Inc. 187 - 181   2015 $250

Association – McCandless, Stanley

Brown, John Mason *George Pierce Baker - a Memorial.* New York: Dramatists Play Service, 1939. First edition, octavo, 46 pages, frontispiece, marbled paper boards, title label on front cover, signed on front free endpaper by all authors, John Mason Brown, Eugene O'Neill, Sidney Howard, Allardyce Nicoll, Stanley R. McCandless, drawing by Gluyas Williams, frontispiece, marbled paper boards, title on label on front cover, covers rubbed at head and tail of spine, corners bruised, very good in chipped and torn original tissue jacket, largely defective at bottom edge.   Peter Ellis, Bookseller   2014 - 018199   2015   £300

Association – McCann, James

Kreymborg, Alfred *Our Singing Strength: an Outline of American Poetry.* New York: Coward McCann, 1929. First edition, spine lettering trifle rubbed, else fine, without dust jacket, inscribed by author for friend James A. McCann. Between the Covers Rare Books, Inc.   187 - 149   2015 $150

Association – McClatchy, J. D.

Smith, William Jay *New and Selected Poems.* New York: Delacorte Press, 1970. First edition, fine in price clipped and rubbed, about very good dust jacket, nicely inscribed by author for J. D. McClatchy.   Between the Covers Rare Books, Inc.   187 - 262   2015 $100

Association – McCleery, Sam

MacKay, Magaret *The Poetic Parrot.* New York: John Day Co., 1951. First edition, illustrations by Kurt Wiese, top of thin spine little bumped and some creases on front fly, else near fine in very good dust jacket with little spine fading, small stain on rear panel and nicks at extremities, inscribed by author Sam McCleery (son of playwright William McCleery), laid in is Christmas card inscribed by McKay to McCleerys.   Between the Covers Rare Books, Inc.   187 - 50   2015 $200

Association – McConnors, Frank

Sterling, George *A Wine of Wizardry and Other Poems.* San Francisco: A. M. Robertson, 1909. First edition, 8vo., signed presentation from author for Frank McConnors, original burgundy red cloth lettered gilt on spine and gilt illustration on front cover, slight fading at spine, otherwise bright, very good+.   Any Amount of Books   2015 - A39601   2015   £220

Association – McCormick, E. Q.

Grubb, Eugene H. *The Potato. A Compilation of Information from Every Available Source.* Doubleday Page & Co., 1912. First edition, inscribed by author for best friend E. Q. McCormick Christmas Day Dec. 25 1922, full leather, raised bands, gilt on spine, half title, frontispiece, numerous illustrations, charts, maps, beautiful copy, fine. Buckingham Books   March 2015 - 15040   2015 $375

Association – McCoy, Tim

Jennings, Al *Number 30664 by Number 31539. A Sketch in the Lives of William Sidney Porter and A. Jennings, The Bandit.* Hollywood: Pioneer Press, 1941. First edition, 8vo., inscribed by Jennings for Col. Tim McCoy, grey printed wrappers, 32 pages, frontispiece, illustrations, rare, fine. Buckingham Books   March 2015 - 32237   2015 $1750

Association – McGahey, D. M.

McClintock, John S. *Pioneer Days in the Black Hills.* Deadwood: John S. McClintock, 1939. First edition, 8vo., very good, inscribed by D. M. McGahey, Curator of Adams Memorial Museum in Deadwood.   Buckingham Books   March 2015 - 24963   2015 $300

Association – McGovern, George

Powell, Colin *My American Journey.* New York: Random House, 1995. First edition, inscribed by author for George McGovern, near fine in near fine dust jacket.   Ed Smith Books   83 - 75   2015 $450

Thompson, Hunter S. *Songs of the Doomed.* New York: Summit, 1990. First edition, remarkable presentation copy with full page inscription from author to friend, Senator George McGovern, near fine in like dust jacket.   Ed Smith Books   83 - 108   2015 $6500

Association – McGuire, Edgar

Lowell, Robert   1917-1977   *The Mills of the Kavanaughs.* New York: Harcourt Brace, 1951. First edition, inscribed by author to Edgar & Janice (McGuire), recipient's bookplate, nice, apparently contemporary inscription, near fine in like dust jacket, slightly spine faded.   Ken Lopez, Bookseller   164 - 124   2015 $1000

Association – McGuire, Janice

Lowell, Robert   1917-1977   *The Mills of the Kavanaughs.* New York: Harcourt Brace, 1951. First edition, inscribed by author to Edgar & Janice (McGuire), recipient's bookplate, nice, apparently contemporary inscription, near fine in like dust jacket, slightly spine faded.   Ken Lopez, Bookseller   164 - 124   2015 $1000

Association – McKee, Louis

Metz, Leon C.   *Robert E. McKee: Master Builder of Structures Beyond the Ordinary.* El Paso: Robert E. & Evelyn McKee Foundation, 1997. First edition, 4to., pictorial silver stamped cloth, illustrations, signed by Metz, Louis McKee (Typography, Design) and editor Nancy Hamilton, fine in fine, original silver stamped slipcase, very scarce, fine.   Baade Books of the West   2014 - 2015 $356

Association – McKinley, William

Paynter, John H.   *Joining the Navy or Abroad with Uncle Sam.* Hartford: American Pub. Co., 1895. First edition, 298 pages, frontispiece, plates, tear on front fly near hinge with little offsetting at top of page and wear at ends of lightly toned spine, very good or better, this copy inscribed by author to President Wm. McKinley, Feb. 20/98.   Between the Covers Rare Books   197 - 93   2015 $4500

Association – McLean, Edward

De Baca, Manuel C.   *Vicente Silva and his 40 Bandits.* Edward McLean, Libros Escogidos, 1947. First edition, 4to., limited of 500 copies, signed by Lane Kauffmann, the translator and Fanita Lanier, who did the illustrations, further inscribed to Carl Hertzog by Edward McLean, the publisher, two-tone cloth, titles in red on front cover, bookplate of Carl Hertzog, illustrations, fine, clean, bright copy in original dust jacket with chips at spine ends and light wear to extremities. Buckingham Books   March 2015 - 35962   2015 $200

Association – McMillan, J. C.

Catich, Edward M. *Letters Redrawn from the Trajan Inscription in Rome.* Davenport: Catfish Press, 1961. 8vo., cloth, with 93 4to. broadside plates, two sections enclosed in cloth bound case specially constructed to hold the two different sized parts, presentation "Dr. J. C. McMillan, E. Catich", preface signed and dated by Dwiggins. Oak Knoll Books   306 - 145   2015 $410

Association – McMurtry, Larry

Kerouac, Jack   1922-1969 *Doctor Sax: Faust Part Three.* New York: Grove Press, 1959. First edition, wrappered issue, Evergreen original E-160, modest rubbing but fresh, near fine, neat ownership signature of author Larry McMurtry dated by him in 1959, interesting association. Between the Covers Rare Books   196 - 84   2015 $750

Louis, Adrian C. *Among the Dog Eaters.* Albuquerque: West End Press, 1992. First edition, paperback original, modest rubbing, else near fine, Advance review copy with promotional material laid in, inscribed by author for Larry McMurtry.   Between the Covers Rare Books, Inc. 187 - 197   2015 $125

Association – McNally, Terry

Zadan, Craig *Sondheim & Co.* New York: Macmillan Pub. Co., 1974. First edition, fine in fine dust jacket, scarce, inscribed by Stephen Sondheim to fellow playwright Terry McNally.   Between the Covers Rare Books, Inc.   187 - 263   2015 $1500

Association – McPherson, Sandra

Bishop, Elizabeth *Questions of Travel.* New York: Farrar, Straus & Giroux, 1965. First edition, trifle rubbed, else fine in price clipped, otherwise fine dust jacket, ownership stamp and signature of poet Sandra McPherson by Bishop who was then studying under Bishop at the University of Washington, two small corrections in text by Bishop and small pencil note, probably in McPherson's hand, beautiful copy.   Between the Covers Rare Books   196 - 68   2015 $2500

Association – Mecus, Laurent

Baouir De Lormian, Pierre Marie Francois Louis *Veillees Poetiques et Morales Suivies Des Plus Beaux Fragmens D'Young en Vers Francais.* Paris: printed by P. Didot for Latour Delanay and Brunot Abbot, 1811. First edition, 156 x 89mm., extremely pretty contemporary green calf, gilt, covers with delicate floral frame enclosing gilt compartments separated by inlaid red morocco bands, two compartments with rose sprig centerpiece and two compartments with densely interlocking rows of circles, red morocco label, turn-ins with decorative gilt roll, marbled endpapers, all edges gilt (lower joint apparently with very neat expert repair at tail), with etched vignette on titlepage and 3 engraved plates, original tissue guards; bookplate of Raoul Simonson, leather bookplate of Laurent Mecus; front joint with very short thin crack at tail, one opening with faintest freckled foxing, otherwise beautiful copy, text exceptionally clean, fresh and bright, scarcely worn, lustrous binding glistening with gold, especially pleasing gold dusted or "Saupoudrage" binding.   Phillip J. Pirages   66 - 78   2015 $1500

Association – Meechi, Irene

Rebello, Stephen *The Art of the Hunchback of Notre Dame.* New York: Hyperion, 1996. First edition, this copy signed by 10 members of the production company, including Gary Trousdale and Kirk Wise, artistic coordinator Randy Fullmer, writers Irene Meechi and Tab Murphy and five animators, numerous full color drawings and sketches in black and white, laid in is announcement for book signing party, fine in fine dust jacket.   Ed Smith Books   83 - 15   2015 $250

Association – Megson, Neil

Ford, Simon *Wreckers of Civilisation....* London: Black Dog Pub., 1999. First edition, original issued as a trade softcover original, this copy rebound by Wiering Books in gray cloth with black titles and rule and original Throbbing Gristle thunderbolt patch inset onto front board, inscribed by COUM founder Genesis P-Orridge (nee Neil Megson), small bindery label to rear pastedown, near fine overall.   Royal Books   46 - 28   2015 $950

Association – Melcher, Frederic

Berry, W. Turner *Catalogue of Specimens of Printing Types by English and Scottish Printers and Founders 1665-1830.* London: Oxford University Press, 1935. First edition, 4to., 24 full page plates, including some foldouts, half cloth over boards, covers rubbed with small mark at bottom of spine where label was removed, bookplate of Frederic Melcher and remnants of another bookplate on front pastedown, supplement is unbound signatures as issued.   Oak Knoll Books   306 - 209   2015 $300

Muir, Percy H. *A. F. Johnson, Selected Essays on Books and Printing.* Amsterdam: Van Gendt & Co., 1970. First edition, thick 4to. cloth, dust jacket, facsimiles, two folding maps, 4 page prospectus loosely inserted, from the Frederic Melcher collection with his bookplate and spot on spine where label was removed.   Oak Knoll Books   306 - 190   2015 $145

Association – Melizer, Ladislai

Burke, Edmund   1729-1797   *Bemerkungen uber die Franzosische Revoluzion und das Betragen Einiger Gesellschafte in London bey Diesen Ereignissne...*   Wien: Joseph Stahel, 1791. First edition in German, 8vo., engraved portrait, tiny localised stain in extreme lower corners of several leaves, contemporary ownership signature of Ladislai Melizer, contemporary German half calf over marbled boards, flat spine with blind lines and three contrasting labels including oval label with Melizer's initials, slight wear to fore edges of boards, else fine in handsome binding.   John Drury Rare Books   2015 - 23546   2015 $1005

Association – Melly, George

Stephen, James   *Lectures on the History of France.*   London: Longman, Brown, Green & Longmans, 1851. First edition, 8vo., original light brown cloth, lettered gilt at spine, signed letter to George Melly 20 August 1830-27 Feb. 1894, Liverpool politician, from the library of Henry A. Bright with attractive armorial bookplate, some rubbing and fraying at spine ends and light scuffing to boards, otherwise sound, close very good or better, clean text and clean boards.   Any Amount of Books   2015 - C11844   2015   £180

Association – Menzies, Robert

Waddington, Samuel   *Arthur Hugh Clough: a Monograph.*   London: George Bell & Sons, 1883. Half title, final ad leaf, original blue cloth, signed by Robert Menzies 1883 and Geoffrey Tillotson.   Jarndyce Antiquarian Booksellers   CCVII - 145   2015   £50

Association – Merecutti

Steinbeck, John Ernst   1902-1968   *Bombs Away.*   New York: Viking Press, 1942. First edition, presentation copy signed and inscribed by author for Lunt (?) and Col. Merecutti, very good plus in very good dust jacket.   Ed Smith Books   83 - 91   2015 $4500

Association – Meredith, Scott

McBain, Ed   *Sadie When She Died.*   Garden City: Doubleday, 1972. First edition, signed by author on titlepage, label of author's literary agent, Scott Meredith Literary agency in NY, fine and unread, fine dust jacket with tiniest pinpoint rubbing at spine ends, remarkable copy, from the collection of Duke Collier.   Royal Books   36 - 185   2015 $450

Association – Meredith, William

Moss, Stanley   *Skull of Adam.*   New York: Horizon, 1979. First edition, hardcover issue, fine in lightly rubbed, near fine dust jacket, warmly inscribed by author to fellow poet, William Meredith.   Between the Covers Rare Books, Inc.   187 - 185   2015 $75

Saroyan, William   *Inhale and Exhale.*   New York: Random House, 1936. First edition, 2 small tears at crown, modest soiling, very good, lacking dust jacket, inscribed by author for William Meredith, signed again on titlepage.   Between the Covers Rare Books, Inc.   187 - 243   2015 $500

Association – Merewether, Henry Alworth

Burn, John Southerden   *Registrum Ecclesiae Parochialis. The History of the Parish Registers in England, also of the Registers of Scotland, Ireland, the East and West Indies...*   London: Edward Suter, 1829. First edition, 8vo., complete with final leaf (errata on recto, imprint on verso), original boards, neatly rebacked, entirely uncut, very good, from the library of Henry Alworth Merewether (1780-1864), the distinguished lawyer, with his signature, notes of purchase in 1829, with ms. notes in text.   John Drury Rare Books   2015 - 14897   2015 $221

Association – Merrill, Louis

Carlson, Raymond   *Arizona Highways. Volume XXII Numbers 1-12 1946.*   Phoenix: Arizona Highways, 1946. First edition, quarto, light blue buckram, titles stamped in gold gilt on front cover and spine, illustrations, full page colored pen and ink drawing by Ross Santee and addressed to Louis P. Merrill (Texas ranchman), fine, bright, tight copy.   Buckingham Books   March 2015 - 28365   2015 $1000

Carlson, Raymond   *Arizona Highways. Volume XXIII Numbers 1-12 1947.*   Phoenix: Arizona Highways, 1947. First edition, quarto, red buckram, titles stamped in gold gilt on front cover and spine, illustrations, full page ink drawing on front flyleaf by Ross Santee and addressed to Louis P. Merrill (noted Texas ranchman), fine, bright, tight copy.   Buckingham Books   March 2015 - 28366   2015 $1000

Carlson, Raymond *Arizona Highways. Volume XXIV. Numbers 1-12 1948.* Phoenix: Arizona Highways, 1948. First edition, quarto, red buckram, titles stamped in gold gilt on front cover and spine, illustrations, full page color pen and ink drawing by Ross Santee addressed to Louis P. Merrill (Texas ranchman), fine, bright, tight copy. Buckingham Books March 2015 - 28367 2015 $1000

Association – Merwin, William

Kessler, Stephen *Nostalgia of the Fortuneteller.* Santa Cruz: Kayak Books, 1975. First edition, octavo, one of 1000 copies, illustrated wrappers, inscribed by poet to fellow poet William Merwin 22 Nov. 1975. Between the Covers Rare Books, Inc. 187 - 146 2015 $50

Association – Metcalf, Eleanor Melville

Melville, Herman 1819-1891 *Melville's Agatha Letter to Hawthorne.* Portland: Southworth Press, 1929. First separate printing, bound in green paper wrapper, spine little discolored, very good, signed on cover by Melville's granddaughter, Eleanor Melville Metcalf, rare. Second Life Books Inc. 190 - 157 2015 $750

Association – Metson, Amy

Coleridge, Sarah *Phantasmion, a Fairy Tale.* Henry S. King & Co., 1874. 8vo., first titlepage spotted, 8vo., original grass green sand grain cloth blocked in silver and gold and lettered in gold on front, ruled and lettered in gold on spine, bevelled boards, some loss to silver on front cover, slight wear to extremities, inner hinges strained, ownership inscription of Sir J(ohn) T(aylor) Coleridge, of Heath's Court, Ottery St. Mary Aril 8 1874 and below this an inscription 'Amy ?Metson with the affectionate regards of her cousin ?Coleridge, Heath's Court, September 1876", good. Blackwell's Rare Books B179 - 31 2015 £750

Association – Meyer, Richard

Nietzsche, Friedrich *Jenseits von gut and Bose. (Beyond Good and Evil).* Leipzig: Naumann, 1886. First edition, octavo, Richard Meyer's (1860-1914) copy, contemporary dark red pebbled boards with most minor wear, half leather spine has seven ribs and gilt titling on red field, Meyer's bookplate to inside front cover, lovely clean copy, remarkable association copy. Athena Rare Books 15 - 41 2015 $9000

Association – Mial, Leonard

Phillips, Harlan B. *Felix Frankfurter Reminiscences.* New York: Reynal, 1960. First edition, 8vo., very good++ with edge spotting, owner bookplate in very good+ supplied dust jacket with mild soil, edgewear, inscribed in year of publication by Frankfurter for Leonard Miall. By the Book, L. C. 44 - 59 2015 $750

Association – Mian, Aristide

White, Elwyn Brooks *The Essays of E. B. White.* New York: Harper & Row, 1977. First edition, inscribed by Helen Thurber (wife of James) to Mary (Mian) and her husband Aristide, near fine in very good, moderately edgeworn dust jacket with one small tape repair. Ken Lopez, Bookseller 164 - 159 2015 $150

Association – Mian, Mary

White, Elwyn Brooks *The Essays of E. B. White.* New York: Harper & Row, 1977. First edition, inscribed by Helen Thurber (wife of James) to Mary (Mian) and her husband Aristide, near fine in very good, moderately edgeworn dust jacket with one small tape repair. Ken Lopez, Bookseller 164 - 159 2015 $150

Association – Michael, John

Catich, Edward M. *Letters Redrawn from the Trajan Inscription in Rome.* Davenport: Catfish Press, 1961. 8vo., cloth, with 93 4to. broadside plates, two sections enclosed in cloth bound case specially constructed to hold the two differently sized parts, signed by Catich, first plate age yellowed as usual from cloth case, presentation from Catich to John Michael. Oak Knoll Books Special Catalogue 24 - 7 2015 $400

Association – Middleton, Richard

Brome, James *An Historical Acccount of Mr. Rogers's Three Years Travels over England and Wales.* London: by J. Moxon and B. Bearwell, 1694. First (unauthorized) edition, 8vo., large folding map of England and Wales (closely trimmed), light dampstain to fore edge of first few leaves, occasional minor worming to blank fore margin, final four leaves browned, early 19th century russia, extremities rubbed, signature of Henry Cope with inscription "given me by Sr. Richard Middleton 1697 H. Cope", (Sir Richard Middleton, 3rd Bart - 1655-1716) of Chirk Castle Co. Denbigh, Wales, label of R. Beckley bookseller, JSC's signature, from the library of James Stevens Cox (1910-1997). Maggs Bros. Ltd. 1447 - 48 2015 £1200

Association – Miles, Bernard

Broadbent, R. J. *Stag Whispers.* London: Simpkin Marshall, 1901. First edition, original blue decorated cloth, dulled, pencil markings and rudimentary index on endpapers, signature of Bernard Miles. Jarndyce Antiquarian Booksellers CCXI - 40 2015 £40

Association – Milford, Frances Elizabeth

Godwin, William   1756-1836   *The Pantheon or Ancient History of the Gods of Greece and Rome for the Use of Schools and Young Persons of Both Sexes...*   London: M(ary) J(ane) Godwin Skinner Street, 1810. Third edition, 12mo., frontispiece and 11 plates in rubbed contemporary calf, large bookplate on endpaper, good, ownership signature of Frances Elizabeth Milford on titlepage.   Second Life Books Inc.   189 - 100   2015 $325

Association – Miller, Keith

Betjeman, John   1906-1984   *A Nip in the Air.*   London: Murray, 1974. Second impression, 16mo., original bright yellow cloth, backstrip gilt lettered, faint, insignificant free endpaper foxing, dust jacket, near fine, inscribed by author for Keith Miller.   Blackwell's Rare Books   B179 - 130   2015   £135

Association – Milne-Thompson, Louis Melville

Muller, Wilhelm   *Mathematische Stromungslehre.*   Berlin: Julius Springer, 1928. 8vo., pencil marginal page 3, ink marginalia pages 30, 52, by Louis Melville Milne-Thompson, original black gilt stamped cloth, some minor wear to extremities, very good.   Jeff Weber Rare Books   178 - 909   2015 $95

Association – Milton, Clifford

McCullers, Carson   1917-1957   *The Mortgaged Heart.*   Boston: Houghton Mifflin, 1971. First edition, about fine in price clipped, very good dust jacket with modest spine faded, nicely inscribed by editor, Margarita Smith (author's sister) to Clifford Milton and Julian Hayes.   Between the Covers Rare Books, Inc.   187 - 175   2015 $450

Association – Minot, George

Osborn, Henry Fairfield   *Fifty-Two Years of Research Observation and Publication 1877-1929: a Life Adventure in Breadth and Depth.*   New York: Charles Scribner's Sons, 1930. 8vo., frontispiece, plates, burgundy cloth, gilt stamped cover and spine titles, dust jacket worn and stained with tape repair, very good, Dr. George Minot's copy with author's presentation.   Jeff Weber Rare Books   178 - 865   2015 $300

Association – Mitchell, Charlotta Amelia

Smith, Hugh   *Letters to Married Women.*   London: printed for the author and sold by G. Kearsly, 1774. Third edition, 12mo., contemporary armorial bookplate of Grant Mitchell on front pastedown and near contemporary signature of Charlotta Amelia Mitchell on titlepage, contemporary plain sheep worn at joints, very good crisp copy.   John Drury Rare Books   2015 - 20556   2015 $1311

Association – Mitchell, Grant

Smith, Hugh   *Letters to Married Women.*   London: printed for the author and sold by G. Kearsly, 1774. Third edition, 12mo., contemporary armorial bookplate of Grant Mitchell on front pastedown and near contemporary signature of Charlotta Amelia Mitchell on titlepage, contemporary plain sheep worn at joints, very good crisp copy.   John Drury Rare Books   2015 - 20556   2015 $1311

Association – Mitchell, Joseph

Hamburger, Philip   *Mayor Watching and Other Pleasures.*   New York: Rinehart & Co., 1958. First edition, first printing, from the library of fellow writer at the New Yorker and friend, Joseph Mitchell, with his ownership stamp, presentation copy inscribed by author to Mitchell and his wife Therese, near fine, very lightly rubbed at extremities, jacket with some light wear rubbing and some light chipping to spine ends, some splitting and some chips along upper front flap, else very good, attractive copy, excellent.   B & B Rare Books, Ltd.   234 - 46   2015 $600

Joyce, James   1882-1941   *A Shorter Finnegans Wake.*   New York: Viking Press, 1967. First American edition edited by Anthony Burgess, octavo, original maroon cloth, original dust jacket, ownership stamps of novelist Jean Stafford and New Yorker writer Joseph Mitchell with his notes pencilled on envelope from his family's tobacco warehouse, laid in.   Honey & Wax Booksellers   2 - 50   2015 $1000

Association – Mitchell, Richard

Mee, Margaret Ursula   *Flowers of the Brazilian Forests Collected and Painted by Margaret Mee.*   London: L. van Leer & Vo. for the Tryon Gallery in association with George Rainbird, 1968. First and only edition, limited to 500 copies, this no. 27 of 100 deluxe copies signed by Mee with original gouache by Mee, folio, original full natural vellum by Zaehnsdorf, gilt facsimile of author's signature blocked on upper board, vignette of a teju-assu lizard after Mee blocked in gilt on lower board, spine lettered gilt, endpapers with printed vignettes of the etju-assu after Mee, top edge gilt, original green cloth slipcase, gilt lettering piece on upper panel, original shipping carton addressed to Richard Mitchell, Aldham, Essex with limitation numbers, title printed in green and black, original gouache over pencil painting on paper watermarked 'Raffaello Fabbriano' signed 'Margaret Mee' and titled 'Aristolochia' and further inscribed '48' mounted as an additional frontispiece, retaining tissue guard, 32 color lithographed plates, including frontispiece, all plates retaining tissue guards, text illustrations, double page map printed in red and black showing Mee's journey and locations where flowers depicted were collected, with loose original prospectus, fine.   Henry Sotheran Ltd.   Natural History: Rarities 2015 - 2015   £7000

Association – Mitchell, S.

Allestree, Richard *The Ladies Calling.* Oxford: printed at the Theater, 1673. First edition, 8vo., 2 parts in 1, early 18th century panelled calf with marbled endpapers, frontispiece, the copy of Barbara Dobell with her signature, and below is "Sally Harrison/June 11th 1797" with note about her marriage and on facing blank is 19th century inscription "the gift of S. Mitchell to her niece Mary Best December 1855, in lower margin of final page of text is note in Dobell's hand about binding and cost charged by a Mr. Double on March 30 1706, edges little rubbed, marbled endpapers have cleanly lifted from boards, firmly held in place by sewing, fine.   The Brick Row Book Shop   Miscellany 67 - 3   2015 $500

Association – Mitchell, Therese

Hamburger, Philip *Mayor Watching and Other Pleasures.* New York: Rinehart & Co., 1958. First edition, first printing, from the library of fellow writer at the New Yorker and friend, Joseph Mitchell, with his ownership stamp, presentation copy inscribed by author to Mitchell and his wife Therese, near fine, very lightly rubbed at extremities, jacket with some light wear rubbing and some light chipping to spine ends, some splitting and some chips along upper front flap, else very good, attractive copy, excellent.   B & B Rare Books, Ltd.   234 - 46   2015 $600

Association – Moffett, Judy

Merrill, James *Mirabell: Books of Number.* New York: Atheneum, 1978. First edition, trifle foxed on fore edge, else fine in fine dust jacket with just touch of rubbing, inscribed by author to Judy Moffett.   Between the Covers Rare Books, Inc.   187 - 177   2015 $200

Association – Molesworth, Spark

Whaley, John *A Collection of Poems.* London: printed for the author by John Willis and Joseph Boddington and sold by Messieurs Innys and Manby...., 1732. First edition, 8vo., contemporary panelled calf, rebacked at early date, red morocco label (some wear to spine and corners, joints cracked), aside from binding wear, very good, signed on titlepage by Spark Molesworth whose name appears in subscriber's list as student at Trinity Hall, Cambridge, later bookplate of Oliver Brett, Viscount Esher.   C. R. Johnson Foxon R-Z - 1128r-z   2015 $460

Association – Monckton, Edward

Chalkhill, John *Thealma and Clarchus. A Pastoral History in Smooth and Easie Verse.* London: for Benj. Tooke, 1683. First edition, second issue with corrected state of title with Edward Spencer corrected to Edmund Spencer, 8vo., small chip from paper flaw at foot of C3 with small piece from lower blank corner of C4 torn away, A3 very closely trimmed along fore-edge, not touching text, 30mm. closed tear from a paper flaw to corner of D3 (touching catchword on recto) and with small stain on H6v, contemporary sheep, worn, covers heavily scuffed and bumped, spine very rubbed and with some worm damage at foot, upper headcap torn away, rear flyleaf torn and beginning to come loose, signature of Hon. Edward Monckton (1744-1823) and armorial bookplate, from the library of James Stevens Cox (1910-1997).   Maggs Bros. Ltd.   1447 - 76   2015   £600

Association – Monclau

Helms, Anthony Zachariah *Travels from Buenos Ayres, by Potsoi to Lima.* London: printed for Richard Phillips, 1806. First English language edition, 1 folding map, illustrations, 16mo., later half calf over marbled boards, red morocco lettering piece, spine decorated in gilt, near fine, from the Coleccion Monclau (bookplate), faint glue mark at hinge, minor foxing.   Kaaterskill Books   19 - 73   2015 $850

Nunez, Ignacio Benito *Noticias Historicas, Politicas y Estadisticas de las Provincias Unidas del Rio de la Plata.* London: Publicado por R. Ackermann, 1825. First edition, 2 folding maps, 8vo., modern full black morocco ruled in gilt, four raised bands, gilt titles, marbled edges, silk book mark sewn in, overall very good or better copy, armorial bookplate, titlepage tender, rear blank with large chip, original contemporary rear wrapper bound in but worn, color map bound upside down, fine modern binding, from the Coleccion Monclau (bookplate).   Kaaterskill Books   19 - 108   2015 $700

Association – Moncrieff, Scott

Proust, Marcel 1871-1922 *Swann's Way: Part One.* London: Chatto & Windus, 1922. First edition in English, octavo, original blue cloth lettered gilt, no dust jacket, initialled in ink by novelist Joseph Conrad, inscribed to Conrad by Proust's translator Scott Moncrieff.   Honey & Wax Booksellers   2 - 62   2015 $3500

Association – Money, Hal

McGinty, Billy *The Old West.* Ripley: privately printed, 1937. First edition, printed wood grain decorated wrappers with stapled binding, 5 1/2 x 8 3/4 inches, pencil inscription by author to Hal Money(?), back cover has old triangular crease at bottom, else very good, very scarce.   Baade Books of the West   2014 - 2015 $750

Association – Monhoff, Frederick

Flanner, Hildegarde *In Native Light.* Calistoga: n.p., 1970. First edition, engravings by Frederick Monhoff, cloth with printed paper spine label toned and rubbed, touch of edgewear to cloth, else near fine, inscribed by Flanner and Monhoff to their editor at the New Yorker, Rachel MacKenzie. Between the Covers Rare Books, Inc. 187 - 99   2015 $100

Association – Moody, Edna

Moody, Ralph *Man of the Family.* New York: W. W. Norton, 1951. First edition, illustrations/drawings, cloth, presentation copy signed by Edna and Ralph Moody 10/25/51 for their friends the Hillaires, fine in chipped but good dust jacket, uncommon now in first edition. Baade Books of the West   2014 - 2015 $172

Association – Moody, Susan

Cody, Liza *Culprit: a Crime Writer's Annual.* London: Chatto & Windus, 1992. First edition, 3 annual volumes, first volume signed by Robert Barnard, Liza Cody, Michael Lewin, Susan Moody and H. R. F. Keating, fine in soft covers and pictorial dust jackets. Mordida Books   March 2015 - 008749   2015 $150

Association – Moore, A. D.

Gibbs, Barbara *The Meeting Place of the Colors. Poems.* West Branch: Cummington Press, 1972. First edition, one of 300 copies printed on Arches text paper, 4 plates from drawings by Ulfert Wilkie, octavo, black cloth with printed spine label, spine slightly sunned, else fine. signed by Wilke, printer' A. D. Moore's copy with gift inscription. Between the Covers Rare Books, Inc.   187 - 109   2015 $150

Association – Moore, Clement C.

Goldsmith, Oliver   1730-1774 *The Miscellaneous Works of Oliver Goldsmith, M.B.* London: printed for Richardson & Co., 1821. Later edition, Volume IV only, later 19th century half leather and cloth, original spine laid down with some loss at extremities, good copy, this the copy of author Clement C. Moore with his ownership signature. Between the Covers Rare Books, Inc.   187 - 110   2015 $1750

Association – Moore, Elvin Roy

Moore, Ben *Random Shots and Tales of Texas.* Seagraves: Pioneer, 1977. First edition, cloth, illustrations, index, inscribed and dated 1978 to friend of Moore's son, Elvin Roy Moore, who edited the book after his father's death, fine in lightly soiled dust jacket, latter has tape reinforcement around top of backstrip, scarce, fine in very good dust jacket. Baade Books of the West   2014 - 2015 $54

Association – Moore, Helen

Fair, A. A. *Traps Need Fresh Bait.* New York: Morrow, 1967. First edition, inscribed "To Helen Moore, my Hollywood Della Street. With love from 'Uncle Erle' Erle Stanley Gardner, fine in dust jacket with short closed tear on front panel. Mordida Books   March 2015 - 011705   2015 $300

Association – Moore, Marianne

Williams, William Carlos   1883-1963 *Make Light of it.* New York: Random House, 1950. First edition, first printing, 8vo., original cloth, fine in custom made slipcase, dust jacket, Marianne Moore's copy with her notes on review slip. James S. Jaffe Rare Books   Modern American Poetry - 322   2015 $2500

Association – Moray, Earl of

Ramsay, Allan   1688-1758 *Poems by Allan Ramsay. (with) Poems by Allan Ramsay. Volume II.* Edinburgh: printed by Thomas Ruddiman, 1721. 1728. First edition, 2 volumes, 4to., contemporary tree calf, spines gilt, red morocco labels and circular numbering pieces (one upper joint cracked, but strong), subscriber's set with armorial bookplate of Earl of Moray in each volume, particularly attractive set, modern booklabels of Douglas Grant, old invoice laid in reveals he acquired the set from John Grant Booksellers, Ltd. of Edinburgh in 1956.   C. R. Johnson   Foxon R-Z - 819r-z   2015 $3831

Association – Mordaunt, John

Thomson, James   1700-1748 *The Seasons.* London: printed for A. Millar, 1752. Second edition, 4 engraved plates and 2 leaves bookseller's ads at end, 12mo., contemporary speckled calf, spine gilt, red morocco label (slight wear to tip of spine), signature of J. Mordant dated 1752, who has inscribed an ode by Shenstone on front flyleaves, armorial bookplate of Sir John Mordaunt, Bart. of Walton in Warwickshire.   C. R. Johnson   Foxon R-Z - 1003r-z   2015 $153

Association – Moreno, Mario Guiral

Bachiller Y Morales, Antonio *Apuntes para la Historia de las Letras y De La Instruction Publica de la Isla de Cuba.* Habana: Impr. de P. Massana/Impr. del Tiempo, 1859-1861. First edition, 8vo., modern quarter speckled calf over green marbled boards, four raised bands, red morocco spine label tilted in gilt, marbled endpapers, very good the copy of Mario Guiral Moreno (1882-1964), titlepage foxed, owner's stamp on margin, few small holes to top edge, notations on few pages, leaves browned and edges foxed, more heavily to first volume, binding quite fine, handsome copy of a rare and important work.   Kaaterskill Books   19 - 11   2015 $1000

Association – Morgan, Peter

Hood, Thomas 1799-1845 *The Letters.* Toronto: University of Toronto Press, 1973. Half title, frontispiece, original dark blue cloth, very good in creased and marked dust jacket, editor (Peter F. Morgan) presentation copy to Kathleen Tillotson, with 2 page ALS from him inserted and inserted notes by her.   Jarndyce Antiquarian Booksellers   CCVII - 303   2015   £35

Jeffrey, Francis *Jeffrey's Criticism: a Selection.* Edinburgh: Scottish Academic Press, 1983. Frontispiece, original blue cloth, very good in slightly marked dust jacket, Kathleen Tillotson's dedication copy with inscription from editor, Peter Morgan with 2 page TLS from him 21 March 1983 at University College Toronto.   Jarndyce Antiquarian Booksellers   CCVII - 326   2015   £25

Association – Morrell, Ottoline

Sedgwick, Anne Douglas *The Old Countess.* Boston and New York: Houghton Mifflin, 1927. First US edition, 8vo., original blue cloth lettered gilt on spine and cover sepia photo of author pasted in at rear, signed presentation to Lady Ottoline Morrell from author, spine slightly dusty and very slightly frayed at top, otherwise sound, near very good copy.   Any Amount of Books   2015 - C3445   2015   £280

Association – Morris, Henry

The London Journal of Arts and Sciences... London: Sherwood, Neely and Jones and W. Newton, 1821-1822. 3 volumes, volumes II-IV only, 8vo., original paper covered boards, labels on spine, top edge gilt, other edges uncut, plates, from the library of Henry Morris who bought them for their information on papermaking, boards and endpapers of volume II separated, spines and labels thereon of all 3 volumes worn, boards of all volumes soiled, some light foxing in text.   Oak Knoll Books   306 - 98   2015 $200

Strouse, Norman *The Passionate Pirate.* North Hills: Bird & Bull Press, 1964. First edition, limited to 200 numbered copies, this written on colophon "No. 1, H.M. copy Bound by myself - I decided binding was not for me - M.M.", printed and bound by Bird and Bull Press, and printed on Mosher handmade paper, loosely inserted is xerxo of small review in NY Times Book Review for this book, two TLS's from Stouse to Morris dated 1967 and 1981, handmade paper has foxed along edges, 8vo., quarter brown morocco, decorated paper over boards.   Oak Knoll Books   306 - 138   2015 $450

Association – Morrow, Brad

Wakoski, Diane *Saturn's Rings.* New York: Targ Editions, 1982. First edition, signed by author, quarter cloth, photographic paper covered boards, fine in slightly age-toned, near fine, unprinted tissue dust jacket, signed by author and inscribed by Wakoski and by Robert Tunney (who took the photo of Wakoski) to author Brad Morrow.   Between the Covers Rare Books, Inc.   187 - 285   2015 $225

Himes, Chester *A Case of Rape.* New York: Targ Editions, 1980. First American edition, fine in quarter cloth and papercovered boards, near fine unprinted glassine dust jacket with small tears at extremities, one of 350 copies, signed by author, warmly inscribed by publisher William Targ to novelist Brad Morrow.   Between the Covers Rare Books, Inc.   187 - 127   2015 $250

Association – Morse, Hugh Whitney

Morse, Charles Fessenden *A Sketch of My Life.* Cambridge: 1927. First edition, cloth, 91 pages, portraits, signed and dated by Hugh Whitney Morse, top edge gilt, cover extremities lightly worn, near very good.   Baade Books of the West   2014 - 2015 $197

Association – Mosley, Penelope

Hutchinson, William *An Excursion to the Lakes in Westmoreland and Cumberland August 1773.* London: J. Wilkie and W. Goldsmith, 1774. First edition, 8vo., engraved vignette on titlepage, slight foxing, first few and final few leaves, contemporary half calf over marbled boards, corners worn, neatly rebacked reusing original label and spine, very good, contemporary armorial bookplate of Sir Ashton Lever and early ownership signature of Penelope Mosley, uncommon.   John Drury Rare Books   2015 - 25681   2015 $830

Association – Moss, Howard

Benedikt, Michael *Serenade in Six Pieces.* Huntington: M. Sabados, 1958. First edition, 24mo., first edition, trifle age toned, corners little bumped, still very near fine in wrappers, one of 55 numbered copies, this copy inscribed by author to poet Howard Moss.   Between the Covers Rare Books, Inc.   187 - 16   2015 $450

Association – Moss, P. Buckley

Rippe, Peter *P. Buckley Moss, Painting the Joy of the Soul.* Cumming: Landauer Books, 1997. First edition, signed by Moss, near fine.   Stephen Lupack   March 2015 - 2015 $100

Association – Mott, John

Hoffman, Conrad *The Prison Camps of Germany.* New York: Associated Press, 1920. First edition, 8o., original green cloth, black lettering, decoration with spine sunned, near fine dust jacket with mild sun spine, minimal edge wear, tipped on f.f.e.p. is TLS by Nobel Laureate, John Mott, discussing this book, scarce thus.   By the Book, L. C. Special List 10 - 42   2015 $350

Association – Mountgarret

Napier, Charles James *Memoir on the Roads of Cefalonia.* London: James Ridgway, 1825. First edition, 8vo., 5 engraved lithographic plates, original boards, uncut, very good with Mountgarret (i.e. Butler family) armorial bookplate, unidentified early 19th century Book Society subscription list on pastedown, rare.   John Drury Rare Books 2015 - 24015   2015 $2185

Association – Moutier, Francois

Sorbin, Arnaud De *Tractatus de Monstris, que a Temporibus Constantini Bucusque Ortum Babuerunt ac ies Quae Circa Eorum te(m)pora Misere Acciderunt, ex Historiarum...* Paris: apud Hieronimum de Marnet & Gulielmum Cavellat sub Pelicano, 1570. First edition, 12mo., 14 woodcut illustrations, woodcut printer's device on titlepage, contemporary limp vellum, bold contemporary mss. title in ink on spine, lower edge with fine contemporary mss. of author and abbreviated title, ties perished, neat 17th century mss. ownership inscription on titlepage P. Marie Boschetti, 18th century unreadable ecclesiastical library stamp on verso of titlepage and verso of final leaf, minute neat mss. ownership inscription, engraved bookplate of Docteur Francois Mouteir, c. 1920, some light browning, but very good.   Maggs Bros. Ltd.   Illustrated Books 2014 - 2015   £2500

Association – Mugnaini, Joe

Bradbury, Ray *The Golden Apples of the Sun.* Garden City: Doubleday and Co., 1953. First edition, octavo, jacket and interior illustrations by Joe Mugnaini, boards, signed by author and artist.   John W. Knott, Bookseller   Selected New Arrivals Jan. 2015 - 16930   2015 $1500

Association – Muir, Frank

Boswell, James 1740-1795 *An Account of Corsica, the Journal of a Tour to that Island and Memoirs of Pascal Paoli...* Glasgow: printed by Robert and Andrew Foulis for Edward and Charles Dilly, 1768. First edition, folding engraved map, little wear at one fold junction and a short handling tear at rear guard invisibly repaired, small abrasion to first two leaves of Introduction (affecting one letter with no loss of sense), engraved vignette on titlepage, half title present, ownership stamp of M.P. Carter to titlepage, 8vo., contemporary speckled calf, red morocco lettering piece, rubbed, little wear to joint ends, pencilled ownership inscription of broadcaster Frank Muir, modern bookplate to flyleaf, very good.   Blackwell's Rare Books   B179 - 13   2015   £1200

Association – Muir, Kenneth

Ellis-Fermor, Una Mary *Shakespeare the Dramatist and Other Papers.* London: Methuen, 1961. Half title, frontispiece, original maroon cloth, slightly faded in torn dust jacket, from the library of Geoffrey & Kathleen Tillotson, signed by Kathleen with few comments, letter from her to Kenneth Muir and his reply, with two papers presented by author to Kathleen and Geoffrey.   Jarndyce Antiquarian Booksellers CCVII - 461   2015   £25

Association – Muirhead, Arnold

Hanway, Jonas *Three Letters on the Subject of the Marine Society, Let. I. On Occasion of their Clothing for the Sea 3097 Men and 2045 Boys to the End of Dec. 1757. II. Pointing Out Several Advantages Accruing to the Nation from this Institution. III. Being a Full Detail of the Rules and Forms of the Marine Society... (Bound with) Two Letters. Let. IV. Being thoughts on the Means of Augmenting the Number of Mariners in These Kingdoms, Upon Principles of Liberty. Let. V. To Robert Dingley, Esq...* London: printed in the year, 1758. Second edition, 4to., fine engraved frontispiece by Cipriani, general title printed in red and black, engraved frontispiece to Letter III, printed throughout on thick paper, contemporary calf, gilt ruled sides, neatly rebacked to match, spine gilt and labelled, fine, sometime in the library of Arnold Muirhead, with his bookplate on front pastedown; evidently bound for a contemporary owner.   John Drury Rare Books   2015 - 25782   2015 $2185

Association – Mulligan, G. G.

Dinsdale, Alfred *Television.* London: Television Press ltd., 1928. Second edition, signed presentation inscribed by John Baird, inventor of TV to G. G. Mulligan 12th April 1929, frontispiece also inscribed "J. H. Baird", octavo, original blue cloth, lightly sunned on spine, title and author embossed in black on front cover and spine, first few leaves bit foxed, lovely copy.   Athena Rare Books   15 - 6   2015 $3800

Association – Munch, Helene

Munch, Caja *The Strange American Way. Letters from Wiota...* Carbondale: Southern Illinois University, 1970. First edition, cloth, 274 pages, signed by translators, Helene and Peter Munch, owner's label, fine in slightly chipped dust jacket, very good+ jacket.   Baade Books of the West   2014 - 2015 $53

Association – Munch, Peter

Munch, Caja *The Strange American Way. Letters from Wiota...* Carbondale: Southern Illinois University, 1970. First edition, cloth, 274 pages, signed by translators, Helene and Peter Munch, owner's label, fine in slightly chipped dust jacket, very good+ jacket.   Baade Books of the West   2014 - 2015 $53

Association – Murphy, Tab

Rebello, Stephen *The Art of the Hunchback of Notre Dame.* New York: Hyperion, 1996. First edition, this copy signed by 10 members of the production company, including Gary Trousdale and Kirk Wise, artistic coordinator Randy Fullmer, writers Irene Meechi and Tab Murphy and five animators, numerous full color drawings and sketches in black and white, laid in is announcement for book signing party, fine in fine dust jacket.   Ed Smith Books   83 - 15   2015 $250

Association – Murphy, William

Dunbar, Paul Laurence *The Jest of Fate.* London: Jarrold & Sons, 1902. First English edition, ownership signature of author's half brother, William L. Murphy, corners little bumped, some slight discoloration at base of spine, still handsome and sound, very good or better, exceptionally uncommon title.   Between the Covers Rare Books   197 - 18   2015 $1500

Association – Murray, Albert

Morris, Wright *What a Way to Go.* New York: Atheneum, 1962. First edition, near fine in modestly worn, very good dust jacket with chips and small tears, African American author, Albert Murray's copy with his ownership signature. Between the Covers Rare Books, Inc.   187 - 184   2015 $100

Association – Murray, David

Philosophical Society of Glasgow *Proceedings of the....* Published for the Society, circa, 1904. 1844., 35 volumes bound in 18, complete handsome, uniform mottled half calf over marbled boards, spines gilt and labelled, all in the finest state of preservation from the library of David Murray (1842-1928) Scottish lawyer, with his bookplate on each pastedown, with 3 ALS's to Murray from Alexander Gardner, Hon. Sec. of the Society.   John Drury Rare Books   2015 - 25818   2015 $3147

Association – Mussenden, William

Crumpe, Samuel *An Essay on the Best Means of Providing Employment for the People.* Dublin: printed by Bonham, published by Mercier & Co., 1793. First edition, 8vo., printed on thick paper with half title and errata leaf, some prelim leaves and several text margins lightly dampstained, but overall fine, crisp copy in contemporary tree calf, spine simply gilt with crimson lettering piece, with 19th century armorial bookplate of William Mussenden.   John Drury Rare Books   March 2015 - 19609   2015 $874

Association – Myers, Cynthia

Plath, Sylvia   1932-1963 *The Colossus. Poems.* London: Heinemann, 1960. First edition, 8vo., original green cloth, dust jacket, inscribed by author for Luke (E. Lucas Myers) and Cynthia, signs of use but very good in worn, soiled dust jacket.   James S. Jaffe Rare Books Modern American Poetry - 224   2015 $45,000

Association – Myers, Luke

Plath, Sylvia   1932-1963 *The Colossus. Poems.* London: Heinemann, 1960. First edition, 8vo., original green cloth, dust jacket, inscribed by author for Luke (E. Lucas Myers) and Cynthia, signs of use but very good in worn, soiled dust jacket.   James S. Jaffe Rare Books Modern American Poetry - 224   2015 $45,000

Association – Neal, Dorothy

Meyer, Tom *Poikilos.* Urbana: Finial Press/Stone Wall Press, 1971. First edition, one of 250 copies, 16mo., black leather grain cloth, gilt rules on front board, silk ribbon marker bound in, fine, inscribed by author in 1973 to Dorothy Neal,.   Between the Covers Rare Books, Inc.   187 - 178   2015 $300

Association – Neal, John

Keese, John *The Poets of America: Illustrated by One of Her Painters...* New York: S. Colman, 1840. First edition, 12mo., contemporary brown half morocco, black cloth boards, gilt lettering, frontispiece, engraved title and 36 wood engravings by John G. Chapman, family copy from one of the contributors, John Neal to his twin sister Rachel, Jan. 1 1840, beneath inscription is later signature in pencil of John Neal's daughter, Margaret Neal and her name gilt stamped at foot of spine, edges little rubbed, some light foxing, very good.   The Brick Row Book Shop   Miscellany 67 - 15   2015 $500

Association – Neal, Margaret

Keese, John *The Poets of America: Illustrated by One of Her Painters...* New York: S. Colman, 1840. First edition, 12mo., contemporary brown half morocco, black cloth boards, gilt lettering, frontispiece, engraved title and 36 wood engravings by John G. Chapman, family copy from one of the contributors, John Neal to his twin sister Rachel, Jan. 1 1840, beneath inscription is later signature in pencil of John Neal's daughter, Margaret Neal and her name gilt stamped at foot of spine, edges little rubbed, some light foxing, very good.   The Brick Row Book Shop   Miscellany 67 - 15   2015 $500

Association – Neal, Rachel

Keese, John *The Poets of America: Illustrated by One of Her Painters...* New York: S. Colman, 1840. First edition, 12mo., contemporary brown half morocco, black cloth boards, gilt lettering, frontispiece, engraved title and 36 wood engravings by John G. Chapman, family copy from one of the contributors, John Neal to his twin sister Rachel, Jan. 1 1840, beneath inscription is later signature in pencil of John Neal's daughter, Margaret Neal and her name gilt stamped at foot of spine, edges little rubbed, some light foxing, very good.   The Brick Row Book Shop   Miscellany 67 - 15   2015 $500

Association – Neale, Henry James Vansittart

Simpson, John Palgrave *Letters from the Danube.* London: Richard Bentley, 1847. First edition, 2 volumes, 12mo., half titles, finely bound in contemporary full tan calf, gilt borders, raised gilt bands, gilt compartments, dark green and brown morocco labels, presentation inscription "Robert Peel from his sincere friend Henry James Vansittart Neale on his leaving Eton, Election 1860', fine, (grandson of Conservative statesman, Sir Robert Peel.   Jarndyce Antiquarian Booksellers   CCXI - 254   2015   £350

Association – Needham, Francis K. W.

Carew, Thomas 1595-1639 *Poems, Songs and Sonnets, Together with a Masque.* London: Henry Herringman, 1670. Fourth edition, 8vo., foxed and browned, heaviest in margins, occasional repairs to fore and upper edge, closely shaved along lower edge, touching catchwords and signatures on a number of leaves, early 20th century half calf and cloth boards, with W(illia)m Gates 18th century signature, pencil signature of H. F. B. Brett Smith (1896-1942), ink inscription March 20th 1922 of Francis K. W. Needham, signature John (?Harr)ison dated 1926, from the library of James Stevens Cox (1910-1997).   Maggs Bros. Ltd.   1447 - 64   2015   £180

Association – Nef, John

Mead, George Herbert *The Philosophy of the Act.* Chicago: University of Chicago Press, 1938. First edition, octavo, frontispiece, publisher's cloth with gilt spine, near fine, without dust jacket, signed and dated by John Nef, noted American historian.   Between the Covers Rare Books, Inc.   187 - 211   2015 $175

Association – Neilson, Meta

Wilkins, Mary E. *The Jamesons.* New York: Doubleday and McClure, 1899. First edition, small octavo, color plates, decorated green cloth, small booklabel, slight wear, spine little toned, else near fine, bears ownership signatures of Meta Neilson dated in 1899 and also of artist, Helen Neilson Armstrong, sister of Margaret Armstrong, dated 1805.   Between the Covers Rare Books   196 - 122   2015 $350

Association – Newbold, H. LeRoy

Lugar, Robert *Villa Architecture: a Collection of Views with Plans of Buildings Executed in England, Scotland, etc.* London: J. Taylor, 1828. First edition, folio, 42 plates of which 26 are hand colored aquatints and 16 floor plans, modern half red morocco, margins of first two leaves bit soiled and with few tiny chips, two leaves of preface moderately foxed, occasional spot of foxing, plates clean and bright and fine, signature of H. LeRoy Newbold, NY 1836.   Joseph J. Felcone Inc.   Science, Medicine and Technology - 1   2015 $4500

Association – Newdigate, Bernard Henry

Drayton, Michael 1563-1631 *Poly-Olbion.* London: printed for M. Lownes, I. Browne, A. Helme, J. Bushbie, 1612-1622. Engraved maps, 19th century half black calf, rubbed with split at head of leading hinge, armorial bookplate of Bernard Henry Newdigate, somewhat defective copy with few pencil marks, from the library of Geoffrey & Kathleen Tillotson.   Jarndyce Antiquarian Booksellers   CCVII - 239   2015   £950

Association – Newell, Peter

Dodgson, Charles Lutwidge 1832-1898 *Through the Looking Glass and What Alice Found There.* New York: Harper, 1902. First edition thus, 8vo., signed and inscribed by the artist, Peter Newell on titlepage, very good+, original white paper covered boards with gilt lettering to spine and front cover, gilt illustration of Alice on front cover, top edge gilt, soil, toning and scuffs to covers, cover edgewear, mild soil to endpapers, binding intact, rare.   By the Book, L. C. 44 - 76   2015 $1000

Association – Newman, Robert William

Cochrane, Basil *An Expose of the Conduct of the Victualling Board to the Honorable Basil Cochrane as Contractor and Agent Victualler to His Majesty's Ships on the East Indian Station.* London: printed by J. Davy, 1824. First and only edition, 8vo., half title, text followed by 5 large folding tables of contract accounts, contingent accounts, abstracts, and disbursements, original boards, printed label (slightly defective) on upper cover, printed spine label, head of spine chipped, upper joint splitting but fine, crisp, presentation copy inscribed by author for Robert Wm. Newman Esq. M.P. (1776-1848), seemingly of great rarity.   John Drury Rare Books   2015 - 25406   2015 $1311

Association – Nichols, Harry Peirce

Stevens, W. Bertrand *Victorious Mountaineer. A Memoir of Harry Peirce Nichols.* Louisville: Cloister Press, 1943. First edition, small 8vo., cloth, 78 pages, drawings, frontispiece, inscribed by Stevens, lightly soiled, very good, very scarce, original black and white photos of Nichols, signed by him.   Baade Books of the West   2014 - 2015 $230

Association – Nichols, Thomas

Balmford, William *The Seaman's Spiritual Companion or Navigation Spirituallized.* London: for Benj. Harris, 1678. First edition, small 8vo., variant state of title with double rule border and price on titlepage, A2 shaved at foot affecting signature and catchword on recto, minor worming in upper outer corner of D4-K8 (affecting end of text in places), stain to B3-E2 affecting three lines, occasional foxing, small hole from paper flaw in lower margin of E2, short tear at foot of F3 slightly affecting last line on recto and catchword on verso, small hole from paper flaw in centre of I2 touching two lines, actually reasonable and much loved copy, contemporary sheep (rubbed, covers scuffed, fore edge of lower cover worn exposing board, corners worn), several pen trials, scribbles, ownership inscriptions John Allab(on) His Booke October ye 24th 16, Charles Canning his book 1679, James Purnell His Booke Anno Domini (deleted), "Thomas Nichols His Book May ye 10 1718", "James Croome His Book March ye 9th 1757" "Jane Hanley", from the library of James Stevens Cox (1910-1997).   Maggs Bros. Ltd.   1447 - 21   2015   £2800

Association – Nicoll, Allardyce

Brown, John Mason *George Pierce Baker - a Memorial.* New York: Dramatists Play Service, 1939. First edition, octavo, 46 pages, frontispiece, marbled paper boards, title label on front cover, signed on front free endpaper by all authors, John Mason Brown, Eugene O'Neill, Sidney Howard, Allardyce Nicoll, Stanley R. McCandless, drawing by Gluyas Williams, frontispiece, marbled paper boards, title on label on front cover, covers rubbed at head and tail of spine, corners bruised, very good in chipped and torn original tissue jacket, largely defective at bottom edge.   Peter Ellis, Bookseller   2014 - 018199   2015   £300

Association – Nicoll, John Ramsay Allardyce

Coppola, Giovanni Carlo *Le Nozze Degli Dei; Favola... Rappresentata in Musica in Firenze nelle Reali Nozze de Serenissimi Gran Duchi di Toschana Ferdinando II e Vittoria Principessa d'Urbino.* Florence: A. Massi & L. Landi, 1637. First edition, 4to., large and handsome copy, etched titlepage and 7 double page etched plates by Stefano della Bella after Alfonso Parigi, 4to., 104 pages, expertly rebound in vellum over pasteboards, bookplate of Professor John Ramsay Allardyce Nicoll (1894-1976).   Maggs Bros. Ltd. Illustrated Books 2014 - 2015   £9000

Association – Nirenberg, Marshall

Watson, James D. *Molecular Biology of the Gene.* Menlo Park: Benjamin Cummings, 1977. Third edition, 4to., signed and dated by Marshall Nirenberg, 4to., near fine, few pages dog eared, original color illustrated cloth.   By the Book, L. C.   Special List 10 - 91   2015 $200

Association – Norfolk, Bernard Edward, 12th Duke of

Hall, Charles *An Enquiry into the Cause of the Present Distress of the People.* London: printed for the author and sold by J. Ridgway, 1820. First edition with this title, 8vo., final ad and errata leaves, contemporary half calf over marbled boards, spine simply gilt with label, very good from the early 19th century library of Bernard Edward, 12th Duke of Norfolk (1765-1842) with his bookplate.   John Drury Rare Books   2015 - 25943   2015 $6119

Association – Norman, Haskell

Bard, Samuel *Enquiry into the Nature, Cause and Cure of the Angina Suffocativa or Sore Throat Distemper....* New York: S. Inslee and A. Car at the New printing Office, 1771. First edition, 12mo., 33 pages, recent cloth backed boards, some folios trimmed, otherwise very nice, Haskell F. Norman bookplate.   M & S Rare Books, Inc.   97 - 18   2015 $4000

Parkinson, James *Organs Remains of a Former World: an Examination of the Mineralized Remains of the Vegetables and Animals of the Antediluvian World: Generally Termed Extraneous Fossils.* London: printed by C. Whittingham and published by J. Robson, J. White and J. Murray, H. D. Symonds, et al, 1804-1811. First edition, 3 volumes, 4to., 54 engraved plates, many hand colored, 2 errata leafs, titlepage vignettes, volume I prelims browned, occasional light foxing and offsetting throughout all volumes, contemporary full tan calf, gilt double ruled covers, 5 raised bands, gilt stamped spines and brown leather spine labels, volume I rebacked with original spine laid down, volume III front cover scratched, extremities rubbed all volumes, bookplate of Haskell Norman, bookplate and signature of J. Walton, 1952, near fine.   Jeff Weber Rare Books   178 - 875   2015 $5000

Upham, Thomas C. *Outlines of Imperfect and Disordered mental Action.* New York: Harper & Brothers, 1840. First edition, 12mo., original cloth some spine wear, with Haskell Norman bookplate.   M & S Rare Books, Inc.   97 - 307   2015 $600

Association – Normand, Mabel

De Acosta, Mercedes *Archways of Life.* New York: Moffat Yard and Co., 1921. First edition, paper covered boards with printed label, small label of Churchill Book and print shop in L, erosion of spine, sunning and corners of board rubbed, good copy, Mabel Normand's copy with her bookplate and inscribed by her to herself, additionally she has made comments at a couple of poems.   Between the Covers Rare Books, Inc.   187 - 71   2015 $3000

Association – Norse, Harold

Williams, William Carlos 1883-1963 *The Desert Music and Other Poems.* New York: Random House, 1954. First trade edition, 8vo., original cloth, very good, inscribed by author to Harold Norse, with Norse's ownership signature.   James S. Jaffe Rare Books   Modern American Poetry - 324   2015 $2500

Association – Northcliffe, Alfred Harmsworth, Lord

Pritchard, Edward William *A Complete Report of the Trial of Dr. E. W. Pritchard for the Alleged Poisoning of His Wife and mother-in-law.* Edinburgh: William Kay, 1865. First edition thus, 8vo., frontispiece, rather later 19th century half calf over marbled boards, spine lettered gilt, original printed yellow upper wrapper bound in, slight wear to joints, else very good, from the library of Alfred Harmsworth, Lord Northcliffe (1865-1922) with his bookplate.   John Drury Rare Books   March 2015 - 21751   2015 $221

Association – Northmont, Baron De

Demidoff, Anatole *Voyage dans la Russie Meridonale & la Crime...* Paris: Dublie par Gihout Freres, 1838-1848. First edition, large folio, half title, lithographed title with plate list on verso and 100 contemporary hand colored lithographed plates by August Raffet, with descriptive text (issued separately) bound in, unusual thus; contemporary half red morocco over marbled boards, boards ruled gilt, spine lettered and decoratively tooled in gilt, minimal wear to extremities, including thumbnail size peeling to bottom edge of front marbled board, overall very clean except for dampstaining to back endpapers and occasionally to upper corner of some plates, but only occurring on title verso, not affecting plates, some light marginal browning and closed crack to upper outer hinge, with no loss, previous owner, Baron de Northmont's armorial bookplate, overall wonderful copy.   Heritage Book Shop   Holiday 2014 - 49   2015 $45,000

Association – Notley, Alice

Ashbery, John *Houseboat Days. Poems.* New York: Viking, 1977. First edition, erratum slip laid in, 8vo., original cloth backed boards, contemporary, presentation copy inscribed by Ashbery for Ted Berrigan and wife Alice Notley, 9/20/77, fine.   James S. Jaffe Rare Books   Many Happy Returns - 352   2015 $3500

Katz, Steve *Cheyenne River Wild Track.* Ithaca: Ithaca House, 1973. First edition, octavo, wrappers illustrated by George Schneeman, trifle rubbed, near fine, inscribed by author to Ted Berrigan and Alice Notley.   Between the Covers Rare Books, Inc.   187 - 144   2015 $125

Association – Nowell-Smith, Simon

Onwhyn, Thomas *Thirty-Two Plates to Illustrate the Cheap edition of Nicholas Nickleby...* London: J. Newman, 1848. 8 parts, plates slightly browned but not foxed, original green printed wrappers to each part, 1 split along spine and slightly chipped, 4 with some splitting, good set, scarce, in brown envelope with notes by Kathleen Tillotson indicating a gift from Simon Nowell-Smith.   Jarndyce Antiquarian Booksellers   CCVII - 219   2015   £180

Association – Noyes, Carleton

McCrae, John *In Flanders Fields and Other Poems.* New York: G. P. Putnam's Sons, 1927. Seventh impression of American edition, ownership signature of editor and critic John S. Mayfield, lightly rubbed, very near fine in very good dust jacket, long inscription from poet and critic Carleton Noyes retelling how McCrae sent him the manuscript of title poem, tipped into back of original mailing envelope from Noyes and copies of correspondence leading up to Noyes signing the book.   Between the Covers Rare Books, Inc.   187 - 174   2015 $500

Association – Noyes, Professor

Dryden, John 1631-1700 *Hymns Attributed to John Dryden.* Berkeley: University of California Press, 1937. Frontispiece, original brown cloth, very good in slightly dusted dust jacket, signed by Geoffrey Tillotson, with pencil notes, copies of his review, correspondence about the questioned ascription, long TLS from Professor Noyes and ms. copy of the reply.   Jarndyce Antiquarian Booksellers CCVII - 248   2015   £30

Association – Nureyev, Rudolf

Bland, Alexander *The Nureyev Iamge.* London: Studio Vista, 1976. First edition, quarto, 288 pages, over 300 photos, boldly signed by Nureyev on half titlepage, loosely inserted is programme for the memorial tribute performance staged at Royal Opera House in 1993, fine in near fine dust jacket with just hint of rubbing to edges.   Peter Ellis, Bookseller   2014 - 010136   2015   £350

Association – O'Bryen, Morough

Denham, John *Poems and Translations with the Sophy.* London: for H. Herringman, 1668. First collected edition, 2nd issue, 8vo., small dampstain and some very minor worming to lower inner margin of A1-K6, 2 small holes in lower part margin of Hh6, with paper flaw in lower corner of M3, 2B1 and lower edge of I2, stain on Aa8, slight rust spotting to Cc3, small slip of paper glued to lower corner of cc4 covering old neat repair, contemporary sheep (20mm. piece torn away from foot of spine, lower corners worn and boards lightly rubbed, old label missing, pastedowns unstuck), Alex Henderson 16?84 signature, early 19th century bookplate of Morough O'Bryen, purple ink oval library stamp of George Stawell, solicitor Torrington, from the library of James Stevens Cox (1910-1997).   Maggs Bros. Ltd.   1447 - 137   2015   £500

Association – O'Byrne, James

Dresser, Christopher *The Art of Decorative Design.* London: Day and Son, Lithographers to the Queen..., 1862. First edition, royal 8vo., original decorated red cloth, gilt with design by author, red edges, recased, armorial bookplates of James O'Byrne.   Marlborough Rare Books   List 54 - 22   2015   £950

Association – O'Donnell, George Marion

Rimbaud, Arthur *A Season in Hell.* Norfolk: New Directions, 1939. First edition, 8vo., original linen backed paper over boards, printed paper label on front cover, dust jacket, presentation copy inscribed by author for George Marion O'Donnell, small ownership signature, otherwise fine.   James S. Jaffe Rare Books   Modern American Poetry - 250   2015 $1500

Association – O'Hara, Frank

Schuyler, James *Locus Solus I - Winter 1961.* Locus Solus Press, 1960. First issue, small octavo, printed wrappers, boxed, Frank O'Hara's personal copy with his ownership signature in ink on first page, he has marked each of his ten included poems with dates of composition.   Honey & Wax Booksellers   1 - 54   2015 $2500

Association – O'Hea, Juliet

Freeling, Nicolas *Valparaiso.* New York: Harper & Row, 1965. First US edition, near fine in dust jacket, very lightly rubbed at extremities and white back panel beginning to uniformly tan, presentation copy from his literary agent, inscribed to Juliet (O'Hea).   Buckingham Books   March 2015 - 27167   2015 $200

Association – O'Neil, Eugene

Tate, James *Hottentot Ossuary.* Cambridge: Temple Bar Bookshop, 1974. First edition, one of 50 specially bound (hardbound) copies numbered and signed by author out of a total edition of 1500 copies, this copy number 1, a presentation copy inscribed on front free endpaper to publisher's James and Eugene O'Neil, with holograph note of provenance from Eugene O'Neil laid in, small 8vo., original black cloth, fine in dust jacket which is slightly rubbed alone one fold.   James S. Jaffe Rare Books   Modern American Poetry - 293   2015 $850

Association – O'Neil, James

Tate, James *Hottentot Ossuary.* Cambridge: Temple Bar Bookshop, 1974. First edition, one of 50 specially bound (hardbound) copies numbered and signed by author out of a total edition of 1500 copies, this copy number 1, a presentation copy inscribed on front free endpaper to publisher's James and Eugene O'Neil, with holograph note of provenance from Eugene O'Neil laid in, small 8vo., original black cloth, fine in dust jacket which is slightly rubbed alone one fold.   James S. Jaffe Rare Books   Modern American Poetry - 293   2015 $850

Association – O'Neill, Eugene

Brown, John Mason *George Pierce Baker - a Memorial.* New York: Dramatists Play Service, 1939. First edition, octavo, 46 pages, frontispiece, marbled paper boards, title label on front cover, signed on front free endpaper by all authors, John Mason Brown, Eugene O'Neill, Sidney Howard, Allardyce Nicoll, Stanley R. McCandless, drawing by Gluyas Williams, frontispiece, marbled paper boards, title on label on front cover, covers rubbed at head and tail of spine, corners bruised, very good in chipped and torn original tissue jacket, largely defective at bottom edge.   Peter Ellis, Bookseller   2014 - 018199   2015   £300

Association – Ober, Harold

Trumbo, Dalton *Johnny Got His Gun.* Philadelphia: J. B. Lippincott, 1939. First edition, light pencilled name, easily erasable (but we think it is of the important author's agent Harold Ober), else fine in handsome very good plus dust jacket with nicks at crown and little light edgewear, from the library of Kate Stettner Lobell and Carl D. Lobell. Between the Covers Rare Books   196 - 35   2015 $2500

Association – Obermayer, Leon

Haley, Alex *The Man Who Wouldn't Quit.* Pleasantville: Reader's Digest Assoc., 1963. First separate edition, offprint from Reader's Digest magazine, one leaf folded to make 6 pages, vertical crease, probably as mailed, one small snag on front page, else very good or better, sent by George Haley to senior law partner Leon J. Obermayer, Washington, signed by Alex Haley, rare.   Between the Covers Rare Books   197 - 24   2015 $3000

Association – Ogilvy, John

Fielding, Henry 1707-1754 *The History of Tom Jones a Foundling.* London: printed for C. Cooke, n.d., 1801. Cooke's edition, 13 super engraved plates, 12mo., 3 volumes, contemporary tree calf, red and green leather labels to spine, blue speckled page edges, title pages present in each volume, letter to George Lyttleton in volume I, two pages of ads in volume III, titles with former owner inscriptions of John Ogilvy, bright and sturdy set with minor rubbing to corners, some hinges worn but secure, pages clean, volume I titlepage with "Printed" misprint, Volume II light staining to margins, small loss to bottom corner of page 51, lacking rear endpapers (appears to have been bound without them, rather than removed), volume III with small touch of loss to head of spine, 18th century set in attractive tree calf, with all 13 plates.   B & B Rare Books, Ltd.   234 - 26   2015 $450

Association – Olson, Charles

Duncan, Robert *As Testimony: the Poem and the Scene.* San Francisco: White Rabbit Press, 1964. First edition, stapled wrappers, about fine, inscribed by author to Charles Olson, Sept. 8 1964.   Between the Covers Rare Books, Inc.   187 - 83   2015 $1750

Association – Onderdonk, Henry Treadwell

Gallagher, Simon Felix *A Brief Reply to a Short Answer to a True Exposition of the Doctrine of the Catholic Church...* New York: printed for the author by Sherman & Pudney, 1815. First edition, disbound, 176 pages, foxing on titlepage, else very good or better, the copy of Bishop Henry Treadwell Onderdonk with his ownership signature twice. Between the Covers Rare Books, Inc.   187 - 106   2015 $300

Association – Ono, Yoko

Solt, Andrew *Imagine: John Lennon.* New York: Macmillan, 1989. First edition, large 4to., 255 pages, original black cloth over grey boards, lettered silver at spine, copiously illustrated in color and black and white throughout, signed presentation from Yoko Ono for Victor Spinetti (1929-2012) actor, poet, author.   Any Amount of Books   March 2015 - C12727   2015   £450

Association – Oppo, Cipriano Efisio

Palanti, Mario *Prima Esposizione Personale d'Architettura nella Republica Argentina.* Milano: Stabilmento di Arti Grafische Rizzoli & Pizzio, 1917. First edition, illustrations with 137 color & black and white plates, folio, brown cloth decorated in blind, gilt titles, presentation copy from author to his fellow Italian painter, art critic and politician Cipriano Efisio Oppo (1891-1962), wear at spine ends and along joints, small tear to top front joint and at middle of spine, remnants of paper revenue stamps on spine, occasional offsetting or light soiling on few leaves, still very good.   Kaaterskill Books   19 - 198   2015 $500

Association – Orlebar, John

Welsted, Leonard *Epistles, Odes, &c.* London: printed for J. Walthoe & J. Peele, 1724. First edition, 8vo., contemporary panelled calf, very slight wear to tips of spine, fine copy, early armorial bookplate of John Orlebar (1697-1765) of the Middle Temple.   C. R. Johnson   Foxon R-Z - 1107r-z   2015 $1149

Association – Orwell, Sonia

Lowell, Robert 1917-1977 *The Dolphin.* London: Faber and Faber, 1973. First US edition, inscribed by author to Sonia Orwell, widow of George Orwell.   Ken Lopez, Bookseller   164 - 125   2015 $750

Association – Osborn, James

Kidgell, John *The Card.* London: printed for the maker and sold by J. Newbery, 1755. First edition, 2 volumes, hand colored engraved frontispiece in volume 1, the word 'Card' in fancy woodcut capitals on both titlepages, frontispiece repaired at inner corners and along fore-edge, loss of the final 'e' in frontispiece, first 2 gatherings in volume i semi-detached, slightly browned, 12mo., contemporary calf, sometime rebacked, tan lettering pieces, joints rubbed, spine of volume ii defective at foot, booklabel of James M. Osborn, sound.   Blackwell's Rare Books   B179 - 57   2015   £1500

Association – Osborne, John

Southey, Robert 1774-1843 *The Life of Nelson.* London: printed for Joh Murray, 1813. First edition, 8vo., full leather lettered gilt on red leather labels, frontispiece of volume on depicts a portrait of Nelson and frontispiece of volume two shows gradual decline of Nelson's handwriting, from the library of playwright John Osborne, some rubbing and slight cracking along spine hinges but holding fast, few missing chips at foot of spines, slight edge wear and rubbing at corner tips, otherwise clean, very good.   Any Amount of Books   2015 - C7943   2015   £300

Association – Owen, Frank

Owen, Ethel *Wish for Tomorrow.* New York: Robert Speller Publishing Corp., 1936. First edition, fine in lightly rubbed, near fine dust jacket with modest chip at crown, inscribed by author to her brother, Frank Owen.   Between the Covers Rare Books, Inc.   187 - 208   2015 $675

Association – Padgett, Ron

Apollinaire, Guillaume *The Poet Assassinated.* New York: Holt Rinehart Winston, 1968. First American edition translated by Ron Padgett, small 4to., original pictorial boards, dust jacket, fine in slightly sunned dust jacket, inscribed by artist, Jim Dine for Burt (Britton) 1978, also inscribed with drawing by Ron Padgett (translator) to same.   James S. Jaffe Rare Books   Many Happy Returns - 192   2015 $50

Berrigan, Ted *Seventeen.* N.P.: Ted Berrigan & Ron Padgett, 1964. First edition, 4to., stapled wrappers, inscribed by Berrigan and signed by Padgett, pages little age darkened, else fine.   James S. Jaffe Rare Books Many Happy Returns - 210   2015 $1250

Berrigan, Ted *Bean Spasms.* New York: Kulchur Press, 1967. First edition, paperback issue, signed by all three (Berrigan, Ron Padgett and artist, Joe Brainard with a note by Berrigan for Burt Britton), fine.   James S. Jaffe Rare Books   Many Happy Returns - 212   2015 $1250

Cendrars, Blaise *Kodak.* New York: Adventures in Poetry, 1976. First edition translated by Ron Padgett, 4to., original black wrappers, inscribed by Padgett for Burt, mint. James S. Jaffe Rare Books   Many Happy Returns - 195 2015 $150

Larbaud, Valery *Ridasedirad les Dicmhypbdf.* New York: Adventures in Poetry, 1973. First edition, one of 250 copies, 4to., original wrappers with cover illustration by Lindsay Stamm Shapiro, inscribed by Padgett for Britton, fine. James S. Jaffe Rare Books   Many Happy Returns - 197 2015 $250

Association – Page, Frederick

Abercrombie, Lascelles *The Art of Wordsworth.* London: Oxford University Press, 1952. Original red cloth, slightly spotted and torn dust jacket, Geoffrey Tillotson's signed copy with correspondence with Frederick Page, review cutting &c., pencil notes.   Jarndyce Antiquarian Booksellers CCVII - 575   2015   £20

Arnold, Matthew 1822-1888 *Poetical Works.* London: Macmillan, 1924. Reprint, half title, original half brown calf, darkened and rubbed, top edge gilt, signed by Geoffrey Tillotson with many ink and pencilled notes and inserted ALS to Tillotson about Arnold from Frederick Page. Jarndyce Antiquarian Booksellers   CCVII - 49   2015   £35

Association – Page, H.

Cooke, James *Mellificium Chirurgiae or the Marrow of Many Good Authors.* London: for Samuel Cartwright, 1648. First edition, 12mo., upper fore corners of B6-7 and P5 torn from paper flaws (affecting rule border not touching text), some worming in inner margin (heavily between Q5-R11), contemporary sheep ruled in blind (rubbed, 30mm piece torn at head of spine, a number of loose gatherings, bumped and rubbed, pastedowns unstuck), early ink initials "E K", late 18th century signature Isaac Webster/Hull, signature Isaac Raines 1802, by descent to Rev. George Francis Twycross-Raines, vicar and antiquary of Hull, with ink inscription, of "H. Page from his old friend G. F. Twycross-Raines Sept. 11, 1911", from the library of James Stevens Cox (1910-1997).   Maggs Bros. Ltd.   1447 - 114   2015 £750

Association – Page, Tim

Thomson, Virgil *A Virgil Thomson Reader.* New York: Alfred A. Knopf, 1948. First edition, about very good without dust jacket, inscribed by author to critic Tim Page and Vanessa Page, 1986.   Between the Covers Rare Books, Inc.   187 - 191   2015 $450

Association – Page, Vanessa

Thomson, Virgil *A Virgil Thomson Reader.* New York: Alfred A. Knopf, 1948. First edition, about very good without dust jacket, inscribed by author to critic Tim Page and Vanessa Page, 1986.   Between the Covers Rare Books, Inc.   187 - 191   2015 $450

Association – Palgrave, Francis Turner

Newman, John Henry 1801-1890 *Hymni Ecclesiae, Excerpti e Breviariis Romano, Salisburiensi, eboracensi...* Oxonii: J. H. Parker, 1838. 4 pages ads, original grey cloth, paper label, spine defective, scarce, inscribed Francis Palgrave from his affectionate NJ and EJJ Jan. 10 1839, from the library of Geoffrey & Kathleen Tillotson.   Jarndyce Antiquarian Booksellers   CCVII - 396   2015   £180

Newman, John Henry 1801-1890 *Loss and Gain.* London: James Burns, 1848. First edition, original black cloth, slightly dulled and rubbed at corners, endpapers replaced, F. T. Palgrave's copy Mar 21:1848 , with postcard photo of author inserted bearing birthday greetings to Geoffrey Tillotson.   Jarndyce Antiquarian Booksellers   CCVII - 390   2015   £180

Tennyson, Alfred Tennyson, 1st Baron 1809-1892 *Lyrical Poems.* London: Maxmillan, 1885. First edition, half title, 6 pages ads, pages 119-20 torn through without loss, uncut in remains of original blue boards, lacking spine strip, last gathering detached, possibly a proof copy, selected and annotated by Francis T. Palgrave, his copy, signed Mch 9 1885, but with no internal marks, from the library of Geoffrey & Kathleen Tillotson, inscribed by them.   Jarndyce Antiquarian Booksellers   CCVII - 487   2015   £45

Association – Palgrave, Gwenllian Florence

Palgrave, Francis Turner 1824-1897 *The Five Days Entertainments at Wentworth Garage.* London: Macmillan & Co., 1868. First edition, half title, plates and illustrations by Arthur Hughes, 2 pages ad, original blue cloth, inner hinges splitting, rubbed and dulled, top edge gilt, with slightly damaged half title and partly obscured presentation to Gwenllian Florence Palgrave 1866-1951, one of the dedicatees from her father 1873, overwritten in pencil with her childish signature, from the library of Geoffrey & Kathleen Tillotson.   Jarndyce Antiquarian Booksellers   CCVII - 404   2015   £60

Association – Palmer, S.

Coleridge, Samuel Taylor 1772-1834 *Biographia Literaria; or Biographical Sketches...* London: Rest Fenner, 1817. First edition, 2 volumes, half titles, without final ad leaf volume II, some spotting, few leaves rather browned, half red calf, spines chipped, hinges weak, signed S. Palmer and with his pencil notes at end of Chapter I, inserted is ALS of inquiry to Geoffrey Tillotson from Geoffrey Grigson.   Jarndyce Antiquarian Booksellers   CCVII - 147   2015   £850

Association – Pares, Martin

Friedman, William F. *The Shakespearean Ciphers Examined: an Analysis of Cryptographic Systems...* Cambridge: Cambridge University Press, 1957. First edition, 8vo., 10 plates, 17 figures, hardback, ownership signature of Martin Pares, with few pages of notes by him loosely inserted, signed presentation to Pares from author, very good+ in like dust jacket with very slight edgewear.   Any Amount of Books   March 2015 - A78928   2015   £350

Association – Parish, Steve

Brandelius, Jerilyn Lee *Grateful Dead Family Album.* New York: Warner Books, 1989. First edition, 'Grateful Dead All Area Access sticker laid down to jacket, this copy signed by band members Jerry Garcia, Mickey Hart and Bob Bralove as well as long time road crew members Ram Rod Shurtliff, Bill 'Kid' Candelario, Steve Parish and Robbie Taylor among others, hundreds of intimate photos and stories, very good plus to near fine with little soil and handling marks, in very good plus to near fine dust jacket with short closed tear to bottom of front flap.   Ed Smith Books   83 - 34   2015 $950

Association – Park, Carlton Moore

Spielmann, M. H., Mrs. *Love Family.* London: George Allen & sons, 1908. First edition, 8vo., cloth backed pictorial boards, 63 pages, some edge wear, very good, illustrations by Carlton Moore Park, 12 color plates, 38 black and white drawings, this copy inscribed by artist to the Chelsea Art Club with signed presentation slip laid in and with artist's own bookplate, special copy.   Aleph-bet Books, Inc.   109 - 340   2015 $250

Association – Park, Darrah

Schuyler, James *The Home Book: Prose and Poems 1951-1970.* Calais: Z Press, 1977. First edition, one of 26 lettered copies signed by Schuyler, out of a total edition of 100 copies, although not called for, this copy signed by Darrah Park who designed covers, 8vo., original wrappers, cover illustration by Darrah Park, spine slightly cocked, otherwise fine.   James S. Jaffe Rare Books   Modern American Poetry - 241   2015 $750

Association – Parnell, Reverend

Young, Edward 1683-1765 *The Force of Religion; or, Vanquish'd Love.* London: printed for E. Curll and J. Pemberton, 1714. First edition, engraved frontispiece, 8vo., half blue morocco, gilt, spine gilt, top edge gilt by Roger de Coverly & sons (traces of rubbing), copy on fine paper, remarkable presentation copy inscribed to Revd. Doct. Pa(rnell) from the author, margins trimmed somewhat close, but not touching text, otherwise very good, bookplate of Oliver Brett, Viscount Esher.   C. R. Johnson   Foxon R-Z - 1187r-z   2015 $1915

Association – Parreno, Alberto

Carbajal Y Lancaster, Isidro De, Bp. of Cuenca *Memorial Ajustado Hecho de Orden del Consejo-Pleno a Instancia de los Senores Fiscales, del Expediente Consultivo Visto por Remision de Su Magestad a el Sobre el Contenido y Expresiones de Diffentes Cartas del Rev. Obispo de Cuenca D. Isidro de Carbajal y Lancaster.* Madrid: En la officina de Joachin de Ibarra, 1768. First edition, 4to., old paper covered boards, crude leather spine, faint dampstain to front board and corner of first few leaves, rare board with larger dampstain as well as last leaves, occasional soil spot on leaves, bookseller label at rear, untrimmed, wide margined, strong impressions, certainly good or better copy, the copy of Alberto Parreno, the Sann Parreno sale 9 Feb. 1978.   Kaaterskill Books   19 - 30   2015 $500

Guia de Forasteros de Siempre fiel Isla de Cuba Para el Ano Economico de 1880-81. Habana: Imprenta del Gobierno y Capitania General, 1880. Small 8vo., 12 in-text zodiac signs, red morocco embossed in blind, gilt onramental borders, marbled endpapers, very good copy, minor rubbing, arorial bookplate from Biblioteca de Alberto Parreno. Kaaterskill Books   19 - 45   2015 $750

Association – Parrish, Maxfield

Saunders, Louise *Knave of Hearts.* New York: Scribner, 1925. First edition, folio, black cloth, pictorial paste-on, some rubbing to cover plate and cloth, very good+ in custom facsimile box, glorious pictorial endpapers plus really magnificent full page color illustrations (printed on rectos only) and numerous rich color illustrations in text, by Maxfield Parrish, all printed on thick, heavy coated paper, laid in is handwritten letter from Parrish to His editor, J. H. Chapin Discussing His Progress on the Knave, written on both sides of 3 1/2 x 5 inch card, dated January 26 1922. Aleph-Bet Books, Inc.   108 - 335   2015 $6000

Association – Parrish, Morris

Shorthouse, H. J. *Sir Percival: a Story of the Past and Present.* London: Macmillan and Co., 1886. First edition, presentation copy inscribed "Edward Shorthouse from his affectionate brother and sister J. Henry & Sarah Shorthouse", original dark blue cloth, gilt strips with embossed design on front over and spine, fine, housed in fine custom half red morocco slipcase, octavo, fine, bookplate of Ohio book collector Paul Lemperly with his inscription stating he received the book as a gift from Morris L. Parrish, with Parrish's letter of presentation inserted.   The Kelmscott Bookshop   11 - 46   2015 $600

Association – Parrish, William

Snell, Charles *The Art of Writing In Its Theory and Practice.* London: Henry Overton, 1712. Oblong 8vo., half leather, marbled paper covered boards, cover scrubbed and scuffed, bookplate on front pastedown, front free endpapers creased, lacks title, one plate and 6 leaves of text (all supplied in Xerox), one leaf torn near center, other leaves with small tears near corners, few ink notations by Wm. Parrish in text.   Oak Knoll Books   Special Catalogue 24 - 51   2015 $500

Association – Parsons, Coleman

Scott, Walter   1771-1832 *The Abbot.* Edinburgh: printed for Longman, Hurst, Rees, Orme and Brown; London and for Archibald Constable and Co. and John Ballantyne, Edinburgh, 1820. First edition, 3 volumes, contemporary calf and marbled paper covered boards, black morocco spine label, titled and spine decorations in gilt, bookplate of Coleman O. Parsons in volume one, moderate rubbing and wear to extremities, half titles lacking in volume one, very good.   Between the Covers Rare Books, Inc.   187 - 254   2015 $250

Association – Parsons, William

Giannone, Pietro *Opera Postume di Pietro Giannone in Difesa Della Sua Storia Civile de Regno di Napoli con la sue Professione di Fede si Aggiungono in Questa Edizione le Annotazioni Critiche del Padre Paoli, Sopra il IX. Libro del Tomo Secondo Della Storia Civile...* Venezia: Giambattista Pasquale, 1768. New edition, volumes, quarto, engraved titlepages, head and tailpieces, contemporary quarter leather with patterned boards, contemporary engraved bookplate of William Parsons on each front pastedown, covers rubbed at spines and edges, very good, internally bright and clean. Peter Ellis, Bookseller   2014 - 016080   2015   £325

Association – Partridge, Frances

Woolf, Virginia   1882-1941 *The Waves.* London: published by Leonard and Virginia Woolf at the Hogarth Press, 1931. First edition, first printing, one of 7113 copies, publisher's purple cloth lettered gilt, printed on laid paper, good with slight lean, two short tears to spine head, rubbing to spine ends, toning and light soiling to spine ends, toning and light soiling to spine, boards slightly bowed, minor soiling and some fading, very light spotting to first few and last pages of text block, pencil correction to page 47, bright and clean pages, housed in custom quarter leather clamshell box, personal copy of author's sister Vanessa Bell, with her ownership signature by descent to her daughter Angelica Garnett, thence to her two surviving daughters Henrietta Coupe and Frances Partridge.   B & B Rare Books, Ltd.   239 - 1   2015 $9500

Association – Passmore, T. H.

Sallustius Crispus, C. *Caius Crispus Salustius ab Ascensio Familiariter Explanatus.* Paris: Jean Petit, 1504. First Badius edition, some light foxing and staining (heavier o titlepage), first leaf of text bound slightly askew and 3 sidenotes copped as a result, 4to., 18th century calf, worn and crackled, rebacked (somewhat crudely), black lettering piece, hinges relined with black cloth tape, bookplates of Wigan public Library, Rev. T. H. Passmore, Sir Robert Shafto Adair and Augustus Frederick, Duke of Sussex, sound.   Blackwell's Rare Books   Greek & Latin Classics VI - 93   2015   £2000

Association – Patten, Nelson Simon

James, William   1842-1910 *The Principles of Psychology.* New York: Henry Holt and Co., 1890. First edition, 2nd printing, octavo, this copy was owned by Simon Nelson Patten (1852-1922), with handwritten signature and date, Patten obviously donated these 2 volumes to University of PA library, although there is no indication of them being treated as library books, other than single blue ink withdrawal notice in each book, original publisher's dark green binding with gilt lettering on spine, covers fairly well preserved with just few hints of spotting and wear, both spines very lightly tattered and torn at top and bottom with one small (half inch) triangular chip missing from top rear volume I, inside front cover volume I is cracked but holding firm, somewhat unsophisticated but perfectly respectable copy.   Athena Rare Books   15 - 15   2015 $1000

Association – Pattenson, William Hodges Tylden

Puffendorf, Samuel, Freiherr Von   1632-1694 *Of the Law of Nature and Nations.* Oxford: printed by L. Lichfield for A. & J. Churchill...., 1703. First edition in English, folio, title printed within double ruled border, this copy with errata leaf at end of introduction, contemporary panelled calf, sometime sympathetically rebacked, spine gilt with raised bands and label, fine, crisp copy, from the mid 19th century library of William Hodges Tylden Pattenson (1857) with ownership inscription on front pastedown.   John Drury Rare Books   2015 - 24994   2015 $6119

Association – Paulin, L.

Examiner, Pseud. *Some Thoughts on Examinations, by an Examiner.* London: privately printed in the Department of English at University College, London, 1936. 4to., original blue printed wrappers, slightly creased, 7 pages, inscribed to Geoffrey Tillotson by Hilda Holme and L. Paulin, with quotation inserted by Tillotson.   Jarndyce Antiquarian Booksellers   CCVII - 268   2015   £60

Association – Paulson, Ronald

Faulkner, William Harrison   1897-1962 *The Unvanquished.* New York: Random House, 1938. First edition, limited to 250 copies signed by author, drawings by Edward Shenton, original publisher's cloth backed patterned boards, from the library of Hogarth scholar Ronald Paulson bearing his bookplate to front pastedown, excellent copy, spine very slightly faded, few small stains to endpaper, else fine, author's scarcest signed limited edition.   B & B Rare Books, Ltd.   234 - 25   2015 $4000

Association – Pears, Tom

Shelton, Richard *Desert Water a Poem.* New York: Monument Press, 1972. First edition, one of 150 copies on Mould Made Rives paper, 12mo., unpaginated in little loose original wrappers, composed in Hunt roman type, lino cuts were printed direction from blocks, this one of 50 copies signed by poet and artist, this is a presentation copy from printer Tom Pears and each of the images signed in pencil.   Second Life Books Inc.   190 - 196   2015 $75

Association – Pearsall, Logan

Bridges, Robert   1844-1930 *Poems.* London: Basil Montagu Pickering, 1873. First edition, original blue cloth, uncut, spine with printed label (rubbed), cloth somewhat soiled, endpapers severely browned as always, otherwise nice, Logan Pearsall's copy, with his ownership signature, from the collection of Gavin H. Fryer.   Bertram Rota Ltd.   308 Part II - 127   2015   £280

Association – Pearson, Hugh

Almack, Henry *A Plea for Deacons.* London: Rivingtons, 1868. First edition, 8vo., well bound fairly recently in linen backed marbled boards lettered, very good, presentation inscribed and initialled by author for Revd. Hugh Pearson, uncommon.   John Drury Rare Books   2015 - 20936   2015 $80

Association – Peel, Robert

Simpson, John Palgrave *Letters from the Danube.* London: Richard Bentley, 1847. First edition, 2 volumes, 12mo., half titles, finely bound in contemporary full tan calf, gilt borders, raised gilt bands, gilt compartments, dark green and brown morocco labels, presentation inscription "Robert Peel from his sincere friend Henry James Vansittart Neale on his leaving Eton, Election 1860', fine, (grandson of Conservative statesman, Sir Robert Peel.   Jarndyce Antiquarian Booksellers   CCXI - 254   2015   £350

Association – Peirce, Charles Anders

Peirce, Benjamin *Physical and Celestial Mechanic's... Developed in Four Systems of Analytic Mechanics, Celestial Mechanics, Potential Physics and Analytic Morphology.* Boston: Little Brown, 1855. First edition, 4to., folding plate, original blindstamped pebbled brown cloth, spine replaced in quarter similarly grained black cloth, extremities lightly rubbed, front corners showing, presentation bookplate from Charles Anders Peirce, institutional holograph inscription to Harvard College, with matching rubber stamps (withdrawn stamp as duplicate), rare, very good.   Jeff Weber Rare Books   178 - 887   2015 $1600

Association – Perceval, William

Herbert, Thomas *A Relation of Some Yeares Travaile Begunne anno 1626.*   London: printed by William Stansby & Jacob Blome, 1634. First edition, 4to., numerous well executed engraved illustrations and maps, contemporary full panelled calf, expertly rebacked raised bands, maroon leather label, from the Maxwell-Perceval Library, with signature of William Perceval, armorial bookplate of John Evans, very good.   Jarndyce Antiquarian Booksellers   CCXI - 137   2015   £1850

Association – Perkins, Maxwell

Wolfe, Thomas Clayton *Look Homeward, Angel.*   New York: Charles Scribner's, 1929. First edition, spine lettering worn but readable, very good in worn, good only first issue dust jacket (with Wolfe portrait on rear panel), lacking bottom couple of inches of spine and several other modest chips and tears, several internal tape repairs, this copy inscribed by author for Fidelia E. Stark, Oct. 30 1929, laid in 4 page carbon manuscript (folded, small breaks at folds, else near fine), unsigned but almost certainly by Maxwell Perkins dated April 17, 1929.   Between the Covers Rare Books   196 - 127   2015 $12,000

Association – Person, Johannes

Thomas A Kempis 1380-1471 *Opera.*   Paris: Iodocus Badius Ascensius, 1523. Second collected edition, first edition printed in France, 330 x 216mm., lacking final blank, fine contemporary London blindstamped calf, covers tooled in panels, outer frame of a roll of Renaisance designs including fountain topped by three heads, central panel composed mainly of five vertical rows of foliage and flowers, raised bands, spine very expertly rebacked to style, two original brass clasps and catches with leather thongs (perhaps later but perhaps not), original vellum tabs marking important textual sections, rear board with contemporaneous inscription (perhaps author and title), rear pastedown comprising a portion of a proclamation dealing with beggars and vagabonds, in recent clamshell box backed with calf, titlepage with woodcut device dated 1520 depicting printer's workshop, large and small woodcut initials in text (few artlessly colored), titlepage with signature of Johannes Person above woodcut vignette and of another member of Person family at top of page, (this inscription dated 1566 with purchase details for the volume), also signature of A. Fletcher, inside cover of box and front pastedown with modern morocco bookplate of Michael Sharpe, lower board with small abraded area, other trivial marks and very small wormholes in leather, thongs bit dried and deteriorating, but expertly restored binding entirely solid and blindstamping still quite sharp, titlepage little dust soiled and with small shadow of turn-in glue at bottom, last three gatherings with minor stains along gutter, final gathering with similar stain at fore-edge, short tears and other trivial imperfections in text, generally quite fine internally, text mostly quite clean, especially fresh and unusually bright.   Phillip J. Pirages   66 - 7   2015 $12,500

Association – Pery, Edmund Sexton, 1st Viscount

Diodorus Siculus *The History of Diodorus Siculus.*   London: by John Macock for Giles Calvert, 1653. First edition in English, small folio, longitudinal half title has been cut-out leaving a stub, 271 pages, small circular stain in inner margins of first few leaves and Kk4-L12, rust spot on Kk4, contemporary sheep, smooth spine ruled in blind and with red morocco and gilt label, covers heavily scuffed, piece missing from top corner of lower cover, upper headcap torn, front pastedown torn away at head, early inscription on flyleaf heavily deleted, early signature Nic. Hare, signature on title Edm. Sex. Pery, 1st and last Viscount Pery (1719-1806) by descent to his elder daughter Diana Jane, Countess of Ranfurly to Earls of Ranfurly, with 19th century bookplate, from the library of James Stevens Cox (1910-1997).   Maggs Bros. Ltd.   1447 - 148   2015   £380

Association – Peters, A. D.

Pritchett, V. S. *When My Girl Comes Home.* London: Chatto & Windus, 1961. First edition, fine, original binding, slightly soiled and frayed dust jacket, with label of literary agent, A.D. Peters, and partly erased signature on front free endpaper, from author's library with posthumous VSP book-label from the collection of Gavin H. Fryer.   Bertram Rota Ltd.   308 Part II - 198   2015   £40

Association – Petit, Philippe

Gerstein, Mordicai   *The Man Who Walked Between the Towers.*   Brookfield: Roaring Brook, 2003. First edition, signed and dated 9/11/11 exactly 10 years after the 9/11 tragedy by Gerstein and with original drawing of a man in top hat on tight rope, additionally signed by the tightrope walker, Philippe Petit with small tight rope drawing, as new in like dust jacket, 4to, no Caldecott medal or mention of award on dust jacket.   By the Book, L. C.   44 - 83   2015 $400

Association – Petre, C. L.

Bronte, Charlotte   1816-1855   *Jane Eyre; an Autobiography.*   London: Smith, Elder and Co., 1848. Second edition, half titles, 3 volumes, slight foxing, some pencil marking in margins, original purple vertical fine grained cloth, boards blocked in blind, spines lettered gilt, faded and slightly rubbed, very carefully recased, nice in original cloth, neat ownership inscription on leading free endpaper of C. L. Petre Jany. 17th 1848 Holly Lodge".   Jarndyce Antiquarian Booksellers   CCXI - 46   2015   £6500

Association – Phelan, James

Barry, Theodore Augustus   *Men and Memories of San Francisco in the "Spring of '50".*   San Francisco: A. L. Bancroft & Co., 1873. First edition, 12mo., green cloth gilt stamped title lettering to spine and front board, green endpapers, withal a good copy, gilt bright, slight lean, small abrasion to cloth at top front joint, foxing to edges, bookplate of James D. Phelan (mayor of San Francisco), ownership signature of Mrs. M. G. Wilson.   Tavistock Books   Bah, Humbug? - 28   2015 $275

Association – Phelipps, John

Gracian y Morales, Baltasar   1601-1658   *The Art of Prudence, or a Companion for a Man of Sense.*   printed for D. Browne... J. Walthoe... and W. Mears and Jonas Browne, 1714. 8vo., contemporary panelled calf, lettered gilt on front cover 'I. Phelipps Y', (Rev. John Phelipps), red lettering piece, cracks at head of spine, very good, delightful copy, this copy from Newton Surmaville, in Somerset, the home of Robert Harbin, it remained in the library which remained untouched for hundreds of years (until it was sold in 2007), when the last member of the family, Sophia Wyndham died.   Blackwell's Rare Books   B179 - 48   2015   £600

Association – Phili, Alexandri

Nilsson, Martin P.   *Primitive Time-Reckoning: a Study in the Origins and First Development of the Art of Counting Time Among the Primitive and Early Peoples.*   Lund: C. W. K. Gleerup; London: Humphrey Milford; Oxford: University Press, 1920. 8vo., original quarter vellum, plain boards, manuscript spine title, ink ownership signatures of Alexandri Phili (192), William Duane Stahlman and David C. Lindberg.   Jeff Weber Rare Books   178 - 846   2015 $45

Association – Pius V, Pope

Johannes Chrysotomus   *Enarratio in Esaiam Prophetam.* (bound with) *Conciones in Celebrioribus Aliquot Anni Festivitatibus Habitae.* (bound with) *Homiliae in Aliquot Veteris Testamenti Loca.*   Antverpiae: in Aedibus Ioan. Seelsii, 1555. 1553. 1553, 165 x 105mm., 3 separately published works bound in one volume, splendid armorial red Roman morocco done for Pope Pius V by Niccolo Franzese, covers gilt with papal arms in central cartouche, front cover with "Pivs V" above arms and initials "P.M." (Pontifex Maximus) below, back cover with "Io Chrys in Esa et Hom" in gilt above and "P.M." below, boards framed by a profusion of acanthus leaves emanating from the brass bosses at corners and with a background stamped with small floral and dot tools, raised bands, spine compartments with interwoven gilt vines and gilt titling, remnants of clasps, all edges gilt and gauffered in pink floral pattern and with Pius' name tooled into head and tail edges and his arms painted on the fore edge (apparently with very expert repairs at spine ends), titlepage with printer's device, bookplate of Carlo Ponzone di Casale and with ink inscription of Ch. Al. Ganora dated 1867, titlepage with ink inscription of a Capuchin convent, hinge separation at first titlepage, majority of the leaves with minor browning (a half dozen gatherings rather browned), other trivial defects but text unsoiled and consistently fresh, front joint with two-inch crack near bottom, leather on spine bit crackled, gilt lost in small area next to one box, but sumptuously decorated binding still quite lustrous showing little wear, and altogether pleasing.   Phillip J. Pirages   66 - 18   2015 $17,500

Association – Planche, James Robinson

Carter, Matthew *Honor Rediviuus (sic) or an Analysis of Honor and Armory.* London: by E(llen) Coates, 1655. First edition, one of two issues, 8vo., engraved frontispiece, 7 etched portraits, numerous armorial woodcuts with four in contemporary hand color, possibly a thick paper copy, some light foxing and occasional staining, contemporary calf, covers ruled in gilt, expertly rebacked, covers worn, chipped especially at corners and edges, mid 19th century endleaves, presentation by author to William Dugdale (1605-1686), the copy of James Robinson Planche (17696-1880) with bookplate, from the library of James Stevens Cox (1910-1997). Maggs Bros. Ltd. 1447 - 66 2015 £3200

Association – Plath, Aurelia

Millay, Edna St. Vincent 1892-1950 *The King's Henchman.* New York and London: Harper & Bros., 1927. First trade edition, early printing, octavo, original black cloth over paper boards, ownership and presentation inscriptions of Aurelia Plath, her ownership inscription (Aurelia Schober, later Plath), inscribed by her for daughter, Sylvia Plath, bookplate of Sylvia Plath inscribed with her name and dated 1950, occasional underlining and marginal notes, no dust jacket, later ink annotations suggest that Aurelia Plath picked up this copy after her daughter's suicide in 1963, exceptional association. Honey & Wax Booksellers 3 - 24 2015 $9500

Association – Plath, Sylvia

Millay, Edna St. Vincent 1892-1950 *The King's Henchman.* New York and London: Harper & Bros., 1927. First trade edition, early printing, octavo, original black cloth over paper boards, ownership and presentation inscriptions of Aurelia Plath, her ownership inscription (Aurelia Schober, later Plath), inscribed by her for daughter, Sylvia Plath, bookplate of Sylvia Plath inscribed with her name and dated 1950, occasional underlining and marginal notes, no dust jacket, later ink annotations suggest that Aurelia Plath picked up this copy after her daughter's suicide in 1963, exceptional association. Honey & Wax Booksellers 3 - 24 2015 $9500

Association – Plomley, Roy

Powell, Michael *200,000 Feet on Foula: the Edge of the World.* London: Faber and Faber, 1938. First edition, inscribed by Powell for Roy Plomley 1942, near fine in very good dust jacket. Royal Books 46 - 4 2015 $4250

Association – Pohl, Frederick

O'Neill, Brian *Easter Week.* New York: International, 1939. First edition, wrappers, near fine, Frederick Pohl's copy with his signature. Beasley Books 2013 - 2015 $45

Association – Poliannovsky, Miriam

Dostoevskii, Fyodor Mikhailovich 1821-1881 *The Grand Inquisitor.* London: Elkin Matthews, 1930. First edition, limited to 300 numbered copies, this no. 267, 4to., original ultra modernist decorated pigskin, lettered black on spine and front cover, signed presentation from S. S. Koteliansky for Raphael Salaman (1906-1993 and wife Miriam Polianovsky, very faint surface soiling, otherwise fine in sound, used slipcases, excellent copy. Any Amount of Books 2015 - C11380 2015 £225

Association – Polwarth, Lord

Buchanan, George 1506-1582 *Octupla; hoc est Octo Paraphrases Poeticae Psalmi CIV.* Edinburgh: Excudebant Haeredes & Successores Andreae Anderson, 1696. One of two reissues, 8vo., contemporary sprinkled panelled calf, spine with gilt crowned orange device of the Earl of Marchmont (joints cracking, spine rubbed), bound for Patrick Hume, 1st Earl of Marchmont, 1641-1724, signature of Lord Polwarth, from the library of James Stevens Cox (1910-1997). Maggs Bros. Ltd. 1447 - 55 2015 £280

Association – Polya, George

Weyl, Hermann *Gruppentheorie and Quatenmechanik.* Leipzig: S. Hirzel, 1931. Second edition, large 8vo., original maroon reddish gilt stamped cloth, bookplate and signature of G(eorge) Polya (1887-1985), near fine. Jeff Weber Rare Books 178 - 1139 2015 $175

Association – Ponzone di Casale, Carlo

Johannes Chrysotomus *Enarratio in Esaiam Prophetam. (bound with) Conciones in Celebrioribus Aliquot Anni Festivitatibus Habitae. (bound with) Homiliae in Aliquot Veteris Testamenti Loca.* Antverpiae: in Aedibus Ioan. Seelsii, 1555. 1553. 1553, 165 x 105mm., 3 separately published works bound in one volume, splendid armorial red Roman morocco done for Pope Pius V by Niccolo Franzese, covers gilt with papal arms in central cartouche, front cover with "Pivs V" above arms and initials "P.M." (Pontifex Maximus) below, back cover with "Io Chrys in Esa et Hom" in gilt above and "P.M." below, boards framed by a profusion of acanthus leaves emanating from the brass bosses at corners and with a background stamped with small floral and dot tools, raised bands, spine compartments with interwoven gilt vines and gilt titling, remnants of clasps, all edges gilt and gauffered in pink floral pattern and with Pius' name tooled into head and tail edges and his arms painted on the fore edge (apparently with very expert repairs at spine ends), titlepage with printer's device, bookplate of Carlo Ponzone di Casale and with ink inscription of Ch. Al. Ganora dated 1867, titlepage with ink inscription of a Capuchin convent, hinge separation at first titlepage, majority of the leaves with minor browning (a half dozen gatherings rather browned), other trivial defects but text unsoiled and consistently fresh, front joint with two-inch crack near bottom, leather on spine bit crackled, gilt lost in small area next to one box, but sumptuously decorated binding still quite lustrous showing little wear, and altogether pleasing. Phillip J. Pirages 66 - 18 2015 $17,500

Association – Pope, S. A.

Browne, Thomas 1605-1682 *Hyrdriotaphia, Urne Buriall or a Discourse of the Sepulchral Urnes Lately found in Norfolk...* London: printed for Hen(rey) Brome, 1658. First edition, 8vo., lacking errata leaf found in some copies, titlepage lightly soiled, spotted, some occasional light foxing, 19th century olive morocco by Ramage, gilt edges, few minor chips to spine, 19th century pencil notes in margins, early 20th century signature S. A. Pope, from the library of James Stevens Cox (1910-1997). Maggs Bros. Ltd. 1447 - 54 2015 £1200

Association – Porter, Bern

Dunbar, Margaret *Bern! Porter! Interview! Conducted by Margaret Dunbar.* N.P.: Dog Ear Press, n.d., First edition, octavo, illustrations, stiff wrappers, front wrapper with one interior tape mend, covers lightly rubbed, else near fine, inscribed by Porter, but unsigned to noted scholar Bertrand Mathieu, Belfast 6.24.90, few annotations by Mathieu in text, five APS's from Porter to Mathieu dated from May 29 1990 to June 25 1991 laid in. Between the Covers Rare Books, Inc. 187 - 218 2015 $375

Association – Portsmouth, Earl of

Campbell, John 1779-1861 *Speeches of Lord Campbell at the Bar and in the House of Commons with an Address to the Irish Bar as Lord Chancellor of Ireland.* Edinburgh: Adam and Charles Black, 1842. 8vo., little foxing of early leaves later 19th century polished calf gilt, raised bands and crimson label, top edge gilt, others uncut, joints worn, still handsome copy, bookplate and inscription "The Early of Portsmouth, Hurstbourne Park Library 1880". John Drury Rare Books March 2015 - 17815 2015 $221

Horsley, Samuel *The Speeches in Parliament of Samuel Horsley....* Dundee: printed by Robert Stephen Rintoul for James Chalmers, 1813. 8vo., half title, prelim leaves lightly foxed, later 19th century polished calf gilt with raised bands, crimson label, top edge gilt, others uncut, fine, from the library of the Earl of Portsmouth, Hurstbourne Park Library. John Drury Rare Books March 2015 - 17809 2015 $221

Huskisson, William *The Speeches of the Right Honourable William Huskisson with a Biographical Memoir...* London: John Murray, 1831. First collected edition, 3 volumes, 8vo., frontispiece in volume I, half titles in volumes II and III, 19th century polished calf gilt with raised bands and contrasting labels, top edge gilt, others uncut, fine, from the 19th century library of the Earl of Portsmouth, with inscription. John Drury Rare Books March 2015 - 17808 2015 £306

Sheil, Richard Lalor *The Speeches of the Right Honourable Richard Lalor Sheil, M.P., with Memoir &c.* Dublin: James Duffy, 1845. First collected edition, 8vo., later 19th century full polished calf, gilt, with raised bands and crimson label, top edge gilt, others uncut, slight wear to upper joint, else fine, form the 19th century library of Earl of Portsmouth with his armorial bookplate and inscription "Earl of Portsmouth Hurstbourne Park Library 1880" on flyleaf. John Drury Rare Books 2015 - 17816 2015 $221

Association – Posner, David

Jarrell, Randall *The Woman at the Washington Zoo Poems & Translations.* New York: Atheneum, 1960. First edition, 8vo., original cloth, dust jacket, fine in lightly worn dust jacket, presentation copy inscribed by author for David Posner. James S. Jaffe Rare Books Modern American Poetry - 149 2015 $2500

Association – Post, Alice Thacher

Jacobi, Mary Putnam *Life and Letters of...* New York: G. P. Putnam's Sons, 1925. First edition, 8vo., stain on pastedown offset from earlier insert, old paperclip stain on endpaper, very good, label on spine very worn, this copy belonged to Alice Thacher Post with her name and address. Second Life Books Inc. 189 - 135 2015 $125

Association – Post, Josephine Fowler

Young, Rose *The Record of the Leslie Woman Suffrage Commission Inc. 1917-1929.* Leslie Commission, 1929. First edition, small 8vo., 94 pages, little soiled, very good inscribed by Carrie Chapman Catt for Josephine Fowler Post.   Second Life Books Inc.   189 - 52   2015 $600

Association – Potter, J. W. S.

Sharpe, James Birch *The Gregorian Oration Delivered Before the Literary, Scientific and Mechanics' Institution of Windsor and Eton, September 1841.* London: Shaw and Sons, 1841. First edition, 8vo.,4 2 pages, sometime in Norwich City library (bookplate and small inkstamp on flyleaf and lower margin of couple of leaves), contemporary green calf, spine fully gilt with raised bands, slight wear to extremities, very good, presentation copy inscribed in ink by author to Mr. J. W. S. Potter, apparently rare.   John Drury Rare Books   2015 - 25557   2015 $168

Association – Potter, William Allen

Great Britian. War Office - 1811 *A List of the Officers of the Local Militia of Great Britain 1811.* London: printed by C. Roworth for the War Office, 30th September, 1811. 8vo., contemporary red morocco with triple gilt borders to spines, flat spine gilt in compartments with Catherine wheel tools and a green morocco lettering piece, inner gilt dentelles and all edges gilt, handsome copy in fine, early 19th century binding, later armorial bookplate of William Allen Potter.   John Drury Rare Books   2015 - 21575   2015 $1049

Association – Preminger, Otto

Moore, Robin *The Country Team.* New York: Crown, 1967. First edition, very good in like dust jacket, rubbed with moderate age wear, inscribed by author to film director Otto Preminger.   Ken Lopez, Bookseller   164 - 231   2015 $125

Association – Preston, Priscilla

Duke, Arthur *The Larke: a Seventeenth Century Poem Ascribed to Dr. Arthur Duke.* London: privately printed in the Department of English at the University College London, 1934. original blue printed wrappers, slightly faded and creased, printed by Geoffrey Tillotson on departmental hand press, inscribed by him to Kathleen Tillotson, inserted is ALS from Priscilla (Preston) to Kathleen.   Jarndyce Antiquarian Booksellers   CCVII - 251   2015   £60

Association – Prevost, Anne Elinor

Harrington, Leicester Fitzgerald Charles Stanhope, 5th Earl of *Greece in 1823 and 1824; Being a Series of letters, and Other Documents on the Greek Revolution, Written during a Visit to that Country...* London: Sherwood Jones and Co., 1824. First edition, 8vo., hand colored frontispiece, 6 facsimiles of documents, contemporary calf, neatly rebacked and labelled to match, gilt lines and lettering, tips of boards worn, mid 19th century armorial bookplate of Anne Elinor Prevost, very good.   John Drury Rare Books   2015 - 23839   2015 $1136

Association – Prevost, Marcel

Proust, Marcel 1871-1922 *A la Recherche du Temps Perdu.* Paris: Bernard Grasset (volume 1), 1913. Librairie Gallimard, Nouvelle revue Francaise (volumes II-XIII) 1918-1927, First edition, 13 volumes, octavo, original wrapper, original glassine, inscribed to fellow writer Marcel Prevost, dedicatee, extraordinary copy.   Honey & Wax Booksellers   2 - 25   2015 $65,000

Association – Price, Charles

Badham, Charles David *The Question concerning the sensibility, Intelligence and Instinctive Actions of Insects by Scarabaeus.* Paris: printed by A. Belin n.d., 1837. First edition, 8vo., with final blank leaf, original upper wrapper preserved, little dust marked, holograph presentation inscription in ink from author to Dr. Charles Price.   John Drury Rare Books   2015 - 15141   2015 $133

Association – Price, Reynolds

Gibbons, Kaye *One the Occasion of My Last Afternoon.* New York: G. P. Putnam's Sons, 1998. First edition, small bump bottom rear board, else fine in fine dust jacket, inscribed by author for Reynolds Price July 1 1998.   Between the Covers Rare Books, Inc.   187 - 108   2015 $350

Linney, Romulus *Heathen Valley.* New York: Atheneum, 1962. First edition, fine, lacking dust jacket, inscribed by author for Reynolds Price.   Between the Covers Rare Books, Inc.   187 - 157   2015 $300

Murray, Albert *South to a Very Old Place.* New York: Modern Library, 1995. First Modern Library edition, fine in fine dust jacket, inscribed by author to writer Reynolds Price.   Between the Covers Rare Books, Inc.   187 - 187   2015 $200

Schiff, James A. *Updike's Version: Rewriting the Scarlet Letter.* Columbia: University of Missouri Press, 1992. First edition, fine in fine dust jacket, inscribed by author to Reynolds Price. Between the Covers Rare Books, Inc. 187 - 245 2015 $125

Association – Price, Thomas

Wotton, Henry *Reliquiae Wottonianae; or a Collection of Lives, Letters, Poems...* London: By T. Roycroft for R. Marriott, 1672. Third edition, portraits, 19th century red morocco, early signatures of J. Grien? 1725, Thomas Price and John Francis Cole 1828, bookplates of J. J. Chapman and Molly Flagg Gibb, very good. Joseph J. Felcone Inc. Science, Medicine and Technology - 57 2015 $900

Association – Pritchett, Dorothy

Pritchett, V. S. *Dead Man Leading.* London: Oxford University Press, 1984. First edition with this introduction by Paul Theroux, wrappers, somewhat browned throughout and some leaves loose, otherwise nice, dedication copy, inscribed by author for wife Dorothy, from author's library with posthumous VSP booklabel, from the collection of Gavin H. Fryer. Bertram Rota Ltd. 308 Part II - 224 2015 £100

Pritchett, V. S. *Dublin: a Portrait.* London: Bodley Head, 1947. First edition, 4to., original binding, fine in creased and torn dust jacket with piece missing, photos in color and black and white by Evelyn Hofer, presentation copy inscribed by author to his wife, Dorothy, with posthumous VSP booklabel, from the collection of Gavin H. Fryer. Bertram Rota Ltd. 308 Part II - 192 2015 £140

Pritchett, V. S. *In My Good Books.* London: Chatto & Windus, 1942. First edition, original binding, spine and covers somewhat marked and worn, hinges weak, otherwise very good, dedication copy inscribed to author's wife, with posthumous VSP booklabel, from the collection of Gavin H. Fryer. Bertram Rota Ltd. 308 Part II - 189 2015 £350

Pritchett, V. S. *It May Never Happen & Other Stories.* London: Chatto & Windus, 1946. First edition, original binding, covers marked, dedication copy, inscribed by author to his wife, posthumous VSP bookplate, from the collection of Gavin H. Fryer. Bertram Rota Ltd. 308 Part II - 190 2015 £350

Pritchett, V. S. *London Perceived.* London: Chatto & Windus and William Heinemann, 1962. First English edition, 4to., photos by Evelyn Hofer, original binding, dust jacket creased, worn, repaired dust jacket for the American edition and cardboard slipcase, presentation copy inscribed by author to his wife, Dorothy, from author's library with posthumous VSP booklabel, from the collection of Gavin H. Fryer. Bertram Rota Ltd. 308 Part II - 199 2015 £160

Pritchett, V. S. *Midnight Oil.* New York: Random House, 1972. First American edition, original binding, edges of covers faded, else very nice in creased and soiled dust jacket, dedication copy inscribed by author for wife Dorothy, from author's library with posthumous VSP booklabel, from the collection of Gavin H. Fryer. Bertram Rota Ltd. 308 Part II - 212 2015 £200

Pritchett, V. S. *On the Edge of the Cliff and Other Stories.* London: Chatto & Windus, 1980. First edition, original binding, fine in dust jacket, dedication copy inscribed by author to his wife, Dorothy, with his autograph signature on titlepage, from author's library with posthumous VSP booklabel, from the collection of Gavin H. Fryer. Bertram Rota Ltd. 308 Part II - 220 2015 £150

Pritchett, V. S. *The Turn of the Years.* Wilton: Michael Russell, 1982. First edition in book form, one of 150 numbered copies, signed by author and Paul Theroux (provided introduction), original binding, fine, presentation copy inscribed by author for wife Dorothy, from author's library with posthumous VSP booklabel, from the collection of Gavin H. Fryer. Bertram Rota Ltd. 308 Part II - 222 2015 £150

Association – Pritchett, V. S.

O'Connor, Frank 1903-1966 *Guests of the Nation: Stories.* London: Macmillan & Co. Ltd., 1931. First edition, original binding, covers faded and marked, endpapers somewhat browned, very good, publisher's review slip tipped in and loosely inserted, V. S. Pritchett's copy, inscribed by him, from the collection of Gavin H. Fryer. Bertram Rota Ltd. 308 Part II - 185 2015 £120

Turgenev, Ivan Sergeevich 1818-1883 *The Torrents of Spring.* London: Hamish Hamilton, 1960. New edition, imperial 8vo., illustrations in color and black and white by Robin Jacques, original binding, top edge gilt, others uncut, fine in original glassine dust jacket and pictorial slipcase, from the library of V. S. Pritchett, with posthumous VSP booklabel, from the collection of Gavin H. Fryer. Bertram Rota Ltd. 308 Part II - 227 2015 £40

Association – Proctor, William Beauchamp

Whaley, John *A Collection of Original Poems and Translations.* London: printed for the author and sold by R. Manby and H. S. cox, 1745. First edition, 8vo., contemporary marbled calf, gilt, spine gilt, red morocco label, just trifle rubbed, wanting flyleaf, else fine, with early armorial bookplate of Sir William Beauchamp Proctor (1722-1773) of Langley Park in Norfolk, recent signature of Margaret Morgan. C. R. Johnson Foxon R-Z - 1129-r-z 2015 $613

Association – Pryce-Jones, Alan

Frost, Robert Lee   1874-1963   *In the Clearing.*   New York: Holt, Rinehart and Winston, 1962. First edition, slightly rubbed bottom of boards, near fine in like dust jacket with little rubbing, bookplate of author Alan Pryce-Jones.   Between the Covers Rare Books, Inc.   187 - 102   2015 $125

Association – Pulsford, Mrs.

MacDonald, George   1824-1905   *Dealings with the Fairies.*   London: Alexander Strahan and Co., 1868. Second edition, 16mo., half title, frontispiece and plates by Arthur Hughes, 4 pages ads (Dec. 1867), few marks, original green cloth, blocked in black and gilt, slightly dulled, small split in leading hinge, all edges gilt, inscribed presentation from author for Mrs. Pulsford.   Jarndyce Antiquarian Booksellers   CCXI - 189   2015   £2250

Association – Purdy, Richard Little

Gray, Thomas   1716-1771   *Poems by Mr. Gray.*   London: printed for J. Murray, 1778. illustrations, full tan calf with raised bands, gilt spine decorations and maroon leather spine label, small bookplate of Yale Professor and Hardy scholar, Richard Little Purdy, very good, little rubbing to board edges, tight clean text.   Stephen Lupack   March 2015 - 2015 $150

Association – Purnell, James

Balmford, William   *The Seaman's Spiritual Companion or Navigation Spiritualized.*   London: for Benj. Harris, 1678. First edition, small 8vo., variant state of title with double rule border and price on titlepage, A2 shaved at foot affecting signature and catchword on recto, minor worming in upper outer corner of D4-K8 (affecting end of text in places), stain to B3-E2 affecting three lines, occasional foxing, small hole from paper flaw in lower margin of E2, short tear at foot of F3 slightly affecting last line on recto and catchword on verso, small hole from paper flaw in centre of I2 touching two lines, actually reasonable and much loved copy, contemporary sheep (rubbed, covers scuffed, fore edge of lower cover worn exposing board, corners worn), several pen trials, scribbles, ownership inscriptions John Allab(on) His Booke October ye 24th 16, Charles Canning his book 1679, James Purnell His Booke Anno Domini (deleted), "Thomas Nichols His Book May ye 10 1718", "James Croome His Book March ye 9th 1757" "Jane Hanley", from the library of James Stevens Cox (1910-1997).   Maggs Bros. Ltd.   1447 - 21   2015   £2800

Association – Purves-Hume-Campbell, William, 6th Baronet

Lambert, Anne Therese De Marguenat De Courcelles, Marchioness De   *Reflexions Nouvelles sur Les Femmes...*   Londres: Paris or The Hague? Chez J. P. Coderc in Little New-port Street, 1730. First edition, 12mo., title printed in red and black engraved armorial bookplate "Sir William Purves-Hume-Campbell" (6th Baronet 1767-1833), early mottled calf, rubbed along extremities, very nice clean copy, with errata slip.   Second Life Books Inc.   189 - 150   2015 $2200

Association – Putman, Charles

Tomlins, Thomas Edlyne   *The Law-Dictionary; Retaining the Rise, Progress and Present state of the British Law...*   London: 1820. Third edition, full brown calf, quarto, 2 volumes, both repaired with modern brown calf spine with black and red spine labels, new calf corners, front and rear endpapers have been replaced and half title to volume I missing, this is Andrew Rainsford Wetmore's copy with his signature to inner margins of titlepage of both volumes, presented to him by his uncle Charles P. Wetmore with his signature stating that they were presented to him from Ralph Ketchum July 1853, it appears the original owner was Charles Putnam.   Schooner Books Ltd.   110 - 28   2015 $275

Association – Putnam, George Haven

Browne, Albert G.   "The Growing Power of the Public of Chile." in Bulletin of the American Geographical Society 1884. No. 1.   New York: printed for the Society, 1884. First edition, small 4to., paper wrappers, inscribed by author to publisher George Haven Putnam, rear wrapper with small repaired tear, else contents fine and unopened, uncut.   Kaaterskill Books   19 - 27   2015 $100

Association – Pym, Barbara

Betjeman, John   1906-1984   *Continual Dew.*   London: Murray, 1937. First edition, printed on pale blue paper, 4 leaves printed on tissue paper in black and red also present, illustrations, signatures strained, 8vo., original black cloth stamped in gilt to front with clasp decoration overlapping onto backstrip, backstrip worn and corners rubbed, all edges gilt foxing to rear free endpaper, sound, from the library of Barbara Pym, signed and dated by Pym, footnote in her hand, 2 further Betjeman poems written out by Pym on blanks at rear.   Blackwell's Rare Books   B179 - 224   2015   £950

Association – Quayle, Eric

Busby, Thomas *The Cries of London. Drawn from Life.* London: Artists' Depository, 21 Charlotte Fitzroy Square and by Simpkin and Marshall..., 1823. First edition, separate engraved pictorial title coloured by hand, 23 hand coloured engraved plates, later half green morocco over marbled boards by Tout, green silk marker, all edges gilt, 16.8 x 10.5cm., bookplate of noted collector Eric Quayle. Marlborough Rare Books   List 53 - 6   2015   £3250

Johns, Joseph *St. George and the Dragon; England and the Drink Traffic.* London: S. W. Partridge, 1907. First edition, half title, frontispiece, illustrations, paper browning, original blue cloth, spine slightly dulled with small mark at foot, booklabel of Eric Quayle on leading pastedown, bright copy.   Jarndyce Antiquarian Booksellers   CCXI - 163   2015   £45

Association – Quick, A. S.

Boyle, Robert 1627-1691 *Some Motives and Incentives to the love of God, pathetically Discorus'd of in a Letter to a friend.* London: for Henry Herringman, 1665. Fourth edition, title browned by turn-ins, one or two wormholes in lower margin, extending to a short trail from C4 to D3 each leaf throughout, H2 trimmed along lower edge, small piece torn away and a close tear I3 (touching text), 8vo., contemporary sheep (heavily worn and scuffed, upper joint split but holding, headcaps missing, pastedowns unstuck torn and stained by turn-ins), from the library of James Stevens Cox (1910-1997), 19th century bookplate William Warren, Bristol, signature A. S. Quick 17 may 1883, number of pencil markings by him.   Maggs Bros. Ltd.   1447 - 44   2015   £150

Association – Quine, W. V. O.

Popper, Karl R. *Objective Knowledge. An Evolutionary Approach.* Oxford: Clarendon Press, 1972. First edition, octavo, inscribed by author to W. V. O. Quine, original dark grey cloth with gilt lettering to spine, bright blue dust jacket with white and black lettering, near fine with just most minor nicks and signs and very slight amount of sunning to spine, preserved in custom clamshell box.   Athena Rare Books 15 - 53   2015 $1800

Association – Quinn, John

Cannan, Gilbert *The Joy of The Theatre.* New York: E. P. Dutton, 1913. First American edition, stamp on front fly, releasing the book from a library, but with no other library markings and corners little rubbed, near fine, bookplate of lawyer and collector John Quinn.   Between the Covers Rare Books, Inc.   187 - 42   2015 $65

Association – Rackham, Arthur

Grimm, The Brothers *Fairy Tales of the Brothers Grimm.* London: Constable, 1909. Limited to 750 copies signed by Rackham, large thick 4to., 325 pages, full vellum with gilt decorations, slight bit of rubbing and soil, else near fine with silk ties, 40 fabulous tipped in color plates with guards plus a profusion of full page and smaller black and whites, 5 inch pen drawing signed by Rackham on half title, extremely rare thus.   Aleph-bet Books, Inc.   109 - 397   2015 $15,000

Association – Raines, Isaac

Cooke, James *Mellificium Chirurgiae or the Marrow of Many Good Authors.* London: for Samuel Cartwright, 1648. First edition, 12mo., upper fore corners of B6-7 and P5 torn from paper flaws (affecting rule border not touching text), some worming in inner margin (heavily between Q5-R11), contemporary sheep ruled in blind (rubbed, 30mm piece torn at head of spine, a number of loose gatherings, bumped and rubbed, pastedowns unstuck), early ink initials "E K", late 18th century signature Isaac Webster/Hull, signature Isaac Raines 1802, by descent to Rev. George Francis Twycross-Raines, vicar and antiquary of Hull, with ink inscription, of "H. Page from his old friend G. F. Twycross-Raines Sept. 11, 1911", from the library of James Stevens Cox (1910-1997).   Maggs Bros. Ltd.   1447 - 114   2015   £750

Association – Ramsay, J.

Bright, Henry Arthur *Free Blacks and Slaves. Would Immediate Abolition be a Blessing?* London: Athur Hall Virtue and Co., 1853. First edition, 8vo., recently well bound in linen backed marbled boards lettered, very good, inscribed in ink "J. Ramsay with author's kind regards". John Drury Rare Books   2015 - 18038   2015 $168

Association – Randall, Margaret

Ferlinghetti, Lawrence *The Mexican Night: Travel Journal.* New York: New Directions, 1970. First edition, trade paperback, very near fine in pictorial wrappers, inscribed by author to fellow poet Margaret Randall, 9 21 78. Between the Covers Rare Books, Inc.   187 - 95   2015 $300

Association – Raney, William

Kelley, William Melvin *A Different Drummer.* Garden City: Doubleday, 1962. First edition, 8vo., author's presentation for William Raney, also author's correction on contents page, paper over boards, cloth spine, very good, tight copy in little scuffed and soiled dust jacket.   Second Life Books Inc.   190 - 143   2015 $225

Association – Ranfurly, Diana Jane, Countes of

Diodorus Siculus *The History of Diodorus Siculus.* London: by John Macock for Giles Calvert, 1653. First edition in English, small folio, longitudinal half title has been cut-out leaving a stub, 271 pages, small circular stain in inner margins of first few leaves and Kk4-L12, rust spot on Kk4, contemporary sheep, smooth spine ruled in blind and with red morocco and gilt label, covers heavily scuffed, piece missing from top corner of lower cover, upper headcap torn, front pastedown torn away at head, early inscription on flyleaf heavily deleted, early signature Nic. Hare, signature on title Edm. Sex. Pery, 1st and last Viscount Pery (1719-1806) by descent to his elder daughter Diana Jane, Countess of Ranfurly to Earls of Ranfurly, with 19th century bookplate, from the library of James Stevens Cox (1910-1997).   Maggs Bros. Ltd.   1447 - 148   2015   £380

Association – Rankin, Miss

Clough, Arthur Hugh *Letters and Remains.* London: Spottiswoode & Co., 1865. Half title, original green patterned cloth, inner hinges rather crudely strengthened, presented to Miss Rankin , sent by her to Joseph Hutton 1888, signed by Geoffrey Tillotson 12.v.47.   Jarndyce Antiquarian Booksellers   CCVII - 141   2015   £40

Association – Ransom, John Crowe

Stevens, Wallace 1879-1955 *Notes Toward a Supreme Fiction.* Cummington: Cummington Press, 1942. Limited first edition, octavo, 45 pages, this copy out of series and marked as a reviewer's copy, this copy belonged to Fugitive poet John Crowe Ransom, then editor of Kenyon Review. Honey & Wax Booksellers   1 - 37   2015 $1500

Association – Rapoport, Kenneth

Plato *(Greek text) Omnia Platonis Opera.* Venice: in aedib. Aldi et Andreae Soceri, Sept, 1513. Editio princeps, 2 volumes, large Aldine anchor device on titlepage (volume i) and on verso of last leaf in volume ii, Greek text (apart from Aldus' dedicatory petition, contents and colophon), titlepage slightly soiled and with hole at inner margin repaired, minor stains on fore-edges, few wormholes in blank lower margin of opening leaves of volumes ii, volume, volume i in contemporary English quartered oak boards, resewn with spine uncovered, modern vellum endleaves, volume ii in contemporary German pigskin over wooden boards, blind tooled to panel design filled in with 'laus deo' and rosette stamps, brass catches and clasps, top of spine worn, inner hinge broken, cord intact, good, binding of the first volume of this copy is subject of 2 page report by Nicholas Pickwoad (printout accompanies the volume), repairs carried out by James Brockman; first volume with signature of Thomas Colm of Oxford dated 1573, 17th century ownership inscription of Hendricus Ffeild, 19th century bookplate and stamp of King Edward's School, Birmingham, plus bookplate of Kenneth Rapoport, the second volume with early ownership inscriptions of Johannes (or Johann?) Lang of Erfurt and Philippus Kleissenius, few early marginalia, inscription 'de bibliotheca Johannis Langi Erphurdiensis.   Blackwell's Rare Books   Greek & Latin Classics VI - 82   2015   £75,000

Polybius *Historiarum Libri Priores Quinque.* Lugduni: Seb. Gryphium, 1554. 178 x 108mm., pleasing contemporary (English?) calf, covers with single gilt fillet border and intricate arabesque centerpiece, raised bands, spine panels with central azured gilt fleur-de-lys or floral spring, apparently original morocco label (perhaps, but perhaps not - with very expert repairs at spine ends), publisher's woodcut griffin device on title and last page, 18th century? engraved armorial bookplate of Sir William Baird and modern bookplate of Kenneth Rapoport, titlepage with early ownership signature of Franciscus T.... (now washed away and consequently very faint), occasional contemporary underlinings and manicules, joints rubbed (and with thin cracks alongside top spine panel on upper and lower joint and along bottom two spine panels on upper joint), lower cover with minor discoloration (perhaps from damp), other trivial defects, binding entirely solid, still quite lustrous and with nothing approaching a major condition problem, without front free endpaper, n3 with branching tear (paper flaw?) from margin into text necessitating, (old) repair, but without loss, isolated faint browning, other small imperfections, but really consistently very fresh and clean, very well preserved, attractive mid 16th century binding.   Phillip J. Pirages   66 - 14   2015 $3200

Association – Rathbone, Theodore

Bates, Henry Walter *The Naturalist on the River Amazon...* London: John Murray, 1863. First edition, 2 volumes, 8vo., original brown cloth lettered gilt on spines and front covers, illustrations, final fold missing from map, browned, chipped at torn edges, ownership signature of Theodore Rathbone and circulating library plates mounted on rear endpapers, top margin of titlepage on volume one torn, edges rough and some leaves loose, rebacked with original spines laid down, inner hinges rubbed and cracked with some foxing to prelims, otherwise good, somewhat used copy. Any Amount of Books 2015 - C14402 2015 £280

Association – Ravensworth, Thomas Henry Liddell, 1st Baron

Sotheby, William *A Tour Through Parts of Wales.* London: printed by J. Smeeton for R. Blamire, 1794. First edition, 295 x 229mm, extremely handsome dark blue straight grain morocco, elaborately decorated in gilt and blind by Lubbock of Newcastle (their ticket on front free endpaper), covers with intricate frame in gilt and blind (featuring stippling, fleurons, drawer handles, wreaths, etc.), large central panel of an unusual design with blind stamped lozenge at center and horizontal blindstamped boards above and below, all enclosed by double gilt fillets (to form a large "I" with a convex vertical element) raised bands, space panels with gilt or blind tooled fleurons, wide densely gilt turn-ins with inlaid red morocco cornerpieces, marbled endpapers, all edges gilt, with modern fore-edge painting showing three landscape vignettes, castle ruins, an arched bridge, and a castle by the sea, surrounded by colored volutes, fruits and cornucopia, 13 sepia tone engravings of Welsh castles and scenery after J. Smith, front pastedown with engraved armorial bookplate of Ravensworth Castle, titlepage with ink ownership inscription of T. H. Liddell, this the copy of (and most likely bound for) Thomas Henry Liddell, 1st Baron Ravensworth; corners and extremities little rubbed joints slightly flaked, but well masked with dye, faint offsetting from engravings, otherwise fine copy, binding lustrous and without significant wear and text and plates with only most trivial imperfections. Phillip J. Pirages 66 - 56 2015 $6500

Association – Rawlett, John

Wemys, Thomas *Beth-Hak-Kodesh, or the Separation and Conservation of Places in God's Public Service and Worship and the Reverence due unto them Vindicated.* London: printed for Thomas Dring at the Harrow over against the inner Temple gate in Fleet Street, 1674. First and only edition, 12mo., with initial imprimatur leaf (A1), wormtracks affect lower margins throughout occasionally with loss of single letter of text, small tear in margin of leaf F4 with loss of single letter on recto, contemporary sheep, unlettered, spine and corners rather worn but sound from the 17th century library of John Rawlett with his signature, scarce. John Drury Rare Books 2015 - 23670 2015 $1136

Association – Rawlinson, S. C.

Lang, Andrew *Ballads of Books.* London: Longmans, 1885. First edition, half title, title in red and black, uncut in original blue bevelled boards, spine slightly faded, cutting removed from endpaper, ticket of Slatter & Rose, Oxford, top edge gilt, signed by S. C. Rawlinson 1889 and with 3 related ms. insertions, from the library of Geoffrey & Kathleen Tillotson. Jarndyce Antiquarian Booksellers CCVII - 355 2015 £85

Association – Ray, Dee

Bryers, Duane *The Bunkhouse Boys from the Lazy Daisy Ranch.* Flagstaff: Northland Press, 1974. First edition, 4to., fine in fine dust jacket, artist has penned portrait of a cowboy on f.e.p. and he and Dee Ray have inscribed this copy. Beasley Books 2013 - 2015 $150

Association – Ray, Joseph

Fischer, E. S. *Elements of Natural Philosophy.* Boston: Hilliard, Gray, Little and Wilkins, 1827. First American edition, quarter cloth, gilt and paper covered boards, dampstain tidemarks on some pages, most pronounced in final quarter of book, one corner of boards worn through, still tight, very good, ownership signature of Joseph Ray, professor of mathematics. Between the Covers Rare Books, Inc. 187 - 97 2015 $375

Association – Rayner, Richard

Ford, Richard *The Sportswriter.* London: Collins Harvill, 1986. First UK edition, 8vo., signed by Richard Rayner, review copy with slip, fine in fine dust jacket. Any Amount of Books 2015 - A97053 2015 £160

Association – Rayner, William

Bacon, Francis, Viscount St. Albans 1561-1626 *Historia Vitae et Mortis.* Amsterdam: Joannem Ravesteinium, 1663. Fifth separate edition, 12mo., contemporary mottled calf covers ruled in gilt, rebacked, new endleaves, old flyleaves preserved, inscription "Guil Rayner Aedis Ch. Alummus 1683" (William Rayner of London 1664-1730), signature of W. Leigh, from the library of James Stevens Cox (1910-1997). Maggs Bros. Ltd. 1447 - 17 2015 £120

Association – Rea, James

Chaucer, Geoffrey 1340-1400 *The Workes of Geffrey Chaucer.* London: imprinted by Jhon Kyngston for John Wight, 1561. First collected edition, first issue, 22 woodcuts in The Prologues, folio, title within woodcut border, 22 woodcuts of Pilgrims in "The Prologues" and woodcut of knight on horse at head of "The Knightes Tale", large and small historiated and decorative initials and other ornaments, Black letter, fifty-six lines, double columns; late 19th century crimson morocco by Riviere, covers with gilt fillet and roll tool border enclosing central olive wreath and elaborate cornerpieces composed of scroll-work and spreading olive branches, remaining field seme with cinquefoils, spine in 7 compartments with six raised bands, lettered gilt in two compartments, rest decoratively tooled gilt with repeated olive leaf motif, board edges and turn-ins decoratively tooled in gilt, all edges gilt, marbled endpapers (pastedowns with decorative gilt tooling), title creased and lightly soiled, small repair to outer blank margin, lower corner of second leaf renewed, affecting catchword on recto and two letters on verso, closed tear through lower half of divisional title to "The Caunterburie Tales", closed tear to A2 of "The Prologues" affecting 8 lines of text to first column and another closed tear at lower margin, F2 with small paper repair to margin and closed tear just touching text, 2U2 with paper fault affecting one word in bottom line of text on recto and verso, few additional small marginal tears or repairs not affecting text, occasional early ink underlining and markings, early signature of James Rea (faded) on title, wonderful copy, from the libraries of C. W. Dyson Perrins and William Foyle, with bookplates.   Heritage Book Shop   Holiday 2014 - 36   2015 $65,000

Association – Redgrave, Evelyn

Kendall, May *Dreams to Sell.* London: Longmans, 1887. First edition, half title in red & black, uncut in original crimson cloth, bevelled boards, spine faded, top edge gilt, presentation inscription to Gilbert Redgrave, bibliographer and art historian from Frances and Evelyn Redgrave 12 may, 1889, note by former of short and apologetic AL from authoress dated Aug. 4th 1892 in another hand: Association books No. 67 and 1945 signature of John Gilman, from the library of Geoffrey & Kathleen Tillotson.   Jarndyce Antiquarian Booksellers   CCVII - 350   2015   £50

Association – Redgrave, Frances

Kendall, May *Dreams to Sell.* London: Longmans, 1887. First edition, half title in red & black, uncut in original crimson cloth, bevelled boards, spine faded, top edge gilt, presentation inscription to Gilbert Redgrave, bibliographer and art historian from Frances and Evelyn Redgrave 12 may, 1889, note by former of short and apologetic AL from authoress dated Aug. 4th 1892 in another hand: Association books No. 67 and 1945 signature of John Gilman, from the library of Geoffrey & Kathleen Tillotson.   Jarndyce Antiquarian Booksellers   CCVII - 350   2015   £50

Association – Redgrave, Gilbert

Kendall, May *Dreams to Sell.* London: Longmans, 1887. First edition, half title in red & black, uncut in original crimson cloth, bevelled boards, spine faded, top edge gilt, presentation inscription to Gilbert Redgrave, bibliographer and art historian from Frances and Evelyn Redgrave 12 may, 1889, note by former of short and apologetic AL from authoress dated Aug. 4th 1892 in another hand: Association books No. 67 and 1945 signature of John Gilman, from the library of Geoffrey & Kathleen Tillotson.   Jarndyce Antiquarian Booksellers   CCVII - 350   2015   £50

Association – Redman, Mary

Anacreon *Anacreon Done into English out of the Original Greek.* Oxford: by L. Litchfield, Printer to the University, for Anthony Stephens, 1683. First edition of this translation, 8vo., leaf (c)1 is duplicated; (c)2 was also duplicated, but the second leaf has been torn away, lightly browned, dampstaining along lower edge of a1-4, corners of K2-L2 and fore margin of P1-2 and in top half of last few leaves, small rust hole in D2 (affecting one letter on each side), marginal rust spot on H1, contemporary calf, spine gilt and lettered (headcap damaged and with upper joint slightly split at head), from the library of James Stevens Cox (1910-1997), inscribed "Sum Philippi Ayresij 1683" on titlepage (Philip Aryes (1638-1712), signature of Madam. Mary Redman, ink signature under bookplate of John Holmes (1702/03-1760) of Holt, Norfolk, Master of Gresham School and writer on education, with his signature, early 19th century circular label with manuscript lot number 12/4 pasted to foot of front flyleaf, the pencil mark of Christie-Miller Britwell Court with pencil shelf mark.   Maggs Bros. Ltd.   1447 - 7   2015   £1500

Association – Reed, Joe

Ellison, Ralph *Invisible Man.* New York: Vintage, 1972. First Paperback edition?, small 8vo., paper wrappers, ink markings on front edges, cover creased and scuffed, but very good, tight copy, author's presentation for Joe Reed family.   Second Life Books Inc.   190 - 73   2015 $700

Association – Reid, A.

Maw & Co. *Patterns Geometrical and Roman Mosaics Encaustic Tile Pavements and Enamelled Wall Decorations.* London: Leighton Bros. 1866, but this copy circa, 1880? Folio, 33 chromolithograph plates, original brown cloth, upper cover overlaid with elaborately decorated chromolithograph sheet by Owen Jones, inscribed by architects "A & W Reid, Elgin".   Marlborough Rare Books   List 54 - 53   2015   £2250

Association – Reid, John

Schnabel, Julian *C.V.J. Nicknames of Maitre D's & Other Exceprts from Life.* New York: Unicorn Publishing Studio, 1987. 4to., original orange cloth, lettered black on acetate dust jacket, illustrations in color and black and white, signed presentation from author to John Reid (rock manger to Queen & Elton John), fine in acetate dust jacket.   Any Amount of Books   2015 - C11092   2015   £320

Association – Reid, W.

Maw & Co. *Patterns Geometrical and Roman Mosaics Encaustic Tile Pavements and Enamelled Wall Decorations.* London: Leighton Bros. 1866, but this copy circa, 1880? Folio, 33 chromolithograph plates, original brown cloth, upper cover overlaid with elaborately decorated chromolithograph sheet by Owen Jones, inscribed by architects "A & W Reid, Elgin".   Marlborough Rare Books   List 54 - 53   2015   £2250

Association – Reilly, James

Rushworth, John *A True Relation of the Storming of Bristoll, and the taking the Town, Castle, Forts, Ordnance, Ammunition and Arms by Sir Thomas Fairfax's army on Thursday the 11 of this instant Septemb. 1645.* London: Edward Husband, 1645. First edition, small 4to., titlepage browned and foxed, some light spotting, closely trimmed in places but with no loss of text, late 19th century calf by Kerr & Richardson, Glasgow, joints and edges rubbed, covers discolored, signature of James Reilly, from the library of James Stevens Cox (1910-1997).   Maggs Bros. Ltd.   1447 - 86   2015   £120

Association – Reinhard, Max

Greene, Graham 1904-1991 *The Revenge.* London: privately printed at the Stellar Press for Bodley Head, 1963. First edition, one of 300 copies, 12mo., original green card sewn wrappers, printed in black, untrimmed, fine, inscribed by Max Reinhardt of Bodley Head to Cambridge University Press printer Brooke Crutchley.   Blackwell's Rare Books   B179 - 158   2015   £325

Association – Renier, Anne

Green, Thomas *Extracts from the Diary of a Lover of Literature.* Ipswich: printed and sold by John Raw, 1810. First edition, 4to., wanting half title, light foxing on titlepage and occasionally elsewhere, author's name in ink on titlepage, original cloth boards, generally boards little soiled and worn, rebacked, good, large copy with bookplates of Thomas Sanderson and Anne and F. G. Renier.   John Drury Rare Books   March 2015 - 25331   2015 $221

Sedley, Charles *Asmodeus; or the Devil's in London: a Sketch.* London: printed by J. Dean, Wardourt Street, Soho for F. F. Hughes 15 Paternsoter Row, 1808. First edition, 3 volumes, 12mo., without half titles, apart from few minor marks in places, clean copy, contemporary green half calf over marbled boards, spines ruled and numbered in gilt, labels missing, chipped at head and rubbed at extremities, still appealing copy, armorial of Felix Booth and Renier booklabels.   Marlborough Rare Books   List 53 - 43   2015   £900

West, Jane *A Tale of the Times.* London: printed for T. N. Longman and O. Rees, 1799. Second edition, 3 volumes, 12mo., 7 pages ads at end volume 3, some foxing, contemporary quarter calf, marbled paper boards, vellum tips, neatly rebacked, spines ruled in gilt, red morocco labels, numbered direct, grey sprinkled edges, bit rubbed, early armorial bookplates of Delapre Abbey, name repeated on each title, lager labels of Anne and F. G. Renier, very good.   Jarndyce Antiquarian Booksellers   CCXI - 283   2015   £280

Association – Renier, Fernand

Green, Thomas *Extracts from the Diary of a Lover of Literature.* Ipswich: printed and sold by John Raw, 1810. First edition, 4to., wanting half title, light foxing on titlepage and occasionally elsewhere, author's name in ink on titlepage, original cloth boards, generally boards little soiled and worn, rebacked, good, large copy with bookplates of Thomas Sanderson and Anne and F. G. Renier.   John Drury Rare Books   March 2015 - 25331   2015 $221

Sedley, Charles *Asmodeus; or the Devil's in London: a Sketch.* London: printed by J. Dean, Wardourt Street, Soho for F. F. Hughes 15 Paternsoter Row, 1808. First edition, 3 volumes, 12mo., without half titles, apart from few minor marks in places, clean copy, contemporary green half calf over marbled boards, spines ruled and numbered in gilt, labels missing, chipped at head and rubbed at extremities, still appealing copy, armorial of Felix Booth and Renier booklabels.   Marlborough Rare Books   List 53 - 43   2015   £900

West, Jane *A Tale of the Times.* London: printed for T. N. Longman and O. Rees, 1799. Second edition, 3 volumes, 12mo., 7 pages ads at end volume 3, some foxing, contemporary quarter calf, marbled paper boards, vellum tips, neatly rebacked, spines ruled in gilt, red morocco labels, numbered direct, grey sprinkled edges, bit rubbed, early armorial bookplates of Delapre Abbey, name repeated on each title, lager labels of Anne and F. G. Renier, very good.   Jarndyce Antiquarian Booksellers   CCXI - 283   2015   £280

Association – Resticaux, Blanche

Procter, Adelaide A. *The Victoria Regia a Volume of Original Contributions in Poetry and Prose.* London: printed and published by Emily Faithfull & Co., Victoria Press for the Employment of Women, 1861. First edition, 8vo. full leather elaborately stamped in gilt, all edges gilt, gilt inner dentelles, designed by John Leighton, some foxing on endpapers, much less in text, some very light wear to boards, still near fine, inscribed by Emily Faithful for Blanche Resticaux, 1862, also inserted a few news clippings about Faithful, very small ALS from Henry Alford and small slip of paper signed yours faithfully Isa Craig.   Second Life Books Inc.   191 - 78   2015 $1500

Association – Rex, Barbara

Bowen, Catherine Drinker *Biography: the Craft and the Calling.* Boston: Little Brown, 1969. First edition, light offsetting to front endpapers from clipping or letter, else fine in near fine dust jacket with little light wear at spinal extremities, inscribed by author for her editor Barbara Rex, with Rex's ownership signature.   Between the Covers Rare Books, Inc.   187 - 22   2015 $350

Association – Reyes, Carlos

Duncan, Robert *Writing Writing.* Portland: Trask House, 1971. First Trask House edition, large 8vo., original stapled printed wrappers, presentation from author for book's publisher Carlos Reyes, with TLS from author to same, with typed receipt signed by Duncan and Reyes for advance royalty, spine portion of book lightly sunned, otherwise book, letter and receipt in fine condition.   James S. Jaffe Rare Books   Modern American Poetry - 73   2015 $2500

Association – Rhoades, Nelson Osgood

Apuntes Para la Historia de la Guerra Entre Mexico y Los Estados-Unidos. Mexico: Tipografia de Manuel Payno, 1848. First edition, 28 litho maps and plates, small 4to., contemporary quarter morocco over marbled boards, four raised bands, gilt title on spine, extremely rare, Nelson Osgood Rhoades bookplate, about very good, small chip to foot of spine, edges worn, scattered foxing, title line on top fore margin of first dozen or so leaves, armorial bookplate on front free endpaper, few leaves with old reinforcement repairs on top inner edge affect a few words, one map with few repairs affecting neat line at one corner and blank areas, one leaf with two wear holes to lower margin, otherwise quite solid.   Kaaterskill Books   19 - 143   2015 $4000

Association – Rhodes, Fairfax

Westall, William *Picturesque Tour of the River Thames.* London: R. Ackerman, 96 Strand, 1828. First edition, 4to., 24 finely hand colored aquatint plates, colored aquatint vignette on title and another to final leaf, contemporary full green crushed morocco, spine decorated and lettered gilt within raised bands, spine faded to brown by Riviere and Son, preserving original cloth at end of work, armorial bookplate of Fairfax Rhodes and C. Robert Bagnold and bookseller tickets of Thomas Thorp and R. D. Steadman, fine.   Marlborough Rare Books   List 54 - 89   2015   £4500

Association – Richards, Helene

Richards, Grant *Vain Pursuit.* London: Grant Richards, 1931. First edition, slight foxing, very good or better with minimal wear in very good dust jacket with modest chipping at crown and some short tears, dedication copy inscribed by author to his daughter Helene, March 1931, scarce in dust jacket.   Between the Covers Rare Books   196 - 107   2015 $850

Association – Richards, Madeleine

Richards, Grant *Bittersweet.* London: Grant Richards, 1915. First edition, original blue green cloth decorated an lettered gilt, positive review of the book from Punch affixed to front fly, corners little bumped, about very good, lacking dust jacket, inscribed by author for his wife Madeleine.   Between the Covers Rare Books   196 - 105   2015 $850

Association – Rickard, Kathryn

Arrelannes, Audrey *Tagore's Fireflies.* Alhambra: Audrey Arrelanes, 1968. Limited to 200 numbered copies, 8.6 x 4.5cm., quarter cloth, paper covered boards, miniature booklabel of Kathryn Rickard.   Oak Knoll Books   306 - 102   2015 $150

Capote, Truman 1924-1985 *The White Rose.* Newton: Tamzaunchale Press, 1987. Limited to 250 numbered copies, miniature book, 6.5 x 4.5 cm., vellum, gilt stamped spine and front cover, all edges gilt frontispiece tissue protected, with miniature bookplate of Kathryn Rickard.   Oak Knoll Books   306 - 104   2015 $210

Christmas. Chicago: Le Petit Oiseau Press, 1963. Limited to 150 copies, frontispiece tipped in, signed by publishers, illustrations in text, half cloth, paper covered boards, paper spine label, miniature bookplate of Kathryn Rickard.   Oak Knoll Books   306 - 105   2015 $150

Christmastide in Ancient Britain. Berkeley: Poole Press, 1987. Limited to 51 numbered copies signed by designer, printer and binder, Maryline Poole Adams, 7.4 x 5.5 cm., quarter leather, decorated paper covered boards, title gilt stamped on spine, illustrated with British postage stamps, miniature bookplate of Kathryn Rickard.   Oak Knoll Books   306 - 106   2015 $350

Edison, Julian I. *Miniature Books.* St. Louis: Julian I. Edison, 1970. Limited to 100 copies, 6.7 x 5.4 cm., leather, title and author gilt stamped on spine, decoration gilt stamped on front board, all edges gilt, black and white illustrations, miniature bookplate of Kathryn Rickard.   Oak Knoll Books   306 - 108   2015 $200

Horatius Flaccus, Quintus *Quintus Horatius Flaccus.* London: Gulielmus, i.e. William Pickering, 1824. Second Pickering edition, 8 x 4.8cm., contemporary full leather, gilt roll pattern on turn-ins, five raised bands on spine, edges gilt, 192 pages, miniature bookplate of Kathryn Rickard.   Oak Knoll Books   306 - 114   2015 $350

Lincoln, Abraham   1809-1865 *Abraham Lincoln President of the United States 1861-1865: selections from His Writings.* Worcester: Achille J. St. Onge, 1950. Limited to 1500 copies, 8 x 5.3cm., leather, gilt stamped covers and spine, all edges gilt, frontispiece, miniature bookplate of Kathryn Rickard.   Oak Knoll Books   306 - 101   2015 $260

Powell, Lawrence Clark *Book Shops.* Los Angeles: Roy V. Boswell, 1965. No limitation given but obviously very small, 6 x 4.3cm., leather, bound by Bela Blau, miniature bookplate of Kathryn Pickard and Raymond A. Smith.   Oak Knoll Books   306 - 121   2015 $200

Van Dyke, Henry *The Tragedy of Little Red Tom: a Contribution to the Fight About Nature Books.* San Diego: Ash Ranch Press, 1988. Limited to 26 numbered copies and 26 lettered and signed by printer, 5.1 x 6.6cm., leather, title and author gilt stamped on spine, edges uncut, cloth slipcase, title and author gilt stamped on spine, miniature bookplate of Kathryn Rickard on front pastedown.   Oak Knoll Books   306 - 122   2015 $150

Association – Ricketts, Edward

James, Charles *A Correction of Abuses in Government, No Encroachment Upon the Constitution of the Country Nobility, although Proper, Not Only Superfluous...* London: printed for H. D. Symonds, 1792. Probably on early edition and certainly very rare, 8vo., emphasis marks in pencil and few annotations, also in pencil, contemporary calf, now neatly rebacked and labelled to match, very good with contemporary ownership signature of G. Ricketts and later armorial bookkplate of Edwards Ricketts on pastedown.   John Drury Rare Books   2015 - 24820   2015 $1311

Association – Ricketts, G.

James, Charles *A Correction of Abuses in Government, No Encroachment Upon the Constitution of the Country Nobility, although Proper, Not Only Superfluous...* London: printed for H. D. Symonds, 1792. Probably on early edition and certainly very rare, 8vo., emphasis marks in pencil and few annotations, also in pencil, contemporary calf, now neatly rebacked and labelled to match, very good with contemporary ownership signature of G. Ricketts and later armorial bookkplate of Edwards Ricketts on pastedown.   John Drury Rare Books   2015 - 24820   2015 $1311

Association – Ricks, Christopher

Palgrave, Francis Turner   1824-1897 *The Golden Treasury of the Best Songs and Lyrical Poems in the English Language.* Cambridge: Macmillan and Co., 1861. First edition, second impression, lacking half title and leading f.e.p., original green glazed cloth by Burn, slightly rubbed, bookseller's ticket of Thomas Brady, York, Kathleen Tillotson's copy with pencil notes above variants, she had written on it sources, with copy of the Penguin Classics edition edited by Christopher Ricks 1991, with ink notes and containing drafts of letter from Kathleen to Ricks about Palgrave's annotated copy of Nightingale Valley.   Jarndyce Antiquarian Booksellers   CCVII - 405   2015   £30

Association – Riley, Stephen

Tate, James *If It Would All Please Hurry. A Poem.* Amherst: Shanachie Press, 1980. First edition, one of only 10 lettered copies reserved for author and artist, this being copy "J" out of a total edition of 35 copies, folio, 10 original etchings and engravings, on Arches Cover white paper, loose sheets in folding box, portfolio lightly soiled, otherwise very fine, rare, presentation from Tale and the artist, Stephen Riley for Stanley Wiater.   James S. Jaffe Rare Books   Modern American Poetry - 294   2015 $4000

Association – Rintoul, Wendy

Knowles, James Sheridan *The Love Chase. A comedy in Five Acts (bound with) Love. A Play.* London: Edward Moxon, 1837. 1839. First edition, and fifth edition respectively, half titles, initial ad leaf in 'Love', titlepage of 'Love Chase' detached and chipped at edges, 2 volumes in 1, early marbled boards, cloth spine rubbed and chipped, inner hinges weakening, 75th birthday gift to Kathleen Tillotson from friend Wendy Rintoul, each play inscribed by author to Mr. Norman.   Jarndyce Antiquarian Booksellers   CCVII - 354   2015   £35

Association – Ritchie, Anne Thackeray

Gaskell, Elizabeth Cleghorn 1810-1865 *Mary Barton: a Tale of Manchester Life.* Leipzig: Bernhard Tauchnitz, 1849. Copyright edition, half title, bookseller's stamps, contemporary half calf, rebacked, retaining original spine strip with red label and initials A.I.T., bookplate of Anthony Philip Martineau Walker, ownership inscription of Anne Thackeray (Ritchie), with note by Kathleen Tillotson that Captain Walker gave her the book. Jarndyce Antiquarian Booksellers CCVII - 273   2015   £50

Association – Ritchie, Thomas

Melville, Herman 1819-1891 *Mardi: and a Voyage Thither.* New York: Harper & Bros., 1849. First American edition, original blue green cloth, decorated in blind, spine in gilt, 2 volumes, excellent, unsophisticated copy with contemporary ownership inscription to front endpapers, volume II with signature of Richmond Enquirer editor, Thomas Ritchie, volume II corners lightly bumped and touch of wear to upper spine some light spotting and minor foxing to pages. B & B Rare Books, Ltd.   234 - 77   2015 $2000

Association – Ritchie, Ward

Preston, Jack *Heil! Hollywood.* Chicago: Reilly & Lee, 1939. First edition, fine in very good dust jacket with small chips and tears, warmly inscribed by Preston for author/printer/publisher Ward Ritchie in 1942. Between the Covers Rare Books, Inc.   187 - 195   2015 $250

Association – Roane, Charles

Aristotle, Pseud. *Aristoteles Master-Piece, or the secrets of Generation Displayed in all Parts Thereof.* London: for J. How and are to be sold next to the Anchor Tavern in Sweeting Rents in Cornhill, 1684. First or second edition, 12mo., woodcut frontispiece (3rd line of text beneath slightly shaved and with catchword 'Jovia' cropped off), 6 woodcuts at end, initial engravings slightly chipped, torn in lower gutter margin and trimmed along lower edge (just touching caption), very light staining to A9-B8, D1-D2, E6v, E12, G4 and H11, 3mm. hole through blank fore-margin of d4, small (20mm.) closed tear to fore-margin of final leaf I6 (just missing text and woodcut) and with a number of edges and corners lightly bumped, otherwise good unsophisticated copy, contemporary sheep (slightly worn), inscriptions "Charles Roane His Booke January ye 15 1697", from the library of James Stevens Cox (1910-1997). Maggs Bros. Ltd.   1447 - 11   2015   £7500

Association – Robartes, Russell

Brown, Thomas *Amusements Serious and Comical, Calculated for the Meridian of London.* London: for John Nutt, 1700. First edition, 8vo., some light dampstaining (Particularly to sheet B), contemporary sprinkled calf, joints split at head and foot of spine, corners bumped and with front flyleaves coming loose), from the library of James Stevens Cox (1910-1997), signature of Russell Robartes, with armorial bookplate, another signature roughly deleted. Maggs Bros. Ltd.   1447 - 51   2015   £220

Association – Roberts, Kenneth

Rose, William Ganson *The Rousing of Parkside.* New York: Duffield & Co., 1914. First edition, 12mo., decorated paper covered boards, spine toned and little worn, very good, bookplate of author Kenneth Roberts, full page poetic inscription from author to Roberts. Between the Covers Rare Books, Inc.   187 - 237   2015 $150

Association – Roberts, Ray

Levine, George *Mindful Pleasures: Essays on Thomas Pynchon.* Boston: Little Brown and Co., 1976. First edition, paperback issue, simultaneous with hardcover, fine in wrappers, Pynchon's editor, Ray Roberts's copy with his book label on front pastedown. Between the Covers Rare Books, Inc.   187 - 227   2015 $125

Association – Robeson, Benjamin

Robeson, Eslanda Goode *Paul Robeson, Negro.* New York: Harper and Bros., 1930. First edition, corners worn and spine has been professionally and neatly seamlessly rebacked, fair copy only, lacking dust jacket, Paul Robeson Jr.'s copy with his bold ownership signature, smaller ownership signature of Rev. Benjamin C. Robeson (Paul Robeson, Sr.'s brother). Between the Covers Rare Books, Inc.   187 - 234   2015 $2500

Association – Robeson, Eslanda Goode

Cocteau, Jean *A Call to Order.* London: Faber and Gwyer, 1926. First English edition, 2 small stains on boards and corners bit bumped, else very good or better, lacking dust jacket, anthropologist, Eslanda Goode Robeson's copy with her ownership signature. Between the Covers Rare Books, Inc.   187 - 58   2015 $350

Association – Robeson, Paul

Robeson, Eslanda Goode *Paul Robeson, Negro.* New York: Harper and Bros., 1930. First edition, corners worn and spine has been professionally and neatly seamlessly rebacked, fair copy only, lacking dust jacket, Paul Robeson Jr.'s copy with his bold ownership signature, smaller ownership signature of Rev. Benjamin C. Robeson (Paul Robeson, Sr.'s brother). Between the Covers Rare Books, Inc. 187 - 234 2015 $2500

Association – Rockefeller, John D.

Andrew, Roy Chapman *On the Trail of Ancient Man.* New York: Putnam, 1926. First edition, 8vo., inscribed by author for John D. Rockefeller, very good++, mild cover edgewear, top edge gilt, in good+ dust jacket with pieces missing along top edge. By the Book, L. C. 44 - 61 2015 $2500

Association – Rodes, John

Sydenham, Thomas *The Whole Works of that Excellent Practical Physician, Dr. Thomas Sydenham...* London: by J. Darby for M. Wellington, 1717. Seventh edition, contemporary panelled calf, extremities worn, two gatherings trifle pulled, numerous contemporary marginal annotations, from the library of Sir John Rodes, with his signature on titlepage. Joseph J. Felcone Inc. Science, Medicine and Technology - 40 2015 $500

Association – Rodgers, Esther Steinbeck

Steinbeck, John Ernst 1902-1968 *Cup of Gold.* New York: McBride, 1929. First edition, first issue, this special copy from author's sister's collection, Esther (Steinbeck) Rodgers and includes bookplates from the library of the Steinbeck Family and "Josephine Rodgers", signed by author, additionally inscribed to Josie, from Emily, near fine with bold lettering to yellow cloth, very good dust jacket with usual spine fading and some slight wear along edges. Ed Smith Books 83 - 101 2015 $45,000

Association – Rodgers, Josephine

Steinbeck, John Ernst 1902-1968 *Cup of Gold.* New York: McBride, 1929. First edition, first issue, this special copy from author's sister's collection, Esther (Steinbeck) Rodgers and includes bookplates from the library of the Steinbeck Family and "Josephine Rodgers", signed by author, additionally inscribed to Josie, from Emily, near fine with bold lettering to yellow cloth, very good dust jacket with usual spine fading and some slight wear along edges. Ed Smith Books 83 - 101 2015 $45,000

Association – Rodman, Selden

Spender, Stephen *Poems.* New York: Random House, 1934. First American edition, rebound, top corner scorched or smoke damaged, good copy, warmly inscribed, ink has feathered a bit, probably from exposure to dampness, although no staining present, inscribed by author to Selden Rodman. Between the Covers Rare Books, Inc. 187 - 265 2015 $300

Spender, Stephen *Returning to Vienna 1947: Nine Sketches.* New York: Banyan Press, 1947. First edition , one of 150 numbered copies for friends of author (out of total of 500), rebound in library style buckram, scorch marks at edges of few pages, clearly the book has been through a fire, else good or better, signed by author inscription by author of Selden Rodman. Between the Covers Rare Books, Inc. 187 - 267 2015 $150

Shaw, T. E. *More Letters from T. E. Shaw to Bruce Rogers.* N.P.: Bruce Rogers, 1936. First edition, one of 300 copies printed by Rogers, rebound in library style buckram, wavieness to pages from dampness but no actual staining, good copy, complimentary slip inscribed by Rogers to Selden Rodman. Between the Covers Rare Books, Inc. 187 - 256 2015 $350

Association – Rogers, Bruce

Shaw, T. E. *More Letters from T. E. Shaw to Bruce Rogers.* N.P.: Bruce Rogers, 1936. First edition, one of 300 copies printed by Rogers, rebound in library style buckram, wavieness to pages from dampness but no actual staining, good copy, complimentary slip inscribed by Rogers to Selden Rodman. Between the Covers Rare Books, Inc. 187 - 256 2015 $350

Association – Rolle

Pownall, Thomas *The Administration of the Colonies.* London: J. Walter, 1768. Fourth edition, collated complete, contemporary full calf slight wear to head of spine and adjacent hinge area, corners mildly worn, light extremity rubbing beautiful copy, internally very fine, crisp and clean, contemporary owner's engraved armorial bookplate and ink signature "Rolle". Argonaut Book Shop Holiday Season 2014 - 11 2015 $3000

Association – Roo-Any, Captain

MacDonald, John D. *Barrier Island.* New York: Alfred A. Knopf, 1986. First edition, inscribed "For Captain Roo-Any, friend of T. Mcgee is a friend of mine! Best regards John D. MacDonald 19 Aug '86", scarce signed, fine in dust jacket. Buckingham Books March 2015 - 30688 2015 $750

Association – Roosevelt, Theodore, III

Keith, Arthur *The Antiquity of Man.* Philadelphia: J. B. Lippincott, 1925. Sixth impression, 2 volumes, blue cloth, gilt, corners little bumped, else near fine, without dust jacket, each volume with attractive Theodore Roosevelt III (grandson of the president). Between the Covers Rare Books, Inc. 187 - 145   2015 $225

Association – Roosevelt, Theodore, Mrs.

MacDonald, Philip *Guest in the House.* Garden City: Doubleday Crime Club, 1955. First edition, small blindstamp of Mrs. Theodore Roosevelt Jr. with her Oyster Bay address, else fine in very good dust jacket with small nicks and tears. Between the Covers Rare Books, Inc.   187 - 194   2015 $125

Association – Rosebery, Archibald Philip, Earl of

Mortimer, John *The Whole Art of Husbandry or the Way of Managing the Improving of Land.* London: printed by J. H. for H. Mortlock at the Phoenix and J. Robinson at the Golden Lion in St. Paul's Church Yard, 1707. First edition, 8vo. several woodcut text figures, contemporary panelled calf with gilt spine label, little wear to extremities and joints but very good in sound, original binding, signature and armorial bookplate of Ambrose Holbech, 18th century signature of Mr. Goodwyn, armorial bookplate 19th century of Archibald Philip (Primrose) Earl of Rosebery, uncommon. John Drury Rare Books   2015 - 25543   2015 $1311

Association – Rosenbach

Congreve, William   1670-1729 *The Way of the World.* London: printed for Jacob Tonson, 1700. First edition, half title, ad verso of last leaf, variant with catchword 'Enter' on page 80, small hole in E3 with loss of two letters on either side of leaf and three more touched on verso (sense recoverable), trifle browned, light staining to upper margin, 4to., half blue morocco (presumably for Rosenbach), spine gilt lettered longitudinally between gilt panels at either end, small leather booklabel on front pastedown, monogram SSB (Silvain S. Bruschwig), offset onto foot of label "From the Rosenbach Collections" with a summary description, later Quaritch collation note inside back cover, good. Blackwell's Rare Books   B179 - 32   2015   £1750

Association – Rosenfeld, Henry

Harris, Joel Chandler   1848-1908 *Sister Jane: Her Friends and Acquaintances.* New York: Houghton Mifflin Co., 1899. Reprint, octavo, green cloth decorated in black and gilt, little spine cocked, small hole on edge of spine, overall very good, inscribed by author for friend Henry Rosenfeld.   Between the Covers Rare Books   196 - 78   2015 $950

Association – Rosenthal, Tom

Coetzee, J. M. *In the Heart of the Country.* London: Secker & Warburg, 1977. First edition, signed by author for publisher, Tom Rosenthal, laid in is ANS signed by Rosenthal dated in 2007 stating "John Coetzee signed this book for me when he came here for dinner...", mild toning to endpages near fine in like dust jacket with original price intact and no sticker, with tanning to spine lettering and trace edge wear, very nice copy.   Ken Lopez, Bookseller 164 - 34   2015 $850

Coetzee, J. M. *Waiting for the Barbarians.* London: Secker & Warburg, 1980. First British edition and true First edition, signed by author, signed by publisher Tom Rosenthal with ANS laid in dated 2007 "John Coetzee signed this book for me when he came here for dinner...", couple of faint spots to top edge, else fine in near fine dust jacket with usual spine fading, text, white faint, still visible and readable, unlike some other copies we have seen. Ken Lopez, Bookseller   164 - 35   2015 $3500

Association – Rosenwald, Lessing

Five on Paper, a Collection of Five Essays on Papermaking, Books and Relevant Matters. North Hills: Bird & Bull Press, 1963. Limited to 169 numbered copies, small 4to., original full morocco, 6 wood engravings, browning along edges of paper and inner margin as is common with all copies presentation from Lessing Rosenwald dated 1963.   Oak Knoll Books   306 - 131 2015 $1000

Association – Ross, Donald

Grafton, Sue *D is for Deadbeat.* London: Macmillan, 1987. First edition, 8vo., signed for collector Donald Ross on titlepage, near fine in like dust jacket with very slight foxspotting to endpapers and dust jacket, excellent condition. Any Amount of Books   2015 - A99152   2015   £220

Association – Rossetti, William Michael

Hayley, William *The Triumphs of Temper. A Poem in six Cantos.* Chichester: printed by F. Seagrave for T. Cadell and W. Davies, 1803. Small 8vo., 19th century full calf gilt, sometime expertly rebacked preserving the original backstrip, preserved in brown cloth covered chemise and quarter brown morocco slipcase, 6 engraved plates by Blake after Maria Flaxman, some offsetting as usual, the copy of William Michael Rossetti, with his ink signature, dated 1868. Henry Sotheran Ltd.   William Blake Exhibition 17th Oct.-7th Nov. 2014 - 67   2015   £625

Tupper, John Lucas *Hiatus: the Void in Modern Education its Cause and Antidote.* London: Macmillan, 1869. 8vo., disbound, 51 page publisher's catalog at rear, presentation copy from author for William Michael Rossetti, last page has a note about errata on 3 pages, possibly in the hand of Rossetti, or Tupper, disbound, otherwise in decent condition with clean text, suitable for rebinding.   Any Amount of Books   2015 - A62731   2015   £220

Swinburne, Algernon Charles   1837-1909 *The Queen Mother. Rosamund. Two Plays.* London: Basil Montagu Pickering, 1860. First edition, first issue in second state with cancel titlepage and addition of half titles to each play, lovely copy, rebound in contemporary three quarter green morocco with red marbled paper boards and endpapers, all edges marbled, slightly rubbed and bumped but very good, interior pages very good with occasional light pencil checks of lines in margins to highlight line or phrase, interesting association copy, very good, inscribed by author for W. M. Rossetti, this is the copy of author and critic John Skelton with his pencil note "Given to me by D. G. Rossetti for review in Fraser's magazine".   The Kelmscott Bookshop   11 - 52   2015 $4500

Association – Rothenberg, Diane

Eshleman, Clayton *Everwhat.* La Laguna: Zasterele, 2003. First edition, illustrated wrappers, inscribed by author to Jerome and Diane Rothenberg.   Between the Covers Rare Books, Inc.   187 - 92   2015 $250

Roditi, Edouard *The Delights of Turkey: Twenty Tales.* New York: New Directions, 1979. First edition, foxing on fore edge, else very near fine in attractive, very good dust jacket with faint dampstains at lower corners, inscribed by author for Diane and Jerry Rothenberg.   Between the Covers Rare Books, Inc.   187 - 236   2015 $275

Rose, Wendy *What Happened when the Hopi Hit New York.* New York: Contact II Publications, 1982. First edition, decorated blue self wrappers, some dampstains along spine and on very margins of leaves, else very good, inscribed by author for Jerome and Diane Rothenberg.   Between the Covers Rare Books, Inc.   187 - 200   2015 $200

Association – Rothenberg, Jerome

Eshleman, Clayton *Everwhat.* La Laguna: Zasterele, 2003. First edition, illustrated wrappers, inscribed by author to Jerome and Diane Rothenberg.   Between the Covers Rare Books, Inc.   187 - 92   2015 $250

Roditi, Edouard *In a Lost World.*   Santa Rosa: Black Sparrow Press Jan., 1978. First edition, stapled printed wrappers (16) pages, dampstain along edge of wrappers, inscribed by author for Jerome Rothenberg.   Between the Covers Rare Books, Inc.   187 - 235   2015 $250

Rose, Wendy *Academic Squaw: Report to the World from the Ivory Tower.* Marvin: Blue Cloud Quarterly, 1977. First edition, stapled illustrated wrappers, near fine, inscribed by author to Jerome Rothenberg.   Between the Covers Rare Books, Inc.   187 - 198   2015 $275

Rose, Wendy *Builder Kachina: a Home Going Cycle.* Marvin: Blue Cloud Quarterly, 1979. First edition, illustrations by author, stapled illustrated wrappers small stain on front wrapper, else near fine, inscribed by author to Jerome Rothenberg.   Between the Covers Rare Books, Inc.   187 - 199   2015 $250

Roditi, Edouard *The Delights of Turkey: Twenty Tales.* New York: New Directions, 1979. First edition, foxing on fore edge, else very near fine in attractive, very good dust jacket with faint dampstains at lower corners, inscribed by author for Diane and Jerry Rothenberg.   Between the Covers Rare Books, Inc.   187 - 236   2015 $275

Rose, Wendy *What Happened when the Hopi Hit New York.* New York: Contact II Publications, 1982. First edition, decorated blue self wrappers, some dampstains along spine and on very margins of leaves, else very good, inscribed by author for Jerome and Diane Rothenberg. Between the Covers Rare Books, Inc.   187 - 200   2015 $200

Association – Roughead, William

Ruffhead, James *The Passions Man.* London: printed for the author, 1746. First edition, 8vo., engraved frontispiece and 3 other plates, contemporary calf, gilt, neatly rebacked, corners worn, very good, scarce, comparatively recent bookplate of William Roughead and booklabel of Ian Jack.   C. R. Johnson   Foxon R-Z - 850r-z   2015 $1302

Association – Roughton, Roger

Jolas, Eugene *Transition Number 19-20 June 1930.* Paris: Transition, 1930. Large 8vo., original illustrated wrappers, 21 plates, sound, slightly used, copy with slight soiling, slight wear at spine hinge and slight browning, ownership signature of British surrealist Roger Roughton.   Any Amount of Books   2015 - C12882   2015   £160

Association – Routledge, Norman

Walpole, Horace 1719-1797 *Horace Walpole's Description of the Villa at Strawberry Hill.* London: Roxburghe Club, 2010. Facsimile edition, limited to 200 copies, large 4to., quarter red leather and red cloth boards, lettered gilt on spine, copiously illustrated, presentation in hand of Nicolas Barker for Norman Routledge, very slight rubbing, else very good+.   Any Amount of Books   March 2015 - C9634   2015   £400

Association – Rowland, Deborah

Rowland, John *The Glorious Mission of the American People. A Thanksgiving Discourse.* Circleville: printed at the Religious Telescope Office, 1850. First edition, 12mo., 24 pages, original printed wrappers lightly soiled and worn, text foxed, with signature on title (smudged) and on following leaf of Mrs. Deborah G. Rowland, Windsor, Ct.   M & S Rare Books, Inc.   97 - 232   2015 $175

Association – Rudd, Donald

Adams, Herbert *Signal for Invasion.* London: Collins - The Crime Club, 1942. First edition, 8vo., 192 pages, original publisher's orange cloth, lettered black on spine, from the Donald Rudd collection of detective fiction, rare, especially in dust jacket, one closed tear and very slight chipping at spine ends and very slightly edge worn, decent copy.   Any Amount of Books   2015 - C8632   2015   £150

Benson, E. F. *Pharisees and Publicans.* London: Hutchinson & Co., n.d. circa, 1926. First edition thus, 8vo., original red cloth, lettered black on spine and cover, from the Donald Rudd collection, publisher's catalog dated Autumn 1926, very slight and faint creasing at spine, otherwise very good+, excellent condition.   Any Amount of Books   2015 - C4965   2015   £300

Conrad, Joseph 1857-1924 *The Secret Agent: a Simple Tale.* London: Methuen, 1907. Second edition, 8vo., original maroon cloth, lettered gilt on spine, very slight rubbing, very slight fading to spine, otherwise sound, clean, very good+, from the Donald Rudd collection.   Any Amount of Books   2015 - A93462   2015   £225

Dexter, Colin *Service for all the Dead.* London: Macmillan, 1979. First edition, 8vo., slight rubbing, slight spotting to fore-edges, otherwise very good+ in like dust jacket, signed presentation from author for Roger, Xmas 1979, from the Donald Rudd collection of detective fiction.   Any Amount of Books   2015 - A93457   2015   £300

Hill, Reginald *A Pinch of Snuff.* London: Collins, 1978. First edition, first impression, 8vo., slight rubbing at edges, fine in near fine dust jacket, excellent condition, from the Donald Rudd collection of detective fiction.   Any Amount of Books   2015 - A96965   2015   £260

Hull, Richard *Invitation to an Inquest.* London: Collins/ Crime Club, 1950. First edition, 8vo., original red cloth lettered black on spine, one pedigree chart, from the Donald Rudd collection of detective fiction, spine slightly faded, had of spine very slightly frayed, cover has faint ring, otherwise near very good, clean text.   Any Amount of Books   2015 - A96879   2015 £160

Rendell, Ruth *The Best Man to Die.* London: John Long, 1969. First edition, 8vo., original brown cloth lettered gilt at spine, ex-library worn, lacking front endpaper, slight rubbing at edges and slight creasing with faint wear at spine ends, otherwise close to very good, in clean dust jacket, from the Donald Rudd collection of detective fiction.   Any Amount of Books   2015 - C11965   2015   £160

Association – Ruesch, Jurgen

Kees, Weldon *Poems 1947-1954.* San Francisco: Adrian Wilson, 1954. First edition, 8vo., original cloth backed pastepaper boards with printed label on spine, wraparound band, presentation copy inscribed by author to Jurgen (Ruesch) collaborator and friend of author, Jan. 1955, very fine.   James S. Jaffe Rare Books   Modern American Poetry - 160   2015 $2500

Association – Russell, Alden

Chapin, Maud H. *Rush-Light Stories.* New York: Duffield and Co., 1918. First edition, octavo, quarter cloth and paper covered boards, gilt, nice gift inscription from American artist Geraldine Spalding to radio pioneer and storyteller Ted Malone (pseudonym of Alden Russell), some cloth eroded on spine, about very good.   Between the Covers Rare Books   196 - 151   2015 $125

Association – Russell, Sidney

England and Wales. Parliament - 1642 *A Declaration of the Lords and Commons Assembled in Parliament, with their Resolution, That if Captaine Catesby, Captaine Lilborne, Captaine Vivers or any Others Which are or shall be Taken Prisoners, by His Majesties Army Shall be Put to Death...* London: Decemb. 19 printed for John Wright, 1642. First edition, small 4to, 8 pages, nasty marks along inner margin of title where a cloth backing has been removed, last leaf stained with white blob obscuring parts of two words, type ornament border at foot of title shaved, disbound, the copy of Sidney Russell, of Fairway, Gorway Rad, Walsall, circa 1936, from the library of James Stevens Cox (1910-1997).   Maggs Bros. Ltd.   1447 - 92   2015   £150

Association – Russell, William

Rich, Henry *What is to Be Done? Or Past, Present and Future.* London: James Ridgway, 1844. First edition, 8vo., recent blue boards, lettered on upper cover, paper label on spine, very good, from the contemporary library of Lord William Russell with his signature, scarce.   John Drury Rare Books   2015 - 4916   2015 $177

Association – Sabin, Joseph

Jones, Horatio Gates *Andrew Bradford, Founder of the Newspaper Press in the Middle States of America.* Philadelphia: King & Baird, 1869. First edition, 24.5cm., folded facsimile, 36 pages, printed wrappers, untrimmed, inscribed by author to Joseph Sabin Esq, neat ink on half titlepage, chipping to edges of wrappers, somewhat darkened and separate at spine, with age toning to text pages, else very good, very scarce.   Between the Covers Rare Books, Inc.   187 - 140   2015 $650

Association – Sachs, Hans

Ehrich, Paul Von *Historisches zur Frage Der Immunisierung per OS.* Wiener: Klinischen Wochenschrift, 1908. First separate edition, offprint, 8vo., very good+, self wrappers, minimal creases and edgewear, inscribed and signed by author to his long time collaborator Hans Sachs.   By the Book, L. C.   44 - 32   2015 $500

Association – Sainte-Beuve, Charles Augustin

Cenac-Moncaut, M. *Histoire Des Chanteurs et Des Artistes Ambulants.* Saint German en Laye: L. Toinon et Cie, 1866. First edition, text in French, printed wrappers, 30 pages, uncut and untrimmed, some foxing, small slits at spine, about very good, inscribed by author to Charles Augustine Sainte-Beuve.   Between the Covers Rare Books, Inc.   187 - 46   2015 $1250

Association – Salaman, Raphael

Dostoevskii, Fyodor Mikhailovich 1821-1881 *The Grand Inquisitor.* London: Elkin Matthews, 1930. First edition, limited to 300 numbered copies, this no. 267, 4to., original ultra modernist decorated pigskin, lettered black on spine and front cover, signed presentation from S. S. Koteliansky for Raphael Salaman (1906-1993 and wife Miriam Polianovsky, very faint surface soiling, otherwise fine in sound, used slipcases, excellent copy.   Any Amount of Books   2015 - C11380   2015   £225

Association – Sampson, George

Boyle, Robert 1627-1691 *Certain Physiological Essays and Other Tracts.* London: Henry Herringman, 1669. Second edition, 4to., without final blank leaf, small wormhole through upper blank margin, long wormtrail in inner margin and into text around line 14 of Pp1(3)E2, leaf B1 dusty at head, small piece torn away from blank corner of T2 and with tear to foot of O3, contemporary sprinkled calf, covers panelled in blind, paper label in second panel of spine, covers affected by worm damage, in particular they have chewed out corner ornaments of panels, early inscription of George Sampson, 18th century signature J. W. Hawker, from the library of James Stevens Cox (1910-1997).   Maggs Bros. Ltd.   1447 - 35   2015   £950

Association – Sampson, Margaret

Howard, John *An Account of the Principal Lazarettos in Europe: with Various Papers Relative to the Plague...* Warrington: printed by William Eyres and sold by T. Cadeel, J. Johnson, C. Dilly and J. Taylor in London, 1789. First edition, 4to., 22 engraved plates (of which 20 are folding), one very large engraved folding table, including half title, some marginal browning, original (probably) marbled boards with original (probably) printed spine label, entirely uncut, minor binding wear, excellent presentation copy, inscribed by author "Mr. Howard requests Mr. Sampson will be kind enough to accept this book from him, as a small mark of his esteem" with Margaret Sampson's ownership signature, later ownership signature of James Froud 1834 on titlepage, in all choice copy, largely in original state.   John Drury Rare Books   2015 - 25837   2015 $2622

Association – Sanders, Ann

Young, Edward 1683-1765 *The Complaint; or Night-Thoughts on Life, Death & Immortality. Nights I-VI. (bound with) Nights VII-IX.* London: printed for J. Dodsley, 1749. 2 volumes in 1, 8vo., contemporary calf, gilt, spine gilt, red morocco label (rather rubbed, some wear to joints and top of spine), aside from binding wear, in very good condition, early signature of Ann Sanders, later signature of James Ford of Heavitree, dated 1837.   C. R. Johnson   Foxon R-Z - 1186r-z   2015 $230

Association – Sanderson, Thomas

Green, Thomas *Extracts from the Diary of a Lover of Literature.* Ipswich: printed and sold by John Raw, 1810. First edition, 4to., wanting half title, light foxing on titlepage and occasionally elsewhere, author's name in ink on titlepage, original cloth boards, generally boards little soiled and worn, rebacked, good, large copy with bookplates of Thomas Sanderson and Anne and F. G. Renier.   John Drury Rare Books   March 2015 - 25331   2015 $221

Association – Sanger, Tom

McWhorter, L. V. *Yellow Wolf - My Story.* Caldwell: Caxton, 1940. First edition, vintage photos, endpaper maps, missing half title leaf after f.f.e.p., worn at edges and corners, but without cloth wearing through, very scarce in first edition, with ownership name of Tom Sanger. Baade Books of the West   2014 - 2015 $75

Association – Santee, Ross

Carlson, Raymond *Arizona Highways. Volume XXII Numbers 1-12 1946.* Phoenix: Arizona Highways, 1946. First edition, quarto, light blue buckram, titles stamped in gold gilt on front cover and spine, illustrations, full page colored pen and ink drawing by Ross Santee and addressed to Louis P. Merrill (Texas ranchman), fine, bright, tight copy. Buckingham Books   March 2015 - 28365   2015 $1000

Carlson, Raymond *Arizona Highways. Volume XXIII Numbers 1-12 1947.* Phoenix: Arizona Highways, 1947. First edition, quarto, red buckram, titles stamped in gold gilt on front cover and spine, illustrations, full page ink drawing on front flyleaf by Ross Santee and addressed to Louis P. Merrill (noted Texas ranchman), fine, bright, tight copy. Buckingham Books   March 2015 - 28366   2015 $1000

Carlson, Raymond *Arizona Highways. Volume XXIV. Numbers 1-12 1948.* Phoenix: Arizona Highways, 1948. First edition, quarto, red buckram, titles stamped in gold gilt on front cover and spine, illustrations, full page color pen and ink drawing by Ross Santee addressed to Louis P. Merrill (Texas ranchman), fine, bright, tight copy. Buckingham Books   March 2015 - 28367   2015 $1000

Association – Saroyan, Aram

Berrigan, Ted *The Sonnets.* New York: Lorenz & Ellen Gude, 1964. First edition, limited to 300 numbered copies 'plus an unspecified number of unnumbered copies, 4to., mimeographed sheets stapled together, original wrappers, presentation copy inscribed by author to Aram (Saroyan), rear wrapper missing as usual, front wrapper lightly foxed and dust soiled, otherwise very good.   James S. Jaffe Rare Books   Many Happy Returns - 3   2015 $4500

Association – Sarton, May

Bishop, John Peale *Selected Poems.* New York: Charles Scribner's Sons, 1941. First edition, top corner bumped, bit of rubbing, very good without dust jacket, Mary Sarton's copy with her ownership signature.   Between the Covers Rare Books, Inc.   187 - 24   2015 $125

Association – Sartre, Jean Paul

Wright, Richard 1908-1960 *Jeunesse Noire. (Black Boy).* Paris: Gallimard, 1947. First French edition, wrappers in glassine dust jacket, pages browned, small chip on last leaf affecting no text, else near fine, inscribed by author to Jean Paul Sartre, magnificent association.   Between the Covers Rare Books   197 - 47   2015 $12,500

Association – Satcher, Herbert Boyce

Sienkiewicz, Henryk *Quo Vadis.* Boston: Little Brown, 1896. First edition, first printing of the American edition with 1896 on titlepage (uncommon thus), small owner label of Herbert Boyce Satcher (book collector, bibliographer), very good, some shelfwear at extremities, green cloth shows little toning, fairly nice, gilt, tight, clean text.   Stephen Lupack   March 2015 - 2015 $95

Association – Satterthwaite, Gilbert

Visser-Hooft, Jenny *Among the Kara-Korum Glaciers in 1925.* London: Edward Arnold, 1926. First edition, 8vo., original blue cloth lettered gilt on spine and cover, pages uncut, frontispiece, 24 plates, 2 maps, neat name on half title "Gilbert Satterthwaite and H. Spencer Jones, stamp on titlepage "Presentation copy",.   Any Amount of Books   2015 - A91390   2015   £220

Association – Saul, Milton

Spender, Stephen *Returning to Vienna 1947: Nine Sketches.* New York: Banyan Press, 1947. First edition, one of 350 numbered copies for sale (out of total edition of 500), tied decorated paper wrappers with printed label, small nicks and splitting along spine, otherwise handsome, very good copy, signed by author, Carl van Vechten's copy with his bookplate, inscribed by him to Milton Saul and Claude Fredericks, publishers at Banyan Press.   Between the Covers Rare Books, Inc.   187 - 266   2015 $250

Association – Saunders, William Henry Radcliffe

Jefferies, Richard 1848-1887 *The Scarlet Shawl.* London: Tinsley Bros., 1874. First edition, text slightly spotted, later half blue morocco by Bumpus, raised bands, compartments decorated in gilt, slightly rubbed, armorial bookplate of William Henry Radcliffe Saunders, top edge gilt, very good.   Jarndyce Antiquarian Booksellers   CCXI - 160   2015   £380

Association – Saunderson, Nicholas

Carleton, George *Astrologomania; the Madnesse of Astrologers.* London: by R. C. for John Hammond, 1651. Second edition, 8vo., first blank leaf (inner margin with old guard), closely shave date head, contemporary sheep ruled in blind, rebacked, corners chewed, upper edge front cover slightly wormed, signature of Ni(cholas?) Saunderson, from the library of James Stevens Cox (1910-1997).   Maggs Bros. Ltd.   1447 - 65   2015   £400

Association – Scherer, Edmond

Arnold, Matthew 1822-1888 *Poems.* London: Longman, Brown, Green and Longmans, 1853. New edition, 8vo., original green cloth lettered gilt at spine and decorated in blind on cover, handwritten signed letter from author to his friend Edmond Scherer the writer, slight splitting at front hinge, minor scuffing to covers, otherwise sound, about very good.   Any Amount of Books   March 2015 - C14214   2015   £350

Association – Schiegel, Glenn

MacDonald, Ross *Blue City.* London: Cassell, 1949. First edition, very good in like dust jacket, some brief soil to boards, jacket moderately worn and creased at extremities, uncommon, early Millar title, inscribed by author Xmas 1951 to Glenn Schiegel, from the collection of Duke Collier.   Royal Books   36 - 79   2015 $1500

Association – Schiff, Harris

Berrigan, Ted *Yo-Yo's With Money.* Hennicker: United Artists (Bernadette Mayer & Lewis Warsh), 1979. First edition, mimeographed, limited to 500 copies, 4to., original pictorial wrappers with cover drawing by Rosina Kuhn and photographs by Rochelle Kraut, fine, presentation copy inscribed by author and Harris Schiff for Steve.   James S. Jaffe Rare Books   Many Happy Returns - 217   2015 $1250

Association – Schiller, F. C. S.

James, William 1842-1910 *A Pluralistic Universe.* New York: Longmans, Green and Co., 1909. First edition, octavo, gift presentation from author to F. C. S. Schiller, with preprinted "From the Author" slip loosely inserted before first half title and Schiller's ownership signature and notation C. Schiller/from W.J." written in upper right corner f.f.e.p., original grayish green covers with green cloth on spine, spine label with just lightest of wear along edges and crease down center, otherwise beautifully preserved and 100 per cent readable label, boards and spine particularly fresh for this book with just bit of white spotting to spine covering on front cover and two small white spots on rear cover, with 4 small pencil notations by Schiller along with occasional pencil lines in margin and even more occasionally underlining.   Athena Rare Books   15 - 20   2015 $1800

James, William 1842-1910 *Pragmatism.* New York: Longmans, Green and Co., 1907. First edition, octavo, presentation from author to F. C. S. Schiller, with preprinted "From the Author" slip loosely inserted before first half title and Schiller's ownership signature and notation, original brown boards with lighter colored cloth spine, spine label with just lightest of wear along right edge and light ding that has removed the letter 's' from "James", otherwise beautiful preserved and 100 per cent readable (rare thing the these books by James), boards and spine particularly fresh for this book, with just one small (3/8") white stain to front cover, gorgeous, well preserved and important presentation copy.   Athena Rare Books   15 - 19   2015 $2200

James, William 1842-1910 *Some Problems of Philosophy.* New York: Longmans, Green and Co., 1911. First edition, octavo, gift from author's wife to F. C. S. Schiller, with Schiller's ownership signature, original green covers with perfectly legible paper spine label and just bit of wear to two top corners, half inch whitish discoloration to lower spine, with Schiller's ownership inscription and notation of presentation, with occasional vertical pencil lines and less frequent underlinings throughout text, some in black, some in blue and others in red, several notations in margins of book by Schiller and his list of relevant pages on inside rear cover, otherwise near fine.   Athena Rare Books   15 - 24   2015 $950

James, William 1842-1910 *The Varieties of Religious Experience.* London: Longmans, Green & Co., 1902. First edition, first issue, octavo, presentation gift from author to F. C. H. Schiller *1864-1937), with preprinted "From the Author" slip glued into inner front cover, this copy has Schiller's sketchy notes on prelim and blank blanks and pencil lines in margins with occasional written comments throughout, otherwise near fine, original green cloth (both boards and spine) unusually bright with just few signs of wear, most especially to rear cover, spine label very lightly worn around edges, with large section of ads which seem to appear in all English first-issues of this book, with enclosed letter attesting to provenance of presentation to Schiller, clean, tight, near fine.   Athena Rare Books   15 - 17   2015 $3500

Association – Schimmel, Stuart

Great Britian. Laws, Statutes, etc. - 1828 *Acts and Votes of Parliament Relating to the British Museum with the Statutes and Rules Thereof and the Succession of Trustees and Officers.* London: G. Woodfall, 1828. Contemporary full dark grey calf, triple ruled gilt borders and additional blind decorated border, raised gilt bands, compartments ruled gilt, slightly rubbed, contemporary inscription, bookplate of Stuart B. Schimmel.   Jarndyce Antiquarian Booksellers   CCXI - 39   2015   £180

Browning, Robert 1812-1889 *Ferishtah's Fancies.* London: Smith, Elder and Co., 1884. First edition, inscribed "To G F Watts From Robert Browning Dec. 1884" not in Browning's hand, in very good original dark brown cloth boards with gilt title to spine and black decoration to front board, rubbing to hinges, edges and corners with short open tear to book along front hinge, foxing to first and last few pages with light pencil bracket marks to text and occasional folded corners, blue endpages, 143 pages plus 8 pages of ads, from the collection of Stuart B. Schimmel, very good. The Kelmscott Bookshop   11 - 7   2015 $450

Association – Schmidt, Harvey

Jones, Tom *The Fantasticks.* New York: Drama Book Shop, 1967. Stated second printing, fine in slightly age toned, near fine dust jacket, inscribed by Jones and co-author Harvey Schmidt, also laid in is unsigned card engraved with initials 'J.F.B.".   Between the Covers Rare Books   196 - 82   2015 $450

Association – Schmidt, Peter

Society of the Framers of the Constitution of the State of Montana *Third and Fourth Reunion of the.... 1911 and 1916.* Butte: 1916. or 1917. First edition thus, pictorial stapled wrappers, 40 pages, illustrations, laid in TLS from Walter Bickford, Asst. sec. & letter of receipt from Peter Schmidt, son of member of constitutional convention, one page creased and section bracketed in pencil, back cover almost detached and tear repaired, unusual, scarce, fair. Baade Books of the West   2014 - 2015 $91

Association – Schneeman, Elio

Bye, Reed *Some Magic at the Dump.* New York: Angel Hair Books, 1978. First edition, one of 500 copies, illustrated wrappers, inscribed by author to the three sons of artist and poet, George Schneeman "for Paul, Elio, Emilio...". Between the Covers Rare Books, Inc.   187 - 40   2015 $225

Association – Schneeman, Emilio

Bye, Reed *Some Magic at the Dump.* New York: Angel Hair Books, 1978. First edition, one of 500 copies, illustrated wrappers, inscribed by author to the three sons of artist and poet, George Schneeman "for Paul, Elio, Emilio...". Between the Covers Rare Books, Inc.   187 - 40   2015 $225

Association – Schneeman, George

Berrigan, Ted *A Feeling for Living.* New York: Frontward Books, 1975. First edition, mimeographed, limited to 400 copies, this one of 25 numbered and signed by author, this numbered '1' an signed by author, 4to., original stapled hand colored pictorial wrappers by Rochelle Kraut, fine, presentation copy inscribed by author for George and Katie (Schneeman), wonderful association.   James S. Jaffe Rare Books   Many Happy Returns - 33   2015 $2500

Schuyler, James *Collabs.* New York: Misty Terrace Press, 1980. First edition, one of 200 copies, 4to., original wrappers with cover design by George Schneeman, stapled as issued, presentation from all contributors, Helena Hughes, Michael Scholnick and signed by small pen and ink self-portrait by Schneeman for Ted Berrigan, fine.   James S. Jaffe Rare Books   Modern American Poetry - 244   2015 $1750

Association – Schneeman, Katie

Berrigan, Ted *A Feeling for Living.* New York: Frontward Books, 1975. First edition, mimeographed, limited to 400 copies, this one of 25 numbered and signed by author, this numbered '1' an signed by author, 4to., original stapled hand colored pictorial wrappers by Rochelle Kraut, fine, presentation copy inscribed by author for George and Katie (Schneeman), wonderful association.   James S. Jaffe Rare Books   Many Happy Returns - 33   2015 $2500

Association – Schneeman, Paul

Bye, Reed *Some Magic at the Dump.* New York: Angel Hair Books, 1978. First edition, one of 500 copies, illustrated wrappers, inscribed by author to the three sons of artist and poet, George Schneeman "for Paul, Elio, Emilio...". Between the Covers Rare Books, Inc.   187 - 40   2015 $225

Association – Schoenberg, David

Chandrasekhar, S. *Stochastic problems in Physics and Astronomy.* Reviews of Modern Physics, 1943. First separate edition, offprint in original orange printed wrappers, small 4to., inscribed by author to David Schoenberg.   By the Book, L. C.   Special List 10 - 53   2015 $250

Association – Scholnick, Michael

Schuyler, James *Collabs.* New York: Misty Terrace Press, 1980. First edition, one of 200 copies, 4to., original wrappers with cover design by George Schneeman, stapled as issued, presentation from all contributors, Helena Hughes, Michael Scholnick and signed by small pen and ink self-portrait by Schneeman for Ted Berrigan, fine.   James S. Jaffe Rare Books   Modern American Poetry - 244   2015 $1750

Association – Schoonover, Frank

Madison, Lucy Foster *Washington.* Philadelphia: Penn Publishing Co., 1925. First edition, 8vo., cloth, illustration inlaid on front cover, illustrated endpapers, this copy signed by illustrator, Frank Schoonover, cover inlaid, endpapers, frontispiece, chapter headers and 7 color plates in text by Schoonover.   Oak Knoll Books   306 - 41   2015 $100

Association – Schott, William

Valeriano, Giovanni Pierio *Hieroglyphica Sive de Sacris Aegyptiorvm Literis Commentarii... A Caelio Augustino Curione Duobus Libris Aucti et Multis Imaginibus Illustrati.* Basileae: Per Thomam Guarinum, 1567. Second edition, 362 x 235mm., excellent contemporary blindstamped pigskin, covers with multiple frames of palmettes, rosettes, floral rolls, and an allegorical roll depicting Fides, Justitia, Caritas and Spes, raised bands, traces of ink titling to spine, intact original brass clasps, small hole at head of rear board where a chain was once attached; woodcut printer's device on title and last page, frontispiece, 12 charts in text, 265 mostly emblematic illustrations, (18th century?) engraved armorial bookplate and 19th century woodcut bookplate of William Schott, titlepage with two early (probably 17th century) inscriptions from monastery library at Kaisersheim; very minor soiling to pigskin, small area of discoloration at top of back board (where chain hasp had been located), front hinge beginning to open at top, final few leaves with minor traces of mildew, barely perceptible diagonal dampstain at upper corner on a number of text leaves, other trivial imperfections, nearly fine contemporary copy, unrestored binding showing almost no signs of use, text bright, clean and fresh with spacious margins.   Phillip J. Pirages   66 - 19   2015 $7500

Association – Schroeder, Barbet

Bukowski, Charles *Shakespeare Never Did This.* San Francisco: City Lights Books, 1979. First edition, numerous photos by Michael Montfort, inscribed by author for Silvanna, with self caricature, with address label of director Barbet Schroeder on inside front cover, along with coffee spot that has been circled, labeled 'Authentic!' and signed by Barbet, laid in is NS from Schroeder to Silvana presenting the book as a birthday gift, near fine wrapper issue.   Ken Lopez, Bookseller   164 - 22   2015 $1250

Association – Schutz, John

Bath, William Pulteney, 1st Earl of   1684-1764   *A Report from the Committee Appointed by Order of the House of Commons to Examine Christopher Layer and Others...* London: printed for Jacob Tonson, Bernard Lintot and William Taylor, 1722. First edition, initial license leaf, stab holes in inner blank margins of last 3 leaves, contemporary calf with double gilt fillets on sides, spine with gilt lines, raised bands and label, minor splits in joints at head and foot but very good, 18th century armorial bookplate of John Schutz, Esq. and armorial bookplate (early 19th century?) of Horace Walpole.   John Drury Rare Books   2015 - 17995   2015 $874

Association – Schuyler, Eugene

Turgenev, Ivan Sergeevich   1818-1883   *Fathers and Sons.* New York: Leypoldt & Holt, 1867. First edition in English, octavo, contemporary red morocco over marbled boards, translator Eugene Schuyler's copy with his bookplate.   Honey & Wax Booksellers   2 - 63   2015 $6000

Association – Schuyler, James

Ashbery, John   *A Nest of Ninnies.* New York: Dutton, 1969. First edition, one of 6000 copies, 8vo., cloth backed boards, dust jacket, small spot of dampstaining at head of spine, spine little cocked, otherwise fine in slightly dust soiled, and nicked dust jacket, with one tiny closed tear and bit of wear to head of spine, presentation from James Schuyler for Trevor Winkfield.   James S. Jaffe Rare Books   Modern American Poetry - 12   2015 $1750

Association – Schwartz, Frances

Zolotow, Charlotte   *The New Friend.* New York: Thomas Y. Crowell, 1981. Reprint of 1968 edition, square octavo, illustrations by Emily Arnold McCully, little foxing, else near fine in near fine dust jacket, dedication copy, inscribed by author to editor and agent Frances Schwartz.   Between the Covers Rare Books, Inc.   187 - 52   2015 $275

Association – Schwerdt

Wilkes, Wetenhall   *Hounslow-Heath, a Poem.* London: printed for C. Corbett and sold at the booksellers in London and Westminster, 1748. First edition, reissue of 1747 printing with date in imprint reset, 4to., 19th century half Roxburghe, purple boards, green morocco spine (rubbed), later bookplates of the celebrated Schwerdt collection and of the Duke of Gloucester, fine.   C. R. Johnson   Foxon R-Z - 1151r-z   2015 $3831

Association – Schwob, Marcel

Whibley, Charles *Studies in Frankness.* London: William Heinemann, 1898. First edition, presentation copy inscribed by author for friend Marcel Schwob Nov.. 1897, original black cloth with rubbing to front cover, bumping to corners and edge of front board, spotting to prelims, otherwise very good. The Kelmscott Bookshop 11 - 62 2015 $250

Association – Scott, A. J., Mrs.

Ruskin, John 1819-1900 *The Queen of the Air: Being a Study of the Greek Myths of Cloud and Storm.* London: Smith, Elder, 1869. Second edition, 8vo., presentation from author for Mrs. A. J. Scott, April 1870, decent clean very good copy in original green cloth lettered gilt at spine, top of titlepage has been cut out to reveal presentation at top of next page, (not affecting text), slight rubbing at spine ends, else very good. Any Amount of Books 2015 - A63060 2015 £200

Association – Scott, Hope Montgomery

John, Augustus *Chiaroscuro: Fragments of Autobiography.* London: Cape, 1952. First edition, of two variants, this copy the variant with red topstain and "AJ" on front board, the Cape imprint on spine (no priority), trifle sunned at crown, corners little bumped, faint tape shadows where address label in John's hand had been affixed and now removed and laid in), this copy inscribed by painter to Hope Montgomery Scott. Between the Covers Rare Books, Inc. 187 - 138 2015 $450

Association – Scott, Joseph

Skutsch, Otto *Alfred Edward Housman 1859-1936.* London: University of London Athlone Press, 1960. Half title, original blue printed wrappers, presentation copy to Geoffrey Tillotson from librarian Joseph Scott, with TLS mentioning omissions from the lecture. Jarndyce Antiquarian Booksellers CCVII - 317 2015 £30

Association – Scott, Laurence

Williams, William Carlos 1883-1963 *Paterson (Books 1-5).* New York: New Directions, 1946-1958. First editions, first four parts limited to 1000 copies, fifth to 3000, 5 volumes, 8vo., original cloth, dust jackets, inscribed by poet to Laurence Scott, fine set. James S. Jaffe Rare Books Modern American Poetry - 325 2015 $8500

Association – Scott, Paul

Grace, Fran *Carry A. Nation: retelling the Life.* Bloomington and Indianapolis: Indiana University Press, 2001. First edition, presentation copy inscribed by author for Paul B. Scott, octavo, original blue cloth, black titles, fine in fine dust jacket. Tavistock Books Temperance - 2015 $50

Association – Scudamore, Joyce

Durrell, Lawrence 1912-1990 *The Tree of Idleness.* London: Faber, 1955. First edition, fine with usual browning of endpapers, near fine dust jacket but for slightly sunned spine, bookplate of Joyce Scudamore, 48 pages. Beasley Books 2013 - 2015 $200

Association – Searle, Monica

Bell, Steve *Steve Bell: Im Auge Des Zeichners; Eine Ausstellung Im Deutschen Museum fur Karikatur und Zeichenkusnt...* Hannover: Wilhelm-Busch, 2011. First edition, oblong 4to., original illustrated matt boards, lettered white on spine and in red on front cover, copiously illustrated in color and black and white, signed presentation from author for Ronald and Monica, written note in Ronald Searle's hand on front endpaper "Rec'd fron Steve 8 April 2011", fine. Any Amount of Books 2015 - C7346 2015 £150

Association – Searle, Ronald

Bell, Steve *Steve Bell: Im Auge Des Zeichners; Eine Ausstellung Im Deutschen Museum fur Karikatur und Zeichenkusnt...* Hannover: Wilhelm-Busch, 2011. First edition, oblong 4to., original illustrated matt boards, lettered white on spine and in red on front cover, copiously illustrated in color and black and white, signed presentation from author for Ronald and Monica, written note in Ronald Searle's hand on front endpaper "Rec'd from Steve 8 April 2011", fine. Any Amount of Books 2015 - C7346 2015 £150

Hancock, H. Irving *Japanese Physical Training.* New York and London: G. P. Putnam's Sons, 1905. First edition, 8vo., original orange cloth lettered black on spine and cover, 19 illustrations, about fine in dust jacket with slight wear and slight chip at head of spine and slight creasing and nick at front corner, from the library of Ronald Searle. Any Amount of Books 2015 - A98969 2015 £180

James, Henry 1843-1916 *The Bostonians.* New York: Modern Library, 1956. First edition thus, 8vo., very good in like dust jacket (price clipped), very clean, bright copy with marginal linings, underlinings and notes of page numbers and one pencil illustration by Ronald Searle, bought from the library of Searle. Any Amount of Books 2015 - C10184 2015 £150

Lacroix, Georges *Chacun Son Chat.* Paris: Edition Fantome Diffusion Glenat, 1987. First edition, limited edition, no. 88 of 350, 4to. original grey cloth, lettered white on spine and cover in gray printed slipcase, Ronald Searle's copy, loosely inserted is card from publisher saying 'examplaire pour R. Searle". Any Amount of Books 2015 - A99118 2015 £175

Association – Sebag-Montefiore, Charles

Trotter, Alexander *A Plan of Communication Between the New and Old Town of Edinburgh, in the Line of the Earthen Mound...* Edinburgh: Oliver & Boyd & Simpkin & Marshall, London and Robertson & Atkinson, Glasgow, 1929. 4to., 6 large folding lithographic plates, fine later binding of half calf gilt over marbled boards, fine, sometime in the library of Charles Sebag-Montefiore with his armorial bookplate. John Drury Rare Books 2015 - 24351 2015 $787

Association – Secker, Martin

Douglas, Norman 1868-1952 *Looking Back: an Autobiographical Excursion.* London: Chatto & Windus, 1934. First edition in one volume, thick large volume, boards bit soiled, thus very good without dust jacket, publisher Martin Secker's copy with his small bookplate. Between the Covers Rare Books, Inc. 187 - 80 2015 $125

Association – Sedgwick, Susan Anne Livingston Ridley

Thorburn, Grant *Forty Years' Residence in America or the Doctrine of a Particular Providence Exemplified in the Life of Grant Thorburn, Seedsman, NY.* Boston: Russell Odiorne & Metcalf, 1834. First edition, publisher's green pebble grain cloth with leather spine label gilt, 264 pages, ownership signature on titlepage of children's book author Susan Anne Livingston Ridley Sedgwick, light scattered foxing, nice, near fine, inscribed by author for Sedgewick. Between the Covers Rare Books, Inc. 187 - 276 2015 $400

Association – Seed, Harris

Bruccoli, Matthew J. *Kenneth Millar/Ross MacDonald: a checklist.* Detroit: Gale Research Co., 1971. First edition, 8vo., photos, inscribed by author to his lawyer Harris Seed, also laid-in is bookmark issued by publisher that prints the poem by author that also bears his holograph signature in ink, fine, bright copy. Buckingham Books March 2015 - 27904 2015 $1250

Association – Segal, David

Ozick,, Cynthia *Trust.* New York: New American Library, 1966. Uncorrected proof copy, tall comb-bound galley sheets, laid in is letter sent by editor, David Segal to author John Barth, with request for opinion, this copy signed by Barth, Ozick's name was left off cover and has been added in ink, mild sunning and curling to covers, small tear at upper spine, about near fine, very scarce proof. Ken Lopez, Bookseller 164 - 163 2015 $1500

Association – Self, William

Dickens, Charles 1812-1870 *Dombey and Son.* London: Bradbury & Evans, 1848. First edition in book form, octavo, engraved frontispiece, engraved titlepage and 38 plates, with two original pen and ink drawings by the artist, Phiz, inserted, each signed "Phiz", extremely rare with drawings, each drawing is on a sheet of onion skin measuring 138 x110mm and then inlaid into later sheet to match size of other leaves, original front wrapper for part iv bound in at end, without half title and list of plates, full olive morocco bound by Sangorski & Sutcliffe, boards decoratively stamped in black, gilt lettered on spine, gilt ruled dentelles, marbled endpapers, top edge gilt, with two previous owner's bookplates, "Kenyon Starling" and "Self" and spine lightly sunned, near fine. Heritage Book Shop Holiday 2014 - 55 2015 $16,500

Association – Selincourt, Ernest De

Arnold, Matthew 1822-1888 *Irish Essays and Other.* London: Smith, Elder, 1891. Popular edition, half title, 2 pages ads, original brown cloth, signature of Ernest de Selincourt Sept. 24 1891, very good. Jarndyce Antiquarian Booksellers CCXI - 14 2015 £25

Association – Senhouse, Roger

Lawrence, David Herbert 1885-1930 *New Poems.* London: Martin Secker, 1919. New edition (reset), paper covered boards with applied spine label, bit of wear to extremities of boards, else near fine, Roger Senhouse's copy with his tiny ownership signature and bookplate. Between the Covers Rare Books, Inc. 187 - 151 2015 $200

Association – Shahn, Ben

Evans, Walker *American Photographs.* New York: Museum of Modern Art, 1962. Second edition, quarto, bookplate designed by Johnathan Shahn, fine in slightly spine toned dust jacket, with tiny tear, otherwise fine, inscribed by author to Ben and Bernarda Shahn, May 1962. Between the Covers Rare Books, Inc. 187 - 214 2015 $5000

Association – Shahn, Bernarda

Evans, Walker *American Photographs.* New York: Museum of Modern Art, 1962. Second edition, quarto, bookplate designed by Johnathan Shahn, fine in slightly spine toned dust jacket, with tiny tear, otherwise fine, inscribed by author to Ben and Bernarda Shahn, May 1962. Between the Covers Rare Books, Inc. 187 - 214 2015 $5000

Association – Shakespear, Olivia

Pound, Ezra Loomis 1885-1972 *Canzoni.* London: Elkin Mathews, 1911. First edition, first issue, one of 1000 copies printed of which 'not more than 500' were later issued as part of the combined volume 'Canzoni & Ripostes' (1913), 12mo., original grey cloth, inscribed for Olivia Shakespear, corners little bumped, spine lightly sunned, faint spot on back cover, otherwise fine. James S. Jaffe Rare Books Modern American Poetry - 230 2015 $2000

Association – Shapiro, Karl

Beloof, Robert *The One Eyed Gunner and Other Portraits: a Book of Poems.* London: Villiers Pub., 1956. First edition, fine in near fine dust jacket with small nicks and tears at crown, inscribed by author to fellow poet, Karl Shapiro. Between the Covers Rare Books, Inc. 187 - 14 2015 $45

Leger, Alexis Saint-Leger *Anabasis.* New York: Harcourt Brace and Co., 1949. Revised edition, modest wear, very good, lacking dust jacket, poet/critic Karl Shapiro's copy with his ownership signature and several ink notes in his hand. Between the Covers Rare Books, Inc. 187 - 210 2015 $250

Manning, Hugo *The Secret Sea.* London: Trigram Press, 1968. One of 500 copies, tiny name inked over, else fine in fine dust jacket, warmly inscribed by author for poet Karl Shapiro. Between the Covers Rare Books, Inc. 187 - 165 2015 $150

Schevill, James *The Black President and Other Plays.* Denver: Alan Swallow, 1965. First edition, wrappered issue, near fine in wrappers, nicely inscribed by poet to Karl Shapiro. Between the Covers Rare Books, Inc. 187 - 243 2015 $150

Slavitt, David R. *Dozens.* Baton Rouge: Louisiana State University Press, 1981. First edition, fine in slightly spine faded, near fine dust jacket, nicely inscribed to poet Karl (and Teri) Shapiro 4/3081. Between the Covers Rare Books, Inc. 187 - 260 2015 $125

Association – Shapiro, Teri

Slavitt, David R. *Dozens.* Baton Rouge: Louisiana State University Press, 1981. First edition, fine in slightly spine faded, near fine dust jacket, nicely inscribed to poet Karl (and Teri) Shapiro 4/3081. Between the Covers Rare Books, Inc. 187 - 260 2015 $125

Association – Sharpe, Fane William

Thomas A Kempis 1380-1471 *The Christian's Pattern; or a Treatise of the Imitation of Jesus Christ...* London: printed for Barker (and others), 1742. 203 x 127mm., animated contemporary black morocco, lavishly gilt, covers with central cottage-roof design enclosed by ornate floral rolls and small tools, the 'roof' frame containing a large and elaborate fleuron within a lozenge of small tools, raised bands, spine gilt in compartments bordered by plain rules and dogtooth rolls, each compartment divided into quarters by gilt diagonal lines, each quarter with a delicate stippled floral tool, red morocco label, gilt turn-ins, marbled endpapers, all edges gilt, engraved frontispiece of Crucifixion, plus engravings of the nativity, Adoration of the Magi, Christ in the Wilderness and the Last Supper; 18th century bookplate of Fane William Sharpe, 18th or 19th century armorial bookplate of W. Combes, spine faded to pleasing hazel brown, little rubbing to joints and extremities, minor chafing to boards, occasional faint foxing, isolated dust soiling to head edge, other trivial imperfections, but fine, nevertheless, leaves clean and fresh and intricately tooled unsophisticated binding very lustrous and showing no significant wear, splendid copy. Phillip J. Pirages 66 - 35 2015 $3200

Association – Sharpe, Michael

Thomas A Kempis 1380-1471 *Opera.* Paris: Iodocus Badius Ascensius, 1523. Second collected edition, first edition printed in France, 330 x 216mm., lacking final blank, fine contemporary London blindstamped calf, covers tooled in panels, outer frame of a roll of Renaissance designs including fountain topped by three heads, central panel composed mainly of five vertical rows of foliage and flowers, raised bands, spine very expertly rebacked to style, two original brass clasps and catches with leather thongs (perhaps later but perhaps not), original vellum tabs marking important textual sections, rear board with contemporaneous inscription (perhaps author and title), rear pastedown comprising a portion of a proclamation dealing with beggars and vagabonds, in recent clamshell box backed with calf, titlepage with woodcut device dated 1520 depicting printer's workshop, large and small woodcut initials in text (few artlessly colored), titlepage with signature of Johannes Person above woodcut vignette and of another member of Person family at top of page, (this inscription dated 1566 with purchase details for the volume), also signature of A. Fletcher, inside cover of box and front pastedown with modern morocco bookplate of Michael Sharpe, lower board with small abraded area, other trivial marks and very small wormholes in leather, thongs bit dried and deteriorating, but expertly restored binding entirely solid and blindstamping still quite sharp, titlepage little dust soiled and with small shadow of turn-in glue at bottom, last three gatherings with minor stains along gutter, final gathering with similar stain at fore-edge, short tears and other trivial imperfections in text, generally quite fine internally, text mostly quite clean, especially fresh and unusually bright. Phillip J. Pirages 66 - 7 2015 $12,500

Association – Shaw, Artie

Dahlberg, Edward *The Flea of Sodom.* Norfolk: New Directions, 1950. First edition, fine in fine dust jacket with little rubbing at spine, inscribed by author for bandleader Artie Shaw. Between the Covers Rare Books, Inc. 187 - 66 2015 $250

Association – Shaw, Joe

Gardner, Erle Stanley *The Case of the Velvet Claws.* First edition, near fine in very good plus example of rare dust jacket, jacket is quite nice with slight loss at crown, just barely touching word 'The' in title, light wear at heel, corners and top of back panel and couple of closed tears, otherwise bright and clean, inscribed by author for Capt. Joe Shaw, editor, from the collection of Duke Collier. Royal Books 36 - 9 2015 $37,500

Association – Sheehan, Neil

Updike, John 1932-2009 *The Music School.* New York: Alfred A. Knopf, 1966. First edition, 2nd state with pages 45-46 as a cancel, slight printer's paper flaw, else fine in dust jacket with offsetting on front panel, otherwise fine, inscribed by author to Susan and Neil Sheehan. Between the Covers Rare Books, Inc. 187 - 282 2015 $1500

Association – Sheehan, Susan

Updike, John 1932-2009 *Bech: a Book.* New York: Alfred A. Knopf, 1970. First edition, ine in fine dust jacket, inscribed by author for Susan Sheehan. Between the Covers Rare Books, Inc. 187 - 283 2015 $950

Updike, John 1932-2009 *The Poorhouse Fair.* New York: Alfred A. Knopf, 1959. First edition, one corner slightly bumped, else fine in fine dust jacket, inscribed by author for Susan Sheehan. Between the Covers Rare Books, Inc. 187 - 271 2015 $3000

Updike, John 1932-2009 *The Music School.* New York: Alfred A. Knopf, 1966. First edition, 2nd state with pages 45-46 as a cancel, slight printer's paper flaw, else fine in dust jacket with offsetting on front panel, otherwise fine, inscribed by author to Susan and Neil Sheehan. Between the Covers Rare Books, Inc. 187 - 282 2015 $1500

Association – Sherburn, George

Smart, Christopher 1722-1771 *Jubilate Agno.* Cambridge: Harvard University Press, 1954. Half title, original green cloth, very good, repaired dust jacket, inscribed by George Sherburn Sept. 1954 for Geoffrey Tilltoson, with inserted postcard. Jarndyce Antiquarian Booksellers CCVII - 472 2015 £25

Association – Sheridan, Marion

Frost, Robert Lee 1874-1963 *A Boy's Will.* New York: Henry Holt, 1934. First edition thus, reissue with minor changes from previous editions, 8vo., original cloth, dust jacket, inscribed by author for Marion Sheridan. James S. Jaffe Rare Books Modern American Poetry - 96 2015 $2500

Association – Shirburn Castle

Bible. Greek - 1590 *Metaphrasis tou Psalteros dia Stichon Heroikon.* Excudebat Georgius Bishop, 1590. First printing in England, ownership embossment to titlepage causing small hole affecting two characters, intermittent light dampmarks to fore-edge, 8vo., contemporary blind ruled sheep, rebacked preserving original spine, few other tidy repairs, hinges lined with printed binder's waste, bookplate of Shirburn Castle, good.   Blackwell's Rare Books   B179 - 9   2015   £600

Association – Shirley, Walter

Ward, Edward   1667-1731 *Nupital Dialogues and Debates; or an Useful Prospect of the Felicities and Discomforts of a Marry'd Life...* London: printed by H. Meere for T. Norris and A. Bettesworth and sold by J. Woodward, 1710. 2 volumes, 8vo., full marbled calf, gilt, spines gilt, brown morocco labels, red edges, traces of rubbing, fine, bookplates of Walter E. Shirley.   C. R. Johnson Foxon R-Z - 1076r-z   2015 $1915

Association – Shivers, Allan

Brewer, J. Mason   *Aunt Dicy Tales: Snuff Dipping Tales of the Texas Negro.*   privately printed for J. Mason Brewer, 1956. Limited to 400 copies, this #39 and signed by Brewer, this copy given as gift by then Governor of Texas Allan Shivers with his gift card laid in and inked presentation, original green gold gilt stamped padded leatherette, beautiful black and white front and rear endpaper, frontispiece on brown enamel stock, illustrations by John Biggers with 13 full page plates, fine, clean, square copy.   Buckingham Books   March 2015 - 37618   2015 $2000

Association – Shore, Mary

Crews, Judson   *The Southern Temper.*   Waco: Motive, 1946. First edition, inscribed by author in 1952 to Mary Shore, painter and friend of Charles Olson, near fine in stapled wrappers and very good, dampstained dust jacket with two small holes on rear panel.   Ken Lopez, Bookseller   164 - 41   2015 $125

Association – Shorthouse, Edward

Shorthouse, H. J.   *Sir Percival: a Story of the Past and Present.*   London: Macmillan and Co., 1886. First edition, presentation copy inscribed "Edward Shorthouse from his affectionate brother and sister J. Henry & Sarah Shorthouse", original dark blue cloth, gilt strips with embossed design on front over and spine, fine, housed in fine custom half red morocco slipcase, octavo, fine, bookplate of Ohio book collector Paul Lemperly with his inscription stating he received the book as a gift from Morris L. Parrish, with Parrish's letter of presentation inserted.   The Kelmscott Bookshop   11 - 46   2015 $600

Association – Shorthouse, John Henry

Shorthouse, H. J.   *Sir Percival: a Story of the Past and Present.*   London: Macmillan and Co., 1886. First edition, presentation copy inscribed "Edward Shorthouse from his affectionate brother and sister J. Henry & Sarah Shorthouse", original dark blue cloth, gilt strips with embossed design on front over and spine, fine, housed in fine custom half red morocco slipcase, octavo, fine, bookplate of Ohio book collector Paul Lemperly with his inscription stating he received the book as a gift from Morris L. Parrish, with Parrish's letter of presentation inserted.   The Kelmscott Bookshop   11 - 46   2015 $600

Association – Shorthouse, Sarah

Shorthouse, H. J.   *Sir Percival: a Story of the Past and Present.*   London: Macmillan and Co., 1886. First edition, presentation copy inscribed "Edward Shorthouse from his affectionate brother and sister J. Henry & Sarah Shorthouse", original dark blue cloth, gilt strips with embossed design on front over and spine, fine, housed in fine custom half red morocco slipcase, octavo, fine, bookplate of Ohio book collector Paul Lemperly with his inscription stating he received the book as a gift from Morris L. Parrish, with Parrish's letter of presentation inserted.   The Kelmscott Bookshop   11 - 46   2015 $600

Association – Shurtliff, Ram Rod

Brandelius, Jerilyn Lee   *Grateful Dead Family Album.*   New York: Warner Books, 1989. First edition, 'Grateful Dead All Area Access sticker laid down to jacket, this copy signed by band members Jerry Garcia, Mickey Hart and Bob Bralove as well as long time road crew members Ram Rod Shurtliff, Bill 'Kid' Candelario, Steve Parish and Robbie Taylor among others, hundreds of intimate photos and stories, very good plus to near fine with little soil and handling marks, in very good plus to near fine dust jacket with short closed tear to bottom of front flap.   Ed Smith Books   83 - 34   2015 $950

Association – Shute, Nevil

Sophocles *Quae Exstant Omnia cum Veterum Grammaticorum Scholiis.* Strasbourg: Apud Joannem Georgium Treuttel, 1786. First Brunck edition, bound without final leaf in volume ii (blank except for colophon on verso, often missing), few minor spots, early ms. date to volume i title, 4to., contemporary russia, boards bordered with gilt roll with torch tools at corners, spines divided by double gilt fillet, second and fourth compartments gilt lettered direct, rest with central gilt tool of mask and instruments, all edges gilt, marbled endpapers, front board of volume I with prize inscription lettered direct in gilt and enclosed on top and sides by gilt flower and pearl tools, old repair to spine ends in slightly different color, some cracking to front joint of volume i, few old scratches and marks, bookplate of author Nevil Shute and lending label of Sandford Press, good. Blackwell's Rare Books   Greek & Latin Classics VI - 97   2015   £750

Association – Sickles, Daniel

Bible. Polyglot - 1554 *Le Noveau Testament De Nostre Seigneur Jesus Christ.* Lyon: Guillaume Rouille, 1554. 127 x 83mm., pleasing contemporary calf decorated in an Entrelac design, boards ornamented in the Lyonnaise style with intricate interlacing strapwork and foliage in dark brown and gray outlined in gilt on a background of tiny gilt dots, flat spine with similar decoration (these 16th century designs expertly laid down onto modern calf), all edges gilt, elaborate historiated woodcut frame enclosing each of the two title pages, some decorative and historiated woodcut initials and headpieces in text, embossed armorial bookplate of Daniel Sickles, covers with trivial marks and worm traces, text printed on inexpensive (and consequently yellowed) paper, first few leaves and last leaf little thumbed, isolated minor soiling, but excellent example, carefully restored binding entirely solid and quite bright and text smooth and fresh. Phillip J. Pirages   66 - 10   2015 $8500

Association – Sifton, Elizabeth

Ashbery, John *Hotel Lautreamont.* New York: Alfred A. Knopf, 1993. First edition, faint sticker shadow on front pastedown, else fine in fine dust jacket, pencil signature of Ashbery's editor Elizabeth Sifton.   Between the Covers Rare Books, Inc.   187 - 4   2015 $65

Association – Simonson, Raoul

Anacreon *Odes.* Paris: Chez Du Pont, 1795. 171 x 102mm., fine contemporary black straight grain morocco gilt by Bozerian (stamp-signed at foot of spine), covers framed with undulating grape vine enclosed by double rules, starburst cornerpieces, raised bands, spine gilt in densely stippled compartments with gilt leaves and flowers emanating from central inlaid red morocco dot, turn-ins with gilt bead and star roll, pink watered silk endleaves embellished with their own cresting floral border, all edges gilt, large paper copy, bookplate of Raoul Simonson (and faint dampstain under it, indicating removal of previous one); one faint scratch on back cover, especially fine, text, clean, smooth and bright, in unworn sparkling binding.   Phillip J. Pirages   66 - 61   2015 $2250

Baouir De Lormian, Pierre Marie Francois Louis *Veillees Poetiques et Morales Suivies Des Plus Beaux Fragmens D'Young en Vers Francais.* Paris: printed by P. Didot for Latour Delanay and Brunot Abbot, 1811. First edition, 156 x 89mm., extremely pretty contemporary green calf, gilt, covers with delicate floral frame enclosing gilt compartments separated by inlaid red morocco bands, two compartments with rose sprig centerpiece and two compartments with densely interlocking rows of circles, red morocco label, turn-ins with decorative gilt roll, marbled endpapers, all edges gilt (lower joint apparently with very neat expert repair at tail), with etched vignette on titlepage and 3 engraved plates, original tissue guards; bookplate of Raoul Simonson, leather bookplate of Laurent Mecus; front joint with very short thin crack at tail, one opening with faintest freckled foxing, otherwise beautiful copy, text exceptionally clean, fresh and bright, scarcely worn, lustrous binding glistening with gold, especially pleasing gold dusted or "Saupoudrage" binding.   Phillip J. Pirages   66 - 78   2015 $1500

Association – Simpson, Harriet

Arnold-Forster, Frances *Studies in Church Dedications; or, England's Patron Saints.* London: Skeffington, 1899. First edition, octavo, 3 volumes, full white buckram lettered in red and black, all edges red, armorial pictorial bookplates and ownership signature of one of the book's subscribers, Harriet A. Simpson, loosely inserted is short ALS to her from author, endpapers little spotted, red lettering on spines slightly faded, still near fine, remarkably bright set.   Peter Ellis, Bookseller   2014 - 005500   2015   £350

Association – Simpson, Tony

Simpson, Louis *The Best Hour of the Night.* New Haven and New York: Ticknor & Fields, 1983. First edition, fine in lightly rubbed, very good dust jacket with bit of wear at head of spine and puncture on front panel, inscribed by poet to his son Tony, Christmas 83.   Between the Covers Rare Books, Inc.   187 - 257   2015 $250

Simpson, Louis *Collected Poems.* New York: Paragon House, 1988. First edition, fine in fine dust jacket, inscribed by author for son Tony, Oct. '88. Between the Covers Rare Books, Inc. 187 - 258 2015 $750

Association – Sipper, Ralph

MacDonald, Ross *Self-Portrait: Ceaselessly into the Past.* Santa Barbara: Capra Press, 1981. First edition, one of 26 lettered copies (this being letter 'J'), signed by author and Eudora Welty who provided introduction and additional inscription by book's publisher, Ralph Sipper, dated 1981, original photo of the two authors laid into pocket tipped on to front pastedown, as issued, fine in black leather, paper covered slipcase as issued, corners of slipcase lightly rubbed, from the collection of Duke Collier. Royal Books 36 - 81 2015 $1500

Association – Skelton, John

Swinburne, Algernon Charles 1837-1909 *The Queen Mother. Rosamund. Two Plays.* London: Basil Montagu Pickering, 1860. First edition, first issue in second state with cancel titlepage and addition of half titles to each play, lovely copy, rebound in contemporary three quarter green morocco with red marbled paper boards and endpapers, all edges marbled, slightly rubbed and bumped but very good, interior pages very good with occasional light pencil checks of lines in margins to highlight line or phrase, interesting association copy, very good, inscribed by author for W. M. Rossetti, this is the copy of author and critic John Skelton with his pencil note "Given to me by D. G. Rossetti for review in Fraser's magazine". The Kelmscott Bookshop 11 - 52 2015 $4500

Association – Skiff, Frederick

Bacheller, Irving *Vergilius: a Tale of the Coming of Christ.* New York: Harper & Bros., 1904. First edition, lightly edge-worn, near fine, without dust jacket, bookplate of collector Frederick W. Skiff and later book label of Estelle Doheny collection, inscribed by Bacheller to Skiff Dec. 22 1916. Between the Covers Rare Books, Inc. 187 - 5 2015 $125

Association – Skinner, Joy

MacKenzie, Faith Compton *The Cardinal's Niece: the Story of Marie Mancini.* London: Martin Secker, 1935. First edition, frontispiece, plates, original binding somewhat marked and spine discolored, but very good, presentation copy inscribed by author for Joy Skinner, from the collection of Gavin H. Fryer. Bertram Rota Ltd. 308 Part II - 183 2015 £60

Association – Slater, Harriet

Rueben Ramble's Travels through the Counties. London: Darton and Clark, Book print and Map Publishers 58 Holborn Hill, 1844. 4to., hand colored lithograph frontispiece, additional title and 40 hand colored lithograph maps with scenic boards of key plates in each county, green half morocco over marbled boards, inscribed "Harriet C. Slater 1 Oakley Crescent 1848". Marlborough Rare Books List 54 - 18 2015 £2850

Association – Sleaford, W.

The History of Tom Jones the Foundling, in His Married State. London: J. Robinson, 1750. (1749). Reissue of sheets of first edition with cancel title and added final chapter, 12mo., half title, small tears to blank fore margin on half title and titlepage, contemporary calf, some small expert repairs, most notably to head of spine, signature on title of W. Sleaford, 1749, very good. Jarndyce Antiquarian Booksellers CCXI - 117 2015 £1100

Association – Smallwood, Steven St. Clair

Callimachus *Callimaco Greco-Italiano Ora Pubblicato.* Parma: Nel Regal Palazzo Co' Tipi Bodiani, 1792. 311 x 229mm., handsome early 19th century red straight grain morocco by Charles Hering (his ticket on verso of front free endpaper), covers with thick and thin gilt rule border, raised bands flanked by gilt rules, gilt titling and turn-ins, all edges gilt, booklabel of Steven St Clair Smallwood; joints bit rubbed and flaked, though refurbished with considerable success, two corners little bumped, spine faded toward rose, few minor marks in morocco, isolated faint marginal foxing, still extremely pleasing copy high quality binding with no serious defects, text printed on thick paper, creamy paper with enormous margins. Phillip J. Pirages 66 - 66 2015 $6500

Association – Smedley, Frances Sarah

Smedley, Frank *Last Leaves from Beechwood.* Enfield: printed by J. H. Meyers, 1867. Photographic portrait of author as frontispiece and one other small photo laid down on page 7, errata slip with two additional corrections in ms., original green cloth blocked in blind, lettered gilt, slightly dulled with small ink mark on front board, presentation inscription "Frances Sarah Smedley 1867 in affectionate remembrance of her beloved son". Jarndyce Antiquarian Booksellers CCXI - 257 2015 £180

Association – Smith, Bernard

Mencken, Henry L. *Supplement One: The American Language.* New York: Alfred A. Knopf, 1945. First edition, fine in moderately age toned, near fine dust jacket with short tear at one fold, nicely in inscribed by author to important literary editor, Bernard Smith. Between the Covers Rare Books 196 - 95 2015 $750

Association – Stafford, Jean

Joyce, James 1882-1941 *A Shorter Finnegans Wake.* New York: Viking Press, 1967. First American edition edited by Anthony Burgess, octavo, original maroon cloth, original dust jacket, ownership stamps of novelist Jean Stafford and New Yorker writer Joseph Mitchell with his notes pencilled on envelope from his family's tobacco warehouse, laid in.   Honey & Wax Booksellers   2 - 50   2015 $1000

Lowell, Robert 1917-1977 *History.* New York: Farrar, Straus & Giroux, 1973. First edition, fine in fine dust jacket, inscribed by author to his first wife Jean Stafford, with short typed letter by one of the proprietors of Argosy bookstore NY city confirming book's provenance.   Between the Covers Rare Books   196 - 88   2015 $4000

Association – Stahlman, William Duane

Nilsson, Martin P. *Primitive Time-Reckoning: a Study in the Origins and First Development of the Art of Counting Time Among the Primitive and Early Peoples.* Lund: C. W. K. Gleerup; London: Humphrey Milford; Oxford: University Press, 1920. 8vo., original quarter vellum, plain boards, manuscript spine title, ink ownership signatures of Alexandri Phili (192), William Duane Stahlman and David C. Lindberg.   Jeff Weber Rare Books   178 - 846   2015 $45

Association – Standard, Paul

Menhart, Oldrich *Menhart 1897-1962.* N.P.: Indiana University, 1966. First edition printed letterpress on Masa and Fabriano papers in an edition limited to 144 numbered copies, 4 volumes, folio, 4 paper wrapper fascicules, slipcase, unpaginated French fold pages, printed in various colors, this copy has loose slip inscribed "Phil, to recall our long years as colleagues & as fellow calligraphers, Paul (Standard) NY, Nov. 1966", some wear along edges of slipcase.   Oak Knoll Books   Special Catalogue 24 - 32   2015 $400

Association – Stark, Fidelia

Wolfe, Thomas Clayton *Look Homeward, Angel.* New York: Charles Scribner's, 1929. First edition, spine lettering worn but readable, very good in worn, good only first issue dust jacket (with Wolfe portrait on rear panel), lacking bottom couple of inches of spine and several other modest chips and tears, several internal tape repairs, this copy inscribed by author for Fidelia E. Stark, Oct. 30 1929, laid in 4 page carbon manuscript (folded, small breaks at folds, else near fine), unsigned but almost certainly by Maxwell Perkins dated April 17, 1929.   Between the Covers Rare Books   196 - 127   2015 $12,000

Association – Starling, Kenyon

Dickens, Charles 1812-1870 *Dombey and Son.* London: Bradbury & Evans, 1848. First edition in book form, octavo, engraved frontispiece, engraved titlepage and 38 plates, with two original pen and ink drawings by the artist, Phiz, inserted, each signed "Phiz", extremely rare with drawings, each drawing is on a sheet of onion skin measuring 138 x110mm and then inlaid into later sheet to match size of other leaves, original front wrapper for part iv bound in at end, without half title and list of plates, full olive morocco bound by Sangorski & Sutcliffe, boards decoratively stamped in black, gilt lettered on spine, gilt ruled dentelles, marbled endpapers, top edge gilt, with two previous owner's bookplates, "Kenyon Starling" and "Self" and spine lightly sunned, near fine.   Heritage Book Shop   Holiday 2014 - 55   2015 $16,500

Association – Starr, Harvey

Outland, Charles F. *Man-Made Disaster: the Story of the St. Francis Dame: Its Place in Southern California's Water System. Its Failure and the Tragedy of March 12 and 13 1928 in the Santa Clara River Valley.* Glendale: Arthur H. Clark Co., 1963. First edition, illustrations, maps, portraits, brown cloth, bookplate, very fine, pictorial dust jacket, presentation inscription signed by author to friend Harvey Starr, very scarce, especially in this condition, one of 2059 copies.   Argonaut Book Shop   Holiday Season 2014 - 219   2015 $500

Association – Starrett, Vincent

Grimm, The Brothers *Home Stories Collected by the Brothers Grimm.* London: Routledge & Co., 1855. First edition, frontispiece and plates, illustrations by George Thompson, slight tear to inner margin of front, not affecting image, binding cracking in places, but still firm, original blue decorated cloth, little rubbed and dulled, bookplate and signature of Vincent Starrett.   Jarndyce Antiquarian Booksellers   CCXI - 128   2015   £125

Doyle, Arthur Conan 1859-1930 *Micah Clarke: His Statement as Made to His Three Grandchildren Joseph, Gervas & Robert during the hard winter of 1734...* London: Longmans, 1889. Half title, final ad leaf, few leaves roughly opened, original navy blue cloth, bevelled boards, little rubbed, booklabel of Christopher Clark Geest on leading pastedown, signature on half title of Vincent Starrett, 1886-1974.   Jarndyce Antiquarian Booksellers   CCXI - 93   2015   £220

Association – Stawell, George

Denham, John *Poems and Translations with the Sophy.* London: for H. Herringman, 1668. First collected edition, 2nd issue, 8vo., small dampstain and some very minor worming to lower inner margin of A1-K6, 2 small holes in lower part margin of Hh6, with paper flaw in lower corner of M3, 2B1 and lower edge of I2, stain on Aa8, slight rust spotting to Cc3, small slip of paper glued to lower corner of cc4 covering old neat repair, contemporary sheep (20mm. piece torn away from foot of spine, lower corners worn and boards lightly rubbed, old label missing, pastedowns unstuck), Alex Henderson 16?84 signature, early 19th century bookplate of Morough O'Bryen, purple ink oval library stamp of George Stawell, solicitor Torrington, from the library of James Stevens Cox (1910-1997). Maggs Bros. Ltd. 1447 - 137 2015 £500

Association – Steadman, Ralph

Bierce, Ambrose 1842-1914 *The Devil's Dictionary.* New York and London: Bloomsbury, 2003. Fourth printing, small 8vo., fine in fine dust jacket, signed and inscribed by Ralph Steadman for Beef (Torrey), he has added a illustration on same page, small blank sheet of stationery laid in from Jerome Hotel in Aspen CO, fine in fine dust jacket. Ed Smith Books 82 - 26 2015 $250

Ingrams, Richard *The Tale of Driver Grope.* London: Dennis Dobson, 1969. First edition, 4to., illustrations in color, signed and dated by artist, Ralph Steadman, about fine in near very good+ slightly browned and slightly soiled and price clipped dust jacket. Any Amount of Books 2015 - A66647 2015 £150

Association – Steeger, Harry

Nebel, Frederick *Fifty Roads to Town.* Boston: Little Brown, 1936. First edition, very good plus in very good plus dust jacket, slightest lean, light toning and faint soil to backstrip and board edges, jacket is as nice as we have seen on this title, only small chip at crown and light edge rubbing to note, attractive copy, from the collection of Duke Collier, inscribed by author for Harry and Shirley Steeger Jan. 24 1936. Royal Books 36 - 216 2015 $1250

Association – Steeger, Shirley

Nebel, Frederick *Fifty Roads to Town.* Boston: Little Brown, 1936. First edition, very good plus in very good plus dust jacket, slightest lean, light toning and faint soil to backstrip and board edges, jacket is as nice as we have seen on this title, only small chip at crown and light edge rubbing to note, attractive copy, from the collection of Duke Collier, inscribed by author for Harry and Shirley Steeger Jan. 24 1936. Royal Books 36 - 216 2015 $1250

Association – Steinbeck, Bea

Steinbeck, John Ernst 1902-1968 *A Russian Journal.* New York: Viking Press, 1948. First edition, special copy inscribed to author's cousin and his wife, Bea and Stanford Steinbeck, very good with some soiling to cloth in very good bright dust jacket. Ed Smith Books 83 - 87 2015 $4500

Association – Steinbeck, Stanford

Steinbeck, John Ernst 1902-1968 *A Russian Journal.* New York: Viking Press, 1948. First edition, special copy inscribed to author's cousin and his wife, Bea and Stanford Steinbeck, very good with some soiling to cloth in very good bright dust jacket. Ed Smith Books 83 - 87 2015 $4500

Association – Stevens, Brooksie

Brooks, Charles Timothy *Bread from God.* Philadelphia: American Sunday School Union, 1869. First edition, 4to., original green cloth, gilt decorations and lettering, all edges gilt, titlepage and 11 chromolithographed pages, printed rectos only, each leaf has decorated gold frame printed border around an onlaid chromolithographed illustrations, in lower margin of each leaf is imprint of F. Moras Lith. Phil.", inscribed by Brooks for Brooksie Stevens, grandchild, edges little rubbed, fine. The Brick Row Book Shop Miscellany 67 - 25 2015 $1500

Association – Stirling-Maxwell, William

Elsum, John *The Art of Painting After the Italian Manner.* London: Printed for D. Brown at the Black Swan Without Temple Bar, 1703. First edition, first issue, 8vo., some browning and foxing, 19th century Spanish calf by J. Leighton, skillfully rebacked to style with red label, lettered gilt, covers embossed with heraldic device of William Stirling Maxwell with his earlier heraldic bookplate, and on rear paste down location label of Keir designated under "Art and Design" press marks 13.3' scored through and relocated at 'D4'. Marlborough Rare Books List 53 - 13 2015 £1350

Association – Stoddard, Charles Warren

Horne, Richard Hengist *Cosmo de' Medici: an Historical Tragedy and Other Poems.* London: George Rivers, 1875. First edition, contemporary red polished half calf gilt and marbled paper covered boards, raised bands and floral decorations in compartments, front joint slightest bit tender, very good or better, inscribed by author to poet Charles Warren Stoddard, Aug. 21 1875. Between the Covers Rare Books, Inc. 187 - 131 2015 $350

Association – Stokes, Whitley

Tennyson, Alfred Tennyson, 1st Baron 1809-1892
Poems, Chiefly Lyrical. London: Effingham Wilson, 1830. Uncut, recased in stiff paper with paper label, signature of Whitley Stokes 14/6/55, from the library of Geoffrey & Kathleen Tillotson.   Jarndyce Antiquarian Booksellers   CCVII - 488   2015   £450

Association – Stone, Dee Wallace

Kotzwinkle, William *E. T. The Extra-Terrestrial.* New York: Putnams, 1982. First edition, signed by three cast members, Dee Wallace Stone, Robert MacNaughton and C. Thomas Howell, near fine in near fine dust jacket.   Ed Smith Books   83 - 57   2015 $175

Association – Stone, John

Austen, Ralph *A Treatise of Fruit-Trees Shewing the Manner of Grafting, Setting, Pruning and Ordering of Them in all Respects.* Oxford: for Tho. Robinson, 1653. First edition, small 4to., engraved title with image of ornamental walled garden, small wormtrail in inner margin L4-T4 (partially repaired M2-R1), contemporary calf, spine stamped with gilt shelf mark '393', spine rubbed and scuffed, boards slightly warped, pastedowns unstuck, with "Robert Stone his book/ Anne Coombar 1677" and various pen trials of his name on front flyleaf and on last blank page, signature John Stone, from the library of James Stevens Cox (1910-1997). Maggs Bros. Ltd.   1447 - 14   2015   £600

Association – Stone, Robert

Austen, Ralph *A Treatise of Fruit-Trees Shewing the Manner of Grafting, Setting, Pruning and Ordering of Them in all Respects.* Oxford: for Tho. Robinson, 1653. First edition, small 4to., engraved title with image of ornamental walled garden, small wormtrail in inner margin L4-T4 (partially repaired M2-R1), contemporary calf, spine stamped with gilt shelf mark '393', spine rubbed and scuffed, boards slightly warped, pastedowns unstuck, with "Robert Stone his book/ Anne Coombar 1677" and various pen trials of his name on front flyleaf and on last blank page, signature John Stone, from the library of James Stevens Cox (1910-1997). Maggs Bros. Ltd.   1447 - 14   2015   £600

Association – Stonehill, Charles

Cleveland, John *The Idol of the Clownes or Insurrection of Wat the Tyler with His Priests Baal and Straw...* London: in the Year, 1654. Second edition, small 8vo., without engraved portrait found in some copies and without final blank, light dampstaining to first few leaves, closely shaved at head (just touching pagination in places), early 19th century calf, covers ruled in gilt, spine tooled in gilt and blind, marbled edges and endpapers, small stain on front cover and minor repair on rear, old front flyleaf preserved, from the library of James Stevens Cox (1910-1997), with late 17th/ early 18th century inscription "Thomas Browne/His booke", not that of Sir Thomas Browne (1605-1682), with bookplate of Albert M. Cohn, posthumous sale, Christie 26/2/1934 lot 176 (as Sir Thomas Browne's copy), £5 to Charles H. Stonehill.   Maggs Bros. Ltd.   1447 - 102   2015   £200

Association – Stout, Fay

Nearing, Scott *Dollar Diplomacy.* New York: B. W. Huebsch and the Viking Press, 1925. First edition, near fine, lacking rare dust jacket, attractive octagonal bookplate, small numeric ink notation to same, at top left corner, inscribed by co-author Joseph Freeman to Rex Stout and his wife Fay, from the collection of Duke Collier.   Royal Books   36 - 125   2015 $1500

Association – Stout, Rex

Nearing, Scott *Dollar Diplomacy.* New York: B. W. Huebsch and the Viking Press, 1925. First edition, near fine, lacking rare dust jacket, attractive octagonal bookplate, small numeric ink notation to same, at top left corner, inscribed by co-author Joseph Freeman to Rex Stout and his wife Fay, from the collection of Duke Collier.   Royal Books   36 - 125   2015 $1500

Association – Strachey, Edward

Strachey, John *The Finances and Public Works of India From 1869-1881.* London: Kegan Paul, Trench & co., 1882. First edition, appealing presentation copy, inscribed by authors, John and Richard Strachey for Sir Edward Strachey, 3rd Baronet, bound in original red cloth with corners slightly bumped and spine faded, text pages clean and binding tight, very good.   The Kelmscott Bookshop   11 - 49   2015 $450

Association – Strachey, Lytton

Colvil, Samuel *Whiggs Supplication.* Edinburgh: by Jo. Reid for Alexander Ogston, 1687. Second edition, 8vo., very small chip from upper fore corner with four minor circular stains on titlepage, some occasional staining throughout, dampstaining just touching corners of F4-F6, some heavy modern pencil markings in a number of margins, and with a number of gatherings beginning to come loose from book block, signed by author sheep (worn, large piece torn away from foot of spine and with upper headcap damaged, boards heavily rubbed and corners bumped, early signature of Geo(rge) Dundas, bookplate of Frederick Locker-Lampson (1821-1895), given by him to Lytton Strachey (1880-1932), from the library of James Stevens Cox (1910-1997). Maggs Bros. Ltd. 1447 - 108 2015 £150

Association – Strachey, Richard

Strachey, John *The Finances and Public Works of India From 1869-1881.* London: Kegan Paul, Trench & co., 1882. First edition, appealing presentation copy, inscribed by authors, John and Richard Strachey for Sir Edward Strachey, 3rd Baronet, bound in original red cloth with corners slightly bumped and spine faded, text pages clean and binding tight, very good. The Kelmscott Bookshop 11 - 49 2015 $450

Association – Strand, Antonia

Justice, Donald *A Local Storm.* Iowa City: Stone Wall Press and the Finial Press, 1963. First edition, limited to 270 copies, tall 8vo., original wrappers, covers somewhat sunned along extremities, edges trifle nicked, two tiny pen marks on back cover, otherwise fine, presentation copy inscribed to poet Mark Strand and Antonia. James S. Jaffe Rare Books Modern American Poetry - 153 2015 $750

Justice, Donald *Night Light.* Middletown: Wesleyan University Press, 1967. First edition, square 8vo., original cloth, dust jacket, presentation copy inscribed by author to poet Mark Strand and Antonia, March 1967, with APCS from Justice to Strand laid in, fine in somewhat rubbed jacket with two short closed tears on back panel. James S. Jaffe Rare Books Modern American Poetry - 154 2015 $850

Justice, Donald *Sixteen Poems.* Iowa City: Stone Wall Press, 1970. First edition, limited to 250 copies, tall 8vo., original wrappers, presentation copy from author to Mark Strand and Antonia, May 1970, tall 8vo., original wrappers, top and bottom edge little nicked, covers trifle sunned, otherwise fine. James S. Jaffe Rare Books Modern American Poetry - 155 2015 $850

Association – Strand, Mark

Justice, Donald *From a Notebook.* Iowa City: Seamark Press, 1972. First edition, limited to 317 copies, 12mo., original green cloth with printed label on spine, fine, presentation copy from author for Mark Strand. James S. Jaffe Rare Books Modern American Poetry - 156 2015 $850

Justice, Donald *A Local Storm.* Iowa City: Stone Wall Press and the Finial Press, 1963. First edition, limited to 270 copies, tall 8vo., original wrappers, covers somewhat sunned along extremities, edges trifle nicked, two tiny pen marks on back cover, otherwise fine, presentation copy inscribed to poet Mark Strand and Antonia. James S. Jaffe Rare Books Modern American Poetry - 153 2015 $750

Justice, Donald *Night Light.* Middletown: Wesleyan University Press, 1967. First edition, square 8vo., original cloth, dust jacket, presentation copy inscribed by author to poet Mark Strand and Antonia, March 1967, with APCS from Justice to Strand laid in, fine in somewhat rubbed jacket with two short closed tears on back panel. James S. Jaffe Rare Books Modern American Poetry - 154 2015 $850

Justice, Donald *Sixteen Poems.* Iowa City: Stone Wall Press, 1970. First edition, limited to 250 copies, tall 8vo., original wrappers, presentation copy from author to Mark Strand and Antonia, May 1970, tall 8vo., original wrappers, top and bottom edge little nicked, covers trifle sunned, otherwise fine. James S. Jaffe Rare Books Modern American Poetry - 155 2015 $850

Levine, Philip *Not This Pig. Poems.* Middletown: Wesleyan University Press, 1968. First edition, 8vo., original cloth, dust jacket, presentation from author for poet Mark Strand, fine in lightly sunned, somewhat rubbed dust jacket with bit of wear to extremities. James S. Jaffe Rare Books Modern American Poetry - 176 2015 $1250

Murray, Les A. *The Boys Who Stole the Funeral.* Sydney: Angus & Robertson Publishers, 1980. First edition, octavo, fine in very good or better dust jacket with moderate chip on rear panel, inscribed by author on titlepage to poet Mark Strand. Between the Covers Rare Books, Inc. 187 - 189 2015 $450

Murray, Les A. *Ethnic Radio. Poems.* Sydney: Angus & Robertson, 1977. First edition, some underscoring and marks in text in Mark Strand's hand, otherwise fine in rubbed and lightly chipped, very good dust jacket, inscribed by author for Mark Strand. Between the Covers Rare Books, Inc. 187 - 188 2015 $450

Association – Strathhallan, William Henry Drummond, 9th Viscount

Charles I, King of England *The King's Maiesties Declaration to His Subjects Concerning Lawfull Sports to Bee Used.* London: Richard Barker and by the Assignes of John Bill, 1633. First edition, 4to., woodcut device on titlepage, large woodcut royal arms on verso, woodcut head and tailpieces, wanting final blank, few minor stains and rust marks, near contemporary ms. annotation in ink, ownership signature of 'Sam. Ware" with 19th century armorial bookplates of Richard Clark Esq. Chamberlain of London (1739-1831) and of William Henry Drummond, 9th Viscount Strathallan (1810-1886), bound, presumably for Richard Clark in late 18th or early 19th century half russia gilt, good copy, wanting only final blank.   John Drury Rare Books   2015 - 25124   2015 $2185

Association – Streatfield, Henry

Gay, John   1685-1732 *Polly. An Opera.* London: printed for the author, 1729. First edition, 4to., contemporary quarter calf marbled paper boards, red leather label, gilt rules and lettering, 31 pages of engraved sheet music, contemporary armorial bookplate of Henry Streatfield, his library was later sold by W. H. Robinson Ltd., bookplate of American collector Charles Walker Andrews, noted in pencil above bookplate that he purchased this from Robinson in 1935, binding bit worn and stained, some light dampstains in text, very good, large copy.   The Brick Row Book Shop   Miscellany 67 - 49   2015 $500

Association – Strode, Thomas

Dary, Michael *The Complete Gauger.* London: for Robert Horne and Nathaniel Ponder, 1678. First and only edition, 12mo., license to print on verso of title, worming to lower inner margin occasionally touching a word and with small stain on D6v and D7r, contemporary sheep, rebacked, later pastedowns, edges lightly rubbed, from the library of James Stevens Cox (1910-1997), the copy of Thomas Strode (d. 1697) by descent to his niece, signature of Abigail Swayne (d. 1723).   Maggs Bros. Ltd.   1447 - 131   2015   £2000

Association – Stroehlin, Gaspard Ernest

Bible. English - 1684   *The Holy Bible. (bound with) The Whole Book of Psalms Collected into English Metre.* London: printed by the Assigns of J. Bill, T. Newcombe and Henr. Hills, 1684. 1683. Printed for the company of stationers, 1683, 127 x 64mm., 2 separately published works bound in 1 volume, 2 leaves (Eee3 and 4) bound in reverse order, very appealing contemporary red morocco, elaborately gilt and painted, covers with an ornate design of drawer handle tools, semi-circle at head and tail and wedge tool at side, both shapes filled with floral tools, top spine end raised, higher than board edges in stylized a la grecque design, marbled endpapers, all edges gilt, velvet lined modern maroon clamshell box with black morocco label, engraved titlepage with architectural frame, engraved bookplate of Gaspard Ernest Stroehlin showing Calvin preaching, with motto "Mente Libera", early (binder's?) pin inserted behind the upper headband; extremities bit rubbed, spine little crackled and with tiny split at bottom, faint faded in several spots, gilt on front cover just slightly dulled but binding still extremely pleasing, with no significant wear, titlepage with minor soil and corner crease, head margin trimmed with little close (no loss), otherwise fine internally, text especially smooth, fresh and clean.   Phillip J. Pirages   66 - 29   2015 $3500

Association – Strum, Clarence

MacDonald, Ross *The Moving Target.* London: Cassell, 1951. First edition, very good plus in very good dust jacket, mild soil to boards, some foxing to page edges, jacket moderately worn at extremities with few small chips and closed tears only signed copy of the UK edition we have encountered, inscribed by author to his in-laws Doogie and Clarence (Strum), from the collection of Duke Collier.   Royal Books   36 - 72   2015 $2000

Association – Strum, Doogie

MacDonald, Ross *The Moving Target.* London: Cassell, 1951. First edition, very good plus in very good dust jacket, mild soil to boards, some foxing to page edges, jacket moderately worn at extremities with few small chips and closed tears only signed copy of the UK edition we have encountered, inscribed by author to his in-laws Doogie and Clarence (Strum), from the collection of Duke Collier.   Royal Books   36 - 72   2015 $2000

Association – Strutt, Joseph

Wollstonecraft, Mary   1759-1797 *Original Stories from Real Life...* London: Johnson, 1791. Second edition, contemporary calf, hinges tender, spine chipped and worn at extremities, good copy, this was issued with and without plates, this has no illustrations, 8vo., some foxing and staining to titlepage and prelim leaf, with ads in rear, with ownership bookplate of Author Joseph Strutt 1749-1802, issued without half title.   Second Life Books Inc.   189 - 271   2015 $2000

Association – Stuart, James

Lucanus, Marcus Annaeus *Pharsalia.* Parisiis: Apud Lefevre Bibliopolam, 1822. 2 volumes, 108 x 76mm., charming contemporary green straight grain morocco covers, panelled with fine gilt and blind raised bands, spine compartments outlined in blind, pretty quatrefoil gilt centerpiece ornament, gilt titling, turn-ins, decorative gilt roll, all edges gilt, each volume with lovely pastoral fore-edge painting, one depicting Fetherstone Castle Northumberland, the other Lowther Castle, Westmorland, in later green cloth chemises and quarter morocco slipcase, spine decorated in much the same fashion as the volumes, front pastedown of both volumes with armorial bookplate of Sir James Stuart, Bart., front free endpaper of both volumes with oval morocco bookplate of R. B. Adam, front free endpaper of first volume with morocco bookplate of Mary Harriman Lecomte du Nouy; joints just slightly rubbed, spines faintly and uniformly darkened, touch of browning to edges of leaves, intermittent light foxing, else fine set, text generally clean and fresh, bindings lustrous and fore edge paintings particularly well preserved with rich colors.   Phillip J. Pirages   66 - 80   2015 $1500

Association – Stuart, Mary Napier

Porter, George Richardson *A Treatise on the Origin, Progressive Improvement and Present State of the Manufacture of Porcelain and Glass.* London: Longman Rees Orme Brown and Green, John Taylor, 1832. First edition, 8vo., 50 text figures, engraved and printed titles, original maroon cloth with printed spine label, spine faded, contemporary number '94' in ink below label, very good, 19th century armorial bookplate of Mary Napier Stuart.   John Drury Rare Books   2015 - 14838   2015 $89

Association – Stuart, William

Davenant, Charles   1656-1714 *An Essay Upon the Probable Methods of making a People Gainers in the Balance of Trade.* London: for James Knapton, 1700. Second edition, five folding tables, few sidenotes slightly shaved, sheet D foxed, occasional minor spotting throughout, late 18th century calf, covers with gilt arms of William Stuart, rebacked, corners repaired, edges worn, new endleaves, arms of William Stuart (1798-1874) on covers, stringently and critically underlined and marked throughout in pencil in early 20th century hand, some occasional longer annotations and mathematical calculations, from the library of James Stevens Cox (1910-1997).   Maggs Bros. Ltd.   1447 - 132   2015   £500

Association – Stull, William

Carver, Raymond *No Heroics Please.* London: Harvill, 1991. True first edition, signed by editor, William Stull fine in fine dust jacket.   Ken Lopez Bookseller   E-list # 82 - 912331   2015 $70

Association – Suffield, Edward Lord

Koran *The Koran, Commonly called the Alcoran of Mohammed.* London: printed by C. Ackers, 1734. First edition translated by George Sale, title printed in red and black, five engraved plates, variable moderate browning, contemporary panelled calf, blind tooling around the central mottled panel, spine gilt in compartments, red lettering piece, gilt Suffield crest in the 5th panel, rebacked preserving original compartments (raised bands showing lighter new calf), engraved armorial bookplate of Edward Lord Suffield, good, well above average copy.   Blackwell's Rare Books   B179 - 59   2015   £1800

Association – Sullivan, Russell

Lowell, Percival *Mars and Its Canals.* New York & London: Macmillan Co., 1906. First edition, frontispiece, 8 plates, 12 maps, 49 figures, original dark green gilt stamped cloth, top edge gilt, lightly rubbed, ownership signatures of Edwin M. Eckard and Russell Sullivan, Indianapolis, bookplate of LA lawyer Herbert Kraus, very good.   Jeff Weber Rare Books   178 - 798   2015 $750

Association – Super, R. H.

Arnold, Matthew   1822-1888 *Friendship's Garland; Being the Conversations, Letters and Opinions of the Late Arminius, Baron von Thunder-Ten-Tronckh.* London: Smith Elder, 1871. First edition, 2 pages ads, half title removed, original white cloth by Hanbury & Simpson, spine sunned, slightly discolored, attractive bookplate of Leonard Courtney, 15 Cheyne Walk, with inserted letters and cuttings including exchange between R. H. Super and Geoffrey Tillotson.   Jarndyce Antiquarian Booksellers   CCVII - 22   2015   £35

Association – Surtees, Robert

Paris, Matthew   1200-1259 *Flores Historiarum per Matthaeum Westmonasteriensem Collecti, Praecipue de Rebus Britannicis ab Exordio Usque ad Annum Domini 1307.* Ex officina Thomae Marshii, 1570. Second printed edition, titlepage trimmed close to woodcut border, final blank leaf discarded, index bound at front of text, one leaf with original paper law affecting few characters, first leaf of index with bottom margin folded over to preserve early manuscript note, verso of title also filled with text in early manuscript (trimmed at bottom), few short notes or marks later on, last dozen leaves showing faint but substantial dampmark, some soiling/minor staining elsewhere, touch of worming to blank fore-edge margin, two leaves remargined, gathering Ttt in earlier (?) state without (and not calling for) the additional unsigned singleton leaf, folio, 18th century mottled calf, spine with five raised bands, red morocco lettering pieces in second and third compartment, rubbed, front joint cracking (but strong), little peeling to leather, light wear to endcaps, marbled endpapers, bookplates of Robert Surtees and his Mainsforth Library, sound.   Blackwell's Rare Books   B179 - 81   2015   £1400

Association – Sussex, Augustus Frederick, Duke of

Sallustius Crispus, C. *Caius Crispus Salustius ab Ascensio Familiariter Explanatus.* Paris: Jean Petit, 1504. First Badius edition, some light foxing and staining (heavier o titlepage), first leaf of text bound slightly askew and 3 sidenotes copped as a result, 4to., 18th century calf, worn and crackled, rebacked (somewhat crudely), black lettering piece, hinges relined with black cloth tape, bookplates of Wigan public Library, Rev. T. H. Passmore, Sir Robert Shafto Adair and Augustus Frederick, Duke of Sussex, sound.   Blackwell's Rare Books   Greek & Latin Classics VI - 93   2015   £2000

Association – Sutcliffe, Fred

Noyes, Alfred *Collected Poems.* Edinburgh and London: William Blackwood and Sons, 1919. Half title, uncut in original green buckram, spine faded, titlepage, signed by Geoffrey Tillotson 29/12/20 "Bought by Uncle Fred Sutcliffe in Bradford Market on Christmas eve 1920", with text of 'A Tale of Old Japan' written neatly in ink by Geoffrey throughout prelims, with few notes in text, 3 cuttings inserted. Jarndyce Antiquarian Booksellers   CCVII - 402   2015 £20

Association – Sutherland

Hilary of Poitiers *Divi Hilarii Pictavorum Episcopi Lucubrationes...* Basel: Io. Frobenius, 1523. First edition, folio, 2 volumes, decorative initials and headpieces, contemporary full calf blindstamped on both sides with design of heraldic devices, rebacked (early) with red and gilt spine label, from the library of Allan Heywood Bright (1862-1941), loosely inserted is an ALS from fellow book collector E. Gordon Duff to Bright thanking him for the loan of the book, front board detached, rear joint and head and foot of spine well worn, armorial bookplate of Sir John Leveson Gower of Trentham, worming from titlepage on decreasing from about 60 holes throughout the first volume, few early ink annotations, ownership inscription of G(eorgius) Folberti(us), pencilled note identifies this book's provenance as "Sutherland Library".   Any Amount of Books   2015 - 12863   2015 £800

Association – Sutherland, George Granville Levenson-Gower, 1st Duke of

Cox, Nicholas *The Gentleman's Recreation.* London: by Jos. Phillips and Hen. Rodes (part 4 Oxford by L. Lichfield for Nicholas Cox), 1685-1686. Third edition, 4 engraved plates, engraved frontispiece by W. Sherwin, large folding engraved plate (old repair to a long tear), double page plate of hawking and double page plate of fish, both by Dolle, lightly browned, light marginal dampstaining throughout, minor worming to top of gatherings C-G that touches the headlines and occasionally the first line of text, contemporary calf, front cover with 19th century arms of Duke of Sutherland and blindstamped to front cover, covers worn, front cover detached, spine split at head and tail; armorial bookplate of Sir John Leveson-Gower (1675-1609) 1st Baron Gower by descent to John Levenson-Gower (1694-1754, 1st Earl Gower with early 19th century armorial bookplate, by descent to George Granville Levenson-Gower, 1st Duke of Sutherland with his arms stamped in blind on front cover, from the library of James Stevens Cox (1910-1997). Maggs Bros. Ltd.   1447 - 121   2015   £1500

Association – Sutro, Alfred

Browning, Robert 1812-1889 *Parleyings with Certain People of Importance in Their Day...* London: Smith, Elder & Co., 1887. First edition, octavo, brick cloth stamped in black and gilt, small leather bookplate of English author and dramatist Alfred Sutro, previous bookplate removed, modest rubbing at extremities, very good or better.   Between the Covers Rare Books, Inc.   187 - 34   2015 $85

Association – Sutro, John

Green, Henry *Loving.* London: Hogarth Press, 1955. Later printing, inscribed to film producer John Sutro. Honey & Wax Booksellers   2 - 55   2015 $2800

Association – Sutton, Ralph

Shacter, James D. *Loose Shoes. The Story of Ralph Sutton.* Chicago: Jaynar, 1994. Updated version, hardcover, quite uncommon signed by author with signed inscription from Sutton tipped in, fine in fine dust jacket.   Beasley Books   2013 - 2015 $85

Association – Svanstrom, Greta

Greene, Graham 1904-1991 *The Virtue of Disloyalty.* London: Bodley Head, 1972. First edition, privately printed in edition of 300 for distribution by author and publisher, ivory paper wrappers, inscribed in year of publication for Ragnar Svanstrom, Greene's Swedish publisher and his wife, Greta, Christmas 1972, fine.   B & B Rare Books, Ltd. 234 - 44   2015 $2000

Association – Svanstrom, Ragnar

Greene, Graham 1904-1991 *The Virtue of Disloyalty.* London: Bodley Head, 1972. First edition, privately printed in edition of 300 for distribution by author and publisher, ivory paper wrappers, inscribed in year of publication for Ragnar Svanstrom, Greene's Swedish publisher and his wife, Greta, Christmas 1972, fine. B & B Rare Books, Ltd. 234 - 44 2015 $2000

Association – Swanson, Gloria

Benefield, Barry *Short Turns.* New York: Century Co., 1926. First edition, spine lettering bit worn, faint dampstain on fore edge, very good plus in very good example of scarce dust jacket with some shallow chipping at spinal extremities, not affecting any lettering, Gloria Swanson's copy with her ownership signature and stamp, this copy was given by Swanson to Van Heflin who later gave it to a friend. Between the Covers Rare Books, Inc. 187 - 17 2015 $475

Association – Swartley, Stanley

Frost, Robert Lee 1874-1963 *New Hampshire.* New York: Henry Holt, 1923. First edition, limited to 350 copies signed by Frost, this copy additionally inscribed by Frost to his friend and Allegheny College English professor, Stanley Swartley, woodcuts by J. J. Lankes, excellent copy with only very minor rubbing to extremities. B & B Rare Books, Ltd. 234 - 38 2015 $3500

Association – Swayne, Abigail

Dary, Michael *The Complete Gauger.* London: for Robert Horne and Nathanel Ponder, 1678. First and only edition, 12mo., license to print on verso of title, worming to lower inner margin occasionally touching a word and with small stain on D6v and D7r, contemporary sheep, rebacked, later pastedowns, edges lightly rubbed, from the library of James Stevens Cox (1910-1997), the copy of Thomas Strode (d. 1697) by descent to his niece, signature of Abigail Swayne (d. 1723). Maggs Bros. Ltd. 1447 - 131 2015 £2000

Association – Sweeney, Anne

Lowell, Robert 1917-1977 *Land of Unlikeness.* Cummington: Cummington Press, 1944. One of 224 copies, of a total edition of 250, inscribed by author to Anne Sweeney, daughter of James John Sweeney, longtime curator of MOMA, spine and cover edges little faded, tips of boards worn, some internal foxing up to titlepage, overall about very good, lacking plain tissue dust jacket, uncommon first book. Ken Lopez, Bookseller 164 - 123 2015 $4500

Association – Swinburne, Alice

Swinburne, Algernon Charles 1837-1909 *A Study of Shakespeare.* London: Chatto & Windus, 1880. First edition, original green cloth, gilt title and author to spine and gilt ruling to front cover, slightly bumped corners and light fraying, but near fine, interior pristine, near fine, presentation copy inscribed by author for sister Alice Swinburne. The Kelmscott Bookshop 11 - 54 2015 $2250

Association – Symons, A. J.

Blake, William 1757-1827 *Auguries of Innocence.* Flansham: Pear Tree Press, 1914. First edition thus, limited to 25 copies, this number '7', scarce title, 8vo., original blue grey card wrappers with printed label to upper corner of upper cover, preserved in recent cloth covered fall downback box, etched frontispiece, titlepage and one other plate, light dust marks to wrappers and f.f.e.p., A. J. Symons with his neat booklabel to verso of upper wrapper. Henry Sotheran Ltd. William Blake Exhibition 17th Oct.-7th Nov. 2014 - 62 2015 £800

Association – Symons, Julian

Milward-Oliver, Edward *Len Deighton: an Annotated Bibliography 1954-1985.* Maidstone: Sammler Press, 1985. First edition, one of 375 copies this one unnumbered, with signed page proof from London match laid in its special folder, inscribed on limitation page for Julian and Kathleen Symons, by author 16-09-1985, fine in dust jacket. Buckingham Books March 2015 - 14532 2015 $750

Association – Symons, Kathleen

Milward-Oliver, Edward *Len Deighton: an Annotated Bibliography 1954-1985.* Maidstone: Sammler Press, 1985. First edition, one of 375 copies this one unnumbered, with signed page proof from London match laid in its special folder, inscribed on limitation page for Julian and Kathleen Symons, by author 16-09-1985, fine in dust jacket. Buckingham Books March 2015 - 14532 2015 $750

Association – Tamworth, Viscount

Smith, John *Poems on Several Occasions.* London: printed for H. Clements, 1713. First edition, 8vo., contemporary panelled calf, spine gilt red morocco label, neatly rebacked, original spine laid down, fine, scarce, early armorial bookplate of Viscount Tamworth. C. R. Johnson Foxon R-Z - 907r-z 2015 $1915

Association – Targ, William

Himes, Chester *A Case of Rape.* New York: Targ Editions, 1980. First American edition, fine in quarter cloth and papercovered boards, near fine unprinted glassine dust jacket with small tears at extremities, one of 350 copies, signed by author, warmly inscribed by publisher William Targ to novelist Brad Morrow.   Between the Covers Rare Books, Inc.   187 - 127   2015 $250

Snodgrass, W. D. *Heart's Needle.* New York: Knopf, 1959. First edition, limited to 1500 copies, 8vo., original red cloth, dust jacket, inscribed by author for William Targ on titlepage.   James S. Jaffe Rare Books   Modern American Poetry - 259   2015 $450

Updike, John   1932-2009   *Ego and Art in Walt Whitman.* New York: Targ Editions, 1980. First edition, fine in fine, unprinted dust jacket, one of 350 copies, signed by author, inscribed by author to publisher William Targ.   Between the Covers Rare Books, Inc.   187 - 284   2015 $150

Association – Tate, Cornelia

Orlovitz, Gil *Concerning Man.* New York: Banyan Press, 1947. First edition, copy 34 of 350 numbered copies, inscribed by author to artist Cornelia Tate, fine in fine dust jacket.   Between the Covers Rare Books, Inc.   187 - 206   2015 $175

Association – Tate, Nahum

Ayres, Philip *Cupids addresse to the Ladies.* London: sold by R. Bently, 5 Tidmarsh, 1683. First edition, small 8vo., engraved throughout, 44 engraved emblem plates, without final blank leaf, small chip torn from fore-margin of titlepage, titlepage lightly soiled, small unobtrusive waterstaining to upper blank margin of first third of the work, short tear to foot of L1, contemporary calf, gilt spine with brown morocco label, corners, head and foot of spine repaired, this copy includes, presumably autograph, 20 line commendatory poem by poet and playwright Nahum Tate addressed "To My Honb. Friend Philip Ayres esqe on his book of Emblems in four Languages", 18th century signature Henry Burt, large bookplate removed, from the library of James Stevens Cox (1910-1997).   Maggs Bros. Ltd.   1447 - 15   2015   £3500

Association – Taylor, Barnard

Carruth, Hayden *Journey to a Known Place.* Norfolk: New Directions, 1961. First edition, large 8vo., original cloth and patterned paper over boards, dust jacket, very fine, presentation copy inscribed by author for Barnard Taylor.   James S. Jaffe Rare Books   Modern American Poetry - 44   2015 $450

Carruth, Hayden *North Winter.* Iowa City: Prairie Press, 1964. first edition in book form, large 8vo., original cloth and patterned paper over boards, dust jacket, very fine, inscribed by author to Barnard Taylor.   James S. Jaffe Rare Books   Modern American Poetry - 46   2015 $400

Association – Taylor, Bruce

Hillerman, Tony *Listening Woman.* New York: Harper and Row, 1978. First edition, near fine in fine dust jacket, inscribed by author for Bruce Taylor, some loss to titling on backstrip (problem endemic to this title), else near fine in like dust jacket with none of the usual spine fading, attractive copy, from the collection of Duke Collier.   Royal Books   36 - 193   2015 $1250

Association – Taylor, Eleanor Ross

Maurer, David *The Dying Place.* New York: Dell, 1986. Second printing, paperback original, near fine, from the library of author Peter Taylor and wife Eleanor Ross Taylor, inscribed by author for Taylor.   Between the Covers Rare Books, Inc.   187 - 166   2015 $50

McCloskey, Michael *Destiny or Death.* N.P.: Michael McCloskey, 1971. First edition, 12mo., stapled printed yellow wrappers, near fine, without dust jacket, from the library of author Peter Taylor and wife Eleanor Ross Taylor, inscribed by author for Taylor.   Between the Covers Rare Books, Inc.   187 - 172   2015 $125

Steiner, George *Tolstoy or Dostoevesky: an Essay in Contrast.* London: Faber, 1959. First edition, bit of foxing on endpapers, near fine, price clipped dust jacket very good or better, inscribed to Peter and Eleanor Ross Taylor, by literary critic E. D. Hirsch and his wife Polly.   Between the Covers Rare Books, Inc.   187 - 270   2015 $175

Warren, Rosanna *Stained Glass.* New York: W. W. Norton & Co., 1993. First edition, 8vo., original cloth, dust jacket, presentation copy inscribed by author to fellow author Peter Taylor and his wife, poet Eleanor Taylor, Warren has corrected one word and supplied a comma in text of poem 'The Broken Pot', very fine.   James S. Jaffe Rare Books   Modern American Poetry - 298   2015 $250

Winner, Anthony *Studies in Joseph Conrad's Major Novels.* Charlottesville: University Press of Virginia, 1988. First edition, slight foxing of endpapers, else fine in fine dust jacket, from the library of author Peter Taylor and wife Eleanor Ross Taylor, inscribed to same by author.   Between the Covers Rare Books, Inc.   187 - 295   2015 $85

Zollinger, Noman *Riders to Cibola.* Santa Fe: Museum of New Mexico Press, 1978. Second printing, small quarto, 258 pages, inscribed and signed by author 11/5/86 for Peter and Eleanor Taylor, near fine in very good price clipped dust jacket with rubbing to front panel and llower corners gently bumped.   Between the Covers Rare Books, Inc.   187 - 301   2015 $100

Association – Taylor, Nathaniel Pendleton

Godwin, William   1756-1836 *Memoirs of the Author of a Vindication of the Rights of Woman.* Philadelphia: James Carey, 1799. First American edition, 8vo., front blank tissued and remounted, bound in new boards with calf spine, some little marginal staining, very good, this copy was owned and annotated by a contemporary American reader, Nathaniel Pendleton Taylor, who signed and dated titlepage, Philadelphia July 17, 1812 and made occasional comments in text and on titlepage.   Second Life Books Inc.   189 - 270   2015 $1500

Association – Taylor, Peter

Maurer, David *The Dying Place.* New York: Dell, 1986. Second printing, paperback original, near fine, from the library of author Peter Taylor and wife Eleanor Ross Taylor, inscribed by author for Taylor.   Between the Covers Rare Books, Inc.   187 - 166   2015 $50

McCloskey, Michael *Destiny or Death.* N.P.: Michael McCloskey, 1971. First edition, 12mo., stapled printed yellow wrappers, near fine, without dust jacket, from the library of author Peter Taylor and wife Eleanor Ross Taylor, inscribed by author for Taylor.   Between the Covers Rare Books, Inc.   187 - 172   2015 $125

Schoenbaum, S. *William Shakespeare: a Documentary Life.* New York: Oxford University Press in Association with the Scolar Press, 1975. First edition, trade issue, folio, slightly musty, else near fine in price clipped, near fine dust jacket, inscribed by author to author Peter Taylor, laid in is TLS for executive director to Pen/Faulkner Award for Fiction presenting the book to Taylor.   Between the Covers Rare Books, Inc.   187 - 247   2015 $125

Steiner, George *Tolstoy or Dostoevesky: an Essay in Contrast.* London: Faber, 1959. First edition, bit of foxing on endpapers, near fine, price clipped dust jacket very good or better, inscribed to Peter and Eleanor Ross Taylor, by literary critic E. D. Hirsch and his wife Polly.   Between the Covers Rare Books, Inc.   187 - 270   2015 $175

Warren, Rosanna *Stained Glass.* New York: W. W. Norton & Co., 1993. First edition, 8vo., original cloth, dust jacket, presentation copy inscribed by author to fellow author Peter Taylor and his wife, poet Eleanor Taylor, Warren has corrected one word and supplied a comma in text of poem 'The Broken Pot', very fine.   James S. Jaffe Rare Books   Modern American Poetry - 298   2015 $250

Winner, Anthony *Studies in Joseph Conrad's Major Novels.* Charlottesville: University Press of Virginia, 1988. First edition, slight foxing of endpapers, else fine in fine dust jacket, from the library of author Peter Taylor and wife Eleanor Ross Taylor, inscribed to same by author.   Between the Covers Rare Books, Inc.   187 - 295   2015 $85

Woodhouse, F. C. *A Manual for Holy Days: a Few Thoughts for Those Week Days for Which the Church Provides Special Services.* London: Wells Gardner Darton & Co., 1889. First edition, small octavo, publisher's green cloth gilt, old pencil ownership signature as well as 1945 signature of novelist Peter Taylor, very scarce.   Between the Covers Rare Books, Inc.   187 - 298   2015 $350

Zollinger, Noman *Riders to Cibola.* Santa Fe: Museum of New Mexico Press, 1978. Second printing, small quarto, 258 pages, inscribed and signed by author 11/5/86 for Peter and Eleanor Taylor, near fine in very good price clipped dust jacket with rubbing to front panel and lower corners gently bumped.   Between the Covers Rare Books, Inc.   187 - 301   2015 $100

Association – Taylor, Robbie

Brandelius, Jerilyn Lee *Grateful Dead Family Album.* New York: Warner Books, 1989. First edition, 'Grateful Dead All Area Access sticker laid down to jacket, this copy signed by band members Jerry Garcia, Mickey Hart and Bob Bralove as well as long time road crew members Ram Rod Shurtliff, Bill 'Kid' Candelario, Steve Parish and Robbie Taylor among others, hundreds of intimate photos and stories, very good plus to near fine with little soil and handling marks, in very good plus to near fine dust jacket with short closed tear to bottom of front flap.   Ed Smith Books   83 - 34   2015 $950

Association – Taylor, Ronald George

Cooper, James Fenimore   1789-1851 *The Deerslayer; a Tale.* London: Richard Bentley, 1841. Second edition, 3 volumes, half titles, original drab boards, brown horizontally ribbed cloth spines, paper labels, slightly chipped, signatures of J. and Elizabeth Bell, recent labels of Ronald George Taylor.   Jarndyce Antiquarian Booksellers   CCXI - 72   2015   £125

Whyte Melville, George John *The Gladiators: a tale of Rome and Judea.* London: Longmans, 1878. New edition, 2 pages ads, 32 page catalog (March 1877), yellowback, original printed paper boards, rubbed and little worn, contemporary signature of A. A. Litten on leading f.e.p., modern booklabel of Ronald George Taylor, good plus copy. Jarndyce Antiquarian Booksellers   CCXI - 289   2015   £65

Association – Taylor, Steve

Moody, Ralph *The Dry Divide.* New York: W. W. Norton, 1963. First edition, cloth, drawings, half page presentation to author's friend, Steve Taylor, fine in very good dust jacket. Baade Books of the West   2014 - 2015 $172

Association – Taylor. H. L.

Oldenburg, Henry *The Correspondence of Henry Oldenburg.* London: University of Wisconsin Press, 1965-1969. 6 volumes, nos. 1-6 (13 have been issued), large 8vo., each volume about 500 pages, illustrations, cloth, dust jackets worn, volume I lower corner bumped bookplates of H. L. Taylor, M.D., good set.   Jeff Weber Rare Books   178 - 858   2015 $150

Association – Teale, Oscar

Houdini, Harry *Elliott's Last Legacy...* New York: Adams Press Print, 1923. First edition, illustrations by Oscar Teale, binding lightly worn at extremities, tidemark from dampstain at top corner of pages throughout, front hinge tender but still sound, very good, Teale's copy, inscribed for him by Houdini, inscribed by Teale for Lester Grimes, Grimes then inscribed the book for friend Gertrude Elliott.   Between the Covers Rare Books, Inc.   187 - 164   2015 $4000

Association – Tennant, Charles

Ariosto, Lodovico *Orlando Furioso.* Birmingham: Da' Torch di G. Baskerville per P. Molini, 1773. One of 100 large paper copies, 4 volumes, with subscriber list at end of volume IV, contemporary red morocco by Derome Le Jeune (his ticket on titlepage of volume I), covers gilt with French fillet borders and with FitzGibbon family arms of Earl of Clare at Center, raised bands, spines gilt in double ruled compartments with simple lozenge centerpiece, gilt titling, densely gilt turn-ins, marbled endpapers, all edges gilt, frontispiece by Eisen after Titian and 46 fine engraved plates, large paper copy, vellum bookplate of Burnham Abbey and engraved armorial bookplate of Charles Tennant, The Glen, spines slightly and evenly sunned, hint of rubbing to extremities, titles faintly browned and with an inch of slightly darker browning to edges from binder's glue), a dozen other leaves with pale browning or spotting, occasional very faint offsetting from plates, isolated light spots of foxing, small marginal smudges or other trivial imperfections with just handful of plates affected, still an elegant set in fine condition, impressive bindings lustrous and scarcely worn, leaves clean and smooth, margins enormous and with strong impressions of the engravings.   Phillip J. Pirages   66 - 49   2015 $19,500

Association – Tennant, Margot

James, Henry 1843-1916 *Stories Revived in Three Volumes.* London: Macmillan, 1885. First edition, 3 volumes, full red leather lettered gilt on spine, 5 raised bands, all edges gilt, bookplate of Margot Tennant in each volume, with 'Margot from Evan Charteris, the Glen 85', little scuffed at edges, covers slightly marked, hinges slightly tender with front board detached on volume 3, overall about very good. Any Amount of Books   March 2015 - A79117   2015   £360

Association – Terry, Reg

Fisher, Leona Weaver *Lemon, Dickens and Mr. Nightingale's Diary a Victorian Farce.* Victoria: University of Victoria, 1988. Original card wrappers, marked, presentation by Reg Terry in 1989 for Kathleen Tillotson.   Jarndyce Antiquarian Booksellers   CCVII - 213   2015   £35

Association – Theobold, Samuel

Howard, Charles F. *Essays on the Age.* London: J. K. Chapman and Co., 1855. First edition, blind embossed brown cloth, gilt stamped spine lettering, small contemporary bookseller's label, very near fine, modest edgewear, corners lightly bumped, inscribed by author for Samuel Theobold, scarce.   Between the Covers Rare Books   196 - 80   2015 $250

Association – Thistlewayte, Alexander

Herodianus *Herodian of Alexandria his History of the Twenty Roman Caesars and Emperors of His Time.* London: printed for Hugh Perry, 1629. Small quarto, cropping affects text of dedication page and list of emperors (sig. b), very light degree of marginal annotation throughout the book, some ink and some pencil, possibly in the hand of Thistlethwayte and or of Allan Heywood Bright (1862-1941) who owned the book in the 20th century, otherwise nice example in slightly faded and worn but very sound, attractive binding, ex-libris Alexandris Thistlewayte, autograph note by Edmond Malone bound in and also bound in are couple of sheets of handwritten notes in later hand, binding by Haines of Liverpool, half red Levant morocco ruled gilt over marbled boards, spine with six compartments, with lettered gilt or bearing crescent and star device, marbled endpapers, top edge gilt,.   Any Amount of Books   2015 - C11789   2015   £2000

Association – Thom, Johannis

Theobald, Lewis *The Cave of Poverty a Poem.* London: printed for Jonas Browne and sold by J. Roberts, n.d., 1715. First edition, 8vo., disbound, half title little soiled, otherwise good, early ownership inscription on title 'Liber Joh(ann)is Thom's" dated 1716.   C. R. Johnson   Foxon R-Z - 977r-z   2015 $919

Association – Thomajan, P. K.

Barnham, Henry D. *The Khoja Tales of Nasr-Ed-Din.* New York: D. Appleton and Co., 1924. First edition, bookplate of designer P. K. Thomajan, some offsetting on front board, about very good, in poor, internally repaired dust jacket with some chips and tears.   Between the Covers Rare Books, Inc.   187 - 7   2015 $65

Association – Thomas, Annibal Fernandes

Porter, Robert Ker *Letters from Portugal and Spain Written during the march of the British Troops Under Sir John Moore...* London: Longman, Hurst, Rees and Orme, 1809. First edition, 8vo, original boards, printed spine label, pages uncut, 335 pages, engraved map, 6 tinted plates, 16 pages Longman's ads at rear dated 1808, boards almost loose, spine chipped and worn, text and plates in excellent state, bookplate of Annibal Fernandes Thomas.   Any Amount of Books   March 2015 - A92910   2015   £450

Association – Thomas, Dylan

Tindall, William York *James Joyce: His Way of Interpreting the Modern World.* New York: Charles Scribner's Sons, 1950. First edition, octavo, original blue cloth, original dust jacket, warmly inscribed to Dylan thomas.   Honey & Wax Booksellers   2 - 49   2015 $450

Association – Thompson, Hunter S.

Kennedy, William 1928- *Legs.* New York: Coward, McCann & Geoghegan, 1975. Uncorrected proof, couple of small smudges or spots on wrappers, else just about fine, ownership signature of Hunter S. Thompson on front blank, TLS from senior editor, Peggy Brooks to Thompson sending the proof and soliciting a blurb from him.   Between the Covers Rare Books   196 - 83   2015 $2500

Association – Thomson, Rose Elisabeth

Thomson, Joseph John *Recollections and Reflections.* London: G. Bell & Sons, 1936. First edition, 8vo., signed and dated by author Dec. 1936, laid in is short note from his wife, Rose Elisabeth Thomson on Trinity Lodge stationery dated Dec. 7 1936, also laid in is review of the book from the Sunday Times Dec. 6 1936, very good+ in very good dust jacket with edge chips and wear, foxing, soil, sun spine, scarce.   By the Book, L. C.   Special List 10 - 65   2015 $1000

Association – Thomson, Virgil

Hill, Edward Burlingame *Modern French Music.* Boston and New York: Houghton Mifflin Co., 1924. First edition, blue cloth gilt, embossed stamp of Virgil Thomson on titlepage, wear and small tears to cloth mostly along bottom extremities, else very good inscribed by author for Thomson, his assistant and friend.   Between the Covers Rare Books, Inc.   187 - 190   2015 $1250

James, William 1842-1910 *Pragmatism: a New Name for some Old Ways of Thinking.* New York: Longmans, Green and Co., 1919. New impression, green publisher's cloth and printed paper spine label, label bit worn and little light fraying at spine ends, else near fine, American composer Virgil Thomson's copy with his pencil ownership signature.   Between the Covers Rare Books, Inc.   187 - 137   2015 $400

Association – Thorogood, Augustine

Thorogood, Augustine H. *The Globe & Laurel. The Journal of the Royal Marines (Volume 37).* Great Britain: Royal Marines, 1929. 12 issues bound in one volume (Volume 37 Numbers 1-12, Jan. - Dec. 1929), photos, full blue cloth, gilt, spine titles, with gilt seal on front board, moderate rubbing to boards and light fading to spine, else fine, presented Sept. 21 1950 by US Marine Commander Augustine Thorogood to boxing champion Gene Tunney.   Between the Covers Rare Books, Inc.   187 - 277   2015 $300

Association – Thrale, Hester Lynch

Bible. Latin - 1726 *Biblia Scacra ex Sebastiani Castellionis Interpretatione Ejusque Postrema Recognitione (Volume I).* Londoni: Excudebat Jacob Bettenham, Impensis J. Knapton, R. Knaplock..., 1726. First edition, volume one only, 12mo., text in Latin, from the library of American book collector Ralph Isham with his engraved bookplate, dust jacket inscription to Mrs. Hester Lynch Thrale from Dr. Samuel Johnson, contemporary full sheep, dark red morocco spine label, gilt edges light cracking to joints, very good, housed in dark red full morocco box, gold silk interior and gold edges, presumably commissioned by Isham, with the Johnston presentation "Bible presented to Mrs. Thrale by Dr. Johnson" in gilt on front cover, front joint of box professionally repaired, very good. Between the Covers Rare Books, Inc.   187 - 44   2015 $3000

Association – Thurber, Anne

White, Elwyn Brooks *The Essays of E. B. White.* New York: Harper & Row, 1977. First edition, inscribed by Helen Thurber (wife of James) to Mary (Mian) and her husband Aristide, near fine in very good, moderately edgeworn dust jacket with one small tape repair.   Ken Lopez, Bookseller   164 - 159   2015 $150

Association – Ticknor, George

Warren, Edward *Some Account of the Letheon; or Who Is the Discoverer.* Boston: Dutton and Wentworth, 1847. First edition, 88 pages, original printed wrappers, ex-library stamps, text foxed, inscribed by author to Prof. G(eorge) Ticknor.   M & S Rare Books, Inc.   97 - 10   2015 $1250

Association – Tillotson, Arthur

Arnold, Matthew 1822-1888 *Essays, Including Essays in Criticism 1865, on Translating Homer.* London: Oxford University Press, 1914. Frontispiece, original red cloth, spine rubbed and dulled, with signature of Arthur Tillotson 1931 and few notes by Geoffrey Tillotson.   Jarndyce Antiquarian Booksellers   CCVII - 15   2015   £20

Defoe, Daniel *The Life and Adventures of Robinson Crusoe.* London & Edinburgh: William & Robert Chambers, circa, 1880? Frontispiece, original green cloth, hinges little rubbed, prize label from All Saints' Schools, Bradford to John H. Tillotson, Christmas 1882 and note from Arthur Tillotson, aged 10 with page of notes inserted, crossed through.   Jarndyce Antiquarian Booksellers   CCVII - 166   2015   £35

Association – Tillotson, Geoffrey

Abercrombie, Lascelles *The Art of Wordsworth.* London: Oxford University Press, 1952. Original red cloth, slightly spotted and torn dust jacket, Geoffrey Tillotson's signed copy with correspondence with Frederick Page, review cutting &c., pencil notes.   Jarndyce Antiquarian Booksellers   CCVII - 575   2015   £20

Addison, Joseph 1672-1719 *The Letters...* Oxford: Clarendon Press, 1941. Half title, frontispiece, plate, original maroon cloth, Geoffrey Tillotson's copy with some pencil and ink notes, typescript review by Donald Bond and contrasting printed review by Marjorie Williams with card from her and from Harold Williams about review.   Jarndyce Antiquarian Booksellers   CCVII - 1   2015   £30

Ainsworth, William Harrison 1805-1882 *Hilary St. Ives.* London: George Routledge & Sons, 1881. Illustrations by Frederick Gilbert, contemporary half red roan, spine faded and slightly rubbed, bookplate with crest of A. J. Constable over another, from the library of Geoffrey & Kathleen Tillotson.   Jarndyce Antiquarian Booksellers   CCVII - 2   2015   £20

Andrewes, Lancelot *Two Sermons of the Resurrection.* Cambridge: University Press, 1932. Half title, Geoffrey Tillotson's copy with corrections and some ms. marginal and inserted notes, GT's paper wrappers made from 18th century Latin printed text, color stained blue,.   Jarndyce Antiquarian Booksellers   CCVII - 6   2015   £25

Annals: Nineteenth Century. n.p.: circa, 1920-1960? Original maroon cloth boards, rubbed and dusted with blue paper ms. title, cloth tabs attached to pages, marking decades, given to Geoffrey Tillotson by Kathleen Tillotson.   Jarndyce Antiquarian Booksellers   CCVII - 7   2015   £45

Arnold, Matthew 1822-1888 *A French Eton.* London: Macmillan, 1892. Half title, original dark blue cloth, endpaper causing some browning, otherwise very good, from the library of Geoffrey & Kathleen Tillotson.   Jarndyce Antiquarian Booksellers   CCVII - 21   2015   £25

Arnold, Matthew 1822-1888 *A French Eton; or Middle-Class Education and the State.* London & Cambridge: Macmillan, 1864. First edition, half title, 6 pages ads, 24 page catalog (25.4.64), original red brown cloth, spine defective, inner hinges splitting, signed by Geoffrey Tillotson Xmas 43, with pencil marginal marks and part of original text from Macmillan's Magazine inserted.   Jarndyce Antiquarian Booksellers   CCVII - 20   2015   £20

Arnold, Matthew   1822-1888   *Culture and Anarchy...* London: Smith, Elder & Co., 1875. Second edition, half title, inserted ad leaf, original brown cloth, slightly dulled, from the library of Geoffrey & Kathleen Tillotson.   Jarndyce Antiquarian Booksellers   CCVII - 12   2015   £85

Arnold, Matthew   1822-1888   *Culture and Anarchy: an Essay In Political and Social Criticism.*   London: Smith, Elder & Co., 1869. First edition, half title, original brown cloth, bevelled boards, spine slightly worn at head and tail, inner hinges splitting, decent copy, from the library of Geoffrey & Kathleen Tillotson.   Jarndyce Antiquarian Booksellers   CCVII - 11   2015   £220

Arnold, Matthew   1822-1888   *Discourses in America.* London: Macmillan, 1885. First edition, half title, original dark green cloth, slightly dulled, few pencil notes, from the library of Geoffrey & Kathleen Tillotson.   Jarndyce Antiquarian Booksellers   CCVII - 14   2015   £65

Arnold, Matthew   1822-1888   *Essays in Criticism.* London: Macmillan, 1865. First edition, half title, 2 pages ads, 32 page catalog, original brown cloth, dark green endpapers, slightly dulled, signed by Geoffrey Tillotson. Jarndyce Antiquarian Booksellers   CCVII - 16   2015   £45

Arnold, Matthew   1822-1888   *Essays in Criticism.* London: Macmillan, 1869. Second edition, half title, 2 pages ads, original brown cloth, dark green endpapers, dulled and rubbed, inner hinges, strengthened with paper, working copy, signed by Geoffrey Tillotson 14 Jan. 142, with numerous ink and pencil notes, insertions, including cuttings, causing slight browning.   Jarndyce Antiquarian Booksellers   CCVII - 17   2015   £75

Arnold, Matthew   1822-1888   *Essays in Criticism: Second Series.*   Leipzig: Tauchnitz, 1892. Copyright edition, without half title, uncut, later red buckram with note 'bound 1942', notes in pencil, ink and red ink, from the library of Geoffrey & Kathleen Tillotson.   Jarndyce Antiquarian Booksellers   CCVII - 18   2015   £60

Arnold, Matthew   1822-1888   *Essays, Including Essays in Criticism 1865, on Translating Homer.*   London: Oxford University Press, 1914. Frontispiece, original red cloth, spine rubbed and dulled, with signature of Arthur Tillotson 1931 and few notes by Geoffrey Tillotson.   Jarndyce Antiquarian Booksellers   CCVII - 15   2015   £20

Arnold, Matthew   1822-1888   *Friendship's Garland.* London: Smith, Elder, 1897. Second edition, half title, 4 pages ads, original white cloth, spine slightly dulled, few spots, bookplate of C. F. Mason, presented to Geoffrey Tillotson by WEB.   Jarndyce Antiquarian Booksellers   CCVII - 23   2015   £30

Arnold, Matthew   1822-1888   *Friendship's Garland...* London: Smith Elder, 1903. Popular edition, 2 pages ads, half title removed, original crimson cloth, spine faded, signed by Geoffrey Tillotson 1932 with few notes.   Jarndyce Antiquarian Booksellers   CCVII - 24   2015   £20

Arnold, Matthew   1822-1888   *Friendship's Garland; Being the Conversations, Letters and Opinions of the Late Arminius, Baron von Thunder-Ten-Tronckh.*   London: Smith Elder, 1871. First edition, 2 pages ads, half title removed, original white cloth by Hanbury & Simpson, spine sunned, slightly discolored, attractive bookplate of Leonard Courtney, 15 Cheyne Walk, with inserted letters and cuttings including exchange between R. H. Super and Geoffrey Tillotson. Jarndyce Antiquarian Booksellers   CCVII - 22   2015   £35

Arnold, Matthew   1822-1888   *God & the Bible: a Review of Objections to 'Literature & Dogma'.*   New York: Macmillan, 1875. First American edition, half title, 2 pages ads, spotting caused by endpapers, name erased from title, original brown cloth, rubbed, inner hinges cracking, signed by Geoffrey Tillotson, with pencil notes and marginal marks. Jarndyce Antiquarian Booksellers   CCVII - 25   2015   £30

Arnold, Matthew   1822-1888   *God and the Bible.* London: Smith, Elder, 1885. Popular edition, initial ad leaf, half title, original brown cloth, signed by Geoffrey Tillotson 1942, with pencil notes and marginal marks.   Jarndyce Antiquarian Booksellers   CCVII - 26   2015   £20

Arnold, Matthew   1822-1888   *Higher Schools and Universities in Germany.*   London: Macmillan, 1874. Second edition, 83 pages, catalog Oct. 1873, browning caused by endpapers, original brown cloth, dulled, signed by Geoffrey Tillotson.   Jarndyce Antiquarian Booksellers   CCVII - 27   2015   £35

Arnold, Matthew   1822-1888   *Irish Essays and Others.* London: Smith, Elder, 1891. Popular edition, half title, 2 pages ads, original crimson cloth, spine slightly faded, few pencil notes, from the library of Geoffrey & Kathleen Tillotson.   Jarndyce Antiquarian Booksellers   CCVII - 28   2015   £20

Arnold, Matthew   1822-1888   *Last Essays on Church and Religion.*   London: Smith, Elder, 1885. First edition, half title, text slightly browned, original brown cloth, signed by Geoffrey Tillotson 25.11.47.   Jarndyce Antiquarian Booksellers   CCVII - 29   2015   £30

Arnold, Matthew   1822-1888   *Literature and Dogma.* London: Smith, Elder & Co., 1900. Popular edition, half title, 4 pages ads, original crimson cloth, spine rubbed, signed by Geoffrey Tillotson Xmas 1924 with ink and pencil notes.   Jarndyce Antiquarian Booksellers   CCVII - 33   2015   £20

Arnold, Matthew 1822-1888 *Literature and Dogma...* London: Smith, Elder & Co., 1873. First edition, half title, inserted slip, final ad leaf, original brown cloth, slight rubbing, signed by Geoffrey Tillotson 6/x/44 with pencil notes.   Jarndyce Antiquarian Booksellers   CCVII - 32   2015   £40

Arnold, Matthew 1822-1888 *Matthew Arnold's Notebooks.* London: Smith Elder, 1902. First edition, half title, frontispiece, facsimile, few spots, original white cloth, marked, spine darkened, signed by Geoffrey Tillotson.   Jarndyce Antiquarian Booksellers   CCVII - 36   2015   £20

Arnold, Matthew 1822-1888 *Merope.* London: Longmans, 1858. First edition, half title, 3 pages ads, 32 page catalog (Nov. 1857), odd spot, original green cloth by Westleys, orange endpapers with printed ad, very good, inscribed "From the author" on verso of leading pastedown and signed by Geoffrey Tillotson.   Jarndyce Antiquarian Booksellers   CCVII - 37   2015   £150

Arnold, Matthew 1822-1888 *Mixed Essays.* London: Smith Elder, 1879. First edition, half title, few spots, original dark blue cloth, dulled, inner hinges splitting, from the library of Geoffrey & Kathleen Tillotson.   Jarndyce Antiquarian Booksellers   CCVII - 38   2015   £20

Arnold, Matthew 1822-1888 *New Poems.* London: Macmillan and Co., 1867. First edition, original green cloth by Burn, slightly marked, following inner hinge slightly cracked, Geoffrey Tillotson's copy.   Jarndyce Antiquarian Booksellers   CCVII - 39   2015   £150

Arnold, Matthew 1822-1888 *On Translating Homer: Last Words a Lecture Given at Oxford.* London: Longmans, 1862. First edition, half title, original turquoise green cloth, slight wear to spine, damp marks on endpapers, pencilled note by Geoffrey Tillotson.   Jarndyce Antiquarian Booksellers   CCVII - 43   2015   £38

Arnold, Matthew 1822-1888 *On Translating Homer: Three Lectures Given at Oxford.* London: Longman, 1861. First edition, half title, 32 page catalog (July 1864), original green cloth, spine torn & chipped at head, signed by Geoffrey Tillotson 1942.   Jarndyce Antiquarian Booksellers   CCVII - 42   2015   £40

Arnold, Matthew 1822-1888 *Passages from the Prose Writings.* London: Smith, Elder, 1880. 2 pages ads, original dark blue cloth, slight marked, signed by Geoffrey Tillotson.   Jarndyce Antiquarian Booksellers   CCVII - 44   2015   £30

Arnold, Matthew 1822-1888 *Poems.* London: Longmans, 1853. New edition, half title, 32 page catalog (March 31 1853), unexplained erasure of edition statement, original green cloth by Westleys, yellow endpapers with printed ads, spine quite worn at head and tail, trace of lending library label, novelist S. R. Crockett's copy, signed by him, H. J. Macrory and Geoffrey Tillotson.   Jarndyce Antiquarian Booksellers   CCVII - 45   2015   £35

Arnold, Matthew 1822-1888 *Poems.* London: Longmans, 1853. New edition, half title, 24 page catalog (Nov. 1854), original green cloth by Westleys, orange endpapers with printed ads, spine faded and worn, hinges splitting, signed by Geoffrey Tillotson, April 1944 with few notes and cuttings inserted.   Jarndyce Antiquarian Booksellers   CCVII - 46   2015   £35

Arnold, Matthew 1822-1888 *Poems. Second Series.* London: Longmans, 1855. First edition, vi & 24 page catalog. (Nov. 1854), original green cloth by Westley's, orange endpapers with printed ads, spine faded, with splits in hinges, bookplate of Oxford Young, signed by Geoffrey Tillotson April 1944.   Jarndyce Antiquarian Booksellers   CCVII - 47   2015   £50

Arnold, Matthew 1822-1888 *Poetical Works.* London: Macmillan, 1924. Reprint, half title, original half brown calf, darkened and rubbed, top edge gilt, signed by Geoffrey Tillotson with many ink and pencilled notes and inserted ALS to Tillotson about Arnold from Frederick Page.   Jarndyce Antiquarian Booksellers   CCVII - 49   2015   £35

Arnold, Matthew 1822-1888 *Reports on Elementary Schools 1852-1882.* London: Macmillan, 1889. First edition, half title, 2 pages ads, original dark blue cloth, dulled, inner hinges splitting, leading f.e.p. slightly chipped, from the library of Geoffrey & Kathleen Tillotson.   Jarndyce Antiquarian Booksellers   CCVII - 52   2015   £25

Arnold, Matthew 1822-1888 *Schools and Universities on the Continent.* Ann Arbor: University of Michigan Press, 1964. Original green cloth, very good in dust jacket, Geoffrey Tillotson's presentation copy with carbon copy of TL presumably from him, sending praise for the project.   Jarndyce Antiquarian Booksellers   CCVII - 54   2015   £20

Arnold, Matthew 1822-1888 *St. Paul and Protestantism...* London: Smith Elder, 1870. First edition, half title, browning caused by endpapers, original brown cloth, small tear on back board, slight rubbing, traces of library label in leading endpapers, from the library of Geoffrey & Kathleen Tillotson.   Jarndyce Antiquarian Booksellers   CCVII - 55   2015   £30

Arnold, Matthew 1822-1888 *The Note-Books.* London: Oxford University Press, 1952. Half title, original red buckram, from the library of Geoffrey & Kathleen Tillotson, inscribed by same, with copy of Geoffrey's review or reviews.   Jarndyce Antiquarian Booksellers   CCVII - 40   2015   £35

Arnold, Matthew 1822-1888 *The Poems.* London: Longmans, 1965. Half title, frontispiece, original turquoise cloth, very good in creased dust jacket, signed by Geoffrey Tillotson 1965 with few notes and few insertions including miscellaneous notes, etc.   Jarndyce Antiquarian Booksellers   CCVII - 48   2015   £25

Austen, Jane 1775-1817 *Jane Austen's Letters to Her Sister Cassandra and Others.* Oxford: Clarendon Press, 1932. 2 volumes, half titles, frontispieces, plates, maps, uncut, original marbled boards, pale blue cloth spines, paper labels, spines slightly faded, from the library of Geoffrey & Kathleen Tillotson.   Jarndyce Antiquarian Booksellers   CCVII - 77   2015   £85

Austen, Jane 1775-1817 *Mansfield Park.* Belfast: Simms & M'Inyre, 1846. Half title, 4 pages ads, original maroon cloth, spine slightly faded, nice, from the library of Geoffrey & Kathleen Tillotson.   Jarndyce Antiquarian Booksellers   CCVII - 78   2015   £200

Balfour, Arthur James *Criticism and Beauty: a Lecture Rewritten...* Oxford: Clarendon press, 1910. publisher's slip, original blue printed wrappers, slightly creased, 48 pages, from the library of Geoffrey & Kathleen Tillotson.   Jarndyce Antiquarian Booksellers   CCVII - 81   2015   £20

Bate, Walter Jackson *Coleridge.* London: Collier MacMillan, 1968. Half title, uncut, original dark green cloth, very good in dust jacket, from the library of Geoffrey & Kathleen Tillotson, presentation from same with inserts.   Jarndyce Antiquarian Booksellers   CCVII - 152   2015   £35

Bible. English - 1875 *Isaiah XL-LXVI with the shorter prophecies ... edited with notes by Matthew Arnold.* London: Macmillan, 1875. First edition, original brown cloth, signed by Geoffrey Tillotson 30.iii.42 with note that it was given to him by Prof. Hermann Levy.   Jarndyce Antiquarian Booksellers   CCVII - 58   2015   £38

Bible. English - 1883 *Isaiah of Jerusalem in the Authorised English Version... notes by Matthew Arnold.* London: Macmillan, 1883. First edition, half title, 32 page catalog (1883), original brown cloth, slightly dulled, from the library of Geoffrey & Kathleen Tillotson.   Jarndyce Antiquarian Booksellers   CCVII - 59   2015   £38

Bond, Richmond P. *English Burlesque Poetry 1700-1750.* Cambridge: Harvard University Press, 1932. Half title original red cloth, spine faded, signed by Geoffrey Tillotson, Mr 1933, with few pencil notes and proof copy of his review.   Jarndyce Antiquarian Booksellers   CCVII - 90   2015   £45

Bose, Amalendu *Chronicles of Life Studies in Early Victorian.* London: Longmans, 1962. Original pale grey cloth, very good in torn and marked dust jacket, Geoffrey Tillotson's copy with typewritten copy of his letter to author.   Jarndyce Antiquarian Booksellers   CCVII - 91   2015   £35

Boswell, James 1740-1795 *Boswell's Life of Johnson...* Oxford: at the Clarendon Press, 1934-1950. Revised and enlarged edition, 6 volumes, half titles, frontispieces, plates, original maroon cloth, very good, volumes I-II with marked dust jacket, Geoffrey Tillotson's copy with cuttings, correspondence and ALS.   Jarndyce Antiquarian Booksellers   CCVII - 339   2015   £125

Boswell, James 1740-1795 *Letters Collected and Edited by Chauncey Brewster Tinker.* Oxford: Clarendon Press, 1924. 2 volumes, half titles, frontispiece volume I, plates, old pencil mark, original brown cloth, from the library of Geoffrey & Kathleen Tillotson, given by Geoffery to Kathleen 3.IV.38, with note and cutting inserted.   Jarndyce Antiquarian Booksellers   CCVII - 93   2015   £35

Brain, Walter Russell, Baron *Some Reflections on Genius and Other Essays.* London: Pitman Medical Pub., 1960. Original purple cloth, illustrations by Norman Smith, half title, very good in slightly spotted dust jacket, from the library of Geoffrey & Kathleen Tillotson, Geoffrey's gift to Kathleen, with AL from Geoffery congratulating Brain on his peerage and Brain's ALS in reply.   Jarndyce Antiquarian Booksellers   CCVII - 96   2015   £20

Bronte, Charlotte 1816-1855 *Shirley.* London: Smith, Elder and Co., 1849. First edition, 3 volumes, 16 page catalog (Oct. 1849) volume I, signed by Geoffrey Tillotson and with pencil notes and marginal marks, card wrappers made by Tillotson retaining original f.e.p., slightly dusty blue ms. paper labels, volumes I and II labelled upside down.   Jarndyce Antiquarian Booksellers   CCVII - 106   2015   £125

Bronte, Charlotte 1816-1855 *Villette.* Boston: Houghton Mifflin Co., 1971. Riverside edition, original printed card wrappers, slightly marked, very good, from the library of Geoffrey & Kathleen Tillotson, edited by Geoffery with inserted correspondence.   Jarndyce Antiquarian Booksellers   CCVII - 109   2015   £20

Bronte, Charlotte 1816-1855 *Villette.* London: Smith Elder & Co., 1853. First edition, 3 volumes, few leaves proud and damaged at fore-edge, from the library of Geoffrey & Kathleen Tillotson, with note by Kathleen, card wrappers made by Geoffrey, many pencil notes and marginal marks.   Jarndyce Antiquarian Booksellers   CCVII - 108   2015   £250

Bronte, Charlotte 1816-1855 *Villette.* Oxford: Clarendon Press, 1984. half title, original dark blue cloth, very good in slightly marked dust jacket, from the library of Geoffrey & Kathleen Tillotson, with 3 page ALS from editor about this edition.   Jarndyce Antiquarian Booksellers   CCVII - 110   2015   £50

Browning, Robert 1812-1889 *Men and Women.* Oxford: Clarendon Press, 1920. Original dark blue cloth, slightly dulled, Geoffrey Tillotson's signed secondhand 'working copy' with some text emendations, notes and insertions.   Jarndyce Antiquarian Booksellers   CCVII - 118   2015   £40

Browning, Robert 1812-1889 *Sordello.* London: Edward Moxon, 1840. First edition, half title, 1 page ads, 15 page catalog Jan. 1840, Geoffrey Tillotson's copy with pencil markings by previous owner, with notes and inserted markers, stiff paper wrappers with paper label made by Geoffrey.   Jarndyce Antiquarian Booksellers   CCVII - 120   2015   £75

Browning, Robert 1812-1889 *The Ring and the Book.* London: Oxford University Press, 1912. Frontispiece, original brown cloth, inner hinge cracking, signed by Geoffrey Tillotson 6.II.45 with notes and marks.   Jarndyce Antiquarian Booksellers   CCVII - 119   2015   £22

Bunyan, John 1628-1688 *The Pilgrim's Progress...* London: Routledge, 1862. New edition, illustrations by John Gilbert, frontispiece and plates, ads on endpapers, original dark green cloth, color paper pasted on by Geoffrey Tilltoson, inner hinge splitting, rubbed, ms. label defective, presentation to Joseph Tillotson, with Kathleen Tillotson's notes and Geoffrey's notes and marginal marks, from the library of Geoffrey & Kathleen Tillotson.   Jarndyce Antiquarian Booksellers   CCVII - 123   2015   £30

Burke, Edmund 1729-1797 *Letters, Speeches and Tracts on Irish Affairs Collected and Arranged by Matthew Arnold.* London: Macmillan, 1881. Half title 2 pages ads, original dark blue cloth, slightly chipped, spine faded, inner hinges cracking, from the library of Geoffrey & Kathleen Tillotson.   Jarndyce Antiquarian Booksellers   CCVII - 60   2015   £35

Butt, John *Dickens at Work.* London: Methuen, 1957. First edition, half title, frontispiece, facsimile, plates, original green cloth, very good in slightly torn and dusted dust jacket, from the library of Geoffrey & Kathleen Tillotson, with Kathleen's presentation to Geoffrey.   Jarndyce Antiquarian Booksellers   CCVII - 208   2015   £35

Caddel, Richard *Burnt Acres and the Shangri-la....* Sunderland: Ceolfrith Press, 1978. Folio, illustrations, ad leaf slightly browned, original grey printed wrappers, from the library of Geoffrey & Kathleen Tillotson, with press cutting of reviews.   Jarndyce Antiquarian Booksellers   CCVII - 129   2015   £85

Cairncross, A. S. *Modern Essays in Criticism.* London: Macmillan, 1938. Half title, final ad leaf, original green cloth, slightly marked, Geoffrey Tillotson's copy with caricature of himself? partly laid down and embellished.   Jarndyce Antiquarian Booksellers   CCVII - 130   2015   £25

Calverley, C. S. *The Complete Works...* London: George Bell & Sons, 1901. Half title, frontispiece, titles in red and black, browning caused by endpapers, original dark brown cloth, signed by Geoffrey Tillotson 1942 with cuttings inserted and 4 page photocopy of original ms. "Lovers and a Reflection".   Jarndyce Antiquarian Booksellers   CCVII - 131   2015   £20

Chambers, E. K. *Shakespearean Gleanings.* London: Oxford University, 1944. Half title, frontispiece, original green cloth, very good, sunned dust jacket, Geoffrey Tillotson's signed copy, with review &c inserted.   Jarndyce Antiquarian Booksellers   CCVII - 460   2015   £20

Chambers, R. W. *Man's Unconquerable Mind: Studies of English Writers from Bede to A. E. Housman and W. P. Ker.* London: Jonathan Cape, 1939. Half title, plates, author's presentation copy to Geoffrey Tillotson and wife, with 2 ALS's from Raymond Wilson Chambers to Geoffrey.   Jarndyce Antiquarian Booksellers   CCVII - 132   2015   £20

Clarke, W. K. Lowther *Eighteenth Century Piety.* London: SPCK, 1944. Half title, plates, original brown cloth, very good in slightly worn dust jacket, Geoffrey Tillotson's review copy with part of his m.s review.   Jarndyce Antiquarian Booksellers   CCVII - 136   2015   £20

Clifford, James L. *Eighteenth Century English Literature: Modern Essays in Criticism.* New York: Oxford University Press, 1959. Half title, original printed card wrappers, from the library of Geoffrey & Kathleen Tillotson, Geoffrey's presentation to Kathleen. Jarndyce Antiquarian Booksellers CCVII - 137   2015   £20

Clough, Arthur Hugh *Emerson-Clough Letters.* Cleveland: Rowfant Club, 1934. No. 52 of 165 copies, half title, original marbled paper boards, paper labels, brief pencil note by Geoffrey Tillotson, but unsigned. Jarndyce Antiquarian Booksellers   CCVII - 140   2015   £40

Clough, Arthur Hugh *Letters and Remains.* London: Spottiswoode & Co., 1865. Half title, original green patterned cloth, inner hinges rather crudely strengthened, presented to Miss Rankin, sent by her to Joseph Hutton 1888, signed by Geoffrey Tillotson 12.v.47. Jarndyce Antiquarian Booksellers   CCVII - 141   2015   £40

Clough, Arthur Hugh *Poems.* London: Macmillan, 1862. First edition, half title, 16 page catalog, original green patterned cloth by Burn, spine darkened with split in leading hinge, Geoffrey Tillotson's copy signed 1944. Jarndyce Antiquarian Booksellers   CCVII - 142   2015 £50

Clough, Arthur Hugh *Poems...* London: Macmillan, 1885. Eleventh edition, half title, full dark green calf, prize binding from Marlborough College, small chip from head of spine, inner hinges splitting, from the library of Geoffrey & Kathleen Tillotson. Jarndyce Antiquarian Booksellers CCVII - 143   2015   £20

Clough, Blanche Athena *A Memoir of Anne Jemima Clough by her niece.* London: Edward Arnold, 1897. Frontispiece and plates, 32 page catalog (Ot. 1897), uncut in original dark green cloth, small split at head of spine, from the library of Geoffrey & Kathleen Tillotson. Jarndyce Antiquarian Booksellers   CCVII - 138   2015   £35

Coleridge, Hartley *Letters.* Oxford University Press, 1941. Half title, frontispiece, from the library of Geoffrey & Kathleen Tillotson, erratum slip, original buff cloth, marked, inscribed by Kathleen for Geoffrey, with original 4 line comic verse, but not signed by him. Jarndyce Antiquarian Booksellers   CCVII - 146   2015   £20

Coleridge, Samuel Taylor 1772-1834 *Biographia Literaria; or Biographical Sketches...* London: Rest Fenner, 1817. First edition, 2 volumes, half titles, without final ad leaf volume II, some spotting, few leaves rather browned, half red calf, spines chipped, hinges weak, signed S. Palmer and with his pencil notes at end of Chapter I, inserted is ALS of inquiry to Geoffrey Tillotson from Geoffrey Grigson. Jarndyce Antiquarian Booksellers   CCVII - 147   2015 £850

Coleridge, Samuel Taylor 1772-1834 *Shakespeare, Ben Jonson, Beaumont and Fletcher: Notes and Lectures.* Liverpool: Edward Howell, 1875. New edition, half title, final ad leaf, original olive green cloth, spine slightly bubbled, signed K. M. Constable, April 1926 with some marginal marks and inserted reviews, from the library of Geoffrey & Kathleen Tillotson. Jarndyce Antiquarian Booksellers CCVII - 149   2015   £35

Coleridge, Samuel Taylor 1772-1834 *The Poems...* London: Oxford University Press, 1924. Half title, frontispiece, original red cloth, spine dulled, Geoffrey Tillotson's copy signed with ms. notes and various insertions. Jarndyce Antiquarian Booksellers   CCVII - 148   2015   £40

Communist Party of Great Britain *Lord and Lady Beavermere ...* London: Communist Party of Great Britain, 1937? 16 pages, illustrations, stabbed as issued, slightly creased, from the library of Geoffrey & Kathleen Tillotson. Jarndyce Antiquarian Booksellers   CCVII - 157   2015 £20

Communist Party of Great Britain *Parade of War.* London: Communist Party of Great Britain, 1937. 16 pages, illustrations, stabbed as issued in original wrappers with caricature, slightly marked and creased, from the library of Geoffrey & Kathleen Tillotson. Jarndyce Antiquarian Booksellers   CCVII - 158   2015   £20

Cory, William *Ionica with Biographical Introduction...* London: George Allen, 1905. Third edition, half title, final colophon leaf, original light blue cloth, marked, top edge gilt, Geoffrey Tillotson's copy May 46 which had belonged to Wilfred Granville. Jarndyce Antiquarian Booksellers CCVII - 159   2015   £120

Cunningham, Valentine *Everywhere Spoken Against: Dissent in the Victorian Novel.* Oxford: Clarendon Press, 1975. Half title, original dark blue cloth, very good in dust jacket, from the library of Geoffrey & Kathleen Tillotson. Jarndyce Antiquarian Booksellers   CCVII - 161   2015 £20

Cussans, John E. *Handbook of Heraldry with Instructions for Tracing Pedigrees and Deciphering Ancient Mss. Rules for the Appointment of Liveries &c.* London: Chatto & Windus, 1893. Fourth edition, 32 page catalog Sept. 1901, half title, frontispiece, illustrations, slightly browned, original olive green cloth, spine faded to brown, from the library of Geoffrey & Kathleen Tillotson. Jarndyce Antiquarian Booksellers   CCVII - 162   2015   £25

Davis, Eliza Jeffries *The University Site, Bloomsbury.* Cambridge: 1936. Reprinted from London Topographical Record Volume XVII, Folding map, photos, maps, plans, uncut in blue paper wrappers, marked, front wrapper detached, presentation by author for Geoffrey Tillotson. Jarndyce Antiquarian Booksellers CCVII - 163 2015 £35

Dawson, William Harbutt *Matthew Arnold and His Relation to the Thought of Our Time...* New York: G. P. Putnam's Sons, 1904. Frontispiece, few marginal marks, original dark blue cloth, from the library of Geoffrey & Kathleen Tillotson. Jarndyce Antiquarian Booksellers CCVII - 62 2015 £20

De Morgan, Augusta *A Budget of Paradoxes.* London: Longmans, 1872. First edition, half title, contemporary half red morocco, spine darkened, scarce, with Geoffrey Tillotson's initials 1953 and Kathleen Tillotson's marker denoting special interest. Jarndyce Antiquarian Booksellers CCVII - 164 2015 £120

Dickens, Charles 1812-1870 *Barnaby Rudge.* Paris: Baudry's European Lib., 1842. 2 volumes, half titles, 4 page catalog volume I, some spotting, original brown paper wrappers, slightly torn, ink mark, original paper labels, nice, from the library of Geoffrey & Kathleen Tillotson. Jarndyce Antiquarian Booksellers CCVII - 169 2015 £85

Dickens, Charles 1812-1870 *Dombey and Son.* Oxford: Clarendon Press, 1974. Half title, frontispiece and illustrations, original dark blue cloth in dusted and slightly torn dust jacket, from the library of Geoffrey & Kathleen Tillotson. Jarndyce Antiquarian Booksellers CCVII - 175 2015 £85

Dickens, Charles 1812-1870 *Great Expectations.* Oxford: Clarendon Press, 1993. Half title, illustrations, original dark blue cloth, very good in slightly torn dust jacket, from the library of Geoffrey & Kathleen Tillotson with Kathleen's note, several inserted letters. Jarndyce Antiquarian Booksellers CCVII - 177 2015 £120

Dickens, Charles 1812-1870 *Hard Times and Pictures from Italy.* London: Chapman & Hall, 1866. Frontispiece, original green pebble grained cloth, few marks on leading pastedown, split in following hinge, otherwise bright, clean copy, from the library of Geoffrey & Kathleen Tillotson. Jarndyce Antiquarian Booksellers CCVII - 179 2015 £45

Dickens, Charles 1812-1870 *Oliver Twist.* Oxford: Clarendon Press, 1966. Half title, frontispiece, illustrations, map, original dark blue cloth in slightly worn dust jacket, from the library of Geoffrey & Kathleen Tillotson. Jarndyce Antiquarian Booksellers CCVII - 189 2015 £120

Dickens, Charles 1812-1870 *Oliver Twist.* Oxford: Clarendon Press, 1966. Half title, frontispiece, illustrations, map, original blue cloth, very good in dust jacket, from the library of Geoffrey & Kathleen Tillotson, inscribed by her for Geoffrey. Jarndyce Antiquarian Booksellers CCVII - 190 2015 £90

Dickens, Charles 1812-1870 *Oliver Twist.* Oxford: Clarendon Press, 1974. Half title, frontispiece, illustrations, map, original blue cloth in slightly torn dust jacket with notes, Kathleen Tillotson's copy, als inserted Geoffrey Tillotson's copy of her paper 'Oliver Twist from Essays and Studies" 1959. Jarndyce Antiquarian Booksellers CCVII - 191 2015 £110

Dickens, Charles 1812-1870 *Sikes and Nancy....* London: Henry Sotheran, 1921. Half title, frontispiece, final ad leaf, original black boards, paper label, dulled, from the library of Geoffrey & Kathleen Tillotson. Jarndyce Antiquarian Booksellers CCVII - 193 2015 £45

Dickens, Charles 1812-1870 *Sketches By Boz.* Philadelphia: Lea and Blanchard, 1842. New edition, from the library of Geoffrey & Kathleen Tillotson, tall 8vo., frontispiece and 18 plates after George Cruikshank, one missing, some browning, lacking pages 29-32, blue paper wrappers made by Geoffrey his note on wrappers, text annotated throughout by Kathleen in ink and pencil. Jarndyce Antiquarian Booksellers CCVII - 197 2015 £45

Dickens, Charles 1812-1870 *Sketches by Boz. First Series.* London: John Macrone, 1837. Third edition, 2 volumes, frontispiece and plates by George Cruikshank, original dark green cloth, slight rubbing, good, clean, attractive copy, from the library of Geoffrey & Kathleen Tillotson. Jarndyce Antiquarian Booksellers CCVII - 196 2015 £350

Dickens, Charles 1812-1870 *Sketches by Boz... (bound with) American Notes for General Circulation.* London: Chapman and Hall, 1850. 1850, 2 volumes in 1, frontispiece, half title, contemporary half maroon calf, spine slightly rubbed and faded, from the library of Geoffrey & Kathleen Tillotson. Jarndyce Antiquarian Booksellers CCVII - 198 2015 £35

Dickens, Charles 1812-1870 *The Adventures of Oliver Twist.* London: Chapman and Hall, 1853. Half title, original light green cloth, one mark, spine slightly sunned, otherwise very good, from the library of Geoffrey & Kathleen Tillotson with note by Kathleen. Jarndyce Antiquarian Booksellers CCVII - 185 2015 £50

Dickens, Charles 1812-1870 *The Adventures of Oliver Twist.* London: Chapman & Hall, 1867? 8 illustrations, half title, frontispiece and plates, original red cloth, spine worn at head and tail, dulled, internally good, from the library of Geoffrey & Kathleen Tillotson. Jarndyce Antiquarian Booksellers   CCVII - 186   2015   £45

Dickens, Charles 1812-1870 *The Letters Volumes I-V (1820-1852).* Oxford: Clarendon, 1965-1988. Pilgrim edition, original pink (volume I) and red cloth, dulled and marbled, volume I with spine strip torn away, volumes III & IV slightly loose, from the library of Geoffrey & Kathleen Tillotson.   Jarndyce Antiquarian Booksellers   CCVII - 199   2015   £480

Dickens, Charles 1812-1870 *The Letters.* Oxford: Clarendon Press, 1969. Pilgrim edition, Volume II 140-1841, original red cloth, very good in very slightly torn dust jacket, from the library of Geoffrey & Kathleen Tillotson.   Jarndyce Antiquarian Booksellers   CCVII - 202   2015   £85

Dickens, Charles 1812-1870 *The Letters.* Oxford: Clarendon Press, 1981. Volume V 1847-1849, original red cloth, very slightly torn dust jacket, from the library of Geoffrey & Kathleen Tillotson.   Jarndyce Antiquarian Booksellers   CCVII - 203   2015   £110

Dickens, Charles 1812-1870 *The Letters.* Oxford: Clarendon Press, 1982? Pilgrim edition, volume I, 1820-1839, original red cloth, near mint in very slightly creased dust jacket, from the library of Geoffrey & Kathleen Tillotson.   Jarndyce Antiquarian Booksellers   CCVII - 200   2015   £85

Dickens, Charles 1812-1870 *The Letters.* Oxford: Clarendon Press, 1989. Volume I 1820-1839, original red cloth, near mint in slightly creased dust jacket, from the library of Geoffrey & Kathleen Tillotson.   Jarndyce Antiquarian Booksellers   CCVII - 201   2015   £85

Dickens, Charles 1812-1870 *The Pickwick Papers.* Oxford: Clarendon Press, Half title, frontispiece, illustrations, original dark blue cloth, very good in creased dust jacket, from the library of Geoffrey & Kathleen Tillotson, relevant papers inserted including browned proof article by Kathleen Tillotson for TLS.   Jarndyce Antiquarian Booksellers   CCVII - 195   2015   £120

Dolby, George *Charles Dickens as I Knew Him...* London: T. Fisher Unwin, 1885. Second thousand, half title, 32 page catalog 1885, pin holes in title, original red cloth, dulled, from the library of Geoffrey & Kathleen Tillotson, press cuttings inserted including obit of Dolby 1900.   Jarndyce Antiquarian Booksellers   CCVII - 212   2015   £40

Donne, John 1571-1631 *The Elegies and Songs and Sonnets.* Oxford: Clarendon Press, 1965. Half title, music, original dark blue cloth, very good in slightly torn and marked dust jacket, with 4 related cuttings inserted, from the library of Geoffrey & Kathleen Tillotson.   Jarndyce Antiquarian Booksellers   CCVII - 2245   2015   £35

Donne, John 1571-1631 *The Extasie.* London: privately printed at the Department of English at University College London, 1934. Unopened, original blue printed wrappers, from the library of Geoffrey & Kathleen Tillotson.   Jarndyce Antiquarian Booksellers   CCVII - 226   2015   £50

Donne, John 1571-1631 *The Poems.* London: Oxford University Press, 1929. Half title, frontispiece, uncut in original blue cloth, covered in thick striped paper, paper label, Kathleen Tillotson's copy 1930 as KMC, Geoffrey Tillotson added 1934, many notes, mostly marginal on endpapers and inserted articles.   Jarndyce Antiquarian Booksellers   CCVII - 228   2015   £50

Donne, John 1571-1631 *The Poems.* Oxford: Clarendon Press, 1912. 2 volumes, original brown buckram, paper labels slightly split at edges, with inserted, notes, probably by J. B. Leishman, the editor to whom correspondence is addressed, from the library of Geoffrey & Kathleen Tillotson.   Jarndyce Antiquarian Booksellers   CCVII - 227   2015   £60

Drayton, Michael 1563-1631 *Endimion and Phoebe. Ideas Lamos.* N.P.: 1870? 4to., privately printed facsimile , original purple wrappers with title, front wrapper detached and creased, spine defective, from the library of Geoffrey & Kathleen Tillotson, with few pencil notes by Geoffrey.   Jarndyce Antiquarian Booksellers   CCVII - 232   2015   £120

Drayton, Michael 1563-1631 *England's Heroical Epistles.* London: printed for J. Johnson, 1788. Some leaves slightly browned, 19th century half dark green morocco, slightly rubbed with scars on marbled boards, with early note on page 308, with names of Geoffrey and Kathleen Tillotson, inserted correspondence shows Kathleen offered this to British Library which in fact had acquired a copy, ALS from John Betjeman probably to Bernard Newdigate.   Jarndyce Antiquarian Booksellers   CCVII - 233   2015   £280

Drayton, Michael 1563-1631 *Minor Poems.* Oxford: Clarendon Press, 1907. 4to., original cream card imitation vellum wrappers, very slightly dusted, very good, signed by Geoffrey Tillotson 1928 with very few pencil notes.   Jarndyce Antiquarian Booksellers   CCVII - 236   2015   £40

Drayton, Michael 1563-1631 *Nimphidia the Court of Fayrie.* Stratford-upon-Avon: printed at the Shakespeare Head Press, 1924. 4to., half title, original decorated paper wrappers, spine slightly browned with small chips, with Christmas greetings from F. H. R. Dix, Hemingford or Stratford-on-Avon sending this poem, from the library of Geoffrey & Kathleen Tillotson. Jarndyce Antiquarian Booksellers CCVII - 237 2015 £50

Drayton, Michael 1563-1631 *Poly-Olbion.* London: printed for M. Lownes, I. Browne, A. Helme, J. Bushbie, 1612-1622. Engraved maps, 19th century half black calf, rubbed with split at head of leading hinge, armorial bookplate of Bernard Henry Newdigate, somewhat defective copy with few pencil marks, from the library of Geoffrey & Kathleen Tillotson. Jarndyce Antiquarian Booksellers CCVII - 239 2015 £950

Drayton, Michael 1563-1631 *The Works.* Oxford: published for the Shakespeare Head Press, 1961. 1941, Volumes I-IV with Volume V 1941, half titles, frontispieces, facsimiles, uncut in original dark blue cloth, very good, from the library of Geoffrey & Kathleen Tillotson. Jarndyce Antiquarian Booksellers CCVII - 231 2015 £300

Dryden, John 1631-1700 *Hymns Attributed to John Dryden.* Berkeley: University of California Press, 1937. Frontispiece, original brown cloth, very good in slightly dusted dust jacket, signed by Geoffrey Tillotson, with pencil notes, copies of his review, correspondence about the questioned ascription, long TLS from Professor Noyes and ms. copy of the reply. Jarndyce Antiquarian Booksellers CCVII - 248 2015 £30

Duke, Arthur *The Larke: a Seventeenth Century Poem Ascribed to Dr. Arthur Duke.* London: privately printed in the Department of English at the University College London, 1934. original blue printed wrappers, slightly faded and creased, printed by Geoffrey Tillotson on departmental hand press, inscribed by him to Kathleen Tillotson, inserted is ALS from Priscilla (Preston) to Kathleen. Jarndyce Antiquarian Booksellers CCVII - 251 2015 £60

Dyson, H. V. D. *Augustans and Romantics 1689-1830.* London: Cresset Press, 1940. Half title, original grey green cloth, inscribed to Geoffrey and Kathleen Tillotson by John Butt. Jarndyce Antiquarian Booksellers CCVII - 253 2015 £20

Eliot, George, Pseud. 1819-1880 *Scenes of Clerical Life.* Edinburgh and London: William Blackwood & Sons, 1859. Second edition, 2 volumes, half titles, 16 page catalog volume II, original burgundy pebble grained cloth by Edmonds & Remnants, little rubbed and dulled with small splits in hinges, lacking leading f.e.p.'s, from the library of Geoffrey & Kathleen Tillotson. Jarndyce Antiquarian Booksellers CCVII - 257 2015 £68

Eliot, George, Pseud. 1819-1880 *Silas Marner, the Weaver of Raveloe.* Edinburgh & London: William Blackwood & Sons, 1861. First edition, 16 page catalog and 4 pages ads, little spotting, original orange brown cloth by Burn, slightly rubbed, one hinge cracking, good, from the library of Geoffrey & Kathleen Tillotson. Jarndyce Antiquarian Booksellers CCVII - 259 2015 £500

Ellis-Fermor, Una Mary *Shakespeare the Dramatist and Other Papers.* London: Methuen, 1961. Half title, frontispiece, original maroon cloth, slightly faded in torn dust jacket, from the library of Geoffrey & Kathleen Tillotson, signed by Kathleen with few comments, letter from her to Kenneth Muir and his reply, with two papers presented by author to Kathleen and Geoffrey. Jarndyce Antiquarian Booksellers CCVII - 461 2015 £25

Ellis-Fermor, Una Mary *The Jacobean Drama: an Interpretation.* London: Methuen, 1936. Half title, original black cloth, crease along spine, with few inserted and marginal pencil notes by Geoffrey Tillotson. Jarndyce Antiquarian Booksellers CCVII - 254 2015 £25

Empson, William *Seven Types of Ambiguity.* London: Chatto & Windus, 1930. First edition, half title, inserted errata list, original orange cloth in torn and dusted dust jacket, with Geoffrey Tillotson's paper label Oxford 1931 and with ms. index compiled by him inserted, pencil marginal corrections by Kathleen Tillotson. Jarndyce Antiquarian Booksellers CCVII - 264 2015 £20

Evison, Vera I. *The Fifth-Century Invasions South of the Thames.* London: University of London, Athlone Press, 1865. 4to., half title, frontispiece, plates, illustrations, maps, original red cloth, very good in dated dust jacket, inscribed by author for Geoffrey Tillotson. Jarndyce Antiquarian Booksellers CCVII - 267 2015 £25

Examiner, Pseud. *Some Thoughts on Examinations, by an Examiner.* London: privately printed in the Department of English at University College, London, 1936. 4to., original blue printed wrappers, slightly creased, 7 pages, inscribed to Geoffrey Tillotson by Hilda Holme and L. Paulin, with quotation inserted by Tillotson. Jarndyce Antiquarian Booksellers CCVII - 268 2015 £60

Galton, Arthur *Two Essays Upon Matthew Arnold with Some of His Letters to the Author.* London: Elkin Mathews, 1897. Uncut in original blue boards, printed cloth spine, slightly marked and dusted, from the library of Geoffrey & Kathleen Tillotson. Jarndyce Antiquarian Booksellers CCVII - 65 2015 £25

Gaskell, Elizabeth Cleghorn 1810-1865 *Mary Barton and Other Tales.* London: Smith, Elder & Co., 1891. New edition, half title, frontispiece, 4 pages ads, from the library of Geoffrey & Kathleen Tillotson, home made paper wrappers with paper label, Kathleen has made few notes in text and marginal marks and inserted handwritten copy of preface to first edition in envelope affixed to half title, with postcard portrait of author.   Jarndyce Antiquarian Booksellers   CCVII - 274   2015   £20

Gissing, George *Thyrza: a Tale.* London: John Murray, 1907. New edition, half title, original pink cloth, little faded, leading f.e.p. cut out, from the library of Geoffrey & Kathleen Tillotson, marked from Kathleen to Geoffrey, 1937 with 2 notes and 2 press cuttings inserted.   Jarndyce Antiquarian Booksellers   CCVII - 278   2015   £20

Gray, Thomas 1716-1771 *An Elegy Written in a Country Churchyard.* London: printed by Edward Walters & Geoffrey Miller at Primrose Hill, 1933. 4to., title in red, uncut in original grey printed boards, cream buckram spine, spine label defective, dusted, complimentary copy of the 125 copies on handmade paper, 125 also on machine paper, from the library of Geoffrey & Kathleen Tillotson, review copy for the TLS with inserted notes by Geoffrey.   Jarndyce Antiquarian Booksellers   CCVII - 285   2015   £50

Gray, Thomas 1716-1771 *An Elegy Wrote in a Country Church Yard (1751) and the Eton College Manuscript...* Los Angeles: William Andrews Clark Memorial Lib., 1951. 4to., plates, facsimiles, original orange printed wrappers, dusted, from the library of Geoffrey & Kathleen Tillotson.   Jarndyce Antiquarian Booksellers   CCVII - 286   2015   £25

Gray, Thomas 1716-1771 *Correspondence.* Oxford: Clarendon Press, 1935. 3 volumes, half titles, frontispieces, original red cloth, spines faded, Geoffrey Tillotson's signed copy with notes, correspondence, copies of his reviews and list of corrections, &c.   Jarndyce Antiquarian Booksellers   CCVII - 287   2015   £65

Gray, Thomas 1716-1771 *The Complete Poems.* Oxford: Clarendon Press, 1966. Half title, frontispiece, original dark blue cloth, very good, strengthened dust jacket, review copy signed by Geoffrey Tillotson, June 1966, with note of his review.   Jarndyce Antiquarian Booksellers   CCVII - 284   2015   £25

Gray, Thomas 1716-1771 *The Poems of Mr. Gray.* London: printed for G. Kearsley, 1786. from the library of Geoffrey & Kathleen Tillotson. red paper covered card wrappers by Geoffrey Tillotson, with calligraphic "prize label" at front "reward of merit Thos. Hodges 1795".   Jarndyce Antiquarian Booksellers   CCVII - 281   2015   £45

Gray, Thomas 1716-1771 *The Poems.* Printed for White, Cochrane & Co. by S. Hamilton, Weybridge, Surrey, 1814. Contemporary half red calf, spine tooled gilt and blind, green labels, attractive copy, few pencil marks, from the library of Geoffrey & Kathleen Tillotson.   Jarndyce Antiquarian Booksellers   CCVII - 282   2015   £45

Gray, Thomas 1716-1771 *The Poetical Works of Gray and Collins.* London: Oxford University Press, 1926. Second edition, frontispiece and plates, original red cloth, rubbed with small split at head of leading hinge, Geoffrey Tillotson's copy 1930 with copious notes and insertions.   Jarndyce Antiquarian Booksellers   CCVII - 283   2015   £45

Greg, Walter Wilson *The Editorial Problem in Shakespeare.* Oxford: Clarendon Press, 1942. Original dark blue cloth, faded, from the library of Geoffrey & Kathleen Tillotson, with her name in Geoffrey's hand and with ink note by Geoffrey, exchange of letters between Greg and Geoffrey preserved in envelope tipped on to following pastedown, with other notes.   Jarndyce Antiquarian Booksellers   CCVII - 462   2015   £25

Grimaldi, Joseph 1779-1837 *Memoirs of Joseph Grimaldi.* London: Richard Bentley, 1846. New edition, Frontispiece, plates slightly spotted or browned, illustrations by George Cruikshank, spotted or browned, original beige cloth, printed in red, spine little sunned, surface slightly rubbed, good, sound, from the library of Geoffrey & Kathleen Tillotson.   Jarndyce Antiquarian Booksellers   CCVII - 182   2015   £75

Grossmith, George *The Diary of a Nobody.* Bristol: J. W. Arrowsmith; London: Simpkin Marshall, Hamilton, Kent and Co., 1910. Binding covered in brown decorated paper by Geoffrey Tillotson, from the library of Geoffrey & Kathleen Tillotson, paper label.   Jarndyce Antiquarian Booksellers   CCVII - 290   2015   £25

Harpsfield, Nicholas *The Life and Death of Sir Thomas Moore...* London: OUP, 1932. Half title, frontispiece and plates, 8 page catalog, handsome full white pigskin with elaborate pattern in blind and gilt, blind and gilt dentelles, marbled endpapers, fine in lined marbled slipcase, from the library of Geoffrey & Kathleen Tillotson, gilt lettered on front from GT, KMC 21XL 33 and with signed inscription from both editors to Tillotson's, with inserted p.c. from R. W. Chambers1933 and ALS from Gertrude Chambers and Edith Batho.   Jarndyce Antiquarian Booksellers   CCVII - 381   2015   £250

Harris, Elizabeth Furlong Skipton *From Oxford ot Rome and How It Fared with Some Who Lately Made the Journey.* London: Longmans, 1847. Original dark brown cloth, worn at head and tail of spine, frontispiece, ownership inscription of JAS Southern? with long note by Geoffrey Tillotson, from the library of Geoffrey & Kathleen Tillotson.   Jarndyce Antiquarian Booksellers   CCVII - 294   2015   £150

Herbert, George *The Works.* Oxford: Clarendon Press, 1941. Half title, frontispiece, facsimiles, uncut, original dark blue cloth, inner hinge cracking, from the library of Geoffrey & Kathleen Tillotson, signed by Geoffrey, ALs from editor, pencil notes, insertions.   Jarndyce Antiquarian Booksellers   CCVII - 297   2015   £35

Holloway, John *The Victorian Sage: Studies in Argument.* London: Macmillan, 1953. Half title, original green cloth, very good in slightly torn dust jacket, from the library of Geoffrey & Kathleen Tillotson, Geoffrey's signed advance review copy with extensive notes, and some insertions.   Jarndyce Antiquarian Booksellers   CCVII - 301   2015   £20

Honan, Park *Jane Austen: Her Life.* London: Weidenfeld & Nicholson, 1987. Half title, plates, original black cloth, very good in dust jacket, from the library of Geoffrey & Kathleen Tillotson, with inserted postcard from Kathleen. Jarndyce Antiquarian Booksellers   CCVII - 79   2015   £45

Hood, Thomas   1799-1845 *Poems.* London: Edward Moxon, 1854. Seventh edition, 8 page catalog (March 1855), half title, frontispiece, original cloth covered with decorated paper by Geoffrey Tillotson, with ms. label, signed by same with few marginal marks.   Jarndyce Antiquarian Booksellers   CCVII - 302   2015   £20

Hopkins, Gerard Manley *The Correspondence of Gerard Manley Hopkins and Richard Watson Dixon.* London: Oxford University Press, 1955. Second impression, half title, frontispiece, plate, original red brown buckram, very good in dust jacket, Geoffrey Tillotson's signed copy with few pencil marks.   Jarndyce Antiquarian Booksellers   CCVII - 308   2015   £20

Hopkins, Gerard Manley *The Journals and Papers.* London: Oxford University Press, 1967. Half title, frontispiece, plates, music, original brown buckram, very good in slightly torn dust jacket, from the library of Geoffrey & Kathleen Tillotson.   Jarndyce Antiquarian Booksellers   CCVII - 306   2015   £25

Hopkins, Gerard Manley *The Letters of Gerard Manley Hopkins to Robert Bridges...*   London: Oxford University Press, 1955. Second edition, half title, frontispiece, folding plate, original red brown buckram, very good in dust jacket, Geoffrey Tillotson's signed copy with pencil marks. Jarndyce Antiquarian Booksellers   CCVII - 307   2015   £20

Hopkins, Gerard Manley *The Poems.* London: Oxford University Press, 1967. Fourth edition, half title, original green cloth, very good in dust jacket, from the library of Geoffrey & Kathleen Tillotson.   Jarndyce Antiquarian Booksellers   CCVII - 304   2015   £25

Hopkins, Gerard Manley *The Sermons and Devotional Writings.* London: Oxford University Press, 1959. Half title, frontispiece, map, original brown buckram, very good in slightly torn dust jacket, Geoffrey Tillotson's signed copy, containing notes by J. B. Leishman, former owner. Jarndyce Antiquarian Booksellers   CCVII - 305   2015   £25

Horatius Flaccus, Quintus *Translating Homer: Thirty Odes Translated...* Oxford: Bruno Cassirer, 1956. Half title, parallel English & Latin text, original light brown cloth, very good in slightly dusted and chipped dust jacket, from the library of Geoffrey & Kathleen Tillotson, signed by both, with signed presentation slip from J. B. Leishman laid in, with ALS's from him to Tillotson's.   Jarndyce Antiquarian Booksellers   CCVII - 309   2015   £20

Hough, Graham *The Last Romantics.* London: Gerald Duckworth & Co., 1949. Half title, original mauve cloth, very good in dusted dust jacket, Geoffrey Tillotson's signed copy with pencil notes, long inserted review from TLS. Jarndyce Antiquarian Booksellers   CCVII - 310   2015   £20

Houghton, Walter E. *The Art of Newman's Apologia.* New Haven: pub. for Wellesley College by Yale University Press, 1945. Frontispiece, original beige cloth, in slightly torn and dusted dust jacket, Geoffrey Tillotson's copy, signed, 25 viii 45, with few marginal notes and marks, with two ALS's from author, proof of Tillotson's review. Jarndyce Antiquarian Booksellers   CCVII - 399   2015   £20

Houghton, Walter E. *The Victorian Frame of Mind 1830-1870.* New Haven: pubished for Wellesley College by Yale University Press, 1957. original black cloth, few pencil marginal marks and notes, signed by Geoffrey Tillotson with part of TLS from author 1938.   Jarndyce Antiquarian Booksellers   CCVII - 311   2015   £20

House, Humphry *All in Due Time.* London: Rupert Hart-Davis, 1955. Half title, original red cloth, torn dust jacket, from the library of Geoffrey & Kathleen Tillotson, inscribed "Tillotson's 1955" with pencil notes, ALS from House's widow Madeline thanking Geoffrey for his review, with note and short review by Kathleen. Jarndyce Antiquarian Booksellers CCVII - 312 2015 £20

House, Humphry *Coleridge, the Clark Lectures 1951-1952.* London: Rupert Hart Davis, 1953. Half title, original decorated boards, very good in slightly dusted dust jacket, Geoffrey Tillotson's copy with TLS from Rupert Hart-Davis 1955 announcing House's sudden death, tipped in, pencil notes, obits, and two ALS's from Madeline House to Geoffrey. Jarndyce Antiquarian Booksellers CCVII - 153 2015 £30

Housman, Alfred Edward 1859-1936 *Last Poems.* London: Grant Richards, 1922. Half title, slight foxing, original dark blue cloth, Geoffrey Tillotson's copy 1926 with a number of inserted cuttings. Jarndyce Antiquarian Booksellers CCVII - 314 2015 £20

James, Henry 1843-1916 *The Notebooks.* New York: Oxford University Press, 1947. Original blue cloth, spine faded, from the library of Geoffrey & Kathleen Tillotson, inscribed by Geoffrey for Kathleen, Harvard 20.II.45, inserted is tatty folded copy of dust jacket containing cuttings of significant reviews of book and about James. Jarndyce Antiquarian Booksellers CCVII - 324 2015 £20

Johnson, Samuel 1709-1784 *Diaries, Prayers and Annals.* New Haven: Yale University Press, 1958. Half title, plates, original blue cloth, very good in slightly torn dust jacket, from the library of Geoffrey & Kathleen Tillotson, signed by Kathleen for Geoffrey 25 De. 59, with inserted long review in TLS and correspondence between Geoffrey and others about revised edition. Jarndyce Antiquarian Booksellers CCVII - 327 2015 £45

Johnson, Samuel 1709-1784 *Lives of the English Poets.* Oxford: at the Clarendon Press, 1905. 3 volumes, original red cloth, hinges little rubbed, from the library of Geoffrey & Kathleen Tillotson, Kathleen's gift to Geoffrey Christmas 1937 with extensive notes and insertions including correspondence with R. W. Chapman and others. Jarndyce Antiquarian Booksellers CCVII - 332 2015 £75

Johnson, Samuel 1709-1784 *The Fountains...* London: Elkin Mathews & Marot, 1927. Number 433 of 500 copies of the first separate edition, uncut, original boards, slight rubbing at corners, signed by Geoffrey Tillotson with few pencil notes. Jarndyce Antiquarian Booksellers CCVII - 328 2015 £35

Johnson, Samuel 1709-1784 *The Idler and the Adventurer.* New Haven: Yale University Press, 1963. Half title, plates, original blue cloth, very good in slightly torn dust jacket, W. J Bate's signed presentation copy to Geoffrey Tillotson, with review of "The Rambler" inserted. Jarndyce Antiquarian Booksellers CCVII - 330 2015 £45

Johnson, Samuel 1709-1784 *The Letters, with Mrs. Thrale's Genuine Letters to Him.* Oxford: Clarendon Press, 1952. 3 volumes, half title, frontispiece, plate, few pencil notes, original maroon cloth in slightly worn dust jacket, with cuttings of review and obits of R. W. Chapman inserted, from the library of Geoffrey & Kathleen Tillotson. Jarndyce Antiquarian Booksellers CCVII - 335 2015 £45

Johnson, Samuel 1709-1784 *The Poems.* Oxford: Clarendon Press, 1941. Half title, original dark blue cloth, Geoffrey Tillotson's copy with notes in text and on following endpapers, much inserted material including reviews and note from R. W. Chapman. Jarndyce Antiquarian Booksellers CCVII - 334 2015 £60

Jones, Enid *Margery Fry: the Essential Amateur.* London: Oxford University Press, 1966. Half title, frontispiece and plates, mark at end of text, original blue cloth, slightly marked in slightly torn dust jacket, from the library of Geoffrey & Kathleen Tillotson with author's presentation inscription pasted to endpaper and ALS from her to Kathleen, and cuttings of 2 reviews inserted. Jarndyce Antiquarian Booksellers CCVII - 271 2015 £25

Keats, John 1795-1821 *Hyperion: a Facsimile of Keats's autograph manuscript.* Oxford: Clarendon Press, 1905. Folio, 27 pages facsimiles, colophon leaf, original green printed boards, beige buckram spine, corners rubbed, dusted, from the library of Geoffrey & Kathleen Tillotson, signed by Geoffrey 1942 with note by Kathleen. Jarndyce Antiquarian Booksellers CCVII - 345 2015 £85

Keats, John 1795-1821 *The Poetical Works.* Oxford: Clarendon Press, 1958. Second edition, half title, frontispiece, original dark blue cloth, very good in slightly torn and dust dust jacket, with review of Keats' 'Letters" 1959 inserted, from the library of Geoffrey & Kathleen Tillotson. Jarndyce Antiquarian Booksellers CCVII - 344 2015 £35

Kellett, E. E. *Ex Libris: Confessions of a Constant Reader.* London: George Allen & Unwin, 1940. Half title, original dark blue cloth, library withdrawn stamps, Geoffrey Tillotson's signed copy with notes and correspondence from author. Jarndyce Antiquarian Booksellers CCVII - 349 2015 £20

Kendall, May *Dreams to Sell.* London: Longmans, 1887. First edition, half title in red & black, uncut in original crimson cloth, bevelled boards, spine faded, top edge gilt, presentation inscription to Gilbert Redgrave, bibliographer and art historian from Frances and Evelyn Redgrave 12 may, 1889, note by former of short and apologetic AL from authoress dated Aug. 4th 1892 in another hand: Association books No. 67 and 1945 signature of John Gilman, from the library of Geoffrey & Kathleen Tillotson.   Jarndyce Antiquarian Booksellers   CCVII - 350   2015   £50

Kent, Charles *Charles Dickens as a Reader.* London: Chapman & Hall, 1872. First edition, plates, original green cloth, dulled, label removed from leading pastedown, stamps and pressmark of Malvern Public Library, from the library of Geoffrey & Kathleen Tillotson, with note by Kathleen.   Jarndyce Antiquarian Booksellers   CCVII - 216   2015   £50

Ketton-Cremer, Robert Wyndham *Thomas Gray: a Biography.* Cambridge: at the University Press, 1955. Half title, frontispiece, marginal pencil marks, original maroon cloth, slightly torn dust jacket, author's signed presentation copy for Geoffrey and Kathleen Tillotson, with accompanying letter laid down and draft of Geoffrey's letter of thanks, other correspondence, typescript of Geoffrey's review and press cuttings.   Jarndyce Antiquarian Booksellers   CCVII - 289   2015   £40

Kipling, Rudyard 1865-1936 *Verse.* London: Hodder & Stoughton, 1930. Fifth impression, half title creased, title in red and black, india paper, original red cloth, inner hinge splitting, top edge gilt, from the library of Geoffrey & Kathleen Tillotson.   Jarndyce Antiquarian Booksellers   CCVII - 352   2015   £30

Knight, George Wilson *The Burning Oracle.* London: Oxford University Press, 1939. Half title, uncut in original maroon cloth, slightly marked, from the library of Geoffrey & Kathleen Tillotson, Kathleen's review copy with ms. and penned review, with ALS from author to Geoffrey 1944 and long TLS article about him as critic.   Jarndyce Antiquarian Booksellers   CCVII - 353   2015   £30

Lang, Andrew *Ballads of Books.* London: Longmans, 1885. First edition, half title, title in red and black, uncut in original blue bevelled boards, spine slightly faded, cutting removed from endpaper, ticket of Slatter & Rose, Oxford, top edge gilt, signed by S. C. Rawlinson 1889 and with 3 related ms. insertions, from the library of Geoffrey & Kathleen Tillotson.   Jarndyce Antiquarian Booksellers   CCVII - 355   2015   £85

Leishman, James Blair *Milton's Minor Poems.* London: Hutchinson, 1969. First edition, half title, original dark green cloth, very good in torn dust jacket, from the library of Geoffrey & Kathleen Tillotson.   Jarndyce Antiquarian Booksellers   CCVII - 377   2015   £38

Leishman, James Blair *The Art of Marvell's Poetry.* Hutchinson University Library, 1968. Second edition, with proof copy of first edition, 1965, few ms. corrections and insertions, dust jacket, from the library of Geoffrey & Kathleen Tillotson.   Jarndyce Antiquarian Booksellers   CCVII - 357   2015   £38

Leishman, James Blair *The Three Paranssus Plays 1598-1601.* London: Ivor Nicholson & Watson, 1949. Half title, original black cloth, very good in torn dust jacket, editor's presentation to Geoffrey and Kathleen Tillotson. Jarndyce Antiquarian Booksellers   CCVII - 358   2015   £30

Leishman, James Blair *Themes and Variations in Shakespeare's Sonnets.* London: Hutchinson, 1961. Half title, original pale maroon cloth slightly knocked, slightly marked dust jacket, this copy with creased Order of Service in Fleishman's memory at St. John's College, Cambridge in 1963 and offprint of his article on Wotton's 'you meaner beauties of the night', inscribed by Geoffrey Tillotson. Jarndyce Antiquarian Booksellers   CCVII - 464   2015   £20

Levin, Harry *Prospectives of Criticism.* Cambridge: Harvard University Press, 1950. Initial catalog, half title, frontispiece, original orange brown cloth, torn dust jacket, Geoffrey Tillotson's signed copy, with few notes by him, including TLS from editor.   Jarndyce Antiquarian Booksellers   CCVII - 359   2015   £20

Lewis, Clive Staples 1898-1963 *The Allegory of Love: a Study in Medieval Tradition.* Oxford: Clarendon Press, 1936. from the library of Geoffrey & Kathleen Tillotson. original dark blue cloth, slightly marked, signed with initials and few pencil notes and marked proof of Kathleen's review. Jarndyce Antiquarian Booksellers   CCVII - 362   2015   £25

Linton, Eliza Lynn *My Literary Life...* London: Hodder & Stoughton, 1899. Title in red and black, uncut in original yellow cloth, rather dulled, from the library of Geoffrey & Kathleen Tillotson.   Jarndyce Antiquarian Booksellers CCVII - 363   2015   £20

Lowery, Margaret Ruth *Windows of the Morning: a Critical Study of William Blake's Poetical Sketches 1783.* New Haven: Yale University Press, 1940. Half title plate, 3 pages ads, signed by Geoffrey Tillotson Oct. 1940 with few notes and inserted cuttings, original card wrappers in typical pasted covering made from printed map with blotched red and green coloring in 18th century style, ms. label. Jarndyce Antiquarian Booksellers   CCVII - 88   2015   £30

MacDonald, George   1824-1905 *Phantastes; a Faerie Romance for Men and Women.* London: Smith, Elder & Co., 1858. First edition, bound without half title, small corner torn form title, few marginal marks, contemporary half calf, rubbed, split in following hinge but sound, bookplate of Augustus Taylor Day, from the library of Geoffrey & Kathleen Tillotson.   Jarndyce Antiquarian Booksellers   CCVII - 368   2015   £520

Mallock, William Hurrell *Lucretius on Life and Death in the Metre of Omar Khayyam...* London: Adam & Charles Black, 1901. Original olive green cloth, embossed head, stab holes in endpapers, slightly marked and rubbed, from the library of Geoffrey & Kathleen Tillotson, undated presentation ANS from author and 2 page ALS from him to Williamson.   Jarndyce Antiquarian Booksellers   CCVII - 372   2015   £20

Marryat, Frederick   1792-1848 *Poor Jack.* London: Longmans, 1840. First edition, frontispiece, plates, illustrations by Clarkson Stanfield, some plates foxed, small portrait of author laid down on leading pastedown, uncut in original dark green cloth blocked in blind and gilt, at some time neatly recased, good, sound copy, from the library of Geoffrey & Kathleen Tillotson.   Jarndyce Antiquarian Booksellers   CCVII - 373   2015   £75

McKillop, Alan Dugald *Restoration and Eighteenth Century Literature...* Chicago: University of Chicago Press for William Marsh Rice University, 1963. Half title, original blue and grey cloth, very good in dust jacket, from the library of Geoffrey & Kathleen Tillotson.   Jarndyce Antiquarian Booksellers   CCVII - 370   2015   £20

Miller, J. Hillis *The Disappearance of God...* Cambridge: Belknap Press of Harvard University Press, 1963. Half title, original brown cloth, very good in marked dust jacket, Geoffrey Tillotson's copy with his notes and drafts for his review for TLS and cutting of printed reviews.   Jarndyce Antiquarian Booksellers   CCVII - 375   2015   £20

Milton, John   1608-1674 *The Poetical Works. Volume I. Paradise Lost.* Oxford: Clarendon Press, 1952. Uncut in original dark blue cloth, very good in slightly creased dust jacket, with printed editor's presentation slip and ALS from editor, Helen Darbishire to Kathleen Tillotson, with review cutting, from the library of Geoffrey & Kathleen Tillotson, signed by both Nov. 8 1952.   Jarndyce Antiquarian Booksellers   CCVII - 376   2015   £20

Monk, Samuel Holt *Studies in Criticism and Aesthetics 1660-1800.* Minneapolis: University of Minnesota Press, 1967. Original green cloth, half title, illustrations, very good in creased dust jacket, signed by Geoffrey Tillotson 22.iii.67 with correspondence with editors about his contribution and with TLS from Samuel Monk thanking him for essay in book. Jarndyce Antiquarian Booksellers   CCVII - 380   2015   £30

Newman, John Henry   1801-1890 *An Essay on the Development of Christian Doctrine.* London: James Tovey, 1845. First edition, later half calf, slightly rubbed and chipped, light brown label, Geoffrey Tillotson's copy 20x43, with notes on leading pastedown and few in text.   Jarndyce Antiquarian Booksellers   CCVII - 388   2015   £110

Newman, John Henry   1801-1890 *Apologia Pro Vita Sua: The Two Versions of 1864 and 1865 Preceded by Newman's and Kingsley's Pamphlets...* London: Oxford University Press, 1931. Second impression, original blue cloth, crease on spine, Geoffrey Tillotson's copy 1 Jan. 1943 with notes, some inserts and marginal marks.   Jarndyce Antiquarian Booksellers   CCVII - 384   2015   £20

Newman, John Henry   1801-1890 *Certain Difficulties Felt by Anglicans in Catholic Teaching Considered...* London: Longmans Green, 1891. 2 volumes, half titles, initial request slip, 2 pages ads volume 2, original maroon cloth, spines slightly chipped at head and tail, annotated by Henry Tristram of Birmingham Oratory, presented to Geoffrey Tillotson, with his annotations.   Jarndyce Antiquarian Booksellers   CCVII - 385   2015   £25

Newman, John Henry   1801-1890 *Correspondence of John Henry Newman with John Keble and others 1839-1845.* London: Longmans, 1917. Half title, odd spot in prelims, original brown cloth, signed by Geoffrey Tillotson 16.xii47, with few notes.   Jarndyce Antiquarian Booksellers   CCVII - 386   2015   £25

Newman, John Henry   1801-1890 *Discussions and Arguments on Various Subjections.* London: Basil Montagu Pickering, 1872. Half title, final ad leaf, initial 8 page catalog, original dark blue cloth, spine faded and worn, hinges repaired, signature of Geoffrey Tillotson with notes. Jarndyce Antiquarian Booksellers   CCVII - 387   2015   £20

Newman, John Henry 1801-1890 *Hymni Ecclesiae, Excerpti e Breviariis Romano, Salisburiensi, eboracensi...* Oxonii: J. H. Parker, 1838. 4 pages ads, original grey cloth, paper label, spine defective, scarce, inscribed Francis Palgrave from his affectionate NJ and EJJ Jan. 10 1839, from the library of Geoffrey & Kathleen Tillotson.   Jarndyce Antiquarian Booksellers   CCVII - 396   2015   £180

Newman, John Henry 1801-1890 *John Henry Newman: Centenary Essays.* London: Burns, Oates & Washbourne, 1945. Half title, original green cloth, very good in torn dust jacket, Geoffrey Tillotson's copy, signed with extensive alterations in text of his essay.   Jarndyce Antiquarian Booksellers   CCVII - 397   2015   £22

Newman, John Henry 1801-1890 *Loss and Gain.* London: James Burns, 1848. First edition, original black cloth, slightly dulled and rubbed at corners, endpapers replaced, F. T. Palgrave's copy Mar 21:1848, with postcard photo of author inserted bearing birthday greetings to Geoffrey Tillotson.   Jarndyce Antiquarian Booksellers CCVII - 390   2015   £180

Newman, John Henry 1801-1890 *Prose and Poetry.* London: Rupert Hart Davis, 1957. Proof copy, half title, uncut in home-made rough paper wrappers, torn dust jacket, Geoffrey Tillotson's last proof 18 Jul 1956 with few notes in text, but with galley proof and few notes inserted. Jarndyce Antiquarian Booksellers   CCVII - 393   2015 £30

Newman, John Henry 1801-1890 *Prose and Poetry.* London: Rupert Hart Davis, 1957. Half title, few pencil notes, original dark blue cloth, bevelled boards, very good in torn dust jacket, from the library of Geoffrey & Kathleen Tillotson, with his inscription to her 25.xii.56 with few inserted notes.   Jarndyce Antiquarian Booksellers   CCVII - 392 2015   £35

Newman, John Henry 1801-1890 *The Idea of a University Defined and Illustrated.* London: Longmans, Green, 1947. New edition, half title, title in red and black, original dark blue cloth in slightly torn dust jacket, signed by Geoffrey Tillotson Feb. 57.   Jarndyce Antiquarian Booksellers   CCVII - 389   2015   £20

Newman, John Henry 1801-1890 *Verses on Religious Subjects.* Dublin: James Duffy, 1853. First edition, contemporary calf, gilt borders and dentelles, spine chipped, boards detached, scarce, John Duke Coleridge's copy signed on original preserved endpaper, from the library of Geoffrey & Kathleen Tillotson.   Jarndyce Antiquarian Booksellers   CCVII - 394   2015   £220

Newman, John Henry 1801-1890 *Verses on Various Occasions.* London: Burns, Oates, 1880. Half title, erratum slip, final ad leaf, Geoffrey Tillotson's copy with signature 1942 indicating Hugh Walker's signature on preserved endpaper with numerous ink and pencil notes in text and inserted, Tillotson's decorated paper casing with ms. label. Jarndyce Antiquarian Booksellers   CCVII - 395   2015 £45

Nicholson, William 1872-1949 *An Almanac of Twelve Sports.* London: William Heinemann, 1898. 4to., illustrations, 1 page ad verso final leaf, original illustrated paper boards, cloth spine repaired, some rubbing to edges and corners, inner hinges strengthened, from the library of Geoffrey & Kathleen Tillotson, with Kathleen's note recording joint purchase.   Jarndyce Antiquarian Booksellers CCVII - 400   2015   £420

Nowell-Smith, Simon *Letters to Macmillan.* London: Macmillan, 1967. Half title, plates, facsimiles, original red cloth, very good in slightly marked dust jacket, editor's signed copy, from the library of Geoffrey & Kathleen Tillotson, presentation inscription to same with note by Kathleen inserted.   Jarndyce Antiquarian Booksellers CCVII - 401   2015   £20

Noyes, Alfred *Collected Poems.* Edinburgh and London: William Blackwood and Sons, 1919. Half title, uncut in original green buckram, spine faded, titlepage, signed by Geoffrey Tillotson 29/12/20 "Bought by Uncle Fred Sutcliffe in Bradford Market on Christmas eve 1920", with text of 'A Tale of Old Japan' written neatly in ink by Geoffrey throughout prelims, with few notes in text, 3 cuttings inserted. Jarndyce Antiquarian Booksellers   CCVII - 402   2015 £20

Ortega Y Gasset, Jose *The Dehumanization of Art and Notes on the Novel.* Princeton: Princeton Univ. Press, 1948. Half title, original brown cloth, very good in darkened dust jacket, from the library of Geoffrey & Kathleen Tillotson, his gift to her Xmas 1949, few pencil notes.   Jarndyce Antiquarian Booksellers   CCVII - 403   2015   £20

Osborn, James M. *John Dryden: Some Biographical facts and Problems.* New York: Columbia University Press, 1940. Frontispiece, original brown cloth, very good in dusted dust jacket, signed by Geoffrey Tillotson Sept. 1941 with few marginal marks, notes on endpapers and proof and printed copy of this review and other items including typescript of a paper by Edwin Rhodes.   Jarndyce Antiquarian Booksellers   CCVII - 249   2015   £30

Pafford, H. H. P. *W. P. Ker 1855-1923: a Bibliography.* London: University of London Press, 1950. Half title, frontispiece and plates, original brown cloth in slightly torn and browned dust jacket, signed by Geoffrey Tillotson 1953 with ms. anecdote of Ker.   Jarndyce Antiquarian Booksellers   CCVII - 351   2015   £25

Palgrave, Francis Turner   1824-1897   *The Five Days Entertainments at Wentworth Garage.*   London: Macmillan & Co., 1868. First edition, half title, plates and illustrations by Arthur Hughes, 2 pages ad, original blue cloth, inner hinges splitting, rubbed and dulled, top edge gilt, with slightly damaged half title and partly obscured presentation to Gwenllian Florence Palgrave 1866-1951, one of the dedicatees from her father 1873, overwritten in pencil with her childish signature, from the library of Geoffrey & Kathleen Tillotson.   Jarndyce Antiquarian Booksellers   CCVII - 404   2015   £60

Palgrave, Francis Turner   1824-1897   *The Visions of England. Second Part.*   London: printed for F. T. Palgrave by Cousins & Co., 1881. First edition, one of 50 copies dated April 1881, marked by Palgrave 'To be returned' with faint address on wrapper and signed by him in pencil on top edge gilt 22 Ap 1881, from the library of Geoffrey & Kathleen Tillotson.   Jarndyce Antiquarian Booksellers   CCVII - 406   2015   £58

Parrish, Stephen Maxwell   *A Concordance to the Poems of Matthew Arnold.*   Ithaca: Cornell University Press, 1959. Original red cloth, half title, presentation to Geoffrey Tillotson with copies of his letters of thanks.   Jarndyce Antiquarian Booksellers   CCVII - 69   2015   £40

A Poetry Book for National Schools.   London: Bell & Daldy, 1857. New edition, frontispiece and numerous engravings, some marginal tears, original brown cloth, rebacked with back cloth, inner hinges strengthened, from the library of Geoffrey & Kathleen Tillotson.   Jarndyce Antiquarian Booksellers   CCVII - 9   2015   £300

A Proper Sonnet from a Gorgeous Gallery of Gallant Inventions.   printed in the Dept. of English at the University College, London, 1935. Small 4to., original orange brown printed wrappers, (2), 4, (2) pages, from the library of Geoffrey & Kathleen Tillotson.   Jarndyce Antiquarian Booksellers   CCVII - 8   2015   £45

Pope, Alexander   1688-1744   *Imitations of Horace with an Epistle to Dr. Arburthnot and The Epilogue to the Satires.*   London: Methuen, 1939. Uncorrected page proofs, half title, from the library of Geoffrey & Kathleen Tillotson, with Geoffrey's pencil marks in introduction only, with Geoffrey's card and decorated paper wrappers with ms. label on spine, staples slightly rusting.   Jarndyce Antiquarian Booksellers   CCVII - 410   2015   £20

Pope, Alexander   1688-1744   *Poetical Works.*   London: Oxford University Press, 1966. half title, frontispiece, original dark blue cloth, very good in dust jacket, review copy sent to Geoffrey Tillotson with cuttings of anonymous review.   Jarndyce Antiquarian Booksellers   CCVII - 414   2015   £20

Pope, Alexander   1688-1744   *Pope's Own Miscellany being a reprint of Poems on Several Occasions 1717...*   London: Nonesuch Press, 1935. One of 750 copies this out of series, Half title, uncut, original green cloth, very good in plain titled dust jacket, Geoffrey Tillotson's copy with 2 copies of his review inserted, with his notes on endpapers, marked by rusting clip.   Jarndyce Antiquarian Booksellers   CCVII - 413   2015   £40

Pope, Alexander   1688-1744   *The Correspondence.*   Oxford: Clarendon Press, 1956. 5 volumes, half titles, frontispieces, original maroon cloth, very slightly torn dust jackets, good set, from the library of Geoffrey & Kathleen Tillotson, with TLS review copies with few pencil notes by Geoffrey, with insertions including letters from editor and offprints.   Jarndyce Antiquarian Booksellers   CCVII - 424   2015   £225

Pope, Alexander   1688-1744   *The Poems.*   London: Methuen & Co., 1963. One volume edition, Half title, original blue cloth, very good in slightly torn and dusted dust jacket, Geoffrey Tillotson's signed copy.   Jarndyce Antiquarian Booksellers   CCVII - 412   2015   £25

Pope, Alexander   1688-1744   *The Rape of the Lock and Other Poems.*   London: Methuen and New Haven: Yale University Press, 1954. Twickenham edition, volume II, half title, frontispiece, original brick red cloth in slightly torn dust jacket, edited by Geoffrey Tillotson with insertions and few notes in text, and long note on leading f.e.p describing the method of production which by his standards did not amount to a revision, note on dust jacket describes it as 'working copy'.   Jarndyce Antiquarian Booksellers   CCVII - 419   2015   £50

Pope, Alexander   1688-1744   *The Rape of the Lock.*   London: John Lane, 1902. Small 4to., half title, frontispiece, plates, illustrations, 4 pages ads, original olive green cloth, spine dulled and rubbed, top edge gilt, Geoffrey Tillotson's signed copy.   Jarndyce Antiquarian Booksellers   CCVII - 415   2015   £15

Pope, Alexander 1688-1744 *The Rape of the Lock.* London: Methuen and New Haven: Yale University Press, 1962. Third Tillotson edition, Twickenham edition volume II, half title frontispiece, plates, original brick red cloth, following inner hinge cracking, slightly dusted, torn dust jacket, from the library of Geoffrey & Kathleen Tillotson, Geoffrey Tillotson's copy signed, with few pencil marks and note by Kathleen on dust jacket stating it was 'Work copy'. Jarndyce Antiquarian Booksellers   CCVII - 421   2015   £40

Ray, Gordon N.   *Books as a Way of Life: Essays...*   New York: Grolier Club, Pierpont Morgan Library, 1988. Frontispiece, original red cloth, from the library of Geoffrey & Kathleen Tillotson, very good in slightly marked dust jacket, with inserted ALS from editor thanking Kathleen for her generous appreciations.   Jarndyce Antiquarian Booksellers   CCVII - 443   2015   £20

Ray, Gordon N.   *Nineteenth Century English Books...*   Urbana: University of Illinois Press, 1952. Half title, title in red and black, original red and grey cloth, from the library of Geoffrey & Kathleen Tillotson, Geoffrey Tillotson's copy for Review of English Studies with pencil notes and copy of his review inserted, and other reviews, TLS from Gordon Ray to Tillotson's Jan. 1953 inserted.   Jarndyce Antiquarian Booksellers   CCVII - 445   2015   £25

Ray, Gordon N.   *Thackeray: the Age of Wisdom 1847-1863.*   New York: McGraw Hill, 1958. Half title, plates, original maroon cloth, very good in torn dust jacket, from the library of Geoffrey & Kathleen Tillotson, author's presentation for them.   Jarndyce Antiquarian Booksellers   CCVII - 501   2015   £20

Richards, Ivor Armstrong   *Practical Criticism: a Study of Literary Judgment.*   London: Kegan Paul, 1929. Half title, folding tables, original red cloth, faded and marked, Geoffrey Tillotson's copy, inserted are 3 postcards to him, Christmas card insertion and note and typed and ms. letter from Richards and his wife Dorothy.   Jarndyce Antiquarian Booksellers   CCVII - 447   2015   £28

Rogers, Robert W.   *The Major Satires of Alexander Pope.*   Urbana: University of Illinois Press, 1955. Half title, original brown printed paper wrappers, marked, spine creased, Geoffrey Tillotson's signed review copy with notes, with copy of his anonymous TLS.   Jarndyce Antiquarian Booksellers CCVII - 426   2015   £30

Ross, Ronald   *In Exile.*   Liverpool: privately printed, 1906. First edition, pencil and occasional ink notes and corrections, original maroon printed paper wrappers, slightly creased with slight loss to upper corner front wrapper, presentation inscription "With Sir Ronald Ross's compliments. Author's working copy see page 6, 22, see especially page 81", from the collection of Kathleen and Geoffrey Tillotson. Jarndyce Antiquarian Booksellers   CCXI - 245   2015   £250

Scriblerus Club   *Memoirs of the Extraordinary Life, Works and Discoveries of Martinus Scriblerus...*   New Haven: for Wellesley College by Yale Univ. Press, 1950. Half title, illustrations, original dark blue cloth, very good in torn dust jacket, Geoffrey Tillotson's signed copy.   Jarndyce Antiquarian Booksellers   CCVII - 454   2015   £20

Shearer, Thomas   *Percy's Relations with Cadell and Davies..*   London: Bibliographical Society, 1934. Reprinted from Transactions of the Bibliographical Society Sept. 1934, Original grey printed wrappers, slightly dusted, from the library of Geoffrey & Kathleen Tillotson.   Jarndyce Antiquarian Booksellers   CCVII - 408   2015   £30

Sherburn, George   *Pope and His Contemporaries: Essays Presented to George Sherburn.*   Oxford: at the Clarendon Press, 1949. Half title, portrait, printed presentation slip, original dark blue cloth in slightly torn and dusted dust jacket, from the library of Geoffrey & Kathleen Tillotson. Jarndyce Antiquarian Booksellers   CCVII - 429   2015   £40

Sherburn, George   *The Early Career of Alexander Pope.*   Oxford: at the Clarendon Press, 1934. Half title, frontispiece, original dark blue cloth, slightly dulled, Geoffrey Tillotson's copy with few pencil notes and inserted letter from author thanking him for favorable review and inserted note thanking him for loan.   Jarndyce Antiquarian Booksellers   CCVII - 428   2015   £25

Shuster, George N.   *The English Ode from Milton to Keats.*   New York: Columbia Univ. Press, 1940. Half title, original blue cloth, very good in slightly torn dust jacket, from the library of Geoffrey & Kathleen Tillotson with inserted notes by Geoffrey.   Jarndyce Antiquarian Booksellers CCVII - 468   2015   £20

Sigdwick, Arthur   *Henry Sidgwick a memoir.*   London: Macmillan & Co., 1906. Half title, frontispiece, plates, final ad leaf, original brown cloth, small split at head of spine, Geoffrey Tillotson's copy Harvard 31.1.48 with pencil notes on leading endpapers and textual marks.   Jarndyce Antiquarian Booksellers   CCVII - 469   2015   £35

Skutsch, Otto *Alfred Edward Housman 1859-1936.* London: University of London Athlone Press, 1960. Half title, original blue printed wrappers, presentation copy to Geoffrey Tillotson from librarian Joseph Scott, with TLS mentioning omissions from the lecture. Jarndyce Antiquarian Booksellers CCVII - 317 2015 £30

Smart, Christopher 1722-1771 *Jubilate Agno.* Cambridge: Harvard University Press, 1954. Half title, original green cloth, very good, repaired dust jacket, inscribed by George Sherburn Sept. 1954 for Geoffrey Tilltoson, with inserted postcard. Jarndyce Antiquarian Booksellers CCVII - 472 2015 £25

Smart, Christopher 1722-1771 *Poems.* Princeton: Princeton Univ.. Press, 1950. Half title, frontispiece, plates, original green cloth, very good in slightly dusted dust jacket, Geoffrey's Tillotson's signed review copy with few notes. Jarndyce Antiquarian Booksellers CCVII - 473 2015 £35

Smart, Christopher 1722-1771 *The Collected Poems.* London: Routledge & Kegan Paul, 1949. 2 volumes, half titles, frontispiece volume I, original dark blue cloth, very good in slightly dusted dust jacket, signed by Geoffrey Tillotson with few notes and 2 inserted letters from publisher. Jarndyce Antiquarian Booksellers CCVII - 471 2015 £20

Smith, David Nichol *Some Observations on Eighteenth Century Poetry.* London: Oxford University Press, printed in Canada by the University of Toronto Press, 1937. Half title, original light brown cloth, slightly dusted in dusted dust jacket, Geoffrey Tillotson's signed copy with initial note, inserted publisher's slip and 2 copies of short review him him. Jarndyce Antiquarian Booksellers CCVII - 474 2015 £20

Spurgeon, Caroline *Shakespeare's Imagery and What It Tells Us.* Cambridge: University Press, 1935. Half title, frontispiece, color folding table, original brown cloth, from the library of Geoffrey & Kathleen Tillotson, with press cutting of review. Jarndyce Antiquarian Booksellers CCVII - 466 2015 £35

Stephen, Leslie *The "Times" on the American War: a Historical Study.* London: William Ridgway, 1865. Disbound and loose in slightly dusted and torn cream paper wrappers, with letter of presentation from Norma Hodgson to Geoffrey Tillotson. Jarndyce Antiquarian Booksellers CCVII - 477 2015 £65

Sutherland, James *Defoe.* London: Methuen, 1937. Half title, plates, original maroon buckram, very good in slightly torn dust jacket, signed by Geoffrey Tillotson 1937, with inserted ink and pencil notes and his printed review. Jarndyce Antiquarian Booksellers CCVII - 167 2015 £20

Swift, Jonathan 1667-1745 *A Tale of a Tub to which is added the Battle of the Books and The Mechanical Operation of the Spirit.* Oxford: at the Clarendon Press, 1920. Half title, facsimiles, original dark blue cloth, worn, following inner hinge strengthened, Geoffrey Tillotson's signed copy with marginalia and inserted notes, notes on endpapers. Jarndyce Antiquarian Booksellers CCVII - 485 2015 £35

Swift, Jonathan 1667-1745 *Irish Tracts 1702-1723 and Sermons...* Oxford: Basil Blackwell, 1948. Half title, frontispiece, facsimiles, original green cloth, very good in slightly torn dust jacket, Geoffrey Tillotson's copy signed with few notes. Jarndyce Antiquarian Booksellers CCVII - 483 2015 £30

Swift, Jonathan 1667-1745 *The Poems of.* Oxford: at the Clarendon Press, 1937. 3 volumes, half titles, frontispieces, original blue cloth slightly torn and dusted dust jackets, Kathleen Tillotson's presentation copies for Geoffrey Tillotson, with few notes and insertions. Jarndyce Antiquarian Booksellers CCVII - 484 2015 £120

Tennyson, Alfred Tennyson, 1st Baron 1809-1892 *In Memoriam.* London: Edward Moxon, 1850. First edition, half title, without initial catalog, brown morocco presentation binding by Budden, Cambridge, little rubbed with small split in leading hinge, all edges gilt, lettered on front board, inscribed to Julain Fane from HAJ, with very poor copy of the 10th edition 1861 in original cloth, heavily annotated with insertions by Geoffrey Tillotson, from the library of Geoffrey & Kathleen Tillotson. Jarndyce Antiquarian Booksellers CCVII - 486 2015 £350

Tennyson, Alfred Tennyson, 1st Baron 1809-1892 *Lyrical Poems.* London: Maximillan, 1885. First edition, half title, 6 pages ads, pages 119-20 torn through without loss, uncut in remains of original blue boards, lacking spine strip, last gathering detached, possibly a proof copy, selected and annotated by Francis T. Palgrave, his copy, signed Mch 9 1885, but with no internal marks, from the library of Geoffrey & Kathleen Tillotson, inscribed by them. Jarndyce Antiquarian Booksellers CCVII - 487 2015 £45

Tennyson, Alfred Tennyson, 1st Baron 1809-1892 *Poems, Chiefly Lyrical.* London: Effingham Wilson, 1830. Uncut, recased in stiff paper with paper label, signature of Whitley Stokes 14/6/55, from the library of Geoffrey & Kathleen Tillotson. Jarndyce Antiquarian Booksellers CCVII - 488 2015 £450

Tennyson, Hallan Tennyson *Materials for a Life of A. T. Collected for My Children.* N.P.: privately printed, 1895? 4 volumes, original blue card wrappers, slight rubbing, from the library of Geoffrey & Kathleen Tillotson, volume I signed by Geoffrey 30 xi 42 with few marginal marks and few pencil notes in each volume, volume I in Geoffrey's paper covers with his notes. Jarndyce Antiquarian Booksellers CCVII - 493   2015   £750

Thackeray, William Makepeace 1811-1863 *The Letters and Private Papers of William Makepeace Thackeray.* London: Oxford University Press, 1945-1946. First edition, 4 volumes, half titles, plates, illustrations, original pink cloth, spines slightly faded, from the library of Geoffrey & Kathleen Tillotson, signed, some notes and markings by both. Jarndyce Antiquarian Booksellers   CCVII - 499   2015   £75

Tillyard, E. M. W. *The Personal Heresy: a Controversy.* London: Oxford University Press, 1939. Half title, from the library of Geoffrey & Kathleen Tillotson, very good in slightly torn dust jacket, Geoffrey Tillotson's signed copy with few notes, and proof of his review, Kathleen' special marker. Jarndyce Antiquarian Booksellers   CCVII - 538   2015   £30

Tucker, Susie I. *Portean Shape: a Study in Eighteenth Century Vocabulary and Usage.* London: University Of London, Athlone Press, 1967. Half title, original olive green cloth, very good, Geoffrey Tillotson's copy with ALs from author.   Jarndyce Antiquarian Booksellers   CCVII - 544   2015   £20

Tuve, Rosamond *Elizabethan and Metaphysical Imagery.* Chicago: University of Chicago Press, 1947. Half title, from the library of Geoffrey & Kathleen Tillotson, original red cloth, inscribed by author of Kathleen Tillotson, signed by Kathleen and Geoffrey, inserted review by Maynard Mack and review by Cleanth Brooks.   Jarndyce Antiquarian Booksellers   CCVII - 546   2015   £25

Tuve, Rosamond *Images and Themes in Five Poems by Milton.* Cambridge: Harvard University Press, 1957. Half title, original green cloth, very good in slightly torn dust jacket, author's signed presentation for Geoffrey and Kathleen Tillotson, with 4 TLS from author.   Jarndyce Antiquarian Booksellers   CCVII - 379   2015   £25

Waddington, Samuel *Arthur Hugh Clough: a Monograph.* London: George Bell & Sons, 1883. Half title, final ad leaf, original blue cloth, signed by Robert Menzies 1883 and Geoffrey Tillotson.   Jarndyce Antiquarian Booksellers CCVII - 145   2015   £50

Wahba, Magdi *Bicentenary Essays on Rasselas.* Cairo: S. O. P. Press, 1959. Plates, original cream printed wrappers marked, signed by Geoffrey Tillotson July 59, with TLS & cards from editor.   Jarndyce Antiquarian Booksellers CCVII - 342   2015   £20

Warmington, Eric Herbert *A History of Birkbeck College, University of London During the Second World War 1939-1945.* 1955. Half title, frontispiece and plates, folding plan, original dark green cloth, presentation by author for Geoffrey Tilltoson.   Jarndyce Antiquarian Booksellers   CCVII - 548 2015   £20

Warren, Alba H. *English Poetic Theory 1825-1865.* Princeton: Princeton University Press, 1950. Half title, original brown cloth, corner knocked, otherwise very good in dust jacket, Geoffrey Tillotson's signed copy with few notes and cutting of TLS review.   Jarndyce Antiquarian Booksellers   CCVII - 549   2015   £20

Wesley, Samuel *Letters to ... Mr. Jacobs Relating to the Introduction into this Country of the Works of John Sebastian Bach.* London: S. W. Partridge & Co., 1875. Blue boards, vellum spine, ink title, armorial bookplate of Charles Buller Heberden, very good, Geoffrey Tillotson's inscription 17.5.1926.   Jarndyce Antiquarian Booksellers CCVII - 554   2015   £20

Williams, Aubrey L. *Pope's Dunciad: a Study of Its Meaning.* London: Methuen, 1955. Half title, map, original brick red cloth, boards, slightly bowed, slightly rubbed, dust jacket marked 'Keep', Geoffrey Tillotson's signed copy. Jarndyce Antiquarian Booksellers   CCVII - 439   2015   £20

Wilson, Frank Percy *Elizabethan and Jacobean Studies Presented to Frank Percy Wilson in Honour of His Seventieth Birthday.* Oxford: Clarendon Press, 1959. Half title, frontispiece, plates, original dark blue cloth, very good in creased and slightly marked dust jacket, from the library of Geoffrey & Kathleen Tillotson.   Jarndyce Antiquarian Booksellers   CCVII - 555   2015   £35

Wimsatt, William Kurtz *Hateful Contraries: Studies in Literature and Criticism.* Lexington: University of Kentucky Press, Half title, original dark brown cloth, very good in slightly rubbed dust jacket, from the library of Geoffrey & Kathleen Tillotson, with Geoffrey's letter of thanks ofr the book.   Jarndyce Antiquarian Booksellers   CCVII - 556 2015   £20

Wimsatt, William Kurtz *The Portraits of Alexander Pope.* New Haven: Yale University Press, 1965. 4to., half title, frontispiece, original brown buckram, very good in slightly torn dust jacket, author's presentation copy for Geoffrey Tillotson, with 2 TLS's from him, Geoffrey's typewritten review and cutting from TLS, related material, ALS from R. Kenton Cremer, photos of Pope's annotations to an edition of "The Pastorals" in worn folder. Jarndyce Antiquarian Booksellers CCVII - 440 2015 £60

Wimsatt, William Kurtz *The Verbal Icon: Studies in the meaning of Poetry...* Lexington: University of Kentucky Press, 1954. Original green cloth, slightly faded in torn dust jacket, half title, Geoffrey Tillotson's copy signed 19.ii 53, with copy of his letter of thanks for the book. Jarndyce Antiquarian Booksellers CCVII - 557 2015 £20

Wodehouse, Pelham Grenville 1881-1975 *Performing Flea: a Self-Portrait in Letters.* London: Herbert Jenkins, 1954. Reprint, from the library of Geoffrey & Kathleen Tillotson, half title, frontispiece, original blue cloth, slightly torn dust jacket, few margin markers and number of press cuttings inserted by Kathleen, press cuttings. Jarndyce Antiquarian Booksellers CCVII - 558 2015 £20

Wordsworth, William 1770-1850 *Lyrical Ballads 1798.* London: Oxford University Press, 1927. Original olive green cloth, signed KMC with ink and pencil notes, from the library of Geoffrey & Kathleen Tillotson. Jarndyce Antiquarian Booksellers CCVII - 150 2015 £20

Wordsworth, William 1770-1850 *Lyrical Ballads 1798-1805.* London: Methuen, 1944. Tenth edition, from the library of Geoffrey & Kathleen Tillotson, color paper wrappers by Geoffrey, with some notes and various inserts. Jarndyce Antiquarian Booksellers CCVII - 573 2015 £50

Wordsworth, William 1770-1850 *Lyrical Ballads.* London: Methuen, 1963. Half title, original green cloth, very good in dust jacket, Geoffrey Tillotson's copy with 2 TLS's from Raymond Brett, Geoffrey adds pencil notes to presentation letter. Jarndyce Antiquarian Booksellers CCVII - 151 2015 £20

Wordsworth, William 1770-1850 *Poems in Two volumes 1807.* Oxford: Clarendon Press, 1942. Original green printed cloth, 2 volumes, spine faded, inner hinges splitting, from the library of Geoffrey & Kathleen Tillotson, signed by them Oxford 26.iv.44 with copious notes and insertions. Jarndyce Antiquarian Booksellers CCVII - 563 2015 £30

Wordsworth, William 1770-1850 *The Poetical Works.* Oxford: Clarendon Press, 1940-1949. Volumes I, III-V, half titles, original dark blue cloth, volume 1 slightly worn, signed by Geoffrey Tillotson with few pencil notes, text and cuttings of reviews and various insertions. Jarndyce Antiquarian Booksellers CCVII - 566 2015 £60

Wordsworth, William 1770-1850 *The Prelude.* Darbishire: Clarendon Press, 1959. Second edition, half title, frontispiece, plates, original dark blue cloth, very good in slightly worn dust jacket, from the library of Geoffrey & Kathleen Tillotson, with few marginal and inserted notes. Jarndyce Antiquarian Booksellers CCVII - 569 2015 £30

Wordsworth, William 1770-1850 *The Prelude; or Growth of a Poet's Mind.* London: Edward Moxon, 1850. First edition, half title, notes page slightly chipped at tail, bust ticket marker causing browning, Geoffrey Tillotson's copy, disbound in Tillotson's characteristic thick paper wrappers, original leather label placed upside down on spine,. Jarndyce Antiquarian Booksellers CCVII - 567 2015 £40

Yeats, William Butler 1865-1939 *Essays.* London: Macmillan, 1924. First edition, from the library of Geoffrey & Kathleen Tillotson, half title, original cloth covered by Geoffrey in handmade paper, spine browned, inner hinges cracking, signed by Geoffrey 3x34 with few pencil notes at end. Jarndyce Antiquarian Booksellers CCVII - 580 2015 £20

Young, George Malcom *Victorian England; Portrait of an Age.* London: OUP, 1937. Plates, facsimiles, original dark green cloth, from the library of Geoffrey & Kathleen Tillotson, inscribed Christmas present from Geoffrey to Kathleen. Jarndyce Antiquarian Booksellers CCVII - 587 2015 £20

Association – Tillotson, John

Defoe, Daniel *The Life and Adventures of Robinson Crusoe.* London & Edinburgh: William & Robert Chambers, circa, 1880? Frontispiece, original green cloth, hinges little rubbed, prize label from All Saints' Schools, Bradford to John H. Tillotson, Christmas 1882 and note from Arthur Tillotson, aged 10 with page of notes inserted, crossed through. Jarndyce Antiquarian Booksellers CCVII - 166 2015 £35

Association – Tillotson, Joseph

Bunyan, John 1628-1688 *The Pilgrim's Progress...* London: Routledge, 1862. New edition, illustrations by John Gilbert, frontispiece and plates, ads on endpapers, original dark green cloth, color paper pasted on by Geoffrey Tilltoson, inner hinge splitting, rubbed, ms. label defective, presentation to Joseph Tillotson, with Kathleen Tillotson's notes and Geoffrey's notes and marginal marks, from the library of Geoffrey & Kathleen Tillotson. Jarndyce Antiquarian Booksellers CCVII - 123 2015 £30

Association – Tillotson, Kathleen

Adrian, Arthur A. *Georgina Hogarth and the Dickens Circle.* London: Oxford University Press, 1957. First edition, half title, frontispiece, plates, original yellow cloth, purple label, dulled and slightly marked, Kathleen Tillotson's copy with notes, given her by OUP. Jarndyce Antiquarian Booksellers CCVII - 204 2015 £30

Ainsworth, William Harrison 1805-1882 *Hilary St. Ives.* London: George Routledge & Sons, 1881. Illustrations by Frederick Gilbert, contemporary half red roan, spine faded and slightly rubbed, bookplate with crest of A. J. Constable over another, from the library of Geoffrey & Kathleen Tillotson. Jarndyce Antiquarian Booksellers CCVII - 2 2015 £20

Allott, Miriam *Novelists on the Novel.* London: Routledge, 1959. Half title, few pencil notes, original brown cloth in slightly torn dust jacket, Kathleen Tillotson's copy with note that she reviewed in review of English Studies in 1960. Jarndyce Antiquarian Booksellers CCVII - 3 2015 £20

Ambulance Train in the Great War: Selections from the Pages of La Vie Sanitaire August 1916 to February 1919. No. 5. Blackburn: Geo. Toulmin & Sons, 1919? frontispiece, illustrations, original black boards with paper label, cream cloth spine, inner hinges cracking, Kathleen Tillotson's copy with signature and 'my father Eric Constable's copy'. Jarndyce Antiquarian Booksellers CCVII - 4 2015 £125

Annals: Nineteenth Century. n.p.: circa, 1920-1960? Original maroon cloth boards, rubbed and dusted with blue paper ms. title, cloth tabs attached to pages, marking decades, given to Geoffrey Tillotson by Kathleen Tillotson. Jarndyce Antiquarian Booksellers CCVII - 7 2015 £45

Arnold, Matthew 1822-1888 *A French Eton.* London: Macmillan, 1892. Half title, original dark blue cloth, endpaper causing some browning, otherwise very good, from the library of Geoffrey & Kathleen Tillotson. Jarndyce Antiquarian Booksellers CCVII - 21 2015 £25

Arnold, Matthew 1822-1888 *Culture and Anarchy...* Cambridge: University Press, 1935. Half title, original orange cloth, dulled, piece cut from leading f.e.p., signed by Kathleen Tillotson Jan. 1940 with ink and pencil notes. Jarndyce Antiquarian Booksellers CCVII - 13 2015 £20

Arnold, Matthew 1822-1888 *Culture and Anarchy...* London: Smith, Elder & Co., 1875. Second edition, half title, inserted ad leaf, original brown cloth, slightly dulled, from the library of Geoffrey & Kathleen Tillotson. Jarndyce Antiquarian Booksellers CCVII - 12 2015 £85

Arnold, Matthew 1822-1888 *Culture and Anarchy: an Essay In Political and Social Criticism.* London: Smith, Elder & Co., 1869. First edition, half title, original brown cloth, bevelled boards, spine slightly worn at head and tail, inner hinges splitting, decent copy, from the library of Geoffrey & Kathleen Tillotson. Jarndyce Antiquarian Booksellers CCVII - 11 2015 £220

Arnold, Matthew 1822-1888 *Discourses in America.* London: Macmillan, 1885. First edition, half title, original dark green cloth, slightly dulled, few pencil notes, from the library of Geoffrey & Kathleen Tillotson. Jarndyce Antiquarian Booksellers CCVII - 14 2015 £65

Arnold, Matthew 1822-1888 *Essays in Criticism: Second Series.* Leipzig: Tauchnitz, 1892. Copyright edition, without half title, uncut, later red buckram with note 'bound 1942', notes in pencil, ink and red ink, from the library of Geoffrey & Kathleen Tillotson. Jarndyce Antiquarian Booksellers CCVII - 18 2015 £60

Arnold, Matthew 1822-1888 *Irish Essays and Others.* London: Smith, Elder, 1891. Popular edition, half title, 2 pages ads, original crimson cloth, spine slightly faded, few pencil notes, from the library of Geoffrey & Kathleen Tillotson. Jarndyce Antiquarian Booksellers CCVII - 28 2015 £20

Arnold, Matthew 1822-1888 *Mixed Essays.* London: Smith Elder, 1879. First edition, half title, few spots, original dark blue cloth, dulled, inner hinges splitting, from the library of Geoffrey & Kathleen Tillotson. Jarndyce Antiquarian Booksellers CCVII - 38 2015 £20

Arnold, Matthew 1822-1888 *On The Study of Celtic Literature.* London: Smith, Elder & Co., 1867. First edition, half title, without ads, original brown cloth, bevelled boards, brick red endpapers, inner hinges noticeably strengthened with blue paper, presentation from H. S. King to the Hon. Mrs. Gordon, with Kathleen Tillotson's booklabel. Jarndyce Antiquarian Booksellers CCVII - 41 2015 £35

Arnold, Matthew 1822-1888 *Reports on Elementary Schools 1852-1882.* London: Macmillan, 1889. First edition, half title, 2 pages ads, original dark blue cloth, dulled, inne
r hinges splitting, leading f.e.p. slightly chipped, from the library of Geoffrey & Kathleen Tillotson.   Jarndyce Antiquarian Booksellers   CCVII - 52   2015   £25

Arnold, Matthew 1822-1888 *St. Paul and Protestantism...* London: Smith Elder, 1870. First edition, half title, browning caused by endpapers, original brown cloth, small tear on back board, slight rubbing, traces of library label in leading endpapers, from the library of Geoffrey & Kathleen Tillotson.   Jarndyce Antiquarian Booksellers   CCVII - 55   2015   £30

Arnold, Matthew 1822-1888 *The Letters of Matthew Arnold to Arthur Hugh Clough.* London: Oxford University Press, 1932. Half title, replacement label at end, uncut in original dark blue cloth, paper label slightly chipped, spine faded, Kathleen Tillotson's copy, signed and heavily annotated with few insertions.   Jarndyce Antiquarian Booksellers   CCVII - 31   2015   £40

Arnold, Matthew 1822-1888 *The Note-Books.* London: Oxford University Press, 1952. Half title, original red buckram, from the library of Geoffrey & Kathleen Tillotson, inscribed by same, with copy of Geoffrey's review or reviews.   Jarndyce Antiquarian Booksellers   CCVII - 40   2015   £35

Austen, Jane 1775-1817 *Jane Austen's Letters to Her Sister Cassandra and Others.* Oxford: Clarendon Press, 1932. 2 volumes, half titles, frontispieces, plates, maps, uncut, original marbled boards, pale blue cloth spines, paper labels, spines slightly faded, from the library of Geoffrey & Kathleen Tillotson.   Jarndyce Antiquarian Booksellers   CCVII - 77   2015   £85

Austen, Jane 1775-1817 *Mansfield Park.* Belfast: Simms & M'Inyre, 1846. Half title, 4 pages ads, original maroon cloth, spine slightly faded, nice, from the library of Geoffrey & Kathleen Tillotson.   Jarndyce Antiquarian Booksellers   CCVII - 78   2015   £200

Balfour, Arthur James *Criticism and Beauty: a Lecture Rewritten...* Oxford: Clarendon press, 1910. publisher's slip, original blue printed wrappers, slightly creased, 48 pages, from the library of Geoffrey & Kathleen Tillotson.   Jarndyce Antiquarian Booksellers   CCVII - 81   2015   £20

Bate, Walter Jackson *Coleridge.* London: Collier MacMillan, 1968. Half title, uncut, original dark green cloth, very good in dust jacket, from the library of Geoffrey & Kathleen Tillotson, presentation from same with inserts.   Jarndyce Antiquarian Booksellers   CCVII - 152   2015   £35

Bate, Walter Jackson *Samuel Johnson.* New York: Harcourt Brace Jovanovich, 1977. Half title, frontispiece and plates, original dark blue cloth, slightly dusted in slightly torn dust jacket, 2 ALS's from author to Kathleen Tillotson with photo, notes and cuttings of her reviews.   Jarndyce Antiquarian Booksellers   CCVII - 338   2015   £45

Beer, Gillian *Darwin's Plots; Evolutionary Narrative in Darwin, George Eliot and Nineteenth Century Fiction.* London: Routledge, 1983. Half title, illustrations, original red cloth, very good in dust jacket, initialled to Kathleen Tillotson with card from her inserted.   Jarndyce Antiquarian Booksellers   CCVII - 83   2015   £20

Beerbohm, Max 1872-1956 *Zuleika Dobson, or an Oxford Love Story.* London: William Heinemann, 1922. New impression, half title, title in brown and black, uncut in original brown cloth, slightly dulled, and marked, signed by Kathleen Tillotson as Constable.   Jarndyce Antiquarian Booksellers   CCVII - 85   2015   £25

Bible. English - 1883 *Isaiah of Jerusalem in the Authorised English Version... notes by Matthew Arnold.* London: Macmillan, 1883. First edition, half title, 32 page catalog (1883), original brown cloth, slightly dulled, from the library of Geoffrey & Kathleen Tillotson.   Jarndyce Antiquarian Booksellers   CCVII - 59   2015   £38

Boswell, James 1740-1795 *Boswell's Journal of a Tour to the Hebrides with Samuel Johnson, LL.D.* London: William Heinemann, 1936. Half title, folding map, plates, original red cloth, spine faded, copy given to Kathleen Tillotson by family members with her name altered from Constable to Tillotson.   Jarndyce Antiquarian Booksellers   CCVII - 92   2015   £35

Boswell, James 1740-1795 *Letters Collected and Edited by Chauncey Brewster Tinker.* Oxford: Clarendon Press, 1924. 2 volumes, half titles, frontispiece volume I, plates, old pencil mark, original brown cloth, from the library of Geoffrey & Kathleen Tillotson, given by Geoffery to Kathleen 3.IV.38, with note and cutting inserted.   Jarndyce Antiquarian Booksellers   CCVII - 93   2015   £35

Brain, Walter Russell, Baron *Some Reflections on Genius and Other Essays.* London: Pitman Medical Pub., 1960. Original purple cloth, illustrations by Norman Smith, half title, very good in slightly spotted dust jacket, from the library of Geoffrey & Kathleen Tillotson, Geoffrey's gift to Kathleen, with AL from Geoffery congratulating Brain on his peerage and Brain's ALS in reply. Jarndyce Antiquarian Booksellers CCVII - 96 2015 £20

Bronte, Charlotte 1816-1855 *Jane Eyre.* Oxford: Clarendon Press, 1969. Half title, original dark blue cloth, very good in slightly marked dust jacket, with ad leaflet, TLS from Ian Jack to Kathleen Tillotson asking for advice and copy of note from Kathleen to Margaret Smith inserted. Jarndyce Antiquarian Booksellers CCVII - 103 2015 £70

Bronte, Charlotte 1816-1855 *Shirley.* Oxford: Clarendon Press, 1979. Half title, original dark blue cloth, very good in slightly marked dust jacket, with note by Kathleen Tillotson. Jarndyce Antiquarian Booksellers CCVII - 107 2015 £50

Bronte, Charlotte 1816-1855 *The Letters... Volume I: 1829-1847.* Oxford: Clarendon Press, 1995. Half title, original dark blue cloth, very good in dust jacket, presentation from editor, Margaret Smith, for Kathleen Tillotson, with earlier card and ALS thanking KT for kind comments, she has made 2 pencil corrections in text. Jarndyce Antiquarian Booksellers CCVII - 104 2015 £50

Bronte, Charlotte 1816-1855 *The Professor.* Oxford: Clarendon Press, 1987. Half title, original dark blue cloth, very good in dust jacket, presentation from editor for Kathleen Tillotson. Jarndyce Antiquarian Booksellers CCVII - 105 2015 £50

Bronte, Charlotte 1816-1855 *Villette.* Boston: Houghton Mifflin Co., 1971. Riverside edition, original printed card wrappers, slightly marked, very good, from the library of Geoffrey & Kathleen Tillotson, edited by Geoffery with inserted correspondence. Jarndyce Antiquarian Booksellers CCVII - 109 2015 £20

Bronte, Charlotte 1816-1855 *Villette.* London: Smith Elder & Co., 1853. First edition, 3 volumes, few leaves proud and damaged at fore-edge, from the library of Geoffrey & Kathleen Tillotson, with note by Kathleen, card wrappers made by Geoffrey, many pencil notes and marginal marks. Jarndyce Antiquarian Booksellers CCVII - 108 2015 £250

Bronte, Charlotte 1816-1855 *Villette.* Oxford: Clarendon Press, 1984. half title, original dark blue cloth, very good in slightly marked dust jacket, from the library of Geoffrey & Kathleen Tillotson, with 3 page ALS from editor about this edition. Jarndyce Antiquarian Booksellers CCVII - 110 2015 £50

Bronte, Emily 1818-1848 *The Complete Poems.* New York: Columbia University Press, 1947. Second printing, half title, frontispiece, original green cloth, signed by Kathleen Tillotson, April 1950, few notes in text and relevant cutting. Jarndyce Antiquarian Booksellers CCVII - 133 2015 £20

Bronte, Emily 1818-1848 *Wuthering Heights.* Oxford: Clarendon press, 1976. Half title, original dark blue cloth, very good in dust jacket, presented to Kathleen Tillotson by Press delegates. Jarndyce Antiquarian Booksellers CCVII - 114 2015 £75

Bunyan, John 1628-1688 *The Pilgrim's Progress...* London: Routledge, 1862. New edition, illustrations by John Gilbert, frontispiece and plates, ads on endpapers, original dark green cloth, color paper pasted on by Geoffrey Tilltoson, inner hinge splitting, rubbed, ms. label defective, presentation to Joseph Tillotson, with Kathleen Tillotson's notes and Geoffrey's notes and marginal marks, from the library of Geoffrey & Kathleen Tillotson. Jarndyce Antiquarian Booksellers CCVII - 123 2015 £30

Burke, Edmund 1729-1797 *Letters, Speeches and Tracts on Irish Affairs Collected and Arranged by Matthew Arnold.* London: Macmillan, 1881. Half title 2 pages ads, original dark blue cloth, slightly chipped, spine faded, inner hinges cracking, from the library of Geoffrey & Kathleen Tillotson. Jarndyce Antiquarian Booksellers CCVII - 60 2015 £35

Butler, Arthur Gray *The Three Friends: a Story of Rugby in the Forties.* London: Henry Frowde, 1900. Original maroon cloth, spine slightly faded, signed by A. F. Buxton, Christmas 1900 and Kathleen Tillotson Oct. 1594, ALS from Dorothy Ward to Kathleen. Jarndyce Antiquarian Booksellers CCVII - 124 2015 £40

Butt, John *Dickens at Work.* London: Methuen, 1957. First edition, half title, frontispiece, facsimile, plates, original green cloth, very good in slightly torn and dusted dust jacket, from the library of Geoffrey & Kathleen Tillotson, with Kathleen's presentation to Geoffrey. Jarndyce Antiquarian Booksellers CCVII - 208 2015 £35

Butt, John *Dickens at Work.* London: Methuen, 1957. First edition, half title, frontispiece, plates, half brown morocco by Sangorski & Sutcliffe, spine in compartments, slight rubbing to leading hinge, top edge gilt, publisher's specially bound copy to Kathleen Tillotson with ANS from Peter Wait inserted. Jarndyce Antiquarian Booksellers CCVII - 207 2015 £40

Butt, John *Imagined Worlds: Essays on Some English Novels and Novelists in Honour of John Butt...* London: Methuen, 1968. Half title, frontispiece, original brown cloth, very good in slightly torn dust jacket, Kathleen Tillotson's copy May 1968, with inserted reviews and correspondence. Jarndyce Antiquarian Booksellers CCVII - 126 2015 £35

Butt, John *Pope, Dickens and Others: Essays and Addresses.* Edinburgh: University Press, 1969. First edition, half title, original pink cloth, very good, with correspondence between editor, Geoffrey Carnall and Kathleen Tillotson. Jarndyce Antiquarian Booksellers CCVII - 127 2015 £25

Byrne, Muriel St. Clair *Somerville College 1879-1921.* London: Oxford University Press, 1922. Frontispiece, illustrations, music, original dark blue cloth, slightly rubbed, Kathleen Tillotson's copy with note 'Helen Darbishire's copy given me by Nesta Clutterbuck, May 1878". Jarndyce Antiquarian Booksellers CCVII - 128 2015 £22

Caddel, Richard *Burnt Acres and the Shangri-la....* Sunderland: Ceolfrith Press, 1978. Folio, illustrations, ad leaf slightly browned, original grey printed wrappers, from the library of Geoffrey & Kathleen Tillotson, with press cutting of reviews. Jarndyce Antiquarian Booksellers CCVII - 129 2015 £85

Chambers, R. W. *Man's Unconquerable Mind: Studies of English Writers from Bede to A. E. Housman and W. P. Ker.* London: Jonathan Cape, 1939. Half title, plates, author's presentation copy to Geoffrey Tillotson and wife, with 2 ALS's from Raymond Wilson Chambers to Geoffrey. Jarndyce Antiquarian Booksellers CCVII - 132 2015 £20

Church of England. Book of Common Prayer *The Book of Common Prayer...* Cambridge: printed by C. J. Clay for SPCK, circa, 1880. small 4to., original full black morocco with embossed device, slight rubbing, stamp of Thomas Davidson, Fritchley Nr. Derby and Kathleen Tillotson's note that he was her grandfather, ink and pencil notes. Jarndyce Antiquarian Booksellers CCVII - 156 2015 £35

Clifford, James L. *Eighteenth Century English Literature: Modern Essays in Criticism.* New York: Oxford University Press, 1959. Half title, original printed card wrappers, from the library of Geoffrey & Kathleen Tillotson, Geoffrey's presentation to Kathleen. Jarndyce Antiquarian Booksellers CCVII - 137 2015 £20

Clough, Arthur Hugh *Poems...* London: Macmillan, 1885. Eleventh edition, half title, full dark green calf, prize binding from Marlborough College, small chip from head of spine, inner hinges splitting, from the library of Geoffrey & Kathleen Tillotson. Jarndyce Antiquarian Booksellers CCVII - 143 2015 £20

Clough, Blanche Athena *A Memoir of Anne Jemima Clough by her niece.* London: Edward Arnold, 1897. Frontispiece and plates, 32 page catalog (Ot. 1897), uncut in original dark green cloth, small split at head of spine, from the library of Geoffrey & Kathleen Tillotson. Jarndyce Antiquarian Booksellers CCVII - 138 2015 £35

Coleridge, Hartley *Letters.* Oxford University Press, 1941. Half title, frontispiece, from the library of Geoffrey & Kathleen Tillotson, erratum slip, original buff cloth, marked, inscribed by Kathleen for Geoffrey, with original 4 line comic verse, but not signed by him. Jarndyce Antiquarian Booksellers CCVII - 146 2015 £20

Coleridge, Samuel Taylor 1772-1834 *Shakespeare, Ben Jonson, Beaumont and Fletcher: Notes and Lectures.* Liverpool: Edward Howell, 1875. New edition, half title, final ad leaf, original olive green cloth, spine slightly bubbled, signed K. M. Constable, April 1926 with some marginal marks and inserted reviews, from the library of Geoffrey & Kathleen Tillotson. Jarndyce Antiquarian Booksellers CCVII - 149 2015 £35

Collins, Wilkie 1824-1889 *The Woman in White.* Boston: Houghton Mifflin, 1969. Riverside edition, half title, illustrations, original card wrappers, slightly creased and marked, Kathleen Tillotson's copy with note, with inserted TLS of appreciation for the loan from Gordon (Haight?) 1987. Jarndyce Antiquarian Booksellers CCVII - 155 2015 £20

Communist Party of Great Britain *Lord and Lady Beavermere ...* London: Communist Party of Great Britain, 1937? 16 pages, illustrations, stabbed as issued, slightly creased, from the library of Geoffrey & Kathleen Tillotson. Jarndyce Antiquarian Booksellers CCVII - 157 2015 £20

Communist Party of Great Britain *Parade of War.* London: Communist Party of Great Britain, 1937. 16 pages, illustrations, stabbed as issued in original wrappers with caricature, slightly marked and creased, from the library of Geoffrey & Kathleen Tillotson.   Jarndyce Antiquarian Booksellers   CCVII - 158   2015   £20

Cunningham, Valentine *Everywhere Spoken Against: Dissent in the Victorian Novel.* Oxford: Clarendon Press, 1975. Half title, original dark blue cloth, very good in dust jacket, from the library of Geoffrey & Kathleen Tillotson.   Jarndyce Antiquarian Booksellers   CCVII - 161   2015   £20

Cussans, John E. *Handbook of Heraldry with Instructions for Tracing Pedigrees and Deciphering Ancient Mss. Rules for the Appointment of Liveries &c.* London: Chatto & Windus, 1893. Fourth edition, 32 page catalog Sept. 1901, half title, frontispiece, illustrations, slightly browned, original olive green cloth, spine faded to brown, from the library of Geoffrey & Kathleen Tillotson.   Jarndyce Antiquarian Booksellers   CCVII - 162   2015   £25

Dawson, William Harbutt *Matthew Arnold and His Relation to the Thought of Our Time...* New York: G. P. Putnam's Sons, 1904. Frontispiece, few marginal marks, original dark blue cloth, from the library of Geoffrey & Kathleen Tillotson.   Jarndyce Antiquarian Booksellers   CCVII - 62   2015   £20

De Morgan, Augusta *A Budget of Paradoxes.* London: Longmans, 1872. First edition, half title, contemporary half red morocco, spine darkened, scarce, with Geoffrey Tillotson's initials 1953 and Kathleen Tillotson's marker denoting special interest.   Jarndyce Antiquarian Booksellers   CCVII - 164   2015   £120

Dickens, Charles 1812-1870 *American Notes.* London: Chapman & Hall, 1842. First edition first issue, 2 volumes, half titles, ad leaf preceding half title volume I, 6 page catalog volume II, few marks in text, original purple cloth, blocked in blind, spines lettered gilt, expertly recased, bought by Kathleen Tillotson.   Jarndyce Antiquarian Booksellers   CCVII - 168   2015   £850

Dickens, Charles 1812-1870 *Barnaby Rudge.* Paris: Baudry's European Lib., 1842. 2 volumes, half titles, 4 page catalog volume I, some spotting, original brown paper wrappers, slightly torn, ink mark, original paper labels, nice, from the library of Geoffrey & Kathleen Tillotson.   Jarndyce Antiquarian Booksellers   CCVII - 169   2015   £85

Dickens, Charles 1812-1870 *Bleak House.* London: Bradbury and Evans, 1853. Frontispiece, added engraved title and plates, contemporary half dark blue calf, crimson label, rather rubbed but sound, internally very clean, Kathleen Tillotson's copy with note.   Jarndyce Antiquarian Booksellers   CCVII - 170   2015   £320

Dickens, Charles 1812-1870 *David Copperfield.* Oxford: Clarendon Press, 1981. Half title, frontispiece, illustrations, original dark blue cloth, very good in torn dust jacket, Kathleen Tillotson's unmarked copy with correspondence inserted.   Jarndyce Antiquarian Booksellers   CCVII - 173   2015   £120

Dickens, Charles 1812-1870 *Dombey and Son.* Oxford: Clarendon Press, 1974. Half title, frontispiece and illustrations, original dark blue cloth in dusted and slightly torn dust jacket, from the library of Geoffrey & Kathleen Tillotson.   Jarndyce Antiquarian Booksellers   CCVII - 175   2015   £85

Dickens, Charles 1812-1870 *Dombey and Son.* Oxford: Clarendon Press, 1974. Half title, frontispiece and illustrations, original dark blue cloth, slightly damp marked in dusted and slightly torn dust jacket, advanced copy signed by Kathleen Tillotson 9 May 1974 with TLS's from Press about publication and note by Kathleen.   Jarndyce Antiquarian Booksellers   CCVII - 174   2015   £100

Dickens, Charles 1812-1870 *Great Expectations.* Oxford: Clarendon Press, 1993. Half title, illustrations, original dark blue cloth, very good in slightly torn dust jacket, from the library of Geoffrey & Kathleen Tillotson with Kathleen's note, several inserted letters.   Jarndyce Antiquarian Booksellers   CCVII - 177   2015   £120

Dickens, Charles 1812-1870 *Hard Times and Pictures from Italy.* London: Chapman & Hall, 1866. Frontispiece, original green pebble grained cloth, few marks on leading pastedown, split in following hinge, otherwise bright, clean copy, from the library of Geoffrey & Kathleen Tillotson.   Jarndyce Antiquarian Booksellers   CCVII - 179   2015   £45

Dickens, Charles 1812-1870 *Hard Times.* London: Bradbury and Evans, 1854. First edition, half title, few spots, original olive green horizontal ribbed cloth, sunned, spine torn and worn at tail, slight damp marking at fore-edge, inner hinges cracking, armorial bookplate of George Jacob Bosanquet, Kathleen Tillotson's copy, signed 1949 with pencil notes , in Kathleen's brown paper wrappers.   Jarndyce Antiquarian Booksellers   CCVII - 178   2015   £350

Dickens, Charles 1812-1870 *Little Dorrit.* London: Bradbury & Evans, 1857. First edition, frontispiece, added engraved title and plates, odd spot, contemporary half dark green calf, rubbed, split in leading hinge, wear at head of spine, clean copy, Kathleen Tillotson's ownership. Jarndyce Antiquarian Booksellers   CCVII - 180   2015   £185

Dickens, Charles 1812-1870 *Martin Chuzzlewit.* Oxford: Clarendon Press, 1982. Half title, frontispiece, illustrations, original dark blue cloth, very good in slightly torn dust jacket, Kathleen Tillotson's copy with few pencil notes.   Jarndyce Antiquarian Booksellers   CCVII - 181   2015   £90

Dickens, Charles 1812-1870 *Oliver Twist.* Oxford: Clarendon Press, 1966. Half title, frontispiece, illustrations, map, original dark blue cloth in slightly worn dust jacket, from the library of Geoffrey & Kathleen Tillotson.   Jarndyce Antiquarian Booksellers   CCVII - 189   2015   £120

Dickens, Charles 1812-1870 *Oliver Twist.* Oxford: Clarendon Press, 1966. Half title, frontispiece, illustrations, map, original blue cloth, very good in dust jacket, from the library of Geoffrey & Kathleen Tillotson, inscribed by her for Geoffrey.   Jarndyce Antiquarian Booksellers   CCVII - 190   2015   £90

Dickens, Charles 1812-1870 *Oliver Twist.* Oxford: Clarendon Press, 1974. Half title, frontispiece, illustrations, map, original blue cloth in slightly torn dust jacket with notes, Kathleen Tillotson's copy, als inserted Geoffrey Tillotson's copy of her paper 'Oliver Twist from Essays and Studies" 1959.   Jarndyce Antiquarian Booksellers   CCVII - 191   2015   £110

Dickens, Charles 1812-1870 *Pickwick Papers.* London: Chapman & Hall, 1837. First edition, early issue with no imprint on plates, Weller title, half title, frontispiece, engraved title, plates by Seymour & Phiz, offsetting and spotting signature of M. Weale, Leamington, pencil notes by Kathleen Tillotson, records loans, with inserted notes.   Jarndyce Antiquarian Booksellers   CCVII - 194   2015   £150

Dickens, Charles 1812-1870 *Sikes and Nancy....* London: Henry Sotheran, 1921. Half title, frontispiece, final ad leaf, original black boards, paper label, dulled, from the library of Geoffrey & Kathleen Tillotson.   Jarndyce Antiquarian Booksellers   CCVII - 193   2015   £45

Dickens, Charles 1812-1870 *Sketches By Boz.* Philadelphia: Lea and Blanchard, 1842. New edition, from the library of Geoffrey & Kathleen Tillotson, tall 8vo., frontispiece and 18 plates after George Cruikshank, one missing, some browning, lacking pages 29-32, blue paper wrappers made by Geoffrey his note on wrappers, text annotated throughout by Kathleen in ink and pencil.   Jarndyce Antiquarian Booksellers   CCVII - 197   2015   £45

Dickens, Charles 1812-1870 *Sketches by Boz. First Series.* London: John Macrone, 1837. Third edition, 2 volumes, frontispiece and plates by George Cruikshank, original dark green cloth, slight rubbing, good, clean, attractive copy, from the library of Geoffrey & Kathleen Tillotson.   Jarndyce Antiquarian Booksellers   CCVII - 196   2015   £350

Dickens, Charles 1812-1870 *Sketches by Boz... (bound with) American Notes for General Circulation.* London: Chapman and Hall, 1850. 1850, 2 volumes in 1, frontispiece, half title, contemporary half maroon calf, spine slightly rubbed and faded, from the library of Geoffrey & Kathleen Tillotson.   Jarndyce Antiquarian Booksellers   CCVII - 198   2015   £35

Dickens, Charles 1812-1870 *The Adventures of Oliver Twist.* London: Chapman and Hall, 1853. Half title, original light green cloth, one mark, spine slightly sunned, otherwise very good, from the library of Geoffrey & Kathleen Tillotson with note by Kathleen.   Jarndyce Antiquarian Booksellers   CCVII - 185   2015   £50

Dickens, Charles 1812-1870 *The Adventures of Oliver Twist.* London: Chapman & Hall, 1867? 8 illustrations, half title, frontispiece and plates, original red cloth, spine worn at head and tail, dulled, internally good, from the library of Geoffrey & Kathleen Tillotson.   Jarndyce Antiquarian Booksellers   CCVII - 186   2015   £45

Dickens, Charles 1812-1870 *The Adventures of Oliver Twist.* London: Chapman and Hall, 1861. illustrations by George Cruikshank, half title, frontispiece and plates, original red cloth spine slightly dulled & rubbed, clean, with few notes by Kathleen Tillotson.   Jarndyce Antiquarian Booksellers   CCVII - 186   2015   £60

Dickens, Charles 1812-1870 *The Adventures of Oliver Twist.* London: Oxford University Press, 1953. Half title, frontispiece and plates, original red cloth, spine worn at head and tail, dulled, internally good, signed by Kathleen Tillotson, TLS about new edition from OUP dated 1955.   Jarndyce Antiquarian Booksellers   CCVII - 188   2015   £25

Dickens, Charles 1812-1870 *The Letters Volumes I-V (1820-1852).* Oxford: Clarendon, 1965-1988. Pilgrim edition, original pink (volume I) and red cloth, dulled and marbled, volume I with spine strip torn away, volumes III & IV slightly loose, from the library of Geoffrey & Kathleen Tillotson.   Jarndyce Antiquarian Booksellers   CCVII - 199   2015   £480

Dickens, Charles 1812-1870 *The Letters.* Oxford: Clarendon Press, 1969. Pilgrim edition, Volume II 140-1841, original red cloth, very good in very slightly torn dust jacket, from the library of Geoffrey & Kathleen Tillotson.   Jarndyce Antiquarian Booksellers   CCVII - 202   2015   £85

Dickens, Charles 1812-1870 *The Letters.* Oxford: Clarendon Press, 1981. Volume V 1847-1849, original red cloth, very slightly torn dust jacket, from the library of Geoffrey & Kathleen Tillotson.   Jarndyce Antiquarian Booksellers   CCVII - 203   2015   £110

Dickens, Charles 1812-1870 *The Letters.* Oxford: Clarendon Press, 1982? Pilgrim edition, volume I, 1820-1839, original red cloth, near mint in very slightly creased dust jacket, from the library of Geoffrey & Kathleen Tillotson.   Jarndyce Antiquarian Booksellers   CCVII - 200   2015   £85

Dickens, Charles 1812-1870 *The Letters.* Oxford: Clarendon Press, 1989. Volume I 1820-1839, original red cloth, near mint in slightly creased dust jacket, from the library of Geoffrey & Kathleen Tillotson.   Jarndyce Antiquarian Booksellers   CCVII - 201   2015   £85

Dickens, Charles 1812-1870 *The Mystery of Edwin Drood.* Oxford: Clarendon Press, 1972. Half title, frontispiece, plates, original dark blue cloth, very good in torn dust jacket, Kathleen Tillotson's spare copy.   Jarndyce Antiquarian Booksellers   CCVII - 184   2015   £75

Dickens, Charles 1812-1870 *The Pickwick Papers.* Oxford: Clarendon Press, Half title, frontispiece, illustrations, original dark blue cloth, very good in creased dust jacket, from the library of Geoffrey & Kathleen Tillotson, relevant papers inserted including browned proof article by Kathleen Tillotson for TLS.   Jarndyce Antiquarian Booksellers   CCVII - 195   2015   £120

Dolby, George *Charles Dickens as I Knew Him...* London: T. Fisher Unwin, 1885. Second thousand, half title, 32 page catalog 1885, pin holes in title, original red cloth, dulled, from the library of Geoffrey & Kathleen Tillotson, press cuttings inserted including obit of Dolby 1900.   Jarndyce Antiquarian Booksellers   CCVII - 212   2015   £40

Domett, Alfred *The Diary of Alfred Dommett 1872-1885.* London: Oxford University Press, 1953. Half title, frontispiece, original green cloth, very good, dust jacket, inscribed by Kathleen Tillotson from EAH.   Jarndyce Antiquarian Booksellers   CCVII - 223   2015   £20

Donne, John 1571-1631 *The Divine Poems.* Oxford: Clarendon Press, 1952. Half title, frontispiece, original dark blue cloth, torn dust jacket, Kathleen Tillotson's copy 1953 with few pencil marginal notes.   Jarndyce Antiquarian Booksellers   CCVII - 224   2015   £30

Donne, John 1571-1631 *The Elegies and Songs and Sonnets.* Oxford: Clarendon Press, 1965. Half title, music, original dark blue cloth, very good in slightly torn and marked dust jacket, with 4 related cuttings inserted, from the library of Geoffrey & Kathleen Tillotson.   Jarndyce Antiquarian Booksellers   CCVII - 2245   2015   £35

Donne, John 1571-1631 *The Extasie.* London: privately printed at the Department of English at University College London, 1934. Unopened, original blue printed wrappers, from the library of Geoffrey & Kathleen Tillotson.   Jarndyce Antiquarian Booksellers   CCVII - 226   2015   £50

Donne, John 1571-1631 *The Poems.* London: Oxford University Press, 1929. Half title, frontispiece, uncut in original blue cloth, covered in thick striped paper, paper label, Kathleen Tillotson's copy 1930 as KMC, Geoffrey Tillotson added 1934, many notes, mostly marginal on endpapers and inserted articles.   Jarndyce Antiquarian Booksellers   CCVII - 228   2015   £50

Donne, John 1571-1631 *The Poems.* Oxford: Clarendon Press, 1912. 2 volumes, original brown buckram, paper labels slightly split at edges, with inserted, notes, probably by J. B. Leishman, the editor to whom correspondence is addressed, from the library of Geoffrey & Kathleen Tillotson.   Jarndyce Antiquarian Booksellers   CCVII - 227   2015   £60

Douton, Agnes May Maud *A Book with Seven Seals.* London: Cayme Press, 1928. Half title, illustrations, original brown boards, brown cloth spine, slight rubbing, given to Kathleen Tillotson by Margaret Blom, with Kathleen's notes of her research included.   Jarndyce Antiquarian Booksellers   CCVII - 229   2015   £110

Drayton, Michael 1563-1631 *Endimion and Phoebe. Ideas Lamos.* N.P.: 1870? 4to., privately printed facsimile, original purple wrappers with title, front wrapper detached and creased, spine defective, from the library of Geoffrey & Kathleen Tillotson, with few pencil notes by Geoffrey.   Jarndyce Antiquarian Booksellers   CCVII - 232   2015   £120

Drayton, Michael 1563-1631 *England's Heroical Epistles.* London: printed for J. Johnson, 1788. Some leaves slightly browned, 19th century half dark green morocco, slightly rubbed with scars on marbled boards, eith early note on page 308, with names of Geoffrey and Kathleen Tillotson, inserted correspondence shows Kathleen offered this to British Library which in fact had acquired a copy, ALS from John Betjeman probably to Bernard Newdigate. Jarndyce Antiquarian Booksellers   CCVII - 233   2015   £280

Drayton, Michael 1563-1631 *Ideas Mirrour.* London: printed by James Roberts for Nicholas Linge, 1928? Facsimile, 4to., photographic facsimile, from Huntington Library copy with label, dark green binder's cloth, signed by Kathleen Tillotson 1928.   Jarndyce Antiquarian Booksellers   CCVII - 234   2015   £40

Drayton, Michael 1563-1631 *Minor Poems...* Oxford: Clarendon Press, 1907. 4to., original cream card imitation vellum wrappers, spine and edges browned, signed, Kathleen M. Constable (Tillotson) may 1927, later pencil notess, letter by Tillotson.   Jarndyce Antiquarian Booksellers   CCVII - 235   2015   £45

Drayton, Michael 1563-1631 *Nimphidia the Court of Fayrie.* Stratford-upon-Avon: printed at the Shakespeare Head Press, 1924. 4to., half title, original decorated paper wrappers, spine slightly browned with small chips, with Christmas greetings from F. H. R. Dix, Hemingford or Stratford-on-Avon sending this poem, from the library of Geoffrey & Kathleen Tillotson.   Jarndyce Antiquarian Booksellers   CCVII - 237   2015   £50

Drayton, Michael 1563-1631 *Poems.* London: Routledge, 1953. 2 volumes, half titles, frontispieces, original dark blue cloth, very good in dust jacket, Kathleen Tillotson's review copy with few pencil notes and galley proof of her favourable review of volume I inserted. Jarndyce Antiquarian Booksellers   CCVII - 238   2015   £20

Drayton, Michael 1563-1631 *Poly-Olbion.* London: printed for M. Lownes, I. Browne, A. Helme, J. Bushbie, 1612-1622. Engraved maps, 19th century half black calf, rubbed with split at head of leading hinge, armorial bookplate of Bernard Henry Newdigate, somewhat defective copy with few pencil marks, from the library of Geoffrey & Kathleen Tillotson.   Jarndyce Antiquarian Booksellers   CCVII - 239   2015   £950

Drayton, Michael 1563-1631 *The Works.* Oxford: printed at Shakespeare Head press, 1931-1941. Tercentary edition, 5 volumes, half titles, frontispieces, facsimiles, uncut, original dark blue cloth, inner hinges volume I splitting, good set, Kathleen Tillotson's copy with notes and insertions.   Jarndyce Antiquarian Booksellers   CCVII - 230   2015   £480

Drayton, Michael 1563-1631 *The Works.* Oxford: published for the Shakespeare Head Press, 1961. 1941, Volumes I-IV with Volume V 1941, half titles, frontispieces, facsimiles, uncut in original dark blue cloth, very good, from the library of Geoffrey & Kathleen Tillotson.   Jarndyce Antiquarian Booksellers   CCVII - 231   2015   £300

Duke, Arthur *The Larke: a Seventeenth Century Poem Ascribed to Dr. Arthur Duke.* London: privately printed in the Department of English at the University College London, 1934. original blue printed wrappers, slightly faded and creased, printed by Geoffrey Tillotson on departmental hand press, inscribed by him to Kathleen Tillotson, inserted is ALS from Priscilla (Preston) to Kathleen.   Jarndyce Antiquarian Booksellers   CCVII - 251   2015   £60

Dyson, H. V. D. *Augustans and Romantics 1689-1830.* London: Cresset Press, 1940. Half title, original grey green cloth, inscribed to Geoffrey and Kathleen Tillotson by John Butt.   Jarndyce Antiquarian Booksellers   CCVII - 253   2015   £20

Eliot, George, Pseud. 1819-1880 *Daniel Deronda.* Oxford: Clarendon Press, 1984. Half title, original black cloth, very good in slightly marked dust jacket, Kathleen Tillotson's copy from the editor, Graham Handley, with TLS of explanation from him inserted 1985, with draft copy of the introduction and notes in response to criticism by General editor, Gordon Haight.   Jarndyce Antiquarian Booksellers   CCVII - 254   2015   £60

Eliot, George, Pseud. 1819-1880 *Romola.* Leipzig: Bernhard Tauchnitz, 1863. Copyright edition, extra illustrated with numerous photos, elaborate gilt binding, contemporary full vellum, bevelled boards, embossed in maroon, finely tooled gilt, gilt endpapers, small bookseller's ticket, G. Giannini, Florence, very good, handsome copy in red cloth jacket now broken red cloth box, presentation by Graham Handley for Kathleen Tillotson, with his inscription, his appreciation, occasional ink marginal notes and accompanying letter and copy of Kathleen's reply.   Jarndyce Antiquarian Booksellers   CCVII - 256   2015   £65

Eliot, George, Pseud. 1819-1880 *Scenes of Clerical Life.* Edinburgh and London: William Blackwood & Sons, 1859. Second edition, 2 volumes, half titles, 16 page catalog volume II, original burgundy pebble grained cloth by Edmonds & Remnants, little rubbed and dulled with small splits in hinges, lacking leading f.e.p.'s, from the library of Geoffrey & Kathleen Tillotson. Jarndyce Antiquarian Booksellers   CCVII - 257   2015   £68

Eliot, George, Pseud. 1819-1880 *Selections from George Eliot's Letters.* New Haven: Yale University Press, 1985. Original olive green cloth, very good in dust jacket, presentation for Kathleen Tillotson, TLS from Gordon Haight for Kathleen. Jarndyce Antiquarian Booksellers   CCVII - 258   2015   £30

Eliot, George, Pseud. 1819-1880 *Silas Marner, the Weaver of Raveloe.* Edinburgh & London: William Blackwood & Sons, 1861. First edition, 16 page catalog and 4 pages ads, little spotting, original orange brown cloth by Burn, slightly rubbed, one hinge cracking, good, from the library of Geoffrey & Kathleen Tillotson. Jarndyce Antiquarian Booksellers   CCVII - 259   2015   £500

Ellis-Fermor, Una Mary *Shakespeare the Dramatist and Other Papers.* London: Methuen, 1961. Half title, frontispiece, original maroon cloth, slightly faded in torn dust jacket, from the library of Geoffrey & Kathleen Tillotson, signed by Kathleen with few comments, letter from her to Kenneth Muir and his reply, with two papers presented by author to Kathleen and Geoffrey. Jarndyce Antiquarian Booksellers   CCVII - 461   2015   £25

Elton, Oliver *Michael Drayton: a Critical Study with Bibliography.* London: Constable & Co., 1905. Half title, frontispiece and plates, original brown cloth, dulled and ink marked, Kathleen Tillotson's copy, signed Kathleen M. Constable Nov. 12 1927, with few notes, bookplate of Sidney Colvin. Jarndyce Antiquarian Booksellers   CCVII - 241   2015   £20

Empson, William *Seven Types of Ambiguity.* London: Chatto & Windus, 1930. First edition, half title, inserted errata list, original orange cloth in torn and dusted dust jacket, with Geoffrey Tillotson's paper label Oxford 1931 and with ms. index compiled by him inserted, pencil marginal corrections by Kathleen Tillotson. Jarndyce Antiquarian Booksellers   CCVII - 264   2015   £20

Fisher, Leona Weaver *Lemon, Dickens and Mr. Nightingale's Diary a Victorian Farce.* Victoria: University of Victoria, 1988. Original card wrappers, marked, presentation by Reg Terry in 1989 for Kathleen Tillotson. Jarndyce Antiquarian Booksellers   CCVII - 213   2015   £35

Forster, John *Dramatic Essays: Reprinted from the 'Examiner' and the 'Leader'.* London: Walter Scott, 1896. Half title, frontispiece, 4 pages ads, original maroon cloth, spine slightly faded, lacking leading free endpaper, stitching slightly weakening, top edge gilt, extensive ms. notes by Kathleen Tillotson. Jarndyce Antiquarian Booksellers   CCVII - 361   2015   £35

Galton, Arthur *Two Essays Upon Matthew Arnold with Some of His Letters to the Author.* London: Elkin Mathews, 1897. Uncut in original blue boards, printed cloth spine, slightly marked and dusted, from the library of Geoffrey & Kathleen Tillotson. Jarndyce Antiquarian Booksellers   CCVII - 65   2015   £25

Gaskell, Elizabeth Cleghorn 1810-1865 *Mary Barton and Other Tales.* London: Smith, Elder & Co., 1891. New edition, half title, frontispiece, 4 pages ads, from the library of Geoffrey & Kathleen Tillotson, home made paper wrappers with paper label, Kathleen has made few notes in text and marginal marks and inserted handwritten copy of preface to first edition in envelope affixed to half title, with postcard portrait of author. Jarndyce Antiquarian Booksellers   CCVII - 274   2015   £20

Gaskell, Elizabeth Cleghorn 1810-1865 *Mary Barton: a Tale of Manchester Life.* Leipzig: Bernhard Tauchnitz, 1849. Copyright edition, half title, bookseller's stamps, contemporary half calf, rebacked, retaining original spine strip with red label and initials A.I.T., bookplate of Anthony Philip Martineau Walker, ownership inscription of Anne Thackeray (Ritchie), with note by Kathleen Tillotson that Captain Walker gave her the book. Jarndyce Antiquarian Booksellers   CCVII - 273   2015   £50

Gettmann, Royal A. *A Victorian Publisher: a Study of the Bentley Papers.* Cambridge: University Press, 1960. Half title, plates, original blue cloth in torn dust jacket, inscribed by Kathleen Tillotson with few internal marks, inserted notes, draft and typescript review. Jarndyce Antiquarian Booksellers   CCVII - 87   2015   £40

Gibson, Colin *Art and Society in the Victorian Novel.* London: Macmillan Press, 1989. Half title, few notes by Kathleen Tillotson, her signed copy, original olive brown cloth, very good in dust jacket, with inserted postcard from Philip (Collins?). Jarndyce Antiquarian Booksellers   CCVII - 277   2015   £25

Gissing, George *Thyrza: a Tale.* London: John Murray, 1907. New edition, half title, original pink cloth, little faded, leading f.e.p. cut out, from the library of Geoffrey & Kathleen Tillotson, marked from Kathleen to Geoffrey, 1937 with 2 notes and 2 press cuttings inserted. Jarndyce Antiquarian Booksellers   CCVII - 278   2015   £20

Godwin, Francis *The Man in the Moone and Nuncius Inanimatus...* Northampton: Smith College, 1937. pages 25-30 torn without loss, original grey printed wrappers, slightly marked with splits at tail of spine, Kathleen Tillotson's marked copy, with typescript proofs and copy of her review.　Jarndyce Antiquarian Booksellers　CCVII - 279　2015　£20

Gray, Thomas　1716-1771 *An Elegy Written in a Country Churchyard.* London: printed by Edward Walters & Geoffrey Miller at Primrose Hill, 1933. 4to., title in red, uncut in original grey printed boards, cream buckram spine, spine label defective, dusted, complimentary copy of the 125 copies on handmade paper, 125 also on machine paper, from the library of Geoffrey & Kathleen Tillotson, review copy for the TLS with inserted notes by Geoffrey.　Jarndyce Antiquarian Booksellers　CCVII - 285　2015　£50

Gray, Thomas　1716-1771 *An Elegy Wrote in a Country Church Yard (1751) and the Eton College Manuscript...* Los Angeles: William Andrews Clark Memorial Lib., 1951. 4to., plates, facsimiles, original orange printed wrappers, dusted, from the library of Geoffrey & Kathleen Tillotson.　Jarndyce Antiquarian Booksellers　CCVII - 286　2015　£25

Gray, Thomas　1716-1771 *The Poems of Mr. Gray.* London: printed for G. Kearsley, 1786. from the library of Geoffrey & Kathleen Tillotson. red paper covered card wrappers by Geoffrey Tillotson, with calligraphic "prize label" at front "rweard of merit Thos. Hodges 1795".　Jarndyce Antiquarian Booksellers　CCVII - 281　2015　£45

Gray, Thomas　1716-1771 *The Poems.* Printed for White, Cochrane & Co. by S. Hamilton, Weybridge, Surrey, 1814. Contemporary half red calf, spine tooled gilt and blind, green labels, attractive copy, few pencil marks, from the library of Geoffrey & Kathleen Tillotson.　Jarndyce Antiquarian Booksellers　CCVII - 282　2015　£45

Greg, Walter Wilson *The Editorial Problem in Shakespeare.* Oxford: Clarendon Press, 1942. Original dark blue cloth, faded, from the library of Geoffrey & Kathleen Tillotson, with her name in Geoffrey's hand and with ink note by Geoffrey, exchange of letters between Greg and Geoffrey preserved in envelope tipped on to following pastedown, with other notes.　Jarndyce Antiquarian Booksellers　CCVII - 462　2015　£25

Grimaldi, Joseph　1779-1837 *Memoirs of Joseph Grimaldi.* London: Richard Bentley, 1846. New edition, Frontispiece, plates slightly spotted or browned, illustrations by George Cruikshank, spotted or browned, original beige cloth, printed in red, spine little sunned, surface slightly rubbed, good, sound, from the library of Geoffrey & Kathleen Tillotson.　Jarndyce Antiquarian Booksellers　CCVII - 182　2015　£75

Grossmith, George *The Diary of a Nobody.* Bristol: J. W. Arrowsmith; London: Simpkin Marshall, Hamilton, Kent and Co., 1910. Binding covered in brown decorated paper by Geoffrey Tillotson, from the library of Geoffrey & Kathleen Tillotson, paper label.　Jarndyce Antiquarian Booksellers　CCVII - 290　2015　£25

Hanson, Lawrence *The Four Brontes: the Lives and Works of Charlotte, Branwell, Emily and Anne Bronte.* London: Oxford University Press, 1949. Half title, frontispiece and plates, original red cloth, signed by Kathleen Tillotson Nov.-Dec. 1949, with many notes in text and insertions.　Jarndyce Antiquarian Booksellers　CCVII - 100　2015　£35

Harpsfield, Nicholas *The Life and Death of Sir Thomas Moore...* London: OUP, 1932. Half title, frontispiece and plates, 8 page catalog, handsome full white pigskin with elaborate pattern in blind and gilt, blind and gilt dentelles, marbled endpapers, fine in lined marbled slipcase, from the library of Geoffrey & Kathleen Tillotson, gilt lettered on front from GT, KMC 21XL 33 and with signed inscription from both editors to Tillotson's, with inserted p.c. from R. W. Chambers1933 and ALS from Gertrude Chambers and Edith Batho.　Jarndyce Antiquarian Booksellers　CCVII - 381　2015　£250

Harris, Elizabeth Furlong Skipton *From Oxford to Rome and How It Fared with Some Who Lately Made the Journey.* London: Longmans, 1847. Original dark brown cloth, worn at head and tail of spine, frontispiece, ownership inscription of JAS Southern? with long note by Geoffrey Tillotson, from the library of Geoffrey & Kathleen Tillotson.　Jarndyce Antiquarian Booksellers　CCVII - 294　2015　£150

Herbert, George *The Works.* Oxford: Clarendon Press, 1941. Half title, frontispiece, facsimiles, uncut, original dark blue cloth, inner hinge cracking, from the library of Geoffrey & Kathleen Tillotson, signed by Geoffrey, ALs from editor, pencil notes, insertions.　Jarndyce Antiquarian Booksellers　CCVII - 297　2015　£35

Holloway, John *The Victorian Sage: Studies in Argument.* London: Macmillan, 1953. Half title, original green cloth, very good in slightly torn dust jacket, from the library of Geoffrey & Kathleen Tillotson, Geoffrey's signed advance review copy with extensive notes, and some insertions. Jarndyce Antiquarian Booksellers   CCVII - 301   2015   £20

Honan, Park *Jane Austen: Her Life.* London: Weidenfeld & Nicholson, 1987. Half title, plates, original black cloth, very good in dust jacket, from the library of Geoffrey & Kathleen Tillotson, with inserted postcard from Kathleen. Jarndyce Antiquarian Booksellers   CCVII - 79   2015   £45

Honan, Park *Matthew Arnold: a Life.* New York: McGraw Hill, 1981. Half title, plates, original grey boards, white cloth spine, very good in creased, dust jacket, author's presentation to Kathleen Tillotson with letters from him and note by her inserted.   Jarndyce Antiquarian Booksellers   CCVII - 66   2015   £30

Hood, Thomas 1799-1845 *The Letters.* Toronto: University of Toronto Press, 1973. Half title, frontispiece, original dark blue cloth, very good in creased and marked dust jacket, editor (Peter F. Morgan) presentation copy to Kathleen Tillotson, with 2 page ALS from him inserted and inserted notes by her.   Jarndyce Antiquarian Booksellers   CCVII - 303   2015   £35

Hopkins, Gerard Manley *The Journals and Papers.* London: Oxford University Press, 1967. Half title, frontispiece, plates, music, original brown buckram, very good in slightly torn dust jacket, from the library of Geoffrey & Kathleen Tillotson.   Jarndyce Antiquarian Booksellers   CCVII - 306   2015   £25

Hopkins, Gerard Manley *The Poems.* London: Oxford University Press, 1967. Fourth edition, half title, original green cloth, very good in dust jacket, from the library of Geoffrey & Kathleen Tillotson.   Jarndyce Antiquarian Booksellers   CCVII - 304   2015   £25

Horatius Flaccus, Quintus *Translating Homer: Thirty Odes Translated...* Oxford: Bruno Cassirer, 1956. Half title, parallel English & Latin text, original light brown cloth, very good in slightly dusted and chipped dust jacket, from the library of Geoffrey & Kathleen Tillotson, signed by both, with signed presentation slip from J. B. Leishman laid in, with ALS's from him to Tillotson's.   Jarndyce Antiquarian Booksellers   CCVII - 309   2015   £20

House, Humphry *All in Due Time.* London: Rupert Hart-Davis, 1955. Half title, original red cloth, torn dust jacket, from the library of Geoffrey & Kathleen Tillotson, inscribed "Tillotson's 1955" with pencil notes, ALS from House's widow Madeline thanking Geoffrey for his review, with note and short review by Kathleen.   Jarndyce Antiquarian Booksellers   CCVII - 312   2015   £20

James, Henry 1843-1916 *The Notebooks.* New York: Oxford University Press, 1947. Original blue cloth, spine faded, from the library of Geoffrey & Kathleen Tillotson, inscribed by Geoffrey for Kathleen, Harvard 20.II.45, inserted is tatty folded copy of dust jacket containing cuttings of significant reviews of book and about James.   Jarndyce Antiquarian Booksellers   CCVII - 324   2015   £20

Jeffrey, Francis *Jeffrey's Criticism: a Selection.* Edinburgh: Scottish Academic Press, 1983. Frontispiece, original blue cloth, very good in slightly marked dust jacket, Kathleen Tillotson's dedication copy with inscription from editor, Peter Morgan with 2 page TLS from him 21 March 1983 at University College Toronto.   Jarndyce Antiquarian Booksellers   CCVII - 326   2015   £25

Johnson, Samuel 1709-1784 *A Journey to the Western Islands of Scotland.* New Haven: Yale University Press, 1971. Half title, folding map, plates, original blue cloth, very good in slightly creased dust jacket, Mary Lascelles (editor) presentation copy to Kathleen Tillotson with one ink correction in Tillotson's hand and inserted reviews.   Jarndyce Antiquarian Booksellers   CCVII - 331   2015   £40

Johnson, Samuel 1709-1784 *Diaries, Prayers and Annals.* New Haven: Yale University Press, 1958. Half title, plates, original blue cloth, very good in slightly torn dust jacket, from the library of Geoffrey & Kathleen Tillotson, signed by Kathleen for Geoffrey 25 De. 59, with inserted long review in TLS and correspondence between Geoffrey and others about revised edition.   Jarndyce Antiquarian Booksellers   CCVII - 327   2015   £45

Johnson, Samuel 1709-1784 *Lives of the English Poets.* Oxford: at the Clarendon Press, 1905. 3 volumes, original red cloth, hinges little rubbed, from the library of Geoffrey & Kathleen Tillotson, Kathleen's gift to Geoffrey Christmas 1937 with extensive notes and insertions including correspondence with R. W. Chapman and others.   Jarndyce Antiquarian Booksellers   CCVII - 332   2015   £75

Johnson, Samuel 1709-1784 *The History of Rasselas, Prince of Abissinia.* London: Oxford University Press, 1971. Half title, original blue cloth, very good in dust jacket, with note at end by Kathleen Tillotson about distribution and some inserted correspondence.   Jarndyce Antiquarian Booksellers   CCVII - 329   2015   £18

Johnson, Samuel 1709-1784 *The Letters, with Mrs. Thrale's Genuine Letters to Him.* Oxford: Clarendon Press, 1952. 3 volumes, half title, frontispiece, plate, few pencil notes, original maroon cloth in slightly worn dust jacket, with cuttings of review and obits of R. W. Chapman inserted, from the library of Geoffrey & Kathleen Tillotson. Jarndyce Antiquarian Booksellers CCVII - 335 2015 £45

Jones, Enid *Margery Fry: the Essential Amateur.* London: Oxford University Press, 1966. Half title, frontispiece and plates, mark at end of text, original blue cloth, slightly marked in slightly torn dust jacket, from the library of Geoffrey & Kathleen Tillotson with author's presentation inscription pasted to endpaper and ALS from her to Kathleen, and cuttings of 2 reviews inserted. Jarndyce Antiquarian Booksellers CCVII - 271 2015 £25

Keats, John 1795-1821 *Hyperion: a Facsimile of Keats's autograph manuscript.* Oxford: Clarendon Press, 1905. Folio, 27 pages facsimiles, colophon leaf, original green printed boards, beige buckram spine, corners rubbed, dusted, from the library of Geoffrey & Kathleen Tillotson, signed by Geoffrey 1942 with note by Kathleen. Jarndyce Antiquarian Booksellers CCVII - 345 2015 £85

Keats, John 1795-1821 *The Poetical Works.* London: Oxford University Press, 1922. Frontispiece, plate, original brown cloth, hinges repaired, signed Kathleen M. Constable (Tillotson) Sept. 1926 with ink and pencil notes, insertions and related cutting. Jarndyce Antiquarian Booksellers CCVII - 343 2015 £25

Keats, John 1795-1821 *The Poetical Works.* Oxford: Clarendon Press, 1958. Second edition, half title, frontispiece, original dark blue cloth, very good in slightly torn and dust jacket, with review of Keats' 'Letters' 1959 inserted, from the library of Geoffrey & Kathleen Tillotson. Jarndyce Antiquarian Booksellers CCVII - 344 2015 £35

Kendall, May *Dreams to Sell.* London: Longmans, 1887. First edition, half title in red & black, uncut in original crimson cloth, bevelled boards, spine faded, top edge gilt, presentation inscription to Gilbert Redgrave, bibliographer and art historian from Frances and Evelyn Redgrave 12 may, 1889, note by former of short and apologetic AL from authoress dated Aug. 4th 1892 in another hand: Association books No. 67 and 1945 signature of John Gilman, from the library of Geoffrey & Kathleen Tillotson. Jarndyce Antiquarian Booksellers CCVII - 350 2015 £50

Kent, Charles *Charles Dickens as a Reader.* London: Chapman & Hall, 1872. First edition, plates, original green cloth, dulled, label removed from leading pastedown, stamps and pressmark of Malvern Public Library, from the library of Geoffrey & Kathleen Tillotson, with note by Kathleen. Jarndyce Antiquarian Booksellers CCVII - 216 2015 £50

Ketton-Cremer, Robert Wyndham *Thomas Gray: a Biography.* Cambridge: at the University Press, 1955. Half title, frontispiece, marginal pencl marks, original maroon cloth, slightly torn dust jacket, author's signed presentation copy for Geoffrey and Kathleen Tillotson, with accompanying letter laid down and draft of Geoffrey's letter of thanks, other correspondence, typescript of Geoffrey's review and press cuttings. Jarndyce Antiquarian Booksellers CCVII - 289 2015 £40

Kipling, Rudyard 1865-1936 *Verse.* London: Hodder & Stoughton, 1930. Fifth impression, half title creased, title in red and black, india paper, original red cloth, inner hinge splitting, top edge gilt, from the library of Geoffrey & Kathleen Tillotson. Jarndyce Antiquarian Booksellers CCVII - 352 2015 £30

Knight, George Wilson *The Burning Oracle.* London: Oxford University Press, 1939. Half title, uncut in original maroon cloth, slightly marked, from the library of Geoffrey & Kathleen Tillotson, Kathleen's review copy with ms. and penned review, with ALS from author to Geoffrey 1944 and long TLS article about him as critic. Jarndyce Antiquarian Booksellers CCVII - 353 2015 £30

Knight, George Wilson *The Imperial Theme.* London: Oxford University Press, 1931. Uncut, half title, original maroon cloth, Kathleen Tillotson's copy as Kathleen M. Constable with 2 pages notes. Jarndyce Antiquarian Booksellers CCVII - 463 2015 £20

Knowles, James Sheridan *The Love Chase. A comedy in Five Acts (bound with) Love. A Play.* London: Edward Moxon, 1837. 1839. First edition, and fifth edition respectively, half titles, initial ad leaf in 'Love', titlepage of 'Love Chase' detached and chipped at edges, 2 volumes in 1, early marbled boards, cloth spine rubbed and chipped, inner hinges weakening, 75th birthday gift to Kathleen Tillotson from friend Wendy Rintoul, each play inscribed by author to Mr. Norman. Jarndyce Antiquarian Booksellers CCVII - 354 2015 £35

Kyd, Joseph Clayton Clark *Characters from Charles Dickens.* London: John Player & Sons, 1889. Set of 50 standard size coloured cigarette cards good clean set, in envelope possibly indicating purchase by Kathleen Tillotson from Dickens House. Jarndyce Antiquarian Booksellers CCVII - 217 2015 £120

Lang, Andrew *Ballads of Books.* London: Longmans, 1885. First edition, half title, title in red and black, uncut in original blue bevelled boards, spine slightly faded, cutting removed from endpaper, ticket of Slatter & Rose, Oxford, top edge gilt, signed by S. C. Rawlinson 1889 and with 3 related ms. insertions, from the library of Geoffrey & Kathleen Tillotson. Jarndyce Antiquarian Booksellers CCVII - 355 2015 £85

Lascelles, Mary Madge *Jane Austen and Her Art.* Oxford: Clarendon Press, 1939. Half title, original dark blue cloth, slightly marked, Kathleen Tillotson's signed copy with her friend's presentation slip. Jarndyce Antiquarian Booksellers CCVII - 80 2015 £40

Leishman, James Blair *Milton's Minor Poems.* London: Hutchinson, 1969. First edition, half title, original dark green cloth, very good in torn dust jacket, from the library of Geoffrey & Kathleen Tillotson. Jarndyce Antiquarian Booksellers CCVII - 377 2015 £38

Leishman, James Blair *The Art of Marvell's Poetry.* Hutchinson University Library, 1968. Second edition, with proof copy of first edition, 1965, few ms. corrections and insertions, dust jacket, from the library of Geoffrey & Kathleen Tillotson. Jarndyce Antiquarian Booksellers CCVII - 357 2015 £38

Leishman, James Blair *The Three Parnassus Plays 1598-1601.* London: Ivor Nicholson & Watson, 1949. Half title, original black cloth, very good in torn dust jacket, editor's presentation to Geoffrey and Kathleen Tillotson. Jarndyce Antiquarian Booksellers CCVII - 358 2015 £30

Lewis, Clive Staples 1898-1963 *The Allegory of Love: a Study in Medieval Tradition.* Oxford: Clarendon Press, 1936. from the library of Geoffrey & Kathleen Tillotson. original dark blue cloth, slightly marked, signed with initials and few pencil notes and marked proof of Kathleen's review. Jarndyce Antiquarian Booksellers CCVII - 362 2015 £25

Linton, Eliza Lynn *My Literary Life...* London: Hodder & Stoughton, 1899. Title in red and black, uncut in original yellow cloth, rather dulled, from the library of Geoffrey & Kathleen Tillotson. Jarndyce Antiquarian Booksellers CCVII - 363 2015 £20

Lowndes, Walter *The Quakers of Fritchley.* Fritchley: Fritchley Preparative Meeting, 1986. Revised reprint, illustrations, original blue illustrated wrappers, slightly marked, title roughly written on spine, Kathleen Tillotson's copy with few notes, inserted letter from Mary Lascelles and letter and notes by Kathleen about new edition, etc. Jarndyce Antiquarian Booksellers CCVII - 366 2015 £25

MacDonald, George 1824-1905 *Phantastes; a Faerie Romance for Men and Women.* London: Smith, Elder & Co., 1858. First edition, bound without half title, small corner torn form title, few marginal marks, contemporary half calf, rubbed, split in following hinge but sound, bookplate of Augustus Taylor Day, from the library of Geoffrey & Kathleen Tillotson. Jarndyce Antiquarian Booksellers CCVII - 368 2015 £520

Mallock, William Hurrell *Lucretius on Life and Death in the Metre of Omar Khayyam...* London: Adam & Charles Black, 1901. Original olive green cloth, embossed head, stab holes in endpapers, slightly marked and rubbed, from the library of Geoffrey & Kathleen Tillotson, undated presentation ANS from author and 2 page ALS from him to Williamson. Jarndyce Antiquarian Booksellers CCVII - 372 2015 £20

Marryat, Frederick 1792-1848 *Poor Jack.* London: Longmans, 1840. First edition, frontispiece, plates, illustrations by Clarkson Stanfield, some plates foxed, small portrait of author laid down on leading pastedown, uncut in original dark green cloth blocked in blind and gilt, at some time neatly recased, good, sound copy, from the library of Geoffrey & Kathleen Tillotson. Jarndyce Antiquarian Booksellers CCVII - 373 2015 £75

McKillop, Alan Dugald *Restoration and Eighteenth Century Literature...* Chicago: University of Chicago Press for William Marsh Rice University, 1963. Half title, original blue and grey cloth, very good in dust jacket, from the library of Geoffrey & Kathleen Tillotson. Jarndyce Antiquarian Booksellers CCVII - 370 2015 £20

Milton, John 1608-1674 *The Poetical Works. Volume I. Paradise Lost.* Oxford: Clarendon Press, 1952. Uncut in original dark blue cloth, very good in slightly creased dust jacket, with printed editor's presentation slip and ALS from editor, Helen Darbishire to Kathleen Tillotson, with review cutting, from the library of Geoffrey & Kathleen Tillotson, signed by both Nov. 8 1952. Jarndyce Antiquarian Booksellers CCVII - 376 2015 £20

Moorman, Mary *William Wordsworth: a biography.* Oxford: Oxford University Press, 1965. Half title, frontispiece, plates, original dark blue cloth, very good in slightly dusted dust jacket, Kathleen Tillotson's copy with inserted markers in text, cuttings of reviews and ALS form author. Jarndyce Antiquarian Booksellers CCVII - 576 2015 £30

Newdigate, Bernard H. *Michael Drayton and His Circle.* Oxford: printed at Shakespeare Head Press, 1941. Half title, frontispiece, addenda & separate corrigenda slip, uncut in original dark blue cloth uniform with Drayton's Works, tipped in is charming presentation note from author to Kathleen Tillotson, inserted are some photos and unsigned account of visit to Polesworth in 1928. Jarndyce Antiquarian Booksellers CCVII - 242 2015 £35

ASSOCIATION COPIES

Newman, John Henry 1801-1890 *Hymni Ecclesiae, Excerpti e Breviariis Romano, Salisburiensi, eboracensi...* Oxonii: J. H. Parker, 1838. 4 pages ads, original grey cloth, paper label, spine defective, scarce, inscribed Francis Palgrave from his affectionate NJ and EJJ Jan. 10 1839, from the library of Geoffrey & Kathleen Tillotson.   Jarndyce Antiquarian Booksellers   CCVII - 396   2015   £180

Newman, John Henry 1801-1890 *Prose and Poetry.* London: Rupert Hart Davis, 1957. Half title, few pencil notes, original dark blue cloth, bevelled boards, very good in torn dust jacket, from the library of Geoffrey & Kathleen Tillotson, with his inscription to her 25.xii.56 with few inserted notes.   Jarndyce Antiquarian Booksellers   CCVII - 392   2015   £35

Newman, John Henry 1801-1890 *Verses on Religious Subjects.* Dublin: James Duffy, 1853. First edition, contemporary calf, gilt borders and dentelles, spine chipped, boards detached, scarce, John Duke Coleridge's copy signed on original preserved endpaper, from the library of Geoffrey & Kathleen Tillotson.   Jarndyce Antiquarian Booksellers   CCVII - 394   2015   £220

Nicholson, William 1872-1949 *An Almanac of Twelve Sports.* London: William Heinemann, 1898. 4to., illustrations, 1 page ad verso final leaf, original illustrated paper boards, cloth spine repaired, some rubbing to edges and corners, inner hinges strengthened, from the library of Geoffrey & Kathleen Tillotson, with Kathleen's note recording joint pruchase.   Jarndyce Antiquarian Booksellers   CCVII - 400   2015   £420

Nowell-Smith, Simon *Letters to Macmillan.* London: Macmillan, 1967. Half title, plates, facsimiles, original red cloth, very good in slightly marked dust jacket, editor's signed copy, from the library of Geoffrey & Kathleen Tillotson, presentation inscription to same with note by Kathleen inserted.   Jarndyce Antiquarian Booksellers   CCVII - 401   2015   £20

Onwhyn, Thomas *Thirty-Two Plates to Illustrate the Cheap edition of Nicholas Nickleby...* London: J. Newman, 1848. 8 parts, plates slightly browned but not foxed, original green printed wrappers to each part, 1 split along spine and slightly chipped, 4 with some splitting, good set, scarce, in brown envelope with notes by Kathleen Tillotson indicating a gift from Simon Nowell-Smith.   Jarndyce Antiquarian Booksellers   CCVII - 219   2015   £180

Ortega Y Gasset, Jose *The Dehumanization of Art and Notes on the Novel.* Princeton: Princeton Univ. Press, 1948. Half title, original brown cloth, very good in darkened dust jacket, from the library of Geoffrey & Kathleen Tillotson, his gift to her Xmas 1949, few pencil notes.   Jarndyce Antiquarian Booksellers   CCVII - 403   2015   £20

Palgrave, Francis Turner 1824-1897 *The Five Days Entertainments at Wentworth Garage.* London: Macmillan & Co., 1868. First edition, half title, plates and illustrations by Arthur Hughes, 2 pages ad, original blue cloth, inner hinges splitting, rubbed and dulled, top edge gilt, with slightly damaged half title and partly obscured presentation to Gwenllian Florence Palgrave 1866-1951, one of the dedicatees from her father 1873, overwritten in pencil with her childish signature, from the library of Geoffrey & Kathleen Tillotson.   Jarndyce Antiquarian Booksellers   CCVII - 404   2015   £60

Palgrave, Francis Turner 1824-1897 *The Golden Treasury of the Best Songs and Lyrical Poems in the English Language.* Cambridge: Macmillan and Co., 1861. First edition, second impression, lacking half title and leading f.e.p., original green glazed cloth by Burn, slightly rubbed, bookseller's ticket of Thomas Brady, York, Kathleen Tillotson's copy with pencil notes above variants, she had written on it sources, with copy of the Penguin Classics edition edited by Christopher Ricks 1991, with ink notes and containing drafts of letter from Kathleen to Ricks about Palgrave's annotated copy of Nightingale Valley.   Jarndyce Antiquarian Booksellers   CCVII - 405   2015   £30

Palgrave, Francis Turner 1824-1897 *The Visions of England. Second Part.* London: printed for F. T. Palgrave by Cousins & Co., 1881. First edition, one of 50 copies dated April 1881, marked by Palgrave 'To be returned' with faint address on wrapper and signed by him in pencil on top edge gilt 22 Ap 1881, from the library of Geoffrey & Kathleen Tillotson.   Jarndyce Antiquarian Booksellers   CCVII - 406   2015   £58

A Poetry Book for National Schools. London: Bell & Daldy, 1857. New edition, frontispiece and numerous engravings, some marginal tears, original brown cloth, rebacked with back cloth, inner hinges strengthened, from the library of Geoffrey & Kathleen Tillotson.   Jarndyce Antiquarian Booksellers   CCVII - 9   2015   £300

A Proper Sonnet from a Gorgeous Gallery of Gallant Inventions. printed in the Dept. of English at the University College, London, 1935. Small 4to., original orange brown printed wrappers, (2), 4, (2) pages, from the library of Geoffrey & Kathleen Tillotson.   Jarndyce Antiquarian Booksellers   CCVII - 8   2015   £45

Pope, Alexander 1688-1744 *Imitations of Horace with an Epistle to Dr. Arbuthnot and The Epilogue to the Satires.* London: Methuen, 1939. Uncorrected page proofs, half title, from the library of Geoffrey & Kathleen Tillotson, with Geoffrey's pencil marks in introduction only, with Geoffrey's card and decorated paper wrappers with ms. label on spine, staples slightly rusting.   Jarndyce Antiquarian Booksellers   CCVII - 410   2015   £20

Pope, Alexander 1688-1744 *The Correspondence.* Oxford: Clarendon Press, 1956. 5 volumes, half titles, frontispieces, original maroon cloth, very slightly torn dust jackets, good set, from the library of Geoffrey & Kathleen Tillotson, with TLS review copies with few pencil notes by Geoffrey, with insertions including letters from editor and offprints.   Jarndyce Antiquarian Booksellers   CCVII - 424   2015   £225

Pope, Alexander 1688-1744 *The Rape of the Lock.* London: Methuen and New Haven: Yale University Press, 1962. Third Tillotson edition, Twickenham edition volume II, half title frontispiece, plates, original brick red cloth, following inner hinge cracking, slightly dusted, torn dust jacket, from the library of Geoffrey & Kathleen Tillotson, Geoffrey Tillotson's copy signed, with few pencil marks and note by Kathleen on dust jacket stating it was 'Work copy'.   Jarndyce Antiquarian Booksellers   CCVII - 421   2015   £40

Praz, Mario *The Hero in Eclipse in Victorian Fiction.* London: Oxford University Press, 1956. Original black cloth, split at tail of spine, half title plates, slightly worn dust jacket, Kathleen Tillotson's review copy with a letter form her to editor of Review of English Studies, with cuttings of her reviews.   Jarndyce Antiquarian Booksellers   CCVII - 441   2015   £35

Purdy, Richard Little *Thomas Hardy: a Bibliographical Study.* London: Oxford University Press, 1954. Half title, plates, original green cloth, inner hinge splitting, marked and slightly distorted by damp, Kathleen Tillotson's copy sent by Oxford press in payment for a report, with inserted correspondence.   Jarndyce Antiquarian Booksellers   CCVII - 293   2015   £25

Raleigh, Walter 1552-1618 *The Poems.* London: Constable & Co., 1929. Half title, uncut, original red buckram, slightly dulled, top edge gilt, Kathleen Tillotson's copy signed Kathleen M. Constable, June 14 1929 with few pencil marks, review from Sat. rev. 1929 and article about new ms. 1925 inserted.   Jarndyce Antiquarian Booksellers   CCVII - 442   2015   £20

Rawnsley, Hardwicke Drummond *Reminiscences of Wordsworth Among the Peasantry of Westmoreland.* London: Dillon's, 1968. Frontispiece, original pink cloth, slightly marked, very good in slightly rubbed dust jacket, Kathleen Tillotson's copy with correspondence, reviews &c. inserted.   Jarndyce Antiquarian Booksellers   CCVII - 578   2015   £30

Ray, Gordon N. *Books as a Way of Life: Essays...* New York: Grolier Club, Pierpont Morgan Library, 1988. Frontispiece, original red cloth, from the library of Geoffrey & Kathleen Tillotson, very good in slightly marked dust jacket, with inserted ALS from editor thanking Kathleen for her generous appreciations.   Jarndyce Antiquarian Booksellers   CCVII - 443   2015   £20

Ray, Gordon N. *Nineteenth Century English Books...* Urbana: University of Illinois Press, 1952. Half title, title in red and black, original red and grey cloth, from the library of Geoffrey & Kathleen Tillotson, Geoffrey Tillotson's copy for Review of English Studies with pencil notes and copy of his review inserted, and other reviews, TLS from Gordon Ray to Tillotson's Jan. 1953 inserted.   Jarndyce Antiquarian Booksellers   CCVII - 445   2015   £25

Ray, Gordon N. *Thackeray: the Age of Wisdom 1847-1863.* New York: McGraw Hill, 1958. Half title, plates, original maroon cloth, very good in torn dust jacket, from the library of Geoffrey & Kathleen Tillotson, author's presentation for them.   Jarndyce Antiquarian Booksellers   CCVII - 501   2015   £20

Ray, Gordon N. *The Illustrator and the Book in England from 1790 to 1914.* New York: Pierpont Morgan Lib., 1976. 4to., color frontispiece, plates, illustrations, original dark wrappers, decorated gilt, spine slightly faded, Kathleen Tillotson's signed copy recording it as gift from author, with cutting of TLS review inserted.   Jarndyce Antiquarian Booksellers   CCVII - 444   2015   £25

Reynolds, Henry *The Tale of Narcissus.* Hull: J. R. Tutin, 1906. One of 666 copies, one page creased, uncut, original printed wrappers, dusted and slightly creased, inscribed on front wrapper from Tutin to Oliver Elton and by Elton to Kathleen Tillotson with compliments.   Jarndyce Antiquarian Booksellers   CCVII - 446   2015   £25

Ross, Ronald *In Exile.* Liverpool: privately printed, 1906. First edition, pencil and occasional ink notes and corrections, original maroon printed paper wrappers, slightly creased with slight loss to upper corner front wrapper, presentation inscription "With Sir Ronald Ross's compliments. Author's working copy see page 6, 22, see especially page 81", from the collection of Kathleen and Geoffrey Tillotson.   Jarndyce Antiquarian Booksellers   CCXI - 245   2015   £250

Shearer, Thomas *Percy's Relations with Cadell and Davies..* London: Bibliographical Society, 1934. Reprinted from Transactions of the Bibliographical Society Sept. 1934, Original grey printed wrappers, slightly dusted, from the library of Geoffrey & Kathleen Tillotson.   Jarndyce Antiquarian Booksellers   CCVII - 408   2015   £30

Sherburn, George *Pope and His Contemporaries: Essays Presented to George Sherburn.* Oxford: at the Clarendon Press, 1949. Half title, portrait, printed presentation slip, original dark blue cloth in slightly torn and dusted dust jacket, from the library of Geoffrey & Kathleen Tillotson. Jarndyce Antiquarian Booksellers   CCVII - 429   2015   £40

Shuster, George N. *The English Ode from Milton to Keats.* New York: Columbia Univ. Press, 1940. Half title, original blue cloth, very good in slightly torn dust jacket, from the library of Geoffrey & Kathleen Tillotson with inserted notes by Geoffrey.   Jarndyce Antiquarian Booksellers   CCVII - 468   2015   £20

Smith, Sheila M. *The Other Nation: the Poor in English Novels of the 1840s and 1850s.* Oxford: Clarendon Press, 1980. Half title, plates, original dark blue cloth, very good in dust jacket, ALS from author inserted thanking her for her review, Kathleen Tillotson's signed copy.   Jarndyce Antiquarian Booksellers   CCVII - 475   2015   £20

Spurgeon, Caroline *Shakespeare's Imagery and What It Tells Us.* Cambridge: University Press, 1935. Half title, frontispiece, color folding table, original brown cloth, from the library of Geoffrey & Kathleen Tillotson, with press cutting of review.   Jarndyce Antiquarian Booksellers   CCVII - 466   2015   £35

Stang, Richard *The Theory of the Novel in England 1850-1870.* London: Routledge & Kegan Paul, 1959. Half title, original red cloth, torn dust jacket, signed by Kathleen Tillotson in 1959 with pencil notes referring the book to Nina Burgis, typescript, proof and printed text inserted. Jarndyce Antiquarian Booksellers   CCVII - 476   2015   £25

Sturge, Helen Winifred *The Mount School, York, 1785 to 1814, 1831 to 1931.* London: J. M. Dent & Sons, 1931. Half title, frontispiece, plates, illustrations, few spots, original blue cloth, faded and slightly rubbed and marked, Kathleen Tillotson's signed copy with ALS asking her for information with typescript copy of her reply.   Jarndyce Antiquarian Booksellers   CCVII - 479   2015   £25

Sturge, Mary Charlotte *Some Little Quakers in their Nursery.* London: Simpkin Marshall, 1906. Half title, illustrations, original yellow cloth, mark on spine, else very good, signed presentation inscription to Nurse Gertrude from author, the Constable family copy, with pencil notes by Kathleen Tillotson inserted.   Jarndyce Antiquarian Booksellers   CCVII - 480   2015   £30

Swift, Jonathan   1667-1745 *The Poems of.* Oxford: at the Clarendon Press, 1937. 3 volumes, half titles, frontispieces, original blue cloth slightly torn and dusted dust jackets, Kathleen Tillotson's presentation copies for Geoffrey Tillotson, with few notes and insertions.   Jarndyce Antiquarian Booksellers   CCVII - 484   2015   £120

Tennyson, Alfred Tennyson, 1st Baron   1809-1892 *In Memoriam.* London: Edward Moxon, 1850. First edition, half title, without initial catalog, brown morocco presentation binding by Budden, Cambridge, little rubbed with small split in leading hinge, all edges gilt, lettered on front board, inscribed to Julain Fane from HAJ, with very poor copy of the 10th edition 1861 in original cloth, heavily annotated with insertions by Geoffrey Tillotson, from the library of Geoffrey & Kathleen Tillotson.   Jarndyce Antiquarian Booksellers CCVII - 486   2015   £350

Tennyson, Alfred Tennyson, 1st Baron   1809-1892 *Lyrical Poems.* London: Maxmillan, 1885. First edition, half title, 6 pages ads, pages 119-20 torn through without loss, uncut in remains of original blue boards, lacking spine strip, last gathering detached, possibly a proof copy, selected and annotated by Francis T. Palgrave, his copy, signed Mch 9 1885, but with no internal marks, from the library of Geoffrey & Kathleen Tillotson, inscribed by them.   Jarndyce Antiquarian Booksellers   CCVII - 487   2015   £45

Tennyson, Alfred Tennyson, 1st Baron   1809-1892 *Poems, Chiefly Lyrical.* London: Effingham Wilson, 1830. Uncut, recased in stiff paper with paper label, signature of Whitley Stokes 14/6/55, from the library of Geoffrey & Kathleen Tillotson.   Jarndyce Antiquarian Booksellers CCVII - 488   2015   £450

Tennyson, Alfred Tennyson, 1st Baron   1809-1892 *The Letters.* Oxford: Clarendon Press, 1987-1990. 3 volumes, half titles, original dark blue cloth, very good, in creased dust jacket, Kathleen Tillotson's copy with few notes, 4 ALS's from Cecil Lang to Kathleen, inserts.   Jarndyce Antiquarian Booksellers   CCVII - 490   2015   £125

Tennyson, Alfred Tennyson, 1st Baron   1809-1892 *The Princess, a Medley.* London: Edward Moxon, 1866. Original dark blue cloth, bevelled boards, embossed in gilt and blind, spine slightly faded, bookseller's ticket of Wm. Mullan, Belfast, all edges gilt, 26 illustrations engraved on wood, attractive larger format edition, Kathleen Tillotson's copy as K. Constable with earlier signature 1867 of great great aunt Anna Waring.   Jarndyce Antiquarian Booksellers CCVII - 489   2015   £85

Thackeray, William Makepeace 1811-1863 *The Letters and Private Papers of William Makepeace Thackeray.* London: Oxford University Press, 1945-1946. First edition, 4 volumes, half titles, plates, illustrations, original pink cloth, spines slightly faded, from the library of Geoffrey & Kathleen Tillotson, signed, some notes and markings by both. Jarndyce Antiquarian Booksellers   CCVII - 499   2015   £75

Thackeray, William Makepeace 1811-1863 *Vanity Fair.* Boston: Houghton Mifflin Co., 1963. Riverside edition, half title, illustrations, original printed boards, Kathleen Tillotson's copy with few alterations indicated to text and appendices, she notes this is first edition.   Jarndyce Antiquarian Booksellers   CCVII - 498   2015   £20

Tillotson, Geoffrey *Essays in Criticism and Research.* Cambridge: University Press, 1942. Half title, original red cloth, paper label, dulled and marked, author's inscription for wife Kathleen, dedication copy, ink corrections, insertions, few ink notes, ALS to Kathleen from Mary Lascelles 1937. Jarndyce Antiquarian Booksellers   CCVII - 520   2015   £50

Tillotson, Geoffrey *Mid-Victorian Studies.* London: Clarendon Press, 1965. Half title, original black cloth, pink paper label, very good in torn and dusted dust jacket, author's signed copy with few notes and insertions, note by co-author Kathleen on wrapper.   Jarndyce Antiquarian Booksellers   CCVII - 529   2015   £20

Tillotson, Geoffrey *On the Poetry of Pope.* Oxford: Clarendon Press, 1938. First edition, half title, original dark blue cloth, paper label slightly marked, inscribed by author for Kathleen Tillotson, with note by Kathleen?, preserved with this is copy made up of page proofs stamped 3 Sep. 1937 with typical GT colored paper casing.   Jarndyce Antiquarian Booksellers   CCVII - 433   2015   £120

Tillotson, Geoffrey *On the Poetry of Pope.* Oxford: Clarendon Press, 1950. Second edition, half title, original dark blue cloth paper label, 2 copies of dust jacket, signed by author, with publisher history by Kathleen on endpaper, inserted related correspondence and notes, from the library of Geoffrey & Kathleen Tillotson.   Jarndyce Antiquarian Booksellers   CCVII - 434   2015   £20

Tillotson, Geoffrey *Pope and Human Nature.* Oxford: Clarendon Press, 1958. Half title, original dark blue cloth, paper label, very good in dust jacket, inscribed to wife Kathleen.   Jarndyce Antiquarian Booksellers   CCVII - 436   2015   £20

Tillotson, Geoffrey *Thackeray the Novelist.* Cambridge: at the University Press, 1954. Half title, plate, original yellow cloth in slightly torn and dusted dust jacket, from the library of Geoffrey & Kathleen Tillotson, his presentationt o her with page of her notes inserted.   Jarndyce Antiquarian Booksellers   CCVII - 502   2015   £20

Tillyard, E. M. W. *The Personal Heresy: a Controversy.* London: Oxford University Press, 1939. Half title, from the library of Geoffrey & Kathleen Tillotson, very good in slightly torn dust jacket, Geoffrey Tillotson's signed copy with few notes, and proof of his review, Kathleen' special marker. Jarndyce Antiquarian Booksellers   CCVII - 538   2015   £30

Tuke, Margaret J. *A History of Bedford College for Women 1849-1937.* London: Oxford University Press, 1939. Half title, frontispiece and plates, folding tables, original purple cloth, slightly marked with split at head of spine, Kathleen Tillotson's copy with inserted material about Tuke. Jarndyce Antiquarian Booksellers   CCVII - 545   2015   £35

Tuve, Rosamond *Elizabethan and Metaphysical Imagery.* Chicago: University of Chicago Press, 1947. Half title, from the library of Geoffrey & Kathleen Tillotson, original red cloth, inscribed by author of Kathleen Tillotson, signed by Kathleen and Geoffrey, inserted review by Maynard Mack and review by Cleanth Brooks.   Jarndyce Antiquarian Booksellers   CCVII - 546   2015   £25

Tuve, Rosamond *Images and Themes in Five Poems by Milton.* Cambridge: Harvard University Press, 1957. Half title, original green cloth, very good in slightly torn dust jacket, author's signed presentation for Geoffrey and Kathleen Tillotson, with 4 TLS from author.   Jarndyce Antiquarian Booksellers   CCVII - 379   2015   £25

Wilson, Frank Percy *Elizabethan and Jacobean Studies Presented to Frank Percy Wilson in Honour of His Seventieth Birthday.* Oxford: Clarendon Press, 1959. Half title, frontispiece, plates, original dark blue cloth, very good in creased and slightly marked dust jacket, from the library of Geoffrey & Kathleen Tillotson.   Jarndyce Antiquarian Booksellers   CCVII - 555   2015   £35

Wimsatt, William Kurtz *Hateful Contraries: Studies in Literature and Criticism.* Lexington: University of Kentucky Press, Half title, original dark brown cloth, very good in slightly rubbed dust jacket, from the library of Geoffrey & Kathleen Tillotson, with Geoffrey's letter of thanks ofr the book.   Jarndyce Antiquarian Booksellers   CCVII - 556   2015   £20

Wodehouse, Pelham Grenville 1881-1975 *Performing Flea: a Self-Portrait in Letters.* London: Herbert Jenkins, 1954. Reprint, from the library of Geoffrey & Kathleen Tillotson, half title, frontispiece, original blue cloth, slightly torn dust jacket, few margin markers and number of press cuttings inserted by Kathleen, press cuttings. Jarndyce Antiquarian Booksellers   CCVII - 558   2015   £20

Wordsworth, William 1770-1850 *Lyrical Ballads 1798.* London: Oxford University Press, 1927. Original olive green cloth, signed KMC with ink and pencil notes, from the library of Geoffrey & Kathleen Tillotson.   Jarndyce Antiquarian Booksellers   CCVII - 150   2015   £20

Wordsworth, William 1770-1850 *Lyrical Ballads 1798-1805.* London: Methuen, 1944. Tenth edition, from the library of Geoffrey & Kathleen Tillotson, color paper wrappers by Geoffrey, with some notes and various inserts. Jarndyce Antiquarian Booksellers   CCVII - 573   2015   £50

Wordsworth, William 1770-1850 *Poems in Two volumes 1807.* Oxford: Clarendon Press, 1942. Original green printed cloth, 2 volumes, spine faded, inner hinges splitting, from the library of Geoffrey & Kathleen Tillotson, signed by them Oxford 26.iv.44 with copious notes and insertions. Jarndyce Antiquarian Booksellers   CCVII - 563   2015   £30

Wordsworth, William 1770-1850 *The Poetical Works.* Oxford: Oxford University Press, 1923. Half title, frontispiece, original blue cloth, battered copy, lacking spine strip, signed by Kathleen Tillotson as Constable and as Tillotson, further note records the gift from E. A. Constable.   Jarndyce Antiquarian Booksellers   CCVII - 565   2015   £30

Wordsworth, William 1770-1850 *The Prelude.* Darbishire: Clarendon Press, 1959. Second edition, half title, frontispiece, plates, original dark blue cloth, very good in slightly worn dust jacket, from the library of Geoffrey & Kathleen Tillotson, with few marginal and inserted notes. Jarndyce Antiquarian Booksellers   CCVII - 569   2015   £30

Wordsworth, William 1770-1850 *The Prelude.* Oxford: Clarendon Press, 1926. Half title, frontispiece, plates, original brown buckram, paper label browned and chipped, inner hinge cracking, Kathleen Tillotson's copy as Kathleen Constable, and name Eric Constable, many pencil notes by Tillotson.   Jarndyce Antiquarian Booksellers   CCVII - 568   2015   £35

Yeats, William Butler 1865-1939 *Essays.* London: Macmillan, 1924. First edition, from the library of Geoffrey & Kathleen Tillotson, half title, original cloth covered by Geoffrey in handmade paper, spine browned, inner hinges cracking, signed by Geoffrey 3x34 with few pencil notes at end.   Jarndyce Antiquarian Booksellers   CCVII - 580   2015   £20

Yonge, Charlotte Mary 1823-1901 *Last Heartsease Leaves.* Bournemouth: pub. at Sydenham's Royal Marine Library, 1900. 16 pages, stabbed as issued, front wrapper detached, small corner torn from title, lightly foxed, Kathleen Tillotson's copy, inserted signed compliments' slip from Margharita (Laski).   Jarndyce Antiquarian Booksellers   CCVII - 582   2015   £65

Yonge, Charlotte Mary 1823-1901 *Reasons Why I am a Catholic and Not a Roman Catholic.* London: Wells Gardner, Darton & Co., 1901. First edition, original crimson cloth, slightly faded, with Kathleen Tillotson's copy with pencilled note and remark, letter to her inserted.   Jarndyce Antiquarian Booksellers   CCVII - 584   2015   £65

Young, George Malcom *Victorian England; Portrait of an Age.* London: OUP, 1937. Plates, facsimiles, original dark green cloth, from the library of Geoffrey & Kathleen Tillotson, inscribed Christmas present from Geoffrey to Kathleen.   Jarndyce Antiquarian Booksellers   CCVII - 587   2015   £20

Association – Tinkle, Brinton

Chardiet, Bernice *C is for Circus.* New York: Walker and Co., 1971. First edition, oblong quarto, slight wear to corners, near fine in like dust jacket with vertical line rubbed on front panel, warmly inscribed by artist Brinton Tinkle to publisher, Beth and Sam Walker.   Between the Covers Rare Books, Inc.   187 - 47   2015 $225

Association – Tocqueville, Alexis De

Aiken, P. F. *A Comparative View of the Constitutions of Great Britain and the United States of America in Six Lectures.* London: Longman and Co., Hamilton Adams and Co., 1842. First edition, 8vo., original green cloth lettered gilt on spine, few scattered white marks to covers, otherwise very good with some light wear, presentation copy from Thomas Kington to Alexis de Tocqueville, very good with some light wear.   Any Amount of Books   2015 - C16194   2015   £160

Association – Todd, Carson

Wheeler, John Archibald *Geons, Black Holes and Quantum Foam: a Life in Physics.* New York: W. W. Norton, 1998. 8vo., photos, quarter gilt stamped black cloth over similar black cloth dust jacket, signed and inscribed by author to Dr. Carson Todd in ink at half title, signed and inscribed black and white photo portrait of Wheeler laid in, TLS from Wheeler to Todd, near fine. Jeff Weber Rare Books 178 - 1140 2015 $450

Wheeler, John Archibald *A Journey into Gravity and Spacetime.* New York: Scientific American Library, 1999. Square 8vo., illustrations, original printed wrappers, signed and inscribed by author to Dr. Carson Todd, very good. Jeff Weber Rare Books 178 - 1141 2015 $125

Association – Topping, John

Crouch, Nathaniel *The English Empire in America.* London: Nath(aniel) Crouch, 1692. Second edition, 12mo., engraved frontispiece map of New England, engraved map of the Caribbean and one of two engraved plates of "Strange Creatures in America", lacking one plate and text leaves D6-7, wormed in gutter throughout, fore-edges chipped and bumped, piece torn away from corner of d4 (touching four lines of text), large stain in inner margin of D4-D5, pencil markings on rear pastedown, contemporary sheep, garment from unidentifiable broadside showing royal arms and "by the Queen (Anne) has been used as front pastedown, 20mm. piece torn away from top of spine, hole lower down spine, covers and spine rubbed, chipped and corners heavily bumped, signature 'John Topping his booke 1710', early 18th century signature Joseph A. Lingom, from the library of James Stevens Cox (1910-1997). Maggs Bros. Ltd. 1447 - 124 2015 £500

Association – Torrey, Beef

Bierce, Ambrose 1842-1914 *The Devil's Dictionary.* New York and London: Bloomsbury, 2003. Fourth printing, small 8vo., fine in fine dust jacket, signed and inscribed by Ralph Steadman for Beef (Torrey), he has added a illustration on same page, small blank sheet of stationery laid in from Jerome Hotel in Aspen CO, fine in fine dust jacket. Ed Smith Books 82 - 26 2015 $250

Brautigan, Richard *Trout Fishing in America, The Pill Versus The Springhill Mine Disaster and In Watermelon Sugar.* New York: Seymour Lawrence/Delacorte Press, 1972. Fifth printing of this edition, signed by author, from the estate of Beef Torrey, friend of author, near fine in very good plus dust jacket (price clipped). Ed Smith Books 82 - 6 2015 $300

Hansen, Ron *Desperadoes.* New York: Knopf, 1979. First edition, signed by author, fine in fine dust jacket, from the estate of Beef Torrey. Ed Smith Books 83 - 39 2015 $150

Harrison, Jim *Braided Creek. A Conversation in Poetry.* Port Towsend: Copper Canyon, 2003. First edition, #117 of 250 numbered copies signed by both poets in two-tone cloth binding (green and black), from the estate of Beef Torrey, fine. Ed Smith Books 83 - 43 2015 $200

Harrison, Jim *Legends of the Fall, Revenge, The Man Who Gave Up His Name.* New York: Delacorte/Seymour Lawrence, 1979. First edition, 3 volumes, white cloth, each volume signed by author, slipcase with Russell Chatham illustration, from the estate of Beef Torrey, all fine in very good plus slipcase and some rubbing to extremities. Ed Smith Books 83 - 41 2015 $450

Harrison, Jim *Plain Song. Poems.* New York: Norton, 1965. First edition, fine in green cloth, very good plus clean jacket, price clipped bottom, with price present on top of front flap, there is a tape pull that affects the N in Plain on top front panel, inscribed by author to friend Beef Torrey. Ed Smith Books 83 - 42 2015 $500

Thompson, Hunter S. *Screwjack.* New York: Simon & Schuster, 2000. First trade edition, signed in full by Thompson on large bookplate mounted to front endpaper, fine in black cloth with silver spine stamping, fine dust jacket, from the estate of Beef Torrey. Ed Smith Books 83 - 102 2015 $400

Association – Torrey, John

Rafinesque, C. S. *Principes Fondamentaux de Somiologie ou les Loix de la Nomenclature et de la Classification de l'Empire Orangique ou des Animaux et des Vegetabux....* Palermo: De l'Imprimerie de Franc. Abate uax depens de l'Auteur, 1814. First edition, 8vo., modern half calf, leather label, top blank portion of title cut away, affecting first line of title, clipping top half of last four letters, otherwise very fine, rare, inscribed in ink by American botanist, J(ohn) Torrey to naturalist & J. E. De Kay. M & S Rare Books, Inc. 97 - 250 2015 $3250

Association – Towle, Tony

Elmslie, Kenward *Album.* New York: Kulchur Press, 1969. First edition, cover and drawings by Joe Brainard, small 4to., original coated patterned paper over boards, photographic endpapers, scarce hardcover issue, presentation copy, inscribed by author for poet Tony Towle, fine. James S. Jaffe Rare Books Many Happy Returns - 248 2015 $450

Padgett, Ron *Summer Balloons.* Tulsa: privately printed, 1960. First edition, inscribed presentation from author to poet Tony Towle, 12mo., original printed wrappers, fine in original envelope addressed by Padgett to Towle, rare. James S. Jaffe Rare Books Many Happy Returns - 138 2015 $3500

Association – Trant, Dominick

Cowley, Abraham 1618-1667 *The Works of Mr. Abraham Cowley.* London: by J(ohn) M(acock) for Henry Herringman, 1668. First edition, small folio, engraved portrait by William Faithorne, stain along lower margin of A1, inksplash on H1, margins of H1-H4 creased (by binder?), uncut corner of (2)Q4 folded, contemporary calf, spine with partial remains of red morocco label (heavily rubbed, covers scuffed and worn, corners worn, endleaves dusty, lower front third of front flyleaf torn away, pastedowns coming loose), ink initials A B H on front flyleaf, handsome engraved bookplate of Dominick Trant has come detached from pastedown and loosely inserted, from the library of James Stevens Cox (1910-1997). Maggs Bros. Ltd. 1447 - 120 2015 £200

Association – Trilling, Diana

Howard, Richard *Findings.* New York: Atheneum, 1971. First edition, fine, inscribed by author to Diana and Lionel Trilling, in 1971. Between the Covers Rare Books, Inc. 187 - 132 2015 $200

Association – Trilling, Lionel

Howard, Richard *Findings.* New York: Atheneum, 1971. First edition, fine, inscribed by author to Diana and Lionel Trilling, in 1971. Between the Covers Rare Books, Inc. 187 - 132 2015 $200

Ranson, John Crowe *Selected Poems.* New York: Alfred A. Knopf, 1963. Second edition, fine in very near fine dust jacket with very slight wear, Lionel Trilling's copy with his ownership signature. Between the Covers Rare Books, Inc. 187 - 229 2015 $85

Association – Trimble, Isaac

Tredgold, Thomas *Elementary Principles of Carpentry; a Treatise on the Pressure and Equilibrium of Timber Framing the Resistence of Timber and Construction of Floors, Roofs, Centres, Bridges.* London: J. Taylor, 1828. Second edition, 4to., 22 engraved plates, contemporary calf backed boards, rubbed at extremities, front hinge beginning to crack, plates moderate foxed, good, signature of Isaac Trimble, Maryland engineer and Civil War general. Joseph J. Felcone Inc. Science, Medicine and Technology - 6 2015 $400

Association – Tristram, Henry

Newman, John Henry 1801-1890 *Certain Difficulties Felt by Anglicans in Catholic Teaching Considered...* London: Longmans Green, 1891. 2 volumes, half titles, initial request slip, 2 pages ads volume 2, original maroon cloth, spines slightly chipped at head and tail, annotated by Henry Tristram of Birmingham Oratory, presented to Geoffrey Tillotson, with his annotations. Jarndyce Antiquarian Booksellers CCVII - 385 2015 £25

Association – Trousdale, Gary

Rebello, Stephen *The Art of the Hunchback of Notre Dame.* New York: Hyperion, 1996. First edition, this copy signed by 10 members of the production company, including Gary Trousdale and Kirk Wise, artistic coordinator Randy Fullmer, writers Irene Meechi and Tab Murphy and five animators, numerous full color drawings and sketches in black and white, laid in is announcement for book signing party, fine in fine dust jacket. Ed Smith Books 83 - 15 2015 $250

Association – Tunney, Gene

Churchward, James *The Children of Mu.* New York: Ives Washburn, 1931. First edition, spine sunned and lettering dull, about very good, without dust jacket, pencilled ownership signature of boxing great Gene Tunney. Between the Covers Rare Books, Inc. 187 - 53 2015 $225

Connolly, James B. *The Book of Gloucester Fisherman.* New York: John Day Co., 1927. First edition, illustrations by Henry O'Connor, publisher's orange cloth, very good or better with light scattered spotting, without dust jacket, with ALS and TLS and one news clipping laid in, the ALS addressed boxer Gene Tunney, from J. T. Holmes. Between the Covers Rare Books, Inc. 187 - 60 2015 $400

Kornitzer, Bela *The Great American Heritage.* New York: Farrar, Straus and Cudahy, 1955. First edition, 22cm., publisher's beige cloth with gilt title, very good with light spotting to endpapers and edges, else near fine in very good dust jacket with scattered spotting and few tiny tears, inscribed by author to Gene Tunney. Between the Covers Rare Books, Inc. 187 - 148 2015 $150

Sloane, Eric *A Reverence for Wood.* New York: Wilfred Funk Inc., 1965. First edition, quarto, fine in fine dust jacket with perhaps slightest of sunning at spine, promotional brochure for Sloane's works laid in, inscribed by Sloane to boxing champion Gene Tunney. Between the Covers Rare Books, Inc. 187 - 3 2015 $650

Shadegg, Stephen *Barry Goldwater: Freedom Is His Flight Plan.* New York: Fleet Pub. Corp., 1962. First edition, fine in fine dust jacket with couple of tiny tears, inscribed by Goldwater to the Gene Tunneys. Between the Covers Rare Books, Inc. 187 - 217 2015 $550

Thorogood, Augustine H. *The Globe & Laurel. The Journal of the Royal Marines (Volume 37).* Great Britain: Royal Marines, 1929. 12 issues bound in one volume (Volume 37 Numbers 1-12, Jan. - Dec. 1929), photos, full blue cloth, gilt, spine titles, with gilt seal on front board, moderate rubbing to boards and light fading to spine, else fine, presented Sept. 21 1950 by US Marine Commander Augustine Thorogood to boxing champion Gene Tunney. Between the Covers Rare Books, Inc. 187 - 277 2015 $300

Association – Tunney, Robert

Wakoski, Diane *Saturn's Rings.* New York: Targ Editions, 1982. First edition, signed by author, quarter cloth, photographic paper covered boards, fine in slightly age-toned, near fine, unprinted tissue dust jacket, signed by author and inscribed by Wakoski and by Robert Tunney (who took the photo of Wakoski) to author Brad Morrow. Between the Covers Rare Books, Inc. 187 - 285 2015 $225

Association – Tutin, J. R.

Reynolds, Henry *The Tale of Narcissus.* Hull: J. R. Tutin, 1906. One of 666 copies, one page creased, uncut, original printed wrappers, dusted and slightly creased, inscribed on front wrapper from Tutin to Oliver Elton and by Elton to Kathleen Tillotson with compliments. Jarndyce Antiquarian Booksellers CCVII - 446 2015 £25

Association – Tuttle, Richard

Berssenbrugge, Mei-Mei *Sphericity.* Berkeley: Kelsey St. Press, 1993. First edition, Deluxe issue, one of 50 numbered copies signed by author and artist from an entire edition of 2000, original hand colored drawing by Richard Tuttle, bound in at back of book, large square 8vo., illustrations, original illustrated wrappers, lower fore-corner of wrappers and text block lightly bumped, otherwise fine. James S. Jaffe Rare Books Modern American Poetry - 35 2015 $1500

Association – Tutu, Naomi

Tutu, Desmond Mpilo *The Words of Desmond Tutu.* New York: Newmarket Press, 1989. First edition, signed and inscribed by author to daughter Naomi Tutu, 8vo., fine in near fine dust jacket with mild sun spine. By the Book, L. C. Special List 10 - 47 2015 $650

Association – Twopenny, William

Capel, Arthur *Excellent Contemplations, Divine and Moral.* London: for Nath(aniel) Crouch, 1683. First edition, 12mo., enraved portrait of Capel (mounted and repaired along inner margin), small piece torn from blank lower margin of F1, small hole (paper flaw?) to blank corner of F6, 19th century sprinkled calf by Bedford, William Twopenny late 19th/early 20th century label, from the library of James Stevens Cox (1910-1997). Maggs Bros. Ltd. 1447 - 63 2015 £350

Association – Twycross-Raines, George Francis

Cooke, James *Mellificium Chirurgiae or the Marrow of Many Good Authors.* London: for Samuel Cartwright, 1648. First edition, 12mo., upper fore corners of B6-7 and P5 torn from paper flaws (affecting rule border not touching text), some worming in inner margin (heavily between Q5-R11), contemporary sheep ruled in blind (rubbed, 30mm piece torn at head of spine, a number of loose gatherings, bumped and rubbed, pastedowns unstuck), early ink initials "E K", late 18th century signature Isaac Webster/Hull, signature Isaac Raines 1802, by descent to Rev. George Francis Twycross-Raines, vicar and antiquary of Hull, with ink inscription, of "H. Page from his old friend G. F. Twycross-Raines Sept. 11, 1911", from the library of James Stevens Cox (1910-1997). Maggs Bros. Ltd. 1447 - 114 2015 £750

Association – Tyler, Winifred

Blatch, Harriot Stanton *Challenging Years: the memoirs of...* New York: Putnams, 1940. First edition, 8vo., very nice in dust jacket, inscribed by Nora Stanton Barney (author's daughter) to Winifred A. Tyler. Second Life Books Inc. 189 - 26 2015 $150

Association – Unger, Norman

Guthrie, A. B. *The Big Sky.* William Sloane Associates, 1947. First edition, 8vo., one of 500 numbered copies with extra leaf signed by Guthrie tipped in, fine, bright, tight copy in both regular grade pictorial dust jacket and the special plain grey printed in brown ink advance dust jacket which bears the limitation number at top of front panel, this copy number 179 some minor wear to top edge of trade jacket, the Norman Unger copy. Buckingham Books March 2015 - 25655 2015 $1000

Association – Upward, Allen

Pound, Ezra Loomis 1885-1972 *Ripostes of Ezra Pound.* London: Stephen Swift & Co., 1912. First edition, first issue, 8vo., original gray cloth, publisher's ads at end present in this copy, covers lightly soiled, spine darkened, some offsetting as usual to endpapers, otherwise very good, presentation copy inscribed by author for Allen Upward. James S. Jaffe Rare Books Modern American Poetry - 233 2015 $6500

Association – Usborne, John

The Bridgewater Treatises: on the Power, Wisdom and Goodness of God as Manifested in the Creation. London: William Pickering, 1833-1839. London: John Murray 1838. Mixed set, Treatises I-IX in 13 volumes, 8vo., all plates and engravings present, occasional light foxing to first and last few pages, contemporary half black calf over marbled paper backed boards, gilt stamped spines and brown leather spine labels, extremities rubbed, some spine labels missing, corners showing, armorial bookplates of Francis Frederick Fox, signature of John Usborne (volume II), very good.   Jeff Weber Rare Books   178 - 779   2015 $1850

Association – Van Beuren, M. M.

Green, Thomas J. *Journal of the Texian Expedition Against Mier; Subsequent Imprisonment of the Author...* Harper Bros., 1845. First edition, presentation copy inscribed in pencil to Col. M. M. Van Beuren by author, finely bound in 20th century half red morocco and cloth gold gilt, raised bands, titles stamped in gold gilt on spine, top edges gilt, 13 plates, 1 folding map, rare, some minor foxing throughout, yet still unusually nice, tight copy, exceptional copy.   Buckingham Books   March 2015 - 30510   2015 $2250

Association – Van Doren, Mark

Berryman, John   1914-1972   *Stephen Crane. The American Men of Letters.*   New York: William Sloane Associates, 1950. First edition, 8vo., original cloth, dust jacket, inscribed by author to his teacher Mark Van Doren, fine, dust jacket neatly reinforced on verso at couple of places along flap folds.   James S. Jaffe Rare Books   Modern American Poetry - 31   2015 $4500

Association – Van Vechten, Carl

Gosse, Edmund   1849-1928   *Some Diversions of a Man of Letters.*   London: William Heinemann, 1919. First edition, cheap paper browned, else near fine, Carl Van Vechten's copy with his bookplate.   Between the Covers Rare Books, Inc.   187 - 111   2015 $150

Pinero, Arthur W.   *A Wife Without a Smile: a comedy in Disguise in Three Acts.*   Boston: Walter H. Baker & Co., 1905. First American edition, flowered cloth, original wrappers bound in, small repair to front wrapper, moderate wear to extremities of boards, good copy, Carl Van Vechten's copy with his ownership signature and bookplate.   Between the Covers Rare Books, Inc.   187 - 215   2015 $150

Spender, Stephen   *Returning to Vienna 1947: Nine Sketches.*   New York: Banyan Press, 1947. First edition, one of 350 numbered copies for sale (out of total edition of 500), tied decorated paper wrappers with printed label, small nicks and splitting along spine, otherwise handsome, very good copy, signed by author, Carl van Vechten's copy with his bookplate, inscribed by him to Milton Saul and Claude Fredericks, publishers at Banyan Press.   Between the Covers Rare Books, Inc.   187 - 266   2015 $250

Association – Van Wert, William

Robbe-Grillet, Alain   *Souvenirs du Triangle d'Or.*   Paris: Les Editions de Minuit, 1978. First edition, inscribed in blue ink by author for novelist and film theorist William Van Wert, very good plus in wrappers, wrappers very lightly soiled, light foxing at spine, rear panel scuffed with single corner crease, slight spine lean.   Royal Books   46 - 27   2015 $750

Association – Vaughan, William

Thomson, James   1700-1748   *Spring. A Poem.*   London: printed and sold by A. Miller, G. Strahan, 1728. First edition, 8vo., recent unlettered half calf, signature of William Vaughan, dated March 18 1730, he has added a crude sketch of author.   C. R. Johnson   Foxon R-Z - 998r-z   2015 $383

Association – Veitch, Tom

Clark, Thomas   *The Sand Burg. Poems by Tom Clark.*   London: Ferry Press, 1966. First edition, limited to 500 copies, 4to., original wrappers with cover by Joe Brainard, fine, presentation copy inscribed by Clark for Tom Veitch.   James S. Jaffe Rare Books   Many Happy Returns - 229   2015 $150

Gallup, Dick   *Where I Hang My Hat.*   New York: Harper & Row, 1970. First edition, large 8vo., original cloth and paper over boards, dust jacket design by George Schneeman, two small dents, one in each cover, that in front cover affecting first few pages of text and adjacent portion of dust jacket, otherwise fine, presentation inscribed by Gallup to fellow author Tom Veitch, with Gallup's accompanying ink drawing.   James S. Jaffe Rare Books   Many Happy Returns - 130   2015 $650

Padgett, Ron   *Antlers in the Treetops.*   Toronto: Coach House Press, 1973. First edition, one of 1000 copies, 8vo., glossy pictorial wrappers by George Schneeman, signed by Padgett and Tom Veitch, who continues the inscription, covers slightly sunned, otherwise fine.   James S. Jaffe Rare Books   Many Happy Returns - 314   2015 $125

Association – Vendeuvre, William Paved

Pascal, Blaise *Pensees de M. Pascal sur la religion et sur Quelques Autres Sujets qui ont Este Trouvees Apres sa Mort Parmy ses Papiers. (Thought of Mr. Pascal on Religion and Some Other Subjects...).* Paris: Guillaume Desprez, 1670. Counterfeit, True Second edition, gorgeous contemporary full leather, spine has five raised bands, gilt lettering and decorations in each compartment, with gilt embossed arms of William Paved Vendeuvre family to center of both front and back covers, lovely marbled endpapers, very handsome, clean, bright, tight copy.   Athena Rare Books   15 - 49   2015 $3000

Association – Vernon, William

Donne, John   1571-1631   *Biathanatos (First word in Greek).*   printed by John Dawson, circa, 1647. First edition, first issue, with undated titlepage, woodcut initials, woodcut and typographic headpieces, initial blank, last 4 leaves with few short marginal tears, light browning at edges of titlepage (offset from binding turn-ins), 4to., contemporary blind ruled calf with corner ornaments, spine gilt, rebacked preserving original spine, lacking lettering piece, preserved in full brown morocco pull-off case, early signature of Wm. Vernon at head of initial blank, engraved bookplate of Henry Greenhill dated 1911, inside front cover, bookplate of H. Bradley Martin inside rear cover, modern bookplate recto of initial blank very good.   Blackwell's Rare Books   B179 - 37   2015   £5000

Association – Vigne, Robert

MacLean, John   *A Compendium of Kafir laws and Customs Including Genealogical Tables of Kafir Chiefs and Various Tribal Cenus Returns.*   Mount Coke: Wesleyan Mission Press, printed for the government of British Kaffaria, 1858. 1st edition, 3 folding tables, original green cloth with printed spine label, label largely defective, old light stain on upper cover, very good, inscribed in ink by Maclean to Robert Vigne, with coy note in contemporary hand at head of title.   John Drury Rare Books   2015 - 26200   2015 $787

Association – Villeneuve, Joannis Petri De

Homerus   (In Greek) *Omerou Ilias Kai Odysseia.* (and) *Homeri Ilias & Odyssea et in landem Scholia & Interpretatio.* Lugduni Batavorum: Apud Franciscum Hackium, 1655-1656. First Schrevelius edited edition, 2 volumes, 248 x 171mm., handsome 18th century red straight grain morocco, cover framed by lovely Neoclassical roll enclosed by double gilt rules, rosette cornerpieces, raised bands flanked by plain gilt rules, spine panels with central gilt medallion containing a narcissus, gilt titling, turn-in with gilt greek key roll purple endpapers, all edges, engraved allegorical title in volume I, woodcut printer's device on title in volume II, engraved armorial bookplate of Joannis Petri de Villeneuve, spines uniformly bit darkened (with slight dulling of some gilt), hint of rubbing to extremities, very minor spotting to covers, but original handsome unrestored bindings generally in fine condition, leather lustrous and with no significant wear, joints almost entirely unworn, vague browning in (ample) margins, isolated trivial rust or wax spots, other minor imperfections but text fresh, clean and generally quite pleasing.   Phillip J. Pirages   66 - 37   2015 $2200

Association – Vincent, Augusta

Hayley, William   *The Triumphs of Temper: a Poem in Six Cantos.*   London: T. Cadell, 1788. Sixth edition, 165 x 102mm., once remarkably attractive and still very pleasing late 18th century citron morocco by Staggemeier & Welcher, covers with inlaid black and red morocco tooled in gilt to a diapered mosaic design, raised bands, spine compartments with central moire silk endleaves, all edges gilt, expertly rejointed, spine label with tiny repairs and some inlays artfully replicated and replaced by Courtland Benson, with 7 engraved plates, silk bookplate of R. M. Trench Chiswell, titlepage and ink ownership inscription of Augusta E. Vincent, inscription from A. Vincent to Blanche Cely-Trevilian, spine little darkened, minor soiling to boards, plates rather foxed, otherwise without any significant defect and, in all, an excellent (albeit restored) specimen, binding with much of its original dramatic appeal reclaimed.   Phillip J. Pirages   66 - 52   2015 $4500

Association – Vizenor, Gerald

Kenny, Maurice   *Dancing Back Strong the Nation.* Marvin: Blue Cloud Quarterly Press, 1979. First edition, stapled wrappers, fine, inscribed by author to fellow author Gerald Vizenor, TLS from Kenny to Vizenor from 1979.   Between the Covers Rare Books, Inc.   187 - 196   2015 $350

Association – Von Puttkamer, Jesco

Marshak, Sondra   *Star Trek: The New Voyages 2.*   New York: Bantam, 1978. First edition, near fine with few creases to wrappers, inscribed by Jesco Von Puttkamer (provided introduction) to Fred Durant with longer typed note from Von Puttkamer to Durant tipped-in.   Between the Covers Rare Books, Inc.   187 - 251   2015 $275

Association – Voorhies, Stephen

Major, Harlan *Fishing Behind the Eight Ball.* Harrisburg: Stackpole Co., 1952. First edition, illustrations by Stephen Voorhies, corners bit bumped, else near fine in price clipped, near fine dust jacket, ownership signature of artist, Voorhies and inscribed by author to him April 1954. Between the Covers Rare Books, Inc.   187 - 98   2015 $250

Association – Wait, Peter

Butt, John *Dickens at Work.* London: Methuen, 1957. First edition, half title, frontispiece, plates, half brown morocco by Sangorski & Sutcliffe, spine in compartments, slight rubbing to leading hinge, top edge gilt, publisher's specially bound copy to Kathleen Tillotson with ANS from Peter Wait inserted.   Jarndyce Antiquarian Booksellers   CCVII - 207   2015   £40

Association – Waite, Arthur Edward

Emmett, George *Captain Jack; or One of the Light Brigade.* London: Hogarth House, 1873? First edition, frontispiece, illustrations, few spots, without wrappers, purple brown binder's cloth, slightly faded, inner hinge splitting, booklabel of Arthur Edward Waite,.   Jarndyce Antiquarian Booksellers   CCXI - 111   2015   £75

Association – Waldman, Anne

Berrigan, Ted *Memorial Day. A Collaboration by Anne Waldman & Ted Berrigan.* London: Aloes Books, 1974. First English edition, limited to 500 copies, although Fischer specifies 479 copies, the projected signed limited edition never having been done, 8vo., original pictorial wrappers, signed by Waldman on titlepage, acidic paper discolored as usual, otherwise fine.   James S. Jaffe Rare Books   Many Happy Returns - 226   2015 $350

Brainard, Joe *Self Portrait.* New York: Siamese Banana Press, 1972. First edition, 4to., original wrappers, fine, signed by Anne Waldman and inscribed by Brainard for Burt Britton.   James S. Jaffe Rare Books   Many Happy Returns - 262   2015 $350

Berrigan, Ted *Memorial Day. A Collaboration by Anne Waldman & Ted Berrigan.* New York: Poetry Project, 1971. First edition, mimeographed, 4to., original stapled wrappers by Donna Dennis, fine, signed by Berrigan and Waldman. James S. Jaffe Rare Books   Many Happy Returns - 224   2015 $750

Association – Waldo, Timothy

Marine Society *The Bye-Laws and Regulations of the Marine Society Inc. in MDCCLXXII with the Several Instructions Forms of Indentures and Other Instruments Used by Them. Also a List of Subscribers from May 1769 to June 1772.* London: 1772. First edition, 12mo., engraved titlepage, contemporary calf, spine fully gilt in compartments with flower and leaf devices within raised bands, red morocco label, just smallest snag at foot of spine, still fine, from the library of Sir Timothy Waldo, one of the original subscribers, with his armorial bookplate on front pastedown, rare. John Drury Rare Books   2015 - 24856   2015 $1661

Association – Wales, Prince of

Co-Operative Wholesale Society *Annual for 1906.* Manchester: Co-operative Wholesale Societies Limited, 1906. Plates, presentation binding of dark green crushed morocco, bevelled boards, bordered gilt, front board elaborately decorated in gilt with inscription, raised bands, spine decorated and lettered gilt with floral gilt dentelles, spine very slightly rubbed at head and tail, front board slightly marked, all edges gilt, very good, inscribed for His Royal Highness Prince of Wales 1906.   Jarndyce Antiquarian Booksellers   CCXI - 74   2015   £125

Association – Walker, Alice

Nathiri, N. Y. *Zora! Zora Neale Hurston: a Woman and Her Community.* Orlando: Orlando Sentinel/Sentinel Communications, 1991. First edition, 4to. this copy signed by Alice Walker, fine in fine dust jacket.   Beasley Books 2013 - 2015 $40

Association – Walker, Amasa

Peace Principles Safe and Right. Boston: American Peace Society, circa, 1859-1865. First edition, small octavo, contemporary green cloth gilt, contemporary bookplate of Frank Batcheller, bit of rubbing on cloth, paper cracking over front hinge but tight and sound, inscribed by abolishionist Amasa Walker for Francis Batcheller.   Between the Covers Rare Books   197 - 107   2015 $650

Association – Walker, Anthony Philip Martineau

Gaskell, Elizabeth Cleghorn 1810-1865 *Mary Barton: a Tale of Manchester Life.* Leipzig: Bernhard Tauchnitz, 1849. Copyright edition, half title, bookseller's stamps, contemporary half calf, rebacked, retaining original spine strip with red label and initials A.I.T., bookplate of Anthony Philip Martineau Walker, ownership inscription of Anne Thackeray (Ritchie), with note by Kathleen Tillotson that Captain Walker gave her the book.   Jarndyce Antiquarian Booksellers CCVII - 273   2015   £50

Association – Walker, Beth

Chardiet, Bernice *C is for Circus.* New York: Walker and Co., 1971. First edition, oblong quarto, slight wear to corners, near fine in like dust jacket with vertical line rubbed on front panel, warmly inscribed by artist Brinton Tinkle to publisher, Beth and Sam Walker. Between the Covers Rare Books, Inc. 187 - 47 2015 $225

Association – Walker, Hugh

Newman, John Henry 1801-1890 *Verses on Various Occasions.* London: Burns, Oates, 1880. Half title, erratum slip, final ad leaf, Geoffrey Tillotson's copy with signature 1942 indicating Hugh Walker's signature on preserved endpaper with numerous ink and pencil notes in text and inserted, Tillotson's decorated paper casing with ms. label. Jarndyce Antiquarian Booksellers CCVII - 395 2015 £45

Association – Walker, J.

Pitman, Isaac *The Reporter; or Phonography Adapted to Verbatim Reporting.* Bath and London: Isaac Pitman, 1846. Second edition, 8vo., old wax splashes on several leaves, few near contemporary annotations in ink, 19th century private stamp of J. Walker on title, contemporary cloth lettered gilt on upper cover, very good. John Drury Rare Books 2015 - 13807 2015 $133

Association – Walker, J. Monro

Bolderwood, Rolf *A Colonial Reformer.* London: Macmillan and Co., 1891. Second edition, half title, contemporary half maroon morocco, little rubbed, bookplate of J. Monro Walker. Jarndyce Antiquarian Booksellers CCXI - 28 2015 £35

Bolderwood, Rolf *The Crooked Stick; or Pollie's Probation.* London: Macmillan and Co., 1895. First edition, half title, contemporary half maroon morocco, little rubbed, bookplate of J. Monro Walker. Jarndyce Antiquarian Booksellers CCXI - 29 2015 £35

Bolderwood, Rolf *A Modern Buccaneer.* London: Macmillan and Co., 1894. Second edition, half titlle, frontispiece, folding map, contemporary half maroon morocco, little rubbed, bookplate of J. Monro Walker. Jarndyce Antiquarian Booksellers CCXI - 30 2015 £35

Bolderwood, Rolf *Nevermore.* London: Macmillan and Co., 1892. First one volume edition, half title, contemporary half maroon morocco, some wear to following hinge, little rubbed, bookplate of J. Monro Walker. Jarndyce Antiquarian Booksellers CCXI - 31 2015 £40

Bolderwood, Rolf *Robbery Under Arms.* London: Macmillan and Co., 1889. Half title, contemporary half maroon morocco, little rubbed, bookplate of J. Monro Walker. Jarndyce Antiquarian Booksellers CCXI - 32 2015 £65

Bolderwood, Rolf *The Squatter's Dream.* London: Macmillan and Co., 1890. New edition, half title, contemporary half maroon morocco, little rubbed, bookplate of J. Monro Walker. Jarndyce Antiquarian Booksellers CCXI - 33 2015 £35

Nisbet, Hume *A Bush Girl's Romance.* London: F. V. White and Co., 1894. Illustrations by author, contemporary half maroon morocco, little rubbed, bookplate of J. Monro Walker. Jarndyce Antiquarian Booksellers CCXI - 217 2015 £50

Nisbet, Hume *The Bushranger's Sweetheart.* London: F. V. White & Co., 1892. First edition, frontispiece and title vignette by author, contemporary half maroon morocco, leading hinge slight worn, little rubbed, bookplate of J. Monro Walker. Jarndyce Antiquarian Booksellers CCXI - 218 2015 £60

Nisbet, Hume *A Desert Bride.* London: F. V. White and Co., 1894. First edition, illustrations by author, contemporary half maroon morocco, little rubbed, bookplate of J. Monro Walker. Jarndyce Antiquarian Booksellers CCXI - 219 2015 £40

Nisbet, Hume *The Great Secret.* London: F.V. White & Co., 1895. First edition, half title, contemporary maroon morocco little rubbed, bookplate of J. Monro Walker. Jarndyce Antiquarian Booksellers CCXI - 220 2015 £125

Nisbet, Hume *Her Loving Slave.* London: Digby, Long & Co., 1894. Second edition, half title, frontispiece, bookplate of J. Monro Walker, contemporary half maroon roan, little rubbed,. Jarndyce Antiquarian Booksellers CCXI - 221 2015 £45

Nisbet, Hume *The "Jolly Roger".* London: Digby, Long & Co., 1891. First edition, frontispiece and title vignette by author, contemporary half marooon morocco, little rubbed, bookplate of J. Monro Walker,. Jarndyce Antiquarian Booksellers CCXI - 222 2015 £125

Nisbet, Hume *My Love Noel.* London: F. V. White & Co., 1896. First edition, half title, contemporary half maroon morocco, little rubbed, bookplate of J. Monro Walker,. Jarndyce Antiquarian Booksellers CCXI - 223 2015 £45

Nisbet, Hume *The Queen's Desire.* London: F. V. White & co., 1893. First edition, frontispiece and title vignette by author, contemporary half maroon morocco, little rubbed, bookplate of bookplate of J. Monro Walker,. Jarndyce Antiquarian Booksellers   CCXI - 224   2015   £50

Nisbet, Hume *The Savage Queen.* London: F. V. White & Co., 1891. First edition, contemporary half maroon morocco little rubbed, bookplate of bookplate of J. Monro Walker,. Jarndyce Antiquarian Booksellers   CCXI - 225   2015   £65

Association – Walker, James

Putnam, Mabel Raef *The Winning of the First Wisconsin Bill of Rights for American Women.* Milwaukee: Frank Putnam, 1924. First edition, 8vo., covers little soiled, very good, scarce, inscribed by author Dec. 7 1923 for Mr. James Walker.   Second Life Books Inc.   189 - 204   2015 $450

Association – Walker, Sam

Chardiet, Bernice *C is for Circus.* New York: Walker and Co., 1971. First edition, oblong quarto, slight wear to corners, near fine in like dust jacket with vertical line rubbed on front panel, warmly inscribed by artist Brinton Tinkle to publisher, Beth and Sam Walker.   Between the Covers Rare Books, Inc.   187 - 47   2015 $225

Association – Wall, June

King, Martin Luther *Where do We Go From Here Chaos or Community?* New York: Harper & Row, 1967. First edition, first printing, presentation copy signed and inscribed by author, additionally signed by his wife, Coretta Scott King to their close friends June & Kelvin Wall, about fine with only crease to one page (173), in excellent and extremely crisp unclipped dust jacket with few minor scuffs to rear panel, lovely copy.   B & B Rare Books, Ltd.   234 - 63   2015 $13,000

Association – Wall, Kelvin

King, Martin Luther *Where do We Go From Here Chaos or Community?* New York: Harper & Row, 1967. First edition, first printing, presentation copy signed and inscribed by author, additionally signed by his wife, Coretta Scott King to their close friends June & Kelvin Wall, about fine with only crease to one page (173), in excellent and extremely crisp unclipped dust jacket with few minor scuffs to rear panel, lovely copy.   B & B Rare Books, Ltd.   234 - 63   2015 $13,000

Association – Wallace, Peter

Comstock, Jim *West Virginia Picture Book West Virginia Heritage Encyclopedia Volume 51.* Richwood: 1978. Tall folio, mild shelf bow, shelf faded to backstrip, gilt bright, else near fine, inscribed by Comstock and co-author Peter Wallace.   Bookworm & Silverfish   2015 - 506605671   2015 $75

Association – Waller, John

Durrell, Lawrence   1912-1990 *On Seeming to Presume.* London: Faber & Faber, 1948. First edition, 8vo. signed presentation from author to John Waller, with Waller ownership signature, fine in slightly darkened else bright, near fine jacket.   Any Amount of Books   2015 - A68493   2015   £270

Association – Waller, Pickford

Walker, Frederick *English Rustic Pictures.* London: George Routledge, 1882. First 'India Proof' edition, small folio, one of 300 numbered copies, 15 proof wood engravings by Walker, and 17 by G. J. Pinwell, decorated gilt parchment, covers with bevelled edges, wood engravings printed from original blocks by Brothers Dalziel on India Proof paper and mounted on rectos, with Agincourt bookplate of Pickford Waller, covers marked and rubbed at corners, very good, engravings in excellent state.   Peter Ellis, Bookseller   2014 - 005239   2015   £350

Association – Wallis, John

Davenant, William   1606-1668 *Gondibert: an Heroick Poem.* London: John Holden, 1651. Second edition, 8vo., marginal browning some spotting and with paper fault in lower margin of O4, contemporary sheep, covers ruled in blind, rebacked, corners repaired, new endleaves, old flyleaves preserved, 17th century inscription of John Wallis, below another deleted signature, from the library of James Stevens Cox (1910-1997).   Maggs Bros. Ltd.   1447 - 133   2015   £240

Association – Wallis, W. M.

Jamieson, Alexander *A Celestial Atlas: Comprising a Systematic Display of the Heavens in a Series of Thirty Maps Illustrated by Scientific Descriptions of their Contents...* London: G. & W. B. Whittaker, 1822. First edition, oblong 4to., engraved title and dedication, 30 engraved plates, 28 are hand colored, original brown paper boards, expertly rebacked in black calf with some neat repair to cornerpieces, boards slightly rubbed and marked, presentation inscription from author for W. M. Wallis, with original recipient scratched away and replaced with W. M. Wallis, very nice, clean, without usual foxing and offsetting.   Jarndyce Antiquarian Booksellers CCXI - 157   2015   £2000

Association – Walmesley, Charles

Welsted, Leonard *Epistles, Odes &c.* London: printed for J. Walthoe and J. Peeple, 1725. Second edition, 12mo., contemporary sheep, rebacked, corners worn, bound without prelim leaf of bookseller's ads, titlepage bit foxed, otherwise good copy, early signature of Charles Walmesley. C. R. Johnson Foxon R-Z - 1108r-z 2015 $153

Association – Walpole, Horace

Bath, William Pulteney, 1st Earl of 1684-1764 *A Report from the Committee Appointed by Order of the House of Commons to Examine Christopher Layer and Others...* London: printed for Jacob Tonson, Bernard Lintot and William Taylor, 1722. First edition, initial license leaf, stab holes in inner blank margins of last 3 leaves, contemporary calf with double gilt fillets on sides, spine with gilt lines, raised bands and label, minor splits in joints at head and foot but very good, 18th century armorial bookplate of John Schutz, Esq. and armorial bookplate (early 19th century?) of Horace Walpole. John Drury Rare Books 2015 - 17995 2015 $874

Association – Walsh, C. C.

Haley, James Evetts *A Log of the Montana Trail as Kept by Ealy Moore.* Russell Stationery Co., 1932. First edition thus, 8vo., inscribed by Haley to C. C. Walsh, printed wrappers, fine, housed in quarter leather and cloth clamshell case with titles stamped in gold, gilt on spine. Buckingham Books March 2015 - 29752 2015 $2000

Association – Walton, J.

Parkinson, James *Organs Remains of a Former World: an Examination of the Mineralized Remains of the Vegetables and Animals of the Antediluvian World: Generally Termed Extraneous Fossils.* London: printed by C. Whittingham and published by J. Robson, J. White and J. Murray, H. D. Symonds, et al, 1804-1811. First edition, 3 volumes, 4to., 54 engraved plates, many hand colored, 2 errata leafs, titlepage vignettes, volume I prelims browned, occasional light foxing and offsetting throughout all volumes, contemporary full tan calf, gilt double ruled covers, 5 raised bands, gilt stamped spines and brown leather spine labels, volume I rebacked with original spine laid down, volume III front cover scratched, extremities rubbed all volumes, bookplate of Haskell Norman, bookplate and signature of J. Walton, 1952, near fine. Jeff Weber Rare Books 178 - 875 2015 $5000

Association – Ward, Dorothy

Butler, Arthur Gray *The Three Friends: a Story of Rugby in the Forties.* London: Henry Frowde, 1900. Original maroon cloth, spine slightly faded, signed by A. F. Buxton, Christmas 1900 and Kathleen Tillotson Oct. 1594, ALS from Dorothy Ward to Kathleen. Jarndyce Antiquarian Booksellers CCVII - 124 2015 £40

Association – Ware, Samuel

Charles I, King of England *The King's Maiesties Declaration to His Subjects Concerning Lawfull Sports to Bee Used.* London: Richard Barker and by the Assignes of John Bill, 1633. First edition, 4to., woodcut device on titlepage, large woodcut royal arms on verso, woodcut head and tailpieces, wanting final blank, few minor stains and rust marks, near contemporary ms. annotation in ink, ownership signature of 'Sam. Ware" with 19th century armorial bookplates of Richard Clark Esq. Chamberlain of London (1739-1831) and of William Henry Drummond, 9th Viscount Strathallan (1810-1886), bound, presumably for Richard Clark in late 18th or early 19th century half russia gilt, good copy, wanting only final blank. John Drury Rare Books 2015 - 25124 2015 $2185

Association – Warga, Wayne

Ambler, Eric *The Mask of Dimitrios.* London: Hodder & Stoughton Ltd., 1939. First edition, signed and inscribed on titlepage in ink by author to fellow mystery writer and journalist Wayne Warga, 25 Feb. 1982, bookplate of mystery collector Adrian Homer Goldstone, near fine, bright, square copy in dust jacket with light professional restoration by expert paper conservationist, housed in cloth clamshell case with leather label on spine and titles stamped in gold gilt, rare. Buckingham Books March 2015 - 37292 2015 $22,500

Association – Waring, Anna

Tennyson, Alfred Tennyson, 1st Baron 1809-1892 *The Princess, a Medley.* London: Edward Moxon, 1866. Original dark blue cloth, bevelled boards, embossed in gilt and blind, spine slightly faded, bookseller's ticket of Wm. Mullan, Belfast, all edges gilt, 26 illustrations engraved on wood, attractive larger format edition, Kathleen Tillotson's copy as K. Constable with earlier signature 1867 of great great aunt Anna Waring. Jarndyce Antiquarian Booksellers CCVII - 489 2015 £85

Association – Warren, William

Boyle, Robert 1627-1691 *Some Motives and Incentives to the love of God, pathetically Discorus'd of in a Letter to a friend.* London: for Henry Herringman, 1665. Fourth edition, title browned by turn-ins, one or two wormholes in lower margin, extending to a short trail from C4 to D3 each leaf throughout, H2 trimmed along lower edge, small piece torn away and a close tear I3 (touching text), 8vo., contemporary sheep (heavily worn and scuffed, upper joint split but holding, headcaps missing, pastedowns unstuck torn and stained by turn-ins), from the library of James Stevens Cox (1910-1997), 19th century bookplate William Warren, Bristol, signature A. S. Quick 17 may 1883, number of pencil markings by him. Maggs Bros. Ltd. 1447 - 44 2015 £150

Association – Warsh, Lewis

Berrigan, Ted *Carrying a Torch.* Brooklyn: Clown War, 1980. First edition, limited to 500 copies, oblong 8vo., illustrated with reproductions of engravings by Jan Vredeman de Vries, original pictorial wrappers, presentation copy inscribed on dedication page (cc#1) to Lewis (Warsh), 25 Jan. 80 NYC, fine. James S. Jaffe Rare Books Many Happy Returns - 52 2015 $1750

Berrigan, Ted *Red Wagon.* Chicago: Yellow Press, 1976. First edition, 8vo., original boards, dust jacket, fine, inscribed by author for Lewis (Warsh), fine. James S. Jaffe Rare Books Many Happy Returns - 36 2015 $1250

Berrigan, Ted *The Sonnets.* New York: United Artists Books, 1982. First of this edition, inscribed by author to one of the publisher's Lewis (Warsh) and wife Bernadette Mayer. James S. Jaffe Rare Books Many Happy Returns - 62 2015 $1250

Association – Washington, Bushrod

Tucker, St. George *Blackstone's Commentaries; with Notes of Reference to the Constitution and Laws of the Federal Government of the United States and of the Commonwealth of Virginia.* Philadelphia: published by William Young Birch and Abraham Small, 1803. First edition, 8vo., folding charts & facsimiles, contemporary calf, leather labels, hinges cracking but sound, scuffed, Bushrod Washington's set with his ink signature at Mount Vernon, in each volume. M & S Rare Books, Inc. 97 - 77 2015 $30,000

Association – Waterhouse, Russell

Graves, John *Goodbye to a River.* New York: Knopf, 1960. First edition, special copy signed by author on titlepage, on second blank page there is original ink drawing by Russell Waterhouse, below drawing is two-line inscription in ink by Waterhouse that is signed by him and dated Sept. 1 1961, very good plus to near fine, nudge to bottom front corner, salmon colored illustrated cloth, in very good plus dust jacket with small closed tear to top of spine fold, some minor wear around edges. Ed Smith Books 83 - 35 2015 $750

Association – Waters, Michael

Levine, Philip *Pili's Wall.* Santa Barbara: Unicorn Press, 1971. First edition, one of 750 copies, entire edition, fine in wrappers, and fine dust jacket, octavo, inscribed by author for Michael Waters. Between the Covers Rare Books, Inc. 187 - 154 2015 $250

Association – Watson, Glegg

Davis, George *Black Life in Corporate America: Swimming in the Mainstream.* Garden City: Anchor/Doubleday, 1982. First edition, fine in near fine dust jacket with usual rubbing, inscribed by Davis and co-author, Glegg Watson for novelist Barry Beckham. Between the Covers Rare Books, Inc. 187 - 68 2015 $250

Association – Watts, G. F.

Browning, Robert 1812-1889 *Ferishtah's Fancies.* London: Smith, Elder and Co., 1884. First edition, inscribed "To G F Watts From Robert Browning Dec. 1884" not in Browning's hand, in very good original dark brown cloth boards with gilt title to spine and black decoration to front board, rubbing to hinges, edges and corners with short open tear to book along front hinge, foxing to first and last few pages with light pencil bracket marks to text and occasional folded corners, blue endpages, 143 pages plus 8 pages of ads, from the collection of Stuart B. Schimmel, very good. The Kelmscott Bookshop 11 - 7 2015 $450

Association – Watts, James

Cobbett, William 1763-1835 *The Woodlands; or a Treatise on the Preparing of Ground for Planting; on the Planting; on the Cultivation; on the Pruning; and on the Cutting Down of Forest Trees and Underwoods...* London: William Cobbett, 1828. Illustrated, 2 pages ads, ads on endpapers, uncut in original olive green cloth, blind double ruled border boards decorated in blind, spine lettered gilt, small mark to spine below 'Cobbett', boards little marked, otherwise very good, handsome, armorial bookplate of James Watts, Cheshire. Jarndyce Antiquarian Booksellers CCXI - 70 2015 £225

Association – Will, Gary

Dexter, Pete *Brotherly Love.* New York: Random House, 1991. First trade edition, fine in very good dust jacket with small chip on rear panel, signed by author, laid in TLS by author to Gary Will.   Between the Covers Rare Books, Inc.   187 - 73   2015 $125

Association – Willan, Anne

Rumford, Benjamin Thompson, Count   1753-1814 *Essays, Political, Economical and Philosophical.* London: printed by Luke Hanford... for T. Cadell Jun. and W. Daives, 1802. 8vo., 7 engraved plates, numerous woodcuts, original full gilt ruled calf, spine heavily restored, extremities worn, hinges neatly mended, bookplates of James T. Bland, and Anne Willan, very good.   Jeff Weber Rare Books   178 - 1059   2015 $350

Association – Willcox, Susan

Lindsay, Vachel   1879-1931 *The Art of the Moving Picture.* New York: Macmillan Co., 1915. First edition, cloth professionally restored at spine ends, white painted background on front board, mostly rubbed away, corners rounded a bit, very good, lacking dust jacket, inscribed by author for Susan Willcox, author's high school English teacher.   Between the Covers Rare Books, Inc.   187 - 96   2015 $2500

Association – Williams, Daniel

Boyle, Robert   1627-1691 *Some considerations Touching the Style of the H. Scriptures.* London: for Henry Herringman, 1663. Second edition, 8vo. in 4's, light marginal browning with some occasional spotting, contemporary sheep ruled in blind, front cover detached, worn, scuffed, bumped and with small pieces missing from upper and lower headcaps, contemporary signature "Dan(ie)l Williams, ex-libris J. Kembler Anno 1755, from the library of James Stevens Cox (1910-1997).   Maggs Bros. Ltd.   1447 - 42   2015   £180

Association – Williams, Galen

Gerber, Dan *The Chinese Poems: Letters to a Distant Friend.* Fremont: Sumac Press, 1978. First edition, number 89 of 300 hardcover copies, signed by author, drawings by Jack Smith, octavo, fine in fine dust jacket, inscribed by poet to Galen Williams, laid in is a brief ANS from Gerber to Williams.   Between the Covers Rare Books, Inc.   187 - 107   2015 $150

Association – Williams, Harold

Addison, Joseph   1672-1719 *The Letters...* Oxford: Clarendon Press, 1941. Half title, frontispiece, plate, original maroon cloth, Geoffrey Tillotson's copy with some pencil and ink notes, typescript review by Donald Bond and contrasting printed review by Marjorie Williams with card from her and from Harold Williams about review.   Jarndyce Antiquarian Booksellers CCVII - 1   2015   £30

Association – Williams, Henry

Stagg, Amos Alonzo *A Scientific and Practical Treatise on American Football for Schools and Colleges.* Hartford: Press of the Case, Lockwood & Brainard Co., 1893. First edition, 12mo., diagrams, blue cloth gilt, illustrations front board, two small contemporary owner's name stamps, modest rubbing and tiny tears at spine ends, handsome, near fine, scarce, signed by Stagg and co-author Henry L. Williams, very scarce, especially signed.   Between the Covers Rare Books   196 - 175   2015 $4800

Association – Williams, Jonathan

Johnstone, William *Paintings by William Johnstone.* Newcastle upon Tyne: Stone Gallery, 1963. Octavo, illustrated wrappers, fine, exhibition pamphlet, inscribed by Hugh MacDiarmid (provided foreword) for Jonathan Williams, 15/8/63.   Between the Covers Rare Books, Inc.   187 - 162   2015 $250

Niedecker, Lorine *My Friend Tree. Poems.* Edinburgh: Wild Hawthorn Press, 1961. First edition, linocuts by Walter Miller, original wrappers, dust jacket, extremely rare, oblong 8vo., original wrappers, dust jacket, fine, inscribed by author for Jonathan Williams Sept. 3 69, extremely rare.   James S. Jaffe Rare Books   Modern American Poetry - 212   2015 $7500

Association – Williams, Marjorie

Addison, Joseph   1672-1719 *The Letters...* Oxford: Clarendon Press, 1941. Half title, frontispiece, plate, original maroon cloth, Geoffrey Tillotson's copy with some pencil and ink notes, typescript review by Donald Bond and contrasting printed review by Marjorie Williams with card from her and from Harold Williams about review.   Jarndyce Antiquarian Booksellers CCVII - 1   2015   £30

Association – Williams, Sidney

Cooper, Merian C. *Grass.* New York: G. P. Putnam's Sons, 1925. First edition, inscribed by author to Sidney Williams, scarce thus, very good plus in very good dust jacket, spine slightly toned and couple of faint smudges to boards, jacket spine and folds toned, few faint dampstains and tiny chips and tears (several cellophane repairs on verso).   Royal Books   46 - 24   2015 $3750

Association – Willington, James Tomkinson

Hamilton, Thomas *Men and Manners in America.* Edinburgh: William Blackwood, 1833. First edition, 12mo., 2 volumes, contemporary half brown calf by J. Seacome, Chester, gilt bands, black and maroon morocco labels, little rubbed, nice, crisp copy, armorial bookplate of James Tomkinson Willington.   Jarndyce Antiquarian Booksellers CCXI - 132   2015   £280

Association – Willis, John

Stillingfleet, Edward *A Discourse Concerning Bonds of resignation of Benefices in Point of law and Conscience.* London: printed by J. H. for Henry Mortlok, 1695. First edition, 8vo., complete with final leaf of ads, contemporary panelled calf rather worn, but very good, crisp copy with original label, early ownership signature on front free endpaper of John Willis of Lymington.   John Drury Rare Books   2015 - 15119   2015 $221

Association – Willis, Mary

Banns, William *The Cabinet of Jewels; or Repository of Truth.* Diss: printed by E. E. Abbott bookseller, 1836. 12mo., half title, original cloth, faded, label removed from upper cover, early signature (Mary Willis 1841), good copy, apparently rare.   John Drury Rare Books   2015 - 23516   2015 $133

Association – Wilmarth, Anna

Ellis, F. S. *Poems Chosen Out of the Works of Samuel Taylor Coleridge.* Hammersmith: Kelmscott Press, 1896. printed in an edition of 308 copies, this being one of 300 copies printed on paper, small 8vo., original publisher's limp vellum with silk ties, ornamented with woodcut borders and six and ten-line initial letters throughout the text, some soiling of vellum along edges, bookplate of Anna H. Wilmarth, some leaves foxed along edges, ribbon ties well preserved.   Oak Knoll Books   306 - 154   2015 $2000

Rossetti, Dante Gabriel   1828-1882 *Hand and Soul.* Hammersmith: Kelmscott Press, 1895. Printed in an edition limited to 546 copies, this one of 225 copies printed on paper for Way and Williams of Chicago, 12mo., original stiff vellum, woodcut borders on facing titlepage and first page of text, ornamented with numerous six line and smaller initial letters throughout text, two small spots along front hinge, bookplate of Anna H. Wilmarth, few foxed spots along outer edge of pages.   Oak Knoll Books   306 - 155   2015 $1500

Association – Wilmarth, Mary Hawes

Rossetti, Dante Gabriel   1828-1882 *The House of Life.* Boston: Copeland and Day, 1894. Limited to 550 copies, 8vo., quarter cloth, paper covered boards, top edge cut, other edges uncut, dust jacket torn at spine and chipped at edges, joints and hinges cracking, 3 borders and 114 initials by Bertram Grosvenor Goodhue, bookplate of Mary Hawes Wilmarth (1837-1919).   Oak Knoll Books   306 - 147   2015 $250

Association – Wilmot, John Eardley

Colquhoun, John Campbell *The System of National Education in Ireland: its Principle and Practice.* Cheltenham: published by William Wight, 1838. First edition, 12mo., original publisher's cloth, sides embossed in blind, spine gilt and lettered, fine, from the 19th century library of John Eardley Wilmot 1783-1847 with his signature.   John Drury Rare Books   March 2015 - 21788   2015   £306

Association – Wilson, Angus

Mishima, Yukio *After the Banquet.* London: Secker & Warburg, 1963. First edition, 8vo. signed presentation from author to Angus (Wilson), very good in like dust jacket.   Any Amount of Books   2015 - C14196   2015   £1400

Mishima, Yukio *Confessions of a Mask.* London: Peter Owen, 1964. Second impression, 8vo., pages 255, original cream cloth lettered gilt at spine, signed presentation from author to novelist Angus Wilson, 23 March 1965, very good+ in faintly used dust jacket, complete and very good with second, slightly chipped jacket underneath.   Any Amount of Books   2015 - C13524   2015   £1200

Mishima, Yukio *Thirst for Love.* New York: Alfred A. Knopf, 1969. First US edition, 8vo., original brown cloth, lettered gilt at spine, signed presentation from author on front endpaper to novelist Angus Wilson, very good+ in very good dust jacket, slight rubbing with slight surface wear and small nicks at top of spine.   Any Amount of Books   2015 - C13525   2015   £1250

Moorcock, Michael *Breakfast in the Ruins: a Novel of Inhumanity.* London: New English Library, 1972. 8vo., original light blue and brown cloth lettered gilt at spine, signed presentation from author on dedication page, dedication for Angus Wilson, very good+ in very good dust jacket slightly rubbed at spine.   Any Amount of Books   2015 - C12515   2015   £225

Spender, Stephen *Engaged in Writing: and the Fool and the Princess.* London: Hamish Hamilton, 1958. First edition, 8vo., original grey cloth lettered gilt at spine, signed presentation from author to writer Angus Wilson, Jan. 1958, very good+ in very slightly discolored but decent, very good dust jacket. Any Amount of Books 2015 - C12512 2015 £160

Torga, Miguel *Lamentation: a Poems.* N.P.: n.p., Printed by Coimbra Editora, 1960. First edition, 8vo., 32 pages, original cream wrappers, lettered blue on front cover, signed presentation from author on front endpaper to author Angus Wilson, slight surface wear, with stain at top of rear wrapper, otherwise sound, near very good. Any Amount of Books 2015 - C12730 2015 £175

Association – Wilson, M. G., Mrs.

Barry, Theodore Augustus *Men and Memories of San Francisco in the "Spring of '50".* San Francisco: A. L. Bancroft & Co., 1873. First edition, 12mo., green cloth gilt stamped title lettering to spine and front board, green endpapers, withal a good copy, gilt bright, slight lean, small abrasion to cloth at top front joint, foxing to edges, bookplate of James D. Phelan (mayor of San Francisco), ownership signature of Mrs. M. G. Wilson. Tavistock Books Bah, Humbug? - 28 2015 $275

Association – Wilson, Rose O'Neill

Wilson, Harry Leon *The Spenders: a Tale of the Third Generation.* Boston: Lothrop Pub. Co., 1902. Stated 'Twenty-six Thousand", illustrations, front hinge little tender, else near fine with light wear at spine ends, this copy inscribed by author for Robert House Mackey, additionally inscribed by the illustrator, the author's wife, Rose O'Neill Wilson. Between the Covers Rare Books 196 - 125 2015 $650

Association – Wilsons, William

Descartes, Rene *Renatus Descartes Excellent Compendium of Musick.* London: by Thomas Harper for Humphrey Moseley and Thomas Heath, 1653. First edition in English, small 4to., later engraved portrait, dampstaining to lower margins throughout, dark ink stain to upper margins of a1-b1- (not touching text), worming to lower margin of I4-M4 and with small piece torn away from margins of B3, G3 and L3 (not touching text), contemporary sheep, covers ruled in blind, spine worn and with some worm damage, edges and corners worn and chewed, 18th century inscription William Wilsons, 19th century signature G. U. Hart, Killderry, from the library of James Stevens Cox (1910-1997). Maggs Bros. Ltd. 1447 - 139 2015 £1500

Association – Wimsey, Matthew

Sayers, Dorothy L. *Papers Relating to the Family of Wimsey.* London: privately printed for the Family by Humphrey Milford, 1936. First edition, one of 500 copies, frontispiece, 1 further plate, 8vo., original blue wrappers printed in black with fading to borders, couple of waterspots at head of front and chipping to edges, 2 cm. loss at head of backstrip, few foxspots to inside front cover and flyleaf, good, inscribed by Matthew Wimsey and Peter Death Bredon Wimsey to Gerard Hopkins, nephew of Gerard Manley Hopkins, with 2 photocopies TLS's from Sayers to Basil Blackwell loosely inserted. Blackwell's Rare Books B179 - 231 2015 £750

Association – Wimsey, Peter

Sayers, Dorothy L. *Papers Relating to the Family of Wimsey.* London: privately printed for the Family by Humphrey Milford, 1936. First edition, one of 500 copies, frontispiece, 1 further plate, 8vo., original blue wrappers printed in black with fading to borders, couple of waterspots at head of front and chipping to edges, 2 cm. loss at head of backstrip, few foxspots to inside front cover and flyleaf, good, inscribed by Matthew Wimsey and Peter Death Bredon Wimsey to Gerard Hopkins, nephew of Gerard Manley Hopkins, with 2 photocopies TLS's from Sayers to Basil Blackwell loosely inserted. Blackwell's Rare Books B179 - 231 2015 £750

Association – Winfield, Trevor

Ashbery, John *A Nest of Ninnies.* New York: Dutton, 1969. First edition, one of 6000 copies, 8vo., cloth backed boards, dust jacket, small spot of dampstaining at head of spine, spine little cocked, otherwise fine in slightly dust soiled, and nicked dust jacket, with one tiny closed tear and bit of wear to head of spine, presentation from James Schuyler for Trevor Winkfield. James S. Jaffe Rare Books Modern American Poetry - 12 2015 $1750

Association – Winn, Clifton

Whitehead, Alfred North 1861-1947 *Process and Reality, an Essay in Cosmology.* New York: Macmillan Co., 1929. First American edition, octavo, former owner's name 'Clifton C. Winn' in ink and typed note crudely taped to inside front cover, given by him to Dr. Donald Kleckner, original navy blue cloth, gilt lettering on slightly sunned spine, inside tight, bright, clean copy. Athena Rare Books 15 - 59 2015 $4000

Association – Winthrop, Bronson

Sterne, Laurence 1713-1768 *Letters of the Late Rev. Mr. Laurence Sterne to His Most Intimate Friends.* London: printed for T. Becket, 1776. New edition, i.e. second edition, 165 x 102mm., extraordinarily pretty contemporary red straight grain morocco, elaborately gilt in style of Roger Payne (though not defintely attributable to him), covers with frame of alternating long stemmed tulips and daisies, corners with floral spring surrounded by dots and stars inside a laurel wreath, flat spines densely gilt in compartments with central lily on a stippled ground, framed by 8 pointed stars and with sunbursts at corners, gilt tiling and turn-ins, marbled endpapers, all edges gilt; with (usually missing) frontispiece in volume I, bookplate of Louis Auchincloss, presentation inscription from Bronson Winthrop dated 23 Feb. 1932, verso of titlepage with pictorial library stamp of Schlossbibliothek Dessau; volume 1 with slight browning, offsetting and foxing (other two volumes only very moderately affected), leaves generally a shade less than bright, uniform faint fading to spines (scarcely noticeable because of abundance of gilt), corners with minor wear but beautiful set, text fresh and clean, bindings lustrous, glittering and so little used as to resist opening. Phillip J. Pirages 66 - 58 2015 $4500

Association – Wise, James

Arness, James *James Arness: an Autobiography.* McFarland & Co., 2001. First edition, first printing, signed and dated in month of publication by Arness and co-author James Wise, also included is T shirt and several promotional leaflets from the signing, and photo of Matt Dillon/Arness, blue cloth, gilt stamped front cover and spine, frontispiece, as new. Buckingham Books March 2015 - 17626 2015 $750

Association – Wise, Kirk

Rebello, Stephen *The Art of the Hunchback of Notre Dame.* New York: Hyperion, 1996. First edition, this copy signed by 10 members of the production company, including Gary Trousdale and Kirk Wise, artistic coordinator Randy Fullmer, writers Irene Meechi and Tab Murphy and five animators, numerous full color drawings and sketches in black and white, laid in is announcement for book signing party, fine in fine dust jacket. Ed Smith Books 83 - 15 2015 $250

Association – Witt-Diamant, Ruth

Broughton, James *Odes for Odd Occasions: Poems 1954-1976.* South San Francisco: Manroot, 1977. First edition, illustrated wrappers, toning on spine, else near fine, Ruth Witt-Diamant's copy, signed by her twice, and signed by Broughton, nice association. Between the Covers Rare Books, Inc. 187 - 33 2015 $100

Association – Woburn Abbey

A Collection of Interesting, Authentic Papers, Relative to the Dispute Between Great Britain and America... London: printed for J. Almon, 1777. First edition, dated bookplate "Woburn Abbey 1873", contemporary three quarter marbled sides, lacking one leaf, corners worn, spine very rough, some scattered light foxing, internally clean overall. Argonaut Book Shop Holiday Season 2014 - 9 2015 $900

Association – Wolfe, Humbert

Pound, Ezra Loomis 1885-1972 *Umbra: the Early Poems of Ezra Pound.* London: Elkin Mathews, 1920. First edition, 8vo., original printed grey boards with cloth spine, slight soiling, slight marks but decent, very good copy, ownership signature of Humbert Wolfe Jan 18 1926. Any Amount of Books 2015 - A45366 2015 £150

Association – Wolseley, A.

Church of England. Book of Common Prayer *The Book of Common Prayer... Together with the Psalter or Psalms of David.* Cambridge: Printed by John Baskerville, 1762. Third edition, 241 x 165mm., excellent contemporary Irish red morocco, very elaborately gilt and inlaid, covers with central white morocco lozenge inlaid and tooled with gilt flowers, plumes and birds beak, whole framed by undulating floral sprigs, raised bands, spine gilt in compartments quartered by a saltire and tooled with roses and other flowers, gilt turn-ins, marbled endpapers, all edges gilt, (small expert repair along top of spine), titlepage with ink inscription of A. Wolseley dated 1772 at top with small decorative printed paper strip pasted over price at bottom, covers less dark than the spine (and so somehow faded?), slight flaking but no cracking to joints, corners little worn, but the once splendid binding still extremely attractive, without serious wear, and with its very animated gilt still bright, despite the loss of color in the morocco background, many leaves with faint browning and muted foxing (one gathering conspicuously toned), some other trivial imperfections, but fresh and clean and generally pleasing internally. Phillip J. Pirages 66 - 40 2015 $12,500

Association – Wood, Audrey

Redgrave, Michael *The Aspern Papers...* London: Heinemann, 1959. First edition, fine in very good dust jacket with some rubbing and small chips and tears, famed literary agent Audrey Wood's ownership stamp on front fly, inscribed by Redgrave for Wood. Between the Covers Rare Books, Inc. 187 - 231 2015 $275

Association – Wood, Sarah Gilbert

Prideaux, Sara T. *An Historical Sketch of Bookbinding.* London: Lawrence & Bullen, 1893. First edition, one of 120 numbered copies printed on handmade paper, square 8vo., original cloth, chip out of bottom of spine, wear along front hinge at top and back hinge bookplate of Sarah Gilbert Wood who has added her ownership inscription dated 1898 on half title.   Oak Knoll Books   306 - 9   2015 $250

Association – Woods, Winnefred

Moore, Marianne   1887-1972 *Collected Poems.* New York: Macmillan, 1951. First American edition, 8vo., original cloth, dust jacket, fine, jacket spine slightly faded as usual, presentation copy inscribed by Moore to Winnefred Woods.   James S. Jaffe Rare Books   Modern American Poetry - 204   2015 $1000

Association – Wool, John Ellis

Cutter, George Washington *Buena Vista and Other Poems.* Cincinnati: Morgan & Overend Printers, 1848. First edition, 12mo., original blindstamped red cloth, gilt decorations and lettering, all edges gilt, frontispiece, fine presentation copy inscribed by author for Maj. Gen'l. John E. Wool (1784-1869), cloth little worn, slight foxing, fine.   The Brick Row Book Shop   Miscellany 67 - 14   2015 $800

Association – Woolf, Leonard

Woolf, Virginia   1882-1941 *Hours in a Library.* New York: Harcourt Brace and Co., 1957. One of 1800 copies, personal copy of author's sister, Vanessa Bell, with presentation from Leonard Woolf Christmas 1957, publisher's royal blue cloth spine over black paper boards, with author's initials stamped in blind to front board, lettered gilt in original publisher's glassine jacket, near fine with hint of wear to extremities, slightest toning to spine, faint hint of light soiling to board edges, glassine tipped in to frontispiece as protective sheet, bright and fresh interior, light toning to glassine with chipping to extremities and some loss to spine ends, light creasing to front panel, rare in any condition, complete copy, custom quarter clamshell box.   B & B Rare Books, Ltd.   239 - 9   2015 $6500

Association – Work, Tom

Steinbeck, John Ernst   1902-1968 *Cannery Row.* New York: Viking Press, 1945. First edition, inscribed by author for Tom Work, irregular sunning to cloth, very good price clipped dust jacket with soiling to rear panel.   Ed Smith Books   83 - 89   2015 $4500

Association – Wright, Stuart

Meredith, William *Hazard the Painter.* New York: Alfred A. Knopf, 1973. First edition, fine in fine dust jacket, inscribed by author to publisher Stuart Wright with two lines of verse.   Between the Covers Rare Books, Inc.   187 - 176   2015 $200

Percy, Walker   1916-1990 *The Moviegoer.* New York: Alfred A. Knopf, 1961. First edition, fine in lightly rubbed, near fine dust jacket with very light edgewear, inscribed by author to publisher and bibliographer Stuart Wright.   Between the Covers Rare Books   196 - 101   2015 $6000

Association – Wyatt, A. J.

Beowulf *The Tale of Beowulf.* Hammersmith: Kelmscott Press, 1895. One of 300 copies printed on Perch paper, quarto, bound in limp vellum, inscribed by translator, A. J. Wyatt to his wife Catherine, custom slipcase, woodcut borders and initials designed by William Morris, "Not to Reader" slip laid in, with pencil annotations to verso, lovely association copy.   Honey & Wax Booksellers   1 - 55   2015 $8200

Association – Wyatt, Catherine

Beowulf *The Tale of Beowulf.* Hammersmith: Kelmscott Press, 1895. One of 300 copies printed on Perch paper, quarto, bound in limp vellum, inscribed by translator, A. J. Wyatt to his wife Catherine, custom slipcase, woodcut borders and initials designed by William Morris, "Not to Reader" slip laid in, with pencil annotations to verso, lovely association copy.   Honey & Wax Booksellers   1 - 55   2015 $8200

Association – Wyatt, Stephen

Powell, Michael *A Life In the Movies: an Autobiography.* London: Heinemann, 1986. First edition, 8vo., original green boards lettered gilt on spine, signed by author, ownership signature of Stephen Wyatt, playwright and author of Doctor Who books, slight lean, slight bumping, otherwise near fine in near fine dust jacket with very slight creasing, spine somewhat faded as always.   Any Amount of Books   2015 - A68824   2015   £225

Association – Wyndham, Greta

Betjeman, John 1906-1984 *An Oxford University Chest, Comprising a Description of the Present State of the Town and University of Oxford...* Miles, 1938. First edition, 54 plates, line drawings by Osbert Lancaster and reproductions of engravings from earlier works, titlepage and frontispiece bordered in red, 4to., original quarter dark blue buckram, lightly faded backstrip gilt blocked, cream, black and red marbled boards, very light tail edge rubbing, very good, very good, with author's presentation inscription on front free endpaper to Greta Wyndham (widow of Richard Wyndham). Blackwell's Rare Books   B179 - 131   2015   £500

Association – Young, Oxford

Arnold, Matthew 1822-1888 *Poems. Second Series.* London: Longmans, 1855. First edition, vi & 24 page catalog. (Nov. 1854), original green cloth by Westley's, orange endpapers with printed ads, spine faded, with splits in hinges, bookplate of Oxford Young, signed by Geoffrey Tillotson April 1944.   Jarndyce Antiquarian Booksellers   CCVII - 47   2015   £50

Association – Zaehnsdorf Company

Maas & Jungvogel *Monogramm Album.* Crefeld: Maas & Jungvogel, n.d. crica 1880's, 4to., original cloth stamped in gilt, all edges gilt, highly decorative titlepage followed by leaves showing combinations of different letters of the alphabet, from the reference library of Zaehnsdorf Company with commemorative booklabel loosely inserted, minor wear along edges.   Oak Knoll Books   Special Catalogue 24 - 34   2015 $650

Association – Zahn, Mabel

Buck, Pearl S. *Of Men and Women.* New York: John Day, 1941. First edition, inscribed by author to Philadelphia bookseller Mabel Zahn, small stain at spine crown corresponding to jacket chip, very good in very good, spine tanned dust jacket with very minor edge loss.   Ken Lopez, Bookseller   164 - 21   2015 $375

Association – Zinn, Howard

Walker, Alice 1944- *Revolutionary Petunias & Other Poems.* New York: Harcourt Brace Jovanovich, 1973. First edition, trifle rubbed at base of spine, else fine in very near fine dust jacket with minimal soiling, warmly inscribed by author to Howard Zinn and his wife Roz, scarce. Between the Covers Rare Books, Inc.   187 - 286   2015 $600

Association – Zinn, Roz

Walker, Alice 1944- *Revolutionary Petunias & Other Poems.* New York: Harcourt Brace Jovanovich, 1973. First edition, trifle rubbed at base of spine, else fine in very near fine dust jacket with minimal soiling, warmly inscribed by author to Howard Zinn and his wife Roz, scarce. Between the Covers Rare Books, Inc.   187 - 286   2015 $600

Fine Bindings

Binding - 15th Century

Thomas Aquinas, Saint *Summa Theologica Pars Secunda; Prima Pars.* Venice: Theodorus de Ragazonibus 31 March, 1490. 324 x 222mm., 200 unnumbered leaves (complete) with first last, and leaf 194 blank, 60 lines, gothic type, excellent contemporary blindstamped Northern Italian calf (perhaps from Venice or Milan), outer border of blind fillets with mitered corners, inner frame formed by chain roll within triple fillets, frame enclosing large central panel dominated by a cross formed by repeated impressions of a diamond tool and with four small crosses composed of same tool in quadrants formed by large cross, background punctuated with small rosettes, raised bands, spine compartments with saltire of blind fillets, the same diamond and rosette tools decorating the quadrants, old paper label with ink year of publication, four original brass catches on lower cover (two along fore edge, one each at top and bottom), top clasp and rawhide thong intact (remnants of the other thongs present), 4 particularly fine 12th century vellum manuscript flyleaves from liturgical ms. in fine Carolingian hand; 8 large decorated initials (most five to seven line, one 14-line) in elaborate vinestem designs in red infilled with yellow, blue and green, one of the initials containing a charming deer, small patch of leather missing from head of front board, exposing wood beneath, upper inner corner of cover solid, without serious wear, still very attractive as an unrestored period artifact, flyleaves with inch or so of discoloration around edges (from binder's glue), vellum slightly rumpled, otherwise manuscript leaves especially fine and well preserved, first four gatherings with small dampstain to upper gutter (quite minor dampstaining and foxing elsewhere), half dozen leaves slightly browned, but really excellent copy internally, mostly very clean and fresh, especially ample margins. Phillip J. Pirages 66 - 1 2015 $95,000

Binding - 16th Century

Baif, Lazare De *Annotationes in L. II. De Captivis et Postiliminio Reversis in Quibus Tractatur de re Navali (and three other works).* Paris: Robert Estienne, 1536. First edition of De Re Navali, first printing of this collection, 216 x 140mm., striking 16th century English calf, heavily and beautifully gilt, covers gilt with border formed by two plain rules flaking a floral roll, this frame enclosing a central field of very many tiny star tools, intricate strapwork cornerpieces and large central arabesque composed of strapwork interspersed with lilies and volutes, flat spine divided into latticed gilt panels by double plain rules and floral bands, newer (17th or 18th century?) black morocco label, binding almost certainly with some restoration (joints probably worked on, though repairs executed with such skill as to make difficult identifying exactly what has been done), old stock used for replacement endpapers 32 fine woodcuts in text, 11 of them full page or nearly so, 4 woodcut diagrams, decorative initials, covers with minor discoloration, little crackling and minor scratching, gilt bit dulled and eroded, one corner somewhat bumped, half a dozen leaves with faint dampstains to lower outer corner, hint of soil in isolated places, but extremely pleasing copy, binding solid, no serious wear, still very attractive, text clean, fresh and bright, margins generous. Phillip J. Pirages 66 - 4 2015 $7500

Catholic Church. Liturgy & Ritual - Hours *Use of Rome (Printed book of Hours on Vellum in Latin and French).* Paris: Thielman Kerver, May, 1510. Calendar covering years 1506-1530, 171 x 108mm., titlepage (A1) in very good paper facsimile (though blank on verso, so lacking Anatomical man engraving that should appear there), pleasing mid 16th century dark calf, gilt, covers framed by multiple blind rules, central panel formed by a gilt fillet with acorn fillet with acorn tools extending obliquely from outer corners, gilt vegetal tools at inner corners, central gilt arabesque, raised bands, expertly rebacked preserving original backstrip (as well as recornered?), spine in blind ruled compartments with saltire, unusual later 17th century?) brass clasps and catches, hardware extending some 90mm. (or three quarters of the way) across each board, extensions held in place by small brass nails, numerous one and two line initials in colors and gold, each page with decorative and/or historiated frames featuring charming and sometimes fascinating scenic metal-cut border panels at bottom and fore edge, 34 small miniatures and 18 richly detailed full page cuts, a diagram explaining the concept of Trinity and Christ with the symbols of the Passion, 17th century engraved and hand painted holy card on vellum by Cornelius Galle tipped in at front, early engraved heraldic bookplate, inkstamp "Kon. Kupferstich Cabinet Stuttgart" on verso of holy card and of last leaf, last (blank) page with early ink ownership signatures and pen trials and dated 1679; spine slightly cocked, backstrip little roughened, but carefully restored binding quite lustrous with very little wear and generally well preserved, trimmed cloth at top, decorative border just touched on several leaves containing full page miniatures, half dozen leaves with faint but noticeable brown stains, minor signs of use, vellum generally not very bright, other trivial imperfections, still reasonable copy internally with many pages quite pleasing, no fatal condition issues. Phillip J. Pirages 66 - 11 2015 $16,000

Gellius, Aulus *Auli Gelii Luculentissimi Scriptoris Noctes Atticae. (Attic Nights).* Lugduni: Apud Antonium Gryphium, 1591. 124 x 76mm., handsome contemporary Venetian red morocco richly gilt in armorial design, upper cover with central coat of arms flanked by oval to right containing an eagle and one to left enclosing a star, the background a riot of foliage, grotesques, crescents and gilt dots, "ALOYS" in a cartouche at top, "ZABAR" at bottom, lower cover with similar design but with different coat of arms, "TIBER" in a cartouche at head, "CINC" at foot, raised bands, spine panels tooled in gilt in a chain pattern, all edges gilt and gauffered in a diapered design, holes for ties (apparently some very expert repairs at spine ends), Printer's griffin device on titlepage, short marginal wormhole to first four leaves, E1 with light (wax?) stain obscuring a couple of words on four lines, text on inferior paper and consequently with light overall browning throughout, occasional minor foxing, other trivial defects but still very good internally, joints and corners little rubbed, but resplendent binding in excellent condition, quite bright and showing only insignificant wear. Phillip J. Pirages 66 - 20 2015 $6500

Plato *(Greek text) Omnia Platonis Opera.* Venice: in aedib. Aldi et Andreae Soceri, Sept, 1513. Editio princeps, 2 volumes, large Aldine anchor device on titlepage (volume I) and on verso of last leaf in volume ii, Greek text (apart from Aldus' dedicatory petition, contents and colophon), titlepage slightly soiled and with hole at inner margin repaired, minor stains on fore-edges, few wormholes in blank lower margin of opening leaves of volumes ii, volume, volume i in contemporary English quartered oak boards, resewn with spine uncovered, modern vellum endleaves, volume ii in contemporary German pigskin over wooden boards, blind tooled to panel design filled in with 'laus deo' and rosette stamps, brass catches and clasps, top of spine worn, inner hinge broken, cord intact, good, binding of the first volume of this copy is subject of 2 page report by Nicholas Pickwood (printout accompanies the volume), repairs carried out by James Brockman; first volume with signature of Thomas Colm of Oxford dated 1573, 17th century ownership inscription of Hendricus Ffeild, 19th century bookplate and stamp of King Edward's School, Birmingham, plus bookplate of Kenneth Rapoport, the second volume with early ownership inscriptions of Johannes (or Johann?) Lang of Erfurt and Philippus Kleissenius, few early marginalia, inscription 'de bibliotheca Johannis Langi Erphurdiensis. Blackwell's Rare Books   Greek & Latin Classics VI - 82   2015   £75,000

Polybius *Historiarum Libri Priores Quinque.* Lugduni: Seb. Gryphium, 1554. 178 x 108mm., pleasing contemporary (English?) calf, covers with single gilt fillet border and intricate arabesque centerpiece, raised bands, spine panels with central azured gilt fleur-de-lys or floral spring, apparently original morocco label (perhaps, but perhaps not - with very expert repairs at spine ends), publisher's woodcut griffin device on title and last page, 18th century? engraved armorial bookplate of Sir William Baird and modern bookplate of Kenneth Rapoport, titlepage with early ownership signature of Franciscus T.... (now washed away and consequently very faint), occasional contemporary underlinings and manicules, joints rubbed (and with thin cracks alongside top spine panel on upper and lower joint and along bottom two spine panels on upper joint), lower cover with minor discoloration (perhaps from damp), other trivial defects, binding entirely solid, still quite lustrous and with nothing approaching a major condition problem, without front free endpaper, n3 with branching tear (paper flaw?) from margin into text necessitating, (old) repair, but without loss, isolated faint browning, other small imperfections, but really consistently very fresh and clean, very well preserved, attractive mid 16th century binding.   Phillip J. Pirages   66 - 14   2015 $3200

Thomas A Kempis   1380-1471 *Opera.* Paris: Iodocus Badius Ascensius, 1523. Second collected edition, first edition printed in France, 330 x 216mm., lacking final blank, fine contemporary London blindstamped calf, covers tooled in panels, outer frame of a roll of Renaissance designs including fountain topped by three heads, central panel composed mainly of five vertical rows of foliage and flowers, raised bands, spine very expertly rebacked to style, two original brass clasps and catches with leather thongs (perhaps later but perhaps not), original vellum tabs marking important textual sections, rear board with contemporaneous inscription (perhaps author and title), rear pastedown comprising a portion of a proclamation dealing with beggars and vagabonds, in recent clamshell box backed with calf, titlepage with woodcut device dated 1520 depicting printer's workshop, large and small woodcut initials in text (few artlessly colored), titlepage with signature of Johannes Person above woodcut vignette and of another member of Person family at top of page, (this inscription dated 1566 with purchase details for the volume), also signature of A. Fletcher, inside cover of box and front pastedown with modern morocco bookplate of Michael Sharpe, lower board with small abraded area, other trivial marks and very small wormholes in leather, thongs bit dried and deteriorating, but expertly restored binding entirely solid and blindstamping still quite sharp, titlepage little dust soiled and with small shadow of turn-in glue at bottom, last three gatherings with minor stains along gutter, final gathering with similar stain at fore-edge, short tears and other trivial imperfections in text, generally quite fine internally, text mostly quite clean, especially fresh and unusually bright.   Phillip J. Pirages   66 - 7   2015 $12,500

Valeriano, Giovanni Pierio *Hieroglyphica Sive de Sacris Aegyptiorvm Literis Commentarii... A Caelio Augustino Curione Duobus Libris Aucti et Multis Imaginibus Illustrati.* Basileae: Per Thomam Guarinum, 1567. Second edition, 362 x 235mm., excellent contemporary blindstamped pigskin, covers with multiple frames of palmettes, rosettes, floral rolls, and an allegorical roll depicting Fides, Justitia, Caritas and Spes, raised bands, traces of ink titling to spine, intact original brass clasps, small hole at head of rear board where a chain was once attached; woodcut printer's device on title and last page, frontispiece, 12 charts in text, 265 mostly emblematic illustrations, (18th century?) engraved armorial bookplate and 19th century woodcut bookplate of William Schott, titlepage with two early (probably 17th century) inscriptions from monastery library at Kaisersheim; very minor soiling to pigskin, small area of discoloration at top of back board (where chain hasp had been located), front hinge beginning to open at top, final few leaves with minor traces of mildew, barely perceptible diagonal dampstain at upper corner on a number of text leaves, other trivial imperfections, nearly fine contemporary copy, unrestored binding showing almost no signs of use, text bright, clean and fresh with spacious margins.   Phillip J. Pirages   66 - 19   2015 $7500

Binding - 17th Century

Bible. English - 1640 *The Holy Bible: Containing the Old Testament and the New. (Bound with) The Whole Book of Pslames.* London: by Robert Barker, 1640. 1639, 191 x 127mm., superb contemporary dark brown morocco, elaborately gilt, covers with intricate frame and central lozenge composed of many fleurons, volutes and other small tools, silver cornerpieces and centerpiece, engraved "Recor/dare/matrem?Johanna Strode" (To Remember Mother, Johanna Strode"), original silver clasps and catches, raised bands, spine densely gilt in compartments with fleurons radiating from concentric circles, marbled pastedowns (apparently lacking marbled free endpapers), all edges gilt, ornate woodcut titles and headpieces for each testament, full page royal coat of arms opposite dedication; slight rubbing to joints and extremities, occasional mild browning, isolated rust spots or small stains, other trivial imperfections, exceptionally fine, clean and fresh internally, sparkling binding. Phillip J. Pirages   66 - 25   2015 $17,500

Bible. English - 1684 *The Holy Bible. (bound with) The Whole Book of Psalms Collected into English Metre.* London: printed by the Assigns of J. Bill, T. Newcombe and Henr. Hills, 1684. 1683. Printed for the company of stationers, 1683, 127 x 64mm., 2 separately published works bound in 1 volume, 2 leaves (Eee3 and 4) bound in reverse order, very appealing contemporary red morocco, elaborately gilt and painted, covers with an ornate design of drawer handle tools, semi-circle at head and tail and wedge tool at side, both shapes filled with floral tools, top spine end raised, higher than board edges in stylized a la grecque design, marbled endpapers, all edges gilt, velvet lined modern maroon clamshell box with black morocco label, engraved titlepage with architectural frame, engraved bookplate of Gaspard Ernest Stroehlin showing Calvin preaching, with motto "Mente Libera", early (binder's?) pin inserted behind the upper headband; extremities bit rubbed, spine little crackled and with tiny split at bottom, faint faded in several spots, gilt on front cover just slightly dulled but binding still extremely pleasing, with no significant wear, titlepage with minor soil and corner crease, head margin trimmed with little close (no loss), otherwise fine internally, text especially smooth, fresh and clean.   Phillip J. Pirages   66 - 29   2015 $3500

Donatus, Alexander *Constantinus Romae Liberator.* Romae: Ex Typographia Manelfi, 1640. First edition, 184 x 121mm., fine contemporary Italian honey brown morocco, ornately gilt, covers framed by multiple plain and dotted rules and elaborate jewel-and-flower roll, central panel with delicate dentelle border enclosing elaborate cornerpieces of scrolling floral vines and central oval with filigree frame formed by fleurons and small tools, at center the 'Sede Vacante' arm of the Holy See comprising crossed keys beneath an umbraculum (i.e. a papal umbrella), this symbol flanked here by the letters "S" and "R", flat spine decorated with a chain of fleurons within an elongated frame of multiple plain and decorative rules, old ink titling, holes for ties (now lacking) all edges gilt (new but suitable endpapers, some small repairs presumably made to joints and corners though obviously with expert hands), extra engraved titlepage with arms of Duke of Etruria and engraved allegorical portrait of Constantine I, just bit of wear to joints and extremities, title page slightly soiled and with careful repairs to edges, faint browning and minor foxing throughout (two gatherings somewhat browned, conspicuous foxing on a dozen or so leaves), little worming to final two (index) leaves, other minor defects, still reasonable copy internally, consistently fresh and clean and splendidly gilt binding lustrous and no serious signs of use.   Phillip J. Pirages   66 - 26   2015 $3900

Guarini, Battista   1538-1612 *Il Pastor Fido: Tragicomedia Pastorale.* Amsterdam: Lodovico Elzevier, 1640. 92 x 54mm. red morocco, covers gilt with french fillet border enlosing a field seme with rows of alternating ciphers "MM" and an interlaced double Phi used by Nicolas Fouquet (1615-1780), (Olivier 1398, fer 4), separated by an "S" ferme, raised bands, spine gilt compartments with double Phi cipher surrounded by small tools, delicately gilt turn-ins, marbled endpapers, all edges gilt (neat repairs to head and tail of spine), engraved vignette by C. C. Dusend on titlepage, one engraved plate and five full page engraved illustrations (blank on verso except for pagination and signature), front pastedown with part of an engraved armorial bookplate, rear pastedown with "HB" bookplate of Heribert Boeder, 9 blank leaves at end of work with ink notations in French in several hands, front joint cracked but still firm, spine slightly cocked, corners little rubbed, occasional mild foxing, final two quires with faint dampstain to upper corner, still very appealing, generally clean and fresh internally. Phillip J. Pirages   66 - 27   2015 $2800

Josephus, Flavius *(in Greek) Philabiou Josepou Hierosolymitou Heireos Ta Heuriskomena, Flavii Josephi Hierosolymitani Sacerdotis Opera Quae Extant. (Works in Greek and Latin).* Geneva: Petrus de la Rouviere, 1611. 362 x 222mm., sumptuous contemporary honey brown morocco richly gilt in modified fanfare design, covers with outer frame of multiple plain and decorative rules and rolls, frame surrounding a central panel formed by multiple plain rules and a filigree roll and featuring oblique fleurons pointing outward at corner, panel with very densely gilt and elaborate cornerpieces and a large central lozenge incorporating olive branch garlands and rosettes, an oval at center of lozenge with contemporary coat of arms of the Abbot of Potigny, either Claude Boucherat, or his cousin Charles, flat spine with a chain roll framing a single elongated panel tooled in a design similar to covers, all edges gilt, holes for ties (perhaps with small, very expert repairs at spine bottom); woodcut printer's device on titlepage, woodcut headpieces and decorative initials, Latin and Greek text printed in parallel columns, front pastedown with partially effaced 17th century ownership inscription of Henry (Becold?) Pembroke College, Oxford dated 1734 and 19th century inscription of D. C. Lewis, blank lower right corner of titlepage neatly replaced (in 19th century?) small, pale dampstain in bottom margin of a few leaves, branching marginal wormholes in half a dozen quires (but these always extremely thin and never intruding on text), minor soiling, browning and foxing here and there, still very good internally, leaves fresh, clean and with good margins; hint of wear to joints and extremities, spine uniformly little darkened (with gilt just slightly less bright tan on boards), covers with trivial discoloration and abrasions, but impressive binding in remarkable condition, entirely solid, only minor signs of use, and with once dazzling gilt nearly as good as it was 400 years ago.   Phillip J. Pirages   66 - 21   2015 $6500

Plutarchus *Vite di Plutarco Cheroneo de gil Huomini Illustri Greci et Romani.* Venetia: Marco Ginami, 1620. Later edition, 2 volumes, 229 x 149mm., extremely pleasing contemporary Italian calf lavishly gilt, covers framed by multiple plain and dotted rules and geometric roll diapered central panel with slender fleuron in each compartment, flat spines with elongated panel formed by multiple plain and dotted rules and floral filigree roll and containing three fleurons, holes for ties (now lacking), all edges gilt (apparently - though not certainly) - with some very expert repairs to spine ends and edges), with 54 ornate woodcut frames and tondo portraits to accompany each biography, printer's device on titlepage, woodcut decorative initials, titlepage of volume II with later ink inscription "A. Barbet/374i, indications of bookplate removal on front pastedowns, four leaves with short marginal tears, occasional faint dampstains to head margin, isolated minor smudges and foxing, otherwise clean, crisp and smooth, joints with minimal rubbing, couple of small stains to boards, other trivial defects, bindings in excellent condition, gilt still bright and generally with minor wear.   Phillip J. Pirages   66 - 24   2015 $4800

Binding - 18th Century

Midnight the Signal. London: sold by Dodsley, 1779. 2 volumes, 165 x 102mm., complete with usual pagination in volume II, pleasing contemporary crimson morocco bound for Jonas Hanway by his second binder, covers gilt with twining border enclosing a frame of roses with sunburst cornerpieces, upper cover with Greek cross at center encircled by motto "O save us from ourselves', lower cover with winged hourglass and motto 'Revere the appointment of nature', raised bands, spine compartments gilt in checkerboard pattern punctuated by daisies, one olive and one black morocco label, gilt turn-ins, marbled endpapers, all edges gilt, engraved titlepage with emblem depicting Death hovering over socializing persons, with a lutist in the background, large paper copy, verso of front free endpapers, with armorial bookplate from which the name has been excised, spines bit darkened with muted gilt leather on covers varying in color (from fading or soiling) but bindings entirely solid and with only trivial wear to joints, leaves with hint of offsetting and isolated soiling, faint dampstain to lower fore edge of one gathering, otherwise extremely pleasing internally, text clean, fresh and bright and with vast margins.   Phillip J. Pirages   66 - 44   2015 $4800

Onomatologia Curiosa Artificiosa et Magica, Oder, Ganz Naturliches Zauber-Lexicon. Ulm: Frankfurt und Leipzig: Auf Kosten der Gaumischen Handlung, 1759. First edition, 216 x 178mm., contemporary multi colored paste paper boards, flat spine, 3 engraved plates, and colophon with woodcut printer's device depicting a printed press, spine somewhat sunned, little chafing to boards and rubbing to extremities, but original fragile paper binding entirely sound and remarkably well preserved, occasional minor browning, foxing or offsetting, four leaves with small marginal inkstain, otherwise clean, fresh copy internally with few signs of use. Phillip J. Pirages   66 - 38   2015 $1500

Poesie Per Le Felicissime Nozze Piovene. Vicenza: per Gio. Battista Vendramini Mosca, 1774. First edition, 305 x 216mm., original pastepaper boards covered in red and green block printed patterned paper, modern red cloth folding box, frontispiece, engraved allegorical vignettes on titlepage and at end, woodcut head and tailpieces and foliated initials, all done with considerable charm, spine and head edge just slightly faded, couple of very small snags in backstrip, one page with mild thumbing, but superb copy, exceptionally clean, fresh and bright, both text and original printed paper wrappers in almost unbelievable state of preservation. Phillip J. Pirages   66 - 43   2015 $2900

Bible. English - 1736 *The Holy Bible Containing the Old and New Testaments.* Edinburgh: Robert Freebairn, 1736. 178 x 144m., animated contemporary red morocco, heavily gilt in characteristically Scottish design, covers framed by dogtooth rolls and densely tooled with gilt flowers, foliage turnips, swirls and dots, central panel with vaguely herringbone design formed by interlocking full and half circles accented by floral tools, fleurons and dots, panel framed by very prominent densely cross-hatched pear shaped ornaments, each containing a stylized thistle within it, raised bands, spine intricately gilt in compartments with scrolling cornerpieces and large fleuron centerpiece incorporating a saltire, patterned paper pastedowns (lacking free endpapers), all edges gilt (boards with shallow, thin blind rules as part of the design or else added later demarcating central panel as well as extending from top to bottom and side to side along exact center of the cover, very expert repairs to head of joints, tiny restoration to corners, bookplate of Hans Furstenberg, hint of splaying to front board, joints and extremities little rubbed (though carefully refurbished), gilt bit muted in places, but once spectacular binding still extremely appealing with nothing approaching a major condition issue, mild browning throughout, occasional trivial foxing, marginal stains, or other trivial imperfections, still excellent copy, internally few signs of use, fresh, clean leaves with comfortable margins. Phillip J. Pirages   66 - 41   2015 $13,000

Bible. English - 1743 *The Holy Bible Containing the Old and New Testaments.* Edinburgh: printed by Richard Watkins, 1743. 140 x 70mm., 2 volumes, extremely pleasing period black morocco, very elaborately gilt in Scottish Herrigbone design, covers bordered by garland roll and double gilt rules, central panel framed by decorative roll and plain rules enclosed by dotted half circles alternating with fleurs-de-lys and with oblique tulip cornerpieces, central panel with herringbone pattern formed by turnip tools and accented by other small ornaments, raised bands, spine gilt in compartments quartered by saltire and tooled with fleurons, small flowers and circlets, gilt turn-ins, Dutch endpapers of green, white and gold, all edges gilt, tiny expert repairs at spine ends, front flyleaf of each volume with 19th century? Ownership inscription of H. Gordon; bit of rubbing to joints and corners, but this well masked with dye, otherwise very appealing set in fine condition, bindings bright and showing no serious wear and especially smooth, clean text with virtually no signs of use.   Phillip J. Pirages   66 - 42   2015 $4500

Bible. German - 1784 *Biblia das ist; Die Ganze Heilige Schrift Alten Und Neuen Testamentes.* Basel: Johann Rudolf Im-Hof und Sohn, 1784. 197 x 121mm., 2 volumes bound 'dos-a-dos', very appealing contemporary red morocco Dos-a-Dos binding, covers gilt with delicate roll border featuring calligraphic flourishes at corners, at center a pineapple like oval ornament flanked by curling acanthus leaves from which a floral garland is draped, flap spines divided into compartments by multiple plain and decorative gilt rules, floral spring centerpiece and small tools at corners and sides, gilt turn-ins, all edges gilt, original (somewhat rubbed) marbled paper pull-off case, front pastedowns with booklabel of Jean Furstenberg, isolated trivial spots of foxing, really excellent specimen and virtually no internal signs of use in very bright binding with only very superficial wear. Phillip J. Pirages   66 - 47   2015 $6500

Catholic Church. Litrugy & Ritual - Breviary *Breviarium Romanum.* Venetiis: Ex Typographia Balleoniana, 1744. 4 volumes, 184 x 121mm., 4 volumes, very attractive contemporary Italian dark brown crushed morocco, handsomely gilt, covers with simple border of plain and stippled gilt rules and fleuron cornerpieces, raised bands intricately and elegantly gilt in compartments formed by plain and decorative gilt rules and featuring cornerpieces of leaves and volutes framing a central curling lozenge incorporating palmettes and a fleur-de-lys, marbled endpapers, all edges gilt with gauffering on top and bottom edges next to endbands, apparently original elaborate ribbon markers comprised of four silk strands held together at top by a large tassel, woodcut tailpieces and floriated initials, engraved printer's device of titlepages, 14 engravings by M. Beylbrouck printed in red and black, one opening with small wax(?) stain, other very trivial imperfections, but nearly flawless copy, binding with only faintest signs of age and clean, fresh and bright text, virtually no signs of use.   Phillip J. Pirages   66 - 36   2015 $1500

Church of England. Book of Common Prayer *The Book of Common Prayer... Together with the Psalter or Psalms of David.* Cambridge: Printed by John Baskerville, 1762. Third edition, 241 x 165mm., excellent contemporary Irish red morocco, very elaborately gilt and inlaid, covers with central white morocco lozenge inlaid and tooled with gilt flowers, plumes and birds beak, whole framed by undulating floral sprigs, raised bands, spine gilt in compartments quartered by a saltire and tooled with roses and other flowers, gilt turn-ins, marbled endpapers, all edges gilt, (small expert repair along top of spine), titlepage with ink inscription of A. Wolseley dated 1772 at top with small decorative printed paper strip pasted over price at bottom, covers less dark than the spine (and so somehow faded?), slight flaking but no cracking to joints, corners little worn, but the once splendid binding still extremely attractive, without serious wear, and with its very animated gilt still bright, despite the loss of color in the morocco background, many leaves with faint browning and muted foxing (one gathering conspicuously toned), some other trivial imperfections, but fresh and clean and generally pleasing internally.   Phillip J. Pirages   66 - 40   2015 $12,500

Ford, St. Clair *Scraps from Indian and Other Journals.* Cheltenham: printed by R. Edwards circa, 1858. (1857), 8vo., headings printed in red, contemporary crushed red morocco, fully gilt, sides with extravagant gilt panelling, spine fully gilt with raised bands, all edges gilt, cream silk doublures, superb but unsigned binding, lettered in gilt "Lady Ford" on upper cover.   John Drury Rare Books   2015 - 25666   2015 $1049

Homerus *The Iliad of Homer. (bound with) The Odyssey of Homer.* London: printed by T. Bensley, 1802. New edition, 5 volumes, 244 x 168mm., very attractive contemporary English red straight grain morocco extravagantly gilt, covers with frame containing alternating drawer handles and lozenges on stippled background with fleuron cornerpieces, central panel with intricate filigree fan cornerpieces, double raised bands, spine panels densely gilt in lacy pattern of small tools, inner gilt dentelles tooled in Oriental motif, turquoise endpapers, pastedowns framed by decorative gilt roll, all edges gilt; 7 engraved plates, including frontispiece in each volume, frontispieces moderately foxed, isolated foxing elsewhere (insignificant on half dozen leaves only, otherwise trivial), frontispiece of one volume with light dampstain affecting half engraved area (faint related discoloration at inner margin of next dozen leaves), otherwise very attractive internally, vast majority of text very clean, fresh and smooth, minor spotting to covers, spines uniformly faded to a pleasing maroon, insignificant rubbing to extremities, but lovely elaborately gilt contemporary bindings, very well preserved, lustrous leather, shining gilt, and only negligible wear. Phillip J. Pirages   66 - 64   2015 $3900

Owen, David Dale 1807-1860 *Report of a Geological Survey of Wisconsin, Iowa and Minnesota and Incidentally of a Portion of Nebraska Territory. (and) Illustrations to the Geological Report of Wisconsin, Iowa and Minnesota.* Philadelphia: Lippincott, Grambo & Co., 1852. First editions, 4to., 27 engraved plates, with captioned tissue guards, 21 maps, all but 3 folding, full elaborately stamped contemporary red morocco (some soiling, but very good), evidently lacks large folding geological map referred to end of volume I, near fine set, spectacular period binding.   M & S Rare Books, Inc. 97 - 25   2015 $750

Binding - 20th Century

Marlowe, Christopher 1564-1593 *Hero and Leander.* Edinburgh: Ballantyne Press, 1909. First edition thus, one of 500 copies, the poem was finished by George Chapman, extra illustrated with two portraits of Chapman, splendidly bound in crushed violet morocco, signed exhibition binding. Honey & Wax Booksellers   1 - 32   2015 $1750

Binding - Adams Bindery

Phillips, Stephen *Dramatic Works: Ulysses, Herod, The Sin of David and Paolo and Francesca.* London and New York: John Lane, Macmillan and Co., 1901-1904. 4 volumes, attractive set in full leather bindings by The Adams Bindery, signed, bindings may be later, possibly 1910's or 1920's, full dark brown morocco with gilt titles and author to spines, each spine has six compartments with gilt rules and raised bands, marbled endpapers and top edge gilt, minor wear to hinges, edges and corners of boards, clean interiors overall, light foxing to few pages, very good.   The Kelmscott Bookshop   11 - 36   2015 $250

Binding - Adams, Maryline Poole

Christmastide in Ancient Britain. Berkeley: Poole Press, 1987. Limited to 51 numbered copies signed by designer, printer and binder, Maryline Poole Adams, 7.4 x 5.5 cm., quarter leather, decorated paper covered boards, title gilt stamped on spine, illustrated with British postage stamps, miniature bookplate of Kathryn Rickard.   Oak Knoll Books 306 - 106   2015 $350

Binding - Aquarius

Markham, Gervase *The Young Sportsman"s Instructor.* London: Apollo Press, 1820. 83 x 57mm., fine contemporary dark green morocco, elaborately gilt by Thomas Gosden, covers intricately gilt in Groliersque design of thick and thin fillets, interlinking strapwork, leafy flourishes and acorn tools, all of these forming a frame enclosing a central oval with gilt hunting horn, flat spine tooled with gilt vine forming 8 rounded compartments, 6 with sport equipment or an animal at center, one with initials "G.M." and one gilt, in excellent later custom made green morocco backed clamshell box by Aquarius of London, woodcut frontispiece, perhaps a breath of wear to leather, leaves shade less than bright with mild offsetting, last two gatherings with slight vertical crease, still very desirable example, text and beautiful binding both clean, fresh and generally well preserved. Phillip J. Pirages   66 - 75   2015 $4500

Young, Edward 1683-1765 *The Complaint and the Consolation or Night Thoughts.* R. Noble, 1797. First edition, large 4to., bound by Aquarius in late 20th century full midnight blue straight grain morocco, period style, boards richly decorated gilt and blind, gilt lettered and decorated backstrip, gilt ruled edges, marbled endpapers, 43 full page engravings by William Blake, very tall, well margined copy, the Coleridge family, with bookplate of Bernard Lord Coleridge and family signatures of J. T., Mary and Jane Coleridge.   Henry Sotheran Ltd.   William Blake Exhibition 17th Oct.-7th Nov. 2014 - 64   2015   £11,150

Binding - Armstrong, Margaret

Dunbar, Paul Laurence *Candle-Lightin' Time.* New York: Dodd, Mead & Co., 1901. First edition, photos, decorative cloth and decorations by Margaret Armstrong, trifle rubbed at bottom of the boards, just about fine in about very good example of rare dust jacket with shallow loss at crown and some slight loss at top of front flap fold, very nice example of fragile dust jacket.   Between the Covers Rare Books   197 - 17   2015 $2500

Dunbar, Paul Laurence *Li'l' Gal.* New York: Dodd, Mead, 1904. First edition thus, large 8vo., frontispiece, 63 photos, olive cloth stamped in gilt, blue, cream and gold designed by Margaret Armstrong, binding little rubbed at extremities, former owner's name in pencil on endpaper, very good, clean copy.   Second Life Books Inc.   190 - 71   2015 $325

Binding - Ashton, R.

Polehampton, Edward *The Gallery of Nature and Art; or a Tour Through Creation and Science.* London: printed for R. N. Rose, 1821. New edition, 6 volumes, attractive contemporary brown polished calf, 216 x 133mm., covers with gilt fleur-de-lys and blindstamped palmette borders, large oblong octagonal panel at center of each board, all volumes with contemporary landscape paintings, three of these signed by R. Ashton, one dated 1821 (but all by the same hand), wide raised bands painted black and tooled gilt, spine panels with central arabesque surrounded by curling vines, gilt titling, marbled edges (very small and expert repairs apparently made to the ends of joints on two of the volumes); 7 illustrations within text and a total of 94 engraved plates, including a frontispiece for each volume one of which is foldout plate and of which two plates are comprised of two illustrations each, front flyleaves with inscription of Barbara Douglas Campbell dated 1st Jan. 1822 and with later indecipherable inscription below; just minor rubbing to joints and extremities (a portion of one joint with shallow damage from an insect), one landscape with small cluster of gouges, superficial scratches to some of the other scenes, variable (mostly faint) offsetting from plates, other trivial imperfections, but still extremely attractive set, text fresh and clean, bindings lustrous with virtually all of the original appeal intact.   Phillip J. Pirages   66 - 79   2015 $7000

Binding - Bartley, Glenn

More, Thomas 1478-1535 *A Frutefull Pleasaunt, and Wittie Worke of the Beste State of a Publique Weale & of the Newe Yle, Called Utopia.* Waltham St. Lawrence: Golden Cockerel Press, 1929. 173/500 copies, title printed in blue and black, woodcut decorations by Eric Gill, small folio, uncut in full navy (almost black) goatskin, full thickness blue and grey goatskin onlays applied to recessed panels edged in blue and grey acrylic, gold and blind tooling, spine lettered in gold doublures of grey goatskin, flyleaves of grey suede and Thai grass paper, edges airbrushed with acrylic by Glenn Bartley (signed inside back over and dated 2011), buckram box with felt lining, recessed navy goatskin label on spine lettered in gold, fine, most attractive binding.   Blackwell's Rare Books   B179 - 132   2015   £1500

Whitfield, Christopher *Together and Alone. Two Short Novels.* Golden Cockerel Press, First edition, 251/400 copies (of an edition of 500 copies), printed on Arnold mouldmade paper, 10 wood engravings by John O'Connor, one small and light spot on title, 8vo., uncut in full black goatskin, full thickness crimson goatskin onlays applied to recessed panels edges in olive green acrylic, doublures of crimson goatskin with black onlays, flyleaves of crimson suede and Thai grass paper, edges airbrushed with acrylic, gold, palladium and blind tooling, by Glen Bartley (signed inside back cover and dated 2011), buckram box with felt lining, recessed label on spine tooled in palladium, fine.   Blackwell's Rare Books   B179 - 133   2015   £1500

Binding - Bathen, Jacob

Ovidius Naso, Publius *Metamorphoseon.* Lugduni: Sebastianius Gryphius, 1553. 178 x 108mm. without final blank, contemporary calf by Jacob Bathen of Louvain with Bathen's elaborately blindstamped "Spes" binder's device and initials "I. B." in lower left, raised bands, spine with simple blind ruling, pastedowns removed exposing construction of the binding, first and last gatherings protected by strips from a 13th century vellum French or Southern Netherlandish Breviary (very expertly rebacked to style with restoration at corners), publisher's woodcut griffin device on titlepage, later (18th century?) ownership inscription of C. N. Cuvier on titlepage, rear flyleaf with early note in Latin, remnants of rear pastedown with signature of (Ro)bertus Camholt; little splaying to upper board, covers with slight crackling, but expertly restored binding entirely solid and details of panel stamps very sharp, faint dampstain cover small portion of many leaves at bottom (another dampstain sometimes at top with about half the page affected in four quires near end), minor soiling, here and there, two leaves with darker, though smaller areas of soiling, not without condition issues, internally but nothing fatal, text both fresh and with ample margins.   Phillip J. Pirages   66 - 13   2015 $4200

Binding - Bayntun

Budden, Maria Elizabeth *True Stories from Ancient History...* London: 1822. First illustrated edition, 2 volumes, 12mo., period style full crushed morocco gilt by Bayntun, 72 hand colored plates. Honey & Wax Booksellers 3 - 8 2015 $2500

Hassell, John *Tour of the Grand Junction, Illustrated in a Series of Engravings with an Historical and Topographical Description of Those Parts of the Counties...* London: J. Hassall, 1819. First edition, 8vo., 24 colored aquatint plates (some occasional offsetting), uncut in modern red straight grained morocco with wide gilt tooled border, spine lettered and decorated in gilt, top edge gilt, by Bayntun, Bath. Marlborough Rare Books List 54 - 39 2015 £1250

Kipling, John Lockwood *Beast and Man in India...* London: Macmillan and Co., 1891. First edition, illustrations, later red half morocco gilt by Bayntun, spine in compartments with raised bands and animal decorations gilt, top edge gilt, upper cover with one small area sunned, some foxing, but nice, from the collection of Gavin H. Fryer. Bertram Rota Ltd. 308 Part II - 152 2015 £200

Binding - Bayntun-Riviere

Bronte, Charlotte 1816-1855 *Shirley.* London: Smith Elder and Co., 1849. First edition, 3 volumes, edges faintly browned, integral ad at end, volume iii present but inserted ads discarded, 8vo., modern dark green morocco by Bayntun-Riviere, backstrips with gilt wavy line-decorated raised bands between double gilt rules, gilt lettered direct in second and fourth compartments, gilt fillet border on sides, wide turn-ins, marbled endpapers, all edges gilt, slipcase, modern bookplate in volume i, very good. Blackwell's Rare Books B179 - 20 2015 £2500

Bronte, Charlotte 1816-1855 *Villette.* London: Smith Elder and Co., 1853. First edition, publisher's ads in volume ii discarded, leaf L1 in volume I remargined, some toning, 8vo., modern green morocco by Bayntun-Riviere, backstrips with gilt wavy line decorate raised bands between double gilt rules, gilt lettered direct to second and fourth compartments, gilt fillet border on both sides, wide turn-ins, marbled endpapers, all edges gilt, slipcase, modern bookplate volume i, very good. Blackwell's Rare Books B179 - 21 2015 £2000

Dickens, Charles 1812-1870 *A Christmas Carol in Prose.* London: Chapman & Hall, 1843. First edition, first issue i.e. 'Stave I', text entirely uncorrected, blue half title and red and blue title, small octavo, four hand colored steel engraved plates by and after Leech and 4 wood engraved illustrations by Linton after Leech, bound by Bayntun Riviere of Bath (stamp signed in gilt on front turn-ins), full red morocco, covers gilt stamped with holly, gilt single rule border, spines decoratively tooled an decorated in gilt compartments, board edges with gilt dotted rule, gilt inner dentelles, all edges gilt, marbled endpapers, original covers bound in rear, a very attractive copy, housed in custom red cloth clamshell. Heritage Book Shop Holiday 2014 - 52 2015 $7500

Dodgson, Charles Lutwidge 1832-1898 *Through the Looking Glass.* London: Macmillan, 1872. First edition, first printing with 'wade' to page 21, illustrations by John Tenniel, finely bound in full crimson morocco by Bayntun-Riviere, gilt, original cloth bound in at rear, about fine, with former owner's 1872 inscription to half title, few hints of scattered light spotting to otherwise fresh pages, book in fine binding. B & B Rare Books, Ltd. 2015 - 2015 $4500

Binding - Bedford

Brome, Alexander *Rump: or an Exact Collection of the Choycest Poems and Songs Relating to the late Times.* London: for Henry Brome and Henry Marsh, 1662. First edition, 8vo., lacking longitudinal half title final blank, Oo4 with added etched titlepage by Wenceslaus Hollar and additional engraved plate, circa 1850, of the Rump bound at front, small burn-hole to gutter of K2 affecting one letter to verso, light discoloration to K3 from burn-hole on preceding leaf, light spotting to O2-O4, small burn-hole to O6 affecting a letter of text on recto, very light dampstain to lower blank margin of gatherings S-X, repaired burn-hole to gutter of X3 affecting three letters on recto, some occasional discoloration, lightly pressed, late 19th century emerald morocco by Bedford, spine lightly sunned, lower edges lightly chipped, couple of minor scrapes to front cover, good copy, from the library of James Stevens Cox (1910-1997). Maggs Bros. Ltd. 1447 - 50 2015 £575

Capel, Arthur *Excellent Contemplations, Divine and Moral.* London: for Nath(aniel) Crouch, 1683. First edition, 12mo., enraved portrait of Capel (mounted and repaired along inner margin), small piece torn from blank lower margin of F1, small hole (paper flaw?) to blank corner of F6, 19th century sprinkled calf by Bedford, William Twopenny late 19th/early 20th century label, from the library of James Stevens Cox (1910-1997). Maggs Bros. Ltd. 1447 - 63 2015 £350

Goldsmith, Oliver 1730-1774 *The Vicar of Wakefield.* Salisbury: printed by B. Collins for F. Newbery, 1766. First edition, a number of variants exist for this book with no priority, this copy with catchword on page 213, volume 1, the incorrected catchword on page 39 volume II and the correctly numbered page 159 in volume II, 2 volumes, 12mo., charming full crushed morocco by Bedford with gilt detailing in spine compartments, all edges gilt, inner gilt dentelles and marbled endpapers, bindings excellent condition, fine but for slight scuff to edge of spine on volume II, internal contents bright and clean with few nearly invisible repaired closed tear in all lovely set, housed in cloth and marbled paper slipcase.   Heritage Book Shop   Holiday 2014 - 68   2015 $4500

Killigrew, Thomas *Comedies and Tragedies.* London: printed for Henry Herringman, 1664. First edition, folio, red full morocco by Bedford, gilt rules, decorations, inner dentelles and lettering, all edges gilt, frontispiece, this copy agrees with Greg's second issue, fine, handsome copy. The Brick Row Book Shop   Miscellany 67 - 62   2015 $4500

Ward, Edward 1667-1731 *The History of the Grand Rebellion; Containing the Most Remark-able Transactions from the Beginning of the Reign of King Charles I to the Happy Restoration....* London: printed for J. Morphew, 1713. First edition, 3 volumes, 84 (of 85) engraved portraits, otherwise fine, 3 folding maps, 8vo., full polished calf panelled in gilt, spines and inner dentelles gilt, red morocco labels, all edges gilt by Bedford, attractive collector's binding.   C. R. Johnson   Foxon R-Z - 1072r-z   2015 $2298

Binding - Bickers

Ainsworth, William Harrison 1805-1882 *Merry England; or Nobles and Serfs.* London: published by Tinsley Brothers, 1874. First edition, 8vo., 16 page publisher's catalog dated March 1873 at end of volume 2 and four page catalog at end of volume 3, the 3 volumes in highly attractive navy blue half leather, marbled boards, raised bands at spine which are richly gilt decorated, top edge gilt, binding by Bickers, original grass green cloth covers and spines laid in on 3 pages at rear of each volume, showing this to be first state with spelling 'Merry' on spines, bright very good+ set in slightly rubbed and slightly scuffed at corners and text very slightly browned.   Any Amount of Books   2015 - A40494   2015   £175

Binding - Bishop, Bonnie

Bishop, Bonnie *Furies. Poetry and Original Prints.* Cornville: 2013. Artist's book, one of 7 copies, all on handmade paper by Katie MacGregor, each copy signed and numbered by artist/author, page size 5 3/4 x 8 1/2 inches, 64 pages, bound by artist, handsewn Coptic style binding, single thread sewn through each of the 8 signatures, red wrappers stiffened with archival paper, title blind embossed on front panel, housed in grey paper box, images printed silkscreen for the vermilion and monoprint in gold gilt, text handset in Optima and printed letterpress by Scott Vile at Ascensius Press, each page spread, gold monoprint textures overprinted with red silkscreens or white pages with gold gilt silkscreens (white page serving as negative space and creating images), highlight the text by allowing printing of text within images of the human form, strong line of silkscreen repeated over three pages, each time on different grounds, provoking different responses.   Priscilla Juvelis - Rare Books   63 - 1   2015 $1250

Binding - Blau, Bela

Powell, Lawrence Clark *Book Shops.* Los Angeles: Roy V. Boswell, 1965. No limitation given but obviously very small, 6 x 4.3cm., leather, bound by Bela Blau, miniature bookplate of Kathryn Pickard and Raymond A. Smith.   Oak Knoll Books   306 - 121   2015 $200

Binding - Bogan, Mary Patrick

Broumas, Olga *Caritas.* N.P.: White Camel Press, 1985. First edition thus, one of 40 copies printed in Romulus Roman and Italic type on Gutenberg laid paper, tall 8vo., original paste paper boards with printed label on spine, signed by binder Mary Patrick Bogan, very fine, lovely edition.   James S. Jaffe Rare Books   Modern American Poetry - 43   2015 $250

Binding - BookLab

Bertolt, Brecht *The Seven Deadly Sins of the Lower Middle Class.* New York: Vincent FitzGerald & Co., 1992. Artist's book, one of 50 copies only, all on rives paper, each signed by artist, Mark Beard, and translator Michael Feingold, over 100 hand collaged and watercolored images of etchings and lithographs, with each of the seven sins a separate gate fold, printed letterpress in Garamond in at least 14 different colors by Dan Keleher at Wild Carrot Letterpress, calligraphy by Jerry Kelly, page size 12 1/2 x 21 inches, bound by Zahra Partovi in association with BookLab, cloth over boards, three quarter leather spine, protective box with game board map of America.   Priscilla Juvelis - Rare Books   62 - 4   2015 $7500

Breuer, Lee *The Warrior Ant.* New York: Vincent FitzGerald & Co., 1992. Artist's book, one of 40 copies, all on handmade paper by Paul Wong of Dieu Donne Papermill, each copy signed by artist, Susan Weil and author, page size 10 x 10 inches, bound in handmade paper wrappers in custom box by BookLab, fine, etchings editioned by Marjorie Van Dyke and Vincent FitzGerald at Printing Workshop and text printed letterpress in Bembo by Dan Keleher at Wild Carrot Letterpress, calligraphy is by Jerry Kelly. Priscilla Juvelis - Rare Books 62 - 5 2015 $3500

Binding - Bourbeau, David

Poe, Edgar Allan 1809-1849 *The Raven.* Easthampton: Cheloniidae Press, 1980. One of 100 copies, from a total of 125 copies all on arches paper, 100 regular issue, 25 deluxe issue, both long out of print, 5 etchings and 2 wood engravings, each of the plates signed and titled in pencil by artist, who printed the etchings as well, in addition, this copy has laid in artist proof of the 'Crow Quill' on titlepage and two proofs on colophon, text is 24 pages, Centaur hand set and printed by master pressman, Harold McGrath, book bound by David Bourbeau in specially painted cloth over boards and housed in black cloth clamshell box, black morocco spine, author, title and press paragraph in gilt, text handset by Harold McGrath in Bruce Rogers lovely 24pt. Centaur type in black and red ink, five full page original etchings and two original wood engravings. Priscilla Juvelis - Rare Books 61 - 5 2015 $3200

Joyce, James 1882-1941 *Epiphanies.* New York: Vincent FitzGerald & Co., 1987. One of 65 copies only, 50 in an edition for sale and 15 Artist's Proofs, all on Moulin du Gue paper and Japanese papers with 62 etchings, employing over 150 plates, original watercolors, collage and hand cutting, collage by Vincent FitzGerald and Zahra Partovi, etchings printed by Marjorie Van Dyke assisted by Maria Luisa Rojo at the printmaking Workshop, lithographs editioned by Marjorie Van Dyke with Rhae Burden, calligraphy by Jerry Kelly, letterpress by Dan Keleher and Bruce Chandler at Wild Carrot Letterpress in 40 colors, type set by Dan Carr and Julia Ferrari at the Golgonooza Letter Foundry, page size 12 x 14 inches, 94 leaves, one printed page loose, two foldout images, loose as issued in original wrappers in handmade box by David Bourbeau at the Thistle Bindery in Japanese handmade silk woven for this box, incised line of Japanese tea paper showing profile of Joyce, spine of box slightly sunned, book fine. Priscilla Juvelis - Rare Books 61 - 14 2015 $12,500

Robinson, Alan James *Cetacea. The Great Whales.* Easthampton: Cheloniidae Press, 1981. One of 100 copies, this copy with original drawing by artist, signed by artist, binders David Bourbeau and Gray Parrot and printer, Harold McGrath, all on Arches Cover Buff from a total issue of 110 (100 copies plus 10 artist's proof copies), this copy with original prospectus laid in as well as separate copy of original wood engraving "Whale Flukes" that also appears on colophon, wood engraving is 5 1/2 x 8 1/2 inches, 27 leaves, page size 22 x 15 inches, bound loose as issued with sheets laid in, black Niger oasis goat over low relief sculpture of Right Whale head by Robinson, then cast in polyester resin and covered by David Bourbeau at the Thistle Bindery, rear panel is lack cloth over board, beautiful folder housed in quarter leather Moroccan goat drop back box by Gray Parrot, bit of wear to box, else fine, 7 bleed etchings by Robinson, two two-color maps, printed in 12 point Garamond with 24 and 36 point Castellar for tilting, each etching protected by a sheet of Japanese tissue, Tomoe Blue, in a wave pattern, used as endsheets. Priscilla Juvelis - Rare Books 63 - 3 2015 $4500

Binding - Bozerian

Anacreon *Odes.* Paris: Chez Du Pont, 1795. 171 x 102mm., fine contemporary black straight grain morocco gilt by Bozerian (stamp-signed at foot of spine), covers framed with undulating grape vine enclosed by double rules, starburst cornerpieces, raised bands, spine gilt in densely stippled compartments with gilt leaves and flowers emanating from central inlaid red morocco dot, turn-ins with gilt bead and star roll, pink watered silk endleaves embellished with their own cresting floral border, all edges gilt, large paper copy, bookplate of Raoul Simonson (and faint dampstain under it, indicating removal of previous one); one faint scratch on back cover, especially fine, text, clean, smooth and bright, in unworn sparkling binding. Phillip J. Pirages 66 - 61 2015 $2250

Bible. Latin - 1785 *Bibliorum Sacorum Vulgatae Versionis Editio.* Parisiis: Excudebat Fr. Amb. Didot, 1785. 2 volumes, 318 x 235mm, superb crimson straight grain morocco by Bozerian, covers with distinctive wide frame incorporating arches, Grecian urns, floral garlands and sunburst cornerpieces, the outer and inner edge of the frame flanked by thick and thin gilt rules and cresting and floral rolls, double raised bands separated by a gilt tooled inlaid strip of black morocco, spines densely gilt in compartments filled with much foliage and many flowers against a stippled background, turn-ins with interlacing flame roll, light green glazed endpapers, all edges gilt, wood engraved bookplate of Ellic Howe (1910-1991) with faint evidence of earlier bookplate removal, verso of rear flyleaf with small engraved heraldic book label; half a dozen or so faint scratches or small spots to boards, occasional mild browning or small marginal spots, couple of gatherings in second volume with faint overall browning, otherwise an excellent copy internally, clean and smooth with generous margins, elegant bindings in fine condition, especially lustrous and with only insignificant wear. Phillip J. Pirages 66 - 62 2015 $6500

Lelille, Jacques *Les Jardins Poeme.* Paris: De L'Imprimerie de P. Didot l'aine, 1801. 152 x 124mm., extremely pretty contemporary green morocco gilt by Bozerian (stamp signed at foot of spine), covers with gilt frame entwined ribbon and leaf roll enclosed within double rules, daisy cornerpieces, flat spine densely gilt in compartments with inlaid red morocco dot at center radiating a profusion of small tools, turn-ins with gilt chain roll, pink watered silk endleaves, pastedowns with delicate gilt border, all edges gilt, 4 charming engraved plates, printed on Papier Velin, bit of fading to covers, but very fine inside and out, binding especially lustrous and entirely unworn, margins very ample and text unusually clean, fresh and bright. Phillip J. Pirages   66 - 63   2015 $4500

Binding - Brockman, James

P., J. *Oeconomica Sacra; or a Paraenetical Discourse of Marriage Together with some Particular Remarks on the Marriage of Isaac and Rebecca.* printed for John Salusbury, 1685. First edition, some browning, last leaf with old repair at foot, lacks initial and terminal blank leaves, 12mo., new calf in contemporary style by James Brockman, some contemporary annotations of interested and attentive reader, ex Wigan public library, blindstamps at beginning and end (that at end straddling repair to foot of page, meaning that the repair was done around or before 1900), good, very rare.   Blackwell's Rare Books   B179 - 70   2015   £2000

Binding - Bumpus

Jefferies, Richard   1848-1887 *The Scarlet Shawl.* London: Tinsley Bros., 1874. First edition, text slightly spotted, later half blue morocco by Bumpus, raised bands, compartments decorated in gilt, slightly rubbed, armorial bookplate of William Henry Radcliffe Saunders, top edge gilt, very good.   Jarndyce Antiquarian Booksellers   CCXI - 160   2015   £380

Binding - Burn

Arnold, Matthew   1822-1888 *New Poems.* London: Macmillan and Co., 1867. First edition, original green cloth by Burn, slightly marked, following inner hinge slightly cracked, Geoffrey Tillotson's copy.   Jarndyce Antiquarian Booksellers   CCVII - 39   2015   £150

Dodgson, Charles Lutwidge   1832-1898 *The Hunting of the Snark.* London: Macmillan, 1876. First edition, unrecorded binding, 8vo., bright red cloth with gilt vignettes on covers, surrounded by 3 gilt ruled circles and triple gilt rules on edges, all edges gilt, some finger soiling on covers and slightest of fraying to spine extremities, else nice, tight copy, binder's ticket Burn and Co., 9 incredibly detailed full page illustrations by Henry Holliday, this copy from the Lewis Carroll collection of Philip C. Blackburn with his notation and note to him laid in.   Aleph-Bet Books, Inc.   108 - 88   2015 $1950

Dresser, Christopher *Popular Manual of Botany...* Edinburgh: Adam and Charles Black, 1860. First edition, 8vo., 12 hand colored plates, original brown cloth, blocked in blind, intertwined leaves, gilt lettered spines, binders ticket on pastedown, bound by Burn, London, clean copy of the colored issue.   Marlborough Rare Books   List 54 - 21   2015   £185

Binding - Campbell-Logan Bindery

Middleton, Bernard C. *Recollections, My Life in Bookbinding.* Newtown: Bird & Bull Press, 1995. First edition, limited to 200 numbered copies, printed by hand on Arches mouldmade paper in Dante types composed by Golgonozza Letter Foundry, bound by Campbell-Logan Bindery, quarter leather, printed paper sides, leather spine label, slipcase, prospectus loosely inserted.   Oak Knoll Books   306 - 135   2015 $350

Waldman, Anne *Makeup on Empty Space.* West Branch: Toothpaste Press, 1984. First edition, 8vo., one of 100 numbered and signed copies, deluxe edition printed on Frankfurt White, quarterbound in cloth and Tokutairei Tanahata, a handmade paper at the Campbell-Logan Bindery, fine in acetate dust jacket.   Second Life Books Inc.   190 - 209   2015 $125

Binding - Campling, C. A., Ltd.

Specimens of Heraldic Painting, Illuminating &c... Great Yarmouth: 1905. Small 4to., 8 illuminations in gold and colors, 8 photographic reproductions, 6 binding samples, 6 endpaper samples, decorating binding sample and crest interleaved in calligraphic manuscript bound in straight grained red roan by C. A. Campling Ltd. binders Gt. Yarmouth, rebacked, lettered gilt on upper cover. Marlborough Rare Books   List 53 - 22   2015   £850

Binding - Carss, J.

The Art Journal Illustrated Catalogue. The Industry of All Nations 1851. London: published for the Proprietors by George Virtue, 1851. Folio, frontispiece, illustrations, final ad leaf, slightly later half maroon calf by J. Carss & Co., Glasgow, leading hinge rubbed, corners slightly bumped, later paper label partially removed.   Jarndyce Antiquarian Booksellers   CCXI - 127   2015   £145

Binding - Cottage Roof

Church of England. Book of Common Prayer *The Book of Common Prayer.* (bound with) *The Whole Book of Psalms Collected into English Metre.* London: John Bill and Christopher Barker, 1676. 184 x 127mm., very animated contemporary black morocco, elaborately gilt and with many inlays and onlays, covers with large central panel framed by citron morocco in a modified cottage-roof design, (including a peaked roof and protruding eaves under vertical supports but with scalloped interruptions on all four sides), vertical sidepieces entwined with gilt and black morocco vines bearing gilt leaves and acorns, panel within filled with lowers and geometrical designs accented with and surrounded by delicate gilt tooling, raised bands, spine compartments gilt and inlaid and either geometric shapes or a rosette, marbled endpapers, all edges gilt and gauffered, with floral vine painted in pinks and blues, fine modern black morocco clamshell box, extra illustrated with 55 hand colored engravings, rear flyleaf with handwritten list of five children born into the Man family between 1745 and 1752 verso of same with pencilled inscription of the eldest child, Robert Man, front flyleaf with pencilled note identifying the family as relatives of Admiral Man, hint of rubbing to joints, very small stain to foot of titlepage, edges of leaves slightly browned, trimmed close at top, isolated minor foxing, other trivial imperfections, but extremely pleasing copy, immensely appealing binding with only insignificant wear and text smooth and clean. Phillip J. Pirages 66 - 28 2015 $22,500

Thomas A Kempis 1380-1471 *The Christian's Pattern; or a Treatise of the Imitation of Jesus Christ...* London: printed for Barker (and others), 1742. 203 x 127mm., animated contemporary black morocco, lavishly gilt, covers with central cottage-roof design enclosed by ornate floral rolls and small tools, the 'roof' frame containing a large and elaborate fleuron within a lozenge of small tools, raised bands, spine gilt in compartments bordered by plain rules and dogtooth rolls, each compartment divided into quarters by gilt diagonal lines, each quarter with a delicate stippled floral tool, red morocco label, gilt turn-ins, marbled endpapers, all edges gilt, engraved frontispiece of Crucifixion, plus engravings of the nativity, Adoration of the Magi, Christ in the Wilderness and the Last Supper; 18th century bookplate of Fane William Sharpe, 18th or 19th century armorial bookplate of W. Combes, spine faded to pleasing hazel brown, little rubbing to joints and extremities, minor chafing to boards, occasional faint foxing, isolated dust soiling to head edge, other trivial imperfections, but fine, nevertheless, leaves clean and fresh and intricately tooled unsophisticated binding very lustrous and showing no significant wear, splendid copy. Phillip J. Pirages 66 - 35 2015 $3200

Binding - Craftsman

Omar Khayyam *The Rubaiyat of Omar Khayyam.* New York: Dodge Pub. Co., 1912. 4to., full leather binding with color embossed Craftsman style design on cover, top edge gilt, fine in publisher's plain felt lined box, 28 tipped in color photos (with tissue guards), text illustrations in black and white, exceptionally fine. Aleph-bet Books, Inc. 109 - 420 2015 $950

Binding - Curtain

Brookshaw, George *Groups of Flowers Drawn and Accurately Coloured after Nature with Full Instructions for the Young Artist.* London: printed for Longman Hurst, Rees, Orme and Brown, 1817. First edition, 343 x 267mm., striking red straight grain morocco gilt in unusual design, covers framed by decorative gilt rules and creating roll, large central lozenge formed by two very elaborately gilt and blind tooled triangular 'curtains', wide bases of which meet at center of each board, large gilt butterfly at peak of each triangle (seeming to pull the curtains upward and downward toward the top and bottom edge of covers), flat spine in densely tooled panels, gilt titling, gilt chain roll on turn-ins, all edges gilt, with 11 (of 12) excellent engravings of flowers in two states, colored and uncolored, without color plate of the Moss Rose, joints and extremities little rubbed, two small abrasions to boards, spine uniformly darkened, touch of faint yellowing to uncolored plates, couple of marginal smudges but still very appealing example in most excellent condition, binding with lustrous covers, and text fresh and smooth, rare example of a 'curtain' binding, based on Spanish style 'cortina' binding. Phillip J. Pirages 66 - 72 2015 $2400

Binding - Davies, H.

Terentius Afer, Publius *The Comedies of Terence.* Dublin: Printed by Boulter Grierson, 1766. First or Second Dublin edition, engraved frontispiece, some light browning, ownership inscription of H. Davies, rector of Llandegfan (177*) to titlepage, 8vo., contemporary calf speckled black and green, green morocco lettering piece, touch rubbed at extremities, front joint just cracking at foot, very good. Blackwell's Rare Books Greek & Latin Classics VI - 100 2015 £200

Binding - De Coverly, Roger

Blake, William 1757-1827 *The Poems of William Blake.* London: Basil Montagu Pickering, 1874. First edition, octavo, early 20th century crimson crushed morocco gilt, bound by Roger De Coverly. Honey & Wax Booksellers 2 - 5 2015 $550

Young, Edward 1683-1765 *The Force of Religion; or, Vanquish'd Love.* London: printed for E. Curll and J. Pemberton, 1714. First edition, engraved frontispiece, 8vo., half blue morocco, gilt, spine gilt, top edge gilt by Roger de Coverly & sons (traces of rubbing), copy on fine paper, remarkable presentation copy inscribed to Revd. Doct. Pa(rnell) from the author, margins trimmed somewhat close, but not touching text, otherwise very good, bookplate of Oliver Brett, Viscount Esher.   C. R. Johnson   Foxon R-Z - 1187r-z   2015 $1915

Binding - De Haas

Senault, Louis *Heures Nouvelles Dediees a Madame La Dauphine.* Paris: chez l'Autheur n.d. circa 1680's, 8vo., full 19th century polished calf with gilt panels, red morocco label, (signed binding by de Haas with his label), joints repaired at head and foot, paper repair to head of titlepage not affecting text, worn at joints, book is printed form engraved plates.   Oak Knoll Books   Special Catalogue 24 - 47   2015 $2250

Binding - Derome

Anacreon *(in Greek) Anakreontos Teiou Mele (then) Anacreontis Teii Odaria (i.e. The Odes).* Parmae: Ex Regio typographeio, 1785. One of 250 copies on 'blue' paper (of a total of 310 copies), 305 x 222mm., splendid contemporary crimson morocco, handsomely gilt by Derome Le Jeune (with his ticket), covers framed with double gilt rules, inner rule with scalloped corners, raised bands, compartments with very appealing all-over diaper pattern, chain pattern (asterisk and four petal flower) on board edges, endleaves of lavender watered silk, very wide and intricate inner dentelles extending (in an unusual way) from turn-ins onto silk pastedowns, all edges gilt, small author portrait in style of ancient coin on titlepage, large and elaborate armorial vignette on dedication page engraved by Cagnoni, tiny bit of wear at spine ends, few leaves with very minor tear or paper flaw at fore edge, especially fine, beautiful book with elegant original binding scarcely worn, text very clean and bright and fresh with margins nothing short of immense.   Phillip J. Pirages   66 - 48   2015 $8500

Ariosto, Lodovico *Orlando Furioso.* Birmingham: Da' Torch di G. Baskerville per P. Molini, 1773. One of 100 large paper copies, 4 volumes, with subscriber list at end of volume IV, contemporary red morocco by Derome Le Jeune (his ticket on titlepage of volume I), covers gilt with French fillet borders and with FitzGibbon family arms of Earl of Clare at Center, raised bands, spines gilt in double ruled compartments with simple lozenge centerpiece, gilt titling, densely gilt turn-ins, marbled endpapers, all edges gilt, frontispiece by Eisen after Titian and 46 fine engraved plates, large paper copy, vellum bookplate of Burnham Abbey and engraved armorial bookplate of Charles Tennant, The Glen, spines slightly and evenly sunned, hint of rubbing to extremities, titles faintly browned and with an inch of slightly darker browning to edges from binder's glue), a dozen other leaves with pale browning or spotting, occasional very faint offsetting from plates, isolated light spots of foxing, small marginal smudges or other trivial imperfections with just handful of plates affected, still an elegant set in fine condition, impressive bindings lustrous and scarcely worn, leaves clean and smooth, margins enormous and with strong impressions of the engravings.   Phillip J. Pirages   66 - 49   2015 $19,500

Binding - Doermaele, Claes Van

Boccaccio, Giovanni 1313-1375 *Amorosa Visione. (bound with) Urbano.* Milan: Zanottie Castiglione per Andrea Calvo 10 Feb., 1521. Bologna: Franciscus Plato de Benedictis circa, 1492-1493. First printing of both works, 210 x 133mm., 2 separately published works in one volume; handsome Renaissance intricately decorated blindstamped calf by Claes Van Doermaele, covers with outer frame of medallion and foliate roll, inner frame of long stemmed lilies and scrolling vines, large central panel containing a medallion with three quarter portrait of Holy Roman Emperor of Charles V, binder's small 'CvD' escutcheon stamp below central panel, raised bands, early ink titled paper label, small paper shelf number of private library at foot of spine, unobtrusive repairs to head of front joint, tail of both joints and upper corners, lacking ties, in (slightly worn) linen clamshell box, 16th century ink ownership inscription of Johannes Hoyel, inscription of A(ndrew) Fletcher (of Saltoun), titlepage just slightly soiled, two leaves with minor browning to lower corners, two tiny marginal stains, otherwise fine, fresh copy in very well preserved binding, leather lustrous and blindstamped details remarkably sharp. Phillip J. Pirages   66 - 6   2015 $35,000

FINE BINDINGS

Binding - Doves Bindery

Hawthorne, Nathaniel 1804-1864 *The Scarlet Letter.* New York: privately printed, 1904. First of this illustrated edition, one of 150 copies on japanese imperial paper, 4to., contemporary navy morocco by the Doves Bindery, signed '19 C-S 10' gilt decorations and lettering, all edges gilt, each of the 15 plates in two states, color and black and white, tipped in to front free endpaper is letter for Cobden-Sanderson dated 23 March 1909 to Charles Walker Andrews, with Andrews bookplate, edges touched up and slightly repaired from wear, fine, handsome copy.   The Brick Row Book Shop   Miscellany 67 - 57   2015 $1750

Binding - Dusel, Philip

The Earwig or an Old Woman's Remarks on the Present Exhibition of Pictures of the Royal Academy. London: printed for G. Kearsly, 1781. First edition, 4to., recent red quarter morocco period style by Philip Dusel, marbled paper boards, gilt rules, decorations and lettering, fine.   The Brick Row Book Shop   Miscellany 67 - 41   2015 $1500

Fuseli, Henry *Remarks on the Writings and Conduct of J. J. Rousseau.* London: printed for T. Cadell, J. Johnson, Be. Davenport and J. Payne, 1767. First edition, 8vo., brown half calf period style by Philip Dusel, marbled paper boards, orange morocco label, gilt rules and lettering, frontispiece engraved by Charles Grignon after Fuseli, fine.   The Brick Row Book Shop   Miscellany 67 - 47   2015 $1500

Loudon, Jane *The Mummy!* London: Henry Colburn, 1828. Second edition, 3 volumes, 8vo., recent brown half morocco period style by Philip Dusel, marbled paper boards, gilt decorations and lettering, 2 pages of publisher's terminal ads in one volume, 2nd edition, some minor spots in text, fine, handsome copy.   The Brick Row Book Shop   Miscellany 67 - 66   2015 $8000

Milton, John 1608-1674 *Paradise Lost.* London: printed by S. Simmons next door to the Golden Lion in Aldersgate St., 1678. Third edition, octavo, full period style crimson morocco gilt, elaborately tooled, fine, bound by Philip Dusel in the Restoration style of Queen's Binder B.   Honey & Wax Booksellers   2 - 2   2015 $4200

Trimmer, Sarah *The Oeconomy of Charity; or an Address to Ladies Concerning Sunday Schools...* London: printed by T. Bensley for T. Longman, G. G. J. and J. Robinson and J. Johnson, 1787. First edition, 12mo., full sheep period style by Philip Dusel, red morocco label, gilt rules, decorations and lettering, 2 folding plates, fine.   The Brick Row Book Shop   Miscellany 67 - 93   2015 $2250

Binding - Edmonds & Remnant

Beste, John Richard *Alcazar; or the Dark Ages.* London: Hurst & Blackett, 1857. 3 volumes, original dark green horizontal fine ribbed moire cloth by Edmonds & Remnants, boards blocked in blind, spine decorated and lettered in gilt, fine, half titles, ownership inscription of Henry Elwell.   Jarndyce Antiquarian Booksellers   CCXI - 25   2015   £480

Darwin, Charles Robert 1809-1882 *Journal of Researches into the Natural History and Geology of the Countries Visited During the Voyage of the HMS Beagle Round the Wold Under the Command of Capt. Fitz Roy.* London: John Murray, 1860. 10th thousand, illustrations, 32 page catalog (Jan. 1863), original green cloth, by Edmonds & Remnant, neatly recased, little dulled, contemporary signature of G. M. Gibson.   Jarndyce Antiquarian Booksellers   CCXI - 84   2015   £580

Eliot, George, Pseud. 1819-1880 *Scenes of Clerical Life.* Edinburgh and London: William Blackwood & Sons, 1859. Second edition, 2 volumes, half titles, 16 page catalog volume II, original burgundy pebble grained cloth by Edmonds & Remnants, little rubbed and dulled with small splits in hinges, lacking leading f.e.p.'s, from the library of Geoffrey & Kathleen Tillotson.   Jarndyce Antiquarian Booksellers   CCVII - 257   2015   £68

Binding - Edwards

Church of England. Book of Common Prayer *The Book of Common Prayer... together with The Psalter or Psalms of David.* Oxford: Clarendon Press, 1783. 1784, 140 x 83mm., very appealing contemporary vellum over boards, almost certainly by Edwards of Halifax, covers bordered by a neoclassical pentaglyph and metope roll against a blue wash, center of each board with large gilt bordered medallion containing gilt monogram "M L C" on a blue background, flat spine divided into panels by gilt pentaglyph and metope border (the one at bottom over blue wash), panels with classical urn centerpiece and volute cornerpieces, second panel with gilt titling on blue background, turn-ins with gilt chain roll, marbled endpapers, all edges gilt, with fine fore-edge painting, very probably by Edwards, depicting Fountains Abbey In Yorkshire, in original (rubbed and soiled but quite intact) soft green leather slipcase, titlepage with ink ownership inscription of M. L. Carey, spine gilt slightly dulled in places, rear turn-in lifting a little at one corner, title and couple of gatherings with moderate foxing, still quite excellent copy binding showing no wear, text clean and fresh and painting well preserved.   Phillip J. Pirages   66 - 46   2015 $5500

Binding - Ely, Tim

Napora, Joseph *Scighte.* New York: Poote Press, 1987. One of 85 copies, on handmade paper by Ruth Lingen and Katherine Kuehn, hand set in Bodoni type, magnesium line cuts, printed by them damp on Vandercook proof press, bound by Tim Ely in coptic binding of paper over boards with original line cut hand colored and green and red morocco over spine stitching, pages pink printed in black, line cuts in yellow, black brown, red and other earth colors, beautiful book.   Priscilla Juvelis - Rare Books   61 - 13   2015 $3000

Binding - Entrelac

Bible. Polyglot - 1554 *Le Noveau Testament De Nostre Seigneur Jesus Christ.*   Lyon: Guillaume Rouille, 1554. 127 x 83mm., pleasing contemporary calf decorated in an Entrelac design, boards ornamented in the Lyonnaise style with intricate interlacing strapwork and foliage in dark brown and gray outlined in gilt on a background of tiny gilt dots, flat spine with similar decoration (these 16th century designs expertly laid down onto modern calf), all edges gilt, elaborate historiated woodcut frame enclosing each of the two title pages, some decorative and historiated woodcut initials and headpieces in text, embossed armorial bookplate of Daniel Sickles, covers with trivial marks and worm traces, text printed on inexpensive (and consequently yellowed) paper, first few leaves and last leaf little thumbed, isolated minor soiling, but excellent example, carefully restored binding entirely solid and quite bright and text smooth and fresh. Phillip J. Pirages   66 - 10   2015 $8500

Lactantius *Des Divines Institutions Contre Les Gentils & Idolatres.*   Lyon: Imprime par Balthazar Arnoullet (pour) Guillaume Gaseau, 1547.   127 x 89mm., without final blank, striking contemporary French calf in Entrelac style, covers with complex strapwork pattern tooled in gilt and painted black and white, design comprising borders, interlaced squares and complex scalloped and spade-like panels with green painted oval at center, original flat diapered spine with each lozenge enclosing a thick dot (covers and spine remounted in 19th century), all edges gilt, titlepage with large woodcut printer's device, historiated opening initial showing a scholar with book and a number of foliated initials throughout, early ink inscription "Bavet?) on titlepage, frequent underlinings and marginal annotations in neat contemporary hand; paint in strapwork decoration slightly eroded in spots, leaves with overall faint yellowing, isolated minor marginal stains or foxing, one page with ink blot obscuring one word, other trivial imperfections, still extremely appealing, splendid animated contemporary binding solid, bright and with only minor wear, nothing approaching significant problem internally.   Phillip J. Pirages   66 - 9   2015 $12,500

Binding - Everson, William

Jeffers, Robinson 1887-1962 *The Californians.*   N.P.: Cayucos Books, 1971. First edition thus, one of 50 numbered copies, specially bound and signed by William Everson (provided introduction), quarter cloth and paper over boards, near fine in original acetate dust jacket.   Ed Smith Books   83 - 50   2015 $250

Binding - Feinstein, Samuel

Grebenstein, Maryanne *Trinity.* Hingham: Maryanne Grebenstein, 2012. Number 3 of 20 copies, one unique hand lettered copy was also issued, 3 x 3 inches, in this limited edition the black text is printed and decorations are hand colored and illuminations in gold or silver pen, each book is hand bound and colored differently so that the 20 copies all have completely different look, this copy bound in lavender leather with inlaid cross to both covers and title in gold, bound by Samuel Feinstein, fine.   The Kelmscott Bookshop   11 - 22   2015 $800

Louys, Pierre *Leda or in Praise of the Blessings of Darkness.*   Easthampton: Cheloniidae Press, 1985. One of 60 copies, from a total edition of 75, each signed and numbered by artist, page size 11 x 8 inches, bound by Samuel Feinstein, full page green buffalo leather from Remy Carriat in France, covers tooled in 23K gold leaf and carbon in single fillets, gold gilt fillet connecting eggshell lacquer ovoid inlays on each of the panels, carbon fillet on back panel only, spine smooth with author and title in gold gilt, small circle surrounded by gold gilt separating them, 'sunken' grey suede doublures with black morocco border with tooled line between black and blue-green leathers, grey pig suede flyleaves, eggshell lacquer panels were inlaid in front and back panels in black and white, top edge gilt, blue and grey silk headbands signed "Samuel Feinstein" in blind on lower edge of back panel, housed in custom made grey cloth over boards clamshell box, with title LEDA a stamped in gold gilt on blue buffalo label affixed to spine of box, 5 drypoint etchings and 7 wood engravings by Alan James Robinson, all housed in custom made cloth and pigskin clamshell box, text printed by Dan Keleher at Wild Carrot Letterpress, wood engravings printed by Harold McGrath, drypoints printed by Alan James Robinson at Cheloniidae Press, type set by Mackenzie-Harris San Francisco. Priscilla Juvelis - Rare Books   61 - 4   2015 $2750

Binding - Fine Bindery

McKitterick, David *Wallpapers by Edward Bawden Printed at the Curwen Press.* Andoversford: The Whittingon Press, 1989. limited to 120 numbered copies, printed by hand on Whittington Press on Oxford mould-made paper binding by Fine Bindery and half tone and color plates printed at Senecio Press, this one of the 40 copies to contain sheets or parts of sheets of seven original wallpapers, folio, quarter cloth with boards covered with a facsimile of a Bawden wall paper design, slipcase, 7 thick leaves on which are mounted foldout specimens of Bawden's wallpaper designs. Oak Knoll Books 306 - 177 2015 $1450

Binding - Four Hands Bindery

Brassai *The Artists of My Life.* New York: Wilken Berley Ltd., 1982. First edition, large 4to., full page reproductions of photos of artists at work, pictorial patterned paper covered boards over cloth lettered silver at spine, special presentation folder housing photogravure, deluxe edition, this number 11 of 150 copies signed and numbered by Brassai, issued with hand pulled dust grained 'photogravure 21 x 15.9cm' also signed by Brassai, book in special binding designed by Sage Reynolds and executed at the Four Hands Bindery, fine in plain buff very good slipcase. Any Amount of Books 2015 - A68259 2015 £750

Binding - Franzese, Niccolo

Johannes Chrysotomus *Enarratio in Esaiam Prophetam.* (bound with) *Conciones in Celebrioribus Aliquot Anni Festivitatibus Habitae.* (bound with) *Homiliae in Aliquot Veteris Testamenti Loca.* Antverpiae: in Aedibus Ioan. Seelsii, 1555. 1553. 1553, 165 x 105mm., 3 separately published works bound in one volume, splendid armorial red Roman morocco done for Pope Pius V by Niccolo Franzese, covers gilt with papal arms in central cartouche, front cover with "Pivs V" above arms and initials "P.M." (Pontifex Maximus) below, back cover with "Io Chrys in Esa et Hom" in gilt above and "P.M." below, boards framed by a profusion of acanthus leaves emanating from the brass bosses at corners and with a background stamped with small floral and dot tools, raised bands, spine compartments with interwoven gilt vines and gilt titling, remnants of clasps, all edges gilt and gauffered in pink floral pattern and with Pius' name tooled into head and tail edges and his arms painted on the fore edge (apparently with very expert repairs at spine ends), titlepage with printer's device, bookplate of Carlo Ponzone di Casale and with ink inscription of Ch. Al. Ganora dated 1867, titlepage with ink inscription of a Capuchin convent, hinge separation at first titlepage, majority of the leaves with minor browning (a half dozen gatherings rather browned), other trivial defects but text unsoiled and consistently fresh, front joint with two-inch crack near bottom, leather on spine bit crackled, gilt lost in small area next to one box, but sumptuously decorated binding still quite lustrous showing little wear, and altogether pleasing. Phillip J. Pirages 66 - 18 2015 $17,500

Binding - Geraty, Peter

Robinson, Alan James *A Wildflower Alphabet.* Easthampton: Cheloniidae Press, 2014. One of 150 copies, all on Innova Smooth Cotton Hight White 110# paper, each copy signed and numbered by artist, page size 5 x 8 1/2 inches, 38 pages, bound by Peter Geraty at Praxis Bindery, accordion style with yellow cloth over boards, title stamped in gold gilt on front panel, housed in green cloth over boards slipcase, with title stamped on front cover of slipcase, designed by Robinson using lettering design by Suzanne Moore. Priscilla Juvelis - Rare Books 63 - 18 2015 $750

Robinson, Alan James *A Wildflower Alphabet.* Easthampton: Cheloniidae Presss, 2014. One of 10 copies (+ 5 AP copies), all on Winsor Newton 908 watercolor paper Hotpress paper, all original watercolors, each copy signed and numbered by artist, Alan James Robinson, page size 5 x 8 1/2 inches, 38 pages, bound by Peter Geraty at Praxis Bindery, accordion style with yellow cloth over boards, title stamped in gold gilt on front panel, housed in custom made cloth over boards clamshell box, title stamped on front cover of slipcase, designed by Robinson using lettering design by Suzanne Moore, original watercolors of the 26 wildflowers and 2 butterflies done free hand. Priscilla Juvelis - Rare Books 63 - 19 2015 $5500

Binding - Gilbert Brothers

Philp, J. M. *Places Worth Seeing in London.* London: Ward and Lock 158 Fleet Street, 1858. 8vo. second engraved illustrations by A. J. Mason, John Bastin and Dalziels, original decorative wood engraved orange covers, slightly chipped at head and tail of spine, generally good copy, binder's ticket and blindstamp "Gilbert Brothers 18 Gracechurch St. & 4 Copthall Buildings. Marlborough Rare Books List 53 - 39 2015 £175

Binding - Glaister, Donald

Beard, Mark *Manhattan Third Year Reader.* New York: Vincent FitzGerald & Co., 1984. First edition, one of only 30 copies, on 28 different papers, each copy signed by artist/author, page size 1 x 11 inches, 16 signatures, unique binding by Donald Glaister, red and black morocco with onlays of goatskin and laminated mylar and gold painted tooling composed to reader a view of the urban landscape, featuring obscured subway cars, altered grid paper imagery and a corregated leather keystone shape that transverses the spine and extends to both boards, doublures of painted cork, top edge gilt with eccentric gold shapes echoing shapes found on covers, binding signed by binder, Glaister, 2014 in blind with usual gold dot on inner rear hinge, housed in black linen clamshell box. Priscilla Juvelis - Rare Books 63 - 5 2015 $15,000

Glaister, Donald *A Few Questions.* Vashon: 2009. Artist's book, one of 10 copies, each signed and numbered by author, page size 8 inches square, 15 pages, bound by artist, Donald Glaister, exposed sewn spine, Mylar and collage, text laser printed in gill sans, pages are Mylar encapsulated, with interior collages of various materials.   Priscilla Juvelis - Rare Books   61 - 21   2015 $3500

Poe, Edgar Allan 1809-1849 *The Bells: a Numerical Exploration.* Vashon Island: 2014. Artist's book, one in a series of 10, on paper, polyester film, and metals, by noted book artist, Donald Glaister who has signed and numbered the book of colophon, page size 14 1/2 x 8 7/8 inches, bound by the artist, Glaister, painted paper over boards, hand sewn with each page on tabs to allow complete opening of each page spread, grey morocco spine, title written in dark grey on aluminum inset on front panel, edges of front and rear panel edges in orange, housed in clamshell box, designed, painted and bound by artist, this book uses paper, various metals and polyester, text printed by laser on mylar, mathematical formulas and equations are hand painted on metal inserts in each of the pages/boards.   Priscilla Juvelis - Rare Books   63 - 7   2015 $3900

Binding - Gosden, Thomas

Markham, Gervase *The Young Sportsman"s Instructor.* London: Apollo Press, 1820. 83 x 57mm., fine contemporary dark green morocco, elaborately gilt by Thomas Gosden, covers intricately gilt in Groliersque design of thick and thin fillets, interlinking strapwork, leafy flourishes and acorn tools, all of these forming a frame enclosing a central oval with gilt hunting horn, flat spine tooled with gilt vine forming 8 rounded compartments, 6 with sport equipment or an animal at center, one with initials "G.M." and one gilt, in excellent later custom made green morocco backed clamshell box by Aquarius of London, woodcut frontispiece, perhaps a breath of wear to leather, leaves shade less than bright with mild offsetting, last two gatherings with slight vertical crease, still very desirable example, text and beautiful binding both clean, fresh and generally well preserved.   Phillip J. Pirages   66 - 75   2015 $4500

Binding - Gouey, Denis

Limited Editions Club *Bibliography of the Fine Books Published by the Limited Editions Club 1929-1985.* New York: Limited Editions Club, 1985. Limited to 800 numbered copies, folio, half Oasis with hand marbled paper covered boards by Faith Harrison, cloth covered slipcase lined in ultrasuede, bound by Denis Gouey.   Oak Knoll Books   25 - 72   2015 $375

Limited Editions Club *Monthly Letters. The First Fifty Monthly Letters, The Limited Editions club 1929-1933.* New York: Limited Editions Club, 1987. Limited to 550 copies, 4to., half Oasis, slipcase, letterpress on Mohawk Superfine, bound by Denis Gouey in Nigerian Oasis goatskin with hand marbled sides.   Oak Knoll Books   25 - 73   2015 $250

Binding - Gray, Earle

Elmslie, Kenward *The Champ.* Los Angeles: Black Sparrow Press, 1968. First edition, one of 26 lettered copies, illustrations by Joe Brainard, handbound in boards by Earle Gray with original ink drawing by Brainard and signed by author and artist, fine.   James S. Jaffe Rare Books   Many Happy Returns - 242   2015 $1250

Elmslie, Kenward *Circus Nerves.* Los Angeles: Black Sparrow, 1971. First edition, one of 26 lettered copies, handbound in boards by Earle Gray, illustrations by Joe Brainard, with original drawing by Brainard and signed by author and artist, original cloth backed boards, fine.   James S. Jaffe Rare Books   Many Happy Returns - 250   2015 $1250

Elmslie, Kenward *Circus Nerves.* Los Angeles: Black Sparrow Press, 1971. First edition, one of 200 numbered copies, handbound in boards by Earle Gray, signed by author, 8vo., original cloth backed boards with front cover illustration by Joe Brainard, acetate dust jacket, fine.   James S. Jaffe Rare Books   Many Happy Returns - 249   2015 $100

Schuyler, James *What's for Dinner?* Santa Barbara: Black Sparrow Press, 1978. First edition, one of 26 lettered copies signed by author, out of a total edition of 226 copies, handbound in boards by Earle Gray, 8vo., original quarter patterned cloth and boards with printed label on spine and front cover, illustrations by Jane Freilicher, acetate dust jacket, fine.   James S. Jaffe Rare Books   Modern American Poetry - 243   2015 $350

Binding - Green Dragon Bindery

McKenney, Thomas Lorraine 1785-1859 *History of the Indian Tribes of North America with Biographical Sketches and Anecdotes of the Principal Chiefs.* Philadelphia: J. T. Bowen, 1848-1849-1850. First octavo edition, royal 8vo., contemporary ornate gilt stamped dark morocco, new spines, text and tissues with light foxing and occasional penciling, plates in excellent condition, binding with only slight wear, spines most appealing, done to match by Green Dragon Bindery.   M & S Rare Books, Inc.   97 - 183   2015 $35,000

Binding - Gross, Roni

Gross, Roni *the same... and yet.* New York: 1999. One of 22 copies, each signed and numbered by artist, all on Somerset and Hiromi papers, 20 copies for sale (2 reserved for the artist), page size 8 x 5 inches, 12 panel accordion, bound in tan Japanese cloth over boards, printed green and black with image of green apple 'the same' printed in black on tan label on front and 'and yet' printed in black on green label on back, in glassine plus green and yellow folding box designed by Peter Schell, text is letterpress from magnesium and polymer plates, designed on a Macintosh and printed in Gill Sans, photography by Yukan Hayashida and text by Ian Ganassi, drawings, printing and binding by Roni Gross.   Priscilla Juvelis - Rare Books   61 - 22   2015 $450

Binding - Haines

Herodianus *Herodian of Alexandria his History of the Twenty Roman Caesars and Emperors of His Time.* London: printed for Hugh Perry, 1629. Small quarto, cropping affects text of dedication page and list of emperors (sig. b), very light degree of marginal annotation throughout the book, some ink and some pencil, possibly in the hand of Thistlethwayte and or of Allan Heywood Bright (1862-1941) who owned the book in the 20th century, otherwise nice example in slightly faded and worn but very sound, attractive binding, ex-libris Alexandris Thistlthwayte, autograph note by Edmond Malone bound in and also bound in are couple of sheets of handwritten notes in later hand, binding by Haines of Liverpool, half red Levant morocco ruled gilt over marbled boards, spine with six compartments, with lettered gilt or bearing crescent and star device, marbled endpapers, top edge gilt,.   Any Amount of Books   2015 - C11789   2015   £2000

Binding - Hammond

Fleetwood, John *The Life of Our Blessed Lord and Saviour Jesus Christ...* London: Thomas Kelly & Co., 1857. 4to., frontispiece, additional engraved title, plates, contemporary full brown crushed morocco by Hammond, inlaid with red morocco cornerpieces, border and diamond shaped central labels initial "GJS" decorated in gilt, raised bands, compartments in gilt with central floral design in red morocco, loss of red morocco & some gilt to one floral cornerpiece of rubbing to edge of front board, all edges gilt, very handsome.   Jarndyce Antiquarian Booksellers   CCXI - 118   2015   £380

Binding - Hanbury & Simpson

Arnold, Matthew 1822-1888 *Friendship's Garland; Being the Conversations, Letters and Opinions of the Late Arminius, Baron von Thunder-Ten-Tronckh.* London: Smith Elder, 1871. First edition, 2 pages ads, half title removed, original white cloth by Hanbury & Simpson, spine sunned, slightly discolored, attractive bookplate of Leonard Courtney, 15 Cheyne Walk, with inserted letters and cuttings including exchange between R. H. Super and Geoffrey Tillotson.   Jarndyce Antiquarian Booksellers   CCVII - 22   2015   £35

Binding - Harcourt Bindery

Dunning, John *Two O'Clock Eastern Wartime.* Santa Barbara: Santa Teresa, 2001. First edition, one of 100 specially bound numbered copies, signed by author, containing one page of the book's original working manuscript which has also been signed and authenticated by Dunning, hand bound by Harcourt Bindery of Boston in quarter leather with marbled boards, very fine in slipcase, without dust jacket as issued.   Mordida Books   March 2015 - 007445   2015 $650

Binding - Hatchards

Charity School at Bamburgh Castle *Rules for the Government of the Charity School for Sixty Poor Girls at Bambrugh Castle, Established on the Appointment of a New Mistress, Asssistant and Usher to the Said School Dec. 1st 1794.* Alnwick: printed by J. Catnach, 1794. First edition, 8vo., light waterstaining throughout, attractively bound in late 19th/early 20th century chocolate morocco by Hatchards with title in gilt on upper cover, mid 19th century ownership inscription in ink on title margin, good, well bound, apparently very rare.   John Drury Rare Books   2015 - 25751   2015 $2622

Morley, John *The Struggle for National Education.* London: Chapman & Hall, 1873. First edition in bookform, 8vo., half title, early 20th century maroon crushed half morocco, spine gilt with raised bands, top edge gilt, silk maker, by Hatchards, fine, from the library of Sir Weetman Dickinson Pearson, first Viscount Cowdray (1856-1927) with his armorial bookplate.   John Drury Rare Books   2015 - 17698   2015 $151

Williams, Philip *Report of the Proceedings in the Case of an Appeal Preferred by the Provost and Scholars of King's College, Cambridge, Against the Provost and fellows of Eton College, to the lord Bishop of Lincoln the Visitor of Both Societies Determined August 15th 1815.* London: J. Butterworth and Son, 1816. First edition, 8vo., early 20th century green half calf, top edge gilt, spine lettered, silk marker by Hatchards very good.   John Drury Rare Books   March 2015 - 12371   2015 $266

Binding - Hayday

Wordsworth, William 1770-1850 *The Poetical Works of William Wordsworth.* London: Edward Moxon, 1846. 7 volumes, octavo, full 19th century polished calf gilt, near fine set bound by Hayday, warmly inscribed to Louisa Fenwick from her friend, the author. Honey & Wax Booksellers 2 - 17 2015 $16,000

Binding - Headlam, Cuthbert

Conrad, Joseph 1857-1924 *The Works of Joseph Conrad.* London: William Heinemann, 1921. 1926. 1927. Limitation leaf signed by Conrad, this no. 658 of 780 sets, 750 for sale, 30 for presentation, 20 volumes, half titles, uncut in original cream boards, cream cloth spines, Conrad's printed signature on front boards, slight rust marking to back board volume 5, slight bump to near edge of front board, volume 6, bookplate of Cuthbert Headlam in all volumes except volumes 11, 12, 19 & 20, overall very good set. Jarndyce Antiquarian Booksellers CCXI - 71 2015 £1500

Binding - Henness, Earl

Griggs, Bob *Elrae: the Littlest printer.* Salem: Beaverdam Press, 1987. Limited to 225 numbered copies, signed by printer/binder, Earl H. Henness on colophon, 8.1 x 6.2cm., cloth, slipcase, illustrations in text by author, miniature bookplate of Kalman Levitan. Oak Knoll Books 306 - 112 2015 $100

Binding - Hering

Callimachus *Callimaco Greco-Italiano Ora Pubblicato.* Parma: Nel Regal Palazzo Co' Tipi Bodiani, 1792. 311 x 229mm., handsome early 19th century red straight grain morocco by Charles Hering (his ticket on verso of front free endpaper), covers with thick and thin gilt rule border, raised bands flanked by gilt rules, gilt titling and turn-ins, all edges gilt, booklabel of Steven St Clair Smallwood; joints bit rubbed and flaked, though refurbished with considerable success, two corners little bumped, spine faded toward rose, few minor marks in morocco, isolated faint marginal foxing, still extremely pleasing copy high quality binding with no serious defects, text printed on thick paper, creamy paper with enormous margins. Phillip J. Pirages 66 - 66 2015 $6500

Gisborne, Thomas *Walks in a Forest.* London: printed by J. Davis for B. and J. White, 1796. Second edition, 191 x 127mm., fine contemporary red straight grain morocco handsomely gilt by Charles Hering Sr. (his ticket), covers with frame of bead and flower roll within thick and thin gilt rules, daisy cornerpieces, scalloped central panel with delicate gilt rule frame inset with garlands at sides and corners, flat spine lavishly gilt in compartments with oval centerpiece surrounded by small circles and many gilt dots, decorative gilt roll to turn-ins, marbled endpapers, all edges gilt, vague hints of soiling to covers, endpapers with minor smudges and faint browning, occasional light spots of foxing leaves a shade less than bright, otherwise excellent internally, text clean and fresh, lovely binding in very fine condition, bright morocco and gilt, virtually no wear. Phillip J. Pirages 66 - 67 2015 $1500

Binding - Hiebert, Helen

Hiebert, Helen *Spring Theory.* Avon: 2010. One of 10 copies, all on handmade abaca paper with string drawings embedded into paper, each copy hand numbered and signed by artist, Helen Hiebert and poet, Carl Adamschick, page size 12 x 18 inches, 6 string drawings plus 1 page text with colophon, loose as issued in black cloth over boards clamshell box designed by Sandy Tilcock with Helen Heibert's string drawings are in red as well as white string and were inspired by knot illustrations in the Ashley Book of Knots, text printed letterpress by Sandy Tilcock, beautiful textured paper is the perfect backdrop for the drawings in string. Priscilla Juvelis - Rare Books 62 - 7 2015 $1800

Binding - Hobson, Charles

Lopez, Barry *The Near Woods. Images and Design by Charles Hobson.* San Francisco: Pacific Editions, 2006. One of 26 lettered copies, each lettered (a to z) and signed in pencil by author and artist, Charles Hobson from a total of 26+ copies which includes few artist proof copies, page size 10 x 7 inches, 10 pages, double page foldout containing monotype image with pastel on German etching paper reproduced as a digital pigment print that has been hand colored with pastel and acrylic paint by the artist and another single page image on verso, the two images signed in pencil by Charles Hobson, bound by Hobson and Alice Shaw in original paper over boards bound in, paper a reproduction of a drawing used to establish land grants in California. Priscilla Juvelis - Rare Books 61 - 40 2015 $850

Binding - Hodgson

Knight, Charles *Passages of a Working Life During Half a Century with a Prelude of Early Reminiscences.* London: Bradbury & Evans, 1865. 1864. First edition, 3 volumes, 8vo., contemporary uniform polished calf, gilt with raised bands, fully gilt in compartments with contrasting labels, all edges marbled by Hodgson of Liverpool, fine set, most attractive binding, with contemporary (unidentified) armorial bookplate.   John Drury Rare Books   March 2015 - 23109   2015 $266

Binding - Holloway

Thackeray, Franciscus St. John *Anthologia Latina.* London: A. M. Bell et Daldy, 1865. First edition, presentation copy, paper lightly toned throughout, few fox spots to first and last leaves, small 8vo., contemporary dark brown morocco by Holloway, boards bordered with double gilt fillet, spine divided by raised bands with gilt fillet borders to compartments, second compartment gilt lettered direct, rest with central fleuron tools and fleur-de-lis cornerpieces, turn-ins decoratively gilt, all edges gilt, marbled endpapers, bookplate of William Thirlwall Bayne, near fine, inscribed by editor for Thirlwall.   Blackwell's Rare Books   Greek & Latin Classics VI - 64   2015   £200

Binding - Jensen Bindery

Faulkner, William Harrison   1897-1962 *Hunting Stories.* N.P.: Limited Editions Club, 1988. Limited to 850 numbered copies signed by artist, 4to., etchings by Neil Welliver, quarter green Nigerian Oasis goatskin, slipcase, well preserved copy, handset at Out of Sorts Letter Foundry on paper Arches paper by Peter Pettengill and Paul and Clary Taylor, bound by Jensen Bindery, with Monthly Letter.   Oak Knoll Books   25 - 57   2015 $350

Binding - Jevne, Jill

Bart, Harriet *The Poetry of Chance Encounters.* Minneapolis: Mnemonic Press, 2003. One of 35 numbered copies, all on Rives BFK, from a total edition of 40, 9 x 6 1/8 inches, 42 pages, bound by Jill Jevne, full brown box calf, matching calf edged and gold paste paper by Claire Mariarcyzk, matching calf over boards slipcase, book contains 16 visual poems on multi-color fields, each imprinted with an icon in 22 karat gold, each printed page has a total of five press runs, including varnish over the icon and field with impression of the gold leaf imparting embossed effect to the icon, basic typeface is Lydian, a stressed sans serif chosen to complement the treatment of image and type throughout the book.   Priscilla Juvelis - Rare Books   61 - 1   2015 $3200

Binding - Joyce, Carol

Kafka, Franz   1883-1924 *In the Penal Colony.* N.P.: Limited Editions Club, 1987. Limited to 800 numbered copies signed by artist, small 4to., limp paper wrappers, cord tied, folding box lined in velvet, paper spine label, text set in Monotype Walbaum at the Out of Sorts letter Foundry and printed on mould made Magnani paper at Shagbark Press, lithographs by Michael Hafftka were printed on handmade Japanese paper at Trestle Editions, bound by Carol Joyce.   Oak Knoll Books   25 - 56   2015 $250

Rattray, David *A Red-Framed Print of the Summer Palace. Poems with Drawings by Peter Thompson.* New York: Vincent FitzGerald & Co., 1983. One of an edition of 150 on Hosho paper, signed in pencil by author and artist, printed at the Wild Carrot Letterpress employing Palatino type, titlepage calligraphy, printed on Moriki paper at Meriden Gravure Co., bound by Gerard Charriere and Carol Joyce, page size 6 x 8 1/2 inches, red linen with gray title label, title printed in silver, fine, titlepage printed in red and black with publisher's monogram VFG facsimiles of four drawings by Peter Thompson in pencil, pen and grey and green washes.   Priscilla Juvelis - Rare Books   61 - 15   2015 $350

Binding - Kalthoeber

Mason, William   1725-1797 *Poems.* York: printed by W. Blanchard, 1796. 191 x 124mm., 2 volumes, handsome contemporary tree calf elaborately gilt by Kalthoeber (ticket on verso of front endpaper), covers bordered with gilt Greek key roll, flat spines ornately gilt in compartments featuring various repeated tools, each spine with black morocco label, gilt turn-ins, marbled endpapers, both volumes with early signature of Elizabeth Hervey; lower compartment of second volume with abrasion and moderate loss of gilt on corner, little rubbing, otherwise only trivial wear, bindings handsome and well preserved, blanks at back of each volume little soiled, otherwise fine and very pretty set, virtually pristine internally.   Phillip J. Pirages   66 - 59   2015 $1800

Binding - Kelliegram

Dickens, Charles   1812-1870 *The Chimes.* London: Chapman & Hall, 1845. First edition, 2nd state with publisher's name outside title vignette, fine, in beautiful Kelliegram binding (so stamped on inside rear cover), full crimson morocco with inlaid leather picture on cover after one of John Leech's illustrations in book, lovely gilt decorative border on both covers, in the six compartments and on the turn-ins as well, all edges gilt. original covers and spine bound in at end, beautiful book.   Aleph-Bet Books, Inc.   108 - 136   2015 $2850

Dodgson, Charles Lutwidge 1832-1898 *Alice's Adventures in Wonderland 1872. and Through the Looking Glass 1877.* London: Macmillan and Co., Later printings, 2 volumes, 8vo., all edges gilt, silk endpapers, original covers bound in rear, illustrations by John Tenniel, each volume in lovely Kelliegram binding stamped inside each rear cover, bound in full green morocco with inlaid leather figure on both covers after Tenniels illustrations, elaborate gilt border featuring crown on both covers and spine compartments, each have a different figure, gilt turn-ins triple ruled with spade motif, except for some darkening on edge of back cover, this fine as well, handsome set.   Aleph-Bet Books, Inc.   108 - 87   2015 $5250

Binding - Kelm, Daniel

Clemens, Samuel Langhorne 1835-1910 *The Jumping Frog.* Easthampton: Cheloniidae Press, 1985. One of 15 Artist Proof copies, with one extra suite of wood engravings plus a suite of 15 state proof engravings, plus one rejected engraving, plus three proofs of portrait etchings of Twain, plus 2 pencil drawings of frogs by the artist, plus one original watercolor of the jumping frog, each signed and numbered by the artist, plus a copy of the prospectus, inscription by artist on front flyleaf below pencil sketch of Jim Smiley by the artist, regular edition was limited to 250 copies and is bound in green paper wrappers, all editions printed on Saunders paper in Centaur and Arighi types at Wild Carrot letterpress with assistance of Arthur Larson, 15 wood engravings printed by Harold Patrick McGrath, page size 6 x 8 1/2 inches, bound by Daniel Kelm, full undyed Oasis with onlays of the frog in repose - before the jump on front panel and after the jump on back panel, with doublures showing the front in mid-jump, onlays in green oasis of the frog, jumping are on front and back pastedowns, housed in linen clamshell box with pull-out portfolio for extra suites and book.   Priscilla Juvelis - Rare Books   61 - 6   2015 $4000

Komunyakaa, Yusef *Love in the Time of War.* Middletown: Robin Price, 2013. Number 36 of 70 copies, signed by author, bound in aluminum boards that are etched in a pattern based on camouflage fabric, spine and endpages are handmade Cave Paper, letterpress printed in silver ink in Adobe Jenson Pro type on hand dyed silk with small pieces of Moriki paper and glassine sewn inside folded sheets, designed, colored and printed by Price in collaboration with Brittney De Nigris, bound by Daniel Kelm of Easthampton MA, housed in archival folding case with printed title label to spine panel, prospectus and insert titled "Visual Backstory", fine.   The Kelmscott Bookshop   11 - 28   2015 $2400

Louys, Pierre *Leda or In Praise of the Blessings of Darkness.* Easthampton: Cheloniidae Press, 1985. State proof edition, copy #1 of 15 deluxe copies, with designer binding by Daniel Kelm, with original drawing, three extra suites, all on Saunders hot press watercolor paper, etchings on hand made Gamp Torinoko paper, one of 15 copies from a total of 75, each signed and numbered by the artist, 60 regular copies and 15 deluxe copies (this copy), page size 8 x 11 inches, 46 pages, five drypoint etchings and 7 wood engravings by Alan James Robinson each signed and numbered, type set by MacKenzie-Harris and printed by Dan Keleher at Wild Carrot Letterpress, wood engravings printed by Harold McGrath and drypoints printed by Alan James Robinson, designed by Robinson and Arthur Larson, bound by Kelm in full white alum-tawed pigskin, front panel with inset bas relief paper casting, in white against blue paper ground with darker blue border, taken from an original wax sculpture by Robinson, torso of nude Leda with swan between her legs, housed in custom made tan cloth clamshell box with blue paper linings, three part foldout with inset in one to accommodate bas relief on binding cover, signed by Kelm on colophon, clamshell box housed original drawing by Robinson, 5 state proof etchings, 13 proofs of wood engravings and extra suite of the 5 etchings and 7 wood engravings as well as a copy of original prospectus, box has some soiling at edges, book and extra suites are fine.   Priscilla Juvelis - Rare Books   61 - 3   2015 $2800

Binding - Kerr & Richardson

Rushworth, John *A True Relation of the Storming of Bristoll, and the taking the Town, Castle, Forts, Ordnance, Ammunition and Arms by Sir Thomas Fairfax's army on Thursday the 11 of this instant Septemb. 1645.* London: Edward Husband, 1645. First edition, small 4to., titlepage browned and foxed, some light spotting, closely trimmed in places but with no loss of text, late 19th century calf by Kerr & Richardson, Glasgow, joints and edges rubbed, covers discolored, signature of James Reilly, from the library of James Stevens Cox (1910-1997).   Maggs Bros. Ltd.   1447 - 86   2015   £120

Binding - Leighton, John

Elsum, John *The Art of Painting After the Italian Manner.* London: Printed for D. Brown at the Black Swan Without Temple Bar, 1703. First edition, first issue, 8vo., some browning and foxing, 19th century Spanish calf by J. Leighton, skillfully rebacked to style with red label, lettered gilt, covers embossed with heraldic device of William Stirling Maxwell with his earlier heraldic bookplate, and on rear paste down location label of Keir designated under "Art and Design" press marks 13.3' scored through and relocated at 'D4'.   Marlborough Rare Books   List 53 - 13   2015   £1350

Procter, Adelaide A. *The Victoria Regia a Volume of Original Contributions in Poetry and Prose.* London: printed and published by Emily Faithfull & Co., Victoria Press for the Employment of Women, 1861. First edition, 8vo. full leather elaborately stamped in gilt, all edges gilt, gilt inner dentelles, designed by John Leighton, some foxing on endpapers, much less in text, some very light wear to boards, still near fine, inscribed by Emily Faithful for Blanche Resticaux, 1862, also inserted a few news clippings about Faithful, very small ALS from Henry Alford and small slip of paper signed yours faithfully Isa Craig.   Second Life Books Inc.   191 - 78   2015 $1500

Binding - Lewis, Charles

Mirror for Magistrates. London: printed for Lackington, Allen & Co. and Longman, Hurst, Rees, Orme & Brown, 1815. One of 150 copies, 248 x 191mm, 5 parts in 3 volumes, remarkably attractive contemporary chocolate brown morocco elaborately decorated in blind and gilt by Charles Lewis, covers with blind tooled frame enclosed by gilt fillets, wide raised bands with decorative gilt rolls, intricately blind tooled panels, gilt titling, turn-ins ruled with gilt, all edges gilt, large paper copy, verso of front free endpaper with pencilled notation, "3 volumes bound by Charles Lewis. £5.50/ Only 150 printed published at £10.10 in bds.", front free endpaper of volume I slightly creased at hinge, occasional light foxing, otherwise in beautiful condition with virtually no signs of use.   Phillip J. Pirages   66 - 69   2015 $3250

Painter, William   *The Palace of Pleasure.* London: reprinted for Robert Triphook by Harding and Wright, 1813. One of 150 copies, 3 volumes, 254 x 197mm., remarkably attractive contemporary chocolate brown morocco elaborately decorated in blind and gilt by Charles Lewis, covers with blind tooled frame enclosed by gilt fillets, wide raised bands, decorative gilt rolls, intricately blind tooled panels, gilt titling, turn-ins ruled in gilt, all edges gilt, large paper copy, verso of front free endpaper in volume I with pencilled notation, "3 volumes bound by Charles Lewis £5.50/Only 150 printed, published at £10.10 in bds.", hint of rubbing to head of one spine, occasional minor foxing and other trivial imperfections, but especially fine set, entirely clean and smooth internally, in lustrous unworn bindings.   Phillip J. Pirages   66 - 70   2015 $3250

Binding - Lewis, William

Dickens, Charles   1812-1870   *Oliver Twist or the Parish Boy's Progress.* London: Richard Bentley, 1838. First edition, first issue, with the 'Fireside' plate and 'Boz' on all three titles, octavo, contemporary full calf by William Lewis (binder's sticker), gilt decorated spines in six compartments, red and green leather labels, gilt ruled boards, gilt dentelles, all edges gilt, with half title to volume I, bound without volume II half title and ads, toning to plates (as often), text generally very clean, only occasional scattered foxing, almost invisible repairs to spine tops and volume 3 label, with 25 plates including 'Fireside' and 'Church' plate.   Manhattan Rare Book Company   Literature 2014 - 2015 $4800

Binding - Lintott, Mark

Bishop, Elizabeth   *12 O'Clock News.* Octon: Verdigris Press, 2006. One of 40 copies fro a total edition of 50, all on Hahemuhle paper, signed by artist, Judith Rothchild and printer/binder, Mark Lintott, 10 of the 50 are deluxe copies with an original copper plate and additional mezzotint, 40 regular copies (this copy) in additional 20 suites of prints from original copper plates were printed, page size 11 1/2 x 16 7/8 inches, bound by Mark Lintott, original gray-green paper over boards, paper has been silkscreened with yellow moon and title printed in khaki green with exposed sewing in ivory linen thread, blood red cloth hinges, red paper spine with title printed in black with author and artist's name, blood red endpapers, housed in publisher's matching slipcase, fine, illustrations by Judith Rothchild and designed by Rothchild and Mark Lintott, including two original mezzotints, pulled from two copper plates, one full page and the other copper plate cut into 8 sections and each of the eight plates separately reprinted and inserted in text.   Priscilla Juvelis - Rare Books   61 - 53   2015 $1300

Leonardo Da Vinci   1452-1519   *Of Light and Shade from the Notebooks of Leonardo Da Vinci. Chapters 118 to 127...* Octon: Verdigris Press, 2009. One of 9 copies, from a total issue of 15 (6 with original copper plate), each only numbered and signed in pencil by artist on colophon as well as initialing each page, page size 9 x 11 3/4 inches, 20 pages, bound by Mark Lintott, loose in wrappers housed in slipcase covered with handmade papers, screen printed by Judith Rothchild in pink, blue and green showing Leonardo's larger sphere on front cover and smaller sphere on rear cover, black front wrapper embossed with circles, squares and triangle, with white label printed in black with title and author, translator and artist on front panel, 6 original full page intaglio prints, endsheets with embossed spheres along bottom edge by Judith Rothchild.   Priscilla Juvelis - Rare Books   62 - 18   2015 $1000

Verne, Jules 1828-1905 *Tempete et Calme. Poeme de Jules Verne.* Octon: Verdigris Press, 2004. One of 38 copies only, all on Hahnemuhle paper, each copy hand numbered and signed by artist, Judith Rothchild, the artist and Mark Lintott, the printer, page size 11 3/4 x 5 15/16 inches, 4 leaves + colophon printed on gray paper mounted on inside rear cover, bound by Lintott Leporello style, but on vertical, original screen prints by Judith Rohchild in subtle shades of gray on front and back boards with gray silk ribbon pull at bottom of front board, housed in publisher's clamshell box of gray paper title printed in black on front panel, lined with screen prints by Rothchild in shades of gray, fine.   Priscilla Juvelis - Rare Books   61 - 55   2015 $750

Binding - Lloyd, Trevor

Charles II, King of England *His Majesties Commission for the Rebuilding of the Cathedral Church of St. Paul in London.* London: printed by the Assignes of John Bill and Christopher Barker ..., 1674. First edition, folio, title printed with double ruled borders, woodcut of royal arms, bound recently in fine old style quarter calf gilt over marbled boards by Trevor Lloyd, fine, very scarce.   John Drury Rare Books   2015 - 25352   2015 $2185

Place, Francis *Illustrations and Proofs of the Principle of Population Including an Examination of Population...* London: Longman, Hurst, Rees, Orme and Brown, 1822. First edition, now in fine but recent old-style half russia gilt over marbled boards, spine fully gilt with raised bands by Trevor Lloyd, fine and handsome copy, uncommon.   John Drury Rare Books   2015 - 25079   2015 $7867

Smith, John *Memoirs of Wool, Woolen Manufacture and Trade (Particularly in England) from the Earliest to the Present Times...* London: printed for the author, 1756-1757. 2 volumes, 4to., little worm damage in blank upper margin of a few leaves in volume II (nowhere near text), marginal dampstain in final few leaves also of volume II, recently bound by Trevor Lloyd in old style half calf, gilt and labelled, very good.   John Drury Rare Books   2015 - 22878 2015 $2185

Smyth, James Carmichael *A Description of the Jail Distemper, as it Appeared Amongst the Spanish Prisoners at Winchester in the year 1780....* London: J. Johnson, 1795. First edition, 8vo., rebound recently in fine 18th century style quarter calf gilt over marbled boards, raised bands, crimson label by Trevor Lloyd, most attractive, uncommon.   John Drury Rare Books   2015 - 22272   2015 $1136

Sophia *Woman Not Inferior to Man; or a Short and Modest Vindication of the Natural Right of the Fair-Sex to a Perfect Equality of Power, Dignity and Esteem with Men.* London: printed for John Hawkins at the Falcon in St. Paul's Church Yard, 1739. First edition, 8vo., half title, without final leaf of ads, half title little soiled, few leaves creased, well bound recently by Trevor Lloyd in contemporary style half calf over marbled boards, spine gilt and lettered with raised bands, very good, uncut.   John Drury Rare Books   2015 - 26113   2015 $6906

Wollstonecraft, Mary 1759-1797 *A Vindication of the Rights of Woman; with Strictures on Political and Moral Subjects.* London: J. Johnson, 1796. 8vo., recently bound in 18th century style half calf gilt by Trevor Lloyd of Ludlow, fine.   John Drury Rare Books   2015 - 24574   2015 $2185

Binding - Lowenstein, Sallie

Lowenstein, Frank L. *Clothed in Bark.* Kensington: Lion Stone Books, 2013. Number 37 of 650 copies, signed by book artist and author, binding, design and illustrations by Sallie Lowenstein, photos of tree bark transformed by drawing on top of each image to accentuate the lines and patterns formed by nature, each copy in unique binding, bound by hand in flexible dark brown leather wrappers decorated with an intricate pattern of circular punches, sewn with medieval long stitch, which is then woven in pattern resembling tree bark housed in cardboard box with velcro closures and plastic bag insert, which holds the book inside box, images from book decorate the exterior of the box, fine.   The Kelmscott Bookshop   11 - 31   2015 $195

Binding - Lubbock

Sotheby, William *A Tour Through Parts of Wales.* London: printed by J. Smeeton for R. Blamire, 1794. First edition, 295 x 229mm, extremely handsome dark blue straight grain morocco, elaborately decorated in gilt and blind by Lubbock of Newcastle (their ticket on front free endpaper), covers with intricate frame in gilt and blind (featuring stippling, fleurons, drawer handles, wreaths, etc.), large central panel of an unusual design with blind stamped lozenge at center and horizontal blindstamped boards above and below, all enclosed by double gilt fillets (to form a large "I" with a convex vertical element) raised bands, space panels with gilt or blind tooled fleurons, wide densely gilt turn-ins with inlaid red morocco cornerpieces, marbled endpapers, all edges gilt, with modern fore-edge painting showing three landscape vignettes, castle ruins, an arched bridge, and a castle by the sea, surrounded by colored volutes, fruits and cornucopia, 13 sepia tone engravings of Welsh castles and scenery after J. Smith, front pastedown with engraved armorial bookplate of Ravensworth Castle, titlepage with ink ownership inscription of T. H. Liddell, this the copy of (and most likely bound for) Thomas Henry Liddell, 1st Baron Ravensworth; corners and extremities little rubbed joints slightly flaked, but well masked with dye, faint offsetting from engravings, otherwise fine copy, binding lustrous and without significant wear and text and plates with only most trivial imperfections.   Phillip J. Pirages 66 - 56   2015 $6500

Binding - Machinchick, Joan

Malmgren, Ebby *Stone Dream and Other Poems by Ebby Malmgren.* Arnold: 2003. Artist's book, one of 18 copies, all on Nepalese Lokta paper and Hiromi Rayon Paper collaged on Indian handmade 'cork' paper, page size 6 1/4 x 10 1/4 inches, 24 pages, bound by Joan Machinchick, hand-sewn in brown paper over boards with title hand lettered and printed Gocco and collaged on front cover, housed in tan linen over boards clamshell box with title printed Gocco from hand lettering on spine and front panel.   Priscilla Juvelis - Rare Books   62 - 09   2015 $750

Binding - MacKenzie, J.

Cole, John *Bookselling Spiritualised. Books and Articles of Stationery Rendered Monitors of Religion.* Scarborough: imprinted by John Cole Newborough St., 1826. First edition, limited impression of only 60 copies, printed on thick paper extended with many blank leaves, contemporary dark red morocco by gilt extra by J. MacKenzie, gilt edges with gilt cypher on each cover and 19th century armorial bookplate of James Cornerford on pastedown, extremities lightly rubbed, fine, handsome.   John Drury Rare Books   2015 - 25207   2015 $830

Binding - Maclehose

Wingfield, Lewis *Abigel Rowe.* London: Richard Bentley & Son, 1883. First edition, 3 volumes, slightly later half crimson calf by Maclehose, Glasgow, raised gilt bands, black and maroon morocco labels, slight rubbing, but very good, ownership signature of Charles F. Grant.   Jarndyce Antiquarian Booksellers   CCXI - 292   2015   £280

Binding - Matthews, Alfred

Flitner, Johann *Nebulo Nebulonum: Hoc Est, loco-Seria Vernaculae Nequitiae Censura Carmine Iambico Depicta Tipisque Exornata Aeneis A Iohanne Flintero.* Leeuwarden: Joanne Coopmans, 1634. Second edition, 8vo., handsome half red leather, marbled boards, five raised bands and lettered gilt at spine, binding by Alfred Matthews, text in Latin, slight rubbing, else very good, exquisite binding.   Any Amount of Books   2015 - C11840   2015   £750

Binding - McKee, Elizabeth

McKee, Elizabeth *Entrance to the Greenhouse.* Moscow: 2006. Artist's book, one of a series of five all on Indian flowered paper, 2 of which are for sale, this copy with last two pages of window-sill gardens highlighted with colored pencils by artist, signed and dated by her on colophon, 6 3/4 x 7 1/2 inches, 38 pages, 4 of which are double-page fold-outs and one of which is a double page pop-up, bound by artist, hand sewn with exposed spine and tape, beige linen over boards, front panel with inlaid linen fabric, Indian flower paper overlay, housed in custom made tan cloth clamshell box with label printed on paper, fine, poem by Joan Finnigan.   Priscilla Juvelis - Rare Books   62 - 13   2015 $1000

Binding - McKibbin, George & Son

Dodgson, Charles Lutwidge 1832-1898 *Alice's Adventures in Wonderland. (with) Through the Looking Glasss and What Alice Found There.* New York: Limited Editions Club, 1912. 1935. Both limited to 1500 numbered copies, signed by the original Alice, Alice Hargraves, signed by Frederic Warde, this copy of the few signed by the 'original Alice', octavo, original text illustrations by Tenniel re-engraved on wood by Bruno Rollitz, printed by members of the LEC by the Printing House of William Edwin Rudge, typography and binding design by Frederic Warde, publisher's full red morocco by George McKibbin & Son, NY. covers decoratively bordered in gilt, smooth spine decoratively tooled and lettered gilt in compartments, some rubbing to spine, near fine, housed in original blue cloth slipcase (some browning and light wear); Looking Glass with original text illustrations by Tenniel, Re-engraved (in metal) by Frederick Warde, publisher's full blue morocco by McKibbin, covers decoratively bordered gilt, smooth spine decoratively tooled and lettered in gilt in compartments, all edges gilt some rubbing, some scuffing to spine, near fine copy, housed in original red cloth slipcase, fine.   Heritage Book Shop Holiday 2014 - 30   2015 $4000

Dickens, Charles 1812-1870 *The Library of Fiction or Family Story-Teller.* London: Chapman and Hall, 1836. 1837. First edition, 2 volumes, octavo, full 19th entury crushed morocco gilt, fine, bound by Ramage, illustrations by George Cruikshank.   Honey & Wax Booksellers   2 - 14   2015 $5000

Binding - Rees, Hugh

Graham, William *Socialism New and Old.* London: Kegan Paul, 1908. Fifth impression, half title, original red cloth by Hugh Rees, boards decorated and lettered in blind, very good, bright copy.   Jarndyce Antiquarian Booksellers   CCXI - 124   2015   £20

Binding - Remnant & Edmonds

Calmet, Augustine *The Phantom World; or the Philosophy of Spirits, Apparitions &c.* London: Richard Bentley, 1850. 2 volumes, occasional slight foxing, small label removed from lower margin of pastedown, volume II, original purple horizontal wavy grained cloth by Remnant & Edmonds, fading to brown, spine embossed in blind, boards slightly rubbed, very good.   Jarndyce Antiquarian Booksellers   CCXI - 58   2015   £485

Binding - Reynolds, Sage

Brassai *The Artists of My Life.* New York: Wilken Berley Ltd., 1982. First edition, large 4to., full page reproductions of photos of artists at work, pictorial patterned paper covered boards over cloth lettered silver at spine, special presentation folder housing photogravure, deluxe edition, this number 11 of 150 copies signed and numbered by Brassai, issued with hand pulled dust grained 'photogravure 21 x 15.9cm' also signed by Brassai, book in special binding designed by Sage Reynolds and executed at the Four Hands Bindery, fine in plain buff very good slipcase.   Any Amount of Books   2015 - A68259   2015   £750

Binding - Richmond & Son

Bentley, Joseph *Health and Wealth: How to Get, Preserve and Enjoy Them or Physical and Industrial Training for the People.* London: Joseph Bentley, 1858. Fifth edition, illustrations, unopened ads pages 299-328, original brown cloth by Richmond & Son, blocked in blind, neat library number foot of spine, ex-libris Manchester & Salford Bank Ltd., very good.   Jarndyce Antiquarian Booksellers   CCXI - 24   2015   £75

Binding - Riley, E., & Son

Tucker, Abraham *Vocal Sounds by Edward Search, Esq.* London: printed by T. Jones and sold by T. Payne, 1773. First edition, small 8vo., 19th century half maroon morocco by E. Riley & Son, very good,.   Blackwell's Rare Books   B179 - 108   2015   £900

Binding - Riviere

Ariosto, Lodovico *Orlando Furiosa in English Heroical Verse.* London: Richard Field, 1607. Second English edition, folio, period style full sprinkled calf gilt, engraved title by Thomas Cockson, 46 plates, bound by Riviere.   Honey & Wax Booksellers   3 - 3   2015 $8500

Austen, Jane 1775-1817 *Northanger Abbey and Persuasion.* London: John Murray, 1818. First edition, 12mo., 4 volumes, bound with old and incorrect half titles, each 20th century full smooth tan morocco by Riviere, covers ruled in gilt, spines decoratively tooled in gilt, gilt turn-ins, black and red morocco gilt lettering labels, all edges gilt, bookplate pastedown of each volume, light foxing throughout, some light rubbing to spine extremities and outer hinge repair to all volumes, all in all handsome set.   Heritage Book Shop   Holiday 2014 - 6   2015 $8500

Austen, Jane 1775-1817 *Pride and Prejudice.* London: printed for T. Egerton, 1813. First edition, 3 volumes, 12mo., fine early 20th century full brown crushed morocco Riviere binding, gilt titles and decorations to spines, all edges gilt, marbled endpapers, gilt inner dentelles, binding shows very minor wear, few light scuffs to corners and few small spots to volume III, while often lacking, half titles present in volumes I and III they appear to be supplied from a second edition; volume 1 with minor chips to pages 143/144 and 15/158 and few minor creases to gatherings M and N, volume II with tiny tear to rear flyleaf, small tear to outer margin of page 77, some very minor scattered spotting, volume III, small repair to upper corner of page 129, repair to lower corner of page 137/138, tiny pin hole to page 259/260, beautiful, clean, very attractive.   B & B Rare Books, Ltd.   234 - 2   2015 $60,000

Brough, Robert B. *The Life of Sir John Falstaff.* London: Longman, Brown, Green, Longmans and Roberts, 1858. Royal 8vo., 20 etched plates and duplicate hand colored set, text illustrations, full red morocco, spine decorated in gilt by Riviere, preserving original wrapper for 'part 1' also upper wrapper for the separate publication, 20 etchings by George Cruikshank and original decorated cloth upper cover and spine for book issue.   Marlborough Rare Books   List 53 - 4   2015   £1100

Brough, Robert B. *The Life of Sir John Falstaff...* London: Longman, Brown, Green, Longmans and Roberts, 1858. Royal 8vo., 20 etched plates and duplicate hand colored set, text illustrations by George Cruickshank, full red morocco, spine decorated gilt by Riviere, preserving the original wrapper for part 1, also upper wrapper for the separate publication 'Twenty Etchings" by Cruikshank, and original decorated cloth, upper cover and spine for book issue.   Marlborough Rare Books   List 54 - 7   2015   £1100

Byron, George Gordon Noel, 6th Baron 1788-1824
Childe Harold's Pilgrimage. London: John Murray, 1841. First extensively illustrated edition, large 8vo., dark red morocco by Riviere, elaborate gilt decorations and inner dentelles, gilt lettering, top edge gilt, frontispiece portrait, engraved title, folding map, 59 engravings binding slightly rubbed, fine. The Brick Row Book Shop Miscellany 67 - 28 2015 $850

Chaucer, Geoffrey 1340-1400 *The Workes of Geffrey Chaucer.* London: imprinted by Jhon Kyngston for Jhon Wight, 1561. First collected edition, first issue, 22 woodcuts in The Prologues, folio, title within woodcut border, 22 woodcuts of Pilgrims in "The Prologues" and woodcut of knight on horse at head of "The Knightes Tale", large and small historiated and decorative initials and other ornaments, Black letter, fifty-six lines, double columns; late 19th century crimson morocco by Riviere, covers with gilt fillet and roll tool border enclosing central olive wreath and elaborate cornerpieces composed of scroll-work and spreading olive branches, remaining field seme with cinquefoils, spine in 7 compartments with six raised bands, lettered gilt in two compartments, rest decoratively tooled gilt with repeated olive leaf motif, board edges and turn-ins decoratively tooled in gilt, all edges gilt, marbled endpapers (pastedowns with decorative gilt tooling), title creased and lightly soiled, small repair to outer blank margin, lower corner of second leaf renewed, affecting catchword on recto and two letters on verso, closed tear through lower half of divisional title to "The Caunterburie Tales", closed tear to A2 of "The Prologues" affecting 8 lines of text to first column and another closed tear at lower margin, F2 with small paper repair to margin and closed tear just touching text, 2U2 with paper fault affecting one word in bottom line of text on recto and verso, few additional small marginal tears or repairs not affecting text, occasional early ink underlining and markings, early signature of James Rea (faded) on title, wonderful copy, from the libraries of C. W. Dyson Perrins and William Foyle, with bookplates. Heritage Book Shop Holiday 2014 - 36 2015 $65,000

Coghlan, Margaret *Memoirs of Mrs. Coghlan... Written by Herself.* New York: T. & J. Swords, 1795. First American edition, 12mo., full brown morocco by Riviere, gilt lettering, all edges gilt, hinges just starting but firm, fine. The Brick Row Book Shop Miscellany 67 - 34 2015 $875

Corbet, Richard *Poems.* London: by J. C for William Crook, 1672. Third edition, 12mo., without first blank leaf, woodcut publisher's device of a dragon on title, some spotting on titlepage, wormed at head up to page 28 then declining to a single tiny pinhole, affecting headlines (repaired on first six leaves), closely shaved (touching some headlines and catchwords), fore margin of A6 (The Table) unevenly trimmed with slight loss on recto), early 20th century brown morocco, tooled in blind, by Riviere, from the library of James Stevens Cox (1910-1997). Maggs Bros. Ltd. 1447 - 116 2015 £240

Dickens, Charles 1812-1870 *The Personal History of David Copperfield.* London: Bradbury & Evans, 1850. First edition in book form, octavo, full 19th century polished calf, gilt, illustrations by Phiz, bound by Riviere. Honey & Wax Booksellers 2 - 16 2015 $2800

Dryden, John 1631-1700 *Of Dramatick Poesie, an Essay.* printed for Henry Heringham, 1668. First edition, uniformly browned, various minor paper repairs, but including a tear in middle of titlepage (very neatly done), 4to., full crushed red morocco by Riviere and Son, lettered in gilt on upper cover and in minuscule letters on spine, gilt edges, cloth slip-in case, upper joint skillfully repaired, lower corners slightly bumped, good. Blackwell's Rare Books B179 - 38 2015 £1500

Riccardi, Pietro *Biblioteca Matematica Italiana.* Modenz: Coi Tipi della Societa Tipografica, Antica Tipografia Soliani, 1873-1928. First editions, 4 volumes, 4to., volumes I-III bound by Riviere & Son in half dark green leather with green cloth sides, gilt stamped spine title with raised bands, top edge gilt, some of the leather discolored to brown (as usual), volume IV bound by another binder, but to match originals very closely, fine, scarce. Jeff Weber Rare Books 178 - 939 2015 $1000

Scriptural Epitaphs. London: Smith Elder and Co., 1947. 12mo., contemporary calf gilt, spine fully gilt with raised bands, red edges, inner gilt dentelles by Riviere, fine, rare. John Drury Rare Books March 2015 - 15838 2015 $266

Shenstone, William 1714-1763 *The Judgment of Hercules, a Poem. Inscrib'd to George Lyttleton, Esq.* London: printed for R. Dodsley and sold by T. Cooper, 1741. First edition, 8vo., full rose morocco, gilt, spine gilt, all edges gilt, by Riviere & Son, bookplate of Oliver Brett, later Viscount Esher. C. R. Johnson Foxon R-Z - 893r-z 2015 $2298

Sheridan, Richard Brinsley Butler 1751-1816 *The Camp.* London: 1795. 8vo., sewn original publisher's plain wrappers (little worn, old catalog entry laid in), housed in cloth chemise and full morocco slipcase by Riviere & Son, former owner's bookplate on inside flap of chemise, fine. Second Life Books Inc. 190 - 197 2015 $325

Shippen, William *Faction Display'd. a poem.* London: printed in the year, 1704. First edition, 4to., full polished calf, gilt, spine and inner dentelles gilt, red morocco label by Riviere and Son, some pale waterstains to lower corners, but very good, large copy, outer edges untrimmed, early owner has identified a passage on page 15 as referring to the bookseller Jacob Tonson. C. R. Johnson Foxon R-Z - 896r-z 2015 $383

Westall, William *Picturesque Tour of the River Thames.* London: R. Ackerman, 96 Strand, 1828. First edition, 4to., 24 finely hand colored aquatint plates, colored aquatint vignette on title and another to final leaf, contemporary full green crushed morocco, spine decorated and lettered gilt within raised bands, spine faded to brown by Riviere and Son, preserving original cloth at end of work, armorial bookplate of Fairfax Rhodes and C. Robert Bagnold and bookseller tickets of Thomas Thorp and R. D. Steadman, fine. Marlborough Rare Books   List 54 - 89   2015   £4500

Young, Edward   1683-1765 *The Complaint or Night-Thoughts on Life, Death & Immortality.* London: printed for R. Dodsley, 1742. First edition, folio, 20 pages, full marbled calf, gilt, spine and inner dentelles gilt, all edges gilt, by Riviere & Son, spine bit worn, upper joint weak, cloth slipcase, very good.   C. R. Johnson   Foxon R-Z - 1178r-z   2015 $7661

Binding - Root

Dodgson, Charles Lutwidge   1832-1898 *Alice's Adventures in Wonderland. (with) Through the Looking-Glass and What Alice Found There.* London: Macmillan, 1870-1873. Later printings, illustrations by John Tenniel, finely bound in full red calf by Root and Son, boards stamped after original cloth bindings with illustrations of Alice and Cheshire Cat and the Red and White Queens, with the original cloth bound into rear of texts, very good with some light wear and rubbing to extremities, minor toning to spine and board edges, light rubbing to spines and hinges, Looking Glass with shallow chip to spine head, bookplates of noted art collector and art historian, J. Frederic Byers, bright and clean pages, overall lovely, finely bound copy.   B & B Rare Books, Ltd.   2015 - 2015 $1500

Sewell, George *Poems on Several Occasions.* London: printed for E. Curll and J. Pemberton, 1719. First edition, 8vo., polished mottled calf, gilt spine and inner dentelles, gilt, by Root & Son, excellent copy, complete with two final leaves of index, sometimes missing, very scarce, bookplate of Oliver Brett, Viscount Esher.   C. R. Johnson   Foxon R-Z - 888r-z   2015 $2298

Shelley, Mary Wollstonecraft Godwin   1797-1851 *Monsieur Nongtongpaw.* London: Alfred Miller, 1830. First illustrated edition, 12mo., 6 engraved plates, contemporary hand coloring, bound in later three quarter morocco and marbled boards by Root, front cover very loose, very clean. Second Life Books Inc.   189 - 230   2015 $600

Binding - Russell, J. C.

Dickens, Charles   1812-1870 *A Christmas Carol.* Philadelphia: Carey & Hart, 1844. First American edition, 12mo. in 6's, four hand colored lithographed plates, including frontispiece and 4 hand colored wood engraved plates, original gilt binding by "J. C. Russell Binder" in dark brown vertically ribbed cloth with front cover decoratively stamped in gilt, rear cover decoratively stamped in blind and spine decoratively stamped and lettered gilt, original buff endpapers, spine gilt lightly rubbed, headcap and tailcap chipped, rear outer hinge repaired, very good in scarce gilt binding, housed in brown cloth clamshell case.   Heritage Book Shop   Holiday 2014 - 54   2015 $10,000

Binding - Salisbury Bookbinders

Rupert, Prince, Count Palatine   1619-1682 *A Declaration of His Hignesse Prince Rupert.* London: Edward Griffin, 1645. 4to. uncut at fore-edge and tail, title browned, edges dusty, small rust spot on E3v and with fore margin of E4 stained, late 20th century calf, ruled in gilt by Salisbury Bookbinders, very light white scuff marks on front board and foot of spine, from the library of James Stevens Cox (1910-1997).   Maggs Bros. Ltd.   1447 - 85   2015   £200

Binding - Sanford, P. B.

Thornbury, George Walter *The Monarchs of the Main; or Adventures of the Buccaneers.* London: Hurst & Blackett, 1855. First edition, 3 volumes, final ad leaf volume III, uncut in early 20th century half red crushed morocco by P. B. Sanford, raised gilt bands, gilt compartments, slight wear to hinges, some slight marking, booklabels of J. B. Troy, Library labels and stamps from St. Charles College Library, Catonsville, attractive copy.   Jarndyce Antiquarian Booksellers   CCXI - 271   2015   £320

Binding - Sangorski

Churchill, Winston Leonard Spencer   1874-1965 *The Second World Ward.* London: Cassell & Co. Ltd., 1948-1954. First edition, 6 volumes, small quarto, numerous maps and diagrams, some folding, throughout, finely bound for Brentano's, probably by Sangorski in full crimson morocco, covers double ruled in gilt, spines decoratively tooled and lettered gilt with five raised bands, gilt stamped with flower motif to compartments, top edge gilt, gilt turn-ins, slightest of sunning to spines, otherwise fine, housed in custom open ended red cloth slipcase, slipcase bit worn and repaired.   Heritage Book Shop   Holiday 2014 - 39   2015 $3500

Binding - Sangorski & Sutcliffe

Blanchard, Jean Pierre *An Exact and Authentic Narrative of M. Blanchard's Third Aerial Voyage.* London: C. Heydigner, 1784. First edition, small folio, frontispiece, early dark brown paper wrappers, housed in dark blue cloth folder by Sangorski & Sutcliffe for E. P. Dutton, gilt lettering on outside of folder, balloon themed bookplate of previous owner William G. Gerhard =, lacking half title, slight offsetting to titlepage from frontispiece and some light foxing to final leaf, very good.   Heritage Book Shop   Holiday 2014 - 18   2015 $2750

Butt, John *Dickens at Work.* London: Methuen, 1957. First edition, half title, frontispiece, plates, half brown morocco by Sangorski & Sutcliffe, spine in compartments, slight rubbing to leading hinge, top edge gilt, publisher's specially bound copy to Kathleen Tillotson with ANS from Peter Wait inserted.   Jarndyce Antiquarian Booksellers   CCVII - 207   2015   £40

Dickens, Charles   1812-1870 *Dombey and Son.* London: Bradbury & Evans, 1848. First edition in book form, octavo, engraved frontispiece, engraved titlepage and 38 plates, with two original pen and ink drawings by the artist, Phiz, inserted, each signed "Phiz", extremely rare with drawings, each drawing is on a sheet of onion skin measuring 138 x110mm and then inlaid into later sheet to match size of other leaves, original front wrapper for part iv bound in at end, without half title and list of plates, full olive morocco bound by Sangorski & Sutcliffe, boards decoratively stamped in black, gilt lettered on spine, gilt ruled dentelles, marbled endpapers, top edge gilt, with two previous owner's bookplates, "Kenyon Starling" and "Self" and spine lightly sunned, near fine.   Heritage Book Shop   Holiday 2014 - 55   2015 $16,500

Keats, John   1795-1821 *The Poems.* Hammersmith: William Morris at the Kelmscott Press, 1894. First edition, one of 300 copies, octavo, full 20th century russet morocco gilt, bound by Sangorski & Sutcliffe, gift inscription by English playwright Henry Arthur Jones.   Honey & Wax Booksellers   2 - 15   2015 $7000

Marvell, Andrew   1621-1678 *A Collection of Poems on Affairs of State. (bound with) The Second Part of the Collection of Poems on Affairs of State. (bound with) The Third Part of the Collection of Poems on Affairs of State.* London: printed in the year, 1689. Second edition of part one, first editions of parts two and three,, 3 parts, 4to., modern red morocco by Sangorski & Sutcliffe, gilt decorations, inner dentelles, rules and lettering, all edges gilt, fine, large copy.   The Brick Row Book Shop   Miscellany 67 - 67   2015 $4750

Omar Khayyam *Rubaiyat.* Siegle: Hill, 1911. 155/550 copies, printed on handmade paper and signed by binders Francis Sangorski & George Sutcliffe, printed text and decorative borders all printed in black and red and several heightened in gold, to a calligraphic design by Alberto Sutcliffe, text interspersed with 12 plates printed on one side only, some plate edges trifle soiled (as usual?), plates carrying color printed illustrations by E. Geddes, large 4to., original full white vellum, backstrip with overall ornate gilt design, gilt lettered green leather label (sunned to brown and trifle chipped), front cover with overall gilt blocked peacock design, others untrimmed, very good.   Blackwell's Rare Books   B179 - 218   2015   £600

Ruskin, John   1819-1900 *King of the Golden River.* London: Harrap, 1932. Number 4 of only 9 special copies (8 for sale) for which Rackham has done a full page watercolor signed by him, book also signed on limitation page and is inscribed by him, 4 fine color plates plus beautiful red and black text illustrations by Arthur Rackham, slim 4to., bound by Sangorski & Sutcliffe for Harrap in full green morocco with gold tooling, raised bands, top edge gilt, marbled endpapers, spine slightly faded, else fine, original pictorial endpapers bound in.   Aleph-Bet Books, Inc.   108 - 380   2015 $25,000

Smedley, Francis *Frank Fairlegh; or Scenes from the Life of a Private Pupil.* London: A. Hall Virtue, 1850. First edition, 30 steel engravings by George Cruikshank, bound by Sangorski & Sutcliffe in three quarter navy leather with fancy gilt decorations to spine, raised bands, top edge gilt, ribbon marker housed in plain slipcase, very good plus, some minor scuffing and scratches to boards, offsetting to endpapers, very solid handsome copy.   Ed Smith Books   82 - 25   2015 $350

Binding - Saupoudrage

Baouir De Lormian, Pierre Marie Francois Louis *Veillees Poetiques et Morales Suivies Des Plus Beaux Fragmens D'Young en Vers Francais.* Paris: printed by P. Didot for Latour Delanay and Brunot Abbot, 1811. First edition, 156 x 89mm., extremely pretty contemporary green calf, gilt, covers with delicate floral frame enclosing gilt compartments separated by inlaid red morocco bands, two compartments with rose sprig centerpiece and two compartments with densely interlocking rows of circles, red morocco label, turn-ins with decorative gilt roll, marbled endpapers, all edges gilt (lower joint apparently with very neat expert repair at tail), with etched vignette on titlepage and 3 engraved plates, original tissue guards; bookplate of Raoul Simonson, leather bookplate of Laurent Mecus; front joint with very short thin crack at tail, one opening with faintest freckled foxing, otherwise beautiful copy, text exceptionally clean, fresh and bright, scarcely worn, lustrous binding glistening with gold, especially pleasing gold dusted or "Saupoudrage" binding.   Phillip J. Pirages   66 - 78   2015 $1500

Binding - Seacome, J.

Hamilton, Thomas *Men and Manners in America.* Edinburgh: William Blackwood, 1833. First edition, 12mo., 2 volumes, contemporary half brown calf by J. Seacome, Chester, gilt bands, black and maroon morocco labels, little rubbed, nice, crisp copy, armorial bookplate of James Tomkinson Willington.   Jarndyce Antiquarian Booksellers   CCXI - 132   2015   £280

Binding - Settle, Smith

Horatius Flaccus, Quintus *The Odes of Horace.* London: Folio Society, 2014. Limited to 980 copies, hand calligraphed illuminated book, beautifully produced facsimile is bound in Indian goatskin with title and five raised bands to spine, edges and doublures and decorated in gilt binding by Smith Settle in Yorkshire, England, printed on Tatami paper in color with gold and silver foil by Castelli Bolis in Bergamo, Italy, the commentary bound in grey paper covered boards, both books housed in cloth clamshell box, titled in silver and gold on front and spine panels, commentary 64 pages, Odes 192 pages, fine.   The Kelmscott Bookshop   11 - 19   2015 $795

Binding - Silver

Spangenberg, Johannes *Postilla. Das Ist: Auslegung Der Episteln Und Evangelien...* Luneburg: Sternische Buchdruckerey, 1794. 219 x 137mm., 3 parts in 1 volume, striking engraved Repousse Silver Binding (probably 18th century German), covers with a beaded border surrounding a broad ornate frame featuring flowers, volutes and cherubs, this frame enclosing a central medallion portraying a scene from the Old Testament, spine divided into three compartments by beaded frames, top with grotesque face surrounded by flowers and arabesques, middle featuring Moses with the Ten Commandments, and the bottom with device for Faith, Hope and Charity framed by volutes, silver head and tail guards (in the form of a winged cherub) extending from the backstrip over a short portion of top and bottom of text block, two silver clasps depicting a male and female saint, presumably recased perhaps in the 19th century; with printer's device on titlepages and 64 woodcut illustrations (measuring approximately 80 x 11mm); titlepage backed, front hinge cracked (causing little looseness, though everything still intact), leaves rather soiled from use, two leaves with tears from fore-edge into text (affecting two lines of text, tears secured at fore edge with transparent tape), third part of the volume bit dampstained, final leaf reattached, its verse with loss of approximately half a column of text along gutter, not without condition problems, but text fresh, and original splendid binding still well preserved, silver lustrous and altogether pleasing.   Phillip J. Pirages   66 - 55   2015 $9500

Binding - Simier

Quintilian *Epitome Fabii Quintiliani Nuper Summo & Ingenio & Diligentia Collecta...* Paris: apud Simonem Colinaeum, 1531. First edition, little minor spotting, early ownership inscription to foot of titlepage (dated 1609 but faded almost beyond eligibility), 8vo., late 19th century burgundy straight grained morocco by Simier, boards bordered with gilt fillet enclosing blind roll, spine divided by raised bands ruled with double gilt fillets, second compartment and foot gilt lettered direct, rest with central tools, marbled endpapers, just touch rubbed at extremities, very good, very pleasant.   Blackwell's Rare Books   Greek & Latin Classics VI - 87   2015   £1500

Binding - Sotheran

Dickens, Charles 1812-1870 *Sketches of Young Couples.* London: Chapman & Hall, n.d. circa, 1870. 12mo., frontispieces, 3 volumes in 1, 6 x 3 3/4 inches, beautifully bound by H. Sotheran in full crimson morocco, decoratively tooled in gilt on covers and spine, original red cloth covers bound in at rear, all edges gilt, gilt turn-ins, bookplate, minor rubbing to spine extremities, else near fine.   Heritage Book Shop   Holiday 2014 - 61   2015 $750

Binding - Staggemeier & Welcher

Fenelon, Francois De Salignac De La Mothe, Abp. 1651-1715 *Les Aventures De Telemaque.* Paris: Imprimerie de Monsieur (i. e. Pierre Francois Didot), 1785. 340 x 264mm., 2 volumes bound in 1, elegant red contemporary straight grain morocco, elaborately gilt by Staggemeier and Welcher, covers with wide gilt border composed of inlaid strips of blue goatskin tooled with Greek-key roll with square green goatskin inlay at corners tooled with a medallion and with inner frame composed of an inlaid citron goatskin band and large, graceful gilt impressions of flowers, foliage and ears of wheat, smooth spine divided into four unequal compartments by a strip of inlaid green goatskin tooled with gilt pentaglyph and metope roll, gilt lettering on green goatskin label in second compartment and directly at foot of backstrip, first compartment tooled with face-in-the-sun, third (elongated) compartment featuring a strange figure with winged helmet holding festoons of flowers, balancing on top of flower issuing from large neoclassical vase, vase in turn perched on candelabrum, edges of boards and turn-ins tooled with gilt rolls, marbled endpapers, all edges gilt; with fore-edge painting very probably contemporary, of two boats sailing on a lake , a stately home in the background; with engraved printer's device on titlepages and two frontispiece portraits and mounted, hint of wear to corners, spine little darkened, slight variation in color of leather covers, other minor defects, but extremely handsome binding entirely solid with nothing approaching a significant fault, and covers especially lustrous with bright gilt, intermittent pale foxing in text (a few gatherings with faint overall browning or more noticeably foxed), but leaves remarkably fresh, they crackle as you turn them, very clean and printed with vast margins.   Phillip J. Pirages   66 - 51   2015 $9500

Hayley, William *The Triumphs of Temper: a Poem in Six Cantos.* London: T. Cadell, 1788. Sixth edition, 165 x 102mm., once remarkably attractive and still very pleasing late 18th century citron morocco by Staggemeier & Welcher, covers with inlaid black and red morocco tooled in gilt to a diapered mosaic design, raised bands, spine compartments with central moire silk endleaves, all edges gilt, expertly rejointed, spine label with tiny repairs and some inlays artfully replicated and replaced by Courtland Benson, with 7 engraved plates, silk bookplate of R. M. Trench Chiswell, titlepage and ink ownership inscription of Augusta E. Vincent, inscription from A. Vincent to Blanche Cely-Trevilian, spine little darkened, minor soiling to boards, plates rather foxed, otherwise without any significant defect and, in all, an excellent (albeit restored) specimen, binding with much of its original dramatic appeal reclaimed.   Phillip J. Pirages   66 - 52   2015 $4500

Binding - Stamper, H.

Richardson, Charles *A New Dictionary of the English Language.* London: William Pickering, 1836-1837. First edition, 2 volumes, half titles, 4to., contemporary polished chestnut calf by H. Stamper, French fillets on sides with an outer roll tooled toothed border, spines richly gilt, gilt edges, spines very slightly faded, cracking to joints (but firm), slight wear to extremities, good.   Blackwell's Rare Books   B179 - 87   2015   £1100

Binding - Star Bookworks

Freind, John *Emmenologia.* London: printed for T. Cox, 1752. Second edition, handsomely bound by Star Bookworks in full modern brown calf with gilt stamped decorations to boards and spine, raised spine bands and red title label, interior pages have waterstaining to first several pages and some foxing and aging throughout, margin cut from endpaper, several ink ownership signatures of Littleton Weatherly, dated 1817, other signatures and stamp to titlepage, very good.   The Kelmscott Bookshop   11 - 20   2015 $400

Binding - Steel, Robert

Fleetwood, William *An Essay Upon Miracles in two discourses.* London: printed for Charles Harper, 1701. First edition, 203 x 146mm., 203 x 146mm., fine contemporary crimson morocco gilt by Robert Steel, covers with French fillet border, central floral frame with triangular filigree sidepieces and oblique fleuron cornerpieces, raised bands, spine heavily gilt in compartments adorned with curls and small tools, black morocco label, gilt rolled turn-ins, marbled endpapers, all edges gilt, large paper copy, front joint bit rubbed and with three very short cracks (spine ends and rear joint minimally worn), darkened areas on front board but binding entirely solid with shining gilt and extraordinarily fine internally, almost preternaturally clean, fresh and bright.   Phillip J. Pirages   66 - 30   2015 $1900

Binding - Stikeman

Hale, George Ellery *The Study of Stellar Evolution, An Account of Some Recent Methods of Astrophysical Research.* Chicago: University of Chicago Press, 1908. First edition, frontispiece, 104 plates, including frontispiece, bound by Stikeman & Co. in half dark green crushed morocco, green cloth, gilt ruled and decorative spine, top edge gilt, marbled endleaves, inner hinge broken, extremities worn (with kozo repairs), bookplate of Katherine Duer Mackay (1880-1930), very good.   Jeff Weber Rare Books   178 - 792   2015 $150

Thoreau, Henry David   1817-1862 *Some Unpublished Letters of Henry D. and Sophie E. Thoreau.* New York: Marion Press, 1899. First edition, number 78 of 150 numbered copies, uncommon, 8vo., contemporary red half morocco by Stikeman, marbled paper boards and matching endpapers, gilt rules and lettering, top edge gilt, others untrimmed, frontispiece and five plates, wear at edges neatly repaired, fine.   The Brick Row Book Shop   Miscellany 67 - 90 2015 $450

Binding - Stuart, R. T.

Art Work of Delaware. N.P.: Charles Madison Co., 1898. First edition, quarto, contemporary leather, 22 pages of text, 70 pages of photos, with ink binding stamp indicating that this copy was bound by R.T. Stuart 615 Shipley Street, Wilmington, Del." and with name "Isaac C. Elliott" stamped in gilt on lower portion of front cover, spine replaced and stamped with author's name and title, professional restoration to original front and rear covers, new front and rear endpapers, some tissues replaced, else near fine, housed in cloth slipcase with leather label on spine and titles stamped in gilt.   Buckingham Books   March 2015 - 23961   2015 $1250

Binding - Thistle Bindery

Joyce, James   1882-1941 *Epiphanies.* New York: Vincent FitzGerald & Co., 1987. One of 65 copies only, 50 in an edition for sale and 15 Artist's Proofs, all on Moulin du Gue paper and Japanese papers with 62 etchings, employing over 150 plates, original watercolors, collage and hand cutting, collage by Vincent FitzGerald and Zahra Partovi, etchings printed by Marjorie Van Dyke assisted by Maria Luisa Rojo at the printmaking Workshop, lithographs editioned by Marjorie Van Dyke with Rhae Burden, calligraphy by Jerry Kelly, letterpress by Dan Keleher and Bruce Chandler at Wild Carrot Letterpress in 40 colors, type set by Dan Carr and Julia Ferrari at the Golgonooza Letter Foundry, page size 12 x 14 inches, 94 leaves, one printed page loose, two foldout images, loose as issued in original wrappers in handmade box by David Bourbeau at the Thistle Bindery in Japanese handmade silk woven for this box, incised line of Japanese tea paper showing profile of Joyce, spine of box slightly sunned, book fine.   Priscilla Juvelis - Rare Books   61 - 14   2015 $12,500

Robinson, Alan James *Cetacea. The Great Whales.* Easthampton: Cheloniidae Press, 1981. One of 100 copies, this copy with original drawing by artist, signed by artist, binders David Bourbeau and Gray Parrot and printer, Harold McGrath, all on Arches Cover Buff from a total issue of 110 (100 copies plus 10 artist's proof copies), this copy with original prospectus laid in as well as separate copy of original wood engraving "Whale Flukes" that also appears on colophon, wood engraving is 5 1/2 x 8 1/2 inches, 27 leaves, page size 22 x 15 inches, bound loose as issued with sheets laid in, black Niger oasis goat over low relief sculpture of Right Whale head by Robinson, then cast in polyester resin and covered by David Bourbeau at the Thistle Bindery, rear panel is lack cloth over board, beautiful folder housed in quarter leather Moroccan goat drop back box by Gray Parrot, bit of wear to box, else fine, 7 bleed etchings by Robinson, tw two-color maps, printed in 12 point Garamond with 24 and 36 point Castellar for tilting, each etching protected by a sheet of Japanese tissue, Tomoe Blue, in a wave pattern, used as endsheets.   Priscilla Juvelis - Rare Books   63 - 3   2015 $4500

Binding - Thouvenin

Corneille, Pierre *Les Chefs-D'Oeuvre De P. Corneille.* Paris: P. Didot l'aine, 1814. 3 volumes, 210 x 165mm., superb contemporary deep blue polished calf by Thouvenin (stamp signed in gilt at foot of spine of volume), covers with triple gilt fillet border, central panel with large blindstamped floral frame, highlighted with gilt, raised bands, spine panels with delicate stippled and tooled cruciform ornament, gilt titling, turn-ins with cresting gilt roll, marbled endpapers, all edges gilt, one gathering somewhat foxed, otherwise splendid set in pristine condition.   Phillip J. Pirages   66 - 76   2015 $1400

Senault, Louis *Petit Office De la Sainte Vierge.* Paris: Chez Senault, circa, 1680. 181 x 127mm., remarkably beautiful black straight grain morocco elegantly and lavishly gilt by Thouvenin (signed at base of spine), covers with elaborate broad frame featuring repeated palmettes, central panel with complex cornerpieces of massed antique tools, raised bands, spine compartments with red cruciform inlay at center and with stylized tulips and multiple stippled leaves emanating from central ornament, very lovely broad inner gilt dentelles featuring 52 additional red morocco inlays (26 inside each cover), these within large 'semis' rectangles with concave sides, dentelles surrounding pink watered silk pastedowns bordered with a neoclaassical foliate and floral roll (facing a free endpaper of the same material and with the same decoration), all edges gilt, small and very expert repair, just top of joints, marbled paper slipcase; engraved throughout with a great variety of immensely charming calligraphic initials, headpieces, tailpieces, borders, flourishes and other decorative elements; bookplate of Hans Furstenberg; just the faintest hint of wear to joints, two minor blemishes on rear cover, discoloration at gutter of free endpapers (apparently from binder's glue), but fine, with extraordinarily handsome binding with glistening and with text nearly pristine.   Phillip J. Pirages   66 - 77   2015 $7500

Binding - Tilcock, Sandy

Hiebert, Helen *Spring Theory.* Avon: 2010. One of 10 copies, all on handmade abaca paper with string drawings embedded into paper, each copy hand numbered and signed by artist, Helen Hiebert and poet, Carl Adamschick, page size 12 x 18 inches, 6 string drawings plus 1 page text with colophon, loose as issued in black cloth over boards clamshell box designed by Sandy Tilcock with Helen Heibert's string drawings are in red as well as white string and were inspired by knot illustrations in the Ashley Book of Knots, text printed letterpress by Sandy Tilcock, beautiful textured paper is the perfect backdrop for the drawings in string.   Priscilla Juvelis - Rare Books   62 - 7   2015 $1800

Binding - Tout

Busby, Thomas *The Cries of London. Drawn from Life.* London: Artists' Depository, 21 Charlotte Fitzroy Square and by Simpkin and Marshall..., 1823. First edition, separate engraved pictorial title coloured by hand, 23 hand coloured engraved plates, later half green morocco over marbled boards by Tout, green silk marker, all edges gilt, 16.8 x 10.5cm., bookplate of noted collector Eric Quayle.   Marlborough Rare Books   List 53 - 6   2015   £3250

Walton, Izaak 1593-1683 *The Complete Angler of Izaak Walton and Charles Cotton...* printed at the Shakespeare Press by W. Nicol for) John Major, 1823. First Major edition, large paper copy, 14 engraved plates, printed upon India paper and mounted, numerous woodcuts in text, some foxing, emanating from leaves upon which plates are mounted and from the binder's endleaves, 8vo. half brown morocco, circa 1920 by Tout, top edge gilt, others uncut, good.   Blackwell's Rare Books   B179 - 115   2015   £600

Binding - Trier Matthiaskloster

Baptista Mantuanus, Giovanni 1448-1516 *De Patientia.* Basel: Johann Bergmann de Olpe, 17 Aug., 1499. First printing of this edition, 222 x 165mm., 118 unnumbered leaves, 30 lines in roman type, pleasing contemporary blind-stamped calf by the Trier Matthiaskloster (Abbey of Saint Matthias in Trier), covers with frames formed by triple blind rules, typographic banners at head and foot of frame, frame and central panel decorated with floral tools and medallions of various sizes containing representations of St. Catherine, the Agnus Dei, crossed halberds, pomegranates, foliage, rosettes and floral sprays, raised bands, original brass fore-edge clasp, front pastedown a vellum manuscript leaf circa 1100, with early form of numbers, rear pastedown removed but with remnants of manuscript text still visible, with 5 large initials written by hand in red, 3 tiny cracks to spine, head of rear joint with quarter inch wormhole exposing band, joints little worn, couple of short worm trails, handful of small patches of lost patina due to insect activity, but contemporary binding still sound, only modest wear and generally very appealing, isolated mild foxing, two pages with small inkblot affecting a couple of letters, other minor defects, almost entirely a fine copy, unusually fresh and clean internally. Phillip J. Pirages 66 - 2 2015 $22,500

Binding - Tuckett

Wordsworth, William 1770-1850 *Yarrow Revisited and Other Poems.* London: Longman, Rees, Orme, Brown, Green & Longman, 1835. First edition, presentation copy inscribed by author for fellow poet Eliz M. Hamilton on a slip of paper pasted on to verso of title and with "From the Author" written on half title by publisher's clerk, erratum slip tipped in, ads discarded, 12mo., slightly later 19th century olive pebble grain morocco by Tuckett ('binder to the Queen'), backstrip panelled and ruled in gilt and infilled with volutes and other tools, lettered gilt in second compartment, sides with triple gilt borders, inner panel with gilt cornerpieces and central panels of curing lines, all edges gilt, marbled endpapers, bookplate of J. O. Edwards, small scrape to upper board, extremities slightly rubbed, good. Blackwell's Rare Books B179 - 121 2015 £2500

Binding - Tushingham, J.

Lauderdale, James Maitland, 8th Earl of 1759-1839 *An Inquiry Into the Nature and Origin of Public Wealth and Into the means and Causes of Its Increase.* Edinburgh: Archibald Constable & Co., 1804. First edition, 8vo., without half title but with folding table, occasional minor foxing and few insignificant rust marks, contemporary half calf over marbled board, spine simply gilt with red morocco lettering piece, very good, binder's ticket of J. Tushingham of Chester. John Drury Rare Books 2015 - 26228 2015 $1136

Binding - Warde, Frederic

Dodgson, Charles Lutwidge 1832-1898 *Alice's Adventures in Wonderland and Through the Looking-Glass.* New York: Limited Editions Club, 1932. Limited to 1500 numbered copies, signed by typographer and binder, Frederic Warde and by Alice Hargreaves, 2 volumes, 8vo., leather, covers and spine gilt stamped, all edges gilt, slipcases, gilt stamped spine, front and rear covers with pictorial vignettes, title, author and publisher on spine. Oak Knoll Books 25 - 7 2015 $5500

Binding - Waschher-James, Sande

Wascher-James, Sande *What Every Woman Needs.* Whidbey Island: 2013. Artist's book, four separate fascicles (books) housed together, one of 5 copies only, each on fine cotton lawn fabric, signed and numbered on colophon by artist, page size 6 1/4 x 8 inches closed, opening when hung to 40 1/2 x 8 inches, bound by artist accordion style for each of the four books, unfolding to make a piece of wall art, housed in box of Red Rose Iris bookcloth, box 17 1/2 x 7 x 1 7/8 inches, box with two storage spaces for books in base and two trays on top to hold the other two books, box with cyanotype of the author, Sophie Tucker, printed on fine lawn cotton on front cover, printed with cyanotype photo on front of each of the four 6-panel books which is bound in Red Rose Iris bookcloth, the six panels contain vintage photos of women. Priscilla Juvelis - Rare Books 62 - 19 2015 $2500

Binding - Watters, T.

Punch; or the Auckland Charivari. Volume I from November 14, 1868 to May 8 1869. Auckland: published by the proprietors Messrs Frank Varley & R. J. Morressey, 1868-1869. Collective titlepage, illustrations, tear to lower fold first leaf not affecting text, slight marking to lower corners, largely good and clean, few gatherings little proud, 24 8 page issues, contemporary full black morocco by T. Watters, Auckland, elaborately decorated in gilt with central royal arms on front board and crown on lower board, gilt dentelles, rubbed, still attractive copy, scarce, elaborate blue and gilt endpapers, armorial bookplate of Coburg Bibliothek. Jarndyce Antiquarian Booksellers CCXI - 232 2015 £480

Binding - Webb & Hunt

Cruikshank, George 1792-1878 *Sir John Falstaff Knight.* London: Longman & Co., 1857. First edition, small oblong 4to., 20 leaves of plates drawn and etched by Cruikshank, contemporary half green morocco green cloth boards lettered gilt on upper cover and spine, all edges gilt by Webb & Hunt, Liverpool, marbled endpapers, extremities little rubbed, some occasional scattered foxing, very good, slight rubbing, some occasional foxing, otherwise very good, tipped in handwritten signed letter from Cruikshank to H. A. Bright. Any Amount of Books March 2015 - C16212 2015 £375

Binding - Westleys

Arnold, Matthew 1822-1888 *Merope.* London: Longmans, 1858. First edition, half title, 3 pages ads, 32 page catalog (Nov. 1857), odd spot, original green cloth by Westleys, orange endpapers with printed ad, very good, inscribed "From the author" on verso of leading pastedown and signed by Geoffrey Tillotson.   Jarndyce Antiquarian Booksellers   CCVII - 37   2015   £150

Arnold, Matthew 1822-1888 *Poems.* London: Longmans, 1853. New edition, half title, 32 page catalog (March 31 1853), unexplained erasure of edition statement, original green cloth by Westleys, yellow endpapers with printed ads, spine quite worn at head and tail, trace of lending library label, novelist S. R. Crockett's copy, signed by him, H. J. Macrory and Geoffrey Tillotson.   Jarndyce Antiquarian Booksellers   CCVII - 45   2015   £35

Arnold, Matthew 1822-1888 *Poems.* London: Longmans, 1853. New edition, half title, 24 page catalog (Nov. 1854), original green cloth by Westleys, orange endpapers with printed ads, spine faded and worn, hinges splitting, signed by Geoffrey Tillotson, April 1944 with few notes and cuttings inserted.   Jarndyce Antiquarian Booksellers   CCVII - 46   2015   £35

Arnold, Matthew 1822-1888 *Poems. Second Series.* London: Longmans, 1855. First edition, vi & 24 page catalog. (Nov. 1854), original green cloth by Westley's, orange endpapers with printed ads, spine faded, with splits in hinges, bookplate of Oxford Young, signed by Geoffrey Tillotson April 1944.   Jarndyce Antiquarian Booksellers   CCVII - 47   2015   £50

Binding - Wiener Werkstatte

Schnitzler, Arthur *Die Hirtenflote.* Wien: Vienna: Deutsch-Osterreichischer Verlag, 1912. First edition, number 261 of 400 copies, small 8vo., original Wiener Werkstatte binding, green full crushed leather gilt patterned and decorated, designed by Josef Hoffmann, clean, tight and unmarked in excellent clean, very good condition, slight rubbing at extremities, 9 original etchings by Ferdinand Schmutzer with tissue guards.   Any Amount of Books   2015 - C9490   2015   £700

Binding - Wotton's Binder "B"

Homerus *Ilias. (The Iliad in Latin).* Parisiis: Apud Martinum Iuuenem Excvdebat Gvil. M., 1550. 121 x 89mm., beautiful and animated contemporary elaborately gilt and painted Parisian calf by Wooton's binder "B", covers with unusual frame of interlacing slender rectangular compartments formed by wide black painted fillets outlined in gilt, center panel with four foliate scrolls arched across frame in each quadrant and forming a centerpiece lozenge, azured curls at head and foot of panel and with stippled lobes, additional azured cornerpieces, stippled circles at top, bottom and either side of the panel, raised bands, spine compartments gilt with centered foliate tool or bull's eye, slightly later red morocco label, all edges gilt, spine ends and corners very artfully renewed, in fleece lined brown buckram clamshell case, with John Roland Abbey's morocco bookplate and large morocco title label on spine, front endpaper with morocco bookplate of Abbey, pastedowns with armorial bookplates of Scrope Berdmore, S.T.P. (dated 1790) at front and of Henry C. Compton esq. at rear, rear endpaper with modern bookplate of Philosophia Hermetica ruled in red throughout, half dozen light ink stains, two or three affecting a few words of text, quite clean and fresh internally, backstrip with minor flaking and few hairline cracks, one corner exposed, otherwise very decorative binding, pleasing and especially well preserved, boards still lustrous.   Phillip J. Pirages   66 - 12   2015 $12,500

Binding - Zaehnsdorf

Cruikshank, George 1792-1878 *George Cruikshank's Omnibus.* London: Tilt and Bogue, 1841-1842. First edition, 100 engravings on steel and wood, half title, frontispiece, plates and illustrations, some plates slightly browned and spotted, illustrations, front wrappers numbers I-IX bound in at front of volume, slightly dusted, some expert paper repair, uncut in later full light brown crushed morocco by Zaehnsdorf, very good, handsome copy, 11 line ALS from Cruikshank to Mr. Eales tipped in.   Jarndyce Antiquarian Booksellers   CCXI - 80   2015   £850

Lovett, Richard *The English Bible in the John Rylands Library.* London: printed for private circulation, 1899. First edition, folio, crushed brown morocco, title gilt stamped on spine with five raised bands, top edge gilt, other edges uncut, 26 facsimile plates and 29 engravings, bound by Zaehnsdorf, richly gilt inner dentelles, printed in red and black, bookplate of Zion Research Library, light rubbing top and bottom of spine and at corners, extremely scarce. Oak Knoll Books   306 - 68   2015 $3500

Mee, Margaret Ursula *Flowers of the Brazilian Forests Collected and Painted by Margaret Mee.* London: L. van Leer & Vo. for the Tryon Gallery in association with George Rainbird, 1968. First and only edition, limited to 500 copies, this no. 27 of 100 deluxe copies signed by Mee with original gouache by Mee, folio, original full natural vellum by Zaehnsdorf, gilt facsimile of author's signature blocked on upper board, vignette of a teju-assu lizard after Mee blocked in gilt on lower board, spine lettered gilt, endpapers with printed vignettes of the etju-assu after Mee, top edge gilt, original green cloth slipcase, gilt lettering piece on upper panel, original shipping carton addressed to Richard Mitchell, Aldham, Essex with limitation numbers, title printed in green and black, original gouache over pencil painting on paper watermarked 'Raffaello Fabbriano' signed 'Margaret Mee' and titled 'Aristolochia' and further inscribed '48' mounted as an additional frontispiece, retaining tissue guard, 32 color lithographed plates, including frontispiece, all plates retaining tissue guards, text illustrations, double page map printed in red and black showing Mee's journey and locations where flowers depicted were collected, with loose original prospectus, fine.   Henry Sotheran Ltd.   Natural History: Rarities 2015 - 2015   £7000

Poe, Edgar Allan   1809-1849 *The Poems of Edgar Allan Poe.* London: Kegan Paul, Trench & Co., 1881. First UK edition thus, one of 50 copies of the large paper edition, numbered and printed October 1881, this #38, signed by printers Ballantyne, Hanson & Co., 8vo., original full leather bound by Zaehnsdorf, raised bands on spine, titles stamped in gold on spine, decorated linen front and rear endpapers, frontispiece, former owner's neat attractive bookplate, bit of minor foxing to few pages, else near fine, bright copy.   Buckingham Books   March 2015 - 29431   2015 $750

Rowlandson, Thomas *Rowlandson's Characteristic Sketches of the Lower Orders Intended as a Companion to the new Picture of London, consisting of Fifty-Four Plates, Neatly Coloured.* London: printed for Samuel Leigh 18 Strand, 1820. First edition, first issue, 12mo., 54 hand colored plates, including frontispiece, later straight ribbed morocco, spine decorated in six compartments, two lettered in gilt, gilt top, silk endpapers, bound by Zaehnsdorf 1902.   Marlborough Rare Books   List 54 - 73   2015   £2500

Williams, Helen Maria *A Narrative of the Events Which Have Taken Place in France from the Landing of Napoleon Bonaparte on the 1st of March 1815 till the Restoration of Louis XVIII.* London: John Murray, 1815. First edition, 8vo., half title, contemporary three quarter morocco by Zaehnsdorf stamped in gilt, little scuffed, very nice, untrimmed.   Second Life Books Inc.   189 - 268   2015 $950

Fore-edge Paintings